LITERATURE
AN INTRODUCTION
TO
CRITICAL READING

COMPACT EDITION

LEE A. JACOBUS

UPPER SADDLE RIVER, NEW JERSEY 07458

Library of Congress Cataloging-in-Publication Data

Literature: an introduction to critical reading / [compiled by] Lee A. Jacobus.–Compact
ed., 1st ed.
    p. cm.
    Includes index.
    1. Literature–Collections.   2. Criticism.   I. Jacobus, Lee A.

PN6014.J22 2001
808–dc21

2001035075

Editor in Chief: Leah Jewell
Senior Acquisitions Editor: Carrie Brandon
Production Editor: Joan E. Foley
Copyeditor: Anne Hebenstreit
Text Permissions Specialist: Mary Dalton-Hoffman
Prepress and Manufacturing Buyer: Sherry Lewis
Marketing Manager: Rachel Falk
Cover Designer: Robert Farrar-Wagner
Cover and Interior Photos: Robert Greg Hill

This book is dedicated
to my teachers,
David Krause
and
Edwin Honig

For permission to use copyrighted material, grateful
acknowledgment is made to the copyright holders
on pages 1385–1395, which are considered an extension of this copyright page.

This book was set in 10/12 Baskerville by PubSet
and was printed and bound by R. R. Donnelley & Sons Company.
Covers were printed by Phoenix Color Corp.

© 2002 by Pearson Education, Inc.
Upper Saddle River, New Jersey 07458

Printed in the United States of America
10   9   8   7   6   5   4   3   2   1

ISBN   0-13-019997-4

Prentice-Hall International (UK) Limited, *London*
Prentice-Hall of Australia Pty. Limited, *Sydney*
Prentice-Hall Canada Inc., *Toronto*
Prentice-Hall Hispanoamericana, S.A., *Mexico*
Prentice-Hall of India Private Limited, *New Delhi*
Prentice-Hall of Japan, Inc., *Tokyo*
Pearson Education Asia Pte. Ltd., *Singapore*
Editora Prentice-Hall do Brasil, Ltda., *Rio de Janeiro*

BRIEF CONTENTS

CONTENTS

PREFACE

Literature: An Introduction to Critical Reading, Compact Edition, is designed for the introduction to literature course and concentrates on developing skills associated with close reading. At the same time, it permits a variety of critical approaches to short fiction, poetry, and drama. The selections engage the interest of the modern student while offering a remarkable range of nationalities, historical periods, and authors: canonical, marginalized, and contemporary. The collection includes 40 short stories, 318 poems, and 11 plays.

CLOSE READING

The primary strategy used in this book is traditional close reading. Close reading begins the process of interpretation and criticism of literature. In this sense, the book encourages us to consider what is truly important in any given work of literature, regardless of its genre. Most of the works that appear in these pages have a strong impact on the reader and all of them benefit from a careful reading and interpretation. In each of the genres of fiction, poetry, and drama, I have spent time detailing a close examination of the primary elements, such as style, theme, plot and narrative structure, point of view, tone, form, imagery, symbol and allegory, figurative language, setting, character, as well as the elements of tragedy, comedy, and tragicomedy. I have chosen works that excite ideas by virtue of their treatment of the elements of literature. I emphasize elements because it is important to see how they intersect, complement each other, and ultimately serve a higher literary purpose: to make a lasting literary statement.

CRITICAL READING

The first chapters of the book explore the importance of critical reading and offer a close examination of Robert Frost's "Fire and Ice." The process of interpretation by means of a sample reading and its resultant notes, outlines, drafts, and final essay completes the first part of the book. The essay on Frost's poem demonstrates one way in which close reading begins the process of interpreting a piece of literature while at the same time pointing to a number of ways in which a critical examination of the poem might be carried out. Naturally, critical reading will differ from reader to reader and the process of interpretation depends in some measure not only on close reading of a text, but on the preparation and background of the reader.

INTERPRETING LITERATURE

Each part of the book dealing with a specific genre begins with the title Interpreting Short Fiction, Interpreting Poetry, or Interpreting Drama. Each of these emphasizes the process of close reading and demonstrates a wide variety of ways in which close reading moves us toward an interpretation of the piece of literature. Interpretation implies a coherent reading that clarifies the work's significance. The examples offered in the book point to a range of interpretations, which reflects the fact that different readers will produce different interpretations depending on their critical approach, whether it is the method of formalist new criticism, historicism, feminism, or any one of a number of cultural criticisms. Making good sense of complex works of art takes time and practice as well as the opportunity to examine useful models of criticism. Each of the parts of the book offers such opportunities and such practice. In short fiction, the close reading and interpretation is developed around William Faulkner's "A Rose for Emily." In poetry several poems are discussed in detail, but the close reading and interpretation is reserved for Robert Frost's "Birches." Susan Glaspell's amusing comedy, *Suppressed Desires,* provides the opportunity for close reading. In each of these cases, short essays illustrate useful interpretations and critical strategies.

THE ELEMENTS OF LITERATURE

Literature: An Introduction to Critical Reading, Compact Edition, gives more emphasis to the elements of each genre than does the fuller edition. For example, three short stories illustrate style and theme, plot and narrative structure, as well as each of the other basic elements of fiction. These stories use their respective elements to wonderful effect and help the reader see how powerful the given elements can be. Poetry and Drama are illustrated in similar fashion, tailored to each genre. For poetry, a group of five to ten poems illustrates their respective elements, such as language, imagery, tone, rhythm, rhyme, figurative language, and form. In the section on drama, a group of plays offers the opportunity to see all the elements at work together.

AUTHORS IN DEPTH

In this new compact edition, several authors are represented in depth with a number of their works as well as commentaries either from the authors themselves or from their critics. Anton Chekhov and Eudora Welty each have three stories in this collection and also a number of commentaries that will help students interpret the stories in relation to one another. This strategy helps readers see how individual writers rework similar ideas and use the elements in a way that determines their individual style. In poetry, generous selections from the works of John Keats, Robert Frost, and Sylvia Plath offer opportunities to see how poetic styles develop and how poets establish their own attitudes toward language and style. Henrik Ibsen is represented by *A Doll House* as well as by his notes on the play. Janet Achurch, the first actress to play Nora, comments on the role while Joan Templeton examines the way critics have treated the play. These critical opportunities offer a model of how outside commentary can shed light on a whole body of writing in addition to the individual piece of writing.

THE ALBUMS OF STORIES, POEMS, AND PLAYS

Each section of the book ends with a representative album of important and exciting stories, poems, and plays. In these albums, students can approach a given work from any angle they choose. Armed with an understanding of how the elements function in short fiction, they may begin with Sarah Orne Jewett, James Joyce, David Wong Louie, or a number of other ranking authors. Each of the nine stories in the album will reward close reading and critical interpretation. In the album of poems, more than two hundred examples, including eight by Emily Dickinson, five by Langston Hughes and Dorothy Parker, and eleven of Shakespeare's sonnets, offer a wide range of style, thought, and technique. The album of plays includes six major dramas: Chekhov's *The Cherry Orchard,* María Irene Fornés's *The Conduct of Life,* Arthur Miller's *Death of a Salesman,* William Shakespeare's *Hamlet, Prince of Denmark,* Tennessee Williams's *The Glass Menagerie,* and August Wilson's *Fences.*

WRITING ABOUT LITERATURE

Supplementing the examples of writing in each of the sections on literary genre, Chapter 21, The Importance of Writing about Literature, details all the steps involved in writing an interpretive essay on a piece of literature. The chapter

takes Percy Bysshe Shelley's "Ozymandias" as its example, then offers an illustration of the process of developing material to support a thorough essay on the
poem. Exercises follow in prewriting, freewriting, outlining, drafting and revising, editing, and the use of outside sources. In addition, the chapter describes
the mechanics of citation and MLA style. Two essays end the chapter, taking two
different critical approaches. The first is a formalist/historicist interpretation,
while the second is essentially a reader response interpretation.

INTERPRETIVE STRATEGIES

The final chapter of the book details some of the most important contemporary approaches to critical examination of texts. The formalist new criticism
approach is followed by considerations of psychoanalytic criticism, reader response criticism, feminist criticism, political-economic criticism, historicist criticism, and a note on how to combine these methods for best effect. A careful
reading of Nikki Giovanni's "Master Charge Blues" shows how a single poem
can yield very different interpretations depending on how one approaches it.

INSTRUCTOR'S MANUAL

An extensive Instructor's Manual of more than 450 pages offers a range of important resources, such as sample syllabi, video and audio recordings of writers in the collection, and detailed treatments of stories, poems, and plays in
the text. Almost every work in the book has questions for close reading appropriate for in-class discussion. A second set of questions for critical interpretation helps engage the student in interpretive consideration of the work.
These questions can be used by directing class discussion or for assignments in
writing. They are open-ended questions designed to stimulate discussion, not
close it down.

I was assisted in the preparation of the first edition of the manual by four
doctoral students at the University of Connecticut: Catherine Nevil Parker, Julie
Pfeiffer, Marianne Sadowski, and Mary Ann Reimann. My own contributions to
the manual are in every section. They are based on my more than 40 years of
teaching, much of that time teaching Introduction to Literature classes at several universities.

TURNITIN.COM

turnitin   www.turnitin.com   This online service makes it easy for teachers
to find out if students are copying their assignments from the Internet, and is
now free to professors using *Literature: An Introduction to Critical Reading, Compact Edition*, by Lee A. Jacobus. In addition to helping educators easily identify

instances of Web-based student plagiarism, Turnitin.com also offers a digital archiving system and an online peer review service. Professors set up a "drop box" at the Turnitin.com Web site where their students submit papers. Turnitin.com then cross-references each submission with millions of possible online sources. Within 24 hours, teachers receive a customized, color-coded "Originality Report," complete with live links to suspect Internet locations, for each submitted paper. To access the site for free, professors must visit the site via the faculty resources of the Jacobus Web site at www.prenhall.com/Jacobus.

ACKNOWLEDGMENTS

The people who contributed to this book are so numerous that I am bound to omit some who have made important contributions. My most important debt is to my editor, Carrie Brandon, whose enthusiasm for this project was sustaining from the very first. She made me see that the compact version of this book could break new ground and be an important instrument in opening literature for careful readers. Her steadiness and encouragement were a key to this project. I have been blessed as well with my developmental editor, Maggie Barbieri, whose wonderful sense of humor and editorial skills kept me on track throughout. I am indebted as well to my copy editor, Anne Hebenstreit; to my permissions editor, Mary Dalton-Hoffman, who steered me through occasionally tricky waters; and to my stalwart production editor, Joan Foley, who spotted and eliminated a number of potential confusions. And while they did not work on this compact edition, I must mention a few of those who contributed to the original edition: Phil Miller, Kate Morgan, Joyce Perkins, Alison Reeves, and Marlane Miriello.

My thanks also to the following reviewers: Ancilla Coleman, Jackson State University; Candis LaPrade, Longwood College; Gay Lyons, Pellissippi State Technical Community College; and Kathleen McHale, Nassau Community College.

Naturally, I owe a great deal to my students, both undergraduates in my Introduction to Literature classes and graduate students in my advanced classes. All helped me understand better the process of interpreting literature. Among my colleagues who offered encouragement are Regina Barreca, Anne Charters, Michael Meyer, Brenda Murphy, Tom Recchio, A. Harris Fairbanks, Lynn Bloom, Margaret Higonnet, Margaret Gibson, Donna Hollenberg, Robert Hasenfratz, and Samuel Pickering. And of course, I owe immense debts to Sharon Jacobus, who first suggested this project, and to my wife Joanna Jacobus, who helped me see it through.

Lee A. Jacobus

I

CRITICAL READING

1

*I*NTRODUCTION

WHAT IS LITERATURE?

What is literature? Nobody has found a universally satisfactory answer to that question. Many people would agree that literature is words artfully arranged to stimulate feelings and impart understanding. Some would also agree that literature can be grouped into three genres: fiction, poetry, and drama. Other kinds of nonfiction prose, such as essays, diaries, journals, newspaper articles, histories, crime reports, wills, deeds, insurance policies, advertisements, and genealogical trees, are at times considered literature too, though some people would exclude all nonfiction prose, including the essay. The criterion used for this book is that a work of literature must both entertain and enlighten the reader; most other kinds of writing, by contrast, aim only at enlightenment. The fiction, poetry, and drama in this collection fulfill those two purposes.

Throughout history, we have valued literature because we believe that the writer is unusually sensitive: in touch with life in a special way and therefore capable of making us more aware ourselves. The writer's skills at metaphor and imagery are highly developed versions of the same skills we all have. The same is true of the whole bag of tricks used to create people and feelings, places and circumstances, that educate our imagination. Literature expands our life because it derives from an enlarged sensibility that is deep and informative. It shows us how rich our world is, how filled with potential we are, and how keen the drama of our life is.

This education succeeds, however, only because it is fused with entertainment of some kind. Whatever else literature does, its primary goal is to give us pleasure. In a short story, we enjoy being taken out of ourselves into other worlds and being given insight into other places, other people, and other ways of living—even when those worlds seem troubled. Likewise, we are amused by witty language, surprised by sharp images, and moved by beautiful sounds and rhythms. It is this element of pleasure that captures us in literature, whatever important "message" the author might have. Some writers inform us about how the world works and what is important ethically, but no reader will pay much attention if the writing is not engaging. For example,

Double, double toil and trouble
Fire burn and cauldron bubble

does not have a great deal of specific meaning or instruction, but in the context of *Macbeth* and spoken by the three witches, the expression becomes almost magical.

Literature, then, does all these things—

* It gives us a special awareness of what we already know.
* It tells us what we don't already know.
* It moves our feelings.
* It gives us pleasure.
* It puts us in another world.
* It uses language in especially powerful ways.

Knowing what literature can do can help you decide whether a specific work is literature. The main question to ask, however, is whether the work tells you something and at the same time delights you; if it does, it is literature.

2

THE IMPORTANCE
OF CRITICAL READING

Literature has many meanings; critical reading is the exploration of those meanings. When responding to a work of literature, people draw on their own understanding, background, and observations. Interpreting literature is nothing more complicated than making those responses available for examination: setting them forth for comparison, discussion, and development. Close reading—the observation of detail, special use of language, and patterns of repetition—not only begins the process but is the basis of interpretation. Interpretive techniques can illuminate a wide variety of values important to the writer and the work itself. Consequently, this book emphasizes a range of interpretive strategies that depend on close reading, which the student of literature can use to achieve greater insight into a work of literature.

CRITICAL READING

Close reading is the exploration of significance. In some works this significance seems clear at first reading; in other works it may seem completely obscure. Obviously, literature that is not self-evident must be interpreted carefully; however, even works that seem clear on first reading can benefit from a deeper consideration because they can have subtle implications that may be uncovered only after more reflection. All literature rewards interpretation by delivering insights into its art.

When you interpret a text—

- You gain a deeper understanding of literature and enjoy it in proportion to your understanding.

- Your interpretation helps others discover what they may have missed or not understood.

- Your interpretation establishes your view of a text's meaning. Since literature can mean many things to many people, your analysis may be unique.

A CLOSE READING OF ROBERT FROST'S "FIRE AND ICE"

Interpretation begins with close reading. In this process, you note specific uses of language, such as imagery, symbols, repeated terms, patterns of expression, the tone of the speaker, and the main ideas the writer introduces. Whether close reading takes the form of writing, discussion, or silent observation, it should be based on a careful questioning of the text. The following pages introduce several different strategies for interpretation, all of which depend on a close reading.

Among other things, close reading requires that you—

- Take the text seriously enough to study it, to read and reread it.
- Search for details that might otherwise go unobserved.
- Examine the text for special words and terms—and refer to the dictionary to be sure of their meaning when necessary.
- Look for symbolic uses of language that might not be evident from a quick reading.
- Ask why certain patterns of behavior or patterns of words repeat themselves: What does their repetition signify?
- Note allusions to other literature.
- Develop and work to answer questions about the text.

Your personal experience helps you interpret a literary text in a slightly different way from anyone else; likewise, others notice details that you might not—everyone has insights and limitations as a reader. Partly because everyone has a unique perspective, the works in this book yield many interpretations. At the same time, however, the value of your interpretation still depends on how well it supports the text. In other words, it has to be convincing.

Any interpretation of Robert Frost's "Fire and Ice" first calls for a close reading.

ROBERT FROST   (1874–1963)

Fire and Ice _____ *1923*

Some say the world will end in fire,
Some say in ice.
From what I've tasted of desire

I hold with those who favor fire.
But if it had to perish twice,   5
I think I know enough of hate
To say that for destruction ice
Is also great
And would suffice.

A close reading uncovers important details and questions like these.

- The poem implies that the world can be destroyed by fire or ice.
- The narrator sees fire and ice as opposing forces.
- Are fire and ice symbols?
- The narrator links fire to desire and ice to hate.
- Has the narrator experienced both desire and hate?
- The destruction of the world by fire seems to be an allusion to the Bible, which promised Noah that the next time the world was destroyed it would be by fire.
- The poem uses three rhyme sounds: "-ice" (*ice, twice, suffice*); "-ire" (*fire, desire, fire*); "-ate" (*hate, great*).
- Who uses the power of fire and ice?

An interpretation of "Fire and Ice" begins by taking into account some or all of the questions and observations uncovered by this reading. At first, fire and ice seem to be gigantic forces of nature that could destroy the planet. But the third line brings these forces down to their human equivalents: to a personal experience with desire, which is compared to fire, and to hate, which is compared to ice. The lines that follow, which explore the potential for destruction by ice, also explore the human emotion of hate. Soon it becomes clear that people are the sources of fire and ice, desire and hate. We realize that Frost has used the forces of fire and ice symbolically to say that human emotions are overwhelming in their power, especially their power to destroy. Frost tells us that the emotions of desire and hate have the power to destroy the world.

THE PROCESS OF INTERPRETATION

The details from a close reading must be brought into an interpretation as evidence to support your views. For example, here is a brief interpretation that grows out of the close reading above.

"Fire and Ice" is a warning to all of us not to permit our emotions to be ungoverned. Robert Frost reminds us that "Some say the world will end in fire" but that ice too "would suffice" to destroy it. We know that a holocaust or an ice age could destroy the world, but he points to something more subtle by symbolically linking fire to desire—such as human lust. He says, "I hold with those who favor fire." But he also symbolically links ice with hate, which can be as destructive as desire, although in a different way. By reminding us of God's biblical promise to Noah that the world will be destroyed by fire, not by water again, Frost suggests that the destruction of the world will depend on our moral behavior. Therefore, controlling desire and hate will be a matter of great importance to the human race.

Close reading examines details; interpretation aims to establish the overall meaning of a work. A work of literature may be interpreted in a number of ways, but some interpretations are more convincing than others. This interpretation of "Fire and Ice" is not the only possible one. Other interpretations might depend on information outside the poem. For example, if you discovered evidence that Frost wrote in response to a long-term hostility with his wife during which he feared lust might destroy his personal world, your interpretation of the poem might change. Suppose, however, that as an animal rights activist you interpret the poem as telling people not to wear fur coats. The first thing you'd hear is, "Where are the textual references to animals, furs, or clothing? Where is anything that points to animal rights?" Even if you suggested in your close reading that *fire* really means "fur" and *ice* really means "eyes," it is unlikely that such an interpretation would be convincing to anyone else. The evidence drawn from a close reading overwhelmingly points in directions other than those needed to support an animal rights interpretation.

Now consider this interpretation.

Frost's poem "Fire and Ice" is about a person's struggle in the kitchen, trying to cook dinner against great odds. Frost tells us that some say they can never create a perfect meal to satisfy their "desire." With the stove, they can apply the "fire" to the meal, even if it has been frozen in "ice" in the "hate"-ful freezer so that it would not "perish." They "desire" a meal that is "great," but the fact is that they "hate" cooking and would not care if the world ended with the destruction of the stove or the refrigerator. Either way would "suffice."

Unlike the animal rights interpreter, this reader uses specific terms from the poem to back up the interpretation. You may consider this interpretation unconvincing, but to make the writer realize how unconvincing it is, you would have to create your own interpretation, explaining that "fire" and "ice" are metaphors representing larger issues than a struggle with a kitchen stove and a refrigerator-freezer (neither of which is mentioned in the poem). If you feel this is not a kitchen lyric but a poem about more cosmic concerns, your work is cut out for you.

One strategy is to go back to the poem and remind the interpreter that Frost starts out talking not about kitchens but about the way the world will end. He chooses the extremes of fire and ice because the Bible tells us after Noah's voyage in Genesis that the world was destroyed by a flood but that the next time destruction will be by fire. On the other hand, some scientists are worried that our civilization may perish in a new ice age. Now, to make a case for this larger interpretation, you might need some specialized knowledge about what the

Bible says and what the scientists say. Interpretations profit from bringing many kinds of knowledge to bear on a piece of literature because all literature intersects with life. Even without specialized knowledge, you can always challenge the kitchen interpreter by pointing out that Frost talks about the world, not the kitchen.

For the sake of argument, suppose the interpreter finds plausible evidence to support the kitchen metaphor as well as the destruction of the world. If the interpretation accounts for all the important elements in the poem—and that is a big *if*—then you would find yourself able, and probably willing, to accept it. The same should be true of your own interpretations. You must demonstrate how all the details support your interpretation.

Interpretation and the Author's Intention

Writers sometimes have a clear intention in writing a story, poem, or play. However, many times the work itself does not reveal the author's intention—it may even seem to contradict its apparent intention. The truth is, we cannot know the author's intention. Once, when Robert Browning was asked what a line from one of his poems meant, he said, "When I wrote that line both I and God knew what I meant. Now, God only knows." William Faulkner responded to a similar question about a story by saying he "was so corned up" when he wrote his piece that he could not be expected to know what he intended.

Some critics assume that the work reveals its own intention, even when it may contradict what the author said about it. Often a difference exists between what we intend a statement to mean and what our audience interprets it to mean. The question is, which takes precedence, interpretation or intention? If interpretation takes precedence, then the job of interpreting a work of literature is very important.

Interpretation and the Search for Meaning

To many people meaning is "in" a work of literature. But modern literary studies quarrel with that view. All works of literature, whether spoken words or printed words, are composed of signs that readers interpret. When a storyteller says, "Marvin walked down the dark hallway," each of us supplies a somewhat different image, a somewhat longer or shorter hallway, a somewhat larger or smaller Marvin. Until we read them, those words have neither a person nor a hallway in them. Were those words to appear here in Chinese, you would realize how important is the reader's role in creating meaning from signs and symbols.

Nonetheless, when we understand the words, they control the meaning we derive from them. For example, most readers reading the words about Marvin would have a general image of a man (not a taxicab) walking down a dark hallway (not a boulevard). Because we know that some interpretations are unconvincing, such as the idea that animal rights is the subject of "Fire and Ice," we also know that every literary text restricts meaning to some extent.

The act of close reading is performed similarly in fiction, poetry, and drama, with distinctions that will show up in the remaining sections of this book. Imagery, tone, language, and action, to name only a few elements of literature, will command our close reading in all forms of literature, but in drama, for example, our attention will be drawn more firmly to plot and action than it might be in, say, a lyric poem. All literary genres have special concerns. Adjusting our attention from genre to genre is one of the most important considerations in close reading. But in all literature, details and patterns need attention. They will add up in many different ways to suggest meaning. The job of close reading is to see how meaning develops and how literature reveals meaning even as we read with great pleasure. Our interpretations of the literature we read will depend on our care in close reading.

II
INTERPRETING
SHORT FICTION

3

READING
THREE STORIES

WHAT IS SHORT FICTION?

Like definitions of *literature,* no definition of **short fiction** can satisfy everyone. Still, some qualities of short fiction can be identified. For one, short fiction is prose storytelling whose incidents are deeply revealing of human values. No length limits have ever been settled on; the stories in this collection range from two pages to dozens of pages. Usually, the reader's sense of satisfaction signals the completion of a story, but you will find that some of the following stories purposely deny you a sense of satisfaction in order to bring you to a point of reflection and questioning. Such stories invite you to round them out in your mind.

No one knows the origins of storytelling, but it began early in human history. In dreams may lie the beginnings of storytelling because people seem to have a universal impulse to tell others their dreams. Or perhaps dreams are the product, not the origin, of fiction. Some dreams have a narrative plot, character, action, setting, and language. They often follow the action/adventure, science fiction, mystery, or other style of narratives found in short fiction. Freud assumed a connection between literature and dreams and felt that literature reflected the subconscious.

Both "The Pot of Basil" and "Two Cents," in this chapter, have dreamlike qualities. In the first story, one character appears to the heroine as a ghost, as if in a dream. In the second story, people behave as if they are detached from themselves—somewhat the way that the "you" in your dreams is detached from the "you" in life. We can say that dreams are interactive with fiction. They may have helped produce it, and in some ways they help sustain it. Scientists tell us we need to dream in order to retain our sanity. If that is true, we may also need fiction to help us maintain a balanced inner life.

For many of us, stories help to form personal values and personal identity. Childhood stories are often moral tales designed to awaken an awareness that we are not alone in the universe, that we have responsibilities to others. They even have the effect of clarifying our sense of ourselves. An influential contemporary literary critic, Stephen J. Greenblatt, tells us this about himself:

> My earliest recollections of "having an identity" or "being a self" are bound up with story-telling—narrating my own life or having it narrated for me by my mother. I suppose that I usually used the personal pronoun "I" in telling my own stories and that my mother used my name, but the heart of the initial experience of selfhood lay in the stories, not in the unequivocal, unmediated possession of an identity.[1]

Greenblatt also remembered going through a terrible period in his life in which he began to "narrate" his existence, saying to himself such things as "He's sitting down, now. He's opening his book." Such behavior gives you an idea of how powerful the typical narrative style of short fiction can become. Ultimately, Greenblatt recognizes one of the most important qualities of fiction: "Pleasure is an important part of my sense of literature—that is, part both of my own response . . . and of what I most wish to understand."

A STORY FROM *THE DECAMERON*

Some people think of the short story as a modern, virtually American invention. The stories and theorizing of Nathaniel Hawthorne (1804–1864) and Edgar Allan Poe (1809–1849) are so influential that such a view is almost supportable. However, the impulse to tell stories is ancient. Among the most important innovators of the short story is Giovanni Boccaccio (1313–1375), whose *Decameron* was designed carefully, almost like a piece of architecture. "I shall narrate a hundred stories or fables or parables or histories or whatever you choose to call them, recited in ten days by a worthy band of seven ladies and three young men, who assembled together during the plague which recently took such heavy toll of life." For ten days, while cloistered away from an epidemic of the Black Death in 1348, these ten young aristocrats tell stories for one another's enjoyment. The hundred stories, some very brief, delve into psychology, inquire into the manners and mores of their culture, and expose the hypocrisy of such institutions as the church, families, and professional societies. Although they are set in the 1300s in Florence, Italy, they are recognizably modern. They touch upon other nations and cultures, such as the Arabic world, which traded with Florence. Their universality shows up in the fact that numerous cultures have raided the stories and adapted them for their own. Like all great literature, they speak to a universal audience.

---

[1] *Learning to Curse* (New York: Routledge, 1990), 6.

"The Pot of Basil" is the fifth story of the fourth day, told by Filomena, who was moved to tell it after hearing the love story that preceded hers. Often retold, this story was popular among the Romantic poets of the early nineteenth century.

GIOVANNI BOCCACCIO   (1313–1375)

The Pot of Basil _____ *1353*

Translated by G. H. McWilliam

When Elissa's story came to an end, the king bestowed a few words of praise upon it and then called upon Filomena to speak next. Being quite overcome with compassion for the hapless Gerbino and his lady-love, she fetched a deep sigh, then began as follows:

This story of mine, fair ladies, will not be about people of so lofty a rank as those of whom Elissa has been speaking, but possibly it will prove to be no less touching, and I was reminded of it by the mention that has just been made of Messina, which was where it all happened.

In Messina, there once lived three brothers, all of them merchants who had been left very rich after the death of their father, whose native town was San Gemignano. They had a sister called Lisabetta, but for some reason or other they had failed to bestow her in marriage, despite the fact that she was uncommonly gracious and beautiful.

In one of their trading establishments, the three brothers employed a young Pisan named Lorenzo, who planned and directed all their operations, and who, being rather dashing and handsomely proportioned, had often attracted the gaze of Lisabetta. Having noticed more than once that she had grown exceedingly fond of him, Lorenzo abandoned all his other amours and began in like fashion to set his own heart on winning Lisabetta. And since they were equally in love with each other, before very long they gratified their dearest wishes, taking care not to be discovered.

In this way, their love continued to prosper, much to their common enjoyment and pleasure. They did everything they could to keep the affair a secret, but one night, as Lisabetta was making her way to Lorenzo's sleeping-quarters, she was observed, without knowing it, by her eldest brother. The discovery greatly distressed him, but being a young man of some intelligence, and not wishing to do anything that would bring discredit upon his family, he neither spoke nor made a move, but spent the whole of the night applying his mind to various sides of the matter.

Next morning he described to his brothers what he had seen of Lisabetta and Lorenzo the night before, and the three of them talked the thing over at considerable length. Being determined that the affair should leave no stain upon the reputation either of themselves or of their sister, he decided that they must pass it over in silence and pretend to have neither seen nor heard anything until such time as it was safe and convenient for them to rid themselves of this ignominy before it got out of hand.

Abiding by this decision, the three brothers jested and chatted with Lorenzo in their usual manner, until one day they pretended they were all going off on a pleasure-trip to the country, and took Lorenzo with them. They bided their time, and on reaching a very remote and lonely spot, they took Lorenzo off his guard, murdered him, and

5

buried his corpse. No one had witnessed the deed, and on their return to Messina they put it about that they had sent Lorenzo away on a trading assignment, being all the more readily believed as they had done this so often before.

Lorenzo's continued absence weighed heavily upon Lisabetta, who kept asking her brothers, in anxious tones, what had become of him, and eventually her questioning became so persistent that one of her brothers rounded on her, and said:

"What is the meaning of this? What business do you have with Lorenzo, that you should be asking so many questions about him? If you go on pestering us, we shall give you the answer you deserve."

From then on, the young woman, who was sad and miserable and full of strange 10 forebodings, refrained from asking questions. But at night she would repeatedly utter his name in a heart-rending voice and beseech him to come to her, and from time to time she would burst into tears because of his failure to return. Nothing would restore her spirits, and meanwhile she simply went on waiting.

One night, however, after crying so much over Lorenzo's absence that she eventually cried herself off to sleep, he appeared to her in a dream, pallid-looking and all dishevelled, his clothes tattered and decaying, and it seemed to her that he said:

"Ah, Lisabetta, you do nothing but call to me and bemoan my long absence, and you cruelly reprove me with your tears. Hence I must tell you that I can never return, because on the day that you saw me for the last time, I was murdered by your brothers."

He then described the place where they had buried him, told her not to call to him or wait for him any longer, and disappeared.

Having woken up, believing that what she had seen was true, the young woman wept bitterly. And when she arose next morning, she resolved to go to the place and seek confirmation of what she had seen in her sleep. She dared not mention the apparition to her brothers, but obtained their permission to make a brief trip to the country for pleasure, taking with her a maidservant who had once acted as her go-between and was privy to all her affairs. She immediately set out, and on reaching the spot, swept aside some dead leaves and started to excavate a section of the ground that appeared to have been disturbed. Nor did she have to dig very deep before she uncovered her poor lover's body, which, showing no sign as yet of decomposition or decay, proved all too clearly that her vision had been true. She was the saddest woman alive, but knowing that this was no time for weeping, and seeing that it was impossible for her to take away his whole body (as she would dearly have wished), she laid it to rest in a more appropriate spot, then severed the head from the shoulders as best she could and enveloped it in a towel. This she handed into her maidservant's keeping whilst she covered over the remainder of the corpse with soil, and then they returned home, having completed the whole of their task unobserved.

Taking the head to her room, she locked herself in and cried bitterly, weeping 15 so profusely that she saturated it with her tears, at the same time implanting a thousand kisses upon it. Then she wrapped the head in a piece of rich cloth, and laid it in a large and elegant pot, of the sort in which basil or marjoram is grown. She next covered it with soil, in which she planted several sprigs of the finest Salernitan basil, and never watered them except with essence of roses or orange-blossom, or with her own teardrops. She took to sitting permanently beside this pot and gazing lovingly at it, concentrating the whole of her desire upon it because it was where her beloved Lorenzo lay concealed. And after gazing raptly for a long while upon it, she would bend over it and begin to cry, and her weeping never ceased until the whole of the basil was wet with her tears.

Because of the long and unceasing care that was lavished upon it, and also because the soil was enriched by the decomposing head inside the pot, the basil grew very thick and exceedingly fragrant. The young woman constantly followed this same routine, and from time to time she attracted the attention of her neighbors. And as they had heard her brothers expressing their concern at the decline in her good looks and the way in which her eyes appeared to have sunk into their sockets, they told them what they had seen, adding:

"We have noticed that she follows the same routine every day."

The brothers discovered for themselves that this was so, and having reproached her once or twice without the slightest effect, they caused the pot to be secretly removed from her room. When she found that it was missing, she kept asking for it over and over again, and because they would not restore it to her she sobbed and cried without a pause until eventually she fell seriously ill. And from her bed of sickness she would call for nothing else except her pot of basil.

The young men were astonished by the persistence of her entreaties, and decided to examine its contents. Having shaken out the soil, they saw the cloth and found the decomposing head inside it, still sufficiently intact for them to recognize it as Lorenzo's from the curls of his hair. This discovery greatly amazed them, and they were afraid lest people should come to know what had happened. So they buried the head, and without breathing a word to anyone, having wound up their affairs in Messina, they left the city and went to live in Naples.

The girl went on weeping and demanding her pot of basil, until eventually she   20
cried herself to death, thus bringing her ill-fated love to an end. But after due process of time, many people came to know of the affair, and one of them composed the song which can still be heard to this day:

Whoever it was,
Whoever the villain
That stole my pot of herbs, etc.

Analyzing the Story

The next chapter explains the elements of fiction—those qualities of the story that are interesting to isolate and analyze: setting and mood, character and psychology, style and theme, plot and structure, point of view, and irony and tone—in detail. "The Pot of Basil" includes each of these elements despite its being so short. The following brief list suggests only some immediate ways the elements figure in an interpretation.

SETTING AND MOOD.   The story does not provide extensive discussions of the setting, the place and time of the action. However, a dark mood, the atmosphere or feelings evoked by the setting, pervades the narrative, especially in regard to the brothers and their behavior.

CHARACTER AND PSYCHOLOGY.   Characters can be fully developed, with recognizable psychological depth, or they can be undeveloped sketches. The characters in this story are sketches: the wicked and self-centered brothers, the innocent and lovelorn Lisabetta, and the industrious, attractive Lorenzo. A single act complicates the psychology of the story immensely: Lisabetta's placing the head of Lorenzo in the pot of basil. This act may imply Lisabetta's insanity.

STYLE AND THEME.   The style, the special use of language, is plain; a major theme, or main idea, is that of thwarted love.

PLOT.   The plot or unraveling of the action is simple enough that Boccaccio summarizes it in a few lines at the beginning. But the central action, placing the head in the basil pot, is anything but simple. It leads us to marvel at the gesture and to wonder what it might mean.

POINT OF VIEW.   The point of view—the control of the story by its teller—is detached. Filomena, the narrator or storyteller, does not interject her evaluation of the story into its telling.

IRONY AND TONE.   The story is told straightforwardly, without irony, or the sense that we are to treat the action as other than what it seems to be, and its tone, the author's attitude toward the subject, seems sincere, however sad the tale itself may be.

Using Interpretive Strategies

Although the individual elements of this story are not extensively developed, and although characterization and plot are limited, the interpretive opportunities are rich and various.

A close reading would concentrate on images that recur in the story, such as the burial of Lorenzo. First, his love for Lisabetta is "buried" because Lisabetta cannot tell her brothers of her love. She loves Lorenzo in secret. Yet her secret is "uncovered." Once Lorenzo is killed and his corpse secretly buried, his ghost "uncovers" the truth about his disappearance. After Lisabetta discovers Lorenzo's body, she gives his head a proper "burial" in a pot of basil. The herb basil has been an emblem of love since ancient times, so Lisabetta is burying her love in several senses. The word *basil* (as an unabridged dictionary tells us) is derived from *basileus,* which means both king and serpent. The serpent is a phallic emblem (also medicinal), perhaps implying Lisabetta's loss of virginity. Finally, taking Lorenzo from her a second time, the brothers bury not only Lisabetta's love (and her emotional life) but kill her from grief in the process. The brothers had buried Lisabetta earlier by not permitting her to marry "for some reason or other." Burial becomes a metaphor for control.

A close reading in terms of character would find this story rich with significance, especially since Lisabetta suffered from a nervous disorder that caused her brothers to express "their concern at the decline in her good looks and the way in which her eyes appeared to have sunk into their sockets." She also behaved in a compulsive fashion when she "constantly followed this same routine" and "attracted the attention of her neighbors." On the one hand, the brothers try to repress Lisabetta's libido, her natural sexual instincts. On the other hand, potting the head of her lover may be an emblem of Lisabetta's own madness. Her sexuality has been repressed once more, and she has sublimated it (given it expression) into the watering and tending of the pot of basil, whose growth now depends on her tears. Her joy is converted into grief by her brothers' repression and there is no healthy outlet that will bring her back to sanity.

The brothers themselves are perverse. They seem to have no love at all in their lives. Even their love for Lisabetta is totally absent. The one brother who speaks to her behaves threateningly, like a vicious tyrant. They are engaged in some form of banking or trade and seem to have sublimated their emotions into a worship of money and position. Their "reputation" takes precedence over any sensitive regard for their sister. They have become sadistic and vicious.

Boccaccio anticipated the reader response approach. When she begins the story, Filomena is "quite overcome with compassion" from hearing the story preceding hers. She suspects that her story might "prove to be no less touching." The three brothers behave like the older sisters of Cinderella. They control Lisabetta and seem unwilling to permit her to have her own life. Such a situation demands an emotional response, especially from those young and in love. Furthermore, the story itself is filled with emotion. Lisabetta cries so much over the loss of Lorenzo that "her weeping never ceased until the whole of the basil was wet with her tears." The story centers on the grief of its main character, who "eventually cried herself to death." However, you may also respond to another emotion: the sense of injustice that you may feel for the fact that the brothers never pay for their terrible behavior. For some readers, that may translate into outrage. Boccaccio, by telling the story matter-of-factly, permits our emotions to take their own shape.

Feminist critics might see in this story an emblem of the brutal dispossession of women. The brothers represent the establishment that exploits women by forcing them into marriages of family or political convenience. The father is dead, but the responsibility for the family falls not on Lisabetta's shoulders but on those of her brothers, who clearly dominate her in every way. They virtually ignore her presence until she threatens their reputation. Her reputation, which is also at stake, is significant only insofar as it might receive a "stain" that would reflect badly on them.

Even Lorenzo falls short in living up to a position of responsibility. He "planned and directed all [the brothers'] operations," yet he seduced her with no mention of the possibility of marriage—which would have saved her honor—nor with any thought of declaring himself to her brothers, which would have preserved the possibility of a totally honorable conclusion. Despite his love for her, Lorenzo profits from her lack of power and her suppression as a woman. Lisabetta's powerlessness is pathetically represented by her quiet grief over the potted head of her beloved. She cannot complain to her brothers; "she locked herself in and cried bitterly." Her grief is the grief of all women dominated by men whose values are determined by family reputation and who regard women as inferior.

In sympathy with the feminist critic, the political-economic or Marxist critic will see Lisabetta as an economic counter. She must marry in a way that enhances the economic status of the family organization. The family itself is identified in terms of "their trading establishment," and the brothers—not Lisabetta—were "merchants who had been left very rich after the death of their father." Money is at the core of the brothers' behavior. Lorenzo may run the business, but he is a Pisan who, apart from being an outsider, is a mere employee, someone from a lower class than Lisabetta. The class distinction keeps Lorenzo from declaring his love in the open. It forces him to sneak behind the backs of the brothers. Although he is good enough to work for them and even, in the manner of servants, to live in their huge household, he is not good enough to merit Lisabetta's hand. The Marxist critic could justifiably see this as a story rooted deep in the class struggle of an emerging merchant-dominated Renaissance Italy. The dominant values are those of the emerging European middle class, the bourgeoisie for whom appearances and "what the neighbors think" are of great importance.

The historicist might begin by examining Italian marriage documents from the fourteenth century to uncover the obligations of one spouse to another at that time. The historicist might also be interested in studying documents of indenture—which fix the responsibilities of young people working for established businesses. It is entirely possible that Lorenzo is indentured to the brothers, in which case he would not have been free either to marry Lisabetta or to sleep with her even if he intended to marry her in the future. In the absence of documents, the historicist would learn something about the history of fourteenth-century Italy to discover as much as possible about the relative position of merchants. Recent studies of everyday life can shed light on what Lisabetta's expectations might have been, or what Lorenzo's opportunities may have been. If Lorenzo is an opportunist—someone who is using Lisabetta for his own purposes to advance his position—then the historical situation could shed light on the nature of his motivations. Reconstructing historical circumstances could be appropriate for you if you have studied Italian history.

CLOSE READING: BEGINNING WITH QUESTIONS

The following story by the Quebec writer Suzanne Jacob shows how much can be accomplished in a page or so. Jacob's stories, characteristically short and intense, are emblems of modern ritual and therefore sometimes mysterious. But once they begin to come clear, they show themselves as full, satisfying, and pleasing. "Two Cents," published in 1989, is recognizably contemporary, but certain aspects are also primeval—referring us to our prehistory—and therefore jarring.

SUZANNE JACOB   (b. 1943)

Two Cents _____ *1989*

Translated by Susanna Finnell

They understood each other. There would be no crying. No tears. There would be no trial, no accounting. Neither one brought accusations: they understood each other.

They invited the few friends with whom they had shared their lives for nine years. The man oiled the two rifles, the woman inspected the photo and chose the place. They started walking.

Drizzle settled softly on the event. Everyone knew Mount Baldy. Everyone knew the Piperock, they knew where to go. As they got closer, their hair seemed to turn a little greyer. Very far away, a train whistled. Someone suggested that it would have been better to have gone in the direction of Envy River. The speaker stumbled over a stump and forgot his suggestion. Everyone gathered dead branches found on the way. That was part of the agreement. The man passed around the flask filled with liquor. No one refused a drink.

They knew the rites and understood the ceremony. They had been initiated to the songs of the monks at a very early age. They built up the fire until it reached new growth on the pine branches. The woman was crouching. The rifle between her legs looked like a soft old animal. As always, the man stood sideways, breathing. This assured the others that he was absent despite appearances.

When the moment came to present the offerings, the friends broke into an old   5
song. Now you could see the dove in its white cage. Everyone was thrilled. The cage was put down near the fire and everyone was hypnotized by the flames. Stupid little things that surfaced in their minds, very ordinary things, resolved themselves, melting away in the heat. They chose not to remember anything, none of the innumerable ecstasies, none of the thresholds crossed. Nothing, by choice they were remembering nothing. In the middle of their forest, they consented absolutely to the evidence of the present.

The man and the woman aimed their rifles. They trusted each other. There was only one bullet and there was no way of knowing which weapon fired the shot that split the fog, the cage and the bird with the necklace. No one ever tried to figure it out.

They went their separate ways. They met children who were running yelling: "We heard shooting!"

They got back to their downtown offices and continued to read the same newspapers without being moved.

Much later, the man met the woman in a tobacco shop. She said she was two cents short for her pack of Camels. The man had them.

Brief as it is, "Two Cents" is a subtle story. It has a clear plot and identifiable but nameless characters. The action of the story is direct and uncomplicated, but nothing explicit seems to emerge from it. The setting is perhaps as rich in detail as any aspect of the story, but it, too, is purposely made imprecise, especially since the time of the action is uncertain.

A close reading begins with some important questions:

- What actually happens in the story?
- Why does the story focus on one woman and one man?
- What is implied by the contrast between the woodsy setting of "Piperock" and the "downtown offices" to which people return?
- The story calls the action a "ritual." What kind of ritual could it be?
- Is the reference to the initiation and the "songs of the monks" a clue to the ritual?
- The dove, an emblem of peace, must be a symbol here. But of what?
- Why is it important that neither the man nor the woman knows which bullet kills the dove? And why does no one ever ask?

• Does the fact that we are told at the beginning, "There would be no trial, no accounting" imply that the action of the story is questionable or possibly outside the normal moral boundaries of these people?

The following close reading answers the questions raised above. It could become the basis of a complete interpretation by demonstrating how the details cohere to produce a sense of unity and how they are all connected significantly to one another. However, this close reading is essentially unfinished to serve as the beginning of an interpretation of the story.

This seems to be a story of an infrequently performed ritual centering on a man and woman who appear to act for the community. By focusing on one man and one woman, the story implies that the ritual is shared equally by both genders. They are both given guns, and in the end they both aim and fire at a dove wearing a symbolic necklace. The necklace implies it is a valued and special bird, and since this is a frequently repeated ritual ("They knew the rites and understood the ceremony"), the dove must be a sacrifice. The ritual takes place in the woods, implying that it is primitive, perhaps seen as related to nature. The closeness of the man and woman in the woods is contrasted by their distance from one another in "downtown," where their only interaction occurs when the man helps the woman out when she is two cents short for her pack of Camels.

This ritual must have religious overtones: "the moment came to present the offerings." Religious sacrifices of "offerings" are common enough in primitive tribes and in the Bible. The ritual in the story is fully understood, performed regularly but not frequently, and involves religious "songs of the monks," which they learned "at a very early age" when they were "initiated." While it is happening all they think about are the "stupid little things that surfaced in their minds." "They consented absolutely to the evidence of the present." Because this is a religious event, they will not have to worry about a "trial" even if they are taking the life of an innocent bird. Since they do not know exactly who killed the bird, it is impossible to single out one of them for trial anyway. If both were prosecuted, one innocent person would be found guilty, making trial impossible even if this were not a familiar religious ritual.

The dove may be a symbol of peace or innocence. It must die for the good of the order of people. Yet no one must be responsible for its death because then the act would be individual rather than collective. All the people who gather at Piperock have an investment in the action of the man and the woman. They act not just for themselves but for the community.

After the ritual, no one thinks much about it. "They went their separate ways. . . . They got back to their downtown offices and continued to read the same newspapers without being moved." So whatever the ritual is, once it is performed it does not weigh on the minds of the man and the woman. They hardly keep the memory of meeting by the pine fire where everyone was "hypnotized by the flames."

Back in the larger community the man and woman have no contact with each other. They apparently go about their work; their only important contact was for the purposes of enacting the ritual. In the community of "downtown offices" they meet only in a tobacco shop—an emblem of petty vice—where the woman smokes a rather powerful cigarette: Camels. The two cents the man helps her out with seems to suggest the depth of his "responsibility" to her outside the setting of ritual sacrifice.

If the dove is a symbol for Christ—the dove is usually the sign of the third person of the Trinity—then the necklace may be a kind of rosary. The ritual might stand for a version of the mass—although a mockery of it—and the essential indifference of the people in their offices after the ritual reveals the separateness of the people from their religious beliefs. As the story implies, they do nothing different when participating in a religious ritual. They read the same papers but do nothing. They are unmoved and content to smoke their Camels. Their faith seems no more important than the "two cents" of the final lines.

MEANING: IMPLIED AND EXPLICIT

Stories such as "Two Cents" imply their meaning rather than state it. However, **fables** (stories using animals with recognizable human qualities), such as those by Aesop or La Fontaine, usually end with a moral tag that contains the meaning of the fable just in case you did not get it.

AESOP (c. 6th century B.C.)

The Rooster and the Precious Gem _____

Jacobus recension from Caxton

As a rooster was searching for seeds and corn in his dunghill one day, he uncovered a precious glittering gem and looked at it startled. "Aha! You are a fair and precious gem lying here in the filth, glittering like the sun. If only a woman who desires such gems were here to find you, she should pick you up and place you on her finger and show you all about to the great acclaim of the multitude of ladies. But, alas! It is I who have found you, and you must know that I, a rooster, have nothing to do with such things as precious gems. I cannot do you any good, and there is certainly no good you can do for me." This fable, said Aesop to those who will read his book, intends you to understand the rooster is like a fool who has no intelligence, no wisdom because, like the rooster who sees a precious gem and can make no use of it, the fool will read this precious book and have no understanding of it.

At first you might think that having the meaning stated outright is better than having it implied. But in fact the opposite is true. If a short story were like a fable of Aesop, with a moral, then it would be like a disposable flashlight. You could use it, but it would not last. Good short stories last. Reread the fable above and note that once you get the message there is no need to go back over it again.

A fable of Aesop is useful for teaching morals to children. All children will get the same message: end of interpretation. However, with a good short story no two people will get precisely the same message: beginning of interpretation.

The story whose meaning is stated outright will not hold your interest long enough for you to read it twice. The more the meaning is implied, the more essential is your own act of interpretation. What, for example, is the meaning of "The Pot of Basil"? If you expect meaning to be reducible to a moral tag, you may find it difficult to accept the answer that the meaning of the story is in your interpretation. Just as you realize your interpretation is likely to account for only part of the meaning of the story, so you realize that the meaning of a successful story is virtually limitless.

The meaning of a short story is inherent in your interpretation, my interpretation, and those of all its readers. There is no ideal collective interpretation that then represents its real meaning. Instead, there are many separable interpretations that may group together to produce what Stanley Fish has called "communities of interpretation." One community of interpreters may think, for example, that "Two Cents" concerns a quasi-religious ritual that, performed mindlessly, shows us how detached people are from their religious roots. Another community of interpreters may think that it shows that religious practice hides primitive acts of violence, sublimating them so they do not interfere with business in the "downtown offices." Yet another community of interpreters will see the story as having nothing to do with religion at all. Although they may seem to start in much the same place and apply much the same methods, and although they may constitute an interpretive community, careful readers may differ sharply. In interpretation there is always room for disagreement.

4

BEGINNING
WITH CLOSE READING

Your first reading of William Faulkner's "A Rose for Emily" should be slow and primarily for enjoyment. During your second reading, underline passages that reveal some of the important details and ideas in the story. Every reader will underline different passages, but the purpose of underlining is to keep track of ideas you think are important. You may want to consider identifying the important elements in the story and establishing what their function may be.

When you read "A Rose for Emily" the second time, note the town's opinions of Miss Emily and her family, her father's role in her life, and her environment. Keep track of details of point of view, important themes, and significant characters. Everything you notice is important. You may compare your observations with the sample close reading and interpretations that follow.

WILLIAM FAULKNER (1897–1962)

William Faulkner, who won the Nobel Prize for literature in 1950, worked on a newspaper in New Orleans after World War I but soon returned to his native Oxford, Mississippi, where he spent most of his life writing. He created Yoknapatawpha, an imaginary Mississippi county, for the setting of most of his stories. Colonel Sartoris, mentioned in "A Rose for Emily," figures in several stories and novels set in Yoknapatawpha, and lives through the post–civil war era, a period of American history that fascinated Faulkner. Faulkner's most important books are The Sound and the Fury *(1929),* As I Lay Dying *(1930),* Sanctuary *(1931),* Light in August *(1932),* Absalom, Absalom! *(1936), and* The Hamlet *(1940). His short stories are usually direct and less complex than his novels, but they are also informed by the history of the American South.*

A Rose for Emily _____ *1924*

I

When Miss Emily Grierson died, our whole town went to her funeral: the men through a sort of respectful affection for a fallen monument, the women mostly out of curiosity to see the inside of her house, which no one save an old manservant—a combined gardener and cook—had seen in at least ten years.

It was a big, squarish frame house that had once been white, decorated with cupolas and spires and scrolled balconies in the heavily lightsome style of the seventies, set on what had once been our most select street. But garages and cotton gins had encroached and obliterated even the august names of that neighborhood; only Miss Emily's house was left, lifting its stubborn and coquettish decay above the cotton wagons and the gasoline pumps—an eyesore among eyesores. And now Miss Emily had gone to join the representatives of those august names where they lay in the cedar-bemused cemetery among the ranked and anonymous graves of Union and Confederate soldiers who fell at the battle of Jefferson.

Alive, Miss Emily had been a tradition, a duty, and a care; a sort of hereditary obligation upon the town, dating from that day in 1894 when Colonel Sartoris, the mayor—he who fathered the edict that no Negro woman should appear on the streets without an apron—remitted her taxes, the dispensation dating from the death of her father on into perpetuity. Not that Miss Emily would have accepted charity. Colonel Sartoris invented an involved tale to the effect that Miss Emily's father had loaned money to the town, which the town, as a matter of business, preferred this way of repaying. Only a man of Colonel Sartoris' generation and thought could have invented it, and only a woman could have believed it.

When the next generation, with its more modern ideas, became mayors and aldermen, this arrangement created some little dissatisfaction. On the first of the year they mailed her a tax notice. February came, and there was no reply. They wrote her a formal letter, asking her to call at the sheriff's office at her convenience. A week later the mayor wrote her himself, offering to call or to send his car for her, and received in reply a note on paper of an archaic shape, in a thin, flowing calligraphy in faded ink, to the effect that she no longer went out at all. The tax notice was also enclosed, without comment.

They called a special meeting of the Board of Aldermen. A deputation waited upon her, knocked at the door through which no visitor had passed since she ceased giving china-painting lessons eight or ten years earlier. They were admitted by the old Negro into a dim hall from which a stairway mounted into still more shadow. It smelled of dust and disuse—a close, dank smell. The Negro led them into the parlor. It was furnished in heavy, leather-covered furniture. When the Negro opened the blinds of one window, they could see that the leather was cracked; and when they sat down, a faint dust rose sluggishly about their thighs, spinning with slow motes in the single sun-ray. On a tarnished gilt easel before the fireplace stood a crayon portrait of Miss Emily's father.

They rose when she entered—a small, fat woman in black, with a thin gold chain descending to her waist and vanishing into her belt, leaning on an ebony cane with a tarnished gold head. Her skeleton was small and spare; perhaps that was why what would have been merely plumpness in another was obesity in her. She looked bloated, like a body long submerged in motionless water, and of that pallid hue. Her eyes, lost in the fatty ridges of her face, looked like two small pieces of coal pressed into a lump of dough as they moved from one face to another while the visitors stated their errand.

5

She did not ask them to sit. She just stood in the door and listened quietly until the spokesman came to a stumbling halt. Then they could hear the invisible watch ticking at the end of the gold chain.

Her voice was dry and cold. "I have no taxes in Jefferson. Colonel Sartoris explained it to me. Perhaps one of you can gain access to the city records and satisfy yourselves."

"But we have. We are the city authorities, Miss Emily. Didn't you get a notice from the sheriff, signed by him?"

"I received a paper, yes," Miss Emily said. "Perhaps he considers himself the sheriff . . . I have no taxes in Jefferson." 10

"But there is nothing on the books to show that, you see. We must go by the—"

"See Colonel Sartoris. I have no taxes in Jefferson."

"But, Miss Emily—"

"See Colonel Sartoris." (Colonel Sartoris had been dead almost ten years.) "I have no taxes in Jefferson. Tobe!" The Negro appeared. "Show these gentlemen out."

II

So she vanquished them, horse and foot, just as she had vanquished their fathers thirty 15 years before about the smell. That was two years after her father's death and a short time after her sweetheart—the one we believed would marry her—had deserted her. After her father's death she went out very little; after her sweetheart went away, people hardly saw her at all. A few of the ladies had the temerity to call, but were not received, and the only sign of life about the place was the Negro man—a young man then—going in and out with a market basket.

"Just as if a man—any man—could keep a kitchen properly," the ladies said; so they were not surprised when the smell developed. It was another link between the gross, teeming world and the high and mighty Griersons.

A neighbor, a woman, complained to the mayor, Judge Stevens, eighty years old.

"But what will you have me do about it, madam?" he said.

"Why, send her word to stop it," the woman said. "Isn't there a law?"

"I'm sure that won't be necessary," Judge Stevens said. "It's probably just a snake 20 or a rat that nigger of hers killed in the yard. I'll speak to him about it."

The next day he received two more complaints, one from a man who came in diffident deprecation. "We really must do something about it, Judge. I'd be the last one in the world to bother Miss Emily, but we've got to do something." That night the Board of Aldermen met—three graybeards and one younger man, a member of the rising generation.

"It's simple enough," he said. "Send her word to have her place cleaned up. Give her a certain time to do it in, and if she don't. . . ."

"Dammit, sir," Judge Stevens said, "will you accuse a lady to her face of smelling bad?"

So the next night, after midnight, four men crossed Miss Emily's lawn and slunk about the house like burglars, sniffing along the base of the brickwork and at the cellar openings while one of them performed a regular sowing motion with his hand out of a sack slung from his shoulder. They broke open the cellar door and sprinkled lime there, and in all the outbuildings. As they recrossed the lawn, a window that had been dark was lighted and Miss Emily sat in it, the light behind her, and her upright torso motionless as that of an idol. They crept quietly across the lawn and into the shadow of the locusts that lined the street. After a week or two the smell went away.

That was when people had begun to feel really sorry for her. People in our town, 25 remembering how old lady Wyatt, her great-aunt, had gone completely crazy at last, believed that the Griersons held themselves a little too high for what they really were. None of the young men were quite good enough to Miss Emily and such. We had long thought of them as a tableau; Miss Emily a slender figure in white in the background, her father a spraddled silhouette in the foreground, his back to her and clutching a horsewhip, the two of them framed by the back-flung front door. So when she got to be thirty and was still single, we were not pleased exactly, but vindicated; even with insanity in the family she wouldn't have turned down all of her chances if they had really materialized.

When her father died, it got about that the house was all that was left to her; and in a way, people were glad. At last they could pity Miss Emily. Being left alone, and a pauper, she had become humanized. Now she too would know the old thrill and the old despair of a penny more or less.

The day after his death all the ladies prepared to call at the house and offer condolence and aid, as is our custom. Miss Emily met them at the door, dressed as usual and with no trace of grief on her face. She told them that her father was not dead. She did that for three days, with the ministers calling on her, and the doctors, trying to persuade her to let them dispose of the body. Just as they were about to resort to law and force, she broke down, and they buried her father quickly.

We did not say she was crazy then. We believed she had to do that. We remembered all the young men her father had driven away, and we knew that with nothing left, she would have to cling to that which had robbed her, as people will.

III

She was sick for a long time. When we saw her again, her hair was cut short, making her look like a girl, with a vague resemblance to those angels in colored church windows— sort of tragic and serene.

The town had just let the contracts for paving the sidewalks, and in the summer 30 after her father's death they began the work. The construction company came with niggers and mules and machinery, and a foreman named Homer Barron, a Yankee—a big, dark, ready man, with a big voice and eyes lighter than his face. The little boys would follow in groups to hear him cuss the niggers, and the niggers singing in time to the rise and fall of picks. Pretty soon he knew everybody in town. Whenever you heard a lot of laughing anywhere about the square, Homer Barron would be in the center of the group. Presently we began to see him and Miss Emily on Sunday afternoons driving in the yellow-wheeled buggy and the matched team of bays from the livery stable.

At first we were glad that Miss Emily would have an interest, because the ladies all said, "Of course a Grierson would not think seriously of a Northerner, a day laborer." But there were still others, older people, who said that even grief could not cause a real lady to forget *noblesse oblige*°—without calling it *noblesse oblige*. They just said, "Poor Emily. Her kinsfolk should come to her." She had some kin in Alabama; but years ago her father had fallen out with them over the estate of old lady Wyatt, the crazy woman, and there was no communication between the two families. They had not even been represented at the funeral.

noblesse oblige: the obligations of the "upper classes" to look after the poor, now regarded as evidence of snobbery

And as soon as the old people said, "Poor Emily," the whispering began. "Do you suppose it's really so?" they said to one another. "Of course it is. What else could. . . ." This behind their hands; rustling of craned silk and satin behind jalousies closed upon the sun of Sunday afternoon as the thin, swift clop-clop-clop of the matched team passed: "Poor Emily."

She carried her head high enough—even when we believed that she was fallen. It was as if she demanded more than ever the recognition of her dignity as the last Grierson; as if it had wanted that touch of earthiness to reaffirm her imperviousness. Like when she bought the rat poison, the arsenic. That was over a year after they had begun to say "Poor Emily," and while the two female cousins were visiting her.

"I want some poison," she said to the druggist. She was over thirty then, still a slight woman, though thinner than usual, with cold, haughty black eyes in a face the flesh of which was strained across the temples and about the eye-sockets as you imagine a lighthouse-keeper's face ought to look. "I want some poison," she said.

"Yes, Miss Emily. What kind? For rats and such? I'd recom—"   35

"I want the best you have. I don't care what kind."

The druggist named several. "They'll kill anything up to an elephant. But what you want is—"

"Arsenic," Miss Emily said. "Is that a good one?"

"Is . . . arsenic? Yes, ma'am. But what you want—"

"I want arsenic."   40

The druggist looked down at her. She looked back at him, erect, her face like a strained flag. "Why, of course," the druggist said. "If that's what you want. But the law requires you to tell what you are going to use it for."

Miss Emily just stared at him, her head tilted back in order to look him eye for eye, until he looked away and went and got the arsenic and wrapped it up. The Negro delivery boy brought her the package; the druggist didn't come back. When she opened the package at home there was written on the box, under the skull and bones: "For rats."

IV

So the next day we all said, "She will kill herself"; and we said it would be the best thing. When she had first begun to be seen with Homer Barron, we had said, "She will marry him." Then we said, "She will persuade him yet," because Homer himself had remarked—he liked men, and it was known that he drank with the younger men in the Elks' Club—that he was not a marrying man. Later we said, "Poor Emily" behind the jalousies as they passed on Sunday afternoon in the glittering buggy, Miss Emily with her head high and Homer Barron with his hat cocked and a cigar in his teeth, reins and whip in a yellow glove.

Then some of the ladies began to say that it was a disgrace to the town and a bad example to the young people. The men did not want to interfere, but at last the ladies forced the Baptist minister—Miss Emily's people were Episcopal—to call upon her. He would never divulge what happened during that interview, but he refused to go back again. The next Sunday they again drove about the streets, and the following day the minister's wife wrote to Miss Emily's relations in Alabama.

So she had blood-kin under her roof again and we sat back to watch developments. At first nothing happened. Then we were sure that they were to be married. We learned that Miss Emily had been to the jeweler's and ordered a man's toilet set in   45 silver, with the letters H. B. on each piece. Two days later we learned that she had bought a complete outfit of men's clothing, including a nightshirt, and we said, "They are married." We were really glad. We were glad because the two female cousins were even more Grierson than Miss Emily had ever been.

So we were not surprised when Homer Barron—the streets had been finished some time since—was gone. We were a little disappointed that there was not a public blowing-off, but we believed that he had gone on to prepare for Miss Emily's coming, or to give her a chance to get rid of the cousins. (By that time it was a cabal, and we were all Miss Emily's allies to help circumvent the cousins.) Sure enough, after another week they departed. And, as we had expected all along, within three days Homer Barron was back in town. A neighbor saw the Negro man admit him at the kitchen door at dusk one evening.

And that was the last we saw of Homer Barron. And of Miss Emily for some time. The Negro man went in and out with the market basket, but the front door remained closed. Now and then we would see her at a window for a moment, as the men did that night when they sprinkled the lime, but for almost six months she did not appear on the streets. Then we knew that this was to be expected too; as if that quality of her father which had thwarted her woman's life so many times had been too virulent and too furious to die.

When we next saw Miss Emily, she had grown fat and her hair was turning gray. During the next few years it grew grayer and grayer until it attained an even pepper-and-salt iron-gray, when it ceased turning. Up to the day of her death at seventy-four it was still that vigorous iron-gray, like the hair of an active man.

From that time on her front door remained closed, save for a period of six or seven years, when she was about forty, during which she gave lessons in china-painting. She fitted up a studio in one of the downstairs rooms, where the daughters and granddaughters of Colonel Sartoris' contemporaries were sent to her with the same regularity and in the same spirit that they were sent to church on Sundays with a twenty-five cent piece for the collection plate. Meanwhile her taxes had been remitted.

Then the newer generation became the backbone and the spirit of the town, and the painting pupils grew up and fell away and did not send their children to her with boxes of color and tedious brushes and pictures cut from the ladies' magazines. The front door closed upon the last one and remained closed for good. When the town got free postal delivery, Miss Emily alone refused to let them fasten the metal numbers above her door and attach a mailbox to it. She would not listen to them.

Daily, monthly, yearly we watched the Negro grow grayer and more stooped, going in and out with the market basket. Each December we sent her a tax notice, which would be returned by the post office a week later, unclaimed. Now and then we would see her in one of the downstairs windows—she had evidently shut up the top floor of the house—like the carven torso of an idol in a niche, looking or not looking at us, we could never tell which. Thus she passed from generation to generation—dear, inescapable, impervious, tranquil, and perverse.

And so she died. Fell ill in the house filled with dust and shadows, with only a doddering Negro man to wait on her. We did not even know she was sick; we had long since given up trying to get any information from the Negro. He talked to no one, probably not even to her, for his voice had grown harsh and rusty, as if from disuse.

She died in one of the downstairs rooms, in a heavy walnut bed with a curtain, her gray head propped on a pillow yellow and moldy with age and lack of sunlight.

50

V

The Negro met the first of the ladies at the front door and let them in, with their hushed, sibilant voices and their quick, curious glances, and then he disappeared. He walked right through the house and out the back and was not seen again.

The two female cousins came at once. They held the funeral on the second day, with the town coming to look at Miss Emily beneath a mass of bought flowers, with the crayon face of her father musing profoundly above the bier and the ladies sibilant and macabre; and the very old men—some in their brushed Confederate uniforms—on the porch and the lawn, talking of Miss Emily as if she had been a contemporary of theirs, believing that they had danced with her and courted her perhaps, confusing time with its mathematical progression, as the old do, to whom all the past is not a diminishing road but, instead, a huge meadow which no winter ever quite touches, divided from them now by the narrow bottle-neck of the most recent decade of years. 55

Already we knew that there was one room in that region above stairs which no one had seen in forty years, and which would have to be forced. They waited until Miss Emily was decently in the ground before they opened it.

The violence of breaking down the door seemed to fill this room with pervading dust. A thin, acrid pall as of the tomb seemed to lie everywhere upon this room decked and furnished as for a bridal: upon the valence curtains of faded rose color, upon the rose-shaded lights, upon the dressing table, upon the delicate array of crystal and the man's toilet things backed with tarnished silver, silver so tarnished that the monogram was obscured. Among them lay a collar and tie, as if they had just been removed, which, lifted, left upon the surface a pale crescent in the dust. Upon a chair hung the suit, carefully folded; beneath it the two mute shoes and the discarded socks.

The man himself lay in the bed.

For a long while we just stood there, looking down at the profound and fleshless grin. The body had apparently once lain in the attitude of an embrace, but now the long sleep that outlasts love, that conquers even the grimace of love, had cuckolded him. What was left of him, rotted beneath what was left of the nightshirt, had become inextricable from the bed in which he lay; and upon him and upon the pillow beside him lay that even coating of the patient and biding dust.

Then we noticed that in the second pillow was the indentation of a head. One of us lifted something from it, and leaning forward, that faint and invisible dust dry and acrid in the nostrils, we saw a long strand of iron-gray hair. 60

A STUDENT INTERPRETATION

Close-reading fiction usually involves taking note of details that may be of significance to an interpretation. Many such details show up in underlining, and making a list of important details helps in the first stages of interpreting a story.

Important Details in "A Rose for Emily"

The whole town went to Miss Emily's funeral
    No one had seen the inside of the house for ten years--except "the old Negro"

Miss Emily lived in a run-down section, but her house had once been nice

When she was alive, she was a "hereditary obligation upon the town"

Colonel Sartoris "remitted her taxes" in a way that did not seem to be charity

She was "a small, fat woman in black"--she was "bloated" as if "submerged"

When the next generation came to explain the taxes she told them to see Colonel Sartoris

Emily had dealt with the authorities before about "the smell" after her lover had "deserted her"

City officials spread lime to counter the smell, which went away in about a week

People felt sorry for Miss Emily; they also thought the Griersons were a little too high and mighty

There was insanity in the family

No man was good enough for her; her father stood in the door with a horsewhip

For three days she refused to believe her father was dead, then she "relented" and "they buried her father quickly"

People remembered "all the young men her father had driven away"

She was sick for a long time

Homer Barron was a Yankee foreman of a construction company who would "cuss the niggers" working for him building streets

People thought Miss Emily was too good for a Yankee like Barron

Miss Emily and Homer Barron were seen together and caused some talk

She bought poison without having to explain what it was for

People thought she would kill herself

Homer had remarked "that he was not a marrying man"

Two cousins were called in by the town to get her to marry Homer

Miss Emily bought Homer "a man's toilet set in silver, with the letters H. B." engraved on them, apparently anticipating marriage

Homer Barron then disappeared; no one was surprised

When he came back to the house, Homer disappeared entirely

For six months Miss Emily did not appear on the streets

People thought that the "quality of her father which had thwarted her woman's life so many times had been too virulent and too furious to die"

Over the years her hair had become iron-gray

For a period of six years she gave china-painting lessons

"She passed from generation to generation--dear, inescapable, impervious, tranquil, and perverse"

When she died no one knew she had been sick

The Negro let the ladies in the house, then disappeared out the back never to be seen again

The two cousins appeared; people knew there was one room in the house that was locked for forty years and would "have to be forced"

When they broke the door in the room was like a "tomb"

The room was "furnished as for a bridal"; the toilet set was there, tarnished

Homer Barron's body "in the attitude of an embrace" lay on the bed

A "long strand of iron-gray hair" lay on the pillow beside the body

Responses for an Interpretation

The following entries from a response journal were written after compiling the list of details above.

> Oct. 14. In some ways this is a creepy story. Miss Emily is some kind of pillar of the community, or her family is. But the house is decaying and there's dust everywhere. Her father is a problem. Nobody is good enough for her to marry, so he keeps all the men away. What's the problem? Why is she so tied down? I wouldn't let my father do that to me. But he wouldn't try, so there's a big difference.
>
> Oct. 17. I reread the story. The whole town protects Miss Emily. I think that's a key to the story. They know she can't pay her taxes, but they cook up a scheme so she doesn't have to. When the new people come in as "aldermen" she stands them down, a lot like her father would have. She's got iron-gray hair, but there's some iron in her, too. She's got enough strength to keep the town in line, but she can't get Homer Barron. He's not the kind of man her father would have liked. In fact, he's supposed to be below her in society. Some people think that way today, but it seems weird to me. Then there is the ending. It's like out of a horror movie. This corpse is on the bed, and she has been lying next to it. Wow. It's creepy.
>
> Oct. 18. I wonder if she killed her father, too. The story doesn't say, but she pretended he wasn't dead. She must have pretended Homer Barron wasn't dead, too. Or could she just be totally crazy? The way she got the poison--doesn't seem like someone crazy. She seems to just want Homer to stick around. She wasn't going to lose him.

After keeping a response journal, this writer tried some freewriting, concentrating on the question of how the town regarded the Grierson family.

Freewriting on "A Rose for Emily"

> Some people thought that the Griersons were too "high and mighty" in the way they thought about themselves. They looked down on people. But the town in the old days thought they were pretty important. Colonel Sartoris protected Miss Emily--even lied to her to save her the embarrassment of not being able to pay her taxes. She inherited almost nothing from her father, just the house. So she had no real status at all. Because she is so strong, she's able to go on as if she really did have some kind of important position. But she can't even hold on to a loud day laborer like Homer. He seemed interested, but he wasn't the marrying type. Okay. So the point is she does what she has to do to survive, at least in her own mind. She wanted to get married, and in a weird way she did. People in the town must have known something was wrong when she got poison and there was that smell after Homer disappeared. How come they didn't investigate? She couldn't get away with that today.

By now, the writer saw a connection between the way the town treated Miss Emily and the decay that attacked her family. She began to think that the story was symbolic, and therefore she prepared to write a critical interpretation emphasizing the symbolic meaning of Miss Emily to the people of Jefferson. The writer wrote some thoughts down in search of a thesis that would guide the entire essay, but she also hoped that some of the paragraphs of the finished essay would develop from some of these statements.

> Miss Emily is probably a symbol for the South. In a way, she represents the South's honor because she kept herself away from committing to change. The town of Jefferson took a special interest in Miss Emily because her family was distinguished in its history. When she was alive, she had been "a tradition, a duty, a care." The town tried its best to preserve her dignity because in a way it was preserving its own dignity at the same time. What they did not seem to see--and neither did she--is that the times were changing.
>
> Miss Emily was the last member of the Grierson family. She had no children because her father did not think there was anyone good enough for her to marry. As a result, the entire family came down to two distant cousins and this one "small, fat woman."
>
> The neighborhood decayed over the years until what was once a nice area was run down and her house was "an eyesore among eyesores." Miss Emily never went out, so she did not notice.
>
> Miss Emily must have been frustrated all her life, with her father keeping the men away, and with her inability to keep hold of Homer Barron. The only man in her life at the end was the old Negro who cooked for her. He disappeared as soon as she died, almost as if her death had released him.

With this much material, the writer decided to make an outline and then write an interpretation.

Outline

"Why Jefferson Protected Miss Emily"

I.   How the town felt about the Griersons
    A.   What they thought of her father
    B.   How they thought about her
        1.   Why they thought she was high and mighty
II.   Miss Emily as a symbol of the South in decline
    A.   Why she was a tradition and duty for the town
    B.   The feelings of the gossips in town
    C.   The decay of the house and neighborhood
    D.   The Negro servant
III.   What Homer Barron meant to Miss Emily
    A.   His character
        1.   His social status
        2.   What he was like
    B.   Her frustration
IV.   The marriage of Emily and Homer
    A.   The bridal "tomb"

A Sample Interpretation of "A Rose for Emily"   Warther 1

Susan Warther
English 109
Paper 3
Mr. Jacobus

Why Jefferson Protected Miss Emily: The "Fallen Monument"

Jefferson protected Miss Emily because she was a symbol for the whole town. She was more than just a person in Jefferson. She was an institution. When she died "our whole town went to her funeral." Most old women who die alone have almost no one at their funeral, so Faulkner is telling us that Miss Emily was very special. The men in town went to her funeral because she was like "a fallen monument," but the women went because they were curious about seeing the "inside of her house."

In the 1890s the town still regarded the family highly. Emily's father was a figure people remembered. He stood in the "back-flung front door" with a whip in his hand as a kind of signal to people to watch out. The town was curious about Emily because, even though there was insanity in the family, they expected she would get married. She might have if her father had not been so mean to her suitors. He kept up appearances as if they were wealthy, even when he knew they were poor. When he died, she did the same.

Faulkner describes Miss Emily as "a tradition, a duty, and a care; a sort of hereditary obligation on the town." Because she was the last of the Griersons (with the exception of her distant cousins), Colonel Sartoris cooked up the scheme of her not paying taxes. Otherwise she would lose the house and become a pauper. But even more important, the town would lose some of its own tradition. The cemetery she is buried in holds the graves of "Union and Confederate soldiers who fell at the battle of Jefferson," so it is clear that during the Civil War this was an important place.

Like Miss Emily and her house, Jefferson seems to have decayed. Nothing is mentioned in the story about positive changes in town. "Garages and cotton gins" have taken over, but the fact that the younger aldermen are so worried about Miss Emily's taxes tells us that it is no longer a prosperous town. The great families whose names are on the streets are all gone. When Miss Emily dies, the town symbolically loses part of its tradition. That is what we learn when some of the men at Miss Emily's funeral show up in Civil War uniforms. They carried on that tradition for a long time. They are like Miss Emily.

The Yankee Homer Barron may stand for signs of change. He came into town to pave sidewalks and he was popular with most people. The town was horrified when they realized Miss Emily was interested in him. They thought she would be above taking up with a Yankee "day laborer." They felt pity for her, and when she bought the poison they "said it would be the best thing" if she used it to commit suicide. But she did not. She killed Homer Barron instead.

People in Jefferson seemed to think they could interfere with the way Miss Emily lived her life. They called Emily's cousins to tell them that she was "a bad example to the young people" because she was seen in public with Homer but was not married. The town ladies sent in the minister, but Miss Emily must have told him off. Finally the cousins came to enforce tradition. Emily then bought the silver toilet set and the man's suit. Homer Barron returned after the cousins left, but he probably did not plan to stay. He was not the marrying kind.

The bridal "tomb" was furnished with rose-colored curtains. The dust was like the dust of tradition. The air was stifling, and Homer's body, in its nightshirt, with its "attitude of an embrace," implies that when he held Miss Emily he was holding a dead tradition, a tradition that killed him, too.

Jefferson protected Miss Emily, but it stifled her, too. It was overprotective. The people were curious about her and thought it was best for her to keep the tradition of the family and the town. In the end she became a frustrated old maid who killed her lover to preserve her honor. The most painful thing about the story is imagining Miss Emily sleeping next to the corpse of a man nobody thought was good enough for her when he was alive. It is almost like a modern horror movie.

Further Strategies for Interpreting "A Rose for Emily"

Susan Warther's essay on "A Rose for Emily" emphasizes the symbolic element in the story. But she also observes that it is "almost like a modern horror movie." The symbolic reading centered on the image of Miss Emily as a "fallen monument." That image related closely to the concept of her being "a tradition, a duty, and a care." The repeated pattern of decay in Miss Emily's house and in the town of Jefferson provided a link to show how the town's own traditions were symbolically connected with those of her family. The writer responded negatively to the people of Jefferson interfering in Miss Emily's life. She interpreted their interference as causing Miss Emily to give in to tradition. That meant killing Homer Barron and keeping him in a "bridal tomb" for the rest of her life.

Other interpretive strategies could have been used for discussing important issues in "A Rose for Emily."

PSYCHOANALYTIC.   Insanity enters the story early: "People in our town" remembered "how old lady Wyatt, her great-aunt, had gone completely crazy at last." When, earlier, Miss Emily is referred to as "a sort of hereditary obligation" of the town, the theme of hereditary insanity is made explicit. But that theme is introduced by the narrator, who, as part of the town, may be unreliable. More important are the images of Miss Emily's father standing in the doorway—blocking the doorway—with his whip in his hand. He becomes the repressive father, much like the repressive brothers in "The Pot of Basil," but once he dies, the town essentially takes over his repressive role. When Miss Emily is attracted to Homer Barron—as everyone else is—she is harshly judged by the town for bad behavior. She is made to feel guilty, which possibly leads her to buy poison while her "female cousins were visiting her." The pressures of her cousins, "who were even more Grierson than Miss Emily had ever been," eventually break her down. Her murder of Homer Barron and her creation of a bridal tomb are direct results of the psychological pressures that both family and society put upon her.

FEMINIST. Miss Emily is without power to direct her life for only one reason: she is a woman. In Jefferson, women must conform to the "rules." When she refuses—by being seen in public with a social inferior, Homer Barron—the town puts pressure on her. They expect her to conform to tradition and marry, even if Barron is beneath her and not the marrying kind. When Emily bought the poison she may have intended to use it on herself. The townspeople pitied her and began to think she would be better off dead. The town feared her father and would never have acted toward him as it did toward her. The town thinks it is "caring" for Miss Emily, but it is actually coercing her into behaving as it thinks she must. In other words, the town expects her to relinquish her freedom and surrender to tradition and duty because she is a woman.

CULTURAL. Colonel Sartoris treats Miss Emily in a special way: he appears to be benevolent on the surface, but he actually causes harm, much as he does when he puts forth "the edict that no Negro woman should appear on the streets without an apron." Jefferson was part of the Confederacy, which among other things fought to preserve the tradition of slavery. That it has not entirely forsaken its tradition is central to the whole story and completely evident in the Confederate uniforms worn at Miss Emily's funeral. Even Homer Barron, the Yankee, would "cuss the niggers," so his views parallel Jefferson's. The unnamed Negro man who remains with Miss Emily is like a shadow. He cooks, he admits people to the house, and he does the marketing and other chores. After a while he "talked to no one, probably not even to her, for his voice had grown harsh and rusty, as if from disuse." Miss Emily is like a "fallen monument," but until she falls entirely, this man is like her slave. After her death, he lets "the first of the ladies" in and then "walked right through the house and out the back and was not seen again." Her death frees him.

These suggestions cover only a few possibilities. You could develop more by considering economic issues as well as different approaches based on details other than those suggested here. You can begin to appreciate how many possibilities for interpretation exist in a story like "A Rose for Emily." Most fine short stories permit multiple interpretations, each of which enriches our understanding and appreciation.

III

CRITICAL APPROACHES
TO
SHORT FICTION

5

ELEMENTS
OF SHORT FICTION

Preparing yourself to interpret a short story involves thinking about what makes a short story work. If part of your responsibility in close reading involves examining details, then in any but a very brief story the details could soon become so overwhelming that a single close reading could become almost a life's work. Therefore, you need to focus on the most important details. A close reading accounts for setting, character, theme, plot, style, action, and other important elements. By identifying those elements and by understanding how they work, you prepare yourself to read closely and interpret well. When you read a short story, all these elements function together. For the sake of analysis, the following stories highlight only a few of those elements at a time so that their function can be examined more closely. The last three stories demonstrate the elements in action together.

We will focus on the following elements and their effects.

SETTING AND MOOD.   Setting refers to the environment, the physical place and time, in which the story takes place. In Boccaccio's "The Pot of Basil," it is the environment of Renaissance Italy in the town of Messina. The **mood**—the feelings communicated by the setting—is usually established by description. In Boccaccio the mood is dark and uneasy, communicated by shadowy description.

CHARACTER AND PSYCHOLOGY.   In Boccaccio's story, the **characters** play recognizable roles: the young suitor, the young girl in love, the evil brothers. Beyond that, their psychological nature is revealed in terms of their action, and especially in terms of Lisabetta's grieving over the pot of basil. In "Two Cents" the characters are nameless in order to emphasize their ordinariness. In some works characters possess a psychological complexity resembling our own. Hamlet, for instance, is one of literature's most psychologically complex characters.

STYLE AND THEME. **Style** refers to artistic decisions in language and narrative techniques. Writers usually develop distinctive personal styles. All stories are about something and therefore have one or more **themes**. One theme of "The Pot of Basil" is frustrated love. One theme of "Two Cents" could be the ritual of sacrifice and what it means in the modern world.

PLOT AND NARRATIVE STRUCTURE. The **plot** is a sequence of actions whose shape produces a **narrative structure** that gives a clear impression and whose ending implies a sense of finality. Everyday life has no plot, which may be why we value carefully plotted fiction. The ending of "The Pot of Basil" produces a sense of satisfaction, even if we are disappointed that Lisabetta must die of grief, because it seems inevitable given the beginning of the story. Stories without a structured plot have characters in action, but the action is much like the life we live ourselves. Plotless stories are often called **"slice of life" stories** because they seem to slice out some moments of the character's life and present them to us as they seem to have been lived. Such stories attempt to achieve the impression of artlessness.

POINT OF VIEW. The question of **point of view** is, Who tells the story? Do you trust the narrator's accuracy? "The Pot of Basil" is narrated by Filomena, about whom you know little. Filomena is not involved in the action of Lisabetta's story, so you can presume she tells things objectively. "Two Cents" is told from a detached point of view by an unnamed narrator who knows everything about the characters and the action. The narrator of "Two Cents" controls everything in the story, including your reactions.

IRONY AND TONE. Some stories are meant to be ironic: they say one thing but mean another. You recognize **irony** by observing the language in which the story is told. In a few cases, you may not be able to tell whether the writer is being sincere or ironic. "Two Cents" may be such a story. Is Suzanne Jacob describing an ironic sacrifice, or is it a serious religious ritual? The **tone** of a story may reveal an author's attitude toward characters or their values. The tone of these stories suggests sympathy for the characters. In some stories the tone is judgmental; in others it is neutral.

WHICH ELEMENTS ARE IMPORTANT?

Most stories possess all the basic elements of short fiction. However, some stories, such as Bharati Mukherjee's "Jasmine," emphasize character more than plot. Mysteries and adventure stories, such as Nathaniel Hawthorne's "Rappaccini's Daughter," depend more on plot. Kate Chopin's "The Story of an Hour" emphasizes action, the death of a husband, and a character's subsequent psychological reaction. In all these stories both character and plot are important, but one may take precedence over the other.

Consequently, one job is to decide which elements are most interesting to talk about in any story you decide to interpret. When you find that character is most important or most challenging, then your discussion may center on character. Other times setting and mood or point of view will provide you with most of your opportunities.

THE ELEMENTS WORKING TOGETHER

Examining the elements separately helps develop a sensitivity to their function. However, it can also give you the illusion that every story has only one element worth looking at. It can also suggest that the individual elements are somehow more important than the whole story. The last story in the following group, Bharati Mukherjee's "Jasmine," shows how you can take into account the interaction of several elements in a story.

Interpretations are usually based on a range of elements and rarely on one. After all, it is extremely difficult to talk about the plot of *Hamlet* as if it were separate from the character of Hamlet or even separate from the setting of the court of Denmark. In addition, since irony is common in Hamlet's speeches to Polonius, Rosenkrantz, Guildenstern, and most of the other characters except for Horatio, one could hardly interpret the play well by ignoring it. The same is true for short stories. Considering the elements separately is a convenience, but nothing more.

SETTING AND MOOD

Stories happen in times and places that evoke feelings associated with history or locale, the physical environment. Historical settings often depend on specialized knowledge of a given period. Very few modern readers will have much specific knowledge of the period of time in which Boccaccio's "The Pot of Basil" took place. The Renaissance is to most of us simply an older time when economic and social structures were recognizable but very different from today. Social structures were more fixed: one born into the peasantry stayed a peasant, aristocrats had privileges, and merchants were only beginning to have influence. More than that we really do not need to know. But even this much gives us great insight into "The Pot of Basil."

Edgar Allan Poe's "The Masque of the Red Death" suggests a similar historical time because its chief character is a prince who behaves as if he has unlimited power. The Renaissance experienced plague—the Black Death—in recurring epidemics that sometimes wiped away a third of the population at a stroke. The locale of Prince Prospero's court is crucial to the story, and thus the reader must be aware that courts similar to the court of Denmark in *Hamlet* were the center of power and influence. Law, religion, and military power all resided at court. Courtiers dressed brilliantly, spoke brilliantly, and threw magnificent parties.

The power of Poe's story lies in the fact that the Red Death is so democratic that it will not excuse such privileged persons. The setting of the story is "the deep seclusion of one of [Prince Prospero's] castellated abbeys." An abbey is a residence for monks and clerics, those who pray and read and retire from the world. Most of Poe's readers associated abbeys with mysterious goings-on.

Poe depends on our having enough associations historically and architecturally to respond to his descriptions of time and place, which establish the setting. However, beyond these Poe also presents us with more immediate and palpable descriptions. One is of the word *masque*, which is unusual and exotic. Poe translates it several times: It is a masked ball and a masquerade. In other words, it is a party, like Halloween, in which everyone is disguised. The disguises, extravagant and amusing, challenge the imagination of the courtiers in a huge, self-indulgent entertainment.

The architecture of the abbey, with its Gothic windows and its seven apartments (rooms) is one of the most carefully described aspects of the setting. Since all the action takes place inside the abbey, Poe describes each of the rooms carefully. He emphasizes details that imply another age: tapestries, candelabra, stained glass, tripods, braziers, and casements. He also emphasizes the colors of these apartments: One is dominated by blue, another by purple, and the next ones by green, orange, white, violet, and finally black.

The setting affects us through Poe's powerful visual description, which makes us aware of special colors, exotic furniture, and materials. Poe also appeals to our sense of touch when he reminds us that the black velvet tapestries fall in heavy folds; we feel the heaviness. He appeals to our sense of sound by describing musicians and introducing the "gigantic clock of ebony" with its "monotonous clang." As Poe says, "It was a voluptuous scene," meaning it awakens the sensual part of ourselves. Setting is presented to us in sensory terms designed to affect our emotional response to locale and its circumstances. Poe is a master of such responses.

EDGAR ALLAN POE (1809–1849)

Edgar Allan Poe's brief but intense and unhappy life was marked by early insecurity. His family was English but lived in Ireland before emigrating to Maryland. His parents died when he was two, and he was adopted by John Allan and his wife, who went to England and sent Poe to school. After they returned to America in 1826, Poe went to the University of Virginia, distinguishing himself with drinking, gambling, and what some called neurotic behavior. After the university his relationship with John Allan deteriorated. Poe joined the army and was recommended to West Point. But there he began his lifelong alcoholism and was not only court-martialed but also disowned by his adoptive father. He made his living as a writer, winning several prizes for short stories and poems. He was a brilliant theorist of poetry and fiction, and his work has been read continuously since his death.

The Masque of the Red Death _____ 1842

The "Red Death" had long devastated the country. No pestilence had ever been so fatal, or so hideous. Blood was its Avatar and its seal—the redness and the horror of blood. There were sharp pains, and sudden dizziness, and then profuse bleeding at the pores, with dissolution. The scarlet stains upon the body and especially upon the face of the victim, were the pest ban which shut him out from the aid and from the sympathy of his fellow-men. And the whole seizure, progress and termination of the disease, were the incidents of half an hour.

But the Prince Prospero was happy and dauntless and sagacious. When his dominions were half depopulated, he summoned to his presence a thousand hale and light-hearted friends from among the knights and dames of his court, and with these retired to the deep seclusion of one of his castellated abbeys. This was an extensive and magnificent structure, the creation of the prince's own eccentric yet august taste. A strong and lofty wall girdled it in. This wall had gates of iron. The courtiers, having entered, brought furnaces and massy hammers and welded the bolts. They resolved to leave means neither of ingress or egress to the sudden impulses of despair or of frenzy from within. The abbey was amply provisioned. With such precautions the courtiers might bid defiance to contagion. The external world could take care of itself. In the meantime it was folly to grieve, or to think. The prince had provided all the appliances of pleasure. There were buffoons, there were improvisatori,° there were ballet-dancers, there were musicians, there was Beauty, there was wine. All these and security were within. Without was the "Red Death."

It was toward the close of the fifth or sixth month of his seclusion, and while the pestilence raged most furiously abroad, that the Prince Prospero entertained his thousand friends at a masked ball of the most unusual magnificence.

It was a voluptuous scene, that masquerade. But first let me tell of the rooms in which it was held. There were seven—an imperial suite. In many palaces, however, such suites form a long and straight vista, while the folding doors slide back nearly to the walls on either hand, so that the view of the whole extent is scarcely impeded. Here the case was very different; as might have been expected from the duke's love of the bizarre. The apartments were so irregularly disposed that the vision embraced but little more than one at a time. There was a sharp turn at every twenty or thirty yards, and at each turn a novel effect. To the right and left, in the middle of each wall, a tall and narrow Gothic window looked out upon a closed corridor which pursued the windings of the suite. These windows were of stained glass whose color varied in accordance with the prevailing hue of the decorations of the chamber into which it opened. That at the eastern extremity was hung, for example, in blue—and vividly blue were its windows. The second chamber was purple in its ornaments and tapestries, and here the panes were purple. The third was green throughout, and so were the casements. The fourth was furnished and lighted with orange—the fifth with white—the sixth with violet. The seventh apartment was closely shrouded in black velvet tapestries that hung all over the ceiling and down the walls, falling in heavy folds upon a carpet of the same material and hue. But in this chamber only, the color of the windows failed to correspond with the decorations. The panes here were scarlet—a deep blood color. Now in no one of the seven apartments was there any lamp or candelabrum, amid the profusion of golden ornaments that lay scattered to and fro or depended from the roof. There was no light of any kind emanating from lamp or candle within the suite of chambers. But in the corridors that followed the suite, there stood, opposite to each window, a heavy tripod, bearing a brazier of fire that projected its rays through the tinted glass and so glaringly illumined the room. And thus were produced a multitude of gaudy and fantastic appearances. But in the western or black chamber the effect of the fire-light

improvisatori: actors who improvised comedies

that streamed upon the dark hangings through the blood-tinted panes, was ghastly in the extreme, and produced so wild a look upon the countenances of those who entered, that there were few of the company bold enough to set foot within its precincts at all.

It was in this apartment, also, that there stood against the western wall, a gigantic clock of ebony. Its pendulum swung to and fro with a dull, heavy, monotonous clang; and when the minute-hand made the circuit of the face, and the hour was to be stricken, there came from the brazen lungs of the clock a sound which was clear and loud and deep and exceedingly musical, but of so peculiar a note and emphasis that, at each lapse of an hour, the musicians of the orchestra were constrained to pause, momentarily, in their performance, to harken to the sound; and thus the waltzers perforce ceased their evolutions; and there was a brief disconcert of the whole gay company; and, while the chimes of the clock yet rang, it was observed that the giddiest grew pale, and the more aged and sedate passed their hands over their brows as if in confused reverie or meditation. But when the echoes had fully ceased, a light laughter at once pervaded the assembly; the musicians looked at each other and smiled as if at their own nervousness and folly, and made whispering vows, each to the other, that the next chiming of the clock should produce in them no similar emotion; and then, after the lapse of sixty minutes (which embrace three thousand and six hundred seconds of the Time that flies), there came yet another chiming of the clock, and then were the same disconcert and tremulousness and meditation as before.

But, in spite of these things, it was a gay and magnificent revel. The tastes of the duke were peculiar. He had a fine eye for colors and effects. He disregarded the *decora* of mere fashion. His plans were bold and fiery, and his conceptions glowed with barbaric luster. There are some who would have thought him mad. His followers felt that he was not. It was necessary to hear and see and touch him to be *sure* that he was not.

He had directed, in great part, the moveable embellishments of the seven chambers, upon occasion of this great féte; and it was his own guiding taste which had given character to the masqueraders. Be sure they were grotesque. There were much glare and glitter and piquancy and phantasm—much of what has been since seen in "Hernani."° There were arabesque figures with unsuited limbs and appointments. There were delirious fancies such as the madman fashions. There was much of the beautiful, much of the wanton, much of the bizarre, something of the terrible, and not a little of that which might have excited disgust. To and fro in the seven chambers there stalked, in fact, a multitude of dreams. And these—the dreams—writhed in and about, taking hue from the rooms, and causing the wild music of the orchestra to seem as the echo of their steps. And, anon, there strikes the ebony clock which stands in the hall of the velvet. And then, for a moment, all is still, and all is silent save the voice of the clock. The dreams are stiff-frozen as they stand. But the echoes of the chime die away— they have endured but an instant—and a light, half-subdued laughter floats after them as they depart. And now again the music swells, and the dreams live, and writhe to and fro more merrily than ever, taking hue from the many tinted windows through which stream the rays from the tripods. But to the chamber which lies most westwardly of the seven, there are now none of the maskers who venture: for the night is waning away; and there flows a ruddier light through the blood-colored panes; and the blackness of the sable drapery appals; and to him whose foot falls upon the sable carpet, there comes from the near clock of ebony a muffled peal more solemnly emphatic

---

"Hernani": a political novel (1830) by Victor Hugo (1802–1885), later dramatized in an opera

than any which reaches *their* ears who indulge in the more remote gaieties of the other apartments.

But these other apartments were densely crowded, and in them beat feverishly the heart of life. And the revel went whirlingly on, until at length there commenced the sounding of midnight upon the clock. And then the music ceased, as I have told; and the evolutions of the waltzers were quieted; and there was an uneasy cessation of all things as before. But now there were twelve strokes to be sounded by the bell of the clock; and thus it happened, perhaps, that more of thought crept, with more of time, into the meditations of the thoughtful among those who revelled. And thus, too, it happened, perhaps, that before the last echoes of the last chime had utterly sunk into silence, there were many individuals in the crowd who had found leisure to become aware of the presence of a masked figure which had arrested the attention of no single individual before. And the rumor of this new presence having spread itself whisperingly around, there arose at length from the whole company a buzz, or murmur, expressive of disapprobation and surprise—then, finally, of terror, of horror, and of disgust.

In an assembly of phantasms such as I have painted, it may well be supposed that no ordinary appearance could have excited such sensation. In truth the masquerade license of the night was nearly unlimited; but the figure in question had out-Heroded Herod,° and gone beyond the bounds of even the prince's indefinite decorum. There are chords in the hearts of the most reckless which cannot be touched without emotion. Even with the utterly lost, to whom life and death are equally jests, there are matters of which no jest can be made. The whole company, indeed, seemed now deeply to feel that in the costume and bearing of the stranger neither wit nor propriety existed. The figure was tall and gaunt, and shrouded from head to foot in the habiliments of the grave. The mask which concealed the visage was made so nearly to resemble the countenance of a stiffened corpse that the closest scrutiny must have had difficulty in detecting the cheat. And yet all this might have been endured, if not approved, by the mad revellers around. But the mummer had gone so far as to assume the type of the Red Death. His vesture was dabbled in *blood*—and his broad brow, with all the features of the face, was besprinkled with the scarlet horror.

When the eyes of Prince Prospero fell upon this spectral image (which with a slow   10
and solemn movement, as if more fully to sustain its rôle, stalked to and fro among the waltzers) he was seen to be convulsed, in the first moment with a strong shudder either of terror or distaste; but, in the next, his brow reddened with rage.

"Who dares?" he demanded hoarsely of the courtiers who stood near him—"who dares insult us with this blasphemous mockery? Seize him and unmask him—that we may know whom we have to hang at sunrise, from the battlements!"

It was in the eastern or blue chamber in which stood the Prince Prospero as he uttered these words. They rang throughout the seven rooms loudly and clearly—for the prince was a bold and robust man, and the music had become hushed at the waving of his hand.

It was in the blue room where stood the prince, with a group of pale courtiers by his side. At first, as he spoke, there was a slight rushing movement of this group in the direction of the intruder, who at the moment was also near at hand, and now, with deliberate and stately step, made closer approach to the speaker. But from a certain nameless awe with which the mad assumptions of the mummer had inspired the whole party, there were found none who put forth hand to seize him; so that, unimpeded, he passed

Herod: ruler of Galilee who sentenced Jesus of Nazareth to crucifixion within a yard of the prince's person; and, while the vast assembly, as if with one impulse, shrank from the centers of the rooms to the walls, he made his way uninterruptedly, but with the same solemn and measured step which had distinguished him from the first, through the blue chamber to the purple—through the purple to the green—through the green to the orange—through this again to the white—and even thence to the violet, ere a decided movement had been made to arrest him. It was then, however, that the Prince Prospero, maddening with rage and the shame of his own momentary cowardice, rushed hurriedly through the six chambers, while none followed him on account of a deadly terror that had seized upon all. He bore aloft a drawn dagger, and had approached, in rapid impetuosity, to within three or four feet of the retreating figure, when the latter, having attained the extremity of the velvet apartment, turned suddenly and confronted his pursuer. There was a sharp cry—and the dagger dropped gleaming upon the sable carpet, upon which, instantly afterwards, fell prostrate in death the Prince Prospero. Then, summoning the wild courage of despair, a throng of the revellers at once threw themselves into the black apartment, and, seizing the mummer, whose tall figure stood erect and motionless within the shadow of the ebony clock, gasped in unutterable horror at finding the grave-cerements and corpse-like mask which they handled with so violent a rudeness, untenanted by any tangible form.

And now was acknowledged the presence of the Red Death. He had come like a thief in the night. And one by one dropped the revellers in the blood-bedewed halls of their revel, and died each in the despairing posture of his fall. And the life of the ebony clock went out with that of the last of the gay. And the flames of the tripods expired. And Darkness and Decay and the Red Death held illimitable dominion over all.

QUESTIONS FOR CLOSE READING OF SETTING AND MOOD

1. How do the visible signs of the Red Death—"profuse bleeding" and "scarlet horror"—contribute to the setting of the story? Which senses does Poe appeal to in order to make us aware of the Red Death's power?

2. The final room in which Prospero encounters the Red Death is described as velvet. How does Poe make a velvet room seem especially frightening?

3. What effects do you perceive in the procession of Prospero from one colored room to another? How expressive or symbolic are the colors?

4. How effective was the masquerade costume of the Red Death?

5. What does the clock add to the power of the story?

6. Why does Poe emphasize that the orchestra plays waltzes?

7. What details of language contribute most powerfully to the setting?

8. Is the "mummer" who portrays the Red Death literally the Red Death, or is he one of the "thousand hale and light-hearted friends" who took sick?

QUESTIONS FOR INTERPRETATION OF SETTING AND MOOD

The Questions for Close reading above imply detailed observation. Your careful reading of the story will produce other important questions that will point to an interpretation of "The Masque of the Red Death." The following questions can also help interpret the story in terms of setting and mood.

1. How does the setting of the story contribute to our understanding of Poe's use of irony? In this story it is ironic that the party-goers wall themselves off from the outside world in order to protect themselves from disease, but that the disease gets in anyway and kills them all. All their partying seems designed to celebrate life but produces death. Prospero's name means "I prosper," but ironically he does not. He dies. Examine the story for the ways in which the rich colors and rich sensual effects of the setting contribute to the irony of the story.

2. The architecture of the abbey is one of the most striking aspects of the setting of the story. In some ways it is similar to nightmare images. The disease invades the abbey in such a way as to lead us to think of the abbey as a female stronghold and the disease as a spermlike thing penetrating a female host. In what ways does the symbolism of male and female exhibit itself in the description of the setting?

3. How do you as a reader respond to the descriptions of the setting of the story? Examine specific descriptions and establish how you think Poe wanted the reader to respond to them. What does he do—in terms of language and description—to achieve specific effects? How well do you think he controls his effects? What emotional moods does the description produce in you? Is this a horror story?

4. The lush description of the abbey and its inhabitants tells us that these are aristocrats and royalty. How are we to regard such people in face of the terror that roams the land? The peasants outside the abbey die horribly in great numbers while the courtiers within "buy" another five or six months of pleasure before they too die. From the point of view of the larger community, do you approve of their behavior? How does the setting and its resultant mood help you develop an answer to that question?

5. In the Renaissance, abbeys were places where men and women retired to spend their time in spiritual meditation. They were often wealthy and self-sufficient and played only a small part in the larger society. Courtiers, by contrast, were power brokers in a secular world. Why do Prince Prospero and the courtiers retire to an abbey? What benefit do they expect? Does Poe imply that the religious community behaved with the same indifference that the courtiers displayed? Does the setting imply moral values right from the start?

DORIS LESSING   (b. 1919)

Although Doris Lessing has lived in London since 1949, her work has been conditioned by her experiences in Africa. She was born in Iran but was raised in Zimbabwe, the setting for much of her writing. She has said, "Writers brought up in Africa have many advantages— being at the center of a modern battlefield; part of a society in rapid, dramatic change. But in a long run it can also be a handicap: to wake up every working day with one's eyes on a fresh evidence of inhumanity . . . can be limiting." African Stories (1981) is a gathering from earlier collections dealing with Africa, many of which examine racial injustice. Her novel The Golden Notebook *(1962) examines another kind of injustice, the sexual attitudes held by men and women. Among her works are* The Grass Is Singing *(1950) and* Martha Quest *(1952), whose title is also the name of the heroine of the Children of Violence series, which includes* A Proper Marriage *(1954),* A Ripple from the Storm *(1958),* Landlocked *(1966), and* The Four-Gated City *(1967). Lessing's writing has often been described as autobiographical, with Martha Quest growing up on an African farm and following in some of Lessing's footsteps.*

To Room 19 _____ 1963

This is a story, I suppose, about a failure in intelligence: the Rawlings' marriage was grounded in intelligence.

They were older when they married than most of their married friends: in their well-seasoned late twenties. Both had had a number of affairs, sweet rather than bitter; and when they fell in love—for they did fall in love—had known each other for some time. They joked that they had saved each other "for the real thing." That they had waited so long (but not too long) for this real thing was to them a proof of their sensible discrimination. A good many of their friends had married young, and now (they felt) probably regretted lost opportunities; while others, still unmarried, seemed to them arid, self-doubting, and likely to make desperate or romantic marriages.

Not only they, but others, felt they were well-matched: their friends' delight was an additional proof of their happiness. They had played the same roles, male and female, in this group or set, if such a wide, loosely connected, constantly changing constellation of people could be called a set. They had both become, by virtue of their moderation, their humor, and their abstinence from painful experience, people to whom others came for advice. They could be, and were, relied on. It was one of those cases of a man and a woman linking themselves whom no one else had ever thought of linking, probably because of their similarities. But then everyone exclaimed: Of course! How right! How was it we never thought of it before!

And so they married amid general rejoicing, and because of their foresight and their sense for what was probable, nothing was a surprise to them.

Both had well-paid jobs. Matthew was a subeditor on a large London newspaper,   5
and Susan worked in an advertising firm. He was not the stuff of which editors or publicized journalists are made, but he was much more than "a subeditor," being one of the essential background people who in fact steady, inspire, and make possible the people in the limelight. He was content with this position. Susan had a talent for commercial drawing. She was humorous about the advertisements she was responsible for, but she did not feel strongly about them one way or the other.

Both, before they married, had had pleasant flats, but they felt it unwise to base a marriage on either flat, because it might seem like a submission of personality on the part of the one whose flat it was not. They moved into a new flat in South Kensington on the clear understanding that when their marriage had settled down (a process they knew would not take long, and was in fact more a humorous concession to popular wisdom than what was due to themselves) they would buy a house and start a family.

And this is what happened. They lived in their charming flat for two years, giving parties and going to them, being a popular young married couple, and then Susan became pregnant, she gave up her job, and they bought a house in Richmond. It was typical of this couple that they had a son first, then a daughter, then twins, son and daughter. Everything right, appropriate, and what everyone would wish for, if they could choose. But people did feel these two had chosen; this balanced and sensible family was no more than what was due to them because of their infallible sense for *choosing* right.

And so they lived with their four children in their gardened house in Richmond and were happy. They had everything they had wanted and had planned for.

And yet . . .

Well, even this was expected, that there must be a certain flatness. . . .   10

Yes, yes, of course, it was natural they sometimes felt like this. Like what?

Their life seemed to be like a snake biting its tail. Matthew's job for the sake of Susan, children, house, and garden—which caravanserai needed a well-paid job to maintain it. And Susan's practical intelligence for the sake of Matthew, the children, the house, and the garden—which unit would have collapsed in a week without her.

But there was no point about which either could say: "For the sake of *this* is all the rest." Children? But children can't be a center of life and a reason for being. They can be a thousand things that are delightful, interesting, satisfying, but they can't be a wellspring to live from. Or they shouldn't be. Susan and Matthew knew that well enough.

Matthew's job? Ridiculous. It was an interesting job, but scarcely a reason for living. Matthew took pride in doing it well, but he could hardly be expected to be proud of the newspaper; the newspaper he read, *his* newspaper, was not the one he worked for.

Their love for each other? Well, that was nearest it. If this wasn't a center, what was?   15

Yes, it was around this point, their love, that the whole extraordinary structure revolved. For extraordinary it certainly was. Both Susan and Matthew had moments of thinking so, of looking in secret disbelief at this thing they had created: marriage, four children, big house, garden, charwomen, friends, cars . . . and this *thing*, this entity, all of it had come into existence, been blown into being out of nowhere, because Susan loved Matthew and Matthew loved Susan. Extraordinary. So that was the central point, the wellspring.

And if one felt that it simply was not strong enough, important enough, to support it all, well whose fault was that? Certainly neither Susan's nor Matthew's. It was in the nature of things. And they sensibly blamed neither themselves nor each other.

On the contrary, they used their intelligence to preserve what they had created from a painful and explosive world: they looked around them, and took lessons. All around them, marriages collapsing, or breaking, or rubbing along (even worse, they felt). They must not make the same mistakes, they must not.

They had avoided the pitfall so many of their friends had fallen into—of buying a house in the country *for the sake of the children,* so that the husband became a weekend husband, a weekend father, and the wife always careful not to ask what went on in the town flat which they called (in joke) a bachelor flat. No, Matthew was a full-time husband, a full-time father, and at night, in the big married bed in the big married bedroom (which had an attractive view of the river), they lay beside each other talking and he told her about his day, and what he had done, and whom he had met; and she told him about her day (not as interesting, but that was not her fault), for both knew of the hidden resentments and deprivations of the woman who has lived her own life—and above all, has earned her own living—and is now dependent on a husband for outside interests and money.

Nor did Susan make the mistake of taking a job for the sake of her independence, which she might very well have done, since her old firm, missing her qualities of humor, balance, and sense, invited her often to go back. Children needed their mother to a certain age, that both parents knew and agreed on; and when these four healthy, wisely brought up children were of the right age, Susan would work again, because she knew, and so did he, what happened to women of fifty at the height of their energy and ability, with grown-up children who no longer needed their full devotion.

So here was this couple, testing their marriage, looking after it, treating it like a   20

small boat full of helpless people in a very stormy sea. Well, of course, so it was. . . . The storms of the world were bad, but not too close—which is not to say they were selfishly felt: Susan and Matthew were both well-informed and responsible people. And the inner storms and quicksands were understood and charted. So everything was all right. Everything was in order. Yes, things were under control.

So what did it matter if they felt dry, flat? People like themselves, fed on a hundred books (psychological, anthropological, sociological), could scarcely be unprepared for the dry, controlled wistfulness which is the distinguishing mark of the intelligent marriage. Two people, endowed with education, with discrimination, with judgment, linked together voluntarily from their will to be happy together and to be of use to others—one sees them everywhere, one knows them, one even is that thing oneself: sadness because so much is after all so little. These two, unsurprised, turned towards each other with even more courtesy and gentle love: this was life, that two people, no matter how carefully chosen, could not be everything to each other. In fact, even to say so, to think in such a way, was banal; they were ashamed to do it.

It was banal, too, when one night Matthew came home late and confessed he had been to a party, taken a girl home and slept with her. Susan forgave him, of course. Except that forgiveness is hardly the word. Understanding, yes. But if you understand something, you don't forgive it, you are the thing itself: forgiveness is for what you *don't* understand. Nor had he *confessed*—what sort of word is that?

The whole thing was not important. After all, years ago they had joked: Of course I'm not going to be faithful to you, no one can be faithful to one other person for a whole lifetime. (And there was the word "faithful"—stupid, all these words, stupid, belonging to a savage old world.) But the incident left both of them irritable. Strange, but they were both bad-tempered, annoyed. There was something unassimilable about it.

Making love splendidly after he had come home that night, both had felt that the idea that Myra Jenkins, a pretty girl met at a party, could be even relevant was ridiculous. They had loved each other for over a decade, would love each other for years more. Who, then, was Myra Jenkins?

Except, thought Susan, unaccountably bad-tempered, she was (is?) the first. In ten years. So either the ten years' fidelity was not important, or she isn't. (No, no, there is something wrong with this way of thinking, there must be.) But if she isn't important, presumably it wasn't important either when Matthew and I first went to bed with each other that afternoon whose delight even now (like a very long shadow at sundown) lays a long, wandlike finger over us. (Why did I say sundown?) Well, if what we felt that afternoon was not important, nothing is important, because if it hadn't been for what we felt, we wouldn't be Mr. and Mrs. Rawlings with four children, et cetera, et cetera. The whole thing is *absurd*—for him to have come home and told me was absurd. For him not to have told me was absurd. For me to care or, for that matter, not to care, is absurd . . . and who is Myra Jenkins? Why, no one at all.

There was only one thing to do, and of course these sensible people did it; they put the thing behind them, and consciously, knowing what they were doing, moved forward into a different phase of their marriage, giving thanks for past good fortune as they did so.

For it was inevitable that the handsome, blond, attractive, manly man, Matthew Rawlings, should be at times tempted (oh, what a word!) by the attractive girls at parties she could not attend because of the four children; and that sometimes he would succumb (a word even more repulsive, if possible) and that she, a good-looking woman in the big well-tended garden at Richmond, would sometimes be pierced as by an arrow from the sky with bitterness. Except that bitterness was not in order, it was out

25

of court. Did the casual girls touch the marriage? They did not. Rather it was they who knew defeat because of the handsome Matthew Rawlings' marriage body and soul to Susan Rawlings.

In that case why did Susan feel (though luckily not for longer than a few seconds at a time) as if life had become a desert, and that nothing mattered, and that her children were not her own?

Meanwhile her intelligence continued to assert that all was well. What if her Matthew did have an occasional sweet afternoon, the odd affair? For she knew quite well, except in her moments of aridity, that they were very happy, that the affairs were not important.

Perhaps that was the trouble? It was in the nature of things that the adventures and delights could no longer be hers, because of the four children and the big house that needed so much attention. But perhaps she was secretly wishing, and even knowing that she did, that the wildness and the beauty could be his. But he was married to her. She was married to him. They were married inextricably. And therefore the gods could not strike him with the real magic, not really. Well, was it Susan's fault that after he came home from an adventure he looked harassed rather than fulfilled? (In fact, that was how she knew he had been *unfaithful,* because of his sullen air, and his glances at her, similar to hers at him: What is it that I share with this person that shields all delight from me?) But none of it by anybody's fault. (But what did they feel ought to be somebody's fault?) Nobody's fault, nothing to be at fault, no one to blame, no one to offer or to take it . . . and nothing wrong, either, except that Matthew never was really struck, as he wanted to be, by joy; and that Susan was more and more often threatened by emptiness. (It was usually in the garden that she was invaded by this feeling: she was coming to avoid the garden, unless the children or Matthew were with her.) There was no need to use the dramatic words "unfaithful," "forgive," and the rest: intelligence forbade them. Intelligence barred, too, quarreling, sulking, anger, silences of withdrawal, accusations and tears. Above all, intelligence forbids tears.

A high price has to be paid for the happy marriage with the four healthy children in the large white gardened house.

And they were paying it, willingly, knowing what they were doing. When they lay side by side or breast to breast in the big civilized bedroom overlooking the wild sullied river, they laughed, often, for no particular reason; but they knew it was really because of these two small people, Susan and Matthew, supporting such an edifice on their intelligent love. The laugh comforted them; it saved them both, though from what, they did not know.

They were now both fortyish. The older children, boy and girl, were ten and eight, at school. The twins, six, were still at home. Susan did not have nurses or girls to help her: childhood is short; and she did not regret the hard work. Often enough she was bored, since small children can be boring; she was often very tired; but she regretted nothing. In another decade, she would turn herself back into being a woman with a life of her own.

Soon the twins would go to school, and they would be away from home from nine until four. These hours, so Susan saw it, would be the preparation for her own slow emancipation away from the role of hub-of-the-family into woman-with-her-own-life. She was already planning for the hours of freedom when all the children would be "off her hands." That was the phrase used by Matthew and by Susan and by their friends, for the moment when the youngest child went off to school. "They'll be off your hands, darling Susan, and you'll have time to yourself." So said Matthew, the intelligent husband, who

30

had often enough commended and consoled Susan, standing by her in spirit during the years when her soul was not her own, as she said, but her children's.

What it amounted to was that Susan saw herself as she had been at twenty-eight, 35 unmarried; and then again somewhere about fifty, blossoming from the root of what she had been twenty years before. As if the essential Susan were in abeyance, as if she were in cold storage. Matthew said something like this to Susan one night: and she agreed that it was true—she did feel something like that. What, then, was this essential Susan? She did not know. Put like that it sounded ridiculous, and she did not really feel it. Anyway, they had a long discussion about the whole thing before going off to sleep in each other's arms.

So the twins went off to their school, two bright affectionate children who had no problems about it, since their older brother and sister had trodden this path so successfully before them. And now Susan was going to be alone in the big house, every day of the school term, except for the daily woman who came in to clean.

It was now, for the first time in this marriage, that something happened which neither of them had foreseen.

This is what happened. She returned, at nine-thirty, from taking the twins to the school by car, looking forward to seven blissful hours of freedom. On the first morning she was simply restless, worrying about the twins "naturally enough" since this was their first day away at school. She was hardly able to contain herself until they came back. Which they did happily, excited by the world of school, looking forward to the next day. And the next day Susan took them, dropped them, came back, and found herself reluctant to enter her big and beautiful home because it was as if something was waiting for her there that she did not wish to confront. Sensibly, however, she parked the car in the garage, entered the house, spoke to Mrs. Parkes, the daily woman, about her duties, and went up to her bedroom. She was possessed by a fever which drove her out again, downstairs, into the kitchen, where Mrs. Parkes was making cake and did not need her, and into the garden. There she sat on a bench and tried to calm herself looking at trees, at a brown glimpse of the river. But she was filled with tension, like a panic: as if an enemy was in the garden with her. She spoke to herself severely, thus: All this is quite natural. First, I spent twelve years of my adult life working, *living my own life*. Then I married, and from the moment I became pregnant for the first time I signed myself over, so to speak, to other people. To the children. Not for one moment in twelve years have I been alone, had time to myself. So now I have to learn to be myself again. That's all.

And she went indoors to help Mrs. Parkes cook and clean, and found some sewing to do for the children. She kept herself occupied every day. At the end of the first term she understood she felt two contrary emotions. First: secret astonishment and dismay that during those weeks when the house was empty of children she had in fact been more occupied (had been careful to keep herself occupied) than ever she had been when the children were around her needing her continual attention. Second: that now she knew the house would be full of them, and for five weeks, she resented the fact she would never be alone. She was already looking back at those hours of sewing, cooking (but by herself) as at a lost freedom which would not be hers for five long weeks. And the two months of term which would succeed the five weeks stretched alluringly open to her—freedom. But what freedom—when in fact she had been so careful *not* to be free of small duties during the last weeks? She looked at herself, Susan Rawlings, sitting in a big chair by the window in the bedroom, sewing shirts or dresses, which she might just as well have bought. She saw herself making cakes for hours at a time in the big family kitchen: yet usually she bought cakes. What she saw was a woman alone, that was true, but she had not felt alone. For instance, Mrs. Parkes was always somewhere in the house. And she did not like being in the garden at all, because of the closeness there of the enemy—irritation, restlessness, emptiness, whatever it was—which keeping her hands occupied made less dangerous for some reason.

Susan did not tell Matthew of these thoughts. They were not sensible. She did not recognize herself in them. What should she say to her dear friend and husband, Matthew? "When I go into the garden, that is, if the children are not there, I feel as if there is an enemy there waiting to invade me." "What enemy, Susan darling?" "Well I don't know, really . . ." "Perhaps you should see a doctor?"

No, clearly this conversation should not take place. The holidays began and Susan welcomed them. Four children, lively, energetic, intelligent, demanding: she was never, not for a moment of her day, alone. If she was in a room, they would be in the next room, or waiting for her to do something for them; or it would soon be time for lunch or tea, or to take one of them to the dentist. Something to do: five weeks of it, thank goodness.

On the fourth day of these so welcome holidays, she found she was storming with anger at the twins: two shrinking beautiful children who (and this is what checked her) stood hand in hand looking at her with sheer dismayed disbelief. This was their calm mother, shouting at them. And for what? They had come to her with some game, some bit of nonsense. They looked at each other, moved closer for support, and went off hand in hand, leaving Susan holding on to the windowsill of the living room, breathing deep, feeling sick. She went to lie down, telling the older children she had a headache. She heard the boy Harry telling the little ones: "It's all right, Mother's got a headache." She heard that *It's all right* with pain.

That night she said to her husband: "Today I shouted at the twins, quite unfairly." She sounded miserable, and he said gently: "Well, what of it?"

"It's more of an adjustment than I thought, their going to school."

"But Susie, Susie darling . . ." For she was crouched weeping on the bed. He comforted her: "Susan, what is all this about? You shouted at them? What of it? If you shouted at them fifty times a day it wouldn't be more than the little devils deserve." But she wouldn't laugh. She wept. Soon he comforted her with his body. She became calm. Calm, she wondered what was wrong with her, and why she should mind so much that she might, just once, have behaved unjustly with the children. What did it matter? They had forgotten it all long ago: Mother had a headache and everything was all right.

It was a long time later that Susan understood that that night, when she had wept and Matthew had driven the misery out of her with his big solid body, was the last time, ever in their married life, that they had been—to use their mutual language—with each other. And even that was a lie, because she had not told him of her real fears at all.

The five weeks passed, and Susan was in control of herself, and good and kind, and she looked forward to the holidays with a mixture of fear and longing. She did not know what to expect. She took the twins off to school (the elder children took themselves to school) and she returned to the house determined to face the enemy wherever he was, in the house, or the garden or—where?

She was again restless, she was possessed by restlessness. She cooked and sewed and worked as before, day after day, while Mrs. Parkes remonstrated: "Mrs. Rawlings, what's the need for it? I can do that, it's what you pay me for."

And it was so irrational that she checked herself. She would put the car into the garage, go up to her bedroom, and sit, hands in her lap, forcing herself to be quiet. She listened to Mrs. Parkes moving around the house. She looked out into the garden and saw the branches shake the trees. She sat defeating the enemy, restlessness. Emptiness. She ought to be thinking about her life, about herself. But she did not. Or perhaps she could not. As soon as she forced her mind to think about Susan (for what else did she want to be alone for?), it skipped off to thoughts of butter or school clothes. Or it thought of Mrs. Parkes. She realized that she sat listening for the movements of the cleaning woman, following her every turn, bend, thought. She followed her in her mind from kitchen to bathroom, from table to oven, and it was as if the duster, the cleaning cloth, the saucepan, were in her own hand. She would hear herself saying: No, not like that, don't put that there. . . . Yet she did not give a damn what Mrs. Parkes did, or if she did it at all. Yet she could not prevent herself from being conscious of her, every minute. Yes, this was what was wrong with her: she needed, when she was alone, to be really alone, with no one near. She could not endure the knowledge that in ten minutes or in half an hour Mrs. Parkes would call up the stairs: "Mrs. Rawlings, there's no silver polish. Madam, we're out of flour."

So she left the house and went to sit in the garden where she was screened from   50
the house by trees. She waited for the demon to appear and claim her, but he did not.

She was keeping him off, because she had not, after all, come to an end of arranging herself.

She was planning how to be somewhere where Mrs. Parkes would not come after her with a cup of tea, or a demand to be allowed to telephone (always irritating, since Susan did not care who she telephoned or how often), or just a nice talk about something. Yes, she needed a place, or a state of affairs, where it would not be necessary to keep reminding herself: In ten minutes I must telephone Matthew about . . . and at half past three I must leave early for the children because the car needs cleaning. And at ten o'clock tomorrow I must remember. . . . She was possessed with resentment that the seven hours of freedom in every day (during weekdays in the school term) were not free, that never, not for one second, ever, was she free from the pressure of time, from having to remember this or that. She could never forget herself; never really let herself go into forgetfulness.

Resentment. It was poisoning her. (She looked at this emotion and thought it was absurd. Yet she felt it.) She was a prisoner. (She looked at this thought too, and it was no good telling herself it was a ridiculous one.) She must tell Matthew—but what? She was filled with emotions that were utterly ridiculous, that she despised, yet that nevertheless she was feeling so strongly she could not shake them off.

The school holidays came round, and this time they were for nearly two months, and she behaved with a conscious controlled decency that nearly drove her crazy. She would lock herself in the bathroom, and sit on the edge of the bath, breathing deep, trying to let go into some kind of calm. Or she went up into the spare room, usually empty, where no one would expect her to be. She heard the children calling "Mother, Mother," and kept silent, feeling guilty. Or she went to the very end of the garden, by herself, and looked at the slow-moving brown river; she looked at the river and closed her eyes and breathed slow and deep, taking it into her being, into her veins.

Then she returned to the family, wife and mother, smiling and responsible, feeling   55
ing as if the pressure of these people—four lively children and her husband—were a painful pressure on the surface of her skin, a hand pressing on her brain. She did not once break down into irritation during these holidays, but it was like living out a prison sentence, and when the children went back to school, she sat on a white stone near the flowing river, and she thought: It is not even a year since the twins went to school, since *they were off my hands* (What on earth did I think I meant when I used that

stupid phrase?), and yet I'm a different person. I'm simply not myself. I don't understand it.

Yet she had to understand it. For she knew that this structure—big white house, on which the mortgage still cost four hundred a year, a husband, so good and kind and insightful; four children, all doing so nicely; and the garden where she sat; and Mrs. Parkes, the cleaning woman—all this depended on her, and yet she could not understand why, or even what it was she contributed to it.

She said to Matthew in their bedroom: "I think there must be something wrong with me."

And he said: "Surely not, Susan? You look marvelous—you're as lovely as ever."

She looked at the handsome blond man, with his clear, intelligent, blue-eyed face, and thought: Why is it I can't tell him? Why not? And she said: "I need to be alone more than I am."

At which he swung his slow blue gaze at her, and she saw what she had been dreading: Incredulity. Disbelief. And fear. An incredulous blue stare from a stranger who was her husband, as close to her as her own breath.

He said: "But the children are at school and off your hands."

She said to herself: I've got to force myself to say: Yes, but do you realize that I never feel free? There's never a moment I can say to myself: There's nothing I have to remind myself about, nothing I have to do in half an hour, or an hour, or two hours. . . .

But she said: "I don't feel well."

He said: "Perhaps you need a holiday."

She said, appalled: "But not without you, surely?" For she could not imagine herself going off without him. Yet that was what he meant. Seeing her face, he laughed, and opened his arms, and she went into them, thinking: Yes, yes, but why can't I say it? And what is it I have to say?

She tried to tell him, about never being free. And he listened and said: "But Susan, what sort of freedom can you possibly want—short of being dead! Am I ever free? I go to the office, and I have to be there at ten—all right, half past ten, sometimes. And I have to do this or that, don't I? Then I've got to come home at a certain time—I don't mean it, you know I don't—but if I'm not going to be back home at six I telephone you. When can I ever say to myself: I have nothing to be responsible for in the next six hours?"

Susan, hearing this, was remorseful. Because it was true. The good marriage, the house, the children, depended just as much on his voluntary bondage as it did on hers. But why did he not feel bound? Why didn't he chafe and become restless? No, there was something really wrong with her and this proved it.

And that word "bondage"—why had she used it? She had never felt marriage, or the children, as bondage. Neither had he, or surely they wouldn't be together lying in each other's arms content after twelve years of marriage.

No, her state (whatever it was) was irrelevant, nothing to do with her real good life with her family. She had to accept the fact that, after all, she was an irrational person and to live with it. Some people had to live with crippled arms, or stammers, or being deaf. She would have to live knowing she was subject to a state of mind she could not own.

Nevertheless, as a result of this conversation with her husband, there was a new regime next holidays.

The spare room at the top of the house now had a cardboard sign saying: PRIVATE! DO NOT DISTURB! on it. (This sign had been drawn in colored chalks by the children, after a discussion between the parents in which it was decided this was psychologically the right thing.) The family and Mrs. Parkes knew this was "Mother's Room" and that she was entitled to her privacy. Many serious conversations took place between Matthew and the children about not taking Mother for granted. Susan overheard the first, between father and Harry, the older boy, and was surprised at her irritation over it. Surely she could have a room somewhere in that big house and retire into it without such a fuss being made? Without it being so solemnly discussed? Why couldn't she simply have announced: "I'm going to fit out the little top room for myself, and when I'm in it I'm not to be disturbed for anything short of fire"? Just that, and finished; instead of long earnest discussions. When she heard Harry and Matthew explaining it to the twins with Mrs. Parkes coming in—"Yes, well, a family sometimes gets on top of a woman"—she had to go right away to the bottom of the garden until the devils of exasperation had finished their dance in her blood.

But now there was a room, and she could go there when she liked, she used it seldom: she felt even more caged there than in her bedroom. One day she had gone up there after a lunch for ten children she had cooked and served because Mrs. Parkes was not there, and had sat alone for a while looking into the garden. She saw the children stream out from the kitchen and stand looking up at the window where she sat behind the curtains. They were all—her children and their friends—discussing Mother's Room. A few minutes later, the chase of children in some game came pounding up the stairs, but ended as abruptly as if they had fallen over a ravine, so sudden was the silence. They had remembered she was there, and had gone silent in a great gale of "Hush! Shhhhhh! Quiet, you'll disturb her. . . ." And they went tiptoeing downstairs like criminal conspirators. When she came down to make tea for them, they all apologized. The twins put their arms around her, from front and back, making a human cage of loving limbs, and promised it would never occur again. "We forgot, Mummy, we forgot all about it!"

What it amounted to was that Mother's Room, and her need for privacy, had become a valuable lesson in respect for other people's rights. Quite soon Susan was going up to the room only because it was a lesson it was a pity to drop. Then she took sewing up there, and the children and Mrs. Parkes came in and out: it had become another family room.

She sighed, and smiled, and resigned herself—she made jokes at her own expense with Matthew over the room. That is, she did from the self she liked, she respected. But at the same time, something inside her howled with impatience, with rage. . . . And she was frightened. One day she found herself kneeling by her bed and praying: "Dear God, keep it away from me, keep him away from me." She meant the devil, for she now thought of it, not caring if she was irrational, as some sort of demon. She imagined him, or it, as a youngish man, or perhaps a middle-aged man pretending to be young. Or a man young-looking from immaturity? At any rate, she saw the young-looking face which, when she drew closer, had dry lines about mouth and eyes. He was thinnish, meager in build. And he had a reddish complexion, and ginger hair. That was he—a gingery, energetic man, and he wore a reddish hairy jacket, unpleasant to the touch.

Well, one day she saw him. She was standing at the bottom of the garden, watching the river ebb past, when she raised her eyes and saw this person, or being, sitting on the white stone bench. He was looking at her, and grinning. In his hand was a long crooked stick, which he had picked off the ground, or broken off the tree above him. He was absentmindedly, out of an absentminded or freakish impulse of spite, using the stick to stir around in the coils of a blindworm or a grass snake (or some kind of snakelike creature: it was whitish and unhealthy to look at, unpleasant). The snake was twisting about, flinging its coils from side to side in a kind of dance of protest against the teasing prodding stick.

Susan looked at him, thinking: Who is the stranger? What is he doing in our garden? Then she recognized the man around whom her terrors had crystallized. As she did so, he vanished. She made herself walk over to the bench. A shadow from a branch lay across thin emerald grass, moving jerkily over its roughness, and she could see why she had taken it for a snake, lashing and twisting. She went back to the house thinking: Right, then, so I've seen him with my own eyes, so I'm not crazy after all—there *is* a danger because I've seen him. He is lurking in the garden and sometimes even in the house, and he wants to *get into me and to take me over.*

She dreamed of having a room or a place, anywhere, where she could go and sit, by herself, no one knowing where she was.

Once, near Victoria, she found herself outside a news agent that had Rooms to Let advertised. She decided to rent a room, telling no one. Sometimes she could take the train in to Richmond and sit alone in it for an hour or two. Yet how could she? A room would cost three or four pounds a week, and she earned no money, and how could she explain to Matthew that she needed such a sum? What for? It did not occur to her that she was taking it for granted she wasn't going to tell him about the room.

Well, it was out of the question, having a room; yet she knew she must.

One day, when a school term was well established, and none of the children had measles or other ailments, and everything seemed in order, she did the shopping early, explained to Mrs. Parkes she was meeting an old school friend, took the train to Victoria, searched until she found a small quiet hotel, and asked for a room for the day. They did not let rooms by the day, the manageress said, looking doubtful, since Susan so obviously was not the kind of woman who needed a room for unrespectable reasons. Susan made a long explanation about not being well, being unable to shop without frequent rests for lying down. At last she was allowed to rent the room provided she paid a full night's price for it. She was taken up by the manageress and a maid, both concerned over the state of her health . . . which must be pretty bad if, living at Richmond (she had signed her name and address in the register), she needed a shelter at Victoria.

The room was ordinary and anonymous, and was just what Susan needed. She put a shilling in the gas fire, and sat, eyes shut, in a dingy armchair with her back to a dingy window. She was alone. She was alone. She was alone. She could feel pressures lifting off her. First the sounds of traffic came very loud; then they seemed to vanish; she might even have slept a little. A knock on the door: it was Miss Townsend, the manageress, bringing her a cup of tea with her own hands, so concerned was she over Susan's long silence and possible illness.

Miss Townsend was a lonely woman of fifty, running this hotel with all the rectitude expected of her, and she sensed in Susan the possibility of understanding companionship. She stayed to talk. Susan found herself in the middle of a fantastic story about her illness, which got more and more impossible as she tried to make it tally with the large house at Richmond, well-off husband, and four children. Suppose she said instead: Miss Townsend, I'm here in your hotel because I need to be alone for a few hours, above all *alone and with no one knowing where I am.* She said it mentally, and saw, mentally, the look that would inevitably come on Miss Townsend's elderly maiden's face. "Miss Townsend, my four children and my husband are driving me insane, do you understand that? Yes, I can see from the gleam of hysteria in your eyes that comes from loneliness controlled but only just contained that I've got everything in the world you've ever

80

longed for. Well, Miss Townsend, I don't want any of it. You can have it, Miss Townsend. I wish I was absolutely alone in the world, like you. Miss Townsend, I'm besieged by seven devils, Miss Townsend, Miss Townsend, let me stay here in your hotel where the devils can't get me. . . ." Instead of saying all this, she described her anemia, agreed to try Miss Townsend's remedy for it, which was raw liver, minced, between whole-meal bread, and said yes, perhaps it would be better if she stayed at home and let a friend do shopping for her. She paid her bill and left the hotel, defeated.

At home Mrs. Parkes said she didn't really like it, no, not really, when Mrs. Rawlings was away from nine in the morning until five. The teacher had telephoned from school to say Joan's teeth were paining her, and she hadn't known what to say; and what was she to make for the children's tea, Mrs. Rawlings hadn't said.

All this was nonsense, of course. Mrs. Parkes's complaint was that Susan had withdrawn herself spiritually, leaving the burden of the big house on her.

Susan looked back at her day of "freedom" which had resulted in her becoming   85
a friend of the lonely Miss Townsend, and in Mrs. Parkes's remonstrances. Yet she remembered the short blissful hour of being alone, really alone. She was determined to arrange her life, no matter what it cost, so that she could have that solitude more often. An absolute solitude, where no one knew her or cared about her.

But how? She thought of saying to her old employer: I want you to back me up in a story with Matthew that I am doing part-time work for you. The truth is that . . . But she would have to tell him a lie, too, and which lie? She could not say: I want to sit by myself three or four times a week in a rented room. And besides, he knew Matthew, and she could not really ask him to tell lies on her behalf, apart from being bound to think it meant a lover.

Suppose she really took a part-time job, which she could get through fast and efficiently, leaving time for herself. What job? Addressing envelopes? Canvassing?

And there was Mrs. Parkes, working widow, who knew exactly what she was prepared to give to the house, who knew by instinct when her mistress withdrew in spirit from her responsibilities. Mrs. Parkes was one of the servers of this world, but she needed someone to serve. She had to have Mrs. Rawlings, her madam, at the top of the house or in the garden, so that she could come and get support from her: "Yes, the bread's not what it was when I was a girl. . . . Yes, Harry's got a wonderful appetite, I wonder where he puts it all. . . . Yes, it's lucky the twins are so much of a size, they can wear each other's shoes, that's a saving in these hard times. . . . Yes, the cherry jam from Switzerland is not a patch on the jam from Poland, and three times the price. . . ." And so on. That sort of talk Mrs. Parkes must have, every day, or she would leave, not knowing herself why she left.

Susan Rawlings, thinking these thoughts, found that she was prowling through the great thicketed garden like a wild cat: she was walking up the stairs, down the stairs, through the rooms into the garden, along the brown running river, back, up through the house, down again. . . . It was a wonder Mrs. Parkes did not think it strange. But, on the contrary, Mrs. Rawlings could do what she liked, she could stand on her head if she wanted, provided she was *there*. Susan Rawlings prowled and muttered through her house, hating Mrs. Parkes, hating poor Miss Townsend, dreaming of her hour of solitude in the dingy respectability of Miss Townsend's hotel bedroom, and she knew quite well she was mad. Yes, she was mad.

She said to Matthew that she must have a holiday. Matthew agreed with her. This   90
was not as things had been once—how they had talked in each other's arms in the marriage bed. He had, she knew, diagnosed her finally as *unreasonable*. She had become

someone outside himself that he had to manage. They were living side by side in this house like two tolerably friendly strangers.

Having told Mrs. Parkes—or rather, asked for her permission—she went off on a walking holiday in Wales. She chose the remotest place she knew of. Every morning the children telephoned her before they went off to school, to encourage and support her, just as they had over Mother's Room. Every evening she telephoned them, spoke to each child in turn, and then to Matthew. Mrs. Parkes, given permission to telephone for instructions or advice, did so every day at lunchtime. When, as happened three times, Mrs. Rawlings was out on the mountainside, Mrs. Parkes asked that she should ring back at such-and-such a time, for she would not be happy in what she was doing without Mrs. Rawlings' blessing.

Susan prowled over wild country with the telephone wire holding her to her duty like a leash. The next time she must telephone, or wait to be telephoned, nailed her to her cross. The mountains themselves seemed trammeled by her unfreedom. Everywhere on the mountains, where she met no one at all, from breakfast time to dusk, excepting sheep, or a shepherd, she came face-to-face with her own craziness, which might attack her in the broadest valleys, so that they seemed too small, or on a mountaintop from which she could see a hundred other mountains and valleys, so that they seemed too low, too small, with the sky pressing down too close. She would stand gazing at a hillside brilliant with ferns and bracken, jeweled with running water, and see nothing but her devil, who lifted inhuman eyes at her from where he leaned negligently on a rock, switching at his ugly yellow boots with a leafy twig.

She returned to her home and family, with the Welsh emptiness at the back of her mind like a promise of freedom.

She told her husband she wanted to have an *au pair* girl.°

They were in their bedroom, it was late at night, the children slept. He sat, shirted and slippered, in a chair by the window, looking out. She sat brushing her hair and watching him in the mirror. A time-hallowed scene in the connubial bedroom. He said nothing, while she heard the arguments coming into his mind, only to be rejected because every one was *reasonable.*

"It seems strange to get one now; after all, the children are in school most of the day. Surely the time for you to have help was when you were stuck with them day and night. Why don't you ask Mrs. Parkes to cook for you? She's even offered to—I can understand if you are tired of cooking for six people. But you know that an *au pair* girl means all kinds of problems; it's not like having an ordinary char° in during the day. . . ."

Finally he said carefully: "Are you thinking of going back to work?"

"No," she said, "no, not really." She made herself sound vague, rather stupid. She went on brushing her black hair and peering at herself so as to be oblivious of the short uneasy glances her Matthew kept giving her. "Do you think we can't afford it?" she went on vaguely, not at all the old efficient Susan who knew exactly what they could afford.

"It's not that," he said, looking out of the window at dark trees, so as not to look at her. Meanwhile she examined a round, candid, pleasant face with clear dark brows and clear grey eyes. A sensible face. She brushed thick healthy black hair and thought: Yet that's the reflection of a madwoman. How very strange! Much more to the point if what looked back at me was the gingery green-eyed demon with his dry meager smile. . . . Why wasn't Matthew agreeing? After all, what else could he do? She was breaking her

95

---

au pair girl: live-in baby-sitter and family helper   *char:* cleaning person

part of the bargain and there was no way of forcing her to keep it: that her spirit, her soul, should live in this house, so that the people in it could grow like plants in water, and Mrs. Parkes remain content in their service. In return for this, he would be a good loving husband, and responsible towards the children. Well, nothing like this had been true of either of them for a long time. He did his duty, perfunctorily; she did not even pretend to do hers. And he had become like other husbands, with his real life in his work and the people he met there, and very likely a serious affair. All this was her fault.

At last he drew heavy curtains, blotting out the trees, and turned to force her at-   100
tention: "Susan, are you really sure we need a girl?" But she would not meet his appeal at all. She was running the brush over her hair again and again, lifting fine black clouds in a small hiss of electricity. She was peering in and smiling as if she were amused at the clinging hissing hair that followed the brush.

"Yes, I think it would be a good idea, on the whole," she said, with the cunning of a madwoman evading the real point.

In the mirror she could see her Matthew lying on his back, his hands behind his head, staring upwards, his face sad and hard. She felt her heart (the old heart of Susan Rawlings) soften and call out to him. But she set it to be indifferent.

He said: "Susan, the children?" It was an appeal that *almost* reached her. He opened his arms, lifting them palms up, empty. She had only to run across and fling herself into them, onto his hard, warm chest, and melt into herself, into Susan. But she could not. She would not see his lifted arms. She said vaguely: "Well, surely it'll be even better for them? We'll get a French or a German girl and they'll learn the language."

In the dark she lay beside him, feeling frozen, a stranger. She felt as if Susan had been spirited away. She disliked very much this woman who lay here, cold and indifferent beside a suffering man, but she could not change her.

Next morning she set about getting a girl, and very soon came Sophie Traub from   105
Hamburg, a girl of twenty, laughing, healthy, blue-eyed, intending to learn English. Indeed, she already spoke a good deal. In return for a room—"Mother's Room"—and her food, she undertook to do some light cooking, and to be with the children when Mrs. Rawlings asked. She was an intelligent girl and understood perfectly what was needed. Susan said: "I go off sometimes, for the morning or for the day—well, sometimes the children run home from school, or they ring up, or a teacher rings up. I should be here, really. And there's the daily woman. . . ." And Sophie laughed her deep fruity fräulein's laugh, showed her fine white teeth and her dimples, and said: "You want some person to play mistress of the house sometimes, not so?"

"Yes, that is just so," said Susan, a bit dry, despite herself, thinking in secret fear how easy it was, how much nearer to the end she was than she thought. Healthy Fräulein Traub's instant understanding of their position proved this to be true.

The *au pair* girl, because of her own common sense, or (as Susan said to herself, with her new inward shudder) because she had been *chosen* so well by Susan, was a success with everyone, the children liking her, Mrs. Parkes forgetting almost at once that she was German, and Matthew finding her "nice to have around the house." For he was now taking things as they came, from the surface of life, withdrawn both as a husband and a father from the household.

One day Susan saw how Sophie and Mrs. Parkes were talking and laughing in the kitchen, and she announced that she would be away until teatime. She knew exactly where to go and what she must look for. She took the District Line to South Kensington, changed to the Circle, got off at Paddington, and walked around looking at the smaller hotels until she was satisfied with one which had FRED'S HOTEL painted on window-panes that needed cleaning. The façade was a faded shiny yellow, like unhealthy skin. A door at the end of a passage said she must knock; she did, and Fred appeared. He was not at all attractive, not in any way, being fattish, and run-down, and wearing a tasteless striped suit. He had small sharp eyes in a white creased face, and was quite prepared to let Mrs. Jones (she chose the farcical name deliberately, staring him out) have a room three days a week from ten until six. Provided of course that she paid in advance each time she came? Susan produced fifteen shillings (no price had been set by him) and held it out, still fixing him with a bold unblinking challenge she had not known until then she could use at will. Looking at her still, he took up a ten-shilling note from her palm between thumb and forefinger, fingered it; then shuffled up two half-crowns, held out his own palm with these bits of money displayed thereon, and let his gaze lower broodingly at them. They were standing in the passage, a red-shaded light above, bare boards beneath, and a strong smell of floor polish rising about them. He shot his gaze up at her over the still-extended palm, and smiled as if to say: What do you take me for? "I shan't," said Susan, "be using this room for the purposes of making money." He still waited. She added another five shillings, at which he nodded and said: "You pay, and I ask no questions." "Good," said Susan. He now went past her to the stairs, and there waited a moment: the light from the street door being in her eyes, she lost sight of him momentarily. Then she saw a sober-suited, white-faced, white-balding little man trotting up the stairs like a waiter, and she went after him. They proceeded in utter silence up the stairs of this house where no questions were asked—Fred's Hotel, which could afford the freedom for its visitors that poor Miss Townsend's hotel could not. The room was hideous. It had a single window, with thin green brocade curtains, a three-quarter bed that had a cheap green satin bedspread on it, a fireplace with a gas fire and a shilling meter by it, a chest of drawers, and a green wicker armchair.

"Thank you," said Susan, knowing that Fred (if this was Fred, and not George, or Herbert or Charlie) was looking at her, not so much with curiosity, an emotion he would not own to, for professional reasons, but with a philosophical sense of what was appropriate. Having taken her money and shown her up and agreed to everything, he was clearly disapproving of her for coming here. She did not belong here at all, so his look said. (But she knew, already, how very much she did belong: the room had been waiting for her to join it.) "Would you have me called at five o'clock, please?" and he nodded and went downstairs.

It was twelve in the morning. She was free. She sat in the armchair, she simply sat, she closed her eyes and sat and let herself be alone. She was alone and no one knew where she was. When a knock came on the door she was annoyed, and prepared to show it: but it was Fred himself; it was five o'clock and he was calling her as ordered. He flicked his sharp little eyes over the room—bed, first. It was undisturbed. She might never have been in the room at all. She thanked him, said she would be returning the day after tomorrow, and left. She was back home in time to cook supper, to put the children to bed, to cook a second supper for her husband and herself later. And to welcome Sophie back from the pictures where she had gone with a friend. All these things she did cheerfully, willingly. But she was thinking all the time of the hotel room; she was longing for it with her whole being.

Three times a week. She arrived promptly at ten, looked Fred in the eyes, gave him twenty shillings, followed him up the stairs, went into the room, and shut the door on him with gentle firmness. For Fred, disapproving of her being here at all, was quite ready to let friendship, or at least acquaintanceship, follow his disapproval, if only she would let him. But he was content to go off on her dismissing nod, with the twenty shillings in his hand.

She sat in the armchair and shut her eyes.

What did she *do* in the room? Why, nothing at all. From the chair, when it had rested her, she went to the window, stretching her arms, smiling, treasuring her anonymity, to look out. She was no longer Susan Rawlings, mother of four, wife of Matthew, employer of Mrs. Parkes and of Sophie Traub, with these and those relations with friends, schoolteachers, tradesmen. She no longer was mistress of the big white house and garden, owning clothes suitable for this and that activity or occasion. She was Mrs. Jones, and she was alone, and she had no past and no future. Here I am, she thought, after all these years of being married and having children and playing those roles of responsibility—and I'm just the same. Yet there have been times I thought that nothing existed of me except the roles that went with being Mrs. Matthew Rawlings. Yes, here I am, and if I never saw any of my family again, here I would still be . . . how very strange that is! And she leaned on the sill, and looked into the street, loving the men and women who passed, because she did not know them. She looked at the downtrodden buildings over the street, and at the sky, wet and dingy, or sometimes blue, and she felt she had never seen buildings or sky before. And then she went back to the chair, empty, her mind a blank. Sometimes she talked aloud, saying nothing—an exclamation, meaningless, followed by a comment about the floral pattern on the thin rug, or a stain on the green satin coverlet. For the most part, she wool-gathered—what word is there for it?—brooded, wandered, simply went dark, feeling emptiness run deliciously through her veins like the movement of her blood.

This room had become more her own than the house she lived in. One morning she found Fred taking her a flight higher than usual. She stopped, refusing to go up, and demanded her usual room, Number 19. "Well, you'll have to wait half an hour, then," he said. Willingly she descended to the dark disinfectant-smelling hall, and sat waiting until the two, man and woman, came down the stairs, giving her swift indifferent glances before they hurried out into the street, separating at the door. She went up to the room, *her* room, which they had just vacated. It was no less hers, though the windows were set wide open, and a maid was straightening the bed as she came in.

After these days of solitude, it was both easy to play her part as mother and wife, and difficult—because it was so easy: she felt an impostor. She felt as if her shell moved here, with her family, answering to Mummy, Mother, Susan, Mrs. Rawlings. She was surprised no one saw through her, that she wasn't turned out of doors, as a fake. On the contrary, it seemed the children loved her more; Matthew and she "got on" pleasantly, and Mrs. Parkes was happy in her work under (for the most part, it must be confessed) Sophie Traub. At night she lay beside her husband, and they made love again, apparently just as they used to, when they were really married. But she, Susan, or the being who answered so readily and improbably to the name of Susan, was not there: she was in Fred's Hotel, in Paddington, waiting for the easing hours of solitude to begin.

Soon she made a new arrangement with Fred and with Sophie. It was for five days a week. As for the money, five pounds, she simply asked Matthew for it. She saw that she was not even frightened he might ask what for: he would give it to her, she knew that, and yet it was terrifying it could be so, for this close couple, these partners, had once known the destination of every shilling they must spend. He agreed to give her five pounds a week. She asked for just so much, not a penny more. He sounded indifferent about it. It was as if he were paying her, she thought: *paying her off*—yes, that was it. Terror came back for a moment when she understood this, but she stilled it: things had gone too far for that. Now, every week, on Sunday nights, he gave her five pounds, turning away from her before their eyes could meet on the transaction. As for Sophie Traub, she was to be somewhere in or near the house until six at night, after which she was free. She was not to cook, or to clean; she was simply to be there. So she gardened or sewed, and asked friends in, being a person who was bound to have a lot of friends. If the children were sick, she nursed them. If teachers telephoned, she answered them sensibly. For the five daytimes in the school week, she was altogether the mistress of the house.

One night in the bedroom, Matthew asked: "Susan, I don't want to interfere—don't think that, please—but are you sure you are well?"

She was brushing her hair at the mirror. She made two more strokes on either side of her head, before she replied: "Yes, dear, I am sure I am well."

He was again lying on his back, his blond head on his hands, his elbows angled up and part-concealing his face. He said: "Then Susan, I have to ask you this question, though you must understand, I'm not putting any sort of pressure on you." (Susan heard the word "pressure" with dismay, because this was inevitable; of course she could not go on like this.) "Are things going to go on like this?"

"Well," she said, going vague and bright and idiotic again, so as to escape: "Well,   120
I don't see why not."

He was jerking his elbows up and down, in annoyance or in pain, and, looking at him, she saw he had got thin, even gaunt; and restless angry movements were not what she remembered of him. He said: "Do you want a divorce, is that it?"

At this, Susan only with the greatest difficulty stopped herself from laughing: she could hear the bright bubbling laughter she *would* have emitted, had she let herself. He could only mean one thing: she had a lover, and that was why she spent her days in London, as lost to him as if she had vanished to another continent.

Then the small panic set in again: she understood that he hoped she did have a lover, he was begging her to say so, because otherwise it would be too terrifying.

She thought this out as she brushed her hair, watching the fine black stuff fly up to make its little clouds of electricity, hiss, hiss, hiss. Behind her head, across the room, was a blue wall. She realized she was absorbed in watching the black hair making shapes against the blue. She should be answering him. "Do *you* want a divorce, Matthew?"

He said: "That surely isn't the point, is it?"   125

"You brought it up, I didn't," she said, brightly, suppressing meaningless tinkling laughter.

Next day she asked Fred: "Have inquiries been made for me?"

He hesitated, and she said: "I've been coming here a year now. I've made no trouble, and you've been paid every day. I have a right to be told."

"As a matter of fact, Mrs. Jones, a man did come asking."

"A man from a detective agency?"   130

"Well, he could have been, couldn't he?"

"I was asking you. . . . Well, what did you tell him?"

"I told him a Mrs. Jones came every weekday from ten until five or six and stayed in Number 19 by herself."

"Describing me?"

"Well, Mrs. Jones, I had no alternative. Put yourself in my place."   135

"By rights I should deduct what that man gave you for the information."

He raised shocked eyes: she was not the sort of person to make jokes like this! Then he chose to laugh: a pinkish wet slit appeared across his white crinkled face; his eyes positively begged her to laugh, otherwise he might lose some money. She remained grave, looking at him.

He stopped laughing and said: "You want to go up now?"—returning to the familiarity, the comradeship, of the country where no questions are asked, on which (and he knew it) she depended completely.

She went up to sit in her wicker chair. But it was not the same. Her husband had searched her out. (The world had searched her out.) The pressures were on her. She was here with his connivance. He might walk in at any moment, here, into Room 19. She imagined the report from the detective agency: "A woman calling herself Mrs. Jones, fitting the description of your wife (et cetera, et cetera, et cetera), stays alone all day in Room No. 19. She insists on this room, waits for it if it is engaged. As far as the proprietor knows, she receives no visitors there, male or female." A report something on these lines Matthew must have received.

Well, of course he was right: things couldn't go on like this. He had put an end   140
to it all simply by sending the detective after her.

She tried to shrink herself back into the shelter of the room, a snail pecked out of its shell and trying to squirm back. But the peace of the room had gone. She was trying consciously to revive it, trying to let go into the dark creative trance (or whatever it was) that she had found there. It was no use, yet she craved it, she was as ill as a suddenly deprived addict.

Several times she returned to the room, to look for herself there, but instead she found the unnamed spirit of restlessness, a pricking fevered hunger for movement, an irritable self-consciousness that made her brain feel as if it had colored lights going on and off inside it. Instead of the soft dark that had been the room's air, were now waiting for her demons that made her dash blindly about, muttering words of hate; she was impelling herself from point to point like a moth dashing itself against a windowpane, sliding to the bottom, fluttering off on broken wings, then crashing into the invisible barrier again. And again and again. Soon she was exhausted, and she told Fred that for a while she would not be needing the room, she was going on holiday. Home she went, to the big white house by the river. The middle of a weekday, and she felt guilty at returning to her own home when not expected. She stood unseen, looking in at the kitchen window. Mrs. Parkes, wearing a discarded floral overall of Susan's, was stooping to slide something into the oven. Sophie, arms folded, was leaning her back against a cupboard and laughing at some joke made by a girl not seen before by Susan—a dark foreign girl, Sophie's visitor. In an armchair Molly, one of the twins, lay curled, sucking her thumb and watching the grown-ups. She must have some sickness, to be kept from school. The child's listless face, the dark circles under her eyes, hurt Susan: Molly was looking at the three grown-ups working and talking in exactly the same way Susan looked at the four through the kitchen window: she was remote, shut off from them.

But then, just as Susan imagined herself going in, picking up the little girl, and sitting in an armchair with her, stroking her probably heated forehead, Sophie did just that: she had been standing on one leg, the other knee flexed, its foot set against the wall. Now she let her foot in its ribbon-tied red shoe slide down the wall, stood solid on two feet, clapping her hands before and behind her, and sang a couple of lines in German, so that the child lifted her heavy eyes at her and began to smile. Then she walked, or rather skipped, over to the child, swung her up, and let her fall into her lap at the same moment she sat herself. She said "Hopla! Hopla! Molly . . ." and began stroking the dark untidy young head that Molly laid on her shoulder for comfort.

Well. . . . Susan blinked the tears of farewell out of her eyes, and went quietly up through the house to her bedroom. There she sat looking at the river through the trees. She felt at peace, but in a way that was new to her. She had no desire to move, to talk, to do anything at all. The devils that had haunted the house, the garden, were not there; but she knew it was because her soul was in Room 19 in Fred's Hotel; she was not really here at all. It was a sensation that should have been frightening: to sit at her own bedroom window, listening to Sophie's rich young voice sing German nursery songs to her child, listening to Mrs. Parkes clatter and move below, and to know that all this had nothing to do with her: she was already out of it.

Later, she made herself go down and say she was home: it was unfair to be here   145
unannounced. She took lunch with Mrs. Parkes, Sophie, Sophie's Italian friend Maria, and her daughter Molly, and felt like a visitor.

A few days later, at bedtime, Matthew said: "Here's your five pounds," and pushed them over at her. Yet he must have known she had not been leaving the house at all.

She shook her head, gave it back to him, and said, in explanation, not in accusation: "As soon as you knew where I was, there was no point."

He nodded, not looking at her. He was turned away from her: thinking, she knew, how best to handle this wife who terrified him.

He said: "I wasn't trying to . . . It's just that I was worried."

"Yes, I know."   150

"I must confess that I was beginning to wonder . . ."

"You thought I had a lover?"

"Yes, I am afraid I did."

She knew that he wished she had. She sat wondering how to say: "For a year now I've been spending all my days in a very sordid hotel room. It's the place where I'm happy. In fact, without it I don't exist." She heard herself saying this, and understood how terrified he was that she might. So instead she said: "Well, perhaps you're not far wrong."

Probably Matthew would think the hotel proprietor lied: he would want to   155
think so.

"Well," he said, and she could hear his voice spring up, so to speak, with relief, "in that case I must confess I've got a bit of an affair on myself."

She said, detached and interested: "Really? Who is she?" and saw Matthew's startled look because of this reaction.

"It's Phil. Phil Hunt."

She had known Phil Hunt well in the old unmarried days. She was thinking: No, she won't do, she's too neurotic and difficult. She's never been happy yet. Sophie's much better. Well, Matthew will see that himself, as sensible as he is.

This line of thought went on in silence, while she said aloud: "It's no point telling   160
you about mine, because you don't know him."

Quick, quick, invent, she thought. Remember how you invented all that nonsense for Miss Townsend.

She began slowly, careful not to contradict herself: "His name is Michael" (*Michael What?*)—"Michael Plant." (What a silly name!) "He's rather like you—in looks, I mean." And indeed, she could imagine herself being touched by no one but Matthew himself. "He's a publisher." (Really? Why?) "He's got a wife already and two children."

She brought out this fantasy, proud of herself.

Matthew said: "Are you two thinking of marrying?"

She said, before she could stop herself: "Good God, *no!*"   165

She realized, if Matthew wanted to marry Phil Hunt, that this was too emphatic, but apparently it was all right, for his voice sounded relieved as he said: "It is a bit impossible to imagine oneself married to anyone else, isn't it?" With which he pulled her to him, so that her head lay on his shoulder. She turned her face into the dark of his flesh, and listened to the blood pounding through her ears saying: I am alone, I am alone, I am alone.

In the morning Susan lay in bed while he dressed.

He had been thinking things out in the night, because now he said: "Susan, why don't we make a foursome?"

Of course, she said to herself, of course he would be bound to say that. If one is sensible, if one is reasonable, if one never allows oneself a base thought or an envious emotion, naturally one says: Let's make a foursome!

"Why not?" she said.   170

"We could all meet for lunch. I mean, it's ridiculous, you sneaking off to filthy hotels, and me staying late at the office, and all the lies everyone has to tell."

What on earth did I say his name was?—she panicked, then said: "I think it's a good idea, but Michael is away at the moment. When he comes back, though—and I'm sure you two would like each other."

"He's away, is he? So that's why you've been . . ." Her husband put his hand to the knot of his tie in a gesture of male coquetry she would not before have associated with him; and he bent to kiss her cheek with the expression that goes with the words: Oh you naughty little puss! And she felt its answering look, naughty and coy, come onto her face.

Inside she was dissolving in horror at them both, at how far they had both sunk from honesty of emotion.

So now she was saddled with a lover, and he had a mistress! How ordinary, how   175
reassuring, how jolly! And now they would make a foursome of it, and go about to theatres and restaurants. After all, the Rawlings could well afford that sort of thing, and presumably the publisher Michael Plant could afford to do himself and his mistress quite well. No, there was nothing to stop the four of them developing the most intricate relationship of civilized tolerance, all enveloped in a charming afterglow of autumnal passion. Perhaps they would all go off on holidays together? She had known people who did. Or perhaps Matthew would draw the line there? Why should he, though, if he was capable of talking about "foursomes" at all?

She lay in the empty bedroom, listening to the car drive off with Matthew in it, off to work. Then she heard the children clattering off to school to the accompaniment of Sophie's cheerfully ringing voice. She slid down into the hollow of the bed, for shelter against her own irrelevance. And she stretched out her hand to the hollow where her husband's body had lain, but found no comfort there: he was not her husband. She curled herself up in a small tight ball under the clothes: she could stay here all day, all week, indeed, all her life.

But in a few days she must produce Michael Plant, and—but how? She must presumably find some agreeable man prepared to impersonate a publisher called Michael Plant. And in return for which she would—what? Well, for one thing they would make love. The idea made her want to cry with sheer exhaustion. Oh, no, she had finished with all that—the proof of it was that the words "make love," or even imagining it, trying hard to revive no more than the pleasures of sensuality, let alone affection, or love, made her want to run away and hide from the sheer effort of the thing. . . . Good Lord, why make love at all? Why make love with anyone? Or if you are going to make love, what does it matter who with? Why shouldn't she simply walk into the street, pick up a man, and have a roaring sexual affair with him? Why not? Or even with Fred? What difference did it make?

But she had let herself in for it—an interminable stretch of time with a lover, called Michael, as part of a gallant civilized foursome. Well, she could not, and she would not.

She got up, dressed, went down to find Mrs. Parkes, and asked her for the loan of a pound, since Matthew, she said, had forgotten to leave her money. She exchanged with Mrs. Parkes variations on the theme that husbands are all the same, they don't think, and without saying a word to Sophie, whose voice could be heard upstairs from the telephone, walked to the underground, traveled to South Kensington, changed to the Inner Circle, got out at Paddington, and walked to Fred's Hotel. There she told Fred that she wasn't going on holiday after all, she needed the room. She would have to wait an hour, Fred said. She went to a busy tearoom-cum-restaurant around the corner, and sat watching the people flow in and out the door that kept swinging open and shut, watched them mingle and merge, and separate, felt her being flow into them, into their movement. When the hour was up, she left a half-crown for her pot of tea, and left the place without looking back at it, just as she had left her house, the big, beautiful white house, without another look, but silently dedicating it to Sophie. She returned to Fred, received the key of Number 19, now free, and ascended the grimy stairs slowly, letting floor after floor fall away below her, keeping her eyes lifted, so that floor after floor descended jerkily to her level of vision, and fell away out of sight.

Number 19 was the same. She saw everything with an acute, narrow, checking   180
glance: the cheap shine of the satin spread, which had been replaced carelessly after the two bodies had finished their convulsions under it; a trace of powder on the glass that topped the chest of drawers; an intense green shade in a fold of the curtain. She stood at the window, looking down, watching people pass and pass and pass until her mind went dark from the constant movement. Then she sat in the wicker chair, letting herself go slack. But she had to be careful, because she did not want, today, to be surprised by Fred's knock at five o'clock.

The demons were not here. They had gone forever, because she was buying her freedom from them. She was slipping already into the dark fructifying dream that seemed to caress her inwardly, like the movement of her blood . . . but she had to think about Matthew first. Should she write a letter for the coroner? But what should she say? She would like to leave him with the look on his face she had seen this morning—banal, admittedly, but at least confidently healthy. Well, that was impossible, one did not look like that with a wife dead from suicide. But how to leave him believing she was dying because of a man—because of the fascinating publisher Michael Plant? Oh, how ridiculous! How absurd! How humiliating! But she decided not to trouble about it, simply not to think about the living. If he wanted to believe she had a lover, he would believe it. And he *did* want to believe it. Even when he had found out that there was no publisher in London called Michael Plant, he would think: Oh poor Susan, she was afraid to give me his real name.

And what did it matter whether he married Phil Hunt or Sophie? Though it ought to be Sophie, who was already the mother of those children . . . and what hypocrisy to sit here worrying about the children, when she was going to leave them because she had not got the energy to stay.

She had about four hours. She spent them delightfully, darkly, sweetly, letting herself slide gently, gently, to the edge of the river. Then, with hardly a break in her consciousness, she got up, pushed the thin rug against the door, made sure the windows were tight shut, put two shillings in the meter, and turned on the gas. For the first time since she had been in the room she lay on the hard bed that smelled stale, that smelled of sweat and sex.

She lay on her back on the green satin cover, but her legs were chilly. She got up, found a blanket folded in the bottom of the chest of drawers, and carefully covered her legs with it. She was quite content lying there, listening to the faint soft hiss of the gas that poured into the room, into her lungs, into her brain, as she drifted off into the dark river.

QUESTIONS FOR CLOSE READING OF SETTING AND MOOD

1. What is the Rawlings' home like? What are its distinguishing features?
2. How does the hotel Room 19 differ from the Rawlings' home? Is it more or less comfortable, more or less middle class?
3. Why does Susan need to put signs up in her own house?
4. How aware of his surroundings is Matthew?
5. The Rawlings talk about "basing a marriage" on a flat (apartment). How could they have based a marriage on their apartment?
6. The narrator talks about the progress of the Rawlings' life as being "typical." What is typical about the way Susan and Matthew live?
7. Consider the environment surrounding the Rawlings. How does it contribute to Susan's unhappiness?
8. Why does Susan go each day to a dingy hotel room? Is she happy there?
9. Why does Susan not give thought to having an affair?
10. Why is suicide her ultimate choice? Why does she think of it as drifting into a river?

QUESTIONS FOR INTERPRETATION OF SETTING AND MOOD

1. Examine the descriptions of space in this story. Consider the space in the Rawlings' house and the space in the dingy hotel and Room 19. Susan needs Room 19 and only Room 19 when she goes to the hotel. What is it about that space that attracts her? Does either physical space correlate with Susan's emotional state of mind? Is there such a thing as "emotional space" implied in the story? How much space does either marriage partner have? Is it enough?
2. The setting in Doris Lessing's "To Room 19" begins to take on significance when the narrator begins to describe "Mother's Room." The sign says "PRIVATE! DO NOT DISTURB!" When you read the story you might ask yourself how the question of "having a room" takes on importance in the lives of the characters. The careful description of the house itself will take on meaning, especially in light of observing which rooms are most carefully described.
3. Examine Susan's state of mind throughout the story. Do you feel she could be the victim of depression? What are the elements of depression in the story and how are they reflected in the setting of Room 19? Does it seem absolutely obvious that Susan is insane on the basis of her having committed suicide?

4. When the narrator talks about the typical nature of Susan's and Matthew's lives, she implies that many, if not most, married couples share their experience. They begin marriage in a flat, then eventually buy a house in Richmond, and soon enough have children. All this is not only typical, but thought of as normal. However, one of the marriage partners is in pain: Susan. She seems to have the sense of having lost something. What is it? How likely is she to find it? Is this story a feminist story revealing the inequalities of marriage? Explain how it critiques marriage and why Susan has the problems she has.

5. How do you react to Susan's situation? Are you sympathetic to her or are you sympathetic to Matthew? Can you tell whether or not Doris Lessing wishes you to sympathize with either of these characters? What kinds of reactions do you feel Doris Lessing wishes you to have? If you are sympathetic to Susan, explain why. If you are sympathetic to Matthew, explain why.

WILLIAM TREVOR (b. 1928)

William Trevor was born in County Cork, Ireland, with the name William Trevor Cox, which he eventually shortened as a way of insulating his family from his success (or possible failure) as a writer. He took his undergraduate degree from Trinity College, Dublin, in 1950 and became a history teacher first in Northern Ireland and then in England. In 1960 he went into advertising copywriting and since 1965 has made his living by writing. His settings are frequently Irish, and though he lives now in rural Devon, England, he is considered among the best living Irish short story writers. His individual collections of short stories include The Day We Got Drunk on Cake, and Other Stories *(1967),* The Ballroom of Romance and Other Stories *(1972),* Angels at the Ritz and Other Stories *(1975), and* Beyond the Pale *(1981). He has published several volumes of collected stories since 1983. Among his novels are* The Old Boys *(1964), which he adapted as a play,* Lovers of Their Time *(1979), and* Other People's Worlds *(1980).* Felicia's Journey *(1999) has been made into a successful film. Trevor's stories are impressive for the evocation of their setting and for the sensitive way he reveals the characters of often inarticulate people. Although his people are often in strange and painful bonds, his writing encourages our sympathy and respect.*

The Ballroom of Romance ———————————————— *1971*

On Sundays, or on Mondays if he couldn't make it and often he couldn't, Sunday being his busy day, Canon O'Connell arrived at the farm in order to hold a private service with Bridie's father, who couldn't get about anymore, having had a leg amputated after gangrene had set in. They'd had a pony and cart then and Bridie's mother had been alive: it hadn't been difficult for the two of them to help her father onto the cart in order to make the journey to Mass. But two years later the pony had gone lame and eventually had to be destroyed; not long after that her mother had died. "Don't worry about it at all," Canon O'Connell had said, referring to the difficulty of transporting her father to Mass. "I'll slip up by the week, Bridie."

The milk lorry called daily for the single churn of milk, Mr. Driscoll delivered groceries and meal in his van, and took away the eggs that Bridie had collected during the week. Since Canon O'Connell had made his offer, in 1953, Bridie's father hadn't left the farm.

As well as Mass on Sundays and her weekly visits to a wayside dance hall Bridie went shopping once every month, cycling to the town early on a Friday afternoon. She bought things for herself, material for a dress, knitting wool, stockings, a newspaper, and paperbacked Wild West novels for her father. She talked in the shops to some of the girls she'd been at school with, girls who had married shop assistants or shopkeepers, or had become assistants themselves. Most of them had families of their own by now. "You're lucky to be peaceful in the hills," they said to Bridie, "instead of stuck in a hole like this." They had a tired look, most of them, from pregnancies and their efforts to organize and control their large families.

As she cycled back to the hills on a Friday Bridie often felt that they truly envied her her life, and she found it surprising that they should do so. If it hadn't been for her father she'd have wanted to work in the town also, in the tinned meat factory maybe, or in a shop. The town had a cinema called the Electric, and a fish-and-chip shop where people met at night, eating chips out of newspaper on the pavement outside. In the evenings, sitting in the farmhouse with her father, she often thought about the town, imagining the shop windows lit up to display their goods and the sweetshops still open so that people could purchase chocolates or fruit to take with them to the Electric cinema. But the town was eleven miles away, which was too far to cycle, there and back, for an evening's entertainment.

"It's a terrible thing for you, girl," her father used to say, genuinely troubled, "tied   5 up to a one-legged man." He would sigh heavily, hobbling back from the fields, where he managed as best he could. "If your mother hadn't died," he'd say, not finishing the sentence.

If her mother hadn't died her mother could have looked after him and the scant acres he owned, her mother could somehow have lifted the milk churn onto the collection platform and attended to the few hens and the cows. "I'd be dead without the girl to assist me," she'd heard her father saying to Canon O'Connell, and Canon O'Connell replied that he was certainly lucky to have her.

"Amn't I as happy here as anywhere?" she'd say herself, but her father knew she was pretending and was saddened because the weight of circumstances had so harshly interfered with her life.

Although her father still called her a girl, Bridie was thirty-six. She was tall and strong: the skin of her fingers and her palms were stained, and harsh to touch. The labor they'd experienced had found its way into them, as though juices had come out of vegetation and pigment out of soil: since childhood she'd torn away the rough scotch grass that grew each spring among her father's mangolds and sugar beet; since childhood she'd harvested potatoes in August, her hands daily rooting in the ground she loosened and turned. Wind had toughened the flesh of her face, sun had browned it; her neck and nose were lean, her lips touched with early wrinkles.

But on Saturday nights Bridie forgot the scotch grass and the soil. In different dresses she cycled to the dance hall, encouraged to make the journey by her father. "Doesn't it do you good, girl?" he'd say, as though he imagined she begrudged herself the pleasure. "Why wouldn't you enjoy yourself?" She'd cook him his tea and then he'd settle down with the wireless, or maybe a Wild West novel. In time, while still she danced, he'd stoke the fire up and hobble his way upstairs to bed.

The dance hall, owned by Mr. Justin Dwyer, was miles from anywhere, a lone build-   10 ing by the roadside with treeless boglands all around and a gravel expanse in front of it. On pink pebbled cement its title was painted in an azure blue that matched the depth of the background shade yet stood out well, unfussily proclaiming *The Ballroom of*

Romance. Above these letters four colored bulbs—in red, green, orange, and mauve—were lit at appropriate times, an indication that the evening rendezvous was open for business. Only the façade of the building was pink, the other walls being a more ordinary gray. And inside, except for pink swing doors, everything was blue.

On Saturday nights Mr. Justin Dwyer, a small, thin man, unlocked the metal grid that protected his property and drew it back, creating an open mouth from which music would later pour. He helped his wife to carry crates of lemonade and packets of biscuits from their car, and then took up a position in the tiny vestibule between the drawn-back grid and the pink swing doors. He sat at a card table, with money and tickets spread out before him. He'd made a fortune, people said: he owned other ballrooms also.

People came on bicycles or in old motorcars, country people like Bridie from remote hill farms and villages. People who did not often see other people met there, girls and boys, men and women. They paid Mr. Dwyer and passed into his dance hall, where shadows were cast on pale blue walls and light from a crystal bowl was dim. The band, known as the Romantic Jazz Band, was composed of clarinet, drums, and piano. The drummer sometimes sang.

Bridie had been going to the dance hall since first she left the Presentation Nuns, before her mother's death. She didn't mind the journey, which was seven miles there and seven miles back: she'd traveled as far every day to the Presentation Nuns on the same bicycle, which had once been the property of her mother, an old Rudge purchased originally in 1936. On Sundays she cycled six miles to Mass, but she never minded either: she'd grown quite used to all that.

"How're you, Bridie?" inquired Mr. Justin Dwyer when she arrived in a new scarlet dress one autumn evening in 1971. She said she was all right and in reply to Mr. Dwyer's second query she said that her father was all right also. "I'll go up one of these days," promised Mr. Dwyer, which was a promise he'd been making for twenty years.

She paid the entrance fee and passed through the pink swing doors. The Romantic Jazz Band was playing a familiar melody of the past, "The Destiny Waltz." In spite of the band's title, jazz was not ever played in the ballroom: Mr. Dwyer did not personally care for that kind of music, nor had he cared for various dance movements that had come and gone over the years. Jiving, rock and roll, twisting, and other such variations had all been resisted by Mr. Dwyer, who believed that a ballroom should be, as much as possible, a dignified place. The Romantic Jazz Band consisted of Mr. Maloney, Mr. Swanton, and Dano Ryan on drums. They were three middle-aged men who drove out from the town in Mr. Maloney's car, amateur performers who were employed otherwise by the tinned-meat factory, the Electricity Supply Board, and the County Council.

"How're you, Bridie?" inquired Dano Ryan as she passed him on her way to the cloakroom. He was idle for a moment with his drums, "The Destiny Waltz" not calling for much attention from him.

"I'm all right, Dano," she said. "Are you fit yourself? Are the eyes better?" The week before he'd told her that he'd developed a watering of the eyes that must have been some kind of cold or other. He'd woken up with it in the morning and it had persisted until the afternoon: it was a new experience, he'd told her, adding that he'd never had a day's illness or discomfort in his life.

"I think I need glasses," he said now, and as she passed into the cloakroom she imagined him in glasses, repairing the roads, as he was employed to do by the County Council. You hardly ever saw a road mender with glasses, she reflected, and she wondered if all the dust that was inherent in his work had perhaps affected his eyes.

15

"How're you, Bridie?" a girl called Eenie Mackie said in the cloakroom, a girl who'd left the Presentation Nuns only a year ago.

"That's a lovely dress, Eenie," Bridie said. "Is it nylon, that?"   20

"Tricel actually. Drip-dry."

Bridie took off her coat and hung it on a hook. There was a small washbasin in the cloakroom above which hung a discolored oval mirror. Used tissues and pieces of cotton wool, cigarette butts, and matches covered the concrete floor. Lengths of green-painted timber partitioned off a lavatory in a corner.

"Jeez, you're looking great, Bridie," Madge Dowding remarked, waiting for her turn at the mirror. She moved towards it as she spoke, taking off a pair of spectacles before endeavoring to apply makeup to the lashes of her eye. She stared myopically into the oval mirror, humming while the other girls became restive.

"Will you hurry up, for God's sake!" shouted Eenie Mackie. "We're standing here all night, Madge."

Madge Dowding was the only one who was older than Bridie. She was thirty-nine,   25
although often she said she was younger. The girls sniggered about that, saying that Madge Dowding should accept her condition—her age and her squint and her poor complexion—and not make herself ridiculous going out after men. What man would be bothered with the like of her anyway? Madge Dowding would do better to give herself over to do Saturday night work for the Legion of Mary: wasn't Canon O'Connell always looking for aid?

"Is that fellow there?" she asked now, moving away from the mirror. "The guy with the long arms. Did anyone see him outside?"

"He's dancing with Cat Bolger," one of the girls replied. "She has herself glued to him."

"Lover boy," remarked Patty Byrne, and everyone laughed because the person referred to was hardly a boy anymore, being over fifty it was said, a bachelor who came only occasionally to the dance hall.

Madge Dowding left the cloakroom rapidly, not bothering to pretend she was not anxious about the conjunction of Cat Bolger and the man with the long arms. Two sharp spots of red had come into her cheeks, and when she stumbled in her haste the girls in the cloakroom laughed. A younger girl would have pretended to be casual.

Bridie chatted, waiting for the mirror. Some girls, not wishing to be delayed, used   30
the mirrors of their compacts. Then in twos and threes, occasionally singly, they left the cloakroom and took their places on upright wooden chairs at one end of the dance hall, waiting to be asked to dance. Mr. Maloney, Mr. Swanton, and Dano Ryan played "Harvest Moon" and "I Wonder Who's Kissing Her Now" and "I'll Be Around."

Bridie danced. Her father would be falling asleep by the fire; the wireless, tuned in to Radio Eireann, would be murmuring in the background. Already he'd have listened to *Faith and Order* and *Spot the Talent*. His Wild West novel, *Three Rode Fast* by Jake Matall, would have dropped from his single knee on to the flagged floor. He would wake with a jerk as he did every night and, forgetting what night it was, might be surprised not to see her, for usually she was sitting there at the table, mending clothes or washing eggs. "Is it time for the news?" he'd automatically say.

Dust and cigarette smoke formed a haze beneath the crystal bowl, feet thudded, girls shrieked and laughed, some of them dancing together for want of a male partner. The music was loud, the musicians had taken off their jackets. Vigorously they played a number of tunes from *State Fair* and then, more romantically, "Just One of Those Things." The tempo increased for a Paul Jones, after which Bridie found herself with a youth who told her he was saving up to emigrate, the nation in his opinion being finished. "I'm up in the hills with the uncle," he said, "laboring fourteen hours a day. Is it any life for a young fellow?" She knew his uncle, a hill farmer whose stony acres were separated from her father's by one other farm only. "He has me gutted with work," the youth told her. "Is there sense in it at all, Bridie?"

At ten o'clock there was a stir, occasioned by the arrival of three middle-aged bachelors who'd cycled over from Carey's public house. They shouted and whistled, greeting other people across the dancing area. They smelt of stout and sweat and whiskey.

Every Saturday at just this time they arrived, and, having sold them their tickets, Mr. Dwyer folded up his card table and locked the tin box that held the evening's takings: his ballroom was complete.

"How're you, Bridie?" one of the bachelors, known as Bowser Egan, inquired. Another one, Tim Daly, asked Patty Byrne how she was. "Will we take the floor?" Eyes Horgan suggested to Madge Dowding, already pressing the front of his navy blue suit against the net of her dress. Bridie danced with Bowser Egan, who said she was looking great.   35

The bachelors would never marry, the girls of the dance hall considered: they were wedded already, to stout and whiskey and laziness, to three old mothers somewhere up in the hills. The man with the long arms didn't drink but he was the same in all other ways: he had the same look of a bachelor, a quality in his face.

"Great," Bowser Egan said, feather-stepping in an inaccurate and inebriated manner. "You're a great little dancer, Bridie."

"Will you lay off that!" cried Madge Dowding, her voice shrill above the sound of the music. Eyes Horgan had slipped two fingers into the back of her dress and was now pretending they'd got there by accident. He smiled blearily, his huge red face streaming with perspiration, the eyes which gave him his nickname protuberant and bloodshot.

"Watch your step with that one," Bowser Egan called out, laughing so that spittle sprayed on to Bridie's face. Eenie Mackie, who was also dancing near the incident, laughed also and winked at Bridie. Dano Ryan left his drums and sang. "Oh, how I miss your gentle kiss," he crooned, "and long to hold you tight."

Nobody knew the name of the man with the long arms. The only words he'd ever been known to speak in the Ballroom of Romance were the words that formed his invitation to dance. He was a shy man who stood alone when he wasn't performing on the dance floor. He rode away on his bicycle afterwards, not saying good night to anyone.   40

"Cat has your man leppin' tonight," Tim Daly remarked to Patty Byrne, for the liveliness that Cat Bolger had introduced into foxtrot and waltz was noticeable.

"I think of you only," sang Dano Ryan. "Only wishing, wishing you were by my side."

Dano Ryan would have done, Bridie often thought, because he was a different kind of bachelor: he had a lonely look about him, as if he'd become tired of being on his own. Every week she thought he would have done, and during the week her mind regularly returned to that thought. Dano Ryan would have done because she felt he wouldn't mind coming to live in the farmhouse while her one-legged father was still about the place. Three could live as cheaply as two where Dano Ryan was concerned because giving up the wages he earned as a road worker would be balanced by the saving made on what he paid for lodgings. Once, at the end of an evening, she'd pretended that there was a puncture in the back wheel of her bicycle and he'd concerned himself with it while Mr. Maloney and Mr. Swanton waited for him in Mr. Maloney's car. He'd blown the tire up with the car pump and had said he thought it would hold.

It was well known in the dance hall that she fancied her chances with Dano Ryan. But it was well known also that Dano Ryan had got into a set way of life and had remained in it for quite some years. He lodged with a widow called Mrs. Griffin and Mrs. Griffin's mentally affected son, in a cottage on the outskirts of the town. He was said to be good to the affected child, buying him sweets and taking him out for rides on the crossbar of his bicycle. He gave an hour or two of his time every week to the Church of Our Lady Queen of Heaven, and he was loyal to Mr. Dwyer. He performed in the two other rural dance halls that Mr. Dwyer owned, rejecting advances from the town's more sophisticated dance hall, even though it was more conveniently situated for him and the fee was more substantial than that paid by Mr. Dwyer. But Mr. Dwyer had discovered Dano Ryan and Dano had not forgotten it, just as Mr. Maloney and Mr. Swanton had not forgotten their discovery by Mr. Dwyer either.

"Would we take a lemonade?" Bowser Egan suggested. "And a packet of biscuits, Bridie?"   45

No alcoholic liquor was ever served in the Ballroom of Romance, the premises not being licensed for this added stimulant. Mr. Dwyer in fact had never sought a license for any of his premises, knowing that romance and alcohol were difficult commodities to mix, especially in a dignified ballroom. Behind where the girls sat on the wooden chairs Mr. Dwyer's wife, a small stout woman, served the bottles of lemonade, with straws, and the biscuits and the crisps. She talked busily while doing so, mainly about the turkeys she kept. She'd once told Bridie that she thought of them as children.

"Thanks," Bridie said, and Bowser Egan led her to the trestle table. Soon it would be the intermission: soon the three members of the band would cross the floor also for refreshment. She thought up questions to ask Dano Ryan.

When first she'd danced in the Ballroom of Romance, when she was just sixteen, Dano Ryan had been there also, four years older than she was, playing the drums for Mr. Maloney as he played them now. She'd hardly noticed him then because of his not being one of the dancers: he was part of the ballroom's scenery, like the trestle table and the lemonade bottles, and Mrs. Dwyer and Mr. Dwyer. The youths who'd danced with her then in their Saturday-night blue suits had later disappeared into the town, or to Dublin or Britain, leaving behind them those who became the middle-aged bachelors of the hills. There'd been a boy called Patrick Grady whom she had loved in those days. Week after week she'd ridden away from the Ballroom of Romance with the image of his face in her mind, a thin face, pale beneath black hair. It had been different, dancing with Patrick Grady, and she'd felt that he found it different dancing with her, although he'd never said so. At night she'd dreamed of him and in the daytime too, while she helped her mother in the kitchen or her father with the cows. Week by week she'd returned to the ballroom, smiling on its pink façade and dancing then in the arms of Patrick Grady. Often they'd stood together drinking lemonade, not saying anything, not knowing what to say. She knew he loved her, and she believed then that he would lead her one day from the dim, romantic ballroom, from its blueness and its pinkness and its crystal bowl of light and its music. She believed he would lead her into sunshine, to the town and the Church of Our Lady Queen of Heaven; to marriage and smiling faces. But someone else had got Patrick Grady, a girl from the town who'd never danced in the wayside ballroom. She'd scooped up Patrick Grady when he didn't have a chance.

Bridie had wept, hearing that. By night she'd lain in her bed in the farmhouse, quietly crying, the tears rolling into her hair and making the pillow damp. When she woke in the early morning the thought was still naggingly with her and it remained with her by day, replacing her daytime dreams of happiness. Someone told her later on that he'd crossed to Britain, to Wolverhampton, with the girl he'd married, and she imagined him there, in a place she wasn't able properly to visualize, laboring in a factory, his children being born and acquiring the accent of the area. The Ballroom of Romance wasn't the same without him, and when no one else stood out for her particularly over the years and when no one offered her marriage, she found herself wondering about Dano Ryan. If you couldn't have love, the next best thing was surely a decent man.

Bowser Egan hardly fell into that category, nor did Tim Daly. And it was plain to everyone that Cat Bolger and Madge Dowding were wasting their time over the man with the long arms. Madge Dowding was already a figure of fun in the ballroom, the way she ran after the bachelors; Cat Bolger would end up the same if she wasn't careful. One way or another it wasn't difficult to be a figure of fun in the ballroom, and you didn't have to be as old as Madge Dowding: a girl who'd just left the Presentation Nuns had once asked Eyes Horgan what he had in his trouser pocket and he told her it was a penknife. She'd repeated this afterwards in the cloakroom, how she'd requested Eyes Horgan not to dance so close to her because his penknife was sticking into her. "Jeez, aren't you the right baby!" Patty Byrne had shouted delightedly: everyone had laughed, knowing that Eyes Horgan only came to the ballroom for stuff like that. He was no use to any girl.

"Two lemonades, Mrs. Dwyer," Bowser Egan said, "and two packets of Kerry Creams. Is Kerry Creams all right, Bridie?"

She nodded, smiling. Kerry Creams would be fine, she said.

"Well, Bridie, isn't that the great outfit you have!" Mrs. Dwyer remarked. "Doesn't the red suit her, Bowser?"

By the swing doors stood Mr. Dwyer, smoking a cigarette that he held cupped in his left hand. His small eyes noted all developments. He had been aware of Madge Dowding's anxiety when Eyes Horgan had inserted two fingers into the back opening of her dress. He had looked away, not caring for the incident, but had it developed further he would have spoken to Eyes Horgan, as he had on other occasions. Some of the younger lads didn't know any better and would dance very close to their partners, who generally were too embarrassed to do anything about it, being young themselves. But that, in Mr. Dwyer's opinion, was a different kettle of fish altogether because they were decent young lads who'd in no time at all be doing a steady line with a girl and would end up as he had himself with Mrs. Dwyer, in the same house with her, sleeping in a bed with her, firmly married. It was the middle-aged bachelors who required the watching: they came down from the hills like mountain goats, released from their mammies and from the smell of animals and soil. Mr. Dwyer continued to watch Eyes Horgan, wondering how drunk he was.

Dano Ryan's song came to an end, Mr. Swanton laid down his clarinet, Mr. Maloney rose from the piano. Dano Ryan wiped sweat from his face and the three men slowly moved towards Mrs. Dwyer's trestle table.

"Jeez, you have powerful legs," Eyes Horgan whispered to Madge Dowding, but Madge Dowding's attention was on the man with the long arms, who had left Cat Bolger's side and was proceeding in the direction of the men's lavatory. He never took refreshments. She moved, herself, towards the men's lavatory, to take up a position outside it, but Eyes Horgan followed her. "Would you take a lemonade, Madge?" he asked. He had a small bottle of whiskey on him: if they went into a corner they could add a drop of it to the lemonade. She didn't drink spirits, she reminded him, and he went away.

"Excuse me a minute," Bowser Egan said, putting down his bottle of lemonade. He crossed the floor to the lavatory. He too, Bridie knew, would have a small bottle of whiskey on him. She watched while Dano Ryan, listening to a story Mr. Maloney was telling, paused in the center of the ballroom, his head bent to hear what was being said. He was a big man, heavily made, with black hair that was slightly touched with grey, and big hands. He laughed when Mr. Maloney came to the end of his story and then bent his head again, in order to listen to a story told by Mr. Swanton.

"Are you on your own, Bridie?" Cat Bolger asked, and Bridie said she was waiting for Bowser Egan. "I think I'll have a lemonade," Cat Bolger said.

Younger boys and girls stood with their arms still around one another, queueing up for refreshments. Boys who hadn't danced at all, being nervous because they didn't know any steps, stood in groups, smoking and making jokes. Girls who hadn't been danced with yet talked to one another, their eyes wandering. Some of them sucked at straws in lemonade bottles.

Bridie, still watching Dano Ryan, imagined him wearing the glasses he'd referred   60
to, sitting in the farmhouse kitchen, reading one of her father's Wild West novels. She imagined the three of them eating a meal she'd prepared, fried eggs and rashers and fried potato cakes and tea and bread and butter and jam, brown bread and soda and shop bread. She imagined Dano Ryan leaving the kitchen in the morning to go out to the fields in order to weed the mangolds, and her father hobbling off behind him, and the two men working together. She saw hay being cut, Dano Ryan with the scythe that she'd learned to use herself, her father using a rake as best he could. She saw herself, because of the extra help, being able to attend to things in the farmhouse, things she'd never had time for because of the cows and the hens and the fields. There were bedroom curtains that needed repairing where the net had ripped, and wallpaper that had become loose and needed to be stuck up with flour paste. The scullery required whitewashing.

The night he'd blown up the tire of her bicycle she'd thought he was going to kiss her. He'd crouched on the ground in the darkness with his ear to the tire, listening for escaping air. When he could hear none he'd straightened up and said he thought she'd be all right on the bicycle. His face had been quite close to hers and she'd smiled at him. At that moment, unfortunately, Mr. Maloney had blown an impatient blast on the horn of his motorcar.

Often she'd been kissed by Bowser Egan, on the nights when he insisted on riding part of the way home with her. They had to dismount in order to push their bicycles up a hill and the first time he'd accompanied her he'd contrived to fall against her, steadying himself by putting a hand on her shoulder. The next thing she was aware of was the moist quality of his lips and the sound of his bicycle as it clattered noisily on the road. He'd suggested then, regaining his breath, that they should go into a field.

That was nine years ago. In the intervening passage of time she'd been kissed as well, in similar circumstances, by Eyes Horgan and Tim Daly. She'd gone into fields with them and permitted them to put their arms about her while heavily they breathed. At one time or another she had imagined marriage with one or other of them, seeing them in the farmhouse with her father, even though the fantasies were unlikely.

Bridie stood with Cat Bolger, knowing that it would be some time before Bowser Egan came out of the lavatory. Mr. Maloney, Mr. Swanton, and Dano Ryan approached, Mr. Maloney insisting that he would fetch three bottles of lemonade from the trestle table.

"You sang the last one beautifully," Bridie said to Dano Ryan. "Isn't it a beauti-   65
ful song?"

Mr. Swanton said it was the finest song ever written, and Cat Bolger said she preferred "Danny Boy," which in her opinion was the finest song ever written.

"Take a suck of that," said Mr. Maloney, handing Dano Ryan and Mr. Swanton bottles of lemonade. "How's Bridie tonight? Is your father well, Bridie?"

Her father was all right, she said.

"I hear they're starting a cement factory," said Mr. Maloney. "Did anyone hear talk of that? They're after striking some commodity in the earth that makes good cement. Ten feet down, over at Kilmalough."

"It'll bring employment," said Mr. Swanton. "It's employment that's necessary in this area."   70

"Canon O'Connell was on about it," Mr. Maloney said. "There's Yankee money involved."

"Will the Yanks come over?" inquired Cat Bolger. "Will they run it themselves, Mr. Maloney?"

Mr. Maloney, intent on his lemonade, didn't hear the questions and Cat Bolger didn't repeat them.

"There's stuff called Optrex," Bridie said quietly to Dano Ryan, "that my father took the time he had a cold in his eyes. Maybe Optrex would settle the watering, Dano."

"Ah sure, it doesn't worry me that much—"   75

"It's terrible, anything wrong with the eyes. You wouldn't want to take a chance. You'd get Optrex in a chemist, Dano, and a little bowl with it so that you can bathe the eyes."

Her father's eyes had become red-rimmed and unsightly to look at. She'd gone into Riordan's Medical Hall in the town and had explained what the trouble was, and Mr. Riordan had recommended Optrex. She told this to Dano Ryan, adding that her father had had no trouble with his eyes since. Dano Ryan nodded.

"Did you hear that, Mrs. Dwyer?" Mr. Maloney called out. "A cement factory for Kilmalough."

Mrs. Dwyer wagged her head, placing empty bottles in a crate. She'd heard references to the cement factory, she said: it was the best news for a long time.

"Kilmalough'll never know itself," her husband commented, joining her in her task with the empty lemonade bottles.   80

"'Twill bring prosperity certainly," said Mr. Swanton. "I was saying just there, Justin, that employment's what's necessary."

"Sure, won't the Yanks—" began Cat Bolger, but Mr. Maloney interrupted her.

"The Yanks'll be in at the top, Cat, or maybe not here at all—maybe only inserting money into it. It'll be local labor entirely."

"You'll not marry a Yank, Cat," said Mr. Swanton, loudly laughing. "You can't catch those fellows."

"Haven't you plenty of homemade bachelors?" suggested Mr. Maloney. He laughed also, throwing away the straw he was sucking through and tipping the bottle into his mouth. Cat Bolger told him to get on with himself. She moved towards the men's lavatory and took up a position outside it, not speaking to Madge Dowding, who was still standing there.   85

"Keep a watch on Eyes Horgan," Mrs. Dwyer warned her husband, which was advice she gave him at this time every Saturday night, knowing that Eyes Horgan was drinking in the lavatory. When he was drunk Eyes Horgan was the most difficult of the bachelors.

"I have a drop of it left, Dano," Bridie said quietly. "I could bring it over on Saturday. The eye stuff."

"Ah, don't worry yourself, Bridie—"

"No trouble at all. Honestly now—"

"Mrs. Griffin has me fixed up for a test with Dr. Cready. The old eyes are no worry,   90
only when I'm reading the paper or at the pictures. Mrs. Griffin says I'm only straining
them due to lack of glasses."

He looked away while he said that, and she knew at once that Mrs. Griffin was arranging to marry him. She felt it instinctively: Mrs. Griffin was going to marry him because she was afraid that if he moved away from her cottage, to get married to someone
else, she'd find it hard to replace him with another lodger who'd be good to her affected son. He'd become a father to Mrs. Griffin's affected son, to whom already he was
kind. It was a natural outcome, for Mrs. Griffin had all the chances, seeing him every
night and morning and not having to make do with weekly encounters in a ballroom.

She thought of Patrick Grady, seeing in her mind his pale, thin face. She might
be the mother of four of his children now, or seven or eight maybe. She might be living in Wolverhampton, going out to the pictures in the evenings, instead of looking
after a one-legged man. If the weight of circumstances hadn't intervened she wouldn't
be standing in a wayside ballroom, mourning the marriage of a road mender she didn't
love. For a moment she thought she might cry, standing there thinking of Patrick Grady
in Wolverhampton. In her life, on the farm and in the house, there was no place for tears.
Tears were a luxury, like flowers would be in the fields where the mangolds grew, or
fresh whitewash in the scullery. It wouldn't have been fair ever to have wept in the
kitchen while her father sat listening to *Spot the Talent:* her father had more right to
weep, having lost a leg. He suffered in a greater way, yet he remained kind and concerned for her.

In the Ballroom of Romance she felt behind her eyes the tears that it would have
been improper to release in the presence of her father. She wanted to let them go, to
feel them streaming on her cheeks, to receive the sympathy of Dano Ryan and of everyone else. She wanted them all to listen to her while she told them about Patrick Grady
who was now in Wolverhampton and about the death of her mother and her own life
since. She wanted Dano Ryan to put his arm around her so that she could lean her head
against it. She wanted him to look at her in his decent way and to stroke with his road
mender's fingers the backs of her hands. She might wake in a bed with him and imagine for a moment that he was Patrick Grady. She might bathe his eyes and pretend.

"Back to business," said Mr. Maloney, leading his band across the floor to their
instruments.

"Tell your father I was asking for him," Dano Ryan said. She smiled and she   95
promised, as though nothing had happened, that she would tell her father that.

She danced with Tim Daly and then again with the youth who'd said he intended to emigrate. She saw Madge Dowding moving swiftly towards the man with
the long arms as he came out of the lavatory, moving faster than Cat Bolger. Eyes Horgan approached Cat Bolger. Dancing with her, he spoke earnestly, attempting to persuade her to permit him to ride part of the way home with her. He was unaware of the
jealousy that was coming from her as she watched Madge Dowding holding close to
her the man with the long arms while they performed a quickstep. Cat Bolger was in
her thirties too.

"Get away out of that," said Bowser Egan, cutting in on the youth who was dancing with Bridie. "Go home to your mammy, boy." He took her into his arms, saying again
that she was looking great tonight. "Did you hear about the cement factory?" he said.
"Isn't it great for Kilmalough?"

She agreed. She said what Mr. Swanton and Mr. Maloney had said: that the cement
factory would bring employment to the neighborhood.

"Will I ride home with you a bit, Bridie?" Bowser Egan suggested, and she pretended not to hear him. "Aren't you my girl, Bridie, and always have been?" he said, a statement that made no sense at all.

His voice went on whispering at her, saying he would marry her tomorrow only   100 his mother wouldn't permit another woman in the house. She knew what it was like herself, he reminded her, having a parent to look after: you couldn't leave them to rot, you had to honor your father and your mother.

She danced to "The Bells Are Ringing," moving her legs in time with Bowser Egan's while over his shoulder she watched Dano Ryan softly striking one of his smaller drums. Mrs. Griffin had got him even though she was nearly fifty, with no looks at all, a lumpish woman with lumpish legs and arms. Mrs. Griffin had got him just as the girl had got Patrick Grady.

The music ceased, Bowser Egan held her hard against him, trying to touch her face with his. Around them, people whistled and clapped: the evening had come to an end. She walked away from Bowser Egan, knowing that not ever again would she dance in the Ballroom of Romance. She'd been a figure of fun, trying to promote a relationship with a middle-aged County Council laborer, as ridiculous as Madge Dowding dancing on beyond her time.

"I'm waiting outside for you, Cat," Eyes Horgan called out, lighting a cigarette as he made for the swing doors.

Already the man with the long arms—made long, so they said, from carrying rocks off his land—had left the ballroom. Others were moving briskly. Mr. Dwyer was tidying the chairs.

In the cloakroom the girls put on their coats and said they'd see one another at   105 Mass the next day. Madge Dowding hurried. "Are you O.K., Bridie?" Patty Byrne asked and Bridie said she was. She smiled at little Patty Byrne, wondering if a day would come for the younger girl also, if one day she'd decide that she was a figure of fun in a wayside ballroom.

"Good night so," Bridie said, leaving the cloakroom, and the girls who were still chatting there wished her good night. Outside the cloakroom she paused for a moment. Mr. Dwyer was still tidying the chairs, picking up empty lemonade bottles from the floor, setting the chairs in a neat row. His wife was sweeping the floor. "Good night, Bridie," Mr. Dwyer said. "Good night, Bridie," his wife said.

Extra lights had been switched on so that the Dwyers could see what they were doing. In the glare the blue walls of the ballroom seemed tatty, marked with hair oil where men had leaned against them, inscribed with names and initials and hearts with arrows through them. The crystal bowl gave out a light that was ineffective in the glare; the bowl was broken here and there, which wasn't noticeable when the other lights weren't on.

"Good night so," Bridie said to the Dwyers. She passed through the swing doors and descended the three concrete steps on the gravel expanse in front of the ballroom. People were gathered on the gravel, talking in groups, standing with their bicycles. She saw Madge Dowding going off with Tim Daly. A youth rode away with a girl on the crossbar of his bicycle. The engines of motorcars started.

"Good night, Bridie," Dano Ryan said.

"Good night, Dano," she said.   110

She walked across the gravel towards her bicycle, hearing Mr. Maloney, somewhere behind her, repeating that no matter how you looked at it the cement factory would be a great thing for Kilmalough. She heard the bang of a car door and knew it was Mr. Swanton banging the door of Mr. Maloney's car because he always gave it the same loud bang. Two other doors banged as she reached her bicycle and then the engine started up and the headlights went on. She touched the two tires of the bicycle to make certain she hadn't a puncture. The wheels of Mr. Maloney's car traversed the gravel and were silent when they reached the road.

"Good night, Bridie," someone called, and she replied, pushing her bicycle towards the road.

"Will I ride a little way with you?" Bowser Egan asked.

They rode together and when they arrived at the hill for which it was necessary to dismount she looked back and saw in the distance the four colored bulbs that decorated the façade of the Ballroom of Romance. As she watched the lights went out, and she imagined Mr. Dwyer pulling the metal grid across the front of his property and locking the two padlocks that secured it. His wife would be waiting with the evening's takings, sitting in the front of their car.

"D'you know what it is, Bridie," said Bowser Egan, "you were never looking bet-   115
ter than tonight." He took from a pocket of his suit the small bottle of whiskey he had. He uncorked it and drank some and then handed it to her. She took it and drank. "Sure, why wouldn't you?" he said, surprised to see her drinking because she never had in his company before. It was an unpleasant taste, she considered, a taste she'd experienced only twice before, when she'd taken whiskey as a remedy for toothache. "What harm would it do you?" Bowser Egan said as she raised the bottle again to her lips. He reached out a hand for it, though, suddenly concerned lest she should consume a greater share than he wished her to.

She watched him drinking more expertly than she had. He would always be drinking, she thought. He'd be lazy and useless, sitting in the kitchen with the *Irish Press*. He'd waste money buying a secondhand motorcar in order to drive into the town to go to the public houses on fair days.

"She's shook these days," he said, referring to his mother. "She'll hardly last two years, I'm thinking." He threw the empty whiskey bottle into the ditch and lit a cigarette. They pushed their bicycles. He said:

"When she goes, Bridie, I'll sell the bloody place up. I'll sell the pigs and the whole damn one and twopence worth." He paused in order to raise the cigarette to his lips. He drew in smoke and exhaled it. "With the cash that I'll get I could improve some place else, Bridie."

They reached a gate on the left-hand side of the road and automatically they pushed their bicycles towards it and leaned them against it. He climbed over the gate into the field and she climbed after him. "Will we sit down here, Bridie?" he said, offering the suggestion as one that had just occurred to him, as though they'd entered the field for some other purpose.

"We could improve a place like your own one," he said, putting his right arm   120
around her shoulders. "Have you a kiss in you, Bridie?" He kissed her, exerting pressure with his teeth. When his mother died he would sell his farm and spend the money in the town. After that he would think of getting married because he'd have nowhere to go, because he'd want a fire to sit at and a woman to cook food for him. He kissed her again, his lips hot, the sweat on his cheeks sticking to her. "God, you're great at kissing," he said.

She rose, saying it was time to go, and they climbed over the gate again. "There's nothing like a Saturday," he said. "Good night to you so, Bridie."

He mounted his bicycle and rode down the hill, and she pushed hers to the top and then mounted it also. She rode through the night as on Saturday nights for years she had ridden and never would ride again because she'd reached a certain age. She would wait now and in time Bowser Egan would seek her out because his mother would have died. Her father would probably have died also by then. She would marry Bowser Egan because it would be lonesome being by herself in the farmhouse.

QUESTIONS FOR CLOSE READING OF SETTING AND MOOD

1. Describe the town that Bridie lives in. What are the principal characteristics that you noticed?
2. What is Bridie's routine in town? What does she do each week?
3. Who visits her regularly?
4. What is life on the farm like for Bridie? Which descriptive passages most intensely communicate the emotional mood of life on the farm?
5. Why are Saturday nights different for Bridie?
6. Which descriptive passages best communicate an emotional mood of the ballroom itself? How sensitive is Bridie to the atmosphere of the ballroom? What are her thoughts about it?
7. What are the men in the ballroom like? Are they typically romantic? Are they cultured and emotionally mature?
8. What are the other women in the ballroom like? What are their hopes and ambitions?
9. In what ways is the ballroom a reflection of life in the larger community? What does the ballroom tell you about the larger community?

QUESTIONS FOR INTERPRETATION OF SETTING AND MOOD

1. In "The Ballroom of Romance" the setting of the ballroom in which Bridie meets Dano Ryan, Eyes Horgan, and Bowser Egan is based on genuine dancehalls in rural Ireland. What does the monotonous, repetitive nature of the setting tell us about the opportunities of the people in it? How does the dull, mediocre band contribute to the setting? What mood does the setting establish, and how does it seem to affect the hopes and ambitions of Bridie and other women, such as Madge Dowding, in the community? What does the setting of this small locale tell you about the community?
2. Is it possible that Bridie and Bowser Egan are examples of arrested emotional development? They both live with their parents, and yet they are both of "a certain age" when most modern individuals are out on their own. Does living with a parent perpetuate juvenile behavior? Is this one of the themes of the story? Are there other examples of arrested development in the story?
3. Does this story imply that women have fewer opportunities in rural Ireland than do men? Are the women in this story victims? Are the men victims? Why does Bridie accept the responsibility of taking care of her one-legged father? Does her decision surprise anyone in the community? What, finally, does the future hold for Bridie? Is it brighter than it is for Bowser Egan?

4. To what extent does this story elicit a sympathetic response from you? Do you find yourself sympathetic to Bridie, or are you critical of her behavior? How does Trevor use the setting to evoke a response from you concerning all these characters?

5. This story portrays an environment and setting that are foreign to most people in North America. The church is a dominant force; poverty or privation is a general condition; the means of earning a living are limited; education is rudimentary. How difficult is it for you to understand the culture of rural Ireland as it is presented here? What cultural characteristics do you have to be especially tolerant of if you are to respond positively to these characters?

CHARACTER AND PSYCHOLOGY

Character is often the central focus of a story, as in Eudora Welty's Phoenix in "A Worn Path," a psychologically powerful portrait of a woman. Some characters, such as Hamlet, are **round,** or psychologically developed, and other characters, such as Lorenzo in "The Pot of Basil," are **flat** or psychologically undeveloped. Some characters, such as Prince Prospero in "The Masque of the Red Death," are **static:** they do not change in the course of the story. Others, such as the narrator in Charlotte Perkins Gilman's "The Yellow Wallpaper," are **dynamic:** they change.

Stock characters are common types we recognize: a gossip who tells tales about people, a soldier who brags about his exploits, a mean stepmother, a young idler. The wicked brothers in "The Pot of Basil" are stock characters who parallel the wicked sisters in "Cinderella." Both Lisabetta and Lorenzo are, on one level, stock characters: young lovers foiled by their elders.

Characters reveal themselves mainly through their actions and their internal reflections. Boccaccio shows us Lisabetta first as a daring young woman becoming the lover of the man she wants to marry. After he is dead, we see her weeping over her lover's head until she is driven mad. Yet we never learn the details of her thoughts and feelings, such as how she can tolerate the injustices of her brothers. Were she a psychologically developed character, we would learn more about her reflections: her thoughts and her inner life. As it is we know only her actions. Similarly, the actions of the characters in "Two Cents" show us all we are permitted to know about them.

The narrator in "The Yellow Wallpaper" reveals herself entirely through her writing, her telling us a diarylike story of events in her three-month summer rental of a home in which the wallpaper has a variety of effects upon her. She wrestles against the paper, with it, and then against it until it has a force of its own. She reveals that her husband is a physician, like her brother, and that they both feel that she is well, while she feels that she is unwell. The style of the story is deeply reflective, almost entirely internalized action. Near the end we are given bits of dialogue, but everything in the story is filtered through the sensibility of a woman who may be enduring a nervous breakdown.

CHARLOTTE PERKINS GILMAN   (1860–1935)

Charlotte Perkins Gilman was born and raised in Hartford, Connecticut, in a circle of distinguished intellectuals. "The Yellow Wallpaper," for example, was written after her separation from her husband, Charles Walter Stetson, her cousin and an artist in Providence, where she had attended the Rhode Island School of Design. They had been married in 1884 and she suffered a mental breakdown after the birth of her daughter in 1885. After a period of separation from her husband, she realized that divorce would be her only salvation and hope for sanity. "The Yellow Wallpaper" was almost certainly a result of her reflection on the experiences during her breakdown. She then began a career as a writer and lecturer, distinguishing herself as an economist in her Women and Economics *(1898). Her autobiography,* The Living of Charlotte Perkins Gilman, *was published after her death in 1935. She is among the most important early American feminist writers.*

The Yellow Wallpaper _____ *1892*

It is very seldom that mere ordinary people like John and myself secure ancestral halls for the summer.

A colonial mansion, a hereditary estate, I would say a haunted house and reach the height of romantic felicity—but that would be asking too much of fate!

Still I will proudly declare that there is something queer about it.

Else, why should it be let so cheaply? And why have stood so long untenanted?

John laughs at me, of course, but one expects that.   5

John is practical in the extreme. He has no patience with faith, an intense horror of superstition, and he scoffs openly at any talk of things not to be felt and seen and put down in figures.

John is a physician, and *perhaps*—(I would not say it to a living soul, of course, but this is dead paper and a great relief to my mind)—*perhaps* that is one reason I do not get well faster.

You see, he does not believe I am sick! And what can one do?

If a physician of high standing, and one's own husband, assures friends and relatives that there is really nothing the matter with one but temporary nervous depression—a slight hysterical tendency—what is one to do?

My brother is also a physician, and also of high standing, and he says the same thing.   10

So I take phosphates or phosphites—whichever it is—and tonics, and air and exercise, and journeys, and am absolutely forbidden to "work" until I am well again.

Personally, I disagree with their ideas.

Personally, I believe that congenial work, with excitement and change, would do me good.

But what is one to do?

I did write for a while in spite of them; but it *does* exhaust me a good deal—having to be so sly about it, or else meet with heavy opposition.   15

I sometimes fancy that in my condition, if I had less opposition and more society and stimulus—but John says the very worst thing I can do is to think about my condition, and I confess it always makes me feel bad.

So I will let it alone and talk about the house.

The most beautiful place! It is quite alone, standing well back from the road, quite three miles from the village. It makes me think of English places that you read about, for there are hedges and walls and gates that lock, and lots of separate little houses for the gardeners and people.

There is a *delicious* garden! I never saw such a garden—large and shady, full of box-bordered° paths, and lined with long grape-covered arbors with seats under them.

There were greenhouses, but they are all broken now.   20

There was some legal trouble, I believe, something about the heirs and co-heirs; anyhow, the place has been empty for years.

That spoils my ghostliness, I am afraid, but I don't care—there is something strange about the house—I can feel it.

I even said so to John one moonlight evening, but he said what I felt was a draught, and shut the window.

I get unreasonably angry with John sometimes. I'm sure I never used to be so sensitive. I think it is due to this nervous condition.

But John says if I feel so I shall neglect proper self-control; so I take pains to con-   25
trol myself—before him, at least, and that makes me very tired.

I don't like our room a bit. I wanted one downstairs that opened onto the piazza and had roses all over the window, and such pretty old-fashioned chintz hangings! But John would not hear of it.

He said there was only one window and not room for two beds, and no near room for him if he took another.

He is very careful and loving, and hardly lets me stir without special direction.

I have a schedule prescription for each hour in the day; he takes all care from me, and so I feel basely ungrateful not to value it more.

He said he came here solely on my account, that I was to have perfect rest and all   30
the air I could get. "Your exercise depends on your strength, my dear," said he, "and your food somewhat on your appetite; but air you can absorb all the time." So we took the nursery at the top of the house.

It is a big, airy room, the whole floor nearly, with windows that look all ways, and air and sunshine galore. It was nursery first, and then playroom and gymnasium, I should judge, for the windows are barred for little children, and there are rings and things in the walls.

The paint and paper look as if a boys' school had used it. It is stripped off—the paper—in great patches all around the head of my bed, about as far as I can reach, and in a great place on the other side of the room low down. I never saw a worse paper in my life. One of those sprawling, flamboyant patterns committing every artistic sin.

It is dull enough to confuse the eye in following, pronounced enough constantly to irritate and provoke study, and when you follow the lame uncertain curves for a little distance they suddenly commit suicide—plunge off at outrageous angles, destroy themselves in unheard-of contradictions.

The color is repellent, almost revolting: a smouldering unclean yellow, strangely faded by the slow-turning sunlight. It is a dull yet lurid orange in some places, a sickly sulphur tint in others.

No wonder the children hated it! I should hate it myself if I had to live in this   35
room long.

There comes John, and I must put this away—he hates to have me write a word.

We have been here two weeks, and I haven't felt like writing before, since that first day.

box-bordered: bordered with boxwood hedges

I am sitting by the window now, up in this atrocious nursery, and there is nothing to hinder my writing as much as I please, save lack of strength.

John is away all day, and even some nights when his cases are serious.

I am glad my case is not serious!   40

But these nervous troubles are dreadfully depressing.

John does not know how much I really suffer. He knows there is no reason to suffer, and that satisfies him.

Of course it is only nervousness. It does weigh on me so not to do my duty in any way!

I meant to be such a help to John, such a real rest and comfort, and here I am a comparative burden already!

Nobody would believe what an effort it is to do what little I am able—to dress and   45
entertain, and order things.

It is fortunate Mary is so good with the baby. Such a dear baby!

And yet I *cannot* be with him, it makes me so nervous.

I suppose John never was nervous in his life. He laughs at me so about this wallpaper!

At first he meant to repaper the room, but afterward he said that I was letting it get the better of me, and that nothing was worse for a nervous patient than to give way to such fancies.

He said that after the wallpaper was changed it would be the heavy bedstead, and   50
then the barred windows, and then that gate at the head of the stairs, and so on.

"You know the place is doing you good," he said, "and really, dear, I don't care to renovate the house just for a three months' rental."

"Then do let us go downstairs," I said. "There are such pretty rooms there."

Then he took me in his arms and called me a blessed little goose, and said he would go down cellar, if I wished, and have it whitewashed into the bargain.

But he is right enough about the beds and windows and things.

It is as airy and comfortable a room as anyone need wish, and, of course, I would   55
not be so silly as to make him uncomfortable just for a whim.

I'm really getting quite fond of the big room, all but that horrid paper.

Out of one window I can see the garden—those mysterious deep-shaded arbors, the riotous old-fashioned flowers, and bushes and gnarly trees.

Out of another I get a lovely view of the bay and a little private wharf belonging to the estate. There is a beautiful shaded lane that runs down there from the house. I always fancy I see people walking in these numerous paths and arbors, but John has cautioned me not to give way to fancy in the least. He says that with my imaginative power and habit of story-making, a nervous weakness like mine is sure to lead to all manner of excited fancies, and that I ought to use my will and good sense to check the tendency. So I try.

I think sometimes that if I were only well enough to write a little it would relieve the press of ideas and rest me.

But I find I get pretty tired when I try.   60

It is so discouraging not to have any advice and companionship about my work. When I get really well, John says we will ask Cousin Henry and Julia down for a long visit; but he says he would as soon put fireworks in my pillow-case as to let me have those stimulating people about now.

I wish I could get well faster.

But I must not think about that. This paper looks to me as if it *knew* what a vicious influence it had!

There is a recurrent spot where the pattern lolls like a broken neck and two bulbous eyes stare at you upside down.

I get positively angry with the impertinence of it and the everlastingness. Up and down and sideways they crawl, and those absurd unblinking eyes are everywhere. There is one place where two breadths didn't match, and the eyes go all up and down the line, one a little higher than the other.

I never saw so much expression in an inanimate thing before, and we all know how much expression they have! I used to lie awake as a child and get more entertainment and terror out of blank walls and plain furniture than most children could find in a toy-store.

I remember what a kindly wink the knobs of our big old bureau used to have, and there was one chair that always seemed like a strong friend.

I used to feel that if any of the other things looked too fierce I could always hop into that chair and be safe.

The furniture in this room is no worse than inharmonious, however, for we had to bring it all from downstairs. I suppose when this was used as a playroom they had to take the nursery things out, and no wonder! I never saw such ravages as the children have made here.

The wallpaper, as I said before, is torn off in spots, and it sticketh closer than a brother—they must have had perseverance as well as hatred.

Then the floor is scratched and gouged and splintered, the plaster itself is dug out here and there, and this great heavy bed, which is all we found in the room, looks as if it had been through the wars.

But I don't mind it a bit—only the paper.

There comes John's sister. Such a dear girl as she is, and so careful of me! I must not let her find me writing.

She is a perfect and enthusiastic housekeeper, and hopes for no better profession. I verily believe she thinks it is the writing which made me sick!

But I can write when she is out, and see her a long way off from these windows.

There is one that commands the road, a lovely shaded winding road, and one that just looks off over the country. A lovely country, too, full of great elms and velvet meadows.

This wallpaper has a kind of subpattern in a different shade, a particularly irritating one, for you can only see it in certain lights, and not clearly then.

But in the places where it isn't faded and where the sun is just so—I can see a strange, provoking, formless sort of figure that seems to skulk about behind that silly and conspicuous front design.

There's sister on the stairs!

Well, the Fourth of July is over! The people are all gone, and I am tired out. John thought it might do me good to see a little company, so we just had Mother and Nellie and the children down for a week.

Of course I didn't do a thing. Jennie sees to everything now.

But it tired me all the same.

John says if I don't pick up faster he shall send me to Weir Mitchell° in the fall.

But I don't want to go there at all. I had a friend who was in his hands once, and she says he is just like John and my brother, only more so!

Weir Mitchell: Dr. S. Weir Mitchell (1829–1914), a Philadelphia physician who developed the "rest cure" for his women patients, including Gilman

Besides, it is such an undertaking to go so far.   85

I don't feel as if it was worthwhile to turn my hand over for anything, and I'm getting dreadfully fretful and querulous.

I cry at nothing, and cry most of the time.

Of course I don't when John is here, or anybody else, but when I am alone.

And I am alone a good deal just now. John is kept in town very often by serious cases, and Jennie is good and lets me alone when I want her to.

So I walk a little in the garden or down that lovely lane, sit on the porch under   90
the roses, and lie down up here a good deal.

I'm getting really fond of the room in spite of the wallpaper. Perhaps *because* of the wallpaper.

It dwells in my mind so!

I lie here on this great immovable bed—it is nailed down, I believe—and follow that pattern about by the hour. It is as good as gymnastics, I assure you. I start, we'll say, at the bottom, down in the corner over there where it has not been touched, and I determine for the thousandth time that I *will* follow that pointless pattern to some sort of a conclusion.

I know a little of the principle of design, and I know this thing was not arranged on any laws of radiation, or alternation, or repetition, or symmetry, or anything else that I ever heard of.

It is repeated, of course, by the breadths, but not otherwise.   95

Looked at in one way, each breadth stands alone; the bloated curves and flourishes—a kind of "debased Romanesque" with dilirium tremens go waddling up and down in isolated columns of fatuity.

But, on the other hand, they connect diagonally, and the sprawling outlines run off in great slanting waves of optic horror, like a lot of wallowing sea-weeds in full chase.

The whole thing goes horizontally, too, at least it seems so, and I exhaust myself trying to distinguish the order of its going in that direction.

They have used a horizontal breadth for a frieze, and that adds wonderfully to the confusion.

There is one end of the room where it is almost intact, and there, when the   100
crosslights fade and the low sun shines directly upon it, I can almost fancy radiation after all—the interminable grotesque seems to form around a common center and rush off in headlong plunges of equal distraction.

It makes me tired to follow it. I will take a nap, I guess.

I don't know why I should write this.

I don't want to.

I don't feel able.

And I know John would think it absurd. But I *must* say what I feel and think in some   105
way—it is such a relief!

But the effort is getting to be greater than the relief.

Half the time now I am awfully lazy, and lie down ever so much. John says I mustn't lose my strength, and has me take cod liver oil and lots of tonics and things, to say nothing of ale and wines and rare meat.

Dear John! He loves me very dearly, and hates to have me sick. I tried to have a real earnest reasonable talk with him the other day, and tell him how I wish he would let me go and make a visit to Cousin Henry and Julia.

But he said I wasn't able to go, nor able to stand it after I got there; and I did not make out a very good case for myself, for I was crying before I had finished.

It is getting to be a great effort for me to think straight. Just this nervous weakness, 110
I suppose.

And dear John gathered me up in his arms, and just carried me upstairs and laid
me on the bed, and sat by me and read to me till it tired my head.

He said I was his darling and his comfort and all he had, and that I must take
care of myself for his sake, and keep well.

He says no one but myself can help me out of it, that I must use my will and self-
control and not let any silly fancies run away with me.

There's one comfort—the baby is well and happy, and does not have to occupy
this nursery with the horrid wallpaper.

If we had not used it, that blessed child would have! What a fortunate escape! 115
Why, I wouldn't have a child of mine, an impressionable little thing, live in such a room
for worlds.

I never thought of it before, but it is lucky that John kept me here after all; I can
stand it so much easier than a baby, you see.

Of course I never mention it to them anymore—I am too wise—but I keep watch
for it all the same.

There are things in the wallpaper that nobody knows about but me, or ever will.

Behind that outside pattern the dim shapes get clearer every day.

It is always the same shape, only very numerous. 120

And it is like a woman stooping down and creeping about behind that pattern. I
don't like it a bit. I wonder—I begin to think—I wish John would take me away from here!

It is so hard to talk with John about my case, because he is so wise, and because
he loves me so.

But I tried it last night.

It was moonlight. The moon shines in all around just as the sun does.

I hate to see it sometimes, it creeps so slowly, and always comes in by one window 125
or another.

John was asleep and I hated to waken him, so I kept still and watched the moonlight on that undulating wallpaper till I felt creepy.

The faint figure behind seemed to shake the pattern, just as if she wanted to
get out.

I got up softly and went to feel and see if the paper *did* move, and when I came
back John was awake.

"What is it, little girl?" he said. "Don't go walking about like that—you'll get cold."

I thought it was a good time to talk, so I told him that I really was not gaining 130
here, and that I wished he would take me away.

"Why, darling!" said he. "Our lease will be up in three weeks, and I can't see how
to leave before."

"The repairs are not done at home, and I cannot possibly leave town just now. Of
course, if you were in any danger, I could and would, but you really are better, dear,
whether you can see it or not. I am a doctor, dear, and I know. You are gaining flesh and
color, your appetite is better, I feel really much easier about you."

"I don't weigh a bit more," said I, "nor as much; and my appetite may be better
in the evening when you are here but it is worse in the morning when you are away!"

"Bless her little heart!" said he with a big hug. "She shall be as sick as she pleases!
But now let's improve the shining hours by going to sleep, and talk about it in
the morning!"

"And you won't go away?" I asked gloomily. 135

"Why, how can I, dear? It is only three weeks more and then we will take a nice little trip for a few days while Jennie is getting the house ready. Really, dear, you are better!"

"Better in body perhaps—" I began, and stopped short, for he sat up straight and looked at me with such a stern, reproachful look that I could not say another word.

"My darling," said he, "I beg you, for my sake and for our child's sake, as well as for your own, that you will never for one instant let that idea enter your mind! There is nothing so dangerous, so fascinating, to a temperament like yours. It is a false and foolish fancy. Can you trust me as a physician when I tell you so?"

So of course I said no more on that score, and we went to sleep before long. He thought I was asleep first, but I wasn't, and lay there for hours trying to decide whether that front pattern and the back pattern really did move together or separately.

On a pattern like this, by daylight, there is a lack of sequence, a defiance of law, 140 that is a constant irritant to a normal mind.

The color is hideous enough, and unreliable enough, and infuriating enough, but the pattern is torturing.

You think you have mastered it, but just as you get well under way in following, it turns a back-somersault and there you are. It slaps you in the face, knocks you down, and tramples upon you. It is like a bad dream.

The outside pattern is a florid arabesque, reminding one of a fungus. If you can imagine a toadstool in joints, an interminable string of toadstools, budding and sprouting in endless convolutions—why, that is something like it.

That is, sometimes!

There is one marked peculiarity about this paper, a thing nobody seems to notice 145 but myself, and that is that it changes as the light changes.

When the sun shoots in through the east window—I always watch for that first long, straight ray—it changes so quickly that I never can quite believe it.

That is why I watch it always.

By moonlight—the moon shines in all night when there is a moon—I wouldn't know it was the same paper.

At night in any kind of light, in twilight, candlelight, lamplight, and worst of all by moonlight, it becomes bars! The outside pattern, I mean, and the woman behind it is as plain as can be.

I didn't realize for a long time what the thing was that showed behind, that dim 150 subpattern, but now I am quite sure it is a woman.

By daylight she is subdued, quiet. I fancy it is the pattern that keeps her so still. It is so puzzling. It keeps me quiet by the hour.

I lie down ever so much now. John says it is good for me, and to sleep all I can.

Indeed he started the habit by making me lie down for an hour after each meal.

It is a very bad habit, I am convinced, for you see, I don't sleep.

And that cultivates deceit, for I don't tell them I'm awake—oh, no!   155

The fact is I am getting a little afraid of John.

He seems very queer sometimes, and even Jennie has an inexplicable look.

It strikes me occasionally, just as a scientific hypothesis, that perhaps it is the paper!

I have watched John when he did not know I was looking, and come into the room suddenly on the most innocent excuses, and I've caught him several times *looking at the paper!* And Jennie too. I caught Jennie with her hand on it once.

She didn't know I was in the room, and when I asked her in a quiet, a very quiet 160 voice, with the most restrained manner possible, what she was doing with the paper, she turned around as if she had been caught stealing, and looked quite angry—asked me why I should frighten her so!

Then she said that the paper stained everything it touched, that she had found yellow smooches on all my clothes and John's and she wished we would be more careful!

Did not that sound innocent? But I know she was studying that pattern, and I am determined that nobody shall find it out but myself!

Life is very much more exciting now than it used to be. You see, I have something more to expect, to look forward to, to watch. I really do eat better, and am more quiet than I was.

John is so pleased to see me improve! He laughed a little the other day, and said I seemed to be flourishing in spite of my wallpaper.

I turned it off with a laugh. I had no intention of telling him it was *because* of the   165
wallpaper—he would make fun of me. He might even want to take me away.

I don't want to leave now until I have found it out. There is a week more, and I think that will be enough.

I'm feeling so much better!

I don't sleep much at night, for it is so interesting to watch developments; but I sleep a good deal during the daytime.

In the daytime it is tiresome and perplexing.

There are always new shoots on the fungus, and new shades of yellow all over it.   170
I cannot keep count of them, though I have tried conscientiously.

It is the strangest yellow, that wallpaper! It makes me think of all the yellow things I ever saw—not beautiful ones like buttercups, but old, foul, bad yellow things.

But there is something else about that paper—the smell! I noticed it the moment we came into the room, but with so much air and sun it was not bad. Now we have had a week of fog and rain, and whether the windows are open or not, the smell is here.

It creeps all over the house.

I find it hovering in the dining-room, skulking in the parlor, hiding in the hall, lying in wait for me on the stairs.

It gets into my hair.   175

Even when I go to ride, if I turn my head suddenly and surprise it—there is that smell!

Such a peculiar odor, too! I have spent hours in trying to analyze it, to find what it smelled like.

It is not bad—at first—and very gentle, but quite the subtlest, most enduring odor I ever met.

In this damp weather it is awful. I wake up in the night and find it hanging over me.

It used to disturb me at first. I thought seriously of burning the house—to reach   180
the smell.

But now I am used to it. The only thing I can think of that it is like is the *color* of the paper! A yellow smell.

There a very funny mark on this wall, low down, near the mopboard. A streak that runs round the room. It goes behind every piece of furniture, except the bed, a long, straight, even *smooch*, as if it had been rubbed over and over.

I wonder how it was done and who did it, and what they did it for. Round and round and round—round and round and round—it makes me dizzy!

I really have discovered something at last.

Through watching so much at night, when it changes so, I have finally found out.   185

The front pattern *does* move—and no wonder! The woman behind shakes it!

Sometimes I think there are a great many women behind, and sometimes only one, and she crawls around fast, and her crawling shakes it all over.

Then in the very bright spots she keeps still, and in the very shady spots she just takes hold of the bars and shakes them hard.

And she is all the time trying to climb through. But nobody could climb through that pattern—it strangles so; I think that is why it has so many heads.

They get through and then the pattern strangles them off and turns them upside   190
down, and makes their eyes white!

If those heads were covered or taken off it would not be half so bad.

I think that woman gets out in the daytime!

And I'll tell you why—privately—I've seen her!

I can see her out of every one of my windows!

It is the same woman, I know, for she is always creeping, and most women do not   195
creep by daylight.

I see her in that long shaded lane, creeping up and down. I see her in those dark grape arbors, creeping all round the garden.

I see her on that long road under the trees, creeping along, and when a carriage comes she hides under the blackberry vines.

I don't blame her a bit. It must be very humiliating to be caught creeping by daylight!

I always lock the door when I creep by daylight. I can't do it at night, for I know John would suspect something at once.

And John is so queer now that I don't want to irritate him. I wish he would take   200
another room! Besides, I don't want anybody to get that woman out at night but myself.

I often wonder if I could see her out of all the windows at once.

But, turn as fast as I can, I can only see out of one at one time.

And though I always see her, she *may* be able to creep faster than I can turn! I have watched her sometimes away off in the open country, creeping as fast as a cloud shadow in a wind.

If only that top pattern could be gotten off from the under one! I mean to try it, little by little.

I have found out another funny thing, but I shan't tell it this time! It does not do   205
to trust people too much.

There are only two more days to get this paper off, and I believe John is beginning to notice. I don't like the look in his eyes.

And I heard him ask Jennie a lot of professional questions about me. She had a very good report to give.

She said I slept a good deal in the daytime.

John knows I don't sleep very well at night, for all I'm so quiet!

He asked me all sorts of questions too, and pretended to be very loving and kind.   210
As if I couldn't see through him!

Still, I don't wonder he acts so, sleeping under this paper for three months.

It only interests me, but I feel sure John and Jennie are affected by it.

Hurrah! This is the last day, but it is enough. John is to stay in town over night, and won't be out until this evening.

Jennie wanted to sleep with me—the sly thing; but I told her I should undoubt-   215
edly rest better for a night all alone.

That was clever, for really I wasn't alone a bit! As soon as it was moonlight and that poor thing began to crawl and shake the pattern, I got up and ran to help her.

I pulled and she shook. I shook and she pulled, and before morning we had peeled off yards of that paper.

A strip about as high as my head and half around the room.

And then when the sun came and that awful pattern began to laugh at me, I declared I would finish it today!

We go away tomorrow, and they are moving all my furniture down again to leave things as they were before.   220

Jennie looked at the wall in amazement, but I told her merrily that I did it out of pure spite at the vicious thing.

She laughed and said she wouldn't mind doing it herself, but I must not get tired.

How she betrayed herself that time!

But I am here, and no person touches this paper but Me—not *alive!*

She tried to get me out of the room—it was too patent! But I said it was so quiet   225
and empty and clean now that I believed I would lie down again and sleep all I could, and not to wake me even for dinner—I would call when I woke.

So now she is gone, and the servants are gone, and the things are gone, and there is nothing left but that great bedstead nailed down, with the canvas mattress we found on it.

We shall sleep downstairs tonight, and take the boat home tomorrow.

I quite enjoy the room, now it is bare again.

How those children did tear about here!

This bedstead is fairly gnawed!   230

But I must get to work.

I have locked the door and thrown the key down into the front path.

I don't want to go out, and I don't want to have anybody come in, till John comes.

I want to astonish him.

I've got a rope up here that even Jennie did not find. If that woman does get out,   235
and tries to get away, I can tie her!

But I forgot I could not reach far without anything to stand on!

This bed will *not* move!

I tried to lift and push it until I was lame, and then I got so angry I bit off a little piece at one corner—but it hurt my teeth.

Then I peeled off all the paper I could reach standing on the floor. It sticks horribly and the pattern just enjoys it! All those strangled heads and bulbous eyes and waddling fungus growths just shriek with derision!

I am getting angry enough to do something desperate. To jump out of the win-   240
dow would be admirable exercise, but the bars are too strong even to try.

Besides I wouldn't do it. Of course not. I know well enough that a step like that is improper and might be misconstrued.

I don't like to *look* out of the windows even—there are so many of those creeping women, and they creep so fast.

I wonder if they all come out of that wallpaper as I did!

But I am securely fastened now by my well-hidden rope—you don't get *me* out in the road there!

I suppose I shall have to get back behind the pattern when it comes night, and that   245
is hard!

It is so pleasant to be out in this great room and creep around as I please!

I don't want to go outside. I won't, even if Jennie asks me to.

For outside you have to creep on the ground, and everything is green instead of yellow.

But here I can creep smoothly on the floor, and my shoulder just fits in that long smooch around the wall, so I cannot lose my way.

Why, there's John at the door!

It is no use, young man, you can't open it!

How he does call and pound!

Now he's crying to Jennie for an axe.

It would be a shame to break down that beautiful door!

"John, dear!" said I in the gentlest voice. "The key is down by the front steps, under a plantain leaf!"

That silenced him for a few moments.

Then he said, very quietly indeed, "Open the door, my darling!"

"I can't," said I. "The key is down by the front door under a plantain leaf!" And then I said it again, several times, very gently and slowly, and said it so often that he had to go and see, and he got it of course, and came in. He stopped short by the door.

"What is the matter?" he cried. "For God's sake, what are you doing!"

I kept on creeping just the same, but I looked at him over my shoulder.

"I've got out at last," said I, "in spite of you and Jane. And I've pulled off most of the paper, so you can't put me back!"

Now why should that man have fainted? But he did, and right across my path by the wall, so that I had to creep over him every time!

QUESTIONS FOR CLOSE READING OF CHARACTER AND PSYCHOLOGY

1. How are the narrator and John contrasted in the first few paragraphs of the story? What happens to this contrast as the story progresses?

2. What is the narrator's "condition"? Does the way she writes reveal the narrator to be psychologically impaired or perhaps suffering a nervous breakdown?

3. How do the narrator's descriptions of and feelings toward the wallpaper change? Why? What symbolic values does the color of the wallpaper take on for the narrator? How does the wallpaper reflect her character?

4. What "conclusion" is the narrator looking for in the wallpaper? What does she find?

5. How does the narrator respond to John's attempts to take care of her? Why? Do you feel John understands the narrator? How much effort does he make to understand her?

6. How does John defend the claim that he knows his wife better than she knows herself? Do you agree that he does?

7. The narrator tells us "it is the pattern that keeps [the woman in the wallpaper] so still." What does the pattern represent? Why is there a woman in the wallpaper instead of a man? Is the woman in the wallpaper a projection of the character of the narrator?

8. The narrator says she is tempted to jump out of the window. Why doesn't she?

9. Who is the "Jane" referred to at the end of the story?

10. Why does John faint? How does the narrator react?

QUESTIONS FOR INTERPRETATION OF CHARACTER AND PSYCHOLOGY

1. The narrator says that she and John are "mere ordinary people." Does the story or narrator imply a social awareness that would categorize people as ordinary or extraordinary? Would extraordinary people be distinguished by their talent? Their money? Their birth? Or does it mean that what happens to John and the narrator can happen to any couple? Would you say that the narrator reveals herself to be "ordinary"? Does the narrator seem to be an ordinary mother, given her relationship with "the baby"? Jennie is John's sister; is she ordinary? How does she compare with the narrator?

2. Do you agree with John that the narrator should not write? What connection is there between her illness and her desire to write? Is the desire to write rooted in psychological necessity? What is the relationship of her writing to the economic security of the family? To what extent is the issue of family important to the narrator?

3. Who is the woman in the wallpaper? What connection does she have to the narrator? Why is yellow wallpaper an appropriate metaphor in this story? Would another color make a difference? How important is the fact that the color seems to come off on the narrator and on John?

4. The narrator's husband is a physician, which implies that he enjoys a relatively high social status. Does the narrator seem to enjoy the same status? The house that they have rented has many rooms, although only one truly figures in this story. Why is that, given the economic position of these characters?

5. Does the narrator become insane? Or does she start that way? What would the "sane" response to her situation have been? Is there a connection between wallpaper and sanity—or wallpaper and ordinariness? Is the question of sanity a significant issue in this story? Examine the story for evidence of compulsive behavior on the part of the narrator. Is this evidence of mental instability? Do you feel her environment—including the people around her—contributes to her "condition"?

RICHARD FORD   (b. 1944)

Primarily a novelist, Richard Ford is often praised for his ability to produce a keen sense of place in his work. His unusual sensitivity to environment is clearly shown in his first novel, A Piece of My Heart *(1976), which is set in Mississippi, where he was born. But Ford also describes exotic environments, such as Oaxaca, Mexico, in* The Ultimate Good Luck *(1981), a high-tension story about a man trying to get his girlfriend's brother out of prison, where he is doing time for a drug deal. His third novel,* The Sportswriter *(1986), portrays a lost soul who has trouble making connections with his own family. As a southern writer, Ford has been inevitably compared with Faulkner, but his style is much more spare and his purposes—examining the surfaces of contemporary life—much different. He has connected himself with Raymond Carver, a friend and mentor.*

Communist _____ *1987*

My mother once had a boyfriend named Glen Baxter. This was in 1961. We—my mother and I—were living in the little house my father had left her up the Sun River, near Victory,

Montana, west of Great Falls. My mother was thirty-two at the time. I was sixteen. Glen Baxter was somewhere in the middle, between us, though I cannot be exact about it.

We were living then off the proceeds of my father's life insurance policies, with my mother doing some part-time waitressing work up in Great Falls and going to the bars in the evenings, which I know is where she met Glen Baxter. Sometimes he would come back with her and stay in her room at night, or she would call up from town and explain that she was staying with him in his little place on Lewis Street by the GN yards. She gave me his number every time, but I never called it. I think she probably thought that what she was doing was terrible, but simply couldn't help herself. I thought it was all right, though. Regular life it seemed, and still does. She was young, and I knew that even then.

Glen Baxter was a Communist and liked hunting, which he talked about a lot. Pheasants. Ducks. Deer. He killed all of them, he said. He had been to Vietnam as far back as then, and when he was in our house he often talked about shooting the animals over there—monkeys and beautiful parrots—using military guns just for sport. We did not know what Vietnam was then, and Glen, when he talked about that, referred to it only as "the Far East." I think now he must've been in the CIA and been disillusioned by something he saw or found out about and been thrown out, but that kind of thing did not matter to us. He was a tall, dark-eyed man with short black hair, and was usually in a good humor. He had gone halfway through college in Peoria, Illinois, he said, where he grew up. But when he was around our life he worked wheat farms as a ditcher, and stayed out of work winters and in the bars drinking with women like my mother, who had work and some money. It is not an uncommon life to lead in Montana.

What I want to explain happened in November. We had not been seeing Glen Baxter for some time. Two months had gone by. My mother knew other men, but she came home most days from work and stayed inside watching television in her bedroom and drinking beers. I asked about Glen once, and she said only that she didn't know where he was, and I assumed they had had a fight and that he was gone off on a flyer back to Illinois or Massachusetts, where he said he had relatives. I'll admit that I liked him. He had something on his mind always. He was a labor man as well as a Communist, and liked to say that the country was poisoned by the rich, and strong men would need to bring it to life again, and I liked that because my father had been a labor man, which was why we had a house to live in and money coming through. It was also true that I'd had a few boxing bouts by then—just with town boys and one with an Indian from Choteau—and there were some girlfriends I knew from that. I did not like my mother being around the house so much at night, and I wished Glen Baxter would come back, or that another man would come along and entertain her somewhere else.

At two o'clock on a Saturday, Glen drove up into our yard in a car. He had had a big brown Harley-Davidson that he rode most of the year, in his black-and-red irrigators° and a baseball cap turned backwards. But this time he had a car, a blue Nash Ambassador.° My mother and I went out on the porch when he stopped inside the olive trees my father had planted as a shelter belt, and my mother had a look on her face of not much pleasure. It was starting to be cold in earnest by then. Snow was down already onto the Fairfield Bench, though on this day a chinook was blowing, and it could as easily have been spring, though the sky above the Divide was turning over in silver and blue clouds of winter.

"We haven't seen you in a long time, I guess," my mother said coldly.

5

---

irrigators: galoshes   *Nash Ambassador:* an expensive automobile

"My little retarded sister died," Glen said, standing at the door of his old car. He was wearing his orange VFW jacket and canvas shoes we called wino shoes, something I had never seen him wear before. He seemed to be in a good humor. "We buried her in Florida near the home."

"That's a good place," my mother said in a voice that meant she was a wronged party in something.

"I want to take this boy hunting today, Aileen," Glen said. "There're snow geese down now. But we have to go right away, or they'll be gone to Idaho by tomorrow."

"He doesn't care to go," my mother said.   10

"Yes I do," I said, and looked at her.

My mother frowned at me. "Why do you?"

"Why does he need a reason?" Glen Baxter said and grinned.

"I want him to have one, that's why." She looked at me oddly. "I think Glen's drunk, Les."

"No, I'm not drinking," Glen said, which was hardly ever true. He looked at both   15
of us, and my mother bit down on the side of her lower lip and stared at me in a way to make you think she thought something was being put over on her and she didn't like you for it. She was very pretty, though when she was mad her features were sharpened and less pretty by a long way. "All right, then I don't care," she said to no one in partic- ular. "Hunt, kill, maim. Your father did that too." She turned to go back inside.

"Why don't you come with us, Aileen?" Glen was smiling still, pleased.

"To do what?" my mother said. She stopped and pulled a package of cigarettes out of her dress pocket and put one in her mouth.

"It's worth seeing."

"See dead animals?" my mother said.

"These geese are from Siberia, Aileen," Glen said. "They're not like a lot of geese.   20
Maybe I'll buy us dinner later. What do you say?"

"Buy what with?" my mother said. To tell the truth, I didn't know why she was so mad at him. I would've thought she'd be glad to see him. But she just suddenly seemed to hate everything about him.

"I've got some money," Glen said. "Let me spend it on a pretty girl tonight."

"Find one of those and you're lucky," my mother said, turning away toward the front door.

"I already found one," Glen Baxter said. But the door slammed behind her, and he looked at me then with a look I think now was helplessness, though I could not see a way to change anything.

My mother sat in the backseat of Glen's Nash and looked out the window while we   25
drove. My double gun was in the seat between us beside Glen's Belgian pump, which he kept loaded with five shells in case, he said, he saw something beside the road he wanted to shoot. I had hunted rabbits before, and had ground-sluiced pheasants and other birds, but I had never been on an actual hunt before, one where you drove out to some special place and did it formally. And I was excited. I had a feeling that something important was about to happen to me, and that this would be a day I would always remember.

My mother did not say anything for a long time, and neither did I. We drove up through Great Falls and out the other side toward Fort Benton, which was on the bench- land where wheat was grown.

"Geese mate for life," my mother said, just out of the blue, as we were driving. "I hope you know that. They're special birds."

"I know that," Glen said in the front seat. "I have every respect for them."

"So where were you for three months?" she said. "I'm only curious."

"I was in the Big Hole for a while," Glen said, "and after that I went over to Doug- las, Wyoming." 30

"What were you planning to do there?" my mother asked.

"I wanted to find a job, but it didn't work out."

"I'm going to college," she said suddenly, and this was something I had never heard about before. I turned to look at her, but she was staring out her window and wouldn't see me.

"I knew French once," Glen said. "*Rosé*'s pink. *Rouge*'s red." He glanced at me and smiled. "I think that's a wise idea, Aileen. When are you going to start?"

"I don't want Les to think he was raised by crazy people all his life," my mother said. 35

"Les ought to go himself," Glen said.

"After I go, he will."

"What do you say about that, Les?" Glen said, grinning.

"He says it's just fine," my mother said.

"It's just fine," I said. 40

Where Glen Baxter took us was out onto the high flat prairie that was disked for wheat and had high, high mountains out to the east, with lower heartbreak hills in be- tween. It was, I remember, a day for blues in the sky, and down in the distance we could see the small town of Floweree, and the state highway running past it toward Fort Ben- ton and the Hi-line. We drove out on top of the prairie on a muddy dirt road fenced on both sides, until we had gone about three miles, which is where Glen stopped.

"All right," he said, looking up in the rearview mirror at my mother. "You wouldn't think there was anything here, would you?"

"*We're* here," my mother said. "You brought us here."

"You'll be glad though," Glen said, and seemed confident to me. I had looked around myself but could not see anything. No water or trees, nothing that seemed like a good place to hunt anything. Just wasted land. "There's a big lake out there, Les," Glen said. "You can't see it now from here because it's low. But the geese are there. You'll see."

"It's like the moon out here, I recognize that," my mother said, "only it's worse." 45 She was staring out at the flat wheatland as if she could actually see something in par- ticular, and wanted to know more about it. "How'd you find this place?"

"I came once on the wheat push," Glen said.

"And I'm sure the owner told you just to come back and hunt anytime you like and bring anybody you wanted. Come one, come all. Is that it?"

"People shouldn't own land anyway," Glen said. "Anybody should be able to use it."

"Les, Glen's going to poach here," my mother said. "I just want you to know that, because that's a crime and the law will get you for it. If you're a man now, you're going to have to face the consequences."

"That's not true," Glen Baxter said, and looked gloomily out over the steering 50 wheel down the muddy road toward the mountains. Though for myself I believed it was true, and didn't care. I didn't care about anything at that moment except seeing geese fly over me and shooting them down.

"Well, I'm certainly not going out there," my mother said. "I like towns better, and I already have enough trouble."

"That's okay," Glen said. "When the geese lift up you'll get to see them. That's all I wanted. Les and me'll go shoot them, won't we, Les?"

"Yes," I said, and I put my hand on my shotgun, which had been my father's and was heavy as rocks.

"Then we should go on," Glen said, "or we'll waste our light."

We got out of the car with our guns. Glen took off his canvas shoes and put on his 55 pair of black irrigators out of the trunk. Then we crossed the barbed wire fence, and walked out into the high, tilled field toward nothing. I looked back at my mother when we were still not so far away, but I could only see the small, dark top of her head, low in the backseat of the Nash, staring out and thinking what I could not then begin to say.

On the walk toward the lake, Glen began talking to me. I had never been alone with him, and knew little about him except what my mother said—that he drank too much, or other times that he was the nicest man she had ever known in the world and that someday a woman would marry him, though she didn't think it would be her. Glen told me as we walked that he wished he had finished college, but that it was too late now, that his mind was too old. He said he had liked the Far East very much, and that people there knew how to treat each other, and that he would go back some day but couldn't go now. He said also that he would like to live in Russia for a while and mentioned the names of people who had gone there, names I didn't know. He said it would be hard at first, because it was so different, but that pretty soon anyone would learn to like it and wouldn't want to live anywhere else, and that Russians treated Americans who came to live there like kings. There were Communists everywhere now, he said. You didn't know them, but they were there. Montana had a large number, and he was in touch with all of them. He said that Communists were always in danger and that he had to protect himself all the time. And when he said that he pulled back his VFW jacket and showed me the butt of a pistol he had stuck under his shirt against his bare skin. "There are people who want to kill me right now," he said, "and I would kill a man myself if I thought I had to." And we kept walking. Though in a while he said, "I don't think I know much about you, Les. But I'd like to. What do you like to do?"

"I like to box," I said. "My father did it. It's a good thing to know."

"I suppose you have to protect yourself too," Glen said.

"I know how to," I said.

"Do you like to watch TV," Glen asked, and smiled. 60

"Not much."

"I love to," Glen said. "I could watch it instead of eating if I had one."

I looked out straight ahead over the green tops of sage that grew to the edge of the disked field, hoping to see the lake Glen said was there. There was an airishness and a sweet smell that I thought might be the place we were going, but I couldn't see it. "How will we hunt these geese?" I said.

"It won't be hard," Glen said. "Most hunting isn't even hunting. It's only shooting. And that's what this will be. In Illinois you would dig holes in the ground and hide and set out your decoys. Then the geese come to you, over and over again. But we don't have time for that here." He glanced at me. "You have to be sure the first time here."

"How do you know they're here now," I asked. And I looked toward the High- 65 wood Mountains twenty miles away, half in snow and half dark blue at the bottom. I could see the little town of Floweree then, looking shabby and dimly lighted in the distance. A red bar sign shone. A car moved slowly away from the scattered buildings.

"They always come November first," Glen said.

"Are we going to poach them?"

"Does it make any difference to you," Glen asked.

"No, it doesn't."

"Well then, we aren't," he said.   70

We walked then for a while without talking. I looked back once to see the Nash far and small in the flat distance. I couldn't see my mother, and I thought that she must've turned on the radio and gone to sleep, which she always did, letting it play all night in her bedroom. Behind the car the sun was nearing the rounded mountains southwest of us, and I knew that when the sun was gone it would be cold. I wished my mother had decided to come along with us, and I thought for a moment of how little I really knew her at all.

Glen walked with me another quarter-mile, crossed another barbed wire fence where sage was growing, then went a hundred yards through wheatgrass and spurge until the ground went up and formed a kind of long hillock bunker built by a farmer against the wind. And I realized the lake was just beyond us. I could hear the sound of a car horn blowing and a dog barking all the way down in the town, then the wind seemed to move and all I could hear then and after then were geese. So many geese, from the sound of them, though I still could not see even one. I stood and listened to the high-pitched shouting sound, a sound I had never heard so close, a sound with size to it—though it was not loud. A sound that meant great numbers and that made your chest rise and your shoulders tighten with expectancy. It was a sound to make you feel separate from it and everything else, as if you were of no importance in the grand scheme of things.

"Do you hear them singing," Glen asked. He held his hand up to make me stand still. And we both listened. "How many do you think, Les, just hearing?"

"A hundred," I said. "More than a hundred."

"Five thousand," Glen said. "More than you can believe when you see them. Go see."   75

I put down my gun and on my hands and knees crawled up the earthwork through the wheatgrass and thistle, until I could see down to the lake and see the geese. And they were there, like a white bandage laid on the water, wide and long and continuous, a white expanse of snow geese, seventy yards from me, on the bank, but stretching far onto the lake, which was large itself—a half-mile across, with thick tules on the far side and wild plums farther and the blue mountain behind them.

"Do you see the big raft?" Glen said from below me, in a whisper.

"I see it," I said, still looking. It was such a thing to see, a view I had never seen and have not since.

"Are any on the land?" he said.

"Some are in the wheatgrass," I said, "but most are swimming."   80

"Good," Glen said. "They'll have to fly. But we can't wait for that now."

And I crawled backwards down the heel of land to where Glen was, and my gun. We were losing our light, and the air was purplish and cooling. I looked toward the car but couldn't see it, and I was no longer sure where it was below the lighted sky.

"Where do they fly to?" I said in a whisper, since I did not want anything to be ruined because of what I did or said. It was important to Glen to shoot the geese, and it was important to me.

"To the wheat," he said. "Or else they leave for good. I wish your mother had come, Les. Now she'll be sorry."

I could hear the geese quarreling and shouting on the lake surface. And I wondered if they knew we were here now. "She might be," I said with my heart pounding, but I didn't think she would be much.   85

It was a simple plan he had. I would stay behind the bunker, and he would crawl on his belly with his gun through the wheatgrass as near to the geese as he could. Then he would simply stand up and shoot all the ones he could close up, both in the air and on the ground. And when all the others flew up, with luck some would turn toward me as they came into the wind, and then I could shoot them and turn them back to him, and he would shoot them again. He could kill ten, he said, if he was lucky, and I might kill four. It didn't seem hard.

"Don't show them your face," Glen said. "Wait till you think you can touch them, then stand up and shoot. To hesitate is lost in this."

"All right," I said. "I'll try it."

"Shoot one in the head, and then shoot another one," Glen said. "It won't be hard." He patted me on the arm and smiled. Then he took off his VFW jacket and put it on the ground, climbed up the side of the bunker, cradling his shotgun in his arms, and slid on his belly into the dry stalks of yellow grass out of my sight.

Then, for the first time in that entire day, I was alone. And I didn't mind it. I sat   90
squat down in the grass, loaded my double gun and took my other two shells out of my pocket to hold. I pushed the safety off and on to see that it was right. The wind rose a little, scuffed the grass and made me shiver. It was not the warm chinook now, but a wind out of the north, the one geese flew away from if they could.

Then I thought about my mother, in the car alone, and how much longer I would stay with her, and what it might mean to her for me to leave. And I wondered when Glen Baxter would die and if someone would kill him, or whether my mother would marry him and how I would feel about it. And though I didn't know why, it occurred to me that Glen Baxter and I would not be friends when all was said and done, since I didn't care if he ever married my mother or didn't.

Then I thought about boxing and what my father had taught me about it. To tighten your fists hard. To strike out straight from the shoulder and never punch backing up. How to cut a punch by snapping your fist inwards, how to carry your chin low, and to step toward a man when he is falling so you can hit him again. And most important, to keep your eyes open when you are hitting in the face and causing damage, because you need to see what you're doing to encourage yourself, and because it is when you close your eyes that you stop hitting and get hurt badly. "Fly all over your man, Les," my father said. "When you see your chance, fly on him and hit him till he falls." That, I thought, would always be my attitude in things.

And then I heard the geese again, their voices in unison, louder and shouting, as if the wind had changed again and put all new sounds in the cold air. And then a *boom.* And I knew Glen was in among them and had stood up to shoot. The noise of geese rose and grew worse, and my fingers burned where I held my gun too tight to the metal, and I put it down and opened my fist to make the burning stop so I could feel the trigger when the moment came. *Boom,* Glen shot again, and I heard him shuck a shell, and all the sounds out beyond the bunker seemed to be rising—the geese, the shots, the air itself going up. *Boom,* Glen shot another time, and I knew he was taking his careful time to make his shots good. And I held my gun and started to crawl up the bunker so as not to be surprised when the geese came over me and I could shoot.

From the top I saw Glen Baxter alone in the wheatgrass field, shooting at a white goose with black tips of wings that was on the ground not far from him, but trying to run and pull into the air. He shot it once more, and it fell over dead with its wings flapping.

Glen looked back at me and his face was distorted and strange. The air around   95
him was full of white rising geese and he seemed to want them all. "Behind you, Les,"

he yelled at me and pointed. "They're all behind you now." I looked behind me, and there were geese in the air as far as I could see, more than I knew how many, moving so slowly, their wings wide out and working calmly and filling the air with noise, though their voices were not as loud or as shrill as I had thought they would be. And they were so close! Forty feet, some of them. The air around me vibrated and I could feel the wind from their wings and it seemed to me I could kill as many as the times I could shoot—a hundred or a thousand—and I raised my gun, put the muzzle on the head of a white goose, and fired. It shuddered in the air, its wide feet sank below its belly, its wings cradled out to hold back air, and it fell straight down and landed with an awful sound, a noise a human would make, a thick, soft, *hump* noise. I looked up again and shot another goose, could hear the pellets hit its chest, but it didn't fall or even break its pattern for flying. *Boom,* Glen shot again. And then again. "Hey," I heard him shout, "Hey, hey." And there were geese flying over me, flying in line after line. I broke my gun and reloaded, and thought to myself as I did: I need confidence here, I need to be sure with this. I pointed at another goose and shot it in the head, and it fell the way the first one had, wings out, its belly down, and with the same thick noise of hitting. Then I sat down in the grass on the bunker and let geese fly over me.

By now the whole raft was in the air, all of it moving in a slow swirl above me and the lake and everywhere, finding the wind and heading out south in long wavering lines that caught the last sun and turned to silver as they gained a distance. It was a thing to see, I will tell you now. Five thousand white geese all in the air around you, making a noise like you have never heard before. And I thought to myself then: this is something I will never see again. I will never forget this. And I was right.

Glen Baxter shot twice more. One he missed, but with the other he hit a goose flying away from him, and knocked it half falling and flying into the empty lake not far from shore, where it began to swim as though it was fine and make its noise.

Glen stood in the stubby grass, looking out at the goose, his gun lowered. "I didn't need to shoot that one, did I, Les?"

"I don't know," I said, sitting on the little knoll of land, looking at the goose swimming in the water.

"I don't know why I shoot 'em. They're so beautiful." He looked at me.   100

"I don't know either," I said.

"Maybe there's nothing else to do with them." Glen stared at the goose again and shook his head. "Maybe this is exactly what they're put on earth for."

I did not know what to say because I did not know what he could mean by that, though what I felt was embarrassment at the great numbers of geese there were, and a dulled feeling like a hunger because the shooting had stopped and it was over for me now.

Glen began to pick up his geese, and I walked down to my two that had fallen close together and were dead. One had hit with such an impact that its stomach had split and some of its inward parts were knocked out. Though the other looked unhurt, its soft white belly turned up like a pillow, its head and jagged bill-teeth, its tiny black eyes looking as they would if they were alive.

"What's happened to the hunters out here?" I heard a voice speak. It was my   105
mother, standing in her pink dress on the knoll above us, hugging her arms. She was smiling though she was cold. And I realized that I had lost all thought of her in the shooting. "Who did all this shooting? Is this your work, Les?"

"No," I said.

"Les is a hunter, though, Aileen," Glen said. "He takes his time." He was holding two white geese by their necks, one in each hand, and he was smiling. He and my mother seemed pleased.

"I see you didn't miss too many," my mother said and smiled. I could tell she admired Glen for his geese, and that she had done some thinking in the car alone. "It *was* wonderful, Glen," she said. "I've never seen anything like that. They were like snow."

"It's worth seeing once, isn't it?" Glen said. "I should've killed more, but I got excited."

My mother looked at me then. "Where's yours, Les?"   110

"Here," I said and pointed to my two geese on the ground beside me.

My mother nodded in a nice way, and I think she liked everything then and wanted the day to turn out right and for all of us to be happy. "Six, then. You've got six in all."

"One's still out there," I said, and motioned where the one goose was swimming in circles on the water.

"Okay," my mother said and put her hand over her eyes to look. "Where is it?"

Glen Baxter looked at me then with a strange smile, a smile that said he wished I   115
had never mentioned anything about the other goose. And I wished I hadn't either. I looked up in the sky and could see the lines of geese by the thousands shining silver in the light, and I wished we could just leave and go home.

"That one's my mistake there," Glen Baxter said and grinned. "I shouldn't have shot that one, Aileen. I got too excited."

My mother looked out on the lake for a minute, then looked at Glen and back again. "Poor goose." She shook her head. "How will you get it, Glen?"

"I can't get that one now," Glen said.

My mother looked at him. "What do you mean?"

"I'm going to leave that one," Glen said.   120

"Well, no. You can't leave one," my mother said. "You shot it. You have to get it. Isn't that a rule?"

"No," Glen said.

And my mother looked from Glen to me. "Wade out and get it, Glen," she said in a sweet way, and my mother looked young then, like a young girl, in her flimsy short-sleeved waitress dress and her skinny, bare legs in the wheatgrass.

"No." Glen Baxter looked down at his gun and shook his head. And I didn't know why he wouldn't go, because it would've been easy. The lake was shallow. And you could tell that anyone could've walked out a long way before it got deep, and Glen had on his boots.

My mother looked at the white goose, which was not more than thirty yards from   125
the shore, its head up, moving in slow circles, its wings settled and relaxed so you could see the black tips. "Wade out and get it, Glenny, won't you, please?" she said. "They're special things."

"You don't understand the world, Aileen," Glen said. "This can happen. It doesn't matter."

"But that's so cruel, Glen," she said, and a sweet smile came on her lips.

"Raise up your own arms, 'Leeny," Glen said. "I can't see any angel's wings, can you, Les?" He looked at me, but I looked away.

"Then you go on and get it, Les," my mother said. "You weren't raised by crazy people." I started to go, but Glen Baxter suddenly grabbed me by my shoulder and pulled me back hard, so hard his fingers made bruises in my skin that I saw later.

"Nobody's going," he said. "This is over with now."   130

And my mother gave Glen a cold look then. "You don't have a heart, Glen," she said. "There's nothing to love in you. You're just a son of a bitch, that's all."

And Glen Baxter nodded at my mother, then, as if he understood something he had not understood before, but something that he was willing to know. "Fine," he said, "that's fine." And he took his big pistol out from against his belly, the big blue revolver I had only seen part of before and that he said protected him, and he pointed it out at the goose on the water, his arm straight away from him, and shot and missed. And then he shot and missed again. The goose made its noise once. And then he hit it dead, because there was no splash. And then he shot it three times more until the gun was empty and the goose's head was down and it was floating toward the middle of the lake where it was empty and dark blue. "Now who has a heart?" Glen said. But my mother was not there when he turned around. She had already started back to the car and was almost lost from sight in the darkness. And Glen smiled at me then and his face had a wild look on it. "Okay, Les?" he said.

"Okay," I said.

"There're limits to everything, right?"

"I guess so," I said.   135

"Your mother's a beautiful woman, but she's not the only beautiful woman in Montana." And I did not say anything. And Glen Baxter suddenly said, "Here," and he held the pistol out at me. "Don't you want this? Don't you want to shoot me? Nobody thinks they'll die. But I'm ready for it right now." And I did not know what to do then. Though it is true that what I wanted to do was to hit him, hit him as hard in the face as I could, and see him on the ground bleeding and crying and pleading for me to stop. Only at that moment he looked scared to me, and I had never seen a grown man scared before—though I have seen one since—and I felt sorry for him, as though he was already a dead man. And I did not end up hitting him at all.

A light can go out in the heart. All of this happened years ago, but I still can feel now how sad and remote the world was to me. Glen Baxter, I think now, was not a bad man, only a man scared of something he'd never seen before—something soft in himself—his life going a way he didn't like. A woman with a son. Who could blame him there? I don't know what makes people do what they do, or call themselves what they call themselves, only that you have to live someone's life to be the expert.

My mother had tried to see the good side of things, tried to be hopeful in the situation she was handed, tried to look out for us both, and it hadn't worked. It was a strange time in her life then and after that, a time when she had to adjust to being an adult just when she was on the thin edge of things. Too much awareness too early in life was her problem, I think.

And what I felt was only that I had somehow been pushed out into the world, into the real life then, the one I hadn't lived yet. In a year I was gone to hard-rock mining and no-paycheck jobs and not to college. And I have thought more than once about my mother saying that I had not been raised by crazy people, and I don't know what that could mean or what difference it could make, unless it means that love is a reliable commodity, and even that is not always true, as I have found out.

Late on the night that all this took place I was in bed when I heard my mother   140
say, "Come outside, Les. Come and hear this." And I went out onto the front porch barefoot and in my underwear, where it was warm like spring, and there was a spring mist in the air. I could see the lights of the Fairfield Coach in the distance, on its way up to Great Falls.

And I could hear geese, white birds in the sky, flying. They made their high-pitched sound like angry yells, and though I couldn't see them high up, it seemed to me they were everywhere. And my mother looked up and said, "Hear them?" I could smell her hair wet from the shower. "They leave with the moon," she said. "It's still half wild out here."

And I said, "I hear them," and I felt a chill come over my bare chest, and the hair stood up on my arms the way it does before a storm. And for a while we listened.

"When I first married your father, you know, we lived on a street called Bluebird Canyon, in California. And I thought that was the prettiest street and the prettiest name. I suppose no one brings you up like your first love. You don't mind if I say that, do you?" She looked at me hopefully.

"No," I said.

"We have to keep civilization alive somehow." And she pulled her little housecoat   145
together because there was a cold vein in the air, a part of the cold that would be on us the next day. "I don't feel part of things tonight, I guess."

"It's all right," I said.

"Do you know where I'd like to go?"

"No," I said. And I suppose I knew she was angry then, angry with life, but did not want to show me that.

"To the Straits of Juan de Fuca.° Wouldn't that be something? Would you like that?"

"I'd like it," I said. And my mother looked off for a minute, as if she could see the   150
Straits of Juan de Fuca out against the line of mountains, see the lights of things alive and a whole new world.

"I know you liked him," she said after a moment. "You and I both suffer fools too well."

"I didn't like him too much," I said. "I didn't really care."

"He'll fall on his face. I'm sure of that," she said. And I didn't say anything because I didn't care about Glen Baxter anymore, and was happy not to talk about him. "Would you tell me something if I asked you? Would you tell me the truth?"

"Yes," I said.

And my mother did not look at me. "Just tell the truth," she said.   155

"All right," I said.

"Do you think I'm still very feminine? I'm thirty-two years old now. You don't know what that means. But do you think I am?"

And I stood at the edge of the porch, with the olive trees before me, looking straight up into the mist where I could not see geese but could still hear them flying, could almost feel the air move below their white wings. And I felt the way you feel when you are on a trestle all alone and the train is coming, and you know you have to decide. And I said, "Yes, I do." Because that was the truth. And I tried to think of something else then and did not hear what my mother said after that.

And how old was I then? Sixteen. Sixteen is young, but it can also be a grown man. I am forty-one years old now, and I think about that time without regret, though my mother and I never talked in that way again, and I have not heard her voice now in a long, long time.

°*Straits of Juan de Fuca:* the long body of water between Canada and Washington State on the West Coast

QUESTIONS FOR CLOSE READING OF CHARACTER AND PSYCHOLOGY

1. What do you learn about the narrator's mother in the early part of the story?
2. How do Les and his mother live? What is the source of their income?
3. How important is it to know that Glen Baxter is a communist? Do you feel it is important to know that he is a communist?
4. What are you meant to understand about Glen Baxter from the information supplied that tells you he rides a Harley-Davidson and a "blue Nash Ambassador"?
5. Why are we told that Glen Baxter hunts pheasants, ducks, and deer, as well as monkeys and parrots in Vietnam?
6. Why does Les's mother, Aileen, assume he does not want to go hunting with Glen? Why does Les want to go?
7. What is Aileen's attitude toward hunting? What do you know about her attitudes?
8. Why does the narrator's mother feel it important to point out that "geese mate for life"? What is the significance of this concept for her? How important is it to Glen?
9. How does the hunting expedition reveal the basic disagreements between Aileen and Glen? Where does Les stand in relation to their disagreements?
10. What kind of effort does Les make toward learning more about Glen Baxter? How successful is he?

QUESTIONS FOR INTERPRETATION OF CHARACTER AND PSYCHOLOGY

1. Richard Ford's "Communist" emphasizes character in a complex fashion. Glen Baxter begins the story as the focus of attention of the narrator when the narrator, Les, was a young boy. But as the story progresses, we see that as we come to know him we also come to know Les and Les's mother. When Glen shoots the goose and refuses to get it, he reveals a personal quality that Les's mother rejects entirely. She reminds Les that there are civilized ways to behave and that Glen's behavior does not qualify as civilized. Do you agree that Glen behaves in an uncivilized fashion? What aspects of his character convince you?
2. Near the end of the story Glen shows Les a pistol that he keeps under his shirt even while he is walking along with a shotgun. He explains that there are people after him, that he might be in danger at any moment. Is this an example of paranoid behavior? Is it an example of an unstable personality? What details in the story suggest to you that Glen may be unstable?
3. Is the difference between Glen and Aileen regarding the hunting and killing of animals typical of the differences between men and women? Does Richard Ford seem to be making a point that suggests gender is at the basis of their general disagreements about life? What details in the story would support or contradict that idea?
4. The narrator of the story explains that he is telling it long after it happened, when he was only a child. What do we learn about Les's development as a young man? Is it possible to determine the extent to which his mother or Glen acts as a role model? What does his mother mean by her statement "I don't want Les to think he was raised by crazy people all his life"? Why would she worry about such a thing?

KATHERINE MANSFIELD (1888–1923)

Katherine Mansfield changed her name from Kathleen Beauchamp when she began writing. She was born in Wellington, New Zealand, and was educated at school in England, where she eventually decided to remain. Her first collection of stories, In a German Pension *(1911), developed mostly in response to a short period spent in Bavaria. Determined to be a writer, Mansfield produced short stories and reviews on a regular basis and eventually married the critic John Middleton Murry in 1918. Her New Zealand background is apparent in her collections* Bliss and Other Stories *(1920) and* The Garden-Party and Other Stories *(1922). Mansfield's writing career was short. She contracted tuberculosis, and after a sickness of several years—during which she worked continuously—she died at the age of thirty-four. Much of her work was published after her death, including stories, letters, criticism, and poems.* Collected Stories *was published in 1945. She has been praised for having given the short story a modern direction away from concentration on plot and more toward development of character through the use of stream of consciousness.*

The Garden-Party ——————————————— *1922*

And after all the weather was ideal. They could not have had a more perfect day for a garden-party if they had ordered it. Windless, warm, the sky without a cloud. Only the blue was veiled with a haze of light gold, as it is sometimes in early summer. The gardener had been up since dawn, mowing the lawns and sweeping them, until the grass and the dark flat rosettes where the daisy plants had been seemed to shine. As for the roses, you could not help feeling they understood that roses are the only flowers that impress people at garden-parties; the only flowers that everybody is certain of knowing. Hundreds, yes, literally hundreds, had come out in a single night; the green bushes bowed down as though they had been visited by archangels.

Breakfast was not yet over before the men came to put up the marquee.

"Where do you want the marquee put, mother?"

"My dear child, it's no use asking me. I'm determined to leave everything to you children this year. Forget I am your mother. Treat me as an honored guest."

But Meg could not possibly go and supervise the men. She had washed her hair   5
before breakfast, and she sat drinking her coffee in a green turban, with a dark wet curl stamped on each cheek. Jose, the butterfly, always came down in a silk petticoat and a kimono jacket.

"You'll have to go, Laura; you're the artistic one."

Away Laura flew, still holding her piece of bread-and-butter. It's so delicious to have an excuse for eating out of doors, and besides, she loved having to arrange things; she always felt she could do it so much better than anybody else.

Four men in their shirt-sleeves stood grouped together on the garden path. They carried staves covered with rolls of canvas, and they had big tool-bags slung on their backs. They looked impressive. Laura wished now that she had not got the bread-and-butter, but there was nowhere to put it, and she couldn't possibly throw it away. She blushed and tried to look severe and even a little bit short-sighted as she came up to them.

"Good morning," she said, copying her mother's voice. But that sounded so fearfully affected that she was ashamed, and stammered like a little girl, "Oh—er—have you come—is it about the marquee?"

"That's right, miss," said the tallest of the men, a lanky, freckled fellow, and he   10
shifted his tool-bag, knocked back his straw hat and smiled down at her. "That's about it."

His smile was so easy, so friendly that Laura recovered. What nice eyes he had, small, but such a dark blue! And now she looked at the others, they were smiling too. "Cheer up, we won't bite," their smile seemed to say. How very nice workmen were! And what a beautiful morning! She mustn't mention the morning; she must be businesslike. The marquee.

"Well, what about the lily-lawn? Would that do?"

And she pointed to the lily-lawn with the hand that didn't hold the bread-and-butter. They turned, they stared in the direction. A little fat chap thrust out his under-lip, and the tall fellow frowned.

"I don't fancy it," said he. "Not conspicuous enough. You see, with a thing like a marquee," and he turned to Laura in his easy way, "you want to put it somewhere where it'll give you a bang slap in the eye, if you follow me."

Laura's upbringing made her wonder for a moment whether it was quite respectful   15 of a workman to talk to her of bangs slap in the eye. But she did quite follow him.

"A corner of the tennis-court," she suggested. "But the band's going to be in one corner."

"H'm, going to have a band, are you?" said another of the workmen. He was pale. He had a haggard look as his dark eyes scanned the tennis court. What was he thinking?

"Only a very small band," said Laura gently. Perhaps he wouldn't mind so much if the band was quite small. But the tall fellow interrupted.

"Look here, miss, that's the place. Against those trees. Over there. That'll do fine."

Against the karakas.° Then the karaka-trees would be hidden. And they were so lovely, with their broad, gleaming leaves, and their clusters of yellow fruit. They were like trees you imagined growing on a desert island, proud, solitary, lifting their leaves and fruits to the sun in a kind of silent splendor. Must they be hidden by a marquee?

They must. Already the men had shouldered their staves and were making for the place. Only the tall fellow was left. He bent down, pinched a sprig of lavender, put his thumb and forefinger to his nose and snuffed up the smell. When Laura saw that gesture she forgot all about the karakas in her wonder at him caring for things like that—caring for the smell of lavender. How many men that she knew would have done such a thing? Oh, how extraordinarily nice workmen were, she thought. Why couldn't she have workmen for friends rather than the silly boys she danced with and who came to Sunday night supper? She would get on much better with men like these.

It's all the fault, she decided, as the tall fellow drew something on the back of an envelope, something that was to be looped up or left to hang, of these absurd class distinctions. Well, for her part, she didn't feel them. Not a bit, not an atom. . . . And now there came the chock-chock of wooden hammers. Someone whistled, someone sang out, "Are you right there, matey?" "Matey!" The friendliness of it, the—the——Just to prove how happy she was, just to show the tall fellow how at home she felt, and how she despised stupid conventions, Laura took a big bite of her bread-and-butter as she stared at the little drawing. She felt just like a work-girl.

"Laura, Laura, where are you? Telephone, Laura!" a voice cried from the house.

"Coming!" Away she skimmed, over the lawn, up the path, up the steps, across the veranda, and into the porch. In the hall her father and Laurie were brushing their hats ready to go to the office.

"I say, Laura," said Laurie very fast, "you might just give a squiz at my coat before   25 this afternoon. See if it wants pressing."

karakas: New Zealand trees somewhat resembling laurels

"I will," said she. Suddenly she couldn't stop herself. She ran at Laurie and gave him a small, quick squeeze. "Oh, I do love parties, don't you?" gasped Laura.

"Ra-ther," said Laurie's warm, boyish voice, and he squeezed his sister too, and gave her a gentle push. "Dash off to the telephone, old girl."

The telephone. "Yes, yes; oh yes. Kitty? Good morning, dear. Come to lunch? Do, dear. Delighted of course. It will only be a very scratch meal—just the sandwich crusts and broken meringue-shells and what's left over. Yes, isn't it a perfect morning? Your white? Oh, I certainly should. One moment—hold the line. Mother's calling." And Laura sat back. "What, mother? Can't hear."

Mrs. Sheridan's voice floated down the stairs. "Tell her to wear that sweet hat she had on last Sunday."

"Mother says you're to wear that *sweet* hat you had on last Sunday. Good. One o'clock.   30
Bye-bye."

Laura put back the receiver, flung her arms over her head, took a deep breath, stretched and let them fall. "Huh," she sighed, and the moment after the sigh she sat up quickly. She was still, listening. All the doors in the house seemed to be open. The house was alive with soft, quick steps and running voices. The green baize door that led to the kitchen regions swung open and shut with a muffled thud. And now there came a long, chuckling absurd sound. It was the heavy piano being moved on its stiff castors. But the air! If you stopped to notice, was the air always like this? Little faint winds were playing chase, in at the tops of the windows, out at the doors. And there were two tiny spots of sun, one on the inkpot, one on a silver photograph frame, playing too. Darling little spots. Especially the one on the inkpot lid. It was quite warm. A warm little silver star. She could have kissed it.

The front door bell pealed, and there sounded the rustle of Sadie's print skirt on the stairs. A man's voice murmured; Sadie answered, careless, "I'm sure I don't know. Wait. I'll ask Mrs. Sheridan."

"What is it, Sadie?" Laura came into the hall.

"It's the florist, Miss Laura."

It was, indeed. There, just inside the door, stood a wide, shallow tray full of pots   35
of pink lilies. No other kind. Nothing but lilies—canna lilies, big pink flowers, wide open, radiant, almost frighteningly alive on bright crimson stems.

"O-oh, Sadie!" said Laura, and the sound was like a little moan. She crouched down as if to warm herself at that blaze of lilies; she felt they were in her fingers, on her lips, growing in her breast.

"It's some mistake," she said faintly. "Nobody ever ordered so many. Sadie, go and find mother."

But at that moment Mrs. Sheridan joined them.

"It's quite right," she said calmly. "Yes, I ordered them. Aren't they lovely?" She pressed Laura's arm. "I was passing the shop yesterday, and I saw them in the window. And I suddenly thought for once in my life I shall have enough canna lilies. The garden-party will be a good excuse."

"But I thought you said you didn't mean to interfere," said Laura. Sadie had gone.   40
The florist's man was still outside at his van. She put her arm round her mother's neck and gently, very gently, she bit her mother's ear.

"My darling child, you wouldn't like a logical mother, would you? Don't do that. Here's the man."

He carried more lilies still, another whole tray.

"Bank them up, just inside the door, on both sides of the porch, please," said Mrs. Sheridan. "Don't you agree, Laura?"

"Oh, I *do*, mother."

In the drawing-room Meg, Jose and good little Hans had at last succeeded in moving the piano. 45

"Now, if we put this chesterfield against the wall and move everything out of the room except the chairs, don't you think?"

"Quite."

"Hans, move these tables into the smoking-room, and bring a sweeper to take these marks off the carpet and—one moment, Hans——" Jose loved giving orders to the servants, and they loved obeying her. She always made them feel they were taking part in some drama. "Tell mother and Miss Laura to come here at once."

"Very good, Miss Jose."

She turned to Meg. "I want to hear what the piano sounds like, just in case I'm asked to sing this afternoon. Let's try over 'This Life is Weary.' " 50

Pom! Ta-ta-ta *Tee*-ta! The piano burst out so passionately that Jose's face changed. She clasped her hands. She looked mournfully and enigmatically at her mother and Laura as they came in.

This Life is *Wee*-ary,
A Tear—a Sigh,
A Love that *Chan*-ges,
  This Life is *Wee*-ary,
A Tear—a Sigh.
A Love that *Chan*-ges,
And then . . . Good-bye!

But at the word "Good-bye," and although the piano sounded more desperate than ever, her face broke into a brilliant, dreadfully unsympathetic smile.

"Aren't I in good voice, mummy?" she beamed.

This Life is *Wee*-ary,
Hope comes to Die.
A Dream—a *Wa*-kening.

But now Sadie interrupted them. "What is it, Sadie?"

"If you please, m'm, cook says have you got the flags for the sandwiches?" 55

"The flags for the sandwiches, Sadie?" echoed Mrs. Sheridan dreamily. And the children knew by her face that she hadn't got them. "Let me see." And she said to Sadie firmly, "Tell cook I'll let her have them in ten minutes."

Sadie went.

"Now, Laura," said her mother quickly. "Come with me into the smoking-room. I've got the names somewhere on the back of an envelope. You'll have to write them out for me. Meg, go upstairs this minute and take that wet thing off your head. Jose, run and finish dressing this instant. Do you hear me, children, or shall I have to tell your father when he comes home to-night? And—and, Jose, pacify cook if you do go into the kitchen, will you? I'm terrified of her this morning."

The envelope was found at last behind the dining-room clock, though how it had got there Mrs. Sheridan could not imagine.

"One of you children must have stolen it out of my bag, because I remember   60
vividly——cream cheese and lemon-curd. Have you done that?"

"Yes."

"Egg and——" Mrs. Sheridan held the envelope away from her. "It looks like mice. It can't be mice, can it?"

"Olive, pet," said Laura, looking over her shoulder.

"Yes, of course, olive. What a horrible combination it sounds. Egg and olive."

They were finished at last, and Laura took them off to the kitchen. She found   65
Jose there pacifying the cook, who did not look at all terrifying.

"I have never seen such exquisite sandwiches," said Jose's rapturous voice. "How many kinds did you say there were, cook? Fifteen?"

"Fifteen, Miss Jose."

"Well, cook, I congratulate you."

Cook swept up crusts with the long sandwich knife, and smiled broadly.

"Godber's has come," announced Sadie, issuing out of the pantry. She had seen   70
the man pass the window.

That meant the cream puffs had come. Godber's were famous for their cream puffs. Nobody ever thought of making them at home.

"Bring them in and put them on the table, my girl," ordered cook.

Sadie brought them in and went back to the door. Of course Laura and Jose were far too grown-up to really care about such things. All the same, they couldn't help agreeing that the puffs looked very attractive. Very. Cook began arranging them, shaking off the extra icing sugar.

"Don't they carry one back to all one's parties?" said Laura.

"I suppose they do," said practical Jose, who never liked to be carried back. "They   75
look beautifully light and feathery, I must say."

"Have one each, my dears," said cook in her comfortable voice. "Yer ma won't know."

Oh, impossible. Fancy cream puffs so soon after breakfast. The very idea made one shudder. All the same, two minutes later Jose and Laura were licking their fingers with that absorbed inward look that only comes from whipped cream.

"Let's go into the garden, out by the back way," suggested Laura. "I want to see how the men are getting on with the marquee. They're such awfully nice men."

But the back door was blocked by cook, Sadie, Godber's man and Hans. Something had happened.   80

"Tuk-tuk-tuk," clucked cook like an agitated hen. Sadie had her hand clapped to her cheek as though she had toothache. Hans's face was screwed up in the effort to understand. Only Godber's man seemed to be enjoying himself; it was his story.

"What's the matter? What's happened?"

"There's been a horrible accident," said cook. "A man killed."

"A man killed! Where? How? When?"

But Godber's man wasn't going to have his story snatched from under his   85
very nose.

"Know those little cottages just below here, miss?" Know them? Of course, she knew them. "Well, there's a young chap living there, name of Scott, a carter. His horse shied at a traction-engine, corner of Hawke Street this morning, and he was thrown out on the back of his head. Killed."

"Dead!" Laura stared at Godber's man.

"Dead when they picked him up," said Godber's man with relish. "They were taking the body home as I come up here." And he said to the cook, "He's left a wife and five little ones."

"Jose, come here." Laura caught hold of her sister's sleeve and dragged her through the kitchen to the other side of the green baize door. There she paused and leaned against it. "Jose!" she said, horrified, "however are we going to stop everything?"

"Stop everything, Laura!" cried Jose in astonishment. "What do you mean?"   90

"Stop the garden-party, of course." Why did Jose pretend?

But Jose was still more amazed. "Stop the garden-party? My dear Laura, don't be so absurd. Of course we can't do anything of the kind. Nobody expects us to. Don't be so extravagant."

"But we can't possibly have a garden-party with a man dead just outside the front gate."

That really was extravagant, for the little cottages were in a lane to themselves at the very bottom of a steep rise that led up to the house. A broad road ran between. True, they were far too near. They were the greatest possible eyesore, and they had no right to be in that neighborhood at all. They were little mean dwellings painted a chocolate brown. In the garden patches there was nothing but cabbage stalks, sick hens and tomato cans. The very smoke coming out of their chimneys was poverty-stricken. Little rags and shreds of smoke, so unlike the great silvery plumes that uncurled from the Sheridans' chimneys. Washer-women lived in the lane and sweeps° and a cobbler, and a man whose house-front was studded all over with minute bird-cages. Children swarmed. When the Sheridans were little they were forbidden to set foot there because of the revolting language and of what they might catch. But since they were grown up, Laura and Laurie on their prowls sometimes walked through. It was disgusting and sordid. They came out with a shudder. But still one must go everywhere; one must see everything. So through they went.

"And just think of what the band would sound like to that poor woman," said Laura.   95

"Oh, Laura!" Jose began to be seriously annoyed. "If you're going to stop a band playing every time some one has an accident, you'll lead a very strenuous life. I'm every bit as sorry about it as you. I feel just as sympathetic." Her eyes hardened. She looked at her sister just as she used to when they were little and fighting together. "You won't bring a drunken workman back to life by being sentimental," she said softly.

"Drunk! Who said he was drunk?" Laura turned furiously on Jose. She said, just as they had used to say on those occasions, "I'm going straight up to tell mother."

"Do, dear," cooed Jose.

"Mother, can I come into your room?" Laura turned the big glass door-knob.

"Of course, child. Why, what's the matter? What's given you such a color?" And   100
Mrs. Sheridan turned round from her dressing-table. She was trying on a new hat.

"Mother, a man's been killed," began Laura.

"*Not* in the garden?" interrupted her mother.

"No, no!"

"Oh, what a fright you gave me!" Mrs. Sheridan sighed with relief, and took off the big hat and held it on her knees.

"But listen, mother," said Laura. Breathless, half-choking, she told the dreadful   105
story. "Of course, we can't have our party, can we?" she pleaded. "The band and everybody arriving. They'd hear us, mother; they're nearly neighbors!"

sweeps: chimney sweeps

To Laura's astonishment her mother behaved just like Jose; it was harder to bear because she seemed amused. She refused to take Laura seriously.

"But, my dear child, use your common sense. It's only by accident we've heard of it. If someone had died there normally—and I can't understand how they keep alive in those poky little holes—we should still be having our party, shouldn't we?"

Laura had to say "yes" to that, but she felt it was all wrong. She sat down on her mother's sofa and pinched the cushion frill.

"Mother, isn't it really terribly heartless of us?" she asked.

"Darling!" Mrs. Sheridan got up and came over to her, carrying the hat. Before   110
Laura could stop her she had popped it on. "My child!" said her mother, "the hat is yours. It's made for you. It's much too young for me. I have never seen you look such a picture. Look at yourself!" And she held up her hand-mirror.

"But, mother," Laura began again. She couldn't look at herself; she turned aside.

This time Mrs. Sheridan lost patience just as Jose had done.

"You are being very absurd, Laura," she said coldly. "People like that don't expect sacrifices from us. And it's not very sympathetic to spoil everybody's enjoyment as you're doing now."

"I don't understand," said Laura, and she walked quickly out of the room into her own bedroom. There, quite by chance, the first thing she saw was this charming girl in the mirror, in her black hat trimmed with gold daisies, and a long black velvet ribbon. Never had she imagined she could look like that. Is mother right? she thought. And now she hoped her mother was right. Am I being extravagant? Perhaps it was extravagant. Just for a moment she had another glimpse of that poor woman and those little children, and the body being carried into the house. But it all seemed blurred, unreal, like a picture in the newspaper. I'll remember it again after the party's over, she decided. And somehow that seemed quite the best plan. . . .

Lunch was over by half-past one. By half-past two they were all ready for the fray.   115
The green-coated band had arrived and was established in a corner of the tennis-court.

"My dear!" trilled Kitty Maitland, "aren't they too like frogs for words? You ought to have arranged them round the pond with the conductor in the middle on a leaf."

Laurie arrived and hailed them on his way to dress. At the sight of him Laura remembered the accident again. She wanted to tell him. If Laurie agreed with the others, then it was bound to be all right. And she followed him into the hall.

"Laurie!"

"Hallo!" He was half-way upstairs, but when he turned round and saw Laura he suddenly puffed out his cheeks and goggled his eyes at her. "My word, Laura! You do look stunning," said Laurie. "What an absolutely topping hat!"

Laura said faintly "Is it?" and smiled up at Laurie, and didn't tell him after all.   120

Soon after that people began coming in streams. The band struck up; the hired waiters ran from the house to the marquee. Wherever you looked there were couples strolling, bending to the flowers, greeting, moving on over the lawn. They were like bright birds that had alighted in the Sheridans' garden for this one afternoon, on their way to—where? Ah, what happiness it is to be with people who all are happy, to press hands, press cheeks, smile into eyes.

"Darling Laura, how well you look!"

"What a becoming hat, child!"

"Laura, you look quite Spanish. I've never seen you look so striking."

And Laura, glowing, answered softly, "Have you had tea? Won't you have an ice?   125
The passion-fruit ices really are rather special." She ran to her father and begged him.
"Daddy darling, can't the band have something to drink?"

And the perfect afternoon slowly ripened, slowly faded, slowly its petals closed.

"Never a more delightful garden-party . . ." "The greatest success . . ." "Quite
the most . . ."

Laura helped her mother with the good-byes. They stood side by side in the porch
till it was all over.

"All over, all over, thank heaven," said Mrs. Sheridan. "Round up the others, Laura.
Let's go and have some fresh coffee. I'm exhausted. Yes, it's been very successful. But
oh, these parties, these parties! Why will you children insist on giving parties!" And they
all of them sat down in the deserted marquee.

"Have a sandwich, daddy dear. I wrote the flag."   130

"Thanks." Mr. Sheridan took a bite and the sandwich was gone. He took another.
"I suppose you didn't hear of a beastly accident that happened today?" he said.

"My dear," said Mrs. Sheridan, holding up her hand, "we did. It nearly ruined the
party. Laura insisted we should put it off."

"Oh, mother!" Laura didn't want to be teased about it.

"It was a horrible affair all the same," said Mr. Sheridan. "The chap was married
too. Lived just below in the lane, and leaves a wife and half a dozen kiddies, so they say."

An awkward little silence fell. Mrs. Sheridan fidgeted with her cup. Really, it was   135
very tactless of father. . .

Suddenly she looked up. There on the table were all those sandwiches, cakes,
puffs, all uneaten, all going to be wasted. She had one of her brilliant ideas.

"I know," she said. "Let's make up a basket. Let's send that poor creature some
of this perfectly good food. At any rate, it will be the greatest treat for the children.
Don't you agree? And she's sure to have neighbors calling in and so on. What a point
to have it all ready prepared. Laura!" She jumped up. "Get me the big basket out of the
stairs cupboard."

"But, mother, do you really think it's a good idea?" said Laura.

Again, how curious, she seemed to be different from them all. To take scraps from
their party. Would the poor woman really like that?

"Of course! What's the matter with you today? An hour or two ago you were in-   140
sisting on us being sympathetic, and now——"

Oh, well! Laura ran for the basket. It was filled, it was heaped by her mother.

"Take it yourself, darling," said she. "Run down just as you are. No, wait, take the
arum lilies too. People of that class are so impressed by arum lilies."

"The stems will ruin her lace frock," said practical Jose.

So they would. Just in time. "Only the basket, then. And, Laura!"—her mother followed her out of the marquee—"don't on any account——"

"What, mother?"   145

No, better not put such ideas into the child's head! "Nothing! Run along."

It was just growing dusky as Laura shut their garden gates. A big dog ran by like
a shadow. The road gleamed white, and down below in the hollow the little cottages
were in deep shade. How quiet it seemed after the afternoon. Here she was going down
the hill to somewhere where a man lay dead, and she couldn't realize it. Why couldn't
she? She stopped a minute. And it seemed to her that kisses, voices, tinkling spoons,
laughter, the smell of crushed grass were somehow inside her. She had no room for

anything else. How strange! She looked up at the pale sky, and all she thought was, "Yes, it was the most successful party."

Now the broad road was crossed. The lane began, smoky and dark. Women in shawls and men's tweed caps hurried by. Men hung over the palings; the children played in the doorways. A low hum came from the mean little cottages. In some of them there was a flicker of light, and a shadow, crab-like, moved across the window. Laura bent her head and hurried on. She wished now she had put on a coat. How her frock shone! And the big hat with the velvet streamer—if only it was another hat! Were the people looking at her? They must be. It was a mistake to have come; she knew all along it was a mistake. Should she go back even now?

No, too late. This was the house. It must be. A dark knot of people stood outside. Beside the gate an old, old woman with a crutch sat in a chair, watching. She had her feet on a newspaper. The voices stopped as Laura drew near. The group parted. It was as though she was expected, as though they had known she was coming here.

Laura was terribly nervous. Tossing the velvet ribbon over her shoulder, she said   150
to a woman standing by, "Is this Mrs. Scott's house?" and the woman, smiling queerly, said, "It is, my lass."

Oh, to be away from this! She actually said, "Help me, God," as she walked up the tiny path and knocked. To be away from those staring eyes, or to be covered up in anything, one of those women's shawls even. I'll just leave the basket and go, she decided. I shan't even wait for it to be emptied.

Then the door opened. A little woman in black showed in the gloom.

Laura said, "Are you Mrs. Scott?" But to her horror the woman answered, "Walk in please, miss," and she was shut in the passage.

"No," said Laura, "I don't want to come in. I only want to leave this basket. Mother sent——"

The little woman in the gloomy passage seemed not to have heard her. "Step this   155
way, please, miss," she said in an oily voice, and Laura followed her.

She found herself in a wretched little low kitchen, lighted by a smoky lamp. There was a woman sitting before the fire.

"Em," said the little creature who had let her in. "Em! It's a young lady." She turned to Laura. She said meaningly, "I'm 'er sister, Miss. You'll excuse 'er, won't you?"

"Oh, but of course!" said Laura. "Please, please don't disturb her. I—I only want to leave——"

But at that moment the woman at the fire turned round. Her face, puffed up, red, with swollen eyes and swollen lips, looked terrible. She seemed as though she couldn't understand why Laura was there. What did it mean? Why was this stranger standing in the kitchen with a basket? What was it all about? And the poor face puckered up again.

"All right, my dear," said the other. "I'll thenk the young lady."   160

And again she began, "You'll excuse her, miss, I'm sure," and her face, swollen too, tried an oily smile.

Laura only wanted to get out, to get away. She was back in the passage. The door opened. She walked straight through into the bedroom, where the dead man was lying.

"You'd like a look at 'im, wouldn't you?" said Em's sister, and she brushed past Laura over to the bed. "Don't be afraid, my lass,—" and now her voice sounded fond and sly, and fondly she drew down the sheet—"'e looks a picture. There's nothing to show. Come along, my dear."

Laura came.

There lay a young man, fast asleep—sleeping so soundly, so deeply, that he was far,   165
far away from them both. Oh, so remote, so peaceful. He was dreaming. Never wake him
up again. His head was sunk in the pillow, his eyes were closed; they were blind under
the closed eyelids. He was given up to his dream. What did garden-parties and baskets
and lace frocks matter to him? He was far from all those things. He was wonderful, beautiful. While they were laughing and while the band was playing, this marvel had come
to the lane. Happy . . . happy. . . . All is well, said that sleeping face. This is just as it
should be. I am content.

But all the same you had to cry, and she couldn't go out of the room without saying something to him. Laura gave a loud childish sob.

"Forgive my hat," she said.

And this time she didn't wait for Em's sister. She found her way out of the door,
down the path, past all those dark people. At the corner of the lane she met Laurie.

He stepped out of the shadow. "Is that you, Laura?"

"Yes."   170

"Mother was getting anxious. Was it all right?"

"Yes, quite. Oh, Laurie!" She took his arm, she pressed up against him.

"I say, you're not crying, are you?" asked her brother.

Laura shook her head. She was.

Laurie put his arm round her shoulder. "Don't cry," he said in his warm, loving   175
voice. "Was it awful?"

"No," sobbed Laura. "It was simply marvellous. But, Laurie——" She stopped, she
looked at her brother. "Isn't life," she stammered, "isn't life——" But what life was she
couldn't explain. No matter. He quite understood.

"*Isn't* it, darling?" said Laurie.

QUESTIONS FOR CLOSE READING OF CHARACTER AND PSYCHOLOGY

1. Why does the mother defer to the children in deciding where to put the party tent?

2. What do you learn about the mother early in the story? Does your first impression
   bear out your ultimate understanding of her character?

3. Apart from learning right away that Laura is "the artistic one," what do you learn
   about her early in the story?

4. How does Laura treat the men who come to erect the tent? What do we learn
   about them?

5. Why does Laura ask the advice of the men rather than making up her mind herself?

6. What does it tell you to hear Laura observe, "Oh, how extraordinarily nice workmen were. . . . Why couldn't she have workmen for friends rather than the silly
   boys she danced with"?

7. How clearly are the class distinctions drawn in the story? How long does it take
   you to become aware of class distinctions?

8. Who does the work in the story? What kind of work is being done? For whom?

9. What is the difference between Laura's and Jose's attitude to the death of the
   man who lived in the cottages?

10. What brings Laura to go down to the cottages and express her concern to the
    widow of the man who was killed? What does her behavior tell you about her
    character?

QUESTIONS FOR INTERPRETATION OF CHARACTER AND PSYCHOLOGY

1. One of the image patterns established in the story is that of flowers. This is a garden party, so flowers would be expected, but is it possible that the flowers are metaphors for a deeper significance in this story? Is Laura like a flower?

2. Katherine Mansfield's "The Garden-Party" presents a portrait of Laura, "the artistic one" in the family whose extravagant and exciting lawn party in New Zealand is a major festive event. Her privileged family contrasts with the working classes who live below in small cottages. When a man named Scott from the cottages is killed, Laura decides that the garden party must be put off, but she finds others in the family disagree. Laura reveals herself as a sympathetic and sensitive person in an environment that condones indulgence. How does she contrast with others in her family? With whom do you sympathize?

3. When the party is over Mother suggests that they take the leftover food down the lane to the house of the man who was killed. Laura thinks it might not be a good idea. What issues are at stake in the argument? Which position best respects the feelings of the widow? Which most respects the feelings of Mother and her family? What is really at stake in the decision to consider sending leftovers down the lane?

4. What does Laura's reaction to visiting the Scotts' household tell you about the relations between the Scotts and her own household? What kind of reaction does she have and why does she have it? How does Laura change in her thinking from the beginning of the story to the end? Does her visit to the Scotts change her any further? In what ways? Is Laura a dynamic character?

5. Is the theme of this story more focused on the development of character of a young woman, or is it more focused on the problems of class distinction in polite society? What seem to be Katherine Mansfield's primary purposes in writing this story? What themes seem most significant?

STYLE AND THEME

Style: Formal, Informal, and Ornamented

Style includes all the verbal qualities of a short story. Therefore, you could isolate virtually any interesting use of language and claim it is a key to understanding the style of a story. For example, you might feel that the style of "The Masque of the Red Death" is dominated by sensuous description, emphasizing colors, light and darkness, and architectural details. You might feel that the **informal style** of everyday conversation is one of the most important aspects of Gilman's story. Some stories impress you with their **formal style:** use of uncommon words, and long sentences. Poe's language is formal, not conversational: telling us that "Prince Prospero was happy and dauntless and sagacious" is exact, and quite unlike anything we would say. It gives us the feeling of being removed from this scene, as if it all happened long ago in a distant place. Most of the stories in this collection reflect a modern informality. However, each in its way uses so many different stylistic choices that you cannot state simply what its style is.

Ornamented styles are those formal or informal styles that depend on special techniques for their success.

- *Metaphor*   A **metaphor** implies much more than it says, usually through a strong image. In "The Yellow Wallpaper," the narrator describes the pattern of the wallpaper: "At night in any kind of light, in twilight, candlelight, lamplight, and worst of all by moonlight, it becomes bars! The outside pattern, I mean, and the woman behind it is as plain as can be." Whatever it is that she sees, the pattern becomes a metaphor for her own sense of imprisonment in a house she does not like with a husband who seems not to understand her, despite his protestations that he knows her better than she knows herself. This metaphor enriches the story for us while also pointing toward some of its deeper meaning.

- *Imagery*   **Images** are rich descriptions that make a strong appeal to our senses of sight, sound, touch, taste, and smell. Occasionally an image will appeal to more than one sense, such as Cheever's reference in "The Swimmer" to cordite—the smell left over after explosions, which, as he uses it, evokes not only a smell but also a sound.

- *Patterns of repetition*   The repetition of Prince Prospero passing from one carefully described apartment to the next is patterned carefully so as to build up suspense. In Cheever's "The Swimmer," we find a curious pattern of repetition right from the first, but it is in the repetition of dialogue: "I *drank* too much last night"; "I *drank* too much"; "we all *drank* too much"; "I *drank* too much of that claret." That message repeats itself through the story, along with the description of one swimming pool after another. We learn that these repetitions—almost refrains—are central to the story's significance.

Theme and Variations

The theme of a short story is its subject matter—what it is about. Until you have given the story a close reading and begun your interpretation, you may not know what that theme is. The theme of "The Pot of Basil" is so complex that probably no two readers will agree on what it is. You might feel that the theme is love confounded by Lisabetta's dominant, insensitive, and criminal brothers. Other readers may emphasize the theme of the feminine response of madness as a technique for coping with a cruel masculine world. If you perceive the theme of this story as rooted in grief, you may imagine many variations on that theme, all relevant to the story. Most stories have several themes. Writers make conscious decisions about most stylistic possibilities; they think they know what their story is about (its theme), but often they find that they, too, have to interpret what they have written to discover their theme.

John Cheever has been praised for writing on the theme of suburban American life. Certainly "The Swimmer" is about suburban New York, with its wealth, privilege, social snobbery, and its indulgences. Neddy Merrill fits the scene perfectly, with his concerns about drinking, about what kind of stroke he uses in the pool, about what distinguishes each of the neighbors whose pools he swims through on his way home. He is conversant about pools, tennis, golf, houses, and investments, although he thinks it vulgar to talk about money. He thinks of himself not only as acceptable but as several rungs up the social ladder.

Neddy lives in a world of illusion. He drinks vastly too much. His scheme of swimming home is at first comical but ultimately mad. His neighbors—and his mistress—regard him with horror. We are left with the question of whether he ever comes to understand reality. "The Swimmer" treats a range of themes all connected by the lifestyle and perceptions of Neddy Merrill, who begins the story with one hand "around a glass of gin."

JOHN CHEEVER   (1912–1982)

For much of his later life, John Cheever drank compulsively—enough to ruin his relationship with his family. Even with psychiatric help, he found it impossible to change his habits. "The Swimmer," with its suburban locale and its compulsive drinking, comes from The Stories of John Cheever *(1964). His first collection,* The Way Some People Live, *was published in 1942, but his reputation was solidified by* The Enormous Radio and Other Stories *(1953).* Collected Stories *was published in 1978. His journals are painfully honest, almost ruthless in their self-judgment. They show a writer tortured by his own weaknesses but aware of every breath he took, every gesture he made, and every hesitation on the part of others. He was an astonishing observer of his own life.*

The Swimmer _____ *1964*

It was one of those midsummer Sundays when everyone sits around saying, "I *drank* too much last night." You might have heard it whispered by the parishioners leaving church, heard it from the lips of the priest himself, struggling with his cassock in the *vestiarium,*° heard it from the golf links and the tennis courts, heard it from the wildlife preserve where the leader of the Audubon group was suffering from a terrible hangover. "I *drank* too much," said Donald Westerhazy. "We all *drank* too much," said Lucinda Merrill. "It must have been the wine," said Helen Westerhazy. "I *drank* too much of that claret."

This was at the edge of the Westerhazys' pool. The pool, fed by an artesian well with a high iron content, was a pale shade of green. It was a fine day. In the west there was a massive stand of cumulus cloud so like a city seen from a distance—from the bow of an approaching ship—that it might have had a name. Lisbon. Hackensack. The sun was hot. Neddy Merrill sat by the green water, one hand in it, one around a glass of gin. He was a slender man—he seemed to have the especial slenderness of youth—and while he was far from young he had slid down his banister that morning and given the bronze backside of Aphrodite° on the hall table a smack, as he jogged toward the smell of coffee in his dining room. He might have been compared to a summer's day, particularly the last hours of one, and while he lacked a tennis racket or a sail bag the impression was definitely one of youth, sport, and clement weather. He had been swimming and now he was breathing deeply, stertorously as if he could gulp into his lungs the components of that moment, the heat of the sun, the intenseness of his pleasure. It all seemed to

---

vestiarium: dressing room   *Aphrodite:* Venus

flow into his chest. His own house stood in Bullet Park, eight miles to the south, where his four beautiful daughters would have had their lunch and might be playing tennis. Then it occurred to him that by taking a dogleg to the southwest he could reach his home by water.

His life was not confining and the delight he took in this observation could not be explained by its suggestion of escape. He seemed to see, with a cartographer's eye, that string of swimming pools, that quasi-subterranean stream that curved across the county. He had made a discovery, a contribution to modern geography; he would name the stream Lucinda after his wife. He was not a practical joker nor was he a fool but he was determinedly original and had a vague and modest idea of himself as a legendary figure. The day was beautiful and it seemed to him that a long swim might enlarge and celebrate its beauty.

He took off a sweater that was hung over his shoulders and dove in. He had an inexplicable contempt for men who did not hurl themselves into pools. He swam a choppy crawl, breathing either with every stroke or every fourth stroke and counting somewhere well in the back of his mind the one-two one-two of a flutter kick. It was not a serviceable stroke for long distances but the domestication of swimming had saddled the sport with some customs and in his part of the world a crawl was customary. To be embraced and sustained by the light green water was less a pleasure, it seemed, than the resumption of a natural condition, and he would have liked to swim without trunks, but this was not possible, considering his project. He hoisted himself up on the far curb—he never used the ladder—and started across the lawn. When Lucinda asked where he was going he said he was going to swim home.

The only maps and charts he had to go by were remembered or imaginary but   5
these were clear enough. First there were the Grahams, the Hammers, the Lears, the Howlands, and the Crosscups. He would cross Ditmar Street to the Bunkers and come, after a short portage, to the Levys, the Welchers, and the public pool in Lancaster. Then there were the Hallorans, the Sachses, the Biswangers, Shirley Adams, the Gilmartins, and the Clydes. The day was lovely, and that he lived in a world so generously supplied with water seemed like a clemency, a beneficence. His heart was high and he ran across the grass. Making his way home by an uncommon route gave him the feeling that he was a pilgrim, an explorer, a man with a destiny, and he knew that he would find friends all along the way; friends would line the banks of the Lucinda River.

He went through a hedge that separated the Westerhazys' land from the Grahams', walked under some flowering apple trees, passed the shed that housed their pump and filter, and came out at the Grahams' pool. "Why, Neddy," Mrs. Graham said, "what a marvelous surprise. I've been trying to get you on the phone all morning. Here, let me get you a drink." He saw then, like any explorer, that the hospitable customs and traditions of the natives would have to be handled with diplomacy if he was ever going to reach his destination. He did not want to mystify or seem rude to the Grahams nor did he have the time to linger there. He swam the length of their pool and joined them in the sun and was rescued, a few minutes later, by the arrival of two carloads of friends from Connecticut. During the uproarious reunions he was able to slip away. He went down by the front of the Grahams' house, stepped over a thorny hedge, and crossed a vacant lot to the Hammers'. Mrs. Hammer, looking up from her roses, saw him swim by although she wasn't quite sure who it was. The Lears heard him splashing past the open windows of their living room. The Howlands and the Crosscups were away. After leaving the Howlands' he crossed Ditmar Street and started for the Bunkers', where he could hear, even at that distance, the noise of a party.

The water refracted the sound of voices and laughter and seemed to suspend it in midair. The Bunkers' pool was on a rise and he climbed some stairs to a terrace where twenty-five or thirty men and women were drinking. The only person in the water was Rusty Towers, who floated there on a rubber raft. Oh, how bonny and lush were the banks of the Lucinda River! Prosperous men and women gathered by the sapphire-colored waters while caterer's men in white coats passed them cold gin. Overhead a red de Haviland trainer was circling around and around and around in the sky with something like the glee of a child in a swing. Ned felt a passing affection for the scene, a tenderness for the gathering, as if it was something he might touch. In the distance he heard thunder. As soon as Enid Bunker saw him she began to scream: "Oh, look who's here! What a marvelous surprise! When Lucinda said that you couldn't come I thought I'd *die*." She made her way to him through the crowd, and when they had finished kissing she led him to the bar, a progress that was slowed by the fact that he stopped to kiss eight or ten other women and shake the hands of as many men. A smiling bartender he had seen at a hundred parties gave him a gin and tonic and he stood by the bar for a moment, anxious not to get stuck in any conversation that would delay his voyage. When he seemed about to be surrounded he dove in and swam close to the side to avoid colliding with Rusty's raft. At the far end of the pool he bypassed the Tomlinsons with a broad smile and jogged up the garden path. The gravel cut his feet but this was the only unpleasantness. The party was confined to the pool, and as he went toward the house he heard the brilliant, watery sound of voices fade, heard the noise of a radio from the Bunkers' kitchen, where someone was listening to a ball game. Sunday afternoon. He made his way through the parked cars and down the grassy border of their driveway to Alewives Lane. He did not want to be seen on the road in his bathing trunks but there was no traffic and he made the short distance to the Levys' driveway, marked with a PRIVATE PROPERTY sign and a green tube for *The New York Times.* All the doors and windows of the big house were open but there were no signs of life; not even a dog barked. He went around the side of the house to the pool and saw that the Levys had only recently left. Glasses and bottles and dishes of nuts were on a table at the deep end, where there was a bathhouse or gazebo, hung with Japanese lanterns. After swimming the pool he got himself a glass and poured a drink. It was his fourth or fifth drink and he had swum nearly half the length of the Lucinda River. He felt tired, clean, and pleased at that moment to be alone; pleased with everything.

It would storm. The stand of cumulus cloud—that city—had risen and darkened, and while he sat there he heard the percussiveness of thunder again. The de Haviland trainer was still circling overhead and it seemed to Ned that he could almost hear the pilot laugh with pleasure in the afternoon; but when there was another peal of thunder he took off for home. A train whistle blew and he wondered what time it had gotten to be. Four? Five? He thought of the provincial station at that hour, where a waiter, his tuxedo concealed by a raincoat, a dwarf with some flowers wrapped in newspaper, and a woman who had been crying would be waiting for the local. It was suddenly growing dark; it was that moment when the pin-headed birds seem to organize their song into some acute and knowledgeable recognition of the storm's approach. Then there was a fine noise of rushing water from the crown of an oak at his back, as if a spigot there had been turned. Then the noise of fountains came from the crowns of all the tall trees. Why did he love storms, what was the meaning of his excitement when the door sprang open and the rain wind fled rudely up the stairs, why had the simple task of shutting the windows of an old house seemed fitting and urgent, why did the first watery notes of a storm wind have for him the unmistakable sound of good news, cheer, glad tidings?

Then there was an explosion, a smell of cordite, and rain lashed the Japanese lanterns that Mrs. Levy had bought in Kyoto the year before last, or was it the year before that?

He stayed in the Levys' gazebo until the storm had passed. The rain had cooled the air and he shivered. The force of the wind had stripped a maple of its red and yellow leaves and scattered them over the grass and the water. Since it was midsummer the tree must be blighted, and yet he felt a peculiar sadness at this sign of autumn. He braced his shoulders, emptied his glass, and started for the Welchers' pool. This meant crossing the Lindleys' riding ring and he was surprised to find it overgrown with grass and all the jumps dismantled. He wondered if the Lindleys had sold their horses or gone away for the summer and put them out to board. He seemed to remember having heard something about the Lindleys and their horses but the memory was unclear. On he went, barefoot through the wet grass, to the Welchers', where he found their pool was dry.

This breach in his chain of water disappointed him absurdly, and he felt like some   10
explorer who seeks a torrential headwater and finds a dead stream. He was disappointed and mystified. It was common enough to go away for the summer but no one ever drained his pool. The Welchers had definitely gone away. The pool furniture was folded, stacked, and covered with a tarpaulin. The bathhouse was locked. All the windows of the house were shut, and when he went around to the driveway in front he saw a FOR SALE sign nailed to a tree. When had he last heard from the Welchers—when, that is, had he and Lucinda last regretted an invitation to dine with them? It seemed only a week or so ago. Was his memory failing or had he so disciplined it in the repression of unpleasant facts that he had damaged his sense of the truth? Then in the distance he heard the sound of a tennis game. This cheered him, cleared away all his apprehensions and let him regard the overcast sky and the cold air with indifference. This was the day that Neddy Merrill swam across the county. That was the day! He started off then for his most difficult portage.

Had you gone for a Sunday afternoon ride that day you might have seen him, close to naked, standing on the shoulders of Route 424, waiting for a chance to cross. You might have wondered if he was the victim of foul play, had his car broken down, or was he merely a fool. Standing barefoot in the deposits of the highway—beer cans, rags, and blowout patches—exposed to all kinds of ridicule, he seemed pitiful. He had known when he started that this was a part of his journey—it had been on his maps—but confronted with the lines of traffic, worming through the summery light, he found himself unprepared. He was laughed at, jeered at, a beer can was thrown at him, and he had no dignity or humor to bring to the situation. He could have gone back, back to the Westerhazys', where Lucinda would still be sitting in the sun. He had signed nothing, vowed nothing, pledged nothing, not even to himself. Why, believing as he did, that all human obduracy was susceptible to common sense, was he unable to turn back? Why was he determined to complete his journey even if it meant putting his life in danger? At what point had this prank, this joke, this piece of horseplay become serious? He could not go back, he could not even recall with any clearness the green water at the Westerhazys', the sense of inhaling the day's components, the friendly and relaxed voices saying that they had *drunk* too much. In the space of an hour, more or less, he had covered a distance that made his return impossible.

An old man, tooling down the highway at fifteen miles an hour, let him get to the middle of the road, where there was a grass divider. Here he was exposed to the ridicule of the northbound traffic, but after ten or fifteen minutes he was able to cross. From here he had only a short walk to the Recreation Center at the edge of the village of Lancaster, where there were some handball courts and a public pool.

The effect of the water on voices, the illusion of brilliance and suspense, was the same here as it had been at the Bunkers' but the sounds here were louder, harsher, and more shrill, and as soon as he entered the crowded enclosure he was confronted with regimentation. "ALL SWIMMERS MUST TAKE A SHOWER BEFORE USING THE POOL. ALL SWIMMERS MUST USE THE FOOTBATH. ALL SWIMMERS MUST WEAR THEIR IDENTIFICATION DISKS." He took a shower, washed his feet in a cloudy and bitter solution, and made his way to the edge of the water. It stank of chlorine and looked to him like a sink. A pair of lifeguards in a pair of towers blew police whistles at what seemed to be regular intervals and abused the swimmers through a public address system. Neddy remembered the sapphire water at the Bunkers' with longing and thought that he might contaminate himself—damage his own prosperousness and charm—by swimming in this murk, but he reminded himself that he was an explorer, a pilgrim, and that this was merely a stagnant bend in the Lucinda River. He dove, scowling with distaste, into the chlorine and had to swim with his head above water to avoid collisions, but even so he was bumped into, splashed, and jostled. When he got to the shallow end both lifeguards were shouting at him: "Hey, you, you without the identification disk, get outa the water." He did, but they had no way of pursuing him and he went through the reek of suntan oil and chlorine out through the hurricane fence and passed the handball courts. By crossing the road he entered the wooded part of the Halloran estate. The woods were not cleared and the footing was treacherous and difficult until he reached the lawn and the clipped beech hedge that encircled their pool.

The Hallorans were friends, an elderly couple of enormous wealth who seemed to bask in the suspicion that they might be Communists. They were zealous reformers but they were not Communists, and yet when they were accused, as they sometimes were, of subversion, it seemed to gratify and excite them. Their beech hedge was yellow and he guessed this had been blighted like the Levys' maple. He called hullo, hullo, to warn the Hallorans of his approach, to palliate his invasion of their privacy. The Hallorans, for reasons that had never been explained to him, did not wear bathing suits. No explanations were in order, really. Their nakedness was a detail in their uncompromising zeal for reform and he stepped politely out of his trunks before he went through the opening in the hedge.

Mrs. Halloran, a stout woman with white hair and a serene face, was reading the *Times*. Mr. Halloran was taking beech leaves out of the water with a scoop. They seemed not surprised or displeased to see him. Their pool was perhaps the oldest in the country, a fieldstone rectangle, fed by a brook. It had no filter or pump and its waters were the opaque gold of the stream.   15

"I'm swimming across the county," Ned said.

"Why, I didn't know one could," exclaimed Mrs. Halloran.

"Well, I've made it from the Westerhazys'," Ned said. "That must be about four miles."

He left his trunks at the deep end, walked to the shallow end, and swam this stretch. As he was pulling himself out of the water he heard Mrs. Halloran say, "We've been *terribly* sorry to hear about all your misfortunes, Neddy."

"My misfortunes?" Ned asked. "I don't know what you mean."   20

"Why, we heard that you'd sold the house and that your poor children . . ."

"I don't recall having sold the house," Ned said, "and the girls are at home."

"Yes," Mrs. Halloran sighed. "Yes . . ." Her voice filled the air with an unseasonable melancholy and Ned spoke briskly. "Thank you for the swim."

"Well, have a nice trip," said Mrs. Halloran.

Beyond the hedge he pulled on his trunks and fastened them. They were loose   25
and he wondered if, during the space of an afternoon, he could have lost some weight. He was cold and he was tired and the naked Hallorans and their dark water had depressed him. The swim was too much for his strength but how could he have guessed this, sliding down the banister that morning and sitting in the Westerhazys' sun? His arms were lame. His legs felt rubbery and ached at the joints. The worst of it was the cold in his bones and the feeling that he might never be warm again. Leaves were falling down around him and he smelled wood smoke on the wind. Who would be burning wood at this time of year?

He needed a drink. Whiskey would warm him, pick him up, carry him through the last of his journey, refresh his feeling that it was original and valorous to swim across the county. Channel swimmers took brandy. He needed a stimulant. He crossed the lawn in front of the Hallorans' house and went down a little path to where they had built a house for their only daughter, Helen, and her husband, Eric Sachs. The Sachses' pool was small and he found Helen and her husband there.

"Oh, *Neddy*," Helen said. "Did you lunch at Mother's?"

"Not *really*," Ned said. "I *did* stop to see your parents." This seemed to be explanation enough. "I'm terribly sorry to break in on you like this but I've taken a chill and I wonder if you'd give me a drink."

"Why, I'd *love* to," Helen said, "but there hasn't been anything in this house to drink since Eric's operation. That was three years ago."

Was he losing his memory, had his gift for concealing painful facts let him forget   30
that he had sold his house, that his children were in trouble, and that his friend had been ill? His eyes slipped from Eric's face to his abdomen, where he saw three pale, sutured scars, two of them at least a foot long. Gone was his navel, and what, Neddy thought, would the roving hand, bed-checking one's gifts at 3 A.M., make of a belly with no navel, no link to birth, this breach in the succession?

"I'm sure you can get a drink at the Biswangers'," Helen said. "They're having an enormous do. You can hear it from here. Listen!"

She raised her head and from across the road, the lawns, the gardens, the woods, the fields, he heard again the brilliant noise of voices over water. "Well, I'll get wet," he said, still feeling that he had no freedom of choice about his means of travel. He dove into the Sachses' cold water and, gasping, close to drowning, made his way from one end of the pool to the other. "Lucinda and I want *terribly* to see you," he said over his shoulder, his face set toward the Biswangers'. "We're sorry it's been so long and we'll call you *very* soon."

He crossed some fields to the Biswangers' and the sounds of revelry there. They would be honored to give him a drink, they would be happy to give him a drink. The Biswangers invited him and Lucinda for dinner four times a year, six weeks in advance. They were always rebuffed and yet they continued to send out their invitations, unwilling to comprehend the rigid and undemocratic realities of their society. They were the sort of people who discussed the price of things at cocktails, exchanged market tips during dinner, and after dinner told dirty stories to mixed company. They did not belong to Neddy's set—they were not even on Lucinda's Christmas-card list. He went toward their pool with feelings of indifference, charity, and some unease, since it seemed to be getting dark and these were the longest days of the year. The party when he joined it was noisy and large. Grace Biswanger was the kind of hostess who asked the optometrist, the veterinarian, the real-estate dealer, and the dentist. No one was swimming and the twilight, reflected on the water of the pool, had a wintry gleam. There was a bar and he started for this. When Grace Biswanger saw him she came toward him, not affectionately as he had every right to expect, but bellicosely.

"Why, this party has everything," she said loudly, "including a gate crasher."

She could not deal him a social blow—there was no question about this and he   35
did not flinch. "As a gate crasher," he asked politely, "do I rate a drink?"

"Suit yourself," she said. "You don't seem to pay much attention to invitations."

She turned her back on him and joined some guests, and he went to the bar and ordered a whiskey. The bartender served him but he served him rudely. His was a world in which the caterer's men kept the social score, and to be rebuffed by a part-time barkeep meant that he had suffered some loss of social esteem. Or perhaps the man was new and uninformed. Then he heard Grace at his back say: "They went for broke overnight—nothing but income—and he showed up drunk one Sunday and asked us to loan him five thousand dollars. . . ." She was always talking about money. It was worse than eating your peas off a knife. He dove into the pool, swam its length and went away.

The next pool on his list, the last but two, belonged to his old mistress, Shirley Adams. If he had suffered any injuries at the Biswangers' they would be cured here. Love—sexual roughhouse in fact—was the supreme elixir, the pain killer, the brightly colored pill that would put the spring back into his step, the joy of life in his heart. They had had an affair last week, last month, last year. He couldn't remember. It was he who had broken it off, his was the upper hand, and he stepped through the gate of the wall that surrounded her pool with nothing so considered as self-confidence. It seemed in a way to be his pool, as the lover, particularly the illicit lover, enjoys the possessions of his mistress with an authority unknown to holy matrimony. She was there, her hair the color of brass, but her figure, at the edge of the lighted, cerulean water, excited in him no profound memories. It had been, he thought, a lighthearted affair, although she had wept when he broke it off. She seemed confused to see him and he wondered if she was still wounded. Would she, God forbid, weep again?

"What do you want?" she asked.

"I'm swimming across the county."   40

"Good Christ. Will you ever grow up?"

"What's the matter?"

"If you've come here for money," she said, "I won't give you another cent."

"You could give me a drink."

"I could but I won't. I'm not alone."   45

"Well, I'm on my way."

He dove in and swam the pool, but when he tried to haul himself up onto the curb he found that the strength in his arms and shoulders had gone, and he paddled to the ladder and climbed out. Looking over his shoulder he saw, in the lighted bathhouse, a young man. Going out onto the dark lawn he smelled chrysanthemums or marigolds—some stubborn autumnal fragrance—on the night air, strong as gas. Looking overhead he saw that the stars had come out, but why should he seem to see Andromeda, Cepheus, and Cassiopeia? What had become of the constellations of midsummer? He began to cry.

It was probably the first time in his adult life that he had ever cried, certainly the first time in his life that he had ever felt so miserable, cold, tired, and bewildered. He could not understand the rudeness of the caterer's barkeep or the rudeness of a mistress who had come to him on her knees and showered his trousers with tears. He had swum too long, he had been immersed too long, and his nose and his throat were sore from the water. What he needed then was a drink, some company, and some clean, dry clothes, and while he could have cut directly across the road to his home he went on to the Gilmartins' pool. Here, for the first time in his life, he did not dive but went down the steps into the icy water and swam a hobbled sidestroke that he might have learned as a youth. He staggered with fatigue on his way to the Clydes' and paddled the length of their pool, stopping again and again with his hand on the curb to rest. He climbed up the ladder and wondered if he had the strength to get home. He had done what he wanted, he had swum the county, but he was so stupefied with exhaustion that his triumph seemed vague. Stooped, holding on to the gateposts for support, he turned up the driveway of his own house.

The place was dark. Was it so late that they had all gone to bed? Had Lucinda stayed at the Westerhazys' for supper? Had the girls joined her there or gone someplace else? Hadn't they agreed, as they usually did on Sunday, to regret all their invitations and stay at home? He tried the garage doors to see what cars were in but the doors were locked and rust came off the handles onto his hands. Going toward the house, he saw that the force of the thunderstorm had knocked one of the rain gutters loose. It hung down over the front door like an umbrella rib, but it could be fixed in the morning. The house was locked, and he thought that the stupid cook or the stupid maid must have locked the place up until he remembered that it had been some time since they had employed a maid or a cook. He shouted, pounded on the door, tried to force it with his shoulder, and then, looking in at the windows, saw that the place was empty.

QUESTIONS FOR CLOSE READING OF STYLE AND THEME

Note: Questions relating to theme immediately get you into interpretation, so some of these questions can also apply to the interpretation of the whole story.

1. Is the style of the story informal (conversational) or formal?

2. In the second paragraph, Cheever says that Neddy Merrill "might have been compared to a summer's day, particularly the last hours of one." Is this a stylistic or thematic detail? In what ways does this metaphoric comparison give us a glimpse of the theme of the story?

3. Early in the story, Neddy sees the gathering cumulus clouds, and "in the distance he heard thunder." How do Cheever's images of the clouds and the weather prepare us for the ending of the story?

4. The descriptions of the Bunkers' crowded pool and the Levys' empty pool contrast sharply with that of the public pool. Which images, appealing to which senses, most effectively establish the contrast that Neddy feels?

5. At one point Neddy thinks with pride, "This was the day that Neddy Merrill swam across the county." Cheever uses the metaphor of swimming from swimming pool to swimming pool to comment on the journey of Neddy's life. How does it begin to reveal the theme or themes of the story?

6. How does the way people speak to Neddy when he begins his swim differ from the way they speak at the end? Are the differences stylistic? What do the differences imply about the way in which people regard Neddy? What do the differences imply about the way Neddy regards his friends and acquaintances? is the theme of the story connected to social isolation?

QUESTIONS FOR INTERPRETATION OF STYLE AND THEME

Note: These questions center on the themes to be found within the story.

1. Examine the imagery of weather, sky, flowers, and nature in the story. How does Cheever use this imagery to reveal the inner nature of Neddy Merrill and the quality of his life? What does the imagery reveal? Cheever commented that the imagery of the constellations near the end of the story was crucial to its understanding. Neddy looks up "to see Andromeda, Cepheus, and Cassiopeia." He asks, "What had become of the constellations of midsummer?" Why does he cry—for the first time in his adult life—when he realizes that summer is gone and the winter constellations have appeared? What is their metaphoric significance? Is it connected only to the changing of seasons, or does it have import in Neddy's life?

2. At one point Neddy's mistress snaps at him, "Good Christ. Will you ever grow up?" What feelings does Neddy have about love or sex? Is his naming the string of swimming pools "Lucinda River" a hint about his psychological problems? What emotional needs does Neddy have? What seem to be his emotional inadequacies? Why does his ex-mistress worry about his ever growing up? Are swimming pools sexual symbols? Is the primary theme of the story connected with Neddy's mental health? Has Neddy's environment driven him insane? Or is Neddy quite sane and, by contrast, are his friends deranged?

3. What emotional response do you have toward Neddy Merrill? Do you think you would like him if you met him? How do stylistic and thematic aspects of the story contribute toward your responses to the lifestyle portrayed in the story? Do you respond positively to any character who appears in the story? How does the central importance of drinking, to Neddy and his friends, affect you? Could the theme of this story be a plea against alcohol abuse? Could Neddy's behavior be an aspect of his personal plea for help? Are you sympathetic to him?

4. In what sense are the genders expected to play specific and traditional roles in Neddy's society? Are women equal partners in the society? Does Neddy expect them to be equal or want them to be equal? How strong are the characters Cheever creates? Do they seem capable of challenging conventional gender roles or do they need the status quo? Is Neddy comfortable in the gender role that society has assigned him? What metaphors in the story convince you one way or the other? What important feminist themes emerge from the metaphors in the story?

5. The style of the story seems to reveal Neddy as sophisticated, judgmental, and snobbish. His friends are wealthy, but the only characters who work in the story are caterers, bartenders, and servants. How might you interpret Neddy's story taking into account the apparent economic inequities he accepts as okay? Does Neddy exploit the laborers in the story? Is the story a critique of a life of privilege?

TONI CADE BAMBARA   (b. 1939)

Toni Cade Bambara is widely known as a social activist. She has studied at universities in New York, Florence (Italy), and Paris, has performed as a dancer and mime, and currently works as a production consultant for television in Philadelphia. "The Lesson" comes from Gorilla, My Love *(1972), which was followed in 1977 by another collection of stories,* The Sea Birds Are Still Alive. *Her novel* The Salt Eaters *was published in 1980, and* If Blessing Comes *was published in 1987. "The Lesson" reveals a gift for language and an ear for the way people speak. In it Bambara captures the voices of bright black children on a makeshift field trip to the Mecca of toy worlds: F.A.O. Schwartz. However, these "babes in toyland" are different from anything conventional American wisdom would have expected. They are there not just to admire fancy toys, but to learn a lesson about why they may look but cannot touch. Another African-American writer, Lucille Clifton, reviewed* Gorilla, My Love *and said, "She has captured it all, how we really talk, how we really are; and done it with both love and respect."*

The Lesson ⎯⎯⎯⎯⎯⎯⎯⎯⎯⎯⎯⎯⎯⎯⎯⎯⎯⎯⎯⎯ 1972

Back in the days when everyone was old and stupid or young and foolish and me and Sugar were the only ones just right, this lady moved on our block with nappy hair and proper speech and no makeup. And quite naturally we laughed at her, laughed the way we did at the junk man who went about his business like he was some big-time president and his sorry-ass horse his secretary. And we kinda hated her too, hated the way we did the winos who cluttered up our parks and pissed on our handball walls and stank up our hallways and stairs so you couldn't halfway play hide-and-seek without a god-damn gas mask. Miss Moore was her name. The only woman on the block with no first name. And she was black as hell, cept for her feet, which were fish-white and spooky. And she was always planning these boring-ass things for us to do, us being my cousin, mostly, who lived on the block cause we all moved North the same time and to the same apartment then spread out gradual to breathe. And our parents would yank our heads into some kinda shape and crisp up our clothes so we'd be presentable for travel with Miss Moore, who always looked like she was going to church, though she never did. Which is just one of things the grown-ups talked about when they talked behind her back like a dog. But when she came calling with some sachet she'd sewed up or some ginger-bread she'd made or some book, why then they'd all be too embarrassed to turn her down and we'd get handed over all spruced up. She'd been to college and said it was only right that she should take responsibility for the young ones' education, and she not even related by marriage or blood. So they'd go for it. Specially Aunt Gretchen. She was the main gofer in the family. You got some ole dumb shit foolishness you want somebody to go for, you send for Aunt Gretchen. She been screwed into the go-along for so long, it's a blood-deep natural thing with her. Which is how she got saddled with me and Sugar and Junior in the first place while our mothers were in a la-de-da apartment up the block having a good ole time.

So this one day Miss Moore rounds us all up at the mailbox and it's puredee hot and she's knockin herself out about arithmetic. And school suppose to let up in summer I heard, but she don't never let up. And the starch in my pinafore scratching the shit outta me and I'm really hating this nappy-head bitch and her goddamn college degree. I'd much rather go to the pool or to the show where it's cool. So me and Sugar leaning on the mailbox being surly, which is a Miss Moore word. And Flyboy checking out what everybody brought for lunch. And Fat Butt already wasting his peanut-butter-and-jelly sandwich like the pig he is. And Junebug punchin on Q.T.'s arm for potato chips. And Rosie Giraffe shifting from one hip to the other waiting for somebody to step on her foot or ask her if she from Georgia so she can kick ass, preferably Mercedes'. And Miss Moore asking us do we know what money is, like we a bunch of retards. I mean real money, she say, like it's only poker chips or monopoly papers we lay on the grocer. So right away I'm tired of this and say so. And would much rather snatch Sugar and go to the Sunset and terrorize the West Indian kids and take their hair ribbons and their money too. And Miss Moore files that remark away for next week's lesson on brotherhood, I can tell. And finally I say we oughta get to the subway cause it's cooler and besides we might meet some cute boys. Sugar done swiped her mama's lipstick, so we ready.

So we heading down the street and she's boring us silly about what things cost and what our parents make and how much goes for rent and how money ain't divided up right in this country. And then she gets to the part about we all poor and live in the slums, which I don't feature. And I'm ready to speak on that, but she steps out in the street and hails two cabs just like that. Then she hustles half the crew in with her and hands me a five-dollar bill and tells me to calculate 10 percent tip for the driver. And we're off. Me and Sugar and Junebug and Flyboy hangin out the window and hollering to everybody, putting lipstick on each other cause Flyboy a faggot anyway, and making farts with our sweaty armpits. But I'm mostly trying to figure how to spend this money. But they all fascinated with the meter ticking and Junebug starts laying bets as to how much it'll read when Flyboy can't hold his breath no more. Then Sugar lays bets as to how much it'll be when we get there. So I'm stuck. Don't nobody want to go for my plan, which is to jump out at the next light and run off to the first bar-b-que we can find. Then the driver tells us to get the hell out cause we there already. And the meter reads eighty-five cents. And I'm stalling to figure out the tip and Sugar say give him a dime. And I decide he don't need it bad as I do, so later for him. But then he tries to take off with Junebug foot still in the door so we talk about his mama something ferocious. Then we check out that we on Fifth Avenue and everybody dressed up in stockings. One lady in a fur coat, hot as it is. White folks crazy.

"This is the place," Miss Moore say, presenting it to us in the voice she uses at the museum. "Let's look in the windows before we go in."

"Can we steal?" Sugar asks very serious like she's getting the ground rules squared   5
away before she plays. "I beg your pardon," say Miss Moore, and we fall out. So she leads us around the windows of the toy store and me and Sugar screamin, "This is mine, that's mine, I gotta have that, that was made for me, I was born for that," till Big Butt drowns us out.

"Hey, I'm goin to buy that there."

"That there? You don't even know what it is, stupid."

"I do so," he say punchin on Rosie Giraffe. "It's a microscope."

"Whatcha gonna do with a microscope, fool?"

"Look at things."   10

"Like what, Ronald?" ask Miss Moore. And Big Butt ain't got the first notion. So here go Miss Moore gabbing about the thousands of bacteria in a drop of water and the somethinorother in a speck of blood and the million and one living things in the air around us is invisible to the naked eye. And what she say that for? Junebug go to town on that "naked" and we rolling. Then Miss Moore ask what it cost. So we all jam into the window smudgin it up and the price tag say $300. So then she ask how long'd take for Big Butt and Junebug to save up their allowances. "Too long," I say. "Yeh," adds

Sugar, "outgrown it by that time." And Miss Moore say no, you never outgrow learning instruments. "Why, even medical students and interns and," blah, blah, blah. And we ready to choke Big Butt for bringing it up in the first damn place.

"This here costs four hundred eighty dollars," say Rosie Giraffe. So we pile up all over her to see what she pointin out. My eyes tell me it's a chunk of glass cracked with something heavy, and different-color inks dripped into the splits, then the whole thing put into a oven or something. But for $480 it don't make sense.

"That's a paperweight made of semi-precious stones fused together under tremendous pressure," she explains slowly, with her hands doing the mining and all the factory work.

"So what's a paperweight?" asks Rosie Giraffe.

"To weigh paper with, dumbbell," say Flyboy, the wise man from the East.   15

"Not exactly," say Miss Moore, which is what she say when you warm or way off too. "It's to weigh paper down so it won't scatter and make your desk untidy." So right away me and Sugar curtsy to each other and then to Mercedes who is more the tidy type.

"We don't keep paper on top of the desk in my class," say Junebug, figuring Miss Moore crazy or lyin one.

"At home, then," she say. "Don't you have a calendar and a pencil case and a blotter and a letter-opener on your desk at home where you do your homework?" And she know damn well what our homes look like cause she nosys around in them every chance she gets.

"I don't even have a desk," say Junebug. "Do we?"

"No. And I don't get no homework neither," say Big Butt.   20

"And I don't even have a home," say Flyboy like he do at school to keep the white folks off his back and sorry for him. Send this poor kid to camp posters, is his specialty.

"I do," says Mercedes. "I have a box of stationery on my desk and a picture of my cat. My godmother bought the stationery and the desk. There's a big rose on each sheet and the envelopes smell like roses."

"Who wants to know about your smelly-ass stationery," say Rosie Giraffe fore I can get my two cents in.

"It's important to have a work area all your own so that . . ."

"Will you look at this sailboat, please," say Flyboy, cuttin her off and pointin to the   25 thing like it was his. So once again we tumble all over each other to gaze at this magnificent thing in the toy store which is just big enough to maybe sail two kittens across the pond if you strap them to the posts tight. We all start reciting the price tag like we in assembly. "Handcrafted sailboat of fiberglass at one thousand one hundred ninety-five dollars."

"Unbelievable," I hear myself say and am really stunned. I read it again for myself just in case the group recitation put me in a trance. Same thing. For some reason this pisses me off. We look at Miss Moore and she lookin at us, waiting for I dunno what.

Who'd pay all that when you can buy a sailboat set for a quarter at Pop's, a tube of glue for a dime, and a ball of string for eight cents? "It must have a motor and a whole lot else besides," I say. "My sailboat cost me about fifty cents."

"But will it take water?" say Mercedes with her smart ass.

"Took mine to Alley Pond Park once," say Flyboy. "String broke, Lost it. Pity."

"Sailed mine in Central Park and it keeled over and sank. Had to ask my father   30 for another dollar."

"And you got the strap," laugh Big Butt. "The jerk didn't even have a string on it. My old man wailed on his behind."

Little Q.T. was staring hard at the sailboat and you could see he wanted it bad. But he too little and somebody'd just take it from him. So what the hell. "This boat for kids, Miss Moore?"

"Parents silly to buy something like that just to get all broke up," say Rosie Giraffe.

"That much money it should last forever," I figure.

"My father'd buy it for me if I wanted it."   35

"Your father, my ass," say Rosie Giraffe getting a chance to finally push Mercedes.

"Must be rich people shop here," say Q.T.

"You are a very bright boy," say Flyboy. "What was your first clue?" And he rap him on the head with the back of his knuckles, since Q.T. the only one he could get away with. Though Q.T. liable to come up behind you years later and get his licks in when you half expect it.

"What I want to know is," I says to Miss Moore though I never talk to her, I wouldn't give the bitch that satisfaction, "is how much a real boat costs? I figure a thousand'd get you a yacht any day."

"Why don't you check that out," she says, "and report back to the group?" Which   40 really pains my ass. If you gonna mess up a perfectly good swim day least you could do is have some answers. "Let's go in," she say like she got something up her sleeve. Only she don't lead the way. So me and Sugar turn the corner to where the entrance is, but when we get there I kinda hang back. Not that I'm scared, what's there to be afraid of, just a toy store. But I feel funny, shame. But what I got to be shamed about? Got as much right to go in as anybody. But somehow I can't seem to get hold of the door, so I step away for Sugar to lead. But she hangs back too. And I look at her and she looks at me and this is ridiculous. I mean, damn, I have never ever been shy about doing nothing or going nowhere. But then Mercedes steps up and then Rosie Giraffe and Big Butt crowd in behind and shove, and next thing we all stuffed into the doorway with only Mercedes squeezing past us, smoothing out her jumper and walking right down the aisle. Then the rest of us tumble in like a glued-together jigsaw done all wrong. And people lookin at us. And it's like the time me and Sugar crashed into the Catholic church on a dare. But once we got in there and everything so hushed and holy and the candles and the bow-in and the handkerchiefs on all the drooping heads, I just couldn't go through with the plan. Which was for me to run up to the altar and do a tap dance while Sugar played the nose flute and messed around in the holy water. And Sugar kept givin me the elbow. Then later teased me so bad I tied her up in the shower and turned it on and locked her in. And she'd be there till this day if Aunt Gretchen hadn't finally figured I was lyin about the boarder takin a shower.

Same thing in the store. We all walkin on tiptoe and hardly touchin the games and puzzles and things. And I watched Miss Moore who is steady watchin us like she waitin for a sign. Like Mama Drewery watches the sky and sniffs the air and takes note of just how much slant is in the bird formation. Then me and Sugar bump smack into each other, so busy gazing at the toys, 'specially the sailboat. But we don't laugh and go into our fat-lady bump-stomach routine. We just stare at that price tag. Then Sugar run a finger over the whole boat. And I'm jealous and want to hit her. Maybe not her, but I sure want to punch somebody in the mouth.

"Watcha bring us here for, Miss Moore?"

"You sound angry, Sylvia. Are you mad about something?" Givin me one of them grins like she tellin a grown-up joke that never turns out to be funny. And she's lookin very closely at me like maybe she plannin to do my portrait from memory. I'm mad, but I won't give her that satisfaction. So I slouch around the store bein very bored and say, "Let's go."

Me and Sugar at the back of the train watchin the tracks whizzin by large then small then gettin gobbled up in the dark. I'm thinkin about this tricky toy I saw in the store. A clown that somersaults on a bar then does chin-ups just cause you yank lightly at his leg. Cost $35. I could see me askin my mother for a $35 birthday clown. "You wanna who that costs what?" she'd say, cocking her head to the side to get a better view of the hole in my head. Thirty-five dollars could buy new bunk beds for Junior and Gretchen's boy. Thirty-five dollars and the whole household could go visit Granddaddy Nelson in the country. Thirty-five dollars would pay for the rent and the piano bill too. Who are these people that spend that much for performing clowns and $1,000 for toy sailboats? What kinda work they do and how they live and how come we ain't in on it? Where we are is who we are, Miss Moore always pointin out. But it don't necessarily have to be that way, she always adds then waits for somebody to say that poor people have to wake up and demand their share of the pie and don't none of us know what kind of pie she talkin about in the first damn place. But she ain't so smart cause I still got her four dollars from the taxi and she sure ain't gettin it. Messin up my day with this shit. Sugar nudges me in my pocket and winks.

Miss Moore lines us up in front of the mailbox where we started from, seem like   45
years ago, and I got a headache for thinkin so hard. And we lean all over each other so we can hold up under the draggy-ass lecture she always finishes us off with at the end before we thank her for borin us to tears. But she just looks at us like she readin tea leaves. Finally she say, "Well, what did you think of F.A.O. Schwartz?"

Rosie Giraffe mumbles, "White folks crazy."

"I'd like to go there again when I get my birthday money," says Mercedes, and we shove her out the pack so she has to lean on the mailbox by herself.

"I'd like a shower. Tiring day," say Flyboy.

Then Sugar surprises me by sayin, "You know, Miss Moore, I don't think all of us here put together eat in a year what that sailboat costs." And Miss Moore lights up like somebody goosed her. "And?" she say, urging Sugar on. Only I'm standin on her foot so she don't continue.

"Imagine for a minute what kind of society it is in which some people can spend   50
on a toy what it would cost to feed a family of six or seven. What do you think?"

"I think," say Sugar pushing me off her feet like she never done before, cause I whip her ass in a minute, "that this is not much of a democracy if you ask me. Equal chance to pursue happiness means an equal crack at the dough, don't it?" Miss Moore is besides herself and I am disgusted with Sugar's treachery. So I stand on her foot one more time to see if she'll shove me. She shuts up, and Miss Moore looks at me, sorrowfully I'm thinkin. And somethin weird is going on, I can feel it in my chest.

"Anybody else learn anything today?" lookin dead at me. I walk away and Sugar has to run to catch up and don't even seem to notice when I shrug her arm off my shoulder.

"Well, we got four dollars anyway," she says.

"Uh hunh."

"We could go to Hascombs and get half a chocolate layer and then go to the Sun-   55
set and still have plenty money for potato chips and ice-cream sodas."

"Uh hunh."

"Race you to Hascombs," she say.

We start down the block and she gets ahead which is O.K. by me cause I'm goin to the West End and then over to the Drive to think this day through. She can run if she want to and even run faster. But ain't nobody gonna beat me at nuthin.

QUESTIONS FOR CLOSE READING OF STYLE AND THEME

1. What is your first impression of the narrator, Sylvia? What do you know about her from the first paragraph of the story?
2. Comment on Sylvia's style of language. What are some of its characteristics?
3. What impression do you get of Miss Moore? How does her style of language differ from Sylvia's? What do you think is implied by the contrast between the way they speak?
4. Why is "surly" a Miss Moore word? How does Sylvia know it?
5. What does Sylvia learn about money in this story? What do you learn about the significance of money to Sylvia? Does she understand the "value of a dollar"?
6. How does Sylvia react to the objects she sees in the store?
7. Why doesn't Sylvia go into the store right away? Why does she hesitate?
8. What patterns of behavior are repeated by Sylvia and her friends? What patterns of behavior are repeated by Miss Moore?
9. Why is the expression "White folks crazy" repeated? What is its significance?
10. What does Miss Moore teach Sylvia and her friends about democracy in this story?

QUESTIONS FOR INTERPRETATION OF STYLE AND THEME

1. One of the persistent motifs of the story is money. Prices of objects and services are mentioned often in the story and begin to take on more significance than just being price tags. Miss Moore engineers the day carefully and leads the children to places that permit them to see things that are outside their normal experience. What is the deeper meaning of the constant references to the cost of things?
2. Miss Moore is very different from Sylvia and her friends. What characterizes her differences? Is Miss Moore a snob? Does she regard the children as less intelligent or worthy than she? Why does she live in the neighborhood and why does she volunteer to take the children on a summer trip into the city? What are her motives? Are they worthy? Will they result in any changes for the children?
3. The children are constantly wising off in the presence of Miss Moore. Sylvia implies that she is usually bored with Miss Moore, but she goes along with the group and seems emotionally moved at various points, such as when she hesitates in going in to the store. She also seems to have been emotionally changed at the end of the story when she lets Sugar run off while Sylvia decides she needs to "think this day through." What does she mean by that expression? How do you react to the behavior of Sylvia and her friends?
4. Miss Moore teaches Sylvia and her friends a lesson in economics. In some parts of the city toys cost more than it might take to feed a family in other parts of the city. Miss Moore does not condemn expensive toys, but she does make a clear point to the children. What does Miss Moore hope Sylvia will learn from this lesson? What do you think Toni Cade Bambara expects you to learn from this lesson?
5. What are the cultural circumstances of the characters in this story? How can you determine what kinds of behavior or what kinds of opinions contribute to establishing a cultural view in this story? Sylvia and Miss Moore do not share precisely the same cultural attitudes. What are their differences, and why does Bambara make us aware of the differences? Consider the behavior of these children. Do you

condone it? Do you disapprove it? Does the story demand that you take a stand on that issue?

RALPH ELLISON   (1914–1998)

Ralph Ellison is among the most celebrated and most influential writers in America. He was born in Oklahoma City and studied music for three years at Tuskegee Institute in Alabama. He joined the Federal Writers' Project in New York in the later 1930s. After serving in the Merchant Marine in World War II, he intended to write a war novel but found himself writing Invisible Man *(1952), one of the most widely read novels of mid-century. Its first chapter, the story appearing here, "Battle Royal," was originally published in* Horizon *under the title "Invisible Man." F. H. Langman has said of the novel that it "has suffered some fierce attacks, survived, and seems now to be taking its place as a classic." Ellison is also a distinguished essayist, with the collection* Shadow and Act *(1964). Both his fiction and his essays concern the experience of African-Americans, depending often on his personal experiences.*

Battle Royal from Invisible Man _____ *1947*

It goes a long way back, some twenty years. All my life I had been looking for something, and everywhere I turned someone tried to tell me what it was. I accepted their answers too, though they were often in contradiction and even self-contradictory. I was naive. I was looking for myself and asking everyone except myself questions which I, and only I, could answer. It took me a long time and much painful boomeranging of my expectations to achieve a realization everyone else appears to have been born with: That I am nobody but myself. But first I had to discover that I am an invisible man!

And yet I am no freak of nature, nor of history. I was in the cards, other things having been equal (or unequal) eighty-five years ago. I am not ashamed of my grandparents for having been slaves. I am only ashamed of myself for having at one time been ashamed. About eighty-five years ago they were told that they were free, united with others of our country in everything pertaining to the common good, and, in everything social, separate like the fingers of the hand. And they believed it. They exulted in it. They stayed in their place, worked hard, and brought up my father to do the same. But my grandfather is the one. He was an odd old guy, my grandfather, and I am told I take after him. It was he who caused the trouble. On his deathbed he called my father to him and said, "Son, after I'm gone I want you to keep up the good fight. I never told you, but our life is a war and I have been a traitor all my born days, a spy in the enemy's country ever since I give up my gun back in the Reconstruction. Live with your head in the lion's mouth. I want you to overcome 'em with yeses, undermine 'em with grins, agree 'em to death and destruction, let 'em swoller you till they vomit or bust wide open." They thought the old man had gone out of his mind. He had been the meekest of men. The younger children were rushed from the room, the shades drawn and the flame of the lamp turned so low that it sputtered on the wick like the old man's breathing. "Learn it to the young-uns," he whispered fiercely; then he died.

But my folks were more alarmed over his last words than over his dying. It was as though he had not died at all, his words caused so much anxiety. I was warned emphatically to forget what he had said and, indeed, this is the first time it has been mentioned outside the family circle. It had a tremendous effect upon me, however, I could never be sure of what he meant. Grandfather had been a quiet old man who never made any trouble, yet on his deathbed he had called himself a traitor and a spy, and he had spoken of his meekness as a dangerous activity. It became a constant puzzle which lay unanswered in the back of my mind. And whenever things went well for me I remembered my grandfather and felt guilty and uncomfortable. It was as though I was carrying out his advice in spite of myself. And to make it worse, everyone loved me for it. I was praised by the most lily-white men of the town. I was considered an example of desirable conduct—just as my grandfather had been. And what puzzled me was that the old man had defined it as *treachery.* When I was praised for my conduct I felt a guilt that in some way I was doing something that was really against the wishes of the white folks, that if they had understood they would have desired me to act just the opposite, that I should have been sulky and mean, and that that really would have been what they wanted, even though they were fooled and thought they wanted me to act as I did. It made me afraid that some day they would look upon me as a traitor and I would be lost. Still I was more afraid to act any other way because they didn't like that at all. The old man's words were like a curse. On my graduation day I delivered an oration in which I showed that humility was the secret, indeed, the very essence of progress. (Not that I believed this—how could I, remembering my grandfather?—I only believed that it worked.) It was a great success. Everyone praised me and I was invited to give the speech at a gathering of the town's leading white citizens. It was a triumph for our whole community.

It was in the main ballroom of the leading hotel. When I got there I discovered that it was on the occasion of a smoker, and I was told that since I was to be there anyway I might as well take part in the battle royal to be fought by some of my schoolmates as part of the entertainment. The battle royal came first.

All of the town's big shots were there in their tuxedoes, wolfing down the buffet foods, drinking beer and whiskey and smoking black cigars. It was a large room with a high ceiling. Chairs were arranged in neat rows around three sides of a portable boxing ring. The fourth side was clear, revealing a gleaming space of polished floor. I had some misgivings over the battle royal, by the way. Not from a distaste for fighting, but because I didn't care too much for the other fellows who were to take part. They were tough guys who seemed to have no grandfather's curse worrying their minds. No one could mistake their toughness. And besides, I suspected that fighting a battle royal might detract from the dignity of my speech. In those pre-invisible days I visualized myself as a potential Booker T. Washington.° But the other fellows didn't care too much for me either, and there were nine of them. I felt superior to them in my way, and I didn't like the manner in which we were all crowded together into the servants' elevator. Nor did they like my being there. In fact, as the warmly lighted floors flashed past the elevator we had words over the fact that I, by taking part in the fight, had knocked one of their friends out of a night's work.

We were led out of the elevator through a rococo hall into an anteroom and told to get into our fighting togs. Each of us was issued a pair of boxing gloves and ushered out into the big mirrored hall, which we entered looking cautiously about us and whispering, lest we might accidentally be heard above the noise of the room. It was foggy with cigar smoke. And already the whiskey was taking effect. I was shocked to see some of the most important men of the town quite tipsy. They were all there—bankers, lawyers,

Booker T. Washington: Negro educator (1856–1915), author of *Up from Slavery* (1901)

judges, doctors, fire chiefs, teachers, merchants. Even one of the more fashionable pastors. Something we could not see was going on up front. A clarinet was vibrating sensuously and the men were standing up and moving eagerly forward. We were a small tight group, clustered together, our bare upper bodies touching and shining with anticipatory sweat; while up front the big shots were becoming increasingly excited over something we still could not see. Suddenly I heard the school superintendent, who had told me to come, yell, "Bring up the shines, gentlemen! Bring up the little shines!"

We were rushed up to the front of the ballroom, where it smelled even more strongly of tobacco and whiskey. Then we were pushed into place. I almost wet my pants. A sea of faces, some hostile, some amused, ringed around us, and in the center, facing us, stood a magnificent blonde—stark naked. There was dead silence. I felt a blast of cold air chill me. I tried to back away, but they were behind me and around me. Some of the boys stood with lowered heads, trembling. I felt a wave of irrational guilt and fear. My teeth chattered, my skin turned to goose flesh, my knees knocked. Yet I was strongly attracted and looked in spite of myself. Had the price of looking been blindness, I would have looked. The hair was yellow like that of a circus kewpie doll, the face heavily powdered and rouged, as though to form an abstract mask, the eyes hollow and smeared a cool blue, the color of a baboon's butt. I felt a desire to spit upon her as my eyes brushed slowly over her body. Her breasts were firm and round as the domes of East Indian temples, and I stood so close as to see the fine skin texture and beads of pearly perspiration glistening like dew around the pink and erected buds of her nipples. I wanted at one and the same time to run from the room, to sink through the floor, or go to her and cover her from my eyes and the eyes of the others with my body; to feel the soft thighs, to caress her and destroy her, to love her and murder her, to hide from her, and yet to stroke where below the small American flag tattooed upon her belly her thighs formed a capital V. I had a notion that of all in the room she saw only me with her impersonal eyes.

And then she began to dance, a slow sensuous movement; the smoke of a hundred cigars clinging to her like the thinnest of veils. She seemed like a fair bird-girl girdled in veils calling to me from the angry surface of some gray and threatening sea. I was transported. Then I became aware of the clarinet playing and the big shots yelling at us. Some threatened us if we looked and others if we did not. On my right I saw one boy faint. And now a man grabbed a silver pitcher from a table and stepped close as he dashed ice water upon him and stood him up and forced two of us to support him as his head hung and moans issued from his thick bluish lips. Another boy began to plead to go home. He was the largest of the group, wearing dark red fighting trunks much too small to conceal the erection which projected from him as though in answer to the insinuating low-registered moaning of the clarinet. He tried to hide himself with his boxing gloves.

And all the while the blonde continued dancing, smiling faintly at the big shots who watched her with fascination, and faintly smiling at our fear. I noticed a certain merchant who followed her hungrily, his lips loose and drooling. He was a large man who wore diamond studs in a shirtfront which swelled with the ample paunch underneath, and each time the blonde swayed her undulating hips he ran his hand through the thin hair of his bald head and, with his arms upheld, his posture clumsy like that of an intoxicated panda, wound his belly in a slow and obscene grind. This creature was completely hypnotized. The music had quickened. As the dancer flung herself about with a detached expression on her face, the men began reaching out to touch her. I could see their beefy fingers sink into the soft flesh. Some of the others tried to stop them and she began to move around the floor in graceful circles, as they gave chase, slipping and sliding over the polished floor. It was mad. Chairs went crashing, drinks were spilt, as they ran laughing and howling after her. They caught her just as she reached a door, raised her from the floor, and tossed her as college boys are tossed at a hazing, and above her red, fixed-smiling lips I saw the terror and disgust in her eyes, almost like my own terror and that which I saw in some of the other boys. As I watched, they tossed her twice and her soft breasts seemed to flatten against the air and her legs flung wildly as she spun. Some of the sober ones helped her to escape. And I started off the floor, heading for the anteroom with the rest of the boys.

Some were still crying and in hysteria. But as we tried to leave we were stopped   10
and ordered to get into the ring. There was nothing to do but what we were told. All ten of us climbed under the ropes and allowed ourselves to be blindfolded with broad bands of white cloth. One of the men seemed to feel a bit sympathetic and tried to cheer us up as we stood with our backs against the ropes. Some of us tried to grin. "See that boy over there?" one of the men said. "I want you to run across at the bell and give it to him right in the belly. If you don't get him, I'm going to get you. I don't like his looks." Each of us was told the same. The blindfolds were put on. Yet even then I had been going over my speech. In my mind each word was as bright as flame. I felt the cloth pressed into place, and frowned so that it would be loosened when I relaxed.

But now I felt a sudden fit of blind terror. I was unused to darkness. It was as though I had suddenly found myself in a dark room filled with poisonous cottonmouths. I could hear the bleary voices yelling insistently for the battle royal to begin.

"Get going in there!"

"Let me at that big nigger!"

I strained to pick up the school superintendent's voice, as though to squeeze some security out of that slightly more familiar sound.

"Let me at those black sonsabitches!" someone yelled.   15

"No, Jackson, no!" another voice yelled. "Here, somebody, help me hold Jack."

"I want to get at that ginger-colored nigger. Tear him limb from limb," the first voice yelled.

I stood against the ropes trembling. For in those days I was what they called ginger-colored, and he sounded as though he might crunch me between his teeth like a crisp ginger cookie.

Quite a struggle was going on. Chairs were being kicked about and I could hear voices grunting as with a terrific effort. I wanted to see, to see more desperately than ever before. But the blindfold was tight as a thick skin-puckering scab and when I raised my gloved hands to push the layers of white aside a voice yelled, "Oh, no you don't, black bastard! Leave that alone!"

"Ring the bell before Jackson kills him a coon!" someone boomed in the sudden   20
silence. And I heard the bell clang and the sound of the feet scuffling forward.

A glove smacked against my head. I pivoted, striking out stiffly as someone went past, and felt the jar ripple along the length of my arm to my shoulder. Then it seemed as though all nine boys had turned upon me at once. Blows pounded me from all sides while I struck out as best I could. So many blows landed upon me that I wondered if I were not the only blindfolded fighter in the ring, or if the man called Jackson hadn't succeeded in getting me after all.

Blindfolded, I could no longer control my motions. I had no dignity. I stumbled about like a baby or a drunken man. The smoke had become thicker and with each new blow it seemed to sear and further restrict my lungs. My saliva became like hot bitter glue. A glove connected with my head, filling my mouth with warm blood. It was everywhere. I could not tell if the moisture I felt upon my body was sweat or blood. A blow landed hard against the nape of my neck. I felt myself going over, my head hitting the floor. Streaks of blue light filled the black world behind the blindfold. I lay prone, pretending that I was knocked out, but felt myself seized by hands and yanked to my feet. "Get going, black boy! Mix it up!" My arms were like lead, my head smarting from blows. I managed to feel my way to the ropes and held on, trying to catch my breath. A glove landed in my mid-section and I went over again, feeling as though the smoke had become a knife jabbed into my guts. Pushed this way and that by the legs milling around me, I finally pulled erect and discovered that I could see the black, sweat-washed forms weaving in the smoky-blue atmosphere like drunken dancers weaving to the rapid drum—like thuds of blows.

Everyone fought hysterically. It was complete anarchy. Everybody fought everybody else. No group fought together for long. Two, three, four, fought one, then turned to fight each other, were themselves attacked. Blows landed below the belt and in the kidney, with the gloves open as well as closed, and with my eye partly opened now there was not so much terror. I moved carefully, avoiding blows, although not too many to attract attention, fighting from group to group. The boys groped about like blind, cautious crabs crouching to protect their mid-sections, their heads pulled in short against their shoulders, their arms stretched nervously before them, with their fists testing the smoke-filled air like the knobbed feelers of hypersensitive snails. In one corner I glimpsed a boy violently punching the air and heard him scream in pain as he smashed his hand against a ring post. For a second I saw him bent over holding his hand, then going down as a blow caught his unprotected head. I played one group against the other, slipping in and throwing a punch then stepping out of range while pushing the others into the melee to take the blows blindly aimed at me. The smoke was agonizing and there were no rounds, no bells at three minute intervals to relieve our exhaustion. The room spun round me, a swirl of lights, smoke, sweating bodies sourrounded by tense white faces. I bled from both nose and mouth, the blood spattering upon my chest.

The men kept yelling, "Slug him, black boy! Knock his guts out!"

"Uppercut him! Kill him! Kill that big boy!"   25

Taking a fake fall, I saw a boy going down heavily beside me as though we were felled by a single blow, saw a sneaker-clad foot shot into his groin as the two who had knocked him down stumbled upon him. I rolled out of range, feeling a twinge of nausea.

The harder we fought the more threatening the men became. And yet, I had begun to worry about my speech again. How would it go? Would they recognize my ability? What would they give me?

I was fighting automatically when suddenly I noticed that one after another of the boys was leaving the ring. I was surprised, filled with panic, as though I had been left alone with an unknown danger. Then I understood. The boys had arranged it among themselves. It was the custom for the two men left in the ring to slug it out for the winner's prize. I discovered this too late. When the bell sounded two men in tuxedoes leaped into the ring and removed the blindfold. I found myself facing Tatlock, the biggest of the gang. I felt sick at my stomach. Hardly had the bell stopped ringing in my ears than it clanged again and I saw him moving swiftly toward me. Thinking of nothing else to do I hit him smash on the nose. He kept coming, bringing the rank sharp violence of stale sweat. His face was a black blank of a face, only his eyes alive—with hate of me and aglow with a feverish terror from what had happened to us all. I became anxious. I wanted to deliver my speech and he came at me as though he meant to beat it out of me. I smashed him again and again, taking his blows as they came. Then on a sudden impulse I struck him lightly and as we clinched, I whispered, "Fake like I knocked you out, you can have the prize."

"I'll break your behind," he whispered hoarsely.

"For *them?*"   30

"For *me,* sonofabitch!"

They were yelling for us to break it up and Tatlock spun me half around with a blow, and as a joggled camera sweeps in a reeling scene, I saw the howling red faces crouching tense beneath the cloud of blue-gray smoke. For a moment the world wavered, unraveled, flowed, then my head cleared and Tatlock bounced before me. The fluttering shadow before my eyes was his jabbing left hand. Then falling forward, my head against his damp shoulder, I whispered,

"I'll make it five dollars more."

"Go to hell!"

But his muscles relaxed a trifle beneath my pressure and I breathed, "Seven?"   35

"Give it to your ma," he said, ripping me beneath the heart.

And while I still held him I butted him and moved away. I felt myself bombarded with punches. I fought back with hopeless desperation. I wanted to deliver my speech more than anything else in the world, because I felt that only these men could judge truly my ability, and now this stupid clown was ruining my chances. I began fighting carefully now, moving in to punch him and out again with my greater speed. A lucky blow to his chin and I had him going too—until I heard a loud voice yell, "I got my money on the big boy."

Hearing this, I almost dropped my guard. I was confused: Should I try to win against the voice out there? Would not this go against my speech, and was not this a moment for humility, for nonresistance? A blow to my head as I danced about sent my right eye popping like a jack-in-the-box and settled my dilemma. The room went red as I fell. It was a dream fall, my body languid and fastidious as to where to land, until the floor became impatient and smashed up to meet me. A moment later I came to. An hypnotic voice said FIVE emphatically. And I lay there, hazily watching a dark red spot of my own blood shaping itself into a butterfly, glistening and soaking into the soiled gray world of the canvas.

When the voice drawled TEN I was lifted up and dragged to a chair. I sat dazed. My eye pained and swelled with each throb of my pounding heart and I wondered if now I would be allowed to speak. I was wringing wet, my mouth still bleeding. We were grouped along the wall now. The other boys ignored me as they congratulated Tatlock and speculated as to how much they would be paid. One boy whimpered over his smashed hand. Looking up front, I saw attendants in white jackets rolling the portable ring away and placing a small square rug in the vacant space surrounded by chairs. Perhaps, I thought, I will stand on the rug to deliver my speech.

Then the M.C. called to us, "Come on up here boys and get your money."   40

We ran forward to where the men laughed and talked in their chairs, waiting. Everyone seemed friendly now.

"There it is on the rug," the man said. I saw the rug covered with coins of all dimensions and a few crumpled bills. But what excited me, scattered here and there, were the gold pieces.

"Boys, it's all yours," the man said. "You get all you grab."

"That's right, Sambo," a blond man said, winking at me confidentially.

I trembled with excitement, forgetting my pain. I would get the gold and the bills,   45
I thought. I would use both hands. I would throw my body against the boys nearest me
to block them from the gold.

"Get down on the rug now," the man commanded, "and don't anyone touch it
until I give the signal."

"This ought to be good," I heard.

As told, we got around the square rug on our knees. Slowly the man raised his
freckled hand as we followed it upward with our eyes.

I heard, "These niggers look like they're about to pray!"

Then, "Ready," the man said, "Go!"   50

I lunged for a yellow coin lying on the blue design of the carpet, touching it and
sending a surprised shriek to join those rising around me. I tried frantically to remove
my hand but could not let go. A hot, violent force tore through my body, shaking me
like a wet rage. The rug was electrified. The hair bristled up on my head as I shook myself free. My muscles jumped, my nerves jangled, writhed. But I saw that this was not
stopping the other boys. Laughing in fear and embarrassment, some were holding back
and scooping up the coins knocked off by the painful contortions of the others. The men
roared above us as we struggled.

"Pick it up, goddamnit, pick it up!" someone called like a bass-voiced parrot. "Go
on, get it!"

I crawled rapidly around the floor, picking up the coins, trying to avoid the cop-
pers and to get greenbacks and the gold. Ignoring the shock by laughing, as I brushed
the coins off quickly, I discovered that I could contain the electricity—a contradiction,
but it works. Then the men began to push us onto the rug. Laughing embarrassedly, we
struggled out of their hands and kept after the coins. We were all wet and slippery and
hard to hold. Suddenly I saw a boy lifted into the air, glistening with sweat like a circus
seal, and dropped, his wet back landing flush upon the charged rug, heard him yell
and saw him literally dance upon his back, his elbows beating a frenzied tattoo upon the
floor, his muscles twitching like the flesh of a horse stung by many flies. When he finally
rolled off, his face was gray and no one stopped him when he ran from the floor amid
booming laughter.

"Get the money," the M.C. called. "That's good hard American cash!"

And we snatched and grabbed, snatched and grabbed. I was careful not to come   55
too close to the rug now, and when I felt the hot whiskey breath descend upon me like
a cloud of foul air I reached out and grabbed the leg of a chair. It was occupied and I
held on desperately.

"Leggo, nigger! Leggo!"

The huge face wavered down to mine as he tried to push me free. But my body
was slippery and he was too drunk. It was Mr. Colcord, who owned a chain of movie
houses and "entertainment palaces." Each time he grabbed me I slipped out of his
hands. It became a real struggle. I feared the rug more than I did the drunk, so I held
on, surprising myself for a moment by trying to topple *him* upon the rug. It was such
an enormous idea that I found myself actually carrying it out. I tried not to be obvious,
yet when I grabbed his leg, trying to tumble him out of the chair, he raised up roaring
with laughter, and, looking at me with soberness dead in the eye, kicked me viciously
in the chest. The chair leg flew out of my hand and I felt myself going and rolled. It
was as though I had rolled through a bed of hot coals. It seemed a whole century would
pass before I would roll free, a century in which I was seared through the deepest

levels of my body to the fearful breath within me and the breath seared and heated to the point of explosion. It'll all be over in a flash, I thought as I rolled clear. It'll all be over in a flash.

But not yet, the men on the other side were waiting, red faces swollen as though from apoplexy as they bent forward in their chairs. Seeing their fingers coming toward me, I rolled away as a fumbled football rolls off the receiver's fingertips, back into the coals. That time I luckily sent the rug sliding out of place and heard the coins ringing against the floor and the boys scuffling to pick them up and the M.C. calling, "All right, boys that's all. Go get dressed and get your money."

I was limp as a dish rag. My back felt as though it had been beaten with wires.

When we had dressed the M.C. came in and gave us each five dollars, except Tat- 60
lock, who got ten for being last in the ring. Then he told us to leave. I was not to get a chance to deliver my speech, I thought. I was going out into the dim alley in despair when I was stopped and told to go back. I returned to the ballroom, where the men were pushing back their chairs and gathering in groups to talk.

The M.C. knocked on a table for quiet. "Gentlemen," he said, "we almost forgot about an important part of the program. A most serious part, gentlemen. This boy was brought here to deliver a speech which he made at his graduation yesterday . . ."

"Bravo!"

"I'm told that he is the smartest boy we've got out there in Greenwood. I'm told that he knows more big words than a pocket-sized dictionary."

Much applause and laughter.

"So now, gentlemen, I want you to give him your attention." 65

There was still laughter as I faced them, my mouth dry, my eye throbbing. I began slowly, but evidently my throat was tense, because they began shouting, "Louder! Louder!"

"We of the younger generation extol the wisdom of that great leader and educator," I shouted, "who first spoke these flaming words of wisdom: 'A ship lost at sea for many days suddenly sighted a friendly vessel. From the mast of the unfortunate vessel was seen a signal: "Water, water; we die of thirst!" The answer from the friendly vessel came back: "Cast down your bucket where you are." The captain of the distressed vessel, at last heeding the injunction, cast down his bucket, and it came up full of fresh sparkling water from the mouth of the Amazon River.' And like him I say, and in his words, 'To those of my race who depend upon bettering their condition in a foreign land, or who underestimate the importance of cultivating friendly relations with the Southern white man, who is his next-door neighbor, I would say: "Cast down your bucket where you are"—cast it down in making friends in every manly way of the people of all races by whom we are surrounded . . .' "

I spoke automatically and with such fervor that I did not realize that the men were still talking and laughing until my dry mouth, filling up with blood from the cut, almost strangled me. I coughed, wanting to stop and go to one of the tall brass, sand-filled spittoons to relieve myself, but a few of the men, especially the superintendent, were listening and I was afraid. So I gulped it down, blood, saliva and all, and continued. (What powers of endurance I had during those days! What enthusiasm! What a belief in the rightness of things!) I spoke even louder in spite of the pain. But still they talked and still they laughed, as though deaf with cotton in dirty ears. So I spoke with greater emotional emphasis. I closed my ears and swallowed blood until I was nauseated. The speech seemed a hundred times as long as before, but I could not leave out a single word. All had to be said, each memorized nuance considered, rendered. Nor was that all. Whenever I uttered a word of three syllables a group of voices would yell for me to repeat it. I used the phrase "social responsibility" and they yelled:

"What's that word you say, boy?"

"Social responsibility," I said.   70

"What?"

"Social . . ."

"Louder."

". . . responsibility."

"More!"   75

"Respon—"

"Repeat!"

"—sibility."

The room filled with the uproar of laughter until, no doubt, distracted by having to gulp down my blood, I made a mistake and yelled a phrase I had often seen denounced in newspaper editorials, heard debated in private.

"Social . . ."   80

"What?" they yelled.

". . . equality—"

The laughter hung smokelike in the sudden stillness. I opened my eyes, puzzled. Sounds of displeasure filled the room. The M.C. rushed forward. They shouted hostile phrases at me. But I did not understand.

A small dry mustached man in the front row blared out, "Say that slowly, son!"

"What, sir?"   85

"What you just said!"

"Social responsibility, sir," I said.

"You weren't being smart, were you, boy?" he said, not unkindly.

"No, sir!"

"You sure that about 'equality' was a mistake?"   90

"Oh, yes sir," I said. "I was swallowing blood."

"Well, you had better speak more slowly so we can understand. We mean to do right by you, but you've got to know your place at all times. All right, now, go on with your speech."

I was afraid. I wanted to leave but I wanted also to speak and I was afraid they'd snatch me down.

"Thank you, sir," I said, beginning where I had left off, and having them ignore me as before.

Yet when I finished there was a thunderous applause. I was surprised to see the   95
superintendent come forth with a package wrapped in white tissue paper, and, gesturing for quiet, address the men.

"Gentlemen, you see that I did not overpraise this boy. He makes a good speech and some day he'll lead his people in the proper paths. And I don't have to tell you that that is important in these days and times. This is a good, smart boy, and so to encourage him in the right direction, in the name of the Board of Education I wish to present him a prize in the form of this . . ."

He paused, removing the tissue paper and revealing a gleaming calfskin brief case.

". . . in the form of this first-class article from Shad Whitmore's shop."

"Boy," he said, addressing me, "take this prize and keep it well. Consider it a badge of office. Prize it. Keep developing as you are and some day it will be filled with important papers that will help shape the destiny of your people."

I was so moved that I could hardly express my thanks. A rope of bloody saliva 100
forming a shape like an undiscovered continent drooled upon the leather and I wiped it quickly away. I felt an importance that I had never dreamed.

"Open it and see what's inside," I was told.

My fingers a-tremble, I complied, smelling the fresh leather and finding an official-looking document inside. It was a scholarship to the state college for Negroes. My eyes filled with tears and I ran awkwardly off the floor.

I was overjoyed; I did not even mind when I discovered that the gold pieces I had scrambled for were brass pocket tokens advertising a certain make of automobile.

When I reached home everyone was excited. Next day the neighbors came to congratulate me. I even felt safe from grandfather, whose deathbed curse usually spoiled my triumphs. I stood beneath his photograph with my brief case in hand and smiled triumphantly into his stolid black peasant's face. It was a face that fascinated me. The eyes seemed to follow everywhere I went.

That night I dreamed I was at a circus with him and that he refused to laugh at 105
the clowns no matter what they did. Then later he told me to open my brief case and read what was inside and I did, finding an official envelope stamped with the state seal; and inside the envelope, I found another and another, endlessly, and I thought I would fall of weariness. "Them's years," he said. "Now open that one." And I did and in it I found an engraved document containing a short message in letters of gold. "Read it," my grandfather said. "Out loud!"

"To Whom It May Concern," I intoned. "Keep This Nigger-Boy Running."

I awoke with the old man's laughter ringing in my ears.

(It was a dream I was to remember and dream again for many years after. But at that time I had no insight into its meaning. First I had to attend college.)

QUESTIONS FOR CLOSE READING OF STYLE AND THEME

1. What does the narrator mean by saying that he was naive in turning to others to discover who he was? Is naiveté a theme of the story?

2. How accurate is the metaphor implied in the expression "a painful boomeranging of my expectations" in the events of this story? Why is the boomerange an appropriate metaphor?

3. Why is the word *ashamed* repeated often in the story?

4. What is the meaning of the message of the narrator's grandfather on his deathbed? What legacy does he leave the narrator?

5. Why do the narrator's parents react negatively to the grandfather's message?

6. The grandfather represents a pattern repeated throughout the story. What is his significance?

7. What are the purposes of the white folks in praising the narrator early in the story?

8. *Humility* is a significant term used early in the story. How does the narrator learn humility? Is it a worthwhile lesson?

9. What characterizes the behavior of the "proper" men of the town? In what ways does the narrator show himself to be "naive" in his expectations of their behavior?

10. Why does the stripper have a "small American flag tattooed on her belly"? What does she symbolize?

11. Why do the men force the boys to fight? What is the symbolism in the electrified money on the rug? Does the symbolism alter when the narrator finds out the gold pieces were "brass pocket tokens advertising a certain make of automobile"?

12. What is the significance of the narrator's "slip" when he says "social equality" instead of "social responsibility" in his speech? Why does it enrage the white audience?

QUESTIONS FOR INTERPRETATION OF STYLE AND THEME

1. Examine the relationship of the narrator and his grandfather. Why is there such a gulf between them in their attitudes about how to live? On the surface there seem to be worlds of difference between the "peasant" grandfather and the narrator, who is heading for college. However, patterns within the story suggest that they have much in common. The dream at the end of the story implies some of those qualities. How does the story emphasize them?

2. Examine the ironies implied in the contrast between the speech the narrator gives and the events surrounding it. What, for you, are the most compelling and bothersome incongruities implied in the speech as it is delivered in this setting? How central are these ironies to the overall theme of the story?

3. The emotional state of the narrator seems to move in several directions very rapidly as he experiences pride, disgust, humiliation, pain, alarm, and eventually more pride. What do you learn about the narrator throughout the course of the story? What are his qualities? What are his values? What makes him go through with his speech at the end of the story? Is his determination a central theme of the story?

4. How do you think Ralph Ellison expected you to react to this story? What are its most alarming moments? What behavior most alarms you? Do you find yourself feeling an emotional reaction to the events in the story that surprises you? Do the events described in the story warrant your responses? Does the story produce a sense of uneasiness in the reader?

5. The story is set in a southern town many decades ago, eighty-five years after emancipation. What seem to be the social circumstances of that era? What kinds of behavior seem to have been acceptable to the "big shots" in the town? Is it fair to call their behavior racist? What odd qualities does their behavior reveal? What contradictions seem to be implied in their behavior? Is it enough to say that racism is the primary theme of the story?

6. One of the most repeated motifs in the story is money. Examine each instance of the reference to money and consider what the larger significance of those references is meant to imply. Why doesn't Tatlock take the money the narrator offers him during their fight? Why do the "big shots" keep referring to the brass tokens as "good hard American cash"? Are they symbolically correct?

PLOT AND NARRATIVE STRUCTURE

Plot in short fiction implies a sequence of actions that hold together by virtue of their causing and shaping the actions that follow. Causality distinguishes carefully plotted stories because the actions seem to logically cause what follows. Certain narrative structures either omit or mute causality to produce a random effect, partly to emphasize the apparent randomness of reality.

Narratives take many shapes. Here are three of the most common.

- *Chronological*   Most stories are **chronological** in that the action follows linear time. As in "The Pot of Basil," events are told to us in the same order as they happen in time.
- *Flashback*   Many modern stories use a popular film technique: the **flashback.** This technique involves a narrative whose present-time action is interrupted to narrate selected past actions.
- *Nonlinear*   Some modern stories defy time and continuity, using instead **nonlinear** action. John Cheever's "The Swimmer" appears at first to be linear and continuous, but soon you realize that it began in the summer and ended in the winter, and Neddy Merrill has lost touch with time and reality. Modern authors who use magical realism, a technique blending realistic details with events that seem impossible (such as Lorenzo's speaking to Lisabetta after death), find this technique useful because it adds to the mystery. Time is fragmented, the sequence of events is fractured, and the reader is responsible for piecing things together.

The plots of short stories have many qualities in common, even if each of them is unique. For example, many stories begin *in medias res*—in the middle of things—and in order to bring us up to date with what has happened, the author must provide exposition. Exposition tells us what has happened so far— at least enough so we can read the story intelligently. "The Swimmer" begins with a paragraph that tells us that "it was one of those midsummer Sundays when everyone sits around saying, 'I *drank* too much last night.' " And the rest of the paragraph fills us in on the usual "scene" before Neddy Merrill enters swimming. Similarly, when Poe opens his story by saying, "The 'Red Death' had long devastated the country," and goes on to speak of the Avatar of blood, he begins the exposition necessary to understand what is about to happen.

The well-plotted story depends also on conflict between the protagonist and the antagonist. The **antagonist**—the villain—is either a character or an abstract force that restricts the action of the **protagonist.** The conflict may be direct, indirect, or merely threatened. In "The Masque of the Red Death" the protagonist is Prince Prospero and the antagonist is the Red Death, the plague that Prospero thinks he can avoid. The conflict between Prospero and the Red Death is threatened from the first line of the story, and its presence builds suspense. Suspense depends upon the anticipation of how the plot will develop. Will Prospero avoid the Red Death? Will the masquers all die? Will Neddy realize he is doing something destructive? Suspense is often part of the **rising action:** the buildup of tension and decription of action that precedes the climax. The **climax** is the point of greatest emotional intensity in the story, and it may take many forms. In Poe's story the climax comes when Prince Prospero races through the carefully described rooms with a "drawn dagger" to kill the uninvited mummer only to fall instantly dead. In "The Swimmer" the climax comes when Neddy is described rudely as a "gate crasher." The suspense in "The Swimmer" builds from swimming pool to swimming pool because the resolution of the action— the **denouement**—is anything but clear. Few readers could predict the story's outcome. The denouement in "The Masque of the Red Death" coincides with the climax and the death of the first masquer. The denouement in "The Swimmer" comes when Neddy for the "first time in his adult life" begins to cry. His tears imply that he finally understands the painful limitations of his life.

Suspense is built in part by the use of **foreshadowing.** Foreshadowing hints at what is to come, but does so without giving away the ending of the story. Poe's references to "the Time that flies" and his intense descriptions all act as foreshadowing of some impending doom. This is especially true in his description of each room, ending with the black room.

Katherine Anne Porter's "The Jilting of Granny Weatherall" begins *in medias res* and is told almost entirely in flashback. You are given a frame to work from: Granny is on her deathbed and her daughter Cornelia and Doctor Harry are with her. Other children arrive. But Granny, in whose mind the entire story takes place, thinks about the past. The exposition reveals that one event in her life has risen to the surface above all others: the day long ago when her fiancé, George, left her standing—jilted—in front of the priest at the altar.

As she is dying that one day takes precedence over the rest of her life. She says repeatedly that she would never trade John, the man she married, for anyone and that he gave her far better children than she expected. But despite that she can think of almost nothing but the day she was jilted.

Porter narrates the events of the day in flashback, interrupted by the occasional demands of father and Cornelia and Granny's irritable responses. Granny remembers the names of everyone, including the priest who was to marry her. The memory of the event is broken now and then by Granny's realization that death is upon her and that she needs to make some specific bequests of land and amethysts.

Typical of some, but not all, flashback narratives, "The Jilting of Granny Weatherall" tells two stories: the events in present time and the events of past time. In present time her children are slowly gathering by her bed, but in past time she is a young girl facing the most humiliating and painful experience of her life. At the end of the story, the two narratives seem to come to one point: The past and the present suddenly and mysteriously merge.

KATHERINE ANNE PORTER (1890–1980)

Katherine Anne Porter was a Texan who spent most of her life in Greenwich Village, Mexico, and Europe. She worked as a newspaper woman and traveled in Mexico at the end of its revolution. She lectured to supplement a meager income until her novel, Ship of Fools, *was published in 1962; money from the sale of the film rights freed Porter financially. After her first collection of stories,* Flowering Judas *(1930), appeared, critics saw her as a master of the craft of short fiction. Most of the stories in the collection concern Mexico and revolution, but on a deeper level they treat the themes of disillusion and loss of innocence, especially on the part of a young American woman, a character in the title story. Porter's* Collected Stories *(1964) is regarded as her major work.*

The Jilting of Granny Weatherall _____ 1930

She flicked her wrist neatly out of Doctor Harry's pudgy careful fingers and pulled the sheet up to her chin. The brat ought to be in knee breeches. Doctoring around the country with spectacles on his nose! "Get along now, take your schoolbooks and go. There's nothing wrong with me."

Doctor Harry spread a warm paw like a cushion on her forehead where the forked green vein danced and made her eyelids twitch. "Now, now, be a good girl, and we'll have you up in no time."

"That's no way to speak to a woman nearly eighty years old just because she's down. I'd have you respect your elders, young man."

"Well, Missy, excuse me." Doctor Harry patted her cheek. "But I've got to warn you, haven't I? You're a marvel, but you must be careful or you're going to be good and sorry."

"Don't tell me what I'm going to be. I'm on my feet now, morally speaking. It's Cornelia. I had to go to bed to get rid of her."   5

Her bones felt loose, and floated around in her skin, and Doctor Harry floated like a balloon around the foot of the bed. He floated and pulled down his waistcoat and swung his glasses on a cord. "Well, stay where you are, it certainly can't hurt you."

"Get along and doctor your sick," said Granny Weatherall. "Leave a well woman alone. I'll call for you when I want you. . . . Where were you forty years ago when I pulled through milk-leg and double pneumonia? You weren't even born. Don't let Cornelia lead you on," she shouted, because Doctor Harry appeared to float up to the ceiling and out. "I pay my own bills, and I don't throw my money away on nonsense!"

She meant to wave good-by, but it was too much trouble. Her eyes closed of themselves, it was like a dark curtain drawn around the bed. The pillow rose and floated under her, pleasant as a hammock in a light wind. She listened to the leaves rustling outside the window. No, somebody was swishing newspapers: no, Cornelia and Doctor Harry were whispering together. She leaped broad awake, thinking they whispered in her ear.

"She was never like this, *never* like this!" "Well, what can we expect?" "Yes, eighty years old. . . ."

Well, and what if she was? She still had ears. It was like Cornelia to whisper around   10
doors. She always kept things secret in such a public way. She was always being tactful and kind. Cornelia was dutiful; that was the trouble with her. Dutiful and good: "So good and dutiful," said Granny, "and I'd like to spank her." She saw herself spanking Cornelia and making a fine job of it.

"What'd you say, Mother?"

Granny felt her face tying up in hard knots.

"Can't a body think, I'd like to know?"

"I thought you might want something."

"I do. I want a lot of things. First off, go away and don't whisper."   15

She lay and drowsed, hoping in her sleep that the children would keep out and let her rest a minute. It had been a long day. Not that she was tired. It was always pleasant to snatch a minute now and then. There was always so much to be done, let me see: tomorrow.

Tomorrow was far away and there was nothing to trouble about. Things were finished somehow when the time came; thank God there was always a little margin over for peace: then a person could spread out the plan of life and tuck in the edges orderly. It was good to have everything clean and folded away, with the hair brushes and tonic bottles sitting straight on the white embroidered linen: the day started without fuss and the pantry shelves laid out with rows of jelly glasses and brown jugs and white stone-china jars with blue whirligigs and words painted on them: coffee, tea, sugar, ginger, cinnamon, allspice: and the bronze clock with the lion on top nicely dusted off. The dust that lion could collect in twenty-four hours! The box in the attic with all those letters tied up, well, she'd have to go through that tomorrow. All those letters—George's letters and John's letters and her letters to them both—lying around for the children to find afterwards made her uneasy. Yes, that would be tomorrow's business. No use to let them know how silly she had been once.

While she was rummaging around she found death in her mind and it felt clammy and unfamiliar. She had spent so much time preparing for death there was no need for bringing it up again. Let it take care of itself now. When she was sixty she had felt very old, finished, and went around making farewell trips to see her children and grand-children, with a secret in her mind: This is the very last of your mother, children! Then she made her will and came down with a long fever. That was all just a notion like a lot of other things, but it was lucky too, for she had once for all got over the idea of dying for a long time. Now she couldn't be worried. She hoped she had better sense now. Her father had lived to be one hundred and two years old and had drunk a noggin of strong hot toddy on his last birthday. He told the reporters it was his daily habit, and he owed his long life to that. He had made quite a scandal and was very pleased about it. She believed she'd just plague Cornelia a little.

"Cornelia! Cornelia!" No footsteps, but a sudden hand on her cheek. "Bless you, where have you been?"

"Here, Mother."   20

"Well, Cornelia, I want a noggin of hot toddy."

"Are you cold, darling?"

"I'm chilly, Cornelia. Lying in bed stops the circulation. I must have told you that a thousand times."

Well, she could just hear Cornelia telling her husband that Mother was getting a little childish and they'd have to humor her. The thing that most annoyed her was that Cornelia thought she was deaf, dumb, and blind. Little hasty glances and tiny gestures tossed around her and over her head saying, "Don't cross her, let her have her way, she's eighty years old," and she sitting there as if she lived in a thin glass cage. Sometimes Granny almost made up her mind to pack up and move back to her own house where nobody could remind her every minute that she was old. Wait, wait, Cornelia, till your own children whisper behind your back!

In her day she had kept a better house and had got more work done. She wasn't   25
too old yet for Lydia to be driving eighty miles for advice when one of the children jumped the track, and Jimmy still dropped in and talked things over: "Now, Mammy, you've a good business head, I want to know what you think of this? . . ." Old. Cornelia couldn't change the furniture around without asking. Little things, little things! They

had been so sweet when they were little. Granny wished the old days were back again with the children young and everything to be done over. It had been a hard pull, but not too much for her. When she thought of all the food she had cooked, and all the clothes she had cut and sewed, and all the gardens she had made—well, the children showed it. There they were, made out of her, and they couldn't get away from that. Sometimes she wanted to see John again and point to them and say, Well, I didn't do so badly, did I? But that would have to wait. That was for tomorrow. She used to think of him as a man, but now all the children were older than their father, and he would be a child beside her if she saw him now. It seemed strange and there was something wrong in the idea. Why, he couldn't possibly recognize her. She had fenced in a hundred acres once, digging the post holes herself and clamping the wires with just a negro boy to help. That changed a woman. John would be looking for a young woman with the peaked Spanish comb in her hair and the painted fan. Digging post holes changed a woman. Riding country roads in the winter when women had their babies was another thing: sitting up nights with sick horses and sick negroes and sick children and hardly ever losing one. John, I hardly ever lost one of them! John would see that in a minute, that would be something he could understand, she wouldn't have to explain anything!

It made her feel like rolling up her sleeves and putting the whole place to rights again. No matter if Cornelia was determined to be everywhere at once, there were a great many things left undone on this place. She would start tomorrow and do them. It was good to be strong enough for everything, even if all you made melted and changed and slipped under your hands, so that by the time you finished you almost forgot what you were working for. What was it I set out to do? she asked herself intently, but she could not remember. A fog rose over the valley, she saw it marching across the creek swallowing the trees and moving up the hill like an army of ghosts. Soon it would be at the near edge of the orchard, and then it was time to go in and light the lamps. Come in, children, don't stay out in the night air.

Lighting the lamps had been beautiful. The children huddled up to her and breathed like little calves waiting at the bars in the twilight. Their eyes followed the match and watched the flame rise and settle in a blue curve, then they moved away from her. The lamp was lit, they didn't have to be scared and hang on to mother any more. Never, never, never more. God, for all my life I thank Thee. Without Thee, my God, I could never have done it. Hail, Mary, full of grace.

I want you to pick all the fruit this year and see that nothing is wasted. There's always someone who can use it. Don't let good things rot for want of using. You waste life when you waste good food. Don't let things get lost. It's bitter to lose things. Now, don't let me get to thinking, not when I am tired and taking a little nap before supper. . . .

The pillow rose about her shoulders and pressed against her heart and the memory was being squeezed out of it: oh, push down the pillow, somebody: it would smother her if she tried to hold it. Such a fresh breeze blowing and such a green day with no threats in it. But he had not come, just the same. What does a woman do when she has put on the white veil and set out the white cake for a man and he doesn't come? She tried to remember. No, I swear he never harmed me but in that. He never harmed me but in that . . . and what if he did? There was the day, the day, but a whirl of dark smoke rose and covered it, crept up and over into the bright field where everything was planted so carefully in orderly rows. That was hell, she knew hell when she saw it. For sixty years she had prayed against remembering him and against losing her soul in the deep pit of hell, and now the two things were mingled in one and the thought of him was a smoky cloud from hell that moved and crept in her head when she had just got rid of Doctor

Harry and was trying to rest a minute. Wounded vanity, Ellen, said a sharp voice in the top of her mind. Don't let your wounded vanity get the upper hand of you. Plenty of girls get jilted. You were jilted, weren't you? Then stand up to it. Her eyelids wavered and let in streamers of blue-gray light like tissue paper over her eyes. She must get up and pull the shades down or she'd never sleep. She was in bed again and the shades were not down. How could that happen? Better turn over, hide from the light, sleeping in the light gave you nightmares. "Mother, how do you feel now?" and a stinging wetness on her forehead. But I don't like having my face washed in cold water!

Hapsy? George? Lydia? Jimmy? No, Cornelia, and her features were swollen and   30
full of little puddles. "They're coming, darling, they'll all be here soon." Go wash your face, child, you look funny.

Instead of obeying, Cornelia knelt down and put her head on the pillow. She seemed to be talking but there was no sound. "Well, are you tongue-tied? Whose birthday is it? Are you going to give a party?"

Cornelia's mouth moved urgently in strange shapes. "Don't do that, you bother me, daughter."

"Oh, no, Mother. Oh, no. . . ."

Nonsense. It was strange about children. They disputed your every word. "No what, Cornelia?"

"Here's Doctor Harry."   35

"I won't see that boy again. He just left five minutes ago."

"That was this morning, Mother. It's night now. Here's the nurse."

"This is Doctor Harry, Mrs. Weatherall. I never saw you look so young and happy!"

"Ah, I'll never be young again—but I'd be happy if they'd let me lie in peace and get rested."

She thought she spoke up loudly, but no one answered. A warm weight on her fore-   40
head, a warm bracelet on her wrist, and a breeze went on whispering, trying to tell her something. A shuffle of leaves in the everlasting hand of God. He blew on them and they danced and rattled. "Mother, don't mind, we're going to give you a little hypodermic." "Look here, daughter, how do ants get in this bed? I saw sugar ants yesterday." Did you send for Hapsy too?

It was Hapsy she really wanted. She had to go a long way back through a great many rooms to find Hapsy standing with a baby on her arm. She seemed to herself to be Hapsy also, and the baby on Hapsy's arm was Hapsy and himself and herself, all at once, and there was no surprise in the meeting. Then Hapsy melted from within and turned flimsy as gray gauze and the baby was a gauzy shadow, and Hapsy came up close and said, "I thought you'd never come," and looked at her very searchingly and said, "You haven't changed a bit!" They leaned forward to kiss, when Cornelia began whispering from a long way off, "Oh, is there anything you want to tell me? Is there anything I can do for you?"

Yes, she had changed her mind after sixty years and she would like to see George. I want you to find George. Find him and be sure to tell him I forgot him. I want him to know I had my husband just the same and my children and my house like any other woman. A good house too and a good husband that I loved and fine children out of him. Better than I hoped for even. Tell him I was given back everything he took away and more. Oh, no, oh, God, no, there was something else besides the house and the man and the children. Oh, surely they were not all? What was it? Something not given back. . . . Her breath crowded down under her ribs and grew into a monstrous frightening shape with cutting edges; it bored up into her head, and the agony was unbelievable: Yes, John, get the doctor now, no more talk, my time has come.

When this one was born it should be the last. The last. It should have been born first, for it was the one she had truly wanted. Everything came in good time. Nothing left out, left over. She was strong, in three days she would be as well as ever. Better. A woman needed milk in her to have her full health.

"Mother, do you hear me?"

"I've been telling you—"   45

"Mother, Father Connolly's here."

"I went to Holy Communion only last week. Tell him I'm not so sinful as all that."

"Father just wants to speak to you."

He could speak as much as he pleased. It was like him to drop in and inquire about her soul as if it were a teething baby, and then stay on for a cup of tea and a round of cards and gossip. He always had a funny story of some sort, usually about an Irishman who made his little mistakes and confessed them, and the point lay in some absurd thing he would blurt out in the confessional showing his struggles between native piety and original sin. Granny felt easy about her soul. Cornelia, where are your manners? Give Father Connolly a chair. She had her secret comfortable understanding with a few favorite saints who cleared a straight road to God for her. All as surely signed and sealed as the papers for the new Forty Acres. Forever . . . heirs and assigns forever. Since the day the wedding cake was not cut, but thrown out and wasted. The whole bottom dropped out of the world, and there she was blind and sweating with nothing under her feet and the walls falling away.

His hand had caught her under the breast, she had not fallen, there was the freshly   50
polished floor with the green rug on it, just as before. He had cursed like a sailor's parrot and said, "I'll kill him for you." Don't lay a hand on him, for my sake leave something to God. "Now, Ellen, you must believe what I tell you. . . ."

So there was nothing, nothing to worry about any more, except sometimes in the night one of the children screamed in a nightmare, and they both hustled out shaking and hunting for the matches and calling, "There, wait a minute, here we are!" John, get the doctor now, Hapsy's time has come. But there was Hapsy standing by the bed in a white cap. "Cornelia, tell Hapsy to take off her cap. I can't see her plain."

Her eyes opened very wide and the room stood out like a picture she had seen somewhere. Dark colors with the shadows rising towards the ceiling in long angles. The tall black dresser gleamed with nothing on it but John's picture, enlarged from a little one, with John's eyes very black when they should have been blue. You never saw him, so how do you know how he looked? But the man insisted the copy was perfect, it was very rich and handsome. For a picture, yes, but it's not my husband. The table by the bed had a linen cover and a candle and a crucifix. The light was blue from Cornelia's silk lampshades. No sort of light at all, just frippery. You had to live forty years with kerosene lamps to appreciate honest electricity. She felt very strong and she saw Doctor Harry with a rosy nimbus around him.

"You look like a saint, Doctor Harry, and I vow that's as near as you'll ever come to it."

"She's saying something."

"I heard you, Cornelia. What's all this carrying on?"   55

"Father Connolly's saying—"

Cornelia's voice staggered and bumped like a cart in a bad road. It rounded corners and turned back again and arrived nowhere. Granny stepped up in the cart very lightly and reached for the reins, but a man sat beside her and she knew him by his hands, driving the cart. She did not look in his face, for she knew without seeing, but looked instead down the road where the trees leaned over and bowed to each other and a thousand birds were singing a Mass. She felt like singing too, but she put her hand in the bosom of her dress and pulled out a rosary, and Father Connolly murmured Latin in a very solemn voice and tickled her feet. My God, will you stop that nonsense? I'm a married woman. What if he did run away and leave me to face the priest by myself? I found another a whole world better. I wouldn't have exchanged my husband for anybody except St. Michael himself, and you may tell him that for me with a thank you in the bargain.

Light flashed on her closed eyelids, and a deep roaring shook her. Cornelia, is that lightning? I hear thunder. There's going to be a storm. Close all the windows. Call the children in. . . . "Mother, here we are, all of us." "Is that you, Hapsy?" "Oh, no, I'm Lydia. We drove as fast as we could." Their faces drifted above her, drifted away. The rosary fell out of her hands and Lydia put it back. Jimmy tried to help, their hands fumbled together, and Granny closed two fingers around Jimmy's thumb. Beads wouldn't do, it must be something alive. She was so amazed her thoughts ran round and round. So, my dear Lord, this is my death and I wasn't even thinking about it. My children have come to see me die. But I can't, it's not time. Oh, I always hated surprises. I wanted to give Cornelia the amethyst set—Cornelia, you're to have the amethyst set, but Hapsy's to wear it when she wants, and, Doctor Harry, do shut up. Nobody sent for you. Oh, my dear Lord, do wait a minute. I meant to do something about the Forty Acres, Jimmy doesn't need it and Lydia will later on, with that worthless husband of hers. I meant to finish the altar cloth and send six bottles of wine to Sister Borgia for her dyspepsia. I want to send six bottles of wine to Sister Borgia, Father Connolly, now don't let me forget.

Cornelia's voice made short turns and tilted over and crashed. "Oh, Mother, oh, Mother, oh, Mother. . . ."

"I'm not going, Cornelia. I'm taken by surprise. I can't go."

60

You'll see Hapsy again. What about her? "I thought you'd never come." Granny made a long journey outward, looking for Hapsy. What if I don't find her? What then? Her heart sank down and down, there was no bottom to death, she couldn't come to the end of it. The blue light from Cornelia's lampshade drew into a tiny point in the center of her brain, it flickered and winked like an eye, quietly it fluttered and dwindled. Granny lay curled down within herself, amazed and watchful, staring at the point of light that was herself, her body was now only a deeper mass of shadow in an endless darkness and this darkness would curl around the light and swallow it up. God, give a sign!

For the second time there was no sign. Again no bridegroom and the priest in the house. She could not remember any other sorrow because this grief wiped them all away. Oh, no, there's nothing more cruel than this—I'll never forgive it. She stretched herself with a deep breath and blew out the light.

QUESTIONS FOR CLOSE READING OF PLOT AND NARRATIVE STRUCTURE

1. When do you first realize that the narrative is of Granny Weatherall dying? What information about her has been imparted by the exposition up to that point?

2. What kind of person was Granny Weatherall when she was young? What does she reveal about herself in her ruminations?

3. Religion takes an important role in the story: "Without Thee, my God, I could never have done it. Hail, Mary, full of grace." During the rising action, what do you learn about Granny's sense of religion?

4. Granny's sense of time is not accurate. What does Porter do to help us see how distorted time has become for her? Why does it matter that time is not clear and distinct to her? How does her sense of time affect the pacing of the plot?

5. Do you think Hapsy is among the children at the bedside, or is she dead? In one paragraph near the end of the story, Granny thinks, "Hapsy's time has come." Did she die?

6. Does the story have a climax? Does it have a denouement?

7. Is Granny Weatherall's name symbolic?

QUESTIONS FOR INTERPRETATION OF PLOT AND NARRATIVE STRUCTURE

1. The last paragraphs of the story seem to narrate Granny's death journey. She is looking for Hapsy but does not find her. At the end of the next-to-last paragraph she seems panicky and says, "God, give a sign!" What does Porter imply when she says, "For the second time there was no sign. Again no bridegroom and the priest in the house"? What would the second jilting of Granny Weatherall amount to? How does the plot reveal the possibility of a second jilting of Granny Weatherall?

2. Granny Weatherall lost her first love at the altar and seems never to have been able to cope with the loss. Is there evidence, either in the structure of the narrative or in the imagery of the story, to suggest that she suffers from an emotional trauma or shock caused by not having been able to deal with her feelings? Why would an incident sixty years earlier not have been resolved? How might that lack of resolution have affected her? Does the plot of this story imply a final and happy resolution of the incident those many years ago?

3. Does the flashback technique of narration intensify this story, or do you feel it is a distraction? Is it used in a way that evokes a clear range of responses from you? Do you find yourself positively impressed by Granny Weatherall? What are her positive and her negative qualities?

4. How would a feminist critic approach this story? Granny Weatherall was left embarrassed at the altar by George. As she speaks she reveals that her fulfillment as a woman came from being a wife and mother. Does the resolution of this story contradict or support feminist desires for independence? Does the structure of the narrative imply a feminine way of telling a story?

5. Examine the story for its religious images. Do they produce suspense? What senses do they appeal to, and in what way are they religious? Are the images a form of foreshadowing? Granny Weatherall thinks about religion much of the time. Do you see her as truly and deeply religious? Does the narrative itself suggest a religious progress of any kind? Could the story be said to be religious?

NATHANIEL HAWTHORNE   (1804–1864)

Nathaniel Hawthorne was among the greatest nineteenth-century American writers, dominating in both short fiction and the novel. His stories in Twice-Told Tales *(1837) and* Mosses on an Old Manse *(1846) helped establish the independence of the American short story. They are dense, filled with atmosphere, and in many ways mysterious. Hawthorne was himself haunted by associations with his place of birth, Salem, Massachusetts, where his relatives presided at the trials of witches who were found guilty and hanged. His novel* The Scarlet Letter *(1850) explores the behavior of the Puritan community that Salem had once been, and* The House of Seven Gables *(1851) examines the moral circumstances of the age succeeding the one that hunted witches. His work is subtle and profound, and his achievement established a tone of high seriousness for short fiction in America.*

Rappaccini's Daughter ——————————————————— *1844*

[*From the Writings of Aubépine.*]°

We do not remember to have seen any translated specimens of the productions of M. de l'Aubépine—a fact the less to be wondered at, as his very name is unknown to many of his own countrymen as well as to the student of foreign literature. As a writer, he seems to occupy an unfortunate position between the Transcendentalists (who, under one name or another, have their share in all the current literature of the world) and the great body of pen-and-ink men who address the intellect and sympathies of the multitude. If not too refined, at all events too remote, too shadowy, and unsubstantial in his modes of development to suit the taste of the latter class, and yet too popular to satisfy the spiritual or metaphysical requisitions of the former, he must necessarily find himself without an audience, except here and there an individual or possibly an isolated clique. His writings, to do them justice, are not altogether destitute of fancy and originality; they might have won him greater reputation but for an inveterate love of allegory, which is apt to invest his plots and characters with the aspect of scenery and people in the clouds, and to steal away the human warmth out of his conceptions. His fictions are sometimes historical, sometimes of the present day, and sometimes, so far as can be discovered, have little or no reference either to time or space. In any case, he generally contents himself with a very slight embroidery of outward manners,—the faintest possible counterfeit of real life,—and endeavors to create an interest by some less obvious peculiarity of the subject. Occasionally a breath of Nature, a raindrop of pathos and tenderness, or a gleam of humor, will find its way into the midst of his fantastic imagery, and make us feel as if, after all, we were yet within the limits of our native earth. We will only add to this very cursory notice that M. de l'Aubépine's productions, if the reader chance to take them in precisely the proper point of view, may amuse a leisure hour as well as those of a brighter man; if otherwise, they can hardly fail to look excessively like nonsense.

Our author is voluminous; he continues to write and publish with as much praiseworthy and indefatigable prolixity as if his efforts were crowned with the brilliant success that so justly attends those of Eugene Sue. His first appearance was by a collection of stories in a long series of volumes entitled "Contes deux fois racontées." The titles of some of his more recent works (we quote from memory) are as follows: "Le Voyage Céleste à Chemin de Fer," 3 tom., 1838; "Le nouveau Père Adam et la nouvelle Mère Eve," 2 tom., 1839; "Roderic; ou le Serpent à l'estomac," 2 tom., 1840; "Le Culte du Feu,"

This introduction is Hawthorne writing about himself in a half-serious, half-playful manner. He pretends he is a European, not American, writer (Aubépine means "hawthorne"), and proceeds to mock himself and his writings, all the time, in subtle ways, making serious statements about his work. Most of the titles refer to his works, such as *Twice-Told Tales*, "The Celestial Railroad," "The New Adam and Eve," "Egotism; or, The Bosom Serpent," "Fire Worship," "Evenings in a Garden of Spain," and "The Artist of the Beautiful," all short stories in the collection with "Rappaccini's Daughter."

a folio volume of ponderous research into the religion and ritual of the old Persian Ghebers, published in 1841; "La Soirée du Chateau en Espagne," 1 tom., 8vo, 1842; and "L'Artiste du Beau; ou le Papillon Mécanique," 5 tom., 4to, 1843. Our somewhat wearisome perusal of this startling catalogue of volumes has left behind it a certain personal affection and sympathy, though by no means admiration, for M. de l'Aubépine; and we would fain do the little in our power towards introducing him favorably to the American public. The ensuing tale is a translation of his "Beatrice; ou la Belle Empoisonneuse," recently published in "La Revue Anti-Aristocratique." This journal, edited by the Comte de Bearhaven, has for some years past led the defense of liberal principles and popular rights with a faithfulness and ability worthy of all praise.

A young man, named Giovanni Guasconti, came, very long ago, from the more southern region of Italy, to pursue his studies at the University of Padua. Giovanni, who had but a scanty supply of gold ducats in his pocket, took lodgings in a high and gloomy chamber of an old edifice which looked not unworthy to have been the palace of a Paduan noble, and which, in fact, exhibited over its entrance the armorial bearings of a family long since extinct. The young stranger, who was not unstudied in the great poem° of his country, recollected that one of the ancestors of this family, and perhaps an occupant of this very mansion, had been pictured by Dante as a partaker of the immortal agonies of his Inferno. These reminiscences and associations, together with the tendency to heartbreak natural to a young man for the first time out of his native sphere, caused Giovanni to sigh heavily as he looked around the desolate and ill-furnished apartment.

"Holy Virgin, signor!" cried old Dame Lisabetta, who, won by the youth's remarkable beauty of person, was kindly endeavoring to give the chamber a habitable air, "what a sigh was that to come out of a young man's heart! Do you find this old mansion gloomy? For the love of Heaven, then, put your head out of the window, and you will see as bright sunshine as you have left in Naples."

Guasconti mechanically did as the old woman advised, but could not quite agree   5 with her that the Paduan sunshine was as cheerful as that of southern Italy. Such as it was, however, it fell upon a garden beneath the window and expended its fostering influences on a variety of plants, which seemed to have been cultivated with exceeding care.

"Does this garden belong to the house?" asked Giovanni.

"Heaven forbid, signor, unless it were fruitful of better pot herbs than any that grow there now," answered old Lisabetta. "No; that garden is cultivated by the own hands of Signor Giacomo Rappaccini, the famous doctor, who, I warrant him, has been heard of as far as Naples. It is said that he distils these plants into medicines that are as potent as a charm. Oftentimes you may see the signor doctor at work, and perchance the signora, his daughter, too, gathering the strange flowers that grow in the garden."

The old woman had now done what she could for the aspect of the chamber; and, commending the young man to the protection of the saints, took her departure.

Giovanni still found no better occupation than to look down into the garden beneath his window. From its appearance, he judged it to be one of those botanic gardens which were of earlier date in Padua than elsewhere in Italy or in the world. Or, not improbably, it might once have been the pleasure-place of an opulent family; for there was the ruin of a marble fountain in the center, sculptured with rare art, but so woefully shattered that it was impossible to trace the original design from the chaos of remaining

---

great poem: Dante's *Inferno,* a poem about a journey through Hell

fragments. The water, however, continued to gush and sparkle into the sunbeams as cheerfully as ever. A little gurgling sound ascended to the young man's window, and made him feel as if the fountain were an immortal spirit that sung its song unceasingly and without heeding the vicissitudes around it, while one century imbodied it in marble and another scattered the perishable garniture on the soil. All about the pool into which the water subsided grew various plants, that seemed to require a plentiful supply of moisture for the nourishment of gigantic leaves, and in some instances, flowers gorgeously magnificent. There was one shrub in particular, set in a marble vase in the midst of the pool, that bore a profusion of purple blossoms, each of which had the lustre and richness of a gem; and the whole together made a show so resplendent that it seemed enough to illuminate the garden, even had there been no sunshine. Every portion of the soil was peopled with plants and herbs, which, if less beautiful, still bore tokens of assiduous care, as if all had their individual virtues, known to the scientific mind that fostered them. Some were placed in urns, rich with old carving, and others in common garden pots; some crept serpent-like along the ground or climbed on high, using whatever means of ascent was offered them. One plant had wreathed itself round a statue of Vertumnus, which was thus quite veiled and shrouded in a drapery of hanging foliage, so happily arranged that it might have served a sculptor for a study.

While Giovanni stood at the window he heard a rustling behind a screen of leaves, and became aware that a person was at work in the garden. His figure soon emerged into view, and showed itself to be that of no common laborer, but a tall, emaciated, sallow, and sickly-looking man, dressed in a scholar's garb of black. He was beyond the middle term of life, with gray hair, a thin, gray beard, and a face singularly marked with intellect and cultivation, but which could never, even in his more youthful days, have expressed much warmth of heart.

Nothing could exceed the intentness with which this scientific gardener examined every shrub which grew in his path: it seemed as if he was looking into their inmost nature, making observations in regard to their creative essence, and discovering why one leaf grew in this shape and another in that, and wherefore such and such flowers differed among themselves in hue and perfume. Nevertheless, in spite of this deep intelligence on his part, there was no approach to intimacy between himself and these vegetable existences. On the contrary, he avoided their actual touch or the direct inhaling of their odors with a caution that impressed Giovanni most disagreeably; for the man's demeanor was that of one walking among malignant influences, such as savage beasts, or deadly snakes, or evil spirits, which, should he allow them one moment of license, would wreak upon him some terrible fatality. It was strangely frightful to the young man's imagination to see this air of insecurity in a person cultivating a garden, that most simple and innocent of human toils, and which had been alike the joy and labor of the unfallen parents of the race. Was this garden, then, the Eden of the present world? And this man, with such a perception of harm in what his own hands caused to grow,—was he the Adam?

The distrustful gardener, while plucking away the dead leaves or pruning the too luxuriant growth of the shrubs, defended his hands with a pair of thick gloves. Nor were these his only armor. When, in his walk through the garden, he came to the magnificent plant that hung its purple gems beside the marble fountain, he placed a kind of mask over his mouth and nostrils, as if all this beauty did but conceal a deadlier malice; but, finding his task still too dangerous, he drew back, removed the mask, and called loudly, but in the infirm voice of a person affected with inward disease,—

"Beatrice! Beatrice!"

"Here am I, my father. What would you?" cried a rich and youthful voice from the window of the opposite house—a voice as rich as a tropical sunset, and which made Giovanni, though he knew not why, think of deep hues of purple or crimson and of perfumes heavily delectable. "Are you in the garden?"

"Yes, Beatrice," answered the gardener, "and I need your help."   15

Soon there emerged from under a sculptured portal the figure of a young girl, arrayed with as much richness of taste as the most splendid of the flowers, beautiful as the day, and with a bloom so deep and vivid that one shade more would have been too much. She looked redundant with life, health, and energy; all of which attributes were bound down and compressed, as it were, and girdled tensely, in their luxuriance, by her virgin zone.° Yet Giovanni's fancy must have grown morbid while he looked down into the garden; for the impression which the fair stranger made upon him was as if here were another flower, the human sister of those vegetable ones, as beautiful as they, more beautiful than the richest of them, but still to be touched only with a glove, nor to be approached without a mask. As Beatrice came down the garden path, it was observable that she handled and inhaled the odor of several of the plants which her father had most sedulously avoided.

"Here, Beatrice," said the latter, "see how many needful offices require to be done to our chief treasure. Yet, shattered as I am, my life might pay the penalty of approaching it so closely as circumstances demand. Henceforth, I fear, this plant must be consigned to your sole charge."

"And gladly will I undertake it," cried again the rich tones of the young lady, as she bent towards the magnificent plant and opened her arms as if to embrace it. "Yes, my sister, my splendor, it shall be Beatrice's task to nurse and serve thee; and thou shalt reward her with thy kisses and perfumed breath, which to her is as the breath of life."

Then, with all the tenderness in her manner that was so strikingly expressed in her words, she busied herself with such attentions as the plant seemed to require; and Giovanni, at his lofty window, rubbed his eyes and almost doubted whether it were a girl tending her favorite flower, or one sister performing the duties of affection to another. The scene soon terminated. Whether Dr. Rappaccini had finished his labors in the garden, or that his watchful eye had caught the stranger's face, he now took his daughter's arm and retired. Night was already closing in; oppressive exhalations seemed to proceed from the plants and steal upward past the open window; and Giovanni, closing the lattice, went to his couch and dreamed of a rich flower and beautiful girl. Flower and maiden were different, and yet the same, and fraught with some strange peril in either shape.

But there is an influence in the light of morning that tends to rectify whatever errors of fancy, or even of judgment, we may have incurred during the sun's decline, or among the shadows of the night, or in the less wholesome glow of moonshine. Giovanni's first movement, on starting from sleep, was to throw open the window and gaze down into the garden which his dreams had made so fertile of mysteries. He was surprised and a little ashamed to find how real and matter-of-fact an affair it proved to be, in the first rays of the sun which gilded the dew-drops that hung upon leaf and blossom, and, while giving a brighter beauty to each rare flower, brought everything within the limits of ordinary experience. The young man rejoiced that, in the heart of the barren city, he had the privilege of overlooking this spot of lovely and luxuriant vegetation. It would serve, he said to himself, as a symbolic language to keep him in communion with   20

virgin zone: a belt worn by unmarried women

Nature. Neither the sickly and thoughtworn Dr. Giacomo Rappaccini, it is true, nor his brilliant daughter, were now visible; so that Giovanni could not determine how much of the singularity which he attributed to both was due to their own qualities and how much to his wonder-working fancy; but he was inclined to take a most rational view of the whole matter.

In the course of the day he paid his respects to Signor Pietro Baglioni, professor of medicine in the university, a physician of eminent repute to whom Giovanni had brought a letter of introduction. The professor was an elderly personage, apparently of genial nature, and habits that might almost be called jovial. He kept the young man to dinner, and made himself very agreeable by the freedom and liveliness of his conversation, especially when warmed by a flask or two of Tuscan wine. Giovanni, conceiving that men of science, inhabitants of the same city, must needs be on familiar terms with one another, took an opportunity to mention the name of Dr. Rappaccini. But the professor did not respond with so much cordiality as he had anticipated.

"Ill would it become a teacher of the divine art of medicine," said Professor Pietro Baglioni, in answer to a question of Giovanni, "to withhold due and well-considered praise of a physician so eminently skilled as Rappaccini; but, on the other hand, I should answer it but scantily to my conscience were I to permit a worthy youth like yourself, Signor Giovanni, the son of an ancient friend, to imbibe erroneous ideas respecting a man who might hereafter chance to hold your life and death in his hands. The truth is, our worshipful Dr. Rappaccini has as much science as any member of the faculty—with perhaps one single exception—in Padua, or all Italy; but there are certain grave objections to his professional character."

"And what are they?" asked the young man.

"Has my friend Giovanni any disease of body or heart, that he is so inquisitive about physicians?" said the professor, with a smile. "But as for Rappaccini, it is said of him—and I, who know the man well, can answer for its truth—that he cares infinitely more for science than for mankind. His patients are interesting to him only as subjects for some new experiment. He would sacrifice human life, his own among the rest, or whatever else was dearest to him, for the sake of adding so much as a grain of mustard seed to the great heap of his accumulated knowledge."

"Methinks he is an awful man indeed," remarked Guasconti, mentally recalling the   25
cold and purely intellectual aspect of Rappaccini. "And yet, worshipful professor, is it not a noble spirit? Are there many men capable of so spiritual a love of science?"

"God forbid," answered the professor, somewhat testily; "at least, unless they take sounder views of the healing art than those adopted by Rappaccini. It is his theory that all medicinal virtues are comprised within those substances which we term vegetable poisons. These he cultivates with his own hands, and is said even to have produced new varieties of poison, more horribly deleterious than Nature, without the assistance of this learned person, would ever have plagued the world withal. That the signor doctor does less mischief than might be expected with such dangerous substances is undeniable. Now and then, it must be owned, he has effected, or seemed to effect, a marvellous cure; but, to tell you my private mind, Signor Giovanni, he should receive little credit for such instances of success,—they being probably the work of chance,—but should be held strictly accountable for his failures, which may justly be considered his own work."

The youth might have taken Baglioni's opinions with many grains of allowance had he known that there was a professional warfare of long continuance between him and Dr. Rappaccini, in which the latter was generally thought to have gained the advantage.

If the reader be inclined to judge for himself, we refer him to certain black-letter tracts on both sides, preserved in the medical department of the University of Padua.

"I know not, most learned professor," returned Giovanni, after musing on what had been said of Rappaccini's exclusive zeal for science,—"I know not how dearly this physician may love his art; but surely there is one object more dear to him. He has a daughter."

"Aha!" cried the professor, with a laugh. "So now our friend Giovanni's secret is out. You have heard of this daughter, whom all the young men in Padua are wild about, though not half a dozen have ever had the good hap to see her face. I know little of the Signora Beatrice save that Rappaccini is said to have instructed her deeply in his science, and that, young and beautiful as fame reports her, she is already qualified to fill a professor's chair. Perchance her father destines her for mine! Other absurd rumors there be, not worth talking about or listening to. So now, Signor Giovanni, drink off your glass of lachryma."

Guasconti returned to his lodgings somewhat heated with the wine he had quaffed, and which caused his brain to swim with strange fantasies in reference to Dr. Rappaccini and the beautiful Beatrice. On his way, happening to pass by a florist's, he bought a fresh bouquet of flowers.   30

Ascending to his chamber, he seated himself near the window, but within the shadow thrown by the depth of the wall, so that he could look down into the garden with little risk of being discovered. All beneath his eye was a solitude. The strange plants were basking in the sunshine, and now and then nodding gently to one another, as if in acknowledgment of sympathy and kindred. In the midst, by the shattered fountain, grew the magnificent shrub, with its purple gems clustering all over it; they glowed in the air, and gleamed back again out of the depths of the pool, which thus seemed to overflow with colored radiance from the rich reflection that was steeped in it. At first, as we have said, the garden was a solitude. Soon, however,—as Giovanni had half hoped, half feared, would be the case,—a figure appeared beneath the antique sculptured portal, and came down between the rows of plants, inhaling their various perfumes as if she were one of those beings of old classic fable that lived upon sweet odors. On again beholding Beatrice, the young man was even startled to perceive how much her beauty exceeded his recollection of it; so brilliant, so vivid, was its character, that she glowed amid the sunlight, and, as Giovanni whispered to himself, positively illuminated the more shadowy intervals of the garden path. Her face being now more revealed than on the former occasion, he was struck by its expression of simplicity and sweetness,—qualities that had not entered into his idea of her character, and which made him ask anew what manner of mortal she might be. Nor did he fail again to observe, or imagine, an analogy between the beautiful girl and the gorgeous shrub that hung its gemlike flowers over the fountain,—a resemblance which Beatrice seemed to have indulged a fantastic humor in heightening, both by the arrangement of her dress and the selection of its hues.

Approaching the shrub, she threw open her arms, as with a passionate ardor, and drew its branches into an intimate embrace—so intimate that her features were hidden in its leafy bosom and her glistening ringlets all intermingled with the flowers.

"Give me thy breath, my sister," exclaimed Beatrice; "for I am faint with common air. And give me this flower of thine, which I separate with gentlest fingers from the stem and place it close beside my heart."

With these words the beautiful daughter of Rappaccini plucked one of the richest blossoms of the shrub, and was about to fasten it in her bosom. But now, unless Giovanni's draughts of wine had bewildered his senses, a singular incident occurred. A small orange-colored reptile, of the lizard or chameleon species, chanced to be creeping along the path, just at the feet of Beatrice. It appeared to Giovanni,—but, at the distance from which he gazed, he could scarcely have seen anything so minute,—it appeared to him, however, that a drop or two of moisture from the broken stem of the flower descended upon the lizard's head. For an instant the reptile contorted itself violently, and then lay motionless in the sunshine. Beatrice observed this remarkable phenomenon, and crossed herself, sadly, but without surprise; nor did she therefore hesitate to arrange the fatal flower in her bosom. There it blushed, and almost glimmered with the dazzling effect of a precious stone, adding to her dress and aspect the one appropriate charm which nothing else in the world could have supplied. But Giovanni, out of the shadow of his window, bent forward and shrank back, and murmured and trembled.

"Am I awake? Have I my senses?" said he to himself. "What is this being? Beautiful shall I call her, or inexpressibly terrible?"

Beatrice now strayed carelessly through the garden, approaching closer beneath Giovanni's window, so that he was compelled to thrust his head quite out of its concealment in order to gratify the intense and painful curiosity which she excited. At this moment there came a beautiful insect over the garden wall; it had, perhaps, wandered through the city, and found no flowers or verdure among those antique haunts of men until the heavy perfumes of Dr. Rappaccini's shrubs had lured it from afar. Without alighting on the flowers, this winged brightness seemed to be attracted by Beatrice, and lingered in the air and fluttered about her head. Now, here it could not be but that Giovanni Guasconti's eyes deceived him. Be that as it might, he fancied that, while Beatrice was gazing at the insect with childish delight, it grew faint and fell at her feet; its bright wings shivered; it was dead—from no cause that he could discern, unless it were the atmosphere of her breath. Again Beatrice crossed herself and sighed heavily as she bent over the dead insect.

An impulsive movement of Giovanni drew her eyes to the window. There she beheld the beautiful head of the young man—rather a Grecian than an Italian head, with fair, regular features, and a glistening of gold among his ringlets—gazing down upon her like a being that hovered in mid air. Scarcely knowing what he did, Giovanni threw down the bouquet which he had hitherto held in his hand.

"Signora," said he, "there are pure and healthful flowers. Wear them for the sake of Giovanni Guasconti."

"Thanks, signor," replied Beatrice, with her rich voice, that came forth as it were like a gush of music, and with a mirthful expression half childish and half woman-like. "I accept your gift, and would fain recompense it with this precious purple flower; but if I toss it into the air it will not reach you. So Signor Guasconti must even content himself with my thanks."

She lifted the bouquet from the ground, and then, as if inwardly ashamed at having stepped aside from her maidenly reserve to respond to a stranger's greeting, passed swiftly homeward through the garden. But few as the moments were, it seemed to Giovanni, when she was on the point of vanishing beneath the sculptured portal, that his beautiful bouquet was already beginning to wither in her grasp. It was an idle thought; there could be no possibility of distinguishing a faded flower from a fresh one at so great a distance.

For many days after this incident the young man avoided the window that looked into Dr. Rappaccini's garden, as if something ugly and monstrous would have blasted his eyesight had he been betrayed into a glance. He felt conscious of having put himself, to a certain extent, within the influence of an unintelligible power by the communication which he had opened with Beatrice. The wisest course would have been, if his heart were in any real danger, to quit his lodgings and Padua itself at once; the next wiser, to have accustomed himself, as far as possible, to the familiar and daylight view of Beatrice—thus bringing her rigidly and systematically within the limits of ordinary experience. Least of all, while avoiding her sight, ought Giovanni to have remained so near this extraordinary being that the proximity and possibility even of intercourse should give a kind of substance and reality to the wild vagaries which his imagination ran riot continually in producing. Guasconti had not a deep heart—or, at all events, its depths were not sounded now; but he had a quick fancy, and an ardent southern temperament, which rose every instant to a higher fever pitch. Whether or no Beatrice possessed those terrible attributes, that fatal breath, the affinity with those so beautiful and deadly flowers which were indicated by what Giovanni had witnessed, she had at least instilled a fierce and subtle poison into his system. It was not love, although her rich beauty was a madness to him; nor horror, even while he fancied her spirit to be imbued with the same baneful essence that seemed to pervade her physical frame; but a wild offspring of both love and horror that had each parent in it, and burned like one and shivered like the other. Giovanni knew not what to dread; still less did he know what to hope; yet hope and dread kept a continual warfare in his breast, alternately vanquishing one another and starting up afresh to renew the contest. Blessed are all simple emotions, be they dark or bright! It is the lurid intermixture of the two that produces the illuminating blaze of the infernal regions.

Sometimes he endeavored to assuage the fever of his spirit by a rapid walk through the streets of Padua or beyond its gates: his footsteps kept time with the throbbings of his brain, so that the walk was apt to accelerate itself to a race. One day he found himself arrested; his arm was seized by a portly personage, who had turned back on recognizing the young man and expended much breath in overtaking him.

"Signor Giovanni! Stay, my young friend!" cried he. "Have you forgotten me? That might well be the case if I were as much altered as yourself."

It was Baglioni, whom Giovanni had avoided ever since their first meeting, from a doubt that the professor's sagacity would look too deeply into his secrets. Endeavoring to recover himself, he stared forth wildly from his inner world into the outer one and spoke like a man in a dream.

"Yes; I am Giovanni Guasconti. You are Professor Pietro Baglioni. Now let me pass!"   45

"Not yet, not yet, Signor Giovanni Guasconti," said the professor, smiling, but at the same time scrutinizing the youth with an earnest glance. "What! did I grow up side by side with your father? and shall his son pass me like a stranger in these old streets of Padua? Stand still, Signor Giovanni; for we must have a word or two before we part."

"Speedily, then, most worshipful professor, speedily," said Giovanni, with feverish impatience. "Does not your worship see that I am in haste?"

Now, while he was speaking there came a man in black along the street, stooping and moving feebly like a person in inferior health. His face was all overspread with a most sickly and sallow hue, but yet so pervaded with an expression of piercing and active intellect that an observer might easily have overlooked the merely physical attributes and have seen only this wonderful energy. As he passed, this person exchanged a cold and distant salutation with Baglioni, but fixed his eyes upon Giovanni with an intentness that seemed to bring out whatever was within him worthy of notice. Nevertheless, there was a peculiar quietness in the look, as if taking merely a speculative, not a human interest, in the young man.

"It is Dr. Rappaccini!" whispered the professor when the stranger had passed. "Has he ever seen your face before?"

"Not that I know," answered Giovanni, starting at the name.

50

"He *has* seen you! he must have seen you!" said Baglioni, hastily. "For some purpose or other, this man of science is making a study of you. I know that look of his! It is the same that coldly illuminates his face as he bends over a bird, a mouse, or a butterfly, which, in pursuance of some experiment, he has killed by the perfume of a flower; a look as deep as Nature itself, but without Nature's warmth of love. Signor Giovanni, I will stake my life upon it, you are the subject of one of Rappaccini's experiments!"

"Will you make a fool of me?" cried Giovanni, passionately. "*That,* signor professor, were an untoward experiment."

"Patience! patience!" replied the imperturbable professor. "I tell thee, my poor Giovanni, that Rappaccini has a scientific interest in thee. Thou hast fallen into fearful hands! And the Signora Beatrice,—what part does she act in this mystery?"

But Guasconti, finding Baglioni's pertinacity intolerable, here broke away, and was gone before the professor could again seize his arm. He looked after the young man intently and shook his head.

"This must not be," said Baglioni to himself. "The youth is the son of my old 55 friend, and shall not come to any harm from which the arcana of medical science can preserve him. Besides, it is too insufferable an impertinence in Rappaccini, thus to snatch the lad out of my own hands, as I may say, and make use of him for his infernal experiments. This daughter of his! It shall be looked to. Perchance, most learned Rappaccini, I may foil you where you little dream of it!"

Meanwhile Giovanni had pursued a circuitous route, and at length found himself at the door of his lodgings. As he crossed the threshold he was met by old Lisabetta, who smirked and smiled, and was evidently desirous to attract his attention; vainly, however, as the ebullition of his feelings had momentarily subsided into a cold and dull vacuity. He turned his eyes full upon the withered face that was puckering itself into a smile, but seemed to behold it not. The old dame, therefore, laid her grasp upon his cloak.

"Signor! signor!" whispered she, still with a smile over the whole breadth of her visage, so that it looked not unlike a grotesque carving in wood, darkened by centuries. "Listen, signor! There is a private entrance into the garden!"

"What do you say?" exclaimed Giovanni, turning quickly about, as if an inanimate thing should start into feverish life. "A private entrance into Dr. Rappaccini's garden?"

"Hush! hush! not so loud!" whispered Lisabetta, putting her hand over his mouth. "Yes; into the worshipful doctor's garden, where you may see all his fine shrubbery. Many a young man in Padua would give gold to be admitted among those flowers."

Giovanni put a piece of gold into her hand.

60

"Show me the way," said he.

A surmise, probably excited by his conversation with Baglioni, crossed his mind, that this interposition of old Lisabetta might perchance be connected with the intrigue, whatever were its nature, in which the professor seemed to suppose that Dr. Rappaccini was involving him. But such a suspicion, though it disturbed Giovanni, was inadequate to restrain him. The instant that he was aware of the possibility of approaching Beatrice, it seemed an absolute necessity of his existence to do so. It mattered not whether she were angel or demon; he was irrevocably within her sphere, and must obey the law that whirled him onward, in ever-lessening circles, towards a result which he did not attempt to foreshadow; and yet, strange to say, there came across him a sudden doubt whether this intense interest on his part were not delusory; whether it were really of so deep and positive a nature as to justify him in now thrusting himself into an incalculable position; whether it were not merely the fantasy of a young man's brain, only slightly or not at all connected with his heart.

He paused, hesitated, turned half about, but again went on. His withered guide led him along several obscure passages, and finally undid a door, through which, as it was opened, there came the sight and sound of rustling leaves, with the broken sunshine glimmering among them. Giovanni stepped forth, and, forcing himself through the entanglement of a shrub that wreathed its tendrils over the hidden entrance, stood beneath his own window in the open area of Dr. Rappaccini's garden.

How often is it the case that, when impossibilities have come to pass and dreams have condensed their misty substance into tangible realities, we find ourselves calm, and even coldly self-possessed, amid circumstances which it would have been a delirium of joy or agony to anticipate! Fate delights to thwart us thus. Passion will choose his own time to rush upon the scene, and lingers sluggishly behind when an appropriate adjustment of events would seem to summon his appearance. So was it now with Giovanni. Day after day his pulses had throbbed with feverish blood at the improbable idea of an interview with Beatrice, and of standing with her, face to face, in this very garden, basking in the Oriental sunshine of her beauty, and snatching from her full gaze the mystery which he deemed the riddle of his own existence. But now there was a singular and untimely equanimity within his breast. He threw a glance around the garden to discover if Beatrice or her father were present, and, perceiving that he was alone, began a critical observation of the plants.

The aspect of one and all of them dissatisfied him; their gorgeousness seemed   65
fierce, passionate, and even unnatural. There was hardly an individual shrub which a wanderer, straying by himself through a forest, would not have been startled to find growing wild, as if an unearthly face had glared at him out of the thicket. Several also would have shocked a delicate instinct by an appearance of artificialness indicating that there had been such commixture, and, as it were, adultery, of various vegetable species, that the production was no longer of God's making, but the monstrous offspring of man's depraved fancy, glowing with only an evil mockery of beauty. They were probably the result of experiment, which in one or two cases had succeeded in mingling plants individually lovely into a compound possessing the questionable and ominous character that distinguished the whole growth of the garden. In fine, Giovanni recognized but two or three plants in the collection, and those of a kind that he well knew to be poisonous. While busy with these contemplations he heard the rustling of a silken garment, and, turning, beheld Beatrice emerging from beneath the sculptured portal.

Giovanni had not considered with himself what should be his deportment; whether he should apologize for his intrusion into the garden, or assume that he was there with the privity at least, if not by the desire, of Dr. Rappaccini or his daughter; but Beatrice's manner placed him at his ease, though leaving him still in doubt by what agency he had gained admittance. She came lightly along the path and met him near the broken fountain. There was surprise in her face, but brightened by a simple and kind expression of pleasure.

"You are a connoisseur in flowers, signor," said Beatrice, with a smile, alluding to the bouquet which he had flung her from the window. "It is no marvel, therefore, if the sight of my father's rare collection has tempted you to take a nearer view. If he were here, he could tell you many strange and interesting facts as to the nature and habits of these shrubs; for he has spent a lifetime in such studies, and this garden is his world."

"And yourself, lady," observed Giovanni, "if fame says true,—you likewise are deeply skilled in the virtues indicated by these rich blossoms and these spicy perfumes. Would you deign to be my instructress, I should prove an apter scholar than if taught by Signor Rappaccini himself."

"Are there such idle rumors?" asked Beatrice, with the music of a pleasant laugh. "Do people say that I am skilled in my father's science of plants? What a jest is there! No; though I have grown up among these flowers, I know no more of them than their hues and perfume; and sometimes methinks I would fain rid myself of even that small knowledge. There are many flowers here, and those not the least brilliant, that shock and offend me when they meet my eye. But pray, signor, do not believe these stories about my science. Believe nothing of me save what you see with your own eyes."

"And must I believe all that I have seen with my own eyes?" asked Giovanni, pointedly, while the recollection of former scenes made him shrink. "No, signora; you demand too little of me. Bid me believe nothing save what comes from your own lips." 70

It would appear that Beatrice understood him. There came a deep flush to her cheek; but she looked full into Giovanni's eyes, and responded to his gaze of uneasy suspicion with a queenlike haughtiness.

"I do so bid you, signor," she replied. "Forget whatever you may have fancied in regard to me. If true to the outward senses, still it may be false in its essence; but the words of Beatrice Rappaccini's lips are true from the depths of the heart outward. Those you may believe."

A fervor glowed in her whole aspect and beamed upon Giovanni's consciousness like the light of truth itself; but while she spoke there was a fragrance in the atmosphere around her, rich and delightful, though evanescent, yet which the young man, from an indefinable reluctance, scarcely dared to draw into his lungs. It might be the odor of the flowers. Could it be Beatrice's breath which thus embalmed her words with a strange richness, as if by steeping them in her heart? A faintness passed like a shadow over Giovanni and flitted away; he seemed to gaze through the beautiful girl's eyes into her transparent soul, and felt no more doubt or fear.

The tinge of passion that had colored Beatrice's manner vanished; she became gay, and appeared to derive a pure delight from her communion with the youth not unlike what the maiden of a lonely island might have felt conversing with a voyager from the civilized world. Evidently her experience of life had been confined within the limits of that garden. She talked now about matters as simple as the daylight or summer clouds, and now asked questions in reference to the city, or Giovanni's distant home, his friends, his mother, and his sisters—questions indicating such seclusion, and such lack of familiarity with modes and forms, that Giovanni responded as if to an infant. Her spirit gushed out before him like a fresh rill that was just catching its first glimpse of the sunlight and wondering at the reflections of earth and sky which were flung into its bosom. There came thoughts, too, from a deep source, and fantasies of a gemlike brilliancy, as if diamonds and rubies sparkled upward among the bubbles of the fountain. Ever and anon there gleamed across the young man's mind a sense of wonder that he should be walking side by side with the being who had so wrought upon his imagination, whom he had idealized in such hues of terror, in whom he had positively witnessed such manifestations of dreadful attributes,—that he should be conversing with Beatrice like a brother, and should find her so human and so maidenlike. But such reflections were only momentary; the effect of her character was too real not to make itself familiar at once.

In this free intercourse they had strayed through the garden, and now, after many turns among its avenues, were come to the shattered fountain, beside which grew the 75 magnificent shrub, with its treasury of glowing blossoms. A fragrance was diffused from it which Giovanni recognized as identical with that which he had attributed to Beatrice's breath, but incomparably more powerful. As her eyes fell upon it, Giovanni beheld her press her hand to her bosom as if her heart were throbbing suddenly and painfully.

"For the first time in my life," murmured she, addressing the shrub, "I had forgotten thee."

"I remember, signora," said Giovanni, "that you once promised to reward me with one of these living gems for the bouquet which I had the happy boldness to fling to your feet. Permit me now to pluck it as a memorial of this interview."

He made a step towards the shrub with extended hand; but Beatrice darted forward, uttering a shriek that went through his heart like a dagger. She caught his hand and drew it back with the whole force of her slender figure. Giovanni felt her touch thrilling through his fibres.

"Touch it not!" exclaimed she, in a voice of agony. "Not for thy life! It is fatal!"

Then, hiding her face, she fled from him and vanished beneath the sculptured   80
portal. As Giovanni followed her with his eyes, he beheld the emaciated figure and pale intelligence of Dr. Rappaccini, who had been watching the scene, he knew not how long, within the shadow of the entrance.

No sooner was Guasconti alone in his chamber than the image of Beatrice came back to his passionate musings, invested with all the witchery that had been gathering around it ever since his first glimpse of her, and now likewise imbued with a tender warmth of girlish womanhood. She was human; her nature was endowed with all gentle and feminine qualities; she was worthiest to be worshipped; she was capable, surely, on her part, of the height and heroism of love. Those tokens which he had hitherto considered as proofs of a frightful peculiarity in her physical and moral system were now either forgotten, or, by the subtle sophistry of passion transmitted into a golden crown of enchantment, rendering Beatrice the more admirable by so much as she was the more unique. Whatever had looked ugly was now beautiful; or, if incapable of such a change, it stole away and hid itself among those shapeless half ideas which throng the dim region beyond the daylight of our perfect consciousness. Thus did he spend the night, nor fell asleep until the dawn had begun to awake the slumbering flowers in Dr. Rappaccini's garden, whither Giovanni's dreams doubtless led him. Up rose the sun in his due season, and, flinging his beams upon the young man's eyelids, awoke him to a sense of pain. When thoroughly aroused, he became sensible of a burning and tingling agony in his hand—in his right hand—the very hand which Beatrice had grasped in her own when he was on the point of plucking one of the gemlike flowers. On the back of that hand there was now a purple print like that of four small fingers, and the likeness of a slender thumb upon his wrist.

Oh, how stubbornly does love,—or even that cunning semblance of love which flourishes in the imagination, but strikes no depth of root into the heart,—how stubbornly does it hold its faith until the moment comes when it is doomed to vanish into thin mist! Giovanni wrapped a handkerchief about his hand and wondered what evil thing had stung him, and soon forgot his pain in a reverie of Beatrice.

After the first interview, a second was in the inevitable course of what we call fate. A third; a fourth; and a meeting with Beatrice in the garden was no longer an incident in Giovanni's daily life, but the whole space in which he might be said to live; for the anticipation and memory of that ecstatic hour made up the remainder. Nor was it otherwise with the daughter of Rappaccini. She watched for the youth's appearance, and flew to his side with confidence as unreserved as if they had been playmates from early infancy—as if they were such playmates still. If, by any unwonted chance, he failed to come at the appointed moment, she stood beneath the window and sent up the rich sweetness of her tones to float around him in his chamber and echo and reverberate throughout his heart: "Giovanni! Giovanni! Why tarriest thou? Come down!" And down he hastened into that Eden of poisonous flowers.

But, with all this intimate familiarity, there was still a reserve in Beatrice's demeanor, so rigidly and invariably sustained that the idea of infringing it scarcely occurred to his imagination. By all appreciable signs, they loved; they had looked love with eyes that conveyed the holy secret from the depths of one soul into the depths of the other, as if it were too sacred to be whispered by the way; they had even spoken love in those gushes of passion when their spirits darted forth in articulated breath like tongues of long-hidden flame; and yet there had been no seal of lips, no clasp of hands, nor any slightest caress such as love claims and hallows. He had never touched one of the gleaming ringlets of her hair; her garment—so marked was the physical barrier between them—had never been waved against him by a breeze. On the few occasions when Giovanni had seemed tempted to overstep the limit, Beatrice grew so sad, so stern, and withal wore such a look of desolate separation, shuddering at itself, that not a spoken word was requisite to repel him. At such times he was startled at the horrible suspicions that rose, monster-like, out of the caverns of his heart and stared him in the face; his love grew thin and faint as the morning mist, his doubts alone had substance. But, when Beatrice's face brightened again after the momentary shadow, she was transformed at once from the mysterious, questionable being whom he had watched with so much awe and horror; she was now the beautiful and unsophisticated girl whom he felt that his spirit knew with a certainty beyond all other knowledge.

A considerable time had now passed since Giovanni's last meeting with Baglioni. One morning, however, he was disagreeably surprised by a visit from the professor, whom he had scarcely thought of for whole weeks, and would willingly have forgotten still longer. Given up as he had long been to a pervading excitement, he could tolerate no companions except upon condition of their perfect sympathy with his present state of feeling. Such sympathy was not to be expected from Professor Baglioni.

The visitor chatted carelessly for a few moments about the gossip of the city and the university, and then took up another topic.

"I have been reading an old classic author lately," said he, "and met with a story that strangely interested me. Possibly you may remember it. It is of an Indian prince, who sent a beautiful woman as a present to Alexander the Great. She was as lovely as the dawn and gorgeous as the sunset; but what especially distinguished her was a certain rich perfume in her breath—richer than a garden of Persian roses. Alexander, as was natural to a youthful conqueror, fell in love at first sight with this magnificent stranger; but a certain sage physician, happening to be present, discovered a terrible secret in regard to her."

"And what was that?" asked Giovanni, turning his eyes downward to avoid those of the professor.

"That this lovely woman," continued Baglioni, with emphasis, "had been nourished with poisons from her birth upward, until her whole nature was so imbued with them that she herself had become the deadliest poison in existence. Poison was her element of life. With that rich perfume of her breath she blasted the very air. Her love would have been poison—her embrace death. Is not this a marvellous tale?"

"A childish fable," answered Giovanni, nervously starting from his chair. "I marvel how your worship finds time to read such nonsense among your graver studies."

85

90

"By the by," said the professor, looking uneasily about him, "what singular fragrance is this in your apartment? Is it the perfume of your gloves? It is faint, but delicious; and yet, after all, by no means agreeable. Were I to breathe it long, methinks it would make me ill. It is like the breath of a flower; but I see no flowers in the chamber."

"Nor are there any," replied Giovanni, who had turned pale as the professor spoke; "nor, I think, is there any fragrance except in your worship's imagination. Odors, being a sort of element combined of the sensual and the spiritual, are apt to deceive us in this manner. The recollection of a perfume, the bare idea of it, may easily be mistaken for a present reality."

"Ay; but my sober imagination does not often play such tricks," said Baglioni; "and, were I to fancy any kind of odor, it would be that of some vile apothecary drug, wherewith my fingers are likely enough to be imbued. Our worshipful friend Rappaccini, as I have heard, tinctures his medicaments with odors richer than those of Araby. Doubtless, likewise, the fair and learned Signora Beatrice would minister to her patients with draughts as sweet as a maiden's breath; but woe to him that sips them!"

Giovanni's face evinced many contending emotions. The tone in which the professor alluded to the pure and lovely daughter of Rappaccini was a torture to his soul; and yet the intimation of a view of her character, opposite to his own, gave instantaneous distinctness to a thousand dim suspicions, which now grinned at him like so many demons. But he strove hard to quell them and to respond to Baglioni with a true lover's perfect faith.

"Signor professor," said he, "you were my father's friend; perchance, too, it is your   95
purpose to act a friendly part towards his son. I would fain feel nothing towards you save respect and deference; but I pray you to observe, signor, that there is one subject on which we must not speak. You know not the Signora Beatrice. You cannot, therefore, estimate the wrong—the blasphemy, I may even say—that is offered to her character by a light or injurious word."

"Giovanni! my poor Giovanni!" answered the professor, with a calm expression of pity, "I know this wretched girl far better than yourself. You shall hear the truth in respect to the poisoner Rappaccini and his poisonous daughter; yes, poisonous as she is beautiful. Listen; for, even should you do violence to my gray hairs, it shall not silence me. That old fable of the Indian woman has become a truth by the deep and deadly science of Rappaccini and in the person of the lovely Beatrice."

Giovanni groaned and hid his face.

"Her father," continued Baglioni, "was not restrained by natural affection from offering up his child in this horrible manner as the victim of his insane zeal for science; for, let us do him justice, he is as true a man of science as ever distilled his own heart in an alembic. What, then, will be your fate? Beyond a doubt you are selected as the material of some new experiment. Perhaps the result is to be death; perhaps a fate more awful still. Rappaccini, with what he calls the interest of science before his eyes, will hesitate at nothing."

"It is a dream," muttered Giovanni to himself; "surely it is a dream."

"But," resumed the professor, "be of good cheer, son of my friend. It is not yet too   100
late for the rescue. Possibly we may even succeed in bringing back this miserable child within the limits of ordinary nature, from which her father's madness has estranged her. Behold this little silver vase! It was wrought by the hands of the renowned Benvenuto Cellini,° and is well worthy to be a love gift to the fairest dame in Italy. But its

Cellini: a famous goldsmith

contents are invaluable. One little sip of this antidote would have rendered the most virulent poisons of the Borgias° innocuous. Doubt not that it will be as efficacious against those of Rappaccini. Bestow the vase, and the precious liquid within it, on your Beatrice, and hopefully await the result."

Baglioni laid a small, exquisitely wrought silver vial on the table and withdrew, leaving what he had said to produce its effect upon the young man's mind.

"We will thwart Rappaccini yet," thought he, chuckling to himself, as he descended the stairs; "but, let us confess the truth of him, he is a wonderful man—a wonderful man indeed; a vile empiric, however, in his practice, and therefore not to be tolerated by those who respect the good old rules of the medical profession."

Throughout Giovanni's whole acquaintance with Beatrice, he had occasionally, as we have said, been haunted by dark surmises as to her character; yet so thoroughly had she made herself felt by him as a simple, natural, most affectionate, and guileless creature, that the image now held up by Professor Baglioni looked as strange and incredible as if it were not in accordance with his own original conception. True, there were ugly recollections connected with his first glimpses of the beautiful girl; he could not quite forget the bouquet that withered in her grasp, and the insect that perished amid the sunny air, by no ostensible agency save the fragrance of her breath. These incidents, however, dissolving in the pure light of her character, had no longer the efficacy of facts, but were acknowledged as mistaken fantasies, by whatever testimony of the senses they might appear to be substantiated. There is something truer and more real than what we can see with the eyes and touch with the finger. On such better evidence had Giovanni founded his confidence in Beatrice, though rather by the necessary force of her high attributes than by any deep and generous faith on his part. But now his spirit was incapable of sustaining itself at the height to which the early enthusiasm of passion had exalted it; he fell down, grovelling among earthly doubts, and defiled therewith the pure whiteness of Beatrice's image. Not that he gave her up; he did but distrust. He resolved to institute some decisive test that should satisfy him, once for all, whether there were those dreadful peculiarities in her physical nature which could not be supposed to exist without some corresponding monstrosity of soul. His eyes, gazing down afar, might have deceived him as to the lizard, the insect, and the flowers; but if he could witness, at the distance of a few paces, the sudden blight of one fresh and healthful flower in Beatrice's hand, there would be room for no further question. With this idea he hastened to the florist's and purchased a bouquet that was still gemmed with the morning dew-drops.

It was now the customary hour of his daily interview with Beatrice. Before descending into the garden, Giovanni failed not to look at his figure in the mirror—a vanity to be expected in a beautiful young man, yet, as displaying itself at that troubled and feverish moment, the token of a certain shallowness of feeling and insincerity of character. He did gaze, however, and said to himself that his features had never before possessed so rich a grace, nor his eyes such vivacity, nor his cheeks so warm a hue of superabundant life.

"At least," thought he, "her poison has not yet insinuated itself into my system. I am no flower to perish in her grasp."

With that thought he turned his eyes on the bouquet, which he had never once laid aside from his hand. A thrill of indefinable horror shot through his frame on

Borgias: an Italian family noted for its cruelty

perceiving that those dewy flowers were already beginning to droop; they wore the aspect of things that had been fresh and lovely yesterday. Giovanni grew white as marble, and stood motionless before the mirror, staring at his own reflection there as at the likeness of something frightful. He remembered Baglioni's remark about the fragrance that seemed to pervade the chamber. It must have been the poison in his breath! Then he shuddered—shuddered at himself. Recovering from his stupor, he began to watch with curious eye a spider that was busily at work hanging its web from the antique cornice of the apartment, crossing and recrossing the artful system of interwoven lines—as vigorous and active a spider as ever dangled from an old ceiling. Giovanni bent towards the insect, and emitted a deep, long breath. The spider suddenly ceased its toil; the web vibrated with a tremor originating in the body of the small artisan. Again Giovanni sent forth a breath, deeper, longer, and imbued with a venomous feeling out of his heart: he knew not whether he were wicked, or only desperate. The spider made a convulsive gripe with his limbs and hung dead across the window.

"Accursed! accursed!" muttered Giovanni, addressing himself. "Hast thou grown so poisonous that this deadly insect perishes by thy breath?"

At that moment a rich, sweet voice came floating up from the garden.

"Giovanni! Giovanni! It is past the hour! Why tarriest thou? Come down!"

"Yes," muttered Giovanni again. "She is the only being whom my breath may not   110 slay! Would that it might!"

He rushed down, and in an instant was standing before the bright and loving eyes of Beatrice. A moment ago his wrath and despair had been so fierce that he could have desired nothing so much as to wither her by a glance; but with her actual presence there came influences which had too real an existence to be at once shaken off: recollections of the delicate and benign power of her feminine nature, which had so often enveloped him in a religious calm; recollections of many a holy and passionate outgush of her heart, when the pure fountain had been unsealed from its depths and made visible in its transparency to his mental eye; recollections which, had Giovanni known how to estimate them, would have assured him that all this ugly mystery was but an earthly illusion, and that, whatever mist of evil might seem to have gathered over her, the real Beatrice was a heavenly angel. Incapable as he was of such high faith, still her presence had not utterly lost its magic. Giovanni's rage was quelled into an aspect of sullen insensibility. Beatrice, with a quick spiritual sense, immediately felt that there was a gulf of blackness between them which neither he nor she could pass. They walked on together, sad and silent, and came thus to the marble fountain and to its pool of water on the ground, in the midst of which grew the shrub that bore gem-like blossoms. Giovanni was affrighted at the eager enjoyment—the appetite, as it were—with which he found himself inhaling the fragrance of the flowers.

"Beatrice," asked he, abruptly, "whence came this shrub?"

"My father created it," answered she, with simplicity.

"Created it! created it!" repeated Giovanni. "What mean you, Beatrice?"

"He is a man fearfully acquainted with the secrets of Nature," replied Beatrice;   115 "and, at the hour when I first drew breath, this plant sprang from the soil, the offspring of his science, of his intellect, while I was but his earthly child. Approach it not!" continued she, observing with terror that Giovanni was drawing nearer to the shrub. "It has qualities that you little dream of. But I, dearest Giovanni,—I grew up and blossomed with the plant and was nourished with its breath. It was my sister, and I loved it with a human affection; for, alas!—hast thou not suspected it?—there was an awful doom."

Here Giovanni frowned so darkly upon her that Beatrice paused and trembled. But her faith in his tenderness reassured her, and made her blush that she had doubted for an instant.

"There was an awful doom," she continued, "the effect of my father's fatal love of science, which estranged me from all society of my kind. Until Heaven sent thee, dearest Giovanni, oh, how lonely was thy poor Beatrice!"

"Was it a hard doom?" asked Giovanni, fixing his eyes upon her.

"Only of late have I known how hard it was," answered she, tenderly. "Oh, yes; but my heart was torpid, and therefore quiet."

Giovanni's rage broke forth from his sullen gloom like a lightning flash out of a   120
dark cloud.

"Accursed one!" cried he, with venomous scorn and anger. "And, finding thy solitude wearisome, thou hast severed me likewise from all the warmth of life and enticed me into thy region of unspeakable horror!"

"Giovanni!" exclaimed Beatrice, turning her large bright eyes upon his face. The force of his words had not found its way into her mind; she was merely thunderstruck.

"Yes, poisonous thing!" repeated Giovanni, beside himself with passion. "Thou hast done it! Thou hast blasted me! Thou hast filled my veins with poison! Thou hast made me as hateful, as ugly, as loathsome and deadly a creature as thyself—a world's wonder of hideous monstrosity! Now, if our breath be happily as fatal to ourselves as to all others, let us join our lips in one kiss of unutterable hatred, and so die!"

"What has befallen me?" murmured Beatrice, with a low moan out of her heart. "Holy Virgin, pity me, a poor heart-broken child!"

"Thou,—dost thou pray?" cried Giovanni, still with the same fiendish scorn. "Thy   125
very prayers, as they come from thy lips, taint the atmosphere with death. Yes, yes; let us pray! Let us to church and dip our fingers in the holy water at the portal! They that come after us will perish as by a pestilence! Let us sign crosses in the air! It will be scattering curses abroad in the likeness of holy symbols!"

"Giovanni," said Beatrice, calmly, for her grief was beyond passion, "why dost thou join thyself with me thus in those terrible words? I, it is true, am the horrible thing thou namest me. But thou,—what hast thou to do, save with one other shudder at my hideous misery to go forth out of the garden and mingle with thy race, and forget there ever crawled on earth such a monster as poor Beatrice?"

"Dost thou pretend ignorance?" asked Giovanni, scowling upon her. "Behold! this power have I gained from the pure daughter of Rappaccini."

There was a swarm of summer insects flitting through the air in search of the food promised by the flower odors of the fatal garden. They circled round Giovanni's head, and were evidently attracted towards him by the same influence which had drawn them for an instant within the sphere of several of the shrubs. He sent forth a breath among them, and smiled bitterly at Beatrice as at least a score of the insects fell dead upon the ground.

"I see it! I see it!" shrieked Beatrice. "It is my father's fatal science! No, no, Giovanni; it was not I! Never! never! I dreamed only to love thee and be with thee a little time, and so to let thee pass away, leaving but thine image in mine heart; for, Giovanni, believe it, though my body be nourished with poison, my spirit is God's creature, and craves love as its daily food. But my father,—he has united us in this fearful sympathy. Yes; spurn me, tread upon me, kill me! Oh, what is death after such words as thine? But it was not I. Not for a world of bliss would I have done it."

Giovanni's passion had exhausted itself in its outburst from his lips. There now   130
came across him a sense, mournful, and not without tenderness, of the intimate and

peculiar relationship between Beatrice and himself. They stood, as it were, in an utter solitude, which would be made none the less solitary by the densest throng of human life. Ought not, then, the desert of humanity around them to press this insulated pair closer together? If they should be cruel to one another, who was there to be kind to them? Besides, thought Giovanni, might there not still be a hope of his returning within the limits of ordinary nature, and leading Beatrice, the redeemed Beatrice, by the hand? O, weak, and selfish, and unworthy spirit, that could dream of an earthly union and earthly happiness as possible, after such deep love had been so bitterly wronged as was Beatrice's love by Giovanni's blighting words! No, no; there could be no such hope. She must pass heavily, with that broken heart, across the borders of Time—she must bathe her hurts in some font of paradise, and forget her grief in the light of immortality, and *there* be well.

But Giovanni did not know it.

"Dear Beatrice," said he, approaching her, while she shrank away as always at his approach, but now with a different impulse, "dearest Beatrice our fate is not yet so desperate. Behold! there is a medicine, potent, as a wise physician has assured me, and almost divine in its efficacy. It is composed of ingredients the most opposite to those by which thy awful father has brought this calamity upon thee and me. It is distilled of blessed herbs. Shall we not quaff it together, and thus be purified from evil?"

"Give it me!" said Beatrice, extending her hand to receive the little silver vial which Giovanni took from his bosom. She added, with a peculiar emphasis, "I will drink; but do thou await the result."

She put Baglioni's antidote to her lips; and, at the same moment, the figure of Rappaccini emerged from the portal and came slowly towards the marble fountain. As he drew near, the pale man of science seemed to gaze with a triumphant expression at the beautiful youth and maiden, as might an artist who should spend his life in achieving a picture or a group of statuary and finally be satisfied with his success. He paused; his bent form grew erect with conscious power; he spread out his hands over them in the attitude of a father imploring a blessing upon his children; but those were the same hands that had thrown poison into the stream of their lives. Giovanni trembled. Beatrice shuddered nervously, and pressed her hand upon her heart.

"My daughter," said Rappaccini, "thou art no longer lonely in the world. Pluck one   135
of those precious gems from thy sister shrub and bid thy bridegroom wear it in his bosom. It will not harm him now. My science and the sympathy between thee and him have so wrought within his system that he now stands apart from common men, as thou dost, daughter of my pride and triumph, from ordinary women. Pass on, then, through the world, most dear to one another and dreadful to all besides!"

"My father," said Beatrice, feebly,—and still as she spoke she kept her hand upon her heart,—"wherefore didst thou inflict this miserable doom upon thy child?"

"Miserable!" exclaimed Rappaccini. "What mean you, foolish girl? Dost thou deem it misery to be endowed with marvellous gifts against which no power nor strength could avail an enemy—misery, to be able to quell the mightiest with a breath—misery, to be as terrible as thou art beautiful? Wouldst thou, then, have preferred the condition of a weak woman, exposed to all evil and capable of none?"

"I would fain have been loved, not feared," murmured Beatrice, sinking down upon the ground. "But now it matters not. I am going, father, where the evil which thou hast striven to mingle with my being will pass away like a dream—like the fragrance of these poisonous flowers, which will no longer taint my breath among the flowers of Eden. Farewell, Giovanni! Thy words of hatred are like lead within my heart; but they, too, will fall away as I ascend. Oh, was there not, from the first, more poison in thy nature than in mine?"

To Beatrice,—so radically had her earthly part been wrought upon by Rappaccini's skill,—as poison had been life, so the powerful antidote was death; and thus the poor victim of man's ingenuity and of thwarted nature, and of the fatality that attends all such efforts of perverted wisdom, perished there, at the feet of her father and Giovanni. Just at that moment Professor Pietro Baglioni looked forth from the window, and called loudly, in a tone of triumph mixed with horror, to the thunderstricken man of science,—

"Rappaccini! Rappaccini! and is *this* the upshot of your experiment!"   140

QUESTIONS FOR CLOSE READING OF PLOT AND NARRATIVE STRUCTURE

1. Why would Hawthorne pretend that this story was translated from a European language and that its author was European instead of American?

2. Examine the early pages of the story for the ways in which Hawthorne builds suspense about the garden and Dr. Rappaccini's daughter. How effective is Hawthorne at building suspense?

3. Which plants seem most important to Giovanni?

4. What kind of mood is established when Giovanni first sees Dr. Rappaccini and Beatrice? How are they described?

5. What does Professor Baglioni mean when he tells Giovanni that Dr. Rappaccini "cares infinitely more for science than for mankind"? Does Baglioni add to the suspense?

6. What happens when Giovanni and Beatrice first speak? What happens to the bouquet he throws to her? Why does Giovanni feel a sense of being poisoned?

7. How does Baglioni know Giovanni is the subject of one of Rappaccini's experiments?

8. What does Giovanni observe when he enters Dr. Rappaccini's garden? What does Beatrice say to him? What happens to his hand when Beatrice stops him from plucking a flower?

9. How does Hawthorne describe the love that grows between Giovanni and Beatrice?

10. How seriously does Giovanni take Professor Baglioni's story about the beautiful woman who was nourished by poison all her life? What is Baglioni telling him? Does he listen?

11. How does Giovanni discover he has been imbued with poison?

12. How does Beatrice learn the secret that Giovanni has come to understand?

13. Why does Beatrice die at the end of the story?

QUESTIONS FOR INTERPRETATION OF PLOT AND NARRATIVE STRUCTURE

1. Frequent references to the Garden of Eden and to Adam and Eve suggest that Rappaccini's garden has symbolic significance. Is it possible that his garden is a parody of the Garden of Eden? Does it make a mockery of the Garden of Eden? Are Giovanni and Beatrice like Adam and Eve? Is there any parallel to the injunction against eating of the tree of knowledge in this story?

2. The plot unfolds slowly to reveal that Dr. Rappaccini is a "vile empiric"—which is to say an experimenter who risks everything on his experiment. Near the end of

the story Beatrice explains to Giovanni in the garden that her "father's fatal love of science . . . estranged me from all society of my kind." Her loneliness was relieved by Giovanni. But at what cost? Is this story a narrative about the risks of science? Or is it about the awful things that scientists can do?

3. Given Professor Baglioni's description of Dr. Rappaccini's behavior, is it possible that Dr. Rappaccini is insane? What aspects of his behavior suggest that he might be unstable or malicious in his intent? Could Hawthorne intend us to understand Dr. Rappaccini as a "mad scientist"?

4. At the end of the story Dr. Rappaccini seems to offer an explanation of his behavior. His "science" has created a companion for Beatrice so that she would not be alone. He says he made her a poisonous woman so that she would not be "a weak woman, exposed to all evil and capable of none." In what sense is this narrative a story of an overprotective and ultimately destructive parent? Is it perhaps an over-bearing parent rather than a "mad scientist" who has caused all this harm?

5. What seems to be the relationship between men and women in this story? Hawthorne does not indicate when the story is set, although he published it in 1844. Can a useful comparison be made between the male-female patterns of behavior in this story with Boccaccio's "Pot of Basil"? Are the men in this story oppressive toward women? What behavior does a daughter owe to a father? Why does Beatrice not realize her condition until Giovanni makes her aware of it? And what does she mean when she says, "was there not, from the first, more poison in thy nature than in mine?"

RAYMOND CARVER   (1938–1988)

Raymond Carver, a legendary hard-drinking writer, is sometimes regarded as a minimalist—one who achieves extraordinary effects with a minimum of language, detail, or fancy literary footwork. Zachary Leader described Carver's second collection of stories, What We Talk about When We Talk about Love *(1981), as "a spare, unsparing collection, grim, minimalist, 'postmodern' in its resistance to depth and the exaggerated blankness of its realism."[1] His first collection,* Will You Please Be Quiet, Please? *(1976), in which the following story appeared, was less "cut to the bone." His third collection,* Cathedral *(1983), returned to the "generosity" of the first collection and established his reputation as a writer of realistic fiction who introduces the reader to dispossessed Americans who are often down and out, wondering what their next move should be.*

Night School ———————————————————————————— *1976*

My marriage had just fallen apart. I couldn't find a job. I had another girl. But she wasn't in town. So I was at a bar having a glass of beer, and two women were sitting a few stools down, and one of them began to talk to me.

  "You have a car?"

  "I do, but it's not here," I said.

[1]"A Chastened Gratitude," *The Times Literary Supplement* (Feb. 28, 1992): 16.

My wife had the car. I was staying at my parents' place. I used their car sometimes. But tonight I was walking.

The other woman looked at me. They were both about forty, maybe older. 5

"What'd you ask him?" the other woman said to the first woman.

"I said did he have a car."

"So do you have a car?" the second woman said to me.

"I was telling her. I have a car. But I don't have it with me," I said.

"That doesn't do us much good, does it?" she said. 10

The first woman laughed. "We had a brainstorm and we need a car to go through with it. Too bad." She turned to the bartender and asked for two more beers.

I'd been nursing my beer along, and now I drank it off and thought they might buy me a round. They didn't.

"What do you do?" the first woman asked me.

"Right now, nothing," I said. "Sometimes, when I can, I go to school."

"He goes to school," she said to the other woman. "He's a student. Where do you 15 go to school?"

"Around," I said.

"I told you," the woman said. "Doesn't he look like a student?"

"What are they teaching you?" the second woman said.

"Everything," I said.

"I mean," she said, "what do you plan to do? What's your big goal in life? Every- 20 body has a big goal in life."

I raised my empty glass to the bartender. He took it and drew me another beer. I counted out some change, which left me with thirty cents from the two dollars I'd started out with a couple of hours ago. She was waiting.

"Teach. Teach school," I said.

"He wants to be a teacher," she said.

I sipped my beer. Someone put a coin in the jukebox and a song that my wife liked began to play. I looked around. Two men near the front were at the shuffleboard. The door was open and it was dark outside.

"We're students too, you know," the first woman said. "We go to school." 25

"We take a night class," the other one said. "We take this reading class on Mon- day nights."

The first woman said, "Why don't you move down here, teacher, so we don't have to yell?"

I picked up my beer and my cigarets and moved down two stools.

"That's better," she said. "Now, did you say you were a student?"

"Sometimes, yes, but not now," I said. 30

"Where?"

"State College."

"That's right," she said. "I remember now." She looked at the other woman. "You ever hear of a teacher over there name of Patterson? He teaches adult-education classes. He teaches this class we take on Monday nights. You remind me a lot of Patterson."

They looked at each other and laughed.

"Don't bother about us," the first woman said. "It's a private joke. Shall we tell 35 him what we thought about doing, Edith? *Shall* we?"

Edith didn't answer. She took a drink of beer and she narrowed her eyes as she looked at herself, at the three of us, in the mirror behind the bar.

"We were thinking," the first woman went on, "if we had a car tonight we'd go over and see him. Patterson. Right, Edith?"

Edith laughed to herself. She finished her beer and asked for a round, one for me included. She paid for the beers with a five-dollar bill.

"Patterson likes to take a drink," Edith said.

"You can say that again," the other woman said. She turned to me. "We talked   40 about it in class one night. Patterson says he always has wine with his meals and a high-ball or two before dinner."

"What class is this?" I said.

"This reading class Patterson teaches. Patterson likes to talk about different things."

"We're learning to read," Edith said. "Can you believe it?"

"I'd like to read Hemingway and things like that," the other woman said. "But Patterson has us reading stories like in *Reader's Digest*."

"We take a test every Monday night," Edith said. "But Patterson's okay. He wouldn't   45 care if we came over for a highball. Wouldn't be much he could do, anyway. We have something on him. On Patterson," she said.

"We're on the loose tonight," the other woman said. "But Edith's car is in the garage."

"If you had a car now, we'd go over and see him," Edith said. She looked at me. "You could tell Patterson you wanted to be a teacher. You'd have something in common."

I finished my beer. I hadn't eaten anything all day except some peanuts. It was hard to keep listening and talking.

"Let's have three more, please, Jerry," the first woman said to the bartender.

"Thank you," I said.   50

"You'd get along with Patterson," Edith said.

"So call him," I said. I thought it was just talk.

"I wouldn't do that," she said. "He could make an excuse. We just show up on his porch, he'll have to let us in." She sipped her beer.

"So let's go!" the first woman said. "What're we waiting for? Where'd you say the car is?"

"There's a car a few blocks from here," I said. "But I don't know."   55

"Do you want to go or don't you?" Edith said.

"He said he does," the first woman said. "We'll get a six-pack to take with us."

"I only have thirty cents," I said.

"Who needs your goddamn money?" Edith said. "We need your goddamn car. Jerry, let's have three more. And a six-pack to go."

"Here's to Patterson," the first woman said when the beer came. "To Patterson and   60 his highballs."

"He'll drop his cookies," Edith said.

"Drink up," the first woman said.

On the sidewalk we headed south, away from town. I walked between the two women. It was about ten o'clock.

"I could drink one of those beers now," I said.

"Help yourself," Edith said.   65

She opened the sack and I reached in and tore a can loose.

"We think he's home," Edith said.

"Patterson," the other woman said. "We don't know for sure. But we think so."

"How much farther?" Edith said.

I stopped, raised the beer, and drained half the can. "The next block," I said. "I'm   70
staying with my parents. It's their place."

"I guess there's nothing wrong with it," Edith said. "But I'd say you're kind of old
for that."

"That's not polite, Edith," the other woman said.

"Well, that's the way I am," Edith said. "He'll have to get used to it, that's all. That's
the way I am."

"That's the way she is," the other woman said.

I finished the beer and tossed the can into some weeds.   75

"Now how far?" Edith said.

"This is it. Right here. I'll try and get the car key," I said.

"Well, hurry up," Edith said.

"We'll wait outside," the other woman said.

"Jesus!" Edith said.   80

I unlocked the door and went downstairs. My father was in his pajamas, watching
television. It was warm in the apartment and I leaned against the jamb for a minute and
ran a hand over my eyes.

"I had a couple of beers," I said. "What are you watching?"

"John Wayne," he said. "It's pretty good. Sit down and watch it. Your mother hasn't
come in yet."

My mother worked the swing shift at Paul's, a *hofbrau*° restaurant. My father
didn't have a job. He used to work in the woods, and then he got hurt. He'd had a settlement, but most of that was gone now. I asked him for a loan of two hundred dollars
when my wife left me, but he refused. He had tears in his eyes when he said no and
said he hoped I wouldn't hold it against him. I'd said it was all right, I wouldn't hold
it against him.

I knew he was going to say no this time too. But I sat down on the other end of the   85
couch and said, "I met a couple of women who asked me if I'd give them a ride home."

"What'd you tell them?" he said.

"They're waiting for me upstairs," I said.

"Just let them wait," he said. "Somebody'll come along. You don't want to get
mixed up with that." He shook his head. "You really didn't show them where we live, did
you? They're not really upstairs?" He moved on the couch and looked again at the television. "Anyway, your mother took the keys with her." He nodded slowly, still looking at
the television.

"That's okay," I said. "I don't need the car. I'm not going anywhere."

I got up and looked into the hallway, where I slept on a cot. There was an ashtray,   90
a Lux clock, and a few old paperbacks on a table beside the cot. I usually went to bed
at midnight and read until the lines of print went fuzzy and I fell asleep with the light
on and the book in my hands. In one of the paperbacks I was reading there was something I remembered telling my wife. It made a terrific impression on me. There's a man
who has a nightmare and in the nightmare he dreams he's dreaming and wakes to see
a man standing at his bedroom window. The dreamer is so terrified he can't move, can
hardly breathe. The man at the window stares into the room and then begins to pry off
the screen. The dreamer can't move. He'd like to scream, but he can't get his breath.

hofbrau: German-style

But the moon appears from behind a cloud, and the dreamer in the nightmare recognizes the man outside. It is his best friend, the best friend of the dreamer but no one the man having the nightmare knows.

Telling it to my wife, I'd felt the blood come to my face and my scalp prickle. But she wasn't interested.

"That's only writing," she said. "Being betrayed by somebody in your own family, *there's* a real nightmare for you."

I could hear them shaking the outside door. I could hear footsteps on the sidewalk over my window.

"Goddamn that bastard!" I heard Edith say.

I went into the bathroom for a long time and then I went upstairs and let myself out. It was cooler, and I did up the zipper on my jacket. I started walking to Paul's. If I got there before my mother went off duty, I could have a turkey sandwich. After that I could go to Kirby's newsstand and look through the magazines. Then I could go to the apartment to bed and read the books until I read enough and I slept.   95

The women, they weren't there when I left, and they wouldn't be there when I got back.

QUESTIONS FOR CLOSE READING OF PLOT AND NARRATIVE STRUCTURE

1. What do you learn about the protagonist in the beginning of the story?
2. Does the protagonist have an antagonist?
3. What do the women want from the narrator?
4. What is the narrator's big goal in life?
5. What kind of class does Patterson teach at the State College?
6. Why does the woman comment that the narrator seems "kind of old" to be staying with his parents?
7. How does the narrator's father react when he asks to use the car? Is his reaction part of a larger pattern?
8. What significance does the narrator's nightmare have?
9. Does this story have a plot?

QUESTIONS FOR INTERPRETATION OF PLOT AND NARRATIVE STRUCTURE

1. This is a "slice of life" story. Describe the action from beginning to end. How does the narrative pattern of the story reveal the character and circumstances of the narrator? How does it reveal the nature of his family and his relationship with his former wife? How does this narrative structure permit you to learn about the important issues in the narrator's life? Is the absence of a detailed plot freeing or restricting?
2. Describe the character of the narrator. What is he like? What values does he hold? How does he interrelate with others? What does he like and dislike? Given the fact that this is a very short story, do you feel you learn a great deal about the character or do you feel you know very little about him? Does he seem stable and in good shape?
3. How do you react to this narrator and the characters in the story? Are you surprised at the way he behaves? Do you feel it is a reasonable way to behave, given

his circumstances? Is there anything about his character that alarms you? Does the absence of a careful plot annoy you in this story? If it does, why do you think Carver wrote the story in this fashion?

4. What are the economic circumstances of the narrator and other characters in the story? Are they in important ways dominated by their economic situation? Would the narrator have acted differently if he had gone out of the house with more than two dollars in his pocket? What is the effect of the fact that the women who walk him home have money to spend and don't worry about the fact that he has only thirty cents?

POINT OF VIEW

Every story is told by a **narrator,** who is created by the author and usually different from the author's voice. The narrator controls the story by talking from a particular **point of view.** Points of view have traditionally been classed as first person, second person, and third person; however, as we shall see, such a classification only begins to describe the mystery of storytelling.

* *First-Person Narrator*   In this strategy, the story is told from the point of view of "I," as in Charles Baxter's "Gryphon." The I-narrator may be part of the action or an observer. As readers, we cannot know or witness anything the narrator does not tell us. We therefore share all the limitations of the narrator. This technique has the advantage of a sharp and precise focus. Moreover, you feel part of the story because the narrator's "I" echoes the "I" already in your own mind.

* *Second-Person Narrator*   This narrator speaks directly to the reader: "You walk in the room and what do you see? It's Mullins again, and you say, 'Out. I've done with him.' " This point of view is rare primarily because it is artificial and self-conscious. It seems to invite identification on the part of the reader with the narrator, but it often fails.

* *Third-Person Narrator*   This is the most common narrative style, illustrated by John Cheever's "The Swimmer": "His life was not confining and the delight he took in this observation could not be explained by its suggestion of escape." Third-person narration permits the author to be **omniscient** (all-knowing) when necessary but also to bring the focus tightly in on the central character by limiting observation only to what that character could possibly witness or recall. One emotional effect of the technique is the acceptance of the authority of the narrator. In essence, the narrator *sounds* like the author.

One of the most significant aspects of point of view is whether it is restricted or unrestricted. This question is important regardless of which point of view is used. The **restricted narrator** does not know everything but restricts his or her observations about thought and feeling to one central character or to a limited physical area, such as the space in which the characters act. When the narrator is the same as a character in the story, this point of view usually respects the character's limitations: The narrator can tell us only what the character knows. Many first-person narrators are restricted in this way, such as the narrator in "Gryphon," who is limited by what a fourth-grader would observe. However, third-person narration can also be restricted. John Cheever uses the third-person *he* to narrate "The Swimmer," but he stays very close to Neddy, and what we know of him is restricted to what Neddy Merrill knows and thinks. Nor does the narrator make any value judgment about Neddy; that is left to us.

The **unrestricted narrator**—usually called omniscient—often resembles the voice of the author and tells us many things: this narrator knows what the characters think, what they say when they are out of sight and hearing, and what they feel. Often this narrator also steps back to comment on the behavior of the characters. Unrestricted narration is usually third person but not always. The voice in Poe's "The Masque of the Red Death" is first person but still seems omniscient: "No pestilence had ever been so fatal, or so hideous." This narrator knows more than any single character; he is an observer, not an actor, and by assuming an authoritative voice appears to speak on behalf of Poe himself. A more traditional, third-person omniscient narration is used by Filomena in "The Pot of Basil"; compared with the character Lisabetta, she is totally unrestricted. However, within the larger group of tales she is only one narrator, and therefore her knowledge may be more restricted than Boccaccio's. Boccaccio may be trying to say something about her character to us, but only a reading of the entire *Decameron* could verify that guess.

Another way of describing narrators is to say that they are reliable or unreliable. The **reliable narrator** can be counted on to know the truth and to reveal it to the reader. The **unreliable narrator** is a character in the story who may tell the truth or not but, like any other character, is beset with limitations and personal prejudices that color his or her values and point of view. The narrators in "The Masque of the Red Death" and in "The Jilting of Granny Weatherall" appear reliable: we can believe what they tell us.

Traditionally, older stories are often told from the point of view of a narrative voice that resembles the author. In other words, that voice is totally authoritative. This is true of Poe's narrator. Charlotte Perkins Gilman presents us with an interesting problem in "The Yellow Wallpaper." Since it is clear that the narrator confides in us and insists that she may be ill and that her illness may be a nervous breakdown, should we consider her a reliable narrator? She tells us that she is, but her husband would certainly argue with that judgment. How can we tell how reliable the narrator is in this story? In essence, that is the important question that Gilman leaves us with in this story. We know the name of Les, the narrator in Richard Ford's "Communist," but since Les tells us a story of events that happened many years ago in his youth, can we depend on the narrator's being reliable? Is it possible his memory of the events distorted them and that they should be judged quite differently from the way Les now judges them? With narrators of this sort, you can see that it is important not to take every word as being the gospel truth. Rather, it is important that we examine the narrator as carefully as we examine other characters in a piece of fiction.

The narrator of Charles Baxter's "Gryphon" is a fourth-grader who watches in awe the performance of his substitute teacher. How much can you trust the narrative of the average fourth-grader? Perhaps this fourth-grader is above average, but he is still a young child. On the other hand, if the narrator were completely restricted to this point of view, the narrative might include limited grammar and vocabulary and other limitations appropriate to the imagination of a fourth-grader. Thus Baxter is really looking back at an earlier time and telling a story of childhood from the point of view of a mature person remembering the distant past. In that way an author can get around the obvious limitations of a child's point of view.

A final question is whether the narrator takes a subjective or objective stance. The **subjective narrator** is given to expressing personal quirks, animosities, and limitations, as in the first-person narrator in "Gryphon." The boy tells us, " 'hope you feel better tomorrow, Mr. Hibler,' Bobby Kryzanowicz, the faultless brown-noser said, and I heard Carol Peterson's evil giggle." Such a narrator makes judgments about characters and events and expects you to accept them. If you feel the narrator is unreliable, you may reject them entirely. The **objective narrator,** on the other hand, seems to present a totally neutral interpretation of events and therefore does not make judgments about characters. For that reason, "Two Cents" by Suzanne Jacob might appear mysterious to you. The third-person objective narrator does not permit you to know what the characters think or feel. You must interpret them objectively, from an emotional distance.

One special form of narration, the **stream-of-consciousness technique,** has become extremely flexible in the hands of modern writers. It recreates the interior of a character's mind so you know and feel what the character knows and feels directly. You learn to think as the character thinks. Katherine Anne Porter's "The Jilting of Granny Weatherall" uses stream of consciousness. However, Porter mixes the point of view in that story by beginning in third person, "She flicked her wrist . . .," and then entering Granny Weatherall's mind after a page, "Tomorrow was far away and there was nothing to trouble about." We learn about the jilting in Granny's recollections, but the point of view shifts from a nameless narrator who tells us what is happening now to the interior of Granny's mind to tell us what happened before and how Granny feels about what happened. The nameless narrator is not a character in the action and is therefore presumably reliable and objective. This mix of narrative point of view is common in early experiments with the stream-of-consciousness technique.

"Gryphon" provides us with special pleasures because we see the action through the eyes of the fourth-grader telling the story. The setting and mood of the grade school classroom dominate the story, and the distance that usually separates the fourth-grader from the teacher is deliciously present. Thus Miss Ferenczi becomes even more exotic than she might be were you to meet her in person.

CHARLES BAXTER   (b. 1947)

Charles Baxter teaches at Wayne State University in Detroit. His short story collections, Harmony of the World *(1984) and* Through the Safety Net *(1985), from which "Gryphon" is taken, have won important writing awards and have caught the attention of both writers and critics. Some of his work falls into the genre of horror stories. The* New York Times *critic Michiko Kakutani has said that Baxter "makes his characters' fears palpable to the reader by slowly drawing us into their day-to-day routines and making us see things through their eyes." That is certainly the case in "Gryphon," which pulls us into the strange yet familiar world of the fourth grade.*

Gryphon _____ *1986*

On Wednesday afternoon, between the geography lesson on ancient Egypt's hand-operated irrigation system and an art project that involved drawing a model city next to a mountain, our fourth-grade teacher, Mr. Hibler, developed a cough. This cough began with a series of muffled throat clearings and progressed to propulsive noises contained within Mr. Hibler's closed mouth. "Listen to him," Carol Peterson whispered to me. "He's gonna blow up." Mr. Hibler's laughter—dazed and infrequent—sounded a bit like his cough, but as we worked on our model cities we would look up, thinking he was enjoying a joke, and see Mr. Hibler's face turning red, his cheeks puffed out. This was not laughter. Twice he bent over, and his loose tie, like a plumb line, hung down straight from his neck as he exploded himself into a Kleenex. He would excuse himself, then go on coughing. "I'll bet you a dime," Carol Peterson whispered, "we get a substitute tomorrow."

Carol sat at the desk in front of mine and was a bad person—when she thought no one was looking she would blow her nose on notebook paper, then crumble it up and throw it into the wastebasket—but at times of crisis she spoke the truth. I knew I'd lose the dime.

"No deal," I said.

When Mr. Hibler stood us up in formation at the door just prior to the final bell, he was almost incapable of speech. "I'm sorry, boys and girls," he said. "I seem to be coming down with something."

"I hope you feel better tomorrow, Mr. Hibler," Bobby Kryzanowicz, the faultless brown-noser said, and I heard Carol Peterson's evil giggle. Then Mr. Hibler opened the door and we walked out to the buses, a clique of us starting noisily to hawk and cough as soon as we thought we were a few feet beyond Mr. Hibler's earshot.   5

Five Oaks being a rural community, and in Michigan, the supply of substitute teachers was limited to the town's unemployed community college graduates, a pool of about four mothers. These ladies fluttered, provided easeful class days, and nervously covered material we had mastered weeks earlier. Therefore it was a surprise when a woman we had never seen came into the class the next day, carrying a purple purse, a checkerboard lunchbox, and a few books. She put the books on one side of Mr. Hibler's desk and the lunchbox on the other, next to the Voice of Music phonograph. Three of us in the back of the room were playing with Heever, the chameleon that lived in the terrarium and on one of the plastic drapes, when she walked in.

She clapped her hands at us. "Little boys," she said, "why are you bent over together like that?" She didn't wait for us to answer. "Are you tormenting an animal? Put it back. Please sit down at your desks. I want no cabals this time of the day." We just stared at her. "Boys," she repeated, "I asked you to sit down."

I put the chameleon in his terrarium and felt my way to my desk, never taking my eyes off the woman. With white and green chalk, she had started to draw a tree on the left side of the blackboard. She didn't look usual. Furthermore, her tree was outsized, disproportionate, for some reason.

"This room needs a tree," she said, with one line drawing the suggestion of a leaf. "A large, leafy, shady, deciduous . . . oak."

Her fine, light hair had been done up in what I would learn years later was called   10
a chignon, and she wore gold-rimmed glasses whose lenses seemed to have the faintest blue tint. Harold Knardahl, who sat across from me, whispered "Mars," and I nodded slowly, savoring the imminent weirdness of the day. The substitute drew another branch with an extravagant arm gesture, then turned around and said, "Good morning. I don't believe I said good morning to all you yet."

Facing us, she was no special age—an adult is an adult—but her face had two prominent lines, descending vertically from the sides of her mouth to her chin. I knew where I had seen those lines before: *Pinocchio*. They were marionette lines. "You may stare at me," she said to us, as a few more kids from the last bus came into the room, their eyes fixed on her, "for a few more seconds, until the bell rings. Then I will permit no more staring. Looking I will permit. Staring, no. It is impolite to stare, and a sign of bad breeding. You cannot make a social effort while staring."

Harold Knardahl did not glance at me, or nudge, but I heard him whisper "Mars" again, trying to get more mileage out of his single joke with the kids who had just come in.

When everyone was seated, the substitute teacher finished her tree, put down her chalk fastidiously on the phonograph, brushed her hands, and faced us. "Good morning," she said. "I am Miss Ferenczi, your teacher for the day. I am fairly new to your community, and I don't believe any of you know me. I will therefore start by telling you a story about myself."

While we settled back, she launched into her tale. She said her grandfather had been a Hungarian prince; her mother had been born in some place called Flanders, had been a pianist, and had played concerts for people Miss Ferenczi referred to as "crowned heads." She gave us a knowing look. "Grieg," she said, "the Norwegian master, wrote a concerto for piano that was," she paused, "my mother's triumph at her debut concert in London." Her eyes searched the ceiling. Our eyes followed. Nothing up there but ceiling tile. "For reasons that I shall not go into, my family's fortunes took us to Detroit, then north to dreadful Saginaw, and now here I am in Five Oaks, as your substitute teacher, for today, Thursday, October the eleventh. I believe it will be a good day: All the forecasts coincide. We shall start with your reading lesson. Take out your reading book. I believe it is called *Broad Horizons*, or something along those lines."

Jeannie Vermeesch raised her hand. Miss Ferenzi nodded at her. "Mr. Hibler al-   15
ways starts the day with the Pledge of Allegiance," Jeannie whined.

"Oh, does he? In that case," Miss Ferenczi said, "you must know it *very* well by now, and we certainly need not spend our time on it. No, no allegiance pledging on the premises today, by my reckoning. Not with so much sunlight coming into the room. A pledge does not suit my mood." She glanced at her watch. "Time *is* flying. Take out *Broad Horizons*."

She disappointed us by giving us an ordinary lesson, complete with vocabulary word drills, comprehension questions, and recitation. She didn't seem to care for the material, however. She sighed every few minutes and rubbed her glasses with a frilly perfumed handkerchief that she withdrew, magician style, from her left sleeve.

After reading we moved on to arithmetic. It was my favorite time of the morning, when the lazy autumn sunlight dazzled its way through ribbons of clouds past the windows on the east side of the classroom, and crept across the linoleum floor. On the playground the first group of children, the kindergartners, were running on the quack grass just beyond the monkey bars. We were doing multiplication tables. Miss Ferenczi had made John Wazny stand up at his desk in the front row. He was supposed to go through the tables of six. From where I was sitting, I could smell the Vitalis soaked into John's plastered hair. He was doing fine until he came to six times eleven and six times twelve. "Six times eleven," he said, "is sixty-eight. Six times twelve is. . . ." He put his fingers to his head, quickly and secretly sniffed his fingertips, and said, "seventy-two." Then he sat down.

"Fine," Miss Ferenczi said. "Well now. That was very good."

"Miss Ferenczi!" One of the Eddy twins was waving her hand desperately in the air.   20
"Miss Ferenczi! Miss Ferenczi!"

"Yes?"

"John said that six times eleven is sixty-eight and you said he was right!"

"*Did* I?" She gazed at the class with a jolly look breaking across her marionette's face. "Did I say that? Well, what *is* six times eleven?"

"It's sixty-six!"

She nodded. "Yes. So it is. But, and I know some people will not entirely agree with   25
me, at some times it is sixty-eight."

"When? When is it sixty-eight?"

We were all waiting.

"In higher mathematics, which you children do not yet understand, six times eleven can be considered to be sixty-eight." She laughed through her nose. "In higher mathematics numbers are . . . more fluid. The only thing a number does is contain a certain amount of something. Think of water. A cup is not the only way to measure a certain amount of water, is it?" We were staring, shaking our heads. "You could use saucepans or thimbles. In either case, the water *would be the same*. Perhaps," she started again, "it would be better for you to think that six times eleven is sixty-eight only when I am in the room."

"Why is it sixty-eight," Mark Poole asked, "when you're in the room?"

"Because it's more interesting that way," she said, smiling very rapidly behind her   30
blue-tinted glasses. "Besides, I'm your substitute teacher, am I not?" We all nodded. "Well, then, think of six times eleven equals sixty-eight as a substitute fact."

"A substitute fact?"

"Yes." Then she looked at us carefully. "Do you think," she asked, "that anyone is going to be hurt by a substitute fact?"

We looked back at her.

"Will the plants on the windowsill be hurt?" We glanced at them. There were sensitive plants thriving in a green plastic tray, and several wilted ferns in small clay pots. "Your dogs and cats, or your moms and dads?" She waited. "So," she concluded, "what's the problem?"

"But it's wrong," Janice Weber said, "isn't it?"   35

"What's your name, young lady?"

"Janice Weber."

"And you think it's wrong, Janice?"

"I was just asking."

"Well, all right. You were just asking. I think we've spent enough time on this mat-   40
ter by now, don't you, class? You are free to think what you like. When your teacher, Mr.
Hibler, returns, six times eleven will be sixty-six again, you can rest assured. And it will
be that for the rest of your lives in Five Oaks. Too bad, eh?" She raised her eyebrows and
glinted herself at us. "But for now, it wasn't. So much for that. Let us go to your assigned
problems for today, as painstakingly outlined, I see, in Mr. Hibler's lesson plan. Take out
a sheet of paper and write your names in the upper left-hand corner."

For the next half hour we did the rest of our arithmetic problems. We handed
them in and went on to spelling, my worst subject. Spelling always came before lunch.
We were taking spelling dictation and looking at the clock. "Thorough," Miss Ferenczi
said. "Boundary." She walked in the aisles between the desks, holding the spelling book
open and looking down at our papers. "Balcony." I clutched my pencil. Somehow,
the way she said those words, they seemed foreign, Hungarian, mis-voweled and mis-
consonanted. I stared down at what I had spelled. *Balconie.* I turned my pencil upside
down and erased my mistake. *Balconey.* That looked better, but still incorrect. I cursed
the world of spelling and tried erasing it again and saw the paper beginning to wear
away. *Balkony.* Suddenly I felt a hand on my shoulder.

"I don't like that word either," Miss Ferenczi whispered, bent over, her mouth
near my ear. "It's ugly. My feeling is, if you don't like a word, you don't have to use it."
She straightened up, leaving behind a slight odor of Clorets.

At lunchtime we went out to get our trays of sloppy joes, peaches in heavy syrup,
coconut cookies, and milk, and brought them back to the classroom, where Miss Ferenczi was sitting at the desk, eating a brown sticky thing she had unwrapped from tightly
rubber-banded wax paper. "Miss Ferenczi," I said, raising my hand. "You don't have to
eat with us. You can eat with the other teachers. There's a teachers' lounge," I ended up,
"next to the principal's office."

"No, thank you," she said. "I prefer it here."

"We've got a room monitor," I said. "Mrs. Eddy." I pointed to where Mrs. Eddy,   45
Joyce and Judy's mother, sat silently at the back of the room, doing her knitting.

"That's fine," Miss Ferenczi said. "But I shall continue to eat here, with you children. I prefer it," she repeated.

"How come?" Wayne Razmer asked without raising his hand.

"I talked with the other teachers before class this morning," Miss Ferenczi said, biting into her brown food. "There was a great rattling of the words for the fewness of
ideas. I didn't care for their brand of hilarity. I don't like ditto machine jokes."

"Oh," Wayne said.

"What's that you're eating?" Maxine Sylvester asked, twitching her nose. "Is   50
it food?"

"It most certainly *is* food. It's a stuffed fig. I had to drive almost down to Detroit
to get it. I also bought some smoked sturgeon. And this," she said, lifting some green
leaves out of her lunchbox, "is raw spinach, cleaned this morning before I came out
here to the Garfield-Murry school."

"Why're you eating raw spinach?" Maxine asked.

"It's good for you," Miss Ferenczi said. "More stimulating than soda pop or
smelling salts." I bit into my sloppy joe and stared blankly out the window. An almost
invisible moon was faintly silvered in the daytime autumn sky. "As far as food is concerned," Miss Ferenczi was saying, "you have to shuffle the pack. Mix it up. Too many
people eat . . . well, never mind."

"Miss Ferenczi," Carol Peterson said, "what are we going to do this afternoon?"

"Well," she said, looking down at Mr. Hibler's lesson plan, "I see that your teacher,   55
Mr. Hibler, has you scheduled for a unit on the Egyptians." Carol groaned. "Yessss," Miss
Ferenczi continued, "that is what we will do: the Egyptians. A remarkable people. Almost
as remarkable as the Americans. But not quite." She lowered her head, did her quick
smile, and went back to eating her spinach.

After noon recess we came back into the classroom and saw that Miss Ferenczi had
drawn a pyramid on the blackboard, close to her oak tree. Some of us who had been playing baseball were messing around in the back of the room, dropping the bats and the
gloves into the playground box, and I think that Ray Schontzeler had just slugged me
when I heard Miss Ferenczi's high-pitched voice quavering with emotion. "Boys," she said,
"come to order right this minute and take your seats. I do not wish to waste a minute of
class time. Take out your geography books." We trudged to our desks and, still sweating,
pulled out *Distant Lands and Their People.* "Turn to page forty-two." She waited for thirty
seconds, then looked over at Kelly Munger. "Young man," she said, "why are you still fos-
sicking in your desk?"

Kelly looked as if his foot had been stepped on. "Why am I what?"

"Why are you . . . burrowing in your desk like that?"

"I'm lookin' for the book, Miss Ferenczi."

Bobby Kryzanowicz, the faultless brown-noser who sat in the first row by choice,   60
softly said, "His name is Kelly Munger. He can't ever find his stuff. He always does that."

"I don't care what his name is, especially after lunch," Miss Ferenczi said. "*Where
is your book?*"

"I just found it." Kelly was peering into his desk and with both hands pulled at the
book, shoveling along in front of it several pencils and crayons, which fell into his lap
and then to the floor.

"I hate a mess," Miss Ferenczi said. "I hate a mess in a desk or a mind. It's . . . un-
sanitary. You wouldn't want your house at home to look like your desk at school, now,
would you?" She didn't wait for an answer. "I should think not. A house at home should
be as neat as human hands can make it. What were we talking about? Egypt. Page forty-
two. I note from Mr. Hibler's lesson plan that you have been discussing the modes of
Egyptian irrigation. Interesting, in my view, but not so interesting as what we are about
to cover. The pyramids and Egyptian slave labor. A plus on one side, a minus on the
other." We had our books open to page forty-two, where there was a picture of a pyramid, but Miss Ferenczi wasn't looking at the book. Instead, she was staring at some object just outside the window.

"Pyramids," Miss Ferenczi said, still looking past the window. "I want you to think
about the pyramids. And what was inside. The bodies of the pharaohs, of course, and their
attendant treasures. Scrolls. Perhaps," Miss Ferenczi said, with something gleeful but un-
smiling in her face, "these scrolls were novels for the pharaohs, helping them to pass the
time in their long voyage through the centuries. But then, I am joking." I was looking at
the lines on Miss Ferenczi's face. "Pyramids," Miss Ferenczi went on, "were the reposi-
tories of special cosmic powers. The nature of a pyramid is to guide cosmic energy forces
into a concentrated point. The Egyptians knew that; we have generally forgotten it. Did
you know," she asked, walking to the side of the room so that she was standing by the coat
closet, "that George Washington had Egyptian blood, from his grandmother? Certain
features of the Constitution of the United States are notable for their Egyptian ideas."

Without glancing down at the book, she began to talk about the movement of   65
souls in Egyptian religion. She said that when people die, their souls return to Earth in

the form of carpenter ants or walnut trees, depending on how they behaved—"well or ill"—in life. She said that the Egyptians believed that people act the way they do because of magnetism produced by tidal forces in the solar system, forces produced by the sun and by its "planetary ally," Jupiter. Jupiter, she said, was a planet, as we had been told, but had "certain properties of stars." She was speaking very fast. She said that the Egyptians were great explorers and conquerors. She said that the greatest of all the conquerors, Genghis Khan, had had forty horses and forty young women killed on the site of his grave. We listened. No one tried to stop her. "I myself have been in Egypt," she said, "and have witnessed much dust and many brutalities." She said that an old man in Egypt who worked for a circus had personally shown her an animal in a cage, a monster, half bird and half lion. She said that this monster was called a gryphon and that she had heard about them but never seen them until she traveled to the outskirts of Cairo. She said that Egyptian astronomers had discovered the planet Saturn, but had not seen its rings. She said that the Egyptians were the first to discover that dogs, when they are ill, will not drink from rivers, but wait for rain, and hold their jaws open to catch it.

"She lies."

We were on the school bus home. I was sitting next to Carl Whiteside, who had bad breath and a huge collection of marbles. We were arguing. Carl thought she was lying. I said she wasn't, probably.

"I didn't believe that stuff about the bird," Carl said, "and what she told us about the pyramids? I didn't believe that either. She didn't know what she was talking about."

"Oh yeah?" I had liked her. She was strange. I thought I could nail him. "If she was lying," I said, "what'd she say that was a lie?"

"Six times eleven isn't sixty-eight. It isn't ever. It's sixty-six, I know for a fact." 70

"She said so. She admitted it. What else did she lie about?"

"I don't know," he said. "Stuff."

"What stuff?"

"Well." He swung his legs back and forth. "You ever see an animal that was half lion and half bird?" He crossed his arms. "It sounded real fakey to me."

"It could happen," I said. I had to improvise, to outrage him. "I read in this news- 75 paper my mom bought in the IGA about this scientist, this mad scientist in the Swiss Alps, and he's been putting genes and chromosomes and stuff together in test tubes, and he combined a human being and a hamster." I waited, for effect. "It's called a humster."

"You never." Carl was staring at me, his mouth open, his terrible bad breath making its way toward me. "What newspaper was it?"

"The *National Enquirer*," I said, "that they sell next to the cash registers." When I saw his look of recognition, I knew I had bested him. "And this mad scientist," I said, "his name was, um, Dr. Frankenbush." I realized belatedly that this name was a mistake and waited for Carl to notice its resemblance to the name of the other famous mad master of permutations, but he only sat there.

"A man and a hamster?" He was staring at me, squinting, his mouth opening in distaste. "Jeez. What'd it look like?"

When the bus reached my stop, I took off down our dirt road and ran up through the back yard, kicking the tire swing for good luck. I dropped my books on the back steps so I could hug and kiss our dog, Mr. Selby. Then I hurried inside. I could smell Brussels sprouts cooking, my unfavorite vegetable. My mother was washing other vegetables in the kitchen sink, and my baby brother was hollering in his yellow playpen on the kitchen floor.

"Hi, Mom," I said, hopping around the playpen to kiss her. "Guess what?"   80

"I have no idea."

"We had this substitute today, Miss Ferenczi, and I'd never seen her before, and she had all these stories and ideas and stuff."

"Well. That's good." My mother looked out the window behind the sink, her eyes on the pine woods west of our house. Her face and hairstyle always reminded other people of Betty Crocker, whose picture was framed inside a gigantic spoon on the side of the Bisquick box; to me, though, my mother's face just looked white. "Listen, Tommy," she said, "go upstairs and pick your clothes off the bathroom floor, then go outside to the shed and put the shovel and ax away that your father left outside this morning."

"She said that six times eleven was sometimes sixty-eight!" I said. "And she said she once saw a monster that was half lion and half bird." I waited. "In Egypt, she said."

"Did you hear me?" my mother asked, raising her arm to wipe her forehead with   85
the back of her hand. "You have chores to do."

"I know," I said. "I was just telling you about the substitute."

"It's very interesting," my mother said, quickly glancing down at me, "and we can talk about it later when your father gets home. But right now you have some work to do."

"Okay, Mom." I took a cookie out of the jar on the counter and was about to go outside when I had a thought. I ran into the living room, pulled out a dictionary next to the TV stand, and opened it to the G's. *Gryphon:* "variant of griffin." *Griffin:* "a fabulous beast with the head and wings of an eagle and the body of a lion." Fabulous was right. I shouted with triumph and ran outside to put my father's tools back in their place.

Miss Ferenczi was back the next day, slightly altered. She had pulled her hair down and twisted it into pigtails, with red rubber bands holding them tight one inch from the ends. She was wearing a green blouse and pink scarf, making her difficult to look at for a full class day. This time there was no pretense of doing a reading lesson or moving on to arithmetic. As soon as the bell rang, she simply began to talk.

She talked for forty minutes straight. There seemed to be less connection be-   90
tween her ideas, but the ideas themselves were, as the dictionary would say, fabulous. She said she had heard of a huge jewel, in what she called the Antipodes, that was so brilliant that when the light shone into it at a certain angle it would blind whoever was looking at its center. She said that the biggest diamond in the world was cursed and had killed everyone who owned it, and that by a trick of fate it was called the Hope diamond. Diamonds are magic, she said, and this is why women wear them on their fingers, as a sign of the magic of womanhood. Men have strength, Miss Ferenczi said, but no true magic. That is why men fall in love with women but women do not fall in love with men: they just love being loved. George Washington had died because of a mistake he made about a diamond. Washington was not the first *true* President, but she did not say who was. In some places in the world, she said, men and women still live in the trees and eat monkeys for breakfast. Their doctors are magicians. At the bottom of the sea are creatures thin as pancakes which have never been studied by scientists because when you take them up to the air, the fish explode.

There was not a sound in the classroom, except for Miss Ferenczi's voice, and Donna DeShano's coughing. No one even went to the bathroom.

Beethoven, she said, had not been deaf; it was a trick to make himself famous, and it worked. As she talked, Miss Ferenczi's pigtails swung back and forth. There are trees in the world, she said, that eat meat: their leaves are sticky and close up on bugs like hands. She lifted her hands and brought them together, palm to palm. Venus, which most people think is the next closest planet to the sun, is not always closer, and, besides, it is the planet of greatest mystery because of its thick cloud cover. "I know what lies underneath those clouds," Miss Ferenczi said, and waited. After the silence, she said, "Angels. Angels live under those clouds." She said that angels were not invisible to everyone and were in fact smarter than most people. They did not dress in robes as was often claimed but instead wore formal evening clothes, as if they were about to attend a concert. Often angels *do* attend concerts and sit in the aisles where, she said, most people pay no attention to them. She said the most terrible angel had the shape of the Sphinx: "There is no running away from that one," she said. She said that unquenchable fires burn just under the surface of the earth in Ohio, and that the baby Mozart fainted dead away in his cradle when he first heard the sound of a trumpet. She said that someone named Narzim al Harrardim was the greatest writer who ever lived. She said that planets control behavior, and anyone conceived during a solar eclipse would be born with webbed feet.

"I know you children like to hear these things," she said, "these secrets, and that is why I am telling you all this." We nodded. It was better than doing comprehension questions for the readings in *Broad Horizons*.

"I will tell you one more story," she said, "and then we will have to do arithmetic." She leaned over, and her voice grew soft. "There is no death," she said. "You must never be afraid. Never. That which is, cannot die. It will change into different earthly and unearthly elements, but I know this as sure as I stand here in front of you, and I swear it: you must not be afraid. I have seen this truth with these eyes. I know it because in a dream God kissed me. Here." And she pointed with her right index finger to the side of her head, below the mouth, where the vertical lines were carved into her skin.

Absent-mindedly we all did our arithmetic problems. At recess the class was out on the playground, but no one was playing. We were all standing in small groups, talking about Miss Ferenczi. We didn't know if she was crazy, or what. I looked out beyond the playground, at the rusted cars piled in a small heap behind a clump of sumac, and I wanted to see shapes there, approaching me.

On the way home, Carl sat next to me again. He didn't say much, and I didn't either. At last he turned to me. "You know what she said about the leaves that close up on bugs?"

"Huh?"

"The leaves," Carl insisted. "The meat-eating plants. I know it's true. I saw it on television. The leaves have this icky glue that the plants have got smeared all over them and the insects can't get off 'cause they're stuck. I saw it." He seemed demoralized. "She's tellin' the truth."

"Yeah."

"You think she's seen all those angels?"

I shrugged.

"I don't think she has," Carl informed me. "I think she made that part up."

"There's a tree," I suddenly said. I was looking out the window at the farms along County Road H. I knew every barn, every broken windmill, every fence, every anhydrous ammonia tank, by heart. "There's a tree that's . . . that I've seen. . . ."

95

100

"Don't you try to do it," Carl said. "You'll just sound like a jerk."

I kissed my mother. She was standing in front of the stove. "How was your day?" [105] she asked.

"Fine."

"Did you have Miss Ferenczi again?"

"Yeah."

"Well?"

"She was fine. Mom," I asked, "can I go to my room?" [110]

"No," she said, "not until you've gone out to the vegetable garden and picked me a few tomatoes." She glanced at the sky. "I think it's going to rain. Skedaddle and do it now. Then you come back inside and watch your brother for a few minutes while I go upstairs. I need to clean up before dinner." She looked down at me. "You're looking a little pale, Tommy." She touched the back of her hand to my forehead and I felt her diamond ring against my skin. "Do you feel all right?"

"I'm fine," I said, and went out to pick the tomatoes.

Coughing mutedly, Mr. Hibler was back the next day, slipping lozenges into his mouth when his back was turned at forty-five-minute intervals and asking us how much of the prepared lesson plan Miss Ferenczi had followed. Edith Atwater took the responsibility for the class of explaining to Mr. Hibler that the substitute hadn't always done exactly what he would have done, but we had worked hard even though she talked a lot. About what? he asked. All kinds of things, Edith said. I sort of forgot. To our relief, Mr. Hibler seemed not at all interested in what Miss Ferenczi had said to fill the day. He probably thought it was woman's talk; unserious and not suited for school. It was enough that he had a pile of arithmetic problems from us to correct.

For the next month, the sumac turned a distracting red in the field, and the sun traveled toward the southern sky, so that its rays reached Mr. Hibler's Halloween display on the bulletin board in the back of the room, fading the scarecrow with a pumpkin head from orange to tan. Every three days I measured how much farther the sun had moved toward the southern horizon by making small marks with my black Crayola on the north wall, ant-sized marks only I knew were there, inching west.

And then in early December, four days after the first permanent snowfall, she appeared again in our classroom. The minute she came in the door, I felt my heart begin [115] to pound. Once again, she was different: this time, her hair hung straight down and seemed hardly to have been combed. She hadn't brought her lunchbox with her, but she was carrying what seemed to be a small box. She greeted all of us and talked about the weather. Donna DeShano had to remind her to take her overcoat off.

When the bell to start the day finally rang, Miss Ferenczi looked out at all of us and said, "Children, I have enjoyed your company in the past, and today I am going to reward you." She held up the small box. "Do you know what this is?" She waited. "Of course you don't. It is a tarot pack."

Edith Atwater raised her hand. "What's a tarot pack, Miss Ferenczi?"

"It is used to tell fortunes," she said. "And that is what I shall do this morning. I shall tell your fortunes, as I have been taught to do."

"What's fortune?" Bobby Kryzanowicz asked.

"The future, young man. I shall tell you what your future will be. I can't do your [120] whole future, of course. I shall have to limit myself to the five-card system, the wands, cups, swords, pentacles, and the higher arcanes. Now who wants to be first?"

There was a long silence. Then Carol Peterson raised her hand.

"All right," Miss Ferenczi said. She divided the pack into five smaller packs and walked back to Carol's desk, in front of mine. "Pick one card from each of these packs," she said. I saw that Carol had a four of cups, a six of swords, but I couldn't see the other cards. Miss Ferenczi studied the cards on Carol's desk for a minute. "Not bad," she said. "I do not see much higher education. Probably an early marriage. Many children. There's something bleak and dreary here, but I can't tell what. Perhaps just the tasks of a housewife life. I think you'll do very well, for the most part." She smiled at Carol, a smile with a certain lack of interest. "Who wants to be next?"

Carl Whiteside raised his hand slowly.

"Yes," Miss Ferenczi said, "let's do a boy." She walked over to where Carl sat. After he picked his five cards, she gazed at them for a long time. "Travel," she said. "Much distant travel. You might go into the Army. Not too much romantic interest here. A late marriage, if at all. Squabbles. But the Sun is in your major arcana, here, yes, that's a very good card." She giggled. "Maybe a good life."

Next I raised my hand, and she told me my future. She did the same with Bobby   125
Kryzanowicz. Kelly Munger, Edith Atwater, and Kim Foor. Then she came to Wayne
Razmer. He picked his five cards, and I could see that the Death card was one of them.

"What's your name?" Miss Ferenczi asked.

"Wayne."

"Well, Wayne," she said, "you will undergo a *great* metamorphosis, the greatest, before you become an adult. Your earthly element will leap away, into thin air, you sweet boy. This card, this nine of swords here, tells of suffering and desolation. And this ten of wands, well, that's certainly a heavy load."

"What about this one?" Wayne pointed to the Death card.

"That one? That one means you will die soon, my dear." She gathered up the   130
cards. We were all looking at Wayne. "But do not fear," she said. "It's not really death,
so much as change." She put the cards on Mr. Hibler's desk. "And now, let's do some
arithmetic."

At lunchtime Wayne went to Mr. Faegre, the principal, and told him what Miss Ferenczi had done. During the noon recess, we saw Miss Ferenczi drive out of the parking lot in her green Rambler. I stood under the slide, listening to the other kids coasting down and landing in the little depressive bowl at the bottom. I was kicking stones and tugging at my hair right up to the moment when I saw Wayne come out to the playground. He smiled, the dead fool, and with the fingers of his right hand he was showing everyone how he had told on Miss Ferenczi.

I made my way toward Wayne, pushing myself past two girls from another class. He was watching me with his little pinhead eyes.

"You told," I shouted at him. "She was just kidding."

"She shouldn't have," he shouted back. "We were supposed to be doing arithmetic."

"She just scared you," I said. "You're a chicken. You're a chicken, Wayne. You are.   135
Scared of a little card," I singsonged.

Wayne fell at me, his two fists hammering down on my nose. I gave him a good one in the stomach and then I tried for his head. Aiming my fist, I saw that he was crying. I slugged him.

"She was right," I yelled. "She was always right! She told the truth!" Other kids were whooping. "You were just scared, that's all!"

And then large hands pulled at us, and it was my turn to speak to Mr. Faegre.

In the afternoon Miss Ferenczi was gone, and my nose was stuffed with cotton clotted with blood, and my lip had swelled, and our class had been combined with Mrs. Mantei's sixth-grade class for a crowded afternoon science unit on insect life in ditches and swamps. I knew where Mrs. Mantei lived: she had a new house trailer just down the road from us, at the Clearwater Park. She was no mystery. Somehow she and Mr. Bodine, the other fourth-grade teacher, had managed to fit forty-five desks into the room. Kelly Munger asked if Miss Ferenczi had been arrested, and Mrs. Mantei said no, of course not. All that afternoon, until the buses came to pick us up, we learned about field crickets and two-striped grasshoppers, water bugs, cicadas, mosquitoes, flies, and moths. We learned about insects' hard outer shell, the exoskeleton, and the usual parts of the mouth, including the labrum, mandible, maxilla, and glossa. We learned about compound eyes and the four-stage metamorphosis from egg to larva to pupa to adult. We learned something, but not much, about mating. Mrs. Mantei drew, very skillfully, the internal anatomy of the grasshopper on the blackboard. We learned about the dance of the honeybee, directing other bees in the hive to pollen. We found out about which insects were pests to man, and which were not. On lined white pieces of paper we made lists of insects we might actually see, then a list of insects too small to be clearly visible, such as fleas; Mrs. Mantei said that our assignment would be to memorize these lists for the next day, when Mr. Hibler would certainly return and test us on our knowledge.

QUESTIONS FOR CLOSE READING OF POINT OF VIEW

1.   Does the narrator sound like a typical fourth-grader? Can you believe that the narrator is a fourth-grader during the telling of this story, or did the narrator recall the events much later?

2.   What picture do you get of Miss Ferenczi through the eyes of the narrator? What do you observe about her that the narrator does not?

3.   Is the point of view omniscient or limited? Does the narrative seem subjective or objective?

4.   Is the narrator reliable or not? How would you support either position?

5.   How much do you know about the narrator? How would you characterize him?

QUESTIONS FOR INTERPRETATION OF POINT OF VIEW

1.   The question of truth in this story seems to depend on one's point of view. The story seems to comment on the nature of truth when Miss Ferenczi talks about facts and substitute facts. Mrs. Mantei has a different point of view when she talks about insects and provides the students with lists to memorize at the end of class. What kind of facts are they, and how do they differ from Miss Ferenczi's? Which character's point of view is more scientific? Which is more truthful? What comment does the story make on these distinctions? To what extent is the story itself a fact or substitute fact?

2.   To what extent is Miss Ferenczi's behavior typical of the teachers you had in the fourth grade? Is it possible that she is mentally unbalanced? If so, what is the narrator's reaction to her odd behavior? For example, she disregards accuracy in spelling and mathematics and she eats lunch with the children. She tells them that God kissed her. Is the gryphon a symbol of madness? Why is the detail of the mad scientist introduced? Was she wrong to tell Wayne he would die?

3. How do you react to Miss Ferenczi? Does the narrator give enough information for you to make a judgment distinct from his or do you feel compelled to accept his point of view? Would you have done what Wayne did at the end of the story if Miss Ferenczi had told your fortune and implied that you would die young? How do you react to a teacher who says there are substitute facts?

4. Consider your own experiences in grade school with substitute teachers. To what extent does this story rely upon your knowledge and your range of responses to the memory of fourth grade for its success? What unspoken playground ethics are at work in the story? Would someone who did not attend a grade school miss anything crucial to understanding this story?

5. The pool of substitute teachers consists of four housewives who went to community college. The narrator's regular teacher is a man. Do the students treat a woman substitute with the same respect they would a man substitute? Is Miss Ferenczi a feminist? Do you think that Miss Ferenczi's point of view in this story is more feminine than Mrs. Mantei's? Is demanding that there be only one set of facts (and no substitutes) a masculine view and not a feminine view?

6. Is there a marked social or cultural difference between Miss Ferenczi and the community she serves in the school? What differences of attitude and outlook seem to exist between them? Education can appeal to the world of facts or to the world of imagination, or both. What position does Miss Ferenczi take toward facts and imagination? Is it shared by the community? What does she awaken in the narrator that his earlier teachers did not?

FAY WELDON   (b. 1933)

Born in England, Fay Weldon now lives in Somerset and London. After a stint in advertising and television, she has had a prolific career writing novels, television scripts, and short stories. Her early work established her as a feminist writer who portrays the lives of women oppressed and manipulated by unworthy men. Novels such as The Fat Woman's Joke *(1967),* Down among the Women *(1971),* Female Friends *(1975), and* Rhode Island Blues *(2000) introduce us to men who want to have everything their own way and who give very little to the women in their lives.* Life and Loves of a She-Devil *(1984), one of her best-known works, details the revenge of a spurned wife on her husband and his mistress. One critic describes some of her male characters as candidates "for sarcastic entombment." Her collections of short stories include* Watching Me, Watching You *(1981),* Polaris and Other Stories *(1985), and* Moon over Minneapolis *(1992). Critic Carol Sternhell has said that Weldon "has been preserving women's lives in brittle, ironic prose; like a feminist Jane Austen, she has a sharp eye and tongue for the least romantic side of human relationships." Fay Weldon herself is as witty as her characters and appears much more tolerant of male foibles.*

Weekend _____ 1978

By seven-thirty they were ready to go. Martha had everything packed into the car and the three children appropriately dressed and in the back seat, complete with educational games and wholewheat biscuits. When everything was ready in the car Martin would switch off the television, come downstairs, lock up the house, front and back, and take the wheel.

Weekend! Only two hours' drive down to the cottage on Friday evenings: three hours' drive back on Sunday nights. The pleasures of greenery and guests in between. They reckoned themselves fortunate, how fortunate!

On Fridays Martha would get home on the bus at six-twelve and prepare tea and sandwiches for the family: then she would strip four beds and put the sheets and quilt covers in the washing machine for Monday: take the country bedding from the airing basket, plus the books and the games, plus the weekend food—acquired at intervals throughout the week, to lessen the load—plus her own folder of work from the office, plus Martin's drawing materials (she was a market researcher in an advertising agency, he a freelance designer) plus hairbrushes, jeans, spare T-shirts, Jolyon's antibiotics (he suffered from sore throats), Jenny's recorder, Jasper's cassette player, and so on— ah, the so on!—and would pack them all, skilfully and quickly, into the boot. Very little could be left in the cottage during the week. ("An open invitation to burglars": Martin) Then Martha would run round the house tidying and wiping, doing this and that, finding the cat at one neighbor's and delivering it to another, while the others ate their tea; and would usually, proudly, have everything finished by the time they had eaten their fill. Martin would just catch the BBC 2 news, while Martha cleared away the tea table, and the children tossed up for the best positions in the car. "Martha," said Martin, tonight, "you ought to get Mrs. Hodder to do more. She takes advantage of you."

Mrs. Hodder came in twice a week to clean. She was over seventy. She charged two pounds an hour. Martha paid her out of her own wages: well, the running of the house was Martha's concern. If Martha chose to go out to work—as was her perfect right, Martin allowed, even though it wasn't the best thing for the children, but that must be Martha's moral responsibility—Martha must surely pay her domestic stand-in. An evident truth, heard loud and clear and frequent in Martin's mouth and Martha's heart.

"I expect you're right," said Martha. She did not want to argue. Martin had had a long hard week, and now had to drive. Martha couldn't. Martha's license had been suspended four months back for drunken driving. Everyone agreed that the suspension was unfair: Martha seldom drank to excess: she was for one thing usually too busy pouring drinks for other people or washing other people's glasses to get much inside herself. But Martin had taken her out to dinner on her birthday, as was his custom, and exhaustion and excitement mixed had made her imprudent, and before she knew where she was, why there she was, in the dock, with a distorted lamppost to pay for and a new bonnet for the car and six months' suspension.

So now Martin had to drive her car down to the cottage, and he was always tired on Fridays, and hot and sleepy on Sundays, and every rattle and clank and bump in the engine she felt to be somehow her fault.

Martin had a little sports car for London and work: it could nip in and out of the traffic nicely: Martha's was an old estate car,° with room for the children, picnic baskets, bedding, food, games, plants, drink, portable television, and all the things required by the middle classes for weekends in the country. It lumbered rather than zipped and made Martin angry. He seldom spoke a harsh word, but Martha, after the fashion of wives, could detect his mood from what he did not say rather than what he did, and from the tilt of his head, and the way his crinkly, merry eyes seemed crinklier and merrier still—and of course from the way he addressed Martha's car.

estate car: station wagon

"Come along, you old banger you! Can't you do better than that? You're too old, that's your trouble. Stop complaining. Always complaining, it's only a hill. You're too wide about the hips. You'll never get through there."

Martha worried about her age, her tendency to complain, and the width of her hips. She took the remarks personally. Was she right to do so? The children noticed nothing: it was just funny lively laughing Daddy being witty about Mummy's car. Mummy, done for drunken driving. Mummy, with the roots of melancholy somewhere deep beneath the bustling, busy, everyday self. Busy: ah so busy!

Martin would only laugh if she said anything about the way he spoke to her car   10
and warn her against paranoia. "Don't get like your mother, darling." Martha's mother had, towards the end, thought that people were plotting against her. Martha's mother had led a secluded, suspicious life, and made Martha's childhood a chilly and a lonely time. Life now, by comparison, was wonderful for Martha. People, children, houses, conversations, food, drink, theatres—even, now, a career. Martin standing between her and the hostility of the world—popular, easy, funny Martin, beckoning the rest of the world into earshot.

Ah, she was grateful: little earnest Martha, with her shy ways and her penchant for passing boring exams—how her life had blossomed out! Three children too—Jasper, Jenny, and Jolyon—all with Martin's broad brow and open looks, and the confidence born of her love and care, and the work she had put into them since the dawning of their days.

Martin drives. Martha, for once, drowses.

The right food, the right words, the right play. Doctors for the tonsils: dentists for the molars. Confiscate guns: censor television: encourage creativity. Paints and paper to hand: books on the shelves: meetings with teachers. Music teachers. Dancing lessons. Parties. Friends to tea. School plays. Open days. Junior orchestra.

Martha is jolted awake. Traffic lights. Martin doesn't like Martha to sleep while he drives.

Clothes. Oh, clothes. Can't wear this: must wear that. Dress shops. Piles of clothes   15
in corners: duly washed, but waiting to be ironed, waiting to be put away.

Get the piles off the floor, into the laundry baskets. Martin doesn't like a mess.

Creativity arises out of order, not chaos. Five years off work while the children were small: back to work with seniority lost. What, did you think something was for nothing? If you have children, mother, that is your reward. It lies not in the world.

Have you taken enough food? Always hard to judge.

Food. Oh, food! Shop in the lunch-hour. Lug it all home. Cook for the freezer on Wednesday evenings while Martin is at his car-maintenance evening class, and isn't there to notice you being unrestful. Martin likes you to sit down in the evenings. Fruit, meat, vegetables, flour for home-made bread. Well, shop bread is full of pollutants. Frozen food, even your own, loses flavor. Martin often remarks on it. Condiments. Everyone loves mango chutney. But the expense!

London Airport to the left. Look, look, children! Concorde? No, idiot, of course   20
it isn't Concorde.

Ah, to be all things to all people: children, husband, employer, friends! It can be done: yes, it can: super woman.

Drink. Home-made wine. Why not? Elderberries grown thick and rich in London: and at least you know what's in it. Store it in high cupboards: lots of room: up and down the step-ladder. Careful! Don't slip. Don't break anything.

No such think as an accident. Accidents are Freudian slips: they are wilful, bad-tempered things.

Martin can't bear bad temper. Martin likes slim ladies. Diet. Martin rather likes his secretary. Diet. Martin admires slim legs and big bosoms. How to achieve them both? Impossible. But try, oh try, to be what you ought to be, not what you are. Inside and out.

Martin brings back flowers and chocolates: whisks Martha off for holiday week-   25
ends. Wonderful! The best husband in the world: look into his crinkly, merry, gentle eyes; see it there. So the mouth slopes away into something of a pout. Never mind. Gaze into the eyes. Love. It must be love. You married him. You. Surely *you* deserve true love?

Salisbury Plain. Stonehenge. Look, children, look! Mother, we've seen Stone-henge a hundred times. Go back to sleep.

Cook! Ah cook. People love to come to Martin and Martha's dinners. Work it out in your head in the lunch-hour. If you get in at six-twelve, you can seal the meat while you beat the egg white while you feed the cat while you lay the table while you string the beans while you set out the cheese, goat's cheese, Martin loves goat's cheese, Martha tries to like goat's cheese—oh, bed, sleep, peace, quiet.

Sex! Ah sex. Orgasm, please. Martin requires it. Well, so do you. And you don't want his secretary providing a passion you neglected to develop. Do you? Quick, quick, the cosmic bond. Love. Married love.

Secretary! Probably a vulgar suspicion: nothing more. Probably a fit of paranoics, à la mother, now dead and gone.

At peace.   30
R.I.P.°
Chilly, lonely mother, following her suspicions where they led.

Nearly there, children. Nearly in paradise, nearly at the cottage. Have another biscuit.

Real roses round the door.

Roses. Prune, weed, spray, feed, pick. Avoid thorns. One of Martin's few harsh words.   35

"Martha, you can't not want roses! What kind of person am I married to? An anti-rose personality?"

Green grass. Oh, God, grass. Grass must be mown. Restful lawns, daisies bobbing, buttercups glowing. Roses and grass and books. Books.

Please, Martin, do we have to have the two hundred books, mostly twenties' first edi-tions, bought at Christie's book sale on one of your afternoons off? Books need dusting.

Roars of laughter from Martin, Jasper, Jenny, and Jolyon. Mummy says we shouldn't have the books: books need dusting!

Roses, green grass, books, and peace.   40

Martha woke up with a start when they got to the cottage, and gave a little shriek which made them all laugh. Mummy's waking shriek, they called it.

Then there was the car to unpack and the beds to make up, and the electricity to connect, and the supper to make, and the cobwebs to remove, while Martin made the fire. Then supper—pork chops in sweet and sour sauce ("Pork is such a *dull* meat if you don't cook it properly": Martin), green salad from the garden, or such green salad as the rabbits had left ("Martha, did you really net them properly? Be honest, now!": Mar-tin), and sauté potatoes. Mash is so stodgy and ordinary, and instant mash unthinkable. The children studied the night sky with the aid of their star map. Wonderful, reward-ing children!

Then clear up the supper: set the dough to prove for the bread: Martin already in bed: exhausted by the drive and lighting the fire. ("Martha, we really ought to get the

R.I.P.: rest in peace

logs stacked properly. Get the children to do it, will you?": Martin) Sweep and tidy: get the TV aerial right. Turn up Jasper's jeans where he has trodden the hem undone. ("He can't go around like *that*, Martha. Not even Jasper": Martin)

Midnight. Good night. Weekend guests arriving in the morning. Seven for lunch and dinner on Saturday. Seven for Sunday breakfast, nine for Sunday lunch. ("Don't fuss, darling. You always make such a fuss": Martin) Oh, God, forgotten the garlic squeezer. That means ten minutes with the back of a spoon and salt. Well, who wants *lumps* of garlic? No one. Not Martin's guests. Martin said so. Sleep.

Colin and Katie. Colin is Martin's oldest friend. Katie is his new young wife. Janet,   45
Colin's other, earlier wife, was Martha's friend. Janet was rather like Martha, quieter and duller than her husband. A nag and a drag, Martin rather thought, and said, and of course she'd let herself go, everyone agreed. No one exactly excused Colin for walking out, but you could see the temptation.

Katie versus Janet.

Katie was languid, beautiful, and elegant. She drawled when she spoke. Her hands were expressive: her feet were little and female. She had no children.

Janet plodded round on very flat, rather large feet. There was something wrong with them. They turned out slightly when she walked. She had two children. She was, frankly, boring. But Martha liked her: when Janet came down to the cottage she would wash up. Not in the way that most guests washed up—washing dutifully and setting everything out on the draining board, but actually drying and putting away too. And Janet would wash the bath and get the children all sat down, with chairs for everyone, even the littlest, and keep them quiet and satisfied so the grown-ups—well, the men—could get on with their conversation and their jokes and their love of country weekends, while Janet stared into space, as if grateful for the rest, quite happy.

Janet would garden, too. Weed the strawberries, while the men went for their walk; her great feet standing firm and square and sometimes crushing a plant or so, but never mind, oh never mind. Lovely Janet; who understood.

Now Janet was gone and here was Katie.   50

Katie talked with the men and went for walks with the men, and moved her ashtray rather impatiently when Martha tried to clear the drinks round it.

Dishes were boring, Katie implied by her manner, and domesticity was boring, and anyone who bothered with that kind of thing was a fool. Like Martha. Ash should be allowed to stay where it was, even if it was in the butter, and conversations should never be interrupted.

Knock, knock. Katie and Colin arrived at one-fifteen on Saturday morning, just after Martha had got to bed. "You don't mind? It was the moonlight. We couldn't resist it. You should have seen Stonehenge! We didn't disturb you? Such early birds!"

Martha rustled up a quick meal of omelettes. Saturday night's eggs. ("Martha makes a lovely omelette": Martin) ("Honey, make one of your mushroom omelettes: cook the mushrooms separately, remember, with lemon. Otherwise the water from the mushrooms gets into the egg, and spoils everything.") Sunday supper mushrooms. But ungracious to say anything.

Martin had revived wonderfully at the sight of Colin and Katie. He brought out   55
the whisky bottle. Glasses. Ice. Jug for water. Wait. Wash up another sinkful, when they're finished. 2 A.M.

"Don't do it tonight, darling."

"It'll only take a sec." Bright smile, not a hint of self-pity. Self-pity can spoil everyone's weekend.

Martha knows that if breakfast for seven is to be manageable the sink must be cleared of dishes. A tricky meal, breakfast. Especially if bacon, eggs, and tomatoes must all be cooked in separate pans. ("Separate pans means separate flavors!": Martin)

She is running around in her nightie. Now if that had been Katie—but there's something so *practical* about Martha. Reassuring, mind; but the skimpy nightie and the broad rump and the thirty-eight years are all rather embarrassing. Martha can see it in Colin and Katie's eyes. Martin's too. Martha wishes she did not see so much in other people's eyes. Her mother did, too. Dear, dead mother. Did I misjudge you?

This was the second weekend Katie had been down with Colin but without Janet.   60
Colin was a photographer: Katie had been his accessorizer. First Colin and Janet: then Colin, Janet, and Katie: now Colin and Katie!

Katie weeded with rubber gloves on and pulled out pansies in mistake for weeds and laughed and laughed along with everyone when her mistake was pointed out to her, but the pansies died. Well, Colin had become with the years fairly rich and fairly famous, and what does a fairly rich and famous man want with a wife like Janet when Katie is at hand?

On the first of the Colin/Janet/Katie weekends Katie had appeared out of the bathroom. "I say," said Katie, holding out a damp towel with evident distaste, "I can only find this. No hope of a dry one?" And Martha had run to fetch a dry towel and amazingly found one, and handed it to Katie who flashed her a brilliant smile and said, "I can't bear damp towels. Anything in the world but damp towels," as if speaking to a servant in a time of shortage of staff, and took all the water so there was none left for Martha to wash up.

The trouble, of course, was drying anything at all in the cottage. There were no facilities for doing so, and Martin had a horror of clothes lines which might spoil the view. He toiled and moiled all week in the city simply to get a country view at the weekend. Ridiculous to spoil it by draping it with wet towels! But now Martha had bought more towels, so perhaps everyone could be satisfied. She would take nine damp towels back on Sunday evenings in a plastic bag and see to them in London.

On this Saturday morning, straight after breakfast, Katie went out to the car— she and Colin had a new Lamborghini; hard to imagine Katie in anything duller—and came back waving a new Yves St. Laurent towel. "See! I brought my own, darlings."

They'd brought nothing else. No fruit, no meat, no vegetables, not even bread,   65
certainly not a box of chocolates. They'd gone off to bed with alacrity, the night before, and the spare room rocked and heaved: well, who'd want to do washing-up when you could do that, but what about the children? Would they get confused? First Colin and Janet, now Colin and Katie?

Martha murmured something of her thoughts to Martin, who looked quite shocked. "Colin's my best friend. I don't expect him to bring anything," and Martha felt mean. "And good heavens, you can't protect the kids from sex for ever, don't be so prudish," so that Martha felt stupid as well. Mean, complaining, and stupid.

Janet had rung Martha during the week. The house had been sold over her head, and she and the children had been moved into a small flat. Katie was trying to persuade Colin to cut down on her allowance, Janet said.

"It does one no good to be materialistic," Katie confided. "I have nothing. No home, no family, no ties, no possessions. Look at me! Only me and a suitcase of clothes." But Katie seemed highly satisfied with the me, and the clothes were stupendous. Katie drank a great deal and became funny. Everyone laughed, including Martha. Katie had been married twice. Martha marvelled at how someone could arrive in their mid-thirties with nothing at all to their name, neither husband, nor children, nor property and not mind.

Mind you, Martha could see the power of such helplessness. If Colin was all Katie had in the world, how could Colin abandon her? And to what? Where would she go? How would she live? Oh, clever Katie.

"My teacup's dirty," said Katie, and Martha ran to clean it, apologizing, and Martin raised his eyebrows, at Martha, not Katie. 70

"I wish *you'd* wear scent," said Martin to Martha, reproachfully. Katie wore lots. Martha never seemed to have time to put any on, though Martin bought her bottle after bottle. Martha leapt out of bed each morning to meet some emergency—miaowing cat, coughing child, faulty alarm clock, postman's knock—when was Martha to put on scent? It annoyed Martin all the same. She ought to do more to charm him.

Colin looked handsome and harrowed and younger than Martin, though they were much the same age. "Youth's catching," said Martin in bed that night. "It's nice he found Katie." Found, like some treasure. Discovered; something exciting and wonderful, in the dreary world of established spouses.

On Saturday morning Jasper trod on a piece of wood ("Martha, why isn't he wearing shoes? It's too bad": Martin) and Martha took him into the hospital to have a nasty splinter removed. She left the cottage at ten and arrived back at one, and they were still sitting in the sun, drinking, empty bottles glinting in the long grass. The grass hadn't been cut. Don't forget the bottles. Broken glass means more mornings at the hospital. Oh, don't fuss. Enjoy yourself. Like other people. Try.

But no potatoes peeled, no breakfast cleared, nothing. Cigarette ends still amongst old toast, bacon rind, and marmalade. "You could have done the potatoes," Martha burst out. Oh, bad temper! Prime sin. They looked at her in amazement and dislike. Martin too.

"Goodness," said Katie. "Are we doing the whole Sunday lunch bit on Saturday? Potatoes! Ages since I've eaten potatoes. Wonderful!" 75

"The children expect it," said Martha.

So they did. Saturday and Sunday lunch shone like reassuring beacons in their lives. Saturday lunch: family lunch: fish and chips. ("So much better cooked at home than bought": Martin) Sunday. Usually roast beef, potatoes, peas, apple pie. Oh, of course. Yorkshire pudding. Always a problem with oven temperatures. When the beef's going slowly, the Yorkshire should be going fast. How to achieve that? Like big bosom and little hips.

"Just relax," said Martin. "I'll cook dinner, all in good time. Splinters always work their own way out: no need to have taken him to hospital. Let life drift over you, my love. Flow with the waves, that's the way."

And Martin flashed Martha a distant, spiritual smile. His hand lay on Katie's slim brown arm, with its many gold bands.

"Anyway, you do too much for the children," said Martin. "It isn't good for them. 80 Have a drink."

So Martha perched uneasily on the step and had a glass of cider, and wondered how, if lunch was going to be late, she would get cleared up and the meat out of the marinade for the rather formal dinner that would be expected that evening. The marinaded lamb ought to cook for at least four hours in a low oven; and the cottage oven was very small, and you couldn't use that and the grill at the same time and Martin liked his fish grilled, not fried. Less cholesterol.

She didn't say as much. Domestic details like this were very boring, and any mild complaint was registered by Martin as a scene. And to make a scene was so ungrateful.

This was the life. Well, wasn't it? Smart friends in large cars and country living and drinks before lunch and roses and bird song—"Don't drink too much," said Martin, and told them about Martha's suspended driving licence.

The children were hungry so Martha opened them a can of beans and sausages and heated that up. ("Martha, do they have to eat that crap? Can't they wait?": Martin)

Katie was hungry: she said so, to keep the children in face. She was lovely with children—most children. She did not particularly like Colin and Janet's children. She said so, and he accepted it. He only saw them once a month now, not once a week.

"Let me make lunch," Katie said to Martha. "You do so much, poor thing!"

And she pulled out of the fridge all the things Martha had put away for the next day's picnic lunch party—Camembert cheese and salad and salami and made a wonderful tomato salad in two minutes and opened the white wine—"Not very cold, darling. Shouldn't it be chilling?"—and had it all on the table in five amazing competent minutes. "That's all we need, darling," said Martin. "You are funny with your fish-and-chip Saturdays! What could be nicer than this? Or simpler?"

Nothing, except there was Sunday's buffet lunch for nine gone, in place of Saturday's fish for six, and would the fish stretch? No. Katie had had quite a lot to drink. She pecked Martha on the forehead. "Funny little Martha," she said. "She reminds me of Janet. I really do like Janet." Colin did not want to be reminded of Janet, and said so. "Darling, Janet's a fact of life," said Katie. "If you'd only think about her more, you might manage to pay her less." And she yawned and stretched her lean, childless body and smiled at Colin with her inviting, naughty little girl eyes, and Martin watched her in admiration.

Martha got up and left them and took a paint pot and put a coat of white gloss on the bathroom wall. The white surface pleased her. She was good at painting. She produced a smooth, even surface. Her legs throbbed. She feared she might be getting varicose veins.

Outside in the garden the children played badminton. They were bad-tempered, but relieved to be able to look up and see their mother working, as usual: making their lives forever better and nicer: organizing, planning, thinking ahead, side-stepping disaster, making preparations, like a mother hen, fussing and irritating: part of the natural boring scenery of the world.

On Saturday night Katie went to bed early: she rose from her chair and stretched and yawned and poked her head into the kitchen where Martha was washing saucepans. Colin had cleared the table and Katie had folded the napkins into pretty creases, while Martin blew at the fire, to make it bright. "Good night," said Katie.

Katie appeared three minutes later, reproachfully holding out her Yves St. Laurent towel, sopping wet. "Oh dear," cried Martha. "Jenny must have washed her hair!" And Martha was obliged to rout Jenny out of bed to rebuke her, publicly, if only to demonstrate that she knew what was right and proper. That meant Jenny would sulk all weekend, and that meant a treat or an outing mid-week, or else by the following week she'd be having an asthma attack. "You fuss the children too much," said Martin. "That's why Jenny has asthma." Jenny was pleasant enough to look at, but not stunning. Perhaps she was a disappointment to her father? Martin would never say so, but Martha feared he thought so.

An egg and an orange each child, each day. Then nothing too bad would go wrong. And it hadn't. The asthma was very mild. A calm, tranquil environment, the doctor said. Ah, smile, Martha smile. Domestic happiness depends on you. 21×52 oranges a year. Each one to be purchased, carried, peeled, and washed up after. And what about potatoes. 12×52 pounds a year? Martin liked his potatoes carefully peeled. He couldn't bear to find little cores of black in the mouthful. ("Well, it isn't very nice, is it?": Martin)

Martha dreamt she was eating coal, by handfuls, and liking it.

Saturday night. Martin made love to Martha three times. Three times? How virile he was, and clearly turned on by the sounds from the spare room. Martin said he loved her. Martin always did. He was a courteous lover; he knew the importance of foreplay. So did Martha. Three times.

Ah, sleep. Jolyon had a nightmare. Jenny was woken by a moth. Martin slept through everything. Martha pottered about the house in the night. There was a moon. She sat at the window and stared out into the summer night for five minutes, and was at peace, and then went back to bed because she ought to be fresh for the morning.

But she wasn't. She slept late. The others went out for a walk. They'd left a note, a considerate note: "Didn't wake you. You looked tired. Had a cold breakfast so as not to make too much mess. Leave everything 'til we get back." But it was ten o'clock, and guests were coming at noon, so she cleared away the bread, the butter, the crumbs, the smears, the jam, the spoons, the spilt sugar, the cereal, the milk (sour by now) and the dirty plates, and swept the floors, and tidied up quickly, and grabbed a cup of coffee, and prepared to make a rice and fish dish, and a chocolate mousse and sat down in the middle to eat a lot of bread and jam herself. Broad hips. She remembered the office work in her file and knew she wouldn't be able to do it. Martin anyway thought it was ridiculous for her to bring work back at the weekends. "It's your holiday," he'd say. "Why should they impose?" Martha loved her work. She didn't have to smile at it. She just did it.

Katie came back upset and crying. She sat in the kitchen while Martha worked and drank glass after glass of gin and bitter lemon. Katie liked ice and lemon in gin. Martha paid for all the drink out of her wages. It was part of the deal between her and Martin— the contract by which she went out to work. All things to cheer the spirit, otherwise depressed by working wife and mother, were to be paid for by Martha. Drink, holidays, petrol, outings, puddings, electricity, heating: it was quite a joke between them. It didn't really make any difference: it was their joint money, after all. Amazing how Martha's wages were creeping up, almost to the level of Martin's. One day they would overtake. Then what?

Work, honestly, was a piece of cake.

Anyway, poor Katie was crying. Colin, she'd discovered, kept a photograph of Janet and the children in his wallet. "He's not free of her. He pretends he is, but he isn't. She has him by a stranglehold. It's the kids. His bloody kids. Moaning Mary and that little creep Joanna. It's all he thinks about. I'm nobody."

But Katie didn't believe it. She knew she was somebody all right. Colin came in, in a fury. He took out the photograph and set fire to it, bitterly, with a match. Up in smoke they went. Mary and Joanna and Janet. The ashes fell on the floor. (Martha swept them up when Colin and Katie had gone. It hardly seemed polite to do so when they were still there.) "Go back to her," Katie said. "Go back to her. I don't care. Honestly, I'd rather be on my own. You're a nice old fashioned thing. Run along then. Do your thing, I'll do mine. Who cares?"

"Christ, Katie, the fuss! She only just happens to be in the photograph. She's not there on purpose to annoy. And I do feel bad about her. She's been having a hard time."

"And haven't you, Colin? She twists a pretty knife, I can tell you. Don't you have rights too? Not to mention me. Is a little loyalty too much to expect?"

They were reconciled before lunch, up in the spare room. Harry and Beryl Elder arrived at twelve-thirty. Harry didn't like to hurry on Sundays; Beryl was flustered with apologies for their lateness. They'd brought artichokes from their garden. "Wonderful," cried Martin. "Fruits of the earth? Let's have a wonderful soup! Don't fret, Martha. I'd do it."

"Don't fret." Martha clearly hadn't been smiling enough. She was in danger, Martin implied, of ruining everyone's weekend. There was an emergency in the garden very shortly—an elm tree which had probably got Dutch elm disease—and Martha finished the artichokes. The lid flew off the blender and there was artichoke purée everywhere. "Let's have lunch outside," said Colin. "Less work for Martha."

Martin frowned at Martha: he thought the appearance of martyrdom in the face of guests to be an unforgivable offense.

Everyone happily joined in taking the furniture out, but it was Martha's experience that nobody ever helped to bring it in again. Jolyon was stung by a wasp. Jasper sneezed and sneezed from hay fever and couldn't find the tissues and he wouldn't use loo paper. ("Surely you remembered the tissues, darling?": Martin)

Beryl Elder was nice. "Wonderful to eat out," she said, fetching the cream for her pudding, while Martha fished a fly from the liquefying Brie ("You shouldn't have bought it so ripe, Martha": Martin)—"except it's just some other woman has to do it. But at least it isn't *me*." Beryl worked too, as a secretary, to send the boys to boarding school, where she'd rather they weren't. But her husband was from a rather grand family, and she'd been only a typist when he married her, so her life was a mass of amends, one way or another. Harry had lately opted out of the stockbroking rat race and become an artist, choosing integrity rather than money, but that choice was his alone and couldn't of course be inflicted on the boys.

Katie found the fish and rice dish rather strange, toyed at it with her fork, and talked about Italian restaurants she knew. Martin lay back soaking in the sun: crying, "Oh, this is the life." He made coffee, nobly, and the lid flew off the grinder and there were coffee beans all over the kitchen especially in amongst the row of cookery books which Martin gave Martha Christmas by Christmas. At least they didn't have to be brought back every weekend. ("The burglars won't have the sense to steal those": Martin)

Beryl fell asleep and Katie watched her, quizzically. Beryl's mouth was open and she had a lot of fillings, and her ankles were thick and her waist was going, and she didn't look after herself. "I love women," sighed Katie. "They look so wonderful asleep. I wish I could be an earth mother."

Beryl woke with a start and nagged her husband into going home, which he clearly didn't want to do, so didn't. Beryl thought she had to get back because his mother was coming round later. Nonsense! Then Beryl tried to stop Harry drinking more homemade wine and was laughed at by everyone. He was driving. Beryl couldn't, and he did have a nasty scar on his temple from a previous road accident. Never mind.

"She does come on strong, poor soul," laughed Katie when they'd finally gone. "I'm never going to get married,"—and Colin looked at her yearningly because he wanted to marry her more than anything in the world, and Martha cleared the coffee cups.

"Oh don't *do* that," said Katie, "do just sit *down,* Martha, you make us all feel bad," and Martin glared at Martha who sat down and Jenny called out for her and Martha went upstairs and Jenny had started her first period and Martha cried and cried and knew she must stop because this must be a joyous occasion for Jenny or her whole future would be blighted, but for once, Martha couldn't.

Her daughter Jenny: wife, mother, friend.

QUESTIONS FOR CLOSE READING OF POINT OF VIEW

1. What is the weekend routine for Martha and Martin? Who gets everyone ready?
2. Compare Martha's and Martin's household responsibilities.
3. What do the middle classes require for weekends in the country?
4. What kinds of comments does Martin make on their drives? Why do they unsettle Martha?
5. What does Martin like?
6. Whose guests come to the house on the weekend?
7. Why is cooking breakfast on the weekend so complex?
8. What do the guests bring with them for the weekend?
9. Why does Martha have a suspended driver's license?
10. How do the children react to seeing their mother working?
11. What does Martha pay for out of her earnings? And why?
12. Why does Martha cry when her daughter Jenny "start[s] her first period"?

QUESTIONS FOR INTERPRETATION OF POINT OF VIEW

1. Examine the point of view in this story. It is essentially third person, but it is not as restricted as in Charles Baxter's "Gryphon." The narrator tells us things that happen out of chronological order, such as the comments made by Martin earlier in time, especially those that criticize Martha. What insights into the situations of these characters does this technique make possible?

2. Fay Weldon is well known as a feminist author. Is this story a feminist story? Does it foreground the inequalities of the relationship of men and women, of husband and wife? How do other women relate to Martha during the weekend meals? Do they have the same expectations that she has? Is Martha afraid that her daughter Jenny will grow up to be like her?

3. What kind of reaction do you suppose Fay Weldon hoped you would have to this story? Do you feel that she would want you to be sympathetic to Martha, or do you feel that she wants you to think Martha gets what she deserves? How do you react to Martin's demand that Martha entertain all his guests during the weekend, take care of the meals and children, and then not do the weekend work she brought along on the grounds that she was on "holiday"? Do you think most readers would react as you do?

4. This is described as a middle-class English family. What seem to be the economic circumstances of this family? How does the fact that both Martin and Martha work at income-producing jobs affect the way they conduct the rest of their lives? Who in this family seems to have the most economic freedom? What objects or activities in this story underscore those freedoms?

5. How does the point of view restrict our understanding of the sexual relations between Martin and Martha? How does it reveal the sexual behavior of the weekend guests? How important is sex in this story? How important is it in the lives of these characters?

BECKY BIRTHA (b. 1948)

Becky Birtha has two collections of short stories: For Nights like This One: Stories of Loving Women and Lovers' Choice. *Her collection* The Forbidden Poems *appeared in 1991. Her work has appeared in feminist and other literary journals, and in Terry Macmillan's anthology* Breaking Ice *(1991), a collection of new black writing by young writers. Birtha currently lives in Philadelphia, where she is working on a novel.*

Johnnieruth _____ *1991*

Summertime. Nighttime. Talk about steam heat. This whole city get like the bathroom when somebody in there taking a shower with the door shut. Nights like that, can't nobody sleep. Everybody be outside, sitting on they steps or else dragging half they furniture out on the sidewalk—kitchen chairs, card tables—even bringing TVs outside.

Womenfolks, mostly. All the grown women around my way look just the same. They all big—stout. They got big bosoms and big hips and fat legs, and they always wearing runover house shoes and them shapeless, flowered numbers with the buttons down the front. 'Cept on Sunday. Sunday morning they all turn into glamour girls, in them big hats and long gloves, with they skinny high heels and they skinny selves in them tight girdles—wouldn't nobody ever know what they look like the rest of the time.

When I was a little kid, I didn't wanna grow up, 'cause I never wanted to look like them ladies. I heard Miz Jenkins down the street one time say she don't mind being fat 'cause that way her husband don't get so jealous. She say it's more than one way to keep a man. Me, I don't have me no intentions of keeping no man. I never understood why they was in so much demand anyway, when it seem like all a woman can depend on 'em for is making sure she keep on having babies.

We got enough children in my neighborhood. In the summertime even the little kids allowed to stay up till eleven or twelve o'clock at night—playing in the street and hollering and carrying on—don't never seem to get tired. Don't nobody care, long as they don't fight.

Me—I don't hang around no front steps no more. Hot nights like that, I get out my ten-speed and I be gone.

5

That's what I like to do more than anything else in the whole world. Feel that wind in my face keeping me cool as a air conditioner, shooting along like a snowball. My bike light as a kite. I can really get up some speed.

All the guys around my way got ten-speed bikes. Some of the girls got 'em, too, but they don't ride 'em at night. They pedal around during the day; but at nighttime they just hang around out front, watching babies and running they mouth. I didn't get my Peugeot° to be no conversation piece.

My mama don't like me to ride at night. I tried to point out to her that she ain't never said nothing to my brothers, and Vincent a year younger than me. (And Langston two years older, in case "old" is the problem.) She say, "That's different, Johnnieruth. You're a girl." Now I wanna know how is anybody gonna know that. I'm skinny as a knifeblade turned sideways, and all I ever wear is blue jeans and a Wrangler jacket. But if I bring that up, she liable to get started in on how come I can't be more of a young

Peugeot: a French-made bicycle

lady, and fourteen is old enough to start taking more pride in my appearance, and she gonna be ashamed to admit I'm her daughter.

I just tell her that my bike be moving so fast can't nobody hardly see me, and couldn't catch me if they did. Mama complain to her friends how I'm wild and she can't do nothing with me. She know I'm gonna do what I want no matter what she say. But she know I ain't getting in no trouble, neither.

Like some of the boys I know stole they bikes, but I didn't do nothing like that.   10 I'd been saving my money ever since I can remember, every time I could get a nickel or a dime outta anybody.

When I was a little kid, it was hard to get money. Seem like the only time they ever give you any was on Sunday morning, and then you had to put it in the offering. I used to hate to do that. In fact, I used to hate everything about Sunday morning. I had to wear all them ruffly dresses—that shiny slippery stuff in the wintertime that got to make a noise every time you move your ass a inch on them hard old benches. And that scratchy starchy stuff in the summertime with all them scratchy crinolines. Had to carry a pocketbook and wear them shiny shoes. And the church we went to was all the way over on Summit Avenue, so the whole damn neighborhood could get a good look. At least all the other kids'd be dressed the same way. The boys think they slick 'cause they get to wear pants, but they still got to wear a white shirt and a tie; and them dumb hats they wear can't hide them baldheaded haircuts, 'cause they got to take the hats off in church.

There was one Sunday when I musta been around eight. I remember it was before my sister Corletta was born, 'cause right around then was when I put my foot down about that whole sanctimonious routine. Anyway, I was dragging my feet along Twenty-fifth Street in back of Mama and Vincent and them, when I spied this lady. I only seen her that one time, but I still remember just how she look. She don't look like nobody I ever seen before. I *know* she don't live around here. She real skinny. But she ain't no real young woman, neither. She could be old as my mama. She ain't nobody's mama—I'm sure. And she ain't wearing Sunday clothes. She got on blue jeans and a man's blue working shirt, with the tail hanging out. She got patches on her blue jeans, and she still got her chin stuck out like she some kinda African royalty. She ain't carrying no shiny pocketbook. It don't look like she care if she got any money or not, or who know it, if she don't. She ain't wearing no house shoes, or stockings or high heels neither.

Mama always speak to everybody, but when she pass by this lady she make like she ain't even seen her. But I get me a real good look, and the lady stare right back at me. She got a funny look on her face, almost like she think she know me from someplace. After she pass on by, I had to turn around to get another look, even though Mama say that ain't polite. And you know what? She was turning around, too, looking back at me. And she give me a great big smile.

I didn't know too much in them days, but that's when I first got to thinking about how it's got to be different ways to be, from the way people be around my way. It's got to be places where it don't matter to nobody if you all dressed up on Sunday morning or you ain't. That's how come I started saving money. So, when I got enough, I could go away to someplace like that.

Afterwhile I begun to see there wasn't no point in waiting around for handouts,   15 and I started thinking of ways to earn my own money. I used to be running errands all the time—mailing letters for old Grandma Whittaker and picking up cigarettes and newspapers up the corner for everybody. After I got bigger, I started washing cars in the summer, and shoveling people sidewalk in the wintertime. Now I got me a newspaper route. Ain't never been no girl around here with no paper route, but I guess everybody got it figured out by now that I ain't gonna be like nobody else.

The reason I got me my Peugeot was so I could start to explore. I figured I better start looking around right now, so when I'm grown, I'll know exactly where I wanna go. So I ride around every chance I get.

Last summer I used to ride with the boys a lot. Sometimes eight or ten of us'd just go cruising around the streets together. All of a sudden my mama decide she don't want me to do that no more. She say I'm too old to be spending so much time with boys. (That's what they tell you half the time, and the other half the time they worried 'cause you ain't interested in spending more time with boys. Don't make much sense.) She want me to have some girl friends, but I never seem to fit in with none of the things the girls doing. I used to think I fit in more with the boys.

But I seen how Mama might be right, for once. I didn't like the way the boys was starting to talk about girls sometimes. Talking about what some girl be like from the neck on down, and talking all up underneath somebody clothes and all. Even though I wasn't really friends with none of the girls, I still didn't like it. So now I mostly just ride around by myself. And Mama don't like that neither—you just can't please her.

This boy that live around the corner on North Street, Kenny Henderson, started asking me one time if I don't ever be lonely, 'cause he always see me by myself. He say don't I ever think I'd like to have me somebody special to go places with and stuff. Like I'd pick him if I did! Made me wanna laugh in his face. I do be lonely, a lotta times, but I don't tell nobody. And I ain't met nobody yet that I'd really rather be with than be by myself. But I will someday. When I find that special place where everybody different, I'm gonna find somebody there I can be friends with. And it ain't gonna be no dumb boy.

I found me one place already that I like to go to a whole lot. It ain't even really that far away—by bike—but it's on the other side of the Avenue. So I don't tell Mama and them I go there, 'cause they like to think I'm right around the neighborhood someplace. But this neighborhood too dull for me. All the houses look just the same—no porches, no yards, no trees—not even no parks around here. Every block look so much like every other block it hurt your eyes to look at afterwhile. So I ride across Summit Avenue and go down that big steep hill there, and then make a sharp right at the bottom and cross the bridge over the train tracks. Then I head on out the boulevard—that's the nicest part, with all them big trees making a tunnel over the top, and lightning bugs shining in the bushes. At the end of the boulevard you get to this place call the Plaza.

It's something like a little park—the sidewalks is all bricks and they got flowers planted all over the place. The same kind my mama grow in that painted-up tire she got out front masquerading like a garden decoration—only seem like they smell sweeter here. It's a big high fountain right in the middle, and all the streetlights is the real old-fashion kind. That Plaza is about the prettiest place I ever been.

Sometimes something going on there. Like a orchestra playing music or some man or lady singing. One time they had a show with some girls doing some kinda foreign dances. They look like they were around my age. They all had on these fancy costumes, with different color ribbons all down they back. I wouldn't wear nothing like that, but it looked real pretty when they was dancing.

I got me a special bench in one corner where I like to sit, 'cause I can see just about everything, but wouldn't nobody know I was there. I like to sit still and think, and I like to watch people. A lotta people be coming there at night—to look at the shows and stuff, or just to hang out and cool off. All different kinda people.

This one night when I was sitting over in that corner where I always be at, there was this lady standing right near my bench. She mostly had her back turned to me and she didn't know I was there, but I could see her real good. She had on this shiny purple shirt and about a million silver bracelets. I kinda liked the way she look. Sorta exotic, like she maybe come from California or one of the islands. I mean she had class—standing there posing with her arms folded. She walk away a little bit. Then turn around and walk back again. Like she waiting for somebody.

Then I spotted this dude coming over. I spied him all the way 'cross the Plaza. Looking real fine. Got on a three-piece suit. One of them little caps sitting on a angle. Look like leather. He coming straight over to this lady I'm watching and then she seen him, too, and she start to smile, but she don't move till he get right up next to her. And then I'm gonna look away, 'cause I can't stand to watch nobody hugging and kissing on each other, but all of a sudden I see it ain't no dude at all. It's another lady.

Now I can't stop looking. They smiling at each other like they ain't seen one another in ten years. Then the one in the purple shirt look around real quick—but she don't look just behind her—and sorta pull the other one right back into the corner where I'm sitting at, and then they put they arms around each other and kiss—for a whole long time. Now I really know I oughtta turn away, but I can't. And I know they gonna see me when they finally open they eyes. And they do.

They both kinda gasp and back up, like I'm the monster that just rose up outta the deep. And then I guess they can see I'm only a girl, and they look at one another—and start to laugh! Then they just turn around and start to walk away like it wasn't nothing at all. But right before they gone, they both look around again, and see I still ain't got my eye muscles and my jaw muscles working right again yet. And the one lady wink at me. And the other one say, "Catch you later."

I can't stop staring at they backs, all the way across the Plaza. And then, all of a sudden, I feel like I got to be doing something, got to be moving.

I wheel on outta the Plaza and I'm just concentrating on getting up my speed. 'Cause I can't figure out what to think. Them two women kissing and then, when they get caught, just laughing about it. And here I'm laughing, too, for no reason at all. I'm sailing down the boulevard laughing like a lunatic, and then I'm singing at the top of my lungs. And climbing that big old hill up to Summit Avenue is just as easy as being on a escalator.

QUESTIONS FOR CLOSE READING OF POINT OF VIEW

1. What can you tell about the narrator from her name?
2. The point of view is first person, with Johnnieruth remembering "when I was a kid." How convinced are you that her memory is reliable?
3. Does Johnnieruth seem to be a reliable narrator? Do you believe her and do you sympathize with her?
4. What does she think of the women in her neighborhood when she "was a kid"?
5. What does she fear will be her future?
6. Why does she think it is unimportant to keep hold of a man?
7. What is the difference in the way her mother treats her and her brothers?
8. Why does Johnnieruth hate Sunday morning?
9. Why does Johnnieruth begin saving her money?

10. What does Johnnieruth not like about the way boys talked about girls?
11. What does Johnnieruth learn when she sees the woman who seems to be dressed like a man come over and sit next to a woman?

QUESTIONS FOR INTERPRETATION OF POINT OF VIEW

1. How does the point of view control the way the story is told? Does Johnnieruth unfold the story in anything close to a chronological order, or does she simply group events in terms of their significance to her?

2. What is the symbolic value of Johnnieruth's saving her money and buying a Peugeot bicycle? What does the bicycle permit her to do? How does it contribute to changing her life? Is there any comparison to be made between the way the story is told and the way the bicycle permits her to roam through the city? How does the bicycle free Johnnieruth?

3. How well do you get to know Johnnieruth in the course of the story? Since no one really comments on her or says anything to her that would reveal her character, you need to rely entirely on what she observes and what she reports. Do you get a good sense of her voice as you read the story? Do you feel you understand who she is?

4. The narrative aims at the moment when Johnnieruth sees two women "kiss for a whole long time." Do you think this implies that Johnnieruth has come to understand something about her own sexuality? Do you feel that Johnnieruth has learned that she is a lesbian? If that is true, what else in the story reinforces that view? Does her development and growing awareness seem reasonable to you?

5. What kind of emotional reaction do you think Becky Birtha expects you to have to this story? What kind of emotional reaction do you actually have? What details in the story seem to prepare you for the reaction you had? What range of reactions can you imagine in different readers?

6. What details does Becky Birtha give you concerning the social circumstances of Johnnieruth's life? Do her social circumstances tend to dictate the way she is to think of herself? Does her environment contribute to who she thinks she is and what her sexual orientation should be? What seem to be the expectations of her mother and those in her neighborhood?

IRONY AND TONE

When Bobby Kryzanowicz told Mr. Hibler to "feel better tomorrow" in "Gryphon," he was using sarcasm, a form of verbal irony. When Carol Peterson laughed at him she indicated that she "got" the irony. Sarcasm, like all verbal irony, depends on diction—the proper choice of words to achieve a given effect.

However, irony goes far beyond sarcasm and attention to diction. **Dramatic irony** depends upon a contradiction of expectations. Characters expect one thing and get another. In Tim O'Brien's "Sweetheart of the Song Tra Bong," the irony begins almost immediately with the completely unlikely story of a soldier in Vietnam having his high school sweetheart flown over to join him. Mary

Anne comes off the plane wearing culottes and a "sexy pink sweater," almost like a cheerleader from home. That irony is almost sufficient, but it is simply a preamble to the ironies that are to come, all based on the fact that we build expectations as we read and that when our expectations do not pan out, or when they are totally turned upside down, as they are in this story, then we experience irony. In the case of the innocent sweetheart who arrives in Vietnam, we can describe it as **dramatic irony** because the irony is built into the character's actions, not just in her words. **Comic irony** implies a humorous situation that contradicts expectations, but with comic effect. Sometimes such comic irony can be rather dark, as when the monkeys begin hitting Mrs. Das's son Bobby in Jhumpa Lahiri's "Interpreter of Maladies." **Tragic irony** has the opposite effect. For example, it is a tragic irony that Prince Prospero walls himself in to avoid the Red Death and then actually pursues the uninvited guest—who *is* the Red Death—and is the first to die. We may not feel a sense of grief because we do not respect Prospero, but from Prospero's point of view the action is tragic. "The Pot of Basil" contains several tragic ironies: Lisabetta ironically ends up with her lover, but the very fact that she has him near her drives her insane. From the point of view of the brothers, their action may have been designed to protect the honor of their sister, but has resulted in her madness. Such ironic contradictions are common not only to drama but to short fiction as well.

Tone is the author's attitude to the subject of the story. One wonders, for example, at the apparently neutral and nonjudgmental tone of John Cheever in "The Swimmer." We know that Neddy Merrill is much like many people Cheever knew and lived with. His tone reveals an understanding, a concern, but nonetheless we ultimately become aware of the shallowness of Neddy's life. Cheever's narrator maintains a neutral tone that guides us but does not force us to a conclusion. The uncertain tone of the narrator of "Gryphon" results from the disjunction between the way a teacher is expected to behave and the way Mrs. Ferenczi actually does behave. The boy's tone is respectful but clearly confused. He is not in a position to make a value judgment the way his parents can.

TIM O'BRIEN   (b. 1946)

Tim O'Brien has made the Vietnam War a major subject. He grew up in Minnesota, went to Macalaster College and Harvard University, and was drafted into the army. He went to Vietnam where he became a sergeant and was eventually wounded and awarded the Purple Heart. Among his books are If I Die in a Combat Zone, Box Me Up and Ship Me Home *(1973), an autobiographical account of some of his experiences in the war, and* Northern Lights *(1974), a novel. He became a widely celebrated writer after the publication of* Going after Cacciato *(1978), a surrealist novel of men searching for one of their unit heading AWOL from Vietnam. It won him the National Book Award in 1979. His stories have appeared in* Esquire *and other national magazines. "Sweetheart of the Song Tra Bong" first appeared in* Esquire *and is collected in* The Things They Carried *(1990). The dedication page of that book reads: "This book is lovingly dedicated to the men of Alpha Company, and in particular to Jimmy Cross, Norman Bowker, Rat Kiley, Mitchell Sanders, Henry Dobbins, and Kiowa."Among his recent books are* TomCat in Love *(1999) and* Northern Lights *(1999).*

Sweetheart of the Song Tra Bong _____ 1987

Vietnam was full of strange stories, some improbable, some well beyond that, but the stories that will last forever are those that swirl back and forth across the border between trivia and bedlam, the mad and the mundane. This one keeps returning to me. I heard it from Rat Kiley, who swore up and down to its truth, although in the end, I'll admit, that doesn't amount to much of a warranty. Among the men in Alpha Company, Rat had a reputation for exaggeration and overstatement, a compulsion to rev up the facts, and for most of us it was normal procedure to discount sixty or seventy percent of anything he had to say. If Rat told you, for example, that he'd slept with four girls one night, you could figure it was about a girl and a half. It wasn't a question of deceit. Just the opposite: he wanted to heat up the truth, to make it burn so hot that you would feel exactly what he felt. For Rat Kiley, I think, facts were formed by sensation, not the other way around, and when you listened to one of his stories, you'd find yourself performing rapid calculations in your head, subtracting superlatives, figuring the square root of an absolute and then multiplying by maybe.

Still, with this particular story, Rat never backed down. He claimed to have witnessed the incident with his own eyes, and I remember how upset he became one morning when Mitchell Sanders challenged him on its basic premise.

"It can't happen," Sanders said. "Nobody ships his honey over to Nam. It don't ring true. I mean, you just can't import your own personal poontang."

Rat shook his head. "I *saw* it, man. I was right there. This guy did it."

"His girlfriend?"   5

"Straight on. It's a fact." Rat's voice squeaked a little. He paused and looked at his hands. "Listen, the guy sends her the money. Flies her over. This cute blonde—just a kid, just barely out of high school—she shows up with a suitcase and one of those plastic cosmetic bags. Comes right out to the boonies. I swear to God, man, she's got on culottes. White culottes and this sexy pink sweater. There she *is.*"

I remember Mitchell Sanders folding his arms. He looked over at me for a second, not quite grinning, not saying a word, but I could read the amusement in his eyes.

Rat saw it, too.

"No lie," he muttered. "Culottes."

When he first arrived in-country, before joining Alpha Company, Rat had been as-   10
signed to a small medical detachment up in the mountains west of Chu Lai, near the village of Tra Bong, where along with eight other enlisted men he ran an aid station that provided basic emergency and trauma care. Casualties were flown in by helicopter, stabilized, then shipped out to hospitals in Chu Lai or Danang. It was gory work, Rat said, but predictable. Amputations, mostly—legs and feet. The area was heavily mined, thick with Bouncing Betties° and homemade booby traps. For a medic, though, it was ideal duty, and Rat counted himself lucky. There was plenty of cold beer, three hot meals a day, a tin roof over his head. No humping at all. No officers, either. You could let your hair grow, he said, and you didn't have to polish your boots or snap off salutes or put

Bouncing Betties: land mines

up with the usual rear-echelon nonsense. The highest ranking NCO was an E-6 named Eddie Diamond, whose pleasures ran from dope to Darvon, and except for a rare field inspection there was no such thing as military discipline.

As Rat described it, the compound was situated at the top of a flat-crested hill along the northern outskirts of Tra Bong. At one end was a small dirt helipad; at the other end, in a rough semicircle, the mess hall and medical hootches overlooked a river called the Song Tra Bong. Surrounding the place were tangled rolls of concertina wire, with bunkers and reinforced firing positions at staggered intervals, and base security was provided by a mixed unit of RFs, PFs, and ARVN° infantry. Which is to say virtually no security at all. As soldiers, the ARVNs were useless; the Ruff-and-Puffs were outright dangerous. And yet even with decent troops the place was clearly indefensible. To the north and west the country rose up in thick walls of wilderness, triple-canopied jungle, mountains unfolding into higher mountains, ravines and gorges and fast-moving rivers and waterfalls and exotic butterflies and steep cliffs and smoky little hamlets and great valleys of bamboo and elephant grass. Originally, in the early 1960s, the place had been set up as a Special Forces outpost, and when Rat Kiley arrived nearly a decade later, a squad of six Green Berets still used the compound as a base of operations. The Greenies were not social animals. Animals, Rat said, but far from social. They had their own hootch at the edge of the perimeter, fortified with sandbags and a metal fence, and except for the bare essentials they avoided contact with the medical detachment. Secretive and suspicious, loners by nature, the six Greenies would sometimes vanish for days at a time, or even weeks, then late in the night they would just as magically reappear, moving like shadows through the moonlight, filing in silently from the dense rain forest off to the west. Among the medics there were jokes about this, but no one asked questions.

While the outpost was isolated and vulnerable, Rat said, he always felt a curious sense of safety there. Nothing much ever happened. The place was never mortared, never taken under fire, and the war seemed to be somewhere far away. On occasion, when casualties came in, there were quick spurts of activity, but otherwise the days flowed by without incident, a smooth and peaceful time. Most mornings were spent on the volleyball court. In the heat of midday the men would head for the shade, lazing away the long afternoons, and after sundown there were movies and card games and sometimes all-night drinking sessions.

It was during one of those late nights that Eddie Diamond first brought up the tantalizing possibility. It was an offhand comment. A joke, really. What they should do, Eddie said, was pool some bucks and bring in a few mama-sans° from Saigon, spice things up, and after a moment one of the men laughed and said, "Our own little EM club," and somebody else said, "Hey, yeah, we pay our fuckin' dues, don't we?" It was nothing serious. Just passing time, playing with the possibilities, and so for a while they tossed the idea around, how you could actually get away with it, no officers or anything, nobody to clamp down, then they dropped the subject and moved on to cars and baseball.

Later in the night, though, a young medic named Mark Fossie kept coming back to the subject.

"Look, if you think about it," he said, "it's not that crazy. You could actually do it."   15

"Do what?" Rat said.

"You know. Bring in a girl. I mean, what's the problem?"

Rat shrugged. "Nothing. A war."

ARVN: South Vietnamese regular troops   *mama-sans:* women

"Well, see, that's the thing," Mark Fossie said. "No war *here*. You could really do it. A pair of solid brass balls, that's all you'd need."

There was some laughter, and Eddie Diamond told him he'd best strap down his   20
dick, but Fossie just frowned and looked at the ceiling for a while and then went off to write a letter.

Six weeks later his girlfriend showed up.

The way Rat told it, she came in by helicopter along with the daily resupply shipment out of Chu Lai. A tall, big-boned blonde. At best, Rat said, she was seventeen years old, fresh out of Cleveland Heights Senior High. She had long white legs and blue eyes and a complexion like strawberry ice cream. Very friendly, too.

At the helipad that morning, Mark Fossie grinned and put his arm around her and said, "Guys, this is Mary Anne."

The girl seemed tired and somewhat lost, but she smiled.

There was a heavy silence. Eddie Diamond, the ranking NCO, made a small mo-   25
tion with his hand, and some of the others murmured a word or two, then they watched Mark Fossie pick up her suitcase and lead her by the arm down to the hootches. For a long while the men were quiet.

"That fucker," somebody finally said.

At evening chow Mark Fossie explained how he'd set it up. It was expensive, he admitted, and the logistics were complicated, but it wasn't like going to the moon. Cleveland to Los Angeles, LA to Bangkok, Bangkok to Saigon. She'd hopped a C-130 up to Chu Lai and stayed overnight at the USO and the next morning hooked a ride west with the resupply chopper.

"A cinch," Fossie said, and gazed down at his pretty girlfriend. "Thing is, you just got to *want* it enough."

Mary Anne Bell and Mark Fossie had been sweethearts since grammar school. From the sixth grade on they had known for a fact that someday they would be married, and live in a fine gingerbread house near Lake Erie, and have three healthy yellow-haired children, and grow old together, and no doubt die in each other's arms and be buried in the same walnut casket. That was the plan. They were very much in love, full of dreams, and in the ordinary flow of their lives the whole scenario might well have come true.

On the first night they set up house in one of the bunkers along the perimeter,   30
near the Special Forces hootch, and over the next two weeks they stuck together like a pair of high school steadies. It was almost disgusting, Rat said, the way they mooned over each other. Always holding hands, always laughing over some private joke. All they needed, he said, were a couple of matching sweaters. But among the medics there was some envy. It was Vietnam, after all, and Mary Anne Bell was an attractive girl. Too wide in the shoulders, maybe, but she had terrific legs, a bubbly personality, a happy smile. The men genuinely liked her. Out on the volleyball court she wore cut-off blue jeans and a black swimsuit top, which the guys appreciated, and in the evenings she liked to dance to music from Rat's portable tape deck. There was a novelty to it; she was good for morale. At times she gave off a kind of come-get-me energy, coy and flirtatious, but apparently it never bothered Mark Fossie. In fact he seemed to enjoy it, just grinning at her, because he was so much in love, and because it was the sort of show that a girl will sometimes put on for her boyfriend's entertainment and education.

Though she was young, Rat said, Mary Anne Bell was no timid child. She was curious about things. During her first days in-country she liked to roam around the compound asking questions: What exactly was a trip flare? How did a Claymore° work? What

Claymore: U.S. military-war personnel mine

was behind those scary green mountains to the west? Then she'd squint and listen quietly while somebody filled her in. She had a good quick mind. She paid attention. Often, especially during the hot afternoons, she would spend time with the ARVNs out along the perimeter, picking up little phrases of Vietnamese, learning how to cook rice over a can of Sterno, how to eat with her hands. The guys sometimes liked to kid her about it—our own little native, they'd say—but Mary Anne would just smile and stick out her tongue. "I'm here," she'd say, "I might as well learn something."

The war intrigued her. The land, too, and the mystery. At the beginning of her second week she began pestering Mark Fossie to take her down to the village at the foot of the hill. In a quiet voice, very patiently, he tried to tell her that it was a bad idea, way too dangerous, but Mary Anne kept after him. She wanted to get a feel for how people lived, what the smells and customs were. It did not impress her that the VC owned the place.

"Listen, it can't be that bad," she said. "They're human beings, aren't they? Like everybody else?"

Fossie nodded. He loved her.

And so in the morning Rat Kiley and two other medics tagged along as security   35
while Mark and Mary Anne strolled through the ville like a pair of tourists. If the girl was nervous, she didn't show it. She seemed comfortable and entirely at home; the hostile atmosphere did not seem to register. All morning Mary Anne chattered away about how quaint the place was, how she loved the thatched roofs and naked children, the wonderful simplicity of village life. A strange thing to watch, Rat said. This seventeen-year-old doll in her goddamn culottes, perky and fresh-faced, like a cheerleader visiting the opposing team's locker room. Her pretty blue eyes seemed to glow. She couldn't get enough of it. On their way back up to the compound she stopped for a swim in the Song Tra Bong, stripping down to her underwear, showing off her legs while Fossie tried to explain to her about things like ambushes and snipers and the stopping power of an AK-47.

The guys, though, were impressed.

"A real tiger," said Eddie Diamond. "D-cup guts, trainer-bra brains."

"She'll learn," somebody said.

Eddie Diamond gave a solemn nod. "There's the scary part. I promise you, this girl will most definitely learn."

In parts, at least, it was a funny story, and yet to hear Rat Kiley tell it you'd almost   40
think it was intended as straight tragedy. He never smiled. Not even at the crazy stuff. There was always a dark, far-off look in his eyes, a kind of sadness, as if he were troubled by something sliding beneath the story's surface. Whenever we laughed, I remember, he'd sigh and wait it out, but the one thing he could not tolerate was disbelief. He'd get edgy if someone questioned one of the details. "She *wasn't* dumb," he'd snap. "I never said that. Young, that's all I said. Like you and me. A *girl*, that's the only difference, and I'll tell you something: it didn't amount to jack. I mean, when we first got here—all of us—we were real young and innocent, full of romantic bullshit, but we learned pretty damn quick. And so did Mary Anne."

Rat would peer down at his hands, silent and thoughtful. After a moment his voice would flatten out.

"You don't believe it?" he'd say. "Fine with me. But you don't know human nature. You don't know Nam."

Then he'd tell us to listen up.

A good sharp mind, Rat said. True, she could be silly sometimes, but she picked up on things fast. At the end of the second week, when four casualties came in, Mary

Anne wasn't afraid to get her hands bloody. At times, in fact, she seemed fascinated by it. Not the gore so much, but the adrenaline buzz that went with the job, that quick hot rush in your veins when the choppers settled down and you had to do things fast and right. No time for sorting through options, no thinking at all; you just stuck your hands in and started plugging up holes. She was quiet and steady. She didn't back off from the ugly cases. Over the next day or two, as more casualties trickled in, she learned how to clip an artery and pump up a plastic splint and shoot in morphine. In times of action her face took on a sudden new composure, almost serene, the fuzzy blue eyes narrowing into a tight, intelligent focus. Mark Fossie would grin at this. He was proud, yes, but also amazed. A different person, it seemed, and he wasn't sure what to make of it.

Other things, too. The way she quickly fell into the habits of the bush. No cos-   45
metics, no fingernail filing. She stopped wearing jewelry, cut her hair short and wrapped it in a dark green bandana. Hygiene became a matter of small consequence. In her second week Eddie Diamond taught her how to disassemble an M-16, how the various parts worked, and from there it was a natural progression to learning how to use the weapon. For hours at a time she plunked away at C-ration cans, a bit unsure of herself, but as it turned out she had a real knack for it. There was a new confidence in her voice, a new authority in the way she carried herself. In many ways she remained naive and immature, still a kid, but Cleveland Heights now seemed very far away.

Once or twice, gently, Mark Fossie suggested that it might be time to think about heading home, but Mary Anne laughed and told him to forget it. "Everything I want," she said, "is right here."

She stroked his arm, and then kissed him.

On one level things remained the same between them. They slept together. They held hands and made plans for after the war. But now there was a new imprecision in the way Mary Anne expressed her thoughts on certain subjects. Not necessarily three kids, she'd say. Not necessarily a house on Lake Erie. "Naturally we'll still get married," she'd tell him, "but it doesn't have to be right away. Maybe travel first. Maybe live together. Just test it out, you know?"

Mark Fossie would nod at this, even smile and agree, but it made him uncomfortable. He couldn't pin it down. Her body seemed foreign somehow—too stiff in places, too firm where the softness used to be. The bubbliness was gone. The nervous giggling, too. When she laughed now, which was rare, it was only when something struck her as truly funny. Her voice seemed to reorganize itself at a lower pitch. In the evenings, while the men played cards, she would sometimes fall into long elastic silences, her eyes fixed on the dark, her arms folded, her foot tapping out a coded message against the floor. When Fossie asked about it one evening, Mary Anne looked at him for a long moment and then shrugged. "It's nothing," she said. "Really nothing. To tell the truth, I've never been happier in my whole life. Never."

Twice, though, she came in late at night. Very late. And then finally she did not   50
come in at all.

Rat Kiley heard about it from Fossie himself. Before dawn one morning, the kid shook him awake. He was in bad shape. His voice seemed hollow and stuffed up, nasal-sounding, as if he had a bad cold. He held a flashlight in his hand, clicking it on and off.

"Mary Anne," he whispered, "I can't *find* her."

Rat sat up and rubbed his face. Even in the dim light it was clear that the boy was in trouble. There were dark smudges under his eyes, the frayed edges of somebody who hadn't slept in a while.

"Gone," Fossie said. "Rat, listen, she's sleeping with somebody. Last night, she didn't even . . . I don't know what to *do*."

Abruptly then, Fossie seemed to collapse. He squatted down, rocking on his heels, still clutching the flashlight. Just a boy—eighteen years old. Tall and blond. A gifted athlete. A nice kid, too, polite and good-hearted, although for the moment none of it seemed to be serving him well. 55

He kept clicking the flashlight on and off.

"All right, start at the start," Rat said. "Nice and slow. Sleeping with who?"

"I don't know who. Eddie Diamond."

"Eddie?"

"Has to be. The guy's always there, always hanging on her." 60

Rat shook his head. "Man, I don't know. Can't say it strikes a right note, not with Eddie."

"Yes, but he's—"

"Easy does it," Rat said. He reached out and tapped the boy's shoulder. "Why not just check some bunks? We got nine guys. You and me, that's two, so there's seven possibles. Do a quick body count."

Fossie hesitated. "But I can't . . . If she's there, I mean, if she's with somebody—"

"Oh, Christ." 65

Rat pushed himself up. He took the flashlight, muttered something, and moved down to the far end of the hootch. For privacy, the men had rigged up curtained walls around their cots, small makeshift bedrooms, and in the dark Rat went quickly from room to room, using the flashlight to pluck out the faces. Eddie Diamond slept a hard deep sleep—the others, too. To be sure, though, Rat checked once more, very carefully, then he reported back to Fossie.

"All accounted for. No extras."

"Eddie?"

"Darvon dreams." Rat switched off the flashlight and tried to think it out. "Maybe she just—I don't know—maybe she camped out tonight. Under the stars or something. You search the compound?"

"Sure I did." 70

"Well, come on," Rat said. "One more time."

Outside, a soft violet light was spreading out across the eastern hillsides. Two or three ARVN soldiers had built their breakfast fires, but the place was mostly quiet and unmoving. They tried the helipad first, then the mess hall and supply hootches, then they walked the entire six hundred meters of perimeter.

"Okay," Rat finally said. "We got a problem."

When he first told the story, Rat stopped there and looked at Mitchell Sanders for a time.

"So what's your vote? Where was she?" 75

"The Greenies," Sanders said.

"Yeah?"

Sanders smiled. "No other option. That stuff about the Special Forces—how they used the place as a base of operations, how they'd glide in and out—all that had to be there for a *reason*. That's how stories work, man."

Rat thought about it, then shrugged.

"All right, sure, the Greenies. But it's not what Fossie thought. She wasn't sleeping with any of them. At least not exactly. I mean, in a way she was sleeping with *all* of 80 them, more or less, except it wasn't sex or anything. They was just lying together, so to speak, Mary Anne and these six grungy weirded-out Green Berets."

"Lying down?" Sanders said.

"You got it."

"Lying down how?"

Rat smiled. "Ambush. All night long, man, Mary Anne's out on fuckin' *ambush.*"

Just after sunrise, Rat said, she came trooping in through the wire, tired-looking   85
but cheerful as she dropped her gear and gave Mark Fossie a brisk hug. The six Green Berets did not speak. One of them nodded at her, and the others gave Fossie a long stare, then they filed off to their hootch at the edge of the compound.

"Please," she said. "Not a word."

Fossie took a half step forward and hesitated. It was as though he had trouble recognizing her. She wore a bush hat and filthy green fatigues; she carried the standard M-16 automatic assault rifle; her face was black with charcoal.

Mary Anne handed him the weapon. "I'm exhausted," she said. "We'll talk later."

She glanced over at the Special Forces area, then turned and walked quickly across the compound toward her own bunker. Fossie stood still for a few seconds. A little dazed, it seemed. After a moment, though, he set his jaw and whispered something and went after her with a hard, fast stride.

"Not later!" he yelled. "Now!"   90

What happened between them, Rat said, nobody ever knew for sure. But in the mess hall that evening it was clear that an accommodation had been reached. Or more likely, he said, it was a case of setting down some new rules. Mary Anne's hair was freshly shampooed. She wore a white blouse, a navy blue skirt, a pair of plain black flats. Over dinner she kept her eyes down, poking at her food, subdued to the point of silence. Eddie Diamond and some of the others tried to nudge her into talking about the ambush—What was the feeling out there? What exactly did she see and hear?—but the questions seemed to give her trouble. Nervously, she'd look across the table at Fossie. She'd wait a moment, as if to receive some sort of clearance, then she'd bow her head and mumble out a vague word or two. There were no real answers.

Mark Fossie, too, had little to say.

"Nobody's business," he told Rat that night. Then he offered a brief smile. "One thing for sure, though, there won't be any more ambushes. No more late nights."

"You laid down the law?"

"Compromise," Fossie said. "I'll put it this way—we're officially engaged."   95

Rat nodded cautiously.

"Well hey, she'll make a sweet bride," he said. "Combat ready."

Over the next several days there was a strained, tightly wound quality to the way they treated each other, a rigid correctness that was enforced by repetitive acts of willpower. To look at them from a distance, Rat said, you would think they were the happiest two people on the planet. They spent the long afternoons sunbathing together, stretched out side by side on top of their bunker, or playing backgammon in the shade of a giant palm tree, or just sitting quietly. A model of togetherness, it seemed. And yet at close range their faces showed the tension. Too polite, too thoughtful. Mark Fossie tried hard to keep up a self-assured pose, as if nothing had ever come between them, or ever could, but there was a fragility to it, something tentative and false. If Mary Anne happened to move a few steps away from him, even briefly, he'd tighten up and force himself not to watch her. But then a moment later he'd be watching.

In the presence of others, at least, they kept on their masks. Over meals they talked about plans for a huge wedding in Cleveland Heights—a two-day bash, lots of flowers. And yet even then their smiles seemed too intense. They were too quick with their banter; they held hands as if afraid to let go.

It had to end, and eventually it did.   100

Near the end of the third week Fossie began making arrangements to send her home. At first, Rat said, Mary Anne seemed to accept it, but then after a day or two she fell into a restless gloom, sitting off by herself at the edge of the perimeter. She would not speak. Shoulders hunched, her blue eyes opaque, she seemed to disappear inside herself. A couple of times Fossie approached her and tried to talk it out, but Mary Anne just stared out at the dark green mountains to the west. The wilderness seemed to draw her in. A haunted look, Rat said—partly terror, partly rapture. It was as if she had come up on the edge of something, as if she were caught in that no-man's-land between Cleveland Heights and deep jungle. Seventeen years old. Just a child, blond and innocent, but then weren't they all?

The next morning she was gone. The six Greenies were gone, too.

In a way, Rat said, poor Fossie expected it, or something like it, but that did not help much with the pain. The kid couldn't function. The grief took him by the throat and squeezed and would not let go.

"Lost," he kept whispering.

It was nearly three weeks before she returned. But in a sense she never returned.   105
Not entirely, not all of her.

By chance, Rat said, he was awake to see it. A damp misty night, he couldn't sleep, so he'd gone outside for a quick smoke. He was just standing there, he said, watching the moon, and then off to the west a column of silhouettes appeared as if by magic at the edge of the jungle. At first he didn't recognize her—a small, soft shadow among six other shadows. There was no sound. No real substance either. The seven silhouettes seemed to float across the surface of the earth, like spirits, vaporous and unreal. As he watched, Rat said, it made him think of some weird opium dream. The silhouettes moved without moving. Silently, one by one, they came up the hill, passed through the wire, and drifted in a loose file across the compound. It was then, Rat said, that he picked out Mary Anne's face. Her eyes seemed to shine in the dark—not blue, though, but a bright glowing jungle green. She did not pause at Fossie's bunker. She cradled her weapon and moved swiftly to the Special Forces hootch and followed the others inside.

Briefly, a light came on, and someone laughed, then the place went dark again.

Whenever he told the story, Rat had a tendency to stop now and then, interrupting the flow, inserting little clarifications or bits of analysis and personal opinion. It was a bad habit, Mitchell Sanders said, because all that matters is the raw material, the stuff itself, and you can't clutter it up with your own half-baked commentary. That just breaks the spell. It destroys the magic. What you have to do, Sanders said, is trust your own story. Get the hell out of the way and let it tell itself.

But Rat Kiley couldn't help it. He wanted to bracket the full range of meaning.

"I know it sounds far-out," he'd tell us, "but it's not like *impossible* or anything. We   110
all heard plenty of wackier stories. Some guy comes back from the bush, tells you he saw the Virgin Mary out there, she was riding a goddamn goose or something. Everybody

buys it. Everybody smiles and asks how fast was they going, did she have spurs on. Well, it's not like that. This Mary Anne wasn't no virgin but at least she was real. I saw it. When she came in through the wire that night, I was right there, I saw those eyes of hers, I saw how she wasn't even the same person no more. What's so impossible about that? She was a girl, that's all. I mean, if it was a guy, everybody'd say, Hey, no big deal, he got caught up in the Nam shit, he got seduced by the Greenies. See what I mean? You got these blinders on about women. How gentle and peaceful they are. All that crap about how if we had a pussy for president there wouldn't be no more wars. Pure garbage. You got to get rid of that sexist attitude."

Rat would go on like that until Mitchell Sanders couldn't tolerate it any longer. It offended his inner ear.

"The story," Sanders would say. "The whole tone, man, you're wrecking it."

"Tone?"

"The *sound*. You need to get a consistent sound, like slow or fast, funny or sad. All these digressions, they just screw up your story's *sound*. Stick to what happened."

Frowning, Rat would close his eyes.   115

"Tone?" he'd say. "I didn't know it was all that complicated. The girl joined the zoo. One more animal—end of story."

"Yeah, fine. But tell it right."

At daybreak the next morning, when Mark Fossie heard she was back, he stationed himself outside the fenced-off Special Forces area. All morning he waited for her, and all afternoon. Around dusk Rat brought him something to eat.

"She has to come out," Fossie said. "Sooner or later, she has to."

"Or else what?" Rat said.   120

"I go get her. I bring her out."

Rat shook his head. "Your decision. I was you, though, no way I'd mess around with any Greenie types, not for nothing."

"It's Mary Anne in there."

"Sure, I know that. All the same, I'd knock real extra super polite."

Even with the cooling night air Fossie's face was slick with sweat. He looked sick.   125
His eyes were bloodshot; his skin had a whitish, almost colorless cast. For a few minutes Rat waited with him, quietly watching the hootch, then he patted the kid's shoulder and left him alone.

It was after midnight when Rat and Eddie Diamond went out to check on him. The night had gone cold and steamy, a low fog sliding down from the mountains, and somewhere out in the dark they heard music playing. Not loud but not soft either. It had a chaotic, almost unmusical sound, without rhythm or form or progression, like the noise of nature. A synthesizer, it seemed, or maybe an electric organ. In the background, just audible, a woman's voice was half singing, half chanting, but the lyrics seemed to be in a foreign tongue.

They found Fossie squatting near the gate in front of the Special Forces area. Head bowed, he was swaying to the music, his face wet and shiny. As Eddie bent down beside him, the kid looked up with dull eyes, ashen and powdery, not quite in register.

"Hear that?" he whispered. "You *hear*? It's Mary Anne."

Eddie Diamond took his arm. "Let's get you inside. Somebody's radio, that's all it is. Move it now."

"Mary Anne. Just listen."   130

"Sure, but—"

"Listen!"

Fossie suddenly pulled away, twisting sideways, and fell back against the gate. He lay there with his eyes closed. The music—the noise, whatever it was—came from the hootch beyond the fence. The place was dark except for a small glowing window, which stood partly open, the panes dancing in bright reds and yellows as though the glass were on fire. The chanting seemed louder now. Fiercer, too, and higher pitched.

Fossie pushed himself up. He wavered for a moment then forced the gate open. "That voice," he said. "Mary Anne."   135

Rat took a step forward, reaching out for him, but Fossie was already moving fast toward the hootch. He stumbled once, caught himself, and hit the door hard with both arms. There was a noise—a short screeching sound, like a cat—and the door swung in and Fossie was framed there for an instant, his arms stretched out, then he slipped inside. After a moment Rat and Eddie followed quietly. Just inside the door they found Fossie bent down on one knee. He wasn't moving.

Across the room a dozen candles were burning on the floor near the open window. The place seemed to echo with a weird deep-wilderness sound—tribal music— bamboo flutes and drums and chimes. But what hit you first, Rat said, was the smell. Two kinds of smells. There was a topmost scent of joss sticks and incense, like the fumes of some exotic smokehouse, but beneath the smoke lay a deeper and much more powerful stench. Impossible to describe, Rat said. It paralyzed your lungs. Thick and numbing, like an animal's den, a mix of blood and scorched hair and excrement and the sweet-sour odor of moldering flesh—the stink of the kill. But that wasn't all. On a post at the rear of the hootch was the decayed head of a large black leopard; strips of yellow-brown skin dangled from the overhead rafters. And bones. Stacks of bones—all kinds. To one side, propped up against a wall, stood a poster in neat black lettering: ASSEMBLE YOUR OWN GOOK!! FREE SAMPLE KIT!! The images came in a swirl, Rat said, and there was no way you could process it all. Off in the gloom a few dim figures lounged in hammocks, or on cots, but none of them moved or spoke. The background music came from a tape deck near the circle of candles, but the high voice was Mary Anne's.

After a second Mark Fossie made a soft moaning sound. He started to get up but then stiffened.

"Mary Anne?" he said.

Quietly then, she stepped out of the shadows. At least for a moment she seemed   140
to be the same pretty young girl who had arrived a few weeks earlier. She was barefoot. She wore her pink sweater and a white blouse and a simple cotton skirt.

For a long while the girl gazed down at Fossie, almost blankly, and in the candlelight her face had the composure of someone perfectly at peace with herself. It took a few seconds, Rat said, to appreciate the full change. In part it was her eyes: utterly flat and indifferent. There was no emotion in her stare, no sense of the person behind it. But the grotesque part, he said, was her jewelry. At the girl's throat was a necklace of human tongues. Elongated and narrow, like pieces of blackened leather, the tongues were threaded along a length of copper wire, one overlapping the next, the tips curled upward as if caught in a final shrill syllable.

Briefly, it seemed, the girl smiled at Mark Fossie.

"There's no sense talking," she said. "I know what you think, but it's not . . . it's not *bad*."

"Bad?" Fossie murmured.

"It's not."   .   145

In the shadows there was laughter.

One of the Greenies sat up and lighted a cigar. The others lay silent.

"You're in a place," Mary Anne said softly, "where you don't belong."

She moved her hand in a gesture that encompassed not just the hootch but everything around it, the entire war, the mountains, the mean little villages, the trails and trees and rivers and deep misted-over valleys.

"You just don't *know*," she said. "You hide in this little fortress, behind wire and   150
sandbags, and you don't know what it's all about. Sometimes I want to *eat* this place. Vietnam. I want to swallow the whole country—the dirt, the death—I just want to eat it and have it there inside me. That's how I feel. It's like . . . this appetite. I get scared sometimes—lots of times—but it's not *bad*. You know? I feel close to myself. When I'm out there at night, I feel close to my own body, I can feel my blood moving, my skin and my fingernails, everything, it's like I'm full of electricity and I'm glowing in the dark— I'm on fire almost—I'm burning away into nothing—but it doesn't matter because I know exactly who I am. You can't feel like that anywhere else."

All this was said softly, as if to herself, her voice slow and impassive. She was not trying to persuade. For a few moments she looked at Mark Fossie, who seemed to shrink away, then she turned and moved back into the gloom.

There was nothing to be done.

Rat took Fossie's arm, helped him up, and led him outside. In the darkness there was that weird tribal music, which seemed to come from the earth itself, from the deep rain forest, and a woman's voice rising up in a language beyond translation.

Mark Fossie stood rigid.

"Do something," he whispered. "I can't just let her go like that."   155

Rat listened for a time, then shook his head.

"Man, you must be deaf. She's already gone."

Rat Kiley stopped there, almost in midsentence, which drove Mitchell Sanders crazy.

"What next?" he said.

"Next?"   160

"The girl. What happened to her?"

Rat made a small, tired motion with his shoulders. "Hard to tell for sure. Maybe three, four days later I got orders to report here to Alpha Company. Jumped the first chopper out, that's the last I ever seen of the place. Mary Anne, too."

Mitchell Sanders stared at him.

"You can't do that."

"Do what?"   165

"Jesus Christ, it's against the *rules*," Sanders said. "Against human *nature*. This elaborate story, you can't say, Hey, by the way, I don't know the *ending*. I mean, you got certain obligations."

Rat gave a quick smile. "Patience, man. Up to now, everything I told you is from personal experience, the exact truth, but there's a few other things I heard secondhand. Thirdhand, actually. From here on it gets to be . . . I don't know what the word is."

"Speculation."

"Yeah, right." Rat looked off to the west, scanning the mountains, as if expecting something to appear on one of the high ridgelines. After a second he shrugged. "Anyhow, maybe two months later I ran into Eddie Diamond over in Bangkok—I was on R&R, just this fluke thing—and he told me some stuff I can't vouch for with my own eyes. Even Eddie didn't really see it. He heard it from one of the Greenies, so you got to take this with a whole shakerful of salt."

Once more, Rat searched the mountains, then he sat back and closed his eyes.   170

"You know," he said abruptly, "I loved her."

"Say again?"

"A lot. We all did, I guess. The way she looked, Mary Anne made you think about those girls back home, how clean and innocent they all are, how they'll never understand any of this, not in a billion years. Try to tell them about it, they'll just stare at you with those big round candy eyes. They won't understand zip. It's like trying to tell somebody what chocolate tastes like."

Mitchell Sanders nodded. "Or shit."

"There it is, you got to taste it, and that's the thing with Mary Anne. She was *there*.   175
She was up to her eyeballs in it. After the war, man, I promise you, you won't find nobody like her."

Suddenly, Rat pushed up to his feet, moved a few steps away from us, then stopped and stood with his back turned. He was an emotional guy.

"Got hooked, I guess," he said. "I loved her. So when I heard from Eddie about what happened, it almost made me . . . Like you say, it's pure speculation."

"Go on," Mitchell Sanders said. "Finish up."

What happened to her, Rat said, was what happened to all of them. You come over clean and you get dirty and then afterward it's never the same. A question of degree. Some make it intact, some don't make it at all. For Mary Anne Bell, it seemed, Vietnam had the effect of a powerful drug: that mix of unnamed terror and unnamed pleasure that comes as the needle slips in and you know you're risking something. The endorphins start to flow, and the adrenaline, and you hold your breath and creep quietly through the moonlit nightscapes; you become intimate with danger; you're in touch with the far side of yourself, as though it's another hemisphere, and you want to string it out and go wherever the trip takes you and be host to all the possibilities inside yourself. Not *bad,* she'd said. Vietnam made her glow in the dark. She wanted more, she wanted to penetrate deeper into the mystery of herself, and after a time the wanting became needing, which turned then to craving.

According to Eddie Diamond, who heard it from one of the Greenies, she took a   180
greedy pleasure in night patrols. She was good at it; she had the moves. All camouflaged up, her face smooth and vacant, she seemed to flow like water through the dark, like oil, without sound or center. She went barefoot. She stopped carrying a weapon. There were times, apparently, when she took crazy, death-wish chances—things that even the Greenies balked at. It was as if she were taunting some wild creature out in the bush, or in her head, inviting it to show itself, a curious game of hide-and-go-seek that was played out in the dense terrain of a nightmare. She was lost inside herself. On occasion, when they were taken under fire, Mary Anne would stand quietly and watch the tracer rounds snap by, a little smile at her lips, intent on some private transaction with the war. Other times she would simply vanish altogether—for hours, for days.

And then one morning, all alone, Mary Anne walked off into the mountains and did not come back.

No body was ever found. No equipment, no clothing. For all he knew, Rat said, the girl was still alive. Maybe up in one of the high mountain villes, maybe with the Montagnard tribes. But that was guesswork.

There was an inquiry, of course, and a week-long air search, and for a time the Tra Bong compound went crazy with MP and CID° types. In the end, however, nothing came of it. It was a war and the war went on. Mark Fossie was busted to PFC, shipped back to

---

MP and CID: Military police and Criminal Investigation Department

a hospital in the States, and two months later received a medical discharge. Mary Anne Bell joined the missing.

But the story did not end there. If you believed the Greenies, Rat said, Mary Anne was still somewhere out there in the dark. Odd movements, odd shapes. Late at night, when the Greenies were out on ambush, the whole rain forest seemed to stare in at them—a watched feeling—and a couple of times they almost saw her sliding through the shadows. Not quite, but almost. She had crossed to the other side. She was part of the land. She was wearing her culottes, her pink sweater, and a necklace of human tongues. She was dangerous. She was ready for the kill.

QUESTIONS FOR CLOSE READING OF IRONY AND TONE

1. How would you describe the tone of Rat's story about Mary Anne? Is it hopeful? Amused? Serious? Alarmed? Amazed? Awed? How does he react when the validity of his story is challenged?

2. The "I" narrator tells us that he heard the story from Rat Kiley. How would you describe the tone of the "I" narrator's opening statements and his interruptions of the story later on?

3. Does the "I" narrator think Rat Kiley is a reliable narrator of the story? Does the "I" narrator seem to change his attitude toward Rat Kiley as the story goes on?

4. Do you feel Rat Kiley is a reliable narrator? What qualities of tone in the story convince you that he is either reliable or unreliable?

5. What ironies are apparent in the assignment that Rat Kiley got when he arrived in Vietnam?

6. Why is Mary Anne Bell's arrival at the base camp in Vietnam ironic?

7. What expectations did you have for Mary Anne Bell upon her arrival to meet her high school sweetheart? How does Rat Kiley build up your expectations?

8. Does Rat Kiley convince the "I" narrator that his story is true? How does Kiley do it? How do you know the "I" narrator is convinced?

9. Does Rat Kiley convince you that the story is true? Or possible?

10. In what ways does the plot of the story seem to defy normal expectations?

QUESTIONS FOR INTERPRETATION OF IRONY AND TONE

1. The contrast between night and day is sharply drawn in the story. A similar contrast is formed between the world of Mark Fossie, Eddie Diamond, and Rat Kiley and the world of the jungle countryside. The contrast resembles an urban/rural distinction at times. But the contrast between the "Greenies," the Green Berets, who crawl in and out of the jungle in the mist of night and dawn, and the regular troops is also enormously profound. Why would it be considered ironic that Mary Anne Bell decides to cast her lot with the special forces who seem most active in the dark? How does the contrast of light and dark imply a moral tone to the story?

2. Rat Kiley describes Mary Anne as having an interesting mind, "a good sharp mind, Rat said." She expresses much more curiosity throughout the story than does Mark or any of the other men in Mark's company. She visits the village and learns enough Vietnamese to communicate with some villagers—something no one else

does. She swims in the Song Tra Bong even though she is warned away from it. She grows curious about the "Greenies" and spends time with them. Eventually Rat Kiley describes her as a totally changed person. What psychological factors seem to have changed her? Do you think that change is typical only of Mary Anne, or would it be true of others who followed her pattern of behavior?

3. How do you respond to the events of the story? Are you horrified by what happens to Mary Anne, or do you feel she did just what was expected of her given the situation of being at war? How does the "I" narrator respond to Rat Kiley's telling of the story? Does Tim O'Brien expect his response to parallel yours? Describe what you feel a typical response to the story might be.

4. What expectations does the story set up in the beginning for the behavior of a high school sweetheart "in-country" in Vietnam during the war? What did Mark Fossie expect of her? What would the other soldiers expect of a woman in this circumstance? Rat Kiley tells us a great deal about the expectations of marriage between Mary Anne and Mark. They plan to marry, have children, even be buried in the same casket. Could this be described as a feminist ambition? Could Mary Anne be described as a feminist early in the story? Could she be described as a feminist at the end of the story? What might be ironic about her feminism?

5. The effectiveness of this story depends in part on the historical circumstances of the Vietnam War and the behavior of American troops. The Green Berets were celebrated in films and in some journals, but in this story they are portrayed as fearsome and animal-like. Comparing the reported behavior of American troops in Vietnam with those in any earlier or later war may help establish why this story functions ironically or why Rat Kiley's story may be convincing to the "I" narrator.

KATE CHOPIN (1850–1904)

Kate Chopin is a feminist writer who was not accepted in her own time. Born in St. Louis, where she enjoyed a prominent place in society, she went with her husband, Oscar Chopin, to live first in New Orleans and later in the bayou region of Louisiana. Her stories and novels reflect her own background as a French Creole descendant and her life among French Creoles in Louisiana. After her husband died, Chopin sold her holdings, returned to St. Louis, and, influenced by Guy de Maupassant and other French writers, decided to write. She began publishing with two collections of stories: Bayou Folk *(1894) and* A Night in Acadie *(1897). Some of her work was rejected for publication on the grounds that its feminist themes were too radical for the times. In 1899, after publication of* The Awakening, *the negative reaction was so great that publishers ignored her work and she died a literary outcast. It took some fifty years for Chopin to begin to get the recognition she deserved.*

The Story of an Hour _____ 1894

Knowing that Mrs. Mallard was afflicted with a heart trouble, great care was taken to break to her as gently as possible the news of her husband's death.

It was her sister Josephine who told her, in broken sentences, veiled hints that revealed in half concealing. Her husband's friend Richards was there, too, near her. It was he who had been in the newspaper office when intelligence of the railroad disaster was received, with Brently Mallard's name leading the list of "killed." He had only taken the time to assure himself of its truth by a second telegram, and had hastened to forestall any less careful, less tender friend in bearing the sad message.

She did not hear the story as many women have heard the same, with a paralyzed inability to accept its significance. She wept at once, with sudden, wild abandonment, in her sister's arms. When the storm of grief had spent itself she went away to her room alone. She would have no one follow her.

There stood, facing the open window, a comfortable, roomy armchair. Into this she sank, pressed down by a physical exhaustion that haunted her body and seemed to reach into her soul.

She could see in the open square before her house the tops of trees that were all   5
aquiver with the new spring life. The delicious breath of rain was in the air. In the street below a peddler was crying his wares. The notes of a distant song which someone was singing reached her faintly, and countless sparrows were twittering in the eaves.

There were patches of blue sky showing here and there through the clouds that had met and piled above the other in the west facing her window.

She sat with her head thrown back upon the cushion of the chair, quite motionless, except when a sob came up into her throat and shook her, as a child who has cried itself to sleep continues to sob in its dreams.

She was young, with a fair, calm face, whose lines bespoke repression and even a certain strength. But now there was a dull stare in her eyes, whose gaze was fixed away off yonder on one of those patches of blue sky. It was not a glance of reflection, but rather indicated a suspension of intelligent thought.

There was something coming to her and she was waiting for it, fearfully. What was it? She did not know; it was too subtle and elusive to name. But she felt it, creeping out of the sky, reaching toward her through the sounds, the scents, the color that filled the air.

Now her bosom rose and fell tumultuously. She was beginning to recognize this   10
thing that was approaching to possess her, and she was striving to beat it back with her will—as powerless as her two white slender hands would have been.

When she abandoned herself a little whispered word escaped her slightly parted lips. She said it over and over under her breath: "Free, free, free!" The vacant stare and the look of terror that had followed it went from her eyes. They stayed keen and bright. Her pulses beat fast, and the coursing blood warmed and relaxed every inch of her body.

She did not stop to ask if it were or were not a monstrous joy that held her. A clear and exalted perception enabled her to dismiss the suggestion as trivial.

She knew that she would weep again when she saw the kind, tender hands folded in death; the face that had never looked save with love upon her, fixed and gray and dead. But she saw beyond that bitter moment a long procession of years to come that would belong to her absolutely. And she opened and spread her arms out to them in welcome.

There would be no one to live for her during those coming years; she would live for herself. There would be no powerful will bending her in that blind persistence with which men and women believe they have a right to impose a private will upon a fellow-creature. A kind intention or a cruel intention made the act seem no less a crime as she looked upon it in that brief moment of illumination.

And yet she had loved him—sometimes. Often she had not. What did it matter!   15
What could love, the unsolved mystery, count for in face of this possession of self-assertion which she suddenly recognized as the strongest impulse of her being!

"Free! Body and soul free!" she kept whispering.

Josephine was kneeling before the closed door with her lips to the keyhole, imploring for admission. "Louise, open the door! I beg; open the door—you will make yourself ill. What are you doing, Louise? For heaven's sake open the door."

"Go away. I am not making myself ill." No; she was drinking in a very elixir of life through that open window.

Her fancy was running riot along those days ahead of her. Spring days, and summer days, and all sorts of days that would be her own. She breathed a quick prayer that life might be long. It was only yesterday she had thought with a shudder that life might be long.

She arose at length and opened the door to her sister's importunities. There was   20
a feverish triumph in her eyes, and she carried herself unwittingly like a goddess of Victory. She clasped her sister's waist, and together they descended the stairs. Richards stood waiting for them at the bottom.

Someone was opening the front door with a latchkey. It was Brently Mallard who entered, a little travel-stained, composedly carrying his grip-sack and umbrella. He had been far from the scene of accident, and did not even know there had been one. He stood amazed at Josephine's piercing cry; at Richards' quick motion to screen him from the view of his wife.

But Richards was too late.

When the doctors came they said she had died of heart disease—of joy that kills.

QUESTIONS FOR CLOSE READING OF IRONY AND TONE

1. Why are we told in the first sentence that Mrs. Mallard has heart trouble?
2. How is she told of her husband's death?
3. How has Richards ascertained the news of Brently Mallard's death?
4. What is Mrs. Mallard's first reaction when she hears the news? Where does she go?
5. Examine the fifth paragraph carefully. How does its tone differ from earlier paragraphs?
6. Describe Mrs. Mallard. She seems at first to resist an emotion. What is it?
7. How does she see the future now that her husband is dead? What does she mean by disregarding "a monstrous joy"?
8. Why does she regard "Spring days, and summer days, and all sorts of days that would be her own"?
9. When she sees that her husband is alive, Mrs. Mallard drops dead; "she had died of heart disease."
10. What is meant by the "joy that kills"? Is that spoken ironically?

QUESTIONS FOR INTERPRETATION OF IRONY AND TONE

1. Are you shocked by the ironic turn of events? We are told that Brently Mallard was on a list in the newspaper as having died in an accident. Further, a telegram reconfirms his death. Yet at the end of the story he walks in without even knowing there had been an accident. Is it ironic that Josephine and others fear heart failure in the beginning of the story? Why does Richards "motion to screen" Brently "from the view of his wife"? What does he know or what does he suspect? Is Mrs. Mallard's death upon the entrance of her husband tragic irony?
2. Much is made of references to the heart and the fact that Mrs. Mallard has "heart trouble." Is it possible that "heart trouble" is symbolic in meaning? Could it imply

trouble with relationships? Can you divine the nature of the relationship between Mr. and Mrs. Mallard from the details of the story? Is theirs a successful marriage? Is it a conventional marriage for 1894?

3. Mrs. Mallard goes through an extreme range of emotional reactions through the course of this short story. Can you tell anything about her emotional stability or her mental state from the details of the story? Does she behave normally when she hears of the death of her husband? Would Josephine, her sister, have thought her reaction to be abnormal? What did Josephine and others expect Mrs. Mallard to do in response to hearing of her husband's death?

4. What does Mrs. Mallard's ultimate reaction to the news that her husband had died tell you about the nature of her marriage? How aware was she herself of the true nature of her marriage before the news came? Is it possible to tell how others regarded her marriage from their attitudes? For example, would you guess that Josephine was married or single? What seems to have been the expectation for a married woman of the era? What would life have been like for Mrs. Mallard if she were a widow?

5. The point of view of the story is tightly controlled so as to represent Mrs. Mallard's views, feelings, and opinions. Would this story be ironic if it were told from Mr. Mallard's point of view? How would the tone of the story change if it were told from Mr. Mallard's point of view? How would he feel if he were told Mrs. Mallard had died in a train crash? Would his reactions be similar or different from Mrs. Mallard's?

URSULA K. LE GUIN   (b. 1929)

Ursula K. Le Guin was born in Berkeley, California, and was educated at Radcliffe College and Columbia University. She has taught writing and has written and edited a large number of books of fantasy and science fiction, for which she has long been acclaimed. One critic has said, "When one enters the world of her fiction, one encounters a distinctive universe of discourse." However, Le Guin herself has said, "I write science fiction because that is what publishers call my books. Left to myself, I should call them novels." Some of her works are interconnected, such as the Hainish cycle—Rocannon (1966), Planet of Exile (1966), City of Illusions (1968), The Left Hand of Darkness (1969), The Dispossessed (1974), and The Word for World Is Forest (1976)—and the Earthsea trilogy, which includes A Wizard of Earthsea (1968), The Tombs of Atuan (1971), and The Farthest Shore (1972). Her most recent novel is The Telling (2000). Among her volumes of short stories are The Wind's Twelve Quarters (1975), also connected with the Hainish cycle; Orsinian Tales (1976); and The Compass Rose (1982). Her background in the sciences and her interest in history are clearly evident in all her stories.

Sur° _____ *1982*

A Summary Report of the Yelcho Expedition to the Antarctic, 1909–10

Although I have no intention of publishing this report, I think it would be nice if a grandchild of mine, or somebody's grandchild, happened to find it some day; so I shall

Sur: south

keep it in the leather trunk in the attic, along with Rosita's christening dress and Juanito's silver rattle and my wedding shoes and finneskos.°

The first requisite for mounting an expedition—money—is normally the hardest to come by. I grieve that even in a report destined for a trunk in the attic of a house in a very quiet suburb of Lima I dare not write the name of the generous benefactor, the great soul without whose unstinting liberality the Yelcho Expedition would never have been more than the idlest excursion into daydream. That our equipment was the best and most modern—that our provisions were plentiful and fine—that a ship of the Chilean government, with her brave officers and gallant crew, was twice sent halfway round the world for our convenience: all this is due to that benefactor whose name, alas!, I must not say, but whose happiest debtor I shall be till death.

When I was little more than a child, my imagination was caught by a newspaper account of the voyage of the *Belgica*, which, sailing south from Tierra del Fuego, was beset by ice in the Bellingshausen Sea and drifted a whole year with the floe, the men aboard her suffering a great deal from want of food and from the terror of the unending winter darkness. I read and reread that account, and later followed with excitement the reports of the rescue of Dr. Nordenskjöld from the South Shetland Islands by the dashing Captain Irizar of the *Uruguay*, and the adventures of the *Scotia* in the Weddell Sea. But all these exploits were to me but forerunners of the British National Antarctic Expedition of 1901–04, in the *Discovery*, and the wonderful account of that expedition by Captain Scott.° This book, which I ordered from London and reread a thousand times, filled me with longing to see with my own eyes that strange continent, last Thule of the South, which lies on our maps and globes like a white cloud, a void, fringed here and there with scraps of coastline, dubious capes, supposititious islands, headlands that may or may not be there: Antarctica. And the desire was as pure as the polar snows: to go, to see—no more, no less. I deeply respect the scientific accomplishments of Captain Scott's expedition, and have read with passionate interest the findings of physicists, meteorologists, biologists, etc.; but having had no training in any science, nor any opportunity for such training, my ignorance obliged me to forgo any thought of adding to the body of scientific knowledge concerning Antarctica, and the same is true for all the members of my expedition. It seems a pity; but there was nothing we could do about it. Our goal was limited to observation and exploration. We hoped to go a little farther, perhaps, and see a little more; if not, simply to go and to see. A simple ambition, I think, and essentially a modest one.

Yet it would have remained less than an ambition, no more than a longing, but for the support and encouragement of my dear cousin and friend Juana————. (I use no surnames, lest this report fall into strangers' hands at last, and embarrassment or unpleasant notoriety thus be brought upon unsuspecting husbands, sons, etc.) I had lent Juana my copy of *The Voyage of the "Discovery,"* and it was she who, as we strolled beneath our parasols across the Plaza de Armas after Mass one Sunday in 1908, said, "Well, if Captain Scott can do it, why can't we?"

It was Juana who proposed that we write Carlota————in Valparaíso. Through Carlota we met our benefactor, and so obtained our money, our ship, and even the plausible pretext of going on retreat in a Bolivian convent, which some of us were forced to employ (while the rest of us said we were going to Paris for the winter season). And it was my Juana who in the darkest moments remained resolute, unshaken in her determination to achieve our goal.

5

finneskos: accessories   *Scott:* Robert Falcon Scott (1868–1912), British Antarctic explorer

And there were dark moments, especially in the spring of 1909—times when I did not see how the Expedition would ever become more than a quarter ton of pemmican gone to waste and a lifelong regret. It was so very hard to gather our expeditionary force together! So few of those we asked even knew what we were talking about—so many thought we were mad, or wicked, or both! And of those few who shared our folly, still fewer were able, when it came to the point, to leave their daily duties and commit themselves to a voyage of at least six months, attended with not inconsiderable uncertainty and danger. An ailing parent; an anxious husband beset by business cares; a child at home with only ignorant or incompetent servants to look after it: these are not responsibilities lightly to be set aside. And those who wished to evade such claims were not the companions we wanted in hard work, risk, and privation.

But since success crowned our efforts, why dwell on the setbacks and delays, or the wretched contrivances and downright lies that we all had to employ? I look back with regret only to those friends who wished to come with us but could not, by any contrivance, get free—those we had to leave behind to a life without danger, without uncertainty, without hope.

On the seventeenth of August, 1909, in Punta Arenas, Chile, all the members of the Expedition met for the first time: Juana and I, the two Peruvians; from Argentina, Zoe, Berta, and Teresa; and our Chileans, Carlota and her friends Eva, Pepita, and Dolores. At the last moment I had received word that María's husband, in Quito, was ill and she must stay to nurse him, so we were nine, not ten. Indeed, we had resigned ourselves to being but eight when, just as night fell, the indomitable Zoe arrived in a tiny pirogue manned by Indians, her yacht having sprung a leak just as it entered the Straits of Magellan.

That night before we sailed we began to get to know one another, and we agreed, as we enjoyed our abominable supper in the abominable seaport inn of Punta Arenas, that if a situation arose of such urgent danger that one voice must be obeyed without present question, the unenviable honor of speaking with that voice should fall first upon myself; if I were incapacitated, upon Carlota; if she, then upon Berta. We three were then toasted as "Supreme Inca," "La Araucana," and "The Third Mate," amid a lot of laughter and cheering. As it came out, to my very great pleasure and relief, my qualities as a "leader" were never tested; the nine of us worked things out amongst us from beginning to end without any orders being given by anybody, and only two or three times with recourse to a vote by voice or show of hands. To be sure, we argued a good deal. But then, we had time to argue. And one way or another the arguments always ended up in a decision, upon which action could be taken. Usually at least one person grumbled about the decision, sometimes bitterly. But what is life without grumbling and the occasional opportunity to say "I told you so"? How could one bear housework, or looking after babies, let alone the rigors of sledge-hauling in Antarctica, without grumbling? Officers—as we came to understand aboard the *Yelcho*—are forbidden to grumble; but we nine were, and are, by birth and upbringing, unequivocally and irrevocably, all crew.

Though our shortest course to the southern continent, and that originally urged   10
upon us by the captain of our good ship, was to the South Shetlands and the Bellingshausen Sea, or else by the South Orkneys into the Weddell Sea, we planned to sail west to the Ross Sea, which Captain Scott had explored and described, and from which the brave Ernest Shackleton° had returned only the previous autumn. More was known

Shackleton: Sir Ernest Shackleton (1874–1922), Irish-born British Antarctic explorer

about this region than any other portion of the coast of Antarctica, and though that more was not much, yet it served as some insurance of the safety of the ship, which we felt we had no right to imperil. Captain Pardo had fully agreed with us after studying the charts and our planned itinerary; and so it was westward that we took our course out of the Straits next morning.

Our journey half round the globe was attended by fortune. The little *Yelcho* steamed cheerily along through gale and gleam, climbing up and down those seas of the Southern Ocean that run unbroken round the world. Juana, who had fought bulls and the far more dangerous cows on her family's *estancia,*° called the ship *la vaca valiente,*° because she always returned to the charge. Once we got over being seasick, we all enjoyed the sea voyage, though oppressed at times by the kindly but officious protectiveness of the captain and his officers, who felt that we were only "safe" when huddled up in the three tiny cabins that they had chivalrously vacated for our use.

We saw our first iceberg much farther south than we had looked for it, and saluted it with Veuve Clicquot° at dinner. The next day we entered the ice pack, the belt of floes and bergs broken loose from the land ice and winter-frozen seas of Antarctica which drifts northward in the spring. Fortune still smiled on us: our little steamer, incapable, with her unreinforced metal hull, of forcing a way into the ice, picked her way from lane to lane without hesitation, and on the third day we were through the pack, in which ships have sometimes struggled for weeks and been obliged to turn back at last. Ahead of us now lay the dark-gray waters of the Ross Sea, and beyond that, on the horizon, the remote glimmer, the cloud-reflected whiteness of the Great Ice Barrier.°

Entering the Ross Sea a little east of Longitude West 160°, we came in sight of the Barrier at the place where Captain Scott's party, finding a bight in the vast wall of ice, had gone ashore and sent up their hydrogen-gas balloon for reconnaissance and photography. The towering face of the Barrier, its sheer cliffs and azure and violet waterworn caves, all were as described, but the location had changed: instead of a narrow bight, there was a considerable bay, full of the beautiful and terrific orca whales playing and spouting in the sunshine of that brilliant southern spring.

Evidently masses of ice many acres in extent had broken away from the Barrier (which—at least for most of its vast extent—does not rest on land but floats on water) since the *Discovery's* passage in 1902. This put our plan to set up camp on the Barrier itself in a new light; and while we were discussing alternatives, we asked Captain Pardo to take the ship west along the Barrier face toward Ross Island and McMurdo Sound. As the sea was clear of ice and quite calm, he was happy to do so and, when we sighted the smoke plume of Mt. Erebus, to share in our celebration—another half case of Veuve Clicquot.

The *Yelcho* anchored in Arrival Bay, and we went ashore in the ship's boat. I cannot describe my emotions when I set foot on the earth, on that earth, the barren, cold gravel at the foot of the long volcanic slope. I felt elation, impatience, gratitude, awe, familiarity. I felt that I was home at last. Eight Adélie penguins immediately came to greet us with many exclamations of interest not unmixed with disapproval. "Where on earth have you been? What took you so long? The Hut is around this way. Please come this way. Mind the rocks!" They insisted on our going to visit Hut Point, where the large structure built by Captain Scott's party stood, looking just as in the photographs and drawings that illustrate his book. The area about it, however, was disgusting—a kind of

15

estancia: small farm   *la vaca valiente:* the valiant cow   *Veuve Clicquot:* expensive champagne   *Great Ice Barrier:* the Ross Ice Shelf that closes the bay

graveyard of seal skins, seal bones, penguin bones, and rubbish, presided over by the mad, screaming skua gulls. Our escorts waddled past the slaughterhouse in all tranquillity, and one showed me personally to the door, though it would not go in.

The interior of the hut was less offensive but very dreary. Boxes of supplies had been stacked up into a kind of room within the room; it did not look as I had imagined it when the *Discovery* party put on their melodramas and minstrel shows in the long winter night. (Much later, we learned that Sir Ernest had rearranged it a good deal when he was there just a year before us.) It was dirty, and had about it a mean disorder. A pound tin of tea was standing open. Empty meat tins lay about; biscuits were spilled on the floor; a lot of dog turds were underfoot—frozen, of course, but not a great deal improved by that. No doubt the last occupants had had to leave in a hurry, perhaps even in a blizzard. All the same, they could have closed the tea tin. But housekeeping, the art of the infinite, is no game for amateurs.

Teresa proposed that we use the hut as our camp. Zoe counterproposed that we set fire to it. We finally shut the door and left it as we had found it. The penguins appeared to approve, and cheered us all the way to the boat.

McMurdo Sound was free of ice, and Captain Pardo now proposed to take us off Ross Island and across to Victoria Land, where we might camp at the foot of the Western Mountains, on dry and solid earth. But those mountains, with their storm-darkened peaks and hanging cirques and glaciers, looked as awful as Captain Scott had found them on his western journey, and none of us felt much inclined to seek shelter among them.

Aboard the ship that night we decided to go back and set up our base as we had originally planned, on the Barrier itself. For all available reports indicated that the clear way south was across the level Barrier surface until one could ascend one of the confluent glaciers to the high plateau that appears to form the whole interior of the continent. Captain Pardo argued strongly against this plan, asking what would become of us if the Barrier "calved"—if our particular acre of ice broke away and started to drift northward. "Well," said Zoe, "then you won't have to come so far to meet us." But he was so persuasive on this theme that he persuaded himself into leaving one of the *Yelcho*'s boats with us when we camped, as a means of escape. We found it useful for fishing, later on.

My first steps on Antarctic soil, my only visit to Ross Island, had not been pleasure unalloyed. I thought of the words of the English poet,   20

Though every prospect pleases,
And only Man is vile.

But then, the backside of heroism is often rather sad; women and servants know that. They know also that the heroism may be no less real for that. But achievement is smaller than men think. What is large is the sky, the earth, the sea, the soul. I looked back as the ship sailed east again that evening. We were well into September now, with eight hours or more of daylight. The spring sunset lingered on the twelve-thousand-foot peak of Erebus and shone rosy-gold on her long plume of steam. The steam from our own small funnel faded blue on the twilit water as we crept along under the towering pale wall of ice.

On our return to "Orca Bay"—Sir Ernest, we learned years later, had named it the Bay of Whales—we found a sheltered nook where the Barrier edge was low enough to provide fairly easy access from the ship. The *Yelcho* put out her ice anchor, and the next long, hard days were spent in unloading our supplies and setting up our camp on the ice, a half kilometre in from the edge: a task in which the *Yelcho*'s crew lent us invaluable aid and interminable advice. We took all the aid gratefully, and most of the advice with salt.

The weather so far had been extraordinarily mild for spring in this latitude; the temperature had not yet gone below −20°F, and there was only one blizzard while we were setting up camp. But Captain Scott had spoken feelingly of the bitter south winds on the Barrier, and we had planned accordingly. Exposed as our camp was to every wind, we built no rigid structures above-ground. We set up tents to shelter in while we dug out a series of cubicles in the ice itself, lined them with hay insulation and pine boarding, and roofed them with canvas over bamboo poles, covered with snow for weight and insulation. The big central room was instantly named Buenos Aires by our Argentineans, to whom the center, wherever one is, is always Buenos Aires. The heating and cooking stove was in Buenos Aires. The storage tunnels and the privy (called Punta Arenas) got some back heat from the stove. The sleeping cubicles opened off Buenos Aires, and were very small, mere tubes into which one crawled feet first; they were lined deeply with hay and soon warmed by one's body warmth. The sailors called them coffins and worm holes, and looked with horror on our burrows in the ice. But our little warren or prairie-dog village served us well, permitting us as much warmth and privacy as one could reasonably expect under the circumstances. If the *Yelcho* was unable to get through the ice in February and we had to spend the winter in Antarctica, we certainly could do so, though on very limited rations. For this coming summer, our base—Sudamérica del Sur, South South America, but we generally called it the Base—was intended merely as a place to sleep, to store our provisions, and to give shelter from blizzards.

To Berta and Eva, however, it was more than that. They were its chief architect-designers, its most ingenious builder-excavators, and its most diligent and contented occupants, forever inventing an improvement in ventilation, or learning how to make skylights, or revealing to us a new addition to our suite of rooms, dug in the living ice. It was thanks to them that our stores were stowed so handily, that our stove drew and heated so efficiently, and that Buenos Aires, where nine people cooked, ate, worked, conversed, argued, grumbled, painted, played the guitar and banjo, and kept the Expedition's library of books and maps, was a marvel of comfort and convenience. We lived there in real amity; and if you simply had to be alone for a while, you crawled into your sleeping hole head first.

Berta went a little farther. When she had done all she could to make South South America livable, she dug out one more cell just under the ice surface, leaving a nearly transparent sheet of ice like a greenhouse roof; and there, alone, she worked at sculptures. They were beautiful forms, some like a blending of the reclining human figure with the subtle curves and volumes of the Weddell seal, others like the fantastic shapes of ice cornices and ice caves. Perhaps they are there still, under the snow, in the bubble in the Great Barrier. There where she made them, they might last as long as stone. But she could not bring them north. That is the penalty for carving in water.

Captain Pardo was reluctant to leave us, but his orders did not permit him to hang about the Ross Sea indefinitely, and so at last, with many earnest injunctions to us to stay put—make no journeys—take no risks—beware of frostbite—don't use edge tools—look out for cracks in the ice—and a heartfelt promise to return to Orca Bay on February 20th, or as near that date as wind and ice would permit, the good man bade us farewell, and his crew shouted us a great goodbye cheer as they weighed anchor. That evening, in the long orange twilight of October, we saw the topmast of the *Yelcho* go down the north horizon, over the edge of the world, leaving us to ice, and silence, and the Pole.

That night we began to plan the Southern Journey.

The ensuing month passed in short practice trips and depot-laying. The life we had led at home, though in its own way strenuous, had not fitted any of us for the kind of strain met with in sledge-hauling at ten or twenty degrees below freezing. We all needed as much working out as possible before we dared undertake a long haul.

My longest exploratory trip, made with Dolores and Carlota, was southwest toward Mt. Markham, and it was a nightmare—blizzards and pressure ice° all the way out, crevasses and no view of the mountains when we got there, and white weather and sastrugi° all the way back. The trip was useful, however, in that we could begin to estimate our capacities; and also in that we had started out with a very heavy load of provisions, which we depoted at a hundred and a hundred and thirty miles southsouthwest of Base. Thereafter other parties pushed on farther, till we had a line of snow cairns and depots right down to Latitude 80° 43′, where Juana and Zoe, on an exploring trip, had found a kind of stone gateway opening on a great glacier leading south. We established these depots to avoid, if possible, the hunger that had bedevilled Captain Scott's Southern Party, and the consequent misery and weakness. And we also established to our own satisfaction—intense satisfaction—that we were sledge-haulers at least as good as Captain Scott's husky dogs. Of course we could not have expected to pull as much or as fast as his men. That we did so was because we were favored by much better weather than Captain Scott's party ever met on the Barrier; and also the quantity and quality of our food made a very considerable difference. I am sure that the fifteen percent of dried fruits in our pemmican helped prevent scurvy; and the potatoes, frozen and dried according to an ancient Andean Indian method, were very nourishing yet very light and compact—perfect sledding rations. In any case, it was with considerable confidence in our capacities that we made ready at last for the Southern Journey.

The Southern Party consisted of two sledge teams: Juana, Dolores, and myself; Carlota, Pepita, and Zoe. The support team of Berta, Eva, and Teresa set out before us with a heavy load of supplies, going right up onto the glacier to prospect routes and leave depots of supplies for our return journey. We followed five days behind them, and met them returning between Depot Ercilla and Depot Miranda. That "night"—of course, there was no real darkness—we were all nine together in the heart of the level plain of ice. It was November 15th, Dolores's birthday. We celebrated by putting eight ounces of pisco in the hot chocolate, and became very merry. We sang. It is strange now to remember how thin our voices sounded in that great silence. It was overcast, white weather, without shadows and without visible horizon or any feature to break the level; there was nothing to see at all. We had come to that white place on the map, that void, and there we flew and sang like sparrows.

After sleep and a good breakfast the Base Party continued north and the Southern Party sledged on. The sky cleared presently. High up, thin clouds passed over very rapidly from southwest to northeast, but down on the Barrier it was calm and just cold enough, five or ten degrees below freezing, to give a firm surface for hauling.   30

pressure ice: ice cracking loudly under pressure created by wind blowing over soft-powder snow dunes   *sastrugi:* short walls of hardened snow

On the level ice we never pulled less than eleven miles (seventeen kilometres) a day, and generally fifteen or sixteen miles (twenty-five kilometres). (Our instruments, being British-made, were calibrated in feet, miles, degrees Fahrenheit, etc., but we often converted miles to kilometres, because the larger numbers sounded more encouraging.) At the time we left South America, we knew only that Mr. Ernest Shackleton had mounted another expedition to the Antarctic in 1907, had tried to attain the Pole but failed, and had returned to England in June of the current year, 1909. No coherent report of his explorations had yet reached South America when we left; we did not know what route he had gone, or how far he had got. But we were not altogether taken by surprise when, far across the featureless white plain, tiny beneath the mountain peaks and the strange silent flight of the rainbow-fringed cloud wisps, we saw a fluttering dot of black. We turned west from our course to visit it: a snow heap nearly buried by the winter's storms—a flag on a bamboo pole, a mere shred of threadbare cloth, an empty oil-can—and a few footprints standing some inches above the ice. In some conditions of weather the snow compressed under one's weight remains when the surrounding soft snow melts or is scoured away by the wind; and so these reversed footprints had been left standing all these months, like rows of cobbler's lasts—a queer sight.

We met no other such traces on our way. In general I believe our course was somewhat east of Mr. Shackleton's. Juana, our surveyor, had trained herself well and was faithful and methodical in her sightings and readings, but our equipment was minimal—a theodolite on tripod legs, a sextant with artificial horizon, two compasses, and chronometers. We had only the wheel meter on the sledge to give distance actually travelled.

In any case, it was the day after passing Mr. Shackleton's waymark that I first saw clearly the great glacier among the mountains to the southwest, which was to give us a pathway from the sea level of the Barrier up to the altiplano, ten thousand feet above. The approach was magnificent: a gateway formed by immense vertical domes and pillars of rock. Zoe and Juana had called the vast ice river that flowed through that gateway the Florence Nightingale Glacier, wishing to honor the British, who had been the inspiration and guide of our Expedition; that very brave and very peculiar lady seemed to represent so much that is best, and strangest, in the island race. On maps, of course, this glacier bears the name Mr. Shackleton gave it: the Beardmore.

The ascent of the Nightingale was not easy. The way was open at first, and well marked by our support party, but after some days we came among terrible crevasses, a maze of hidden cracks, from a foot to thirty feet wide and from thirty to a thousand feet deep. Step by step we went, and step by step, and the way always upward now. We were fifteen days on the glacier. At first the weather was hot—up to 20°F—and the hot nights without darkness were wretchedly uncomfortable in our small tents. And all of us suffered more or less from snow blindness just at the time when we wanted clear eyesight to pick our way among the ridges and crevasses of the tortured ice, and to see the wonders about and before us. For at every day's advance more great, nameless peaks came into view in the west and southwest, summit beyond summit, range beyond range, stark rock and snow in the unending noon.

We gave names to these peaks, not very seriously, since we did not expect our discoveries to come to the attention of geographers. Zoe had a gift for naming, and it is thanks to her that certain sketch maps in various suburban South American attics bear such curious features as "Bolívar's Big Nose," "I Am General Rosas," "The Cloudmaker," "Whose Toe?," and "Throne of Our Lady of the Southern Cross." And when at last we got up onto the altiplano, the great interior plateau, it was Zoe who called it the pampa, and maintained that we walked there among vast herds of invisible cattle, transparent cattle pastured on the spindrift snow, their gauchos the restless, merciless winds. We were by then all a little crazy with exhaustion and the great altitude—twelve thousand feet—and the cold and the wind blowing and the luminous circles and crosses surrounding the suns, for often there were three or four suns in the sky, up there.

That is not a place where people have any business to be. We should have turned back; but since we had worked so hard to get there, it seemed that we should go on, at least for a while.

A blizzard came, with very low temperatures, so we had to stay in the tents, in our sleeping bags, for thirty hours—a rest we all needed, though it was warmth we needed most, and there was no warmth on that terrible plain anywhere at all but in our veins. We huddled close together all that time. The ice we lay on is two miles thick.

It cleared suddenly and became, for the plateau, good weather: twelve below zero and the wind not very strong. We three crawled out of our tent and met the others crawling out of theirs. Carlota told us then that her group wished to turn back. Pepita had been feeling very ill; even after the rest during the blizzard, her temperature would not rise above 94°. Carlota was having trouble breathing. Zoe was perfectly fit, but much preferred staying with her friends and lending them a hand in difficulties to pushing on toward the Pole. So we put the four ounces of pisco that we had been keeping for Christmas into the breakfast cocoa, and dug out our tents, and loaded our sledges, and parted there in the white daylight on the bitter plain.

Our sledge was fairly light by now. We pulled on to the south. Juana calculated our position daily. On the twenty-second of December, 1909, we reached the South Pole. The weather was, as always, very cruel. Nothing of any kind marked the dreary whiteness. We discussed leaving some kind of mark or monument, a snow cairn, a tent pole and flag; but there seemed no particular reason to do so. Anything we could do, anything we were, was insignificant, in that awful place. We put up the tent for shelter for an hour and made a cup of tea, and then struck "90° Camp."

Dolores, standing patient as ever in her sledging harness, looked at the snow; it   40
was so hard frozen that it showed no trace of our footprints coming, and she said, "Which way?"

"North," said Juana.

It was a joke, because at that particular place there is no other direction. But we did not laugh. Our lips were cracked with frostbite and hurt too much to let us laugh. So we started back, and the wind at our backs pushed us along, and dulled the knife edges of the waves of frozen snow.

All that week the blizzard wind pursued us like a pack of mad dogs. I cannot describe it. I wished we had not gone to the Pole. I think I wish it even now. But I was glad even then that we had left no sign there, for some man longing to be first might come some day, and find it, and know then what a fool he had been, and break his heart.

We talked, when we could talk, of catching up to Carlota's party, since they might be going slower than we. In fact they used their tent as a sail to catch the following wind and had got far ahead of us. But in many places they had built snow cairns or left some sign for us; once, Zoe had written on the lee side of a ten-foot sastruga, just as children write on the sand of the beach at Miraflores, "This Way Out!" The wind blowing over the frozen ridge had left the words perfectly distinct.

In the very hour that we began to descend the glacier, the weather turned warmer,   45
and the mad dogs were left to howl forever tethered to the Pole. The distance that had taken us fifteen days going up we covered in only eight days going down. But the good weather that had aided us descending the Nightingale became a curse down on the

Barrier ice, where we had looked forward to a kind of royal progress from depot to depot, eating our fill and taking our time for the last three hundred-odd miles. In a tight place on the glacier I lost my goggles—I was swinging from my harness at the time in a crevasse—and then Juana broke hers when we had to do some rock-climbing coming down to the Gateway. After two days in bright sunlight with only one pair of snow goggles to pass amongst us, we were all suffering badly from snow blindness. It became acutely painful to keep lookout for landmarks or depot flags, to take sightings, even to study the compass, which had to be laid down on the snow to steady the needle. At Concolorcorvo Depot, where there was a particularly good supply of food and fuel, we gave up, crawled into our sleeping bags with bandaged eyes, and slowly boiled alive like lobsters in the tent exposed to the relentless sun. The voices of Berta and Zoe were the sweetest sound I ever heard. A little concerned about us, they had skied south to meet us. They led us home to Base.

We recovered quite swiftly, but the altiplano left its mark. When she was very little, Rosita asked if a dog "had bitted Mama's toes." I told her yes—a great, white, mad dog named Blizzard! My Rosita and my Juanito heard many stories when they were little, about that fearful dog and how it howled, and the transparent cattle of the invisible gauchos, and a river of ice eight thousand feet high called Nightingale, and how Cousin Juana drank a cup of tea standing on the bottom of the world under seven suns, and other fairy tales.

We were in for one severe shock when we reached Base at last. Teresa was pregnant. I must admit that my first response to the poor girl's big belly and sheepish look was anger—rage—fury. That one of us should have concealed anything, and such a thing, from the others! But Teresa had done nothing of the sort. Only those who had concealed from her what she most needed to know were to blame. Brought up by servants, with four years' schooling in a convent, and married at sixteen, the poor girl was still so ignorant at twenty years of age that she had thought it was "the cold weather" that made her miss her periods. Even this was not entirely stupid, for all of us on the Southern Journey had seen our periods change or stop altogether as we experienced increasing cold, hunger, and fatigue. Teresa's appetite had begun to draw general attention; and then she had begun, as she said pathetically, "to get fat." The others were worried at the thought of all the sledge-hauling she had done, but she flourished, and the only problem was her positively insatiable appetite. As well as could be determined from her shy references to her last night on the hacienda with her husband, the baby was due at just about the same time as the *Yelcho*, February 20th. But we had not been back from the Southern Journey two weeks when, on February 14th, she went into labor.

Several of us had borne children and had helped with deliveries, and anyhow most of what needs to be done is fairly self-evident; but a first labor can be long and trying, and we were all anxious, while Teresa was frightened out of her wits. She kept calling for her José till she was as hoarse as a skua. Zoe lost all patience at last and said, "By God, Teresa, if you say 'José!' once more, I hope you have a penguin!" But what she had, after twenty long hours, was a pretty little red-faced girl.

Many were the suggestions for that child's name from her eight proud midwife aunts: Polita, Penguina, McMurdo, Victoria . . . But Teresa announced, after she had had a good sleep and a large serving of pemmican, "I shall name her Rosa—Rosa del Sur," Rose of the South. That night we drank the last two bottles of Veuve Clicquot (having finished the pisco at 88° 60′ South) in toasts to our little Rose.

On the nineteenth of February, a day early, my Juana came down into Buenos   50
Aires in a hurry. "The ship," she said, "the ship has come," and she burst into tears—
she who had never wept in all our weeks of pain and weariness on the long haul.

Of the return voyage there is nothing to tell. We came back safe.

In 1912 all the world learned that the brave Norwegian Amundsen° had reached
the South Pole; and then, much later, we heard the accounts of how Captain Scott and
his men had come there after him but did not come home again.

Just this year, Juana and I wrote to the captain of the *Yelcho*, for the newspapers
have been full of the story of his gallant dash to rescue Sir Ernest Shackleton's men
from Elephant Island, and we wished to congratulate him, and once more to thank him.
Never one word has he breathed of our secret. He is a man of honor, Luis Pardo.

I add this last note in 1929. Over the years we have lost touch with one another.
It is very difficult for women to meet, when they live as far apart as we do. Since Juana
died, I have seen none of my old sledgemates, though sometimes we write. Our little Rosa
del Sur died of the scarlet fever when she was five years old. Teresa had many other children. Carlota took the veil in Santiago ten years ago. We are old women now, with old
husbands, and grown children, and grandchildren who might some day like to read
about the Expedition. Even if they are rather ashamed of having such a crazy grandmother, they may enjoy sharing in the secret. But they must not let Mr. Amundsen°
know! He would be terribly embarrassed and disappointed. There is no need for him
or anyone else outside the family to know. We left no footprints, even.

QUESTIONS FOR CLOSE READING OF IRONY AND TONE

1. Why does the narrator tell us that her report is not intended for publication?
2. How would you describe the tone of the first pages of the story? How do the
   naming of names and the specific references to places and events contribute to
   the tone?
3. Why doesn't the narrator use the proper names of the women in her expeditionary force?
4. Some women could not go along with the force. Why?
5. In what ways is the ambition of the expeditionary force ironic? Does the narrator
   represent it as ironic?
6. Is the description of the journey on the *Yelcho* convincing? Why?
7. What does the narrator think of the housekeeping of Ernest Shackleton's hut
   when she arrives? Why does Zoe want to set fire to it? What do they finally do?
8. Is the narrator being ironic when she tells us that the weather was mild and had
   "not yet gone below −20°F"?
9. What are we to make of Captain Pardo's advice when he leaves the party behind
   and promises to come back close to February 20?
10. What makes the description of the journey of the sledge teams convincing?
11. In paragraph 35 the narrator explains how they named the places they encoun-
    tered. What is ironic about their procedure?

Amundsen: Roald Amundsen (1872–1928), the first man to reach the South Pole (1911)

12. When the team actually reaches the South Pole it does not leave any markers or any evidence of its having been there. Why? Why is that an ironic decision?

13. What does the narrator tell her children happened to her frostbitten toes?

14. Why is it ironic that a girl should be born during the expedition?

15. Why must Roald Amundsen never know of the success of the narrator's expedition?

QUESTIONS FOR INTERPRETATION OF IRONY AND TONE

1. Ursula Le Guin's "Sur" has an ironic center and a whimsical tone. The name is Spanish for "South," and the story tells of a team of women who conquered the South Pole two years before the Norwegian explorer Roald Amundsen. The team included a pregnant woman who gave birth only two weeks after returning from the South Pole. The tone of the story is similar to what one would expect from a *National Geographic*-style account of a successful exploration. However, the story is a piece of ironic fiction designed to stimulate thought concerning people's attitudes toward women and exploration. In what ways does it contradict your expectations of the behavior of women?

2. What is the primary irony in this story? It purports to be a genuine record of an exploration written in a style consonant with all the formal reports made to geographical societies during the early years of the twentieth century. Why would we find it ironic in tone rather than simply a fraud? Do you think many readers would assume the story is true? How would those who know it to be false detect its irony?

3. What do you learn about the character of the narrator during the course of the story? What do you learn about the other women in the party? How fully are these characters developed? What are their expressed motives in taking part in such a risky venture? Is it possible that they operate out of a sense of competition with men? If so, is it especially ironic that they do not even leave footprints behind?

4. How should a reader respond to this story? Did your response change as you read through the story? Describe as best you can your responses and how they alter. Would you expect many readers to respond as you did? Can you tell what Ursula Le Guin expected her readers to feel as they read the story? Does she do anything to control their responses?

5. If we assume this is a feminist story, what would make it so? The women in the story have utmost regard for men explorers and even go to great lengths to avoid hurting their feelings. With that being the case, how could we call this a feminist story? What are its feminist elements? Does irony contribute to the story's being feminist in tone?

HOW THE ELEMENTS WORK TOGETHER

Examining one element of a short story constrains you by a limitation you may not have chosen. For example, you may have wanted to ignore point of view in Charles Baxter's "Gryphon" in favor of discussing its theme or the psychology of its characters. You may have wanted to discuss the setting of "The Swimmer" instead of focusing on style and theme. Or you may have wanted to talk about several elements rather than just one in relation to all the stories. Well, the good news is that interpretations of short fiction offer you a wide range of choices. You can discuss all or none of the elements of the short story as you like.

When a story impresses you as good, something has caused it to do so. Your responses are caused not by one element but rather by a combination. A good interpretation of a short story may therefore move from setting to character to theme to style and tone and back again at will. Great short stories succeed because all their elements work together and create a powerful effect. Bharati Mukherjee's "Jasmine" is such a story. The setting is economical, the characters are rich and complex, and the style imparts subtle contrasts, some of them ironic, with the thematic concerns of a young woman making her way in a strange and unexpected world. The straightforward action is told with no flashbacks, and the point of view is consistent with the most conventional storytelling techniques. Conventional simplicities add to the richness and complexity of the story because they help us contrast the simplicity of certain characters' perceptions with the enormous subtleties of the environment.

"Jasmine," told from a third-person point of view, never veers from what Jasmine saw, thought, and experienced. The reader sees the world through her eyes because the narrative stays entirely within her sphere of understanding; it is restricted. The setting is recognizable to any contemporary North American, especially one who has visited large cities like Detroit or who has experienced college towns like Ann Arbor. However, the experiences are unusual because of the perceptions of the character, for whom they are exotic. Jasmine is an East Indian who had been living in Trinidad and who has now come to the United States through Canada. She is illegal. She is also eager and excited by her opportunities.

BHARATI MUKHERJEE   (b. 1940)

Born in Calcutta, India, Bharati Mukherjee came to the United States when she was twenty-one and then moved in 1968 to Canada. Partly in reaction to prejudice against Indians in Canada, she returned to the United States in 1980 and became a permanent resident. Mukherjee has written several novels: The Tiger's Daughter *(1972);* Wife *(1975); and* Jasmine *(1989), which further treats the character in this story. Her short stories are collected in* Darkness *(1980) and* The Middleman and Other Stories *(1988). She has also written some personal reminiscences,* Days and Nights in Calcutta *and* The Sorrow and the Terror. *Mukherjee is a powerful writer in the early stages of her career.*

Jasmine ————————————————————— *1988*

Jasmine came to Detroit from Port-of-Spain, Trinidad, by way of Canada. She crossed the border at Windsor in the back of a gray van loaded with mattresses and box springs. The plan was for her to hide in an empty mattress box if she heard the driver say, "All bad weather seems to come down from Canada, doesn't it?" to the customs man. But she didn't have to crawl into a box and hold her breath. The customs man didn't ask to look in.

The driver let her off at a scary intersection on Woodward Avenue and gave her instructions on how to get to the Plantations Motel in Southfield. The trick was to keep changing vehicles, he said. That threw off the immigration guys real quick.

Jasmine took money for cab fare out of the pocket of the great big raincoat that the van driver had given her. The raincoat looked like something that nuns in Port-of-Spain sold in church bazaars. Jasmine was glad to have a coat with wool lining, though; and anyway, who would know in Detroit that she was Dr. Vassanji's daughter?

All the bills in her hand looked the same. She would have to be careful when she paid the cabdriver. Money in Detroit wasn't pretty the way it was back home, or even in Canada, but she liked this money better. Why should money be pretty, like a picture? Pretty money is only good for putting on your walls maybe. The dollar bills felt businesslike, serious. Back home at work, she used to count out thousands of Trinidad dollars every day and not even think of them as real. Real money was worn and green, American dollars. Holding the bills in her fist on a street corner meant she had made it in okay. She'd outsmarted the guys at the border. Now it was up to her to use her wits to do something with her life. As her Daddy kept saying, "Girl, is opportunity come only once." The girls she'd worked with at the bank in Port-of-Spain had gone green as bananas when she'd walked in with her ticket on Air Canada. Trinidad was too tiny. That was the trouble. Trinidad was an island stuck in the middle of nowhere. What kind of place was that for a girl with ambition?

The Plantations Motel was run by a family of Trinidad Indians who had come   5 from the tuppenny-ha'penny° country town, Chaguanas. The Daboos were nobodies back home. They were lucky, that's all. They'd gotten here before the rush and bought up a motel and an ice cream parlor. Jasmine felt very superior when she saw Mr. Daboo in the motel's reception area. He was a pumpkin-shaped man with very black skin and Elvis Presley sideburns turning white. They looked like earmuffs. Mrs. Daboo was a bumpkin, too; short, fat, flapping around in house slippers. The Daboo daughters seemed very American, though. They didn't seem to know that they were nobodies, and kept looking at her and giggling.

She knew she would be short of cash for a great long while. Besides, she wasn't sure she wanted to wear bright leather boots and leotards like Viola and Loretta. The smartest move she could make would be to put a down payment on a husband. Her Daddy had told her to talk to the Daboos first chance. The Daboos ran a service fixing up illegals with islanders who had made it in legally. Daddy had paid three thousand back in Trinidad, with the Daboos and the mattress man getting part of it. They should throw in a good-earning husband for that kind of money.

The Daboos asked her to keep books for them and to clean the rooms in the new wing, and she could stay in 16B as long as she liked. They showed her 16B. They said she could cook her own roti;° Mr. Daboo would bring in a stove, two gas rings that you could fold up in a metal box. The room was quite grand, Jasmine thought. It had a double bed, a TV, a pink sink and matching bathtub. Mrs. Daboo said Jasmine wasn't the big-city Port-of-Spain type she'd expected. Mr. Daboo said that he wanted her to stay because it was nice to have a neat, cheerful person around. It wasn't a bad deal, better than stories she'd heard about Trinidad girls in the States.

tuppenny-ha'penny: equivalent to nickel-and-dime in American slang   *roti:* a kind of bread

All day every day except Sundays Jasmine worked. There wasn't just the book-keeping and the cleaning up. Mr. Daboo had her working on the match-up marriage service. Jasmine's job was to check up on social security cards, call clients' bosses for references, and make sure credit information wasn't false. Dermatologists and engineers living in Bloomfield Hills, store owners on Canfield and Woodward: she treated them all as potential liars. One of the first things she learned was that Ann Arbor was a magic word. A boy goes to Ann Arbor and gets an education, and all the barriers come crashing down. So Ann Arbor was the place to be.

She didn't mind the work. She was learning about Detroit, every side of it. Sunday mornings she helped unload packing crates of Caribbean spices in a shop on the next block. For the first time in her life, she was working for a black man, an African. So what if the boss was black? This was a new life, and she wanted to learn everything. Her Sunday boss, Mr. Anthony, was a courtly, Christian, church-going man, and paid her the only wages she had in her pocket. Viola and Loretta, for all their fancy American ways, wouldn't go out with blacks.

One Friday afternoon she was writing up the credit info on a Guyanese Muslim   10
who worked in an assembly plant when Loretta said that enough was enough and that there was no need for Jasmine to be her father's drudge.

"Is time to have fun," Viola said. "We're going to Ann Arbor."

Jasmine filed the sheet on the Guyanese man who probably now would never get a wife and got her raincoat. Loretta's boyfriend had a Cadillac parked out front. It was the longest car Jasmine had ever been in and louder than a country bus. Viola's boyfriend got out of the front seat. "Oh, oh, sweet things," he said to Jasmine. "Get in front." He was a talker. She'd learned that much from working on the matrimonial match-ups. She didn't believe him for a second when he said that there were dudes out there dying to ask her out.

Loretta's boyfriend said, "You have eyes I could leap into, girl."

Jasmine knew he was just talking. They sounded like Port-of-Spain boys of three years ago. It didn't surprise her that these Trinidad country boys in Detroit were still behind the times, even of Port-of-Spain. She sat very stiff between the two men, hands on her purse. The Daboo girls laughed in the back seat.

On the highway the girls told her about the reggae night in Ann Arbor. Kevin   15
and the Krazee Islanders. Malcolm's Lovers. All the big reggae groups in the Midwest were converging for the West Indian Students Association fall bash. The ticket didn't come cheap but Jasmine wouldn't let the fellows pay. She wasn't that kind of girl.

The reggae and steel drums brought out the old Jasmine. The rum punch, the dancing, the dreadlocks, the whole combination. She hadn't heard real music since she got to Detroit, where music was supposed to be so famous. The Daboo girls kept turning on rock stuff in the motel lobby whenever their father left the area. She hadn't danced, really *danced,* since she'd left home. It felt so good to dance. She felt hot and sweaty and sexy. The boys at the dance were more than sweet talkers; they moved with assurance and spoke of their futures in America. The bartender gave her two free drinks and said, "Is ready when you are, girl." She ignored him but she felt all hot and good deep inside. She knew Ann Arbor was a special place.

When it was time to pile back into Loretta's boyfriend's Cadillac, she just couldn't face going back to the Plantations Motel and to the Daboos with their accounting books and messy files.

"I don't know what happen, girl," she said to Loretta. "I feel all crazy inside. Maybe is time for me to pursue higher studies in this town."

"This Ann Arbor, girl, they don't just take you off the street. It cost like hell."

She spent the night on a bashed-up sofa in the Student Union. She was a well-dressed, respectable girl, and she didn't expect anyone to question her right to sleep on the furniture. Many others were doing the same thing. In the morning, a boy in an army parka showed her the way to the Placement Office. He was a big, blond, clumsy boy, not bad-looking except for the blond eyelashes. He didn't scare her, as did most Americans. She let him buy her a Coke and a hotdog. That evening she had a job with the Moffitts.

Bill Moffitt taught molecular biology and Lara Hatch-Moffitt, his wife, was a performance artist. A performance artist, said Lara, was very different from being an actress, though Jasmine still didn't understand what the difference might be. The Moffitts had a little girl, Muffin, whom Jasmine was to look after, though for the first few months she might have to help out with the housework and the cooking because Lara said she was deep into performance rehearsals. That was all right with her, Jasmine said, maybe a little too quickly. She explained she came from a big family and was used to heavy-duty cooking and cleaning. This wasn't the time to say anything about Ram, the family servant. Americans like the Moffitts wouldn't understand about keeping servants. Ram and she weren't in similar situations. Here mother's helpers, which is what Lara had called her—Americans were good with words to cover their shame—seemed to be as good as anyone.

Lara showed her the room she would have all to herself in the finished basement. There was a big, old TV, not in color like the motel's and a portable typewriter on a desk which Lara said she would find handy when it came time to turn in her term papers. Jasmine didn't say anything about not being a student. She was a student of life, wasn't she? There was a scary moment after they'd discussed what she could expect as salary, which was three times more than anything Mr. Daboo was supposed to pay her but hadn't. She thought Bill Moffitt was going to ask her about her visa or her green card number and social security. But all Bill did was smile and smile at her—he had a wide, pink, baby face—and play with a button on his corduroy jacket. The button would need sewing back on, firmly.

Lara said, "I think I'm going to like you, Jasmine. You have a something about you. A something real special. I'll just bet you've acted, haven't you?" The idea amused her, but she merely smiled and accepted Lara's hug. The interview was over.

Then Bill opened a bottle of Soave and told stories about camping in northern Michigan. He'd been raised there. Jasmine didn't see the point in sleeping in tents; the woods sounded cold and wild and creepy. But she said, "Is exactly what I want to try out come summer, man. Campin and huntin."

Lara asked about Port-of-Spain. There was nothing to tell about her hometown that wouldn't shame her in front of nice white American folk like the Moffitts. The place was shabby, the people were grasping and cheating and lying and life was full of despair and drink and wanting. But by the time she finished, the island sounded romantic. Lara said, "It wouldn't surprise me one bit if you were a writer, Jasmine."

Ann Arbor was a huge small town. She couldn't imagine any kind of school the size of the University of Michigan. She meant to sign up for courses in the spring. Bill brought home a catalogue bigger than the phonebook for all of Trinidad. The university had courses in everything. It would be hard to choose; she'd have to get help from Bill. He wasn't like a professor, not the ones back home where even high school teachers called themselves professors and acted like little potentates. He wore blue jeans and thick sweaters with holes in the elbows and used phrases like "in vitro" as he watched her curry up fish. Dr. Parveen back home—he called himself "doctor" when everybody knew he didn't have even a Master's degree—was never seen without his cotton jacket which had gotten really ratty at the cuffs and lapel edges. She hadn't learned anything in the two years she'd put into college. She'd learned more from working in the bank for two months than she had at college. It was the assistant manager, Personal Loans Department, Mr. Singh, who had turned her on to the Daboos and to smooth, bargain-priced emigration.

Jasmine liked Lara. Lara was easygoing. She didn't spend the time she had between rehearsals telling Jasmine how to cook and clean American-style. Mrs. Daboo did that in 16B. Mrs. Daboo would barge in with a plate of stale samosas and snoop around giving free advice on how mainstream Americans did things. As if she were dumb or something! As if she couldn't keep her own eyes open and make her mind up for herself. Sunday mornings she had to share the butcher-block workspace in the kitchen with Bill. He made the Sunday brunch from new recipes in *Gourmet* and *Cuisine*. Jasmine hadn't seen a man cook who didn't have to or wasn't getting paid to do it. Things were topsy-turvy in the Moffitt house. Lara went on two- and three-day road trips and Bill stayed home. But even her Daddy, who'd never poured himself a cup of tea, wouldn't put Bill down as a woman. The mornings Bill tried out something complicated, a Cajun shrimp, sausage, and beans dish, for instance, Jasmine skipped church services. The Moffitts didn't go to church, though they seemed to be good Christians. They just didn't talk church talk, which suited her fine.

Two months passed. Jasmine knew she was lucky to have found a small, clean, friendly family like the Moffitts to build her new life around. "Man!" she'd exclaim as she vacuumed the wide-plank wood floors or ironed (Lara wore pure silk or pure cotton). "In this country Jesus givin out good luck only!" By this time they knew she wasn't a student, but they didn't care and said they wouldn't report her. They never asked if she was illegal on top of it.

To savor her new sense of being a happy, lucky person, she would put herself through a series of "what ifs": what if Mr. Singh in Port-of-Spain hadn't turned her on to the Daboos and loaned her two thousand! What if she'd been ugly like the Mintoo girl and the manager hadn't even offered! What if the customs man had unlocked the door of the van! Her Daddy liked to say, "You is a helluva girl, Jasmine."

"Thank you, Jesus," Jasmine said, as she carried on.   30

Christmas Day the Moffitts treated her just like family. They gave her a red cashmere sweater with a V neck so deep it made her blush. If Lara had worn it, her bosom wouldn't hang out like melons. For the holiday weekend Bill drove her to the Daboos in Detroit. "You work too hard," Bill said to her. "Learn to be more selfish. Come on, throw your weight around." She'd rather not have spent time with the Daboos, but that first afternoon of the interview she'd told Bill and Lara that Mr. Daboo was her mother's first cousin. She had thought it shameful in those days to have no papers, no family, no roots. Now Loretta and Viola in tight, bright pants seemed trashy like girls at Two-Johnny Bissoondath's Bar back home. She was stuck with the story of the Daboos being family. Village bumpkins, ha! She would break out. Soon.

Jasmine had Bill drop her off at the RenCen. The Plantations Motel, in fact, the whole Riverfront area, was too seamy. She'd managed to cut herself off mentally from anything too islandy. She loved her Daddy and Mummy, but she didn't think of them that often anymore. Mummy had expected her to be homesick and come flying right back home. "Is blowin sweat-of-brow money is what you doin, Pa," Mummy had scolded.

She loved them, but she'd become her own person. That was something that Lara said: "I am my own person."

The Daboos acted thrilled to see her back. "What you drinkin, Jasmine girl?" Mr. Daboo kept asking. "You drinkin sherry or what?" Pouring her little glasses of sherry instead of rum was a sure sign he thought she had become whitefolk-fancy. The Daboo sisters were very friendly, but Jasmine considered them too wild. Both Loretta and Viola had changed boyfriends. Both were seeing black men they'd danced with in Ann Arbor. Each night at bedtime, Mr. Daboo cried. "In Trinidad we stayin we side, they stayin they side. Here, everything mixed up. Is helluva confusion, no?"

On New Year's Eve the Daboo girls and their black friends went to a dance. Mr. and Mrs. Daboo and Jasmine watched TV for a while. Then Mr. Daboo got out a brooch from his pocket and pinned it on Jasmine's red sweater. It was a Christmasy brooch, a miniature sleigh loaded down with snowed-on mistletoe. Before she could pull away, he kissed her on the lips. "Good luck for the New Year!" he said. She lifted her head and saw tears. "Is year for dreams comin true."

Jasmine started to cry, too. There was nothing wrong, but Mr. Daboo, Mrs. Daboo, she, everybody was crying.   35

What for? This is where she wanted to be. She'd spent some damned uncomfortable times with the assistant manager to get approval for her loan. She thought of Daddy. He would be playing poker and fanning himself with a magazine. Her married sisters would be rolling out the dough for stacks and stacks of roti, and Mummy would be steamed purple from stirring the big pot of goat curry on the stove. She missed them. But. It felt strange to think of anyone celebrating New Year's Eve in summery clothes.

In March Lara and her performing group went on the road. Jasmine knew that the group didn't work from scripts. The group didn't use a stage, either; instead, it took over supermarkets, senior citizens' centers, and school halls, without notice. Jasmine didn't understand the performance world. But she was glad that Lara said, "I'm not going to lay a guilt trip on myself. Muffie's in super hands," before she left.

Muffie didn't need much looking after. She played Trivial Pursuit all day, usually pretending to be two persons, sometimes Jasmine, whose accent she could imitate. Since Jasmine didn't know any of the answers, she couldn't help. Muffie was a quiet, precocious child with see-through blue eyes like her dad's, and red braids. In the early evenings Jasmine cooked supper, something special she hadn't forgotten from her island days. After supper she and Muffie watched some TV, and Bill read. When Muffie went to bed, Bill and she sat together for a bit with their glasses of Soave. Bill, Muffie, and she were a family, almost.

Down in her basement room that late, dark winter, she had trouble sleeping. She wanted to stay awake and think of Bill. Even when she fell asleep it didn't feel like sleep because Bill came barging into her dreams in his funny, loose-jointed, clumsy way. It was mad to think of him all the time, and stupid and sinful; but she couldn't help it. Whenever she put back a book he'd taken off the shelf to read or whenever she put his clothes through the washer and dryer, she felt sick in a giddy, wonderful way. When Lara came back things would get back to normal. Meantime she wanted the performance group miles away.

Lara called in at least twice a week. She said things like, "We've finally obliterated   40 the margin between realspace and performancespace." Jasmine filled her in on Muffie's doings and the mail. Bill always closed with, "I love you. We miss you, hon."

One night after Lara had called—she was in Lincoln, Nebraska—Bill said to Jasmine, "Let's dance."

She hadn't danced since the reggae night she'd had too many rum punches. Her toes began to throb and clench. She untied her apron and the fraying, knotted-up laces of her running shoes.

Bill went around the downstairs rooms turning down lights. "We need atmosphere," he said. He got a small, tidy fire going in the living room grate and pulled the Turkish scatter rug closer to it. Lara didn't like anybody walking on the Turkish rug, but Bill meant to have his way. The hissing logs, the plants in the dimmed light, the thick patterned rug: everything was changed. This wasn't the room she cleaned every day.

He stood close to her. She smoothed her skirt down with both hands.

"I want you to choose the record," he said.   45

"I don't know your music."

She brought her hand high to his face. His skin was baby smooth.

"I want *you* to pick," he said. "You are your own person now."

"You got island music?"

He laughed, "What do you think?" The stereo was in a cabinet with albums   50
packed tight alphabetically into the bottom three shelves. "Calypso has not been a force in my life."

She couldn't help laughing. "Calypso? Oh, man." She pulled dust jackets out at random. Lara's records. The Flying Lizards. The Violent Fems. There was so much still to pick up on!

"This one," she said, finally.

He took the record out of her hand. "God! he laughed. "Lara must have found this in a garage sale!" He laid the old record on the turntable. It was "Music for Lovers," something the nuns had taught her to foxtrot to way back in Port-of-Spain.

They danced so close that she could feel his heart heaving and crashing against her head. She liked it, she liked it very much. She didn't care what happened.

"Come on," Bill whispered. "If it feels right, do it." He began to take her clothes   55
off.

"Don't, Bill," she pleaded.

"Come on, baby," he whispered again. "You're a blossom, a flower."

He took off his fisherman's knit pullover, the corduroy pants, the blue shorts. She kept pace. She'd never had such an effect on a man. He nearly flung his socks and Adidas into the fire. "You feel so good," he said. "You smell so good. You're really something, flower of Trinidad."

"Flower of Ann Arbor," she said, "not Trinidad."

She felt so good she was dizzy. She'd never felt this good on the island where men   60
did this all the time, and girls went along with it always for favors. You couldn't feel really good in a nothing place. She was thinking this as they made love on the Turkish carpet in front of the fire: she was a bright, pretty girl with no visa, no papers, and no birth certificate. No nothing other than what she wanted to invent and tell. She was a girl rushing wildly into the future.

His hand moved up her throat and forced her lips apart and it felt so good, so right, that she forgot all the dreariness of her new life and gave herself up to it.

QUESTIONS FOR CLOSE READING OF HOW THE ELEMENTS
WORK TOGETHER

1. Jasmine's entrance into Detroit was illegal. What was her emotional state upon entry? Did she feel guilty? Should she? How does the initial setting contribute to her feelings? How do you respond to her arrival?

2. What was Jasmine's background before she arrived in Detroit? What was her attitude toward herself in relation to the society around her?

3. Is Jasmine ambitious? What is her relationship to the Daboos? What does she mean when she thinks, "The Daboos were nobodies back home"? How do the Daboos treat her?

4. Jasmine thinks room 16B is "quite grand." How do you react to the setting of 16B? Does Mukherjee rely on irony for effect here?

5. How do the characters react to those of other races? What is Jasmine's attitude toward blacks? Toward whites? Toward other Indians? Is racial prejudice a major theme of the story?

6. In what ways is the contrast between Lara Hatch-Moffitt and Jasmine ironic? Why does Jasmine think, "Things were topsy-turvy in the Moffitt house"? Is she right?

7. One of the central themes of the story is the disjunction between traditional Indian social style and the American style of the Moffitts. What chief distinctions does Jasmine notice? Is the disjunction ironic?

8. What stylistic contrasts in the use of language do you feel are most important in the story? How would you describe the major differences in the ways in which characters speak? What do the differences add to the story?

9. How does the narrative unfold? How does the third-person point of view limit what the reader must understand about the situation that Jasmine finds herself in? Do you as a reader understand more about the situation than Jasmine does? If you do, how is this possible?

10. Although a young girl, Jasmine responds in a complex fashion to her environment, beginning with the Daboos. How much do you feel you know about her? How fully does Mukherjee develop her character in the story? What important values does she hold?

11. The story ends with a metaphor when Bill calls her "flower of Trinidad." What is the force of this metaphor when Jasmine responds by correcting him: " 'Flower of Ann Arbor,' she said, 'not Trinidad.' " What does this imply for Jasmine's future?

QUESTIONS FOR INTERPRETATION OF HOW THE ELEMENTS
WORK TOGETHER

1. How appropriate is the restricted third-person point of view to the telling of Jasmine's story? Is the action of the story more satisfying because of the point of view, or less satisfying? How effective is this point of view for revealing Jasmine's personality? What overall effect does this point of view have on making you understand her emotional and moral circumstances?

2. At the end of the story, as Bill undresses Jasmine, he says, "If it feels right, do it." This is an ethical statement. What has Jasmine done throughout the story to prepare her to accept and act upon that statement? Has Bill's ethical view always been one Jasmine could share? When, in the story, does she seem to have begun accepting it? Does the story make a judgment in approval or disapproval of this ethical view? Is Bill's comment ironic or sincere? Is the story ironic?

3. Are you sympathetic or unsympathetic to Jasmine and her situation? Does she do things that annoy you? Or please you? How do you feel about Bill and Lara Moffitt? Are your responses to them positive or not? What about the Daboos and their daughters, Viola and Loretta? To what extent are your sympathies controlled by Jasmine's experiences? To what extent are your sympathies controlled by your own views on illegal immigrants?

4. What is the position of women in the story? How many different women are important in the story? What are their approximate ages? What is expected of them, and how free or independent are they? Are women oppressed in "Jasmine"? Is Jasmine oppressed? Was Jasmine right in going along with Bill's seduction at the end of the story? What does it mean to say, "She was a girl rushing wildly into the future"? Does Bill exploit Jasmine?

5. One theme of the story is emigration—a theme common to much of Mukherjee's writing. What significance does the story have for us regarding emigration to America, especially of nonwhites? What cultural disjunctions does Jasmine experience? What does Jasmine mean by the reference to "all the dreariness of her new life" on the last page of the story?

6. Comment on the way in which the theme of the story is reinforced by the settings both discussed in the story and presented directly in the narration. How is the theme revealed in the course of the developing narrative? What interesting uses of metaphor or language help you interpret the theme of the story?

ERNEST HEMINGWAY   (1899–1961)

Ernest Hemingway came to symbolize the "Lost Generation" of writers, those who, like Hemingway, spent much of their early productive lives in Europe between the world wars. He first arrived in Italy as a Red Cross ambulance driver and was wounded in 1918 while carrying a wounded Italian soldier to safety. His period of recovery in an Italian hospital was the basis of his novel A Farewell to Arms *(1929). Before that, he wrote several books that established his reputation as an innovative and significant writer. His story collections,* In Our Time *(1925) and* Men without Women *(1927), signaled a powerful approach to language and subject matter.* The Sun Also Rises *(1926) made him famous. Hemingway spent the early 1920s in Paris, where he met Ezra Pound, Gertrude Stein, and James Joyce, the major modernist writers. His style is marked by an unusual economy of language: simple words, and few of them. He observed details closely and portrayed nuances of emotion with great clarity. His notebooks indicate the care with which he observed people, especially his friends. After the success of his novels, he published short stories in numerous magazines. "Hills like White Elephants" appeared in 1938 in* The Fifth Column and the First Forty-nine Stories.

Hills like White Elephants _____ *1938*

The hills across the valley of the Ebro were long and white. On this side there was no
shade and no trees and the station was between two lines of rails in the sun. Close against
the side of the station there was the warm shadow of the building and a curtain, made
of strings of bamboo beads, hung across the open door into the bar, to keep out flies.
The American and the girl with him sat at a table in the shade, outside the building. It
was very hot and the express from Barcelona would come in forty minutes. It stopped
at this junction for two minutes and went on to Madrid.

"What should we drink?" the girl asked. She had taken off her hat and put it on
the table.

"It's pretty hot," the man said.

"Let's drink beer."

"*Dos cervezas,*"° the man said into the curtain.   5

"Big ones?" a woman asked from the doorway.

"Yes. Two big ones."

The woman brought two glasses of beer and two felt pads. She put the felt pads and
the beer glasses on the table and looked at the man and the girl. The girl was looking off
at the line of hills. They were white in the sun and the country was brown and dry.

"They look like white elephants," she said.

"I've never seen one," the man drank his beer.   10

"No, you wouldn't have."

"I might have," the man said. "Just because you say I wouldn't have doesn't prove
anything."

The girl looked at the bead curtain. "They've painted something on it," she said.
"What does it say?"

"Anis del Toro. It's a drink."

"Could we try it?"   15

The man called "Listen" through the curtain. The woman came out from the bar.

"Four reales."

"We want two Anis del Toro."

"With water?"

"Do you want it with water?"   20

"I don't know," the girl said. "Is it good with water?"

"It's all right."

"You want them with water?" asked the woman.

"Yes, with water."

"It tastes like licorice," the girl said and put the glass down.   25

"That's the way with everything."

"Yes," said the girl. "Everything tastes of licorice. Especially all the things you've
waited so long for, like absinthe."

"Oh, cut it out."

"You started it," the girl said. "I was being amused. I was having a fine time."

"Well, let's try and have a fine time."   30

"All right. I was trying. I said the mountains looked like white elephants. Wasn't
that bright?"

dos cervezas: two beers

"That was bright."

"I wanted to try this new drink: That's all we do, isn't it—look at things and try new drinks?"

"I guess so."

The girl looked across at the hills.   35

"They're lovely hills," she said. "They don't really look like white elephants. I just meant the coloring of their skin through the trees."

"Should we have another drink?"

"All right."

The warm wind blew the bead curtain against the table.

"The beer's nice and cool," the man said.   40

"It's lovely," the girl said.

"It's really an awfully simple operation, Jig," the man said. "It's not really an operation at all."

The girl looked at the ground the table legs rested on.

"I know you wouldn't mind it, Jig. It's really not anything. It's just to let the air in."

The girl did not say anything.   45

"I'll go with you and I'll stay with you all the time. They just let the air in and then it's all perfectly natural."

"Then what will we do afterward?"

"We'll be fine afterward. Just like we were before."

"What makes you think so?"

"That's the only thing that bothers us. It's the only thing that's made us unhappy." 50

The girl looked at the bead curtain, put her hand out and took hold of two of the strings of beads.

"And you think then we'll be all right and be happy."

"I know we will. You don't have to be afraid. I've known lots of people that have done it."

"So have I," said the girl. "And afterward they were all so happy."

"Well," the man said, "if you don't want to you don't have to. I wouldn't have you   55
do it if you didn't want to. But I know it's perfectly simple."

"And you really want to?"

"I think it's the best thing to do. But I don't want you to do it if you don't really want to."

"And if I do it you'll be happy and things will be like they were and you'll love me?"

"I love you now. You know I love you."

"I know. But if I do it, then it will be nice again if I say things are like white ele- 60
phants, and you'll like it?"

"I'll love it. I love it now but I just can't think about it. You know how I get when I worry."

"If I do it you won't ever worry?"

"I won't worry about that because it's perfectly simple."

"Then I'll do it. Because I don't care about me."

"What do you mean?"   65

"I don't care about me."

"Well, I care about you."

"Oh, yes. But I don't care about me. And I'll do it and then everything will be fine."

"I don't want you to do it if you feel that way."

The girl stood up and walked to the end of the station. Across, on the other side, 70
were fields of grain and trees along the banks of the Ebro. Far away, beyond the river,
were mountains. The shadow of a cloud moved across the field of grain and she saw the
river through the trees.

"And we could have all this," she said. "And we could have everything and every
day we make it more impossible."

"What did you say?"

"I said we could have everything."

"We can have everything."

"No, we can't." 75

"We can have the whole world."

"No, we can't."

"We can go everywhere."

"No, we can't. It isn't ours any more."

"It's ours." 80

"No, it isn't. And once they take it away, you never get it back."

"But they haven't taken it away."

"We'll wait and see."

"Come on back in the shade," he said. "You mustn't feel that way."

"I don't feel any way," the girl said. "I just know things." 85

"I don't want you to do anything that you don't want to do——"

"Nor that isn't good for me," she said. "I know. Could we have another beer?"

"All right. But you've got to realize——"

"I realize," the girl said. "Can't we maybe stop talking?"

They sat down at the table and the girl looked across at the hills on the dry side 90
of the valley and the man looked at her and at the table.

"You've got to realize," he said, "that I don't want you to do it if you don't want
to. I'm perfectly willing to go through with it if it means anything to you."

"Doesn't it mean anything to you? We could get along."

"Of course it does. But I don't want anybody but you. I don't want anyone else.
And I know it's perfectly simple."

"Yes, you know it's perfectly simple."

"It's all right for you to say that, but I do know it." 95

"Would you do something for me now?"

"I'd do anything for you."

"Would you please please please please please please please stop talking?"

He did not say anything but looked at the bags against the wall of the station.
There were labels on them from all the hotels where they had spent nights.

"But I don't want you to," he said, "I don't care anything about it." 100

"I'll scream," the girl said.

The woman came out through the curtains with two glasses of beer and put them
down on the damp felt pads. "The train comes in five minutes," she said.

"What did she say?" asked the girl.

"That the train is coming in five minutes."

The girl smiled brightly at the woman, to thank her. 105

"I'd better take the bags over to the other side of the station," the man said. She
smiled at him.

"All right. Then come back and we'll finish the beer."

He picked up the two heavy bags and carried them around the station to the other tracks. He looked up the tracks but could not see the train. Coming back, he walked through the barroom, where people waiting for the train were drinking. He drank an Anis at the bar and looked at the people. They were all waiting reasonably for the train. He went out through the bead curtain. She was sitting at the table and smiled at him.

"Do you feel better?" he asked.

"I feel fine," she said. "There's nothing wrong with me. I feel fine.   110

QUESTIONS FOR CLOSE READING OF HOW THE ELEMENTS WORK TOGETHER

1. How does Hemingway describe the landscape at the beginning of the story?

2. Where does the story take place?

3. What is the tone of the exchange of dialogue when the girl says the hills look like white elephants? Why does the American react as he does?

4. What does Hemingway imply about the way the two characters live when the girl says, "That's all we do, isn't it—look at things and try new drinks?" What does the girl mean by saying this?

5. The American says the operation is simple, just to let the air in. Why does the girl not reply to him?

6. He says they will be together and that they will be fine afterward. Does she agree?

7. The American says her pregnancy "is the only thing that's made us unhappy." What is the girl's opinion on this point?

8. What does she mean when she says, "But if I do it, then it will be nice again if I say things are like white elephants, and you'll like it?" He says, "I'll love it." Does the tone of the conversation convince you that's true?

9. What is the theme of the story? How does the progress of the narrative reveal the theme?

10. Why does the girl say that they can't have everything any more?

11. The American constantly says he doesn't want her to do anything she doesn't want to do, but do you believe him?

QUESTIONS FOR INTERPRETATION OF HOW THE ELEMENTS WORK TOGETHER

1. The elements of setting, character, style, and theme work coherently in Ernest Hemingway's "Hills like White Elephants." Hemingway's style is extremely spare. His characters speak in something close to a shorthand. In this story they sit at a barren railroad station in Spain waiting for a train that will take the girl to Madrid where she will have an abortion. The dialogue, spare and barren as the setting, eventually reveals not only the ultimate subject of discussion, but also the limitations of the American's character. When the girl looks "off at the line of hills" she sees them "like white elephants." The question we ask is: why does the American not see them the same way? What does this disjunction reveal about these people and their situation?

2. The American says several times that he wants only the girl, nobody else, in his life. "I don't want anyone else. And I know it's perfectly simple." Does this statement

mean that he is very selfish, or does it mean that he is very much in love? What can you tell from the girl's reaction to his statements regarding her getting an abortion?

3. What details in the story suggest that the American is trying to force his will on the girl? Certain images of animals—the elephants, the bull (del toro)—take on importance in the story. Do they contribute to the feeling that the girl is being pushed to do something she does not want to do? What does the girl mean when she says that all "all the things you've waited so long for" taste like licorice? Why is she disappointed? Is disappointment a theme of the story?

4. What is your reaction to the situation of these characters? How do you find your sympathies directed? Are you more sympathetic to the American or to the girl? Where do Hemingway's sympathies seem to lie? What does he think of these characters? Would he want the girl to do what the American wants her to do?

5. How does the style of the story function to reveal its central issues? What are the strengths of this style? How does the simplicity of the language finally add up to such a significant complexity? Consider the ways in which the dialogue implies more than it says. Consider, too, the way the description of the landscape and the bar contribute to the significance of the story.

ANN BEATTIE   (b. 1947)

Ann Beattie writes about characters who often experience changes in "normal" social structures. "The Cinderella Waltz" explores a divorce in which one partner has gone off with his homosexual lover. Louise, the wise child of this marriage, seems adult in many ways, yet it is hard to tell how much she understands. Beattie's stories have appeared constantly since 1972, often in the New Yorker. Distortions, *a book of stories, and* Chilly Scenes of Winter, *a novel, were both published in 1976.* Secrets and Surprises *and* The Burning House, *from which this story comes, were published in 1982.* Picturing Will *(1989) concerns a woman making her living after a divorce by becoming a photographer.* What Is Mine *(1991) is a collection of stories.*

The Cinderella Waltz _____ 1982

Milo and Bradley are creatures of habit. For as long as I've known him, Milo has worn his moth-eaten blue scarf with the knot hanging so low on his chest that the scarf is useless. Bradley is addicted to coffee and carries a Thermos with him. Milo complains about the cold, and Bradley is always a little edgy. They come out from the city every Saturday—this is not habit but loyalty—to pick up Louise. Louise is even more unpredictable than most nine-year-olds; sometimes she waits for them on the front step, sometimes she hasn't even gotten out of bed when they arrive. One time she hid in a closet and wouldn't leave with them.

Today Louise has put together a shopping bag full of things she wants to take with her. She is taking my whisk and my blue pottery bowl, to make Sunday breakfast for Milo and Bradley; Beckett's *Happy Days,* which she has carried around for weeks, and which she looks through, smiling—but I'm not sure she's reading it; and a coleus growing out of a conch shell. Also, she has stuffed into one side of the bag the fancy

Victorian-style nightgown her grandmother gave her for Christmas, and into the other she has tucked her octascope. Milo keeps a couple of dresses, a nightgown, a toothbrush, and extra sneakers and boots at his apartment for her. He got tired of rounding up her stuff to pack for her to take home, so he has brought some things for her that can be left. It annoys him that she still packs bags, because then he has to go around making sure that she has found everything before she goes home. She seems to know how to manipulate him, and after the weekend is over she calls tearfully to say that she has left this or that, which means that he must get his car out of the garage and drive all the way out to the house to bring it to her. One time, he refused to take the hour-long drive, because she had only left a copy of Tolkien's *The Two Towers*. The following weekend was the time she hid in the closet.

"I'll water your plant if you leave it here," I say now.

"I can take it," she says.

"I didn't say you couldn't take it. I just thought it might be easier to leave it, because if the shell tips over the plant might get ruined."   5

"O.K.," she says. "Don't water it today, though. Water it Sunday afternoon."

I reach for the shopping bag.

"I'll put it back on my window sill," she says. She lifts the plant out and carries it as if it's made of Steuben glass. Bradley bought it for her last month, driving back to the city, when they stopped at a lawn sale. She and Bradley are both very choosy, and he likes that. He drinks French-roast coffee; she will debate with herself almost endlessly over whether to buy a coleus that is primarily pink or lavender or striped.

"Has Milo made any plans for this weekend?" I ask.

"He's having a couple of people over tonight, and I'm going to help them make   10
crêpes for dinner. If they buy more bottles of that wine with the yellow flowers on the label, Bradley is going to soak the labels off for me."

"That's nice of him," I say. "He never minds taking a lot of time with things."

"He doesn't like to cook, though. Milo and I are going to cook. Bradley sets the table and fixes flowers in a bowl. He thinks it's frustrating to cook."

"Well," I say, "with cooking you have to have a good sense of timing. You have to coordinate everything. Bradley likes to work carefully and not be rushed."

I wonder how much she knows. Last week she told me about a conversation she'd had with her friend Sarah. Sarah was trying to persuade Louise to stay around on the weekends, but Louise said she always went to her father's. Then Sarah tried to get her to take her along, and Louise said that she couldn't. "You could take her if you wanted to," I said later. "Check with Milo and see if that isn't right. I don't think he'd mind having a friend of yours occasionally."

She shrugged. "Bradley doesn't like a lot of people around," she said.   15

"Bradley likes you, and if she's your friend I don't think he'd mind."

She looked at me with an expression I didn't recognize; perhaps she thought I was a little dumb, or perhaps she was just curious to see if I would go on. I didn't know how to go on. Like an adult, she gave a little shrug and changed the subject.

At ten o'clock Milo pulls into the driveway and honks his horn, which makes a noise like a bleating sheep. He knows the noise the horn makes is funny, and he means to amuse us. There was a time just after the divorce when he and Bradley would come here and get out of the car and stand around silently, waiting for her. She knew that she had to watch for them, because Milo wouldn't come to the door. We were both bitter then, but I got over it. I still don't think Milo would have come into the house again, though, if Bradley hadn't thought it was a good idea. The third time Milo came to pick her up after he'd left home, I went out to invite them in, but Milo said nothing. He was standing there with his arms at his sides like a wooden soldier, and his eyes were as dead to me as if they'd been painted on. It was Bradley whom I reasoned with. "Louise is over at Sarah's right now, and it'll make her feel more comfortable if we're all together when she comes in," I said to him, and Bradley turned to Milo and said, "Hey, that's right. Why don't we go in for a quick cup of coffee?" I looked into the back seat of the car and saw his red Thermos there; Louise had told me about it. Bradley meant that they should come in and sit down. He was giving me even more than I'd asked for.

It would be an understatement to say that I disliked Bradley at first. I was actually afraid of him, afraid even after I saw him, though he was slender, and more nervous than I, and spoke quietly. The second time I saw him, I persuaded myself that he was just a stereotype, but someone who certainly seemed harmless enough. By the third time, I had enough courage to suggest that they come into the house. It was embarrassing for all of us, sitting around the table—the same table where Milo and I had eaten our meals for the years we were married. Before he left, Milo had shouted at me that the house was a farce, that my playing the happy suburban housewife was a farce, that it was un-conscionable of me to let things drag on, that I would probably kiss him and say, "How was your day, sweetheart?" and that he should bring home flowers and the evening paper. "Maybe I would!" I screamed back. "Maybe it would be nice to do that, even if we were pretending, instead of you coming home drunk and not caring what had hap-pened to me or to Louise all day." He was holding on to the edge of the kitchen table, the way you'd hold on to the horse's reins in a runaway carriage. "I care about Louise," he said finally. That was the most horrible moment. Until then, until he said it that way, I had thought that he was going through something horrible—certainly something was terribly wrong—but that, in his way, he loved me after all. "*You don't love me?*" I had whis-pered at once. It took us both aback. It was an innocent and pathetic question, and it made him come and put his arms around me in the last hug he ever gave me. "I'm sorry for you," he said, "and I'm sorry for marrying you and causing this, but you know who I love. I told you who I love." "But you were kidding," I said. "You didn't mean it. You were kidding."

When Bradley sat at the table that first day, I tried to be polite and not look at him much. I had gotten it through my head that Milo was crazy, and I guess I was expecting Bradley to be a horrible parody—Craig Russell doing Marilyn Monroe. Bradley did not spoon sugar into Milo's coffee. He did not even sit near him. In fact, he pulled his chair a little away from us, and in spite of his uneasiness he found more things to start con-versations about than Milo and I did. He told me about the ad agency where he worked; he is a designer there. He asked if he could go out on the porch to see the brook—Milo had told him about the stream in the back of our place that was as thin as a pencil but still gave us our own watercress. He went out on the porch and stayed there for at least five minutes, giving us a chance to talk. We didn't say one word until he came back. Louise came home from Sarah's house just as Bradley sat down at the table again, and she gave him a hug as well as us. I could see that she really liked him. I was amazed that I liked him, too. Bradley had won and I had lost, but he was as gentle and low-key as if none of it mattered. Later in the week, I called him and asked him to tell me if any free-lance jobs opened in his advertising agency. (I do a little free-lance artwork, whenever I can arrange it.) The week after that, he called and told me about another agency, where they were looking for outside artists. Our calls to each other are always brief and for a purpose, but lately they're not just calls about business. Before Bradley left to scout

20

some picture locations in Mexico, he called to say that Milo had told him that when the two of us were there years ago I had seen one of those big circular bronze Aztec calendars and I had always regretted not bringing it back. He wanted to know if I would like him to buy a calendar if he saw one like the one Milo had told him about.

Today, Milo is getting out of his car, his blue scarf flapping against his chest. Louise, looking out the window, asks the same thing I am wondering: "Where's Bradley?"

Milo comes in and shakes my hand, gives Louise a one-armed hug.

"Bradley thinks he's coming down with a cold," Milo says. "The dinner is still on, Louise. We'll do the dinner. We have to stop at Gristede's° when we get back to town, unless your mother happens to have a tin of anchovies and two sticks of unsalted butter."

"Let's go to Gristede's," Louise says. "I like to go there."

"Let me look in the kitchen," I say. The butter is salted, but Milo says that will do,   25
and he takes three sticks instead of two. I have a brainstorm and cut the cellophane on a leftover Christmas present from my aunt—a wicker plate that holds nuts and foil-wrapped triangles of cheese—and, sure enough: one tin of anchovies.

"We can go to the museum instead," Milo says to Louise. "Wonderful."

But then, going out the door, carrying her bag, he changes his mind. "We can go to America Hurrah, and if we see something beautiful we can buy it," he says.

They go off in high spirits. Louise comes up to his waist, almost, and I notice again that they have the same walk. Both of them stride forward with great purpose. Last week, Bradley told me that Milo had bought a weathervane in the shape of a horse, made around 1800, at America Hurrah, and stood it in the bedroom, and then was enraged when Bradley draped his socks over it to dry. Bradley is still learning what a perfectionist Milo is, and how little sense of humor he has. When we were first married, I used one of our pottery casserole dishes to put my jewelry in, and he nagged me until I took it out and put the dish back in the kitchen cabinet. I remember his saying that the dish looked silly on my dresser because it was obvious what it was and people would think we left our dishes lying around. It was one of the things that Milo wouldn't tolerate, because it was improper.

When Milo brings Louise back on Sunday night they are not in a good mood. The dinner was all right, Milo says, and Griffin and Amy and Mark were amazed at what a good hostess Louise had been, but Bradley hadn't been able to eat.

"Is he still coming down with a cold?" I ask. I was still a little shy about asking   30
questions about Bradley.

Milo shrugs. "Louise made him take megadoses of vitamin C all weekend."

Louise says, "Bradley said that taking too much vitamin C was bad for your kidneys, though."

"It's a rotten climate," Milo says, sitting on the living-room sofa, scarf and coat still on. "The combination of cold and air pollution . . ."

Louise and I look at each other, and then back at Milo. For weeks now, he has been talking about moving to San Francisco, if he can find work there. (Milo is an architect.) This talk bores me, and it makes Louise nervous. I've asked him not to talk to her about it unless he's actually going to move, but he doesn't seem to be able to stop himself.

"O.K.," Milo says, looking at us both. "I'm not going to say anything about San   35
Francisco."

"*California* is polluted," I say. I am unable to stop myself, either.

Gristede's: a grocery store, part of an eastern chain of upscale markets

Milo heaves himself up from the sofa, ready for the drive back to New York. It is the same way he used to get off the sofa that last year he lived here. He would get up, dress for work, and not even go into the kitchen for breakfast—just sit, sometimes in his coat as he was sitting just now, and at the last minute he would push himself up and go out to the driveway, usually without a goodbye, and get in the car and drive off either very fast or very slowly. I liked it better when he made the tires spin in the gravel when he took off.

He stops at the doorway now, and turns to face me. "Did I take all your butter?" he says.

"No," I say. "There's another stick." I point into the kitchen.

"I could have guessed that's where it would be," he says, and smiles at me.   40

When Milo comes the next weekend, Bradley is still not with him. The night before, as I was putting Louise to bed, she said that she had a feeling he wouldn't be coming.

"I had that feeling a couple of days ago," I said. "Usually Bradley calls once during the week."

"He must still be sick," Louise said. She looked at me anxiously. "Do you think he is?"

"A cold isn't going to kill him," I said. "If he has a cold, he'll be O.K."

Her expression changed; she thought I was talking down to her. She lay back in   45
bed. The last year Milo was with us, I used to tuck her in and tell her that everything was all right. What that meant was that there had not been a fight. Milo had sat listening to music on the phonograph, with a book or the newspaper in front of his face. He didn't pay very much attention to Louise, and he ignored me entirely. Instead of saying a prayer with her, the way I usually did, I would say to her that everything was all right. Then I would go downstairs and hope that Milo would say the same thing to me. What he finally did say one night was "You might as well find out from me as some other way."

"Hey, are you an old bag lady again this weekend?" Milo says now, stooping to kiss Louise's forehead.

"Because you take some things with you doesn't mean you're a bag lady," she says primly.

"Well," Milo says, "you start doing something innocently, and before you know it it can take you over."

He looks angry, and acts as though it's difficult for him to make conversation, even when the conversation is full of sarcasm and double-entendres.

"What do you say we get going?" he says to Louise.   50

In the shopping bag she is taking is her doll, which she has not played with for more than a year. I found it by accident when I went to tuck in a loaf of banana bread that I had baked. When I saw Baby Betsy, deep in the bag, I decided against putting the bread in.

"O.K.," Louise says to Milo. "Where's Bradley?"

"Sick," he says.

"Is he too sick to have me visit?"

"Good heavens, no. He'll be happier to see you than to see me."   55

"I'm rooting some of my coleus to give him," she says. "Maybe I'll give it to him like it is, in water, and he can plant it when it roots."

When she leaves the room, I go over to Milo. "Be nice to her," I say quietly.

"I'm nice to her," he says. "Why does everybody have to act like I'm going to grow fangs every time I turn around?"

"You were quite cutting when you came in."

"I was being self-deprecating." He sighs. "I don't really know why I come here and   60
act this way," he says.

"What's the matter, Milo?"

But now he lets me know he's bored with the conversation. He walks over to the
table and picks up a *Newsweek* and flips through it. Louise comes back with the coleus
in a water glass.

"You know what you could do," I say. "Wet a napkin and put it around that cutting
and then wrap it in foil, and put it in water when you get there. That way, you wouldn't
have to hold a glass of water all the way to New York."

She shrugs. "This is O.K.," she says.

"Why don't you take your mother's suggestion," Milo says. "The water will slosh   65
out of the glass."

"Not if you don't drive fast."

"It doesn't have anything to do with my driving fast. If we go over a bump in the
road, you're going to get all wet."

"Then I can put on one of my dresses at your apartment."

"Am I being unreasonable?" Milo says to me.

"I started it," I say. "Let her take it in the glass."   70

"Would you, as a favor, do what your mother says?" he says to Louise.

Louise looks at the coleus, and at me.

"Hold the glass over the seat instead of over your lap, and you won't get wet," I say.

"Your first idea was the best," Milo says.

Louise gives him an exasperated look and puts the glass down on the floor, pulls   75
on her poncho, picks up the glass again and says a sullen goodbye to me, and goes out
the front door.

"Why is this my fault?" Milo says. "Have I done anything terrible? I—"

"Do something to cheer yourself up," I say, patting him on the back.

He looks as exasperated with me as Louise was with him. He nods his head yes,
and goes out the door.

"Was everything all right this weekend?" I ask Louise.

"Milo was in a bad mood, and Bradley wasn't even there on Saturday," Louise says.   80
"He came back today and took us to the Village for breakfast."

"What did you have?"

"I had sausage wrapped in little pancakes and fruit salad and a rum bun."

"Where was Bradley on Saturday?"

She shrugs. "I didn't ask him."

She almost always surprises me by being more grownup than I give her credit for.   85
Does she suspect, as I do, that Bradley has found another lover?

"Milo was in a bad mood when you two left here Saturday," I say.

"I told him if he didn't want me to come next weekend, just to tell me." She looks
perturbed, and I suddenly realize that she can sound exactly like Milo sometimes.

"You shouldn't have said that to him, Louise," I say. "You know he wants you. He's
just worried about Bradley."

"So?" she says. "I'm probably going to flunk math."

"No, you're not, honey. You got a C-plus on the last assignment."   90

"It still doesn't make my grade average out to a C."

"You'll get a C. It's all right to get a C."

She doesn't believe me.

"Don't be a perfectionist, like Milo," I tell her. "Even if you got a D, you wouldn't fail."

Louise is brushing her hair—thin, shoulder-length, auburn hair. She is already so 95 pretty and so smart in everything except math that I wonder what will become of her. When I was her age, I was plain and serious and I wanted to be a tree surgeon. I went with my father to the park and held a stethoscope—a real one—to the trunks of trees, listening to their silence. Children seem older now.

"What do you think's the matter with Bradley?" Louise says. She sounds worried.

"Maybe the two of them are unhappy with each other right now."

She misses my point. "Bradley's sad, and Milo's sad that he's unhappy."

I drop Louise off at Sarah's house for supper. Sarah's mother, Martine Cooper, looks like Shelley Winters, and I have never seen her without a glass of Galliano on ice in her hand. She has a strong candy smell. Her husband has left her, and she professes not to care. She has emptied her living room of furniture and put up ballet bars on the walls, and dances in a purple leotard to records by Cher and Mac Davis. I prefer to have Sarah come to our house, but her mother is adamant that everything must be, as she puts it, "fifty-fifty." When Sarah visited us a week ago and loved the chocolate pie I had made, I sent two pieces home with her. Tonight, when I left Sarah's house, her mother gave me a bowl of Jell-O fruit salad.

The phone is ringing when I come in the door. It is Bradley.   100

"Bradley," I say at once, "whatever's wrong, at least you don't have a neighbor who just gave you a bowl of maraschino cherries in green Jell-O with a Reddi-Whip flower squirted on top."

"Jesus," he says. "You don't need me to depress you, do you?"

"What's wrong?" I say.

He sighs into the phone. "Guess what?" he says.

"What?"   105

"I've lost my job."

It wasn't at all what I was expecting to hear. I was ready to hear that he was leaving Milo, and I had even thought that that would serve Milo right. Part of me still wanted him punished for what he did. I was so out of my mind when Milo left me that I used to go over and drink Galliano with Martine Cooper. I even thought seriously about forming a ballet group with her. I would go to her house in the afternoon, and she would hold a tambourine in the air and I would hold my leg rigid and try to kick it.

"That's awful," I say to Bradley. "What happened?"

"They said it was nothing personal—they were laying off three people. Two other people are going to get the ax at the agency within the next six months. I was the first to go, and it was nothing personal. From twenty thousand bucks a year to nothing, and nothing personal, either."

"But your work is so good. Won't you be able to find something again?"   110

"Could I ask you a favor?" he says. "I'm calling from a phone booth. I'm not in the city. Could I come talk to you?"

"Sure," I say.

It seems perfectly logical that he should come alone to talk—perfectly logical until I actually see him coming up the walk. I can't entirely believe it. A year after my husband has left me, I am sitting with his lover—a man, a person I like quite well—and trying to cheer him up because he is out of work. ("Honey," my father would say, "listen to Daddy's heart with the stethoscope, or you can turn it toward you and listen to your own heart. You won't hear anything listening to a tree." Was my persistence will-fulness, or belief in magic? Is it possible that I hugged Bradley at the door because I'm secretly glad he's down and out, the way I used to be? Or do I really want to make things better for him?)

He comes into the kitchen and thanks me for the coffee I am making, drapes his coat over the chair he always sits in.

"What am I going to do?" he asks.   115

"You shouldn't get so upset, Bradley," I say. "You know you're good. You won't have trouble finding another job."

"That's only half of it," he says. "Milo thinks I did this deliberately. He told me I was quitting on him. He's very angry at me. He fights with me, and then he gets mad that I don't enjoy eating dinner. My stomach's upset, and I can't eat anything."

"Maybe some juice would be better than coffee."

"If I didn't drink coffee, I'd collapse," he says.

I pour coffee into a mug for him, coffee into a mug for me.   120

"This is probably very awkward for you," he says. "That I come here and say all this about Milo."

"What does he mean about your quitting on him?"

"He said . . . he actually accused me of doing badly deliberately, so they'd fire me. I was so afraid to tell him the truth when I was fired that I pretended to be sick. Then I really *was* sick. He's never been angry at me this way. Is this always the way he acts? Does he get a notion in his head for no reason and then pick at a person because of it?"

I try to remember. "We didn't argue much," I say. "When he didn't want to live here, he made me look ridiculous for complaining when I knew something was wrong. He expects perfection, but what that means is that you do things his way."

"I *was*. I never wanted to sit around the apartment, the way he says I did. I even   125
brought work home with me. He made me feel so bad all week that I went to a friend's apartment for the day on Saturday. Then he said I had walked out on the problem. He's a little paranoid. I was listening to the radio, and Carole King was singing 'It's Too Late,' and he came into the study and looked very upset, as though I had planned for the song to come on. I couldn't believe it."

"Whew," I say, shaking my head. "I don't envy you. You have to stand up to him. I didn't do that. I pretended the problem would go away."

"And now the problem sits across from you drinking coffee, and you're being nice to him."

"I know it. I was just thinking we look like two characters in some soap opera my friend Martine Cooper would watch."

He pushes his coffee cup away from him with a grimace.

"But anyway, I like you now," I say. "And you're exceptionally nice to Louise."   130

"I took her father," he says.

"Bradley—I hope you don't take offense, but it makes me nervous to talk about that."

"I don't take offense. But how can you be having coffee with me?"

"You invited yourself over so you could ask that?"

"Please," he says, holding up both hands. Then he runs his hands through his   135
hair. "Don't make me feel illogical. He does that to me, you know. He doesn't under-stand it when everything doesn't fall right into line. If I like fixing up the place, keep-ing some flowers around, therefore I can't like being a working person, too, therefore I deliberately sabotage myself in my job." Bradley sips his coffee.

"I wish I could do something for him," he says in a different voice.

This is not what I expected, either. We have sounded like two wise adults, and then suddenly he has changed and sounds very tender. I realize the situation is still the same. It is two of them on one side and me on the other, even though Bradley is in my kitchen.

"Come and pick up Louise with me, Bradley," I say. "When you see Martine Cooper, you'll cheer up about your situation."

He looks up from his coffee. "You're forgetting what I'd look like to Martine Cooper," he says.

Milo is going to California. He has been offered a job with a new San Francisco architectural firm. I am not the first to know. His sister, Deanna, knows before I do, and mentions it when we're talking on the phone. "It's middle-age crisis," Deanna says sniffily. "Not that I need to tell you." Deanna would drop dead if she knew the way things are. She is scandalized every time a new display is put up in Bloomingdale's window. ("Those mannequins had eyes like an Egyptian princess, and *rags*. I swear to you, they had mops and brooms and ragged gauze dresses on, with whores' shoes—stiletto heels that prostitutes wear.")

I hang up from Deanna's call and tell Louise I'm going to drive to the gas station for cigarettes. I go there to call New York on their pay phone.

"Well, I only just knew," Milo says. "I found out for sure yesterday, and last night Deanna called and so I told her. It's not like I'm leaving tonight."

He sounds elated, in spite of being upset that I called. He's happy in the way he used to be on Christmas morning. I remember him once running into the living room in his underwear and tearing open the gifts we'd been sent by relatives. He was looking for the eight-slice toaster he was sure we'd get. We'd been given two-slice, four-slice, and six-slice toasters, but then we got no more. "Come out, my eight-slice beauty!" Milo crooned, and out came an electric clock, a blender, and an expensive electric pan.

"When are you leaving?" I ask him.

"I'm going out to look for a place to live next week."

"Are you going to tell Louise yourself this weekend?"

"Of course," he says.

"And what are you going to do about seeing Louise?"

"Why do you act as if I don't like Louise?" he says. "I will occasionally come back East, and I will arrange for her to fly to San Francisco on her vacations."

"It's going to break her heart."

"No it isn't. Why do you want to make me feel bad?"

"She's had so many things to adjust to. You don't have to go to San Francisco right now, Milo."

"It happens, if you care, that my own job here is in jeopardy. This is a real chance for me, with a young firm. They really want me. But anyway, all we need in this happy group is to have you bringing in a couple of hundred dollars a month with your graphic work and me destitute and Bradley so devastated by being fired that of course he can't even look for work."

"I'll bet he is looking for a job," I say.

"Yes. He read the want ads today and then fixed a crab quiche."

"Maybe that's the way you like things, Milo, and people respond to you. You forbade me to work when we had a baby. Do you say anything encouraging to him about finding a job, or do you just take it out on him that he was fired?"

There is a pause, and then he almost seems to lose his mind with impatience.

"I can hardly *believe*, when I am trying to find a logical solution to all our problems, that I am being subjected, by telephone, to an unflattering psychological analysis by my ex-wife." He says this all in a rush.

"All right, Milo. But don't you think that if you're leaving so soon you ought to call her, instead of waiting until Saturday?"

Milo sighs very deeply. "I have more sense than to have important conversations   160
on the telephone," he says.

Milo calls on Friday and asks Louise whether it wouldn't be nice if both of us came in and spent the night Saturday and if we all went to brunch together Sunday. Louise is excited. I never go into town with her.

Louise and I pack a suitcase and put it in the car Saturday morning. A cutting of ivy for Bradley has taken root, and she has put it in a little green plastic pot for him. It's heartbreaking, and I hope that Milo notices and has a tough time dealing with it. I am relieved I'm going to be there when he tells her, and sad that I have to hear it at all.

In the city, I give the car to the garage attendant, who does not remember me. Milo and I lived in the apartment when we were first married, and moved when Louise was two years old. When we moved, Milo kept the apartment and sublet it—a sign that things were not going well, if I had been one to heed such a warning. What he said was that if we were ever rich enough we could have the house in Connecticut *and* the apartment in New York. When Milo moved out of the house, he went right back to the apartment. This will be the first time I have visited there in years.

Louise strides in in front of me, throwing her coat over the brass coatrack in the entranceway—almost too casual about being there. She's the hostess at Milo's, the way I am at our house.

He has painted the walls white. There are floor-length white curtains in the living   165
room, where my silly flowered curtains used to hang. The walls are bare, the floor has been sanded, a stereo as huge as a computer stands against one wall of the living room, and there are four speakers.

"Look around," Milo says. "Show your mother around, Louise."

I am trying to remember if I have ever told Louise that I used to live in this apartment. I must have told her, at some point, but I can't remember it.

"Hello," Bradley says, coming out of the bedroom.

"Hi, Bradley," I say. "Have you got a drink?"

Bradley looks sad. "He's got champagne," he says, and looks nervously at Milo.   170

"No one *has* to drink champagne," Milo says. "There's the usual assortment of liquor."

"Yes," Bradley says. "What would you like?"

"Some bourbon, please."

"Bourbon." Bradley turns to go into the kitchen. He looks different; his hair is different—more wavy—and he is dressed as though it were summer, in straight-legged-white pants and black leather thongs.

"I want Perrier water with strawberry juice," Louise says, tagging along after   175
Bradley. I have never heard her ask for such a thing before. At home, she drinks too many Cokes. I am always trying to get her to drink fruit juice.

Bradley comes back with two drinks and hands me one. "Did you want anything?" he says to Milo.

"I'm going to open the champagne in a moment," Milo says. "How have you been this week, sweetheart?"

"O.K.," Louise says. She is holding a pale-pink, bubbly drink. She sips it like a cocktail.

Bradley looks very bad. He has circles under his eyes, and he is ill at ease. A red light begins to blink on the phone-answering device next to where Bradley sits on the sofa, and Milo gets out of his chair to pick up the phone.

"Do you really want to talk on the phone right now?" Bradley asks Milo quietly.   180

Milo looks at him. "No, not particularly," he says, sitting down again. After a moment, the red light goes out.

"I'm going to mist your bowl garden," Louise says to Bradley, and slides off the sofa and goes to the bedroom. "Hey, a little toadstool is growing in here!" she calls back. "Did you put it there, Bradley?"

"It grew from the soil mixture, I guess," Bradley calls back. "I don't know how it got there."

"Have you heard anything about a job?" I ask Bradley.

"I haven't been looking, really," he says. "You know."   185

Milo frowns at him. "Your choice, Bradley," he says. "I didn't ask you to follow me to California. You can stay here."

"No," Bradley says. "You've hardly made me feel welcome."

"Should we have some champagne—all four of us—and you can get back to your bourbons later?" Milo says cheerfully.

We don't answer him, but he gets up anyway and goes to the kitchen. "Where have you hidden the tulip-shaped glasses, Bradley?" he calls out after a while.

"They should be in the cabinet on the far left," Bradley says.   190

"You're going with him?" I say to Bradley. "To San Francisco?"

He shrugs, and won't look at me. "I'm not quite sure I'm wanted," he says quietly.

The cork pops in the kitchen. I look at Bradley, but he won't look up. His new hairdo makes him look older. I remember that when Milo left me I went to the hairdresser the same week and had bangs cut. The next week, I went to a therapist who told me it was no good trying to hide from myself. The week after that, I did dance exercises with Martine Cooper, and the week after that the therapist told me not to dance if I wasn't interested in dancing.

"I'm not going to act like this is a funeral," Milo says, coming in with the glasses. "Louise, come in here and have champagne! We have something to have a toast about."

Louise comes into the living room suspiciously. She is so used to being refused   195
even a sip of wine from my glass or her father's that she no longer even asks. "How come I'm in on this?" she asks.

"We're going to drink a toast to me," Milo says.

Three of the four glasses are clustered on the table in front of the sofa. Milo's glass is raised. Louise looks at me, to see what I'm going to say. Milo raises his glass even higher. Bradley reaches for a glass. Louise picks up a glass. I lean forward and take the last one.

"This is a toast to me," Milo says, "because I am going to be going to San Francisco."

It was not a very good or informative toast. Bradley and I sip from our glasses. Louise puts her glass down hard and bursts into tears, knocking the glass over. The champagne spills onto the cover of a big art book about the Unicorn Tapestries. She runs into the bedroom and slams the door.

Milo looks furious. "Everybody lets me know just what my insufficiencies are,   200
don't they?" he says. "Nobody minds expressing himself. We have it all right out in the open."

"He's criticizing me," Bradley murmurs, his head still bowed. "It's because I was offered a job here in the city and I didn't automatically refuse it."

I turn to Milo. "Go say something to Louise, Milo," I say. "Do you think that's what somebody who isn't brokenhearted sounds like?"

He glares at me and stomps into the bedroom, and I can hear him talking to Louise reassuringly. "It doesn't mean you'll *never* see me," he says. "You can fly there, I'll come here. It's not going to be that different."

"You lied!" Louise screams. "You said we were going to brunch."

"We are. We are. I can't very well take us to brunch before Sunday, can I?"   205

"You didn't say you were going to San Francisco. What *is* San Francisco, anyway?"

"I just said so. I bought us a bottle of champagne. You can come out as soon as I get settled. You're going to like it there."

Louise is sobbing. She has told him the truth and she knows it's futile to go on.

By the next morning, Louise acts the way I acted—as if everything were just the same. She looks calm, but her face is small and pale. She looks very young. We walk into the restaurant and sit at the table Milo has reserved. Bradley pulls out a chair for me, and Milo pulls out a chair for Louise, locking his finger with hers for a second, raising her arm above her head, as if she were about to take a twirl.

She looks very nice, really. She has a ribbon in her hair. It is cold, and she should   210
have worn a hat, but she wanted to wear the ribbon. Milo has good taste: the dress she is wearing, which he bought for her, is a hazy purple plaid, and it sets off her hair.

"Come with me. Don't be sad," Milo suddenly says to Louise, pulling her by the hand. "Come with me for a minute. Come across the street to the park for just a second, and we'll have some space to dance, and your mother and Bradley can have a nice quiet drink."

She gets up from the table and, looking long-suffering, backs into her coat, which he is holding for her, and the two of them go out. The waitress comes to the table, and Bradley orders three Bloody Marys and a Coke, and eggs Benedict for everyone. He asks the waitress to wait awhile before she brings the food. I have hardly slept at all, and having a drink is not going to clear my head. I have to think of things to say to Louise later, on the ride home.

"He takes so many *chances*," I say. "He pushes things so far with people. I don't want her to turn against him."

"No," he says.

"Why are you going, Bradley? You've seen the way he acts. You know that when you   215
get out there he'll pull something on you. Take the job and stay here."

Bradley is fiddling with the edge of his napkin. I study him. I don't know who his friends are, how old he is, where he grew up, whether he believes in God, or what he usually drinks. I'm shocked that I know so little, and I reach out and touch him. He looks up.

"Don't go," I say quietly.

The waitress puts the glasses down quickly and leaves, embarrassed because she thinks she's interrupted a tender moment. Bradley pats my hand on his arm. Then he says the thing that has always been between us, the thing too painful for me to envision or think about.

"I love him," Bradley whispers.

We sit quietly until Milo and Louise come into the restaurant, swinging hands. She   220
is pretending to be a young child, almost a baby, and I wonder for an instant if Milo and Bradley and I haven't been playing house, too—pretending to be adults.

"Daddy's going to give me a first-class ticket," Louise says. "When I go to California we're going to ride in a glass elevator to the top of the Fairman Hotel."

"The Fairmont," Milo says, smiling at her.

Before Louise was born, Milo used to put his ear to my stomach and say that if the baby turned out to be a girl he would put her into glass slippers instead of bootees. Now he is the prince once again. I see them in a glass elevator, not long from now, going up and up, with the people below getting smaller and smaller, until they disappear.

QUESTIONS FOR CLOSE READING OF HOW THE ELEMENTS WORK TOGETHER

1. How does Louise react to Milo and Bradley's visits to pick her up?
2. Has the narrator told Louise that Milo and Bradley are homosexual partners?
3. Does the narrator dislike Bradley? Is she jealous of him?
4. What do these characters do to make a living?
5. Describe the setting of the story? Where does it take place? What is the environment like?
6. How is the narrative structured? Is the action linear, without flashbacks?
7. Comment on the point of view. How does the narrator control your judgments of the characters? Does the narrator seem fair in her judgments?
8. Why does Bradley come to talk to the narrator when he loses his job?
9. How does the narrator react when she hears Milo is moving to California?
10. How does Louise behave in Milo's apartment?
11. What does Louise do when she learns that Milo and Bradley are going to San Francisco?

QUESTIONS FOR INTERPRETATION OF HOW THE ELEMENTS WORK TOGETHER

1. The circumstances of Ann Beattie's "The Cinderella Waltz" reveal themselves slowly: The narrator and Milo were once married, and Louise is their child. Now, the narrator lives alone with Louise, and Milo lives with his lover, Bradley. The narrative technique permits us to know how things were in the past by virtue of the narrator's recalling earlier events. The style of the story is marked not just by description and recollection, but by the recounting of dialogue, which itself tends to reveal the character of those other than the narrator. Much of the story is dialogue, and through it we learn that another break—echoing the earlier divorce—is likely to take place in the lives of the characters. Critical questions for interpretation might center on the nature of love and how it survives the breaks and ruptures that these characters experience.

2. In what sense is Milo at the center of this story? What do Louise, Bradley, and the narrator have in common in their relationship with Milo? Is Milo the kind of person who deserves such admiration and love? What can you tell about him from this story? What values does he seem to have in terms of respecting and establishing a sense of family?

3. In what ways are Bradley and the narrator alike? Why do they spend so much time in conversations—vastly more than, for example, the narrator spends with Milo? Do they seem to like each other? Why is the narrator not as angry at Bradley as Bradley expects her to be? What does it mean that she likes him as much as she does?

4. Louise and the narrator have many qualities in common. They take the same respective roles in Milo's homes, the narrator in Connecticut and Louise in New York. What are we to understand by these similarities? Do Louise and the narrator simply assume stereotypically feminine roles? How do Milo and Bradley determine their respective roles in their relationship?

5. This story represents middle-class people dealing with an unusual pattern of relationships. Is the primary theme of the story connected with the cultural implications of the ways in which these characters respond to their situation? Even Bradley is surprised at the "civilized" way in which the narrator handles the situation of his having stolen her husband from her. If Bradley were a woman, would the kinds of conversations the narrator had with him have happened? Consider the complex interrelationships these characters have with one another.

6

READING ANTON CHEKHOV IN DEPTH

Anton Chekhov (1860–1904) struggled to become a doctor and began to support his family while his father was unable to find decent jobs. He supplemented his income by writing short comic pieces, less than 1,000 words, at the rate of sometimes a hundred or more a year. Eventually, he found his voice in the short story, which he is credited with having revolutionized by drawing on personal observation and experience. His stories are penetrating studies of character and circumstance. His first important literary publication was in 1888 and after he moved from Moscow during what is called his Melikhovo period, 1892–1898, he wrote the bulk of his most well known stories, including two of the three stories included below. These stories have a seriousness to them born of experience, but they also have a subtext of humor born of his earlier writing and his special way of seeing the world. He is considered the first genius of the modern short story, in part because of the depth of his understanding of people and life and in part because of his style of permitting the reader to make the judgments of the characters rather than having him do so as the author. Today his work can be found in a complete edition, *The Oxford Chekhov* (1964–80), but the short stories were published in single volumes: *The Black Monk and Other Stories* (1903), *The Kiss and Other Stories* (1908), *The Lady with the Dog and Other Stories* (1917), and numerous others after his death.

The Darling ———————————————— *1899*

Translated by Constance Garnett

Olenka, the daughter of the retired collegiate assessor, Plemyanniakov, was sitting in her back porch, lost in thought. It was hot, the flies were persistent and teasing, and it was pleasant to reflect that it would soon be evening. Dark rainclouds were gathering from the east, and bringing from time to time a breath of moisture in the air.

Kukin, who was the manager of an open-air theatre called the Tivoli, and who lived in the lodge, was standing in the middle of the garden looking at the sky.

"Again!" he observed despairingly. "It's going to rain again! Rain every day, as though to spite me. I might as well hang myself! It's ruin! Fearful losses every day."

He flung up his hands, and went on, addressing Olenka:

"There! that's the life we lead, Olga Semyonovna. It's enough to make one cry. One works and does one's utmost; one wears oneself out, getting no sleep at night, and racks one's brain what to do for the best. And then what happens? To begin with, one's public is ignorant, boorish. I give them the very best operetta, a dainty masque, first rate music-hall artists. But do you suppose that's what they want! They don't understand anything of that sort. They want a clown; what they ask for is vulgarity. And then look at the weather! Almost every evening it rains. It started on the tenth of May, and it's kept it up all May and June. It's simply awful! The public doesn't come, but I've to pay the rent just the same, and pay the artists."   5

The next evening the clouds would gather again, and Kukin would say with an hysterical laugh:

"Well, rain away, then! Flood the garden, drown me! Damn my luck in this world and the next! Let the artists have me up! Send me to prison!—to Siberia!—the scaffold! Ha, ha, ha!"

And next day the same thing.

Olenka listened to Kukin with silent gravity, and sometimes tears came into her eyes. In the end his misfortunes touched her; she grew to love him. He was a small thin man, with a yellow face, and curls combed forward on his forehead. He spoke in a thin tenor; as he talked his mouth worked on one side, and there was always an expression of despair on his face; yet he aroused a deep and genuine affection in her. She was always fond of some one, and could not exist without loving. In earlier days she had loved her papa, who now sat in a darkened room, breathing with difficulty; she had loved her aunt who used to come every other year from Bryansk; and before that, when she was at school, she had loved her French master. She was a gentle, soft-hearted, compassionate girl, with mild, tender eyes and very good health. At the sight of her full rosy cheeks, her soft white neck with a little dark mole on it, and the kind, naïve smile, which came into her face when she listened to anything pleasant, men thought, "Yes, not half bad," and smiled too, while lady visitors could not refrain from seizing her hand in the middle of a conversation, exclaiming in a gush of delight, "You darling!"

The house in which she had lived from her birth upwards, and which was left her   10 in her father's will, was at the extreme end of the town, not far from the Tivoli. In the evenings and at night she could hear the band playing, and the crackling and banging of fireworks, and it seemed to her that it was Kukin struggling with his destiny, storming the entrenchments of his chief foe, the indifferent public; there was a sweet thrill at her heart, she had no desire to sleep, and when he returned home at daybreak, she tapped softly at her bedroom window, and showing him only her face and one shoulder through the curtain, she gave him a friendly smile. . . .

He proposed to her, and they were married. And when he had a closer view of her neck and her plump, fine shoulders, he threw up his hands, and said:

"You darling!"

He was happy, but as it rained on the day and night of his wedding, his face still retained an expression of despair.

They get on very well together. She used to sit in his office, to look after things in the Tivoli, to put down the accounts and pay the wages. And her rosy cheeks, her sweet, naïve, radiant smile, were to be seen now at the office window, now in the refreshment bar or behind the scenes of the theatre. And already she used to say to her acquaintances that the theatre was the chief and most important thing in life, and that it was only through the drama that one could derive true enjoyment and become cultivated and humane.

"But do you suppose the public understands that?" she used to say. "What they want is a clown. Yesterday we gave 'Faust Inside Out,' and almost all the boxes were empty; but if Vanitchka and I had been producing some vulgar thing, I assure you the theatre would have been packed. Tomorrow Vanitchka and I are doing 'Orpheus in Hell.' Do come."

And what Kukin said about the theatre and the actors she repeated. Like him she despised the public for their ignorance and their indifference to art; she took part in the rehearsals, she corrected the actors, she kept an eye on the behavior of the musicians, and when there was an unfavorable notice in the local paper, she shed tears, and then went to the editor's office to set things right.

The actors were fond of her and used to call her "Vanitchka and I," and "the darling"; she was sorry for them and used to lend them small sums of money, and if they deceived her, she used to shed a few tears in private, but did not complain to her husband.

They got on well in the winter too. They took the theatre in the town for the whole winter, and let it for short terms to a Little Russian company, or to a conjurer, or to a local dramatic society. Olenka grew stouter, and was always beaming with satisfaction, while Kukin grew thinner and yellower, and continually complained of their terrible losses, although he had not done badly all the winter. He used to cough at night, and she used to give him hot raspberry tea or lime-flower water, to rub him with eau-de-Cologne and to wrap him in her warm shawls.

"You're such a sweet pet!" she used to say with perfect sincerity, stroking his hair. "You're such a pretty dear!"

Towards Lent he went to Moscow to collect a new troupe, and without him she could not sleep, but sat all night at her window, looking at the stars, and she compared herself with the hens, who are awake all night and uneasy when the cock is not in the hen-house. Kukin was detained in Moscow, and wrote that he would be back at Easter, adding some instructions about the Tivoli. But on the Sunday before Easter, late in the evening, came a sudden ominous knock at the gate; some one was hammering on the gate as though on a barrel—boom, boom, boom! The drowsy cook went flopping with her bare feet through the puddles, as she ran to open the gate.

"Please open," said some one outside in a thick bass. "There is a telegram for you."

Olenka had received telegrams from her husband before, but this time for some reason she felt numb with terror. With shaking hands she opened the telegram and read as follows:

"Ivan Petrovitch died suddenly to-day. Awaiting immate instructions fufuneral Tuesday."

That was how it was written in the telegram—"fufuneral," and the utterly incomprehensible word "immate." It was signed by the stage manager of the operatic company.

15

20

"My darling!" sobbed Olenka. "Vanitchka, my precious, my darling! Why did I ever meet you! Why did I know you and love you! Your poor heart-broken Olenka is all alone without you!"

Kukin's funeral took place on Tuesday in Moscow, Olenka returned home on Wednesday, and as soon as she got indoors she threw herself on her bed and sobbed so loudly that it could be heard next door, and in the street.

"Poor darling!" the neighbors said, as they crossed themselves. "Olga Semyonovna, poor darling! How she does take on!"

Three months later Olenka was coming home from mass, melancholy and in deep mourning. It happened that one of her neighbors, Vassily Andreitch Pustovalov, returning home from church, walked back beside her. He was the manager at Babakayev's the timber merchant's. He wore a straw hat, a white waistcoat, and a gold watch-chain, and looked more like a country gentleman than a man in trade.

"Everything happens as it is ordained, Olga Semyonovna," he said gravely, with a sympathetic note in his voice; "and if any of our dear ones die, it must be because it is the will of God, so we ought to have fortitude and bear it submissively."

After seeing Olenka to her gate, he said good-bye and went on. All day afterwards she heard his sedately dignified voice, and whenever she shut her eyes she saw his dark beard. She liked him very much. And apparently she had made an impression on him too, for not long afterwards an elderly lady, with whom she was only slightly acquainted, came to drink coffee with her, and as soon as she was seated at table began to talk about Pustovalov, saying that he was an excellent man whom one could thoroughly depend upon, and that any girl would be happy to marry him. Three days later Pustovalov came himself. He did not stay long, only about ten minutes, and he did not say much, but when he left, Olenka loved him—loved him so much that she lay awake all night in a perfect fever, and in the morning she sent for the elderly lady. The match was quickly arranged, and then came the wedding.

Pustovalov and Olenka got on very well together when they were married.

Usually he sat in the office till dinner-time, then he went out on business, while Olenka took his place, and sat in the office till evening, making up accounts and booking orders.

"Timber gets dearer every year; the price rise twenty per cent," she would say to her customers and friends. "Only fancy we used to sell local timber, and now Vassitchka always has to go for wood to the Mogilev district. And the freight!" she would add, covering her cheeks with her hands in horror. "The freight!"

It seemed to her that she had been in the timber trade for ages and ages, and that the most important and necessary thing in life was timber; and there was something intimate and touching to her in the very sound of words such as "baulk," "post," "beam," "pole," "scantling," "batten," "lath," "plank," etc.

At night when she was asleep she dreamed of perfect mountains of planks and boards, and long strings of wagons, carting timber somewhere far away. She dreamed that a whole regiment of six-inch beams forty feet high, standing on end, was marching upon the timber-yard; that logs, beams, and boards knocked together with the resounding crash of dry wood, kept falling and getting up again, piling themselves on each other. Olenka cried out in her sleep, and Pustovalov said to her tenderly: "Olenka, what's the matter, darling? Cross yourself!"

Her husband's ideas were hers. If he thought the room was too hot, or that business was slack, she thought the same. Her husband did not care for entertainments, and on holidays he stayed at home. She did likewise.

"You are always at home or in the office," her friends said to her. "You should go to the theatre, darling, or to the circus."

"Vassitchka and I have no time to go to theatres," she would answer sedately. "We have no time for nonsense. What's the use of these theatres?"

On Saturdays Pustovalov and she used to go to the evening service; on holidays to early mass, and they walked side by side with softened faces as they came home from church. There was a pleasant fragrance about them both, and her silk dress rustled agreeably. At home they drank tea, with fancy bread and jams of various kinds, and afterwards they ate pie. Every day at twelve o'clock there was a savory smell of beet-root soup and of mutton or duck in their yard, and on fast-days of fish, and no one could pass the gate without feeling hungry. In the office the samovar was always boiling, and customers were regaled with tea and cracknels. Once a week the couple went to the baths and returned side by side, both red in the face.

"Yes, we have nothing to complain of, thank God," Olenka used to say to her acquaintances. "I wish every one were as well off as Vassitchka and I."

When Pustovalov went away to buy wood in the Mogilev district, she missed him   40
dreadfully, lay awake and cried. A young veterinary surgeon in the army, called Smirnin, to whom they had left their lodge, used sometimes to come in in the evening. He used to talk to her and play cards with her, and this entertained her in her husband's absence. She was particularly interested in what he told her of his home life. He was married and had a little boy, but was separated from his wife because she had been unfaithful to him, and now he hated her and used to send her forty rubles a month for the maintenance of their son. And hearing of all this, Olenka sighed and shook her head. She was sorry for him.

"Well, God keep you," she used to say to him at parting, as she lighted him down the stairs with a candle. "Thank you for coming to cheer me up, and may the Mother of God give you health."

And she always expressed herself with the same sedateness and dignity, the same reasonableness, in imitation of her husband. As the veterinary surgeon was disappearing behind the door below, she would say:

"You know, Vladimir Platonitch, you'd better make it up with your wife. You should forgive her for the sake of your son. You may be sure the little fellow understands."

And when Pustovalov came back, she told him in a low voice about the veterinary surgeon and his unhappy home life, and both sighed and shook their heads and talked about the boy, who, no doubt, missed his father, and by some strange connection of ideas, they went up to the holy icons, bowed to the ground before them, and prayed that God would give them children.

And so the Pustovalovs lived for six years quietly and peaceably in love and com-   45
plete harmony.

But behold! one winter day after drinking hot tea in the office, Vassily Andreitch went out into the yard without his cap on to see about sending off some timber, caught cold, and was taken ill. He had the best doctors, but he grew worse and died after four months' illness. And Olenka was a widow once more.

"I've nobody, now you've left me, my darling," she sobbed, after her husband's funeral. "How can I live without you, in wretchedness and misery! Pity me, good people, all alone in the world!"

She went about dressed in black with long "weepers," and gave up wearing hat and gloves for good. She hardly ever went out, except to church, or to her husband's grave, and led the life of a nun. It was not till six months later that she took off the weepers and opened the shutters of the windows. She was sometimes seen in the mornings, going with her cook to market for provisions, but what went on in her house and how she lived now could only be surmised. People guessed, from seeing her drinking tea in her garden with the veterinary surgeon, who read the newspaper aloud to her, and from the fact that, meeting a lady she knew at the post-office, she said to her:

"There is no proper veterinary inspection in our town, and that's the cause of all sorts of epidemics. One is always hearing of people's getting infection from the milk supply, or catching diseases from horses and cows. The health of domestic animals ought to be as well cared for as the health of human beings."

She repeated the veterinary surgeon's words, and was of the same opinion as he about everything. It was evident that she could not live a year without some attachment, and had found new happiness in the lodge. In any one else this would have been censured, but no one could think ill of Olenka; everything she did was so natural. Neither she nor the veterinary surgeon said anything to other people of the change in their relations, and tried, indeed, to conceal it, but without success, for Olenka could not keep a secret. When he had visitors, men serving in his regiment, and she poured out tea or served the supper, she would begin talking of the cattle plague, of the foot and mouth disease, and of the municipal slaughter-houses. He was dreadfully embarrassed, and when the guests had gone, he would seize her by the hand and hiss angrily:

"I've asked you before not to talk about what you don't understand. When we veterinary surgeons are talking among ourselves, please don't put your word in. It's really annoying."

And she would look at him with astonishment and dismay, and ask him in alarm: "But, Voloditchka, what *am* I to talk about?"

And with tears in her eyes she would embrace him, begging him not to be angry, and they were both happy.

But this happiness did not last long. The veterinary surgeon departed, departed for ever with his regiment, when it was transferred to a distant place—to Siberia, it may be. And Olenka was left alone.

Now she was absolutely alone. Her father had long been dead, and his armchair lay in the attic, covered with dust and lame of one leg. She got thinner and plainer, and when people met her in the street they did not look at her as they used to, and did not smile to her; evidently her best years were over and left behind, and now a new sort of life had begun for her, which did not bear thinking about. In the evening Olenka sat in the porch, and heard the band playing and the fireworks popping in the Tivoli, but now the sound stirred no response. She looked into her yard without interest, thought of nothing, wished for nothing, and afterwards, when night came on she went to bed and dreamed of her empty yard. She ate and drank as it were unwillingly.

And what was worst of all, she had no opinions of any sort. She saw the objects about her and understood what she saw, but could not form any opinion about them, and did not know what to talk about. And how awful it is not to have any opinions! One sees a bottle, for instance, or the rain, or a peasant driving in his cart, but what the bottle is for, or the rain, or the peasant, and what is the meaning of it, one can't say, and could not even for a thousand rubles. When she had Kukin, or Pustovalov, or the veterinary surgeon, Olenka could explain everything, and gave her opinion about anything you like, but now there was the same emptiness in her brain and in her heart as there was in her yard outside. And it was as harsh and as bitter as wormwood in the mouth.

Little by little the town grew in all directions. The road became a street, and where the Tivoli and the timber-yard had been, there were new turnings and houses. How rapidly time passes! Olenka's house grew dingy, the roof got rusty, the shed sank on one side, and the whole yard was overgrown with docks and stinging-nettles. Olenka herself had grown plain and elderly; in summer she sat in the porch, and her soul, as before, was empty and dreary and full of bitterness. In winter she sat at her window and looked at the snow. When she caught the scent of spring, or heard the chime of the church bells, a sudden rush of memories from the past came over her, there was a tender ache in her heart, and her eyes brimmed over with tears; but this was only for a minute, and then came emptiness again and the sense of the futility of life. The black kitten, Briska, rubbed against her and purred softly, but Olenka was not touched by these feline caresses. That was not what she needed. She wanted a love that would absorb her whole being, her whole soul and reason—that would give her ideas and an object in life, and would warm her old blood. And she would shake the kitten off her skirt and say with vexation:

"Get along; I don't want you!"

And so it was, day after day and year after year, and no joy, and no opinions. Whatever Mavra, the cook, said she accepted.

One hot July day, towards evening, just as the cattle were being driven away, and 60
the whole yard was full of dust, some one suddenly knocked at the gate. Olenka went to open it herself and was dumbfounded when she looked out; she saw Smirnin, the veterinary surgeon, grey-headed, and dressed as a civilian. She suddenly remembered everything. She could not help crying and letting her head fall on his breast without uttering a word, and in the violence of her feeling she did not notice how they both walked into the house and sat down to tea.

"My dear Vladimir Platonitch! What fate has brought you?" she muttered, trembling with joy.

"I want to settle here for good, Olga Semyonovna," he told her. "I have resigned my post, and have come to settle down and try my luck on my own account. Besides, it's time for my boy to go to school. He's a big boy. I am reconciled with my wife, you know."

"Where is she?" asked Olenka.

"She's at the hotel with the boy, and I'm looking for lodgings."

"Good gracious, my dear soul! Lodgings? Why not have my house? Why shouldn't 65
that suit you? Why, my goodness, I wouldn't take any rent!" cried Olenka in a flutter, beginning to cry again. "You live here, and the lodge will do nicely for me. Oh dear! how glad I am!"

Next day the roof was painted and the walls were whitewashed, and Olenka, with her arms akimbo, walked about the yard giving directions. Her face was beaming with her old smile, and she was brisk and alert as though she had waked from a long sleep. The veterinary's wife arrived—a thin, plain lady, with short hair and a peevish expression. With her was her little Sasha, a boy of ten, small for his age, blue-eyed, chubby, with dimples in his cheeks. And scarcely had the boy walked into the yard when he ran after the cat, and at once there was the sound of his gay, joyous laugh.

"Is that your puss, auntie?" he asked Olenka. "When she has little ones, do give us a kitten. Mamma is awfully afraid of mice."

Olenka talked to him, and gave him tea. Her heart warmed and there was a sweet ache in her bosom, as though the boy had been her own child. And when he sat at the table in the evening, going over his lessons, she looked at him with deep tenderness and pity as she murmured to herself:

"You pretty pet! . . . my precious! . . . Such a fair little thing, and so clever."

" 'An island is a piece of land which is entirely surrounded by water,' " he read 70
aloud.

"An island is a piece of land," she repeated, and this was the first opinion to which she gave utterance with positive conviction after so many years of silence and dearth of ideas.

Now she had opinions of her own, and at supper she talked to Sasha's parents, saying how difficult the lessons were at the high schools, but that yet the high school was better than a commercial one, since with a high-school education all careers were open to one, such as being a doctor or an engineer.

Sasha began going to the high school. His mother departed to Harkov to her sister's and did not return; his father used to go off every day to inspect cattle, and would often be away from home for three days together, and it seemed to Olenka as though Sasha was entirely abandoned, that he was not wanted at home, that he was being starved, and she carried him off to her lodge and gave him a little room there.

And for six months Sasha had lived in the lodge with her. Every morning Olenka came into his bedroom and found him fast asleep, sleeping noiselessly with his hand under his cheek. She was sorry to wake him.

"Sashenka," she would say mournfully, "get up darling. It's time for school."   75

He would get up, dress and say his prayers, and then sit down to breakfast, drink three glasses of tea, and eat two large cracknels and half a buttered roll. All this time he was hardly awake and a little ill-humored in consequence.

"You don't quite know your fable, Sashenka," Olenka would say, looking at him as though he were about to set off on a long journey. "What a lot of trouble I have with you! You must work and do your best, darling, and obey your teachers."

"Oh, do leave me alone!" Sasha would say.

Then he would go down the street to school, a little figure, wearing a big cap and carrying a satchel on his shoulder. Olenka would follow him noiselessly.

"Sashenka!" she would call after him, and she would pop into his hand a date or   80
a caramel. When he reached the street where the school was, he would feel ashamed of being followed by a tall, stout woman; he would turn round and say:

"You'd better go home, auntie. I can go the rest of the way alone."

She would stand still and look after him fixedly till he had disappeared at the school-gate.

Ah, how she loved him! Of her former attachments not one had been so deep; never had her soul surrendered to any feeling so spontaneously, so disinterestedly, and so joyously as now that her maternal instincts were aroused. For this little boy with the dimple in his cheek and the big school cap, she would have given her whole life, she would have given it with joy and tears of tenderness. Why? Who can tell why?

When she had seen the last of Sasha, she returned home, contented and serene, brimming over with love; her face, which had grown younger during the last six months, smiled and beamed; people meeting her looked at her with pleasure.

"Good-morning, Olga Semyonovna, darling. How are you, darling?"   85

"The lessons at the high school are very difficult now," she would relate at the market. "It's too much; in the first class yesterday they gave him a fable to learn by heart, and a Latin translation and a problem. You know it's too much for a little chap."

And she would begin talking about the teachers, the lessons, and the school books, saying just what Sasha said.

At three o'clock they had dinner together: in the evening they learned their lessons together and cried. When she put him to bed, she would stay a long time making the Cross over him and murmuring a prayer; then she would go to bed and dream of that far-away misty future when Sasha would finish his studies and become a doctor or an engineer, would have a big house of his own with horses and a carriage, would get married and have children. . . . She would fall asleep still thinking of the same thing, and tears would run down her cheeks from her closed eyes, while the black cat lay purring beside her: "Mrr, mrr, mrr."

Suddenly there would come a loud knock at the gate.

Olenka would wake up breathless with alarm, her heart throbbing. Half a minute later would come another knock.   90

"It must be a telegram from Harkov," she would think, beginning to tremble from head to foot. "Sasha's mother is sending for him from Harkov. . . . Oh, mercy on us!"

She was in despair. Her head, her hands, and her feet would turn chill, and she would feel that she was the most unhappy woman in the world. But another minute would pass, voices would be heard: it would turn out to be the veterinary surgeon coming home from the club.

"Well, thank God!" she would think.

And gradually the load in her heart would pass off, and she would feel at ease. She would go back to bed thinking of Sasha, who lay sound asleep in the next room, sometimes crying out in his sleep:

"I'll give it you! Get away! Shut up!"   95

QUESTIONS FOR CLOSE READING

1. How does the weather work in conjunction with the setting to establish the tone of the story?

2. Why do people call Olenka "the darling"? What do you know of her nature?

3. Of her second husband, Pustovalov, we are told, "Her husband's ideas were hers." What is the significance of this comment?

4. When Smirnin the veterinary surgeon leaves, the narrator tells us that Olenka has no opinions. Why is that a problem? And why has she no opinions?

5. When Smirnin and his family return, Olenka finds comfort in treating Sasha as something close to her own child. Why, then, does she develop opinions? What are those opinions?

QUESTIONS FOR INTERPRETATION

1. Olenka is a lovable woman, as we learn from her experiences in the theater with her first husband, and from her experiences with Pustovalov, the timber merchant, her second husband. Even Smirnin finds her warm and affectionate. What are the qualities of this woman that make her so lovable? Why does Sasha have such a difficult time in seeing her in the same light as did her husbands and the townspeople? What significance does the final outburst of Sasha in his sleep imply? Are the words directed at Olenka?

2. The question of opinions is central to this story. Why does Olenka have no opinions except when she has a man in her life to care for? What seems to be the source of her happiness? Is she suffering a fate similar to that of other women in the story? Is her fate a Russian woman's fate, or is she simply very different from other people in the story?

Concerning Love _____ *1898*

Translated by Ronald Hingley

For lunch next day delicious pasties, crayfish and mutton rissoles were served. During the meal Nikanor the cook came upstairs to ask what the guests wanted for dinner. He was a man of average height with a puffy face and small eyes—and so clean-shaven that his whiskers seemed to have been plucked out rather than cut off.

Alyokhin explained that the fair Pelageya was in love with this cook. He was a drunkard and a bit of a hooligan, so she didn't want to marry him, but she didn't mind "just living with him." He was very pious, though, and his religion forbade his just living with her. He insisted on marriage, didn't want her otherwise. He swore at her in his cups, and even beat her. She would hide upstairs, weeping, when he was drunk, while Alyokhin and his servants stayed at home to protect her if necessary.

The conversation turned to love.

"What makes people fall in love?" asked Alyokhin. "Why couldn't Pelageya love someone else more suited to her intellectually and physically? Why must she love this Nikanor—'Fat-face,' everyone calls him round here—seeing that personal happiness is an important factor in love? It's all very mysterious, there are any number of possible interpretations. So far we've only heard one incontrovertible truth about love: the biblical 'this is a great mystery.' Everything else written and spoken about love has offered no solution, but has just posed questions which have simply remained unanswered. What seems to explain one instance doesn't fit a dozen others. It's best to interpret each instance separately, in my view, without trying to generalize. We must isolate each individual case, as doctors say."

"Very true," agreed Burkin.   5

"Your ordinary decent Russian has a weakness for these unsolved problems. Where other peoples romanticize their love, garnishing it with roses and nightingales, we Russians bedizen ours with dubious profundities—and the most tedious available, at that. Back in my student days in Moscow I had a 'friend': a lovely lady who, when I held her in my arms, was always wondering what monthly allowance I would give her, and what was the price of a pound of beef. We're just the same. When we're in love we're for ever questioning ourselves. Are we being honorable or dishonorable? Wise or stupid? How will it end, this love? And so on. Whether this attitude is right or wrong I don't know, but that it is a nuisance, that it is unsatisfactory and frustrating—that I do know."

He seemed to have some story he wanted to tell. People who live alone always do have things on their minds that they are keen to talk about. Bachelors deliberately go to the public baths, and to restaurants in town, just to talk, and they sometimes tell bath attendants or waiters the most fascinating tales. In the country, though, it is their guests to whom they usually unbosom themselves. Grey sky and rain-soaked trees could be seen through the windows. There was nowhere to go in such weather—and nothing to do except swap yarns.

I've been living and farming in Sofyino for some time—since I took my degree (Alyokhin began). By upbringing I'm the armchair type, my leanings are academic. But this estate was badly in debt when I came here, and since it was partly through spending so much on my education that Father had run up those debts, I decided to stay on and work until I'd paid them off. I made my decision and started working here: not without a certain repugnance, frankly. The land isn't all that productive hereabouts, and if you don't want to farm at a loss you either have to use hired hands—slave labor, practically—or else you have to run the place peasant-fashion: do your own field work, that is, yourself and your family. There's no other way. But I hadn't gone into these subtleties at the time. Not one single plot of earth did I leave in peace, I corralled all the nearby villagers and their women, and I had us all working away like billy-o. I ploughed myself, I sowed and I reaped myself—bored stiff the while, and frowning fastidiously like a village cat eating gherkins in the vegetable patch because it's starving. My body ached, I was nearly dead on my feet. At first I thought I could easily combine this drudgery with the cultured life—all I had to do, thought I, was to observe a certain routine. I moved into the best rooms up here, I arranged for coffee and liqueurs to be served after lunch and dinner, and I read the *European Herald* in bed at night. But one day our priest, Father Ivan, turned up and scoffed my whole stock of liquor at a sitting. The priest also ran off with my *European Heralds,* or rather his daughters did, because I never managed to get as far as my bed in summer, especially during haymaking, but slept in the bar, in a sledge, or in some woodman's hut—hardly conducive to reading, that. I gradually moved downstairs, I began having my meals with the servants, and there's nothing left of my former gracious living but these same servants who once worked for my father, and whom I hadn't the heart to dismiss.

Quite early on I was elected an honorary justice of the peace, and had to go to town and then to take part in sessions and sit at the assizes, which I found entertaining. When you've been cooped up here for a couple of months, especially in winter, you end up yearning for a black frock-coat. Now, at the assizes you had your frock-coats, your uniforms, your tail-coats. They were all lawyers there, all educated men. They were the sort of people you could talk to. To sit in an arm-chair wearing clean underwear and light boots with your watch-chain on your chest . . . after sleeping in a sledge and eating with servants, that really was the height of luxury.

I was always welcome in town, and I liked meeting new people. Now, among these new friendships the most serious—and, quite honestly, the most pleasant—was with Luganovich, the Deputy Chairman of Assize. You both know him: a most charming individual. This happened just after the famous arson case. The proceedings had lasted two days, we were worn out, and Luganovich looked in my direction.

"How about dinner at my place?"

I was surprised, barely knowing the man, and then only in an official capacity—I had never visited his home. After calling briefly at my hotel to change, I set off. This dinner led to my first meeting with Luganovich's wife, Anne. She was still very young, not more than twenty-two, and her first child had been born six months previously. It all happened so long ago that I'd be hard put to it, now, to define precisely what it was about her that so much attracted me. But at that dinner it was abundantly clear. I saw a woman—young, handsome, kind, intellectual and captivating—unlike any I had ever met before. I at once sensed that this creature was dear to me, I seemed to know her already—rather as if I'd once seen that face, those eager, intelligent eyes, when I was a little boy looking at the album on my mother's chest-of-drawers.

At the arson trial four Jews had been found guilty and it had been made a conspiracy charge: quite indefensibly in my view. I became rather agitated at dinner—most distressed, in fact—and I've forgotten what I said, now, except that Anne kept shaking her head and telling her husband that "I just can't believe it, Dmitry."

Luganovich is a good fellow, one of those simple-minded chaps who have got it into their heads that the man in the dock is always guilty, and that a sentence may be

10

challenged only in writing, through the proper channels—most certainly not at a private dinner-table.

"You and I didn't start that fire," he said gently. "Which is why you and I aren't   15
being tried and sent to prison."

Husband and wife both pressed food and drink on me. From several details—the way they made coffee together, the way they understood each other almost without words—I concluded that they lived in peace and harmony, that they were pleased to be entertaining a guest. We played piano duets after dinner. Then it grew dark and I went to my lodgings.

This happened in early spring, after which I was stuck in Sofyino all summer. I didn't even think of town, I was so busy. But I was haunted all along by the memory of that slender, fair-haired woman. Not directly present in my consciousness, she seemed rather to cast a faint shadow over it.

In late autumn a charity performance was staged in town. I went into the Governor's box (having been invited in the interval), and there was Anne Luganovich seated by the Governor's wife. Again I was struck by that same irresistible vibrant beauty, by that charming, friendly expression in her eyes. And again I sensed an intimacy shared.

We sat next to each other, we walked in the foyer, and she told me that I had grown thinner. Had I been ill?

"Yes. I've had a bad shoulder, and I sleep poorly when it rains."   20

"You look worn out. When you came to dinner in the spring you seemed younger, more sure of yourself. You were a bit carried away at the time, you talked a lot, you were quite fascinating. I couldn't help being a bit taken with you, actually. I've often thought of you during the summer for some reason, and when I was getting ready for the theatre tonight I felt sure I should see you."

She laughed. "But today you look worn out," she repeated. "It makes you seem older."

I lunched at the Luganoviches' next day. Afterwards they drove out to their holiday cottage to put it in shape for the winter. I went with them, I came back to town with them, and at midnight I had tea with them in the peaceful setting of their home: by a blazing fire, with the young mother going out from time to time to see if her little girl was asleep. After that I always made a point of seeing the Luganoviches when I was in town. We got to know each other, and I used to call unannounced. I was just like one of the family.

"Who is that?" I would hear her ask from the back of the house in the slow drawl which I found so attractive.

"It's Mr. Alyokhin," the maid or nanny would answer, and Anne would appear   25
looking worried. Why hadn't I been to see them sooner? Had anything happened?

Her gaze, the clasp of her fine, delicate hand, the clothes which she wore about the house, the way she did her hair, her voice, her steps . . . they always made me feel as if something new and out of the ordinary, something significant, had happened to me. We enjoyed long conversations—and long silences, each wrapt in his own thoughts. Or she would play the piano for me. When there was no one at home I would wait, I'd talk to nanny, play with baby, or lie on the study ottoman reading the newspaper. When Anne came in I would meet her in the hall and take her shopping off her. I always carried that shopping so fondly and triumphantly, somehow—just like a little boy.

It was a bit like the farmer's wife in the story, the one who had no troubles—not, that is, until she went and bought herself a pig! The Luganoviches had no troubles—

so they went and chummed up with me! If I hadn't been to town recently, then I must be ill or something must have happened to me, and both would be genuinely alarmed. What worried them was that I—an educated man who knew foreign languages—didn't devote myself to learning or letters, but lived in the country, going round and round the same old treadmill, that I worked so much but was always hard up. I was bound to be unhappy, they felt, and if they saw me talking, laughing or having a meal, I must be doing so merely to conceal my anguish. Even when I was happy and relaxed I could feel them viewing me with concern. They were particularly touching when I really was in a bit of a fix: when some creditor was pressing me, when I couldn't meet some payment on time. Husband and wife would then whisper together by the window, and he would approach me looking very solemn.

"If you're a bit short, Paul, my wife and I would like to lend you something. Please don't hesitate to ask." His ears would flush with embarrassment.

Or else he would come up with his red ears after one of those whispering sessions by the window, and say that he and his wife "do most urgently beg you to accept this gift." He would then present me with some studs, a cigarette-case or a lamp. In return I would send them something from the country: a bird for the table, butter, flowers. Both of them, incidentally, had money of their own. Now, I was always borrowing in the early days, and I wasn't particularly choosy about it—I took my loans where I could get them. But no power on earth would have induced me to borrow from the Luganoviches. Need I say more?

I was unhappy. At home, in my fields and in my barn my thoughts were of her. I tried to plumb the mystery of a young, handsome, intelligent woman, the wife of an unattractive, almost elderly husband (the man was over forty) and the mother of his children. I also tried to plumb the mystery of this same unattractive husband, this good sort, this easy-going fellow with his boring, common-sensical views, who (when attending a party or dance) always cultivated the local fuddy-duddies, this listless misfit with his submissive air of being a spectator or a bale of goods put up for auction . . . of this man who still believed in his right to be happy and to have children by her. Why ever, I kept wondering, had she met him instead of me? To what purpose so drastic an error in our lives?

On my visits to town I could always tell from her eyes that she was expecting me, and she'd admit having had a special feeling all day—she'd guessed I'd be coming. We enjoyed our long conversations and silences, not declaring our love for each other but concealing it fearfully and jealously. We feared anything which might betray our secret to ourselves. Deep and tender though my love was, I tried to be sensible about it, speculating what the upshot might be if we should lack the strength to fight our passions. It seemed incredible that a love so quiet, so sad as mine could suddenly and crudely disrupt the happy tenor of her husband's and children's lives: disrupt an entire household where I was so loved and trusted. Was that the way for a decent man to behave? She would have gone away with me—but where to? Where could I take her? Things would have been different if my life had been romantic and enterprising: if I'd been fighting for my country's freedom, for instance, if I'd been a distinguished scholar, actor or artist. As it was I should be conveying her from one humdrum, colorless milieu into another equally humdrum, or even worse. How long would our happiness last? What would happen to her if I became ill or died? What if we just fell out of love?

Her reflections were evidently similar. She thought about her husband and children, thought about her mother who loved her husband like a son. If she yielded to her passions she would either have to lie or tell the truth, but both courses would be equally alarming and difficult to one in her situation. Would her love bring me happiness, she wondered agonizingly. Wouldn't it complicate my life: irksome enough anyway, and beset with all sorts of tribulations? She felt she was too old for me, that she lacked the drive and energy to start a new life. She often told her husband that I ought to marry some decent, intelligent girl who would be a good housewife and helpmeet— but she would add at once that such a paragon was unlikely to be found anywhere in town.

Meanwhile the years were passing. Anne now had two children. Whenever I visited the family the servants smiled their welcome, the children shouted that Uncle Paul had arrived and clung round my neck, and everyone rejoiced. Not understanding my innermost feelings, they thought I was rejoicing with them. They all saw me as the embodiment of integrity. Adults and children alike, they felt that integrity incarnate was walking about the room—which imparted a special charm to their relations with me, as if my presence made their lives purer and finer. Anne and I used to go to the theatre together, always on foot. We would sit beside each other in the stalls, our shoulders touching, and I'd silently take the opera glasses from her, sensing her nearness to me, sensing that she was mine, that we couldn't live without each other. But through some strange lack of *rapport* we always said good-bye when we left the theatre, and we parted like strangers. People were saying goodness knows what about us in town, but not one word of truth was there in all their gossip.

Anne had begun going away to her mother's and sister's more often in recent years. She had become subject to depressions: moods in which she was conscious that her life was unfulfilled and wasted. She didn't want to see her husband and children at such times. She was under treatment for a nervous condition.

And still we did not speak our minds. In company she would feel curiously   35
exasperated with me. She would disagree with everything I said, and if I became involved in an argument she would take my opponent's side. If I chanced to drop something she would coldly offer her "congratulations." If I forgot the opera glasses when we went to the theatre, she'd tell me she had "known very well I'd forget those."

Luckily or unluckily, there is nothing in our lives which doesn't end sooner or later. The time had now come for us to part: Luganovich had been appointed to a judgeship in the west country. They had to sell their furniture, horses and cottage. We drove out to the cottage, and as we turned back for one last look at the garden and green roof everyone was sad, and I knew that it was time for me to take my leave of rather more than a mere cottage. It had been decided that we should see Anne off to the Crimea (where her doctors had advised her to stay) at the end of August, and that Luganovich would take the children to the west a little later.

A large crowd of us went to see Anne off. She had already said good-bye to her husband and children, and the train was due to leave at any moment, when I dashed into her compartment to put a basket—which she had nearly left behind—on the luggage rack. It was my turn to say good-bye. Our eyes met there in the compartment, and we could hold back no longer. I put my arms around her, she pressed her face against my breast, and the tears flowed. Kissing her face, her shoulders, her tear-drenched hands— we were both so unhappy—I declared my love. With a burning pain in my heart, I saw how inessential, how trivial, how illusory it was . . . everything which had frustrated our love. I saw that, if you love, you must base your theory of love on something loftier and more significant than happiness or unhappiness, than sin or virtue as they are commonly understood. Better, otherwise, not to theorize at all.

I kissed her for the last time, I clasped her hand, and we parted—for ever. The train had already started. I sat down in the next compartment, which was empty . . . sat there, weeping, until the first stop. Then I walked home to Sofyino.

It had stopped raining while Alyokhin was telling his story, and the sun had peeped out. Burkin and Ivan Ivanovich went on to the balcony, which had a superb view of the garden, and of the river which now gleamed, mirror-like, in the sun. As they admired the view they felt sorry that this man with the kind, intelligent eyes—who had spoken with such sincere feeling—really was going round and round the same old treadmill, doing neither academic work nor anything else capable of making his life more pleasant. And they imagined how stricken that young woman must have looked when he had said good-bye to her in the train, kissing her head and shoulders. Both of them had met her in town. Burkin, indeed, had been a friend of hers and had thought her very good-looking.

QUESTIONS FOR CLOSE READING

1. Why do Nikanor and Pelageya seem unsuited for each other at the beginning of the story?

2. What is the structure of the narrative? How does the story start and what leads Alyokhin to tell his friends his story? What is the effect on the reader of having the story told this way?

3. What attracts Alyokhin to Anne Luganovich? Does she seem attracted to him? Is it love?

4. How do the circumstances of their lives control the behavior of Alyokhin and Anne?

5. Alyokhin's friends feel sorry for him once his story is told. What further reactions do they have? What would they have wanted Alyokhin to do instead of what he did when he last saw Anne?

QUESTIONS FOR INTERPRETATION

1. Explain what Alyokhin means when he says at the end of the story that "if you love, you must base your theory of love on something loftier and more significant than happiness or unhappiness, than sin or virtue as they are commonly understood"? What does he seem to feel a theory of love should be based on? Does he seem to base his theory of love on that theory?

2. What are the fundamental differences between the love of Nikanor and Pelageya and the love of Alyokhin and Anne? What seems to be the point of comparing these people? Does Alyokhin seem to be aware of the comparison? What is the reader to understand about love by comparing the circumstances of the two sets of lovers?

3. The reader is placed in the same position as Burkin and Ivan Ivanovich at the end of the story. What seems to have been Chekhov's expectation for the reaction of the reader? How would you have wanted Alyokhin's story to turn out? Do you as reader agree that there is a theory of love that people adhere to? Should happiness be part of that theory? Is there happiness anywhere in the story? What does that tell us about Chekhov's conception of love?

The Lady with the Dog ————————————————— *1898*

Translated by Constance Garnett

I

It was said that a new person had appeared on the sea-front: a lady with a little dog. Dmitri Dmitritch Gurov, who had by then been a fortnight at Yalta, and so was fairly at home there, had begun to take an interest in new arrivals. Sitting in Verney's pavilion, he saw, walking on the sea-front, a fair-haired young lady of medium height, wearing a *béret;* a white Pomeranian dog was running behind her.

And afterwards he met her in the public gardens and in the square several times a day. She was walking alone, always wearing the same *béret,* and always with the same white dog; no one knew who she was, and every one called her simply "the lady with the dog."

"If she is here alone without a husband or friends, it wouldn't be amiss to make her acquaintance," Gurov reflected.

He was under forty, but he had a daughter already twelve years old, and two sons at school. He had been married young, when he was a student in his second year, and by now his wife seemed half as old again as he. She was a tall, erect woman with dark eyebrows, staid and dignified, and, as she said of herself, intellectual. She read a great deal, used phonetic spelling, called her husband, not Dmitri, but Dimitri, and he secretly considered her unintelligent, narrow, inelegant, was afraid of her, and did not like to be at home. He had begun being unfaithful to her long ago—had been unfaithful to her often, and, probably on that account, almost always spoke ill of women, and when they were talked about in his presence, used to call them "the lower race."

It seemed to him that he had been so schooled by bitter experience that he might call them what he liked, and yet he could not get on for two days together without "the lower race." In the society of men he was bored and not himself, with them he was cold and uncommunicative; but when he was in the company of women he felt free, and knew what to say to them and how to behave; and he was at ease with them even when he was silent. In his appearance, in his character, in his whole nature, there was something attractive and elusive which allured women and disposed them in his favour; he knew that, and some force seemed to draw him, too, to them.

Experience often repeated, truly bitter experience, had taught him long ago that with decent people, especially Moscow people—always slow to move and irresolute—every intimacy, which at first so agreeably diversifies life and appears a light and charming adventure, inevitably grows into a regular problem of extreme intricacy, and in the long run the situation becomes unbearable. But at every fresh meeting with an interesting woman this experience seemed to slip out of his memory, and he was eager for life, and everything seemed simple and amusing.

One evening he was dining in the gardens, and the lady in the *béret* came up slowly to take the next table. Her expression, her gait, her dress, and the way she did her hair told him that she was a lady, that she was married, that she was in Yalta for the first time and alone, and that she was dull there. . . . The stories told of the immorality in such places as Yalta are to a great extent untrue; he despised them, and knew that such stories were for the most part made up by persons who would themselves have been glad to sin if they had been able; but when the lady sat down at the next table three paces from him, he remembered these tales of easy conquests, of trips to the mountains, and

5

the tempting thought of a swift, fleeting love affair, a romance with an unknown woman, whose name he did not know, suddenly took possession of him.

He beckoned coaxingly to the Pomeranian, and when the dog came up to him he shook his finger at it. The Pomeranian growled: Gurov shook his finger at it again.

The lady looked at him and at once dropped her eyes.

"He doesn't bite," she said, and blushed.   10

"May I give him a bone?" he asked; and when she nodded he asked courteously, "Have you been long in Yalta?"

"Five days."

"And I have already dragged out a fortnight here."

There was a brief silence.

"Times goes fast, and yet it is so dull here!" she said, not looking at him.   15

"That's only the fashion to say it is dull here. A provincial will live in Belyov or Zhidra and not be dull, and when he comes here it's 'Oh, the dullness! Oh the dust!' One would think he came from Grenada."

She laughed. Then both continued eating in silence, like strangers, but after dinner they walked side by side; and there sprang up between them the light jesting conversation of people who are free and satisfied, to whom it does not matter where they go or what they talk about. They walked and talked of the strange light on the sea: the water was of a soft warm lilac hue, and there was a golden streak from the moon upon it. They talked of how sultry it was after a hot day. Gurov told her that he came from Moscow, that he had taken his degree in Arts, but had a post in a bank; that he had trained as an opera-singer, but had given it up, that he owned two houses in Moscow. . . . And from her he learnt that she had grown up in Petersburg, but had lived in S— since her marriage two years before, and that she was staying another month in Yalta, and that her husband, who needed a holiday too, might perhaps come and fetch her. She was not sure whether her husband had a post in a Crown Department or under the Provincial Council—and was amused by her own ignorance. And Gurov learnt, too, that she was called Anna Sergeyevna.

Afterwards he thought about her in his room at the hotel—thought she would certainly meet him next day; it would be sure to happen. As he got into bed he thought how lately she had been a girl at school, doing lessons like his own daughter; he recalled the diffidence, the angularity, that was still manifest in her laugh and her manner of talking with a stranger. This must have been the first time in her life she had been alone in surroundings in which she was followed, looked at, and spoken to merely from a secret motive which she could hardly fail to guess. He recalled her slender, delicate neck, her lovely grey eyes.

"There's something pathetic about her, anyway," he thought, and fell asleep.

II

A week had passed since they had made acquaintance. It was a holiday. It was sultry indoors, while in the street the wind whirled the dust round and round, and blew people's   20
hats off. It was a thirsty day, and Gurov often went into the pavilion, and pressed Anna Sergeyevna to have syrup and water or an ice. One did not know what to do with oneself.

In the evening when the wind had dropped a little, they went out on the groyne° to see the steamer come in. There were a great many people walking about the harbour;

groyne: stone pier

they had gathered to welcome some one, bringing bouquets. And two peculiarities of a well-dressed Yalta crowd were very conspicuous: the elderly ladies were dressed like young ones, and there were great numbers of generals.

Owing to the roughness of the sea, the steamer arrived late, after the sun had set, and it was a long time turning about before it reached the groyne. Anna Sergeyevna looked through her lorgnette° at the steamer and the passengers as though looking for acquaintances, and when she turned to Gurov her eyes were shining. She talked a great deal and asked disconnected questions, forgetting next moment what she had asked; then she dropped her lorgnette in the crush.

The festive crowd began to disperse; it was too dark to see people's faces. The wind had completely dropped, but Gurov and Anna Sergeyevna still stood as though waiting to see some one else come from the steamer. Anna Sergeyevna was silent now, and sniffed the flowers without looking at Gurov.

"The weather is better this evening," he said. "Where shall we go now? Shall we drive somewhere?"

She made no answer.   25

The he looked at her intently, and all at once put his arm round her and kissed her on the lips, and breathed in the moisture and the fragrance of the flowers; and he immediately looked round him, anxiously wondering whether any one had seen them.

"Let us go to your hotel," he said softly. And both walked quickly.

The room was close and smelt of the scent she had bought at the Japanese shop. Gurov looked at her and thought: "What different people one meets in the world!" From the past he preserved memories of careless, good-natured women, who loved cheerfully and were grateful to him for the happiness he gave them, however brief it might be; and of women like his wife who loved without any genuine feeling, with superfluous phrases, affectedly, hysterically, with an expression that suggested that it was not love nor passion, but something more significant; and of two or three others, very beautiful, cold women, on whose faces he had caught a glimpse of a rapacious expression—an obstinate desire to snatch from life more than it could give, and these were capricious, unreflecting, domineering, unintelligent women not in their first youth, and when Gurov grew cold to them their beauty excited his hatred, and the lace on their linen seemed to him like scales.

But in this case there was still the diffidence, the angularity of inexperienced youth, an awkward feeling; and there was a sense of consternation as though some one had suddenly knocked at the door. The attitude of Anna Sergeyevna—"the lady with the dog"—to what had happened was somehow peculiar, very grave, as though it were her fall—so it seemed, and it was strange and inappropriate. Her face dropped and faded, and on both sides of it her long hair hung down mournfully; she mused in a dejected attitude like "the woman who was a sinner" in an old-fashioned picture.

"It's wrong," she said. "You will be the first to despise me now."   30

There was a water-melon on the table. Gurov cut himself a slice and began eating it without haste. There followed at least half an hour of silence.

Anna Sergeyevna was touching; there was about her the purity of a good, simple woman who had seen little of life. The solitary candle burning on the table threw a faint light on her face, yet it was clear that she was very unhappy.

"How could I despise you?" asked Gurov. "You don't know what you are saying."

"God forgive me," she said, and her eyes filled with tears. "It's awful."

lorgnette: hand-held eyeglasses

"You seem to feel you need to be forgiven."   35

"Forgiven? No. I am a bad, low woman; I despise myself and I don't attempt to justify myself. It's not my husband but myself I have deceived. And not only just now; I
have been deceiving myself for a long time. My husband may be a good, honest man,
but he is a flunkey! I don'' know what he does there, what his work is, but I know he is
a flunkey! I was twenty when I was married to him. I have been tormented by curiosity;
I wanted something better. 'There must be a different sort of life,' I said to myself. I
wanted to live! To live, to live! . . . I was fired by curiosity . . . you don't understand it,
but, I swear to God, I could not control myself, something happened to me: I could not
be restrained. I told my husband I was ill, and came here. . . . And here I have been
walking about as though I were dazed, like a mad creature; . . . and now I have become
a vulgar, contemptible woman whom any one may despise."

Gurov felt bored already, listening to her. He was irritated by the naive tone, by
this remorse, so unexpected and inopportune; but for the tears in her eyes, he might
have thought she was jesting or playing a part.

"I don't understand," he said softly. "What is it you want?"

She hid her face on his breast and pressed close to him.

"Believe me, believe me, I beseech you . . ." she said. "I love a pure, honest life,   40
and sin is loathsome to me. I don't know what I am doing. Simple people say: 'The Evil
One has beguiled me.' And I may say of myself now that the Evil One has beguiled me."

"Hush, hush! . . ." he muttered.

He looked at her fixed, scared eyes, kissed her, talked softly and affectionately, and
by degrees she was comforted, and her gaiety returned; they both began laughing.

Afterwards when they went out there was not a soul on the sea-front. The town with
its cypresses had quite a deathlike air, but the sea still broke noisily on the shore; a single barge was rocking on the waves, and a lantern was blinking sleepily on it.

They found a cab and drove to Oreanda.

"I found out your surname in the hall just now: it was written on the board—Von   45
Diderits," said Gurov. "Is your husband a German?"

"No, I believe his grandfather was a German, but he is an Orthodox Russian
himself."

At Oreanda they sat on a seat not far from the church, looked down at the sea,
and were silent. Yalta was hardly visible through the morning mist; white clouds stood
motionless on the mountain-tops. The leaves did not stir on the trees, grasshoppers
chirruped, and the monotonous hollow sound of the sea rising up from below, spoke
of the peace, of the eternal sleep awaiting us. So it must have sounded when there was
no Yalta, no Oreanda here; so it sounds now, and it will sound as indifferently and mo-
notonously when we are all no more. And in this constancy, in this complete indifference to the life and death of each of us, there lies hid, perhaps a pledge of our eternal
salvation, of the unceasing movement of life upon earth, of unceasing progress towards
perfection. Sitting beside a young woman who in the dawn seemed so lovely, soothed
and spellbound in these magical surroundings—the sea, mountains, clouds, the open
sky—Gurov thought how in reality everything is beautiful in this world when one reflects: everything except what we think or do ourselves when we forget our human dignity and the higher aims of our existence.

A man walked up to them—probably a keeper—looked at them and walked away.
And this detail seemed mysterious and beautiful, too. They saw a steamer come from
Theodosia, with its lights out in the glow of dawn.

"There is dew on the grass," said Anna Sergeyevna, after a silence.

"Yes. It's time to go home." 50

They went back to the town.

Then they met every day at twelve o'clock on the sea-front, lunched and dined together, went for walks, admired the sea. She complained that she slept badly, that her heart throbbed violently; asked the same questions, troubled now by jealousy and now by the fear that he did not respect her sufficiently. And often in the square or gardens, where there was no one near them, he suddenly drew her to him and kissed her passionately. Complete idleness, these kisses in broad daylight while he looked round in dread of some one's seeing them, the heat, the smell of the sea, and the continual passing to and fro before him of idle, well-dressed, well-fed people, made a new man of him; he told Anna Sergeyevna how beautiful she was, how fascinating. He was impatiently passionate, he would not move a step away from her, while she was often pensive and continually urged him to confess that he did not respect her, did not love her in the least, and thought of her as nothing but a common woman. Rather late almost every evening they drove somewhere out of town, to Oreanda or to the waterfall; and the expedition was always a success, the scenery invariably impressed them as grand and beautiful.

They were expecting her husband to come, but a letter came from him, saying that there was something wrong with his eyes, and he entreated his wife to come home as quickly as possible. Anna Sergeyevna made haste to go.

"It's a good thing I am going away," she said to Gurov. "It's the finger of destiny!"

She went by coach and he went with her. They were driving the whole day. When she 55 had got into a compartment of the express, and when the second bell had rung, she said:

"Let me look at you once more . . . look at you once again. That's right."

She did not shed tears, but was so sad that she seemed ill, and her face was quivering.

"I shall remember you . . . think of you," she said. "God be with you; be happy. Don't remember evil against me. We are parting forever—it must be so, for we ought never to have met. Well, God be with you."

The train moved off rapidly, its lights soon vanished from sight, and a minute later there was no sound of it, as though everything had conspired together to end as quickly as possible that sweet delirium, that madness. Left alone on the platform, and gazing into the dark distance, Gurov listened to the chirrup of the grasshoppers and the hum of the telegraph wires, feeling as though he had only just waked up. And he thought, musing, that there had been another episode or adventure in his life, and it, too, was at an end, and nothing was left of it but a memory. . . . He was moved, sad, and conscious of a slight remorse. This young woman whom he would never meet again had not been happy with him; he was genuinely warm and affectionate with her, but yet in his manner, his tone, and his caresses there had been a shade of light irony, the coarse condescension of a happy man who was, besides, almost twice her age. All the time she had called him kind, exceptional, lofty; obviously he had seemed to her different from what he really was, so he had unintentionally deceived her. . . .

Here at the station was already a scent of autumn; it was a cold evening. 60

"It's time for me to go north," thought Gurov as he left the platform. "High time!"

III

At home in Moscow everything was in its winter routine; the stoves were heated, and in the morning it was still dark when the children were having breakfast and getting ready for school, and the nurse would light the lamp for a short time. The frosts had begun already. When the first snow has fallen, on the first day of sledge-driving it is pleasant to see the white earth, the white roofs, to draw soft, delicious breath, and the season brings back the days of one's youth. The old limes and birches, white with hoar-frost, have a good-natured expression; they are nearer to one's heart than cypresses and palms, and near them one doesn't want to be thinking of the sea and the mountains.

Gurov was Moscow born; he arrived in Moscow on a fine frosty day, and when he put on his fur coat and warm gloves, and walked along Petrovka, and when on Saturday evening he heard the ringing of the bells, his recent trip and the places he had seen lost all charm for him. Little by little he became absorbed in Moscow life, greedily read three newspapers a day, and declared he did not read the Moscow papers on principle! He already felt a longing to go to restaurants, clubs, dinner-parties, anniversary celebrations and he felt flattered at entertaining distinguished lawyers and artists, and at playing cards with a professor at the doctors' club. He could already eat a whole plateful of salt fish and cabbage. . . .

In another month, he fancied, the image of Anna Sergeyevna would be shrouded in a mist in his memory, and only from time to time would visit him in his dreams with a touching smile as others did. But more than a month passed, real winter had come, and everything was still clear in his memory as though he had parted with Anna Sergeyevna only the day before. And his memories glowed more and more vividly. When in the evening stillness he heard from his study the voices of his children, preparing their lessons, or when he listened to a song or the organ at the restaurant, or the storm howled in the chimney, suddenly everything would rise up in his memory: what had happened on the groyne, and the early morning with the mist on the mountains, and the steamer coming from Theodosia and the kisses. He would pace a long time about his room, remembering it all and smiling; then his memories passed into dreams, and in his fancy the past was mingled with what was to come. Anna Sergeyevna did not visit him in dreams, but followed him about everywhere like a shadow and haunted him. When he shut his eyes he saw her as though she were living before him, and she seemed to him lovelier, younger, tenderer than she was; and he imagined himself finer than he had been in Yalta. In the evenings she peeped out at him from the bookcase, from the fireplace, from the corner—he heard her breathing, the caressing rustle of her dress. In the street he watched the women, looking for some one like her.

He was tormented by an intense desire to confide his memories to some one. But   65
in his home it was impossible to talk of his love, and he had no one outside; he could not talk to his tenants nor to any one at the bank. And what had he to talk of? Had he been in love, then? Had there been anything beautiful, poetical, or edifying or simply interesting in his relations with Anna Sergeyevna? And there was nothing for him but to talk vaguely of love, of woman, and no one guessed what it meant; only his wife twitched her black eyebrows, and said: "The part of a lady-killer does not suit you at all, Dimitri."

One evening, coming out of the doctors' club with an official with whom he had been playing cards, he could not resist saying:

"If only you knew what a fascinating woman I made the acquaintance of in Yalta!"

The official got into his sledge and was driving away, but turned suddenly and shouted:

"Dmitri Dmitritch!"

"What?"   70

"You were right this evening: the sturgeon was a bit too strong!"

These words, so ordinary, for some reason moved Gurov to indignation, and struck him as degrading and unclean. What savage manners, what people! What senseless nights, what uninteresting, uneventful days! The rage for card-playing, the gluttony, the drunkenness, the continual talk always about the same thing. Useless pursuits and conversations always about the same things absorb the better part of one's time, the better part of one's strength, and in the end there is left a life grovelling and curtailed, worthless and trivial, and there is no escaping or getting away from it—just as though one were in a madhouse or a prison.

Gurov did not sleep all night, and was filled with indignation. And he had a headache all next day. And the next night he slept badly; he sat up in bed, thinking, or paced up and down his room. He was sick of his children, sick of the bank; he had no desire to go anywhere or to talk of anything.

In the holidays in December he prepared for a journey, and told his wife he was going to Petersburg to do something in the interests of a young friend—and he set off for S—. What for? He did not very well know himself. He wanted to see Anna Sergeyevna and to talk with her—to arrange a meeting, if possible.

He reached S— in the morning, and took the best room at the hotel, in which the   75
floor was covered with grey army cloth, and on the table was an inkstand, grey with dust and adorned with a figure on horseback, with its hat and its hand and its head broken off. The hotel porter gave him the necessary information; Von Diderits lived in a house of his own in Old Gontcharny Street—it was not far from the hotel: he was rich and lived in good style and had his own horses; every one in town knew him. The porter pronounced the name "Dridirits."

Gurov went without haste to Old Gontcharny Street and found the house. Just opposite the house stretched a long grey fence adorned with nails.

"One would run away from a fence like that," thought Gurov, looking from the fence to the windows of the house and back again.

He considered: to-day was a holiday, and the husband would probably be at home. And in any case it would be tactless to go into the house and upset her. If he were to send her a note it might fall into her husband's hands, and then it might ruin everything. The best thing was to trust to chance. And he kept walking up and down the street by the fence, waiting for the chance. He saw a beggar go in at the gate and dogs fly at him; then an hour later he heard a piano, and the sounds were faint and indistinct. Probably it was Anna Sergeyevna playing. The front door suddenly opened and an old woman came out, followed by the familiar white Pomeranian. Gurov was on the point of calling to the dog, but his heart began beating violently, and in his excitement he could not remember the dog's name.

He walked up and down, and loathed the grey fence more and more and by now he thought irritably that Anna Sergeyevna had forgotten him and was perhaps already amusing herself with some one else, and that that was very natural in a young woman who had nothing to look at from morning till night but that confounded fence. He went back to his hotel room and sat for a long while on the sofa, not knowing what to do, then he had dinner and a long nap.

"How stupid and worrying it is!" he thought when he woke and looked at the   80
dark windows: it was already evening. "Here I've had a good sleep for some reason. What shall I do in the night?"

He sat on the bed, which was covered by a cheap grey blanket, such as one sees in hospitals, and he taunted himself in his vexation:

"So much for the lady with the dog . . . so much for the adventure. . . . You're in a nice fix. . . ."

That morning at the station a poster in large letters had caught his eye. "The Geisha" was to be performed for the first time. He thought of this and went to the theater.

"It's quite possible she may go to the first performance," he thought.

The theatre was full. As in all provincial theatres, there was a fog above the chandelier, the gallery was noisy and restless; in the front row the local dandies were standing up before the beginning of the performance, with their hands behind them; in the Governor's box the Governor's daughter, wearing a boa, was sitting in the front seat, while the Governor himself lurked modestly behind the curtain with only his hands visible; the orchestra was a long time tuning up; the stage curtain swayed. All the time the audience were coming in and taking their seats Gurov looked at them eagerly.

Anna Sergeyevna, too, came in. She sat down in the third row, and when Gurov looked at her his heart contracted, and he understood clearly that for him there was in the whole world no creature so near, so precious, and so important to him; she, this little woman, in no way remarkable, lost in a provincial crowd, with a vulgar lorgnette in her hand, filled his whole life now, was his sorrow and his joy, the one happiness that he now desired for himself, and to the sounds of the inferior orchestra, of the wretched provincial violins, he thought how lovely she was. He thought and dreamed.

A young man with small side-whiskers, tall and stooping, came in with Anna Sergeyevna, and sat down beside her; he bent his head at every step and seemed to be continually bowing. Most likely this was the husband whom at Yalta, in a rush of bitter feeling, she had called a flunkey. And there really was in his long figure, his side-whiskers, and the small bald patch on his head, something of the flunkey's obsequiousness; his smile was sugary, and in his buttonhole there was some badge of distinction like the number on a waiter.

During the first interval the husband went away to smoke; she remained alone in her stall. Gurov, who was sitting in the stalls, too, went up to her and said in a trembling voice, with a forced smile:

"Good-evening."

She glanced at him and turned pale, then glanced again with horror, unable to believe her eyes, and tightly gripped her fan and the lorgnette in her hands, evidently struggling with herself not to faint. Both were silent. She was sitting, he was standing, frightened by her confusion and not venturing to sit down beside her. The violins and the flute began tuning up. He felt suddenly frightened; it seemed as though all the people in the boxes were looking at them. She got up and went quickly to the door; he followed her, and both walked senselessly along passages, and up and down stairs, and figures in legal, scholastic, and civil service uniforms, all wearing badges, flitted before their eyes. They caught glimpses of ladies, of fur coats hanging on pegs; the draughts blew on them, bringing a smell of stale tobacco. And Gurov, whose heart was beating violently, thought:

"Oh, heavens! Why are these people her and this orchestra! . . ."

And at that instant he recalled how when he had seen Anna Sergeyevna off at the station he had thought that everything was over and they would never meet again. But how far they were still from the end!

On the narrow, gloomy staircase over which was written "To the Amphitheatre," she stopped.

"How you have frightened me!" she said, breathing hard, still pale and overwhelmed. "Oh, how you have frightened me! I am half dead. Why have you come? Why?"

"But do understand, Anna, do understand . . ." he said hastily in a low voice. "I entreat you to understand. . . ."

She looked at him with dread, with entreaty, with love; she looked at him intently, to keep his features more distinctly in her memory.

"I am so unhappy," she went on, not heeding him. "I have thought of nothing but you all the time; I live only in the thought of you. And I wanted to forget, to forget you; but why, oh, why, have you come?"

On the landing above them two schoolboys were smoking and looking down, but that was nothing to Gurov; he drew Anna Sergeyevna to him, and began kissing her face, her cheeks, and her hands.

"What are you doing, what are you doing!" she cried in horror, pushing him away. "We are mad. Go away to-day; go away at once. . . . I beseech you by all that is sacred, I implore you. . . . There are people coming this way!"

Some one was coming up the stairs.   100

"You must go away," Anna Sergeyevna went on in a whisper. "Do you hear, Dmitri Dmitritch? I will come and see you in Moscow. I have never been happy; I am miserable now, and I never, never shall be happy, never. Don't make me suffer still more! I swear I'll come to Moscow. But now let us part. My precious, good, dear one, we must part!"

She pressed his hand and began rapidly going downstairs, looking round at him, and from her eyes he could see that she really was unhappy. Gurov stood for a little while, listened, then, when all sound had died away he found his coat and left the theatre.

IV

And Anna Sergeyevna began coming to see him in Moscow. Once in two or three months she left S—, telling her husband that she was going to consult a doctor about an internal complaint—and her husband believed her, and did not believe her. In Moscow she stayed at the Slaviansky Bazaar hotel, and at once sent a man in a red cap to Gurov. Gurov went to see her, and no one in Moscow knew of it.

Once he was going to see her in this way on a winter morning (the messenger had come the evening before when he was out). With him walked his daughter, whom he wanted to take to school: it was on the way. Snow was falling in big wet flakes.

"It's three degrees above freezing-point, and yet it is snowing," said Gurov to his   105
daughter. "The thaw is only on the surface of the earth; there is quite a different temperature at a greater height in the atmosphere."

"And why are there no thunderstorms in the winter, father?"

He explained that, too. He talked, thinking all the while that he was going to see *her,* and no living soul knew of it, and probably never would know. He had two lives: one, open, seen and known by all who cared to know, full of relative truth and of relative falsehood, exactly like the lives of his friends and acquaintances; and another life running its course in secret. And through some strange, perhaps accidental, conjunction of circumstances, everything that was essential, of interest and of value to him, everything in which he was sincere and did not deceive himself, everything that made the kernel of his life, was hidden from other people; and all that was false in him, the sheath in which he hid himself to conceal the truth—such, for instance, as his work in the bank, his discussions at the club, his "lower race," his presence with his wife at anniversary festivities—all that was open. And he judged of others by himself, not believing in what he saw, and always believing that every man had his real, most interesting life under the cover of secrecy and under the cover of night. All personal life rested on secrecy, and possibly it was partly on that account that civilised man was so nervously anxious that personal privacy should be respected.

After leaving his daughter at school, Gurov went on to the Slaviansky Bazaar. He took off his fur coat below, went upstairs, and softly knocked at the door. Anna Sergeyevna, wearing his favourite grey dress, exhausted by the journey and the suspense, had been expecting him since the evening before. She was pale; she looked at him, and did not smile, and he had hardly come in when she fell on his breast. Their kiss was slow and prolonged, as though they had not met for two years.

"Well, how are you getting on there?" he asked. "What news?"

"Wait; I'll tell you directly. . . . I can't talk." 110

She could not speak; she was crying. She turned away from him, and pressed her handkerchief to her eyes.

"Let her have her cry out. I'll sit down and wait," he thought, and he sat down in an arm-chair.

Then he rang and asked for tea to be brought him, and while he drank his tea she remained standing at the window with her back to him. She was crying from emotion, from the miserable consciousness that their life was so hard for them; they could only meet in secret, hiding themselves from people, like thieves! Was not their life shattered?

"Come, do stop!" he said.

It was evident to him that this love of theirs would not soon be over, that he could not see the end of it. Anna Sergeyevna grew more and more attached to him. She adored him, and it was unthinkable to say to her that it was bound to have an end some day; besides, she would not have believed it!

He went up to her and took her by the shoulders to say something affectionate 115 and cheering, and at that moment he saw himself in the looking-glass.

His hair was already beginning to turn grey. And it seemed strange to him that he had grown so much older, so much plainer during the last few years. The shoulders on which his hands rested were warm and quivering. He felt compassion for this life, still so warm and lovely, but probably already not far from beginning to fade and wither like his own. Why did she love him so much? He always seemed to women different from what he was, and they loved in him not himself, but the man created by their imagination, whom they had been eagerly seeking all their lives; and afterwards, when they noticed their mistake, they loved him all the same. And not one of them had been happy with him. Time passed, he had made their acquaintance, got on with them, parted, but he had never once loved; it was anything you like, but not love.

And only now when his head was grey he had fallen properly, really in love—for the first time in his life.

Anna Sergeyevna and he loved each other like people very close and akin, like husband and wife, like tender friends; it seemed to them that fate itself had meant them for one another, and they could not understand why he had a wife and she a husband; and it was as though they were a pair of birds of passage, caught and forced to live in different cages. They forgave each other for what they were ashamed of in their past, they forgave everything in the present, and felt that this love of theirs had changed them both.

In moments of depression in the past he had comforted himself with any arguments that came into his mind, but now he no longer cared for arguments; he felt profound compassion, he wanted to be sincere and tender. . . .

"Don't cry, my darling," he said. "You've had your cry; that's enough. . . . Let us 120 talk now, let us think of some plan."

Then they spent a long while taking counsel together, talked of how to avoid the necessity for secrecy, for deception, for living in different towns and not seeing each other for long at a time. How could they be free from this intolerable bondage?

"How? How?" he asked, clutching his head. "How?"

And it seemed as though in a little while the solution would be found, and then a new and splendid life would begin; and it was clear to both of them that they had still a long, long road before them, and that the most complicated and difficult part of it was only just beginning.

QUESTIONS FOR CLOSE READING

1. What are Gurov's views on the subject of women? Why can't he get along without them? How do women treat him and what do they seem to think of him?

2. What has Gurov's experience taught him about love affairs?

3. How does Anna, the lady with the dog, react after their affair begins? How does Gurov react to her? What bothers each of them?

4. What is Gurov's life like in Moscow? How does it contrast with his experiences in Yalta?

5. How does Anna react when she sees Gurov again in her home town at the theater? Why does she want him to leave?

6. What do Gurov and Anna hope for at the end of the story? How do they envision their problem in life? "How could they be free from this intolerable bondage?"

QUESTIONS FOR INTERPRETATION

1. At the beginning of the story, Gurov reveals that he thinks of women as a "lower race." Yet he has peculiar powers over them and has had many affairs, none of which have lasted. What makes his relationship with Anna different? Would he consider Anna to be of a "lower race"? Does she seem aware of his basic feelings toward women? Examine the story in terms of the ways in which women and men seem expected to behave with one another in this society. Consider what makes Gurov and Anna different.

2. The story seems to be set in a culture in which marriage and love have some basic differences. What seems to be the relationship between the two? Does this story take a stand on whether the relationship between Gurov and Anna is immoral? What position does Chekhov seem to take on the potential success of a love affair in this environment? What view do you hold of its potential success?

RESOURCES FOR READING CHEKHOV

ANTON CHEKHOV

Chekhov described himself as suffering from a disease: "autobiographophobia," the fear of writing one's autobiography. When asked by an editor for details about himself, he wrote the first letter that follows, much of it tongue in cheek, especially the reference to having taken part in "an orgy" with the editor to whom he was writing. In other letters he says some interesting things about how one ought to write.

Letters on Writing (1888–1892)

To V. A. Tikhonov, Moscow _____ *Feb. 22, 1892*

Translated by Constance Garnett

Do you want my biography? Here it is. I was born in Taganrog in 1860. I finished the course at Taganrog High School in 1879. In 1884 I took my degree in medicine at the University of Moscow. In 1888 I received the Pushkin Prize. In 1890 I made a journey to Sakhalin across Siberia and back by sea. In 1891 I made a tour of Europe, where I drank excellent wine and ate oysters. In 1892 I took part in an orgy in the company of V. A. Tikhonov at a name-day party. I began writing in 1879. The published collections of my works are: "Motley Tales," "In the Twilight," "Stories," "Surly People," and a novel, "The Duel." I have sinned in the dramatic line too, though with moderation. I have been translated into all the languages with the exception of the foreign ones, though I have indeed long ago been translated by the Germans. The Czechs and the Serbs approve of me also, and the French are not indifferent. The mysteries of love I fathomed at the age of thirteen. With my colleagues, doctors, and literary men alike, I am on the best of terms. I am a bachelor. I should like to receive a pension. I practise medicine, and so much so that sometimes in the summer I perform postmortems, though I have not done so for two or three years. Of authors my favorite is Tolstoy, of doctors, Zakharin.

All that is nonsense though. Write what you like. If you haven't facts, substitute lyricism.

To A. S. Souvorin, Sumi _____ *May 30, 1888*

What you say about "Lights" is quite just. You write that neither the conversation on pessimism, nor the story of Kisochka helps in the least to solve the problem of pessimism. It seems to me that the writer of fiction should not try to solve such questions as those of God, pessimism, etc. His business is but to describe those who have been speaking or thinking about God and pessimism, how, and under what circumstances. The artist should be, not the judge of his characters and their conversations, but only an unbiassed witness. I once overheard a desultory conversation about pessimism between two Russians; nothing was solved,—and my business is to report the conversation exactly as I heard it, and let the jury,—that is, the readers, estimate its value. My business is merely to be talented, i.e., to be able to distinguish between important and unimportant statements, to be able to illuminate the characters and speak their language. Shcheglov-Leontyev finds fault with me because I concluded the story with the phrase: "There's no way of making things out in this world!" In his opinion an artist-psychologist *must* work things out, for this is just why he is a psychologist. But I do not agree with him. The time has come for writers, especially those who are artists, to admit that in this world one cannot make anything out, just as Socrates once admitted it, just as Voltaire admitted it. The mob think they know and understand everything; the more stupid they are, the wider, I think, do they conceive their horizon to be. And if an artist in whom the crowd has faith decides to declare what he understands nothing of what he sees,—this in itself constitutes a considerable clarity in the realm of thought, and a great step forward.

To A. S. Souvorin, Moscow _____ *October 27, 1888*

In conversation with my literary colleagues I always insist that it is not the artist's business to solve problems that require a specialist's knowledge. It is a bad thing if a writer tackles a subject he does not understand. We have specialists for dealing with special questions: it is their business to judge of the commune, of the future, of capitalism, of the evils of drunkenness, of boots, of the diseases of women. An artist may judge only of what he understands, his field is just as limited as that of any other specialist—I repeat this and insist on it always. That in his sphere there are no questions, but only answers, can be maintained only by those who have never written and have had no experience of thinking in images. An artist observes, selects, guesses, combines—and this in itself presupposes a problem: unless he had set himself a problem from the very first there would be nothing to conjecture and nothing to select. To put it briefly, I will end by using the language of psychiatry: if one denies that creative work involves problems and purposes, one must admit that an artist creates without premeditation or intention, in a state of aberration; therefore, if an author boasted to me of having written a novel without a preconceived design, under a sudden inspiration, I should call him mad.

You are right in demanding that an artist should take an intelligent attitude in his work, but you confuse two things: *solving a problem* and *stating a problem correctly*. It is only the second that is obligatory for the artist. In "Anna Karenina" and "Evgeni Onegin" not a single problem is solved, but they satisfy you completely because all the problems in these works are correctly stated. It is the business of the judge to put the right questions, but the answers must be given by the jury according to their own lights.

LEO TOLSTOY   (1828–1910)

Tolstoy is sometimes considered the greatest Russian novelist. His War and Peace *(1865–1869) continues to set a standard for novels that attempt to deal with great events and historical moments. He was also known during his life as an upholder of moral views. His approach to Chekhov's short story is highly personal and reveals his moral attitudes. They may or may not be in line with the reader's or with Chekhov's. Tolstoy's position may be one you will wish to argue with.*

Chekhov's Intent in "The Darling" _____ *1905*

Translated by Constance Garnett

There is a story of profound meaning in the Book of Numbers which tells how Balak, the King of the Moabites, sent for the prophet Balaam to curse the Israelites who were on his borders. Balak promised Balaam many gifts for this service, and Balaam, tempted, went to Balak, and went with him up the mountain, where an alter was prepared with calves and sheep sacrificed in readiness for the curse. Balak waited for the curse, but instead of cursing, Balaam blessed the people of Israel.

> And Balak said unto Balaam, What hast thou done unto me? I took thee to curse mine enemies, and, behold, thou hast blessed them altogether.

And he answered and said, Must I not take heed to speak that which the Lord hath put in my mouth?

And Balak said unto him, Come, I pray thee, with me into another place . . . and curse me them from thence.

But again, instead of cursing, Balaam blessed. And so it was the third time also.

And Balak's anger was kindled against Balaam, and he smote his hands together: And Balak said unto Balaam, I called thee to curse my enemies, and, behold, thou hast altogether blessed them these three times.

Therefore now fell thee to thy place: I thought to promote thee unto great honour; but, lo, the Lord hast kept thee back from honour.

And so Balaam departed without having received the gifts, because, instead of cursing, he had blessed the enemies of Balak. [Numbers 23:11–13; 24:10–11]

What happened to Balaam often happens to real poets and artists. Tempted by Balak's gifts, popularity, or by false preconceived ideas, the poet does not see the angel barring his way, thought the ass sees him, and he means to curse, and yet, behold, he blesses.

This is just what happened to the true poet and artist Chekhov when he wrote this charming story "The Darling."

The author evidently means to mock at the pitiful creature—as he judges her with his intellect, but not with his heart—the Darling, who after first sharing Kukin's anxiety about his theater, then throwing herself into the interests of the timber trade, then under the influence of the veterinary surgeon regarding the campaign against the foot and mouth disease as the most important matter in the world, is finally engrossed in the grammatical questions and the interests of the little schoolboy in the big cap. Kukin's surname is absurd, even his illness and the telegram announcing his death, the timber merchant with his respectability, the veterinary surgeon, even the boy—all are absurd, but the soul of the Darling, with her faculty of devoting herself with her whole being to any one she loves, is not absurd, but marvelous and holy.

I believe that while he was writing "The Darling," the author had in his mind, though not in his heart, a vague image of a new woman; of her equality with man; of a woman mentally developed, learned, working independently for the good of society as well as, if not better than, a man; of the woman who has raised and upholds the woman question; and in writing "The Darling" he wanted to show what woman ought not to be. The Balak of public opinion bade Chekhov curse the weak, submissive undeveloped woman devoted to man; and Chekhov went up the mountain, and the calves and sheep were laid upon the altar, but when he began to speak, the poet blessed what he had come to curse. In spite of its exquisite gay humor, I at least cannot read without tears some passages of this wonderful story. I am touched by the description of her complete devotion and love for Kukin and all that he cares for, and for the timber merchant and for the veterinary surgeon, and even more of her sufferings when she is left alone and has no one to love; and finally the account of how with all the strength of womanly, motherly feelings (of which she has no experience in her own life) she devotes herself with boundless love to the future man, the schoolboy in the big cap.

The author makes her love the absurd Kukin, the insignificant timber merchant, and the unpleasant veterinary surgeon, but love is no less sacred whether its object is a Kukin or a Spinoza, a Pascal, or a Schiller,° and whether the objects of it change as

Baruch Spinoza (1632–1677): Dutch philosopher; *Blaise Pascal* (1623–1662): French scientist and philosopher; *Johann Christoph Friedrich von Schiller* (1759–1805): German poet, playwright, and critic

rapidly as with the Darling, or whether the object of it remains the same throughout the whole life.

Some time ago I happened to read in the *Novoe Vremya* an excellent article upon woman. The author has in this article expressed a remarkably clever and profound idea about woman. "Women," he says, "are trying to show us they can do everything we men can do. I don't contest it; I am prepared to admit women can do everything men can do, and possibly better than men; but the trouble is that men cannot do anything faintly approaching to what women can do."

Yes, that is undoubtedly true, and it is true not only with regard to birth, nurture, and early education of children. Men cannot do that highest, best work which brings man nearest to God—the work of love, and complete devotion to the loved object, which good women have done, do, and will do so well and so naturally. What would become of the world, what would become of us men if women had not that faculty and did not exercise it? We could get on without women doctors, women telegraph clerks, women lawyers, women scientists, women writers, but life would be a sorry affair without mothers, helpers, friends, comforters, who love in men the best in them, and imperceptibly instill, evoke, and support it. There would have been no Magdalen with Christ, no Claire with St. Francis; there would have been no wives of the Dekabrists° in Siberia; there would not have been among the Duhobors° those wives who, instead of holding their husbands back, supported them in their martyrdom for truth; there would not have been those thousands and thousands of unknown women—the best of all, as the unknown always are—the comforters of the drunken, the weak, and the dissolute, who, more than any, need the comfort of love. That love, whether devoted to a Kukin or to Christ, is the chief, grand, unique strength of woman.

What an amazing misunderstanding it is—all this so-called woman question, which as every vulgar idea is bound to do, has taken possession of the majority of women, and even of men.

"Woman longs to improve herself"—what can be more legitimate and just than that?

But a woman's work is from her very vocation different from man's, and so the ideal of feminine perfection cannot be the same as the ideal of masculine perfection. Let us admit that we do not know what that ideal is; it is quite certain in any case that it is not the ideal of masculine perfection. And yet it is to the attainment of that masculine ideal that the whole and the absurd and evil activity of the fashionable woman movement, which is such a stumbling-block to woman, is directed.

I am afraid that Chekhov was under the influence of that misunderstanding when he wrote "The Darling."

He, like Balaam, intended to curse, but the god of poetry forbade him, and commanded him to bless. And he did bless, and unconsciously clothed this sweet creature in such an exquisite radiance that she will always remain a type of what a woman can be in order to be happy herself, and to make the happiness of those with whom destiny throws her.

What makes the story so excellent is that the effect is unintentional.

I learned to ride a bicycle in a hall large enough to drill a division of soldiers. At the end of the hall a lady was learning. I thought I must be careful to avoid getting into

---

Dekabrists (Decembrists): members of the unsuccessful December 1825 uprising against Czar Nicholas I   *Duhobors:* members of the Christian sect that advocated following inner spirituality instead of church or government doctrine

her way, and began looking at her. And as I looked at her I began unconsciously getting nearer and nearer to her, and in spite of the fact that, noticing the danger, she hastened to retreat, I rode down upon her and knocked her down—that is, I did the very opposite of what I wanted to do, simply because I concentrated my attention upon her.

The same thing has happened to Chekhov, but in an inverse sense: He wanted to knock the Darling down, and concentrating upon her the close attention of the poet, he raised her up.

EUDORA WELTY   (b. 1909)

Eudora Welty, herself a major short story writer, observes some interesting aspects of both plot and character in Chekhov's "The Darling." Her analysis offers us an interesting portrait of Olenka, suggesting that her ultimate mission is her maternal affection for Sasha. This reading offers an interesting contrast with Tolstoy's.

Chekhov's "The Darling" _____ 1977

Clearly, the fact that stories have plots in common is of no more account than that many people have blue eyes. Plots are, indeed, what the story writer sees with, and so do we as we read. The plot is the Why. Why? is asked and replied to at various depths; the fishes in the sea are bigger the deeper we go. To learn that character is a more awe-inspiring fish and (in a short story, though not, I think, in a novel) one some degrees deeper down than situation, we have only to read Chekhov. What constitutes the reality of his characters is what they reveal to us. And the possibility that they may indeed reveal everything is what makes fictional characters differ so greatly from us in real life; yet isn't it strange that they don't really *seem* to differ? This is one clue to the extraordinary magnitude of character in fiction. Characters in the plot connect us with the vastness of our secret life, which is endlessly explorable. This is their role. What happens to them is what they have been put here to show.

In his story "The Darling," the darling's first husband, the theatre manager, dies suddenly *because* of the darling's sweet passivity; this is the causality of fiction. In everyday or real life he might have held on to his health for years. But under Chekhov's hand he is living and dying in dependence on, and in revelation of, Olenka's character. He can only last a page and a half. Only by force of the story's circumstance is he here at all; Olenka took him up to begin with because he lived next door.

> Olenka listened to Kukin with silent gravity, and sometimes tears came into her eyes. In the end his misfortunes touched her; she grew to love him. He was a small thin man, with a yellow face; as he talked his mouth worked on one side, and there was always an expression of despair on his face; yet he aroused a deep and genuine affection in her. She was always fond of someone, and could not exist without loving. In earlier days she had loved her papa, who now sat in a darkened room, breathing with difficulty; she had loved her aunt, who used to come every other year from Bryansk; and before that, when she was at school, she had loved her French master. She was a gentle, soft-hearted, compassionate girl, with mild, tender eyes and very good health. At the sight of her fully rosy cheeks, her soft

> white neck with a little dark mole on it, and the kind, naïve smile, which came into her face when she listened to anything pleasant, men thought, "Yes, not half bad," and smiled too, while lady-visitors could not refrain from seizing her hand in the middle of a conversation, exclaiming in a gush of delight, "You darling!"

Kukin proposes and they are married.

> And when he had a closer view of her neck and her plump, fine shoulders, he threw up his hand and said "You darling!" . . . And what Kukin said about the theatre and the actors she repeated. Like him she despised the public for their ignorance and indifference to art; she took part in the rehearsals, she corrected the actors, she kept an eye on the behavior of the musicians, and when there was an unfavorable notice in the local paper, she shed tears and then water to the editor's office to set things right . . .

And when Kukin dies, Olenka's cry of heartbreak is this: "Vanitchka, my precious, my darling! Why did I ever meet you! Why did I know you and love you! Your poor broken-hearted Olenka is all alone without you!"

With variations the pattern is repeated, and we are made to feel it as plot, aware of its clear upon stress, the variations all springing from Chekhov's boundless and minute perception of character. The timber-merchant, another neighbor, is the one who walks home from the funeral with Olenka. The outcome follows tenderly, is only natural. After three days, he calls. "He did not stay long, only about ten minutes, and he did not say much, but when he left, Olenka loved him—loved him so much that she lay awake all night in a perfect fever."

Olenka and Pustovalov get along very well together when they are married.

> "Timber gets dearer every year; the price rises twenty per cent," she would say to her customers and friends . . . "And the freight!" she would add, covering her cheeks with her hands in horror, "the freight!" . . . It seemed to her that she had been in the timber trade for ages and ages; and that the most important and necessary thing in life was timber; and there was something intimate and touching to her in the very sound of words such as "post," "beam," "pole," "batten," "lath," "plank," and the like.

Even in her dreams Olenka is in the timber business, dreaming of "perfect mountains of planks and boards," and cries out in her sleep, so that Pustovalov says to her tenderly, "Olenka, what's the matter, darling? Cross yourself!" But the timber merchant inevitably goes out in the timber yard one day without his cap on; he catches cold and dies, to leave Olenka a widow once more. "I've nobody, now you've left me, my darling," she sobs after the funeral. "How can I live without you?"

And the timber merchant is succeeded by a veterinary surgeon—who gets transferred to Siberia. But the plot is not repetition—it is direction. The love which Olenka bears to whatever is nearest her reaches its final and, we discover, its truest mold in maternalism: for there it is most naturally innocent of anything but formless, thoughtless, blameless *embracing;* the true innocence is in never perceiving. Only mother love could endure in a pursuit of such blind regard, caring so little for the reality of either life involved so long as love wraps them together, Chekhov tells us—unpretentiously, as he tells everything, and with the simplest of concluding episodes. Olenka's character is seen purely then for what it is: limpid reflection, mindless and purposeless regard, love that falls like the sun and rain on all alike, vacant when there is nothing to reflect.

We know this because, before her final chance to love, Olenka is shown to us truly alone:

> [She] got thinner and plainer; and when people met her in the street they did not look at her as they used to, and did not smile to her; evidently her best years were over and left behind, and now a new sort of life had begun for her, which did not bear thinking about . . . And what was worst of all, she had no opinions of any sort. She saw the objects about her and understood what she saw, but could not form any opinions about them, and did not know what to talk about. And how awful it is not to have any opinions! She wanted a love that would absorb her whole being, her whole soul and reason—that would give her ideas and an object in life, and would warm her old blood.

The answer is Sasha, the ten-year-old son of the veterinary surgeon, an unexpected blessing from Siberia—a schoolchild. The veterinarian has another wife now, but this no longer matters. "Olenka, with arms akimbo, walked about the yard giving directions. Her face was beaming, and she was brisk and alert, as though she had waked from a long sleep . . ." "An island is a piece of land entirely surrounded by water," Sasha reads aloud. " 'An island is a piece of land,' she repeated, and this was the first opinion to which she gave utterance with positive conviction, after so many years of silence and dearth of ideas." She would follow Sasha halfway to school, until he told her to go back. She would go to bed thinking blissfully of Sasha, "who lay sound asleep in the next room, sometimes crying out in his sleep, 'I'll give it to you! Get away! Shut up!'"

The darling herself *is* the story; all else is sacrificed to her; deaths and departures are perfunctory and to be expected. The last words of the story are the child's and a protest, but they are delivered in sleep, as indeed protest to the darlings of this world will always be—out of inward and silent rebellion alone, as this master makes plain.

VLADIMIR NABOKOV   (1899–1977)

> *Nabokov, an American author and professor of Russian Literature, was born in St. Petersburg, Russia, and emigrated after the October Revolution of 1917. He is best known for his 1955 novel* Lolita. *On the other hand, he taught at Cornell University and was also well known as a critic of literature. His interpretation of "The Lady with the Dog" attempts to explain why "it is one of the greatest stories ever written."*

A Reading of Chekhov's "The Lady with the Little Dog" _____ 1971

Chekhov comes into the story "The Lady with the Little Dog" without knocking. There is no dilly-dallying. The very first paragraph reveals the main character, the young fair-haired lady followed by her white Spitz dog on the waterfront of a Crimean resort, Yalta, on the Black Sea. And immediately after, the male character Gurov appears. His wife, whom he has left with the children in Moscow, is vividly depicted: her solid frame, her thick black eyebrows, and the way she had of calling herself "a woman who thinks." One notes the magic of the trifles the author collects—the wife's manner of dropping a certain mute letter in spelling and her calling her husband by the longest and fullest form of his name, both traits in combination with the impressive dignity of her beetle-browed face and rigid poise forming exactly the necessary impression. A hard woman with the strong feminist and social ideas of her time, but one whom her husband finds in his heart of hearts to be narrow, dull-minded, and devoid of grace. The natural transition is to Gurov's constant unfaithfulness to her, to his general attitude toward women—"that inferior race" is what he calls them, but without this inferior race he could not exist. It is hinted that these Russian romances were not altogether as light-winged as in the Paris of Maupassant. Complications and problems are unavoidable with those decent hesitating people of Moscow who are slow heavy starters but plunge into tedious difficulties when once they start going.

Then with the same neat and direct method of attack, with the bridging formula "and so . . .", we slide back to the lady with the dog. Everything about her, even the way her hair was done, told him that she was bored. The spirit of adventure—though he realized perfectly well that his attitude toward a lone woman in a fashionable sea town was based on vulgar stories, generally false—this spirit of adventure prompts him to call the little dog, which thus becomes a link between her and him. They are both in a public restaurant.

"He beckoned invitingly to the Spitz, and when the dog approached him, shook his finger at it. The Spitz growled; Gurov threatened it again.

"The lady glanced at him and at once dropped her eyes.

" 'He doesn't bite,' she said and blushed.

" 'May I give him a bone?' he asked; and when she nodded he inquired affably, 'Have you been in Yalta long?'

" 'About five days.' "

They talk. The author has hinted already that Gurov was witty in the company of women; and instead of having the reader take it for granted (you know the old method of describing the talk as "brilliant" but giving no samples of the conversation), Chekhov makes him joke in a really attractive, winning way. "Bored, are you? An average citizen lives in . . . (here Chekhov lists the names of beautifully chosen, super-provincial towns) and is not bored, but when he arrives here on his vacation it is all boredom and dust. One could think he came from Grenada" (a name particularly appealing to the Russian imagination). The rest of their talk, for which this sidelight is richly sufficient, is conveyed indirectly. Now comes a first glimpse of Chekhov's own system of suggesting atmosphere by the most concise details of nature, "the sea was of a warm lilac hue with a golden path for the moon"; whoever has lived in Yalta knows how exactly this conveys the impression of a summer evening there. This first movement of the story ends with Gurov alone in his hotel room thinking of her as he goes to sleep and imagining her delicate weak-looking neck and her pretty gray eyes. It is to be noted that only now, through the medium of the hero's imagination, does Chekhov give a visible and definite form to the lady, features that fit in perfectly with her listless manner and expression of boredom already known to us.

"Getting into bed he recalled that she had been a schoolgirl only recently, doing lessons like his own daughter; he thought how much timidity and angularity there was still in her laugh and her manner of talking with a stranger. It must have been the first time in her life that she was alone in a setting in which she was followed, looked at, and spoken to for one secret purpose alone, which she could hardly fail to guess. He thought of her slim, delicate throat, her lovely gray eyes.

" 'There's something pathetic about her, though,' he thought, and dropped off.'"

The next movement (each of the four diminutive chapters or movements of which the story is composed is not more than four or five pages long), the next movement starts a week later with Gurov going to the pavilion and bringing the lady iced lemonade on a hot windy day, with the dust flying; and then in the evening when the sirocco subsides, they go on the pier to watch the incoming steamer. "The lady lost her lorgnette in the crowd," Chekhov notes shortly, and this being so casually worded, without any direct influence on the story—just a passing statement—somehow fits in with that helpless pathos already alluded to.

Then in her hotel room her awkwardness and tender angularity are delicately conveyed. They have become lovers. She was now sitting with her long hair hanging down on both sides of her face in the dejected pose of a sinner in some old picture. There was a watermelon on the table. Gurov cut himself a piece and began to eat unhurriedly. This realistic touch is again a typical Chekhov device.

She tells him about her existence in the remote town she comes from and Gurov is slightly bored by her naiveté, confusion, and tears. It is only now that we learn her husband's name: von Dideritz—probably of German descent.

They roam about Yalta in the early morning mist. "At Oreanda they sat on a bench not far from the church, looked down at the sea, and were silent. Yalta was barely visible through the morning mist; white clouds rested motionlessly on the mountain-tops. The leaves did not stir on the trees, the crickets chirped, and the monotonous muffled sound of the sea that rose from below spoke of the peace, the eternal sleep awaiting us. So it rumbled below when there was no Yalta, no Oreanda here; so it rumbles now, and it will rumble as indifferently and hollowly when we are no more. . . . Sitting beside a young woman who in the dawn seemed so lovely, Gurov, soothed and spellbound by these magical surroundings—the sea, the mountains, the clouds, the wide sky—thought how everything is really beautiful in this world when one reflects: everything except what we think or do ourselves when we forget the higher aims of life and our own human dignity.

"A man strolled up to them—probably a watchman—looked at them and walked away. And this detail, too, seemed so mysterious and beautiful. They saw a steamer arrive from Feodosia, its lights extinguished in the glow of dawn.

" 'There is dew on the grass,' said Anna Sergeievna, after a silence.

" 'Yes, it's time to go home.' " Then several days pass and then she has to go back to her home town.

" 'Time for me, too, to go North,' thought Gurov as he returned after seeing her off." And there the chapter ends.

The third movement plunges us straight into Gurov's life in Moscow. The richness of a gay Russian winter, his family affairs, the dinners at clubs and restaurants, all this is swiftly and vividly suggested. Then a page is devoted to a queer thing that has happened to him: he cannot forget the lady with the little dog. He has many friends, but the curious longing he has for talking about his adventure finds no outlet. When he happens to speak in a very general way of love and women, nobody guesses what he means, and only his wife moves her dark eyebrows and says: "Stop that fatuous posing; it does not suit you."

And now comes what in Chekhov's quiet stories may be called the climax. There is something that your average citizen calls romance and something he calls prose—though both are the meat of poetry for the artist. Such a contrast has already been hinted at by the slice of watermelon which Gurov crunched in a Yalta hotel room at a most romantic moment, sitting heavily and munching away. This contrast is beautifully followed up when at last Gurov blurts out to a friend late at night as they come out of the club: If you knew what a delightful woman I met in Yalta! His friend, a bureaucratic civil servant, got into his sleigh, the horses moved, but suddenly he turned and called back to Gurov. Yes? asked Gurov, evidently expecting some reaction to what he had just mentioned. By the way, said the man, you were quite right. That fish at the club was decidedly smelly.

This is a natural transition to the description of Gurov's new mood, his feeling that he lives among savages where cards and food are life. His family, his bank, the whole trend of his existence, everything seems futile, dull, and senseless. About Christmas he tells his wife he is going on a business trip to St. Petersburg, instead of which he travels to the remote Volga town where the lady lives.

Critics of Chekhov in the good old days when the mania for the civic problem flourished in Russia were incensed with his way of describing what they considered to be trivial unnecessary matters instead of thoroughly examining and solving the problems of bourgeois marriage. For as soon as Gurov arrives in the early hours to that town and takes the best room at the local hotel, Chekhov, instead of describing his mood or intensifying his difficult moral position, gives what is artistic in the highest sense of the word: he notes the gray carpet, made of military cloth, and the inkstand, also gray with dust, with a horseman whose hand waves a hat and whose head is gone. That is all: it is nothing but it is everything in authentic literature. A feature in the same line is the phonetic transformation which the hotel porter imposes on the German name von Dideritz. Having learned the address Gurov goes there and looks at the house. Opposite was a long gray fence with nails sticking out. An unescapable fence, Gurov says to himself, and here we get the concluding note in the rhythm of drabness and grayness already suggested by the carpet, the ink-stand, the illiterate accent of the porter. The unexpected little turns and the lightness of the touches are what places Chekhov, above all Russian writers of fiction, on the level of Gogol and Tolstoy.

Presently he saw an old servant coming out with the familiar little white dog. He wanted to call it (by a kind of conditional reflex), but suddenly his heart began beating fast and in his excitement he could not remember the dog's name—another delightful touch. Later on he decides to go to the local theatre, where for the first time the operetta *The Geisha* is being given. In sixty words Chekhov paints a complete picture of a provincial theatre, not forgetting the town-governor who modestly hid in his box behind a plush curtain so that only his hands were visible. Then the lady appeared. And he realized quite clearly that now in the whole world there was none nearer and dearer and more important to him than this slight woman, lost in a small-town crowd, a woman perfectly unremarkable, with a vulgar lorgnette in her hand. He saw her husband and remembered her qualifying him as a flunkey—he distinctly resembled one.

A remarkably fine scene follows when Gurov manages to talk to her, and then their mad swift walk up all kinds of staircases and corridors, and down again, and up again, amid people in the various uniforms of provincial officials. Neither does Chekhov forget "two schoolboys who smoked on the stairs and looked down at him and her."

" 'You must leave,' Anna Sergeievna went on in a whisper. 'Do you hear, Dmitri Dmitrich? I will come and see you in Moscow. I have never been happy; I am unhappy now, and I never, never shall be happy, never! So don't make me suffer still more! I swear I'll come to Moscow. But now let us part. My dear, good, precious one, let us part!'

"She pressed his hand and walked rapidly downstairs, turning to look round at him, and from her eyes he could see that she really was unhappy. Gurov stood for a while, listening, then when all grew quiet, he found his coat and left the theatre."

The fourth and last little chapter gives the atmosphere of their secret meetings in Moscow. As soon as she would arrive she used to send a red-capped messenger to Gurov. One day he was on his way to her and his daughter was with him. She was going to school, in the same direction as he. Big damp snowflakes were slowly coming down.

The thermometer, Gurov was saying to his daughter, shows a few degrees above freezing point (actually 37° above, fahrenheit), but nevertheless snow is falling. The explanation is that this warmth applies only to the surface of the earth, while in the higher layers of the atmosphere the temperature is quite different.

And as he spoke and walked, he kept thinking that not a soul knew or would ever know about these secret meetings.

What puzzled him was that all the false part of his life, his bank, his club, his conversations, his social obligations—all this happened openly, while the real and interesting part was hidden.

"He had two lives: an open one, seen and known by all who needed to know it, full of conventional truth and conventional falsehood, exactly like the lives of his friends and acquaintances; and another life that went on in secret. And through some strange, perhaps accidental, combination of circumstances, everything that was of interest and importance to him, everything that was essential to him, everything about which he felt sincerely and did not deceive himself, everything that constituted the core of his life, was going on concealed from others; while all that was false, the shell in which he hid to cover the truth—his work at the bank for instance, his discussions at the club, his references to the 'inferior race,' his appearances at anniversary celebrations with his wife—all that went on in the open. Judging others by himself, he did not believe what he saw, and always fancied that every man led his real, most interesting life under cover of secrecy as under cover of night. The personal life of every individual is based on secrecy, and perhaps it is partly for that reason that civilized man is so nervously anxious that personal privacy should be respected."

The final scene is full of that pathos which has been suggested in the very beginning. They meet, she sobs, they feel that they are the closest of couples, the tenderest of friends, and he sees that his hair is getting a little gray and knows that only death will end their love.

"The shoulders on which his hands rested were warm and quivering. He felt compassion for this life, still so warm and lovely, but probably already about to begin to fade and wither like his own. Why did she love him so much? He always seemed to women different from what he was, and they loved in him not himself, but the man whom their imagination had created and whom they had been eagerly seeking all their lives; and afterwards, when they saw their mistake, they loved him nevertheless. And not one of them had been happy with him. In the past he had met women, come together with them, parted from them, but he had never once loved; it was anything you please, but not love. And only now when his head was gray he had fallen in love, really, truly—for the first time in his life."

They talk, they discuss their position, how to get rid of the necessity of this sordid secrecy, how to be together always. They find no solution and in the typical Chekhov way the tale fades out with no definite full-stop but with the natural motion of life.

"And it seemed as though in a little while the solution would be found, and then a new and glorious life would begin; and it was clear to both of them that the end was still far off, and that what was to be most complicated and difficult for them was only just beginning."

All the traditional rules of story telling have been broken in this wonderful short story of twenty pages or so. There is no problem, no regular climax, no point at the end. And it is one of the greatest stories ever written.

We will now repeat the different features that are typical for this and other Chekhov tales.

First: The story is told in the most natural way possible, not beside the after-dinner fireplace as with Turgenev or Maupassant but in the way one person relates to another the most important things in his life, slowly and yet without a break, in a slightly subdued voice.

Second: Exact and rich characterization is attained by a careful selection and careful distribution of minute but striking features, with perfect contempt for the sustained description, repetition, and strong emphasis of ordinary authors. In this or that description one detail is chosen to illume the whole setting.

Third: There is no special moral to be drawn and no special message to be received. Compare this to the special delivery stories of Gorki or Thomas Mann.

Fourth: The story is based on a system of waves, on the shades of this or that mood. If in Gorki's world the molecules forming it are matter, here, in Chekhov, we get a world of waves instead of particles of matter, which, incidentally, is a nearer approach to the modern scientific understanding of the universe.

Fifth: The contrast of poetry and prose stressed here and there with such insight and humor is, in the long run, a contrast only for the heroes; in reality we feel, and this is again typical of authentic genius, that for Chekhov the lofty and the base are *not* different, that the slice of watermelon and the violet sea, and the hands of the town-governor, are essential points of the "beauty plus pity" of the world.

Sixth: The story does not really end, for as long as people are alive, there is no possible and definite conclusion to their troubles or hopes or dreams.

Seventh: The storyteller seems to keep going out of his way to allude to trifles, every one of which in another type of story would mean a signpost denoting a turn in the action—for instance, the two boys at the theatre would be eavesdroppers, and rumors would spread, or the inkstand would mean a letter changing the course of the story; but just because these trifles are meaningless, they are all-important in giving the real atmosphere of this particular story.

CHARLES E. MAY

Charles May, one of the important theorists of the modern short story, comments briefly on character and mood in Chekhov's short stories. His view is that Chekhov uses character to establish mood in the story rather than simply maintaining a realistic portrayal of a person in action.

Character and Mood in Chekhov[1] _____ 1985

Anton Chekhov's short stories were first welcomed in England and America just after the turn of the century as examples of late nineteenth-century realism, but since they did not embody the social commitment or political convictions of the realist novel, they

[1]Charles E. May. From "Chekhov and the Modern Short Story" in A CHEKHOV COMPANION, ed. Toby W. Clyman. Copyright © 1985 by Toby W. Clyman. Reproduced with permission of Greenwood Publishing Group, Inc., Westport, CT.

were termed "realistic" primarily because they seemed to focus on fragments of every-day reality. Consequently, they were characterized as "sketches," "slices of life," "cross-sections of Russian life," and were often said to be lacking every element which constitutes a really good short story. However, at the same time, other critics saw that Chekhov's ability to dispense with a striking incident, his impressionism, and his free-dom from the literary conventions of the highly plotted and formalized short story marked the beginnings of a new or "modern" kind of short fiction that combined the specific detail of realism with the poetic lyricism of romanticism.

The primary characteristics of this new hybrid form are: character as mood rather than as either symbolic projection or realistic depiction; story as minimal lyricized sketch rather than as elaborately plotted tale; atmosphere as an ambiguous mixture of both ex-ternal details and psychic projections; and a basic impressionistic apprehension of re-ality itself as a function of perspectival point of view. The ultimate result of these characteristics is the modernist and postmodernist focus on reality itself as a fictional con-struct and the contemporary trend to make fictional assumptions and techniques both the subject matter and theme of the novel and the short story.

Character as Mood

The most basic problem in understanding the Chekhovian shift to the "mod-ern" short story involves a new definition of the notion of "story" itself, which, in turn, involves not only a new understanding of the kind of "experience" to be embodied in story but a new conception of character as well. Primarily this shift to the modern is marked by a transition from the romantic focus on a projective fiction, in which char-acters are functions in an essentially code-bound parabolic or ironic structure, to an apparently realistic episode in which plot is subordinate to "as-if-real" character. How-ever, it should be noted that Chekhov's fictional figures are not realistic in the way that characters in the novel usually are. The short story is too short to allow for character to be created by the kind of dense detail and social interaction through duration typ-ical of the novel.

Conrad Aiken was perhaps the first critic to recognize the secret of Chekhov's creation of character. Noting that Chekhov's stories offer an unparalleled "range of states of consciousness," Aiken says that whereas Poe manipulates plot and James ma-nipulates thought, Chekhov "manipulates feeling or mood." If, says Aiken, we find his characters have a strange way of evaporating, "it is because our view of them was never permitted for a moment to be external—we saw them only as infinitely fine and truth-ful sequences of mood." This apprehension of character as mood is closely related to D. S. Mirsky's understanding of the Chekhovian style, which he described as "bathed in a perfect and uniform haze," and the Chekhovian narrative method, which Mirsky says "allows nothing to 'happen,' but only smoothly and imperceptibly to 'become.' "

Such a notion of character as mood and story as a hazy "eventless" becoming is characteristic of the modern artistic understanding of story. It is like Conrad's con-ception in *Heart of Darkness,* for to his story-teller Marlowe, "the meaning of an episode was not inside like a kernel but outside, enveloping the tale which brought it out only as a glow brings out a haze." More recently, Eudora Welty has suggested that the first thing we notice about the short story is "that we can't really see the solid outlines of it—it seems bathed in something of its own. It is wrapped in an atmosphere." Once we see that the short story, by its very shortness, cannot deal with the denseness of detail and the duration of time typical of the novel, but rather focuses on a revelatory break-up of the rhythm of everyday reality, we can see how the form, striving to accommodate "realism" at the end of the nineteenth century, focused on an experience under the influence of a particular mood and therefore depended more on tone than on plot as a principle of unity.

In fact, "an experience" phenomenologically encountered, rather than "experience" discursively understood, is the primary focus of the modern short story, and, as John Dewey makes clear, "an experience" is recognized as such precisely because it has a unity, "a single *quality* that pervades the entire experience in spite of the variation of its constituent parts." Rather than plot, what unifies the modern short story is an atmosphere, a certain tone of significance. The problem is to determine the source of this significance. On the one hand, it may be the episode itself, which, to use Henry James's phrase, seems to have a "latent value" that the artist tries to unveil. It is this point of view that governs James Joyce's notion of the epiphany—"a sudden spiritual manifestation, whether in the vulgarity of speech or of gesture or in a memorable phase of the mind itself."

On the other hand, it may be the subjectivity of the teller, his perception that what seems trivial and everyday has, from his point of view, significance and meaning. There is no way to distinguish between these two views of the source of the so-called "modern" short story, for it is the teller's very choice of seemingly trivial details and his organization of them into a unified pattern that lyricizes the story and makes it seem natural and realistic even as it resonates with meaning. As Georg Lukács has suggested, lyricism in the short story is pure selection which hides itself behind the hard outlines of the event; it is "the most purely artistic form; it expresses the ultimate meaning of all artistic creation as *mood.*"

Although Chekhov's conception of the short story as a lyrically charged fragment in which characters are less fully rounded realistic figures than they are embodiments of mood has influenced all twentieth-century practitioners of the form, his most immediate impact has been on the three writers of the early twenties who have received the most critical attention for fully developing the so-called "modern" short story—James Joyce, Katherine Mansfield, and Sherwood Anderson. And because of the widespread influence of the stories of these three writers, Chekhov has thus had an effect on the works of such major twentieth-century short story writers as Katherine Anne Porter, Franz Kafka, Bernard Malamud, Ernest Hemingway, and Raymond Carver.

7

READING EUDORA WELTY IN DEPTH

EUDORA WELTY   (b. 1909)

Eudora Welty has lived most of her life in her birthplace, Jackson, Mississippi, and has set most of her works—including those presented here—in the American South. She is part of a generation of writers who have given the South a distinctive literary voice. Welty has said that she has been careful to include nothing, including names, that would not be normal and expected in the environment of her stories. Among her novels are Delta Wedding *(1946),* The Ponder Heart *(1954), and* The Optimist's Daughter *(1972). Her collections of stories include* Curtain of Green and Other Stories *(1941),* The Wide Net *(1943), and* The Bride of Inishfallen and Other Stories *(1955). She has also written essays on writing.*

Cleanth Brooks has said of Eudora Welty that she "is the author of works that make use of the resources of our language at its highest level. The interior life, the world of fantasy and imagination, is the subject matter of much of her fiction." Some critics have also insisted that Welty is not naturally a novelist, but a short story writer at heart. Her novels, they suggest, are merely extended stories, and her true achievement is as a short story writer. Welty's skill in this literary form is certainly considerable. Most of her famous stories were written in her earliest collections, when, as she explains, writing came easily and naturally. They are realistic, apparently simple, and uncluttered; once examined, however, they open up and reveal inner depths. As critic Jonathan Yardley put it, "Reading her best work, one peels off layer after layer of mood and meaning, each more subtle and more difficult to find than its predecessor."

A Worn Path _____ 1941

It was December—a bright frozen day in the early morning. Far out in the country there was an old Negro woman with her head tied in a red rag, coming along a path through the pinewoods. Her name was Phoenix Jackson. She was very old and small and she walked slowly in the dark pine shadows, moving a little from side to side in her steps, with the balanced heaviness and lightness of a pendulum in a grandfather clock. She carried a thin, small cane made from an umbrella, and with this she kept tapping the frozen earth in front of her. This made a grave and persistent noise in the still air, that seemed meditative like the chirping of a solitary little bird.

She wore a dark striped dress reaching down to her shoe tops, and an equally long apron of bleached sugar sacks, with a full pocket: all neat and tidy, but every time she took a step she might have fallen over her shoelaces, which dragged from her unlaced shoes. She looked straight ahead. Her eyes were blue with age. Her skin had a pattern all of its own of numberless branching wrinkles and as though a whole little tree stood in the middle of her forehead, but a golden color ran underneath, and the two knobs of her cheeks were illumined by a yellow burning under the dark. Under the red rag her hair came down on her neck in the frailest of ringlets, still black, and with an odor like copper.

Now and then there was a quivering in the thicket. Old Phoenix said, "Out of my way, all you foxes, owls, beetles, jack rabbits, coons and wild animals! . . . Keep out from under these feet, little bob-whites. Keep the big wild hogs out of my path. Don't let none of those come running my direction. I got a long way." Under her small black-freckled hand her cane, limber as a buggy whip, would switch at the brush as if to rouse up any hiding things.

On she went. The woods were deep and still. The sun made the pine needles almost too bright to look at, up where the wind rocked. The cones dropped as light as feathers. Down in the hollow was the mourning dove—it was not too late for him.

The path ran up a hill. "Seem like there is chains about my feet, time I get this far,"   5
she said, in the voice of argument old people keep to use with themselves. "Something always take a hold of me on this hill—pleads I should stay."

After she got to the top she turned and gave a full, severe look behind her where she had come. "Up through pines," she said at length. "Now down through oaks."

Her eyes opened their widest, and she started down gently. But before she got to the bottom of the hill a bush caught her dress.

Her fingers were busy and intent, but her skirts were full and long, so that before she could pull them free in one place they were caught in another. It was not possible to allow the dress to tear. "I in the thorny bush," she said. "Thorns, you doing your appointed work. Never want to let folks pass, no sir. Old eyes thought you was a pretty little *green* bush."

Finally, trembling all over, she stood free, and after a moment dared to stoop for her cane.

"Sun so high!" she cried, leaning back and looking, while the thick tears went   10
over her eyes. "The time getting all gone here."

At the foot of this hill was a place where a log was laid across the creek.

"Now comes the trial," said Phoenix.

Putting her right foot out, she mounted the log and shut her eyes. Lifting her skirt, leveling her cane fiercely before her, like a festival figure in some parade, she began to march across. Then she opened her eyes and she was safe on the other side.

"I wasn't as old as I thought," she said.

But she sat down to rest. She spread her skirts on the bank around her and folded   15
her hands over her knees. Up above her was a tree in a pearly cloud of mistletoe. She did not dare to close her eyes, and when a little boy brought her a plate with a slice of marble-cake on it she spoke to him. "That would be acceptable," she said. But when she went to take it there was just her own hand in the air.

So she left that tree, and had to go through a barbed-wire fence. There she had to creep and crawl, spreading her knees and stretching her fingers like a baby trying to climb the steps. But she talked loudly to herself: she could not let her dress be torn now, so late in the day, and she could not pay for having her arm or her leg sawed off if she got caught fast where she was.

At last she was safe through the fence and risen up out in the clearing. Big dead trees, like black men with one arm, were standing in the purple stalks of the withered cotton field. There sat a buzzard.

"Who you watching?"

In the furrow she made her way along.

"Glad this not the season for bulls," she said, looking sideways, "and the good   20
Lord made his snakes to curl up and sleep in the winter. A pleasure I don't see no two-headed snake coming around that tree, where it come once. It took a while to get by him, back in the summer."

She passed through the old cotton and went into a field of dead corn. It whispered and shook and was taller than her head. "Through the maze now," she said, for there was no path.

Then there was something tall, black, and skinny there, moving before her.

At first she took it for a man. It could have been a man dancing in the field. But she stood still and listened, and it did not make a sound. It was as silent as a ghost.

"Ghost," she said sharply, "who be you the ghost of? For I have heard of nary death close by."

But there was no answer—only the ragged dancing in the wind.   25

She shut her eyes, reached out her hand, and touched a sleeve. She found a coat and inside that an emptiness, cold as ice.

"You scarecrow," she said. Her face lighted. "I ought to be shut up for good," she said with laughter. "My senses is gone. I too old. I the oldest people I ever know. Dance, old scarecrow," she said, "while I dancing with you."

She kicked her foot over the furrow, and with mouth drawn down, shook her head once or twice in a little strutting way. Some husks blew down and whirled in streamers about her skirts.

Then she went on, parting her way from side to side with the cane, through the whispering field. At last she came to the end, to a wagon track where the silver grass blew between the red ruts. The quail were walking around like pullets, seeming all dainty and unseen.

"Walk pretty," she said. "This the easy place. This the easy going."   30

She followed the track, swaying through the quiet bare fields, through the little strings of trees silver in their dead leaves, past cabins silver from weather, with the doors and windows boarded shut, all like old women under a spell sitting there. "I walking in their sleep," she said, nodding her head vigorously.

In a ravine she went where a spring was silently flowing through a hollow log. Old Phoenix bent and drank. "Sweet-gum makes the water sweet," she said, and drank more. "Nobody know who made this well, for it was here when I was born."

The track crossed a swampy part where the moss hung as white as lace from every limb. "Sleep on, alligators, and blow your bubbles." Then the track went into the road.

Deep, deep the road went down between the high green-colored banks. Overhead the live-oaks met, and it was as dark as a cave.

A black dog with a lolling tongue came up out of the weeds by the ditch. She was   35
meditating, and not ready, and when he came at her she only hit him a little with her cane. Over she went in the ditch, like a little puff of milkweed.

Down there, her senses drifted away. A dream visited her, and she reached her hand up, but nothing reached down and gave her a pull. So she lay there and presently went to talking. "Old woman," she said to herself, "that black dog come up out of the weeds to stall you off, and now there he sitting on his fine tail, smiling at you."

A white man finally came along and found her—a hunter, a young man, with his dog on a chain.

"Well, Granny!" he laughed. "What are you doing there?"

"Lying on my back like a June-bug waiting to be turned over, mister," she said, reaching up her hand.

He lifted her up, gave her a swing in the air, and set her down. "Anything broken,   40
Granny?"

"No sir, them old dead weeds is springy enough," said Phoenix, when she had got her breath. "I thank you for your trouble."

"Where do you live, Granny?" he asked, while the two dogs were growling at each other.

"Away back yonder, sir, behind the ridge. You can't even see it from here."

"On your way home?"

"No sir, I going to town."   45

"Why, that's too far! That's as far as I walk when I come out myself, and I get something for my trouble." He patted the stuffed bag he carried, and there hung down a little closed claw. It was one of the bob-whites, with its beak hooked bitterly to show it was dead. "Now you go on home, Granny!"

"I bound to go to town, mister," said Phoenix. "The time come around."

He gave another laugh, filling the whole landscape. "I know you old colored people! Wouldn't miss going to town to see Santa Claus!"

But something held old Phoenix very still. The deep lines in her face went into a fierce and different radiation. Without warning, she had seen with her own eyes a flashing nickel fall out of the man's pocket onto the ground.

"How old are you, Granny?" he was saying.   50

"There is no telling, mister," she said, "no telling."

Then she gave a little cry and clapped her hands and said, "Git on away from here, dog! Look! Look at that dog!" She laughed as if in admiration. "He ain't scared of nobody. He a big black dog." She whispered, "Sic him!"

"Watch me get rid of that cur," said the man. "Sic him, Pete! Sic him!"

Phoenix heard the dogs fighting, and heard the man running and throwing sticks. She even heard a gunshot. But she was slowly bending forward by that time, further and further forward, the lids stretched down over her eyes, as if she were doing this in her sleep. Her chin was lowered almost to her knees. The yellow palm of her hand came out from the fold of her apron. Her fingers slid down and along the ground under the piece of money with the grace and care they would have in lifting an egg from under a setting hen. Then she slowly straightened up, she stood erect, and the nickel was in her apron pocket. A bird flew by. Her lips moved. "God watching me the whole time. I come to stealing."

The man came back, and his own dog panted about them. "Well, I scared him off   55
that time," he said, and then he laughed and lifted his gun and pointed it at Phoenix.

She stood straight and faced him.

"Doesn't the gun scare you?" he said, still pointing it.

"No, sir, I seen plenty go off closer by, in my day, and for less than what I done," she said, holding utterly still.

He smiled, and shouldered the gun. "Well, Granny," he said, "you must be a hundred years old, and scared of nothing. I'd give you a dime if I had any money with me. But you take my advice and stay home, and nothing will happen to you."

"I bound to go on my way, mister," said Phoenix. She inclined her head in the red rag. Then they went in different directions, but she could hear the gun shooting again and again over the hill.   60

She walked on. The shadows hung from the oak trees to the road like curtains. Then she smelled wood-smoke, and smelled the river, and she saw a steeple and the cabins on their steep steps. Dozens of little black children whirled around her. There ahead was Natchez shining. Bells were ringing. She walked on.

In the paved city it was Christmas time. There were red and green electric lights strung and crisscrossed everywhere, and all turned on in the daytime. Old Phoenix would have been lost if she had not distrusted her eyesight and depended on her feet to know where to take her.

She paused quietly on the sidewalk where people were passing by. A lady came along in the crowd, carrying an armful of red-, green- and silver-wrapped presents; she gave off perfume like the red roses in hot summer, and Phoenix stopped her.

"Please, missy, will you lace up my shoe?" She held up her foot.

"What do you want, Grandma?"   65

"See my shoe," said Phoenix. "Do all right for out in the country, but wouldn't look right to go in a big building."

"Stand still then, Grandma," said the lady. She put her packages down on the sidewalk beside her and laced and tied both shoes tightly.

"Can't lace 'em with a cane," said Phoenix. "Thank you, missy. I doesn't mind asking a nice lady to tie up my shoe, when I gets out on the street."

Moving slowly and from side to side, she went into the big building, and into a tower of steps, where she walked up and around and around until her feet knew to stop.

She entered a door, and there she saw nailed up on the wall the document that   70
had been stamped with the gold seal and framed in the gold frame, which matched the dream that was hung up in her head.

"Here I be," she said. There was a fixed and ceremonial stiffness over her body.

"A charity case, I suppose," said an attendant who sat at the desk before her.

But Phoenix only looked above her head. There was sweat on her face, the wrinkles in her skin shone like a bright net.

"Speak up, Grandma," the woman said. "What's your name? We must have your history, you know. Have you been here before? What seems to be the trouble with you?"

Old Phoenix only gave a twitch to her face as if a fly were bothering her.   75

"Are you deaf?" cried the attendant.

But then the nurse came in.

"Oh, that's just old Aunt Phoenix," she said. "She doesn't come for herself—she has a little grandson. She makes these trips just as regular as clockwork. She lives away back off the Old Natchez Trace." She bent down. "Well, Aunt Phoenix, why don't you just take a seat? We won't keep you standing after your long trip." She pointed.

The old woman sat down, bolt upright in the chair.

"Now, how is the boy?" asked the nurse.   80

Old Phoenix did not speak.

"I said, how is the boy?"

But Phoenix only waited and stared straight ahead, her face very solemn and withdrawn into rigidity.

"Is his throat any better?" asked the nurse. "Aunt Phoenix, don't you hear me? Is your grandson's throat any better since the last time you came for the medicine?"

With her hands on her knees, the old woman waited, silent, erect and motionless,   85
just as if she were in armor.

"You mustn't take up on our time this way, Aunt Phoenix," the nurse said. "Tell us quickly about your grandson, and get it over. He isn't dead, is he?"

At last there came a flicker and then a flame of comprehension across her face, and she spoke.

"My grandson. It was my memory had left me. There I sat and forgot why I made my long trip."

"Forgot?" The nurse frowned. "After you came so far?"

Then Phoenix was like an old woman begging a dignified forgiveness for waking   90
up frightened in the night. "I never did go to school, I was too old at the Surrender," she said in a soft voice. "I'm an old woman without an education. It was my memory fail me. My little grandson, he is just the same, and I forgot it in the coming."

"Throat never heals, does it?" said the nurse, speaking in a loud, sure voice to old Phoenix. By now she had a card with something written on it, a little list. "Yes. Swallowed lye. When was it?—January—two-three years ago—"

Phoenix spoke unasked now. "No, missy, he not dead, he just the same. Every little while his throat begin to close up again, and he not able to swallow. He not get his breath. He not able to help himself. So the time come around, and I go on another trip for the soothing medicine."

"All right. The doctor said as long as you came to get it, you could have it," said the nurse. "But it's an obstinate case."

"My little grandson, he sit up there in the house all wrapped up, waiting by himself," Phoenix went on. "We is the only two left in the world. He suffer and it don't seem to put him back at all. He got a sweet look. He going to last. He wear a little patch quilt and peep out holding his mouth open like a little bird. I remembers so plain now. I not going to forget him again, no, the whole enduring time. I could tell him from all the others in creation."

"All right." The nurse was trying to hush her now. She brought her a bottle of   95
medicine. "Charity," she said, making a check mark in a book.

Old Phoenix held the bottle close to her eyes, and then carefully put it into her pocket.

"I thank you," she said.

"It's Christmas time, Grandma," said the attendant. "Could I give you a few pennies out of my purse?"

"Five pennies is a nickel," said Phoenix stiffly.

"Here's a nickel," said the attendant.   100

Phoenix rose carefully and held out her hand. She received the nickel and then fished the other nickel out of her pocket and laid it beside the new one. She stared at her palm closely, with her head on one side.

Then she gave a tap with her cane on the floor.

"This is what come to me to do," she said. "I going to the store and buy my child a little windmill they sells, made out of paper. He going to find it hard to believe there such a thing in the world. I'll march myself back where he waiting, holding it straight up in this hand."

She lifted her free hand, gave a little nod, turned around, and walked out of the doctor's office. Then her slow step began on the stairs, going down.

QUESTIONS FOR CLOSE READING

1. How does the setting of the story during the Christmas season contribute to your reaction to Phoenix Jackson?
2. What is Phoenix Jackson's relationship with her natural surroundings?
3. What significance does the white hunter have for Phoenix? How does she relate to him?
4. How does the nurse treat Phoenix once she arrives at the hospital?
5. What seems to be the general attitude of people toward Phoenix?

QUESTIONS FOR INTERPRETATION

1. The story is filled with physical obstacles. Examine the nature of these obstacles and comment on how they help interpret the nature of the experience that Phoenix Jackson had in her past and has now during the story. What do you feel are the most important obstacles that Phoenix faces in this story?
2. The story is set in the late 1930s. What appears to be the attitude of the white population toward African-Americans? What is Phoenix's attitude toward the white people she meets? What is the nature of her economic situation and how does it compare with others in the story? Is her situation a factor in her repeated journeys? Is the theme of this story primarily concerned with race or with economics? Or is it both?

Livvie _____ *1942*

Solomon carried Livvie twenty-one miles away from her home when he married her. He carried her away up on the Old Natchez Trace into the deep country to live in his house. She was sixteen—an only girl, then. Once people said he thought nobody would ever come along there. He told her himself that it had been a long time, and a day she did not know about, since that road was a traveled road with *people* coming and going. He was good to her, but he kept her in the house. She had not thought that she could not get back. Where she came from, people said an old man did not want anybody in the world to ever find his wife, for fear they would steal her back from him. Solomon asked her before he took her, "Would she be happy?"—very dignified, for he was a colored man that owned his land and had it written down in the courthouse; and she said, "Yes, sir," since he was an old man and she was young and just listened and answered. He asked her, if she was choosing winter, would she pine for spring, and she said, "No indeed." Whatever she said, always, was because he was an old man . . . while nine years went by. All the time, he got old, and he got so old he gave out. At last he slept the whole day in bed, and she was young still.

It was a nice house, inside and outside both. In the first place, it had three rooms. The front room was papered in holly paper, with green palmettos from the swamp spaced at careful intervals over the walls. There was fresh newspaper cut with fancy borders on the mantel-shelf, on which were propped photographs of old or very young men printed in faint yellow—Solomon's people. Solomon had a houseful of furniture. There was a double settee, a tall scrolled rocker and an organ in the front room, all around a three-legged table with a pink marble top, on which was set a lamp with three gold feet, besides a jelly glass with pretty hen feathers in it. Behind the front room, the other room had the bright iron bed with the polished knobs like a throne, in which Solomon slept all day. There were snow-white curtains of wiry lace at the window, and a lace bed-spread belonged on the bed. But what old Solomon slept so sound under was a big feather-stitched piece-quilt in the pattern "Trip Around the World," which had twenty-one different colors, four hundred and forty pieces, and a thousand yards of thread, and that was what Solomon's mother made in her life and old age. There was a table holding the Bible, and a trunk with a key. On the wall were two calendars, and a diploma from somewhere in Solomon's family, and under that Livvie's one possession was nailed, a picture of the little white baby of the family she worked for, back in Natchez before she was married. Going through that room and on to the kitchen, there was a big wood stove and a big round table always with a wet top and with the knives and forks in one jelly glass and the spoons in another, and a cut-glass vinegar bottle between, and going out from those, many shallow dishes of pickled peaches, fig preserves, watermelon pickles and blackberry jam always sitting there. The churn sat in the sun, the doors of the safe were always both shut, and there were four baited mouse-traps in the kitchen, one in every corner.

The outside of Solomon's house looked nice. It was not painted, but across the porch was an even balance. On each side there was one easy chair with high springs, looking out, and a fern basket hanging over it from the ceiling, and a dishpan of zinnia seedlings growing at its foot on the floor. By the door was a plow-wheel, just a pretty iron circle, nailed up on one wall and a square mirror on the other, a turquoise-blue comb stuck up in the frame, with the wash stand beneath it. On the door was a wooden knob with a pearl in the end, and Solomon's black hat hung on that, if he was in the house.

Out front was a clean dirt yard with every vestige of grass patiently uprooted and the ground scarred in deep whorls from the strike of Livvie's broom. Rose bushes with tiny blood-red roses blooming every month grew in threes on either side of the steps. On one side was a peach tree, on the other a pomegranate. Then coming around up the path from the deep cut of the Natchez Trace below was a line of bare crape-myrtle trees with every branch of them ending in a colored bottle, green or blue. There was no word that fell from Solomon's lips to say what they were for, but Livvie knew that there could be a spell put in trees, and she was familiar from the time she was born with the way bottle trees kept evil spirits from coming into the house—by luring them inside the colored bottles, where they cannot get out again. Solomon had made the bottle trees with his own hands over the nine years, in labor amounting to about a tree a year, and without a sign that he had any uneasiness in his heart, for he took as much pride in his precautions against spirits coming in the house as he took in the house, and sometimes in the sun the bottle trees looked prettier than the house did.

It was a nice house. It was in a place where the days would go by and surprise anyone that they were over. The lamplight and the firelight would shine out the door after dark, over the still and breathing country, lighting the roses and the bottle trees, and all was quiet there.

But there was nobody, nobody at all, not even a white person. And if there had been anybody, Solomon would not have let Livvie look at them, just as he would not let her look at a field hand, or a field hand look at her. There was no house near, except for the cabins of the tenants that were forbidden to her, and there was no house as far as she had been, stealing away down the still, deep Trace. She felt as if she waded a river when she went, for the dead leaves on the ground reached as high as her knees, and when she was all scratched and bleeding she said it was not like a road that went

5

anywhere. One day, climbing up the high bank, she had found a graveyard without a church, with ribbon-grass growing about the foot of an angel (she had climbed up because she thought she saw angel wings), and in the sun, trees shining like burning flames through the great caterpillar nets which enclosed them. Scarey thistles stood looking like the prophets in the Bible in Solomon's house. Indian paint brushes° grew over her head, and the mourning dove made the only sound in the world. Oh for a stirring of the leaves, and a breaking of the nets! But not by a ghost, prayed Livvie, jumping down the bank. After Solomon took to his bed, she never went out, except one more time.

Livvie knew she made a nice girl to wait on anybody. She fixed things to eat on a tray like a surprise. She could keep from singing when she ironed, and to sit by a bed and fan away the flies, she could be so still she could not hear herself breathe. She could clean up the house and never drop a thing, and wash the dishes without a sound, and she would step outside to churn, for churning sounded too sad to her, like sobbing, and if it made her home-sick and not Solomon, she did not think of that.

But Solomon scarcely opened his eyes to see her, and scarcely tasted his food. He was not sick or paralyzed or in any pain that he mentioned, but he was surely wearing out in the body, and no matter what nice hot thing Livvie would bring him to taste, he would only look at it now, as if he were past seeing how he could add anything more to himself. Before she could beg him, he would go fast asleep. She could not surprise him anymore, if he would not taste, and she was afraid that he was never in the world going to taste another thing she brought him—and so how could he last?

But one morning it was breakfast time and she cooked his eggs and grits, carried them in on a tray, and called his name. He was sound asleep. He lay in a dignified way with his watch beside him, on his back in the middle of the bed. One hand drew the quilt up high, though it was the first day of spring. Through the white lace curtains a little puffy wind was blowing as if it came from round cheeks. All night the frogs had sung out in the swamp, like a commotion in the room, and he had not stirred, though she lay wide awake and saying "Shh, frogs!" for fear he would mind them.

He looked as if he would like to sleep a little longer, and so she put back the tray and waited a little. When she tiptoed and stayed so quiet, she surrounded herself with a little reverie, and sometimes it seemed to her when she was so stealthy that the quiet she kept was for a sleeping baby, and that she had a baby and was its mother. When she stood at Solomon's bed and looked down at him, she would be thinking, "He sleeps so well," and she would hate to wake him up. And in some other way, too, she was afraid to wake him up because even in his sleep he seemed to be such a strict man.

Of course, nailed to the wall over the bed—only she would forget who it was—there was a picture of him when he was young. Then he had a fan of hair over his forehead like a king's crown. Now his hair lay down on his head, the spring had gone out of it. Solomon had a lightish face, with eyebrows scattered but rugged, the way privet grows, strong eyes, with second sight, a strict mouth, and a little gold smile. This was the way he looked in his clothes, but in bed in the daytime he looked like a different and smaller man, even when he was wide awake, and holding the Bible. He looked like somebody kin to himself. And then sometimes when he lay in sleep and she stood fanning the flies away, and the light came in, his face was like new, so smooth and clear that it was like a glass of jelly held to the window, and she could almost look through his forehead and see what he thought.

10

Indian paint brushes: a type of flaming red flower

She fanned him and at length he opened his eyes and spoke her name, but he would not taste the nice eggs she had kept warm under a pan.

Back in the kitchen she ate heartily, his breakfast and hers, and looked out the open door at what went on. The whole day, and the whole night before, she had felt the stir of spring close to her. It was as present in the house as a young man would be. The moon was in the last quarter and outside they were turning the sod and planting peas and beans. Up and down the red fields, over which smoke from the brush-burning hung showing like a little skirt of sky, a white horse and a white mule pulled the plow. At intervals hoarse shouts came through the air and roused her as if she dozed neglectfully in the shade, and they were telling her, "Jump up!" She could see how over each ribbon of field were moving men and girls, on foot and mounted on mules, with hats set on their heads and bright with tall hoes and forks as if they carried streamers on them and were going to some place on a journey—and how as if at a signal now and then they would all start at once shouting, hollering, cajoling, calling and answering back, running, being leaped on and breaking away, flinging to earth with a shout and lying motionless in the trance of twelve o'clock. The old women came out of the cabins and brought them the food they had ready for them, and then all worked together, spread evenly out. The little children came too, like a bouncing stream overflowing the fields, and set upon the men, the women, the dogs, the rushing birds, and the wave-like rows of earth, their little voices almost too high to be heard. In the middle distance like some white and gold towers were the haystacks, with black cows coming around to eat their edges. High above everything, the wheel of fields, house, and cabins, and the deep road surrounding like a moat to keep them in, was the turning sky, blue with long, far-flung white mare's-tail clouds, serene and still as high flames. And sound asleep while all this went around him that was his, Solomon was like a little still spot in the middle.

Even in the house the earth was sweet to breathe. Solomon had never let Livvie go any farther than the chicken house and the well. But what if she would walk now into the heart of the fields and take a hoe and work until she fell stretched out and drenched with her efforts, like other girls, and laid her cheek against the laid-open earth, and shamed the old man with her humbleness and delight? To shame him! A cruel wish could come in uninvited and so fast while she looked out the back door. She washed the dishes and scrubbed the table. She could hear the cries of the little lambs. Her mother, that she had not seen since her wedding day, had said one time, "I rather a man be anything, than a woman be mean."

So all morning she kept tasting the chicken broth on the stove, and when it was right she poured off a nice cup-ful. She carried it in to Solomon, and there he lay having a dream. Now what did he dream about? For she saw him sigh gently as if not to disturb some whole thing he held round in his mind, like a fresh egg. So even an old man dreamed about something pretty. Did he dream of her, while his eyes were shut and sunken, and his small hand with the wedding ring curled close in sleep around the quilt? He might be dreaming of what time it was, for even through his sleep he kept track of it like a clock, and knew how much of it went by, and waked up knowing where the hands were even before he consulted the silver watch that he never let go. He would sleep with the watch in his palm, and even holding it to his cheek like a child that loves a plaything. Or he might dream of journeys and travels on a steamboat to Natchez. Yet she thought he dreamed of her; but even while she scrutinized him, the rods of the foot of the bed seemed to rise up like a rail fence between them, and she could see that people never could be sure of anything as long as one of them was asleep and the other awake. To look at him dreaming of her when he might be going to die frightened her

15

a little, as if he might carry her with him that way, and she wanted to run out of the room. She took hold of the bed and held on, and Solomon opened his eyes and called her name, but he did not want anything. He would not taste the good broth.

Just a little after that, as she was taking up the ashes in the front room for the last time in the year, she heard a sound. It was somebody coming. She pulled the curtains together and looked through the slit.

Coming up the path under the bottle trees was a white lady. At first she looked young, but then she looked old. Marvelous to see, a little car stood steaming like a kettle out in the field-track—it had come without a road.

Livvie stood listening to the long, repeated knockings at the door, and after a while she opened it just a little. The lady came in through the crack, though she was more than middle-sized and wore a big hat.

"My name is Miss Baby Marie," she said.

Livvie gazed respectfully at the lady and at the little suitcase she was holding close   20
to her by the handle until the proper moment. The lady's eyes were running over the room, from palmetto to palmetto, but she was saying, "I live at home . . . out from Natchez . . . and get out and show these pretty cosmetic things to the white people and the colored people both . . . all around . . . years and years. . . . Both shades of powder and rouge. . . . It's the kind of work a girl can do and not go clear 'way from home . . ." And the harder she looked, the more she talked. Suddenly she turned up her nose and said, "It is not Christian or sanitary to put feathers in a vase," and then she took a gold key out of the front of her dress and began unlocking the locks on her suitcase. Her face drew the light, the way it was covered with intense white and red, with a little patty-cake of white between the wrinkles by her upper lip. Little red tassels of hair bobbed under the rusty wires of her picture-hat, as with an air of triumph and secrecy she now drew open her little suitcase and brought out bottle after bottle and jar after jar, which she put down on the table, the mantel-piece, the settee, and the organ.

"Did you ever see so many cosmetics in your life?" cried Miss Baby Marie.

"No'm," Livvie tried to say, but the cat had her tongue.

"Have you ever applied cosmetics?" asked Miss Baby Marie next.

"No'm," Livvie tried to say.

"Then look!" she said, and pulling out the last thing of all, "Try this!" she said. And   25
in her hand was unclenched a golden lipstick which popped open like magic. A fragrance came out of it like incense, and Livvie cried out suddenly, "Chinaberry flowers!"

Her hand took the lipstick, and in an instant she was carried away in the air through the spring, and looking down with a half-drowsy smile from a purple cloud she saw from above a chinaberry tree, dark and smooth and neatly leaved, neat as a guinea hen in the dooryard, and there was her home that she had left. On one side of the tree was her mama holding up her heavy apron, and she could see it was loaded with ripe figs, and on the other side was her papa holding a fish-pole over the pond, and she could see it transparently, the little clear fishes swimming up to the brim.

"Oh no, not chinaberry flowers—secret ingredients," said Miss Baby Marie. "My cosmetics have secret ingredients—not chinaberry flowers."

"It's purple," Livvie breathed, and Miss Baby Marie said, "Use it freely. Rub it on."

Livvie tiptoed out to the wash stand on the front porch and before the mirror put the paint on her mouth. In the wavery surface her face danced before her like a flame. Miss Baby Marie followed her out, took a look at what she had done, and said, "That's it."

Livvie tried to say "Thank you" without moving her parted lips where the paint lay   30
so new.

By now Miss Baby Marie stood behind Livvie and looked in the mirror over her
shoulder, twisting up the tassels of her hair. "The lipstick I can let you have for only two
dollars," she said, close to her neck.

"Lady, but I don't have no money, never did have," said Livvie.

"Oh, but you don't pay the first time. I make another trip, that's the way I do. I
come back again—later."

"Oh," said Livvie, pretending she understood everything so as to please the lady.

"But if you don't take it now, this may be the last time I'll call at your house," said   35
Miss Baby Marie sharply. "It's far away from anywhere, I'll tell you that. You don't live
close to anywhere."

"Yes'm. My husband, he keep the *money*," said Livvie, trembling. "He is strict as he
can be. He don't know *you* walk in here—Miss Baby Marie!"

"Where is he?"

"Right now, he in yonder sound asleep, an old man. I wouldn't ever ask him for
anything."

Miss Baby Marie took back the lipstick and packed it up. She gathered up the jars
for both black and white and got them all inside the suitcase, with the same little fuss
of triumph with which she had brought them out. She started away.

"Goodbye," she said, making herself look grand from the back, but at the last   40
minute she turned around in the door. Her old hat wobbled as she whispered, "Let me
see your husband."

Livvie obediently went on tiptoe and opened the door to the other room. Miss
Baby Marie came behind her and rose on her toes and looked in.

"My, what a little tiny old, old man!" she whispered, clasping her hands and shaking her head over them. "What a beautiful quilt! What a tiny old, old man!"

"He can sleep like that all day," whispered Livvie proudly.

They looked at him awhile so fast asleep, and then all at once they looked at each
other. Somehow that was as if they had a secret, for he had never stirred. Livvie then politely, but all at once, closed the door.

"Well! I'd certainly like to leave you with a lipstick!" said Miss Baby Marie viva-   45
ciously. She smiled in the door.

"Lady, but I told you I don't have no money, and never did have."

"And never will?" In the air and all around, like a bright halo around the white
lady's nodding head, it was a true spring day.

"Would you take eggs, lady?" asked Livvie softly.

"No, I have plenty of eggs—plenty," said Miss Baby Marie.

"I still don't have no money," said Livvie, and Miss Baby Marie took her suitcase   50
and went on somewhere else.

Livvie stood watching her go, and all the time she felt her heart beating in her left
side. She touched the place with her hand. It seemed as if her heart beat and her whole
face flamed from the pulsing color of her lips. She went to sit by Solomon and when he
opened his eyes he could not see a change in her. "He's fixin' to die," she said inside.
That was the secret. That was when she went out of the house for a little breath of air.

She went down the path and down the Natchez Trace a way, and she did not
know how far she had gone, but it was not far, when she saw a sight. It was a man, looking like a vision—she standing on one side of the Old Natchez Trace and he standing
on the other.

As soon as this man caught sight of her, he began to look himself over. Starting at the bottom with his pointed shoes, he began to look up, lifting his peg-top pants the higher to see fully his bright socks. His coat long and wide and leaf-green he opened like doors to see his high-up tawny pants and his pants he smoothed downward from the points of his collar, and he wore a luminous baby-pink satin shirt. At the end, he reached gently above his wide platter-shaped round hat, the color of a plum, and one finger touched at the feather, emerald green, blowing in the spring winds.

No matter how she looked, she could never look so fine as he did, and she was not sorry for that, she was pleased.

He took three jumps, one down and two up, and was by her side.   55

"My name is Cash," he said.

He had a guinea pig in his pocket. They began to walk along. She stared on and on at him, as if he were doing some daring spectacular thing, instead of just walking beside her. It was not simply the city way he was dressed that made her look at him and see hope in its insolence looking back. It was not only the way he moved along kicking the flowers as if he could break through everything in the way and destroy anything in the world, that made her eyes grow bright. It might be, if he had not appeared the way he did appear that day she would never have looked so closely at him, but the time people come makes a difference.

They walked through the still leaves of the Natchez Trace, the light and the shade falling through trees about them, the white irises shining like candles on the banks and the new ferns shining like green stars up in the oak branches. They came out at Solomon's house, bottle trees and all. Livvie stopped and hung her head.

Cash began whistling a little tune. She did not know what it was, but she had heard it before from a distance, and she had a revelation. Cash was a field hand. He was a transformed field hand. Cash belonged to Solomon. But he had stepped out of his overalls into this. There in front of Solomon's house he laughed. He had a round head, a round face, all of him was young, and he flung his head up, rolled it against the mare's-tail sky in his round hat, and he could laugh just to see Solomon's house sitting there. Livvie looked at it, and there was Solomon's black hat hanging on the peg on the front door, the blackest thing in the world.

"I been to Natchez," Cash said, wagging his head around against the sky. "*I* taken   60
a trip, *I* ready for Easter!"

How was it possible to look so fine before the harvest? Cash must have stolen the money, stolen it from Solomon. He stood in the path and lifted his spread hand high and brought it down again and again in his laughter. He kicked up his heels. A little chill went through her. It was as if Cash was bringing that strong hand down to beat a drum or to rain blows upon a man, such an abandon and menace were in his laugh. Frowning, she went closer to him and his swinging arm drew her in at once and the fright was crushed from her body, as a little match-flame might be smothered out by what it lighted. She gathered the folds of his coat behind him and fastened her red lips to his mouth, and she was dazzled by herself then, the way he had been dazzled at himself to begin with.

In that instant she felt something that could not be told—that Solomon's death was at hand, that he was the same to her as if he were dead now. She cried out, and uttering little cries turned and ran for the house.

At once Cash was coming, following after, he was running behind her. He came close, and halfway up the path he laughed and passed her. He even picked up a stone and sailed it into the bottle trees. She put her hands over her head, and sounds clattered through the bottle trees like cries of outrage. Cash stamped and plunged zigzag up the front steps and in at the door.

When she got there, he had stuck his hands in his pockets and was turning slowly about in the front room. The little guinea pig peeped out. Around Cash, the pinned-up palmettos looked as if a lazy green monkey had walked up and down and around the walls leaving green prints of his hands and feet.

She got through the room and his hands were still in his pockets, and she fell   65
upon the closed door to the other room and pushed it open. She ran to Solomon's bed, calling "Solomon! Solomon!" The little shape of the old man never moved at all, wrapped under the quilt as if it were winter still.

"Solomon!" She pulled the quilt away, but there was another one under that, and she fell on her knees beside him. He made no sound except a sigh, and then she could hear in the silence the light springy steps of Cash walking and walking in the front room, and the ticking of Solomon's silver watch, which came from the bed. Old Solomon was far away in his sleep, his face looked small, relentless, and devout, as if he were walking somewhere where she could imagine the snow falling.

Then there was a noise like a hoof pawing the floor, and the door gave a creak, and Cash appeared beside her. When she looked up, Cash's face was so black it was bright, and so bright and bare of pity that it looked sweet to her. She stood up and held up her head. Cash was so powerful that his presence gave her strength even when she did not need any.

Under their eyes Solomon slept. People's faces tell of things and places not known to the one who looks at them while they sleep, and while Solomon slept under the eyes of Livvie and Cash his face told them like a mythical story that all his life he had built, little scrap by little scrap, respect. A beetle could not have been more laborious or more ingenious in the task of its destiny. When Solomon was young, as he was in his picture overhead, it was the infinite thing with him, and he could see no end to the respect he would contrive and keep in a house. He had built a lonely house, the way he would make a cage, but it grew to be the same with him as a great monumental pyramid and sometimes in his absorption of getting it erected he was like the builder-slaves of Egypt who forgot or never knew the origin and meaning of the thing to which they gave all the strength of their bodies and used up all their days. Livvie and Cash could see that as a man might rest from a life-labor he lay in his bed, and they could hear how, wrapped in his quilt, he sighed to himself comfortably in sleep, while in his dreams he might have been an ant, a beetle, a bird, an Egyptian, assembling and carrying on his back and building with his hands, or he might have been an old man of India or a swaddled baby, about to smile and brush all away.

Then without warning old Solomon's eyes flew wide open under the hedge-like brows. He was wide awake.

And instantly Cash raised his quick arm. A radiant sweat stood on his temples.   70
But he did not bring his arm down—it stayed in the air, as if something might have taken hold.

It was not Livvie—she did not move. As if something said "Wait," she stood waiting. Even while her eyes burned under motionless lids, her lips parted in a stiff grimace, and with her arms stiff at her sides she stood above the prone old man and the panting young one, erect and apart.

Movement when it came came in Solomon's face. It was an old and strict face, a frail face, but behind it, like a covered light, came an animation that could play hide and seek, that would dart and escape, had always escaped. The mystery flickered in him, and invited from his eyes. It was that very mystery that Cash with his quick arm would have to strike, and that Livvie could not weep for. But Cash only stood holding his arm in the air, when the gentlest flick of his great strength, almost a puff of his breath, would have been enough, if he had known how to give it, to send the old man over the obstruction that kept him away from death.

If it could not be that the tiny illumination in the fragile and ancient face caused a crisis, a mystery in the room that would not permit a blow to fall, at least it was certain that Cash, throbbing in his Easter clothes, felt a pang of shame that the vigor of a man would come to such an end that he could not be struck without warning. He took down his hand and stepped back behind Livvie, like a round-eyed schoolboy on whose unsuspecting head the dunce cap has been set.

"Young ones can't wait," said Solomon.

Livvie shuddered violently, and then in a gush of tears she stooped for a glass of   75
water and handed it to him, but he did not see her.

"So here come the young man Livvie wait for. Was no prevention. No prevention. Now I lay eyes on young man and it come to be somebody I know all the time, and been knowing since he were born in a cotton patch, and watched grow up year to year, Cash McCord, growed to size, growed up to come in my house in the end—ragged and barefoot."

Solomon gave a cough of distaste. Then he shut his eyes vigorously, and his lips began to move like a chanter's.

"When Livvie married, her husband were already somebody. He had paid great cost for his land. He spread sycamore leaves over the ground from wagon to door, day he brought her home, so her foot would not have to touch ground. He carried her through his door. Then he growed old and could not lift her, and she were still young."

Livvie's sobs followed his words like a soft melody repeating each thing as he stated it. His lips moved for a little without sound, or she cried too fervently, and unheard he might have been telling his whole life, and then he said, "God forgive Solomon for sins great and small. God forgive Solomon for carrying away too young girl for wife and keeping her away from her people and from all the young people would clamor for her back."

Then he lifted up his right hand toward Livvie where she stood by the bed and   80
offered her his silver watch. He dangled it before her eyes, and she hushed crying; her tears stopped. For a moment the watch could be heard ticking as it always did, precisely in his proud hand. She lifted it away. Then he took hold of the quilt; then he was dead.

Livvie left Solomon dead and went out of the room. Stealthily, nearly without noise, Cash went beside her. He was like a shadow, but his shiny shoes moved over the floor in spangles, and the green downy feather shone like a light in his hat. As they reached the front room, he seized her deftly as a long black cat and dragged her hanging by the waist round and round him, while he turned in a circle, his face bent down to hers. The first moment, she kept one arm and its hand stiff and still, the one that held Solomon's watch. Then the fingers softly let go, all of her was limp, and the watch fell somewhere on the floor. It ticked away in the still room, and all at once there began outside the full song of a bird.

They moved around and around the room and into the brightness of the open door, then he stopped and shook her once. She rested in silence in his trembling arms, unprotesting as a bird on a nest. Outside the redbirds were flying and crisscrossing, the sun was in all the bottles on the prisoned trees, and the young peach was shining in the middle of them with the bursting light of spring.

QUESTIONS FOR CLOSE READING

1. What are the circumstances of Livvie's marriage? What do we know about Solomon? Why is he so possessive?
2. Why is the interior of the house so carefully described?
3. What is the meaning of "Livvie knew she made a nice girl to wait on anybody"? What does that tell you about Livvie?
4. Solomon said people did not come around the house. What brings Miss Baby Marie to the house? How does Livvie react to her arrival and her effort to sell cosmetics?
5. How does meeting Cash McCord transform Livvie? How does she then think of Solomon?
6. How true are the words that Solomon says near the end of the story, when he wakes to see Cash standing with Livvie?

QUESTIONS FOR INTERPRETATION

1. Welty relies on several interesting symbols in this story. Examine them in terms of how they help impart a deeper significance to Livvie's experiences. One symbol concerns the seasons, with Solomon comparing himself to winter and a young man to spring. How appropriate is this symbol for what happens in the story? Another symbol is the bottle tree, in which Solomon "bottles" all the dangerous spirits near his house. His house is also a symbol, compared at one point with a cage. Finally, the watch that Solomon gives Livvie is yet another symbol. How do these symbols function to help reveal the meaning of this story?
2. One theme of the story is freedom and its absence. In what ways is Livvie a free woman and in what ways is her freedom limited by her marriage to Solomon? How does Livvie react to her situation before she meets Miss Baby Marie? How does meeting a stranger change her attitude toward herself? Is her situation a result of the normal expectations of marriage in the community in which she lives, or is it more a result of Livvie's being the kind of person she is? Explain how the circumstances of the story clarify the nature of personal freedom in a marital relationship.
3. Another theme of the story is youth and age. How is age portrayed in "Livvie" and how is youth portrayed? How does Miss Baby Marie figure in a portrayal of youth and age? Is there a sense of inevitability built into the story on the basis of the simple fact that age implies weakness and youth implies strength? If so, how does it manifest itself in the most interesting descriptive passages in the story? How do the descriptive passages help reveal the story's deeper significance?

Lily Daw and the Three Ladies _____ *1941*

Mrs. Watts and Mrs. Carson were both in the post office in Victory when the letter came from the Ellisville Institute for the Feeble-Minded of Mississippi. Aimee Slocum, with her hand still full of mail, ran out in front and handed it straight to Mrs. Watts, and they all three read it together. Mrs. Watts held it taut between her pink hands, and Mrs. Carson underscored each line slowly with her thimbled finger. Everybody else in the post office wondered what was up now.

"What will Lily say," beamed Mrs. Carson at last, "when we tell her we're sending her to Ellisville!"

"She'll be tickled to death," said Mrs. Watts, and added in a guttural voice to a deaf lady, "Lily Daw's getting in at Ellisville!"

"Don't you all dare go off and tell Lily without me!" called Aimee Slocum, trotting back to finish putting up the mail.

"Do you suppose they'll look after her down there?" Mrs. Carson began to carry on a conversation with a group of Baptist ladies waiting in the post office. She was the Baptist preacher's wife. 5

"I've always heard it was lovely down there, but crowded," said one.

"Lily lets people walk over her so," said another.

"Last night at the tent show—" said another, and then popped her hand over her mouth.

"Don't mind me, I know there are such things in the world," said Mrs. Carson, looking down and fingering the tape measure which hung over her bosom.

"Oh, Mrs. Carson. Well, anyway, last night at the tent show, why, the man was just before making Lily buy a ticket to get in." 10

"A ticket!"

"Till my husband went up and explained she wasn't bright, and so did everybody else."

The ladies all clucked their tongues.

"Oh, it was a very nice show," said the lady who had gone. "And Lily acted so nice. She was a perfect lady—just set in her seat and stared."

"Oh, she can be a lady—she can be," said Mrs. Carson, shaking her head and turning her eyes up. "That's just what breaks your heart." 15

"Yes'm, she kept her eyes on—what's that thing makes all the commotion?—the xylophone," said the lady. "Didn't turn her head to the right or to the left the whole time. Set in front of me."

"The point is, what did she do after the show?" asked Mrs. Watts practically. "Lily has gotten so she is very mature for her age."

"Oh, Etta!" protested Mrs. Carson, looking at her wildly for a moment.

"And that's how come we are sending her to Ellisville," finished Mrs. Watts.

"I'm ready, you all," said Aimee Slocum, running out with white powder all over her face. "Mail's up. I don't know how good it's up." 20

"Well, of course, I do hope it's for the best," said several of the other ladies. They did not go at once to take their mail out of their boxes; they felt a little left out.

The three women stood at the foot of the water tank.

"To find Lily is a different thing," said Aimee Slocum.

"Where in the wide world do you suppose she'd be?" It was Mrs. Watts who was carrying the letter.

"I don't see a sign of her either on this side of the street or on the other side," Mrs. Carson declared as they walked along. 25

Ed Newton was stringing Redbird school tablets on the wire across the store.

"If you're after Lily, she come in here while ago and tole me she was fixin' to git married," he said.

"Ed Newton!" cried the ladies all together, clutching one another. Mrs. Watts began to fan herself at once with the letter from Ellisville. She wore widow's black, and the least thing made her hot.

"Why she is not. She's going to Ellisville, Ed," said Mrs. Carson gently. "Mrs. Watts and I and Aimee Slocum are paying her way out of our own pockets. Besides, the boys of Victory are on their honor. Lily's not going to get married, that's just an idea she's got in her head."

"More power to you, ladies," said Ed Newton, spanking himself with a tablet.   30

When they came to the bridge over the railroad tracks, there was Estelle Mabers, sitting on a rail. She was slowly drinking an orange Ne-Hi.

"Have you seen Lily?" they asked her.

"I'm supposed to be out here watching for her now," said the Mabers girl, as though she weren't there yet. "But for Jewel—Jewel says Lily come in the store while ago and picked out a two-ninety-eight hat and wore it off. Jewel wants to swap her something else for it."

"Oh, Estelle, Lily says she's going to get married!" cried Aimee Slocum.

"Well, I declare," said Estelle; she never understood anything.   35

Loralee Adkins came riding by in her Willys-Knight, tooting the horn to find out what they were talking about.

Aimee threw up her hands and ran out into the street. "Loralee, Loralee, you got to ride us up to Lily Daw's. She's up yonder fixing to get married!"

"Hop in, my land!"

"Well, that just goes to show you right now," said Mrs. Watts, groaning as she was helped into the back seat. "What we've got to do is persuade Lily it will be nicer to go to Ellisville."

"Just to think!"   40

While they rode around the corner Mrs. Carson was going on in her sad voice, sad as the soft noises in the hen house at twilight. "We buried Lily's poor defenseless mother. We gave Lily all her food and kindling and every stitch she had on. Sent her to Sunday school to learn the Lord's teachings, had her baptized a Baptist. And when her old father commenced beating her and tried to cut her head off with the butcher knife, why, we went and took her away from him and gave her a place to stay."

The paintless frame house with all the weather vanes was three stories high in places and had yellow and violet stained-glass windows in front and gingerbread around the porch. It leaned steeply to one side, toward the railroad, and the front steps were gone. The car full of ladies drew up under the cedar tree.

"Now Lily's almost grown up," Mrs. Carson continued. "In fact, she's grown," she concluded, getting out.

"Talking about getting married," said Mrs. Watts disgustedly. "Thanks, Loralee, you run on home."

They climbed over the dusty zinnias onto the porch and walked through the open   45
door without knocking.

"There certainly is always a funny smell in this house. I say it every time I come," said Aimee Slocum.

Lily was there, in the dark of the hall, kneeling on the floor by a small open trunk. When she saw them she put a zinnia in her mouth, and held still.

"Hello, Lily," said Mrs. Carson reproachfully.

"Hello," said Lily. In a minute she gave a suck on the zinnia stem that sounded ex-   50
actly like a jay bird. There she sat, wearing a petticoat for a dress, one of the things Mrs. Carson kept after her about. Her milky-yellow hair streamed freely down from under a new hat. You could see the wavy scar on her throat if you knew it was there.

Mrs. Carson and Mrs. Watts, the two fattest, sat in the double rocker. Aimee Slocum sat on the wire chair donated from the drugstore that burned.

"Well, what are you doing, Lily?" asked Mrs. Watts, who led the rocking.

Lily smiled.

The trunk was old and lined with yellow and brown paper, with an asterisk pattern showing in darker circles and rings. Mutely the ladies indicated to each other that they did not know where in the world it had come from. It was empty except for two bars of soap and a green washcloth, which Lily was now trying to arrange in the bottom.

"Go on and tell us what you're doing, Lily," said Aimee Slocum.   55

"Packing, silly," said Lily.

"Where are you going?"

"Going to get married, and I bet you wish you was me now," said Lily. But shyness overcame her suddenly, and she popped the zinnia back into her mouth.

"Talk to me, dear," said Mrs. Carson. "Tell old Mrs. Carson why you want to get married."

"No," said Lily, after a moment's hesitation.   60

"Well, we've thought of something that will be so much nicer," said Mrs. Carson. "Why don't you go to Ellisville!"

"Won't that be lovely?" said Mrs. Watts. "Goodness, yes."

"It's a lovely place," said Aimee Slocum uncertainly.

"You've got bumps on your face," said Lily.

"Aimee, dear, you stay out of this, if you don't mind," said Mrs. Carson anxiously.   65
"I don't know what it is comes over Lily when you come around her."

Lily stared at Aimee Slocum meditatively.

"There! Wouldn't you like to go to Ellisville now?" asked Mrs. Carson.

"No'm," said Lily.

"Why not?" All the ladies leaned down toward her in impressive astonishment.

"'Cause I'm goin' to get married," said Lily.   70

"Well, and who are you going to marry, dear?" asked Mrs. Watts. She knew how to pin people down and make them deny what they'd already said.

Lily bit her lip and began to smile. She reached into the trunk and held up both cakes of soap and wagged them.

"Tell us," challenged Mrs. Watts. "Who you're going to marry, now."

"A man last night."

There was a gasp from each lady. The possible reality of a lover descended sud-   75
denly like a summer hail over their heads. Mrs. Watts stood up and balanced herself.

"One of those show fellows! A musician!" she cried.

Lily looked up in admiration.

"Did he—did he do anything to you?" In the long run, it was still only Mrs. Watts who could take charge.

"Oh, yes'm," said Lily. She patted the cakes of soap fastidiously with the tips of her small fingers and tucked them in with the washcloth.

"What?" demanded Aimee Slocum, rising up and tottering before her scream.   80
"What?" she called out in the hall.

"Don't ask her what," said Mrs. Carson, coming up behind. "Tell me, Lily—just yes or no—are you the same as you were?"

"He had a red coat," said Lily graciously. "He took little sticks and went *ping-pong!*
ding-dong!"

"Oh, I think I'm going to faint," said Aimee Slocum, but they said, "No, you're not." 85

"The xylophone!" cried Mrs. Watts. "The xylophone player! Why, the coward, he ought to be run out of town on a rail!"

"Out of town? He is out of town, by now," cried Aimee. "Can't you read?—the sign in the café—Victory on the ninth, Como on the tenth? He's in Como. Como!" 85

"All right! We'll bring him back!" cried Mrs. Watts. "He can't get away from me!"

"Hush," said Mrs. Carson. "I don't think it's any use following that line of reasoning at all. It's better in the long run for him to be gone out of our lives for good and all. That kind of a man. He was after Lily's body alone and he wouldn't ever in this world make the poor little thing happy, even if we went out and forced him to marry her like he ought—at the point of a gun."

"Still—" began Aimee, her eyes widening.

"Shut up," said Mrs. Watts. "Mrs. Carson, you're right, I expect."

"This is my hope chest—see?" said Lily politely in the pause that followed. "You 90 haven't even looked at it. I've already got soap and a washrag. And I have my hat—on. What are you all going to give me?"

"Lily," said Mrs. Watts, starting over, "we'll give you lots of gorgeous things if you'll only go to Ellisville instead of getting married."

"What will you give me?" asked Lily.

"I'll give you a pair of hemstitched pillowcases," said Mrs. Carson.

"I'll give you a big caramel cake," said Mrs. Watts.

"I'll give you a souvenir from Jackson—a little toy bank," said Aimee Slocum. 95 "Now will you go?"

"No," said Lily.

"I'll give you a pretty little Bible with your name on it in real gold," said Mrs. Carson.

"What if I was to give you a pink crêpe de Chine brassière with adjustable shoulder straps?" asked Mrs. Watts grimly.

"Oh, Etta."

"Well, she needs it," said Mrs. Watts. "What would they think if she ran all over El- 100 lisville in a petticoat looking like a Fiji?"

"I wish *I* could go to Ellisville," said Aimee Slocum luringly.

"What will they have for me down there?" asked Lily softly.

"Oh! lots of things. You'll have baskets to weave, I expect. . . ." Mrs. Carson looked vaguely at the others.

"Oh, yes indeed, they will let you make all sorts of baskets," said Mrs. Watts; then her voice too trailed off.

"No'm, I'd rather get married," said Lily. 105

"Lily Daw! Now that's just plain stubbornness!" cried Mrs. Watts. "You almost said you'd go and then you took it back!"

"We've all asked God, Lily," said Mrs. Carson finally, "and God seemed to tell us— Mr. Carson, too—that the place where you ought to be, so as to be happy, was Ellisville."

Lily looked reverent, but still stubborn.

"We've really just got to get her there—now!" screamed Aimee Slocum all at once. "Suppose—! She can't stay here!"

"Oh, no, no, no," said Mrs. Carson hurriedly. "We mustn't think that." 110

They sat sunken in despair.

"Could I take my hope chest—to go to Ellisville?" asked Lily shyly, looking at them sidewise.

"Why, yes," said Mrs. Carson blankly.

Silently they rose once more to their feet.

"Oh, if I could just take my hope chest!"   115

"All the time it was just her hope chest," Aimee whispered.

Mrs. Watts struck her palms together. "It's settled!"

"Praise the fathers," murmured Mrs. Carson.

Lily looked up at them, and her eyes gleamed. She cocked her head and spoke out in a proud imitation of someone—someone utterly unknown.

"O.K.—Toots!"   120

The ladies had been nodding and smiling and backing away toward the door.

"I think I'd better stay," said Mrs. Carson, stopping in her tracks. "Where—where could she have learned that terrible expression?"

"Pack up," said Mrs. Watts. "Lily Daw is leaving for Ellisville on Number One."

In the station the train was puffing. Nearly everyone in Victory was hanging around waiting for it to leave. The Victory Civic Band had assembled without any orders and was scattered through the crowd. Ed Newton gave false signals to start on his bass horn. A crate full of baby chickens got loose on the platform. Everybody wanted to see Lily all dressed up, but Mrs. Carson and Mrs. Watts had sneaked her into the train from the other side of the tracks.

The two ladies were going to travel as far as Jackson to help Lily change trains   125
and be sure she went in the right direction.

Lily sat between them on the plush seat with her hair combed and pinned up into a knot under a small blue hat which was Jewel's exchange for the pretty one. She wore a traveling dress made out of part of Mrs. Watts's last summer's mourning. Pink straps glowed through. She had a purse and a Bible and a warm cake in a box, all in her lap.

Aimee Slocum had been getting the outgoing mail stamped and bundled. She stood in the aisle of the coach now, tears shaking from her eyes.

"Good-bye, Lily," she said. She was the one who felt things.

"Good-bye, silly," said Lily.

"Oh, dear, I hope they get our telegram to meet her in Ellisville!" Aimee cried   130
sorrowfully, as she thought how far away it was. "And it was so hard to get it all in ten words, too."

"Get off, Aimee, before the train starts and you break your neck," said Mrs. Watts, all settled and waving her dressy fan gaily. "I declare, it's so hot, as soon as we get a few miles out of town I'm going to slip my corset down."

"Oh, Lily, don't cry down there. Just be good, and do what they tell you—it's all because they love you." Aimee drew her mouth down. She was backing away, down the aisle.

Lily laughed. She pointed across Mrs. Carson's bosom out the window toward a man. He had stepped off the train and just stood there, by himself. He was a stranger and wore a cap.

"Look," she said, laughing softly through her fingers.

"Don't—look," said Mrs. Carson very distinctly, as if, out of all she had ever spo-   135
ken, she would impress these two solemn words upon Lily's soft little brain. She added, "Don't look at anything till you get to Ellisville."

Outside, Aimee Slocum was crying so hard she almost ran into the stranger. He wore a cap and was short and seemed to have on perfume, if such a thing could be.

"Could you tell me, madam," he said, "where a little lady lives in this burg name of Miss Lily Daw?" He lifted his cap—and he had red hair.

"What do you want to know for?" Aimee asked before she knew it.

"Talk louder," said the stranger. He almost whispered, himself.

"She's gone away—she's gone to Ellisville!"   140

"Gone?"

"Gone to Ellisville!"

"Well, I like that!" The man stuck out his bottom lip and puffed till his hair jumped.

"What business did you have with Lily?" cried Aimee suddenly.

"We was only going to get married, that's all," said the man.   145

Aimee Slocum started to scream in front of all those people. She almost pointed to the long black box she saw lying on the ground at the man's feet. Then she jumped back in fright.

"The xylophone! The xylophone!" she cried, looking back and forth from the man to the hissing train. Which was more terrible? The bell began to ring hollowly, and the man was talking.

"Did you say Ellisville? That in the state of Mississippi?" Like lightning he had pulled out a red notebook entitled, "Permanent Facts & Data." He wrote down something. "I don't hear well."

Aimee nodded her head up and down, and circled around him.

Under "Ellis-Ville Miss" he was drawing a line; now he was flicking it with two lit-   150 tle marks. "Maybe she didn't say she would. Maybe she said she wouldn't." He suddenly laughed very loudly, after the way he had whispered. Aimee jumped back. "Women!—Well, if we play anywheres near Ellisville, Miss., in the future I may look her up and I may not," he said.

The bass horn sounded the true signal for the band to begin. White steam rushed out of the engine. Usually the train stopped for only a minute in Victory, but the engineer knew Lily from waving at her, and he knew this was her big day.

"Wait!" Aimee Slocum did scream. "Wait, mister! I can get her for you. Wait, Mister Engineer! Don't go!"

Then there she was back on the train, screaming in Mrs. Carson's and Mrs. Watts's faces.

"The xylophone player! The xylophone player to marry her! Yonder he is!"

"Nonsense," murmured Mrs. Watts, peering over the others to look where Aimee   155 pointed. "If he's there I don't see him. Where is he? You're looking at One-Eye Beasley."

"The little man with the cap—no, with the red hair! Hurry!"

"Is that really him?" Mrs. Carson asked Mrs. Watts in wonder. "Mercy! He's small, isn't he?"

"Never saw him before in my life!" cried Mrs. Watts. But suddenly she shut up her fan.

"Come on! This is a train we're on!" cried Aimee Slocum. Her nerves were all unstrung.

"All right, don't have a conniption fit, girl," said Mrs. Watts. "Come on," she said   160 thickly to Mrs. Carson.

"Where are we going now?" asked Lily as they struggled down the aisle.

"We're taking you to get married," said Mrs. Watts. "Mrs. Carson, you'd better phone up your husband right there in the station."

"But I don't want to git married," said Lily, beginning to whimper. "I'm going to Ellisville."

"Hush, and we'll all have some ice-cream cones later," whispered Mrs. Carson.

Just as they climbed down the steps at the back end of the train, the band went   165 into "Independence March."

The xylophone player was still there, patting his foot. He came up and said, "Hello, Toots. What's up—tricks?" and kissed Lily with a smack, after which she hung her head.

"So you're the young man we've heard so much about," said Mrs. Watts. Her smile was brilliant. "Here's your little Lily."

"What say?" asked the xylophone player.

"My husband happens to be the Baptist preacher of Victory," said Mrs. Carson in a loud, clear voice. "Isn't that lucky? I can get him here in five minutes: I know exactly where he is."

They were in a circle around the xylophone player, all going into the white waiting room. 170

"Oh, I feel just like crying, at a time like this," said Aimee Slocum. She looked back and saw the train moving slowly away, going under the bridge at Main Street. Then it disappeared around the curve.

"Oh, the hope chest!" Aimee cried in a stricken voice.

"And whom have we the pleasure of addressing?" Mrs. Watts was shouting, while Mrs. Carson was ringing up the telephone.

The band went on playing. Some of the people thought Lily was on the train, and some swore she wasn't. Everybody cheered, though, and a straw hat was thrown into the telephone wires.

QUESTIONS FOR CLOSE READING

1. What do you learn about the community in the opening of the story? What do people think of Lily Daw?

2. Why is this story told so completely in dialogue form? What do you learn from the dialogue of the three women?

3. How much concern do people have for what Lily wants?

4. What is your reaction to Lily once she enters the story?

5. What is your impression of the xylophone player?

6. How do the women react when the xylophone player really wants to marry Lily Daw?

QUESTIONS FOR INTERPRETATION

1. Decide on the basis of what you know in the story whether or not Lily Daw will get married. If she does, will the marriage be successful? What qualities do the potential bride and groom have that would suggest to you that they will succeed or fail in marriage?

2. What do you learn about the character of Lily Daw? Comment on her childhood and her upbringing and the way in which Mrs. Carson and others have cared for her. What has been the result of her having been so carefully watched over by Mrs. Watts, Aimee, and Mrs. Carson? To what extent has Lily Daw's personal freedom been put in jeopardy by this community?

3. Considering that the women want Lily Daw to go to Ellisville and spend so much time convincing her to go, why do they all change their minds when they discover that the xylophone player really intends to marry her? Why is marriage an acceptable alternative to Ellisville? To what extent could it be said that Lily Daw's fate, whichever it is, is the result of antifeminist thinking in this community?

RESOURCES FOR READING WELTY

EUDORA WELTY

> *Eudora Welty recollects, in this brief excerpt from* One Writer's Beginnings, *some of the moments of childhood that led her toward writing as a career. Most important was her intense curiosity, which made her listen for stories.*

One Writer's Beginnings _____ *1984*

This was a day when ladies' and children's clothes were very often made at home. My mother cut out all the dresses and her little boys' rompers, and a sewing woman would come and spend the day upstairs in the sewing room fitting and stitching them all. This was Fannie. This old black sewing woman, along with her speed and dexterity, brought along a great provision of up-to-the-minute news. She spent her life going from family to family in town and worked right in its bosom, and nothing could stop her. My mother would try, while I stood being pinned up. "Fannie, I'd rather Eudora didn't hear that." "That" would be just what I was longing to hear, whatever it was. "I don't want her exposed to gossip"—as if gossip were measles and I could catch it. I did catch some of it but not enough. "Mrs. O'Neil's oldest daughter she had her wedding dress *tried on,* and all her fine underclothes featherstitched and ribbon run in and then—" "I think that will do, Fannie," said my mother. It was tantalizing never to be exposed long enough to hear the end.

Fannie was the worldliest old woman to be imagined. She could do whatever her hands were doing without having to stop talking; and she could speak in a wonderfully derogatory way with any number of pins stuck in her mouth. Her hands steadied me like claws as she stumped on her knees around me, tacking me together. The gist of her tale would be lost on me, but Fannie didn't bother about the ear she was telling it to; she just liked telling. She was like an author. In fact, for a good deal of what she said, I daresay she *was* the author.

Long before I wrote stories, I listened for stories. Listening *for* them is something more acute than listening to them. I suppose it's an early form of participation in what goes on. Listening children know stories are *there.* When their elders sit and begin, children are just waiting and hoping for one to come out, like a mouse from its hole.

It was taken entirely for granted that there wasn't any lying in our family, and I was advanced in adolescence before I realized that in plenty of homes where I played with schoolmates and went to their parties, children lied to their parents and parents lied to their children and to each other. It took me a long time to realize that these very same everyday lies, and the stratagems and jokes and tricks and dares that went with them, were in fact the basis of the *scenes* I so well loved to hear about and hoped for and treasured in the conversation of adults.

My instinct—the dramatic instinct—was to lead me, eventually, on the right track for a storyteller: the *scene* was full of hints, pointers, suggestions, and promises of things to find out and know about human beings. I had to grow up and learn to listen for the unspoken as well as the spoken—and to know a truth, I also had to recognize a lie.

EUDORA WELTY

This essay by Eudora Welty from The Eye of the Story: Selected Essays and Reviews *was designed to answer questions that came so frequently from readers of "A Worn Path" that she realized a public statement was necessary. In it Welty gives us a rare glimpse of how she decides on a problem of meaning in her work.*

"Is Phoenix Jackson's Grandson Really Dead?" _____ *1974*

A story writer is more than happy to be read by students; the fact that these serious readers think and feel something in response to his work he finds life-giving. At the same time he may not always be able to reply to their specific questions in kind. I wondered if it might clarify something, for both the questioners and myself, if I set down a general reply to the question that comes to me most often in the mail, from both students and their teachers, after some classroom discussion. The unrivaled favorite is this: "Is Phoenix Jackson's grandson really *dead?*"

It refers to a short story I wrote years ago called "A Worn Path," which tells of a day's journey an old woman makes on foot from deep in the country into town and into a doctor's office on behalf of her little grandson; he is at home, periodically ill, and periodically she comes for his medicine; they give it to her as usual, she receives it and starts the journey back.

I had not meant to mystify readers by withholding any fact; it is not a writer's business to tease. The story is told through Phoenix's mind as she undertakes her errand. As the author at one with the character as I tell it, I must assume that the boy is alive. As the reader, you are free to think as you like, of course: the story invites you to believe that no matter what happens, Phoenix for as long as she is able to walk and can hold to her purpose will make her journey. The *possibility* that she would keep on even if he were dead is there in her devotion and its single-minded, single-track errand. Certainly the *artistic* truth, which should be good enough for the fact, lies in Phoenix's own answer to that question. When the nurse asks, "He isn't dead, is he?" she speaks for herself: "He still the same. He going to last."

The grandchild is the incentive. But it is the journey, the going of the errand, that is the story, and the question is not whether the grandchild is in reality alive or dead. It doesn't affect the outcome of the story or its meaning from start to finish. But it is not the question itself that has struck me as much as the idea, almost without exception implied in the asking, that for Phoenix's grandson to be dead would somehow make the story "better."

It's *all right,* I want to say to the students who write to me, for things to be what they appear to be, and for words to mean what they say. It's all right, too, for words and appearances to mean more than one thing—ambiguity is a fact of life. A fiction writer's responsibility covers not only what he presents as the facts of a given story but what he chooses to stir up as their implications; in the end, these implications, too, become facts, in the larger, fictional sense. But it is not all right, not in good faith, for things *not* to mean what they say.

The grandson's plight was real and it made the truth of the story, which is the story of an errand of love carried out. If the child no longer lived, the truth would persist in the "wornness" of the path. But his being dead can't increase the truth of the story, can't affect it one way or the other. I think I signal this, because the end of the story has been reached before old Phoenix gets home again: she simply starts back. To the question "Is the grandson really dead?" I could reply that it doesn't make any difference. I could also say that I did not make him up in order to let him play a trick on Phoenix. But my best answer would be: "*Phoenix* is alive."

The origin of a story is sometimes a trustworthy clue to the author—or can provide him with the clue—to its key image; maybe in this case it will do the same for the reader. One day I saw a solitary old woman like Phoenix. She was walking; I saw her, at middle distance, in a winter country landscape, and watched her slowly make her way across my line of vision. That sight of her made me write the story. I invented an errand for her, but that only seemed a living part of the figure she was herself: what errand other than for someone else could be making her go? And her going was the first thing, her persisting in her landscape was the real thing, and the first and the real were what I wanted and worked to keep. I brought her up close enough, by imagination, to describe her face, make her present to the eyes, but the full-length figure moving across the winter fields was the indelible one and the image to keep, and the perspective extending into the vanishing distance the true one to hold in mind.

I invented for my character, as I wrote, some passing adventures—some dreams and harassments and a small triumph or two, some jolts to her pride, some flights of fancy to console her, one or two encounters to scare her, a moment that gave her cause to feel ashamed, a moment to dance and preen—for it had to be a *journey,* and all these things belonged to that, parts of life's uncertainty.

A narrative line is in its deeper sense, of course, the tracing out of a meaning, and the real continuity of a story lies in this probing forward. The real dramatic force of a story depends on the strength of the emotion that has set it going. The emotional value is the measure of the reach of the story. What gives any such content to "A Worn Path" is not its circumstances but its *subject:* the deep-grained habit of love.

What I hoped would come clear was that in the whole surround of this story, the world it threads through, the only certain thing at all is the worn path. The habit of love cuts through confusion and stumbles or contrives its way out of difficulty, it remembers the way even when it forgets, for a dumbfounded moment, its reason for being. The path is the thing that matters.

Her victory—old Phoenix's—is when she sees the diploma in the doctor's office, when she finds "nailed up on the wall the document that had been stamped with the gold seal and framed in the gold frame, which matched the dream that was hung up in her head." The return with the medicine is just a matter of retracing her own footsteps. It is the part of the journey, and of the story, that can now go without saying.

In the matter of function, old Phoenix's way might even do as a sort of parallel to your way of work if you are a writer of stories. The way to get there is the all-important, all-absorbing problem, and this problem is your reason for undertaking the story. Your only guide, too, is your sureness about your subject, about what this subject is. Like Phoenix, you work all your life to find your way, through all the obstructions and the false appearances and the upsets you may have brought on yourself, to reach a meaning—using inventions of your imagination, perhaps helped out by your dreams and bits of good luck. And finally too, like Phoenix, you have to assume that what you are working in aid of is life, not death.

But you would make the trip anyway—wouldn't you?—just on hope.

RUTH M. VANDE KIEFT

Ruth M. Vande Kieft is one of the best-known critics of Eudora Welty. Her discussion of "Livvie" from Eudora Welty, *revised edition, gives us insight into the potential meanings of details and names in the story, especially those that connect us to the Bible.*

Technique in "Livvie" _____ 1987

. . . In the story "Livvie," however, we find the reverse: a narrative method disarmingly simple and clear, but a thematic structure far more complex and subtly adjusted to the ambiguities of human experience. The beautiful balance of the opposing values, their easy, natural embodiment in character and situation, the purity of the language, and the sympathy and detachment of the vision, give this story a deservedly high place among Eudora Welty's works.

Livvie's return to life (the original title of the story was "Livvie Is Back") through the death of her old husband, Solomon, and her surrender to Cash, the field hand who comes to claim her, is an obvious but not a complete and clear gain; for there is a corresponding loss and destruction of certain positive values.

As his name implies, Solomon stands for order, control, wisdom, security. His house is "nice"—neat and orderly. Patterns are delightfully worked out in groups of twos, threes, and fours. On each side of the porch, in perfect balance, is an easy chair with overhanging fern and a dishpan of seedlings growing at its foot; a plow-wheel hanging on one side of the door is balanced by a square mirror on the other side. In the house are three rooms; in the living room is a three-legged table with a pink marble top, and on it is a lamp with three gold feet; on the kitchen table are three objects: two jelly glasses holding spoons, knives, and forks, with a cut-glass vinegar bottle between them; even the tiny blood-red roses that bloom on the bushes outside grow in threes on either side of the steps. And there are four baited mouse-traps in the kitchen, one in every corner. Each pictured detail of the house, inside and out, speaks of the balance and symmetry that characterize a dignified, well-disciplined, quiet and peaceful mode of existence.

Safety and security are suggested by the two safedoors that are always kept shut and by the bottled branches of the crape-myrtle trees, a precaution taken, as Livvie knows, to keep "evil spirits from coming into the house—by luring them inside the colored bottles, where they cannot get out again." Solomon's life is moral and pious—he seems to Livvie "such a strict man"; he has his Bible on the bedside table (and uses it); he keeps track of time like a clock, sleeping with his silver watch in his palm "and even holding it to his cheek like a child that loves a plaything."

As mistress of Solomon's golden palace, Livvie passes her days in serenity and comfort; in a sense she shares in Solomon's kingly opulence, though she serves her now-ancient, fragile master by waiting on him in his illness. But since the "nice house" has also been her gilded cage for nine years, she is vaguely restless and discontent, unconsciously oppressed by the wintry atmosphere, by her barren and lonely existence. Once she had ventured forth through the dead leaves in the deep Trace, and there, over a bank in a graveyard, she had had a vision both of her bondage and her possible release. She had seen "in the sun, trees shining like burning flames through the great caterpillar nets which enclosed them," even though "scary thistles stood looking like the prophets in the Bible in Solomon's house." And she had thought, "Oh for a stirring of the leaves, and a breaking of the nets!"

Her release comes on the first day of spring, which brings a "little puffy wind," and on it the sounds of the distant shouts of men and girls plowing in the red fields and of the small piping cries of children playing. The harbinger of Livvie's release is Miss Baby-Marie, an amusingly vulgar, red-haired woman who travels around selling cosmetics to "white and colored" and is herself covered with "intense white and red" makeup. Livvie is tempted to apply some lipstick, and when she looks in the mirror, her face "dance[s] before her like a flame." The outside world has impinged on her secure, withdrawn world in a form crassly commercial, but its effect is romantically exciting. Pulsating with her new self-consciousness, Livvie is stirred to a further insight which she shares, unspoken, with Miss Baby-Marie as the two of them look at Solomon sleeping: he is about to die. Livvie rushes out for air.

Then Cash comes in his fine Easter clothes, and Livvie is purely dazzled. Cash is, as Robert Penn Warren has suggested, a black buck, a kind of field god; but that identification overlooks the fact that his gaudy clothes have been purchased with money stolen from Solomon, the fact that his luminous baby-pink shirt is the color of Miss Baby-Marie's lipstick. He is a commercially transformed field god, dressed in "the city way"; and if he destroys the nets that are binding Livvie, he is also destroying a certain decency and reserve, even a certain moral order. As she walks beside him, Livvie senses this threat in "the way he move[s] along kicking the flowers as if he could break through everything in the way and destroy anything in the world." Her eyes grow bright at that; she sees "hope in its insolence looking back"; but a little chill goes through her when he lifts his spread hand and laughingly brings it down, "as if Cash was bringing that strong hand down to beat a drum or to rain blows upon a man, such an abandon and menace were in his laugh." Soon afterwards when Cash sends a stone sailing through the bottle trees, the sounds of broken glass clatter "like cries of outrage"—the outrage perpetrated against Solomon's prevention and protection. Surely, by implication, a few more evil spirits have been released to wander freely and work their mischief in the world.

When Livvie rushes in to Solomon's bedside, she hears his watch ticking and sees him withdrawn in sleep, his old face looking "small, relentless, and devout, as if he were walking somewhere where she could imagine the snow falling." She feels the strength of his austerity, his pure dedication; and that is why the sight of Cash's bright, pitiless black face is "sweet" to her: she would have to be cruel to break with Solomon. Now as Solomon sleeps under the eyes of Cash and Livvie, his face tells them "like a mythical story that all his life he had built, little scrap by little scrap, respect." The images used to describe his purpose and method—that of an ant or beetle collecting, or an Egyptian builder-slave industriously working on the pyramid, so absorbed in his pursuit that he forgets the origins and meaning of his work—imply a curious blend of sympathy and criticism. Respectability, as Robert Penn Warren states, is "the dream, the idea, which has withered"; but nonetheless a simple wisdom and nobility characterize the process of this old man's life, the achievement of which is not entirely vitiated by the dubious value of its goal.

When Solomon wakes up, Cash raises his arm to strike; but the arm is fixed in midair as if held. A mysterious illumination flickers across Solomon's face: "It was that very mystery that Cash with his quick arm would have to strike, and that Livvie could not weep for." Though Cash is an impatiently pawing buck, he is momentarily stayed—if not by the sense of Solomon's mystery, at least because he feels "a pang of shame that the vigor of a man would come to such an end that he could not be struck without warning." Cash is sufficiently human to realize human vulnerability, if not dignity: he could not, without ceasing to be human, do violence to Solomon—push him over the trembling edge of life—in this moment of the old man's greatest strength and helplessness. Solomon must be permitted to surrender his ghost, and he does so with beautiful candor and dignity. Gently he reviews his own purpose for Livvie; without rebellion he faces the disagreeable fact of his failure (since there was "no prevention"), and the irony of its being Cash who has come to claim Livvie: "somebody I know all the time, and been knowing since he was born in a cotton patch, . . . Cash McCord, growed to size, growed up to come in my house in the end." With humility he confesses his fault: "God forgive Solomon for carrying away too young girl for wife and keeping her away from . . . all the young people would clamor for her back." Finally he offers to Livvie his most valued possession, the symbol of his very life, his dignified, orderly existence; and the moment she receives the silver watch from his hand, Solomon dies.

The denouement is swift and joyful. Back in the front room, Cash seizes Livvie and drags her round him and out toward the door in a whirling embrace. As a final fleeting gesture of loyalty, Livvie keeps stiff and still the arm and hand holding Solomon's watch; then her fingers relax, the watch falls somewhere on the floor, all at once "the full song of a bird" is heard, and outside "the sun was in all the bottles on the prisoned trees, and the young peach was shining in the middle of them with the bursting light of spring."

The triumph of life, youth, passion would appear to be complete. But Eudora Welty has shown us that just as Solomon's death is a necessary prelude to Livvie's new life with Cash, so all of Solomon's values and achievements must suffer a death. The new freedom and joy are not the uncomplicated pagan sort embodied in Don McInnis; they are, in part, a "cash" purchase, and their characteristic hue is a gaudy pink.

RUTH D. WESTON

In the following brief discussion from Eudora Welty: Eye of the Storyteller *(ed. Dawn Trouard), Ruth D. Weston points to folk tale elements in "Lily Daw and the Three Ladies." She emphasizes the imagery of restraint common to folk tales. The folk tale repetition—three times for everything—has a ritual significance that deepens the significance of the story. The charm is designed to help Lily Daw escape from the bondage of the three ladies, whose power is akin to that of witches.*

Lily Daw and the Three Ladies _____ *1989*

Mrs. Carson carries a tape measure on her bosom. Mrs. Watts knows how to "pin people down." Aimee Slocum makes her living stamping and bundling mail, and she even observes the ten-word limit in her telegram to Ellisville. Mrs. Watts is confined in a tight corset from which she plans to free herself as soon as the train pulls out, while she attempts to restrict even Lily's view from the train. Lily's stranger is limited too and confesses that he doesn't hear well. And in the crowd of representatively limited folk are those described as small, as one-eyed, and finally as cheering without knowing why.

More serious implications of limitation result from the grotesque comparisons of humans with animals and inanimate objects. Aimee wonders which is more terrible, "the man [or] the hissing train"; and the narrator implies a connection as "the bell began to ring hollowly, and the man was talking." The ladies cluck their tongues and make noises "sad as the soft noises in the henhouse at twilight"; people and chicks run wild on the station platform; and Lily, named for a jackdaw and sucking on a zinnia between her teeth, makes a sound "exactly like a jaybird." Pictures of redbirds on a school tablet adorn wires inside the store, while Estelle perches outside on a rail fence. The story reads like the script for an absurdist comedy in which the silent and controlled pantomime of modern dance alternates with the apparent randomness of what was called in the 1960s a theatrical happening.

In "Lily Daw," Welty has utilized the rhetorical patterning of a folk or fairy tale, in which things often happen in threes. She combines mnemonic qualities of the oral folk tradition with the rhythms and shapes of the drama and of the plastic and painterly folk and fine arts. Her story depicts a lyric and individual impulse toward freedom in Lily's carefree bestowal of favor and unconventional behavior. And it portrays the culture's limitation of such freedom because of its threat to safe conventions and its attempt to hide the other than normal (that which cannot be neatly stamped and bundled) behind institutional walls. And, not least, it reveals the ironic situation of women who, blessed and limited by fertility, must therefore be controlled when they are "mature for [their] age." It portrays a community tangle of women who close in around a little innocent wild life to see it safely entrusted to one institution or another—to the asylum or to marriage. The flat (unrealistic), yet hauntingly real, characters are effective metaphors for the flat, unreal roles that Ruth Vande Kieft has noted are not only assumed by men but that are often forced by men on women in Welty's South; but in "Lily Daw," as in other Welty stories, these stereotypical roles are forced on women by other women who have become so rigid in their assigned roles that they do not realize they are performing. In their own way, like Fay in *The Optimist's Daughter,* Welty's three ladies are "making a scene."

While such human concerns are important in the story, the piece itself is less a social treatise than an abstract design that evokes a sense of grotesque human limitation. Its treatment in spatial, more than temporal, terms underscores its metaphoric confining lines and spaces. Even the language itself functions as a metaphor for limitation. For, as Welty has said, "We start from scratch, and words don't," her own critical vocabulary suggesting a linguistic dimension of the concept of limitation. Language is loaded with accumulated meanings; it is a grotesquely limited and delimiting automatism that Welty extends by creating the illusion of spatiality. "Lily Daw and the Three Ladies" is Welty's earliest portrait of the virtual confinement of women in society by their inscription in its linguistic and cultural codes. Lily herself symbolizes the victim of such limitation as well as the hope of escape; and the circling, threatening, talking ladies reveal woman's own complicity in what Michel Foucault has called a "carceral society," one that not only supervises criminal incarceration but also incorporates a series of enclosing devices, a network of forces, including "walls, space, institution, rules, discourse," all intended to normalize human beings in accord with the prevailing cultural mythos. The few props in the setting for "Lily Daw" contribute to the sense of a "bare stage" on which Lily is cruelly exposed to the elements in her world that threaten her freedom, investing her small figure, however deflated, with dramatic monumentality.

At the story's end, Lily understandably hangs her head, for her hope chest is gone on the train to Ellisville, while she herself is as trapped as the hat thrown into the electric wires. Welty leaves us with an image as graphic and functional as the fused sword and plow that she admires in Cather's *My Antonia.* For, in the final scene, those electric lines, like the lines of perspective in a painting, now draw our attention past Lily to the focal point that represents her: the hat itself, an object caught.

PETER SCHMIDT

Peter Schmidt raises some feminist issues in "Lily Daw and the Three Ladies," from The Heart of the Story, Eudora Welty's Short Fiction, *and shows us the ways in which life is circumscribed for women in the environment of Victory, Mississippi. Schmidt's approach introduces some of the psychological elements that drive the action.*

Lily Daw and the Three Ladies _____ *1991*

Of all the stories in *A Curtain of Green,* "Lily Daw and the Three Ladies" represents most clearly the choice open to white southern women in Welty's early stories. (Perhaps it is for this reason that Welty chose it to open her first collection.) That choice is suggested by the story's title: a woman may be either a married and respectable lady, like Mrs. Carter and her friend Mrs. Watts, or she may be eccentric like the retarded girl Lily Daw, continually threatened by scandal, madness, and confinement.

Lily grew up as a ward of the ladies of Victory, Mississippi, but now, in her teens, she has suddenly begun acting independently, talking back to her elders, sneaking away to circuses, and showing an interest in the opposite sex. The town's matriarchs first decide that confinement in an asylum can be the only remedy, but then, in a comic reversal caused partly by Lily's boyfriend's faithfulness and partly by the rebellion of one of their own members, Aimee Slocum, they decide that Lily's marrying her boyfriend must be accepted after all. By juxtaposing marriage and madness in such an exaggerated way, Welty's story comically subverts the ladies' authority. Their ideal of marriage comes to seem a kind of confining madness, whereas Lily's unconscious defiance of the community's standards becomes a liberating sanity, an escape and transformation. Yet even this twist is not the last the story has in store for us. Our euphoria over Lily's apparent victory over the ladies fades slightly when the story is reread: even as she is united with her lover we can see the ladies extending their control over her again. The story's acerbity and exuberance hardly suggest anxiety on Welty's part, yet its pointed linking of rebelliousness and madness provides an appropriate entry into the other, darker stories in *A Curtain of Green* about the potentially disastrous consequences of nonconformity.

Lily Daw's defection from the ladies' rule comes very suddenly; they hear that she went to a traveling circus the night before and became entranced with the red-headed boy playing the xylophone.

> "Oh, it was a very nice show," said the lady who had gone. "And Lily acted so nice. She was a perfect lady—just set in her seat and stared."

> "Oh, she can be a lady—she can be," said Mrs. Carson, shaking her head and turning her eyes up. "That's just what breaks your heart."

> "Yes'm, she kept her eyes on—what's that thing makes all the commotion?—the xylophone," said the lady. "Didn't turn her head to the right or to the left the whole time. Set in front of me."

"The point is, what did she do after the show?" asked Mrs. Watts practically. "Lily has gotten so she is very mature for her age."

"Oh, Etta!" protested Mrs. Carson, looking at her wildly for a moment.

"And that's how come we are sending her to Ellisville," finished Mrs. Watts.

Here, acting the part of a "perfect lady" means a careful suppression of what Mrs. Watts delicately calls "maturity." Mrs. Carson and her cohorts recognize that Lily's retardedness means that she will never learn to play the part of a lady well; she is too susceptible to "commotion"—to the excitement of music, the xylophone player's red hair and racy slang. When Mrs. Carson, Mrs. Watts, and Aimee Slocum hear about what happened at the circus, they realize that they have arranged just in time to entomb her permanently within propriety at the Institute for the Feeble-Minded at Ellisville: "Lily Daw's getting in at Ellisville," they whisper to the other women in the post office, as if she had graduated from high school and been accepted at the prestigious college of her choice.

Welty's portrayal of the three ladies in the story's opening scene shows how they have carefully repressed the sensual, "natural" Lily within themselves in order to construct their status as "ladies." Mrs. Carson is a prim, self-righteous Baptist minister's wife. Other women in the town are embarrassed even to mention the circus in her presence, but when they do, she unctuously replies, " 'Don't mind me, I know there are such things in the world,' . . . looking down and fingering the tape measure which hung over her bosom." Mrs. Watts, the most authoritative of the three, wears "widow's black, and the least thing made her hot." The third woman in the group, a spinster named Aimee Slocum, has distinctly less success in turning herself into a lady. Not only is she addressed by her first name, as Lily is, but she works in the post office and is bumbling and ugly—even Lily can see that. She is the only one of the three ladies whom Lily dares to insult.

Welty deftly demonstrates the stature that these three women hold in the town by setting the first scene in the town's post office while the day's mail is being put up in everyone's boxes. The post office is a major gathering place in any small southern town (hence Sister's proud retreat to it in "Why I Live at the P.O."), and the hour that the mail is put up is naturally a social highlight of the day. During this time, Mrs. Carson and Mrs. Watts reign supreme. The ladies' power, however, is hardly absolute. It is dependent upon the institution of marriage; they could not achieve their eminence in society without it. This is why Mrs. Carson murmurs "praise the fathers" when Lily finally consents to give up her plans to marry and go to Ellisville: she sees herself as defending the standards of God the Father and the male representatives of His authority on earth, including her husband. Thus the near absence of males in the story does not mean that the town is run by women, but rather that the women's power would be impossible unless sanctioned by the "fathers." The story is thus not a satire of women with too much power but of women self-righteously acting on behalf of the "fathers"—the patriarchal authority that defines "proper" roles for both men and women to play.

Throughout the narrative, the third-person narrator appears to side with the ladies' point of view towards the events, imitating their language and adopting their reasoning. The narrator takes their opinions and presents them as objective fact, as when it is said of one of the women in the town, "she never understood anything." As the story develops and the women's tyrannization over Lily becomes more obvious, however, a reader cannot help but notice ironic parallels between their ideas of marriage and confinement in a madhouse. Lily's retardation means that the women can bribe her into going to Ellisville by offering to give her presents for her bridal "hope chest" and threatening to refuse to give her anything if she goes through with her plan to marry the xylophonist, but the fact that Lily and her lady's hope chest will be sent to Ellisville suggests an ironic link between getting married and getting institutionalized in an insane asylum. How different, in fact, is Mrs. Carson's and Mrs. Watts's position? After all, they are dependent on an institution for their status, possessions, power, and even their names. Welty's story raises this question, but her readers are the only ones who hear it asked; Mrs. Carson and Mrs. Watts certainly do not, nor do the townspeople. They greet the train that will carry Lily to Ellisville and even arrange for a band to play a comically inappropriate piece called the "Independence March" to honor Lily's departure.

The story of Lily Daw of course turns out differently from what the three ladies expect: the xylophonist shows up in the crowd at the last minute, just as the train is about to pull out of the station, and Aimee Slocum defects and decides to rescue Lily, eventually persuading her to give up her "gift" of the train ride to Ellisville. Lily's seeming passivity and shyness during this final scene should not mislead us: Lily's own earlier acts of rebellion in the story have apparently awakened Aimee's own dormant sense of independence, and she arranges a reunion that seems to force the ladies of Victory to accept Lily's marrying the man she loves as the "right" and "proper" ending. Even Mrs. Watts must smile and greet the musician cordially.

Yet Welty's story leaves several issues unresolved, repressed for the sake of the comic ending and the narrative's gentle mockery of the three ladies. The first is the fact of Lily's anger. It surfaces only once in the story, when Lily lashes out at Aimee Slocum's ugliness, but it is ever-present and powerful, just as male power is. We feel it in Lily's flight from the ladies and in her frenzied efforts to gather her belongings together when they finally catch up with her at her house and entrap her. We also sense it in Welty's description of Lily's house, the first of many Gothic portraits of decrepit and rambling houses of women in *A Curtain of Green*. The house lacks front steps, as if it, like Lily, will not easily accommodate visitors from the town, and it "leaned steeply to one side, toward the railroad," as if desiring to flee. (This latter detail was added when Welty revised the story, thus drawing its hidden undercurrents closer to the surface.)

The second issue that the comic ending of the story does not confront is the question of why Mrs. Carson and Mrs. Watts suddenly capitulate to Aimee Slocum's demands and let Lily marry. They seem startled by the musician's presence and Aimee's unprecedented resoluteness, but why should they not simply override Aimee, as they often have before? One answer that suggests itself is that they are afraid that they may be sending a pregnant woman to Ellisville; once the musician appears they realize that marrying Lily off may very well be the safer course. Another is that they realize that their power over Lily once she is married may very well increase rather than diminish. Mrs. Carson's first comment when she sees Lily's future husband in the crowd, before they have agreed to let Lily get off the train ("Mercy! He's small, isn't he?"), implies a victory for the ladies of Victory: Lily may yet be forced to conform to the standards of the "fathers" for being a lady. Despite her sometimes unconventional behavior and instinctive distrust of the three ladies, Lily has fully absorbed her society's standards for what a proper lady is: her treasured hope chest contains two bars of soap and a washcloth, and she is delighted when the ladies promise her other items associated with proper femininity, such as a Bible, hemstitched pillowcases, and a brassiere. The most revealing gift the women have bestowed on Lily is associated with mourning, not marriage: throughout the story Mrs. Watts wears "widow's black," and the dress she gives Lily to cover up the petticoat Lily prefers wearing in public is "made out of part of Mrs. Watts's last summer's mourning." Lily thus wears second-hand mourning to her wedding. There is something funereal about everything the three ladies do, in spite of their frantic energy, and the rite of marriage as they conceive it is more an act of entombment than of metamorphosis.

The complexities of the story's comic ending parallel the complexities of the story's narrative voice. Standard critical labels that may be used to define the narrative voice, such as "third-person" and "omniscient," are misleading. Recently the work of M. M. Bakhtin has advanced beyond Wayne Booth's classic *The Rhetoric of Fiction,* teaching us new ways of conceiving of the ironic play of meanings possible within a "third-person" voice. We must learn to notice the irony and the unspoken in Welty's narrative voices in *A Curtain of Green* and her later fiction; in Bakhtin's sense, these narrative voices are always dialogical, ironically quoting the language of social authority so that it can be questioned, can be engaged in dialogue rather than treated as a monologue. Apparent praise of the "fathers" (or of the ladies) is thus not necessarily praise. Just as importantly, we must learn to see how "omniscient" narrators in Welty always have blind spots and that the alleged unity of her "third-person" narrators is in practice fractured and multivocal. Indeed, Welty's third-person narrators are really no more unified than the "three ladies" in "Lily Daw": they may appear to speak in a single voice, but actually they are in perpetual contention with themselves and with opposing voices such as Lily's that they can so vividly imagine.

8

AN ALBUM
OF SHORT FICTION

STRATEGIES FOR CLOSE READING
AND INTERPRETATION OF STORIES IN THIS ALBUM

The following stories represent a variety of approaches to short fiction. Working with these stories will be more interesting if you keep the following suggestions in mind as you read.

Annotate the Stories

This means underlining the passages you think are important to developing a deeper understanding of the story. By underlining or highlighting as you go along, you will make it easier for yourself to see what is important and to review the entire story once you finish it.

Write Down Your Questions for Close Reading

Keep a list of questions for close reading as you read the stories. Try to develop questions similar to the ones you have seen in stories above. Consider this checklist for questions:

- Ask yourself what the title means. In Mary Lavin's "Happiness," for example, you might decide that part of the theme of the story will deal with happiness, just as Anton Chekhov's story "Concerning Love" will treat the theme of love.

- Question the setting of the story and ask yourself how the setting establishes a mood or a tone for the story. Is the setting urban or rural? Is it contemporary or historical? Is it marked by political issues, such as unequal economic opportunity or ideological struggles?

- Who is telling the story and what do you learn about the narrator? Is the narrator reliable or does the narrator seem to distort the story for his or her own benefit? Is the story about the narrator, as in Charlotte Perkins Gilman's "The Yellow Wallpa-per," or about a character in the story, as in Richard Ford's "Communist"? What kind of voice does the narrator have?

- Ask yourself about the style of the story. Is it told in dialogue, as in Eudora Welty's "Lily Daw and the Three Ladies"? Or is it carefully descriptive, as in Sarah Orne Jewett's "The White Heron"? Is the story marked by careful comparisons, symbols, or metaphors, as in Welty's "A Worn Path"?

- Is the plot or narrative the most important aspect of the story? In Edgar Allan Poe's "The Masque of the Red Death," individual characters seem less important than what happens to all of them. Is that the case in the story you are reading? How carefully shaped is the plot? Is the story a "slice of life" story in which the narra-tive is revealing, but not necessarily central, as for instance in Raymond Carver's "Night School"?

- Is the story ironic in tone? In James Joyce's "Araby," the unnamed boy finds that his long-awaited visit to an exotic bazaar is so disappointing that he thinks of himself in an ironic fashion, accusing himself of vanity. There is irony in this story, but not necessarily where the boy thinks it is.

- Always look for the ways in which the elements of the short story work together. In a story such as D. H. Lawrence's "The Horse-Dealer's Daughter," the elements fuse into one, with setting, character, plot, and tone all functioning at high levels to make the touching ending significant.

Questions for Interpretation of Stories in the Album

- Look for patterns of repetition: items that show up often, such as birds, clouds, flowers, or other details. They may have a symbolic significance, as in Hawthorne's "Rappaccini's Daughter."

- Look also for repeated actions, such as the repetition of different swimming pools in John Cheever's "The Swimmer." These actions may give a clue to the inner mean-ing of the story.

- Observe the nature of the narrator or the main character in the story. Ask yourself what he or she is like and whether you can truly rely on what the character says or reports. Is the protagonist emotionally stable? If unstable, do we know why? Is the protagonist a victim of someone else's actions?

- What are the gender issues in the story? Is the theme of the story connected to rigid expectations of gender behavior? Is the situation in the story dependent on un-derstanding how the characters accept their attitudes toward gender, as in Becky Birtha's "Johnnieruth"? Or in Ann Beattie's "The Cinderella Waltz"?

- Are there cultural issues dominating the story? David Wong Louie's "Pangs of Love" and Jhumpa Lahiri's "Interpreter of Maladies" both reveal certain cultural expec-tations that are frustrated by circumstances. That is true, too; of Bharati Mukherjee's "Jasmine."

- What are the economic issues at stake in the story? In Poe's "Masque of the Red Death," the economic independence of the courtiers makes it possible to do what they do. Is it important to know that they did not try to help their poorer brethren?

- Is the most interesting aspect of the story connected to its setting in time? Is the story interesting because of its historical setting, as in Kate Chopin's "The Story of an Hour"? What role does history play in the story?

By reviewing these questions as you read the stories that follow, you will have a good chance of being able to provide yourself with excellent opportunities for close reading and good interpretations. These are stories by some of the world's best writers. They are meant to be enjoyed.

SARAH ORNE JEWETT (1849–1909)

Sarah Orne Jewett was born in South Berwick, Maine, close to the Atlantic Ocean, and has long been regarded as one of the most interesting American writers of local color. Her characters are drawn from the tight-lipped New England people who were her neighbors. Her most famous books are Deep Haven *(1877), her first collection of short stories, and* The Country of the Pointed Firs and Other Stories *(1896). Because she lived close to Boston, the center of publishing during her lifetime, her early work received notice and established her as an important writer early in her career.*

A White Heron _____ 1886

The woods were already filled with shadows one June evening, just before eight o'clock, though a bright sunset still glimmered faintly among the trunks of the trees. A little girl was driving home her cow, a plodding, dilatory, provoking creature in her behavior, but a valued companion for all that. They were going away from the western light, and striking deep into the dark woods, but their feet were familiar with the path, and it was no matter whether their eyes could see it or not.

There was hardly a night the summer through when the old cow could be found waiting at the pasture bars; on the contrary, it was her greatest pleasure to hide herself away among the high huckleberry bushes, and though she wore a loud bell she had made the discovery that if one stood perfectly still it would not ring. So Sylvia had to hunt for her until she found her, and call Co'! Co'! with never an answering Moo, until her childish patience was quite spent. If the creature had not given good milk and plenty of it, the case would have seemed very different to her owners. Besides, Sylvia had all the time there was, and very little use to make of it. Sometimes in pleasant weather it was a consolation to look upon the cow's pranks as an intelligent attempt to play hide and seek, and as the child had no playmates she lent herself to this amusement with a good deal of zest. Though this chase had been so long that the wary animal herself had given an unusual signal of her whereabouts, Sylvia had only laughed when she came upon Mistress Moolly at the swamp-side, and urged her affectionately homeward with a twig of birch leaves. The old cow was not inclined to wander further, she even turned in the right direction for once as they left the pasture, and stepped along the road at a good pace. She was quite ready to be milked now, and seldom stopped to browse.

Sylvia wondered what her grandmother would say because they were so late. It was a great while since she had left home at half-past five o'clock, but everybody knew the difficulty of making this errand a short one. Mrs. Tilley had chased the horned torment too many summer evenings herself to blame any one else for lingering, and was only thankful as she waited that she had Sylvia, nowadays, to give such valuable assistance. The good woman suspected that Sylvia loitered occasionally on her own account; there never was such a child for straying about out-of-doors since the world was made! Everybody said that it was a good change for a little maid who had tried to grow for eight years in a crowded manufacturing town, but, as for Sylvia herself, it seemed as if she never had been alive at all before she came to live at the farm. She thought often with wistful compassion of a wretched dry geranium that belonged to a town neighbor.

" 'Afraid of folks,' " old Mrs. Tilley said to herself, with a smile, after she had made the unlikely choice of Sylvia from her daughter's houseful of children, and was returning to the farm. " 'Afraid of folks,' they said! I guess she won't be troubled no great with 'em up to the old place!" When they reached the door of the lonely house and stopped to unlock it, and the cat came to purr loudly, and rub against them, a deserted pussy, indeed, but fat with young robins, Sylvia whispered that this was a beautiful place to live in, and she never should wish to go home.

The companions followed the shady wood-road, the cow taking slow steps, and the   5 child very fast ones. The cow stopped long at the brook to drink, as if the pasture were not half a swamp, and Sylvia stood still and waited, letting her bare feet cool themselves in the shoal water, while the great twilight moths struck softly against her. She waded on through the brook as the cow moved away, and listened to the thrushes with a heart that beat fast with pleasure. There was a stirring in the great boughs overhead. They were full of little birds and beasts that seemed to be wide awake, and going about their world, or else saying good-night to each other in sleepy twitters. Sylvia herself felt sleepy as she walked along. However, it was not much farther to the house, and the air was soft and sweet. She was not often in the woods so late as this, and it made her feel as if she were a part of the gray shadows and the moving leaves. She was just thinking how long it seemed since she first came to the farm a year ago, and wondering if everything went on in the noisy town just the same as when she was there; she thought of the great red-faced boy who used to chase and frighten her made her hurry along the path to escape from the shadow of the trees.

Suddenly this little woods-girl is horror-stricken to hear a clear whistle not very far away. Not a bird's-whistle, which would have a sort of friendliness, but a boy's whistle, determined, and somewhat aggressive. Sylvia left the cow to whatever sad fate might await her, and stepped discreetly aside into the bushes, but she was just too late. The enemy had discovered her, and called out in a very cheerful and persuasive tone, "Halloa, little girl, how far is it to the road?" and trembling Sylvia answered almost inaudibly, "A good ways."

She did not dare to look boldly at the tall young man, who carried a gun over his shoulder, but she came out of her bush and again followed the cow, while he walked alongside.

"I have been hunting for some birds," the stranger said kindly, "and I have lost my way, and need a friend very much. Don't be afraid," he added gallantly. "Speak up and tell me what your name is, and whether you think I can spend the night at your house, and go out gunning early in the morning."

Sylvia was more alarmed than before. Would not her grandmother consider her much to blame? But who could have foreseen such an accident as this? It did not seem to be her fault, and she hung her head as if the stem of it were broken, but managed to answer "Sylvy," with much effort when her companion again asked her name.

Mrs. Tilley was standing in the doorway when the trio came into view. The cow gave   10 a loud moo by way of explanation.

"Yes, you'd better speak up for yourself, you old trial! Where'd she tucked herself away this time, Sylvy?" But Sylvia kept an awed silence; she knew by instinct that her grandmother did not comprehend the gravity of the situation. She must be mistaking the stranger for one of the farmer-lads of the region.

The young man stood his gun beside the door, and dropped a lumpy game-bag beside it; then he bade Mrs. Tilley good-evening, and repeated his wayfarer's story, and asked if he could have a night's lodging.

"Put me anywhere you like," he said. "I must be off early in the morning, before day; but I am very hungry, indeed. You can give me some milk at any rate, that's plain."

"Dear sakes, yes," responded the hostess, whose long slumbering hospitality seemed to be easily awakened. "You might fare better if you went out on the main road a mile or so, but you're welcome to what we've got. I'll milk right off, and you make yourself at home. You can sleep on husks or feathers," she proffered graciously. "I raised them all myself. There's good pasturing for geese just below here towards the ma'sh. Now step round and set a plate for the gentlemen, Sylvy!" And Sylvia promptly stepped. She was glad to have something to do, and she was hungry herself.

It was a surprise to find so clean and comfortable a little dwelling in this New   15
England wilderness. The young man had known the horrors of its most primitive house-keeping, and the dreary squalor of that level of society which does not rebel at the companionship of hens. This was the best thrift of an old-fashioned farmstead, though on such a small scale that it seemed like a hermitage. He listened eagerly to the old woman's quaint talk, he watched Sylvia's pale face and shining gray eyes with ever growing enthusiasm, and insisted that this was the best supper he had eaten for a month; and afterward the new-made friends sat down in the door-way together while the moon came up.

Soon it would be berry-time, and Sylvia was a great help at picking. The cow was a good milker, though a plaguy thing to keep track of, the hostess gossiped frankly, adding presently that she had buried four children, so Sylvia's mother, and a son (who might be dead) in California were all the children she had left. "Dan, my boy, was a great hand to go gunning," she explained sadly. "I never wanted for pa'tridges or gray squer'ls while he was to home. He's been a great wand'rer, I expect, and he's no hand to write letters. There, I don't blame him, I'd ha' seen the world myself if it had been so I could."

"Sylvy takes after him," the grandmother continued affectionately, after a minute's pause. "There ain't a foot o' ground she don't know her way over, and the wild creaturs counts her one o' themselves. Squer'ls she'll tame to come an' feed right out o' her hands, and all sorts o' birds. Last winter she got the jay birds to bangeing here, and I believe she'd 'a' scanted herself of her own meals to have plenty to throw out amongst 'em, if I hadn't kep' watch. Anything but crows, I tell her, I'm willin' to help support— though Dan he had a tamed one o' them that did seem to have reason same as folks. It was round here a good spell after he went away. Dan an' his father they didn't hitch,— but he never held up his head ag'in after Dan had dared him an' gone off."

The guest did not notice this hint of family sorrows in his eager interest in something else.

"So Sylvy knows all about birds, does she?" he exclaimed, as he looked around at the little girl who sat, very demure but increasingly sleepy, in the moonlight. "I am making a collection of birds myself. I have been at it ever since I was a boy." (Mrs. Tilley smiled.) "There are two or three very rare ones I have been hunting for these five years. I mean to get them on my own ground if they can be found."

"Do you cage 'em up?" asked Mrs. Tilley doubtfully, in response to this enthusi-   20
astic announcement.

"Oh, no, they're stuffed and preserved, dozens and dozens of them," said the ornithologist, "and I have shot or snared every one myself. I caught a glimpse of a white heron three miles from here on Saturday, and I have followed it in this direction. They have never been found in this district at all. The little white heron, it is," and he turned again to look at Sylvia with the hope of discovering that the rare bird was one of her acquaintances.

But Sylvia was watching a hop-toad in the narrow footpath.

"You would know the heron if you saw it," the stranger continued eagerly. "A queer tall white bird with soft feathers and long thin legs. And it would have a nest perhaps in the top of a high tree, made of sticks, something like a hawk's nest."

Sylvia's heart gave a wild beat; she knew that strange white bird, and had once stolen softly near where it stood in some bright green swamp grass, away over at the other side of the woods. There was an open place where the sunshine always seemed strangely yellow and hot, where tall, nodding rushes grew, and her grandmother had warned her that she might sink in the soft black mud underneath and never be heard of more. Not far beyond were the salt marshes just this side the sea itself, which Sylvia wondered and dreamed about, but never had seen, whose great voice could sometimes be heard above the noise of the woods on stormy nights.

"I can't think of anything I should like so much as to find that heron's nest," the   25
handsome stranger was saying. "I would give ten dollars to anybody who could show it to me," he added desperately, "and I mean to spend my whole vacation hunting for it if need be. Perhaps it was only migrating, or had been chased out of its own region by some bird of prey."

Mrs. Tilley gave amazed attention to all this, but Sylvia still watched the toad, not divining, as she might have done at some calmer time, that the creature wished to get to its hole under the door-step, and was much hindered by the unusual spectators at that hour of the evening. No amount of thought, that night, could decide how many wished-for treasures the ten dollars, so lightly spoken of, would buy.

The next day the young sportsman hovered about the woods, and Sylvia kept him company, having lost her first fear of the friendly lad, who proved to be most kind and sympathetic. He told her many things about the birds and what they knew and where they lived and what they did with themselves. And he gave her a jack-knife, which she thought as great a treasure as if she were a desert-islander. All day long he did not once make her troubled or afraid except when he brought down some unsuspecting singing creature from its bough. Sylvia would have liked him vastly better without his gun; she could not understand why he killed the very birds he seemed to like so much. But as the day waned, Sylvia still watched the young man with loving admiration. She had never seen anybody so charming and delightful; the woman's heart, asleep in the child, was vaguely thrilled by a dream of love. Some premonition of that great power stirred and swayed these young creatures who traversed the solemn woodlands with soft-footed silent care. They stopped to listen to a bird's song; they pressed forward again eagerly, parting the branches—speaking to each other rarely and in whispers; the young man going first and Sylvia following, fascinated, a few steps behind, with her gray eyes dark with excitement.

She grieved because the longed-for white heron was elusive, but she did not lead the guest, she only followed, and there was no such thing as speaking first. The sound of her own unquestioned voice would have terrified her—it was hard enough to answer yes or no when there was need of that. At last evening began to fall, and they drove the cow together, and Sylvia smiled with pleasure when they came to the place where she heard the whistle and was afraid only the night before.

II

Half a mile from home, at the farther edge of the woods, where the land was highest, a great pine-tree stood, the last of its generation. Whether it was left for a boundary mark, or for what reason, no one could say; the woodchoppers who had felled its mates were dead and gone long ago, and a whole forest of sturdy trees, pines and oaks and maples, had grown again. But the stately head of this old pine towered above them all and made a landmark for sea and shore miles and miles away. Sylvia knew it well. She had always believed that whoever climbed to the top of it could see the ocean; and the little girl had often laid her hand on the great rough trunk and looked up wistfully at those dark boughs that the wind always stirred, no matter how hot and still the air might be below. Now she thought of the tree with a new excitement, for why, if one climbed it at break of day, could not one see all the world, and easily discover from whence the white heron flew, and mark the place, and find the hidden nest?

What a spirit of adventure, what wild ambition! What fancied triumph and de-   30 light and glory for the later morning when she could make known the secret! It was almost too real and too great for the childish heart to bear.

All night the door of the little house stood open, and the whippoorwills came and sang upon the very step. The young sportsman and his old hostess were sound asleep, but Sylvia's great design kept her broad awake and watching. She forgot to think of sleep. The short summer night seemed as long as the winter darkness, and at least when the whippoorwills ceased, and she was afraid the morning would after all come too soon, she stole out of the house and followed the pasture path through the woods, hastening toward the open ground beyond, listening with a sense of comfort and companionship to the drowsy twitter of a half-awakened bird, whose perch she had jarred in passing. Alas, if the great wave of human interest which flooded for the first time this dull little life should sweep away the satisfactions of an existence heart to heart with nature and the dumb life of the forest!

There was the huge tree asleep yet in the paling moonlight, and small and silly Sylvia began with utmost bravery to mount to the top of it, with tingling, eager blood coursing the channels of her whole frame, with her bare feet and fingers, that pinched and held like bird's claws to the monstrous ladder reaching up, up, almost to the sky itself. First she must mount the white oak tree that grew alongside, where she was almost lost among the dark branches and the green leaves heavy and wet with dew; a bird fluttered off its nest, and a red squirrel ran to and fro and scolded pettishly at the harmless housebreaker. Sylvia felt her way easily. She had often climbed there, and knew that higher still one of the oak's upper branches chafed against the pine trunk, just where its lower boughs were set close together. There, when she made the dangerous pass from one tree to the other, the great enterprise would really begin.

She crept out along the swaying oak limb at last, and took the daring step across into the old pine-tree. The way was harder than she thought; she must reach far and hold fast, the sharp dry twigs caught and held her and scratched her like angry talons, the pitch made her thin little fingers clumsy and stiff as she went round and round the tree's great stem, higher and higher upward. The sparrows and robins in the woods below were beginning to wake and twitter to the dawn, yet it seemed much lighter there aloft in the pine tree, and the child knew that she must hurry if her project were to be of any use.

The tree seemed to lengthen itself out as she went up, and to reach farther and farther upward. It was like a great main-mast to the voyaging earth; it must truly have been amazed that morning through all its ponderous frame as it felt this determined spark of human spirit wending its way from higher branch to branch. Who knows how steadily the least twigs held themselves to advantage this light, weak creature on her way! The old pine must have loved his new dependent. More than all the hawks, and bats, and moths, and even the sweet voiced thrushes, was the brave, beating heart of the solitary gray-eyed child. And the tree stood still and frowned away the winds that June morning while the dawn grew bright in the east.

Sylvia's face was like a pale star, if one had seen it from the ground, when the last thorny bough was past, and she stood trembling and tired but wholly triumphant, high in the tree-top. Yes, there was the sea with the dawning sun making a golden dazzle over it, and toward that glorious east flew two hawks with slow-moving pinions. How low they looked in the air from that height when one had only seen them before far up, and dark against the blue sky. Their gray feathers were as soft as moths; they seemed only a little way from the tree, and Sylvia felt as if she too could go flying away among the clouds. Westward, the woodlands and farms reached miles and miles into the distance; here and there were church steeples, and white villages; truly it was a vast and awesome world!   35

The birds sang louder and louder. At last the sun came up bewilderingly bright. Sylvia could see the white sails of ships out at sea, and the clouds that were purple and rose-colored and yellow at first began to fade away. Where was the white heron's nest in the sea of green branches, and was this wonderful sight and pageant of the world the only reward for having climbed to such a giddy height? Now look down again, Sylvia, where the green marsh is set among the shining birches and dark hemlocks; there where you saw the white heron once you will see him again; look, look! a white spot of him like a single floating feather comes up from the dead hemlock and grows larger, and rises, and comes close at last, and goes by the landmark pine with steady sweep of wing and outstretched slender neck and crested head. And wait! wait! do not move a foot or a finger, little girl, do not send an arrow of light and consciousness from your two eager eyes, for the heron has perched on a pine bough not far beyond yours, and cries back to his mate on the nest and plumes his feathers for the new day!

The child gives a long sigh a minute later when a company of shouting cat-birds comes also to the tree, and vexed by their fluttering and lawlessness the solemn heron goes away. She knows his secret now, the wild, light, slender bird that floats and wavers, and goes back like an arrow presently to his home in the green world beneath. Then Sylvia, well satisfied, makes her perilous way down again, not daring to look far below the branch she stands on, ready to cry sometimes because her fingers ache and her lamed feet slip. Wondering over and over again what the stranger would say to her, and what he would think of when she told him how to find his way straight to the heron's nest.

"Sylvy, Sylvy!" called the busy old grandmother again and again, but nobody answered, and the small husk bed was empty, and Sylvia had disappeared.

The guest waked from a dream, and remembering his day's pleasure hurried to dress himself that it might sooner begin. He was sure from the way the shy little girl looked once or twice yesterday that she had at least seen the white heron, and now she must really be made to tell. Here she comes now, paler than ever, and her worn old frock is torn and tattered, and smeared with pine pitch. The grandmother and the sportsman stand in the door together and question her, and the splendid moment has come to speak of the dead hemlock-tree by the green marsh.

But Sylvia does not speak after all, though the old grandmother fretfully rebukes her, and the young man's kind appealing eyes are looking straight in her own. He can make them rich with money; he has promised it, and they are poor now. He is so well worth making happy, and he waits to hear the story she can tell.

40

No, she must keep silence! What is it that suddenly forbids her and makes her dumb? Has she been nine years growing, and now, when the great world for the first time puts out a hand to her, must she thrust it aside for a bird's sake? The murmur of the pine's green branches is in her ears, she remembers how the white heron came flying through the golden air and how they watched the sea and the morning together, and Sylvia cannot speak; she cannot tell the heron's secret and give its life away.

Dear loyalty, that suffered a sharp pang as the guest went away disappointed later in the day, that could have served and followed him and loved him as a dog loves! Many a night Sylvia heard the echo of his whistle haunting the pasture path as she came home with the loitering cow. She forgot even her sorrow at the sharp report of his gun and the piteous sight of thrushes and sparrows dropping silent to the ground, their songs hushed and their pretty feathers stained and wet with blood. Were the birds better friends than their hunter might have been,—who can tell? Whatever treasures were lost to her, woodlands and summertime, remember! Bring your gifts and graces and tell your secrets to this lonely country child!

JAMES JOYCE (1882–1941)

Born in Dublin on February 2, 1882, James Joyce became the ranking English-language novelist of the twentieth century. His short stories appeared in a volume called Dubliners *in 1914, but the path to their publication was problematic. He began the stories in 1904, publishing the first of them in a new journal called* The Irish Homestead *and using the nom de plume Stephen Daedalus (later Dedalus) for the first three stories. The first printing of* Dubliners *in 1906 was destroyed because of fear of libel over Joyce's realistic technique of referring to actual businesses by their name.*

Joyce's method was to create in painstaking detail the realistic surfaces of experience in his stories. He is known for the use of stream of consciousness—the direct recording of his characters' thoughts. "Araby" reveals the main character's inner life most thoroughly.

Araby _____ *1914*

North Richmond Street, being blind,° was a quiet street except at the hour when the Christian Brothers' School set the boys free. An uninhabited house of two stories stood at the blind end, detached from its neighbors in a square ground. The other houses of the street, conscious of decent lives within them, gazed at one another with brown imperturbable faces.

blind: a dead-end street

The former tenant of our house, a priest, had died in the back drawing-room. Air, musty from having been long enclosed, hung in all the rooms, and the waste room behind the kitchen was littered with old useless papers. Among these I found a few paper-covered books, the pages of which were curled and damp: *The Abbot,*° by Walter Scott, *The Devout Communicant* and *The Memoirs of Vidocq.*° I liked the last best because its leaves were yellow. The wild garden behind the house contained a central apple-tree and a few straggling bushes under one of which I found the late tenant's rusty bicycle-pump. He had been a very charitable priest; in his will he had left all his money to institutions and the furniture of his house to his sister.

When the short days of winter came dusk fell before we had well eaten our dinners. When we met in the street the houses had grown somber. The space of sky above us was the color of ever-changing violet and towards it the lamps of the street lifted their feeble lanterns. The cold air stung us and we played till our bodies glowed. Our shouts echoed in the silent street. The career of our play brought us through the dark muddy lanes behind the houses where we ran the gauntlet of the rough tribes from the cottages, to the back doors of the dark dripping gardens where odors arose from the ashpits, to the dark odorous stables where a coachman smoothed and combed the horse or shook music from the buckled harness. When we returned to the street light from the kitchen windows had filled the areas. If my uncle was seen turning the corner we hid in the shadow until we had seen him safely housed. Or if Mangan's sister came out on the doorstep to call her brother in to his tea we watched her from our shadow peer up and down the street. We waited to see whether she would remain or go in and, if she remained, we left our shadow and walked up to Mangan's steps resignedly. She was waiting for us, her figure defined by the light from the half-opened door. Her brother always teased her before he obeyed and I stood by the railings looking at her. Her dress swung as she moved her body and the soft rope of her hair tossed from side to side.

Every morning I lay on the floor in the front parlor watching her door. The blind was pulled down to within an inch of the sash so that I could not be seen. When she came out on the doorstep my heart leaped. I ran to the hall, seized my books and followed her. I kept her brown figure always in my eye and, when we came near the point at which our ways diverged, I quickened my pace and passed her. This happened morning after morning. I had never spoken to her, except for a few casual words, and yet her name was like a summons to all my foolish blood.

Her image accompanied me even in places the most hostile to romance. On Saturday evenings when my aunt went marketing I had to go to carry some of the parcels. We walked through the flaring streets, jostled by drunken men and bargaining women, amid the curses of laborers, the shrill litanies of shop-boys who stood on guard by the barrels of pigs' cheeks, the nasal chanting of street-singers, who sang a *come-all-you* about O'Donovan Rossa,° or a ballad about the troubles in our native land. These noises converged in a single sensation of life for me: I imagined that I bore my chalice safely through a throng of foes. Her name sprang to my lips at moments in strange prayers and praises which I myself did not understand. My eyes were often full of tears (I could not tell why) and at times a flood from my heart seemed to pour itself out into my bosom. I thought little of the future. I did not know whether I would ever speak to her or not

5

The Abbot: a popular historical romance by Sir Walter Scott (1771–1832)   *The Devout Communicant:* a book of meditations   *The Memoirs of Vidocq:* a story based on the life of a Paris police detective   *O'Donovan Rossa:* a leader of the Fenians, a secret revolutionary group formed in New York and Ireland to free Ireland from British rule

or, if I spoke to her, how I could tell her of my confused adoration. But my body was like a harp and her words and gestures were like fingers running upon the wires.

One evening I went into the back drawing-room in which the priest had died. It was a dark rainy evening and there was no sound in the house. Through one of the broken panes I heard the rain impinge upon the earth, the fine incessant needles of water playing in the sodden beds. Some distant lamp or lighted window gleamed below me. I was thankful that I could see so little. All my senses seemed to desire to veil themselves and, feeling that I was about to slip from them, I pressed the palms of my hands together until they trembled, murmuring: "*O love! O love!*" many times.

At last she spoke to me. When she addressed the first words to me I was so confused that I did not know what to answer. She asked me was I going to *Araby.*° I forgot whether I answered yes or no. It would be a splendid bazaar, she said; she would love to go.

"And why can't you?" I asked.

While she spoke she turned a silver bracelet round and round her wrist. She could not go, she said, because there would be a retreat that week in her convent. Her brother and two other boys were fighting for their caps and I was alone at the railings. She held one of the spikes, bowing her head towards me. The light from the lamp opposite our door caught the white curve of her neck, lit up her hair that rested there and, falling, lit up the hand upon the railing. It fell over one side of her dress and caught the white border of a petticoat, just visible as she stood at ease.

"It's well for you," she said.   10

"If I go," I said, "I will bring you something."

What innumerable follies laid waste my waking and sleeping thoughts after that evening! I wished to annihilate the tedious intervening days. I chafed against the work of school. At night in my bedroom and by day in the classroom her image came between me and the page I strove to read. The syllables of the word *Araby* were called to me through the silence in which my soul luxuriated and cast an Eastern enchantment over me. I asked for leave to go to the bazaar on Saturday night. My aunt was surprised and hoped it was not some Freemason° affair. I answered few questions in class. I watched my master's face pass from amiability to sternness; he hoped I was not beginning to idle. I could not call my wandering thoughts together. I had hardly any patience with the serious work of life which, now that it stood between me and my desire, seemed to me child's play, ugly monotonous child's play.

On Saturday morning I reminded my uncle that I wished to go to the bazaar in the evening. He was fussing at the hallstand, looking for the hat-brush, and answered me curtly:

"Yes, boy, I know."

As he was in the hall I could not go into the front parlor and lie at the window. I   15
felt the house in bad humor and walked slowly towards the school. The air was pitilessly raw and already my heart misgave me.

When I came home to dinner my uncle had not yet been home. Still it was early. I sat staring at the clock for some time and, when its ticking began to irritate me, I left the room. I mounted the staircase and gained the upper part of the house. The high cold empty gloomy rooms liberated me and I went from room to room singing. From the front window I saw my companions playing below in the street. Their cries reached

Araby: a bazaar that was held in Dublin in May 1894. The attraction was its oriental (therefore exotic and romantic) theme   *Freemason:* a secret international Protestant brotherhood emphasizing charity and mutual aid

me weakened and indistinct and, leaning my forehead against the cool glass, I looked over at the dark house where she lived. I may have stood there for an hour, seeing nothing but the brown-clad figure cast by my imagination, touched discreetly by the lamplight at the curved neck, at the hand upon the railings and at the border below the dress.

When I came downstairs again I found Mrs. Mercer sitting at the fire. She was an old garrulous woman, a pawnbroker's widow, who collected used stamps for some pious purpose. I had to endure the gossip of the tea-table. The meal was prolonged beyond an hour and still my uncle did not come. Mrs. Mercer stood up to go: she was sorry she couldn't wait any longer, but it was after eight o'clock and she did not like to be out late, as the night air was bad for her. When she had gone I began to walk up and down the room, clenching my fists. My aunt said:

"I'm afraid you may put off your bazaar for this night of Our Lord."

At nine o'clock I heard my uncle's latchkey in the halldoor. I heard him talking to himself and heard the hallstand rocking when it had received the weight of his overcoat. I could interpret these signs. When he was midway through his dinner I asked him to give me the money to go to the bazaar. He had forgotten.

"The people are in bed and after their first sleep now," he said.   20

I did not smile. My aunt said to him energetically:

"Can't you give him the money and let him go? You've kept him late enough as it is."

My uncle said he was very sorry he had forgotten. He said he believed in the old saying: "All work and no play makes Jack a dull boy." He asked me where I was going and, when I had told him a second time he asked me did I know *The Arab's Farewell to his Steed.* When I left the kitchen he was about to recite the opening lines of the piece to my aunt.

I held a florin tightly in my hand as I strode down Buckingham Street towards the station. The sight of the streets thronged with buyers and glaring with gas recalled to me the purpose of my journey. I took my seat in a third-class carriage of a deserted train. After an intolerable delay the train moved out of the station slowly. It crept onward among ruinous houses and over the twinkling river. At Westland Row Station a crowd of people pressed to the carriage doors; but the porters moved them back, saying that it was a special train for the bazaar. I remained alone in the bare carriage. In a few minutes the train drew up beside an improvised wooden platform. I passed out on to the road and saw by the lighted dial of a clock that it was ten minutes to ten. In front of me was a large building which displayed the magical name.

I could not find any sixpenny entrance and, fearing that the bazaar would be   25
closed, I passed in quickly through a turnstile, handing a shilling to a weary-looking man. I found myself in a big hall girdled at half its height by a gallery. Nearly all the stalls were closed and the greater part of the hall was in darkness. I recognized a silence like that which pervades a church after a service. I walked into the center of the bazaar timidly. A few people were gathered about the stalls which were still open. Before a curtain, over which the words *Café Chantant* were written in colored lamps, two men were counting money on a salver. I listened to the fall of the coins.

Remembering with difficulty why I had come I went over to one of the stalls and examined porcelain vases and flowered tea-sets. At the door of the stall a young lady was talking and laughing with two young gentlemen. I remarked their English accents and listened vaguely to their conversation.

"O, I never said such a thing!"

"O, but you did!"

"O, but I didn't!"

"Didn't she say that?"   30

"Yes. I heard her."

"O, there's a . . . fib!"

Observing me the young lady came over and asked me did I wish to buy anything. The tone of her voice was not encouraging; she seemed to have spoken to me out of a sense of duty. I looked humbly at the great jars that stood like eastern guards at either side of the dark entrance to the stall and murmured:

"No, thank you."

The young lady changed the position of one of the vases and went back to the two   35
young men. They began to talk of the same subject. Once or twice the young lady glanced at me over her shoulder.

I lingered before her stall, though I knew my stay was useless, to make my interest in her wares seem the more real. Then I turned away slowly and walked down the middle of the bazaar. I allowed the two pennies to fall against the sixpence in my pocket. I heard a voice call from one end of the gallery that the light was out. The upper part of the hall was now completely dark.

Gazing up into the darkness I saw myself as a creature driven and derided by vanity; and my eyes burned with anguish and anger.

FRANZ KAFKA   (1883–1924)

Kafka, famous for novels in which unknown forces persecute his protagonists, was born in Prague, to a family in which his father was an overbearing shopkeeper. Kafka wrote a letter that he never sent in which he blamed his father for having stunted his life and having made it all but impossible for him to have an independent life and family of his own. He began writing early but received no support from his family. Much of his life he supported himself by working in an insurance company. The stress of trying to write and also keep his job eventually undid him. He died of tuberculosis, which had weakened him much of his life. He is best known for two novels published after he died: The Trial *(1925) and* The Castle *(1926).*

A Hunger Artist _____ *1924*

Translated by Willa and Edwin Muir

During these last decades the interest in professional fasting has markedly diminished. It used to pay very well to stage such great performances under one's own management, but today that is quite impossible. We live in a different world now. At one time the whole town took a lively interest in the hunger artist; from day to day of his fast the excitement mounted; everybody wanted to see him at least once a day; there were people who bought season tickets for the last few days and sat from morning till night in front of his small barred cage; even in the nighttime there were visiting hours, when the whole effect was heightened by torch flares; on fine days the cage was set out in the open air, and then it was the children's special treat to see the hunger artist; for their elders he was often just a joke that happened to be in fashion, but the children stood open-mouthed, holding each other's hands for greater security, marveling at him as he sat there pallid in black tights, with his ribs sticking out so prominently, not even on a seat but down among straw on the ground, sometimes giving a courteous nod, answering questions with a constrained smile, or perhaps stretching an arm through the bars so that one might feel how thin it was, and then again withdrawing deep into himself, paying no attention to anyone or anything, not even to the all-important striking of the clock that was the only piece of furniture in his cage, but merely staring into vacancy with half-shut eyes, now and then taking a sip from a tiny glass of water to moisten his lips.

Besides casual onlookers there were also relays of permanent watchers selected by the public, usually butchers, strangely enough, and it was their task to watch the hunger artist day and night, three of them at a time, in case he should have some secret recourse to nourishment. This was nothing but a formality, instituted to reassure the masses, for the initiates knew well enough that during his fast the artist would never in any circumstances, not even under forcible compulsion, swallow the smallest morsel of food; the honor of his profession forbade it. Not every watcher, of course, was capable of understanding this, there were often groups of night watchers who were very lax in carrying out their duties and deliberately huddled together in a retired corner to play cards with great absorption, obviously intending to give the hunger artist the chance of a little refreshment, which they supposed he could draw from some private hoard. Nothing annoyed the artist more than such watchers; they made him miserable; they made his fast seem unendurable; sometimes he mastered his feebleness sufficiently to sing during their watch for as long as he could keep going, to show them how unjust their suspicions were. But that was of little use; they only wondered at his cleverness in being able to fill his mouth even while singing. Much more to his taste were the watchers who sat close up to the bars, who were not content with the dim night lighting of the hall but focused him in the full glare of the electric pocket torch given them by the impresario. The harsh light did not trouble him at all, in any case he could never sleep properly, and he could always drowse a little, whatever the light, at any hour, even when the hall was thronged with noisy onlookers. He was quite happy at the prospect of spending a sleepless night with such watchers; he was ready to exchange jokes with them, to tell them stories out of his nomadic life, anything at all to keep them awake and demonstrate to them again that he had no eatables in his cage and that he was fasting as not one of them could fast. But his happiest moment was when the morning came and an enormous breakfast was brought them, at his expense, on which they flung themselves with the keen appetite of healthy men after a weary night of wakefulness. Of course there were people who argued that this breakfast was an unfair attempt to bribe the watchers, but that was going rather too far, and when they were invited to take on a night's vigil without a breakfast, merely for the sake of the cause, they made themselves scarce, although they stuck stubbornly to their suspicions.

Such suspicions, anyhow, were a necessary accompaniment to the profession of fasting. No one could possibly watch the hunger artist continuously, day and night, and so no one could produce the first-hand evidence that the fast had really been rigorous and continuous; only the artist himself could know that, he was therefore bound to be the sole completely satisfied spectator of his own fast. Yet for other reasons he was never satisfied; it was not perhaps mere fasting that had brought him to such skeleton thinness that many people had regretfully to keep away from his exhibitions, because the sight of him was too much for them, perhaps it was dissatisfaction with himself that had worn him down. For he alone knew, what no other initiate knew, how easy it was to fast. It was the easiest thing in the world. He made no secret of this, yet people did not believe him, at the best they set him down as modest, most of them, however, thought he was out for publicity or else was some kind of cheat who found it easy to fast because he had discovered a way of making it easy, and then had the impudence to admit the fact, more or less. He had to put up with all that, and in the course of time had got used to it, but his inner dissatisfaction always rankled, and never yet, after any term of fasting—this must be granted to his credit—had he left the cage of his own free will. The longest period of fasting was fixed by his impresario at forty days, beyond that term he was not allowed to go, not even in great cities, and there was good reason for it, too. Experience had proved that for about forty days the interest of the public could be stimulated by a steadily increasing pressure of advertisement, but after that the town began to lose interest, sympathetic support began notably to fall off; there were of course local variations as between one town and another or one country and another, but as a general rule forty days marked the limit. So on the fortieth day the flower-bedecked cage was opened, enthusiastic spectators filled the hall, a military band played, two doctors entered the cage to measure the results of the fast, which were announced through a megaphone, and finally two young ladies appeared blissful at having been selected for the honor, to help the hunger artist down the few steps leading to a small table on which was spread a carefully chosen invalid repast. And at this very moment the artist always turned stubborn. True, he would entrust his bony arms to the outstretched helping hands of the ladies bending over him, but stand up he would not. Why stop fasting at this particular moment, after forty days of it? He had held out for a long time, an illimitably long time; why stop now, when he was in his best fasting form, or rather, not yet quite in his best fasting form? Why should he be cheated of the fame he would get for fasting longer, for being not only the record hunger artist of all time, which presumably he was already, but for beating his own record by a performance beyond human imagination, since he felt that there were no limits to his capacity for fasting? His public pretended to admire him so much, why should it have so little patience with him; if he could endure fasting longer, why shouldn't the public endure it? Besides, he was tired, he was comfortable sitting in the straw, and now he was supposed to lift himself to his full height and go down to a meal the very thought of which gave him a nausea that only the presence of the ladies kept him from betraying, and even that with an effort. And he looked up into the eyes of the ladies who were apparently so friendly and in reality so cruel, and shook his head, which felt too heavy on its strengthless neck. But then there happened yet again what always happened. The impresario came forward, without a word—for the band made speech impossible—lifted his arms in the air above the artist, as if inviting Heaven to look down upon its creature here in the straw, this suffering martyr, which indeed he was, although in quite another sense; grasped him around the emaciated waist, with exaggerated caution, so that the frail condition he was in might be appreciated; and committed him to the care of the blenching ladies, not without secretly giving him a shaking so that his legs and body tottered and swayed. The artist now submitted completely; his head lolled on his breast as if it had landed there by chance; his body was hollowed out; his legs in a spasm of self-preservation clung close to each other at the knees, yet scraped on the ground as if it were not really solid ground, as if they were only trying to find solid ground; and the whole weight of his body, a featherweight after all, relapsed onto one of the ladies, who, looking around for help and panting a little—this post of honor was not at all what she had expected it to be—first stretched her neck as far as she could to keep her face at least free from contact with the artist, then finding this impossible, and her more fortunate companion not coming to her aid but merely holding extended in her own trembling hand the little bunch of knucklebones that was the artist's, to the great delight of the spectators that burst into tears and had to be replaced by an attendant who had long been stationed in readiness. Then came the food, a little of which the impresario managed to get between the artist's lips, while he sat in a kind of half-fainting trance, to the accompaniment of cheerful patter designed to distract the public's attention from the artist's condition; after that, a toast was drunk to the public, supposedly prompted by a whisper from the artist in the impresario's ear; the band confirmed it with a mighty flourish, the spectators melted away, and no one had any cause to be dissatisfied with the proceedings, no one except the hunger artist himself, he only, as always.

So he lived for many years, with small regular intervals of recuperation, in visible glory, honored by the world, yet in spite of that troubled in spirit, and all the more troubled because no one would take his trouble seriously. What comfort could he possibly need? What more could he possibly wish for? And if some good-natured person, feeling sorry for him, tried to console him by pointing out that his melancholy was probably caused by fasting, it could happen, especially when he had been fasting for some time, that he reacted with an outburst of fury and to the general alarm began to shake the bars of his cage like a wild animal. Yet the impresario had a way of punishing these outbreaks which he rather enjoyed putting into operation. He would apologize publicly for the artist's behavior, which was only to be excused, he admitted, because of the irritability caused by fasting; a condition hardly to be understood by well-fed people; then by natural transition he went on to mention the artist's equally incomprehensible boast that he could fast for much longer than he was doing; he praised the high ambition, the good will, the great self-denial undoubtedly implicit in such a statement; and then quite simply countered it by bringing out photographs, which were also on sale to the public, showing the artist on the fortieth day of a fast lying in bed almost dead from exhaustion. This perversion of the truth, familiar to the artist though it was, always unnerved him afresh and proved too much for him. What was a consequence of the premature ending of his fast was here presented as the cause of it! To fight against this lack of understanding, against a whole world of nonunderstanding, was impossible. Time and again in good faith he stood by the bars listening to the impresario, but as soon as the photographs appeared he always let go and sank with a groan back onto his straw, and the reassured public could once more come close and gaze at him.

A few years later when the witnesses of such scenes called them to mind, they   5
often failed to understand themselves at all. For meanwhile the aforementioned change in public interest had set in; it seemed to happen almost overnight; there may have been profound causes for it, but who was going to bother about that; at any rate the pampered hunger artist suddenly found himself deserted one fine day by the amusement-seekers, who went streaming past him to other more-favored attractions. For the last time the impresario hurried him over half Europe to discover whether the old interest might still survive here and there; all in vain; everywhere, as if by secret agreement, a positive revulsion from professional fasting was in evidence. Of course it could not really have sprung up so suddenly as all that, and many premonitory symptoms which had not been sufficiently remarked or suppressed during the rush and glitter of success now came retrospectively to mind, but it was now too late to take any countermeasures. Fasting would surely come into fashion again at some future date, yet there was no comfort for those living in the present. What, then, was the hunger artist to do? He had been applauded by thousands in his time and could hardly come down to showing himself in a street booth at village fairs, and as for adopting another profession, he was not only too old for that but too fanatically devoted to fasting. So he took leave of his impresario, his partner in an unparalleled career, and hired himself to a large circus; in order to spare his own feelings he avoided reading the conditions of his contract.

A large circus with its enormous traffic in replacing and recruiting men, animals, and apparatus can always find a use for people at any time, even for a hunger artist, provided of course that he does not ask for too much, and in this particular case anyhow it was not only the artist who was taken on but his famous and long-known name as well, indeed considering the peculiar nature of his performance, which was not impaired by advancing age, it could not be objected that here was an artist past his prime, no longer at the height of his professional skill, seeking a refuge in some quiet corner of a circus; on the contrary, the hunger artist averred that he could fast as well as ever, which was entirely credible, he even alleged that if he were allowed to fast as he liked and this was at once promised him without more ado, he could astound the world by establishing a record never yet achieved, a statement that certainly provoked a smile among the other professionals, since it left out of account the change in public opinion, which the hunger artist in his zeal conveniently forgot.

He had not, however, actually lost his sense of the real situation and took it as a matter of course that he and his cage should be stationed, not in the middle of the ring as a main attraction, but outside, near the animal cages, on a site that was after all easily accessible. Large and gaily painted placards made a frame for the cage and announced what was to be seen inside it. When the public came thronging out in the intervals to see the animals, they could hardly avoid passing the hunger artist's cage and stopping there for a moment, perhaps they might even have stayed longer had not those pressing behind them in the narrow gangway, who did not understand why they should be help up on their way toward the excitements of the menagerie, made it impossible for anyone to stand gazing quietly for any length of time. And that was the reason why the hunger artist, who had of course been looking forward to these visiting hours as the main achievement of his life, began instead to shrink from them. At first he could hardly wait for the intervals; it was exhilarating to watch the crowds come streaming his way, until only too soon—not even the most obstinate self-deception, clung to almost consciously, could hold out against the fact—the conviction was borne in upon him that these people, most of them, to judge from their actions, again and again, without exception, were all on their way to the menagerie. And the first sight of them from the distance remained the best. For when they reached his cage he was at once deafened by the storm of shouting and abuse that arose from the two contending factions, which renewed themselves continuously, of those who wanted to stop and stare at him—he began to dislike them more than the others—not out of real interest but only out of obstinate self-assertiveness, and those who wanted to go straight on to the animals. When the first great rush was past, the stragglers came along, and these, whom nothing could have prevented from stopping to look at him as long as they had breath, raced past with long strides, hardly even glancing at him, in their haste to get to the menagerie in time. And all too rarely did it happen that he had a stroke of luck, when some father of a family fetched up before him with his children, pointed a finger at the hunger artist, and explained at length what the phenomenon meant, telling stories of earlier years when he himself had watched similar but much more thrilling performances, and the children, still rather uncomprehending, since neither inside nor outside school had they been sufficiently prepared for this lesson—what did they care about fasting?—yet showed by the brightness of their intent eyes that new and better times might be coming. Perhaps, said the hunger artist to himself many a time, things would be a little better if his cage were set not quite so near the menagerie. That made it too easy for people to make their choice, to say nothing of what he suffered from the stench of the menagerie, the animals' restlessness by night, the carrying past of raw lumps of flesh for the beasts of prey, the roaring at feeding times, which depressed him continually. But he did not dare to lodge a complaint with the management; after all, he had the animals to thank for the troops of people who passed his cage, among whom there might always be one here and there to take an interest in him, and who could tell where they might seclude him if he called attention to his existence and thereby to the fact that, strictly speaking, he was only an impediment on the way to the menagerie.

A small impediment, to be sure, one that grew steadily less. People grew familiar with the strange idea that they could be expected, in times like these, to take an interest in a hunger artist, and with this familiarity the verdict went out against him. He might fast as much as he could, and he did so; but nothing could save him now, people passed him by. Just try to explain to anyone the art of fasting! Anyone who has no feeling for it cannot be made to understand it. The fine placards grew dirty and illegible, they were torn down; the little notice board telling the number of fast days achieved, which at first was changed carefully every day, had long stayed at the same figure, for after the first few weeks even this small task seemed pointless to the staff; and so the artist simply fasted on and on, as he had once dreamed of doing, and it was no trouble to him, just as he had always foretold, but no one counted the days, not one, not even the artist himself, knew what records he was already breaking and his heart grew heavy. And when once in a while some leisurely passer-by stopped, made merry over the old figure on the board, and spoke of swindling, that was in its way the stupidest lie ever invented by indifference and inborn malice, since it was not the hunger artist who was cheating, he was working honestly, but the world was cheating him of his reward.

Many more days went by, however, and that too came to an end. An overseer's eye fell on the cage one day and he asked the attendants why this perfectly good cage should be left standing there unused with dirty straw inside it; nobody knew, until one man, helped out by the notice board, remembered about the hunger artist. They poked into the straw with sticks and found him in it. "Are you still fasting?" asked the overseer, "when on earth do you mean to stop?" "Forgive me, everybody," whispered the hunger artist; only the overseer, who had his ear to the bars, understood him. "Of course," said the overseer, and tapped his forehead with a finger to let the attendants know what state the man was in, "we forgive you." "I always wanted you to admire my fasting," said the hunger artist. "We do admire it," said the overseer, affably. "But you shouldn't admire it," said the hunger artist. "Well then we don't admire it," said the overseer, "but why shouldn't we admire it?" "Because I have to fast, I can't help it," said the hunger artist. "What a fellow you are," said the overseer, "and why can't you help it?" "Because," said the hunger artist, lifting his head a little and speaking, with his lips pursed, as if for a kiss, right into the overseer's ear, so that no syllable might be lost, "because I couldn't find the food I liked. If I had found it, believe me, I should have made no fuss and stuffed myself like you or anyone else." These were his last words, but in his dimming eyes remained the firm though no longer proud persuasion that he was still continuing to fast.

"Well, clear this out now!" said the overseer, and they buried the hunger artist, straw and all. Into the cage they put a young panther. Even the most insensitive felt it refreshing to see this wild creature leaping around the cage that had so long been dreary. The panther was all right. The food he liked was brought him without hesitation by the attendants; he seemed not even to miss his freedom; his noble body, furnished almost to the bursting point with all that it needed, seemed to carry freedom around with it too; somewhere in his jaws it seemed to lurk; and the joy of life streamed with such ardent

10

passion from his throat that for the onlookers it was not easy to stand the shock of it. But they braced themselves, crowded around the cage, and did not want ever to move away.

JHUMPA LAHIRI   (b. 1967)

Jhumpa Lahiri was born in London to parents who were born in India. They moved to Rhode Island, where she grew up. She graduated from Barnard College with a degree in English literature and went to work in Cambridge, Massachusetts, for a nonprofit agency. Soon after, she decided to get a Ph.D. in English from Boston University, with an emphasis on Renaissance studies. Her short stories have been published in The New Yorker *and other literary magazines. Her first book,* Interpreter of Maladies *(1999), won the Pulitzer Prize for fiction, 2000.*

Interpreter of Maladies _____ *1998*

At the tea stall Mr. and Mrs. Das bickered about who should take Tina to the toilet. Eventually Mrs. Das relented when Mr. Das pointed out that he had given the girl her bath the night before. In the rearview mirror Mr. Kapasi watched as Mrs. Das emerged slowly from his bulky white Ambassador, dragging her shaved, largely bare legs across the back seat. She did not hold the little girl's hand as they walked to the restroom.

They were on their way to see the Sun Temple at Konarak. It was a dry, bright Saturday, the mid-July heat tempered by a steady ocean breeze, ideal weather for sightseeing. Ordinarily Mr. Kapasi would not have stopped so soon along the way, but less than five minutes after he'd picked up the family that morning in front of Hotel Sandy Villa, the little girl had complained. The first thing Mr. Kapasi had noticed when he saw Mr. and Mrs. Das, standing with their children under the portico of the hotel, was that they were very young, perhaps not even thirty. In addition to Tina they had two boys, Ronny and Bobby, who appeared very close in age and had teeth covered in a network of flashing silver wires. The family looked Indian but dressed as foreigners did, the children in stiff, brightly colored clothing and caps with translucent visors. Mr. Kapasi was accustomed to foreign tourists; he was assigned to them regularly because he could speak English. Yesterday he had driven an elderly couple from Scotland, both with spotted faces and fluffy white hair so thin it exposed their sunburnt scalps. In comparison, the tanned, youthful faces of Mr. and Mrs. Das were all the more striking. When he'd introduced himself, Mr. Kapasi had pressed his palms together in greeting, but Mr. Das squeezed hands like an American so that Mr. Kapasi felt it in his elbow. Mrs. Das, for her past, had flexed one side of her mouth, smiling dutifully at Mr. Kapasi without displaying any interest in him.

As they waited at the tea stall, Ronny, who looked like the older of the two boys, clambered suddenly out of the back seat, intrigued by a goat tied to a stake in the ground. "Don't touch it," Mr. Das said. He glanced up from his paperback tour book, which said "INDIA" in yellow letters and looked as if it had been published abroad. His voice, somehow tentative and a little shrill, sounded as though it had not yet settled into maturity.

"I want to give it a piece of gum," the boy called back as he trotted ahead.   5

Mr. Das stepped out of the car and stretched his legs by squatting briefly to the ground. A clean-shaven man, he looked exactly like a magnified version of Ronny. He had a sapphire-blue visor and was dressed in shorts, sneakers, and a T-shirt. The camera slung around his neck, with an impressive telephoto lens and numerous buttons and markings, was the only complicated thing he wore. He frowned, watching as Ronny rushed toward the goat, but appeared to have no intention of intervening. "Bobby, make sure that your brother doesn't do anything stupid."

"I don't feel like it," Bobby said, not moving. He was sitting in the front seat beside Mr. Kapasi, studying a picture of the elephant god taped to the glove compartment.

"No need to worry," Mr. Kapasi said. "They are quite tame." Mr. Kapasi was forty-six years old, with receding hair that had gone completely silver, but his butterscotch complexion and his unlined brow, which he treated in spare moments to dabs of lotus-oil balm, made it easy to imagine what he must have looked like at an earlier age. He wore gray trousers and a matching jacket-style shirt, tapered at the waist, with short sleeves and a large pointed collar, made of a thin but durable synthetic material. He had specified both the cut and the fabric to his tailor—it was his preferred uniform for giving tours because it did not get crushed during his long hours behind the wheel. Through the windshield he watched as Ronny circled around the goat, touched it quickly on its side, then trotted back to the car.

"You left India as a child?" Mr. Kapasi asked when Mr. Das had settled once again into the passenger seat.

"Oh, Mina and I were both born in America," Mr. Das announced with an air of sudden confidence. "Born and raised. Our parents live here now, in Assansol. They retired. We visit them every couple years." He turned to watch as the little girl ran toward the car, the wide purple bows of her sundress flopping on her narrow brown shoulders. She was holding to her chest a doll with yellow hair that looked as if it had been chopped, as a punitive measure, with a pair of dull scissors. "This is Tina's first trip to India, isn't it, Tina?" 10

"I don't have to go the bathroom anymore," Tina announced.

"Where's Mina?" Mr. Das asked.

Mr. Kapasi found it strange that Mr. Das should refer to his wife by her first name when speaking to the little girl. Tina pointed to where Mrs. Das was purchasing something from one of the shirtless men who worked at the tea stall. Mr. Kapasi heard one of the shirtless men sing a phrase from a popular Hindi love son as Mrs. Das walked back to the car, but she did not appear to understand the words of the song, for she did not express irritation, or embarrassment, or react in any other way to the man's declarations.

He observed her. She wore a red-and-white-checkered skirt that stopped above her knees, slip-on shoes with square wooden heels, and a close-fitting blouse styled like a man's undershirt. The blouse was decorated at chest level with a calico appliqué in the shape of a strawberry. She was a short woman, with small hands like paws, her frosty pink fingernails painted to match her lips, and was slightly plump in her figure. Her hair, shorn only a little longer than her husband's, was parted far to one side. She was wearing large dark brown sunglasses with a pinkish tint to them, and carried a big straw bag, almost as big as her torso, shaped like a bowl, with a water bottle poking out of it. She walked slowly, carrying some puffed rice tossed with peanuts and chili peppers in a large packet made from newspapers. Mr. Kapasi turned to Mr. Das.

"Where in America do you live?" 15

"New Brunswick, New Jersey."

"Next to New York?"

"Exactly. I teach middle school there."

"What subject?"

"Science. In fact, every year I take my students on a trip to the Museum of Nat- 20
ural History if New York City. In a way we have a lot in common, you could say, you and
I. How long have you been a tour guide, Mr. Kapasi?"

"Five years."

Mrs. Das reached the car. "How long's the trip?" she asked, shutting the door.

"About two and a half hours," Mr. Kapasi replied.

At this Mrs. Das gave an impatient sigh, as if she had been traveling her whole
life without pause. She fanned herself with a folded Bombay film magazine written
in English.

"I thought that the Sun Temple is only eighteen miles north of Puri," Mr. Das 25
said, tapping on the tour book.

"The roads to Konarak are poor. Actually it is a distance of fifty-two miles," Mr. Kapasi explained.

Mr. Das nodded, readjusting the camera strap where it had begun to chafe the
back of his neck.

Before starting the ignition, Mr. Kapasi reached back to make sure the cranklike
locks on the inside of each of the back doors were secured. As soon as the car began to
move the little girl began to play with the lock on her side, clicking it with some effort
forward and backward, but Mrs. Das said nothing to stop her. She sat a bit slouched
at one end of the back seat, not offering her puffed rice to anyone. Ronny and Tina sat
on either side of her, both snapping bright green gum.

"Look," Bobby said as the car began to gather speed. He pointed with his finger
to the tall trees that lined the road. "Look."

"Monkeys!" Ronny shrieked. "Wow!" 30

They were seated in groups along the branches, with shining black faces, silver bodies, horizontal eyebrows, and crested heads. Their long gray tails dangled like a series
of ropes among the leaves. A few scratched themselves with black leathery hands, or
swung their feet, staring as the car passed.

"We call them the hanuman," Mr. Kapasi said. "They are quite common in
the area."

As soon as he spoke, one of the monkeys leaped into the middle of the road, causing Mr. Kapasi to brake suddenly. Another bounded onto the hood of the car, then
sprang away. Mr. Kapasi beeped his horn. The children began to get excited, sucking in
their breath and covering their faces partly with their hands. They had never seen monkeys outside of a zoo, Mr. Das explained. He asked Mr. Kapasi stop the car so that he
could take a picture.

While Mr. Das adjusted his telephoto lens, Mrs. Das reached into her straw bag and
pulled out a bottle of colorless nail polish, which she proceeded to stroke on the tip of
her index finger.

The little girl stuck out a hand. "Mine too. Mommy, do mine too." 35

"Leave me alone," Mrs. Das said, blowing on her nail and turning her body slightly.
"You're make me mess up."

The little girl occupied herself by buttoning and unbuttoning a pinafore on the
doll's plastic body.

"All set," Mr. Das said, replacing the lens cap.

The car rattled considerably as it raced along the dusty road, causing them all to
pop up from their seats every now and then, but Mrs. Das continued to polish her
nails. Mr. Kapasi eased up on the accelerator, hoping to produce a smoother ride.
When he reached for the gearshift the boy in front accommodated him by swinging his

hairless knees out of the way. Mr. Kapasi noted that this boy was slightly paler than the other children. "Daddy, why is the driver sitting on the wrong side in this car too?" the boy asked.

"They all do that here, dummy," Ronny said.   40

"Don't call your brother a dummy," Mr. Das said. He turned to Mr. Kapasi. "In America, you know . . . it confuses them."

"Oh yes, I am well aware," Mr. Kapasi said. As delicately as he could, he shifted gears again, accelerating as they approached a hill in the road. "I see it on *Dallas,* the steering wheels are on the left-hand side."

"What's *Dallas?*" Tina asked, banging her now naked doll on the seat behind Mr. Kapasi.

"It went off the air," Mr. Das explained. "It's a television show."

They were all like siblings, Mr. Kapasi thought as they passed a row of date trees.   45
Mr. and Mrs. Das behaved like an older brother and sister, not parents. It seemed that they were in charge of the children only for the day; it was hard to believe they were regularly responsible for anything other than themselves. Mr. Das tapped on his lens cap and his tour book, dragging his thumbnail occasionally across the pages so that they made a scraping sound. Mrs. Das continued to polish her nails. She had still not removed her sunglasses. Every now and then Tina renewed her plea that she wanted her nails done too, and so at one point Mrs. Das flicked a drop of polish on the little girl's finger before depositing the bottle back inside her straw bag.

"Isn't this an air-conditioned car?" she asked, still blowing on her hand. The window on Tina's side was broken and could not be rolled down.

"Quit complaining," Mr. Das said. "It isn't so hot."

"I told you to get a car with air conditioning," Mrs. Das continued. "Why do you do this, Raj, just to save a few stupid rupees? What are you saving us, fifty cents?"

Their accents sounded just like the ones Mr. Kapasi heard on American television programs, though not like the ones on *Dallas.*

"Doesn't it get tiresome, Mr. Kapasi, showing people the same thing every day?"   50
Mr. Das asked, rolling down his own window all the way. "Hey, do you mind stopping the car? I just want to get a shot of this guy."

Mr. Kapasi pulled over to the side of the road as Mr. Das took a picture of a barefoot man, his head wrapped in a dirty turban, seated on top of a cart of grain sacks pulled by a pair of bullocks. Both the man and the bullocks were emaciated. In the back seat Mrs. Das gazed out another window at the sky, where nearly transparent clouds passed quickly in front of one another.

"I look forward to it, actually," Mr. Kapasi said as they continued on their way. "The Sun Temple is one of my favorite places. In that way it is a reward for me. I give tours on Fridays and Saturdays only. I have another job during the week."

"Oh? Where?" Mr. Das asked.

"I work in a doctor's office."

"You're a doctor?"   55

"I am not a doctor. I work with one. As an interpreter."

"What does a doctor need an interpreter for?"

"He has a number of Gujarati patients. My father was Gujarati, but many people do not speak Gujarati in this area, including the doctor. And so the doctor asked me to work in his office, interpreting what the patients say."

"Interesting. I've never heard of anything like that," Mr. Das said.

Mr. Kapasi shrugged. "It is a job like any other."   60

"But so romantic," Mrs. Das said dreamily, breaking her extended silence. She lifted her pinkish brown sunglasses and arranged them on top of her head like a tiara. For the first time, her eyes met Mr. Kapasi's in the rearview mirror: pale, a bit small, their gaze fixed but drowsy.

Mr. Das craned to look at her. "What's so romantic about it?"

"I don't know. Something." She shrugged, knitting her brows together for an instant. "Would you like a piece of gum, Mr. Kapasi?" she asked brightly. She reached into her straw bag and handed him a small square wrapped in green-and-white-striped paper. As soon as Mr. Kapasi put the gum in his mouth a thick sweet liquid burst onto his tongue.

"Tell us more about your job, Mr. Kapasi," Mrs. Das said.

"What would you like to know, madam?"

"I don't know." She shrugged again, munching on some puffed rice and licking the mustard oil from the corners of her mouth. "Tell us a typical situation." She settled back in her seat, her head tilted in a patch of sun, and closed her eyes. "I want to picture what happens."

"Very well. The other day a man came in with a pain in his throat."

"Did he smoke cigarettes?"

"No. It was very curious. He complained that he felt as if there were long pieces of straw stuck in his throat. When I told the doctor, he was able to prescribe the proper medication."

"That's so neat."

"Yes," Mr. Kapasi agreed, after some hesitation.

"So these patients are totally dependent on you," Mrs. Das said. She spoke slowly, as if she were thinking aloud. "In a way, more dependent on you than the doctor."

"How do you mean? How could it be?"

"Well, for example, you could tell the doctor that the pain felt like a burning, not straw. The patient would never know what you had told the doctor, and the doctor wouldn't know that you had told the wrong thing. It's a big responsibility."

"Yes, a big responsibility you have there, Mr. Kapasi," Mr. Das agreed.

Mr. Kapasi had never thought of his job in such complimentary terms. To him it was a thankless occupation. He found nothing noble in interpreting people's maladies, assiduously translating the symptoms of so many swollen bones, countless cramps of bellies and bowels, spots on people's palms that changed color, shape, or size. The doctor, nearly half his age, had an affinity for bell-bottom trousers and made humorless jokes about the Congress party. Together they worked in a stale little infirmary where Mr. Kapasi's smartly tailored clothes clung to him in the heat, in spite of the blackened blades of a ceiling fan churning over their heads.

The job was a sign of his failings. In his youth he'd been a devoted scholar of foreign languages, the owner of an impressive collection of dictionaries. He had dreamed of being an interpreter for diplomats and dignitaries, resolving conflicts between people and nations, settling disputes of which he alone could understand both sides. He was a self-educated man. In a series of notebooks, in the evenings before his parents settled his marriage, he had listed the common etymologies of words, and at one point in his life he was confident that he could converse, if given the opportunity, in English, French, Russian, Portuguese, and Italian, not to mention Hindi, Bengali, Orissi, and Gujarati. Now only a handful of European phrases remained in his memory, scattered words for things like saucers and chairs. English was the only non-Indian language he spoke fluently anymore. Mr. Kapasi knew it was not a remarkable talent. Sometimes he feared that his children knew better English than he did, just from watching television. Still, it came in handy for the tours.

65

70

75

He had taken the job as an interpreter after his first son, at the age of seven, contracted typhoid—that was how he had first made the acquaintance of the doctor. At the time Mr. Kapasi had been teaching English in a grammar school, and he bartered his skills as an interpreter to pay the increasingly exorbitant medical bills. In the end the boy had died one evening in his mother's arms, his limbs burning with fever, but then there was the funeral to pay for, and the other children who were born soon enough, and the newer, bigger house, and the good schools and tutors, and the fine shoes and the television, and the countless other ways he tried to console his wife and to keep her from crying in her sleep, and so when the doctor offered to pay him twice as much as he earned at the grammar school, he accepted. Mr. Kapasi knew that his wife had little regard for his career as an interpreter. He knew it reminded her of the son she'd lost, and that she resented the other lives he helped, in his own small way, to save. If ever she referred to his position, she used the phrase "doctor's assistant," as if the process of interpretation were equal to taking someone's temperature, or changing a bedpan. She never asked him about the patients who came to the doctor's office, or said that his job was a big responsibility.

For this reason it flattered Mr. Kapasi that Mrs. Das was so intrigued by his job. Unlike his wife, she had reminded him of its intellectual challenges. She had also used the word *romantic*. She did not behave in a romantic way toward her husband, and yet she had used the word to describe him. He wondered if Mr. and Mrs. Das were a bad match, just as he and his wife were. Perhaps they too had little in common apart from three children and a decade of their lives. The signs he recognized from his own marriage were there—the bickering, the indifference, the protracted silences. Her sudden interest in him, an interest she did not express in either her husband or her children, was mildly intoxicating. When Mr. Kapasi thought once again about how she had said "romantic," the feeling of intoxication grew.

He began to check his reflection in the rearview mirror as he drove, feeling grateful that he had chosen the gray suit that morning and not the brown one, which tended to sag a little in the knees. From time to time he glanced in the mirror at Mrs. Das. In addition to glancing at her face, he glanced at the strawberry between her breasts and the golden brown hollow in her throat. He decided to tell Mrs. Das about another patient, and another: the young woman who had complained of a sensation of raindrops in her spine, the gentleman whose birthmark had begun to sprout hairs. Mrs. Das listened attentively, stroking her hair with a small plastic brush that resembled an oval bed of nails, asking more questions, for yet another example. The children were quiet, intent on spotting more monkeys in the trees, and Mr. Das was absorbed by his tour book, so it seemed like a private conversation between Mr. Kapasi and Mrs. Das. In this manner the next half hour passed, and when they stopped for lunch at a roadside restaurant that sold fritters and omelette sandwiches, usually something Mr. Kapasi looked forward to on his tours so that he could sit in peace and enjoy some hot tea, he was disappointed. As the Das family settled together under a magenta umbrella fringed with white and orange tassels, and placed their orders with one of the waiters who marched about in tricornered caps, Mr. Kapasi reluctantly headed toward a neighboring table.

80

"Mr. Kapasi, wait. There's room here," Mrs. Das called out. She gathered Tina onto her lap, insisting that he accompany them. And so together they had bottled mango juice and sandwiches and plates of onions and potatoes deep-fried in graham-flour batter. After finishing two omelette sandwiches, Mr. Das took more pictures of the group as they ate.

"How much longer?" he asked Mr. Kapasi as he paused to load a new roll of film in the camera.

"About half an hour more."

By now the children had gotten up from the table to look at more monkeys perched in a nearby tree, so there was a considerable space between Mrs. Das and Mr. Kapasi. Mr. Das placed the camera to his face and squeezed one eye shut, his tongue exposed at one corner of his mouth. "This looks funny. Mina, you need to lean in closer to Mr. Kapasi."

She did. He could smell a scent on her skin, like a mixture of whiskey and rose-water. He worried suddenly that she could smell his perspiration, which he knew had collected beneath the synthetic material of his shirt. He polished off his mango juice in one gulp and smoothed his silver hair with his hands. A bit of the juice dripped onto his chin. He wondered if Mrs. Das had noticed.

She had not. "What's your address, Mr. Kapasi?" she inquired, fishing for something insider her straw bag.

"You would like my address?"

"So we can send you copies," she said. "Of the pictures." She handed him a scrap of paper which she had hastily ripped from a page of her film magazine. The blank portion was limited, for the narrow strip was crowded by lines of text and a tiny picture of a hero and heroine embracing under a eucalyptus tree.

The paper curled as Mr. Kapasi wrote his address in clear, careful letters. She would write to him, asking about his days interpreting at the doctor's office, and he would respond eloquently, choosing only the most entertaining anecdotes, ones that would make her laugh out loud as she read them in her house in New Jersey. In time she would reveal the disappointment of her marriage, and he his. In this way their friendship would grow, and flourish. He would possess a picture of the two of them, eating fried onions under a magenta umbrella, which he would keep, he decided, safely tucked between the pages of his Russian grammar. As his mind raced, Mr. Kapasi experienced a mild and pleasant shock. It was similar to a feeling he used to experience long ago when, after months of translating with the aid of a dictionary, he would finally read a passage from a French novel, or an Italian sonnet, and understand the words, one after another, unencumbered by his own efforts. In those moments Mr. Kapasi used to believe that all was right with the world, that all struggles were rewarded, that all of life's mistakes made sense in the end. The promise that he would hear from Mrs. Das now filled him with the same belief.

When he finished writing his address Mr. Kapasi handed her the paper, but as soon as he did so he worried that he had either misspelled his name or accidentally reversed the numbers of his postal code. He dreaded the possibility of a lost letter, the photograph never reaching him, hovering somewhere in Orissa, close but ultimately unattainable. He thought of asking for the slip of paper again, just to make sure he had written his address accurately, but Mrs. Das had already dropped it into the jumble of her bag.

They reached Konarak at two-thirty. The temple, made of sandstone, was a massive pyramid-like structure in the shape of a chariot. It was dedicated to the great master of life, the sun, which struck three sides of the edifice as it made its journey each day across the sky. Twenty-four giant wheels were carved on the north and south sides of the plinth. The whole thing was drawn by a team of seven horses, speeding as if through the heavens. As they approached, Mr. Kapasi explained that the temple had been built between A.D. 1243 and 1255, with the efforts of twelve hundred artisans, by the great ruler of the Ganga dynasty, King Narasimhadeva the First, to commemorate his victory against the Muslim army.

"It says the temple occupies about a hundred and seventy acres of land," Mr. Das said, reading from his book.

"It's like a desert," Ronny said, his eyes wandering across the sand that stretched on all sides beyond the temple.

"The Chandrabhaga River once flowed one mile north of here. It is dry now," Mr. Kapasi said, turning off the engine.

They got out and walked toward the temple, posing first for pictures by the pair   95
of lions that flanked the steps. Mr. Kapasi led them next to one of the wheels of the chariot, higher than any human being, nine feet in diameter.

" 'The wheels are supposed to symbolize the wheel of life,' " Mr. Das read. " 'They depict the cycle of creation, preservation, and achievement of realization.' Cool." He turned the page of his book. " Each wheel is divided into eight thick and thin spokes, dividing the day into eight equal parts. The rims are carved with designs of birds and animals, whereas the medallions in the spokes are carved with women in luxurious poses, largely erotic in nature.' "

What he referred to were the countless friezes of entwined naked bodies making love in various positions, women clinging to the necks of men, their knees wrapped eternally around their lovers' thighs. In addition to these were assorted scenes from daily life, of hunting and trading, of deer being killed with bows and arrows and marching warriors holding swords in their hands.

It was no longer possible to enter the temple, for it had filled with rubble years ago, but they admired the exterior, as did all the tourists Mr. Kapasi took there, slowing strolling along each of its sides. Mr. Das trailed behind, taking pictures. The children ran ahead, pointing to figures of naked people, intrigued in particular by the Nagamithunas, the half-human, half-serpentine couples who were said, Mr. Kapasi told them, to live in the deepest waters of the sea. Mr. Kapasi was pleased that they liked the temple, pleased especially that it appealed to Mrs. Das. She stopped every three or four paces, staring silently at the carved lovers, and the processions of elephants, and the topless female musicians beating on two-sided drums.

Though Mr. Kapasi had been to the temple countless times, it occurred to him, as he too gazed at the topless women, that he had never seen his own wife fully naked. Even when they had made love she kept the panels of her blouse hooked together, the string of her petticoat knotted around her waist. He had never admired the backs of his wife's legs the way he now admired those of Mrs. Das, walking as if for his benefit alone. He had, of course, seen plenty of bare limbs before, belonging to the American and European ladies who took his tours. But Mrs. Das was different. Unlike the other women, who had an interest only in the temple and kept their noses buried in a guidebook or their eyes behind the lens of a camera, Mrs. Das had taken an interest in him.

Mr. Kapasi was anxious to be alone with her, to continue their private conversa-   100
tion, yet he felt nervous to walk at her side. She was lost behind her sunglasses, ignoring her husband's requests that she pose for another picture, walking past her children as if they were strangers. Worried that he might disturb her, Mr. Kapasi walked ahead, to admire, as he always did, the three life-sized bronze avatars of Surya, the sun god, each emerging from its own niche on the temple façade to greet the sun at dawn, noon, and evening. They wore elaborate headdresses, their languid, elongated eyes closed, their bare chests draped with carved chains and amulets. Hibiscus petals, offerings from

pervious visitors, were strewn at their gray-green feet. The last statue, on the northern wall of the temple, was Mr. Kapasi's favorite. This Surya had a tired expression, weary after a hard day of work, sitting astride a horse with folded legs. Even his horse's eyes were drowsy. Around his body were smaller sculptures of women in pairs, their hips thrust to one side.

"Who's that?" Mrs. Das asked. He was startled to see that she was standing beside him.

"He is the Astachala-Surya," Mr. Kapasi said. "The setting sun."

"So in a couple of hours the sun will set right here?" She slipped a foot out of one of her square-heeled shoes, rubbed her toes on the back of her other leg.

"That is correct."

She raised her sunglasses for a moment, then put them back on again. "Neat." 105

Mr. Kapasi was not certain exactly what the word suggested, but he had a feeling it was a favorable response. He hoped that Mrs. Das had understood Surya's beauty, his power. Perhaps they would discuss it further in their letters. He would explain things to her, things about India, and she would explain things to her, things about India, and she would explain things to him about America. In its own way this correspondence would fulfill his dream of serving as an interpreter between nations. He looked at her straw bag, delighted that his address lay nestled among its contents. When he pictured her so many thousands of miles away he plummeted, so much so that he had an overwhelming urge to wrap his arms around her, to freeze with her, even for an instant, in an embrace witnessed by his favorite Surya. But Mrs. Das had already started walking.

"When do you return to America?" he asked, trying to sound placid.

"In ten days."

He calculated: a week to settle in, a week to develop the pictures, a few days to compose her letter, two weeks to get to India by air. According to his schedule, allowing room for delays, he would hear from Mrs. Das in approximately six weeks' time.

The family was silent as Mr. Kapasi drove them back, a little past four-thirty, to 110
Hotel Sandy Villa. The children had bought miniature granite versions of the chariot's wheels at a souvenir stand, and they turned them round in their hands. Mr. Das continued to read his book. Mrs. Das untangled Tina's hair with her brush and divided it into two little ponytails.

Mr. Kapasi was beginning to dread the thought of dropping them off. He was not prepared to begin his six-week wait to hear from Mrs. Das. As he stole glances at her in the rearview mirror, wrapping elastic bands around Tina's hair, he wondered how he might make the tour last a little longer. Ordinarily he sped back to Puri using a shortcut, eager to return home, scrub his feet and hands with sandalwood soap, and enjoy the evening newspaper and a cup of tea that his wife would serve him in silence. The thought of that silence, something to which he'd long been resigned, now oppressed him. It was then that he suggested visiting the hills at Udayagiri and Khandagiri, where a number of monastic dwellings were hewn out of the ground, facing one another across a defile. It was some miles away, but well worth seeing, Mr. Kapasi told them.

"Oh yeah, there's something mentioned about it in this book," Mr. Das said. "Built by a Jain king or something."

"Shall we go then?" Mr. Kapasi asked. He paused at a turn in the road. "It's to the left."

Mr. Das turned to look at Mrs. Das. Both of them shrugged.

"Left, left," the children chanted. 115

Mr. Kapasi turned the wheel, almost delirious with relief. He did not know what he would do or say to Mrs. Das once they arrived at the hills. Perhaps he would tell her what a pleasing smile she had. Perhaps he would compliment her strawberry shirt, which he found irresistibly becoming. Perhaps, when Mr. Das was busy taking a picture, he would take her hand.

He did not have to worry. When they got to the hills, divided by a steep path thick with trees, Mrs. Das refused to get out of the car. All along the path, dozens of monkeys were seated on stones, as well as on the branches of the trees. Their hind legs were stretched out in front and raised to shoulder level, their arms resting on their knees.

"My legs are tired," she said, sinking low in her seat. "I'll stay here."

"Why did you have to wear those stupid shoes?" Mr. Das said. "You won't be in the pictures."

"Pretend I'm there."   120

"But we could use one of those pictures for our Christmas card this year. We didn't get one of all five of us at the Sun Temple. Mr. Kapasi could take it."

"I'm not coming. Anyway, those monkeys give me the creeps."

"But they're harmless," Mr. Das said. He turned to Mr. Kapasi. "Aren't they?"

"They are more hungry than dangerous," Mr. Kapasi said. "Do not provoke them with food, and they will not bother you."

Mr. Das headed up the defile with the children, the boys at his side, the little girl   125
on his shoulders. Mr. Kapasi watched as they crossed paths with a Japanese man and woman, the only other tourists there, who paused for a final photograph, then stepped into a nearby car and drove away. As the car disappeared out of view some of the monkeys called out, emitting soft whooping sounds, and then walked on their flat black hands and feet up the path. At one point a group of them formed a little ring around Mr. Das and the children. Tina screamed in delight. Ronny ran in circles around his father. Bobby bent down and picked up a fat stick on the ground. When he extended it, one of the monkeys approached him and snatched it, then briefly beat the ground.

"I'll join them," Mr. Kapasi said, unlocking the door on his side. "There is much to explain about the caves."

"No. Stay a minute," Mrs. Das said. She got out of the back seat and slipped in beside Mr. Kapasi. "Raj has his dumb book anyway." Together, through the windshield, Mrs. Das and Mr. Kapasi watched as Bobby and the monkey passed the stick back and forth between them.

"A brave little boy," Mr. Kapasi commented.

"It's not so surprising," Mrs. Das said.

"No?"   130

"He's not his."

"I beg your pardon?"

"Raj's. He's not Raj's son."

Mr. Kapasi felt a prickle on his skin. He reached into his shirt pocket for the small tin of lotus-oil balm he carried with him at all times, and applied it to three spots on his forehead. He knew that Mrs. Das was watching him, but he did not turn to face her. Instead he watched as the figures of Mr. Das and the children grew smaller, climbing up the steep path, pausing every now and then for a picture, surrounded by a growing number of monkeys.

"Are you surprised?" The way she put it made him choose his words with care.   135

"It's not the type of thing one assumes," Mr. Kapasi replied slowly. He put the tin of lotus-oil balm back in his pocket.

"No, of course not. And no one knows, of course. No one at all. I've kept it a secret for eight whole years." She looked at Mr. Kapasi, tilting her chin as if to gain a fresh
perspective. "But now I've told you."

Mr. Kapasi nodded. He felt suddenly parched, and his forehead was warm and
slightly numb from the balm. He considered asking Mrs. Das for a sip of water, then decided against it.

"We met when we were very young," she said. She reached into her straw bag in
search of something, then pulled out a packet of puffed rice. "Want some?"

"No, thank you."   140

She put a fistful in her mouth, sank into the seat a little, and looked away from
Mr. Kapasi, out the window on her side of the car. "We married when we were still in college. We were in high school when he proposed. We went to the same college, of course.
Back then we couldn't stand the thought of being separated, not for a day, not for a
minute. Our parents were best friends who lived in the same town. My entire life I saw
him every weekend, either at our house or theirs. We were sent upstairs to play together
while our parents joked about our marriage. Imagine! They never caught us at anything, though in a way I think it was all more or less a setup. The things we did those
Friday and Saturday nights, while our parents sat downstairs drinking tea . . . I could
tell you stories, Mr. Kapasi."

As a result of spending all her time in college with Raj, she continued, she did not
make many close friends. There was no one to confide in about him at the end of a difficult day, or to share a passing thought or a worry. Her parents now lived on the other
side of the world, but she had never been very close to them anyway. After marrying so
young she was overwhelmed by it all, having a child so quickly, and nursing, and warming up bottles of milk and testing their temperature against her wrist while Raj was at
work, dressed in sweaters and corduroy pants, teaching his students about rocks and di-
nosaurs. Raj never looked cross or harried, or plump as she had become after the first baby.

Always tired, she declined invitations from her one or two college girlfriends to
have lunch or shop in Manhattan. Eventually the friends stopped calling her, so that
she was left at home all day with the baby, surrounded by toys that made her trip when she
walked or wince when she sat, always cross and tired. Only occasionally did they go out
after Ronny was born, and even more rarely did they entertain. Raj didn't mind; he
looked forward to coming home from teaching and watching television and bouncing
Ronny on his knee. She had been outraged when Raj told her that a Punjabi friend,
someone whom she had once met but did not remember, would be staying with them
for a week for some job interviews in the New Brunswick area.

Bobby was conceived in the afternoon, on a sofa littered with rubber teething
toys, after the friend learned that a London pharmaceutical company had hired him,
while Ronny cried to be freed from his playpen. She made no protest when the friend
touched the small of her back as she was about to make a pot of coffee, then pulled her
against his crisp navy suit. He made love to her swiftly, in silence, with an expertise she
had never known, without the meaningful expressions and smiles Raj always insisted
on afterward. The next day Raj drove the friend to JFK. He was married now, to a Punjabi girl, and they lived in London still, and every year they exchanged Christmas cards
with Raj and Mina, each couple tucking photos of their families into the envelopes. He
did not know that he was Bobby's father. He never would.

"I beg your pardon, Mrs. Das, but why have you told me this information?"   145
Mr. Kapasi asked when she had finally finished speaking and had turned to face him
once again.

"For God's sake, stop calling me Mrs. Das. I'm twenty-eight. You probably have children my age."

"Not quite." It disturbed Mr. Kapasi to learn that she thought of him as a parent. The feeling he had had toward her, that had make him check his reflection in the rearview mirror as they drove, evaporated a little.

"I told you, because of your talents." She put the packet of puffed rice back into her bag without folding over the top.

"I don't understand," Mr. Kapasi said.

"Don't you see? For eight years I haven't been able to express this to anybody, not   150
to friends, certainly not to Raj. He doesn't even suspect it. He thinks I'm still in love with him. Well, don't you have anything to say?"

"About what?"

"About what I've just told you. About my secret, and about how terrible it makes me feel. I feel terrible looking at my children, and at Raj, always terrible. I have terrible urges, Mr. Kapasi, to throw things away. One day I had the urge to throw everything I own out the window—the television, the children, everything. Don't you think it's unhealthy?"

He was silent.

"Mr. Kapasi, don't you have anything to say? I thought that was your job."

"My job is to give tours, Mrs. Das."   155

"Not that. Your other job. As an interpreter."

"But we do not face a language barrier. What need is there for an interpreter?"

"That's not what I mean. I would never have told you otherwise. Don't you realize what it means for me to tell you?"

"What does it mean?"

"It means that I'm tired of feeling so terrible all the time. Eight years, Mr. Kapasi,   160
I've been in pain eight years. I was hoping you could help me feel better, say the right thing. Suggest some kind of remedy."

He looked at her, in her red plaid skirt and strawberry T-shirt, a woman not yet thirty, who loved neither her husband nor her children, who had already fallen out of love with life. Her confession depressed him, depressed him all the more when he thought of Mr. Das at the top of the path, Tina clinging to his shoulders, taking pictures of ancient monastic cells cut into the hills to show his students in America, unsuspecting and unaware that one of his sons was not his own. Mr. Kapasi felt insulted that Mrs. Das should ask him to interpret her common, trivial little secret. She did not resemble the patients in the doctor's office, those who came glassy-eyed and desperate, unable to sleep or breathe or urinate with ease, unable, above all, to give words to their pains. Still, Mr. Kapasi believed it was his duty to assist Mrs. Das. Perhaps he ought to tell her to confess the truth to Mr. Das. He would explain that honesty was the best policy. Honesty, surely, would help her feel better, as she'd put it. Perhaps he would offer to preside over the discussion, as a mediator. He decided to begin with the most obvious question, to get to the heart of the matter, and so he asked, "Is it really pain you feel, Mrs. Das, or is it guilt?"

She turned to him and glared, mustard oil thick on her frosty pink lips. She opened her mouth to say something, but as she glared at Mr. Kapasi some certain knowledge seemed to pass before her eyes, and she stopped. It crushed him; he knew at that moment that he was not even important enough to be properly insulted. She opened the car door and began walking up the path, wobbling a little on her square wooden heels, reaching into her straw bag to eat handfuls of puffed rice. It fell through her fingers, leaving a zigzagging trail, causing a monkey to leap down from a tree and devour the little white grains. In search of more, the monkey began to follow Mrs. Das. Others joined him, so that she was soon being followed by about half a dozen of them, their velvety tails dragging behind.

Mr. Kapasi stepped out of the car. He wanted to holler, to alert her in some way, but he worried that if she knew they were behind her, she would grow nervous. Perhaps she would lose her balance. Perhaps they would pull at her bag or her hair. He began to jog up the path, taking a fallen branch in his hand to scare away the monkeys. Mrs. Das continued walking, oblivious, trailing grains of puffed rice. Near the top of the incline, before a group of cells fronted by a row of squat stone pillars, Mr. Das was kneeling on the ground, focusing the lens of his camera. The children stood under the arcade, now hiding, now emerging from view.

"Wait for me," Mrs. Das called out. "I'm coming."

Tina jumped up and down. "Here comes Mommy!"   165

"Great," Mr. Das said without looking up. "Just in time. We'll get Mr. Kapasi to take a picture of the five of us."

Mr. Kapasi quickened his pace, waving his branch so that the monkeys scampered away, distracted, in another direction.

"Where's Bobby?" Mrs. Das asked when she stopped.

Mr. Das looked up from the camera. "I don't know. Ronny, where's Bobby?"

Ronny shrugged. "I thought he was right here."   170

"Where is he?" Mrs. Das repeated sharply. "What's wrong with all of you?"

They began calling his name, wandering up and down the path a bit. Because they were calling, they did not initially hear the boy's screams. When they found him, a little farther down the path under a tree, he was surrounded by a group of monkeys, over a dozen of them, pulling at his T-shirt with their long black fingers. The puffed rice Mrs. Das had spilled was scattered at his feet, raked over by the monkeys' hands. The boy was silent, his body frozen, swift tears running down his startled face. His bare legs were dusty and red with welts from where one of the monkeys struck him repeatedly with the stick he had given to it earlier.

"Daddy, the monkey's hurting Bobby," Tina said.

Mr. Das wiped his palms on the front of his shorts. In his nervousness he accidentally pressed the shutter on his camera; the whirring noise of the advancing film excited the monkeys, and the one with the stick began to beat Bobby more intently. "What are we supposed to do? What if they start attacking?"

"Mr. Kapasi," Mrs. Das shrieked, noticing him standing to one side. "Do some-   175
thing, for God's sake, do something!"

Mr. Kapasi took his branch and shooed them away, hissing at the ones that remained, stomping his feet to scare them. The animals retreated slowly, with a measured gait, obedient but unintimidated. Mr. Kapasi gathered Bobby in his arms and brought him back to where his parents and siblings were standing. As he carried him, he was tempted to whisper a secret into the boy's ear. But Bobby was stunned, and shivering with fright, his legs bleeding slightly where the stick had broken the skin. When Mr. Kapasi delivered him to his parents, Mr. Das brushed some dirt off the boy's T-shirt and put the visor on him the right way. Mrs. Das reached into her straw bag to find a bandage, which she taped over the cut on his knee. Ronny offered his brother a fresh piece of gum. "He's fine. Just a little scared, right, Bobby?" Mr. Das said, patting the top of his head.

"God, let's get out of here," Mrs. Das said. She folded her arms across the strawberry on her chest. "This place gives me the creeps."

"Yeah. Back to the hotel, definitely," Mr. Das agreed.

"Poor Bobby," Mrs. Das said. "Come here a second. Let Mommy fix your hair." Again she reached into her straw bag, this time for her hairbrush, and began to run it around the edges of the translucent visor. When she whipped out the hairbrush, the slip of paper with Mr. Kapasi's address on it fluttered away in the wind. No one but Mr. Kapasi noticed. He watched as it rose, carried higher and higher by the breeze, into the trees where the monkeys now sat, solemnly observing the scene below. Mr. Kapasi observed it too, knowing that this was the picture of the Das family he would preserve forever in his mind.

MARY LAVIN   (1912–1996)

Mary Lavin was born in Massachusetts, but she returned to Ireland with her parents at an early age and is thus an Irish short story writer. She has said that both of her novels, The House in Clewe Street *(1945) and* Mary O'Grady *(1950), might have been better as short stories. Among her numerous collections of stories are* Tales from Bective Bridge *(1942),* The Becker Wives and Other Stories *(1946),* The Great Wave and Other Stories *(1961),* Happiness and Other Stories *(1969), and several important collections published in the 1980s. Lavin's work has a universal appeal, and its settings are not limited to Ireland. She has a keen wit, a powerful gift of observation, and deep feeling for the circumstances of her characters.*

Happiness _____ *1969*

Mother had a lot to say. This does not mean she was always talking but that we children felt the wells she drew upon were deep, deep, deep. Her theme was happiness: what it was, what it was not; where we might find it, where not; and how, if found, it must be guarded. Never must we confound it with pleasure. Nor think sorrow its exact opposite.

"Take Father Hugh," Mother's eyes flashed as she looked at him. "According to him, sorrow is an ingredient of happiness—a *necessary* ingredient, if you please!" And when he tried to protest she put up her hand. "There may be a freakish truth in the theory—for some people. But not for me. And not, I hope, for my children." She looked severely at us three girls. We laughed. None of us had had much experience with sorrow. Bea and I were children and Linda only a year old when our father died suddenly after a short illness that had not at first seemed serious. "I've known people to make sorrow a *substitute* for happiness," Mother said.

Father Hugh protested again. "You're not putting me in that class, I hope?"

Father Hugh, ever since our father died, had been the closest of anyone to us as a family, without being close to any one of us in particular—even to Mother. He lived in a monastery near our farm in County Meath, and he had been one of the celebrants at the Requiem High Mass our father's political importance had demanded. He met us that day for the first time, but he took to dropping in to see us, with the idea of filling the crater of loneliness left at our center. He did not know that there was a cavity in his own life, much less that we would fill it. He and Mother were both young in those days, and perhaps it gave scandal to some that he was so often in our house, staying till late into the night and, indeed, thinking nothing of stopping all night if there was any special reason, such as one of us being sick. He had even on occasion slept there if the night was too wet for tramping home across the fields.

When we girls were young, we were so used to having Father Hugh around that we never stood on ceremony with him but in his presence dried our hair and pared our nails and never minded what garments were strewn about. As for Mother—she thought nothing of running out of the bathroom in her slip, brushing her teeth or combing her hair, if she wanted to tell him something she might otherwise forget. And she brooked no criticism of her behavior. "Celibacy was never meant to take all the warmth and homeliness out of their lives," she said.

On this point, too, Bea was adamant. Bea, the middle sister, was our oracle. "I'm so glad he *has* Mother," she said, "as well as her having him, because it must be awful the way most women treat them—priests, I mean—as if they were pariahs. Mother treats him like a human being—that's all!"

And when it came to Mother's ears that there had been gossip about her making free with Father Hugh, she opened her eyes wide in astonishment. "But he's only a priest!" she said.

Bea giggled. "It's a good job he didn't hear *that*," she said to me afterwards. "It would undo the good she's done him. You'd think he was a eunuch."

"Bea!" I said. "Do you think he's in love with her?"

"If so, he doesn't know it," Bea said firmly. "It's her soul he's after! Maybe he wants to make sure of her in the next world!"

But thoughts of the world to come never troubled Mother. "If anything ever happens to me, children," she said, "suddenly, I mean, or when you are not near me, or I cannot speak to you, I want you to promise you won't feel bad. There's no need! Just remember that I had a happy life—and that if I had to choose my kind of heaven I'd take it on this earth with you again, no matter how much you might annoy me!"

You see, annoyance and fatigue, according to Mother, and even illness and pain, could coexist with happiness. She had a habit of asking people if they were happy at times and in places that—to say the least of it—seemed to us inappropriate. "But are you happy?" she'd probe as one lay sick and bathed in sweat, or in the throes of a jumping toothache. And once in our presence she made the inquiry of an old friend as he lay upon his deathbed.

"Why not?" she said when we took her to task for it later. "Isn't it more important than ever to be happy when you're dying? Take my own father! You know what he said in his last moments? On his deathbed, he defied me to name a man who had enjoyed a better life. In spite of dreadful pain, his face *radiated* happiness!" Mother nodded her head comfortably. "Happiness drives out pain, as fire burns out fire."

Having no knowledge of our own to pit against hers, we thirstily drank in her rhetoric. Only Bea was sceptical. "Perhaps you *got* it from him, like spots, or fever," she said. "Or something that could at least be slipped from hand to hand."

"Do you think I'd have taken it if that were the case!" Mother cried. "Then, when he needed it most?"

"Not there and then!" Bea said stubbornly. "I meant as a sort of legacy."

"Don't you think in *that* case," Mother said, exasperated, "he would have felt obliged to leave it to your grandmother?"

Certainly we knew that in spite of his lavish heart our grandfather had failed to provide our grandmother with enduring happiness. He had passed that job on to Mother. And Mother had not made too good a fist of it, even when Father was living and she had him—and, later, us children—to help.

As for Father Hugh, he had given our grandmother up early in the game. "God Almighty couldn't make that woman happy," he said one day, seeing Mother's face, drawn and pale with fatigue, preparing for the nightly run over to her own mother's flat that would exhaust her utterly.

There were evenings after she came home from the library where she worked   20
when we saw her stand with the car keys in her hand, trying to think which would be worse—to slog over there on foot, or take out the car again. And yet the distance was short. It was Mother's day that had been too long.

"Weren't you over to see her this morning?" Father Hugh demanded.

"No matter!" said Mother. She was no doubt thinking of the forlorn face our grandmother always put on when she was leaving. ("Don't say good night, Vera," Grandmother would plead. "It makes me feel too lonely. And you never can tell—you might slip over again before you go to bed!")

"Do you know the time?" Bea would say impatiently, if she happened to be with Mother. Not indeed that the lateness of the hour counted for anything, because in all likelihood Mother *would* go back, if only to pass by under the window and see that the lights were out, or stand and listen and make sure that as far as she could tell all was well.

"I wouldn't mind if she was happy," Mother said.

"And how do you know she's not?" we'd ask.   25

"When people are happy, I can feel it. Can't you?"

We were not sure. Most people thought our grandmother was a gay creature, a small birdy being who even at a great age laughed like a girl, and—more remarkably— sang like one, as she went about her day. But beak and claw were of steel. She'd think nothing of sending Mother back to a shop three times if her errands were not exactly right. "Not sugar like that—that's *too* fine; it's not castor sugar I want. But *not* as coarse as *that,* either. I want an in-between kind."

Provoked one day, my youngest sister, Linda, turned and gave battle. "You're mean!" she cried. "You love ordering people about!"

Grandmother preened, as if Linda had acclaimed an attribute. "I was always hard to please," she said. "As a girl, I used to be called Miss Imperious."

And Miss Imperious she remained as long as she lived, even when she was a great   30
age. Her orders were then given a wry twist by the fact that as she advanced in age she took to calling her daughter Mother, as we did.

There was one great phrase with which our grandmother opened every sentence: "if only." "If only," she'd say, when we came to visit her—"if only you'd come earlier, before I was worn out expecting you!" Or if we were early, then if only it was later, after she'd had a rest and could enjoy us, be *able* for us. And if we brought her flowers, she'd sigh to think that if only we'd brought them the previous day she'd have had a visitor to appreciate them, or say it was a pity the stems weren't longer. If only we'd picked a few green leaves, or included some buds, because, she said disparagingly, the poor flowers we'd brought were already wilting. We might just as well not have brought them! As the years went on, Grandmother had a new bead to add to her rosary: if only her friends were not all dead! By their absence, they reduced to nil all *real* enjoyment in anything. Our own father—her son-in-law—was the one person who had ever gone close to pleasing her. But even here there had been a snag. "If only he was my real son!" she used to say, with a sigh.

Mother's mother lived on through our childhood and into our early maturity (though she outlived the money our grandfather left her), and in our minds she was a complicated mixture of valiance and defeat. Courageous and generous within the limits of her own life, her simplest demand was yet enormous in the larger frame of Mother's life, and so we never could see her with the same clarity of vision with which we saw our grandfather, or our own father. Them we saw only through Mother's eyes.

"Take your grandfather!" she'd cry, and instantly we'd see him, his eyes burning upon us—yes, upon *us,* although in his day only one of us had been born: me. At another time, Mother would cry, "Take your own father!" and instantly we'd see *him*—tall, handsome, young, and much more suited to marry one of us than poor bedraggled Mother.

Most fascinating of all were the times Mother would say "Take me!" By magic then, staring down the years, we'd see blazingly clear a small girl with black hair and buttoned boots, who, though plain and pouting, burned bright, like a star. "I was happy, you see," Mother said. And we'd strain hard to try and understand the mystery of the light that still radiated from her. "I used to lean along a tree that grew out over the river," she said, "and look down through the gray leaves at the water flowing past below, and I used to think it was not the stream that flowed but me, spread-eagled over it, who flew through the air! Like a bird! That I'd found the secret!" She made it seem there might *be* such a secret, just waiting to be found. Another time she'd dream that she'd be a great singer.

"We didn't know you sang, Mother!"   35

She had to laugh. "Like a crow," she said.

Sometimes she used to think she'd swim the Channel.

"Did you swim *that* well, Mother?"

"Oh, not really—just the breaststroke," she said. "And then only by the aid of two pig bladders blown up by my father and tied around my middle. But I used to throb—yes, throb—with happiness."

Behind Mother's back, Bea raised her eyebrows.   40

What was it, we used to ask ourselves—that quality that she, we felt sure, misnamed? Was it courage? Was it strength, health, or high spirits? Something you could not give or take—a conundrum? A game of catch-as-catch-can?

"I know," cried Bea. "A sham!"

Whatever it was, we knew that Mother would let no wind of violence from within or without tear it from her. Although, one evening when Father Hugh was with us, our astonished ears heard her proclaim that there might be a time when one had to slacken hold on it—let go—to catch at it again with a surer hand. In the way, we supposed, that the high-wire walker up among the painted stars of his canvas sky must wait to fling himself through the air until the bar he catches at has started to sway perversely from him. Oh no, no! That downward drag at our innards we could not bear, the belly swelling to the shape of a pear. Let happiness go by the board. "After all, lots of people seem to make out without it," Bea cried. It was too tricky a business. And might it not be that one had to be born with a flair for it?

"A flair would not be enough," Mother answered. "Take Father Hugh. He, if anyone, had a flair for it—a natural capacity! You've only to look at him when he's off guard, with you children, or helping me in the garden. But he rejects happiness! He casts it from him."

"That is simply not true, Vera," cried Father Hugh, overhearing her. "It's just that   45
I don't place an inordinate value on it like you. I don't think it's enough to carry one all the way. To the end, I mean—and after."

"Oh, don't talk about the end when we're only in the middle," cried Mother. And, indeed, at that moment her own face shone with such happiness it was hard to believe that her earth was not her heaven. Certainly it was her constant contention that of happiness she had had a lion's share. This, however, we, in private, doubted. Perhaps there

were times when she had had a surplus of it—when she was young, say, with her redoubtable father, whose love blazed circles around her, making winter into summer and
ice into fire. Perhaps she did have a brimming measure in her early married years. By
straining hard, we could find traces left in our minds from those days of milk and honey.
Our father, while he lived, had cast a magic over everything, for us as well as for her. He
held his love up over us like an umbrella and kept off the troubles that afterwards came
down on us, pouring cats and dogs!

   But if she did have more than the common lot of happiness in those early days,
what use was that when we could remember so clearly how our father's death had
ravaged her? And how could we forget the distress it brought on us when, afraid to
let her out of our sight, Bea and I stumbled after her everywhere, through the woods
and along the bank of the river, where, in the weeks that followed, she tried vainly to
find peace.

   The summer after Father died, we were invited to France to stay with friends, and
when she went walking on the cliffs at Fécamp our fears for her grew frenzied, so that
we hung on to her arm and dragged at her skirt, hoping that like leaded weights we'd
pin her down if she went too near to the edge. But at night we had to abandon our
watch, being forced to follow the conventions of a family still whole—a home still intact—
and go to bed at the same time as the other children. It was at that hour, when the coast
guard was gone from his rowing boat offshore and the sand was as cold and gray as the
sea, that Mother liked to swim. And when she had washed, kissed, and left us, our hearts
almost died inside us and we'd creep out of bed again to stand in our bare feet at the
mansard and watch as she ran down the shingle, striking out when she reached the water
where, far out, wave and sky and mist were one, and the grayness closed over her. If we
took our eyes off her for an instant, it was impossible to find her again.

   "Oh, make her turn back, God, please!" I prayed out loud one night.

   Startled, Bea turned away from the window. "She'll *have* to turn back sometime,   50
won't she? Unless. . . ?"

   Locking our damp hands together, we stared out again. "She wouldn't!" I whispered. "It would be a sin!"

   Secure in the deterring power of sin, we let out our breath. Then Bea's breath
caught again. "What if she went out so far she used up all her strength? She couldn't swim
back! It wouldn't be a sin then!"

   "It's the intention that counts," I whispered.

   A second later, we could see an arm lift heavily up and wearily cleave down, and
at last Mother was in the shallows, wading back to shore.

   "Don't let her see us!" cried Bea. As if our chattering teeth would not give us away   55
when she looked in at us before she went to her own room on the other side of the corridor, where, later in the night, sometimes the sound of crying would reach us.

   What was it worth—a happiness bought that dearly.

   Mother had never questioned it. And once she told us, "On a wintry day, I brought
my own mother a snowdrop. It was the first one of the year—a bleak bud that had come
up stunted before its time—and I meant it for a sign. But do you know what your grandmother said? 'What good are snowdrops to me now?' Such a thing to say! What good is
a snowdrop at all if it doesn't hold its value always, and never lose it! Isn't that the whole
point of a snowdrop? And that is the whole point of happiness, too! What good would
it be if it could be erased without trace? Take me and those daffodils!" Stooping, she
buried her face in a bunch that lay on the table waiting to be put in vases. "If they didn't

hold their beauty absolute and inviolable, do you think I could bear the sight of them after what happened when your father was in hospital?"

It was a fair question. When Father went to hospital, Mother went with him and stayed in a small hotel across the street so she could be with him all day from early to late. "Because it was so awful for him—being in Dublin!" she said. "You have no idea how he hated it."

That he was dying neither of them realized. How could they know, as it rushed through the sky, that their star was a falling star! But one evening when she'd left him asleep Mother came home for a few hours to see how we were faring, and it broke her heart to see the daffodils out all over the place—in the woods, under the trees, and along the sides of the avenue. There had never been so many, and she thought how awful it was that Father was missing them. "You sent up little bunches to him, you poor dears!" she said. "Sweet little bunches, too—squeezed tight as posies by your little fists! But stuffed into vases they couldn't really make up to him for not being able to see them growing!"

So on the way back to the hospital she stopped her car and pulled a great bunch— the full of her arms. "They took up the whole back seat," she said, "and I was so excited at the thought of walking into his room and dumping them on his bed—you know—just plomping them down so he could smell them, and feel them, and look and look! I didn't mean them to be put in vases, or anything ridiculous like that—it would have taken a rainwater barrel to hold them. Why, I could hardly see over them as I came up the steps; I kept tripping. But when I came into the hall, that nun—I told you about her—that nun came up to me, sprang out of nowhere it seemed, although I know now that she was waiting for me, knowing that somebody had to bring me to my senses. But the way she did it! Reached out and grabbed the flowers, letting lots of them fall—I remember them getting stood on. 'Where are you going with those foolish flowers, you foolish woman?' she said. 'Don't you know your husband is dying? Your prayers are all you can give him now!'

"She was right. I *was* foolish. But I wasn't cured. Afterwards, it was nothing but foolishness the way I dragged you children after me all over Europe. As if any one place was going to be different from another, any better, any less desolate. But there was great satisfaction in bringing you places your father and I had planned to bring you—although in fairness to him I must say that he would not perhaps have brought you so young. And he would not have had an ulterior motive. But above all, he would not have attempted those trips in such a dilapidated car."

Oh, that car! It was a battered and dilapidated red sports car, so depleted of accessories that when, eventually, we got a new car Mother still stuck out her hand on bends, and in wet weather jumped out to wipe the windscreen with her sleeve. And if fussed, she'd let down the window and shout at people, forgetting she now had a horn. How we had ever fitted into it with all our luggage was a miracle.

"You were never lumpish—any of you!" Mother said proudly. "But you were very healthy and very strong." She turned to me. "Think of how you got that car up the hill in Switzerland!"

"The Alps are not hills, Mother!" I pointed out coldly, as I had done at the time, when, as actually happened, the car failed to make it on one of the inclines. Mother let it run back until it wedged against the rock face, and I had to get out and push till she got going again in first gear. But when it got started it couldn't be stopped to pick me up until it got to the top, where they had to wait for me, and for a very long time.

"Ah, well," she said, sighing wistfully at the thought of those trips. "You got something out of them, I hope. All that traveling must have helped you with your geography and your history."

60

65

We looked at each other and smiled, and then Mother herself laughed. "Remember the time," she said, "when we were in Italy, and it was Easter, and all the shops were chock-full of food? The butchers' shops had poultry and game hanging up outside the doors, fully feathered, and with their poor heads dripping blood, and in the windows they had poor little lambs and suckling pigs and young goats, all skinned and hanging by their hind feet." Mother shuddered. "They think so much about food. I found it revolting. I had to hurry past. But Linda, who must have been only four then, dragged at me and stared and stared. You know how children are at that age; they have a morbid fascination for what is cruel and bloody. Her face was flushed and her eyes were wide. I hurried her back to the hotel. But next morning she crept into my room. She crept up to me and pressed against me. 'Can't we go back, just once, and look again at that shop?' she whispered. 'The shop where they have the little children hanging up for Easter!' It was the young goats, of course, but I'd said 'kids,' I suppose. How we laughed." But her face was grave. "You were *so* good on those trips, all of you," she said. "You were really very good children in general. Otherwise I would never have put so much effort into rearing you, because I wasn't a bit maternal. You brought out the best in me! I put an unnatural effort into you, of course, because I was taking my standards from your father, forgetting that his might not have remained so inflexible if he had lived to middle age and was beset by life, like other parents."

"Well, the job is nearly over now, Vera," said Father Hugh. "And you didn't do so badly."

"That's right, Hugh," said Mother, and she straightened up, and put her hand to her back the way she sometimes did in the garden when she got up from her knees after weeding. "I didn't go over to the enemy anyway! We survived!" Then a flash of defiance came into her eyes. "And we were happy. That's the main thing!"

Father Hugh frowned. "There you go again!" he said.

Mother turned on him. "I don't think you realize the onslaughts that were made 70 upon our happiness! The minute Robert died, they came down on me—cohorts of relatives, friends, even strangers, all draped in black, opening their arms like bats to let me pass into their company. 'Life is a vale of tears,' they said. 'You are privileged to find it out so young!' Ugh! After I staggered onto my feet and began to take hold of life once more, they fell back defeated. And the first day I gave a laugh—pouff, they were blown out like candles. They weren't living in a real world at all; they belonged to a ghostly world where life was easy: all one had to do was sit and weep. It takes effort to push back the stone from the mouth of the tomb and walk out."

Effort. Effort. Ah, but that strange-sounding word could invoke little sympathy from those who had not learned yet what it meant. Life must have been hardest for Mother in those years when we older ones were at college—no longer children, and still dependent on her. Indeed, we made more demands on her than ever then, having moved into new areas of activity and emotion. And our friends! Our friends came and went as freely as we did ourselves, so that the house was often like a café—and one where pets were not prohibited but took their places on our chairs and beds, as regardless as the people. And anyway it was hard to have sympathy for someone who got things into such a state as Mother. All over the house there was clutter. Her study was like the returned-letter department of a post office, with stacks of paper everywhere, bills paid and unpaid, letters answered and unanswered, tax returns, pamphlets, leaflets. If by mistake we left the door open on a windy day, we came back to find papers flapping through the air like frightened birds. Efficient only in that she managed eventually to conclude every task she began, it never seemed possible to outsiders that by Mother's methods anything whatever could be accomplished. In an attempt to keep order else-where, she made her own room the clearinghouse into which the rest of us put everything: things to be given away, things to be mended, things to be stored, things to be treasured, things to be returned—even things to be thrown out! By the end of the year, the room resembled an obsolescence dump. And no one could help her; the chaos of her life was as personal as an act of creation—one might as well try to finish another person's poem.

As the years passed, Mother rushed around more hectically. And although Bea and I had married and were not at home anymore, except at holiday time and for occasional weekends, Linda was noisier than the two of us put together had been, and for every fol-lower we had brought home she brought twenty. The house was never still. Now that we were reduced to being visitors, we watched Mother's tension mount to vertigo, knowing that, like a spinning top, she could not rest till she fell. But now at the smallest pretext Father Hugh would call in the doctor and Mother would be put on the mail boat and dispatched for London. For it was essential that she get far enough away to make phon-ing home every night prohibitively costly.

Unfortunately, the thought of departure often drove a spur into her and she re-doubled her effort to achieve order in her affairs. She would be up until the early hours ransacking her desk. To her, as always, the shortest parting entailed a preparation as for death. And as if it were her end that was at hand, we would all be summoned, al-though she had no time to speak a word to us, because five minutes before departure she would still be attempting to reply to letters that were the acquisition of weeks and would have taken whole days to dispatch.

"Don't you know the taxi is at the door, Vera?" Father Hugh would say, running his hand through his gray hair and looking very disheveled himself. She had him at times as distracted as herself. "You can't do any more. You'll have to leave the rest till you come back."

"I can't, I can't!" Mother would cry. "I'll have to cancel my plans." 75

One day, Father Hugh opened the lid of her case, which was strapped up in the hall, and with a swipe of his arm he cleared all the papers on the top of the desk pell-mell into the suitcase. "You can sort them on the boat," he said, "or the train to London!"

Thereafter, Mother's luggage always included an empty case to hold the unfinished papers on her desk. And years afterwards a steward on the Irish Mail told us she was a familiar figure, working away at letters and bills nearly all the way from Holyhead to Euston. "She gave it up about Rugby or Crewe," he said. "She'd get talking to someone in the compartment." He smiled. "There was one time coming down the train I was just in time to see her close up the window with a guilty look. I didn't say anything, but I think she'd emptied those papers of hers out the window!"

Quite likely. When we were children, even a few hours away from us gave her com-posure. And in two weeks or less, when she'd come home, the well of her spirit would be freshened. We'd hardly know her—her step so light, her eye so bright, and her love and patience once more freely flowing. But in no time at all the house would fill up once more with the noise and confusion of too many people and too many animals, and again we'd be fighting our corner with cats and dogs, bats, mice, bees, and even wasps. "Don't kill it!" Mother would cry if we raised a hand to an angry wasp. "Just catch it, dear, and put it outside. Open the window and let it fly away!" But even this treatment could at times be deemed too harsh. "Wait a minute. Close the window!" she'd cry. "It's too cold outside. It will die. That's why it came in, I suppose! Oh dear, what will we do?" Life would be going full blast again.

There was only one place Mother found rest. When she was at breaking point and fit to fall, she'd go out into the garden—not to sit or stroll around but to dig, to drag up weeds, to move great clumps of corms or rhizomes, or indeed quite frequently to haul huge rocks from one place to another. She was always laying down a path, building a dry wall, or making compost heaps as high as hills. However jaded she might be going out, when dark forced her in at last her step had the spring of a daisy. So if she did not succeed in defining happiness to our understanding, we could see that whatever it was, she possessed it to the full when she was in her garden.

One of us said as much one Sunday when Bea and I had dropped round for the   80
afternoon. Father Hugh was with us again. "It's an unthinking happiness, though," he caviled. We were standing at the drawing-room window, looking out to where in the fading light we could see Mother on her knees weeding, in the long border that stretched from the house right down to the woods. "I wonder how she'd take it if she were stricken down and had to give up that heavy work!" he said. Was he perhaps a little jealous of how she could stoop and bend? He himself had begun to use a stick. I was often a little jealous of her myself, because although I was married and had children of my own, I had married young and felt the weight of living as heavy as a weight of years. "She doesn't take enough care of herself," Father Hugh said sadly. "Look at her out there with nothing under her knees to protect her from the damp ground." It was almost too dim for us to see her, but even in the drawing room it was chilly. "She should not be let stay out there after the sun goes down."

"Just you try to get her in then!" said Linda, who had come into the room in time to hear him. "Don't you know by now anyway that what would kill another person only seems to make Mother thrive?"

Father Hugh shook his head again. "You seem to forget it's not younger she's getting!" He fidgeted and fussed, and several times went to the window to stare out apprehensively. He was really getting quite elderly.

"Come and sit down, Father Hugh," Bea said, and to take his mind off Mother she turned on the light and blotted out the garden. Instead of seeing through the window, we saw into it as into a mirror, and there between the flower-laden tables and the lamps it was ourselves we saw moving vaguely. Like Father Hugh, we, too, were waiting for her to come in before we called an end to the day.

"Oh, this is ridiculous!" Father Hugh cried at last. "She'll have to listen to reason." And going back to the window he threw it open. "Vera!" he called. "Vera!"—sternly, so sternly that, more intimate than an endearment, his tone shocked us. "She didn't hear me," he said, turning back blinking at us in the lighted room. "I'm going out to get her." And in a minute he was gone from the room. As he ran down the garden path, we stared at each other, astonished; his step, like his voice, was the step of a lover. "I'm coming, Vera!" he cried.

Although she was never stubborn except in things that mattered, Mother had not   85
moved. In the wholehearted way she did everything, she was bent down close to the ground. It wasn't the light only that was dimming; her eyesight also was failing, I thought, as instinctively I followed Father Hugh.

But halfway down the path I stopped. I had seen something he had not: Mother's hand that appeared to support itself in a forked branch of an old tree peony she had planted as a bride was not in fact gripping it but impaled upon it. And the hand that appeared to be grubbing in the clay in fact was sunk into the soft mold. "Mother!" I screamed, and I ran forward, but when I reached her I covered my face with my hands. "Oh Father Hugh!" I cried. "Is she dead?"

It was Bea who answered, hysterical. "She is! She is!" she cried, and she began to pound Father Hugh on the back with her fists, as if his pessimistic words had made this happen.

But Mother was not dead. And at first the doctor even offered hope of her pulling through. But from the moment Father Hugh lifted her up to carry her into the house we ourselves had no hope, seeing how effortlessly he, who was not strong, could carry her. When he put her down on her bed, her head hardly creased the pillow. Mother lived for four more hours.

Like the days of her life, those four hours that Mother lived were packed tight with concern and anxiety. Partly conscious, partly delirious, she seemed to think the counterpane was her desk, and she scrabbled her fingers upon it as if trying to sort out a muddle of bills and correspondence. No longer indifferent now, we listened, anguished, to the distracted cries that had for all our lifetime been so familiar to us. "Oh, where is it? Where is it? I had it a minute ago! Where on earth did I put it?"

"Vera, Vera, stop worrying," Father Hugh pleaded, but she waved him away and went on sifting through the sheets as if they were sheets of paper. "Oh, Vera!" he begged. "Listen to me. Do you not know—"

Bea pushed between them. "You're not to tell her!" she commanded. "Why frighten her?"

"But it ought not to frighten her," said Father Hugh. "This is what I was always afraid would happen—that she'd be frightened when it came to the end."

At that moment, as if to vindicate him, Mother's hands fell idle on the coverlet, palm upward and empty. And turning her head she stared at each of us in turn, beseechingly. "I cannot face it," she whispered. "I can't! I can't! I can't!"

"Oh, my God!" Bea said, and she started to cry.

"Vera. For God's sake listen to me," Father Hugh cried, and pressing his face to hers, as close as a kiss, he kept whispering to her, trying to cast into the dark tunnel before her the light of his own faith.

But it seemed to us that Mother must already be looking into God's exigent eyes. "I can't!" she cried. "I can't!"

Then her mind came back from the stark world of the spirit to the world where her body was still detained, but even that world was now a whirling kaleidoscope of things which only she could see. Suddenly her eyes focused, and, catching at Father Hugh, she pulled herself up a little and pointed to something we could not see. "What will be done with them?" Her voice was anxious. "They ought to be put in water anyway," she said, and, leaning over the edge of the bed, she pointed to the floor. "Don't step on that one!" she said sharply. Then, more sharply still, she addressed us all. "Have them sent to the public ward," she said peremptorily. "Don't let that nun take them; she'll only put them on the altar. And God doesn't want them! He made them for *us*—not for Himself!"

It was the familiar rhetoric that all her life had characterized her utterances. For a moment we were mystified. Then Bea gasped. "The daffodils!" she cried. "The day Father died!" And over her face came the light that had so often blazed over Mother's. Leaning across the bed, she pushed Father Hugh aside. And, putting out her hands, she held Mother's face between her palms as tenderly as if it were the face of a child. "It's all right, Mother. You don't *have* to face it! It's over!" Then she who had so fiercely forbade Father Hugh to do so blurted out the truth. "You've finished with this world, Mother," she said, and, confident that her tidings were joyous, her voice was strong.

90

95

Mother made the last effort of her life and grasped at Bea's meaning. She let out a sigh, and, closing her eyes, she sank back, and this time her head sank so deep into the pillow that it would have been dented had it been a pillow of stone.

D. H. LAWRENCE   (1885–1930)

One of the giants of twentieth-century literature, D. H. Lawrence was born in Eastwood, Nottinghamshire, England, and knew the coal miner's life well. He avoided that fate by going to Nottingham University College. His early fiction, influenced by Freudianism and the psychoanalytic movement, rejected rationalism and celebrated dark, fiery spirits associated with the libido—the sex drive. After marriage to Frieda von Richthofen, he traveled widely in Europe, Australia, Mexico, and the American Southwest. His major novels are the autobiographical Sons and Lovers *(1913),* The Rainbow *(1915), and* Women in Love *(1920).* Lady Chatterley's Lover *(1928) became famous because it was banned for its sexual frankness. His short stories, collected after his death, establish him as an important innovator. Critic Frank Amon has said of his stories that they "all depend, as stories, upon subtle psychological changes of character."*

The Horse Dealer's Daughter _____ 1922

"Well, Mabel, and what are you going to do with yourself?" asked Joe, with foolish flippancy. He felt quite safe himself. Without listening for an answer, he turned aside, worked a grain of tobacco to the tip of his tongue, and spat it out. He did not care about anything, since he felt safe himself.

The three brothers and the sister sat round the desolate breakfast-table, attempting some sort of desultory consultation. The morning's post had given the final tap to the family fortunes, and all was over. The dreary dining-room itself, with its heavy mahogany furniture, looked as if it were waiting to be done away with.

But the consultation amounted to nothing. There was a strange air of ineffectuality about the three men, as they sprawled at table, smoking and reflecting vaguely on their own condition. The girl was alone, a rather short, sullen-looking young woman of twenty-seven. She did not share the same life as her brothers. She would have been good-looking, save for the impassive fixity of her face, "bull-dog," as her brothers called it.

There was a confused tramping of horses' feet outside. The three men all sprawled round in their chairs, to watch. Beyond the dark holly-bushes that separated the strip of lawn from the high road, they could see a cavalcade of shire horses swinging out of their own yard, being taken for exercise. This was the last time. These were the last horses that would go through their hands. The young men watched with critical, callous look. They were all frightened at the collapse of their lives, and the sense of disaster in which they were involved left them no inner freedom.

Yet they were three fine, well-set fellows enough. Joe, the eldest, was a man of thirty-three, broad and handsome in a hot, flushed way. His face was red, he twisted his black moustache over a thick finger, his eyes were shallow and restless. He had a sensual way of uncovering his teeth when he laughed, and his bearing was stupid. Now he watched the horses with a glazed look of helplessness in his eyes, a certain stupor of downfall.

5

The great draft-horses° swung past. They were tied head to tail, four of them, and they heaved along to where a lane branched off from the high road, planting their great hoofs floutingly in the fine black mud, swinging their great rounded haunches sumptuously, and trotting a few sudden steps as they were led into the lane, round the corner. Every movement showed a massive, slumbrous strength, and a stupidity which held them in subjection. The groom at the head looked back, jerking the leading rope. And the cavalcade moved out of sight up the lane, the tail of the last horse, bobbed up tight and stiff, held out taut from the swinging great haunches as they rocked behind the hedges in a motion like sleep.

Joe watched with glazed, hopeless eyes. The horses were almost like his own body to him. He felt he was done for now. Luckily he was engaged to a woman as old as himself, and therefore her father, who was steward of a neighboring estate, would provide him with a job. He would marry and go into harness. His life was over, he would be a subject animal now.

He turned uneasily aside, the retreating steps of the horses echoing in his ears. Then, with foolish restlessness, he reached for the scraps of bacon-rind from the plates, and, making a faint whistling sound, flung them to the terrier that lay against the fender. He watched the dog swallow them, and waited till the creature looked into his eyes. Then a faint grin came on his face, and in a high, foolish voice he said:

"You won't get much more bacon, shall you, you little b——?"

The dog faintly and dismally wagged its tail, then lowered its haunches, circled round, and lay down again.   10

There was another helpless silence at the table. Joe sprawled uneasily in his seat, not willing to go till the family conclave was dissolved. Fred Henry, the second brother, was erect, clean-limbed, alert. He had watched the passing of the horses with more *sang-froid*. If he was an animal, like Joe, he was an animal which controls, not one which is controlled. He was master of any horse, and he carried himself with a well-tempered air of mastery. But he was not master of the situations of life. He pushed his coarse brown moustache upwards, off his lip, and glanced irritably at his sister, who sat impassive and inscrutable.

"You'll go and stop with Lucy for a bit, shan't you?" he asked. The girl did not answer.

"I don't see what else you can do," persisted Fred Henry.

"Go as a skivvy,"° Joe interpolated laconically.

The girl did not move a muscle.   15

"If I was her, I should go in for training for a nurse," said Malcolm, the youngest of them all. He was the baby of the family, a young man of twenty-two, with a fresh, jaunty *museau*.°

But Mabel did not take any notice of him. They had talked at her and round her for so many years, that she hardly heard them at all.

The marble clock on the mantelpiece softly chimed the half-hour, the dog rose uneasily from the hearthrug and looked at the party at the breakfast-table. But still they sat on in ineffectual conclave.

"Oh all right," said Joe suddenly, *à propos* of nothing. "I'll get a move on."

He pushed back his chair, straddled his knees with a downward jerk, to get them   20
free, in horsey fashion, and went to the fire. Still he did not go out of the room, he was

---

draft-horses: large work horses   *skivvy:* a contemptuous term for housemaid   *museau:*
French for nose; used as slang for face

curious to know what the others would do or say. He began to charge his pipe, looking down at the dog and saying, in a high, affected voice:

"Going wi' me? Going wi' me are ter? Tha'rt goin' further than tha counts on just now, dost hear?"

The dog faintly wagged its tail, the man stuck out his jaw and covered his pipe with his hands, and puffed intently, losing himself in the tobacco, looking down all the while at the dog, with an absent brown eye. The dog looked up at him in mournful distrust. Joe stood with his knees stuck out, in real horsey fashion.

"Have you had a letter from Lucy?" Fred Henry asked of his sister.

"Last week," came the neutral reply.

"And what does she say?"   25

There was no answer.

"Does she *ask* you to go and stop there?" persisted Fred Henry.

"She says I can if I like."

"Well, then, you'd better. Tell her you'll come on Monday."

This was received in silence.   30

"That's what you'll do then, is it?" said Fred Henry, in some exasperation.

But she made no answer. There was a silence of futility and irritation in the room. Malcolm grinned fatuously.

"You'll have to make up your mind between now and next Wednesday," said Joe loudly, "or else find yourself lodgings on the curbstone."

The face of the young woman darkened, but she sat on immutable.

"Here's Jack Fergusson!" exclaimed Malcolm, who was looking aimlessly out of   35
the window.

"Where?" exclaimed Joe loudly.

"Just gone past."

"Coming in?"

Malcolm craned his neck to see the gate.

"Yes," he said.   40

There was a silence. Mabel sat on like one condemned, at the head of the table. Then a whistle was heard from the kitchen. The dog got up and barked sharply. Joe opened the door and shouted:

"Come on."

After a moment, a young man entered. He was muffled up in overcoat and a purple woollen scarf, and his tweed cap, which he did not remove, was pulled down on his head. He was of medium height, his face was rather long and pale, his eyes looked tired.

"Hallo, Jack! Well, Jack!" exclaimed Malcolm and Joe. Fred Henry merely said "Jack!"

"What's doing?" asked the newcomer, evidently addressing Fred Henry.   45

"Same. We've got to be out by Wednesday.—Got a cold?"

"I have—got it bad, too."

"Why don't you stop in?"

"*Me* stop in? When I can't stand on my legs, perhaps I shall have a chance." The young man spoke huskily. He had a slight Scotch accent.

"It's a knock-out, isn't it," said Joe boisterously, "if a doctor goes round croaking   50
with a cold. Looks bad for the patients, doesn't it?"

The young doctor looked at him slowly.

"Anything the matter with you, then?" he asked sarcastically.

"Not as I know of. Damn your eyes, I hope not. Why?"

"I thought you were very concerned about the patients, wondered if you might be one yourself."

"Damn it, no, I've never been patient to no flaming doctor, and hope I never shall be," returned Joe.

At this point Mabel rose from the table, and they all seemed to become aware of her existence. She began putting the dishes together. The young doctor looked at her, but did not address her. He had not greeted her. She went out of the room with the tray, her face impassive and unchanged.

"When are you off then, all of you?" asked the doctor.

"I'm catching the eleven-forty," replied Malcolm. "Are you goin' down wi' th' trap,° Joe?"

"Yes, you young b——, I've told you I'm going down wi' th' trap, haven't I?"

"We'd better be getting her in then.—So long, Jack, if I don't see you before I go," said Malcolm, shaking hands.

He went out, followed by Joe, who seemed to have his tail between his legs.

"Well, this is the devil's own," exclaimed the doctor when he was left alone with Fred Henry. "Going before Wednesday, are you?"

"That's the orders," replied the other.

Where, to Northampton?"

"That's it."

"The devil!" exclaimed Fergusson with quiet chagrin.

And there was silence between the two.

"All settled up, are you?" asked Fergusson.

"About."

There was another pause.

"Well, I shall miss yer, Freddy boy," said the young doctor.

"And I shall miss thee, Jack," returned the other.

"Miss you like Hell," mused the doctor.

Fred Henry turned aside. There was nothing to say. Mabel came in again, to finish clearing the table.

"What are *you* going to do then, Miss Pervin?" asked Fergusson. "Going to your sister's, are you?"

Mabel looked at him with her steady, dangerous eyes, that always made him uncomfortable, unsettling his superficial ease.

"No," she said.

"Well, what in the name of fortune *are* you going to do? Say what you *mean* to do," cried Fred Henry with futile intensity.

But she only averted her head and continued her work. She folded the white tablecloth, and put on the chenille cloth.

"The sulkiest bitch that ever trod!" muttered her brother.

But she finished her task with perfectly impassive face, the young doctor watching her interestedly all the while. Then she went out.

Fred Henry stared after her, clenching his lips, his blue eyes fixing in sharp antagonism, as he made a grimace of sour exasperation.

"You could bray her into bits, and that's all you'd get out of her," he said in a small, narrowed tone.

The doctor smiled faintly.

trap: a light, two-wheeled carriage

"What's she *going* to do then?" he asked.   85
"Strike me if *I* know!" returned the other.
There was a pause. Then the doctor stirred.
"I'll be seeing you to-night, shall I?" he said to his friend.
"Ay—where's it to be? Are we going over to Jessdale?"
"I don't know. I've got such a cold on me. I'll come round to the Moon and Stars,°   90
anyway."
"Let Lizzie and May miss their night for once, eh?"
"That's it—if I feel as I do now."
"All's one——"

The two young men went through the passage and down to the back door together. The house was large, but it was servantless now, and desolate. At the back was a small bricked house-yard, and beyond that a big square, gravelled fine and red, and having stables on two sides. Sloping, dank, winter-dark fields stretched away on the open sides.

But the stables were empty. Joseph Pervin, the father of the family, had been a man   95
of no education, who had become a fairly large horse-dealer. The stables had been full of horses, there was a great turmoil and come-and-go of horses and of dealers and grooms. Then the kitchen was full of servants. But of late things had declined. The old man had married a second time, to retrieve his fortunes. Now he was dead and everything was gone to the dogs, there was nothing but debt and threatening.

For months Mabel had been servantless in the big house, keeping the home together in penury for her ineffectual brothers. She had kept house for ten years. But previously it was with unstinted means. Then, however brutal and coarse everything was, the sense of money had kept her proud, confident. The men might be foul-mouthed, the women in the kitchen might have bad reputations, her brothers might have illegitimate children. But so long as there was money, the girl felt herself established, and brutally proud, reserved.

No company came to the house, save dealers and coarse men. Mabel had no associates of her own sex, after her sister went away. But she did not mind. She went regularly to church, she attended to her father. And she lived in the memory of her mother, who had died when she was fourteen, and whom she had loved. She had loved her father too, in a different way, depending upon him, and feeling secure in him, until at the age of fifty-four he married again. And then she had set hard against him. Now he had died and left them all hopelessly in debt.

She had suffered badly during the period of poverty. Nothing, however, could shake the curious sullen, animal pride that dominated each member of the family. Now, for Mabel, the end had come. Still she would not cast about her. She would follow her own way just the same. She would always hold the keys of her own situation. Mindless and persistent, she endured from day to day. Why should she think? Why should she answer anybody? It was enough that this was the end, and there was no way out. She need not pass anymore darkly along the main street of the small town, avoiding every eye. She need not demean herself anymore, going into the shops and buying the cheapest food. This was at an end. She thought of nobody, not even of herself. Mindless and persistent, she seemed in a sort of ecstasy to be coming nearer to her fulfilment, her own glorification, approaching her dead mother, who was glorified.

In the afternoon she took a little bag, with shears and sponge and a small scrubbing brush, and went out. It was a grey, wintry day, with saddened, dark-green fields

---

Moon and Stars: a local tavern

and an atmosphere blackened by the smoke of foundries not far off. She went quickly, darkly along the causeway, heeding nobody, through the town to the churchyard.

There she always felt secure, as if no one could see her, although as a matter of fact   100
she was exposed to the stare of everyone who passed along under the churchyard wall. Nevertheless, once under the shadow of the great looming church, among the graves, she felt immune from the world, reserved within the thick churchyard wall as in another country.

Carefully she clipped the grass from the grave, and arranged the pinky-white, small chrysanthemums in the tin cross. When this was done, she took an empty jar from a neighboring grave, brought water, and carefully, most scrupulously sponged the marble head-stone and the coping-stone.°

It gave her sincere satisfaction to do this. She felt in immediate contact with the world of her mother. She took minute pains, went through the work in a state bordering on pure happiness, as if in performing this task she came into a subtle, intimate connection with her mother. For the life she followed here in the world was far less real than the world of death she inherited from her mother.

The doctor's house was just by the church. Fergusson, being a mere hired assistant, was slave to the countryside. As he hurried now to attend to the out-patients in the surgery, glancing across the graveyard with his quick eye he saw the girl at her task at the grave. She seemed so intent and remote, it was like looking into another world. Some mystical element was touched in him. He slowed down as he walked, watching her as if spellbound.

She lifted her eyes, feeling him looking. Their eyes met. And each looked away again at once, each feeling in some way found out by the other. He lifted his cap and passed on down the road. There remained distinct in his consciousness, like a vision, the memory of her face, lifted from the tombstone in the churchyard, and looking at him with slow, large, portentous eyes. It *was* portentous, her face. It seemed to mesmerize him. There was a heavy power in her eyes which laid hold of his whole being, as if he had drunk some powerful drug. He had been feeling weak and done before. Now the life came back into him, he felt delivered from his own fretted, daily self.

He finished his duties at the surgery as quickly as might be, hastily filling up the   105
bottles of the waiting people with cheap drugs. Then, in perpetual haste, he set off again to visit several cases in another part of his round before tea-time. At all times he preferred to walk, if he could, but particularly when he was not well. He fancied the motion restored him.

The afternoon was falling. It was grey, deadened, and wintry, with a slow, moist, heavy coldness sinking in and deadening all the faculties. But why should he think or notice? He hastily climbed the hill and turned across the dark-green fields, following the black cinder-track. In the distance, across a shallow dip in the country, the small town was clustered like smoldering ash, a tower, a spire, a heap of low, raw, extinct houses. And on the nearest fringe of the town, sloping into the dip, was Oldmeadow, the Pervins' house. He could see the stables and the outbuildings distinctly, as they lay towards him on the slope. Well, he would not go there many more times! Another resource would be lost to him, another place gone: the only company he cared for in the alien, ugly little town, he was losing. Nothing but work, drudgery, constant hastening from dwelling to dwelling among the colliers and the iron-workers. It wore him out, but at the same time he had a craving for it. It was a stimulant to him to be in the homes of the working people, moving, as it were, through the innermost body of their life. His nerves

coping-stone: uppermost layer of stones under the headstone

were excited and gratified. He could come so near, into the very lives of the rough, inarticulate, powerfully emotional men and women. He grumbled, he said he hated the hellish hole. But as a matter of fact it excited him, the contact with the rough, strongly-feeling people was a stimulant applied direct to his nerves.

Below Oldmeadow, in the green, shallow, soddened hollows of fields, lay a square deep pond. Roving across the landscape, the doctor's quick eye detected a figure in black passing through the gates of the field, down towards the pond. He looked again. It would be Mabel Pervin. His mind suddenly became alive and attentive.

Why was she going down there? He pulled up on the path on the slope above, and stood staring. He could just make sure of the small black figure moving in the hollow of the failing day. He seemed to see her in the midst of such obscurity, that he was like a clairvoyant, seeing rather with the mind's eye than with ordinary sight. Yet he could see her positively enough, whilst he kept his eye attentive. He felt, if he looked away from her, in the thick, ugly, falling dusk, he would lose her altogether.

He followed her minutely as she moved, direct and intent, like something transmitted rather than stirring in voluntary activity, straight down the field towards the pond. There she stood on the bank for a moment. She never raised her head. Then she waded slowly into the water.

He stood motionless as the small black figure walked slowly and deliberately towards   110
the center of the pond, very slowly, gradually moving deeper into the motionless water, and still moving forward as the water got up to her breast. Then he could see her no more in the dusk of the dead afternoon.

"There!" he exclaimed. "Would you believe it?"

And he hastened straight down, running over the wet, soddened fields, pushing through the hedges, down into the depression of callous wintry obscurity. It took him several minutes to come to the pond. He stood on the bank, breathing heavily. He could see nothing. His eyes seemed to penetrate the dead water. Yes, perhaps that was the dark shadow of her black clothing beneath the surface of the water.

He slowly ventured into the pond. The bottom was deep, soft clay; he sank in, and the water clasped dead cold round his legs. As he stirred he could smell the cold, rotten clay that fouled up into the water. It was objectionable in his lungs. Still, repelled and yet not heeding, he moved deeper into the pond. The cold water rose over his thighs, over his loins, upon his abdomen. The lower part of his body was all sunk in the hideous cold element. And the bottom was so deeply soft and uncertain, he was afraid of pitching with his mouth underneath. He could not swim, and was afraid.

He crouched a little, spreading his hands under the water and moving them round, trying to feel for her. The dead cold pond swayed upon his chest. He moved again, a little deeper, and again, with his hands underneath, he felt all around under the water. And he touched her clothing. But it evaded his fingers. He made a desperate effort to grasp it.

And so doing he lost his balance and went under, horribly, suffocating in the foul,   115
earthy water, struggling madly for a few moments. At last, after what seemed an eternity, he got his footing, rose again into the air and looked around. He gasped, and knew he was in the world. Then he looked at the water. She had risen near him. He grasped her clothing, and, drawing her nearer, turned to take his way to land again.

He went very slowly, carefully, absorbed in the slow progress. He rose higher, climbing out of the pond. The water was now only about his legs; he was thankful, full of relief to be out of the clutches of the pond. He lifted her and staggered on to the bank, out of the horror of wet grey clay.

He laid her down on the bank. She was quite unconscious and running with water. He made the water come from her mouth, he worked to restore her. He did not have to work very long before he could feel the breathing begin again in her, she was breathing naturally. He worked a little longer. He could feel her live beneath his hands, she was coming back. He wiped her face, wrapped her in his overcoat, looked round into the dim, dark-grey world, then lifted her and staggered down the bank and across the fields.

It seemed an unthinkably long way, and his burden so heavy he felt he would never get to the house. But at last he was in the stable-yard, and then in the house-yard. He opened the door and went into the house. In the kitchen he laid her down on the hearthrug, and called. The house was empty. But the fire was burning in the grate.

Then again he kneeled to attend to her. She was breathing regularly, her eyes were wide open and as if conscious, but there seemed something missing in her look. She was conscious in herself, but unconscious of her surroundings.

He ran upstairs, took blankets from a bed, and put them before the fire to warm.   120
Then he removed her saturated, earthy-smelling clothing, rubbed her dry with a towel, and wrapped her naked in the blankets. Then he went into the dining-room to look for spirits. There was a little whisky. He drank a gulp himself, and put some into her mouth.

The effect was instantaneous. She looked full into his face, as if she had been seeing him for some time, and yet had only just become conscious of him.

"Dr. Fergusson?" she said.

"What?" he answered.

He was divesting himself of his coat, intending to find some dry clothing upstairs. He could not bear the smell of the dead, clayey water, and he was mortally afraid for his own health.

"What did I do?" she asked.   125

"Walked into the pond," he replied. He had begun to shudder like one sick, and could hardly attend to her. Her eyes remained full on him; he seemed to be going dark in his mind, looking back at her helplessly. The shuddering became quieter in him, his life came back in him, dark and unknowing, but strong again.

"Was I out of my mind?" she asked, while her eyes were fixed on him all the time.

"Maybe, for the moment," he replied. He felt quiet, because his strength had come back. The strange fretful strain had left him.

"Am I out of my mind now?" she asked.

"Are you?" he reflected a moment. "No," he answered truthfully, "I don't see that   130
you are." He turned his face aside. He was afraid, now, because he felt dazed, and felt dimly that her power was stronger than his, in this issue. And she continued to look at him fixedly all the time. "Can you tell me where I shall find some dry things to put on?" he asked.

"Did you dive into the pond for me?" she asked.

"No," he answered. "I walked in. But I went in overhead as well."

There was silence for a moment. He hesitated. He very much wanted to go upstairs to get into dry clothing. But there was another desire in him. And she seemed to hold him. His will seemed to have gone to sleep, and left him, standing there slack before her. But he felt warm inside himself. He did not shudder at all, though his clothes were sodden on him.

"Why did you?" she asked.

"Because I didn't want you to do such a foolish thing," he said.   135

"It wasn't foolish," she said, still gazing at him as she lay on the floor, with a sofa cushion under her head. "It was the right thing to do. *I* knew best, then."

"I'll go and shift these wet things," he said. But still he had not the power to move out of her presence, until she sent him. It was as if she had the life of his body in her hands, and he could not extricate himself. Or perhaps he did not want to.

Suddenly she sat up. Then she became aware of her own immediate condition. She felt the blankets about her, she knew her own limbs. For a moment it seemed as if her reason were going. She looked round, with wild eye, as if seeking something. He stood still with fear. She saw her clothing lying scattered.

"Who undressed me?" she asked, her eyes resting full and inevitable on his face. "I did," he replied, "to bring you round."   140

For some moments she sat and gazed at him awfully, her lips parted.

"Do you love me then?" she asked.

He only stood and stared at her fascinated. His soul seemed to melt.

She shuffled forward on her knees, and put her arms round him, round his legs, as he stood there, pressing her breasts against his knees and thighs, clutching him with strange, convulsive certainty, pressing his thighs against her, drawing him to her face, her throat, as she looked up at him with flaring, humble eyes of transfiguration, triumphant in first possession.

"You love me," she murmured, in strange transport, yearning and triumphant   145 and confident. "You love me. I know you love me, I know."

And she was passionately kissing his knees through the wet clothing, passionately and indiscriminately kissing his knees, his legs, as if unaware of everything.

He looked down at the tangled wet hair, the wild, bare, animal shoulders. He was amazed, bewildered, and afraid. He had never thought of loving her. He had never wanted to love her. When he rescued her and restored her, he was a doctor and she was a patient. He had had no single personal thought of her. Nay, this introduction of the personal element was very distasteful to him, a violation of his professional honor. It was horrible to have her there embracing his knees. It was horrible. He revolted from it violently. And yet—and yet—he had not the power to break away.

She looked at him again, with the same supplication of powerful love, and that same transcendent, frightening light of triumph. In view of the delicate flame which seemed to come from her face like a light, he was powerless. And yet he had never intended to love her. He had never intended. And something stubborn in him could not give way.

"You love me," she repeated, in a murmur of deep, rhapsodic assurance. "You love me."

Her hands were drawing him, drawing him down to her. He was afraid, even   150 a little horrified. For he had really no intention of loving her. Yet her hands were drawing him towards her. He put out his hand quickly to steady himself, and grasped her bare shoulder. A flame seemed to burn the hand that grasped her soft shoulder. He had no intention of loving her: his whole will was against his yielding. It was horrible—— And yet wonderful was the touch of her shoulder, beautiful the shining of her face. Was she perhaps mad? He had a horror of yielding to her. Yet something in him ached also.

He had been staring away at the door, away from her. But his hand remained on her shoulder. She had gone suddenly very still. He looked down at her. Her eyes were now wide with fear, with doubt, the light was dying from her face, a shadow of terrible greyness was returning. He could not bear the touch of her eyes' question upon him, and the look of death behind the question.

With an inward groan he gave way, and let his heart yield towards her. A sudden gentle smile came on his face. And her eyes, which never left his face, slowly, slowly filled with tears. He watched the strange water rise in her eyes, like some slow fountain coming up. And his heart seemed to burn and melt in his breast.

He could not bear to look at her anymore. He dropped on his knees and caught her head with his arm and pressed her face against his throat. She was very still. His heart, which seemed to have broken, was burning with a kind of agony in his breast. And he felt her slow, hot tears wetting his throat. But he could not move.

He felt the hot tears wet his neck and the hollows of his neck, and he remained motionless, suspended through one of man's eternities. Only now it had become indispensable to him to have her face pressed close to him, he could never let her go again. He could never let her head go away from the close clutch of his arm. He wanted to remain like that for ever, with his heart hurting him in a pain that was also life to him. Without knowing, he was looking down on her damp, soft brown hair.

Then, as it were suddenly, he smelt the horrid stagnant smell of that water. And   155
at the same moment she drew away from him and looked at him. Her eyes were wistful and unfathomable. He was afraid of them, and he fell to kissing her, not knowing what he was doing. He wanted her eyes not to have that terrible wistful, unfathomable look.

When she turned her face to him again, a faint delicate flush was glowing, and there was again dawning that terrible shining of joy in her eyes, which really terrified him, and yet which he now wanted to see, because he feared the look of doubt still more.

"You love me?" she said, rather faltering.

"Yes." The word cost him a painful effort. Not because it wasn't true. But because it was too newly true, the *saying* seemed to tear open again his newly-torn heart. And he hardly wanted it to be true, even now.

She lifted her face to him, and he bent forward and kissed her on the mouth, gently, with the one kiss that is an eternal pledge. And as he kissed her his heart strained again in his breast. He never intended to love her. But now it was over. He had crossed over the gulf to her, and all that he had left behind had shrivelled and become void.

After the kiss, her eyes again slowly filled with tears. She sat still, away from   160
him, with her face dropped aside, and her hands folded in her lap. The tears fell very slowly. There was complete silence. He too sat there motionless and silent on the hearthrug. The strange pain of his heart that was broken seemed to consume him. That he should love her! That this was love! That he should be ripped open in this way!—him, a doctor!—How they would all jeer if they knew!—It was agony to him to think they might know.

In the curious naked pain of the thought he looked again to her. She was sitting there drooped into a muse. He saw a tear fall, and his heart flared hot. He saw for the first time that one of her shoulders was quite uncovered, one arm bare, he could see one of her small breasts; dimly, because it had become almost dark in the room.

"Why are you crying?" he asked in an altered voice.

She looked up at him, and behind her tears the consciousness of her situation for the first time brought a dark look of shame to her eyes.

"I'm not crying, really," she said, watching him half frightened.

He reached his hand, and softly closed it on her bare arm.   165

"I love you! I love you!" he said in a soft, low, vibrating voice, unlike himself.

She shrank, and dropped her head. The soft, penetrating grip of his hand on her arm distressed her. She looked up at him.

"I want to go," she said, "I want to go and get you some dry things."

"Why?" he said. "I'm all right."

"But I want to go," she said. "And I want you to change your things."   170

He released her arm, and she wrapped herself in the blanket, looking at him rather frightened. And still she did not rise.

"Kiss me," she said wistfully.

He kissed her, but briefly, half in anger.

Then, after a second, she rose nervously, all mixed up in the blanket. He watched her in her confusion, as she tried to extricate herself and wrap herself up so that she could walk. He watched her relentlessly, as she knew. And as she went, the blanket trailing, and as he saw a glimpse of her feet and her white leg, he tried to remember her as she was when he had wrapped her in the blanket. But he didn't want to remember, because she had been nothing to him then, and his nature revolted from remembering what she was when she was nothing to him.

A tumbling, muffled noise from within the dark house startled him. Then he   175
heard her voice:—"There are clothes." He rose and went to the foot of the stairs, and gathered up the garments she had thrown down. Then he came back to the fire, to rub himself down and dress. He grinned at his own appearance when he had finished.

The fire was sinking, so he put on coal. The house was now quite dark, save for the light of a street-lamp that shone in faintly from beyond the holly trees. He lit the gas with matches he found on the mantelpiece. Then he emptied the pockets of his own clothes, and threw all his wet things in a heap into the scullery. After which he gathered up her sodden clothes, gently, and put them in a separate heap on the copper-top in the scullery.

It was six o'clock on the clock. His own watch had stopped. He ought to go back to the surgery. He waited, and still she did not come down. So he went to the foot of the stairs and called:

"I shall have to go."

Almost immediately he heard her coming down. She had on her best dress of black voile, and her hair was tidy, but still damp. She looked at him—and, in spite of herself, smiled.

"I don't like you in those clothes," she said.   180

"Do I look a sight?" he answered.

They were shy of one another.

"I'll make you some tea," she said.

"No, I must go."

"Must you?" And she looked at him again with the wide, strained, doubtful eyes.   185
And again, from the pain of his breast, he knew how he loved her. He went and bent to kiss her, gently, passionately, with his heart's painful kiss.

"And my hair smells so horrible," she murmured in distraction. "And I'm so awful, I'm so awful! Oh, no, I'm too awful," and she broke into bitter, heart-broken sobbing. "You can't want to love me, I'm horrible."

"Don't be silly, don't be silly," he said, trying to comfort her, kissing her, holding her in his arms. "I want you, I want to marry you; we're going to be married, quickly, quickly—tomorrow if I can."

But she only sobbed terribly, and cried:

"I feel awful. I feel awful. I feel I'm horrible to you."

"No, I want you, I want you," was all he answered, blindly, with that terrible into-   190
nation which frightened her almost more than her horror lest he should *not* want her.

DAVID WONG LOUIE (b. 1954)

David Wong Louie has taught creative writing at Vassar College, where he was himself an undergraduate. He was born in Rockville Center, New York, and went to graduate school at the University of Iowa. He has published a number of stories in literary magazines and in collections, such as The Best American Short Stories 1989. *His new novel,* The Barbarians Are Coming, *was published in March 2000. It is a comic treatment of cultural expectations, disappointments, and confusions.*

Pangs of Love _____ *1991*

Each night, like most Americans, my mother watches hours of TV. She loves Lucy and Carol Burnett, then switches to cable for the Chinese channel, but always concludes the broadcast day with the local news and Johnny Carson. She doesn't understand what Johnny says, but when the studio audience laughs, she laughs too, as if invisible wires run between her and the set.

My mother has lived in this country for forty years and, through what must be a monumental act of will, has managed not to learn English. This does no one any good, though I suppose when it comes to TV her linguistic shortcomings can't be anything but a positive evolutionary adaptation; dumb to the prattle that fills the airwaves, maybe her brain will wither proportionately less than the average American's.

I am thirty-five years old, and for the past nine months have lived with my mother in a federally subsidized high-rise in the lower reaches of Chinatown. After my father died, my siblings convened a secret meeting during which they unanimously elected me our mother's new apartment mate. They moved her things from Long Island, carpeted her floors, bought prints for the walls, imported me for company, then returned to their lives. I work for a midsize corporation that manufactures synthetic flavors and fragrances. We are the soul of hundreds of household products: the tobacco taste in low-tar cigarettes, the pine forests in aerosol cans, the minty pizzazz of toothpastes. We have sprays that simulate the smell of new cars; in fact, we have honed the olfactory art to a level of sophistication that enables us to distinguish between makes and models. Our mission is to make the chemical world, an otherwise noxious, foul-tasting, polysyllabic ocean of consumer dread, a cozier place for the deserving noses and tastebuds of America.

My mother's in her pajamas, he hair in a net that seems to scar her forehead. I'm sitting up with her, putting in time. I flip through the day's paper, Johnny in the background carrying on a three-way with Ed and Doc, when my mother's laugh starts revving like a siren. I shoot her a look—fat-lipped, pellet-eyed—that says, What business do you have laughing, Mrs. Pang? My mother's a sweet, blockish woman whom people generally like. She's chatty with her friends in her loud Cantonese voice and keeps her cabinets and refrigerator jammed tight with food, turning her kitchen into a mini grocery store—she's prepared for a long famine or a state of siege. Now, feeling the stab of my glare, she holds in her laughter, hand over mouth schoolgirl-style, hiding those gold caps that liven up her smiles, eyes moist and shifty dancing.

I roll my eyes the way Johnny does and return to the paper. The world's going through its usual contortions: bigger wars, emptier stomachs, more roofless lives; so many unhappy, complicated acres. As a responsible citizen of the planet, I slip into my doom swoon, a mild but satisfying funk over the state of the world. But then she starts again. Fist on cheek blocking my view of her gold mine. Her round shoulders quivering with joy. I click my tongue to let her know she has spoiled my dark mood. She turns toward me, sees the sour expression hanging on my face like dough, points at the screen where Johnny's in a turban the size of a prize pumpkin, then waves me off, swatting at flies. Ed's "ho-ho-ho" erupts from the box, the siren in her throat winds up, and all I see is the dark cave of her mouth.

What I need is a spray that smells of mankind's worst fears, something on the order of canned Hiroshima, a mist of organic putrefaction, that I'll spritz whenever the audience laughs. That'll teach her.

I stumble over my own meanness. Some son I am. What does she know about such things anyway? It's fair to say she's as innocent as a child. Her mind isn't cluttered with worries that extend beyond food and family. When she talks about the Japanese raids on her village back home, for instance, it's as a personal matter; the larger geopolitical landscape escapes her. She blinks her weary eyes. She's fighting sleep, hanging on to Johnny for one more guest before turning in. Suddenly, I have the urge to wrap my arms around her solid bulk and protect her, only she'd think I'm crazy, as I would if she did the same to me. "Go to bed," I say. "I'm not tired yet," she says. I cup my hands over my face, my fingers stinking of toilet-tissue lilacs and roses, and think things that should never enter a son's mind: a bomb explodes over the Empire State, forty blocks due north on a straight line from where we are seated, and glass shatters, and she's thrown back, the net on her hair, her pajamas, her beaded slippers on fire, and she hasn't a clue how such a thing can happen in this world. And I imagine I'll never see her again.

I fetch the newspaper, go to the couch where my mother's seated, and splashland down beside her. I'm all set to translate the headlines, to wake her up to the world, when I stop, my tongue suddenly lead. I don't have the words for this task. Once I went to school, my Chinese vocabulary stopped growing; in conversation with my mother I'm a linguistic dwarf. When I talk Chinese, I'm at best a precocious five-year-old, and what five-year-old chats about the military budget? Still, I'm determined and gather my courage. "What's that?" I ask, pointing at the dim photo on the front page. An Afghan guerrilla, eyes to sky, on the lookout for planes, crouches near the twisted body of a government soldier; in the desolate background there's a tank, busted up in pieces. My mother pulls on the glasses she bought at the drugstore and takes a closer look. "A monkey?" she says. I finger the body. She gives up. "That's a dead person," I say, pulling the paper away. "People are dying everywhere."

"You think I don't know. Your father just died." Her voice is quivering, but combative.

I realize I'm on shaky ground. "This man's killed by another man," I say. I'm supposed to talk about freedom, about self-determination, but with my vocabulary that's a task equal to digging a grave without a shovel. "People are killing people and all you worry about is your next bowl of rice."   10

"You don't need to eat?" she snaps. "Fine, don't eat. It costs money to put food on the table."

She keeps talking this way, but I tune her out, giving my all to Johnny. That guy from the San Diego Zoo's on, and with him is the fleshy pink offspring of an endangered species of wild boar. It knocks over Johnny's coffee, and Johnny jumps. The audience roars; I laugh too, but it's forced a forgery; my mother's still sore and just sits there, holding herself in like a bronze Buddha.

While I am at work the next day, she calls me. She wants to know whether I've rented a car yet. My youngest brother owns a house on the Island, and we're invited out for the weekend. My mother and I have gone over our plans many times already, so when she starts in now I lose patience in a wink. But I catch myself—with my mother repetition is a necessity, as it is when teaching a child to speak. The rental car is my idea. She says we'll save money by taking the train. But she keeps forgetting there's three of us traveling—me, my mother, and my friend Deborah. Once we agree to go in a rental car, she then tells me I should get a small model in order, again, to save money. "I'll ask for one with three wheels," I say. And she says anything's fine, but cheaper is better.

Later the same day, my boss, Kyoto, comes to my office with a problem. Every time we meet he sizes me up, eyes crawling across my body, and lots of sidelong glances. *Who is this guy?* It's the same going-over I get when I enter a sushi joint, when the chefs with their long knives and blood-red headbands stop work and take my measure, colonizers amused by the native's hunger for their superior culture. Kyoto says a client in the personal-hygiene business wants a "new and improved" scent for its men's deodorant.

"They want to change Musk 838/Lot No. i9144375941-3e?"   15

He bows his head, chin to chest. "You take care for Kyoto, okay?" Kyoto says.

I nod, slow and low, as if in mourning. He nods his head. I nod again.

Musk 838/Lot No. i9144375941-3e. Palm trees and surf, hibachied hotdogs topped with mustard, relish, and a tincture of Musk 838/Lot No. i9144375941-3e. Amanda Miller. Mandy Millstein. She was my love, and I followed her to Los Angeles. Within a year, about the time Sony purchased Columbia Pictures, she fell for someone named Ito, and broke off our engagement. When that happened, my siblings rushed to fill the void Mandy's leaving left in my life, and decided I should be my newly widowed mother's apartment mate. My mother had grown accustomed to Mandy. She spoke Chinese, a stunning Mandarin that she learned at Vassar, and while that wasn't my mother's dialect Mandy picked up enough Cantonese to hold an adult conversation, and what she couldn't bridge verbally she wrote in notes. They conspired together to celebrate Chinese festivals and holidays, making coconut-filled sweet-potato dumplings, lotus-seed cookies, daikon and green onion soup, tiny bowls of monk's food for New Year's Day. Beyond all that, Mandy had a ladylike manner of dressing that appealed to my mother's own vanity, and to her notions of what an American ("If you're going to marry a non-Chinese, she might as well look the part") should be: skirt, nylons, high-heel shoes.

Kyoto's request saddens me. Musk 838/Lot No. i9144375941-3e, a synthetic hybrid of natural deer and mink musks, spiced with a twist of mint, was, and always will be, our special scent. Taken internally, it had an aphrodisiacal effect on Mandy. One night, as was my custom, I had brought samples of our latest flavors and fragrances home from the lab. As usual, Mandy eagerly sniffed the tiny corked vials; when she tried the musk, she said it smelled dirty. I told her that to fully appreciate its essence it needed to come in contact with the heat of one's skin. She, of course, refused to experiment with her own flesh, so I volunteered my hand; as she poured, I warned her that this was a concentrate, each drop equal in potency to the glandular secretions of a herd of buck deer. Clearly my warnings unsettled her, because the next thing I know Mandy had dumped the whole works onto my palm. Later that evening, as planned, I made pizza, working the dough with my well-scrubbed hands, but Ivory soap, as it turned out, was no match for the oily compounds in Musk 838/Lot No. i9144375941-3e. The baking pie filled the apartment with a scent reminiscent of horses. But the pizza itself was a sensation, every bite bearing a snootful of joy: tomato sauce that seemed to have fangs, cheese as virile as steak, onions so pungent they ripped our eyes from our heads. "It tastes alive," Mandy said.

"Wild," I said.   20

"It's the basil," she said.

Her eyes caught mine. I shook my head. "Not basil," I said, "not oregano."

She creased her second slice and dipped her fingertip in the reservoir of orange grease that pooled in the resulting valley. She touched her glistening orange finger to the gap between my eyebrows, then let it slide south down the bridge of my nose, stopping at the fleshy tip of my northernmost lip. At that moment I realized we'd been eating Musk 838/Lot No. i9144375941-3e. If it had any toxic properties, it hardly mattered then. Mandy started giggling, as if she were high on grass, and I laughed to keep her company. She drew circles on my cheeks with the orange musk-laced oils. A regular pizza face. She cackled in the manner of chimps, and when I returned the favor and greased her with gleaming polka dots, I got the joke: no doubt I looked as dopey as she did then.

After that we spiked our food and beverages with Musk 838/Lot No. i9144375941-3e whenever Mandy was feeling amorous but needed a jump start.

I wonder how she has managed since she left. When she needs that little extra, does she do the same trick with Ito? Has he noticed that his California rolls smell funny—not fishy, but gamy like a herd of deer? If Mandy wants to recapture that old magic she had with me, she'll have to act quickly. Kyoto says it's time for a change. The manly scent of musk is no longer manly enough.   25

It's a sad day for love, Mandy, everywhere.

This is a fancy car," my mother says in Chinese as we stop-and-go up Third Avenue. "It must've cost you a bundle. Tell me, *how mucha cents*," she says conspiratorially. I look at her and say nothing.

"Isn't this nice of Bagel," my mother says a few minutes later. My youngest brother, the landowner in Bridgehampton, has always been called "Bagel" in the family. His real name is Billy, and God help him who drops "Bagel" in front of Bagel's friends. My mother's the lone exception. When she says Bagel, he knows his friends simply think that's her immigrant tongue mangling "Billy." "Out of you four brothers and sisters," she adds, "only Bagel asks me to visit."

"What are you saying? How can I invite you over when I live with you?"

"That's right. You're a good son."   30

"I didn't say I was a good son, but didn't I bring you out to California?"

"*Ah-mahn-da* invited me."

"I told *Amanda* to invite you while she was talking to you on the phone."

"That's right, that's right. You're a good son," she says. "Good son who doesn't know how to talk to his own mother. His American girl speaks better Chinese."

"*Forget it*," I say, waving her off.   35

"That's right. Always '*fo-gellit, fo-gellit.*' Ah-mahn-da never uses such words."

I swing across Twenty-third heading for Park. "Look at so many Puerto Ricans," she says. "Just like in California."

My brain stops, wrapped around a telephone pole that is my mother. I tell myself, *Try*. Explain the difference to your mother, who knows next to nothing: in Los Angeles what she thinks are Puerto Ricans are Mexicans and Chicanos. But I don't even know the words for Mexico, so how do I begin? In Chinese I'm as geography-poor as my mother, who knows only the streets and fields she's walked. Maybe I should use my hands. This is California, Amanda and I lived here, and over here—by my right hand—is another country Americans call Mexico. But that requires the patience of a special-ed teacher. In her mental maps, California is a few hours' drive from New York. That's what I'm up against.

Deborah is a bean pole. As a joke, my mother calls her "Mah-ti," water chestnut, the squat, bulbous tuber that tapers to a point like a mini dunce cap. She has hips that flare like the fins of an old Cadillac, but no rump to speak of. She wears glasses with a rhinestone frame—she's had the same ones since the eighth grade; this is not a stab at style here—and photosensitive lenses that have the annoying quality of never being dark enough or clear enough; she's always in a haze. On the rare occasions she's visited me at my mother's, she's come dressed in a most unladylike fashion: penny loafers or running shoes, chinos, and shirts bought in a boys' department. Today is no exception. I stop the rental car, a big Chevy four-door, at Park and Thirty-third. She grabs the front-passenger-side handle and stands there expecting my mother to climb into the backseat like a dog. I hit the power window switches. "You can sit in front when we stop to pee," I say.

Deborah slams the door behind her. She leans forward in her seat. "How are you, Mrs. Pang?" I've heard her speak more warmly to the bald mice she tends at Sloan-Kettering. That's where we met. At the lab we had had a small-scale scare, a baby version of the Red Dye No. 3 controversy a few years back, that forced Kyoto to send me, his right-hand slave, across town to have the stuff tested in Deborah's mice.

"*Goot*," my mother says. "*How you?*"

Deborah doesn't answer. Won't waste her breath on someone who can't take the conversation the next step. Mrs. Pang, the linguistic dead-end street. Barbarian, I think. But a savage in bed she is, even without Musk 838/Lot No. i9144375941-3e. Early on, my mother caught us in the sack—her sack, in fact—bony Deborah, with breasts like thimbles, on all fours. At that moment, as my mother's eyes burned holes through our nakedness, I meant to say, "What are you looking at?" full of indignation, but it came out a meek, "What do you see?" Fine, Deborah, I think, trash my mother; you're not a keeper anyway, as the fishermen say. She's the rebound among rebounds; only somehow she's stuck. If I had the words I'd straighten my mother out, allay her fears. What is she so fond of saying? "Are you planning to marry Mah-ti?" To which I tell her, emphatically, no. "So why," she says back, "you always hugging that scrawny thing?"

The trouble between Deborah and my mother runs deeper than the fact that my mother's seen the glare of Deborah's glassy bare rump. There are things I can do to soften their feelings toward each other. I might buy Deborah a pair of high-heel shoes, or register her at Hunter for Cantonese classes, or rent videos of the Frugal Gourmet cooking Chinese; I might ask my mother to stop calling Deborah Mah-ti and teach her, with patient repetition, the difficult syllables of Deborah's given name. But Deborah wants me to move out of my mother's place, says I'm a mama's boy, calls me that even as we make love; and my mother's still sad about the loss of Mandy, her surrogate Chinese daughter-in-law. My mother is subtle about this: "Mah-ti has no smell," she says, "like paper." That is to say, she misses Mandy, who made a point of showering herself with the perfumes I brought home from the lab whenever she visited my mother. There's no clean dealing with either of them.

When we pass the gas tanks along the Expressway, my mother tells me this is the very route Bagel always takes to his house. She says this with a measure of pride; I can tell what's going on in her head: I'm driving the same road my brother has driven, and to my mother's way of thinking that's not only a remarkable coincidence but a confirmation of

40

the common thread between us, our genes, our good blood—ah, her boys, her talented womb! So why bother telling her the Expressway is the only reasonable route out to Bagel's?

Her last time out, she says, she drove with Bagel and his friend "*Ah-Jay-mee*" in the   45
latter's two-seater, with Bagel folded into the rear storage area, best suited for umbrellas and tennis rackets. Then she wistfully adds that Bagel's former apartment mate Dennis had a car that had an entire backseat, but that luxury is "washed up" since he moved out.

After a while Deborah taps me on the shoulder. "What's she saying? She's talking about me, right? I heard her say my name."

"She said Dennis."

"*Dennis-ah cah bik,*" my mother tells Deborah, spreading her hand to show size.

"Tell her this is a 'bik' pain in the you-know-what," Deborah says in a huff. "Tell her I'm tired of your secrecy, of being gossiped about in front of my face."

I say, "Slow down, okay? We're discussing my brother."   50

"What's Mah-ti saying?" my mother asks.

"She's saying her parents have a big car. She wants to take you on a drive someday."

My mother turns to Deborah and says, "*Goot!*"

There's not much traffic eastbound on a Saturday, not at this hour. Deborah's listening to her Walkman; I take the tinny *scrape scrape scrape* of the headphone's overflow as a token of peace. My mother stares out the windshield. Her eyes look glazed, uncomprehending. She seems out of place in a car, near machines, a woman from another culture, of another time, at ease with needle and thread, around pigs and horses. When I think of my mother's seventy-five-year-old body hurtling forward at eighty miles an hour, I think of our country's first astronaut, a monkey strapped into the Mercury capsule, all wires and restraints and electricity, shot screaming into outer space.

With Deborah occupied, I figure it's safe to talk. A chance to humanize the speed,   55
the way pharmaceutical companies sweeten their chemicals with Cherry 12/Lot No. x362-4d so a new mother will eyedropper the stuff into her baby's mouth.

We speak at the same time.

"Ah-Vee-ah," she says my Chinese name in a whisper, "why is it that *Ba-ko* has no girlfriends? You have too many. You should marry. Look at Ah-yo. See how content he is?"

Poor Ray! If she only knew half of his troubles.

"Why is *Bak-ko* so stubborn?" she asks. "I tell you something, when I offer to take him to Hong Kong to find a bride, you know what he says? He says he's already married to his cat. Ah-Vee-ah," she says, touching my hand, "he upsets me so, I wouldn't even mind if he dated your Mah-ti."

I laugh a little; she shows her gold mischievously. "Tell me," she says (we're confidants now), "what do you make of your youngest brother?"   60

I shrug my shoulders. "*I don't know,*" I say, turning palms up. "Ask him."

"I'm talking to you now."

"Talk to Bagel."

"*Fo-gellit!*" she says.

At some time or other, my mother's offered to take all the boys on bride safaris   65
in Hong Kong. Ray's the only one to take her up on it, and came back to the States with a Nikon and telephoto lenses and horror stories about pigeon restaurants. He's married to a Catholic girl named Polly, who insisted, probably to get back at her parents for some past sins, on taking his name—Polly Pang. Even Ray tried to dissuade her. Following my example, Bagel has turned my mother down every time. Once after a family

dinner, I overheard my mother working on Bagel. She said, "I want to see Hong Kong again before I die. I first went there in 1939 because of the Japanese. How proud I'd be returning to old friends with such a fine young son! 'An overseas bandit,' they call you. They line the prettiest girls up for you. Whatever you like. You pick. Take her out. If you don't like her, you try another. *Too muchee Chinee girl.*"

My brother said, "I'm too busy for a wife."

"She cook for you."

"I won't be able to talk to her."

"They're all very modern. They're learning English. If you take a young one, you can teach her yourself."

"I'm already married to my cat."   70

"Such crazy talk," she said. "What kind of life is that, hugging a cat all the time. She give you babies?"

"*Forget it,*" he said. "Too much trouble."

"You're killing me," she said. "Soon I'll be lying next to your father. You crazy juksing, you do as I say. Before it's too late, marry a Chinese girl who will remember my grave and come with food and spirit money. Left up to you, I'll starve when I'm dead."

Bagel's house is white. Even the oak floors have been bleached white. A stranger in a white turtleneck and white pleated trousers opens the door. He's very blond, with dazzling teeth and a jawline that's an archeologist's dream. "Well, look who's here," he says, "the brother, et al." We shake hands, and he says his name's Nino. Nino leads us to the sun-washed living room and introduces us to Mack, who's sprawled over a couch with the *Times*. My mother whispers that she'd warned my brother against buying a white couch because it wouldn't "withstand the dirt," but she's surprised at how clean it looks. Mack's dressed like Deborah, and this depresses me. "Billy," Nino says in a loud singsong, "big bro and Mommy's here."

Jamie of the two-seater comes into the living room. He hugs my mother, shakes   75
my hand, and nods at Deborah. He's in a white terry-cloth robe and Italian loafers, and offers us coffee. Down the hallway someone starts to run a shower.

While Jamie grinds coffee beans in the kitchen, Nino says, "I had the worst night's sleep." He's stretched out on the other couch, his hand cupped over his eyes. "What a shock to the system, it was so damn quiet. How do the chipmunks stand it?" Then my brother makes his entrance decked out in hound's-tooth slacks, tight turquoise tennis shirt, and black-and-white saddle shoes. "God, Billy," Nino says, "you always look so pulled together."

Hugs and kisses all the way around. Bagel's got bulk. He pumps iron. I feel as if I'm holding a steer.

"*Ah-Ba-ko,*" my mother says, once we have resettled in our seats, "come and see." She leans forward in her easy chair, a white plastic shopping bag of goodies from Chinatown at her feet. "I told her not to," I say as she unloads bundles of raw greens and paper boats of dumplings onto the armrests. When she magically lifts the roast duck from the bag, soy sauce drips from the take-out container and lands on the chair, spotting the off-white fabric. Bagel has a fit: "I invite you to dinner and you bring dinner."

"So what else is new?" I hear Deborah say.

Within seconds, Nino, Mack, Jamie, and Bagel converge on the stains with sponges,   80
Palmolive dishwashing detergent, paper towels, and a pot of water. An eight-armed upholstery patrol.

Soon after, we're having Jamie's coffee and nibbling on my mother's dumplings, which Bagel has arranged beautifully on a Chinese-looking platter, as much a conciliatory gesture as it is his way of doing things.

"Bette Davis was buried yesterday," Mack says, from behind the paper.

"Really?" says Nino. "God, now there's a lady. Hollywood heaven, open your gates. May she rest . . . in . . . peace."

"What eyes she had," says Jamie, "like two full moons."

"Old bug eyes," Deborah says.   85

Nino makes a hissing sound. We all look at Deborah. "Oh, hell," Nino finally says, "what does she know?"

"How old was she?" my brother asks before Deborah can answer Nino back.

"Who knows? I saw her on Johnny Carson and she looked like hell."

"*Johnny Cahson?* He said *Johnny Cahson,* right?" My mother giggles, thrilled she understood a bit of our conversation.

Bagel rolls his eyes at me like Johnny. I shrug my shoulders as if to say, I didn't invite her to the party.   90

"I wanted so badly for Bette to be beautiful, but she looked like leftovers that even the cat won't touch. I swear I cried, she was such a mess."

"He did," says Mack. "Poor Nino, it was tragic. He cried the biggest tears ever. But you have to admit, she still had those fabulous eyes."

"Sure, eyes. The rest of her head has been run over by Hurricane Hugo."

"I saw that show," Jamie says. "Her mind was still there. She was very sharp."

"Oh sure," says Nino, "so's broken glass."   95

Deborah laughs; then my mother laughs. "What is she laughing about?" my mother asks through her own laughter. I shake my head to quiet her down.

Bagel holds up a gray-skinned dumpling to the ceiling. A toast: he says, "*What Ever Happened to Baby Jane?*"

"*Jezebel,*" says Jamie.

"*All About Eve.*"

"*Kid Galahad,*" I say.   100

"Oooo, that has Edward G. Robinson in it," Nino says.

Bagel's cat, Judy, and her husband, Vavoom, enter the living room, led by their noses. My mother surreptitiously plunks a shrimp dumpling on each armrest. She sees I see her doing this, and I scowl at her and she scowls back, then covers her gold mine with her hand as she breaks into a smile. She's surrounded by cats. "Look! What an adorable picture!" says Nino. "Judy, Vavoom, and Mrs. Pang, the goddess of treats." Then he adds, "Truthfully, I wouldn't give away any of these delicacies to cats; I wouldn't give any to Bette, even if she begged from her deathbed. Mrs. Pang, you've made lifelong friends." My mother, hearing her name, looks up from the cats, but the dim heat of her eyes tells everyone she's understood little else. "Silly me," Nino says, "did I say something?"

Bagel's a commercial artist, Nino's a jewelry designer, Mack's a book editor, Jamie's a city attorney. During a lull in the conversation, which we fill by watching the cats walk across my mother's lap from one armrest to the other, Jamie asks what's new at my job. I consider the Kyoto-Musk 838/Lot No. i9144375941-3e affair, but I realize if I mention Mandy's name my mother will start in on me. So, instead, I improvise: "The rumor going around the lab," I begin, "says the chemists are developing a spray for the homeless, a time-release formula that'll simulate, in succession, the smell of a living room in a Scarsdale Tudor, a regular coffee (cream and one sugar), a roast-beef dinner, and fresh sheets washed in Tide."

"How ingenious!" Nino says. "The nose is such an amazing organ."

"When someone asks you for change," says Mack, "you give him a squirt of the comforts of home." 105

"Picture this, a panhandler in a subway car: 'Spare spray, spare spray?' "

"This is sick," says Deborah.

"I'm just giving you the latest gossip," I say. "The other rumor is that the city plans to distribute the stuff to the homeless."

"Cheaper than shelters, I suppose," Mack says.

"This is news to me," says Jamie, the city attorney. "But I wouldn't put it past the 110 mayor's office. Remember those prints of potted flowers the city put in the windows of abandoned buildings up in Harlem?"

He pours himself a cup of coffee. "I'm working on a homeless case right now," he says. "This couple, the Montezumas, show up at Bellevue one day. They're carrying one of those Express Mail envelopes and inside there's a baby, hot and sticky from being born, the cord still on. She's purple, in real trouble. The doctors hook her up to machines, but in a few days she dies. Only she doesn't look dead. The machines pump air into her lungs, and somehow her heart keeps beating."

"Then she's alive," I say.

"No, she *looks* alive, but that's what Montezuma claims. Her chest goes up and down. But her brain doesn't register a single blip on the screen. Specialists are called in, and they tell Montezuma the same story. But Montezuma says God is testing us all, and he won't let the hospital pull the plug. Meanwhile the city is footing the bill. More specialists are consulted; Montezuma still refuses to sign the forms, so finally the city steps in and turns off the juice. The next thing you know, half the attorneys in town are fighting for the chance to sue the city, and I have lots of work."

Bagel, Jamie, and I spend the afternoon playing tennis while my mother watches us from the car. The others take a drive around the "countryside."

We eat dinner late. Jamie barbecues chicken. My mother chops her duck into rec- 115 tangular chunks. We drink three bottles of chardonnay. Afterward, we're in the kitchen, slicing pies, making coffee, putting away leftovers, washing dishes.

I hear my mother calling for Bagel. We find each other in the busy kitchen, and he asks me to see what she wants.

She's in the master bedroom standing in front of the TV set. It's turned on; the screen's filled with pink and blue snow.

"What are you doing?" I say. "This is Saturday. There's no Johnny Carson."

"You think I don't know," she says. "Saturday night has to have wrestling."

I flip through the stations with the remote control. For as long as I can remem- 120 ber, my mother has been a wrestling fan. It's good pitted against evil; the clean-shaven, self-effacing, play-by-the-rules good guy versus the strutting, loudmouthed, eye-gouger. No language skills required here. A dialogue of dropkicks, forearm smashes, and body slams. It's a big fake but my mother believes. And for a long time, as a kid, our family gathered in front of the set Saturday nights, drinking sodas and cracking red pistachio nuts, true believers all.

In one of my strongest memories, a man from ringside wearing a pea coat and knit cap, with a duffel bag slung over his shoulder, leapt into the ring where the champ, a vicious long-haired blond, was taking a post-victory strut on his victim's chest. The fans in the arena, my mother beside me, were voicing their indignation when this mystery man, who looked as if he had walked in off the streets, caught the champ unawares, lifted him onto his shoulder, and applied a backbreaker, soon recognized as his signature hold. What joy, what gratitude, what relief we all felt! Justice restored! Later in the program, the ringside announcer interviewed our hero. He was an Italian sailor, he said, in heavily accented English, a recent immigrant to U.S. shores.

It was myth in action. The American Dream in all its muscle-bound splendor played out before our faithful eyes.

My mother and I sit at the edge of the king-size bed. On the screen, a match is about to begin between a doe-faced boy named Bubby Arnold and the Samurai Warrior. The All-American Boy meets the Yellow Peril. The outcome is obvious to everyone except my mother. She yells encouragement to Bubby, "Kill him, kill the little Jap boy!" as he bounds across the ring, all grit and determination, but promptly collapses to the mat when he runs into the Samurai Warrior's lethal, upraised foot. I shake my head. By then my thoughts are full of Kyoto and Mandy's Ito. My Musk 838/Lot No. i9144375941-3e, testament to our love, and my tenuous hold on Mandy are crumbling, going the way of Bubby Arnold under the Samurai Warrior's assault. I ache for Bubby, the poor schnook. I can't bear to watch. But my mother hasn't given up. She screams for her man to step on his opponent's bare toes, to yank on his goatee. But that isn't in the script. He isn't paid to be resourceful, no Yankee ingenuity here. No one, not my mother and her frantic heart, can change the illusion.

At the commercial break my mother says, "The Japanese are so cruel. He almost killed that poor boy." She goes on that way, recounting the mugging, and I tell her not to take it so seriously. "It's all a fake," I say. "He's not really hurt."

"I have eyes," she says. "I know what I just saw."   125

I'm surprised by the sudden heat in her voice, by the wound beneath the words. The fights matter: in them, she believes her heart's desire, her words of encouragement have currency. What *she* wants counts. But the truth is she doesn't believe what she has seen. The good guy should win. Somewhere in that mind of hers she carries hope for the impossible. Bubby Arnold triumphant, Mandy back in our lives again. I look at her, a woman against the odds. What a life of disappointment!

I won't let her down as Bubby Arnold has. She needs to hear the truth: there is no Santa; the Communists aren't leaving China. Her beloved Amanda is gone for good.

"I have to tell you something." I take a deep breath and say, "Amanda," and as anticipated, she's startled, expectant, hanging on my next word.

I regret I ever started. That hope is flickering in her irises, and it's poison to my enterprise. But I have no recourse but to get on with it; as my mother likes to say at such a juncture, "You wet your hair, you might as well cut it."

I know what I want to say in English. My mind's stuffed full with the words. I pull   130
one sentence at a time from the elegant little speech I've devised over the months for just this occasion, and try to piece together a word-for-word translation into Chinese. Yielding nonsense. I abandon this approach and opt for the shorter path, the one of reduction, simplicity, lowest common denominator. "*Ah-mahn-da*, what? Talk if you have talk." There's music in her voice I haven't heard in years.

"I like *Amanda*," I say.

My mother nods. On the TV, wrestlers being interviewed snarl into the camera and holler threats that seem directed not so much at future opponents, but at the viewers themselves.

"She doesn't like me," I say.

"Crazy boy. Like? What is this "like"? I lived all those years without your father—who worried about who liked which one? Tomorrow, you call her back here."

Samurai Warrior's grinning face fills the screen. In the background his manager   135
carries on about the mysteries of the Orient, tea ceremonies, karate, brown rice, and his
client's Banzai Death Grip.

"Look it, look it. He's so brutal, that one is," my mother says. She touches my
cheek, her hand warm but leathery. I can't remember this happening before. "You say
you like her, so call her back."

"What's wrong with your ears? I said she doesn't like me. She likes him." I point
at the TV.

"Crazy boy. What are you saying?" She dismisses me, her fingers pushing off my
cheek, as if they have springs.

"*Amanda* likes a Japanese."

"That one?" she says, meaning the wrestler.   140

I pound my fists against my thighs. "No, not him." I stand up and pace the carpet
between my mother and the TV set. "*Amanda*," I begin, "*Amanda* . . ." And each time
I say her name and hesitate, my mother sucks in breath and inflates with new hope. I
stop pacing. She looks up at me from her seat at the edge of the bed. I touch her cheeks
with both hands. I don't know where the gesture comes from, movies or TV, but it has
nothing to do with what went on in our household. I am on strange ground. In my
palms her face is a glass bowl, open and cool. "*Amanda* likes you. She doesn't like me.
She likes a Japanese boy in *California*. I can call her, but she's not coming back."

My mother pulls away, not just from my hands, but receding, a filament inside
her dimming. "*Ah-mahn-da* makes a delicious dumpling," she says in a small, distant
voice. "She rolls the skins so delicately."

During the next match she is uncharacteristically subdued. The fight has left her.
On the screen two masked wrestlers beat up Bubby Arnold clones. Nothing issues from
her, no encouragement, no outrage, no hope. I've robbed my mother of her pleasure,
of her flimsy faith in Americans, in America, and in me. And I don't have the words for
I am sorry, or fine sentences that would resurrect her faith and put things back in order.
I'm the pebble in her shoe, the stone in her kidney. Now I see that she's Montezuma from
Jamie's story: she would hold on to the slimmest hope, while I, as I have just done, would
rush in and pull the plug on her.

At the next commercial time-out she turns to me and says, "Ah-Vee-ah, all the
men in this house have good jobs, they have money, why don't they have women? Why
is your brother that way? What does he tell you? I don't understand." She speaks
somberly, with difficulty, as she had when she described the raids.

Her eyes, I see, are filled with tears. I know that she cries easily and often since my   145
father's death. I've heard her in her room late at night.

I put my hand on her back, as round as a turtle's, but hot and meaty. "I don't
know," I tell her, and for the first time I am stunned by my deception of her. "I don't know
why there's no women here."

Bagel comes to the bedroom announcing coffee and dessert. He turns off the
set. I can read his mind. He doesn't want his friends to know he dropped from the womb
of one who loves something as low as wrestling. "Come eat *pie*," he says.

"*Pie*. Who made them?" she asks.

"I did, who else? I stayed up last night baking pies for you. Come on."

"Yours I won't eat," she says. "I want to taste your girlfriend's baking."   150

"You crazy? I don't have a girlfriend," he says. "She's driving me crazy!" he ex-
claims, then leaves the bedroom, and we follow.

"*Ca-lay-zee.* Who's *ca-lay-zee?* You hammerhead. Hug your dead cat the rest of your life. How fragrant is that?"

"*Forget it,* Ma," I say. I touch her shoulder, but she flicks me off.

"Ah-Ma," she says. "How can I be your mother if nobody listens to what I say?"

At the table we are confronted with big wedges of apple pie. My mother's still   155
upset. She stares at the pie as if it were a form of torture.

"Where've you two been?" Deborah asks.

"In the bedroom, watching wrestling."

"God, how retro," she says. "What's happening to you?"

"Bagel," I say, stopping his hand as he's about to spoon sugar into my mother's coffee.

"Bagels?" Jamie says. "You're hungry for bagels? We're having bagels for breakfast."   160

I say nothing. I pull from my pocket gold-foil packets the size and shape of condoms. Inside each is a tablet developed at the lab. You dissolve it in your mouth, and it will disguise the sourness of whatever you drink or eat. I pass them to everyone at the table.

They won't know what has happened. They will laugh, delighted by the tricks of their tongues. But soon the old bitterness in our mouths will be forgotten, and from this moment on, our words will come out sweet.

GABRIEL GARCÍA MÁRQUEZ   (b. 1928)

Born in Colombia, Gabriel García Márquez won the Nobel Prize for fiction in 1982. Like other great Latin American writers, he creates a unique blend of realism and fantasy in his stories, many of which take place in the fictional town Macondo, based on his native Aracataca. Among his novels are One Hundred Years of Solitude *(1967),* The Autumn of the Patriarch *(1976), and* Love in the Time of Cholera *(1988), all impressive successes. When* One Hundred Years of Solitude *was published, his usual print run for a book was seven hundred copies, but the publisher had so much faith in it that he printed eight thousand. To date, this book has sold over ten million copies in thirty languages. García Márquez's collections of stories include* No One Writes to the Colonel and Other Stories *(1968),* Leaf Storm and Other Stories *(1972), and* Innocent Erendira and Other Stories *(1978). His early years were spent as a journalist, and he has said, "I'm fascinated by the relationship between literature and journalism. I began my career as a journalist in Colombia, and a reporter is something I have never stopped being."*

Eyes of a Blue Dog ————————————————————— 1968

Then she looked at me. I thought that she was looking at me for the first time. But then, when she turned around behind the lamp and I kept feeling her slippery and oily look in back of me, over my shoulder, I understood that it was I who was looking at her for the first time. I lit a cigarette. I took a drag on the harsh, strong smoke, before spinning in the chair, balancing on one of the rear legs. After that I saw her there, as if she'd been standing beside the lamp looking at me every night. For a few brief minutes that's all we did: look at each other. I looked from the chair, balancing on one of the rear legs. She stood, with a long and quiet hand on the lamp, looking at me. I saw her eyelids lighted up as on every night. It was then that I remembered the usual thing, when

I said to her: "Eyes of a blue dog." Without taking her hand off the lamp she said to me: "That. We'll never forget that." She left the orbit, sighing: "Eyes of a blue dog. I've written it everywhere."

I saw her walk over to the dressing table. I watched her appear in the circular glass of the mirror looking at me now at the end of a back and forth of mathematical light. I watched her keep on looking at me with her great hot-coal eyes: looking at me while she opened the little box covered with pink mother of pearl. I saw her powder her nose. When she finished, she closed the box, stood up again, and walked over to the lamp once more, saying: "I'm afraid that someone is dreaming about this room and revealing my secrets." And over the flame she held the same long and tremulous hand that she had been warming before sitting down at the mirror. And she said: "You don't feel the cold." And I said to her: "Sometimes." And she said to me: "You must feel it now." And then I understood why I couldn't have been alone in the seat. It was the cold that had been giving me the certainty of my solitude. "Now I feel it," I said. "And it's strange because the night is quiet. Maybe the sheet fell off." She didn't answer. Again she began to move toward the mirror and I turned again in the chair, keeping my back to her. Without seeing her, I knew what she was doing. I knew that she was sitting in front of the mirror again, seeing my back, which had had time to reach the depths of the mirror and be caught by her look, which had also had just enough time to reach the depths and return—before the hand had time to start the second turn—until her lips were anointed now with crimson, from the first turn of her hand in front of the mirror. I saw, opposite me, the smooth wall, which was like another blind mirror in which I couldn't see her—sitting behind me—but could imagine her where she probably was as if a mirror had been hung in place of the wall. "I see you," I told her. And on the wall I saw what was as if she had raised her eyes and had seen me with my back turned toward her from the chair, in the depths of the mirror, my face turned toward the wall. Then I saw her lower her eyes again and remain with her eyes always on her brassiere, not talking. And I said to her again: "I see you." And she raised her eyes from her brassiere again. "That's impossible," she said. I asked her why. And she, with her eyes quiet and on her brassiere again: "Because your face is turned toward the wall." Then I spun the chair around. I had the cigarette clenched in my mouth. When I stayed facing the mirror she was back by the lamp. Now she had her hands open over the flame, like the two wings of a hen, toasting herself, and with her face shaded by her own fingers. "I think I'm going to catch cold," she said. "This must be a city of ice." She turned her face to profile and her skin, from copper to red, suddenly became sad. "Do something about it," she said. And she began to get undressed, item by item, starting at the top with the brassiere. I told her: "I'm going to turn back to the wall." She said: "No. In any case, you'll see me the way you did when your back was turned." And no sooner had she said it than she was almost completely undressed, with the flame licking her long copper skin. "I've always wanted to see you like that, with the skin of your belly full of deep pits, as if you'd been beaten." And before I realized that my words had become clumsy at the sight of her nakedness, she became motionless, warming herself on the globe of the lamp, and she said: "Sometimes I think I'm made of metal." She was silent for an instant. The position of her hands over the flame varied slightly. I said: "Sometimes, in other dreams, I've thought you were only a little bronze statue in the corner of some museum. Maybe that's why you're cold." And she said: "Sometimes, when I sleep on my heart, I can feel my body growing hollow and my skin is like plate. Then, when the blood beats inside me, it's as if someone were calling by knocking on my stomach and I can feel my own copper sound in the bed. It's like—what do you call it—laminated metal." She drew closer to the lamp. "I would have liked to hear you," I said. And she said: "If we find each other sometime, put your ear to my ribs when I sleep on the left side and you'll hear me echoing. I've always wanted you to do it sometime." I heard her breathe heavily as she talked. And she said that for years she'd done nothing different. Her life had been dedicated to finding me in reality, through that identifying phrase: "Eyes of a blue dog." And she went along the street saying it aloud, as a way of telling the only person who could have understood her:

"I'm the one who comes into your dreams every night and tells you: 'Eyes of a blue dog.' " And she said that she went into restaurants and before ordering said to the waiters: "Eyes of a blue dog." But the waiters bowed reverently, without remembering ever having said that in their dreams. Then she would write on the napkins and scratch on the varnish of the tables with a knife: "Eyes of a blue dog." And on the steamed-up windows of hotels, stations, all public buildings, she would write with her forefinger: "Eyes of a blue dog." She said that once she went into a drugstore and noticed the same smell that she had smelled in her room one night after having dreamed about me. "He must be near," she thought, seeing the clean, new tiles of the drugstore. Then she went over to the clerk and said to him: "I always dream about a man who says to me: 'Eyes of a blue dog.' " And she said the clerk had looked at her eyes and told her: "As a matter of fact, miss, you do have eyes like that." And she said to him: "I have to find the man who told me those very words in my dreams." And the clerk started to laugh and moved to the other end of the counter. She kept on seeing the clean tile and smelling the odor. And she opened her purse and on the tiles, with her crimson lipstick, she wrote in red letters: "Eyes of a blue dog." The clerk came back from where he had been. He told her: "Madam, you have dirtied the tiles." He gave her a damp cloth, saying: "Clean it up." And she said, still by the lamp, that she had spent the whole afternoon on all fours, washing the tiles and saying: "Eyes of a blue dog," until people gathered at the door and said she was crazy.

Now, when she finished speaking, I remained in the corner, sitting, rocking in the chair. "Every day I try to remember the phrase with which I am to find you," I said. "Now I don't think I'll forget it tomorrow. Still, I've always said the same thing and when I wake up I've always forgotten what the words I can find you with are." And she said: "You invented them yourself on the first day." And I said to her: "I invented them because I saw your eyes of ash. But I never remember the next morning." And she, with clenched fists, beside the lamp, breathed deeply: "If you could at least remember now what city I've been writing it in."

Her tightened teeth gleamed over the flame. "I'd like to touch you now," I said. 5 She raised the face that had been looking at the light; she raised her look, burning, roasting, too, just like her, like her hands, and I felt that she saw me, in the corner where I was sitting, rocking in the chair. "You'd never told me that," she said. "I tell you now and it's the truth," I said. From the other side of the lamp she asked for a cigarette. The butt had disappeared between my fingers. I'd forgotten that I was smoking. She said: "I don't know why I can't remember where I wrote it." And I said to her: "For the same reason that tomorrow I won't be able to remember the words." And she said sadly: "No. It's just that sometimes I think that I've dreamed that too." I stood up and walked toward the lamp. She was a little beyond, and I kept on walking with the cigarettes and matches in my hand, which would not go beyond the lamp. I held the cigarette out to her. She squeezed it between her lips and leaned over to reach the flame before I had time to light the match. "In some city in the world, on all the walls, those words have to appear in writing: 'Eyes of a blue dog,' " I said. "If I remembered them tomorrow I could find you." She raised her head again and now the lighted coal was between her lips. "Eyes of a blue dog," she sighed, remembered, with the cigarette drooping over her chin and one eye half closed. Then she sucked in the smoke with the cigarette between her fingers and exclaimed: "This is something else now. I'm warming up." And she said it with her voice a little lukewarm and fleeting, as if she hadn't really said it, but as if she had written it on a piece of paper and had brought the paper close to the flame while I read: "I'm warming," and she had continued with the paper between her thumb and forefinger, turning it around as it was being consumed and I had just read ". . . up," before the paper was completely consumed and dropped all wrinkled to the floor, diminished, converted into light ash dust. "That's better," I said. "Sometimes it frightens me to see you that way. Trembling beside a lamp."

We had been seeing each other for several years. Sometimes, when we were already together, somebody would drop a spoon outside and we would wake up. Little by little we'd been coming to understand that our friendship was subordinated to things, to the simplest of happenings. Our meetings always ended that way, with the fall of a spoon early in the morning.

Now, next to the lamp, she was looking at me. I remembered that she had also looked at me in that way in the past, from that remote dream where I made the chair spin on its back legs and remained facing a strange woman with ashen eyes. It was in that dream that I asked her for the first time: "Who are you?" And she said to me: "I don't remember." I said to her: "But I think we've seen each other before." And she said, indifferently: "I think I dreamed about you once, about this same room." And I told her: "That's it. I'm beginning to remember now." And she said: "How strange. It's certain that we've met in other dreams."

She took two drags on the cigarette. I was still standing, facing the lamp, when suddenly I kept looking at her. I looked her up and down and she was still copper; no longer hard and cold metal, but yellow, soft, malleable copper. "I'd like to touch you," I said again. And she said: "You'll ruin everything." I said: "It doesn't matter now. All we have to do is turn the pillow over in order to meet again." And I held my hand out over the lamp. She didn't move. "You'll ruin everything," she said again before I could touch her. "Maybe, if you come around behind the lamp, we'd wake up frightened in who knows what part of the world." But I insisted: "It doesn't matter." And she said: "If we turned over the pillow, we'd meet again. But when you wake up you'll have forgotten." I began to move toward the corner. She stayed behind, warming her hands over the flame. And I still wasn't beside the chair when I heard her say behind me: "When I wake up at midnight, I keep turning in bed, with the fringe of the pillow burning my knee, and repeating until dawn: 'Eyes of a blue dog.' "

Then I remained with my face toward the wall. "It's already dawning," I said without looking at her. "When it struck two I was awake and that was a long time back." I went to the door. When I had the knob in my hand, I heard her voice again, the same, invariable. "Don't open that door," she said. "The hallway is full of difficult dreams." And I asked her: "How do you know?" And she told me: "Because I was there a moment ago and I had to come back when I discovered I was sleeping on my heart." I had the door half opened. I moved it a little and a cold, thin breeze brought me the fresh smell of vegetable earth, damp fields. She spoke again. I gave the turn, still moving the door, mounted on silent hinges, and I told her: "I don't think there's any hallway outside here. I'm getting the smell of country." And she, a little distant, told me: "I know that better than you. What's happening is that there's a woman outside dreaming about the country." She crossed her arms over the flame. She continued speaking: "It's that woman

who always wanted to have a house in the country and was never able to leave the city."
I remembered having seen the woman in some previous dream, but I knew, with the door
ajar now, that within half an hour I would have to go down for breakfast. And I said: "In
any case, I have to leave here in order to wake up."

Outside the wind fluttered for an instant, then remained quiet, and the breath-   10
ing of someone sleeping who had just turned over in bed could be heard. The wind from
the fields had ceased. There were no more smells. "Tomorrow I'll recognize you
from that," I said. "I'll recognize you when on the street I see a woman writing 'Eyes of
a blue dog' on the walls." And she, with a sad smile—which was already a smile of surrender to the impossible, the unreachable—said: "Yet you won't remember anything
during the day." And she put her hands back over the lamp, her features darkened by
a bitter cloud. "You're the only man who doesn't remember anything of what he's
dreamed after he wakes up."

ALICE MUNRO   (b. 1931)

> *Alice Munro, born and raised in Canada, still lives in southwestern Ontario. Although her*
> *stories usually reflect the circumstances of life in Canada, their subject matter is contempo-*
> *rary and universal in appeal. Her work in fiction has been almost entirely in the short story,*
> *and she describes her novel* Lives of Girls and Women *(1971) as a series of connected sto-*
> *ries. Among her collections are* Dance of the Happy Shades *(1968),* Who Do You Think
> You Are? *(1978),* The Moons of Jupiter *(1983),* The Progress of Love *(1986),* Se-
> lected Stories *(1997), and* The Love of a Good Woman *(1999). Joyce Carol Oates has*
> *said that Munro "writes stories that have the density—moral, emotional, sometimes histor-*
> *ical—of other writers' novels," and Munro herself has said, "I want to write the story that*
> *will zero in and give you intense, but not connected, moments of experience. I guess that's*
> *the way I see life."*

The Moons of Jupiter ———————————————————— *1983*

I found my father in the heart wing, on the eighth floor of Toronto General Hospital. He
was in a semi-private room. The other bed was empty. He said that his hospital insurance
covered only a bed in the ward, and he was worried that he might be charged extra.

"I never asked for a semi-private," he said.

I said the wards were probably full.

"No. I saw some empty beds when they were wheeling me by."

"Then it was because you had to be hooked up to that thing," I said. "Don't worry.   5
If they're going to charge you extra, they tell you about it."

"That's likely it," he said. "They wouldn't want those doohickeys set up in the
wards. I guess I'm covered for that kind of thing."

I said I was sure he was.

He had wires taped to his chest. A small screen hung over his head. On the screen
a bright jagged line was continually being written. The writing was accompanied by a nervous electronic beeping. The behavior of his heart was on display. I tried to ignore it. It
seemed to me that paying such close attention—in fact, dramatizing what ought to be

a most secret activity—was asking for trouble. Anything exposed that way was apt to flare up and go crazy.

My father did not seem to mind. He said they had him on tranquillizers. You know, he said, the happy pills. He did seem calm and optimistic.

It had been a different story the night before. When I brought him into the hospital, to the emergency room, he had been pale and closemouthed. He had opened the car door and stood up and said quietly, "Maybe you better get me one of those wheelchairs." He used the voice he always used in a crisis. Once, our chimney caught on fire; it was on a Sunday afternoon and I was in the dining room pinning together a dress I was making. He came in and said in that same matter-of-fact, warning voice, "Janet. Do you know where there's some baking powder?" He wanted it to throw on the fire. Afterwards he said, "I guess it was your fault—sewing on Sunday."

I had to wait for over an hour in the emergency waiting room. They summoned a heart specialist who was in the hospital, a young man. He called me out into the hall and explained to me that one of the valves of my father's heart had deteriorated so badly that there ought to be an immediate operation.

I asked him what would happen otherwise.

"He'd have to stay in bed," the doctor said.

"How long?"

"Maybe three months."

"I meant, how long would he live?"

"That's what I meant, too," the doctor said.

I went to see my father. He was sitting up in bed in a curtained-off corner. "It's bad, isn't it?" he said. "Did he tell you about the valve?"

"It's not as bad as it could be," I said. Then I repeated, even exaggerated, anything hopeful the doctor had said. "You're not in any immediate danger. Your physical condition is good, otherwise."

"Otherwise," said my father, gloomily.

I was tired from the drive—all the way up to Dalgleish, to get him, and back to Toronto since noon—and worried about getting the rented car back on time, and irritated by an article I had been reading in a magazine in the waiting room. It was about another writer, a woman younger, better-looking, probably more talented than I am. I had been in England for two months and so I had not seen this article before, but it crossed my mind while I was reading that my father would have. I could hear him saying, Well, I didn't see anything about you in *Maclean's*.° And if he had read something about me he would say, Well, I didn't think too much of that writeup. His tone would be humorous and indulgent but would produce in me a familiar dreariness of spirit. The message I got from him was simple: Fame must be striven for, then apologized for. Getting or not getting it, you will be to blame.

I was not surprised by the doctor's news. I was prepared to hear something of the sort and was pleased with myself for taking it calmly, just as I would be pleased with myself for dressing a wound or looking down from the frail balcony of a high building. I thought, Yes, it's time; there has to be something, here it is. I did not feel any of the protest I would have felt twenty, even ten, years before. When I saw from my father's face that he felt it—that refusal leapt up in him as readily as if he had been thirty or forty years

Maclean's: popular Canadian magazine

younger—my heart hardened, and I spoke with a kind of badgering cheerfulness. "Otherwise is plenty," I said.

The next day he was himself again.

That was how I would have put it. He said it appeared to him now that the young fellow, the doctor, might have been a bit too eager to operate. "A bit knife-happy," he said. He was both mocking and showing off the hospital slang. He said that another doctor had examined him, an older man, and had given it as his opinion that rest and medication might do the trick.

I didn't ask what trick.   25

"He says I've got a defective valve, all right. There's certainly some damage. They wanted to know if I had rheumatic fever when I was a kid. I said I didn't think so. But half the time then you weren't diagnosed what you had. My father was not one for getting the doctor."

The thought of my father's childhood, which I always pictured as bleak and dangerous—the poor farm, the scared sisters, the harsh father—made me less resigned to his dying. I thought of him running away to work on the lake boats, running along the railway tracks, toward Goderich, in the evening light. He used to tell about that trip. Somewhere along the track he found a quince tree. Quince trees are rare in our part of the country; in fact, I have never seen one. Not even the one my father found, though he once took us on an expedition to look for it. He thought he knew the crossroad it was near, but we could not find it. He had not been able to eat the fruit, of course, but he had been impressed by its existence. It made him think he had got into a new part of the world.

The escaped child, the survivor, an old man trapped here by his leaky heart. I didn't pursue these thoughts. I didn't care to think of his younger selves. Even his bare torso, thick and white—he had the body of a workingman of his generation, seldom exposed to the sun—was a danger to me; it looked so strong and young. The wrinkled neck, the age-freckled hands and arms, the narrow, courteous head, with its thin gray hair and mustache, were more what I was used to.

"Now, why would I want to get myself operated on?" said my father reasonably. "Think of the risk at my age, and what for? A few years at the outside. I think the best thing for me to do is go home and take it easy. Give in gracefully. That's all you can do, at my age. Your attitude changes, you know. You go through some mental changes. It seems more natural."

"What does?" I said.   30

"Well, death does. You can't get more natural than that. No, what I mean, specifically, is not having the operation."

"That seems more natural?"

"Yes."

"It's up to you," I said, but I did approve. This was what I would have expected of him. Whenever I told people about my father I stressed his independence, his self-sufficiency, his forbearance. He worked in a factory, he worked in his garden, he read history books. He could tell you about the Roman emperors or the Balkan wars. He never made a fuss.

Judith, my younger daughter, had come to meet me at Toronto Airport two days   35
before. She had brought the boy she was living with, whose name was Don. They were driving to Mexico in the morning, and while I was in Toronto I was to stay in their

apartment. For the time being, I live in Vancouver. I sometimes say I have my head-quarters in Vancouver.

"Where's Nichola?" I said, thinking at once of an accident or an overdose. Nichola is my older daughter. She used to be a student at the Conservatory, then she became a cocktail waitress, then she was out of work. If she had been at the airport, I would probably have said something wrong. I would have asked her what her plans were, and she would have gracefully brushed back her hair and said, "Plans?"—as if that was a word I had invented.

"I knew the first thing you'd say would be about Nichola," Judith said.

"It wasn't. I said hello and I—"

"We'll get your bag," Don said neutrally.

"Is she all right?"   40

"I'm sure she is," said Judith, with a fabricated air of amusement. "You wouldn't look like that if I was the one who wasn't here."

"Of course I would."

"You wouldn't. Nichola is the baby of the family. You know, she's four years older than I am."

"I ought to know."

Judith said she did not know where Nichola was exactly. She said Nichola had   45
moved out of her apartment (that dump!) and had actually telephoned (which is quite a deal, you might say, Nichola phoning) to say she wanted to be incommunicado for a while but she was fine.

"I told her you would worry," said Judith more kindly on the way to their van. Don walked ahead carrying my suitcase. "But don't. She's all right, believe me."

Don's presence made me uncomfortable. I did not like him to hear these things. I thought of the conversations they must have had, Don and Judith. Or Don and Judith and Nichola, for Nichola and Judith were sometimes on good terms. Or Don and Judith and Nichola and others whose names I did not even know. They would have talked about me. Judith and Nichola comparing notes, relating anecdotes; analyzing, regretting, blaming, forgiving. I wished I'd had a boy and a girl. Or two boys. They wouldn't have done that. Boys couldn't possibly know so much about you.

I did the same thing at that age. When I was the age Judith is now I talked with my friends in the college cafeteria or, late at night, over coffee in our cheap rooms. When I was the age Nichola is now I had Nichola herself in a carry-cot or squirming in my lap, and I was drinking coffee again all the rainy Vancouver afternoons with my one neighborhood friend, Ruth Boudreau, who read a lot and was bewildered by her situation, as I was. We talked about our parents, our childhoods, though for some time we kept clear of our marriages. How thoroughly we dealt with our fathers and mothers, deplored their marriages, their mistaken ambitions or fear of ambition, how competently we filed them away, defined them beyond any possibility of change. What presumption.

I looked at Don walking ahead. A tall ascetic-looking boy, with a St. Francis cap of black hair, a precise fringe of beard. What right did he have to hear about me, to know things I myself had probably forgotten? I decided that his beard and hairstyle were affected.

Once, when my children were little, my father said to me, "You know those years   50
you were growing up—well, that's all just a kind of a blur to me. I can't sort out one year from another." I was offended. I remembered each separate year with pain and clarity. I could have told how old I was when I went to look at the evening dresses in the window of Benbow's Ladies' Wear. Every week through the winter a new dress, spotlit—the

sequins and tulle, the rose and lilac, sapphire, daffodil—and me a cold worshipper on the slushy sidewalk. I could have told how old I was when I forged my mother's signature on a bad report card, when I had measles, when we papered the front room. But the years when Judith and Nichola were little, when I lived with their father—yes, blur is the word for it. I remember hanging out diapers, bringing in and folding diapers; I can recall the kitchen counters of two houses and where the clothesbasket sat. I remember the television programs—*Popeye the Sailor, The Three Stooges, Funorama.* When *Funorama* came on it was time to turn on the lights and cook supper. But I couldn't tell the years apart. We lived outside Vancouver in a dormitory suburb: Dormir, Dormer, Dormouse—something like that. I was sleepy all the time then; pregnancy made me sleepy, and the night feedings, and the West Coast rain falling. Dark dripping cedars, shiny dripping laurel; wives yawning, napping, visiting, drinking coffee, and folding diapers; husbands coming home at night from the city across the water. Every night I kissed my homecoming husband in his wet Burberry° and hoped he might wake me up; I served up meat and potatoes and one of the four vegetables he permitted. He ate with a violent appetite, then fell asleep on the living-room sofa. We had become a cartoon couple, more middle-aged in our twenties than we would be in middle age.

Those bumbling years are the years our children will remember all their lives. Corners of the yards I never visited will stay in their heads.

"Did Nichola not want to see me?" I said to Judith.

"She doesn't want to see anybody, half the time," she said. Judith moved ahead and touched Don's arm. I knew that touch—an apology, an anxious reassurance. You touch a man that way to remind him that you are grateful, that you realize he is doing for your sake something that bores him or slightly endangers his dignity. It made me feel older than grandchildren would to see my daughter touch a man—a boy—this way. I felt her sad jitters, could predict her supple attentions. My blunt and stocky, blonde and candid child. Why should I think she wouldn't be susceptible, that she would always be straightforward, heavy-footed, self-reliant? Just as I go around saying that Nichola is sly and solitary, cold, seductive. Many people must know things that would contradict what I say.

In the morning Don and Judith left for Mexico. I decided I wanted to see somebody who wasn't related to me, and who didn't expect anything in particular from me. I called an old lover of mine, but his phone was answered by a machine: "This is Tom Shepherd speaking. I will be out of town for the month of September. Please record your message, name, and phone number."

Tom's voice sounded so pleasant and familiar that I opened my mouth to ask him   55
the meaning of this foolishness. Then I hung up. I felt as if he had deliberately let me down, as if we had planned to meet in a public place and then he hadn't shown up. Once, he had done that, I remembered.

I got myself a glass of vermouth, though it was not yet noon, and I phoned my father.

"Well, of all things," he said. "Fifteen more minutes and you would have missed me."

"Were you going downtown?"

"Downtown Toronto."

He explained that he was going to the hospital. His doctor in Dalgleish wanted   60
the doctors in Toronto to take a look at him, and had given him a letter to show them in the emergency room.

"Emergency room?" I said.

Burberry: raincoat

"It's not an emergency. He just seems to think this is the best way to handle it. He knows the name of a fellow there. If he was to make me an appointment, it might take weeks."

"Does your doctor know you're driving to Toronto?" I said.

"Well, he didn't say I couldn't."

The upshot of this was that I rented a car, drove to Dalgleish, brought my father back to Toronto, and had him in the emergency room by seven o'clock that evening.

Before Judith left I said to her, "You're sure Nichola knows I'm staying here?"

"Well, I told her," she said.

Sometimes the phone rang, but it was always a friend of Judith's.

"Well, it looks like I'm going to have it," my father said. This was on the fourth day. He had done a complete turnaround overnight. "It looks like I might as well."

I didn't know what he wanted me to say. I thought perhaps he looked to me for a protest, an attempt to dissuade him.

"When will they do it?" I said.

"Day after tomorrow."

I said I was going to the washroom. I went to the nurses' station and found a woman there who I thought was the head nurse. At any rate, she was gray-haired, kind, and serious-looking.

"My father's having an operation the day after tomorrow?" I said.

"Oh, yes."

"I just wanted to talk to somebody about it. I thought there'd been a sort of decision reached that he'd be better not to. I thought because of his age."

"Well, it's his decision and the doctor's." She smiled at me without condescension. "It's hard to make these decisions."

"How were his tests?"

"Well, I haven't seen them all."

I was sure she had. After a moment she said, "We have to be realistic. But the doctors here are very good."

When I went back into the room my father said, in a surprised voice, "*Shore*less seas."

"What?" I said. I wondered if he had found out how much, or how little, time he could hope for. I wondered if the pills had brought on an untrustworthy euphoria. Or if he had wanted to gamble. Once, when he was talking to me about his life, he said, "The trouble was I was always afraid to take chances."

I used to tell people that he never spoke regretfully about his life, but that was not true. It was just that I didn't listen to it. He said that he should have gone into the Army as a tradesman—he would have been better off. He said he should have gone on his own, as a carpenter, after the war. He should have got out of Dalgleish. Once, he said, "A wasted life, eh?" But he was making fun of himself, saying that, because it was such a dramatic thing to say. When he quoted poetry, too, he always had a scoffing note in his voice, to excuse the showing-off and the pleasure.

"Shoreless seas," he said again. " 'Behind him lay the gray Azores, / Behind the Gates of Hercules; / Before him not the ghost of shores, / Before him only shoreless seas.' That's what was going through my head last night. But do you think I could remember what kind of seas? I could not. Lonely seas? Empty seas? I was on the right track but I couldn't get it. But there now when you came into the room and I wasn't thinking about it at all, the word popped into my head. That's always the way, isn't it? It's not all that surprising. I ask my mind a question. The answer's there, but I can't see all the connections my mind's making to get it. Like a computer. Nothing out of the way. You know, in my situation the thing is, if there's anything you can't explain right away, there's a great temptation to—well, to make a mystery out of it. There's a great temptation to believe in—You know."

"The soul?" I said, speaking lightly, feeling an appalling rush of love and recognition.   85

"Oh, I guess you could call it that. You know, when I first came into this room there was a pile of papers here by the bed. Somebody had left them here—one of those tabloid sort of things I never looked at. I started reading them. I'll read anything handy. There was a series running in them on personal experiences of people who had died, medically speaking—heart arrest, mostly—and had been brought back to life. It was what they remembered of the time when they were dead. Their experiences."

"Pleasant or un-?" I said.

"Oh, pleasant. Oh yes. They'd float up to the ceiling and look down on themselves and see the doctors working on them, on their bodies. Then float on further and recognize some people they knew who had died before them. Not see them exactly but sort of sense them. Sometimes there would be a humming and sometimes a sort of— what's that light that there is or color around a person?"

"Aura?"

"Yes. But without the person. That's about all they'd get time for; then they found   90 themselves back in the body and feeling all the mortal pain and so on—brought back to life."

"Did it seem—convincing?"

"Oh, I don't know. It's all in whether you want to believe that kind of thing or not. And if you are going to believe it, take it seriously, I figure you've got to take everything else seriously that they print in those papers."

"What else do they?"

"Rubbish—cancer cures, baldness cures, bellyaching about the younger generation and the welfare bums. Tripe about movie stars."

"Oh, yes. I know."   95

"In my situation you have to keep a watch," he said, "or you'll start playing tricks on yourself." Then he said, "There's a few practical details we ought to get straight on," and he told me about his will, the house, the cemetery plot. Everything was simple.

"Do you want me to phone Peggy?" I said. Peggy is my sister. She is married to an astronomer and lives in Victoria.

He thought about it. "I guess we ought to tell them," he said finally. "But tell them not to get alarmed."

"All right."

"No, wait a minute. Sam is supposed to be going to a conference the end of this   100 week, and Peggy was planning to go along with him. I don't want them wondering about changing their plans."

"Where is the conference?"

"Amsterdam," he said proudly. He did take pride in Sam, and kept track of his books and articles. He would pick one up and say, "Look at that, will you? And I can't understand a word of it!" in a marvelling voice that managed nevertheless to have a trace of ridicule.

"Professor Sam," he would say. "And the three little Sams." This is what he called his grandsons, who did resemble their father in braininess and in an almost endearing pushiness—an innocent energetic showing-off. They went to a private school that favored old-fashioned discipline and started calculus in Grade Five. "And the dogs," he might enumerate further, "who have been to obedience school. And Peggy . . ."

But if I said, "Do you suppose she has been to obedience school, too?" he would play the game no further. I imagine that when he was with Sam and Peggy he spoke of me in the same way—hinted at my flightiness just as he hinted at their stodginess, made mild jokes at my expense, did not quite conceal his amazement (or pretended not to conceal his amazement) that people paid money for things I had written. He had to do this so that he might never seem to brag, but he would put up the gates when the joking got too rough. And of course I found later, in the house, things of mine he had kept—a few magazines, clippings, things I had never bothered about.

Now his thoughts travelled from Peggy's family to mine. "Have you heard from Judith?" he said.   105

"Not yet."

"Well, it's pretty soon. Were they going to sleep in the van?"

"Yes."

"I guess it's safe enough, if they stop in the right places."

I knew he would have to say something more and I knew it would come as a joke.   110

"I guess they put a board down the middle, like the pioneers?"

I smiled but did not answer.

"I take it you have no objections?"

"No," I said.

"Well, I always believed that, too. Keep out of your children's business. I tried not   115
to say anything. I never said anything when you left Richard."

"What do you mean, 'said anything'? Criticize?"

"It wasn't any of my business."

"No."

"But that doesn't mean I was pleased."

I was surprised—not just at what he said but at his feeling that he had any right, even   120
now, to say it. I had to look out the window and down at the traffic to control myself.

"I just wanted you to know," he added.

A long time ago, he said to me in his mild way, "It's funny. Richard when I first saw him reminded me of what my father used to say. He'd say if that fellow was half as smart as he thinks he is, he'd be twice as smart as he really is."

I turned to remind him of this, but found myself looking at the line his heart was writing. Not that there seemed to be anything wrong, any difference in the beeps and points. But it was there.

He saw where I was looking. "Unfair advantage," he said.

"It is," I said. "I'm going to have to get hooked up, too."   125

We laughed, we kissed formally; I left. At least he hadn't asked me about Nichola, I thought.

The next afternoon I didn't go to the hospital, because my father was having some more tests done, to prepare for the operation. I was to see him in the evening instead. I found myself wandering through the Bloor Street dress shops, trying on clothes. A preoccupation with fashion and my own appearance had descended on me like a raging headache. I looked at the women in the street, at the clothes in the shops, trying to discover how a transformation might be made, what I would have to buy. I recognized this obsession for what it was but had trouble shaking it. I've had people tell me that waiting for life-or-death news they've stood in front of an open refrigerator eating any-thing in sight—cold boiled potatoes, chili sauce, bowls of whipped cream. Or have been unable to stop doing crossword puzzles. Attention narrows in on something—some dis-traction—grabs on, becomes fanatically serious. I shuffled clothes on the racks, pulled them on in hot little changing rooms in front of cruel mirrors. I was sweating; once or twice I thought I might faint. Out on the street again, I thought I must remove myself from Bloor Street, and decided to go to the museum.

I remembered another time, in Vancouver. It was when Nichola was going to Kindergarten and Judith was a baby. Nichola had been to the doctor about a cold, or maybe for a routine examination, and the blood test revealed something about her white blood cells—either that there were too many of them or that they were enlarged. The doctor ordered further tests, and I took Nichola to the hospital for them. Nobody mentioned leukemia but I knew, of course, what they were looking for. When I took Nichola home I asked the babysitter who had been with Judith to stay for the after-noon and I went shopping. I bought the most daring dress I ever owned, a black silk sheath with some laced-up arrangement in front. I remembered that bright spring af-ternoon, the spike-heeled shoes in the department store, the underwear printed with leopard spots.

I also remembered going home from St. Paul's Hospital over the Lions Gate Bridge on the crowded bus and holding Nichola on my knee. She suddenly recalled her baby name for bridge and whispered to me, "Whee—over the whee." I did not avoid touching my child—Nichola was slender and graceful even then, with a pretty back and fine dark hair—but realized I was touching her with a difference, though I did not think it could ever be detected. There was a care—not a withdrawal exactly but a care—not to feel anything much. I saw how the forms of love might be maintained with a condemned person but with the love in fact measured and disciplined, because you have to survive. It could be done so discreetly that the object of such care would not suspect, any more than she would suspect the sentence of death itself. Nichola did not know, would not know. Toys and kisses and jokes would come tumbling over her; she would never know, though I worried that she would feel the wind between the cracks of the manufactured holidays, the manufactured normal days. But all was well. Nichola did not have leukemia. She grew up—was still alive, and possibly happy. Incommunicado.

I could not think of anything in the museum I really wanted to see, so I walked   130
past it to the planetarium. I had never been to a planetarium. The show was due to start in ten minutes. I went inside, bought a ticket, got in line. There was a whole class of schoolchildren, maybe a couple of classes, with teachers and volunteer mothers riding herd on them. I looked around to see if there were any other unattached adults. Only one—a man with a red face and puffy eyes, who looked as if he might be here to keep himself from going to a bar.

Inside, we sat on wonderfully comfortable seats that were tilted back so that you lay in a sort of hammock, attention directed to the bowl of the ceiling, which soon turned dark blue, with a faint rim of light all around the edge. There was some splen-did, commanding music. The adults all around were shushing the children, trying to make them stop crackling their potato-chip bags. Then a man's voice, an eloquent pro-fessional voice, began to speak slowly, out of the walls. The voice reminded me a little of the way radio announcers used to introduce a piece of classical music or describe the progress of the Royal Family to Westminster Abbey on one of their royal occasions. There was a faint echo-chamber effect.

The dark ceiling was filling with stars. They came out not all at once but one after another, the way the stars really do come out at night, though more quickly. The Milky Way appeared, was moving closer; stars swam into brilliance and kept on going, disappearing beyond the edges of the sky-screen or behind my head. While the flow of light continued, the voice presented the stunning facts. A few light-years away, it announced, the sun appears as a bright star, and the planets are not visible. A few dozen light-years away, the sun is not visible, either, to the naked eye. And that distance—a few dozen light-years—is only about a thousandth part of the distance from the sun to the center of our galaxy, one galaxy, which itself contains about two hundred billion suns. And is, in turn, one of millions, perhaps billions, of galaxies. Innumerable repetitions, innumerable variations. All this rolled past my head, too, like balls of lightning.

Now realism was abandoned, for familiar artifice. A model of the solar system was spinning away in its elegant style. A bright bug took off from the earth, heading for Jupiter. I set my dodging and shrinking mind sternly to recording facts. The mass of Jupiter two and a half times that of all the other planets put together. The Great Red Spot. The thirteen moons. Past Jupiter, a glance at the eccentric orbit of Pluto, the icy rings of Saturn. Back to Earth and moving in to hot and dazzling Venus. Atmospheric pressure ninety times ours. Moonless Mercury rotating three times while circling the sun twice; an odd arrangement, not as satisfying as what they used to tell us—that it rotated once as it circled the sun. No perpetual darkness after all. Why did they give out such confident information, only to announce later that it was quite wrong? Finally, the picture already familiar from magazines: the red soil of Mars, the blooming pink sky.

When the show was over I sat in my seat while the children clambered across me, making no comments on anything they had just seen or heard. They were pestering their keepers for eatables and further entertainments. An effort had been made to get their attention, to take it away from canned pop and potato chips and fix it on various knowns and unknowns and horrible immensities, and it seemed to have failed. A good thing, too, I thought. Children have a natural immunity, most of them, and it shouldn't be tampered with. As for the adults who would deplore it, the ones who promoted this show, weren't they immune themselves to the extent that they could put in the echo-chamber effects, the music, the churchlike solemnity, simulating the awe that they supposed they ought to feel? Awe—what was that supposed to be? A fit of the shivers when you looked out the window? Once you knew what it was, you wouldn't be courting it.

Two men came with brooms to sweep up the debris the audience had left behind. They told me that the next show would start in forty minutes. In the meantime, I had to get out.

"I went to the show at the planetarium," I said to my father. "It was very exciting—about the solar system." I thought what a silly word I had used: "exciting." "It's like a slightly phony temple," I added.

He was already talking. "I remember when they found Pluto. Right where they thought it had to be. Mercury, Venus, Earth, Mars," he recited. "Jupiter, Saturn, Nept—no, Uranus, Neptune, Pluto. Is that right?"

"Yes," I said. I was just as glad he hadn't heard what I said about the phony temple. I had meant that to be truthful, but it sounded slick and superior. "Tell me the moons of Jupiter."

"Well, I don't know the new ones. There's a bunch of new ones, isn't there?"

"Two. But they're not new."

"New to us," said my father. "You've turned pretty cheeky now I'm going under the knife."

" 'Under the knife.' What an expression."

He was not in bed tonight, his last night. He had been detached from his apparatus, and was sitting in a chair by the window. He was bare-legged, wearing a hospital dressing gown, but he did not look self-conscious or out of place. He looked thoughtful but good-humored, an affable host.

"You haven't even named the old ones," I said.

" Give me time. Galileo named them. Io."   145

"That's a start."

"The moons of Jupiter were the first heavenly bodies discovered with the telescope." He said this gravely, as if he could see the sentence in an old book. "It wasn't Galileo named them, either; it was some German. Io, Europa, Ganymede, Callisto. There you are."

"Yes."

"Io and Europa, they were girlfriends of Jupiter's, weren't they? Ganymede was a boy. A shepherd? I don't know who Callisto was."

"I think she was a girlfriend, too," I said. "Jupiter's wife—Jove's wife—changed   150
her into a bear and stuck her up in the sky. Great Bear and Little Bear. Little Bear was her baby."

The loudspeaker said that it was time for visitors to go.

"I'll see you when you come out of the anesthetic," I said.

"Yes."

When I was at the door, he called to me, "Ganymede wasn't any shepherd. He was Jove's cupbearer."

When I left the planetarium that afternoon, I had walked through the museum   155
to the Chinese garden. I saw the stone camels again, the warriors, the tomb. I sat on a bench looking toward Bloor Street. Through the evergreen bushes and the high grilled iron fence I watched people going by in the late-afternoon sunlight. The planetarium show had done what I wanted it to after all—calmed me down, drained me. I saw a girl who reminded me of Nichola. She wore a trenchcoat and carried a bag of groceries. She was shorter than Nichola—not really much like her at all—but I thought that I might see Nichola. She would be walking along some street maybe not far from here—burdened, preoccupied, alone. She was one of the grownup people in the world now, one of the shoppers going home.

If I did see her, I might just sit and watch, I decided. I felt like one of those people who have floated up to the ceiling, enjoying a brief death. A relief, while it lasts. My father had chosen and Nichola had chosen. Someday, probably soon, I would hear from her, but it came to the same thing.

I meant to get up and go over to the tomb, to look at the relief carvings, the stone pictures, that go all the way around it. I always mean to look at them and I never do. Not this time, either. It was getting cold out, so I went inside to have coffee and something to eat before I went back to the hospital.

IV

INTERPRETING

POETRY

9

READING SIX POEMS

Poetry defies definition and mocks those who attempt to pin it down. To some extent it is mysterious, linked as it is in prehistory with religious chants and mystic prayers. Since ancient times, poets have talked about being inspired by the muse, a power of divine origin greater than themselves. When poets have written poems much better than they knew they could, their only explanation was that they were inspired. Some poets write only when they can induce in themselves a feeling of being moved to write—which is to say, the psychological condition of being inspired.

Although Robert Frost said that poetry was what was lost in the translation, good translators have given us versions of poems from other languages that preserve their poetic nature. But Frost's point is that poetry is a condition of language. If painting represents a way of seeing, then poetry represents a way of saying. All poetry has language at its heart.

Fortunately, as with many things that cannot be defined, poetry is almost instantly recognizable. Some of its qualities are special uses of language and rhythm: rhyme, imagery, metaphor, symbol, onomatopoeia, meter, and repetition. Some are special visual tips on the printed page: stanzas, and forms such as couplets, quatrains, sonnets, capitalized first lines, and short lines. Others are compression of language, tension, tone, seriousness of ideas, or utter playfulness. The poems in this collection illustrate all of these qualities and more. Some poems masquerade as prose, or advertisements, or even shapes, increasing the pleasures of poetry by increasing its possibilities.

POETRY AND PERFORMANCE

Rap poets make their living by performing their work. They excite audiences not just because they say something interesting, but because they say it with a beat, a lilting rhyme, and the illusion that they are talking spontaneously, making it up as they go along. Some rappers do improvise, but most are like other poets: they work out the details in advance, write them down, then memorize them. Rappers are also like songwriters in that their work is much more interesting in performance than in reading.

Many poets, such as T. S. Eliot, Langston Hughes, Robert Frost, Dylan Thomas, Adrienne Rich, and Marge Piercy, have recorded their poems. Their performances vary because some of them are better readers than others. But they have a special authority: They wrote the poetry they read. On the other hand, many recordings feature actors such as Richard Burton and Siobhan McKenna. Listening to them also helps us develop an ear for poetry.

Poetry is always amenable to performance even without the original poets or actors. Reciting them yourself is one of the best ways to perform poems. All the poems in this collection need recitation, which may range from memorization and dramatic interpretation—through modulation of voice or gesture—to the simple act of saying them out loud. The following anonymous poem is a somewhat waggish rhyme that seems to demand to be said aloud:

It isn't the cough
That carries you off.
It's the coffin
They carry you off in.

The poem's gallows humor is intensified by some lovely tricks of rhyme and language. The connection between cough and coffin was always there, of course, but never perceived so fully as after one recites this poem. Even the different senses of the expression "carry you off" resonate in the air after a recitation. One of the most amusing aspects of the poem may be its portability: it is brief, compressed, complete.

Built into the act of recitation is another aspect of performance: rereading. Poetry is a language artifact intended to be reread. That is not true of all literature; mystery stories are usually of no interest after the first reading. Poetry needs rereading because its compression of language, its fireworks of metaphor and imagery, and its tension and play of rhythm and meter all work simultaneously, making it almost impossible to interpret everything at first reading. A poem is like a brilliant high-action sequence in a film that moves so fast you want to rewind and see it again.

A POEM BY EMILY DICKINSON

Emily Dickinson (1830–1886) remains one of the most read, most enjoyed, and most respected American poets of the nineteenth century. She was something of a recluse, living at home without visiting friends or taking part in most family rituals. She published a few of her poems early in life, but the vast majority of her poems were found in desk drawers, sometimes written on the backs of envelopes or on scrap paper. Yet her work is careful, disciplined, and finished.

The act of interpreting a poem involves a number of things. One is a knowledge, however limited, of the poet's life and milieu. Another is a knowledge, again however limited, of the circumstances and the history of the times in which the poet lived and, when possible, the locale in which the poems were written. We cannot always have this information, and even when we feel that the information is largely available, it is always incomplete. Therefore, most people depend on a close reading of the text itself when interpreting a poem. In general, that will be our approach in reading the poems that follow.

Interpreting Dickinson's "A Narrow Fellow in the Grass"

One of Emily Dickinson's best-known poems, "A Narrow Fellow in the Grass," stands somewhat apart from the background information of biography and history. It records the memory of the narrator—in this case, a boy—and his recollections of meeting a snake in the grass. The effect of the poem depends on a universal feeling, the surprise of perceiving a rope or whip in the grass only to find it a snake moving rapidly away. Even those who are not frightened by snakes will be able to understand the fundamental message of Dickinson's poem.

EMILY DICKINSON   (1830–1886)

A Narrow Fellow in the Grass (986) _____ *1865; 1866*

A narrow Fellow in the Grass
Occasionally rides—
You may have met Him—did you not
His notice sudden is—

The Grass divides as with a Comb—   5
A spotted shaft is seen—
And then it closes at your feet
And opens further on—

He likes a Boggy Acre
A Floor too cool for Corn—   10
Yet when a Boy, and Barefoot—
I more than once at Noon
Have passed, I thought, a Whip lash
Unbraiding in the Sun
When stooping to secure it   15
It wrinkled, and was gone—

Several of Nature's People
I know, and they know me—
I feel for them a transport
Of cordiality—   20

But never met this Fellow
Attended, or alone
Without a tighter breathing
And Zero at the Bone—

The effect of this poem depends in part on our ability to refer to the universal experience of being surprised by a snake. Such an experience is more common for those who live in the country or those who have spent time hiking or camping. But even those of us who grew up in the city will instinctively respond to the shock of seeing a snake move suddenly in front of us.

However, another reason we respond to this poem depends on its poetic strategies. The first stanzas, like the last stanzas, are four lines each. However, the first stanzas are not rhymed, while the last stanzas present strong rhymes in *me, cordiality,* and *alone, bone.* When you read the poem aloud to yourself, you see that the rhymes of the final stanzas represent a powerful conclusiveness that might not be possible without rhyme.

The opening of the poem implies that the snake is essentially a familiar figure, called "A narrow Fellow." The narrator speaks to the reader directly, "You may have met Him," implying again a familiarity. Even the suggestion that the snake parts the grass like a "Comb" continues the sense that seeing snakes is commonplace and normal. The central stanza describes the snake's habits and appearance, reminding us that it is common for the boy to reach down for what appears to be a "Whip lash" only to find it zip away suddenly. The next-to-last stanza tells us that the boy is used to nature, expressing a comfortable relationship with various animals. But the last stanza also tells us that the sudden appearance of the snake produces a powerful physiological reaction that is akin to fear. The "Zero at the bone" implies an emotional iciness just as the "tighter breathing" implies uncertainty and fear. Most—but not all—people share these feelings.

On one level the poem is literal. It tells us that the appearance of a snake is cause for some alarm, even if we are used to being in the country and are familiar with nature and its denizens. Some people insist that we respond to a primeval fear of snakes because they are sometimes poisonous and have represented a threat through the ages. Others suggest that the proliferation of mythic stories about Typhon and other gigantic snakes, like the snake in the Bible's Garden of Eden, have penetrated our unconscious and made themselves resident echoes of fear. Still others, using symbology developed by psychiatrists, suggest that the snake is a phallic emblem and represents a sexual threat or a sexual force. Emily Dickinson, by having a boy as her narrator, either intensifies the sexual implication or else defuses it. Only the reader can make that decision based on a fuller interpretation of the poem.

Any interpretation of this poem will depend on what you decide must be the meaning of the situation and in this case the snake itself. To begin with, is the snake a symbol, or is it just a snake? In either case the poem works exceptionally well. A poem about a real snake, it informs us about the emotions involved in the boy's encounters even when the boy tells us that he has seen snakes "more than once at Noon." The inclusion of the time of day helps us on a literal level because it implies that these sightings are not dreams, and not symbols. They are facts.

However, facts in poems have a way of taking on special significance. This poem tells us of an experience that ought to be something in the range of normal for the boy. He suggests that he is close to nature, that he has seen many snakes, even reached down to touch them. He also tells us that he feels a sense of "cordiality" for "Nature's People." They know him, too. But there is something special about the snake. When he meets one whether "Attended, or alone"—with another person or alone—he has a deep and fearful response. In essence, he tells us that the response is irrational. He knows enough about snakes to make them seem familiar. Yet they shock him and frighten him to "the Bone." Symbolically, the snake seems to stand for things that evoke fear, such as sudden and unexpected death in familiar surroundings. In the Garden of Eden the snake represents evil, but that is not the case in this poem. Rather, the snake represents all aspects of a normal environment that can unexpectedly become a threat to security, a source of terror. Interestingly, it does so not only for the narrator as a boy but for the narrator grown up, as the last two stanzas imply.

This short poem offers us some interesting opportunities. It shows us that even short poems that appear simply to describe a common experience have depths of significance that a careful reading can delve into. This poem seems to have two levels on which it can be interpreted, something common to many poems. One level is the level of action, and another is the level of symbol. Both levels have something to tell us. Both what the poem tells us and how it tells it combine to intensify our understanding and experience. That will be true for most of the poems we will encounter.

CLOSE READING: BEGINNING WITH QUESTIONS

As in the case of reading fiction, close reading of a poem involves careful attention to detail within the poem. However, in part because poems are usually brief forms of literature, close reading also involves paying attention to things that lie outside the text itself. When Wordsworth talks about London in his sonnet (p. 481) or John Milton refers to the slaughter of the Waldensians by the Piedmontese in 1655 (p. 498), they expect you to understand their references. Judith Rodriguez expects you to know what an Eskimo is in "Eskimo Occasion" (p. 460). When A. E. Housman refers to "rue," "brooks," and "roses" (p. 468), he expects you to have referents drawn from outside the poem to make sense of the words he uses. Even nonsense poems like "Jabberwocky" (p. 423) and "Anyone Lived in a Pretty How Town" (p. 469) point outside themselves to general experience. Most poems demand a wide repertory of experience from us, and the richer our experience, the richer our interpretation.

Close reading of the poetic texts involves a careful examination of details and the way the elements of the poem function. As much as possible, it begins from a holistic reading of the poem. Your first impression, derived from a careful reading, guides your early responses. Rereading helps you evaluate the qualities within the poem that help produce your initial impression. If your first reading produces no distinct response, then you must rely upon rereading with an eye toward examining specific elements, such as imagery, ideas, and use of language.

Once you have read a poem closely, larger interpretive issues begin to take over and direct your understanding. The relationship of part to whole—the image to the overall form, for example—may play an extensive role in an interpretation of a poem examining the ways the poem achieves unity. Social issues expressed, implied, or altogether omitted may take clues from certain details, such as symbols or special use of language. Whatever the significance that your close reading begins to uncover, your interpretation will grow from your earliest questions and your continued observation and awareness of how details begin to cluster into meaningfulness.

Robert Browning, "My Last Duchess"

In Robert Browning's "My Last Duchess," we have a poem that poses a number of interesting questions for close reading. In terms of form, the poem is a dramatic monologue, which means it is like a speech in a play. A monologue implies that the speaker holds forth alone, not expecting a response (or dialogue) from the listener. In this case, the duke of Ferrara speaks to a person unfamiliar with his court, presumably an important visitor, and tells that visitor the story behind the interesting painting of his wife. In the process the duke reveals a great deal about his wife, but he also reveals perhaps more than he intends about himself. As you read this poem jot down the kinds of questions you might ask of the poem as you perform a close reading. Then compare them with the questions that follow the poem.

ROBERT BROWNING (1812–1889)

My Last Duchess _____ *1842*

> *Ferrara°*

That's my last Duchess painted on the wall,
Looking as if she were alive. I call
That piece a wonder, now: Frà Pandolf's° hands
Worked busily a day, and there she stands.

Ferrara: This poem may be based on the life of an Italian nobleman, the duke of Ferrara, whose first wife is believed to have been poisoned.   3 *Frà Pandolf:* a fictitious painter.

Will't please you sit and look at her? I said   5
"Frà Pandolf" by design, for never read
Strangers like you that pictured countenance,
The depth and passion of its earnest glance,
But to myself they turned (since none puts by
The curtain I have drawn for you, but I)   10
And seemed as they would ask me, if they durst,
How such a glance came there; so, not the first
Are you to turn and ask thus. Sir, 'twas not
Her husband's presence only, called that spot
Of joy into the Duchess' cheek; perhaps   15
Frà Pandolf chanced to say "Her mantle laps
Over my lady's wrist too much," or "Paint
Must never hope to reproduce the faint
Half-flush that dies along her throat": such stuff
Was courtesy, she thought, and cause enough   20
For calling up that spot of joy. She had
A heart—how shall I say?—too soon made glad,
Too easily impressed; she liked whate'er
She looked on, and her looks went everywhere.
Sir, 'twas all one! My favor at her breast,   25
The dropping of the daylight in the West,
The bough of cherries some officious fool
Broke in the orchard for her, the white mule
She rode with round the terrace—all and each
Would draw from her alike the approving speech,   30
Or blush, at least. She thanked men,—good! but thanked
Somehow—I know not how—as if she ranked
My gift of a nine-hundred-years-old name
With anybody's gift. Who'd stoop to blame
This sort of trifling? Even had you skill   35
In speech—(which I have not)—to make your will
Quite clear to such an one, and say, "Just this
Or that in you disgusts me; here you miss,
Or there exceed the mark"—and if she let
Herself be lessoned so, nor plainly set   40
Her wits to yours, forsooth, and made excuse,
—E'en then would be some stooping; and I choose
Never to stoop. Oh sir, she smiled, no doubt,
Whene'er I passed her; but who passed without
Much the same smile? This grew; I gave commands;   45
Then all smiles stopped together. There she stands
As if alive. Will't please you rise? We'll meet
The company below, then. I repeat,
The Count your master's known munificence
Is ample warrant that no just pretense   50
Of mine for dowry will be disallowed;
Though his fair daughter's self, as I avowed

At starting, is my object. Nay, we'll go
Together down, sir. Notice Neptune, though,
Taming a sea-horse, thought a rarity,   55
Which Claus of Innsbruck° cast in bronze for me!

56 *Claus of Innsbruck:* a fictitious sculptor.

QUESTIONS FOR CLOSE READING

1. Why is the duke showing the "stranger" the picture of his wife?

2. Why does the duke call his wife his "last" duchess? Why doesn't he use her name?

3. Is the stranger supposed to understand that Fra Pandolf is a famous painter?

4. Why is it important that "'twas not / Her husband's presence only, called that spot / Of joy into the Duchess' cheek"? Is the duke jealous?

5. Why does the duke tell the stranger that his duchess had a heart "too soon made glad"? Why does he think she was "Too easily impressed"?

6. The duke is annoyed that so many things gladdened her, and that she did not discriminate among gifts. Why should his "nine-hundred-years-old name" gladden her more than anything else?

7. Apparently he could not train her to value what he thought important (lines 35–45). Why?

8. When he "gave commands" "all smiles stopped together." What does the duke mean by this?

9. In line 51 there is mention of a "dowry," but the duke implies that "The Count your master's" daughter is enough. The duke plans a new marriage. Is it likely to be successful? Is money involved?

10. On the way downstairs the duke pauses to show the stranger a bronze sculpture. Why? Does he hold it on the same level as Fra Pandolf's painting of his "last Duchess"?

Beginning an Interpretation

The questions for close reading can begin the process of interpretation by demanding answers that open up the meaning of the poem. For example, once we reread the poem it becomes clear that the stranger is in court as the representative of a count who plans to marry his daughter to the duke of Ferrara. On the surface, one would think this is a desirable marriage. The duke is wealthy and has a "nine-hundred-years-old name," which implies that he will remain in power for a long time more and that the count's daughter will benefit from wealth and security. However, a careful observation of the way the duke talks about his "last Duchess" tells us that he values her only as the subject of a painting that reveals a lively, happy woman. The fact that he does not even grace her with a name tells us that he treats her as a trophy, as an object of admiration. She was less a person to him than a beautiful object.

The duke's pride reveals itself when he tells the stranger that the painting was done by a famous painter—something he repeats at the end of the conversation when he points to the bronze by Claus of Innsbruck. All this is to impress the stranger. As a result, the duke reveals his insecurity. In the process, the duke tells the stranger that his "last Duchess" was pleased by little things as much as by important things, and that her pleasures were, in his estimation, inappropriate. Everyone pleased her as much as he did, and he did not care for that behavior. As a result he gave her commands to behave as he wished—then her smiles, and, presumably, her happiness—disappeared altogether. The duke sees nothing wrong with his behavior, but it is clear that he has crushed her spirit with regulations. At the end of the monologue, he reminds the stranger that he is counting on his master's "munificence"—which is to say, he expects a very large dowry to come with the count's daughter. Finally, we realize how limited the duke is and also how destructive he has been to the willing and joyous spirit of his most recent wife. Can his new wife expect happiness? The stranger should realize that would be impossible.

MEANING: IMPLIED AND EXPLICIT

Most good poems have at least two kinds of meaning. One is implied, or hidden, as for example Emily Dickinson's poem implies that some otherwise normal things in our environment can be dangerous. Another is explicit, or obvious, as for the example in Emily Dickinson's poem we understand that snakes are potentially dangerous and can frighten us. Usually the explicit meaning of a poem is obvious to most careful readers and needs little deep interpretation. However, implied meanings may not become clear to us except after numerous readings. In "My Last Duchess," Robert Browning implies that the marriage of the duke of Ferrara to the count's daughter will not end well for the daughter. Because the portrait of the last duchess is of a very young woman, Browning also implies that the duke was responsible for the early death of his wife. If she had lived longer the portrait might have been more mature. While the duke thinks his monologue reveals his wealth and taste in art, he actually, and unintentionally, reveals that he is a possessive, prideful monster.

Lewis Carroll, "Jabberwocky"

In the following poem the problem of meaning is complicated by the fact that the explicit level seems characterized by nonsense. The pleasure of hearing the words and listening to the rhymes and rhythms is so great that our attention is drawn away from the possibility of an implied meaning. This poem by Lewis Carroll appeared in *Through the Looking Glass,* the story of Alice in Wonderland, and has been entertaining us for more than a century.

LEWIS CARROLL   (1832–1898)

Jabberwocky ————————————————————— *1871*

'Twas brillig, and the slithy toves
   Did gyre and gimble in the wabe:
All mimsy were the borogoves,
   And the mome raths outgrabe.

"Beware the Jabberwock, my son!   5
   The jaws that bite, the claws that catch!
Beware the Jubjub bird, and shun
   The frumious Bandersnatch!"

He took his vorpal sword in hand:
   Long time the manxome foe he sought—   10
So rested he by the Tumtum tree,
   And stood awhile in thought.

And, as in uffish thought he stood,
   The Jabberwock, with eyes of flame,
Came whiffling through the tulgey wood,   15
   And burbled as it came!

One, two! One, two! And through and through
   The vorpal blade went snicker-snack!
He left it dead, and with its head
   He went galumphing back.   20

"And hast thou slain the Jabberwock?
   Come to my arms, my beamish boy!
O frabjous day! Callooh! Callay!"
   He chortled in his joy.

'Twas brillig, and the slithy toves   25
   Did gyre and gimble in the wabe:
All mimsy were the borogoves,
   And the mome raths outgrabe.

Humpty Dumpty tells Alice, "I can explain all the poems that ever were invented—and a good many that haven't been invented yet." After she recites the first verse, Humpty "explains" it:

> "That's enough to begin with," Humpty Dumpty interrupted: "there are plenty of hard words there. '*Brillig*' means four o'clock in the afternoon—the time when you begin *broiling* things for dinner."
>
> "That'll do very well," said Alice "and '*slithy*'?"
>
> "Well, '*slithy*' means 'lithe and slimy.' 'Lithe' is the same as 'active.' You see it's like a portmanteau—there are two meanings packed up into one word."
>
> "I see it now," Alice remarked thoughtfully: "and what are '*toves*'?"

"Well, '*toves*' are something like badgers—they're something like lizards—and they're something like corkscrews."

"They must be very curious-looking creatures."

"They are that," said Humpty Dumpty; "also they make their nests under sun-dials—also they live on cheese."

"And what's to '*gyre*' and to '*gimble*'?"

"To '*gyre*' is to go round and round like a gyroscope. To '*gimble*' is to make holes like a gimlet."

"And '*the wabe*' is the grass-plot round a sun-dial, I suppose?" said Alice, surprised at her own ingenuity.

"Of course, it is. It's called '*wabe*' you know, because it goes a long way before it, and a long way behind it—"

"And a long way beyond it on each side," Alice added.

"Exactly so. Well, then, '*mimsy*' is 'flimsy and miserable' (there's another portmanteau for you). And a '*borogove*' is a thin shabby-looking bird with its feathers sticking out all round—something like a live mop."

"And then '*mome raths*'?" said Alice. "I'm afraid I'm giving you a great deal of trouble."

"Well, a '*rath*' is a sort of green pig: but '*mome*' I'm not certain about. I think it's short for 'from home'—meaning that they'd lost their way, you know."

"And what does '*outgrabe*' mean?"

"Well, '*outgribing*' is something between bellowing and whistling, with a kind of sneeze in the middle; however, you'll hear it done, maybe—down in the wood yonder—and, when you've once heard it, you'll be *quite* content. Who's been repeating all that hard stuff to you?"

"I read it in a book," said Alice.

Lewis Carroll delights us by treating nonsense as if it were a serious subject. Humpty Dumpty's "interpretation" is as much fun as the poem itself because it, too, of course, is nonsense. The general narrative of the poem is classic: a young man goes out to fight the Jabberwock, equivalent to the dragon of old. With his vorpal blade he kills the beast, to the delight of the speaker, who calls him "my beamish boy!" More than this about the "plot" we really do not need to know. The poem has a classic narrative, a happy ending, and plenty of linguistic amusement along the way.

Humpty Dumpty offers a gloss on the poem, by which is meant a word-by-word explanation. He interprets the poem on the most literal and explicit level. He shows that the unusual language of the poem results from the conjunction of two different words, as in "lithe and slimy." But he might also have said that many of the words gather an apparent meaning from our sense of sound association. For example, when the Jabberwock "Came whiffling through the tulgey wood" we understand the action even though some words are not in the dictionary. "Whiffling" is a motion that has a peculiar sound, like the wind through trees, while "tulgey" implies a wood that is none too pleasant to see. Perhaps it is dark and dank. Each of us will have some associations to connect with the word. Any associations we have are implied in the poem, but in this case we might ask who has done the implying. "Tulgey" may or may not have meant something specific to Lewis Carroll, but today different readers will bring different meanings to the word, although they may all be closely related.

On the surface, we might feel that the poem is generally nonsensical. It is fun and humorous. On another level, though, we can also see that the poem is a parody of the great epic poems of adventure, such as the story of King George and the dragon, which was told in Edmund Spenser's (1552–1599) *The Faerie Queene* (1596), an enormously long poem. In seven short stanzas, Carroll tells the story of a young and unlikely hero who, despite being warned of the danger of the terrifying Jabberwock, sets out to rid the world of the monster and restore order to the community. Implied in this short poem is the story of all adventurers who risk their lives and come back as heroes. But what Carroll has also done is made the story delightful and avoided the high seriousness that characterizes epics such as Homer's *Iliad* or his *Odyssey* or John Milton's *Paradise Lost*. In the process he has not ridiculed epic, simply made it more portable (like a portmanteau suitcase) and amusing.

BEGINNING WITH CLOSE READING

The following two poems need to be examined carefully. The techniques of close reading are especially valuable in approaching them because more is there than meets the eye—or ear. In the case of John Masefield's "Cargoes," the sounds are so enticing as to make the reader revel in its music, while perhaps overlooking some of its meaning. In the case of W. S. Merwin's "Fly," the circumstances of the poem are such that only after questioning it carefully can one hope to appreciate its subtlety.

John Masefield, "Cargoes"

John Masefield was the poet laureate of Great Britain for much of his life, and his poems were read by schoolchildren and their parents for decades. One of his most celebrated poems is "Cargoes," a poem whose separate stanzas treat separate moments in history in terms of the cargoes that were carried in trade from one part of the world to another.

JOHN MASEFIELD   (1878–1967)

Cargoes _____ *1902*

Quinquireme° of Nineveh from distant Ophir,°
Rowing home to haven in sunny Palestine,
With a cargo of ivory,
And apes and peacocks,
Sandalwood, cedarwood, and sweet white wine.   5

Stately Spanish galleon coming from the Isthmus,
Dipping through the Tropics by the palm-green shores,
With a cargo of diamonds,
Emeralds, amethysts,
Topazes, and cinnamon, and gold moidores.°   10

Dirty British coaster with a salt-caked smoke stack,
Butting through the Channel in the mad March days,
With a cargo of Tyne° coal,
Road-rails, pig-lead,
Firewood, iron-ware, and cheap tin trays.   15

1 *Quinquireme:* a large ship, with five men at each rowing station.   *Ophir:* probably a city in Africa, mentioned as having gold in the Bible.   *10* moidores: Renaissance coins used in coastal trade in Africa and China.   13 *Tyne:* Newcastle-upon-Tyne was a coal-producing center in England.

This poem has long been a favorite because it reads magnificently. Masefield had a sense of both language and sound. The way one must assume a stately tone when saying "Quinquireme of Nineveh from distant Ophir" charmed most readers. The rhythms of each first line are insistent:

Quinquireme of I Nine I veh from I distant I Ophir

Stately I Spanish I galleon I coming I from the I Isthmus,

Dirty I British I coaster I with a I salt-caked I smoke stack,

The hammering rhythm of these lines reinforces the sense of labor involved in the activities described. But even more interesting is the shift in language from stanza to stanza. Masefield maintains a high, sonorous tone in the first stanza that is dependent on repetition of *n* and half-open vowel sounds (*-eh*, *O*), then moves to a smooth-sounding language relying on the repetition of soft, sibilant *s* sounds. Finally, in the last stanza come the brutal plosives of *D-*, *Bri-*, *co-* and the one-syllable combinations of *s-k* sounds. These are all admirable formal qualities of the poem: its stanza structure, its rhythms, its word choices, and its sounds.

Any interpretation of this poem that examines only its formal elements has to praise it as a tour de force. The first stanza conjures up ancient riches in terms of marvelous imagery appealing to the sense of touch ("ivory"), sight ("peacocks"), smell ("sandalwood"), and taste ("sweet white wine"). The riches of the second stanza conjure up images of jewels and treasure. But the last stanza, of contemporary times, is couched in terms of unpleasant images of "coal," "pig-lead," and "cheap tin trays." The dominant idea of the poem is that the modern age has not lived up to the glories of the past. Modern British trade is ghastly in comparison with the greatness of the Assyrians of Nineveh in the seventh century B.C. or the Spaniards of the Golden Age of the sixteenth and seventeenth centuries A.D. The sounds and the imagery of this poem argue for the grandness of the past and the tawdriness of the present, as seen through the emblems of its worldwide trade.

All this works well in this poem unless the reader brings to bear some knowledge of the historical circumstances that Masefield does not want to discuss. A politically sensitive interpretation would point out the following important facts.

- The quinquiremes were huge five-level ships that were rowed by slaves won in battle. Each level had ten to forty slaves rowing on each side of the ship. The slaves rarely lasted more than a few months chained to their seats. When they died they were cast overboard like garbage. The Assyrian government in Nineveh was harsh, violent, tyrannical, and absolute. Those receiving the treasures on this quinquireme were absolute and terrible rulers.

- The stately Spanish galleon was sailing from the New World with the treasures it had essentially stolen. The crew of the galleon was largely impounded from foreign ports, and the death rate on board was high. The diamonds, topazes, and amethysts were destined for royalty and the church hierarchy. Again, the government was aristocratic and antidemocratic, and held human life as cheap.

- The dirty British coaster of the late nineteenth century brought goods for a more democratic society. It was not a classless society; Masefield's attitude tells us that much, since he looks down on the ordinary people who need the wares the coaster carries ("cheap tin trays"). However, none of the hands on board this coaster were slaves.

This historical information comes from outside the poem, but it is all implied inside it. Masefield seems to have intended that we ignore the negative values connected with the quinquireme and the galleon, but not the coaster. For years readers did so, but contemporary critics have observed that Masefield ends up praising obnoxious social systems on questionable grounds.

Feminist critics might point out that women will eventually be given some of the products being shipped in these boats, but if so they will be given them by men. Women have no role in the governments indirectly praised by Masefield and become little more than ornaments of the society. Moreover, feminists who critique the masculine quest for domination over people, nature, and social systems would see this poem as representative of the point of view that maintains dominance over women as well. Masefield's worldview is also backward-looking, a "retro-spect," which feminists have condemned.

These antagonistic interpretations of the poem rely on ideas implied in the poem but obviously pressed into the background by the poet. Some readers will feel this view does the poem injustice because it focuses on issues that the poem expressly ignores. It seems to contradict the author's intentions. On the other hand, feminist and political interpreters remind us that their methods are effective with poems that disguise the truth or ignore the crucial issues in the poem. In light of their interpretation, one might think twice before praising the grandeur of ancient Assyria and Renaissance Spain in contrast with more modern Great Britain.

W. S. Merwin, "Fly"

Elements such as rhythm, meter, imagery, rhyme, and metaphor work so effectively in "Cargoes" that most of its original readers ignored Masefield's distortions. On the other hand, many poems do not handle the elements in a virtuoso fashion. Sometimes readers trained in responding to the elements of poetry tend to overlook or undervalue poems that do not give imagery, rhyme, metaphor, or other elements a prominent position. Yet every poem can respond to an analysis through its elements; after all, all poems use language and have ideas, and most employ imagery. However, a poem whose elements are subtly developed can be momentarily puzzling. In terms of interpretation, one might feel there is little or nothing to do or say. Consider the interpretive approaches possible in reading W. S. Merwin's "Fly."

W. S. MERWIN   (b. 1929)

Fly _____ *1974*

I have been cruel to a fat pigeon
Because he would not fly
All he wanted was to live like a friendly old man

He had let himself become a wreck filthy and confiding
Wild for his food beating the cat off the garbage   5
Ignoring his mate perpetually snotty at the beak
Smelling waddling having to be
Carried up the ladder at night content

Fly I said throwing him into the air
But he would drop and run back expecting to be fed   10
I said it again and again throwing him up
As he got worse
He let himself be picked up every time
Until I found him in the dovecote dead
Of the needless effort   15

So this is what I am

Pondering his eye that could not
Conceive that I was a creature to run from

I who have always believed too much in words

QUESTIONS FOR CLOSE READING

1. When you first read the title of the poem, what did you think it meant? If you thought the title was the name of an insect, what were your expectations?

2. What constitutes the poet's "cruelty" to the pigeon? Can you tell what the poet's emotional state is in response to the events of the poem?

3. What does the poet expect of pigeons in a dovecote?

4. How would you characterize the desires of the pigeon? How do they contrast with those of the poet?

5. In the relationship between the poet and the pigeon, who has the power? What is the power? Is the power expressed as an important element in the poem?

6. What poetic elements are important in the poem?

7. How is the pigeon described? Why is the description unflattering and negatively critical?

8. Why did the pigeon die?

9. Why does the poet say he "always believed too much in words"?

Interpretations of this poem can lead in many directions. First, one may begin with the question of emotional response. The poem describes the poet's demanding that the pigeon "fly" rather than "waddling" around after food "like a friendly old man." The poet tosses the bird in the air and the bird drops to the ground. After enough of this, the bird dies, apparently of the trauma of being thrown. The poet then feels guilt for his cruelty and blames himself for demanding something of the bird that the bird could not give. He feels he believed in words too much because to him the concept of "fly" was an essential quality of pigeons.

The second stanza is not pleasant description. The poet "stacks the deck" against the pigeon by describing it in negative terms. It has become a "wreck," "beating the cat off the garbage," "perpetually snotty," "smelling," and needing to be "Carried up the ladder at night." The poet makes all these qualities seem undesirable, offensive, and ugly. Because they produce in him a sense of revulsion, he wants to force the pigeon to fly. As you interpret this poem, you might ask whether the description causes you to feel revulsion as well. Or do you feel sympathy for the pigeon? The poet has described things to make us feel that the pigeon would be much better off if it lost some weight and flew back into its cage on its own and paid some attention to its mate. To respond any other way takes immense effort on our part.

The negative description of the pigeon gives way in the third stanza. The poet simply tells us what he did and what its results were, and in the process builds up some sympathy for the pigeon, who patiently dropped and ran "back expecting to be fed." After the pigeon's death, the word *needless* takes on special force. The words is the poet's admission that his efforts were wrong, and in the last lines of the poem, that the pigeon's trust was misplaced. The pigeon would have been better off if it had stayed away from the poet, if it had never trusted him. When the poet says, "So that is what I am," he is saying many things: that he is cruel and untrustworthy. He realizes that he makes demands based not on what the pigeon's needs are but on what he has presumed the pigeon's nature is. Instead of paying attention to the pigeon, he has paid attention to his ideal of the pigeon. It is a false ideal, but the pigeon must die before the poet realizes he is wrong.

In the process of offering a close reading of the poem, we have also begun an interpretation. The two are often inseparable because close readings depend on interpretation of details. However, a close reading is preparatory to a higher-level interpretation. For example, nothing has been said in this commentary about the significance of the action the poet has described or the lesson, if any, that the poet has learned. Further, nothing has been said about the meaning that a careful reader might take away from the poem. Here are two ways in which a reading may be developed and the significance of the poem established.

A Cultural Interpretation

One way of looking at this poem is to think of how individuals establish expectations of others, whether the others are pigeons, people, institutions, or nations. The poem focuses on a very special relationship between a nominally wild animal, a pigeon, and a poet who is a keeper of that animal. The act of keeping it in a "dovecote" alters the nature of the animal and erases part of its wildness, but not all of it (the pigeon can still be wild in relation to the cat). But the poet is unable to see, until it is vastly too late, that the relationship he has established has altered the nature of the pigeon dramatically. The word *Fly* is italicized because it is in the imperative mood: it is a command. The command is followed by physical abuse: tossing an overweight old pigeon up in the air until it dies. The poet simply does not get the message until it is too late, and only then will he understand that he paid more attention to his presumptions than to the realities of a situation that he himself created and for which he himself is responsible.

It should not be difficult to move from the example of this pigeon to other examples of relationships in which a dependence is established and then blindly ignored. When parents rob children of independence by overparenting, they sometimes expect the children to grow up instantly and "fly" on their own. When they do not, the results can be painful. Extending this model to social programs involving any minority group in relation to the majority can produce a similar situation. When a society permits one group to become dependent on another, the results may follow the model established in "Fly."

A Reader Response Interpretation

Readers will respond variously to the poem, possibly depending on their experience with a trusting pet. Anyone who has had the responsibility of a pet will realize the depth to which pets will trust even a brutalizing master. The very word *master*, used in this way, will cause a painful response, since it is clear that the unpleasant associations that come with the word can be operative in the poem. The narrator attempts to master the pigeon, to master its nature and direct its behavior no matter what the cost. However, even those who have had no pet will sense an injustice in the poem. The claim that the master has been "cruel" is partly based on his having been unjust. Why not let the pigeon be? Why not respect its wishes? True, the pigeon is slothful, lazy, fat, and filthy, but why worry? Who is responsible for its current condition if not the "master"?

A reader-based reading of this poem involves much more than an examination of possible emotional responses to its narrative. For one thing, the pigeon might be a symbol for something else (as well as being a pigeon). Even thinking in terms of one's pet, a reader begins to think symbolically. But moving to a larger symbolic issue, such as any situation in which the pigeon might represent dependent social groups like people on welfare, people in prison, or native Americans on a reservation, demands an act of will on the part of the reader. Where in the poem, for example, is the evidence that such a symbolic reading is reasonable? Does the poem invite this interpretation? Is there specific evidence to support such a reading? Many poems have much more specific symbolism than this one. However, Merwin's poem is more bare-bones. There is no rhyme, no meter, no predictable stanzas, no regular line length. The poem does without most of the elements of poetry. Nevertheless, its last line implies that it has important ideas and that the poet has learned a lesson.

One clue to a larger meaning is the fact that few readers keep pigeons in a dovecote; so the poem must mean more than this. However, the poet leaves it to the reader to decide just what the meaning might be. Is it possible we believe too much in words? If so, what do we learn from this pigeon? The poem pushes us toward a symbolic interpretation by taking this narrative so seriously that it becomes a story with a moral. In a sense, then, it is like a fable from *Aesop's Fables,* whose barnyard anecdotes become moral fables demanding a symbolic interpretation. The fable of the rooster discovering a precious gem is not really about roosters. Ultimately, the decision that a fable is symbolic or possesses greater significance is the responsibility of the reader who can "read between the lines." "Fly's" seriousness invites such a reading.

A STUDENT INTERPRETATION
OF ROBERT FROST'S "BIRCHES"

Robert Frost's "Birches" is in the deceptively simple style that helped make him America's first poet laureate. Frost (1874–1963) portrays himself as a New Englander with experiences tied to the land and to the world of farmers: simple people, hard living, and a reverent regard for life. The actual facts tend to contradict this portrait and reveal a pattern of self-constructed identity that has fascinated Frost's biographers. For example, Frost was not born a New England farmer. He was born in San Francisco, where his father was a journalist on the *San Francisco Bulletin,* and he lived there until he was eleven. His father died in 1885, and his family moved to Lawrence, Massachusetts, where his father wanted to be buried. They did not live on a farm, but in an industrial

mill town. His father had been born in New Hampshire, so there was a legitimate family connection with the state that Frost enjoyed and with which he associated himself. Frost shaped himself carefully as a poet, coming to know the
most important English-language poets of his time: Amy Lowell, W. B. Yeats,
Ezra Pound, and T. S. Eliot. His work contrasted with theirs, and his image as
a poet has survived as a grand old philosopher of the land.

ROBERT FROST   (1874–1963)

Birches _____ *1916*

When I see birches bend to left and right
Across the lines of straighter darker trees,
I like to think some boy's been swinging them.
But swinging doesn't bend them down to stay
As ice storms do. Often you must have seen them   5
Loaded with ice a sunny winter morning
After a rain. They click upon themselves
As the breeze rises, and turn many-colored
As the stir cracks and crazes their enamel.
Soon the sun's warmth makes them shed crystal shells   10
Shattering and avalanching on the snow crust—
Such heaps of broken glass to sweep away
You'd think the inner dome of heaven had fallen.
They are dragged to the withered bracken by the load,
And they seem not to break; though once they are bowed   15
So low for long, they never right themselves
You may see their trunks arching in the woods
Years afterwards, trailing their leaves on the ground
Like girls on hands and knees that throw their hair
Before them over their heads to dry in the sun.   20
But I was going to say when Truth broke in
With all her matter of fact about the ice storm,
I should prefer to have some boy bend them
As he went out and in to fetch the cows—
Some boy too far from town to learn baseball,   25
Whose only play was what he found himself,
Summer or winter, and could play alone.
One by one he subdued his father's trees
By riding them down over and over again
Until he took the stiffness out of them,   30
And not one but hung limp, not one was left
From him to conquer. He learned all there was
To learn about not launching out too soon
And so not carrying the tree away
Clear to the ground. He always kept his poise   35
To the top branches, climbing carefully

With the same pains you use to fill a cup
Up to the brim, and even above the brim.
Then he flung outward, feet first, with a swish,
Kicking his way down through the air to the ground.   40
So was I once myself a swinger of birches.
And so I dream of going back to be.
It's when I'm weary of considerations,
And life is too much like a pathless wood
Where your face burns and tickles with the cobwebs   45
Broken across it, and one eye is weeping
From a twig's having lashed across it open.
I'd like to get away from earth awhile
And then come back to it and begin over.
May no fate willfully misunderstand me   50
And half grant what I wish and snatch me away
Not to return. Earth's the right place for love:
I don't know where it's likely to go better.
I'd like to go by climbing a birch tree,
And climb black branches up a snow-white trunk   55
Toward heaven, till the tree could bear no more,
But dipped its top and set me down again.
That would be good both going and coming back.
One could do worse than be a swinger of birches.

Beginning with Close Reading

Many of our examples of close reading have begun with a series of questions. However, a response journal can also help begin the close-reading process. The following is a freewriting passage recording first impressions of the poem.

> The poem seems to be about the birch trees. I've never been in New England, so I have to take Frost's word for what happens in a storm when they get iced up. They get bent over and don't straighten up. Ice storms do a lot of damage. Frost says he'd rather see a boy do the damage than the ice storm. I get the feeling he was a boy who liked to ride the birches. There's a lot here about how the boy learned not to ruin the trees entirely, so he's probably thinking about his own experience. You know that for sure when he tells us that he was once a swinger of birches. The end of the poem turns philosophical and even makes you think that the poet is worried about dying. Riding up the birches is like reaching for heaven, and maybe Frost has that on his mind in this poem. Generally, it's the kind of poem that you can read and pretty much understand, but you also know that it's got something going on beneath the surface that will take a little getting into to figure out.

Just as close reading concentrated on the details of the short story, it always helps to examine the poem and take note of its important details. The following is one person's listing of details.

In the first five lines the narrator tells us he likes to imagine that birches that sway "left and right" were bent by boys having fun riding them. There are "darker trees" in background that are not as flexible as the birches--and I guess not as much fun for boys. They don't bend.

There's a choice: boys can bend them, or ice storms can do it, but ice storms make them bend so "they never right themselves."

The imagery in lines 6 to 16 is strong. Frost uses sound: "click"; vision: "many-colored," "crazes their enamel." He also uses metaphor when he calls the fallen ice "heaps of broken glass." The same happens when he talks about "the inner dome of heaven" in line 13. That's when you know he's talking about more than kids and trees.

The simile of the trees "Like girls on hands and knees that throw their hair / Before them" is nice, but is it supposed to mean that the poem is about something sexual? Boys and girls, not just trees?

"Truth" has a capital T, so something is happening in line 21. Maybe he means that dreaming about boys bending the trees is fantasy because the truth is that the trees were bent by nature.

The description of the boy beginning on line 25 is pretty clearly a description of the narrator, or so it seems. Frost makes a special point of telling us that the boy learned how to climb trees without hurting them. It's a skill like filling the cup "Up to the brim" as he says in line 38. But it's also basic to growing up, and when "not one was left / For him to conquer" maybe he was already grown up.

In line 41 the poem shifts. He says he was once a swinger of birches "And so I dream of going back to be." That's a key line in the poem, I think. I need to figure out what this is supposed to mean.

He talks about getting tired of things in line 44 and maybe reaching up off the earth. But then he's worried that "fate" will "misunderstand me" and "snatch me away." He doesn't want that. He wants to climb up on the tree, "<u>Toward</u> heaven," but he wants to come back to earth because "That would be good both going and coming back."

The last line makes you realize that what he did as a boy is still good to do now that he's a man.

Much of the work of brainstorming has been done by the notes above. One of the realities of writing about poetry is that since a poem is much shorter than a story, play, or essay, a close reading that accounts for details will sometimes get you in a position to think about writing. You can devote some of your freewriting to examining the important elements that the poet uses.

Analyzing the Elements

It is not always necessary to take each element of poetry by itself, but it helps to note how the most important elements function in the poem. Certainly the language, imagery, metaphor, and symbolism are important enough to warrant special notice. While detailed discussion of the elements of poetry will come in the next chapter, this student had time to take them into account here. The terms mentioned, *iambic pentameter, metaphor,* and *simile,* are somewhat technical, but they figure in this student's reading. You will find more information on them and many other basic elements of poetry in the following pages.

There are no unusual terms and no complicated language. Frost talks the way most people do--or at least the way an older New Englander might.

The poem is not sarcastic or ironic. The narrator speaks so honestly that you get the feeling it is Frost himself talking. Maybe it is.

Frost doesn't rhyme the poem, so it has an easygoing style. But the lines are metrical, or seem so. They seem to have ten syllables and most of the feet I've scanned are iambic, so the poem is probably iambic pentameter. That helps give a sense of shape and form to it, although it doesn't allow for any sudden shift in meaning or emotion. Maybe it doesn't need it.

Metaphor is pretty well developed here. The birches have to be a metaphor for something; maybe they are symbolic. They're natural, so they must stand for something good: maybe reaching for something, like ambition or something. Climbing without breaking them is a challenge, so the boy learns a skill. The man must be much too big to climb a birch tree, but since he wants to do it again it must stand for something important.

One simile that's odd is the trees bent like girls after the ice storm has broken them: "Years afterwards, trailing their leaves on the ground." I'm not so sure there's anything sexual about that. It might actually be sexist.

The ideas are interesting, and I'm not sure I've got them fully under control. The birches represent a challenge and the chance to become skilled. That's something a man can benefit from throughout life. So the narrator says he'd like to be able to climb birches now just so long as he doesn't die trying. So he must think of swinging on birches as being risky, challenging, and dangerous.

Freewriting

One of the best ways to begin an interpretation is to take some important details discussed above and freewrite to develop a thesis. Several important ideas have already been raised in the notes above, so it makes sense to examine them. The writer took several of those details and wrote without self-censorship for three minutes on each one, hoping to develop material that could be used in an interpretation.

> One thing that gets me is that Frost really talks about little boys and not little girls. The idea of jumping up on the birches and swinging them down is a real challenge to him as a boy, and the grown-up narrator tells you that it's important. It is not a bad thing to be a swinger of birches. The idea that you "conquer" the birches is probably the most important detail there. Boys like to conquer things. It's part of the masculine mystique, I guess. But they also want to be sure they can take chances and not necessarily get wiped out. I think that's what Frost means when he says at the end that he'd like to be able to swing on birches again but not necessarily risk "fate," which might think he is reaching for the heavens because he wants to die. That's the trick: take the risk, but succeed.

The writer took the question of conquering the trees, mentioned in line 32, and developed it in connection with the description of boys growing up. Below, the writer takes another approach to freewriting. Instead of focusing on a detail and working up ideas about it, the writer has chosen to answer one basic question. He spent three minutes without censorship trying to answer it.

> What do the birches symbolize?
>
> The birches could symbolize any challenge, anything that is difficult and worth doing. But they also symbolize challenges that help build skill in men. The birches have to be climbed, so that means the boy has to reach beyond "mother earth" and reach for the heavens. But Frost makes it clear that he hopes to try to do something challenging like reaching for the heavens, but he doesn't want to get to heaven--not yet. He wants to end up back on earth because that's where "love" goes best. Maybe the birches symbolize something like the challenge of writing poetry or being imaginative or creative. I say that because little children are more naturally creative than adults. It takes an effort for a man to take the risks that children accept as normal.

Dealing with the symbolism of the birches offers an interesting way into the poem, since the writer has sensed that much more is implied in the imagery of the birches than just trees. Even the boy swinging on birches seems to be doing more than just having fun in the woods.

A Sample Interpretation

Going over annotation, notes, and freewriting, the writer began to see that it was possible to talk about feminist issues in the poem while also taking into account some of the formal elements implied in the oppositions that seemed important to Frost. On the basis of the writing above, the writer created these potential statements, hoping to use one for a thesis.

> Although the narrator in the poem seems to be talking only about birches, he is actually talking about the opportunities boys have in childhood to learn how to be men.
>
> The "birches" in this poem represent the challenges life offers for boys to grow up as conquerors, as men who use power carefully.
>
> "Birches" talks about two kinds of power. One is the terrible power of nature's ice storms, which permanently damage trees so they resemble girls. The other is the power of boys who learn to be skilled enough to subdue nature but not permanently damage it.

The writer decided to try to work with the third of these statements, keeping the other two in reserve as supporting statements in later paragraphs. The job was to write a three-page interpretation without using outside references, so the writer set about to construct a working outline, knowing that it would change as the writing progressed. The basic outline, after some false starts and revision, came out this way.

"Boys, Birches, and Power"

    I.   Boys and birches
        A.   Birches bend
            1.   Boys bend them through swinging
            2.   Or, ice storms permanently bend them

    B.   The poet prefers boys to swing the birches
          1.   The poet constructs a fantasy of boys swinging
          2.   Truth, with a capital T, breaks in on the fantasy

II.   Ice storms and birches
    A.   Ice storms are beautiful
          1.   Beautiful visual images
          2.   Beautiful sounds
    B.   Ice storms are destructive
          1.   They are the power of nature
          2.   Their effect is permanent
          3.   Damaged birches look like bent-over girls

III.   The portrait of the lonely boy
    A.   Poet imagines the boy as a dairy farmer
          1.   He manages cows--a symbol for the female
          2.   Not a city boy, doesn't play team sports
          3.   Learns to play alone
    B.   The boy is "privileged"
          1.   The trees are his "father's"
          2.   The boy will inherit them when he is grown

IV.   Conquering trees is a skill for boys
    A.   By learning the proper skill, the boy conquers the trees
          1.   Conquering controls but does not destroy
          2.   Ice storms conquer but destroy
    B.   The skills of the boy imply the skills of the man
          1.   Life now is "too much like a pathless wood"
              a.   He feels too many "considerations," presumably for others
              b.   Swinging birches is solitary and something he would like to do again
          2.   "Earth's the right place for love"
              a.   As a grown man he would like to swing up toward heaven alone
              b.   But he wants to be sure to come back to earth
          3.   Being a swinger of birches is a fantasy wish
              a.   Recalls childhood independence
              b.   It's not a bad thing

The actual paper, based on this outline, came out like this.

Marcus Hemphill
Professor Jacobus
English 109-03

Boys, Birches, and Power

    Two kinds of power exist in Robert Frost's "Birches," the power of man symbolized by the growing boy, and the power of nature symbolized by the ice storm. Of the two kinds of trees in the poem, one is the white birch and the other is the "straighter darker" tree, mysterious and not good for climbing. Ice storms do not bother them, either. But birches bend, and you can either see them bent by boys who are trying out their skills as conquerors, or see them bent to the ground by ice storms. Boys do not ruin the trees, but the ice storms do.

The narrator begins by imagining a fantasy about boys swinging birches. The darker reality of nature permanently bending the birches--the narrator calls it "Truth" "With all her matter of fact"--"broke in" on his fantasy. The ice storm is beautiful but destructive, just as Truth is bothersome to the imagery of boys swinging birches. Frost uses beautiful imagery and description for birches in the ice storm: "They click upon themselves," "turn many-colored," and have "crystal shells." This beauty is destructive and leaves the birches useless, "Like girls." The image of the bent-over birches suggests that girls are not as strong or adventurous as boys, and the fact that Truth is a "her" suggests that the narrator might be annoyed with females. He never says so, but the imagery makes you wonder.

The narrator paints a portrait of an ideal boy who manages cows, another female symbol, and who lives in the country. He's lonely and doesn't play games with other kids. He plays alone, so swinging birches is ideal. The birches the boy swings belong to his father and will someday probably belong to him. So in a way you could say that the swinging he does on the trees gets him ready to take over the farm and his father's role. The boy the narrator describes in lines 23 to 41 begins as an imaginary boy, but pretty soon you realize the narrator is describing himself. "He learned all there was / To learn about not launching out too soon," and "he always kept his poise."

In line 32 the narrator tells us the trees were there for "him to conquer," and from that you get the impression that the whole thing about growing up the way the boy does is to learn how to conquer things without ruining them. If you leave things bent over "Like girls" that is not good. It is interesting that girls do not swing on birches. Only boys. It's as if the narrator was saying that this conquering game is appropriate only for boys and helps them become men.

Now that he is a man looking back on himself ("So was I once myself a swinger of birches"), he no longer swings birches. He would like to try because now,

> life is too much like a pathless wood
> Where your face burns and tickles with the cobwebs
> Broken across it, and one eye is weeping
> From a twig's having lashed across it open. (44–47)

He wants to "climb black branches up a snow-white trunk / Toward heaven" again, but he does not want to get to heaven just yet. He wants to come back because "Earth's the right place for love: / I don't know where it's likely to go better" (52–53). Then he says, "I'd like to go by climbing a birch tree," but it is not clear what he means by "go" in this sentence. Does he mean die? Or does he mean something related to the previous line in "go better"? It is heard to tell.

Another thing that is hard to tell is what kind of love he means in line 52. The way he seems to idealize the independence of his boyhood and his negative imagery about women makes you wonder if the problems of being "weary of considerations" (43) might have something to do with adjusting to living with a woman. It is easy to be a conqueror when a boy is swinging birches, but a man cannot behave the way a boy does. In the end, I think the nostalgia the narrator feels for the simplicity of his childhood has to do with the fact that he mastered the skills he needed then, and now looks back at that time as one when he had a great deal of power. Now as a man there are too many "considerations" and he has to learn to live with them and accept their pain. Maybe he also has to accept the fact that he has less power.

Further Strategies for Interpretation

FEMINIST. The imagery of ice-damaged trees resembling girls on their hands and knees and the constant reference to boys and their development suggests an approach to the poem through a potentially feminist reading. Such a reading would consider Frost's emphasis on boys and their efforts to develop skill, while essentially ignoring girls and their growing up. However, a balanced reading would take into account the fact that Frost is a male and has a right to discuss growing up from the point of view of a man. An important question is whether the imagery of the damaged trees is a demeaning reference to femaleness. Frost in his later years carefully presented himself as a white-haired patriarch of poetry. A feminist reading of this poem might ask whether his true posture was patriarchic in the negative sense of dominating and conquering the environment.

FORMALIST. A formalist approach to the poem might concentrate on the regularity of the meter of the lines, pointing out that iambic pentameter is one of the most historically durable lines in English. Shakespeare's plays, Milton's *Paradise Lost,* and almost every sonnet use that line. The poem is built on obvious oppositions: boy and man; boys and ice storms; rural and urban; heaven and earth; boys and girls; conquering and not conquering. The formalist reading would attempt to clarify these oppositions and the meaning of birches for the narrator. It assumes that the reader's job is to study the formal qualities along with the poem's explicit language to see how the form clarifies, reinforces, and creates meaning.

POLITICAL-ECONOMIC. One could suggest a political-economic interpretation by studying the childhood relationship to the land and seeing that it has now become uncertain for the adult narrator. If he was a dairy farmer's son once, he seems not to have grown to be a dairy farmer himself, and so he is not as connected to the earth as he had been. He is obviously wistful for earlier times. An economic discussion would question the kind of skill that the boy learned in riding the birches and what the man grew up to conquer. The description of being "weary of considerations" and of his present life being like a "pathless wood" (line 44) and painful suggests that he is no longer in the immediate relationships to the earth's economy as he once was.

READER RESPONSE. A reader response approach might examine how the style is designed to put the reader at ease and to make the experience of reading the poem especially nonthreatening. We all know that some poets need unusual complexity of language to sustain their thinking or depend on allusion to other literature to establish a special audience for their poetry. In contrast, the style of this poem suggests that one can get right in and understand everything without much effort. But we know that is not the case. Frost puts the reader at ease, but he also gives the reader more than the reader expects: the language, though simple, hides complex meanings. The poem sucks the reader in almost like quicksand. Analyzing how Frost answers a reader's expectations and then frustrates them could produce a fascinating interpretation. Another approach—and a good way to begin discussing the poem—would be to use one's personal experience with birches, the country, and even childhood. What experiences does Frost expect the reader to bring to the poem? The narrator is clearly aware of the audience when he says, "Often you have seen them / Loaded with ice a sunny winter morning." Well, not everyone has seen ice-covered birches, but those who have not will probably be able to imagine them without difficulty. The reader is led carefully in this poem, and Frost never loses sight of the reader's potential response to the imagery, the narrative, or the narrator's personality.

When deciding what kind of strategy to use to interpret "Birches," one must think about the poem and its overall effect. For some readers a feminist or political-economic reading might appear to distort the poem. This is not to rule out such readings, only to suggest they might treat issues peripheral to the poem. Some readers may feel the same way about a reader response or even a formalist reading. You will have to decide how to approach any poem on the basis of your reading and rereading and your impression of the poem's overall purposes. Your job will be to decide what approach is most reasonable for you, most responsible to the poem itself, and most capable of producing an insightful reading.

V

CRITICAL APPROACHES
TO
POETRY

10

ELEMENTS OF POETRY

Most poets do not think about their poem's separate elements (although some do); they are too busy orchestrating feelings, ideas, and whatever else they feel will work. Because of this, examining elements separately is an artificial critical exercise. Nevertheless, it is useful, especially if you remember to put the poem back together again. A good close reading of a poem will depend on observing specific elements as they serve the purpose of the poet. Likewise, all interpretive strategies depend on the ability to be specific, to note special uses of language and special effects.

We can talk about two general kinds of poems: the **lyric** and the **narrative.** The lyric originates from ancient poems sung to a lyre, and the narrative was probably chanted with the accompaniment of a similar stringed instrument. Lyrics are short, such as Aphra Behn's "Song" (p. 466). Narratives are longer, such as Frost's "Home Burial" (p. 577). Included under the general class of lyrics are special forms such as sonnets, odes, and villanelles, discussed in this chapter. Poems such as *Paradise Lost*—much too long to be included here—are epics and therefore narrative poems. However, some of the longer poems in the album are clearly narratives, such as Anne Sexton's "Red Riding Hood" (p. 762). The line between lyric and narrative often blurs in longer forms such as ballads, but both kinds of poems rely upon the same elements.

We will focus on eight elements and their effects.

LANGUAGE. Poets often become poets because they love language and are able to use it creatively and imaginatively. Carroll's "Jabberwocky" reveals a powerful interest in language, going to the extreme of inventing new words such as "slithey," "mome raths," and "outgrabe." In the poem "Jabberwocky" Lewis Carroll has fun with language, and so do we. Some poems, such as "Letter to the Local Police" by June Jordan (p. 711), are more *discursive* than imagistic;

that is, they depend on the language of discourse—*telling* us something—more than on the use of imagery, which *shows* us something. Poetic language can be formal or informal, and it often plays on the connotations of words. The poet usually controls language not only through meaning but also through sound. **Euphony** is the term for words that sound good together. It is present in the first line of John Masefield's "Cargoes": "Quinquireme of Nineveh from distant Ophir." One hardly cares what the words mean because they sound so musical. **Cacophony** refers to sounds that grate, annoy, or create a sense of distaste. John Milton, in *Paradise Lost,* uses cacophony to intensify the transformation of the devils into serpents in hell:

> dreadful was the din
> Of hissing through the Hall, thick swarming now
> With complicated monsters, head and tail,
> Scorpion and Asp, and *Amphisbaena* dire,
> *Cerastes* horn'd, *Hydrus,* and *Ellops* drear,
> And *Dipsas* (not so thick swarm'd once the Soil
> Bedropt with blood of *Gorgon,* or the Isle
> *Ophiusa*)
>
>   (X. 521–28)

Onomatopoeia implies an effort to make the words imitate the sound of the thing or action they refer to. Individual expressions, such as "ruff-ruff," "chirp-chirp," or "buzz," are common examples from everyday speech. One of the most-well known poetic examples is from Alfred Lord Tennyson's "The Princess": "The moan of doves in immemorial elms, / And the murmuring of innumerable bees."

IMAGERY.   **Images** appeal directly to one of the senses: touch, sight, hearing, smell, or taste. Imagist poets make every effort to excite our responses through images rather than through discursive language. They want us to react to images in poetry the way we do in life. When we see a flower in nature, we respond directly to it, and when poets describe a flower as if it were in front of us, they expect us to recreate the image in our imagination and respond as directly as possible. When an image, such as Ezra Pound's "petals on a wet, black bough," appeals to two or more senses at the same time, it is said to possess **synaesthesia.**

TONE.   **Tone** may be thought of as arising from the voice the poet projects. Poems can adopt any of the tones of voice that we use in conversation. They can be ironic, conversational, angry, satirical, or judgmental. The varieties of tone are virtually unlimited, and every poem must be examined on its own terms.

RHYTHM AND RHYME.   For many poets and readers the core of a poem is its rhythm, and some want all poems to have a regular beat. For other readers a poem is not a poem until it **rhymes.** We often refer to rhymed and metrical poetry as **verse** in order to make a cautious distinction between poetry in general and poems that have regular rhythms and rhymes. Although this term is used derisively by some important poets and critics, be aware that contemporary poetry often depends upon rhyme for its power and prose poetry depends on rhythm to signal that it is poetry.

METAPHOR AND FIGURATIVE LANGUAGE.   For many people **metaphor,** the implied comparison of two unlike things, instantly evokes the idea of poetry, since poetry achieves so many of its effects metaphorically. We often use metaphor in conversation: "You're chicken!" implies a comparison between "you" and the spineless chicken. Other devices related to metaphor are the simile, allegory, and symbol, discussed in this chapter. All of these function by means of comparisons that depend on the careful selection of certain qualities. For example, "You're chicken!" ignores the laying of eggs, the roosterly crowing in the morning, and all other qualities except the quality of cowardice. The chicken's scurrying away in haste is an emblem of fear, the quality we metaphorize. Metaphor is a kind of **figurative language,** which also includes such wordplays as puns and **oxymorons** (a contradiction such as "black light," or "hot ice"), as well as other devices.

SYMBOL AND ALLEGORY.   **Symbols** are special forms of metaphor. A symbol may be universal in its nature, as when we say that "sailing westward" usually symbolizes preparation for death. But a symbol can also be more private, as in Robert Frost's "The Road Not Taken" (p. 580). For Frost, the symbol of the road may represent a professional path he might have chosen but did not. For the reader, it may suggest something similar, but not exactly the same thing. Symbols, unlike **allegories,** are not fixed. Gerard Manley Hopkins uses allegory in "The Windhover," (p. 702) in which the falcon is an allegory for Christ. Symbols tend to respond to the context in which they are found, and consequently they are not always easy to identify. However, everyone uses symbols in language much of the time. Recognizing their use in poetry will help you see them in daily language, either spoken or written.

FORM.   All poems have form, but some forms are more specific than others. **Sonnets** have fourteen lines and usually rhyme according to one of several patterns. In some rare instances, a sonnet will have thirteen or even sixteen lines, and will rhyme or not rhyme. **Quatrains** are groups of four rhyming lines, and although they do not usually function as whole poems, they are important forms within a poem. Some specialized forms, such as the **sestina** and the **villanelle,** depend on repeated lines, words, phrases, or rhymes to satisfy their formal requirements. Some forms are very tight and demanding, such as **haiku** (seventeen syllables in three lines of five, seven, and five syllables) and **terza rima** (three-line stanzas rhyming *aba, bcb, cdc,* and so on); others are relatively loose, such as the **epigram** (a short, pithy poem) and the **ode** (a long, irregular poem). Some poets feel they work best when the form is tight; others feel that tight forms limit creativity. Most of these forms are discussed beginning on page 491.

IDEAS. Most poems contain ideas; very few do not. When we interpret a poem, we usually attempt to establish the nature of its ideas and their significance. Aristotle used the term *thought* and some critics use the term *theme* to describe the ideas the poet works with. **Theme** may be reductive because it implies that the poem has one idea, whereas most poems concerned with ideas have many. Although poems usually have a focus, sometimes even a "message," they sometimes ruminate on an idea, looking at it from several perspectives.

The most important point to remember is that poets use all these elements in most of their poems, and looking at only one of them represents a kind of distortion. Our efforts will be to attain a balance that will permit us to examine specific elements of a poem without losing sight of how they interact. The achievement of a poem results from the subtle cooperation of all of its elements.

LANGUAGE

Language is the stuff of poetry, and the love of words is probably as basic to the poet as love of color or form is to a painter. Poets love the way words sound, the way they surprise a reader with their shape or their many syllables, and the way words build up meanings through modern associations and an understanding of ancient roots. Some poets like uncommon words, like *vetch* or *gorse*, names for undergrowth and grasses. Some like words that have many possible meanings, such as *score*, which can mean something related to a sports event, a sexual event, or a manufacturing event, depending on its context.

In some poems the language is quite **formal;** in others it is very **informal.** The difference is in tone. Edward Hirsch's "Fast Break" (p. 529) begins informally with a description: "A hook shot kisses the rim and / Hangs there helplessly, but doesn't drop." It continues as if it were telling us about any special play in a basketball game. By contrast, William Wordsworth (1770–1850) is much more formal when he addresses the dead poet whom he most admired: "Milton! thou shouldst be living at this hour: / England hath need of thee: she is a fen / Of stagnant waters." The formality sets a tone of respect and admiration, whereas in Edward Hirsch's poem the tone is somewhat the opposite. Hirsch relies on the informal language of basketball and the easy tone of the sports buff.

Individual words can excite humorous or sad responses. Sometimes a poet uses a word with a special emotional association, like "Balaclava," the site of a battle, or "Aghadoe," a place in Ireland that had meaning for the Irish poet John Todhunter (1839–1916). The first stanza of "Aghadoe" is as follows:

There's a glade in Aghadoe, Aghadoe, Aghadoe,
   There's a green and silent glade in Aghadoe,
Where we met, my love and I, Lover's fair planet in the sky,
   O'er that sweet and silent glade in Aghadoe.

Every stanza thereafter repeats *Aghadoe* at least four times while the lover tells the story of hiding her sweetheart from the British redcoats only to have him betrayed by her own brother. Through this repetition, the word *Aghadoe* builds up a melancholy power.

Repetition is not the primary device of John Skelton (1460–1529). Instead, he uses a form of listing, placing one phrase or one word in a line, following with another, adding them up for effect. Moreover, he uses words in such an unusual way that the modern reader needs footnotes to interpret their meaning. The overall purpose of the poem is to celebrate the nobility and courtliness of a woman. Skelton's delight in finding and rhyming the right words has made this a poem that has delighted readers since the eighteenth century.

JOHN SKELTON   (1460–1529)

To Mistress Margaret Hussey _____ *1523*

Merry Margaret
As midsummer flower,
Gentle as falcon
Or hawk of the tower;°
    With solace and gladness,   5
Much mirth and no madness,°
All good and no badness,
So joyously,
So maidenly,
So womanly   10
Her demeaning°
In every thing,
Far, far passing
That I can indite°
Or suffice to write   15
Of merry Margaret
As midsummer flower,
Gentle as falcon
Or hawk of the tower;
    As patient and as still   20
And as full of good will
As fair Isaphil;°
Coliander,°
Sweet pomander,°
Good Cassander;   25
Steadfast of thought,

4 *Gentle . . . hawk:* the falcon was a symbol of gentility, as was the hawk. Skelton means he thinks of Mistress Hussey as being an aristocrat.   6 *madness:* silliness or foolishness.   11 *demeaning:* demeanor, or behavior.   14 *indite:* write.   22–25 *Isaphil . . . Cassander:* classical ladies.   23 *Coliander:* coriander, a spice.   24 *pomander:* a spicy perfumed ball.

Well made, well wrought;
Far may be sought
Erst° that ye can find
So cortays,° so kind   30
As merry Margaret,
This midsummer flower,
Gentle as falcon
Or hawk of the tower.

29 *Erst:* until, or before.   30 *cortays:* courtly or courteous.

The following poem uses language with exuberance and delight and with
a mixture of formal and informal expressions. It links high seriousness with the
preposterous, addressing itself to "Sir Beelzebub," the "Lord of the Flies," another name for Satan. Instead of being fearful, however, the author is at times
almost silly. Clearly Edith Sitwell's exuberance is reserved for the pleasure of her
language. She apparently does not fear the devil.

EDITH SITWELL   (1887–1964)

Sir Beelzebub _____ *1922*

When
Sir
Beelzebub called for his syllabub in the hotel in Hell
        Where Proserpine first fell,
Blue as the gendarmerie were the waves of the sea   5

        (Rocking and shocking the bar-maid).

Nobody comes to give him his rum but the
Rim of the sky hippopotamus-glum
Enhances the chances to bless with a benison
Alfred Lord Tennyson crossing the bar laid   10
With cold vegetation from pale deputations
Of temperance workers (all signed In Memoriam)
Hoping with glory to trip up the Laureate's feet

        (Moving in classical metres) . . .

Like Balaclava, the lava came down from the   15
Roof, and the sea's blue wooden gendarmerie
Took them in charge while Beelzebub roared for his rum.

        . . . None of them come!

The slow opening lines, each consisting of one word, prepare us for seriousness, but then the third line moves embarrassingly fast, with an internal rhyme
in *Beelzebub* and *syllabub* and a reference to a "hotel in Hell," another internal
rhyme. These are here for fun. A syllabub is a frothy dessert made of wine and

cream and not likely to hold up to the rigors of Hell's weather. What is it doing here? It's rhyming. That is its entire function, and we enjoy it on that level. Even the comparison of the "gendarmerie"—the French police, who wear dark blue uniforms—with the sea is silly. The "bar-maid" seems out of place, too, but it reveals another function of language: **allusion** (reference to another work of literature). Not every reader will know Alfred Lord Tennyson (1809–1892), the poet laureate of England, but those who do may recognize the allusion to his poems "Crossing the Bar" (1889) (thus getting in the "bar-maid") and "In Memoriam" (1850), about the death of a friend. Because they are about death, Tennyson's poems credit the underworld with power (Proserpine is the classical goddess of the underworld, Hades). But Sitwell refers to them after complaining that Beelzebub sits "hippopotamus-glum" because no one brings him his rum. Then, what does "Like Balaclava, the lava" really mean? Balaclava is another allusion to Tennyson, this time through the site of the cavalry madness memorialized in Tennyson's "Charge of the Light Brigade" (1854), but it has little to do with lava, except for the rhyme. Thus Sitwell manages to be funny and serious at the same time.

A final distinction of language is that of connotation and denotation. A word's **denotation** is what it means on the dictionary level: a *rat* is a rodent. **Connotation** is what it means on an emotional level: a *rat* is a person you don't trust. Poems often exploit the double meanings of connotation and denotation.

In the following poem, note how snatches of common phrases are juxtaposed for satirical effect. While you first read it, examine the unusual uses of conversational tone and voice as well as the background voice which interrupts from time to time. Moreover, the reliance on juxtaposing informal with formal language as well as playing with denotation and connotation make this poem both challenging and amusing to read.

E. E. CUMMINGS   (1894–1962)

Poem, or Beauty Hurts Mr. Vinal _____ *1926*

take it from me kiddo
believe me
my country, 'tis of

you, land of the Cluett
Shirt Boston Garter and Spearmint   5
Girl With The Wrigley Eyes(of you
land of the Arrow Ide
and Earl &
Wilson
Collars)of you i   10
sing: land of Abraham Lincoln and Lydia E. Pinkham,°
land above all of Just Add Hot Water And Serve—
from every B.V.D.

---

11 *Lydia E. Pinkham:* inventor of a woman's patent medicine for anemia.

let freedom ring

amen. i do however protest,anent the un   15
-spontaneous and otherwise scented merde which
greets one(Everywhere Why)as divine poesy per
that and this radically defunct periodical. i would

suggest that certain ideas gestures
rhymes,like Gillette Razor Blades   20
having been used and reused
to the mystical moment of dullness emphatically are
Not To Be Resharpened. (Case in point

if we are to believe these gently O sweetly
melancholy trillers amid the thrillers   25
these crepuscular violinists among my and your
skyscrapers—Helen & Cleopatra were Just Too Lovely,
The Snail's On The Thorn° enter Morn and God's°
In His andsoforth

do you get me?)according   30
to such supposedly indigenous
throstles° Art is O World O Life
a formula:example,Turn Your Shirttails Into
Drawers and If It Isn't An Eastman It Isn't A
Kodak therefore my friends let   35
us now sing each and all fortissimo A-
mer
i

ca,I
love,   40
You. And there're a
hun-dred-mil-lion-oth-ers,like
all of you successfully if
delicately gelded(or spaded)
gentlemen(and ladies)—pretty   45

littleliverpill-
hearted-Nujolneeding°-There's-A-Reason
americans(who tensetendoned and with
upward vacant eyes,painfully
perpetually crouched,quivering,upon the   50
sternly allotted sandpile
—how silently
emit a tiny violetflavoured nuisance:Odor?

ono.
comes out like a ribbon lies flat on the brush   55

28 *Snail's . . . Thorn:* parody of second-rate poetry.   32 *throstles:* thrush, or songbird.   47 *Nujol-*
needing: patent medicine, a tonic.

QUESTIONS FOR CLOSE READING

1. Find the echoes of "My Country, 'tis of Thee," which begin in the third line and which continue to break through every so often. Does Cummings make it difficult for you to "hear" the echoes in this poem?

2. Identify the different kinds of language Cummings uses. Which lines are conversational and colloquial, like the first? Which lines suggest the language of advertising, like the last?

3. Some lines suggest an artificiality, a kind of hoity-toity tone, such as "Art is O World O Life." Find other examples of that tone. What is the point of using such language?

4. Cummings uses the obsolete word *anent*, meaning "regarding." In the next line he uses a French word for shit: *merde*. What effect does he get by using these words?

5. Advertising is basic to the poem. What product names can you find? Which ones are still being advertised? Why does Cummings emphasize advertising to such an extent?

Bessie Smith is known throughout the world as a blues singer. The blues, which is related to jazz, was extremely popular in the United States during the depression of the 1930s. At that time it was thought to be a basically disreputable kind of music and was therefore inappropriate for "polite" society. Bessie Smith usually sang with a very small group, piano, drums, and guitar, and she wrote many of her own tunes. "Empty Bed Blues" is typical of her songs. Its language is informal, virtually conversational, sometimes casual speech. The use of connotation—"coffee grinder" and "brand new grind" rely on double meaning for effect—is a chief linguistic element of the poem.

BESSIE SMITH   (1894–1937)

Empty Bed Blues _____ *1928*

I woke up this mornin'
With an awful achin' head,
I woke up this mornin'
With an awful achin' head,
My new man had left me,   5
Just a room and an empty bed.

Bought me a coffee grinder,
The best one I could find.
Bought me a coffee grinder,
The best one I could find.   10
Oh, he could grind my coffee,
'Cause he had a brand-new grind.

He's deep, deep diver,
With a stroke that can't go wrong.
He's deep, deep diver,   15

With a stroke that can't go wrong.
Oh, he can touch the bottom,
And his wind holds out so long.

He knows how to thrill me,
And he thrills me night and day.   20
He knows how to thrill me,
And he thrills me night and day.
He's got a new way of lovin',
Almost takes my breath away.

Lord, he's got that sweet somethin',   25
And I told my gal-friend Lu.
He's got that sweet somethin',
And I told my gal-friend Lu.
For the way she's ravin',
She must have gone and tried it too.   30

When my bed is empty,
Makes me feel awful mean and blue.
When my bed is empty,
Makes me feel awful mean and blue.
My springs are getting rusty,   35
Living single like I do.

Bought him a blanket,
Pillow for his head at night.
Bought him a blanket,
Pillow for his head at night.   40
Then I bought him a mattress,
So he could lay just right.

He came home one ev'nin',
With his spirit way up high.
He came home one ev'nin',   45
With his spirit way up high.
What he had to give me
Made we wring my hands and cry.

He gave me a lesson
That I never had before.   50
He gave me a lesson
That I never had before.
When he got through teachin',
From my elbows down was sore.

He boiled first my cabbage,   55
And he made it awful hot.
He boiled first my cabbage,
And he made it awful hot.
When he put in the bacon,
It overflowed the pot.   60

When you get good lovin',
Never go and spread the news.
When you get good lovin',
Never go and spread the news.
Else he'll double-cross you   65
And leave you with them empty bed blues.

QUESTIONS FOR CLOSE READING

1. Which language in the poem is especially formal or informal? What qualities establish it one way or the other?

2. Because this is a song, each stanza is sung to the same melody. What special uses of language help you identify the poem as appropriate for singing? Would you find it possible to "invent" a tune and sing it just from looking at the words?

3. The blues and jazz music always contained sexual overtones. The title of this poem directly introduces a sexual theme. However, most of the poem depends on double entendre—or the difference between denotation and connotation—for its effect. Go through the poem stanza by stanza. Does every stanza make use of the difference between denotation and connotation? Which stanzas do so most effectively?

4. To some readers, this poem might be immoral. Why? What is the "moral" in the last stanza of the poem?

IMAGERY

Some poems depend upon **images** for their effect: they impress us with a visual, aural, or tactile description much like a painting or melody. Images are said to be "concrete" because they cause us to imagine a sensation on the basis of our personal experience. Poets who use images rely on their knowledge of the reader's experience, but they also try to control the reader's responses. Thus when Carol Rumens mentions "cellophaned flowers," she does not tell us what kind they are, but we imagine floral colors showing through a crinkly, shiny cellophane.

The imagist poets of the early twentieth century felt that no poem was truly poetic unless it expressed itself entirely through images. They discounted discursive poetry because it argued with the reader, discoursed on philosophy, or told instead of showed what something meant. In other words, discursive poetry depended on abstract language, language that is not rooted in a sensory experience. To say, "my heart is sad and weary" is to use abstract language, since no one can perceive a heart being sad and weary. One of the most famous of the imagist poems is by the American Ezra Pound. Its title refers to a subway platform in Paris, where the subway is called the Metro.

EZRA POUND   (1885–1972)

In a Station of the Metro _____ *1916*

The apparition of these faces in the crowd;
Petals on a wet, black bough.

By reading Chinese poets, Pound found a way of compressing his language, focusing his vision, and suggesting his emotional state through images. Each line offers a visual image. The first is straightforward: faces in a crowd, something we would expect in a subway station. However, by using the word *apparition,* Pound gives the image a special quality, suggesting the ghostlike passing of faces. The second line, in using the word *wet,* appeals to our sense of touch as well as sight. We can imagine the petals of a recently flowered tree on wet, springtime branches. They resemble the faces in the crowd, but Pound does not tell us that they are "like" the faces. Instead, he provides two separate images that we can relate in our own mind. The poem says what it has to say in terms of imagery. We are not told what to think about the images, nor how to link them.

Ordinarily, images do not constitute an entire poem but rather appear within it. In Carol Rumens's "An Easter Garland," images such as flowers are focal points. The reader recreates the flowers in the imagination and then explores their implications.

CAROL RUMENS   (b. 1944)

An Easter Garland _____ *1983*

I

The flowers did not seem to unfurl from slow bulbs.
They were suddenly there,
shivering swimmers on the edge of a gala
—nude whites and yellows shocking the raw air.
They'd switched themselves on like streetlamps   5
waking at dawn, feeling wrong,
to blaze nervously all day at the chalky sky.
Are they masks, the frills on bruised babies?
I can't believe in them,
as I can't believe in the spruces and lawns and bricks   10
they publicize, the misted light of front lounges
twinned all the way down the road,
twinned like their occupants, little weather-house people
who hide inside and do not show their tears
—the moisture that drives one sadly to a doorway.   15

II

My father explained the workings of the weather-house
as if he seriously loved such things,
told me why Grandpa kept a blackening tress
of seaweed in the hall.
He was an expert on atmosphere,   20
having known a weight of dampness
—the fog in a sick brother's lungs

where he lost his childhood; later, the soft squalls
of marriage and the wordier silences.
In the atmosphere of the fire   25
that took him back to bone
and beyond bone, he smiled.
The cellophaned flowers outside
went a slower way, their sweat
dappling the linings of their glassy hoods.   30

III

My orphaned grass
is standing on tiptoe to look for you.
Your last gift to a work-shy daughter
was to play out and regather
the slow thread of your breath   35
behind the rattling blades,
crossing always to darker green,
till the lawn was a well-washed quilt
drying, the palest on the line,
and you rested over the handlebars   40
like a schoolboy, freewheeling
through your decades of green-scented, blue,
suburban English twilights.

IV

In the lonely garden of the page,
something has happened to your silence.   45
The stone cloud has rolled off.
You make yourself known,
as innocently abrupt
as the flared wings of the almond,
cherry, magnolia;   50
and I, though stupid with regret,
would not be far wrong
if I took you for the gardener.

The title of the poem reveals that the season is spring, and the flowers, because they come from bulbs, are daffodils and/or tulips. The image of the bulb
is carried over into the image of the streetlamps, and the flowers "switched
themselves on," suggesting an electric image. Rumens explores the possibilities
of her imagery in surprising and refreshing ways. The sky is not just overcast but
"chalky," a term that gives us a concrete impression. She sees the flowers as
swimmers in the air: "nude whites and yellows." A tactile image is evoked with
"the raw air." The flowers "blaze" all day, like confused streetlamps. They "publicize" "spruces and lawns and bricks."

The appeal to the senses continues throughout the poem. In line 13, Rumens evokes a new image, that of "weather-house people," figures in a mechanical house that come out to indicate a change: a figure in a raincoat for rain, a figure in a sun suit for sunny days. The second stanza focuses on weather, making the abstract quality of "dampness" concrete by giving it "weight" (line 21). Dampness is a "fog" in a "brother's lungs." All these are perceptible images. Even the arguments of marriage, the "soft squalls," are expressed in weather imagery. The third stanza evokes memories of the speaker's father, who mowed the lawn until it looked like a "well-washed quilt." The final stanza refers to "the page"—presumably the page on which she writes—as being a kind of garden similar to the garden her father tended for decades. The image of the "stone cloud" can refer to the stony-colored overcast sky or to the stone that may be the father's headstone. The father makes himself "known," much as the flowers of the first stanza: abruptly, without warning, coming up of a sudden—but here in the imagination of the speaker. She associates him with the "almond, cherry, magnolia" trees blossoming in this Easter scene. When she thinks of him as "the gardener," she implies that she, too, has been tended by his hand.

The following poem uses unusual images.

HENRI COULETTE   (1927–1988)

Correspondence _____ *1990*

The letter lies unanswered, thus free of lies.
The light all day has travelled the crowded pages,
Shifting the shadows, changing the hue of ink.
The truths, if truths there are, are stationary.

Now night comes on, from your time zone to mine.   5
The moon is tentative, not wholly herself,
And the owl bells, and the owl's mate bells back,
A dialogue of sorts, question and answer,

The answer being but the question asked.
East of your sleep, deep in the zodiac,   10
Tomorrow is already chronicled.
Oh, I shall write you what you want to hear.

QUESTIONS FOR CLOSE READING

1. What images are suggested by the second line? Are they purely visual, or do they suggest other sensory experience?

2. If the word *stationary* is a pun on *stationery,* would it then be an image?

3. What imagery do you recreate in line 6: "The moon is tentative, not wholly herself"? What is suggested by making the moon's gender female? Is that an image?

4. Are there any images in the third stanza?

Many poems refer to paintings or visual artists, and sometimes they attempt to interpret a painting or work of art. The following poem is about the impressionist painter Paul Gauguin (1848–1903), who spent part of his life as a painter in France.

ANDREW HUDGINS   (b. 1951)

Gauguin: The Yellow Christ ————————————————— *1990*

After the last harvest, when the fields
are stripped of grain and trees blaze orange,
three peasant women walk
out of their blue-roofed houses, trudge

through barren fields and kneel, heads bowed,   5
before the yellow Christ. Gauguin has chosen
a dying meadow near their village
to paint his last cross, spread his arms

and nail himself to its
enormous dark-brown reaching. Gauguin: 10
there's no mistaking that thin beard,
that face, that tilt of head. But even

the artist knows it isn't he
the women walk so far to worship.
He is no longer Paul Gauguin.   15
Bright yellow tinged with green—just like

the autumn fields stretched out behind him—
he's Christ. He's harvested: cut, bundled,
and, like a last shock of late wheat,
left in the field past gathering.   20

And this Christ knows he's dying. He yearns
to return—budding, green—to blossom,
seed, wither, die, and come again.
The women gathered at his feet

pray they will live the winter through,   25
pray they will eat, keep warm, and prosper.
But Christ, who was once Paul Gauguin,
sags on his cross. The yellow hills,

the yellow valleys and the gleaned,
dry yellow hills—all dying—call,   30

O Son of Man, we're coming back.
Put down your soul and follow us.

QUESTIONS FOR CLOSE READING

1. Which images are most dependent on colors? Which colors are mentioned, and how do you feel they would work in a painting?
2. Gauguin is described in stanza 3. How effective is that imagery? How "concrete" is it?
3. The poem is filled with imagery associated with harvest and autumn. Which of those images strikes you as most powerful?
4. Identify the religious images. Which ones work best for you? Why might some readers think the line "But Christ, who was once Paul Gauguin" would be in bad taste? What does Hudgins mean by it? Is that line an example of imagery?

The author of the following poem was a pilot in the U.S. Air Force from 1957 to 1971, through the Vietnam War. "The Food Pickers of Saigon," which contrasts many images, is set on the edges of Tan Son Nhut, the largest airfield in South Vietnam and the center of most U.S. air activity during the war.

WALTER McDONALD   (b. 1934)

The Food Pickers of Saigon _____ *1987*

Rubbish like compost heaps burned every hour
of my days and nights at Tan Son Nhut.
Ragpickers scoured the edges of our junk,
risking the flames, bent over,
searching for food. A ton of tin cans   5

piled up each month, sharp-edged, unlabeled.
Those tiny anonymous people could stick
their hands inside and claw out whatever
remained, scooping it into jars, into their
mouths. No one went hungry. At a distance,   10

the dump was like a coal mine fire burning
out of control, or Moses' holy bush
which was not consumed. Watching them labor
in the field north of my barracks, trying
to think of something good to write my wife,   15

I often thought of bears in Yellowstone
our first good summer in a tent. I wrote
about the bears, helping us both focus
on how they waddled to the road and begged,
and came some nights into the campground   20

so long ago and took all food they found.
We sat helplessly naive outside our tent
and watched them, and one night rolled
inside laughing when one great bear
turned and shoulder-swayed his way toward us.   25

Through the zipped mosquito netting
we watched him watching us. Slack-jawed,
he seemed to grin, to thank us for all
he was about to receive from our table.
We thought how lovely, how much fun   30

to be this close to danger. No campers
had died in that Disneyland national park
for years. Now, when my children
eat their meat and bread and leave
good broccoli or green beans   35

on their plates, I call them back
and growl, I can't help it. It's like hearing
my father's voice again. I never tell them
why they have to eat it. I never say
they're like two beautiful children   40

I found staring at me one night
through the screen of my window,
at Tan Son Nhut, bone-faced. Or that
when I crawled out of my stifling monsoon
dream to feed them, they were gone.   45

QUESTIONS FOR CLOSE READING

1. Some stanzas concentrate on a powerful image. Which words in the first stanza produce images for you? Is the imagery purely descriptive, or does it suggest comparisons like the *bulb-streetlamps* comparisons in Carol Rumens's poem?

2. What imagery does the verb *claw* produce for you in stanza 2?

3. In stanza 3, McDonald thinks of a religious image, the burning bush in Genesis that flamed but was not burned up. Is a religious image appropriate? What is its effect?

4. What effect is gained by the bear imagery in stanzas 4, 5, and 6? This imagery introduces a comic element. Is that appropriate for this poem? Disneyland calls up many images. How does it work in stanza 7?

5. Two contrasting images of children dominate the last three stanzas. Why does McDonald present them to us? To what extent do images haunt him?

TONE

The manner in which something is said—its **tone**—controls much of what we perceive in a poem. Some poems are ironic, in that they seem to speak of their subject approvingly only to reveal at the last minute that they do not approve at all. Laments, usually questioning the death of a loved one, can be sad, angry, resigned, or distressed. Conversational poems imitate various tones we hear in people's voices: joy, irritation, despair, agony, and grief. Other poems are explicitly satirical. They may satirize a person, an office, an institution, or society by being scornful or by ridiculing its faults.

Irish poets have been so famous for their satirical wit that kings were careful of their behavior when in the company of a satirist to avoid being attacked in a poem that might outlast them for generations. No one wanted to be the butt of an Irish satirist. The following is an adaptation from a seventeenth-century Irish poet named David O'Bruadair from Limerick. Stephens reshaped the poem so as to attack a barmaid who "cut him off" from his drink. In Stephens's hands, satire becomes a weapon.

JAMES STEPHENS   (1880–1950)

A Glass of Beer _____ *1918*

The lanky hank of a she in the inn over there
Nearly killed me for asking the loan of a glass of beer;
May the devil grip the whey-faced slut by the hair,
And beat bad manners out of her skin for a year.

That parboiled ape, with the toughest jaw you will see   5
On virtue's path, and a voice that would rasp the dead,
Came roaring and raging the minute she looked at me,
And threw me out of the house on the back of my head!

If I asked her master he'd give me a cask a day;
But she, with the beer at hand, not a gill would arrange!   10
May she marry a ghost and bear him a kitten, and may
The High King of Glory permit her to get the mange.

Part of the vehemence of the poem comes from Stephens's ability to cast a curse on "the whey-faced slut" who refused him a glass of beer. He insults her in every way he can. This phrase casts doubt on her morals; her ape-like jaw is emblematic of her toughness; and her voice would raise the dead. Her physical size is implied by the fact that she threw him out of the inn on his head. The last two lines are typical of the terrible curses the Irish poets could cast on their victims. The voice of the poet railing against the barmaid is so loud that it nearly masks the regularity of the lines and the rhyme scheme. Of course, this version and O'Bruadair's both conveniently omit any discussion of what their behavior might have been in the inn and why the barmaid responded so fiercely.

The tone of the following poem is totally different: it is whimsical, filled with anticipation, joy, and the enthusiastic use of ritual cries.

JUDITH RODRIGUEZ   (b. 1936)

Eskimo Occasion _____ *1976*

I am in my Eskimo-hunting-song mood,
Aha!
The lawn is tundra   the car will not start
the sunlight is an avalanche   we are avalanche-struck at our
                                                                              breakfast   5
struck with sunlight through glass   me and my spoon-fed
                                                                   daughters
out of this world in our kitchen.

I will sing the song of my daughter-hunting,
Oho!   10
The waves lay down   the ice grew strong
I sang the song   of dark water under ice
the song of winter fishing   the magic for seal rising
among the ancestor-masks.

I waited by water to dream new spirits,   15
Hoo!
The water spoke   the ice shouted
the sea opened   the sun made young shadows
they breathed my breathing   I took them from deep water
I brought them fur-warmed home.   20

I am dancing the years of the two great hunts,
Ya-hay!
It was I who waited   cold in the wind-break
I stamp like the bear   I call like the wind of the thaw
I leap like the sea spring-running.   My sunstruck daughters   25
                                                                   splutter
and chuckle and bang their spoons:

Mummy is singing at breakfast and dancing!
So big!

    The Australian Judith Rodriguez is a poet of many moods, and as she says
in this poem, "I am in my Eskimo-hunting-song mood." The tone depends on
certain devices. The interjection of the dance cries, "Aha!", "Oho!", "Hoo!",
"Ya-hay!", and the final cry, "So big!", are amusing and light spirited. They also
remind those who have seen Inuit dances of the joy of the "tundra." The lines
are broken into **hemistichs;** that is, each line is separated in the middle by a
pause. Much of the tone seems formal, perhaps because the Eskimo culture is
foreign to most readers. Rodriguez adopts an Eskimo persona because she is in
the right "mood" and can adopt any persona she wishes. Now that we have her
model we can do so ourselves.

    A. E. Housman, the author of the next poem, was a classics professor at
University College, London, and later at Cambridge. The title of his poem,

"Terence, This Is Stupid Stuff," seems at first to allude to the Roman play-wright Terence, but in fact it refers to the persona Housman invented for his volume of poems *A Shropshire Lad,* which was going to be called *The Poems of Terence Hearsay.* In other words, Housman is satirizing himself, as well as other things along the way. The poem's most famous lines are "Malt does more than Milton can / To justify God's ways to man," which indirectly, of course, satirizes John Milton, who wrote the great epic *Paradise Lost* to justify the ways of God to man.

A. E. HOUSMAN   (1859–1936)

Terence, This Is Stupid Stuff ————————————————— *1896*

"Terence, this is stupid stuff:
You eat your victuals fast enough;
There can't be much amiss, 'tis clear,
To see the rate you drink your beer.
But oh, good Lord, the verse you make,   5
It gives a chap the belly-ache.
The cow, the old cow, she is dead;
It sleeps well, the horned head:
We poor lads, 'tis our turn now
To hear such tunes as killed the cow.   10
Pretty friendship 'tis to rhyme
Your friends to death before their time
Moping melancholy mad:
Come, pipe a tune to dance to, lad."

Why, if 'tis dancing you would be,   15
There's brisker pipes than poetry.
Say, for what were hop-yards meant,
Or why was Burton built on Trent?°
Oh many a peer of England brews
Livelier liquor than the Muse,   20
And malt does more than Milton can
To justify God's ways to man.
Ale, man, ale's the stuff to drink
For fellows whom it hurts to think:
Look into the pewter pot   25
To see the world as the world's not.
And faith, 'tis pleasant till 'tis past:
The mischief is that 'twill not last.
Oh I have been to Ludlow fair
And left my necktie God knows where,   30
And carried half-way home, or near,

18 *Burton . . . Trent:* Burton-on-Trent was famous for its breweries.

Pints and quarts of Ludlow beer:
Then the world seemed none so bad,
And I myself a sterling lad;
And down in lovely muck I've lain,   35
Happy till I woke again.
Then I saw the morning sky:
Heigho, the tale was all a lie;
The world, it was the old world yet,
I was I, my things were wet,   40
And nothing now remained to do
But begin the game anew.

   Therefore, since the world has still
Much good, but much less good than ill,
And while the sun and moon endure   45
Luck's a chance, but trouble's sure,
I'd face it as a wise man would,
And train for ill and not for good.
'Tis true, the stuff I bring for sale
Is not so brisk a brew as ale: 50
Out of a stem that scored the hand°
I wrung it in a weary land.
But take it: if the smack is sour,
The better for the embittered hour;
It should do good to heart and head   55
When your soul is in my soul's stead;
And I will friend you, if I may,
In the dark and cloudy day.

   There was a king reigned in the East:
There, when kings will sit to feast,   60
They get their fill before they think
With poisoned meat and poisoned drink.
He gathered all that springs to birth
From the many-venomed earth;
First a little, thence to more,   65
He sampled all her killing store;
And easy, smiling, seasoned sound,
Sate the king when healths went round.
They put arsenic in his meat
And stared aghast to watch him eat;   70
They poured strychnine in his cup
And shook to see him drink it up:
They shook, they stared as white's their shirt:
Them it was their poison hurt.
—I tell the tale that I heard told.   75
Mithridates,° he died old.

---

51 *stem . . . hand:* Housman implies the pen that scores the hand.   75 *Mithridates:* Mithridates VI
(c. 132–63 B.C.) was king of Pontus, an ancient kingdom in Asia Minor.

QUESTIONS FOR CLOSE READING

1. The first stanza, which addresses Terence, assesses Terence's poetry. What is that assessment? What apparently is the effect of his poetry on others? Why does the speaker establish in lines 1 and 2 that Terence is eating well?

2. The second stanza, which begins Terence's reply, talks about the effects of beer and ale on Terence, who is well experienced with them both. What are those effects, and in what tone does Terence inform us of them?

3. The tone alters in stanza 3. Is this stanza more or less serious than the first two? Is it more or less optimistic about the world?

4. Stanza 4 tells of Mithridates VI, who made himself immune to poison by taking it in small quantities. What is the relationship between Mithridates and Terence? What is the relationship between the speaker of the first stanza and "Them" in "Them it was their poison hurt"?

5. Compare the tone of the first stanza with the tone of the last stanza. Would you conclude that the overall tone of the poem is one of seriousness? Satire? Light humor?

The next poem has yet another tone. Ben Jonson, the first English poet laureate, made a living with his pen and knew Shakespeare. Venerated as "rare Ben," he lived a life of robust adventure in and out of the social world of king and court. He killed a man in a duel, got into trouble for political innuendoes in his dramatic work, and wrote gala entertainments in the royal courts of Queen Elizabeth and King James. "On My First Son," however, was written for a private occasion.

BEN JONSON   (1572–1637)

On My First Son ————————————————————————— *1616 (1603?)*

Farewell, thou child of my right hand, and joy;
My sin was too much hope of thee, loved boy,
Seven years thou wert lent to me, and I thee pay,
Exacted by thy fate, on the just day.°
O, could I lose all father,° now. For why   5
Will man lament the state he should envy?
To have so soon 'scaped world's, and flesh's rage,
And, if no other misery, yet age!
Rest in soft peace, and, asked, say here doth lie
Ben Jonson his best piece of poetry.   10
For whose sake, henceforth, all his vows be such,
As what he loves may never like too much.

---

4 *Exacted . . . day:* His son is a "loan" he must repay God. His son died on his seventh birthday.   5 *could . . . father:* Now he could renounce fatherhood entirely.

QUESTIONS FOR CLOSE READING

1. The poem addresses Jonson's dead son. What tone of voice does Jonson seem to be using? Is there an unusual tone of frankness to his mode of address? Is he sad, resigned, content, dissatisfied? Can you tell from the tone of the poem how he feels?

2. Jonson's child was named Benjamin, meaning "child of my right hand." But the expression "to sit at my right hand" also implies offering someone a favorite spot, and therefore recognizes the child's importance. How would you describe the tone of the first line? Does it evoke a response in you?

3. This poem is a lament. However, in lines 5–6 the poet questions his reasons for lamenting his son's death. How does this questioning affect the tone?

4. Why does Jonson call his son "his best piece of poetry"? What is his resolution now that he has lost his son? Is his resolution offered in a different tone?

Of course, tone also suggests a certain actual tone of voice, and the poet has great power to suggest how a poem should be read aloud, just as dramatists can control the tone of their dialogues. **Dramatic monologues** present one side of a conversation, one voice that the reader "hears." There are several examples of this convention in this book. Sometimes it narrates an event, as in Robert Frost's "Mending Wall" (p. 486) and "Birches" (p.432). But it may also be a conversation with oneself, as in Housman's "Terence, This Is Stupid Stuff" (p. 461), which appears to be a lighthearted tongue-lashing of the poet by himself: "There can't be much amiss, 'tis clear, / To see the rate you drink your beer." E. E. Cummings's "Poem, or Beauty Hurts Mr. Vinal" (p. 448), is another monologue, one side of an imaginary conversation: "take it from me kiddo / believe me." One of the most famous examples of the dramatic monologue is Robert Browning's "My Last Duchess" (p. 419). In this poem, a man shows a guest a painting of his late wife, all the while explaining his attitudes toward her in a way that reveals his own shortcomings and limitations. An **internal dramatic monologue**—a stream-of-consciousness version of the dramatic monologue—is used in Judith Rodriguez's "Eskimo Occasion" (p. 460). Finally, Allen Ginsburg's "Howl" (p. 671) may represent a special form of dramatic monologue in the form of an angry poet ranting against the culture that oppresses him. The varieties of tone possible in dramatic monologue are unlimited.

RHYTHM AND RHYME

The spellings of *rhythm* and *rhyme* indicate their close relationship and imply their importance to the poet. **Rhythm** is the pacing, from slow to fast, and the pauses, stops, and starts that we perceive as we speak or read the words and lines of a poem. When read aloud, some lines demand a slow, stately, even tempo. Other lines lurch and jostle, hip and hop, or bounce and lope. Some poems demand a slow beginning, a fast middle, and a slower ending.

End-stopped lines have a pause at the end of the line, usually indicated by punctuation. **Run-on lines** force you to read beyond their end into the beginning of the next line; the use of these lines is called enjambment. When Andrew Marvell (1621–1678) wrote the following lines, he had survived the English Civil War and was looking back on prewar England as a peaceful, paradisal garden. However, his recollections of soldiers and sentinels still produced a march-like movement:

See how the flowers, as at parade,	*a*
Under their colors stand displayed;	*a*
Each regiment in order grows,	*b*
That of the tulip, pink, and rose.	*b*

All these lines are end-stopped, some more completely than others. The lines that end with a comma are pauses; those that end with a semicolon or period are full stops. Breaks within the lines are called **caesuras.** The first line has a caesura after the comma, just as the commas in the last lines provide more pauses. Sometimes a caesura brings you to a complete halt, but more often it simply indicates a pause, as in these lines. In Marvell's time, end-stopped lines were the norm for English poetry.

These four lines also illustrate **rhyme,** or regular sound patterns. The two couplets rhyme in the pattern *aa, bb.* Marvell uses masculine rhyme (see below), in which only the last syllable of the first line echoes the last syllable of the next line: *-ade, -played* and *grows, rose.*

Types of Rhyme

MASCULINE RHYME.	One syllable rhymes: *still, fill.*
FEMININE RHYME.	Two syllables rhyme: *Balaclava, lava.*
SLANT RHYME.	Sounds almost echo each other: *mousse, clues.*
ASSONANTAL RHYME.	Vowels echo each other: *tube, mood.*
CONSONANTAL RHYME.	Consonants echo each other: *klutz, blitz.*
INTERNAL RHYME.	End word rhymes with a word in the middle of the same line or another nearby line: *turned the air, a prayer.*
EYE RHYME.	Words look alike but do not sound alike: *blood, food.*

All but the first two of these are **off-rhymes,** not quite true rhymes. Specialized versions of these off-rhymes exist, such as rhyming only the first or last consonant in rhyme words. Many poets want to avoid the closure or end-stopping of Marvell's rhymes but still maintain the discipline of rhyme by using slant, assonantal, or consonantal rhyme techniques.

Aphra Behn, the first professional woman playwright in England, led an adventurous life and is rumored to have been a spy in Europe. She visited South America with her husband and wrote a novel about her adventures called *Oroonoko* (c. 1688). Her "Song" is typical of the late seventeenth century in its rhythm and its rhyme. The lines maintain a regular **meter:** they measure their syllables into units or **metrical feet.** The usual metrical foot in English is iambic: an unaccented syllable followed by an accented syllable: ˘ ´. The word *begin* follows that pattern: its first syllable is unaccented and its second syllable is accented. Sometimes it is difficult to know which syllable receives an accent, but one reliable guide is the dictionary, which usually breaks words into their syllables: *be-gin´.* Since poets shift accents from their normal place usually only for humorous effect, it is safe to assume that competent poets will rely on normal pronunciation.

APHRA BEHN   (1640–1689)

Song ——————————————————————————————— *1665*

Love in fantastic triumph sat	*a*	
Whilst bleeding hearts around him flowed,	*b*	
For whom fresh pains he did create	*a*	
And strange tyrranic power he showed:	*b*	
From thy bright eyes he took his fires,	*c*	5
Which round about in sport he hurled;	*d*	
But 'twas from mine he took desires	*c*	
Enough t'undo the amorous world.	*d*	
From me he took his sighs and tears,	*e*	
From thee his pride and cruelty;	*f*	10
From me his languishments and fears,	*e*	
And every killing dart from thee.	*f*	
Thus thou and I the god° have armed	*g*	
And set him up a deity;	*h*	
But my poor heart alone is harmed,	*g*	15
Whilst thine the victor is, and free!	*h*	

13 *god:* cupid

In order to **scan** a poem, or determine its meter, the best procedure is to sound out one of the middle lines of the first verse. In this case, the third line will do:

    For whom | fresh pains | he did | cre ate

The bars separate each metrical foot in this **scansion.** This line has four metrical feet. Each foot is iambic; therefore, this line is *iambic tetrameter.*

Number of Metrical Feet in a Line

one foot per line: monometer

two feet per line: dimeter

three feet per line: trimeter

four feet per line: tetrameter

five feet per line: pentameter

six feet per line: hexameter

seven feet per line: septameter

eight feet per line: octameter

Aphra Behn's poem is written entirely in four-foot lines, and most of its metrical feet are iambic; therefore, we say the poem is written in iambic tetrameter, one of the most common metrical patterns in English poetry.

However, not all Behn's metrical feet are iambs. Before we examine her differences, consider this table of the normal metrical feet you will encounter in this book. Those with two syllables are called **duple meter,** and those with three syllables are **triple meter.**

METRICAL FOOT	PATTERN	EXAMPLE
iambic (iamb)	˘ ´	in-sist´
trochaic (trochee)	´ ˘	pen-´cil
anapestic (anapest	˘ ˘ ´	in a fix´
dactylic (dactyl)	´ ˘ ˘	im-´pli-cate
spondaic (spondee)	´ ´	top´ gun´
pyrrhic (pyrrhic)	˘ ˘	of a
amphribrachic (amphibrach)	˘ ´ ˘	in-ter-´nal
cretic (cretic)	´ ˘ ´	med-´i-tate´

The iamb and anapest are usually called **rising rhythms** because they begin with an unstressed syllable and proceed to a final stress. The trochee and dactyl, referred to as **falling rhythms,** begin with a stressed syllable and end on an unstressed syllable.

The opening lines of poems are usually the most difficult to scan because in those lines the poet aims at diversity and attention-getting rhythms. Here is one way of scanning the opening lines of Behn's poem:

´ ˘ | ˘ ´ | ˘ ´ | ˘ ´
Love in | fantas | tic tri | umph sat

˘ ´ | ˘ ´ | ˘ ´ | ˘ ´
Whilst bleed | ing hearts | around | him flowed,

The device Behn uses in the first two feet, a trochee followed by an iamb, is common in the first lines of poems. The rhythm of this combination moves the reader rapidly into the line. The succeeding iambs establish the poem as highly regular iambic tetrameter. Scan the rest of the poem, and you will find its meter identical with the second and third lines. The only substitute foot is the opening trochee. Poems with such regularity risk dullness, but Behn expects this poem to be sung aloud. The music thrives on the regularity of meter and stress and provides another layer to the poem.

Like the meter, the ideas of the poem are also familiar and expected. Behn tells how the behavior of lovers establishes the god of love as their deity. Their own experiences, her "languishments and fears," her lover's "pride and cruelty," have "armed" the deity, or given it its powers. In this case, the cost is borne by the woman: "my poor heart alone is harmed." Behn strongly implies that this is the usual outcome.

Some poets poke fun at the demands of meter and rhyme. Algernon Swinburne's "Nephelidia" does this. In this poem Swinburne uses triple meter, or three syllables for each foot, and depends on **alliteration,** the repetition of consonant sounds at the beginning of words, to intensify the beat of the accents. He does this partly to show off and partly to ridicule those who put too much emphasis on metrical virtuosity. Here is a scansion of the first two lines.

From the depth | of the dream | y decline | of the dawn

   through a no | table nim | bus of neb | ulous noonshine,

Pallid | and pink | as the palm | of the flag | -flower that

   flick | ers with fear | of the flies | as they float,

Each line has eight mostly anapestic feet; therefore, the meter of the poem is anapestic octameter. The first half of line 1 alliterates *d-*, and the last half *n-*, the last consonant of *dawn*. The second line alliterates *p-* for the first half, employing *f-*, the consonant in *of*, to finish the alliteration of the line. This method is followed throughout.

The following poem shows the effectiveness of simple rhyme and rhythm. Such simplicity is a memory aid.

A. E. HOUSMAN   (1859–1936)

With Rue My Heart Is Laden _____ *1922*

With rue my heart is laden
For golden friends I had,
For many a rose-lipped maiden
And many a lightfoot lad.

By brooks too broad for leaping   5
The lightfoot boys are laid;
The rose-lipped girls are sleeping
In fields where roses fade.

QUESTIONS FOR CLOSE READING

1. Both stanzas use both feminine and masculine rhyme. Which is which?
2. What is the primary metrical foot of this verse? How many metrical feet are in each line? What, then, do we call the meter of this verse?
3. Scan the entire poem after you have spoken it out loud to identify the accented syllables. Do the accents fall on the most important words in the poem or on the least important words? How do the accents help bring the point of the poem home?
4. The verse is simple, light, and direct. What is the relationship of your metrical description to the ideas in the poem? What is Housman saying about his friends?

The next poem mixes several different kinds of rhyme, and although the lines look metrical and regular to the eyes, they are free verse: irregular and not metrical. Some lines seem conversational and unmetrical, and others seem as regularly iambic as Aphra Behn's. Cummings mixes the lines liberally and repeats certain basic lines with variations: "spring summer autumn winter" and "sun moon stars rain." It would be difficult to see either of those lines as metrical and regular, despite their accented and unaccented syllables.

E. E. CUMMINGS   (1894–1962)

anyone lived in a pretty how town _____ *1940*

anyone lived in a pretty how town
(with up so floating many bells down)
spring summer autumn winter
he sang his didn't he danced his did.

Women and men(both little and small)   5
cared for anyone not at all
they sowed their isn't they reaped their same
sun moon stars rain

children guessed(but only a few
and down they forgot as up they grew   10
autumn winter spring summer)
that noone loved him more by more

when by now and tree by leaf
she laughed his joy she cried his grief
bird by snow and stir by still   15
anyone's any was all to her

someones married their everyones
laughed their cryings and did their dance
(sleep wake hope and then)they
said their nevers they slept their dream   20

stars rain sun moon
(and only the snow can begin to explain

how children are apt to forget to remember
with up so floating many bells down)

one day anyone died i guess   25
(and noone stooped to kiss his face)
busy folk buried them side by side
little by little and was by was

all by all and deep by deep
and more by more they dream their sleep   30
noone and anyone earth by april
wish by spirit and if by yes.

Women and men(both dong and ding)
summer autumn winter spring
reaped their sowing and went their came   35
sun moon stars rain

QUESTIONS FOR CLOSE READING

1. Scan the fourth line of the first stanza: "he sang his didn't he danced his did." Is
    this a metrically regular line? Does this line indicate the general metrical character
    of the poem?

2. The first thing a reader may notice is that the poem seems to verge on nonsense.
    The expression "pretty how town" has no denotative meaning, although it may
    suggest many connotations to you. Making "anyone" a character who "sang his
    didn't" and "danced his did" is also unusual. Does the rhythm of the poem help
    you interpret these expressions as significant? In other words, does it contribute
    to the poem's meaning?

3. Compare this poem with Lewis Carroll's "Jabberwocky" (p. 423). What do these
    poems have in common rhythmically? How would you summarize the general
    structure of Cummings's narrative? How does it compare with the narrative in
    "Jabberwocky"? Does Cummings express emotion over the deaths of anyone
    and noone?

4. The rhyme patterns vary throughout the poem. In stanza 1 the first two lines are
    full rhyme: *town* and *down*. Lines 3 and 4 are assonantal rhyme: *winter* and *did*.
    The same is true for the second stanza. In the third stanza the *m*'s are consonan-
    tal rhymes in the third and fourth lines: *summer* and *more*. What are the rhyming
    techniques of the rest of the stanzas? Look for slant rhyme, assonantal rhyme,
    consonantal rhyme, and internal rhyme.

The following poem gives a portrait of a seventh-grade teacher, "Miss Arbuckle," who taught about the Romantic poets. The rhyme scheme uses many
off-rhyming techniques and then ends purposely and surprisingly with a very
clichéd full rhyme: *June, moon.*

PETER MEINKE   (b. 1932)

Miss Arbuckle _____ *1981*

Miss Arbuckle taught seventh grade.
She hid her lips against her teeth:
her bottom like the ace of spades
was guarded by the virgin queen.

Miss Arbuckle wore thick-soled shoes,   5
blue dresses with white polka dots.
She followed and enforced the rules:
what she was paid to teach, she taught.

She said that Wordsworth liked the woods,
that Blake had never seen a tiger,   10
that Byron was not always good
but died in Greece, a freedom-fighter.

She gave her students rigid tests
and when the school let out in June,
she painted rings around her breasts   15
and danced by the light of the moon.

QUESTIONS FOR CLOSE READING

1. Scan the second line of the poem. What is the basic metrical foot, and how many are there? Scan the third line. What would you say the basic meter of the poem is?

2. Scan the first line of the poem. The name *Miss Arbuckle* will give you trouble. Meinke knows this, so what is his point? How well does *Miss Arbuckle* fit into this poem?

3. Examine the rhymes in stanza 1. What kind of rhymes are *grade, spades* and *teeth, queen?* Examine stanzas 2 and 3. They rhyme *abab,* as do all the stanzas. What kinds of rhymes does Meinke prefer? Can you see the reasons for his preference?

4. Identify the end-stopped lines by putting a mark at the end of each. Identify the run-on lines by connecting the end of one line with the beginning of the next. What rhythmic effects do you find interesting in the first three stanzas?

5. The last stanza surprises us with full rhyme: *tests, breasts* and *June, moon.* What else is surprising? Does the rhyme or the meter help reinforce what Meinke tells us of Miss Arbuckle?

The next short poem also uses rhyme and meter to reinforce its ideas.

HOWARD NEMEROV   (b. 1920)

Because You Asked about the Line between Prose and Poetry _____ *1980*

Sparrows were feeding in a freezing drizzle
That while you watched turned into pieces of snow
Riding a gradient invisible
From silver aslant to random, white, and slow.

There came a moment that you couldn't tell.   5
And then they clearly flew instead of fell.

QUESTIONS FOR CLOSE READING

1. What kinds of rhymes does Nemerov use?
2. What kind of change is taking place in the weather Nemerov describes? What
    changes take place in the rhyming and metrical qualities of the lines from the
    first stanza to the second?
3. Is the mix of run-on and end-stopped lines effective in light of what Nemerov
    talks about?
4. When do you become aware that this poem is becoming a poem?

Nemerov seems to be talking about the distinction between ordinary
workaday prose, such as what we see in magazines and newspapers, and poetry.
However, some poems, such as Carolyn Forché's "The Colonel" (p. 506), are not
set up in a recognizable system of individual lines. These are known as **prose
poems.** Although they do not appear to be poems, they still "fly" because of
their fusion of language, imagery, and idea, as well as, quite often, their rhythm.
    The following poem shows some unique uses of rhyme and meter. ("Dust-
bins" are what the British call garbage cans.)

STEVIE SMITH   (1902–1971)

Mother, among the Dustbins _____ *1976*

Mother, among the dustbins and the manure
I feel the measure of my humanity, an allure
As of the presence of God. I am sure

In the dustbins, in the manure, in the cat at play,
Is the presence of God, in a sure way   5
He moves there. Mother, what do you say?

I too have felt the presence of God in the broom
I hold, in the cobwebs in the room,
But most of all in the silence of the tomb.

Ah! but that thought that informs the hope of our kind   10

Is but an empty thing, what lies behind?—
Naught but the vanity of a protesting mind

That would not die. This is the thought that bounces
Within a conceited head and trounces
Inquiry. Man is most frivolous when he pronounces.   15

Well Mother, I shall continue to think as I do,
And I think you would be wise to do so too,
Can you question the folly of man in the creation of God?
    Who are you?

QUESTIONS FOR CLOSE READING

1. Scan lines 2 and 3 of stanza 1. Do you have a clear sense of the metrical character of the poem?

2. Examine the rhyme scheme. The poem rhymes *aaa, bbb, ccc, ddd, eee, fff*. Triple rhyme is unusual in English. What is Smith's reason for using it? When do you become aware of her reason?

3. Examine the meter of the last line, scanning it syllable by syllable. How does it connect with the rhyme scheme?

The word *prosody* is used to define particular systems of rhyme and meter, as well as the *study* of how rhyme and meter function in a poem. We have only begun such a study, and there are many more metrical feet and details of rhythm and meter than those given here. Nonetheless, these definitions should help you make good sense of most of the poems in this volume and most that you are likely to read. In an effective poem the prosody contributes to the overall purpose; it does not function as a separate layer. Thus Peter Meinke uses interesting variations in rhyme and meter to point up the problems that Miss Arbuckle presented to him as a young poet. Aphra Behn makes a light song out of a very serious issue partly to ensure that her poem will be received by people in her own time. Its innocent and ordinary prosody is like camouflage; only after reading and thinking about the poem would her audience begin to see the nature of her critical position. E. E. Cummings uses the most ordinary of rhythms to tell a story that we realize we already have within us. Like the "plot" of "Jabberwocky," the narrative of anyone meeting noone and getting married and living happily ever after is already built into our expectations. Cummings uses the most comfortable rhythms and is able to make a moving poem out of very common details. Whenever you find the rhythms of a poem exciting and interesting, examine them for their relationship to the overall effect of the poem.

METAPHOR AND FIGURATIVE LANGUAGE

Metaphor is one of the greatest resources of poetic language. A **metaphor** evokes a comparison between two things: one is usually the subject at hand, and the other is something associated with it. The comparison is not stated directly but implied. The purpose of the association is to use some qualities of the distant "something" to illuminate an unsuspected quality of the subject at hand. There are several varieties of metaphor.

NOUN METAPHOR.   "Love is a sickness full of woes." You are not told love is *like* a sickness; you are told it is one. Thus we have a metaphor comparing the subject *love* with the noun *sickness.* "Come, Sleep; O Sleep! the certain knot of peace." The comparison is with *Sleep,* the subject at hand, and the noun *knot.* Sleep is a knot that unites the speaker with peace.

VERB METAPHOR.   "Love guards the roses of thy lips." Guards is a verb comparing *Love* with a sentinel; *roses* is a noun metaphor compared with *lips.*

IMPLIED METAPHOR.   When the metaphor is not stated directly, it may be implied. Instead of saying "This is the autumn of my life," which would be a clear metaphor, Shakespeare implies the same idea when he begins Sonnet 73 with the following:

That time of year thou mayst in me behold
When yellow leaves, or none, or few, do hang
Upon those boughs which shake against the cold,
Bare, ruined choirs, where late the sweet birds sang.

Implied metaphors are often so subtle that they are not recognized right away. This is also an example of **extended metaphor,** in which the same metaphor is continued over several lines.

PREPOSITIONAL METAPHOR.   "The winter of our discontent." The comparison is the prepositional phrase of *our discontent* with the *year,* which has seasons. This metaphor implies that *discontent* could have a summer or other season, although *winter* fits perfectly with discontent. "She was the apple of my eye." *Apple* is a metaphor of something important in relation to the *eye,* which is also a metaphor for admiration or desire. The prepositional phrase is *of my eye.*

A **simile** is like a metaphor except that it makes the comparison explicit by using *like, as,* or *as if.* In the line "My love is like a red red rose," the simile is open-ended. Love is said to share some of the qualities of the rose—beauty, perishability, and rarity—but you can also add your own qualities to the list. In "Beauty, sweet Love, is like the morning dew," beauty shares the qualities of freshness and perishability with dew. This comes from an **extended simile,** in which the comparison is stretched over several lines:

Beauty, sweet Love, is like the morning dew,
Whose short refresh upon the tender green
Cheers for a time, but till the sun doth show,
And straight 'tis gone as it had never been.

Metaphor and simile are subtle in their effect, penetrating the subconscious and operating there "out of sight." Often one's most powerful response to poetry depends upon the power of metaphor because the comparisons are open-ended and resonant. You may read a metaphoric poem one day and respond to one set of felt comparisons, and then later you may perceive an entirely new set. Metaphors are filled with surprises and constitute one of the richest resources of poetry. Shakespeare's sonnets, for example, use powerful metaphoric language, as in this poem.

WILLIAM SHAKESPEARE   (1564–1616)

Sonnet 73: That Time of Year Thou Mayst in Me Behold _____ *1609*

That time of year thou mayst in me behold
When yellow leaves, or none, or few, do hang
Upon those boughs which shake against the cold,
Bare, ruined choirs, where late the sweet birds sang.
In me thou seest the twilight of such day   5
As after sunset fadeth in the west,
Which by and by black night doth take away,
Death's second self, that seals up all in rest.
In me thou seest the glowing of such fire
That on the ashes of his youth doth lie,   10
As the death-bed whereon it must expire,
Consumed with that which it was nourished by.
   This thou perceiv'st, which makes thy love more strong,
   To love that well, which thou must leave ere long.

The poet talks about himself to another person, someone for whom he cares. This is a sonnet (discussed shortly), which has several distinct units: three quatrains and a couplet. The first four lines are a unit (quatrain) ending with a period. The same is true of the next four lines and the next four. The last two lines (couplet) end with a period. In each of these units Shakespeare develops metaphors. The first quatrain begins with a metaphor of the season: the "time of year" we "behold" in him must be autumn, implied by the "yellow leaves." But the emphasis shifts to the boughs, high in the air (the choir is high in a church and these boughs shake against "Bare, ruined choirs"). Shakespeare invites a comparison of his head and hair—presumably growing thin in his autumn years—with boughs in which birds sang. He as a poet sang, as well. The second quatrain suggests another noun metaphor, but the comparison moves from a season to a single day: "the twilight of such day." In this quatrain Shakespeare evokes "black night," "Death's second self," thus introducing a menacing idea. The day ends with sleep, as life ends with death. The third quatrain evokes a new metaphor: a fire, but one that is fed with "the ashes of his youth." This prepositional metaphor likens youth to a timber that is in limited supply and can be consumed. Life is like a fire that burns itself. These three quatrains, dominated by three extended metaphors, constitute a powerful argument to "prove" the message of the couplet: love that well which you must leave soon. In other words, love life; it does not last. The power of metaphor in this poem is largely subliminal. The images of a person's autumn or twilight years and of being consumed by flames of time are very compelling. We do not have to think hard to grasp and feel these comparisons.

The next four-stanza song uses metaphors in every stanza. (A *canción* is a song.)

DENISE LEVERTOV   (b. 1923)

Canción _____ *1975*

When I am the sky
a glittering bird
slashes at me with the knives of song.

When I am the sea
fiery clouds plunge into my mirrors,   5
fracture my smooth breath with crimson sobbing.

When I am the earth
I feel my flesh of rock wearing down:
pebbles, grit, finest dust, nothing.

When I am a woman—O, when I am   10
a woman,
my wells of salt brim and brim,
poems force the lock of my throat.

These metaphors are often violent and tortured, such as the opening comparison of song with knives. The description is clear enough: birds do "slash" the sky and seem knifelike if seen from one point of view. This violent metaphor contrasts with the calmness of "When I am the sky," also a metaphor. Some of the metaphors in the second stanza are surrealistic: "fiery clouds plunge into my mirrors / fracture my smooth breath with crimson sobbing." The clouds metaphorically "plunge," "fracture," and sob. In the third stanza, when the speaker is the earth, she feels "the flesh of rock wearing down." Finally, in the last stanza, when "I" is a woman, the "wells of salt brim and brim;" a metaphor for her eyes producing salt tears. She expresses herself by forcing "the lock of [her] throat." The underlying violence of all these metaphors makes this poem function like a volcano. The pressure builds and builds until we become aware that the poem has realized its message: it has forced the locks and expressed itself. Levertov invokes all four elements—air, earth, fire, and water—to encompass the entire universe of experience.

The next poem is an example of an extended and implied metaphor; note also how rhythm contributes to its meaning.

E. E. CUMMINGS (1894–1962)

she being Brand / -new _____ *1926*

she being Brand

-new; and you
know consequently a
little stiff i was
careful of her and(having   5

thoroughly oiled the universal
joint tested my gas felt of
her radiator made sure her springs were O.

K.)i went right to it flooded-the-carburetor cranked her

up, slipped the   10
clutch(and then somehow got into reverse she
kicked what
the hell)next
minute i was back in neutral tried and

again slo-wly;bare,ly nudg.   ing(my   15

lev-er Right-
oh and her gears being in
A 1 shape passed
from low through

second-in-to-high like   20
greasedlightning)just as we turned the corner of Divinity

avenue i touched the accelerator and give

her the juice,good

               (it
was the first ride and believe i we was   25
happy to see how nice she acted right up to
the last minute coming back down by the Public
Gardens i slammed on
the

internalexpanding   30
&
externalcontracting
brakes Bothatonce and

brought allofher tremB
-ling   35
to a:dead.

stand-
;Still)

QUESTIONS FOR CLOSE READING

1. Read the poem silently and mark those passages that need to be read quickly
    and those that should be read slowly or haltingly. Then read the poem aloud.
    The poem is not metrical, but it does have rhythm. How would you describe the
    rhythm? How does the movement of the lines operate metaphorically to suggest
    the movement of an automobile?

2. The extended metaphor works in terms of the distinction between denotative
    and connotative language. Are there any noun, verb, or prepositional metaphors
    in the text of the poem? What connotations do you perceive in the language of
    the poem? What metaphorically could the automobile be compared with?

3. Some readers may not "get" this comparison right away. This raises the question,
    To what extent does the double meaning depend on the reader? Who is respon-
    sible for the interpretation of a metaphoric comparison?

The author of the next poem was in the air force in World War II, so its
imagery and details have a special authenticity. The power of the controlling
metaphor has made this brief poem one of the most memorable to come from
that war.

RANDALL JARRELL   (1914–1965)

The Death of the Ball Turret° Gunner _____ *1945*

From my mother's sleep I fell into the State,
And I hunched in its belly till my wet fur froze,
Six miles from earth, loosed from its dream of life,
I woke to black flak° and the nightmare fighters.
When I died they washed me out of the turret with a hose.   5

Ball Turret: the transparent capsule under a bomber where the machine gunner sat, sometimes upside down.   5 *flak:* antiaircraft fire: explosions in the air.

QUESTIONS FOR CLOSE READING

1. What metaphor is implied in the first line of the poem? Why is *State* capitalized?

2. In the second line the gunner says he "hunched in its belly." What metaphor is im-
    plied in that expression? Why is it effective?

3. The third line refers to "its dream of life." Is "dream of life" a prepositional
    metaphor? What is being compared to a dream? Who is the "its" in this line?

4. Is the last line metaphoric? The entire poem is an extended metaphor, but of what?

The following poem employs an extended simile. We are like the great princes of old, who, after a day's work in the field hunting stags or other noble beasts, came back to the palace to live a life that was appropriate for royalty. Honig's simile is a commentary on the way we live now.

EDWIN HONIG (b. 1919)

As a Great Prince _____ *1955*

As a great prince after the hunt comes
Stomping through the antlered spear-hung hall
Of his overnourished leisure, flopping his weight
    Of rich self-certitude to dream in thick
    Bearskin the teasing horror of a beast   5
Outstaring axe blows, questioning the onslaught,
In immortal posture gazing and uncaught,

So we inhabit a drowsy movie dark,
Amid love's trophies deliberating self-content,
Moist anticipants of the overplayed crescendo   10
    Clutching the smoking guns of pleasure,
    Till suddenly blond beast removes a robe
And pulsing reel relaxes to a still
Of smiling passion frozen in our death of will.

QUESTIONS FOR CLOSE READING

1. The metaphors of lines 3 and 4 point to physical qualities of the "great prince." What are they? Why is metaphor an effective means of making us aware of the physicality of the prince?

2. The second half of the poem invites a metaphoric comparison: for us the prince's great hall has become a darkened "movie." How, then, does this metaphor compare us with the prince?

3. What are the "smoking guns of pleasure"?

4. What metaphors do you see at work in the final line?

OTHER FIGURATIVE LANGUAGE. Poetry has many special kinds of figurative language besides metaphoric techniques. You will encounter some of them in the poetry in this section, but you will already have seen some of them in other kinds of literature. Here is a list of the most important techniques.

IRONY.   **Irony** is saying one thing but meaning another, or giving an apparently innocent comparison that reveals the shortcoming of the subject. For example, Edwin Honig's "As a Great Prince" compares today's householder with a great prince of old, only to make us aware of how puny the contemporary householder is in relation to the nobility of the prince.

Verbal irony is commonly used in conversation, as when someone claims to be "bad," intending the listener to know that exactly the opposite is meant. Advertisers recognize the value of such irony when they recommend "killer" systems for audio, video, or computer equipment. Verbal irony does not always connote the opposite of what it says, but it always connotes something different from the literal meaning of the words used.

Dramatic irony is not limited to words but spills over into actions. It is not only found in plays. In poetic or other narratives, dramatic irony heightens suspense and the reader's anticipation. When a character wishes for something desirable, gets it, then discovers it to be the source of ruin or damnation, the poet has used dramatic irony. In *Oedipus Rex* Oedipus constantly vows to avenge the murder of Laios, no matter who the murderer is. In that play, Oedipus's quest is not just dramatic irony, but **tragic irony** because the result is the tragic end of a great hero.

Irony is a subtle resource for the poet because it has many links with life, which is filled with ironies. In literature such ironies are controlled to produce maximum psychological effect. One of the pleasures of irony is that the audience usually understands the ironic circumstances when the characters do not. For example, in *Hamlet* Claudio kneels to pray only to realize his conscience is not clear. Hamlet hesitates in killing him because he thinks his prayer is genuine and that Claudio would be dispatched to Heaven instead of Hell if he were to be killed then. The audience knows otherwise.

Edwin Arlington Robinson's "Richard Cory" (p. 757) may be an example of **cosmic irony,** in that the man admired by all who knew him turns out to be so miserable as to commit suicide. Cosmic irony shows fate reaching from the heavens to make an otherwise admirable person—Richard Cory, the man who has everything—so unhappy as to cause his death. In every case irony functions in terms of a reversal of appearances. Usually the reader is aware of the irony before the characters, and so is in a special relation to the action.

PARADOX.   A **paradox** is an apparently impossible circumstance, situation, or condition. The line in Denise Levertov's poem, "I feel my flesh of rock," is paradoxical. It cannot be explained rationally.

PERSONIFICATION.   **Personification** is giving a nonbeing the characteristics of a person, as when Jarrell suggests that the "State" has a "belly" or Honig tells us that a "reel relaxes." The entire effect of "she being Brand / -new" is achieved by personifying an automobile as a woman.

Pun. A **pun** is a play on words that usually depends on a word's having several meanings or sounding like another word with a different meaning. The reference to "death-bed" in Shakespeare's Sonnet 73 (p. 475) is a pun on the bed of ashes (as in "bed of coals").

Metonymy. When you use one thing in place of something closely related to it, you use **metonymy**. Calling an athlete a "jock," referring to a casino as "the house," and calling the police "the heat" are examples of metonymy.

Synecdoche. **Synecdoche,** closely related to metonymy, uses a part for the whole, as when one uses *wheels* to mean an automobile, *wings* to mean an airplane, *rifles* to mean a regiment of soldiers, or *hands* to mean sailors in "all hands on deck."

Hyperbole. **Hyperbole is overstatement** for effect. "I fell into the State" is a form of hyperbole which Jarrell depends upon for part of the power of his poem. The last line, "When I died they washed me out of the turret with a hose," may seem to be hyperbole, but unfortunately it may be a literal description, given the nature of World War II bombing missions.

Litotes. The opposite of overstatement, **litotes,** is **understatement** (a word we sometimes use instead of *litotes*): it downplays for effect. When one refers to World War II as a "pretty little squabble," one uses litotes. Litotes often relies on a negative structure, as in "it was not unpopular" when one means it was wildly popular, or as in "it did not go unappreciated" for something that may have won general appreciation and high regard.

Some of these figures may be seen at work in William Wordsworth's sonnet "London, 1802." The poem invokes the memory of Wordsworth's greatest influence, John Milton (1608–1672), the revolutionary poet who supported the defeat and beheading of Charles I during the English Civil War. When Wordsworth wrote, France had undergone the most important revolution of modern times, and Wordsworth was excited by the rise of democracy and Europe's potential for overthrowing kings, princes, and all backward systems of government. He saw Milton as the spiritual leader in the fight for republicanism.

WILLIAM WORDSWORTH (1770–1850)

London, 1802 _____ *1807 (1802?)*

Milton! thou should'st be living at this hour:
England hath need of thee: she is a fen
Of stagnant waters: altar, sword, and pen,
Fireside, the heroic wealth of hall and bower,

Have forfeited their ancient English dower   5
Of inward happiness. We are selfish men;
Oh! raise us up, return to us again;
And give us manners, virtue, freedom, power.
Thy soul was like a star, and dwelt apart:
Thou hadst a voice whose sound was like the sea: ·   10
Pure as the naked heavens, majestic, free,
So didst thou travel on life's common way,
In cheerful godliness; and yet thy heart
The lowliest duties on herself did lay.

Wordsworth uses paradox in addressing Milton in the first place, since Milton had been long dead. He uses hyperbole in lines 2 and 3 in claiming that England is a fen of stagnant waters. In "altar, sword, and pen" he uses metonymy to allude to religious leaders, military leaders, and writers (politicians). "Hall and bower" are synecdoches for the English manor house, from which traditional stability and government had come. In light of England's problems, the half-line "We are selfish men" may be thought of as an instance of litotes. Wordsworth's praise of Milton in the latter part of the poem—"Thy soul was like a star," "Thou hadst a voice . . . like the sea"—is hyperbole. "Heart" in line 13 is metonymy, just as "soul" in line 9 may be metonymic for Milton's spiritual nature. Even in a relatively brief poem, such figurative devices operate quite forcefully. They contribute an emotional density to the poem, especially as they synchronize with its imagery and metaphors.

The following poem derives its entire effect from the use of figurative language.

GERALD COSTANZO   (b. 1945)

At Irony's Picnic _____ *1974*

Silence is sight-reading
Swahili. Sin lumbers by on

stilts. Where did he get
that Hawaiian shirt? those

rose-colored glasses? Down   5
by the lake Desire is fondling

Regret's mother. Jealousy
and Happiness dance the mazurka.

Justice, wearing the same
old swimsuit, is cutting the   10

ballyhoo. Irony himself
isn't even here.

QUESTIONS FOR CLOSE READING

1. What is the primary irony in this poem?
2. Which pun is most effective?
3. How many examples of personification does Costanzo use?
4. Why is personification so important to Costanzo?
5. Which personification does Costanzo most extensively develop? Do the attributes Costanzo links with that figure give us a better understanding, or do they contribute to confusion?
6. Are the "rose-colored glasses" an example of imagery, metaphor, metonymy, synecdoche, or a combination of these figures? What do rose-colored glasses signify?

Poets do not always know which figures they will use in a poem, and when you begin examining a poem for its use of figures you may not know what you will find. In a poem titled "Irony's Picnic," one would expect to find irony, and Costanzo does not disappoint us (or does he?). Is Irony's absence at the picnic ironic? Or if it is ironic, does that mean irony is present in the poem? Costanzo is not just having fun; he is making a point about poetry, language, and life. All figurative language contributes to the subtle effect of a poem, no matter what its significance or purpose may be.

SYMBOL AND ALLEGORY

A **symbol** is a specialized use of metaphor. It begins with a comparison, but the reader is not always immediately aware that the comparison is important. Without saying so, the poet makes one thing—the thing he or she specifically talks about—stand for another—something not specifically talked about. The poet does not substitute the subject for the symbol but instead speaks about both simultaneously. The reader gradually becomes aware that the subject of the poem is taking on larger meanings, larger associations, and suggestions of meaning than was first apparent. For example, the scarlet letter A, which stands for adultery in Nathaniel Hawthorne's novel *The Scarlet Letter,* is supposed to identify Hester Prynne's shame among her Puritan citizens. However, it soon begins to symbolize the shame of the community that has treated her as outcast.

Certain conventional symbols abound in literature. The sun symbolizes masculinity; the moon symbolizes femininity. Fire symbolizes passion; air symbolizes the spirit; water symbolizes rejuvenation; earth symbolizes the mother. Some points of the compass are symbols: north symbolizes the devil; west, death; east, beginnings. These are age-old symbols and are by no means rigid or fixed. Water, for example, can symbolize life, but in too great abundance it can also mean death. Poets use symbols in a variety of ways, sometimes relying on tradition and sometimes breaking with it.

William Blake's poem "The Tiger" demonstrates how a symbol slowly gathers meaning. In its original published form, the poem was accompanied by

Blake's drawing of a tiger, and the reader would have expected the poem to concern a tiger, and not necessarily something beyond that.

WILLIAM BLAKE   (1757–1827)

The Tiger _____ *1794*

Tiger, tiger, burning bright
In the forests of the night,
What immortal hand or eye
Could frame thy fearful symmetry?

In what distant deeps or skies   5
Burnt the fire of thine eyes?
On what wings dare he aspire?
What the hand dare seize the fire?

And what shoulder and what art
Could twist the sinews of thy heart?   10
And when thy heart began to beat,
What dread hand? And what dread feet?

What the hammer? What the chain?
In what furnace was thy brain?
What the anvil? What dread grasp   15
Dare its deadly terrors clasp?

When the stars threw down their spears
And watered Heaven with their tears,
Did he smile his work to see?
Did he who made the Lamb make thee?   20

Tiger, tiger, burning bright
In the forests of the night,
What immortal hand or eye
Dare frame thy fearful symmetry?

That this is no ordinary tiger seems clear in the opening stanza, in which Blake tells us that it burns and that its fire illumines the forests of the night. Modern psychologists would see "forests of the night" as symbolic of the unconscious world of dreams. The dream world is forested because it is uncleared, dark, and threatening. The tiger becomes part of that unconscious because it stands for an elemental violence and predatory behavior that may be in every person as a result of evolutionary forces. Blake meditates on the creation of the tiger in the second stanza, imagining a creator in some "distant deeps" seizing the fire of the tiger's eyes, the spark of its creation. Building on this idea in the third and fourth stanzas, Blake imagines a creator in the guise of a blacksmith forging the shape of this terrifying predator. We see at the end of stanza 4 that whoever created the tiger must somehow be greater even than that beast: "What dread grasp / Dare its deadly terrors clasp?" But then, in stanza 5, Blake wonders if the tiger pleased the creator. He further wonders if the same creator made both the ferocious tiger and the peaceful, defenseless lamb. He capitalizes "Lamb," which many commentators assume is a symbolic reference to Jesus.

Symbols imply a range of significance, not a single significance. Therefore, the tiger of this poem can be seen to symbolize the terrors of nature as present in predators and violent death. The lamb can be seen to symbolize innocence, mildness, and the gentleness of nature, as well as the gentleness and innocence associated with God and godliness. But then the tiger can symbolize the wrath of God and the terror associated with an angry God. The fact that both the tiger and the lamb exist in the same universe, whether physical or spiritual, is the central, and possibly paradoxical, idea in this poem.

Blake works with elemental ideas and elemental forces, but he does not pin them down. By contrast, when you make a symbol stand for only one thing, you have created an **allegory.** Allegory is related to metaphor because it implies a comparison, but the emphasis is usually on the hidden meaning, not both parts. Allegory is a form of "other-speak," in which the language on the surface must be translated according to a kind of key to get the true meaning. In George Orwell's novel *Animal Farm,* certain animals allegorically represented certain governments. The French, for example, were allegorized as roosters, the English as bulls (John Bull), and the Russians as bears. These are age-old allegories that Orwell appropriated. "Jabberwocky" (p. 423), is an allegory for all the dragons and dangerous beasts who lie in the way of the virtuous young hero. In Stevie Smith's poem "Mother, among the Dustbins" (p. 472), the dustbins may be an allegory for the dust we all become at death. E. E. Cummings expects us to see the allegorical relationship between a new car and a young virgin in "she being Brand/-new." Once one gets the key to this poem, one basically forgets about the car and concentrates on the woman and all the details that precisely fit that meaning. Allegory is highly useful in situations in which free and open speech is not possible, and so was useful for Cummings in 1926.

E. E. Cummings plays with both symbol and allegory in the following poem.

E. E. CUMMINGS   (1894–1962)

l(a _____ *1958*

l(a
le
af
fa

ll   5

s)
one
l

iness

QUESTIONS FOR CLOSE READING

1. What does the shape of the poem resemble?
2. The poem consists of two parts: one is an image. What is the image?
3. The second part of the poem is a single, long, word. What is that word?
4. Why does one part of the poem interrupt the other?
5. What symbolism do you see at work here?

Cummings seems to have had a good time exploring the resources of shape in this poem. If you were to take a pencil and follow the curved and vertical lines of the typography, you would have a diagram of something like a leaf falling. Note the way the parentheses imply a swirling motion and the way the *af, fa* lines resemble a twist in a falling spiral (pencil a line through the *a*'s and another through the *f*'s. The last line is like the recumbent leaf. Then look at the repetition of the concept of "one." First, the opening l on the typewriter is the same as the number 1 (this poem is also number 1 in its original collection). The first letter after the parenthesis is *a*, the first letter of the alphabet. In French, *le* means premier, or first. The two *l*'s in line 5 emphasize the oneness; then *one* (line 7) is reinforced by l in the next line; and finally, *iness* may be taken as *oneness* or *I-ness,* which are closely related.

The primary image of the poem is in parentheses, broken into spiraling parts, and it reads: "a leaf falls." This image interrupts—and in so doing illustrates—a single word: *loneliness.* But Cummings explores that single word by breaking it into several parts, all of which reinforce the basic idea of oneness. That leaf, when it was in the tree, was part of a vast community. However, when it died, when it fell from the tree, it did so alone, and every swirl, every downward move, reinforced its oneness. If the leaf is symbolic, then we can see it reinforcing our sense of community with other people but reminding us of our individuality, which for better or worse will assert itself when we die. The falling leaf is an allegory for loneliness; but it is a symbol for humanity.

Robert Frost often worked with materials from New England farming country, finding in them significances that we may think of as symbolic. When he speaks of apple-picking or of a road not taken, we begin with what seem to be straightforward descriptions of experience that gain meaning as we examine them. The following poem is typical of Frost's method.

ROBERT FROST   (1874–1963)

Mending Wall _____ *1914*

Something there is that doesn't love a wall,
That sends the frozen-ground-swell under it
And spills the upper boulders in the sun,
And makes gaps even two can pass abreast.
The work of hunters is another thing: 5

I have come after them and made repair
Where they have left not one stone on a stone,
But they would have the rabbit out of hiding,
To please the yelping dogs. The gaps I mean,
No one has seen them made or heard them made,   10
But at spring mending-time we find them there.
I let my neighbor know beyond the hill;
And on a day we meet to walk the line
And set the wall between us once again.
We keep the wall between us as we go.   15
To each the boulders that have fallen to each.
And some are loaves and some so nearly balls
We have to use a spell to make them balance:
"Stay where you are until our backs are turned!"
We wear our fingers rough with handling them.   20
Oh, just another kind of outdoor game,
One on a side. It comes to little more:
There where it is we do not need the wall:
He is all pine and I am apple orchard.
My apple trees will never get across   25
And eat the cones under his pines, I tell him.
He only says, "Good fences make good neighbors."
Spring is the mischief in me, and I wonder
If I could put a notion in his head:
"*Why* do they make good neighbors? Isn't it   30
Where there are cows? But here there are no cows.
Before I built a wall I'd ask to know
What I was walling in or walling out,
And to whom I was like to give offense.
Something there is that doesn't love a wall,   35
That wants it down." I could say "Elves" to him,
But it's not elves exactly, and I'd rather
He said it for himself. I see him there,
Bringing a stone grasped firmly by the top
In each hand, like an old-stone savage armed.   40
He moves in darkness as it seems to me,
Not of woods only and the shade of trees.
He will not go behind his father's saying,
And he likes having thought of it so well
He says again, "Good fences make good neighbors."   45

QUESTIONS FOR CLOSE READING

1. When do you become aware that the wall is more than a specific pile of stones? Is there a line that begins to suggest a symbolic significance? What clues do you get to suggest such a significance?

2. What does Frost seem to mean by saying he and his neighbor "set the wall between us once again"?

3. Are the words *loaves* and *balls* in line 17 symbolic? Are they images? Are they metaphors?

4. Is line 27 meant to be symbolic? What does the neighbor seem to mean by it? How does the speaker of the poem seem to interpret it?

5. The speaker of the poem repeats the first line in line 35. Why? What has happened in the poem to make him reconsider the possibility that "Something there is that doesn't love a wall"?

6. What does Frost gain by the way he says line 35? Would it be better to say, "There is something that doesn't like a wall"? Is it really different?

7. In line 40, the speaker sees his neighbor as "like an old-stone savage armed." Why? What is the meaning of such a simile?

8. What does the neighbor's repetition of "Good fences make good neighbors" achieve at the end of the poem? What thoughts are you left with? What do you think walls symbolize?

Patrick Kavanagh, the author of the next poem, grew up in Ireland in a farming county. His father was a cobbler and for a time he took up the trade, but he soon abandoned it for the literary life. Some of his early poetry resembles Frost's in that its imagery is drawn from the land and its surfaces often suggest a deeper meaning. The horse-drawn machine referred to in this poem is designed to break up the ground to prepare it for seeding. The harrow is also associated with Jesus Christ, who after his crucifixion was said to have gone into Hell and harrowed it, bringing out the souls who had been waiting for his coming and who deserved to be in Heaven. Thus some of the imagery of the poem depends on a familiarity with the Bible as well as with farming.

PATRICK KAVANAGH   (1905–1967)

To the Man after the Harrow _____ *1936*

Now leave the check-reins slack,
The seed is flying far to-day—
The seed like stars against the black
Eternity of April clay.

This seed is potent as the seed   5
Of knowledge in the Hebrew Book,
So drive your horses in the creed
Of God the Father as a stook.°

Forget the men on Brady's° hill.
Forget what Brady's boy may say.   10
For destiny will not fulfill
Unless you let the harrow play.

---

8 *stook:* a bundle of sheaves of straw.   9 *Brady's:* his neighbor's hill.

Forget the worm's opinion too
Of hooves and pointed harrow-pins,
For you are driving your horses through   15
The mist where Genesis begins.

QUESTIONS FOR CLOSE READING

1. April is a possible allegory for both spring and Easter, an agricultural and religious time. How does Kavanagh make you aware of their relationship in stanza 1?
2. The seed is "like stars," but it is set "against the black / Eternity of April clay."
   What effect do this simile and this metaphor have? How might they prepare you
   to read the poem symbolically?
3. The seed that the farmer sows is compared to "the seed / Of knowledge" in the
   Bible. How can Kavanagh make that comparison? What does the farmer share
   with God the Father? Is their relationship symbolic, metaphoric, or both?
4. How does Kavanagh elevate the farmer's importance in stanza 3? What does "destiny" imply? Whose destiny is the subject of this stanza?
5. What does the worm symbolize in the last stanza? Is it appropriate in this poem?
6. Mists are vague. "The mist where Genesis begins" is also vague in that one cannot
   pin it down, but it is rich in associations. What are they? What is mist meant to symbolize for the farmer driving the harrow? How does it enrich the significance of
   the poem?.

The next poem creates a symbol of modern life. At first it is difficult to interpret the tone, but eventually the reader wonders just how serious the author
is in describing an action that we are pretty sure he did not commit. However,
the fact that we are not 100 percent sure tells us something. If we were Freudian
psychologists, we might interpret this poem as a wish fulfillment dream.

WILLIAM CARPENTER (b. 1940)

Fire _____ *1987*

This morning, on the opposite shore of the river,
I watch a man burning his own house.
It is a cold day, and the man wears thick gloves
and a fur hat that gives him a Russian look.
I envy his energy, since I'm still on the sunporch   5
in my robe, with morning coffee, my day not
even begun, while my neighbor has already piled
spruce boughs against his house and poured
flammable liquids over them to send a ribbon
of black smoke into the air, a column surrounded   10
by herring gulls, who think he's having a barbecue
or has founded a new dump. I hadn't known what labor
it took to burn something. Now the man's working

at such speed, he's like the criminal in a silent
movie, as if he had a deadline, as if he had   15
to get his house burned by a certain time, or it
would be all over. I see his kids helping, bringing
him matches and kindling, and I'd like to help out
myself, I'd like to bring him coffee and a bagel,
but the Penobscot River separates us, icebergs   20
the size of small ships drifting down the tide.
Moreover, why should I help him when I have a house
myself, which needs burning as much as anyone's?
It has begun to leak. I think it has carpenter ants.
I hear them making sounds at night like writing, only   25
they aren't writing, they are building small tubular
cities inside the walls. I start burning in the study,
working from within so it will go faster, so I can
catch up, and soon there's a smoke column on either
side, like a couple of Algonquins having a dialogue   30
on how much harder it is to destroy than to create.
I shovel books and poems into the growing fire. If
I burn everything, I can start over, with a future
like a white rectangle of paper. Then I notice
my neighbor has a hose, that he's spraying his house   35
with water, the coward, he has bailed out, but I
keep throwing things into the fire: my stamps,
my Berlioz collection, my photos of nude people,
my correspondence dating back to grade school.
Over there, the fire engines are reaching his home.   40
His wife is crying with relief, his fire's extinguished.
He has walked down to the shore to see the ruins
of the house across the river, the open cellar,
the charred timbers, the man laughing and singing
in the snow, who has been finally freed from his   45
possessions, who has no clothes, no library, who has
gone back to the beginning, when we lived in nature:
no refuge from the elements, no fixed address.

QUESTIONS FOR CLOSE READING

1. The speaker of the poem talks about the "labor / it took to burn something" as if it were a challenge. What has Carpenter done to prepare you to accept this point of view? Do you find yourself receptive to it?

2. When the speaker says he has a house "which needs burning as much as anyone's," what does he seem to mean? Has he begun to speak symbolically at this point of the poem, or is he still being literal?

3. What does the speaker think about the condition of his home when he begins to burn it too? Why does he compare himself and his neighbor to two Algonquin Indians having a dialogue with smoke signals?

4. The speaker explicitly mentions shoveling "books and poems into the growing fire." Why are these items mentioned?

5. What do you make of all the special "collectibles" that he piles onto his fire? Do they give you a clue to his character?

6. Why did his neighbor put out the fire? Why didn't the speaker put out his?

7. Symbolically, what has the speaker achieved? What has the fire done for him? Is he a happy man at the end of the poem?

FORM

One of the fascinating qualities of poetry is that it thrives amid constraints. The constraint to rhyme, for example, has produced many surprising and magical moments. The constraint to maintain a metrical pattern is so powerful that for most readers it identifies what poetry is. Free verse, which uses neither rhyme nor meter, is for many people simply not poetry. That is an extreme position, but the point is that one of the great resources of poetry comes from its capacity not just to resist constraints but to overcome them brilliantly.

The form of some poems is even more constraining than most rhyme and meter because it is established before the poet begins. A couplet is two rhyming lines, a tercet is three rhyming lines, a quatrain is four rhyming lines, and so on. The metrical pattern is also usually decided on in advance. The poet's job is to use these beforehand decisions to best advantage. However, these small forms are relatively simple to work with. Much more elaborate forms have interested poets, and their success has inspired other poets throughout history.

Verse refers to any poem that is metrical in character, as well as a line or a stanza of such poetry. In common use, it also refers to a stanza of a song, as in the first or second verse of "Old Man River." Although modern poets do not regard verse as highly as did the poets of earlier centuries, the general public normally expects a poem to be a form of verse, with established rhyme and meter. A. E. Housman's poems (see pp. 461 and 468) are good examples of what is commonly called verse.

Blank verse is unrhymed iambic pentameter (five iambic feet) and takes on special importance because it is the line that Shakespeare used for most of his plays and that Milton used for *Paradise Lost, Paradise Regained,* and *Samson Agonistes.* It is a highly flexible line especially suited for dramatic narrative.

Free verse avoids preestablished rhyme, stanza pattern, or meter. You have seen several examples in earlier discussions, such as Ezra Pound's "In a Station of the Metro" (p. 452), Judith Rodriguez's "Eskimo Occasion" (p. 460), Denise Levertov's "Canción" (p. 476), E. E. Cummings's "She Being Brand/-New" (p. 477), and Gerald Costanzo's "At Irony's Picnic" (p.482). Modern poets have been fond of free verse since the time of Walt Whitman in the 1850s, but many poets in the 1990s have rediscovered the virtues of poetry that uses fixed forms.

Most **fixed forms** depend upon a predetermined **rhyme scheme,** a pattern of sounds at the ends of lines of verse that sound alike, look alike, or sound very close to one another. In describing a rhyme scheme we assign a letter to the end sound of each line, using the same letter when that sound repeats:

The explosive sound above the hill	*a*
Made me stop with climber's skill;	*a*
Holding on where goats once walked	*b*
I listened as if God had talked.	*b*

The first *a* refers to *hill,* the second to its rhyme word, *skill.* The first *b* refers to *walked,* the second to its rhyme word, *talked.* As discussed earlier, often the rhyme will not be the entire end word but only its last syllable (see p. 465). Sometimes it will be more than one syllable. The predetermined form for the rhyme in this example is the **couplet:** each line rhymes with the next line. When lines fall into units of four, we call them **quatrains,** which might rhyme *abab* or *abba.* **Tercets** are units of three lines, which might rhyme *aaa, aba,* or *abc* (in the last case, the next tercet will also be *abc*). As you will see, the sonnet is normally composed of groupings of quatrains, tercets, and/or couplets. Fixed forms sometimes establish patterns of rhyme, stanza length, and repetition of lines, as in the villanelle, discussed below.

The Song

Not all lyric poems are set to music, but songs enjoy a life involved with musical settings. Generally songs are simple and short, emotional and rhythmic. They have been written in all ages, including our own. Some of the most memorable were songs in plays, such as those of Shakespeare. The following is from Shakespeare's play *The Tempest:*

Full fathom five thy father lies;
    Of his bones are coral made;
Those are pearls that were his eyes.
    Nothing of him that doth fade
But doth suffer a sea-change
Into something rich and strange.
Sea-nymphs hourly ring his knell:
    Burden [within]. Ding-Dong.
Hark, now I hear them—Ding-dong, bell.

5

Ariel, a wood-sprite, is the singer of the song, telling Ferdinand that his father has drowned. However, Ariel is not telling the truth. He wishes only to mystify Ferdinand so as to change him. The idea of a "sea-change" has fascinated poets and writers ever since this song was written. It has always implied a massive, significant change on a psychological level.

Richard Lovelace was a seventeenth-century poet who lived during the troubling times of the English Civil War. His poem has been sung to many different melodies. Its last two lines have been quoted frequently as an emblem of the honorable soldier off to do his duty.

RICHARD LOVELACE 1618–1657)

Song: To Lucasta, Going to the Wars _____ *1649*

Tell me not, sweet, I am unkind,
   That from the nunnery
Of thy chaste breast and quiet mind
   To war and arms I fly.

True, a new mistress now I chase,   5
   The first foe in the field;
And with a stronger faith embrace
   A sword, a horse, a shield.

Yet this inconstancy is such
   As you too shall adore;   10
I could not love thee, dear, so much,
   Loved I not honor more.

     Edmund Waller, another seventeenth-century poet, also lived through the tumult of the Civil War and enjoyed an extraordinary popularity as a poet. His "Go, Lovely Rose" is also addressed indirectly to a woman. The direct address of this song is to the rose itself, which Waller urges to tell his young woman that she is something like a rose. He knows that the rose he sends is beautiful, and so is the woman. He knows that soon the rose will die, and so will the woman. He expects the woman will get the message of the song: not to waste "her time and me." In other words, "gather ye rosebuds while ye may." This song belongs to a tradition called *carpe diem*, Latin for "seize the day." This song, like the song of Richard Lovelace, was intended to be sung to a lute or a guitar.

EDMUND WALLER (1606–1687)

Go, Lovely Rose _____ *1645*

  Go, lovely rose
Tell her that wastes her time and me
  That now she knows,
When I resemble her to thee,
  How sweet and fair she seems to be.   5

  Tell her that's young,
And shuns to have her graces spied,

That hadst thou sprung
In deserts, where no men abide,
   Thou must have uncommended died.   10

Small is the worth
Of beauty from the light retired;
   Bid her come forth,
Suffer herself to be desired,
   And not blush so to be admired.   15

Then die, that she
The common fate of all things rare
   May read in thee:
How small a part of time they share,
   That are so wondrous sweet and fair.   20

The Sonnet

Sonnets are fourteen lines of iambic pentameter: ˘ ´ | ˘ ´ | ˘ ´ | ˘ ´ | ˘ ´.
These lines are not always regular, and substitute feet normally occur. Sonnets also follow certain patterns of structure and rhyme, each of which has its own name.

PETRARCHAN, OR ITALIAN.   The **Petrarchan,** or **Italian, sonnet** (named after the fourteenth-century poet Petrarch) is divided into an eight-line segment called an **octave** rhyming *abbaabba,* followed by a six-line segment called a **sestet** rhyming *cdecde, cdcdcd, cdcdee,* or *cdedce.* The normal pattern is to state the main idea in the first four lines of the octave and then elaborate that idea in the next four lines. Between the octave and the sestet is a "turn": a change of tone, action, or concept. The first part of the sestet sometimes has an example or complication of the idea developed in the octave, and the last three lines conclude the poem. The lines of both octave and sestet are usually end-stopped, with very strong stops after most rhymes. The end-stopped lines reinforce the individual treatment of ideas in each segment of the sonnet.

SHAKESPEAREAN, OR ENGLISH.   The **Shakespearean,** or **English, sonnet** establishes three quatrains rhyming *abab, cdcd, efef* and ends with a couplet: *gg.* It spends the first twelve lines elaborating on an idea or a problem with details and examples. The last two lines of the poem resolve the issues raised by the first three quatrains. The couplet usually sounds like a tag or resolution, and sometimes adopts the form of a moral, as with Shakespeare's Sonnet 73: "This thou perceiv'st, which makes thy love more strong, / To love that well, which thou must leave ere long."

Sir Philip Sidney was among the most accomplished of English sonneteers. His sonnet cycle, *Astrophel and Stella* (1591), is the first of several important Elizabethan collections of sonnets that narrate a complex story. The title means "starlover and star," a reference to his (the starlover's) devotion to Penelope

Devereaux Rich, the "star" whom he admired. Many of the poems reflect on the skies, the stars, or, like the following, the moon. This is a type of Petrarchan sonnet popular in his day.

SIR PHILIP SIDNEY   (1554–1586)

Sonnet 31: With How Sad Steps Oh Moon, Thou Climb'st the Skies! _____ *1591 (1582?)*

With how sad steps Oh Moon, thou climb'st the skies!	a
How silently, and with how wan a face!	b
What, may it be that even in heavenly place	b
That busy archer° his sharp arrows tries?	a
Sure,° if that long-with-love-acquainted eyes	a
Can judge of love, thou feel'st a lover's case,	b
I read it in thy looks; thy languished grace,	b
To me, that feel the like, thy state descries.°	a
Then, even of fellowship, Oh Moon, tell me,	c
Is constant love deemed there but want of wit?	d
Are beauties there as proud as here they be?	c
Do they above love to be loved, and yet	d
Those lovers scorn whom that love doth possess?	e
Do they call virtue there ungratefulness?	e

5

10

4 *archer:* cupid.   5 *Sure:* surely.   8 *descries:* makes known.

The octave compares the speaker to the moon. The moon has a wan face, as he does; it languishes, as he does; it seems to be love-struck, as he is. Having established that, the sestet turns, and, making a friend of the moon, asks questions: Is there love in the heavens? Does being faithful to one's lover in heaven win contempt (as he has presumably done)? Do the proud beauties of heaven scorn those who love them? Is ungratefulness a virtue in heaven, as it seems to be in his world? The tone of the sestet is ironic, especially in the last line, when virtue and gratefulness, contradictions, are equated.

Sidney's reliance on rhetorical questions (which expect no answer), along with the relative absence of imagery, establishes the poem as discursive. The Petrarchan sonnet frequently complained about the pangs of love in an argumentative fashion. The sonnet argues that Sidney had been stung by inconstancy (implied in the moon's changeableness) and ingratitude (implied in the moon's cool light). He asks, reasonably, Is this the way things are done in heaven? Is that why the moon looks so glum? The moon is the most complex image in the poem, and its qualities are employed in whatever way Sidney needs them.

William Shakespeare's Sonnet 29 is also from an extensive cycle, one of whose themes is love. Though this sonnet follows the Shakespearean structure, the turn of thought occurs at the end of the octave, as in the Petrarchan sonnet.

WILLIAM SHAKESPEARE   (1564–1616)

Sonnet 29: When in Disgrace with Fortune and Men's Eyes _____ *1609*

When in disgrace with Fortune and men's eyes	*a*
I all alone beweep my outcast state,	*b*
And trouble deaf heaven with my bootless° cries,	*a*
And look upon myself and curse my fate,	*b*
Wishing me like to one more rich in hope,	*c*
Featured like him, like him with friends possessed	*d*
Desiring this man's art, and that man's scope,	*c*
With what I most enjoy contented least;	*d*
Yet in these thoughts myself almost despising,	*e*
Haply I think on thee, and then my state	*f*
(Like to the lark at break of day arising	*e*
From sullen° earth) sings hymns at heaven's gate,	*f*
For thy sweet love remembered such wealth brings,	*g*
That then I scorn to change my state with kings.	*g*

5

10

3 *bootless:* useless.   12 *sullen:* dull, heavy.

    The octave tells us how the speaker feels when he is emotionally down. He describes moments when he feels outcast and envies all others' successes. Even the things he most likes displease him. The turn comes, however, at the darkest moment ("myself almost despising"); he shifts his attention to his beloved and realizes in the sestet how much he has to be grateful for. The images of the sestet—the lark rising, and singing "hymns at heaven's gate"—have been extremely memorable and uplifting to many readers. This poem begins on an emotional downslide, a virtual avalanche, only to turn again upward, rising to a sublimity resembling the status of the monarch. Thus in fourteen lines, an overwhelming transformation has taken place.

    John Donne wrote a relatively brief series of holy sonnets which do not constitute a cycle, although they are on religious subjects. The most famous of those follows.

JOHN DONNE   (1573–1631)

Holy Sonnet 10: Death, Be Not Proud _____ *1633*

Death, be not proud, though some have called thee
Mighty and dreadful, for thou art not so;
For those whom thou think'st thou dost overthrow
Die not, poor Death, nor yet canst thou kill me.
From rest and sleep, which but thy pictures be,
Much pleasure; then from thee much more must flow,
And soonest our best men with thee do go,

5

Rest of their bones, and soul's delivery.
Thou art slave to fate, chance, kings, and desperate men,
And dost with poison, war, and sickness dwell,   10
And poppy° or charms can make us sleep as well
And better than thy stroke; why swell'st° thou then?
One short sleep past, we wake eternally
And death shall be no more; Death, thou shalt die.

11 *poppy:* opium.   12 *swell'st:* puff out your chest with pride (a reference to the first line of
the poem).

QUESTIONS FOR CLOSE READING

1. The first quatrain establishes Donne's argument about death. What, essentially, does he say?

2. The second quatrain compares death with rest and sleep. What is the point of these comparisons?

3. The third quatrain clinches the argument against death. What is its basis? To what extent is this quatrain derived from the first two?

4. The final couplet establishes the point of the poem. How does well does it fit with the first twelve lines?

5. Examine the lines for their rhythm. Mark the end-stopped lines with a pencil. Which lines have a break, or caesura, in the middle? What is the effect of the caesura? Examine the lines for the relative strength of the breaks or end-stops. Are some more powerful than others? Is there any relation between them and death (another form of end-stopping)?

MILTONIC.   The **Miltonic sonnet,** named for John Milton (1608–1672), uses the same rhyme pattern as the Petrarchan for the octave but varies the rhyme scheme of the sestet and places the turn, or change of development, after the ninth, tenth, or eleventh line of the poem, if it occurs at all. The result is that the Miltonic sonnet feels less segmented and develops its main idea straight through with a special intensity. William Wordsworth's "London, 1802" (p. 481) is an example of the Miltonic sonnet, with its sestet rhyming *cddece.* Like Milton, Wordsworth uses some end-stopped lines, but he depends on enjambed, or run-on lines, especially in the last part of the sestet. If there is a turn, it comes between the octave and the sestet, but there may be no turn at all, since the poem moves intensely forward, developing a single idea.

Many of Milton's sonnets treated personal matters, such as his blindness, his memory of his dead wife, and his anxiety about his own talent. Other sonnets examine public matters, such as his concern for the behavior of parliament, his admiration of friends, and his anger at atrocities against innocent citizens. The sonnet below concerns the murder of a Protestant religious group called the Waldensians who lived peacefully in Italian Piedmont until 1655, when Catholic Piedmontese troops with the church's approval attacked them. Milton, working for the Protestant government of England at the time, was outraged.

JOHN MILTON   (1608–1672)

On the Late Massacre in Piedmont _____ *1655*

Avenge, O Lord, thy slaughtered Saints, whose bones
   Lie scattered on the Alpine mountains cold,
   Ev'n them who kept thy truth so pure of old
   When all our Fathers worshipped Stocks and Stones,
Forget not: in thy book record their groans   5
   Who were thy Sheep and in their ancient Fold
   Slain by the bloody *Piemontese* that rolled
   Mother with Infant down the Rocks. Their moans
The Vales redoubled to the Hills, and they
   To Heav'n. Their martyred blood and ashes sow   10
   O'er all th' Italian fields where still doth sway
The triple Tyrant:° that from these may grow
   A hundredfold, who having learnt thy way
   Early may fly the Babylonian woe.°

12 *triple Tyrant:* a reference to the triple tiara of the Pope.   14 *Babylonian woe:* the Roman
Catholic church.

QUESTIONS FOR CLOSE READING

1. Are the breaks in rhythm primarily made with end-stopped lines or with caesuras?
    How many can you identify?
2. The quatrains and tercets are clearly marked by indentation. Are they also units
    of thought in the poem? What is the function of the indentation?
3. To whom is the poem addressed? Why?
4. How does the rhythmic movement of the lines help intensify Milton's emotional
    expression?
5. To what extent do you see the form of a sonnet as compressing and intensifying
    emotion?

    Many modern poets have also used the sonnet. The following poem com-
bines an analysis of the resources of the sonnet with the sonnet itself.

PETER MEINKE   (b. 1932)

The Poet, Trying to Surprise God _____ *1981*

The poet, trying to surprise his God
composed new forms from secret harmonies,
tore from his fiery vision galaxies
of unrelated shapes, both even & odd.
But God just smiled, and gave His know-all nod   5
saying, "There's no surprising One who sees

the acorn, root, and branch of centuries;
I swallow all things up, like Aaron's rod.°

So hold this thought beneath your poet-bonnet:
no matter how free-seeming flows your sample   10
God is by definition the Unsurprised."
"Then I'll return," the poet sighed, "to sonnets
of which this is a rather pale example."

"Is that right?" said God. "I hadn't realized. . . ."

8 *Aaron's rod:* Aaron was Moses's older brother. His rod, a symbol of authority, alone among the rods
of other priests, bloomed.

QUESTIONS FOR CLOSE READING

1. What does Meinke mean in line 2 by "secret harmonies"? What is secret about them?
2. What makes this poem different from the ones discussed earlier?
3. Is this an Italian or an English sonnet?
4. Is this sonnet a "pale example"?
5. What is surprising about it?

The Ballad

The general widespread use of the term *ballad* implies a song, usually sung slowly and lyrically. In poetry a **ballad** is a form sometimes sung or recited to a guitar or lute. Traditionally, the ballad told a story, often one filled with love, promises, war, and disappointment. Ballads often depend on the repetition of key lines for their effect. Some examples in the album include Robert Creeley's "Ballad of the Despairing Husband" (p. 647) which depends on couplet rhyme: "Oh wife, oh wife—I tell you true, / I never loved no one but you." It also uses colloquial language and careful repetition, as in the repeated phrases "Oh lovely lady" and "Oh loveliest of ladies." Langston Hughes's "Ballad of the Land-lord" tells a story familiar to some who live in the city:

Landlord, landlord
My roof has sprung a leak.
Don't you 'member I told you about it
Way last week?

Hughes wrote many ballads concerning the lives of African-Americans in the 1930s and 1940s. His sensitivity to music and his ear for local dialect and conversational language make his ballads among the most touching of modern examples.

The Ode

The **ode,** a long irregular poem, was originally meant to be a form of sublime poetic utterance inspired by the gods: lyric in nature and exalted in tone. The text of *Oedipus Rex* shows that the ode in ancient Greek drama depended on strophe, antistrophe, and epode. The **strophe** was chanted walking to the right, the **antistrophe** while walking to the left, and the **epode** while standing still in the center. Similarly, odes are usually predicated on oppositions; the subject of one stanza (the antistrophe) may sometimes re-evaluate the subject of the previous stanza (the strophe). The end of the ode (epode) usually attempts to resolve the tensions raised by the body of the poem.

The ode exists in two basic forms. The first, the **Horatian ode,** is usually composed of two or more long stanzas of the same or similar form; its rhyme pattern and meter vary, although most in English rely on rhyming couplets. It tends to be meditative and philosophical. The second, the **Pindaric ode,** is somewhat more flamboyant in that its stanza patterns are highly imaginative and singular. Pindaric odes use rhyme but rarely rely on couplets, and they often mix very short and very long lines in the same stanza.

Some of these forms are also maintained in modern odes. The following modern ode is Horatian (John Keats's "Ode to a Nightingale" [p. 538] is Pindaric). The author does a kind of literary history emphasizing the figures she feels shaped English and American literary modernism.

ANNE STEVENSON   (b. 1933)

*The Fiction-Makers*_____ *1982*

We were the wrecked elect,
the ruined few. Youth,
youth, the Café Iruña
and the bullfight set,
looped on Lepanto brandy   5
but talking "truth"—
Hem,° the 4 A.M. wisecrack,
the hard way in,
that story we were all at the end of
and couldn't begin—   10
we thought we were living now,
but we were living then.

Sanctified Pound,° a knot
of nerves in his fist,
squeezing the Goddamn iamb   15
out of our verse,
making it new in his
archaeological plot—
to maintain "the sublime"

7 *Hem:* Ernest Hemingway (1899–1961), American novelist of the "Lost Generation"; the Café Iruña was one of his literary hangouts.   13 *Pound:* Ezra Pound (1885–1972), American poet: the *Pisan Cantos* were written while he was in an American military prison after World War II.

in the factive?° Couldn't be done.   20
Something went wrong
with "new" in the Pisan pen.
He thought he was making now,
but he was making then.

Virginia, Vanessa,°   25
a teapot, a Fitzroy° fuss,
"Semen?" asks Lytton,
eyeing a smudge on a dress.
How to educate England
and keep a correct address   30
on the path to the river through
Auschwitz? Belsen?
Auden and Isherwood°
stalking glad boys in Berlin—
they thought they were suffering now,   35
but they were suffering then.

Out of pink-cheeked Cwmdonkin,
Dylan° with his Soho grin.
Planted in the fiercest of flames,
gold ash on a stem.   40
When Henry jumped out of his joke,
Mr. Bones sat in.
Even you, with your breakable heart
in your ruined skin,
those poems all written   45
that have to be you, dear friend,
you guessed you were dying now,
but you were dying then.

Here is a table with glasses,
ribbed cages tipped back,   50
or turned on a hinge to each other
to talk, to talk,
mouths that are drinking or smiling
or quoting some book,
or laughing out laughter as candletongues   55
lick at the dark—
so bright in this fiction
forever becoming its end,
we think we are laughing now,
but we are laughing then.   60

20 *factive:* concerned with making.   25 *Virginia, Vanessa:* Virginia Woolf (1882–1941), English novelist; her sister Vanessa Bell, English painter; and Lytton Strachey (1880–1932), English historian
(see line 27); all were members of the Bloomsbury Group, which flourished in London in the
1930s.   26 *Fitzroy:* reference to controversial "Fitzroy St. Nude," painting by Sir Matthew
Smith (1879–1959).   33 *Auden, Isherwood:* W. H. Auden (1970–1973), poet, and Christopher
Isherwood (1904–1980), novelist, were homosexual modernists.   38 *Dylan:* Dylan Thomas
(1914–1953), Welsh poet from Cwmdonkin, drank regularly in Soho's White Horse Tavern.

Stevenson's modern interpretation of the ode is elevated, meditative, and lyric. Each stanza treats an aspect of her theme: the modern fiction-makers who dominated her literary world. The poem does not rhyme, but every stanza ends with variations on the same refrain: "we think we are laughing now, / but we are laughing then." The poem does not maintain an exact meter, but individual lines can be scanned and are metrical. The stanzas all have twelve lines, some short, some long. Each stanza treats an aspect of modernist literature, meditating on its scope and success.

The Epitaph

Except in the sense that it usually needs to be short enough to appear on a tombstone or plaque, the epitaph is not so much a form of poetry as a type of poem. The epitaph can take many forms, although it usually refers specifically to the person memorialized and sometimes it mentions details of his or her death. One famous epitaph, obviously designed for a memorial stone is: "O rare Ben Jonson." There may be a pun on the Latin verb *orare*, to pray for, in which case this is an elegant line.

Some modern epitaphs commemorate the dead, as in W. H. Auden's "In Memory of W. B. Yeats" (p. 622), which uses a famous verse form associated with Yeats. Sharon Olds's "The Death of Marilyn Monroe" not only memorializes the death of the film star but examines the effect her death had on the men who discovered her body. In part because Marilyn Monroe was famous because of the beauty of her body, the poem takes on a dark, almost ironic quality.

SHARON OLDS   (b. 1942)

The Death of Marilyn Monroe _____ *c. 1983*

The ambulance men touched her cold
body, lifted it, heavy as iron,
onto the stretcher, tried to close the
mouth, closed the eyes, tied the
arms to the sides, moved a caught   5
strand of hair, as if it mattered,
saw the shape of her breasts, flattened by
gravity, under the sheet,
carried her, as if it were she,
down the steps.   10

These men were never the same. They went out
afterwards, as they always did,
for a drink or two, but they could not meet
each other's eyes.
               Their lives took
a turn—one had nightmares, strange   15

pains, impotence, depression. One did not
like his work, his wife looked
different, his kids. Even death
seemed different to him—a place where she
would be waiting,   20

and one found himself standing at night
in the doorway to a room of sleep, listening to a
woman breathing, just an ordinary
woman
breathing.   25

Some other important epitaphs in this collection are Anne Bradstreet's "In Memory of My Dear Grandchild" (p. 634), and Wing Tek Lum's "At a Chinaman's Grave" (p. 726). The **elegy** is a related type of poem. It, too, has no specific form but is identifiable by its subject matter. Originally, the elegy was written in a specific Greek meter, but in English the elegy is simply a thoughtful, meditative poem, often on the subject of death, as in the case of Theodore Roethke's "Elegy for Jane" (p.758), which meditates on the death of one of the poet's students. Thomas Gray's "Elegy in a Country Churchyard" (p. 688) is another famous example.

The Verse Epistle

An epistle is a letter, and therefore a **verse epistle** is a letter in the form of a poem, often rhymed, sometimes even dated, as is conventional with most letters. The verse epistle is an ancient kind of poem, often written as if it were meant to be mailed, but not in fact always mailed. Often, the verse epistle to a distant loved one, as in the case of Anne Finch's "A Letter to Daphnis, April 2, 1685," urges an early return.

ANNE FINCH   (1661–1720)

A Letter to Daphnis,° April 2, 1685 _____ *1864; 1903*

This to the crown and blessing of my life,
The much loved husband of a happy wife,
To him whose constant passion found the art
To win a stubborn and ungrateful heart;
And to the world by tenderest proof discovers   5
They err, who say that husbands can't be lovers.
With such return of passion, as is due,
Daphnis I love, Daphnis my thoughts pursue,
Daphnis, my hopes, my joys, are bounded all in you:
Even I, for Daphnis, and my promise sake,   10

Daphnis: Poetic name for Finch's husband, Heneage Finch.

What I in women censure,° undertake.
But this from love, not vanity, proceeds;
You know who writes; and I who 'tis that reads.
Judge not my passion by my want of skill,
Many love well, though they express it ill;   15
And I your censure could with pleasure bear,
Would you but soon return, and speak it here.

11 *censure:* disapprove.

QUESTIONS FOR CLOSE READING

1. Do you see any evidence that Anne Finch may be ironic in this poem? If you do,
    would you think the poem would have been sent to her husband?
2. What do you think the line "They err, who say that husbands can't be lovers" tells
    us about the state of marriage in late-seventeenth-century England?
3. Why might Anne Finch censure women who write poetry? How does she excuse
    her own efforts at poetry?
4. What does she request of her husband? Why do you think she calls him "Daphnis"?
    Look up the story of Daphnis and Chloe in a classical dictionary or encyclopedia.

The Villanelle

The **villanelle** is not a common fixed form, but it is one of the most surprising. Originally French, a language rich in rhymes, the villanelle is extremely
difficult in English. The following poem, however, appears to be effortless.

DYLAN THOMAS   (1914–1953)

Do Not Go Gentle into That Good Night _____ *1951, 1952*

Do not go gentle into that good night,
Old age should burn and rave at close of day;
Rage, rage against the dying of the light.

Though wise men at their end know dark is right,
Because their words had forked no lightning they   5
Do not go gentle into that good night.

Good men, the last wave by, crying how bright
Their frail deeds might have danced in a green bay,
Rage, rage against the dying of the light.

Wild men who caught and sang the sun in flight,   10
And learn, too late, they grieved it on its way,
Do not go gentle into that good night.

Grave men, near death, who see with blinding sight
Blind eyes could blaze like meteors and be gay,
Rage, rage against the dying of the light.   15

And you, my father, there on the sad height,
Curse, bless, me now with your fierce tears, I pray.
Do not go gentle into that good night.
Rage, rage against the dying of the light.

Villanelles have six stanzas of iambic pentameter: five with three lines,
and the last with four lines. There are only two rhymes, in this case, *night* and
day. Thomas chose those purposely for their opposition. The first line and the
third line of the first stanza repeat throughout the poem: stanza 2 ends with line
1; stanza 3 ends with line 3; stanza 4 ends with line 1; stanza 5 ends with line 3;
stanza 6 ends with lines 1 and 3.

Any villanelle is a major achievement, but a poem such as Dylan Thomas's
is especially remarkable. Because it is so moving, many readers are totally unaware that it is so tightly patterned. Its emotional qualities and sincerity seem
evident in every line, demonstrating Thomas's outstanding technical abilities.
He often chose extremely demanding forms because they helped him in his
composition.

The Sestina

One of the most difficult of verse forms, the **sestina** was invented in French
poetry, although it is not normally a rhymed form. Instead of rhyme, the poet
depends on the repetition of the last word of each six lines. The sestina uses six
six-line stanzas followed by a final stanza of three lines. The end words of each
line repeat themselves 1-2-3-4-5-6 in stanza 1 and 6-1-5-2-4-3 in stanza 2, then
3-6-4-1-2-5 in stanza 3, and so on. The three-line final stanza includes all the six
end words but uses 5-3-1 as its own end words. Candace Warne handles this difficult form brilliantly in "Blackbird Sestina."

CANDACE WARNE (b. 1945)

Blackbird Sestina _____

Below me on the road, the blackbirds
have awaited my descent; the town
is darkened by them, starting like a wind
up the hill to meet me, shaking trees
like dry bones to conjure a new snow.   5
My road will be trackless, going down.

No one will have seen me going down;
there is only myself, and blackbirds
are the only movement except the snow
falling, like white hair, past to the town.   10
Coming up through the rattling trees,
I hear the quick ascension of a wind.

Some vague expectation of this wind
has veiled my hesitation to go down,
or perhaps it is the hope these trees   15
will hide me from the crying of blackbirds.
They have left the unfamiliar town
to look for me in their whirling snow.

There is an indifference in this snow;
it moves only in accord with wind,   20
confusing my footsteps toward town,
closing in behind as I move down,
showing my movements to the blackbirds
that are coming closer through the trees.

I have lost sight of all but the trees   25
nearest me; all else is hid by snow.
Still, I hear the approach of blackbirds
and their confusing talk in the wind
sounds practically human, blowing down
toward me. I can not find the town.   30

It is too dark to look for the town.
Dark sleep falls from the gathering trees.
Cold has numbed to warmth; my falling down
cannot be undone; the weight of snow
blankets me from the rasping of wind,   35
muffling the sound of the blackbirds.

The lost town is singing in the snow;
The trees run away in the mad wind.
The stars fall down to become blackbirds.

The Prose Poem

The **prose poem** offers readers of poetry a puzzle. Generally, a prose poem is defined as a piece of writing that is shaped like prose—without stanzas, regular or irregular line lengths, rhyme, or meter. In practice the prose poem is visually prose. Because even ordinary prose usually has a cadence and rhythm of its own, one cannot determine the prose poem on the basis of a lack of meter. Therefore, the visual form dictates what we call a poem such as Carolyn Forché's "The Colonel."

CAROLYN FORCHÉ   (b. 1950)

The Colonel _____ *1978*

What you have heard is true. I was in his house. His wife carried
a tray of coffee and sugar. His daughter filed her nails, his son went

out for the night. There were daily papers, pet dogs, a pistol on the
cushion beside him. The moon swung bare on its black cord over
the house. On the television was a cop show. It was in English.   5
Broken bottles were embedded in the walls around the house to
scoop the kneecaps from a man's legs or cut his hands to lace. On
the windows there were gratings like those in liquor stores. We had
dinner, rack of lamb, good wine, a gold bell was on the table for
calling the maid. The maid brought green mangoes, salt, a type of   10
bread. I was asked how I enjoyed the country. There was a brief
commercial in Spanish. His wife took everything away. There was
some talk then of how difficult it had become to govern. The parrot
said hello on the terrace. The colonel told it to shut up, and pushed
himself from the table. My friend said to me with his eyes: say   15
nothing. The colonel returned with a sack used to bring groceries
home. He spilled many human ears on the table. They were like
dried peach halves. There is no other way to say this. He took one
of them in his hands, shook it in our faces, dropped it into a water
glass. It came alive there. I am tired of fooling around he said. As   20
for the rights of anyone, tell your people they can go fuck themselves.
He swept the ears to the floor with his arm and held the last
of his wine in the air. Something for your poetry, no? he said. Some
of the ears on the floor caught this scrap of his voice. Some of the
ears on the floor were pressed to the ground.   25

QUESTIONS FOR CRITICAL READING

1. Does the form of the poem convince you that it is both prose and poetry? Do you feel it is possible that "The Colonel" is both prose and poetry?
2. What qualities of this poem alarm you? What do you make of the politeness of the colonel and his wife?
3. Can you establish this as a political poem? How? Is the prose form appropriate to the kind of politics implied in the poem?
4. Where do you think the colonel collected the ears he shows the poet? In what nation, or what part of the world, does the colonel do his collecting?
5. Why would this poem qualify as ironic?

Some other prose poems include Joy Harjo's "Santa Fe" and "Nine Lives" (pp. 693–694). These poems distinguish themselves slightly from Carolyn Forché's in that they are both left- and right-justified. "The Colonel" is only left-justified, which might leave the reader the option of deciding it is not a prose poem at all, just an irregular-line poem. Because the prose poem is an essentially late-nineteenth-century invention, and because it is very rarely employed, we can only with difficulty conclude that it is a definitive form. Yet the effect on the reader of the relaxation of line and rhyme constraints is such that poets will probably continue to experiment in this manner, looking for opportunities to achieve new effects.

Free Verse

Just as the prose poem is difficult to define, **free verse** often defies definition. Language always places restrictions on the poet or prose writer, so it is unlikely that any verse is absolutely free. However, what we think of as free verse developed in the nineteenth century in reaction to the overstrict requirements of certain forms, such as the sonnet, the villanelle, the sestina, and various couplet and quatrain forms. The demands of blank verse, which ignored rhyme but maintained a ten-syllable iambic meter, also became constraining for some poets. Free verse essentially tries to avoid regular meter, regular rhythm, regular line length, and regular rhyme. Perhaps one of the best examples is in the work of Walt Whitman (pp. 796–802). The beginning of "Song of Myself" announced a break with formal traditions of the past:

I celebrate myself, and sing myself,
And what I assume you shall assume,
For every atom belonging to me as good belongs to you.

I loaf and invite my soul,
I lean and loaf at my ease observing a spear of summer grass.   5

Yet you can see that even in this small sample, certain qualities develop that hold these words and lines together as recognizable poetry. The repetition of words and phrases imparts the same kind of inevitability as one expects from rhyme and meter. When you read his poetry later in the following album, ask yourself how free his verse really is. The same question can be asked of other poets whose work appears to be free, such as Marcia Southwick's "Owning a Dead Man" (p. 776), W. S. Merwin's "For a Coming Extinction" (p. 734), or Cathy Song's "The Youngest Daughter" (p. 775).

Part of our delight in poetry is being surprised. Peter Meinke reminds us that form can be surprising. Dylan Thomas and Candace Warne remind us that tight formal demands do not rob a poem of its importance or significance. To some extent, we admire the poet who can employ a dazzling technique: after all, poetry, like other literature, demands technique or else it fails. But we are also suspicious of writers whose only virtue is a flashy technique. Poets who use free verse or the appearance of prose feel the same way. Ultimately, what we admire most is the combination of serious motives and competent formal technique.

11

STYLE AND THEME

The use of various poetic elements combined with formal opportunities is a key part of the style of any poet. However, the poet's style is also often connected directly to the themes and ideas that the poet employs. All poems are, after all, about something. Occasionally they are about language itself; sometimes they are about poetry; sometimes they are about political issues; sometimes they are about the human condition in general. When a poet such as E. E. Cummings composes a complex structure such as "l(a" (p. 485), he shows us that a poem can focus on a single theme, loneliness, and come close to "performing" the underlying idea of loneliness. When we interpret a poem we look at both style and theme in an effort to see them as one.

When we examine poems for their ideas we need not always be judgmental. For example, the main idea of Cummings's poem "l(a" is definitely loneliness. In that sense the theme is an element of the poem. But whether the poem implies that loneliness is good, bad, inevitable, avoidable, or even neutral is a question of interpretation. Some poems naturally demand more interpretation than others, but all poems can stand up under close scrutiny. Readers may evaluate themes or ideas in the same fashion they evaluate metaphors, rhyme patterns, imagery, or any other element of a poem.

The following poem is from a tradition called *carpe diem*, which means "seize the day." Carpe Diem poems remind us that we are not going to live forever, and they exhort us to live now because tomorrow we may die. Such poems have been with us from the most ancient times.

ROBERT HERRICK   (1591–1674)

To the Virgins, to Make Much of Time _____ *1648*

Gather ye rosebuds while ye may,
  Old time is still a-flying;
And this same flower that smiles today
  Tomorrow will be dying.

The glorious lamp of heaven, the sun,   5
  The higher he's a-getting;
The sooner will his race be run,
  And nearer he's to setting.

That age is best which is the first,
  When youth and blood are warmer;   10
But being spent, the worse and worst
  Times still succeed the former.

Then be not coy, but use your time;
  And while ye may, go marry:
For, having lost but once your prime,   15
  You may for ever tarry.

Like a sonnet, this poem is segmented: each stanza treats an issue relative
to the overall idea of seizing the day, and all these stanzas have a cumulative
effect. The main idea is that we are like flowers who bloom in our youth for only
a short time, then fade quickly; therefore, we should make the most of our
youth and get married. The first stanza uses flowers in two ways. First, they are
the rewards our youth can bring us—"Gather ye rosebuds." Second, the smiling, dying flower is metaphorically ourselves. The second stanza tells us that
the sun rises and sets, and like Shakespeare in his Sonnet 73 (p. 475), Herrick
uses the day as a metaphor for our entire life. Each stanza presents us with evidence that we can examine from nature around us, and we conclude that we,
like all natural things, will age and die. The third stanza argues that old age is
not much good, whereas youth is not only first but "best." The last stanza urges
the reader not to hold back ("be not coy") but "go marry." If you miss your
chance, "You may for ever tarry."

The historical circumstances of the poem need to be taken into account
primarily because all the life expectancy in the seventeenth century was not
comparable to ours. And, since medical science was primitive and based on erroneous theories, old age would have been painful and tormented by a wide
variety of sicknesses and agonies. Consequently, it is not difficult to see why Herrick would have urged the young to take advantage of their youth, even to the
point of rushing things. The idea that one should seize the day is clearly expressed in the form of an argument, and one that has been convincing enough
to make this poem famous. Andrew Marvell and many others have used the

same idea, and its appeal is not likely to diminish. Of course, any poem that presents its ideas in the form of an argument is susceptible to counter-argument, as when Sir Walter Ralegh's "The Nymph's Reply to the Shepherd" (p.752) contradicts Christopher Marlowe's "The Passionate Shepherd to His Love" (p. 732).

Parody is a mimic of another poem implying a reinterpretation of one poet's work by another poet. Thus all parodies use the same form as the poem they parody, with perhaps some variations. Often the purpose is to have fun; sometimes it is to mock; sometimes it is to show respect. Parodies critique both a poem's form and its ideas. Several parodies follow in the album of poems. Marilyn Nelson Waniek shows respect both to Emily Dickinson and E. E. Cummings in her "Emily Dickinson's Defunct" (p. 793), which parodies Cummings's "Buffalo Bill's Defunct" (p. 648). It has often been said that only good poems can be successfully parodied, so in a way a parody is a form of praise.

The next poem, written in 1867, explores quite different ideas, which modern readers have seen as prophetic of the coming wars on the European continent in 1914 and 1939. Arnold believed that the modern world had abandoned important values of religious faith and that the results would be terrifying.

MATTHEW ARNOLD (1822–1888)

Dover Beach _____ *1867*

The sea is calm to-night.
The tide is full, the moon lies fair
Upon the straits;—on the French coast the light
Gleams and is gone; the cliffs of England stand,
Glimmering and vast, out in the tranquil bay.   5
Come to the window, sweet is the night-air!

Only, from the long line of spray
Where the sea meets the moon-blanch'd land,
Listen! you hear the grating roar
Of pebbles which the waves draw back, and fling,   10
At their return, up the high strand,
Begin, and cease, and then again begin,
With tremulous cadence slow, and bring
The eternal note of sadness in.

Sophocles long ago   15
Heard it on the Aegean, and it brought
Into his mind the turbid ebb and flow
Of human misery; we
Find also in the sound a thought,
Hearing it by this distant northern sea.   20

The Sea of Faith
Was once, too, at the full, and round earth's shore
Lay like the folds of a bright girdle furl'd.
But now I only hear
Its melancholy, long, withdrawing roar, 25
Retreating, to the breath
Of the night-wind, down the vast edges drear
And naked shingles° of the world.

Ah, love, let us be true
To one another! for the world, which seems 30
To lie before us like a land of dreams,
So various, so beautiful, so new,
Hath really neither joy, nor love, nor light,
Nor certitude, nor peace, nor help for pain;
And we are here as on a darkling plain 35
Swept with the confused alarms of struggle and flight,
Where ignorant armies clash by night.

28 *shingles:* pebbly beaches.

    The reader becomes slowly aware that the narrator of the poem is speaking to his beloved while looking out from Dover, where the English Channel, only twenty miles wide, is close enough to see lights in French towns. The narrator hears the sounds of the waves drawing the pebbles back along the beach, and the steadiness of the sea reminds him of the normal rhythms of change, the ebb and flow of history, as Sophocles knew it in his play *Antigone,* when its memory "brought / Into his mind the turbid ebb and flow / Of human misery." The rhythm of ebb and flow pertains to "The Sea of Faith" as well, and Arnold's point is that faith is ebbing: "now I only hear / Its melancholy, long, withdrawing roar." He sees the new age as having "neither joy, nor love, nor light, / Nor certitude, nor peace, nor help for pain." In consequence, he implores himself and his beloved to "be true / To one another!" It is their only assurance in a world in which armies struggle relentlessly for command of the world. These armies are metaphors for forces that command individuals' belief in political, economic, or religious systems. The image of Arnold and his beloved on a "darkling plain" has had special power in part because so many decisive battles of history, since ancient times, have been fought on plains.

    In some poems an ironic tone cloaks a serious theme, although some readers might miss the point if they remain unaware of the irony. One famous poem that depends on irony for its effect is Arthur Hugh Clough's (1819–1861) "The Latest Decalogue." As you read it, keep in mind that it is an ironic parody of the Ten Commandments. How difficult is it to know what Clough really believes in this poem? What is the main theme?

ARTHUR HUGH CLOUGH   (1819–1861)

The Latest Decalogue° _____ *1862*

Thou shalt have one God only; who
Would be at the expense of two?
No graven images may be
Worshipped, except the currency.
Swear not at all; for, for the curse   5
Thine enemy is none the worse.
At church on Sunday to attend
Will serve to keep the world they friend.
Honor they parents; that is, all
From whom advancement may befall.   10
Thou shalt not kill; but need'st not strive
Officiously to keep alive
Do not adultery commit;
Advantage rarely comes of it.
Thou shalt not steal; an empty feat,   15
When it's so lucrative to cheat.
Bear not false witness; let the lie
Have time on its own wings to fly.
Thou shalt not covet, but tradition
Approves all forms of competition.   20

Decalogue: the Ten Commandments.

Clough lived in a period in which religion was foremost in the minds of those close to him in society. The Victorian age appeared to maintain a high moral standard and preached the Ten Commandments even when those in society did not live up to them. Clough, in providing his age with a new Decalogue (Ten Commandments), chides them with his irony.

Ishmael Reed, an African-American poet, sometimes writes polemical, idea-laden poems and often finds surprising connections between popular culture and the most serious concerns of civilization. The main idea behind the poem that follows is a theory of literary criticism: that the reader and the poem are not totally separate.

ISHMAEL REED   (b. 1938)

Beware : Do Not Read This Poem _____ *1968*

tonite, thriller was
abt an ol woman, so vain she

surrounded herself w/
    many mirrors

it got so bad that finally she   5
locked herself indoors & her
whole life became the
    mirrors

one day the villagers broke
into her house , but she was too   10
swift for them . she disappeared
    into a mirror
each tenant who bought the house
after that , lost a loved one to
    the ol woman in the mirror :   15
    first a little girl
    then a young woman
    then   the   young   woman/s   husband

the hunger of this poem is legendary
it has taken in many victims   20
back off from this poem
it has drawn in yr feet
back off from this poem
it has drawn in yr legs

back off from this poem   25
it is a greedy mirror
you are into this poem   .   from
    the waist down
nobody can hear you can they ?
this poem has had you up to here   30
    belch
this poem aint got no manners
you cant call out frm this poem
relax now & go w/ this poem

move & roll on to this poem   35
do not resist this poem
this poem has yr eyes
this poem has his head
this poem has his arms
this poem has his fingers   40
this poem has his fingertips

this poem is the reader & the
reader this poem

    Marilyn Chin uses a much less formal style in "How I Got That Name." Her conversational approach puts the reader at ease and makes her poem involving and immediate. But in the process of telling us how she got her name, she also introduces an interesting analysis of what she calls "the model minority," the general prejudices of our society toward Asian people.

MARILYN CHIN   (b. 1955)

How I Got That Name _____ *1990*

An essay on assimilation—
or: Den Xiao Ping,° are we not your children?

I am Marilyn Mei Ling Chin.
Oh, how I love the resoluteness
of that first person singular
followed by that stalwart indicative
of "be," without the uncertain i-n-g   5
of "becoming." Of course,
the name had been changed
somewhere between Angel Island and the sea,
when my father the paperson
in the late 1950s   10
obsessed with some bombshell blonde
transliterated "Mei Ling" to "Marilyn."
And nobody dared question
his initial impulse—for we all know
lust drove men to greatness,   15
not goodness, not decency,
And there I was, a wayward pink baby,
named after some tragic
white woman, swollen with gin and Nembutal.°
My mother couldn't pronounce the "r."   20
She dubbed me "Numba one female offshoot"
for brevity: henceforth, she will live and die
in sublime ignorance, flanked
by loving children and the "kitchen deity."
While my father dithers,   25
a tomcat in Hong Kong trash—
a gambler, a petty thug,
who bought a chain of chopsuey joints
in Piss River, Oregon
with bootlegged Gucci cash.   30
Nobody dared question his integrity given
his nice, devout daughters
and his bright industrious sons.
As if filial piety were the standard
with which all earthly men were measured.   35

Deng Xiao Ping (b. 1904): Chinese Communist leader; resigned 1987.   19 *gin and Nembutal:* reference to Marilyn Monroe's supposed dependency on drugs and alcohol.

Oh, how trustworthy our daughters,
how thrifty our sons!
How we've managed to fool the experts
in education, statistics and demography—
We're not very creative but not adverse to rote-learning.   40
Indeed, you can *use* us.
But the "Model Minority" is a tease.
We know you are watching now,
so we refuse to give you any!
Oh, bamboo shoots, bamboo shoots!   45
The further west we go, we'll hit east;
The deeper down we dig, we'll find China.
History has turned its stomach
on a black, polluted beach—
where life doesn't hinge   50
on that red, red wheelbarrow,
but on whether or not our new lover
in the final episode of "Santa Barbara"°
will lean over a scented candle
and call us a "bitch."   55
Oh god, where have we gone wrong?
We have no inner resources!

Then, one redolent spring morning
the Great Patriarch Chin
peered down from his kiosk in heaven   60
and saw that his descendants were ugly.
One had a squarish head and a nose without a bridge.
Another's profile—long and knobbed as a gourd.
A third, the sad, brutish one
may never, never marry.   65
And I, his least favorite—
"not quite boiled, not quite cooked,"
a plump pomfret simmering in my juices—
too listless to fight for my people's destiny.
"To kill without resistance is not slaughter"   70
says the proverb. So, I wait for imminent death.
The fact that this death is also metaphorical
is testament to my lethargy.

So, here lies Marilyn Mei Ling Chin,
married once, twice to so-and-so, a Lee and a Wong,   75
granddaughter of Jack "the patriarch" Chin
and the brooding Suilin Fong,
daughter of the virtuous Yuet Kuen Wong
and G. G. Chin the infamous,
sister of a dozen, cousin of a billion,   80
survived by everybody and forgotten by all.

53 *"Santa Barbara":* TV series about trendy Californians.

She was neither black nor white,
neither cherished nor vanquished,
just another squatter in her own bamboo grove
minding her poetry—   85
when one day heaven was unmerciful,
And a chasm opened where she then stood.
Like the jowls of a mighty white whale,
or the daws of a metaphysical Godzilla,
it swallowed her whole.   90
She did not flinch nor writhe,
nor fret about the afterlife,
but stayed! Solid as wood, happily
a little gnawed, tattered, mesmerized
by all that was lavished upon her   95
and all that was taken away!

for Gwendolyn Brooks

QUESTIONS FOR CRITICAL READING

1. What ironies are implied in the fact that Marilyn Chin was "named after some tragic / white woman, swollen with gin and Nembutal"?

2. The devotion of children to their parents is also treated ironically in this poem. Why does Chin use such an ironic style?

3. In what ways do the cultures of China and the United States intermingle in this poem? What point does Marilyn Chin make by examining both cultures as she does?

Like Marilyn Chin, Maya Angelou becomes slightly confrontational in "These Yet to Be United States." She constructs her poem in three stanzas, the first two of which end with rhetorical questions, "What more do you long for?", "Why do your children cry?" The last stanza make a careful observation about the youthful generation of 1990. Angelou uses rhyme in all three stanzas, achieving a more formal effect than Marilyn Chin. The point of the poem, in part, is to unsettle the reader by pointing out that the possession of such power as the United States wields does not necessarily produce happiness and satisfaction.

MAYA ANGELOU (b. 1928)

These Yet to Be United States _____ *1990*

Tremors of your network
cause kings to disappear.
Your open mouth in anger
makes nations bow in fear.
Your bombs can change the seasons,   5
obliterate the spring.

What more do you long for?
Why are you suffering?

You control the human lives
in Rome and Timbuktu.   10
Lonely nomads wandering
owe Telstar to you.
Seas shift at your bidding,
your mushrooms fill the sky.
Why are you unhappy?   15
Why do your children cry?

They kneel alone in terror
with dread in every glance.
Their nights are threatened daily
by a grim inheritance.   20
You dwell in whitened castles
with deep and poisoned moats
and cannot hear the curses
which fill your children's throats.

QUESTIONS FOR CRITICAL READING

1. Does Maya Angelou seem to include herself among the citizens of the "yet to be United States"? How does she seem to see herself?
2. What are the main themes in this poem? Do you agree with Angelou's treatment of these themes?
3. Do you feel the form of the poem makes an ironic comment on its themes?

ANONYMOUS

Sumer Is Icumen In _____ *Medieval*

Sumer is icumen in,°
Lhude° sing, cuccu!°
Groweth sed° and bloweth° med°
And springth the wude° nu.°
Sing, cuccu!   5

Awe° bleteth after lomb,
Lhouth° after calve° cu,°
Bulluc sterteth,° bucke ferteth.°
Murie° sing, cuccu!
Cuccu, cuccu,   10

---

1 *Sumer is icumen in:* Summer has come in.   2 *Lhude:* loudly.   *cuccu:* cuckoo.   3 *sed:* seed.
bloweth: blooms.   *med:* meadow.   4 *wude:* wood.   *nu:* now.   6 *Awe:* ewe.   7 *Lhouth:* lows.
calve: calif.   *cu:* cow.   8 *sterteth:* leaps up.   *ferteth:* farts.   9 *Murie:* merrily.

Wel singes thu, cuccu.
Ne swik° thu naver° nu!

Sing cuccu nu, sing cuccu!
Sing cuccu, sing cuccu nu!

12 *swik:* cease.   *naver:* never.

When Muriel Rukeyser wrote "From *Letter to the Front*" the world was at war and the Nazis were gassing Jews in huge numbers in Germany and Poland. The fate of Jews in Europe was sealed by Hitler and his legions. Rukeyser's poem is a sonnet, but a sonnet with a grave range of ideas. As you read, ask yourself how effective the form of this poem is considering its profound themes.

MURIEL RUKEYSER   (1913–1980)

From *Letter to the Front* _____ *1944*

To be a Jew in the twentieth century
Is to be offered a gift. If you refuse,
Wishing to be invisible, you choose
Death of the spirit, the stone insanity.
Accepting, take full life. Full agonies: 5
Your evening deep in labyrinthine blood
Of those who resist, fail, and resist; and God
Reduced to a hostage among hostages.

The gift is torment. Not alone the still
Torture, isolation; or torture of the flesh.   10
That may come also. But the accepting wish,
The whole and fertile spirit as guarantee
For every human freedom, suffering to be free,
Daring to live for the impossible.

The form of a poem contributes to its themes and in some cases conditions our responses to the thematic material in the poem. The style of a poem involves the use of the elements of a poem, and among those elements are the ideas and themes developed within the poem. All the poets in this book take seriously the responsibilities of finding a language and means by which to express their ideas and involve the reader in that expression.

12

~

THE ELEMENTS
WORKING TOGETHER

Close reading means seeing many elements of poetry at work in combination to produce a total effect. We learn about language, imagery, tone, rhythms and rhymes, metaphor and figurative language, symbol, form, and ideas so we can recognize them at work, but they work together. When you read a poem, any one of these elements may strike you first as very important, but only if you know what the elements of a poem are in the first place. Otherwise, your impression of a poem may be vague and imprecise: you may have the sense that you like or dislike a poem but have no concrete idea why, or even what it is that you like or dislike. Understanding what the components of a poem are helps you clarify your impressions and solidify your understanding.

Before beginning to work on the following poem, read it through and develop an overall impression; then consider the commentary that follows.

PATRICIA GOEDICKE   (b. 1931)

Wise Owl _____ *1968*

An old black bird on a strand of silk,
Sidewise my father walks the white ice
Between two fields of snow.
It is night. The air is like thin milk,
Icicles click in the wind like dice,   5
His steps are crabbed and slow,

But dapper as a magpie with a game leg
The old brave gambler bets his hide
Against the glittering street,

Though the moon is a bright metallic egg,   10
The cold snaps at his twisted side,
And the snow flusters his feet.

Beside him the languorous featherbed fields
Dovecall comfort to the old crow:
If he would stop he would stay,   15
Lose and find himself softly concealed,
Sunk in the mothering mounded snow,
Nested the easiest way

But no. Not for this wise owl. The road
May dwindle away to an icy thread   20
But the dream of a new design
Mumbles and broods in his hunched head
Better luck next time, the gambler's goad
That keeps him along the lifeline.

So like a sparrow on a telephone wire   25
He balances down the tightrope track,
The road that must narrow as the night
Must finally constrict the flow of fire,
Harden, pinch the heart, and crack:
Ahead is the home light.   30

Before discussing the poem in detail, we will take a brief look at some of
its most obvious elements.

LANGUAGE.   The language is conversational, easy. Goedicke speaks to a
friend (or to herself) with little or no artificiality. The key words all connect
with key images: "crabbed," "dapper," "languorous."

IMAGERY.   The setting of the poem is a snowy pathway at night, so much
of the description is relevant to snow, ice, the moon, and darkness.

TONE.   The tone of the poem is not easy to discern, since there seems to
be at once a reverence toward the subject, "my father," and at the same time a critical attitude, implied in all the references to him as a gambler who "bets his hide."

RHYTHM AND RHYME.   The rhythm of the poem is not unusual: the lines
are often end-stopped and sometimes run-on. They rarely break in the middle, except in line 4. The rhyme pattern is consistent: *abcabc*, and so on. However, the lines are not metrically regular; the accents fall freely and the lines vary
in length.

An old | black bird | on a strand | of silk,

Sidewise | my fa | ther walks | the white ice

METAPHOR AND FIGURATIVE LANGUAGE.   The poem makes many references to birds that seem to be metaphoric. Even the title is an important metaphor. The use of dice and the reference to gambling may be metaphoric.

SYMBOL.   The "wise owl" seems to be a symbolic reference to the poet's father. The track down which the father travels seems to be symbolic of the path of life, especially since it "must narrow as the night."

FORM.   The poem is strophic; its six-line stanzas are all alike in form. These stanzas have no special name; however, poems which use such strophic stanzas are often odes, as this one seems to be.

IDEAS.   The main idea seems to be connected with the risk taking involved in pursuing the path of life. Survival is a key issue in the poem.

Working with these elements together helps us get a full grasp of the poem. The regularity of the repeated stanza structure reassures us, since we know we can rely upon the repetition and completion of the pattern. The structure of the ode implies that the poem will meditate on a serious subject, one that can be reflected upon from two points of view. The poet's father is a "wise owl"—a phrase that most people would have amended to say, "wise old owl." The owl is a symbol of wisdom, so the title reinforces itself and also makes us aware of its relevance as a descriptor of the father. The father, cautious as he gets older, walks sidewise ("crabbed and slow") along the ice. He is like "An old black bird" (it is night) and the "Icicles click in the wind like dice" because the old father takes his chances. When he is called the "old brave gambler," the tone becomes one of respect and admiration because the father continues taking his chances in life even though the snow "flusters his feet."

The imagery associated with the path implies that the father has to struggle. Things are not easy for him, not even walking. The season has placed impediments before him, and some of them are dangerous. The poet's admiration continues in her descriptive imagery of him as "dapper as a magpie," implying that he is trim, self-aware (maybe even a bit vain), and roguish (the magpie is often characterized as thieving). In stanza 3 a new idea enters in the metaphoric comparison of the snow field: "featherbed fields / Dovecall comfort to the old crow." We remember that it is winter, and as in Shakespeare's sonnet, winter symbolizes the end of life. Here the poet points out that the end of life implies rest. Were her father to stop on his path, he could rest in the "mothering mounded snow." He could find peace and comfort. When we encounter this image, we realize the meaning of the first rhyme in the poem: *silk* with *milk*. Both imply softness, perhaps mothering, perhaps comfort. By the time we have read through the third stanza, we can see that the other early rhymes—*ice, dice* and *snow, slow*—reinforce the main ideas of the poem.

Once it is plain, in stanza 5, that the father will not stop, will not rest, we realize that the power of the rhythms of line 19 reinforce the entire poem: "But no. Not for this wise owl. The road / May dwindle" contains two caesuras with strong periods breaking the line twice. When the line continues, it runs on powerfully into the next line. Every successive line is a run-on line, implying the need to continue moving, to keep on the "road" that has become a "lifeline." The stanza enacts the idea of continuous motion.

The last stanza recognizes, however, that the journey must someday be over. "The road . . . must narrow as the night," but when it does, what is "Ahead is the home light." The poet thus prepares for the inevitable death of her father, but only after seeing him as persisting in his struggle, taking his chances, refusing to give up. The bird of the last stanza is a sparrow, perhaps alluding to Hamlet's "There is special providence in the fall of a sparrow" (V.II.192–93), by which he means that God takes notice even of the slightest of his creatures when they die. Like Hamlet, Goedicke's narrator is prepared for death because she has observed life so closely. By watching her father, she has become a wise owl herself.

John Keats, famous for his great odes, used a poetic strategy that may have inspired Patricia Goedicke. His "Ode on a Grecian Urn" also has five strophic stanzas. His rhyme scheme is *ababcdedce,* and his lines follow a regular meter: iambic pentameter. Like Goedicke, Keats focuses entirely on something outside himself. Goedicke focuses on her father making his way through difficult snowy paths; Keats focuses on a genuine Grecian urn that still exists in the British Museum. When he addresses the urn (Goedicke never addresses her father), he points to the scenes that are on its surface with the understanding that they represent a life that is long gone, the life of ancient Greece. The scenes are equivalent to a language; they function in the same way that a letter from ancient times would function. Keats turns the urn about and regards its different scenes, calling the urn a "sylvan historian" because it tells the history of rural (sylvan) life.

JOHN KEATS (1795–1821)

Ode on a Grecian Urn ——————————————————————— *1819*

                    I
Thou° still unravished bride of quietness,
Thou foster-child of silence and slow time,
Sylvan historian, who canst thus express
A flowery tale more sweetly than our rhyme:
What leaf-fringed legend haunts about thy shape   5
Of deities or mortals, or of both,
In Tempe or the dales of Arcady?
What men or gods are these? What maidens loth?°
What mad pursuit? What struggle to escape?
What pipes and timbrels? What wild ecstasy?   10

———————————————
1 *Thou:* the urn itself.   8 *loth:* reluctant.

II

Heard melodies are sweet, but those unheard
Are sweeter;° therefore, ye soft pipes, play on;
Not to the sensual ear, but, more endeared,
Pipe to the spirit ditties of no tone:
Fair youth, beneath the trees, thou canst not leave   15
Thy song, nor ever can those trees be bare;
Bold lover, never, never canst thou kiss,
Though winning near the goal—yet, do not grieve;
She cannot fade, though thou hast not thy bliss,
Forever wilt thou love, and she be fair!   20

III

Ah, happy, happy boughs! that cannot shed
Your leaves, nor ever bid the spring adieu;
And, happy melodist, unwearied,
Forever piping songs forever new;
More happy love! more happy, happy love!   25
Forever warm and still to be enjoyed,
Forever panting, and forever young;
All breathing human passion far above,
That leaves a heart high-sorrowful and cloyed,
A burning forehead, and a parching tongue.   30

IV

Who are these coming to the sacrifice?
To what green altar, O mysterious priest,
Lead'st thou that heifer lowing at the skies,
And all her silken flanks with garlands drest?
What little town by river or sea shore,   35
Or mountain-built with peaceful citadel,
Is emptied of this folk, this pious morn?
And, little town, thy streets forevermore
Will silent be; and not a soul to tell
Why thou art desolate, can e'er return.   40

V

O Attic° shape! Fair attitude! with brede°
Of marble men and maidens overwrought,
With forest branches and the trodden weed;
Thou, silent form, dost tease us out of thought
As doth eternity: Cold Pastoral!   45
When old age shall this generation waste,
Thou shalt remain, in midst of other woe

11–12 *Heard . . . sweeter:* Platonic theory held that the inaudible "music of the spheres" was the
most beautiful sound in the universe.   41 *Attic:* referring to Athens.   *brede:* woven pattern.

Than ours, a friend to man, to whom thou say'st,
"Beauty is truth, truth beauty,"—that is all
Ye know on earth, and all ye need to know.°   50

49–50 "Beauty . . . know: An early edition closed the quotation after "know," thus making the urn's message the entire last two lines.

Again, it will help to perform a simple listing of the poem's elements.

LANGUAGE.   Keats uses a number of interesting word combinations for effect: *foster-child, leaf-fringed,* and *high-sorrowful* to raise the emotional pitch of the poem. He also repeats key words, as in the six repetitions of *happy* in stanza 3. Another key use of language is the rhetorical question (a question which expects no answer), as in the end of stanza 1 and the beginning of stanza 4. The entire poem is a direct address to the urn itself.

IMAGERY.   Several kinds of imagery are at work in the poem. First, there is the imagery associated with the urn as an urn, as when it is called a "still unravished bride" or "sylvan historian." Then there is the imagery of the scenes pictured on the urn, in the classical "dales of Arcady," the Greek paradise. In stanza 2 there is some aural imagery ("soft pipes").

TONE.   The tone is established in the reverence of the poet's questions and the solemnity of Keats's address in the opening two lines. If one may be said to hold an object in awe, Keats seems to do so in this poem.

RHYTHM AND RHYME.   The lines are metrical:

Thou still | unrav | ished bride | of qui | etness,

with each line essentially iambic pentameter: five feet (ten syllables). Most of the lines are end-stopped, with often the first and second lines of a stanza running on to keep the rhythm intense and swift.

METAPHOR AND FIGURATIVE LANGUAGE.   The most important metaphor may be the urn itself as "sylvan historian." It tells a tale from ancient days, revealing the continuity of life.

SYMBOL.   The urn may be a symbol of perfection or of beauty. For Keats, who was dying of tuberculosis, it was a symbol of the endurance of art.

FORM.   The ode has five strophic stanzas of exactly the same form, with each stanza meditating on an aspect of the urn.

IDEAS.   Implied throughout the poem is a contrast of the "Cold Pastoral" of the scenes around the urn with "A burning forehead, and a parching tongue" of the feverish, tubercular world in which Keats lived. The idea of the endurance of art possesses Keats's imagination. Finally, the message that the urn speaks to us: "Beauty is truth, truth beauty," is a key idea in the poem. The question of whether or not it "is all / Ye know on earth, and all ye need to know" is central to all discussions of the poem.

Any interpretation of the poem would need to take into account an expansion of these issues. In addition, each of the scenes on the urn needs to be examined for its imagery, its contribution to the poem. Keats says that the urn tells a "tale more sweetly than our rhyme," and it is important for us to examine each of its scenes of shepherds and priests of ancient Greece ("deities or mortals"). The word *legend* has two meanings: one refers to what is written on the object before us (Keats's first meaning), and the other to mythic story, Keats's important secondary meaning.

Implied in the poem is a contrast of the present with the ancient Greek world. Keats and other Romantic poets were deeply touched by the struggle of the Greeks to free their homeland, and many English poets visited Greece. One, Lord Byron, died there hoping to fight for Greek independence. Keats offers us a Romantic view of Greece by centering only on the imagery of the dancers and musicians in stanza 1, the shepherd boy with his shepherd's pipes and the lovers about to kiss in stanza 2, and the priests bringing the heifer to the altar of their gods in stanza 4, thus creating an ideal world.

Keats also concentrates on the mystery of the urn by reminding us that it cannot speak, and that we divine its meaning from its scenes. Its shape is an ideal form of beauty as Keats understands it. Upon it are "overwrought" "marble men and maidens" representing people who once lived and loved and prayed. They remind him that "old age shall this generation waste," so the urn becomes not just a thing of beauty but a *memento mori*—a reminder of death. Since Keats knew he was dying as he wrote the poem, the urn had a special meaning.

A full interpretation should take into account the fact that there are two versions of the poem. The other version has the urn speaking both last lines, thus telling us that its message is all we know on earth or need to know. No one has successfully unriddled this confusion, although theories are numerous. An interpretation might consider that mystery; it also should ask why Keats tells us in the beginning that the urn is silent and then goes on to make it talk.

Perhaps the question of why Keats demands that the urn speak would be answered by analysis from a psychoanalytic perspective, regarding the urn as a parent in the artistic sense. Some of these comments refer to Keats's dying of tuberculosis, and an interpretation of the poem in light of his illness would depend on research. A detailed historical interpretation would also involve research into the influence of Greek culture in the world of the educated English citizen of the early 1800s. Keats wrote after Napoleon's defeat at Waterloo (1814) and after the huge military campaigns that introduced northeastern Europe to the then exotic worlds of Egypt, Greece, and the Middle East. A critical view that took economics into account might quarrel with Keats's idealizing the scenes on the urn, venerating the perfection of its shape, and then focusing on a limited aesthetic message assigning truth to beauty and nothing else. The political critic would find the treatment of power in this poem unsatisfying. How, for example, do the priests wield their power, and who gives it to them? However complex any of these interpretations may be, they will depend on a close reading of the text. Since this has been a favorite of formalist critics, one may profitably reflect on the possibility that Keats is himself a formalist critic in dealing with the form of the urn itself and interpreting its implied narrative.

The next poem is in the tradition of John Donne's *Holy Sonnets*. Like Donne, Hopkins was a priest. He was part of a religious revival among British intellectuals in the second half of the nineteenth century, and he taught in University College Dublin. In some ways his poem is antiurban and what we might call today "environmentalist." But Hopkins's environment is spiritual, not just physical.

GERARD MANLEY HOPKINS   (1844–1889)

God's Grandeur _____ *1877*

The world is charged with the grándeur of God.
  It will flame out, like shining from shook foil;
  It gathers to a greatness, like the ooze of oil
Crushed. Why do men then now not reck his rod?
Génerátions have trod, have trod, have trod;   5
  And all is seared with trade; bleared, smeared, with toil;
  And wears man's smudge and shares man's smell: the soil
Is bare now, nor can foot feel, being shod.

Ánd, for all this, náture is never spent;
  There lives the dearest freshness deep down things;   10
And though the last lights off the black West went
  Oh, morning, at the brown brink eastward, springs—
Because the Holy Ghost óver the bent
  World broods with warm breast and with ah! bright wings.

LANGUAGE.   Hopkins uses language in special ways: repetition in lines 5 and 6, alliteration in *ooze of oil, reck his rod, foot feel,* and especially the *w* sounds in the last line.

IMAGERY.   The images appeal to many senses: the sense of sight—"shining from shook foil"; touch—"ooze of oil," "nor can foot feel"; and smell—"shares man's smell." Flame imagery, associated with God, is also associated in "seared" with trade and industry. The final image of the Holy Ghost as a bird brooding over the world, as if it were an egg, is quite powerful.

TONE. At first the tone is magisterial, proclaiming that "The world is charged with the grandeur of God." But it becomes almost chastening when it asks why people do "not reck his rod," that is, pay attention and behave themselves. The octave ends with the sense that we have ruined planet earth; the sestet returns with the hopeful message that it will renew itself, and the tone becomes reverent and filled with hope in describing the Holy Ghost.

RHYTHM AND RHYME. The lines are metrical:

The world | is charged | with the | grandeur | of God.

Each line is essentially iambic pentameter: five feet (ten syllables), as in all traditional sonnets. Most of the lines are end-stopped, with the last four lines of the poem run-on so as to exploit the emotional intensity of the final imagery. Certain syllables are accented to help the reader find the stresses Hopkins intended, and the arcs over words in line 3 indicate rapid movement, so *gathers* and *to a* must be spoken as if they were one-syllable words. Hopkins had his own system of scansion, sometimes referred to as "sprung rhythm," reminiscent of school rhymes. The marks over words in this poem help us see his method. The rhymes are very interesting: *God* and *rod* suggest that God can punish as well as love. *Foil, oil, toil, soil* are very unusual rhymes, but all relate to one another. Hopkins also depends on internal rhyme, such as *seared, bleared, smeared* in line 6.

METAPHOR AND FIGURATIVE LANGUAGE. The metaphor of the world being charged as if it were a battery (or explosive) is dominant in the octave, and the metaphor of nature as something that can be spent, either as in one's energy or one's money, is dominant in the sestet.

SYMBOL. One might ask if nature is a symbol for God, but answering such a question poses interesting difficulties.

FORM. This is a Petrarchan sonnet rhyming *abbaabba,* then *cdcdcd.* Relying on so few rhymes increases the challenge. The octave establishes what man has done to the world in modern times. The sestet explains why, even in the darkest night, the sunrise spells hope and a new beginning.

IDEAS. It may be that the first line contains the primary ideas of the poem, in which case it is a statement of faith in the power of nature and God. Hopkins tells us that nature is never spent, but he predicates this view on a highly spiritual belief. His God is the conventional God of his time and religion, and he expects us to treat this as a religious poem. One can also see this as an environmental plea to save the earth, but one would have to keep God in the picture to be true to the poem.

QUESTIONS FOR CLOSE READING

1. Which elements work best together in reinforcing the idea that the "world is charged with the grandeur of God"?

2. How do the limits of iambic pentameter and only four rhymes contribute to the idea expressed in line 9 that "nature is never spent"?

3. Do the elements function well in this poem in light of its demand that it be considered a religious poem? What does it mean for a poem to be religious? Do you feel it is religious?

4. How do the elements of the poem reinforce its main ideas?

The author of the following poem, Edward Hirsch, is an American poet whose poem uses the American game of basketball as its basis. Just as Patricia Goedicke focuses on her father as a wise owl, John Keats focuses on the Grecian urn, and Gerard Manley Hopkins focuses on the "grandeur of God," Hirsch focuses on a fast break to meditate on an important aspect of life.

EDWARD HIRSCH   (b. 1950)

Fast Break _____ *1985*

In memory of Dennis Turner, 1946–1984

A hook shot kisses the rim and
hangs there, helplessly, but doesn't drop,

and for once our gangly starting center
boxes out his man and times his jump

perfectly, gathering the orange leather   5
from the air like a cherished possession

and spinning around to throw a strike
to the outlet who is already shoveling

an underhand pass toward the other guard
scissoring past a flat-footed defender   10

who looks stunned and nailed to the floor
in the wrong direction, trying to catch sight

of a high, gliding dribble and a man
letting the play develop in front of him

in slow motion, almost exactly   15
like a coach's drawing on the blackboard,

both forwards racing down the court
the way that forwards should, fanning out

and filling the lanes in tandem, moving
together as brothers passing the ball   20

between them without a dribble, without
a single bounce hitting the hardwood

until the guard finally lunges out
and commits to the wrong man

while the power-forward explodes past them   25
in a fury, taking the ball into the air

by himself now and laying it gently
against the glass for a lay-up,

but losing his balance in the process,
inexplicably falling, hitting the floor   30

with a wild, headlong motion
for the game he loved like a country

and swiveling back to see an orange blur
floating perfectly through the net.

QUESTIONS FOR CLOSE READING

1. Examine the form of the poem, especially the end-stopped and run-on lines, and the rhythmic qualities. Are they especially appropriate to the game of basketball?
2. Do two-line stanzas contribute to the overall power of the poem?
3. The language of the poem depends on a knowledge of basketball. If you are unfamiliar with it, ask a knowledgeable friend to explain terms like *fast break, outlet, power-forward, boxes out his man,* and *dribble.*
4. The poem is dedicated to "Dennis Turner, 1946–1984." What ideas are thus implied? Why would Hirsch dedicate a poem about basketball to a dead friend?
5. How do the elements of the poem give the fast break larger significance? How do they impart importance to this fast break?
6. Do the elements work together to give the fast break a symbolic importance?

Countee Cullen (1903–1946) was a member of the school of poetry associated with the Harlem Renaissance of the 1920s, 1930s, and 1940s, along with Langston Hughes (1902–1967), Jean Toomer(1894–1967), Claude McKay (1890–1948), and Arna Bontemps (1902–1973). During the period following World War I, African-American writers reawakened their interest in Africa and tried to examine it—and their feelings about it—from a fresh viewpoint.

COUNTEE CULLEN   (1903–1946)

Heritage _____ *1925*

(For Harold Jackman)

What is Africa to me:
Copper sun or scarlet sea,

Jungle star or jungle track,
Strong bronzed men, or regal black
Women from whose loins I sprang   5
When the birds of Eden sang?
One three centuries removed
From the scenes his fathers loved,
Spicy grove, cinnamon tree,
What is Africa to me?   10

So I lie, who all day long
Want no sound except the song
Sung by wild barbaric birds
Goading massive jungle herds,
Juggernauts of flesh that pass   15
Trampling tall defiant grass
Where young forest lovers lie,
Plighting troth beneath the sky.
So I lie, who always hear,
Though I cram against my ear   20
Both my thumbs, and keep them there,
Great drums throbbing through the air.
So I lie, whose fount of pride,
Dear distress, and joy allied,
Is my somber flesh and skin,   25
With the dark blood dammed within
Like great pulsing tides of wine
That, I fear, must burst the fine
Channels of the chafing net
Where they surge and foam and fret.   30

Africa? A book one thumbs
Listlessly, till slumber comes.
Unremembered are her bats
Circling through the night, her cats
Crouching in the river reeds,   35
Stalking gentle flesh that feeds
By the river brink; no more
Does the bugle-throated roar
Cry that monarch claws have leapt
From the scabbards where they slept.   40
Silver snakes that once a year
Doff the lovely coats you wear,
Seek no covert in your fear
Lest a mortal eye should see;
What's your nakedness to me?   45
Here no leprous flowers rear
Fierce corollas in the air;
Here no bodies sleek and wet,
Dripping mingled rain and sweat,
Tread the savage measures of   50

Jungle boys and girls in love.
What is last year's snow to me,
Last year's anything? The tree
Budding yearly must forget
How its past arose or set—   55
Bough and blossom, flower, fruit,
Even what shy bird with mute
Wonder at her travail there,
Meekly labored in its hair.
One three centuries removed   60
From the scenes his fathers loved,
Spicy grove, cinnamon tree,
What is Africa to me?

So I lie, who find no peace
Night or day, no slight release   65
From the unremittent beat
Made by cruel padded feet
Walking through my body's street.
Up and down they go, and back,
Treading out a jungle track.   70
So I lie, who never quite
Safely sleep from rain at night—
I can never rest at all
When the rain begins to fall;
Like a soul gone mad with pain   75
I must match its weird refrain;
Ever must I twist and squirm,
Writhing like a baited worm,
While its primal measures drip
Through my body, crying, "Strip!   80
Doff this new exuberance.
Come and dance the Lover's Dance!"
In an old remembered way
Rain works on me night and day.
Quaint, outlandish heathen gods   85
Black men fashion out of rods,
Clay, and brittle bits of stone,
In a likeness like their own,
My conversion came high-priced;
I belong to Jesus Christ,   90
Preacher of humility;
Heathen gods are naught to me.

Father, Son, and Holy Ghost,
So I make an idle boast;
Jesus of the twice-turned cheek,   95
Lamb of God, although I speak
With my mouth thus, in my heart
Do I play a double part.

Ever at Thy glowing altar
Must my heart grow sick and falter,   100
Wishing He I served were black,
Thinking then it would not lack
Precedent of pain to guide it,
Let who would or might deride it;
Surely then this flesh would know   105
Yours had borne a kindred woe.
Lord, I fashion dark gods, too,
Daring even to give You
Dark despairing features where,
Crowned with dark rebellious hair,   110
Patience wavers just so much as
Mortal grief compels, while touches
Quick and hot, of anger, rise
To smitten cheek and weary eyes.
Lord, forgive me if my need   115
Sometimes shapes a human creed.

All day long and all night through,
One thing only must I do:
Quench my pride and cool my blood,
Lest I perish in the flood.   120
Lest a hidden ember set
Timber that I thought was wet
Burning like the dryest flax,
Melting like the merest wax,
Lest the grave restore its dead.   125
Not yet has my heart or head
In the least way realized
They and I are civilized.

QUESTIONS FOR CLOSE READING

1. Examine some of the unusual words in the poem: "Goading," "Juggernauts,"
   "Plighting troth." How would you characterize the language of the poem? Is Cullen
   ironic in tone?

2. How important is the imagery of the poem? Which images seem to you most intense? Consider the lines: "Does the bugle-throated roar / Cry that monarch claws
   have leapt / From the scabbards where they slept." What is the significance of
   the images in those lines to the overall theme of the poem?

3. Examine the rhythm and rhyme of the poem. Scan the following lines:

   Here no leprous flowers rear
   Fierce corollas in the air;
   Here no bodies sleep and wet,
   Dripping mingled rain and sweat,
   Tread the savage measures of
   Jungle boys and girls in love.

You may notice that there are seven syllables and four accents, an unusual combination. An unaccented syllable is missing either before the first accent or after the last. Technically, this is called **tetrameter catalectic,** four metrical feet with an omitted syllable. Why is this meter effective for this poem?

4. The form of the poem is similar to many verse epistles, which often constitute a series of rhymed couplets, as in "Heritage." The couplet is usually effective for a meditative, philosophical poem. Is that the case here? How would you interpret Cullen's philosophy?

5. The ideas in the poem represent a range of thought and consideration. The opening line is a question: "What is Africa to me." Cullen begins with the idea of origins, his own origins in the lost history of Africa, but it extends to the present and to his considerations about religion and worship. His "conversion" to Christianity came, as he says, at a high price. Does he regret his being Christian? How does he describe his attitudes toward God?

6. What does Africa mean to Countee Cullen?

Louise Glück (b. 1943) is an American poet teaching at Williams College. Her work has been deeply personal and highly valued by lovers of poetry. In her volume *Wild Iris* (1992) many of her poems aim at addressing spiritual issues, sometimes in relatively conventional ways, such as in her poems titled "Matins" and "Vespers," which have the quality of both prayers and psalms. Her love of gardening and flowers shows up in an interesting and complex way in the following poem, whose title refers to religious ceremonies held in the late afternoon or early evening.

LOUISE GLÜCK   (b. 1943)

Vespers _____ *1992*

Even as you appeared to Moses, because
I need you, you appear to me, not
often, however. I live essentially
in darkness. You are perhaps training me to be
responsive to the slightest brightening. Or, like the poets,   5
are you stimulated by despair, does grief
move you to reveal your nature? This afternoon,
in the physical world to which you commonly
contribute your silence, I climbed
the small hill above the wild blueberries, metaphysically   10
descending, as on all my walks: did I go deep enough
for you to pity me, as you have sometimes pitied
others who suffer, favoring those
with theological gifts? As you anticipated,
I did not look up. So you came down to me: 15
at my feet, not the wax
leaves of the wild blueberry but your fiery self, a whole

pasture of fire, and beyond, the red sun neither falling
    nor rising—
I was not a child; I could take advantage of illusions.

QUESTIONS FOR CLOSE READING

1. To whom is the poem addressed? How would you describe Glück's relationship with the person whom she addresses?

2. What can you say about the formal qualities of the poem? Is it metrical? Does it seem to follow the pattern of any of the forms we discussed? How effective is the form of this poem?

3. What images seem strongest and most significant in light of the ideas within the poem?

4. Glück refers to people with "theological gifts." Do you think she is one of those people? What would it mean to be a person with "theological gifts"?

5. What is the "fiery self" alluded to in line 17?

6. What does Glück mean by saying, in the last line, "I could take advantage of illusions"? What does she feel she has seen at the end of this poem?

7. Is this a religious poem? How do the language, images, and form of the poem work together to make the ideas palpable and significant? Does the poem touch you in the sense of making you reflect on your own experiences in nature?

This entire section on the elements of poetry should serve to help you develop close readings basic to any interpretation of a poem. Not all the elements will be of great importance all the time, but whatever elements the poem chooses to rely upon will work—and work together—to produce whatever power the poem has.

13

READING JOHN KEATS
IN DEPTH

Except in anthologies, the normal way to read poetry is either in a poetry journal in which two or more of the poet's works will appear, or in a "slim" volume in which a group of the poet's works is published. When you find a poet who is especially important to you, you have the option of finding that poet's book or books. When you read a group of poems by the same poet, you will find that elements of style that you might not have noticed in one poem become obvious and valued. You also notice that there is sometimes a similarity of concern in certain themes and in certain approaches to language and formal techniques.

In this and the following chapters you will find the work of three poets whose styles differ, but who have all been extremely influential on poetry today. Their work is singular, stylistically distinct, and thematically significant. Following their poetry is a selection of letters and materials that will help you develop a further understanding of what they have achieved in their poetry.

A COMMENTARY ON KEATS'S CAREER

John Keats was one of the most important of the English Romantic poets, who flourished from 1798 to 1832. Their work was distinctive for several things. One was an effort to make their language close to the way people spoke and therefore to do away with previous formal poetic flourishes. Another was an effort to move away from formal rhymed couplets, such as those Alexander Pope (1688–1744) had used in the previous age of Neo-Classicism. The Romantic poets used rhyme, but they also used imaginative stanzaic forms, sometimes of considerable complexity. John Keats is especially interesting in this regard. In

"The Eve of St. Agnes," he uses the Spenserian stanza (named for Edmund Spenser [1552–1599], an important influence on Keats). Many poets have used the Spenserian stanza, but very few have achieved the ease and sensitivity of Keats. His stanzas in the great odes are also imaginative and original and quite different from the forms used in poetry before him.

The Romantics also meditated on nature more than had the earlier Neo-Classic poets. Their interest in politics and in the development of the individual were also heightened. Some of the Romantics took a special interest in the supernatural, often seeing God in nature, and sometimes seeing ghosts or spirits in the world around them. They also emphasized a deeply personal emotional expression in their work. Sometimes the Romantics affected an archaic style—in part to distinguish them from earlier poets of the eighteenth century. Keats sometimes uses archaic language in "The Eve of St. Agnes" as a means of implying that what happened in the poem happened long ago. John Keats was one of the best loved of the Romantic poets, and much that was true of all the Romantics was true of him.

He was born on October 21, 1795, to a family that owned a London livery business renting and caring for horses. His father died when he was eight as a result of a fall from a horse, and his mother died from tuberculosis when he was fourteen. His guardian apprenticed him to a medical man, and by the time he was twenty, Keats qualified as something of a combination of physician and pharmacist. However, as soon as he could, he abandoned medicine and began to write poetry. He was fortunate in meeting another important writer, Leigh Hunt (1784–1859), whose connections helped Keats get published and who placed him in contact with most of the important writers in London at the time.

By 1817 Keats published his first book of poetry and had begun to establish himself as a popular and well-regarded poet. But eventually hostile critics attacked him on the basis of poetry that he himself considered experimental. In 1818 his younger brother Tom contracted tuberculosis, and in treating him, Keats himself developed the disease. At this time he also fell in love with Fanny Brawne and intended to marry her. But because he was still very poor and now beginning to be ill, he held off. He wrote virtually all of his best work in one year, 1819. In 1820 his best work was published: all of the great odes, "The Eve of St. Agnes," and "La Belle Dame sans Merci."

In February 1820 he knew he was dying from his disease. Even earlier in his life he had significant presentiments of an early death, perhaps because of the early death of his parents. In his last year he was convinced that he needed to go to a warmer climate and traveled with a friend to Italy. He died in Rome on February 23, 1821. One can only wonder what great works he might have produced if he had lived longer. He had begun writing poetry at the age of eighteen and stopped when he was twenty-four. The greatest of English poets, Geoffrey Chaucer, William Shakespeare, and John Milton, would hardly have been known if they had died at that age.

Ode to a Nightingale _____ *1820*

I

My heart aches, and a drowsy numbness pains
  My sense, as though of hemlock I had drunk,
Or emptied some dull opiate to the drains
  One minute past, and Lethe-wards° had sunk:
'Tis not through envy of thy happy lot,   5
  But being too happy in thine happiness,—
    That thou, light-wingèd Dryad of the trees,
      In some melodious plot
Of beechen green, and shadows numberless,
    Singest of summer in full-throated ease.   10

II

O, for a draught of vintage! that hath been
Cooled a long age in the deep-delvèd earth,
Tasting of Flora° and the country green,
  Dance, and Provençal song, and sunburnt mirth!
O for a beaker full of the warm South,   15
  Full of the true, the blushful Hippocrene,
    With beaded bubbles winking at the brim,
      And purple-stainèd mouth;
That I might drink, and leave the world unseen,
  And with thee fade away into the forest dim: 20

III

Fade far away, dissolve, and quite forget
  What thou among the leaves hast never known,
The weariness, the fever, and the fret
  Here, where men sit and hear each other groan;
Where palsy shakes a few, sad, last gray hairs,   25
  Where youth grows pale, and specter-thin, and dies;
    Where but to think is to be full of sorrow
      And leaden-eyed despairs,
Where Beauty cannot keep her lustrous eyes,
  Or new Love pine at them beyond tomorrow.   30

IV

Away! away! for I will fly to thee,
  Not charioted by Bacchus and his pards,°
But on the viewless wings of Poesy,
  Though the dull brain perplexes and retards:
Already with thee! tender is the night,   35
  And haply the Queen-Moon is on her throne,

---

4 *Lethe-wards:* toward Lethe in Greek mythology the river of forgetfulness, oblivion.   13 *Flora:*
Roman goddess of flowers.   32 *Bacchus and his pards:* the Greek god of wine and his leopards
(which pulled his chariot).

Clustered around by all her starry Fays;
　　But here there is no light,
Save what from heaven is with the breezes blown
Through verdurous glooms and winding mossy ways.　　　　　40

V

I cannot see what flowers are at my feet,
　Nor what soft incense hangs upon the boughs,
But, in embalmèd darkness, guess each sweet
　Wherewith the seasonable month endows
The grass, the thicket, and the fruit-tree wild;　　　　　45
　White hawthorn, and the pastoral eglantine;
　　Fast fading violets covered up in leaves;
　　　And mid-May's eldest child,
　The coming musk-rose, full of dewy wine,
　　The murmurous haunt of flies on summer eves.　　　　　50

VI

Darkling I listen; and, for many a time
　I have been half in love with easeful Death,
Called him soft names in many a musèd rhyme,
　To take into the air my quiet breath;
Now more than ever seems it rich to die,　　　　　55
　To cease upon the midnight with no pain,
　　While thou art pouring forth thy soul abroad
　　　In such an ecstasy!
　Still wouldst thou sing, and I have ears in vain—
　To thy high requiem become a sod.　　　　　60

VII

Thou wast not born for death, immortal Bird!
　No hungry generations tread three down;
The voice I hear this passing night was heard
　In ancient days by emperor and clown:
Perhaps the self-same song that found a path　　　　　65
　Through the sad heart of Ruth,° when, sick for home,
　　She stood in tears amid the alien corn;
　　　The same that oft-times hath
　Charmed magic casements, opening on the foam
　Of perilous seas, in faery lands forlorn.　　　　　70

VIII

Forlorn! the very word is like a bell
　To roll me back from thee to my sole self!
Adieu! the fancy cannot cheat so well
　As she is famed to do, deceiving elf.
Adieu! adieu! thy plaintive anthem fades　　　　　75

66 *Ruth:* In the biblical book of Ruth, the heroine leaves her home to work in a strange land.

Past the near meadows, over the still stream,
   Up the hill-side; and now 'tis buried deep
      In the next valley-glades:
Was it a vision, or a waking dream?
Fled is that music:—Do I wake or sleep?   80

La Belle Dame Sans Merci° ————————————————— *1820*

A Ballad

I

O what can ail thee, knight at arms,
   Alone and palely loitering?
The sedge has withered from the lake,
   And no birds sing.

II

O what can ail thee, knight at arms,   5
   So haggard and so woe-begone?
The squirrel's granary is full,
   And the harvest's done.

III

I see a lily on thy brow
   With anguish moist and fever dew,   10
And on thy cheeks a fading rose
   Fast withereth too.

IV

I met a lady in the meads,
   Full beautiful, a fairy's child;
Her hair was long, her foot was light,   15
   And her eyes were wild.

V

I made a garland for her head,
   And bracelets too, and fragrant zone;°
She looked at me as she did love,
   And made sweet moan.   20

VI

I set her on my pacing steed,
   And nothing else saw all day long,
For sidelong would she bend, and sing
   A fairy's song.

La Belle Dame sans Merci: "The Beautiful Lady without Pity."   18 *zone:* belt, girdle.

VII

She found me roots of relish sweet,   25
  And honey wild, and manna dew,
And sure in language strange she said—
    "I love thee true."

VIII

She took me to her elfin grot,
  And there she wept, and sighed full sore,   30
And there I shut her wild wild eyes
    With kisses four.

IX

And there she lullèd me asleep,
  And there I dreamed—Ah! woe betide!
The latest dream I ever dreamed   35
    On the cold hill's side.

X

I saw pale kings, and princes too,
  Pale warriors, death pale were they all;
They cried—"La belle dame sans merci
    Hath thee in thrall!"   40

XI

I saw their starved lips in the gloam
  With horrid warning gapèd wide,
And I awoke and found me here
    On the cold hill's side.

XII

And this is why I sojourn here,   45
  Alone and palely loitering,
Though the sedge is withered from the lake,
    And no birds sing.

When I Have Fears That I May Cease to Be ———————— *1818; 1848*

When I have fears that I may cease to be
  Before my pen has gleaned my teeming brain,
Before high piled books, in charactery,
  Hold like rich garners the full ripened grain;
When I behold, upon the night's starred face,   5
  Huge cloudy symbols of a high romance,
And think that I may never live to trace
  Their shadows, with the magic hand of chance;
And when I feel, fair creature of an hour,

That I shall never look upon thee more,   10
Never have relish in the fairy power
    Of unreflecting love;—then on the shore
Of the wide world I stand alone, and think
Till love and fame to nothingness do sink.

On First Looking into Chapman's Homer° _____ 1816

Much have I traveled in the realms of gold,
    And many goodly states and kingdoms seen;
    Round many western islands have I been
Which bards in fealty to Apollo hold.
Oft of one wide expanse had I been told   5
    That deep-browed Homer ruled as his demesne;
    Yet did I never breathe its pure serene°
Till I heard Chapman speak out loud and bold:
Then felt I like some watcher of the skies
    When a new planet swims into his ken;   10
Or like stout Cortez° when with eagle eyes
    He stared at the Pacific—and all his men
Looked at each other with a wild surmise—
    Silent, upon a peak in Darien.°

Chapman's Homer: Keats had never read the Greek epic poet Homer until he read Chapman's translations.   7 *serene:* often interpreted to mean air; could also mean serenity, clarity, grandeur.   11 *Cortez:* a famous error; the Pacific was discovered by Balboa.   14 *Darien:* the old name for the Isthmus of Panama.

On Seeing the Elgin Marbles° _____ 1817

My spirit is too weak—mortality
    Weighs heavily on me like unwilling sleep,
    And each imagined pinnacle and steep
Of godlike hardship, tells me I must die.
Like a sick Eagle looking at the sky.   5
    Yet 'tis a gentle luxury to weep
    That I have not the cloudy winds to keep
Fresh for the opening of the morning's eye.
Such dim-conceived glories of the brain
    Bring round the heart an undescribable feud;   10
So do these wonders a most dizzy pain,
    That mingles Grecian grandeur with the rude
Wasting of old Time—with a billowy main—
A sun—a shadow of a magnitude.

Elgin Marbles: Lord Elgin had purchased the great sculptures and the frieze (a continuous sculptural relief that went around the main room) from the Parthenon in Greece in 1806 when it was in control of the Ottoman Turks. The marble sculptures were shown in London when the British Museum bought them in 1816.

The Eve of St. Agnes° ————————————————————— *1819; 1820*

I

St. Agnes' Eve—Ah, bitter chill it was!
The owl, for all his feathers, was a-cold;
The hare limp'd trembling through the frozen grass,
And silent was the flock in woolly fold:
Numb were the Beadsman's° fingers, while he told   5
His rosary, and while his frosted breath,
Like pious incense from a censer old
Seem'd taking flight for heaven, without a death,
Past the sweet Virgin's picture, while his prayer he saith.

II

His prayer he saith, this patient, holy man;   10
Then takes his lamp, and riseth from his knees,
And back returneth, meagre, barefoot, wan,
Along the chapel aisle by slow degrees:
The sculptur'd dead, on each side, seem to freeze,
Emprison'd in black, purgatorial rails: 15
Knights, ladies, praying in dumb orat'ries,°
He passeth by; and his weak spirit fails
To think how they may ache in icy hoods and mails.

III

Northward he turneth through a little door,
And scarce three steps, ere Music's golden tongue   20
Flatter'd to tears this aged man and poor;
But no—already had his deathbell rung;
The joys of all his life were said and sung:
His was harsh penance on St. Agnes' Eve:
Another way he went, and soon among   25
Rough ashes sat he for his soul's reprieve,
And all night kept awake, for sinner's sake to grieve.

IV

That ancient Beadsman heard the prelude soft;
And so it chanc'd, for many a door was wide,
From hurry to and fro. Soon, up aloft,   30
The silver, snarling trumpets 'gan to chide:
The level chambers, ready with their pride,
Were glowing to receive a thousand guests:
The carved angels, ever eager-eyed,
Star'd, where upon their heads the cornice rests   35
With hair blown back, and wings put cross-wise on their breasts.

St. Agnes: January 21 is St. Agnes' day. The evening before was traditionally a time when a young girl, performing a specific ritual, might dream of her future husband.   5 *Beadsman:* a man hired to pray with his rosary beads.   16 *dumb orat'ries:* silent chapels.

V

At length burst in the argent revelry,°
With plume, tiara, and all rich array,
Numerous as shadows haunting fairily
The brain, new stuff'd, in youth, with triumphs gay   40
Of old romance. These let us wish away,
And turn, sole-thoughted, to one Lady there,
Whose heart had brooded, all that wintry day,
On love, and wing'd St. Agnes' saintly care,
As she had heard old dames full many times declare.   45

VI

They told her how, upon St. Agnes' Eve,
Young virgins might have visions of delight,
And soft adorings from their loves receive
Upon the honey'd middle of the night,
If ceremonies due they did aright;   50
As, supperless to bed they must retire,
And couch supine their beauties, lily white;
Nor look behind, nor sideways, but require
Of heavens with upward eyes for all that they desire.

VII

Full of this whim was thoughtful Madeline: 55
The music, yearning like a god in pain,
She scarcely heard: her maiden eyes divine,
Fix'd on the floor, saw many a sweeping train
Pass by—she heeded not at all: in vain
Came many a tiptoe, amorous cavalier,   60
And back retir'd, not cool'd by high disdain;
But she saw not: her heart was otherwhere:
She sigh'd for Agnes' dreams, the sweetest of the year.

VIII

She danc'd along with vague, regardless eyes,
Anxious her lips, her breathing quick and short: 65
The hallow'd hour was near at hand: she sighs
Amid the timbrels°, and the throng'd resort
Of whisperers in anger, or in sport;
'Mid looks of love, defiance, hate, and scorn,
Hoodwink'd with faery fancy; all amort,°   70
Save to St. Agnes and her lambs unshorn,
And all the bliss to be before to-morrow morn.

IX

So, purposing each moment to retire,
She linger'd still. Meantime, across the moors,

---

37 *argent revelry:* glittering, brilliant partyers. *Argent* means silvery.   67 *timbrels:* tambourines.
70 *amort:* unaware.

Had come young Porphyro, with heart on fire   75
For Madeline. Beside the portal doors,
Buttress'd° from moonlight, stands he, and implores
All saints to give him sight of Madeline,
But for one moment in the tedious hours,
That he might gaze and worship all unseen;   80
Perchance speak, kneel, touch, kiss—in sooth such things have been.

X

He ventures in: let no buzz'd whisper tell:
All eyes be muffled, or a hundred swords
Will storm his heart, Love's fev'rous citadel:
For him, those chambers held barbarian hordes,   85
Hyena foemen, and hot-blooded lords,
Whose very dogs would execrations howl
Against his lineage: not one breast affords
Him any mercy, in that mansion foul,
Save one old beldame,° weak in body and in soul.   90

XI

Ah, happy chance! the aged creature came,
Shuffling along with ivory-headed wand,
To where he stood, hid from the torch's flame,
Behind a broad hall-pillar, far beyond
The sound of merriment and chorus bland: 95
He startled her; but soon she knew his face,
And grasp'd his fingers in her palsied hand,
Saying, "Mercy, Porphyro! hie thee from this place;
They are all here to-night, the whole blood-thirsty race!

XII

"Get hence! get hence! there's dwarfish Hildebrand;   100
He had a fever late, and in the fit
He cursed thee and thine, both house and land:
Then there's that old Lord Maurice, not a whit
More tame for his gray hair—Alas me! flit!
Flit like a ghost away."—"Ah, Gossip dear,   105
We're safe enough; here in this arm-chair sit,
And tell me how"—"Good Saints! not here, not here;
Follow me, child, or else these stones will be thy bier."

XIII

He follow'd through a lowly arched way,
Brushing the cobwebs with his lofty plume,   110
And as she mutter'd "Well-a—well-a-day"
He found him in a little moonlight room,
Pale, lattic'd, chill, and silent as a tomb.

77 *Buttress'd:* shaded.   90 *beldame:* old woman.

"Now tell me where is Madeline," said he,
"O tell me, Angela, by the holy loom   115
Which none but secret sisterhood may see,
When they St. Agnes' wool are weaving piously."

XIV

"St. Agnes! Ah! it is St. Agnes' Eve—
Yet men will murder upon holy days:
Thou must hold water in a witch's sieve,   120
And be liege-lord of all the Elves and Fays,
To venture so:° it fills me with amaze
To see thee, Porphyro!—St. Agnes' Eve!
God's help! my lady fair the conjuror plays
This very night: good angels her deceive!   125
But let me laugh awhile, I've mickle° time to grieve."

XV

Feebly she laugheth in the languid moon,
While Porphyro upon her face doth look,
Like puzzled urchin on an aged crone
Who keepeth clos'd a wond'rous riddle-book,   130
As spectacled she sits in chimney nook.
But soon his eyes grew brilliant, when she told
His lady's purpose; and he scarce could brook°
Tears, at the thought of those enchantments cold,
And Madeline asleep in lap of legends old.   135

XVI

Sudden a thought came like a full-blown rose,
Flushing his brow, and in his pained heart
Made purple riot: then doth he propose
A strategem, that makes the beldame start:
"A cruel man and impious thou art: 140
Sweet lady, let her pray, and sleep, and dream
Alone with her good angels, far apart
From wicked men like thee. Go, go!—I deem
Thou canst not surely be the same that thou didst seem."

XVII

"I will not harm her, by all saints I swear,"   145
Quoth Porphyro: "O may I ne'er find grace
When my weak voice shall whisper its last prayer,
If one of her soft ringlets I displace.
Or look with ruffian passion in her face:
Good Angela, believe me by these tears;   150

---

122 *To venture so:* To achieve his ends, Porphyro needs be a magician.   126 *mickle:* much.
133 *brook:* hold back.

Or I will, even in a moment's space,
    Awake, with horrid shout, my foemen's ears,
And beard them, though they be more fang'd than wolves and bears."

XVIII

"Ah! why wilt thou affright a feeble soul?
    A poor, weak, palsy-stricken, churchyard thing,   155
    Whose passing-bell° may ere the midnight toll;
    Whose prayers for thee, each morn and evening,
    Were never miss'd."—Thus plaining,° doth she bring
    A gentler speech from burning Porphyro;
    So woful, and of such deep sorrowing,   160
    That Angela gives promise she will do
Whatever he shall wish, betide her weal or woe.

XIX

Which was, to lead him, in close secrecy,
    Even to Madeline's chamber, and there hide
    Him in a closet, of such privacy   165
    That he might see her beauty unespied,
    And win perhaps that night a peerless bride,
    While legion'd fairies pac'd the coverlet,
    And pale enchantment held her sleepy-eyed,
    Never on such a night have lovers met.   170
Since Merlin paid his Demon all the monstrous debt.°

XX

"It shall be as thou wishest," said the Dame:
    "All cates° and dainties shall be stored there
    Quickly on this feast-night: by the tambour frame°
    Her own lute thou wilt see: no time to spare,   175
    For I am slow and feeble, and scarce dare
    On such a catering trust my dizzy head.
    Wait here, my child, with patience; kneel in prayer
    The while: Ah! thou must needs the lady wed,
Or may I never leave my grave among the dead."   180

XXI

So saying, she hobbled off with busy fear.
    The lover's endless minutes slowly pass'd;
    The dame return'd, and whisper'd in his ear
    To follow her; with aged eyes aghast
    From fright of dim espial. Safe at last   185
    Through many a dusky gallery, they gain
    The maiden's chamber, silken, hush'd and chaste;

---

156 *passing bell:* church-bell rung at death.   158 *plaining:* explaining   171 *Merlin . . . debt:* a
reference to King Arthur's great magician.   173 *cates:* fancy foods.   174 *tambour frame:* embroidery frame.

Where Porphyro took covert, pleas'd amain.°
His poor guide hurried back with agues in her brain.

XXII

Her falt'ring hand upon the balustrade,   190
Old Angela was feeling for the stair,
When Madeline, St. Agnes' charmed maid,
Rose, like a mission'd spirit, unaware:
With silver taper's light and pious care,
She turn'd, and down the aged gossip led   195
To a safe level matting. Now prepare,
Young Porphyro, for gazing on that bed;
She comes, she comes again, like ring-dove fray'd° and fled.

XXIII

Out went the taper as she hurried in;
Its little smoke, in pallid moonshine, died: 200
She clos'd the door, she panted, all akin
To spirits of the air, and visions wide:
No uttered syllable, or, woe betide!
But to her heart, her heart was voluble,
Paining with eloquence her balmy side;   205
As though a tongueless nightingale should swell
Her throat in vain, and die, heart-stifled, in her dell.

XXIV

A casement high and triple-arch'd there was,
All garlanded with carven imag'ries
Of fruits, and flowers, and bunches of knot-grass,   210
And diamonded with panes of quaint device,
Innumerable of stains and splendid dyes,
As are the tiger-moth's deep-damasked° wings;
And in the midst, 'mong thousand heraldries,
And twilight saints, and dim emblazonings,°   215
A shielded scutcheon blush'd with blood of queens and kings.°

XXV

Full on this casement shone the wintry moon.
And threw warm gules° on Madeline's fair breast,
As down she knelt for heaven's grace and boon;
Rose-bloom fell on her hands, together prest,   220
And on her silver cross soft amethyst,
And on her hair a glory, like a saint:
She seem'd a splendid angel, newly drest,
Save wings, for heaven:—Porphyro grew faint:
She knelt, so pure a thing, so free from mortal taint.   225

---

188 *amain:* mightily.   *198* fray'd: frightened.   213 *deep-damasked:* brilliant markings.   215 *em-blazonings:* royal designs.   216 *kings:* a reference to royal coats of arms.   218 *gules:* red (in a coat of arms).

XXVI

Anon his heart revives: her vespers done,
Of all its wreathed pearls her hair she frees;
Unclasps her warmed jewels one by one;
Loosens her fragrant boddice; by degrees
Her rich attire creeps rustling to her knees; 230
Half-hidden, like a mermaid in sea-weed,
Pensive awhile she dreams awake, and sees,
In fancy, fair St. Agnes in her bed,
But dares not look behind, or all the charm is fled.

XXVII

Soon, trembling in her soft and chilly nest, 235
In sort of wakeful swoon, perplex'd she lay.
Until the poppied warmth of sleep oppress'd
Her soothed limbs, and soul fatigued away;
Flow, like a thought, until the morrow-day;
Blissfully haven'd both from joy and pain; 240
Clasp'd like a missal where swart Paynims° pray;
Blinded alike from sunshine and from rain,
As though a rose should shut, and be a bud again.

XXVIII

Stol'n to this paradise, and so entranced,
Porphyro gazed upon her empty dress, 245
And listen'd to her breathing, if it chanced
To wake into a slumberous tenderness;
Which when he heard, that minute did he bless,
And breath'd himself: then from the closet crept,
Noiseless as fear in a wide wilderness, 250
And over the hush'd carpet, silent, stept,
And 'tween the curtains peep'd, where lo!—how fast she slept.

XXIX

Then by the bed-side, where the faded moon
Made a dim, silver twilight, soft he set
A table, and, half anguish'd, threw thereon 255
A cloth of woven crimson, gold, and jet:—
O for some drowsy Morphean° amulet!
The boisterous, midnight, festive clarion,
The kettle-drum, and far-heard clarionet,
Affray his ears, though but in dying tone:— 260
The hall door shuts again, and all the noise is gone.

XXX

And still she slept an azure-lidded sleep,
In blanched linen, smooth, and lavender'd,

241 *Paynims:* pagans.   257 *Morphean:* possibly a sleeping potion.

While he from forth the closet brought a heap
Of candied apple, quince, and plum, and gourd;   265
With jellies soother than the creamy curd,
And lucent syrops, tinct with cinnamon;
Manna and dates, in argosy transferr'd
From Fez; and spiced dainties, every one,
From silken Samarcand to cedar'd Lebanon.°   270

XXXI

These delicates he heap'd with glowing hand
On golden dishes and in baskets bright
Of wreathed silver: sumptuous they stand
In the retired quiet of the night,
Filling the chilly room with perfume light.—   275
"And now, my love, my seraph fair, awake!
Thou art my heaven, and I thine eremite:°
Open thine eyes, for meek St. Agnes' sake,
Or I shall drowse beside thee, so my soul doth ache."

XXXII

Thus whispering, his warm, unnerved arm   280
Sank in her pillow. Shaded was her dream
By the dusk curtains:—'twas a midnight charm
Impossible to melt as iced stream:
The lustrous salvers° in the moonlight gleam;
Broad golden fringe upon the carpet lies: 285
It seem'd he never, never could redeem
From such a stedfast spell his lady's eyes;
So mus'd awhile, entoil'd in woofed phantasies.°

XXXIII

Awakening up, he took her hollow lute,—
Tumultuous,—and, in chords that tenderest be,   290
He play'd an ancient ditty, long since mute,
In Provence call'd, "La belle dame sans mercy":
Close to her ear touching the melody;—
Wherewith disturb'd, she utter'd a soft moan:
He ceased—she panted quick—and suddenly   295
Her blue affrayed eyes wide open shone:
Upon his knees he sank, pale as smooth-sculptured stone.

XXXIV

Her eyes were open, but she still beheld,
Now wide awake, the vision of her sleep:
There was a painful change, that nigh expell'd   300

---

270 *Lebanon:* This stanza describes the exotic meal the husband-to-be will provide his loved one.
277 *eremite:* religious hermit.   284 *lustrous salvers:* shiny serving plates.   288 *woofed phantasies:* woven fantasies.

The blisses of her dream so pure and deep:
At which fair Madeline began to weep,
And moan forth witless words with many a sigh;
While still her gaze on Porphyro would keep;
Who knelt, with joined hands and piteous eye   305
Fearing to move or speak, she look'd so dreamingly.

XXXV

"Ah, Porphyro!" said she, "but even now
Thy voice was at sweet tremble in mine ear,
Made tuneable with every sweetest vow;
And those sad eyes were spiritual and clear: 310
How chang'd thou art! how pallid, chill, and drear!
Give me that voice again, my Porphyro,
Those looks immortal, those complainings dear!
Oh leave me not in this eternal woe,
For if thou diest, my love, I know not where to go."   315

XXXVI

Beyond a mortal man impassion'd far
At these voluptuous accents, he arose,
Ethereal, flush'd, and like a throbbing star
Seen mid the sapphire heaven's deep repose;
Into her dream he melted, as the rose   320
Blendeth its odour with the violet,—
Solution sweet: meantime the frost-wind blows
Like Love's alarum pattering the sharp sleet
Against the window-panes; St. Agnes' moon hath set.

XXXVII

'Tis dark: quick pattereth the flaw-blown° sleet: 325
"This is no dream, my bride, my Madeline!"
'Tis dark: the iced gusts still rave and beat:
"No dream, alas! alas! and woe is mine!
Porphyro will leave me here to fade and pine.—
Cruel! what traitor could thee hither bring?   330
I curse not, for my heart is lost in thine,
Though thou forsakest a deceived thing;—
A dove forlorn and lost with sick unpruned wing."

XXXVIII

"My Madeline! sweet dreamer! lovely bride!
Say, may I be for aye thy vassal blest?   335
Thy beauty's shield, heart-shap'd and vermeil° dyed?
Ah, silver shrine, here will I take my rest
After so many hours of toil and quest,
A famish'd pilgrim,—saved by miracle.

325 *flaw-blown:* gust-blown.   336 *vermeil:* deep red, vermilion.

Though I have found, I will not rob thy nest   340
    Saving of thy sweet self; if thou think'st well
To trust, fair Madeline, to no rude infidel.

XXXIX
"Hark! 'tis an elfin-storm faery land,
    Of haggard° seeming, but a boon indeed:
    Arise—arise! the morning is at hand;—   345
    The bloated wassaillers° will never heed:—
    Let us away, my love, with happy speed;
    There are no ears to hear, or eyes to see,—
    Drown'd all in Rhenish and the sleepy mead:°
    Awake! arise! my love, and fearless be,   350
For o'er the southern moors I have a home for thee."

XL
She hurried at his words, beset with fears,
    For there were sleeping dragons all around,
    At glaring watch, perhaps, with ready spears—
    Down the wide stairs a darkling way they found.—   355
    In all the house was heard no human sound.
    A chain-droop'd lump was flickering by each door;
    The arras°, rich with horseman, hawk, and hound,
    Flutter'd in the besieging wind's uproar;
And the long carpets rose along the gusty floor.   360

XLI
They glide, like phantoms, into the wide hall;
    Like phantoms, to the iron porch, they glide;
    Where lay the Porter, in uneasy sprawl,
    With a huge empty flaggon by his side:
    The wakeful bloodhound rose, and shook his hide,   365
    But his sagacious eye an inmate owns:°
    By one, and one, the bolts full easy slide:—
    The chains lie silent on the footworn stores;—
The key turns, and the door upon its hinges groans.

XLII
And they are gone; ay, ages long ago   370
    These lovers fled away into the storm.
    That night the Baron dreamt of many a woe,
    And all his warrior-guests, with shade and form
    Of witch, and demon, and large coffin-worm,
    Were long be-nightmar'd. Angela the old.   375
    Died palsy-twitch'd, with meagre face deform;
    The Beadsman, after thousand aves° told,
For aye unsought for slept among his ashes cold.

344 *haggard:* wild, untamed.   346 *wassaillers:* heavy drinkers.   349 *Rhenish . . . mead:* Rhine wine and a honeyed liquor.   358 *arras:* tapestry covering the wall.   366 *inmate owns:* He recognizes one of the household (an inmate).   377 *aves:* Hail Marys.

Ode to Psyche° _____ *1819; 1820*

O Goddess! hear these tuneless numbers, wrung
　By sweet enforcement and remembrance dear,
And pardon that thy secrets should be sung
　Even into thine own soft-conched ear:
Surely I dreamt to-day, or did I see   5
　The winged Psyche with awaken'd eyes?
I wander'd in a forest thoughtlessly,
　And, on the sudden, fainting with surprise,
Saw two fair creatures, crouched side by side
　In deepest grass, beneath the whisp'ring roof   10
Of leaves and trembled blossoms, where there ran
　　A brooklet, scarce espied:
'Mid hush'd, cool-rooted flowers, fragrant-eyed,
　Blue, silver-white, and budded Tyrian,
They lay calm-breathing on the bedded grass;   15
　Their arms embraced, and their pinions° too;
　Their lips touch'd not, but had not bade adieu,
As if disjoined by soft-handed slumber,
And ready still past kisses to outnumber
　At tender eye-drawn of aurorean love:°   20
　　The winged boy I knew;
But who wast thou, O happy, happy dove?
　　His Psyche true!

O latest born and loveliest vision far
　Of all Olympus' faded hierarchy!   25
Fairer than Phoebe's sapphire-region'd star,°
　Or Vesper,° amorous glow-worm of the sky;
Fairer than these, though temple thou hast none,
　　Nor altar heap'd with flowers;
Nor virgin-choir to make delicious moan   30
　　Upon the midnight hours;
No voice, no lute, no pipe, no incense sweet
　From chain-swing censer teeming;
No shrine, no grove, no oracle, no heat
　Of pale-mouth'd prophet dreaming.   35

O brightest! though too late for antique vows,
　Too, too late for the fond believing lyre,
When holy were the haunted forest boughs,
　Holy the air, the water, and the fire;
yet even in these days so far retir'd   40
　From happy pieties, thy lucent fans,
　Fluttering among the faint Olympians,
I see, and sing, by my own eyes inspired.

Psyche: a goddess beloved of Cupid. The word in Greek means soul.　16 *pinions:* wings.　20 *aurorean love:* early-morning love.　26 *Sapphire-region'd star:* the moon.　27 *Vesper:* the evening star.

So let me be thy choir, and make a moan
    Upon the midnight hours;   45
Thy voice, thy lute, thy pipe, thy incense sweet
    From swinged censer teeming;
Thy shrine, thy grove, thy oracle, thy heat
    Of pale-mouth'd prophet dreaming.

Yes, I will be thy priest, and build a fane°   50
    In some untrodden region of my mind,
Where branched thoughts, new grown with pleasant pain,
    Instead of pines shall murmur in the wind:
Far, far around shall those dark-cluster'd trees
    Fledge° the wild-ridged mountains steep by steep;   55
And there by zephyrs, streams, and birds, and bees,
    The moss-lain Dryads° shall be lull'd to sleep;
And in the midst of this wide quietness
    A rosy sanctuary will I dress
With the wreath'd trellis of a working brain,   60
    With buds, and bells, and stars without a name,
With all the gardener Fancy e'er could feign,
    Who breeding flowers, will never breed the same;
And there shall be for thee all soft delight
    That shadowy thought can win   65
A bright torch, and a casement ope at night,
    To let the warm Love in!

50 *fane:* a temple.   55 *Fledge:* feather.   57 *Dryads:* wood nymphs.

Ode on Melancholy _____ *1819; 1820*

I

No, no, go not to Lethe,° neither twist
Wolf's-bane, tight-rooted, for its poisonous wine;
Nor suffer thy pale forehead to be kiss'd
By nightshade, ruby grape of Proserpine;
Make not your rosary of yew-berries,°   5
Nor let the beetle,° nor the death-moth be
Your mournful Psyche,° nor the downy owl
A partner in your sorrow's mysteries;
For shade to shade will come too drowsily,
And drown the wakeful anguish of the soul.   10

II

But when the melancholy fit shall fall
Sudden from heaven like a weeping cloud,

1 *Lethe:* river of forgetfulness in the classical Hades.   4 *Proserpine:* classical queen of Hades.
5 *yew-berries:* berries associated with mortuaries.   6 *beetle:* symbol of death.   7 *Psyche:* soul; but here he means don't let yourself fall in love with death (as Cupid fell in love with Psyche).

That fosters the droop-headed flowers all,
And hides the green hill in an April shroud;
Then glut thy sorrow on a morning rose,   15
Or on the rainbow of the salt sand-wave,
Or on the wealth of globed peonies;
Or if the mistress some rich anger shows,
Emprison her soft hand, and let her rave,
And feed deep, deep upon her peerless eyes.   20

III

She dwells with Beauty—Beauty that must die;
And Joy, whose hand is ever at his lips
Bidding adieu; and aching Pleasure nigh,
Turning to poison while the bee-mouth sips:
Ay, in the very temple of Delight   25
Veil'd Melancholy has her sovran shrine,
Though seen of none save him whose strenuous tongue
Can burst Joy's grape against his palate fine;°
His soul shall taste the sadness of her might,
And be among her cloudy trophies hung.   30

28 *palate fine:* educated taste.

To Autumn _____ *1819; 1820*

I

Season of mists and mellow fruitfulness,
    Close bosom-friend of the maturing sun;
Conspiring with him how to load and bless
    With fruit the vines that round the thatch-eves run;
To bend with apples the moss'd cottage-trees,   5
    And fill all fruit with ripeness to the core;
        To swell the gourd, and plump the hazel shells
    With a sweet kernel; to set budding more,
And still more, later flowers for the bees,
Until they think warm days will never cease.   10
        For summer has o'er-brimm'd their clammy cells.

II

Who hath not seen thee oft amid thy store?
    Sometimes whoever seeks abroad may find
Thee sitting careless on a granary floor,
    Thy hair soft-lifted by the winnowing wind;   15
Or on a half-reap'd furrow sound asleep,
    Drows'd with the fume of poppies, while thy hook°
        Spares the next swath and all its twined flowers:

17 *hook:* scythe.

And sometimes like a gleaner° thou dost keep
   Steady thy laden head across a brook;   20
   Or by a cyder-press, with patient look,
      Thou watchest the last oozings hours by hours.

III

Where are the songs of spring? Ay, where are they?
   Think not of them, thou hast thy music too,—
While barred clouds bloom the soft-dying day,   25
   And touch the stubble-plains with rosy hue;
Then in a wailful choir the small gnats mourn
   Among the river sallows,° borne aloft
      Or sinking as the light wind lives or dies;
And full-grown lambs loud bleat from hilly bourn;°   30
   Hedge-crickets sing; and now with treble soft
   The red-breast whistles from a garden-croft;°
      And gathering swallows twitter in the skies.

19 *gleaner:* man who picks up grain left behind.   28 *sallows:* willow trees.   30 *bourn:* region.
32 *garden-croft:* small vegetable garden.

QUESTIONS FOR CRITICAL READING

1. Keats's command of rhythmic effects represents one of his greatest strengths. Examine "Ode to a Nightingale" and read the first stanza aloud. How does Keats use the pauses and line breaks to good effect? How does the speaker of the poem contrast himself with the nightingale (the "light-wingèd Dryad of the trees")? How does the movement of the lines contrast the speaker and the bird? Scan the opening lines to help you deal with this issue.

2. Why is the speaker of the poem envious of the nightingale?

3. Is "Ode to a Nightingale" a melancholy poem? What would make it melancholy? What effect does the poem have on you as reader?

4. What are the most important elements at work in "La Belle Dame sans Merci"? Keats describes it as a ballad. What balladic qualities are apparent in the poem? Try to sing the poem in a ballad style. How effective is it?

5. Choose one of Keats's sonnets and examine his use of imagery, symbol, rhythm, and rhyme. What stylistic qualities most impress you as making his sonnets distinctive?

6. The story told in "The Eve of St. Agnes" is said to have occurred long ago. What uses of language help us believe that the story is ancient? The stanza form of the poem is Spenserian, which rhymes: *a, b, a, b, b, c, b, c, c.* This, too, is an older form, dating from the late sixteenth and early seventeenth centuries. How does the form of the stanza help qualify the emotional impact of the poem?

7. What makes the narrative structure of "The Eve of St. Agnes" effective? Keats is usually thought of as a lyric poet; however, this poem is a narrative. Comment on the richness of imagery, description, and appeals to the senses within the poem. Do they distract from the narrative or do they contribute to its effectiveness?

8. Which stanza of "The Eve of St. Agnes" has for you the most intense and sensuous language? How does Keats achieve such an effect?

9. The three odes in this collection of poems seem highly personal. Which, for you, is the most personal of these odes? Does it have the most intense expression of personal emotion on the part of Keats? How would you describe that emotion? Comment on the elements of poetry that make the emotion distinctive.

10. When Keats wrote the final odes in this collection, he knew he was dying of tuberculosis. What evidence in the poems suggests that his awareness was somehow expressed in the poems?

RESOURCES FOR READING KEATS

The following materials are designed to expand our knowledge of Keats and his work. The letters that follow discuss poetry, poetic problems, and attitudes toward the art of writing. Keats was generous in his comments on his work and his calling, and some of what he has to say may help clarify his thinking in his poetry.

The two critical comments, which come from modern critical biographies of the poet, focus on "The Eve of St. Agnes" and "Ode to Psyche," both poems that can benefit from critical consideration. Both commentaries offer interesting interpretations of the poems.

Letters[1] of John Keats

Keats was a remarkable correspondent in his last years, before his illness made it difficult or impossible for him to write. He wrote often to his brothers George and Thomas as well as to his sister Fanny. He also wrote to his close friend John Hamilton Reynolds. His letters to John Taylor and Richard Woodhouse are significant for what they reveal about his attitudes toward his writing. He discusses his work and his objectives in poetry. But late in his correspondence he reveals that as his illness became totally apparent he resolved to write some prose pieces that might earn him some money. His first letter to Taylor lays down some axioms for poetry that he says he followed. His famous letter to his brothers discusses a theory of "negative capability," a capacity to accept mystery when certainty cannot be had. In his letter to Reynolds, Keats muses on poetry and writes an original sonnet as a way of articulating his thoughts. His letter to Woodhouse became famous for its pronouncement on the absence of the poet's identity. To an extent this observation implies that the poet is inspired and an instrument rather than a personality. Even in his letter he remarks that he may not be "speaking from myself, but from some character in whose soul I now live." Such a view elevates both poet and poetry in a fashion that would have pleased some Romantic poets.

[1] These letters are from the edition of H. Buxton Forman (London, 1889), vol. 4.

To *George and Thomas Keats, Teignmouth*

Hampstead
22nd December, 1817.

My dear Brothers,

I must crave your pardon for not having written ere this. * * * I saw Kean[1] return to the public in "Richard III.," and finely he did it, and, at the request of Reynolds, I went to criticize his Duke. The critique is in to-day's "Champion," which I send you, with the "Examiner," in which you will find very proper lamentation on the obsoletion of Christmas gambols and pastimes: but it was mixed up with so much egotism of that drivelling nature that all pleasure is entirely lost. Hone, the publisher's trial, you must find very amusing, and, as Englishmen, very encouraging; his *Not Guilty* is a thing, which not to have been, would have dulled still more Liberty's emblazoning. Lord Ellenborough has been paid in his own coin. Wooler and Hone have done us an essential service. I have had two very pleasant evenings with Dilke, yesterday and to-day, and am at this moment just come from him, and feel in the humour to go on with this, begun in the morning, and from which he came to fetch me. I spent Friday evening with Wells,[2] and went next morning to see "Death on the Pale Horse." It is a wonderful picture, when West's[3] age is considered; but there is nothing to be intense upon, no women one feels mad to kiss, no face swelling into reality. The excellence of every art is its intensity, capable of making all disagreeables evaporate from their being in close relationship with beauty and truth. Examine "King Lear," and you will find this exemplified throughout: but in this picture we have unpleasantness without any momentous depth of speculation excited, in which to bury its repulsiveness. The picture is larger than "Christ Rejected."

I dined with Haydon[4] the Sunday after you left, and had a very pleasant day. I dined too (for I have been out too much lately) with Horace Smith, and met his two brothers, with Hill and Kingston, and one Du Bois. They only served to convince me how superior humour is to wit, in respect to enjoyment. These men say things which make one start, without making one feel; they are all alike; their manners are alike; they all know fashionables; they have all a mannerism in their very eating and drinking, in their mere handling a decanter. They talked of Kean and his low company. "Would I were with that company instead of yours," said I to myself! I know such like acquaintance will never do for me, and yet I am going to Reynolds on Wednesday. Brown and Dilke walked with me and back to the Christmas pantomime. I had not a dispute, but a disquisition, with Dilke upon various subjects; several things dove-tailed in my mind, and at once it struck me what quality went to form a man of achievement, especially in literature, and which Shakespeare possessed so enormously—I mean *negative capability*, that is, when a man is capable of being in uncertainties, mysteries, doubts, without any irritable reaching after fact and reason. Coleridge, for instance, would let go by a fine isolated verisimilitude caught from the penetralium of Mystery, from being incapable of remaining content with half-knowledge. This pursued through volumes would perhaps take us no further than this, that with a great Poet the sense of Beauty

---

[1] Kean, the great English actor Edmund Kean (1789–1833).
[2] Charles Wells, the author of *Stories after Nature* and *Joseph and His Brethren.*
[3] West, the American painter Benjamin West (1738–1820).
[4] Haydon, Benjamin Haydon, one of Keats's close friends and a painter.

overcomes every other consideration, or rather obliterates all consideration. Shelley's poem[5] is out, and there are words about its being objected to as much as "Queen Mab" was. Poor Shelley, I think he has his quota of good qualities. * * * Write soon to your most sincere friend and affectionate brother,   John.

[5]Shelley's poem, *Laon and Cythna* (1817), dealing with the theme of incest.

To *John Hamilton Reynolds*

[Postmark, *Hampstead, 19 February 1818.*]

My dear Reynolds,
    I had an idea that a Man might pass a very pleasant life in this manner—let him on a certain day read a certain Page of full Poesy or distilled Prose, and let him wander with it, and muse upon it, and reflect upon it, and bring home to it, and prophesy upon it, and dream upon it, until it becomes stale—but when will it do so? Never. When Man has arrived at a certain ripeness in intellect any one grand and spiritual passage serves him as a starting-post towards all "the two-and-thirty Palaces." How happy is such a voyage of conception, what delicious diligent Indolence! A doze upon a sofa does not hinder it, and a nap upon Clover engenders ethereal finger-pointings—the prattle of a child gives it wings, and the converse of middle-age a strength to beat them—a strain of music conducts to "an odd angle of the isle," and when the leaves whisper it puts a girdle round the earth. Nor will this sparing touch of noble Books by any irreverence to their Writers—for perhaps the honors paid by Man to Man are trifles in comparison to the Benefit done by great Works to the Spirit and pulse of good by their mere passive existence. Memory should not be called knowledge. Many have original minds who do not think it—they are led away by Custom. Now it appears to me that almost any Man may like the spider spin from his own inwards his own airy Citadel—the points of leaves and twigs on which the spider begins her work are few, and she fills the air with a beautiful circuiting. Man should be content with as few points to tip with the fine Web of his Soul, and weave a tapestry empyrean full of symbols for her spiritual eye, of softness for his spiritual touch, of space for his wandering, of distinctness for his luxury. But the Minds of Mortals are so different and bent on such diverse journeys that it may at first appear impossible for any common taste and fellowship to exist between two or three under these suppositions. It is however quite the contrary. Minds would leave each other in contrary directions, traverse each other in numberless points, and at last greet each other at the journey's end. An old Man and a child would talk together and the old Man be led on his path and the child left thinking. Man should not dispute or assert but whisper results to his neighbour and thus by every germ of spirit sucking the sap from mould ethereal every human [being] might become great, and Humanity instead of being a wide heath of Furze and Briars with here and there a remote Oak or Pine, would become a grand democracy of Forest Trees! It has been an old comparison for our urging on—the Beehive; however, it seems to me that we should rather be the flower than the Bee—for it is a false notion that more is gained by receiving than giving—no, the receiver and the giver are equal in their benefits. The flower, I doubt not, receives a fair guerdon from the Bee—its leaves blush deeper in the next spring—and who shall say between Man and Woman which is the most delighted? Now it is more noble to sit like Jove than to fly like Mercury—let us not therefore go hurrying about and collecting honey, bee-like buzzing here and there impatiently from a knowledge of what is to be aimed at; but let us open

our leaves like a flower and be passive and receptive—budding patiently under the eye of Apollo and taking hints from every noble insect that favours us with a visit—sap will be given us for meat and dew for drink. I was led into these thoughts, my dear Reynolds, by the beauty of the morning operating on a sense of Idleness—I have not read any Books—the Morning said I was right—I had no idea but of the morning, and the thrush said I was right—seeming to say,

O thou whose face hath felt the Winter's wind,
Whose eye has seen the snow-clouds hung in mist,
And the black elm-tops 'mong the freezing stars,
To thee the Spring will be a harvest-time.
O thou, whose only book has been the light
Of supreme darkness which thou feddest on
Night after night when Phœbus was away,
To thee the Spring shall be a triple morn.
O fret not after knowledge—I have none,
And yet my song comes native with the warmth.
O fret not after knowledge—I have none,
And yet the Evening listens. He who saddens
At thought of idleness cannot be idle,
And he's awake who thinks himself asleep.

Now I am sensible all this is a mere sophistication (however it may neighbour to any truths), to excuse my own indolence—so I will not deceive myself that Man should be equal with Jove—but think himself very well off as a sort of scullion-Mercury, or even a humble Bee. It is no matter whether I am right or wrong, either one way or another, if there is sufficient to lift a little time from your shoulders.

Your affectionate friend
John Keats—

To *John Taylor*[1]

Hampstead,
27 February [1818].

My dear Taylor,
Your alteration strikes me as being a great improvement. And now I will attend to the punctuation you speak of. The comma should be at *soberly,* and in the other passage the comma should follow *quiet.* I am extremely indebted to you for this alteration, and also for your after admonitions. It is a sorry thing for me that any one should have to overcome prejudices in reading my verses. That affects me more than any hypercriticism on any particular passage. In "Endymion," I have most likely but moved into the go-cart from the leading strings. In poetry I have a few axioms, and you will see how far I am from their centre.
1st.   I think poetry should surprise by a fine excess, and not by singularity; it should strike the reader as a wording of his own highest thoughts, and appear almost a remembrance.

---

[1]John Taylor, Keats's editor at the publisher Taylor & Hessey.

2nd.   Its touches of beauty should never be half-way, thereby making the reader breathless, instead of content. The rise, the progress, the setting of imagery, should, like the sun, come natural to him, shine over him, and set soberly, although in magnificence, leaving him in the luxury of twilight. But it is easier to think what poetry should be, than to write it. And this leads me to

Another axiom—That if poetry comes not as naturally as the leaves to a tree, it had better not come at all. However it may be with me, I cannot help looking into new countries with "Oh, for a muse of fire to ascent!" If "Endymion" serves me as a pioneer, perhaps I ought to be content, for, thank God, I can read, and perhaps understand, Shakespeare to his depths; and I have, I am sure, many friends who, if I fail, will attribute any change in my life and temper to humbleness rather than pride—to a cowering under the wings of great poets, rather than to a bitterness that I am not appreciated.[2] I am anxious to get "Endymion" printed that I may forget it, and proceed. I have copied the Third Book, and begun the Fourth. I will take care the printer shall not trip up my heels.

Remember me to Percy Street.

Your sincere and obliged friend
John Keats

P.S.—I shall have a short preface in good time.

[2]"Mr. Bailey has informed me," says Lord Houghton, "that one of Keats's favourite topics of conversation was the principle of melody in verse, which he believed to consist in the adroit management of open and close vowels. He had a theory that vowels could be as skilfully combined and interchanged as differing notes of music, and that all sense of monotony was to be avoided, except when expressive of a special purpose. Uniformity of metre is so much the rule of English poetry, that, undoubtedly, the carefully varied harmonies of Keats's verse were disagreeable, even to cultivated readers, often producing exactly the contrary impression from what was intended, and, combined as they were with rare and curious rhymes, diverted the attention from the beauty of the thoughts and the force of the imagery. In 'Endymion,' indeed, there was much which not only seemed, but was, experimental; and it is impossible not to observe the superior mastery of melody, and sure-footedness of the poetic paces, in 'Hyperion.' "
[H. Buxton Forman's note. Benjamin Bailey was one of Keats's closest friends.]

To Richard Woodhouse[1]

[Postmark, *Hampstead, 27 October 1818.*]

My dear Woodhouse,

Your letter gave me great satisfaction, more on account of its friendliness than any relish of that matter in it which is accounted so acceptable in the "genus irritabile." The best answer I can give you is in a clerklike manner to make some observations on two principal points which seem to point like indices into the midst of the whole *pro* and *con* about genius, and views, and achievements, and ambition, *et cetera.* 1st. As to the poetical character itself (I mean that sort, of which, if I am anything, I am a member; that sort distinguished from the Wordworthian, or egotistical sublime; which a thing *per se,* and stands alone), it is not itself—it has no self—it is every thing and nothing—it has no character—it enjoys light and shade—it lives in gusto, be it foul or fair, high or low, rich or poor, mean or elevated,—it has as much delight in conceiving an Iago as an Imogen.

[1]Richard Woodhouse, a lawyer who preserved many of Keats's manuscripts. He encouraged Keats's early efforts.

What shocks the virtuous philosopher delights the cameleon poet. It does no harm from its relish of the dark side of things, any more than from its taste for the bright one, because they both end in speculation. A poet is the most unpoetical of anything in existence, because he has no identity; he is continually in for, and filling, some other body. The sun, the moon, the sea, and men and women, who are creatures of impulse, are poetical, and have about them as unchangeable attribute; the poet has none, no identity. He is certainly the most unpoetical of all God's creatures. If, then, he has no self, and if I am a poet, where is the wonder that I should say I would write no more? Might I not at that very instant have been cogitating on the characters of Saturn and Ops? It is a wretched thing to confess, but it is a very fact, that not one word I ever utter can be taken for granted as an opinion growing out of my identical nature. How can it, when I have no nature? When I am in a room with people, if I ever am free from speculating on creations of my own brain, then, not myself goes home to myself, but the identity of every one in the room begins to press upon me, [so] that I am in a very little time annihilated—not only among men; it would be the same in a nursery of children. I know not whether I make myself wholly understood: I hope enough so to let you see that no dependence is to be placed on what I said that day.

In the second place, I will speak of my views, and of the life I purpose to myself. I am ambitious of doing the world some good: if I should be spared, that may be the work of maturer years—in the interval I will assay to reach to as high a summit in poetry as the nerve bestowed upon me will suffer. The faint conceptions I have of poems to come bring the blood frequently into my forehead. All I hope is, that I may not lose all interest in human affairs—that the solitary indifference I feel for applause, even from the finest spirits, will not blunt any acuteness of vision I may have. I do not think it will. I feel assured I should write from the mere yearning and fondness I have for the beautiful, even if my night's labours should be burnt every morning, and no eye ever shine upon them. But even now I am perhaps not speaking from myself, but from some character in whose soul I now live.

I am sure, however, that this next sentence is from myself.—I feel your anxiety, good opinion, and friendship, in the highest degree, and am

Yours most sincerely,
John Keats.

To *John Taylor*

Winchester, 23 August, 1819.

My dear Taylor,

I feel every confidence that, if I choose, I may be a popular writer. That I will never be; but for all that I will get a livelihood. I equally dislike the favour of the public with the love of a woman. They are both a cloying treacle to the wings of independence. I shall ever consider them (the people) as debtors to me for verses, not myself to them for admiration, which I can do without. I have of late been indulging my spleen by composing a preface AT them; after all resolving never to write a preface at all. "There are so many verses," would I have said to them; "give so much means for me to buy pleasure with, as a relief to my hours of labour." You will observe at the end of this, if you put down the letter, "How a solitary life engenders pride and egotism!" True—I know it does: but this pride and egotism will enable me to write finer things than anything else could, so I will indulge it. Just so much as I am humbled by the genius above my grasp, am I exalted and look with hate and contempt upon the literary world. A drummer-boy who holds out his hand familiarly to a field-marshal,—that drummer-boy with me is the good word and favour of the public. Who could wish to be among the common-place crowd of the little-famous, who are each individually lost in a throng made up of themselves? Is this worth louting or playing the hypocrite for? To beg suffrages for a seat on the benches of a myriad-aristocracy in letters? This is not wise—I am not a wise man. 'Tis pride. I will give you a definition of a proud man. He is a man who has neither vanity nor wisdom—one filled with hatreds cannot be vain, neither can he be wise. Pardon me for hammering instead of writing. Remember me to Woodhouse, Hessey, and all in Percy Street.

Ever yours sincerely
John Keats

Aileen Ward, "The Eve of St. Agnes"

In her biography of Keats, Ward connects Keats's romance with Fanny Brawne with the narrative of "The Eve of St. Agnes." Ward refers to the poem as Keats's "Epithalamion," which connects Keats with one of his favorite poets, Edmund Spenser. One of Spenser's most famous poems is his "Epithalamion," whose title means a poem on marriage or to celebrate a marriage. Spenser's poem celebrated his own marriage. Ward sees "The Eve of St. Agnes" as celebrating an imaginary marriage to Fanny.

. . . During the day Keats was free to work. He had brought down some thin paper which Haslam° had given him for his long letters to America, but he still found it impossible to begin his new journal. Instead his thoughts turned finally in the direction toward which they had been veering ever since Christmas. On Haslam's "thin genteel sheets" he drafted a poem into which he poured all the feelings and sensations of the last month. From his impressions of Chichester and Stansted—light and shadow, sumptuous colour and texture and intricate architectural line—he built up a great duskygalleried house in which two young lovers, beset by a dark and hostile world, meet and escape to their freedom together.

The Eve of St. Agnes is Keats's "Epithalamion"° in narrative form, celebrating the joys of a first love fulfilled in a runaway marriage. The abstract tone and superhuman drama of *Hyperion*° are exchanged for a medieval world, remote enough for romance but as real as the cathedral and cloisters of Chichester, and peopled with beings of flesh and blood—the Beadsman telling his rosary with numb fingers, the dim-sighted Angela groping for the balustrade, Madeline unclasping the warm jewels from her white throat. The actual germ of the story seems to have been a recent suggestion of Isabella Jones's— the superstition that a maiden would see her future husband in a dream if she fasted on St. Agnes' Eve. And if one listens for them, echoes of the whole gamut of Keats's reading may be heard throughout the poem, from Spenser and Shakespeare and Milton to Boccaccio and Mrs. Radcliffe and the Arabian Nights. Still, these are not the real sources of the poem. What matters in *The Eve of St. Agnes,* as in all Keats's other work, is the poetic intention at the front of his mind which called up the words and images from his memory—the felt emotion, the actual experience, the sense of reality which he wished

From Aileen Ward, *John Keats: The Making of a Poet* (New York: Viking, 1963), 244–246.

Haslam: William Haslam, a young lawyer who watched over Tom Keats when he was ill. *Epithalamion:* a poem celebrating marriage. *Hyperion:* an epic poem by Keats.

to express. We can only surmise his adventure with Fanny Brawne, though we know something of the actual circumstances of these weeks, from which he could not as yet disentangle his feelings: the frozen fields and the Christmas festivities at Hampstead; his elderly companions and medieval surroundings in Chichester; the baroque splendour of Stansted and the remote quiet of Bedhampton. And yet these very circumstances of warmth and cold, youth and age, sound and silence, all counterpointed against each other, perfectly project the emotion he felt at the unexpected birth of a new love in his time of sorrow after Tom's death. *The Eve of St. Agnes* is Keats's first great achievement in what he later called "the knowledge of contrast, feeling for light and shade" which he thought essential to a poem: the stillness of Madeline's room, "silken, hush'd, and chaste," balanced against the noisy celebrations in the hall below; the warmth of her bed contrasted with the chilly night; the pallid moon outside the triple-arched window casting soft amethyst and rose on Madeline's breast as she knelt in prayer. The light almost without shade of *Endymion* and the deep shadows of *Hyperion* here vivify and brighten each other. It is significant that *Romeo and Juliet* is the source echoed most frequently in this poem—knowing what symbolic value Keats set on Juliet. Yet the contrast between the fever heat of midsummer Verona and the aching cold of Keats's castle is striking, for he chose to intensify the passion of his story by an almost Spenserian insistence on its purity. In the authentic feeling of his first master, this is a "song made in lieu of many ornaments" in honour of his love.

Walter Jackson Bate, "The Odes of April and May, 1819"

Professor Bate offers some interesting insights concerning Keats's "Ode to Psyche." Bate's discussion is detailed and probing, connecting it to the theme of love, which underlies the poem in Keats's version and in the sources that inspired him.

THE ODES OF APRIL AND MAY, 1819

No single interpretation of any of the odes—still less of the odes as a group—satisfies anyone except the interpreter. Too many different elements converge. This, of course, is one explanation for their success, as it is for the success of any great work of art. That commonplace is one of those truths of which, as Johnson said, though we may not need to be informed, we need to be reminded. For, while few of us deny it in principle, most of us tend to betray it in practice. To seek relief in particular details is inevitable to a finite being. In reading a poem, in contemplating any work of art, we may genuinely feel the active coalescence of the diverse. But when we come to speak about it, we have to proceed consecutively: one thing has to be mentioned before another; in the process of noticing them individually, we find some considerations striking us more than others, if only because in our own phrasing of them we begin to tap essential concerns within ourselves; and we are led by the momentum of our own cooperating eloquence to narrow our interpretation. (A great work, of course, not only permits but invites that eager subjective response to different parts of it.) Moreover, the existence of previous commentary further specializes our attitude if we feel called upon to contribute our mite. For in the heat of debate, or even in the honest desire to return to the amplitude

From Walter Jackson Bate, *John Keats* (Belknap Press of Harvard University Press, 1963), 486–495.

of the work of art, our recoil from what we consider to be partial, single-minded interpretations encourages us to champion those details that we feel were overlooked, and to contradict or minimize considerations that we might otherwise have wished only to supplement.

Whatever else we may say of the odes of late April and May, 1819, we do them little justice unless we also see them—not wholly, but partly—in the mainstream of Keats's thought as it had begun to clarify itself in the letter to Reynolds (May 3, 1818) about the "Chamber of Maiden-Thought." He was now, after a difficult but fertile year, going back to that sonnet-length "Ode to Maia" which he had written on the previous May Day— the fragment that he had said he would finish "all in good time." In his long journal letter to George and Georgiana in America, begun back in February, he wrote (April 30), as this new May Day, the final one of his active career, approached:

> The following Poem—the last I have written is the first and the only one with which I have taken even moderate pains—I have for the most part dash'd of[f] my lines in a hurry—This I have done leisurely—I think it reads the more richly for it and will I hope encourage me to write other thing[s] in even a more peaceable and healthy spirit.

2

The sixty-seven lines of the new poem, an "Ode to Psyche," have always puzzled readers. It is justly felt that the ode may be something of a prototype for the others that follow it within the next month—that Keats was trying to do something in this first ode that he develops or redirects in the later ones. But, finding the poem so elusive, we return to it only after we know the others far better. If we had hoped to use them as keys, we discover they do not quite fit the lock. Meanwhile they have given us a standard hard to equal. hence we either feel a disappointment about the "Ode to Psyche" or else, remembering the care Keats supposedly gave it, we once more put the poem aside for future consideration.

Our puzzlement extends to technical details, partly again because we know that he worked on the poem in a more "leisurely" way than on most of his earlier poetry. The later odes were probably written much more rapidly (at least the first draft of the "Ode to a Nightingale" was completed in one morning); but the structure of the "Ode to Psyche" seems much less firm. Moreover, from *Hyperion* on, sureness of phrase had become habitual to him, even in his most rapid writing. Yet in the opening stanzas of this new ode (and to some extent in the third book of *Hyperion,* on which he had been recently working) we encounter banalities of diction that carry us back to *Endymion:* "Fainting with surprise"; "tender eye-dawn of aurorean love"" or, until it was later changed, "O Bloomiest." A few of them come from Mary Tighe's° *Psyche* (1805), which he had read as a youth, and only four months ago he mentioned to George: "Mrs. Tighe and Beattie° once delighted me—now I see through them and can find nothing in them—or weakness." That he was relatively uncritical, as such phrases came back to his mind, suggests how preoccupied he was, in these first stanzas, with something else.

On what part or aspect of the poem, then, were the new "pains" and "leisure" bestowed? He probably refers to the general effort (which is partly technical) to find some

---

Mary Tighe (1772–1810): an Irish poet whose *Psyche or The Legend of Love* impressed Keats.
James Beattie (1735–1803): one of the Pre-Romantic English poets.

way shorter than narrative, or dramatic tragedy, of capturing the drama of that "greeting of the Spirit" and its object about which he had once written to Benjamin Bailey. The "march of intellect" since the age of Milton had disclosed or created new complexities and doubts that embarrassed the confidence and completeness of this "greeting." Whether one liked it or not, poetry—if it was to retain its honesty—would have to become more inward. This at least had been his feeling exactly a year before. For on the one hand was the majestic confidence of classical and Renaissance poetry—poetry that rested on "seeming sure" points of reasoning; and on the other hand were the growing uncertainties, the impact of further knowledge, that he had suggested in his image of the darkening "Chamber of Maiden-Thought," the doors of which are gradually opening but all leading to dark passages ("We see not the balance of good and evil. . . . *We* are now in that state"). Here Wordsworth, though he may have "martyred" himself in the process and been forced to surrender epic grandeur by circumscribing his effort, had been honest before this demand; "and it seems to me that his Genius is explorative of those dark Passages. Now if we live, and go on thinking, we too shall explore them."

The challenge ahead included the further exploration of the human psyche as it tries to come to terms with life, and especially with increasing knowledge. Reading again about the goddess Psyche in Lemprière, and then turning directly from Lemprière to Apuleius and finding that Psyche was made a goddess only after the Augustan age— after the era of "Olympus' [now] faded hierarchy" was already coming to an end—he was struck by the relevance of this "late" deity to what seemed to him now the proper object of poetry and of his own efforts. He goes on, in his letter to George, before copying the new ode:

> You must recollect that Psyche was not embodied as a goddess before the time of Apuleius the Platonist who lived after the A[u]gustan age, and consequently the Goddess was never worshipped or sacrificed to with any of the ancient fervour—and perhaps never thought of in the old religion—I am more orthodox tha[n] to let a he[a]then Goddess be so neglected.

The story of Psyche and Cupid, which Keats read in William Adlington's translation (1566) of Apuleius (chapter 22), also had a potential moral that caught his imagination and, to some extent, merged with the general thought of the poem. Psyche, the youngest and most beautiful of three princesses, arouses the jealousy of Venus, who then commands her son Cupid—or Eros—to force Psyche to fall in love with the "most poore, most crooked, and the most vile" creature he can find. Meanwhile, all of Psyche's admirers, owing to the intervention of Venus, withdraw. Her bewildered father consults the oracle of Apollo, and is told to clothe her in mourning and leave her on a barren rock: she will in time be wed by a serpent. Seeing no alternative, the unhappy Psyche assents. "Then they brought her to the appointed rocks of the high hill . . . and so departed. The Torches and lights were put out." At length, however, the gentle Zephyrus carries the weeping Psyche "downe into a deepe valley," where she lies "sweetly couched . . . as in a bed of sweet and fragrant flowers" (some of Adlington's phrases and images reappear in the poem). Rested, she wanders for a while and then comes to a palace. A voice tells her it is the palace of her husband. She is waited on by invisible servants. At night her unknown husband comes; and so the days pass.

What has happened, of course, is that Love—hitherto mischievous and vagrant—has been won over to the mind or soul: Eros or Cupid, sent to make Psyche infatuated with the vilest and "most crooked" of objects, has himself fallen in love with her. But he can meet her only secretly and in the dark. Never seeing her husband, the curious Psyche pines with uncertainty. Her sisters, whom she is allowed to visit, persuade her that her husband is indeed the serpent predicted by Apollo's oracle. Following their advice, she hides a burning oil lamp, then brings it out as soon as her husband is asleep, and prepares to cut off his head with a razor. But seeing the form of Cupid, she falls trembling to her knees and hides her razor. A drop of burning oil falls from the lamp onto the shoulder of the god; he awakens, wounded with the burn, and flees. She tries to follow. Her wanderings are many and painful (one of them takes her to the precarious "ridge" of a "mountain"—echoed in Keats's phrase, "the wild-ridged mountains"). In time Cupid himself, healed of his wound, escapes through "a window of the chamber where hee was inclosed" and joins Psyche. Jupiter, at Cupid's petition, sanctions the marriage and makes Psyche immortal; and Love may thus be said to have rescued the mind.

3

A "greeting of the Spirit" and its object was still possible, in other words—and a greeting by the spirit of something not fully known or explored in that earlier age of what Keats now calls "happy pieties." With a sort of credo in mind—and so many of his poems had consisted of credos—he tried to face the subject directly: he addressed the poem to Psyche herself.

The latter, climactic part of the new poem was to be one more assertion of intention, like "Sleep and Poetry," the sonnet "On Sitting Down to Read *King Lear* Once Again," or the "Lines on Seeing a Lock of Milton's Hair." But the ode, he plainly hoped, would consist of more than the credo, the statement of intention: it was to have a more objective and if possible a more nearly dramatic structure. The new leisure and "pains" may well have included his effort to follow up the story of Psyche and Cupid in Apuleius, and then to think over its possible use. But the care was also technical in the strict sense. Reverting to the lyric after the narrative—or quasi-epic—*Hyperion,* which had not succeeded, he was attempting, as we have seen, to circumvent the sonnet (now so habitual to him) and to develop a longer, more flexible form.

With an uncertainty that extends for almost half the poem, he begins. Love (Eros or Cupid) could approach Psyche—as the myth went—only in darkness. But the poet (though it may have been merely a dream) now sees the two together in daylight. Could the sight have been genuine, and have come to him through a new understanding and through "awaken'd eyes"? The question, familiar in the earlier poems, is now basic in almost all the odes, especially the "Nightingale," "Indolence," and, in another way, the "Grecian Urn":

> O Goddess! hear these tuneless numbers, wrung
>   By sweet enforcement and remembrance dear,
> And pardon that thy secrets should be sung
>   Even into thine own soft-conchèd ear:
>
> Surely I dreamt today, or did I see
>   The wingèd Psyche with awaken'd eyes?

I wander'd in a forest thoughtlessly,
    And, on the sudden, fainting with surprise,
Saw two fair creatures, couchèd side by side.

The figures, like those on the Grecian urn, are somewhat apart: "Their lips touch'd not, but had not bade adieu." The poet could hardly help recognizing Cupid. His own situation is analogous (however far he is from being a god): he himself has been vagrant, if only through ignorance; he has been won over to the mind; he is ready to build a palace for this new subject, this new demand of conscience, as Cupid (in the tale by Apuleius) built one for Psyche. But he is so eager to get on to that resolve that the quick, feigned hesitation about the other figure is expressed in the banal phrasing of his early poems ("O happy, happy dove"), and the rapid transition, the acknowledgment, is effected in three words of mere exclamation:

    The wingèd boy I knew;
But who wast thou, O happy, happy dove?
    His Psyche true!

The twenty-three lines thus far consist of little more than filler: they are there to provide a setting. Three years before, in his primitive attempt at Guy's Hospital to write the "Specimen of an Induction," he had found descriptive setting inevitably usurping his attention; and after the setting, the poem then dwindled. Trying to overcome this temptation in his youthful second attempt at narrative, "Calidore," he had made his hero—after the descriptive opening—dart ludicrously cross the lake to a castle and then "leap along" the halls. The present quick recognition and bow, "His Psyche true!" derives from that effort. The "pains" bestowed on the "Ode to Psyche" affect the first third of it only in so far as they helped to keep down the sheer length of the preface, the setting. Such prefaces are dropped in the next three odes: setting is dispensed with, or merely implied. The modern, respectful attitude toward this ode is deserved. But the itch for novelty has encouraged a few critics to suggest that the poem, in some dark but fundamental way, has more to it as a whole than do the later odes. Among the many interests of the ode, the principal one is that, through writing it, Keats learned better how to proceed.

    With the setting condensed to twenty-three lines, he is now able to turn to what he wants to say. The real preface to the long, expanded sentence that makes up the close of the ode is put in the two next stanzas. Those two stanzas are parallel in form and wording, but somewhat antithetic in emphasis. The first stresses the nonacknowledgment thus far of this "latest born" yet "loveliest" among all "Olympus' faded hierarchy." This personification of the mind, of human understanding, far exceeds those simpler conceptions in the Olympian hierarchy, Diana and Venus:

Fairer than these, though temple thou hast none,
    Nor altar heap'd with flowers;
Nor virgin-choir to make delicious moan
    Upon the midnight hours;
No voice, no lute, no pipe, no incense sweet
    From chain-swung censer teeming;
No shrine, no grove, no oracle, no heat
    Of pale-mouth'd prophet dreaming.

The catalogue, however lyrically chanted, is deprecatory, by its very excess, and is put with mock nostalgia. It is only the externals, the ceremonial trappings, that have been denied Psyche because she came too late. (Perhaps unconsciously he remembers and echoes the phrases about the pagan deities in Milton's "On the Morning of Christ's Nativity.") Used in this way, the list permits the rhetoric of the following stanza: the catalogue of apparatus—which would have seemed sentimental and hyperbolic had it appeared there for the first time—can now be repeated as an answering assertion. Writing hastily—not even noticing when he copied out the poem for George that he begins the stanza "O Bloomiest! though too late for antique vows"—he continues, in what is the finished draft:

O brightest! though too late for antique vows,
  Too, too late for the fond believing lyre,
When holy were the haunted forest boughs,
  Holy the air, the water, and the fire.

The regret, though genuine, is not complete. The "pieties" by which the elements were regarded as holy were indeed "happy pieties"; and we think ahead to the "happiness" of the nightingale and the "happy" boughs and figures on the Grecian urn. But the word "fond," in "fond believing lyre," also includes the older meaning of "foolish." However far removed the present may be from that era of simple, happy belief, he can now see ("by my own eyes inspired"—the insight has to be self-won), among the faint shadows of the Olympians, the living, fluttering movement of the wings of Psyche, who was traditionally represented by the butterfly:

Yet even in these days so far retir'd
  From happy pieties, thy lucent fans,
  Fluttering among the faint Olympians,
I see, and sing, by my own eyes inspired.
So let me be thy choir, and make a moan
    Upon the midnight hours;
Thy voice thy lute, thy pipe, thy incense sweet
  From swingèd censer teeming;
Thy shrine, thy grove, thy oracle, thy heat
  Of pale-mouth'd prophet dreaming.

4

The essential part now follows—the reassertion of aim that was in his mind when he began the poem, the commitment to explore the "dark Passages," the "untrodden region"; and if phrases from Mary Tighe's *Psyche* ("untrodden forests," "paths untrodden") return to him, he is also echoing his own sonnet "To Homer":

Aye, on the shores of darkness there is light,
And precipices show untrodden green.

For the "untrodden region" of the mind, in this closing credo of the "Ode to Psyche," is also associated with precipices and steep mountainsides. Back in "Sleep and Poetry" he had spoken of his hope and anxiety, his "ardent prayer" and sense of inadequacy, in approaching the "very fane . . . of Poesy." But both the fear and the hope had been simply conceived. The "fane," in this new region he now hopes to explore, is not there to be discovered. It has to be built. And he now promises to do just that in this place where "branchèd thoughts" reach upward and fledge the surrounding hills (we recall the "labyrinth" of speculation he had described to Reynolds in the letter about the "Chamber of Maiden-Thought"—"My branchings out therefrom have been numerous"). The growth in awareness will bring new pain as well as pleasure, or rather unforeseen combinations of both.

Yes, I will be thy priest, and build a fane
   In some untrodden region of my mind,
Where branchèd thoughts, new grown with pleasant pain,
   Instead of pines shall murmur in the wind:
Far, far around shall those dark-cluster'd trees
   Fledge the wild-ridgèd mountains steep by steep.

In this protective labyrinth, still to be explored, there will be a "sanctuary" with all that a "working brain" may find or construct. And Fancy, seen as a "gardender," will, as Woodhouse had tried to assure Keats six months before, grow plants completely unknown and "without a name." "I understood you to say," Woodhouse had written (October 21, 1818), "that there was now nothing original to be written in poetry; that its riches were already exhausted." And Woodhouse went on to stress that the combination of ideas possible is almost infinite; that the development of "reflection & the moral sense" can, in an active mind, open new doors; that the complaint that there is nothing left to write is a rationalization of one's subjective fears and of one's "own dull brain" (a phrase that Keats within two weeks was to use in his "Ode to a Nightingale"). The ode continues:

And in the midst of this wide quietness
A rosy sanctuary will I dress
With the wreath'd trellis of a working brain,
   With buds, and bells, and stars without a name,
With all the gardener Fancy e'er could feign,
   Who breeding flowers, will never breed the same.

Naturally there will be uncertainty. The word "feign" is double-edged: there is the possibility of mere illusion as well as creativity. And he also thinks back to the lines from "The Recluse" that Wordsworth had printed as a "Prospectus" to his great endeavor, and from which Keats had quoted in the letter on the "Chamber of Maiden-Thought" ("the Mind of Man— / My haunt, and the main region of my song"). Wordsworth, for the task ahead, had invoked the aid of "a greater Muse" than Milton's: "For I must tread on shadowy ground." In Keats's own prospect, thought will inevitably be "shadowy" ("We see not the ballance of good and evil. We are in a Mist"). Nor can there be promise of the epic passion Wordsworth himself had to sacrifice, nor of dramatic intensity. The "delight" may be only "soft." But there will at least be whatever "shadowy thought can *win*." The spirit, in short, will include a devotion and commitment that can only be called Love. And from the tale by Apuleius, he perhaps recalls the passage where poor Psyche was left abandoned on the rocks of a high hill; and as the people departed "The Torches . . . were put out." He may even have thought of that window by which Cupid, near the end of the story, escaped from the chamber in which he was enclosed, though the open window had long since become an habitual image to Keats. In any case, a torch will now be burning brightly, and the window will be altogether open:

And there shall be for thee all soft delight
That shadowy thought can win,
A bright torch, and a casement ope at night,
To let the warm Love in!

And, as he finishes copying out the new poem for George, he writes, with a playfulness released by satisfaction and sudden confidence: "Here endethe ye Ode to Psyche."

14

READING ROBERT FROST IN DEPTH

A COMMENTARY ON FROST'S CAREER

Robert Frost (1874–1963) began his career slowly. His father was a journalist in San Francisco, where Frost was born. But after his father died, and when he was ten, the family moved to Lawrence, Massachusetts, to be closer to his mother's people. In his childhood he was close to the farming community, and his poetry has been indelibly marked by his love of the New England countryside. He spent a while at Dartmouth College but disliked the academic experience. Later he spent time at Harvard, but he drifted away to various kinds of work, mostly in trades involving some craftsmanship.

In 1912 he moved to England for three years. His first book of poetry, *A Boy's Will* (1913), was published in England. Some of his best-known poetry was published in *North of Boston* (1914), by which time Frost was established as a poet. He returned to the United States and settled on a farm in New Hampshire. His next book, *Mountain Interval* (1916), continued his development as a poet close to the soil. "The Road Not Taken" and "Birches" appeared in that volume. By this time he was fully recognized as an important American poet. His first *Collected Poems* (1930) won the Pulitzer Prize for Literature.

Frost taught sporadically at Amherst, Harvard, and the University of Michigan, but all the while he wrote and published poems and some verse plays. He won three more Pulitzer Prizes for his work. Late in his life, he became regarded as the American equivalent of a poet laureate. John Fitzgerald Kennedy invited him to read a poem at his inauguration as president in January, 1960.

Frost carefully cultivated the persona connected with farm life and New England seasons. But in his personal life he had great difficulties. Psychological instability and the eventual suicide of one of his children haunted his late years. The major biography of Lawrence Thompson (1966–1976) cast a shadow on Frost's reputation because it revealed unpleasant aspects of Frost's personality: professional jealousy and a manner that made life very difficult for his family. However, Frost's work reveals a deeply sympathetic man as well as a man capable of serious philosophical reflection. His work is characterized by accessible language, concrete experiences, and direct expression. In many ways he had a difficult life, as he reveals in some of his letters, and paid a personal price for his health and his successes, neither of which were bequeathed to his children. At times he felt personally responsible for their problems. However, he maintained a deep commitment to his work, and contemporary critics have been much kinder to him than was his biographer.

The Death of the Hired Man _____ *1914*

Mary sat musing on the lamp-flame at the table,
Waiting for Warren. When she heard his step,
She ran on tiptoe down the darkened passage
To meet him in the doorway with the news
And put him on his guard. "Silas is back."   5
She pushed him outward with her through the door
And shut it after her. "Be kind," she said.
She took the market things from Warren's arms
And set them on the porch, then drew him down
To sit beside her on the wooden steps.   10

"When was I ever anything but kind to him?
But I'll not have the fellow back," he said.
"I told him so last haying, didn't I?
If he left then, I said, that ended it.
What good is he? Who else will harbor him   15
At his age for the little he can do?
What help he is there's no depending on.
Off he goes always when I need him most.
He thinks he ought to earn a little pay,
Enough at least to buy tobacco with,   20
So he won't have to beg and be beholden.
'All right,' I say, 'I can't afford to pay
Any fixed wages, though I wish I could.'
'Someone else can.' 'Then someone else will have to.'
I shouldn't mind his bettering himself   25
If that was what it was. You can be certain,
When he begins like that, there's someone at him
Trying to coax him off with pocket money—
In haying time, when any help is scarce.
In winter he comes back to us. I'm done."   30

"Sh! not so loud: he'll hear you," Mary said.

"I want him to: he'll have to soon or late."

"He's worn out. He's asleep beside the stove.
When I came up from Rowe's I found him here,
Huddled against the barn door fast asleep,   35
A miserable sight, and frightening, too—
You needn't smile—I didn't recognize him—
I wasn't looking for him—and he's changed.
Wait till you see."

                    "Where did you say he'd been?"

"He didn't say. I dragged him to the house,   40
And gave him tea and tried to make him smoke.
I tried to make him talk about his travels.
Nothing would do: he just kept nodding off."

"What did he say? Did he say anything?"

"But little."

                    "Anything? Mary, confess   45
He said he'd come to ditch the meadow for me."

"Warren!"

                    "But did he? I just want to know."

"Of course he did. What would you have him say?
Surely you wouldn't grudge the poor old man
Some humble way to save his self-respect.   50
He added, if you really care to know,
He meant to clear the upper pasture, too.
That sounds like something you have heard before?
Warren, I wish you could have heard the way
He jumbled everything. I stopped to look   55
Two or three times—he made me feel so queer—
To see if he was talking in his sleep.
He ran on Harold Wilson—you remember—
The boy you had in haying four years since.
He's finished school, and teaching in his college.   60
Silas declares you'll have to get him back.
He says they two will make a team for work:
Between them they will lay this farm as smooth!
The way he mixed that in with other things.
He thinks young Wilson a likely lad, though daft   65
On education—you know how they fought
All through July under the blazing sun,
Silas up on the cart to build the load,
Harold along beside to pitch it on."

"Yes, I took care to keep well out of earshot."   70

"Well, those days trouble Silas like a dream.
You wouldn't think they would. How some things linger!

Harold's young college-boy's assurance piqued him.
After so many years he still keeps finding
Good arguments he sees he might have used. 75
I sympathize. I know just how it feels
To think of the right thing to say too late.
Harold's associated in his mind with Latin.
He asked me what I thought of Harold's saying
He studied Latin, like the violin, 80
Because he liked it—that an argument!
He said he couldn't make the boy believe
He could find water with a hazel prong—
Which showed how much good school had ever done him.
He wanted to go over that. But most of all 85
He thinks if he could have another chance
To teach him how to build a load of hay——"

"I know, that's Silas' one accomplishment.
He bundles every forkful in its place,
And tags and numbers it for future reference, 90
So he can find and easily dislodge it
In the unloading. Silas does that well.
He takes it out in bunches like big birds' nests.
You never see him standing on the hay
He's trying to lift, straining to lift himself." 95

"He thinks if he could teach him that, he'd be
Some good perhaps to someone in the world.
He hates to see a boy the fool of books.
Poor Silas, so concerned for other folk,
And nothing to look backward to with pride, 100
And nothing to look forward to with hope,
So now and never any different."

Part of a moon was falling down the west,
Dragging the whole sky with it to the hills.
Its light poured softly in her lap. She saw it 105
And spread her apron to it. She put out her hand
Among the harplike morning-glory strings,
Taut with the dew from garden bed to eaves,
As if she played unheard some tenderness
That wrought on him beside her in the night. 110
"Warren," she said, "he has come home to die:
You needn't be afraid he'll leave you this time."

"Home," he mocked gently.

               "Yes, what else but home?
It all depends on what you mean by home.
Of course he's nothing to us, any more 115
Than was the hound that came a stranger to us
Out of the woods, worn out upon the trail."

"Home is the place where, when you have to go there,
They have to take you in."

                                "I should have called it
Something you somehow haven't to deserve."   120

Warren leaned out and took a step or two,
Picked up a little stick, and brought it back
And broke it in his hand and tossed it by.
"Silas has better claim on us you think
Than on his brother? Thirteen little miles   125
As the road winds would bring him to his door.
Silas has walked that for no doubt today.
Why doesn't he go there? His brother's rich,
A somebody—director in the bank."

"He never told us that."

                              "We know it, though."   130

"I think his brother ought to help, of course.
I'll see to it that if there is need. He ought of right
To take him in, and might be willing to—
He may be better than appearances.
But have some pity on Silas. Do you think   135
If he had any pride in claiming kin
Or anything he looked for from his brother,
He'd keep so still about him all this time?"

"I wonder what's between them."

                            "I can tell you.
Silas is what he is—we wouldn't mind him—   140
But just the kind that kinsfolk can't abide.
He never did a thing so very bad.
He don't know why he isn't quite as good
As anybody. Worthless though he is,
He won't be made ashamed to please his brother."   145

"*I* can't think Si ever hurt anyone."

"No, but he hurt my heart the way he lay
And rolled his old head on that sharp-edged chair-back.
He wouldn't let me put him on the lounge.
You must go in and see what you can do.   150
I made the bed up for him there tonight.
You'll be surprised at him—how much he's broken.
His working days are done; I'm sure of it."

"I'd not be in a hurry to say that."

"I haven't been. Go, look, see for yourself.   155
But, Warren, please remember how it is:
He's come to help you ditch the meadow.

He has a plan. You mustn't laugh at him.
He may not speak of it, and then he may.
I'll sit and see if that small sailing cloud   160
Will hit or miss the moon."

                 It hit the moon.
Then there were three there, making a dim row,
The moon, the little silver cloud, and she.

Warren returned—too soon, it seemed to her—
Slipped to her side, caught up her hand and waited.   165

"Warren?" she questioned.

              "Dead," was all he answered.

Home Burial _____ *1914*

He saw her from the bottom of the stairs
Before she saw him. She was starting down,
Looking back over her shoulder at some fear.
She took a doubtful step and then undid it
To raise herself and look again. He spoke   5
Advancing toward her: "What is it you see
From up there always?—for I want to know."
She turned and sank upon her skirts at that,
And her face changed from terrified to dull.
He said to gain time: "What is it you see?"   10
Mounting until she cowered under him.
"I will find out now—you must tell me, dear."
She, in her place, refused him any help,
With the least stiffening of her neck and silence.
She let him look, sure that he wouldn't see,   15
Blind creature; and awhile he didn't see.
But at last he murmured, "Oh," and again, "Oh."

"What is it—what?" she said.
                  "Just that I see."

"You don't," she challenged. "Tell me what it is."

"The wonder is I didn't see at once.   20
I never noticed it from here before.
I must be wonted to it—that's the reason.
The little graveyard where my people are!
So small the window frames the whole of it.
Not so much larger than a bedroom, is it?   25
There are three stones of slate and one of marble,
Broad-shouldered little slabs there in the sunlight
On the sidehill. We haven't to mind *those*.
But I understand: it is not the stones,

But the child's mound——"

        "Don't, don't, don't, don't," she cried.   30

She withdrew, shrinking from beneath his arm
That rested on the banister, and slid downstairs;
And turned on him with such a daunting look,
He said twice over before he knew himself:
"Can't a man speak of his own child he's lost?"   35

"Not you!—Oh, where's my hat? Oh, I don't need it!
I must get out of here. I must get air.—
I don't know rightly whether any man can."

"Amy! Don't go to someone else this time.
Listen to me. I won't come down the stairs."   40
He sat and fixed his chin between his fists.
"There's something I should like to ask you, dear."

"You don't know how to ask it."

        "Help me, then."

Her fingers moved the latch for all reply.

"My words are nearly always an offense.   45
I don't know how to speak of anything
So as to please you. But I might be taught,
I should suppose. I can't say I see how.
A man must partly give up being a man
With womenfolk. We could have some arrangement   50
By which I'd bind myself to keep hands off
Anything special you're a-mind to name.
Though I don't like such things 'twixt those that love.
Two that don't love can't live together without them.
But two that do can't live together with them."   55
She moved the latch a little. "Don't—don't go.
Don't carry it to someone else this time.
Tell me about it if it's something human.
Let me into your grief. I'm not so much
Unlike other folks as your standing there   60
Apart would make me out. Give me my chance.
I do think, though, you overdo it a little.
What was it brought you up to think it the thing
To take your mother-loss of a first child
So inconsolably—in the face of love.   65
You'd think his memory might be satisfied——"

"There you go sneering now!"

        "I'm not, I'm not!
You make me angry. I'll come down to you.
God, what a woman! And it's come to this,
A man can't speak of his own child that's dead."   70

"You can't because you don't know how to speak.
If you had any feelings, you that dug
With your own hand—how could you?—his little grave;
I saw you from that very window there,
Making the gravel leap and leap in air,   75
Leap up, like that, like that, and land so lightly
And roll back down the mound beside the hole.
I thought, Who is that man? I didn't know you.
And I crept down the stairs and up the stairs
To look again, and still your spade kept lifting.   80
Then you came in. I heard your rumbling voice
Out in the kitchen, and I don't know why,
But I went near to see with my own eyes.
You could sit there with the stains on your shoes
Of the fresh earth from your own baby's grave   85
And talk about your everyday concerns.
You had stood the spade up against the wall
Outside there in the entry, for I saw it."

"I shall laugh the worst laugh I ever laughed.
I'm cursed. God, if I don't believe I'm cursed."   90

"I can repeat the very words you were saying:
'Three foggy mornings and one rainy day
Will rot the best birch fence a man can build.'
Think of it, talk like that at such a time!
What had how long it takes a birch to rot   95
To do with what was in the darkened parlor?
You *couldn't* care! The nearest friends can go
With anyone to death, comes so far short
They might as well not try to go at all.
No, from the time when one is sick to death,   100
One is alone, and he dies more alone
Friends make pretense of following to the grave,
But before one is in it, their minds are turned
And making the best of their way back to life
And living people, and things they understand.   105
But the world's evil. I won't have grief so
If I can change it. Oh, I won't, I won't!"

"There, you have said it all and you feel better.
You won't go now. You're crying. Close the door.
The heart's gone out of it: why keep it up?   110
Amy! There's someone coming down the road!"

"*You*—oh, you think the talk is all. I must go—
Somewhere out of this house. How can I make you——"

"If—you—do!" She was opening the door wider.
"Where do you mean to go? First tell me that.   115
I'll follow and bring you back by force. I *will!*—"

After Apple-Picking ———————————————————————— *1914*

My long two-pointed ladder's sticking through a tree
Toward heaven still,
And there's a barrel that I didn't fill
Beside it, and there may be two or three
Apples I didn't pick upon some bough.   5
But I am done with apple-picking now.
Essence of winter sleep is on the night,
The scent of apples: I am drowsing off.
I cannot rub the strangeness from my sight
I got from looking through a pane of glass   10
I skimmed this morning from the drinking trough
And held against the world of hoary grass.
It melted, and I let it fall and break.
But I was well
Upon my way to sleep before it fell,   15
And I could tell
What form my dreaming was about to take.
Magnified apples appear and disappear,
Stem end and blossom end,
And every fleck of russet showing clear.   20
My instep arch not only keeps the ache,
It keeps the pressure of a ladder-round.
I feel the ladder sway as the boughs bend.
And I keep hearing from the cellar bin
The rumbling sound   25
Of load on load of apples coming in.
For I have had too much
Of apple-picking: I am overtired
Of the great harvest I myself desired.
There were ten thousand thousand fruit to touch,   30
Cherish in hand, lift down, and not let fall.·
For all
That struck the earth,
No matter if not bruised or spiked with stubble,
Went surely to the cider-apple heap   35
As of no worth.
One can see what will trouble
This sleep of mine, whatever sleep it is.
Were he not gone,
The woodchuck could say whether it's like his   40
Long sleep, as I describe its coming on,
Or just some human sleep.

The Road Not Taken ———————————————————————— *1916*

Two roads diverged in a yellow wood,
And sorry I could not travel both

And be one traveler, long I stood
And looked down one as far as I could
To where it bent in the undergrowth;   5

Then took the other, as just as fair,
And having perhaps the better claim,
Because it was grassy and wanted wear;
Though as for that, the passing there
Had worn them really about the same,   10

And both that morning equally lay
In leaves no step had trodden black.
Oh, I kept the first for another day!
Yet knowing how way leads on to way,
I doubted if I should ever come back.   15

I shall be telling this with a sigh
Somewhere ages and ages hence:
Two roads diverged in a wood, and I—
I took the one less traveled by,
And that has made all the difference.   20

The Oven Bird _____ *1916*

There is a singer everyone has heard,
Loud, a mid-summer and a mid-wood bird,
Who makes the solid tree trunks sound again.
He says that leaves are old and that for flowers
Mid-summer is to spring as one to ten.   5
He says the early petal-fall is past,
When pear and cherry bloom went down in showers
On sunny days a moment overcast;
And comes that other fall we name the fall.
He says the highway dust is over all.   10
The bird would cease and be as other birds
But that he knows in singing not to sing.
The question that he frames in all but words
Is what to make of a diminished thing.

"Out, Out—" _____ *1916*

The buzz saw snarled and rattled in the yard
And made dust and dropped stove-length sticks of wood,
Sweet-scented stuff when the breeze drew across it.
And from there those that lifted eyes could count
Five mountain ranges one behind the other   5
Under the sunset far into Vermont.
And the saw snarled and rattled, snarled and rattled,

As it ran light, or had to bear a load.
And nothing happened: day was all but done.
Call it a day, I wish they might have said   10
To please the boy by giving him the half hour
That a boy counts so much when saved from work.
His sister stood beside them in her apron
To tell them "Supper." At the word, the saw,
As if to prove saws knew what supper meant,   15
Leaped out at the boy's hand, or seemed to leap—
He must have given the hand. However it was,
Neither refused the meeting. But the hand!
The boy's first outcry was a rueful laugh,
As he swung toward them holding up the hand,   20
Half in appeal, but half as if to keep
The life from spilling. Then the boy saw all—
Since he was old enough to know, big boy
Doing a man's work, though a child at heart—
He saw all spoiled. "Don't let him cut my hand off—   25
The doctor, when he comes. Don't let him, sister!"
So. But the hand was gone already.
The doctor put him in the dark of ether.
He lay and puffed his lips out with his breath.
And then—the watcher at his pulse took fright.   30
No one believed. They listened at his heart.
Little—less—nothing!—and that ended it.
No more to build on there. And they, since they
Were not the one dead, turned to their affairs.

Stopping by Woods on a Snowy Evening _____ 1923

Whose woods these are I think I know.
His house is in the village, though;
He will not see me stopping here
To watch his woods fill up with snow.

My little horse must think it queer   5
To stop without a farmhouse near
Between the woods and frozen lake
The darkest evening of the year.

He gives his harness bells a shake
To ask if there is some mistake.   10
The only other sound's the sweep
Of easy wind and downy flake.

The woods are lovely, dark, and deep,
But I have promises to keep,
And miles to go before I sleep,   15
And miles to go before I sleep.

Acquainted with the Night ———————————————————— *1928*

I have been one acquainted with the night.
I have walked out in rain—and back in rain.
I have outwalked the furthest city light.

I have looked down the saddest city lane.
I have passed by the watchman on his beat   5
And dropped my eyes, unwilling to explain.

I have stood still and stopped the sound of feet
When far away an interrupted cry
Came over houses from another street,

But not to call me back or say good-by;   10
And further still at an unearthly height
One luminary clock against the sky

Proclaimed the time was neither wrong nor right.
I have been one acquainted with the night.

West-Running Brook ———————————————————— *1928*

"Fred, where is north?" "North?

                              North is there, my love.
The brook runs west."

                    "West-Running Brook then call it."
(West-Running Brook men call it to this day.)
"What does it think it's doing running west
When all the other country brooks flow east   5
To reach the ocean? It must be the brook
Can trust itself to go by contraries
The way I can with you—and you with me—
Because we're—we're—I don't know what we are.
What are we?"

           "Young or new?"

                              "We must be something   10
We've said we two. Let's change that to we three.
As you and I are married to each other,
We'll both be married to the brook. We'll build
Our bridge across it, and the bridge shall be
Our arm thrown over it asleep beside it.   15
Look, look, it's waving to us with a wave
To let us know it hears me."

                         "Why, my dear,
That wave's been standing off this jut of shore—"
(The black stream, catching on a sunken rock,

Flung backward on itself in one white wave,   20
And the white water rode the black forever,
Not gaining but not losing, like a bird
White feathers from the struggle of whose breast
Flecked the dark stream and flecked the darker pool
Below the point, and were at last driven wrinkled   25
In a white scarf against the far-shore alders.)
"That wave's been standing off this jut of shore
Ever since rivers, I was going to say,
Were made in heaven. It wasn't waved to us."

"It wasn't, yet it was. If not to you,   30
It was to me—in an annunciation."

"Oh, if you take it off to lady-land,
As't were the country of the Amazons
We men must see you to the confines of
And leave you there, ourselves forbid to enter—   35
It is your brook! I have no more to say."

"Yes, you have, too. Go on. You thought of something."

"Speaking of contraries, see how the brook
In that white wave runs counter to itself.
It is from that in water we were from   40
Long, long before we were from any creature.
Here we, in our impatience of the steps,
Get back to the beginning of beginnings,
The stream of everything that runs away.
Some say existence like a Pirouot   45
And Pirouette, forever in one place,
Stands still and dances, but it runs away;
It seriously, sadly, runs away
To fill the abyss's void with emptiness.
It flows beside us in this water brook,   50
But it flows over us. It flows between us
To separate us for a panic moment.
It flows between us, over us, and *with* us.
And it is time, strength, tone, light, life, and love—
And even substance lapsing unsubstantial;   55
The universal cataract of death
That spends to nothingness—and unresisted,
Save by some strange resistance in itself,
Not just a swerving, but a throwing back,
As if regret were in it and were sacred.   60
It has this throwing backward on itself
So that the fall of most of it is always
Raising a little, sending up a little.
Our life runs down in sending up the clock.
The brook runs down in sending up our life.   65
The sun runs down in sending up the brook.

And there is something sending up the sun.
It is this backward motion toward the source,
Against the stream, that most we see ourselves in,
The tribute of the current to the source.   70
It is from this in nature we are from.
It is most us."

    "Today will be the day
You said so."

    "No, today will be the day
You said the brook was called West-Running Brook."

"Today will be the day of what we both said."   75

Neither Out Far nor In Deep _____ *1936*

The people along the sand
All turn and look one way.
They turn their back on the land.
They look at the sea all day.

As long as it takes to pass   5
A ship keeps raising its hull;
The wetter ground like glass
Reflects a standing gull.

The land may vary more;
But wherever the truth may be—   10
The water comes ashore,
And the people look at the sea.

They cannot look out far.
They cannot look in deep.
But when was that ever a bar   15
To any watch they keep?

Provide, Provide _____ *1936*

The witch that came (the withered hag)
To wash the steps with pail and rag
Was once the beauty Abishag,°

The picture pride of Hollywood.
Too many fall from great and good   5
For you to doubt the likelihood.

3 *Abishag:* King David's concubine (1 Kings, 1).

Die early and avoid the fate.
Or if predestined to die late,
Make up your mind to die in state.

Make the whole stock exchange your own!   10
If need be occupy a throne,
Where nobody can call *you* crone.

Some have relied on what they knew,
Others on being simply true.
What worked for them might work for you.   15

No memory of having starred
Atones for later disregard
Or keeps the end from being hard.

Better to go down dignified
With boughten friendship at your side   20
Than none at all. Provide, provide!

Auspex _____ *1960*

Once in a California Sierra
I was swooped down upon when I was small,
And measured, but not taken after all,
By a great eagle bird in all its terror.

Such auspices are very hard to read.   5
My parents when I ran to them averred
I was rejected by the royal bird
As one who would not make a Ganymede.°

Not find a barkeep unto Jove in me?
I have remained resentful to this day   10
When any but myself presumed to say
That there was anything I couldn't be.

8 *Ganymede:* cupbearer to Jove, chief of Roman gods.

QUESTIONS FOR CRITICAL READING

1. Frost has often been complimented for his having found rhythms appropriate to the New England experience. Examine "The Death of the Hired Man" for its rhythmic qualities. What is the meter of the poem? How does Frost treat breaks or the lack of them at the end of lines? Does he often use a caesura in the middle of lines?

2. What seems to be the most common metrical pattern in this group of poems?

3. How important is the psychological or interior life of the characters in these poems? Is it characteristic of Frost to probe the interior life of people in his poems? Why?

4. How would you describe the dramatic situations that Frost sometimes examines? What is the source of the dramatic tension in his poetry?

5. Which of the images in the poems seem most powerful to you? What is the source of Frost's imagery? Is it consistent throughout this sample of his work?

6. Which symbols are most powerful in these poems? How obvious are Frost's symbols? Would it be possible for readers to read the poetry and not notice the symbols?

7. When Frost rhymes, does he seem to have a special purpose? Comment on the power of rhyme in any of these poems. Is it decoration, or is it a structural and emotional necessity?

8. What seems to be Frost's attitude toward women in these poems? Would you call him a feminist in his sympathies?

9. Frost spent much of his life concerned with making a living. Is there evidence in these poems of an awareness of economic realities? What seems to be Frost's attitude toward economics?

10. What stylistic qualities tend to identify all these poems as Frost's? What are the hallmarks of Frost's style?

RESOURCES FOR READING FROST

Letters of Robert Frost to Louis Untermeyer

The poet and critic Louis Untermeyer (1885–1977) began a correspondence with Robert Frost in 1915 after having read and written a review of *North of Boston*. At that time Untermeyer lived in Newark, New Jersey, managing a family business. But he also wrote poetry, had begun a career as a critic, and eventually became well known for his often revised anthology *Modern American Poetry*, first published in 1919. The correspondence between the two writers was lively and often very personal. The excerpts that appear here concern two things: first, some of Frost's most interesting comments about poetry and his own methods, and second, some interesting personal comments late in his life about his career. Untermeyer wanted some information about the various jobs and duties Frost had when he was younger, and two interesting letters in 1950 resulted. Frost talks about his early life with considerable frankness.

To *Louis Untermeyer, 1916*

No, I didn't read the book. I'll tell you what I did do, though. I took the Midnight Horror out of Littleton not long ago, and on the train with me I had about as many good-looking boys and girls as there are great poets in the book. They were of the Lisbon High School which had just beaten at basket-ball for a second time the Littleton High School. And they were yelling glad. And this is what they kept saying all together and out loud: it came somewhere near expressing my feelings, though at the same time it shocked me: since as you know I am not a swearing man: I couldn't help liking the liberty taken in the rhyme: all the old rhyme pairs are so worn out that I'm ready to permit anything for the sake of a fresh combination: this was a new one to me—It may not be to you: well here goes: I mustn't put you off any longer: this is what the good looking children said:

Lisbon *once*—Lisbon *twice!*
Holy jumping Jesus Christ!

Maybe you don't like me to talk this way. I can see that I am going to make enemies if I keep on. Still that won't be anything new or strange. I had nothing but enemies three years ago this Christmas.

Why go into details? Granted that there are a few good poems in the book—I read yours and liked it because it *says* something, first felt and then unfolded in thought as the poem wrote itself. That's what makes a poem. A poem is never a put-up job so to speak. It begins as a lump in the throat, a sense of wrong, a homesickness, a lovesickness. It is never a thought to begin with. It is at its best when it is a tantalizing vagueness. It finds its thought and succeeds, or doesn't find it and comes to nothing. It finds its thought or makes its thought. I suppose it finds it lying around with others not so much to its purpose in a more or less full mind. That's why it oftener comes to nothing in youth before experience has filled the mind with thoughts. It may be a big big emotion then and yet finds nothing it can embody in. It finds the thought and the thought finds the words. Let's say again: A poem particularly must not begin with thought first.

To *Louis Untermeyer, 1929*

Nothing was a solution for you. You had no idea I thought it was. It's lucky you haven't been seeing me or hearing from me the last two years or you would have had as many false solutions as I have had phases. I can't help seeking a solution for anybody in your predicament. But it's just as well I shouldn't be where I could propose every solution I think of. I mean I shouldn't be encouraged or allowed to propose everyone. I don't believe in myself as a problem-solver. Honestly. Though I can't help thinking at this moment that if Jean only had the self-respect to act out in good faith her independence of you you might, left to your own freedom of movement, find that she was the only girl you wanted to live with. She drains you insensible with her desperate demands on you. I told her that. I ought not to be telling it to you: it might make the remedy less effective for you to know about it. But never mind: nothing I say matters in a situation that I thought in the first place was none of my business and have now pretty well proved to have been none of my business. I'd just like to see you adopting four children to run your Adirondack farm with. But you wouldn't gratify me that much. You'd be afraid you were amusing me.

Well, to hell with nearly everything—with everything but poetry, politics, and true religion—and a few friends and relatives—a very few. And I forgot farming. I bought a farm for myself for Christmas. One hundred and fifty three acres in all, fifty in woods. The house a poor little cottage of five rooms, two ordinary fireplaces, and one large kitchen fireplace in all in one central chimney as it was in the beginning. The central chimney is the best part of it—that and the woods. You mustn't be jealous, though jealousy is a passion I approve of and attribute to angels. May I be guarded and watched over always by the jealousy of a strong nature. It is better than arms around the body. Jealousy alone gives me the sense of being held. My farm probably doesn't compare with yours for view. But it looks away to the north so that you would know you were in the mountains. We have no trout brook, but there is a live spring that I am told should be made into a trout pond. There is a small grove of white paper birches doubling daylight. The woods are a little too far from the house. I must bring them nearer by the power of music like Amphion or Orpheus. It is an old occupation with me. The trees have learned that they have to come where I play them to. I enjoy the power I find I have over them. You must see us together, the trees dancing obedience to the poet (so called). You'll exclaim.

I ain't going to mention books this time.

Ever yours
Robert Frost

[South Shaftsbury, Vt.
August 12, 1929]

Dear Louis:

My farm is fast going back to wilderness—as fast as can be expected, the doctor and nurse would say. How is your farm? I ask out of politeness more than any real interest. My farm has got a considerable start of the cows in its pasture trees. Give it a year or two more unpastured and I doubt if I will ever be overtaken. Seventy-five years from now it will show a sugar bush to match yours. You wait! You are younger than I am, so I leave it to you to do the waiting. Meanwhile you ought to have to see all the H—L hinges there are in our farm house. In those we XL. In those we superiorate. Our barns are coming down little by little, a board at a time as the mood comes over Wade our poet in labour—at, I mean. And as the barns come down the view comes out. Our trickle (as compared with your torrent) has held its own through the drought with pristine vitality. Some are in favor of calling the farm The Trickle. Marjorie wants it called Nine Barns in memory of the barns it once had. But Prescott[1] has become accustomed to The Gully, and one hates to undeceive a child.

We're to meet then on and around the 27th. I had difficulty in fixing on a date because I hate to face eventualities at this time of year.

I'll have to write you out a copy of The Egg and the Machine: I have no one to type for me.

Lankes[2] is over at the Gully camping out. But I am afraid we are not giving him just the company he wants in Wade Van Dore.[3]

[1]Prescott, christened William Prescott after his grandfather and great-grandfather, was the son of Carol and Lillian La Batt Frost.
[2]J. Lankes, engraver, made many woodcuts for Robert's poems, including those in the limited edition of *New Hampshire.*
[3]Wade Van Dore, one of Robert's "boys," was a sort of disciple who, at that time, earned his keep as Robert's part-time hired man.

Box 100– Route 2
South Miami, Florida
February 15, 1950

Dear Louis:

I am glad you reminded me of the colleges. We must try to get a true picture of me with them—of course in your own words—I'm not trying to write your biographic preface to *The Road Not Taken* (as you call it). My special stays have been at Dartmouth, Amherst, and Michigan, but I have belonged longest, nearly twenty-five years of the last thirty-five, and belong now to Amherst. Amherst is the only place where I have had *markable* classes. I have made almost a practice of lingering round for several days at a time to lecture and visit with the faculty and students at many other colleges. And as you haven't failed to notice I have had honorary degrees from many.

Perhaps that's enough about me as teacher. Still perhaps you might find it grist to your mill that I was most really and truly an all-out teacher back at Salem, New Hampshire, where I presided over twelve barefoot children under twelve in a district school by the woods and often sitting on the lid of the woodbox by the stove wrote poetry (some of it the poetry of *A Boy's Will*) on the window sill for my table. I worked the hardest at teaching for my five years at Pinkerton Academy in Derry, New Hampshire. I got invited in there on the strength of "A Tuft of Flowers" read aloud at a village banquet not by me but by someone else with me sitting by with my head hung down. I liked the job. I never hated anything new and strange enough to give me ideas.

The way to speak so as to get a true picture of the odd jobs I took from time to time to help get along with would be to call them merely makeshift, I suppose. We have to be careful not to claim for me that I originated as a bobbin boy, cobbler, or like poor Clare and Bloomfield[1] as a farm hand. I simply turned my hand to most and turned it good (or pretty good) in various situations, as Kipling has it, and never mind what so long as I got by while furtively fooling with poetry. One year I was up on a ten foot ladder trimming the carbon-pencil lamps over the mule frames in the Arlington Textile Mills. But one year I was editing all by myself the old *Lawrence Sentinel* newspaper. Another I was writing paragraphs as a sort of columnist on *The Lawrence American*. But before all that I was getting an audience and hiring a hall in Boston for a Shakespearean reader. I seemed without pride or even without self-respect in those days; I didn't care what I was looked down on for doing. You see the danger of distorting me into too humble a beginning. I always had the keys of the city to play with so as not to take big things too seriously. I walked out of two colleges like nothing at all. I was no rebel. I must have left from failure to see the difference between being intellectual in college and being intellectual outside of college. I got suspicious that it was very much up to me to find out for myself whether I had it in me to write and think. I was shifting my dependence you might say from teachers to writers who had written before me.

You might like to hear a little about the first poem I wrote. I read my first book *Scottish Chiefs* in my fourteenth year. I wrote my first poem in my fifteenth. It must have spring full grown, forty four-line stanzas from Prescott's *Conquest of Mexico*. I gave it to the senior editing our high school Bulletin and saw it in print that month. It exists at the Jones Library in Amherst to this day. The theme was the bad night the Indians gave the Spaniards to my gratification when they drove them temporarily back from Tenochtitlan. There's a lot of history in it and a lot of excitement but not much else. I wrote about ten pieces in rhyme and blank verse in the next two years and then I wrote "My Butterfly," and sent it to *The Independent*. And in the ten lines there beginning "The grey grass scarce dappled with the snow" I found myself. Don't you think so?

Expect a second installment of this dictation to K. by the next mail but one (or two). But seriously I mean it. I'll do some more tomorrow. Then we may mention a few poems for you to bring in if you want to indulge us.

Ever yours
Robert

---

[1]Robert Bloomfield, author of *The Farmer's Boy*, published in 1800, was often compared to John Clare, a far superior poet.

(Written in great haste before train time)

Box 100–Route 2
South Miami, Florida.
February 21, 1950

Dear Louis:

All right let's have some sort of chronology for your guidance: I helped elect Grover Cleveland in San Francisco in 1884—marched in torchlight processions—rode on a fire engine—pulled by one or two hundred men in one procession. My father was chairman of the democratic city committee. I campaigned through all the saloons with him—plastered their ceilings with campaign literature, using a silver dollar to drive in the tack. I didn't go to school much till I came East in 1885 right after my father's death.

Came to Lawrence in 1885 and started school there in a grade that would have got me into the Lawrence High School at sixteen or seventeen. In '86 my mother went to teach district school at Salem Depot, New Hampshire. After one year and a half of up-graded school there I went eight miles down to Lawrence and passed by examination into the Lawrence High School from which I graduated valedictorian in 1892 about the time I would have entered if my bad luck had kept me in the city graded schools. My year and a half of the district school and my four years in the Lawrence High School were the heart of my education. They suited me perfectly.

I nailed shanks (drove six nails into the hollow of the sole of the shoes) in a shoe shop and had a mouthful of nails all the summer of my twelfth year. It was piece work and I earned better pay than I was to earn for ten years. That was my cobbling.

From then on I spent all my vacations either in a shoe shop or on a farm as a hired hand till I got through High School. The summer of 1891 I left a farm for a job pushing a bobbin wagon in a textile mill in Lawrence—a mistake for my health.

Passed first half of entrance exams for Harvard in 1891 but was sent in 1892 to Dartmouth by my grandmother whose idea was to save me from drink. Tended gate at a textile mill summer of '92—the year Lizzie Borden was being tried. At Christmas or just after left Dartmouth to come home and take my mother's room in the grammar school at Methuen, Massachusetts. She had been having a hard time with some rough boys. I was feeling pretty rough myself from hazing and all that at college. I asked the school committee to let me see what I could do with the boys. My victory over them though decisive was Pyrrhic and I quit after one term. I spent the summer of '93 farming for myself after a fashion on a rented place near Canobie Lake, New Hampshire. Read advertisements looking for what to do next. Set out to promote a Shakespearean reader but gave him up as not distinguished enough after trying him on a small Boston audience I got together for him—I don't know how. One of the audience was Rolfe the old scholar, another was the dramatic critic of the *Transcript.*

In '93 began my stretch at trimming lights and tending dynamos in the Arlington Mills in Lawrence, Massachusetts. Must have gone out to teach a spring term of '94 at District School No. 9 (I think) in Salem. See "A Lone Striker."

Spent the summer of '94 alone with a dog in an abandoned farmhouse, the last house away up Ossippee Mountain. Had to get rid of the dog because he was gun shy and jumped on me in bed at the first roll of thunder.

In '94 began as a reporter on the Lawrence *American* but gravitated to the editorial page where I wrote "paragraphs" some of which though in prose were really eclogues. I remember the subject of two or three. Out of them came "Mending Wall," "The Woodpile," and "Two Look at Two."

Married in 1895 right after Elinor graduated from St. Lawrence University.

For the next five years I took more or less part in my mother's private and tutorial school in Lawrence though I was doing regular work at Harvard for two of the years, '97 and '98. I was of the class of 1901 along with Wallace Stevens but I never heard of him till long afterward. I had a course with Santayana. I ran all to Latin, Greek, and Philosophy till I ran away.

My mother died in 1900 and her school might have fallen to me if I had felt executive enough for the responsibility.

My grandfather helped me to go to college both times. Elinor now asked him to buy me a farm for my health. I farmed exclusively for five years and then began part-time teaching at Pinkerton Academy to supplement my farming. The extra money enabled us to make our summer trips to Bethlehem New Hampshire to get away from hay fever. I ended up a full time teacher at Pinkerton and was even urged to be the principal. That scared me for my freedom and put me to flight. I was only induced to stay on teaching by the novelty offered of teaching psychology at The State Normal School at Plymouth. It was agreed that my stay should be no longer than a year. From Plymouth we sailed for Glasgow in August of 1912 (might be 1911) in a small boat out of Boston with a very few passengers on board at that time of year. Fifty dollars was the fare. There were six of us. The children all under fare—Lesley, Carol, Irma and Marjorie. The captain hated us all because he was seasick and believed us all of the servant class going back to England to find a coat of arms for ourselves. To show you how little I knew where I was going, I almost got into a duel with a Scotch schoolmaster on board by miscalling some of the British navy we saw. I called it the English navy.

I had not a relative or an acquaintance to look up in England. 1912 was right, for it was then soon after we got there that I carried a sheaf of poems to David Nutt. As you know they appeared and were rather well received in 1913. I never even knew who read them for Mrs David Nutt who was the owner of the publishing house. Almost immediately on top of *A Boy's Will* I gave her the manuscript of *North of Boston*. She liked it better. She didn't seem very literary herself. I was curious about her advisors. She would never tell me who they were. *A Boy's Will* had made me friends who began to ask "What next?" I let one and another have copies of "The Death of the Hired Man," "The Code," and "The Black Cottage." They got into circulation round London and prepared the way for book success. Ezra imposed "The Code" on Harriet Monroe. He failed to get *The Smart Set* to take "The Death of the Hired Man."

As you probably know, everything from then on—that is May 1914—went rather fine. *North of Boston* was one of the most reviewed books of the year. Massingham the editor of *The Nation* in summing up the year said so. Edward Thomas was one of my warmest advocates. We were thrown together very closely for the rest of our time over there.

15

READING SYLVIA PLATH
IN DEPTH

A COMMENTARY ON PLATH'S CAREER

When Sylvia Plath (1932–1963) committed suicide, she had published only one book of poetry, *The Colossus* (1962). Her most famous book of poems, *Ariel* (1965), was published posthumously. Her autobiographical novel *The Bell Jar* (1967), written originally under a pseudonym, details much of her life at Smith College, where she was an outstanding student, Phi Beta Kappa, graduating *summa cum laude*. Even in 1963 Plath was known among poets and writers for the power of her work. Among her early successes was a prize story for *Mademoiselle* magazine, with a $500 check, as much as she would earn that summer waiting on tables in a resort hotel on Cape Cod. Perhaps her most pleasant honor was having been selected as an editor for *Mademoiselle*'s annual college edition, which necessitated a summer working in New York.

Plath's early death made her in some ways a cult figure. She had a reputation for being supersensitive, a careful and sometimes mysterious writer, always striving for excellence and recognition. She has left behind a remarkable collection of almost seven hundred letters to her mother Aurelia, much of them discussing her work and her ambitions as a writer. Her husband, the British poet Ted Hughes, lived for a year early in their marriage in Northampton, Massachusetts, while she taught at Smith. Her letters to her mother in this period describe anxieties about domestic life and her role in relation to a husband.

Teaching took too much of her writing time, and Hughes and Plath first moved to Boston, where Plath took odd jobs and also attended a poetry class run by Robert Lowell at Boston University. Lowell's poetry, especially his "Skunk Hour," had an important influence on her at this time. When she became pregnant, she and Hughes moved to England, where they eventually had two children, Frieda and Nicholas. They lived at first in London during a period in which

Ted Hughes began to publish and receive important recognition through prizes and offers of readings. Plath was an energetic supporter of Hughes's work, acting as his typist, secretary, and agent. Biographers have pointed out that she accepted the same kind of role in relation to her husband as her mother had done with her father. Both her parents were German in background, and they accepted the traditional roles of husband and wife. Plath, knowing full well the risks she ran, did the same. Eventually, she and Ted bought a thatched-roof house in Devon in the English countryside, where they felt they would have space in which to write and a place to raise their children.

Her marriage began to fail in 1962, when Ted began seeing another woman. Hughes left and she busied herself with the children and with learning to ride her horse Ariel. But after a period of extraordinary productivity in her writing, Sylvia began to feel depressed in the countryside and in need of the stimulation of literary London. She moved back into London without her husband. Those who knew only her work were shocked when she committed suicide on February 11, 1963, barely thirty years old. However, her letters, some poems, recollections of close friends, an earlier breakdown and suicide attempt, and her novel *The Bell Jar* all provide signs that might have been better understood by those who could have helped.

Unfortunately, no adequate biography exists, nor is it likely to for many years. The emphasis critics have placed on her personal life in some ways distracts from the work, which is demanding and complex. Yet her poems sometimes point directly at her own life, as does "Daddy," which describes a recollection of her father, Otto Plath, a German-speaking immigrant from Poland who taught German at Boston University and who published a book on bumblebees in 1934. He died in 1940, so Sylvia's memories stem from early childhood, and the poem reflects the influence of the general anxiety of the United States in the early 1940s regarding the Nazis and Hitler's threat to world security. The violence of the language and imagery of the poem is totally unexpected given everything we know about Plath's early experiences with her father.

Sylvia Plath's work is rich, inventive, and filled with the ambition of one who wished to be recognized as an important writer. Critics attracted to Plath regard her from numerous angles. The biographical-historicist approach is certainly common; because of the existence of a detailed journal, extensive letters, and many personal recollections of friends, information about Sylvia Plath's personal life is widely available, even if it is not always complete. Plath's work also demands close attention to the formalist elements of image, rhythm, the narrator or persona of the poem, and the many shocking disjunctions that bring a reader up short. Feminist approaches have also been used. Whatever their angle, critics agree that her poems are engaging and deeply moving.

Daddy _____ *1963*

You do not do, you do not do
Any more, black shoe

In which I have lived like a foot
For thirty years, poor and white,
Barely daring to breathe or Achoo.   5

Daddy, I have had to kill you.
You died before I had time——
Marble-heavy, a bag full of God,
Ghastly statue with one grey toe
Big as a Frisco seal   10

And a head in the freakish Atlantic
Where it pours bean green over blue
In the waters off beautiful Nauset.°
I used to pray to recover you.
Ach, du.°   15

In the German tongue, in the Polish town°
Scraped flat by the roller
Of wars, wars, wars.
But the name of the town is common.
My Polack friend   20

Says there are a dozen or two.
So I never could tell where you
Put your foot, your root,
I never could talk to you.
The tongue stuck in my jaw.   25

It stuck in a barb wire snare.
Ich, ich, ich, ich,°
I could hardly speak.
I thought every German was you.
And the language obscene   30

An engine, an engine
Chuffing me off like a Jew.
A Jew to Dachau, Auschwitz, Belsen.
I began to talk like a Jew.
I think I may well be a Jew.   35

The snows of the Tyrol, the clear beer of Vienna
Are not very pure or true.
With my gypsy ancestress and my weird luck
And my Taroc pack and my Taroc pack
I may be a bit of a Jew.   40

I have always been scared of *you*,
With your Luftwaffe, your gobbledygoo.
And your neat moustache
And your Aryan eye, bright blue.
Panzer-man, panzer-man, O You——   45

13 *Nauset:* an inlet on Cape Cod.   15 *Ach du:* Oh, you.   16 *Polish town:* where he was
born.   27 *Ich:* I.

Not God but a swastika
So black no sky could squeak through.
Every woman adores a Fascist,
The boot in the face, the brute
Brute heart of a brute like you.   50

You stand at the blackboard, daddy,
In the picture I have of you,
A cleft in your chin instead of your foot
But no less a devil for that, no not
Any less the black man who   55

Bit my pretty red heart in two.
I was ten when they buried you.
At twenty I tried to die
And get back, back, back to you.
I thought even the bones would do   60

But they pulled me out of the sack,
And they stuck me together with glue.
And then I knew what to do.
I made a model of you,
A man in black with a Meinkampf° look   65

And a love of the rack and the screw.
And I said I do, I do.
So daddy, I'm finally through.
The black telephone's off at the root,
The voices just can't worm through.   70

If I've killed one man, I've killed two——
The vampire who said he was you
And drank my blood for a year,
Seven years,° if you want to know.
Daddy, you can lie back now.   75

There's a stake in your fat black heart
And the villagers never liked you.
They are dancing and stamping on you.
They always *knew* it was you.
Daddy, daddy, you bastard, I'm through.   80

65 *Meinkampf:* an allusion to Hitler's autobiography *Mein Kampf (My Struggle).*   74 *Seven years:* Plath was married to Ted Hughes for seven years.

Ariel° _____ *1963*

Stasis in darkness.
Then the substanceless blue
Pour of tor and distances.

Ariel: the name of Plath's horse. It comes from the attendant spirit in Shakespeare's *The Tempest.* Ariel is a spirit with supernatural powers.

God's lioness,
How one we grow,   5
Pivot of heels and knees!—The furrow

Splits and passes, sister to
The brown arc
Of the neck I cannot catch,

Nigger-eye   10
Berries cast dark
Hooks——

Black sweet blood mouthfuls,
Shadows.
Something else   15

Hauls me through air——
Thighs, hair;
Flakes from my heels.

White
Godiva, I unpeel——   20
Dead hands, dead stringencies.

And now I
Foam to wheat, a glitter of seas.
The child's cry

Melts in the wall.   25
And I
Am the arrow,

The dew that flies
Suicidal, at one with the drive
Into the red   30

Eye, the cauldron of morning.

Elm _____ *1965*

   For Ruth Fainlight

I know the bottom, she says. I know it with my great tap root:
It is what you fear.
I do not fear it: I have been there.

Is it the sea you hear in me,
Its dissatisfactions?   5
Or the voice of nothing, that was your madness?

Love is a shadow.
How you lie and cry after it.
Listen: these are its hooves: it has gone off, like a horse.

All night I shall gallop thus, impetuously,   10
Till your head is a stone, your pillow a little turf,
Echoing, echoing.

Or shall I bring you the sound of poisons?
This is rain now, this big hush.
And this is the fruit of it: tin-white, like arsenic.   15

I have suffered the atrocity of sunsets.
Scorched to the root
My red filaments burn and stand, a hand of wires.

Now I break up in pieces that fly about like clubs.
A wind of such violence   20
Will tolerate no bystanding: I must shriek.

The moon, also, is merciless: she would drag me
Cruelly, being barren.
Her radiance scathes me. Or perhaps I have caught her.

I let her go. I let her go   25
Diminished and flat, as after radical surgery.
How your bad dreams possess and endow me.

I am inhabited by a cry.
Nightly it flaps out
Looking, with its hooks, for something to love.   30

I am terrified by this dark thing
That sleeps in me;
All day I feel its soft, feathery turnings, its malignity.

Clouds pass and disperse.
Are those the faces of love, those pale irretrievables?   35
Is it for such I agitate my heart?

I am incapable of more knowledge.
What is this, this face
So murderous in its strangle of branches?

Its snaky acids kiss.   40
It petrifies the will. These are the isolate, slow faults
That kill, that kill, that kill.

Metaphors _____ *1960*

I'm a riddle in nine syllables,
An elephant, a ponderous house,
A melon strolling on two tendrils.
O red fruit, ivory, fine timbers!
This loaf's big with its yeasty rising.   5
Money's new-minted in this fat purse.
I'm a means, a stage, a cow in calf.

I've eaten a bag of green apples,
Boarded the train there's no getting off.

Mirror ——————————————————————————— *1963*

I am silver and exact. I have no preconceptions.
Whatever I see I swallow immediately
Just as it is, unmisted by love or dislike.
I am not cruel, only truthful—
The eye of a little god, four-cornered.   5
Most of the time I meditate on the opposite wall.
It is pink, with speckles. I have looked at it so long
I think it is a part of my heart. But it flickers.
Faces and darkness separate us over and over.

Now I am a lake. A woman bends over me,   10
Searching my reaches for what she really is.
Then she turns to those liars, the candles or the moon.
I see her back, and reflect it faithfully.
She rewards me with tears and an agitation of hands.
I am important to her. She comes and goes.   15
Each morning it is her face that replaces the darkness.
In me she has drowned a young girl, and in me an old woman
Rises toward her day after day, like a terrible fish.

Morning Song ——————————————————————— *1965*

Love set you going like a fat gold watch.
The midwife slapped your footsoles, and your bald cry
Took its place among the elements.

Our voices echo, magnifying your arrival. New statue.
In a drafty museum, your nakedness   5
Shadows our safety. We stand round blankly as walls.

I'm no more your mother
Than the cloud that distils a mirror to reflect its own slow
Effacement at the wind's hand.

All night your moth-breath   10
Flickers among the flat pink roses. I wake to listen:
A far sea moves in my ear.

One cry, and I stumble from bed, cow-heavy and floral
In my Victorian nightgown.
Your mouth opens clean as a cat's. The window square   15

Whitens and swallows its dull stars. And now you try
Your handful of notes;
The clear vowels rise like balloons.

Tulips _____ *1962*

The tulips are too excitable, it is winter here.
Look how white everything is, how quiet, how snowed-in.
I am learning peacefulness, lying by myself quietly
As the light lies on these white walls, this bed, these hands.
I am nobody; I have nothing to do with explosions.   5
I have given my name and my day-clothes up to the nurses
And my history to the anaesthetist and my body to surgeons.

They have propped my head between the pillow and the sheet-cuff
Like an eye between two white lids that will not shut.
Stupid pupil, it has to take everything in.   10
The nurses pass and pass, they are no trouble,
They pass the way gulls pass inland in their white caps,
Doing things with their hands, one just the same as another,
So it is impossible to tell how many there are.

My body is a pebble to them, they tend it as water   15
Tends to the pebbles it must run over, smoothing them gently.
They bring me numbness in their bright needles, they bring me sleep.
Now I have lost myself I am sick of baggage
My patent leather overnight case like a black pillbox,
My husband and child smiling out of the family photo;   20
Their smiles catch onto my skin, little smiling hooks.

I have let things slip, a thirty-year-old cargo boat
Stubbornly hanging on to my name and address.
They have swabbed me clear of my loving associations.
Scared and bare on the green plastic-pillowed trolley   25
I watched my tea-set, my bureaus of linen, my books
Sink out of sight, and the water went over my head.
I am a nun now, I have never been so pure.

I didn't want any flowers, I only wanted
To lie with my hands turned up and be utterly empty.   30
How free it is, you have no idea how free——
The peacefulness is so big it dazes you,
And it asks nothing, a name tag, a few trinkets.
It is what the dead close on, finally; I imagine them
Shutting their mouths on it, like a Communion tablet.   35

The tulips are too red in the first place, they hurt me.
Even through the gift paper I could hear them breathe
Lightly, through their white swaddlings, like an awful baby.
Their redness talks to my wound, it corresponds.
They are subtle: they seem to float, though they weigh me down,   40
Upsetting me with their sudden tongues and their color,
A dozen red lead sinkers round my neck.

Nobody watched me before, now I am watched.
The tulips turn to me, and the window behind me

Where once a day the light slowly widens and slowly thins,   45
And I see myself, flat, ridiculous, a cut-paper shadow
Between the eye of the sun and the eyes of the tulips,
And I have no face, I have wanted to efface myself.
The vivid tulips eat my oxygen.

Before they came the air was calm enough,   50
Coming and going, breath by breath, without any fuss.
Then the tulips filled it up like a loud noise.
Now the air snags and eddies round them the way a river
Snags and eddies round a sunken rust-red engine.
They concentrate my attention, that was happy   55
Playing and resting without committing itself.

The walls, also, seem to be warming themselves.
The tulips should be behind bars like dangerous animals;
They are opening like the mouth of some great African cat,
And I am aware of my heart: it opens and closes   60
Its bowl of red blooms out of sheer love of me.
The water I taste is warm and salt, like the sea,
And comes from a country far away as health.

The Colossus _____ *1960*

I shall never get you put together entirely,
Pieced, glued, and properly jointed.
Mule-bray, pig-grunt and bawdy cackles
Proceed from your great lips.
It's worse than a barnyard.   5

Perhaps you consider yourself an oracle,
Mouthpiece of the dead, or of some god or other.
Thirty years now I have labored
To dredge the silt from your throat.
I am none the wiser.   10

Scaling little ladders with gluepots and pails of lysol
I crawl like an ant in mourning
Over the weedy acres of your brow
To mend the immense skull plates and clear
The bald, white tumuli of your eyes.   15

A blue sky out of the Oresteia°
Arches above us. O father, all by yourself
You are pithy and historical as the Roman Forum.
I open my lunch on a hill of black cypress.
Your fluted bones and acanthine hair are littered   20

16 *Oresteia*: three tragedies by Aeschylus (525?–456 B.C.)—*Agamemnon, The Libation Bearers, The Eumenides*—all concerning the murder of Agamemnon and the revenge of his son Orestes on his mother Clytemnestra.

In their old anarchy to the horizon-line.
It would take more than a lightning-stroke
To create such a ruin.
Nights, I squat in the cornucopia
Of your left ear, out of the wind,   25

Counting the red stars and those of plum-color.
The sun rises under the pillar of your tongue.
My hours are married to shadow.
No longer do I listen for the scrape of a keel
On the blank stones of the landing.   30

The Moon and the Yew Tree _____ 1963

This is the light of the mind, cold and planetary.
The trees of the mind are black. The light is blue.
The grasses unload their griefs on my feet as if I were God,
Prickling my ankles and murmuring of their humility.
Fumy, spiritous mists inhabit this place   5
Separated from my house by a row of headstones.
I simply cannot see where there is to get to.

The moon is no door. It is a face in its own right,
White as a knuckle and terribly upset.
It drags the sea after it like a dark crime; it is quiet   10
With the O-gape of complete despair.° I live here.
Twice on Sunday, the bells startle the sky——
Eight great tongues affirming the Resurrection.
At the end, they soberly bong out their names.

The yew tree points up. It has a Gothic shape.   15
The eyes lift after it and find the moon.
The moon is my mother. She is not sweet like Mary.
Her blue garments unloose small bats and owls.
How I would like to believe in tenderness——
The face of the effigy, gentled by candles,   20
Bending, on me in particular, its mild eyes.

I have fallen a long way. Clouds are flowering
Blue and mystical over the face of the stars.
Inside the church, the saints will be all blue,
Floating on their delicate feet over the cold pews,   25
Their hands and faces stiff with holiness.
The moon sees nothing of this. She is bald and wild.
And the message of the yew tree is blackness—blackness and silence.

11 *despair:* the gape of despair is from Queen Niobe's mourning her murdered children as Keats
describes her in one of his poems.

Lady Lazarus ⸻ *1963*

I have done it again.
One year in every ten
I manage it——

A sort of walking miracle, my skin
Bright as a Nazi lampshade,   5
My right foot

A paperweight,
My face a featureless, fine
Jew linen.

Peel off the napkin   10
O my enemy.
Do I terrify?——

The nose, the eye pits, the full set of teeth?
The sour breath
Will vanish in a day.   15

Soon, soon the flesh
The grave cave ate will be
At home on me

And I a smiling woman.
I am only thirty.   20
And like the cat I have nine times to die.

This is Number Three.
What a trash
To annihilate each decade.

What a million filaments.   25
The peanut-crunching crowd
Shoves in to see

Them unwrap me hand and foot——
The big strip tease.
Gentleman, ladies,   30

These are my hands,
My knees.
I may be skin and bone,

Nevertheless, I am the same, identical woman.
The first time it happened I was ten.   35
It was an accident.

The second time I meant
To last it out and not come back at all.
I rocked shut

As a seashell.   40
They had to call and call
And pick the worms off me like sticky pearls.

Dying
Is an art, like everything else.
I do it exceptionally well.   45

I do it so it feels like hell.
I do it so it feels real.
I guess you could say I've a call.

It's easy enough to do it in a cell.
It's easy enough to do it and stay put.   50
It's the theatrical

Comeback in broad day
To the same place, the same face, the same brute
Amused shout:

"A miracle!"   55
That knocks me out.
There is a charge

For the eyeing of my scars, there is a charge
For the hearing of my heart——
It really goes.   60

And there is a charge, a very large charge,
For a word or a touch
Or a bit of blood

Or a piece of my hair or my clothes.
So, so, Herr Doktor.   65
So, Herr Enemy.

I am your opus,
I am your valuable,
The pure gold baby

That melts to a shriek.   70
I turn and burn.
Do not think I underestimate your great concern.

Ash, ash——
You poke and stir.
Flesh, bone, there is nothing there——   75

A cake of soap,
A wedding ring,
A gold filling.

Herr God, Herr Lucifer,
Beware   80
Beware.

Out of the ash
I rise with my red hair
And I eat men like air.

Paralytic ——————————————————————— *1965*

It happens. Will it go on?——
My mind a rock,
No fingers to grip, no tongue,
My god the iron lung

That loves me, pumps   5
My two
Dust bags in and out,
Will not

Let me relapse
While the day outside glides by like ticker tape.   10
The night brings violets,
Tapestries of eyes,

Lights,
The soft anonymous
Talkers: "You all right?"   15
The starched, inaccessible breast.

Dead egg, I lie
Whole
On a whole world I cannot touch,
At the white, tight   20

Drum of my sleeping couch
Photographs visit me——
My wife, dead and flat, in 1920 furs,
Mouth full of pearls,

Two girls   25
As flat as she, who whisper "We're your daughters."
The still waters
Wrap my lips,

Eyes, nose and ears,
A clear   30
Cellophane I cannot crack.
On my bare back

I smile, a buddha, all
Wants, desire
Falling from me like rings   35
Hugging their lights.

The claw
Of the magnolia,

Drunk on its own scents,
Asks nothing of life.

Mary's Song —————————————————————————— *1963*

The Sunday lamb cracks in its fat.
The fat
Sacrifices its opacity. . . .

A window, holy gold.
The fire makes it precious,   5
The same fire

Melting the tallow heretics,
Ousting the Jews.
Their thick palls float

Over the cicatrix of Poland, burnt-out   10
Germany.
They do not die.

Grey birds obsess my heart,
Mouth-ash, ash of eye.
They settle. On the high   15

Precipice
That emptied one man into space
The ovens glowed like heavens, incandescent.

It is a heart,
This holocaust I walk in,   20
O golden child the world will kill and eat.

QUESTIONS FOR CRITICAL READING:

1. The word *Daddy* in the poem of that name seems to gather meaning beyond any simple association with Plath's own father. In what sense is "Daddy" all men? In what sense is "Daddy" Plath's—and our—heritage?

2. Examine the meter and the rhymes in "Daddy." The rhyme sound *you* is common throughout; why? To what extent is the meter or rhyme regular or irregular? How does the metrical quality contribute to the effectiveness of the poem?

3. In "Ariel" what or who do you think "I" is? How do the images in the poem reinforce the idea of a horse or horselike movement? Why does the arrow fly "suicidal"?

4. The "I" persona in "Elm" is the tree. How effectively does Plath handle this point of view? What insight into trees (or into Plath's own consciousness) does the poem provide? Why is *kill* repeated three times at the end of the poem?

5. In "Metaphors" and "Mirror" Plath employs a considerable number of metaphors and comparisons. Which, for you, are the most powerful? Which seem to provide insight into the psychology of the poet? To what extent does Plath convince you that the poet is a mirror?

6. Can "Morning Song" be interpreted as a hymn to motherhood? What image does Plath give of the child in relation to the mother? How would this image contrast with conventional images of the Madonna and child?

7. Which metaphors and images in "Tulips" seem most powerful? How does the poet see herself in the hospital, and why do the tulips produce such a profound reaction from her?

8. "The Colossus" makes reference to family turmoil and murder in Greek tragedy. How do you interpret the poet's relationship with her "father" in stanza 4? Is this a personal poem or a poem aimed at critiquing the poet's culture?

9. What references in "The Moon and the Yew Tree" echo images or metaphors in other poems by Plath? The yew tree is a conventional symbol associated with death. Is death a primary theme in this poem?

10. Lazarus was raised from the dead by Jesus in the Bible (John 11:18, 30, 32, 38). In what sense is the poet speaking in "Lady Lazarus" concerned about death and returning from the dead? How many of these poems treat death as a theme? Does "Lady Lazarus" take a position markedly different from that taken in other poems? Is the poem positive in tone at the end?

11. "Paralytic" portrays a man in an iron lung. Describe the emotional situation in the poem? Which images seem most powerful in communicating the condition of the man?

12. Is "Mary's Song" a religious poem? Who is the "Sunday lamb"? Is the poem about the Holocaust?

13. What themes and images seem to recur in Plath's poems? Would you call Plath a feminist writer? What is her attitude toward world events? To what extent does Plath seem to portray herself in her poems? Does she convince you that the narrator of some of her poems is Plath herself rather than a dramatic persona?

RESOURCES FOR READING PLATH

Plath's suicide contributed to making her a cult figure in poetry, much the way John Keats's early death in the previous century did the same for him. Her journal, kept at Smith College in the early 1950s, offers insight into her psychological state as she grew up. This passage reveals her capacity to explore her emotions, then to pull back, examine her circumstances as a beginning writer, then respond and move on.

From The Journal of Sylvia Plath: *On Suicide* _____

NORTHAMPTON

November 3. God, if ever I have come close to wanting to commit suicide, it is now, with the groggy sleepless blood dragging through my veins, and the air thick and gray with rain and the damn little men across the street pounding on the roof with picks and axes and chisels, and the acrid hellish stench of tar. I fell into bed again this morning, begging for sleep, withdrawing into the dark, warm, fetid escape from action, from responsibility. No good. The mail bell rang and I jerked myself up to answer it. A letter from Dick.° Sick with envy, I read it, thinking of him lying up there, rested, fed, taken care of, free to explore books and thoughts at any whim. I thought of the myriad of physical duties I had to perform: write Prouty°; *Life* back to Cal; write-up Press Board; call Marcia. The list mounted obstacle after fiendish obstacle; they jarred, they leered, they fell apart in chaos, and the revulsion, the desire to end the pointless round of objects, of things, of actions, rose higher. To annihilate the world by annihilation of one's self is the deluded height of desperate egoism. The simple way out of all the little brick dead ends we scratch our nails against. Irony it is to see Dick raised, lifted to the pinnacles of irresponsibility to anything but care of his body—to feel his mind soaring, reaching, and mine caged, crying, impotent, self-reviling, and imposter. How to justify myself, my bold, brave humanitarian faith? My world falls apart, crumbles, "the centre cannot hold." There is no integrating force, only the naked fear, the urge of self-preservation.

I am afraid. I am not solid, but hollow. I feel behind my eyes a numb, paralyzed cavern, a pit of hell, a mimicking nothingness. I never thought. I never wrote, I never suffered. I want to kill myself, to escape from responsibility, to crawl back abjectly into the womb. I do not know who I am, where I am going—and I am the one who has to decide the answers to these hideous questions. I long for a noble escape from freedom—I am weak, tired, in revolt from the strong constructive humanitarian faith which presupposes a healthy, active intellect and will. There is nowhere to go—not home, where I would blubber and cry, a grotesque fool, into my mother's skirts—not to men, where I want more than ever now their stern, final, paternal directive—not to church, which is liberal, free—no, I turn wearily to the totalitarian dictatorship where I am absolved of all personal responsibility and can sacrifice myself in a "splurge of altruism" on the altar of the Cause with a capital "C."

Now I sit here, crying almost, afraid, seeing the finger writing my hollow futility on the wall, damning me—God, where is the integrating force going to come from? My life up till now seems messy, inconclusive, disorganized: I arranged my courses wrong, played my strategy without unifying rules—got excited at my own potentialities, yet amputated some to serve others. I am drowning in negativism, self-hate, doubt, madness—and even I am not strong enough to deny the routine, the rote, to simplify. No, I go plodding on, afraid that the blank hell in back of my eyes will break through, spewing forth like a dark pestilence, afraid that the disease which eats away the pith of my body with merciless impersonality will break forth in obvious sores and warts, screaming "Traitor, sinner, imposter."

I can begin to see the compulsion for admitting original sin, for adoring Hitler, for taking opium. I have long wanted to read and explore the theories of philosophy, psychology, national, religious, and primitive consciousness, but it seems now too late for anything—I am a conglomerate garbage heap of loose ends—selfish, scared, contemplating devoting the rest of my life to a cause—going naked to send clothes to the needy, escaping to a convent, into hypochondria, into religious mysticism, into the waves—anywhere, anywhere, where the burden, the terrifying hellish weight of self-responsibility and ultimate self-judgment, is lifted. I can see ahead only into dark, sordid alleys, where the dregs, the sludge, the filth of my life lies, unglorified, unchanged—transfigured by nothing: no nobility, not even the illusion of a dream.

Reality is what I make it. That is what I have said I believed. Then I look at the hell I am wallowing in, nerves paralyzed, action nullified—fear, envy, hate: all the corrosive

---

Dick: Dick Norton, a close friend who was recuperating from tuberculosis.
Prouty: Olive Higgins Prouty, a novelist and friend. She sponsored Plath's scholarship at Smith College.

emotions of insecurity biting away at my sensitive guts. Time, experience: the colossal wave, sweeping tidal over me, drowning, drowning. How can I ever find that permanence, that continuity with past and future, that communication with other human beings that I crave? Can I ever honestly accept an artificial imposed solution? How can I justify, how can I rationalize the rest of my life away?

The most terrifying realization is that so many millions in the world would like to be in my place: I am not ugly, not an imbecile, not poor, not crippled—I am, in fact, living in the free, spoiled, pampered country of America and going for hardly any money at all to one of the best colleges. I have earned $1000 in the last three years by writing. Hundreds of dreaming ambitious girls would like to be in my place. They write me letters, asking if they may correspond with me. Five years ago, if I could have seen myself now: at Smith (instead of Wellesley) with seven acceptances from *Seventeen* and one from *Mlle*, with a few lovely clothes, and one intelligent, handsome boy—I would have said: that is all I could ever ask!

And there is the fallacy of existence: the idea that one would be happy forever and age with a given situation or series of accomplishments. Why did Virginia Woolf commit suicide? Or Sara Teasdale or the other brilliant women? Neurotic? Was their writing sublimation (oh, horrible word) of deep, basic desires? If only I knew. If only I knew how high I could set my goals, my requirements for my life! I am in the position of a blind girl playing with a slide rule of values. I am now at the nadir of my calculating powers.

The future? God—will it get worse and worse? Will I never travel, never integrate my life, never have purpose, meaning? Never have time—long stretches, to investigate ideas, philosophy—to articulate the vague seething desires in me? Will I be a secretary—a self-rationalizing, uninspired housewife, secretly jealous of my husband's ability to grow intellectually and professionally while I am impeded? Will I submerge my embarrassing desires and aspirations, refuse to face myself, and go either mad or become neurotic?

Whom can I talk to? Get advice from? No one. A psychiatrist is the god of our age. But they cost money. And I won't take advice, even if I want it. I'll kill myself. I am beyond help. No one here has time to probe, to aid me in understanding myself . . . so many others are worse off than I. How can I selfishly demand help, solace, guidance? No, it is my own mess, and even if now I have lost my sense of perspective, thereby my creative sense of humor, I will not let myself get sick, go mad, or retreat like a child into blubbering on someone else's shoulder. Masks are the order of the day—and the least I can do is cultivate the illusion that I am gay, serene, not hollow and afraid. Someday, god knows when, I will stop this absurd, self-pitying, idle, futile despair. I will begin to think again, and to act according to the way I think. Attitude is a pitifully relative and capricious quality to base a faith on. Like the proverbial sand, it slides, founders, sucks me down to hell.

At present, the last thing I can do is be objective, self-critical, diagnostic—but I *do* know that my philosophy is too subjective, relative and personal to be strong and creative in all circumstances. It is fine in fair weather, but it dissolves when the forty-day rains come. I must submerge it before a larger, transcending goal or craft; what that is I cannot now imagine.

Sylvia Plath wrote hundreds of letters to her mother while she was in college. Most of them talk about her personal psychology, her wishes, anxieties, and dreams. Many of them talk about her ambitions as a writer. When Plath won $500 in a prize for young writers in Mademoiselle *magazine, she was ecstatic. Several of her letters, signed "Sivvy," give a very clear sense of her response and her hopes for the future.*

Sylvia Plath's *From Letters to Her Mother:*
On the Mademoiselle *Prize* _____ *1952*

THE BELMONT HOTEL, CAPE COD

JUNE 11, 1952

Your amazing telegram [*telegram announcing $500* Mademoiselle *prize for "Sunday at the Mintons', " which I forwarded*] came just as I was scrubbing tables in the shady interior of The Belmont dining room. I was so excited that I screamed and actually threw my arms around the head waitress who no doubt thinks I am rather insane! Anyhow, psychologically, the moment couldn't have been better. I felt tired—first night's sleep in new places never are peaceful—and I didn't get much! To top it off, I was the only girl waitress here, and had been scrubbing furniture, washing dishes and silver, lifting tables, etc. since 8 a.m. Also, I just learned since I am completely inexperienced, I am not going to be working in the main dining room, but in the "side hall" where the managers and top hotel brass eat. So, tips will no doubt net much less during the summer and the company be less interesting. So I was beginning to worry about money when your telegram came. God! To think "Sunday at the Mintons'" is *one* of *two* prize stories to be put in a big national slick!!! Frankly, I can't believe it!

The first thing I thought of was: Mother can keep her intersession money and buy some pretty clothes and a special trip or something! At least I get a winter coat and extra special suit out of the Mintons. I think the prize is $500!!!!!!!!!

ME! Of all people! . . .

So it's really looking up around here, now that I don't have to be scared stiff about money . . . Oh, I say, even if my feet kill me after this first week, and I drop 20 trays, I will have the beach, boys to bring me beer, sun, and young gay companions. What a life.

Love, your crazy old daughter. (Or as Eddie said: "One hell of a sexy dame"!)

x x x Sivvy

JUNE 12, 1952

No doubt after I catch up on sleep, and learn to balance trays high on my left hand, I'll feel much happier. As it is now, I feel stuck in the midst of a lot of loud, brassy Irish Catholics, and the only way I can jolly myself is to say, "Oh, well, it's only for a summer, and I can maybe write about them all." At least I've got a new name for my next protagonist—Marley, a gabby girl who knows her way around but good. The ratio of boys to girls has gotten less and less, so I'll be lucky if I get tagged by the youngest kid here. Lots of the girls are really wise, drinking flirts. As for me, being the conservative, quiet, gracious type, I don't stand much chance of dating some of the cutest ones . . . If I can only get "in" as a pal with these girls, and never for a minute let them know I'm the gentle intellectual type, it'll be O.K.

As for the *Mlle* news, I don't think it's really sunk in yet. I felt sure they made a mistake, or that you'd made it up to cheer me. The big advantage will be that I won't have to worry about earning barely $300 this summer. I would really have been sick otherwise. I can't wait till August when I can go casually down to the drug store and pick up a slick copy of *Mlle,* flip to the index, and see ME, one of two college girls in the U.S.!

Really, when I think of how I started it over spring vacation, polished it at school, and sat up till midnight in the Haven House kitchen typing it amidst noise and chatter, I can't get over how the story soared to where it did. One thing about *Mlle* college fiction—although that great one last year by the Radcliffe girl was tremendous and realistic—I remembered the first issue I read where there were two queer part-fantasies, one about the hotel the woman kept for queer people, and the other about an elderly married couple. So I guess the swing of the pendulum dictated something like good old Henry and Elizabeth Minton. Elizabeth has been floating around in my head in her lavender dress, giggling very happily about her burst into the world of print. She always wanted to show Henry she could be famous if she ever worked at it!

One thing I am partly scared and partly curious about is Dick's° reaction when he reads the story in print. I'm glad Dick hasn't read it yet, but Henry started out by being him and Elizabeth me (and they grew old and related in the process). But nevertheless I wonder if Dick will recognize his dismembered self! It's funny how one always, some-where, has the germ of reality in a story, no matter how fantastic . . .

I get great pleasure out of sharing it [*her feeling about the story*] with *you*, who really understand how terribly much it means as a tangible testimony that I *have* got a germ of writing ability even if *Seventeen* has forgotten about it. The only thing, I probably won't have a chance to win *Mlle* again, so I'll try for a guest editorship maybe next year or my senior year, and set my sights for the *Atlantic*. God, I'm glad I can talk about it with you—probably you're the only outlet that I'll have that won't get tired of my talking about writing . . .

Speaking again of Henry and Liz, it was a step for me to a story where the pro-tagonist isn't always ME, and proved that I am beginning to use imagination to transform the actual incident. I was scared that would never happen, but I think it's an indication that my perspective is broadening.

Sometimes I think—heck, I don't know why I didn't stay home all summer, writ-ing, doing physical science, and having a small part-time job. I could "afford" to now, but it doesn't do much good to yearn about that, I guess. Although it would have been nice. Oh well, I'll cheer up. I love you.

Your own Sivvy

June 15, 1952

Dear Mother,

. . . Do write me letters, Mommy, because I am in a very dangerous state of feel-ing sorry for myself . . . Just at present, life is awful. *Mademoiselle* seems quite unreal, and I am exhausted, scared, incompetent, unenergetic and generally low in spirits . . . Work-ing in side hall puts me apart, and I feel completely uprooted and clumsy. The more I see the main hall girls expertly getting special dishes, fixing shaved ice and fruit, etc., the more I get an inferiority complex and feel that each day in side hall leaves me fur-ther behind . . . But as tempted as I am to be a coward and escape by crawling back home, I have resolved to give it a good month's trial—till July 10 . . . Don't worry about me, but do send me little pellets of advice now and then.

Dick: Dick Norton.

16

An Album of Poems

**STRATEGIES FOR CLOSE READING
AND INTERPRETATION OF POEMS IN THIS ALBUM**

The poems in this collection represent a wide variety of approaches. They demonstrate the incredible variety of styles available to the poet. The forms, themes, and ideas in the poems cover an enormous range. Some of the poems in the album are classics, some contemporary, and many are ethnically diverse. They offer insights into the human condition in an emotionally engaging fashion.

Annotate the Poems

The first step in working with these poems will probably be to read the poem aloud. Then, in a rereading, underline the passages you think are important to developing a deeper understanding of the poem. By underlining or highlighting as you go along, you will make it easier for yourself to see what is important and to review the entire poem once you finish it. Write a note in the margin describing the form of the poem or the form of the stanzas. Spend a moment in scanning the opening lines of the poem to get a sense of its metrical character. Beyond its meter, examine the poem for its rhythmic qualities. See where the breaks in the rhythm come and how the lines stop or run on.

Write Down Your Questions for Close Reading

Keep a list of questions for close reading as you read the poems. Try to develop questions similar to the ones you have seen following the poems above. Consider this checklist for questions:

- Ask yourself what the title means. In Diane Ackerman's "On Looking into Sylvia Plath's Copy of Goethe's *Faust*" you need to look for connections with Sylvia Plath, whose work you may have read just before encountering this poem. Further, you may want to look up Goethe's *Faust* in a literary (or regular) encyclopedia to get a quick fix on how it might relate to Plath.

- Read the poem aloud. If possible, have someone read the poem aloud to you. Experiment with ways in which the lines can be expressed.
- Look at the whole poem. Decide whether it is metrical or free verse. Is it a formal or informal poem? How will that affect your reading?
- What are the primary ideas in the poem? If you feel it has a clear theme, try to identify it. What is the poet concerned with and how do you connect to it?
- Who is speaking in the poem? Is the speaker the poet—in a generalized way—or is it a dramatically conceived character, as in Browning's "My Last Duchess"?
- Examine the poem for its use of language. What unusual words appear in the poem? Is the poet playing with language? Do you like the way the poem expresses itself? Is the poem conversational or discursive?
- What images are most powerful? Which of the senses does the poet appeal to most carefully? Is there a pattern to the imagery? Are the images logically or emotionally connected to one another so as to produce a sense of unity in the poem?
- How would you describe the tone of the poem? Is the poet ironic? Is the poet writing a parody? Is the poet earnest and sincere? How does the tone contribute to your understanding and appreciation of the poem?
- Examine the metrical qualities of the poem as well as its rhythmic qualities. Examine its rhyme patterns. How does rhyme contribute to the power of the poem? Does rhyme achieve a sense of definiteness or inevitability?
- Does the poem use metaphor effectively? What figurative language, such as irony, does the poem employ?
- Examine the poem for its use of symbol or allegory. Is the poem entirely literal in its meaning, or, like Adrienne Rich's "Diving into the Wreck," is it symbolic in significance?
- What do you notice about the poem's form? Is it a sonnet? A song? An ode? Is it a form demanding special technical skill, or is it an open form that permits more freedom to the poet? How does the form of the poem intensify your experience?
- Comment in the margins on the style of the poem. Jot down your observations for review later. How does the style of the poem connect with its themes and ideas? How are those ideas better conveyed as a result of the poet's style?
- How do the elements of the poem work together? Which elements are most important in the poem, and how do they interact? Again, consider the poem as a whole and try to experience it all together.

Questions for Interpretation of Poems in the Album

- Look for patterns of repetition: descriptions and imagery that show up often, such as references to horses, birds, clouds, flowers, or other details. They may have a symbolic significance, as in Juanita Casey's "Pegasus." The horse Pegasus was a classical symbol for the power of poetry.
- Look also for repeated words and lines, such as the repetition of "I've known rivers" and similar line openers in Langston Hughes's "The Negro Speaks of Rivers." These

repetitions may give a clue to the inner meaning of the poem. How does their emphatic repetition build emotional power in the poem?

● Observe the nature of the narrator or the main character in the poem. Ask yourself what he or she is like and whether you can truly rely on the narrator. Does the narrator reveal qualities that are believable and recognizable as deeply human? How does the psychological nature of the narrator affect the perceptions revealed in the poem?

● What are the gender issues in the poem? Is the situation in the poem connected to rigid expectations of gender behavior? Does the poem depend on understanding how the characters accept their attitudes toward gender, as in Adrienne Rich's "Trying to Talk with a Man," or Simon Ortiz's "Juanita, Wife of Manuelito"?

● Do cultural issues dominate the poem? Cathy Song's "The Youngest Daughter" and Win Tek Lum's, "At a Chinaman's Grave" both reveal certain cultural expectations determined by circumstances. That is true, too, of Langston Hughes's "Theme for English B" and for Mazisi Kunene's "The Political Prisoner."

● What are the economic issues at stake in the poem? In Browning's "My Last Duchess," the economic independence of the duke makes it possible for him to be arrogant. Is it important to know how the economic or social circumstances of the characters or narrator affect the outcome of the poem?

● Is the most interesting aspect of the poem connected to its setting? Is the poem interesting because of its historical setting, as in John Keats's "The Eve of St. Agnes"? You might ask that question of David Wagoner's "The Shooting of John Dillinger outside the Biograph Theater, July 22, 1934." What role does history play in these poems?

● Finally, one thing you can do more easily with poems than with other kinds of literature is make comparisons, or read one poem in relation to another. Marilyn Nelson Waniek's "Emily Dickinson's Defunct" can be read in relation to the poems of Emily Dickinson, but also in relation to E. E. Cummings's "Buffalo Bill's Defunct." You may also read poems of the same kind, such as sonnets, poems on death, or poems about art and artifacts, in relation to one another. Paired poems, such as Philip Dacey's "Jack, Afterwards" and "Jill, Afterwards," as well as Christopher Marlowe's "The Passionate Shepherd to His Love" and Sir Walter Ralegh's "The Nymph's Reply to the Shepherd," offer interesting opportunities for interpretation.

By reviewing these questions as you read the poems in the album, you may provide yourself with excellent opportunities for close reading and good interpretations. These are poems by some of the world's best poets. They are meant to be enjoyed.

DIANE ACKERMAN   (b. 1948)

On Looking into Sylvia Plath's° Copy of Goethe's Faust° _____ *1991*

You underlined the "jugglery of flame"
with ink sinewy and black as an ocelot.

Sylvia Plath: a major poet who committed suicide when very young. See section on Plath, p. 593.   *Faust:* Johann Wolfgang von Goethe (1749–1832) wrote the dramatic poem *Faust* in two parts (1808; 1832). It is a Romantic portrait of a man who defied God.

Pensive about ash, you ran to detail,
you ran the mad sweetshop of the soul,
keen for Faust's appetite, not Helen's° beauty.   5
No stranger to scalpel or garden,
you collected bees, knew how to cook,
dressed simply, and undressed the flesh
in word mirrors. Armed and dangerous
with the nightstick of desire,   10
you became the doll of insight we knew
to whom nearly all lady poets write,
a morbid Santa Claus who could die on cue.
You had the gift of rage, and a savage wistfulness.
You wanted life to derange you,   15
to sample its real muscle, you wanted
to be a word on the lips of the abyss.
You wanted to unlock the weather system
in your cells, and one day you did.

I never loved the pain you wore as a shroud,   20
but your keen naturalist's eye,
avid and roaming, your nomad curiosity,
and the cautionless ease with which your mind
slid into the soft flesh of an idea.
I thought you found serenity in the plunge   25
of a hot image into cool words.
I thought you took the pledge
that sunlight makes to living things,
could be startled to joy
by the green epaulets of a lily.   30
But you were your own demonology,
balancing terror's knife on one finger,
until you numbed, and the edge fell free.

5 *Helen:* Helen of Troy, whom Faust conjured from the dead.

DIANE ACKERMAN   (b. 1948)

Letter to Wallace Stevens° _____ *1991*

Heartless in a Hartford long dissolved,
    you were the axis
        of my revolving world

when, at nineteen, I desired your gift
    and Dylan Thomas's: 5
        his voluptousness of mind,
            your sensuous rigor.

Wallace Stevens: an important modern poet, in this collection. See p. 778. Stevens lived in Hartford, Connecticut.

I didn't know then that Art
  is the best one rises to,
    a momentary privilege.   10

I didn't know that bad men
  could write good poems,
    be spiteful to all,

cruel to their children,
  but wholly compassionate   15
    to ideal compassion.

Rude, icy, alert to advantage,
  rapt but condescending,
    terrified to be cornered
      into a friendship,   20

you knew the dollar each lily concealed
  and fantasized a Paris
    laminated by distance,

whose essence you took
  in strong, cunning draughts.   25
    Few speak well of you,
      the glacial man in the baggy suit.

The new biography makes me a fortuneteller
  in reverse. I watch you weaken
    in your garden robust with peonies   30

where you ushered in the world
  and escaped your wife (whose face, on the liberty dime,°
    sat in your pants pocket all day).

But your poems, what madrigals,
  canny and luscious, in which the Sinbads   35
    of thought wear twirling knives,

and you steer by the polestar
  of your own invention. Your nomadic eye
    roamed the seven seas
      of the seven senses.   40

By heart, and by law,
  you could toss a bucketful of light
    onto any dim object, make ideas fluoresce,

and stain the willows with a glance.
  You named the chaos.   45
    You could dry out the sun.

I wish you'd reveled in the deserts—
  Egypt, Africa, the Southwest—
    but it wasn't your fault

---

32 *dime:* Elsie Moll, Stevens's wife, modeled for the face of Liberty.

that world is ampler than you knew.   50
   Anyway, a coral key can be played
      to the absolute,

and desert bluffs arrive by ship in New England,
   where tide can be touched
      and night is a leopard.   55

DIANE ACKERMAN   (b. 1948)

Anne Donne° to Her Husband _____ *1978*

   Come to bed, Jack, the candle's shed
to its waxy skirt, and I can read
   your straying wits by the moon.
A brain-fly must be buzzing your head!
   What is it now, that new ice, sheeting   5
the pond like a scald on hot milk? The swoon
   of dam-water, like a silent diphthong?
Lucky pond, to hold your gaze so long.

   My eiderdown is greener than a glade;
you gave it me yourself, high   10
   when you dubbed me your *new found land,*
and swore, my continents your quest, you'd trade
   along the shores of my dark timbered eyes,
where unwooed lusheries of life meander,
   and time drops sail like a ketch in a lagoon.   15
Well, then, what keeps you?

   Come away from the window!
You get ideas like other men catch cold.
   Mid-morning, a trifle waylaid you again,
and now your eyes, like twin hyenas,   20
   pick dinner in the silvery light
from the moon. Enough of your lyric flight!
   Enough peeking under the night's black shirt!
All day, you've been sickening with a verse.

   For God's sake, quit gaming   25
with love, in poems abstruse, or as physical
   as if you were a physical
man. Maybe this one you'll title "Love's Dynasty,"
   and begin with a sunset, lying
on the horizon like an eel   30
   twitching its thick brown hide,
then hint at things matrimonial.

Anne Donne: wife of poet John Donne, in this collection. This poem parodies the love poems Donne
wrote to his wife, which often expressed an impatient desire to get on with physical lovemaking,
as in "The Flea," p. 663.

And who'll guess that tonight, upright as an easel,
you've earth on the brain, not me.
    Though I'd tie you in lawless knots   35
if I could, my heart knows
    no rhetoric but your name,
Jack, that, like a doomed colonial,
    sails out with a seed-chest full of hope,
and raises so little crop.   40

    How can I compete with a vision?
What holy logic could my wiles defy?
    Your muse that's fat and sassy
as a cow, could I stint her even one
    of her piquancies? Her powwows? Her sprees?   45
What would it cost, in hard daily coin,
    if I shook you loose from this reverie?
I am not love's barrister (wish I were),

    but an offput woman on a night growing bleaker,
and night was never longer, or woman weaker.   50

BELLA AKHMADULINA   (b. 1937)

Volcanoes _____ *1963*

Translated from Russian by W. H. Auden

Extinct volcanoes are silent:
Ash chokes craters and vent.
There giants hide from the sun
After the evil they have done.

Realms ever denser and colder   5
Weigh on each brutal shoulder,
But the old wicked visions keep
Visiting them in their sleep.

They behold a city, sure
Here summer will endure,   10
Though columns carved from congealed
Lava frame garden and field.

It is long ago: in sunlit hours
Girls gather armfuls of flowers
And Bacchantes° give a meaning sign   15
To men as they sip their wine.

A feast is in progress: louder
The diners grow, more heated and lewder . . .

15 *Bacchantes:* priestesses of Bacchus, god of wine.

O my Pompei in your cindery grave,
Child of a princess and a slave!   20

What future did you assume,
What were you thinking of and whom
When you leaned your elbow thus
Thoughtlessly on Vesuvius?

Were you carried away by his stories?   25
Did you gaze with astonished eyes?
Didn't you guess—were you *that* innocent?—
Passion can be violent?

And then, when that day ended,
Did he lay a knowing forehead   30
At your dead feet? Did he, didn't he,
Bellow: "Forgive me!"?

AGHA SHAHID ALI   (b. 1949)

Homage to Faiz Ahmed Faiz° _____ *1987*

(*d. 20 November 1984*)
"You are welcome to make your adaptations of my poems."

I

You wrote this from Beirut, two years before
the Sabra-Shatila massacres.° That city's
refugee air was open, torn
by jets and the voices of reporters.
As always, you were witness to "rains of stones,"   5

though you were away from Pakistan, from
the laws of home which said: the hands
of thieves will be surgically
amputated. But the subcontinent always spoke
to you: in Ghalib's Urdu,° and sometimes through   10

the old masters who sang of twilight
but didn't live, like Ghalib, to see the wind
rip the collars of the dawn: the summer
of 1857,° the trees of Delhi
became scaffolds: 30,000 men   15

Faiz Ahmed Faiz (1911–1984): well-known Pakistani political activist and poet (see "Before You Came," p. 667) who spent time in solitary confinement for his views.   2 *Sabra-Shatila massacres:* 1982 massacre of refugees in Beirut by Christian phalangists.   10 *Ghalib's Urdu:* Ghalib: Mirzā Asadullāh Khān Naushāh (d. 1869), most influential of Delhi poets, wrote mostly in Persian, but his Urdu—the primary language of Pakistan—was widely praised.   14 *1857:* In this year Indian regulars rose against their British superiors and were brutally crushed. The event marked the beginning of British national rule over India.

were hanged. Wherever you were, Faiz, that
language spoke to you; and when you heard it,
you were alone—in Tunis, Beirut,
London, or Moscow. Those poets' laments
concealed, as yours revealed, the sorrows   20

of a broken time. You knew Ghalib was right:
blood must not merely follow routine, must not
just flow as the veins' uninterrupted
river. Sometimes it must flood the eyes,
surprise them by being clear as water.   25

II

I didn't listen when my father
recited your poems to us
by heart. What could it mean to a boy

that you had redefined the cruel
beloved, that figure who already   30
was Friend, Woman, God? In your hands

she was Revolution. You gave
her silver hands, her lips were red.
Impoverished lovers waited all

night every night, but she remained   35
only a glimpse behind
light. When I learned of her,

I was no longer a boy, and Urdu
a silhouette traced
by the voices of singers,   40

by Begum Akhtar,° who wove your couplets
into ragas: both language and music
were sharpened. I listened:

and you became, like memory,
necessary. *Dast-e-Saba,*°   45
I said to myself. And quietly

the wind opened its palms: I read
there of the night: the secrets
of lovers, the secrets of prisons.

III

When you permitted my hands to turn to stone,   50
as must happen to a translator's hands,

I thought of you writing *Zindan-Nama*°
on prison walls, on cigarette packages,

41 *Begum Akhtar:* famous Indian singer. Ali memorialized her in another poem.   45 *Dast-e-*
Saba: present thoughts.   52 *Zindan-Nama:* Faiz's book, *Hands of the Morning Breeze.*

on torn envelopes. Your lines were measured
so carefully to become in our veins   55

the blood of prisoners. In the free verse
of another language I imprisoned

each line—but I touched my own exile.
This hush, while your ghazals° lay in my palms,

was accurate, as is this hush that falls   60
at news of your death over Pakistan

and India and over all of us no
longer there to whom you spoke in Urdu.

Twenty days before your death you finally
wrote, this time from Lahore, that after the sack   65

of Beirut you had no address . . . I
had gone from poem to poem, and found

you once, terribly alone, speaking
to yourself: "Bolt your doors, Sad heart! Put out

the candles, break all cups of wine. No one,   70
now no one will ever return." But you

still waited, Faiz, for that God, that Woman,
that Friend, that Revolution, to come
at last. And because you waited,
I listen as you pass with some song,   75

a memory of musk, the rebel face of hope.

59 *ghazals:* a form of rhyming lyric poetry.

W. H. AUDEN (1907–1973)

Musée des Beaux Arts° _____ *1938*

About suffering they were never wrong,
The Old Masters: how well they understood
Its human position; how it takes place
While someone else is eating or opening a window or just walking dully along;
How, when the aged are reverently, passionately waiting   5
For the miraculous birth,° there always must be
Children who did not specially want it to happen, skating
On a pond at the edge of the wood:
They never forgot
That even the dreadful martyrdom must run its course   10
Anyhow in a corner, some untidy spot

Musée des Beaux Arts: Museum of Fine Arts.   6 *miraculous birth: The Nativity,* a painting by Breughel.

Where the dogs go on with their doggy life and the torturer's horse
Scratches its innocent behind on a tree.

In Breughel's *Icarus*,° for instance: how everything turns away
Quite leisurely from the disaster; the ploughman may   15
Have heard the splash, the forsaken cry,
But for him it was not an important failure; the sun shone
As it had to on the white legs disappearing into the green
Water; and the expensive delicate ship that must have seen
Something amazing, a boy falling out of the sky,   20
Had somewhere to get to and sailed calmly on.

14 *Breughel's Icarus:* A painting entitled *Landscape with the Fall of Icarus,* by Pieter Breughel the Elder
(c. 1525–1569). In the legend, when Icarus flew too close to the sun his wings melted and he fell
into the sea.

W. H. AUDEN   (1907–1973)

In Memory of W. B. Yeats ———————————————————————— *1940*

d. Jan. 1939

I

He disappeared in the dead of winter:
The brooks were frozen, the airports almost deserted,
And snow disfigured the public statues;
The mercury sank in the mouth of the dying day.
What instruments we have agree   5
The day of his death was a dark cold day.

Far from his illness
The wolves ran on through the evergreen forests,
The peasant river was untempted by the fashionable quays;
By mourning tongues   10
The death of the poet was kept from his poems.

But for him it was his last afternoon as himself,
An afternoon of nurses and rumors;
The provinces of his body revolted,
The squares of his mind were empty,   15
Silence invaded the suburbs,
The current of his feeling failed; he became his admirers.

Now he is scattered among a hundred cities
And wholly given over to unfamiliar affections;
To find his happiness in another kind of wood   20
And be punished under a foreign code of conscience.
The words of a dead man
Are modified in the guts of the living.

But in the importance and noise of tomorrow
When the brokers are roaring like beasts on the floor of the Bourse,° 25
And the poor have the sufferings to which they are fairly accustomed,
And each in the cell of himself is almost convinced of his freedom,
A few thousand will think of this day
As one thinks of a day when one did something slightly unusual.

What instruments we have agree 30
The day of his death was a dark cold day.

II

You were silly like us; your gift survived it all;
The parish of rich women, physical decay,
Yourself: mad Ireland hurt you into poetry.
Now Ireland has her madness and her weather still, 35
For poetry makes nothing happen: it survives
In the valley of its saying where executives
Would never want to tamper; it flows south
From ranches of isolation and the busy griefs,
Raw towns that we believe and die in; it survives, 40
A way of happening, a mouth.

III

Earth, receive an honored guest:
William Yeats is laid to rest.
Let the Irish vessel lie
Emptied of its poetry. 45

In the nightmare of the dark
All the dogs of Europe bark,
And the living nations wait,
Each sequestered in its hate;

Intellectual disgrace 50
Stares from every human face,
And the seas of pity lie
Locked and frozen in each eye.

Follow, poet, follow right
To the bottom of the night, 55
With your unconstraining voice
Still persuade us to rejoice;

With the farming of a verse
Make a vineyard of the curse,
Sing of human unsuccess 60
In a rapture of distress;

25 *Bourse:* the Paris Stock Exchange.

In the deserts of the heart
Let the healing fountain start,
In the prison of his days
Teach the free man how to praise.   65

IMAMU AMIRI BARAKA   (b. 1934)

In Memory of Radio ——————————————————————— *1961*

Who has ever stopped to think of the divinity of Lamont Cranston?°
(Only Jack Kerouac,° that I know of: & me.
The rest of you probably had on WCBS and Kate Smith,°
Or something equally unattractive.)

What can I say?   5
It is better to have loved and lost
Than to put linoleum in your living rooms?

Am I a sage or something?
Mandrake's hypnotic gesture of the week?°
(Remember, I do not have the healing powers of Oral Roberts . . .   10
I cannot, like F. J. Sheen,° tell you how to get saved *& rich!*
I cannot even order you to gaschamber satori like Hitler or
      Goody Knight°

& Love is an evil word.
Turn it backwards/see, see what I mean?
An evol word. & besides   15
who understands it?
I certainly wouldn't like to go out on that kind of limb.

Saturday mornings we listened to *Red Lantern*° & his undersea folk.
At 11, *Let's Pretend*°/& we did/&I, the poet, still do, Thank God!

What was it he° used to say (after the transformation, when he was safe 20
& invisible & the unbelievers couldn't throw stones?) "Heh, heh, heh,
Who knows what evil lurks in the hearts of men? The Shadow knows."

O, yes he does
O, yes he does.
An evil word it is,   25
This Love.

1 *Lamont Cranston:* fictional radio character who became the Shadow.   2 *Jack Kerouac:* writer (1922–1969), one of the Beats, known for *On the Road.*   3 *Kate Smith:* popular American singer.   9 *Mandrake's . . . week:* Mandrake the Magician, a weekly comic feature.   11 *F. J. Sheen:* Fulton J. Sheen, popular radio evangelist.   13 *Goody Knight:* Goodwin J. Knight, governor of California in the 1950s.   18 *Red Lantern:* comic book hero.   19 *Let's Pretend:* radio program.   20 *he:* the Shadow.

GRACE BAUER

Eve Recollecting the Garden _____ *1990*

Was it your nakedness
or the knack you had

for naming I learned
to love? *Crow,* you whispered

and wings flapped black   5
as satin in the sky

Bee, and sweetness thickened
on my tongue, *Lion*

and something roared beneath
the ribs you claimed   10

you sacrificed. Our first quarrel
arose about the beast

I thought deserved a nobler tag
than *Dog.* And *Orchid*—

a sound more delicate. Admit it!   15
Dolphin, Starling, Antelope

were syllables you stole
from me, and you

were the one who swore
we'd have to taste those blood   20

red globes of fruit
before we'd find the right word

for that god-forsaken tree.

ELIZABETH BISHOP   (1911–1979)

Poem _____ *1976*

About the size of an old-style dollar bill,
American or Canadian,
mostly the same whites, gray greens, and steel grays
—this little painting (a sketch for a larger one?)
has never earned any money in its life.   5
Useless and free, it has spent seventy years
as a minor family relic
handed along collaterally to owners

who looked at it sometimes, or didn't bother to.
It must be Nova Scotia; only there   10
does one see gabled wooden houses
painted that awful shade of brown.
The other houses, the bits that show, are white.
Elm trees, low hills, a thin church steeple
—that gray-blue wisp—or is it? In the foreground   15
a water meadow with some tiny cows,
two brushstrokes each, but confidently cows;
two minuscule white geese in the blue water,
back-to-back, feeding, and a slanting stick.
Up closer, a wild iris, white and yellow,   20
fresh-squiggled from the tube.
The air is fresh and cold; cold early spring
clear as gray glass; a half inch of blue sky
below the steel-gray storm clouds.
(They were the artist's specialty.)   25
A specklike bird is flying to the left.
Or is it a flyspeck looking like a bird?

Heavens, I recognize the place, I know it!
It's behind—I can almost remember the farmer's name.
His barn backed on that meadow. There it is,   30
titanium white, one dab. The hint of steeple,
filaments of brush-hairs, barely there,
must be the Presbyterian church.
Would that be Miss Gillespie's house?
Those particular geese and cows   35
are naturally before my time.

A sketch done in an hour, "in one breath,"
once taken from a trunk and handed over.
Would you like this? I'll probably never
have room to hang these things again.   40
Your Uncle George, no, mine, my Uncle George,
he'd be your great-uncle, left them all with Mother
when he went back to England.
You know, he was quite famous, an R.A.°

I never knew him. We both knew this place,   45
apparently, this literal small backwater,
looked at it long enough to memorize it,
our years apart. How strange. And it's still loved,
or its memory is (it must have changed a lot).

Our visions coincided—"visions" is   50
too serious a word—our looks, two looks:

44 *R.A.:* member of the Royal Academy, therefore an important recognized painter.

art "copying from life" and life itself,
life and the memory of it so compressed
they've turned into each other. Which is which?
Life and the memory of it cramped,   55
dim, on a piece of Bristol board,
dim, but how live, how touching in detail
—the little that we get for free,
the little of our earthly trust. Not much.
About the size of our abidance   60
along with theirs: the munching cows,
the iris, crisp and shivering, the water
still standing from spring freshets,
the yet-to-be-dismantled elms, the geese.

WILLIAM BLAKE   (1757–1827)

Introduction _____ *1789*

From *Songs of Innocence*°

Piping down the valleys wild,
Piping songs of pleasant glee,
On a cloud I saw a child.
And he laughing said to me,

Pipe a song about a Lamb;   5
So I piped with merry cheer.
Piper pipe that song again—
So I piped; he wept to hear.

Drop thy pipe, thy happy pipe;
Sing thy songs of happy cheer.   10
So I sung the same again
While he wept with joy to hear.

Piper sit thee down and write
In a book that all may read—
So he vanished from my sight.   15
And I plucked a hollow reed.

And I made a rural pen,
And I stained the water clear,
And I wrote my happy songs
Every child may joy to hear.   20

Songs of Innocence: These poems were published both separately and with *Songs of Experience.* Together they were intended to show "the two contrary states of the human soul."

WILLIAM BLAKE   (1757–1827)

The Chimney Sweeper ——————————————————————— *1789*

From *Songs of Innocence°*

When my mother died I was very young,
And my father sold me° while yet my tongue,
Could scarcely cry 'weep 'weep 'weep 'weep.°
So your chimneys I sweep and in soot I sleep.

There's little Tom Dacre, who cried when his head   5
That curled like a lamb's back, was shaved, so I said,
Hush, Tom, never mind it, for when your head's bare,
You know that the soot cannot spoil your white hair.

And so he was quiet, and that very night,
As Tom was a-sleeping he had such a sight,   10
That thousands of sweepers, Dick, Joe, Ned, and Jack,
Were all of them locked up in coffins of black.

And by came an Angel who had a bright key,
And he opened the coffins and set them all free.
Then down a green plain leaping, laughing, they run   15
And wash in a river and shine in the Sun.

Then naked and white, all their bags left behind,
They rise upon clouds, and sport in the wind.
And the Angel told Tom, if he'd be a good boy,
He'd have God for his father and never want joy.   20

And so Tom awoke and we rose in the dark
And got with our bags and our brushes to work.
Though the morning was cold, Tom was happy and warm;
So if all do their duty, they need not fear harm.

Songs of Innocence: See note to "Introduction."   2 *sold me:* a reference to the church's use of child
labor under the guise of charity.   3 *weep:* The child is trying to say "sweep."

WILLIAM BLAKE   (1757–1827)

The Little Boy Lost ——————————————————————— *1789*

From *Songs of Innocence*

Father, father, where are you going?
O, do not walk so fast.
Speak, father, speak to your little boy,
Or else I shall be lost.

The night was dark, no father was there,   5
The child was wet with dew.

The mire was deep, and the child did weep,
And away the vapor flew.

WILLIAM BLAKE   (1757–1827)

The Little Boy Found _____ *1789*

From *Songs of Innocence*

The little boy lost in the lonely fen,
Led by the wand'ring light,
Began to cry, but God ever nigh,
Appeared like his father in white.

He kissed the child and by the hand led   5
And to his mother brought,
Who in sorrow pale, through the lonely dale
Her little boy weeping sought.

WILLIAM BLAKE   (1757–1827)

The Clod and the Pebble _____ *1794*

From *Songs of Experience*

Love seeketh not Itself to please,
Nor for itself hath any care;
But for another gives its ease,
And builds a Heaven in Hell's despair.

　　So sang a little Clod of Clay,   5
　　Trodden with the cattles' feet:
　　But a Pebble of the brook,
　　Warbled out these meters meet:°

Love seeketh only Self to please,
To bind another to its delight;   10
Joys in another's loss of ease,
And builds a Hell in Heaven's despite.°

8 *meet:* fitting, suitable.   12 *despite:* scorn, anger, defiance.

WILLIAM BLAKE   (1757–1827)

The Chimney Sweeper _____ *1794*

From *Songs of Experience*

A little black thing among the snow:
Crying " 'weep, weep" in notes of woe!

"Where are thy father and mother? say?"
"They are both gone up to the church to pray.

"Because I was happy upon the heath,"   5
And smiled among the winter's snow:
They clothed me in the clothes of death,
And taught me to sing the notes of woe.

"And because I am happy, and dance and sing,
They think they have done me no injury: 10
And are gone to praise God and his Priest and King,
Who make up a heaven of our misery."

WILLIAM BLAKE   (1757–1827)

The Garden of Love ————————————————— *1794*

From *Songs of Experience*

I went to the Garden of Love,
And saw what I never had seen:
A Chapel° was built in the midst,
Where I used to play on the green.

And the gates of this Chapel were shut,   5
And "Thou shalt not" writ over the door;
So I turned to the Garden of Love,
That so many sweet flowers bore;

And I saw it was filled with graves,
And tomb-stones where flowers should be: 10
And Priests in black gowns were walking their rounds,
And binding with briars my joys and desires.

3 *Chapel:* See notes to "The Chimney Sweeper," p. 628.

WILLIAM BLAKE   (1757–1827)

London ——————————————————————— *1794*

From *Songs of Experience*

I wander through each chartered° street,
Near where the chartered Thames does flow,
And mark in every face I meet
Marks of weakness, marks of woe.

1 *chartered:* defined or licensed by written law. This meaning becomes ironic when used with a river in the next line because a river is free-flowing and cannot be chartered.

In every cry of every Man,   5
In every Infant's cry of fear,
In every voice, in every ban,
The mind-forged manacles I hear—

How the Chimney-sweeper's cry
Every black'ning Church° appalls,   10
And the hapless Soldier's sigh
Runs in blood down Palace walls.

But most through midnight streets I hear
How the youthful Harlot's curse
Blasts the new-born Infant's tear   15
And blights with plagues the Marriage hearse.

10 *Church:* See notes to "The Chimney Sweeper," p. 628.

LOUISE BOGAN   (1897–1970)

Medusa° _____ *1923*

I had come to the house, in a cave of trees,
Facing a sheer sky.
Everything moved,—a bell hung ready to strike,
Sun and reflection wheeled by.

When the bare eyes were before me   5
And the hissing hair,
Held up at a window, seen through a door.
The stiff bald eyes, the serpents on the forehead
Formed in the air.

This is a dead scene forever now.   10
Nothing will ever stir.
The end will never brighten it more than this,
Nor the rain blur.

Medusa: In classical literature a Gorgon, a female with snakes for hair. Any man who looked on
her was turned to stone.

LOUISE BOGAN   (1897–1970)

Women _____ *1923*

Women have no wilderness in them,
They are provident instead,
Content in the tight hot cell of their hearts
To eat dusty bread.

They do not see cattle cropping red winter grass,   5
They do not hear
Snow water going down under culverts
Shallow and clear.

They wait, when they should turn to journeys,
They stiffen, when they should bend.   10
They use against themselves that benevolence
To which no man is friend.

They cannot think of so many crops to a field
Or of clean wood cleft by an axe.
Their love is an eager meaninglessness   15
Too tense, or too lax.

They hear in every whisper that speaks to them
A shout and a cry.
As like as not, when they take life over their door-sills
They should let it go by.   20

ARNA BONTEMPS   (1902–1973)

A Black Man Talks of Reaping _____ *1940*

I have sown beside all waters in my day.
I planted deep, within my heart the fear
That wind or fowl would take the grain away.
I planted safe against this stark, lean year.

I scattered seed enough to plant the land   5
In rows from Canada to Mexico,
But for my reaping only what the hand
Can hold at once is all that I can show.

Yet what I sowed and what the orchard yields
My brother's sons are gathering stalk and root,   10
Small wonder then my children glean in fields
They have not sown, and feed on bitter fruit.

ANNE BRADSTREET   (1612–1672)

To My Dear and Loving Husband _____ *1678*

If ever two were one, then surely we.
If ever man were loved by wife, then thee;

If ever wife was happy in a man,
Compare with me ye women if you can.
I prize thy love more than whole Mines of gold,   5
Or all the riches that the East doth hold.
My love is such that Rivers cannot quench,
Nor ought° but love from thee, give recompense.
Thy love is such I can no way repay;
The heavens reward thee manifold, I pray.   10
Then while we live, in love let's so persevere,
That when we live no more, we may live ever.

8 *ought:* aught; anything whatever.

ANNE BRADSTREET   (1612–1672)

The Author to Her Book ———————————————— *1678*

Thou ill-formed offspring of my feeble brain,
Who after birth did'st by my side remain,
Till snatched from thence by friends, less wise than true,
Who thee abroad, exposed to public view,
Made thee in rags, halting to the press to trudge,   5
Where errors were not lessened (all may judge).
At thy return my blushing was not small,
My rambling brat (in print) should mother call,
I cast thee by as one unfit for light,
Thy visage was so irksome in my sight;   10
Yet being mine own, at length affection would
Thy blemishes amend, if so I could:
I washed thy face, but more defects I saw,
And rubbing off a spot still made a flaw.
I stretched thy joints to make thee even feet,°   15
Yet still thou run'st more hobbling than is meet;°
In better dress to trim thee was my mind,
But nought save° homespun cloth in the house I find.
In this array 'mongst vulgars may'st thou roam.
In critic's hands beware thou dost not come,   20
And take thy way where yet thou art not known.
If for thy father asked, say thou hadst none;
And for thy mother, she alas is poor,
Which caused her thus to send thee out of door.

15 *feet:* Metaphorically she "stretched" the book's hinges in order to make its "feet"—meter—more
regular and even.   16 *meet:* fitting, suitable.   18 *nought save:* nothing but.

ANNE BRADSTREET   (1612–1672)

*In Memory of My Dear Grandchild Anne Bradstreet Who Deceased
June 20, 1669, Being Three Years and Seven Months Old* _____ 1678

With troubled heart and trembling hand I write,
The heavens have changed to sorrow my delight.
How oft with disappointment have I met,
When I on fading things my hopes have set?
Experience might 'fore this have made me wise,   5
To value things according to their price.
Was ever stable joy yet found below?
Or perfect bliss without mixture of woe?
I knew she was but as a withering flower,
That's here today, perhaps gone in an hour;   10
Like as a bubble, or the brittle glass,
Or like a shadow turning as it was.
More fool then I to look on that was lent
As if mine own, when thus impermanent.
Farewell dear child, thou ne'er shall come to me,   15
But yet a while, and I shall go to thee;
Mean time my throbbing heart's cheered up with this:
Thou with thy Savior art in endless bliss.

GWENDOLYN BROOKS   (1917–2000)

The Mother _____ 1953

Abortions will not let you forget.
You remember the children you got that you did not get,
The damp small pulps with a little or with no hair,
The singers and workers that never handled the air.
You will never neglect or beat   5
Them, or silence or buy with a sweet.
You will never wind up the sucking-thumb
Or scuttle off ghosts that come.
You will never leave them, controlling your luscious sigh,
Return for a snack of them, with gobbling mother-eye.   10

I have heard in the voices of the wind the voices of my dim killed children.
I have contracted. I have eased
My dim dears at the breasts they could never suck.
I have said, Sweets, if I sinned, if I seized
Your luck   15
And your lives from your unfinished reach,
If I stole your births and your names,
Your straight baby tears and your games,
Your stilted or lovely loves, your tumults, your marriages, aches, and your deaths,

If I poisoned the beginnings of your breaths,   20
Believe that even in my deliberateness I was not deliberate.
Though why should I whine,
Whine that the crime was other than mine?—
Since anyhow you are dead.
Or rather, or instead,   25
You were never made.

But that too, I am afraid,
Is faulty: oh, what shall I say, how is the truth to be said?
You were born, you had body, you died.
It is just that you never giggled or planned or cried.   30

Believe me, I loved you all.
Believe me, I knew you, though faintly, and I loved, I loved you
All.

GWENDOLYN BROOKS   (1917–2000)

We Real Cool ———————————————————————— *1959*

The Pool Players.
Seven at the Golden Shovel.

We real cool. We
Left school. We

Lurk late. We
Strike straight. We

Sing sin. We   5
Thin gin. We

Jazz June. We
Die soon.

ELIZABETH BARRETT BROWNING   (1806–1861)

To George Sand° ————————————————————————— *1844*

A Desire

Thou large-brained woman and large-hearted man,
Self-called George Sand! whose soul, amid the lions
Of thy tumultuous senses, moans defiance
And answers roar for roar, as spirits can:

George Sand: pen name of Amandine Aurore Lucie Dupin, Baroness Dudevant (1804–1876). Sand was a French novelist who scandalized society by living and loving as she pleased. She ordinarily dressed like a man so as to move and behave more freely.

I would some mild miraculous thunder ran   5
Above the applauded circus, in appliance
Of thine own nobler nature's strength and science,
Drawing two pinions, white as wings of swan,
From thy strong shoulders, to amaze the place
With holier light! that thou to woman's claim   10
And man's, mightst join beside the angel's grace
Of a pure genius sanctified from blame,
Till child and maiden pressed to thine embrace
To kiss upon thy lips a stainless fame.

ELIZABETH BARRETT BROWNING   (1806–1861)

To George Sand ———————————————————— *1844*

A Recognition

True genius, but true woman! dost deny
The woman's nature with a manly scorn,
And break away the gauds and armlets worn
By weaker women in captivity?
Ah, vain denial! that revolted cry   5
Is sobbed in by a woman's voice forlorn,—
Thy woman's hair, my sister, all unshorn
Floats back dishevelled strength in agony,
Disproving thy man's name: and while before
The world thou burnest in a poet-fire,   10
We see thy woman-heart beat evermore
Through the large flame. Beat purer, heart, and higher,
Till God unsex thee on the heavenly shore
Where unincarnate spirits purely aspire!

JOSÉ ANTONIO BURCIAGA   (b. 1940)

Berta Crocker's Bicentennial Recipe ——————————— *1976*

Con tu filero°
. . . . cut along the dotted line . . . .
Don't wait for the light to change to brown.
Adentro°
You will find   5
Tres paquetes:
         One Red
         One White
         One Blue

1 *Con tu filero:* for your file.   4 *Adentro:* first.

Mézclalos°.   10

                    Pero con huevos.°

Stick it in the oven for 200 years
And let it rise and propagate

And you will have a beautiful brown cake.

10 *Mézclalos:* mix.   11 *Pero con huevos:* but with eggs.

JOSÉ ANTONIO BURCIAGA   (b. 1940)

World Premiere _____ *1976*

To the sergeant who told me,
   "At least you admit it."

To a neighbor down the street who told me,
   "You don't even belong here.
   Go back where you came from."   5

To the honky tonk from Mineral Wells, Texas, who said,
   "We caint help it.
   We was raised to hate Meskins."

To the Redwood City California Chief of Police
Who told his flunky,   10
   "Stay here till the last DOG leaves."

To the flunky who answered,
   "Yes Chief, till the laaaaaaast DOG leaves."

To Herbert Hoover who warned the nation,
   "Mexicans are bad shots but watch out if they have a knife."   15

To the U.S. Senator from California
Whose name I forgot, but said,
   "Mexicans were built low to the ground for picking."

To Frito Lay
   Who made a mascot of a people   20
   And millions from their staple.

To the Dallas policeman
   Who shot a defenceless,
       handcuffed,
       12 year old,   25
       Santos Rodrigues.

To Officer Michael Cogley of the Oakland Police Farce,
   Who shot José Barlow Benavides with a shotgun,
   When José was spread eagled against a squad car.

KATHRYN STRIPLING BYER (b. 1944)

Chestnut Flat Mine ———————————————————— *1992*

They say the fringe of her shawl clung
like lichen to creek rock
and under the laurel her sash looked
for all the sad world like a garter snake.

Farther on something so sheer   5
it was almost invisible floated away
on the Toe River. Red
said the woman who watched it go by,

baby-blue said her little girl stoning
the water with acorns. (Did he stroke   10
her silken leg after he'd unlaced
her tiny black shoe? Did he say Little

Darling, you're mine and what good
are your fancy ways now?) God Almighty,
the way they heard screams floating   15
downhill like what I imagine a town woman

wears underneath all her finery,
but when they came to the old mine by late
afternoon, they found only her gloves
thrown aside in the larkspur. Her dress   20

was laid out like a corpse with a rose
in its lap, on its lily-white bosom
a bird's nest of wrinkles as if a man's
head had lain ever so gently there.

JUANITA CASEY (b. 1925)

Pegasus° ———————————————————————— *1964*

Do you sometimes hear
A sound
Of great wings overhead?
Many people who see nothing
Tell me they do.   5

And have you seen,
Even if you are no horseman,
This horse
Which paces from the valley

Pegasus: In Greek mythology, Pegasus is the winged horse symbolizing poetic inspiration.

On the chalk road to the uplands,   10
Watching you as he climbs,
First with one eye,
Then the other,
As horses will.
It will be   15
One of those special moments
When it is like the first morning.
The mist lingering
Like threads laid by night
For her return at cockcrow.   20
Can you hold
The bold onyx eye
Of the horse approaching,
Unafraid
If unaccustomed to horses,   25
Without sense of inferiority,
Or if a horseman,
Without flinching
From so redoubtable a stallion,
Who, breasting the proud light,   30
Challenges the sun
As rival to his own blood.
You are aware this is Horse.
Everything is,
The bay-brown river,   35
Piebald and roan mountains,
Branded hills moving against the sky
Like Oncus' mares.
And unknowingly, you know
That this astonishing animal   40
Is coming quite unbidden
To your hand.

When it happened to me,
He greeted me,
Because although I am a woman   45
And no poet,
He knew I had my kingdom amongst his nation.
I told him
Women cannot be poets.
If they try   50
They become masculine apologies,
Or apologies for women.
They must be content
To be spiritual and physical bran tubs
For real poets,   55
Who by a lucky delve may now and then
Find a pearl
Amongst all the bran.

When he came to me,
There was in his eye   60
A look which some earth-bound horses show.
But they are rare these days,
The singing blood is deadened,
And should honor be sought
Amongst the conditioned?   65
They stand
Like falcons chained° to an ignoble hand.
And they stand,
Shining out of the dark
Like Blake's tiger.°   70
While the warnings rustle like rats in straw,
A rogue. He killed a man.° Beware.
Waiting for one
To step out of the centuries
And greet him,   75
Ho, my good horse.
And they search great horizons
Past our heads,
Back over Babylon,
Tigris and Thessaly,   80
They look for those Twins
Or for him who carried Wisdom's bridle
To the spring that day.
How sweetly
They would step under that hand,   85
Guided by the traditional
Silken thread
Between mind, not metal.
Good Horse,
Do you too search for someone worthy of your blood,   90
Who would not slide off ignominiously
At the first clap of wings
As though you'd crowed as well!
Or taking the harshest curb
Bend you to impossible propriety   95
In classes designed
To exhibit the exhibitor.
And no one would wish these days to drink with you
From Hippocrene.°
There would be mention   100
Of worms, bacteria, hygiene.

---

67 *Falcons obtained:* Trained falcons are usually kept on a leash tied to the wrist.   70 *Blake's
tiger:* a reference to the poem "The Tiger" by William Blake; which begins, "Tiger, Tiger, burning
bright / In the forests of the night."   72 *man:* Ben Jonson (1572–1637), the poet's
poet.   99 *Hippocrene:* fountain of the Muses, thus the inspiration of the poet—it rose from a
spot struck by the hoof of Pegasus.

(Hygeia, girl, blush for them)
Perhaps he knows I could ride him,
But will not.
It would be an insult.   105
I'm surprised at those who did.
Perseus°—
Though due to possible artistic misinterpretation—
Coal-bucket on head as though
All set for a celestial scramble,   110
And nothing to do with horses,
Cretinous shield in hand,
And all smirk and sandals.
Or Bellerophon.°
Whose appalling horsemanship   115
Ended in degradation
And an arseful of brambles.

Now he is up with me, what a horse this is.
How are you bred,
Horse?   120
Sired by the Mind
Out of Light,
Or a cloud covering the night?
A Horse
From a handful of Libyan wind?   125
Or from Poseidon's° line of sea-thrown winners,
By the stallion Ocean,
Put him to the mare Demeter,°
She is a black,
A wild one, snake-headed and uncertain.   130
But she could go the distance
In Time's stakes.
She'd scorch the last lap of Eternity
Though her heart burst . . .
However you're bred, Horse,   135
No matter.
Pedigree unknown, they might write.
But there is no disguising that in form
And spirit
You were tempered   140
By that old Damascene, Truth.

I am glad he came,
Just this once.
That for a moment
I scratched that place under the mane   145

107 *Perseus:* hero who slew Medusa, from whose trunk sprang Pegasus.   114 *Bellerophon:* hero
who killed the Chimera with the help of Pegasus.   126 *Poseidon:* The horse was sacred to Poseidon, god of the sea.   128 *Demeter:* goddess of architecture and fertility.

Which entrances all horses,
And made the immortal lip bunch and twitch.
I saw his teeth unringed
And ageless,
Time cannot bishop him.   150
I told him
Go back,
Back to his lusher centuries,
Away from
This close cropped age.   155
Back
Good horse,
Here you will be a freak, and it is better
To return
Even though you graze Time bare.   160

LADY MARY CHUDLEIGH   (1656–1710)

To the Ladies _____ *1703*

Wife and servant are the same,
But only differ in the name:
For when that fatal knot is tied,
Which nothing, nothing can divide:
When she the word *obey* has said,   5
And man by law supreme has made,
Then all that's kind is laid aside,
And nothing left but state° and pride:
Fierce as an Eastern prince he grows,
And all his innate rigor shows: 10
Then but to look, to laugh, or speak,
Will the nuptual contract break.
Like mutes she signs alone must make,
And never any freedom take:
But still be governed by a nod,   15
And fear her husband as her God:
Him still must serve, him still obey,
And nothing act, and nothing say,
But what her haughty lord thinks fit,
Who with the power, has all the wit.   20
Then shun, oh! shun that wretched state,
And all the fawning flatterers hate:
Value your selves, and men despise,
You must be proud, if you'll be wise.

8 *state:* stateliness; ceremony.

AMY CLAMPITT   (1920–1994)

Beach Glass _____ *1983*

While you walk the water's edge,
turning over concepts
I can't envision, the honking buoy
serves notice that at any time
the wind may change,   5
the reef-bell clatters
its treble monotone, deaf as Cassandra°
to any note but warning. The ocean,
cumbered by no business more urgent
than keeping open old accounts   10
that never balanced,
goes on shuffling its millenniums
of quartz, granite, basalt.
                    It behaves
toward the permutations of novelty—
driftwood and shipwreck, last night's   15
beer cans, spilt oil, the coughed-up
residue of plastic—with random
impartiality, playing catch or tag
or touch-last like a terrier,
turning the same thing over and over,   20
over and over. For the ocean, nothing
is beneath consideration.
                    The houses
of so many mussels and periwinkles
have been abandoned here, it's hopeless
to know which to salvage. Instead   25
I keep a lookout for beach glass—
amber of Budweiser, chrysoprase
of Almadén and Gallo, lapis
by way of (no getting around it,
I'm afraid) Phillips'   30
Milk of Magnesia, with now and then a rare
translucent turquoise or blurred amethyst
of no known origin.
                    The process
goes on forever: they came from sand,
they go back to gravel,   35
along with the treasuries
of Murano,° the buttressed
astonishments of Chartres,°
which even now are readying

7 *Cassandra:* prophetess in Aeschylus' *Agamemnon.*   40 *Murano:* island near Venice renowned
for its glassware.   41 *Chartres:* reference to the cathedral in Chartres (France), which has flying buttresses and astonishing stained-glass windows.

for being turned over and over as gravely   40
and gradually as an intellect
engaged in the hazardous
redefinition of structures
no one has yet looked at.

SAMUEL TAYLOR COLERIDGE   (1772–1834)

Kubla Khan° _____ *1816*

In Xanadu did Kubla Khan
A stately pleasure-dome decree:
Where Alph,° the sacred river, ran
Through caverns measureless to man
   Down to a sunless sea.   5
So twice five miles of fertile ground
With walls and towers were girdled round:
And there were gardens bright with sinuous rills,
Where blossomed many an incense-bearing tree;
And here were forests ancient as the hills,   10
Enfolding sunny spots of greenery.

But oh! that deep romantic chasm which slanted
Down the green hill athwart a cedarn cover!°
A savage place! as holy and enchanted
As e'er beneath a waning moon was haunted   15
By woman wailing for her demon-lover!
And from this chasm, with ceaseless turmoil seething,
As if this earth in fast thick pants were breathing,
A mighty fountain momently was forced:
Amid whose swift half-intermitted burst   20
Huge fragments vaulted like rebounding hail,
Or chaffy grain beneath the thresher's flail:
And 'mid these dancing rocks at once and ever
It flung up momently the sacred river.
Five miles meandering with a mazy motion   25
Through wood and dale the sacred river ran,
Then reached the caverns measureless to man,
And sank in tumult to a lifeless ocean:
And 'mid this tumult Kubla heard from far
Ancestral voices prophesying war!   30

Kubla Khan: Coleridge relates that he was reading about the palace and gardens of Kublai Khan (1216–1294), the founder of the Mongol dynasty in China, when he fell asleep under the influence of some opium and dreamed the following dream. When he awoke he began writing quickly but lost his concentration when he was interrupted by a visitor. The poem therefore is unfinished, a "fragment."   3 *Alph:* This is Alpheus, the river in John Milton's *Lycidas* and in Greek myth.   13 *athwart . . . cover:* across a forest of cedars.

The shadow of the dome of pleasure
Floated midway on the waves;
Where was heard the mingled measure
From the fountain and the caves.
It was a miracle of rare device,   35
A sunny pleasure-dome with caves of ice!

A damsel with a dulcimer
In a vision once I saw:
It was an Abyssinian maid,
And on her dulcimer she played,   40
Singing of Mount Abora.
Could I revive within me
Her symphony and song,
To such a deep delight 'twould win me,
That with music loud and long,   45
I would build that dome in air,
That sunny dome! those caves of ice!
And all who heard should see them there,
And all should cry, Beware! Beware!
His flashing eyes, his floating hair!   50
Weave a circle round him thrice,
And close your eyes with holy dread,
For he on honey-dew hath fed,
And drunk the milk of Paradise.

JOHN COTTON   (b. 1925)

Report Back —————————————————————— *1971*

> "O dark dark dark. They all go into the dark,
> *The vacant interstellar spaces*"
> —T. S. Eliot, *East Coker*

Galactic probe seven-thousand and four
Reports an uneventful journey, free
From any serious meteoric collisions.
Geological and radiation
Surveys are now being prepared, though our first   5
Instrumentation suggests little, if
Any, difficulty in setting up
The usual research apparatus.

> And looking into the void
> From the far edge of our empire   10
> We see the next galaxy
> A rapidly receding
> Thumb-smudge of light in a mid-
> Night violet sky pierced by the

> Dead-lights of a handful of planets,   15
> Red-tinged and steady like the
> Eyes of disappointed lovers,
> And our perspective's gone.

Gravity repulsion is now reduced
To a minimum, while preliminary   20
Spectrascopic analysis suggests
Possible vegetation, though we seem,
At present, on what is clearly a desert.

> Pock-marked with small craters
> To the edge of a ragged   25
> Horizon, and long-shadowed
> In what passes for a moon
> On the galactic periphery,
> Here is an austere beauty,
> Barren, uncompromising,   30
> Like that which must have been
> Experienced by men
> On the ice-caps and deserts
> As they once existed on earth
> Before their urbanization.   35
> Harsh and unambiguous
> It throws, as it were, a man
> Into himself. Is this what
> The early poets wrote about?

Our first extra-craft exploration has   40
Returned with specimens, one of which may
Be a new mineral. We are working
On the uranium breakdown now.
We have found, also, what appear to be
Pebbles, which suggest the action of seas,   45
Suggesting life, if not now, at some time.
With the spectrascopic analysis
This could prove most interesting. We will
Begin work radio-gravitation
Project immediate first light. Meanwhile,   50
We are now occupied with lab. work as
It is eighty hours until the next "dawn."
The darkness, as expected, is intense.

> O the dark, the deep hard dark
> Of these galactic nights!   55
> Even the planets have set
> Leaving it slab and impenetrable,
> As dark and directionless
> As those long nights of the soul
> The ancient mystics spoke of.   60
> Beyond there is nothing,

Nothing we have known or experienced.
It is such a dark
To be lost in which a man
Might, perhaps, find himself.   65

Excessive hyperwarp has set up
A fault in our auxiliary booster,
Could you contact the depot-ship asking
To send a supply-cruiser with a spare?
And, while they are at it, some playing-cards   70
Or a set of Galaxtopoly with
A few of the latest girlie magazines.
Anything to kill the time.

If a man could stare out
Such a darkness and endure,   75
In such a darkness a man
Might, perhaps, find himself,
Scoured to the quick
In the timeless sands of the void.

Anything, as I said, to kill the time.   80

ROBERT CREELEY   (b. 1926)

Ballad of the Despairing Husband _____ *1982*

My wife and I lived all alone,
contention was our only bone.
I fought with her, she fought with me,
and things went on right merrily.

But now I live here by myself   5
with hardly a damn thing on the shelf,
and pass my days with little cheer
since I have parted from my dear.

Oh come home soon, I write to her.
Go fuck yourself, is her answer.   10
Now what is that, for Christian word?
I hope she feeds on dried goose turd.

But still I love her, yes I do.
I love her and the children too.
I only think it fit that she   15
should quickly come right back to me.

Ah no, she says, and she is tough,
and smacks me down with her rebuff.
Ah no, she says, I will not come
after the bloody things you've done.   20

Oh wife, oh wife—I tell you true,
I never loved no one but you.
I never will, it cannot be
another woman is for me.

That may be right, she will say then,   25
but as for me, there's other men.
And I will tell you I propose
to catch them firmly by the nose.

And I will wear what dresses I choose!
And I will dance, and what's to lose!   30
I'm free of you, you little prick,
and I'm the one can make it stick.

Was this the darling I did love?
Was this that mercy from above
did open violets in the spring—   35
and made my own worn self to sing?

She was. I know. And she is still,
and if I love her? then so I will.
And I will tell her, and tell her right . . .

Oh lovely lady, morning or evening or afternoon.   40
Oh lovely lady, eating with or without a spoon.
Oh most lovely lady, whether dressed or undressed or partly.
Oh most lovely lady, getting up or going to bed or sitting only.

Oh loveliest of ladies, than whom none is more fair, more gracious,
    more beautiful.
Oh loveliest of ladies, whether you are just or unjust, merciful,
    indifferent, or cruel.   45
Oh most loveliest of ladies, doing whatever, seeing whatever, being
    whatever.
Oh most loveliest of ladies, in rain, in shine, in any weather.

Oh lady, grant me time,
please, to finish my rhyme.

E. E. CUMMINGS   (1894–1962)

Buffalo Bill's defunct _____ *1923*

Buffalo Bill's
defunct
        who used to
        ride a watersmooth-silver
                            stallion   5
and break onetwothreefourfive pigeonsjustlikethat
                        Jesus

he was a handsome man
                     and what i want to know is
how do you like your blueeyed boy   10
Mister Death

E. E. CUMMINGS (1894–1962)

my sweet old etcetera ————————————————————— *1926*

my sweet old etcetera
aunt lucy during the recent

war could and what
is more did tell you just
what everybody was fighting   5

for,
my sister

isabel created hundreds
(and
hundreds)of socks not to   10
mention shirts fleaproof earwarmers

etcetera wristers etcetera, my
mother hoped that

i would die etcetera
bravely of course my father used   15
to become hoarse talking about how it was
a privilege and if only he
could meanwhile my

self etcetera lay quietly
in the deep mud et   20

cetera
(dreaming,
et
   cetera, of
Your smile   25
eyes knees and of your Etcetera)

PHILIP DACEY (b. 1939)

Jack, Afterwards° ————————————————————— *1977*

It's difficult to say what it all meant.
The whole experience, in memory,

Jack, Afterwards: reference to Jack in "Jack and the Beanstalk."

Seems like a story someone might invent
Who was both mad and congenitally cheery.
I have to remind myself, it happened to me.   5
The stalk's gone now, and Alma, the old cow;
And I fear only the dream with the shadow.

My mother had a lot to do with it.
In fact, you might say it was her beanstalk—
She scattered the seeds, I didn't, when she hit   10
My full hand and said all I was good for was talk.
She haunted me in those days: I couldn't walk
Anywhere without seeing her face,
Even on the crone in the giant's palace.

Throughout this whole time, my father was dead.   15
I think I must have felt his not-being-there
More than I would have his being-there. Instead
Of his snoring, his absence was everywhere.
So the old man with the beans, poor and threadbare
As he was, became the more important   20
To my boyish needs. Not to mention the giant.

Oddly enough, the beanstalk itself, which some
Might think the most wonderful part of all this,
Pales in time's perspective. Though my true home
Between the earth and sky, and though no less   25
Than magic, that stalk, in the last analysis,
Was but a means to an end. Yet, I must say,
I still recall the beanflowers' sweet bouquet.

Then there's the giant. What can be said? Nothing
And everything. Or this: if the truth be known   30
About someone so great, it was surprising
How vulnerable he seemed, and how alone.
Not that I wasn't frightened. I was, to the bone—
But it was his weakness, joined to such power,
I feared most, and fear now, any late hour.   35

The fruits of it all were gold, a hen, and a harp.
I wish I could say I miss my poverty,
When my appetite, if not my wit, was sharp,
But I don't. A little fat hasn't hurt me
Much. Still it's that strange harp's melody,   40
Beauty willing itself, not golden eggs,
Whose loss would leave me, I hope, one who begs.

Of everything, the strangest was to see
Alma the cow come back home at the end,
Her two horns wreathed in wild briony   45
And traveler's joy. Did the old man send
Her as a gift? She seemed, somehow, lightened.

I'd like to think I traded her away
To get her back, sea-changed, in such array.

So I sit here, my dying, blind mother   50
To tend to, and wonder how it was
I escaped, smiling, from such an adventure.
If events in those days conformed to laws,
I'd like to know—not least, nor only, because
What happened then still makes me ask, Why me?   55
Not even my mother knew, when she could see.

PHILIP DACEY (b. 1939)

Jill, Afterwards° _____ *1977*

He had this idea about the hill,
How at the top there would be water
Sweeter than any in any pail
Lugged previously, and to come down
Would be the easiest part of all.   5
I told him it was a kids' story.

Before I had knockers that story
Was making the rounds in my gang. Hell,
We laughed at it even then. We all
Knew better than to think sweet water   10
Could be had for the price of a pail
And a little leg-work up and down

A hill that had been standing there, dawn
To dreary dawn, our whole life's story
Long. Not to mention the probabil-   15
ity such a thing as sweet water,
Hill or no hill, didn't exist. I'll
Give him credit for this, though: a wall

Couldn't have been more stubborn. He'd call
Me late at night even, to break down   20
My resistance. Okay, I said, I'll
Go. The truth is, he was cute. Starry-
eyed, but cute. And I wondered whether
He had anything in his pants. Pale

Dawn found us taking turns with the pail   25
As we rose above the town. Not all
The money down there beats the water
We'll find, he said. Now I was poor, down

Jill, Afterwards: reference to Jill in "Jack and Jill went up the hill" nursery rhyme.

To a few bucks. It's no mystery
Money talks. Loud. But I climbed the hill.   30

To the top. And there was this big hole.
And deep. I got dizzy to look down
It. He had rope and let the pail fall
Yards and yards. "Got something," he yelled, pull-
ing the catch in. Later, the story   35
He told, back in town, was the water

Spilled out. But the fact of the matter
Is I saw what he had. Nothing. Damn
If he didn't claim different, though. Al-
ways. Damn, too, if his pants weren't full.   40
I've got these kids to prove that story.
When they whine, I tell them: climb a hill.

BERNARD DADIÉ   (b. 1916)

In Memoriam _____ *1975*

> *From* Africa Arise!
> *Translated by Ellen Conroy Kennedy*

"Starved to death,"
He died of hunger,
but it won't be written on his tomb
for they put him in an unmarked grave,
it won't be written there in stone   5
for the government rejects the truth.

He had gone to all the offices,
the factories, the farms:
no jobs . . .

And thread by thread, his clothing turned to rags.   10
This, with a thousand bales of surplus cloth nearby . . .
He slept beneath the stars.

And he was a man like you
a man like me,
a man like them,   15
and he lay beneath the stars,
this man, on the bare ground
before the palaces,
while on the docks mountains of cement were growing hard.
It won't be written there on stone   20
that he died
beside a palace
with hunger in his belly,

cold gnawing at his bones,
his flesh grown colorless and limp, his ribs collapsing,   25
the sockets of his bones rebelling.

It won't be written on his tomb
that he died of hunger, slowly,
slowly, while flour mildewed in the stores,
while behind the counters with the iron grills,   30
behind warehouses filled with goods
they were pulling in the profits . . .
A man is dying.
A man like you,
a man like me,   35
a man like them.
A man is dying of hunger,
starving, in the midst of plenty.

"Starved to Death"
won't be written on his tomb.   40
Dishonor on the government
that degrades mankind and brings him low.
It won't be written on his grave
"Dead, of Hunger."

But you, remember   45
that he starved to death,
slowly
died of hunger,

a man like them
a man like you   50
slowly
died of hunger
bit by bit
in the midst of plenty
staring at deaf heaven.   55

This was a man
like you,
like them,
a man . . .
Remember!   60

BERNARD DADIÉ   (b. 1916)

I Thank You, Lord _____ *1975*

Translated by Ellen Conroy Kennedy

I thank you, Lord, for having made me Black,
for having made me

the sum of all griefs,
for having put upon my head
the World.   5
I wear the livery of the Centaur°
and I have carried the World since the first morning.

White is the color of the great occasions.
Black the color of everyday.
And I have carried the World since the first evening.   10

I am content
with the shape of my head
made to carry the World.
Satisfied
with the shape of my nose   15
made to inhale the four winds of the World.
Pleased
with the shape of my legs
ready to run to the end of the Earth.

I thank you, Lord, for having made me Black,   20
for having made me
the sum of all pain.
A thousand swords have pierced my heart.
A thousand brands have burned me.
And my blood has reddened the snow of all the calvaries,   25
and my blood, at each dawn, has reddened all horizons.

Yet I am content
to carry the World.

Happy with my short arms
with my long arms   30
with my thick lips.

I thank you, Lord, for having made me Black.
I have carried the World since the dawn of time
and in the night my laughter at the World
creates the day.   35

6 *Centaur:* in Greek mythology, half-man, half-horse, one who bridges nature and humanity.

CARL DENNIS   (b. 1939)

Oedipus the King _____ *1990*

Hard to forgive Freud,° the exposer of fictions,
When he borrows the name of a great mythical king

1 *Freud:* Sigmund Freud (1856–1939), founder of psychoanalysis, who believed the story of Oedipus (see Sophocles, *Oedipus the King,* in this volume) illustrated every man's desire to sleep with his mother.

To cover our common wish not to share mom
With anyone, not even with dad.

Oedipus, solver of riddles too hard for us,   5
Freud's inspiration and mentor,
Teacher and pupil of one mind with the sphinx
That man is the mystery,
Three people at least in one.
But even Freud, with all his interpreting,   10
Didn't manage to save a city, as Oedipus did.
Vienna could have done without him,
He knew, and would go on as before,
Winning and wasting.

We never imagine Oedipus one of us   15
Except for a moment, just after the plague arrives,
When he vows to rid the city of its pollution,
To root the murderer out, no matter where.
We too could have made a mistake like that.
But when the question changes slowly   20
To who exactly his parents are
We would have stopped, as the prophet advises,
While the King, suspecting the worst, presses on.

Freud may have taken the facts, however painful,
As evidence he was only human,   25
Alive and desiring.
But Oedipus chooses to be guilty,
To blind himself, to banish himself
And go the gods one better, the father gods
Who didn't love him as a father should.   30

As for his mother, if he has one then,
It's the earth, who feels him tapping
Her breast with his cane
As he hobbles along outside the walls.
"Where are you going, dear Son?" she calls.   35
"For you the door to my dark house stands open.
No other house will take you in."

JAMES DICKEY (b. 1923)

On the Hill Below the Lighthouse _____ *1967*

Now I can be sure of my sleep;
I have lost the blue sea in my eyelids.
From a place in the mind too deep
For thought, a light like a wind is beginning.
 Now I can be sure of my sleep.   5

When the moon is held strongly within it,
The eye of the mind opens gladly.
Day changes to dark, and is bright,
And miracles trust to the body,
 When the moon is held strongly within it.   10

A woman comes true when I think her.
Her eyes on the window are closing.
She has dressed the stark wood of a chair.
Her form and my body are facing.
 A woman comes true when I think her.   15

Shade swings, and she lies against me.
The lighthouse has opened its brain.
A browed light travels the sea.
Her clothes on the chair spread their wings.
 Shade swings, and she lies against me.   20

Let us lie in returning light,
As a bright arm sweeps through the moon.
The sun is dead, thinking of night
Swung round like a thing on a chain.
 Let us lie in returning light.   25

Let us lie where your angel is walking
In shadow, from wall onto wall,
Cast forth from your off-cast clothing
To pace the dim room where we fell.
 Let us lie where your angel is walking.   30

Coming back, coming back, going over.
An arm turns the light world around
The dark. Again we are waiting to hover
In a blaze in the mind like a wind.
 Coming back, coming back, going over.   35

 Now I can be sure of my sleep;
 The moon is held strongly within it.
 A woman comes true when I think her.
 Shade swings, and she lies against me.
 Let us lie in returning light;   40
 Let us lie where your angel is walking,
 Coming back, coming back, going over.

EMILY DICKINSON   (1830–1886)

One of the most mysterious of poets, Emily Dickinson was educated at Amherst Academy in Amherst, Massachusetts, and spent a year at Mount Holyoke, seven miles from home. She left as a result of homesickness and spent the rest of her life unmarried in her home with a small circle of friends. She rarely greeted visitors, and often sat behind her bedroom door while she talked with them. She traveled very little and not at all in mid and later life. She dressed in white as a sign of her celibacy and in her twenties sometimes took part in local agricultural fairs. No one knows why she remained at home in seclusion, although she refers in 1860 to an event, "a terror," about which she could speak to no one. Most biographers have speculated that she had an unhappy romance.

Emily's father was a strict Calvinist, virtually a Puritan in his beliefs. He was treasurer of Amherst College and a man of commanding physical and psychological presence. In some ways, he dominated her life. For a time, she shared his religious beliefs, but she ceased attending church early in life. When her father died in 1874, she did not attend the funeral, which was downstairs in her home. Biographers do not regard her action as a form of denial or rejection because she listened to the funeral upstairs through her bedroom door. At that point in her life, she saw very few people.

Emily devoted most of her adult life to writing poems. We have almost eighteen hundred, some of which were included in letters to friends. Yet she published only eight in her lifetime and was not truly discovered as an important poet until the twentieth century. Therefore, this highly original, distinctive imagination could not have affected the poetry of her own time. She has been regarded, along with her older contemporary, Walt Whitman, as one of the founders of modern American poetry. Her work follows no pattern. Most of her poems are short lyrics, usually punctuated with dashes (she punctuated her recipes this way, too), sometimes fully rhymed, sometimes slant rhymed, and sometimes unrhymed. Her images are striking, rooted in everyday experience, and intensely memorable.

Emily Dickinson may not have lived an adventurous life, but she lived a thoroughly examined life. As she says, "Inebriate of Air—am I— / And Debauchee of Dew—." Little things such as air (if these are little) were of profound importance to her and stirred rich emotions. In "I felt a Funeral, in my Brain," she describes a common occurrence in her time, a funeral. This one may have been real or imagined—the poem is dated close to 1861, when she was thirty-one,—but it was deeply felt. She also speaks with extraordinary authority in "After great pain, a formal feeling comes—," or so we imagine from what little we know of her life. This, too, is a poem from her early thirties, and in her imagination of death—"This is the Hour of Lead—"—she brings considerable imaginative conviction.

In one of her few published poems, "A Narrow Fellow in the Grass," Dickinson writes from a point of view that baffles biography, since the narrator is clearly "a Boy, and Barefoot." Thus what we have in Emily Dickinson is a mystery that invites readers to imagine solutions. Why did she write so many poems when she knew they would not be published? Why did she stay by herself and avoid the normal social pleasures of a bustling Amherst, filled with interesting people? What was the "terror" or disappointment in her life? We may never know the answers to these questions. However, those who pursue them have the poetry for clues, and it is very tempting to leave the poem behind in an effort to solve the problems of biography. The same is true for many poets. Emily Dickinson is one of the most fascinating because her work is so powerful, so personal, so modern in sensibility, that we think of her more as one of us than as a reclusive nineteenth-century spinster.

Success Is Counted Sweetest _____ *1878 (c. 1859)*

(67)

Success is counted sweetest
By those who ne'er succeed.
To comprehend a nectar
Requires sorest need.

Not one of all the purple Host   5
Who took the Flag today
Can tell the definition
So clear of Victory

As he defeated—dying—
On whose forbidden ear   10
The distant strains of triumph
Burst agonized and clear!

EMILY DICKINSON   (1830–1886)

I Taste a Liquor Never Brewed _____ *1861 (c. 1860)*

(214)

I taste a liquor never brewed—
From Tankards scooped in Pearl—
Not all the Vats upon the Rhine
Yield such an Alcohol!

Inebriate of Air—am I—   5
And Debauchee of Dew—
Reeling—thro endless summer days—
From inns of Molten Blue—

When "Landlords" turn the drunken Bee
Out of the Foxglove's door—   10
When Butterflies—renounce their "drams"—
I shall but drink the more!

Till Seraphs swing their snowy Hats—
And Saints—to windows run—
To see the little Tippler   15
Leaning against the—Sun—

EMILY DICKINSON   (1830–1886)

I Felt a Funeral, in My Brain _____ *1896 (c. 1861)*

(280)

I felt a Funeral, in my Brain,
And Mourners to and fro
Kept treading—treading—till it seemed
That Sense was breaking through—

And when they all were seated,   5
A Service, like a Drum—
Kept beating—beating—till I thought
My Mind was going numb—

And then I heard them lift a Box
And creak across my Soul   10
With those same Boots of Lead, again,
Then Space—began to toll,

As all the Heavens were a Bell,
And Being, but an Ear,
And I, and Silence, some strange Race   15
Wrecked, solitary, here—

And then a Plank in Reason, broke,
And I dropped down, and down—
And hit a World, at every plunge,
And Finished knowing—then—   20

EMILY DICKINSON   (1830–1886)

After Great Pain, a Formal Feeling Comes —————— *1929 (c. 1862)*

(341)
After great pain, a formal feeling comes—
The Nerves sit ceremonious, like Tombs—
The stiff Heart questions was it He, that bore,
And Yesterday, or Centuries before?

The Feet, mechanical, go round—   5
Of Ground, or Air, or Ought—
A Wooden way
Regardless grown,
A Quartz contentment, like a stone—

This is the Hour of Lead—   10
Remembered, if outlived,
As Freezing persons, recollect the Snow—
First—Chill—then Stupor—then the letting go—

EMILY DICKINSON   (1830–1886)

I Heard a Fly Buzz—When I Died —————— *1896 (c. 1862)*

(465)
I heard a Fly buzz—when I died—
The Stillness in the Room
Was like the Stillness in the Air—
Between the Heaves of Storm—

The Eyes around—had wrung them dry—   5
And Breaths were gathering firm
For that last Onset—when the King
Be witnessed—in the Room—

I willed my Keepsakes—Signed away
What portion of me be   10

Assignable—and then it was
There interposed a Fly—

With Blue—uncertain stumbling Buzz—
Between the light—and me—
And then the Windows failed—and then   15
I could not see to see—

EMILY DICKINSON   (1830–1886)

Because I Could Not Stop for Death _____ *1890 (c. 1863)*

(712)

Because I could not stop for Death—
He kindly stopped for me—
The Carriage held but just Ourselves—
And Immortality.

We slowly drove—He knew no haste   5
And I had put away
My labor and my leisure too,
For His Civility—

We passed the School, where Children strove
At Recess—in the Ring—   10
We passed the Fields of Gazing Grain—
We passed the Setting Sun—

Or rather—He passed Us—
The Dews drew quivering and chill—
For only Gossamer, my Gown—   15
My Tippet—only Tulle—

We paused before a House that seemed
A Swelling of the Ground—
The Roof was scarcely visible—
The Cornice—in the Ground—   20

Since then—'tis Centuries—and yet
Feels shorter than the Day
I first surmised the Horses' Heads
Were toward Eternity—

EMILY DICKINSON   (1830–1886)

Tell All the Truth but Tell It Slant _____ *1945 (c. 1868)*

(1129)

Tell all the Truth but tell it slant—
Success in Circuit lies

Too bright for our infirm Delight
The Truth's superb surprise
As Lightning to the Children eased   5
With explanation kind
The Truth must dazzle gradually
Or every man be blind—

SHEILA DIETZ   (b. 1949)

Not Remembering More _____ *1992*

That Christmas Eve, the train derailed between St. Louis
        grandparents and my mother's parents in Springfield,
Illinois. In the dark, Mom and Dad hauled luggage

through swirling snow, had us kids hold hands stepping
        over iced tracks. Sliding doors hissed back so Dad   5
could lift each child into the white haired conductor's

navy blue arms. This train promised we'd be there
        by Christmas, and, sure enough, hours later,
squeezed onto jump seats in Grandfather's black

"Checker," I counted Christmas trees flickering   10
        from houses we passed in the still dark hours
of Christmas morning. So many it would have

been easier to count the few dark homes. Back
        then I counted colored lights as joy. But later,
at Grandma's Christmas party, he pulled me—It was   15

Uncle Ed, not a real uncle, who lifted me onto his
        lap, scared. Then his wet mouth on mine, too long,
but gone before my parents turned around. Smoothing

his hair he said "Let's go to the playhouse." Mother's
        big playhouse in the backyard. No. It's too cold. I   20
don't want to. Didn't anyone hear me? Or did someone

say, "Sheila, why don't you go?" Out the door, crunching
        across snow. I used to pretend I was waiting for someone
to come home. I'd push little red curtains aside, look

out the window. No—not here yet. Time to make dinner.   25
        Is anybody coming? Open the cabinet doors wide,
use the best china dishes decorated with blue flowers.

Set the table. The fork goes here, the knife, put it
        down there. Close the curtains. No one's coming. Him
over my shoulder. The wooden floor? Then the party,   30

and scraps of a dream. Bluberry children from Grandma's
    Scandinavian storybooks. Big red and black candy, red
for cinnamon, black licorice, and deep in the woods,

a candy house. Hansel and Gretel. After Christmas, riding
    to the train station in the same Checker, back down   35
the same streets. Back, past one dark house after another.

BIRAGO DIOP   (1906–1989)

Viaticum° _____ *1967 (tr. 1977)*

Translated by Ellen Conroy Kennedy

Into one of three pots,
three pots to which on certain evenings
souls serene and satisfied return—
the breathing of ancestors,
ancestors who were men,   5
forefathers who were sages—
Mother dipped three fingers,
three fingers of her left hand:
the thumb, the first and middle fingers.

With her three fingers red with blood   10
with dog's blood,
with bull's blood,
with goat's blood,
three times Mother touched me.
With her thumb she touched my brow,   15
with her index my left breast,
and my navel with her third.

I, I held my fingers red with blood
with dog's blood,
with bull's blood,   20
with goat's blood,
I held these three fingers to the winds,
to the North winds, to the winds of the rising sun,
to the South winds, to the winds of the setting sun;
and I raised my three fingers toward the moon,   25
the full moon, the full and naked moon,
reflected in the bottom of the biggest pot.

Then I put these three fingers in the sand,
into the sand that had grown cold,

Viaticum: Latin for preparation for a journey.

and Mother said: "Go, go into the World!   30
They will follow in your steps for life."

Since then I go my way
along the pathways,
the pathways and the roads,
across the sea and farther, farther still   35
beyond the sea and farther than beyond.
And when evil ones draw near,
men with black hearts,
when I approach the envious,
men with black hearts   40
before me move the Spirits of the Elders.

JOHN DONNE   (1572–1631)

The Flea ⎯⎯⎯⎯⎯⎯⎯⎯⎯⎯⎯⎯⎯⎯⎯⎯⎯⎯⎯ *1633*

Mark but° this flea, and mark in this,
How little that which thou deniest me is;
Me it sucked first, and now sucks thee,
And in this flea our two bloods mingled be;
Thou know'st that this cannot be said   5
A sin, or shame, or loss of maidenhead,
   Yet this enjoys before it woo,
    And pampered swells with one blood made of two,
    And this, alas, is more than we would do.

Oh stay, three lives in one flea spare,   10
Where we almost, nay more than married, are.
This flea is you and I, and this
Our marriage bed and marriage temple is;
Though parents grudge, and you, we are met,
And cloistered in these living walls of jet,   15
   Though use° make you apt to kill me
   Let not to that, self-murder added be,
   And sacrilege, three sins in killing three.

Cruel and sudden, hast thou since
Purpled thy nail, in blood of innocence?   20
Wherein could this flea guilty be,
Except in that drop which it sucked from thee?
Yet thou triumph'st, and say'st that thou
Find'st not thy self nor me the weaker now;
   'Tis true, then learn how false tears be;   25
   Just so much honor, when thou yield'st to me,
   Will waste, as this flea's death took life from thee.

1 *Mark but:* note only.   16 *use:* habit.

JOHN DONNE   (1572–1631)

A Valediction: Forbidding Mourning ———————————————— 1633

As virtuous men pass mildly away,
   And whisper to their souls to go,
Whilst some of their sad friends do say
   The breath goes now, and some say, No;

So let us melt, and make no noise,   5
   No tear-floods, nor sigh-tempests move,
'Twere profanation of our joys
   To tell the laity our love.

Moving of th' earth° brings harms and fears,
   Men reckon what it did and meant;   10
But trepidation of the spheres,
   Though greater far, is innocent.°

Dull sublunary° lovers' love
   (Whose soul is sense) cannot admit
Absence, because it doth remove   15
   Those things which elemented° it.

But we by a love so much refined
   That our selves know not what it is,
Inter-assurèd of the mind,
   Care less, eyes, lips, and hands to miss.   20

Our two souls therefore, which are one,
   Though I must go, endure not yet
A breach, but an expansion,
   Like gold to airy thinness beat.

If they be two, they are two so   25
   As stiff twin compasses are two;
Thy soul, the fixed foot, makes no show
   To move, but doth, if th' other do.

And though it in the center sit,
   Yet when the other far doth roam,   30
It leans and hearkens after it,
   And grows erect, as that comes home.

Such wilt thou be to me, who must
   Like th' other foot, obliquely run;
Thy firmness makes my circle just,   35
   And makes me end where I begun.

---

9 *Moving of th' earth:* earthquakes.   11–12 *trepidation of the spheres . . . innocent:* According to Ptolemaic astronomy, the planets rocked, but this motion was not felt on earth.   13 *sublunary:* below the moon, that is, on earth.   16 *elemented:* composed.

JOHN DONNE   (1572–1631)

Holy Sonnet 14 _____ *1633*

Batter my heart, three-personed God; for you
As yet but knock, breathe, shine, and seek to mend;
That I may rise, and stand, o'erthrow me, and bend
Your force, to break, blow, burn, and make me new.
I, like an usurped town, to another due,   5
Labor to admit you, but oh, to no end,
Reason, your viceroy in me, me should defend,
But is captived, and proves weak or untrue.
Yet dearly I love you, and would be loved fain,
But am betrothed unto your enemy: 10
Divorce me, untie, or break that knot again,
Take me to you, imprison me, for I,
Except you enthral me, never shall be free,
Nor ever chaste, except you ravish me.

H.D. (HILDA DOOLITTLE)   (1886–1961)

Heat _____ *1916*

O wind, rend open the heat,
cut apart the heat,
rend it to tatters.

Fruit cannot drop
through this thick air—   5
fruit cannot fall into heat
that presses up and blunts
the points of pears
and rounds the grapes.

Cut the heat—   10
plough through it,
turning it on either side
of your path.

H.D. (HILDA DOOLITTLE)   (1886–1961)

Helen° _____ *1925*

All Greece hates
the still eyes in the white face,

the lustre as of olives
where she stands,
and the white hands.   5

All Greece reviles
the wan face when she smiles,
hating it deeper still
when it grows wan and white,
remembering past enchantments   10
and past ills.

Greece sees unmoved,
God's daughter, born of love,
the beauty of cool feet
and slenderest knees,   15
could love indeed the maid,
only if she were laid,
white ash amid funereal cypresses.

RITA DOVE   (b. 1952)

Used _____ *c. 1989*

The conspiracy's to make us thin. Size three's
all the rage, and skirts ballooning above twinkling knees
are every man-child's preadolescent dream.
Tabula rasa. No slate's *that* clean—

we've earned the navels sunk in grief   5
when the last child emptied us of their brief
interior light. Our muscles say *We have been used.*

Have you ever tried silk sheets? I did,
persuaded by postnatal dread
and a Macy's clerk to bargain for more zip.   10
We couldn't hang on, slipped
to the floor and by morning the quilts
had slid off, too. Enough of guilt—
It's hard work staying cool.

GRETEL EHRLICH   (b. 1946)

The Orchard _____ *c. 1981*

We go into it at night.
In Wyoming an orchard is the
only city around—so many blossoms going up
into trees like lights

and windfall apples like lives   5
coming down.

In the pickup, heads on the tailgate,
we lie on last year's hay and wait
for the orchard to bloom.

A great horned owl sweeps between   10
trees as if to cropdust the rising
sap with white for the flowers.

"The first blossom to come," you say,
"I'll give the apple that grows there to you."

Another owl lands   15
on a bare branch and drops
a plug of micebones to the roots.
Under him, the tree does not think of
the sap's struggle.
I listen to your heart. Divided by   20
beats and rests, it says yes, then no, then yes.

Above us the Milky Way seams the sky and is
stirred by a hand too big to see.
We watch the stars.

Tonight so many of them fall.   25

FAIZ AHMED FAIZ° (1914–1984)

Before You Came _____ *1988*

Translated by Agha Shahid Ali

Before you came,
things were as they should be:
the sky was the dead-end of sight,
the road was just a road, wine merely wine—

Now everything is like my heart,   5
a color at the edge of blood:
the grey of your absence, the color of poison, of thorns,
the gold when we meet, the season ablaze,
the yellow of autumn, the red of flowers, of flames,
and the black when you cover the earth   10
with the coal of dead fires.

And the sky, the road, the glass of wine?
The sky is a shirt wet with tears,

Faiz Ahmed Faiz: See notes to "Homage to Faiz Ahmed Faiz," p. 619.

the road a vein about to break,
and the glass of wine a mirror in which   15
the sky, the road, the world keep changing.

Don't leave now that you're here—
the world will become like itself again:
the sky will be the sky,
the road a road,   20
and the glass of wine not a mirror, just a glass of wine.

ANNE FINCH   (1661–1720)

A Song of the Cannibals ————————————————— *c. 1689*

Lovely viper, haste not on,
Nor curl, in various folds along,
Till from that figur'd coat of thine,
Which ev'ry motion, makes more fine.
I take, as near as art can do,   5
A draught, of what I wond'ring view;
Which, in a bracelet, for my Love
Shall be with careful mixtures wove.
So may'st thou find they beauties last,
As thou doest not, retard thy haste.   10
So, may'st thou, above all the snakes,
That harbour, in the neigh'bring brakes,°
Be honour'd; and where thou do'st pass
The shades be close, and fresh the grass.

12 *brakes:* a thicket, overgrown area.

MARGARET GIBSON   (b. 1944)

Out in the Open ————————————————————— *1989*

In memory of R. H. B. M.

                    I.
The first signs of your illness I misread.
A change in character, I thought, annoyed
at the stubborn frequency of your needs.
Like a dog, you snapped at strangers.
Like a child, you had me up at night.   5
You'd want to go outside at any hour,
and you'd go, you'd stare at the moon
or the hard shell of snow left in the yard.
Sudden things far away seemed near.

You'd fix on them, stare off. Too fond,   10
you'd follow me about, insist some part
of your body towards mine, just touch.
Then the sheer fact of distance wore
you out. The tree in the open field
we'd walk to—too far. No memory   15
moved you from the quiet you slid into.
But when your skin seemed to loosen
and slur, when it slipped like an ill-
fitting cap down towards your eyes,
I called the doctors. They tested,   20
I bargained, made promises, pressed
down on hope as if hope were a seal
of eventual success. I held you, talked
nonsense, and sense, tried to tempt
you with food. I force-fed you, a tube   25
in the side of your slack jaw. Then
the shots, the intervals, the hours.
I'd go off to calm myself, come back
to find you'd managed to pull yourself
slowly over to the wall, find the corner,   30
a blind meeting, and stand there without
any sign of what it was you wanted,
as if you were pulled to an invisible
threshold, as of course you were.

II.

Before any of this, months before, an echo   35
of the unforeseen spun out of the blind spot
in my eye and made itself visible. I made
note of it, logged it in a journal of dreams,
more taken frankly by other things—a new
word, *piezoelectric,*° and the fact that the bow   40
of a violin drawn deftly across the edge of
a metal plate shows the pattern of that note
in white powder on the surface of the metal.
That I magnified, forgetting the sand
that blew across the path of my dream, the dust   45
that insisted itself into all the open crevices
of my clothes and into my watch; forgetting
how I called you to me, hoarse, wanting
you to stay, at the same time distracted
by a replica of bird, long-legged and blue,   50
by shells and other artful surfaces that took
my fancy, ignoring the point of steep descent,
the black hole we stood at the edge of—

---

40 *piezoelectric:* electricity created by pressure—usually on crystals. Here, connected to the pressure
of the violin on metal shifting patterns of powder, it is an emblem of mysterious cause and effect
like a form of life.

a dense space where night felt like justice,
and more—the sense that the bird of the dream   55
had that emptiness for its nest.

III.

Today, putting to rights your things,
fully aware of the elsewhere that sinks
through the edges of everything I touch,
I recall that dream, in the mood for echoes.   60
The doorbell rings, and I open to a kid
up the street who loved you, too. Unsteady
on his roller skates, he's brought down
an envelope sealed tight. He touches
the threshold for balance, letting air out   65
shy between the spaces of his teeth.
The note says everything simply and right,
if transformed by the code of his spelling.
You he's drawn underneath the tree in the open
field, beneath a squat yellow sun and a deft   70
V of birds drawn into a distant vanishing
point beyond paper. He watches me read
and laugh through tears and praise his art—
but neither of us, I think, can think to see
the dark blue silhouette of bird he's put   75
in the branches of the tree, long-legged,
for what it is. We hug, he skates off
on the shifting winter sand of the road,
and for one brief moment, watching him go,
I see everything out in the open—not knowing   80
which to bless more—your life, life itself,
or the patterns, blind in time, we learn to see.

MARGARET GIBSON   (b. 1944)

Unborn Child Elegy _____ 1982

Tell me a story
                whispers my always unborn child
and I pause, listening. Whenever a word
shapes itself outward in speech
there's a hush.   5
                In the beginning, I tell her, nothing—
if you can imagine nothing. Just so, and patiently, the ancient
stories begin.
                Once, lying down in the backseat of my parents'
car—their heads dark on the windshield, telephone poles   10
outside and the heads of trees blown back against the stars—
I tried to imagine nothing. Warm air rushed on my eyes

erasing the car, the trees, the stars. I inched across
a bridge of thread called emptiness, cold.

Then I knew you were there inside,   15
asleep in one of the body's seedbeds.
I could hold my breath and find
you, small as a syllable,
a grain like pearled barley in the hourglass of my brain,
a stitch in my side.   20

We made a pact. I'd bring the world inside,
the moon your heart,
a dark plum your eyesight.
You'd bring me so close to the unspoken I'd shake,
some of the mystery spilling like salt.   25

Today snow sparks the air like mica—the sun's
just so, cocked right angles to the wind.
I bring you the snow and it isn't enough.
You whisper you want to be born.

I study your whisper, I study my fear.   30
You're bound, my mother said, to pain.
Each child pries you open.

No one will believe
how alive and present to me you are if I refuse
you a body. But I believe in nothing, a transparent   35
breath from which all form and color rise
in a passion of wings and leaves.

In the ancient stories, the world begins by surprise
when zero speaks, from mere words
weaving sun and moon, the fire   40
the flash of snow.

Be the zero who speaks for me.
Be birth and death, the emptiness
only a child, and never a child, can fill.

ALLEN GINSBERG   (b. 1926)

Howl _____ *1956*

> *San Francisco 1955–1956*
> *For Carl Solomon°*

I

I saw the best minds of my generation destroyed by madness, starving
      hysterical naked,

Carl Solomon (b. 1928): Ginsberg met Solomon while they were patients in Columbia Psychiatric Institute in 1949.

dragging themselves through the negro streets at dawn looking for an
    angry fix,
angelheaded hipsters burning for the ancient heavenly connection to
    the starry dynamo in the machinery of night,
who poverty and tatters and hollow-eyed and high sat up smoking in
    the supernatural darkness of cold-water flats floating across the
    tops of cities contemplating jazz,
who bared their brains to Heaven under the El° and saw
    Mohammedan angels staggering on tenement roofs illuminated,   5
who passed through universities with radiant cool eyes hallucinating
    Arkansas° and Blake-light tragedy among the scholars of war,
who were expelled from the academies for crazy & publishing obscene
    odes on the windows of the skull,
who cowered in unshaven rooms in underwear, burning their money
    in wastebaskets and listening to the Terror through the wall,
who got busted in their pubic beards returning through Laredo with a
    belt of marijuana for New York,
who ate fire in paint hotels or drank turpentine in Paradise Alley,°
    death, or purgatoried their torsos night after night   10
with dreams, with drugs, with waking nightmares, alcohol and cock
    and endless balls,
incomparable blind streets of shuddering cloud and lightning in the
    mind leaping toward poles of Canada & Paterson,° illuminating
    all the motionless world of Time between,
Peyote solidities of halls, backyard green tree cemetery dawns, wine
    drunkenness over the rooftops, storefront boroughs of teahead
    joyride neon blinking traffic light, sun and moon and tree
    vibrations in the roaring winter dusks of Brooklyn, ashcan
    rantings and kind king light of mind,
who chained themselves to subways for the endless ride from Battery
    to holy Bronx on benzedrine until the noise of wheels and
    children brought them down shuddering mouth-wracked and
    battered bleak of brain all drained of brilliance in the drear light
    of Zoo,°
who sank all night in submarine light of Bickford's° floated out and sat
    through the stale beer afternoon in desolate Fugazzi's,°
    listening to the crack of doom on the hydrogen jukebox,   15
who talked continuously seventy hours from park to pad to bar to
    Bellevue° to museum to the Brooklyn Bridge,
a lost battalion of platonic conversationalists jumping down the stoops
    off fire escapes off windowsills off Empire State out of the
    moon,

5 *El:* the elevated railway.   6 *Arkansas:* reference to various drug-induced hallucinations, including the voice of poet William Blake.   10 *Paradise Alley:* in the Lower East Side of New York,
setting for one of Beat writer Jack Kerouac's novels.   10 *Paterson:* Ginsberg's birthplace in New
Jersey.   14 *Zoo:* the Bronx Zoo in New York City.   15 *Bickford's:* a cafeteria where Ginsberg
once worked. *Fugazzi's:* a Greenwich village bar.   16 *Bellevue:* a hospital often associated with
care for the insane.

yacketayakking screaming vomiting whispering facts and memories and
    anecdotes and eyeball kicks and shocks of hospitals and jails and
    wars,

whole intellects disgorged in total recall for seven days and nights with
    brilliant eyes, meat for the Synagogue cast on the pavement,

who vanished into nowhere Zen° New Jersey leaving a trail of
    ambiguous picture postcards of Atlantic City Hall,   20

suffering Eastern sweats and Tangerian bone-grindings and migraines
    of China under junk-withdrawal in Newark's bleak furnished
    room,

who wandered around and around at midnight in the railroad yard
    wondering where to go, and went, leaving no broken hearts,

who lit cigarettes in boxcars boxcars boxcars racketing through snow
    toward lonesome farms in grandfather night,

who studied Plotinus Poe St. John of the Cross telepathy and bop
    kabbalah° because the cosmos instinctively vibrated at their feet
    in Kansas,

who loned it through the streets of Idaho seeking visionary indian
    angels who were visionary indian angels,   25

who thought they were only mad when Baltimore gleamed in
    supernatural ecstasy,

who jumped in limousines with the Chinaman of Oklahoma on the
    impulse of winter midnight streetlight smalltown rain,

who lounged hungry and lonesome through Houston seeking jazz or
    sex or soup, and followed the brilliant Spaniard to converse
    about America and Eternity, a hopeless task, and so took ship
    to Africa,

who disappeared into the volcanoes of Mexico leaving behind nothing
    but the shadow of dungarees and the lava and ash of poetry
    scattered in fireplace Chicago,

who reappeared on the West Coast investigating the FBI in beards and
    shorts with big pacifist eyes sexy in their dark skin passing out
    incomprehensible leaflets,   30

who burned cigarette holes in their arms protesting the narcotic
    tobacco haze of Capitalism,

who distributed Supercommunist pamphlets in Union Square weeping
    and undressing while the sirens of Los Alamos wailed them
    down, and wailed down Wall, and the Staten Island ferry also
    wailed,

who broke down crying in white gymnasiums naked and trembling
    before the machinery of other skeletons,

who bit detectives in the neck and shrieked with delight in policecars
    for committing no crime but their own wild cooking pederasty
    and intoxication,

who howled on their knees in the subway and were dragged off the
    roof waving genitals and manuscripts,   35

20 *Zen:* Zen Buddhism, important to Beat generation in 1950s.   24 *Plotinus . . . kabbalah:* All
these people and texts are associated with mysticism and visionary religious experience.

who let themselves be fucked in the ass by saintly motorcyclists, and
    screamed with joy,
who blew and were blown by those human seraphim, the sailors,
    caresses of Atlantic and Caribbean love,
who balled in the morning in the evenings in rosegardens and the
    grass of public parks and cemeteries scattering their semen
    freely to whomever come who may,
who hiccuped endlessly trying to giggle but wound up with a sob
    behind a partition in a Turkish Bath when the blond & naked
    angel° came to pierce them with a sword,
who lost their loveboys to the three old shrews of fate the one eyed
    shrew of the heterosexual dollar the one eyed shrew that winks
    out of the womb and the one eyed shrew that does nothing but
    sit on her ass and snip the intellectual golden threads of the
    craftsman's loom,   40
who copulated ecstatic and insatiate with a bottle of beer a sweetheart
    a package of cigarettes a candle and fell off the bed, and
    continued along the floor and down the hall and ended fainting
    on the wall with a vision of ultimate cunt and come eluding the
    last gyzym° of consciousness,
who sweetened the snatches of a million girls trembling in the sunset,
    and were red eyed in the morning but prepared to sweeten the
    snatch of the sunrise, flashing buttocks under barns and naked
    in the lake,
who went out whoring through Colorado in myriad stolen night-cars,
    N.C.,° secret hero of these poems, cocksman and Adonis of
    Denver—joy to the memory of his innumerable lays of girls in
    empty lots & diner backyards, moviehouses' rickety rows, on
    mountaintops in caves or with gaunt waitresses in familiar
    roadside lonely petticoat upliftings & especially secret gas-
    station solipsisms of johns, & hometown alleys too,
who faded out in vast sordid movies, were shifted in dreams, woke on
    a sudden Manhattan, and picked themselves up out of
    basements hungover with heartless Tokay and horrors of Third
    Avenue iron dreams & stumbled to unemployment offices,
who walked all night with their shoes full of blood on the snowbank
    docks waiting for a door in the East River to open to a room
    full of steamheat and opium,   45
who created great suicidal dramas on the apartment cliff-banks of the
    Hudson under the wartime blue floodlight of the moon & their
    heads shall be crowned with laurel in oblivion,
who ate the lamb stew of the imagination or digested the crab at the
    muddy bottom of the rivers of Bowery,°
who wept at the romance of the streets with their pushcarts full of
    onions and bad music,

39 *angel:* possible reference to the ecstasy of St. Theresa, who was pierced by an angel. 41 *gyzym:* slang
for sperm.   43 *N.C.:* Neal Cassady (1926–1968), who traveled with Jack Kerouac (as Dean Mori-
arty) and was memorialized in *On the Road* (1957).   47 *Bowery:* famous in New York for its al-
coholics and down-and-outers.

who sat in boxes breathing in the darkness under the bridge, and rose
    up to build harpsichords in their lofts,

who coughed on the sixth floor of Harlem crowned with flame under
    the tubercular sky surrounded by orange crates of theology,   50

who scribbled all night rocking and rolling over lofty incantations
    which in the yellow morning were stanzas of gibberish,

who cooked rotten animals lung heart feet tail borsht & tortillas
    dreaming of the pure vegetable kingdom,

who plunged themselves under meat trucks looking for an egg,

who threw their watches off the roof to cast their ballot for Eternity
    outside of Time, & alarm clocks fell on their heads every day
    for the next decade,

who cut their wrists three times successively unsuccessfully, gave up
    and were forced to open antique stores where they thought
    they were growing old and cried,   55

who were burned alive in their innocent flannel suits on Madison
    Avenue amid blasts of leaden verse & the tanked-up clatter of
    the iron regiments of fashion & the nitroglycerine shrieks of the
    fairies of advertising & the mustard gas of sinister intelligent
    editors, or were run down by the drunken taxicabs of Absolute
    Reality,

who jumped off the Brooklyn Bridge this actually happened and
    walked away unknown and forgotten into the ghostly daze of
    Chinatown soup alleyways & firetrucks, not even one free beer,

who sang out of their windows in despair, fell out of the subway
    window, jumped in the filthy Passaic,° leaped on negroes, cried
    all over the street, danced on broken wineglasses barefoot
    smashed phonograph records of nostalgic European 1930s
    German jazz finished the whiskey and threw up groaning into
    the bloody toilet, moans in their ears and the blast of colossal
    steamwhistles,

who barreled down the highways of the past journeying to each
    other's hotrod-Golgotha jail-solitude watch or Birmingham
    jazz incarnation,

who drove crosscountry seventytwo hours to find out if I had a vision
    or you had a vision or he had a vision to find out Eternity,   60

who journeyed to Denver, who died in Denver, who came back to
    Denver & waited in vain, who watched over Denver & brooded
    & loned in Denver and finally went away to find out the Time,
    & now Denver is lonesome for her heroes,

who fell on their knees in hopeless cathedrals praying for each other's
    salvation and light and breasts, until the soul illuminated its hair
    for a second,

who crashed through their minds in jail waiting for impossible
    criminals with golden heads and the charm of reality in their
    hearts who sang sweet blues to Alcatraz,

who retired to Mexico to cultivate a habit, or Rocky Mount to tender
    Buddha or Tangiers to boys or Southern Pacific to the black

58 *Passaic:* a river in New Jersey.

locomotive or Harvard to Narcissus to Woodlawn° to the
daisychain or grave,

who demanded sanity trials accusing the radio of hypnotism & were
left with their insanity & their hands & a hung jury,   65

who threw potato salad at CCNY lecturers on Dadaism° and
subsequently presented themselves on the granite steps of the
madhouse with shaven heads and harlequin speech of suicide,
demanding instantaneous lobotomy,

and who were given instead the concrete void of insulin Metrazol°
electricity hydrotherapy psychotherapy occupational therapy
pingpong & amnesia,

who in humorless protest overturned only one symbolic pingpong
table, resting briefly in catatonia,

returning years later truly bald except for a wig of blood, and tears
and fingers, to the visible madman doom of the wards of the
madtowns of the East,

Pilgrim State's Rockland's and Greystone's° foetid halls, bickering
with the echoes of the soul, rocking and rolling in the midnight
solitude-bench dolmen-realms of love, dream of life a
nightmare, bodies turned to stone as heavy as the moon,   70

with mother finally ******°, and the last fantastic book flung out of
the tenement window, and the last door closed at 4 a.m. and the
last telephone slammed at the wall in reply and the last furnished
room emptied down to the last piece of mental furniture, a
yellow paper rose twisted on a wire hanger in the closet, and even
that imaginary nothing but a hopeful little bit of hallucination—

ah, Carl, while you are not safe I am not safe, and now you're really in
the total animal soup of time—

and who therefore ran through the icy streets obsessed with a sudden
flash of the alchemy of the use of the ellipse the catalog the
meter & the vibrating plane,

who dreamt and made incarnate gaps in Time & Space through
images juxtaposed, and trapped the archangel of the soul
between 2 visual images and joined the elemental verbs and set
the noun and dash of consciousness together jumping with
sensation of Pater Omnipotens Aeterna Deus°

to recreate the syntax and measure of poor human prose and stand
before you speechless and intelligent and shaking with shame,
rejected yet confessing out the soul to conform to the rhythm
of thought in his naked and endless head,   75

the madman bum and angel beat in Time, unknown, yet putting down
here what might be left to say in time come after death,

and rose reincarnate in the ghostly clothes of jazz in the goldhorn
shadow of the band and blew the suffering of America's naked

---

64 *Narcissus to Woodlawn:* Ginsberg refers to quests by Beats John Burroughs (1914–1997), Kerouac, and himself for drugs, sex, and even death: Woodlawn is a cemetery.   66 *Dadaism:* absurdist avant-garde art movement following World War I.   67 *Metrazol:* shock therapy induced
chemically.   70 *Pilgrim . . . Greystone's:* mental hospitals.   71 ******: Ginsberg's mother Naomi
was hospitalized for paranoia and died in 1956.   74 *Pater Omnipoteus Aeterna Deus:* "Father om-
nipotent, eternal God." From a letter by the painter Paul Cézanne (1839–1906).

mind for love into an eli eli lamma lamma sabacthani°
saxophone cry that shivered the cities down to the last radio
with the absolute heart of the poem of life butchered out of their own
    bodies good to eat a thousand years.

II

What sphinx of cement and aluminum bashed open their skulls and ate
    up their brains and imagination?
Moloch!° Solitude! Filth! Ugliness! Ashcans and unobtainable dollars!
    Children screaming under the stairways! Boys sobbing in
    armies! Old men weeping in the parks!   80
Moloch! Moloch! Nightmare of Moloch! Moloch the loveless! Mental
    Moloch! Moloch the heavy judger of men!
Moloch the incomprehensible prison! Moloch the crossbone soulless
    jailhouse and Congress of sorrows! Moloch whose buildings are
    judgment! Moloch the vast stone of war! Moloch the stunned
    governments!
Moloch whose mind is pure machinery! Moloch whose blood is
    running money! Moloch whose fingers are ten armies! Moloch
    whose breast is a cannibal dynamo! Moloch whose ear is a
    smoking tomb!
Moloch whose eyes are a thousand blind windows! Moloch whose
    skyscrapers stand in the long streets like endless Jehovahs!
    Moloch whose factories dream and croak in the fog! Moloch
    whose smokestacks and antennae crown the cities!
Moloch whose love is endless oil and stone! Moloch whose soul is
    electricity and banks! Moloch whose poverty is the specter of
    genius! Moloch whose fate is a cloud of sexless hydrogen!
    Moloch whose name is the Mind!   85
Moloch in whom I sit lonely! Moloch in whom I dream Angels! Crazy
    in Moloch! Cocksucker in Moloch! Lacklove and manless in
    Moloch!
Moloch who entered my soul early! Moloch in whom I am a
    consciousness without a body! Moloch who frightened me out
    of my natural ecstasy! Moloch whom I abandon! Wake up in
    Moloch! Light streaming out of the sky!
Moloch! Moloch! Robot apartments! invisible suburbs! skeleton
    treasuries! blind capitals! demonic industries! spectral nations!
    invincible madhouses! granite cocks! monstrous bombs!
They broke their backs lifting Moloch to Heaven! Pavements, trees,
    radios, tons! lifting the city to Heaven which exists and is
    everywhere about us!
Visions! omens! hallucinations! miracles! ecstasies! gone down the
    American river!   90
Dreams! adorations! illuminations! religions! the whole boatload of
    sensitive bullshit!

---

77 *eli eli lamma . . . sabacthani:* "My God, my God, why have you forsaken me?"—Christ's words on
the cross.   80 *Moloch:* an ancient god worshiped with human sacrifices.

Breakthroughs! over the river! flips and crucifixions! gone down the
    flood! Highs! Epiphanies! Despairs! Ten years' animal screams
    and suicides! Minds! New loves! Mad generation! down on the
    rocks of Time!
Real holy laughter in the river! They saw it all! the wild eyes! the holy
    yells! They bade farewell! They jumped off the roof! to
    solitude! waving! carrying flowers! Down to the river! into the
    street!

III

Carl Solomon! I'm with you in Rockland°
    where you're madder than I am
I'm with you in Rockland
    where you must feel very strange   95
I'm with you in Rockland
    where you imitate the shade of my mother
I'm with you in Rockland
    where you've murdered your twelve secretaries
I'm with you in Rockland
    where you laugh at this invisible humor
I'm with you in Rockland
    where we are great writers on the same dreadful typewriter
I'm with you in Rockland
    where your condition has become serious and is reported on
    the radio   100
I'm with you in Rockland
    where the faculties of the skull no longer admit the worms of
    the senses
I'm with you in Rockland
    where you drink the tea of the breasts of the spinsters of Utica°
I'm with you in Rockland
    where you pun on the bodies of your nurses the harpies of the
    Bronx
I'm with you in Rockland
    where you scream in a straightjacket that you're losing the
    game of the actual pingpong of the abyss
I'm with you in Rockland
    where you bang on the catatonic piano the soul is innocent and
    immortal it should never die ungodly in an armed madhouse   105
I'm with you in Rockland
    where fifty more shocks will never return your soul to its body
    again from its pilgrimage to a cross in the void
I'm with you in Rockland
    where you accuse your doctors of insanity and plot the Hebrew
    socialist revolution against the fascist national Golgotha

95 *Rockland:* New York psychiatric hospital.   102 *spinsters of Utica:* reference to Solomon's
birthplace (?).

I'm with you in Rockland
    where you will split the heavens of Long Island and resurrect
    your living human Jesus from the superhuman tomb
I'm with you in Rockland
    where there are twentyfive thousand mad comrades all together
    singing the final stanzas of the Internationale°
I'm with you in Rockland
    where we hug and kiss the United States under our bedsheets
    the United States that coughs all night and won't let us sleep   110
I'm with you in Rockland
    where we wake up electrified out of the coma by our own souls'
    airplanes roaring over the roof they've come to drop angelic
    bombs the hospital illuminates itself imaginary walls collapse O
    skinny legions run outside O starry-spangled shock of mercy the
    eternal war is here O victory forget your underwear we're free
I'm with you in Rockland
    in my dreams you walk dripping from a sea-journey on the
    highway across America in tears to the door of my cottage in
    the Western night

109 *Internationale:* Communist anthem.

LOUISE GLÜCK   (b. 1943)

Brown Circle ——————————————————————— *c. 1990*

My mother wants to know
why, if I hate
family so much,
I went ahead and
had one. I don't   5
answer my mother.
What I hated
was being a child,
having no choice about
what people I loved.   10

I don't love my son
the way I meant to love him.
I thought I'd be
the lover of orchids who finds
red trillium growing   15
in the pine shade, and doesn't
touch it, doesn't need
to possess it. What I am
is the scientist,
who comes to that flower   20
with a magnifying glass

and doesn't leave, though
the sun burns a brown
circle of grass around
the flower. Which is   25
more or less the way
my mother loved me.

I must learn
to forgive my mother,
now that I'm helpless   30
to spare my son.

LOUISE GLÜCK (b. 1943)

Brooding Likeness ——————————————————— *c. 1981*

I was born in the month of the bull,°
the month of heaviness,
or of the lowered, the destructive head,
or of purposeful blindness. So I know, beyond the shadowed
patch of grass, the stubborn one, the one who doesn't look up,   5
still senses the rejected world. It is
a stadium, a well of dust. And you who watch him
looking down in the face of death, what do you know
of commitment? If the bull lives
one controlled act of revenge, be satisfied   10
that in the sky, like you, he is always moving,
not of his own accord but through the black field
like grit caught on a wheel, like shining freight.

1 *month of the bull:* April 21–May 21; Taurus.

LOUISE GLÜCK (b. 1943)

Matins° ——————————————————————— *1992*

Forgive me if I say I love you: the powerful
are always lied to since the weak are always
driven by panic. I cannot love
what I can't conceive, and you disclose
virtually nothing: are you like the hawthorn tree,   5
always the same thing in the same place,
or are you more the foxglove, inconsistent, first springing up
a pink spike on the slope behind the daisies,
and the next year, purple in the rose garden? You must see

Matins: early morning prayer usually recited aloud at daybreak. The poem is addressed to God.

it is useless to us, this silence that promotes belief   10
you must be all things, the foxglove and the hawthorn tree,
the vulnerable rose and tough daisy—we are left to think
you couldn't possibly exist. Is this
what you mean us to think, does this explain
the silence of the morning,   15
the crickets not yet rubbing their wings, the cats
not fighting in the yard?

LORNA GOODISON   (b. 1947)

My Last Poem _____ *1980*

I once wrote poems
that emerged so fine
with a rough edge for honing
a soft cloth for polishing
and a houseproud eye   5
I'd pride myself in making them shine.
But in this false winter
with the real cold to come
no, this season's shift
there are no winters here,   10
well call it what you will but the cold time is here
with its memorial crosses to mark
my father's dying
and me wondering where next year will find me
in whose vineyard toiling.   15
I gave my son
to a kind woman to keep
and walked down through the valley
on my scarred feet,
across the river   20
and into the guilty town
in search of bread
but they had closed the bakery down.
So I returned and said child
there was no bread   25
I'll write you my last poem instead.
My last poem is not my best
all things weaken towards the end.
O but it should be laid out
and chronicled, crazy like my life   30
with a place for all my several lives
daughter, sister, mistress, friend, warrior
wife
and a high holy ending for the blessed

one   35
me as mother to a man.
There should be a place for
messages and replies
you are too tightly bound, too whole
he said   40
I loosened my hair and I bled
now you send conflicting signals they said
divided I turned both ways and fled.
There should be a place for all this
but I'm almost at the end of my last poem   45
and I'm almost a full woman.
I warm my son's clothes
in this cold time
in the deep of my bosom
and I'm not afraid of love.   50
In fact, should it be
that these are false signals I'm receiving
and not a real unqualified ending
I'm going to keep the word love
and use it in my next poem.   55
I know it's just the wordsmith's failing
to forge a new metal to ring like its rhyme
but I'll keep its fool's gold
for you see it's always bought me time.
And if I write another poem   60
I'm going to use it
for it has always used me
and if I ever write another poem
I'm going to return that courtesy.

LORNA GOODISON   (b. 1947)

Jamaica 1980 _____ *1980*

It trails always behind me
a webbed seine with a catch of fantasy
a penance I pay for being me
who took the order of poetry.
Always there with the gaping holes   5
and the mended ones, and the stand-in words.
But this time my Jamaica
my green-clad muse
this time your callings are of no use
I am spied on by your mountains   10
wire-tapped by your secret streams

your trees dripping blood-leaves
and jasmine selling tourist-dreams.

For over all this edenism
hangs the smell of necromancy   15
and each man eats his brother's flesh
Lord, so much of the cannibal left
in the jungle on my people's tongues.

We've sacrificed babies
and burnt our mothers   20
as payment to some viridian-eyed God dread
who works in cocaine under hungry men's heads.

And mine the task of writing it down
as I ride in shame round this blood-stained town.
And when the poem refuses to believe   25
and slimes to aloes in my hands
mine is the task of burying the dead
I the late madonna of barren lands.

LORNA GOODISON   (b. 1947)

My Last Poem (Again) _____ *1987*

I'm approaching the end of my penance of poems.
I can tell because the rosary beads are colder
and it's becoming harder to hold them.

So then, let them go! I'll be glad to see the last of them
once born they sometimes evoked (like most babies)   5
wonderment. But the delivery of them!
Good-bye poems, you bled me shiny bottles of red feelings.
Poems, you were blood leeches attaching yourself to me
in my should-have-been-brighter moments.
You put to flight lovers who could not compete   10
you forced yourself into my birthing bed
so I delivered one son and a poem.
When the King of Swords° gutted me
and left me for dead, in my insides were found
clots of poems, proving that poets are made of poems   15
and poems are truth demanding punctuation of light
and your all, and that makes my head vie with night all day.
I don't want to live this way anymore.
Somewhere there is a clean kind man
with a deep and wide understanding   20

13 *King of Swords:* a card in the Tarot deck implying danger.

of the mercy and the peace and the infinity.
And we will, if we are lucky, live by the sea
and serve and heal eating of life's salt and bread
and at night lie close to each other and read poems
for which somebody else besides me bled . . .   25
and that will make me want to write poems.

GEORGE GORDON, LORD BYRON   (1788–1824)

Song ————————————————————————————————— *1810*

     Ζώη μοῦ, σάς α'γαπώ
     Athens, 1810

            I.

Maid of Athens, ere we part,
Give, oh, give me back my heart!
Or, since that has left my breast,
Keep it now, and take the rest!
Hear my vow before I go,   5
Ζώη μοῦ, σάς α'γαπώ

           II.

By those tresses unconfined,
Wooed by each Aegean wind;
By those lids whose jetty fringe
Kiss thy soft cheeks' blooming tinge;   10
By those wild eyes like the roe,
Ζώη μοῦ, σάς α'γαπώ

           III.

By that lip I long to taste;
By that zone° encircled waist;
By all the token-flowers that tell   15
What words can never speak so well;
By Love's alternate joy and woe,
Ζώη μοῦ, σάς α'γαπώ

           IV.

Maid of Athens! I am gone:
Think of me, sweet! when alone.   20
Though I fly to Istambul,
Athens holds my heart and soul:
Can I cease to love thee? No!
Ζώη μοῦ, σάς α'γαπώ

Ζώη μοῦ, σάς α'γαπώ (pronounced "zoe mon tas agapo"): "My Life, I Love You"; also used as the
refrain.   14 *zone:* a belt worn by virgins.

GEORGE GORDON, LORD BYRON (1788–1824)

She Walks in Beauty ———————————————————— *1814*

I.

She walks in beauty, like the night
  Of cloudless climes and starry skies;
And all that's best of dark and bright
  Meet in her aspect and her eyes:
Thus mellowed to that tender light   5
  Which heaven to gaudy day denies.

II.

One shade the more, one ray the less,
  Had half impaired the nameless grace
Which waves in every raven tress,
  Or softly lightens o'er her face;   10
Where thoughts serenely sweet express
  How pure, how dear their dwelling place.

III.

And on that cheek, and o'er that brow,
  So soft, so calm, yet eloquent,
The smiles that win, the tints that glow,   15
  But tell of days in goodness spent,
A mind at peace with all below,
  A heart whose love is innocent!

JORIE GRAHAM   (b. 1951)

The Hiding Place ———————————————————— *1991*

  The last time I saw it was 1968.
Paris, France. The time of the *disturbances*.
  We had claims. Schools shut down.
Three million *workers* and *students* on strike.°
  Marches, sit-ins, helicopters, gas.   5
They stopped you at gunpoint asking for papers.

  I spent eleven nights sleeping in the halls. Arguments.
  Negotiations.
Hurrying in the dawn looking for a certain leader,
  I found his face above an open street fire.   10
No, he said, tell them *no concessions.*
  His voice above the fire as if there were no fire—

---

4 *strike:* Graham was educated at the Sorbonne in Paris during a period of great political unrest in France and the United States. Some of the protest was against the war in Vietnam.

language floating everywhere above the sleeping bodies;
    and crates of fruit donated in secret;
and torn sheets (for tear gas) tossed down from shuttered windows;   15
    and bread; and blankets, stolen from the firehouse.
The CRS (the government police) would swarm in around dawn
    in small blue vans and round us up.
Once I watched the searchbeams play on some flames.
    The flames push up into the corridor of light.   20

In the cell we were so crowded no one could sit or lean.
    People peed on each other. I felt a girl
vomiting gently onto my back.
    I found two Americans rounded up by chance,
their charter left that morning, they screamed, what were they
    going to do?   25

    Later a man in a uniform came in with a stick.
He started beating here and there, found the girl in her eighth
    month.
He beat her frantically over and over.
He pummelled her belly. Screaming aren't you ashamed?

    I remember the cell vividly,   30
but is it from a photograph? I think the shadows as I
    see them still—the slatted brilliant bits
against the wall—I think they're true—but are they from a photograph?
    Do I see it from inside now—his hands, her face—or

is it from the news account?   35
    The strangest part of getting out again was *streets*.
The light running down them.
    Everything spilling whenever the wall breaks.
And the air—thick with dwellings—the air filled—doubled—
    as if the open   40

had been made to render—
    the open squeezed for space until the hollows spill out,
story upon story of them
    starting to light up as I walked out.
How thick was the empty meant to be?   45
    What were we finding in the air?

What were we meant to find?
I went home slowly, sat in my rented room.
    Sat for a long time the window open,

    watched the white gauze curtain sluff this way then that a bit—   50
    watched the air suck it out, push it back in. Lung
of the room with street cries in it. Watched until the lights
    outside made it gold, pumping gently.
Was I meant to get up again? I was inside. The century clicked by.
    The woman below called down *not to forget the*   55

loaf. Crackle of helicopters. Voice on a loudspeaker issuing warnings.
    They made agreements, we all returned to work.
The government fell but then it was all right again.
    The man above the fire, listening to my question,

the red wool shirt he wore: where is it? who has it?   60
    He looked straight back into the century: no concessions.
I took the message back.
    The look in his eyes—shoving out—into the open—
    expressionless with thought:
no—tell them *no*—   65

JORIE GRAHAM   (b. 1951)

History ———————————————————— *1983*

Into whose ear the deeds are spoken. The only
listener. So I believed
he would remember everything, the murmuring trees,
the sunshine's zealotry, its deep
unevenness. For history   5
is the opposite
of the eye
for whom, for instance, six million bodies in portions
of hundreds and
the flowerpots broken by a sudden wind stand as   10
equivalent. What more
is there
than fact? *I'll give ten thousand dollars to the man*
who proves the holocaust really
occurred said the exhausted solitude   15
in San Francisco
in 1980. Far in the woods
in a faded photograph
in 1942 the man with his own
genitalia in his mouth and hundreds of   20
slow holes
a pitchfork has opened
over his face
grows beautiful. The ferns and deepwood
lilies catch   25
the eye. Three men in ragged uniforms
with guns keep laughing
nervously. They share the day
with him. A bluebird
sings. The feathers of the shade touch every inch   30
of skin—the hand holding down the delicate gun,
the hands holding down the delicate

hips. And the sky
is visible between the men, between
the trees, a blue spirit   35
enveloping
anything. Late in the story, in Northern Italy,
a man cuts down some trees for winter
fuel. We read this in the evening
news. Watching the fire burn late   40
one night, watching it change and change, a hand grenade,
lodged in the pulp the young tree
grew around, explodes, blinding the man, killing
his wife. Now who
will tell the children   45
fairytales? The ones where simple
crumbs over the forest
floor endure
to help us home?

THOMAS GRAY   (1716–1771)

Elegy Written in a Country Churchyard ————————— *1753*

The Curfew tolls the knell of parting day,
The lowing herd wind slowly o'er the lea,
The plowman homeward plods his weary way,
And leaves the world to darkness and to me.

Now fades the glimmering landscape on the sight,   5
And all the air a solemn stillness holds,
Save where the beetle wheels his droning flight,
And drowsy tinklings lull the distant folds;

Save° that from yonder ivy-mantled tower
The moping owl does to the moon complain   10
Of such, as wandering near her secret bower,
Molest her ancient solitary reign.

Beneath those rugged elms, that yew-tree's shade,
Where heaves the turf in many a moldering heap,
Each in his narrow cell forever laid,   15
The rude Forefathers of the hamlet sleep.

The breezy call of incense-breathing Morn,
The swallow twittering from the straw-built shed,
The cock's shrill clarion, or the echoing horn,
No more shall rouse them from their lowly bed.   20

For them no more the blazing hearth shall burn,
Or busy housewife ply her evening care:

7 *Save:* except.

No children run to lisp their sire's return,
Or climb his knees the envied kiss to share.

Oft did the harvest to their sickle yield,   25
Their furrow oft the stubborn glebe has broke;
How jocund did they drive their team afield!
How bowed the woods beneath their sturdy stroke!

Let not Ambition mock their useful toil,
Their homely joys, and destiny obscure;   30
Nor Grandeur hear with a disdainful smile,
The short and simple annals of the poor.

The boast of heraldry, the pomp of power,
And all that beauty, all that wealth e'er gave,
Awaits alike the inevitable hour.   35
The paths of glory lead but to the grave.

Nor you, ye Proud, impute to These the fault,
If Memory o'er their Tomb no Trophies raise,
Where through the long-drawn isle and fretted vault
The pealing anthem swells the note of praise.   40

Can storied urn or animated bust
Back to its mansion call the fleeting breath?
Can Honor's voice provoke the silent dust,
Or Flattery sooth the dull cold ear of Death?

Perhaps in this neglected spot is laid   45
Some heart once pregnant with celestial fire,
Hands, that the rod of empire might have swayed,
Or waked to ecstasy the living lyre.

But Knowledge to their eyes her ample page
Rich with the spoils of time did ne'er unroll;   50
Chill Penury repressed their noble rage,
And froze the genial current of the soul.

Full many a gem of purest ray serene,
The dark unfathomed caves of ocean bear:
Full many a flower is born to blush unseen,   55
And waste its sweetness on the desert air.

Some village-Hampden,° that with dauntless breast
The little Tyrant of his fields withstood;
Some mute inglorious Milton° here may rest,
Some Cromwell° guiltless of his country's blood.   60

The applause of listening senates to command,
The threats of pain and ruin to despise,

---

57 *Hampden:* John Hampden (1594–1643), English parliamentarian who protested King Charles I's method of taxation.   59 *Milton:* John Milton, in this volume.   60 *Cromwell:* Oliver Cromwell (1599–1658), English revolutionary leader.

To scatter plenty o'er a smiling land,
And read their history in a nation's eyes

Their lot forbade: nor circumscribed alone°   65
Their growing virtues, but their crimes confined;
Forbade to wade through slaughter to a throne,
And shut the gates of mercy on mankind,

The struggling pangs of conscious truth to hide,
To quench the blushes of ingenuous shame,   70
Or heap the shrine of Luxury and Pride
With incense kindled at the Muse's flame.

Far from the madding crowd's ignoble strife,
Their sober wishes never learned to stray;
Along the cool sequestered vale of life   75
They kept the noiseless tenor of their way.

Yet even these bones from insult to protect
Some frail memorial still erected nigh,
With uncouth rhymes and shapeless sculpture decked,
Implores the passing tribute of a sigh.   80

Their name, their years, spelt by the unlettered muse,
The place of fame and elegy supply:
And many a holy text around she strews,
That teach the rustic moralist to die.

For who, to dumb Forgetfulness a prey,   85
This pleasing anxious being e'er resigned,
Left the warm precincts of the cheerful day,
Nor cast one longing lingering look behind?

On some fond breast the parting soul relies,
Some pious drops the closing eye requires;   90
Even from the tomb the voice of Nature cries,
Even in our Ashes live their wonted Fires.

For thee,° who mindful of the unhonored Dead
Dost in these lines their artless tale relate;
If chance, by lonely contemplation led,   95
Some kindred Spirit shall inquire thy fate,

Haply some hoary-headed Swain may say,
"Oft have we seen him at the peep of dawn
Brushing with hasty steps the dews away
To meet the sun upon the upland lawn.   100

"There at the foot of yonder nodding beech
That wreathes its old fantastic roots so high,
His listless length at noontide would he stretch,
And pore upon the brook that babbles by.

---

65 *nor . . . alone:* not only.   93 *thee:* the poet who is writing these lines.

"Hard by yon wood, now smiling as in scorn,   105
Muttering his wayward fancies he would rove,
Now drooping, woeful wan, like one forlorn,
Or crazed with care, or crossed in hopeless love.

"One morn I missed him on the customed° hill,
Along the heath and near his favorite tree;   110
Another came; nor yet beside the rill,
Nor up the lawn, nor at the wood was he,

"The next with dirges due in sad array
Slow through the church-way path we saw him borne.
Approach and read (for thou canst read) the lay,   115
Graved on the stone beneath yon agèd thorn."

                    THE EPITAPH
Here rests his head upon the lap of Earth
A Youth to Fortune and to Fame unknown,
Fair Science° frowned not on his humble birth,
And Melancholy marked him for her own.   120

Large was his bounty, and his soul sincere,
Heaven did a recompense as largely send:
He gave to Misery all he had, a tear,
He gained from Heaven ('twas all he wished) a friend.

No farther seek his merits to disclose,   125
Or draw his frailties from their dread abode,
(There they alike in trembling hope repose)
The bosom of his Father and his God.

109 *customed:* accustomed, usual.   119 *Science:* learning, education. In other words, he was
uneducated.

LINDA GREGG   (b. 1942)

Whole and without Blessing ———————————————— *c. 1981*

What is beautiful alters, has undertow.
Otherwise I have no tactics to begin with.
Femininity is a sickness. I open my eyes
out of this fever and see the meaning
of my life clearly. A thing like a hill.   5
I proclaim myself whole and without blessing,
or need to be blessed. A fish of my own
spirit. I belong to no one. I do not move.
Am not required to move. I lie naked on a sheet
and the indifferent sun warms me.   10
I was bred for slaughter, like the other

animals. To suffer exactly at the center,
where there are no clues except pleasure.

MARILYN HACKER   (b. 1942)

Did You Love Well What Very Soon You Left?° _____ *c. 1986*

Did you love well what very soon you left?
Come home and take me in your arms and take
away this stomach ache, headache, heartache.
Never so full, I never was bereft
so utterly. The winter evenings drift   5
dark to the window. Not one word will make
you, where you are, turn in your day, or wake
from your night toward me. The only gift
I got to keep or give is what I've cried,
floodgates let down to mourning for the dead   10
chances, for the end of being young,
for everyone I loved who really died.
I drank our one year out in brine instead
of honey from the seasons of your tongue.

Did you love . . . left: a play on Shakespeare's Sonnet 73, which ends, "To love that well which thou
must leave ere long."

MARILYN HACKER   (b. 1942)

Sonnet Ending with a Film Subtitle° _____ *1980*

> *For Judith Landry*

Life has its nauseating ironies:
The good die young, as often has been shown;
Chaste spouses catch Venereal Disease;
And feminists sit by the telephone.
Last night was rather bleak, tonight is starker.   5
I may stare at the wall till half-past-one.
My friends are all convinced Dorothy Parker
Lives, but is not well, in Marylebone.°
I wish that I could imitate my betters
And fortify my rhetoric with guns.   10
Some day we women all will break our fetters
And raise our daughters to be Lesbians.
(I wonder if the bastard kept my letters?)
Here follow untranslatable French puns.

Film Subtitle: the translation projected in foreign films.   7–8 *Dorothy Parker . . . Marylebone:* Parker,
poet and writer in this collection. Marylebone is a London suburb.

THOMAS HARDY   (1840–1928)

The Darkling Thrush _____ *1900; 1902*

I leant upon a coppice gate
   When Frost was spectre-gray
And Winter's dregs made desolate
   The weakening eye of day.
The tangled bine-stems scored the sky   5
   Like strings of broken lyres,
And all mankind that haunted nigh
   Had sought their household fires.

The land's sharp features seemed to be
   The Century's corpse outleant,   10
His crypt the cloudy canopy,
   The wind his death-lament.
The ancient pulse of germ and birth
   Was shrunken hard and dry,
And every spirit upon earth   15
   Seemed fervourless as I.

At once a voice arose among
   The bleak twigs overhead
In a full-hearted evensong
   Of joy illimited;   20
An aged thrush, frail, gaunt, and small,
   In blast-beruffled plume,
Had chosen thus to fling his soul
   Upon the growing gloom.

So little cause for carolings   25
   Of such ecstatic sound
Was written on terrestrial things
   Afar or nigh around,
That I could think there trembled through
   His happy good-night air   30
Some blessed Hope, whereof he knew
   And I was unaware.

JOY HARJO   (b. 1951)

Santa Fe _____ *1990*

The wind blows lilacs out of the east. And it isn't lilac season. And I am walking the street
in front of St. Francis Cathedral in Santa Fe. Oh, and it's a few years earlier and more.
That's how you tell real time. It is here, it is there. The lilacs have taken over everything:
the sky, the narrow streets, my shoulders, my lips. I talk lilac. And there is nothing else
until a woman the size of a fox breaks through the bushes, breaks the purple web. She

is tall and black and gorgeous. She is the size of a fox on the arm of a white man who looks and tastes like cocaine. She lies for cocaine, dangles on the arm of cocaine. And lies to me now from a room in the DeVargas Hotel, where she has eaten her lover, white powder on her lips. That is true now; it is not true anymore. Eventually space curves, walks over and taps me on the shoulder. On the sidewalk I stand near St. Francis; he has been bronzed, a perpetual tan, with birds on his hand, his shoulder, deer at his feet. I am Indian and in this town I will never be a saint. I am seventeen and shy and wild. I have been up until three at a party, but there is no woman in the DeVargas Hotel, for that story hasn't yet been invented. A man whose face I will never remember, and never did, drives up on a Harley-Davidson. There are lilacs on his arm; they spill out from the spokes of his wheels. He wants me on his arm, on the back of his lilac bike touring the flower kingdom of San Francisco. And for a piece of time the size of a nickel, I think, maybe. But maybe is vapor, has no anchor here in the sun beneath St. Francis Cathedral. And space is as solid as the bronze statue of St. Francis, the fox breaking through the lilacs, my invention of this story, the wind blowing.

JOY HARJO   (b. 1951)

Nine Lives ————————————————————————— *1990*

A storm tangles in the east and will disappear in a paradise of midnight. The moon is a stripped lizard half here and half visible by the eye on the other side of the world. Someone up the alley is singing Happy Birthday to a packed house. I am downwind of the beer foam, the laughter. Death with its coat of tender wings is close to my shoulder, while the neighbor's cat fights for one of its nine lives. In the morning the winner will be grinning at the door of my sleep. I know you can understand the structure of the spiraled world in an ordinary moment, or by falling through the crack of a perfumed nightmare. Cicadas climb out of the carcasses their voices make, into their wings of fragile promises to glide over the wet grass. We are all spun within a crescendo of abalone light, unseen beneath the wild storm. What spins us now, in this neighborhood chrysalis at exactly midnight? Don't tell me unless it will turn me into something as perfect as a perfect monarch butterfly.

MICHAEL HARPER   (b. 1938)

Last Affair: Bessie's° Blues Song ———————————————— *1972*

Disarticulated
arm torn out,
large veins cross
her shoulder intact,
her tourniquet
her blood in all-white big bands:

5

Bessie: Bessie Smith, blues singer in this collection. The refrain is similar to those she sang.

Can't you see
what love and heartache's done to me
I'm not the same as I used to be
this is my last affair   10

Mail truck or parked car
in the fast lane,
afloat at forty-three
on a Mississippi road,
Two-hundred-pound muscle on her ham bone,   15
'nother nigger dead 'fore noon:

Can't you see
what love and heartache's done to me
I'm not the same as I used to be
this is my last affair   20

Fifty-dollar record
cut the vein in her neck,
fool about her money
toll her black train wreck,
white press missed her fun'ral   25
in the same stacked deck:

Can't you see
what love and heartache's done to me
I'm not the same as I used to be
this is my last affair   30

Loved a little blackbird
heard she could sing,
Martha in her vineyard
pestle in her spring,
Bessie had a bad mouth   35
made my chimes ring:

Can't you see
what love and heartache's done to me
I'm not the same as I used to be
this is my last affair   40

SEAMUS HEANEY   (b. 1939)

Punishment° _____ *1975*

I can feel the tug
of the halter at the nape

Punishment: Heaney refers to a female corpse from the bogs, imagining her as having been punished for a crime.

of her neck, the wind
on her naked front.

It blows her nipples   5
to amber beads,
it shakes the frail rigging
of her ribs.

I can see her drowned
body in the bog,   10
the weighing stone,
the floating rods and boughs.

Under which at first
she was a barked sapling
that is dug up   15
oak-bone, brain-firkin:

her shaved head
like a stubble of black corn,
her blindfold a soiled bandage,
her noose a ring   20

to store
the memories of love.
Little adulteress,
before they punished you

you were flaxen-haired,   25
undernourished, and your
tar-black face was beautiful.
My poor scapegoat,

I almost love you
but would have cast, I know,   30
the stones of silence.
I am the artful voyeur

of your brain's exposed
and darkened combs,
your muscles' webbing   35
and all your numbered bones:

I who have stood dumb
when your betraying sisters,
cauled in tar,
wept by the railings,   40

who would connive
in civilized outrage
yet understand the exact
and tribal, intimate revenge.

SEAMUS HEANEY   (b. 1939)

The Tollund Man° ————————————————————— *1972*

I

Some day I will go to Aarhus°
To see his peat-brown head,
The mild pods of his eye-lids,
His pointed skin cap.

In the flat country nearby   5
Where they dug him out,
His last gruel of winter seeds
Caked in his stomach,

Naked except for
The cap, noose and girdle,   10
I will stand a long time.
Bridegroom to the goddess,

She tightened her torc° on him
And opened her fen,
Those dark juices working   15
Him to a saint's kept body,°

Trove of the turfcutters'
Honeycombed workings.
Now his stained face
Reposes at Aarhus.   20

II

I could risk blasphemy,
Consecrate the cauldron bog
Our holy ground and pray
Him to make germinate

The scattered, ambushed   25
Flesh of laborers,
Stockinged corpses
Laid out in the farmyards,

Tell-tale skin and teeth
Flecking the sleepers   30
Of four young brothers, trailed
For miles along the lines.

III

Something of his sad freedom
As he rode the tumbril°

Tollund Man: a body preserved in a peat bog in Denmark.   1 *Aarhus:* town in Denmark.
13 *torc:* necklace, choker.   16 *saint's kept body:* saints' bodies are said not to decay.   34 *tumbril:* cart transporting him to death.

Should come to me, driving,   35
Saying the names

Tollund, Grauballe, Nebelgard,°
Watching the pointing hands
Of country people,
Not knowing their tongue.   40

Out there in Jutland
In the old man-killing parishes
I will feel lost,
Unhappy and at home.

37 *Grauballe, Nebelgard:* other places where such bodies have been found.

GEORGE HERBERT   (1593–1633)

The Altar° _____ *1633*

A broken A L T A R, Lord, thy servant rears,
Made of a heart, and cemented with tears:
  Whose parts are as they hand did frame;
  No workman's tool hath touched the same.
      A   H E A R T   alone   5
      Is   such   a   stone,
      As   nothing   but
      Thy   Power   doth   cut.
      Wherefore   each   part
      Of   my   hard   heart   10
      Meets   in   this   frame,
      To   praise   thy   name.
  That if I chance to hold my peace,
  These stones to praise thee may not cease.
O let thy blessed S A C R I F I C E be mine,   15
And sanctify this A L T A R to be thine:

The Altar: The shape of this poem resembles an altar.

GEORGE HERBERT   (1593–1633)

Easter Wings _____ *1633*

Lord, who createdst man in wealth and store,
  Though foolishly he lost the same,
    Decaying   more   and   more,

<pre>
          Till   he   became
             Most   poor: 5
             With   thee
          O   let   me   rise
       As   larks,   harmoniously,
    And   sing   this   day   thy   victories:
Then shall the fall further the flight° in me   10

My   tender   age   in   sorrow   did   begin:
    And   still   with   sicknesses   and   shame
       Thou   didst   so   punish   sin,
          That   I   became
             Most   thin.   15
             With   thee
          Let   me   combine,
       And   feel   this   day   thy   victory:
    For,   if   I   imp°   my   wing   on   thine,
Affliction   shall   advance   the   flight   in   me.   20
</pre>

10 *fall* ... *flight:* The fall into sin and weakness allows for his redemption by Christ
(flight).   19 *imp:* graft.

GEOFFREY HILL   (b. 1932)

September Song ——————————————————————— *1986*

   born 19.6.32—deported 24.9.42

Undesirable you may have been, untouchable
you were not. Not forgotten
or passed over at the proper time.

As estimated, you died. Things marched,
sufficient, to that end.   5
Just so much Zyklon° and leather, patented
terror, so many routine cries.

(I have made
an elegy for myself it
is true)   10

September fattens on vines. Roses
flake from the wall. The smoke
of harmless fires drifts to my eyes.

This is plenty. This is more than enough.

6 *Zyklon:* poison gas Nazis used to kill Jews in Auschwitz and other camps.

CHRISTINE HOLBO

Gomorrah° —————————————————————————— *1992*

Also, in Gomorrah, there were plays,
a life of the mind;
there were the schools
and the quiet temples; Sodom
and "the new theatre"   5
were conveniently located,
just an hour's ride away. There
the wife of Lot held her
gatherings, "my *petites*
soirées," for the priests   10
and the politicians
and the intellectual élite.

> *And in the hills the wild dogs cried*
> *And the sand shifted on the desert stones.*

But Gomorrah was mostly as you will have heard: 15
litigious, polyglot, city of worlds; a scene
from a favorite story frequently told.
There was the traffic, the market banter—
merchants crying catalogues of marvels: uncut
rubies, silver mirrors, porcelain,   20
parrots, olives at discount, clocks and
sea salt, carbuncles, pearls—the streets
full of crowds, the dirty gypsies,
the quick brown-ankled girls,
the old men smoking on the temple   25
stoop, the smells of hashish and tanneries,
the bellowing herds.

> *And in the hills the wild dogs cried*
> *And the desert gods shifted sand across the stones.*

The wife of Lot   30
was not *so* young anymore.
She didn't laugh like
the brown-ankled girls;
the wife of Lot wore a veil in public,
and held her tongue.   35
And she kept the books
in the family establishment,
was quick with an abacus
or a bon mot or advice about money;
knew how to cook   40

Gomorrah: See Gen. 19:1–26. God warned Lot and his family to flee Sodom and Gomorrah before
he destroyed them by fire for their wickedness. Lot's wife looked back as she fled and was turned
into a pillar of salt.

wild duck with rice, how to
pack a camel—and the best caterers
in town "just like old friends,"
and most of the city councilmen.
The wife of Lot   45
did what she thought
fitting and appropriate
for the wife of a public figure
and a pillar of the community.

> *And the gods ran along the desert*   50
> *And a voice echoed across the stones.*

Also, the forenamed woman kept
the books from "my schoolgirl days"
at the Temple. She remembered
learning how to pray,   55
and the philosophers, taught
by an old and frightening priest
at the gilded knees of an idol.
"Someday I'll get back to
them," she would say.   60

The wife of Lot
had two pretty daughters,
"the very image of their mother";
they were sent, like the mother,
to the Temple school, the very best,   65
and were taught French
and the philosophers, and could
quite intelligently discuss
"the name of God" or, alternatively,
"the common good."   70
            They were only young girls,
of course; they liked best to laugh
and they were beautifully dressed
and were like all girls silly.
            She asked, "Who am I   75
thus to be blessed?"

> *And a spirit cried, "Atone, atone,"*
> *And the wind ran along the desert stone.*

Once in a generation or so,
a war or an epiphany occurs,   80
or a transformation, or a revolution,
or a waiting God stirs; a name
comes into a city, a word
is passed down—an Idea seeks
ten righteous men to save,   85
the rest, the evidently lost, to reap;
to separate those who have kept

her faith from the too far gone,
and from those who have lost
what they'd sought to keep.   90
Once in a generation
a warning is heard—

> *Flee, flee to the hills, flee to the valleys,*
> *The cities. Abandon. Atone.*

Lot consulted his in-laws,   95
And the two daughters wept,
And the wife of Lot packed, asking
herself, "How much should we keep?
How much can be kept?"
                  They made   100
the abandoning leap—
but you know the rest: how
Lot and his daughters fled
from that place, how they passed
the test. And how   105
a moment's recollection,
a sudden grief, a backward
glance revealed what she
had quietly foreseen: a pocky
and astringent silent thing.   110

GERARD MANLEY HOPKINS   (1844–1889)

The Windhover° _____ *1918*

      To Christ our Lord

I caught this morning morning's minion,° king-
   dom of daylight's dauphin,° dapple-dawn-drawn Falcon, in his riding
   Of the rolling level underneath him steady air, and striding
High there, how he rung upon the rein° of a wimpling wing
In his ecstasy! then off, off forth on swing,   5
   As a skate's heel sweeps smooth on a bow-bend: the hurl and gliding
   Rebuffed the big wind. My heart in hiding
Stirred for a bird,—the achieve of, the mastery of the thing!

Brute beauty and valor and act, oh, air, pride, plume here
   Buckle!° and the fire that breaks from thee then, a billion   10
   Times told lovelier, more dangerous, O my chevalier!

Windhover: sparrow-hawk, or kestrel, so named because it can hover motionless in the face of a
wind.   1 *minion:* darling, beloved.   2 *dauphin:* prince.   4 *rung upon the rein:* an image
from horse training: to hold steady at the end of a rein.   10 *Buckle:* various possible meanings:
to prepare for battle, to make a dive.

No wonder of it: shéer plód makes plough down sillion°
Shine, and blue-bleak embers, ah my dear,
Fall, gall themselves, and gash gold-vermilion.

12 *sillion:* ridge or strip between two furrows often glinting with mica.

GERARD MANLEY HOPKINS (1844–1889)

Pied Beauty _____ *1918*

Glory be to God for dappled things—
   For skies of couple-color as a brinded° cow;
     For rose-moles all in stipple upon trout that swim;
Fresh-firecoal chestnut-falls,° finches' wings;
   Landscape plotted and pieced—fold, fallow, and plough;   5
     And áll trádes, their gear and tackle and trim.

All things counter, original, spare, strange;
   Whatever is fickle, freckled (who knows how?)
     With swift, slow; sweet, sour; adazzle, dim;
He fathers-forth whose beauty is past change: 10
                Praise him.

2 *brinded:* streaked.   4 *chestnut-falls:* roasted chestnuts stripped of their husks.

LANGSTON HUGHES (1902–1967)

Harlem _____ *1951*

What happens to a dream deferred?

   Does it dry up
   like a raisin in the sun?
   Or fester like a sore—
   And then run?
   Does it stink like rotten meat?   5
   Or crust and sugar over—
   like a syrupy sweet?

   Maybe it just sags
   like a heavy load.   10

   Or does it explode?

LANGSTON HUGHES (1902–1967)

The Negro Speaks of Rivers _____ *1926*

I've known rivers:
I've known rivers ancient as the world and older than the flow of
   human blood in human veins.

My soul has grown deep like the rivers.

I bathed in the Euphrates when dawns were young.
I built my hut near the Congo and it lulled me to sleep.   5
I looked upon the Nile and raised the pyramids above it.
I heard the singing of the Mississippi when Abe Lincoln went down to
    New Orleans, and I've seen its muddy bosom turn all golden in
    the sunset.

I've known rivers:
Ancient, dusky rivers.

My soul has grown deep like the rivers.   10

LANGSTON HUGHES   (1902–1967)

The Weary Blues ————————————————————— *1926*

Droning a drowsy syncopated tune,
Rocking back and forth to a mellow croon,
    I heard a Negro play.
Down on Lenox Avenue the other night
By the pale dull pallor of an old gas light   5
    He did a lazy sway. . . .
    He did a lazy sway. . . .
To the tune o' those Weary Blues.
With his ebony hands on each ivory key
He made that poor piano moan with melody.   10
    O Blues!
Swaying to and fro on his rickety stool
He played that sad raggy tune like a musical fool.
    Sweet Blues!
Coming from a black man's soul.   15
    O Blues!
In a deep song voice with a melancholy tone
I heard that Negro sing, that old piano moan—
    "Ain't got nobody in all this world,
    Ain't got nobody but ma self.   20
    I's gwine to quit ma frownin'
    And put ma troubles on the shelf."
Thump, thump, thump, went his foot on the floor.
He played a few chords then he sang some more—
    "I got the Weary Blues   25
    And I can't be satisfied.
    Got the Weary Blues
    And can't be satisfied—

I ain't happy no mo'
    And I wish that I had died."   30
And far into the night he crooned that tune.
The stars went out and so did the moon.
The singer stopped playing and went to bed
While the Weary Blues echoed through his head.
He slept like a rock or a man that's dead.   35

LANGSTON HUGHES   (1902–1967)

Madam and the Rent Man —————————————————————— *1949*

The rent man knocked.
He said, Howdy-do?
I said, What
Can I do for you?
He said, You know   5
Your rent is due.

I said, Listen,
Before I'd pay
I'd go to Hades
And rot away!   10

The sink is broke,
The water don't run,
And you ain't done a thing
You promised to've done.

Back window's cracked,   15
Kitchen floor squeaks,
There's rats in the cellar,
And the attic leaks.

He said, Madam,
It's not up to me.   20
I'm just the agent,
Don't you see?

I said, Naturally,
You pass the buck.
If it's money you want   25
You're out of luck.

He said, Madam,
I ain't pleased!
I said, Neither am I.

So we agrees!   30

LANGSTON HUGHES   (1902–1967)

Theme for English B _____ *1959*

The instructor said,

> *Go home and write*
> *a page tonight.*
> *And let that page come out of you—*
> *Then, it will be true.*   5

I wonder if it's that simple?
I am twenty-two, colored, born in Winston-Salem.
I went to school there, then Durham, then here
to this college on the hill above Harlem.
I am the only colored student in my class.   10
The steps from the hill lead down into Harlem,
through a park, then I cross St. Nicholas,
Eighth Avenue, Seventh, and I come to the Y,
the Harlem Branch Y, where I take the elevator
up to my room, sit down, and write this page: 15

It's not easy to know what is true for you or me
at twenty-two, my age. But I guess I'm what
I feel and see and hear, Harlem, I hear you:
hear you, hear me—we two—you, me, talk on this page.
(I hear New York, too.) Me—who?   20

Well, I like to eat, sleep, drink, and be in love.
I like to work, read, learn, and understand life.
I like a pipe for a Christmas present,
or records—Bessie, bop, or Bach.
I guess being colored doesn't make me not like   25
the same things other folks like who are other races.
So will my page be colored that I write?
Being me, it will not be white.
But it will be
a part of you, instructor.   30
You are white—
yet a part of me, as I am a part of you.
That's American.
Sometimes perhaps you don't want to be a part of me.
Nor do I often want to be a part of you.   35
But we are, that's true!
As I learn from you,
I guess you learn from me—
although you're older—and white—
and somewhat more free.   40

This is my page for English B.

TED HUGHES   (1930–1998)

Examination at the Womb-Door _____ *1970*

Who owns these scrawny little feet?   *Death.*
Who owns this bristly scorched-looking face?   *Death.*
Who owns these still-working lungs?   *Death.*
Who owns this utility coat of muscles?   *Death.*
Who owns these unspeakable guts?   *Death.*   5
Who owns these questionable brains?   *Death.*
All this messy blood?   *Death.*
These minimum-efficiency eyes?   *Death.*
This wicked little tongue?   *Death.*
This occasional wakefulness?   *Death.*   10

Given, stolen, or held pending trial?   *Held.*

Who owns the whole rainy, stony earth?   *Death.*
Who owns all of space?   *Death.*

Who is stronger than hope?   *Death.*
Who is stronger than the will?   *Death.*   15
Stronger than love?   *Death.*
Stronger than life?   *Death.*

But who is stronger than   death?
                                        Me, evidently.

Pass, Crow.°

21 *Crow:* a frequent figure in Hughes's poetry. *Crow* (1971) explores nature with Crow as a main character.

TED HUGHES   (1930–1998)

Crow's First Lesson _____ *1970*

God tried to teach Crow° how to talk.
"Love," said God. "Say, Love."
Crow gaped, and the white shark crashed into the sea
And went rolling downwards, discovering its own depth.

"No, no," said God, "Say Love. Now try it. LOVE."   5
Crow gaped, and a bluefly, a tsetse, a mosquito
Zoomed out and down
To their sundry flesh-pots.

"A final try," said God. "Now, LOVE."
Crow convulsed, gaped, retched and   10

1 *Crow:* See note to "Examination at the Womb-Door."

Man's bodiless prodigious head
Bulbed out onto the earth, with swiveling eyes,
Jabbering protest—

And Crow retched again, before God could stop him.
And woman's vulva dropped over man's neck and tightened.   15
The two struggled together on the grass.
God struggled to part them, cursed, wept—

Crow flew guiltily off.

LYNDA HULL   (1954–1994)

Midnight Reports _____ *1991*

That's how billboards give up their promises—
they look right into your window, then whisper
sex, success. The Salem girl's smoke plume
marries the gulf between the high-rise projects,
the usual knife's edge ballet enacted nightly there   5
for the benefit of no one. It's just that
around midnight every love I've known flicks open
like a switchblade and I have to start talking,
talking to drown out the man in the radio
who instructs me I'm on the edge of a new day   10
in this city of Newark which is not a city

of roses, just one big hockshop. I can't tell you
how it labors with its grilled storefronts, air
rushing over the facts of diamonds, appliances,
the trick carnations. But you already know that.   15
The M-16 Vinnie sent—piece by piece—from Vietnam
is right where you left it the day you skipped town
with the usherette of the Paradise Triple-X Theater.
You liked the way she played her flashlight down
those rows of men, plaster angels flanked around   20
that screen. Sometimes you'd go fire rounds over
the landfill, said it felt better than crystal meth,°
a hit that leaves a trail of neon, ether.

I keep it clean, oiled, and some nights it seems
like a good idea to simply pick up that rifle   25
and hold it, because nothing's safe. You know
how it is: one minute you're dancing, the next you're flying
through plate glass and the whole damn town is burning
again with riots and looters, the bogus politicians.
We'd graduated that year, called the city ours,   30
a real bed of Garden State roses. I've drawn x's

22 *meth:* methamphetamine, a drug.

over our eyes in the snapshot Vinnie took commencement
night, a line of x's over our linked hands. The quartet
onstage behind us sang a cappella°—four brothers
from Springfield Ave. spinning in sequined tuxedos,   35

palms outstretched to the crowd, the Latin girls
from Ironbound shimmering in the brief conflagration
of their beauty, before the kids, before
the welfare motels, corridors of cries and exhalations.
I wore the heels you called my blue suede shoes,   40
and you'd given yourself a new tattoo, my name across
your bicep, in honor of finishing, in honor of the future
we were arrogant enough to think would turn out right.
I was laughing in that picture, laughing when the rain
caught us later and washed the blue dye from my shoes—   45
blue, the color of bruises, of minor regrets.

34 *a cappella:* without instrumental accompaniment.

T. R. HUMMER   (b. 1950)

The Rural Carrier Discovers That Love Is Everywhere _____ 1982

A registered letter for the Jensens. I walk down their drive
Through the gate of their thick-hedged yard, and by God there they are,
On a blanket in the grass, asleep, buck-naked, honeymooners
Not married a month. I smile, turn to leave,
But can't help looking back. Lord, they're a pretty sight,   5
Both of them, tangled up in each other, easy in their skin—
It's their own front yard, after all, perfectly closed in
By privet hedge and country. Maybe they were here all night.

I want to believe they'd do that, not thinking of me
Or anyone but themselves, alone in the world   10
Of the yard with its clipped grass and fresh-picked fruit trees.
Whatever this letter says can wait. To hell with the mail.
I slip through the gate, silent as I came, and leave them
Alone. There's no one they need to hear from.

T. R. HUMMER   (b. 1950)

The Rural Carrier Stops to Kill a Nine-Foot Cottonmouth _____ 1982

Lord God, I saw the son-of-a-bitch uncoil
In the road ahead of me, uncoil and squirm
For the ditch, squirm a hell of a long time.
Missed him with the car. When I got back to him, he was all

But gone, nothing left on the road but the tip-end   5
Of his tail, and that disappearing into Johnson grass.
I leaned over the ditch and saw him, balled up now, hiss.
I aimed for the mouth and shot him. And shot him again.

Then I got a good strong stick and dragged him out.
He was long and evil, thick as the top of my arm.   10
There are things in this world a man can't look at without
Wanting to kill. Don't ask me why. I was calm
Enough, I thought. But I felt my spine
Squirm suddenly. I admit it. It was mine.

ELIZABETH JENNINGS   (b. 1926)

Fragment for the Dark _____ *1977*

Let it not come near me, let it not
Fold round or over me. One weak hand
Clutches a foot of air, asks the brisk buds
To suffer grey winds, spear through
Fog I feel in me. Give me the magic   5
To see grounded starlings, their polish
As this threat of all-day night. Mind, mind
In me, make thoughts candles to light me
Out of the furthest reach of possible nights.
Lantern me, stars, if I look up through wet hands,   10
Show assurance in blurred shining. I have
Put every light in the house on.
May their filaments last till true morning.

ELIZABETH JENNINGS   (b. 1926)

The Child's Story _____ *1985*

When I was small and they talked about love I laughed
But I ran away and I hid in a tall tree
Or I lay in asparagus beds
But I still listened.
The blue dome sang with the wildest birds   5
And the new sun sang in the idle noon
But then I heard love, love, rung from the steeples, each belfry,
And I was afraid and I watched the cypress trees
Join the deciduous chestnuts and oaks in a crowd of shadows
And then I shivered and ran and ran to the tall   10
White house with the green shutters and dark red door
And I cried "Let me in even if you must love me"

And they came and lifted me up and told me the name
Of the near and the far stars,
And so my first love was.   15

JUNE JORDAN   (b. 1936)

Letter to the Local Police _____ *1977–1980*

Dear Sirs:

I have been enjoying the law and order of our
community throughout the past three months since
my wife and I, our two cats, and miscellaneous
photographs of the six grandchildren belonging to
our previous neighbors (with whom we were very   5
close) arrived in Saratoga Springs which is clearly
prospering under your custody

Indeed, until yesterday afternoon and despite my
vigilant casting about, I have been unable to discover
a single instance of reasons for public-spirited concern,   10
much less complaint

You may easily appreciate, then, how it is that
I write to your office, at this date, with utmost
regret for the lamentable circumstances that force
my hand   15

Speaking directly to the issue of moment:

I have encountered a regular profusion of certain
unidentified roses, growing to no discernible purpose,
and according to no perceptible control, approximately
one quarter mile west of the Northway, on the southern   20
side

To be specific, there are practically thousands of
aforementioned abiding in perpetual near riot
of wild behavior, indiscriminate coloring, and only
the Good Lord Himself can say what diverse soliciting   25
of promiscuous cross-fertilization

As I say, these roses, no matter what the apparent
background, training, tropistic tendencies, age,
or color, do not demonstrate the least inclination
toward categorization, specified allegiance, resolute   30
preference, consideration of the needs of others, nor
any other minimal traits of decency

May I point out that I did not assiduously seek out
this colony, as it were, and that these certain

unidentified roses remain open to viewing even by   35
children, with or without suitable supervision

(My wife asks me to append a note as regards the
seasonal but nevertheless seriously licentious
phenomenon of honeysuckle under the moon that one may
apprehend at the corner of Nelson and Main   40

However, I have recommended that she undertake direct
correspondence with you, as regards this: yet
another civic disturbance in our midst)

I am confident that you will devise and pursue
appropriate legal response to the roses in question   45
If I may aid your efforts in this respect, please
do not hesitate to call me into consultation

                              Respectfully yours,

JENNY JOSEPH   (b. 1932)

Warning _____ *1974*

When I am an old woman I shall wear purple
With a red hat which doesn't go, and doesn't suit me.
And I shall spend my pension on brandy and summer gloves
And satin sandals, and say we've no money for butter.
I shall sit down on the pavement when I'm tired   5
And gobble up samples in shops and press alarm bells
And run my stick along the public railings
And make up for the sobriety of my youth.
I shall go out in my slippers in the rain
And pick the flowers in other people's gardens   10
And learn to spit.

You can wear terrible shirts and grow more fat
And eat three pounds of sausages at a go
Or only bread and pickle for a week
And hoard pens and pencils and beermats and things in boxes.   15

But now we must have clothes that keep us dry
And pay our rent and not swear in the street
And set a good example for the children.
We must have friends to dinner and read the papers.

But maybe I ought to practise a little now?   20
So people who know me are not too shocked and surprised
When suddenly I am old, and start to wear purple.

DONALD JUSTICE   (b. 1925)

A Map of Love ————————————————————————— *1959*

Your face more than others' faces
Maps the half-remembered places
I have come to while I slept—
Continents a dream had kept
Secret from all waking folk   5
Till to your face I awoke,
And remembered then the shore,
And the dark interior.

BRIGIT PEGEEN KELLY   (b. 1951)

Young Wife's Lament ————————————————————— *c. 1988*

The mule that lived on the road
where I was married
would bray to wake the morning,
but could not wake me.
How many summers I slept   5
lost in my hair. How many
mules on how many hills singing.
Back of a deep ravine
he lived, above a small river
on a beaten patch of land.   10
I walked up in the day and walked down,
having been given nothing
else to do. The road grew no longer,
I grew no wiser, my husband
was away selling things to people who buy.   15
He went up the road, too, but
the road was full of doors for him,
the road was his belt and,
one notch at a time, he loosened it
on his way. I would sit   20
on the hill of stones and look down
on the trees, on the lake
far away with its boats and those
who ride in boats
and I could not pray. Some of us   25
have mule minds,
are foolish as sails whipping
in the wind, senseless
as sheets rolling through the fields,
some of us are not given   30

even a wheel of the tinker's cart
upon which to pray.
When I came back I pumped water
in the yard under the trees
by the fence where the cows came up,   35
but water is not wisdom
and change is not made by wishes.
Else I would have ridden something,
even a mule, over
those hills and away.   40

DOLORES KENDRICK   (b. 1927)

Leah: In Freedom _____ *1989*

I run away
          I keep runnin' away
                    they won't let me alone
                              they won't let me bear
my misery to the river   5
          and out
                    over the sky
                              or even
                                        under the trees
in moles' holes   10
          and wolves' caves
                    and blackberry patches
                              with my feet
skiddin' and bleedin'
          on the thorns   15
                    and then it rains
                              on my run
as quick as my momma's voice
          on the slippery road
                    to freedom.   20
They catch me
          all the time they catch me
                    and bring me back
and whip me
          till I'm blind and deaf   25
                    and dumb,
     and put me in the cabin
                    where the blood soak my back
like scaldin' water
                    and take me out to the fields   30
and whip me some more.
               Oh! the sky is so big!
               Ain't it?

The trees are so tall!
Ain't they?   35

The river's so wide!
Ain't it?

Don't you hear?
Cain't you hear

all that callin', Leah?   40
Leah's gotta go!

And I run again
        all twenty-three years of me
                        all white and black of me
all the angels in me   45
                and the wings
                        growing out of my armpits
flapping against my thighs
                    makin' me move
                            when I can't,   50
when I don't want to,
                when my back is so sore
                        and painful
that every flight
        makes my wings stick to my side sometimes   55
                        and keep me slow
and earthbound;
        all my momma in me.
                    So soon they catch me again
and beat me again.   60
            That was the last time for that.
                            I lay here
on the hard floor on my back
            only place that's soft:
                        guess it's the flesh,   65
the wounds that do it,
                guess it's the salt, too.
                        So much pain
it don't pain no more,
            only the want of freedom pains,   70
                    only the fear
of dyin' before I'm free.
            Yesterday they took out
                    one of my front teeth
to identify me   75
            in case I 'scape again
                    and now when I ain't doin'
the housework
        they put me in an iron collar.
                        Three days they gives me   80

three days I got for my wings
                              to heal
                                        but they's bent and dirty
and tattered, need washin'
                    they's not the same   85
                                    don't round themselves right
somehow.
            I can see the roots of trees now,
                              don't see the tops no more.
The mole and me   90
            we's on our own.
                        These days I go
                                    to my mistress' room
sew her clothes and cloaks
                    though the wounds be still breakin' through my shawl   95
                    and I be sore.
                              She got lots of holes
                                        under her armpits
of her dresses:
                    that makes me shiver,   100
                                    think of my momma.
Mistress say, "good mawnin', Leah"
                              (won't look at me)
and tell me about faith
                    and Jesus.   105

RACHEL KORN   (1898–1987)

Keep Hidden from Me ————————————————————— *1967*

        Translated from Yiddish by Carolyn Kizer

Keep from me all that I might comprehend!
O God, I ripen toward you in my unknowing.

The barely burgeoning leaf on the roadside tree
Limns innocence: here endeth the first lesson.

Keep from me, God, all forms of certainty: 5
The steady tread that paces off the self

And forms it, seamless, ignorant of doubt
Or failure, hell-bent for fulfilment.

To know myself: is not that the supreme disaster?
To know Thee, one must sink on trembling knees.   10

To hear Thee, only the terrified heart may truly listen;
To see Thee, only the gaze half-blind with dread.

Though the day darken, preserve my memory
From Your bright oblivion. Erase not my faulty traces.

If I aspire again to make four poor walls my house,   15
Let me pillow myself on the book of my peregrinations.

God, grant me strength to give over false happiness,
And the sense that suffering has earned us Your regard.

Elohim! Though sorrow fill me to the brim,
Let me carefully bear the cup of myself to Thee.   20

MAZISI KUNENE   (b. 1930)

From the Ravages of Life We Create _____ *1970*

And the suns are torn from the cord of the skies
And fall to the ground humiliated by the cluster of leaves.
The eternal feet travel on on their journey.
The bars of iron pierce through, feeding on their blood.
The wedding party walks proudly   5
And catches a glimpse of the moon disintegrating.
Beyond this aberration in the land of the hostile winds,
The tall woman is seized by madness.
She covers her face with a black cloth
Imitating the dance of the ecstatic children.   10
Then the ruined man of time fondles her
Until she gives birth, and gives birth to the infants of stone.
We are their kin whose ribs are wide with their power,
We are one with those who wander everywhere.
A man enters and marks down our generation   15
And tells us how suddenly summer has come
And makes us sing though our hearts are bleeding

Knowing how because of us,
We who are the locusts with broken wings,
Our shadows shelter the earth from the sun.   20

MAZISI KUNENE   (b. 1930)

Place of Dreams _____ *1970*

There is a place
Where the dream is dreaming us,
We who are the shepherds of the stars.
It stands towering as tall as the mountains
Spreading its fire over the sun   5
Until when we take one great stride

We speed with the eagle on our journey.
It is the eagle that plays its wings on our paths,
Wakening another blind dream.
Together with other generations hereafter   10
They shall dream them like us.
When they wake on their journeys they will say:
Someone, somewhere, is dreaming us, in the ruins.

MAZISI KUNENE   (b. 1930)

The Political Prisoner _____ *1970*

I desired to talk
And talk with words as numerous as sands,
The other side of the wire,
The other side of the fortress of stone.

I found a widow travelling   5
Passing the prisoners with firewood.
It is this woman who forbade me to sleep
Who filled me with dreams.

The dream is always the same.
It turns on an anchor   10
Until it finds a place to rest:
It builds its cobwebs from the hours.

One day someone arrives and opens the gate.
The sun explodes its fire
Spreading its flames over the earth,   15
Touching the spring of mankind.

Behind us there are mountains
Where the widow is abandoned.
She remains there unable to give birth
Priding herself only in the shadows of yesterdays.   20

PHILIP LARKIN   (1922–1992)

Faith Healing _____ *1979*

Slowly the women file to where he stands
Upright in rimless glasses, silver hair,
Dark suit, white collar. Stewards tirelessly
Persuade them onwards to his voice and hands,
Within whose warm spring rain of loving care   5
Each dwells some twenty seconds. *Now, dear child,*

What's wrong, the deep American voice demands,
And, scarcely pausing, goes into a prayer
Directing God about this eye, that knee.
Their heads are clasped abruptly; then, exiled   10

Like losing thoughts, they go in silence; some
Sheepishly stray, not back into their lives
Just yet; but some stay stiff, twitching and loud
With deep hoarse tears, as if a kind of dumb
And idiot child within them still survives   15
To re-awake at kindness, thinking a voice
At last calls them alone, that hands have come
To lift and lighten; and such joy arrives
Their thick tongues blort, their eyes squeeze grief, a crowd
Of huge unheard answers jam and rejoice—   20

What's wrong! Moustached in flowered frocks they shake:
By now, all's wrong. In everyone there sleeps
A sense of life lived according to love.
To some it means the difference they could make
By loving others, but across most it sweeps   25
As all they might have done had they been loved.
That nothing cures. An immense slackening ache,
As when, thawing, the rigid landscape weeps,
Spreads slowly through them—that, and the voice above
Saying *Dear child,* and all time has disproved.   30

PHILIP LARKIN   (1922–1992)

Church Going _____ *1955*

Once I am sure there's nothing going on
I step inside, letting the door thud shut.
Another church: matting, seats, and stone,
And little books; sprawlings of flowers, cut
For Sunday, brownish now; some brass and stuff   5
Up at the holy end; the small neat organ;
And a tense, musty, unignorable silence,
Brewed God knows how long. Hatless, I take off
My cycle-clips in awkward reverence,

Move forward, run my hand around the font.   10
From where I stand, the roof looks almost new—
Cleaned, or restored? Someone would know: I don't.
Mounting the lectern, I peruse a few
Hectoring large-scale verses, and pronounce
"Here endeth" much more loudly than I'd meant.   15
The echoes snigger briefly. Back at the door

I sign the book, donate an Irish sixpence,
Reflect the place was not worth stopping for.

Yet stop I did: in fact I often do,
And always end much at a loss like this,   20
Wondering what to look for; wondering, too,
When churches fall completely out of use
What we shall turn them into, if we shall keep
A few cathedrals chronically on show,
Their parchment, plate and pyx° in locked cases,   25
And let the rest rent-free to rain and sheep.
Shall we avoid them as unlucky places?

Or, after dark, will dubious women come
To make their children touch a particular stone;
Pick simples° for a cancer; or on some   30
Advised night see walking a dead one?
Power of some sort or other will go on
In games, in riddles, seemingly at random;
But superstition, like belief, must die,
And what remains when disbelief has gone?   35
Grass, weedy pavement, brambles, buttress, sky,

A shape less recognizable each week,
A purpose more obscure. I wonder who
Will be the last, the very last, to seek
This place for what it was; one of the crew   40
That tap and jot and know what rood-lofts° were?
Some ruin-bibber, randy for antique,°
Or Christmas-addict, counting on a whiff
Of gown-and-bands and organ-pipes and myrrh?
Or will he be my representative,   45

Bored, uninformed, knowing the ghostly silt
Dispersed, yet tending to this cross of ground
Through suburb scrub because it held unspilt
So long and equably what since is found
Only in separation—marriage, and birth,   50
And death, and thoughts of these—for whom was built
This special shell? For, though I've no idea
What this accoutred frowsty barn is worth,
It pleases me to stand in silence here;

A serious house on serious earth it is,   55
In whose blent air all our compulsions meet,
Are recognized, and robed as destinies.
And that much never can be obsolete,
Since someone will forever be surprising

---

25 *pyx:* box for communion wafers.   30 *simples:* herbs for medicine.   41 *rood-lofts:* where the
crucifix is erected in a church.   42 *Some ruin-bibber, randy for antique:* someone who "drinks in"
ruins, lusts for antiques.

A hunger in himself to be more serious,   60
And gravitating with it to this ground,
Which, he once heard, was proper to grow wise in,
If only that so many dead lie round.

DENISE LEVERTOV (1923–1997)

O Taste and See ——————————————————————— *1964*

The world is
not with us enough.°
O taste and see

the subway Bible poster said,
meaning *The Lord,* meaning   5
if anything all that lives
to the imagination's tongue,

grief, mercy, language,
tangerine, weather, to
breathe them, bite,   10
savor, chew, swallow, transform

into our flesh our
deaths, crossing the street, plum, quince,
living in the orchard and being
hungry, and plucking   15
the fruit.

1–2 *The world . . . enough:* a play on Wordsworth's poem "The World Is Too Much with Us," p. 804.

DENISE LEVERTOV (1923–1997)

Matins ———————————————————————————————— *1961*

I

The authentic! Shadows of it
sweep past in dreams, one could say imprecisely,
evoking the almost-silent
ripping apart of giant
sheets of cellophane. No.   5
It thrusts up close. Exactly in dreams
it has you off-guard, you
recognize it before you have time.
For a second before waking
the alarm bell is a red conical hat, it   10
takes form.

II

The authentic! I said
rising from the toilet seat.
The radiator in rhythmic knockings
spoke of the rising steam.   15
The authentic, I said
breaking the handle of my hairbrush as I
brushed my hair in
rhythmic strokes: That's it,
that's joy, it's always   20
a recognition, the known
appearing fully itself, and
more itself than one knew.

III

The new day rises
as heat rises,
knocking in the pipes   25
with rhythms it seizes for its own
to speak of its invention—
the real, the new-laid
egg whose speckled shell
the poet fondles and must break   30
if he will be nourished.

IV

A shadow painted where
yes, a shadow must fall.
The cow's breath   35
not forgotten in the mist, in the
words. Yes,
verisimilitude draws up
heat in us, zest
to follow through,   40
follow through,
follow
transformations of day
in its turning, in its becoming.

V

Stir the holy grains, set   45
the bowls on the table and
call the child to eat.

While we eat we think,
as we think an undercurrent
of dream runs through us   50
faster than thought
towards recognition.

Call the child to eat,
send him off, his mouth
tasting of toothpaste, to go down   55
into the ground, into a roaring train
and to school.

His cheeks are pink
his black eyes hold his dreams, he has left
forgetting his glasses.   60

Follow down the stairs at a clatter
to give them to him and save
his clear sight.

Cold air
comes in at the street door.   65

VI

The authentic! It rolls
just out of reach, beyond
running feet and
stretching fingers, down
the green slope and into   70
the black waves of the sea.
Speak to me, little horse, beloved,
tell me
how to follow the iron ball,
how to follow through to the country   75
beneath the waves
to the place where I must kill you and you step out
of your bones and flystrewn meat
tall, smiling, renewed,
formed in your own likeness   80

VII

Marvelous Truth, confront us
at every turn,
in every guise, iron ball,
egg, dark horse, shadow,
cloud   85
of breath on the air,

dwell
in our crowded hearts
our steaming bathrooms, kitchens full of
things to be done, the   90
ordinary streets.

Thrust close your smile
that we know you, terrible joy.

JAN HELLER LEVI   (b. 1954)

Sex Is Not Important _____ *1990*

I

Sex is not important. That's why
we have conversation. In the dark,
the unforgivable dark, it's hope
that's important, and hope
is something I do alone.   5

II

So here comes the unfortunate part.
Sisters, forgive me:
what we always love about the other
man is that he doesn't
care;   10
he's got an itch he's going to scratch;
he's going to lick you like a puppy
hungry for salt;
he's going to cry out and he's going to fall,
sweating and flushed and finished,   15
beside your trembling.
He's going to keep his eyes open and his mouth shut.
And he's going to leave you, not knowing what he's left.

III

It's not your body, is it,
that glows in the night,   20
and it's not me,
that woman in that hotel room,
doing all that wanting?

It can't be. I'm too smart
for all this;   25
too smart to disturb
those hospital corners
with all this unaccountable thrashing.

It must be my mind.
It's oozing.   30
It's evaluated the situation
and suggested
that my back should arch,
arch, arch. Oh!,

you're so interesting.   35
When we're ourselves
again, we really should
talk about this.

Have you ever seen
those teenagers clenched   40

on street corners
and repetitively touching lips?
I think it's because
they have nothing to say.

But you and I   45
have so much in common,
as I seem to recall.

                    IV
Sex is not important. That's why
we have everything else: friends,
husband, work, books, politics,   50
postcards, art, and poetry.
That's why, when the telephone rings,
we answer. That's why
we wake up in the morning,
sick to our stomach with dreams,   55
and ready to live.

                    V
That's why I have my circle game:
no one here but me and my abstract fame.

Everything unspoken
an endearment.   60

A woman's nipple—mine—
finds a finger.

AMY LOWELL   (1874–1925)

Venus Transiens° _____ *1919*

Tell me,
Was Venus more beautiful
Than you are,
When she topped
The crinkled waves,   5
Drifting shoreward
On her plaited shell?
Was Botticelli's vision
Fairer than mine;
And were the painted rosebuds   10

He tossed his lady,
Of better worth
Than the words I blow about you
To cover your too great loveliness
As with a gauze   15
Of misted silver?
For me,
You stand poised
In the blue and buoyant air,
Cinctured by bright winds,   20
Treading the sunlight.
And the waves which precede you
Ripple and stir
The sands at my feet.

ROBERT LOWELL   (1917–1977)

Robert Frost ———————————————————————— 1969

Robert Frost at midnight, the audience gone
to vapor, the great act laid on the shelf in mothballs,
his voice musical, raw and raw—he writes in the flyleaf:
"Robert Lowell from Robert Frost, his friend in the art."
"Sometimes I feel too full of myself," I say.   5
And he, misunderstanding, "When I am low,
I stray away. My son° wasn't your kind. The night
we told him Merrill Moore° would come to treat him,
he said, 'I'll kill him first.' One of my daughters thought things,
knew every male she met was out to make her;   10
the way she dresses, she couldn't make a whorehouse."
And I, "Sometimes I'm so happy I can't stand myself."
And he, "When I am too full of joy, I think
how little good my health did anyone near me."

7 *Son:* Frost's son committed suicide.   8 *Moore:* a psychoanalyst.

WING TEK LUM   (b. 1946)

At a Chinaman's Grave ———————————————————— 1987

> *"Kingston, too, looked critically at it ['Chinaman'] as not being meaningful for her. . . .*
> *She said she even tried 'Chinaperson' and 'Chinawoman' and found they didn't work*
> *either, the first sounding 'terrible' and the second being inaccurate."*
> —The Honolulu Advertiser, *July 22, 1978*

My grandmother's
brother here
died all alone, wife

and children back
in the village. He   5
answered to
"Chinaman" like all
the others
of our race back then.
The Demons hired   10
only lonely
men, not their
sweethearts,
tai pos, baby
daughters. They laid   15
ties, cut cane, but
could not
proliferate. They took
on woman's
work, by default,   20
washing shirts,
frying eggs and sausages.
Granduncle cooked.
From what he earned
he sent   25
money home,
gambled perhaps, maybe hid
some away—all for
one purpose. Those old men:
they lived   30
their whole
lives with souls
somewhere else, their hearts
burdened of
hopes, waiting to   35
be reunited.
Some succeeded
and we
are the fruits of those
reunions. Some   40
did not,
and they are
now forgotten, but for
these tombstones,
by the rest.   45

WING TEK LUM   (b. 1946)

Minority Poem _____ *1987*

Why
we're just as American

as apple pie—
that is, if you count
the leftover peelings   5
lying on the kitchen counter
which the cook has forgotten about
or doesn't know
quite what to do with
except hope that the maid   10
when she cleans off the chopping block
will chuck them away
into a garbage can she'll take out
on leaving for the night.

GEORGE ELLA LYON   (b. 1949)

Salvation _____ *1982*

> *"What does the Lord want with Virgil's heart?*
> *And what is Virgil going to do without one?"*

O Lord, spare him the Call.
You're looking for bass
in a pond stocked with catfish.
Pass him by.
You got our best.   5
You took Mammy and the truck and the second hay.
What do you want with Virgil's heart?

Virgil, he comes in of a night
so wore out he can hardly chew
blacked with dust   10
that don't come off at the bathhouse.
He washes again
eats onions and beans with the rest of us
then gives the least one a shoulder ride to bed
slow and singing   15

> Down in some lone valley
> in some lonesome place
> where the wild birds do whistle . . .

After that, he sags like a full feed sack
on a couch alongside the TV   20
and watches whatever news Your waves are giving.
His soul sifts out
like feed from a slit in that sack
and he's gone—
wore out and give out and plumb used up, Lord.   25
What do You want with his heart?

GEORGE ELLA LYON   (b. 1949)

Progress ————————————————————————————— *1984*

I reckon it was in the early Fifties
when they finally got the electric up at Smith.
I was hired to go behind the linemen
selling stoves, washers, frigidaires.

Anyway, there was this one woman   5
I saw as I came around a bend
with her washtub set up by a poplar
singing like a bird at first light.

She seemed awful glad to see me—
took my hand in her soapy hand—   10
but it wasn't any washer that she wanted.
No sir, she wanted a hi-fi.

Paid cash, a hundred and some dollars,
set the cabinet on the dirt floor.
Full blast, Nashville filled the holler   15
and saved her all the drudgery of song.

MEKEEL McBRIDE   (b. 1950)

If I'd Been Born in Tennessee ————————————————— *1988*

I'd have long ago married somebody
named Sweet Pea Russell. Sour mash, shoot,
I guess. And my name'd be Rita Louise.
I'd find me a Chinaberry to sit up in
with old blind Henry's monkey and maybe   5
I'd play the banjo and maybe I'd just talk
monkey talk and wait for Sweet Pea to come looking.

There'd be no trouble telling how God's
got hold of the mockingbird's throat
making it tell its kinda repeat truth   10
just in a way you can't quite get hold of.
Or how the Lord's slinked his way
up the spine of the sunflower that leans over
eavesdropping on everything.

Reading aloud would be easier, too; vowels,   15
those old wheels going no place special
spinning their worn-outness on the red cart
those idiot twins drive around in,
their over-alls so dusty you ain't never
gonna tell what color they was to begin with.   20
There's rules. There's always rules.

But then there's what's got to be done.
And if I went out into the honeysuckle-
soaked night with someone I ain't naming.
And if we laid down on Double Wedding Ring   25
quilts and never slept the whole time and
never made much mind of if we got caught.
Well, I guess that's my own business.
I could give up

reading altogether and look for Jesus   30
in the garden with his gold scissors
cutting June-bugs and poke brush, black
snakes outta my way. I could say
God damn, just like that and be old,
the oldest woman ever was, without getting tired   35
of discoursing with whatever passes by—

three legged mongrel, hunter's moon,
or the reverend who wears the eye patch,
although the Lord ain't taken no sight
out of that eye. Holy past all telling, he talks   40
with no patience for the primrose path
which I do believe I have walked
all my life. Sour mash, shoot, I guess.

WALTER McDONALD   (b. 1934)

Father's Straight Razor _____ *1990*

This old razor loves a beard, the subtle
scrape of flesh all it asks for.
It glides the moist, soaped stubble
like a water spider, sharp enough
to puncture flesh, balanced on the stretched   5
surface tension of skin.

I remember its touch along my jaw,
the cold Toledo steel slicing me
squeegee clean, before I grew a beard.
Unfolded, sharpened back and forth   10
on my father's stiff, black leather strop,
it smoothed my honeymoon face twice daily,

leaving no shadow to burn my bride.
I remember my father's face when I flew home
after his attack, the nights in CCU,   15
the first wave of his hand, his last request,
to shave him before he saw Mother.
I remember his eyes barely wavering,

his scalp buried in the pillow
exposing the slack stretch of his face,   20
when I touched him, the soft prickle of a week's
white growth under my nervous thumb
and fingers, the willing tilt of his chin,
the short, slick flicks of the blade

on his throat and jaw, floating   25
over his blue-veined skin and bone, his face
coming clean and true through the lather,
my own eyes barely wavering, like nothing
I'd ever get to do again, nothing
I wouldn't have done to save him.   30

CLAUDE McKAY (1890–1948)

The Harlem Dancer ——————————————————————— *1922*

Applauding youths laughed with young prostitutes
And watched her perfect, half-clothed body sway;
Her voice was like the sound of blended flutes
Blown by black players upon a picnic day.
She sang and danced on gracefully and calm,   5
The light gauze hanging loose about her form;
To me she seemed a proudly-swaying palm
Grown lovelier for passing through a storm.
Upon her swarthy neck black shiny curls
Luxuriant fell; and tossing coins in praise,   10
The wine-flushed, bold-eyed boys, and even the girls,
Devoured her shape with eager, passionate gaze;
But looking at her falsely-smiling face,
I knew her self was not in that strange place.

NAOMI LONG MADGETT (b. 1923)

Midway ————————————————————————————— *1959*

I've come this far to freedom and I won't turn back.
I'm climbing to the highway from my old dirt track.
    I'm coming and I'm going
    And I'm stretching and I'm growing
And I'll reap what I've been sowing or my skin's not black.   5

I've prayed and slaved and waited and I've sung my song.
You've bled me and you've starved me but I've still grown strong.
    You've lashed me and you've treed me

And you've everything but freed me
But in time you'll know you need me and it won't be long.   10

I've seen the daylight breaking high above the bough.
I've found my destination and I've made my vow;
    So whether you abhor me
    Or deride me or ignore me,
Mighty mountains loom before me and I won't stop now.   15

NAOMI LONG MADGETT   (b. 1923)

The Race Question ————————————————— *1963*

    (For one whose fame depends on keeping The Problem a problem)

Would it please you if I strung my tears
In pearls for you to wear?
Would you like a gift of my hands' endless beating
Against old bars?
This time I can forget my Otherness,   5
Silence my drums of discontent awhile
And listen to the stars.

Wait in the shadows if you choose.
Stand alert to catch
The thunder and first sprinkle of unrest   10
Your insufficiency demands.
But you will find no comfort.
I will not feed your hunger with my blood
Nor crown your nakedness
With jewels of my elegant pain.   15

CHRISTOPHER MARLOWE   (1564–1593)

The Passionate Shepherd to His Love ————————— *1599*

    [Six-stanza version from Englands Helicon*]*

Come live with me, and be my love,
And we will all the pleasures prove,
That Valleys, groves, hills, and fields,
Woods, or steepy mountain yields.

And we will sit upon the Rocks,   5
Seeing the Shepherds feed their flocks,
By shallow Rivers, to whose falls,
Melodious birds sing Madrigals.

And I will make thee beds of Roses,
And a thousand fragrant posies,
A cap of flowers, and a kirtle, 10
Imbroidered all with leaves of Myrtle.

A gown made of the finest wool,
Which from our pretty Lambs we pull,
Fair lined slippers for the cold: 15
With buckles of the purest gold.

A belt of straw, and Ivy buds,
With Coral clasps and Amber studs,
And if these pleasures may thee move,
Come live with me, and be my love. 20

The Shepherds' Swains shall dance and sing,
For thy delight each May-morning.
If these delights thy mind may move;
Then live with me, and be my love.

ANDREW MARVELL (1621–1678)

To His Coy Mistress —————————————————— *1681*

Had we but world enough, and time,
This coyness, Lady, were no crime.
We would sit down, and think which way
To walk, and pass our long love's day.
Thou by the Indian Ganges' side 5
Shouldst rubies find: I by the tide
Of Humber would complain. I would
Love you ten years before the flood:
And you should, if you please, refuse
Till the conversion of the Jews. 10
My vegetable love should grow
Vaster than empires, and more slow.
An hundred years should go to praise
Thine eyes, and on thy forehead gaze.
Two hundred to adore each breast: 15
But thirty thousand to the rest.
An age at least to every part,
And the last age should show your heart:
For, Lady, you deserve this state;
Nor would I love at lower rate. 20
    But at my back I always hear
Time's wingèd chariot hurrying near:
And yonder all before us lie
Deserts of vast eternity.
Thy beauty shall no more be found; 25

Nor, in thy marble vault, shall sound
My echoing song: then worms shall try
That long-preserved virginity:
And your quaint honor turn to dust;
And into ashes all my lust.   30
The grave's a fine and private place,
But none, I think, do there embrace.
   Now, therefore, while the youthful glue
Sits on thy skin like morning dew,
And while thy willing soul transpires   35
At every pore with instant fires,
Now let us sport us while we may;
And now, like amorous birds of prey,
Rather at once our time devour,
Than languish in his slow-chapped° power.   40
Let us roll all our strength, and all
Our sweetness, up into one ball:
And tear our pleasures with rough strife,
Thorough° the iron gates of life.
Thus, though we cannot make our sun   45
Stand still, yet we will make him run.

40 *Chapped:* jawed.   44 *Thorough:* through.

W. S. MERWIN   (b. 1927)

For a Coming Extinction ———————————————————————— *1974*

Gray whale
Now that we are sending you to The End
That great god
Tell him
That we who follow you invented forgiveness   5
And forgive nothing

I write as though you could understand
And I could say it
One must always pretend something
Among the dying   10
When you have left the seas nodding on their stalks
Empty of you
Tell him that we were made
On another day

The bewilderment will diminish like an echo   15
Winding along your inner mountains
Unheard by us
And find its way out
Leaving behind it the future

Dead   20
And ours

When you will not see again
The whale calves trying the light
Consider what you will find in the black garden
And its court   25
The sea cows the Great Auks the gorillas
The irreplaceable hosts ranged countless
And fore-ordaining as stars
Our sacrifices
Join your word to theirs   30
Tell him
That it is we who are important

EDNA ST. VINCENT MILLAY   (1892–1950)

Childhood Is the Kingdom Where Nobody Dies _____ *1934*

Childhood is not from birth to a certain age and at a certain age
The child is grown, and puts away childish things.
Childhood is the kingdom where nobody dies.

Nobody that matters, that is. Distant relatives of course
Die, whom one never has seen or has seen for an hour,   5
And they gave one candy in a pink-and-green striped bag, or a jack-knife,
And went away, and cannot really be said to have lived at all.

And cats die. They lie on the floor and lash their tails,
And their reticent fur is suddenly all in motion
With fleas that one never knew were there,   10
Polished and brown, knowing all there is to know,
Trekking off into the living world.
You fetch a shoe-box, but it's much too small, because she won't curl up now:
So you find a bigger box, and bury her in the yard, and weep.

But you do not wake up a month from then, two months,   15
A year from then, two years, in the middle of the night
And weep, with your knuckles in your mouth, and say Oh, God! Oh, God!
Childhood is the kingdom where nobody dies that matters,—mothers
    and fathers don't die.

And if you have said, "For heaven's sake, must you always be kissing a person?"
Or, "I do wish to gracious you'd stop tapping on the window with your thimble!"   20
Tomorrow, or even the day after tomorrow if you're busy having fun,
Is plenty of time to say, "I'm sorry, mother."

To be grown up is to sit at the table with people who have died, who neither
    listen nor speak;
Who do not drink their tea, though they always said
Tea was such a comfort.   25

Run down into the cellar and bring up the last jar of raspberries;
      they are not tempted.
Flatter them, ask them what was it they said exactly
That time, to the bishop, or to the overseer, or to Mrs. Mason;

They are not taken in.
Shout at them, get red in the face, rise,   30
Drag them up out of their chairs by their stiff shoulders and shake them
      and yell at them;
They are not startled, they are not even embarrassed; they slide back
      into their chairs.
Your tea is cold now.
You drink it standing up,
And leave the house.   35

JOHN MILTON   (1608–1674)

How Soon Hath Time, the Subtle Thief of Youth _____ *1632*

How soon hath Time, the subtle thief of youth,
    Stolen on his wing my three and twentieth year!
    My hasting days fly on with full career,
    But my late spring no bud or blossom showeth.°
Perhaps my semblance might deceive the truth   5
    That I to manhood am arrived so near,
    And inward ripeness doth much less appear,
    That some more timely-happy spirits endueth.°
Yet be it less or more, or soon or slow,
    It shall be still° in strictest measure even°   10
    To that same lot, however mean or high,
Toward which Time leads me, and the will of Heaven;
    All is, if I have grace to use it so,
    As ever in my great task-master's eye.

4 *my late . . . showeth:* I haven't accomplished much yet.   7–8 *And inward . . . endueth:* His spiritual (inward) ripeness is much less apparent than physical maturity in others.   10 *still:* always. *even:* equivalent, regular.

JOHN MILTON   (1608–1674)

Sonnet 19: When I Consider How My Light Is Spent _____ *1655*

When I consider how my light is spent,°
    Ere half my days in this dark world and wide,
    And that one Talent which is death to hide
    Lodged with me useless, though my Soul more bent

1 *how my light is spent:* Milton was completely blind by 1651.

To serve therewith my Maker, and present   5
   My true account, lest he returning chide,°
   "Doth God exact day labor, light denied?"°
I fondly° ask. But patience, to prevent
That murmur, soon replies, "God doth not need
   Either man's work or his own gifts. Who best   10
   Bear his mild yoke,° they serve him best. His State
Is Kingly. Thousands at his bidding speed
   And post o'er Land and Ocean without rest:
   They also serve who only stand and wait."

3–6 *And that one Talent . . . returning chide:* See the parable in Matt. 25:14–30, in which the "sloth-ful" servant, out of fear, hides his one talent (unit of money) rather than investing it, for which he is rebuked and punished.   7 *Doth . . . denied:* See John 9:4–5 and 12:35.   8 *fondly:* fool-ishly.   11 *yoke:* See Matt. 11:28–30, especially "For my yoke is easy."

JOHN MILTON   (1608–1674)

Sonnet 23: Methought I Saw My Late Espousèd Saint ————————— *1658*

Methought I saw my late espousèd Saint°
   Brought to me like Alcestis from the grave,
   Whom Jove's great Son to her glad Husband gave,
   Rescued from death by force though pale and faint.
Mine, as whom washed from spot of childbed taint,   5
   Purification in the old Law did save,°
   And such, as yet once more I trust to have
   Full sight of her° in Heaven without restraint,
Came vested all in white, pure as her mind:
   Her face was veiled, yet to my fancied sight,   10
   Love, sweetness, goodness, in her person shined
So clear, as in no face with more delight.
   But O, as to embrace me she inclined,
   I waked, she fled, and day brought back my night.

1 *late espousèd Saint:* spirit of his dead wife.   5–6 *Mine, as whom washed . . . Law did save:* In the Old Testament, women are considered unclean after childbirth and must be purified. Milton's first wife, Mary, died in childbirth; his second wife, Katherine, died after the feast of the Purification of the Virgin. Reference could be to either one.   8 *full sight of her:* If Milton is speaking of Kather-ine, he was blind when he married her.

CHENG MIN   (b. 1924)

Student ——————————————————————————————— *1972*

Translated from Chinese by Kenneth Rexroth and Ling Chung

I go one step forward,
Then stumble one step back.

I join the march
And then slip away to the sidelines.
I look at the posters on the left wall,   5
And the people gathered around them.
I look at the posters on the right wall,
And the people gathered around them.
They are like soldiers in two bunkers,
Shooting at one another   10
With arrows that fly away over my head.
O Socrates of the streets,
Where are you?
I heard that you can bring the young to face the truth
Like a shepherd who herds his sheep   15
Onto the right path,
Like a kind passerby
Who returns a lost child to its mother.
But why have you forgotten
This country more baffled than any other country,   20
This time more doubtful
Than any other time?
Here yes and no are indistinguishable
Like East and West at the Poles.
Here truth is a puppet   25
That doubles in two roles.
One self says, "Whatever is mine must be truth."
The other says, "When your 'whatever'
Becomes my 'whatever', then it is truth."
Truth becomes a tasty bait   30
To lure fish obsessed with books.
In their short-sighted, round eyes
They cannot see the many hooks of fraud.
Socrates, if you cannot reappear
In the network of streets   35
Of the Twentieth Century,
Why cannot truth become simply a baby
That laughs when it is happy,
And cries when it is hurt,
As if to tell me which is itself?   40

N. SCOTT MOMADAY   (b. 1934)

Comparatives _____ *1976*

Sunlit sea,
the drift of fronds,
and banners
of bobbing boats—
the seaside   5

of any day—
except: this
cold, bright body
of the fish
upon the planks,   10
the coil and
crescent of flesh
extending
just into death.

Even so,   15
in the distant,
inland sea,
a shadow runs,
radiant,
rude in the rock: 20
fossil fish,
fissure of bone
forever.

It is perhaps
the same thing,   25
an agony
twice perceived.

It is most like
wind on waves—
mere commotion,   30
mute and mean,
perceptible—
that is all.

MARIANNE MOORE   (1887–1972)

Poetry _____ *1924*

I, too, dislike it.
   Reading it, however, with a perfect contempt for it, one dis-
                                     covers in
   it, after all, a place for the genuine.

LARRY NEAL   (1938–1981)

Ghost Poem #1 _____ *1989*

You would never shoot smack°
or lay in one of these Harlem

1 *smack:* heroin.

doorways pissing on yourself
that is not your way not the
way of Alabama boys groomed slick   5
for these wicked cities momma
warned us of

You were always swifter than that:
the fast money was the Murphy game°
or the main supply before the cutting—   10
so now you lean with the shadows
(at the dark end of Turk's bar)
aware that the hitman is on your ass

You know that there is something inevitable
about it   15
You know that he will come as sure as shit
snorting blow° for courage
and he will burn° you at the peak of your peacocking
glory
And when momma gets the news   20
she will shudder over the evening meal
and moan: "Is that my Junie Boy runnin
with that fast crowd?"

9 *Murphy game:* being a dealer or merchant in drugs.   17 *blow:* cocaine.   18 *burn:* shoot.

SHARON OLDS   (b. 1942)

Things That Are Worse Than Death ———————————————— *1982*

> *For Margaret Randall*

You are speaking of Chile,
of the woman who was arrested
with her husband and their five-year-old son.
You tell how the guards tortured the woman, the man, the child,
in front of each other,   5
"as they like to do."
Things that are worse than death.
I can see myself taking my son's ash-blond hair in my fingers,
tilting back his head before he knows what is happening,
slitting his throat, slitting my own throat   10
to save us that. Things that are worse than death:
this new idea enters my life.
The guard enters my life, the sewage of his body,
"as they like to do." The eyes of the five-year-old boy, Dago,
watching them with his mother. The eyes of his mother   15
watching them with Dago. And in my living room as a child,
the word, Dago. And nothing I experienced was worse than death,

life was beautiful as our blood on the stone floor
to save us that—my son's eyes on me,
my eyes on my son—the ram-boar on our bodies   20
making us look at our old enemy and bow in welcome,
gracious and eternal death
who permits departure.

SHARON OLDS (b. 1942)

The One Girl at the Boys Party ————————————— *c. 1983*

When I take my girl to the swimming party
I set her down among the boys. They tower and
bristle, she stands there smooth and sleek,
her math scores unfolding in the air around her.
They will strip to their suits, her body hard and   5
indivisible as a prime number,
they'll plunge in the deep end, she'll subtract
her height from ten feet, divide it into
hundreds of gallons of water, the numbers
bouncing in her mind like molecules of chlorine   10
in the bright blue pool. When they climb out,
her ponytail will hang its pencil lead
down her back, her narrow silk suit
with hamburgers and french fries printed on it
will glisten in the brilliant air, and they will   15
see her sweet face, solemn and
sealed, a factor of one, and she will
see their eyes, two each,
their legs, two each, and the curves of their sexes,
one each, and in her head she'll be doing her   20
wild multiplying, as the drops
sparkle and fall to the power of a thousand from her body.

MARY OLIVER (b. 1935)

Some Questions You Might Ask ————————————— *1990*

Is the soul solid, like iron?
Or is it tender and breakable, like
the wings of a moth in the beak of the owl?
Who has it, and who doesn't?
I keep looking around me.   5
The face of the moose is as sad
as the face of Jesus.
The swan opens her white wings slowly.

In the fall, the black bear carries leaves into the darkness.
One question leads to another.   10
Does it have a shape? Like an iceberg?
Like the eye of a hummingbird?
Does it have one lung, like the snake and the scallop?
Why should I have it, and not the anteater
who loves her children?   15
Why should I have it, and not the camel?
Come to think of it, what about the maple trees?
What about the blue iris?
What about all the little stones, sitting alone in the moonlight?
What about roses, and lemons, and their shining leaves?   20
What about the grass?

MARY OLIVER   (b. 1935)

The Summer Day _____ *1990*

Who made the world?
Who made the swan, and the black bear?
Who made the grasshopper?
This grasshopper, I mean—
the one who has flung herself out of the grass,   5
the one who is eating sugar out of my hand,
who is moving her jaws back and forth instead of up and down—
who is gazing around with her enormous and complicated eyes.
Now she lifts her pale forearms and thoroughly washes her face.
Now she snaps her wings open, and floats away.   10
I don't know exactly what a prayer is.
I do know how to pay attention, how to fall down
into the grass, how to kneel down in the grass,
how to be idle and blessed, how to stroll through the fields,
which is what I have been doing all day.   15
Tell me, what else should I have done?
Doesn't everything die at last, and too soon?
Tell me, what is it you plan to do
with your one wild and precious life?

SIMON ORTIZ   (b. 1941)

Juanita, Wife of Manuelito _____ *c. 1976*

> *after seeing a photograph of her in Dine Baa-Hani*

I can see by your eyes
the gray in them like by Sonsela Butte,

the long ache
that comes about when I think
about where the road climbs   5
up onto the Roof Butte.

I can see
the whole sky
when it is ready to rain
over Whiskey Creek,   10
and a small girl
driving her sheep
and she looks so pretty
her hair tied up
with a length of yarn.   15

I can see
by the way you stare
out of a photograph
that you are a stern woman
informed by the history   20
of a long walk
and how it must have felt
to leave the canyons
and the mountains of your own land.

I can see, Navajo woman,   25
that it is possible for dreams
to occur, the prayers full of the mystery
of children, laughter, the dances,
my own humanity, so it can last unto forever.

That is what I want to teach my son.   30

WILFRED OWEN   (1893–1918)

Dulce et Decorum Est° _____ *1917*

Bent double, like old beggars under sacks,
Knock-kneed, coughing like hags, we cursed through sludge,
Till on the haunting flares we turned our backs
And towards our distant rest began to trudge.
Men marched asleep. Many had lost their boots   5
But limped on, blood-shod. All went lame; all blind;
Drunk with fatigue; deaf even to the hoots
Of tired, outstripped Five-Nines° that dropped behind.

Dulce et decorum est a phrase from Horace's line *Dulce et decorum est pro patria mori*—"It is sweet and fitting to die for one's country." Owen died fighting in World War I.   8 *Five-Nines:* shells containing poison gas.

Gas! GAS! Quick, boys!—An ecstasy of fumbling,
Fitting the clumsy helmets just in time;   5
But someone still was yelling out and stumbling,
And flound'ring like a man in fire or lime . . .
Dim, through the misty panes and thick green light,
As under a green sea, I saw him drowning.

In all my dreams, before my helpless sight,   10
He plunges at me, guttering, choking, drowning.

If in some smothering dreams you too could pace
Behind the wagon that we flung him in,
And watch the white eyes writhing in his face,
His hanging face, like a devil's sick of sin;   15
If you could hear, at every jolt, the blood
Come gargling from the froth-corrupted lungs,
Obscene as cancer, bitter as the cud
Of vile, incurable sores on innocent tongues,—
My friend, you would not tell with such high zest   20
To children ardent for some desperate glory,
The old Lie: Dulce et decorum est
Pro patria mori.

WILFRED OWEN   (1893–1918)

Arms and the Boy° _____ *1917*

Let the boy try along this bayonet-blade
How cold steel is, and keen with hunger of blood;
Blue with all malice, like a madman's flash;
And thinly drawn with famishing for flesh.

Lend him to stroke these blind, blunt bullet-leads,   5
Which long to nuzzle in the hearts of lads,
Or give him cartridges whose fine zinc teeth
Are sharp with sharpness of grief and death.

For his teeth seem for laughing round an apple.
There lurk no claws behind his fingers supple;   10
And God will grow no talons at his heels,
Nor antlers through the thickness of his curls.

Arms and the Boy: a play on a line from Virgil's heroic war poem the *Aeneid:* "Of arms and the man
I sing."

WILFRED OWEN   (1893–1918)

Spring Offensive _____ *1917*

Halted against the shade of a last hill
They fed, and eased of pack-loads, were at ease;

And leaning on the nearest chest or knees
Carelessly slept.
       But many there stood still
To face the stark blank sky beyond the ridge,   5
Knowing their feet had come to the end of the world.
Marvelling they stood, and watched the long grass swirled
By the May breeze, murmurous with wasp and midge;
And though the summer oozed into their veins
Like an injected drug for their bodies' pains,   10
Sharp on their souls hung the imminent ridge of grass,
Fearfully flashed the sky's mysterious glass.

Hour after hour they ponder the warm field
And the far valley behind, where buttercups
Had blessed with gold their slow boots coming up;   15
When even the little brambles would not yield
But clutched and clung to them like sorrowing arms.
They breathe like trees unstirred.

Till like a cold gust thrills the little word
At which each body and its soul begird   20
And tighten them for battle. No alarms
Of bugles, no high flags, no clamorous haste,—
Only a lift and flare of eyes that faced
The sun, like a friend with whom their love is done.
O larger shone that smile against the sun,—   25
Mightier than his whose bounty these have spurned.

So, soon they topped the hill, and raced together
Over an open stretch of herb and heather
Exposed. And instantly the whole sky burned
With fury against them; earth set sudden cups   30
In thousands for their blood; and the green slope
Chasmed and deepened sheer to infinite space.

Of them who running on that last high place
Breasted the surf of bullets, or went up
On the hot blast and fury of hell's upsurge,   35
Or plunged and fell away past this world's verge,
Some say God caught them even before they fell.

But what say such as from existence' brink
Ventured but drave° too swift to sink,
The few who rushed in the body to enter hell,   40
And there out-fiending all its fiends and flames
With superhuman inhumanities,
Long-famous glories, immemorial shames—
And crawling slowly back, have by degrees
Regained cool peaceful air in wonder—   45
Why speak not they of comrades that went under?

40 *drave:* drove.

DOROTHY PARKER (1893–1967)

General Review of the Sex Situation —————————————— *1926*

Woman wants monogamy;
Man delights in novelty.
Love is woman's moon and sun;
Man has other forms of fun.
Woman lives but in her lord;   5
Count to ten, and man is bored.
With this the gist and sum of it,
What earthly good can come of it?

DOROTHY PARKER (1893–1967)

Incurable —————————————————— *1928*

And if my heart be scarred and burned,
The safer, I, for all I learned;
The calmer, I, to see it true
That ways of love are never new—
The love that sets you daft and dazed   5
Is every love that ever blazed;
The happier, I, to fathom this:
A kiss is every other kiss.
The reckless vow, the lovely name,
When Helen° walked, were spoke the same;   10
The weighted breast, the grinding woe,
When Phaon° fled, were ever so.
Oh, it is sure as it is sad
That any lad is every lad,
And what's a girl, to dare implore   15
Her dear be hers forevermore?
Though he be tried and he be bold,
And swearing death should he be cold,
He'll run the path the others went. . . .
But you, my sweet, are different.   20

10 *Helen:* Helen of Troy, whose beauty started the Trojan War.   12 *Phaon:* supposedly a romantic interest of the poet Sappho.

DOROTHY PARKER (1893–1967)

Men —————————————————————— *1926*

They hail you as their morning star
Because you are the way you are.

If you return the sentiment,
They'll try to make you different;
And once they have you, safe and sound,   5
They want to change you all around.
Your moods and ways they put a curse on;
They'd make of you another person.
They cannot let you go your gait;
They influence and educate.   10
They'd alter all that they admired.
They make me sick, they make me tired.

DOROTHY PARKER   (1893–1967)

Observation _____ *1926*

If I don't drive around the park,
I'm pretty sure to make my mark.
If I'm in bed each night by ten,
I may get back my looks again.
If I abstain from fun and such,   5
I'll probably amount to much;
But I shall stay the way I am,
Because I do not give a damn.

DOROTHY PARKER   (1893–1967)

Symptom Recital _____ *1926*

I do not like my state of mind;
I'm bitter, querulous, unkind.
I hate my legs, I hate my hands,
I do not yearn for lovelier lands.
I dread the dawn's recurrent light;   5
I hate to go to bed at night.
I snoot at simple, earnest folk.
I cannot take the gentlest joke.
I find no peace in paint or type.
My world is but a lot of tripe.   10
I'm disillusioned, empty-breasted.
For what I think, I'd be arrested.
I am not sick, I am not well.
My quondam dreams are shot to hell.
My soul is crushed, my spirit sore;   15
I do not like me any more.
I cavil, quarrel, grumble, grouse.
I ponder on the narrow house.

I shudder at the thought of men. . . .
I'm due to fall in love again.   20

MARGE PIERCY (b. 1936)

The Secretary Chant ———————————————————— *1971*

My hips are a desk.
From my ears hang
chains of paper clips.
Rubber bands form my hair.
My breasts are wells of mimeograph ink.   5
My feet bear casters.
Buzz. Click.
My head
is a badly organized file.
My head is a switchboard   10
where crossed lines crackle.
My head is a wastebasket
of worn ideas.
Press my fingers
and in my eyes appear   15
credit and debit.
Zing. Tinkle.
My navel is a reject button.
From my mouth issue canceled reams.
Swollen, heavy, rectangular   20
I am about to be delivered
of a baby
xerox machine.
File me under W
because I wonce   25
was
a woman.

KATHA POLLITT (b. 1949)

The Old Neighbors ———————————————————— *1990*

The weather's turned, and the old neighbors creep out
from their crammed rooms to blink in the sun, as if
surprised to find they've lived through another winter.
Though steam heat's left them pale and shrunken
like old root vegetables,   5
Mr. and Mrs. Tozzi are already
hard at work on their front-yard mini-Sicily:

a Virgin-Mary birdbath, a thicket of roses,
and the only outdoor aloes in Manhattan.
It's the old immigrant story,   10
the beautiful babies
grown up into foreigners. Nothing's
turned out the way they planned
as sweethearts in the sinks of Palermo. Still,
each waves a dirt-caked hand   15
in geriatric fellowship with Stanley,
the former tattoo king of the Merchant Marine,
turning the corner with his shaggy collie,
who's hardly three but trots
arthritically in sympathy. It's only   20
the young who ask if life's worth living, not
Mrs. Sansanowitz, who for the last hour
has been inching her way down the sidewalk, lifting and placing
her new aluminum walker as carefully
as a spider testing its web. On days like these,   25
I stand for a long time
under the wild gnarled root of the ancient wisteria,
dry twigs that in a week
will manage a feeble shower of purple blossom,
and I believe it: this is all there is,   30
all history's brought us here to our only life
to find, if anywhere,
our hanging gardens° and our street of gold:
cracked stoops, geraniums, fire escapes, these old
stragglers basking in their bit of sun.   35

33 *hanging gardens:* a reference to biblical gardens of Babylon.

KATHA POLITT   (b. 1949)

In Memory ————————————————————— *c. 1982–1985*

> *"But can we not sometimes speak of a darkening (for example) of our memory-image?"*
> —*Wittgenstein*

Over the years, they've darkened, like old paintings
or wainscoting in a damp house in the country,
until now the streets where you roller-skated brim with twilight,
your mother drinks morning coffee from a cup of shadows,
and out in the garden, the hardest August noon   5
is washed with a tender, retrospective blue—
like woodsmoke, or the shade of an unseen lilac.
Upstairs, you can hardly make yourself out, a child
peering out the window, speechless with happiness,
reciting your future in an endless summer dusk.   10

At first, this maddened you. You wanted to see
your life as a rope of diamonds: permanent, flashing.
Strange, then, how lately this darkening of memory moves you,
as though what it claimed it also made more true,
the way discoloring varnish on a portrait   15
little by little engulfs the ornate background—
the overstuffed sofa, the velvet-and-gold festoons
framing an elegant vista—but only deepens
the calm and serious face. The speaking eyes.

ALEXANDER POPE   (1688–1744)

Ode on Solitude° _____ *c. 1700–1709*

Happy the man, whose wish and care
A few paternal acres bound,
Content to breathe his native air,
              In his own ground.

Whose herds with milk, whose fields with bread,   5
Whose flocks supply him with attire,
Whose trees in summer yield him shade,
              In winter fire.

Blest! who can unconcern'dly find
Hours, days, and years slide soft away,   10
In health of body, peace of mind,
              Quiet by day,

Sound sleep by night; study and ease
Together mixed; sweet recreation,
And innocence, which most does please,   15
              With meditation.

Thus let me live, unseen, unknown;
Thus unlamented let me die;
Steal from the world, and not a stone
              Tell where I lie.   20

Ode on Solitude: Pope said he wrote this when he was twelve (1700), but the manuscript dates to 1709.

EZRA POUND   (1885–1972)

Ancient Music _____ *1909(?)*

Winter is icummen in,°
Lhude sing Goddamm,

This is not folk music, but Dr. Ker writes that the tune is to be found under the Latin words of a
very ancient canon. [Pound's note]   1 *Winter is icummen in:* See "Sumer is icumen in," p. 518.

Raineth drop and staineth slop,
And how the wind doth ramm!
                    Sing: Goddamm.   5
Skiddeth bus and sloppeth us,
An ague hath my ham.
Freezeth river, turneth liver,
                    Damn you, sing: Goddamm.
Goddamm, Goddamm, 'tis why I am, Goddamm,   10
                    So 'gainst the winter's balm.
Sing goddamm, damm, sing Goddamm.
Sing goddamm, sing goddamm, DAMM.

EZRA POUND   (1885–1972)

The River-Merchant's Wife: A Letter° _____ *1915*

> *By Rihaku (Li T'ai Po)*

While my hair was still cut straight across my forehead
Played I about the front gate, pulling flowers.
You came by on bamboo stilts, playing horse,
You walked about my seat, playing with blue plums.
And we went on living in the village of Chōkan: 5
Two small people, without dislike or suspicion.

At fourteen I married My Lord you.
I never laughed, being bashful.
Lowering my head, I looked at the wall.
Called to, a thousand times, I never looked back.   10

At fifteen I stopped scowling,
I desired my dust to be mingled with yours
Forever and forever and forever.
Why should I climb the look out?

At sixteen you departed,   15
You went into far Ku-tō-en, by the river of swirling eddies,
And you have been gone five months.
The monkeys make sorrowful noise overhead.

You dragged your feet when you went out.
By the gate now, the moss is grown, the different mosses,   20
Too deep to clear them away!
The leaves fall early this autumn, in wind.
The paired butterflies are already yellow with August
Over the grass in the West garden;
They hurt me. I grow older.   25
If you are coming down through the narrows of the river Kiang,

Please let me know beforehand,
And I will come out to meet you
           As far as Chō-fū-Sa.

SIR WALTER RALEGH   (1552–1618)

The Nymph's Reply to the Shepherd° _____ *1600*

If all the world and love were young,
And truth in every shepherd's tongue,
These pretty pleasures might me move,
To live with thee and be thy love.

Time drives the flocks from field to fold,   5
When rivers rage, and rocks grow cold,
And Philomel° becometh dumb,
The rest complains of cares to come.

The flowers do fade, and wanton fields,
To wayward winter reckoning yields,   10
A honey tongue, a heart of gall,
Is fancy's spring, but sorrow's fall.

Thy gowns, thy shoes, thy beds of roses,
Thy cap, thy kirtle, and thy posies,
Soon break, soon wither, soon forgotten,   15
In folly ripe, in reason rotten.

The belt of straw and ivy buds,
Thy coral clasps and amber studs,
All these in me no means can move,
To come to thee, and be thy love.   20

But could youth last, and love still breed,
Had joys no date, nor age no need,
Then these delights my mind might move,
To live with thee, and be thy love.

The Nymph's Reply to the Shepherd: See Christopher Marlowe, "The Passionate Shepherd to His Love,"
p. 732.   7 *Philomel:* In Greek mythology, the princess whom the gods changed into a nightingale
after her brother-in-law raped her and cut out her tongue.

HENRY REED   (1914–1986)

Naming of Parts _____ *1946*

Today we have naming of parts. Yesterday,
We had daily cleaning. And tomorrow morning,
We shall have what to do after firing. But today,

Today we have naming of parts. Japonica
Glistens like coral in all of the neighboring gardens,   5
    And today we have naming of parts.

This is the lower sling swivel. And this
Is the upper sling swivel, whose use you will see,
When you are given your slings. And this is the piling swivel,
Which in your case you have not got. The branches   10
Hold in the gardens their silent, eloquent gestures,
    Which in our case we have not got.

This is the safety-catch, which is always released
With an easy flick of the thumb. And please do not let me
See anyone using his finger. You can do it quite easy   15
If you have any strength in your thumb. The blossoms
Are fragile and motionless, never letting anyone see
    Any of them using their finger.

And this you can see is the bolt. The purpose of this
Is to open the breech, as you see. We can slide it   20
Rapidly backwards and forwards: we call this
Easing the spring. And rapidly backwards and forwards
The early bees are assaulting and fumbling the flowers:
    They call it easing the Spring.

They call it easing the Spring: it is perfectly easy   25
If you have any strength in your thumb: like the bolt,
And the breech, and the cocking-piece, and the point of balance,
Which in our case we have not got; and the almond-blossom
Silent in all of the gardens and the bees going backwards and forwards,
    For today we have naming of parts.   30

CARTER REVARD   (b. 1931)

What the Eagle Fan Says° _____ *1992*

(For Bob and Evelyne Voelker, Dale and Arlene Besse, and the St. Louis Gourd Dancers.)

I strung dazzling thrones   of thunder beings
on a spiraling thread   of spinning flight,
beading dawn's blood   and blue of noon
to the gold and dark   of day's leaving,

What the Eagle Fan Says: This poem offers thanks for the honor of being given eagle feathers, which
were then set into a beaded fan. It tells how the eagle in flight pierces clouds just as a beadworker's
needle goes through beads and buckskin, spiraling round sky and fan-handle; and how the eagle
flies from dawn to sunset, linking day and night colors as they are linked on a Gourd Dancer's
blanket (half crimson, half blue), and just as they are beaded onto the handle of this eagle fan. In
such "riddles" ordinary things receive mysterious names: tree leaves are green *light-dancers,* wood
is *tree-heart* or *ash-heart,* clouds are *thrones of thunder beings.* Readers will decipher for themselves the
one-eyed serpent. [Revard's note]

circling with Sun
over turquoise eyes
her silver veins,
heard human relatives
calling me down,
that I bring them closer
and I turned from heaven
When the bullet came
the hunter's hands
loosened light beings
toward the sacred center
but fixed us first
that green light-dancers
ash-heart in hiding where
and a one-eyed serpent
strung tiny rattles
in beaded harmonies
now I move lightly
above dancing feet
around old songs
on human breath,

the soaring heaven   5
of Earth below,
her sable fur,
    hunting beneath
crying their need
    to Wakonda's° ways,   10
    to help them then.
it caught my heart,
gave earth its blood,
    and let us float
    of song in the drum,   15
firm in tree-heart
    gave to men's knives,
    a deer's heart had beat,
    with silver-straight head
around white softness   20
    of blue and red—
in a man's left hand,
follow the sun
soaring toward heaven
and I help them rise.   25

10 *Wakonda:* A spirit god.

ADRIENNE RICH (b. 1929)

Trying to Talk with a Man _____ *1971*

Out in this desert we are testing bombs,

that's why we came here.

Sometimes I feel an underground river
forcing its way between deformed cliffs
an acute angle of understanding   5
moving itself like a locus of the sun
into this condemned scenery.

What we've had to give up to get here—
whole LP collections, films we starred in
playing in the neighborhoods, bakery windows   10
full of dry, chocolate-filled Jewish cookies,
the language of love-letters, of suicide notes,
afternoons on the riverbank
pretending to be children

Coming out to this desert   15
we meant to change the face of
driving among dull green succulents

walking at noon in the ghost town
surrounded by a silence

that sounds like the silence of the place   20
except that it came with us
and is familiar
and everything we were saying until now
was an effort to blot it out—
coming out here we are up against it   25

Out here I feel more helpless
with you than without you
You mention the danger
and list the equipment
we talk of people caring for each other   30
in emergencies—laceration, thirst—
but you look at me like an emergency

Your dry heat feels like power
your eyes are stars of a different magnitude
they reflect lights that spell out: EXIT   35
when you get up and pace the floor

talking of the danger
as if it were not ourselves
as if we were testing anything else.

ADRIENNE RICH (b. 1929)

Diving into the Wreck° _____ *1973*

First having read the book of myths,
and loaded the camera,
and checked the edge of the knife-blade,
I put on
the body-armor of black rubber   5
the absurd flippers
the grave and awkward mask.
I am having to do this
not like Cousteau with his
assiduous team   10
aboard the sun-flooded schooner
but here alone.

There is a ladder.
The ladder is always there
hanging innocently   15
close to the side of the schooner.

We know what it is for,
we who have used it.
Otherwise
it's a piece of maritime floss   20
some sundry equipment.

I go down.
Rung after rung and still
the oxygen immerses me
the blue light   25
the clear atoms
of our human air.
I go down.
My flippers cripple me,
I crawl like an insect down the ladder   30
and there is no one
to tell me when the ocean
will begin.

First the air is blue and then
it is bluer and then green and then   35
black I am blacking out and yet
my mask is powerful
it pumps my blood with power
the sea is another story
the sea is not a question of power   40
I have to learn alone
to turn my body without force
in the deep element.

And now: it is easy to forget
what I came for   45
among so many who have always
lived here
swaying their crenellated fans
between the reefs
and besides   50
you breathe differently down here.

I came to explore the wreck.
The words are purposes.
The words are maps.
I came to see the damage that was done   55
and the treasures that prevail.
I stroke the beam of my lamp
slowly along the flank
of something more permanent
than fish or weed   60

the thing I came for:
the wreck and not the story of the wreck

the thing itself and not the myth
the drowned face always staring
toward the sun   65
the evidence of damage
worn by salt and sway into this threadbare beauty
the ribs of the disaster
curving their assertion
among the tentative haunters.   70

This is the place.
And I am here, the mermaid whose dark hair
streams black, the merman in his armored body
We circle silently
about the wreck   75
we dive into the hold.
I am she: I am he

whose drowned face sleeps with open eyes
whose breasts still bear the stress
whose silver, copper, vermeil cargo lies   80
obscurely inside barrels
half-wedged and left to rot
we are the half-destroyed instruments
that once held to a course
the water-eaten log   85
the fouled compass

We are, I am, you are
by cowardice or courage
the one who find our way
back to this scene   90
carrying a knife, a camera
a book of myths
in which
our names do not appear.

EDWIN ARLINGTON ROBINSON   (1869–1935)

Richard Cory _____ *1897*

Whenever Richard Cory went down town,
We people on the pavement looked at him:
He was a gentleman from sole to crown,
Clean favored, and imperially slim.

And he was always quietly arrayed,   5
And he was always human when he talked;
But still he fluttered pulses when he said,
"Good-morning," and he glittered when he walked.

And he was rich—yes, richer than a king—
And admirably schooled in every grace: 10
In fine, we thought that he was everything
To make us wish that we were in his place.

So on we worked, and waited for the light,
And went without the meat, and cursed the bread;
And Richard Cory, one calm summer night,   15
Went home and put a bullet through his head.

THEODORE ROETHKE   (1907–1963)

Elegy for Jane ———————————————————————— *1953*

My Student, Thrown by a Horse

I remember the neckcurls, limp and damp as tendrils;
And her quick look, a sidelong pickerel smile;
And how, once startled into talk, the light syllables leaped for her,
And she balanced in the delight of her thought,
A wren, happy, tail into the wind,   5
Her song trembling the twigs and small branches.
The shade sang with her;
The leaves, their whispers turned to kissing;
And the mold sang in the bleached valleys under the rose.

Oh, when she was sad, she cast herself down into such a pure depth,   10
Even a father could not find her:
Scraping her cheek against straw;
Stirring the clearest water.

My sparrow, you are not here,
Waiting like a fern, making a spiny shadow.   15
The sides of wet stones cannot console me,
Nor the moss, wound with the last light.

If only I could nudge you from this sleep,
My maimed darling, my skittery pigeon.
Over this damp grave I speak the words of my love: 20
I, with no rights in this matter,
Neither father nor lover.

THEODORE ROETHKE   (1907–1963)

My Papa's Waltz ———————————————————————— *1948*

The whiskey on your breath
Could make a small boy dizzy;

But I hung on like death:
Such waltzing was not easy.

We romped until the pans   5
Slid from the kitchen shelf;
My mother's countenance
Could not unfrown itself.

The hand that held my wrist
Was battered on one knuckle;   10
At every step you missed
My right ear scraped a buckle.

You beat time on my head
With a palm caked hard by dirt,
Then waltzed me off to bed   15
Still clinging to your shirt.

CHRISTINA ROSSETTI (1830–1894)

Song ———————————————————————— *1848*

When I am dead, my dearest,
   Sing no sad songs for me;
Plant thou no roses at my head,
   Nor shady cypress tree:
Be the green grass above me   5
   With showers and dewdrops wet:
And if thou wilt, remember,
   And if thou wilt, forget.

I shall not see the shadows,
   I shall not feel the rain;   10
I shall not hear the nightingale
   Sing on as if in pain:
And dreaming through the twilight
   That doth not rise nor set,
Haply I may remember,   15
   And haply may forget.

CHRISTINA ROSSETTI (1830–1894)

Remember ———————————————————————— *1849*

Remember me when I am gone away,

   Gone far away into the silent land;
   When you can no more hold me by the hand,

Nor I half turn to go yet turning stay.
Remember me when no more day by day 5
   You tell me of our future that you planned:
   Only remember me: you understand
It will be late to counsel then or pray.
Yet if you should forget me for a while
   And afterwards remember, do not grieve: 10
   For if the darkness and corruption leave
   A vestige of the thoughts that once I had,
Better by far you should forget and smile
   Than that you should remember and be sad.

CHRISTINA ROSSETTI   (1830–1894)

Echo _____ *1854*

Come to me in the silence of the night;
   Come in the sleeping silence of a dream;
Come with soft rounded cheeks and eyes as bright
   As sunlight on a stream;
      Come back in tears, 5
O memory, hope, love of finished years.

O dream how sweet, too sweet, too bitter sweet,
   Whose wakening should have been in Paradise,
Where souls brimfull of love abide and meet,
   Where thirsting longful eyes 10
      Watch the slow door
That opening, letting in, lets out no more.

Yet come to me in dreams, that I may live
   My very life again though cold in death:
Come back to me in dreams, that I may give 15
   Pulse for pulse, breath for breath:
      Speak low, lean low,
As long ago, my love, how long ago.

CHRISTINA ROSSETTI   (1830–1894)

In an Artist's Studio _____ *1856*

One face looks out from all his canvases,
   One selfsame figure sits or walks or leans:
   We found her hidden just behind those screens,
That mirror gave back all her loveliness.
A queen in opal or in ruby dress, 5
   A nameless girl in freshest summer-greens,

A saint, an angel—every canvas means
The same one meaning, neither more nor less.
He feeds upon her face by day and night,
    And she with true kind eyes looks back on him,   10
Fair as the moon and joyful as the light:
    Not wan with waiting, not with sorrow dim;
Not as she is, but was when hope shone bright;
    Not as she is, but as she fills his dream.

MURIEL RUKEYSER (1913–1980)

Myth ———————————————————————————— *1973*

Long afterward, Oedipus,° old and blinded, walked the
roads.   He smelled a familiar smell.   It was
the Sphinx.   Oedipus said, "I want to ask one question.
Why didn't I recognize my mother?"   "You gave the
wrong answer," said the Sphinx.   "But that was what   5
made everything possible," said Oedipus.   "No," she said.
"When I asked, What walks on four legs in the morning,
two at noon, and three in the evening, you answered,
Man.   You didn't say anything about woman."
"When you say Man," said Oedipus, "you include women   10
too. Everyone knows that."   She said, "That's what
you think."

1 *Oedipus:* See Sophocles' *Oedipus Rex* in the section on drama. By solving the riddle of the Sphinx, Oedipus moved closer to his fate, which was to marry his own mother.

LÉOPOLD SÉDAR SENGHOR (b. 1906)

Night of Sine° ———————————————————————— *1975*

    Translated by Ellen Conroy Kennedy

Woman, rest your balsam hands upon my brow, softer your hands are
    than fur.
Above, the swaying palms rustle faintly in the evening breeze.
Not quite a lullaby.
May the rhythmic silence cradle us.
Let us listen to its song, listen to our dark blood beat,   5
Let us listen to it beat, the deep pulse beat of Africa in the mist of lost
    villages.

Lazily the moon inclines into her slack sea bed.
Laughter dies away, and even storytellers

Sine: a river; also the province where Senghor was born.

Begin to nod their heads like sleepy children dozing on their mothers'
    backs.
The dancers' feet grow heavy now, as the alternating choirs cease.   10

It's star time, and dreamily the Night leans her elbows on this cloudy
    hill, draped in her long, milky robe.
Tenderly the rooftops gleam. What are they confiding to the stars?
Within, the fire burns low in the privacy of odors sharp and sweet.
Woman, light the limpid butter lamp, so around it ancestors can come
    to chat like parents when their children are in bed.
Let us listen to the ancients of Elissa.° Exiled, like us.   15
They did not wish to die, or lose their fertile torrent in the sands.
Let me listen in the smoky hut where friendly souls have come to visit,
My head upon your breast, warm as couscous newly steaming from the
    fire.
Let me breathe the odor of our Dead, let me gather and repeat their
    living voices, let me learn
To live before I sink, deeper than a diver, into the lofty depths of
    sleep.   20

15 *Elissa:* the home of Senghor's ancestors.

ANNE SEXTON (1928–1974)

Red Riding Hood ——————————————————— *1971*

Many are the deceivers:

The suburban matron,
proper in the supermarket,
list in hand so she won't suddenly fly,
buying her Duz and Chuck Wagon dog food,   5
meanwhile ascending from earth,
letting her stomach fill up with helium,
letting her arms go loose as kite tails,
getting ready to meet her lover
a mile down Apple Crest Road   10
in the Congregational Church parking lot.

Two seemingly respectable women
come up to an old Jenny
and show her an envelope
full of money   15
and promise to share the booty
if she'll give them ten thou
as an act of faith.
Her life savings are under the mattress
covered with rust stains   20
and counting.

They are as wrinkled as prunes
but negotiable.
The two women take the money and disappear.
Where is the moral?   25
Not all knives are for
stabbing the exposed belly.
Rock climbs on rock
and it only makes a seashore.
Old Jenny has lost her belief in mattresses   30
and now she has no wastebasket in which
to keep her youth.

The standup comic
on the "Tonight" show
who imitates the Vice President   35
and cracks up Johnny Carson
and delays sleep for millions
of bedfellows watching between their feet,
slits his wrist the next morning
in the Algonquin's° old-fashioned bathroom,   40
the razor in his hand like a toothbrush,
wall as anonymous as a urinal,
the shower curtain his slack rubberman audience,
and then the slash
as simple as opening a letter   45
and the warm blood breaking out like a rose
upon the bathtub with its claw and ball feet.

And I. I too.
Quite collected at cocktail parties,
meanwhile in my head   50
I'm undergoing open-heart surgery.
The heart, poor fellow,
pounding on his little tin drum
with a faint death beat.
The heart, that eyeless beetle,   55
enormous that Kafka beetle,°
running panicked through his maze,
never stopping one foot after the other
one hour after the other
until he gags on an apple   60
and it's all over.

And I. I too again.
I built a summer house on Cape Ann.
A simple A-frame and this too was
a deception—nothing haunts a new house.   65

40 *Algonquin:* a hotel in New York's theater district.   56 *Kafka beetle:* Franz Kafka's *Metamorphosis* begins with a character who wakes up as a cockroach.

When I moved in with a bathing suit and tea bags
the ocean rumbled like a train backing up
and at each window secrets came in
like gas. My mother, that departed soul,
sat in my Eames chair° and reproached me   70
for losing her keys to the old cottage.
Even in the electric kitchen there was
the smell of a journey. The ocean
was seeping through its frontiers
and laying me out on its wet rails.   75
The bed was stale with my childhood
and I could not move to another city
where the worthy make a new life.

Long ago
there was a strange deception: 80
a wolf dressed in frills,
a kind of transvestite.
But I get ahead of my story.
In the beginning
there was just little Red Riding Hood,   85
so called because her grandmother
made her a red cape and she was never without it.
It was her Linus blanket, besides
it was red, as red as the Swiss flag,
yes it was red, as red as chicken blood.   90
But more than she loved her riding hood
she loved her grandmother who lived
far from the city in the big wood.

This one day her mother gave her
a basket of wine and cake   95
to take to her grandmother
because she was ill.
Wine and cake?
Where's the aspirin? The penicillin?
Where's the fruit juice?   100
Peter Rabbit got camomile tea.
But wine and cake it was.

On her way in the big wood
Red Riding Hood met the wolf.
Good day, Mr. Wolf, she said,   105
thinking him no more dangerous
than a streetcar or a panhandler.
He asked where she was going
and she obligingly told him.
There among the roots and trunks   110
with the mushrooms pulsing inside the moss

70 *Eames chair:* expensive metal and leather designer chair by Charles Eames.

he planned how to eat them both,
the grandmother an old carrot
and the child a shy budkin
in a red red hood.   115
He bade her to look at the bloodroot,
the small bunchberry and the dogtooth
and pick some for her grandmother.
And this she did.
Meanwhile he scampered off   120
to Grandmother's house and ate her up
as quick as a slap.
Then he put on her nightdress and cap
and snuggled down into the bed.
A deceptive fellow.   125

Red Riding Hood
knocked on the door and entered
with her flowers, her cake, her wine.
Grandmother looked strange,
a dark and hairy disease it seemed.   130
Oh Grandmother, what big ears you have,
ears, eyes, hands and then the teeth.
The better to eat you with, my dear.
So the wolf gobbled Red Riding Hood down
like a gumdrop. Now he was fat.   135
He appeared to be in his ninth month
and Red Riding Hood and her grandmother
rode like two Jonahs up and down with
his every breath. One pigeon. One partridge.

He was fast asleep,   140
dreaming in his cap and gown
wolfless.
Along came a huntsman who heard
the loud contented snores
and knew that was no grandmother.   145
He opened the door and said,
So it's you, old sinner.
He raised his gun to shoot him
when it occurred to him that maybe
the wolf had eaten up the old lady.   150
So he took a knife and began cutting open
the sleeping wolf, a kind of caesarian section.

It was a carnal knife that let
Red Riding Hood out like a poppy,
quite alive from the kingdom of the belly.   155
And grandmother too
still waiting for cakes and wine.
The wolf, they decided, was too mean

to be simply shot so they filled his belly
with large stones and sewed him up. 160
He was as heavy as a cemetery
and when he woke up and tried to run off
he fell over dead. Killed by his own weight.
Many a deception ends on such a note.

The huntsman and the grandmother and Red Riding Hood 165
sat down by his corpse and had a meal of wine and cake.
Those two remembering
nothing naked and brutal
from that little death,
that little birth, 170
from their going down
and their lifting up.

WILLIAM SHAKESPEARE   (1564–1616)

Sonnet 18: Shall I Compare Thee to a Summer's Day? _____ *1609*

Shall I compare thee to a summer's day?
Thou art more lovely and more temperate:
Rough winds do shake the darling buds of May,
And summer's lease hath all too short a date;
Sometime too hot the eye of heaven shines, 5
And often is his gold complexion dimmed,
And every fair from fair° sometime declines,
By chance or nature's changing course untrimmed:
But thy eternal summer shall not fade,
Nor lose possession of that fair thou ow'st,° 10
Nor shall Death brag thou wand'rest in his shade,
When in eternal lines to time thou grow'st.
　　So long as men can breathe or eyes can see,
　　So long lives this, and this gives life to thee.

7 *fair . . . fair:* Every beautiful thing ceases to be beautiful.　　10 *ow'st:* ownest.

WILLIAM SHAKESPEARE   (1564–1616)

Sonnet 30: When to the Sessions of Sweet Silent Thought _____ *1609*

When to the sessions° of sweet silent thought
I summon up remembrance of things past,
I sigh the lack of many a thing I sought,
And with old woes new wail my dear time's waste;

1 *sessions:* sessions of a law court.

Then can I drown an eye (unused to flow)   5
For precious friends hid in death's dateless° night,
And weep afresh love's long since cancelled° woe,
And moan the expense° of many a vanished sight;
Then can I grieve at grievances foregone,
And heavily° from woe to woe tell o'er   10
The sad account of fore-bemoanèd moan,
Which I new pay as if not paid before:
    But if the while I think on thee, dear friend,
    All losses are restored, and sorrows end.

6 *dateless:* timeless.   7 *cancelled:* paid for.   8 *expense:* loss.   10 *heavily:* sadly.

WILLIAM SHAKESPEARE   (1564–1616)

Sonnet 64: When I Have Seen by Time's Fell Hand Defaced _____ *1609*

When I have seen by Time's fell hand defaced
The rich proud cost of outworn buried age;
When sometime lofty towers I see down-razed
And brass eternal slave to mortal rage;
When I have seen the hungry ocean gain   5
Advantage on the kingdom of the shore,
And the firm soil win of the wat'ry main
Increasing store with loss and loss with store;
When I have seen such interchange of state,
Or state itself confounded to decay,   10
Ruin hath taught me thus to ruminate
That Time will come and take my love away.
    This thought is as a death, which cannot choose
    But weep to have that which it fears to lose.

WILLIAM SHAKESPEARE   (1564–1616)

Sonnet 106: When in the Chronicle of Wasted Time _____ *1609*

When in the chronicle of wasted time
I see descriptions of the fairest wights,
And beauty making beautiful old rhyme
In praise of ladies dead and lovely knights,
Then in the blazon of sweet beauty's best,   5
Of hand, of foot, of lip, of eye, of brow,
I see their antique pen would have expressed
Even such a beauty as you master now.
So all their praises are but prophecies
Of this our time, all you prefiguring,   10

And for° they looked but with divining° eyes,
They had not still enough your worth to sing:
   For we which now behold these present days
   Have eyes to wonder, but lack tongues to praise.

11 *for:* because.   *divining:* guessing.

WILLIAM SHAKESPEARE   (1564–1616)

Sonnet 116: Let Me Not to the Marriage of True Minds _____ *1609*

Let me not to the marriage of true minds
Admit impediments; love is not love
Which alters when it alteration finds,
Or bends with the remover to remove.
O no, it is an ever-fixèd mark   5
That looks on tempests and is never shaken;
It is the star to every wandering bark,
Whose worth's unknown, although his height be taken.
Love's not Time's fool, though rosy lips and cheeks
Within his bending sickle's compass come;   10
Love alters not with his brief hours and weeks,
But bears it out even to the edge of doom.
   If this be error and upon me proved,
   I never writ, nor no man ever loved.

WILLIAM SHAKESPEARE   (1564–1616)

Sonnet 129: The Expense of Spirit in a Waste of Shame _____ *1609*

The expense of spirit° in a waste of shame
Is lust in action, and till action,° lust
Is perjured, murderous, bloody, full of blame,
Savage, extreme, rude, cruel, not to trust,
Enjoyed no sooner but despisèd straight,°   5
Past reason° hunted, and no sooner had,
Past reason hated as a swallowed bait
On purpose laid to make the taker mad:
Mad in pursuit and in possession so,
Had, having, and in quest to have, extreme,   10
A bliss in proof,° and proved, a very woe,
Before, a joy proposed; behind, a dream.
   All this the world well knows, yet none knows well
   To shun the heaven that leads men to this hell.

1 *expense of spirit:* ejaculation of semen, or any waste of vitality.   2 *till action:* until consummation.   5 *straight:* immediately.   6 *past reason:* madly.   11 *in proof:* while being experienced, tested.

WILLIAM SHAKESPEARE   (1564–1616)

Sonnet 130: My Mistress' Eyes Are Nothing like the Sun _____ *1609*

My mistress' eyes are nothing like the sun;
Coral is far more red than her lips' red;
If snow be white, why then her breasts are dun;
If hairs be wires, black wires grow on her head.
I have seen roses damasked, red and white,   5
But no such roses see I in her cheeks;

And in some perfumes is there more delight
Than in the breath that from my mistress reeks.
I love to hear her speak, yet well I know
That music hath a far more pleasing sound.   10
I grant I never saw a goddess go;
My mistress, when she walks, treads on the ground.
　　And yet, by heaven, I think my love as rare
　　As any she belied with false compare.

WILLIAM SHAKESPEARE   (1564–1616)

Sonnet 135: Whoever Hath Her Wish, Thou Hast Thy Will _____ *1609*

Whoever hath her wish, thou hast thy Will,°
And Will to boot,° and Will in overplus;
More than enough am I that vex thee still,
To thy sweet will making addition thus.°
Wilt thou, whose will is large and spacious,   5
Not once vouchsafe to hide my will in thine?
Shall will in others seem right gracious,
And in my will no fair acceptance shine?
The sea, all water, yet receives rain still,
And in abundance addeth to his store,   10
So thou being rich in Will add to thy Will
One will of mine to make thy large Will more.
　　Let no unkind, no fair beseechers kill;
　　Think all but one, and me in that one Will.

1 *Will:* Shakespeare puns on his name, on will as lustful desire.   2 *to boot:* in addition.   4 *making addition thus:* that is, by adding him.

WILLIAM SHAKESPEARE   (1564–1616)

Sonnet 144: Two Loves I Have of Comfort and Despair _____ *1609*

Two loves I have of comfort and despair,
Which like two spirits do suggest me still:°

2 *suggest me still:* always tempt me.

The better angel is a man right fair,
The worser spirit a woman colored ill.°
To win me soon to hell, my female evil   5
Tempteth my better angel from my side,
And would corrupt my saint to be a devil,
Wooing his purity with her foul pride.°
And whether that my angel be turned fiend
Suspect I may, yet not directly tell,   10
But being both from me, both to each friend,°
I guess one angel in another's hell.
Yet this shall I ne'er know, but live in doubt,
Till my bad angel fire my good one out.°

4 *colored ill:* a brunette.   8 *pride:* sexual desire.   11 *both to each friend:* friends to one
another.   14 *fire . . . out:* reject, or give venereal disease to (which would prove they slept
together).

FILY-DABO SISSOKO   (1900–1964)

Brush Fire ————————————————————————— *1964*

Translated by Ellen Conroy Kennedy

At the onset of its sprint, the blazing circle climbs straight ahead, flood-
    ing the sky with globules of fire, dancing a saraband to dazzled eyes.

Beaten down in the last strong gusts, grasses carpet the underbrush in
    yellow. Shivering beneath, one feels the teeming life of animals and
    serpents, wild and small.

Come hunter or honey-seeker, the brush fire lights.

From crackling to crackling, closer and closer it tongues its way. Green
    grasshoppers, dizzy butterflies take flight. The wind rises, the trees
    howl death. Sheets of flame, suddenly tall, spring in gusts to storm
    the summits.

Nothing will stop the brush fire's furious race. Jumping over the thin
    curtain of greenery that runs along the riverbanks, it crosses streams,
    frightening does and palm-squirrels, pythons and panthers, cobras
    and elk.   5

Up to the naked foot of cliffs it creeps, to do final battle there with some
    fallen veteran whose ashes, dragged afar, will whiten the burnt earth.

Then, at night, here and there along the length of the horizon, one sees
    upon the slopes great spots of flame flickering in the debris.

For long days, brush fire has overcome the steppe.

CHARLOTTE SMITH   (1749–1806)

Pressed by the Moon, Mute Arbitress of Tides _____ *1786*

Written in the churchyard at Middleton in Sussex

Pressed by the moon, mute arbitress of tides,
   While the loud equinox° its power combines,
   The sea no more its swelling surge confines,
But o'er the shrinking land sublimely rides.
The wild blast, rising from the western cave,   5
   Drives the huge billows from their heaving bed,
   Tears from their grassy tombs the village dead,
And breaks the silent sabbath° of the grave!
With shells and seaweed mingled, on the shore
   Lo! their bones whiten in the frequent wave;   10
   But vain to them the winds and waters rave;
They hear the warring elements no more:
While I am doomed—by life's long storm oppressed,
To gaze with envy on their gloomy rest.

2 *equinox:* March 21 or September 21, when days and nights are equal. The March equinox is often marked by strong winds in England.   8 *sabbath:* peace, rest.

STEVIE SMITH   (1902–1971)

The Galloping Cat _____ *1966*

Oh I am a cat that likes to
Gallop about doing good
So
One day when I was
Galloping about doing good, I saw   5
A Figure in the path; I said:
Get off! (Be-
cause
I am a cat that likes to
Gallop about doing good)   10
But he did not move, instead
He raised his hand as if
To land me a cuff
So I made to dodge so as to
Prevent him bringing it orf,   15
Un-for-tune-ately I slid
On a banana skin
Some Ass had left instead
Of putting in the bin. So
His hand caught me on the cheek   20

I tried
To lay his arm open from wrist to elbow
With my sharp teeth
Because I am
A cat that likes to gallop about doing good.   25
Would you believe it?
He wasn't there
My teeth met nothing but air,
But a Voice said: Poor cat,
(Meaning me) and a soft stroke   30
Came on me head
Since when
I have been bald.
I regard myself as
A martyr to doing good.   35
Also I heard a swoosh
As of wings, and saw
A halo shining at the height of
Mrs Gubbins's backyard fence,
So I thought: What's the good   40
Of galloping about doing good
When angels stand in the path
And do not do as they should
Such as having an arm to be bitten off
All the same I   45
Intend to go on being
A cat that likes to
Gallop about doing good
So
Now with my bald head I go,   50
Chopping the untidy flowers down, to and fro,
An' scooping up the grass to show
Underneath
The cinder path of wrath
Ha ha ha ha, ho,   55
Angels aren't the only ones who do not know
What's what and that
Galloping about doing good
Is a full-time job
That needs   60
An experienced eye of earthly
Sharpness, worth I dare say
(If you'll forgive a personal note)
A good deal more
Than all that skyey stuff   65
Of angels that make so bold as
To pity a cat like me that
Gallops about doing good.

STEVIE SMITH   (1902–1971)

Scorpion _____ *1971*

"This night shall thy soul be required of thee"°
My soul is never required of *me*
It always has to be somebody else of course
Will my soul be required of me tonight perhaps?

(I often wonder what it will be like   5
To have one's soul required of one
But all I can think of is the Out-Patients' Department—
"Are you Mrs. Briggs, dear?"
No, I am Scorpion.)

I should like my soul to be required of me, so as   10
To waft over grass till it comes to the blue sea

I am very fond of grass, I always have been, but there must
Be no cow, person or house to be seen.

Sea and *grass* must be quite empty
Other souls can find somewhere else.   15

O Lord God please come
And require the soul of thy Scorpion

Scorpion so wishes to be gone.

1 *"This night . . . thee":* Christ's parable of the rich man, Luke 12:13–21, reminding him that his death may be imminent.

STEVIE SMITH   (1902–1971)

Away, Melancholy _____ *1957*

Away, melancholy,
Away with it, let it go.

Are not the trees green,
The earth as green?
Does not the wind blow,   5
Fire leap and the rivers flow?
Away melancholy.

The ant is busy
He carrieth his meat,
All things hurry   10
To be eaten or eat.
Away, melancholy.

Man, too, hurries,
Eats, couples, buries,
He is an animal also   15
With a hey ho melancholy,
Away with it, let it go.

Man of all creatures
Is superlative
(Away melancholy)   20
He of all creatures alone
Raiseth a stone
(Away melancholy)
Into the stone, the god,
Pours what he knows of good   25
Calling good, God.
Away melancholy, let it go.

Speak not to me of tears,
Tyranny, pox, wars,
Saying, Can God   30
Stone of man's thought, be good?

Say rather it is enough
That the stuffed
Stone of man's good, growing,
By man's called God.   35
Away, melancholy, let it go.

Man aspires
To good,
To love
Sighs;   40

Beaten, corrupted, dying
In his own blood lying
Yet heaves up an eye above
Cries, Love, love.
It is his virtue needs explaining,   45
Not his failing.

Away, melancholy,
Away with it, let it go.

GARY SNYDER   (b. 1930)

Riprap _____ *1965*

Lay down these words
Before your mind like rocks
            placed solid, by hands

In choice of place, set
Before the body of the mind   5
        in space and time:
Solidity of bark, leaf, or wall
        riprap of things:
Cobble of milky way,
        straying planets,   10
These poems, people,
        lost ponies with
Dragging saddles
        and rocky sure-foot trails.
The worlds like an endless   15
        four-dimensional
Game of *Go*.
        ants and pebbles
In the thin loam, each rock a word
        a creek-washed stone   20
Granite: ingrained
        with torment of fire and weight
Crystal and sediment linked hot
        all change, in thoughts,
As well as things.   25

CATHY SONG   (b. 1955)

The Youngest Daughter —————————————— *c. 1983*

The sky has been dark
for many years.
My skin has become as damp
and pale as rice paper
and feels the way   5
mother's used to before the drying sun
parched it out there in the fields.

    Lately, when I touch my eyelids,
my hands react as if
I had just touched something   10
hot enough to burn.
My skin, aspirin colored,
tingles with migraine. Mother
has been massaging the left side of my face
especially in the evenings   15
when the pain flares up.

This morning
her breathing was graveled,
her voice gruff with affection

when I wheeled her into the bath.   20
She was in a good humor,
making jokes about her great breasts,
floating in the milky water
like two walruses,
flaccid and whiskered around the nipples.   25
I scrubbed them with a sour taste
in my mouth, thinking:
six children and an old man
have sucked from these brown nipples.

I was almost tender   30
when I came to the blue bruises
that freckle her body,
places where she has been injecting insulin
for thirty years. I soaped her slowly,
she sighed deeply, her eyes closed.   35
It seems it has always
been like this: the two of us
in this sunless room,
the splashing of the bathwater.

In the afternoons   40
when she has rested,
she prepares our ritual of tea and rice,
garnished with a shred of gingered fish,
a slice of pickled turnip,
a token for my white body.   45
We eat in the familiar silence.
She knows I am not to be trusted,
even now planning my escape.
As I toast to her health
with the tea she has poured,   50
a thousand cranes curtain the window,
fly up in a sudden breeze.

MARCIA SOUTHWICK   (b. 1949)

Owning a Dead Man ——————————————————————— *c. 1980*

The geese fly off, but sometimes they don't take
their voices with them. Stretched out like this,
I think my future is simple, like a cornfield
filling with light. I'm happy,
because of the way the geese have left their shadows   5
drying on the lawn around me, and the way
the long docks lean out into the water,
letting the unpainted boats knock against them.
Once, my mother told me, a woman came to this place

with an urn that held her dead husband's ashes.   10
The woman's pale hands tossed bits of gray-white
bone and soot onto the marsh, where the quail hid.
My mother was angry that the bones had trespassed
her land. *In a way,* she said, *I own a dead man.*

Now as I lie here, I think of the coming winter,   15
of his bones, mixed with the bones of the mouse
and the gull, cleansed and shining in the new snow,
but if I try to think too deeply, it's as if a bird
were pulling straws from a dried out nest!
So I wonder if I have ever witnessed the middle   20
of winter: the birch trees' inability to lose
anything more, or if I have ever seen myself
as more irrelevant than in December—
In that cold and stillness, my blood
and my muscles contracting as I tramp through the snow   25
couldn't possibly mean anything. And there are days
when a landscape feels nothing for its real trees,
only for what lies still in the snow,
or only for what has been.

MAURA STANTON   (b. 1946)

Childhood _____ *1984*

I used to lie on my back, imagining
A reverse house on the ceiling of my house
Where I could walk around in empty rooms
All by myself. There was no furniture
Up there, only a glass globe in the floor,   5
And knee-high barriers at every door.
The low silled windows opened on blue air.
Nothing hung in the closet; even the kitchen
Seemed immaculate, a place for thought.
I liked to walk across the swirling plaster   10
Into the parts of the house I couldn't see.
The hum from the other house, now my ceiling,
Reached me only faintly. I'd look up
To find my brothers watching old cartoons,
Or my mother vacuuming the ugly carpet.   15
I'd stare amazed at unmade beds, the clutter,
Shoes, half-dressed dolls, the telephone,
Then return dizzily to my perfect floorplan
Where I never spoke or listened to anyone.

I must have turned down the wrong hall,   20
Or opened a door that locked shut behind me,

For I live on the ceiling now, not the floor.
This is my house, room after empty room.
How do I ever get back to the real house
Where my sisters spill milk, my father calls,   25
And I am at the table, eating cereal?
I fill my white rooms with furniture,
Hang curtains over the piercing blue outside.
I lie on my back. I strive to look down.
This ceiling is higher than it used to be,   30
The floor so far away I can't determine
Which room I'm in, which year, which life.

GEORGE STARBUCK   (b. 1931)

On First Looking In On Blodgett's Keats's "Chapman's Homer"°___ *1960*

(Sum. ½C. M9–II)°

Mellifluous as bees,° these brittle men
droning of Honeyed Homer give me hives.
I scratch, yawn like a bear, my arm arrives
at yours—oh, Honey, and we're back again,
me the Balboa, you the Darien,   5
lording the loud Pacific sands, our lives
as hazarded as when a petrel dives
to yank the dull sea's coverlet, or when,

breaking from me across the sand that's rink
and record of our weekend boning up   10
on *The Romantic Agony,*° you sink
John Keats a good surf-fisher's cast out—plump
in the sun's wake—and the parched pages drink
that great whales' blanket party hump and hump.

On First . . . "Chapman's Homer": Blodgett is an edition of Keats.   *(Sum. ½C. M9–II):* a comic reference to the source of the poem.   1 *Mellifluous as bees:* buzzing like busy bees.   11 *The
Romantic Agony:* a critical study of the Romantics by Mario Praz.

WALLACE STEVENS   (1879–1955)

The Emperor of Ice-Cream _____ *1923*

Call the roller of big cigars,
The muscular one, and bid him whip
In kitchen cups concupiscent curds.
Let the wenches dawdle in such dress
As they are used to wear, and let the boys   5

Bring flowers in last month's newspapers.
Let be be finale of seem.
The only emperor is the emperor of ice-cream.

Take from the dresser of deal,°
Lacking the three glass knobs, that sheet   10
On which she embroidered fantails once
And spread it so as to cover her face.
If her horny feet protrude, they come
To show how cold she is, and dumb.
Let the lamp affix its beam.   15
The only emperor is the emperor of ice-cream.

9 *deal:* fir or pine wood.

WALLACE STEVENS   (1879–1955)

The Idea of Order at Key West ——————————————— *1935*

She sang beyond the genius of the sea.
The water never formed to mind or voice,
Like a body wholly body, fluttering
Its empty sleeves; and yet its mimic motion
Made constant cry, caused constantly a cry,   5
That was not ours although we understood,
Inhuman, of the veritable ocean.

The sea was not a mask. No more was she.
The song and water were not medleyed sound
Even if what she sang was what she heard,   10
Since what she sang was uttered word by word.
It may be that in all her phrases stirred
The grinding water and the gasping wind;
But it was she and not the sea we heard.

For she was the maker of the song she sang.   15
The ever-hooded, tragic-gestured sea
Was merely a place by which she walked to sing.
Whose spirit is this? we said, because we knew
It was the spirit that we sought and knew
That we should ask this often as she sang.   20

If it was only the dark voice of the sea
That rose, or even colored by many waves;
If it was only the outer voice of sky
And cloud, of the sunken coral water-walled,
However clear, it would have been deep air,   25
The heaving speech of air, a summer sound
Repeated in a summer without end

And sound alone. But it was more than that,
More even than her voice, and ours, among
The meaningless plungings of water and the wind,   30
Theatrical distances, bronze shadows heaped
On high horizons, mountainous atmospheres
Of sky and sea.
                    It was her voice that made
The sky acutest at its vanishing.
She measured to the hour its solitude.   35
She was the single artificer of the world
In which she sang. And when she sang, the sea,
Whatever self it had, became the self
That was her song, for she was the maker. Then we,
As we beheld her striding there alone,   40
Knew that there never was a world for her
Except the one she sang and, singing, made.

Ramon Fernandez, tell me, if you know,
Why, when the singing ended and we turned
Toward the town, tell why the glassy lights,   45
The lights in the fishing boats at anchor there,
As the night descended, tilting in the air,
Mastered the night and portioned out the sea,
Fixing emblazoned zones and fiery poles,
Arranging, deepening, enchanting night.   50

Oh! Blessed rage for order, pale Ramon,
The maker's rage to order words of the sea,
Words of the fragrant portals, dimly-starred,
And of ourselves and of our origins,
In ghostlier demarcations, keener sounds.   55

ANNE STEVENSON   (b. 1933)

Cain° ————————————————————————— *1977*

Lord have mercy upon the angry.
The anguished can take care of each other.
The angels will take care of themselves.
But the angry have no daughters or mothers;
only brute brothers, themselves.   5
Hearing that faint "Abel, Abel" they stop their ears.
Watching that approved flame snake to the sky
they beat stubby blades out of ploughshares,°

Cain: In Genesis 4, Cain, the oldest son of Adam and Eve, murdered his brother Abel because the "approved flame" (line 7) of Abel's sacrifice to God was accepted and Cain's was not.   8 *blades out of ploughshares:* a reversal of the biblical phrase *to beat swords into ploughshares,* that is, turn instruments of war into instruments of peace.

cut the sun out of the air,
Stamp on small fires they might have seen by.   10

ANNE STEVENSON   (b. 1933)

By the Boat House, Oxford _____ *1977*

They belong here in their own quenched country.
I had forgotten nice women could be so nice,
smiling beside large sons on the makeshift quay,
frail, behind pale faces and hurt eyes.

Their husbands are plainly superior, with them, without them.   5
Their boys wear privilege like a clear inheritance, easily.
(Now a swan's neck couples with its own reflection,
making in the simple water a perfect 3.)

The punts° seem resigned to an unexciting mooring.
But the women? It's hard to tell. Do their fine grey hairs   10
and filament lips approve or disdain the loving
that living alone, or else lonely in pairs, impairs?

9 *punts:* flat-bottomed boats.

RUTH STONE   (b. 1915)

Where I Came From _____ *c. 1987*

My father put me in my mother
but he didn't pick me out.
I am my own quick woman.
What drew him to my mother?
Beating his drumsticks   5
he thought—why not?
And he gave her an umbrella.
Their marriage was like that.
She hid ironically in her apron.
Sometimes she cried into the biscuit dough.   10
When she wanted to make a point
she would sing a hymn or an old song.
He was loose-footed. He couldn't be counted on
until his pockets were empty.
When he was home the kettle drums,   15
the snare drum, the celeste,
the triangle throbbed.
While he changed their heads,
the drum skins soaked in the bathtub.

Collapsed and wrinkled, they floated   20
like huge used condoms.

MARK STRAND   (b. 1934)

Where Are the Waters of Childhood? _____ *1978*

See where the windows are boarded up,
where the gray siding shines in the sun and salt air
and the asphalt shingles on the roof have peeled or fallen off,
where tiers of oxeye daisies float on a sea of grass?
That's the place to begin.   5

Enter the kingdom of rot,
smell the damp plaster, step over the shattered glass,
the pockets of dust, the rags, the soiled remains of a mattress,
look at the rusted stove and sink, at the rectangular stain
on the wall where Winslow Homer's *Gulf Stream* hung.   10

Go to the room where your father and mother
would let themselves go in the drift and pitch of love,
and hear, if you can, the creak of their bed,
then go to the place where you hid.

Go to your room, to all the rooms whose cold, damp air you breathed,   15
to all the unwanted places where summer, fall, winter, spring,
seem the same unwanted season, where the trees you knew have died
and other trees have risen. Visit that other place
you barely recall, that other house half hidden.

See the two dogs burst into sight. When you leave,   20
they will cease, snuffed out in the glare of an earlier light.
Visit the neighbors down the block; he waters his lawn,
she sits on her porch, but not for long.
When you look again they are gone.

Keep going back, back to the field, flat and sealed in mist.   25
On the other side, a man and a woman are waiting;
they have come back, your mother before she was gray,
your father before he was white.

Now look at the North West Arm, how it glows a deep cerulean blue.
See the light on the grass, the one leaf burning, the cloud   30
that flares. You're almost there, in a moment your parents
will disappear, leaving you under the light of a vanished star,
under the dark of a star newly born. Now is the time.

Now you invent the boat of your flesh and set it upon the waters
and drift in the gradual swell, in the laboring salt.   35
Now you look down. The waters of childhood are there.

JONATHAN SWIFT   (1667–1745)

The Progress of Beauty _____ *1719–1720*

When first Diana° leaves her Bed,
Vapors and Steams her Looks disgrace;
A frowzy dirty-colored red
Sits on her cloudy wrinkled Face.

But by degrees when mounted high   5
Her artificial Face appears,
Down from her Window in the Sky,
Her Spots are gone, her Visage clears.

'Twixt earthly Females and the Moon
All Parallels exactly run;   10
If Celia° should appear too soon,
Alas, the Nymph would be undone.

To see her from her Pillow rise
All reeking in a cloudy Steam,
Cracked Lips, foul Teeth, and gummy Eyes,   15
Poor Strephon, how would he blaspheme!

The Soot or Powder which was wont
To make her Hair look black as Jet,
Falls from her Tresses on her Front,
A mingled Mass of Dirt and Sweat.   20

Three Colors, Black, and Red, and White,
So graceful in their proper Place,
Remove them to a different Light—
They form a frightful hideous Face,

For instance: when the Lily slips   25
Into the Precincts of the Rose,
And takes Possession of the Lips,
Leaving the Purple to the Nose.

So Celia went entire to bed,
All her Complexions safe and sound,   30
But when she rose, the black and red,
Though still in Sight, had changed their Ground.

The Black, which would not be confined,
A more inferior Station seeks,
Leaving the fiery red behind,   35
And mingles in her muddy Cheeks.

The Paint by Perspiration cracks,
And falls in Rivulets of Sweat;

---

1 *Diana:* the moon.   11 *Celia:* a lady of fashion.

On either Side you see the Tracks,
While at her Chin the Confluents met.   40

   A Skillful Housewife thus her Thumb
With Spittle while she spins, anoints,
And thus the brown Meanders come
In trickling Streams betwixt her Joints.

   But Celia can with ease reduce   45
By help of Pencil, Paint and Brush
Each Color to its Place and Use,
And teach her Cheeks again to blush.

   She knows her Early self no more,
But filled with Admiration, stands,   50
As Other Painters oft adore
The Workmanship of their own Hands.

   Thus after four important Hours
Celia's the Wonder of her Sex;
Say, which among the Heavenly Powers   55
Could cause such wonderful Effects.

   Venus, indulgent to her Kind,
Gave Women all their Hearts could wish
When first she taught them where to find
White Lead, and Lusitanian Dish.°   60

   Love with White lead cements his Wings,
White lead was sent us to repair
Two brightest, brittlest, earthly Things:
A Lady's Face, and China ware.

   She ventures now to lift the Sash;   65
The Window is her proper Sphere;
Ah, Lovely Nymph, be not too rash,
Nor let the Beaux approach too near.

   Take Pattern by your Sister Star:
Delude at once and Bless our Sight;   70
When you are seen, be seen from far,
And chiefly choose to shine by Night.

   In the Pellmell when passing by,
Keep up the Glasses of your Chair;°
Then each transported Fop will cry,   75
G—d d—m me, Jack, she's wondrous fair.

   But, Art no longer can prevail
When the Materials all are gone;

---

60 *Lusitanian Dish:* Portuguese dish holding her makeup.   74 *Glasses of your Chair:* windows on
the chair she's carried in.

The best Mechanic Hand must fail
Where Nothing's left to work upon.   80

    Matter, as wise Logicians say,
Cannot without a Form subsist,
And Form, say I, as well as They,
Must fail if Matter brings no Grist.

    And this is fair Diana's Case,   85
For, all Astrologers maintain
Each Night a Bit drops off her Face
When Mortals say she's in her Wane.

    While Partridge wisely shows the Cause
Efficient of the Moon's Decay,   90
That Cancer with his poisonous Claws
Attacks her in the Milky Way:

    But Gadbury in Art profound
From her pale Cheeks pretends to show
That Swain Endymion is not sound,   95
Or else, that Mercury's her Foe.

    But, let the Cause be what it will,
In half a Month she looks so thin
That Flamstead° can with all his Skill
See but her Forehead and her Chin.   100

    Yet as she wastes, she grows discreet,
Till Midnight never shows her Head;
So rotting Celia strolls the Street
When sober Folks are all abed.

    For sure if this be Luna's° Fate,   105
Poor Celia, but of mortal Race,
In vain expects a longer Date
To the Materials of Her Face.

    When Mercury her Tresses mows,
To think of Oil and Soot is vain;   110
No Painting can restore a Nose,
Nor will her Teeth return again.

    Two Balls of Glass may serve for Eyes;
White Lead can plaster up a Cleft,
But these, alas, are poor Supplies   115
If neither Cheeks nor Lips be left.

    Ye Powers who over Love preside,
Since mortal Beauties drop so soon,
If you would have us well supplied,
Send us new Nymphs with each new Moon.   120

99 *Flamstead:* John Flamstead (1646–1719), an astronomer.   105 *Luna:* the moon.

ALFRED, LORD TENNYSON   (1809–1892)

Ulysses° _____ *1833*

It little profits that an idle king,
By this still hearth, among these barren crags,
Matched with an agèd wife, I mete and dole
Unequal laws unto a savage race,
That hoard, and sleep, and feed, and know not me.   5

I cannot rest from travel: I will drink
Life to the lees: all times I have enjoyed
Greatly, have suffered greatly, both with those
That loved me, and alone; on shore, and when
Through scudding drifts the rainy Hyades°   10
Vexed the dim sea: I am become a name;
For always roaming with a hungry heart
Much have I seen and known; cities of men
And manners, climates, councils, governments,
Myself not least, but honored of them all;   15
And drunk delight of battle with my peers,
Far on the ringing plains of windy Troy.
I am a part of all that I have met;
Yet all experience is an arch wherethrough
Gleams that untravelled world, whose margin fades   20
For ever and for ever when I move.
How dull it is to pause, to make an end,
To rust unburnished, not to shine in use!
As though to breathe were life. Life piled on life
Were all too little, and of one° to me   25
Little remains: but every hour is saved
From that eternal silence, something more,
A bringer of new things; and vile it were
For some three suns to store and hoard myself,
And this gray spirit yearning in desire   30
To follow knowledge like a sinking star,
Beyond the utmost bound of human thought.

    This is my son, mine own Telemachus,
To whom I leave the scepter and the isle—
Well-loved of me, discerning to fulfil   35
This labor, by slow prudence to make mild
A rugged people, and through soft degrees
Subdue them to the useful and the good.
Most blameless is he, centered in the sphere,
Of common duties, decent not to fail   40
In offices of tenderness, and pay

Ulysses: the hero whose sea adventures form Homer's *Odyssey.* Tennyson here pictures Ulysses back
home and bored.   10 *Hyades:* a cluster of stars supposed to signal coming storms.   25 *of
one:* of time. Ulysses is old.

Meet adoration to my household gods,
When I am gone. He works his work, I mine.

   There lies the port; the vessel puffs her sail:
There gloom the dark broad seas. My mariners,   45
Souls that have toiled, and wrought, and thought with me—
That ever with a frolic welcome took
The thunder and the sunshine, and opposed
Free hearts, free foreheads—you and I are old;
Old age hath yet his honor and his toil;   50
Death closes all: but something ere the end,
Some work of noble note, may yet be done,
Not unbecoming men that strove with Gods.
The lights begin to twinkle from the rocks:
The long day wanes: the slow moon climbs: the deep   55
Moans round with many voices. Come, my friends,
'Tis not too late to seek a newer world.
Push off, and sitting well in order smite
The sounding furrows; for my purpose holds
To sail beyond the sunset, and the baths   60
Of all the western stars, until I die.
It may be that the gulfs will wash us down:
It may be we shall touch the Happy Isles,°
And see the great Achilles, whom we knew.
Though much is taken, much abides; and though   65
We are not now that strength which in old days
Moved earth and heaven; that which we are, we are;
One equal temper of heroic hearts,
Made weak by time and fate, but strong in will
To strive, to seek, to find, and not to yield.   70

63 *Happy Isles:* the paradise for heroes after death.

DYLAN THOMAS   (1914–1953)

Fern Hill _____ *1946*

Now as I was young and easy under the apple boughs
About the lilting house and happy as the grass was green,
   The night above the dingle starry,
    Time let me hail and climb
   Golden in the heydays of his eyes,   5
And honored among wagons I was prince of the apple towns
And once below a time I lordly had the trees and leaves
   Trail with daisies and barley
   Down the rivers of the windfall light.

And as I was green and carefree, famous among the barns   10
About the happy yard and singing as the farm was home,

In the sun that is young once only,
　　Time let me play and be
　　Golden in the mercy of his means,
And green and golden I was huntsman and herdsman, the calves　　　　15
Sang to my horn, the foxes on the hills barked clear and cold,
　　　And the sabbath rang slowly
　　In the pebbles of the holy streams.

All the sun long it was running, it was lovely, the hay
Fields high as the house, the tunes from the chimneys, it was air　　20
　　And playing, lovely and watery
　　　And fire green as grass.
　　And nightly under the simple stars
As I rode to sleep the owls were bearing the farm away,
All the moon long I heard, blessed among stables, the nightjars　　25
　　Flying with the ricks, and the horses
　　　Flashing into the dark.

And then to awake, and the farm, like a wanderer white
With the dew, come back, the cock on his shoulder: it was all
　　Shining, it was Adam and maiden,　　　　　　　　　　　　　30
　　　The sky gathered again
　　And the sun grew round that very day.
So it must have been after the birth of the simple light
In the first, spinning place, the spellbound horses walking warm
　　Out of the whinnying green stable　　　　　　　　　　　　35
　　　On to the fields of praise.

And honored among foxes and pheasants by the gay house
Under the new made clouds and happy as the heart was long,
　　In the sun born over and over,
　　　I ran my heedless ways,　　　　　　　　　　　　　　　40
　　My wishes raced through the house-high hay
And nothing I cared, at my sky blue trades, that time allows
In all his tuneful turning so few and such morning songs
　　Before the children green and golden
　　　Follow him out of grace,　　　　　　　　　　　　　　45

Nothing I cared, in the lamb white days, that time would take me
Up to the swallow thronged loft by the shadow of my hand,
　　In the moon that is always rising,
　　　Nor that riding to sleep
　　I should hear him fly with the high fields　　　　　　　　50
And wake to the farm forever fled from the childless land.
Oh as I was young and easy in the mercy of his means,
　　Time held me green and dying
　　Though I sang in my chains like the sea.

DYLAN THOMAS   (1914–1953)

Poem in October _____ *1944*

It was my thirtieth year to heaven
Woke to my hearing from harbor and neighbor wood
    And the mussel pooled and the heron
            Priested shore
        The morning beckon   5
With water praying and call of seagull and rook
And the knock of sailing boats on the net webbed wall
        Myself to set foot
            That second
In the still sleeping town and set forth.   10

    My birthday began with the water-
Birds and the birds of the winged trees flying my name
    Above the farms and the white horses
            And I rose
        In rainy autumn   15
And walked abroad in a shower of all my days.
High tide and the heron dived when I took the road
        Over the border
            And the gates
Of the town closed as the town awoke.   20

    A springful of larks in a rolling
Cloud and the roadside bushes brimming with whistling
    Blackbirds and the sun of October
            Summery
        On the hill's shoulder,   25
Here were fond climates and sweet singers suddenly
Come in the morning where I wandered and listened
        To the rain wringing
            Wind blow cold
In the wood faraway under me.   30

    Pale rain over the dwindling harbor
And over the sea wet church the size of a snail
    With its horns through mist and the castle
            Brown as owls
        But all the gardens   35
Of spring and summer were blooming in the tall tales
Beyond the border and under the lark full cloud.
        There could I marvel
            My birthday
Away but the weather turned around.   40

It turned away from the blithe country
And down the other air and the blue altered sky
    Streamed again a wonder of summer
            With apples
      Pears and red currants   45
And I saw in the turning so clearly a child's
Forgotten mornings when he walked with his mother
      Through the parables
          Of sun light
And the legends of the green chapels   50

  And the twice told fields of infancy
That his tears burned my cheeks and his heart moved in mine.
    These were the woods the river and sea
        Where a boy
      In the listening   55
Summertime of the dead whispered the truth of his joy
To the trees and the stones and the fish in the tide.
      And the mystery
        Sang alive
Still in the water and singingbirds.   60

  And there could I marvel my birthday
Away but the weather turned around. And the true
    Joy of the long dead child sang burning
        In the sun.
      It was my thirtieth   65
Year to heaven stood there then in the summer noon
Though the town below lay leaved with October blood.
      O may my heart's truth
        Still be sung
On this high hill in a year's turning.   70

DAVID WAGONER   (b. 1926)

The Shooting of John Dillinger° outside the Biograph Theater,
July 22, 1934 _____ *1969*

Chicago ran a fever of a hundred and one that groggy Sunday.
A reporter fried an egg on a sidewalk; the air looked shaky.
And a hundred thousand people were in the lake like shirts in a
    laundry.
Why was Johnny lonely?
Not because two dozen solid citizens, heat-struck, had keeled over
    backward.   5
Not because those lawful souls had fallen out of their sockets and
    melted.

John Dillinger (1902–1934): notorious American bank robber.

But because the sun went down like a lump in a furnace or a bull in
    the Stockyards.
Where was Johnny headed?
Under the Biograph Theater sign that said, "Our Air is Refrigerated."
Past seventeen FBI men and four policemen who stood in doorways
    and sweated.   10
Johnny sat down in a cold seat to watch Clark Gable get
    electrocuted.
Had Johnny been mistreated?
Yes, but Gable told the D. A. he'd rather fry than be shut up forever.
Two women sat by Johnny. One looked sweet, one looked like J.
    Edgar Hoover.
Polly Hamilton made him feel hot, but Anna Sage made him shiver.   15
Was Johnny a good lover?
Yes, but he passed out his share of squeezes and pokes like a jittery
    masher.
While Agent Purvis sneaked up and down the aisle like an extra
    usher,
Trying to make sure they wouldn't slip out till the show was over.
Was Johnny a fourflusher?   20
No, not if he knew the game. He got it up or got it back.
But he liked to take snapshots of policemen with his own Kodak,
And once in a while he liked to take them with an automatic.
Why was Johnny frantic?
Because he couldn't take a walk or sit down in a movie   25
Without being afraid he'd run smack into somebody
Who'd point at his rearranged face and holler, "Johnny!"
Was Johnny ugly?
Yes, because Dr. Wilhelm Loeser had given him a new profile
With a baggy jawline and squint eyes and an erased dimple,   30
With kangaroo-tendon cheekbones and a gigolo's mustache that
    should've been illegal.
Did Johnny love a girl?
Yes, a good-looking, hard-headed Indian named Billie Frechette.
He wanted to marry her and lie down and try to get over it,
But she was locked in jail for giving him first-aid and comfort.   35
Did Johnny feel hurt?
He felt like breaking a bank or jumping over a railing
Into some panicky teller's cage to shout, "Reach for the ceiling!"
Or like kicking some vice president in the bum checks and smiling.
What was he really doing?   40
Going up the aisle with the crowd and into the lobby
With Polly saying, "Would *you* do what Clark done?" And Johnny
    saying, "Maybe."
And Anna saying, "If he'd been smart, he'd of acted like Bing
    Crosby."
Did Johnny look flashy?
Yes, his white-on-white shirt and tie were luminous.   45
His trousers were creased like knives to the tops of his shoes,

And his yellow straw hat came down to his dark glasses.
Was Johnny suspicious?
Yes, and when Agent Purvis signalled with a trembling cigar,
Johnny ducked left and ran out of the theater,   50
And innocent Polly and squealing Anna were left nowhere.
Was Johnny a fast runner?
No, but he crouched and scurried past a friendly liquor store
Under the coupled arms of double-daters, under awnings, under
    stars,
To the curb at the mouth of an alley. He hunched there.   55
Was Johnny a thinker?
No, but he was thinking more or less of Billie Frechette
Who was lost in prison for longer than he could possibly wait,
And then it was suddenly too hard to think around a bullet.
Did anyone shoot straight?   60
Yes, but Mrs. Etta Natalsky fell out from under her picture hat.
Theresa Paulus sprawled on the sidewalk, clutching her left foot.
And both of them groaned loud and long under the streetlight.
Did Johnny like that?
No, but he lay down with those strange women, his face in the
    alley,   65
One shoe off, cinders in his mouth, his eyelids heavy.
When they shouted questions at him, he talked back to nobody.
Did Johnny lie easy?
Yes, holding his gun and holding his breath as a last trick,
He waited, but when the Agents came close, his breath wouldn't
    work.   70
Clark Gable walked his last mile; Johnny ran half a block.
Did he run out of luck?
Yes, before he was cool, they had him spread out on dished-in marble
In the Cook County Morgue, surrounded by babbling people
With a crime reporter presiding over the head of the table.   75
Did Johnny have a soul?
Yes, and it was climbing his slippery wind-pipe like a trapped burglar.
It was beating the inside of his ribcage, hollering, "Let me out of
    here!"
Maybe it got out, and maybe it just stayed there.
Was Johnny a money-maker?   80
Yes, and thousands paid 25¢ to see him, mostly women,
And one said, "I wouldn't have come, except he's a moral lesson,"
And another, "I'm disappointed. He feels like a dead man."
Did Johnny have a brain?
Yes, and it always worked best through the worst of dangers,   85
Through flat-footed hammerlocks, through guarded doors, around
    corners,
But it got taken out in the morgue and sold to some doctors.
Could Johnny take orders?
No, but he stayed in the wicker basket carried by six men

Through the bulging crowd to the hearse and let himself be locked
    in,   90
And he stayed put as it went driving south in a driving rain.
And he didn't get stolen?
No, not even after his old hard-nosed dad refused to sell
The quick-drawing corpse for $10,000 to somebody in a carnival.
He figured he'd let Johnny decide how to get to Hell.   95
Did anyone wish him well?
Yes, half of Indiana camped in the family pasture,
And the minister said, "With luck, he could have been a minister."
And up the sleeve of his oversized gray suit, Johnny twitched a
    finger.
Does anyone remember?   100
Everyone still alive. And some dead ones. It was a new kind of
    holiday
With hot and cold drinks and hot and cold tears. They planted
    him in a cemetery
With three unknown vice presidents, Benjamin Harrison, and
    James Whitcomb Riley,
Who never held up anybody.

MARILYN NELSON WANIEK   (b. 1946)

Emily Dickinson's Defunct —————————————————— *1978*

She used to
pack poems
in her hip pocket.
Under all the
gray old lady   5
clothes she was
dressed for action.
She had hair,
imagine,
in certain places, and   10
believe me
she smelled human
on a hot summer day.
Stalking snakes
or counting   15
the thousand motes
in sunlight
she walked just
like an Indian.
She was New England's   20
favorite daughter,

she could pray
like the devil.
She was a
two-fisted woman,   25
this babe.
All the flies
just stood around
and buzzed
when she died.   30

BELLE WARING   (b. 1951)

What Hurts _____ *1990*

is waking up flung cold across
the bed, right where I left myself, these eyes
spooked, like my father's after a binge.
Just what the hell is he doing in my face?
I don't booze. I'm not like him.   5
But that scared and blowsy stare
I recognize after this stark dream of looking
for Max, my hopeless ex, world without end.
Some nights my father spent stripped in a cell
to sober up. I learned to sleep in my clothes.   10
Sentry. Night watch. Mother by a sickbed.
Doctor on call. No surprise. Ready for
a shit storm. Praying for a cool sunrise.

BELLE WARING   (b. 1951)

Children Must Have Manners _____ *1990*

Not morals. Manners. Grist for the guests.
They suck up the Scotch. Daddy
rattles my school report under their snouts.
See. I'm his prize piggie.
But soon as they exit,   5
he slaps my fat face
'cause I dropped a whole fifth.
Twelve years old.
The praise must have gone
to my head, Daddy says.   10

"Pig," he spits.
But when company's here,

pig's to smile till it splits.
One jangled day I'll forget
this face. Show up for breakfast   15
pig scraped to the bone.
Nights, alone with my face,
I peel it away, wring out the grin,
rinse it in pilfered rosewater.
While I sleep, let it work its roots.   20

JOHN WEINERS   (b. 1934)

The Eagle Bar —————————————————————— *1986*

A lamp lit in the corner
the Chinese girl talks to her lover
At bar, saxophone blares—

blue music, while boy in white turtleneck sweater
seduces the polka player from Poland   5
left over from Union party.

Janet sits beside me,
Barbra Streisand sings on Juke box
James tends bar

It's the same old scene   10
in Buffalo or Boston
yen goes on, continues in the glare

of night, searching for its lover
oh will we go
where will we search   15

between potato chips and boys,
for impeccable one—
that impossible lover

who does not come in,
with fresh air and sea   20
off Lake Erie

but stays home, hidden in the sheets
with his wife and child, alone
ah, the awful ache

as cash register rings   25
and James the bartender sweeps
bottles off the bar.

WALT WHITMAN   (1819–1892)

From *Song of Myself°* _____ *1855–1891*

I

I celebrate myself, and sing myself,
And what I assume you shall assume,
For every atom belonging to me as good belongs to you.

I loaf and invite my soul,
I lean and loaf at my ease observing a spear of summer grass.   5

My tongue, every atom of my blood, formed from this soil, this air,
Born here of parents born here from parents the same, and their
    parents the same,
I, now thirty-seven years old in perfect health begin,
Hoping to cease not till death.

Creeds and schools in abeyance,   10
Retiring back a while sufficed at what they are, but never forgotten,
I harbor for good or bad, I permit to speak at every hazard,
Nature without check with original energy.

II

Houses and rooms are full of perfumes, the shelves are crowded with
    perfumes,
I breathe the fragrance myself and know it and like it,   15
The distillation would intoxicate me also, but I shall not let it.
The atmosphere is not a perfume, it has no taste of distillation, it is
    odorless,
It is for my mouth forever, I am in love with it,
I will go to the bank by the wood and become undisguised and
    naked,
I am mad for it to be in contact with me.   20

The smoke of my own breath,
Echoes, ripples, buzzed whispers, love-root, silk-thread, crotch and
    vine,
My respiration and inspiration, the beating of my heart, the passing
    of blood and air through my lungs,
The sniff of green leaves and dry leaves, and of the shore and dark-
    colored sea-rocks, and of hay in the barn,
The sound of the belched words of my voice loosed to the eddies of
    the wind,   25
A few light kisses, a few embraces, a reaching around of arms,
The play of shine and shade on the trees as the supple boughs wag,
The delight alone or in the rush of the streets, or along the fields
    and hillsides,
The feeling of health, the full-noon trill, the song of me rising from
    bed and meeting the sun.

Have you reckoned a thousand acres much? Have you reckoned the
    earth much?   30
Have you practiced so long to learn to read?
Have you felt so proud to get at the meaning of poems?

Stop this day and night with me and you shall possess the origin of
    all poems,
You shall possess the good of the earth and sun (there are millions
    of suns left),
You shall no longer take things at second or third hand, nor look
    through the eyes of the dead, nor feed on the specters in
    books,   35
You shall not look through my eyes either, nor take things from me,
You shall listen to all sides and filter them from your self.

III

I have heard what the talkers were talking, the talk of the beginning
    and the end,
But I do not talk of the beginning or the end.

There was never any more inception than there is now,   40
Nor any more youth or age than there is now,
And will never be any more perfection than there is now,
Nor any more heaven or hell than there is now.

Urge and urge and urge,
Always the procreant urge of the world.   45
Out of the dimness opposite equals advance, always substance and
    increase, always sex,
Always a knit of identity, always distinction, always a breed of life.

To elaborate is no avail, learned and unlearned feel that it is so.

Sure as the most certain sure, plumb in the uprights, well
    entretied,° braced in the beams,
Stout as a horse, affectionate, haughty, electrical,   50
I and this mystery here we stand.

Clear and sweet is my soul, and clear and sweet is all that is not my
    soul.
Lack one lacks both, and the unseen is proved by the seen,
Till that becomes unseen and receives proof in its turn.

Showing the best and dividing it from the worst age vexes age,   55
Knowing the perfect fitness and equanimity of things, while they
    discuss I am silent, and go bathe and admire myself.

Welcome is every organ and attribute of me, and of any man hearty
    and clean,
Not an inch nor a particle of an inch is vile, and none shall be less
    familiar than the rest.

49 *entretied:* plastered.

I am satisfied—I see, dance, laugh, sing;
As the hugging and loving bedfellow sleeps at my side through the
    night, and withdraws at the peep of the day with stealthy
    tread,   60
Leaving me baskets covered with white towels swelling the house
    with their plenty,
Shall I postpone my acceptation and realization and scream at my
    eyes,
That they turn from gazing after and down the road,
And forthwith cipher and show me to a cent,
Exactly the value of one and exactly the value of two, and which is
    ahead?   65

IV

Trippers and askers surround me,
People I meet, the effect upon me of my early life or the ward and
    city I live in, or the nation,
The latest dates, discoveries, inventions, societies, authors old and
    new,
My dinner, dress, associates, looks, compliments, dues,
The real or fancied indifference of some man or woman I love,   70
The sickness of one of my folks or of myself, or ill-doing or loss or
    lack of money, or depressions or exaltations,
Battles, the horrors of fratricidal war, the fever of doubtful news, the
    fitful events;
These come to me days and nights and go from me again,
But they are not the Me myself.

Apart from the pulling and hauling stands what I am,   75
Stands amused, complacent, compassionating, idle, unitary,
Looks down, is erect, or bends an arm on an impalpable certain rest,
Looking with side-curved head curious what will come next,
Both in and out of the game and watching and wondering at it.
Backward I see in my own days where I sweated through fog with
    linguists and contenders,   80
I have no mockings or arguments, I witness and wait.

V

I believe in you my soul, the other I am must not abase itself to you,
And you must not be abased to the other.

Loaf with me on the grass, loose the stop from your throat,
Not words, not music or rhyme I want, not custom or lecture, not
    even the best,   85
Only the lull I like, the hum of your valvèd voice.

I mind how once we lay such a transparent summer morning,
How you settled your head athwart my hips and gently turned over
    upon me,
And parted the shirt from my bosom-bone, and plunged your
    tongue to my bare-stripped heart,

And reached till you felt my beard, and reached till you held my
    feet.   90

Swiftly arose and spread around me the peace and knowledge that
    pass all the argument of the earth,
And I know that the hand of God is the promise of my own,
And I know that the spirit of God is the brother of my own,
And that all the men ever born are also my brothers, and the women
    my sisters and lovers,
And that a kelson of the creation is love,   95
And limitless are leaves stiff or drooping in the fields,
And brown ants in the little wells beneath them,
And mossy scabs of the worm fence, heaped stones, elder, mullein
    and poke-weed.

VI

A child said *What is the grass?* fetching it to me with full hands;
How could I answer the child? I do not know what it is any more
    than he.   100

I guess it must be the flag of my disposition, out of hopeful green
    stuff woven.

Or I guess it is the handkerchief of the Lord,
A scented gift and remembrancer designedly dropped,
Bearing the owner's name someway in the corners, that we may see
    and remark, and say *Whose?*
Or I guess the grass is itself a child, the produced babe of the
    vegetation.   105

Or I guess it is a uniform hieroglyphic,
And it means, Sprouting alike in broad zones and narrow zones,
Growing among black folks as among white,
Kanuck, Tuckahoe, Congressman, Cuff, I give them the same, I
    receive them the same.

And now it seems to me the beautiful uncut hair of graves.   110

Tenderly will I use you curling grass,
It may be you transpire from the breasts of young men,
It may be if I had known them I would have loved them,
It may be you are from old people, or from offspring taken soon
    out of their mothers' laps,
And here you are the mothers' laps.   115

This grass is very dark to be from the white heads of old mothers,
Darker than the colorless beards of old men,
Dark to come from under the faint red roofs of mouths.

O I perceive after all so many uttering tongues,
And I perceive they do not come from the roofs of mouths for
    nothing.   120

I wish I could translate the hints about the dead young men and
    women,
And the hints about old men and mothers, and the offspring taken
    soon out of their laps.

What do you think has become of the young and old men?
And what do you think has become of the women and children?

They are alive and well somewhere,   125
The smallest sprout shows there is really no death,
And if ever there was it led forward life, and does not wait at the
    end to arrest it,
And ceased the moment life appeared.

All goes onward and outward, nothing collapses,
And to die is different from what any one supposed, and luckier.   130

VII

Has any one supposed it lucky to be born?
I hasten to inform him or her it is just as lucky to die, and I know
    it.

I pass death with the dying and birth with the new-washed babe,
    and am not contained between my hat and boots,
And peruse manifold objects, no two alike and every one good,
The earth good and the stars good, and their adjuncts all good.   135

I am not an earth nor an adjunct of an earth,
I am the mate and companion of people, all just as immortal and
    fathomless as myself
(They do not know how immortal, but I know).

Every kind for itself and its own, for me mine male and female,
For me those that have been boys and that love women,   140
For me the man that is proud and feels how it stings to be
    slighted,
For me the sweetheart and the old maid, for me mothers and the
    mothers of mothers,
For me lips that have smiled, eyes that have shed tears,
For me children and the begetters of children.

Undrape! you are not guilty to me, nor stale nor discarded,   145
I see through the broadcloth and gingham whether or no,
And am around, tenacious, acquisitive, tireless, and cannot be
    shaken away.

VIII

The little one sleeps in its cradle,
I lift the gauze and look a long time, and silently brush away flies
    with my hand.

The youngster and the red-faced girl turn aside up the bushy hill,   150
I peeringly view them from the top.

The suicide sprawls on the bloody floor of the bedroom,
I witness the corpse with its dabbled hair, I note where the pistol
    has fallen.

The blab of the pave,° tires of carts, sluff of boot-soles, talk of the
    promenaders,
The heavy omnibus, the driver with his interrogating thumb, the
    clank of the shod horses on the granite floor,   155
The snow-sleighs, clinking, shouted jokes, pelts of snowballs,
The hurrahs for popular favorites, the fury of roused mobs,
The flap of the curtained litter, a sick man inside borne to the
    hospital,
The meeting of enemies, the sudden oath, the blows and fall,
The excited crowd, the policeman with his star quickly working his
    passage to the center of the crowd,   160
The impassive stones that receive and return so many echoes,
What groans of over-fed or half-starved who fall sunstruck or in fits,
What exclamations of women taken suddenly who hurry home and
    give birth to babes,
What living and buried speech is always vibrating here, what howls
    restrained by decorum,
Arrests of criminals, slights, adulterous offers made, acceptances,
    rejections with convex lips,   165
I mind them or the show or resonance of them—I come and I
    depart.

IX

The big doors of the country barn stand open and ready,
The dried grass of the harvest-time loads the slow-drawn wagon,
The clear light plays on the brown gray and green intertinged,
The armfuls are packed to the sagging mow.   170

I am there, I help, I came stretched atop of the load,
I felt its soft jolts, one leg reclined on the other,
I jump from the crossbeams and seize the clover and timothy,
And roll head over heels and tangle my hair full of wisps.

X

Alone far in the wilds and mountains I hunt,   175
Wandering amazed at my own lightness and glee,
In the late afternoon choosing a safe spot to pass the night,
Kindling a fire and broiling the fresh-killed game,
Falling asleep on the gathered leaves with my dog and gun by my
    side.

The Yankee clipper is under her sky-sails, she cuts the sparkle and
    scud,   180
My eyes settle the land, I bend at her prow or shout joyously from
    the deck.

154 *blab of the pave:* the sound of the pavement, the streets.

The boatmen and clam-diggers arose early and stopped for me,
I tucked my trowser-ends in my boots and went and had a good
        time;
You should have been with us that day round the chowder-kettle.

I saw the marriage of the trapper in the open air in the far west,
        the bride was a red girl,   185
Her father and his friends sat near cross-legged and dumbly
        smoking, they had moccasins to their feet and large thick
        blankets hanging from their shoulders,
On a bank lounged the trapper, he was dressed mostly in skins,
        his luxuriant beard and curls protected his neck, he held his
        bride by the hand,
She had long eyelashes, her head was bare, her coarse straight locks
        descended upon her voluptuous limbs and reached to her feet.

The runaway slave came to my house and stopped outside,
I heard his motions crackling the twigs of the woodpile,   190
Through the swung half-door of the kitchen I saw him limpsy and
        weak,
And went where he sat on a log and led him in and assured him,
And brought water and filled a tub for his sweated body and
        bruised feet,
And gave him a room that entered from my own, and gave him
        some coarse clean clothes,
And remember perfectly well his revolving eyes and his
        awkwardness,   195
And remember putting plasters on the galls of his neck and ankles;
He stayed with me a week before he was recuperated and passed
        north,
I had him sit next me at table, my fire-lock leaned in the corner.

WILLIAM CARLOS WILLIAMS   (1883–1963)

The Red Wheelbarrow _____ *1923*

so much depends
upon

a red wheel
barrow

glazed with rain   5
water

beside the white
chickens.

WILLIAM CARLOS WILLIAMS   (1883–1963)

Danse Russe _____ *1944*

If when my wife is sleeping
and the baby and Kathleen
are sleeping
and the sun is a flame-white disc
in silken mists   5
above shining trees,—
if I in my north room
dance naked, grotesquely
before my mirror
waving my shirt round my head   10
and singing softly to myself:
"I am lonely, lonely.
I was born to be lonely,
I am best so!"
If I admire my arms, my face,   15
my shoulders, flanks, buttocks
against the yellow drawn shades,—

Who shall say I am not
the happy genius of my household?

TERENCE WINCH   (b. 1945)

The Meanest Gang in the Bronx _____ *1985*

once when I was in the fifth grade
I heard a rumor that the Fordham Baldies
were going to invade my school during the lunch hour
I was terrified   everybody knew the Baldies
were the meanest gang in the Bronx   5
who not only killed people but were known
to carve tic tac toe with their knives
on the bellies of their girl victims
since my father was custodian of the school
I tried to warn him about the attack   10
so that he could shut the school down
but he didn't pay me any mind
and the Fordham Baldies never showed up
once they did come into our neighborhood
looking for the Elsmere Tims   our local gang   15
but the brave Tims were no where to be found

TERENCE WINCH   (b. 1945)

Six Families of Puerto Ricans ————————————— *1985*

I guess it was the summer of nineteen
fifty five   I just got back from Rockaway°
the first thing I heard when I got back
was the news that
six families of Puerto Ricans had moved   5
into nineteen fifteen Daly Avenue   the Mitchells'
building   as time went on
more and more pee ars moved into
the neighborhood   there was great hostility
on both sides   once on the fourth of July   10
Martin Conlon threw some cherry bombs
and ash cans through the windows of the Puerto
Ricans   they were just spics to us
I remember a Puerto Rican shooting
at me and some friends with a bee bee gun   15
from his roof   you could hear the bee bees
bouncing off the cars   bodegas opened
on Tremont Avenue   Spanish kids dropped
water balloons on Irish kids   there was
a Sunday mass in Spanish in the church basement   20
this was worse than a potato famine
and the Irish started moving out
Mr. Zayas moved in next door to us
where the Gormans had lived   Mr. Zayas
had a son named Efrain who married   25
a beautiful girl named Carmen   Puerto Rican men
played dominoes on the sidewalk
when me and my father left the block
in the fall of nineteen sixty eight
we were among a handful of Irish still   30
in the neighborhood   things were so bad
by then that even the respectable Puerto Ricans
like Mr. Zayas were long gone
we used to think Puerto Ricans
weren't too far from being animals   35
even if they were Catholics

2 *Rockaway:* a town in Long Island.

WILLIAM WORDSWORTH   (1770–1850)

The World Is Too Much with Us ————————————— *1807*

The world is too much with us; late and soon,
Getting and spending, we lay waste our powers:

Little we see in nature that is ours;
We have given our hearts away, a sordid boon!
This Sea that bares her bosom to the moon;   5
The Winds that will be howling at all hours
And are upgathered now like sleeping flowers;
For this, for everything, we are out of tune;
It moves us not—Great God! I'd rather be
A Pagan suckled in a creed outworn;   10
So might I, standing on this pleasant lea,
Have glimpses that would make me less forlorn;
Have sight of Proteus coming from the sea;
Or hear old Triton blow his wreathèd horn.

WILLIAM WORDSWORTH   (1770–1850)

Lines Composed a Few Miles above Tintern Abbey° ———————— *1798*

On Revisiting the Banks of the Wye during a Tour, July 13, 1798

Five years have passed; five summers, with the length
Of five long winters! and again I hear
These waters, rolling from their mountain-springs
With a sweet inland murmur.—Once again
Do I behold these steep and lofty cliffs,   5
Which on a wild secluded scene impress
Thoughts of more deep seclusion; and connect
The landscape with the quiet of the sky.
The day is come when I again repose
Here, under this dark sycamore, and view   10
These plots of cottage-ground, these orchard-tufts,
Which, at this season, with their unripe fruits,
Among the woods and copses lose themselves,
Nor, with their green and simple hue, disturb
The wild green landscape. Once again I see   15
These hedge-rows, hardly hedge-rows, little lines
Of sportive wood run wild; these pastoral farms
Green to the very door; and wreaths of smoke
Sent up, in silence, from among the trees,
With some uncertain notice, as might seem,   20
Of vagrant dwellers in the houseless woods,
Or of some hermit's cave, where by his fire
The hermit sits alone.

　　　　　　Though absent long,
These forms of beauty have not been to me,
As is a landscape to a blind man's eye: 25

But oft, in lonely rooms, and mid the din
Of towns and cities, I have owed to them,
In hours of weariness, sensations sweet,
Felt in the blood, and felt along the heart,
And passing even into my purer mind   30
With tranquil restoration:—feelings too
Of unremembered pleasure; such, perhaps,
As may have had no trivial influence
On that best portion of a good man's life;
His little, nameless, unremembered acts   35
Of kindness and of love. Nor less, I trust,
To them I may have owed another gift,
Of aspect more sublime; that blessed mood,
In which the burden of the mystery,
In which the heavy and the weary weight   40
Of all this unintelligible world
Is lightened:—that serene and blessed mood,
In which the affections gently lead us on,
Until, the breath of this corporeal frame,
And even the motion of our human blood   45
Almost suspended, we are laid asleep
In body, and become a living soul:
While with an eye made quiet by the power
Of harmony, and the deep power of joy,
We see into the life of things.   50
                    If this
Be but a vain belief, yet, oh! how oft,
In darkness, and amid the many shapes
Of joyless daylight; when the fretful stir
Unprofitable, and the fever of the world,
Have hung upon the beatings of my heart,   55
How oft, in spirit, have I turned to thee
O sylvan Wye! Thou wanderer through the woods,
How often has my spirit turned to thee!
And now, with gleams of half-extinguished thought,
With many recognitions dim and faint,   60
And somewhat of a sad perplexity,
The picture of the mind revives again:
While here I stand, not only with the sense
Of present pleasure, but with pleasing thoughts
That in this moment there is life and food   65
For future years. And so I dare to hope
Though changed, no doubt, from what I was, when first
I came among these hills; when like a roe
I bounded o'er the mountains, by the sides
Of the deep rivers, and the lonely streams,   70
Wherever nature led; more like a man
Flying from something that he dreads, than one
Who sought the thing he loved. For nature then

(The coarser pleasures of my boyish days,
And their glad animal movements all gone by)   75
To me was all in all.—I cannot paint
What then I was. The sounding cataract
Haunted me like a passion: the tall rock,
The mountain, and the deep and gloomy wood,
Their colors and their forms, were then to me   80
An appetite: a feeling and a love,
That had no need of a remoter charm,
By thought supplied, or any interest
Unborrowed from the eye.—That time is past,
And all its aching joys are now no more,   85
And all its dizzy raptures. Not for this
Faint I, nor mourn nor murmur: other gifts
Have followed, for such loss, I would believe,
Abundant recompence. For I have learned
To look on nature, not as in the hour   90
Of thoughtless youth, but hearing oftentimes
The still, sad music of humanity,
Not harsh nor grating, though of ample power
To chasten and subdue. And I have felt
A presence that disturbs me with the joy   95
Of elevated thoughts; a sense sublime
Of something far more deeply interfused,
Whose dwelling is the light of setting suns,
And the round ocean, and the living air,
And the blue sky, and in the mind of man,   100
A motion and a spirit, that impels
All thinking things, all objects of all thought,
And rolls through all things. Therefore am I still
A lover of the meadows and the woods,
And mountains; and of all that we behold   105
From this green earth; of all the mighty world
Of eye and ear, both what they half-create,
And what perceive; well pleased to recognize
In nature and the language of the sense,
The anchor of my purest thoughts, the nurse,   110
The guide, the guardian of my heart, and soul
Of all my moral being.
                                  Nor, perchance,
If I were not thus taught, should I the more
Suffer my genial spirits to decay:
For thou art with me, here, upon the banks   115
Of this fair river; thou, my dearest Friend,
My dear, dear Friend, and in thy voice I catch
The language of my former heart, and read
My former pleasures in the shooting lights
Of thy wild eyes. Oh! yet a little while   120
May I behold in thee what I was once,

My dear, dear Sister! And this prayer I make,
Knowing that Nature never did betray
The heart that loved her; 'tis her privilege,
Through all the years of this our life, to lead 125
From joy to joy: for she can so inform
The mind that is within us, so impress
With quietness and beauty, and so feed
With lofty thoughts, that neither evil tongues,
Rash judgments, nor the sneers of selfish men, 130
Nor greetings where no kindness is, nor all
The dreary intercourse of daily life,
Shall e'er prevail against us, or disturb
Our cheerful faith that all which we behold
Is full of blessings. Therefore let the moon 135
Shine on thee in thy solitary walk;
And let the misty mountain winds be free
To blow against thee: and in after years,
When these wild ecstasies shall be matured
Into a sober pleasure, when thy mind 140
Shall be a mansion for all lovely forms,
Thy memory be as a dwelling-place
For all sweet sounds and harmonies; Oh! then,
If solitude, or fear, or pain, or grief,
Should be thy portion, with what healing thoughts 145
Of tender joy wilt thou remember me,
And these my exhortations! Nor, perchance,
If I should be, where I no more can hear
Thy voice, nor catch from thy wild eyes these gleams
Of past existence, wilt thou then forget 150
That on the banks of this delightful stream
We stood together; and that I, so long
A worshipper of Nature, hither came,
Unwearied in that service: rather say
With warmer love, oh! with far deeper zeal 155
Of holier love. Nor wilt thou then forget,
That after many wanderings, many years
Of absence, these steep woods and lofty cliffs,
And this green pastoral landscape, were to me
More dear, both for themselves, and for thy sake. 160

JAMES WRIGHT (1927–1980)

At the Executed Murderer's Grave _____ 1971

(for J.L.D.)
"Why should we do this? What good is it to us? Above all, how can we do such a
thing? How can it possibly be done?"

—Freud

I

My name is James A. Wright, and I was born
Twenty-five miles from this infected grave,
In Martins Ferry, Ohio, where one slave
To Hazel-Atlas Glass became my father.
He tried to teach me kindness. I return   5
Only in memory now, aloof, unhurried,
To dead Ohio, where I might lie buried,
Had I not run away before my time.
Ohio caught George Doty. Clean as lime,
His skull rots empty here. Dying's the best   10
Of all the arts men learn in a dead place.
I walked here once. I made my loud display,
Leaning for language on a dead man's voice.
Now sick of lies, I turn to face the past.
I add my easy grievance to the rest: 15

II

Doty, if I confess I do not love you,
Will you let me alone? I burn for my own lies.
The nights electrocute my fugitive,
My mind. I run like the bewildered mad
At St. Clair Sanitarium, who lurk,   20
Arch and cunning, under the maple trees,
Pleased to be playing guilty after dark.
Staring to bed, they croon self-lullabies.
Doty, you make me sick. I am not dead.
I croon my tears at fifty cents per line.   25

III

Idiot, he demanded love from girls,
And murdered one. Also, he was a thief.
He left two women, and a ghost with child.
The hair, foul as a dog's upon his head,
Made such revolting Ohio animals   30
Fitter for vomit than a kind man's grief.
I waste no pity on the dead that stink,
And no love's lost between me and the crying
Drunks of Belaire, Ohio, where police
Kick at their kidneys till they die of drink.   35
Christ may restore them whole, for all of me.
Alive and dead, those giggling muckers who
Saddled my nightmares thirty years ago
Can do without my widely printed sighing
Over their pains with paid sincerity.   40
I do not pity the dead, I pity the dying.

IV

I pity myself, because a man is dead.
If Belmont County killed him, what of me?

His victims never loved him. Why should we?
And yet, nobody had to kill him either.   45
It does no good to woo the grass, to veil
The quicklime hole of a man's defeat and shame.
Nature-lovers are gone. To hell with them.
I kick the clods away, and speak my name.

                                V

This grave's gash festers. Maybe it will heal,   50
When all are caught with what they had to do
In fear of love, when every man stands still
By the last sea,
And the princes of the sea come down
To lay away their robes, to judge the earth   55
And its dead, and we dead stand undefended everywhere,
And my bodies—father and child and unskilled criminal—
Ridiculously kneel to bare my scars,
My sneaking crimes, to God's unpitying stars.

                                VI

Staring politely, they will not mark my face   60
From any murderer's, buried in this place.
Why should they? We are nothing but a man.

                                VII

Doty, the rapist and the murderer,
Sleeps in a ditch of fire, and cannot hear;
And where, in earth or hell's unholy peace,   65
Men's suicides will stop, God knows, not I.
Angels and pebbles mock me under trees.
Earth is a door I cannot even face.
Order be damned, I do not want to die,
Even to keep Belaire, Ohio, safe.   70
The hackles on my neck are fear, not grief.
(Open, dungeon! Open, roof of the ground!)
I hear the last sea in the Ohio grass,
Heaving a tide of gray disastrousness.
Wrinkles of winter ditch the rotted face   75
Of Doty, killer, imbecile, and thief:
Dirt of my flesh, defeated, underground.

WILLIAM BUTLER YEATS   (1865–1939)

Sailing to Byzantium° ————————————————————————— *1927*

                                I

That is no country for old men. The young
In one another's arms, birds in the trees

Byzantium: Now Istanbul, Yeats's ideal city.

—Those dying generations—at their song,
The salmon-falls, the mackerel-crowded seas,
Fish, flesh, or fowl, commend all summer long   5
Whatever is begotten, born, and dies.
Caught in that sensual music all neglect
Monuments of unageing intellect.

II

An aged man is but a paltry thing,
A tattered coat upon a stick, unless   10
Soul clap its hands and sing, and louder sing
For every tatter in its mortal dress,
Nor is there singing school but studying
Monuments of its own magnificence;
And therefore I have sailed the seas and come   15
To the holy city of Byzantium.

III

O sages standing in God's holy fire
As in the gold mosaic of a wall,
Come from the holy fire, perne in a gyre,°
And be the singing-masters of my soul.   20
Consume my heart away; sick with desire
And fastened to a dying animal
It knows not what it is; and gather me
Into the artifice of eternity.

IV

Once out of nature I shall never take   25
My bodily form from any natural thing,
But such a form as Grecian goldsmiths make
Of hammered gold and gold enamelling
To keep a drowsy Emperor awake;
Or set upon a golden bough to sing   30
To lords and ladies of Byzantium
Of what is past, or passing, or to come.

19 *perne in a gyre:* spin in a whirling vortex; a perne is a spool on which yarn is wound.

WILLIAM BUTLER YEATS (1865–1939)

The Lake Isle of Innisfree _____ *1892*

I will arise and go now, and go to Innisfree,
And a small cabin build there, of clay and wattles made:
Nine bean-rows will I have there, a hive for the honeybee,
And live alone in the bee-loud glade.

And I shall have some peace there, for peace comes dropping slow,   5
Dropping from the veils of the morning to where the cricket sings;
There midnight's all a glimmer, and noon a purple glow,
And evening full of the linnet's wings.

I will arise and go now, for always night and day
I hear lake water lapping with low sounds by the shore;   10
While I stand on the roadway, or on the pavements grey,
I hear it in the deep heart's core.

VI

Interpreting
Drama

17

ℛEADING A ℙLAY

Like all literature, drama invites interpretation. However, unlike other forms of literature, drama is live action, so there are many things beyond the text to interpret. For example, vocal inflection or physical movement can suggest meanings invisible in the text. Despite these problems, you can still interpret dramatic texts without having seen full-scale productions if you take the time to recreate them as you read.

A good reading of a play provides the basis of a good interpretation. It includes paying close attention to stage directions and trying to translate those directions into an imaginative structure. Reading the key lines aloud can also help. In plays, you cannot always rely on description and authorial comment for a clue to character. Instead, you need to rely on your powers of observation. For example, in Anton Chekhov's *The Cherry Orchard*, it is up to you to decide whether the decision to turn a beautiful old cherry orchard into a housing development is a good thing or a bad thing. Even Konstantin Stanislavsky (1865–1938), the original director, disagreed with Chekhov's basic attitude toward the play, proving that the text can be interpreted in various important ways. On the other hand, the director's decision in how to present the main characters can cause us to decide this matter one way or another and therefore represents an interpretation in its own right. Reading a play should be accompanied by an effort at imaginative reconstruction of the action.

A close reading examines the text for its use of the elements of drama, such as plot, characterization, style, and setting. The stage directions usually provide enough clues to imagine the actors in motion. For some plays that require more theatricality than others, of course, a close reading of the text alone might yield less than an analysis of a performance. However, close reading is always essential to an interpretation.

Because drama is performed for an audience, it is much more likely to be concerned with audience response than other kinds of literature. For that reason, close reading usually aims at uncovering the elements that most clearly affect the audience. It raises questions about the portrayal of character, the believability of a dramatic situation, the genre of the play (tragedy, comedy, tragicomedy), the use of dramatic irony, thematic questions (especially if it is a "message" play), and style. In certain plays close reading needs to account for imagery, symbolism, and patterns of repetition. Since every play is unique, every play requires a certain kind of attention. For example, in *The Glass Menagerie* the language, because it attempts to recreate the way people in St. Louis spoke, has a special hypnotic effect on the audience, something like the effect of poetry. If you are to understand the power of this play, then, you need to hear this poetry as you read.

The first question in a drama is: What happens? Thus, the first thing to examine is the action, or plot. Then one needs to examine the role of character. Some plays, especially raucous comedies, rely entirely on action and do not need much character development. On the other hand, some of the most important plays concentrate on developing the psychological depth of the character. Sophocles' *Oedipus Rex* starts out like a mystery. A king has been murdered and there is a curse on the land. To release the curse Oedipus must find the murderer. The tragic irony in that play is that he himself, without knowing it, is the murderer. During the course of the play not only do we learn more and more about Oedipus, but Oedipus has his own character revealed to him.

William Shakespeare's *Hamlet* resembles *Oedipus Rex* in many ways. Both are tragedies. Both begin with an unsolved murder, except that in the case of *Hamlet* no one knows there has been a murder until old Hamlet comes back as a ghost to tell his son that he must avenge his death. Action is handled peculiarly in *Hamlet:* it almost stops in the middle of the play. Instead of hurrying to avenge his father's death by killing Claudius, his usurping uncle, Hamlet begins a course of meditation that examines crime, guilt, inaction, and his inner life. Few characters in the history of drama have ever been presented in such depth as Hamlet.

The ideas presented within a play, sometimes described as its themes, are also of importance in the drama presented in this book. August Wilson's *Fences* uses the idea of fences to suggest that black Americans have been hemmed in by limited opportunity. The father in *Fences* could have been a major league baseball player, but in his time only white players were allowed in the major leagues. In Irene Fornés's *Conduct of Life* the problems of tyranny and torture in South America are dealt with directly. The audience is meant to feel the agony and terror of life in a society that dominates its people.

The setting of plays contributes to our understanding. For example, Anton Chekhov set *The Cherry Orchard* in a place that was said to be among the most beautiful spots in Russia. He set it at a time of social change, when the great landowners—who did not work because they collected rents from the land—were facing intractable financial problems. They had formerly depended on serfs, essentially slaves, to do the work on the land. But with emancipation, they found themselves unable to do the work that would keep them independent. With the new economic situations at hand, the aristocratic owners of the beautiful cherry orchard must watch as a new social class, more attuned to money and its value, takes over. This play is so complex and ambiguous that some Russians saw it as a tragedy, while others saw it as a comedy.

INTERPRETIVE STRATEGIES

As with fiction, drama can sustain interpretation from many viewpoints. The imagery, language, and structure of the action can be the basis of a good interpretation, especially when these qualities are unusual and sensitively organized. Patterns such as the many references to the imagery of weeds, flowers, and gardens in *Hamlet* can sometimes be missed by an audience, even an audience of readers. Therefore, a close reading of such details can help us understand the meaning of such a rich play. Symbols, such as the glass figurines in *A Glass Menagerie*, or even the title of a play such as *A Doll House* can also form the basis of a good interpretation. The same kinds of elements that constitute the most interesting aspects of fiction and poetry can sometimes provide a good starting point for a careful close reading.

Because drama is often so close to the experience of life, and because it is usually action presented in the context of a social setting—a specific time and place—we can also look closely at the social issues that qualify the action. Arthur Miller's *Death of a Salesman* was written in the 1950s in a period of rising material gain in America. After World War II, the economic opportunities in the United States changed. Before the war the Great Depression robbed a generation of its chances for material success. After the war things were different. However, in the scramble for economic success many people seemed to adopt materialist values and lose the spiritual values that had guided them earlier. Willy Loman held on to values that were false, thinking that education was unimportant, that being well liked was the key to success. Miller examines the idea in such depth as to make the play not only reveal the nature of American materialism, but that of virtually every nation in which the play has been performed.

The economic situation of the Ranevskys in Chekhov's *The Cherry Orchard* contrasts sharply with that of the developer Lopahin. One could approach this play from the point of view of examining its economic issues. What Chekhov observed about the nature of society in his Russia depends entirely on how he interprets the influence of money, work, and independence in contemporary Russia.

In the play that follows, Susan Glaspell's *Suppressed Desires*, the questions of setting and therefore of economic or social issues are not central to the action. Even the development of character is somewhat limited. We do not get to know the main characters very well in this short play, primarily because their inner lives were not the major interest of Susan Glaspell. Here is a play with a limited plot and with limited interest in the psychological development of character, yet what it centers on is the process of psychological analysis. In Glaspell's time psychoanalysis was the rage, a topic of cocktail parties and popular magazines. What interests Glaspell is the idea of psychoanalysis, and examining this play with that in mind helps us appreciate its appeal.

A STUDENT INTERPRETATION

The following sections describe the development of an interpretation of Susan Glaspell's brief comedy *Suppressed Desires*. Susan Glaspell (1876–1948) founded the most important theater movement in early twentieth-century American drama: the Provincetown Playhouse. After graduating from Drake University, she began a career in journalism. Soon she published her first novel, *The Glory of the Conquered* (1909), which was followed with a collection of stories, *Lifted Masks* (1912), and a second novel, *Fidelity* (1915). She went to Paris on the earnings of her first novel and returned to meet and marry the novelist George Cram Cook. Cook, known as Jig, kidded Glaspell about her serious interest in Freudian psychology, and their joking produced so many good lines of dialogue that they suddenly realized they might have an amusing play. In this way *Suppressed Desires* was formed. Jig Cook helped develop the idea, and Susan Glaspell finished the dialogue. The Provincetown Playhouse began in Susan Glaspell's living room, where the play was first read. Eventually a stage was found in Provincetown for full productions, and soon it moved to New York.

Susan Glaspell wrote a letter to the editor of the *New York Times* (February 15, 1920) in response to a review of *Suppressed Desires* in which she explains her purposes in writing.

> It seems to me that in calling *Suppressed Desires* a jeering travesty on psychoanalysis you are forgetting what the play is leveled at. It is having fun with the people who went off their heads about psychoanalysis—went "bugs"—when this subject reached the first circle in New York to know of it—some years in advance of reaching other circles. If you had known some of those people as we knew them you would certainly have felt them legitimate game for some form of comic treatment. The psychoanalysts knew them, and writers on psychoanalysis and practicing analysts have been among the play's best friends. Surely there is a real distinction here. You are not making fun of a thing when you make fun of people who are absurdly uncritical about that thing.
>
> Mr. Cook and I have been students of psychoanalysis for a number of years and we feel it a bit unfair to put us in the light of people unaware of its significance.

Glaspell wrote several more plays and won the Pulitzer Prize for playwriting in 1930 for *Alison's House,* a play about Emily Dickinson.

SUSAN GLASPELL   (1876–1948)

Suppressed Desires —————————————————————————— *1914*

with the collaboration of George Cram Cook

Characters
    Henrietta Brewster
    Stephen Brewster
    Mabel
    (Place: a New York apartment. Time: today.)
    (A period of two weeks is supposed to elapse between the first and second scenes.)

SCENE I

(The stage represents a studio, used as living and dining room in an upper story, Washington Square South. Through an immense north window in the back wall appear tree tops and the upper part of the Washington Arch. Beyond it you look up Fifth Avenue. There are rugs, bookcases, a divan. Near the window is a big table, loaded at one end with serious-looking books and austere scientific periodicals. At the other end are architect's drawings, blueprints, dividing compasses, square, ruler, etc. There is a door in each side wall. Near the one to the spectator's right stands a costumer with hats and coats masculine and feminine. There is a breakfast table set for three but only two seated at it—namely Henrietta and Stephen Brewster. As the curtains withdraw Steve pushes back his coffee cup and sits dejected.)

HENRIETTA.   It isn't the coffee, Steve dear. There's nothing the matter with the coffee. There's something the matter with *you.*

STEVE *(doggedly).*   There may be something the matter with my stomach.

HENRIETTA *(scornfully).*   Your stomach! The trouble is not with your stomach but in your subconscious mind.

STEVE.   Subconscious piffle! *(Takes morning paper and tries to read.)*

HENRIETTA.   Steve, you never used to be so disagreeable. You certainly have got some sort of a complex. You're all inhibited. You're no longer open to new ideas. You won't listen to a word about psychoanalysis.

STEVE.   A word! I've listened to volumes!

HENRIETTA.   You've ceased to be creative in architecture—your work isn't going well. You're not sleeping well——

STEVE.   How can I sleep, Henrietta, when you're always waking me up in the night to find out what I'm dreaming?

HENRIETTA.   But dreams are so important, Steve.

STEVE.   There's nothing wrong with me.

HENRIETTA.   You don't even talk as well as you used to.

STEVE.   Talk? I can't say a thing without you looking at me in that dark fashion you have when you're on the trail of a complex.

HENRIETTA.   This very irritability indicates that you're suffering from some suppressed desire.

STEVE.   I'm suffering from a suppressed desire for a little peace.

HENRIETTA.   Dr. Russell is doing simply wonderful things with nervous cases. Won't you go to him, Steve?

STEVE *(slamming down his newspaper).*   No, Henrietta, I won't!

HENRIETTA.   But, Stephen—!

STEVE.   Tst! I hear Mabel coming. Let's not be at each other's throats the first day of her visit. *(He takes out cigarettes. Enter Mabel from door left, the side opposite Steve, so that he is facing her. She is wearing a rather fussy negligee and breakfast cap in contrast to Henrietta, who wears "radical" clothes. Mabel is what is called plump.)*

MABEL.   Good morning.

HENRIETTA.   Oh, here you are, little sister.

STEVE.   Good morning, Mabel. *(Mabel nods to him and turns, her face lighting up, to Henrietta.)*

HENRIETTA *(giving Mabel a hug as she leans against her).*   It's so good to have you here.

MABEL.   It's so good to be here—with you.

HENRIETTA.   I was going to let you sleep, thinking you'd be tired after the long trip. Sit down. There'll be fresh toast in a few minutes and *(rising from her chair)* will you have——

MABEL.   Oh, I ought to have told you, Henrietta. Don't get anything for me. I'm not eating any breakfast.

HENRIETTA *(at first in mere surprise).*   Not eating breakfast? *(She sits down, then leans toward Mabel and scrutinizes her.)*

STEVE *(half to himself).*   The psychoanalytical look!

HENRIETTA.   Mabel, why are you not eating any breakfast?

MABEL *(a little startled).*   Why, no particular reason. I just don't care much for breakfast, and they say it keeps down—that is, it's a good thing to go without it.

HENRIETTA.   Don't you sleep well? Did you sleep well last night?

MABEL.   Oh, yes, I slept all right. Yes, I slept fine last night, only *(laughing)* I did have the funniest dream!

STEVE.   S—h! S—t!

HENRIETTA *(moving closer).*   And what did you dream, Mabel?

STEVE.   Look-a-here, Mabel, I feel it's my duty to put you on. Don't tell Henrietta your dreams. If you do she'll find out that you have an underground desire to kill your father and marry your mother.

HENRIETTA.   Don't be absurd, Stephen Brewster. *(Sweetly to Mabel.)* What was your dream, dear?

MABEL *(laughing).*   Well, I dreamed I was a hen.

HENRIETTA.   A hen?

STEVE *(solemnly).*   A hen.

MABEL.   Yes; and I was pushing along through a crowd as fast as I could, but being a hen I couldn't walk very fast—it was like having a tight skirt, you know; and there was some sort of creature in a blue cap—you know how mixed up dreams are—and it kept shouting after me and saying, "Step, Hen! Step, Hen!" until I got all excited and just couldn't move at all.

HENRIETTA *(resting chin in palm and peering).*   You say you became much excited?

MABEL *(laughing).*   Oh, yes; I was in a terrible state.

HENRIETTA *(leaning back, murmurs).*   This is significant.

STEVE.   She dreams she's a hen. She is told to step lively. She becomes violently agitated. What can it mean?

HENRIETTA *(turning impatiently from him).*   Mabel, do you know anything about psychoanalysis?

MABEL *(feebly)*. Oh—not much. No—I—*(Brightening.)* It's something about the war, isn't it?

STEVE. Not that kind of war.

MABEL *(abashed)*. I thought it might be the name of a new explosive.

STEVE. It *is*.

MABEL *(apologetically to Henrietta, who is frowning)*. You see, Henrietta, I—we do not live in touch with intellectual things, as you do. Bob being a dentist—somehow—our friends—

STEVE *(softly)*. Oh, to be a dentist! *(Goes to window and stands looking out.)*

HENRIETTA. Don't you ever see anything more of that editorial writer—what was his name?

MABEL. Lyman Eggleston?

HENRIETTA. Yes, Eggleston. He was in touch with things. Don't you see him?

MABEL. Yes, I see him once in a while. Bob doesn't like him very well.

HENRIETTA. Your husband does not like Lyman Eggleston? *(Mysteriously.)* Mabel, are you perfectly happy with your husband?

STEVE *(sharply)*. Oh, come now, Henrietta—that's going a little strong!

HENRIETTA. Are you perfectly happy with him, Mabel? *(Steve goes to worktable.)*

MABEL. Why—yes—I guess so. Why—of course I am!

HENRIETTA. Are you happy? Or do you only think you are? Or do you only think you *ought* to be?

MABEL. Why, Henrietta, I don't know what you mean!

STEVE *(seizes stack of books and magazines and dumps them on the breakfast table)*. This is what she means, Mabel. Psychoanalysis. My worktable groans with it. Books by Freud, the new Messiah; books by Jung, the new St. Paul; the *Psychoanalytical Review*—back numbers two-fifty per.

MABEL. But what is it all about?

STEVE. All about your sub, un, nonconscious mind and desires you know not of. They may be doing you a great deal of harm. You may go crazy with them. Oh, yes! People are doing it right and left. Your dreaming you're a hen—— *(Shakes his head darkly.)*

MABEL *(hastily, to avert a quarrel)*. But what do you say it is, Henrietta?

STEVE *(looking at his watch)*. Oh, if Henrietta's going to start that! *(He goes to his worktable, and during Henrietta's next speech settles himself and sharpens a lead pencil.)*

HENRIETTA. It's like this, Mabel. You want something. You think you can't have it. You think it's wrong. So you try to think you don't want it. Your mind protects you—avoids pain—by refusing to think the forbidden thing. But it's there just the same. It stays there shut up in your unconscious mind, and it festers.

STEVE. Sort of an ingrowing mental toenail.

HENRIETTA. Precisely. The forbidden impulse is there full of energy which has simply got to do something. It breaks into your consciousness in disguise, masks itself in dreams, makes all sorts of trouble. In extreme cases it drives you insane.

MABEL *(with a gesture of horror)*. Oh!

HENRIETTA *(reassuring)*. But psychoanalysis has found out how to save us from that. It removes the obstruction, brings into consciousness the suppressed desire that was making all the trouble. In a word psychoanalysis is simply the latest scientific method of preventing and curing insanity.

STEVE *(from his table)*. It is also the latest scientific method of separating families.

HENRIETTA *(mildly)*. Families that ought to be separated.

STEVE.   The Dwights, for instance. You must have met them, Mabel, when you were here before. Helen was living, apparently, in peace and happiness with good old Joe. Well—she went to this psychoanalyzer she was "psyched," and biff!—bang!—home she comes with an unsuppressed desire to leave her husband. *(He starts work, drawing lines on a drawing board with a T-square.)*

MABEL.   How terrible! Yes, I remember Helen Dwight. But—but did she have such a desire?

STEVE.   First she'd known of it.

MABEL.   And she *left* him?

HENRIETTA *(coolly).*   Yes, she did.

MABEL.   Wasn't he good to her?

HENRIETTA.   Why yes, good enough.

MABEL.   Wasn't he kind to her?

HENRIETTA.   Oh, yes—kind to her.

MABEL.   And she left her good, kind husband—!

HENRIETTA.   Oh, Mabel! "Left her good, kind husband!" How naive—forgive me, dear, but how bourgeois you are! She came to know herself. And she had the courage!!

MABEL.   I may be very naive and—bourgeois—but I don't see the good of a new science that breaks up homes. *(Steve claps hands, applauding.)*

STEVE.   In enlightening Mabel, we mustn't neglect to mention the case of Art Holden's private secretary, Mary Snow, who has just been informed of her suppressed desire for her employer.

MABEL.   Why, I think it is terrible, Henrietta! It would be better if we didn't know such things about ourselves.

HENRIETTA.   No, Mabel, that is the old way.

MABEL.   But—but her employer? Is he married?

STEVE *(grunts).*   Wife and four children.

MABEL.   Well, then, what good does it do the girl to be told she has a desire for him? There's nothing that can be done about it.

HENRIETTA.   Old institutions will have to be reshaped so that something can be done in such cases. It happens, Mabel, that this suppressed desire was on the point of landing Mary Snow in the insane asylum. Are you so tight-minded that you'd rather have her in the insane asylum than break the conventions?

MABEL.   But—but have people always had these awful suppressed desires?

HENRIETTA.   Always.

STEVE.   But they've just been discovered.

HENRIETTA.   The harm they do has just been discovered. And free, sane people must face the fact that they have to be dealt with.

MABEL *(stoutly).*   I don't believe they have them in Chicago.

HENRIETTA *(business of giving Mabel up).*   People "have them" wherever the living Libido—the center of the soul's energy—is in conflict with petrified moral codes. That means everywhere in civilization. Psychoanalysis—

STEVE.   Good God! I've got the roof in the cellar! *(Holds plan at arm's length.)*

HENRIETTA.   The roof in the cellar! That's what psychoanalysis could undo. *(To Mabel.)* Is it any wonder I'm concerned about Steve? He dreamed the other night that the walls of his room melted away and he found himself alone in a forest. Don't you see how significant it is for an architect to have *walls* slip away from him like that? It symbolizes his loss of grip in his work. There's some suppressed desire——

STEVE *(hurling his ruined plan viciously to the floor).*   Suppressed hell!

HENRIETTA.   You speak more truly than you know. It is through suppressions that hells are formed in us.

MABEL *(looking at Steve, who is tearing his hair).*   Don't you think it would be a good thing, Henrietta, if we went somewhere else? *(They rise and begin to pick up the dishes. Mabel drops a plate which breaks. Henrietta draws up short and looks at her—the psychoanalytic look.)* I'm sorry, Henrietta. One of the Spode plates, too. *(Surprised and resentful as Henrietta continues to peer at her.)* Don't take it so to heart, Henrietta.

HENRIETTA.   I can't help taking it to heart.

MABEL.   I'll get you another. *(Pause. More sharply as Henrietta does not answer.)* I said I'll get you another plate, Henrietta.

HENRIETTA.   It's not the plate.

MABEL.   For heaven's sake, what is it then?

HENRIETTA.   It's the significant little false movement once in a while.

MABEL.   Well, I suppose everyone makes a false movement once in a while.

HENRIETTA.   Yes, Mabel, but these false movements all mean something.

MABEL *(about to cry).*   I don't think that's very nice! It was just because I happened to think of Mabel Snow you were talking about——

HENRIETTA.   *Mabel Snow!*

MABEL.   Snow—Snow—Well, what was her name, then?

HENRIETTA.   Her name is Mary.

MABEL.   Well, *Mary* Snow, then; *Mary* Snow. I never heard her name but once. I don't see anything to make such a fuss about.

HENRIETTA *(gently).*   Mabel dear—mistakes like that in names——

MABEL *(desperately).*   They don't mean something, too, do they?

HENRIETTA *(gently).*   I am sorry, but they do.

MABEL.   But I am always doing that!

HENRIETTA *(after a start of horror).*   My poor little sister, tell me all about it.

MABEL.   About what?

HENRIETTA.   About your not being happy. About your yearnings for another sort of life.

MABEL.   But I *don't.*

HENRIETTA.   Ah, I understand these things, dear. You feel Bob is limiting you to a life which you do not feel free——

MABEL.   Henrietta! When did I ever say such a thing?

HENRIETTA.   You said you are not in touch with things intellectual. You showed your feelings that it is Bob's profession—that has engendered a resentment which has colored your whole life with him.

MABEL.   Why—Henrietta!

HENRIETTA.   Don't be afraid, little sister. There's nothing can shock me or turn me from you. I am not like that. I wanted you to come for this visit because I had a feeling that you needed more from life than you were getting. No one of these things I have seen would excite my suspicion. It's the combination. You don't eat breakfast; you make false moves; you substitute your own name for the name of another *whose love is misdirected.* You're nervous; you look queer; in your eyes there's a frightened look that is most unlike you. And this dream. A *hen*—Come with me this afternoon to Dr. Russell! Your whole life may be at stake, Mabel.

MABEL *(gasping).*   Henrietta, I—you—you always were the smartest in the family, and all that, but—this is terrible! I don't think we *ought* to think such things, and—*(Brightening.)* Why, I'll tell you why I dreamed I was a hen. It was because last night, telling about that time in Chicago, you said I was as mad as a wet hen.

HENRIETTA *(superior)*.   Did you dream you were a *wet* hen?

MABEL *(forced to admit it)*.   No.

HENRIETTA.   No. You dreamed you were a *dry* hen. And why, being a hen, were you urged to step?

MABEL.   Maybe it's because when I am getting on a street-car it always irritates me to have them call "Step lively."

HENRIETTA.   No, Mabel, that is only a child's view of it—if you will forgive me. You see merely the elements used in the dream. You do not see into the dream; you do not see its meaning. This dream of the hen——

STEVE.   Hen—hen—wet hen—dry hen—mad hen! *(Jumps up in a rage.)* Let me out of this!

HENRIETTA *(hastily picking up dishes, speaks soothingly)*.   Just a minute, dear, and we'll have things so you can work in quiet. Mabel and I are going to sit in my room. *(She goes out with both hands full of dishes.)*

STEVE *(seizing hat and coat from the costumer)*.   I'm going to be psychoanalyzed. I'm going now! I'm going straight to that infallible doctor of hers—that priest of this new religion. If he's got honesty enough to tell Henrietta there's nothing the matter with my unconscious mind, perhaps I can be let alone about it, and then I will be all right. *(From the door in a low voice.)* Don't tell Henrietta I'm going. It might take weeks, and I couldn't stand all the talk. *(Exit desperately.)*

(Enter Henrietta.)

HENRIETTA.   Where's Steve? Gone? *(With hopeless gesture.)* You see how impatient he is!—how unlike himself! I tell you, Mabel, I am nearly distracted about Steve.

MABEL.   I think he's a little distracted, too.

HENRIETTA.   Well, if he's gone—you might as well stay in this room. I have a committee meeting at the bookshop, and will have to leave you to yourself for an hour or two. *(As she puts her hat on, her eye, lighting up almost carnivorously, falls on an enormous volume on the floor beside the worktable. The book has been half hidden from the audience by the wastebasket. She picks it up and carries it around the table toward Mabel.)* Here, dear, this is one of the simplest statements of psychoanalysis. You read it and then we can talk more intelligently. *(Mabel takes volume and staggers back under its weight to chair rear center; Henrietta goes to outer door, stops and asks abruptly:)* How old is Lyman Eggleston?

MABEL *(promptly)*.   He isn't forty yet. Why, what made you ask that, Henrietta? *(As she turns her head to look at Henrietta her hands move toward the upper corners of the book balanced on her knees.)*

HENRIETTA.   Oh, nothing. Au revoir. *(Exit.)*

(Mabel stares at the ceiling. The book slides to the floor. She starts; looks at the book, then at the broken plate on the table.) The plate! The book! *(She lifts her eyes, leans forward elbow on knee, chin on knuckles and plaintively queries:)* Am I unhappy?

SCENE II

(The stage is set as in Scene I except that the breakfast table has been removed and set back against the wall. During the first few minutes the dusk of a winter afternoon deepens. Out of the darkness spring rows of double street-lights almost meeting in the distance. Henrietta is disclosed at the psychoanalytical end of Steve's worktable. Surrounded by open books and periodicals, she is writing. Steve enters briskly.)

STEVE.   What are you doing, my dear?

HENRIETTA.   My paper for the Liberal Club.

STEVE.   Your paper on——?

HENRIETTA.   On a subject which does not have your sympathy.

STEVE.   Oh, I'm not sure I'm wholly out of sympathy with psychoanalysis, Henrietta. You worked it so hard. I couldn't even take a bath without it's meaning something.

HENRIETTA *(loftily)*.   I talked it because I knew you needed it.

STEVE.   You haven't said much about it these last two weeks. Uh—your faith in it hasn't weakened any?

HENRIETTA.   Weakened? It's grown stronger with each new thing I've come to know. And Mabel. She is with Dr. Russell now. Dr. Russell is wonderful. From what Mabel tells me I believe he is going to prove that I was right. Today I discovered a remarkable confirmation of my theory in the hen-dream.

STEVE.   What is your theory?

HENRIETTA.   Well, you know about Lyman Eggleston. I've wondered about him from the first. I've never seen him, but I know he's less bourgeois than Mabel's other friends—more intellectual—and *(significantly)* she doesn't see much of him because Bob doesn't like him.

STEVE.   But what's the confirmation?

HENRIETTA.   Today I noticed the first syllable of his name.

STEVE.   Ly?

HENRIETTA.   No—egg.

STEVE.   Egg?

HENRIETTA *(patiently)*.   Mabel dreamed she was a *hen*. *(Steve laughs.)* You wouldn't laugh if you knew how important names are in interpreting dreams. Freud is full of just such cases in which a whole hidden complex is revealed by a single significant syllable— like this egg.

STEVE.   Doesn't the traditional relation of hen and egg suggest rather a maternal feeling?

HENRIETTA.   There is something maternal in Mabel—love, of course, but that's only one element.

STEVE.   Well, suppose Mabel hasn't a suppressed desire to be this gentleman's mother, but his beloved. What's to be done about it? What about Bob? Don't you think it's going to be a little rough on him?

HENRIETTA.   That can't be helped. Bob, like everyone else, must face the facts of life. If Dr. Russell should arrive independently at this same interpretation I shall not hesitate to tell Mabel to leave her present husband.

STEVE.   Um—um! *(The lights go up on Fifth Avenue. Steve goes to the window and looks out.)* How long is it we've lived here, Henrietta?

HENRIETTA.   Why, this is the third year, Steve.

STEVE.   I—we—one would miss this view if one went away, wouldn't one?

HENRIETTA.   How strangely you speak! Oh, Stephen, I *wish* you'd go to Dr. Russell. Don't think my fears have abated because I have been able to restrain myself. I felt I must on account of Mabel. It wouldn't do for her to hear you discrediting it while she was being analyzed. But now, dear—won't you go?

STEVE.   I—*(He breaks off, turns on the light, then comes and sits beside Henrietta.)* How long have we been married, Henrietta?

HENRIETTA.   Stephen, I don't understand you! You must go to Dr. Russell.

STEVE.   I *have* gone.

HENRIETTA.   You—what?

STEVE *(jauntily).*   Yes, Henrietta, I've been psyched.

HENRIETTA.   You went to Dr. Russell?

STEVE.   The same.

HENRIETTA.   And what did he say?

STEVE.   He said—I—I was a little surprised by what he said, Henrietta.

HENRIETTA *(breathlessly).*   Of course—one can so seldom anticipate. But tell me—your dream, Stephen? It means——?

STEVE.   It means—I was considerably surprised by what it means.

HENRIETTA.   *Don't* be so exasperating!

STEVE.   It means—you really want to know, Henrietta?

HENRIETTA.   Stephen, you'll drive me mad!

STEVE.   He said—Of course he may be wrong in what he said.

HENRIETTA.   He *isn't* wrong. *Tell* me!

STEVE.   He said my dream of the walls receding and leaving me alone in a forest indicates a suppressed desire—

HENRIETTA.   Yes—yes!

STEVE.   To be freed from——

HENRIETTA.   Yes—freed from——?

STEVE.   Marriage.

HENRIETTA *(crumples. Stares).*   Marriage!

STEVE.   He—he may be mistaken, you know.

HENRIETTA.   *May* be mistaken!

STEVE.   I—well, of course, I haven't taken any stock in it myself. It was only your great confidence——

HENRIETTA.   Stephen, are you telling me that Dr. Russell—Dr. A. R. Russell—told you this? *(Steve nods.)* Told you you have a suppressed desire to separate from me?

STEVE.   That's what he said.

HENRIETTA.   Did he know who you were?

STEVE.   Yes.

HENRIETTA.   That you were married to me?

STEVE.   Yes, he knew that.

HENRIETTA *(rising).*   And he told you to leave me?

STEVE.   It seems he must be wrong, Henrietta.

HENRIETTA.   And I've sent him more patients—! *(Catches herself and resumes coldly.)* What reason did he give for this analysis?

STEVE.   He says the confining walls are a symbol of my feeling about marriage and that their fading away is a wish-fulfillment.

HENRIETTA *(gulping).*   Well, is it? Do you want our marriage to end?

STEVE.   Well, it was a surprise to me that I did, Henrietta—a great surprise. You see I hadn't known what was in my unconscious mind.

HENRIETTA *(flaming).*   What did you tell Dr. Russell about me? What did you tell him to make him think you were not happy?

STEVE.   I never told him a thing, Henrietta. He got it all from his confound-clever inferences. I—I tried to refute them, but he said that was only part of my self-protective lying.

HENRIETTA.   And that's why you were so—happy—when you came in just now!

STEVE.   Why, Henrietta, how can you say such a thing? I was *sad.* Didn't I speak sadly of—of the view? Didn't I ask you how long we had been married?

HENRIETTA *(rising).*   Stephen Brewster, have you no sense of the seriousness of this? Dr. Russell doesn't know what our marriage has been. You do. You should have laughed him down! Confined—in life with me? Why didn't you tell him that I believed in freedom?

STEVE.   I very emphatically told him that his results were a great surprise to me.

HENRIETTA.   But you accepted them.

STEVE.   Oh, not at all. I merely couldn't refute his arguments. I'm not a psychologist. I came home to talk it over with you. You being a disciple of psychoanalysis——

HENRIETTA *(whirling).*   If you are going, I wish you would go tonight!

STEVE.   Oh, my dear! I—surely couldn't do that! Think of my feelings. And my laundry hasn't come home yet.

HENRIETTA.   I ask you to go tonight. Some women would falter at this, Steve, but I am not such a woman. I leave you free. I do not repudiate psychoanalysis, I say again that it has done great things. It has also made mistakes, of course. But since you accept this analysis—*(She sits down and pretends to begin work.)* I have to finish this paper. I wish you would leave me.

STEVE *(scratches his head, goes to the inner door).*   I'm sorry, Henrietta, about my unconscious mind. *(Exit.) (Henrietta's face betrays her outraged state of mind—disconcerted, resentful, trying to pull herself together. She attains an air of bravely bearing an outrageous thing. Mabel enters in great excitement.)*

MABEL *(breathless).*   Henrietta, I'm so glad you're here. And alone? *(Looks toward the inner door.)* Are you alone, Henrietta?

HENRIETTA *(with reproving dignity).*   Very much so.

MABEL *(rushing to her).*   Henrietta, he's found it!

HENRIETTA *(aloof).*   Who has found what?

MABEL.   Who has found what? Dr. Russell has found my suppressed desire.

HENRIETTA.   That is interesting.

MABEL.   He finished with me today—he got hold of my complex—in the most amazing way! But, oh, Henrietta—it is so terrible!

HENRIETTA.   Do calm yourself, Mabel. Surely there's no occasion for all this agitation.

MABEL.   But there is! And when you think of the lives that are affected—the readjustments that must be made in order to bring the suppressed hell out of me and save me from the insane asylum——!

HENRIETTA.   The insane asylum!

MABEL.   You said that's where these complexes brought people?

HENRIETTA.   What did the doctor tell you, Mabel?

MABEL.   Oh, I don't know how I can tell you—it is so awful—so unbelievable. Henrietta, who would ever have thought it? How can it be true? But the doctor is perfectly certain that I have a suppressed desire for——*(Looks at Henrietta, unable to go on.)*

HENRIETTA.   Oh, go on, Mabel. I'm not unprepared for what you have to say.

MABEL.   Not unprepared? You mean you have suspected it?

HENRIETTA.   From the first. It's been my theory all along.

MABEL.   But, Henrietta, I didn't know myself that I had this secret desire for Stephen.

HENRIETTA *(jumps up).*   Stephen!

MABEL.   My brother-in-law! My own sister's husband!

HENRIETTA.   *You* have a suppressed desire for *Stephen!*

MABEL.   Oh, Henrietta, aren't these unconscious selves terrible? They seem so unlike us!

HENRIETTA.   What insane things are you driving at?

MABEL *(blubbering).*   Henrietta, don't you use that word to me. I don't want to go to the insane asylum.

HENRIETTA *(stonily).*   What did Dr. Russell say?

MABEL.   Well, you see—oh, it's the strangest thing! But you know the voice in my dream that called "Step, Hen!" Dr. Russell found out today that when I was a little girl I had a story-book in words of one syllable and I read the name Stephen wrong. I used to read it S-t-e-p, step, h-e-n, hen. *(Dramatically.)* Step Hen is Stephen. *(Enter Stephen, his head bent over a time-table.)* Stephen is Step Hen!

STEVE.   I? Step Hen!

MABEL *(triumphantly).*   S-t-e-p, step, H-e-n, hen, Stephen!

HENRIETTA *(exploding).*   Well, what if Stephen is Step Hen? *(Scornfully.)* Step Hen! Step Hen! For that ridiculous coincidence——

MABEL.   Coincidence! But it's so childish to look at the mere elements of a dream. You have to look into it—you have to see what it means!

HENRIETTA.   And do you mean to say that on account of that trivial, meaningless play on syllables—on that flimsy basis—you are ready—*(Wails.)* O-h!

STEVE.   What on earth's the matter? What has happened? Suppose I am Step Hen? What about it? What does it mean?

MABEL *(crying).*   It means—that I—have a suppressed desire for *you!*

STEVE.   For me! The deuce you have? *(Feebly.)* What—er—makes you think so?

MABEL.   Dr. Russell has worked it out scientifically.

HENRIETTA.   Yes. Through the amazing discovery that Step Hen equals Stephen!

MABEL *(tearfully).*   Oh, that isn't all—that isn't near all. Henrietta won't give me a chance to tell it. She'd rather I'd go to the insane asylum than be unconventional.

HENRIETTA.   We'll all go there if you can't control yourself. We are still waiting for some rational report.

MABEL *(drying her eyes).*   Oh, there's such a lot about names. *(With some pride.)* I don't see how I ever did it. It all works in together. I dreamed I was a hen because that's the first syllable of *Hen*-rietta's name, and when I dreamed I was a hen, I was putting myself in Henrietta's place.

HENRIETTA.   With Stephen?

MABEL.   With Stephen.

HENRIETTA *(outraged).*   Oh! *(Turns in rage upon Stephen, who is fanning himself with the time-table.)* What are you doing with that time-table?

STEVE.   Why—I thought—you were so keen to have me go tonight—I thought I'd just take a run up to Canada, and join Billy—a little shooting—but——

MABEL.   But there's more about the names.

HENRIETTA.   Mabel, have you thought of Bob—dear old Bob—your good, kind husband?

MABEL.   Oh, Henrietta, "my good kind husband"!

HENRIETTA.   Just think of him out there in Chicago, working his head off, fixing people's teeth—for you!

MABEL.   Yes, but think of the living Libido—in conflict with petrified moral codes! And think of the perfectly wonderful way the names all prove it. Dr. Russell said he's never seen anything more convincing. Just look at Stephen's last name—Brewster. I dream I'm a hen, and the name Brewster—you have to say its first letter by itself—and then the hen, that's me, she says to him: "Stephen, Be Rooster!"

(Henrietta and Stephen both collapse on chair and divan.)

MABEL.   I think it's perfectly wonderful! Why, if it wasn't for psychoanalysis you'd never find out how wonderful your own mind is!

STEVE *(begins to chuckle).*   Be Rooster, Stephen, Be Rooster!

HENRIETTA.   You think it's funny, do you?

STEVE.   Well, what's to be done about it? Does Mabel have to go away with me?

HENRIETTA.   Do you *want* Mabel to go away with you?

STEVE.   Well, but Mabel herself—her complex—her suppressed desire—!

HENRIETTA.   Mabel, are you going to insist on going away with Stephen?

MABEL.   I'd rather go with Stephen than go to the insane asylum!

HENRIETTA.   For heaven's sake, Mabel, drop that insane asylum! If you *did* have a suppressed desire for Stephen hidden away in you—God knows it isn't hidden *now.* Dr. Russell has brought it into consciousness—with a vengeance. That's all that's necessary to break up a complex. Psychoanalysis doesn't say you have to *gratify* every suppressed desire.

STEVE *(softly).*   Unless it's for Lyman Eggleston.

HENRIETTA *(turning on him).*   Well, if it comes to that, Stephen Brewster, I'd like to know why that interpretation of mine isn't as good as this one? Step, Hen!

STEVE.   But Be Rooster! *(He pauses, chuckling to himself.)* Step-Hen B-rooster *and* Henrietta. Pshaw, my dear, Doc Russell's got you beat a mile! *(He turns away and chuckles.)* Be rooster!

MABEL.   What has Lyman Eggleston got to do with it?

STEVE.   According to Henrietta's interpretation, you, the hen, have a suppressed desire for Lyman Eggleston, the egg.

MABEL.   Henrietta, I think that's indecent of you! He is bald as an egg and little and fat—the idea of you thinking such a thing of me!

HENRIETTA.   Well, Bob isn't little and bald and fat! Why don't you stick to your own husband? *(Turns on Stephen.)* What if Dr. Russell's interpretation has got mine "beat a mile"? *(Resentful look at him.)* It would only mean that Mabel doesn't want Eggleston and does want you. Does that mean she is to have you?

MABEL.   But you said Mabel Snow——

HENRIETTA.   *Mary* Snow!! You're not as much like her as you think—substituting your name for hers! The cases are entirely different. Oh, I wouldn't have believed this of you, Mabel. I brought you here for a pleasant visit—thought you needed brightening up—wanted to be nice to you—and now you—my husband—you insist—*(Begins to cry. Makes a movement which brushes to the floor some sheets from the psychoanalytical table.)*

STEVE *(with solicitude).*   Careful, dear. Your paper on psychoanalysis! *(Gathers up sheets and offers them to her.)*

HENRIETTA *(crying).*   I don't want my paper on psychoanalysis! I'm sick of psychoanalysis!

STEVE *(eagerly).*   Do you mean that, Henrietta?

HENRIETTA.   Why shouldn't I mean it? Look at all I've done for psychoanalysis—and—what has psychoanalysis done for me?

STEVE.   Do you mean, Henrietta, that you're going to stop taking psychoanalysis?

HENRIETTA.   Why shouldn't I stop taking it? Haven't I seen what it does to people? Mabel has gone crazy about psychoanalysis! *(At the word "crazy" Mabel sinks with a moan into the armchair and buries her face in her hands.)* I'm done with it!

STEVE *(solemnly).*   Do you swear never to wake me up in the night to find out what I'm dreaming?

HENRIETTA.   Dream what you please—I don't care what you're dreaming.

STEVE.   Will you clear off my worktable so that the *Journal of Morbid Psychology* doesn't stare me in the face when I'm trying to plan a house?

HENRIETTA *(pushing a stack of periodicals off the table)*.   I'll *burn* the *Journal of Morbid Psychology!*

STEVE.   My dear Henrietta, if you're going to separate from psychoanalysis, there's no reason why I should separate from you. *(They embrace ardently. Mabel lifts her head and looks at them woefully.)*

MABEL *(jumping up and going toward them)*.   But what about me? What am I to do with my suppressed desire?

STEVE *(with one arm still around Henrietta, gives Mabel a brotherly hug)*.   Mabel, you just keep right on suppressing it.

Beginning with Close Reading

One of the first steps in close reading is to keep track of some of the play's most important details. Here is one person's list.

The play opens with Henrietta "henpecking" Steve about psychoanalysis.
Steve is an architect.
Henrietta tells Steve his dreams are important.
She interprets his irritability as rooted in a suppressed desire.
Mabel is Henrietta's sister; she enters in a "fussy negligee."
Henrietta assumes there is a "reason" that Mabel does not eat breakfast.
She discovers that Mabel had a dream.
The dream involves a hen and a shout: "Step, Hen!"
Henrietta assumes the dream means something important.
She finds out Mabel's husband does not like Lyman Eggleston.
Henrietta asks if Mabel is happy or only thinks she is.
Henrietta explains psychoanalysis as the modern way of preventing insanity.
Henrietta mentions several examples of women acting on suppressed desires and leaving their husbands.
Henrietta says "old institutions will have to be reshaped."
When Steve dreams about walls, "walls" suddenly have important meaning, a suppressed desire.
Henrietta sees significance in "little false movements" and in mistakes of names-- these are Freudian slips.
Henrietta was "always the smartest in the family."
Steve decides to go to the doctor to get psychoanalyzed.
Henrietta gives Mabel a huge book on psychoanalysis.
Mabel ends Scene I wondering if she is happy.
Scene II opens with Henrietta preparing a paper on psychoanalysis.
She interprets Mabel's dream to suggest she is in love with Lyman Eggleston.
The reversal takes place when Steve explains he has been "psyched" and has a suppressed desire to be freed from marriage.
Henrietta tries to conceal her shock.
The doctor's analysis was based on "confound-clever inferences."
Steve did not accept the doctor's arguments; he "merely couldn't refute them."
Henrietta suggests he leave immediately; she does not "repudiate psychoanalysis."
Stage directions indicate that she is more upset than she reveals.

Mabel enters and tells her that Dr. Russell has uncovered her suppressed desire: it is for Stephen.

Henrietta tries to remind her of her "good, kind husband" Bob.

Mabel sees great meaning in names, as in "Be Rooster" for Brewster.

Henrietta finally says that the important thing is not to "gratify every suppressed desire"--bringing it up in the consciousness is all that is needed to "break up a complex."

Henrietta interprets Mabel's dream differently than Dr. Russell.

Finally she breaks down and repudiates psychoanalysis, casting her paper to the floor.

She accuses Mabel of "going crazy over psychoanalysis."

Steve gets Henrietta to give up psychoanalysis and then tells Mabel to keep on suppressing her desires.

Different readers will produce different lists of details or may want to add to this one. You may find it useful to discuss *Suppressed Desires* with other readers to see which details impress them.

Keeping a Response Journal

The following entries from a response journal concentrate on an overview of the play.

Feb. 26. I thought the play was funny. It is a comedy, not a tragicomedy because everything works out all right and nobody suffers for anything. Henrietta is a dominating kind of person and Steve seems to be easygoing and a little overwhelmed. Not much actually happens on stage--people basically sit or stand and talk, and the "action" occurs in the ideas that they talk about. There is a conflict. The conflict is between Henrietta and everyone else. She assumes that dreams, mistakes, and other slips of language all have meaning and the meaning reveals the deep desires people have. Suppressed desires. All the ones in this play seem to be involved in sexual freedom. Obviously that makes you wonder if Susan Glaspell doesn't have some of the same desires. Apparently Glaspell's husband decided to live in Delphi, Greece, on a hillside like a Greek peasant. He died there in the late 1920s and she was with him most of the time. Maybe she had a suppressed desire of her own.

Feb. 27. A thought occurred to me. Steve says he's going to go to the doctor to get "psyched" but I wonder if he really went at all. He says he's going, but that could be a smokescreen. I wonder. Henrietta is all in favor of other women acting on their suppressed desires, but not Mabel. When Mabel says the doctor told her she had a desire for Stephen, Henrietta reacts. At first she is a "disciple" of psychoanalysis—as long as it doesn't affect her. But when it backfires, she gets rid of it. This reversal is one source of its comedy.

Feb. 28. One thing seems to be that the play is about interpreting things. Dreams are like stories, and Henrietta interprets them. There's that line near the end about Dr. Russell's interpretation being better than Henrietta's. That's a lot like interpreting a text. The dream is a text. The way it's interpreted is what counts.

Freewriting

The writer has found a number of interesting points. One is that the source of the comedy is in the reversal of Henrietta's beliefs in psychoanalysis when the interpretations of dreams begin to affect her negatively. Another point is that interpretation is one theme of the play, and may be a useful beginning for discussing the play. However, before going further, the writer sat down and did some freewriting, hoping to make a discovery or two that would be useful later.

> Lots of things going on in the play. Glaspell was a feminist and she has Henrietta say a lot of things that feminists might say. For example, she says that there are worn-out moral principles that keep women from fulfilling themselves—or something to that effect. She must mean marriages that don't work. In the beginning of the play she says right away that people have to act on their suppressed desires or else go insane, and she has some examples—Helen Dwight and Mary Snow. They both acted on their desires and got out of a bad situation. In the beginning of the play psychoanalysis is like a religion. She's a disciple. Freud is the Messiah and Jung the St. Paul, so it's a religion. That must mean it should reveal the truth even about what you can't see. Like Moses tells us what God said, but we can't see God. The subconscious is not "seeable" either and psychoanalysis is the only way we can get in touch with it. Henrietta believes it all as long as only other people are affected by it. Even Steve says he feels sorry for Helen Dwight's decent husband. She never feels anything for him. Then when things are reversed, she loses it.

By now the reader was ready to try out some paragraphs for the essay. One fact was clear: *Suppressed Desires* could be approached in several ways. For example, the strong feminist concern in the play could be one focus, and psychoanalysis could be another. One could also examine this play as a comedy, and perhaps study its use of dramatic irony. The writer began to develop some paragraphs in an effort to find the best interpretive strategy.

> Henrietta is an idealist. By that I mean she is committed to ideas that she thinks should tell people how to live. For example, she believes in being up to date and not suppressing desires even when that involves breaking up with a "good, kind husband," as Helen Dwight did. She believes that "old institutions have to be reshaped" so as to avoid insanity, one of the results of suppressing strong desires.
>
> Her husband, Steve, is a practical type. He has heard a lot about psychoanalysis, but he does not have any faith in it. The reason is that he thinks Helen Dwight was wrong in running off from her husband. He also agrees with Mabel, who thinks Mary Snow should have suppressed her desire for her employer because her employer had a wife and four children. Steve is also a good, kind husband. But it is also clear that he is just tolerating Henrietta's commitment to psychoanalysis in the hopes that it will go away. He does not believe in it in Scene I. But Henrietta spends a great deal of time in amateur psychology trying to find the significance of Mabel's dream.

> Amateur psychology is basically nothing more than interpretation. The play gets most interesting when the interpretations of individuals conflict. For example, when Henrietta interprets Mabel's dream as indicating a symbolic yearning for Lyman Eggleston, she relies on the syllable "Egg" in his name. When Dr. Russell interprets it, the object of her desire suddenly becomes Steve because "Step hen" is his name. Henrietta's name could also be involved, and so could Mabel's idea that being called "a wet hen" might have triggered the dream. I think the point of the play is that you can't go around choosing one set of evidence just because it is convenient. You can see the results of that when things go against Henrietta in Scene II. Suddenly she is an idealist who doesn't like the ideas she has to deal with.

The writer went over this material and saw that there was enough to begin an interpretation. Several important points emerged from the prewriting process, and either separately or together, they could be used as the basis of a good interpretation.

> 1. The play is about interpreting behavior so as to reveal hidden meanings. But Henrietta, who believes in psychoanalysis, is happy only when she is in control of the interpretation.
> 2. Henrietta's feminism is as important to her as her belief in psychoanalysis. However, in both cases she is happy only when the ideas work to her advantage.
> 3. *Suppressed Desires* shows us how difficult it is to believe in ideas that are worthwhile but which can sometimes work against us. To be an idealist is very difficult if the idealist does not have some practicality.

The writer decided to work with the first point and compose an opening paragraph.

> *Suppressed Desires* is a study of how new ideas affect people. Henrietta is a "disciple" of psychoanalysis, and her husband Steve has been hearing so much about it that he is getting tired. He compares it to a religion. But he does not mean that it is good. When Henrietta tells him he is suffering from some kind of suppressed desire, a bad sign in psychoanalysis, he says, "a suppressed desire for a little peace." He wants some peace because Henrietta has found a new idea that gives her power over other people. She sees that everything they dream and every mistake they make, especially a mistake in a name, has a hidden meaning. But she is the only one who can interpret that meaning. That gives her power.

Developing an Outline

At this point the writer decided to try to use this as an opening and prepare an outline for the rest of the interpretation. This assignment was to write a three-page essay without using outside sources or help. Class discussion had provided some background biographical information on Susan Glaspell, but apart from general comments, no special critical studies.

Outline: "Interpretation as Power in Suppressed Desires"
I. Introduction: Interpretation is power
   A. Henrietta controls the new idea: psychoanalysis
   B. Steve is subservient
II. Henrietta dominates Mabel
   A. Mabel's dream
   B. Mabel's interpretation
   C. Harriet's interpretation
III. Henrietta explains psychoanalysis
   A. Her examples: Helen and Mary
   B. Feminism and suppressed desires
IV. Steve and Mabel go to Dr. Russell
   A. Conflict
      1. Dr. Russell's interpretation
         a. Steve's suppressed desires
         b. Mabel's suppressed desires
   B. Henrietta's reaction to Dr. Russell
V. The reversal: Henrietta's ideas backfire
   A. Her reaction to Steve
      1. How she holds to feminist principles
   B. Her reaction to Mabel
      2. How she reconsiders her attitude toward husbands
VI. Conclusion: How hard it is to be an idealist

The writer moved on from here to do a draft of the essay, using the first paragraph above and referring to earlier notes. After a waiting period, the writer went back to the first draft, revised it, and produced the essay that follows.

**SAMPLE ESSAY: AN INTERPRETATION
OF *SUPPRESSED DESIRES***

Muriello 1

Tina Muriello
English 109–08
Paper Four
Prof. Jacobus

Interpretation as Power in *Suppressed Desires*

Susan Glaspell shows that the person who can interpret the meaning of things has power over others. She also shows that there can be conflicts between interpreters, and when that happens the loser sometimes gives up the new ideas that made the interpretation possible to begin with. The first conflict in the play is between Henrietta and her husband Steve. She is a "disciple" of psychoanalysis, and Steve, an architect, has been hearing so much about it he is getting worn out. He compares it to a religion, "with books by Freud, the new Messiah." But he does not mean this positively. He is fed up with Henrietta and psychoanalysis. When she tells him he is suffering from a suppressed desire, he tells her it is "a suppressed desire for a little peace." He's tired because Henrietta uses psychoanalysis as a weapon to get power over people. She tells them what their dreams mean, what their mistakes in language mean, and what their hidden desires are. Someone like this could be very annoying. One reason Henrietta has so much power is that she's an expert in psychoanalysis. But another reason is that Steve is henpecked and gives in to her.

Henrietta even dominates her sister Mabel, who is visiting from Chicago, where her husband is a dentist. When she begins to tell people her "funniest" dream, Steve tries to shush her up. He tells her that Henrietta will uncover an Oedipus complex: "she'll find out that you have an underground desire to kill your father and marry your mother." Mabel interprets her dream of "being a hen" told by a creature in a "blue cap" to "step, hen" as about being on a street car and being told to step lively. She says the dream was suggested by Henrietta calling her a "wet hen" earlier in the evening. Henrietta ridicules that interpretation by calling it "only a child's view."

Henrietta interprets the dream as concealing a suppressed desire for an old boyfriend, Lyman Eggleston. Her interpretation depends on the first syllable of his last name. Henrietta explains how Helen Dwight and Mary Snow both had suppressed desires that were driving them insane. Psychoanalysis, she tells them, "is simply the latest scientific method of preventing and curing insanity." Henrietta's examples both involve breaking up a marriage in order to express the suppressed desires. She approves both women's behavior on feminist grounds. The "old institutions will have to be reshaped" if women are to be free.

The conflict grows when Steve and Mabel go to Dr. Russell. He "psyches" them and interprets their suppressed desires. Steve supposedly wants to be free from Henrietta, and Mabel supposedly wants Steve. Henrietta is "alarmed" at this interpretation. But she has already said, "If Dr. Russell should arrive independently at this same interpretation I shall not hesitate to advise Mabel to leave her present husband." But when she is told what Dr. Russell says, she can hardly believe it. The stage directions, "*Catches herself and resumes coldly*" and "*gulping*," show that she is not able to accept what he says, but she puts on a good front.

The reversal puts Henrietta in an ironic position. If she keeps her faith in psychoanalysis her marriage is gone. If she keeps her faith in feminism Mabel gets her husband. She says, "What if Dr. Russell's interpretation has got mine 'beat a mile'?" She doesn't care. She realizes that the interpretation does not matter when it goes against her. What matters is that she should keep her husband and that Mabel should go back to hers. Finally, Henrietta rejects psychoanalysis by pushing over a stack of journals. She and Steve "*embrace ardently.*" Henrietta gives up her power in order to save her family.

Henrietta shows how interpretation can make life uncomfortable sometimes. In psychoanalysis, if you have the power to control the interpretation (because you have more knowledge), things are fine. Otherwise you become a potential victim, like Henrietta. I wondered if Steve and Mabel might not have made up the story of going to Dr. Russell and just made up their interpretations to spite Henrietta. The play does not say so, but I think it would be even more ironic if they did.

Further Strategies for Interpretation

This interpretation focuses on one element of the play, the theme of domination, which provides the material for analysis. The writer was interested in seeing how Henrietta's commitment to ideals worked as long as they were to her advantage. What the writer uncovered was an all too human tendency to hold on to ideals as long as they are useful, then to abandon them when they get threatening. The writer might have said so more directly and clearly, but the implication is present in the essay. There are, however, some other strategies that could also work well in interpreting the play.

IRONY.   One could emphasize the basic irony that the very ideas Henrietta holds most dear come back to torment her. The irony is not that she thinks psychoanalysis is powerful or true, but that she thinks anyone can practice it after reading a few books about it. One marvelous irony would be the verification of the writer's suspicion above: that Steve and Mabel "invented" the story about going to Dr. Russell. If you could, from a study of the play, establish that Steve and Mabel made up their stories to "cure" Henrietta, that would add a powerful ironic twist by giving them the same kind of power over Henrietta that she had over them. Small ironic details would also figure into a reading of the play. For example, the book Henrietta gives Mabel is supposed to be a small treatise on psychoanalysis, but it is so heavy it almost knocks Mabel down. Ironically, it is much too heavy for anyone in the play.

FEMINIST.   Feminist issues in this play are problematic. Henrietta seems to be a feminist and seems to believe strongly that women should be free to express themselves. She appears to be willing to accept the fact that marriages may have to be shattered for feminists to realize themselves. However, her beliefs are shaken when she becomes the victim of one woman, her sister, who threatens to take Steve away from her. Either this means that Henrietta is not as strong a feminist as she says she is or that Susan Glaspell's own beliefs in feminism are limited. An essay on this subject would have to account for the change at the end of the play: Henrietta's dominance by Steve and his "striking a deal" with her about psychoanalysis. Because the play was written in 1914, you might be able to argue that early feminists risked exactly what Henrietta could not face. She may be a model for all early feminists. But it may also be argued that the conventional American theatergoers of 1914 were not yet ready for the full force of feminism. Consequently the play had to be rendered conventional and acceptable by having Steve, the husband, end up victorious.

READER RESPONSE.   Responses to the play will be quite individual. However, one response may be impatience with how both Steve and Mabel tolerate Henrietta's dominance over them. The fact that the audience is probably uniformly pleased when Henrietta gets her comeuppance may also annoy those who are feminists or people who feel that Freudian psychology has provided the world with important insights. Why, such viewers might ask, should we feel pleased to see the defeat of a character holding such views? Perhaps Glaspell knew well in advance that her audience would not tolerate approving such a character. Therefore, to get the audience to listen to *any* feminist or psychoanalytic theories, she had to reward them with the response they wanted and maybe the only response they could tolerate: delight at seeing someone whose theories they disagreed with get "shot down." This interpretation would then propose the theory that Susan Glaspell was not selling out feminism or Freudian psychology, both positions that she personally championed. Instead, she was being realistic and taking the ideas as far as they would go, but no further. If Henrietta's dominance had gone unchallenged, the audience would have rejected the entire play. Given the way Glaspell handled the play, the audience had a great deal to think about after having had the superficial pleasure of rejecting Henrietta and her ideas.

These suggestions represent only a few possibilities. By using combinations and variations on patterns of interpretation, you can develop a highly personal approach. The point is to develop the interpretive strategy that you think works best.

VII

CRITICAL APPROACHES
TO
DRAMA

18

ELEMENTS OF DRAMA

The critic Martin Esslin has said that drama is the "most social of the art forms," reminding us that **drama** is storytelling by actors performing before our eyes, speaking words, and enacting moments in imaginary lives. Today audiences respond to the physical presence of actors such as Anthony Hopkins, Meryl Streep, and James Earl Jones. Before theaters had artificial lighting, audiences could also see each other and interact. Sometimes players were prompted by audience members when they forgot their lines, and often they played to the audience, depending on their relationship with it, which was usually based on their reputation. In most plays, then and now, the audience reacts together, laughing, crying, in suspense or awe.

Because of its social character, most people find drama impossible to resist. One of the basic functions of human socialization is the capacity to empathize with others. In drama, that capacity is the most important element used by the playwright. Witnessing the suffering or joy of others causes us to share those feelings, and sharing helps educate our emotional life. Indeed, this may be one of the chief functions of literature. However, in drama it is more immediate simply because audiences see another human being experiencing something that they can personally respond to with ease.

ELEMENTS OF DRAMA

Some elements of drama, such as plot, characterization, setting, dialogue, and theme, overlap those of short fiction. Others, such as stage directions, are specific to drama. In certain kinds of plays specific elements may dominate. In plays such as Susan Glaspell's *Suppressed Desires,* the plot is more important than character, but in tragedies such as *Hamlet,* character shares importance with plot. In some plays scenery dominates, although such plays are rarely significant enough to study. In most good plays the elements balance one another. We will focus on seven elements of drama.

Plot

The **plot** of a play is the pattern of the characters' actions. Tragedies and tragicomedies usually have a single plot with a beginning, middle, and end. Not all plays follow this pattern, but most tragedies begin by introducing the characters with an **exposition** of previous action that reveals their current circumstances. The **rising action** introduces the **conflict:** the problems that must be solved or the trials that must be faced. The rising action in *Hamlet* begins with the appearance of the ghost, and the **exciting force** is the ghost's revelation that he has been murdered and that Hamlet must avenge him. The middle of the drama includes the conflicts facing the hero. Among them in *Hamlet* are Hamlet's mixed feelings regarding his mother, Claudius's attempt to get Hamlet to stop mourning his father, the plot to spy on Hamlet, and Hamlet's own efforts to discover the truth about his father's death. All of these constitute the rising action, the period in which the hero is in ascendancy.

The **falling action** includes the elements of the plot in which the hero moves steadily toward the inevitable conclusion. The **climax** occurs when the forces of the hero and the antagonist meet head-on. In some plays it occurs simultaneously with the crisis, the moment in which the rising action changes to the falling action. In *Hamlet* the climax occurs when Hamlet forces Claudius's hand during the play-within-a-play scene and Claudius rises in guilt at watching an enactment of the murder of Gonzago. The crisis, or falling action, begins when Hamlet erroneously kills Polonius. He was within reach of achieving his end of avenging his father, but after the death of Polonius and the entrance of Rosencrantz and Guildenstern, he suffers a **reversal (peripeteia)**, when his fortunes change. The coincidence of climax, crisis, and reversal all within a short space of time builds great dramatic tension into the middle of the play.

The **conclusion** includes the remaining falling action. In *Hamlet*, Hamlet returns to face Laertes, Polonius's son bent on revenge for his own father's death. Eventually he faces Laertes in a rigged duel, kills both Laertes and Claudius, watches his mother die from poison, and then dies himself. This section of the play is called the **denouement**, which means an untying or unraveling. One description of a dramatic plot is the tying of a knot: the beginning and middle of the play tie things into knots; the denouement unties the knot or unravels the plot. In a tragedy, the denouement is often called the **catastrophe.**

In comedy, many of the same plot details apply. For example, the concept of a plot as a knot tied and then untied is common in comedy. The rising action often accompanies a misunderstanding or a mix-up in identities. One common pattern, especially in romantic comedies, is that of young, worthy lovers frustrated in their desire for marriage by **blocking characters**, usually parents, stepparents, or guardians. The action thwarts the blocking characters by revealing their weaknesses or by revealing the true identities of the prospective lovers. The denouement usually includes a marriage or several marriages.

Many of these plot elements are at work in tragicomedies as well, as in Anton Chekhov's *The Cherry Orchard*. In this play the beauty of the setting is frequently alluded to, implying that the passing age possessed both charm and beauty and that the coming age was more invested in material values. Lopahin sees the beautiful cherry orchard on the Ranevsky estate as an opportunity for development. He is the son of a peasant who now has entrepreneurial skills and considerable economic imagination. On the other hand, Madame Ranevsky is foolish with her money. When she has virtually none, she gives a gold coin away as a gift. Her brother Gaev is no wiser. They lose their cherry orchard because they cannot change and cannot see how the world is changing before them. All this comes out through careful exposition and through the characters' dialogue. We learn right from the first that Madame Ranevsky is generous and that she befriended Lopahin. Yet it is Lopahin who ends the play in triumph, while she leaves for an uncertain future.

The middle of the play produces the rising action, the movement toward a moment of great dramatic tension. When the tension reaches its greatest point the drama reaches its climax, when, in a sense, there is a showdown, usually between the protagonist, in this case Madame Ranevsky, and the antagonist, Lopahin. The climax in this play coincides with Lopahin's inability to convince Madame Ranevsky to save her estate by changing her ways. The point, to some extent, demonstrates how the landed aristocrats adapted to the old ways but fossilized in those ways and perished in the face of changing values. Chekhov does not by any means let us feel that the new values are better. He simply clarifies their significance.

Characterization

Characterization is the creation of the persons of the drama, such as Hamlet in *Hamlet* or Willy Loman in *Death of a Salesman*. Characterization is achieved through several methods. In some plays the exposition establishes character through dialogue—speech between two or more characters that describes one of them or an absent character. Often several minor players perform this function, as in the encounter with Rosencrantz and Guildenstern in *Hamlet*. Another way is through a soliloquy, a speech by a character alone on stage that describes himself or herself. But character can also be revealed gradually through dialogue and action. This is the method chosen by Henrik Ibsen in *A Doll House*. Nora Helmer is characterized largely by the way she conducts herself and interacts with others.

As in fiction, drama depends on **flat characters**—those who are developed only minimally and who behave predictably—and **round characters**—those who are fleshed out and fully developed. In *Fences*, Troy Maxson and his son Cory are both round characters. They are complex, many-sided, and not totally predictable. Bono, on the other hand, is relatively flat and obvious in his attitudes and his needs. **Type characters** (also called **stock characters**), such as the mechanicals in *A Midsummer Night's Dream,* behave true to their type, or what we expect of them.

The *Cherry Orchard* provides us with a range of characterization. The most important characters are Madame Ranevsky and Lopahin. They reveal themselves partly in terms of contrast, one born to privilege, unable to work, the other risen from a low station through hard work. Gaev has tried work and finds himself adapting, but slowly. Some of the characters are types. Trofimov is the eternal student, impractical, dreamy. Firs is one of the most interesting of characters. He is the family valet, formerly a serf, and one who, because of his age, cannot accept the responsibilities of complete freedom. He ends the play with a touching farewell.

Types, Stereotypes, and Archetypes

Dramatists often rely on the economy achieved by using quickly recognizable types. We all recognize the miser, the spoiled brat, the wallflower, the bully, the snob. Sometimes these types are gender-specific, such as the shrew, the witch, or the hysteric for women and the braggart soldier, the drunk, or the tough guy for men. However, dramatists usually use types only with minor characters. When a character such as Laura in *The Glass Menagerie* takes a central role, the limitations of type fall away, and we begin to see the wallflower developed into a complex human being.

Although most good drama develops central characters as individuals, not types, some plays are developed successfully around the concept of the type. *The Glass Menagerie* and *Hamlet* are both built on types: Amanda is the over-ambitious mother, Laura is the wallflower, and Hamlet is the melancholy intellectual. Hamlet, however, develops far beyond any superficial concepts of the type. Although we sometimes call him the Melancholy Dane, we also recognize that such a term does not sum him up. The same may be said of both Amanda and Laura. In contrast, the minor characters in *Hamlet* sometimes do not develop beyond their type. Osric is the sleazy courtier who will say anything to please; Polonius is the fatherly busybody who keeps giving advice even when it is not welcome; Fortinbras is the warrior who lives to fight; Laertes is the rash young man; and Ophelia may be the hysteric.

A stereotype is even less complex than a type character. The differences may be a matter of degree. For example, Polonius, although a type character, is somewhat individuated. A stereotype, however, is usually an uncomplicated—and uninteresting—two-dimensional shadow of a person. Racial stereotypes are common in drama as well as in life: the greedy Jew, lazy black, Mafia-owned Italian, drunken Irishman, dumb Polack, stingy Scot, and fanatical Arab are all popular stereotypes. They are oversimple, the product of prejudice.

Laura Wingfield, in *The Glass Menagerie,* is an archetypal smothering mother, the mother who lives her life through her children. The best type characters have a complexity and dimension that makes them individuals, but at the same time they establish patterns that many others follow. In some ways Troy Maxson becomes an archetypal father in August Wilson's *Fences.*

His inability to communicate with his son will be recognizable to many young men in the audience.

Types, stereotypes, and archetypes work because they are recognizable. We respond to types and stereotypes in part because the playwright depends on our inbuilt prejudices and in part because experience has taught us that some aspects of types are reliable some of the time. Archetypes are more difficult to recognize as such, but once we do we see in them the patterns of behavior that we know guide many people. The archetypal father-figure, the archetypal mother, the archetypal adventurer and seeker—all these are patterns that many people will follow in their own lives. Types and stereotypes are reductive and simplifying. But archetypes, such as Oedipus or Hamlet, are complex and in-clusive. Archetypes do not limit a range of behavior, they merely demonstrate its range so that we can tell when we—or others—take part in similar behavior.

Setting

The **setting** of the play includes the scenery, the historical time of the ac-tion, and the props. Some settings are very simple, sometimes only a bare stage, as in many productions of *Hamlet*. When August Wilson's *Fences* was produced the stage was transformed into a neighborly backyard, realistically recreated to look as it might have looked in the period of the play. Arthur Miller's set for *Death of a Salesman* was more expressionist, with regions of the stage assigned various locales and with a cross-sectioned house for the Lomans. As the lights fell or rose on specific areas of the set, we knew where the action took place. In plays produced before the late nineteenth century, such effects were im-possible. However, Shakespeare overcame the problems of lighting—and often the absence of props and elaborate furniture—by having the audience use its imagination. Shakespeare's dialogue would reveal the setting if it had not been otherwise established. However, modern editors of Shakespeare, lacking the visual clues supplied to Shakespeare's audience by costumes, gestures, and in-struments such as burning torches (indicating nighttime), cannot always be sure where certain scenes take place. Shakespeare's stage directions are few and rudimentary.

Dialogue

Dialogue is the conversation or speech of two or more characters. Since a drama is a story told in dialogue, the playwright's choices for dialogue are crit-ical to the success of the drama. Dialogue has several tasks in a play: (1) to ad-vance the action of the drama in a natural way, (2) to embody the ideas or theme of the play without sending a blatant "message" to the audience, (3) to reveal the personality of each character, (4) to vary with each character so as to preserve the character's individuality, and (5) to resemble normal speech be-tween persons so as to preserve the illusion of reality.

Some dialogue consists of rapid exchanges, such as some of the inter-changes with Hallie and Sam in *"Master Harold"* . . . *and the boys*. Some dialogue is very informal and conversational, as in *Fences*. Some is slightly more formal, as in Henrik Ibsen's *A Doll House*, in which the dialogue reveals the more distant and "correct" ways of speaking in the polite society represented by the drama. In poetic drama, such as *Oedipus Rex, A Midsummer Night's Dream*, and *Hamlet*, the language takes on a greater significance than it might in, say, Irene Fornés's *Conduct of Life*, in which the theme seems to take precedence over language. The great **soliloquies** of Hamlet are curious kinds of dialogue because they represent a character speaking to himself (or sometimes to the audience). It is a one-way form of speech designed to reveal the inner life of the character.

Stage Directions

Not every playwright supplies **stage directions**. In the case of Shakespeare's plays, we have very few directions for how the action of the play is to be performed, and most of them seem to come from those who produced the plays. Some stage directions seem to attempt an introduction to the entire play, as in the case of Tennessee Williams's elaborate and poetical commentaries on the action. The purpose of stage directions is to help guide the actors in their interpretation of character as well as to give them an idea how their physical movements should coordinate with the dialogue. However, most directors study the play they produce carefully and decide on many of those issues independently of the author's wishes. In the case of classic plays with little or no stage direction, the tradition of performance is handed down and substitutes, in some cases, for the absent stage directions.

Theme

Like short stories, dramas have many **themes,** or main ideas. *Hamlet* may have for a major theme the idea of revenge, but in the process of the play a great many other important ideas are raised. Incest, betrayal, lost love, courage, and self-examination all figure hugely in *Hamlet* and it would be very difficult (and unnecessary) to pin it down to a single theme. Ibsen's *A Doll House* has been seen as a feminist drama, an examination of the ways in which an insensitive and unyielding husband can wield absolute power over his essentially helpless wife. In many ways it is an examination of the condition of being a wife in late-nineteenth-century society.

Style

Dramas can use numerous **styles,** ways of presenting their material. Aristotle said that drama was mimetic, by which he meant that it mirrored life and gave us insight into who we are. Realistic approaches to mimesis depend on answering the expectations of probability: people are expected to behave as they do in life, with all the limitations we assume are normal. Characters are human, not immortal; they do not become invisible or defy gravity; they often work for a living; they often live in environments much like our own and conduct their lives as the audience does. In the 1880s, when Ibsen's *A Doll House* was performed, many people in the audience lived lives that resembled that of the Helmers. Indeed, a great many married women lived lives as stifled as that of Nora Helmer. Ibsen was the first of the modern realistic dramatists, and his realism shocked his world so severely as to make him infamous in many parts of Europe and the Americas. And while essentially realistic, Tennessee Williams's *The Glass Menagerie* has a dreamlike quality accentuated by Tom's long, poetic speeches recapitulating the past. On the other hand, Shakespeare's *A Midsummer Night's Dream* is a fantasy in which his audience takes great delight, suspending disbelief long enough to enjoy the show.

REALISM. The primary style of modern drama is probably best described as **realism:** the action is kept faithful to events that are probable. The details of everyday activity in Chekhov's *The Cherry Orchard* are probable and realistic. We recognize the characters as living in a world similar to ours, doing things we might do were we living in their time and place. The term **naturalism** was a special kind of realism associated at first with the Swedish playwright August Strindberg. It is the kind of drama that includes sordid details of life, something like the details of rape and torture that Irene Fornés includes in *The Conduct of Life.* These are details that would never appear in a play by Ibsen, Chekhov, or Shaw.

EXPRESSIONISM. **Expressionism** depends on nonrealistic details, settings, or situations to express an emotional value or to intensify an emotional effect. None of the plays in this collection are explicitly expressionistic, but aspects of Fornés's *The Conduct of Life,* properly staged, might come close. The thought of having a young girl downstairs being tortured while the army lieutenant Orlando struts threateningly upstairs keeping his wife Leticia in the dark about his activities is hardly realistic. The depraved sadism of the play seems somewhat over the top, thus producing an expressionistic quality. The horror of the violence in the play is meant to mirror the actual horror of the Latin American country in which it is set. The distortion of reality, as well as the discontinuity of the play's scenes, intensifies the emotional impact of the play.

GENRES OF DRAMA: TRAGEDY, COMEDY, TRAGICOMEDY

Itself a genre of literature, drama can also be divided into two main genres: **tragedy** and **comedy.** These two genres, along with the satyr play, a quasi-pornographic **farce,** constituted the forms of drama known to the Greeks. Successive ages have added the genre **tragicomedy,** a mixed form. For instance, the Elizabethan stage added **histories** and **romances,** which sometimes combined tragedy and comedy. Later ages have relied on these distinctions, with modern plays such as Henrik Ibsen's *A Doll House,* Anton Chekhov's *The Cherry*

Orchard, Tennessee Williams's *The Glass Menagerie,* and Athol Fugard's *"Master Harold"* . . . *and the boys* continuing the development of tragicomedy.

TRAGEDY

Like most interesting concepts in literature, **tragedy** is difficult to define. Perhaps it will help to list some of its most important traditional qualities.

* Tragedy tells of the fall of a worthwhile, usually noble, character. Greek and Elizabethan tragedies relied on a **protagonist**—the hero, or primary character—who was of high station, but modern tragedies also use protagonists of low or middle station as a means of exploring their worthiness.
* Traditionally, tragic heroes or heroines faced an unexpected fate. Fate, or destiny, dominates tragedy, and the plot reveals the protagonist resisting fate before finally yielding to it. Fate in classical tragedy was determined by the will of the gods; in modern tragedy it is sometimes determined by inherent characteristics of the heroes, by the force of the environment, or by both.
* Tragic heroes and heroines face their fate with determination, courage, and bravery. Thus, they are worthy of our respect.
* Tragedy hinges on **hamartia,** the wrong action that leads to the tragic fall. This is sometimes referred to as the character's **tragic flaw,** but it is not always a flaw of character.
* The **peripeteia** is the tragic hero's **reversal** of fortune. Before the peripeteia the protagonist seems to make favorable progress, but as he or she seeks knowledge—**recognition** or **anagnorisis**—the peripeteia or reversal ironically pushes the protagonist to his or her fate.
* The ancient Greek philosopher Aristotle recommended that tragedy have a single plot that follows the actions of a single character or set of characters without the distraction of a secondary plot (especially avoiding a comic subplot).

As we have come to use the term, *tragedy* is, above all, serious in tone and importance. It focuses on a hero or heroine whose potential is great but whose efforts to realize that potential are thwarted by fate: circumstances beyond his or her control. Traditionally, the tragic hero has been of royal blood, like Oedipus. Thus the fall from such a height can be terrifying. Sophocles' *Oedipus Rex* was, for Aristotle, the model of what a tragedy should be. It is the quintessential tragedy and has established the tragic genre in the minds of most successive playwrights.

Because the classical tragedy insisted on a protagonist of high station, usually a king or queen, some critics have felt that in our modern age of relatively democratic institutions there can be no true tragedy. However, modern plays such as Arthur Miller's *Death of a Salesman* find enough greatness in a peasant or average person to justify calling them tragedies. Despite the fact that the Shakespearean critic Sigurd Burckhardt said, "A tragedy—to define it very simply—is a *killing poem,*" the hero or heroine need not die. Oedipus does not die in *Oedipus Rex*. On the other hand, Antigone, King Lear, Hamlet, and Macbeth all die at the end of their plays.

The Emotions of Pity and Terror

The earliest efforts to examine tragedy defined the kinds of emotions that were or should be evoked in the audience. In essence, Aristotle focused on a form of reader response criticism. If the tragic hero or heroine was well drawn, sympathetic, and touching, then the audience felt the emotion of pity. Such an emotion stems from the audience's capacity to emphathize with the tragic hero. The emotion of terror, watching the hero's fall, also stems from empathy, since the audience can imagine being in the same situation.

Aristotle claimed that tragic drama not only produced such emotions in the audience but also purged the audience of them. It is not clear what he meant. However, he may have referred to the anxiety audiences felt about their own security and their own fate. If one thinks of the anxiety Elizabethan Calvinists felt when they were told God had decided beforehand whether they were saved or not, then one can imagine how Greeks may have felt knowing their fate was ordained. Their anxiety might have made them neurotic or dysfunctional. Examining their emotions—just releasing them—would help them immensely. Even today audiences respond powerfully to the tragic ironies deep in the heart of *Oedipus Rex*.

Tragedies produce anticipation because the audience knows that the main character will fall. However, there is no sense in which it is absolutely obvious that the tragic hero or heroine will die at the end of the play. First viewers of *Hamlet*, if they have not read the play, have no reason to suspect he will die at the end. In the case of Arthur Miller's *Death of a Salesman*, many early theatergoers insisted that Willy Loman should not have died. In other times, such as the eighteenth century, tragedies such as *King Lear* were successfully played with happy endings. Greek tragedies, such as *Oedipus Rex*, depended on a highborn figure, such as a king, falling from his station. Sometimes that meant death, and sometimes it meant, as it does in *Oedipus Rex*, that the tragic hero became an object of pity.

Certain ingredients associated with tragedy often show up in modern plays. The emotions of terror and dread are often reinforced by a supernatural element. Hamlet sees a ghost, Oedipus relies on a blind seer, Willy Loman in *Death of a Salesman* hears voices. Thus even in some modern plays, the "other world"—the world we do not understand, whether it comes from without or within—often seems to reach into the ordinariness of the characters' lives, calling attention to their fear and giving it good reason.

Oedipus Rex was for Aristotle the epitome of tragedy. The play involves a search for the truth and a reverence for the gods and for the ineluctable force of fate. Sophocles gives us a portrait of a man—modern in many ways—struggling with forces that he thinks will bend to his will, but which defy him. In that sense, Sophocles is as much a man of our time as he is of the golden age of Greece.

A CLASSIC TRAGEDY

SOPHOCLES   c. 496–406 B.C.

Sophocles lived in Athens during the last Persian invasion and its defeat. The great age of Athens began in 480 B.C., and before Sophocles died, Pericles and Phidias had rebuilt the Acropolis and erected the Parthenon. Sophocles, unlike his predecessors, was not an actor. He broke with tradition by writing plays but not acting in them. Although we know he wrote at least ninety plays, only a few have survived. We have the great Oedipus trilogy: Antigone *(441 B.C.),* Oedipus Rex *(c. 430–27 B.C.), and* Oedipus at Colonus *(401 B.C.). Besides these are* Ajax, Philoctetes, Trachiniae, *and* Elektra.

Sophocles's tragedies, like all Greek plays, were produced during great celebrations. The audience at the outdoor theaters numbered fifteen thousand people, and the acoustics were designed so carefully that everyone in the theater could hear the action on stage. The actors and the chorus, fifteen citizens of Thebes in this play, held large masks in front of their faces. The masks identified their characters and helped emphasize the text of the play by preventing charismatic actors from distracting the audience.

Aristotle considered Oedipus Rex *the masterpiece of Greek drama and used it to illustrate the perfection of tragedy. He praised its unities: it tells only one story and has no distracting subplot; the action takes place in the time it takes to perform the play, with no break for an intermission; and all the action takes place in front of Oedipus's palace. The tension of the play rises constantly until Oedipus realizes that he is responsible for the plague. At that moment the action falls sharply toward the conclusion. Aristotle felt that this combination—simultaneous recognition and reversal—made for perfection in tragedy.*

Oedipus Rex *is the story of a man who attempts to flee his fate. It was prophesied that he would kill his father, King Laios, and marry his mother, Iokaste. Knowing this, Laios had him left to die in a remote area, his feet pierced and bound. But the shepherd assigned this task took pity on the infant and gave him to a childless couple. When he grew up, Oedipus heard about the prophecy and determined to leave home to avoid hurting his parents. Ironically, however, he headed directly toward his true home, Thebes, murdering Laios along the way.*

When the play opens, Oedipus has married Iokaste and become king because he has solved the riddle of the Sphinx. But Thebes now suffers a plague brought on by the failure of the Thebans to solve the murder of Laios. Oedipus, the source of the plague, begins the action by vowing to find the murderer and punish him no matter who he is. The irony is that he has no way of knowing where that search will lead him. In pride, he demands that people tell him what they know no matter what the cost. But the closer he gets to the truth, the less his pride permits him to believe it. This prideful resistance builds both suspense and tension throughout the rising action. Finally, however, Oedipus displays his nobility by facing the truth squarely. The play does not end with his death—not all tragedies do—but he suffers the twin pains of blindness and exile. Blindness is emblematic of his inability to see the truth about himself, and exile is emblematic of his condition before he returned to Thebes. His ultimate fate, the humbling of his pride, is in some ways worse than death.

Oedipus Rex _____ *c. 430 B.C.*

Translated by Dudley Fitts and Robert Fitzgerald

Characters

    Oedipus, *King of Thebes, supposed son of Polybos and Merope, King and Queen of Corinth*

    Iokaste, *wife of Oedipus and widow of the late King Laios*

Kreon, *brother of Iokaste, a prince of Thebes*
Teiresias, *a blind seer who serves Apollo*
Priest
Messenger, *from Corinth*
Shepherd, *former servant of Laios*
Second Messenger, *from the palace*
Chorus of Theban Elders
Choragos, *leader of the Chorus*
Antigone *and* Ismene, *young daughters of Oedipus and Iokaste. They appear in the*
Exodos but do not speak.
Suppliants, Guards, Servants
(Scene: Before the palace of Oedipus, King of Thebes. A central door and two lateral
doors open onto a platform which runs the length of the facade. On the platform, right
and left, are altars; and three steps lead down into the orchestra, or chorus-ground. At
the beginning of the action these steps are crowded by suppliants who have brought
branches and chaplets of olive leaves and who sit in various attitudes of despair.
Oedipus enters.)

PROLOGUE°

OEDIPUS.   My children, generations of the living
    In the line of Kadmos,° nursed at his ancient hearth:
    Why have you strewn yourselves before these altars
    In supplication, with your boughs and garlands?
    The breath of incense rises from the city   5
    with a sound of prayer and lamentation.
                          Children,
    I would not have you speak through messengers,
    and therefore I have come myself to hear you—
    I, Oedipus, who bear the famous name.   10
    (To a Priest.) You, there, since you are eldest in the company,
    Speak for them all, tell me what preys upon you,
    Whether you come in dread, or crave some blessing:
    Tell me, and never doubt that I will help you
    In every way I can; I should be heartless   15
    Were I not moved to find you suppliant here.
PRIEST.   Great Oedipus, O powerful king of Thebes!
    You see how all the ages of our people
    Cling to your altar steps: here are boys
    Who can barely stand alone, and here are priests   20
    By weight of age, as I am a priest of God,
    And young men chosen from those yet unmarried;
    As for the others, all that multitude,
    They wait with olive chaplets in the squares,

Prologue: portion of the play explaining the background and current action.   2 *Kadmos:* founder
of Thebes.

At the two shrines of Pallas,° and where Apollo°   25
Speaks in the glowing embers.
                                        Your own eyes
Must tell you: Thebes is tossed on a murdering sea
And cannot lift her head from the death surge.
A rust consumes the buds and fruits of the earth;   30
The herds are sick; children die unborn,
And labor is vain. The god of plague and pyre
Raids like detestable lightning through the city,
And all the house of Kadmos is laid waste,
All emptied, and all darkened: Death alone   35
Battens upon the misery of Thebes.

You are not one of the immortal gods, we know;
Yet we have come to you to make our prayer
As to the man surest in mortal ways
And wisest in the ways of God. You saved us   40
From the Sphinx,° that flinty singer, and the tribute
We paid to her so long; yet you were never
Better informed than we, nor could we teach you:
A god's touch, it seems, enabled you to help us.

Therefore, O mighty power, we turn to you: 45
Find us our safety, find us a remedy,
Whether by counsel of the gods or of men.
A king of wisdom tested in the past
Can act in a time of troubles, and act well.
Noblest of men, restore   50
Life to your city! Think how all men call you
Liberator for your boldness long ago;
Ah, when your years of kingship are remembered,
Let them not say *We rose, but later fell*—
Keep the State from going down in the storm!   55
Once, years ago, with happy augury,
You brought us fortune; be the same again!
No man questions your power to rule the land:
But rule over men, not over a dead city!
Ships are only hulls, high walls are nothing,   60
When no life moves in the empty passageways.
OEDIPUS.   Poor children! You may be sure I know
All that you longed for in your coming here.
I know that you are deathly sick; and yet,
Sick as you are, not one is as sick as I.   65
Each of you suffers in himself alone
His anguish, not another's; but my spirit
Groans for the city, for myself, for you.

---

25 *Pallas:* Pallas Athene, daughter of Zeus and goddess of wisdom.   *Apollo:* son of Zeus and
god of the sun, of light and truth.   41 *Sphinx:* a winged monster with the body of a lion and the
face of a woman, the Sphinx had tormented Thebes with her riddle, killing those who could not
solve it. When Oedipus solved the riddle, the Sphinx killed herself.

I was not sleeping, you are not waking me.
No, I have been in tears for a long while   70
And in my restless thought walked many ways.
In all my search I found one remedy,
And I have adopted it: I have sent Kreon,
Son of Menoikeus, brother of the queen,
To Delphi,° Apollo's place of revelation,   75
To learn there, if he can,
What act or pledge of mine may save the city.
I have counted the days, and now, this very day,
I am troubled, for he has overstayed his time.
What is he doing? He has been gone too long.   80
Yet whenever he comes back, I should do ill
Not to take any action the god orders.
PRIEST.   It is a timely promise. At this instant
     They tell me Kreon is here.
OEDIPUS.   O Lord Apollo!   85
     May his news be fair as his face is radiant!
PRIEST.   Good news, I gather! he is crowned with bay,
     The chaplet is thick with berries.
OEDIPUS.   We shall soon know;
     He is near enough to hear us now. *(Enter Kreon.)* O prince: 90
     Brother: son of Menoikeus:
     What answer do you bring us from the god?
KREON.   A strong one. I can tell you, great afflictions
     Will turn out well, if they are taken well.
OEDIPUS.   What was the oracle? These vague words   95
     Leave me still hanging between hope and fear.
KREON.   Is it your pleasure to hear me with all these
     Gathered around us? I am prepared to speak,
     But should we not go in?
OEDIPUS.   Speak to them all,   100
     It is for them I suffer, more than for myself.
KREON.   Then I will tell you what I heard at Delphi.
     In plain words
     The god commands us to expel from the land of Thebes
     An old defilement we are sheltering.   105
     It is a deathly thing, beyond cure;
     We must not let it feed upon us longer.
OEDIPUS.   What defilement? How shall we rid ourselves of it?
KREON.   By exile or death, blood for blood. It was
     Murder that brought the plague-wind on the city.   110
OEDIPUS.   Murder of whom? Surely the god has named him?
KREON.   My Lord: Laios once ruled this land,
     Before you came to govern us.

75 *Delphi:* site of the oracle, source of religious authority and prophecy, under the protection of
Apollo.

OEDIPUS.   I know;
    I learned of him from others; I never saw him.   115
KREON.   He was murdered; and Apollo commands us now
    To take revenge upon whoever killed him.
OEDIPUS.   Upon whom? Where are they? Where shall we find a clue
    To solve that crime, after so many years?
KREON.   Here in this land, he said. Search reveals   120
    Things that escape an inattentive man.
OEDIPUS.   Tell me: Was Laios murdered in his house,
    Or in the fields, or in some foreign country?
KREON.   He said he planned to make a pilgrimage.
    He did not come home again.   125
OEDIPUS.   And was there no one,
    No witness, no companion, to tell what happened?
KREON.   They were all killed but one, and he got away
    So frightened that he could remember one thing only.
OEDIPUS.   What was that one thing? One may be the key   130
    To everything, if we resolve to use it.
KREON.   He said that a band of highwaymen attacked them,
    Outnumbered them, and overwhelmed the king.
OEDIPUS.   Strange, that a highwayman should be so daring—
    Unless some faction here bribed him to do it.   135
KREON.   We thought of that. But after Laios' death
    New troubles arose and we had no avenger.
OEDIPUS.   What troubles could prevent your hunting down the killers?
KREON.   The riddling Sphinx's song
    Made us deaf to all mysteries but her own.   140
OEDIPUS.   Then once more I must bring what is dark to light.
    It is most fitting that Apollo shows,
    As you do, this compunction for the dead.
    You shall see how I stand by you, as I should,
    Avenging this country and the god as well,   145
    And not as though it were for some distant friend,
    But for my own sake, to be rid of evil.
    Whoever killed King Laios might—who knows?—
    Lay violent hands even on me—and soon.
    I act for the murdered king in my own interest.   150

    Come, then, my children: leave the altar steps,
    Lift up your olive boughs!
                 One of you go
    And summon the people of Kadmos to gather here.
    I will do all that I can; you may tell them that.   155

(Exit a Page.)

    So, with the help of God,
    We shall be saved—or else indeed we are lost.
PRIEST.   Let us rise, children. It was for this we came,
    and now the king has promised it.   160

Phoibos° has sent us an oracle; may he descend
Himself to save us and drive out the plague.

(*Exeunt° Oedipus and Kreon into the palace by the central door. The Priest and the Suppliants disperse right and left. After a short pause the Chorus enters the orchestra.*)

161 *Phoibos:* Apollo.   163 *Exeunt:* Latin for "they go out."

PARODOS°

Strophe° 1

CHORUS.   What is God singing in his profound
        Delphi of gold and shadow?
    What oracle for Thebes, the Sunwhipped city?
    Fear unjoints me, the roots of my heart tremble.
    Now I remember, O Healer, your power, and wonder: 5
    Will you send doom like a sudden cloud, or weave it
    Like nightfall of the past?
    Speak to me, tell me, O
    Child of golden Hope, immortal Voice.

Antistrophe° 1

    Let me pray to Athene, the immortal daughter of Zeus,   10
    And to Artemis° her sister
    Who keeps her famous throne in the market ring,
    And to Apollo, archer from distant heaven—
    O gods, descend! Like three streams leap against
    The fires of our grief, the fires of darkness;   15
    Be swift to bring us rest!
    As in the old time from the brilliant house
    Of air you stepped to save us, come again!

Strophe 2

    Now our afflictions have no end,
    Now all our stricken host lies down   20
    And no man fights off death with his mind;
    The noble plowland bears no grain,
    And groaning mothers cannot bear—
    See, how our lives like birds take wing,

Parodos: the song or ode chanted by the Chorus on their entry.   *Strophe:* song sung by the Chorus as they danced from stage right to stage left.   *Antistrophe:* song sung by the Chorus following the Strophe, as they danced back from stage left to stage right.   11 *Artemis:* the huntress, daughter of Zeus, twin sister of Apollo.

Like sparks that fly when a fire soars,   25
To the shore of the god of evening.

Antistrophe 2

The plague burns on, it is pitiless,
Though pallid children laden with death
Lie unwept in the stony ways,
And old gray women by every path   30
Flock to the strand about the altars
There to strike their breasts and cry
Worship of Phoibos in wailing prayers:
Be kind, God's golden child!

Strophe 3

There are no swords in this attack by fire,   35
No shields, but we are ringed with cries.
Send the besieger plunging from our homes
Into the vast sea-room of the Atlantic
Or into the waves that foam eastward of Thrace—
For the day ravages what the night spares—   40
Destroy our enemy, lord of the thunder!
Let him be riven by lightning from heaven!

Antistrophe 3

Phoibos Apollo, stretch the sun's bowstring,
That golden cord, until it sing for us,
Flashing arrows in heaven!   45
                              Artemis, Huntress,
Race with flaring lights upon our mountains!
O scarlet god,° O golden-banded brow,
O Theban Bacchos in a storm of Maenads,°

(Enter Oedipus, center.)   50

Whirl upon Death, that all the Undying hate!
Come with blinding torches, come in joy!

48 *scarlet god:* Bacchus, god of wine and revelry; also called Dionysus.   49 *Maenads:* female wor-
shipers of Bacchus (Dionysus).

SCENE 1

OEDIPUS.   Is this your prayer? It may be answered. Come,
    Listen to me, act as the crisis demands,

And you shall have relief from all these evils.
Until now I was a stranger to this tale,
As I had been a stranger to the crime.   5
Could I track down the murderer without a clue?
But now, friends,
As one who became a citizen after the murder,
I make this proclamation to all Thebans:
If any man knows by whose hand Laios, son of Labdakos,   10
Met his death, I direct that man to tell me everything,
No matter what he fears for having so long withheld it.
Let it stand as promised that no further trouble
Will come to him, but he may leave the land in safety.
Moreover: If anyone knows the murderer to be foreign,   15
Let him not keep silent: he shall have his reward from me.
However, if he does conceal it; if any man
Fearing for his friend or for himself disobeys this edict,
Hear what I propose to do:

I solemnly forbid the people of this country,   20
Where power and throne are mine, ever to receive that man
Or speak to him, no matter who he is, or let him
Join in sacrifice, lustration, or in prayer.
I decree that he be driven from every house,
Being, as he is, corruption itself to us: the Delphic   25
Voice of Apollo has pronounced this revelation.
Thus I associate myself with the oracle
And take the side of the murdered king.

As for the criminal, I pray to God—
Whether it be a lurking thief, or one of a number—   30
I pray that that man's life be consumed in evil and wretchedness.
And as for me, this curse applies no less
If it should turn out that the culprit is my guest here,
Sharing my hearth.
                     You have heard the penalty.   35
I lay it on you now to attend to this
For my sake, for Apollo's, for the sick
Sterile city that heaven has abandoned.
Suppose the oracle had given you no command:
Should this defilement go uncleansed for ever?   40
You should have found the murderer: your king,
A noble king, had been destroyed!
                     Now I,
Having the power that he held before me,
Having his bed, begetting children there   45
Upon his wife, as he would have, had he lived—
Their son would have been my children's brother,
If Laios had had luck in fatherhood!
(And now his bad fortune has struck him down)—
I say I take the son's part, just as though   50

I were his son, to press the fight for him
And see it won! I'll find the hand that brought
Death to Labdakos' and Polydoros' child,
Heir of Kadmos' and Agenor's line.°
And as for those who fail me,   55
May the gods deny them the fruit of the earth,
Fruit of the womb, and may they rot utterly!
Let them be wretched as we are wretched, and worse!

For you, for loyal Thebans, and for all
Who find my actions right, I pray the favor   60
Of justice, and of all the immortal gods.
CHORAGOS.°   Since I am under oath, my lord, I swear
I did not do the murder, I cannot name
The murderer. Phoibos ordained the search;
Why did he not say who the culprit was?   65
OEDIPUS.   An honest question. But no man in the world
Can make the gods do more than the gods will.
CHORAGOS.   There is an alternative, I think—
OEDIPUS.   Tell me.
Any or all, you must not fail to tell me.   70
CHORAGOS.   A lord clairvoyant to the lord Apollo,
As we all know, is the skilled Teiresias.
One might learn much about this from him, Oedipus.
OEDIPUS.   I am not wasting time:
Kreon spoke of this, and I have sent for him—   75
Twice, in fact; it is strange that he is not here.
CHORAGOS.   The other matter—that old report—seems useless.
OEDIPUS.   What was that? I am interested in all reports.
CHORAGOS.   The king was said to have been killed by highwaymen.
OEDIPUS.   I know. But we have no witnesses to that.   80
CHORAGOS.   If the killer can feel a particle of dread,
Your curse will bring him out of hiding!
OEDIPUS.   No.
The man who dared that act will fear no curse.

(Enter the blind seer Teiresias, led by a Page.)   85

CHORAGOS.   But there is one man who may detect the criminal.
This is Teiresias, this is the holy prophet
In whom, alone of all men, truth was born.
OEDIPUS.   Teiresias: seer: student of mysteries,
Of all that's taught and all that no man tells,   90
Secrets of Heaven and secrets of the earth:
Blind though you are, you know the city lies
Sick with plague; and from this plague, my lord,
We find that you alone can guard or save us.

53–54 *Labdakos, Polydoros, Kadmos, and Agenor:* father, grandfather, great-grandfather, and great-
great-grandfather of Laios.   62 *Choragos:* leader of the Chorus.

Possibly you did not hear the messengers?   95
Apollo, when we sent to him,
Sent us back word that this great pestilence
Would lift, but only if we established clearly
The identity of those who murdered Laios.
They must be killed or exiled.   100
                              Can you use
Birdflight° or any part of divination
To purify yourself, and Thebes, and me
From this contagion? We are in your hands.
There is no fairer duty   105
Than that of helping others in distress.
TEIRESIAS.   How dreadful knowledge of the truth can be
    When there's no help in truth! I knew this well,
    But did not act on it; else I should not have come.
OEDIPUS.   What is troubling you? Why are your eyes so cold?   110
TEIRESIAS.   Let me go home. Bear your own fate, and I'll
    Bear mine. It is better so: trust what I say.
OEDIPUS.   What you say is ungracious and unhelpful
    To your native country. Do not refuse to speak.
TEIRESIAS.   When it comes to speech, your own is neither temperate   115
    Nor opportune. I wish to be more prudent.
OEDIPUS.   In God's name, we all beg you—
TEIRESIAS.   You are all ignorant.
    No; I will never tell you what I know.
    Now it is my misery; then, it would be yours.   120
OEDIPUS.   What! You do know something, and will not tell us?
    You would betray us all and wreck the State?
TEIRESIAS.   I do not intend to torture myself, or you.
    Why persist in asking? You will not persuade me.
OEDIPUS.   What a wicked old man you are! You'd try a stone's   125
    Patience! Out with it! Have you no feeling at all?
TEIRESIAS.   You call me unfeeling. If you could only see
    The nature of your own feelings . . .
OEDIPUS.   Why,
    Who would not feel as I do? Who could endure   130
    Your arrogance toward the city?
TEIRESIAS.   What does it matter?
    Whether I speak or not, it is bound to come.
OEDIPUS.   Then, if "it" is bound to come, you are bound to tell me.
TEIRESIAS.   No, I will not go on. Rage as you please.   135
OEDIPUS.   Rage? Why not!
                              And I'll tell you what I think:
    You planned it, you had it done, you all but
    Killed him with your own hands: if you had eyes,
    I'd say the crime was yours, and yours alone.   140
TEIRESIAS.   So? I charge you, then,
    Abide by the proclamation you have made:

102 *Birdflight:* Prophets used the flight of birds to predict the future.

From this day forth
Never speak again to these men or to me;
You yourself are the pollution of this country.   145
OEDIPUS.   You dare say that! Can you possibly think you have
    Some way of going free, after such insolence?
TEIRESIAS.   I have gone free. It is the truth sustains me.
OEDIPUS.   Who taught you shamelessness? It was not your craft.
TEIRESIAS.   You did. You made me speak. I did not want to.   150
OEDIPUS.   Speak what? Let me hear it again more clearly.
TEIRESIAS.   Was it not clear before? Are you tempting me?
OEDIPUS.   I did not understand it. Say it again.
TEIRESIAS.   I say that you are the murderer whom you seek.
OEDIPUS.   Now twice you have spat out infamy. You'll pay for it!   155
TEIRESIAS.   Would you care for more? Do you wish to be really angry?
OEDIPUS.   Say what you will. Whatever you say is worthless.
TEIRESIAS.   I say you live in hideous shame with those
    Most dear to you. You cannot see the evil.
OEDIPUS.   Can you go on babbling like this for ever?   160
TEIRESIAS.   I can, if there is power in truth.
OEDIPUS.   There is:
    But not for you, not for you,
    You sightless, witless, senseless, mad old man!
TEIRESIAS.   You are the madman. There is no one here   165
    Who will not curse you soon, as you curse me.
OEDIPUS.   You child of total night! I would not touch you;
    Neither would any man who sees the sun.
TEIRESIAS.   True: it is not from you my fate will come.
    That lies within Apollo's competence,   170
    As it is his concern.
OEDIPUS.   Tell me, who made
    These fine discoveries? Kreon? or someone else?
TEIRESIAS.   Kreon is no threat. You weave your own doom.
OEDIPUS.   Wealth, power, craft of statemanship!   175
    Kingly position, everywhere admired!
    What savage envy is stored up against these,
    If Kreon, whom I trusted, Kreon my friend,
    For this great office which the city once
    Put in my hands unsought—if for this power   180
    Kreon desires in secret to destroy me!

    He has bought this decrepit fortune-teller, this
    Collector of dirty pennies, this prophet fraud—
    Why, he is no more clairvoyant than I am!
                                       Tell us: 185
    Has your mystic mummery ever approached the truth?
    When that hellcat the Sphinx was performing here,
    What help were you to these people?
    Her magic was not for the first man who came along:
    It demanded a real exorcist. Your birds—   190
    What good were they? or the gods, for the matter of that?

But I came by,
Oedipus, the simple man, who knows nothing—
I thought it out for myself, no birds helped me!
And this is the man you think you can destroy,   195
That you may be close to Kreon when he's king!
Well, you and your friend Kreon, it seems to me,
Will suffer most. If you were not an old man,
You would have paid already for your plot.

CHORAGOS.   We cannot see that his words or yours   200
Have been spoken except in anger, Oedipus,
And of anger we have no need. How to accomplish
The god's will best: that is what most concerns us.

TEIRESIAS.   You are a king. But where argument's concerned
I am your man, as much a king as you.   205
I am not your servant, but Apollo's.
I have no need of Kreon or Kreon's name.

Listen to me. You mock my blindness, do you?
But I say that you, with both your eyes, are blind:
You cannot see the wretchedness of your life,   210
Nor in whose house you live, no, nor with whom.
Who are your father and mother? Can you tell me?
You do not even know the blind wrongs
That you have done them, on earth and in the world below.
But the double lash of your parents' curse will whip you   215
Out of this land some day, with only night
Upon your precious eyes.
Your cries then—where will they not be heard?
What fastness of Kithairon° will not echo them?
And that bridal-descant of yours—you'll know it then,   220
The song they sang when you came here to Thebes
And found your misguided berthing.
All this, and more, that you cannot guess at now,
Will bring you to yourself among your children.

Be angry, then. Curse Kreon. Curse my words.   225
I tell you, no man that walks upon the earth
Shall be rooted out more horribly than you.

OEDIPUS.   Am I to bear this from him?—Damnation
Take you! Out of this place! Out of my sight!

TEIRESIAS.   I would not have come at all if you had not asked me.   230

OEDIPUS.   Could I have told that you'd talk nonsense, that you'd come
here to make a fool of yourself, and of me?

TEIRESIAS.   A fool? Your parents thought me sane enough.

OEDIPUS.   My parents again!—Wait: who were my parents?

TEIRESIAS.   This day will give you a father, and break your heart.   235

OEDIPUS.   Your infantile riddles! Your damned abracadabra!

TEIRESIAS.   You were a great man once at solving riddles.

OEDIPUS.   Mock me with that if you like; you will find it true.

219 *Kithairon:* the mountain where Oedipus was abandoned as an infant.

TEIRESIAS.   It was true enough. It brought about your ruin.

OEDIPUS.   But if it saved this town?   240

TEIRESIAS *(to the Page).*   Boy, give me your hand.

OEDIPUS.   Yes, boy; lead him away.—

                    While you are here

   We can do nothing. Go; leave us in peace.

TEIRESIAS.   I will go when I have said what I have to say.   245

   How can you hurt me? And I tell you again:

   The man you have been looking for all this time,

   The damned man, the murderer of Laios,

   That man is in Thebes. To your mind he is foreign-born,

   But it will soon be shown that he is a Theban,   250

   A revelation that will fail to please.

                   A blind man,

   Who has his eyes now; a penniless man, who is rich now;

   And he will go tapping the strange earth with his staff.

   To the children with whom he lives now he will be   255

   Brother and father—the very same; to her

   Who bore him, son and husband—the very same

   Who came to his father's bed, wet with his father's blood.

   Enough. Go think that over.

   If later you find error in what I have said,   260

   You may say that I have no skill in prophecy.

(Exit Teiresias, led by his Page. Oedipus goes into the palace.)

ODE° 1

Strophe 1

CHORUS.   The Delphic stone of prophecies

   Remembers ancient regicide

   And a still bloody hand.

   That killer's hour of flight has come.

   He must be stronger than riderless   5

   Coursers of untiring wind,

   For the son of Zeus° armed with his father's thunder

   Leaps in lightning after him;

   And the Furies° hold his track, the sad Furies.

Antistrophe 1

   Holy Parnassos'° peak of snow   10

   Flashes and blinds that secret man,

Ode: song sung by the Chorus.   7 *son of Zeus:* Apollo.   9 *Furies:* spirits called upon to avenge
crimes, especially against kin.   10 *Parnassos:* mountain sacred to Apollo.

That all shall hunt him down:
Though he may roam the forest shade
Like a bull gone wild from pasture
To rage through glooms of stone. 15
Doom comes down on him; flight will not avail him;
For the world's heart calls him desolate,
And the immortal voices follow, for ever follow.

Strophe 2

But now a wilder thing is heard
From the old man skilled at hearing Fate in the wing-beat of a bird. 20
Bewildered as a blown bird, my soul hovers and cannot find
Foothold in this debate, or any reason or rest of mind.
But no man ever brought—none can bring
Proof of strife between Thebes' royal house,
Labdakos' line, and the son of Polybos;° 25
And never until now has any man brought word
Of Laios' dark death staining Oedipus the king.

Antistrophe 2

Divine Zeus and Apollo hold
Perfect intelligence alone of all tales ever told;
And well though this diviner works, he works in his own night; 30
No man can judge that rough unknown or trust in second sight,
For wisdom changes hands among the wise.
Shall I believe my great lord criminal
At a raging word that a blind old man let fall?
I saw him, when the carrion woman° faced him of old, 35
Prove his heroic mind. These evil words are lies.

SCENE 2

KREON.   Men of Thebes:
    I am told that heavy accusations
    Have been brought against me by King Oedipus.

    I am not the kind of man to bear this tamely. 40

    If in these present difficulties
    He holds me accountable for any harm to him
    Through anything I have said or done—why, then,
    I do not value life in this dishonor.

---

25 *Polybos:* king who adopted Oedipus.   35 *woman:* the Sphinx.

It is not as though this rumor touched upon   45
Some private indiscretion. The matter is grave.
The fact is that I am being called disloyal
   To the State, to my fellow citizens, to my friends.
CHORAGOS.   He may have spoken in anger, not from his mind.
KREON.   But did you not hear him say I was the one   50
   Who seduced the old prophet into lying?
CHORAGOS.   The thing was said; I do not know how seriously.
KREON.   But you were watching him! Were his eyes steady?
   Did he look like a man in his right mind?
CHORAGOS.   I do not know.   55
   I cannot judge the behavior of great men.
   But here is the king himself.

(Enter Oedipus.)

OEDIPUS.   So you dared come back.
   Why? How brazen of you to come to my house,   60
   You murderer!
   Do you think I do not know
   That you plotted to kill me, plotted to steal my throne?
   Tell me, in God's name: am I coward, a fool,
   That you should dream you could accomplish this?   65
   A fool who could not see your slippery game?
   A coward, not to fight back when I saw it?
   You are the fool, Kreon, are you not? hoping
   Without support or friends to get a throne?
   Thrones may be won or bought: you could do neither.   70
KREON.   Now listen to me. You have talked; let me talk, too.
   You cannot judge unless you know the facts.
OEDIPUS.   You speak well: there is one fact; but I find it hard
   To learn from the deadliest enemy I have.
KREON.   That above all I must dispute with you.   75
OEDIPUS.   That above all I will not hear you deny.
KREON.   If you think there is anything good in being stubborn
   Against all reason, then I say you are wrong.
OEDIPUS.   If you think a man can sin against his own kind
   And not be punished for it, I say you are mad.   80
KREON.   I agree. But tell me: what have I done to you?
OEDIPUS.   You advised me to send for that wizard, did you not?
KREON.   I did. I should do it again.
OEDIPUS.   Very well. Now tell me:
   How long has it been since Laios—   85
KREON.   What of Laios?
OEDIPUS.   Since he vanished in that onset by the road?
KREON.   It was long ago, a long time.
OEDIPUS.   And this prophet,
   Was he practicing here then?   90
KREON.   He was; and with honor, as now.
OEDIPUS.   Did he speak of me at that time?

KREON.   He never did,
     At least, not when I was present,
OEDIPUS.   But . . . the enquiry?   95
     I suppose you held one?
KREON.   We did, but we learned nothing.
OEDIPUS.   Why did the prophet not speak against me then?
KREON.   I do not know; and I am the kind of man
     Who holds his tongue when he has no facts to go on.   100
OEDIPUS.   There's one fact that you know, and you could tell it.
KREON.   What fact is that? If I know it, you shall have it.
OEDIPUS.   If he were not involved with you, he could not say
     That it was I who murdered Laios.
KREON.   If he says that, you are the one that knows it!—   105
     But now it is my turn to question you.
OEDIPUS.   Put your questions. I am no murderer.
KREON.   First, then: You married my sister?
OEDIPUS.   I married your sister.
KREON.   And you rule the kingdom equally with her?
OEDIPUS.   Everything that she wants she has from me.
KREON.   And I am the third, equal to both of you?
OEDIPUS.   That is why I call you a bad friend.
KREON.   No. Reason it out, as I have done.
     Think of this first: would any sane man prefer   115
     Power, with all a king's anxieties,
     To that same power and the grace of sleep?
     Certainly not I.
     I have never longed for the king's power—only his rights.
     Would any wise man differ from me in this?   120
     As matters stand, I have my way in everything
     With your consent, and no responsibilities.
     If I were king, I should be a slave to policy.
     How could I desire a scepter more
     Than what is now mine—untroubled influence?   125
     No, I have not gone mad; I need no honors,
     Except those with the perquisites I have now.
     I am welcome everywhere; every man salutes me,
     And those who want your favor seek my ear,
     Since I know how to manage what they ask.   130
     Should I exchange this ease for that anxiety?
     Besides, no sober mind is treasonable.
     I hate anarchy
     And never would deal with any man who likes it.

     Test what I have said. Go to the priestess   135
     At Delphi, ask if I quoted her correctly.
     And as for this other thing: if I am found
     Guilty of treason with Teiresias,
     Then sentence me to death. You have my word
     It is a sentence I should cast my vote for—   140
     But not without evidence!

You do wrong

When you take good men for bad, bad men for good.
A true friend thrown aside—why, life itself
Is not more precious!   145
In time you will know this well:
For time, and time alone, will show the just man,
Though scoundrels are discovered in a day.
CHORAGOS.   This is well said, and a prudent man would ponder it.
Judgments too quickly formed are dangerous.   150
OEDIPUS.   But is he not quick in his duplicity?
And shall I not be quick to parry him?
Would you have me stand still, hold my peace, and let
This man win everything, through my inaction?
KREON.   And you want—what is it, then? To banish me?   155
OEDIPUS.   No, not exile. It is your death I want,
So that all the world may see what treason means.
KREON.   You will persist, then? You will not believe me?
OEDIPUS.   How can I believe you?
KREON.   Then you are a fool.   160
OEDIPUS.   To save myself?
KREON.   In justice, think of me.
OEDIPUS.   You are evil incarnate.
KREON.   But suppose that you are wrong?
OEDIPUS.   Still I must rule.   165
KREON.   But not if you rule badly.
OEDIPUS.   O city, city!
KREON.   It is my city, too!
CHORAGOS.   Now, my lords, be still. I see the queen,
Iokaste, coming from her palace chambers;   170
And it is time she came, for the sake of you both.
This dreadful quarrel can be resolved through her.

(Enter Iokaste.)

IOKASTE.   Poor foolish men, what wicked din is this?
With Thebes sick to death, is it not shameful   175
That you should rake some private quarrel up?
(To Oedipus.) Come into the house.
—And you, Kreon, go now:
Let us have no more of this tumult over nothing.
KREON.   Nothing? No, sister: what your husband plans for me   180
Is one of two great evils: exile or death.
OEDIPUS.   He is right.
Why, woman I have caught him squarely
Plotting against my life.
KREON.   No! Let me die   185
Accurst if ever I have wished you harm!
IOKASTE.   Ah, believe it, Oedipus!
In the name of the gods, respect this oath of his
For my sake, for the sake of these people here!

Strophe 1

CHORAGOS.   Open your mind to her, my lord. Be ruled by her, I beg you!   190
OEDIPUS.   What would you have me do?
CHORAGOS.   Respect Kreon's word. He has never spoken like a fool,
    And now he has sworn an oath.
OEDIPUS.   You know what you ask?
CHORAGOS.   I do.   195
OEDIPUS.   Speak on, then.
CHORAGOS.   A friend so sworn should not be baited so,
    In blind malice, and without final proof.
OEDIPUS.   You are aware, I hope, that what you say
    Means death for me, or exile at the least.   200

Strophe 2

CHORAGOS.   No, I swear by Helios, first in heaven!
      May I die friendless and accurst,
    The worst of deaths, if ever I meant that!
    It is the withering fields
      That hurt my sick heart: 205
    Must we bear all these ills,
      And now your bad blood as well?
OEDIPUS.   Then let him go. And let me die, if I must,
    Or be driven by him in shame from the land of Thebes.
    It is your unhappiness, and not his talk,   210
    That touches me.
             As for him—
    Wherever he goes, hatred will follow him.
KREON.   Ugly in yielding, as you were ugly in rage!
    Natures like yours chiefly torment themselves.   215
OEDIPUS.   Can you not go? Can you not leave me?
KREON.   I can.
    You do not know me; but the city knows me,
    And in its eyes I am just, if not in yours.

(Exit Kreon.)   220

Antistrophe 1

CHORAGOS.   Lady Iokaste, did you not ask the king to go to his chambers?
IOKASTE.   First tell me what has happened.
CHORAGOS.   There was suspicion without evidence; yet it rankled
    As even false charges will.
IOKASTE.   On both sides?   225
CHORAGOS.   On both.
IOKASTE.   But what was said?

CHORAGOS.   Oh let it rest, let it be done with!
  Have we not suffered enough?
OEDIPUS.   You see to what your decency has brought you: 230
  You have made difficulties where my heart saw none.

Antistrophe 2

CHORAGOS.   Oedipus, it is not once only I have told you—
  You must know I should count myself unwise
  To the point of madness, should I now forsake you—
    You, under whose hand,   235
      In the storm of another time,
        Our dear land sailed out free.
  But now stand fast at the helm!
IOKASTE.   In God's name, Oedipus, inform your wife as well:
  Why are you so set in this hard anger?   240
OEDIPUS.   I will tell you, for none of these men deserves
  My confidence as you do. It is Kreon's work,
  His treachery, his plotting against me.
IOKASTE.   Go on, if you can make this clear to me.
OEDIPUS.   He charges me with the murder of Laios.   245
IOKASTE.   Has he some knowledge? Or does he speak from hearsay?
OEDIPUS.   He would not commit himself to such a charge,
  But he has brought in that damnable soothsayer
  To tell his story.
IOKASTE.   Set your mind at rest.   250
  If it is a question of soothsayers, I tell you
  That you will find no man whose craft gives knowledge
  Of the unknowable.
                Here is my proof:
  An oracle was reported to Laios once   255
  (I will not say from Phoibos himself, but from
  His appointed ministers, at any rate)
  That his doom would be death at the hands of his own son—
  His son, born of his flesh and of mine!

  Now, you remember the story: Laios was killed   260
  By marauding strangers where three highways meet;
  But his child had not been three days in this world
  Before the king had pierced the baby's ankles
  And left him to die on a lonely mountainside.

  Thus, Apollo never caused that child   265
  To kill his father, and it was not Laios' fate
  To die at the hands of his son, as he had feared.
  This is what prophets and prophecies are worth!
  Have no dread of them.
                It is God himself   270
  Who can show us what he wills, in his own way.

OEDIPUS.   How strange a shadowy memory crossed my mind,
    Just now while you were speaking; it chilled my heart.
IOKASTE.   What do you mean? What memory do you speak of?
OEDIPUS.   If I understand you, Laios was killed   275
    At a place where three roads meet.
IOKASTE.   So it was said;
    We have no later story.
OEDIPUS.   Where did it happen?
IOKASTE.   Phokis, it is called: at a place where the Theban Way   280
    Divides into the roads toward Delphi and Daulia.
OEDIPUS.   When?
IOKASTE.   We had the news not long before you came
    And proved the right to your succession here.
OEDIPUS.   Ah, what net has God been weaving for me?   285
IOKASTE.   Oedipus! Why does this trouble you?
OEDIPUS.   Do not ask me yet.
    First, tell me how Laios looked, and tell me
    How old he was.
IOKASTE.   He was tall, his hair just touched   290
    With white; his form was not unlike your own.
OEDIPUS.   I think that I myself may be accurst
    By my own ignorant edict.
IOKASTE.   You speak strangely.
    It makes me tremble to look at you, my king.   295
OEDIPUS.   I am not sure that the blind man cannot see.
    But I should know better if you were to tell me—
IOKASTE.   Anything—though I dread to hear you ask it.
OEDIPUS.   Was the king lightly escorted, or did he ride
    With a large company, as a ruler should?   300
IOKASTE.   There were five men with him in all: one was a herald;
    And a single chariot, which he was driving.
OEDIPUS.   Alas, that makes it plain enough!
                                    But who—
    Who told you how it happened?   305
IOKASTE.   A household servant,
    The only one to escape.
OEDIPUS.   And is he still
    A servant of ours?
IOKASTE.   No; for when he came back at last   310
    And found you enthroned in the place of the dead king,
    He came to me, touched my hand with his, and begged
    That I would send him away to the frontier district
    Where only the shepherds go—
    As far away from the city as I could send him.   315
    I granted his prayer; for although the man was a slave,
    He had earned more than this favor at my hands.
OEDIPUS.   Can he be called back quickly?
IOKASTE.   Easily.
    But why?

OEDIPUS.   I have taken too much upon myself   320
   Without enquiry; therefore I wish to consult him.
IOKASTE.   Then he shall come.
                         But am I not one also
   To whom you might confide these fears of yours?   325
OEDIPUS.   That is your right; it will not be denied you,
   Now least of all; for I have reached a pitch
   Of wild foreboding. Is there anyone
   To whom I should sooner speak?

   Polybos of Corinth is my father.   330
   My mother is a Dorian: Merope.
   I grew up chief among the men of Corinth
   Until a strange thing happened—
   Not worth my passion, it may be, but strange.
   At a feast, a drunken man maundering in his cups   335
   Cries out that I am not my father's son!

   I contained myself that night, though I felt anger
   And a sinking heart. The next day I visited
   My father and mother, and questioned them.
   They stormed,   340
   Calling it all the slanderous rant of a fool;
   And this relieved me. Yet the suspicion
   Remained always aching in my mind;
   I knew there was talk; I could not rest;
   And finally, saying nothing to my parents,   345
   I went to the shrine at Delphi.

   The god dismissed my question without reply;
   He spoke of other things.
                      Some were clear,
   Full of wretchedness, dreadful, unbearable: 350
   As, that I should lie with my own mother, breed
   Children from whom all men would turn their eyes;
   And that I should be my father's murderer.

   I heard all this, and fled. And from that day
   Corinth to me was only in the stars   355
   Descending in that quarter of the sky,
   As I wandered farther and farther on my way
   To a land where I should never see the evil
   Sung by the oracle. And I came to this country
   Where, so you say, King Laios was killed.   360

   I will tell you all that happened there, my lady.
   There were three highways
   Coming together at a place I passed;
   And there a herald came toward me, and a chariot
   Drawn by horses, with a man such as you describe   365
   Seated in it. The groom leading the horses

Forced me off the road at his lord's command;
But as this charioteer lurched over toward me
I struck him in my rage. The old man saw me
And brought his double goad down upon my head   370
As I came abreast.

            He was paid back, and more!
Swinging my club in this right hand I knocked him
Out of his car, and he rolled on the ground.

                       I killed him.   375
I killed them all.
Now if that stranger and Laios were—kin,
Where is a man more miserable than I?
More hated by the gods? Citizen and alien alike
Must never shelter me or speak to me—   380
I must be shunned by all.

               And I myself
Pronounced this malediction upon myself!

Think of it: I have touched you with these hands,
These hands that killed your husband. What defilement!   385

Am I all evil, then? It must be so,
Since I must flee from Thebes, yet never again
See my own countrymen, my own country,
For fear of joining my mother in marriage
And killing Polybos, my father.   390

                 Ah,
If I was created so, born to this fate,
Who could deny the savagery of God?

O holy majesty of heavenly powers!
May I never see that day! Never!   395
Rather let me vanish from the race of men
Than know the abomination destined me!

CHORAGOS.   We too, my lord, have felt dismay at this.
    But there is hope: you have yet to hear the shepherd.
OEDIPUS.   Indeed, I fear no other hope is left me.   400
IOKASTE.   What do you hope from him when he comes?
OEDIPUS.   This much:
    If his account of the murder tallies with yours,
    Then I am cleared.
IOKASTE.   What was it that I said   405
    Of such importance?
OEDIPUS.   Why, "marauders," you said,
    Killed the king, according to this man's story.
    If he maintains that still, if there were several,
    Clearly the guilt is not mine: I was alone.   410
    But if he says one man, singlehanded, did it,
    Then the evidence all points to me.
IOKASTE.   You may be sure that he said there were several;

And can he call back that story now? He cannot.
The whole city heard it as plainly as I.   415
But suppose he alters some detail of it:
He cannot ever show that Laios' death
Fulfilled the oracle: for Apollo said
My child was doomed to kill him; and my child—
Poor baby!—it was my child that died first.   420

No. From now on, where oracles are concerned,
I would not waste a second thought on any.
OEDIPUS.   You may be right.
                                    But come: let someone go
For the shepherd at once. This matter must be settled.   425
IOKASTE.   I will send for him.
I would not wish to cross you in anything,
And surely not in this.—Let us go in.

(Exeunt into the palace.)

ODE 2

Strophe 1

CHORUS.   Let me be reverent in the ways of right,
        Lowly the paths I journey on;
        Let all my words and actions keep
        The laws of the pure universe
        From highest Heaven handed down.   5
        For Heaven is their bright nurse,
        Those generations of the realms of light;
        Ah, never of mortal kind were they begot,
        Nor are they slaves of memory, lost in sleep:
        Their Father is greater than Time, and ages not.   10

Antistrophe 1

        The tyrant is a child of Pride
        Who drinks from his great sickening cup
        Recklessness and vanity,
        Until from his high crest headlong
        He plummets to the dust of hope.   15
        That strong man is not strong.
        But let no fair ambition be denied;
        May God protect the wrestler for the State
        In government, in comely policy,
        Who will fear God, and on his ordinance wait.   20

Strophe 2

Haughtiness and the high hand of disdain
Tempt and outrage God's holy law;
And any mortal who dares hold
No immortal Power in awe
Will be caught up in a net of pain: 25
The price for which his levity is sold.
Let each man take due earnings, then,
And keep his hands from holy things,
And from blasphemy stand apart—
Else the crackling blast of heaven   30
Blows on his head, and on his desperate heart.
Though fools will honor impious men,
In their cities no tragic poet sings.

Antistrophe 2

Shall we lose faith in Delphi's obscurities,
We who have heard the world's core   35
Discredited, and the sacred wood
Of Zeus at Elis° praised no more?
The deeds and the strange prophecies
Must make a pattern yet to be understood.
Zeus, if indeed you are lord of all,   40
Throned in light over night and day,
Mirror this in your endless mind:
Our masters call the oracle
Words on the wind, and the Delphic vision blind!
Their hearts no longer know Apollo,   45
And reverence for the gods has died away.

37 *Elis:* ancient country where Olympia was reputed to have existed.

SCENE 3

(Enter Iokaste.)

IOKASTE.   Princes of Thebes, it has occurred to me
    To visit the altars of the gods, bearing
    These branches as a suppliant, and this incense.
    Our king is not himself: his noble soul
    Is overwrought with fantasies of dread,   5
    Else he would consider
    The new prophecies in the light of the old.
    He will listen to any voice that speaks disaster,
    And my advice goes for nothing. *(She
    approaches the altar, right.)*   10

To you, then, Apollo,
Lycean lord, since you are nearest, I turn in prayer.
Receive these offerings, and grant us deliverance
From defilement. Our hearts are heavy with fear
When we see our leader distracted, as helpless sailors   15
Are terrified by the confusion of their helmsman.

(Enter Messenger.)

MESSENGER.   Friends, no doubt you can direct me:
    Where shall I find the house of Oedipus,
    Or, better still, where is the king himself?   20
CHORAGOS.   It is this very place, stranger; he is inside.
    This is his wife and mother of his children.
MESSENGER.   I wish her happiness in a happy house,
    Blest in all the fulfillment of her marriage.
IOKASTE.   I wish as much for you: your courtesy   25
    Deserves a like good fortune. But now, tell me:
    Why have you come? What have you to say to us?
MESSENGER.   Good news, my lady, for your house and your husband.
IOKASTE.   What news? Who sent you here?
MESSENGER.   I am from Corinth.   30
    The news I bring ought to mean joy for you,
    Though it may be you will find some grief in it.
IOKASTE.   What is it? How can it touch us in both ways?
MESSENGER.   The word is that the people of the Isthmus
    Intend to call Oedipus to be their king.   35
IOKASTE.   But old King Polybos—is he not reigning still?
MESSENGER.   No. Death holds him in his sepulchre.
IOKASTE.   What are you saying? Polybos is dead?
MESSENGER.   If I am not telling the truth, may I die myself.
IOKASTE *(to a Maidservant).*   Go in, go quickly; tell this to your master.   40
    O riddlers of God's will, where are you now!
    This was the man whom Oedipus, long ago,
    Feared so, fled so, in dread of destroying him—
    But it was another fate by which he died.

(Enter Oedipus, center.)   45

OEDIPUS.   Dearest Iokaste, why have you sent for me?
IOKASTE.   Listen to what this man says, and then tell me
    What has become of the solemn prophecies.
OEDIPUS.   Who is this man? What is his news for me?
IOKASTE.   He has come from Corinth to announce your father's death!   50
OEDIPUS.   Is it true, stranger? Tell me in your own words.
MESSENGER.   I cannot say it more clearly: the king is dead.
OEDIPUS.   Was it by treason? Or by an attack of illness?
MESSENGER.   A little thing brings old men to their rest.
OEDIPUS.   It was sickness, then?   55
MESSENGER.   Yes, and his many years.

OEDIPUS.   Ah!
    Why should a man respect the Pythian hearth,° or
    Give heed to the birds that jangle above his head?
    They prophesied that I should kill Polybos,   60
    Kill my own father; but he is dead and buried,
    And I am here—I never touched him, never,
    Unless he died of grief for my departure,
    And thus, in a sense, through me. No. Polybos
    Has packed the oracles off with him underground.   65
    They are empty words.
IOKASTE.   Had I not told you so?
OEDIPUS.   You had; it was my faint heart that betrayed me.
IOKASTE.   From now on never think of those things again.
OEDIPUS.   And yet—must I not fear my mother's bed?   70
IOKASTE.   Why should anyone in this world be afraid,
    Since Fate rules us and nothing can be foreseen?
    A man should live only for the present day.

    Have no more fear of sleeping with your mother:
    how many men, in dreams, have lain with their mothers!   75
    No reasonable man is troubled by such things.
OEDIPUS.   That is true; only—
    If only my mother were not still alive!
    But she is alive. I cannot help my dread.
IOKASTE.   Yet this news of your father's death is wonderful.   80
OEDIPUS.   Wonderful. But I fear the living woman.
MESSENGER.   Tell me, who is this woman that you fear?
OEDIPUS.   It is Merope, man; the wife of King Polybos.
MESSENGER.   Merope? Why should you be afraid of her?
OEDIPUS.   An oracle of the gods, a dreadful saying.   85
MESSENGER.   Can you tell me about it or are you sworn to silence?
OEDIPUS.   I can tell you, and I will.
    Apollo said through his prophet that I was the man
    Who should marry his own mother, shed his father's blood
    With his own hands. And so, for all these years   90
    I have kept clear of Corinth, and no harm has come—
    Though it would have been sweet to see my parents again.
MESSENGER.   And is this the fear that drove you out of Corinth?
OEDIPUS.   Would you have me kill my father?
MESSENGER.   As for that   95
    You must be reassured by the news I gave you.
OEDIPUS.   If you could reassure me, I would reward you.
MESSENGER.   I had that in mind, I will confess: I thought
    I could count on you when you returned to Corinth.
OEDIPUS.   No: I will never go near my parents again.   100
MESSENGER.   Ah, son, you still do not know what you are doing—
OEDIPUS.   What do you mean? In the name of God tell me!
MESSENGER.   —If these are your reasons for not going home.

58 *Pythian hearth:* Delphi.

OEDIPUS.   I tell you, I fear the oracle may come true.

MESSENGER.   And guilt may come upon you through your parents?   105

OEDIPUS.   That is the dread that is always in my heart.

MESSENGER.   Can you not see that all your fears are groundless?

OEDIPUS.   Groundless? Am I not my parents' son?

MESSENGER.   Polybos was not your father.

OEDIPUS.   Not my father?   110

MESSENGER.   No more your father than the man speaking to you.

OEDIPUS.   But you are nothing to me!

MESSENGER.   Neither was he.

OEDIPUS.   Then why did he call me son?

MESSENGER.   I will tell you: 115

  Long ago he had you from my hands, as a gift.

OEDIPUS.   Then how could he love me so, if I was not his?

MESSENGER.   He had no children, and his heart turned to you.

OEDIPUS.   What of you? Did you buy me? Did you find me by chance?

MESSENGER.   I came upon you in the woody vales of Kithairon.   120

OEDIPUS.   And what were you doing there?

MESSENGER.   Tending my flocks.

OEDIPUS.   A wandering shepherd?

MESSENGER.   But your savior, son, that day.

OEDIPUS.   From what did you save me?   125

MESSENGER.   Your ankles should tell you that.

OEDIPUS.   Ah, stranger, why do you speak of that childhood pain?

MESSENGER.   I pulled the skewer that pinned your feet together.

OEDIPUS.   I have had the mark as long as I can remember.

MESSENGER.   That was why you were given the name you bear.   130

OEDIPUS.   God! Was it my father or my mother who did it?
  Tell me!

MESSENGER.   I do not know. The man who gave you to me
  Can tell you better than I.

OEDIPUS.   It was not you that found me, but another?   135

MESSENGER.   It was another shepherd gave you to me.

OEDIPUS.   Who was he? Can you tell me who he was?

MESSENGER.   I think he was said to be one of Laios' people.

OEDIPUS.   You mean the Laios who was king here years ago?

MESSENGER.   Yes; King Laios; and the man was one of his herdsmen.   140

OEDIPUS.   Is he still alive? Can I see him?

MESSENGER.   These men here
  Know best about such things.

OEDIPUS.   Does anyone here
  Know this shepherd that he is talking about?   145
  Have you seen him in the fields, or in the town?
  If you have, tell me. It is time things were made plain.

CHORAGOS.   I think the man he means is that same shepherd
  You have already asked to see. Iokaste perhaps
  Could tell you something.   150

OEDIPUS.   Do you know anything
  About him, Lady? Is he the man we have summoned?

Is that the man this shepherd means?

IOKASTE.   Why think of him?
    Forget this herdsman. Forget it all.   155
    This talk is a waste of time.

OEDIPUS.   How can you say that,
    When the clues to my true birth are in my hands?

IOKASTE.   For God's love, let us have no more questioning!
    Is your life nothing to you?   160
    My own is pain enough for me to bear.

OEDIPUS.   You need not worry. Suppose my mother a slave,
    And born of slaves: no baseness can touch you.

IOKASTE.   Listen to me, I beg you: do not do this thing!

OEDIPUS.   I will not listen; the truth must be made known.   165

IOKASTE.   Everything that I say is for your own good!

OEDIPUS.   My own good
    Snaps my patience, then; I want none of it.

IOKASTE.   You are fatally wrong! May you never learn who you are!

OEDIPUS.   Go, one of you, and bring the shepherd here.   170
    Let us leave this woman to brag of her royal name.

IOKASTE.   Ah, miserable!
    That is the only word I have for you now.
    That is the only word I can ever have.

(Exit into the palace.)   175

CHORAGOS.   Why has she left us, Oedipus? Why has she gone
    In such a passion of sorrow? I fear this silence:
    Something dreadful may come of it.

OEDIPUS.   Let it come!
    However base my birth, I must know about it.   180
    The queen, like a woman, is perhaps ashamed
    To think of my low origin. But I
    Am a child of Luck; I cannot be dishonored.
    Luck is my mother; the passing months, my brothers,
    Have seen me rich and poor.   185
                         If this is so,
    How could I wish that I were someone else?
    How could I not be glad to know my birth?

ODE 3

Strophe

CHORUS.   If ever the coming time were known
    To my heart's pondering,
    Kithairon, now by Heaven I see the torches
    At the festival of the next full moon,
    And see the dance, and hear the choir sing   5

A grace to your gentle shade:
Mountain where Oedipus was found,
O mountain guard of a noble race!
May the god° who heals us lend his aid,
And let that glory come to pass   10
For our king's cradling-ground.

Antistrophe

Of the nymphs that flower beyond the years,
Who bore you,° royal child,
To Pan° of the hills or the timberline Apollo,
Cold in delight where the upland clears,   15
Or Hermes° for whom Kyllene's° heights are piled?
Or flushed as evening cloud,
Great Dionysos,° roamer of mountains,
He—was it he who found you there,
And caught you up in his own proud   20
Arms from the sweet god-ravisher
Who laughed by the Muses'° fountains?

9 *god:* Apollo.   13 *Who bore you:* The Chorus is asking if Oedipus is the son of an immortal nymph and a god: Pan, Apollo, Hermes, or Dionysus.   14 *Pan:* god of nature, forests, flocks, and shepherds, depicted as half-man and half-goat.   16 *Hermes:* son of Zeus, messenger of the gods.   *Kyllene:* mountain reputed to be the birthplace of Hermes; also the center of a cult to Hermes.   18 *Dionysos* (Dionysus): god of wine around whom wild, orgiastic rituals developed; also called Bacchus.   22 *Muses:* nine sister goddesses who presided over poetry and music, art and sciences.

SCENE 4

OEDIPUS.   Sirs: though I do not know the man,
    I think I see him coming, this shepherd we want:
    He is old, like our friend here, and the men
    Bringing him seem to be servants of my house.
    But you can tell, if you have ever seen him.   5

(Enter Shepherd escorted by Servants.)

CHORAGOS.   I know him, he was Laios' man. You can trust him.
OEDIPUS.   Tell me first, you from Corinth: is this the shepherd
    We were discussing?
MESSENGER.   This is the very man.   10
OEDIPUS *(to Shepherd).*   Come here. No, look at me. You must answer
    Everything I ask.—You belonged to Laios?
SHEPHERD.   Yes: born his slave, brought up in his house.
OEDIPUS.   Tell me: what kind of work did you do for him?
SHEPHERD.   I was a shepherd of his, most of my life.   15
OEDIPUS.   Where mainly did you go for pasturage?

SHEPHERD.   Sometimes Kithairon, sometimes the hills nearby.

OEDIPUS.   Do you remember ever seeing this man out there?

SHEPHERD.   What would he be doing there? This man?

OEDIPUS.   This man standing here. Have you ever seen him before?   20

SHEPHERD.   No. At least, not to my recollection.

MESSENGER.   And that is not strange, my lord. But I'll refresh
    His memory: he must remember when we two
    Spent three whole seasons together, March to September,
    On Kithairon or thereabouts. He had two flocks;   25
    I had one. Each autumn I'd drive mine home
    And he would go back with his to Laios' sheepfold.—
    Is this not true, just as I have described it?

SHEPHERD.   True, yes; but it was all so long ago.

MESSENGER.   Well, then: do you remember, back in those days,   30
    That you gave me a baby boy to bring up as my own?

SHEPHERD.   What if I did? What are you trying to say?

MESSENGER.   King Oedipus was once that little child.

SHEPHERD.   Damn you, hold your tongue!

OEDIPUS.   No more of that!   35
    It is your tongue needs watching, not this man's.

SHEPHERD.   My king, my master, what is it I have done wrong?

OEDIPUS.   You have not answered his question about the boy.

SHEPHERD.   He does not know . . . He is only making trouble . . .

OEDIPUS.   Come, speak plainly, or it will go hard with you.   40

SHEPHERD.   In God's name, do not torture an old man!

OEDIPUS.   Come here, one of you; bind his arms behind him.

SHEPHERD.   Unhappy king! What more do you wish to learn?

OEDIPUS.   Did you give this man the child he speaks of?

SHEPHERD.   I did.   45
    And I would to God I had died that very day.

OEDIPUS.   You will die now unless you speak the truth.

SHEPHERD.   Yet if I speak the truth, I am worse than dead.

OEDIPUS *(to Attendant)*.   He intends to draw it out, apparently—

SHEPHERD.   No! I have told you already that I gave him the boy.   50

OEDIPUS.   Where did you get him? From your house? From somewhere else?

SHEPHERD.   Not from mine, no. A man gave him to me.

OEDIPUS.   Is that man here? Whose house did he belong to?

SHEPHERD.   For God's love, my king, do not ask me any more!

OEDIPUS.   You are a dead man if I have to ask you again.   55

SHEPHERD.   Then . . . Then the child was from the palace of Laios.

OEDIPUS.   A slave child? or a child of his own line?

SHEPHERD.   Ah, I am on the brink of dreadful speech!

OEDIPUS.   And I of dreadful hearing. Yet I must hear.

SHEPHERD.   If you must be told, then . . .   60
                                        they said it was Laios' child;
    But it is your wife who can tell you about that.

OEDIPUS.   My wife—Did she give it to you?

SHEPHERD.   My lord, she did.

OEDIPUS.   Do you know why?   65

SHEPHERD.   I was told to get rid of it.

OEDIPUS.   Oh heartless mother!

SHEPHERD.   But in dread of prophecies . . .

OEDIPUS.   Tell me.

SHEPHERD.   It was said that the boy would kill his own father.   70

OEDIPUS.   Then why did you give him over to this old man?

SHEPHERD.   I pitied the baby, my king,
    And I thought that this man would take him far away
    To his own country.
                  He saved him—but for what a fate!   75
    For if you are what this man says you are,
    No man living is more wretched than Oedipus.

OEDIPUS.   Ah God! It was true!
                All the prophecies!—
                        Now   80
    O Light, may I look on you for the last time!
    I, Oedipus,
    Oedipus, damned in his birth, in his marriage damned,
    Damned in the blood he shed with his own hand!

(He rushes into the palace.)   85

ODE 4

Strophe 1

CHORUS.   Alas for the seed of men.
    What measure shall I give these generations
    That breathe on the void and are void
    And exist and do not exist?
    Who bears more weight of joy   5
    Than mass of sunlight shifting in images,
    Or who shall make his thought stay on
    That down time drifts away?
    Your splendor is all fallen.
    O naked brow of wrath and tears,   10
    O change of Oedipus!
    I who saw your days call no man blest—
    Your great days like ghosts gone.

Antistrophe 1

    That mind was a strong bow.
    Deep, how deep you drew it then, hard archer,   15
    At a dim fearful range,

And brought dear glory down!
You overcame the stranger°—
The virgin with her hooking lion claws—
And though death sang, stood like a tower   20
To make pale Thebes take heart.
Fortress against our sorrow!
True king, giver of laws,
Majestic Oedipus!
No prince in Thebes had ever such renown,   25
No prince won such grace of power.

Strophe 2

And now of all men ever known
Most pitiful is this man's story:
His fortunes are most changed; his state
Fallen to a low slave's   30
Ground under bitter fate.
O Oedipus, most royal one!
The great door° that expelled you to the light
Gave at night—ah, gave night to your glory:
As to the father, to the fathering son.   35
All understood too late.
How could that queen whom Laios won,
The garden that he harrowed at his height,
Be silent when that act was done?

Antistrophe 2

But all eyes fail before time's eye,   40
All actions come to justice there.
Though never willed, though far down the deep past,
Your bed, your dread sirings,
Are brought to book at last.
Child by Laios doomed to die,   45
Then doomed to lose that fortunate little death,
Would God you never took breath in this air
That with my wailing lips I take to cry:
For I weep the world's outcast.
I was blind, and now I can tell why: 50
Asleep, for you had given ease of breath
To Thebes, while the false years went by.

18 *stranger:* the Sphinx.   33 *door:* Iokaste's womb.

EXODOS°

(Enter, from the palace, Second Messenger.)

SECOND MESSENGER.   Elders of Thebes, most honored in this land,
What horrors are yours to see and hear, what weight
Of sorrow to be endured, if, true to your birth,
You venerate the line of Labdakos!   5
I think neither Istros nor Phasis, those great rivers,
Could purify this place of all the evil
It shelters now, or soon must bring to light—
Evil not done unconsciously, but willed.

The greatest griefs are those we cause ourselves.   10
CHORAGOS.   Surely, friend, we have grief enough already;
What new sorrow do you mean?
SECOND MESSENGER.   The queen is dead.
CHORAGOS.   O miserable queen! But at whose hand?
SECOND MESSENGER.   Her own.   15
The full horror of what happened you cannot know,
For you did not see it; but I, who did, will tell you
As clearly as I can how she met her death.

When she had left us,
In passionate silence, passing through the court,   20
She ran to her apartment in the house,
Her hair clutched by the fingers of both hands.
She closed the doors behind her; then, by that bed
Where long ago the fatal son was conceived—
That son who should bring about his father's death—   25
We heard her call upon Laios, dead so many years,
And heard her wail for the double fruit of her marriage,
A husband by her husband, children by her child.

Exactly how she died I do not know:
For Oedipus burst in moaning and would not let us   30
Keep vigil to the end: it was by him
As he stormed about the room that our eyes were caught.
From one to another of us he went, begging a sword,
Hunting the wife who was not his wife, the mother
Whose womb had carried his own children and himself.   35
I do not know: it was none of us aided him,
But surely one of the gods was in control!
For with a dreadful cry
He hurled his weight, as though wrenched out of himself,

Exodos: final scene.

At the twin doors: the bolts gave, and he rushed in.   40
And there we saw her hanging, her body swaying
From the cruel cord she had noosed about her neck.
A great sob broke from him, heartbreaking to hear,
As he loosed the rope and lowered her to the ground.

I would blot out from my mind what happened next!
For the king ripped from her gown the golden brooches   45
That were her ornament, and raised them, and plunged them down
Straight into his own eyeballs, crying, "no more,
No more shall you look on the misery about me,
The horrors of my own doing! Too long you have known   50
The faces of those whom I should never have seen,
Too long been blind to those for whom I was searching!
From this hour, go in darkness!" And as he spoke,
He struck at his eyes—not once, but many times;
And the blood spattered his beard,   55
Bursting from his ruined sockets like red hail.

So from the unhappiness of two this evil has sprung,
A curse on the man and woman alike. The old
Happiness of the house of Labdakos
Was happiness enough: where is it today?   60
It is all wailing and ruin, disgrace, death—all
The misery of mankind that has a name—
And it is wholly and for ever theirs.
CHORAGOS.   Is he in agony still? Is there no rest for him?
SECOND MESSENGER.   He is calling for someone to open the doors wide   65
So that all the children of Kadmos may look upon
His father's murderer, his mother's—no,
I cannot say it!
              And then he will leave Thebes,
Self-exiled, in order that the curse   70
Which he himself pronounced may depart from the house.
He is weak, and there is none to lead him,
So terrible is his suffering.
                        But you will see:
Look, the doors are opening; in a moment   75
You will see a thing that would crush a heart of stone.

(The central door is opened; Oedipus, blinded, is led in.)

CHORAGOS.   Dreadful indeed for men to see.
Never have my own eyes
Looked on a sight so full of fear.   80

Oedipus!
What madness came upon you, what demon
Leaped on your life with heavier
Punishment than a mortal man can bear?
No: I cannot even   85

Look at you, poor ruined one.
And I would speak, question, ponder,
If I were able. No.
You make me shudder.
OEDIPUS.   God. God.   90
Is there a sorrow greater?
Where shall I find harbor in this world?
My voice is hurled far on a dark wind.
What has God done to me?
CHORAGOS.   Too terrible to think of, or to see.   95

Strophe 1

OEDIPUS.   O cloud of night,
Never to be turned away: night coming on,
I cannot tell how: night like a shroud!
My fair winds brought me here.
                                    O God. Again   100
The pain of the spikes where I had sight,
The flooding pain
Of memory, never to be gouged out.
CHORAGOS.   This is not strange.
You suffer it all twice over, remorse in pain,   105
Pain in remorse.

Antistrophe 1

OEDIPUS.   Ah dear friend
Are you faithful even yet, you alone?
Are you still standing near me, will you stay here,
Patient, to care for the blind?   110
                              The blind man!
Yet even blind I know who it is attends me,
By the voice's tone—
Though my new darkness hide the comforter.
CHORAGOS.   Oh fearful act!   115
What god was it drove you to rake black
Night across your eyes?

Strophe 2

OEDIPUS.   Apollo. Apollo. Dear
Children, the god was Apollo.
He brought my sick, sick fate upon me.   120
But the blinding hand was my own!
How could I bear to see
When all my sight was horror everywhere?

CHORAGOS.   Everywhere; that is true.
OEDIPUS.   And now what is left?   125
    Images? Love? A greeting even,
    Sweet to the senses? Is there anything?
    Ah, no, friends: lead me away.
    Lead me away from Thebes.
    Lead the great wreck   130
    And hell of Oedipus, whom the gods hate.
CHORAGOS.   Your misery, you are not blind to that.
    Would God you had never found it out!

Antistrophe 2

OEDIPUS.   Death take the man who unbound
    My feet on that hillside   135
    And delivered me from death to life! What life?
    If only I had died,
    This weight of monstrous doom
    Could not have dragged me and my darlings down.
CHORAGOS.   I would have wished the same.   140
OEDIPUS.   Oh never to have come here
    With my father's blood upon me! Never
    To have been the man they call his mother's husband!
    Oh accurst! Oh child of evil,
    To have entered that wretched bed—   145
                    the selfsame one!
    More primal than sin itself, this fell to me.
CHORAGOS.   I do not know what words to offer you.
    You were better dead than alive and blind.
OEDIPUS.   Do not counsel me anymore. This punishment   150
    That I have laid upon myself is just.
    If I had eyes,
    I do not know how I could bear the sight
    Of my father, when I came to the house of Death,
    Or my mother: for I have sinned against them both   155
    So vilely that I could not make my peace
    By strangling my own life.
                  Or do you think my children,
    Born as they were born, would be sweet to my eyes?
    Ah never, never! Nor this town with its high walls, 160
    Nor the holy images of the gods.
                For I,
    Thrice miserable!—Oedipus, noblest of all the line
    Of Kadmos, have condemned myself to enjoy
    These things no more, by my own malediction   165
    Expelling that man whom the gods declared
    To be a defilement in the house of Laios.
    After exposing the rankness of my own guilt,

How could I look men frankly in the eyes?
No, I swear it,   170
If I could have stifled my hearing at its source,
I would have done it and made all this body
A tight cell of misery, blank to light and sound:
So I should have been safe in my dark mind
Beyond external evil.   175
                Ah Kithairon!
Why did you shelter me? When I was cast upon you,
Why did I not die? Then I should never
Have shown the world my execrable birth.

Ah Polybos! Corinth, city that I believed   180
The ancient seat of my ancestors: how fair
I seemed, your child! And all the while this evil
Was cancerous within me!
                For I am sick
In my own being, sick in my origin.   185

O three roads, dark ravine, woodland and way
Where three roads met; you, drinking my father's blood,
My own blood, spilled by my own hand: can you remember
The unspeakable things I did there, and the things
I went on from there to do?   190
                O marriage, marriage!
The act that engendered me, and again the act
Performed by the son in the same bed—
                Ah, the net
Of incest, mingling fathers, brothers, sons,   195
With brides, wives, mothers: the last evil
That can be known by men: no tongue can say
How evil!
        No. For the Love of God, conceal me
Somewhere far from Thebes; or kill me; or hurl me   200
Into the sea, away from men's eyes for ever.

Come, lead me. You need not fear to touch me.
Of all men, I alone can bear this guilt.

(Enter Kreon.)

CHORAGOS.   Kreon is here now. As to what you ask,   205
    He may decide the course to take. He only
    Is left to protect the city in your place.
OEDIPUS.   Alas, how can I speak to him? What right have I
    To beg his courtesy whom I have deeply wronged?
KREON.   I have not come to mock you, Oedipus,   210
    Or to reproach you, either.—
    (To Attendants)   You, standing there:
    if you have lost all respect for man's dignity,
    At least respect the flame of Lord Helios:

Do not allow this pollution to show itself   215
Openly here, an affront to the earth
And Heaven's rain and the light of day. No, take him
Into the house as quickly as you can.
For it is proper
That only the close kindred see his grief.   220
OEDIPUS.   I pray you in God's name, since your courtesy
Ignores my dark expectation, visiting
With mercy this man of all men most execrable:
Give me what I ask—for your good, not for mine.
KREON.   And what is it that you turn to me begging for?   225
OEDIPUS.   Drive me out of this country as quickly as may be
To a place where no human voice can ever greet me.
KREON.   I should have done that before now—only,
God's will had not been wholly revealed to me.
OEDIPUS.   But his command is plain: the parricide   230
Must be destroyed. I am that evil man.
KREON.   That is the sense of it, yes; but as things are,
We had best discover clearly what is to be done.
OEDIPUS.   You would learn more about a man like me?
KREON.   You are ready now to listen to the god.   235
OEDIPUS.   I will listen. But it is to you
That I must turn for help. I beg you, hear me.
The woman is there—
Give her whatever funeral you think proper:
She is your sister.   240
                    —but let me go, Kreon!
Let me purge my father's Thebes of the pollution
Of my living here, and go out to the wild hills,
To Kithairon, that has won such fame with me,
The tomb my mother and father appointed for me,   245
And let me die there, as they willed I should.
And yet I know
Death will not ever come to me through sickness
Or in any natural way: I have been preserved
For some unthinkable fate. But let that be.   250

As for my sons, you need not care for them.
They are men, they will find some way to live.
But my poor daughters, who have shared my table,
Who never before have been parted from their father—
Take care of them, Kreon; do this for me.   255

And will you let me touch them with my hands
A last time, and let us weep together?
Be kind, my lord,
Great prince, be kind!
                    Could I but touch them,   260
They would be mine again, as when I had my eyes.

(Enter Antigone and Ismene, attended.)

Ah, God!
Is it my dearest children I hear weeping?
Has Kreon pitied me and sent my daughters?   265
KREON.   Yes, Oedipus: I knew that they were dear to you
In the old days, and know you must love them still.
OEDIPUS.   May God bless you for this—and be a friendlier
Guardian to you than he has been to me!

Children, where are you?   270
Come quickly to my hands: they are your brother's—
Hands that have brought your father's once clear eyes
To this way of seeing—
             Ah dearest ones,
I had neither sight nor knowledge then, your father   275
By the woman who was the source of his own life!
And I weep for you—having no strength to see you—,
I weep for you when I think of the bitterness
That men will visit upon you all your lives.
What homes, what festivals can you attend   280
Without being forced to depart again in tears?
And when you come to marriageable age,
Where is the man, my daughters, who would dare
Risk the bane that lies on all my children?
Is there any evil wanting? Your father killed   285
His father; sowed the womb of her who bore him;
Engendered you at the fount of his own existence!
That is what they will say of you.
                 Then, whom
Can you ever marry? There are no bridegrooms for you,   290
And your lives must wither away in sterile dreaming.

O Kreon, son of Menoikeus!
You are the only father my daughters have,
Since we, their parents, are both of us gone for ever.
They are your own blood: you will not let them   295
Fall into beggary and loneliness;
You will keep them from the miseries that are mine!
Take pity on them; see, they are only children,
Friendless except for you. Promise me this,
Great prince, and give me your hand in token of it.   300

(Kreon clasps his right hand.)

Children:
I could say much, if you could understand me,
But as it is, I have only this prayer for you:
Live where you can, be as happy as you can—   305
Happier, please God, than God has made your father.
KREON.   Enough. You have wept enough. Now go within.
OEDIPUS.   I must; but it is hard.
KREON.   Time eases all things.

OEDIPUS.   You know my mind, then?   310
KREON.   Say what you desire.
OEDIPUS.   Send me from Thebes!
KREON.   God grant that I may!
OEDIPUS.   But since God hates me . . .
KREON.   No, he will grant your wish.   315
OEDIPUS.   You promise?
KREON.   I cannot speak beyond my knowledge.
OEDIPUS.   Then lead me in.
KREON.   Come now, and leave your children.
OEDIPUS.   No! Do not take them from me!   320
KREON.   Think no longer
   That you are in command here, but rather think
   How, when you were, you served your own destruction.

(Exeunt into the house all but the Chorus; the Choragos chants directly to the audience.)   325

CHORAGOS.   Men of Thebes: look upon Oedipus.
   This is the king who solved the famous riddle
   And towered up, most powerful of men.
   No mortal eyes but looked on him with envy,
   Yet in the end ruin swept over him.   330

   Let every man in mankind's frailty
   Consider his last day; and let none
   Presume on his good fortune until he find
   Life, at his death, a memory without pain.

QUESTIONS FOR CRITICAL READING

1. What evidence of personal pride does Oedipus give at the beginning of the play?

2. A great deal of the language of the Priest at the beginning of the play refers to God and to the rituals of worship. However, the Priest does not ask God to relieve Thebes from its plague but instead asks Oedipus: "Therefore, O mighty power, we turn to you" (Prologue, 45). Does Oedipus seem to be a godly man? Is he appropriately reverent?

3. What was the oracle that Oedipus heard? Does he believe it?

4. Apollo, Kreon tells us (Prologue, 116–17), demands revenge upon whoever killed Laios. What do you make of a god or a religion that demands such revenge? What does that tell you about the culture in which Oedipus lived?

5. Part of the dramatic irony of the play develops in Scene 1 when Oedipus demands that the killer of Laios be found and treated harshly. Examine his speech for its ironic content (see lines 29 ff.).

6. Oedipus has little faith in the capacity of Teiresias to know the truth. Why does he consult him? How does he treat him once Teiresias has told him what he knows? What is Teiresias's attitude toward Apollo?

7. What is the dramatic effect of Teiresias's telling Oedipus's fortune (Sc. 1, 245 ff.)?

8. Why, in Scene 2, has Oedipus accused Kreon of misbehavior? What does Kreon tell Oedipus regarding his attitude toward kingly power?

9. Examine the beginning of Oedipus's recognition (anagnorisis) in Scene 2, lines 272–73. How does Oedipus's growing understanding affect your response to his character?

10. When Oedipus realizes he may have killed Laios, he demands verification. He calls back the servant who witnessed the killing. Why does he do this? What does he hope for? How does he treat the servant?

11. How does Oedipus react when he discovers that Polybos was not his real father? See Scene 3, line 109. What truths does Oedipus discover about himself?

12. In Scene 4 why does the Shepherd refuse to carry out the orders of Iokaste when she told him to take her baby and kill it? What dramatic irony is involved in the Shepherd's decision to let the baby live?

13. Is Oedipus's last speech in Scene 4 the peripeteia of the play, the dramatic reversal? Is it also the moment of ultimate recognition on Oedipus's part of his guilt?

14. Iokaste kills herself when she realizes what has happened. Why doesn't Oedipus do the same?

15. Oedipus is fated to spend his life in exile. Is exile a fate similar to death? Does Oedipus suffer enough to rouse the feelings of both terror and pity in the audience?

QUESTIONS FOR INTERPRETATION

1. Sigmund Freud developed the concept of the Oedipus complex—the desire of the child to murder the parent of the same sex and marry the parent of the opposite sex—from this play. One interesting approach to interpretation would be an examination of the psychological forces at work in the drama. Oedipus seems to be going through a process of self-discovery. How relevant is his journey into understanding to the journey that each of us takes in life? What can we learn from his search?

2. The play is obviously riddled with moments of dramatic irony. One of the strongest interpretations might develop from an analysis of the most important moments of dramatic irony. In this play, the ironies are tragic, so it may be useful to establish how *Oedipus Rex* defines tragic irony, as opposed to ordinary irony.

3. This play is also valuable for its examination of the role of force in government. Iokaste, Kreon, and Oedipus are the essential governors of Thebes. What is their attitude toward political force? How do they involve religion as an element of that force? Is religion a political force, or is it a force that reaches beyond politics?

4. How does fate function in this play? Consider the role of prophecy and the power of the oracle. Is Oedipus attempting to be a modern man when he reveals his uncertainty about the value of Teiresias's testimony? What is Oedipus's attitude toward fate?

5. An interesting interpretation of this play might begin with a consideration of the play as a formal legal hearing, like a court trial. What resemblance does the structure of the play have to a trial? What legal issues are being resolved? What is the nature of the law that these people seem to respect?

COMEDY

Comedy is a less serious kind of drama than tragedy. It is not always funny, nor do things always end absolutely happily, but the resolution is brighter than in tragedies. Comedies are also more amusing and do not excite the emotions of pity and terror. Again, some of the qualities of comedy can be listed.

- A comedy generally presents characters of middle social station, rather than noble or serious characters. For the Greeks, who originated the genre, comedy was defined in part by its reliance on ordinary citizens for its characters.
- Comedy often relies on complications that center on mistaken identity, conflicts between generations, and numerous misunderstandings.
- Comedy usually relies on wit and humor for its effect.
- Comedy frequently ends in marriage or marriages.
- The subject of comedy is often the weakness of human ambition or the pretenses of characters who think they are better than others.
- Comedy often relies on the dynamics of multiple plots, often contrasting the actions of characters in high station with those in low station.

Among the many subgenres of comedy several are well known. **Burlesque** is a form of exaggerated ridicule in which people, usually of high station, are made to look asinine. **Parody** is a form of comedy in which a playwright pokes fun at a specific play or specific action. **Travesty** makes fun of an entire kind of drama; for example, many TV skits travesty film noir and other dramatic genres.

Satire is ridicule with a moral purpose; thus it is not always comic, since it usually intends to improve the manners or habits of its audience. Susan Glaspell's *Suppressed Desires,* a good example of comic satire, makes fun of the extreme interpretations of Freudian psychology then prevalent in popular publications and in literary society. **Farce** is a form of comedy built on a joke or a gag. The comedy of the Three Stooges and of the Marx Brothers is farce.

High comedy is a term applied to comedies with serious themes such as Susan Glaspell's *Suppressed Desires* and possibly *The Cherry Orchard.* **Low comedy** is a term reserved for farce and burlesque, such as *Pyramus and Thisby,* the rude mechanicals' play in *A Midsummer Night's Dream.* Low comedy uses many **sight gags:** visual tricks such as mugging (making weird faces), pratfalls, and mimicking of other characters on stage. Early films, such as those by Charlie Chaplin and the Keystone Kops, gave rise to the term **slapstick comedy,** which looked for every conceivable opportunity to include a sight gag, pratfall, or preposterous piece of **stage business**—extra action that is not in the script. Some of the devices associated with low comedy can be used in productions of plays such as *A Midsummer Night's Dream.* They are up to the discretion of the director.

However, unless the playwright has included stage directions in the play itself, the reader will miss such additions.

Types of Comedy

The plot of a **romantic comedy** pits the young lovers struggling against artificial difficulties created by parents. Often the difficulties are resolved by the discovery of the "true" identity of one of the lovers; for example, an unworthy suitor may turn out to be worthy after all. This dramatic formula still works, despite our modern age's relative indifference to the social status of young people about to marry. The parents in such comedies are **blocking characters.** Despite many changes in culture and style, parents have tried to block marriages or liaisons between children for the last twenty-five hundred years and more. But there are also many other kinds of blocking characters: misers, tyrants, bosses, fools, and do-gooders. The pleasure of comedy often derives from watching these characters get their comeuppance.

The oldest comedy—the **comedy of situation**—seems to have depended on ridiculous situations for its energy. Men forced to dress up as women, a poor man mistaken for a millionaire, women forcing peace by withholding sex from their warrior husbands—all have been popular. Such plays, originating with the Greeks, have come to be known as **Old Comedy.** They verge on slapstick and farce and survive today in sitcoms (situation comedies) on commercial television. Television classics such as *The Honeymooners, I Love Lucy, The Carol Burnett Show, Seinfeld,* and many more reveal the continuing power of comedies of situation.

The **comedy of manners** expanded situation comedy by aiming at a critique of the way people lived. It then became an instrument of social criticism, often poking fun at people who are hypocrites, stuffed shirts, or intellectually pretentious. This is the case with *Suppressed Desires.*

The **comedy of intrigue** involves the manipulation of characters by another character or characters, usually for ends that are less than noble. Susan Glaspell's *Suppressed Desires* is partly a comedy of intrigue, since the husband, Stephen Brewster, intrigues to trick his wife, Henrietta, back into what he thinks is common-sense behavior. He tricks her by using her own method of interpreting everything according to Freudian symbols—but this time to her disadvantage. Comedies of intrigue have a durability not because they suggest social reform or because they show the preposterousness of the situations people get into, but because they amuse us with the ingenuity of the ways in which characters manipulate each other.

Comedies have turned out to be extremely effective instruments in helping societies see themselves as they really are. It is easier to accept criticism if one can laugh at the same time. Of course, serious plays often include social commentary. Most of the plays in the album combine social commentary with dramatic action.

A SHAKESPEAREAN COMEDY

WILLIAM SHAKESPEARE   (1564–1616)

Shakespeare wrote and produced A Midsummer Night's Dream *probably in 1595 or1596, early in his career, but at a time when he was already well known and successful. He probably wrote* Romeo and Juliet *close to the same time. By 1597 he had earned enough money to purchase a considerable property in his home town of Stratford. He was renowned for his history plays, which entertained thousands of Londoners while imparting something of the history of kings such as* Henry VI, Richard II, Richard III, *and* Henry IV. *Among his comedies by that time were* The Comedy of Errors *and* The Taming of the Shrew.

A Midsummer Night's Dream *satisfies most of the demands of comedy as set down in ancient Greece, in which the play is set. The characters are noble in the case of Oberon and Titania, although they are noble fairies rather than noble citizens. Among the noble citizens are Theseus, duke of Athens, and his bride-to-be, Hippolyta, the queen of the Amazons. The complications that beset the play are naturally those of mistaken identity, as when Puck mistakes Lysander for Demetrius (Act II, Sc. ii, line 80) and pours the love-juice into his eyes, thus making him fall in love with the wrong woman. There is a great deal of wit and humor in* A Midsummer Night's Dream, *especially in the amusing subplot of the country bumpkins who intend to put on a play for Theseus and Hippolyta. Peter Quince, Snug the joiner, and Bottom the weaver are characters of low social station, but of such ingratiating qualities that they are laughed at affectionately by all.*

The blocking character in this comedy is Egeus, Hermia's father, who wishes her to marry Demetrius, whom she does not love. As a result of Egeus's stubbornness, Hermia flees to the forest, where Oberon and Titania rule, and the natural complications flesh out the story with a touch of hilarity. Most comedies end in marriage, and A Midsummer Night's Dream *ends in not only one, but three marriages, as well as a reconciliation between Oberon and Titania. The essence of this comedy is optimism, borne out by the resolution of all complications.*

A Midsummer Night's Dream° _____ *c. 1596*

Dramatis Personae
  Theseus, *Duke of Athens*
  Egeus, *father to Hermia*
  Lysander, ⎱ *in love with Hermia*
  Demetrius, ⎰
  Philostrate, *Master of the Revels to Theseus*
  Quince, *a carpenter*
  Snug, *a joiner*
  Bottom, *a weaver*
  Flute, *a bellows-mender*
  Snout, *a tinker*
  Starveling, *a tailor*
  Hippolyta, Queen of the Amazons, *betrothed to Theseus*
  Hermia, *daughter to Egeus, in love with Lysander*

The text of *A Midsummer Night's Dream* has come down to us in different versions—such as the first quarto, the second quarto, and the first folio. The copy of the text used here is largely drawn from the first quarto. Passages enclosed in square brackets are taken from one of the other versions.

Helena, *in love with Demetrius*
Oberon, *King of the Fairies*
Titania, *Queen of the Fairies*
Puck, *or Robin Goodfellow*
Peaseblossom, ⎫
Cobweb,   ⎬ *fairies*
Moth,   ⎪
Mustardseed, ⎭
Other Fairies *attending their king and queen*
Attendants *on Theseus and Hippolyta*
Scene: Athens, and a wood near it.

ACT I

Scene I°

(Enter Theseus, Hippolyta, [Philostrate,] with others.)

THESEUS.   Now, fair Hippolyta, our nuptial hour
    Draws on apace. Four happy days bring in
    Another moon; but, O, methinks, how slow
    This old moon wanes! She lingers° my desires
    Like to step-dame° or a dowager°   5
    Long withering out a young man's revenue.
HIPPOLYTA.   Four days will quickly steep themselves in night,
    Four nights will quickly dream away the time;
    And then the moon, like to a silver bow
    New-bent in heaven, shall behold the night   10
    Of our solemnities.
THESEUS.   Go, Philostrate,
    Stir up the Athenian youth to merriments,
    Awake the pert and nimble spirit of mirth,
    Turn melancholy forth to funerals;
    The pale companion° is not for our pomp.°   15

[Exit Philostrate.]

    Hippolyta, I woo'd thee with my sword,°
    And won they love doing thee injuries;
    But I will wed thee in another key,
    With pomp, with triumph,° and with reveling.

(Enter Egeus and his daughter Hermia, and Lysander, and Demetrius.)

1 *Location:* the palace of Theseus.   4 *lingers:* lengthens, protects.   5 *step-dame:* stepmother.   *dowager:* widow with a jointure or dower (an estate or title from her deceased husband).   15 *companion:* fellow.   *pomp:* ceremonial magnificence.   16 *with my sword:* in a
military engagement against the Amazons, when Hippolyta was taken captive.   19 *triumph:* public festivity.

EGEUS.   Happy be Theseus, our renowned Duke!   20
THESEUS.   Thanks good Egeus. What's the news with thee?
EGEUS.   Full of vexation come I, with complaint
    Against my child, my daughter Hermia.
    Stand forth, Demetrius. My noble lord,
    This man hath consent to marry her.   25
    Stand forth, Lysander. And, my gracious Duke,
    This man hath bewitch'd the bosom of my child.
    Thou, thou, Lysander, thou hast given her rhymes
    And interchang'd love tokens with my child.
    Thou hast by moonlight at her window sung   30
    With feigning voice verses of feigning love,°
    And stol'n the impression of her fantasy,°
    With bracelets of thy hair, rings, gauds,° conceits,°
    Knacks,° trifles, nosegays, sweetmeats—messengers
    Of strong prevailment in unhardened youth.   35
    With cunning hast thou filch'd my daughter's heart,
    Turn'd her obedience, which is due to me,
    To stubborn harshness. And, my gracious Duke,
    Be it so she will not here before your Grace
    Consent to marry with Demetrius   40
    I beg the ancient privilege of Athens:
    As she is mine, I may dispose of her,
    Which shall be either to this gentleman
    Or to her death, according to our law
    Immediately° provided in that case.   45
THESEUS.   What say you, Hermia? Be advis'd, fair maid.
    To you your father should be as a god—
    One that compos'd your beauties, yea, and one
    To whom you are but as a form in wax
    By him imprinted and within his power   50
    To leave° the figure or disfigure° it.
    Demetrius is a worthy gentleman.
HERMIA.   So is Lysander.
THESEUS.   In himself he is;
    But in this kind,° wanting° your father's voice,°
    The other must be held the worthier.   55
HERMIA.   I would my father look'd but with my eyes.
THESEUS.   Rather your eyes must with his judgment look.
HERMIA.   I do entreat your Grace to pardon me.
    I know not by what power I am made bold,
    Nor how it may concern° my modesty,   60
    In such a presence here to plead my thoughts;
    But I beseech your Grace that I may know

31 *feigning:* (1) counterfeiting, (2) faining, desirous.   32 *And . . . fantasy:* and made her fall in love with you (imprinting your image on her imagination) by stealthy and dishonest means. 33 *gauds:* playthings.   *conceits:* fanciful trifles.   34 *Knacks:* knickknacks.   45 *Immediately:* expressly.   51 *leave:* leave unaltered.   *disfigure:* obliterate.   54 *kind:* respect.   *wanting:* lacking.   *voice:* approval.   60 *concern:* befit.

The worst that may befall me in this case,
If I refuse to wed Demetrius.

THESEUS. Either to die the death, or to abjure   65
Forever the society of men.
Therefore, fair Hermia, question your desires,
Know of your youth, examine well your blood,°
Whether, if you yield not to your father's choice,
You can endure the livery° of a nun,   70
For aye° to be in shady cloister mew'd,°
To live a barren sister all your life,
Chanting faint hymns to the cold fruitless moon.
Thrice blessed they that master so their blood
To undergo such maiden pilgrimage,   75
But earthlier happy° is the rose distill'd,
Than that which withering on the virgin thorn
Grows, lives, and dies in single blessedness.

HERMIA. So will I grow, so live, so die, my lord,
Ere I will yield my virgin patent° up   80
Unto his lordship, whose unwished yoke
My soul consents not to give sovereignty.

THESEUS. Take time to pause; and, by the next new moon—
The sealing-day betwixt my love and me
For everlasting bond of fellowship—   85
Upon that day either prepare to die
For disobedience to your father's will,
Or° else to wed Demetrius, as he would,
Or on Diana's altar° to protest°
For aye austerity and single life.   90

DEMETRIUS. Relent, sweet Hermia, and, Lysander, yield
Thy crazed° title to my certain right.

LYSANDER. You have her father's love, Demetrius;
Let me have Hermia's. Do you marry him.

EGEUS. Scornful Lysander! True, he hath my love,   95
And this is mine my love shall render him.
And she is mine, and all my right of her
I do estate unto° Demetrius.

LYSANDER. I am, my lord, as well deriv'd° as he,
As well possess'd;° my love is more than his;   100
My fortunes every way as fairly° rank'd,
If not with vantage,° as Demetrius';
And, which is more than all these boasts can be,
I am belov'd of beauteous Hermia.
Why should not I then prosecute my right?   105

---

68 *blood:* passions.   70 *livery:* habit.   71 *aye:* ever.   *mew'd:* shut in (said of a hawk, poultry, etc.).   76 *earthlier happy:* happier as respects this world.   80 *patent:* privilege.   88 *Or:*
either.   89 *Diana's altar:* Diana was a virgin goddess.   *protest:* vow.   92 *crazed:* cracked,
unsound.   98 *estate unto:* settle or bestow upon.   99 *deriv'd:* descended, i.e., "as well born."
100 *possess'd:* endowed with wealth.   101 *fairly:* handsomely.   102 *vantage:* superiority.

Demetrius, I'll avouch it to his head,°
Made love to Nedar's daughter, Helena,
And won her soul; and she, sweet lady, dotes,
Devoutly dotes, dotes in idolatry,
Upon this spotted° and inconstant man.   110
THESEUS.   I must confess that I have heard so much,
And with Demetrius thought to have spoke thereof;
But, being over-full of self-affairs,
My mind did lose it. But, Demetrius, come,
And come, Egeus, you shall go with me;   115
I have some private schooling for you both.
For you, fair Hermia, look you arm° yourself
To fit your fancies° to your father's will;
Or else the law of Athens yields you up—
Which by no means we may extenuate°—   120
To death, or to a vow of single life.
Come, my Hippolyta. What cheer, my love?
Demetrius and Egeus, go° along.
I must employ you in some business
Against° our nuptial, and confer with you   125
Of something nearly that° concerns yourselves.
EGEUS.   With duty and desire we follow you.

(Exeunt° [all but Lysander and Hermia].)

LYSANDER.   How now, my love, why is your cheek so pale?
How chance the roses there do fade so fast?
HERMIA.   Belike° for want of rain, which I could well   130
Beteem° them from the tempest of my eyes.
LYSANDER.   Ay me! for aught that I could ever read,
Could ever hear by tale or history,
The course of true love never did run smooth;
But either it was different in blood°—   135
HERMIA.   O cross,° too high to be enthrall'd to low!
LYSANDER.   Or else misgraffed° in respect of years—
HERMIA.   O spite, too old to be engag'd to young!
LYSANDER.   Or else it stood upon the choice of friends°—
HERMIA.   O hell, to choose love by another's eyes!   140
LYSANDER.   Or, if there were a sympathy in choice,
War, death, or sickness did lay siege to it,
Making it momentany° as a sound,
Swift as a shadow, short as any dream,
Brief as the lightning in the collied° night,   145
That, in a spleen,° unfolds° both heaven and earth,

106 *head:* face.   110 *spotted:* morally stained.   117 *look you arm:* take care you prepare. 118 *fancies:* likings, thoughts of love.   120 *extenuate:* mitigate.   123 *go:* come.   125 *Against:* in preparation for.   126 *nearly that:* that closely.   127 [S.D.] *Exeunt:* Latin for "they go out." 130 *Belike:* very likely.   131 *Beteem:* grant, afford.   135 *blood:* hereditary station.   136 *cross:* vexation.   137 *misgraffed:* ill grafted, badly matched.   139 *friends:* relatives.   143 *momentany:* lasting but a moment.   145 *collied:* blackened (as with coal dust), darkened.   146 *in a spleen:* in a swift impulse in a violent flash.   *unfolds:* discloses.

And ere a man hath power to say "Behold!"
The jaws of darkness do devour it up.
So quick° bright things come to confusion.°
HERMIA.   If then true lovers have been ever cross'd,°   150
It stands as an edict in destiny.
Then let us teach our trial patience,°
Because it is a customary cross,
As due to love as thoughts and dreams and sighs,
Wishes and tears, poor fancy's° followers.   155
LYSANDER.   A good persuasion. Therefore, hear me, Hermia.
I have a widow aunt, a dowager
Of great revenue, and she hath no child.
From Athens is her house remote seven leagues;
And she respects° me as her only son,   160
There, gentle Hermia, may I marry thee,
And to that place the sharp Athenian law
Cannot pursue us. If thou lovest me, then,
Steal forth thy father's house tomorrow night;
And in the wood, a league without the town,   165
Where I did meet thee once with Helena
To do observance to a morn of May,°
There will I stay for thee.
HERMIA.   My good Lysander!
I swear to thee, by Cupid's strongest bow,
By his best arrow with the golden head,°   170
By the simplicity° of Venus' doves,°
By that which knitteth souls and prospers loves,
And by that fire which burn'd the Carthage queen,
When the false Troyan° under sail was seen,
By all the vows that ever men have broke,   175
In number more than ever women spoke,
In that same place thou hast appointed me
Tomorrow truly will I meet with thee.
LYSANDER.   Keep promise, love. Look, here comes Helena.

(Enter Helena.)

HERMIA.   God speed fair° Helena, whither away?   180
HELENA.   Call you me fair? That fair again unsay.
Demetrius loves your fair.° O happy fair!°
Your eyes are lodestars,° your tongue's sweet air°

---

149 *quick:* quickly; or, perhaps, living, alive.   *confusion:* ruin.   150 *ever cross'd:* always
thwarted.   152 *teach . . . patience:* teach ourselves patience in this trial.   155 *fancy's:* amorous
passion's.   160 *respects:* regards.   167 *do . . . May:* peform the ceremonies of May Day.
170 *best arrow . . . golden head:* Cupid's best gold-pointed arrows were supposed to induce love, his
blunt leaden arrows aversion.   171 *simplicity:* innocence.   *doves:* those that drew Venus's chariot.   173–74 *by that fire . . . false Troyan:* Dido, queen of Carthage, immolated herself on a funeral pyre after having been deserted by the Trojan hero Aeneas.   180 *fair:* fair-complexioned
(generally regarded by the Elizabethans as more beautiful than dark-complexioned).   182 *your
fair:* your beauty (even though Hermia is dark-complexioned).   *happy fair:* lucky fair one.
183 *lodestars:* guiding stars.   *air:* music.

More tuneable° than lark to shepherd's ear
When wheat is green, when hawthorn buds appear.   185
Sickness is catching. O, were favor° so,
Yours would I catch, fair Hermia, ere I go;
My ear should catch your voice, my eye your eye,
My tongue should catch your tongue's sweet melody.
Were the world mine, Demetrius being bated,°   190
The rest I'd give to be to you translated.°
O, teach me how you look, and with what art
You sway the motion° of Demetrius heart.

HERMIA.   I frown upon him, yet he loves me still.
HELENA.   O that your frowns would teach my smiles such skill!   195
HERMIA.   I give him curses, yet he gives me love.
HELENA.   O that my prayers could such affection° move!°
HERMIA.   The more I hate, the more he follows me.
HELENA.   The more I love, the more he hateth me.
HERMIA.   His folly, Helena, is no fault of mine.   200
HELENA.   None, but your beauty. Would that fault were mine!
HERMIA.   Take comfort. He no more shall see my face.
Lysander and myself will fly this place.
Before the time I did Lysander see,
Seem'd Athens as a paradise to me.   205
O, then, what graces in my love do dwell,
That he hath turn'd a heaven unto a hell!

LYSANDER.   Helen, to you our minds we will unfold.
Tomorrow night, when Phoebe° doth behold   •
Her silver visage in the wat'ry glass,°   210
Decking with liquid pearl the bladed grass,
A time that lovers' flights doth still° conceal,
Through Athens' gates have we devis'd to steal.

HERMIA.   And in the wood, where often you and I
Upon faint° primrose beds were wont to lie,   215
Emptying our bosoms of their counsel° sweet,
There my Lysander and myself shall meet;
And thence from Athens turn away our eyes,
To seek new friends and stranger companies.
Farewell, sweet playfellow. Pray thou for us,   220
And good luck grant thee thy Demetrius!
Keep word, Lysander. We must starve our sight
From lovers' food till morrow deep midnight.

LYSANDER.   I will, my Hermia.

(Exit Hermia.)

Helena, adieu.
As you on him, Demetrius dote on you!   225

---

184 *tuneable:* tuneful, melodious.   186 *favor:* appearance, looks.   190 *bated:* excepted. 191 *translated:* transformed.   193 *motion:* impulse.   197 *affection:* passion.   *move:* arouse.
209 *Phoebe:* Diana, the moon.   210 *glass:* mirror.   212 *still:* always.   215 *faint:* pale.
216 *counsel:* secret thought.

(Exit Lysander.)

HELENA.   How happy some o'er other some can be!°
 Through Athens I am thought as fair as she.
 But what of that? Demetrius thinks not so;
 He will not know what all but he do know.
 And as he errs, doting on Hermia's eyes,   230
 So I, admiring of° his qualities.
 Things base and vile, holding no quantity,°
 Love can transpose to form and dignity.
 Love looks not with the eyes, but with the mind,
 And therefore is wing'd Cupid painted blind.   235
 Nor hath Love's mind of any judgment taste;°
 Wings, and no eyes, figure° unheedy haste.
 And therefore is Love said to be a child,
 Because in choice he is so oft beguil'd.
 As waggish boys in game° themselves forswear,   240
 So the boy Love is perjur'd everywhere.
 For ere Demetrius look'd on Hermia's eyne,°
 He hail'd down oaths that he was only mine;
 And when this hail some heat from Hermia felt,
 So he dissolv'd, and show'rs of oaths did melt.   245
 I will go tell him of fair Hermia's flight.
 then to the wood will he tomorrow night
 Pursue her; and for this intelligence°
 If I have thanks, it is a dear° expense.°
 But herein mean I to enrich my pain,   250
 To have his sight thither and back again.

(Exit.)

Scene II°

(Enter Quince the Carpenter, and Snug the Joiner, and Bottom the Weaver, and Flute the Bellows-Mender, and Snout the Tinker, and Starveling the Tailor.)

QUINCE.   Is all our company here?
BOTTOM.   You were best to call them generally,° man by man, according to the scrip.°
QUINCE.   Here is the scroll of every man's name which is thought fit, through all
   Athens, to play in our interlude before the Duke and the Duchess on his
   wedding-day at night.   5
BOTTOM.   First, good Peter Quince, say what the play treats on, then read the names
   of the actors, and so grow to° a point.
QUINCE.   Marry,° our play is "The most lamentable comedy and most cruel death of
   Pyramus and Thisby."

226 *o'er . . . can be:* can be in comparison to some others.   231 *admiring of:* wondering at. 232 *holding no quantity:* unsubstantial, unshapely.   236   *Nor . . . taste:* Nor has love, which dwells in the fancy or imagination, any *taste* or least bit of judgment or reason.   237 *figure:* are a symbol of.   240 *game:* sport, jest.   242 *dear:* costly.   *a dear expense:* a trouble worth taking.   I. II *Location:* Athens. Quince's house(?).   2 *generally:* Bottom's blunder for *individually. scrip:* script, written list.   7 *grow to:* come to.   8 *Marry:* a mild oath, originally the name of the Virgin Mary.

BOTTOM.   A very good piece of work, I assure you, and a merry. Now, good Peter   10
Quince, call forth your actors by the scroll. Masters, spread yourselves.
QUINCE.   Answer as I call you. Nick Bottom, the weaver.
BOTTOM.   Ready. Name what part I am for, and proceed.
QUINCE.   You, Nick Bottom, are set down for Pyramus.
BOTTOM.   What is Pyramus? A lover, or a tyrant?   15
QUINCE.   A lover, that kills himself most gallant for love.
BOTTOM.   That will ask some tears in the true performing of it. If I do it, the
audience look to their eyes. I will move storms; I will condole° in some
measure. To the rest—yet my chief humor° is for a tyrant. I could play
Ercles° rarely, or a part to tear a cat° in, to make all split.°   20
"The raging rocks
And shivering shocks
Shall break the locks
Of prison gates;
And Phibbus' car°   25
Shall shine from far
And make and mar
The foolish Fates."
This was lofty! Now name the rest of the players. This is Ercles' vein, a tyrant's
vein. A lover is more condoling.   30
QUINCE.   Francis Flute, the bellows-mender.
FLUTE.   Here, Peter Quince.
QUINCE.   Flute, you must take Thisby on you.
FLUTE.   What is Thisby? A wand'ring knight?
QUINCE.   It is the lady that Pyramus must love.   35
FLUTE.   Nay, faith, let not me play a woman. I have a beard coming.
QUINCE.   That's all one.° You shall play it in a mask, and you may speak as small° as
you will.
BOTTOM.   An° I may hide my face, let me play Thisby too. I'll speak in a monstrous
little voice, "Thisne, Thisne!" Ah Pyramus, my lover dear! Thy Thisby dear,   40
and lady dear!"
QUINCE.   No, no; you must play Pyramus; and, Flute, you Thisby.
BOTTOM.   Well, proceed.
QUINCE.   Robin Starveling, the tailor.
STARVELING.   Here, Peter Quince.   45
QUINCE.   Robin Starveling, you must play Thisby's mother. Tom Snout, the tinker.
SNOUT.   Here, Peter Quince.
QUINCE.   You, Pyramus' father; myself, Thisby's father; Snug, the joiner, you, the
lion's part; and I hope here is a play fitted.
SNUG.   Have you the lion's part written? Pray you, if it be, give it me, for I am slow   50
of study.
QUINCE.   You may do it extempore, for it is nothing but roaring.
BOTTOM.   Let me play the lion too. I will roar that I will do any man's heart good to
hear me. I will roar that I will make the Duke say, "Let him roar again, let
him roar again."   55

18 *condole:* lament, arouse pity.   19 *humor:* inclination, whim.   20 *Ercles:* Hercules (the tradition of ranting came from Seneca's *Hercules Furens*).   *tear a cat:* rant.   *make all split:* cause a stir, bring the house down.   25 *Phibbus' car:* Phoebus's, the sun-god's, chariot.   37 *That's all one:* It makes no difference.   *small:* high-pitched.   39 *An:* if.

QUINCE.   An you should do it too terribly, you would fright the Duchess and the
　　　ladies, that they would shriek; and that were enough to hang us all.
ALL.   That would hang us, every mother's son.
BOTTOM.   I grant you, friends, if you should fright the ladies out of their wits, they
　　　would have no more discretion but to hang us; but I will aggravate° my   60
　　　voice so that I will roar you° as gently as any sucking dove; I will roar you
　　　an 'twere any nightingale.
QUINCE.   You can play no part but Pyramus; for Pyramus is a sweet-fac'd man, a
　　　proper° man as one shall see in a summer's day, a most lovely gentleman-
　　　like man. Therefore you must needs play Pyramus.   65
BOTTOM.   Well, I will undertake it. What beard were I best to play it in?
QUINCE.   Why, what you will.
BOTTOM.   I will discharge° it in either your° straw-colored beard, your orange-tawny
　　　beard, your purple-in-grain° beard, or your French-crown-color° beard,
　　　your perfect yellow.   70
QUINCE.   Some of your French crowns° have no hair at all, and then you will play
　　　barefac'd. But, masters, here are your parts. *[He distributes parts.]* And I am
　　　to entreat you, request you, and desire you, to con° them by tomorrow
　　　night; and meet me in the palace wood, a mile without the town, by
　　　moonlight. There will we rehearse; for if we meet in the city, we shall be   75
　　　dogg'd with company, and our devices° known. In the meantime I will
　　　draw a bill° of properties, such as our play wants. I pray you, fail me not.
BOTTOM.   We will meet, and there we may rehearse most obscenely° and
　　　courageously. Take pains, be perfect;° adieu.
QUINCE.   At the Duke's oak we meet.   80
BOTTOM.   Enough. Hold, or cut bow-strings.°

(Exeunt.)

60 *aggravate:* Bottom's blunder for *diminish.*   61 *roar you:* roar for you.   64 *proper:* handsome.   68 *discharge:* perform.   *your:* i.e., you know the kind I mean.   69 *purple-in-grain:* dyed
a very deep red (from *grain,* the name applied to the dried insect used to make the dye).
69 *French-crown-color:* color of a French crown, a gold coin.   71 *crowns:* heads bald from syphilis,
the "French disease."   73 *con:* learn by heart.   76 *devices:* plans.   77 *bill:* list.   78 *ob-
scenely:* an unintentionally funny blunder, whatever Bottom meant to say.   79 *perfect:* letter-
perfect in memorizing your parts.   81 *Hold . . . bowstrings:* an archer's expression not definitely
explained, but probably meaning here "keep your promises, or give up the play."

ACT II

Scene I°

(Enter a Fairy at one door, and Robin Goodfellow [Puck] at another.)

PUCK.   How now, spirit, Whither wander you?
FAIRY.   Over hill, over dale,
　　　Thorough° bush, thorough brier,
　　　Over park, over pale,°
　　　Thorough flood, thorough fire,
　　　I do wander every where,   5

II. I. *Location:* a wood near Athens.   3 *Thorough:* through.   4 *pale:* enclosure.

Swifter than the moon's sphere;
And I serve the Fairy Queen,
To dew her orbs° upon the green.
The cowslips tall her pensioners° be.   10
In their gold coats spots you see;
Those be rubies, fairy favors,°
In those freckles live their savors.°
I must go seek some dewdrops here
And hang a pearl in every cowslip's ear.   15
Farewell, thou lob° of spirits; I'll be gone.
Our Queen and all her elves come here anon.°
PUCK.   The King doth keep his revels here tonight.
Take heed the Queen come not within his sight.
For Oberon is passing fell° and wrath,°   20
Because that she was her attendant hath
A lovely boy, stolen from an Indian king;
She never had so sweet a changeling.°
And jealous Oberon would have the child
Knight of his train, to trace° the forests wild.   25
But she perforce° withholds the loved boy,
Crowns him with flowers and makes him all her joy.
And now they never meet in grove or green,
By fountain° clear, or spangled starlight sheen,
But they do square,° that all their elves for fear   30
Creep into acorn-cups and hide them there.
FAIRY.   Either I mistake your shape and making quite,
Or else you are that shrewd° and knavish sprite°
Call'd Robin Goodfellow. Are not you he
That frights the maidens of the villagery,   35
Skim milk, and sometimes labor in the quern,°
And bootless° make the breathless huswife churn,
And sometime make the drink to bear no harm°
Mislead night-wanderers, laughing at their harm?
Those that Hobgoblin call you and sweet Puck,   40
You do their work, and they shall have good luck.
Are you not he?
PUCK.   Thou speakest aright;
I am that merry wanderer of the night.
I jest to Oberon and make him smile
When I a fat and bean-fed horse beguile,   45
Neighing in likeness of a filly foal;
And sometime lurk I in a gossip's° bowl,
In very likeness of a roasted crab,°
And when she drinks, against her lips I bob

9 *orbs:* circles, i.e., fairy rings.   10 *pensioners:* retainers, members of the royal bodyguard.
12 *favors:* love tokens.   13 *savors:* sweet smells.   16 *lob:* country bumpkin.   17 *anon:* at
once.   20 *passing fell:* exceedingly angry.   *wrath:* wrathful.   23 *changeling:* child exchanged
for another by the fairies.   25 *trace:* range through.   26 *perforce:* forcibly.   29 *fountain:* spring.
30 *square:* quarrel.   33 *shrewd:* mischievous.   *sprite:* spirit.   36 *quern:* handmill.   37 *bootless:* in vain.   38 *barm:* yeast, head on the ale.   47 *gossip's:* old woman's.   48 *crab:* crabapple.

And on her withered dewlap° pour the ale.   50
The wisest aunt,° telling the saddest° tale,
Sometime for three-foot stool mistaketh me;
Then slip I from her bum, down topples she,
And "tailor"° cries, and falls into a cough;
And then the whole quire° hold their hips and laugh,   55
And waxen° in their mirth and neeze° and swear°
A merrier hour was never wasted there.
But, room, fairy! Here comes Oberon.
FAIRY.   And here my mistress. Would that he were gone!

(Enter [Oberon] the King of Fairies at one door, with his train; and [Titania] the Queen at another, with hers.)

OBERON.   Ill met by moonlight, proud Titania.
TITANIA.   What, jealous Oberon? Fairies, skip hence.
I have forsworn his bed and company.
OBERON.   Tarry, rush wanton.° Am not I thy lord?°
TITANIA.   Then I must be thy lady; but I know
When thou hast stolen away from fairy land,   65
And in the shape of Corin° sat all day,
Playing on pipes of corn° and versing love
To amorous Phillida.° Why art thou here,
Come from the farthest steep° of India,
But that, forsooth, the bouncing Amazon,   70
Your buskin'd° mistress and your warrior love,°
To Theseus must be wedded, and you come
To give their bed joy and prosperity.
OBERON.   How canst thou thus for shame, Titania,
Glance at my credit with Hippolyta,°   75
Knowing I know thy love to Theseus?
Didst not thou lead him through the glimmering night
From Perigenia,° whom he ravished?
And make him with fair Aegles° break his faith,
With Ariadne° and Antiopa?°   80
TITANIA.   These are the forgeries of jealousy;
And never, since the middle summer's spring,°
Met we on hill, in dale, forest, or mead,

---

50 *dewlap:* loose skin on neck.   51 *aunt:* old woman.   *saddest:* most serious.   54 *tailor:* possibly because she ends up sitting cross-legged on the floor, looking like a tailor. 55 *quire:* company.   56 *waxen:* increase.   *neeze:* sneeze.   63 *wanton:* headstrong creature.   66, 68 *Corin, Phillida:* conventional names of pastoral lovers.   67 *corn:* here, oat stalks.   69 *steep:* mountain range.   71 *buskin'd:* wearing half-boots called buskins. 75 *Glance . . . Hippolyta:* make insinuations about my favored relationship with Hippolyta. 78 *Perigenia:* Perigouna, one of Theseus's conquests. (This and the following women are named in Thomas North's translation of Plutarch's *Life of Theseus*.)   79 *Aegles:* Aegle, for whom Theseus deserted Ariadne according to some accounts.   80 *Ariadne:* the daughter of Minos, King of Crete, who helped Theseus escape the labyrinth after killing the Minotaur; later she was abandoned by Theseus.   *Antiopa:* queen of the Amazons and wife of Theseus; elsewhere identified with Hippolyta, but here thought of as a separate woman.   82 *middle summer's spring:* beginning of midsummer.

By paved° fountain or by rushy° brook,
Or in° the beached margent° of the sea,   85
To dance our ringlets° to the whistling wind,
But with thy brawls thou hast disturb'd our sport.
Therefore the winds, piping to us in vain,
As in revenge, have suck'd up from the sea
Contagious° fogs; which falling in the land   90
Hath every pelting° river made so proud
That they have overborne their continents.°
The ox hath therefore stretch'd his yoke in vain,
The ploughman lost his sweat, and the green corn°
Hath rotted ere his youth attain'd a beard;   95
The fold° stands empty in the drowned field,
And crows are fatted with the murrion° flock;
The nine men's morris° is fill'd up with mud,
And the quaint mazes° in the wanton° green
For lack of tread are undistinguishable.   100
The human mortals want° their winter° here;
No night is now with hymn or carol bless'd.
Therefore° the moon, the governess of floods,
Pale in her anger, washes all the air,
That rehumatic diseases° do abound.   105
And thorough this distemperature° we see
The seasons alter: hoary-headed frosts
Fall in the fresh lap of the crimson rose,
And on old Hiems'° thin and icy crown
An odorous chaplet of sweet summer buds   110
Is, as in mockery, set. The spring, the summer,
The childing° autumn, angry winter, change
Their wonted liveries,° and the mazed° world,
By their increase,° now knows not which is which.
And this same progeny of evils comes   115
From our debate,° from our dissension;
We are their parents and original.°
OBERON.   Do you amend it then; it lies in you.
Why should Titania cross her Oberon?
I do but beg a little changeling boy,   120
To be my henchman.°

84 *paved:* with pebbled bottom.   *rushy:* bordered with rushes.   85 *in:* on.   *margent:* edge,
border.   86 *ringlets:* dances in a ring (see *orbs* in line 9).   90 *Contagious:* noxious.   91 *pelt-
ing:* paltry; or striking, moving forcefully.   92 *continents:* banks that contain them.   94 *corn:*
grain of any kind.   96 *fold:* pen for sheep or cattle.   97 *murrion:* having died of the murrain,
plague.   98 *nine men's morris:* portion of the village green marked out in a square for a game
played with nine pebbles or pegs.   99 *quaint mazes:* intricate paths marked out on the village
green to be followed rapidly on foot as a kind of contest.   *wanton:* luxuriant.
101 *want:* lack.   *winter:* regular winter season; or proper observances of winter, such as the *hymn
or carol* in the next line (?).   103 *Therefore:* i.e., as a result of our quarrel.   105 *rheumatic diseases:* colds, flu, and other respiratory infections.   106 *distemperature:* disturbance in nature.
109 *Hiems:* the winter god.   112 *childing:* fruitful, pregnant.   113 *wonted liveries:* usual apparel.   *mazed:* bewildered.   114 *their increase:* their yield, what they produce.   116 *debate:* quarrel.   117 *original:* origin.   121 *henchman:* attendant, page.

TITANIA.   Set your heart at rest.
   The fairy land buys not the child of me.
   His mother was a vot'ress° of my order,
   And, in the spiced Indian air, by night,
   Full often hath she gossip'd by my side,   125
   And sat with me on Neptune's yellow sands,
   Marking th' embarked traders° on the flood,°
   When we have laugh'd to see the sails conceive
   And grow big-bellied with the wanton° wind;
   Which she, with pretty and with swimming gait,   130
   Following—her womb then rich with my young squire—
   Would imitate, and sail upon the land
   To fetch me trifles, and return again,
   As from a voyage, rich with merchandise.
   But she, being mortal, of that boy did die;   135
   And for her sake do I rear up her boy,
   And for her sake I will not part with him.
OBERON.   How long within this wood intend you stay?
TITANIA.   Perchance till after Theseus' wedding-day.
   If you will patiently dance in our round°   140
   And see our moonlight revels, go with us;
   If not, shun me, and I will spare° your haunts.
OBERON.   Give me that boy, and I will go with thee.
TITANIA.   Not for thy fairy kingdom. Fairies, away!
   We shall chide downright, if I longer stay.   145

(Exeunt [Titania with her train].)

OBERON.   Well, go thy way. Thou shalt not from° this grove
   Till I torment thee for this injury.
   My gentle Puck, come hither. Thou rememb'rest
   Since° once I sat upon a promontory,
   And heard a mermaid on a dolphin's back   150
   Uttering such dulcet and harmonious breath°
   That the rude sea grew civil at her song
   And certain stars shot madly from their spheres,
   To hear the sea-maid's music.
PUCK.   I remember.
OBERON.   That very time I saw, but thou consider not,   155
   Flying between the cold moon and the earth,
   Cupid all° arm'd. A certain aim he took
   At a fair vestal° throned by the west,
   And loos'd his love-shaft smartly from his bow,
   As° it should pierce a hundred thousand hearts;   160
   But I might° see young Cupid's fiery shaft

---

123 *vot'ress:* female votary; devotee; worshiper.   127 *traders:* trading vessels.   *flood:* flood
tide.   129 *wanton:* sportive.   140 *round:* circular dance.   142 *spare:* shun.   146 *from:* go
from.   149 *Since:* when.   151 *breath:* voice, song.   157 *all:* fully.   158 *vestal:* vestal virgin (contains a complimentary allusion to Queen Elizabeth as a votaress of Diana and probably
refers to an actual entertainment in her honor at Elvetham in 1591).   160 *As:* as
if.   161 *might:* could.

Quench'd in the chaste beams of the wat'ry moon,
And the imperial vot'ress passed on,
In maiden meditation, fancy-free.°
Yet mark'd I where the bolt of Cupid fell: 165
It fell upon a little western flower,
Before milk-white, now purple with love's wound,
And maidens call it love-in-idleness.°
Fetch me that flow'r; the herb I showed thee once.
The juice of it on sleeping eyelids laid   170
Will make or man or° woman madly dote
Upon the next live creature that it sees.
Fetch me this herb, and be thou here again
Ere the leviathan° can swim a league.
PUCK. I'll put a girdle round about the earth   175
In forty° minutes.

(Exit.)

OBERON. Having once this juice,
I'll watch Titania when she is asleep,
And drop the liquor of it in her eyes.
The next thing then she waking looks upon,
Be it on lion, bear, or wolf, or bull,   180
On meddling monkey, or on busy ape,
She shall pursue it with the soul of love.
And ere I take this charm from off her sight,
As I can take it with another herb,
I'll make her render up her page to me.   185
But who comes here? I am invisible,
And I will overhear their conference.

(Enter Demetrius, Helena following him.)

DEMETRIUS. I love thee not, therefore pursue me not.
Where is Lysander and fair Hermia?
The one I'll slay, the other slayeth me.   190
Thou told'st me they were stol'n unto this wood;
And here am I, and wode° within this wood,
Because I cannot meet my Hermia.
Hence, get thee gone, and follow me no more.
HELENA. You draw me, you hard-hearted adamant;°   195
But yet you draw not iron, for my heart
Is true as steel. Leave° you your power to draw,
And I shall have no power to follow you.
DEMETRIUS. Do I entice you? Do I speak you fair?°
Or, rather, do I not in plainest truth   200

164 *fancy-free:* free of love's spell.   168 *love-in-idleness:* pansy, heartsease.   171 *or . . . or:* either . . .
or.   174 *leviathan:* sea monster, whale.   176 *forty:* used indefinitely.   192 *wode:* mad (pronounced "wood" and often spelled so).   195 *adamant:* lodestone, magnet (with pun on *hard-hearted,* since adamant was also thought to be the hardest of all stones and was confused with the diamond).   197 *leave:* give up.   199 *fair:* courteously.

Tell you I do not nor I cannot love you?
HELENA.   And even for that do I love you the more.
    I am your spaniel; and, Demetrius,
    The more you beat me, I will fawn on you.
    Use me but as your spaniel, spurn me, strike me,   205
    Neglect me, lose me; only give me leave,
    Unworthy as I am, to follow you.
    What worser place can I beg in your love—
    And yet a place of high respect with me—
    Than to be used as you use your dog?   210
DEMETRIUS.   Tempt not too much the hatred of my spirit.
    For I am sick when I do look on thee.
HELENA.   And I am sick when I look not on you.
DEMETRIUS.   You do impeach° your modesty too much
    To leave the city and commit yourself   215
    Into the hands of one that loves you not,
    To trust the opportunity of night
    And the ill counsel of a desert° place
    With the rich worthy of your virginity.
HELENA.   Your virtue° is my privilege.° For that°   220
    It is not night when I do see your face,
    Therefore I think I am not in the night;
    Nor doth this wood lack worlds of company,
    For you in my respect° are all the world.
    Then how can it be said I am alone,   225
    When all the world is here to look on me?
DEMETRIUS.   I'll run from thee and hide me in the brakes,°
    And leave thee to the mercy of wild beasts.
HELENA.   The wildest hath not such a heart as you.
    Run when you will, the story shall be chang'd: 230
    Apollo flies and Daphne holds the chase,°
    The dove pursues the griffin,° the mild hind°
    Makes speed to catch the tiger—bootless° speed,
    When cowardice pursues and valor flies.
DEMETRIUS.   I will not stay° thy questions.° Let me go!   235
    Or if thou follow me, do not believe
    But I shall do thee mischief in the wood.
HELENA.   Ay, in the temple, in the town, the field,
    You do me mischief. Fie, Demetrius!
    Your wrongs do set a scandal on my sex.   240
    We cannot fight for love, as men may do;
    We should be woo'd and were not made to woo.

---

214 *impeach:* call into question.   218 *desert:* deserted.   220 *virtue:* goodness or power to attract.   *privilege:* safeguard, warrant.   *For that:* because.   224 *in my respect:* as far as I am concerned.   227 *brakes:* thickets.   231 *Apollo . . . chase:* In the ancient myth, Daphne fled from Apollo and was saved from rape by being transformed into a laurel tree; here it is the female who *holds the chase,* or pursues, instead of the male.   232 *griffin:* a fabulous monster with the head of an eagle and the body of a lion.   *hind:* female deer.   233 *bootless:* fruitless.   235 *stay:* wait for.   *questions:* talk or argument.

(Exit Demetrius.]

    I'll follow thee and make a heaven of hell,
    To die upon° the hand I love so well.

(Exit.)

OBERON.   Fare thee well, nymph. Ere he do leave this grove,   245
    Thou shalt fly him and he shall seek thy love.

(Enter Puck.)

    Hast thou the flower there? Welcome, wanderer.
PUCK.   Ay, there it is.   *[Offers the flower.]*
OBERON.   I pray thee, give it me.
    I know a bank where the wild thyme blows,°
    Where oxlips° and the nodding violet grows,   250
    Quite over-canopied with luscious woodbine,°
    With sweet musk-roses° and with eglantine.°
    There sleeps Titania sometime of the night
    Lull'd in these flowers with dances and delight;
    And there the snake throws° her enamel'd skin,   255
    Weed° wide enough to wrap a fairy in.
    And with the juice of this I'll streak° her eyes,
    And make her full of hateful fantasies.
    Take thou some of it, and seek through this
        grove.   *[Gives some love-juice.]*
    A sweet Athenian lady is in love   260
    With a disdainful youth. Anoint his eyes,
    But do it when the next thing he espies
    May be the lady. Thou shalt know the man
    By the Athenian garments he hath on.
    Effect it with some care, that he may prove   265
    More fond on° her than she upon her love;
    And look thou meet me ere the first cock crow.
PUCK.   Fear not, my lord, your servant shall do so.

(Exeunt.)

Scene II°

(Enter Titania, Queen of Fairies, with her train.)

TITANIA.   Come, now a roundel° and a fairy song;
    Then, for the third part of a minute, hence—
    Some to kill cankers° in the musk-rose buds,
    Some war with rere-mice° for their leathern wings,

---

244 *upon:* by.   249 *blows:* blooms.   250 *oxlips:* flowers resembling cowslip and primrose.
251 *woodbine:* honeysuckle.   252 *musk-roses:* a kind of large, sweet-scented rose.   *eglantine:*
sweetbriar, another kind of rose.   255 *throws:* sloughs off, shed.   256 *Weed:* garment.   257 *streak:* anoint, touch gently.   266 *fond on:* doting on.   II, I. *Location:* the
wood.   1 *roundel:* dance in a ring.   3 *cankers:* cankerworms.   4 *rere-mice:* bats.

To make my small elves coats, and some keep back   5
The clamorous owl, that nightly hoots and wonders
At our quaint° spirits. Sing me now asleep.
Then to your offices and let me rest.

(Fairies sing.)

FIRST FAIRY.   You spotted snakes with double° tongue,
    Thorny hedgehogs, be not seen;   10
Newts° and blindworms, do no wrong,
    Come not near our Fairy Queen.
    [Chorus.] Philomel,° with melody
    Sing in our sweet lullaby;
    Lulla, lulla, lullaby, lulla, lulla, lullaby.   15
      Never harm,
      Nor spell nor charm,
    Come our lovely lady nigh.
    So, good night, with lullaby.
FIRST FAIRY.   Weaving spiders, come not here;   20
    Hence, you long-legg'd spinners, hence!
Beetles black, approach not near;
    Worm nor snail, do no offense.
    [Chorus.] Philomel, with melody, etc.
SECOND FAIRY.   Hence, away! Now all is well.   25
    One aloof stand sentinel.

(Exeunt Fairies. Titania sleeps.)

(Enter Oberon [and squeezes the flower on Titania's eyelids].)

OBERON.   What thou seest when thou dost wake,
    Do it for thy true-love take;
    Love and languish for his sake.
    Be it ounce,° or cat, or bear,   30
    Pard,° or boar with bristled hair,
    In thy eye that shall appear
    When thou wak'st, it is thy dear
Wake when some vile thing is near.

(Exit.)

(Enter Lysander and Hermia.)

LYSANDER.   Fair love, you faint with wand'ring in the wood;   35
    And to speak troth,° I have forgot our way.
    We'll rest us, Hermia, if you think it good,
    And tarry for the comfort of the day.
HERMIA.   Be 't so, Lysander. Find you out a bed,
    For I upon this bank will rest my head.   40

---

7 *quaint:* dainty.   9 *double:* forked.   11 *Newts:* water lizards (considered poisonous, as were
blindworms—small snakes with tiny eyes—and spiders).   13 *Philomel:* the nightingale. (Philo-
mela, daughter of King Pandion, was transformed into a nightingale, according to Ovid's *Metamorphoses,* after she had been raped by her sister Procne's husband, Tereus.)   30 *ounce:*
lynx.   31 *Pard:* leopard.   36 *troth:* truth.

LYSANDER.   One turf shall serve as pillow for us both,
    One heart, one bed, two bosoms, and one troth.°
HERMIA.   Nay, good Lysander; for my sake, my dear,
    Lie further off yet, do not lie so near.
LYSANDER.   O, take the sense, sweet, of my innocence!°   45
    Love takes the meaning in love's conference.°
    I mean, that my heart unto yours is knit
    So that but one heart we can make of it;
    Two bosoms interchained with an oath—
    So then two bosoms and a single troth.   50
    Then by your side no bed-room me deny,
    For lying so, Hermia, I do not lie.°
HERMIA.   Lysander riddles very prettily.
    Now much beshrew° my manners and my pride
    If Hermia meant to say Lysander lied.   55
    But, gentle friend, for love and courtesy
    Lie further off, in human° modesty;
    Such separation as may well be said
    Becomes a virtuous bachelor and a maid,
    So far be distant; and, good night, sweet friend.   60
    Thy love ne'er alter till thy sweet life end!
LYSANDER.   Amen, amen, to that fair prayer, say I,
    And then end life when I end loyalty!
    Here is my bed. Sleep give thee all his rest!
HERMIA.   With half that wish the wisher's eyes be press'd!°   65
    [They sleep, separated by a short distance.]

(Enter Puck.)

PUCK.   Through the forest have I gone,
    But Athenian found I none
    On whose eyes I might approve°
    This flower's force in stirring love.
    Night and silence.—Who is here?   70
    Weeds of Athens he doth wear.
    This is he, my master said,
    Despised the Athenian maid;
    And here the maiden, sleeping sound,
    On the dank and dirty ground.   75
    Pretty soul! She durst not lie
    Near this lack-love, this kill-courtesy.
    Churl, upon thy eyes I throw
    All the power this charm doth owe.°
    [Applies the love-juice.]
    When thou wak'st, let love forbid   80

---

42 *troth:* faith, troth-plight.   45 *take . . . innocence:* interpret my intention as innocent.   46 *Love . . . conference:* When lovers confer, love teaches each lover to interpret the other's meaning lovingly.   52 *lie:* tell a falsehood (with a riddling pun on *lie,* recline).   54 *beshrew:* curse (but mildly meant).   57 *human:* courteous.   65 *With . . . press'd:* May we share your wish, so that your eyes too are *press'd,* closed, in sleep.   68 *approve:* test.   79 *owe:* own.

Sleep his seat on they eyelid.
So awake when I am gone,
For I must now to Oberon.

(Exit.)

(Enter Demetrius and Helena, running.)

HELENA.   Stay, though thou kill me, sweet Demetrius.
DEMETRIUS.   I charge thee, hence, and do not haunt me thus.   85
HELENA.   O, wait thou darkling° leave me? Do not so.
DEMETRIUS.   Stay, on they peril!° I alone will go.

(Exit.)

HELENA.   O, I am out of breath in this fond° chase!
    The more my prayer, the lesser is my grace.°
    Happy is Hermia, wheresoe'er she lies,°   90
    For she hath blessed and attractive eyes.
    How came her eyes so bright? Not with salt tears;
    If so, my eyes are oft'ner wash'd thus hers.
    No, no, I am as ugly as a bear;
    For beasts that meet me run away for fear.   95
    Therefore no marvel though Demetrius
    Do, as a monster, fly my presence thus.
    What wicked and dissembling glass of mine
    Made me compare with Hermia's sphery eyne?°
    But who is here? Lysander, on the ground?   100
    Dead, or asleep? I see no blood, no wound.
    Lysander, if you live, good sir, awake.
LYSANDER *[awaking]*.   And run through fire I will for thy sweet sake.
    Transparent° Helena! Nature shows art,
    That through thy bosom makes me see thy heart.   105
    Where is Demetrius? O, how fit a word
    Is that vile name to perish on my sword!
HELENA.   Do not say so, Lysander, say not so.
    What though he love your Hermia? Lord, what though?
    Yet Hermia still loves you. Then be content.   110
LYSANDER.   Content with Hermia? No! I do repent
    The tedious minutes I with her have spent.
    Not Hermia but Helena I love.
    Who will not change a raven for a dove?
    The will of man is by his reason sway'd,   115
    And reason says you are the worthier maid.
    Things growing are not ripe until their season;
    So I, being young, till now ripe not° to reason.
    And touching° now the point° of human skill,°

---

86 *darkling:* in the dark.   87 *on thy peril:* on pain of danger to you if you don't obey me and
stay.   88 *fond:* doting.   89 *my grace:* the favor I obtain.   90 *lies:* dwells.   99 *sphery eyne:* eyes
as bright as stars in their spheres.   104 *transparent:* (1) Radiant; (2) able to be seen through.
118 *ripe not:* (am) not ripened.   119 *touching:* reaching.   *point:* summit.   *skill:* judgment.

Reason becomes the marshal to my will   120
And leads me to your eyes, where I o'erlook°
Love's stories written in love's richest book.

HELENA.   Wherefore was I to this keen mockery born?
When at your hands did I deserve this scorn?
Is 't not enough, is 't not enough, young man,   125
That I did never, no, nor never can,
Deserve a sweet look from Demetrius' eye,
But you must flout my insufficiency?
Good troth,° you do me wrong, good sooth,° you do,
In such disdainful manner me to woo,   130
But fare you well. Perforce I must confess
I thought you lord of° more true gentleness.
O, that a lady, of° one man refus'd,
Should of another therefore be abus'd!°

(Exit.)

LYSANDER.   She sees not Hermia. Hermia, sleep thou there,   135
And never mayst thou come Lysander near!
For as a surfeit of the sweetest things
The deepest loathing to the stomach brings,
Or as the heresies that men do leave
Are hated most of those they did deceive,   140
So thou, my surfeit and my heresy,
Of all be hated, but the most of me!
And, all my powers, address your love and might
To honor Helen and to be her knight!

(Exit.)

HERMIA *[awaking].*   Help me, Lysander, help me! Do thy best 145
To pluck this crawling serpent from my breast!
Ay me, for pity! What a dream was here!
Lysander, look how I do quake with fear.
Methought a serpent eat° my heart away,
And you sat smiling at his cruel prey.°   150
Lysander! What, remov'd? Lysander! Lord!
What, out of hearing? Grone? No sound, no word?
Alack, where are you? Speak, an if you hear,
Speak, of all loves!° I swoon almost with fear.
No? Then I well perceive you are not night.   155
Either death, or you, I'll find immediately.

(Exit. [Manet° Titania lying asleep.])

---

121 *o'erlook:* read.   129 *Good troth, good sooth:* indeed, truly.   132 *lord of:* possessor of.   *gen-*
tleness: courtesy.   133 *of:* by.   134 *abus'd:* ill treated.   149 *eat:* ate (pronounced "et").
150 *prey:* act of preying.   154 *of all loves:* for all love's sake.   156. [S.D.] *Manet:* Latin for "she
remains."

ACT III

Scene I°

(Enter the Clowns [Quince, Snug, Bottom, Flute, Snout, and Starveling].)

BOTTOM. Are we all met?

QUINCE. Pat, pat; and here's a marvailes° convenient
place for our rehearsal. This green plot shall be our
stage, this hawthorn brake° our tiring-house,° and
we will do it in action as we will do it before the   5
Duke.

BOTTOM. Peter Quince?

QUINCE. What sayest thou, bully° Bottom?

BOTTOM. There are things in this comedy of Pyramus
and Thisby that will never please. First, Pyramus   10
must draw a sword to kill himself, which the ladies
cannot abide. How answer you that?

SNOUT. By 'r lakin,° a parlous° feat.

Starveling. I believe we must leave the killing out,
when all is done.°   15

BOTTOM. Not a whit. I have a device to make all well.
Write me° a prologue; and let the prologue seem to
say, we will do no harm with our swords and that
Pyramus is not kill'd indeed; and, for the more better
assurance, tell them that I Pyramus am not Pyramus,   20
but Bottom the weaver. This will put them out of
fear.

QUINCE. Well, we will have such a prologue, and it shall be written in
eight and six.°

BOTTOM. No, make it two more; let it be written in eight   25
and eight.

SNOUT. Will not the ladies be afeard of the lion?

Starveling. I fear it, I promise you.

BOTTOM. Masters, you ought to consider with yourselves,
to bring in—God shield us!—a lion among   30
ladies,° is a most dreadful thing. For there is not a more
fearful° wild-fowl than your lion living; and we ought
to look to 't.

SNOUT. Therefore another prologue must tell he is not
a lion.   35

III. I. *Location:* scene continues.   2 *marvailes:* marvelous.   4 *brake:* thicket.   *tiring-house:* at-
tiring area, hence backstage.   8 *bully:* worthy, jolly, fine fellow.   13 *By 'r lakin:* by our ladykin,
the Virgin Mary.   *parlous:* perilous.   15 *when all is done:* when all is said and done.   17 *write
me:* write at my suggestion.   24 *eight and six:* alternate lines of eight and six syllables, a common
ballad measure.   30–31 *lion among ladies:* A contemporary pamphlet tells how at the christening in 1594 of Prince Henry, eldest son of King James VI of Scotland, later James I of England, a
"blackmoor" instead of a lion drew the triumphal chariot, since the lion's presence might have
"brought some fear to the nearest."   32 *fearful:* fear-inspiring.

BOTTOM.   Nay, you must name his name, and half his
face must be seen through the lion's neck, and he
himself must speak through, saying thus, or to the
same defect:° "Ladies"—or "Fair ladies—I
would wish you"—or "I would request you"—   40
or "I would entreat you—not to fear, not to tremble;
my life for yours.° If you think I come hither as a
lion, it were pity of my life.° No, I am no such thing,
I am a man as other men are." And there indeed
let him name his name, and tell them plainly he is   45
Snug the joiner.
QUINCE.   Well, it shall be so. But there is two hard things:
that is, to bring the moonlight into a chamber;
for, you know, Pyramus and Thisby meet by
moonlight.   50
SNOUT.   Doth the moon shine that night we play our
play?
BOTTOM.   A calendar, a calendar! Look in the almanac.
Find out moonshine, find out moonshine.

(They consult an almanac.)

QUINCE.   Yes, it doth shine that night.   55
BOTTOM.   Why then may you leave a casement of the
great chamber window, where we play, open, and
the moon may shine in at the casement.
QUINCE.   Ay; or else one must come in with a bush of
thorns° and a lantern, and say he comes to   60
disfigure,° or to present,° the person of Moonshine.
Then there is another thing: we must have a wall
in the great chamber; for Pyramus and Thisby, says
the story, did talk through the chink of a wall.
SNOUT.   You can never bring in a wall. What say you,   65
Bottom?
BOTTOM.   Some man or other must present Wall. And
let him have some plaster, or some loam, or some
rought-cast° about him, to signify wall; and let him
hold his fingers thus, and through that cranny shall   70
Pyramus and Thisby whisper.
QUINCE.   If that may be, then all is well. Come, sit down,
every mother's son, and rehearse your parts.
Pyramus, you begin. When you have spoken your
speech, enter into that brake, and so every one   75
according to his cue.

---

39 *defect:* Bottom's blunder for *effect.*   42 *my life for yours:* I pledge my life to make your lives
safe.   43 *it were . . . life:* My life would be endangered.   59–60 *bush of thorns:* bundle of thorn-
bush faggots (part of the accoutrements of the man in the moon, according to the popular notions
of the time, along with his lantern and his dog).   61 *disfigure:* Quince's blunder for *prefig-
ure.   present:* represent.   69 *rough-cast:* a mixture of lime and gravel used to plaster the outside of buildings.

(Enter Robin [Puck].)

PUCK.   What hempen° home-spuns have we
    swagg'ring here,
    So near the cradle of the Fairy Queen?
    What, a play toward?° I'll be an auditor;°
    An actor too perhaps, if I see cause.   80
QUINCE.   Speak, Pyramus. Thisby, stand forth.
BOTTOM.   "Thisby, the flowers of odious savors
    sweet,"—
QUINCE.   Odors, odors.
BOTTOM.   —"Odors savors sweet;
    So hath thy breath, my dearest Thisby dear.   85
    But hark, a voice! Stay thou but here awhile,
    And by and by I will to thee appear."

(Exit.)

PUCK.   A strange Pyramus than e'er played here.°

(Exit.)

FLUTE.   Must I speak now?
QUINCE.   Ay, marry, must you; for you must understand   90
    he goes but to see a noise that he heard, and
    is to come again.
FLUTE.   "Most radiant Pyramus, most lily-white of hue,
    Of color like the red rose on triumphant brier,
    Most brisky juvenal° and eke° most lovely Jew,°   95
    As true as truest horse that yet would never tire.
    I'll meet thee, Pyramus, at Ninny's womb."
QUINCE.   "Ninus'° tomb," man. Why, you must not speak that yet.
    That you answer to Pyramus. You speak all your part
    at once, cues and all. Pyramus enter. Your cue is past;   100
    it is, "never tire."
FLUTE.   O—"As true as truest horse, that yet would never tire."

(Enter Puck, and Bottom as Pyramus with the ass head.)°

BOTTOM.   "If I were fair,° Thisby, I were° only thine."
QUINCE.   O monstrous! O strange! We are haunted. Pray, masters!
    Fly, masters! Help!   105

(Exeunt Quince, Snug, Flute, Snout, and Starveling.)

PUCK.   I'll follow you, I'll lead you about a round,°
    Through bog, through bush, through brake, through brier.

---

77 *hempen:* made of hemp, a rough fiber.   79 *toward:* about to take place.   *auditor:* one who listens, i.e., part of the audience.   88 *here:* In this theater (?).   95 *brisky juvenal:* brisk youth.   *eke:* also.   *Jew:* probably an absurd repetition of the first syllable of *juvenal.* 98 *Ninus:* mythical founder of Nineveh (whose wife, Semiramis, was supposed to have built the walls of Babylon where the story of Pyramus and Thisby takes place).   102 [S.D.] *with the ass head:* This stage direction, taken from the Folio, presumably refers to a standard stage property. 103 *fair:* handsome.   *were:* would be.   106 *about a round:* roundabout.

Sometime a horse I'll be, sometime a hound,
A hog, a headless bear, sometime a fire,°
And neigh, and bark, and grunt, and roar, and burn,
Like horse, hound, hog, beat, fire, at every turn.   110

(Exit.)

BOTTOM.   Why do they run away? This is a knavery of them
   to make me afeard.
   (Enter Snout.)
SNOUT.   O Bottom, thou art chang'd! What do I see on
   thee?   115
BOTTOM.   What do you see? You see an ass-head of your own,
   do you?

(Exit Snout.)

(Enter Quince.)

QUINCE.   Bless thee, Bottom, bless thee! Thou art
   translated.°

(Exit.)

BOTTOM.   I see their knavery. This is to make an ass of me,   120
   to fright me, if they could. But I will not stir from
   this place, do what they can. I will walk up and down
   here, and I will sing, that they shall hear I am
   not afraid.   *[Sings.]*
The woosel cock° so black of hue,   125
  With orange-tawny bill,
The throstle° with his note so true,
  The wren with little quill°—
TITANIA *[awaking]*.   What angel wakes me from my flow'ry bed?
BOTTOM *[sings]*.   The finch, the sparrow, and the lark,   130
  The plain-song° cuckoo grey,
Whose note full many a man doth mark,
  And dares not answer nay°—
For, indeed, who would set his wit to so foolish
  a bird? Who would give a bird the lie,° though he cry   135
  "cuckoo" never so?°
TITANIA.   I pray thee, gentle mortal, sing again.
Mine ear is much enamored of thy note;
So is mine eye enthralled to thy shape;
And they fair virtue's force° perforce doth move me   140
On the first view to say, to swear, I love thee.
BOTTOM.   Methinks, mistress, you should have little
   reason for that. And yet, to say the truth, reason

---

109 *fire:* will-o'-the-wisp.   119 *translated:* transformed.   125 *woosel cock:* male ousel or ouzel,
blackbird.   127 *throstle:* song thrush.   128 *quill:* literally, a reed pipe; hence, the bird's piping
song.   131 *plain-song:* singing a melody without variations.   133 *dares . . . nay:* cannot deny that
he is a cuckold.   135 *give . . . lie:* call the bird a liar.   136 *never so:* ever so much.   140 *thy . . .
force:* the power of your beauty.

and love keep little company together nowadays.
The more the pity that some honest neighbors will   145
not make them friends. Nay, I can gleek° upon
occasion.
TITANIA.   Thou art as wise as thou art beautiful.
BOTTOM.   Not so, neither. But if I had wit enough to
get out of this wood, I have enough to serve mine   150
over turn.°
TITANIA.   Out of this wood do not desire to go.
Thou shalt remain here, whether thou wilt or no.
I am a spirit of no common rate.°
The summer still° doth tend upon my state;°   155
And I do love thee. Therefore, go with me.
I'll give thee fairies to attend on thee,
And they shall fetch thee jewels from the deep,
And sing while thou on pressed flowers dost sleep.
And I will purge thy mortal grossness so   160
That thou shalt like an airy spirit go.
Peaseblossom, Cobweb, Moth,° and Mustardseed!

(Enter four Fairies [Peaseblossom, Cobweb, Moth, and Mustardseed].)

PEASEBLOSSOM.   Ready.
COBWEB.   And I.
MOTH.   And I.
MUSTARDSEED.   And I.
ALL.   Where shall we go?
TITANIA.   Be kind and courteous to this gentleman.   165
Hop in his walks and gambol in his eyes;
Feed him with apricocks and dewberries,
With purple grapes, green figs, and mulberries;
The honey-bags steal from the humble-bees,
And for night-tapers crop their waxen thighs   170
And light them at the fiery glow-worm's eyes,
To have my love to bed and to arise;
And pluck the wings from painted butterflies
To fan the moonbeams from his sleeping eyes.
Nod to him, elves, and do him courtesies.   175
PEASEBLOSSOM.   Hail, mortal!
COBWEB.   Hail!
MOTH.   Hail!
MUSTARDSEED.   Hail!
BOTTOM.   I cry your worship's mercy, heartily. I beseech your   180
worship's name.
COBWEB.   Cobweb.
BOTTOM.   I shall desire you of more acquantance, good

---

146 *gleek:* scoff, jest.   150–51 *serve ... turn:* answer my purpose.   154 *rate:* rank, value.   155 *still:* ever always.   *doth ... state:* waits upon me as part of my royal retinue.   162 *Moth:* mote, speck. (The two words *moth* and *mote* were pronounced alike.)

Master Cobweb.   If I cut my finger, I shall make bold
with you.° Your name, honest gentleman?   185
PEASEBLOSSOM.   Peaseblossom.
BOTTOM.   I pray you, commend me to Mistress
Squash,° your mother, and to Master Peascod,°
your father. Good Master Peaseblossom, I shall
desire you of more acquaintance too. Your name,   190
I beseech you, sir?
MUSTARDSEED.   Mustardseed.
BOTTOM.   Good Master Mustardseed, I know your
patience° well. That same cowardly, giant-like ox-beef
hath devour'd many a gentleman of your house.   195
I promise you your kindred hath made my eyes
water ere now. I desire you of more acquaintance,
good Master Mustardseed.
TITANIA.   Come wait upon him; lead him to my bower.
The moon methinks looks with a wat'ry eye;   200
And when she weeps,° weeps every little flower,
Lamenting some enforced° chastity.
Tie up my lover's tongue, bring him silently.

(Exeunt.)

Scene II°

(Enter [Oberon,] King of Fairies.)

OBERON.   I wonder if Titania be awak'd;
Then, what it was that next came in her eye,
Which she must dote on in extremity.

([Enter] Robin Goodfellow [Puck].)

Here comes my messenger. How now, mad spirit?
What night-rule° now about this haunted° grove?   5
PUCK.   My mistress with a monster is in love.
Near to her close° and consecrated bower,
While she was in her dull° and sleeping hout,
A crew of patches,° rude mechanicals,°
That work for bread upon Athenian stalls,   10
Were met together to rehearse a play
Intended for great Theseus' nuptial day.
The shallowest thick-skin of that barren sort,°
Who Pyramus presented,° in their sport

184–85 *If . . . you:* Cobwebs were used to stanch bleeding.   187 *Squash:* unripe pea pod.
188 *Peascod:* ripe pea pod.   193–94 *your patience:* what you have endured.   201 *she weeps:* i.e.,
she causes dew.   202 *enforced:* forced, violated; or, possibly, constrained (since Titania at this
moment is hardly concerned about chastity). III. II. *Location:* the wood.   5 *night-rule:* diversion
for the night.   *haunted:* much frequented.   7 *close:* secret, private.   8 *dull:* drowsy.
9 *patches:* clowns, fools.   *rude mechanicals:* ignorant artisans.   13 *barren sort:* stupid company
or crew.   14 *presented:* acted.

Forsook his scene° and ent'red in a brake.   15
When I did him at this advantage take,
An ass's nole° I fixed on his head.
Anon his Thisby must be answered,
And forth my mimic° comes. When they him spy,
As wild geese that the creeping fowler eye,   20
Or russet-pated choughs,° many in sort,°
Rising and cawing at the gun's report,
Sever° themselves and madly sweep the sky,
So, at his sight, away his fellows fly;
And, at our stamp, here o'er and o'er one falls;   25
He murder cries and help from Athens calls.
Their sense thus weak, lost with their fears thus strong,
Made senseless things begin to do them wrong,
For briers and thorns at their apparel snatch;
Some, sleeves—some, hats; from yielders all things catch.   30
I led them on in this distracted fear
And left sweet Pyramus translated there,
When in that moment, so it came to pass,
Titania wak'd and straightway lov'd an ass.

OBERON.   This falls out better than I could devise   35
But hast thou yet latch'd° the Athenian's eyes
With the love-juice, as I did bid thee do?
PUCK.   I took him sleeping—that is finish'd too—
And the Athenian woman by his side,
That, when he wak'd, of force° she must be ey'd.   40

(Enter Demetrius and Hermia.)

OBERON.   Stand close. This is the same Athenian.
PUCK.   This is the woman, but not this the man.
                                    [They stand aside.]
DEMETRIUS.   O, why rebuke you him that loves you so?
Lay breath so bitter on your bitter foe.
HERMIA.   How I but chide; but I should use thee worse,   45
For thou, I fear, hast given me cause to curse.
If thou hast slain Lysander in his sleep,
Being o'er shoes in blood, plunge in the deep,
And kill me too.
The sun was not so true unto the day   50
As he to me. Would he have stolen away
From sleeping Hermia? I'll believe as soon
This whole° earth may be bor'd and that the moon
May through the center creep and so displease
Her brother's° noontide with th' Antipodes.°   55
It cannot be but thou has murd'red him;

15 *scene:* playing area.   17 *nole:* noddle, head.   19 *mimic:* burlesque actor.   21 *russet-pated choughs:* gray-headed jackdaws.   *in sort:* in a flock.   23 *Sever:* scatter.   36 *latch'd:* moistened, anointed.   40 *of force:* perforce.   53 *whole:* solid.   55 *Her brother's:* i.e., the sun's.   *th' Antipodes:* the people on the opposite side of the earth.

So should a murderer look, so dead,° so grim.

DEMETRIUS.   So should the murdered look, and so should I,
Pierc'd through the heart with your sterm cruelty.
Yet you, the murderer, look as bright, as clear,   60
As yonder Venus in her glimmering sphere.

HERMIA.   What's this to my Lysander? Where is he?
Ah, good Demetrius, wilt thou give him me?

DEMETRIUS.   I had rather give his carcass to my hounds.

HERMIA.   Out dog! Out cur! Thou driv'st me past the bounds   65
Of maiden's patience. Hast thou slain him, then?
Henceforth be never numb'red among men!
O, once tell true, tell true, even for my sake!
Durst thou have look'd upon him being awake,
And hast thou kill'd him sleeping? O brave touch!°   70
Could not a worm,° an adder, do so much?
An adder did it, for with doubler tongue
Than thine, thou serpent, never adder stung.

DEMETRIUS.   You spend your passion° on a mispris'd mood.°
I am not guilty of Lysander's blood,   75
Nor is he dead, for aught that I can tell.

HERMIA.   I pray thee, tell me then that he is well.

DEMETRIUS.   An if I could, what should I get therefore?

HERMIA.   A privilege never to see me more.
And from they hated presense part I so.   80
See me no more, whether he be dead or no.

(Exit.)

DEMETRIUS.   There is no following her in this fierce vein.
Here therefore for a while I will remain.
So sorrow's heaviness doth heavier° grow
For debt that bankrupt° sleep doth sorrow owe;   85
Which now in some slight measure it will pay,
If for his tender here I make some stay.°

(Lie down [and sleep].)

OBERON.   What has thou done? Thou hast mistaken quite
And laid the love-juice on some true-lover's sight.
Of thy misprision° must perforce ensue   90
Some true love turn'd and not a false turn'd true.

PUCK.   Then fate o'er-rules, that, one man holding troth,°
A million fail, confounding oath on oath.°

OBERON.   About the wood go swifter than the wind,
And Helena of Athens look thou find.   95

---

57 *dead:* deadly, or deathly pale.   70 *brave touch:* noble exploit (said ironically).   71 *worm:* serpent.   74 *passion:* violent feelings.   *mispris'd mood:* anger based on misconceptions.
84 *heavier:* (1) harder to bear, (2) drowsier.   85 *bankrupt:* Demetrius is saying that his sleepiness adds to the weariness caused by sorrow.   86–87 *Which . . . stay:* To a small extent I will be able to "pay back" and hence find some relief from sorrow, if I pause here a while (*make some stay*) while sleep "tenders" or offers itself by way of paying the debt owed to sorrow.   90 *misprision:* mistake.   92 *troth:* faith.   93 *confounding . . . oath:* invalidating one oath with another.

All fancy-sick° she is and pale of cheer°
With sighs of love, that cost the fresh blood° dear.
By some illusion see thou bring her here.
I'll charm his eyes against she do appear.°

PUCK.   I go, I go; look how I go   100
    Swifter than arrow from the Tartar's bow.°

(Exit.)

OBERON.   Flower of this purple dye,
    Hit with Cupid's archery.
    Sink in angle of his eye.
        [Applies love-juice to Demetrius' eyes.]
    When his love he doth espy,   105
    Let her shine as gloriously
    As the Venus of the sky.
    When thou wak'st, if she be by,
    Beg of her for remedy.

(Enter Puck.)

PUCK.   Captain of our fairy band,   110
    Helena is here at hand,
    And the youth, mistook by me,
    Pleading for a lover's fee.°
    Shall we their fond pageant° see?
    Lord, what fools these mortals be!   115

OBERON.   Stand aside. The noise they make
    Will cause Demetrius to awake.

PUCK.   Then will two at once woo one;
    That must needs be sport alone;°
    And those things do best please me   120
    That befall prepost'rously.°
        [They stand aside.]

(Enter Lysander and Helena.)

LYSANDER.   Why should you think that I should woo in scorn?
    Scorn and derision never come in tears.
    Look when° I vow, I weep; and vows so born,
    In their nativity all truth appears.°   125
    How can these things in me seem scorn to you,
    Bearing the badge° of faith, to prove them true?

HELENA.   You do advance° your cunning more and more.
    When truth kills truth,° O devilish-holy fray!

---

96 *fancy-sick:* lovesick.   *cheer:* face.   97 *sighs . . . blood:* an allusion to the physiological theory
that each sigh costs the heart a drop of blood.   99 *against . . . appear:* in anticipation of her coming.   101 *Tartar's bow:* Tartars were famed for their skill with the bow.   113 *fee:* privilege, reward.   114 *fond pageant:* foolish exhibition.   119 *alone:* unequaled.   121 *prepost'rously:* out
of the natural order.   124 *Look when:* whenever.   124–25 *vows . . . appears:* Vows made by one
who is weeping give evidence thereby of their sincerity.   127 *badge:* identifying device such as that
worn on servants' livery.   128 *advance:* carry forward, display.   129 *truth kills truth:* One of
Lysander's vows must invalidate the other.

These vows are Hermia's. Will you give her o'er   130
Weigh oath with oath, and you will nothing weigh.
Your vows to her and me, put in two scales
Will even weigh, and both as light as tales.°
LYSANDER.   I had no judgment when to her I swore.
HELENA.   Nor none, in my mind, now you give her o'er.   135
LYSANDER.   Demetrius loves her, and he loves not you.
DEMETRIUS *[awaking].*   O Helen, goddess, nymph, perfect, divine!
To what, my love, shall I compare thine eyne?
Crystal is muddy. O, how ripe in show°
Thy lips, those kissing cherries, tempting grow!   140
That pure congealed white, high Taurus'° snow,
Fann'd with the eastern wind, turns to a crow°
When thou hold'st up thy hand. O, let me kiss
This princess of pure white, this seal° of bliss!
HELENA.   O spite! O hell! I see you all are bent   145
To set against me for your merriment.
If you were civil and knew courtesy,
You would not do me thus much injury.
Can you not hate me, as I know you do,
But you must join in souls to mock me too?   150
If you were men, as men you are in show,
You would not use a gentle lady so—
To vow, and swear, and superpraise° my parts,°
When I am sure you hate me with your hearts.
You both are rivals, and love Hermia;   155
And now both rivals, to mock Helena.
A trim° exploit, a manly enterprise,
To conjure tears up in a poor maid's eyes
With your derision! None of noble sort
Would so offend a virgin and extort°   160
A poor soul's patience, all to make you sport.
LYSANDER.   You are unkind, Demetrius. Be not so;
For you love Hermia; this you know I know.
And here, with all good will, with all my heart,
In Hermia's love I yield you up my part;   165
And yours of Helena to me bequeath,
Whom I do love and will do till my death.
HELENA.   Never did mockers waste more idle breath.
DEMETRIUS.   Lysander, keep thy Hermia; I will none.°
If e'er I lov'd her, all that love is gone.   170
My heart to her but as guest-wise sojourn'd,
There to remain.
LYSANDER.   Helen, it is not so.
DEMETRIUS.   Disparage not the faith thou dost not know.

---

133 *tales:* lies.   139 *show:* appearance.   141 *Taurus:* a lofty mountain range in Asia Minor.   142 *turns to a crow:* seems black by contrast.   144 *seal:* pledge.   153 *superpraise:* overpraise.   *parts:* qualities.   157 *trim:* pretty, fine (said ironically).   160 *extort:* twist, torture.   169 *will none:* wish none of her.

Lest, to thy peril, thou aby° it dear.   175
Look where thy love comes; yonder is thy dear.

(Enter Hermia.)

HERMIA.   Dark night, that from the eye his° function takes,
  The ear more quick of apprehension makes;
  Wherein it doth impair the seeing sense,
  It pays the hearing double recompense.   180
  Thou art not by mine eye, Lysander, found;
  Mine ear, I thank it, brought me to thy sound.
  But why unkindly didst thou leave me so?
LYSANDER.   Why should he stay, whom love doth press to go?
HERMIA.   What love could press Lysander from my side?   185
LYSANDER.   Lysander's love, that would not let him bide,
  Fair Helena, who more engilds the night
  Than all you fiery oes° and eyes of light.
  Why seek'st thou me? Could not this make thee know,
  The hate I bear thee made me leave thee so?   190
HERMIA.   You speak not as you think. It cannot be.
HELENA.   Lo, she is one of this confederacy!
  Now I perceive they have conjoin'd all three
  To fashion this false sport, in spite of me.°
  Injurious Hermia, most ungrateful maid!   195
  Have you conspir'd, have you with these contriv'd°
  To bait° me with this foul derision?
  Is all the counsel° that we two have shar'd,
  The sisters' vows, the hours that we have spent,
  When we have child the hasty-footed time   200
  For parting us—O, is all forgot?
  All school-days friendship, childhood innocence?
  We, Hermia, like two artificial° gods,
  Have with our needles created both one flower,
  Both on one sampler, sitting on one cushion,   205
  Both warbling of one song, both in one key,
  As if our hands, our sides, voices, and minds
  Had been incorporate. So we grew together,
  Like to a double cherry, seeming parted,
  But yet an union in partition;   210
  Two lovely° berries molded on one stem;
  So, with two seeming bodies, but one heart;
  Two of the first, like costs in heraldry,
  Due but to one and crowned with one crest.°
  And will you rent° our ancient love asunder,   215
  To join with men in scorning your poor friend?

---

175 *aby:* pay for.   177 *his:* its.   188 *oes:* circles, orbs, stars.   194 *in spite of me:* to vex me.
196 *contriv'd:* plotted.   197 *bait:* torment, as one sets on dogs to bait a bear.   198 *counsel:* con-
fidential talk.   203 *artificial:* skilled in art or creation.   211 *lovely:* loving.   213–14 *Two . . .
crest:* We have two separate bodies, just as a coat of arms in heraldry can be represented twice on
a shield but surmounted by a single crest.   215 *rent:* rend.

It is not friendly, 'tis not maidenly.
Our sex, as well as I, may chide you for it,
Though I alone do feel the injury.

HERMIA.   I am amazed at your passionate words.   220
I scorn you not. It seems that you scorn me.

HELENA.   Have you not set Lysander, as in scorn,
To follow me and praise my eyes and face?
And made your other love, Demetrius,
Who even but now did spurn me with his foot,   225
To call me goddess, nymph, divine and rare,
Precious, celestial? Wherefore speaks he this
To her he hates? And wherefore doth Lysander
Deny your love, so rich within his soul,
And tender° me, forsooth, affection,   230
But by your setting on, by your consent?
What though I be not so in grace° as you,
So hung upon with love, so fortunate,
But miserable most, to love unlov'd?
This you should pity rather than despise.   235

HERMIA.   I understand not what you mean by this.

HELENA.   Ay, do! Persever, counterfeit sad° looks,
Make mouths° upon° me when I turn my back,
Wink each at other, hold the sweet jest up.
This sport, well carried,° shall be chronicled.   240
If you have any pity, grace, or manners,
You would not make me such an argument.°
But fare ye well. 'Tis partly my own fault,
Which death, or absence, soon shall remedy.

LYSANDER.   Stay, gentle Helena; hear my excuse,   245
My love, my life, my soul, fair Helena!

HELENA.   O excellent!

HERMIA.   Sweet, do not scorn her so.

DEMETRIUS.   If she cannot entreat,° I can compel.

LYSANDER.   Thou canst compel no more than she entreat.
Thy threats have no more strength than her weak prayers.   250
Helen, I love thee, by my life, I do!
I swear by that which I will lose for thee,
To prove him false that says I love thee not.

DEMETRIUS.   I say I love thee more than he can do.

LYSANDER.   If thou say so, withdraw, and prove it too.   255

DEMETRIUS.   Quick, come!

HERMIA.   Lysander, whereto tends all this?

LYSANDER.   Away, you Ethiope!°   *[He tries to break away from Hermia.]*

DEMETRIUS.   No, no; he'll
Seem to break loose; take on as you would follow,

---

230 *tender:* offer.   232 *grace:* favor.   237 *sad:* grave, serious.   238 *mouths:* maws, faces, grimaces.   *upon:* at.   240 *carried:* managed.   242 *argument:* subject for a jest.   248 *entreat:* succeed by entreaty.   257 *Ethiope:* referring to Hermia's relatively dark hair and complexion; see also *tawny Tartar* six lines later.

But yet come not. You are a tame man, go!

LYSANDER.   Hang off,° thou cat, thou burr! Vile thing, let loose,   260
Or I will shake thee from me like a serpent!

HERMIA.   Why are you grown so rude? What change is this,
Sweet love?

LYSANDER.   Thy love? Out, tawny Tartar, out!
Out, loathed med'cine!° O hated potion, hence!

HERMIA.   Do you not jest?

HELENA.   Yes, sooth,° and so do you.   265

LYSANDER.   Demetrius, I will keep my word with thee.

DEMETRIUS.   I would I had your bond, for I perceive
A weak bond° holds you. I'll not trust your word.

LYSANDER.   What, should I hurt her, strike her, kill her dead?
Although I hate her, I'll not harm her so.   270

HERMIA.   What, can you do me greater harm than hate?
Hate me? Wherefore? O me, what news,° my love?
Am not I Hermia? Are not you Lysander?
I am as fair now as I was erewhile.°
Since night you lov'd me; yet since night you left me.   275
Why, then you left me—O, the gods forbid!—
In earnest, shall I say?

LYSANDER.   Ay, by my life!
And never did desire to see thee more.
Therefore be out of hope, of question, of doubt;
Be certain, nothing truer. 'Tis no jest   280
That I do hate thee and love Helena.

HERMIA.   O me! You juggler? You cankerblossom!°
You thief of love! What, have you come by night
And stol'n my love's heart from him?

HELENA.   Fine, i' faith!
Have you no modesty, no maiden shame,   285
No touch of bashfulness? What, will you tear
Impatient answers from my gentle tongue?
Fie, fie! You counterfeit, you puppet,° you!

HERMIA.   Puppet? Why so? Ay, that way goes the game.
Now I perceive that she hath made compare   290
Between our statures; she hath urg'd her height,
And with her personage, her tall personage,
Her height, forsooth, she hath prevail'd with him.
And are you grown so high in his esteem,
Because I am so dwarfish and so low?   295
How low am I, thou painted maypole? Speak!
How low am I? I am not yet so low
But that my nails can reach unto thine eyes.

[She flails at Helena but is restrained.]

260 *Hang off:* let go.   264 *med'cine:* poison.   265 *sooth:* truly.   268 *weak bond:* Hermia's arm
(with a pun on *bond,* oath, in the previous line).   272 *what is the matter.*   274 erewhile: just now.
282 *cankerblossom:* worm that destroys the flower bud (?).   288 *puppet:* (1) counterfeit, (2)
dwarfish woman (in reference to Hermia's smaller stature).

HELENA.   I pray you, though you mock me, gentleman,
    Let her not hurt me. I was never curst;°   300
    I have no gift at all in shrewishness;
    I am a right° maid for my cowardice.
    Let her not strike me. You perhaps may think,
    Because she is something° lower than myself,
    That I can match her.
HERMIA.   Lower! Hark, again!   305
HELENA.   Good Hermia, do not be so bitter with me.
    I evermore did love you, Hermia,
    Did ever keep your counsels, never wrong'd you;
    Save that, in love unto Demetrius,
    I told him of your stealth° unto this wood.   310
    He followed you; for love I followed him.
    But he hath chid me hence and threat'ned me
    To strike me, spurn me, nay, to kill me too.
    And now, so° you will let me quiet go,
    To Athens will I bear my folly back   315
    And follow you no further. Let me go.
    You see how simple and how fond° I am.
HERMIA.   Why, get you gone. Who is 't that hinders you?
HELENA.   A foolish heart, that I leave here behind.
HERMIA.   What, with Lysander?
HELENA.   With Demetrius.   320
LYSANDER.   Be not afraid, she shall not harm thee, Helena.
DEMETRIUS.   No, sir, she shall not, though you take her part.
HELENA.   O, when she is angry, she is keen and shrewd!°
    She was a vixen when she went to school;
    And though she be but little she is fierce.   325
HERMIA.   "Little" again! Nothing but "low" and "little"!
    Why will you suffer her to flout me thus?
    Let me come to her.
LYSANDER.   Get you gone, you dwarf!
    You minimus,° of hind'ring knot-grass° made!
    You bead, you acorn!
DEMETRIUS.   You are too officious   330
    In her behalf that scorns your services.
    Let her alone. Speak not of Helena;
    Take not her part. For, if thou dost intend°
    Never so little show of love to her,
    Thou shalt aby° it.
LYSANDER.   Now she holds me not;   335
    Now follow, if thou dar'st, to try whose right,
    Of thine or mine, is most in Helena.

(Exit.)

---

300 *curst:* shrewish.   302 *right:* true.   304 *something:* somewhat.   310 *stealth:* stealing away.   314 *so:* if only.   317 *fond:* foolish.   323 *shrewd:* shrewish.   329 *minimus:* diminutive creature.   *knot-grass:* a weed, an infusion of which was thought to stunt the growth.   333 *intend:* give sign of.   335 *aby:* pay for.

DEMETRIUS.   Follow? Nay, I'll go with thee, cheek by jowl.°

(Exit, following Lysander.)

HERMIA.   You, mistress, all this coil° is 'long of° you.
    Nay, go not back.°
HELENA.   I will not trust you, I,   340
    Nor longer stay in your curst company.
    Your hands than mine are quicker for a fray;
    My legs are longer, though, to run away.

(Exit.)

HERMIA.   I am amaz'd, and know not what to say.

(Exit.)

OBERON.   This is thy negligence. Still thou mistak'st,   345
    Or else committ'st thy knaveries willfully.
PUCK.   Believe me, king of shadows, I mistook.
    Did not you tell me I should know the man
    By the Athenian garments he had on?
    And so far blameless proves my enterprise   350
    That I have 'nointed an Athenian's eyes;
    And so far am I glad it so did sort°
    As this their jangling I esteem a sport.
OBERON.   Thou see'st these lovers seek a place to fight.
    Hie therefore, Robin, overcast the night;   355
    The starry welkin° cover thou anon
    With drooping fog as black as Acheron,°
    And lead these testy rivals so astray
    As° one come not within another's way.
    Like to Lysander sometime frame they tongue,   360
    Then stir Demetrius up with bitter wrong;°
    And sometime rail thou like Demetrius.
    And from each other look thou lead them thus,
    Till o'er their brows death-counterfeiting sleep
    With leaden legs and batty° wings doth creep.   365
    Then crush this herb° into Lysander's eye,
                     [Gives herb.]
    Whose liquor hath this virtuous° property,
    To take from thence all error with his° might
    And make his eyeballs roll with wonted° sight.
    When they next wake, all this derision°   370
    Shall seem a dream and fruitless vision,
    And back to Athens shall the lovers wend

---

338 *cheek by jowl:* side by side.   339 *coil:* turmoil, dissension.   *'long of:* on account of.   340 *go not back:* Don't retreat. (Hermia is again proposing a fight.)   352 *sort:* turn out.   356 *welkin:* sky.   357 *Acheron:* river of Hades (here representing Hades itself).   359 *As:* that.   361 *wrong:* insults.   365 *batty:* batlike.   366 *this herb:* the antidote (mentioned in II. I. 184) to love-in-idleness.   367 *virtuous:* efficacious.   368 *his:* its.   369 *wonted:* accustomed.   370 *derision:* laughable business.

With league whose date° till death shall never end.
Whiles I in this affair do thee employ,
I'll to my queen and beg her Indian boy;   375
And then I will her charmed eye release
From monster's view, and all things shall be peace.

PUCK.   My fairy lord, this must be done with haste,
For night's swift dragons° cut the clouds full fast,
And yonder shines Aurora's harbinger,°   380
At whose approach, ghosts, wand'ring her and there,
Troop home to churchyards. Damned spirits all,
That in crossways and floods have burial,°
Already to their wormy beds are gone.
For fear lest day should look their shames upon,   385
They willfully themselves exile from light
And must for aye° consort with black-brow'd night.

OBERON.   But we are spirits of another sort.
I with the Morning's love° have oft made sport,
And, like a forester,° the groves may tread   390
Even till the eastern gate, all fiery-red,
Opening on Neptune with fair blessed beams,
Turns into yellow gold his salt green streams.
But, notwithstanding, haste; make no delay.
We may effect this business yet ere day.

(Exit.)

PUCK.   Up and down, up and down,
I will lead them up and down.
I am fear'd in field and town.
Goblin, lead them up and down.
Here comes one.   400

(Enter Lysander.)

LYSANDER.   Where art thou, proud Demetrius? Speak thou now.
PUCK *[mimicking Demetrius]*.   Here, villain, drawn° and ready. Where are thou?
LYSANDER.   I will be with thee straight.°
PUCK.   Follow me, then,
To plainer° ground.
                    [Lysander wanders about, following the voice.]°

(Enter Demetrius.)

DEMETRIUS.   Lysander! Speak again!

---

373 *date:* term of existence.   379 *dragons:* supposed to be yoked to the car of the goddess of
night.   380 *Aurora's harbinger:* the morning star, precursor of dawn.   383 *crossways . . . burial:* Those who had committed suicide were buried at crossways, with a stake driven through them;
those drowned, i.e., buried in floods or great waters, were condemned to wander disconsolate for
want of burial rites.   387 *for aye:* forever.   389 *Morning's love:* Cephalus, a beautiful youth
beloved by Aurora; or perhaps the goddess of the dawn herself.   390 *forester:* keeper of a royal
forest.   402 *drawn:* with drawn sword.   403 *straight:* immediately.   404 *plainer:* smoother.
404 [S.D.] *Lysander wanders about:* It is not clearly necessary that Lysander exit at this point; neither
exit nor reentrance is indicated in the early texts.

Thou runaway, thou coward, art thou fled?   405
Speak! In some bush? Where dost thou hide thy head?
PUCK *[mimicking Lysander].*   Thou coward, art thou bragging to the stars,
    Telling the bushes that thou look'st for wars,
    And wilt not come? Come, recreant;° come, thou child,
    I'll whip thee with a rod. he is defil'd   410
    That draws a sword on thee.
DEMETRIUS.   Yea, art thou there?
PUCK.   Follow my voice. We'll try° no manhood here.

(Exeunt.)

(Lysander returns.)

LYSANDER.   He goes before me and still dares me on.
    When I come where he calls, then he is gone.
    The villain is much lighter-heel'd than I.   415
    I followed fast, but faster he did fly,
    That fallen am I in dark uneven way,
    And here will rest me. *[Lies down.]* Come, thou gentle day!
    For if but once thou show me thy gray light,
    I'll find Demetrius and revenge this spite.   *[Sleeps.]*   420

([Enter] Robin [Puck] and Demetrius.)

PUCK.   Ho, ho, ho! Coward, why com'st thou not?
DEMETRIUS.   Abide me, if thou dar'st; for well I wot°
    Thou runn'st before me, shifting every place,
    And dar'st not stand not look me in the face.
    Where art thou now?
PUCK.   Come hither. I am here.   425
DEMETRIUS.   Nay, then, thou mock'st me. Thou shalt buy° this dear,°
    If ever I thy face by daylight see.
    Now, go thy way. Faintness constraineth me
    To measure out my length on this cold bed.
    By day's approach look to be visited.   430
                   [Lies down and sleeps.]

(Enter Helena.)

HELENA.   O weary night, O long and tedious night,
    Abate° thy hours! Shine, comforts, from the east,
    That I may back to Athens by daylight,
    From these that my poor company detest;
    And sleep, that sometimes shuts up sorrow's eye,   435
    Steal me awhile from mine own company.
                  [Lies down and] sleep[s].
PUCK.   Yet but three? Come one more;
    Two of both kinds makes up four.
    Here she comes, curst and sad.

409 *recreant:* cowardly wretch.   412 *try:* test.   422 *wot:* know.   426 *buy:* pay for.   *dear:*
dearly.   432 *Abate:* lessen, shorten.

Cupid is a knavish lad,   440
Thus to make poor females mad.

(Enter Hermia.)

HERMIA.   Never so weary, never so in woe,
    Bedabbled with the dew and torn with briers,
    I can no further crawl, no further go;
    My legs can keep no pace with my desires.   445
    Here will I rest me till the break of day.
    Heavens shield Lysander, if they mean a fray!
                            [Lies down and sleeps.]
PUCK.   On the ground
    Sleep sound.
    I'll apply   450
        To your eye,
    Gentle lover, remedy.
                [Squeezing the juice on Lysander's eyes.]
        When thou wak'st,
        Thou tak'st
        True delight   455
        In the sight
    Of thy former lady's eye;
    And the country proverb known,
    That every man should take his own,
    In your waking shall be shown: 460
        Jack shall have Jill;
        Nought shall go ill;
    The man shall have his mare again, and all shall be well.

[Exit. Manent the four lovers.]

ACT IV

Scene I°

*(Enter [Titania,] Queen of Fairies, and [Bottom the] Clown, and Fairies; and [Oberon,]
the King, behind them.)*

TITANIA.   Come, sit thee down upon this flow'ry bed,
    While I thy amiable° cheeks do coy,°
    And stick musk-roses in they sleek smooth head,
    And kiss thy fair large ears, my gentle joy.
                            [They recline.]
BOTTOM.   Where's Peaseblossom?   5
PEASEBLOSSOM.   Ready.

IV. I. *Location:* scene continues. The four lovers are still asleep onstage.   2 *amiable:*
lovely.   *coy:* caress.

BOTTOM.   Scratch my head, Peaseblossom. Where's Monsieur
Cobweb?

COBWEB.   Ready.

BOTTOM.   Mounsieur Cobweb, good mounsieur, get you   10
your weapons in your hand, and kill me a red-
hipp'd humble-bee on the top of a thistle; and,
good mounsieur, bring me the honey-bag. Do not
fret yourself too much in the action, mounsieur;
and, good mounsieur, have a care the honey-bag   15
break not; I would be loath to have you overflown
with a honey-bag, signior. Where's Mounsieur
Mustardseed?

MUSTARDSEED.   Ready.

BOTTOM.   Give me your neaf,° Mounsieur Mustardseed.   20
Pray you, leave your curtsy,° good mounsieur.

MUSTARDSEED.   What's your will?

BOTTOM.   Nothing, good mounsieur, but to help
Cavalery° Cobweb° to scratch. I must to the barber's,
mounsieur; for methinks I am marvailes hairy   25
about the face; and I am such a tender ass, if my
hair do but tickle me, I must scratch.

TITANIA.   What, wilt thou hear some music, my sweet love?

BOTTOM.   I have a reasonable good ear in music. Let's
have the tongs and the bones.°   30

[Music: tongs, rural music.]°

TITANIA.   Or say, sweet love, what thou desirest to eat.

BOTTOM.   Truly, a peck of provender. I could munch
your good dry oats. Methinks I have a great desire
to a bottle° of hay. Good hay, sweet hay, hath no
fellow.°   35

TITANIA.   I have a venturous fairy that shall seek
The squirrel's hoard, and fetch thee new nuts.

BOTTOM.   I had rather have a handful or two of dried
peas. But, I pray you, let none of your people stir
me. I have an exposition° of sleep come upon me.   40

TITANIA.   Sleep thou, and I will wind thee in my arms.
Fairies, be gone, and be all ways° away.

(Exeunt fairies.)

So doth the woodbine the sweet honeysuckle
Gently entwist; the female ivy so
Enrings the barky fingers of the elm.   45
Oh, how I love thee! How I dote on thee!

[They sleep.]

---

20 *neaf:* fist.   21 *leave your curtsy:* put on your hat.   23–24 *Cavalery:* cavalier; form of address for
a gentleman.   24 *Cobweb:* seemingly in error, since Cobweb has been sent to bring honey while
Peaseblossom has been asked to scratch.   30 *tongs . . . bones:* instruments for rustic music. (The
tongs were played like a triangle, whereas the bones were held between the fingers and used as clap-
pers.)   30 [S.D.] *Music . . . music:* This stage direction is added from the Folio.   34 *bottle:* bundle.   35 *fellow:* equal.   40 *exposition:* Bottom's word for *disposition.*   42 *all ways:* in all directions.

(Enter Robin Goodfellow [Puck].)

OBERON *[advancing].*   Welcome, good Robin. See'st thou this sweet sight?
    Her dotage now I do begin to pity.
    For, meeting her of late behind the wood,
    Seeking sweet favors° for this hateful fool,   50
    I did upbraid her and fall out with her.
    For she his hairy temples then had rounded
    With coronet of fresh and fragrant flowers;
    And that same dew, which sometime° on the buds
    Was wont to swell like round and orient pearls,°   55
    Stood now within the pretty flouriets'° eyes
    Like tears that did their own disgrace bewail.
    When I had at my pleasure taunted her,
    And she in mild terms begg'd my patience,
    I then did ask of her her changeling child;   60
    Which straight she gave me, and her fairy sent
    To bear him to my bower in fairy land.
    And, now I have the boy, I will undo
    This hateful imperfection of her eyes.
    And, gentle Puck, take this transformed scalp   65
    From off the head of this Athenian swain,
    That, he awaking when the other° do,
    May all to Athens back again repair,
    And think no more of this night's accidents
    But as the fierce vexation of a dream.   70
    But first I will release the Fairy Queen.
                   [Squeezes juice in her eyes.]
    Be as thou wast wont to be;
    See as thou wast wont to see.
    Dian's bud° o'er Cupid's flower
    Hath such force and blessed power.   75
    Now, my Titania, wake you, my sweet queen.
TITANIA *[waking].* My Oberon! What visions have I seen!
    Methought I was enamor'd of an ass.
OBERON.   There lies your love.
TITANIA.   How came these things to pass?
    O, how mine eyes do loathe his visage now!   80
OBERON.   Silence awhile. Robin, take off this head.
    Titania, music call, and strike more dead
    Than common sleep of all these five° the sense.
TITANIA.   Music, ho! Music, such as charmeth sleep!   *[Music.]*
PUCK *[removing the ass's head].* Now, when thou wak'st, with thine
        own fool's eyes peep.   85

---

50 *favors:* i.e., gifts of flowers.   54 *sometime:* formerly.   55 *orient pearls:* the most beautiful of all pearls, those coming from the Orient.   56 *flouriets':* flowerets'.   67 *other:* others.   74 *Dian's bud:* perhaps the flower of the *agnus castus* or chaste-tree, supposed to preserve chastity; or perhaps referring simply to Oberon's herb by which he can undo the effects of "Cupid's flower," the love-in-idleness of II. I. 166–68.   83 *these five:* i.e., the four lovers and Bottom.

OBERON. Sound, music! Come, my queen, take hands with me,
  And rock the ground whereon these sleepers be. *[Dance.]*
  Now thou and I are new in amity,
  And will tomorrow midnight solemnly°
  Dance in Duke Theseus' house triumphantly   90
  And bless it to all fair prosperity.
  There shall the pairs of faithful lovers be
  Wedded, with Theseus, all in jollity.
PUCK. Fairy King, attend, and mark:
  I do hear the morning lark.   95
OBERON. Then, my queen, in silence sad,°
  Trip we after night's shade.
  We the globe can compass soon,
  Swifter than the wand'ring moon.
TITANIA. Come, my lord, and in our flight   100
  Tell me how it came this night
  That I sleeping here was found
  With these mortals on the ground.

(Exeunt.)   *(Wind horn [within].)*

(Enter Theseus and all his train; [Hippolyta, Egeus].)

THESEUS. Go, one of you, find out the forester,
  For now our observation° is perform'd;   105
  And since we have the vaward° of the day,
  My love shall hear the music of my hounds.
  Uncouple in the western valley; let them go.
  Dispatch, I say, and find the forester.

(Exit an Attendant.)

  We will, fair queen, up to the mountain's top   110
  And mark the musical confusion
  Of hounds and echo in conjunction.
HIPPOLYTA. I was with Hercules and Cadmus° once,
  When in a wood of Crete they bay'd° the bear
  With hounds of Sparta.° Never did I hear   115
  Such gallant chiding; for, besides the groves,
  The skies, the fountains, every region near
  Seem'd all one mutual cry. I never heard
  So musical a discord, such sweet thunder.
THESEUS. My hounds are bred out of the Spartan kind,   120
  So flew'd,° so sanded;° and their heads are hung
  With ears that sweep away the morning dew;
  Crook-knee'd, and dewlapp'd° like Thessalian bulls;

---

89 *solemnly:* ceremoniously.   96 *sad:* sober.   105 *observation:* observance to a morn of May (I.
I. 167).   106 *vaward:* vanguard, i.e., earliest part.   113 *Cadmus:* Mythical founder of Thebes.
(This story about him is unknown.)   114 *bay'd:* brought to bay.   115 *hounds of Sparta:* breed
famous in antiquity for their hunting skill.   121 *So flew'd:* similarly having large hanging chaps
or fleshy covering of the jaw.   *sanded:* of sandy color.   123 *dewlapp'd:* having pendulous folds
of skin under the neck.

Slow in pursuit, but match'd in mouth like bells,
Each under each.° A cry° more tuneable°   125
Was never holla'd to, nor cheer'd with horn,
In Crete, in Sparta, nor in Thessaly.
Judge when you hear. *[Sees the sleepers.]* But, soft! What nymphs are these?
EGEUS.   My lord, this' my daughter here asleep;
And this, Lysander; this Demetrius is;   130
This Helena, old Nedar's Helena.
I wonder of their being here together.
THESEUS.   No doubt they rose up early to observe
The rite of May, and, hearing our itnent,
Came here in grace of our solemnity.°   135
But speak, Egeus. Is not this the day
That Hermia should give answer of her choice?
EGEUS.   It is, my lord.
THESEUS.   Go, bid the huntsmen wake them with their horns.

(Exit an Attendant.)   *(Shout within. Wind horns. They all start up.)*

Good morrow, friends. Saint Valentine° is past.   140
Begin these wood-birds but to couple now?
LYSANDER.   Pardon, my lord.   *[They kneel.]*
THESEUS.   I pray you all, stand up.
I know you two are rival enemies;
How comes this gentle concord in the world,
That hatred is so far from jealousy   145
To sleep by hate and fear no enmity?
LYSANDER.   My lord, I shall reply amazedly,
Half sleep, half waking; but as yet, I swear,
I cannot truly say how I came here.
But, as I think—for truly would I speak,   150
And now I do bethink me, so it is—
I came with Hermia hither. Our intent
Was to be gone from Athens, where° we might,
Without° the peril of the Athenian law—
EGEUS.   Enough, enough, my lord; you have enough.   155
I beg the law, the law, upon his head.
They would have stol'n away; they would, Demetrius,
Thereby to have defeated you and me,
You of your wife and me of my consent,
Of my consent that she should be your wife.   160
DEMETRIUS.   My lord, fair Helen told me of their stealth,
Of this their purpose hither to this wood,
And I in fury hither followed them,
Fair Helena in fancy following me.

124–25 *match'd . . . under each:* harmoniously matched in their various cries like a set of bells, from treble down to bass.   125 *cry:* pack of hounds.   *tuneable:* well tuned, melodius.   135 *solemnity:* observance of these same rites of May.   140 *Saint Valentine:* Birds were supposed to choose their mates on St. Valentine's Day.   153 *where:* wherever; or to where.   154 *Without:* outside of, beyond.

But, my good lord, I wot not by what power— 165
But by some power it is—my love to Hermia,
Melted as the snow, seems to me now
As the remembrance of an idle gaud.°
Which in my childhood I did dote upon;
And all the faith, the virtue of my heart, 170
The object and the pleasure of mine eye,
Is only Helena. To her, my lord,
Was I betroth'd ere I saw Hermia,
But like a sickness did I loathe this food;
But, as in health, come to my natural taste, 175
Now I do wish it, love it, long for it,
And will for evermore be true to it.
THESEUS. Fair lovers, you are fortunately met.
Of this discourse we more will hear anon.
Egeus, I will overbear your will; 180
For in the temple, by and by, with us
These couples shall eternally be knit.
And, for° the morning now is something° worn,
Our purpos'd hunting shall be set aside.
Away with us to Athens. Three and three, 185
We'll hold a feast in great solemnity.
Come, Hippolyta.

(Exeunt Theseus, Hippolyta, Egeus, and train.)

DEMETRIUS. These things seem small and undistinguishable,
Like far-off mountains turned into clouds.
HERMIA. Methinks I see these things with parted° eye, 190
When every thing seems double.
HELENA. So methinks;
And I have found Demetrius like a jewel,
Mine own, and not mine own.°
DEMETRIUS. Are you sure
That we are awake? It seems to me
That yet we sleep, we dream. Do not you think 195
The Duke was here, and bid us follow him?
HERMIA. Yea, and my father.
HELENA. And Hippolyta.
LYSANDER. And he did bid us follow to the temple.
DEMETRIUS. Why, then, we are awake. Let's follow him,
And by the way let us recount our dreams. 200

(Exeunt.)

BOTTOM *[awaking]*. When my cue comes, call me
and I will answer. My next is, "Most fair Pyramus."
Heigh-ho! Peter Quince! Flute, the bellowsmender.

---

168 *idle gaud:* worthless trinket.   183 *for:* since.   *something:* somewhat.   190 *parted:* improperly focused.   192–93 *like . . . not mine own:* like a jewel that one finds by chance and therefore possesses but cannot certainly consider one's own property.

Snout, the tinker! Starveling! God's my life,
stol'n hence, and left me asleep! I have had a   205
most rare vision. I have had a dream, past the wit
of man to say what dream it was. Man is but an
ass, if he go about° to expound this dream.
Methought I was—there is no man can tell what.
Methought I was—and methought I had—but   210
man is but a patch'd fool, if he will offer° to say
what me-thought I had. The eye of man hath not
heard, the ear of man hath not seen, man's hand is
not able to taste, his tongue to conceive, nor his
heart to report, what my dream was. I will get Peter   215
Quince to write a ballad of this dream. It shall be
call'd "Bottom's Dream," because it hath no bottom;
and I will sing it in the latter end of a play, before
the Duke. Peradventure, to make it the more gracious,
I shall sing it at her° death.   220

(Exit.)

Scene II°

(Enter Quince, Flute, [Snout, and Starveling].)

QUINCE.   Have you sent to Bottom's house? Is he come
         home yet?
STARVELING.   He cannot be heard of. Out of doubt he
         is transported.°
FLUTE.   If he come not, then the play is marr'd. It goes   5
         not forward, doth it?
QUINCE.   It is not possible. You have not a man in all
         Athens able to discharge° Pyramus but he.
FLUTE.   No, he hath simply the best wit of any handicraft
         man in Athens.   10
QUINCE.   Yea, and the best person too; and he is a very paramour
         for a sweet voice.
FLUTE.   You must say "paragon." A paramour is, God bless us,
         a thing of naught.

(Enter Snug the Joiner.)

SNUG.   Masters, the Duke is coming from the temple,   15
         and there is two or three lords and ladies more
         married. If our sport had gone forward, we had all
         been made men.
FLUTE.   O sweet bully Bottom! Thus hath he lost

---

208 *go about:* attempt.   211 *patch'd:* wearing motley, i.e., a dress of various colors.   *offer:* venture.   220 *her:* Thisby's (?). IV. II. *Location:* Athens, Quince's house (?).   4 *transported:* carried off by fairies; or, possibly, transformed.   8 *discharge:* perform.

sixpence a day° during his life; he could not   20
have scap'd sixpence a day. An the Duke had not given
him sixpence a day for playing Pyramus, I'll be
hang'd. He would have deserv'd it. Sixpence a day
in Pyramus, or nothing.

(Enter Bottom.)

BOTTOM.   Where are these lads? Where are these hearts?°   25
QUINCE.   Bottom! O most courageous day! O most happy hour!
BOTTOM.   Masters, I am to discourse wonders.° But ask
me not what; for if I tell you, I am no true Athenian.
I will tell you everything, right as it fell out.   30
QUINCE.   Let us hear, sweet Bottom.
BOTTOM.   Not a word of° me. All that I will tell you
is, that the Duke hath din'd. Get your apparel
together, good strings° to your beards, new ribands°
to your pumps, meet presently° at the palace, every   35
man look o'er his part; for the short and the long
is, our play is preferr'd.° In any case, let Thisby
have clean linen; and let not him that plays the lion
pare his nails, for they shall hang out for the lion's
claws. And, most dear actors, eat no onions nor   40
garlic, for we are to utter sweet breath; and I do
not doubt but to hear them say, it is a sweet comedy.
No more words. Away! go, away!

(Exeunt.)

ACT V

Scene 1°

(Enter Theseus, Hippolyta, and Philostrate, [Lords, and Attendants].)

HIPPOLYTA.   'Tis strange, my Theseus, that° these lovers speak of.
THESEUS.   More strange than true. I never may° believe
These antic° fables, nor these fairy toys.°
Lovers and madmen have such seething brains
Such shaping fantasies,° that apprehend   5
More than cool reason ever comprehends.
The lunatic, the lover, and the poet

---

20 *sixpence a day:* as a royal pension.   25 *hearts:* good fellows.   28 *am . . . wonders:* have wonders to relate.   33 *of:* out of.   35 *strings:* to attach the beards.   *ribands:* ribbons. 36 *presently:* immediately.   38 *preferr'd:* selected for consideration. V. I. *Location:* Athens, the palace of Theseus.   1 *that:* that which.   2 *may:* can.   3 *antic:* strange, grotesque (with additional punning sense of *antique,* ancient).   *fairy toys:* trifling stories about fairies.   5 *fantasies:* imaginations.

Are of imagination all compact.°
One sees more devils than vast hell can hold;
That is the madman. The lover, all as frantic,   10
Sees Helen's° beauty in a brow of Egypt.°
The poet's eye, in a fine frenzy rolling,
Doth glance from heaven to earth, from earth to heaven;
And as imagination bodies forth
The forms of things unknown, the poet's pen   15
Turns them to shapes and gives to airy nothing
A local habitation and a name.
Such tricks hath strong imagination
That, if it would but apprehend some joy,
It comprehends some bringer° of that joy;   20
Or in the night, imagining some fear,°
How easy is a bush suppos'd a bear!

HIPPOLYTA.   But all the story of the night told over,
And all their minds transfigur'd so together,
More witnesseth than fancy's images°   25
And grows to something of great constancy;°
But, however,° strange and admirable.°

(Enter lovers: Lysander, Demetrius, Hermia, and Helena.)

THESEUS.   Here come the lovers, full of joy and mirth.
Joy, gentle friends! Joy and fresh days of love
Accompany your hearts!

LYSANDER.   More than to us   30
Wait in your royal walks, your board, your bed!

THESEUS.   Come now, what masques, what dances shall we have.
To wear away this long age of three hours
Between our after-supper and bed-time?
Where is our usual manager of mirth?   35
What revels are in hand? Is there no play,
To ease the anguish of a torturing hour?
Call Philostrate.

PHILOSTRATE.   Here, mighty Theseus.

THESEUS.   Say, what abridgement° have you for this evening?
What masque? What music? How shall we beguile   40
The lazy time, if not with some delight?

PHILOSTRATE.   There is a brief° how many sports are ripe.
Make choice of which your Highness will see first.

[Giving a paper.]

THESEUS *[reads].* "The battle with the Centaurs,° to be sung

---

8 *compact:* formed, composed.   11 *Helen's:* of Helen of Troy, pattern of beauty.   *brow of Egypt:* face of a gypsy.   20 *bringer:* source.   21 *fear:* object of fear.   25 *More . . . images:* testifies to something more substantial than mere imaginings.   26 *constancy:* certainty.   27 *howsoever:* in any case.   *admirable:* a source of wonder.   39 *abridgement:* pastime (to abridge or shorten the evening).   42 *brief:* short written statement, list.   44 *"battle . . Centaurs":* probably refers to the battle of the Centaurs and the Lapithae, when the Centaurs attempted to carry off Hippodamia, bride of Theseus's friend Pirothous.

By an Athenian eunuch to the harp." 45
We'll none of that. That have I told my love,
In glory of my kinsman° Hercules.
[Reads.] "The riot of the tipsy Bacchanals,
Tearing the Thracian singer in their rage."°
That is an old device; and it was play'd 50
When I from Thebes came last a conqueror.
[Reads.] "The thrice three Muses mourning for the death
Of Learning, late deceas'd in beggary."°
That is some satire, keen and critical,
Not sorting with° a nuptial ceremony. 55
[Reads.] "A tedious brief scene of young Pyramus
And his love Thisby; very tragical mirth."
Merry and tragical? Tedious and brief?
That is, hot ice and wondrous strange° snow.
How shall we find the concord of this discord? 60
PHILOSTRATE.   A play there is, my lord, some ten words long,
But by ten words, my lord, it is too long,
Which makes it tedious. For in all the play
There is not one word apt, one player fitted. 65
And tragical, my noble lord, it is,
For Pyramus therein doth kill himself.
Which, when I saw rehears'd, I must confess,
Made mine eyes water, but more merry tears
The passion of loud laughter never shed. 70
THESEUS.   What are they that do play it?
PHILOSTRATE.   Hard-handed men that work in Athens here,
Which never labor'd in their minds till now,
And now have toil'd° their unbreathed° memories
With this same play, against° your nuptial. 75
THESEUS.   And we will hear it.
PHILOSTRATE.   No, my noble lord,
It is not for you. I have heard it over,
And it is nothing, nothing in the world;
Unless you can find sport in their intents,
Extremely stretch'd° and conn'd° with cruel pain, 80
To do you service.
THESEUS.   I will hear that play;
For never anything can be amiss.
When simpleness and duty tender it.
Go, bring them in; and take your places, ladies.

---

47 *kinsman:* Plutarch's *Life of Theseus* states that Hercules and Theseus were near-kinsmen. Theseus is referring to a version of the battle of the Centaurs in which Hercules was said to be present.   48–49 *"The riot . . . rage":* This was the story of the death of Orpheus, as told in *Metamorphoses.*   52–53 *"The thrice . . . beggary":* possibly an allusion to Spenser's *Teares of the Muses* (1591), through "satires" deploring the neglect of learning and the creative arts were commonplace.   55 *sorting with:* befitting.   59 *strange:* seemingly an error for some adjective that would contrast with *snow,* just as *hot* contrasts with *ice.*   74 *toil'd:* taxed.   *unbreathed:* unexercised.   75 *against:* in preparation for.   80 *stretch'd:* strained.   *conn'd:* memorized.

(Philostrate goes to summon the players.)

HIPPOLYTA.   I love not to see wretchedness o'ercharg°d°   85
    And duty in his service° perishing.
THESEUS.   Why gentle sweet, you shall see no such thing.
HIPPOLYTA.   He says they can do nothing in this kind.°
THESEUS.   The kinder we, to give them thanks for nothing.
    Our sport shall be to take what they mistake;   90
    And what poor duty cannot do, noble respect
    Takes it in might, not merit.°
    Where I have come, great clerks° have purposed
    To greet me with premeditated welcomes;
    Where I have seen them shiver and look pale,   95
    Make periods in the midst of sentences,
    Throttle their practic'd accent° in their fears,
    And in conclusion dumbly have broke off,
    Not paying me a welcome. Trust me, sweet,
    Out of this silence yet I pick'd a welcome;   100
    And in the modesty of fearful duty
    I read as much as from the rattling tongue
    Of saucy and audacious eloquence.
    Love, therefore, and tongue-tied simplicity
    In least° speak most, to my capacity.°   105

(Philostrate returns.)

PHILOSTRATE.   So please your Grace, the Prologue° is address'd.°
THESEUS.   Let him approach.   *[Flourish of trumpets.]*

(Enter the Prologue [Quince].)

PROLOGUE.   If we offend, it is with our good will.
    That you should think, we come not to offend,
    But with good will. To show our simple skill,   110
    That is the true beginning of our end.
    Consider, then, we come but in despite.
    We do not come, as minding° to content you,
    Our true intent is. All for your delight
    We are not here. That you should here repent you,   115
    The actors are at hand; and, by their show,
    You shall know all that you are like to know.
THESEUS.   This fellow doth not stand upon points.°
LYSANDER.   He hath rid his prologue like a rough°
    colt; he knows not the stop.° A good moral, my   120

---

85 *wretchedness o'ercharg'd:* incompetence overburdened.   86 *his service:* its attempt to serve.
88 *kind:* kind of thing.   92 *Takes . . . merit:* values it for the effort made rather than for the excellence achieved.   93 *clerks:* learned men.   97 *practic'd accent:* rehearsed speech; or usual
way of speaking.   105 *least:* saying least.   *to my capacity:* in my judgment and undersanding.
106 *Prologue:* speaker   of   the   prologue.   *address'd:* ready.   113 *minding:* intending.
118 *stand upon points:* (1) heed niceties or small points, (2) pay attention to punctuation in his
reading. (The humor of Quince's speech is in the blunders of its punctuation.)   119 *rough:* unbroken.   120 *stop:* (1) the stopping of a colt by reining it in, (2) punctuation mark.

lord: it is not enough to speak, but to speak true.

HIPPOLYTA.   Indeed he hath play'd on his prologue like
a child on a recorder;° a sound, but not in
government.°

THESEUS.   His speech was like a tangled chain, nothing°   125
impair'd, but all disorder'd. Who is next?

(Enter Pyramus and Thisby, and Wall, and Moonshine, and Lion.)

PROLOGUE.   Gentles, perchance you wonder at this show;
But wonder on, till truth make all things plain.
This man is Pyramus, if you would know;
This beauteous lady Thisby is certain.   130
This man, with lime and rough-cast, doth present
Wall, that vile Wall which did these lovers sunder;
And through Wall's chink, poor souls, they are content
To whisper. At the which let no man wonder.
This man, with lantern, dog, and bush of thorn,   135
Presenteth Moonshine; for, if you will know,
By moonshine did these lovers think no scorn°
To meet at Ninus' tomb, there, there to woo.
This grisly beast, which Lion hight° by name,
And trusty Thisby, coming first by night,   140
Did scare away, or rather did affright;
And, as she fled, her mantle she did fall,°
Which Lion vile with bloody mouth did stain.
Anon comes Pyramus, sweet youth and tall,°
And finds his trusty Thisby's mantle slain;   145
Whereat, with blade, with bloody blameful blade,
He bravely broach'd° his boiling bloody breast.
And Thisby, tarrying in mulberry shade,
His dagger drew, and died. For all the rest,
Let Lion, Moonshine, Wall, and lovers twain   150
At large° discourse, while here they do remain.

(Exeunt Lion, Thisby, and Moonshine.)

THESEUS.   I wonder if the lion be to speak.

DEMETRIUS.   No wonder, my lord. One lion may, when many
asses do.

WALL.   In this same interlude it doth befall   155
That I, one Snout by name, present a wall;
And such a wall, as I would have you think,
That had in it a crannied hole or chink,
Through which the lovers, Pyramus and Thisby,
Did whisper often very secretly.   160
This loam, this rough-cast, and this stone doth show
That I am that same wall; the truth is so.

123 *recorder:* a wind instrument like a flute.   124 *government:* control.   125 *nothing:* not at all.
137 *think no scorn:* think it no disgraceful matter.   139 *hight:* is called.   142 *fall:* let
fall.   144 *tall:* courageous.   147 *broach'd:* stabbed.   151 *at large:* in full, at length.

And this the cranny is, right and sinister,°
Through which the fearful lovers are to whisper.
THESEUS. Would you desire lime and hair to speak better?   165
DEMETRIUS. It is the wittiest partition° that ever I heard
    discourse, my lord.   *[Pyramus comes forward.]*
THESEUS. Pyramus draws near the wall. Silence!
PYRAMUS. O grim-look'd° night! O night with hue
    so black!   170
  O night, which ever art when day is not!
  O night, O night! Alack, alack, alack,
  I fear my Thisby's promise is forgot.
  And thou, O wall, O sweet, O lovely wall,
  That stand'st between her father's ground and mine,   175
  Thou wall, O wall, O sweet and lovely wall,
  Show me thy chink, to blink through with mine
    eyne!   *[Wall holds up his fingers.]*
  Thanks, courteous wall. Jove shield thee well for this!
  But what see I? No Thisby do I see.
  O wicked wall, through whom I see no bliss!   180
  Curs'd be thy stones for thus deceiving me!
THESEUS. The wall, methinks, being sensible,° should curse again.
PYRAMUS. No, in truth, sir, he should not. "Deceiving
    me" is Thisby's cue: she is to enter now, and I am   185
    to spy her through the wall. You shall see, it will
    fall pat as I told you. Yonder she comes.

(Enter Thisby.)

THISBY. O wall, full often hast thou heard my moans,
  For parting my fair Pyramus and me.
  My cherry lips have often kiss'd thy stones,   190
  Thy stones with lime and hair knit up in thee.
PYRAMUS. I see a voice. Now will I to the chink,
  To spy an° I can hear my Thisby's face.
  Thisby!
THISBY. My love! Thou art my love, I think.   195
PYRAMUS. Think what thou wilt, I am thy lover's grace;°
  And, like Limander° am I trusty still.
THISBY. And I like Helen,° till the Fates me kill.
PYRAMUS. Not Shafalus° to Procrus° was so true.
THISBY. As Shafalus to Procrus, I to you.   200
PYRAMUS. O, kiss me through the hole of this vile wall!
THISBY. I kiss the wall's hole, not your lips at all.
PYRAMUS. Wilt thou at Ninny's tomb meet me straightway?
THISBY. 'Tide° life, 'tide death, I come without delay.

---

163 *right and sinister:* the right side of it and the left (sinister); or running from right to left, horizontally.   167 *partition:* (1) wall, (2) section of a learned treatise or oration.   170 *grim-look'd:* grim-looking.   182 *sensible:* capable of feeling.   193 *an:* if.   196 *lover's grace:* gracious love.   197 *Limander:* blunder for *Leander.*   198 *Helen:* blunder for *Hero.*   199 *Shafalus, Procrus:* blunders for *Cephalus* and *Procris,* also famous lovers.   204 *'Tide:* betide, come.

(Exeunt Pyramus and Thisby.)

WALL. Thus have I, Wall, my part discharged so;   205
    And, being done, thus Wall away doth go.

(Exit.)

THESEUS. Now is the mural down between the two
    neighbors.
DEMETRIUS. No remedy, my lord, when walls are so
    willful to hear° without warning.°   210
HIPPOLYTA. This is the silliest stuff that ever I heard.
THESEUS. The best in this kind° are but shadows;°
    and the worst are no worse, if imagination amend
    them.
HIPPOLYTA. It must be your imagination then, and not   215
    theirs.
THESEUS. If we imagine no worse of them than they of
    themselves, they may pass for excellent men. Here
    come two noble beasts in, a man and a lion.
    (Enter Lion and Moonshine.)
LION. You, ladies, you, whose gentle hearts do fear   220
    The smallest monstrous mouse that creeps on floor,
    May now perchance both quake and tremble here,
    When lion rough in wildest rage doth roar.
    Then know that I, as Snug the joiner, am
    A lion fell,° nor else no lion's dam;   225
    For, if I should as lion come in strife
    Into this place, 'twere pity on my life.
THESEUS. A very gentle beast, and of a good conscience.
DEMETRIUS. The very best at a beast, my lord, that e'er
    I saw.   230
LYSANDER. This lion is a very fox for his valor.°
THESEUS. True; and a goose for his discretion.°
DEMETRIUS. Not so, my lord; for his valor cannot
    carry his discretion; and the fox carries the goose.
THESEUS. His discretion, I am sure, cannot carry his   235
    valor, for the goose carries not the fox. It is well.
    Leave it to his discretion, and let us listen to the
    moon.
MOON. This lanthorn° doth the horned moon present—
DEMETRIUS. He should have worn the horns on his   240
    head.°

---

210 *to hear:* as to hear. *without warning:* without warning the parents. 212 *in this kind:* of this sort. *shadows:* likenesses, representations. 225 *lion fell:* fierce lion (with a play on the idea of *lion skin*). 231 *is . . . valor:* His valor consists of craftiness and discretion. 232 *goose . . . discretion:* as discreet as a goose, that is, more foolish than discreet. 239 *lanthorn:* This original spelling may suggest a play on the *horn* of which lanterns were made and also on a cuckold's horns; but the spelling *lanthorn* is not used consistently for comic effect in this play or elsewhere. In V. I. 135, for example, the word is *lantern* in the original. 240–41 *on his head:* as a sign of cuckoldry.

THESEUS.   He is no crescent, and his horns are invisible
           within the circumference.
MOON.   This lanthorn doth the horned moon
        present;
   Myself the man i' th' moon do seem to be.   245
THESEUS.   This is the greatest error of all the rest. The
           man should be put into the lanthorn. How is it else
           the man i' th' moon?
DEMETRIUS.   He dares not come there for the° candle;
           for, you see, it is already in snuff.°   250
HIPPOLYTA.   I am aweary of this moon. Would he
           would change!
THESEUS.   It appears, by his small light of discretion,
           that he is in the wane; but yet, in courtesy, in all
           reason, we must stay the time.   255
LYSANDER.   Proceed, Moon.
MOON.   All that I have to say is to tell you that the
        lanthorn is the moon, I, the man in the moon, this
        thorn-bush my thorn-bush, and this dog my dog.
DEMETRIUS.   Why, all these should be in the lanthorn;   260
           for all these are in the moon. But silence! Here
           comes Thisby.

(Enter Thisby.)

THISBY.   This is old Ninny's tomb. Where is my love?
LION *[roaring]*. Oh—

(Thisby runs off.)

DEMETRIUS.   Well roar'd, Lion.   265
THESEUS.   Well run, Thisby.
HIPPOLYTA.   Well shone, Moon. Truly, the moon shines
           with a good grace.

[The Lion shakes Thisby's mantle, and exit.]

THESEUS.   Well mous'd,° Lion.
DEMETRIUS.   And then came Pyramus.   270
LYSANDER.   And so the lion vanish'd.

(Enter Pyramus.)

PYRAMUS.   Sweet Moon, I thank thee for thy sunny beams;
   I thank thee, Moon, for shining now so bright;
   For, by thy gracious, golden, glittering gleams,
   I trust to take of truest Thisby sight.   275
      But stay, O spite!
    But mark, poor knight,
   What dreadful dole° is here!

---

249 *for the:* because of the.   250 *in snuff:* (1) offended, (2) in need of snuffing.   269 *mous'd:*
shaken.   278 *dole:* grievous event.

Eyes, do you see?
How can it be?   280
O dainty duck! O dear!
Thy mantle good,
What, stain'd with blood!
Approach, ye Furies fell!°
O Fates, come, come,   285
Cut thread and thrum;°
Quail,° crush, conclude, and quell!°

THESEUS.   This passion, and the death of a dear friend,
would go near to make a man look sad.°

HIPPOLYTA.   Beshrew my heart, but I pity the man.   290

PYRAMUS.   O wherefore, Nature, didst thou lions frame?
Since lion vile hath here deflow'r'd my dear,
Which is—no, no—which was the fairest dame
That liv'd, that lov'd, that lik'd, that look'd with cheer.°
Come, tears, confound,   295
Out, sword, and wound
The pap of Pyramus;
Ay, that left pap,
Where heart doth hop.   *[Stabs himself.]*
Thus die I, thus, thus, thus.   300
Now am I dead,
Now am I fled;
My soul is in the sky.
Tongue, lose thy light;
Moon, take thy flight.   305

(Exit Moonshine.)

Now die, die, die, die, die.   *[Dies.]*

DEMETRIUS.   No die, but an ace,° for him; for he is but
one.°

LYSANDER.   Less than an ace, man; for he is dead, he is
nothing.   310

THESEUS.   With the help of a surgeon he might yet
recover, and yet prove an ass.°

HIPPOLYTA.   How chance Moonshine is gone before
Thisby comes back and finds her lover?

THESEUS.   She will find him by starlight. Here she
comes; and her passion ends the play.   315

(Enter Thisby.)

HIPPOLYTA.   Methinks she should not use a long one

---

284 *fell:* fierce.   286 *thread and thrum:* the warp in weaving and the loose end of the
warp.   287 *Quail:* overpower.   *quell:* kill, destroy.   288–89 *This . . . sad:* If one had other reason to grieve, one might be sad, but not from this absurd portrayal of passion.   294 *cheer:* countenance.   307 *ace:* The side of the die featuring the single pip, or spot. (The pun is on *die* as a
singular of *dice;* Bottom's performance is not worth a whole *die* but rather one single face of it,
one small portion.)   308 *one:* (1) an individual person, (2) unique.   312 *ass:* with a pun on *ace.*

for such a Pyramus. I hope she will be brief.

DEMETRIUS.   A mote will turn the balance, which Pyramus,
    which° Thisby, is the better: he for a man   320
    God warr'nt us; she for a woman, God bless us.

LYSANDER.   She hath spied him already with those
    sweet eyes.

DEMETRIUS.   And thus she means,° videlicet:°

THISBY.   Asleep, my love?   325
    What, dead, my dove?
    O Pyramus, arise!
        Speak, speak. Quite dumb?
    Dead, dead? A tomb
    Must cover thy sweet eyes.   330
        These lily lips,
        This cherry nose,
    These yellow cowslip cheeks,
        Are gone, are gone!
        Lovers, make moan.   335
    His eyes were green as leeks.
        O Sisters Three,°
        Come, come to me,
    With hands as pale as milk;
        Lay them in gore,   340
        Since you have shore°
    With shears his thread of silk.
        Tongue, not a word.
        Come, trusty sword,
    Come, blade, my breast imbrue!°   *[Stabs herself.]*   345
        And farewell, friends.
        Thus Thisby ends.
    Adieu, adieu, adieu.   *[Dies.]*

THESEUS.   Moonshine and Lion are left to bury the
    dead.   350

DEMETRIUS.   Ay, and Wall too.

BOTTOM *[starting up]*. No, I assure you; the wall is
    down that parted their fathers. Will it please you
    to see the epilogue, or to hear a Bergomask dance°
    between two of our company?   355

THESEUS.   No epilogue, I pray you; for your play needs
    no excuse. Never excuse; for when the players are
    all dead, there need none to be blam'd. Marry, if
    he that writ it had play'd Pyramus and hang'd
    himself in Thisby's garter, it would have been a fine   360
    tragedy; and so it is, truly, and very notably
    discharg'd. But, come, your Bergomask. Let your
    epilogue alone.   *[A dance.]*

319–20 *which . . . which:* whether . . . or.   324 *means:* moans, laments.   *videlicet:* to wit.   337 *Sisters Three:*   the Fates.   *341* shore: shorn.   345 *imbrue:* stain with blood.   354 *Bergomask dance:* a rustic dance named for Bergamo, a province in the state of Venice.

The iron tongue of midnight hath told° twelve.
Lovers, to bed; 'tis almost fairy time.   365
I fear we shall outsleep the coming morn
As much as we this night have overwatch'd.°
This palpable-gross° play hath well beguil'd
The heavy° gait of night. Sweet friends, to bed.
A fortnight hold we this solemnity,   370
In nightly revels and new jollity.

(Exeunt.)

(Enter Puck)

PUCK.   Now the hungry lion roars,
 And the wolf behowls the moon;
Whilst the heavy ploughman snores,
 All with weary task fordone.°   375
Now the wasted brands° do glow,
 Whilst the screech-owl, screeching loud,
Puts the wretch that lies in woe
 In remembrance of a shroud.
Now it is the time of night   380
 That the graves, all gaping wide,
Every one lets forth his sprite,°
 In the churchway paths to glide.
And we fairies, that do run
 By the triple Hecate's° team   385
From the presence of the sun,
 Following darkness like a dream,
Now are frolic.° Not a mouse
Shall disturb this hallowed house.
I am sent with broom before,   390
To sweep the dust behind° the door.

(Enter [Oberon and Titania,] King and Queen of Fairies, with all their train.)

OBERON.   Through the house give glimmering light,
 By the dead and drowsy fire;
Every elf and fairy sprite
 Hop as light as bird from brier;   395
And this ditty, after me,
 Sing, and dance it trippingly.
TITANIA.   First, rehearse your song by rote,
 To each word a warbling note.
Hand in hand, with fairy grace,   400

---

364 *told:* counted, struck ("tolled").   367 *overwatch'd:* stayed up too late.   368 *palpable-gross:* obviously crude.   369 *heavy:* drowsy, dull.   375 *fordone:* exhausted.   376 *wasted brand:* burned-out logs.   382 *Every . . . sprite:* Every grave lets forth its ghost.   385 *triple Hecate's:* Hecate ruled in three capacities: as Luna or Cynthia in heaven, as Diana on earth, and as Proserpina in hell.   388 *frolic:* merry.   391 *behind:* from behind. (Robin Goodfellow was a household spirit who helped good housemaids and punished lazy ones.)

Will we sing, and bless this place.

[Song and dance.]

OBERON.   Now, until the break of day,
Through this house each fairy stray.
To the best bride-bed will we,
Which by us shall blessed be;   405
And the issue there create°
Ever shall be fortunate.
So shall all the couples three
Ever true in loving be;
And the blots of Nature's hand   410
Shall not in their issue stand;
Never mole, hare lip, nor scar,
Nor mark prodigious,° such as are
Despised in nativity,
Shall upon their children be.   415
With this field-dew consecrate,°
Every fairy take his gait,°
And each several° chamber bless,
Through this palace, with sweet peace;
And the owner of its blest   420
Ever shall in safety rest.
Trip away; make no stay;
Meet me all by break of day.

(Exeunt [Oberon, Titania, and train].)

PUCK.   If we shadows have offended,
Think but this, and all is mended,   425
That you have but slumb'red here°
While these visions did appear.
And this weak and idle theme,
No more yielding but° a dream,
Gentles, do not reprehend.   430
If you pardon, we will mend.
And, as I am an honest Puck,
If we have unearned luck
Now to scape the serpent's tongue,°
We will make amends ere long;   435
Else the Puck a liar call.
So, good night unto you all.
Give me your hands,° if we be friends,
And Robin shall restore amends.

(Exit.)

---

406 *create:* created.   413 *prodigious:* monstrous, unnatural.   416 *consecrate:* consecrated.
417 *take his gait:* go his way.   418 *several:* separate.   426 *That . . . here:* that it is a "midsummer
night's dream."   429 *No . . . but:* yielding no more than.   434 *serpent's tongue:* hissing.
438 *Give . . . hands:* applaud.

QUESTIONS FOR CRITICAL READING

1. What is the social station of Egeus in this play? What is the social station of Hermia, Helena, Lysander, and Demetrius? What can you tell about the social structure of Shakespeare's Athens?

2. What is the nature of Hermia's situation in Act I? What are her options if she refuses to honor her father's wishes? Why does her father hold to his views? Does he not love his daughter? Does Hermia do wrong in disobeying her father?

3. In Act I, Scene ii, the "rude mechanicals," Peter Quince and Bottom, are introduced. Are they immediately funny? What is their function at the end of Act I?

4. Act II introduces the fairies. What is the source of disagreement between Oberon and Titania? Who seems to have more power? Titania talks of a boy's mother being a "vot'ress of my order," which implies that the mother treated her as a kind of goddess. Do these fairies resemble gods? Is the fairy world a spiritual world?

5. What problems does Puck provoke for the humans at the end of Act II?

6. What can you tell of the plans of the "mechanicals" at the beginning of Act III? What are the comic elements in their presentation?

7. In Act III, Scene ii, what problems does Puck provoke for Titania? What is the source of the subsequent humor?

8. Why is it funny in Act III, Scene ii, that both Lysander and Demetrius profess love for Hermia? How does Helena react? Does she think it funny? Does Hermia?

9. How are the problems of Hermia resolved in Act IV, Scene i? Is the resolution satisfying?

10. In what ways is the "mechanicals'" play of Pyramus and Thisbe similar to the action of the lovers, Helena, Hermia, Lysander, and Demetrius?

11. How completely do the multiple marriages at the end of the play satisfy your need for a thorough resolution of the action?

QUESTIONS FOR INTERPRETATION

1. An interesting approach to the play could be to examine it for its portrait of love. The play presents love among aristocrats, ordinary mortals, and fairies. It presents love between the very young and the middle-aged. Oberon's demand that Titania hand over the boy she treasures may even imply a "Greek" love, or homosexuality. How does love function in this play, and how does the play help define the idea and the forces of love?

2. Examine the social structure of the play. Because the play is set in ancient Athens, it is not clear that Shakespeare is mimicking the social structure of Elizabethan England. Instead, he has imagined a structure that the play defines as it goes along. How do you see it? What kinds of laws and social expectations seem to dominate the play? Does fate play a role in this play?

3. The story of Pyramus and Thisbe is drawn from Greek myth. It depends on mistaken identity and ends tragically. In *A Midsummer Night's Dream* mistaken identity dominates portions of the play and provides much of the play's amusement. Why is it not tragic in outcome? What is the difference between the primary story of *A Midsummer Night's Dream* and the story of Pyramus and Thisbe?

4. How well do women fare in this play? Can we reasonably suggest that Hermia is the heroine of the drama? How does she fare in relation to Hippolyta and Titania? Is Shakespeare's Athens a man's world?

5. The source of humor concerning the rude mechanicals is their contrast with the social world of Theseus and Hippolyta as well as that of Helena, Hermia, Lysander, and Demetrius. Describe the contrast as carefully as possible and explain why the contrast should produce a sense of comic humor. Is the humor in the scenes in which the mechanicals perform a humor at their expense, or is it a humor that somehow ennobles the mechanicals? How do you feel about Peter Quince, Bottom, Snug, Flute, Snout, and Starveling? Consider the comic value of their names, but also consider the quality of their acting and the nature of their trades.

TRAGICOMEDY

Tragedy usually ends with exile, death, or a similar resolution. Comedy usually ends with a new beginning: a marriage or another chance of some sort. But **tragicomedy** often ends with no clear resolution: the circumstances are so complex that the audience may feel perplexed at the ending. For example, in *"Master Harold"* . . . *and the boys* the ending does not clearly point to a bright future. Although characters and relationships have been permanently changed, it is not absolutely clear that the results implied by this change are entirely hopeful.

Tragicomedy cannot be described in terms of nameable emotions such as pity and fear or ridicule and contempt. Every tragicomedy explores a range of emotions that may include all these and more. Thus the audience response to tragicomedy is usually complex and unsettling. Drama reflects not only the values but also the presumptions and beliefs of the time. Tragicomedy today reflects the modern sense that experience is shaped by forces beyond our control, such as fate, and that life has no convenient or meaningful resolutions.

Some of the qualities of tragicomedy are as follows.

*   Tragicomedy mixes aspects of tragedy with aspects of comedy.
*   Tragicomedy usually begins in seriousness and seems to veer toward the tragic, but is relieved by actions that permit the play to end on a happy or neutral note.
*   Clear resolutions are often not possible in tragicomedy. The complexities of circumstances are such that the audience is left in a form of suspension, often hopeful, but sometimes uncertain of the long-term future of the characters.
*   Some tragicomedies begin comically, almost farcically, and slowly move toward a greater and greater seriousness.
*   Most tragicomedies rely on a single plot.

Modern dramatists whose work seems most concerned with respecting the complexity of modern experience—such as Henrik Ibsen, Tennessee Williams, Irene Fornés, and August Wilson, all of whom appear in this book—avoid convenient and reassuring resolutions. Their plays are tragicomedies and continue to help define the genre.

A MODERN TRAGICOMEDY

Athol Fugard is one of Africa's most important playwrights. His plays include *Boesman and Lena* (1969), *Sizwe Banzi Is Dead* (1972), *A Lesson from Aloes* (1978), and *The Road to Mecca* (1984). In the 1950s and 1960s he worked with interracial theater groups in Johannesburg, South Africa, when such activities were illegal, and there he established a close theatrical relationship with Zakes Mokae, who played Sam in *"Master Harold" . . . and the boys* (1982). Fugard, himself an actor in films and on stage, played opposite Mokae when Fugard's *The Blood Knot* (1961) premiered in Johannesburg. This play concerns two brothers, one black and one white, who meet and discuss their separate conditions. It created a powerful stir in South Africa and toured throughout the world.

Fugard's concern for racial justice is a constant in his work, and his notebooks reveal that Hally in *Master Harold* could have been modeled on his own personal experience. His parents owned a hotel where a waiter named Sam became, says Fugard, "the most significant—the only—friend of my boyhood years." Yet, for reasons that he cannot unravel, Fugard once spat in Sam's face. The shame that overwhelmed him as a result of that willful act of disdain lived with Fugard and may have been the seed from which *Master Harold* grew. Fugard remains committed to undoing the damage apartheid has caused the entire society of South Africa.

"Master Harold" . . . and the boys is a tragicomedy that begins on a comic note and ends on a tragic note. It is not clear how the characters will be able to continue after Hally's racist outburst. In many ways, the circumstances of the play reflect those of modern South Africa.

ATHOL FUGARD   (b. 1932)

"Master Harold" . . . and the boys ————————————————— *1982*

Characters
    Willy
    Sam
    Hally
    (Scene: The St. George's Park Tea Room on a wet and windy Port Elizabeth afternoon.)
    (Tables and chairs have been cleared and are stacked on one side except for one which stands apart with a single chair. On this table a knife, fork, spoon and side plate in anticipation of a simple meal, together with a pile of comic books.)
    (Other elements: a serving counter with a few stale cakes under glass and a not very impressive display of sweets, cigarettes and cool drinks, etc.; a few cardboard advertising handouts—Cadbury's Chocolate, Coca-Cola—and a blackboard on which an untrained hand has chalked up the prices of Tea, Coffee, Scones, Milkshakes—all flavors—and Cool Drinks; a few sad ferns in pots; a telephone; an old-style jukebox.)
    (There is an entrance on one side and an exit into a kitchen on the other.)
    (Leaning on the solitary table, his head cupped in one hand as he pages through one of the comic books, is Sam. A black man in his mid-forties. He wears the white coat

of a waiter. Behind him on his knees, mopping down the floor with a bucket of water and a rag, is Willie. Also black and about the same age as Sam. He has his sleeves and trousers rolled up.)

(The year: 1950.)

WILLIE *(singing as he works).*   "She was scandalizin' my name, she took my money, she called me honey but she was scandalizin' my name. Called it love but was playin' a game. . . ."

(He gets up and moves the bucket. Stands thinking for a moment, then, raising his arms to hold an imaginary partner, he launches into an intricate ballroom dance step. Although a mildly comic figure, he reveals a reasonable degree of accomplishment.)

Hey, Sam.

(Sam, absorbed in the comic book, does not respond.)

Hey, Boet° Sam!

(Sam looks up.)

I'm getting it. The quickstep. Look now and tell me. *(He repeats the step.)* Well?

SAM *(encouragingly).*   Show me again.

WILLIE.   Okay, count for me.

SAM.   Ready?

WILLIE.   Ready.

SAM.   Five, six, seven, eight. . . . *(Willie starts to dance.)* A-n-d one two three four . . . and one two three four. . . . *(Ad libbing as Willie dances.)* Your shoulders, Willie . . . your shoulders! Don't look down! Look happy, Willie! Relax, Willie!

WILLIE *(desperate but still dancing).*   I am relax.

SAM.   No, you're not.

WILLIE *(he falters).*   Ag no man, Sam! Mustn't talk. You make me make mistakes.

SAM.   But you're stiff.

WILLIE.   Yesterday I'm not straight . . . today I'm too stiff!

SAM.   Well, you are. You asked me and I'm telling you.

WILLIE.   Where?

SAM.   Everywhere. Try to glide through it.

WILLIE.   Glide?

SAM.   Ja, make it smooth. And give it more style. It must look like you're enjoying yourself.

WILLIE *(emphatically).*   I wasn't.

SAM.   Exactly.

WILLIE.   How can I enjoy myself? Not straight, too stiff and now it's also glide, give it more style, make it smooth. . . . Haai! Is hard to remember all those things, Boet Sam.

SAM.   That's your trouble. You're trying too hard.

WILLIE.   I try hard because it is hard.

SAM.   But don't let me see it. The secret is to make it look easy. Ballroom must look happy, Willie, not like hard work. It must. . . . Ja! . . . it must look like romance.

WILLIE.   Now another one! What's romance?

SAM.   Love story with happy ending. A handsome man in tails, and in his arms, smiling at him, a beautiful lady in evening dress!

WILLIE.   Fred Astaire, Ginger Rogers.

Boet: brother.

SAM.   You got it. Tapdance or ballroom, it's the same. Romance. In two weeks' time when the judges look at you and Hilda, they must see a man and a woman who are dancing their way to a happy ending. What I saw was you holding her like you were frightened she was going to run away.

WILLIE.   Ja! Because that is what she wants to do! I got no romance left for Hilda anymore, Boet Sam.

SAM.   Then pretend. When you put your arms around Hilda, imagine she is Ginger Rogers.

WILLIE.   With no teeth? You try.

SAM.   Well, just remember, there's only two weeks left.

WILLIE.   I know, I know! *(To the jukebox.)* I do it better with music. You got six-pence for Sarah Vaughan?

SAM.   That's a slow foxtrot. You're practicing the quickstep.

WILLIE.   I'll practice slow foxtrot.

SAM *(shaking his head).*   It's your turn to put money in the jukebox.

WILLIE.   I only got bus fare to go home. *(He returns disconsolately to his work.)* Love story and happy ending! She's doing it all right, Boet Sam, but is not me she's giving happy endings. Fuckin' whore! Three nights now she doesn't come practice. I wind up gramophone, I get record ready and I sit and wait. What happens? Nothing. Ten o'clock I start dancing with my pillow. You try and practice romance by yourself, Boet Sam. Struesgod, she doesn't come tonight I take back my dress and ballroom shoes and I find me new partner. Size twenty-six. Shoes size seven. And now she's also making trouble for me with the baby again. Reports me to Child Wellfed, that I'm not giving her money. She lies! Every week I am giving her money for milk. And how do I know is my baby? Only his hair looks like me. She's fucking around all the time I turn my back. Hilda Samuels is a bitch! *(Pause.)* Hey, Sam!

SAM.   Ja.

WILLIE.   You listening?

SAM.   Ja.

WILLIE.   So what you say?

SAM.   About Hilda?

WILLIE.   Ja.

SAM.   When did you last give her a hiding?

WILLIE *(reluctantly).*   Sunday night.

SAM.   And today is Thursday.

WILLIE *(he knows what's coming).*   Okay.

SAM.   Hiding on Sunday night, then Monday, Tuesday, and Wednesday she doesn't come to practice . . . and you are asking me why?

WILLIE.   I said okay, Boet Sam!

SAM.   You hit her too much. One day she's going to leave you for good.

WILLIE.   So? She makes me the hell-in too much.

SAM *(emphasizing his point).*   Too much and too hard. You had the same trouble with Eunice.

WILLIE.   Because she also make the hell-in, Boet Sam. She never got the steps right. Even the waltz.

SAM.   Beating her up every time she makes a mistake in the waltz? *(Shaking his head.)* No, Willie! That takes the pleasure out of ballroom dancing.

WILLIE.   Hilda is not too bad with the waltz, Boet Sam. Is the quickstep where the trouble starts.

SAM *(teasing him gently).*   How's your pillow with the quickstep?

WILLIE *(ignoring the tease).*   Good! And why? Because it got no legs. That's her trouble. She can't move them quick enough, Boet Sam. I start the record and before halfway Count Basie is already winning. Only time we catch up with him is when gramophone runs down. *(Sam laughs.)* Haaikona, Boet Sam, is not funny.

SAM *(snapping his fingers).*   I got it! Give her a handicap.

WILLIE.   What's that?

SAM.   Give her a ten-second start and then let Count Basie go. Then I put my money on her. Hot favorite in the Ballroom Stakes: Hilda Samuels ridden by Willie Malopo.

WILLIE *(turning away).*   I'm not talking to you no more.

SAM *(relenting).*   Sorry, Willie. . . .

WILLIE.   It's finish between us.

SAM.   Okay, okay . . . I'll stop.

WILLIE.   You can also fuck off.

SAM.   Willie, listen! I want to help you!

WILLIE.   No more jokes?

SAM.   I promise.

WILLIE.   Okay. Help me.

SAM *(his turn to hold an imaginary partner).*   Look and learn. Feet together. Back straight. Body relaxed. Right hand placed gently in the small of her back and wait for the music. Don't start worrying about making mistakes or the judges or the other competitors. It's just you, Hilda and the music, and you're going to have a good time. What Count Basie do you play?

WILLIE.   "You the cream in my coffee, you the salt in my stew."

SAM.   Right. Give it to me in strict tempo.

WILLIE.   Ready?

SAM.   Ready.

WILLIE.   A-n-d . . . *(Singing.)* "You the cream in my coffee. You the salt in my stew. You will always be my necessity. I'd be lost without you. . . ." *(etc.)*

(Sam launches into the quickstep. He is obviously a much more accomplished dancer than Willie. Hally enters. A seventeen-year-old white boy. Wet raincoat and school case. He stops and watches Sam. The demonstration comes to an end with a flourish. Applause from Hally and Willie.)

HALLY.   Bravo! No question about it. First place goes to Mr. Sam Semela.

WILLIE *(in total agreement).*   You was gliding with style, Boet Sam.

HALLY *(cheerfully).*   How's it, chaps?

SAM.   Okay, Hally.

WILLIE *(springing to attention like a soldier and saluting).*   At your service, Master Harold!

HALLY.   Not long to the big event, hey!

SAM.   Two weeks.

HALLY.   You nervous?

SAM.   No.

HALLY.   Think you stand a chance?

SAM.   Let's just say I'm ready to go out there and dance.

HALLY.   It looked like it. What about you, Willie?

(Willie groans.)

What's the matter?

SAM.   He's got leg trouble.

HALLY *(innocently)*.   Oh, sorry to hear that, Willie.

WILLIE.   Boet Sam! You promised. *(Willie returns to his work.)*

(Hally deposits his school case and takes off his raincoat. His clothes are a little neglected and untidy: black blazer with school badge, gray flannel trousers in need of an ironing, khaki shirt and tie, black shoes. Sam has fetched a towel for Hally to dry his hair.)

HALLY.   God, what a lousy bloody day. It's coming down cats and dogs out there. Bad for business, chaps. . . . *(Conspiratorial whisper.)* . . . but it also means we're in for a nice quiet afternoon.

SAM.   You can speak loud. Your Mom's not here.

HALLY.   Out shopping?

SAM.   No. The hospital.

HALLY.   But it's Thursday. There's no visiting on Thursday afternoons. Is my Dad okay?

SAM.   Sounds like it. In fact, I think he's going home.

HALLY *(stopped short by Sam's remark)*.   What do you mean?

SAM.   The hospital phoned.

HALLY.   To say what?

SAM.   I don't know. I just heard your Mom talking.

HALLY.   So what makes you say he's going home?

SAM.   It sounded as if they were telling her to come and fetch him.

(Hally thinks about what Sam has said for a few seconds.)

HALLY.   When did she leave?

SAM.   About an hour ago. She said she would phone you. Want to eat?

(Hally doesn't respond.)

Hally, want your lunch?

HALLY.   I suppose so. *(His mood has changed.)* What's on the menu? . . . as if I don't know.

SAM.   Soup, followed by meat pie and gravy.

HALLY.   Today's?

SAM.   No.

HALLY.   And the soup?

SAM.   Nourishing pea soup.

HALLY.   Just the soup. *(The pile of comic books on the table.)* And these?

SAM.   For your Dad. Mr. Kempston brought them.

HALLY.   You haven't been reading them, have you?

SAM.   Just looking.

HALLY *(examining the comics)*.   Jungle Jim . . . Batman and Robin . . . Tarzan . . . God, what rubbish! Mental pollution. Take them away.

(Sam exits waltzing into the kitchen. Hally turns to Willie.)

HALLY.   Did you hear my Mom talking on the telephone, Willie?

WILLIE.   No, Master Hally. I was at the back.

HALLY.   And she didn't say anything to you before she left?

WILLIE.   She said I must clean the floors.

HALLY.   I mean about my Dad.

WILLIE.   She didn't say nothing to me about him, Master Hally.

HALLY *(with conviction).*   No! It can't be. They said he needed at least another three weeks of treatment. Sam's definitely made a mistake. *(Rummages through his school case, finds a book and settles down at the table to read.)* So, Willie!

WILLIE.   Yes, Master Hally! Schooling okay today?

HALLY.   Yes, okay . . . . *(He thinks about it.)* . . . No, not really. Ag, what's the difference? I don't care. And Sam says you've got problems.

WILLIE.   Big problems.

HALLY.   Which leg is sore?

(Willie groans.)

Both legs.

WILLIE.   There is nothing wrong with my legs. Sam is just making jokes.

HALLY.   So then you will be in the competition.

WILLIE.   Only if I can find a partner.

HALLY.   But what about Hilda?

SAM *(returning with a bowl of soup).*   She's the one who's got trouble with her legs.

HALLY.   What sort of trouble, Willie?

SAM.   From the way he describes it, I think the lady has gone a bit lame.

HALLY.   Good God! Have you taken her to see a doctor?

SAM.   I think a vet would be better.

HALLY.   What do you mean?

SAM.   What do you call it again when a racehorse goes very fast?

HALLY.   Gallop?

SAM.   That's it!

WILLIE.   Boet Sam!

HALLY.   "A gallop down the homestretch to the winning post." But what's that got to do with Hilda?

SAM.   Count Basie always gets there first.

(Willie lets fly with his slop rag. It misses Sam and hits Hally.)

HALLY *(furious).*   For Christ's sake, Willie! What the hell do you think you're doing?

WILLIE.   Sorry, Master Hally, but it's him. . . .

HALLY.   Act your bloody age! *(Hurls the rag back at Willie.)* Cut out the nonsense now and get on with your work. And you too, Sam. Stop fooling around.

(Sam moves away.)

No. Hang on. I haven't finished! Tell me exactly what my Mom said.

SAM.   I have. "When Hally comes, tell him I've gone to the hospital and I'll phone him."

HALLY.   She didn't say anything about taking my Dad home?

SAM.   No. It's just that when she was talking on the phone. . . .

HALLY *(interrupting him).*   No, Sam. They can't be discharging him. She would have said so if they were. In any case, we saw him last night and he wasn't in good shape at all. Staff nurse even said there was talk about taking more X-rays. And now suddenly today he's better? If anything, it sounds more like a bad turn to me . . . which I sincerely hope it isn't. Hang on . . . how long ago did you say she left?

SAM.   Just before two . . . *(his wrist watch)* . . . hour and a half.

HALLY.   I know how to settle it. *(Behind the counter to the telephone. Talking as he dials.)* Let's give her ten minutes to get to the hospital, ten minutes to load him up, another ten, at the most, to get home, and another ten to get him inside. Forty minutes. They should have been home for at least half an hour already. *(Pause—he waits with the receiver to his ear.)* No reply, chaps. And you know why? Because she's at his bedside in hospital helping him pull through a bad turn. You definitely heard wrong.

SAM.   Okay.

(As far as Hally is concerned, the matter is settled. He returns to his table, sits down, and divides his attention between the book and his soup. Sam is at his school case and picks up a textbook.)

Modern Graded Mathematics for Standards Nine and Ten. (Opens it at random and laughs at something he sees.) Who is this supposed to be?

HALLY.   Old fart-face Prentice.

SAM.   Teacher?

HALLY.   Thinks he is. And believe me, that is not a bad likeness.

SAM.   Has he seen it?

HALLY.   Yes.

SAM.   What did he say?

HALLY.   Tried to be clever, as usual. Said I was no Leonardo da Vinci and that bad art had to be punished. So, six of the best, and his are bloody good.

SAM.   On your bum?

HALLY.   Where else? The days when I got them on my hands are gone forever, Sam.

SAM.   With your trousers down!

HALLY.   No. He's not quite that barbaric.

SAM.   That's the way they do it in jail.

HALLY *(flicker of morbid interest).*   Really?

SAM.   Ja. When the magistrate sentences you to "strokes with a light cane."

HALLY.   Go on.

SAM.   They make you lie down on a bench. One policeman pulls down your trousers and holds your ankles, another one pulls your shirt over your head and holds your arms. . . .

HALLY.   Thank you! That's enough.

SAM.   . . . and the one that gives you the strokes talks to you gently and for a long time between each one. *(He laughs.)*

HALLY.   I've heard enough, Sam! Jesus! It's a bloody awful world when you come to think of it. People can be real bastards.

SAM.   That's the way it is, Hally.

HALLY.   It doesn't *have* to be that way. There is something called progress, you know. We don't exactly burn people at the stake anymore.

SAM.   Like Joan of Arc.

HALLY.   Correct. If she was captured today, she'd be given a fair trial.

SAM.   And then the death sentence.

HALLY *(a world-weary sigh).*   I know, I know! I oscillate between hope and despair for this world as well, Sam. But things will change, you wait and see. One day somebody is going to get up and give history a kick up the backside and get it going again.

SAM.   Like who?

HALLY *(after thought).*   They're called social reformers. Every age, Sam, has got its social reformer. My history book is full of them.

SAM.   So where's ours?

HALLY.   Good question. And I hate to say it, but the answer is. I don't know. Maybe he hasn't even been born yet. Or is still only a babe in arms at his mother's breast. God, what a thought.

SAM.   So we just go on waiting.

HALLY.   Ja, looks like it. *(Back to his soup and the book.)*

SAM *(reading from the textbook)*.   "Introduction: In some mathematical problems only the magnitude. . . ." *(He mispronounces the word "magnitude.")*

HALLY *(correcting him without looking up)*.   Magnitude.

SAM.   What's it mean?

HALLY.   How big it is. The size of the thing.

SAM *(reading)*.   ". . . magnitude of the quantities is of importance. In other problems we need to know whether these quantities are negative or positive. For example, whether there is a debit or credit bank balance . . ."

HALLY.   Whether you're broke or not.

SAM.   ". . . whether the temperature is above or below Zero. . . ."

HALLY.   Naught degrees. Cheerful state of affairs! No cash and you're freezing to death. Mathematics won't get you out of that one.

SAM.   "All these quantities are called . . ." *(spelling the word)* . . . s-c-a-l. . . .

HALLY.   Scalars.

SAM.   Scalars! *(Shaking his head with a laugh.)* You understand all that?

HALLY *(turning a page)*.   No. And I don't intend to try.

SAM.   So what happens when the exams come?

HALLY.   Failing a maths exam isn't the end of the world, Sam. How many times have I told you that examination results don't measure intelligence?

SAM.   I would say about as many times as you've failed one of them.

HALLY *(mirthlessly)*.   Ha, ha, ha.

SAM *(simultaneously)*.   Ha, ha, ha.

HALLY.   Just remember Winston Churchill didn't do particularly well at school.

SAM.   You've also told me that one many times.

HALLY.   Well, it just so happens to be the truth.

SAM *(enjoying the word)*.   Magnitude! Magnitude! Show me how to use it.

HALLY *(after thought)*.   An intrepid social reformer will not be daunted by the magnitude of the task he has undertaken.

SAM *(impressed)*.   Couple of jaw-breakers in there!

HALLY.   I gave you three for the price of one. Intrepid, daunted, and magnitude. I did that once in an exam. Put five of the words I had to explain in one sentence. It was half a page long.

SAM.   Well, I'll put my money on you in the English exam.

HALLY.   Piece of cake. Eighty percent without even trying.

SAM *(another textbook from Hally's case)*.   And history?

HALLY.   So-so. I'll scrape through. In the fifties if I'm lucky.

SAM.   You didn't do too badly last year.

HALLY.   Because we had World War One. That at least has some action. You try to find that in the South African Parliamentary system.

SAM *(reading from the history textbook)*.   "Napoleon and the principle of equality." Hey! This sounds interesting. "After concluding peace with Britain in 1802, Napoleon used a brief period of calm to in-sti-tute . . ."

HALLY.   Introduce.

SAM.   ". . . many reforms. Napoleon regarded all people as equal before the law and wanted them to have equal opportunities for advancement. All ves-ti-ges of the feudal sys-tem with its oppression of the poor were abol-ished." Vestiges, feudal system, and abolished. I'm all right on oppression.

HALLY.   I'm thinking. He swept away . . . abolished . . . the last remains . . . vestiges . . . of the bad old days . . . feudal system.

SAM.   Ha! There's the social reformer we're waiting for. He sounds like a man of some magnitude.

HALLY.   I'm not so sure about that. It's a damn good title for a book, though. A man of magnitude!

SAM.   He sounds pretty big to me, Hally.

HALLY.   Don't confuse historical significance with greatness. But maybe I'm being a bit prejudiced. Have a look in there and you'll see he's two chapters long. And hell! . . . has he only got dates, Sam, all of which you've got to remember! This campaign and that campaign, and then, because of all the fighting, the next thing is we get Peace Treaties all over the place. And what's the end of the story? Battle of Waterloo, which he loses. Wasn't worth it. No, I don't know about him as a man of magnitude.

SAM.   Then who would you say was?

HALLY.   To answer that, we need a definition of greatness, and I suppose that would be somebody who . . . somebody who benefited all mankind.

SAM.   Right. But like who?

HALLY.   *(he speaks with total conviction):* Charles Darwin. Remember him? That big book from the library. *The Origin of the Species.*

SAM.   Him?

HALLY.   Yes. For his Theory of Evolution.

SAM.   You didn't finish it.

HALLY.   I ran out of time. I didn't finish it because my two weeks was up. But I'm going to take it out again after I've digested what I read. It's safe. I've hidden it away in the Theology section. Nobody ever goes in there. And anyway who are you to talk? You hardly even looked at it.

SAM.   I tried. I looked at the chapters in the beginning and I saw one called "The Struggle for an Existence." Ah ha, I thought. At last! But what did I get? Something called the mistiltoe which needs the apple tree and there's too many seeds and all are going to die except one . . . ! No, Hally.

HALLY *(intellectually outraged).*   What do you mean, No! The poor man had to start somewhere. For God's sake, Sam, he revolutionized science. Now we know.

SAM.   What?

HALLY.   Where we come from and what it all means.

SAM.   And that's a benefit to mankind? Anyway, I still don't believe it.

HALLY.   God, you're impossible. I showed it to you in black and white.

SAM.   Doesn't mean I got to believe it.

HALLY.   It's the likes of you that kept the Inquisition in business. It's called bigotry. Anyway, that's my man of magnitude. Charles Darwin! Who's yours?

SAM *(without hesitation).*   Abraham Lincoln.

HALLY.   I might have guessed as much. Don't get sentimental, Sam. You've never been a slave, you know. And anyway we freed your ancestors here in South Africa long before the Americans. But if you want to thank somebody on their behalf, do it to Mr. William Wilberforce.° Come on. Try again. I want a real genius.

(Now enjoying himself, and so is Sam. Hally goes behind the counter and helps himself to a chocolate.)

Mr. William Wilberforce (1759–1833): British statesman who supported a bill outlawing the slave trade and suppressing slavery in the British Empire.

SAM.   William Shakespeare.

HALLY *(no enthusiasm)*.   Oh. So you're also one of them, are you? You're basing that opinion on only one play, you know. You've only read my *Julius Caesar* and even I don't understand half of what they're talking about. They should do what they did with the old Bible: bring the language up to date.

SAM.   That's all you've got. It's also the only one you've read.

HALLY.   I know. I admit it. That's why I suggest we reserve our judgment until we've checked up on a few others. I've got a feeling, though, that by the end of this year one is going to be enough for me, and I can give you the names of twenty-nine other chaps in the Standard Nine class of the Port Elizabeth Technical College who feel the same. But if you want him, you can have him. My turn now. *(Pacing.)* This is a damned good exercise, you know! It started off looking like a simple question and here it's got us really probing into the intellectual heritage of our civilization.

SAM.   So who is it going to be?

HALLY.   My next man . . . and he gets the title on two scores: social reform and literary genius . . . is Leo Nikolaevich Tolstoy.

SAM.   That Russian.

HALLY.   Correct. Remember the picture of him I showed you?

SAM.   With the long beard.

HALLY *(Trying to look like Tolstoy)*.   And those burning, visionary eyes. My God, the face of a social prophet if ever I saw one! And remember my words when I showed it to you? Here's a man, Sam!

SAM.   Those were words, Hally.

HALLY.   Not many intellectuals are prepared to shovel manure with the peasants and then go home and write a "little book" called *War and Peace*. Incidentally, Sam, he was somebody else who, to quote, ". . . did not distinguish himself scholastically."

SAM.   Meaning?

HALLY.   He was also no good at school.

SAM.   Like you and Winston Churchill.

HALLY *(mirthlessly)*.   Ha, ha, ha.

SAM *(simultaneously)*.   Ha, ha, ha.

HALLY.   Don't get clever, Sam. That man freed his serfs of his own free will.

SAM.   No argument. He was a somebody, all right. I accept him.

HALLY.   I'm sure Count Tolstoy will be very pleased to hear that. Your turn. Shoot. *(Another chocolate from behind the counter.)* I'm waiting, Sam.

SAM.   I've got him.

HALLY.   Good. Submit your candidate for examination.

SAM.   Jesus.

HALLY *(stopped dead in his tracks)*.   Who?

SAM.   Jesus Christ.

HALLY.   Oh, come on, Sam!

SAM.   The Messiah.

HALLY.   Ja, but still . . . No, Sam. Don't let's get started on religion. We'll just spend the whole afternoon arguing again. Suppose I turn around and say Mohammed?

SAM.   All right.

HALLY.   All right.

HALLY.   You can't have them both on the same list!

SAM.   Why not? You like Mohammed, I like Jesus.

HALLY.   I *don't* like Mohammed. I never have. I was merely being hypothetical. As far as I'm concerned, the Koran is as bad as the Bible. No. Religion is out! I'm not going to waste my time again arguing with you about the existence of God. You know perfectly well I'm an atheist . . . and I've got homework to do.

SAM.   Okay, I take him back.

HALLY.   You've got time for one more name.

SAM *(after thought)*.   I've got one I know we'll agree on. A simple straightforward great Man of Magnitude . . . and no arguments. And *he* really *did* benefit all mankind.

HALLY.   I wonder. After your last contribution I'm beginning to doubt whether anything in the way of an intellectual agreement is possible between the two of us. Who is he?

SAM.   Guess.

HALLY.   Socrates? Alexandre Dumas? Karl Marx, Dostoevsky? Nietzsche?

(Sam shakes his head after each name.)

Give me a clue.

SAM.   The letter *P* is important. . . .

HALLY.   Plato!

SAM.   . . . and his name begins with an *F*.

HALLY.   I've got it. Freud and Psychology.

SAM.   No. I didn't understand him.

HALLY.   That makes two of us.

SAM.   Think of moldy apricot jam.

HALLY *(after a delighted laugh)*.   Penicillin and Sir Alexander Fleming! And the title of the book: *The Microbe Hunters. (Delighted.)* Splendid, Sam! Splendid. For once we are in total agreement. The major breakthrough in medical science in the Twentieth Century. If it wasn't for him, we might have lost the Second World War. It's deeply gratifying, Sam, to know that I haven't been wasting my time in talking to you. *(Strutting around proudly.)* Tolstoy may have educated his peasants, but I've educated you.

SAM.   Standard Four to Standard Nine.

HALLY.   Have we been at it as long as that?

SAM.   Yep. And my first lesson was geography.

HALLY *(intrigued)*.   Really? I don't remember.

SAM.   My room there at the back of the old Jubilee Boarding House. I had just started working for your Mom. Little boy in short trousers walks in one afternoon and asks me seriously: "Sam, do you want to see South Africa?" Hey man! Sure I wanted to see South Africa!

HALLY.   Was that me?

SAM.   . . . So the next thing I'm looking at a map you had just done for homework. It was your first one and you were very proud of yourself.

HALLY.   Go on.

SAM.   Then came my first lesson. "Repeat after me, Sam: Gold in the Transvaal, mealies° in the Free State, sugar in Natal, and grapes in the Cape." I still know it!

HALLY.   Well, I'll be buggered. So that's how it all started.

SAM.   And your next map was one with all the rivers and the mountains they came from. The Orange, the Vaal, the Limpopo, the Zambezi. . . .

---

mealies: corn.

HALLY.   You've got a phenomenal memory!

SAM.   You should be grateful. That is why you started passing your exams. You tried to be better than me.

(They laugh together. Willie is attracted by the laughter and joins them.)

HALLY.   The old Jubilee Boarding House. Sixteen rooms with board and lodging, rent in advance and one week's notice. I haven't thought about it for donkey's years . . . and I don't think that's an accident. God, was I glad when we sold it and moved out. Those years are not remembered as the happiest ones of an unhappy childhood.

WILLIE *(knocking on the table and trying to imitate a woman's voice)*.   "Hally, are you there?"

HALLY.   Who's that supposed to be?

WILLIE.   "What you doing in there, Hally? Come out at once!"

HALLY *(to Sam)*.   What's he talking about?

SAM.   Don't you remember?

WILLIE.   "Sam, Willie . . . is he in there with you boys?"

SAM.   Hiding away in our room when your mother was looking for you.

HALLY *(another good laugh)*.   Of course! I used to crawl and hide under your bed! But finish the story, Willie. Then what used to happen? You chaps would give the game away by telling her I was in there with you. So much for friendship.

SAM.   We couldn't lie to her. She knew.

HALLY.   Which meant I got another rowing for hanging around the "servants' quarters." I think I spent more time in there with you chaps than anywhere else in that dump. And do you blame me? Nothing but bloody misery wherever you went. Somebody was always complaining about the food, or my mother was having a fight with Micky Nash because she'd caught her with a petty officer in her room. Maud Meiring was another one. Remember those two? They were prostitutes, you know. Soldiers and sailors from the troopships. Bottom fell out of the business when the war ended. God, the flotsam and jetsam that life washed up on our shores! No joking, if it wasn't for your room, I would have been the first certified ten-year-old in medical history. Ja, the memories are coming back now. Walking home from school and thinking: "What can I do this afternoon?" Try out a few ideas, but sooner or later I'd end up in there with you fellows. I bet you I could still find my way to your room with my eyes closed. *(He does exactly that.)* Down the corridor . . . telephone on the right, which my Mom keeps locked because somebody is using it on the sly and not paying . . . past the kitchen and unappetizing cooking smells . . . around the corner into the backyard, hold my breath again because there are more smells coming when I pass your lavatory, then into that little passageway, first door on the right and into your room. How's that?

SAM.   Good. But, as usual, you forgot to knock.

HALLY.   Like that time I barged in and caught you and Cynthia . . . at it. Remember? God, was I embarrassed! I didn't know what was going on at first.

SAM.   Ja, that taught you a lesson.

HALLY.   And about a lot more than knocking on doors, I'll have you know, and I don't mean geography either. Hell, Sam, couldn't you have waited until it was dark?

SAM.   No.

HALLY.   Was it that urgent?

SAM.   Yes, and if you don't believe me, wait until your time comes.

HALLY.   No, thank you. I am not interested in girls. *(Back to his memories. . . . Using a few chairs he re-creates the room as he lists the items.)* A gray little room with a cold cement floor. Your bed against that wall . . . and I now know why the mattress sags so much! . . . Willie's bed . . . it's propped up on bricks because one leg is broken . . . that wobbly little table with the washbasin and jug of water . . . Yes! . . . stuck to the wall above it are some pin-up pictures from magazines. Joe Louis. . . .

WILLIE.   Brown Bomber. World Title. *(Boxing pose.)* Three rounds and knockout.

HALLY.   Against who?

SAM.   Max Schmeling.

HALLY.   Correct. I can also remember Fred Astaire and Ginger Rogers, and Rita Hayworth in a bathing costume which always made me hot and bothered when I looked at it. Under Willie's bed is an old suitcase with all his clothes in a mess, which is why I never hide there. Your things are neat and tidy in a trunk next to your bed, and on it there is a picture of you and Cynthia in your ballroom clothes, your first silver cup for third place in a competition and an old radio which doesn't work anymore. Have I left out anything?

SAM.   No.

HALLY.   Right, so much for the stage directions. Now the characters. *(Sam and Willie move to their appropriate positions in the bedroom.)* Willie is in bed, under his blankets with his clothes on, complaining nonstop about something, but we can't make out a word of what he's saying because he's got his head under the blankets as well. You're on your bed trimming your toenails with a knife—not a very edifying sight—and as for me. . . . What am I doing?

SAM.   You're sitting on the floor giving Willie a lecture about being a good loser while you get the checkerboard and pieces ready for a game. Then you go to Willie's bed, pull off the blankets and make him play with you first because you know you're going to win, and that gives you the second game with me.

HALLY.   And you certainly were a bad loser, Willie!

WILLIE.   Haai!

HALLY.   Wasn't he, Sam? And so slow! A game with you almost took the whole afternoon. Thank God I gave up trying to teach you how to play chess.

WILLIE.   You and Sam cheated.

HALLY.   I never saw Sam cheat, and mine were mostly the mistakes of youth.

WILLIE.   Then how is it you two was always winning?

HALLY.   Have you ever considered the possibility, Willie, that it was because we were better than you?

WILLIE.   Every time better?

HALLY.   Not every time. There were occasions when we deliberately let you win a game so that you would stop sulking and go on playing with us. Sam used to wink at me when you weren't looking to show me it was time to let you win.

WILLIE.   So then you two didn't play fair.

HALLY.   It was for your benefit, Mr. Malopo, which is more than being fair. It was an act of self-sacrifice. *(To Sam.)* But you know what my best memory is, don't you?

SAM.   No.

HALLY.   Come on, guess. If your memory is so good, you must remember it as well.

SAM.   We got up to a lot of tricks in there, Hally.

HALLY.   This one was special, Sam.

SAM.   I'm listening.

HALLY.   It started off looking like another of those useless nothing-to-do afternoons. I'd already been down to Main Street looking for adventure, but nothing had happened. I didn't feel like climbing trees in the Donkin Park or pretending I was a private eye and following a stranger . . . so as usual: See what's cooking in Sam's room. This time it was you on the floor. You had two thin pieces of wood and you were smoothing them down with a knife. It didn't look particularly interesting, but when I asked you what you were doing, you just said, "Wait and see, Hally. Wait . . . and see" . . . in that secret sort of way of yours, so I knew there was a surprise coming. You teased me, you bugger, by being deliberately slow and not answering my questions!

(Sam laughs.)

And whistling while you worked away! God, it was infuriating! I could have brained you! It was only when you tied them together in a cross and put that down on the brown paper that I realized what you were doing. "Sam is making a kite?" And when I asked you and you said "Yes" . . . ! *(Shaking his head with disbelief.)* The sheer audacity of it took my breath away. I mean, seriously, what the hell does a black man know about flying a kite? I'll be honest with you, Sam, I had no hopes for it. If you think I was excited and happy, you got another guess coming. In fact, I was shit-scared that we were going to make fools of ourselves. When we left the boarding house to go up onto the hill, I was praying quietly that there wouldn't be any other kids around to laugh at us.

SAM *(enjoying the memory as much as Hally).*   Ja, I could see that.

HALLY.   I made it obvious, did I?

SAM.   Ja. You refused to carry it.

HALLY.   Do you blame me? Can you remember what the poor thing looked like? Tomato-box wood and brown paper! Flour and water for glue! Two of my mother's old stockings for a tail, and then all those bits and pieces of string you made me tie together so that we could fly it! Hell, no, that was now only asking for a miracle to happen.

SAM.   Then the big argument when I told you to hold the string and run with it when I let go.

HALLY.   I was prepared to run, all right, but straight back to the boarding house.

SAM *(knowing what's coming).*   So what happened?

HALLY.   Come on, Sam, you remember as well as I do.

SAM.   I want to hear it from you.

(Hally pauses. He wants to be as accurate as possible.)

HALLY.   You went a little distance from me down the hill, you held it up ready to let it go. . . . "This is it," I thought. "Like everything else in my life, here comes another fiasco." Then you shouted, "Go, Hally!" and I started to run. *(Another pause.)* I don't know how to describe it, Sam. Ja! The miracle happened! I was running, waiting for it to crash to the ground, but instead suddenly there was something alive behind me at the end of the string, tugging at it as if it wanted to be free. I looked back . . . *(Shakes his head.)* . . . I still can't believe my eyes. It was flying! Looping around and trying to climb even higher into the sky. You shouted to me to let it have more string. I did, until there was none left and I was just holding that piece of wood we had tied it to. You came up and joined me. You were laughing.

SAM.   So were you. And shouting, "It works, Sam! We've done it!"

HALLY.   And we had! I was so proud of us! It was the most splendid thing I had ever seen. I wished there were hundreds of kids around to watch us. The part that scared me, though, was when you showed me how to make it dive down to the ground and then just when it was on the point of crashing, swoop up again!

SAM.   You didn't want to try yourself.

HALLY.   Of course not! I would have been suicidal if anything had happened to it. Watching you do it made me nervous enough. I was quite happy just to see it up there with its tail fluttering behind it. You left me after that, didn't you? You explained how to get it down, we tied it to the bench so that I could sit and watch it, and you went away. I wanted you to stay, you know. I was a little scared of having to look after it by myself.

SAM *(quietly).*   I had work to do, Hally.

HALLY.   It was sort of sad bringing it down, Sam. And it looked sad again when it was lying there on the ground. Like something that had lost its soul. Just tomato-box wood, brown paper and two of my mother's old stockings! But, hell, I'll never forget that first moment when I saw it up there. I had a stiff neck the next day from looking up so much.

(Sam laughs. Hally turns to him with a question he never thought of asking before.)

Why did you make that kite, Sam?

SAM *(evenly).*   I can't remember.

HALLY.   Truly?

SAM.   Too long ago, Hally.

HALLY.   Ja, I suppose it was. It's time for another one, you know.

SAM.   Why do you say that?

HALLY.   Because it feels like that. Wouldn't be a good day to fly it, though.

SAM.   No. You can't fly kites on rainy days.

HALLY *(he studies Sam. Their memories have made him conscious of the man's presence in his life).*   How old are you, Sam?

SAM.   Two score and five.

HALLY.   Strange, isn't it?

SAM.   What?

HALLY.   Me and you.

SAM.   What's strange about it?

HALLY.   Little white boy in short trousers and a black man old enough to be his father flying a kite. It's not every day you see that.

SAM.   But why strange? Because the one is white and the other black?

HALLY.   I don't know. Would have been just as strange, I suppose, if it had been me and my Dad . . . cripple man and a little boy! Nope! There's no chance of me flying a kite without it being strange. *(Simple statement of fact—no self-pity.)* There's a nice little short story there. "The Kite-Flyers." But we'd have to find a twist in the ending.

SAM.   Twist?

HALLY.   Yes. Something unexpected. The way it ended with us was too straightforward . . . me on the bench and you going back to work. There's no drama in that.

WILLIE.   And me?

HALLY.   You?

WILLIE.   Yes me.

HALLY.   You want to get into the story as well, do you? I got it! Change the title: "Afternoons in Sam's Room" . . . expand it and tell all the stories. It's on its way to being a novel. Our days in the old Jubilee. Sad in a way that they're over. I almost wish we were still in that little room.

SAM.   We're still together.

HALLY.   That's true. It's just that life felt the right size in there . . . not too big and not too small. Wasn't so hard to work up a bit of courage. It's got so bloody complicated since then.

(The telephone rings. Sam answers it.)

SAM.   St. George's Park Tea Room . . . Hello, Madam. . . Yes, Madam, he's here. . . . Hally, it's your mother.

HALLY.   Where is she phoning from?

SAM.   Sounds like the hospital. It's a public telephone.

HALLY *(relieved).*   You see! I told you. *(The telephone.)* Hello, Mom . . . Yes . . . Yes no fine. Everything's under control here. How's things with poor old Dad? . . . Has he had a bad turn? . . . What? . . . Oh, God! . . . Yes, Sam told me, but I was sure he'd made a mistake. But what's this all about, Mom? He didn't look at all good last night. How can he get better so quickly? . . . Then very obviously you must say no. Be firm with him. You're the boss. . . . You know what it's going to be like if he comes home. . . . Well then, don't blame me when I fail my exams at the end of the year. . . . Yes! How am I expected to be fresh for school when I spend half the night massaging his gammy leg? . . . So am I! . . . So tell him a white lie. Say Dr. Colley wants more X-rays of his stump. Or bribe him. We'll sneak in double tots of brandy in future. . . . What? . . . Order him to get back into bed at once! If he's going to behave like a child, treat him like one. . . . All right, Mom! I was just trying to . . . I'm sorry. . . . I said I'm sorry. . . . Quick, give me your number. I'll phone you back. *(He hangs up and waits a few seconds.)* Here we go again! *(He dials.)* I'm sorry, Mom. . . . Okay. . . . But now listen to me carefully. All it needs is for you to put your foot down. Don't take no for an answer. . . . Did you hear me? And whatever you do, don't discuss it with him. . . . Because I'm frightened you'll give in to him. . . . Yes, Sam gave me lunch. . . . I ate all of it! . . . No, Mom, not a soul. It's still raining here. . . . Right, I'll tell them. I'll just do some homework and then lock up. . . . But remember now, Mom. Don't listen to anything he says. And phone me back and let me know what happens. . . . Okay. Bye, Mom. *(He hangs up. The men are staring at him.)* My Mom says that when you're finished with the floors you must do the windows. *(Pause.)* Don't misunderstand me, chaps. All I want is for him to get better. And if he was, I'd be the first person to say: "Bring him home." But he's not, and we can't give him the medical care and attention he needs at home. That's what hospitals are there for. *(Brusquely.)* So don't just stand there! Get on with it!

(Sam clears Hally's table.)

You heard right. My Dad wants to go home.

SAM.   Is he better?

HALLY *(sharply).*   No! How the hell can he be better when last night he was groaning with pain? This is not an age of miracles!

SAM.   Then he should stay in hospital.

HALLY *(seething with irritation and frustration).*   Tell me something I don't know, Sam. What the hell do you think I was saying to my Mom? All I can say is fuck-it-all.

SAM.   I'm sure he'll listen to your Mom.

HALLY.   You don't know what she's up against. He's already packed his shaving kit and pajamas and is sitting on his bed with his crutches, dressed and ready to go. I know him when he gets in that mood. If she tries to reason with him, we've had it. She's no match for him when it comes to a battle of words. He'll tie her up in knots. *(Trying to hide his true feelings.)*

SAM.   I suppose it gets lonely for him in there.

HALLY.   With all the patients and nurses around? Regular visits from the Salvation Army? Balls! It's ten times worse for him at home. I'm at school and my mother is here in the business all day.

SAM.   He's at least got you at night.

HALLY *(before he can stop himself).*   And we've got him! Please! I don't want to talk about it anymore. *(Unpacks his school case, slamming down books on the table.)* Life is just a plain bloody mess, that's all. And people are fools.

SAM.   Come on, Hally.

HALLY.   Yes, they are! They bloody well deserve what they get.

SAM.   Then don't complain.

HALLY.   Don't try to be clever, Sam. It doesn't suit you. Anybody who thinks there's nothing wrong with this world needs to have his head examined. Just when things are going along all right, without fail someone or something will come along and spoil everything. Somebody should write that down as a fundamental law of the Universe. The principle of perpetual disappointment. If there is a God who created this world, he should scrap it and try again.

SAM.   All right, Hally, all right. What you got for homework?

HALLY.   Bullshit, as usual. *(Opens an exercise book and reads.)* "Write five hundred words describing an annual event of cultural or historical significance."

SAM.   That should be easy enough for you.

HALLY.   And also plain bloody boring. You know what he wants, don't you? One of their useless old ceremonies. The commemoration of the landing of the 1820 Settlers, or if it's going to be culture, Carols by Candlelight every Christmas.

SAM.   It's an impressive sight. Make a good description, Hally. All those candles glowing in the dark and the people singing hymns.

HALLY.   And it's called religious hysteria. *(Intense irritation.)* Please, Sam! Just leave me alone and let me get on with it. I'm not in the mood for games this afternoon. And remember my Mom's orders . . . you're to help Willie with the windows. Come on now, I don't want any more nonsense in here.

SAM.   Okay, Hally, okay.

(Hally settles down to his homework; determined preparations . . . pen, ruler, exercise book, dictionary, another cake . . . all of which will lead to nothing.)

(Sam waltzes over to Willie and starts to replace tables and chairs. He practices a ballroom step while doing so. Willie watches. When Sam is finished, Willie tries.)

Good! But just a little bit quicker on the turn and only move in to her after she's crossed over. What about this one?

(Another step. When Sam is finished, Willie again has a go.)

Much better. See what happens when you just relax and enjoy yourself? Remember that in two weeks' time and you'll be all right.

WILLIE.   But I haven't got partner, Boet Sam.

SAM.   Maybe Hilda will turn up tonight.

WILLIE.   No, Boet Sam. *(Reluctantly.)* I gave her a good hiding.

SAM.   You mean a bad one.

WILLIE.   Good bad one.

SAM.   Then you mustn't complain either. Now you pay the price for losing your temper.

WILLIE.   I also pay two pounds ten shilling entrance fee.

SAM.   They'll refund you if you withdraw now.

WILLIE *(appalled)*.   You mean, don't dance?

SAM.   Yes.

WILLIE.   No! I wait too long and I practice too hard. If I find me a new partner, you think I can be ready in two weeks? I ask Madam for my leave now and we practice every day.

SAM.   Quickstep nonstop for two weeks. World record, Willie, but you'll be mad at the end.

WILLIE.   No jokes, Boet Sam.

SAM.   I'm not joking.

WILLIE.   So then what?

SAM.   Find Hilda. Say you're sorry and promise you won't beat her again.

WILLIE.   No.

SAM.   Then withdraw. Try again next year.

WILLIE.   No.

SAM.   Then I give up.

WILLIE.   Haaikona, Boet Sam, you can't.

SAM.   What do you mean, I can't? I'm telling you: I give up.

WILLIE *(adamant)*.   No! *(Accusingly.)* It was you who start me ballroom dancing.

SAM.   So?

WILLIE.   Before that I use to be happy. And is you and Miriam who bring me to Hilda and say here's partner for you.

SAM.   What are you saying, Willie?

WILLIE.   You!

SAM.   But me what? To blame?

WILLIE.   Yes.

SAM.   Willie . . . ? *(Bursts into laughter.)*

WILLIE.   And now all you do is make jokes at me. You wait. When Miriam leaves you is my turn to laugh. Ha! Ha! Ha!

SAM *(he can't take Willie seriously any longer)*.   She can leave me tonight! I know what to do. *(Bowing before an imaginary partner.)* May I have the pleasure? *(He dances and sings.)*

"Just a fellow with his pillow . . .

Dancin' like a willow . . .

In an autumn breeze. . . ."

WILLIE.   There you go again!

(Sam goes on dancing and singing.)

Boet Sam!

SAM.   There's the answer to your problem! Judges' announcement in two weeks' time: "Ladies and gentlemen, the winner in the open section . . . Mr. Willie Malopo and his pillow!"

(This is too much for a now really angry Willie. He goes for Sam, but the latter is too quick for him and puts Hally's table between the two of them.)

HALLY *(exploding)*.   For Christ's sake, you two!

WILLIE *(still trying to get at Sam)*.   I donner you, Sam! Struesgod!

SAM *(still laughing)*.   Sorry, Willie . . . Sorry. . . .

HALLY.   Sam! Willie! *(Grabs his ruler and gives Willie a vicious whack on the bum.)* How the hell am I supposed to concentrate with the two of you behaving like bloody children!

WILLIE.   Hit him too!

HALLY.   Shut up, Willie.

WILLIE.   He started jokes again.

HALLY.   Get back to your work. You too, Sam. *(His ruler.)* Do you want another one, Willie?

(Sam and Willie return to their work. Hally uses the opportunity to escape from his unsuccessful attempt at homework. He struts around like a little despot, ruler in hand, giving vent to his anger and frustration.)

Suppose a customer had walked in then? Or the Park Superintendent. And seen the two of you behaving like a pair of hooligans. That would have been the end of my mother's license, you know. And your jobs? Well, this is the end of it. From now on there will be no more of your ballroom nonsense in here. This is a business establishment, not a bloody New Brighton dancing school. I've been far too lenient with the two of you. *(Behind the counter for a green cool drink and a dollop of ice cream. He keeps up his tirade as he prepares it.)* But what really makes me bitter is that I allow you chaps a little freedom in here when business is bad and what do you do with it? The foxtrot! Specially you, Sam. There's more to life than trotting around a dance floor and I thought at least you knew it.

SAM.   It's a harmless pleasure, Hally. It doesn't hurt anybody.

HALLY.   It's also a rather simple one, you know.

SAM.   You reckon so? Have you ever tried?

HALLY.   Of course not.

SAM.   Why don't you? Now.

HALLY.   What do you mean? Me dance?

SAM.   Yes. I'll show you a simple step—the waltz—then you try it.

HALLY.   What will that prove?

SAM.   That it might not be as easy as you think.

HALLY.   I didn't say it was easy. I said it was simple—like in simple-minded, meaning mentally retarded. You can't exactly say it challenges the intellect.

SAM.   It does other things.

HALLY.   Such as?

SAM.   Make people happy.

HALLY.   *(the glass in his hand):* So do American cream sodas with ice cream. For God's sake, Sam, you're not asking me to take ballroom dancing serious, are you?

SAM.   Yes.

HALLY.   *(sigh of defeat):* Oh, well, so much for trying to give you a decent education. I've obviously achieved nothing.

SAM.   You still haven't told me what's wrong with admiring something that's beautiful and then trying to do it yourself.

HALLY.   Nothing. But we happen to be talking about a foxtrot, not a thing of beauty.

SAM.   But that is just what I'm saying. If you were to see two champions doing, two masters of the art . . . !

HALLY.   Oh God, I give up. So now it's also art!

SAM.   Ja.

HALLY.   There's a limit, Sam. Don't confuse art and entertainment.

SAM.   So then what is art?

HALLY.   You want a definition?

SAM.   Ja.

HALLY *(he realizes he has got to be careful. He gives the matter a lot of thought before answering):* Philosophers have been trying to do that for centuries. What is Art? What is Life? But basically I suppose it's . . . the giving of meaning to matter.

SAM.   Nothing to do with beautiful?

HALLY.   It goes beyond that. It's the giving of form to the formless.

SAM.   Ja, well, maybe it's not art, then. But I still say it's beautiful.

HALLY.   I'm sure the word you mean to use is entertaining.

SAM *(adamant).*   No. Beautiful. And if you want proof come along to the Centenary Hall in New Brighton in two weeks' time.

(The mention of the Centenary Hall draws Willie over to them.)

HALLY.   What for? I've seen the two of you prancing around in here often enough.

SAM *(he laughs).*   This isn't the real thing, Hally. We're just playing around in here.

HALLY.   So? I can use my imagination.

SAM.   And what do you get?

HALLY.   A lot of people dancing around and having a so-called good time.

SAM.   That all?

HALLY.   Well, basically it is that, surely.

SAM.   No, it isn't. Your imagination hasn't helped you at all. There's a lot more to it than that. We're getting ready for the championships, Hally, not just another dance. There's going to be a lot of people, all right, and they're going to have a good time, but they'll only be spectators, sitting around and watching. It's just the competitors out there on the dance floor. Party decorations and fancy lights all around the walls! The ladies in beautiful evening dresses!

HALLY.   My mother's got one of those, Sam, and, quite frankly, it's an embarrassment every time she wears it.

SAM *(undeterred).*   Your imagination left out the excitement.

(Hally scoffs.)

Oh, yes. The finalists are not going to be out there just to have a good time. One of those couples will be the 1950 Eastern Province Champions. And your imagination left out the music.

WILLIE.   Mr. Elijah Gladman Guzana and his Orchestral Jazzonions.

SAM.   The sound of the big band, Hally. Trombone, trumpet, tenor and alto sax. And then, finally, your imagination also left out the climax of the evening when the dancing is finished, the judges have stopped whispering among themselves and the Master of Ceremonies collects their scorecards and goes up onto the stage to announce the winners.

HALLY.   All right. So you make it sound like a bit of a do. It's an occasion. Satisfied?

SAM *(victory).*   So you admit that!

HALLY.   Emotionally yes, intellectually no.

SAM.   Well, I don't know what you mean by that, all I'm telling you is that it is going to be *the* event of the year in New Brighton. It's been sold out for two weeks already. There's only standing room left. We've got competitors coming from Kingwilliamstown, East London, Port Alfred.

(Hally starts pacing thoughtfully.)

HALLY.   Tell me a bit more.

SAM.   I thought you weren't interested . . . intellectually.

HALLY *(mysteriously).*   I've got my reasons.

SAM.   What do you want to know?

HALLY.   It takes place every year?

SAM.   Yes. But only every third year in New Brighton. It's East London's turn to have the championships next year.

HALLY.   Which, I suppose, makes it an even more significant event.

SAM.   Ah ha! We're getting somewhere. Our "occasion" is now a "significant event."

HALLY.   I wonder.

SAM.   What?

HALLY.   I wonder if I would get away with it.

SAM.   But what?

HALLY *(to the table and his exercise book).*   "Write five hundred words describing an annual event of cultural or historical significance." Would I be stretching poetic license a little too far if I called your ballroom championships a cultural event?

SAM.   You mean . . . ?

HALLY.   You think we could get five hundred words out of it, Sam?

SAM.   Victor Sylvester has written a whole book on ballroom dancing.

WILLIE.   You going to write about it, Master Hally?

HALLY.   Yes, gentlemen, that is precisely what I am considering doing. Old Doc Bromely—he's my English teacher—is going to argue with me, of course. He doesn't like natives. But I'll point out to him that in strict anthropological terms the culture of a primitive black society includes its dancing and singing. To put my thesis in a nutshell: The war-dance has been replaced by the waltz. But it still amounts to the same thing: the release of primitive emotions through movement. Shall we give it a go?

SAM.   I'm ready.

WILLIE.   Me also.

HALLY.   Ha! This will teach the old bugger a lesson. *(Decision taken.)* Right. Let's get ourselves organized. *(This means another cake on the table. He sits.)* I think you've given me enough general atmosphere, Sam, but to build the tension and suspense I need facts. *(Pencil poised.)*

WILLIE.   Give him facts, Boet Sam.

HALLY.   What you called the climax . . . how many finalists?

SAM.   Six couples.

HALLY *(making notes).*   Go on. Give me the picture.

SAM.   Spectators seated right around the hall. *(Willie becomes a spectator.)*

HALLY.   . . . and it's a full house.

SAM.   At one end, on the stage, Gladman and his Orchestral Jazzonions. At the other end is a long table with the three judges. The six finalists go onto the dance floor and take up their positions. When they are ready and the spectators have settled down, the Master of Ceremonies goes to the microphone. To start with, he makes some jokes to get people laughing. . . .

HALLY.   Good touch. *(As he writes.)* ". . . creating a relaxed atmosphere which will change to one of tension and drama as the climax is approached."

SAM *(onto a chair to act out the M.C.).*   "Ladies and gentlemen, we come now to the great moment you have all been waiting for this evening. . . . The finals of the 1950 Eastern Province Open Ballroom Dancing Championships. But first let me introduce the finalists! Mr. and Mrs. Welcome Tchabalala from Kingwilliamstown . . ."

WILLIE *(he applauds after every name).*   Is when the people clap their hands and whistle and make a lot of noise, Master Hally.

SAM.   "Mr. Mulligan Njikelane and Miss Nomhle Nkonyeni of Grahamstown; Mr. and Mrs. Norman Nchinga from Port Alfred; Mr. Fats Bokolane and Miss Dina Plaatjies from East London; Mr. Sipho Dugu and Mrs. Mable Magada from Peddie; and from New Brighton our very own Mr. Willie Malopo and Miss Hilda Samuels."

(Willie can't believe his ears. He abandons his role as spectator and scrambles into position as a finalist.)

WILLIE.   Relaxed and ready to romance!

SAM.   The applause dies down. When everybody is silent, Gladman lifts up his sax, nods at the Orchestral Jazzonions. . . .

WILLIE.   Play the jukebox please, Boet Sam!

SAM.   I also only got bus fare, Willie.

HALLY.   Hold it, everybody. *(Heads for the cash register behind the counter.)* How much is in the till, Sam?

SAM.   Three shillings. Hally . . . Your Mom counted it before she left.

(Hally hesitates.)

HALLY.   Sorry, Willie. You know how she carried on the last time I did it. We'll just have to pool our combined imaginations and hope for the best. *(Returns to the table.)* Back to work. How are the points scored, Sam?

SAM.   Maximum of ten points each for individual style, deportment, rhythm, and general appearance.

WILLIE.   Must I start?

HALLY.   Hold it for a second, Willie. And penalties?

SAM.   For what?

HALLY.   For doing something wrong. Say you stumble or bump into somebody . . . do they take off any points?

SAM *(aghast)*.   Hally . . . !

HALLY.   When you're dancing. If you and your partner collide into another couple.

(Hally can get no further. Sam has collapsed with laughter. He explains to Willie.)

SAM.   If me and Miriam bump into you and Hilda. . . .

(Willie joins him in another good laugh.)

Hally, Hally . . . !

HALLY *(perplexed)*.   Why? What did I say?

SAM.   There's no collisions out there, Hally. Nobody trips or stumbles or bumps into anybody else. That's what that moment is all about. To be one of those finalists on that dance floor is like . . . like being in a dream about a world in which accidents don't happen.

HALLY *(genuinely moved by Sam's image)*.   Jesus, Sam! That's beautiful!

WILLIE *(can endure waiting no longer)*.   I'm starting!

(Willie dances while Sam talks.)

SAM.   Of course it is. That's what I've been trying to say to you all afternoon. And it's beautiful because that is what we want life to be like. But instead, like you said, Hally, we're bumping into each other all the time. Look at the three of us this afternoon: I've bumped into Willie, the two of us have bumped into you, you've bumped into your mother, she bumping into your Dad. . . . None of us knows the steps and there's no music playing. And it doesn't stop with us. The whole world is doing it all the time. Open a newspaper and what do you read? America has bumped into Russia, England is bumping into India, rich man bumps into poor man. Those are big collisions, Hally. They make for a lot of bruises. People get hurt in all that bumping, and we're sick and tired of it now. It's been going on for too long. Are we never going to get it right? . . . Learn to dance life like champions instead of always being just a bunch of beginners at it?

HALLY *(deep and sincere admiration of the man)*.   You've got a vision, Sam!

SAM.   Not just me. What I'm saying to you is that everybody's got it. That's why there's only standing room left for the Centenary Hall in two weeks' time. For as long as the music lasts, we are going to see six couples get it right, the way we want life to be.

HALLY.   But is that the best we can do, Sam . . . watch six finalists dreaming about the way it should be?

SAM.   I don't know. But it starts with that. Without the dream we won't know what we're going for. And anyway I reckon there are a few people who have got past just dreaming about it and are trying for something real. Remember that thing we read once in the paper about the Mahatma Gandhi? Going without food to stop those riots in India?

HALLY.   You're right. He certainly was trying to teach people to get the steps right.

SAM.   And the Pope.

HALLY.   Yes, he's another one. Our old General Smuts° as well, you know. He's also out there dancing. You know, Sam, when you come to think of it, that's what the United Nations boils down to . . . a dancing school for politicians!

SAM.   And let's hope they learn.

HALLY *(a little surge of hope).*   You're right. We mustn't despair. Maybe there's some hope for mankind after all. Keep it up, Willie. *(Back to his table with determination.)* This is a lot bigger than I thought. So what have we got? Yes, our title: "A World Without Collisions."

SAM.   That sounds good! "A World Without Collisions."

HALLY.   Subtitle: "Global Politics on the Dance Floor." No. A bit too heavy, hey? What about "Ballroom Dancing as a Political Vision"?

(The telephone rings. Sam answers it.)

SAM.   St. George's Park Tea Room . . . Yes, Madam . . . Hally, it's your Mom.

HALLY *(back to reality).*   Oh, God, yes! I'd forgotten all about that. Shit! Remember my words, Sam! Just when you're enjoying yourself, someone or something will come along and wreck everything.

SAM.   You haven't heard what she's got to say yet.

HALLY.   Public telephone?

SAM.   No.

HALLY.   Does she sound happy or unhappy?

SAM.   I couldn't tell. *(Pause.)* She's waiting, Hally.

HALLY *(to the telephone).*   Hello, Mom . . . No, everything is okay here. Just doing my homework. . . . What's your news? . . . You've what? . . . *(Pause. He takes the receiver away from his ear for a few seconds. In the course of Hally's telephone conversation, Sam and Willie discreetly position the stacked tables and chairs. Hally places the receiver back to his ear.)* Yes, I'm still here. Oh, well, I give up now. Why did you do it, Mom? . . . Well, I just hope you know what you've let us in for. . . . *(Loudly.)* I said I hope you know what you've let us in for! It's the end of the peace and quiet we've been having. *(Softly.)* Where is he? *(Normal voice.)* He can't hear us from in there. But for God's sake, Mom, what happened? I told you to be firm with him. . . . Then you and the nurses should have held him down, taken his crutches away. . . . I know only too well he's my father! . . . I'm not being disrespectful, but I'm sick and tired of emptying stinking chamber pots full of phlegm and piss. . . . Yes, I do! When you're not there, he asks *me* to do it. . . . If you really want to know the truth, that's why I've got no appetite for my food. . . . Yes! There's a lot of

General Smuts (1870–1950): South African statesman who fought the British in the Boer War in 1899, was instrumental in forming the Union of South Africa in 1910, and was active in the creation of the United Nations.

things you don't know about. For your information, I still haven't got that science text-book I need. And you know why? He borrowed the money you gave me for it. . . . Because I didn't want to start another fight between you two. . . . He says that every time. . . . All right, Mom! *(Viciously.)* Then just remember to start hiding your bag away again, because he'll be at your purse before long for money for booze. And when he's well enough to come down here, you better keep an eye on the till as well, because that is also going to develop a leak. . . . Then don't complain to me when he starts his old tricks. . . . Yes, you do. I get it from you on one side and from him on the other, and it makes life hell for me. I'm not going to be the peacemaker anymore. I'm warning you now: when the two of you start fighting again, I'm leaving home. . . . Mom, if you start crying, I'm going to put down the receiver. . . . Okay. . . . *(Lowering his voice to a vicious whisper.)* Okay, Mom, I heard you. *(Desperate.)* No. . . . Because I don't want to. I'll see him when I get home! Mom! . . . *(Pause. When he speaks again, his tone changes completely. It is not simply pretense. We sense a genuine emotional conflict.)* Welcome home, chum! . . . What's that? . . . Don't be silly, Dad. You being home is just about the best news in the world. . . . I bet you are. Bloody depressing there with everybody going on about their ailments, hey! . . . How you feeling? . . . Good. . . . Here as well, pal. Coming down cats and dogs. . . . That's right. Just the day for a kip° and a toss in your old Uncle Ned. . . . Everything's just hunky-dory on my side, Dad. . . . Well, to start with, there's a nice pile of comics for you on the counter. . . . Yes, old Kemple brought them in. *Batman and Robin, Submariner* . . . just your cup of tea. . . . I will. . . . Yes, we'll spin a few yarns tonight. . . . Okay, chum, see you in a little while. . . . No, I promise. I'll come straight home. . . . *(Pause—his mother comes back on the phone.)* Mom? Okay. I'll lock up now. . . . What? . . . Oh, the brandy . . . Yes, I'll remember! . . . I'll put it in my suitcase now, for God's sake. I know well enough what will happen if he doesn't get it. . . . *(Places a bottle of brandy on the counter.)* I was kind to him, Mom. I didn't say anything nasty! . . . All right. Bye. *(End of telephone conversation. A desolate Hally doesn't move. A strained silence.)*

SAM *(quietly).*   That sounded like a bad bump, Hally.

HALLY *(having a hard time controlling his emotions. He speaks carefully).*   Mind your own business, Sam.

SAM.   Sorry. I wasn't trying to interfere. Shall we carry on? Hally? *(He indicates the exercise book. No response from Hally.)*

WILLIE *(also trying).*   Tell him about when they give out the cups, Boet Sam.

SAM.   Ja! That's another big moment. The presentation of the cups after the winners have been announced. You've got to put that in.

(Still no response from Hally.)

WILLIE.   A big silver one, Master Hally, called floating trophy for the champions.

SAM.   We always invite some big-shot personality to hand them over. Guest of honor this year is going to be His Holiness Bishop Jabulani of the All African Free Zionist Church.

(Hally gets up abruptly, goes to his table, and tears up the page he was writing on.)

HALLY.   So much for a bloody world without collisions.

SAM.   Too bad. It was on its way to being a good composition.

HALLY.   Let's stop bullshitting ourselves, Sam.

SAM.   Have we been doing that?

HALLY.   Yes! That's what all our talk about a decent world has been . . . just so much bullshit.

kip: nap.

SAM.   We did say it was still only a dream.

HALLY.   And a bloody useless one at that. Life's a fuckup and it's never going to change.

SAM.   Ja, maybe that's true.

HALLY.   There's no maybe about it. It's a blunt and brutal fact. All we've done this afternoon is waste our time.

SAM.   Not if we'd got your homework done.

HALLY.   I don't give a shit about my homework, so, for Christ's sake, just shut up about it. *(Slamming books viciously into his school case.)* Hurry up now and finish your work. I want to lock up and get out of here. *(Pause.)* And then go where? Home-sweet-fucking-home. Jesus, I hate that word.

(Hally goes to the counter to put the brandy bottle and comics in his school case. After a moment's hesitation, he smashes the bottle of brandy. He abandons all further attempts to hide his feelings. Sam and Willie work away as unobtrusively as possible.)

Do you want to know what is really wrong with your lovely little dream, Sam? It's not just that we are all bad dancers. That does happen to be perfectly true, but there's more to it than just that. You left out the cripples.

SAM.   Hally!

HALLY *(now totally reckless)*.   Ja! Can't leave them out, Sam. That's why we always end up on our backsides on the dance floor. They're also out there dancing . . . like a bunch of broken spiders trying to do the quickstep! *(An ugly attempt at laughter.)* When you come to think of it, it's a bloody comical sight. I mean, it's bad enough on two legs . . . but one and a pair of crutches! Hell, no, Sam. That's guaranteed to turn that dance floor into a shambles. Why you shaking your head? Picture it, man. For once this afternoon let's use our imaginations sensibly.

SAM.   Be careful, Hally.

HALLY.   Of what? The truth? I seem to be the only one around here who is prepared to face it. We've had the pretty dream, it's time now to wake up and have a good long look at the way things really are. Nobody knows the steps, there's no music, the cripples are also out there tripping up everybody and trying to get into the act, and it's all called the All-Comers-How-to-Make-a-Fuckup-of-Life Championships. *(Another ugly laugh.)* Hang on, Sam! The best bit is still coming. Do you know what the winner's trophy is? A beautiful big chamber pot with roses on the side, and it's full to the brim with piss. And guess who I think is going to be this year's winner.

SAM *(almost shouting)*.   Stop now!

HALLY *(suddenly appalled by how far he has gone)*.   Why?

SAM.   Hally? It's your father you're talking about.

HALLY.   So?

SAM.   Do you know what you've been saying?

(Hally can't answer. He is rigid with shame. Sam speaks to him sternly.)

No, Hally, you mustn't do it. Take back those words and ask for forgiveness! It's a terrible sin for a son to mock his father with jokes like that. You'll be punished if you carry on. Your father is your father, even if he is a . . . cripple man.

WILLIE.   Yes, Master Hally. Is true what Sam say.

SAM.   I understand how you are feeling, Hally, but even so. . . .

HALLY.   No, you don't!

SAM.   I think I do.

HALLY.   And I'm telling you you don't. Nobody does. *(Speaking carefully as his shame turns to rage at Sam.)* It's your turn to be careful, Sam. Very careful! You're treading on dangerous ground. Leave me and my father alone.

SAM.   I'm not the one who's been saying things about him.

HALLY.   What goes on between me and my Dad is none of your business!

SAM.   Then don't tell me about it. If that's all you've got to say about him, I don't want to hear.

(For a moment Hally is at loss for a response.)

HALLY.   Just get on with your bloody work and shut up.

SAM.   Swearing at me won't help you.

HALLY.   Yes, it does! Mind your own fucking business and shut up!

SAM.   Okay. If that's the way you want it, I'll stop trying.

(He turns away. This infuriates Hally even more.)

HALLY.   Good. Because what you've been trying to do is meddle in something you know nothing about. All that concerns you in here, Sam, is to try and do what you get paid for—keep the place clean and serve the customers. In plain words, just get on with your job. My mother is right. She's always warning me about allowing you to get too familiar. Well, this time you've gone too far. It's going to stop right now.

(No response from Sam.)

You're only a servant in here, and don't forget it.

(Still no response. Hally is trying hard to get one.)

And as far as my father is concerned, all you need to remember is that he is your boss.

SAM *(needled at last)*.   No, he isn't. I get paid by your mother.

HALLY.   Don't argue with me, Sam!

SAM.   Then don't say he's my boss.

HALLY.   He's a white man and that's good enough for you.

SAM.   I'll try to forget you said that.

HALLY.   Don't! Because you won't be doing me a favor if you do. I'm telling you to remember it.

(A pause. Sam pulls himself together and makes one last effort.)

SAM.   Hally, Hally . . . ! Come on now. Let's stop before it's too late. You're right. We are on dangerous ground. If we're not careful, somebody is going to get hurt.

HALLY.   It won't be me.

SAM.   Don't be so sure.

HALLY.   I don't know what you're talking about, Sam.

SAM.   Yes, you do.

HALLY *(furious)*.   Jesus, I wish you would stop trying to tell me what I do and what I don't know.

(Sam gives up. He turns to Willie.)

SAM.   Let's finish up.

HALLY.   Don't turn your back on me! I haven't finished talking.

(He grabs Sam by the arm and tries to make him turn around. Sam reacts with a flash of anger.)

SAM.   Don't do that, Hally! *(Facing the boy.)* All right, I'm listening. Well? What do you want to say to me?

HALLY *(pause as Hally looks for something to say).*   To begin with, why don't you also start calling me Master Harold, like Willie.

SAM.   Do you mean that?

HALLY.   Why the hell do you think I said it?

SAM.   And if I don't?

HALLY.   You might just lose your job.

SAM *(quietly and very carefully).*   If you make me say it once, I'll never call you anything else again.

HALLY.   So? *(The boy confronts the man.)* Is that meant to be a threat?

SAM.   Just telling you what will happen if you make me do that. You must decide what it means to you.

HALLY.   Well, I have. It's good news. Because that is exactly what Master Harold wants from now on. Think of it as a little lesson in respect, Sam, that's long overdue, and I hope you remember it as well as you do your geography. I can tell you now that somebody who will be glad to hear I've finally given it to you will be my Dad. Yes! He agrees with my Mom. He's always going on about it as well. "You must teach the boys to show you more respect, my son."

SAM.   So now you can stop complaining about going home. Everybody is going to be happy tonight.

HALLY.   That's perfectly correct. You see, you mustn't get the wrong idea about me and my Dad, Sam. We also have our good times together. Some bloody good laughs. He's got a marvelous sense of humor. Want to know what our favorite joke is? He gives out a big groan, you see, and says: "It's not fair, is it, Hally?" Then I have to ask: "What, chum?" And then he says: "A nigger's arse" . . . and we both have a good laugh.

(The men stare at him with disbelief.)

What's the matter, Willie? Don't you catch the joke? You always were a bit slow on the uptake. It's what is called a pun. You see, fair means both light in color and to be just and decent. *(He turns to Sam.)* I thought you would catch it, Sam.

SAM.   Oh ja, I catch it all right.

HALLY.   But it doesn't appeal to your sense of humor.

SAM.   Do you really laugh?

HALLY.   Of course.

SAM.   To please him? Make him feel good?

HALLY.   No, for heaven's sake! I laugh because I think it's a bloody good joke.

SAM.   You're really trying hard to be ugly, aren't you? And why drag poor old Willie into it? He's done nothing to you except show you the respect you want so badly. That's also not being fair, you know . . . and I mean just or decent.

WILLIE.   It's all right, Sam. Leave it now.

SAM.   It's me you're after. You should just have said "Sam's arse" . . . because that's the one you're trying to kick. Anyway, how do you know it's not fair? You've never seen it. Do you want to? *(He drops his trousers and underpants and presents his backside for Hally's inspection.)* Have a good look. A real Basuto arse . . . which is about as nigger as they can come. Satisfied? *(Trousers up.)* Now you can make your Dad even happier when you go home tonight. Tell him I showed you my arse and he is quite right. It's not fair. And if it will give him an even better laugh next time, I'll also let *him* have a look. Come, Willie, let's finish up and go.

(Sam and Willie start to tidy up the tea room. Hally doesn't move. He waits for a moment when Sam passes him.)

HALLY *(quietly).* Sam . . .

(Sam stops and looks expectantly at the boy. Hally spits in his face. A long and heartfelt groan from Willie. For a few seconds Sam doesn't move.)

SAM *(taking out a handkerchief and wiping his face).* It's all right, Willie.

(To Hally.)

Ja, well, you've done it . . . Master Harold. Yes, I'll start calling you that from now on. It won't be difficult anymore. You've hurt yourself, Master Harold. I saw it coming. I warned you, but you wouldn't listen. You've just hurt yourself *bad.* And you're a coward, Master Harold. The face you should be spitting in is your father's . . . but you used mine, because you think you're safe inside your fair skin . . . and this time I don't mean just or decent. *(Pause, then moving violently toward Hally.)* Should I hit him, Willie?

WILLIE *(stopping Sam).* No, Boet Sam.

SAM *(violently).* Why not?

WILLIE. It won't help, Boet Sam.

SAM. I don't want to help! I want to hurt him.

WILLIE. You also hurt yourself.

SAM. And if he had done it to you, Willie?

WILLIE. Me? Spit at me like I was a dog? *(A thought that had not occurred to him before. He looks at Hally.)* Ja. Then I want to hit him. I want to hit him hard!

(A dangerous few seconds as the men stand staring at the boy. Willie turns away, shaking his head.)

But maybe all I do is go cry at the back. He's little boy, Boet Sam. Little white boy. Long trousers now, but he's still little boy.

SAM *(his violence ebbing away into defeat as quickly as it flooded).* You're right. So go on, then: groan again, Willie. You do it better than me. *(To Hally.)* You don't know all of what you've just done . . . Master Harold. It's not just that you've made me feel dirtier than I've ever been in my life . . . I mean, how do I wash off yours and your father's filth? . . . I've also failed. A long time ago I promised myself I was going to try and do something, but you've just shown me . . . Master Harold . . . that I've failed. *(Pause.)* I've also got a memory of a little white boy when he was still wearing short trousers and a black man, but they're not flying a kite. It was the old Jubilee days, after dinner one night. I was in my room. You came in and just stood against the wall, looking down at the ground, and only after I'd asked you what you wanted, what was wrong, I don't know how many times, did you speak and even then so softly I almost didn't hear you. "Sam, please help me to go and fetch my Dad." Remember? He was dead drunk on the floor of the Central Hotel Bar. They'd phoned for your Mom, but you were the only one at home. And do you remember how we did it? You went in first by yourself to ask permission for me to go into the bar. Then I loaded him onto my back like a baby and carried him back to the boarding house with you following behind carrying his crutches. *(Shaking his head as he remembers.)* A crowded Main Street with all the people watching a little white boy following his drunk father on a nigger's back! I felt for that little boy . . . Master Harold. I felt for him. After that we still had to clean him up, remember? He'd messed in his trousers, so we had to clean him up and get him into bed.

HALLY *(great pain).* I love him, Sam.

SAM. I know you do. That's why I tried to stop you from saying these things about him. It would have been so simple if you could have just despised him for being a weak man. But he's your father. You love him and you're ashamed of him. You're ashamed of so much! . . . And now that's going to include yourself. That was the promise I made to myself: to try and stop that happening. *(Pause.)* After we got him to bed you came back with me to my room and sat in a corner and carried on just looking down at the ground. And for days after that! You hadn't done anything wrong, but you went around as if you owed the world an apology for being alive. I didn't like seeing that! That's not the way a boy grows up to be a man! . . . But the one person who should have been teaching you what that means was the cause of your shame. If you really want to know, that's why I made you that kite. I wanted you to look up, be proud of something, of yourself . . . *(bitter smile at the memory)* . . . and you certainly were that when I left you with it up there on the hill. Oh, ja . . . something else! . . . If you ever do write it as a short story, there was a twist in our ending. I couldn't sit down there and stay with you. It was a "Whites Only" bench. You were too young, too excited to notice then. But not anymore. If you're not careful . . . Master Harold . . . you're going to be sitting up there by yourself for a long time to come, and there won't be a kite in the sky. *(Sam has got nothing more to say. He exits into the kitchen, taking off his waiter's jacket.)*

WILLIE.   Is bad. Is all bad in here now.

HALLY *(books into his school case, raincoat on).*   Willie . . . *(It is difficult to speak.)* Will you lock up for me and look after the keys?

WILLIE.   Okay.

(Sam returns. Hally goes behind the counter and collects the few coins in the cash register. As he starts to leave . . . .)

SAM.   Don't forget the comic books.

(Hally returns to the counter and puts them in his case. He starts to leave again.)

SAM *(to the retreating back of the boy).*   Stop . . . Hally. . . .

(Hally stops, but doesn't turn to face him.)

Hally . . . I've got no right to tell you what being a man means if I don't behave like one myself, and I'm not doing so well at that this afternoon. Should we try again, Hally?

HALLY.   Try what?

SAM.   Fly another kite, I suppose. It worked once, and this time I need it as much as you do.

HALLY.   It's still raining, Sam. You can't fly kites on rainy days, remember.

SAM.   So what do we do? Hope for better weather tomorrow?

HALLY *(helpless gesture).*   I don't know. I don't know anything anymore.

SAM.   You sure of that, Hally? Because it would be pretty hopeless if that was true. It would mean nothing has been learnt in here this afternoon, and there was a hell of a lot of teaching going on . . . one way or the other. But anyway, I don't believe you. I reckon there's one thing you know. You don't have to sit up there by yourself. You know what that bench means now, and you can leave it any time you choose. All you've got to do is stand up and walk away from it.

(Hally leaves. Willie goes up quietly to Sam.)

WILLIE.   Is okay, Boet Sam. You see. Is . . . *(he can't find any better words)* . . . is going to be okay tomorrow. *(Changing his tone.)* Hey, Boet Sam! *(He is trying hard.)* You right. I think about it and you right. Tonight I find Hilda and say sorry. And make promise I won't beat her no more. You hear me, Boet Sam?

SAM.   I hear you, Willie.

WILLIE.   And when we practice I relax and romance with her from beginning to end. Nonstop! You watch! Two weeks' time: "First prize for promising newcomers: Mr. Willie Malopo and Miss Hilda Samuels." *(Sudden impulse.)* To hell with it! I walk home. *(He goes to the jukebox, puts in a coin and selects a record. The machine comes to life in the gray twilight, blushing its way through a spectrum of soft, romantic colors.)* How did you say it, Boet Sam? Let's dream. *(Willie sways with the music and gestures for Sam to dance.)*

(Sarah Vaughan sings.)

"Little man you're crying,
I know why you're blue,
Someone took your kiddy car away;
Better go to sleep now,
Little man you've had a busy day." *(etc., etc.)*
You lead. I follow.

(The men dance together.)

"Johnny won your marbles,
Tell you what we'll do;
Dad will get you new ones right away;
Better go to sleep now,
Little man you've had a busy day."

QUESTIONS FOR CLOSE READING

1. Describe the setting, "St. George's Park Tea Room." Who was St. George?
2. What do we learn about Sam and Willie early in the play?
3. What kind of dances does Willie rehearse? Why?
4. What is the difference between Willie's attitude toward Hilda Samuels at the beginning of the play and his attitude at the end?
5. What differences between Willie and Sam and Hally seem most important?
6. How does Hally treat his father? What do we know about his father?
7. What is Sam reading from the history book?
8. What is Hally learning in school? Did Willie and Sam learn the same things?
9. What was Hally doing hiding in Willie's room when he was little?
10. What games do Hally and Willie play? Why don't they play chess?
11. When does Hally become most irritated at Sam?
12. What is the difference between Sam's and Willie's reaction to Hally's insults?
13. What are Hally's insults? What does he say that hurts Sam? How do his insults alter their relationship?
14. Why does Sam want to fly a kite at the end of the play?

QUESTIONS FOR INTERPRETATION

1. Hally's attitudes toward his mother and father are quite different. Is the difference significant? Given the nature of the play, what importance should we place on the fact that women are talked about but not present in the action?

2. Why does Willie place so much importance on the upcoming dance that he is rehearsing for? What significance could dancing have for the overall drama? Is dancing symbolic of another kind of activity?

3. Sam taught Hally how to fly a kite properly. Why does Hally describe the action in such detail in the middle of the play? Is flying a kite a symbol of a larger action? The entire issue is raised again at the end of the play. Why?

4. What is the significance of Hally's always beating Willie at games? They explore the reasons for his winning; why does Fugard emphasize the issue?

5. Compare the three characters for evidence of selfishness in any of them. Who seems most selfish in the play? What does selfishness have to do with the main action of the drama?

6. To what extent is Hally's attitude toward his father similar to his attitude toward Willie and Sam? Are Willie and Sam portrayed as substitute fathers? What has been their relation to Hally since Hally's childhood?

7. Hally's anger at Sam and Willie erupts when Sam tries to tell Hally that he should be more respectful of his father. Why does Hally become so angry? Why does he challenge Sam by telling him to remember he is only a servant? A profound change takes place when Hally says, "You're only a servant in here, and don't forget it." What are the implications of Hally's demanding to be called Master Harold? Is his behavior racist? Is his behavior marked by a class distinction?

8. Should Sam have hit Hally at the end of the play? Why does Willie hold him back? Would it have been just to hit Hally?

9. How do you interpret the ending of the play? To what extent is the future hopeful? To what extent is it hopeless?

19

HENRIK IBSEN
IN DEPTH

The work of Henrik Ibsen (1828–1906) was not immediately successful. Among the reasons for his early failures was his inability to write verse plays in the accepted style of the time. His early life centered on the new National Theater in what is now Oslo, Norway, and by the 1850s he was writing and producing plays, most of which were generally unnoticed. His first success came in 1866 with *Brand,* a verse play about a fiery preacher who rejected the New Testament god of love in favor of the Old Testament god of wrath. Brand is last seen on a mountaintop in his Ice Church facing an avalanche that will destroy him. Even though this play made Ibsen well known in Norway, it was not until 1877 that he began to have an important place in the world theater.

Ibsen's great work began with *The Pillars of Society* (1877), a study of the corruption of the merchant class. This was the first of his realistic plays. For Ibsen, realism meant showing his audience the problems they faced in their daily lives, both individually and as members of society. In an environment that preferred sentimental comedies and fluffy dramas, Ibsen's plays cut through like a cleaver. His work was shocking and thrilling. It was also difficult for many theatergoers to accept, and Europe took sides for and against Ibsen. In the early 1900s William Butler Yeats thought Ibsen damaging to all that was literary, but the younger approving James Joyce learned enough Dano-Norwegian to write Ibsen a letter proclaiming his genius. Realism sensed heartless and soulless to Yeats, but it was a breath of honesty to Joyce. Whatever it was, realism swept other dramatic styles aside, and Ibsen became known as the father of modern drama.

Although *A Doll House* (1879) established Ibsen as a critic of society, its feminist theme was acceptable in Norway in the late 1870s because a strong feminist movement was already in place. The rest of Europe found it shocking. Later, *Ghosts* (1881) shocked Norway and Europe because it discussed a subject never publicly mentioned: syphilis. The primary character, Oswald Alving, has inherited syphilis from his seagoing father. Moreover, Captain Alving's illegitimate daughter Regina falls in love with Oswald, raising the specter of incest. Such subject matter was so unusual and so shocking that Ibsen became ostracized and felt he had to go into temporary exile. *Hedda Gabler* (1890) continued his analysis of the European middle class, but added to it a rich psychological portrait of a woman dissatisfied with her role in society.

Ibsen treated social issues with relentless honesty and directness. He was also a skilled dramatic craftsman and an interpreter of character, and his work has guided the major dramatists of the twentieth century. Arthur Miller paid homage to Ibsen by adapting *An Enemy of the People* (original version 1882; Miller's version 1992) for the modern American stage.

When Ibsen produced *A Doll House,* Europe had begun to see a major movement toward women's rights. Women could not vote, nor could they exercise many of their political rights independently of their husband, who in most marriages expected to be served, to be patronized, and to make all the important decisions. But modern women, living in an age of rapid industrialization and change, saw opportunities for change and began to assert themselves in a variety of organizations. *A Doll House* has often been described as an important stimulus for change, and Nora's slamming of the household door at the end of the play has been regarded as resounding throughout the modern world.

Torvald Helmer and his wife Nora are in many ways models of the comfortable upper middle class of Europe and the Americas. Their world is family centered, the house is a special protected environment, and as far as Torvald is concerned everything is perfect. Throughout the early part of the play, Nora is compared to a singing bird or a busy squirrel—a pet to amuse Torvald and to keep his life smooth and functioning. She seems to him an empty-headed woman, a decoration in his life. His own empty-headedness is at times almost overwhelming.

The problems begin when Nora tries to help her husband in a manifest way by borrowing money to take a trip to Italy to save Torvald's health. In order to pay back her loan, which she got by forging her father's signature, Nora has to take in work. She discovers that work is congenial, and it gives her an entirely new sense of her own worth. She now feels some of the pleasures that had been reserved only for men. For Ibsen, this was part of the crux of the play, since he was interested not only in the feminist question but also in how people fulfill their talent. Unfortunately, these issues were not evident in the first critics in Copenhagen, and they were generally negative. However, audiences were curious and flocked to the theater, making the play a resounding success.

The play's ending, with Nora storming out of the house into a totally uncertain future, disturbed audiences and theater people alike. In some versions in 1880 and after, a "happy ending" was inserted into the play because actresses would not play the part as written, insisting that no woman would willingly leave her children as Nora did. Even today critics debate the degree to which the play is feminist and the extent to which Nora can be praised. Ibsen has left us with a great many challenging questions.

HENRIK IBSEN   (1828–1906)

A Doll House ——————————————————— *1879*

Translated by Eva LeGallienne

Characters

    Torvald Helmer, *a lawyer*
    Nora, *his wife*
    Doctor Rank
    Mrs. Kristine Linde
    Nils Krogstad, *an attorney*
    Helmer's Three Small Children
    Anne-Marie,° *nurse at the Helmers'*
    Helene, *maid at the Helmers'*
    A Porter
    The action takes place in the Helmer residence.

ACT I

(Scene: A comfortable room furnished with taste, but not expensively. In the back wall a door on the right leads to the hall; another door on the left leads to Helmer's study. Between the two doors a piano. In the left wall, center, a door; farther downstage a window. Near the window a round table with an armchair and a small sofa. In the right wall upstage a door, and further downstage a porcelain stove round which are grouped a couple of armchairs and a rocking chair. Between the stove and the door stands a small table. Engravings on the walls. A whatnot with china objects and various bric-a-brac. A small bookcase with books in fancy bindings. The floor is carpeted; a fire burns in the stove. A winter day.)

    NORA.   Be sure and hide the Christmas tree carefully, Helene, the children mustn't see it till this evening, when it's all decorated. *(To the Porter, taking out her purse.)* How much?
    PORTER.   Fifty, Ma'am.
    NORA.   Here you are. No—keep the change.

(The Porter thanks her and goes. Nora closes the door. She laughs gaily to herself as she takes off her outdoor things. Takes a bag of macaroons out of her pocket and eats a couple, then she goes cautiously to the door of her husband's study and listens.) Yes—he's home. *(She goes over to the table right, humming to herself again.)*

    HELMER *(from his study).*   Is that my little lark twittering out there?
    NORA *(busily undoing the packages).*   Yes, it is.
    HELMER.   Is that my little squirrel bustling about?
    NORA.   Yes.
    HELMER.   When did my squirrel get home?
    NORA.   Just this minute. *(She puts the bag of macaroons back in her pocket and wipes her mouth.)* Oh, Torvald, do come in here! You must see what I have bought.

Anne-Marie: for stage purposes, often *Anna-Maria.*

HELMER.   Now, don't disturb me! *(A moment afterwards he opens the door and looks in—pen in hand.)* Did you say "bought"? That—all *that?* Has my little spendthrift been flinging money about again?

NORA.   But, Torvald, surely this year we ought to let ourselves go a bit! After all, it's the first Christmas we haven't had to be careful.

HELMER.   Yes, but that doesn't mean we can afford to *squander* money.

NORA.   Oh, Torvald, we can squander a bit, can't we? Just a little tiny bit? You're going to get a big salary and you'll be making lots and lots of money.

HELMER.   After the first of the year, yes. But remember there'll be three whole months before my salary falls due.

NORA.   We can always borrow in the meantime.

HELMER.   Nora! *(Goes to her and pulls her ear playfully.)* There goes my little feather-brain! Let's suppose I borrowed a thousand crowns today, you'd probably squander it all during Christmas week; and then let's suppose that on New Year's Eve a tile blew off the roof and knocked my brains out—

NORA *(puts her hand over his mouth).*   Don't say such frightful things!

HELMER.   But let's suppose it happened—then what?

NORA.   If anything as terrible as *that* happened, I shouldn't care whether I owed money or not.

HELMER.   But what about the people I'd borrowed from?

NORA.   Who cares about them? After all they're just strangers.

HELMER.   Oh, Nora, Nora! What a little woman you are! But seriously, Nora, you know my feelings about such things. I'll have no borrowing—I'll have no debts! There can be no freedom—no, nor beauty either—in a home based upon loans and credit. We've held out bravely up to now, and we shall continue to do so for the short time that remains.

NORA *(goes toward the stove).*   Just as you like, Torvald.

HELMER *(following her).*   Come, come; this little lark mustn't droop her wings. Don't tell me my little squire is sulking! *(He opens his purse.)* Nora! Guess what I have here!

NORA *(turns quickly).*   Money!

HELMER.   There you are! *(He hands her some notes.)* Don't you suppose I know that money is needed at Christmas time.

NORA *(counts the notes).*   Ten, twenty, thirty, forty. Oh thank you, thank you, Torvald—this'll last me a long time!

HELMER.   Better see that it does!

NORA.   Oh, it will—I know. But do come here. I want to show you everything I've bought, and all so cheap too! Here are some new clothes for Ivar, and a little sword—and this horse and trumpet are for Bob, and here's a doll for Emmy—and a doll's bed. They're not worth much, but she's sure to tear them to pieces in a minute anyway. This is some dress material and handkerchiefs for the maids. Old Anne-Marie really should have had something better.

HELMER.   And what's in that other parcel?

NORA *(with a shriek).*   No, Torvald! You can't see that until this evening!

HELMER.   I can't eh? But what about you—you little squanderer? Have you thought of anything for yourself?

NORA.   Oh, there's nothing I want, Torvald.

HELMER.   Of course there is!—now tell me something sensible you'd really like to have.

NORA.   But there's nothing—really! Except of course—

HELMER.   Well?

NORA *(she fingers the buttons on his coat; without looking at him).*   Well—If you really want to give me something—you might—you might—

HELMER.   Well, well, out with it!

NORA *(rapidly).*   You might give me some money, Torvald—just anything you feel you could spare; and then one of these days I'll buy myself something with it.

HELMER.   But Nora—

NORA.   Oh, please do, dear Torvald—I beg you to! I'll wrap it up in beautiful gold paper and hang it on the Christmas tree. Wouldn't that be fun?

HELMER.   What's the name of the bird that eats up money?

NORA.   The Spendthrift bird—I know! But do let's do as I say, Torvald!—it will give me a chance to choose something I really need. Don't you think that's a sensible idea? Don't you?

HELMER *(smiling).*   Sensible enough—providing you really *do* buy something for yourself with it. But I expect you'll fritter it away on a lot of unnecessary household expenses, and before I know it you'll be coming to me for more.

NORA.   But, Torvald—

HELMER.   You can't deny it, Nora dear. *(Puts his arm round her waist.)* The Spendthrift is a sweet little bird—but it costs a man an awful lot of money to support one!

NORA.   How can you say such nasty things—I save all I can!

HELMER.   Yes, I dare say—but that doesn't amount to much!

NORA *(hums softly and smiles happily).*   You don't know, Torvald, what expenses we larks and squirrels have!

HELMER.   You're a strange little creature; exactly like your father. You'll go to any lengths to get a sum of money—but as soon as you have it, it just slips through your fingers. You don't know yourself what's become of it. Well, I suppose one must just take you as you are. It's in your blood. Oh, yes! such things are hereditary, Nora.

NORA.   I only wish I had inherited a lot of Father's qualities.

HELMER.   And I wouldn't wish you any different than you are, my own sweet little lark. But Nora, it's just occurred to me—isn't there something a little—what shall I call it—a little guilty about you this morning?

NORA.   About me?

HELMER.   Yes. Look me straight in the eye.

NORA *(looking at him).*   Well?

HELMER *(wags a threatening finger at her).*   Has my little sweet-tooth been breaking rules today?

NORA.   No! What makes you think that?

HELMER.   Are you sure the sweet-tooth didn't drop in at the confectioner's?

NORA.   No, I assure you, Torvald—

HELMER.   She didn't nibble a little candy?

NORA.   No, really not.

HELMER.   Not even a macaroon or two?

NORA.   No, Torvald, I assure you—really—

HELMER.   There, there! Of course I'm only joking.

NORA *(going to the table right).*   It would never occur to me to go against your wishes.

HELMER.   Of course I know that—and anyhow—you've given me your word— *(Goes to her.)* Well, my darling, I won't pry into your little Christmas secrets. They'll be unveiled tonight under the Christmas tree.

NORA.   Did you remember to ask Dr. Rank?

HELMER.   No, it really isn't necessary. He'll take it for granted he's to dine with us. However, I'll ask him, when he stops by this morning. I've ordered some specially good wine. I am so looking forward to this evening, Nora, dear!

NORA.   So am I—And the children will have such fun!

HELMER.   Ah! How nice it is to feel secure; to look forward to a good position with an ample income. It's a wonderful prospect—isn't it, Nora?

NORA.   It's simply marvelous!

HELMER.   Do you remember last Christmas? For three whole weeks—you locked yourself up every evening until past midnight—making paper flowers for the Christmas tree—and a lot of other wonderful things you wanted to surprise us with. I was never so bored in my life!

NORA.   I wasn't a bit bored.

HELMER *(smiling)*.   But it all came to rather a sad end, didn't it, Nora?

NORA.   Oh, do you have to tease me about that again? How could I help the cat coming in and tearing it all to pieces?

HELMER.   Of course you couldn't help it, you poor darling! You meant to give us a good time—that's the main thing. But it's nice to know those lean times are over.

NORA.   It's wonderful!

HELMER.   Now I don't have to sit here alone, boring myself to death; and you don't have to strain your dear little eyes, and prick your sweet little fingers—

NORA *(claps her hands)*.   No, I don't—do I, Torvald! Oh! How lovely it all is. *(Takes his arm.)* I want to tell you how I thought we'd arrange things after Christmas. *(The doorbell rings.)* Oh there's the bell. *(Tidies up the room a bit.)* It must be a visitor—how tiresome!

HELMER.   I don't care to see any visitors, Nora—remember that.

HELENE *(in the doorway)*.   There's a lady to see you, Ma'am.

NORA.   Well, show her in.

HELENE *(to Helmer)*.   And the Doctor's here too, Sir.

HELMER.   Did he go straight to my study?

HELENE.   Yes, he did, Sir.

(Helmer goes into his study. Helene ushers in Mrs. Linde, who is dressed in traveling clothes, and closes the door behind her.)

MRS. LINDE *(in subdued and hesitant tone)*.   How do you do, Nora?

NORA *(doubtfully)*.   How do you do?

MRS. LINDE.   You don't recognize me, do you?

NORA.   No, I don't think—and yet—I seem to—*(With a sudden outburst.)* Kristine! Is it really you?

MRS. LINDE.   Yes, it's really I!

NORA.   Kristine! And to think of my not knowing you! But how could I when— *(More softly.)* You've changed so, Kristine!

MRS. LINDE.   Yes I suppose I have. After all—it's nine or ten years—

NORA.   Is it *that* long since we met? Yes, so it is. Oh, these last eight years have been such happy ones! Fancy your being in town! And imagine taking that long trip in midwinter! How brave you are!

MRS. LINDE.   I arrived by the morning boat.

NORA.   You've come for the Christmas holidays, I suppose—what fun! Oh, what a good time we'll have! Do take off your things. You're not cold, are you? *(Helping her.)*

There; now we'll sit here by the stove. No, you take the armchair; I'll sit here in the rocker. *(Seizes her hands.)* Now you look more like yourself again. It was just at first— you're a bit paler, Kristine—and perhaps a little thinner.

MRS. LINDE.   And much, much older, Nora.

NORA.   Well, perhaps a *little* older—a tiny, tiny bit—not much, though. *(She suddenly checks herself; seriously:)* Oh, but, Kristine! What a thoughtless wretch I am, chattering away like that—Dear, darling Kristine, do forgive me!

MRS. LINDE.   What for, Nora, dear?

NORA *(softly)*.   You lost your husband, didn't you, Kristine! You're a widow.

MRS. LINDE.   Yes, my husband died three years ago.

NORA.   Yes, I remember; I saw it in the paper. Oh, I *did* mean to write to you, Kristine! But I kept on putting it off, and all sorts of things kept coming in the way.

MRS. LINDE.   I understand, dear Nora.

NORA.   No, it was beastly of me, Kristine! Oh, you poor darling! What you must have gone through—And he died without leaving you anything, didn't he?

MRS. LINDE.   Yes.

NORA.   And you have no children?

MRS. LINDE.   No.

NORA.   Nothing then?

MRS. LINDE.   Nothing—Not even grief, not even regret.

NORA *(looking at her incredulously)*.   But how is that possible, Kristine?

MRS. LINDE *(smiling sadly and stroking her hair)*.   It sometimes happens, Nora.

NORA.   Imagine being so utterly alone! It must be dreadful for you, Kristine! I have three of the loveliest children! I can't show them to you just now, they're out with their nurse. But I want you to tell me all about yourself—

MRS. LINDE.   No, no; I'd rather hear about you, Nora—

NORA.   No, I want you to begin. I'm not going to be selfish today. I'm going to think only of you. Oh! but one thing I *must* tell you. You haven't heard about the wonderful thing that's just happened to us, have you?

MRS. LINDE.   No. What is it?

NORA.   My husband's been elected president of the Joint Stock Bank!

MRS. LINDE.   Oh, Nora—How splendid!

NORA.   Yes, isn't it? you see, a lawyer's position is so uncertain, especially if he refuses to handle any cases that are in the least bit—shady; Torvald is very particular about such things—and I agree with him, of course! You can imagine how glad we are. He's to start at the Bank right after the New Year; he'll make a big salary and all sorts of percentages. We'll be able to live quite differently from then on—we'll have everything we want. Oh, Kristine! I'm so happy and excited! Won't it be wonderful to have lots and lots of money, and nothing to worry about!

MRS. LINDE.   It certainly would be wonderful to have enough for one's needs.

NORA.   Oh, not just for one's *needs*, Kristine! But heaps and heaps of money!

MRS. LINDE *(with a smile)*.   Nora, Nora, I see you haven't grown up yet! I remember at school you were a frightful spendthrift.

NORA *(quietly; smiling)*.   Yes; that's what Torvald always says. *(Holding up her forefinger.)* But I haven't had much chance to be a spendthrift. We have had to work hard— both of us.

MRS. LINDE.   You too?

NORA.   Oh yes! I did all sorts of little jobs: needlework, embroidery, crochet—that sort of thing. *(Casually.)* And other things as well. I suppose you know that Torvald left the Government service right after we were married. There wasn't much chance of promotion in his department, and of course he had to earn more money when he had me to support. But that first year he overworked himself terribly. He had to undertake all sorts of odd jobs, worked from morning till night. He couldn't stand it; his health gave way and he become deathly ill. The doctors said he absolutely *must* spend some time in the South.

MRS. LINDE.   Yes, I heard you spent a whole year in Italy.

NORA.   Yes, we did. I wasn't easy to arrange, I can tell you. It was just after Ivar's birth. But of course we had to go. It was a wonderful trip, and it saved Torvald's life. But it cost a fearful lot of money, Kristine.

MRS. LINDE.   Yes, it must have.

NORA.   Twelve hundred dollars! Four thousand eight hundred crowns! That's an awful lot of money, you know.

MRS. LINDE.   You were lucky to have it.

NORA.   Well, you see, we got it from Father.

MRS. LINDE.   Oh, I see. Wasn't it just about that time that your father died?

NORA.   Yes, it was, Kristine. Just think! I wasn't able to go to him—I couldn't be there to nurse him! I was expecting Ivar at the time and then I had my poor sick Torvald to look after. Dear, darling Papa! I never saw him again, Kristine. It's the hardest thing I have had to go through since my marriage.

MRS. LINDE.   I know you were awfully fond of him. And after that you went to Italy?

NORA.   Yes; then we had the money, you see; and the doctors said we must lose no time; so we started a month later.

MRS. LINDE.   And your husband came back completely cured?

NORA.   Strong as an ox!

MRS. LINDE.   But—what about the doctor then?

NORA.   How do you mean?

MRS. LINDE.   Didn't the maid say something about a doctor, just as I arrived?

NORA.   Oh, yes; Dr. Rank. He's our best friend—it's not a professional call; he stops in to see us every day. No, Torvald hasn't had a moment's illness since; and the children are strong and well, and so am I. *(Jumps up and claps her hands.)* Oh Kristine, Kristine! How lovely it is to be alive and happy! But how disgraceful of me! Here I am talking about nothing but myself! *(Seats herself upon a footstool close to Kristine and lays her arms on her lap.)* Please don't be cross with me—Is it really true, Kristine, that you didn't love your husband? Why did you marry him, then?

MRS. LINDE.   Well, you see—Mother was still alive; she was bedridden: completely helpless; and I had my two younger brothers to take care of. I didn't think it would be right to refuse him.

NORA.   No, I suppose not. I suppose he had money then?

MRS. LINDE.   Yes, I believe he was quite well off. But his business was precarious, Nora. When he died it all went to pieces, and there was nothing left.

NORA.   And then—?

MRS. LINDE.   Then I had to struggle along as best I could. I had a small shop for a while, and then I started a little school. These last three years have been one long battle—but it is over now, Nora. My dear mother is at rest—She doesn't need me any more. And my brothers are old enough to work, and can look after themselves.

NORA.   You must have such a free feeling!

MRS. LINDE.   No—only one of complete emptiness. I haven't a soul to live for! *(Stands up restlessly.)* I suppose that's why I felt I had to get away. I should think here it would be easier to find something to do—something to occupy one's thoughts. I might be lucky enough to get a steady job here—some office work, perhaps—

NORA.   But that's so terribly tiring, Kristine; and you look so tired already. What you need is a rest. Couldn't you go to some nice watering-place?°

MRS. LINDE *(going to the window)*.   I have no father to give me the money, Nora.

NORA *(rising)*.   Oh, please don't be cross with me!

MRS. LINDE *(goes to her)*.   My dear Nora, you mustn't be cross with me! In my sort of position it's hard not to become bitter. One has no one to work for, and yet one can't give up the struggle. One must go on living, and it makes one selfish. I'm ashamed to admit it—but, just now, when you told me the good news about your husband's new position—I was glad—not so much for your sake as for mine.

NORA.   How do you mean? Oh of course—I see! You think Torvald might perhaps help you.

MRS. LINDE.   That's what I thought, yes.

NORA.   And so he shall, Kristine. Just you leave it to me. I'll get him in a really good mood—and then bring it up quite casually. Oh, it would be such fun to help you!

MRS. LINDE.   How good of you, Nora dear, to bother on my account! It's especially good of you—after all, you've never had to go through any hardship.

NORA.   I? Not go through any—?

MRS. LINDE *(smiling)*.   Well—good heavens—a little needlework, and so forth—You're just a child, Nora.

NORA *(tosses her head and paces the room)*.   You needn't be so patronizing!

MRS. LINDE.   No?

NORA.   You're just like all the rest. You all think I'm incapable of being serious—

MRS. LINDE.   Oh, come now—

NORA.   You seem to think I've had no troubles—that I've been through nothing in my life!

MRS. LINDE.   But you've just told me all your troubles, Nora dear.

NORA.   I've only told you trifles! *(Softly.)* I haven't mentioned the important thing.

MRS. LINDE.   Important thing? What do you mean?

NORA.   I know you look down on me, Kristine; but you really shouldn't. You take pride in having worked so hard and so long for your mother.

MRS. LINDE.   I don't look down on anyone, Nora; I can't help feeling proud and happy too, to have been able to make Mother's last days a little easier—

NORA.   And you're proud of what you did for your brothers, too.

MRS. LINDE.   I think I have a right to be.

NORA.   Yes, so do I. But I want you to know, Kristine—that I, too, have something to be proud of.

MRS. LINDE.   I don't doubt that. But what are you referring to?

NORA.   Hush! We must talk quietly. It would be dreadful if Torvald overheard us! He must never know about it! No one must know about it, except you.

MRS. LINDE.   And what is it, Nora?

NORA.   Come over here. *(Draws her down beside her on sofa.)* Yes, I have something to be proud and happy about too. I saved Torvald's life, you see.

MRS. LINDE.   Saved his life? But how?

NORA.   I told you about our trip to Italy. Torvald would never have recovered if it hadn't been for that.

watering-place: a beach resort.

MRS. LINDE.   Yes, I know—and your father gave you the necessary money.

NORA *(smiling)*.   That's what everyone thinks—Torvald too; but—

MRS. LINDE.   Well—?

NORA.   Papa never gave us a penny. I raised the money myself.

MRS. LINDE.   All that money! You?

NORA.   Twelve hundred dollars. Four thousand eight hundred crowns. What do you think of that?

MRS. LINDE.   But, Nora, how on earth did you do it? Did you win it in the lottery?

NORA *(contemptuously)*.   The lottery! Of course not! Any fool could have done that!

MRS. LINDE.   Where did you get it then?

NORA *(hums and smiles mysteriously)*.   H'm; tra-la-la-la.

MRS. LINDE.   You certainly couldn't have borrowed it.

NORA.   Why not?

MRS. LINDE.   A wife can't borrow without a husband's consent.

NORA *(tossing her head)*.   Oh, I don't know! If a wife has a good head on her shoulders—and has a little sense of business—

MRS. LINDE.   I don't in the least understand, Nora—

NORA.   Well, you needn't. I never said I borrowed the money. I may have got it some other way. *(Throws herself back on the sofa.)* Perhaps I got it from some admirer. After all when one is as attractive as I am—!

MRS. LINDE.   What a mad little creature you are!

NORA.   I'm sure you're dying of curiosity, Kristine—

MRS. LINDE.   Nora, are you sure you haven't been a little rash?

NORA *(sitting upright again)*.   Is it rash to save one's husband's life?

MRS. LINDE.   But mightn't it be rash to do such a thing behind his back?

NORA.   But I couldn't tell him—don't you understand that! He wasn't even supposed to know how ill he was. The doctors didn't tell him—they came to me privately, told me his life was in danger and that he could only be saved by living in the South for a while. At first I tried persuasion; I cried, I begged, I cajoled—I said how much I longed to take a trip abroad like other young wives; I reminded him of my condition and told him he ought to humor me—and finally, I came right out and suggested that we borrow the money. But then, Kristine, he was almost angry; he said I was being frivolous and that it was his duty as my husband not to indulge my whims and fancies—I think that's what he called them. Then I made up my mind he must be saved in spite of himself—and I thought of a way.

MRS. LINDE.   But didn't he ever find out from your father that the money was not from him?

NORA.   No; never. You see, Papa died just about that time. I was going to tell him all about it and beg him not to give me away. But he was so very ill—and then, it was no longer necessary—unfortunately.

MRS. LINDE.   And you have never confided all this to your husband?

NORA.   Good heavens, no! That's out of the question! He's much too strict in manners of that sort. And besides—Torvald could never bear to think of owing anything to me! It would hurt his self-respect—wound his pride. It would ruin everything between us. Our whole marriage would be wrecked by it!

MRS. LINDE.   Don't you think you'll ever tell him?

NORA *(thoughtfully; half-smiling)*.   Perhaps some day—a long time from now when I'm no longer so pretty and attractive. No! Don't laugh! Some day when Torvald is no longer as much in love with me as he is now; when it no longer amuses him to see me dance and dress up and act for him—then it might be useful to have something in reserve. *(Breaking off.)* Oh, what nonsense! That time will never come! Well—what do you think of my great secret, Kristine? Haven't I something to be proud of too? It's caused me endless worry, though. It hasn't been easy to fulfill my obligations. You know, in business there are things called installments, and quarterly interest—and they're dreadfully hard to meet on time. I've had to save a little here and there, wherever I could I couldn't save much out of the housekeeping, for of course Torvald had to live well. And I couldn't let the children go about badly dressed; any money I got for them, I spent on them, the darlings!

MRS. LINDE.   Poor Nora! I suppose it had to come out of your own allowance.

NORA.   Yes, of course. But after all, the whole thing was my doing. Whenever Torvald gave me money to buy some new clothes, or other things I needed, I never spent more than half of it; I always picked out the simplest cheapest dresses. It's a blessing that almost anything looks well on me—so Torvald never knew the difference. But it's been hard sometimes, Kristine. It's so nice to have pretty clothes—isn't it?

MRS. LINDE.   I suppose it is.

NORA.   And I made money in other ways too. Last winter I was lucky enough to get a lot of copying to do. I shut myself up in my room every evening and wrote far into the night. Sometimes I was absolutely exhausted—but it was fun all the same—working like that and earning money. It made me feel almost like a man!

MRS. LINDE.   How much have you managed to pay off?

NORA.   Well, I really don't know exactly. It's hard to keep track of things like that. All I know is—I've paid every penny I could scrape together. There were times when I didn't know which way to turn! *(Smiles.)* Then I used to sit here and pretend that some rich old gentleman had fallen madly in love with me—

MRS. LINDE.   What are you talking about? *What* old gentleman?

NORA.   I'm just joking! And then he was to die and when they opened his will, there in large letters were to be the words: "I leave all my fortune to that charming Nora Helmer to be handed over to her immediately."

MRS. LINDE.   But who *is* this old gentleman?

NORA.   Good heavens, can't you understand? There never *was* any such old gentleman; I just used to make him up, when I was at the end of my rope and didn't know where to turn for money. But it doesn't matter now—the tiresome old fellow can stay where he is as far as I am concerned. I no longer need him nor his money; for now my troubles are over. *(Springing up.)* Oh, isn't it wonderful to think of, Kristine. No more troubles! No more worry! I'll be able to play and romp about with the children; I'll be able to make a charming lovely home for Torvald—have everything just as he likes it. And soon spring will be here, with its great blue sky. Perhaps we might take a little trip—I might see the ocean again. Oh, it's so marvelous to be alive and to be happy!

(The hall doorbell rings.)

MRS. LINDE *(rising).*   There's the bell. Perhaps I had better go.

NORA.   No, no; do stay! It's probably just someone for Torvald.

HELENE *(in the doorway).*   Excuse me, Ma'am; there's a gentleman asking for Mr. Helmer—but the doctor's in there—and I didn't know if I should disturb him—

NORA.   Who is it?

KROGSTAD *(in the doorway).*   It is I, Mrs. Helmer.

(Mrs. Linde starts and turns away to the window.)

NORA (*goes a step toward him, anxiously; in a low voice*).   You? What is it? Why do you want to see my husband?

KROGSTAD.   It's to do with Bank business—more or less. I have a small position in the Joint Stock Bank, and I hear your husband is to be the new president.

NORA.   Then it's just—?

KROGSTAD.   Just routine business, Mrs. Helmer; nothing else.

NORA.   Then, please be good enough to go into his study.

(*Krogstad goes. She bows indifferently while she closes the door into the hall. Then she goes to the stove and tends the fire.*)

MRS. LINDE.   Who was that man, Nora?

NORA.   A Mr. Krogstad—he's a lawyer.

MRS. LINDE.   I was right, then.

NORA.   Do you know him?

MRS. LINDE.   I used to know him—many years ago. He worked in a law office in our town.

NORA.   Yes, so he did.

MRS. LINDE.   How he has changed!

NORA.   He was unhappily married, they say.

MRS. LINDE.   Is he a widower now?

NORA.   Yes—with lots of children. There! That's better! (*She closes the door of the stove and moves the rocking chair a little to one side.*)

MRS. LINDE.   I'm told he's mixed up in a lot of rather questionable business.

NORA.   He may be; I really don't know. But don't let's talk about business—it's so tiresome.

(*Dr. Rank comes out of Helmer's room.*)

RANK (*still in the doorway*).   No, no, I won't disturb you. I'll go in and see your wife for a moment. (*Sees Mrs. Linde.*) Oh, I beg your pardon. I seem to be in the way here, too.

NORA.   Of course not! (*Introduces them.*) Dr. Rank—Mrs. Linde.

RANK.   Well, well, I've often heard that name mentioned in this house; didn't I pass you on the stairs when I came in?

MRS. LINDE.   Yes; I'm afraid I climb them very slowly. They wear me out!

RANK.   A little on the delicate side—eh?

MRS. LINDE.   No; just a bit overtired.

RANK.   I see. So I suppose you've come to town for a good rest—on a round of dissipation!

MRS. LINDE.   I have come to look for work.

RANK.   Is that the best remedy for tiredness?

MRS. LINDE.   One has to live, Doctor.

RANK.   Yes, I'm told that's necessary.

NORA.   Oh, come now, Dr. Rank! You're not above wanting to live yourself!

RANK.   That's true enough. No matter how wretched I may be, I still want to hang on as long as possible. All my patients have that feeling too. Even the *morally* sick seem to share it. There's a wreck of a man in there with Helmer now—

MRS. LINDE (*softly*).   Ah!

NORA.   Whom do you mean?

RANK.   A fellow named Krogstad, he's a lawyer—you wouldn't know anything about him. He's thoroughly depraved—rotten to the core—Yet even he declared, as though it were a matter of paramount importance, that he must live.

NORA.   Really? What did he want with Torvald?

RANK.   I have no idea; I gathered it was some Bank business.

NORA.   I didn't know that Krog—that this man Krogstad had anything to do with the Bank?

RANK.   He seems to have some sort of position there. *(To Mrs. Linde.)* I don't know if this is true in your part of the country—but there are men who make it a practice of prying about in other people's business, searching for individuals of doubtful character—and having discovered their secret, place them in positions of trust, where they can keep an eye on them, and make use of them at will. Honest men—men of strong moral fiber—they leave out in the cold.

MRS. LINDE.   Perhaps the weaklings need more help.

RANK *(shrugs his shoulders)*.   That point of view is fast turning society into a clinic.

(Nora, deep in her own thoughts, breaks into half-stifled laughter and claps her hands.)

RANK.   Why should that make you laugh? I wonder if you've any idea what "society" is?

NORA.   Why should I care about your tiresome old "society"? I was laughing at something quite different—something frightfully amusing. Tell me, Dr. Rank—will all the employees at the Bank be dependent on Torvald now?

RANK.   Is *that* what strikes you as so amusing?

NORA *(smiles and hums)*.   Never you mind! Never you mind! *(Walks about the room.)* What fun to think that we—that Torvald—has such power over so many people. *(Takes the bag from her pocket.)* Dr. Rank, how about a macaroon?

RANK.   Well, well!—Macaroons, eh? I thought they were forbidden here.

NORA.   These are some Kristine brought—

MRS. LINDE.   What! I—

NORA.   Now, you needn't be so frightened. How could you possibly know that Torvald had forbidden them? He's afraid they'll spoil my teeth. Oh, well—just for once! Don't you agree, Dr. Rank? There you are! *(Puts a macaroon into his mouth.)* You must have one, too, Kristine. And I'll have just one—just a tiny one, or at most two. *(Walks about again.)* Oh dear, I am so happy! There's just one thing in all the world that would give me the greatest pleasure.

RANK.   What's that?

NORA.   It's something I long to say in front of Torvald.

RANK.   What's to prevent you?

NORA.   Oh, I don't dare; it isn't nice.

MRS. LINDE.   Not nice?

RANK.   It might be unwise, then; but you can certainly say it to us. What is it you so long to say in front of Torvald?

NORA.   I'd so love to say "Damn!—damn!—damn it all!"

RANK.   Have you gone crazy?

MRS. LINDE.   Good gracious, Nora—

RANK.   Go ahead and say it—here he comes!

NORA *(hides the macaroons)*.   Hush—sh—sh.

(Helmer comes out of his room; he carries his hat and overcoat.)

NORA *(going to him)*.   Well, Torvald, dear, did you get rid of him?

HELMER.   He has just gone.

NORA.   Let me introduce you—this is Kristine, who has just arrived in town—

HELMER.   Kristine? I'm sorry—but I really don't—

NORA.   Mrs. Linde, Torvald, dear—Kristine Linde.

HELMER.   Oh yes! I suppose you're one of my wife's school friends?

MRS. LINDE.   Yes; we knew each other as children.

NORA.   Imagine, Torvald! She came all that long way just to talk to you.

HELMER.   How do you mean?

MRS. LINDE.   Well, it wasn't exactly—

NORA.   Kristine is tremendously good at office work, and her great dream is to get a position with a really clever man—so she can improve still more, you see—

HELMER.   Very sensible, Mrs. Linde.

NORA.   And when she heard that you had become president of the Bank—it was in the paper, you know—she started off at once; you *will* try and do something for Kristine, won't you, Torvald? For my sake?

HELMER.   It's by no means impossible. You're a widow, I presume?

MRS. LINDE.   Yes.

HELMER.   And you've already had business experience?

MRS. LINDE.   A good deal.

HELMER.   Then, I think it's quite likely I may be able to find a place for you.

NORA *(clapping her hands).*   There, you see! You see!

HELMER.   You have come at a good moment, Mrs. Linde.

MRS. LINDE.   How can I ever thank you—?

HELMER *(smiling).*   Don't mention it. *(Puts on his overcoat.)* But just now, I'm afraid you must excuse me—

RANK.   I'll go with you. *(Fetches his fur coat from the hall and warms it at the stove.)*

NORA.   Don't be long, Torvald, dear.

HELMER.   I shan't be more than an hour.

NORA.   Are you going too, Kristine?

MRS. LINDE *(putting on her outdoor things).*   Yes; I must go and find a place to live.

HELMER.   We can all go out together.

NORA *(helping her).*   How tiresome that we're so cramped for room, Kristine; otherwise—

MRS. LINDE.   Oh, you mustn't think of that! Good-bye, dear Nora, and thanks for everything.

NORA.   Good-bye for the present. Of course you'll come back this evening. And you too, Dr. Rank—eh? If you're well enough? But of course you'll be well enough! Wrap up warmly now! *(They go out talking, into the hall; children's voices are heard on the stairs.)* Here they come! Here they come! *(She runs to the outer door and opens it. The nurse, Anne-Marie, enters the hall with the children.)* Come in, come in—you darlings! Just look at them, Kristine. Aren't they sweet?

RANK.   No chattering in this awful draught!

HELMER.   Come along, Mrs. Linde; you have to be a mother to put up with this!

(Dr. Rank, Helmer, and Mrs. Linde go down the stairs; Anne-Marie enters the room with the children; Nora comes in too, shutting the door behind her.)

NORA.   How fresh and bright you look! And what red cheeks! Like apples and roses. *(The children chatter to her during what follows.)* Did you have a good time? Splendid! You gave Emmy and Bob a ride on your sled? Both at once? You *are* a clever boy, Ivar!

Let me hold her for a bit, Anne-Marie. My darling little doll-baby. *(Takes the smallest from the nurse and dances with her.)* All right, Bobbie! Mama will dance with you too. You threw snowballs, did you? I should have been in on that! Never mind, Anne; I'll undress them myself—oh, do let me—it's such fun. Go on into the nursery, you look half-frozen. There's some hot coffee in there on the stove. *(The nurse goes into the room on the left. Nora takes off the children's things and throws them down anywhere, while the children all talk together.)* Not really! You were chased by a big dog? But he didn't bite you? No; dogs don't bite tiny little doll-babies! Don't touch the packages, Ivar. What's in them? Wouldn't you like to know! No. No! Careful! It might bite! Come on, let's play. What will we play? Hide-and-seek? Let's play hide-and seek. Bob, you hide first! Do you want me to? All right! I'll hide first then.

(She and the children play, laughing and shouting, all over the room and in the adjacent room the left. Finally, Nora hides under the table; the children come rushing in, look for her, but cannot find her, hear her half-suppressed laughter, rush to the table, lift up the cover and see her. Loud shouts of delight. She creeps out, as though to frighten them. More shouts. Meanwhile there has been a knock at the door leading into the hall. No one has heard it. Now the door is half-opened and Krogstad appears. He waits a little—the game continues.)

KROGSTAD.   I beg your pardon, Mrs. Helmer—

NORA *(with a stifled scream, turns round and half jumps up).*   Oh! What do you want?

KROGSTAD.   Excuse me; the outer door was ajar—someone must have forgotten to close it—

NORA *(standing up).*   My husband is not at home, Mr. Krogstad.

KROGSTAD.   I know that.

NORA.   Then, what do you want here?

KROGSTAD.   I want a few words with you.

NORA.   With—? *(To the children, softly.)* Go in Anne-Marie. What? No—the strange man won't do Mama any harm; when he's gone we'll go on playing. *(She leads the children into the right hand room, and shuts the door behind them; uneasy, in suspense.)* You want to speak to me?

KROGSTAD.   Yes, I do.

NORA.   Today? But it's not the first of the month yet—

KROGSTAD.   No, it is Christmas Eve. It's up to you whether your Christmas is a merry one.

NORA.   What is it you want? Today I can't possibly—

KROGSTAD.   That doesn't concern me for the moment. This is about something else. You have a few minutes, haven't you?

NORA.   I suppose so; although—

KROGSTAD.   Good. I was sitting in the restaurant opposite, and I saw your husband go down the street—

NORA.   Well?

KROGSTAD.   —with a lady.

NORA.   What of it?

KROGSTAD.   May I ask if that lady was a Mrs. Linde?

NORA.   Yes.

KROGSTAD.   She's just come to town, hasn't she?

NORA.   Yes. Today.

KROGSTAD.   Is she a good friend of yours?

NORA.   Yes, she is. But I can't imagine—

KROGSTAD.   I used to know her too.

NORA.   Yes, I know you did.

KROGSTAD.   Then you know all about it. I thought as much. Now, tell me: is Mrs. Linde to have a place in the Bank?

NORA.   How dare you question me like this, Mr. Krogstad—you, one of my husband's employees! But since you ask—you might as well know. Yes, Mrs. Linde is to have a position at the Bank, and it is I who recommended her. Does that satisfy you, Mr. Krogstad?

KROGSTAD.   I was right, then.

NORA *(walks up and down).*   After all, one has a little influence, now and then. Even if one is only a woman it doesn't always follow that—people in subordinate positions, Mr. Krogstad, ought really to be careful how they offend anyone who—h'm—

KROGSTAD.   —has influence?

NORA.   Precisely.

KROGSTAD *(taking another tone).*   Then perhaps you'll be so kind, Mrs. Helmer, as to use your influence on *my* behalf?

NORA.   What? How do you mean?

KROGSTAD.   Perhaps you'll be good enough to see that I *retain* my subordinate position?

NORA.   But, I don't understand. Who wants to take it from you?

KROGSTAD.   Oh, don't try and play the innocent! I can well understand that it would be unpleasant for your friend to associate with me; and I understand too, whom I have to thank for my dismissal.

NORA.   But I assure you—

KROGSTAD.   Never mind all that—there is still time. But I advise you to use your influence to prevent this.

NORA.   But, Mr. Krogstad, I *have* no influence—absolutely none!

KROGSTAD.   Indeed! I thought you just told me yourself—

NORA.   You misunderstood me—*really* you did! You must know my husband would never be influenced by me!

KROGSTAD.   Your husband and I were at the University together—I know him well. I don't suppose he's any more inflexible than other married men.

NORA.   Don't you dare talk disrespectfully about my husband, or I'll show you the door!

KROGSTAD.   The little lady's plucky.

NORA.   I'm no longer afraid of you. I'll soon be free of all this—after the first of the year.

KROGSTAD *(in a more controlled manner).*   Listen to me, Mrs. Helmer. This is a matter of life and death to me. I warn you I shall fight with all my might to keep my position in the Bank.

NORA.   So it seems.

KROGSTAD.   It's not just the salary; that is the least important part of it—It's something else—Well, I might as well be frank with you. I suppose you know, like everyone else, that once—a long time ago—I got into quite a bit of trouble.

NORA.   I have never heard something about it, I believe.

KROGSTAD.   The matter never came to court; but from that time on, all doors were closed to me. I then went into the business with which you are familiar. I had to do something; and I don't think I've been among the worst. But now I must get away from all that. My sons are growing up, you see; for their sake I'm determined to recapture my good name. This position in the Bank was to be the first step; and now your husband wants to kick me back into the mud again.

NORA.   But I tell you, Mr. Krogstad, it's not in my power to help you.

KROGSTAD.   Only because you don't really want to; but I can compel you to do it, if I choose.

NORA.   You wouldn't tell my husband that I owe you money?

KROGSTAD.   And suppose I were to?

NORA.   But that would be an outrageous thing to do! *(With tears in her voice.)* My secret—that I've guarded with such pride—such joy! I couldn't bear to have him find it out in such an ugly, hateful way—to have him find it out from you! I couldn't bear it! It would be too horribly unpleasant!

KROGSTAD.   Only unpleasant, Mrs. Helmer?

NORA *(vehemently)* But just you do it! You'll be the one to suffer; for then my husband will *really* know the kind of man you are—there'll be no chance of keeping your job then!

KROGSTAD.   Didn't you hear my question? I asked if it were only unpleasantness you feared?

NORA.   If my husband got to know about it, he'd naturally pay you off at once, and then we'd have nothing more to do with you.

KROGSTAD *(takes a step towards her).*   Listen, Mrs. Helmer: Either you have a very bad memory, or you know nothing about business. I think I'd better make the position clear to you.

NORA.   What do you mean?

KROGSTAD.   When your husband fell ill, you came to me to borrow twelve hundred dollars.

NORA.   I didn't know what else to do.

KROGSTAD.   I promised to find you the money—

NORA.   And you did find it.

KROGSTAD.   I promised to find you the money, on certain conditions, At that time you were so taken up with your husband's illness and so anxious to procure the money for your journey, that you probably did not give much thought to details. Perhaps I'd better remind you of them. I promised to find you the amount in exchange for a note, which I drew up.

NORA.   Yes, and I signed it.

KROGSTAD.   Very good. But then I added a clause, stating that your father would stand sponsor for the debt. This clause your father was to have signed.

NORA.   Was to—? He did sign it.

KROGSTAD.   I left the date blank, so that your father himself should date his signature. You recall that?

NORA.   Yes, I believe—

KROGSTAD.   Then I gave you the paper, and you were to mail to your father. Isn't that so?

NORA.   Yes.

KROGSTAD.   And you must have mailed it at once; for five or six days later you brought me back the document with your father's signature; and then I handed you the money.

NORA.   Well? Haven't I made my payments punctually?

KROGSTAD.   Fairly—yes. But to return to the point: That was a sad time for you, wasn't it, Mrs. Helmer?

NORA. It was indeed!

KROGSTAD. Your father was very ill, I believe?

NORA. Yes—he was dying.

KROGSTAD. And he did die soon after, didn't he?

NORA. Yes.

KROGSTAD. Now tell me, Mrs. Helmer: Do you happen to recollect the date of your father's death: the day of the month, I mean?

NORA. Father died on the 29th of September.

KROGSTAD. Quite correct. I have made inquiries. Now here is a strange thing, Mrs. Helmer—*(Produces a paper.)* something rather hard to explain.

NORA. What do you mean? What strange thing?

KROGSTAD. The strange thing about it is, that your father seems to have signed this paper three days after his death!

NORA. I don't understand—

KROGSTAD. Your father died on the 29th of September. But look at this: his signature is dated October 2nd! Isn't that rather strange, Mrs. Helmer? *(Nora is silent.)* Can you explain that to me? *(Nora continues silent.)* It is curious, too, that the words "October 2nd" and the year are not in your father's handwriting, but in a handwriting I seem to know. This could easily be explained, however; your father might have forgotten to date his signature, and someone might have added the date at random, before the fact of your father's death was known. There is nothing wrong in that. It all depends on the signature itself. It is of course genuine, Mrs. Helmer? It was your father himself who wrote his name here?

NORA *(after a short silence, throws her head back and looks defiantly at him).* No, it wasn't. *I* wrote Father's name.

KROGSTAD. I suppose you realize, Mrs. Helmer, what a dangerous confession that is?

NORA. Why should it be dangerous? You will get your money soon enough!

KROGSTAD. I'd like to ask you a question: Why didn't you send the paper to your father?

NORA. It was impossible. Father was too ill. If I had asked him for his signature, he'd have wanted to know what the money was for. In his condition I simply could not tell him that my husband's life was in danger. That's why it was impossible.

KROGSTAD. Then wouldn't it have been wiser to give up the journey?

NORA. How could I? That journey was to save my husband's life. I simply couldn't give it up.

KROGSTAD. And it never occurred to you that you weren't being honest with me?

NORA. I really couldn't concern myself with that. You meant nothing to me—In fact I couldn't help disliking you for making it all so difficult—with your cold, businesslike clauses and conditions—when you knew my husband's life was at stake.

KROGSTAD. You evidently haven't the faintest idea, Mrs. Helmer, what you have been guilty of. Yet let me tell you that it was nothing more and nothing worse that made me an outcast from society.

NORA. You don't expect me to believe that you ever did a brave thing to save your wife's life?

KROGSTAD. The law takes no account of motives.

NORA. It must be a very bad law, then!

KROGSTAD. Bad or not, if I produce this document in court, you will be condemned according to the law.

NORA.   I don't believe that for a minute. Do you mean to tell me that a daughter has no right to spare her dying father worry and anxiety? Or that a wife has no right to save her husband's life? I may not know much about it—but I'm sure there must be something or other in the law that permits such things. You as a lawyer should be aware of that. You don't seem to know very much about the law, Mr. Krogstad.

KROGSTAD.   Possibly not. But business—the kind of business we are concerned with—I *do* know something about. Don't you agree? Very well, then; do as you please. But I warn you: if I am made to suffer a second time, you shall keep me company. *(Bows and goes out through the hall.)*

NORA *(stands a while thinking, then tosses her head)*.   What nonsense! He's just trying to frighten me. I'm not such a fool as all that! *(Begins folding the children's clothes. Pauses.)* And yet?— No, it's impossible! After all—I only did it for love's sake.

CHILDREN *(at the door, left)*. Mamma, the strange man has gone now.

NORA.   Yes, yes, I know. But don't tell anyone about the strange man. Do you hear? Not even Papa!

CHILDREN.   No, Mamma; now will you play with us again?

NORA.   No, not just now.

CHILDREN.   But Mamma! You promised!

NORA.   But I can't just now. Run back to the nursery; I have so much to do. Run along now! Run along, my darlings! *(She pushes them gently into the inner room, and closes the door behind them. She sits on the sofa, embroiders a few stitches, but soon pauses.)* No! *(Throws down the work, rises, goes to the hall door and calls out.)* Helene, bring the tree in to me, will you? *(Goes to table, right, and opens the drawer; again pauses.)* No, it's utterly impossible!

HELENE *(carries in the Christmas tree)*.   Where shall I put it, Ma'am?

NORA.   Right there; in the middle of the room.

HELENE.   Is there anything else you need?

NORA.   No, thanks; I have everything.

(Helene, having put down the tree, goes out.)

NORA *(busy dressing the tree)*.   We'll put a candle here—and some flowers here—that dreadful man! But it's just nonsense! There's nothing to worry about. The tree will be lovely. I'll do everything to please you, Torvald; I'll sing for you, I'll dance for you—

(Enter Helmer by the hall door, with a bundle of documents.)

NORA.   Oh! You're back already?

HELMER.   Yes. Has somebody been here?

NORA.   No. Nobody.

HELMER.   That's odd. I just saw Krogstad leave the house.

NORA.   Really? Well—as a matter of fact—Krogstad was here for a moment.

HELMER.   Nora—I can tell by your manner—he came here to ask you to put in a good word for him, didn't he?

NORA.   Yes, Torvald.

HELMER.   And you weren't supposed to tell me he'd been here—You were to do it as if of your own accord—isn't that it?

NORA.   Yes, Torvald; but—

HELMER.   Nora, Nora! How could you consent to such a thing! To have dealings with a man like that—make him promises! And then to lie about it too!

NORA.   Lie!

HELMER.   Didn't you tell me that nobody had been here? *(Threatens with his finger.)* My little bird must never do that again! A songbird must sing clear and true! No false notes! *(Puts arm around her.)* Isn't that the way it should be? Of course it is! *(Lets her go.)* And now we'll say no more about it. *(Sits down before the fire.)* It's so cozy and peaceful here! *(Glances through the documents.)*

NORA *(busy with the tree, after a short silence).*   Torvald!

HELMER.   Yes.

NORA.   I'm so looking forward to the Stenborgs' fancy dress party, day after tomorrow.

HELMER.   And I can't wait to see what surprise you have in store for me.

NORA.   Oh, it's so awful, Torvald!

HELMER.   *What* is?

NORA.   I can't think of anything amusing. Everything seems so silly, so pointless.

HELMER.   Has my little Nora come to *that* conclusion?

NORA *(behind his chair, with her arms on the back).*   Are you very busy, Torvald?

HELMER.   Well—

NORA.   What are all those papers?

HELMER.   Just Bank business.

NORA.   Already!

HELMER.   The board of directors has given me full authority to do some reorganizing—to make a few necessary changes in the staff. I'll have to work on it during Christmas week. I want it all settled by the New Year.

NORA.   I see. So that was why that poor Krogstad—

HELMER.   H'm.

NORA *(still leaning over the chair-back and slowly stroking his hair).*   If you weren't so very busy, I'd ask you to do me a great, great favor, Torvald.

HELMER.   Well, let's hear it! Out with it!

NORA.   You have such a perfect taste, Torvald; and I do so want to look well at the fancy dress ball. Couldn't you take me in hand, and decide what I'm to be, and arrange my costume for me?

HELMER.   Well, well! So we're not so self-sufficient after all! We need a helping hand, do we?

NORA.   Oh, please, Torvald! I know I shall *never* manage without your help!

HELMER.   I'll think about it; we'll hit on something.

NORA.   Oh, how sweet of you! *(Goes to the tree again; pause.)* Those red flowers show up beautifully! Tell me, Torvald; did that Krogstad do something very wrong?

HELMER.   He committed forgery. Have you any idea of what that means?

NORA.   Perhaps he did it out of necessity?

HELMER.   Or perhaps he was just foolhardy, like so many others. I am not so harsh as to condemn a man irrevocably for one mistake.

NORA.   No, of course not!

HELMER.   A man has a chance to rehabilitate himself, if he honestly admits his guilt and takes his punishment.

NORA.   Punishment—

HELMER.   But that wasn't Krogstad's way. He resorted to tricks and evasions; became thoroughly demoralized.

NORA.   You really think it would—?

HELMER.   When a man has that sort of thing on his conscience his life becomes a tissue of lies and deception. He's forced to wear a mask—even with those nearest to him—his own wife and children even. And the children—that's the worst part of it, Nora.

NORA.   Why?

HELMER.   Because the whole atmosphere of the home would be contaminated. The very air the children breathed would be filled with evil.

NORA *(closer behind him).*   Are you sure of that?

HELMER.   As a lawyer, I know it from experience. Almost all cases of early delinquency can be traced to dishonest mothers.

NORA.   Why—only mothers?

HELMER.   It usually stems from the mother's side; but of course it can come from the father too. We lawyers know a lot about such things. And this Krogstad has been deliberately poisoning his own children for years, by surrounding them with lies and hypocrisy—that is why I call him demoralized. *(Holds out both hands to her.)* So my sweet little Nora must promise not to plead his cause. Shake hands on it. Well? What's the matter? Give me your hand. There! That's all settled. I assure you it would have been impossible for me to work with him. It literally gives me a feeling of physical discomfort to come in contact with such people. *(Nora draws her hand away, and moves to the other side of the Christmas tree.)*

NORA.   It's so warm here. And I have such a lot to do.

HELMER *(rises and gathers up his papers).*   I must try and look through some of these papers before dinner. I'll give some thought to your costume too. Perhaps I may even find something to hang in gilt paper on the Christmas tree! *(Lays his hand on her head.)* My own precious little songbird! *(He goes into his study and closes the door after him.)*

NORA *(softly, after a pause).*   It can't be—! It's impossible. Of course it's impossible!

ANNE-MARIE *(at the door, left).*   The babies keep begging to come in and see Mamma.

NORA.   No, no! Don't let them come to me! Keep them with you, Anne-Marie.

ANN-MARIE.   Very well, Ma'am *(Shuts the door.)*

NORA *(pale with terror).*   Harm my children!—Corrupt my home! *(Short pause. She throws back her head.)* It's not true! I know it's not! It could never, never be true!

ACT II

(Scene: The same room. In the corner, beside the piano, stands the Christmas tree, stripped and with the candles burnt out. Nora's outdoor things lie on the sofa. Nora, alone, is walking about restlessly. At last she stops by the sofa, and picks up her cloak.)

NORA *(puts the cloak down again).*   Did someone come in? *(Goes to the hall and listens.)* No; no one; of course no one will come today, Christmas Day; nor tomorrow either. But perhaps—*(Opens the door and looks out.)* No, there's nothing in the mailbox; it's quite empty. *(Comes forward.)* Oh nonsense! He only meant to frighten me. There won't be any trouble. It's all impossible! Why, I—I have three little children!

(Anne-Marie enters from the left, with a large cardboard box.)

ANNE-MARIE.   Well—I found the box with the fancy dress clothes at last, Miss Nora.

NORA.   Thanks; put it on the table.

ANNE-MARIE *(does so).*   I'm afraid they're rather shabby.

NORA.   If I had my way I'd tear them into a thousand pieces!

ANNE-MARIE.   Good gracious! They can be repaired—just have a little patience.

NORA. I'll go and get Mrs. Linde to help me.

ANNE-MARIE. I wouldn't go out again in this awful weather! You might catch cold, Miss Nora, and get sick.

NORA. Worse things might happen—How are the children?

ANNE-MARIE. The poor little things are playing with their Christmas presents; but—

NORA. Have they asked for me?

ANNE-MARIE. They're so used to having Mamma with them.

NORA. I know; but, you see, Anne-Marie, I won't be able to be with them as much as I used to.

ANNE-MARIE. Well, little children soon get used to anything.

NORA. You really think so? Would they forget me if I went away for good?

ANNE-MARIE. Good gracious!—for good!

NORA. Tell me something, Anne-Marie—I've so often wondered about it—how could you bear to part with your child—give it up to strangers?

ANNE-MARIE. Well, you see, I had to—when I came to nurse my little Nora.

NORA. Yes—but how could you *bear* to do it?

ANNE-MARIE. I couldn't afford to say "no" to such a good position. A poor girl who's been in trouble must take what comes. Of course *he* never offered to help me—the wicked sinner!

NORA. Then I suppose your daughter has forgotten all about you.

ANNE-MARIE. No—indeed she hasn't! She even wrote to me—once when she was confirmed and again when she was married.

NORA *(embracing her)*. Dear old Anne-Marie—you were a good mother to me when I was little.

ANNE-MARIE. But then my poor little Nora *had* no mother of her own!

NORA. And if ever my little ones were left without—you'd look after them, wouldn't you?—Oh, that's just nonsense! *(Opens the box.)* Go back to them. Now I must—Just you wait and see how lovely I'll look tomorrow!

ANNE-MARIE. My Miss Nora will be the prettiest person there! *(She goes into the room on the left.)*

NORA *(takes the costume out of the box, but soon throws it down again)*. I wish I dared go out—I'm afraid someone might come. I'm afraid something might happen while I'm gone. That's just silly! No one will come. I must try not to think—This muff needs cleaning. What pretty gloves—they're lovely! I must put it out of my head! One, two, three, four, five, six—*(With a scream.)* Ah! They're here!

(Goes toward the door, then stands irresolute. Mrs. Linde enters from the hall, where she has taken off her things.)

NORA. Oh, it's you, Kristine! There's no one else out there, is there? I'm so glad you have come!

MRS. LINDE. I got a message you'd been asking for me.

NORA. Yes, I just happened to be passing by. There's something I want you to help me with. Sit down here on the sofa. Now, listen: There's to be a fancy dress ball at the Stenborgs' tomorrow evening—they live just overhead—and Torvald wants me to go as a Neapolitan peasant girl, and dance the tarantella; I learned it while we were in Capri.

MRS. LINDE. So you're going to give a real performance, are you?

NORA. Torvald wants me to. Look, here's the costume; Torvald had it made for me down there. But it's all torn, Kristine, and I don't know whether—

MRS. LINDE. Oh, we'll soon fix that. It's only the trimming that has come loose here and there. Have you a needle and thread? Oh, yes. Here's everything I need.

NORA. It's awfully good of you!

MRS. LINDE *(sewing)*. So you're going to be all dressed up, Nora—what fun! You know—I think I'll run in for a moment—just to see you in your costume—I haven't really thanked you for last night. I had such a happy time!

NORA *(rises and walks across the room)*. Somehow it didn't seem as nice to me as usual. I wish you'd come to town a little earlier, Kristine. Yes—Torvald has a way of making things so gay and cozy.

MRS. LINDE. No; last night it was worse than usual. He's terribly ill, you see—tuberculosis of the spine, or something. His father was a frightful man, who kept mistresses and all that sort of thing—that's why his son has been an invalid from birth—

MRS. LINDE *(lets her sewing fall into her lap)*. Why, Nora! what do you know about such things?

NORA *(moving about the room)*. After all—I've had three children; and those women who look after one at childbirth know almost as much as doctors; and they love to gossip.

MRS. LINDE *(goes on sewing; a short pause)*. Does Doctor Rank come here every day?

NORA. Every single day. He's Torvald's best friend, you know—always has been; and he's *my* friend too. He's almost like one of the family.

MRS. LINDE. Do you think he's quite sincere, Nora? I mean—isn't he inclined to flatter people?

NORA. Quite the contrary. What gave you that impression?

MRS. LINDE. When you introduced us yesterday he said he had often heard my name mentioned here; but I noticed afterwards that your husband hadn't the faintest notion who I was. How could Doctor Rank—?

NORA. He was quite right, Kristine. You see Torvald loves me so tremendously that he won't share me with anyone; he wants me all to himself, he says. At first he used to get terribly jealous if I even mentioned any of my old friends back home; so naturally I gave up doing it. But I often talk to Doctor Rank about such things—he likes to hear about them.

MRS. LINDE. Listen to me, Nora! In many ways you are still a child. I'm somewhat older than you, and besides, I've had much more experience. I think you ought to put a stop to all this with Dr. Rank.

NORA. Put a stop to what?

MRS. LINDE. To the whole business. You said something yesterday about a rich admirer who was to give you money—

NORA. One who never existed, unfortunately. Go on.

MRS. LINDE. Has Doctor Rank money?

NORA. Why yes, he has.

MRS. LINDE. And he has no one dependent on him?

NORA. No, no one. But—

MRS. LINDE. And he comes here every single day?

NORA. Yes—I've just told you so.

MRS. LINDE. It's surprising that a sensitive man like that should be so importunate.

NORA. I don't understand you—

MRS. LINDE. Don't try to deceive me, Nora. Don't you suppose I can guess who lent you the twelve hundred dollars?

NORA. You must be out of your mind! How could you ever think such a thing? Why, he's a friend of ours; he comes to see us every day! The situation would have been impossible!

MRS. LINDE.   So it wasn't he, then?

NORA.   No, I assure you. Such a thing never even occurred to me. Anyway, he didn't have any money at that time; he came into it later.

MRS. LINDE.   Perhaps that was just as well, Nora, dear.

NORA.   No—it would never have entered my head to ask Dr. Rank—Still—I'm sure that if I did ask him—

MRS. LINDE.   But you won't, of course.

NORA.   No, of course not. Anyway—I don't see why it should be necessary. But I'm sure that if I talked to Doctor Rank—

MRS. LINDE.   Behind your husband's back?

NORA.   I want to get that thing cleared up; after all, that's behind his back too. I must get clear of it.

MRS. LINDE.   That's just what I said yesterday; but—

NORA *(walking up and down)*.   It's so much easier for a man to manage things like that—

MRS. LINDE.   One's own husband, yes.

NORA.   Nonsense. *(Stands still.)*.   Surely if you pay back everything you owe—the paper is returned to you?

MRS. LINDE.   Naturally.

NORA.   Then you can tear it into a thousand pieces, and burn it up—the nasty, filthy thing!

MRS. LINDE *(looks at her fixedly, lays down her work, and rises slowly)*.   Nora, you are hiding something from me.

NORA.   You can see it in my face, can't you?

MRS. LINDE.   Something's happened to you since yesterday morning, Nora, what is it?

NORA *(going towards her)*.   Kristine—! *(Listens.)* Hush! Here comes Torvald! Go into the nursery for a little while. Torvald hates anything to do with sewing. Get Anne-Marie to help you.

MRS. LINDE *(gathers the things together)*.   Very well; but I shan't leave until you have told me all about it. *(She goes out to the left, as Helmer enters from the hall.)*

NORA *(runs to meet him)*.   Oh, I've missed you so, Torvald, dear!

HELMER.   Was that the dressmaker—?

NORA.   No, it was Kristine. She's helping me fix my costume. It's going to look so nice.

HELMER.   Wasn't that a good idea of mine?

NORA.   Splendid! But don't you think it was good of me to let you have your way?

HELMER.   Good of you! To let your own husband have his way! There, there, you crazy little thing; I'm only teasing. Now I won't disturb you. You'll have to try the dress on, I suppose.

NORA.   Yes—and I expect you've work to do.

HELMER.   I have. *(Shows her a bundle of papers.)* Look. I've just come from the Bank—*(Goes toward his room.)*

NORA.   Torvald.

HELMER *(stopping)*.   Yes?

NORA.   If your little squirrel were to beg you—with all her heart—

HELMER.   Well?

NORA.   Would you do something for her?

HELMER.   That depends on what it is.

NORA.   Be a darling and say "Yes," Torvald! Your squirrel would skip about and play all sorts of pretty tricks—

HELMER.   Well—out with it!

NORA.   Your little lark would twitter all day long—

HELMER.   She does that anyway!

NORA.   I'll pretend to be an elf and dance for you in the moonlight, Torvald.

HELMER.   Nora—you're surely not getting back to what we talked about this morning?

NORA *(coming nearer).*   Oh, Torvald, dear, I do most humbly beg you—!

HELMER.   You have the temerity to bring that up again?

NORA.   You must give in to me about this, Torvald! You *must* let Krogstad keep his place!

HELMER.   I'm giving his place to Mrs. Linde.

NORA.   That's awfully sweet of you. But instead of Krogstad—couldn't you dismiss some other clerk?

HELMER.   This is the most incredible obstinacy! Because you were thoughtless enough to promise to put in a good word for him, am I supposed to—?

NORA.   That's not the reason, Torvald. It's for your own sake. Didn't you tell me yourself he writes for the most horrible newspapers? He can do you no end of harm. Oh! I'm so afraid of him—

HELMER.   I think I understand; you have some unpleasant memories—that's why you're frightened.

NORA.   What do you mean?

HELMER.   Aren't you thinking of your father?

NORA.   Oh, yes!—of course! You remember how those awful people slandered poor Father in the newspapers? If you hadn't been seen to investigate the matter, and been so kind and helpful—he might have been dismissed.

HELMER.   My dear Nora, there is a distinct difference between your father and me. Your father's conduct was not entirely unimpeachable. But mine is; and I trust it will remain so.

NORA.   You never know what evil-minded people can think up. We could be so happy now, Torvald, in our lovely, peaceful home—you and I and the children! Oh! I implore you, Torvald—!

HELMER.   The more you plead his cause the less likely I am to keep him on. It's already known at the Bank that I intend to dismiss Krogstad. If I were to change my mind, people might say I'd done it at the insistence of my wife—

NORA.   Well—what of that?

HELMER.   Oh, nothing, of course! As long as the obstinate little woman gets her way! I'd simply be the laughingstock of the whole staff; they'd think I was weak and easily influenced—I should soon be made to feel the consequences. Besides—there is one factor that makes it quite impossible for Krogstad to work at the Bank as long as I'm head there.

NORA.   What could that be?

HELMER.   His past record I might be able to overlook—

NORA.   Yes, you might, mightn't you, Torvald—?

HELMER.   And I'm told he's an excellent worker. But unfortunately we were friendly during our college days. It was one of those impetuous friendships that subsequently often prove embarrassing. He's tactless enough to call me by my first name—regardless of the circumstances—and feels quite justified in taking a familiar tone with me. At any moment he comes out with "Torvald" this, and "Torvald" that! It's acutely irritating. It would make my position at the Bank intolerable.

NORA.   You're surely not serious about this, Torvald?

HELMER.   Why not?

NORA.   But—it's all so petty.

HELMER.   Petty! So you think I'm petty!

NORA.   Of course not, Torvald—just the opposite; that's why—

HELMER.   Never mind; you call my motives petty; so I must be petty too! Petty! Very well!—We'll put an end to this now—once and for all. *(Helmer goes to the door into the hall and calls Helene.)*

NORA.   What do you want?

HELMER *(searing among his papers).*   I want this thing settled. *(Helene enters.)* Take this letter, will you? Get a messenger and have him deliver it at once! It's urgent. Here's some money.

HELENE.   Very good, Sir. *(Goes with the letter.)*

HELMER *(putting his papers together).*   There, little Miss Obstinacy.

NORA *(breathless).*   Torvald—what was in that letter?

HELMER.   Krogstad's dismissal.

NORA.   Call her back, Torvald! There's still time. Call her back! For my sake, for your own sake, for the sake of the children, don't send that letter! Torvald, do you hear? You don't realize what may come of this!

HELMER.   It's too late.

NORA.   Too late, yes.

HELMER.   Nora, dear; I forgive your fears—though it's not exactly flattering to me to think I could ever be afraid of any spiteful nonsense Krogstad might choose to write about me! But I forgive you all the same—it shows how much you love me. *(Takes her in his arms.)* And that's the way it should be, Nora darling. No matter what happens, you'll see—I have strength and courage for us both. My shoulders are broad—I'll bear the burden.

NORA *(terror-struck).*   How do you mean?

HELMER.   The whole burden, my darling. Don't you worry any more.

NORA *(with decision).*   No! You mustn't—I won't let you!

HELMER.   Then we'll share it, Nora, as man and wife. That is as it should be. *(Petting her.)* Are you happy now? There! Don't look at me like a frightened little dove! You're just imagining things, you know—Now don't you think you ought to play the tarantella through—and practice your tambourine? I'll go into my study and close both doors, then you won't disturb me. You can make all the noise you like! *(Turns round in doorway.)* And when Rank comes, just tell him where I am. *(He nods to her, and goes with his papers to his room, closing the door.)*

NORA *(bewildered with terror, stands as though rooted to the ground, and whispers).*   He'd do it too! He'd do it—in spite of anything! But he mustn't—never, never! Anything but that! There must be some way out! What shall I do? *(The hall bell rings.)* Dr. Rank—! Anything but that—anything, *any*thing but that!

(Nora draws her hands over her face, pulls herself together, goes to the door and opens it. Rank stands outside hanging up his fur coat. During the following scene, darkness begins to fall.)

NORA.   How are you, Doctor Rank? I recognized your ring. You'd better not go in to Torvald just now; I think he's busy.

RANK.   How about you? *(Enters and closes the door.)*

NORA.   You know I always have an hour to spare for you.

RANK.   Many thanks. I'll make use of that privilege as long as possible.

NORA.   What do you mean—as long as possible?

RANK.   Does that frighten you?

NORA.   No—but it's such a queer expression. Has anything happened?

RANK.   I've been expecting it for a long time; but I never thought it would come quite so soon.

NORA.   What is it you have found out? Doctor Rank, please tell me!

RANK *(sitting down by the stove)*.   I haven't much time left. There's nothing to do about it.

NORA *(with a sigh of relief)*.   Oh! Then—it's about you—?

RANK.   Of course. What did you think? It's no use lying to one's self. I am the most miserable of all my patients, Mrs. Helmer. These past few days I've been taking stock of my position—and I find myself completely bankrupt. Within a month, I shall be rotting in the churchyard.

NORA.   What a ghastly way to talk!

RANK.   The whole business is pretty ghastly, you see. And the worst of it is, there are so many ghastly things to be gone through before it's over. I've just one last examination to make, then I shall know approximately when the final dissolution will begin. There's something I want to say to you: Helmer's sensitive nature is repelled by anything ugly. I couldn't bear to have him near me when—

NORA.   But Doctor Rank—

RANK.   No, I couldn't bear it! I won't have him there—I shall bar my door against him—As soon as I am absolutely certain of the worst, I'll send you my visiting-card marked with a black cross; that will mean that the final horror has begun.

NORA.   Doctor Rank—you're absolutely impossible today! And I did so want you to be in a good humor.

RANK.   With death staring me in the face? And why should I have to expiate another's sins! What justice is there in that? Well—I suppose in almost every family there are some such debts that have to be paid.

NORA *(her hands over her ears)*.   Don't talk such nonsense! Come along! Cheer up!

RANK.   One might as well laugh. It's really very funny when you come to think of it—that my poor innocent spine should be made to suffer for my father's exploits!

NORA *(at table, left)*.   He was much addicted to asparagus tips and paté de foie gras, wasn't he?

RANK.   Yes; and truffles.

NORA.   Oh, of course—truffles, yes. And I suppose oysters too?

RANK.   Oh, yes! Masses of oysters, certainly!

NORA.   And all the wine and champagne that went with them! It does seem a shame that all these pleasant things should be so damaging to the spine, doesn't it?

RANK.   Especially when it's a poor miserable spine that never had any of the fun!

NORA.   Yes, that's the biggest shame of all!

RANK *(gives her a searching look)*.   H'm—

NORA *(a moment later)*.   Why did you smile?

RANK.   No; you were the one that laughed.

NORA.   No; you were the one that smiled, Doctor Rank!

RANK *(gets up)*.   You're more of a rogue than I thought you were.

NORA.   I'm full of mischief today.

RANK.   So it seems.

NORA *(with her hands on his shoulders)*.   Dear, dear Doctor Rank, don't go and die and leave Torvald and me.

RANK. Oh, you won't miss me long! Those who go away—are soon forgotten.

NORA *(looks at him anxiously).* You really believe that?

RANK. People develop new interests, and soon—

NORA. What do you mean—new interests?

RANK. That'll happen to you and Helmer when I am gone. you seem to have made a good start already. What was that Mrs. Linde doing here last evening?

NORA. You're surely not jealous of poor old Kristine!

RANK. Yes, I am. She will be my successor in this house. When I'm gone she'll probably—

NORA. Sh—hh! She's in there.

RANK. She's here again today? You see!

NORA. She's just helping me with my costume. Good heavens, you *are* in an unreasonable mood! *(Sits on sofa.)* Now do try to be good, Doctor Rank. Tomorrow you'll see how beautifully I'll dance; and then you can pretend I'm doing it all to please you—and Torvald too, of course—that's understood.

RANK *(after a short silence).* You know—sitting here talking to you so informally—I simply can't imagine what would have become of me, if I had never had this house to come to.

NORA *(smiling).* You really *do* feel at home with us, don't you?

RANK *(in a low voice—looking straight before him).* And to be obliged to leave it all—

NORA. Nonsense! You're not going to leave anything.

RANK *(in the same tone).* And not to be able to leave behind one even the smallest proof of gratitude; at most a fleeting regret—an empty place to be filled by the first person who comes along.

NORA. And supposing I were to task you for—? No—

RANK. For what?

NORA. For a great proof of your friendship.

RANK. Yes?—Yes?

NORA. No, I mean—if I were to ask you to do me a really tremendous favor—

RANK. You'd really, for once, give me that great happiness?

NORA. Oh, but you don't know what it is.

RANK. Then tell me.

NORA. I don't think I can, Doctor Rank. It's much too much to ask—it's not just a favor—I need your help and advice as well—

RANK. So much the better. I've no conception of what you mean. But tell me about it. You trust me, don't you?

NORA. More than anyone. I know you are my best and truest friend—that's why I can tell you. Well then, Doctor Rank, there is something you must help me prevent. You know how deeply, how intensely Torvald loves me; he wouldn't hesitate for a moment to give up his life for my sake.

RANK *(bending towards her).* Nora—do you think he is the only one who—?

NORA *(with a slight start).* Who—what?

RANK. Who would gladly give his life for you?

NORA *(sadly).* I see.

RANK. I was determined that you should know this before I—went away. There'll never be a better chance to tell you. Well, Nora, now you know, and you must know too that you can trust me as you can no one else.

NORA *(standing up; simply and calmly).* Let me get by—

RANK *(makes way for her, but remains sitting).* Nora—

NORA *in the doorway).*   Bring in the lamp, Helene. *(Crosses to the stove.)* Oh, dear Doctor Rank, that was really horrid of you.

RANK *(rising).*   To love you just as deeply as—as someone else does; is that horrid?

NORA.   No—but the fact of your telling me. There was no need to do that.

RANK.   What do you mean? Did you know—?

(Helene enters with the lamp; sets it on the table and goes out again.)

RANK.   Nora—Mrs. Helmer—tell me, did you know?

NORA.   Oh, how do I know what I knew or didn't know. I really can't say—How could you be so clumsy, Doctor Rank? It was all so nice.

RANK.   Well, at any rate, you know now that I stand ready to serve you body and soul. So—tell me.

NORA *(looking at him).*   After this?

RANK.   I beg you to tell me what it is.

NORA.   I can't tell you anything now.

RANK.   But you must! Don't punish me like that! Let me be of use to you; I'll do anything for you—anything within human power.

NORA.   You can do nothing for me now. Anyway—I don't really need help. I was just imagining things, you see. Really! That's all it was. *(Sits in the rocking chair, looks at him and smiles.)* Well—you're a nice one, Doctor Rank! Aren't you a bit ashamed, now that the lamp's been lit?

RANK.   No; really not. But I suppose I'd better go now—for good?

NORA.   You'll do no such thing! You must come here just as you always have. Torvald could never get on without you!

RANK.   But how about *you?*

NORA.   You know I always love to have you here.

RANK.   Yes—I suppose that's what misled me. I can't quite make you out. I've often felt you liked being with me almost as much as being with Helmer.

NORA.   Well—you see—There are the people one loves best—and yet there are others one would almost rather *be* with.

RANK.   Yes—there's something in that.

NORA.   When I was still at home, it was of course Papa whom I loved best. And yet whenever I could, I used to slip down to the servants' quarters. I loved being with them. To begin with, they never lectured me a bit, and it was such fun to hear them talk.

RANK.   I see; and now you have me instead!

NORA *(jumps up and hurries toward him).*   Oh, dear, Doctor Rank. I didn't mean it like that! It's just that now, Torvald comes first—the way Papa did. *You* understand—!

(Helene enters from the hall.)

HELENE.   I beg your pardon, Ma'am—*(Whispers to Nora, and gives her a card.)*

NORA *(glancing at card).*   Ah! *(Puts it in her pocket.)*

RANK.   Anything wrong?

NORA.   No, nothing! It's just—it's my new costume—

RANK.   Isn't that your costume—there?

NORA.   Oh, that one, yes. But this is a different one. It's one I've ordered—Torvald mustn't know—

RANK.   So *that's* the great secret!

NORA.   Yes, of course it is! Go in and see him, will you? He's in his study. Be sure and keep him there as long as—

RANK. Don't worry; he shan't escape me. *(Goes into Helmer's room.)*

NORA *(to Helene).* He's waiting in the kitchen?

HELENE. Yes, he came up the back stairs—

NORA. Why didn't you tell him I was busy?

HELENE. I did, but he insisted.

NORA. He won't go away?

HELENE. Not until he has spoken to you, Ma'am.

NORA. Very well, then; show him in; but quietly, Helene—and don't say a word to anyone; it's about a surprise for my husband.

HELENE. I understand, Ma'am. *(She goes out.)*

NORA. It's coming! It's going to happen after all! No, no! It can't happen. It *can't!*

(She goes to Helmer's door and locks it. Helene opens the hall door for Krogstad, and shuts it after him. He wears a traveling coat, boots, and a fur cap.)

NORA *(goes towards him).* Talk quietly; my husband is at home.

KROGSTAD. What's that to me?

NORA. What is it you want?

KROGSTAD. I want to make sure of something.

NORA. Well—what is it? Quickly!

KROGSTAD. I suppose you know I've been dismissed.

NORA. I couldn't prevent it, Mr. Krogstad. I did everything in my power, but it was useless.

KROGSTAD. So that's all your husband cares about you! He must realize what I can put you through, and yet, in spite of that, he dares to—

NORA. You don't imagine my husband knows about it?

KROGSTAD. No—I didn't really suppose he did. I can't imagine my friend Torvald Helmer showing that much courage.

NORA. I insist that you show respect when speaking of my husband, Mr. Krogstad!

KROGSTAD. With all due respect, I assure you! But am I right in thinking—since you are so anxious to keep the matter secret—that you have a clearer idea today than you had yesterday, of what you really did?

NORA. Clearer than *you* could ever give me!

KROGSTAD. Of course! I who know so little about the law—!

NORA. What do you want of me?

KROGSTAD. I just wanted to see how you were getting on, Mrs. Helmer. I've been thinking about you all day. You see—even a mere moneylender, a cheap journalist—in short, someone like me—is not entirely without feeling.

NORA. Then prove it; think of my little children.

KROGSTAD. Did you or your husband think of mine? But that's not the point. I only wanted to tell you not to take his matter too seriously. I shan't take any action—for the present, at least.

NORA. You won't will you? I was sure you wouldn't!

KROGSTAD. It can all be settled quite amicably. It needn't be made public. It needn't go beyond us three.

NORA. But, my husband must never know.

KROGSTAD. How can you prevent it? Can you pay off the balance?

NORA. No, not immediately.

KROGSTAD. Have you any way of raising the money within the next few days?

NORA. None—that I will make use of.

KROGSTAD. And if you had, it would have made no difference. Even if you were to offer me the entire sum in cash—I still wouldn't give you back your note.

NORA. What are you going to do with it?

KROGSTAD. I shall simply keep it—I shall guard it carefully. No one, outside the three of us, shall know a thing about it. So, if you have any thought of doing something desperate—

NORA. I shall.

KROGSTAD. —of running away from home, for instance—

NORA. I shall!

KROGSTAD. —or perhaps even something worse—

NORA. How could you guess that?

KROGSTAD. —then put all such thoughts out of your head.

NORA. How did you know I had thought of *that?*

KROGSTAD. Most of us think of *that,* at first. I thought of it, too; but I didn't have the courage—

NORA *(tonelessly).* I haven't either.

KROGSTAD *(relieved).* No; you haven't the courage for it either, have you?

NORA. No! I haven't, I haven't!

KROGSTAD. Besides, it would be a very foolish thing to do. You'll just have to get through one domestic storm—and then it'll all be over. I have a letter for your husband, here in my pocket—

NORA. Telling him all about it?

KROGSTAD. Sparing you as much as possible.

NORA *(quickly).* He must never read the letter. Tear it up, Mr. Krogstad! I will manage to get the money somehow—

KROGSTAD. Excuse me, Mrs. Helmer, but I thought I just told you—

NORA. Oh, I'm not talking about the money I owe you. Just tell me how much money you want from my husband—I will get it somehow!

KROGSTAD. I want no money from your husband?

NORA. What *do* you want then?

KROGSTAD. Just this: I want a new start; I want to make something of myself; and your husband shall help me do it. For the past eighteen months my conduct has been irreproachable. It's been a hard struggle—I've lived in abject poverty; still, I was content to work my way up gradually, step by step. But now I've been kicked out, and now I shall not be satisfied to be merely reinstated—taken back on sufferance. I'm determined to make something of myself, I tell you. I intend to continue working in the Bank—but I expect to be promoted. Your husband shall create a new position for me—

NORA. He'll never do it!

KROGSTAD. Oh, yes he will; I know him—he'll do it without a murmur; he wouldn't dare do otherwise. And then—you'll see! Within a year I'll be his right hand man. It'll be Nils Krogstad, not Torvald Helmer, who'll run the Joint Stock Bank.

NORA. That will never happen.

KROGSTAD. No? Would you, perhaps—?

NORA. Yes! I have the courage for it now.

KROGSTAD. You don't frighten me! A dainty, pampered little lady such as you—

NORA. You'll see, you'll see!

KROGSTAD. Yes, I dare say! How would you like to lie there under the ice—in that freezing, pitch-black water? And in the spring your body would be found floating on the surface—hideous, hairless, unrecognizable—

NORA.   You can't frighten me!

KROGSTAD.   You can't frighten me either. People don't do that sort of thing, Mrs. Helmer. And, anyway, what would be the use? I'd still have your husband in my power.

NORA.   You mean—afterwards? Even if I were no longer—?

KROGSTAD.   Remember—I'd still have your reputation in my hands! *(Nora stands speechless and looks at him.)* Well, I've given you fair warning. I wouldn't do anything foolish, if I were you. As soon as Helmer receives my letter, I shall expect to hear from him. And just remember this: I've been forced back into my former way of life—and your husband is responsible. I shall never forgive him for it. Good-bye, Mrs. Helmer.

(Goes out through the hall. Nora hurries to the door, opens it a little, and listens.)

NORA.   He's gone. He didn't leave the letter. Of course he didn't—that would be impossible! *(Opens the door further and further.)* What's he doing? He's stopped outside the door. He's not going down the stairs. Has he changed his mind? Is he—? *(A letter falls into the box. Krogstad's footsteps are heard gradually receding down the stairs. Nora utters a suppressed shriek, and rushes forward toward the sofa table; pause.)* It's in the letter-box! *(Slips shrinkingly up to the hall door.)* It's there!—Torvald, Torvald—now we are lost!

(Mrs. Linde enters from the left with the costume.)

MRS. LINDE.   There, I think it's all right now. If you'll just try it on—?

NORA *(hoarsely and softly)*.   Come here, Kristine.

MRS. LINDE *(throws down the dress on the sofa)*.   What's the matter with you? You look upset.

NORA.   Come here. Do you see that letter? Do you see it—in the letter-box?

MRS. LINDE.   Yes, yes, I see it.

NORA.   It's from Krogstad—

MRS. LINDE.   Nora—you don't mean Krogstad lent you the money!

NORA.   Yes; and now Torvald will know everything.

MRS. LINDE.   It'll be much the best thing for you both, Nora.

NORA.   But you don't know everything. I committed forgery—

MRS. LINDE.   Good heavens!

NORA.   Now, listen to me, Kristine; I want you to be my witness—

MRS. LINDE.   How do you mean "witness"? What am I to—?

NORA.   If I should go out of my mind—that might easily happen—

MRS. LINDE.   Nora!

NORA.   Or if something should happen to me—something that would prevent my being here—!

MRS. LINDE.   Nora, Nora, you're quite beside yourself!

NORA.   In case anyone else should insist on taking all the blame upon himself—the whole blame—you understand—

MRS. LINDE.   Yes, but what makes you think—?

NORA.   Then you must bear witness to the fact that that isn't true. I'm in my right mind now; I know exactly what I'm saying; and I tell you nobody else knew anything about it; I did the whole thing on my own. Just remember that.

MRS. LINDE.   Very well—I will. But I don't understand at all.

NORA.   No—of course—you couldn't. It's the wonderful thing—It's about to happen, don't you see?

MRS. LINDE.   What "wonderful thing"?

NORA.   The wonderful—wonderful thing! But it must never be allowed to happen—never. It would be too terrible.

MRS. LINDE.   I'll go and talk to Krogstad at once.

NORA.   No, don't go to him! He might do you some harm.

MRS. LINDE.   There was a time—he would have done anything in the world for me.

NORA.   He?

MRS. LINDE.   Where does he live?

NORA.   How do I know—? Yes—*(Feels in her pocket.)* Here's his card. But the letter, the letter—!

HELMER *(from his study; knocking on the door).*   Nora!

NORA *(shrieks in terror).*   Oh! What is it? What do you want?

HELMER.   Don't be frightened! We're not coming in; anyway, you've locked the door. Are you trying on?

NORA.   Yes, yes, I'm trying on. I'm going to look so pretty, Torvald.

MRS. LINDE *(who has read the card).*   He lives just round the corner.

NORA.   But it won't do any good. It's too late now. The letter is in the box.

MRS. LINDE.   I suppose your husband has the key?

NORA.   Of course.

MRS. LINDE.   Krogstad must ask for his letter back, unread. He must make up some excuse—

NORA.   But this is the time that Torvald usually—

MRS. LINDE.   Prevent him. Keep him occupied. I'll come back as quickly as I can. *(She goes out hastily by the hall door.)*

NORA *(opens Helmer's door and peeps in).*   Torvald!

HELMER *(in the study).*   Well? May one venture to come back into one's own living room? Come along, Rank—now we shall see—*(In the doorway.)* Why—what's this?

NORA.   What, Torvald, dear?

HELMER.   Rank led me to expect some wonderful disguise.

RANK *(in the doorway).*   That's what I understood. I must have been mistaken.

NORA.   Not till tomorrow evening! Then I shall appear in all my splendor!

HELMER.   But you look quite tired, Nora, dear. I'm afraid you've been practicing too hard.

NORA.   Oh, I haven't practiced at all yet.

HELMER.   You ought to, though—

NORA.   Yes—I really should, Torvald! But I can't seem to manage without your help. I'm afraid I've forgotten all about it.

HELMER.   Well—we'll see what we can do. It'll soon come back to you.

NORA.   You will help me, won't you, Torvald? Promise! I feel so nervous—all those people! You must concentrate on me this evening—forget all about business. *Please*, Torvald, dear—promise me you will!

HELMER.   I promise. This evening I'll be your slave—you sweet, helpless little thing—! Just one moment, though—I want to see—*(Going to hall door.)*

NORA.   What do you want out there?

HELMER.   I just want to see if there are any letters.

NORA.   Oh, don't, Torvald! Don't bother about that now!

HELMER.   Why not?

NORA.   *Please* don't, Torvald! There aren't any.

HELMER.   Just let me take a look—*(Starts to go.)*

(Nora, at the piano, plays the first bars of the tarantella.)

HELMER *(stops in the doorway).*   Aha!

NORA.   I shan't be able to dance tomorrow if I don't rehearse with you!

HELMER *(going to her).*   Are you really so nervous, Nora, dear?

NORA.   Yes, I'm terrified! Let's rehearse right away. We've plenty of time before dinner. Sit down and play for me, Torvald, dear; direct me—guide me; you know how you do!

HELMER.   With pleasure, my darling, if you wish me to. *(Sits at piano.)*

(Nora snatches the tambourine out of the box, and hurriedly drapes herself in a long parti-colored shawl; then, with a bound, stands in the middle of the floor and cries out.)

NORA.   Now play for me! Now I'll dance!

(Helmer plays and Nora dances. Rank stands at the piano behind Helmer and looks on.)

HELMER *(playing).*   Too fast! Too fast!

NORA.   I can't help it!

HELMER.   Don't' be so violent, Nora!

NORA.   That's the way it *should* be!

HELMER *(stops).*   No, no; this won't do at all!

NORA *(laughs and swings her tambourine).*   You see? What did I tell you?

RANK.   I'll play for her.

HELMER *(rising).*   Yes, do—then I'll be able to direct her.

(Rank sits down at the piano and plays; Nora dances more and more wildly. Helmer stands by the stove and addresses frequent corrections to her; she seems not to hear. Her hair breaks loose, and falls over her shoulders. She does not notice it, but goes on dancing. Mrs. Linde enters and stands spellbound in the doorway.)

MRS. LINDE.   Ah—!

NORA *(dancing).*   We've having such fun, Kristine!

HELMER.   Why, Nora, dear, you're dancing as if your life were at stake!

NORA.   It is! It is!

HELMER.   Rank, stop! This is absolute madness. Stop, I say!

(Rank stops playing, and Nora comes to a sudden standstill.)

HELMER *(going toward her).*   I never would have believed it. You've forgotten everything I ever taught you.

HELMER.   This needs an immense amount of work.

NORA.   That's what I said; you see how important it is! You must work with me up to the very last minute. Will you promise me, Torvald?

HELMER.   I most certainly will!

NORA.   This evening and all day tomorrow you must think of nothing but me. You mustn't open a single letter—mustn't even *look* at the mailbox.

HELMER.   Nora! I believe you're still worried about that wretched man—

NORA.   Yes—yes, I am!

HELMER.   Nora—Look at me—there's a letter from him in the box, isn't there?

NORA.   Maybe—I don't know; I believe there is. But you're not to read anything of that sort now; nothing must come between us until the party's over.

RANK *(softly, to Helmer).*   Don't go against her.

HELMER *(putting his arm around her).*   Very well! The child shall have her way. But tomorrow night, when your dance is over—

NORA.   Then you'll be free.

(Helene appears in the doorway, right.)

HELENE.   Dinner is served, Ma'am.

NORA.   We'll have champagne, Helene.

HELENE.   Very good, Ma'am. *(Goes out.)*

HELMER.   Quite a feast, I see!

NORA.   Yes—a real feast! We'll stay up till dawn drinking champagne! *(Calling out.)* Oh, and we'll have macaroons, Helene—lots of them! Why not—for once?

HELMER *(seizing her hand).*   Come, come! Not so violent! Be my own little lark again.

NORA.   I will, Torvald. But now—both of you go in—while Kristine helps me with my hair.

RANK *(softly, as they go).*   Is anything special the matter? I mean anything—?

HELMER.   No, no; nothing at all. It's just this childish fear I was telling you about. *(They go out to the right.)*

NORA.   Well?

MRS. LINDE.   He's gone out of town.

NORA.   I saw it in your face.

MRS. LINDE.   He'll be back tomorrow evening. I left a note for him.

NORA.   You shouldn't have bothered. You couldn't prevent it anyway. After all, there's a kind of joy in waiting for the wonderful thing to happen.

MRS. LINDE.   I don't understand. What *is* this thing you're waiting for?

NORA.   I can't explain. Go in and join them. I'll be there in a moment.

(Mrs. Linde goes into the dining room. Nora stands for a moment as though pulling herself together; then looks at her watch.)

NORA.   Five o'clock. Seven hours till midnight. Twenty-four hours till the next midnight and then the tarantella will be over. Twenty-four and seven? I've thirty-one hours left to live.

(Helmer appears at the door, right.)

HELMER.   Well! What has become of the little lark?

NORA *(runs to him with open arms).*   Here she is!

ACT III

(Scene: The same room. The table, with the chairs around it, has been moved to stage-center. A lighted lamp on the table. The hall door is open. Dance music is heard from the floor above. Mrs. Linde sits by the table absent-mindedly turning the pages of a book. She tries to read, but seems unable to keep her mind on it. Now and then she listens intently and glances towards the hall door.)

MRS. LINDE *(looks at her watch).*   Where can he be? The time is nearly up. I hope he hasn't—*(Looks again.)* Here he is now. *(She goes into the hall and cautiously opens the outer door; cautious footsteps are heard on the stairs; she whispers.)* Come in, there is no one here.

KROGSTAD *(in the doorway).*   I found a note from you at home. What does it mean?

MRS. LINDE.   I simply *must* speak to you.

KROGSTAD.   Indeed? But why here? Why in this house?

MRS. LINDE.   I couldn't see you at my place. My room has no separate entrance. Come in; we're quite alone. The servants are asleep, and the Helmers are upstairs at a party.

KROGSTAD *(coming into the room).*   Well, well! So the Helmers are dancing tonight, are they?

MRS. LINDE.   Why shouldn't they?

KROGSTAD.   Well—why not!

MRS. LINDE.   Let's have a talk, Krogstad.

KROGSTAD.   Have we two anything to talk about?

MRS. LINDE.   Yes. A great deal.

KROGSTAD.   I shouldn't have thought so.

MRS. LINDE.   But then, you see—you have never really understood me.

KROGSTAD.   There wasn't much to understand, was there? A woman is heartless enough to break off with a man, when a better match is offered; it's quite an ordinary occurrence.

MRS. LINDE.   You really think me heartless? Did you think it was so easy for me?

KROGSTAD.   Wasn't it?

MRS. LINDE.   You really believed that, Krogstad?

KROGSTAD.   If not, why should you have written to me as you did?

MRS. LINDE.   What else could I do? Since I was forced to break with you, I felt it was only right to try and kill your love for me.

KROGSTAD *(clenching his hands together).*   So that was it! And you did this for money!

MRS. LINDE.   Don't forget I had my mother and two little brothers to think of. We couldn't wait for you, Krogstad; things were so unsettled for you then.

KROGSTAD.   That may be; but, even so, you had no right to throw me over—not even for their sake.

KROSTAD *(more softly).*   When I had lost you, I felt the ground crumble beneath my feet. Look at me. I'm like a shipwrecked man clinging to a raft.

MRS. LINDE.   Help may be nearer than you think.

KROGSTAD.   Help was here! Then you came and stood in the way.

MRS. LINDE.   I knew nothing about it, Krogstad. I didn't know until today that I was to replace *you* at the Bank.

KROGSTAD.   Very well—I believe you. But now that you do know, will you withdraw?

MRS. LINDE.   No; I'd do you no good by doing that.

KROGSTAD.   "Good" or not—I'd withdraw all the same.

MRS. LINDE.   I have learnt to be prudent, Krogstad—I've had to. The bitter necessities of life have taught me that.

KROGSTAD.   And life has taught me not to believe in phrases.

MRS. LINDE.   Then life has taught you a very wise lesson. But what about deeds? Surely you must still believe in them?

KROGSTAD.   How do you mean?

MRS. LINDE.   You just said you were like a shipwrecked man, clinging to a raft.

KROGSTAD.   I have good reason to say so.

MRS. LINDE.   Well—I'm like a shipwrecked *woman* clinging to a raft. I have no one to mourn for, no one to care for.

KROGSTAD.   You made your choice.

MRS. LINDE.   I *had* no choice, I tell you!

KROGSTAD.   What then?

MRS. LINDE.   Since we're both of us shipwrecked, couldn't we join forces, Krogstad?

KROGSTAD.   You don't mean—?

MRS. LINDE.   Two people on a raft have a better chance than one.

KROGSTAD. Kristine!

MRS. LINDE. Why do you suppose I came here to the city?

KROGSTAD. You mean—you thought of me?

MRS. LINDE. I can't live without work; all my life I've worked, as far back as I can remember; it's always been my one great joy. Now I'm quite alone in the world; my life is empty—aimless. There's not much joy in working for one's self. You could help me, Nils; you could give me something and someone to work for.

KROGSTAD. I can't believe all this. It's an hysterical impulse—a woman's exaggerated craving for self-sacrifice.

MRS. LINDE. When have you ever found me hysterical?

KROGSTAD. You'd really be willing to do this? Tell me honestly—do you quite realize what my past has been?

MRS. LINDE. Yes.

KROGSTAD. And you know what people think of me?

MRS. LINDE. Didn't you just say you'd have been a different person if you'd been with me?

KROGSTAD. I'm sure of it.

MRS. LINDE. Mightn't that still be true?

KROGSTAD. You really mean this, Kristine, don't you? I can see it in your face. Are you sure you have the courage—?

MRS. LINDE. I need someone to care for, and your children need a mother. We two need each other, Nils. I have faith in your fundamental goodness. I'm not afraid.

KROGSTAD *(seizing her hands)*. Thank you—thank you, Kristine. I'll make others believe in me too—I won't fail you! But—I'd almost forgotten—

MRS. LINDE *(listening)*. Hush! The tarantella! You must go!

KROGSTAD. Why? What is it?

MRS. LINDE. Listen! She's begun her dance; as soon as she's finished dancing, they'll be down.

KROGSTAD. Yes—I'd better go. There'd have been no need for all that—but, of course, you don't know what I've done about the Helmers.

MRS. LINDE. Yes, I do, Nils.

KROGSTAD. And yet you have the courage to—?

MRS. LINDE. I know you are desperate—I understand.

KROGSTAD. I'd give anything to undo it!

MRS. LINDE. You can. Your letter's still in the mailbox.

KROGSTAD. Are you sure?

MRS. LINDE. Quite, but—

KROGSTAD *(giving her a searching look)*. Could that be it? You're doing all this to save your friend? You might as well be honest with me! Is that it?

MRS. LINDE. I sold myself once for the sake of others, Nils; I'm not likely to do it again.

KROGSTAD. I'll ask for my letter back unopened.

MRS. LINDE. No, no.

KROGSTAD. Yes, of course. I'll wait till Helmer comes; I'll tell him to give me back the letter—I'll say it refers to my dismissal—and ask him not to read it—

MRS. LINDE. No, Nils; don't ask for it back.

KROGSTAD. But wasn't that actually your reason for getting me to come here?

MRS. LINDE. Yes, in my first moment of fear. But that was twenty-four hours ago, and since then I've seen incredible things happening here. Helmer must know the truth; this wretched business must no longer be kept secret; it's time those two came to a thorough understanding; there's been enough deceit and subterfuge.

KROGSTAD.   Very well, if you like to risk it. But there's one thing I can do, and at once—

MRS. LINDE *(listening).*   You must go now. Make haste! The dance is over; we're not safe here another moment.

KROGSTAD.   I'll wait for you downstairs.

MRS. LINDE.   Yes, do; then you can see me home.

KROGSTAD.   Kristine! I've never been so happy! *(Krogstad goes out by the outer door. The door between the room and the hall remains open.)*

MRS. LINDE *(arranging the room and getting her outdoor things together).*   How different things will be! Someone to work for, to live for; a home to make happy! How wonderful it will be to try!—I wish they'd come—*(Listens.)* Here they are! I'll get my coat—*(Takes bonnet and cloak. Helmer's and Nora's voices are heard outside, a key is turned in the lock, and Helmer drags Nora almost by force into the hall. She wears the Italian costume with a large black shawl over it. He is in evening dress and wears a black domino, open.)*

NORA *(struggling with him in the doorway).*   No, no! I don't want to come home; I want to go upstairs again; I don't want to leave so early!

HELMER.   Come—Nora dearest!

NORA.   I beg you, Torvald! Please, *please*—just one hour more!

HELMER.   Not one single minute more, Nora darling; don't you remember our agreement? Come along in, now; you'll catch cold. *(He leads her gently into the room in spite of her resistance.)*

MRS. LINDE.   Good evening.

NORA.   Kristine!

HELMER.   Why, Mrs. Linde! What are you doing here so late?

MRS. LINDE.   Do forgive me. I did so want to see Nora in her costume.

NORA.   Have you been waiting for me all this time?

MRS. LINDE.   Yes; I came too late to catch you before you went upstairs, and I didn't want to go away without seeing you.

HELMER *(taking Nora's shawl off).*   And you *shall* see her, Mrs. Linde! She's worth looking at I can tell you! Isn't she lovely?

MRS. LINDE.   Oh, Nora! How perfectly—!

HELMER.   Absolutely exquisite, isn't she? That's what everybody said. But she's obstinate as a mule, is my sweet little thing! I don't know what to do with her! Will you believe it, Mrs. Linde, I had to drag her away by force?

NORA.   You'll see—you'll be sorry, Torvald, you didn't let me stay, if only for another half-hour.

HELMER.   Did you hear that, Mrs. Linde? Now, listen to this: She danced her tarantella to wild applause, and she deserved it, too, I must say—though, perhaps, from an artistic point of view, her interpretation was a bit too realistic. But never mind—the point is, she made a great success, a phenomenal success. Now—should I have allowed her to stay on and spoil the whole effect? Certainly not! I took my sweet little Capri girl—my capricious little Capri girl, I might say—in my arms; a rapid whirl round the room, a low curtsey to all sides, and—as they say in novels—the lovely apparition vanished! An exit should always be effective, Mrs. Linde; but I can't get Nora to see that. Phew! It's warm here. *(Throws his domino on a chair and opens the door to his room.)* Why—there's no light on in here! Oh no, of course—Excuse me—*(Goes in and lights candles.)*

NORA *(whispers breathlessly).*   Well?

MRS. LINDE *(softly)*.   I've spoken to him.

NORA.   And—?

MRS. LINDE.   Nora—you must tell your husband everything—

NORA *(tonelessly)*.   I knew it!

MRS. LINDE.   You have nothing to fear from Krogstad; but you must speak out.

NORA.   I shan't.

MRS. LINDE.   Then the letter will.

NORA.   Thank you, Kristine. Now I know what I must do. Hush—!

HELMER *(coming back)*.   Well, have you finished admiring her, Mrs. Linde?

MRS. LINDE.   Yes, and now I must say good night.

HELMER.   Oh—must you be going already? Does this knitting belong to you?

MRS. LINDE *(takes it)*.   Oh, thank you; I almost forgot it.

HELMER.   So you knit, do you?

MRS. LINDE.   Yes.

HELMER.   Why don't you do embroidery instead?

MRS. LINDE.   Why?

HELMER.   Because it's so much prettier. Now watch! You hold the embroidery in the left hand—so—and then, in the right hand, you hold the needle, and guide it—so—in a long graceful curve—isn't that right?

MRS. LINDE.   Yes, I suppose so—

HELMER.   Whereas, knitting can never be anything but ugly. Now, watch! Arms close to your sides, needles going up and down—there's something Chinese about it!— That really was splendid champagne they gave us.

MRS. LINDE.   Well, good night, Nora; don't be obstinate any more.

HELMER.   Well said, Mrs. Linde!

MRS. LINDE.   Good night, Mr. Helmer.

HELMER *(accompanying her to the door)*.   Good night, good night; I hope you get home safely. I'd be only too glad to—but you've such a short way to go. Good night, good night. *(She goes; Helmer shuts the door after her and comes forward again.)* Well—thank God we've got rid of her; she's a dreadful bore, that woman.

NORA.   You must be tired, Torvald.

HELMER.   I? Not in the least.

NORA.   But aren't you sleepy?

HELMER.   Not a bit. On the contrary, I feel exceedingly lively. But what about you? You seem to be very tired and sleepy.

NORA.   Yes, I am very tired. But I'll soon sleep now.

HELMER.   You see! I was right not to let you stay there any longer.

NORA.   Everything you do is always right, Torvald.

HELMER *(kissing her forehead)*.   There's my sweet, sensible little lark! By the way, did you notice how gay Rank was this evening?

NORA.   Was he? I didn't get a chance to speak to him.

HELMER.   I didn't either, really; but it's a long time since I've seen him in such a jolly mood. *(Gazes at Nora for a while, then comes nearer her.)* It's so lovely to be home again— to be here alone with you. You glorious, fascinating creature!

NORA.   Don't look at me like that, Torvald.

HELMER.   Why shouldn't I look at my own dearest treasure?—at all this loveliness that is mine, wholly and utterly mine—mine alone!

NORA *(goes to the other side of the table)*.   You mustn't talk to me like that tonight.

HELMER *(following).* You're still under the spell of the tarantella—and it makes you even more desirable. Listen! The other guests are leaving now. *(More softly.)* Soon the whole house will be still, Nora.

NORA. I hope so.

HELMER. Yes, you do, don't you, my beloved? Do you know something—when I'm out with you among a lot of people—do you know why it is I hardly speak to you, why I keep away from you, and only occasionally steal a quick glance at you; do you know why that is? It's because I pretend that we love each other in secret, that we're secretly engaged, and that no one suspects there is anything between us.

NORA. Yes, yes; I know your thoughts are always round me.

HELMER. Then, when it's time to leave, and I put your shawl round your smooth, soft, young shoulders—round that beautiful neck of yours—I pretend that you are my young bride, that we've just come from the wedding, and that I'm taking you home for the first time—that for the first time I shall be alone with you—quite alone with you, in all your tremulous beauty. All evening I have been filled with longing for you. As I watched you swaying and whirling in the tarantella—my pulses began to throb until I thought I should go mad; that's why I carried you off—made you leave so early—

NORA. Please go, Torvald! Please leave me. I don't want you like this.

HELMER. What do you mean? You're teasing me, aren't you, little Nora? Not want me—! Aren't I your husband—?

(A knock at the outer door.)

NORA *(starts).* Listen—!

HELMER *(going toward the hall).* Who is it?

RANK *(outside).* It is I; may I come in a moment?

HELMER *(in a low tone, annoyed).* Why does he have to bother us now! *(Aloud.)* Just a second! *(Opens door.)* Well! How nice of you to look in.

RANK. I heard your voice, and I thought I'd like to stop in a minute. *(Looks round.)* These dear old rooms! You must be so cozy and happy here, you two!

HELMER. I was just saying how gay and happy you seemed to be, upstairs.

RANK. Why not? Why shouldn't I be? One should get all one can out of life; all one can, for as long as one can. That wine was excellent—

HELMER. Especially the champagne.

RANK. You noticed that, did you? It's incredible how much I managed to get down.

NORA. Torvald drank plenty of it too.

RANK. Oh?

NORA. It always puts him in such a jolly mood.

RANK. Well, why shouldn't one have a jolly evening after a well-spent day?

HELMER. Well-spent! I'm afraid mine wasn't much to boast of!

RANK *(slapping him on the shoulder).* But mine was, you see?

NORA. Did you by any chance make a scientific investigation, Doctor Rank?

RANK. Precisely.

HELMER. Listen to little Nora, talking about scientific investigations!

NORA. Am I to congratulate you on the result?

RANK. By all means.

NORA. It was good then?

RANK. The best possible, both for the doctor and the patient—certainty.

NORA *(quickly and searchingly).* Certainty?

RANK.   Absolute certainty. Wasn't I right to spend a jolly evening after that?

NORA.   You were quite right, Doctor Rank.

HELMER.   I quite agree! Provided you don't have to pay for it, tomorrow.

RANK.   You don't get anything for nothing in this life.

NORA.   You like masquerade parties, don't you, Dr. Rank?

RANK.   Very much—when there are plenty of amusing disguises—

NORA.   What shall we two be at our next masquerade?

HELMER.   Listen to her! Thinking of the next party already!

RANK.   We two? I'll tell you. You must go as a precious talisman.

HELMER.   How on earth would you dress that!

RANK.   That's easy. She'd only have to be herself.

HELMER.   Charmingly put. But what about you? Have you decided what you'd be?

RANK.   Oh, definitely.

HELMER.   Well?

RANK.   At the next masquerade party I shall be invisible.

HELMER.   That's a funny notion!

RANK.   There's a large black cloak—you've heard of the invisible cloak, haven't you? You've only to put it around you and no one can see you any more.

HELMER *(with a suppressed smile)*.   Quite true!

RANK.   But I almost forgot what I came for. Give me a cigar, will you, Helmer? One of the dark Havanas.

HELMER.   Of course—with pleasure. *(Hands cigar case.)*

RANK *(takes one and cuts the end off)*.   Thanks.

NORA *(striking a wax match)*.   Let me give you a light.

RANK.   I thank you. *(She holds the match. He lights his cigar at it.)* And now, I'll say good-bye!

HELMER.   Good-bye, good-bye, my dear fellow.

NORA.   Sleep well, Doctor Rank.

RANK.   Thanks for the wish.

NORA.   Wish me the same.

RANK.   You? Very well, since you ask me—Sleep well. And thanks for the light. *(He nods to them both and goes out.)*

HELMER *(in an undertone)*.   He's had a lot to drink.

NORA *(absently)*.   I dare say. *(Helmer takes his bunch of keys from his pocket and goes into the hall.)* Torvald! What do you want out there?

HELMER.   I'd better empty the mailbox; it's so full there won't be room for the papers in the morning.

NORA.   Are you going to work tonight?

HELMER.   No—you know I'm not.—Why, what's this? Someone has been at the lock.

NORA.   The lock—?

HELMER.   Yes—that's funny! I shouldn't have thought that the maids would— Here's a broken hairpin. Why—it's one of yours, Nora.

NORA *(quickly)*.   It must have been the children—

HELMER.   You'll have to stop them doing that—There! I got it open at last. *(Takes contents out and calls out towards the kitchen.)* Helene?—Oh, Helene; put out the lamp in the hall, will you? *(He returns with letters in his hand, and shuts the door to the hall.)* Just look how they've stacked up. *(Looks through them.)* Why, what's this?

NORA *(at the window)*.   The letter! Oh, Torvald! No!

HELMER.   Two visiting cards—from Rank.

NORA.   From Doctor Rank?

HELMER *(looking at them).*   Doctor Rank, physician. They were right on top. He must have stuck them in just now, as he left.

NORA.   Is there anything on them?

HELMER.   There's a black cross over his name. Look! What a gruesome thought. Just as if he were announcing his own death.

NORA.   And so he is.

HELMER.   What do you mean? What do you know about it? Did he tell you anything?

NORA.   Yes. These cards mean that he has said good-bye to us for good. Now he'll lock himself up to die.

HELMER.   Oh, my poor friend! I always knew he hadn't long to live, but I never dreamed it would be quite so soon—! And to hide away like a wounded animal—

NORA.   When the time comes, it's best to go in silence. Don't you think so, Torvald?

HELMER *(walking up and down).*   He'd become so a part of us. I can't imagine his having gone for good. With his suffering and loneliness he was like a dark, cloudy background to our lives—it made the sunshine of our happiness seem even brighter—Well, I suppose it's for the best—for him at any rate. *(Stands still.)* And perhaps for us too, Nora. Now we are more than ever dependent on each other. *(Takes her in his arms.)* Oh, my beloved wife; I can't seem to hold you close enough. Do you know something, Nora? I often wish you were in some great danger—so I could risk body and soul—my whole life—everything, everything, for your sake.

NORA *(tears herself from him and says firmly).*   Now you must read your letters, Torvald.

HELMER.   No, no; not tonight. I want to be with you, my beloved wife.

NORA.   With the thought of your dying friend—?

HELMER.   Of course—You are right. It's been a shock to both of us. A hideous shadow has come between us—thoughts of death and decay. We must try and throw them off. Until then—we'll stay apart.

NORA *(her arms round his neck).*   Torvald! Good night! good night!

HELMER *(Kissing her forehead).*   Good night, my little songbird; sleep well! Now I'll go and read my letters. *(He goes with the letters in his hand into his room and shuts the door.)*

NORA *(with wild eyes, gropes about her, seizes Helmer's domino, throws it round her, and whispers quickly, hoarsely, and brokenly).*   I'll never see him again. Never, never, never. *(Throws her shawl over her head.)* I'll never see the children again. I'll never see them either—Oh the thought of that black, icy water! That fathomless—! If it were only over! He has it now; he's reading it. Oh, not yet—please! Not yet! Torvald, good-bye—! Good-bye to you and the children!

(She is rushing out by the hall; at the same moment Helmer flings his door open, and stands there with an open letter in his hand.)

HELMER.   Nora!

NORA *(shrieks).*   Ah—!

HELMER.   What does this mean! Do you know what is in this letter?

NORA.   Yes, yes, I know. Let me go! Let me out!

HELMER *(holds her back).*   Where are you going?

NORA *(tries to break away from him).*   Don't try to save me, Torvald!

HELMER *(falling back).*   So it's true! It's true what he writes! It's too horrible! It's impossible—it can't be true.

NORA.   It *is* true. I've loved you more than all the world.

HELMER.   Oh, come now! Let's have no silly nonsense!

NORA *(a step nearer him)*.   Torvald—!

HELMER.   Do you realize what you've done?

NORA.   Let me go—I won't have you suffer for it! I won't have you take the blame!

HELMER.   Will you stop this play-acting! *(Locks the outer door.)* You'll stay here and give an account of yourself. Do you understand what you have done? Answer me! Do you understand it?

NORA *(looks at him fixedly, and says with a stiffening expression)*.   I think I'm beginning to understand for the first time.

HELMER *(walking up and down)*.   God! What an awakening! After eight years to discover that you have been my pride and joy—are no better than a hypocrite, a liar—worse than that—a criminal! It's too horrible to think of! *(Nora says nothing, and continues to look fixedly at him.)* I might have known what to expect. I should have foreseen it. You've inherited all your father's lack of principle—be silent!—all of your father's lack of principle, I say!—no religion, no moral code, no sense of duty. This is my punishment for shielding him! I did it for your sake; and this is my reward!

NORA.   I see.

HELMER.   You've destroyed my happiness. You've ruined my whole future. It's ghastly to think of! I'm completely in the power of this scoundrel; he can force me to do whatever he likes, demand whatever he chooses; order me about at will; and I shan't dare open my mouth! My entire career is to be wrecked and all because of a lawless, unprincipled woman!

NORA.   If I were no longer alive, then you'd be free.

HELMER.   Oh yes! You're full of histrionics! Your father was just the same. Even if you "weren't alive," as you put it, what good would that do me? None whatever! He could publish the story all the same; I might even be suspected of collusion. People might say I was behind it all—that I had prompted you to do it. And to think I have you to thank for all this—you whom I've done nothing but pamper and spoil since the day of our marriage. Now do you realize what you've done to me?

NORA *(with cold calmness)*.   Yes.

HELMER.   It's all so incredible, I can't grasp it. But we must try and come to some agreement. Take off that shawl. Take it off, I say! Of course, we must find some way to appease him—the matter must be hushed up at any cost. As far as we two are concerned, there must be no change in our way of life—in the eyes of the world, I mean. You'll naturally continue to live here. But you won't be allowed to bring up the children—I'd never dare trust them to you—God! to have to say this to the woman I've loved so tenderly—There can be no further thought of happiness between us. We must save what we can from the ruins—we can save appearances, at least—*(A ring; Helmer starts.)* What can that be? At this hour! You don't suppose he—! Could he—? Hide yourself, Nora; say you are ill.

(Nora stands motionless. Helmer goes to the door and opens it.)

HELENE *(Half dressed, in the hall)*.   It's a letter for Mrs. Helmer.

HELMER.   Give it to me. *(Seizes the letter and shuts the door.)* It's from him. I shan't give it to you. I'll read it myself.

NORA.   Very well.

HELMER *(by the lamp)*.   I don't dare open it; this may be the end—for both of us. Still—I must know. *(Hastily tears the letter open; reads a few lines, looks at an enclosure; with a cry of joy.)* Nora! *(Nora looks inquiringly at him.)* Nora!—I can't believe it—I must read it again. But it's true—it's really true! Nora, I am saved! I'm saved!

NORA.   What about me?

HELMER.   You too, of course; we are both of us saved, both of us. Look!—he's sent you back your note—he says he's sorry for what he did and apologizes for it—that due to a happy turn of events he— Oh, what does it matter what he says! We are saved, Nora! No one can harm you now. Oh, Nora, Nora—; but let's get rid of this hateful thing. I'll just see—*(Glances at the I.O.U.)* No, no—I won't even look at it; I'll pretend it was all a horrible dream. *(Tears the I.O.U. and both letters in pieces. Throws them into the fire and watches them burn.)* There! Now it's all over—He said in his letter you've known about this since Christmas Eve—you must have had three dreadful days, Nora!

NORA.   Yes. It's been very hard.

HELMER.   How you must have suffered! And you saw no way out but— No! We'll forget the whole ghastly business. We'll just thank God and repeat again and again: It's over; all over! Don't you understand, Nora? You don't seem to grasp it: It's over. What's the matter with you? Why do you look so grim? My poor darling little Nora, I understand; but you mustn't worry—beause I've forgiven you, Nora; I swear I have; I've forgiven everything. You did what you did because you loved me—I see that now.

NORA.   Yes—that's true.

HELMER.   You loved me as a wife should love her husband. You didn't realize what you were doing—you weren't able to judge how wrong it was. Don't think this makes you any less dear to me. Just you lean on me; let me guide you and advise you; I'm not a man for nothing! There's something very endearing about a woman's help-lessness. And try and forget those harsh things I said just now. I was frantic; my whole world seemed to be tumbling about my ears. Believe me, I've forgiven you, Nora—I swear it—I've forgiven everything.

NORA.   Thank you for your forgiveness, Torvald. *(Goes out, to the right.)*

HELMER.   No! Don't go. *(Looking through the doorway.)* Why do you have to go in there?

NORA *(inside).*   I want to get out of these fancy-dress clothes.

HELMER *(in the doorway).*   Yes, do, my darling. Try to calm down now, and get back to normal, my poor frightened little songbird. Don't you worry—you'll be safe under my wings—they'll protect you. *(Walking up and down near the door.)* How lovely our home is, Nora! You'll be sheltered here; I'll cherish you as if you were a little dove I'd rescued from the claws of some dreadful hawk. You'll see—your poor fluttering little heart will soon grow calm again. Tomorrow all this will appear in quite a different light— things will be just as they were. I won't have to keep on saying I've forgiven you—you'll be able to sense it. You don't really think I could ever drive you away, do you? That I could even so much as reproach you for anything? You'd understand if you could see into my heart. When a man forgives his wife whole-heartedly—as I have you—it fills him with such tenderness, such peace. She seems to belong to him in a double sense; it's as though he'd brought her to life again; she's become more than his wife—she's become his child as well. That's how it will be with us, Nora—my own bewildered, helpless little darling. From now on you mustn't worry about anything; just open your heart to me; just let me be both will and conscience to you. *(Nora enters in everyday dress.)* What's all this? I thought you were going to bed. You've changed your dress?

NORA.   Yes, Torvald; I've changed my dress.

HELMER.   But what for? At this hour?

NORA.   I shan't sleep tonight.

HELMER.   But, Nora dear—

NORA *(looking at her watch)*.   It's not so very late—Sit down, Torvald; we have a lot to talk about. *(She sits on one side of the table.)*

HELMER.   Nora—what does this mean? Why that stern expression?

NORA.   Sit down. It'll take some time. I have a lot to say to you.

(Helmer sits at the other side of the table.)

HELMER.   You frighten me, Nora. I don't understand you.

NORA.   No, that's just it. You don't understand me; and I have never understood you either—until tonight. No, don't interrupt me. Just listen to what I have to say. This is to be a final settlement, Torvald.

HELMER.   How do you mean?

NORA *(after a short silence)*.   Doesn't anything special strike you as we sit here like this?

HELMER.   I don't think so—why?

NORA.   It doesn't occur to you, does it, that though we've been married for eight years, this is the first time that we two—man and wife—have sat down for a serious talk?

HELMER.   What do you mean by serious?

NORA.   During eight whole years, no—more than that—ever since the first day we met—we have never exchanged so much as one serious word about serious things.

HELMER.   Why should I perpetually burden you with all my cares and problems? How could you possibly help me to solve them?

NORA.   I'm not talking about cares and problems. I'm simply saying we've never once sat down seriously and tried to get to the bottom of anything.

HELMER.   But, Nora, darling—why should you be concerned with serious thoughts?

NORA.   That's the whole point! You've never understood me—A great injustice has been done me, Torvald; first by Father, and then by you.

HELMER.   What a thing to say! No two people on earth could ever have loved you more than we have!

NORA *(shaking her head)*.   You never loved me. You just thought it was fun to be in love with me.

HELMER.   This is fantastic!

NORA.   Perhaps. But it's true all the same. While I was still at home I used to hear Father airing his opinions and they became my opinions; or if I didn't happen to agree, I kept it to myself—he would have been displeased otherwise. He used to call me his doll-baby, and played with me as I played with my dolls. Then I came to live in your house—

HELMER.   What an expression to use about our marriage!

NORA *(undisturbed)*.   I mean—from Father's hands I passed into yours. You arranged everything according to your tastes, and I acquired the same tastes, or I pretended to—I'm not sure which—a little of both, perhaps. Looking back on it all, it seems to me I've lived here like a beggar, from hand to mouth. I've lived by performing tricks for you, Torvald. But that's the way you wanted it. You and Father have done me a great wrong. You've prevented me from becoming a real person.

HELMER.   Nora, how can you be so ungrateful and unreasonable! Haven't you been happy here?

NORA.   No, never. I thought I was; but I wasn't really.

HELMER.   Not—not happy!

NORA.   No; only merry. You've always been so kind to me. But our home has never been anything but a play-room. I've been your doll-wife, just as at home I was

Papa's doll-child. And the children in turn, have been my dolls. I thought it fun when you played games with me, just as they thought it fun when I played games with them. And that's been our marriage, Torvald.

HELMER.   There may be a grain of truth in what you say, even though it is distorted and exaggerated. From now on things will be different. Playtime is over now; tomorrow lessons begin!

NORA.   Whose lessons? Mine, or the children's?

HELMER.   Both, if you wish it, Nora, dear.

NORA.   Torvald, I'm afraid you're not the man to teach me to be a real wife to you.

HELMER.   How can you say that?

NORA.   And I'm certainly not fit to teach the children.

HELMER.   Nora!

NORA.   Didn't you just say, a moment ago, you didn't dare trust them to me?

HELMER.   That was in the excitement of the moment! You mustn't take it so seriously!

NORA.   But you were right, Torvald. That job is beyond me; there's another job I must do first: I must try and educate myself. You could never help me to do that; I must do it quite alone. So, you see—that's why I'm going to leave you.

HELMER *(jumping up)*.   What did you say—?

NORA.   I shall never get to know myself—I shall never learn to face reality—unless I stand alone. So I can't stay with you any longer.

HELMER.   Nora! Nora!

NORA.   I am going at once. I'm sure Kristine will let me stay with her tonight—

HELMER.   But, Nora—this is madness! I shan't allow you to do this. I shall forbid it!

NORA.   You no longer have the power to forbid me anything. I'll only take a few things with me—those that belong to me. I shall never again accept anything from you.

HELMER.   Have you lost your senses?

NORA.   Tomorrow I'll go home—to what *was* my home, I mean. It might be easier for me there, to find something to do.

HELMER.   You talk like an ignorant child, Nora—!

NORA.   Yes. That's just why I must educate myself.

HELMER.   To leave your home—to leave your husband, and your children! What do you suppose people would say to that?

NORA.   It makes no difference. This is something I *must* do.

HELMER.   It's inconceivable! Don't you realize you'd be betraying your most sacred duty?

NORA.   What do you consider that to be?

HELMER.   Your duty towards your husband and your children—I surely don't have to tell you that!

NORA.   I've another duty just as sacred.

HELMER.   Nonsense! What duty do you mean?

NORA.   My duty towards myself.

HELMER.   Remember—before all else you are a wife and mother.

NORA.   I don't believe that anymore. I believe that before all else I am a human being, just as you are—or at least that I should try and become one. I know that most people would agree with you, Torvald—and that's what they say in books. But I can no longer be satisfied with what most people say—or what they write in books. I must think things out for myself—get clear about them.

HELMER.   Surely your position in your home is clear enough? Have you no sense of religion? Isn't that an infallible guide to you?

NORA.   But don't you see, Torvald—I don't really know what religion is.

HELMER.   Nora! How *can* you!

NORA.   All I know about it is what Pastor Hansen told me when I was confirmed. He taught me what he thought religion was—said it was *this* and *that*. As soon as I get away by myself, I shall have to look into that matter too, try and decide whether what he taught me was right—or whether it's right for *me*, at least.

HELMER.   A nice way for a young woman to talk! It's unheard of! If religion means nothing to you, I'll appeal to your conscience; you must have some sense of ethics, I suppose? Answer me! Or have you none?

NORA.   It's hard for me to answer you, Torvald. I don't think I know—all these things bewilder me. But I *do* know that I think quite differently from you about them. I've discovered that the law, for instance, is quite different from what I had imagined; but I find it hard to believe it can be right. It seems it's criminal for a woman to try and spare her old, sick, father, or save her husband's life! I can't agree with that.

HELMER.   You talk like a child. You have no understanding of the society we live in.

NORA.   No, I haven't. But I'm going to try and learn. I want to find out which of us is right—society or I.

HELMER.   You are ill, Nora; you have a touch of fever; you're quite beside yourself.

NORA.   I've never felt so sure—so clear-headed—as I do tonight.

HELMER.   "Sure and clear-headed" enough to leave your husband and your children?

NORA.   Yes.

HELMER.   Then there is only one explanation possible.

NORA.   What?

HELMER.   You don't love me any more.

NORA.   No; that is just it.

HELMER.   Nora!—What are you saying!

NORA.   It makes me so unhappy, Torvald; for you've always been so kind to me. But I can't help it. I don't love you any more.

HELMER *(mastering himself with difficulty)*.   You feel "sure and clear-headed" about this too?

NORA.   Yes, utterly sure. That's why I can't stay here any longer.

HELMER.   And can you tell me how I lost your love?

NORA.   Yes, I can tell you. It was tonight—when the wonderful thing didn't happen; I knew then you weren't the man I always thought you were.

HELMER.   I don't understand.

NORA.   For eight years I've been waiting patiently; I knew, of course, that such things don't happen every day. Then, when this trouble came to me—I thought to myself: Now! Now the wonderful thing will happen! All the time Krogstad's letter was out there in the box, it never occurred to me for a single moment that you'd think of submitting to his conditions. I was absolutely convinced that you'd defy him—that you'd tell him to publish the thing to all the world; and that then—

HELMER.   You mean you thought I'd let my wife be publicly dishonored and disgraced?

NORA.   No. What I thought you'd do, was to take the blame upon yourself.

HELMER.   Nora—!

NORA.   I know! You think I never would have accepted such a sacrifice. Of course I wouldn't! But my word would have meant nothing against yours. That was the wonderful thing I hoped for, Torvald, hoped for with such terror. And it was to prevent that, that I chose to kill myself.

HELMER.   I'd gladly work for you day and night, Nora—go through suffering and want, if need be—but one doesn't sacrifice one's honor for love's sake.

NORA.   Millions of women have done so.

HELMER.   You think and talk like a silly child.

NORA.   Perhaps. But you neither think nor talk like the man I want to share my life with. When you'd recovered from your fright—and you never thought of me, only of yourself—when you had nothing more to fear—you behaved as though none of this had happened. I was your little lark again, your little doll—whom you would have to guard more carefully than ever, because she was so weak and frail. *(Stands up.)* At that moment it suddenly dawned on me that I had been living here for eight years with a stranger and that I'd borne him three children. I can't bear to think about it! I could tear myself to pieces!

HELMER *(sadly)*.   I see, Nora—I understand; there's suddenly a great void between us—Is there no way to bridge it?

NORA.   Feeling as I do now, Torvald—I could never be a wife to you.

HELMER.   But, if I were to change? Don't you think I'm capable of that?

NORA.   Perhaps—when you no longer have your doll to play with.

HELMER.   It's inconceivable! I *can't* part with you, Nora. I can't endure the thought.

NORA *(going into room on the right)*.   All the more reason it should happen. *(She comes back with outdoor things and a small traveling-bag, which she places on a chair.)*

HELMER.   But not at once, Nora—not now! At least wait till tomorrow.

NORA *(putting on cloak)*.   I can't spend the night in a strange man's house.

HELMER.   Couldn't we go on living here together? As brother and sister, if you like—as friends.

NORA *(fastening her hat)*.   You know very well that wouldn't last, Torvald. *(Puts on the shawl.)* Good-bye. I won't go in and see the children. I know they're in better hands than mine. Being what I am—how can I be of any use to them?

HELMER.   But surely, some day, Nora—?

NORA.   How can I tell? How do I know what sort of person I'll become?

HELMER.   You are my wife, Nora, now and always!

NORA.   Listen to me, Torvald—I've always heard that when a wife deliberately leaves her husband as I am leaving you, he is legally freed from all responsibility towards her. At any rate, I release you now from all responsibility. You mustn't feel yourself bound, any more than I shall. There must be complete freedom on both sides. Here is your ring. Now give me mine.

HELMER.   That too?

NORA.   That too.

HELMER.   Here it is.

NORA.   So—it's all over now. Here are the keys. The servants know how to run the house—better than I do. I'll ask Kristine to come by tomorrow, after I've left town; there are a few things I brought with me from home; she'll pack them up and send them on to me.

HELMER.   You really mean it's over, Nora? *Really* over? You'll never think of me again?

NORA.   I expect I shall often think of you; of you—and the children, and this house.

HELMER.   May I write to you?

NORA.   No—never. you mustn't! Please!

HELMER.   At least, let me send you—

NORA.   Nothing!

HELMER.   But, you'll let me help you, Nora—

NORA.   No, I say! I can't accept anything from strangers.

HELMER.   Must I always be a stranger to you, Nora?

NORA *(taking her traveling bag)*.   Yes. Unless it were to happen—the most wonderful thing of all—

HELMER.   What?

NORA.   Unless we both could change so that—Oh, Torvald! I no longer *believe* in miracles, you see!

HELMER.   Tell me! Let *me* believe! Unless we both could change so that—?

NORA.   —So that our life together might truly be a marriage. Good-bye. *(She goes out by the hall door.)*

HELMER *(sinks into a chair by the door with his face in his hands)*.   Nora! Nora! *(He looks around the room and rises.)* She is gone! How empty it all seems! *(A hope springs up in him.)* The most wonderful thing of all—?

(From below is heard the reverberation of a heavy door closing.)

QUESTIONS FOR CLOSE READING

1. The play opens with plans for a Christmas celebration. Why is this detail important in light of the rest of the play?

2. Helmer calls Nora his "little lark" and wonders if she is "twittering out there." What is the significance of the imagery of Nora as a little singing bird? Helmer also refers to her as "my little squirrel." How are we to take this kind of language?

3. What is Helmer's attitude toward Nora when the play opens? How does she see herself?

4. Why does Helmer emphasize his financial difficulties? He is a lawyer with prospects, but what are those prospects?

5. Who is Mrs. Linde and what does her arrival imply for Nora and Helmer?

6. Nora did something technically illegal. What were her motives? Do you feel, as Helmer ultimately does, that what she did was unforgivable?

7. What are Krogstad's motives in regard to Nora? What kind of man is Krogstad? What power does he have over Nora?

8. How does Nora try to get Helmer to do what she wants? What are her strategies?

9. What is Dr. Rank's role in Nora's and Helmer's lives?

10. In Act III Helmer rails against Nora, calling her "no better than a hypocrite." What do you learn about Helmer's character in this act? What is Nora's reaction?

11. Nora says in Act III that she must educate herself. How has she changed? What does she mean by saying she must educate herself? Nora says "a great injustice has been done me, Torvald; first by Father, and then by you." What does she mean? Is she right?

QUESTIONS FOR AN INTERPRETATION

1. What are the feminist issues at stake in this play? Ibsen was seen as a prominent feminist during his lifetime. Scandinavia was very active in the debate in the late nineteenth century over women's rights. What assumptions about the role of women are revealed in this play? In what ways does Nora behave in a stereotypical fashion as a housewife? Does her behavior please her husband? How does Mrs. Linde react to it?

2. An interesting interpretation of the action of the drama could arise from a comparison between the two prominent women in the play, Nora Helmer and Kristine Linde. In what ways are they similar and in what ways different? Mrs. Linde repeatedly regards Nora as being childlike. Is she right? In what ways does she seem more grown-up? How does her life differ from Nora's?

3. Nora's behavior seems self-determined in the early part of the play. However, an interesting interpretation could arise from an examination of the way in which she reacts to Torvald Helmer's expectations and suggestions. How does Torvald manipulate her to make her the kind of woman he wishes her to be? And what kind of woman is that?

4. Is Torvald Helmer as high-minded and moral as he says and thinks he is? What does he say about moral behavior? How does his own behavior carry out his ideals? In what ways does he fall short? Why is it so difficult for him to see the change in Nora at the end of the play? How much do you respect him at the end of the play?

5. Examine the animal imagery in the play. What is it doing here and how does it affect your interpretation of the main action? How does it affect your interpretation of the characters?

6. What economic circumstances have the most serious effect on the action of the play? Is this play essentially about economics and its domination of people's lives? Who is most seriously hurt by the economic limitations described in the play? How wise is Torvald in his attitudes toward money and how to earn it? Is there an irony implied in the fact that Torvald is to become the new president of the Joint Stock Bank?

7. The behavior of some of the characters may strike you as annoying, alarming, or distasteful. How carefully do you feel Ibsen controls your attitudes toward the main characters in the play? How does he want you to feel toward Nora? Does he wish you to be sympathetic or unsympathetic? How about Torvald Helmer or Krogstad? Can you see a growth and development in your attitudes toward these characters?

RESOURCES FOR READING IBSEN

HENRIK IBSEN

Notes on *A Doll House* _____ *1878*

Ibsen's journals and notes (from Playwrights on Playwrighting, *ed. Toby Cole) give us insight into some of his key beliefs. In his notes to* A Doll House, *for example, he says that men and women are very different and that a woman cannot be herself because she lives in a masculine society. This selection also shows how Ibsen planned the play, thus giving us a glimpse of the creative process at work. Note that Nora and Torvald first had the name of Stenborg.*

NOTES FOR THE MODERN TRAGEDY.   There are two kinds of spiritual law, two kinds of conscience, one in man and another, altogether different, in woman. They do not understand each other; but in practical life the woman is judged by man's law, as though she were not a woman but a man.

The wife in the play ends by having no idea of what is right or wrong; natural feeling on the one hand and belief in authority on the other have altogether bewildered her.

A woman cannot be herself in the society of the present day, which is an exclusively masculine society, with laws framed by men and with a judicial system that judges feminine conduct from a masculine point of view.

She has committed forgery, and she is proud of it; for she did it out of love for her husband, to save his life. But this husband with his commonplace principles of honor is on the side of the law and looks at the question from the masculine point of view.

Spiritual conflicts. Oppressed and bewildered by the belief in authority, she loses faith in her moral right and ability to bring up her children. Bitterness. A mother in modern society, like certain insects who go away and die when she has done her duty in the propagation of the race. Love of life, of home, of husband and children and family. Now and then a womanly shaking off of her thoughts. Sudden return of anxiety and terror. She must bear it all alone. The catastrophe approaches, inexorably, inevitably. Despair, conflict, and destruction.

(Krogstad has acted dishonorably and thereby become well-to-do; now his prosperity does not help him, he cannot recover his honor.)

SCENARIO: FIRST ACT.   A room comfortably, but not showily, furnished. A door to the right in the back leads to the hall; another door to the left in the back leads to the room or office of the master of the house, which can be seen when the door is opened. A fire in the stove. Winter day.

She enters from the back, humming gaily; she is in outdoor dress and carries several parcels, has been shopping. As she opens the door, a porter is seen in the hall, carrying a Christmas tree. *She:* Put it down there for the present. (Taking out her purse) How much? *Porter:* Fifty öre. *She:* Here is a crown. No, keep the change. The porter thanks her and goes. She continues humming and smiling contentedly as she opens several of the parcels she has brought. Calls off to find out if he is home. Yes! At first, conversation through the closed door; then he opens it and goes on talking to her while continuing to work most of the time, standing at his desk. There is a ring at the hall door; he does not want to be disturbed; shuts himself in. The maid opens the door to her mistress's friend, just arrived in town. Happy surprise. Mutual explanation of the state of affairs. He has received the post of manager in the new joint-stock bank and is to begin at New Year's; all financial worries are at an end.

The friend has come to town to look for some small employment in an office or whatever may present itself. Mrs. Stenborg encourages her, is certain that all will turn out well. The maid opens the front door to the debt collector. Mrs. Stenborg terrified; they exchange a few words; he is shown into the office. Mrs. Stenborg and her friend; the circumstances of the collector are touched upon. Stenborg enters in his overcoat; has sent the collector out the other way. Conversation about the friend's affairs; hesitation on his part. He and the friend go out; his wife follows them into the hall; the Nurse enters with the children. Mother and children play. The collector enters. Mrs. Stenborg sends the children out to the left. Big scene between her and him. He goes. Stenborg enters; has met him on the stairs; displeased; wants to know what he came back for? Her support? No intrigues. His wife cautiously tries to pump him. Strict legal answers. Exit to his room. *She:* (repeating her words when the collector went out) But that's impossible. Why, I did it from love!

SECOND ACT.   The last day of the year. Midday. Nora and the old Nurse. Nora, driven by anxiety, is putting on her things to go out. Anxious random questions of one kind and another intimate that thoughts of death are in her mind. Tries to banish these thoughts, to make light of it, hopes that something or other may intervene. But what? The Nurse goes off to the left. Stenborg enters from his room. Short dialogue between him and Nora. The Nurse re-enters; looks for Nora; the youngest child is crying. Annoyance and questioning on Stenborg's part; exit the Nurse; Stenborg is going in to the children. Doctor enters. Scene between him and Stenborg. Nora soon re-enters; she has turned back; anxiety has driven her home again. Scene between her, the Doctor, and Stenborg. Stenborg goes into his room. Scene between Nora and the Doctor. The Doctor goes out. Nora alone. Mrs. Linde enters. Scene between her and Nora. Lawyer Krogstad enters. Short scene between him, Mrs. Linde, and Nora. Mrs. Linde in to the children. Scene between Krogstad and Nora. She entreats and implores him for the sake of her little children; in vain. Krogstad goes out. The letter is seen to fall from outside into the letter box. Mrs. Linde re-enters after a short pause. Scene between her and Nora. Half confession. Mrs. Linde goes out. Nora alone. Stenborg enters. Scene between him and Nora. He wants to empty the letter box. Entreaties, jests, half-playful persuasion. He promises to let business wait till after New Year's Day; but at 12 o'clock midnight...! Exit. Nora alone. *Nora:* (looking at the clock) It is five o'clock. Five; seven hours till midnight. Twenty-four hours till the next midnight. Twenty-four and seven—thirty-one. Thirty-one hours to live.

THIRD ACT.   A muffled sound of dance music is heard from the floor above. A lighted lamp on the table. Mrs. Linde sits in an armchair and absently turns the pages of a book, tries to read, but seems unable to fix her attention; once or twice she looks at her watch. Nora comes down from the party; so disturbed she was compelled to leave; surprise at finding Mrs. Linde, who pretends that she wanted to see Nora in her costume. Helmer, displeased at her going away, comes to fetch her back. The Doctor also enters, to say good-by. Meanwhile Mrs. Linde has gone into the side room on the right. Scene between the Doctor, Helmer, and Nora. He is going to bed, he says, never to get up again; they are not to come and see him; there is ugliness about a deathbed. He goes out. Helmer goes upstairs again with Nora, after the latter has exchanged a few words of farewell with Mrs. Linde. Mrs. Linde alone. Then Krogstad. Scene and explanation between them. Both go out. Nora and the children. Then she alone. Then Helmer. He takes the letters out of the letter box. Short scene; good night; he goes into his room. Nora in despair prepares for the final step, is already at the door when Helmer enters with the open letter in his hand. Big scene. A ring. Letter to Nora from Krogstad. Final scene. Divorce. Nora leaves the house.

JANET ACHURCH

On Being Nora ————————————————————— *1889*

In this interview (from The Pall Mall Gazette, *1889) actress Janet Achurch compares the part of Nora with that of Hamlet in terms of its demands on her talent. She also reveals that she likes the role of Nora better than any other she has played. Interestingly, the interviewer's concerns for the children parallel those of the general audience. Janet Achurch feels the children will be taken care of and disregards the charge of "reckless abandonment."*

It is not often that any young actress achieves the phenomenal success with which Miss Janet Achurch has brought to a temporary close her dramatic career in the old country. Before *A Doll House* was brought out at the Novelty Theatre almost every one predicted that the attempt would result in disastrous failure. Ibsen as a dramatist had never been brought before the London playgoer, and it was a somewhat daring experiment to begin with such a dish of strong meat as the drama in which the Norwegian poet laid the axe to the root of the conventional idea of matrimonial fine-ladyism. You will be fortunate, very fortunate, said sympathizing friends, if you can keep it running a week, and no doubt but for Miss Achurch's brilliant rendering of the arduous role of the heroine the play would have been numbered among the numerous failures which make up so large a part of the history of the attempts to acclimatize the higher drama on the London stage. Thanks, however, to the extraordinary fidelity with which Miss Achurch represented Ibsen's Nora, the play has had a run of three weeks, and has only been withdrawn because it was impossible to postpone any longer the departure of Miss Achurch and Mr. Charrington for Australia. They start to-day for Brindisi, where they meet the *Ballarat* and take ship for Melbourne. Seldom has any actress had a more brilliant "send off" than that which the creation as the English Nora Helmer has supplied to Miss Achurch; and the following interview will be read with interest by many who usually regard with supreme indifference the sayings and doings of the stars of the London stage.

"Yes," said Miss Achurch, in reply to a question from our representative, "*A Doll House* has been a great success. But it has taken a great deal out of me, and if it had gone on much longer I should have broken down. It is the hardest part I have ever played. Nora is never off the stage for a single moment during the whole of the first and second acts, and in the third act she is only absent for five minutes. The part is heavier than that of Hamlet, and to go through it eight times a week is too great a strain."

"Eight times a week?"

"Yes. We had a morning performance every Wednesday and Saturday, and to go through such a piece twice a day twice a week has told somewhat seriously on me. I shall be delighted to get rest on the voyage out, before beginning again on the Australian boards. As soon as we land in Melbourne we have four months' engagement before us in that city. Then we go to Adelaide and Sydney and perhaps to Brisbane. It will be eighteen months at the least, and two years at the most, before we return home."

"But Nora, how do you like the character?"

"I like Nora better than about 200 roles I have filled since I first appeared on the stage. After Nora I think on the whole I prefer Lady Macbeth. But Nora is a wonderful conception, into the realization of which one can throw one's whole soul."

"Tell me, what is your reading of what Nora will do afterwards?"

"Ibsen leaves every one to form their own idea as to the sequel of his play. It is left an interrogation which every one can answer as he pleases. I think she will come back after a time and try again the experiment of living with Helmer. But it will fail. That man is impossible, utterly impossible. She did right to leave him."

"But the children?"

"Ah! that is another matter. I don't think that was right, but you should remember that it was partly for the sake of the children she went away. She felt herself so utterly unworthy of undertaking their education, and she left them in the hands of a very good nurse."

"At the same time don't you think it was a mistake, the last and crowning illustration of the extent to which her doll-like upbringing worked out its dismal harvest of wrongdoing? Even when she caught a glimpse of a higher ideal and aspired after a nobler life, at that very moment the impulsive weakness of the untrained mind asserted itself, and her frantic plunge at the last was as natural an outcome of the moral atmosphere of a doll's house as her forgery or any other of her heedless acts of impulsive ignorance."

"Possibly you are right, but the moral is plain enough in any case. For men the play can hardly be accused of being anything but good. To open their eyes to the consequences of ignoring the moral and intellectual nature of the human being with whom they have allied themselves is surely excellent. For the women, if I may judge from the letters I have received, it has been also useful, nor do I think that it will tend, as some say, to more easy divorce and reckless abandonment of home. What it ought to do is to make them much less reckless about marrying, by showing that a plunge into matrimony in the mere fever of a passionate attachment, without any similarity of taste or common interest in the serious work of life, is to prepare for yourself a terrible awakening."

JOAN TEMPLETON

The Doll House Backlash: Criticism, Feminism, and Ibsen _____ *1989*

In this excerpt from a longer article (in PMLA, January 1989), Joan Templeton gives us insight into the range of negative criticism of Nora Helmer's actions. Critics of Nora, both men and women, have seen her as problematic not only because of her problems with her role in society but also because of her psychological instability, her "hysteria." Their responses have often been quite personal.

> *A Doll House* is no more about women's rights than Shakespeare's *Richard II* is about the divine right of kings, or *Ghosts* about syphilis. . . . Its theme is the need of every individual to find out the kind of person he or she is and to strive to become that person.
>
> (M. Meyer 457)

Ibsen has been resoundingly saved from feminism, or, as it was called in his day, "the woman question." His rescuers customarily cite a statement the dramatist made on 26 May 1898 at a seventieth-birthday banquet given in his honor by the Norwegian Women's Rights League:

> I thank you for the toast, but must disclaim the honor of having consciously worked for the women's rights movement. . . . True enough, it is desirable to solve the woman problem, along with all the others; but that has not been the whole purpose. My task has been the description of humanity.
>
> (Ibsen, *Letters* 337)

Ibsen's champions like to take this disavowal as a precise reference to his purpose in writing *A Doll House* twenty years earlier, his "original intention," according to Maurice Valency. Ibsen's biographer Michael Meyer urges all reviewers of *Doll House* revivals to learn Ibsen's speech by heart, and James McFarlane, editor of *The Oxford Ibsen*, includes it in his explanatory material on *A Doll House*, under "Some Pronouncements of the Author," as though Ibsen had been speaking of the play. Whatever propaganda feminists may have made of *A Doll House*, Ibsen, it is argued, never meant to write a play about the highly topical subject of women's rights; Nora's conflict represents something other than, or something more than, woman's. In an article commemorating the half century of Ibsen's death, R. M. Adams explains, "*A Doll House* represents a woman imbued with the idea of becoming a person, but it proposes nothing categorical about women becoming people; in fact, its real theme has nothing to do with the sexes." Over twenty years later, after feminism had resurfaced as an international movement, Einar Haugen, the doyen of American Scandinavian studies, insisted that "Ibsen's Nora is not just a woman arguing for female liberation; she is much more. She embodies the comedy as well as the tragedy of modern life." In the Modern Language Association's *Approaches to Teaching* A Doll House, the editor speaks disparagingly of "reductionist views of [*A Doll House*] as a feminist drama." Summarizing a "major theme" in the volume as "the need for a broad view of the play and a condemnation of a static approach," she warns that discussions of the play's "connection with feminism" have value only if they are monitored, "properly channeled and kept firmly linked to Ibsen's text."

Removing the woman question from *A Doll House* is presented as part of a corrective effort to free Ibsen from his erroneous reputation as a writer of thesis plays, a wrongheaded notion usually blamed on Shaw, who, it is claimed, mistakenly saw Ibsen as the nineteenth century's greatest iconoclast and offered that misreading to the public as *The Quintessence of Ibsenism.* Ibsen, it is now de rigueur to explain, did not stoop to "issues." He was a poet of the truth of the human soul. That Nora's exit from her dollhouse has long been the principle international symbol for women's issues, including many that far exceed the confines of her small world, is irrelevant to the essential meaning of *A Doll House,* a play, in Richard Gilman's phrase, "pitched beyond sexual difference." Ibsen, explains Robert Brustein, "was completely indifferent to [the woman question] except as a metaphor for individual freedom." Discussing the relation of *A Doll House* to feminism, Halvdan Koht, author of the definitive Norwegian Ibsen life, says in summary, "Little by little the topical controversy died away; what remained was the work of art, with its demand for truth in every human relation."

Thus, it turns out, the *Uncle Tom's Cabin* of the women's rights movement is not really about women at all. "Fiddle-faddle," pronounced R. M. Adams, dismissing feminist claims for the play. Like angels, Nora has no sex. Ibsen meant her to be Everyman.

THE DEMON IN THE HOUSE

[Nora is] a daughter of Eve. . . . [A]n irresistibly bewitching piece of femininity. . . . [Her] charge that in all the years of their marriage they have never exchanged one serious word about serious things is incorrect: she has quite forgotten how seriously Torvald lectured her on the subjects of forgery and lying less than three days ago.

The a priori dismissal of women's rights as the subject of *A Doll House* is a gentlemanly backlash, a refusal to acknowledge the existence of a tiresome reality, "the hoary problem of women's rights," as Michael Meyer has it; the issue is decidedly *vieux jeu,°* and its importance has been greatly exaggerated.

vieux jeu: old hat.

In Ibsen's timeless world of Everyman, questions of gender can only be tedious intrusions.

But for over a hundred years, Nora has been under direct siege as exhibiting the most perfidious characteristics of her sex; the original outcry of the 1880s is swollen now to a mighty chorus of blame. She is denounced as an irrational and frivolous narcissist; an "abnormal" woman, a "hysteric"; a vain, unloving egoist who abandons her family in a paroxysm of selfishness. The proponents of the last view would seem to think Ibsen had in mind a housewife Medea, whose cruelty to husband and children he tailored down to fit the framed, domestic world of realist drama.

The first attacks were launched against Nora on moral grounds and against Ibsen, ostensibly, on "literary" ones. The outraged reviewers of the premiere claimed that *A Doll House* did not have to be taken as a serious statement about women's rights because the heroine of Act III is an incomprehensible transformation of the heroine of Acts I and II. This reasoning provided an ideal way to dismiss Nora altogether; nothing she said needed to be taken seriously, and her door slamming could be written off as silly theatrics.

The argument for the two Noras, which still remains popular, has had its most determined defender in the Norwegian scholar Else Høst, who argues that Ibsen's carefree, charming "lark" could never have become the "newly fledged feminist." In any case it is the "childish, expectant, ecstatic, broken-hearted Nora" who makes *A Doll House* immortal; the other one, the unfeeling woman of Act III who coldly analyzes the flaws in her marriage, is psychologically unconvincing and wholly unsympathetic.

The most unrelenting attempt on record to trivialize Ibsen's protagonist, and a favorite source for Nora's later detractors, is Hermann Weigand's. In a classic 1925 study, Weigand labors through forty-nine pages to demonstrate that Ibsen conceived of Nora as a silly, lovable female. At the beginning, Weigand confesses, he was, like all men, momentarily shaken by the play: "Having had the misfortune to be born of the male sex, we slink away in shame, vowing to mend our ways." The chastened critic's remorse is short-lived, however, as a "clear male voice, irreverently breaking the silence," stuns with its critical acumen: " 'The meaning of the final scene,' the voice says, 'is epitomized by Nora's remark: "Yes, Torvald. Now I have changed my dress." ' " With this epiphany as guide, Weigand spends the night poring over the "little volume." Dawn arrives, bringing with it the return of "masculine self-respect." For there is only one explanation for the revolt of "this winsome little woman" and her childish door slamming: Ibsen meant *A Doll House* as comedy. Nora's erratic behavior at the curtain's fall leaves us laughing heartily, for there is no doubt that she will return home to "revert, imperceptibly, to her role of songbird and charmer." After all, since Nora is

> an irresistibly bewitching piece of femininity, an extravagant poet and romancer, utterly lacking in sense of fact, and endowed with a natural gift for play-acting

which makes her instinctively dramatize her experiences: how can the settlement fail of a fundamentally comic appeal?

The most popular way to render Nora inconsequential has been to attack her morality; whatever the vocabulary used, the arguments have remained much the same for over a century. Oswald Crawford, writing in the *Fortnightly Review* in 1891, scolded that while Nora may be "charming as doll-women may be charming," she is "unprincipled." A half century later, after Freudianism had produced a widely accepted "clinical" language of disapproval, Nora could be called "abnormal." Mary McCarthy lists Nora as one of the "neurotic" women whom Ibsen, she curiously claims, was the first playwright to put on stage. For Maurice Valency, Nora is a case study of female hysteria, a willful, unwomanly woman: "Nora is a carefully studied example of what we have come to know as the hysterical personality—bright, unstable, impulsive, romantic, quite immune from feelings of guilt, and, at bottom, not especially feminine."

More recent assaults on Nora have argued that her forgery to obtain the money to save her husband's life proves her irresponsibility and egotism. Brian Johnston condemns Nora's love as "unintelligent" and her crime as "a trivial act which nevertheless turns to evil because it refused to take the universal ethical realm into consideration at all"; Ibsen uses Torvald's famous pet names for Nora—lark, squirrel—to give her a "strong 'animal' identity" and to underscore her inability to understand the ethical issues faced by human beings. Evert Sprinchorn argues that Nora had only to ask her husband's kindly friends (entirely missing from the play) for the necessary money: ". . . any other woman would have done so. But Nora knew that if she turned to one of Torvald's friends for help, she would have had to share her role of savior with someone else."

Even Nora's sweet tooth is evidence of her unworthiness, as we see her "surreptitiously devouring the forbidden [by her husband] macaroons," even "brazenly offer[ing] macaroons to Doctor Rank, and finally lying in her denial that the macaroons are hers"; eating macaroons in secret suggests that "Nora is deceitful and manipulative from the start" and that her exit thus "reflects only a petulant woman's irresponsibility." As she eats the cookies, Nora adds insult to injury by declaring her hidden wish to say "death and damnation" in front of her husband, thus revealing, according to Brian Downs, of Christ's College, Cambridge, "something a trifle febrile and morbid" in her nature.

Much has been made of Nora's relationship with Doctor Rank, the surest proof, it is argued, of her dishonesty. Nora is revealed as *la belle dame sans merci*° when she "suggestively queries Rank whether a pair of silk stockings will fit her"; she "flirts cruelly with [him] and toys with his affection for her, drawing him on to find out how strong her hold over him actually is."

---

la belle dame sans merci: the beautiful lady without mercy.

Nora's detractors have often been, from the first, her husband's defenders. In an argument that claims to rescue Nora and Torvald from "the campaign for the liberation of women" so that they "become vivid and disturbingly real," Evert Sprinchorn pleads that Torvald "has given Nora all the material things and all the sexual attention that any young wife could reasonably desire. He loves beautiful things, and not least his pretty wife." Nora is incapable of appreciating her husband because she "is not a normal woman. She is compulsive, highly imaginative, and very much inclined to go to extremes." Since it is she who has acquired the money to save his life, Torvald, and not Nora, is really the "wife in the family," although he "has regarded himself as the breadwinner . . . the main support of his wife and children, as any decent husband would like to regard himself." In another defense, John Chamberlain argues that Torvald deserves our sympathy because he is no "mere common or garden chauvinist." If Nora were less the actress Weigand has proved her to be, "the woman in her might observe what the embarrassingly naive feminist overlooks or ignores, namely, the indications that Torvald, for all his faults, is taking her at least as seriously as he can—and perhaps even as seriously as she deserves."

20

AN ALBUM OF PLAYS

STRATEGIES FOR CLOSE READING AND
INTERPRETATION OF PLAYS IN THIS ALBUM

The plays in this collection represent a wide variety of approaches. Some of the plays are conventionally realistic, some dreamlike. The styles, themes, and ideas in the plays cover a considerable range. Some of the plays in the album are classics, some contemporary, and some are ethnically diverse. They offer insights into the human condition and invite us to question some of the values that we and others hold. In many ways, these plays center on plot, character, and values in an effort to illuminate us at the same time they entertain us.

Annotate the Plays

Initially, the best approach will probably be to read the play quickly, then, in a rereading, underline the passages you think are important to developing a deeper understanding of the play. At the same time, you should try to visualize the characters in action as if you were watching the play performed. If possible, it will help to watch a video performance of the play while reading along with it, taking notes on how the performers interpret the lines. Using a video playback system with a pause button will help with that process. By underlining or highlighting as you go along, you will make it easier for yourself to remember the important lines and situations and to review the entire play later.

Most of the plays in the album are of the mixed genre of tragicomedy. *Hamlet* and *Death of a Salesman* are tragedies. As you read the plays try to decide whether they help you define the genres of drama. The first director of Chekhov's *The Cherry Orchard* thought it was a comedy, while Chekhov thought it was a tragedy. It is not always a simple matter to decide what the proper genre of a play may be.

Write Down Your Questions for Close Reading

Keep a list of questions for close reading as you read the plays. Try to develop questions similar to the ones you have seen following the plays above. Consider this checklist for questions:

- Ask yourself what the title means. *Hamlet*'s title implies that the play is centered on one character. *The Cherry Orchard* implies that a geographic detail will be of central importance. As you read, jot down some questions related to the title.
- If possible, read some of the scenes aloud, with another reader/actor. With a friend or in a group, discuss the action of the scene and how it fits into the play.
- Consider the structure of the drama and the pacing of the action. Is the play plot-centered in the sense that the plot takes on special importance? How does the author pace the action?
- The conventional five-act structure of Shakespeare permits the development of exposition, rising action, and falling action. Examine *Hamlet* for the moments of most important action. What can you predict about the development of each act?
- Chekhov uses a four-act structure and Fornés a nineteen-scene structure. How does that affect the way in which the dramatic action rises and falls?
- Determine the significance of character in the plays you read. Does the importance of character tend to eclipse the importance of the action? Is character more important than plot?
- In some plays the ideas will take precedence over plot and character. If you sense that is the case, keep track of the ideas that are presented in the play. Use the margins to annotate the primary ideas that you detect in the play.
- Consider the setting of the drama. Where and when is the play set? What are the social conditions in that place and time? How are they the same or how do they differ from what you observe about our own time?
- Keep track of details, such as allusions to animals, flowers, gardens, or any other pattern of repetition. Sometimes these offer clues that point toward a deeper meaning than one might see on the surface.
- Identify the protagonist and the antagonist as soon as possible. In the case of plays in which the antagonist is a force rather than a person, ask what kind of force it is and how it functions in the life of the community and the individual characters.
- Where relevant, study the stage directions. Do they reveal qualities of character that the dialogue does not reveal? Do the stage directions color your interpretation of the play?

Questions for Interpretation of Plays in the Album

- Look for patterns of repetition: descriptions and imagery that show up often, such as references to gardens, flowers, or other similar details. They may have a symbolic significance, as does the unweeded garden in Shakespeare's *Hamlet*. The garden becomes a metaphor for all of Denmark, perhaps all of humanity.
- Look also for the symbolic use of objects in plays. The glass animals that Laura plays with in *The Glass Menagerie* have considerable significance, but exactly what is that significance? The same will be true of the fences in August Wilson's *Fences*.

Such objects take on importance, but only through a careful interpretive study can we determine what the importance might be.

- One important question to ask of every drama is: How well do we know the main character or characters? Do the characters reveal themselves truly to one another, or do they hide the truth? There are times when Hamlet tells the truth and times when he hides it. Why is this the case and how can we tell when he is being truthful and when he is being false? Does his hiding the truth about himself make him any less worthy? Such a question is reasonable about most important characters in a drama.

- What are the gender issues in the play? Is the situation in the poem connected to rigid expectations of gender behavior? Does our interpretation of the play depend on understanding how the characters accept or reject society's attitudes toward gender, as in Ibsen's *A Doll House?*

- Do cultural or ethnic issues dominate the play? Apartheid and racial inequities dominate the action in *"Master Harold" . . . and the boys.* Any interpretation of this play would find it difficult to ignore those issues. The same should be true of August Wilson's *Fences,* which concerns unequal economic opportunities.

- What are the economic issues at stake in the play? Willy Loman is driven by the need to appear extremely successful, but his economic failure drives him to despair. This play, like Chekhov's *The Cherry Orchard,* concerns money at one important level. A careful interpretation could base itself in the economic issues implied in these plays.

- Comparative interpretations are always possible. Some of the obvious pairings of plays that could produce useful and interesting interpretations are:

    Oedipus Rex and *Hamlet*

    Oedipus Rex and *Death of a Salesman*

    "Master Harold" . . . and the boys and *Fences*

    A Doll House and *Conduct of Life*

ANTON CHEKHOV   (1860–1904)

Anton Chekhov seems to have been inspired to write plays by having seen a production of Uncle Tom's Cabin *in 1877, shortly before he went to medical school. During his early years of practice, he gained fame as a writer by publishing many short stories in Russian newspapers. In the mid-1880s his plays began to attract attention. After some failures, he produced* The Seagull *(1896), which was followed by* Uncle Vanya *(1897). Three Sisters (1901) and* The Cherry Orchard *(1903), usually regarded as his best plays, came at the end of his life.*

The Moscow Art Theatre, led by Konstantin Stanislavsky (the director/actor whose writings inspired method acting, a style in which the actor uses personal psychological experience for inspiration), produced Chekhov's plays but sometimes disagreed on whether they were comedies or tragedies. The Cherry Orchard *is a case in point. Chekhov saw the play as a comedy, but Stanislavsky thought the destruction of the cherry orchard implied that it was a tragedy. This disagreement results from the value placed upon the beauty of the orchard in contrast with the value of the social rise of Lopahin, the merchant who buys and develops the property. The question of interpretation remains with us, especially in light of the general success of twentieth-century real estate developers.*

Chekhov derives his power from personal observation. The surfaces of his plays are detailed and realistic, whereas the deep structure is tragic.

The Cherry Orchard ——————————————————— *1903*

Translated by Constance Garnett

Characters

> Madame Ranevsky (Lyubov Andreyevna), *the owner of the cherry orchard*
> Semyonov-Pishtchik, *a landowner*
> Charlotta Ivanovna, *a governess*
> Anya, *her daughter, age seventeen*
> Varya, *her adopted daughter, age twenty four*
> Gaev (Leonid Andreyevitch), *brother of Madame Ranevsky*
> Lopahin (Yermolay Alexeyevitch), *a merchant*
> Trofimov (Pyotr Sergeyevitch), *a student*
> Epihodov (Semyon Pantaleyevitch), *a clerk*
> Dunyasha, *a maid*
> Firs, *an old valet, age eighty-seven*
> Yasha, *a young valet*
> A Wayfarer
> The Stationmaster
> A Post-Office Clerk
> Visitors, Servants
> *The action takes place on the estate of Madame Ranevsky.*

ACT I

(Scene: A room, which has always been called the nursery. One of the doors leads into Anya's room. Dawn, sun rises during the scene. May, the cherry trees in flower, but it is cold in the garden with the frost of early morning. Windows closed.)

(Enter Dunyasha with a candle and Lopahin with a book in his hand.)

LOPAHIN.   The train's in, thank God. What time is it?

DUNYASHA.   Nearly two o'clock. *(Puts out the candle.)* It's daylight already.

LOPAHIN.   The train's late! Two hours, at least. *(Yawns and stretches.)* I'm a pretty one; what a fool I've been. Came here on purpose to meet them at the station and dropped asleep. . . . Dozed off as I sat in the chair. It's annoying. . . . You might have waked me.

DUNYASHA.   I thought you had gone. *(Listens.)* There, I do believe they're coming!

LOPAHIN (LISTENS).   No, what with the luggage and one thing and another. *(A pause.)* Lyubov Andreyevna has been abroad five years; I don't know what she is like now. . . . She's a splendid woman. A good-natured, kind-hearted woman. I remember when I was a lad of fifteen, my poor father—he used to keep a little shop here in the vil-lage in those days—gave me a punch in the face with his fist and made my nose bleed. We were in the yard here, I forget what we'd come about—he had had a drop. Lyubov Andreyevna—I can see her now—she was a slim young girl then—took me to wash my face, and then brought me into this very room, into the nursery. "Don't cry, little peasant," says she, "it will be well in time for your wedding day." . . . *(A pause.)* Little peas-ant. . . . My father was a peasant, it's true, but here am I in a white waistcoat and brown shoes, like a pig in a bun shop. Yes, I'm a rich man, but for all my money, come to think, a peasant I was, and a peasant I am. *(Turns over the pages of the book.)* I've been reading this book and I can't make head or tail of it. I fell asleep over it.

(A pause.)

DUNYASHA.   The dogs have been awake all night, they feel that the mistress is coming.

LOPAHIN.   Why, what's the matter with you, Dunyasha?

DUNYASHA.   My hands are all of a tremble. I feel as though I should faint.

LOPAHIN.   You're a spoilt soft creature, Dunyasha. And dressed like a lady too, and your hair done up. That's not the thing. One must know one's place.

(Enter Epihodov with a nosegay; he wears a pea jacket and highly polished creaking top boots; he drops the nosegay as he comes in.)

EPIHODOV *(picking up the nosegay).*   Here! the gardener's sent this, says you're to put it in the dining room. *(Gives Dunyasha the nosegay.)*

LOPAHIN.   And bring me some kvass.

DUNYASHA.   I will. *(Goes out.)*

EPIHODOV.   It's chilly this morning, three degrees of frost, though the cherries are all in flower. I can't say much for our climate. *(Sighs.)* I can't. Our climate is not often propitious to the occasion. Yermolay Alexeyevitch, permit me to call your attention to the fact that I purchased myself a pair of boots the day before yesterday, and they creak, I venture to assure you, so that there's no tolerating them. What ought I to grease them with?

LOPAHIN.   Oh, shut up! Don't bother me.

EPIHODOV.   Every day some misfortune befalls me. I don't complain, I'm used to it, and I wear a smiling face. *(Dunyasha comes in, hands Lopahin the kvass.)* I am going. *(Stumbles against a chair, which falls over.)* There! *(As though triumphant.)* There you see now, excuse the expression, an accident like that among others. . . . It's positively remarkable. *(Goes out.)*

DUNYASHA.   Do you know, Yermolay Alexeyevitch, I must confess, Epihodov has made me a proposal.

LOPAHIN.   Ah!

DUNYASHA.   I'm sure I don't know. . . . He's a harmless fellow, but sometimes when he begins talking, there's no making anything of it. It's all very fine and expressive, only there's no understanding it. I've a sort of liking for him too. He loves me to distraction. He's an unfortunate man; every day there's something. They tease him about it—two and twenty misfortunes they call him.

LOPAHIN *(listening).*   There! I do believe they're coming.

DUNYASHA.   They are coming! What's the matter with me? . . . I'm cold all over.

LOPAHIN.   They really are coming. Let's go and meet them. Will she know me? It's five years since I saw her.

DUNYASHA *(in a flutter).*   I shall drop this very minute. . . . Ah, I shall drop.

(There is a sound of two carriages driving up to the house. Lopahin and Dunyasha go out quickly. The stage is left empty. A noise is heard in the adjoining rooms. Firs, who has driven to meet Madame Ranevsky, crosses the stage hurriedly leaning on a stick. He is wearing old-fashioned livery and a high hat. He says something to himself, but not a word can be distinguished. The noise behind the scenes goes on increasing. A voice: "Come, let's go in here." Enter Lyubov Andreyevna, Anya, and Charlotta Ivanovna with a pet dog on a chain, all in traveling dresses. Varya in an outdoor coat with a kerchief over her head, Gaev, Semyonov-Pishtchik, Lopahin, Dunyasha with bag and parasol, servants with other articles. All walk across the room.)

ANYA.   Let's come in here. Do you remember what room this is, mamma?

LYUBOV *(joyfully, through her tears).*   The nursery!

VARYA.   How cold it is, my hands are numb. *(To Lyubov Andreyevna.)* Your rooms, the white room and the lavender one, are just the same as ever, mamma.

LYUBOV.   My nursery, dear delightful room. . . . I used to sleep here when I was little. . . . *(Cries.)* And here I am, like a little child. . . . *(Kisses her brother and Varya, and then her brother again.)* Varya's just the same as ever, like a nun. And I knew Dunyasha. *(Kisses Dunyasha.)*

GAEV.   The train was two hours late. What do you think of that? Is that the way to do things?

CHARLOTTA *(to Pishtchik).*   My dog eats nuts, too.

PISHTCHIK *(wonderingly).*   Fancy that!

(They all go out except Anya and Dunyasha.)

DUNYASHA.   We've been expecting you so long. *(Takes Anya's hat and coat.)*

ANYA.   I haven't slept for four nights on the journey. I feel dreadfully cold.

DUNYASHA.   You set out in Lent, there was snow and frost, and now? My darling! *(Laughs and kisses her.)* I *have* missed you, my precious, my joy. I must tell you . . . I can't put it off a minute. . . .

ANYA *(wearily).*   What now?

DUNYASHA.   Epihodov, the clerk, made me a proposal just after Easter.

ANYA.   It's always the same thing with you. . . . *(Straightening her hair.)* I've lost all my hairpins. *(She is staggering from exhaustion.)*

DUNYASHA.   I don't know what to think, really. He does love me, he does love me so!

ANYA *(looking toward her door, tenderly).*   My own room, my windows just as though I had never gone away. I'm home! Tomorrow morning I shall get up and run into the garden. . . . Oh, if I could get to sleep! I haven't slept all the journey, I was so anxious and worried.

DUNYASHA.   Pyotr Sergeyevitch came the day before yesterday.

ANYA *(joyfully).*   Petya!

DUNYASHA.   He's asleep in the bath house, he has settled in there. I'm afraid of being in their way, says he. *(Glancing at her watch.)* I was to have waked him, but Varvara Mihalovia told me not to. Don't you wake him, says she.

(Enter Varya with a bunch of keys at her waist.)

VARYA.   Dunyasha, coffee and make haste. . . . Mamma's asking for coffee.

DUNYASHA.   This very minute. *(Goes out.)*

VARYA.   Well, thank God, you've come. You're home again. *(Petting her.)* My little darling has come back! My precious beauty has come back again!

ANYA.   I have had a time of it!

VARYA.   I can fancy.

ANYA.   We set off in Holy Week—it was so cold then, and all the way Charlotta would talk and show off her tricks. What did you want to burden me with Charlotta for?

VARYA.   You couldn't have traveled all alone, darling. At seventeen!

ANYA.   We got to Paris at last, it was cold there—snow. I speak French shockingly. Mamma lives on the fifth floor, I went up to her and there were a lot of French people, ladies, an old priest with a book. The place smelt of tobacco and so comfortless. I felt sorry, oh! so sorry for mamma all at once, I put my arms round her neck, and hugged her and wouldn't let her go. Mamma was as kind as she could be, and she cried. . . .

VARYA *(through her tears)*.   Don't speak of it, don't speak of it!

ANYA.   She had sold her villa at Mentone, she had nothing left, nothing. I hadn't a farthing left either, we only just had enough to get here. And mamma doesn't understand! When we had dinner at the stations, she always ordered the most expensive things and gave the waiters a whole ruble. Charlotta's just the same. Yasha too must have the same as we do; it's simply awful. You know Yasha is mamma's valet now, we brought him here with us.

VARYA.   Yes, I've seen the young rascal.

ANYA.   Well, tell me—have you paid the arrears on the mortgage?

VARYA.   How could we get the money?

ANYA.   Oh, dear! Oh, dear!

VARYA.   In August the place will be sold.

ANYA.   My goodness!

LOPAHIN *(peeps in at the door and moos like a cow)*.   Moo! *(Disappears.)*

VARYA *(weeping)*.   There, that's what I could do to him. *(Shakes her fist.)*

ANYA *(embracing Varya, softly)*.   Varya, has he made you an offer? *(Varya shakes her head.)* Why, but he loves you. Why is it you don't come to an understanding? What are you waiting for?

VARYA.   I believe that there never will be anything between us. He has a lot to do, he has no time for me . . . and takes no notice of me. Bless the man, it makes me miserable to see him. . . . Everyone's talking of our being married, everyone's congratulating me, and all the while there's really nothing in it; it's all like a dream. *(In another tone.)* You have a new brooch like a bee.

ANYA *(mournfully)*.   Mamma bought it. *(Goes into her own room and talks in a light-hearted childish tone.)* And you know, in Paris I went up in a balloon!

VARYA.   My darling's home again! My pretty is home again!

(Dunyasha returns with the coffeepot and is making the coffee.)

VARYA *(standing at the door)*.   All day long, darling, as I go about looking after the house, I keep dreaming all the time. If only we could marry you to a rich man, then I should feel more at rest. Then I would go off by myself on a pilgrimage to Kiev, to Moscow . . . and so I would spend my life going from one holy place to another. . . . I would go on and on. . . . What bliss!

ANYA.   The birds are singing in the garden. What time is it?

VARYA.   It must be nearly three. It's time you were asleep, darling. *(Going into Anya's room.)* What bliss!

(Yasha enters with a rug and a traveling bag.)

YASHA *(crosses the stage, mincingly)*.   May one come in here, pray?

DUNYASHA.   I shouldn't have known you, Yasha. How you have changed abroad.

YASHA.   H'm! . . . And who are you?

DUNYASHA.   When you went away, I was that high. *(Shows distance from floor.)* Dunyasha, Fyodor's daughter. . . . You don't remember me!

YASHA.   H'm! . . . You're a peach! *(Looks round and embraces her: she shrieks and drops a saucer. Yasha goes out hastily.)*

VARYA *(in the doorway, in a tone of vexation)*.   What now?

DUNYASHA *(through her tears)*.   I have broken a saucer.

VARYA.   Well, that brings good luck.

ANYA *(coming out of her room)*.   We ought to prepare mamma: Petya is here.

VARYA.   I told them not to wake him.

ANYA *(dreamily)*. It's six years since father died. Then only a month later little brother Grisha was drowned in the river, such a pretty boy he was, only seven. It was more than mamma could bear, so she went away, went away without looking back. *(Shuddering.)* . . . How well I understand her, if only she knew! *(A pause.)* And Petya Trofimov was Grisha's tutor, he may remind her.

(Enter Firs; he is wearing a pea jacket and a white waistcoat.)

FIRS *(goes up to the coffeepot, anxiously)*. The mistress will be served here. *(Puts on white gloves.)* Is the coffee ready? *(Sternly to Dunyasha.)* Girl! Where's the cream?

DUNYASHA. Ah, mercy on us! *(Goes out quickly.)*

FIRS *(fussing round the coffeepot)*. Ech! you good-for-nothing! *(Muttering to himself.)* Come back from Paris. And the old master used to go to Paris too . . . horses all the way. *(Laughs.)*

LYUBOV. Can it really be me sitting here? *(Laughs.)* I want to dance about and clap my hands. *(Covers her face with her hands.)* And I could drop asleep in a moment! God knows I love my country, I love it tenderly; I couldn't look out of the window in the train, I kept crying so. *(Through her tears.)* But I must drink my coffee, though. Thank you, Firs, thanks, dear old man. I'm so glad to find you still alive.

FIRS. The day before yesterday.

GAEV. He's rather deaf.

LOPAHIN. I have to set off for Harkov directly, at five o'clock. . . . It is annoying! I wanted to have a look at you, and a little talk. . . . You are just as splendid as ever.

PISHTCHIK *(breathing heavily)*. Handsomer, indeed. . . . Dressed in Parisian style . . . completely bowled me over.

LOPAHIN. Your brother, Leonid Andreyevitch here, is always saying that I'm a low-born knave, that I'm a money-grubber, but I don't care one straw for that. Let him talk. Only I do want you to believe in me as you used to. I do want your wonderful tender eyes to look at me as they used to in the old days. Merciful God! My father was a serf of your father and of your grandfather, but you—you—did so much for me once, that I've forgotten all that; I love you as though you were my kin . . . more than my kin.

LYUBOV. I can't sit still, I simply can't. . . . *(Jumps up and walks about in violent agitation.)* This happiness is too much for me. . . . You may laugh at me, I know I'm silly. . . . My own bookcase. *(Kisses the bookcase.)* My little table.

GAEV. Nurse died while you were away.

LYUBOV *(sits down and drinks coffee)*. Yes, the Kingdom of Heaven be hers! You wrote me of her death.

GAEV. And Anastasy is dead. Squinting Petruchka has left me and is in service now with the police captain in the town. *(Takes a box of caramels out of his pocket and sucks one.)*

PISHTCHIK. My daughter, Dashenka, wishes to be remembered to you.

LOPAHIN. I want to tell you something very pleasant and cheering. *(Glancing at his watch.)* I'm going directly . . . there's no time to say much . . . well, I can say it in a couple of words. I needn't tell you your cherry orchard is to be sold to pay your debts; the 22nd of August is the date fixed for the sale; but don't you worry, dearest lady, you may sleep in peace, there is a way of saving it. . . . This is what I propose. I beg your attention! Your estate is not twenty miles from the town, the railway runs close by it, and if the cherry orchard and the land along the river bank were cut up into building plots and then let on lease for summer villas, you would make an income of at least 25,000 rubles a year out of it.

GAEV. That's all rot, if you'll excuse me.

LYUBOV. I don't quite understand you, Yermolay Alexeyevitch.

LOPAHIN. You will get a rent of at least twenty-five rubles a year for a three-acre plot from summer visitors, and if you say the word now, I'll bet you what you like there won't be one square foot of ground vacant by the autumn, all the plots will be taken up. I congratulate you; in fact, you are saved. It's a perfect situation with that deep river. Only, of course, it must be cleared—all the old buildings, for example, must be removed, this house too, which is really good for nothing, and the old cherry orchard must be cut down.

LYUBOV. Cut down? My dear fellow, forgive me, but you don't know what you are talking about. If there is one thing interesting—remarkable indeed—in the whole province, it's just our cherry orchard.

LOPAHIN. The only thing remarkable about the orchard is that it's a very large one. There's a crop of cherries every alternate year, and then there's nothing to be done with them, no one buys them.

GAEV. This orchard is mentioned in the *Encyclopedia.*

LOPAHIN *(glancing at his watch).* If we don't decide on something and don't take some steps, on the 22nd of August the cherry orchard and the whole estate too will be sold at auction. Make up your minds! There is no other way of saving it, I'll take my oath on that. No, no!

FIRS. In old days, forty or fifty years ago, they used to dry the cherries, soak them, pickle them, make jam too, and they used—

GAEV. Be quiet, Firs.

FIRS. And they used to send the preserved cherries to Moscow and to Markov by the wagonload. That brought the money in! And the preserved cherries in those days were soft and juicy, sweet and fragrant. . . . They knew the way to do them then. . . .

LYUBOV. And where is the recipe now?

FIRS. It's forgotten. Nobody remembers it.

PISHTCHIK *(to Lyubov Andreyevna).* What's it like in Paris? Did you eat frogs there?

LYUBOV. Oh, I ate crocodiles.

PISHTCHIK. Fancy that now!

LOPAHIN. There used to be only the gentlefolks and the peasants in the country, but now there are these summer visitors. All the towns, even the small ones, are surrounded, nowadays by these summer villas. And one may say for sure, that in another twenty years there'll be many more of these people and that they'll be everywhere. At present the summer visitor only drinks tea in his veranda, but maybe he'll take to working his bit of land too, and then your cherry orchard would become happy, rich and prosperous. . . .

GAEV *(indignant).* What rot!

(Enter Varya and Yasha.)

VARYA. There are two telegrams for you, mamma. *(Takes out keys and opens an old-fashioned bookcase with a loud crack.)* Here they are.

LYUBOV. From Paris. *(Tears the telegrams, without reading them.)* I have done with Paris.

GAEV. Do you know, Lyuba, how old that bookcase is? Last week I pulled out the bottom drawer and there I found the date branded on it. The bookcase was made just a hundred years ago. What do you say to that? We might have celebrated its jubilee. Though it's an inanimate object, still it is a *book*case.

PISHTCHIK *(amazed).*   A hundred years! Fancy that now.

GAEV.   Yes. . . . It is a thing. . . . *(Feeling the bookcase.)* Dear, honored bookcase! Hail to thee who for more than a hundred years hast served the pure ideals of good and justice; thy silent call to fruitful labor has never flagged in those hundred years, maintaining *(in tears)* in the generations of man, courage and faith in a brighter future and fostering in us ideals of good and social consciousness.

(A pause.)

LOPAHIN.   Yes . . .

LYUBOV.   You are just the same as ever, Leonid.

GAEV *(a little embarrassed).*   Cannon off the right into the pocket!°

LOPAHIN *(looking at his watch).*   Well, it's time I was off.

YASHA *(handing Lyubov Andreyevna medicine).*   Perhaps you will take your pills now.

PISHTCHIK.   You shouldn't take medicines, my dear madam . . . they do no harm and no good. Give them here . . . honored lady. *(Takes the pillbox, pours the pills into the hollow of his hand, blows on them, puts them in his mouth and drinks off some kvass.)* There!

LYUBOV *(in alarm).*   Why, you must be out of your mind!

PISHTCHIK.   I have taken all the pills.

LOPAHIN.   What a glutton!

(All laugh.)

FIRS.   His honor stayed with us in Easter week, ate a gallon and a half of cucumbers. . . . *(Mutters.)*

LYUBOV.   What is he saying?

VARYA.   He has taken to muttering like that for the last three years. We are used to it.

YASHA.   His declining years!

(Charlotta Ivanovna, a very thin, lanky figure in a white dress with a lorgnette in her belt, walks across the stage.)

LOPAHIN.   I beg your pardon, Charlotta Ivanovna, I have not had time to greet you. *(Tries to kiss her hand.)*

CHARLOTTA *(pulling away her hand).*   If I let you kiss my hand, you'll be wanting to kiss my elbow, and then my shoulder.

LOPAHIN.   I've no luck today! *(All laugh.)* Charlotta Ivanovna, show us some tricks!

LYUBOV.   Charlotta, do show us some tricks!

CHARLOTTA.   I don't want to. I'm sleepy. *(Goes out.)*

LOPAHIN.   In three weeks' time we shall meet again. *(Kisses Lyubov Andreyevna's hand.)* Good-by till then—I must go. *(To Gaev.)* Good-by. *(Kisses Pishtchik.)* Good-by. *(Gives his hand to Varya, then to Firs and Yasha.)* I don't want to go. *(To Lyubov Andreyevna.)* If you think over my plan for the villas and make up your mind, then let me know; I will lend you 50,000 rubles. Think of it seriously.

VARYA *(angrily).*   Well, do go, for goodness' sake.

LOPAHIN.   I'm going, I'm going. *(Goes out.)*

GAEV.   Low-born knave! I beg pardon, though . . . Varya is going to marry him, he's Varya's fiancé.

VARYA.   Don't talk nonsense, uncle.

LYUBOV.   Well, Varya, I shall be delighted. He's a good man.

Cannon . . . pocket: Throughout the play Gaev interjects phrases from billiards.

PISHTCHIK.   He is, one must acknowledge, a most worthy man. And my Dashenka . . . says too that . . . she says . . . various things. *(Snores, but at once wakes up.)* But all the same, honored lady, could you oblige me . . . with a loan of 240 rubles . . . to pay the interest on my mortgage tomorrow?

VARYA *(dismayed)*.   No, no.

LYUBOV.   I really haven't any money.

PISHTCHIK.   It will turn up. *(Laughs.)* I never lose hope. I thought everything was over, I was a ruined man, and lo and behold—the railway passed through my land and . . . they paid me for it. And something else will turn up again, if not today, then tomorrow . . . Dashenka'll win two hundred thousand . . . she's got a lottery ticket.

LYUBOV.   Well, we've finished our coffee, we can go to bed.

FIRS *(brushes Gaev, reprovingly)*.   You have got on the wrong trousers again! What am I to do with you?

VARYA *(softly)*.   Anya's asleep. *(Softly opens the window.)* Now the sun's risen, it's not a bit cold. Look, mamma, what exquisite trees! My goodness! And the air! The starlings are singing!

GAEV *(opens another window)*.   The orchard is all white. You've not forgotten it, Lyuba? That long avenue that runs straight, straight as an arrow, how it shines on a moonlight night. You remember? You've not forgotten?

LYUBOV *(looking out of the window into the garden)*.   Oh, my childhood, my innocence! It was in this nursery I used to sleep, from here I looked out into the orchard, happiness waked with me every morning and in those days the orchard was just the same, nothing has changed. *(Laughs with delight.)* All, all white! Oh, my orchard! After the dark gloomy autumn, and the cold winter; you are young again and full of happiness, the heavenly angels have never left you. . . . If I could cast off the burden that weighs on my heart, if I could forget the past!

GAEV.   H'm! and the orchard will be sold to pay our debts; it seems strange. . . .

LYUBOV.   See, our mother walking . . . all in white, down the avenue! *(Laughs with delight.)* It is she!

GAEV.   Where?

VARYA.   Oh, don't, mamma!

LYUBOV.   There is no one. It was my fancy. On the right there, by the path to the arbor, there is a white tree bending like a woman. . . . *(Enter Trofimov wearing a shabby student's uniform and spectacles.)* What a ravishing orchard! White masses of blossom, blue sky. . . .

TROFIMOV.   Lyubov Andreyevna! *(She looks round at him.)* I will just pay my respects to you and then leave you at once. *(Kisses her hand warmly.)* I was told to wait until morning, but I hadn't the patience to wait any longer. . . .

(Lyubov Andreyevna looks at him in perplexity.)

VARYA *(through her tears)*.   This is Petya Trofimov.

TROFIMOV.   Petya Trofimov, who was your Grisha's tutor. . . . Can I have changed so much?

(Lyubov Andreyevna embraces him and weeps quietly.)

GAEV *(in confusion)*.   There, there, Lyuba.

VARYA *(crying)*.   I told you, Petya, to wait till tomorrow.

LYUBOV.   My Grisha . . . my boy . . . Grisha . . . my son!

VARYA.   We can't help it, mamma, it is God's will.

TROFIMOV *(softly through his tears).*   There . . . there.

LYUBOV *(weeping quietly).*   My boy was lost . . . drowned. Why? Oh, why, dear Petya? *(More quietly.)* Anya is asleep in there, and I'm talking loudly . . . making this noise. . . . But, Petya? Why have you grown so ugly? Why do you look so old?

TROFIMOV.   A peasant-woman in the train called me a mangy-looking gentleman.

LYUBOV.   You were quite a boy then, a pretty little student, and now your hair's thin—and spectacles. Are you really a student still? *(Goes toward the door.)*

TROFIMOV.   I seem likely to be a perpetual student.

LYUBOV *(kisses her brother, then Varya).*   Well, go to bed. . . . You are older too, Leonid.

PISHTCHIK *(follows her).*   I suppose it's time we were asleep. . . . Ugh! my gout. I'm staying the night! Lyubov Andreyevna, my dear soul, if you could . . . tomorrow morning . . . 240 rubles.

GAEV.   That's always his story.

PISHTCHIK.   240 rubles . . . to pay the interest on my mortgage.

LYUBOV.   My dear man, I have no money.

PISHTCHIK.   I'll pay it back, my dear . . . a trifling sum.

LYUBOV.   Oh, well, Leonid will give it you. . . . You give him the money, Leonid.

GAEV.   Me give it him! Let him wait till he gets it!

LYUBOV.   It can't be helped, give it him. He needs it. He'll pay it back.

(Lyubov Andreyevna, Trofimov, Pishtchik, and Firs go out. Gaev, Varya, and Yasha remain.)

GAEV.   Sister hasn't got out of the habit of flinging away her money. *(To Yasha.)* Get away, my good fellow, you smell of the henhouse.

YASHA *(with a grin).*   And you, Leonid Andreyevitch, are just the same as ever.

GAEV.   What's that? *(To Varya.)* What did he say?

VARYA *(to Yasha).*   Your mother has come from the village; she has been sitting in the servants' room since yesterday, waiting to see you.

YASHA.   Oh, bother her!

VARYA.   For shame!

YASHA.   What's the hurry? She might just as well have come tomorrow. *(Goes out.)*

VARYA.   Mamma's just the same as ever, she hasn't changed a bit. If she had her own way, she'd give away everything.

GAEV.   Yes. *(A pause.)* If a great many remedies are suggested for some disease, it means that the disease is incurable. I keep thinking and racking my brains; I have many schemes, a great many, and that really means none. If we could only come in for a legacy from somebody, or marry our Anya to a very rich man, or we might go to Yaroslavl and try our luck with our old aunt, the Countess. She's very, very rich, you know.

VARYA *(weeps).*   If God would help us.

GAEV.   Don't blubber. Aunt's very rich, but she doesn't like us. First, sister married a lawyer instead of a nobleman. . . . *(Anya appears in the doorway.)* And then her conduct, one can't call it virtuous. She is good, and kind, and nice, and I love her, but, however one allows for extenuating circumstances, there's no denying that she's an immoral woman. One feels it in her slightest gesture.

VARYA *(in a whisper).*   Anya's in the doorway.

GAEV.   What do you say? *(A pause.)* It's queer, there seems to be something wrong with my right eye. I don't see as well as I did. And on Thursday when I was in the district Court . . .

(Enter Anya.)

VARYA.   Why aren't you asleep, Anya?

ANYA.   I can't get to sleep.

GAEV.   My pet. *(Kisses Anya's face and hands.)* My child. *(Weeps.)* You are not my niece, you are my angel, you are everything to me. Believe me, believe. . . .

ANYA.   I believe you, uncle. Everyone loves you and respects you . . . but, uncle dear, you must be silent . . . simply be silent. What were you saying just now about my mother, about your own sister? What made you say that?

GAEV.   Yes, yes. . . . *(Puts his hand over his face.)* Really, that was awful! My God, save me! And today I made a speech to the bookcase . . . so stupid! And only when I had finished, I saw how stupid it was.

VARYA.   It's true, uncle, you ought to keep quiet. Don't talk, that's all.

ANYA.   If you could keep from talking, it would make things easier for you, too.

GAEV.   I won't speak. *(Kisses Anya's and Varya's hands.)* I'll be silent. Only this is about business. On Thursday I was in the district Court; well, there was a large party of us there and we began talking of one thing and another, and this and that, and do you know, I believe that it will be possible to raise a loan on an I.O.U. to pay the arrears on the mortgage.

VARYA.   If the Lord would help us!

GAEV.   I'm going on Tuesday; I'll talk of it again. *(To Varya.)* Don't blubber. *(To Anya.)* Your mamma will talk to Lopahin; of course, he won't refuse her. And as soon as you're rested you shall go to Yaroslavl to the Countess, your great-aunt. So we shall all set to work in three directions at once, and the business is done. We shall pay off arrears. I'm convinced of it. *(Puts a caramel in his mouth.)* I swear on my honor, I swear by anything you like, the estate shan't be sold. *(Excitedly.)* By my own happiness, I swear it! Here's my hand on it, call me the basest, vilest of men, if I let it come to an auction! Upon my soul I swear it!

ANYA *(her equanimity has returned, she is quite happy)*.   How good you are, uncle, and how clever! *(Embraces her uncle.)* I'm at peace now! Quite at peace! I'm happy!

(Enter Firs.)

FIRS *(reproachfully)*.   Leonid Andreyevitch, have you no fear of God? When are you going to bed?

GAEV.   Directly, directly. You can go, Firs. I'll . . . yes, I will undress myself. Come, children, by-by. We'll go into details tomorrow, but now go to bed. *(Kisses Anya and Varya.)* I'm a man of the eighties. They run down that period, but still I can say I have had to suffer not a little for my convictions in my life, it's not for nothing that the peasant loves me. One must know the peasant! One must know how. . . .

ANYA.   At it again, uncle!

VARYA.   Uncle dear, you'd better be quiet!

FIRS *(angrily)*.   Leonid Andreyevitch!

GAEV.   I'm coming. I'm coming. Go to bed. Potted the shot—there's a shot for you! A beauty! *(Goes out, Firs hobbling after him.)*

ANYA.   My mind's at rest now. I don't want to go to Yaroslavl, I don't like my great-aunt, but still my mind's at rest. Thanks to uncle. *(Sits down.)*

VARYA.   We must go to bed. I'm going. Something unpleasant happened while you were away. In the old servants' quarters there are only the old servants, as you know—Efimyushka, Polya and Yevstigney—and Karp too. They began letting stray people in to spend the night—I said nothing. But all at once I heard they had been spreading a report that I gave them nothing but pease pudding to eat. Out of stinginess, you know. . . .

And it was all Yevstigney's doing. . . Very well, I said to myself. . . . If that's how it is, I thought, wait a bit. I sent for Yevstigney. . . *(Yawns.)* He comes. . . . "How's this, Yevstigney," I said, "you could be such a fool as to?. . ." *(Looking at Anya.)* Anitchka! *(A pause.)* She's asleep. *(Puts her arm around Anya.)* Come to bed . . . come along! *(Leads her.)* My darling has fallen asleep! Come . . . *(They go. Far away beyond the orchard a shepherd plays on a pipe. Trofimov crosses the stage and, seeing Varya and Anya, stands still.)* Sh! asleep, asleep. Come, my own.

ANYA *(softly, half asleep).* I'm so tired. Still those bells. Uncle . . . dear . . . mamma and uncle. . . .

VARYA. Come, my own, come along.

(They go into Anya's room.)

TROFIMOV *(tenderly).* My sunshine! My spring.

ACT II

(Scene: The open country. An old shrine, long abandoned and fallen out of the perpendicular; near it a well, large stones that have apparently once been tombstones, and an old garden seat. The road to Gaev's house is seen. On one side rise dark poplars; and there the cherry orchard begins. In the distance a row of telegraph poles and far, far away on the horizon there is faintly outlined a great town, only visible in very fine clear weather. It is near sunset. Charlotta, Yasha, and Dunyasha are sitting on the seat. Epihodov is standing near, playing something mournful on a guitar. All sit plunged in thought. Charlotta wears an old forage cap; she has taken a gun from her shoulder and is tightening the buckle on the strap.)

CHARLOTTA *(musingly).* I haven't a real passport of my own, and I don't know how old I am, and I always feel that I'm a young thing. When I was a little girl, my father and mother used to travel about to fairs and give performances—very good ones. And I used to do *salto mortale°* and all sorts of things. And when papa and mamma died, a German lady took me and had me educated. And so I grew up and became a governess. But where I came from, and who I am, I don't know. . . . Who my parents were, very likely they weren't married. . . . I don't know. *(Takes a cucumber out of her pocket and eats.)* I know nothing at all. *(A pause.)* One wants to talk and has no one to talk to. . . . I have nobody.

EPIHODOV *(plays on the guitar and sings).* "What care I for the noisy world! What care I for friends or foes!" How agreeable it is to play on the mandolin!

DUNYASHA. That's a guitar, not a mandolin. *(Looks in a hand-mirror and powders herself.)*

EPIHODOV. To a man mad with love, it's a mandolin. *(Sings.)* "Were her heart but aglow with love's mutual flame."

(Yasha joins in.)

CHARLOTTA. How shockingly these people sing! Foo! Like jackals!

DUNYASHA *(to Yasha).* What happiness, though, to visit foreign lands.

YASHA. Ah, yes! I rather agree with you there. *(Yawns, then lights a cigar.)*

EPIHODOV. That's comprehensible. In foreign lands everything has long since reached full complexion.

---

salto mortale: a standing somersault.

YASHA.   That's so, of course.

EPIHODOV.   I'm a cultivated man, I read remarkable books of all sorts, but I can never make out the tendency I am myself precisely inclined for, whether to live or to shoot myself, speaking precisely, but nevertheless I always carry a revolver. Here it is. . . . *(Shows revolver.)*

CHARLOTTA.   I've had enough, and now I'm going. *(Puts on the gun.)* Epihodov, you're a very clever fellow, and a very terrible one too, all the women must be wild about you. Br-r-r! *(Goes.)* These clever fellows are all so stupid; there's not a creature for me to speak to. . . . Always alone, alone, nobody belonging to me . . . and who I am, and why I'm on earth, I don't know. *(Walks away slowly.)*

EPIHODOV.   Speaking precisely, not touching upon other subjects, I'm bound to admit about myself, that destiny behaves mercilessly to me, as a storm to a little boat. If, let us suppose, I am mistaken, then why did I wake up this morning, to quote an example, and look round, and there on my chest was a spider of fearful magnitude . . . like this. *(Shows with both hands.)* And then I take up a jug of kvass, to quench my thirst, and in it there is something in the highest degree unseemly of the nature of a cockroach. (A pause.) Have you read Buckle?° *(A pause.)* I am desirous of troubling you, Dunyasha, with a couple of words.

DUNYASHA.   Well, speak.

EPIHODOV.   I should be desirous to speak with you alone. *(Sighs.)*

DUNYASHA *(embarrassed).*   Well—only bring me my mantle first. It's by the cupboard. It's rather damp here.

EPIHODOV.   Certainly. I will fetch it. Now I know what I must do with my revolver. *(Takes guitar and goes off playing on it.)*

YASHA.   Two and twenty misfortunes! Between ourselves, he's a fool. *(Yawns.)*

DUNYASHA.   God grant he doesn't shoot himself! *(A pause.)* I am so nervous, I'm always in a flutter. I was a little girl when I was taken into our lady's house, and now I have quite grown out of peasant ways, and my hands are white, as white as a lady's. I'm such a delicate, sensitive creature, I'm afraid of everything. I'm so frightened. And if you deceive me, Yasha, I don't know what will become of my nerves.

YASHA *(kisses her).*   You're a peach! Of course a girl must never forget herself; what I dislike more than anything is a girl being flighty in her behavior.

DUNYASHA.   I'm passionately in love with you, Yasha; you are a man of culture—you can give your opinion about anything.

(A pause.)

YASHA *(yawns).*   Yes, that's so. My opinion is this: if a girl loves anyone, that means that she has no principles. *(A pause.)* It's pleasant smoking a cigar in the open air. *(Listens.)* Someone's coming this way . . . it's the gentlefolk. *(Dunyasha embraces him impulsively.)* Go home, as though you had been to the river to bathe; go by that path, or else they'll meet you and suppose I have made an appointment with you here. That I can't endure.

DUNYASHA *(coughing softly).*   The cigar has made my head ache. . . .

(Goes off. Yasha remains sitting near the shrine. Enter Lyubov Andreyevna, Gaev, and Lopahin.)

LOPAHIN.   You must make up your mind once for all—there's no time to lose. It's quite a simple question, you know. Will you consent to letting the land for building or not? One word in answer: Yes or no? Only one word!

Buckle: Thomas Henry Buckle (1821–1862), a historian with radical theories about climate, agriculture, population, and wealth.

LYUBOV.   Who is smoking such horrible cigars here? *(Sits down.)*

GAEV.   Now the railway line has been brought near, it's made things very convenient. *(Sits down.)* Here we have been over and lunched in town. Cannon off the white! I should like to go home and have a game.

LYUBOV.   You have plenty of time.

LOPAHIN.   Only one word! *(Beseechingly.)* Give me an answer!

GAEV *(yawning).*   What do you say?

LYUBOV *(looks in her purse).*   I had quite a lot of money here yesterday, and there's scarcely any left today. My poor Varya feeds us all on milk soup for the sake of economy; the old folks in the kitchen get nothing but pease pudding, while I waste my money in a senseless way. *(Drops purse, scattering gold pieces.)* There, they have all fallen out! *(Annoyed.)*

YASHA.   Allow me. I'll soon pick them up. *(Collects the coins.)*

LYUBOV.   Pray do, Yasha. And what did I go off to the town to lunch for? Your restaurant's a wretched place with its music and the tablecloth smelling of soap. . . . Why drink so much, Leonid? And eat so much? And talk so much? Today you talked a great deal again in the restaurant, and all so inappropriately. About the era of the seventies, about the decadents. And to whom? Talking to waiters about decadents!

LOPAHIN.   Yes.

GAEV *(waving his hand).*   I'm incorrigible; that's evident. *(Irritably to Yasha.)* Why is it you keep fidgeting about in front of us!

YASHA *(laughs).*   I can't help laughing when I hear your voice.

GAEV *(to his sister).*   Either I or he. . . .

LYUBOV.   Get along! Go away, Yasha.

YASHA *(gives Lyubov Andreyevna her purse).*   Directly. *(Hardly able to suppress his laughter.)* This minute. . . . *(Goes off.)*

LOPAHIN.   Deriganov, the millionaire, means to buy your estate. They say he is coming to the sale himself.

LYUBOV.   Where did you hear that?

LOPAHIN.   That's what they say in town.

GAEV.   Our aunt in Yaroslavl has promised to send help; but when, and how much she will send, we don't know.

LOPAHIN.   How much will she send? A hundred thousand? Two hundred?

LYUBOV.   Oh, well! . . . Ten or fifteen thousand, and we must be thankful to get that.

LOPAHIN.   Forgive me, but such reckless people as you are—such queer, unbusinesslike people—I never met in my life. One tells you in plain Russian your estate is going to be sold, and you seem not to understand it.

LYUBOV.   What are we to do? Tell us what to do.

LOPAHIN.   I do tell you every day. Every day I say the same thing. You absolutely must let the cherry orchard and the land on building leases; and do it at once, as quick as may be—the auction's close upon us! Do understand! Once make up your mind to build villas, and you can raise as much money as you like, and then you are saved.

LYUBOV.   Villas and summer visitors—forgive me saying so—it's so vulgar.

GAEV.   There I perfectly agree with you.

LOPAHIN.   I shall sob, or scream, or fall into a fit. I can't stand it! You drive me mad! *(To Gaev.)* You're an old woman!

GAEV.   What do you say?

LOPAHIN.   An old woman! *(Gets up to go.)*

LYUBOV *(in dismay).*   No, don't go! Do stay, my dear friend! Perhaps we shall think of something.

LOPAHIN.   What is there to think of?

LYUBOV.   Don't go, I entreat you! With you here it's more cheerful, anyway. *(A pause.)* I keep expecting something, as though the house were going to fall about our ears.

GAEV *(in profound dejection).*   Potted the white! It fails—a kiss.

LYUBOV.   We have been great sinners. . . .

LOPAHIN.   You have no sins to repent of.

GAEV *(puts a caramel in his mouth).*   They say I've eaten up my property in caramels. *(Laughs.)*

LYUBOV.   Oh, my sins! I've always thrown my money away recklessly like a lunatic. I married a man who made nothing but debts. My husband died of champagne—he drank dreadfully. To my misery I loved another man, and immediately—it was my first punishment—the blow fell upon me, here, in the river . . . my boy was drowned and I went abroad—went away forever, never to return, not to see that river again. . . . I shut my eyes, and fled, distracted, and he after me . . . pitilessly, brutally. I bought a villa at Mentone, for he fell ill there, and for three years I had no rest day or night. His illness wore me out, my soul was dried up. And last year, when my villa was sold to pay my debts, I went to Paris and there he robbed me of everything and abandoned me for another woman; and I tried to poison myself. . . . So stupid, so shameful! . . . And suddenly I felt a yearning for Russia, for my country, for my little girl. . . . *(Dries her tears.)* Lord, Lord, be merciful! Forgive my sins! Do not chastise me more! *(Takes a telegram out of her pocket.)* I got this today from Paris. He implores forgiveness, entreats me to return. *(Tears up the telegram.)* I fancy there is music somewhere. *(Listens.)*

GAEV.   That's our famous Jewish orchestra. You remember, four violins, a flute and a double bass.

LYUBOV.   That still in existence? We ought to send for them one evening, and give a dance.

LOPAHIN *(listens).*   I can't hear. . . . *(Hums softly.)* "For money the Germans will turn a Russian into a Frenchman." *(Laughs.)* I did see such a piece at the theater yesterday! It was funny!

LYUBOV.   And most likely there was nothing funny in it. You shouldn't look at plays, you should look at yourselves a little oftener. How gray your lives are! How much nonsense you talk.

LOPAHIN.   That's true. One may say honestly, we live a fool's life. *(Pause.)* My father was a peasant, an idiot; he knew nothing and taught me nothing, only beat me when he was drunk, and always with his stick. In reality I am just such another blockhead and idiot. I've learned nothing properly. I write a wretched hand. I write so that I feel ashamed before folks, like a pig.

LYUBOV.   You ought to get married, my dear fellow.

LOPAHIN.   Yes . . . that's true.

LYUBOV.   You should marry our Varya, she's a good girl.

LOPAHIN.   Yes.

LYUBOV.   She's a good-natured girl, she's busy all day long, and what's more, she loves you. And you have liked her for ever so long.

LOPAHIN.   Well? I'm not against it. . . . She's a good girl.

(Pause.)

GAEV.   I've been offered a place in the bank: 6,000 rubles a year. Did you know?

LYUBOV.   You would never do for that! You must stay as you are.

(Enter Firs with overcoat.)

FIRS.   Put it on, sir, it's damp.

GAEV *(putting it on)*.   You bother me, old fellow.

FIRS.   You can't go on like this. You went away in the morning without leaving word. *(Looks him over.)*

LYUBOV.   You look older, Firs!

FIRS.   What is your pleasure?

LOPAHIN.   You look older, she said.

FIRS.   I've had a long life. They were arranging my wedding before your papa was born. . . . *(Laughs.)* I was the head footman before the emancipation came. I wouldn't consent to be set free then; I stayed on with the old master. . . . *(A pause.)* I remember what rejoicings they made and didn't know themselves what they were rejoicing over.

LOPAHIN.   Those were fine old times. There was flogging anyway.

FIRS *(not hearing)*.   To be sure! The peasants knew their place, and the masters knew theirs; but now they're all at sixes and sevens, there's no making it out.

GAEV.   Hold your tongue, Firs. I must go to town tomorrow. I have been promised an introduction to a general, who might let us have a loan.

LOPAHIN.   You won't bring that off. And you won't pay your arrears, you may rest assured of that.

LYUBOV.   That's all his nonsense. There is no such general.

(Enter Trofimov, Anya, and Varya.)

GAEV.   Here come our girls.

ANYA.   There's mamma on the seat.

LYUBOV *(tenderly)*.   Come here, come along. My darlings! *(Embraces Anya and Varya.)* If you only knew how I love you both. Sit beside me, there, like that. *(All sit down.)*

LOPAHIN.   Our perpetual student is always with the young ladies.

TROFIMOV.   That's not your business.

LOPAHIN.   He'll soon be fifty, and he's still a student.

TROFIMOV.   Drop your idiotic jokes.

LOPAHIN.   Why are you so cross, you queer fish?

TROFIMOV.   Oh, don't persist!

LOPAHIN *(laughs)*.   Allow me to ask you what's your idea of me?

TROFIMOV.   I'll tell you my idea of you. Yermolay Alexeyevitch; you are a rich man, you'll soon be a millionaire. Well, just as in the economy of nature a wild beast is of use, who devours everything that comes in his way, so you too have your use.

(All laugh.)

VARYA.   Better tell us something about the planets, Petya.

LYUBOV.   No, let us go on with the conversation we had yesterday.

TROFIMOV.   What was it about?

GAEV.   About pride.

TROFIMOV.   We had a long conversation yesterday, but we came to no conclusion. In pride, in your sense of it, there is something mystical. Perhaps you are right from your point of view; but if one looks at it simply, without subtlety, what sort of pride can there be, what sense is there in it, if man in his physiological formation is very imperfect, if in the immense majority of cases he is coarse, dull-witted, profoundly unhappy? One must give up glorification of self. One should work, and nothing else.

GAEV.   One must die in any case.

TROFIMOV.   Who knows? And what does it mean—dying? Perhaps man has a hundred senses, and only the five we know are lost at death, while the other ninety-five remain alive.

LYUBOV.   How clever you are, Petya!

LOPAHIN *(ironically).*   Fearfully clever!

TROFIMOV.   Humanity progresses, perfecting its powers. Everything that is beyond its ken now will one day become familiar and comprehensible; only we must work, we must with all our powers aid the seeker after truth. Here among us in Russia the workers are few in number as yet. The vast majority of the intellectual people I know seek nothing, do nothing, are not fit as yet for work of any kind. They call themselves intellectual, but they treat their servants as inferiors, behave to the peasants as though they were animals, learn little, read nothing seriously, do practically nothing, only talk about science and know very little about art. They are all serious people, they all have severe faces, they all talk of weighty matters and air their theories, and yet the vast majority of us—ninety-nine per cent—live like savages, at the least thing fly to blows and abuse, eat piggishly, sleep in filth and stuffiness, bugs everywhere, stench and damp and moral impurity. And it's clear all our fine talk is only to divert our attention and other people's. Show me where to find the *crèches*° there's so much talk about, and the reading-rooms? They only exist in novels: in real life there are none of them. There is nothing but filth and vulgarity and Asiatic apathy.° I fear and dislike very serious faces. I'm afraid of serious conversation. We should do better to be silent.

LOPAHIN.   You know, I get up at five o'clock in the morning, and I work from morning to night; and I've money, my own and other people's, always passing through my hands, and I see what people are made of all round me. One has only to begin to do anything to see how few honest decent people there are. Sometimes when I lie awake at night, I think: "Oh! Lord, thou hast given us immense forests, boundless plains, the widest horizons, and living here we ourselves ought really to be giants."

LYUBOV.   You ask for giants! They are no good except in storybooks; in real life they frighten us.

(Epihodov advances in the background, playing on the guitar.)

LYUBOV *(dreamily).*   There goes Epihodov.

ANYA *(dreamily).*   There goes Epihodov.

GAEV.   The sun has set, my friends.

TROFIMOV.   Yes.

GAEV *(not loudly, but, as it were, declaiming).*   O nature, divine nature, thou art bright with eternal luster, beautiful and indifferent! Thou, whom we call mother, thou dost unite within thee life and death! Thou dost give life and dost destroy!

VARYA *(in a tone of supplication).*   Uncle!

ANYA.   Uncle, you are at it again!

TROFIMOV.   You'd much better be cannoning off the red!

GAEV.   I'll hold my tongue, I will.

(All sit plunged in thought. Perfect stillness. The only thing audible is the muttering of Firs. Suddenly there is a sound in the distance, as it were from the sky—the sound of a breaking harp-string, mournfully dying away.)

LYUBOV.   What is that?

___

crèches: day nurseries.   *Asiatic apathy:* The common prejudice was that Asians were apathetic.

LOPAHIN.   I don't know. Somewhere far away a bucket fallen and broken in the pits. But somewhere very far away.

GAEV.   It might be a bird of some sort—such as a heron.

TROFIMOV.   Or an owl.

LYUBOV *(shudders)*.   I don't know why, but it's horrid.

(A pause.)

FIRS.   It was the same before the calamity—the owl hooted and the samovar hissed all the time.

GAEV.   Before what calamity?

FIRS.   Before the emancipation.

(A pause.)

LYUBOV.   Come, my friends, let us be going; evening is falling. *(To Anya.)* There are tears in your eyes. What is it, darling? *(Embraces her.)*

ANYA.   Nothing, mamma; it's nothing.

TROFIMOV.   There is somebody coming.

(The Wayfarer appears in a shabby white forage cap and an overcoat; he is slightly drunk.)

WAYFARER.   Allow me to inquire, can I get to the station this way?

GAEV.   Yes. Go along that road.

WAYFARER.   I thank you most feelingly. *(Coughing.)* The weather is superb. *(Declaims.)* My brother, my suffering brother!. . . Come out to the Volga! Whose groan do you hear? . . . *(To Varya.)* Mademoiselle, vouchsafe a hungry Russian thirty kopecks.

(Varya utters a shriek of alarm.)

LOPAHIN *(angrily)*.   There's a right and a wrong way of doing everything!

LYUBOV *(hurriedly)*.   Here, take this. *(Looks in her purse.)* I've no silver. No matter—here's gold for you.

WAYFARER.   I thank you most feelingly! *(Goes off.)*

(Laughter.)

VARYA *(frightened)*.   I'm going home—I'm going. . . . Oh, mamma, the servants have nothing to eat, and you gave him gold!

LYUBOV.   There's no doing anything with me. I'm so silly! When we get home, I'll give you all I possess, Yermolay Alexeyevitch, you will lend me some more! . . .

LOPAHIN.   I will.

LYUBOV.   Come, friends, it's time to be going. And Varya, we have made a match of it for you. I congratulate you.

VARYA *(through her tears)*.   Mamma, that's not a joking matter.

LOPAHIN.   "Ophelia, get thee to a nunnery!"°

GAEV.   My hands are trembling; it's a long while since I had a game of billiards.

LOPAHIN.   "Ophelia! Nymph, in thy orisons be all my sins remember'd."

LYUBOV.   Come, it will soon be supper-time.

VARYA.   How he frightened me! My heart's simply throbbing.

LOPAHIN.   Let me remind you, ladies and gentlemen: on the 22nd of August the cherry orchard will be sold. Think about that! Think about it!

(All go off, except Trofimov and Anya.)

Ophelia . . . nunnery: Lopahin starts quoting from *Hamlet.*

ANYA *(laughing).*   I'm grateful to the wayfarer! He frightened Varya and we are left alone.

TROFIMOV.   Varya's afraid we shall fall in love with each other, and for days together she won't leave us. With her narrow brain she can't grasp that we are above love. To eliminate the petty and transitory which hinder us from being free and happy—that is the aim and meaning of our life. Forward! We go forward irresistibly toward the bright star that shines yonder in the distance. Forward! Do not lag behind, friends.

ANYA *(claps her hands).*   How well you speak! *(A pause.)* It is divine here today.

TROFIMOV.   Yes, it's glorious weather.

ANYA.   Somehow, Petya, you've made me so that I don't love the cherry orchard as I used to. I used to love it so dearly. I used to think that there was no spot on earth like our garden.

TROFIMOV.   All Russia is our garden. The earth is great and beautiful—there are many beautiful places in it. *(A pause.)* Think only, Anya, your grandfather, and great-grandfather, and all your ancestors were slaveowners—the owners of living souls—and from every cherry in the orchard, from every leaf, from every trunk there are human creatures looking at you. Cannot you hear their voices? Oh, it is awful! Your orchard is a fearful thing, and when in the evening or at night one walks about the orchard, the old bark on the trees glimmers dimly in the dusk, and the old cherry trees seem to be dreaming of centuries gone by and tortured by fearful visions. Yes! We are at least two hundred years behind, we have really gained nothing yet, we have no definite attitude to the past, we do nothing but theorize or complain of depression or drink vodka. It is clear that to begin to live in the present, we must first expiate our past; we must break with it; and we can expiate it only by suffering, by extraordinary unceasing labor. Understand that, Anya.

ANYA.   The house we live in has long ceased to be our own, and I shall leave it, I give you my word.

TROFIMOV.   If you have the house keys, fling them into the well and go away. Be free as the wind.

ANYA *(in ecstasy).*   How beautifully you said that!

TROFIMOV.   Believe me, Anya, believe me! I am not thirty yet. I am young. I am still a student, but I have gone through so much already! As soon as winter comes I am hungry, sick, careworn, poor as a beggar, and what ups and downs of fortune have I not known! And my soul was always, every minute, day and night, full of inexplicable forebodings. I have a foreboding of happiness, Anya. I see glimpses of it already.

ANYA *(pensively).*   The moon is rising.

(Epihodov is heard playing still the same mournful song on the guitar. The moon rises. Somewhere near the poplars Varya is looking for Anya and calling "Anya! Where are you?")

TROFIMOV.   Yes, the moon is rising. *(A pause.)* Here is happiness—here it comes! It is coming nearer and nearer; already I can hear its footsteps. And if we never see it—if we may never know it—what does it matter? Others will see it after us.

VARYA'S VOICE.   Anya! Where are you?

TROFIMOV.   That Varya again! *(Angrily.)* It's revolting!

ANYA.   Well, let's go down to the river. It's lovely there.

TROFIMOV.   Yes, let's go.

(They go.)

VARYA'S VOICE.   Anya! Anya!

ACT III

(Scene: A drawing room divided by an arch from a larger drawing room. A chandelier burning. The Jewish orchestra, the same that was mentioned in Act II, is heard playing in the anteroom. It is evening. In the larger drawing room they are dancing the grand chain. The voice of Semyonov-Pishtchik: "Promenade à une paire!"° They enter the drawing room in couples, first Pishtchik and Charlotta Ivanovna, then Trofimov and Lyubov Andreyevna, thirdly Anya with the Post-Office Clerk, fourthly Varya with the stationmaster, and other guests. Varya is quietly weeping and wiping away her tears as she dances. In the last couple is Dunyasha. They move across the drawing room. Pishtchik shouts: "Grand rond, balancez!" and "Les Cavaliers à genou et remerciez vos dames."°)

(Firs in a swallowtail coat brings in seltzer water on a tray. Pishtchik and Trofimov enter the drawing room.)

PISHTCHIK.   I am a full-blooded man; I have already had two strokes. Dancing's hard work for me, but as they say, if you're in the pack, you must bark with the rest. I'm as strong, I may say, as a horse. My parent, who would have his joke—may the Kingdom of Heaven be his!—used to say about our origin that the ancient stock of the Semyonov-Pishtchiks was derived from the very horse that Caligula° made a member of the senate. *(Sits down.)* But I've no money, that's where the mischief is. A hungry dog believes in nothing but meat. *(Snores, but at once wakes up.)* That's like me. . . . I can think of nothing but money.

TROFIMOV.   There really is something horsy about your appearance.

PISHTCHIK.   Well . . . a horse is a fine beast . . . a horse can be sold.

(There is the sound of billiards being played in an adjoining room. Varya appears in the arch leading to the larger drawing room.)

TROFIMOV *(teasing)*.   Madame Lopahin! Madame Lopahin!

VARYA *(angrily)*.   Mangy-looking gentleman!

TROFIMOV.   Yes, I am a mangy-looking gentleman, and I'm proud of it!

VARYA *(pondering bitterly)*.   Here we have hired musicians and nothing to pay them! *(Goes out.)*

TROFIMOV *(to Pishtchik)*.   If the energy you have wasted during your lifetime in trying to find the money to pay your interest had gone to something else, you might in the end have turned the world upside down.

PISHTCHIK.   Nietzsche, the philosopher, a very great and celebrated man . . . of enormous intellect . . . says in his works, that one can make forged banknotes.

TROFIMOV.   Why, have you read Nietzsche?

PISHTCHIK.   What next . . . Dashenka told me. . . . And now I am in such a position, I might just as well forge banknotes. The day after tomorrow I must pay 310 rubles—130 I have procured. *(Feels in his pockets, in alarm.)* The money's gone! I have lost my money! *(Through his tears.)* Where's the money? *(Gleefully.)* Why, here it is behind the lining. . . . It has made me hot all over.

(Enter Lyubov Andreyevna and Charlotta Ivanovna.)

"Promenade à une paire!": "Walk in pairs" (French).   *"Grand rond . . . vos dames"*: "Form a large circle" and "Gentlemen kneel and thank your ladies."   *Caligula*: Roman emperor (A.D. 37–41) who reputedly put a horse in the Senate.

LYUBOV *(hums the Lezginka°)*. Why is Leonid so long? What can he be doing in town? *(To Dunyasha.)* Offer the musicians some tea.

TROFIMOV. The sale hasn't taken place, most likely.

LYUBOV. It's the wrong time to have the orchestra, and the wrong time to give a dance. Well, never mind. *(Sits down and hums softly.)*

CHARLOTTA *(gives Pishtchik a pack of cards)*. Here's a pack of cards. Think of any card you like.

PISHTCHIK. I've thought of one.

CHARLOTTA. Shuffle the pack now. That's right. Give it here, my dear Mr. Pishtchik. *Ein, zwei, drei°*—now look, it's in your breast pocket.

PISHTCHIK *(taking a card out of his breast pocket)*. The eight of spades! Perfectly right! *(Wonderingly.)* Fancy that now!

CHARLOTTA *(holding pack of cards in her hands, to Trofimov)*. Tell me quickly which is the top card.

TROFIMOV. Well, the queen of spades.

CHARLOTTA. It is! *(To Pishtchik.)* Well, which card is uppermost?

PISHTCHIK. The ace of hearts.

CHARLOTTA. It is! *(Claps her hands, pack of cards disappears.)* Ah! what lovely weather it is today! *(A mysterious feminine voice which seems coming out of the floor answers her.* "Oh, yes, it's magnificent weather, madam.")! You are my perfect ideal.

VOICE. And I greatly admire you too, madam.

STATIONMASTER *(applauding)*. The lady ventriloquist—bravo!

PISHTCHIK *(wonderingly)*. Fancy that now! Most enchanting, Charlotta Ivanovna. I'm simply in love with you.

CHARLOTTA. In love? *(Shrugging shoulders.)* What do you know of love, *guter Mensch, aber schlechter Musikant.°*

TROFIMOV *(pats Pishtchik on the shoulder)*. You dear old horse. . . .

CHARLOTTA. Attention, please! Another trick! *(Takes a traveling rug from a chair.)* Here's a very good rug; I want to sell it. *(Shaking it out.)* Doesn't anyone want to buy it?

PISHTCHIK *(wonderingly)*. Fancy that!

CHARLOTTA. *Ein, zwei, drei!*

(Quickly picks up rug she has dropped; behind the rug stands Anya; she makes a curtsey, runs to her mother, embraces her and runs back into the larger drawing room amidst general enthusiasm.)

LYUBOV *(applauds)*. Bravo! Bravo!

CHARLOTTA. Now again; *Ein, zwei, drei!*

(Lifts up the rug; behind the rug stands Varya, bowing.)

PISHTCHIK *(wonderingly)*. Fancy that now!

CHARLOTTA. That's the end. *(Throws the rug at Pishtchik, makes a curtsey, runs into the larger drawing room.)*

PISHTCHIK *(hurries after her)*. Mischievous creature! Fancy! *(Goes out.)*

LYUBOV. And still Leonid doesn't come. I can't understand what he's doing in the town so long! Why, everything must be over by now. The estate is sold, or the sale has not taken place. Why keep us so long in suspense?

VARYA *(trying to console her)*. Uncle's bought it. I feel sure of that.

Lezginka: a Russian dance tune. *Ein, zwei, drei:* one, two, three. *guter Mensch, aber schlechter Musikant:* good person but terrible musician (German).

TROFIMOV *(ironically).* Oh, yes!

VARYA. Great-aunt sent him an authorization to buy it in her name, and transfer the debt. She's doing it for Anya's sake, and I'm sure God will be merciful. Uncle will buy it.

LYUBOV. My aunt in Yaroslavl sent fifteen thousand to buy the estate in her name, she doesn't trust us—but that's not enough even to pay the arrears. *(Hides her face in her hands.)* My fate is being sealed today, my fate. . . .

TROFIMOV *(teasing Varya).* Madame Lopahin.

Varya *(angrily).* Perpetual student! Twice already you've been sent down from the University.

LYUBOV. Why are you angry, Varya? He's teasing you about Lopahin. Well, what of that? Marry Lopahin if you like, he's a good man, and interesting; if you don't want to, don't! Nobody compels you, darling.

VARYA. I must tell you plainly, mamma, I look at the matter seriously; he's a good man, I like him.

LYUBOV. Well, marry him. I can't see what you're waiting for.

VARYA. Mamma. I can't make him an offer myself. For the last two years, everyone's been talking to me about him. Everyone talks; but he says nothing or else makes a joke. I see what it means. He's growing rich, he's absorbed in business, he has no thoughts for me. If I had money, were it ever so little, if I had only a hundred rubles, I'd throw everything up and go far away. I would go into a nunnery.

TROFIMOV. What bliss!

VARYA *(to Trofimov).* A student ought to have sense! *(In a soft tone with tears.)* How ugly you've grown, Petya! How old you look! *(To Lyubov Andreyevna, no longer crying.)* But I can't do without work, mamma; I must have something to do every minute.

(Enter Yasha.)

YASHA *(hardly restraining his laughter).* Epihodov has broken a billiard cue! *(Goes out.)*

VARYA. What is Epihodov doing here? Who gave him leave to play billiards? I can't make these people out. *(Goes out.)*

LYUBOV. Don't tease her, Petya. You see she has grief enough without that.

TROFIMOV. She is so very officious, meddling in what's not her business. All the summer she's given Anya and me no peace. She's afraid of a love affair between us. What's it to do with her? Besides, I have given no grounds for it. Such triviality is not in my line. We are above love!

LYUBOV. And I suppose I am beneath love. *(Very uneasily.)* Why is it Leonid's not here? If only I could know whether the estate is sold or not! It seems such an incredible calamity that I really don't know what to think. I am distracted. . . . I shall scream in a minute. . . . I shall do something stupid. Save me, Petya, tell me something, talk to me!

TROFIMOV. What does it matter whether the estate is sold today or not? That's all done with long ago. There's no turning back, the path is overgrown. Don't worry yourself, dear Lyubov Andreyevna. You mustn't deceive yourself; for once in your life you must face the truth!

LYUBOV. What truth? You see where the truth lies, but I seem to have lost my sight, I see nothing. You settle every great problem so boldly, but tell me, my dear boy, isn't it because you're young—because you haven't yet understood one of your problems through suffering? You look forward boldly, and isn't it that you don't see and don't expect anything dreadful because life is still hidden from your young eyes?

You're bolder, more honest, deeper than we are, but think, be just a little magnani-mous, have pity on me. I was born here, you know, my father and mother lived here, my grandfather lived here, I love this house. I can't conceive of life without the cherry orchard, and if it really must be sold, then sell me with the orchard. *(Embraces Trofi-mov, kisses him on the forehead.)* My boy was drowned here. *(Weeps.)* Pity me, my dear kind fellow.

TROFIMOV.   You know I feel for you with all my heart.

LYUBOV.   But that should have been said differently, so differently. *(Takes out her handkerchief, telegram falls on the floor.)* My heart is so heavy today. It's so noisy here, my soul is quivering at every sound, I'm shuddering all over, but I can't go away; I'm afraid to be quiet and alone. Don't be hard on me, Petya . . . I love you as though you were one of ourselves. I would gladly let you marry Anya—I swear I would—only, my dear boy, you must take your degree, you do nothing—you're simply tossed by fate from place to place. That's so strange. It is, isn't it? And you must do something with your beard to make it grow somehow. *(Laughs.)* You look so funny!

TROFIMOV *(picks up the telegram).*   I've no wish to be a beauty.

LYUBOV.   That's a telegram from Paris. I get one every day. One yesterday and one today. That savage creature is ill again, he's in trouble again. He begs forgiveness, be-seeches me to go, and really I ought to go to Paris to see him. You look shocked, Petya. What am I to do, my dear boy, what am I to do? He is ill, he is alone and unhappy, and who'll look after him, who'll keep him from doing the wrong thing, who'll give him his medicine at the right time? And why hide it or be silent? I love him, that's clear. I love him! I love him! He's a millstone about my neck, I'm going to the bottom with him, but I love that stone and can't live without it. *(Presses Trofimov's hand.)* Don't think ill of me, Petya, don't tell me anything, don't tell me. . . .

TROFIMOV *(through his tears).*   For God's sake forgive my frankness: why, he robbed you!

LYUBOV.   No! No! No! You mustn't speak like that. *(Covers her ears.)*

TROFIMOV.   He is a wretch! You're the only person that doesn't know it! He's a worthless creature! A despicable wretch!

LYUBOV *(getting angry, but speaking with restraint).*   You're twenty-six or twenty-seven years old, but you're still a schoolboy.

TROFIMOV.   Possibly.

LYUBOV.   You should be a man at your age! You should understand what love means! And you ought to be in love yourself. You ought to fall in love! *(Angrily.)* Yes, yes, and it's not purity in you, you're simply a prude, a comic fool, a freak.

TROFIMOV *(in horror).*   The things she's saying!

LYUBOV.   I am above love! You're not above love, but simply as our Firs here says, "You are a good-for-nothing." At your age not to have a mistress!

TROFIMOV *(in horror).*   This is awful! The things she is saying! *(Goes rapidly into the larger drawing room clutching his head.)* This is awful! I can't stand it! I'm going. *(Goes off, but at once returns.)* All is over between us! *(Goes off into the anteroom.)*

LYUBOV *(shouts after him).*   Petya! Wait a minute! You funny creature! I was joking! Petya! *(There is a sound of somebody running quickly downstairs and suddenly fall-ing with a crash, Anya and Varya scream, but there is a sound of laughter at once.)* What has happened?

(Anya runs in.)

ANYA *(laughing).*   Petya's fallen downstairs! *(Runs out.)*

LYUBOV.   What a queer fellow that Petya is! *(The Stationmaster stands in the middle of the larger room and reads* The Magdalene, *by Alexey Tolstoy.° They listen to him, but before he has recited many lines strains of a waltz are heard from the anteroom and the reading is broken off. All dance. Trofimov, Anya, Varya, and Lyubov Andreyevna come in from the anteroom.)* Come, Petya—come, pure heart! I beg your pardon. Let's have a dance!

(Dances with Petya. Anya and Varya dance. Firs comes in, puts his stick down near the side door. Yasha also comes into the drawing room and looks on at the dancing.)

YASHA.   What is it, old man?

FIRS.   I don't feel well. In old days we used to have generals, barons and admirals dancing at our balls, and now we send for the post-office clerk and the stationmaster and even they're not overanxious to come. I am getting feeble. The old master, the grandfather, used to give sealing-wax for all complaints. I have been taking sealing-wax for twenty years or more. Perhaps that's what's kept me alive.

YASHA.   You bore me, old man! *(Yawns.)* It's time you were done with.

FIRS.   Ach, you're a good-for-nothing! *(Mutters.)*

(Trofimov and Lyubov Andreyevna dance in larger room and then on to the stage.)

LYUBOV.   Merci. I'll sit down a little. *(Sits down.)* I'm tired.

(Enter Anya.)

ANYA *(excitedly).*   There's a man in the kitchen has been saying that the cherry orchard's been sold today.

LYUBOV.   Sold to whom?

ANYA.   He didn't say to whom. He's gone away.

(She dances with Trofimov, and they go off into the larger room.)

YASHA.   There was an old man gossiping there, a stranger.

FIRS.   Leonid Andreyevitch isn't here yet, he hasn't come back. He has his light overcoat on, *demi-saison,°* he'll catch cold for sure. *Ach!* Foolish young things!

LYUBOV.   I feel as though I should die. Go, Yasha, find out to whom it has been sold.

YASHA.   But he went away long ago, the old chap. *(Laughs.)*

LYUBOV *(with slight vexation).*   What are you laughing at? What are you pleased at?

YASHA.   Epihodov is so funny. He's a silly fellow, two and twenty misfortunes.

LYUBOV.   Firs, if the estate is sold, where will you go?

FIRS.   Where you bid me, there I'll go.

LYUBOV.   Why do you look like that? Are you ill? You ought to be in bed.

FIRS.   Yes. *(Ironically.)* Me go to bed and who's to wait here? Who's to see to things without me? I'm the only one in all the house.

YASHA *(to Lyubov Andreyevna).*   Lyubov Andreyevna, permit me to make a request of you; if you go back to Paris again, be so kind as to take me with you. It's positively impossible for me to stay here. *(Looking about him; in an undertone.)* There's no need to say it, you see for yourself—an uncivilized country, the people have no morals, and then the dullness! The food in the kitchen's abominable, and then Firs runs after one muttering all sorts of unsuitable words. Take me with you, please do!

(Enter Pishtchik.)

Alexey Tolstoy (1817–1875): Russian novelist, dramatist, and poet.   *demi-saison:* between seasons.

PISHTCHIK.   Allow me to ask you for a waltz, my dear lady. *(Lyubov Andreyevna goes with him.)* Enchanting lady, I really must borrow of you just 180 rubles, *(dances)* only 180 rubles.

(They pass into the larger room. In the larger drawing room, a figure in a gray top hat and in checked trousers is gesticulating and jumping about. Shouts of "Bravo, Charlotta Ivanovna.")

DUNYASHA *(she has stopped to powder herself).*   My young lady tells me to dance. There are plenty of gentlemen, and too few ladies, but dancing makes me giddy and makes my heart beat. Firs, the post-office clerk said something to me just now that quite took my breath away.

(Music becomes more subdued.)

FIRS.   What did he say to you?
DUNYASHA.   He said I was like a flower.
YASHA *(yawns).*   What ignorance! *(Goes out.)*
DUNYASHA.   Like a flower. I am a girl of such delicate feelings, I am awfully fond of soft speeches.
FIRS.   Your head's being turned.

(Enter Epihodov.)

EPIHODOV.   You have no desire to see me, Dunyasha. I might be an insect. *(Sighs.)* Ah! life!
DUNYASHA.   What is it you want?
EPIHODOV.   Undoubtedly you may be right. *(Sighs.)* But, of course, if one looks at it from that point of view, if I may so express myself, you have, excuse my plain speaking, reduced me to a complete state of mind. I know my destiny. Every day some misfortune befalls me and I have long ago grown accustomed to it, so that I look upon my fate with a smile. You gave me your word, and though I—
DUNYASHA.   Let us have a talk later, I entreat you, but now leave me in peace, for I am lost in reverie. *(Plays with her fan.)*
EPIHODOV.   I have a misfortune every day, and if I may venture to express myself, I merely smile at it, I even laugh.

(Varya enters from the larger drawing room.)

VARYA.   You still have not gone, Epihodov. What a disrespectful creature you are, really! *(To Dunyasha.)* Go along, Dunyasha! *(To Epihodov.)* First you play billiards and break the cue, then you go wandering about the drawing room like a visitor!
EPIHODOV.   You really cannot, if I may so express myself, call me to account like this.
VARYA.   I'm not calling you to account, I'm speaking to you. You do nothing but wander from place to place and don't do your work. We keep you as a counting-house clerk, but what use you are I can't say.
EPIHODOV *(offended).*   Whether I work or whether I walk, whether I eat or whether I play billiards, is a matter to be judged by persons of understanding and my elders.
VARYA.   You dare to tell me that! *(Firing up.)* You dare! You mean to say I've no understanding. Begone from here! This minute!
EPIHODOV *(intimidated).*   I beg you to express yourself with delicacy.
VARYA *(beside herself with anger).*   This moment! get out! away! *(He goes toward the door, she following him.)* Two and twenty misfortunes! Take yourself off! Don't let me set eyes on you! *(Epihodov has gone out, behind the door his voice,* "I shall lodge a complaint against you.") What! You're coming back? *(Snatches up the stick Firs has put down near the

door.) Come! Come! Come! I'll show you! What! you're coming? Then take that! *(She swings the stick, at the very moment that Lopahin comes in.)*

LOPAHIN.   Very much obliged to you!

VARYA *(angrily and ironically)*.   I beg your pardon!

LOPAHIN.   Not at all! I humbly thank you for your kind reception!

VARYA.   No need of thanks for it. *(Moves away, then looks round and asks softly.)* I haven't hurt you?

LOPAHIN.   Oh, no! Not at all! There's an immense bump coming up, though!

VOICES FROM LARGER ROOM.   Lopahin has come! Yermolay Alexeyevitch!

PISHTCHIK.   What do I see and hear? *(Kisses Lopahin.)* There's a whiff of cognac about you, my dear soul, and we're making merry here too!

(Enter Lyubov Andreyevna.)

LYUBOV.   Is it you, Yermolay Alexeyevitch? Why have you been so long? Where's Leonid?

LOPAHIN.   Leonid Andreyevitch arrived with me. He is coming.

LYUBOV *(in agitation)*.   Well! Well! Was there a sale? Speak!

LOPAHIN *(embarrassed, afraid of betraying his joy)*.   The sale was over at four o'clock. We missed our train—had to wait till half-past nine. *(Sighing heavily.)* Ugh! I feel a little giddy.

(Enter Gaev. In his right hand he has purchases, with his left hand he is wiping away his tears.)

LYUBOV.   Well, Leonid? What news? *(Impatiently, with tears.)* Make haste, for God's sake!

GAEV *(makes her no answer, simply waves his hand. To Firs, weeping)*.   Here, take them; there's anchovies, Kertch herrings. I have eaten nothing all day. What I have been through! *(Door into the billiard room is open. There is heard a knocking of balls and the voice of Yasha saying* "Eighty-seven." *Gaev's expression changes, he leaves off weeping.)* I am fearfully tired. Firs, come and help me change my things. *(Goes to his own room across the larger drawing room.)*

PISHTCHIK.   How about the sale? Tell us, do!

LYUBOV.   Is the cherry orchard sold?

LOPAHIN.   It is sold.

LYUBOV.   Who has bought it?

LOPAHIN.   I have bought it. *(A pause. Lyubov is crushed; she would fall down if she were not standing near a chair and table. Varya takes keys from her waistband, flings them on the floor in middle of drawing room and goes out.)* I have bought it! Wait a bit, ladies and gentlemen, pray. My head's a bit muddled, I can't speak. *(Laughs.)* We came to the auction. Deriganov was there already. Leonid Andreyevitch only had 15,000 and Deriganov bid 30,000, besides the arrears, straight off. I saw how the land lay. I bid against him. I bid 40,000, he bid 45,000, I said 55, and so he went on, adding 5 thousands and I adding 10. Well . . . So it ended. I bid 90, and it was knocked down to me. Now the cherry orchard's mine! Mine! *(Chuckles.)* My God, the cherry orchard's mine! Tell me that I'm drunk, that I'm out of my mind, that it's all a dream. *(Stamps with his feet.)* Don't laugh at me! If my father and my grandfather could rise from their graves and see all that has happened! How their Yermolay, ignorant, beaten Yermolay, who used to run about barefoot in winter, how that very Yermolay has bought the finest estate in the world! I have bought the estate where my father and grandfather were slaves, where they weren't even admitted into the kitchen. I am asleep, I am dreaming! It is all fancy, it is the work of your imagination plunged in the darkness of ignorance. *(Picks up keys, smiling fondly.)* She threw away the keys; she means to show she's not the housewife now. *(Jingles the keys.)* Well, no matter. *(The orchestra is heard tuning up.)* Hey, musicians! Play! I want to hear you. Come, all of you, and look how Yermolay Lopahin will take the ax to the cherry orchard, how the trees will fall to the ground! We will build houses on it and our grandsons and great-grandsons will see a new life springing up there. Music! Play up!

(Music begins to play. Lyubov Andreyevna has sunk into a chair and is weeping bitterly.)

LOPAHIN *(reproachfully)*.   Why, why didn't you listen to me? My poor friend! Dear lady, there's no turning back now. *(With tears.)* Oh, if all this could be over, oh, if our miserable disjointed life could somehow soon be changed!

PISHTCHIK *(takes him by the arm, in an undertone)*.   She's weeping, let us go and leave her alone. Come. *(Takes him by the arm and leads him into the larger drawing room.)*

LOPAHIN.   What's that? Musicians, play up! All must be as I wish it. *(With irony.)* Here comes the new master, the owner of the cherry orchard! *(Accidentally tips over a little table, almost upsetting the candelabra.)* I can pay for everything!

(Goes out with Pishtchik. No one remains on the stage or in the larger drawing room except Lyubov, who sits huddled up, weeping bitterly. The music plays softly. Anya and Trofimov come in quickly. Anya goes up to her mother and falls on her knees before her. Trofimov stands at the entrance to the larger drawing room.)

ANYA.   Mamma! Mamma, you're crying, dear, kind, good mamma! My precious! I love you! I bless you! The cherry orchard is sold, it is gone, that's true, that's true! But don't weep, mamma! Life is still before you, you have still your good, pure heart! Let us go, let us go, darling, away from here! We will make a new garden, more splendid than this one; you will see it, you will understand. And joy, quiet, deep joy, will sink into your soul like the sun at evening! And you will smile, mamma! Come, darling, let us go!

ACT IV

(Scene: Same as in Act I. There are neither curtains on the windows nor pictures on the walls: only a little furniture remains piled up in a corner as if for sale. There is a sense of desolation; near the outer door and in the background of the scene are packed trunks, traveling bags, etc. On the left the door is open, and from here the voices of Varya and Anya are audible. Lopahin is standing waiting. Yasha is holding a tray with glasses full of champagne. In front of the stage Epihodov is tying up a box. In the background behind the scene a hum of talk from the peasants who have come to say good-by. The voice of Gaev: "Thanks, brothers, thanks!")

YASHA.   The peasants have come to say good-by. In my opinion, Yermolay Alexeyevitch, the peasants are good-natured, but they don't know much about things.

(The hum of talk dies away. Enter across front of stage. Lyubov Andreyevna and Gaev. She is not weeping, but is pale; her face is quivering—she cannot speak.)

GAEV.   You gave them your purse, Lyuba. That won't do—that won't do!

LYUBOV.   I couldn't help it! I couldn't help it!

(Both go out.)

LOPAHIN *(in the doorway, calls after them)*.   You will take a glass at parting? Please do. I didn't think to bring any from the town, and at the station I could only get one bottle. Please take a glass. *(A pause.)* What? You don't care for any? *(Comes away from the door.)* If I'd known, I wouldn't have bought it. Well, and I'm not going to drink it. *(Yasha carefully sets the tray down on a chair.)* You have a glass, Yasha, anyway.

YASHA.   Good luck to the travelers, and luck to those that stay behind! *(Drinks.)* This champagne isn't the real thing, I can assure you.

LOPAHIN.   It cost eight rubles the bottle. *(A pause.)* It's devilish cold here.

YASHA.   They haven't heated the stove today—it's all the same since we're going. *(Laughs.)*

LOPAHIN.   What are you laughing for?

YASHA.   For pleasure.

LOPAHIN.   Though it's October, it's as still and sunny as though it were summer. It's just right for building! *(Looks at his watch; says in doorway:)* Take note, ladies and gentlemen, the train goes in forty-seven minutes; so you ought to start for the station in twenty minutes. You must hurry up!

(Trofimov comes in from out of doors wearing a great-coat.)

TROFIMOV.   I think it must be time to start, the horses are ready. The devil only knows what's become of my galoshes; they're lost. *(In the doorway.)* Anya! My galoshes aren't here. I can't find them.

LOPAHIN.   And I'm getting off to Harkov. I am going in the same train with you. I'm spending all the winter at Harkov. I've been wasting all my time gossiping with you and fretting with no work to do. I can't get on without work. I don't know what to do with my hands, they flap about so queerly, as if they didn't belong to me.

TROFIMOV.   Well, we're just going away, and you will take up your profitable labors again.

LOPAHIN.   Do take a glass.

TROFIMOV.   No, thanks.

LOPAHIN.   Then you're going to Moscow now?

TROFIMOV.   Yes. I shall see them as far as the town, and tomorrow I shall go on to Moscow.

LOPAHIN.   Yes, I dare say, the professors aren't giving any lectures, they're waiting for your arrival.

TROFIMOV.   That's not your business.

LOPAHIN.   How many years have you been at the University?

TROFIMOV.   Do think of something newer than that—that's stale and flat. *(Hunts for galoshes.)* You know we shall most likely never see each other again, so let me give you one piece of advice at parting: don't wave your arms about—get out of the habit. And another thing, building villas, reckoning up that the summer visitors will in time become independent farmers—reckoning like that, that's not the thing to do either. After all, I am fond of you: you have fine delicate fingers like an artist, you've a fine delicate soul.

LOPAHIN *(embraces him).*   Good-by, my dear fellow. Thanks for everything. Let me give you money for the journey, if you need it.

TROFIMOV.   What for? I don't need it.

LOPAHIN.   Why, you haven't got a half-penny.

TROFIMOV.   Yes, I have, thank you. I got some money for a translation. Here it is in my pocket, *(anxiously)* but where can my galoshes be!

VARYA *(from the next room).*   Take the nasty things! *(Flings a pair of galoshes onto the stage.)*

TROFIMOV.   Why are you so cross, Varya? h'm! . . . but those aren't my galoshes.

LOPAHIN.   I sowed three thousand acres with poppies in the spring, and now I have cleared forty thousand profit. And when my poppies were in flower, wasn't it a picture! So here, as I say, I made forty thousand, and I'm offering you a loan because I can afford to. Why turn up your nose? I am a peasant—I speak bluntly.

TROFIMOV.   Your father was a peasant, mine was a chemist—and that proves absolutely nothing whatever. *(Lopahin takes out his pocketbook.)* Stop that—stop that. If you were to offer me two hundred thousand I wouldn't take it. I am an independent man, and everything that all of you, rich and poor alike, prize so highly and hold so dear, hasn't the slightest power over me—it's like so much fluff fluttering in the air. I can get on without you. I can pass by you. I am strong and proud. Humanity is advancing toward the highest truth, the highest happiness which is possible on earth, and I am in the front ranks.

LOPAHIN.   Will you get there?

TROFIMOV.   I shall get there. *(A pause.)* I shall get there, or I shall show others the way to get there.

(In the distance is heard the strike of an ax on a tree.)

LOPAHIN.   Good-by, my dear fellow; it's time to be off. We turn up our noses at one another, but life is passing all the while. When I am working hard without resting, then my mind is more at ease, and it seems to me as though I too know what I exist for; but how many people are in Russia, my dear boy, who exist, one doesn't know what for. Well, it doesn't matter. That's not what keeps things spinning. They tell me Leonid Andreyevitch has taken a situation. He is going to be a clerk at the bank—6,000 rubles a year. Only, of course, he won't stick to it—he's too lazy.

ANYA *(in the doorway)*.   Mamma begs you not to let them chop down the orchard until she's gone.

TROFIMOV.   Yes, really, you might have the tact. *(Walks out across the front of the stage.)*

LOPAHIN.   I'll see to it! I'll see to it! Stupid fellows! *(Goes out after him.)*

ANYA.   Has Firs been taken to the hospital?

YASHA.   I told them this morning. No doubt they have taken him.

ANYA *(to Epihodov, who passes across the drawing room)*.   Semyon Pantaleyevitch, inquire, please, if Firs has been taken to the hospital.

YASHA *(in a tone of offense)*.   I told Yegor this morning—why ask a dozen times?

EPIHODOV.   Firs is advanced in years. It's my conclusive opinion no treatment would do him good; it's time he was gathered to his fathers. And I can only envy him. *(Puts a trunk down on a cardboard hatbox and crushes it.)* There, now, of course—I knew it would be so.

YASHA *(jeeringly)*.   Two and twenty misfortunes!

VARYA *(through the door)*.   Has Firs been taken to the hospital?

ANYA.   Yes.

VARYA.   Why wasn't the note for the doctor taken too?

ANYA.   Oh, then, we must send it after them. *(Goes out.)*

VARYA *(from the adjoining room)*.   Where's Yasha? Tell him his mother's come to say good-by to him.

YASHA *(waves his hand)*.   They put me out of all patience!

(Dunyasha has all this time been busy about the luggage. Now, when Yasha is left alone, she goes up to him.)

DUNYASHA.   You might just give me one look, Yasha. You're going away. You're leaving me. *(Weeps and throws herself on his neck.)*

YASHA.   What are you crying for? *(Drinks the champagne.)* In six days I shall be in Paris again. Tomorrow we shall get into the express train and roll away in a flash. I can scarcely believe it! Vive la France! It doesn't suit me here—it's not the life for me; there's no doing anything. I have seen enough of the ignorance here. I have had enough of it. *(Drinks champagne.)* What are you crying for? Behave yourself properly, and then you won't cry.

DUNYASHA *(powders her face, looking in a pocket-mirror)*.   Do send me a letter from Paris. You know how I loved you, Yasha—how I loved you! I am a tender creature, Yasha.

YASHA.   Here, they are coming!

(Busies himself about the trunks, humming softly. Enter Lyubov Andreyevna, Gaev, Anya and Charlotta Ivanovna.)

GAEV.   We ought to be off. There's not much time now. *(Looking at Yasha.)* What a smell of herrings!

LYUBOV.   In ten minutes we must get into the carriage. *(Casts a look about the room.)* Farewell, dear house, dear old home of our fathers! Winter will pass and spring will come, and then you will be no more; they will tear you down! How much those walls have seen! *(Kisses her daughter passionately.)* My treasure, how bright you look! Your eyes are sparkling like diamonds! Are you glad? Very glad?

ANYA.   Very glad! A new life is beginning, mamma.

GAEV.   Yes, really, everything is all right now. Before the cherry orchard was sold, we were all worried and wretched, but afterward, when once the question was settled conclusively, irrevocably, we all felt calm and even cheerful. I am a bank clerk now—I am a financier—cannon off the red. And you, Lyuba, after all, you are looking better; there's no question of that.

LYUBOV.   Yes. My nerves are better, that's true. *(Her hat and coat are handed to her.)* I'm sleeping well. Carry out my things, Yasha. It's time. *(To Anya.)* My darling, we shall soon see each other again. I am going to Paris. I can live there on the money your Yaroslavl auntie sent us to buy the estate with—hurrah for auntie!—but that money won't last long.

ANYA.   You'll come back soon, mamma, won't you? I'll be working up for my examination in the high school, and when I have passed that, I shall set to work and be a help to you. We will read all sorts of things together, mamma, won't we? *(Kisses her mother's hands.)* We will read in the autumn evenings. We'll read lots of books, and a new wonderful world will open out before us. *(Dreamily.)* Mamma, come soon.

LYUBOV.   I shall come, my precious treasure.

(Embraces her. Enter Lopahin. Charlotta softly hums a song.)

GAEV.   Charlotta's happy; she's singing!

CHARLOTTA *(picks up a bundle like a swaddled baby)*.   By, by, my baby. *(A baby is heard crying: "Ooah! ooah!")* Hush, hush, my pretty boy! *("Ooah! ooah!")* Poor little thing! *(Throws the bundle back.)* You must please find me a situation. I can't go on like this.

LOPAHIN.   We'll find you one, Charlotta Ivanovna. Don't worry yourself.

GAEV.   Everyone's leaving us. Varya's going away. We have become of no use all at once.

CHARLOTTA.   There's nowhere for me to be in the town. I must go away. *(Hums.)* What care I . . .

(Enter Pishtchik.)

LOPAHIN.   The freak of nature.

PISHTCHIK *(gasping).*   Oh . . . Let me get my breath. . . . I'm worn out . . . my most honored . . . Give me some water.

GAEV.   Want some money, I suppose? Your humble servant! I'll go out of the way of temptation. *(Goes out.)*

PISHTCHIK.   It's a long while since I have been to see you . . . dearest lady. *(To Lopahin.)* You are here . . . glad to see you . . . a man of immense intellect . . . take . . . here. *(Gives to Lopahin.)* 400 rubles. That leaves me owing 840.

LOPAHIN *(shrugging his shoulders in amazement).*   It's like a dream. Where did you get it?

PISHTCHIK.   Wait a bit . . . I'm hot . . . a most extraordinary occurrence! Some Englishmen came along and found in my land some sort of white clay. *(To Lyubov Andreyevna.)* And 400 for you . . . most lovely . . . wonderful. *(Gives money.)* The rest later. *(Sips water.)* A young man in the train was telling me just now that a great philosopher advises jumping off a house-top. "Jump!" says he; "the whole gist of the problem lies in that." *(Wonderingly.)* Fancy that, now! Water, please!

LOPAHIN.   What Englishmen?

PISHTCHIK.   I have made over to them the rights to dig the clay for twenty-four years . . . and now, excuse me . . . I can't stay . . . I must be trotting on. I'm going to Znoikovo . . . to Kardamanovo. . . . I'm in debt all round. *(Sips.)* . . . To your very good health! . . . I'll come in on Thursday.

LYUBOV.   We are just off to the town, and tomorrow I start for abroad.

PISHTCHIK.   What! *(In agitation.)* Why to the town? Oh, I see the furniture . . . the boxes. No matter . . . *(Through his tears.)* . . . no matter . . . men of enormous intellect . . . these Englishmen. . . . Never mind . . . be happy. God will succor you . . . no matter . . . everything in this world must have an end. *(Kisses Lyubov Andreyevna's hand.)* If the rumor reaches you that my end has come, think of this . . . old horse, and say: "There once was such a man in the world . . . Semyonov-Pishtchik . . . the Kingdom of Heaven be his!" . . . most extraordinary weather . . . yes. *(Goes out in violent agitation, but at once returns and says in the doorway:)* Dashenka wishes to be remembered to you. *(Goes out.)*

LYUBOV.   Now we can start. I leave with two cares in my heart. The first is leaving Firs ill. *(Looking at her watch.)* We have still five minutes.

ANYA.   Mamma, Firs has been taken to the hospital. Yasha sent him off this morning.

LYUBOV.   My other anxiety is Varya. She is used to getting up early and working; and now, without work, she's like a fish out of water. She is thin and pale, and she's crying, poor dear! *(A pause.)* You are well aware, Yermolay Alexeyevitch, I dreamed of marrying her to you, and everything seemed to show that you would get married. *(Whispers to Anya and motions to Charlotta and both go out.)* She loves you—she suits you. And I don't know—I don't know why it is you seem, as it were, to avoid each other. I can't understand it!

LOPAHIN.   I don't understand it myself, I confess. It's queer somehow, altogether. If there's still time, I'm ready now at once. Let's settle it straight off, and go ahead; but without you, I feel I shan't make her an offer.

LYUBOV.   That's excellent. Why, a single moment's all that's necessary. I'll call her at once.

LOPAHIN.   And there's champagne all ready too. *(Looking into the glasses.)* Empty! Someone's emptied them already. *(Yasha coughs.)* I call that greedy.

LYUBOV *(eagerly)*.   Capital! We will go out. Yasha, *allez!* I'll call her in. *(At the door.)* Varya, leave all that; come here. Come along! *(Goes out with Yasha.)*

LOPAHIN *(looking at his watch)*.   Yes.

(A pause. Behind the door, smothered laughter and whispering, and, at last, enter Varya.)

VARYA *(looking a long while over the things)*.   It is strange, I can't find it anywhere.

LOPAHIN.   What are you looking for?

VARYA.   I packed it myself, and I can't remember.

(A pause.)

LOPAHIN.   Where are you going now, Varvara Mihailova?

VARYA.   I? To the Ragulins. I have arranged to go to them to look after the house—as a housekeeper.

LOPAHIN.   That's in Yashnovo? It'll be seventy miles away. *(A pause.)* So this is the end of life in this house!

VARYA *(looking among the things)*.   Where is it? Perhaps I put it in the trunk. Yes, life in this house is over—there will be no more of it.

LOPAHIN.   And I'm just off to Harkov—by this next train. I've a lot of business there. I'm leaving Epihodov here, and I've taken him on.

VARYA.   Really!

LOPAHIN.   This time last year we had snow already, if you remember; but now it's so fine and sunny. Though it's cold, to be sure—three degrees of frost.

VARYA.   I haven't looked. *(A pause.)* And besides, our thermometer's broken.

(A pause. Voice at the door from the yard: "Yermolay Alexeyevitch!")

LOPAHIN *(as though he had long been expecting this summons)*.   This minute!

(Lopahin goes out quickly. Varya sitting on the floor and laying her head on a bag full of clothes, sobs quietly. The door opens, Lyubov Andreyevna comes in cautiously.)

LYUBOV.   Well? *(A pause.)* We must be going.

VARYA *(has wiped her eyes and is no longer crying)*.   Yes, mamma, it's time to start. I shall have time to get to the Ragulins today, if only you're not late for the train.

LYUBOV *(in the doorway)*.   Anya, put your things on. *(Enter Anya, then Gaev and Charlotta Ivanovna. Gaev has on a warm coat with a hood. Servants and cabmen come in. Epihodov bustles about the luggage.)* Now we can start on our travels.

ANYA *(joyfully)*.   On our travels!

GAEV.   My friends—my dear, my precious friends! Leaving this house forever, can I be silent? Can I refrain from giving utterance at leave-taking to those emotions which now flood all my being?

ANYA *(supplicatingly)*.   Uncle!

VARYA.   Uncle, you mustn't!

GAEV *(dejectedly)*.   Cannon and into the pocket . . . . I'll be quiet. . . .

(Enter Trofimov and afterward Lopahin.)

TROFIMOV.   Well, ladies and gentlemen, we must start.

LOPAHIN.   Epihodov, my coat!

LYUBOV.   I'll stay just one minute. It seems as though I have never seen before what the walls, what the ceilings in this house were like, and now I look at them with greediness, with such tender love.

allez!: go! (French).

GAEV.   I remember when I was six years old sitting in that window on Trinity Day watching my father going to church.

LYUBOV.   Have all the things been taken?

LOPAHIN.   I think all. *(Putting on overcoat, to Epihodov.)* You, Epihodov, mind you see everything is right.

EPIHODOV *(in a husky voice)*.   Don't you trouble, Yermolay Alexeyevitch.

LOPAHIN.   Why, what's wrong with your voice?

EPIHODOV.   I've just had a drink of water, and I choked over something.

YASHA *(contemptuously)*.   The ignorance!

LYUBOV.   We are going—and not a soul will be left here.

LOPAHIN.   Not till the spring.

VARYA *(pulls a parasol out of a bundle, as though about to hit someone with it. Lopahin makes a gesture as though alarmed)*.   What is it? I didn't mean anything.

TROFIMOV.   Ladies and gentlemen, let us get into the carriage. It's time. The train will be in directly.

VARYA.   Petya, here they are, your galoshes, by that box. *(With tears.)* And what dirty old things they are!

TROFIMOV *(putting on his galoshes)*.   Let us go, friends!

GAEV *(greatly agitated, afraid of weeping)*.   The train—the station! Double balk, ah!

LYUBOV.   Let us go!

LOPAHIN.   Are we all here? *(Locks the side door on left.)* The things are all here. We must lock up. Let us go!

ANYA.   Good-by, home! Good-by to the old life!

TROFIMOV.   Welcome to the new life!

(Trofimov goes out with Anya. Varya looks round the room and goes out slowly. Yasha and Charlotta Ivanovna, with her dog, go out.)

LOPAHIN.   Till the spring, then! Come, friends, till we meet! *(Goes out.)*

(Lyubov Andreyevna and Gaev remain alone. As though they had been waiting for this, they throw themselves on each other's necks, and break into subdued smothered sobbing, afraid of being overheard.)

GAEV *(in despair)*.   Sister, my sister!

LYUBOV.   Oh, my orchard!—my sweet, beautiful orchard! My life, my youth, my happiness, good-by! good-by!

VOICE OF ANYA *(calling gaily)*.   Mamma!

VOICE OF TROFIMOV *(gaily, excitedly)*.   Aa—oo!

LYUBOV.   One last look at the walls, at the windows. My dear mother loved to walk about this room.

GAEV.   Sister, sister!

VOICE OF ANYA.   Mamma!

VOICE OF TROFIMOV.   Aa—oo!

LYUBOV.   We are coming.

(They go out. The stage is empty. There is the sound of the doors being locked up, then of the carriages driving away. There is silence. In the stillness there is the dull stroke of an ax in a tree, clanging with a mournful lonely sound. Footsteps are heard. Firs appears in the doorway on the right. He is dressed as always—in a pea jacket and white waistcoat, with slippers on his feet. He is ill.)

FIRS *(goes up to the doors, and tries the handles)*.   Locked! They have gone. . . . *(Sits down on sofa.)* They have forgotten me. . . . Never mind . . . I'll sit here a bit. . . . I'll be bound Leonid Andreyevitch hasn't put his fur coat on and has gone off in his thin over-coat. *(Sighs anxiously.)* I didn't see after him. . . . These young people . . . *(Mutters something that can't be distinguished.)* Life has slipped by as though I hadn't lived. *(Lies down.)* I'll lie down a bit. . . . There's no strength in you, nothing left you—all gone! Ech! I'm good for nothing.

(Lies motionless. A sound is heard that seems to come from the sky, like a breaking harp-string, dying away mournfully. All is still again, and there is heard nothing but the strokes of the ax far away in the orchard.)

MARÍA IRENE FORNÉS   (b. 1930)

María Irene Fornés was born in Havana, Cuba, but came to the United States in 1945. She studied art and spent some time as a painter, but in 1957 she read Henrik Ibsen's play Hedda Gabler *and became inspired. Her first play,* Tango Palace, *came directly from that experience, and from that time Fornés became active in theater. She spent many years in the experimental, Off-Off-Broadway theater in New York, but she also produced plays in Havana, London, and San Francisco. Some of her work at the Padua Hills Theatre in Claremont, California, has been widely influential.* The Conduct of Life *is one of those plays. It is experimental in structure, composed in nineteen scenes rather than acts and scenes. The issues raised in the play, sadism, terror, sexual molestation, and tyranny, are handled with a shocking directness in part because the origin of the play derives from real events in Latin America. One of Fornés's principal concerns in her plays has been the role of women in society. That concern is evident in* The Conduct of Life.

The Conduct of Life _____ *1985*

Characters

> Orlando, a*n army lieutenant at the start of the play. A lieutenant commander soon after.*
> Leticia, *his wife, ten years his elder.*
> Alejo, *a lieutenant commander. Their friend.*
> Nena, *a destitute girl of twelve.*
> Olimpia, *a middle-aged, somewhat retarded servant.*

Time and Place: *The present. A Latin American country.*

To Julian Beck°

> *in memory of his courageous life*
> *(1925–1985)*

(The floor is divided in four horizontal planes. Downstage is the living room, which is about ten feet deep. Center stage, eighteen inches high, is the dining room, which is about ten feet deep. Further upstage, eighteen inches high, is a hallway which is about four feet deep. At each end of the hallway there is a door. The one to the right leads to the servants' quarters, the one to the left to the cellar. Upstage, three feet lower than the hallway (the same level as the living room), is the cellar, which is twenty feet wide and sixteen feet deep. Most of the cellar is occupied by two platforms,

---

Julian Beck: With Julian Malina, Beck developed The Living Theatre, an influential experimental group flourishing off Broadway in the 1960s and 1970s.

which are eight feet wide, eight feet deep, and three feet high. There is a space four feet wide around each platform. Upstage of the cellar are steps leading upstairs. Approximately ten feet above the cellar is another level, extending from the extreme left to the extreme right, which represents a warehouse. There is a door on the left of the warehouse. On the left and the right of the living room there are archways that lead to hallways or antechambers. The floors of these hallways are the same level as the dining room. On the left and the right of the dining room there is a second set of archways that lead to hallways or antechambers, the floors of which are the same level as the hallways. All along the edge of each level there is a step that leads to the next level. All floors and steps are black marble. In the living room there are two chairs. One is to the left, next to a table with a telephone on it. The other is on the right. In the dining room there are a large green marble table and three chairs. On the right cellar platform there is a mattress, on the left cellar platform there is a chair. In the warehouse there is a table and a chair to the left, and a chair and some crates and boxes to the right.)

Scene 1

(Before the lights come up one hears Orlando doing jumping-jacks. He is in the upper left corner of the dining room. A light slowly comes up on him. He wears military breeches held by suspenders, and riding boots. He continues doing jumping-jacks as long as the actor can endure it. When he stops, the lights come up on the center area. There is a chair upstage of the table. There is a linen towel on the left side of the table. Orlando dries his face with the towel and sits as he puts the towel around his neck.)

ORLANDO.   Thirty-three and I'm still a lieutenant. In two years I'll receive a promotion or I'll leave the military. I promise I will not spend time feeling sorry for myself.—Instead I will study the situation and draw an effective plan of action. I must eliminate all obstacles.—I will make the acquaintance of people in high power. If I cannot achieve this on my own merit, I will marry a woman in high circles. Leticia must not be an obstacle.—Man must have an ideal, mine is to achieve maximum power. That is my destiny.—No other interest will deter me from this.—My sexual drive is detrimental to my ideals. I must no longer be overwhelmed by sexual passion or I will be degraded beyond hope of recovery.

(Lights fade to black.)

Scene 2

(Alejo sits to the right of the dining-room table. Orlando stands to Alejo's left. He is now a lieutenant commander. He wears an army tunic, breeches, and boots. Leticia stands to the left. She wears a dress that suggests 1940s fashion.)

LETICIA.   What! Me go hunting? Do you think I'm going to shoot a deer, the most beautiful animal in the world? Do you think I'm going to destroy a deer? On the contrary, I would run in the field and scream and wave my arms like a mad woman and try to scare them away so the hunters could not reach them. I'd run in front of the bullets and let the mad hunters kill me—stand in the way of the bullets—and stop the bullets with my body. I don't see how anyone can shoot a deer.

ORLANDO *(to Alejo).*   Do you understand that? You, who are her friend, can you understand that? You don't think that is madness? She's mad. Tell her that—she'll think it's you who's mad. *(To Leticia.)* Hunting is a sport! A skill! Don't talk about something you know nothing about. Must you have an opinion about every damn thing! Can't you keep your mouth shut when you don't know what you're talking about? *(He exits right.)*

LETICIA.   He told me he didn't love me, and that his sole relationship to me was simply a marital one. What he means is that I am to keep this house, and he is to provide for it. That's what he said. That explains why he treats me the way he treats me. I never understood why he did, but now it's clear. He doesn't love me. I thought he loved me and that he stayed with me because he loved me and that's why I didn't understand his behavior. But now I know, because he told me that he sees me as a person who runs the house. I never understood that because I would have never—and if he had said, "Would you marry me to run my house even if I don't love you." I would have never— I would have never believed what I was hearing. I would have never believed that these words were coming out of his mouth. Because I loved him.

(Orlando has reentered. Leticia sees him and exits left. Orlando sits center.)

ORLANDO.   I didn't say any of that. I told her that she's not my heir. That's what I said. I told her that she's not in my will, and she will not receive a penny of my money if I die. That's what I said. I didn't say anything about running the house. I said she will not inherit a penny from me because I would be humiliated by how she'd put it to use. She is capable of foolishness beyond belief. Ask her what she would do if she were rich and could do anything she wants with her money.

(Leticia reenters.)

LETICIA.   I would distribute it among the poor.

ORLANDO.   She has no respect for money.

LETICIA.   That is not true. If I had money I would give it to those who need it. I know what money is, what money can do. It can feed people, it can put a roof over their heads. Money can do that. It can clothe them. What do you know about money? What does it mean to you? What do you do with money? Buy rifles? To shoot deer?

ORLANDO.   You're foolish—You're foolish! You're a foolish woman! *(He exits. His voice becomes faint as he walks into the distance.)* Foolish! Foolish! Foolish!

LETICIA.   He has no respect for me. He is insensitive. He doesn't listen. You cannot reach him. He is deaf. He is an animal. Nothing touches him except sensuality. He responds to food, to the flesh. To music sometimes, if it is romantic. To the moon. He is romantic but he is not aware of what you are feeling. I can't change him.—I'll tell you why I asked you to come. Because I want something from you.—I want you to educate me. I want to study. I want to study so I am not an ignorant person. I want to go to the university. I want to be knowledgeable. I'm tired of being ignored. I want to study political science. Is political science what diplomats study? Is that what it is? You have to teach me elemental things because I never finished grammar school. I would have to study a great deal. A great deal so I could enter the university. I would have to go through all the subjects. I would like to be a woman who speaks in a group and have others listen.

ALEJO.   Why do you want to worry about any of that? What's the use? Do you think you can change anything? Do you think anyone can change anything?

LETICIA.   Why not? *(Pause.)* Do you think I'm crazy?—He can't help it.—Do you think I'm crazy?—Because I love him?

(He looks away. Lights fade to black.)

Scene 3

(Orlando enters the warehouse holding Nena close to him. She wears a gray overlarge uniform. She is barefoot. She resists him. She is tearful and frightened. She pulls away and runs to the right wall. He follows her.)

ORLANDO *(softly)*.   You called me a snake.
NENA.   No, I didn't.

(He tries to reach her. She pushes his hands away from her.)

I was kidding.—I swear I was kidding.

(He grabs her and pushes her against the wall. He pushes his pelvis against her. He moves to the chair dragging her with him. She gets away from him and crawls to the left. He goes after her. She goes behind the table. He goes after her. She goes under the table. He grabs her foot and pulls her out toward the downstage side. He opens his fly and pushes his pelvis against her. She screams. Lights fade to black.)

Scene 4

(Olimpia is wiping crumbs off the dining-room table. She wears a plain gray uniform. Leticia sits to the left of the table facing front. She wears a dressing gown. She writes in a notebook. There is some silverware on the table. Olimpia has a speech defect.)

LETICIA.   Let's do this.
OLIMPIA.   Okay. *(She continues wiping the table.)*
LETICIA *(still writing)*.   What are you doing?
OLIMPIA.   I'm doing what I always do.
LETICIA.   Let's do this.
OLIMPIA *(in a mumble)*.   As soon as I finish doing this. You can't just ask me to do what you want me to do, and interrupt what I'm doing. I don't stop from the time I wake up in the morning to the time I go to sleep. You can't interrupt me whenever you want, not if you want me to get to the end of my work. I wake up at 5:30. I wash. I put on my clothes and make my bed. I go to the kitchen. I get the milk and the bread from outside and I put them on the counter. I open the icebox. I put one bottle in and take the butter out. I leave the other bottle on the counter. I shut the refrigerator door. I take the pan that I use for water and put water in it. I know how much. I put the pan on the stove, light the stove, cover it. I take the top off the milk and pour it in the milk pan except for a little. (Indicating with her finger.) Like this. For the cat. I put the pan on the stove, light the stove. I put coffee in the thing. I know how much. I light the oven and put bread in it. I come here, get the tablecloth and I lay it on the table. I shout "Breakfast." I get the napkins. I take the cups, the saucers, and the silver out and set the table. I go to the kitchen. I put the tray on the counter, put the butter on the tray. The water and the milk are getting hot. I pick up the cat's dish. I wash it. I pour the milk I left in the bottle in the milk dish. I put it on the floor for the cat. I shout "Breakfast." The water boils. I pour it in the thing. When the milk boils I turn off the gas and cover the milk. I get the bread from the oven. I slice it down the middle and butter it. Then I cut it in pieces *(indicating)* this big. I set a piece aside for me. I put the rest of the bread in the bread dish and shout "Breakfast." I pour the coffee in the coffee pot and the milk in the milk pitcher, except I leave *(indicating)* this much for me. I put them on

the tray and bring them here. If you're not in the dining room I call again. "Breakfast." I go to the kitchen, I fill the milk pan with water and let it soak. I pour my coffee, sit at the counter and eat my breakfast. I go upstairs to make your bed and clean your bathroom. I come down here to meet you and figure out what you want for lunch and dinner. And try to get you to think quickly so I can run to the market and get it bought before all the fresh stuff is bought up. Then, I start the day.

LETICIA. So?

OLIMPIA. So I need a steam pot.

LETICIA. What is a steam pot?

OLIMPIA. A pressure cooker.

LETICIA. And you want a steam pot? Don't you have enough pots?

OLIMPIA. No.

LETICIA. Why do you want a steam pot?

OLIMPIA. It cooks faster.

LETICIA. How much is it?

OLIMPIA. Expensive.

LETICIA. How much?

OLIMPIA. Twenty.

LETICIA. Too expensive.

(Olimpia throws the silver on the floor. Leticia turns her eyes up to the ceiling.)

Why do you want one more pot?

OLIMPIA. I don't have a steam pot.

LETICIA. A pressure cooker.

OLIMPIA. A pressure cooker.

LETICIA. You have too many pots.

(Olimpia goes to the kitchen and returns with an aluminum pan. She shows it to Leticia.)

OLIMPIA. Look at this.

(Leticia looks at it.)

LETICIA. What?

(Olimpia hits the pan against the back of a chair, breaking off a piece of it.)

OLIMPIA. It's not good.

LETICIA. All right! *(She takes money from her pocket and gives it to Olimpia.)* Buy it!— What are we having for lunch?

OLIMPIA. Fish.

LETICIA. I don't like fish.—What else?

OLIMPIA. Boiled plantains.

LETICIA. Make something I like.

OLIMPIA. Avocados.

(Leticia looks at Olimpia with resentment.)

LETICIA. Why can't you make something I like?

OLIMPIA. Avocados.

LETICIA. Something that needs cooking.

OLIMPIA. Bread pudding.

LETICIA. And for dinner?

OLIMPIA.   Pot roast.
LETICIA.   What else?
OLIMPIA.   Rice.
LETICIA.   What else?
OLIMPIA.   Salad.
LETICIA.   What kind?
OLIMPIA.   Avocado.
LETICIA.   Again.

(Olimpia looks at Leticia.)

LETICIA.   Not again.—Tomatoes. *(Olimpia mumbles.)* What's wrong with tomatoes besides that you don't like them? *(Olimpia mumbles.)* Get some. *(Olimpia mumbles.)* What does that mean? *(Olimpia doesn't answer.)* Buy tomatoes.—What else?
OLIMPIA.   That's all.
LETICIA.   We need a green.
OLIMPIA.   Watercress.
LETICIA.   What else.
OLIMPIA.   Nothing.
LETICIA.   For dessert.
OLIMPIA.   Bread pudding.
LETICIA.   Again.
OLIMPIA.   Why not?
LETICIA.   Make a flan.
OLIMPIA.   No flan.
LETICIA.   Why not?
OLIMPIA.   No good.
LETICIA.   Why no good?—Buy some fruit then.
OLIMPIA.   What kind?
LETICIA.   Pineapple. *(Olimpia shakes her head.)* Why not? *(Olimpia shakes her head.)* Mango.
OLIMPIA.   No mango.
LETICIA.   Buy some fruit! That's all. Don't forget bread.

(Leticia hands Olimpia money. Olimpia holds her hand out for more. Leticia hands her one more bill. Lights fade to black.)

Scene 5

(The warehouse table is propped against the door. The chair on the left faces right. The door is pushed and the table falls to the floor. Orlando enters. He wears an undershirt with short sleeves, breeches with suspenders and boots. He looks around the room for Nena. Believing she has escaped, he becomes still and downcast. He turns to the door and stands there for a moment. He takes a few steps to the right and stands there for a moment staring fixedly. He hears a sound from behind the boxes, walks to them and takes a box off. Nena is there. Her head is covered with a blanket. He pulls the blanket off. Nena is motionless and staring into space. He looks at her for a while, then walks to the chair and sits facing right staring into space. A few moments pass. Lights fade to black.)

Scene 6

(Leticia speaks on the telephone to Mona.)

LETICIA.   Since they moved to the new department he's different. *(Brief pause.)* He's distracted. I don't know where he goes in his mind. He doesn't listen to me. He worries. When I talk to him he doesn't listen. He's thinking about the job. He says he worries. What is there to worry about? Do you think there is anything to worry about? *(Brief pause.)* What meeting? *(Brief pause.)* Oh, sure. When is it? *(Brief pause.)* At what time? What do you mean I knew? No one told me.—I don't remember. Would you pick me up? *(Brief pause.)* At 1:00? Isn't 1:00 early? *(Brief pause.)* Orlando may still be home at 1:00. Sometimes he's here a little longer than usual. After lunch he sits and smokes. Don't you think 1:30 will give us enough time? *(Brief pause.)* No. I can't leave while he's smoking . . . I'd rather not. I'd rather wait till he leaves. *(Brief pause.)* 1:30, then. Thank you, Mona. *(Brief pause.)* See you then. Bye.

(Leticia puts down the receiver and walks to the stage right area. Orlando's voice is heard offstage left. He and Alejo enter halfway through the following speech.)

ORLANDO.   He made loud sounds, not high-pitched like a horse. He sounded like a whale, like a wounded whale. He was pouring liquid from everywhere, his mouth, his noise, his eyes. He was not a horse but a sexual organ.—Helpless. A viscera.—Screaming. Making strange sounds. He collapsed on top of her. She wanted him off but he collapsed on top of her and stayed there on top of her. Like gum. He looked more like a whale than a horse. A seal. His muscles were soft. What does it feel like to be without shape like that. Without pride. She was indifferent. He stayed there for a while and then lifted himself off her and to the ground. *(Pause.)* He looked like a horse again.

LETICIA.   Alejo, how are you?

(Alejo kisses Leticia's hand.)

ORLANDO *(as he walks to the living room).*   Alejo is staying for dinner. *(He sits left facing front.)*

LETICIA.   Would you like some coffee?

ALEJO.   Yes, thank you.

LETICIA.   Would you like some coffee, Orlando?

ORLANDO.   Yes, thank you.

LETICIA *(in a loud voices towards the kitchen).*   Olimpia . . .

OLIMPIA.   What?

LETICIA.   Coffee . . .

(Leticia sits to the right of the table. Alejo sits center.)

ALEJO.   Have you heard?

LETICIA.   Yes, he's dead and I'm glad he's dead. An evil man. I knew he'd be killed. Who killed him?

ALEJO.   Someone who knew him.

LETICIA.   What is there to gain? So he's murdered. Someone else will do the job. Nothing will change. To destroy them all is to say we destroy us all.

ALEJO.   Do you think we're all rotten?

LETICIA.   Yes.

ORLANDO.   A bad germ?

LETICIA.   Yes.

ORLANDO.   In our hearts?

LETICIA.   Yes.—In our eyes.

ORLANDO.   You're silly

LETICIA.   We're blind. We can't see beyond an arm's reach. We don't believe our life will last beyond the day. We only know what we have in our hand to put in our mouth, to put in our stomach, and to put in our pocket. We take care of our pocket, but not of our country. We take care of our stomachs but not of our hungry. We are primitive. We don't believe in the future. Each night when the sun goes down we think that's the end of life—so we have one last fling. We don't think we have a future. We don't think we have a country. Ask anybody, "Do you have a country?" They'll say, "Yes." Ask them, "What is your country?" They'll say, "My bed, my dinner plate." But, things can change. They can. I have changed. You have changed. He has changed.

ALEJO.   Look at me. I used to be an idealist. Now I don't have any feeling for anything. I used to be strong, healthy, I looked at the future with hope.

LETICIA.   Now you don't?

ALEJO.   Now I don't. I know what viciousness is.

ORLANDO.   What is viciousness?

ALEJO.   You.

ORLANDO.   Me?

ALEJO.   The way you tortured Felo.

ORLANDO.   I never tortured Felo.

ALEJO.   You did.

ORLANDO.   Boys play that way. You did too.

ALEJO.   I didn't.

ORLANDO.   He was repulsive to us.

ALEJO.   I never hurt him.

ORLANDO.   Well, you never stopped me.

ALEJO.   I didn't know how to stop you. I didn't know anyone could behave the way you did. It frightened me. It changed me. I became hopeless.

(Orlando walks to the dining room.)

ORLANDO.   You were always hopeless.

(Orlando exits. Olimpia enters carrying three demitasse coffees on a tray. She places them on the table and exits.)

ALEJO.   I am sexually impotent. I have no feelings. Things pass through me which resemble feelings but I know they are not. I'm impotent.

LETICIA.   Nonsense.

ALEJO.   It's not nonsense. How can you say it's nonsense?—How can one live in a world that festers the way ours does and take any pleasure in life?

(Lights fade to black.)

Scene 7

(Nena and Orlando stand against the wall in the warehouse. She is fully dressed. He is barechested. He pushes his pelvis against her gently. His lips touch her face as she speaks. The words are inaudible to the audience. On the table there is a tin plate with food and a tin cup with milk.)

ORLANDO.   Look this way. I'm going to do something to you.

(She makes a move away from him.)

Don't do that. Don't move away. *(As he slides his hand along her side.)* I just want to put my hand here like this. *(He puts his lips on hers softly and speaks at the same time.)* Don't hold your lips so tight. Make them soft. Let them loose. So I can do this. *(She whimpers.)* Don't cry. I won't hurt you. This is all I'm going to do to you. Just hold your lips soft. Be nice. Be a nice girl. *(He pushes against her and reaches an orgasm. He remains motionless for a moment; then steps away from her still leaning his hand on the wall.)* Go eat. I brought you food.

(She goes to the table. He sits on the floor and watches her eat. She eats voraciously. She looks at the milk.)

Drink it. It's milk. It's good for you.

(She drinks the milk, then continues eating. Lights fade to black.)

Scene 8

(Leticia stands left of the dining-room table. She speaks words she has memorized. Olimpia sits to the left of the table. She holds a book close to her eyes. Her head moves from left to right along the written words as she mumbles the sound of imaginary words. She continues doing this through the rest of the scene.)

LETICIA.   The impact of war is felt particularly in the economic realm. The destruction of property, private as well as public, may paralyze the country. Foreign investment is virtually . . . *(To Olimpia.)* Is that right? *(Pause.)* Is that right!
OLIMPIA.   What a moment. *(She continues mumbling and moving her head.)*
LETICIA.   What for? *(Pause.)* You can't read. *(Pause.)* You can't read!
OLIMPIA.   Wait a moment. *(She continues mumbling and moving her head.)*
LETICIA *(slapping the book out of Olimpia's hand).*   Why are you pretending you can read?

(Olimpia slaps Leticia's hands. They slap each other's hands. Lights fade to black.)

Scene 9

(Orlando sits in the living room. He smokes. He faces front and is thoughtful. Leticia and Olimpia are in the dining room. Leticia wears a hat and jacket. She tries to put a leather strap through the loops of a suitcase. There is a smaller piece of luggage on the floor.)

LETICIA.   This strap is too wide. It doesn't fit through the loop. *(Orlando doesn't reply.)* Is this the right strap? Is this the strap that came with this suitcase? Did the strap that came with the suitcase break? If so, where is it? And when did it break? Why doesn't this strap fit the suitcase and how did it get here? Did you buy this strap, Orlando?
ORLANDO.   I may have.
LETICIA.   It doesn't fit.
ORLANDO.   Hm.
LETICIA.   It doesn't fit through the loops.
ORLANDO.   Just strap it outside the loops.

(Leticia stands. Olimpia tries to put the strap through the loop.)

LETICIA.   No. You're supposed to put it through the loops. That's what the loops are for. What happened to the other strap?

ORLANDO.   It broke.

LETICIA.   How?

ORLANDO.   I used it for something.

LETICIA.   What! *(He looks at her.)* You should have gotten me one that fit. What did you use it for?—Look at that.

ORLANDO.   Strap it outside the loops.

LETICIA.   That wouldn't look right.

ORLANDO *(going to look at the suitcase)*.   Why do you need the straps?

LETICIA.   Because they come with it.

ORLANDO.   You don't need them.

LETICIA.   And travel like this?

ORLANDO.   Use another suitcase.

LETICIA.   What other suitcase. I don't have another.

(Orlando looks at his watch.)

ORLANDO.   You're going to miss your plane.

LETICIA.   I'm not going. I'm not traveling like this.

ORLANDO.   Go without it. I'll send it to you.

LETICIA.   You'll get new luggage, repack it and send it to me?—All right. *(She starts to exit left.)* It's nice to travel light. *(Offstage.)* Do I have everything?—Come, Olimpia.

(Olimpia follows with the suitcases. Orlando takes the larger suitcase from Olimpia. She exits. Orlando puts the suitcase down on the floor. He goes up the hallway and exits through the left door. A moment later he enters holding Nena close to him. She is pale, disheveled and has black circles around her eyes. She has a high fever and is almost unconscious. Her dress is torn and soiled. She is barefoot. He carries a new cotton dress on his arm. He takes her to the chair in the living room. He takes off the soiled dress and puts the new dress on her over a soiled slip.)

ORLANDO.   That's nice. You look nice.

(Leticia's voice is heard. He hurriedly takes Nena out the door, closes it, and leans on it.)

LETICIA *(offstage)*.   It would take but a second. you run to the garage and get the little suitcase and I'll take out the things I need.

(Leticia and Olimpia reenter left. Olimpia exits right.)

Hurry. Hurry. It would take but a second. *(Seeing Orlando.)* Orlando, I came back because I couldn't leave without anything at all. I came to get a few things because I have a smaller suitcase where I can take a few things.

(Leticia puts the suitcase she left behind on the table and opens it. Olimpia reenters right with a small suitcase.)

OLIMPIA.   Here.

LETICIA *(taking out the things she mentions)*.   A pair of shoes. A nightgown. A robe. Underwear. A dress. A sweater.

OLIMPIA *(overlapping Leticia's lines, packing the things she mentions in the small suitcase)*.   A robe. A dress. A nightgown. Underwear. A sweater. A pair of shoes.

(Leticia closes the large suitcase. Olimpia closes the small suitcase.)

LETICIA *(starting to exit)*.   Good-bye.

OLIMPIA *(following Leticia).* Good-bye.
ORLANDO. Good-bye.

(Lights fade to black.)

Scene 10

(In the cellar, Nena is curled up on the mattress. Orlando sits on the mattress using Nena as a back support. Alejo sits on the chair. He holds a green paper in his hand. Olimpia sweeps on the floor.)

ORLANDO. Tell them to check him. See if there's a scratch on him. There's not a scratch on that body. Why the fuss! Who was he and who's making a fuss? Why is he so important?

ALEJO. He was in deep. He knew names.

ORLANDO. I was never told that. But it wouldn't have mattered if they had because he died before I touched him.

ALEJO. you have to go to headquarters. They want you there.

ORLANDO. He came in screaming and he wouldn't stop. I had to wait for him to stop screaming before I could even pose a question to him. He wouldn't stop. I had put the poker to his neck to see if he would stop. Just to see if he would shut up. He just opened his eyes wide and started shaking and screamed even louder and fell over dead. Maybe he took something. I didn't do anything to him. If I didn't get anything from him it's because he died before I could get to him. He died of fear, not from anything I did to him. Tell them to do an autopsy. I'm telling you the truth. That's the truth. Why the fuss.

ALEJO *(starting to put the paper in his pocket).* I'll tell them what you said.

ORLANDO. Let me see that.

(Alejo takes it to him. Orlando looks at it and puts it back in Alejo's hands.)

Okay so it's a trap. So what side are you on? *(Pause. Alejo says nothing.)* So what do they want? *(Pause.)* Who's going to question me? That's funny. That's very funny. They want to question me. They want to punch my eyes out? I knew something was wrong because they were getting nervous. Antonio was getting nervous. I went to him and I asked him if something was wrong. He said, no, nothing was wrong. But I could tell something was wrong. He looked at Velez and Velez looked back at him. They are stupid. They want to conceal something from me and they look at each other right in front of me, as if I'm blind, as if I can't tell that they are worried about something. As if there's something happening right in front of my nose but I'm blind and I can't see it. *(He grabs the paper from Alejo's hand.)* You understand? *(He goes up the steps.)*

OLIMPIA. Like an alligator, big mouth and no brains. Lots of teeth but no brains. All tongue.

(Orlando enters through the left hallway door, and sits at the dining-room table. Alejo enters a few moments later. He stands to the right.)

ORLANDO. What kind of way is this to treat me?—After what I've done for them?—Is this a way to treat me?—I'll come up . . . as soon as I can—I haven't been well.—Okay. I'll come up. I get depressed because things are bad and they are not going to improve. There's something malignant in the world. Destructiveness, aggressiveness.—Greed. People take what is not theirs. There is greed. I am depressed, disillusioned . . . with life . . . with work . . . family. I don't see hope. *(He sits. He speaks more to himself than to Alejo.)* Some people get a cut in a finger and die. Because their veins are right next to their skin. There are people who, if you punch them in their stomach, the skin around the stomach bursts and the bowels fall out. Other people, you cut them open and you don't see any veins. You can't find their intestines. There are people who don't even bleed. There are people who bleed like pigs. There are people who have the nerves right on their skins. You touch them and they scream. They have their vital organs close to the surface. You hit them and they burst an organ. I didn't even touch this one and he died. He died of fear.

(Lights fade to black.)

Scene 11

(Nena, Alejo and Olimpia sit cross-legged on the mattress. Nena sits right, Alejo center, Olimpia left. Nena and Olimpia play patty-cake. Orlando enters. He goes close to them.)

ORLANDO.   What are you doing?

OLIMPIA.   I'm playing with her.

ORLANDO *(to Alejo)*.   What are you doing here? *(Alejo looks at him as a reply. He speaks sarcastically.)* They're playing patty-cake. *(He goes near Nena.)* So? *(Short pause. Nena giggles.)* Stop laughing!

(Nena is frightened. Olimpia holds her.)

OLIMPIA.   Why do you have to spoil everything. We were having a good time.

ORLANDO.   Shut up! *(Nena whimpers.)* Stop whimpering. I can't stand your whimpering. I can't stand it. *(Timidly, she tries to speak words as she whimpers.)* Speak up. I can't hear you! She's crazy! Take her to the crazy house!

OLIMPIA.   She's not crazy! She's a baby!

ORLANDO.   She's not a baby! She's crazy! You think she's a baby? She's older than you think! How old do you think she is.—Don't tell me that.

OLIMPIA.   She's sick. Don't you see she's sick? Let her cry! *(To Nena.)* Cry!

ORLANDO.   You drive me crazy too with your . . .

(Orlando imitates Olimpia's speech defect. She punches him repeatedly.)

OLIMPIA.   You drive me crazy! *(He pushes her off.)* You drive me crazy! You are a bastard! One day I'm going to kill you when you're asleep! I'm going to open you up and cut your entrails and feed them to the snakes. *(She tries to strangle him.)* I'm going to tear your heart out and feed it to the dogs! I'm going to cut your head open and have the cats eat your brain! *(Reaching for his fly.)* I'm going to cut your peepee and hang it on a tree and feed it to the birds!

ORLANDO.   Get off me! I'm getting rid of you too! *(He starts to exit.)* I can't stand you!

OLIMPIA.   Oh, yeah! I'm getting rid of you.

ORLANDO.   I can't stand you!

OLIMPIA.   I can't stand you!

ORLANDO.   Meddler! *(To Alejo.)* I can't stand you either. *(He exits.)*

OLIMPIA *(going to the stairs.)*.   Tell the boss! Tell her! She won't get rid of me! She'll get rid of you! What good are you! Tell her! *(She goes to Nena.)* Don't pay any attention to him. He's a coward.—You're pretty.

(Orlando enters through the hallway left door. He sits center at the dining-room table and leans his head on it. Leticia enters. He turns to look at her.)

LETICIA.   You didn't send it.

(Lights fade to black.)

Scene 12

(Leticia sits next to the phone. Without holding the phone, she speaks to an imaginary Mona.)

LETICIA.   I walk through the house and I know where he's made love to her I think I hear his voice making love to her. Saying the same things he says to me, the same words. *(There is a pause.)* There is someone here. He keeps someone here in the house. *(Pause.)* I don't dare look. *(Pause.)* No, there's nothing I can do. I can't do anything.

(Leticia walks to the hallway. She hears footsteps. She moves rapidly to the left and hides behind a pillar. Olimpia enters from right. She takes a few steps down the hallway. She carries a plate of food. She sees Leticia and stops. She takes a few steps in various directions, then stops.)

OLIMPIA.   Here kitty, kitty.

(Leticia walks to Olimpia, looks closely at the plate, then up at her.)

LETICIA.   What is it?
OLIMPIA.   Food.
LETICIA.   Who is it for?

(Olimpia turns her eyes away and doesn't answer. Leticia decides to go the cellar door. She stops halfway there.)

Who is it?
OLIMPIA.   A cat.

(Leticia opens the cellar door.)

LETICIA.   It's not a cat. I'm going down. *(She opens the door to the cellar and starts to go down.)* I want to see who is there.

ORLANDO *(offstage from the cellar)*.   What is it you want?

(Lights fade to black.)

Scene 13

(Orlando lies back in the chair in the cellar. His legs are outstretched. His eyes are bloodshot. His tunic is open. Nena is curled on the floor. Orlando speaks quietly. He is deeply absorbed.)

ORLANDO.   What I do to you is out of love. Out of want. It's not what you think. I wish you didn't have to be hurt. I don't do it out of hatred. It is not out of rage. It is love. It is a quiet feeling. It's a pleasure. It is quiet and it pierces my insides in the most internal way. It is my most private self. And this I give to you.—Don't be afraid.—It is a desire to destroy and to see things destroyed and to see the inside of them.—It's my nature. I must hide this from others. But I don't feel remorse. I was born this way and I must have this.—I need love. I wish you did not feel hurt and re-coil from me.

(Lights fade to black.)

Scene 14

(Orlando sits to the right and Leticia sits to the left of the table.)

LETICIA.   Don't make her scream.

(There is a pause.)

ORLANDO.   You're crazy.

LETICIA.   Don't I give you enough?

ORLANDO *(he's calm)*.   Don't start.

LETICIA.   How long is she going to be here?

ORLANDO.   Not long.

LETICIA.   Don't make her cry. *(He looks at her.)* I can't stand it. *(Pause.)* Why do you make her scream?

ORLANDO.   I don't make her scream.

LETICIA.   She screams.

ORLANDO.   I can't help it.

(Pause.)

LETICIA.   I tell you I can't stand it. I'm going to ask Mona to come and stay with me.

ORLANDO.   No.

LETICIA.   I want someone here with me.

ORLANDO.   I don't want her here.

LETICIA.   Why not?

ORLANDO.   I don't.

LETICIA.   I need someone here with me.

ORLANDO.   Not now.

LETICIA.   When?

ORLANDO.   Soon enough.—She's going to stay here for a while. She's going to work for us. She'll be a servant here.

LETICIA.   . . . No.

ORLANDO.   She's going to be a servant here.

(Lights fade to black.)

Scene 15

(Olimpia and Nena are sitting at the dining-room table. They are separating stones and other matter from dried beans.)

NENA.   I used to clean beans when I was in the home. And also string beans. I also pressed clothes. The days were long. Some girls did hand sewing. They spent the day doing that. I didn't like it. When I did that, the day was even longer and there were times when I couldn't move even if I tried. And they said I couldn't go there anymore, that I had to stay in the yard. I didn't mind sitting in the yard looking at the birds. I went to the laundry room and watched the women work. They let me go in and sit there. And they showed me how to press. I liked to press because my mind wanders and I find satisfaction. I can iron all day. I like the way the wrinkles come out and things look nice. It's a miracle isn't it? I could earn a living pressing clothes. And I could find my grandpa and take care of him.

OLIMPIA. Where is your grandpa?

NENA. I don't know.

(They work a little in silence.)

He sleeps in the streets. Because he's too old to remember where he lives. He needs a person to take care of him. And I can take care of him. But I don't know where he is.—He doesn't know where I am.—He doesn't know who he is. He's too old. He doesn't know anything about himself. He only knows how to beg. And he knows that only because he's hungry. He walks around and begs for food. He forgets to go home. He lives in the camp for the homeless and he has his own box. It's not an ugly box like the others. It is a real box. I used to live there with him. He took me with him when my mother died till they took me to the home. It is a big box. It's big enough for two. I could sleep in the front where it's cold. And he could sleep in the back where it's warmer. And he could lean on me. The floor is hard for him because he's skinny and it's hard on his poor bones. He could sleep on top of me if that would make him feel comfortable. I wouldn't mind. Except that he may pee on me because he pees in his pants. He doesn't know not to. He is incontinent. He can't hold it. His box was a little smelly. But that doesn't matter because I could clean it. All I would need is some soap. I could get plenty of water from the public faucet. And I could borrow a brush. You know how clean I could get it? As clean as new. You know what I would do? I would make holes in the floor so the pee would go down to the ground. And you know what else I would do?

OLIMPIA. What?

NENA. I would get straw and put it on the floor for him and for me and it would make it comfortable and clean and warm. How do you like that? Just as I did for my goat.

OLIMPIA. You have a goat?

NENA. . . . I did.

OLIMPIA. What happened to him?

NENA. He died. They killed him and ate him. Just like they did Christ.

OLIMPIA. Nobody ate Christ.

NENA. . . . I thought they did. My goat was eaten though.—In the home we had clean sheets. But that doesn't help. You can't sleep on clean sheets, not if there isn't someone watching over you while you sleep. And since my ma died there just wasn't anyone watching over me. Except you.—Aren't you? In the home they said guardian angels watch your sleep, but I didn't see any there. There weren't any. One day I heard my grandpa calling me and I went to look for him. And I didn't find him. I got tired and I slept in the street, and I was hungry and I was crying. And then he came to me and he spoke to me very softly so as not to scare me and he said he would give me something to eat and he said he would help me look for my grandpa. And he put me in the back of his van. . . . And he took me to a place. And he hurt me. I fought with him but I stopped fighting—because I couldn't fight anymore and he did things to me. And he locked me in. And sometimes he brought me food and sometimes he didn't. And he did things to me. And he beat me. And he hung me on the wall. And I got sick. And sometimes he brought me medicine. And then he said he had to take me somewhere. And he brought me here. And I am glad to be here because you are here. I only wish my grandpa were here too. He doesn't beat me so much anymore.

OLIMPIA. Why does he beat you? I hear him at night. He goes down the steps and I hear you cry. Why does he beat you?

NENA. Because I'm dirty.

OLIMPIA. You are not dirty.

NENA.   I am. That's why he beats me. The dirt won't go away from inside me.— He comes downstairs when I'm sleeping and I hear him coming and it frightens me. And he takes the covers off me and I don't move because I'm frightened and because I feel cold and I think I'm going to die. And he puts his hand on me and he recites poetry. And he is almost naked. He wears a robe but he leaves it open and he feels himself as he recites. He touches himself and he touches his stomach and his breast and his behind. He puts his fingers in my parts and he keeps reciting. Then he turns me on my stomach and puts himself inside me. And he says I belong to him. *(There is a pause.)* I want to conduct each day of my life in the best possible way. I should value the things I have. And I should value all those who are near me. And I should value the kindness that others bestow upon me. And if someone should treat me unkindly, I should not blind myself with rage, but I should see them and receive them, since maybe they are in worse pain than me.

(Lights fade to black.)

Scene 16

(Leticia speaks on the telephone with Mona. She speaks rapidly.)

LETICIA.   He is violent. He has become more so. I sense it. I feel it in him.—I understand his thoughts. I know what he thinks.—I raised him. I practically did. He was a boy when I met him. I saw him grow. I was the first woman he loved. That's how young he was. I have to look after him, make sure it doesn't get into trouble. He's not wise. He's trusting. They are changing him.—He tortures people. I know he does. He tells me he doesn't but I know he does. I know it. How could I not. Sometimes he comes from headquarters and his hands are shaking. Why should he shake? What do they do there?—He should transfer. Why do that? He says he doesn't do it himself. That the officers don't do it. He says that people are not being tortured. That that is questionable.—Everybody knows it. How could he not know it when everybody knows it. Sometimes you see blood in the streets. Haven't you seen it? Why do they leave the bodies in the streets—how evil, to frighten people? They tear their fingernails off and their poor hands are bloody and destroyed. And they mangle their genitals and expose them and they tear their eyes out and you can see the empty eyesockets in the skull. How awful, Mona. He mustn't do it. I don't care if I don't have anything! What's money! I don't need a house as big as this! He's doing it for money! What other reason could he have! What other reason could he have!! He shouldn't do it. I cannot look at him without thinking of it. He's doing it. I know he's doing it.—Shhhh! I hear steps. I'll call you later. Bye, Mona. I'll talk to you.

(She hangs up the receiver. Lights fade to black.)

Scene 17

(The living room. Olimpia sits to the right, Nena to the left.)

OLIMPIA.   I don't wear high heels because they hurt my feet. I used to have a pair but they hurt my feet and also *(pointing to her calf)* here in my legs. So I don't wear them anymore even if they were pretty. Did you ever wear high heels? *(Nena shakes her head.)*

Do you have ingrown nails? *(Nena looks at her questioningly.)* Nails that grow twisted into the flesh. *(Nena shakes her head.)* I don't either. Do you have sugar in the blood? *(Nena shakes her head.)* My mother had sugar in the blood and that's what she died of but she lived to be eighty-six which is very old even if she had many things wrong with her. She had glaucoma and high blood pressure.

(Leticia enters and sits center at the table. Nena starts to get up. Olimpia signals her to be still. Leticia is not concerned with them.)

> LETICIA.   So, what are you talking about?
> OLIMPIA.   Ingrown nails.

(Nena turns to Leticia to make sure she may remain seated there. Leticia is involved with her own thoughts. Nena turns front. Lights fade to black.)

Scene 18

(Orlando is sleeping on the dining-room table. The telephone rings. He speaks as someone having a nightmare.)

> ORLANDO.   Ah! Ah! Get off me! Get off! I said get off!

(Leticia enters.)

> LETICIA *(going to him).*   Orlando! What's the matter? What are you doing here!
> ORLANDO.   Get off me! Ah! Ah! Get off me!
> LETICIA.   Why are you sleeping here! On the table. *(Holding him close to her.)* Wake up.
> ORLANDO.   Let go of me. *(He slaps her hands as she tries to reach him.)* Get away from me. *(He goes to the floor on his knees. He staggers to the telephone.)* Yes. Yes, it's me.—You did?—So?—It's true then.—What's the name?—Yes, sure.—Thanks.—Sure.

(Orlando hangs up the receiver. He turns to look at Leticia. Lights fade to black.)

Scene 19

(Two chairs are placed side by side facing front in the center of the living room. Leticia sits on the right. Orlando stands in the down left corner. Nena sits to the left of the dining-room table facing front. She covers her face. Olimpia stands behind her, holding Nena and leaning her head on her.)

> ORLANDO.   Talk.
> LETICIA.   I can't talk like this.
> ORLANDO.   Why not?
> LETICIA.   In front of everyone.
> ORLANDO.   Why not?
> LETICIA.   It is personal. I don't need the whole world to know.
> ORLANDO.   Why not?
> LETICIA.   Because it's private. My life is private.
> ORLANDO.   Are you ashamed?
> LETICIA.   Yes, I am ashamed!
> ORLANDO.   What of . . . ? What of . . . ?—I want you to tell us—about your lover.
> LETICIA.   I don't have a lover.

(Orlando grabs Leticia by the hair. Olimpia holds on to Nena. Olimpia and Nena hide their faces.)

ORLANDO.   You have a lover.

LETICIA.   That's a lie.

ORLANDO *(moving closer to Leticia)*.   It's not a lie. Come on tell us. *(He pulls her hair.)* What's his name? *(Leticia emits a sound of pain. He pulls harder, leans toward her and speaks in a low tone.)* What's his name?

LETICIA.   Albertico.

(Orlando takes a moment to release Leticia.)

ORLANDO.   Tell us about it.

(There is silence. Orlando pulls Leticia's hair.)

LETICIA.   All right.

(Orlando releases Leticia.)

ORLANDO.   What's his name?

LETICIA.   Albertico.

ORLANDO.   Go on. *(Pause.)* Sit up! *(She does.)* Albertico what?

LETICIA.   Estévez.

(Orlando sits next to Leticia.)

ORLANDO.   Go on. *(Silence.)* Where did you first meet him?

LETICIA.   At . . . I . . .

ORLANDO *(he grabs Leticia by the hair)*.   In my office.

LETICIA.   Yes.

ORLANDO.   Don't lie.—When?

LETICIA.   You know when.

ORLANDO.   When! *(Silence.)* How did you meet him?

LETICIA.   You introduced him to me.

(Orlando lets Leticia go.)

ORLANDO.   What else? *(Silence.)* Who is he!

LETICIA.   He's a lieutenant.

ORLANDO *(he stands)*.   When did you meet with him?

LETICIA.   Last week.

ORLANDO.   When!

LETICIA.   Last week.

ORLANDO.   When!

LETICIA.   Last week. I said last week.

ORLANDO.   Where did you meet him?

LETICIA.   . . . In a house of rendezvous . . .

ORLANDO.   How did you arrange it?

LETICIA.   . . . I wrote to him

ORLANDO.   Did he approach you?

LETICIA.   No.

ORLANDO.   Did he!

LETICIA.   No.

ORLANDO *(He grabs Leticia's hair again.)*.   He did! How!

LETICIA.   I approached him.

ORLANDO.   How!

LETICIA *(aggressively).*   I looked at him! I looked at him! I looked at him!

(Orlando lets Leticia go.)

ORLANDO.   When did you look at him?
LETICIA.   Please stop . . . !
ORLANDO.   Where! When!
LETICIA.   In your office!
ORLANDO.   When?
LETICIA.   I asked him to meet me!
ORLANDO.   What did he say?
LETICIA *(aggressively).*   He walked away! He walked away! He walked away! I asked
him to meet me.
ORLANDO.   What was he like?
LETITIA.   . . . Oh . . .
ORLANDO.   Was he tender? Was he tender to you!

(Leticia doesn't answer. Orlando puts his hand inside her blouse. She lets out an excruciating scream. He lets her go and walks to the right of the dining room. She goes to the telephone table, opens the drawer, takes a gun and shoots Orlando. Orlando falls dead. Nena runs to downstage of the table. Leticia is disconcerted, then puts the revolver in Nena's hand, hoping she will take the blame. Leticia steps away from Nena.)

LETICIA.   Please . . .

(Nena is in a state of terror and numb acceptance. She looks at the gun. Then, up. The lights fade.)

ARTHUR MILLER   (b. 1915)

By the time his first major play, Death of a Salesman *(1949), established him as one of the great American playwrights, Arthur Miller had already been writing radio plays, screenplays, articles, and fiction for ten years. Political issues, especially anti-Semitism and the red-scare blacklisting and paranoia surrounding communism, became some of his central themes.* All My Sons *(1947) ran on Broadway for almost a year. It concerns a manager of a defense plant who knew that flaws in the parts he built for warplanes would cause some of the fliers to crash.* The Crucible *(1953), about witch hunts in the seventeenth century, invited comparison with the communist witch hunts of the 1950s.* A View from the Bridge *(1955) treats immigrants and their hopes in America. Miller's personal life became tabloid material when he married Marilyn Monroe; and* The Misfits *(1960), from his script, remains one of her most interesting films. Once his marriage ended he wrote* After the Fall *(1964), about a divorced writer getting his thinking together while considering a third marriage.* Incident at Vichy *(1964) and* The Price *(1967) were both successful. Miller's later plays have been well received in England, including a musical,* The American Clock *(1980). His play,* Broken Glass *(1994), is about a crisis in the life of a Jewish immigrant couple in Brooklyn in 1938.* The Ride Down Mount Morgan *(1991 London; 1998 New York) examines the life of a Reaganite go-getter whose car crash exposes him as a man with two wives—in a sense too much of everything. His work continues to explore issues of significance and to set a standard for American drama.*

Death of a Salesman ———————————————————————— *1949*

Characters

Willy Loman	Charley
Biff	Uncle Ben
Happy	Howard Wagner
Bernard	Jenny
The Woman	Stanley
	Miss Forsythe

(Scene: The action takes place in Willy Loman's house and yard and in various places he visits in the New York and Boston of today.)

(Throughout the play, in the stage directions, left and right mean stage left and stage right.)

ACT I

(A melody is heard, played upon a flute. It is small and fine, telling of grass and trees and the horizon. The curtain rises.)

(Before us is the Salesman's house. We are aware of towering, angular shapes behind it, surrounding it on all sides. Only the blue light of the sky falls upon the house and forestage; the surrounding area shows an angry glow of orange. As more light appears, we see a solid vault of apartment houses around the small, fragile-seeming home. An air of the dream clings to the place, a dream rising out of reality. The kitchen at center seems actual enough, for there is a kitchen table with three chairs, and a refrigerator. But no other fixtures are seen. At the back of the kitchen there is a draped entrance, which leads to the living room. To the right of the kitchen, on a level raised two feet, is a bedroom furnished only with a brass bedstead and a straight chair. On a shelf over the bed a silver athletic trophy stands. A window opens onto the apartment house at the side.)

(Behind the kitchen, on a level raised six and a half feet, is the boys' bedroom, at present barely visible. Two beds are dimly seen, and at the back of the room a dormer window. [This bedroom is above the unseen living room.] At the left a stairway curves up to it from the kitchen.)

(The entire setting is wholly or, in some places, partially transparent. The roofline of the house is one-dimensional; under and over it we see the apartment buildings. Before the house lies an apron, curving beyond the forestage into the orchestra. This forward area serves as the back yard as well as the locale of all Willy's imaginings and of his city scenes. Whenever the action is in the present the actors observe the imaginary wall-lines, entering the house only through its door at the left. But in the scenes of the past these boundaries are broken, and characters enter or leave a room by stepping "through" a wall onto the forestage.)

(From the right, Willy Loman, the Salesman, enters, carrying two large sample cases. The flute plays on. He hears but is not aware of it. He is past sixty years of age, dressed quietly. Even as he crosses the stage to the doorway of the house, his exhaustion is apparent. He unlocks the door, comes into the kitchen, and thankfully lets his burden down, feeling the soreness of his palms. A word-sigh escapes his lips—it might be "Oh, boy, oh, boy." He closes the door, then carries his cases out into the living room, through the draped kitchen doorway.)

(Linda, his wife, has stirred in her bed at the right. She gets out and puts on a robe, listening. Most often jovial, she has developed an iron repression of her exceptions to Willy's behavior— she more than loves him, she admires him, as though his mercurial nature, his temper, his massive dreams and little cruelties, served her only as sharp reminders of the turbulent longings within him, longings which she shares but lacks the temperament to utter and follow to their end.)

LINDA *(hearing Willy outside the bedroom, calls with some trepidation).* Willy!

WILLY. It's all right. I came back.

LINDA. Why? What happened? *(Slight pause.)* Did something happen, Willy?

WILLY. No, nothing happened.

LINDA. You didn't smash the car, did you?

WILLY *(with casual irritation).* I said nothing happened. Didn't you hear me?

LINDA. Don't you feel well?

WILLY. I'm tired to the death. *(The flute has faded away. He sits on the bed beside her, a little numb.)* I couldn't make it. I just couldn't make it, Linda.

LINDA *(very carefully, delicately).* Where were you all day? You look terrible.

WILLY. I got as far as a little above Yonkers. I stopped for a cup of coffee. Maybe it was the coffee.

LINDA. What?

WILLY *(after a pause).* I suddenly couldn't drive anymore. The car kept going off onto the shoulder, y'know?

LINDA *(helpfully).* Oh. Maybe it was the steering again. I don't think Angelo knows the Studebaker.

WILLY. No, it's me, it's me. Suddenly I realize I'm goin' sixty miles an hour and I don't remember the last five minutes. I'm—I can't seem to—keep my mind to it.

LINDA. Maybe it's your glasses. You never went for your new glasses.

WILLY. No, I see everything. I came back ten miles an hour. It took me nearly four hours from Yonkers.

LINDA *(resigned).* Well, you'll just have to take a rest, Willy, you can't continue this way.

WILLY. I just got back from Florida.

LINDA. But you didn't rest your mind. Your mind is overactive, and the mind is what counts, dear.

WILLY. I'll start out in the morning. Maybe I'll feel better in the morning. *(She is taking off his shoes.)* These goddam arch supports are killing me.

LINDA. Take an aspirin. Should I get you an aspirin? It'll soothe you.

WILLY *(with wonder).* I was driving along, you understand? And I was fine. I was even observing the scenery. You can imagine, me looking at scenery, on the road every week of my life. But it's so beautiful up there, Linda, the trees are so thick, and the sun is warm. I opened the windshield and just let the warm air bathe over me. And then all of a sudden I'm goin' off the road! I'm tellin' ya, I absolutely forgot I was driving. If I'd've gone the other way over the white line I might've killed somebody. So I went on again—and five minutes later I'm dreamin' again, and I nearly—*(He presses two fingers against his eyes.)* I have such thoughts, I have such strange thoughts.

LINDA. Willy, dear. Talk to them again. There's no reason why you can't work in New York.

WILLY. They don't need me in New York. I'm the New England man. I'm vital in New England.

LINDA.   But you're sixty years old. They can't expect you to keep traveling every week.

WILLY.   I'll have to send a wire to Portland. I'm supposed to see Brown and Morrison tomorrow morning at ten o'clock to show the line. Goddammit, I could sell them! *(He starts putting on his jacket.)*

LINDA *(taking the jacket from him).*   Why don't you go down to the place tomorrow and tell Howard you've simply got to work in New York? You're too accommodating, dear.

WILLY.   If old man Wagner was alive I'd a been in charge of New York now! That man was a prince, he was a masterful man. But that boy of his, that Howard, he don't appreciate. When I went north the first time, the Wagner Company didn't know where New England was!

LINDA.   Why don't you tell those things to Howard, dear?

WILLY *(encouraged).*   I will, I definitely will. Is there any cheese?

LINDA.   I'll make you a sandwich.

WILLY.   No, go to sleep. I'll take some milk. I'll be up right away. The boys in?

LINDA.   They're sleeping. Happy took Biff on a date tonight.

WILLY *(interested).*   That so?

LINDA.   It was so nice to see them shaving together, one behind the other, in the bathroom. And going out together. You notice? The whole house smells of shaving lotion.

WILLY.   Figure it out. Work a lifetime to pay off a house. You finally own it, and there's nobody to live in it.

LINDA.   Well, dear, life is a casting off. It's always that way.

WILLY.   No, no, some people—some people accomplish something. Did Biff say anything after I went this morning?

LINDA.   You shouldn't have criticized him, Willy, especially after he just got off the train. You mustn't lose your temper with him.

WILLY.   When the hell did I lose my temper? I simply asked him if he was making any money. Is that a criticism?

LINDA.   But, dear, how could he make any money?

WILLY *(worried and angered).*   There's such an undercurrent in him. He became a moody man. Did he apologize when I left this morning?

LINDA.   He was crestfallen, Willy. You know how he admires you. I think if he finds himself, then you'll both be happier and not fight anymore.

WILLY.   How can he find himself on a farm? Is that a life? A farmhand? In the beginning, when he was young, I thought, well, a young man, it's good for him to tramp around, take a lot of different jobs. But it's more than ten years now and he has yet to make thirty-five dollars a week!

LINDA.   He's finding himself, Willy.

WILLY.   Not finding yourself at the age of thirty-four is a disgrace!

LINDA.   Shh!

WILLY.   The trouble is he's lazy, goddammit!

LINDA.   Willy, please!

WILLY.   Biff is a lazy bum!

LINDA.   They're sleeping. Get something to eat. Go on down.

WILLY.   Why did he come home? I would like to know what brought him home.

LINDA.   I don't know. I think he's still lost, Willy. I think he's very lost.

WILLY.   Biff Loman is lost. In the greatest country in the world a young man with such—personal attractiveness, gets lost. And such a hard worker. There's one thing about Biff—he's not lazy.

LINDA.   Never.

WILLY *(with pity and resolve).*   I'll see him in the morning; I'll have a nice talk with him. I'll get him a job selling. He could be big in no time. My God! Remember how they used to follow him around in high school? When he smiled at one of them their faces lit up. When he walked down the street . . . *(He loses himself in reminiscences.)*

LINDA *(trying to bring him out of it).*   Willy, dear, I got a new kind of American-type cheese today. It's whipped.

WILLY.   Why do you get American when I like Swiss?

LINDA.   I just thought you'd like a change—

WILLY.   I don't want a change! I want Swiss cheese. Why am I always being contradicted?

LINDA *(with a covering laugh).*   I thought it would be a surprise.

WILLY.   Why don't you open a window in here, for God's sake?

LINDA *(with infinite patience).*   They're all open, dear.

WILLY.   The way they boxed us in here. Bricks and windows, windows and bricks.

LINDA.   We should've bought the land next door.

WILLY.   The street is lined with cars. There's not a breath of fresh air in the neighborhood. The grass don't grow anymore, you can't raise a carrot in the back yard. They should've had a law against apartment houses. Remember those two beautiful elm trees out there? When I and Biff hung the swing between them?

LINDA.   Yeah, like being a million miles from the city.

WILLY.   They should've arrested the builder for cutting those down. They massacred the neighborhood. *(Lost.)* More and more I think of those days, Linda. This time of year it was lilac and wisteria. And then the peonies would come out, and the daffodils. What fragrance in this room!

LINDA.   Well, after all, people had to move somewhere.

WILLY.   No, there's more people now.

LINDA.   I don't think there's more people. I think—

WILLY.   There's more people! That's what's ruining this country! Population is getting out of control. The competition is maddening! Smell the stink from that apartment house! And another one on the other side . . . How can they whip cheese?

(On Willy's last line, Biff and Happy raise themselves up in their beds, listening.)

LINDA.   Go down, try it. And be quiet.

WILLY *(turning to Linda, guiltily).*   You're not worried about me, are you, sweetheart?

BIFF.   What's the matter?

HAPPY.   Listen!

LINDA.   You've got too much on the ball to worry about.

WILLY.   You're my foundation and my support, Linda.

LINDA.   Just try to relax, dear. You make mountains out of molehills.

WILLY.   I won't fight with him anymore. If he wants to go back to Texas, let him go.

LINDA.   He'll find his way.

WILLY.   Sure. Certain men just don't get started till later in life. Like Thomas Edison, I think. Or B. F. Goodrich. One of them was deaf. *(He starts for the bedroom doorway.)* I'll put my money on Biff.

LINDA.   And Willy—if it's warm Sunday we'll drive in the country. And we'll open the windshield, and take lunch.

WILLY.   No, the windshields don't open on the new cars.

LINDA.   But you opened it today.

WILLY.   Me? I didn't. *(He stops.)* Now isn't that peculiar! Isn't that a remarkable— *(He breaks off in amazement and fright as the flute is heard distantly.)*

LINDA.   What, darling?

WILLY.   That is the most remarkable thing.

LINDA.   What, dear?

WILLY.   I was thinking of the Chevvy. *(Slight pause.)* Nineteen twenty-eight . . . when I had that red Chevvy—*(Breaks off.)* That funny? I coulda sworn I was driving that Chevvy today.

LINDA.   Well, that's nothing. Something must've reminded you.

WILLY.   Remarkable. Ts. Remember those days? The way Biff used to simonize that car? The dealer refused to believe there was eighty thousand miles on it. *(He shakes his head.)* Heh! *(To Linda.)* Close your eyes, I'll be right up. *(He walks out of the bedroom.)*

HAPPY *(to Biff)*.   Jesus, maybe he smashed up the car again!

LINDA *(calling after Willy)*.   Be careful on the stairs, dear! The cheese is on the middle shelf! *(She turns, goes over to the bed, takes his jacket, and goes out of the bedroom.)*

(Light has risen on the boys' room. Unseen, Willy is heard talking to himself, "Eighty thousand miles," and a little laugh. Biff gets out of bed, comes downstage a bit, and stands attentively. Biff is two years older than his brother Happy, well built, but in these days bears a worn air and seems less self-assured. He has succeeded less, and his dreams are stronger and less acceptable than Happy's. Happy is tall, powerfully made. Sexuality is like a visible color on him, or a scent that many women have discovered. He, like his brother, is lost, but in a different way, for he has never allowed himself to turn his face toward defeat and is thus more confused and hard-skinned, although seemingly more content.)

HAPPY *(getting out of bed)*.   He's going to get his license taken away if he keeps that up. I'm getting nervous about him, y'know, Biff?

BIFF.   His eyes are going.

HAPPY.   No, I've driven with him. He sees all right. He just doesn't keep his mind on it. I drove into the city with him last week. He stops at a green light and then it turns red and he goes. *(He laughs.)*

BIFF.   Maybe he's color-blind.

HAPPY.   Pop? Why he's got the finest eye for color in the business. You know that.

BIFF *(sitting down on his bed)*.   I'm going to sleep.

HAPPY.   You're not still sour on Dad, are you, Biff?

BIFF.   He's all right, I guess.

WILLY *(underneath them, in the living room)*.   Yes, sir, eighty thousand miles—eighty-two thousand!

BIFF.   You smoking?

HAPPY *(holding out a pack of cigarettes)*.   Want one?

BIFF *(taking a cigarette)*.   I can never sleep when I smell it.

WILLY.   What a simonizing job, heh!

HAPPY *(with deep sentiment)*.   Funny, Biff, y'know? Us sleeping in here again? The old beds. *(He pats his bed affectionately.)* All the talk that went across those two beds, huh? Our whole lives.

BIFF.   Yeah. Lotta dreams and plans.

HAPPY *(with a deep and masculine laugh)*.   About five hundred women would like to know what was said in this room.

(They share a soft laugh.)

BIFF.   Remember that big Betsy something—what the hell was her name—over on Bushwick Avenue?

HAPPY *(combing his hair)*.   With the collie dog!

BIFF.   That's the one. I got you in there, remember?

HAPPY.   Yeah, that was my first time—I think. Boy, there was a pig. *(They laugh, almost crudely.)* You taught me everything I know about women. Don't forget that.

BIFF.   I bet you forgot how bashful you used to be. Especially with girls.

HAPPY.   Oh, I still am, Biff.

BIFF.   Oh, go on.

HAPPY.   I just control it, that's all. I think I got less bashful and you got more so. What happened, Biff? Where's the old humor, the old confidence? *(He shakes Biff's knee. Biff gets up and moves restlessly about the room.)* What's the matter?

BIFF.   Why does Dad mock me all the time?

HAPPY.   He's not mocking you, he—

BIFF.   Everything I say there's a twist of mockery on his face. I can't get near him.

HAPPY.   He just wants you to make good, that's all. I wanted to talk to you about Dad for a long time, Biff. Something's—happening to him. He—talks to himself.

BIFF.   I noticed that this morning. But he always mumbled.

HAPPY.   But not so noticeable. It got so embarrassing I sent him to Florida. And you know something? Most of the time he's talking to you.

BIFF.   What's he say about me?

HAPPY.   I can't make it out.

BIFF.   What's he say about me?

HAPPY.   I think the fact that you're not settled, that you're still kind of up in the air . . .

BIFF.   There's one or two other things depressing him, Happy.

HAPPY.   What do you mean?

BIFF.   Never mind. Just don't lay it all to me.

HAPPY.   But I think if you just got started—I mean—is there any future for you out there?

BIFF.   I tell ya, Hap, I don't know what the future is. I don't know—what I'm supposed to want.

HAPPY.   What do you mean?

BIFF.   Well, I spent six or seven years after high school trying to work myself up. Shipping clerk, salesman, business of one kind or another. And it's a measly manner of existence. To get on that subway on the hot mornings in summer. To devote your whole life to keeping stock, or making phone calls, or selling or buying. To suffer fifty weeks of the year for the sake of a two-week vacation, when all you really desire is to be outdoors, with your shirt off. And always to have to get ahead of the next fella. And still—that's how you build a future.

HAPPY.   Well, you really enjoy it on a farm? Are you content out there?

BIFF *(with rising agitation)*.   Hap, I've had twenty or thirty different kinds of jobs since I left home before the war, and it always turns out the same. I just realized it lately. In Nebraska when I herded cattle, and the Dakotas, and Arizona, and now in Texas. It's why I came home now, I guess, because I realized it. This farm I work on, it's spring there now, see? And they've got about fifteen new colts. There's nothing more inspiring or—beautiful than the sight of a mare and a new colt. And it's cool there now, see? Texas is cool now, and it's spring. And whenever spring comes to where I am, I suddenly get the feeling, my God, I'm not gettin' anywhere! What the hell am I doing, playing around with horses, twenty-eight dollars a week! I'm thirty-four years old, I oughta be makin' my future. That's when I come running home. And now, I get here, and I don't know what to do with myself. *(After a pause.)* I've always made a point of not wasting my life, and every time I come back here I know that all I've done is to waste my life.

HAPPY.   You're a poet, you know that, Biff? You're a—you're an idealist!

BIFF.   No, I'm mixed up very bad. Maybe I oughta get married. Maybe I oughta get stuck into something. Maybe that's my trouble. I'm like a boy. I'm not married, I'm not in business, I just—I'm like a boy. Are you content, Hap? You're a success, aren't you? Are you content?

HAPPY.   Hell, no!

BIFF.   Why? You're making money, aren't you?

HAPPY *(moving about with energy, expressiveness).*   All I can do now is wait for the merchandise manager to die. And suppose I get to be merchandise manager? He's a good friend of mine, and he just built a terrific estate on Long Island. And he lived there about two months and sold it, and now he's building another one. He can't enjoy it once it's finished. And I know that's just what I would do. I don't know what the hell I'm workin' for. Sometimes I sit in my apartment—all alone. And I think of the rent I'm paying. And it's crazy. But then, it's what I always wanted. My own apartment, a car, and plenty of women. And still, goddammit, I'm lonely.

BIFF *(with enthusiasm).*   Listen, why don't you come out West with me?

HAPPY.   You and I, heh?

BIFF.   Sure, maybe we could buy a ranch. Raise cattle, use our muscles. Men built like we are should be working out in the open.

HAPPY *(avidly).*   The Loman Brothers, heh?

BIFF *(with vast affection).*   Sure, we'd be known all over the counties!

HAPPY *(enthralled).*   That's what I dream about, Biff. Sometimes I want to just rip my clothes off in the middle of the store and outbox that goddam merchandise manager. I mean I can outbox, outrun, and outlift anybody in that store, and I have to take orders from those common, petty sons-of-bitches till I can't stand it anymore.

BIFF.   I'm tellin' you, kid, if you were with me I'd be happy out there.

HAPPY *(enthused).*   See, Biff, everybody around me is so false that I'm constantly lowering my ideals . . .

BIFF.   Baby, together we'd stand up for one another, we'd have someone to trust.

HAPPY.   If I were around you—

BIFF.   Hap, the trouble is we weren't brought up to grub for money. I don't know how to do it.

HAPPY.   Neither can I!

BIFF.   Then let's go!

HAPPY.   The only thing is—what can you make out there?

BIFF.   But look at your friend. Builds an estate and then hasn't the peace of mind to live in it.

HAPPY.   Yeah, but when he walks into the store the waves part in front of him. That's fifty-two thousand dollars a year coming through the revolving door, and I got more in my pinky finger than he's got in his head.

BIFF.   Yeah, but you just said—

HAPPY.   I gotta show some of those pompous, self-important executives over there that Hap Loman can make the grade. I want to walk into the store the way he walks in. Then I'll go with you, Biff. We'll be together yet, I swear. But take those two we had tonight. Now weren't they gorgeous creatures?

BIFF. Yeah, yeah, most gorgeous I've had in years.

HAPPY. I get that any time I want, Biff. Whenever I feel disgusted. The only trouble is, it gets like bowling or something. I just keep knockin' them over and it doesn't mean anything. You still run around a lot?

BIFF. Naa. I'd like to find a girl—steady, somebody with substance.

HAPPY. That's what I long for.

BIFF. Go on! You'd never come home.

HAPPY. I would! Somebody with character, with resistance! Like Mom, y'know? You're gonna call me a bastard when I tell you this. That girl Charlotte I was with tonight is engaged to be married in five weeks. *(He tries on his new hat.)*

BIFF. No kiddin'!

HAPPY. Sure, the guy's in line for the vice-presidency of the store. I don't know what gets into me, maybe I just have an overdeveloped sense of competition or something, but I went and ruined her, and furthermore I can't get rid of her. And he's the third executive I've done that to. Isn't that a crummy characteristic? And to top it all, I go to their weddings! *(Indignantly, but laughing.)* Like I'm not supposed to take bribes. Manufacturers offer me a hundred-dollar bill now and then to throw an order their way. You know how honest I am, but it's like this girl, see. I hate myself for it. Because I don't want the girl, and, still, I take it and—I love it!

BIFF. Let's go to sleep.

HAPPY. I guess we didn't settle anything, heh?

BIFF. I just got one idea that I think I'm going to try.

HAPPY. What's that?

BIFF. Remember Bill Oliver?

HAPPY. Sure, Oliver is very big now. You want to work for him again?

BIFF. No, but when I quit he said something to me. He put his arm on my shoulder, and he said, "Biff, if you ever need anything, come to me."

HAPPY. I remember that. That sounds good.

BIFF. I think I'll go to see him. If I could get ten thousand or even seven or eight thousand dollars I could buy a beautiful ranch.

HAPPY. I bet he'd back you. 'Cause he thought highly of you, Biff. I mean, they all do. You're well liked, Biff. That's why I say to come back here, and we both have the apartment. And I'm tellin' you, Biff, any babe you want . . .

BIFF. No, with a ranch I could do the work I like and still be something. I just wonder though. I wonder if Oliver still thinks I stole that carton of basketballs.

HAPPY. Oh, he probably forgot that long ago. It's almost ten years. You're too sensitive. Anyway, he didn't really fire you.

BIFF. Well, I think he was going to. I think that's why I quit. I was never sure whether he knew or not. I know he thought the world of me, though. I was the only one he'd let lock up the place.

WILLY *(below)*. You gonna wash the engine, Biff?

HAPPY. Shh!

(Biff looks at Happy, who is gazing down, listening. Willy is mumbling in the parlor.)

HAPPY. You hear that?

(They listen. Willy laughs warmly.)

BIFF *(growing angry)*. Doesn't he know Mom can hear that?

WILLY. Don't get your sweater dirty, Biff!

(A look of pain crosses Biff's face.)

HAPPY. Isn't that terrible? Don't leave again, will you? You'll find a job here. You gotta stick around. I don't know what to do about him, it's getting embarrassing.

WILLY. What a simonizing job!

BIFF. Mom's hearing that!

WILLY. No kiddin', Biff, you got a date? Wonderful!

HAPPY. Go on to sleep. But talk to him in the morning, will you?

BIFF *(reluctantly getting into bed).* With her in the house. Brother!

HAPPY *(getting into bed).* I wish you'd have a good talk with him.

(The light on their room begins to fade.)

BIFF *(to himself in bed).* That selfish, stupid . . .

HAPPY. Sh . . . Sleep, Biff.

(Their light is out. Well before they have finished speaking, Willy's form is dimly seen below in the darkened kitchen. He opens the refrigerator, searches in there, and takes out a bottle of milk. The apartment houses are fading out, and the entire house and surroundings become covered with leaves. Music insinuates itself as the leaves appear.)

WILLY. Just wanna be careful with those girls, Biff, that's all. Don't make any promises. No promises of any kind. Because a girl, y'know, they always believe what you tell 'em, and you're very young, Biff, you're too young to be talking seriously to girls. *(Light rises on the kitchen. Willy, talking, shuts the refrigerator door and comes downstage to the kitchen table. He pours milk into a glass. He is totally immersed in himself, smiling faintly.)* Too young entirely, Biff. You want to watch your schooling first. Then when you're all set, there'll be plenty of girls for a boy like you. *(He smiles broadly at a kitchen chair.)* That so? The girls pay for you? *(He laughs.)* Boy, you must really be makin' a hit. *(Willy is gradually addressing—physically—a point offstage, speaking through the wall of the kitchen, and his voice has been rising in volume to that of a normal conversation.)* I been wondering why you polish the car so careful. Ha! Don't leave the hubcaps, boys. Get the chamois to the hubcaps. Happy, use newspaper on the windows, it's the easiest thing. Show him how to do it, Biff! You see, Happy? Pad it up, use it like a pad. That's it, that's it, good work. You're doin' all right, Hap. *(He pauses, then nods in approbation for a few seconds, then looks upward.)* Biff, first thing we gotta do when we get time is clip that big branch over the house. Afraid it's gonna fall in a storm and hit the roof. Tell you what. We get a rope and sling her around, and then we climb up there with a couple of saws and take her down. Soon as you finish the car, boys, I wanna see ya. I got a surprise for you, boys.

BIFF *(offstage).* Whatta ya got, Dad?

WILLY. No, you finish first. Never leave a job till you're finished—remember that. *(Looking toward the "big trees.")* Biff, up in Albany I saw a beautiful hammock. I think I'll buy it next trip, and we'll hang it right between those two elms. Wouldn't that be something? Just swingin' there under those branches. Boy, that would be . . .

(Young Biff and Young Happy appear from the direction Willy was addressing. Happy carries rags and a pail of water. Biff, wearing a sweater with a block "S," carries a football.)

BIFF *(pointing in the direction of the car offstage).* How's that, Pop, professional?

WILLY. Terrific. Terrific job, boys. Good work, Biff.

HAPPY. Where's the surprise, Pop?

WILLY. In the back seat of the car.

HAPPY. Boy! *(He runs off.)*

BIFF.   What is it, Dad? Tell me, what'd you buy?

WILLY. *(laughing, cuffs him).*   Never mind, something I want you to have.

BIFF. *(turns and starts off).*   What is it, Hap?

HAPPY. *(offstage).*   It's a punching bag!

BIFF.   Oh, Pop!

WILLY.   It's got Gene Tunney's signature on it!

(Happy runs onstage with a punching bag.)

BIFF.   Gee, how'd you know we wanted a punching bag?

WILLY.   Well, it's the finest thing for the timing.

HAPPY. *(lies down on his back and pedals with his feet).*   I'm losing weight, you notice, Pop?

WILLY. *(to Happy).*   Jumping rope is good too.

BIFF.   Did you see the new football I got?

WILLY. *(examining the ball).*   Where'd you get a new ball?

BIFF.   The coach told me to practice my passing.

WILLY.   That so? And he gave you the ball, heh?

BIFF.   Well, I borrowed it from the locker room. *(He laughs confidentially.)*

WILLY *(laughing with him at the theft).*   I want you to return that.

HAPPY.   I told you he wouldn't like it!

BIFF. *(angrily).*   Well, I'm bringing it back!

WILLY *(stopping the incipient argument, to Happy).*   Sure, he's gotta practice with a regulation ball, doesn't he? *(To Biff.)* Coach'll probably congratulate you on your initiative!

BIFF.   Oh, he keeps congratulating my initiative all the time, Pop.

WILLY.   That's because he likes you. If somebody else took that ball there'd be an uproar. So what's the report, boys, what's the report?

BIFF.   Where'd you go this time, Dad? Gee we were lonesome for you.

WILLY *(pleased, puts an arm around each boy and they come down to the apron).*   Lonesome, heh?

BIFF.   Missed you every minute.

WILLY.   Don't say? Tell you a secret, boys. Don't breathe it to a soul. Someday I'll have my own business, and I'll never have to leave home anymore.

HAPPY.   Like Uncle Charley, heh?

WILLY.   Bigger than Uncle Charley! Because Charley is not—liked. He's liked, but he's not—well liked.

BIFF.   Where'd you go this time, Dad?

WILLY.   Well, I got on the road, and I went north to Providence. Met the Mayor.

BIFF.   The Mayor of Providence!

WILLY.   He was sitting in the hotel lobby.

BIFF.   What'd he say?

WILLY.   He said, "Morning!" And I said, "You got a fine city here, Mayor." And then he had coffee with me. And then I went to Waterbury. Waterbury is a fine city. Big clock city, the famous Waterbury clock. Sold a nice bill there. And then Boston—Boston is the cradle of the Revolution. A fine city. And a couple of other towns in Mass., and on to Portland and Bangor and straight home!

BIFF.   Gee, I'd love to go with you sometime, Dad.

WILLY.   Soon as summer comes.

HAPPY.   Promise?

WILLY.   You and Hap and I, and I'll show you all the towns. America is full of beautiful towns and fine, upstanding people. And they know me, boys, they know me up and down New England. The finest people. And when I bring you fellas up, there'll be open sesame for all of us, 'cause one thing, boys: I have friends. I can park my car in any street in New England, and the cops protect it like their own. This summer, heh?

BIFF AND HAPPY *(together)*.   Yeah! You bet!

WILLY.   We'll take our bathing suits.

HAPPY.   We'll carry your bags, Pop!

WILLY.   Oh, won't that be something! Me comin' into the Boston stores with you boys carryin' my bags. What a sensation! *(Biff is prancing around, practicing passing the ball.)* You nervous, Biff, about the game?

BIFF.   Not if you're gonna be there.

WILLY.   What do they say about you in school, now that they made you captain?

HAPPY.   There's a crowd of girls behind him every time the classes change.

BIFF *(taking Willy's hand)*.   This Saturday, Pop, this Saturday—just for you, I'm going to break through for a touchdown.

HAPPY.   You're supposed to pass.

BIFF.   I'm takin' one play for Pop. You watch me, Pop, and when I take off my helmet, that means I'm breakin' out. Then you watch me crash through that line!

WILLY *(kisses Biff)*.   Oh, wait'll I tell this in Boston!

(Bernard enters in knickers. He is younger than Biff, earnest and loyal, a worried boy.)

BERNARD.   Biff, where are you? You're supposed to study with me today.

WILLY.   Hey, looka Bernard. What're you lookin' so anemic about, Bernard?

BERNARD.   He's gotta study, Uncle Willy. He's got Regents next week.

HAPPY. *(tauntingly, spinning Bernard around)*.   Let's box, Bernard!

BERNARD.   Biff! *(He gets away from Happy.)* Listen, Biff, I heard Mr. Birnbaum say that if you don't start studyin' math he's gonna flunk you, and you won't graduate. I heard him!

WILLY.   You better study with him, Biff. Go ahead now.

BERNARD.   I heard him!

BIFF.   Oh, Pop, you didn't see my sneakers! *(He holds up a foot for Willy to look at.)*

WILLY.   Hey, that's a beautiful job of printing!

BERNARD *(wiping his glasses)*.   Just because he printed University of Virginia on his sneakers doesn't mean they've got to graduate him, Uncle Willy!

WILLY *(angrily)*.   What're you talking about? With scholarships to three universities they're gonna flunk him?

BERNARD.   But I heard Mr. Birnbaum say—

WILLY.   Don't be a pest, Bernard! *(To his boys.)* What an anemic!

BERNARD.   Okay, I'm waiting for you in my house, Biff.

(Bernard goes off. The Lomans laugh.)

WILLY.   Bernard is not well liked, is he?

BIFF.   He's liked, but he's not well liked.

HAPPY.   That's right, Pop.

WILLY.   That's just what I mean. Bernard can get the best marks in school, y'understand, but when he gets out in the business world, y'understand, you are going to be five times ahead of him. That's why I thank Almighty God you're both built like Adonises. Because the man who makes an appearance in the business world, the man who creates personal interest, is the man who gets ahead. Be liked and you will never want. You take me, for instance. I never have to wait in line to see a buyer. "Willy Loman is here!" That's all they have to know, and I go right through.

BIFF.   Did you knock them dead, Pop?

WILLY.   Knocked 'em cold in Providence, slaughtered 'em in Boston.

HAPPY *(on his back, pedaling again)*.   I'm losing weight, you notice, Pop?

(Linda enters as of old, a ribbon in her hair, carrying a basket of washing.)

LINDA *(with youthful energy)*.   Hello, dear!

WILLY.   Sweetheart!

LINDA.   How'd the Chevvy run?

WILLY.   Chevrolet, Linda, is the greatest car ever built. *(To the boys.)* Since when do you let your mother carry wash up the stairs?

BIFF.   Grab hold there, boy!

HAPPY.   Where to, Mom?

LINDA.   Hang them up on the line. And you better go down to your friends, Biff. The cellar is full of boys. They don't know what to do with themselves.

BIFF.   Ah, when Pop comes home they can wait!

WILLY *(laughs appreciatively)*.   You better go down and tell them what to do, Biff.

BIFF.   I think I'll have them sweep out the furnace room.

WILLY.   Good work, Biff.

BIFF *(goes through wall-line of kitchen to doorway at back and calls down)*.   Fellas! Everybody sweep out the furnace room! I'll be right down!

VOICES.   All right! Okay, Biff.

BIFF.   George and Sam and Frank, come out back! We're hangin' up the wash! Come on, Hap, on the double! *(He and Happy carry out the basket.)*

LINDA.   The way they obey him!

WILLY.   Well, that's training, the training. I'm tellin' you, I was sellin' thousands and thousands, but I had to come home.

LINDA.   Oh, the whole block'll be at that game. Did you sell anything?

WILLY.   I did five hundred gross in Providence and seven hundred gross in Boston.

LINDA.   No! Wait a minute, I've got a pencil. *(She pulls pencil and paper out of her apron pocket.)* That makes your commission . . . Two hundred—my God! Two hundred and twelve dollars!

WILLY.   Well, I didn't figure it yet, but . . .

LINDA.   How much did you do?

WILLY.   Well, I—I did—about a hundred and eighty gross in Providence. Well, no—it came to—roughly two hundred gross on the whole trip.

LINDA *(without hesitation)*.   Two hundred gross. That's . . . *(She figures.)*

WILLY.   The trouble was that three of the stores were half-closed for inventory in Boston. Otherwise I woulda broke records.

LINDA.   Well, it makes seventy dollars and some pennies. That's very good.

WILLY.   What do we owe?

LINDA.   Well, on the first there's sixteen dollars on the refrigerator—

WILLY.   Why sixteen?

LINDA.   Well, the fan belt broke, so it was a dollar eighty.

WILLY.   But it's brand new.

LINDA.   Well, the man said that's the way it is. Till they work themselves in, y'know.

(They move through the wall-line into the kitchen.)

WILLY.   I hope we didn't get stuck on that machine.

LINDA.   They got the biggest ads of any of them!

WILLY.   I know, it's a fine machine. What else?

LINDA.   Well, there's nine-sixty for the washing machine. And for the vacuum cleaner there's three and a half due on the fifteenth. Then the roof, you got twenty-one dollars remaining.

WILLY.   It don't leak, does it?

LINDA.   No, they did a wonderful job. Then you owe Frank for the carburetor.

WILLY.   I'm not going to pay that man! That goddam Chevrolet, they ought to prohibit the manufacture of that car!

LINDA.   Well, you owe him three and a half. And odds and ends, comes to around a hundred and twenty dollars by the fifteenth.

WILLY.   A hundred and twenty dollars! My God, if business don't pick up I don't know what I'm gonna do!

LINDA.   Well, next week you'll do better.

WILLY.   Oh, I'll knock 'em dead next week. I'll go to Hartford. I'm very well liked in Hartford. You know, the trouble is, Linda, people don't seem to take to me.

(They move onto the forestage.)

LINDA.   Oh, don't be foolish.

WILLY.   I know it when I walk in. They seem to laugh at me.

LINDA.   Why? Why would they laugh at you? Don't talk that way, Willy.

(Willy moves to the edge of the stage. Linda goes into the kitchen and starts to darn stockings.)

WILLY.   I don't know the reason for it, but they just pass me by. I'm not noticed.

LINDA.   But you're doing wonderful, dear. You're making seventy to a hundred dollars a week.

WILLY.   But I gotta be at it ten, twelve hours a day. Other men—I don't know—they do it easier. I don't know why—I can't stop myself—I talk too much. A man oughta come in with a few words. One thing about Charley. He's a man of few words, and they respect him.

LINDA.   You don't talk too much, you're just lively.

WILLY *(smiling)*.   Well, I figure, what the hell, life is short, a couple of jokes. *(To himself.)* I joke too much! *(The smile goes.)*

LINDA.   Why? You're—

WILLY.   I'm fat. I'm very—foolish to look at, Linda. I didn't tell you, but Christmas time I happened to be calling on F. H. Stewarts, and a salesman I know, as I was going in to see the buyer I heard him say something about—walrus. And I—I cracked him right across the face. I won't take that. I simply will not take that. But they do laugh at me. I know that.

LINDA.   Darling . . .

WILLY.   I gotta overcome it. I know I gotta overcome it. I'm not dressing to advantage, maybe.

LINDA.   Willy, darling, you're the handsomest man in the world—

WILLY.   Oh, no, Linda.

LINDA.   To me you are. *(Slight pause.)* The handsomest. *(From the darkness is heard the laughter of a woman. Willy doesn't turn to it, but it continues through Linda's lines.)* And the boys, Willy. Few men are idolized by their children the way you are.

(Music is heard as behind a scrim, to the left of the house, The Woman, dimly seen, is dressing.)

WILLY *(with great feeling).* You're the best there is, Linda, you're a pal, you know that? On the road—on the road I want to grab you sometimes and just kiss the life outa you. *(The laughter is loud now, and he moves into a brightening area at the left, where The Woman has come from behind the scrim and is standing, putting on her hat, looking into a "mirror" and laughing.)* 'Cause I get so lonely—especially when business is bad and there's nobody to talk to. I get the feeling that I'll never sell anything again, that I won't make a living for you, or a business, a business for the boys. *(He talks through The Woman's subsiding laughter; The Woman primps at the "mirror.")* There's so much I want to make for—

THE WOMAN. Me? You didn't make me, Willy. I picked you.

WILLY *(pleased).* You picked me?

THE WOMAN *(who is quite proper-looking, Willy's age).* I did. I've been sitting at that desk watching all the salesmen go by, day in, day out. But you've got such a sense of humor, and we do have such a good time together, don't we?

WILLY. Sure, sure. *(He takes her in his arms.)* Why do you have to go now?

THE WOMAN. It's two o'clock . . .

WILLY. No, come on in! *(He pulls her.)*

THE WOMAN. . . . my sisters'll be scandalized. When'll you be back?

WILLY. Oh, two weeks about. Will you come up again?

THE WOMAN. Sure thing. You do make me laugh. It's good for me. *(She squeezes his arm, kisses him.)* And I think you're a wonderful man.

WILLY. You picked me, heh?

THE WOMAN. Sure. Because you're so sweet. And such a kidder.

WILLY. Well, I'll see you next time I'm in Boston.

THE WOMAN. I'll put you right through to the buyers.

WILLY *(slapping her bottom).* Right. Well, bottoms up!

THE WOMAN *(slaps him gently and laughs).* You just kill me, Willy. *(He suddenly grabs her and kisses her roughly.)* You kill me. And thanks for the stockings. I love a lot of stockings. Well, good night.

WILLY. Good night. And keep your pores open!

THE WOMAN. Oh, Willy!

(The Woman bursts out laughing, and Linda's laughter blends in. The Woman disappears into the dark. Now the area at the kitchen table brightens. Linda is sitting where she was at the kitchen table, but now is mending a pair of her silk stockings.)

LINDA. You are, Willy. The handsomest man. You've got no reason to feel that—

WILLY *(coming out of The Woman's dimming area and going over to Linda).* I'll make it all up to you, Linda, I'll—

LINDA. There's nothing to make up, dear. You're doing fine, better than—

WILLY *(noticing her mending).* What's that?

LINDA. Just mending my stockings. They're so expensive—

WILLY *(angrily, taking them from her).* I won't have you mending stockings in this house! Now throw them out!

(Linda puts the stockings in her pocket.)

BERNARD *(entering on the run).* Where is he? If he doesn't study!

WILLY *(moving to the forestage, with great agitation).* You'll give him the answers!

BERNARD. I do, but I can't on a Regents! That's a state exam! They're liable to arrest me!

WILLY. Where is he? I'll whip him, I'll whip him!

LINDA. And he'd better give back that football, Willy, it's not nice.

WILLY.   Biff! Where is he? Why is he taking everything?

LINDA.   He's too rough with the girls, Willy. All the mothers are afraid of him!

WILLY.   I'll whip him!

BERNARD.   He's driving the car without a license!

(The Woman's laugh is heard.)

WILLY.   Shut up!

LINDA.   All the mothers—

WILLY.   Shut up!

BERNARD *(backing quietly away and out).*   Mr. Birnbaum says he's stuck up.

WILLY.   Get outa here!

BERNARD.   If he doesn't buckle down he'll flunk math! *(He goes off.)*

LINDA.   He's right, Willy, you've gotta—

WILLY *(exploding at her).*   There's nothing the matter with him! You want him to be a worm like Bernard? He's got spirit, personality . . . *(As he speaks, Linda, almost in tears, exits into the living room. Willy is alone in the kitchen, wilting and staring. The leaves are gone. It is night again, and the apartment houses look down from behind.)* Loaded with it. Loaded! What is he stealing? He's giving it back, isn't he? Why is he stealing? What did I tell him? I never in my life told him anything but decent things.

(Happy in pajamas has come down the stairs; Willy suddenly becomes aware of Happy's presence.)

HAPPY.   Let's go now, come on.

WILLY *(sitting down at the kitchen table).*   Huh! Why did she have to wax the floors herself? Everytime she waxes the floors she keels over. She knows that!

HAPPY.   Shh! Take it easy. What brought you back tonight?

WILLY.   I got an awful scare. Nearly hit a kid in Yonkers. God! Why didn't I go to Alaska with my brother Ben that time! Ben! That man was a genius, that man was success incarnate! What a mistake! He begged me to go.

HAPPY.   Well, there's no use in—

WILLY.   You guys! There was a man started with the clothes on his back and ended up with diamond mines!

HAPPY.   Boy, someday I'd like to know how he did it.

WILLY.   What's the mystery? The man knew what he wanted and went out and got it! Walked into a jungle, and comes out, the age of twenty-one, and he's rich! The world is an oyster, but you don't crack it open on a mattress!

HAPPY.   Pop, I told you I'm gonna retire you for life.

WILLY.   You'll retire me for life on seventy goddam dollars a week? And your women and your car and your apartment, and you'll retire me for life! Christ's sake, I couldn't get past Yonkers today! Where are you guys, where are you? The woods are burning! I can't drive a car!

(Charley has appeared in the doorway. He is a large man, slow of speech, laconic, immovable. In all he says, despite what he says, there is pity, and, now, trepidation. He has a robe over pajamas, slippers on his feet. He enters the kitchen.)

CHARLEY.   Everything all right?

HAPPY.   Yeah, Charley, everything's . . .

WILLY.   What's the matter?

CHARLEY.   I heard some noise. I thought something happened. Can't we do something about the walls? You sneeze in here, and in my house hats blow off.

HAPPY.   Let's go to bed, Dad. Come on.

(Charley signals to Happy to go.)

WILLY.   You go ahead, I'm not tired at the moment.

HAPPY *(to Willy)*.   Take it easy, huh? *(He exits.)*

WILLY.   What're you doin' up?

CHARLEY *(sitting down at the kitchen table opposite Willy)*.   Couldn't sleep good. I had a heartburn.

WILLY.   Well, you don't know how to eat.

CHARLEY.   I eat with my mouth.

WILLY.   No, you're ignorant. You gotta know about vitamins and things like that.

CHARLEY.   Come on, let's shoot. Tire you out a little.

WILLY *(hesitantly)*.   All right. You got cards?

CHARLEY *(taking a deck from his pocket)*.   Yeah, I got them. Someplace. What is it with those vitamins?

WILLY *(dealing)*.   They build up your bones. Chemistry.

CHARLEY.   Yeah, but there's no bones in a heartburn.

WILLY.   What are you talkin' about? Do you know the first thing about it?

CHARLEY.   Don't get insulted.

WILLY.   Don't talk about something you don't know anything about.

(They are playing. Pause.)

CHARLEY.   What're you doin' home?

WILLY.   A little trouble with the car.

CHARLEY.   Oh. *(Pause.)* I'd like to take a trip to California.

WILLY.   Don't say.

CHARLEY.   You want a job?

WILLY.   I got a job. I told you that. *(After a slight pause.)* What the hell are you offering me a job for?

CHARLEY.   Don't get insulted.

WILLY.   Don't insult me.

CHARLEY.   I don't see no sense in it. You don't have to go on this way.

WILLY.   I got a good job. *(Slight pause.)* What do you keep comin' in here for?

CHARLEY.   You want me to go?

WILLY *(after a pause, withering)*.   I can't understand it. He's going back to Texas again. What the hell is that?

CHARLEY.   Let him go.

WILLY.   I got nothin' to give him, Charley, I'm clean, I'm clean.

CHARLEY.   He won't starve. None a them starve. Forget about him.

WILLY.   Then what have I got to remember?

CHARLEY.   You take it too hard. To hell with it. When a deposit bottle is broken you don't get your nickel back.

WILLY.   That's easy enough for you to say.

CHARLEY.   That ain't easy for me to say.

WILLY.   Did you see the ceiling I put up in the living room?

CHARLEY.   Yeah, that's a piece of work. To put up a ceiling is a mystery to me. How do you do it?

WILLY.   What's the difference?

CHARLEY.   Well, talk about it.

WILLY.   You gonna put up a ceiling?

CHARLEY.   How could I put up a ceiling?

WILLY.   Then what the hell are you bothering me for?

CHARLEY.   You're insulted again.

WILLY.   A man who can't handle tools is not a man. You're disgusting.

CHARLEY.   Don't call me disgusting, Willy.

(Uncle Ben, carrying a valise and an umbrella, enters the forestage from around the right corner of the house. He is a stolid man, in his sixties, with a mustache and an authoritative air. He is utterly certain of his destiny, and there is an aura of far places about him. He enters exactly as Willy speaks.)

WILLY.   I'm getting awfully tired, Ben.

(Ben's music is heard. Ben looks around at everything.)

CHARLEY.   Good, keep playing; you'll sleep better. Did you call me Ben?

(Ben looks at his watch.)

WILLY.   That's funny. For a second there you reminded me of my brother Ben.

BEN.   I only have a few minutes. *(He strolls, inspecting the place. Willy and Charley continue playing.)*

CHARLEY.   You never heard from him again, heh? Since that time?

WILLY.   Didn't Linda tell you? Couple of weeks ago we got a letter from his wife in Africa. He died.

CHARLEY.   That so.

BEN *(chuckling)*.   So this is Brooklyn, eh?

CHARLEY.   Maybe you're in for some of his money.

WILLY.   Naa, he had seven sons. There's just one opportunity I had with that man . . .

BEN.   I must make a train, William. There are several properties I'm looking at in Alaska.

WILLY.   Sure, sure! If I'd gone with him to Alaska that time, everything would've been totally different.

CHARLEY.   Go on, you'd froze to death up there.

WILLY.   What're you talking about?

BEN.   Opportunity is tremendous in Alaska, William. Surprised you're not up there.

WILLY.   Sure, tremendous.

CHARLEY.   Heh?

WILLY.   There was the only man I ever met who knew the answers.

CHARLEY.   Who?

BEN.   How are you all?

WILLY *(taking a pot, smiling)*.   Fine, fine.

CHARLEY.   Pretty sharp tonight.

BEN.   Is Mother living with you?

WILLY.   No, she died a long time ago.

CHARLEY.   Who?

BEN.   That's too bad. Fine specimen of a lady, Mother.

WILLY *(to Charley)*.   Heh?

BEN.   I'd hoped to see the old girl.

CHARLEY.   Who died?

BEN.   Heard anything from Father, have you?

WILLY *(unnerved)*.   What do you mean, who died?

CHARLEY *(taking a pot)*.   What're you talkin' about?

BEN *(looking at his watch).*   William, it's half-past eight!

WILLY *(as though to dispel his confusion he angrily stops Charley's hand).*   That's my build!

CHARLEY.   I put the ace—

WILLY.   If you don't know how to play the game I'm not gonna throw my money away on you!

CHARLEY *(rising).*   It was my ace, for God's sake!

WILLY.   I'm through, I'm through!

BEN.   When did Mother die?

WILLY.   Long ago. Since the beginning you never knew how to play cards.

CHARLEY *(picks up the cards and goes to the door).*   All right! Next time I'll bring a deck with five aces.

WILLY.   I don't play that kind of game!

CHARLEY *(turning to him).*   You ought to be ashamed of yourself!

WILLY.   Yeah?

CHARLEY.   Yeah! *(He goes out.)*

WILLY *(slamming the door after him).*   Ignoramus!

BEN *(as Willy comes toward him through the wall-line of the kitchen).*   So you're William.

WILLY *(shaking Ben's hand).*   Ben! I've been waiting for you so long! What's the answer? How did you do it?

BEN.   Oh, there's a story in that.

(Linda enters the forestage, as of old, carrying the wash basket.)

LINDA.   Is this Ben?

BEN *(gallantly).*   How do you do, my dear.

LINDA.   Where've you been all these years? Willy's always wondered why you—

WILLY *(pulling Ben away from her impatiently).*   Where is Dad? Didn't you follow him? How did you get started?

BEN.   Well, I don't know how much you remember.

WILLY.   Well, I was just a baby, of course, only three or four years old—

BEN.   Three years and eleven months.

WILLY.   What a memory, Ben!

BEN.   I have many enterprises, William, and I have never kept books.

WILLY.   I remember I was sitting under the wagon in—was it Nebraska?

BEN.   It was South Dakota, and I gave you a bunch of wild flowers.

WILLY.   I remember you walking away down some open road.

BEN *(laughing).*   I was going to find Father in Alaska.

WILLY.   Where is he?

BEN.   At that age I had a very faulty view of geography, William. I discovered after a few days that I was heading due south, so instead of Alaska, I ended up in Africa.

LINDA.   Africa!

WILLY.   The Gold Coast!

BEN.   Principally diamond mines.

LINDA.   Diamond mines!

BEN.   Yes, my dear. But I've only a few minutes—

WILLY.   No! Boys! Boys! *(Young Biff and Happy appear.)* Listen to this. This is your Uncle Ben, a great man! Tell my boys, Ben!

BEN.   Why, boys, when I was seventeen I walked into the jungle, and when I was twenty-one I walked out. *(He laughs.)* And by God I was rich.

WILLY *(to the boys).*   You see what I been talking about? The greatest things can happen!

BEN *(glancing at his watch).*   I have an appointment in Ketchikan Tuesday week.

WILLY.   No, Ben! Please tell about Dad. I want my boys to hear. I want them to know the kind of stock they spring from. All I remember is a man with a big beard, and I was in Mamma's lap, sitting around a fire, and some kind of high music.

BEN.   His flute. He played the flute.

WILLY.   Sure, the flute, that's right!

(New music is heard, a high, rollicking tune.)

BEN.   Father was a very great and a very wild-hearted man. We would start in Boston, and he'd toss the whole family into the wagon, and then he'd drive the team right across the country; through Ohio, and Indiana, Michigan, Illinois, and all the Western states. And we'd stop in the towns and sell the flutes that he'd made on the way. Great inventor, Father. With one gadget he made more in a week than a man like you could make in a lifetime.

WILLY.   That's just the way I'm bringing them up, Ben—rugged, well liked, all-around.

BEN.   Yeah? *(To Biff.)* Hit that, boy—hard as you can. *(He pounds his stomach.)*

BIFF.   Oh, no, sir!

BEN *(taking boxing stance).*   Come on, get to me! *(He laughs.)*

WILLY.   Go to it, Biff! Go ahead, show him!

BIFF.   Okay! *(He cocks his fists and starts in.)*

LINDA *(to Willy).*   Why must he fight, dear?

BEN *(sparring with Biff).*   Good boy! Good boy!

WILLY.   How's that, Ben, heh?

HAPPY.   Give him the left, Biff!

LINDA.   Why are you fighting?

BEN.   Good boy! *(Suddenly comes in, trips Biff, and stands over him, the point of his umbrella poised over Biff's eye.)*

LINDA.   Look out, Biff!

BIFF.   Gee!

BEN *(patting Biff's knee).*   Never fight fair with a stranger, boy. You'll never get out of the jungle that way. *(Taking Linda's hand and bowing.)* It was an honor and a pleasure to meet you, Linda.

LINDA *(withdrawing her hand coldly, frightened).*   Have a nice—trip.

BEN *(to Willy).*   And good luck with your—what do you do?

WILLY.   Selling.

BEN.   Yes. Well . . . *(He raises his hand in farewell to all.)*

WILLY.   No, Ben, I don't want you to think . . . *(He takes Ben's arm to show him.)* It's Brooklyn, I know, but we hunt too.

BEN.   Really, now.

WILLY.   Oh, sure, there's snakes and rabbits and—that's why I moved out here. Why, Biff can fell any one of these trees in no time! Boys! Go right over to where they're building the apartment house and get some sand. We're gonna rebuild the entire front stoop right now! Watch this, Ben!

BIFF.   Yes, sir! On the double, Hap!

HAPPY *(as he and Biff run off).*   I lost weight, Pop, you notice?

(Charley enters in knickers, even before the boys are gone.)

CHARLEY.   Listen, if they steal anymore from that building the watchman'll put the cops on them!

LINDA *(to Willy).* Don't let Biff . . .

(Ben laughs lustily.)

WILLY. You shoulda seen the lumber they brought home last week. At least a dozen six-by-tens worth all kinds a money.

CHARLEY. Listen, if that watchman—

WILLY. I gave them hell, understand. But I got a couple of fearless characters there.

CHARLEY. Willy, the jails are full of fearless characters.

BEN *(clapping Willy on the back, with a laugh at Charley).* And the stock exchange, friend!

WILLY *(joining in Ben's laughter).* Where are the rest of your pants?

CHARLEY. My wife bought them.

WILLY. Now all you need is a golf club and you can go upstairs and go to sleep. *(To Ben.)* Great athlete! Between him and his son Bernard they can't hammer a nail!

BERNARD *(rushing in).* The watchman's chasing Biff!

WILLY *(angrily).* Shut up! He's not stealing anything!

LINDA *(alarmed, hurrying off left).* Where is he? Biff, dear! *(She exits.)*

WILLY *(moving toward the left, away from Ben).* There's nothing wrong. What's the matter with you?

BEN. Nervy boy. Good!

WILLY *(laughing).* Oh, nerves of iron, that Biff!

CHARLEY. Don't know what it is. My New England man comes back and he's bleedin', they murdered him up there.

WILLY. It's contacts, Charley, I got important contacts!

CHARLEY *(sarcastically).* Glad to hear it, Willy. Come in later, we'll shoot a little casino. I'll take some of your Portland money. *(He laughs at Willy and exits.)*

WILLY *(turning to Ben).* Business is bad, it's murderous. But not for me, of course.

BEN. I'll stop by on my way back to Africa.

WILLY *(longingly).* Can't you stay a few days? You're just what I need, Ben, because I—I have a fine position here, but I—well, Dad left when I was such a baby and I never had a chance to talk to him and I still feel—kind of temporary about myself.

BEN. I'll be late for my train.

(They are at opposite ends of the stage.)

WILLY. Ben, my boys—can't we talk? They'd go into the jaws of hell for me, see, but I—

BEN. William, you're being first-rate with your boys. Outstanding, manly chaps!

WILLY *(hanging on to his words).* Oh, Ben, that's good to hear! Because sometimes I'm afraid that I'm not teaching them the right kind of—Ben, how should I teach them?

BEN *(giving great weight to each word, and with a certain vicious audacity).* William, when I walked into the jungle, I was seventeen. When I walked out I was twenty-one. And, by God, I was rich! *(He goes off into darkness around the right corner of the house.)*

WILLY. . . . was rich! That's just the spirit I want to imbue them with! To walk into a jungle! I was right! I was right! I was right!

(Ben is gone, but Willy is still speaking to him as Linda, in nightgown and robe, enters the kitchen, glances around for Willy, then goes to the door of the house, looks out and sees him. Comes down to his left. He looks at her.)

LINDA. Willy, dear? Willy?

WILLY. I was right!

LINDA.   Did you have some cheese? *(He can't answer.)* It's very late, darling. Come to bed, heh?

WILLY *(looking straight up)*.   Gotta break your neck to see a star in this yard.

LINDA.   You coming in?

WILLY.   Whatever happened to that diamond watch fob? Remember? When Ben came from Africa that time? Didn't he give me a watch fob with a diamond in it?

LINDA.   You pawned it, dear. Twelve, thirteen years ago. For Biff's radio correspondence course.

WILLY.   Gee, that was a beautiful thing. I'll take a walk.

LINDA.   But you're in your slippers.

WILLY *(starting to go around the house at the left)*.   I was right! I was! *(Half to Linda, as he goes, shaking his head.)* What a man! There was a man worth talking to. I was right!

LINDA *(calling after Willy)*.   But in your slippers, Willy!

(Willy is almost gone when Biff, in his pajamas, comes down the stairs and enters the kitchen.)

BIFF.   What is he doing out there?

LINDA.   Sh!

BIFF.   God Almighty, Mom, how long has he been doing this?

LINDA.   Don't, he'll hear you.

BIFF.   What the hell is the matter with him?

LINDA.   It'll pass by morning.

BIFF.   Shouldn't we do anything?

LINDA.   Oh, my dear, you should do a lot of things, but there's nothing to do, so go to sleep.

(Happy comes down the stair and sits on the steps.)

HAPPY.   I never heard him so loud, Mom.

LINDA.   Well, come around more often; you'll hear him. *(She sits down at the table and mends the lining of Willy's jacket.)*

BIFF.   Why didn't you ever write me about this, Mom?

LINDA.   How would I write to you? For over three months you had no address.

BIFF.   I was on the move. But you know I thought of you all the time. You know that, don't you, pal?

LINDA.   I know, dear, I know. But he likes to have a letter. Just to know that there's still a possibility for better things.

BIFF.   He's not like this all the time, is he?

LINDA.   It's when you come home he's always the worst.

BIFF.   When I come home?

LINDA.   When you write you're coming, he's all smiles, and talks about the future, and—he's just wonderful. And then the closer you seem to come, the more shaky he gets, and then, by the time you get here, he's arguing, and he seems angry at you. I think it's just that maybe he can't bring himself to—to open up to you. Why are you so hateful to each other? Why is that?

BIFF *(evasively)*.   I'm not hateful, Mom.

LINDA.   But you no sooner come in the door than you're fighting!

BIFF.   I don't know why. I mean to change. I'm tryin', Mom, you understand?

LINDA.   Are you home to stay now?

BIFF.   I don't know. I want to look around, see what's doin'.

LINDA.   Biff, you can't look around all your life, can you?

BIFF.   I just can't take hold, Mom. I can't take hold of some kind of a life.

LINDA.   Biff, a man is not a bird, to come and go with the springtime.

BIFF.   Your hair . . . *(He touches her hair.)* Your hair got so gray.

LINDA.   Oh, it's been gray since you were in high school. I just stopped dyeing it, that's all.

BIFF.   Dye it again, will ya? I don't want my pal looking old. *(He smiles.)*

LINDA.   You're such a boy! You think you can go away for a year and . . . You've got to get it into your head now that one day you'll knock on this door and there'll be strange people here—

BIFF.   What are you talking about? You're not even sixty, Mom.

LINDA.   But what about your father?

BIFF *(lamely)*.   Well, I meant him too.

HAPPY.   He admires Pop.

LINDA.   Biff, dear, if you don't have any feeling for him, then you can't have any feeling for me.

BIFF.   Sure I can, Mom.

LINDA.   No. You can't just come to see me, because I love him. *(With a threat, but only a threat, of tears.)* He's the dearest man in the world to me, and I won't have anyone making him feel unwanted and low and blue. You've got to make up your mind now, darling, there's no leeway anymore. Either he's your father and you pay him that respect, or else you're not to come here. I know he's not easy to get along with—nobody knows that better than me—but . . .

WILLY *(from the left, with a laugh)*.   Hey, hey, Biffo!

BIFF *(starting to go out after Willy)*.   What the hell is the matter with him? *(Happy stops him.)*

LINDA.   Don't—don't go near him!

BIFF.   Stop making excuses for him! He always, always wiped the floor with you. Never had an ounce of respect for you.

HAPPY.   He's always had respect for—

BIFF.   What the hell do you know about it?

HAPPY *(surlily)*.   Just don't call him crazy!

BIFF.   He's got no character—Charley wouldn't do this. Not in his own house— spewing out that vomit from his mind.

HAPPY.   Charley never had to cope with what he's got to.

BIFF.   People are worse off than Willy Loman. Believe me, I've seen them!

LINDA.   Then make Charley your father, Biff. You can't do that, can you? I don't say he's a great man. Willy Loman never made a lot of money. His name was never in the paper. He's not the finest character that ever lived. But he's a human being, and a terrible thing is happening to him. So attention must be paid. He's not to be allowed to fall into his grave like an old dog. Attention, attention must be finally paid to such a person. You called him crazy—

BIFF.   I didn't mean—

LINDA.   No, a lot of people think he's lost his—balance. But you don't have to be very smart to know what his trouble is. The man is exhausted.

HAPPY.   Sure!

LINDA.   A small man can be just as exhausted as a great man. He works for a company thirty-six years this March, opens up unheard-of territories to their trademark, and now in his old age they take his salary away.

HAPPY *(indignantly)*.   I didn't know that, Mom.

LINDA.   You never asked, my dear! Now that you get your spending money some-place else you don't trouble your mind with him.

HAPPY.   But I gave you money last—

LINDA.   Christmas time, fifty dollars! To fix the hot water it cost ninety-seven fifty! For five weeks he's been on straight commission, like a beginner, an unknown!

BIFF.   Those ungrateful bastards!

LINDA.   Are they any worse than his sons? When he brought them business, when he was young, they were glad to see him. But now his old friends, the old buyers that loved him so and always found some order to hand him in a pinch—they're all dead, retired. He used to be able to make six, seven calls a day in Boston. Now he takes his valises out of the car and puts them back and takes them out again and he's exhausted. Instead of walking he talks now. He drives seven hundred miles, and when he gets there no one knows him anymore, no one welcomes him. And what goes through a man's mind, driving seven hundred miles home without having earned a cent? Why shouldn't he talk to himself? Why? When he has to go to Charley and borrow fifty dollars a week and pretend to me that it's his pay? How long can that go on? How long? You see what I'm sitting here and waiting for? And you tell me he has no character? The man who never worked a day but for your benefit? When does he get the medal for that? Is this his reward—to turn around at the age of sixty-three and find his sons, who he loved better than his life, one a philandering bum—

HAPPY.   Mom!

LINDA.   That's all you are, my baby! *(To Biff.)* And you! What happened to the love you had for him? You were such pals! How you used to talk to him on the phone every night! How lonely he was till he could come home to you!

BIFF.   All right, Mom. I'll live here in my room, and I'll get a job. I'll keep away from him, that's all.

LINDA.   No, Biff. You can't stay here and fight all the time.

BIFF.   He threw me out of this house, remember that.

LINDA.   Why did he do that? I never knew why.

BIFF.   Because I know he's a fake and he doesn't like anybody around who knows!

LINDA.   Why a fake? In what way? What do you mean?

BIFF.   Just don't lay it all at my feet. It's between me and him—that's all I have to say. I'll chip in from now on. He'll settle for half my pay check. He'll be all right. I'm going to bed. *(He starts for the stairs.)*

LINDA.   He won't be all right.

BIFF *(turning on the stairs, furiously)*.   I hate this city and I'll stay here. Now what do you want?

LINDA.   He's dying, Biff.

(Happy turns quickly to her, shocked.)

BIFF *(after a pause)*.   Why is he dying?

LINDA.   He's been trying to kill himself.

BIFF *(with great horror)*.   How?

LINDA.   I live from day to day.

BIFF.   What're you talking about?

LINDA.   Remember I wrote you that he smashed up the car again? In February?

BIFF.   Well?

LINDA.   The insurance inspector came. He said that they have evidence. That all these accidents in the last year—weren't—weren't—accidents.

HAPPY.   How can they tell that? That's a lie.

LINDA.   It seems there's a woman . . . *(She takes a breath as)*

BIFF *(sharply but contained).* | What woman?

LINDA *(simultaneously).* | . . . . and this woman . . .

LINDA.   What?

BIFF.   Nothing. Go ahead.

LINDA.   What did you say?

BIFF.   Nothing. I just said what woman?

HAPPY.   What about her?

LINDA.   Well, it seems she was walking down the road and saw his car. She says that he wasn't driving fast at all, and that he didn't skid. She says he came to that little bridge, and then deliberately smashed into the railing, and it was only the shallowness of the water that saved him.

BIFF.   Oh, no, he probably just fell asleep again.

LINDA.   I don't think he fell asleep.

BIFF.   Why not?

LINDA.   Last month . . . *(With great difficulty.)* Oh, boys, it's so hard to say a thing like this! He's just a big stupid man to you, but I tell you there's more good in him than in many other people. *(She chokes, wipes her eyes.)* I was looking for a fuse. The lights blew out, and I went down the cellar. And behind the fuse box—it happened to fall out—was a length of rubber pipe—just short.

HAPPY.   No kidding!

LINDA.   There's a little attachment on the end of it. I knew right away. And sure enough, on the bottom of the water heater there's a new little nipple on the gas pipe.

HAPPY *(angrily).*   That—jerk.

BIFF.   Did you have it taken off?

LINDA.   I'm—I'm ashamed to. How can I mention it to him? Every day I go down and take away that little rubber pipe. But, when he comes home, I put it back where it was. How can I insult him that way? I don't know what to do. I live from day to day, boys. I tell you, I know every thought in his mind. It sounds so old-fashioned and silly, but I tell you he put his whole life into you and you've turned your backs on him. *(She is bent over in the chair, weeping, her face in her hands.)* Biff, I swear to God! Biff, his life is in your hands!

HAPPY *(to Biff).*   How do you like that damned fool!

BIFF *(kissing her).*   All right, pal, all right. It's all settled now. I've been remiss. I know that, Mom. But now I'll stay, and I swear to you, I'll apply myself. *(Kneeling in front of her, in a fever of self-reproach.)* It's just—you see, Mom, I don't fit in business. Not that I won't try. I'll try, and I'll make good.

HAPPY.   Sure you will. The trouble with you in business was you never tried to please people.

BIFF.   I know, I—

HAPPY.   Like when you worked for Harrison's. Bob Harrison said you were tops, and then you go and do some damn fool thing like whistling whole songs in the elevator like a comedian.

BIFF *(against Happy).*   So what? I like to whistle sometimes.

HAPPY.   You don't raise a guy to a responsible job who whistles in the elevator!

LINDA.   Well, don't argue about it now.

HAPPY.   Like when you'd go off and swim in the middle of the day instead of taking the line around.

BIFF *(his resentment rising).* Well, don't you run off? You take off sometimes, don't you? On a nice summer day?

HAPPY. Yeah, but I cover myself!

LINDA. Boys!

HAPPY. If I'm going to take a fade the boss can call any number where I'm supposed to be and they'll swear to him that I just left. I'll tell you something that I hate to say, Biff, but in the business world some of them think you're crazy.

BIFF *(angered).* Screw the business world!

HAPPY. All right, screw it! Great, but cover yourself!

LINDA. Hap, Hap!

BIFF. I don't care what they think! They've laughed at Dad for years, and you know why? Because we don't belong in this nuthouse of a city! We should be mixing cement on some open plain, or—or carpenters. A carpenter is allowed to whistle!

(Willy walks in from the entrance of the house, at left.)

WILLY. Even your grandfather was better than a carpenter. *(Pause. They watch him.)* You never grew up. Bernard does not whistle in the elevator, I assure you.

BIFF *(as though to laugh Willy out of it).* Yeah, but you do, Pop.

WILLY. I never in my life whistled in an elevator! And who in the business world thinks I'm crazy?

BIFF. I didn't mean it like that, Pop. Now don't make a whole thing out of it, will ya?

WILLY. Go back to the West! Be a carpenter, a cowboy, enjoy yourself!

LINDA. Willy, he was just saying—

WILLY. I heard what he said!

HAPPY *(trying to quiet Willy).* Hey, Pop, come on now . . .

WILLY *(continuing over Happy's line).* They laugh at me, heh? Go to Filene's, go to the Hub, go to Slattery's, Boston. Call out the name Willy Loman and see what happens! Big shot!

BIFF. All right, Pop.

WILLY. Big!

BIFF. All right!

WILLY. Why do you always insult me?

BIFF. I didn't say a word. *(To Linda.)* Did I say a word?

LINDA. He didn't say anything, Willy.

WILLY *(going to the doorway of the living room).* All right, good night, good night.

LINDA. Willy, dear, he just decided . . .

WILLY *(to Biff).* If you get tired hanging around tomorrow, paint the ceiling I put up in the living room.

BIFF. I'm leaving early tomorrow.

HAPPY. He's going to see Bill Oliver, Pop.

WILLY *(interestedly).* Oliver? For what?

BIFF *(with reserve, but trying, trying).* He always said he'd stake me. I'd like to go into business, so maybe I can take him up on it.

LINDA. Isn't that wonderful?

WILLY. Don't interrupt. What's wonderful about it? There's fifty men in the City of New York who'd stake him. *(To Biff.)* Sporting goods?

BIFF. I guess so. I know something about it and—

WILLY. He knows something about it! You know sporting goods better than Spalding, for God's sake! How much is he giving you?

BIFF.   I don't know, I didn't even see him yet, but—

WILLY.   Then what're you talkin' about?

BIFF *(getting angry)*.   Well, all I said was I'm gonna see him, that's all!

WILLY *(turning away)*.   Ah, you're counting your chickens again.

BIFF *(starting left for the stairs)*.   Oh, Jesus, I'm going to sleep!

WILLY *(calling after him)*.   Don't curse in this house!

BIFF *(turning)*.   Since when did you get so clean?

HAPPY *(trying to stop them)*.   Wait a . . .

WILLY.   Don't use that language to me! I won't have it!

HAPPY *(grabbing Biff, shouts)*.   Wait a minute! I got an idea. I got a feasible idea. Come here, Biff, let's talk this over now, let's talk some sense here. When I was down in Florida last time, I thought of a great idea to sell sporting goods. It just came back to me. You and I, Biff—we have a line, the Loman Line. We train a couple of weeks, and put on a couple of exhibitions, see?

WILLY.   That's an idea!

HAPPY.   Wait! We form two basketball teams, see? Two water polo teams. We play each other. It's a million dollars' worth of publicity. Two brothers, see? The Loman Brothers. Displays in the Royal Palms—all the hotels. And banners over the ring and the basketball court: "Loman Brothers." Baby, we could sell sporting goods!

WILLY.   That is a one-million-dollar idea!

LINDA.   Marvelous!

BIFF.   I'm in great shape as far as that's concerned.

HAPPY.   And the beauty of it is, Biff, it wouldn't be like a business. We'd be out playin' ball again . . .

BIFF *(enthused)*.   Yeah, that's . . .

WILLY.   Million-dollar . . .

HAPPY.   And you wouldn't get fed up with it, Biff. It'd be the family again. There'd be the old honor, and comradeship, and if you wanted to go off for a swim or somethin'—well, you'd do it! Without some smart cooky gettin' up ahead of you!

WILLY.   Lick the world! You guys together could absolutely lick the civilized world.

BIFF.   I'll see Oliver tomorrow. Hap, if we could work that out . . .

LINDA.   Maybe things are beginning to—

WILLY *(wildly enthused, to Linda)*.   Stop interrupting! *(To Biff.)* But don't wear sport jacket and slacks when you see Oliver.

BIFF.   No, I'll—

WILLY.   A business suit, and talk as little as possible, and don't crack any jokes.

BIFF.   He did like me. Always liked me.

LINDA.   He loved you!

WILLY *(to Linda)*.   Will you stop! *(To Biff.)* Walk in very serious. You are not applying for a boy's job. Money is to pass. Be quiet, fine, and serious. Everybody likes a kidder, but nobody lends him money.

HAPPY.   I'll try to get some myself, Biff. I'm sure I can.

WILLY.   I see great things for you kids, I think your troubles are over. But remember, start big and you'll end big. Ask for fifteen. How much you gonna ask for?

BIFF.   Gee, I don't know—

WILLY.   And don't say "Gee." "Gee" is a boy's word. A man walking in for fifteen thousand dollars does not say "Gee!"

BIFF.   Ten, I think, would be top though.

WILLY.   Don't be so modest. You always started too low. Walk in with a big laugh. Don't look worried. Start off with a couple of your good stories to lighten things up. It's not what you say, it's how you say it—because personality always wins the day.

LINDA.   Oliver always thought the highest of him—

WILLY.   Will you let me talk?

BIFF.   Don't yell at her, Pop, will ya?

WILLY *(angrily)*.   I was talking, wasn't I?

BIFF.   I don't like you yelling at her all the time, and I'm tellin' you, that's all.

WILLY.   What're you, takin' over this house?

LINDA.   Willy—

WILLY *(turning to her)*.   Don't take his side all the time, goddammit!

BIFF *(furiously)*.   Stop yelling at her!

WILLY *(suddenly pulling on his cheek, beaten down, guilt ridden)*.   Give my best to Bill Oliver—he may remember me. *(He exits through the living room doorway.)*

LINDA *(her voice subdued)*.   What'd you have to start that for? *(Biff turns away.)* You see how sweet he was as soon as you talked hopefully? *(She goes over to Biff.)* Come up and say good night to him. Don't let him go to bed that way.

HAPPY.   Come on, Biff, let's buck him up.

LINDA.   Please, dear. Just say good night. It takes so little to make him happy. Come. *(She goes through the living room doorway, calling upstairs from within the living room.)* Your pajamas are hanging in the bathroom, Willy!

HAPPY *(looking toward where Linda went out)*.   What a woman! They broke the mold when they made her. You know that, Biff?

BIFF.   He's off salary. My God, working on commission!

HAPPY.   Well, let's face it: he's no hot-shot selling man. Except that sometimes, you have to admit, he's a sweet personality.

BIFF *(deciding)*.   Lend me ten bucks, will ya? I want to buy some new ties.

HAPPY.   I'll take you to a place I know. Beautiful stuff. Wear one of my striped shirts tomorrow.

BIFF.   She got gray. Mom got awful old. Gee, I'm gonna go in to Oliver tomorrow and knock him for a—

HAPPY.   Come on up. Tell that to Dad. Let's give him a whirl. Come on.

BIFF *(steamed up)*.   You know, with ten thousand bucks, boy!

HAPPY *(as they go into the living room)*.   That's the talk, Biff, that's the first time I've heard the old confidence out of you! *(From within the living room, fading off.)* You're gonna live with me, kid, and any babe you want just say the word . . . *(The last lines are hardly heard. They are mounting the stairs to their parents' bedroom.)*

LINDA *(entering her bedroom and addressing Willy, who is in the bathroom. She is straightening the bed for him)*.   Can you do anything about the shower? It drips.

WILLY *(from the bathroom)*.   All of a sudden everything falls to pieces. Goddam plumbing, oughta be sued, those people. I hardly finished putting it in and the thing . . . *(His words rumble off.)*

LINDA.   I'm just wondering if Oliver will remember him. You think he might?

WILLY *(coming out of the bathroom in his pajamas)*.   Remember him? What's the matter with you, you crazy? If he'd've stayed with Oliver he'd be on top by now! Wait'll Oliver gets a look at him. You don't know the average caliber anymore. The average young man today—*(he is getting into bed)*—is got a caliber of zero. Greatest thing in the world for him was to bum around.

(Biff and Happy enter the bedroom. Slight pause.)

WILLY *(stops short, looking at Biff)*.   Glad to hear it, boy.

HAPPY.   He wanted to say good night to you, sport.

WILLY *(to Biff)*.   Yeah. Knock him dead, boy. What'd you want to tell me?

BIFF.   Just take it easy, Pop. Good night. *(He turns to go.)*

WILLY *(unable to resist)*.   And if anything falls off the desk while you're talking to him—like a package or something—don't you pick it up. They have office boys for that.

LINDA.   I'll make a big breakfast—

WILLY.   Will you let me finish? *(To Biff.)* Tell him you were in the business in the West. Not farm work.

BIFF.   All right, Dad.

LINDA.   I think everything—

WILLY *(going right through her speech)*.   And don't undersell yourself. No less than fifteen thousand dollars.

BIFF *(unable to bear him)*.   Okay. Good night, Mom. *(He starts moving.)*

WILLY.   Because you got a greatness in you, Biff, remember that. You got all kinds of greatness . . . *(He lies back, exhausted. Biff walks out.)*

LINDA *(calling after Biff)*.   Sleep well, darling!

HAPPY.   I'm gonna get married, Mom. I wanted to tell you.

LINDA.   Go to sleep, dear.

HAPPY *(going)*.   I just wanted to tell you.

WILLY.   Keep up the good work. *(Happy exits.)* God . . . remember that Ebbets Field game? The championship of the city?

LINDA.   Just rest. Should I sing to you?

WILLY.   Yeah. Sing to me. *(Linda hums a soft lullaby.)* When that team came out—he was the tallest, remember?

LINDA.   Oh, yes. And in gold.

(Biff enters the darkened kitchen, takes a cigarette, and leaves the house. He comes downstage into a golden pool of light. He smokes, staring at the night.)

WILLY.   Like a young god. Hercules—something like that. And the sun, the sun all around him. Remember how he waved to me? Right up from the field, with the representatives of three colleges standing by? And the buyers I brought, and the cheers when he came out—Loman, Loman, Loman! God Almighty, he'll be great yet. A star like that, magnificent, can never really fade away!

(The light on Willy is fading. The gas heater begins to glow through the kitchen wall, near the stairs, a blue flame beneath red coils.)

LINDA *(timidly)*.   Willy dear, what has he got against you?

WILLY.   I'm so tired. Don't talk anymore.

(Biff slowly returns to the kitchen. He stops, stares toward the heater.)

LINDA.   Will you ask Howard to let you work in New York?

WILLY.   First thing in the morning. Everything'll be all right. *(Biff reaches behind the heater and draws out a length of rubber tubing. He is horrified and turns his head toward Willy's room, still dimly lit, from which the strains of Linda's desperate but monotonous humming rise. Staring through the window into the moonlight.)*   Gee, look at the moon moving between the buildings!

(Biff wraps the tubing around his hand and quickly goes up the stairs.)

ACT II

(Music is heard, gay and bright. The curtain rises as the music fades away. Willy, in shirt sleeves, is sitting at the kitchen table, sipping coffee, his hat in his lap. Linda is filling his cup when she can.)

WILLY.   Wonderful coffee. Meal in itself.

LINDA.   Can I make you some eggs?

WILLY.   No. Take a breath.

LINDA.   You look so rested, dear.

WILLY.   I slept like a dead one. First time in months. Imagine, sleeping till ten on a Tuesday morning. Boys left nice and early, heh?

LINDA.   They were out of here by eight o'clock.

WILLY.   Good work!

LINDA.   It was so thrilling to see them leaving together. I can't get over the shaving lotion in this house!

WILLY *(smiling)*.   Mmm—

LINDA.   Biff was very changed this morning. His whole attitude seemed to be hopeful. He couldn't wait to get downtown to see Oliver.

WILLY.   He's heading for a change. There's no question, there simply are certain men that take longer to get—solidified. How did he dress?

LINDA.   His blue suit. He's so handsome in that suit. He could be a—anything in that suit!

(Willy gets up from the table. Linda holds his jacket for him.)

WILLY.   There's no question, no question at all. Gee, on the way home tonight I'd like to buy some seeds.

LINDA *(laughing)*.   That'd be wonderful. But not enough sun gets back there. Nothing'll grow anymore.

WILLY.   You wait, kid, before it's all over we're gonna get a little place out in the country, and I'll raise some vegetables, a couple of chickens . . .

LINDA.   You'll do it yet, dear.

(Willy walks out of his jacket. Linda follows him.)

WILLY.   And they'll get married, and come for a weekend. I'd build a little guest house. 'Cause I got so many fine tools, all I'd need would be a little lumber and some peace of mind.

LINDA *(joyfully)*.   I sewed the lining . . .

WILLY.   I could build two guest houses, so they'd both come. Did he decide how much he's going to ask Oliver for?

LINDA *(getting him into the jacket)*.   He didn't mention it, but I imagine ten or fifteen thousand. You going to talk to Howard today?

WILLY.   Yeah. I'll put it to him straight and simple. He'll just have to take me off the road.

LINDA.   And Willy, don't forget to ask for a little advance, because we've got the insurance premium. It's the grace period now.

WILLY.   That's a hundred . . . ?

LINDA.   A hundred and eight, sixty-eight. Because we're a little short again.

WILLY.   Why are we short?

LINDA.   Well, you had the motor job on the car . . .

WILLY.   That goddam Studebaker!

LINDA.   And you got one more payment on the refrigerator . . .

WILLY.   But it just broke again!

LINDA.   Well, it's old, dear.

WILLY.   I told you we should've bought a well-advertised machine. Charley bought a General Electric and it's twenty years old and it's still good, that son-of-a-bitch.

LINDA.   But, Willy—

WILLY.   Whoever heard of a Hastings refrigerator? Once in my life I would like to own something outright before it's broken! I'm always in a race with the junkyard! I just finished paying for the car and it's on its last legs. The refrigerator consumes belts like a goddamn maniac. They time those things. They time them so when you finally paid for them, they're used up.

LINDA *(buttoning up his jacket as he unbuttons it).*   All told, about two hundred dollars would carry us, dear. But that includes the last payment on the mortgage. After this payment, Willy, the house belongs to us.

WILLY.   It's twenty-five years!

LINDA.   Biff was nine years old when we bought it.

WILLY.   Well, that's a great thing. To weather a twenty-five year mortgage is—

LINDA.   It's an accomplishment.

WILLY.   All the cement, the lumber, the reconstruction I put in this house! There ain't a crack to be found in it anymore.

LINDA.   Well, it served its purpose.

WILLY.   What purpose? Some stranger'll come along, move in, and that's that. If only Biff would take this house, and raise a family . . . *(He starts to go.)* Good-by, I'm late.

LINDA *(suddenly remembering).*   Oh, I forgot! You're supposed to meet them for dinner.

WILLY.   Me?

LINDA.   At Frank's Chop House on Forty-eighth near Sixth Avenue.

WILLY.   Is that so! How about you?

LINDA.   No, just the three of you. They're gonna blow you to a big meal!

WILLY.   Don't say! Who thought of that?

LINDA.   Biff came to me this morning, Willy, and he said, "Tell Dad, we want to blow him to a big meal." Be there six o'clock. You and your two boys are going to have dinner.

WILLY.   Gee whiz! That's really somethin'. I'm gonna knock Howard for a loop, kid. I'll get an advance, and I'll come home with a New York job. Goddammit, now I'm gonna do it!

LINDA.   Oh, that's the spirit, Willy!

WILLY.   I will never get behind a wheel the rest of my life!

LINDA.   It's changing, Willy, I can feel it changing!

WILLY.   Beyond a question. G'by, I'm late. *(He starts to go again.)*

LINDA *(calling after him as she runs to the kitchen table for a handkerchief).*   You got your glasses?

WILLY *(feels for them, then comes back in).*   Yeah, yeah, got my glasses.

LINDA *(giving him the handkerchief).*   And a handkerchief.

WILLY.   Yeah, handkerchief.

LINDA.   And your saccharine?

WILLY.   Yeah, my saccharine.

LINDA.   Be careful on the subway stairs.

(She kisses him, and a silk stocking is seen hanging from her hand. Willy notices it.)

WILLY.   Will you stop mending stockings? At least while I'm in the house. It gets me nervous. I can't tell you. Please.

(Linda hides the stocking in her hand as she follows Willy across the forestage in front of the house.)

LINDA.   Remember, Frank's Chop House.

WILLY *(passing the apron).*   Maybe beets would grow out there.

LINDA *(laughing).*   But you tried so many times.

WILLY.   Yeah. Well, don't work hard today. *(He disappears around the right corner of the house.)*

LINDA.   Be careful! *(As Willy vanishes, Linda waves to him. Suddenly the phone rings. She runs across the stage and into the kitchen and lifts it.)* Hello? Oh, Biff! I'm so glad you called, I just . . . Yes, sure, I just told him. Yes, he'll be there for dinner at six o'clock, I didn't forget. Listen, I was just dying to tell you. You know that little rubber pipe I told you about? That he connected to the gas heater? I finally decided to go down the cellar this morning and take it away and destroy it. But it's gone! Imagine? He took it away himself, it isn't there! *(She listens.)* When? Oh, then you took it. Oh—nothing, it's just that I'd hoped he'd taken it away himself. Oh, I'm not worried, darling, because this morning he left in such high spirits, it was like the old days! I'm not afraid anymore. Did Mr. Oliver see you? . . . Well, you wait there then. And make a nice impression on him, darling. Just don't perspire too much before you see him. And have a nice time with Dad. He may have big news too! . . . That's right, a New York job. And be sweet to him tonight, dear. Be loving to him. Because he's only a little boat looking for a harbor. *(She is trembling with sorrow and joy.)* Oh, that's wonderful, Biff, you'll save his life. Thanks, darling. Just put your arm around him when he comes into the restaurant. Give him a smile. That's the boy . . . Good-by, dear. . . . You got your comb? . . . That's fine. Good-by, Biff dear.

(In the middle of her speech, Howard Wagner, thirty-six, wheels in a small typewriter table on which is a wire-recording machine and proceeds to plug it in. This is on the left forestage. Light slowly fades on Linda as it rises on Howard. Howard is intent on threading the machine and only glances over his shoulder as Willy appears.)

WILLY.   Pst! Pst!

HOWARD.   Hello, Willy, come in.

WILLY.   Like to have a little talk with you, Howard.

HOWARD.   Sorry to keep you waiting. I'll be with you in a minute.

WILLY.   What's that, Howard?

HOWARD.   Didn't you ever see one of these? Wire recorder.

WILLY.   Oh. Can we talk a minute?

HOWARD.   Records things. Just got delivery yesterday. Been driving me crazy, the most terrific machine I ever saw in my life. I was up all night with it.

WILLY.   What do you do with it?

HOWARD.   I bought it for dictation, but you can do anything with it. Listen to this. I had it home last night. Listen to what I picked up. The first one is my daughter. Get this. *(He flicks the switch and "Roll out the Barrel" is heard being whistled.)* Listen to that kid whistle.

WILLY.   That is lifelike, isn't it?

HOWARD.   Seven years old. Get that tone.

WILLY.   Ts, ts. Like to ask a little favor if you . . .

(The whistling breaks off, and the voice of Howard's daughter is heard.)

HIS DAUGHTER. "Now you, Daddy."

HOWARD.   She's crazy for me! *(Again the same song is whistled.)* That's me! Ha! *(He winks.)*

WILLY.   You're very good!

(The whistling breaks off again. The machine runs silent for a moment.)

HOWARD.   Sh! Get this now, this is my son.

HIS SON.   "The capital of Alabama is Montgomery; the capital of Arizona is Phoenix; the capital of Arkansas is Little Rock; the capital of California is Sacramento . . ." (and on, and on)

HOWARD *(holding up five fingers)*.   Five years old, Willy!

WILLY.   He'll make an announcer someday!

HIS SON *(continuing)*.   "The capital . . ."

HOWARD.   Get that—alphabetical order! *(The machine breaks off suddenly.)* Wait a minute. The maid kicked the plug out.

WILLY.   It certainly is a—

HOWARD.   Sh, for God's sake!

HIS SON.   "It's nine o'clock, Bulova watch time. So I have to go to sleep."

WILLY.   That really is—

HOWARD.   Wait a minute! The next is my wife.

(They wait.)

HOWARD'S VOICE.   "Go on, say something." *(Pause.)* "Well, you gonna talk?"

HIS WIFE.   "I can't think of anything."

HOWARD'S VOICE.   "Well, talk—it's turning."

HIS WIFE *(shyly, beaten)*.   "Hello." *(Silence.)* "Oh, Howard, I can't talk into this . . ."

HOWARD *(snapping the machine off)*.   That was my wife.

WILLY.   That is a wonderful machine. Can we—

HOWARD.   I tell you, Willy, I'm gonna take my camera, and my bandsaw, and all my hobbies, and out they go. This is the most fascinating relaxation I ever found.

WILLY.   I think I'll get one myself.

HOWARD.   Sure, they're only a hundred and a half. You can't do without it. Supposing you wanna hear Jack Benny, see? But you can't be at home at that hour. So you tell the maid to turn the radio on when Jack Benny comes on, and this automatically goes on with the radio . . .

WILLY.   And when you come home you . . .

HOWARD.   You can come home twelve o'clock, one o'clock, any time you like, and you get yourself a Coke and sit yourself down, throw the switch, and there's Jack Benny's program in the middle of the night!

WILLY.   I'm definitely going to get one. Because lots of times I'm on the road, and I think to myself, what I must be missing on the radio!

HOWARD.   Don't you have a radio in the car?

WILLY.   Well, yeah, but who ever thinks of turning it on?

HOWARD.   Say, aren't you supposed to be in Boston?

WILLY.   That's what I want to talk to you about, Howard. You got a minute? *(He draws a chair in from the wing.)*

HOWARD.   What happened? What're you doing here?

WILLY.   Well . . .

HOWARD.   You didn't crack up again, did you?

WILLY.   Oh, no. No . . .

HOWARD.   Geez, you had me worried there for a minute. What's the trouble?

WILLY.   Well, tell you the truth, Howard. I've come to the decision that I'd rather not travel anymore.

HOWARD.   Not travel! Well, what'll you do?

WILLY.   Remember, Christmas time, when you had the party here? You said you'd try to think of some spot for me here in town.

HOWARD.   With us?

WILLY.   Well, sure.

HOWARD.   Oh, yeah, yeah. I remember. Well, I couldn't think of anything for you, Willy.

WILLY.   I tell ya, Howard. The kids are all grown up, y'know. I don't need much anymore. If I could take home—well, sixty-five dollars a week, I could swing it.

HOWARD.   Yeah, but Willy, see I—

WILLY.   I tell ya why, Howard. Speaking frankly and between the two of us, y'know—I'm just a little tired.

HOWARD.   Oh, I could understand that, Willy. But you're a road man, Willy, and we do a road business. We've only got a half-dozen salesmen on the floor here.

WILLY.   God knows, Howard, I never asked a favor of any man. But I was with the firm when your father used to carry you in here in his arms.

HOWARD.   I know that, Willy, but—

WILLY.   Your father came to me the day you were born and asked me what I thought of the name Howard, may he rest in peace.

HOWARD.   I appreciate that, Willy, but there just is no spot here for you. If I had a spot I'd slam you right in, but I just don't have a single solitary spot.

(He looks for his lighter. Willy has picked it up and gives it to him. Pause.)

WILLY *(with increasing anger)*.   Howard, all I need to set my table is fifty dollars a week.

HOWARD.   But where am I going to put you, kid?

WILLY.   Look, it isn't a question of whether I can sell merchandise, is it?

HOWARD.   No, but it's business, kid, and everybody's gotta pull his own weight.

WILLY *(desperately)*.   Just let me tell you a story, Howard—

HOWARD.   'Cause you gotta admit, business is business.

WILLY *(angrily)*.   Business is definitely business, but just listen for a minute. You don't understand this. When I was a boy—eighteen, nineteen—I was already on the road. And there was a question in my mind as to whether selling had a future for me. Because in those days I had a yearning to go to Alaska. See, there were three gold strikes in one month in Alaska, and I felt like going out. Just for the ride, you might say.

HOWARD *(barely interested)*.   Don't say.

WILLY.   Oh, yeah, my father lived many years in Alaska. He was an adventurous man. We've got quite a little streak of self-reliance in our family. I thought I'd go out with my older brother and try to locate him, and maybe settle in the North with the old man. And I was almost decided to go, when I met a salesman in the Parker House. His name was Dave Singleman. And he was eighty-four years old, and he'd drummed merchandise in thirty-one states. And old Dave, he'd go up to his room, y'understand, put on his green velvet slippers—I'll never forget—and pick up his phone and call the buyers, and without ever leaving his room, at the age of eighty-four, he made his living. And when

I saw that, I realized that selling was the greatest career a man could want. 'Cause what could be more satisfying than to be able to go, at the age of eighty-four, into twenty or thirty different cities, and pick up a phone, and be remembered and loved and helped by so many different people? Do you know? When he died—and by the way he died the death of a salesman, in his green velvet slippers in the smoker of the New York, New Haven and Hartford, going into Boston—when he died, hundreds of salesmen and buyers were at his funeral. Things were sad on a lotta trains for months after that. *(He stands up. Howard has not looked at him.)* In those days there was personality in it, Howard. There was respect, and comradeship, and gratitude in it. Today, it's all cut and dried, and there's no chance for bringing friendship to bear—or personality. You see what I mean? They don't know me anymore.

HOWARD *(moving away, to the right).* That's just the thing, Willy.

WILLY. If I had forty dollars a week—that's all I'd need. Forty dollars, Howard.

HOWARD. Kid, I can't take blood from a stone, I—

WILLY *(desperation is on him now).* Howard, the year Al Smith was nominated, your father came to me and—

HOWARD *(starting to go off).* I've got to see some people, kid.

WILLY *(stopping him).* I'm talking about your father! There were promises made across this desk! You mustn't tell me you've got people to see—I put thirty-four years into this firm, Howard, and now I can't pay my insurance! You can't eat the orange and throw the peel away—a man is not a piece of fruit! *(After a pause.)* Now pay attention. Your father—in 1928 I had a big year. I averaged a hundred and seventy dollars a week in commissions.

HOWARD *(impatiently).* Now, Willy, you never averaged—

WILLY *(banging his hand on the desk).* I averaged a hundred and seventy dollars a week in the year of 1928! And your father came to me—or rather, I was in the office here—it was right over this desk—and he put his hand on my shoulder—

HOWARD *(getting up).* You'll have to excuse me, Willy, I gotta see some people. Pull yourself together. *(Going out.)* I'll be back in a little while.

(On Howard's exit, the light on his chair grows very bright and strange.)

WILLY. Pull myself together! What the hell did I say to him? My God, I was yelling at him! How could I? *(Willy breaks off, staring at the light, which occupies the chair, animating it. He approaches this chair, standing across the desk from it.)* Frank, Frank, don't you remember what you told me that time? How you put your hand on my shoulder, and Frank . . . *(He leans on the desk and as he speaks the dead man's name he accidentally switches on the recorder, and instantly:)*

HOWARD'S SON. ". . . of New York is Albany. The capital of Ohio is Cincinnati, the capital of Rhode Island is . . ." *(The recitation continues.)*

WILLY *(leaping away with fright, shouting).* Ha! Howard! Howard! Howard!

HOWARD *(rushing in).* What happened?

WILLY *(pointing at the machine, which continues nasally, childishly, with the capital cities).* Shut it off! Shut it off!

HOWARD *(pulling the plug out).* Look, Willy . . .

WILLY *(pressing his hands to his eyes).* I gotta get myself some coffee. I'll get some coffee . . .

(Willy starts to walk out. Howard stops him.)

HOWARD *(rolling up the cord).* Willy, look . . .

WILLY. I'll go to Boston.

HOWARD.   Willy, you can't go to Boston for us.

WILLY.   Why can't I go?

HOWARD.   I don't want you to represent us. I've been meaning to tell you for a long time now.

WILLY.   Howard, are you firing me?

HOWARD.   I think you need a good long rest, Willy.

WILLY.   Howard—

HOWARD.   And when you feel better, come back, and we'll see if we can work something out.

WILLY.   But I gotta earn money, Howard. I'm in no position to—

HOWARD.   Where are your sons? Why don't your sons give you a hand?

WILLY.   They're working on a very big deal.

HOWARD.   This is no time for false pride, Willy. You go to your sons and you tell them that you're tired. You've got two great boys, haven't you?

WILLY.   Oh, no question, no question, but in the meantime . . .

HOWARD.   Then that's that, heh?

WILLY.   All right, I'll go to Boston tomorrow.

HOWARD.   No, no.

WILLY.   I can't throw myself on my sons. I'm not a cripple!

HOWARD.   Look, kid, I'm busy this morning.

WILLY (*grasping Howard's arm*).   Howard, you've got to let me go to Boston!

HOWARD (*hard, keeping himself under control*).   I've got a line of people to see this morning. Sit down, take five minutes, and pull yourself together, and then go home, will ya? I need the office, Willy. (*He starts to go, turns, remembering the recorder, starts to push off the table holding the recorder.*) Oh, yeah. Whenever you can this week, stop by and drop off the samples. You'll feel better, Willy, and then come back and we'll talk. Pull yourself together, kid, there's people outside.

(*Howard exits, pushing the table off left. Willy stares into space, exhausted. Now the music is heard—Ben's music—first distantly, then closer, closer. As Willy speaks, Ben enters from the right. He carries valise and umbrella.*)

WILLY.   Oh, Ben, how did you do it? What is the answer? Did you wind up the Alaska deal already?

BEN.   Doesn't take much time if you know what you're doing. Just a short business trip. Boarding ship in an hour. Wanted to say good-by.

WILLY.   Ben, I've got to talk to you.

BEN (*glancing at his watch*).   Haven't the time, William.

WILLY (*crossing the apron to Ben*).   Ben, nothing's working out. I don't know what to do.

BEN.   Now, look here, William. I've bought timberland in Alaska and I need a man to look after things for me.

WILLY.   God, timberland! Me and my boys in those grand outdoors!

BEN.   You've a new continent at your doorstep, William. Get out of these cities, they're full of talk and time payments and courts of law. Screw on your fists and you can fight for a fortune up there.

WILLY.   Yes, yes! Linda, Linda!

(*Linda enters as of old, with the wash.*)

LINDA.   Oh, you're back?

BEN.   I haven't much time.

WILLY. No, wait! Linda, he's got a proposition for me in Alaska.

LINDA. But you've got—*(To Ben.)* He's got a beautiful job here.

WILLY. But in Alaska, kid, I could—

LINDA. You're doing well enough, Willy!

BEN *(to Linda).* Enough for what, my dear?

LINDA *(frightened of Ben and angry at him).* Don't say those things to him! Enough to be happy right here, right now. *(To Willy, while Ben laughs.)* Why must everybody conquer the world? You're well liked, and the boys love you, and someday—*(to Ben)*—why, old man Wagner told him just the other day that if he keeps it up he'll be a member of the firm, didn't he, Willy?

WILLY. Sure, sure. I am building something with this firm, Ben, and if a man is building something he must be on the right track, mustn't he?

BEN. What are you building? Lay your hand on it. Where is it?

WILLY *(hesitantly).* That's true, Linda, there's nothing.

LINDA. Why? *(To Ben.)* There's a man eighty-four years old—

WILLY. That's right, Ben, that's right. When I look at that man I say, what is there to worry about?

BEN. Bah!

WILLY. It's true, Ben. All he has to do is go into any city, pick up the phone, and he's making his living and you know why?

BEN *(picking up his valise).* I've got to go.

WILLY *(holding Ben back).* Look at this boy! *(Biff, in his high school sweater, enters carrying suitcase. Happy carries Biff's shoulder guards, gold helmet, and football pants.)* Without a penny to his name, three great universities are begging for him, and from there the sky's the limit, because it's not what you do, Ben. It's who you know and the smile on your face! It's contacts, Ben, contacts! The whole wealth of Alaska passes over the lunch table at the Commodore Hotel, and that's the wonder, the wonder of this country, that a man can end with diamonds here on the basis of being liked! *(He turns to Biff.)* And that's why when you get out on that field today it's important. Because thousands of people will be rooting for you and loving you. *(To Ben, who has again begun to leave.)* And Ben! when he walks into a business office his name will sound out like a bell and all the doors will open to him! I've seen it, Ben, I've seen it a thousand times! You can't feel it with your hand like timber, but it's there!

BEN. Good-by, William.

WILLY. Ben, am I right? Don't you think I'm right? I value your advice.

BEN. There's a new continent at your doorstep, William. You could walk out rich. Rich! *(He is gone.)*

WILLY. We'll do it here, Ben! You hear me? We're gonna do it here!

(Young Bernard rushes in. The gay music of the Boys is heard.)

BERNARD. Oh, gee, I was afraid you left already!

WILLY. Why? What time is it?

BERNARD. It's half-past one!

WILLY. Well, come on, everybody! Ebbets Field next stop! Where's the pennants? *(He rushes through the wall-line of the kitchen and out into the living room.)*

LINDA *(to Biff).* Did you pack fresh underwear?

BIFF *(who has been limbering up).* I want to go!

BERNARD. Biff, I'm carrying your helmet, ain't I?

HAPPY. No, I'm carrying the helmet.

BERNARD. Oh, Biff, you promised me.

HAPPY. I'm carrying the helmet.

BERNARD. How am I going to get in the locker room?

LINDA. Let him carry the shoulder guards. *(She puts her coat and hat on in the kitchen.)*

BERNARD. Can I, Biff? 'Cause I told everybody I'm going to be in the locker room.

HAPPY. In Ebbets Field it's the clubhouse.

BERNARD. I meant the clubhouse. Biff!

HAPPY. Biff!

BIFF *(grandly, after a slight pause).* Let him carry the shoulder guards.

HAPPY *(as he gives Bernard the shoulder guards).* Stay close to us now.

(Willy rushes in with the pennants.)

WILLY *(handing them out).* Everybody wave when Biff comes out on the field. *(Happy and Bernard run off.)* You set now, boy?

(The music has died away.)

BIFF. Ready to go, Pop. Every muscle is ready.

WILLY *(at the edge of the apron).* You realize what this means?

BIFF. That's right, Pop.

WILLY *(feeling Biff's muscles).* You're comin' home this afternoon captain of the All-Scholastic Championship Team of the City of New York.

BIFF. I got it, Pop. And remember, pal, when I take off my helmet, that touchdown is for you.

WILLY. Let's go! *(He is starting out, with his arm around Biff, when Charley enters, as of old, in knickers.)* I got no room for you, Charley.

CHARLEY. Room? For what?

WILLY. In the car.

CHARLEY. You goin' for a ride? I wanted to shoot some casino.

WILLY. *(furiously).* Casino! *(Incredulously.)* Don't you realize what today is?

LINDA. Oh, he knows, Willy. He's just kidding you.

WILLY. That's nothing to kid about!

CHARLEY. No, Linda, what's goin' on?

LINDA. He's playing in Ebbets Field.

CHARLEY. Baseball in this weather?

WILLY. Don't talk to him. Come on, come on! *(He is pushing them out.)*

CHARLEY. Wait a minute, didn't you hear the news?

WILLY. What?

CHARLEY. Don't you listen to the radio? Ebbets Field just blew up.

WILLY. You go to hell! *(Charley laughs. Pushing them out.)* Come on, come on! We're late.

CHARLEY *(as they go).* Knock a homer, Biff, knock a homer!

WILLY *(the last to leave, turning to Charley).* I don't think that was funny, Charley. This is the greatest day of his life.

CHARLEY. Willy, when are you going to grow up?

WILLY. Yeah, heh? When this game is over, Charley, you'll be laughing out of the other side of your face. They'll be calling him another Red Grange. Twenty-five thousand a year.

CHARLEY *(kidding).* Is that so?

WILLY. Yeah, that's so.

CHARLEY.   Well, then, I'm sorry, Willy. But tell me something.

WILLY.   What?

CHARLEY.   Who is Red Grange?

WILLY.   Put up your hands. Goddam you, put up your hands! *(Charley, chuckling, shakes his head and walks away, around the left corner of the stage. Willy follows him. The music rises to a mocking frenzy.)* Who the hell do you think you are, better than everybody else? You don't know everything, you big, ignorant, stupid . . . Put up your hands!

(Light rises, on the right side of the forestage, on a small table in the reception room of Charley's office. Traffic sounds are heard. Bernard, now mature, sits whistling to himself. A pair of tennis rackets and an overnight bag are on the floor beside him.)

WILLY *(offstage)*.   What are you walking away for? Don't walk away! If you're going to say something say it to my face! I know you laugh at me behind my back. You'll laugh out of the other side of your goddam face after this game. Touchdown! Touchdown! Eighty thousand people! Touchdown! Right between the goal posts.

(Bernard is a quiet, earnest, but self-assured young man. Willy's voice is coming from right upstage now. Bernard lowers his feet off the table and listens. Jenny, his father's secretary, enters.)

JENNY *(distressed)*.   Say, Bernard, will you go out in the hall?

BERNARD.   What is that noise? Who is it?

JENNY.   Mr. Loman. He just got off the elevator.

BERNARD *(getting up)*.   Who's he arguing with?

JENNY.   Nobody. There's nobody with him. I can't deal with him anymore, and your father gets all upset everytime he comes. I've got a lot of typing to do, and your father's waiting to sign it. Will you see him?

WILLY *(entering)*.   Touchdown! Touch—*(He sees Jenny.)* Jenny, Jenny, good to see you. How're ya? Workin'? Or still honest?

JENNY.   Fine. How've you been feeling?

WILLY.   Not much anymore, Jenny. Ha, ha! *(He is surprised to see the rackets.)*

BERNARD.   Hello, Uncle Willy.

WILLY *(almost shocked)*.   Bernard! Well, look who's here! *(He comes quickly, guiltily, to Bernard and warmly shakes his hand.)*

BERNARD.   How are you? Good to see you.

WILLY.   What are you doing here?

BERNARD.   Oh, just stopped by to see Pop. Get off my feet till my train leaves. I'm going to Washington in a few minutes.

WILLY.   Is he in?

BERNARD.   Yes, he's in his office with the accountant. Sit down.

WILLY *(sitting down)*.   What're you going to do in Washington?

BERNARD.   Oh, just a case I've got there, Willy.

WILLY.   That so? *(Indicating the rackets.)* You going to play tennis there?

BERNARD.   I'm staying with a friend who's got a court.

WILLY.   Don't say. His own tennis court. Must be fine people, I bet.

BERNARD.   They are, very nice. Dad tells me Biff's in town.

WILLY *(with a big smile)*.   Yeah, Biff's in. Working on a very big deal, Bernard.

BERNARD.   What's Biff doing?

WILLY.   Well, he's been doing very big things in the West. But he decided to establish himself here. Very big. We're having dinner. Did I hear your wife had a boy?

BERNARD.   That's right. Our second.

WILLY.   Two boys! What do you know!

BERNARD.   What kind of a deal has Biff got?

WILLY.   Well, Bill Oliver—very big sporting-goods man—he wants Biff very badly. Called him in from the West. Long distance, carte blanche, special deliveries. Your friends have their own private tennis court?

BERNARD.   You still with the old firm, Willy?

WILLY *(after a pause).*   I'm—I'm overjoyed to see how you made the grade, Bernard, overjoyed. It's an encouraging thing to see a young man really—really—Looks very good for Biff—very—*(He breaks off, then.)* Bernard—*(He is so full of emotion, he breaks off again.)*

BERNARD.   What is it, Willy?

WILLY *(small and alone).*   What—what's the secret?

BERNARD.   What secret?

WILLY.   How—how did you? Why didn't he ever catch on?

BERNARD.   I wouldn't know that, Willy.

WILLY *(confidentially, desperately).*   You were his friend, his boyhood friend. There's something I don't understand about it. His life ended after that Ebbets Field game. From the age of seventeen nothing good ever happened to him.

BERNARD.   He never trained himself for anything.

WILLY.   But he did, he did. After high school he took so many correspondence courses. Radio mechanics; television; God knows what, and never made the slightest mark.

BERNARD *(taking off his glasses).*   Willy, do you want to talk candidly?

WILLY *(rising, faces Bernard).*   I regard you as a very brilliant man, Bernard. I value your advice.

BERNARD.   Oh, the hell with the advice, Willy. I couldn't advise you. There's just one thing I've always wanted to ask you. When he was supposed to graduate, and the math teacher flunked him—

WILLY.   Oh, that son-of-a-bitch ruined his life.

BERNARD.   Yeah, but, Willy, all he had to do was go to summer school and make up that subject.

WILLY.   That's right, that's right.

BERNARD.   Did you tell him not to go to summer school?

WILLY.   Me? I begged him to go. I ordered him to go!

BERNARD.   Then why wouldn't he go?

WILLY.   Why? Why! Bernard, that question has been trailing me like a ghost for the last fifteen years. He flunked the subject, and laid down and died like a hammer hit him!

BERNARD.   Take it easy, kid.

WILLY.   Let me talk to you—I got nobody to talk to. Bernard, Bernard, was it my fault? Y'see? It keeps going around in my mind, maybe I did something to him. I got nothing to give him.

BERNARD.   Don't take it so hard.

WILLY.   Why did he lay down? What is the story there? You were his friend!

BERNARD.   Willy, I remember, it was June, and our grades came out. And he'd flunked math.

WILLY.   That son-of-a-bitch!

BERNARD.   No, it wasn't right then. Biff just got very angry, I remember, and he was ready to enroll in summer school.

WILLY *(surprised).*   He was?

BERNARD.   He wasn't beaten by it at all. But then, Willy, he disappeared from the block for almost a month. And I got the idea that he'd gone up to New England to see you. Did he have a talk with you then? *(Willy stares in silence.)* Willy?

WILLY *(with a strong edge of resentment in his voice)*.   Yeah, he came to Boston. What about it?

BERNARD.   Well, just that when he came back—I'll never forget this, it always mystifies me. Because I'd thought so well of Biff, even though he'd always taken advantage of me. I loved him, Willy, y'know? And he came back after that month and took his sneakers—remember those sneakers with "University of Virginia" printed on them? He was so proud of those, wore them every day. And he took them down in the cellar, and burned them up in the furnace. We had a fist fight. It lasted at least half an hour. Just the two of us, punching each other down the cellar, and crying right through it. I've often thought of how strange it was that I knew he'd given up his life. What happened in Boston, Willy? *(Willy looks at him as at an intruder.)* I just bring it up because you asked me.

WILLY *(angrily)*.   Nothing. What do you mean, "What happened?" What's that got to do with anything?

BERNARD.   Well, don't get sore.

WILLY.   What are you trying to do, blame it on me? If a boy lays down is that my fault?

BERNARD.   Now, Willy, don't get—

WILLY.   Well, don't—don't talk to me that way! What does that mean, "What happened?"

(Charley enters. He is in his vest, and he carries a bottle of bourbon.)

CHARLEY.   Hey, you're going to miss that train. *(He waves the bottle.)*

BERNARD.   Yeah, I'm going. *(He takes the bottle.)*Thanks, Pop. *(He picks up his rackets and bag.)* Good-by, Willy, and don't worry about it. You know, "If at first you don't succeed . . ."

WILLY.   Yes, I believe in that.

BERNARD.   But sometimes, Willy, it's better for a man just to walk away.

WILLY.   Walk away?

BERNARD.   That's right.

WILLY.   But if you can't walk away?

BERNARD *(after a slight pause)*.   I guess that's when it's tough. *(Extending his hand.)* Good-by, Willy.

WILLY *(shaking Bernard's hand)*.   Good-by, boy.

CHARLEY *(an arm on Bernard's shoulder)*.   How do you like this kid? Gonna argue a case in front of the Supreme Court.

BERNARD *(protesting)*.   Pop!

WILLY *(genuinely shocked, pained, and happy)*.   No! The Supreme Court!

BERNARD.   I gotta run. 'By, Dad!

CHARLEY.   Knock 'em dead, Bernard!

(Bernard goes off.)

WILLY *(as Charley takes out his wallet)*.   The Supreme Court! And he didn't even mention it!

CHARLEY *(counting out money on the desk)*.   He don't have to—he's gonna do it.

WILLY.   And you never told him what to do, did you? You never took any interest in him.

CHARLEY.   My salvation is that I never took any interest in anything. There's some money—fifty dollars. I got an accountant inside.

WILLY.   Charley, look . . . *(With difficulty.)* I got my insurance to pay. If you can manage it—I need a hundred and ten dollars. *(Charley doesn't reply for a moment; merely stops moving.)* I'd draw it from my bank but Linda would know, and I . . .

CHARLEY.   Sit down, Willy.

WILLY *(moving toward the chair).*   I'm keeping an account of everything, remember. I'll pay every penny back. *(He sits.)*

CHARLEY.   Now listen to me, Willy.

WILLY.   I want you to know I appreciate . . .

CHARLEY *(sitting down on the table).*   Willy, what're you doin'? What the hell is goin' on in your head?

WILLY.   Why? I'm simply . . .

CHARLEY.   I offered you a job. You make fifty dollars a week. And I won't send you on the road.

WILLY.   I've got a job.

CHARLEY.   Without pay? What kind of a job is a job without pay? *(He rises.)* Now, look, kid, enough is enough. I'm no genius but I know when I'm being insulted.

WILLY.   Insulted!

CHARLEY.   Why don't you want to work for me?

WILLY.   What's the matter with you? I've got a job.

CHARLEY.   Then what're you walkin' in here every week for?

WILLY *(getting up).*   Well, if you don't want me to walk in here—

CHARLEY.   I'm offering you a job.

WILLY.   I don't want your goddam job!

CHARLEY.   When the hell are you going to grow up?

WILLY *(furiously).*   You big ignoramus, if you say that to me again I'll rap you one! I don't care how big you are! *(He's ready to fight.)*

(Pause.)

CHARLEY *(kindly, going to him).*   How much do you need, Willy?

WILLY.   Charley, I'm strapped. I'm strapped. I don't know what to do. I was just fired.

CHARLEY.   Howard fired you?

WILLY.   That snotnose. Imagine that? I named him. I named him Howard.

CHARLEY.   Willy, when're you gonna realize that them things don't mean anything? You named him Howard, but you can't sell that. The only thing you got in this world is what you can sell. And the funny thing is that you're a salesman, and you don't know that.

WILLY.   I've always tried to think otherwise, I guess. I always felt that if a man was impressive, and well liked, that nothing—

CHARLEY.   Why must everybody like you? Who liked J. P. Morgan?° Was he impressive? In a Turkish bath he'd look like a butcher. But with his pockets on he was very well liked. Now listen, Willy, I know you don't like me, and nobody can say I'm in love with you, but I'll give you a job because—just for the hell of it, put it that way. Now what do you say?

WILLY.   I—I just can't work for you, Charley.

J. P. Morgan (1837–1913): wealthy financier and art collector whose money was made chiefly in banking, railroads, and steel.

CHARLEY. What're you, jealous of me?

WILLY. I can't work for you, that's all, don't ask me why.

CHARLEY *(angered, takes out more bills)*. You been jealous of me all your life, you dammed fool! Here, pay your insurance. *(He puts the money in Willy's hand.)*

WILLY. I'm keeping strict accounts.

CHARLEY. I've got some work to do. Take care of yourself. And pay your insurance.

WILLY *(moving to the right)*. Funny, y'know? After all the highways, and the trains, and the appointments, and the years, you end up worth more dead than alive.

CHARLEY. Willy, nobody's worth nothin' dead. *(After a slight pause.)* Did you hear what I said? *(Willy stands still, dreaming.)* Willy!

WILLY. Apologize to Bernard for me when you see him. I didn't mean to argue with him. He's a fine boy. They're all fine boys, and they'll end up big—all of them. Someday they'll all play tennis together. Wish me luck, Charley. He saw Bill Oliver today.

CHARLEY. Good luck.

WILLY *(on the verge of tears)*. Charley, you're the only friend I got. Isn't that a remarkable thing? *(He goes out.)*

CHARLEY. Jesus!

(Charley stares after him a moment and follows. All light blacks out. Suddenly raucous music is heard, and a red glow rises behind the screen at right. Stanley, a young waiter, appears, carrying a table, followed by Happy, who is carrying two chairs.)

STANLEY *(putting the table down)*. That's all right, Mr. Loman, I can handle it myself. *(He turns and takes the chairs from Happy and places them at the table.)*

HAPPY *(glancing around)*. Oh, this is better.

STANLEY. Sure, in the front there you're in the middle of all kinds of noise. Whenever you got a party, Mr. Loman, you just tell me and I'll put you back here. Y'know, there's a lotta people they don't like it private, because when they go out they like to see a lotta action around them because they're sick and tired to stay in the house by theirself. But I know you, you ain't from Hackensack. You know what I mean?

HAPPY *(sitting down)*. So how's it coming, Stanley?

STANLEY. Ah, it's a dog life. I only wish during the war they'd a took me in the Army. I coulda been dead by now.

HAPPY. My brother's back, Stanley.

STANLEY. Oh, he come back, heh? From the Far West.

HAPPY. Yeah, big cattle man, my brother, so treat him right. And my father's coming too.

STANLEY. Oh, your father too!

HAPPY. You got a couple of nice lobsters?

STANLEY. Hundred percent, big.

HAPPY. I want them with the claws.

STANLEY. Don't worry, I don't give you no mice. *(Happy laughs.)* How about some wine? It'll put a head on the meal.

HAPPY. No. You remember, Stanley, that recipe I brought you from overseas? With the champagne in it?

STANLEY. Oh, yeah, sure. I still got it tacked up yet in the kitchen. But that'll have to cost a buck apiece anyways.

HAPPY. That's all right.

STANLEY. What'd you, hit a number or somethin'?

HAPPY. No, it's a little celebration. My brother is—I think he pulled off a big deal today. I think we're going into business together.

STANLEY.   Great! That's the best for you. Because a family business, you know what I mean?—that's the best.

HAPPY.   That's what I think.

STANLEY.   'Cause what's the difference? Somebody steals? It's in the family. Know what I mean? *(Sotto voce.°)* Like this bartender here. The boss is goin' crazy what kinda leak he's got in the cash register. You put it in but it don't come out.

HAPPY *(raising his head).*   Sh!

STANLEY.   What?

HAPPY.   You notice I wasn't lookin' right or left, was I?

STANLEY.   No.

HAPPY.   And my eyes are closed.

STANLEY.   So what's the—?

HAPPY.   Strudel's comin'.

STANLEY *(catching on, looks around).*   Ah, no, there's no—*(He breaks off as a furred, lavishly dressed girl enters and sits at the next table. Both follow her with their eyes.)* Geez, how'd ya know?

HAPPY.   I got radar or something. *(Staring directly at her profile.)* Oooooooooo . . . Stanley.

STANLEY.   I think that's for you, Mr. Loman.

HAPPY.   Look at that mouth. Oh, God. And the binoculars.

STANLEY.   Geez, you got a life, Mr. Loman.

HAPPY.   Wait on her.

STANLEY *(going to the Girl's table).*   Would you like a menu, ma'am?

GIRL.   I'm expecting someone, but I'd like a—

HAPPY.   Why don't you bring her—excuse me, miss, do you mind? I sell champagne, and I'd like you to try my brand. Bring her a champagne, Stanley.

GIRL.   That's awfully nice of you.

HAPPY.   Don't mention it. It's all company money. *(He laughs.)*

GIRL.   That's a charming product to be selling, isn't it?

HAPPY.   Oh, gets to be like everything else. Selling is selling, y'know.

GIRL.   I suppose.

HAPPY.   You don't happen to sell, do you?

GIRL.   No, I don't sell.

HAPPY.   Would you object to a compliment from a stranger? You ought to be on a magazine cover.

GIRL *(looking at him a little archly).*   I have been.

(Stanley comes in with a glass of champagne.)

HAPPY.   What'd I say before, Stanley? You see? She's a cover girl.

STANLEY.   Oh, I could see, I could see.

HAPPY *(to the Girl).*   What magazine?

GIRL.   Oh, a lot of them. *(She takes the drink.)* Thank you.

HAPPY.   You know what they say in France, don't you? "Champagne is the drink of the complexion"—Hya, Biff!

(Biff has entered and sits with Happy.)

BIFF.   Hello, kid. Sorry I'm late.

HAPPY.   I just got here. Uh, Miss—?

Sotto voce: in a soft voice or stage whisper.

GIRL.   Forsythe.

HAPPY.   Miss Forsythe, this is my brother.

BIFF.   Is Dad here?

HAPPY.   His name is Biff. You might've heard of him. Great football player.

GIRL.   Really? What team?

HAPPY.   Are you familiar with football?

GIRL.   No, I'm afraid I'm not.

HAPPY.   Biff is quarterback with the New York Giants.

GIRL.   Well, that is nice, isn't it? *(She drinks.)*

HAPPY.   Good health.

GIRL.   I'm happy to meet you.

HAPPY.   That's my name. Hap. It's really Harold, but at West Point they called me Happy.

GIRL *(now really impressed).*   Oh, I see. How do you do? *(She turns her profile.)*

BIFF.   Isn't Dad coming?

HAPPY.   You want her?

BIFF.   Oh, I could never make that.

HAPPY.   I remember the time that idea would never come into your head. Where's the old confidence, Biff?

BIFF.   I just saw Oliver—

HAPPY.   Wait a minute. I've got to see that old confidence again. Do you want her? She's on call.

BIFF.   Oh, no. *(He turns to look at the Girl.)*

HAPPY.   I'm telling you. Watch this. *(Turning to the Girl).*   Honey? *(She turns to him.)* Are you busy?

GIRL.   Well, I am . . . but I could make a phone call.

HAPPY.   Do that, will you, honey? And see if you can get a friend. We'll be here for a while. Biff is one of the greatest football players in the country.

GIRL *(standing up).*   Well, I'm certainly happy to meet you.

HAPPY.   Come back soon.

GIRL.   I'll try.

HAPPY.   Don't try, honey, try hard. *(The Girl exits. Stanley follows, shaking his head in bewildered admiration.)* Isn't that a shame now? A beautiful girl like that? That's why I can't get married. There's not a good woman in a thousand. New York is loaded with them, kid!

BIFF.   Hap, look—

HAPPY.   I told you she was on call!

BIFF *(strangely unnerved).*   Cut it out, will ya? I want to say something to you.

HAPPY.   Did you see Oliver?

BIFF.   I saw him all right. Now look, I want to tell Dad a couple of things and I want you to help me.

HAPPY.   What? Is he going to back you?

BIFF.   Are you crazy? You're out of your goddam head, you know that?

HAPPY.   Why? What happened?

BIFF *(breathlessly).*   I did a terrible thing today, Hap. It's been the strangest day I ever went through. I'm all numb, I swear.

HAPPY.   You mean he wouldn't see you?

BIFF.   Well, I waited six hours for him, see? All day. Kept sending my name in. Even tried to date his secretary so she'd get me to him, but no soap.

HAPPY.   Because you're not showin' the old confidence, Biff. He remembered you, didn't he?

BIFF *(stopping Happy with a gesture).*   Finally, about five o'clock, he comes out. Didn't remember who I was or anything. I felt like such an idiot, Hap.

HAPPY.   Did you tell him my Florida idea?

BIFF.   He walked away. I saw him for one minute. I got so mad I could've torn the walls down! How the hell did I ever get the idea I was a salesman there? I even believed myself that I'd been a salesman for him! And then he gave me one look and—I realized what a ridiculous lie my whole life has been! We've been talking in a dream for fifteen years. I was a shipping clerk.

HAPPY.   What'd you do?

BIFF *(with great tension and wonder).*   Well, he left, see. And the secretary went out. I was all alone in the waiting room. I don't know what came over me, Hap. The next thing I know I'm in his office—paneled walls, everything. I can't explain it. I—Hap, I took his fountain pen.

HAPPY.   Geez, did he catch you?

BIFF.   I ran out. I ran down all eleven flights. I ran and ran and ran.

HAPPY.   That was an awful dumb—what'd you do that for?

BIFF *(agonized).*   I don't know, I just—wanted to take something, I don't know. You gotta help me, Hap. I'm gonna tell Pop.

HAPPY.   You crazy? What for?

BIFF.   Hap, he's got to understand that I'm not the man somebody lends that kind of money to. He thinks I've been spiting him all these years and it's eating him up.

HAPPY.   That's just it. You tell him something nice.

BIFF.   I can't.

HAPPY.   Say you got a lunch date with Oliver tomorrow.

BIFF.   So what do I do tomorrow.

HAPPY.   You leave the house tomorrow and come back at night and say Oliver is thinking it over. And he thinks it over for a couple of weeks, and gradually it fades away and nobody's the worse.

BIFF.   But it'll go on forever!

HAPPY.   Dad is never so happy as when he's looking forward to something! *(Willy enters.)* Hello, scout!

WILLY.   Gee, I haven't been here in years!

(Stanley has followed Willy in and sets a chair for him. Stanley starts off but Happy stops him.)

HAPPY.   Stanley!

(Stanley stands by, waiting for an order.)

BIFF *(going to Willy with guilt, as to an invalid).*   Sit down, Pop. You want a drink?

WILLY.   Sure, I don't mind.

BIFF.   Let's get a load on.

WILLY.   You look worried.

BIFF.   N-no. *(To Stanley.)* Scotch all around. Make it doubles.

STANLEY.   Doubles, right. *(He goes.)*

WILLY.   You had a couple already, didn't you?

BIFF.   Just a couple, yeah.

WILLY.   Well, what happened, boy? *(Nodding affirmatively, with a smile.)* Everything go all right?

BIFF *(takes a breath, then reaches out and grasps Willy's hand).*   Pal . . . *(He is smiling bravely, and Willy is smiling too.)* I had an experience today.

HAPPY.   Terrific, Pop.

WILLY.   That so? What happened?

BIFF *(high, slightly alcoholic, above the earth).*   I'm going to tell you everything from first to last. It's been a strange day. *(Silence. He looks around, composes himself as best he can, but his breath keeps breaking the rhythm of his voice.)* I had to wait quite a while for him, and—

WILLY.   Oliver?

BIFF.   Yeah, Oliver. All day, as a matter of cold fact. And a lot of—instances— facts, Pop, facts about my life came back to me. Who was it, Pop? Who ever said I was a salesman with Oliver?

WILLY.   Well, you were.

BIFF.   No, Dad, I was a shipping clerk.

WILLY.   But you were practically—

BIFF *(with determination).*   Dad, I don't know who said it first, but I was never a sales- man for Bill Oliver.

WILLY.   What're you talking about?

BIFF.   Let's hold on to the facts tonight, Pop. We're not going to get anywhere bullin' around. I was a shipping clerk.

WILLY *(angrily).*   All right, now listen to me—

BIFF.   Why don't you let me finish?

WILLY.   I'm not interested in stories about the past or any crap of that kind be- cause the woods are burning, boys, you understand? There's a big blaze going on all around. I was fired today.

BIFF *(shocked).*   How could you be?

WILLY.   I was fired, and I'm looking for a little good news to tell your mother, be- cause the woman has waited and the woman has suffered. The gist of it is that I haven't got a story left in my head, Biff. So don't give me a lecture about facts and aspects. I am not interested. Now what've you got to say to me? *(Stanley enters with three drinks. They wait until he leaves.)* Did you see Oliver?

BIFF.   Jesus, Dad!

WILLY.   You mean you didn't go up there?

HAPPY.   Sure he went up there.

BIFF.   I did. I—saw him. How could they fire you?

WILLY *(on the edge of his chair).*   What kind of a welcome did he give you?

BIFF.   He won't even let you work on commission?

WILLY.   I'm out! *(Driving.)* So tell me, he gave you a warm welcome?

HAPPY.   Sure, Pop, sure!

BIFF *(driven).*   Well, it was kind of—

WILLY.   I was wondering if he'd remember you. *(To Happy.)* Imagine, man doesn't see him for ten, twelve years and gives him that kind of a welcome!

HAPPY.   Damn right!

BIFF *(trying to return to the offensive).*   Pop, look—

WILLY.   You know why he remembered you, don't you? Because you impressed him in those days.

BIFF.   Let's talk quietly and get this down to the facts, huh?

WILLY *(as though Biff had been interrupting).*   Well, what happened? It's great news, Biff. Did he take you into his office or'd you talk in the waiting room?

BIFF. Well, he came in, see, and—

WILLY *(with a big smile).* What'd he say? Betcha he threw his arm around you.

BIFF. Well, he kinda—

WILLY. He's a fine man. *(To Happy.)* Very hard man to see, y'know.

HAPPY *(agreeing).* Oh, I know.

WILLY *(to Biff).* Is that where you had the drinks?

BIFF. Yeah, he gave me a couple of—no, no!

HAPPY *(cutting in).* He told him my Florida idea.

WILLY. Don't interrupt. *(To Biff.)* How'd he react to the Florida idea?

BIFF. Dad, will you give me a minute to explain?

WILLY. I've been waiting for you to explain since I sat down here! What happened? He took you into his office and what?

BIFF. Well—I talked. And—and he listened, see.

WILLY. Famous for the way he listens, y'know. What was his answer?

BIFF. His answer was—*(He breaks off, suddenly angry.)* Dad, you're not letting me tell you what I want to tell you!

WILLY *(accusing, angered).* You didn't see him, did you?

BIFF. I did see him!

WILLY. What'd you insult him or something? You insulted him, didn't you?

BIFF. Listen, will you let me out of it, will you just let me out of it!

HAPPY. What the hell!

WILLY. Tell me what happened!

BIFF *(to Happy).* I can't talk to him!

(A single trumpet note jars the ear. The light of green leaves stains the house, which holds the air of night and a dream. Young Bernard enters and knocks on the door of the house.)

YOUNG BERNARD *(frantically).* Mrs. Loman, Mrs. Loman!

HAPPY. Tell him what happened!

BIFF *(to Happy).* Shut up and leave me alone!

WILLY. No, no! You had to go and flunk math!

BIFF. What math? What're you talking about?

YOUNG BERNARD. Mrs. Loman, Mrs. Loman!

(Linda appears in the house, as of old.)

WILLY *(wildly).* Math, math, math!

BIFF. Take it easy, Pop!

YOUNG BERNARD. Mrs. Loman!

WILLY *(furiously).* If you hadn't flunked you'd've been set by now!

BIFF. Now, look, I'm gonna tell you what happened, and you're going to listen to me.

YOUNG BERNARD. Mrs. Loman!

BIFF. I waited six hours—

HAPPY. What the hell are you saying?

BIFF. I kept sending in my name but he wouldn't see me. So finally he . . . *(He continues unheard as light fades low on the restaurant.)*

YOUNG BERNARD. Biff flunked math!

LINDA. No!

YOUNG BERNARD. Birnbaum flunked him! They won't graduate him!

LINDA. But they have to. He's gotta go to the university. Where is he? Biff! Biff!

YOUNG BERNARD.   No, he left. He went to Grand Central.

LINDA.   Grand—You mean he went to Boston!

YOUNG BERNARD.   Is Uncle Willy in Boston?

LINDA.   Oh, maybe Willy can talk to the teacher. Oh, the poor, poor boy!

(Light on house area snaps out.)

BIFF *(at the table, now audible, holding up a gold fountain pen).*   . . . so I'm washed up with Oliver, you understand? Are you listening to me?

WILLY *(at a loss).*   Yeah, sure. If you hadn't flunked—

BIFF.   Flunked what? What're you talking about?

WILLY.   Don't blame everything on me! I didn't flunk math—you did! What pen?

HAPPY.   That was awful dumb, Biff, a pen like that is worth—

WILLY *(seeing the pen for the first time).*   You took Oliver's pen?

BIFF *(weakening).*   Dad, I just explained it to you.

WILLY.   You stole Bill Oliver's fountain pen!

BIFF.   I didn't exactly steal it! That's just what I've been explaining to you!

HAPPY.   He had it in his hand and just then Oliver walked in, so he got nervous and stuck it in his pocket!

WILLY.   My God, Biff!

BIFF.   I never intended to do it, Dad!

OPERATOR'S VOICE.   Standish Arms, good evening!

WILLY *(shouting).*   I'm not in my room!

BIFF *(frightened).*   Dad, what's the matter? *(He and Happy stand up.)*

OPERATOR.   Ringing Mr. Loman for you!

WILLY.   I'm not there, stop it!

BIFF *(horrified, gets down on one knee before Willy).*   Dad, I'll make good, I'll make good. *(Willy tries to get to his feet. Biff holds him down.)* Sit down now.

WILLY.   No, you're no good, you're no good for anything.

BIFF.   I am, Dad, I'll find something else, you understand? Now don't worry about anything. *(He holds up Willy's face.)* Talk to me, Dad.

OPERATOR.   Mr. Loman does not answer. Shall I page him?

WILLY *(attempting to stand, as though to rush and silence the Operator).*   No, no, no!

HAPPY.   He'll strike something, Pop.

WILLY.   No, no . . .

BIFF *(desperately, standing over Willy).*   Pop, listen! Listen to me! I'm telling you something good. Oliver talked to his partner about the Florida idea. You listening? He—he talked to his partner, and he came to me . . . I'm going to be all right, you hear? Dad, listen to me, he said it was just a question of the amount!

WILLY.   Then you . . . got it?

HAPPY.   He's gonna be terrific, Pop!

WILLY *(trying to stand).*   Then you got it, haven't you? You got it! You got it!

BIFF *(agonized, holds Willy down).*   No, no. Look, Pop. I'm supposed to have lunch with them tomorrow. I'm just telling you this so you'll know that I can still make an impression, Pop. And I'll make good somewhere, but I can't go tomorrow, see?

WILLY.   Why not? You simply—

BIFF.   But the pen, Pop!

WILLY.   You give it to him and tell him it was an oversight!

HAPPY.   Sure, have lunch tomorrow!

BIFF.   I can't say that—

WILLY.   You were doing a crossword puzzle and accidentally used his pen!

BIFF.   Listen, kid, I took those balls years ago, now I walk in with his fountain pen? That clinches it, don't you see? I can't face him like that! I'll try elsewhere. *(Page's Voice: Paging Mr. Loman!)*

WILLY.   Don't you want to be anything?

BIFF.   Pop, how can I go back?

WILLY.   You don't want to be anything, is that what's behind it?

BIFF *(now angry at Willy for not crediting his sympathy)*.   Don't take it that way! You think it was easy walking into that office after what I'd done to him? A team of horses couldn't have dragged me back to Bill Oliver!

WILLY.   Then why'd you go?

BIFF.   Why did I go? Why did I go! Look at you! Look at what's become of you!

(Off left, The Woman laughs.)

WILLY.   Biff, you're going to go to that lunch tomorrow, or—

BIFF.   I can't go. I've got no appointment!

HAPPY.   Biff, for . . . !

WILLY.   Are you spiting me?

BIFF.   Don't take it that way! Goddammit!

WILLY *(strikes Biff and falters away from the table)*.   You rotten little louse! Are you spiting me?

THE WOMAN.   Someone's at the door, Willy!

BIFF.   I'm no good, can't you see what I am?

HAPPY *(separating them)*.   Hey, you're in a restaurant! Now cut it out, both of you! *(The girls enter.)* Hello, girls, sit down.

(The Woman laughs, off left.)

MISS FORSYTHE.   I guess we might as well. This is Letta.

THE WOMAN.   Willy, are you going to wake up?

BIFF *(ignoring Willy)*.   How're ya, miss, sit down. What do you drink?

MISS FORSYTHE.   Letta might not be able to stay long.

LETTA.   I gotta get up very early tomorrow. I got jury duty. I'm so excited! Were you fellows ever on a jury?

BIFF.   No, but I been in front of them! *(The girls laugh.)* This is my father.

LETTA.   Isn't he cute? Sit down with us, Pop.

HAPPY.   Sit him down, Biff!

BIFF *(going to him)*.   Come on, slugger, drink us under the table. To hell with it! Come on, sit down, pal.

(On Biff's last insistence, Willy is about to sit.)

THE WOMAN *(now urgently)*.   Willy, are you going to answer the door!

(The Woman's call pulls Willy back. He starts right, befuddled.)

BIFF.   Hey, where are you going?

WILLY.   Open the door.

BIFF.   The door?

WILLY.   The washroom . . . the door . . . where's the door?

BIFF *(leading Willy to the left)*.   Just go straight down.

(Willy moves left.)

THE WOMAN.   Willy, Willy, are you going to get up, get up, get up, get up?

(Willy exits left.)

LETTA.   I think it's sweet you bring your daddy along.

MISS FORSYTHE.   Oh, he isn't really your father!

BIFF *(at left, turning to her resentfully)*.   Miss Forsythe, you've just seen a prince walk by. A fine, troubled prince. A hard-working, unappreciated prince. A pal, you understand? A good companion. Always for his boys.

LETTA.   That's so sweet.

HAPPY.   Well, girls, what's the program? We're wasting time. Come on, Biff. Gather round. Where would you like to go?

BIFF.   Why don't you do something for him?

HAPPY.   Me!

BIFF.   Don't you give a damn for him, Hap?

HAPPY.   What're you talking about? I'm the one who—

BIFF.   I sense it, you don't give a good goddam about him. *(He takes the rolled-up hose from his pocket and puts it on the table in front of Happy.)* Look what I found in the cellar, for Christ's sake. How can you bear to let it go on?

HAPPY.   Me? Who goes away? Who runs off and—

BIFF.   Yeah, but he doesn't mean anything to you. You could help him—I can't! Don't you understand what I'm talking about? He's going to kill himself, don't you know that?

HAPPY.   Don't I know it! Me!

BIFF.   Hap, help him! Jesus . . . help him . . . Help me, help me, I can't bear to look at his face! *(Ready to weep, he hurries out, up right.)*

HAPPY *(starting after him)*.   Where are you going?

MISS FORSYTHE.   What's he so mad about?

HAPPY.   Come on, girls, we'll catch up with him.

MISS FORSYTHE *(as Happy pushes her out)*.   Say, I don't like that temper of his!

HAPPY.   He's just a little overstrung, he'll be all right!

WILLY *(off left, as The Woman laughs)*.   Don't answer! Don't answer!

LETTA.   Don't you want to tell your father—

HAPPY.   No, that's not my father. He's just a guy. Come on, we'll catch Biff, and, honey, we're going to paint this town! Stanley, where's the check! Hey, Stanley!

(They exit. Stanley looks toward left.)

STANLEY *(calling to Happy indignantly)*.   Mr. Loman! Mr. Loman!

(Stanley picks up a chair and follows them off. Knocking is heard off left. The Woman enters, laughing. Willy follows her. She is in a black slip; he is buttoning his shirt. Raw, sensuous music accompanies their speech.)

WILLY.   Will you stop laughing? Will you stop?

THE WOMAN.   Aren't you going to answer the door? He'll wake the whole hotel.

WILLY.   I'm not expecting anybody.

THE WOMAN.   Whyn't you have another drink, honey, and stop being so damn self-centered?

WILLY.   I'm so lonely.

THE WOMAN.   You know you ruined me, Willy? From now on, whenever you come to the office, I'll see that you go right through to the buyers. No waiting at my desk anymore, Willy. You ruined me.

WILLY.   That's nice of you to say that.

THE WOMAN.   Gee, you are self-centered! Why so sad? You are the saddest, self-centeredest soul I ever did see-saw. *(She laughs, He kisses her.)* Come on inside, drummer boy. It's silly to be dressing in the middle of the night. *(As knocking is heard.)* Aren't you going to answer the door?

WILLY.   They're knocking on the wrong door.

THE WOMAN.   But I felt the knocking. And he heard us talking in here. Maybe the hotel's on fire!

WILLY *(his terror rising).*   It's a mistake.

THE WOMAN.   Then tell him to go away!

WILLY.   There's nobody there.

THE WOMAN.   It's getting on my nerves, Willy. There's somebody standing out there and it's getting on my nerves!

WILLY *(pushing her away from him).*   All right, stay in the bathroom here, and don't come out. I think there's a law in Massachusetts about it, so don't come out. It may be that new room clerk. He looked very mean. So don't come out. It's a mistake, there's no fire.

(The knocking is heard again. He takes a few steps away from her, and she vanishes into the wing. The light follows him, and now he is facing Young Biff, who carries a suitcase. Biff steps toward him. The music is gone.)

BIFF.   Why didn't you answer?

WILLY.   Biff! What are you doing in Boston?

BIFF.   Why didn't you answer? I've been knocking for five minutes, I called you on the phone—

WILLY.   I just heard you. I was in the bathroom and had the door shut. Did anything happen home?

BIFF.   Dad—I let you down.

WILLY.   What do you mean?

BIFF.   Dad . . .

WILLY.   Biffo, what's this about? *(Putting his arm around Biff.)* Come on, let's go downstairs and get you a malted.

BIFF.   Dad, I flunked math.

WILLY.   Not for the term?

BIFF.   The term. I haven't got enough credits to graduate.

WILLY.   You mean to say Bernard wouldn't give you the answers?

BIFF.   He did, he tried, but I only got a sixty-one.

WILLY.   And they wouldn't give you four points?

BIFF.   Birnbaum refused absolutely. I begged him, Pop, but he won't give me those points. You gotta talk to him before they close the school. Because if he saw the kind of man you are, and you just talked to him in your way, I'm sure he'd come through for me. The class came right before practice, see, and I didn't go enough. Would you talk to him? He'd like you, Pop. You know the way you could talk.

WILLY.   You're on. We'll drive right back.

BIFF.   Oh, Dad, good work! I'm sure he'll change it for you!

WILLY.   Go downstairs and tell the clerk I'm checkin' out. Go right down.

BIFF.   Yes, sir! See, the reason he hates me, Pop—one day he was late for class so I got up at the blackboard and imitated him. I crossed my eyes and talked with a lithp.

WILLY *(laughing).*   You did? The kids like it?

BIFF.   They nearly died laughing!

WILLY.   Yeah? What'd you do?

BIFF.   The thquare root of thixthy twee is . . . *(Willy bursts out laughing; Biff joins.)*
And in the middle of it he walked in!

(Willy laughs and The Woman joins in offstage.)

WILLY *(without hesitation).*   Hurry downstairs and—

BIFF.   Somebody in there?

WILLY.   No, that was next door.

(The Woman laughs offstage.)

BIFF.   Somebody got in your bathroom!

WILLY.   No, it's the next room, there's a party—

THE WOMAN *(enters, laughing. She lisps this).*   Can I come in? There's something in
the bathtub, Willy, and it's moving!

(Willy looks at Biff, who is staring open-mouthed and horrified at The Woman.)

WILLY.   Ah—you better go back to your room. They must be finished painting by
now. They're painting her room so I let her take a shower here. Go back, go back . . .
(He pushes her.)

THE WOMAN *(resisting).*   But I've got to get dressed, Willy, I can't—

WILLY.   Get out of here! Go back, go back . . . *(Suddenly striving for the ordinary.)*
This is Miss Francis, Biff, she's a buyer. They're painting her room. Go back, Miss Francis, go back . . .

THE WOMAN.   But my clothes, I can't go out naked in the hall!

WILLY *(pushing her offstage).*   Get outa here! Go back, go back!

(Biff slowly sits down on his suitcase as the argument continues offstage.)

THE WOMAN.   Where's my stockings? You promised me stockings, Willy!

WILLY.   I have no stockings here!

THE WOMAN.   You had two boxes of size nine sheers for me, and I want them!

WILLY.   Here, for God's sake, will you get outa here!

THE WOMAN *(enters holding a box of stockings).*   I just hope there's nobody in the hall.
That's all I hope. *(To Biff.)* Are you football or baseball?

BIFF.   Football.

THE WOMAN *(angry, humiliated).*   That's me too. G'night. *(She snatches her clothes
from Willy, and walks out.)*

WILLY *(after a pause).*   Well, better get going. I want to get to the school first thing
in the morning. Get my suits out of the closet. I'll get my valise. *(Biff doesn't move.)* What's
the matter! *(Biff remains motionless, tears falling.)* She's a buyer. Buys for J. H. Simmons. She
lives down the hall—they're painting. You don't imagine—*(He breaks off. After a pause.)* Now
listen, pal, she's just a buyer. She sees merchandise in her room and they have to keep it
looking just so . . . *(Pause. Assuming command.)* All right, get my suits. *(Biff doesn't move.)*
Now stop crying and do as I say. I gave you an order. Biff, I gave you an order! Is that what
you do when I give you an order? How dare you cry! *(Putting his arm around Biff.)* Now
look, Biff, when you grow up you'll understand about these things. You mustn't—you
mustn't overemphasize a thing like this. I'll see Birnbaum first thing in the morning.

BIFF.   Never mind.

WILLY *(getting down beside Biff).*   Never mind! He's going to give you those points.
I'll see to it.

BIFF.   He wouldn't listen to you.

WILLY.   He certainly will listen to me. You need those points for the U. of Virginia.

BIFF.   I'm not going there.

WILLY.   Heh? If I can't get him to change that mark you'll make it up in summer school. You've got all summer to—

BIFF *(his weeping breaking from him)*.   Dad . . .

WILLY *(infected by it)*.   Oh, my boy . . .

BIFF.   Dad . . .

WILLY.   She's nothing to me, Biff. I was lonely, I was terribly lonely.

BIFF.   You—you gave her Mama's stockings! *(His tears break through and he rises to go.)*

WILLY *(grabbing for Biff)*.   I gave you an order!

BIFF.   Don't touch me, you—liar!

WILLY.   Apologize for that!

BIFF.   You fake! You phony little fake! You fake! *(Overcome, he turns quickly and weeping fully goes out with his suitcase. Willy is left on the floor on his knees.)*

WILLY.   I gave you an order! Biff, come back here or I'll beat you! Come back here! I'll whip you! *(Stanley comes quickly in from the right and stands in front of Willy.)* *(shouts at Stanley)*.   I gave you an order . . .

STANLEY.   Hey, let's pick it up, pick it up, Mr. Loman. *(He helps Willy to his feet.)* Your boys left with the chippies. They said they'll see you home.

(A second waiter watches some distance away.)

WILLY.   But we were supposed to have dinner together.

(Music is heard, Willy's theme.)

STANLEY.   Can you make it?

WILLY.   I'll—sure, I can make it. *(Suddenly concerned about his clothes.)* Do I—I look all right?

STANLEY.   Sure, you look all right. *(He flicks a speck off Willy's lapel.)*

WILLY.   Here—here's a dollar.

STANLEY.   Oh, your son paid me. It's all right.

WILLY *(putting it in Stanley's hand)*.   No, take it. You're a good boy.

STANLEY.   Oh, no, you don't have to . . .

WILLY.   Here—here's some more, I don't need it anymore. *(After a slight pause.)* Tell me—is there a seed store in the neighborhood?

STANLEY.   Seeds? You mean like to plant?

(As Willy turns, Stanley slips the money back into his jacket pocket.)

WILLY.   Yes. Carrots, peas . . .

STANLEY.   Well, there's hardware stores on Sixth Avenue, but it may be too late now.

WILLY *(anxiously)*.   Oh, I'd better hurry. I've got to get some seeds. *(He starts off to the right.)* I've got to get some seeds, right away. Nothing's planted. I don't have a thing in the ground.

(Willy hurries out as the light goes down. Stanley moves over to the right after him, watches him off. The other waiter has been staring at Willy.)

STANLEY *(to the waiter)*.   Well, whatta you looking at?

(The waiter picks up the chairs and moves off right. Stanley takes the table and follows him. The light fades on this area. There is a long pause, the sound of the flute coming over. The light gradually rises

on the kitchen, which is empty. Happy appears at the door of the house, followed by Biff. Happy is carrying a large bunch of long-stemmed roses. He enters the kitchen, looks around for Linda. Not seeing her, he turns to Biff, who is just outside the house door, and makes a gesture with his hands, indicating "Not here, I guess." He looks into the living room and freezes. Inside, Linda, unseen, is seated, Willy's coat on her lap. She rises ominously and quietly and moves toward Happy, who backs up into the kitchen, afraid.)

HAPPY.   Hey, what're you doing up? *(Linda says nothing but moves toward him implacably.)* Where's Pop? *(He keeps backing to the right, and now Linda is in full view in the doorway to the living room.)* Is he sleeping?

LINDA.   Where were you?

HAPPY *(trying to laugh it off).*   We met two girls, Mom, very fine types. Here, we brought you some flowers. *(Offering them to her.)* Put them in your room, Ma. *(She knocks them to the floor at Biff's feet. He has now come inside and closed the door behind him. She stares at Biff, silent.)* Now what'd you do that for? Mom, I want you to have some flowers—

LINDA *(cutting Happy off, violently to Biff).*   Don't you care whether he lives or dies?

HAPPY *(going to the stairs).*   Come upstairs, Biff.

BIFF *(with a flare of disgust, to Happy).*   Go away from me! *(To Linda.)* What do you mean, lives or dies? Nobody's dying around here, pal.

LINDA.   Get out of my sight! Get out of here!

BIFF.   I wanna see the boss.

LINDA.   You're not going near him!

BIFF.   Where is he? *(He moves into the living room and Linda follows.)*

LINDA *(shouting after Biff).*   You invite him for dinner. He looks forward to it all day—*(Biff appears in his parents' bedroom, looks around, and exits)*—and then you desert him there. There's no stranger you'd do that to!

HAPPY.   Why? He had a swell time with us. Listen, when I—*(Linda comes back into the kitchen)*—desert him I hope I don't outlive the day!

LINDA.   Get out of here!

HAPPY.   Now look, Mom . . .

LINDA.   Did you have to go to women tonight? You and your lousy rotten whores!

(Biff reenters the kitchen.)

HAPPY.   Mom, all we did was follow Biff around trying to cheer him up! *(To Biff.)* Boy, what a night you gave me!

LINDA.   Get out of here, both of you, and don't come back! I don't want you tormenting him anymore. Go on now, get your things together! *(To Biff.)* You can sleep in his apartment. *(She starts to pick up the flowers and stops herself.)* Pick up this stuff, I'm not your maid anymore. Pick it up, you bum, you! *(Happy turns his back to her in refusal. Biff slowly moves over and gets down on his knees, picking up the flowers.)* You're a pair of animals! Not one, not another living soul would have had the cruelty to walk out on that man in a restaurant!

BIFF *(not looking at her).*   Is that what he said?

LINDA.   He didn't have to say anything. He was so humiliated he nearly limped when he came in.

HAPPY.   But, Mom, he had a great time with us—

BIFF *(cutting him off violently).*   Shut up!

(Without another word, Happy goes upstairs.)

LINDA.   You! You didn't even go in to see if he was all right!

BIFF *(still on the floor in front of Linda, the flowers in his hand; with self-loathing).* No. Didn't. Didn't do a damned thing. How do you like that, heh? Left him babbling in a toilet.

LINDA. You louse, you . . .

BIFF. Now you hit it on the nose! *(He gets up, throws the flowers in the wastebasket.)* The scum of the earth, and you're looking at him!

LINDA. Get out of here!

BIFF. I gotta talk to the boss, Mom. Where is he?

LINDA. You're not going near him. Get out of this house!

BIFF *(with absolute assurance, determination).* No. We're gonna have an abrupt conversation, him and me.

LINDA. You're not talking to him.

(Hammering is heard from outside the house, off right. Biff turns toward the noise.)

LINDA *(suddenly pleading).* Will you please leave him alone?

BIFF. What's he doing out there?

LINDA. He's planting the garden!

BIFF *(quietly).* Now? Oh, my God!

(Biff moves outside, Linda following. The light dies down on them and comes up on the center of the apron as Willy walks into it. He is carrying a flashlight, a hoe, and a handful of seed packets. He raps the top of the hoe sharply to fix it firmly, and then moves to the left, measuring off the distance with his foot. He holds the flashlight to look at the seed packets, reading off the instructions. He is in the blue of night.)

WILLY. Carrots . . . quarter-inch apart. Rows . . . one-foot rows. *(He measures it off.)* One foot. *(He puts down a package and measures off.)* Beets. *(He puts down another package and measures again.)* Lettuce. *(He reads the package, puts it down.)* One foot—*(He breaks off as Ben appears at the right and moves slowly down to him.)* What a proposition, ts, ts. Terrific, terrific. 'Cause she's suffered, Ben, the woman has suffered. You understand me? A man can't go out the way he came in, Ben, a man has got to add up to something. You can't, you can't—*(Ben moves toward him as though to interrupt.)* You gotta consider, now. Don't answer so quick. Remember, it's a guaranteed twenty-thousand-dollar proposition. Now look, Ben, I want you to go through the ins and outs of this thing with me. I've got nobody to talk to, Ben, and the woman has suffered, you hear me?

BEN *(standing still, considering).* What's the proposition?

WILLY. It's twenty thousand dollars on the barrelhead. Guaranteed, gilt-edged, you understand?

BEN. You don't want to make a fool of yourself. They might not honor the policy.

WILLY. How can they dare refuse? Didn't I work like a coolie to meet every premium on the nose? And now they don't pay off? Impossible!

BEN. It's called a cowardly thing, William.

WILLY. Why? Does it take more guts to stand here the rest of my life ringing up a zero?

BEN *(yielding).* That's a point, William. *(He moves, thinking, turns.)* And twenty thousand—that is something one can feel with the hand, it is there.

WILLY *(now assured, with rising power).* Oh, Ben, that's the whole beauty of it! I see it like a diamond, shining in the dark, hard and rough, that I can pick up and touch in my hand. Not like—like an appointment! This would not be another damned-fool appointment, Ben, and it changes all the aspects. Because he thinks I'm nothing, see, and so he spites me. But the funeral—*(Straightening up.)* Ben, that funeral will be massive! They'll come from Maine, Massachusetts, Vermont, New Hampshire! All the old-timers with the strange license plates—that boy will be thunderstruck, Ben, because he never realized—I am known! Rhode Island, New York, New Jersey—I am known, Ben, and he'll see it with his eyes once and for all. He'll see what I am, Ben! He's in for a shock, that boy!

BEN *(coming down to the edge of the garden).*　He'll call you a coward.

WILLY *(suddenly fearful).*　No, that would be terrible.

BEN.　Yes. And a damned fool.

WILLY.　No, no, he mustn't, I won't have that! *(He is broken and desperate.)*

BEN.　He'll hate you, William.

(The gay music of the Boys is heard.)

WILLY.　Oh, Ben, how do we get back to all the great times? Used to be so full of light, and comradeship, the sleigh-riding in winter, and the ruddiness on his cheeks. And always some kind of good news coming up, always something nice coming up ahead. And never even let me carry the valises in the house, and simonizing, simonizing that little red car! Why, why can't I give him something and not have him hate me?

BEN.　Let me think about it. *(He glances at his watch.)* I still have a little time. Remarkable proposition, but you've got to be sure you're not making a fool of yourself.

(Ben drifts off upstage and goes out of sight. Biff comes down from the left.)

WILLY *(suddenly conscious of Biff, turns and looks up at him, then begins picking up the packages of seeds in confusion).*　Where the hell is that seed? *(Indignantly.)* You can't see nothing out here! They boxed in the whole goddam neighborhood!

BIFF.　There are people all around here. Don't you realize that?

WILLY.　I'm busy. Don't bother me.

BIFF *(taking the hoe from Willy).*　I'm saying good-by to you, Pop. *(Willy looks at him, silent, unable to move.)* I'm not coming back anymore.

WILLY.　You're not going to see Oliver tomorrow?

BIFF.　I've got no appointment, Dad.

WILLY.　He put his arm around you, and you've got no appointment?

BIFF.　Pop, get this now, will you? Everytime I've left it's been a fight that sent me out of here. Today I realized something about myself and I tried to explain it to you and I—I think I'm just not smart enough to make any sense out of it for you. To hell with whose fault it is or anything like that. *(He takes Willy's arm.)* Let's just wrap it up, heh? Come on in, we'll tell Mom. *(He gently tries to pull Willy to left.)*

WILLY *(frozen, immobile, with guilt in his voice).*　No, I don't want to see her.

BIFF.　Come on! *(He pulls again, and Willy tries to pull away.)*

WILLY *(highly nervous).*　No, no, I don't want to see her.

BIFF *(tries to look into Willy's face, as if to find the answer there).*　Why don't you want to see her?

WILLY *(more harshly now).*　Don't bother me, will you?

BIFF.　What do you mean, you don't want to see her? You don't want them calling you yellow, do you? This isn't your fault; it's me, I'm a bum. Now come inside! *(Willy strains to get away.)* Did you hear what I said to you?

(Willy pulls away and quickly goes by himself into the house. Biff follows.)

LINDA *(to Willy).*　Did you plant, dear?

BIFF *(at the door, to Linda).*   All right, we had it out. I'm going and I'm not writing anymore.

LINDA *(going to Willy in the kitchen).*   I think that's the best way, dear. 'Cause there's no use drawing it out, you'll just never get along.

(Willy doesn't respond.)

BIFF.   People ask where I am and what I'm doing, you don't know, and you don't care. That way it'll be off your mind and you can start brightening up again. All right? That clears it, doesn't it? *(Willy is silent, and Biff goes to him.)* You gonna wish me luck, scout? *(He extends his hand.)* What do you say?

LINDA.   Shake his hand, Willy.

WILLY *(turning to her, seething with hurt).*   There's no necessity to mention the pen at all, y'know.

BIFF *(gently).*   I've got no appointment, Dad.

WILLY *(erupting fiercely).*   He put his arm around . . . ?

BIFF.   Dad, you're never going to see what I am, so what's the use of arguing? If I strike oil I'll send you a check. Meantime forget I'm alive.

WILLY *(to Linda).*   Spite, see?

BIFF.   Shake hands, Dad.

WILLY.   Not my hand.

BIFF.   I was hoping not to go this way.

WILLY.   Well, this is the way you're going. Good-by.

(Biff looks at him a moment, then turns sharply and goes to the stairs.)

WILLY *(stops him with).*   May you rot in hell if you leave this house!

BIFF *(turning).*   Exactly what is it that you want from me?

WILLY.   I want you to know, on the train, in the mountains, in the valleys, wherever you go, that you cut down your life for spite!

BIFF.   No, no.

WILLY.   Spite, spite, is the word of your undoing! And when you're down and out, remember what did it. When you're rotting somewhere beside the railroad tracks, remember, and don't you dare blame it on me!

BIFF.   I'm not blaming it on you!

WILLY.   I won't take the rap for this, you hear?

(Happy comes down the stairs and stands on the bottom step, watching.)

BIFF.   That's just what I'm telling you!

WILLY *(sinking into a chair at a table, with full accusation).*   You're trying to put a knife in me—don't think I don't know what you're doing!

BIFF.   All right, phony! Then let's lay it on the line. *(He whips the rubber tube out of his pocket and puts it on the table.)*

HAPPY.   You crazy . . .

LINDA.   Biff! *(She moves to grab the hose, but Biff holds it down with his hand.)*

BIFF.   Leave it there! Don't move it!

WILLY *(not looking at it).*   What is that?

BIFF.   You know goddam well what that is.

WILLY *(caged, wanting to escape).*   I never saw that.

BIFF.   You saw it. The mice didn't bring it into the cellar! What is this supposed to do, make a hero out of you? This supposed to make me sorry for you?

WILLY.   Never heard of it.

BIFF.   There'll be no pity for you, you hear it? No pity!

WILLY *(to Linda)*.   You hear the spite!

BIFF.   No, you're going to hear the truth—what you are and what I am!

LINDA.   Stop it!

WILLY.   Spite!

HAPPY *(coming down toward Biff)*.   You cut it now!

BIFF *(to Happy)*.   The man don't know who we are! The man is gonna know! *(To Willy.)* We never told the truth for ten minutes in this house!

HAPPY.   We always told the truth!

BIFF *(turning on him)*.   You big blow, are you the assistant buyer? You're one of the two assistants to the assistant, aren't you?

HAPPY.   Well, I'm practically . . .

BIFF.   You're practically full of it! We all are! and I'm through with it. *(To Willy.)* Now hear this, Willy, this is me.

WILLY.   I know you!

BIFF.   You know why I had no address for three months? I stole a suit in Kansas City and I was in jail. *(To Linda, who is sobbing.)* Stop crying. I'm through with it.

(Linda turns away from them, her hands covering her face.)

WILLY.   I suppose that's my fault!

BIFF.   I stole myself out of every good job since high school!

WILLY.   And whose fault is that?

BIFF.   And I never got anywhere because you blew me so full of hot air I could never stand taking orders from anybody! That's whose fault it is!

WILLY.   I hear that!

LINDA.   Don't, Biff!

BIFF.   It's goddam time you heard that! I had to be boss big shot in two weeks, and I'm through with it!

WILLY.   Then hang yourself! For spite, hang yourself!

BIFF.   No! Nobody's hanging himself, Willy! I ran down eleven flights with a pen in my hand today. And suddenly I stopped, you hear me? And in the middle of that office building, do you hear this? I stopped in the middle of that building and I saw—the sky. I saw the things that I love in this world. The work and the food and time to sit and smoke. And I looked at the pen and said to myself, what the hell am I grabbing this for? Why am I trying to become what I don't want to be? What am I doing in an office, making a contemptuous, begging fool of myself, when all I want is out there, waiting for me the minute I say I know who I am! Why can't I say that, Willy? *(He tries to make Willy face him, but Willy pulls away and moves to the left.)*

WILLY *(with hatred, threateningly)*.   The door of your life is wide open!

BIFF.   Pop! I'm a dime a dozen, and so are you!

WILLY *(turning on him now in an uncontrolled outburst)*.   I am not a dime a dozen! I am Willy Loman, and you are Biff Loman!

(Biff starts for Willy, but is blocked by Happy. In his fury, Biff seems on the verge of attacking his father.)

BIFF.   I am not a leader of men, Willy, and neither are you. You were never anything but a hard-working drummer who landed in the ash can like all the rest of them! I'm one dollar an hour, Willy! I tried seven states and couldn't raise it. A buck an hour!

Do you gather my meaning? I'm not bringing home any prizes anymore, and you're going to stop waiting for me to bring them home!

WILLY *(directly to Biff).* You vengeful, spiteful mutt!

(Biff breaks from Happy. Willy, in fright, starts up the stairs. Biff grabs him.)

BIFF *(at the peak of his fury).* Pop, I'm nothing! I'm nothing, Pop. Can't you understand that? There's no spite in it anymore. I'm just what I am, that's all.

(Biff's fury has spent itself and he breaks down, sobbing, holding on to Willy, who dumbly fumbles for Biff's face.)

WILLY *(astonished).* What're you doing? What're you doing? *(To Linda.)* Why is he crying?

BIFF *(crying, broken).* Will you let me go, for Christ's sake? Will you take that phony dream and burn it before something happens? *(Struggling to contain himself he pulls away and moves to the stairs.)* I'll go in the morning. Put him—put him to bed. *(Exhausted, Biff moves up the stairs to his room.)*

WILLY *(after a long pause, astonished, elevated).* Isn't that—isn't that remarkable? Biff—he likes me!

LINDA. He loves you, Willy!

HAPPY *(deeply moved).* Always did, Pop.

WILLY. Oh, Biff! *(Staring wildly.)* He cried! Cried to me. *(He is choking with his love, and now cries out his promise.)* That boy—that boy is going to be magnificent!

(Ben appears in the light just outside the kitchen.)

BEN. Yes, outstanding, with twenty thousand behind him.

LINDA *(sensing the racing of his mind, fearfully, carefully).* Now come to bed, Willy. It's all settled now.

WILLY *(finding it difficult not to rush out of the house).* Yes, we'll sleep. Come on. Go to sleep, Hap.

BEN. And it does take a great kind of a man to crack the jungle.

(In accents of dread, Ben's idyllic music starts up.)

HAPPY *(his arm around Linda).* I'm getting married, Pop, don't forget it. I'm changing everything. I'm gonna run that department before the year is up. You'll see, Mom. *(He kisses her.)*

BEN. The jungle is dark but full of diamonds, Willy.

(Willy turns, moves, listening to Ben.)

LINDA. Be good. You're both good boys, just act that way, that's all.

HAPPY. 'Night, Pop. *(He goes upstairs.)*

LINDA *(to Willy).* Come, dear.

BEN *(with greater force).* One must go in to fetch a diamond out.

WILLY *(to Linda, as he moves slowly along the edge of kitchen, toward the door).* I just want to get settled down, Linda. Let me sit alone for a little.

LINDA *(almost uttering her fear).* I want you upstairs.

WILLY *(taking her in his arms).* In a few minutes, Linda. I couldn't sleep right now. Go on, you look awful tired. *(He kisses her.)*

BEN. Not like an appointment at all. A diamond is rough and hard to the touch.

WILLY. Go on now. I'll be right up.

LINDA. I think this is the only way, Willy.

WILLY.   Sure, it's the best thing.

BEN.   Best thing!

WILLY.   The only way. Everything is gonna be—go on, kid, get to bed. You look so tired.

LINDA.   Come right up.

WILLY.   Two minutes. *(Linda goes into the living room, then reappears in her bedroom. Willy moves just outside the kitchen door.)* Loves me. *(Wonderingly.)* Always loved me. Isn't that a remarkable thing? Ben, he'll worship me for it!

BEN *(with promise).*   It's dark there, but full of diamonds.

WILLY.   Can you imagine that magnificence with twenty thousand dollars in his pocket?

LINDA *(calling from her room).*   Willy! Come up!

WILLY *(calling into the kitchen).*   Yes! yes. Coming! It's very smart, you realize that, don't you, sweetheart? Even Ben sees it. I gotta go, baby. 'By! 'By! *(Going over to Ben, almost dancing.)* Imagine? When the mail comes he'll be ahead of Bernard again!

BEN.   A perfect proposition all around.

WILLY.   Did you see how he cried to me? Oh, if I could kiss him, Ben!

BEN.   Time, William, time!

WILLY.   Oh, Ben, I always knew one way or another we were gonna make it, Biff and I!

BEN *(looking at his watch).*   The boat. We'll be late. *(He moves slowly off into the darkness.)*

WILLY *(elegiacally, turning to the house).*   Now when you kick off, boy, I want a seventy-yard boot, and get right down the field under the ball, and when you hit, hit low and hit hard, because it's important, boy. *(He swings around and faces the audience.)* There's all kinds of important people in the stands, and the first thing you know . . . *(Suddenly realizing he is alone.)* Ben! Ben, where do I . . . ? *(He makes a sudden movement of search.)* Ben, how do I . . . ?

LINDA *(calling).*   Willy, you coming up?

WILLY *(uttering a gasp of fear, whirling about as if to quiet her).*   Sh! *(He turns around as if to find his way; sounds, faces, voices, seem to be swarming in upon him and he flicks at them, crying, Sh! Sh! Suddenly music, faint and high, stops him. It rises in intensity, almost to an unbearable scream. He goes up and down on his toes, and rushes off around the house.)* Shhh!

LINDA.   Willy?

(There is no answer. Linda waits. Biff gets up off his bed. He is still in his clothes. Happy sits up. Biff stands listening.)

LINDA *(with real fear).*   Willy, answer me! Willy! *(There is the sound of a car starting and moving away at full speed.)* No!

BIFF *(rushing down the stairs).*   Pop!

(As the car speeds off, the music crashes down in a frenzy of sound, which becomes the soft pulsation of a single cello string. Biff slowly returns to his bedroom. He and Happy gravely don their jackets. Linda slowly walks out of her room. The music has developed into a dead march. The leaves of day are appearing over everything. Charley and Bernard, somberly dressed, appear and knock on the kitchen door. Biff and Happy slowly descend the stairs to the kitchen as Charley and Bernard enter. All stop a moment when Linda, in clothes of mourning, bearing a little bunch of roses, comes through the draped doorway into the kitchen. She goes to Charley and takes his arm. Now all move toward the audience, through the wall-line of the kitchen. At the limit of the apron, Linda lays down the flowers, kneels, and sits back on her heels. All stare down at the grave.)

REQUIEM

CHARLEY. It's getting dark, Linda.

(Linda doesn't react. She stares at the grave.)

BIFF. How about it, Mom? Better get some rest, heh? They'll be closing the gate soon.

(Linda makes no move. Pause.)

HAPPY *(deeply angered).* He had no right to do that. There was no necessity for it. We would've helped him.

CHARLEY *(grunting).* Hmmm.

BIFF. Come along, Mom.

LINDA. Why didn't anybody come?

CHARLEY. It was a very nice funeral.

LINDA. But where are all the people he knew? Maybe they blame him.

CHARLEY. Naa. It's a rough world, Linda. They wouldn't blame him.

LINDA. I can't understand it. At this time especially. First time in thirty-five years we were just about free and clear. He only needed a little salary. He was even finished with the dentist.

CHARLEY. No man only needs a little salary.

LINDA. I can't understand it.

BIFF. There were a lot of nice days. When he'd come home from a trip; or on Sundays, making the stoop; finishing the cellar; putting on the new porch; when he built the extra bathroom; and put up the garage. You know something, Charley, there's more of him in that front stoop than in all the sales he ever made.

CHARLEY. Yeah. He was a happy man with a batch of cement.

LINDA. He was so wonderful with his hands.

BIFF. He had the wrong dreams. All, all, wrong.

HAPPY *(almost ready to fight Biff).* Don't say that!

BIFF. He never knew who he was.

CHARLEY *(stopping Happy's movement and reply. To Biff).* Nobody dast blame this man. You don't understand: Willy was a salesman. And for a salesman, there is no rock bottom to the life. He don't put a bolt to a nut, he don't tell you the law or give you medicine. He's a man way out there in the blue, riding on a smile and a shoeshine. And when they start not smiling back—that's an earthquake. And then you get yourself a couple of spots on your hat, and you're finished. Nobody dast blame this man. A salesman is got to dream, boy. It comes with the territory.

BIFF. Charley, the man didn't know who he was.

HAPPY *(infuriated).* Don't say that!

BIFF. Why don't you come with me, Happy?

HAPPY. I'm not licked that easily. I'm staying right in this city, and I'm gonna beat this racket! *(He looks at Biff, his chin set.)* The Loman Brothers!

BIFF. I know who I am, kid.

HAPPY. All right, boy. I'm gonna show you and everybody else that Willy Loman did not die in vain. He had a good dream. It's the only dream you can have—to come out number-one man. He fought it out here, and this is where I'm gonna win it for him.

BIFF *(with a hopeless glance at Happy, bends toward his mother).* Let's go, Mom.

LINDA.   I'll be with you in a minute. Go on, Charley. *(He hesitates.)* I want to, just for a minute. I never had a chance to say good-by. *(Charley moves away, followed by Happy. Biff remains a slight distance up and left of Linda. She sits there, summoning herself. The flute begins, not far away, playing behind her speech.)* Forgive me, dear. I can't cry. I don't know what it is, but I can't cry. I don't understand it. Why did you ever do that? Help me, Willy, I can't cry. It seems to me that you're just on another trip. I keep expecting you. Willy, dear, I can't cry. Why did you do it? I search and search and I search, and I can't understand it, Willy. I made the last payment on the house today. Today, dear. And there'll be nobody home. *(A sob rises in her throat.)* We're free and clear. *(Sobbing more fully, released.)* We're free. *(Biff comes slowly toward her.)* We're free . . . We're free . . .

(Biff lifts her to her feet and moves out up right with her in his arms. Linda sobs quietly. Bernard and Charley come together and follow them, followed by Happy. Only the music of the flute is left on the darkening stage as over the house the hard towers of the apartment buildings rise into sharp focus, and the curtain falls.)

WILLIAM SHAKESPEARE   (1564–1616)

Hamlet is a scholar returned from Wittenberg, where he presumably studies theology, the main curriculum available to one his age. Everything he does has a moral impact, and the evidence of his father's ghostly return from the grave makes him aware that his own actions may also be fatal. He learns that he risks not only his life, but his soul as well.

The form of this play follows convention, but also moves beyond tradition. It is a revenge tragedy, which usually requires the revenge of a relative—especially a father avenged by a son, the appearance of a ghost, hesitation on the part of the hero, real or pretended insanity, suicide, political intrigue, a spy, soliloquies especially philosophic in content, and sensational horror and gore. In addition to following convention, Shakespeare manages to give his major characters a lively psychological dimension.

Hamlet has been described as one of the most psychologically complex of all literary characters. His self-analysis, expressed in extensive soliloquies, implies total honesty, and reveals a mind whose vision is almost limitless. Unlike Greek characters, inexorably drawn to their fate, Hamlet seems to wander toward it. He surveys his options until he takes action.

In contrast to Hamlet, certain characters are flat and almost undeveloped. Polonius is the stereotypical pompous old fool. Laertes is his eager-to-please son. Then, characters such as Gertrude and Ophelia, who might have become a stereotypical mother and girlfriend, become astonishingly complex by virtue of their struggle to understand Hamlet. Gertrude is torn between her loyalty to her husband and her love for her son. Part of the tension of the drama is Hamlet's effort to warn her of Claudius and to make her see that his father was a better man than the brother who married her. The institution of marriage in Elizabethan times was such that even a queen owed absolute loyalty to her husband, so Gertrude's struggle between two loyalties is profound. Ophelia owes her allegiance to her father, but she loves Hamlet. Given the way she is used, it is hardly a wonder that she becomes insane.

The circumstances of Hamlet's return to court are so dangerous that he sees quickly that something is wrong. The ghost begins to confirm his suspicions, and the "mousetrap," the play he puts on to expose the king, reveals the truth to him at last. As the audience, we can sense his fears, his danger, and the threats that make him cautious.

Hamlet, Prince of Denmark _____ *c. 1600*

[Dramatis Personae

Claudius, *king of Denmark*
Hamlet, *son to the late King*
   Hamlet, and nephew to
   the present king
Polonius, *Lord Chamberlain*
Horatio, *friend to Hamlet*
Laertes, *son to Polonius*
Voltimand,
Cornelius,
Rosencrantz,
Guildenstern, } *courtiers*
Osric,
Gentleman,
Priest, or Doctor of Divinity
Marcellus, } *officers*
Bernardo,
Scene: Denmark.]

Francisco, *a soldier*
Reynaldo, *servant to Polonius*
Players
Two Clowns, *grave-diggers*
Fortinbras, *Prince of Norway*
Captain
English Ambassadors

Gertrude, *queen of Denmark,*
   mother to Hamlet
Ophelia, *daughter to Polonius*

Lords, Ladies, Officers, Soldiers,
   Sailors, Messengers, and other
   Attendants
Ghost of Hamlet's father

[ACT I

Scene I]°

(Enter Bernardo and Francisco, two sentinels, [meeting].)

BERNARDO.   Who's there?
FRANCISCO.   Nay, answer me.° Stand and unfold yourself.
BERNARDO.   Long live the King!
FRANCISCO.   Bernardo?
BERNARDO.   He.   5
FRANCISCO.   You come most carefully upon your hour.
BERNARDO.   'Tis now struck twelve. Get thee to bed, Francisco.
FRANCISCO.   For this relief much thanks. 'Tis bitter cold,
   And I am sick at heart.
BERNARDO.   Have you had quiet guard?
FRANCISCO.   Not a mouse stirring.   10
BERNARDO.   Well, good night.
   If you do meet Horatio and Marcellus,
   The rivals° of my watch, bid them make haste.

The text of Hamlet has come down to us in different versions—such as the first quarto, the second quarto, and the first Folio. The copy of the text used here is largely drawn from the second quarto. Passages enclosed in square brackets are taken from one of the other versions, in most cases the first Folio.   I. I. *Location:* Elsinore castle; a guard platform.   2 *me:* Francisco emphasizes that he is the sentry currently on watch.   13 *rivals:* partners.

(Enter Horatio and Marcellus.)

FRANCISCO.   I think I hear them. Stand, ho! Who is there?

HORATIO.   Friends to this ground.

MARCELLUS.   And liegemen to the Dane.°   15

FRANCISCO.   Give you° good night.

MARCELLUS.   O, farewell, honest soldier.
    Who hath relieved you?

FRANCISCO.   Bernardo hath my place.
    Give you good night.   *(Exit Francisco.)*

MARCELLUS.   Holla, Bernardo!

BERNARDO.   Say,
    What, is Horatio there?

HORATIO.   A piece of him.

BERNARDO.   Welcome, Horatio. Welcome, good Marcellus.   20

HORATIO.   What, has this thing appear'd again tonight?

BERNARDO.   I have seen nothing.

MARCELLUS.   Horatio says 'Tis but our fantasy,
    And will not let belief take hold of him
    Touching this dreaded sight, twice, seen of us.   25
    Therefore I have entreated him along
    With us to watch the minutes of this night,
    That if again this apparition come
    He may approve° our eyes and speak to it.

HORATIO.   Tush, tush, 'twill not appear.

BERNARDO.   Sit down awhile,   30
    And let us once again assail your ears,
    That are so fortified against our story,
    What we have two nights seen.

HORATIO.   Well, sit we down,
    And let us hear Bernardo speak of this.

BERNARDO.   Last night of all,   35
    When yond same star that's westward from the pole°
    Had made his° course t'illume that part of heaven
    Where now it burns, Marcellus and myself,
    The bell then beating one—

(Enter Ghost.)

MARCELLUS.   Peace, break thee off! Look where it comes again!   40

BERNARDO.   In the same figure, like the King that's dead.

MARCELLUS.   Thou art a scholar.° Speak to it, Horatio.

BERNARDO.   Looks 'a° not like the King? Mark it, Horatio.

HORATIO.   Most like. It harrows me with fear and wonder.

BERNARDO.   It would be spoke to.°

MARCELLUS.   Speak to it, Horatio.   45

HORATIO.   What art thou that usurp'st this time of night,
    Together with that fair and warlike form

---

15 *liegemen to the Dane:* men sworn to serve the Danish king.   16 *Give you:* God give you.   29 *approve:* corroborate.   36 *pole:* polestar.   37 *his:* its.   42 *scholar:* one learned in Latin and able to address spirits.   43 *'a:* he.   45 *It … to:* a ghost could not speak until spoken to.

In which the majesty of buried Denmark°
Did sometimes° march? By heaven I charge thee speak!
MARCELLUS.   It is offended.
BERNARDO.   See, it stalks away.   50
HORATIO.   Stay! Speak, speak. I charge thee, speak.

                                                        (Exit Ghost.)

MARCELLUS.   'Tis gone, and will not answer.
BERNARDO.   How now, Horatio? You tremble and look pale.
   Is not this something more than fantasy?
   What think you on 't?   55
HORATIO.   Before my God, I might not this believe
   Without the sensible° and true avouch
   Of mine own eyes.
MARCELLUS.   Is it not like the King?
HORATIO.   As thou art to thyself.
   Such was the very armor he had on   60
   When he the ambitious Norway° combated.
   So frown'd he once when, in an angry parle,°
   He smote the sledded° Polacks° on the ice.
   'Tis strange.
MARCELLUS.   Thus twice before, and jump° at this dead hour,   65
   With martial stalk hath he gone by our watch.
HORATIO.   In what particular thought to work I know not,
   But, in the gross and scope° of mine opinion,
   This bodes some strange eruption to our state.
MARCELLUS.   Good now,° sit down, and tell me, he that knows,   70
   Why this same strict and most observant watch
   So nightly toils° the subject° of the land,
   And why such daily cast° of brazen cannon,
   And foreign mart° for implements of war,
   Why such impress° of shipwrights, whose sore task   75
   Does not divide the Sunday from the week.
   What might be toward,° that this sweaty haste
   Doth make the night joint-laborer with the day?
   Who is 't that can inform me?
HORATIO.   That can I,
   At least, the whisper goes so. Our last king   80
   Whose image even but now appear'd to us,
   Was, as you know, by Fortinbras of Norway,
   Thereto prick'd on° by a most emulate° pride,
   Dar'd to the combat; in which our valiant Hamlet—
   For so this side of our known world esteem'd him—   85

48 *buried Denmark:* the buried king of Denmark.   49 *sometimes:* formerly.   57 *sensible:* confirmed by the senses.   61 *Norway:* King of Norway.   62 *parle:* parley.   63 *sledded:* traveling on sleds.   *Polacks:* Poles.   65 *jump:* exactly.   68 *gross and scope:* general view.   70 *good now:* an expression denoting entreaty or expostulation.   72 *toils:* causes to toil.   *subject:* subjects.   73 *cast:* casting.   74 *mart:* buying and selling.   75 *impress:* impressment, conscription.   77 *toward:* in preparation.   83 *prick'd on:* incited.   *emulate:* ambitious.

Did slay this Fortinbras; who, by a seal'd compact,
Well ratified by law and heraldry,
Did forfeit, with his life, all those his lands
Which he stood seiz'd° of, to the conqueror;
Against the° which a moi'ty competent°   90
Was gaged° by our king, which had return'd
To the inheritance of Fortinbras
Had he been vanquisher, as, by the same comart°
And carriage° of the article design'd,
His fell to Hamlet. Now, sir, young Fortinbras,   95
Of unimproved° mettle hot and full,
Hath in the skirts° of Norway here and there
Shark'd up° a list of lawless resolutes°
For food and diet° to some enterprise
That hath a stomach° in 't, which is no other—   100
As it doth well appear unto our state—
But to recover of us, by strong hand
And terms compulsatory, those foresaid lands
So by his father lost. And this, I take it,
Is the main motive of our preparations,   105
The source of this our watch, and the chief head°
Of this post-haste and romage° in the land.
BERNARDO.   I think it be no other but e'en so.
Well may it sort° that this portentous figure
Comes armed through our watch so like the King   110
That was and is the question of these wars.
HORATIO.   A mote° it is to trouble the mind's eye.
In the most high and palmy° state of Rome,
A little ere the mightiest Julius fell,
The graves stood tenantless and the sheeted° dead   115
Did squeak and gibber in the Roman streets;
As° stars with trains of fire and dews of blood,
Disasters° in the sun; and the moist star°
Upon whose influence Neptune's° empire stands°
Was sick almost to doomsday° with eclipse.   120
And even the like precurse° of fear'd events,
As harbingers° preceding still° the fates
And prologue to the omen° coming on,

---

89 *seiz'd:* possessed.   90 *Against the:* in return for.   *moi'ty competent:* sufficient portion.
91 *gaged:* engaged, pledged.   93 *comart:* joint bargain (?).   94 *carriage:* import, bearing.
96 *unimproved:* not turned to account (?) or untested (?).   97 *skirts:* outlying regions, outskirts.   98 *shark'd up:* got together in haphazard fashion.   *resolutes:* desperadoes.   99 *food
and diet:* no pay but their keep.   100 *stomach:* relish of danger.   106 *head:* source.   107 *ro-
mage:* bustle, commotion.   109 *sort:* suit.   112 *mote:* speck of dust.   113 *palmy:* flourishing.   115 *sheeted:* shrouded.   117 *As:* This abrupt transition suggests that matter is possibly
omitted between lines 116 and 117.   118 *Disasters:* unfavorable signs of aspects.   *moist
star:* moon, governing tides.   119 *Neptune:* god of the sea.   *stands:* depends.   120 *sick . . .
doomsday:* See Matt. 24:29 and Rev. 6:12.   121 *precurse:* heralding, foreshadowing.   122 *har-
bingers:* forerunners.   *still:* continually.   123 *omen:* calamitous event.

Have heaven and earth together demonstrated
Unto our climatures° and countrymen.   125

(Enter Ghost.)

But soft, behold! Lo where it comes again!
I'll cross° it, though it blast me. Stay, illusion!
If thou hast any sound, or use of voice,
Speak to me!   *(It spreads his arms.)*
If there be any good thing to be done   130
That may to thee do ease and grace to me,
Speak to me!
If thou art privy to thy country's fate,
Which, happily,° foreknowing may avoid,
O, speak!   135
Or if thou hast uphoarded in thy life
Extorted treasure in the womb of earth,
For which, they say, you spirits oft walk in death,

(The cock crows.)

Speak of it. Stay, and speak! Stop it, Marcellus.
MARCELLUS.   Shall I strike at it with my partisan?°   140
HORATIO.   Do, if it will not stand.*[They strike at it.]*
BERNARDO.   'Tis here!
HORATIO.   'Tis here!
MARCELLUS.   'Tis gone.   *[Exit Ghost.]*
We do it wrong, being so majestical,
To offer it the show of violence;
For it is, as the air, invulnerable,   145
And our vain blows malicious mockery.
BERNARDO.   It was about to speak when the cock crew.
HORATIO.   And then it started like a guilty thing
Upon a fearful summons. I have heard,
The cock, that is the trumpet to the morn,   150
Doth with his lofty and shrill-sounding throat
Awake the god of day, and, at his warning,
Whether in sea or fire, in earth or air,
Th' extravagant and erring° spirit hies
To his confine; and of the truth herein   155
This present object made probation.°
MARCELLUS.   It faded on the crowing of the cock.
Some say that ever 'gainst° that season comes
Wherein our Savior's birth is celebrated,
The bird of dawning singeth all night long,   160
And then, they say, no spirit dare stir abroad;
The nights are wholesome, then no planets strike,°

125 *climatures:* regions.   127 *cross:* meet, face directly.   134 *happily:* haply, perchance.
140 *partisan:* long-handled spear.   154 *extravagant and erring:* wandering. (The words have similar
meaning.)   156 *probation:* proof.   158 *'gainst:* just before.   162 *strike:* exert evil influence.

No fairy takes,° nor witch hath power to charm,
So hallowed and so gracious° is that time.
HORATIO.   So have I heard and do in part believe it.   165
But, look, the morn, in russet mantle clad,
Walks o'er the dew of yon high eastward hill.
Break we our watch up, and by my advice
Let us impart what we have seen tonight
Unto young Hamlet; for, upon my life,   170
This spirit, dumb to us, will speak to him.
Do you consent we shall acquaint him with it,
As needful in our loves, fitting our duty?
MARCELLUS.   Let's do 't, I pray, and I this morning know
Where we shall find him most conveniently.   175

(*Exeunt.*) °

163 *takes:* bewitches.   164 *gracious:* full of goodness.   175 *Exeunt:* Latin for "they go out."

[*Scene II*]°

(*Flourish. Enter Claudius, King of Denmark, Gertrude the Queen, Councilors, Polonius
and his son Laertes, Hamlet, cum aliis° [including Voltimand and Cornelius].*)

KING.   Though yet of Hamlet our dear brother's death
The memory be green, and that it us befitted
To bear our hearts in grief and our whole kingdom
To be contracted in one brow of woe,
Yet so far hath discretion fought with nature   5
That we with wisest sorrow think on him,
Together with remembrance of ourselves.
Therefore our sometime sister, now our queen,
Th' imperial jointress° to this warlike state,
Have we, as 'twere with a defeated joy—   10
With an auspicious and a dropping eye,
With mirth in funeral and with dirge in marriage,
In equal scale weighing delight and dole—
Taken to wife. Nor have we herein barr'd
Your better wisdoms, which have freely gone   15
With this affair along. For all, our thanks.
Now follows that you know° young Fortinbras,
Holding a weak supposal° of our worth,
Or thinking by our late dear brother's death
Our state to be disjoint and out of frame,   20
Colleagued with° this dream of his advantage,°
He hath not fail'd to pester us with message
Importing° the surrender of those lands

I. II. *Location:* The castle.   *cum aliis:* with others.   9 *jointress:* woman possessed of a joint tenancy of an estate.   17 *know:* be informed (that).   18 weak supposal: low estimate.
21 *colleagued with:* joined to, allied with.   *dream . . . advantage:* illusory hope of success.   23 *importing:* pertaining to.

Lost by his father, with all bands° of law,
To our most valiant brother. So much for him.   25
Now for ourself and for this time of meeting.
Thus much the business is: we have here writ
To Norway, uncle of young Fortinbras—
Who, impotent and bed-rid, scarcely hears
Of this his nephew's purpose—to suppress   30
His° further gait° herein, in that the levies,
The lists, and full proportions are all made
Out of his Subject;° and we here dispatch
You, good Cornelius, and you, Voltimand,
For bearers of this greeting to old Norway,   35
Giving to you no further personal power
To business with the King, more than the Scope
Of these delated° articles allow   *[Gives a paper.]*
Farewell, and let your haste commend your duty.

CORNELIUS, VOLTIMAND: In that, and all things, will we show our duty.   40
KING.   We doubt it nothing. Heartily farewell.

[Exit Voltimand and Cornelius.]

And now, Laertes, what's the news with you?
You told us of some suit; what is 't, Laertes?
You cannot speak of reason to the Dane°
And lose your voice.° What wouldst thou beg, Laertes,   45
That shall not be my offer, not thy asking?
The head is not more native° to the heart,
The hand more instrumental° to the mouth,
Than is the throne of Denmark to thy father.
What wouldst thou have, Laertes?
LAERTES.   My dread lord,   50
Your leave and favor to return to France,
From whence though willingly I came to Denmark
To show my duty in your coronation,
Yet now I must confess, that duty done,
My thoughts and wishes bend again toward France   55
And bow them to your gracious leave and pardon.°
KING.   Have you your father's leave? What says Polonius?
POLONIUS.   H'ath,° my lord, wrung from me my slow leave
By laborsome petition, and at last
Upon his will I seal'd my hard° consent.   60
I do beseech you, give him leave to go.
KING.   Take thy fair hour, Laertes. Time be thine,
And thy best graces spend it at thy will!
But now, my cousin° Hamlet, and my son—

24 *bands:* contracts.   31 *his:* Fortinbras's.   *gait:* proceeding.   31-33 *in that ... Subject:* since
the levying of troops and supplies is drawn entirely from the king of Norway's own sub-
ject.   38 *delated:* detailed. (variant of dilated.)   44 *the Dane:* The Danish king.   45 *lose your*
voice: waste your speech.   47 *native:* closely connected, related.   48 *instrumental:* serviceable.
56 *leave and pardon:* permission to depart.   58 *h'ath:* he hath (has).   60 *hard:* reluctant.
64 *cousin:* any kin not of the immediate family.

HAMLET.   A little more than kin, and less than kind.°   65
KING.   How is it that the clouds still hang on you?
HAMLET.   Not so, my lord. I am too much in the sun.°
QUEEN.   Good Hamlet, cast thy nighted color off,
    And let thine eye look like a friend on Denmark.
    Do not forever with thy vailed° lids   70
    Seek for thy noble father in the dust.
    Thou know'st 'tis common,° all that lives must die,
    Passing through nature to eternity.
HAMLET.   Ay, madam, it is common.
QUEEN.   If it be,
    Why seems it so particular with thee?   75
HAMLET.   Seems, madam! Nay, it is. I know not "seems."
    'Tis not alone my inky cloak, good mother,
    Nor customary suits of solemn black,
    Nor windy suspiration of forc'd breath,
    No, nor the fruitful° river in the eye   80
    Nor the dejected havior° of the visage,
    Together with all forms, moods, shapes of grief,
    That can denote me truly. These indeed seem,
    For they are actions that a man might play.
    But I have that within which passes show;   85
    These but the trappings and the suits of woe.
KING.   'Tis sweet and commendable in your nature, Hamlet,
    To give these mourning duties to your father.
    But you must know your father lost a father,
    That father lost, lost his, and the survivor bound   90
    In filial obligation for some term
    To do obsequious° sorrow. But to persever°
    In obstinate condolement° is a course
    Of impious stubbornness. 'Tis unmanly grief.
    It shows a will most incorrect to heaven,   95
    A heart unfortified, a mind impatient,
    An understanding simple and unschool'd.
    For what we know must be and is as common
    As any the most vulgar thing to sense,°
    Why should we in our peevish opposition   100
    Take it to heart? Fie, 'tis a fault to heaven,
    A fault against the dead, a fault to nature,
    To reason most absurd, whose common theme
    Is death of fathers, and who still hath cried,
    From the first corse° till he that died today,   105
    "This must be so." We pray you, throw to earth

---

65 *a little ... kind:* closer than an ordinary nephew (since I am stepson), and yet more separated in
natural feeling (with pun on kind, meaning affectionate and natural, lawful. This line is often read
as an aside, but it need not be.)   67 *sun:* the sunshine of the King's royal favor (with pun on
son).   70 *vailed:* downcast.   72 *common:* of universal occurrence. (But Hamlet plays on the
sense of vulgar in line 72.)   80 *fruitful:* abundant.   81 *havior:* appearance.   92 *obse-*
quious: suited to obsequies or funerals.   persever: persevere.   93 *condolement:* sorrowing.
99 *as . . . sense:* as the most ordinary experience.   105 *corse:* corpse.

This unprevailing° woe, and think of us
As of a father; for let the world take note,
You are the most immediate° to our throne,
And with no less nobility of love   110
Than that which dearest father bears his son
Do I impart toward you. For your intent
In going back to school in Wittenberg,°
It is most retrograde° to our desire,
And we beseech you, bend you° to remain   115
Here in the cheer and comfort of our eye,
Our chiefest courtier, cousin, and our son.
QUEEN.   Let not thy mother lose her prayers, Hamlet.
I pray thee stay with us, go not to Wittenberg.
HAMLET.   I shall in all my best obey you, madam.   120
KING.   Why, 'tis a loving and a fair reply.
Be as ourself in Denmark. Madam, come.
This gentle and unforc'd accord of Hamlet
Sits smiling to my heart, in grace whereof
No jocund° health that Denmark drinks today   125
But the great cannon to the clouds shall tell,
And the King's rouse° the heaven shall bruit again,°
Respeaking earthly thunder.° Come away.

(Flourish. Exeunt all but Hamlet.)

HAMLET.   O, that this too too sullied° flesh would melt,
Thaw, and resolve itself into a dew!   130
Or that the Everlasting had not fix'd
His canon° 'gainst self-slaughter! O God, God,
How weary, stale, flat, and unprofitable
Seem to me all the uses of this world!
Fie on 't, ah, fie! 'Tis an unweeded garden   135
That grows to seed. Things rank and gross in nature
Possess it merely.° That it should come to this!
But two months dead—nay, not so much, not two.
So excellent a king, that was to° this
Hyperion° to a satyr; so loving to my mother   140
That he might not beteem° the winds of heaven
Visit her face too roughly. Heaven and earth,
Must I remember? Why, she would hang on him
As if increase of appetite had grown
By what it fed on, and yet, within a month—   145
Let me not think on 't. Frailty, thy name is woman!—
A little month, or ere those shoes were old

---

107 *unprevailing:* unavailing.   109 *most immediate:* next in succession.   113 *Wittenberg:* famous
German university founded in 1502.   114 *retrograde:* contrary.   115 *bend you:* incline yourself.   125 *jocund:* merry.   127 *rouse:* draft of liquor.   *bruit again:* loudly echo.   128 *thunder:* of trumpet and kettledrum, sounded when the King drinks; see I. iv. 8-12.   129 *sullied:*
defiled. (the early quartos read sallied, the folio solid.)   132 *canon:* law.   137 *merely:* completely.   139 *to:* in comparison to.   140 *Hyperion:* Titan sun-god, father of Helios.   141 *beteem:* allow.

With which she followed my poor father's body,
Like Niobe,° all tears, why she, even she—
O God, a beast, that wants discourse of reason,°   150
Would have mourn'd longer—married with my uncle,
My father's brother, but no more like my father
Than I to Hercules. Within a month,
Ere yet the salt of most unrighteous tears
Had left the flushing in her galled° eyes,   155
She married. O, most wicked speed, to post
With such dexterity to incestuous° sheets!
It is not nor it cannot come to good.
But break, my heart, for I must hold my tongue.

(Enter Horatio, Marcellus, and Bernardo.)

HORATIO.   Hail to your lordship!
HAMLET.   I am glad to see you well.   160
    Horatio!—or I do forget myself.
HORATIO.   The same, my lord, and your poor servant ever.
HAMLET.   Sir, my good friend; I'll change° that name with you.
    And what make° you from Wittenberg, Horatio?
    Marcellus?   165
MARCELLUS.   My good lord.
HAMLET.   I am very glad to see you.   *[To Bernardo.]*
    Good even, sir.—
    But what, in faith, make you from Wittenberg?
HORATIO.   A truant disposition, good my lord.
HAMLET.   I would not hear your enemy say so,   170
    Nor shall you do my ear that violence
    To make it truster of your own report
    Against yourself. I know you are no truant.
    But what is your affair in Elsinore?
    We'll teach you to drink deep ere you depart.   175
HORATIO.   My lord, I came to see your father's funeral.
HAMLET.   I prithee do not mock me, fellow student;
    I think it was to see my mother's wedding.
HORATIO.   Indeed, my lord, it followed hard° upon.
HAMLET.   Thrift, thrift, Horatio! The funeral bak'd meats   180
    Did coldly furnish forth the marriage tables.
    Would I had met my dearest° foe in heaven
    Or° ever I had seen that day, Horatio!
    My father!— Methinks I see my father.
HORATIO.   Where, my lord?
HAMLET.   In my mind's eye, Horatio.   185

149 *Niobe:* Tantalus's daughter, Queen of Thebes, who boasted that she had more sons and daughters than Leto; for this, Apollo and Artemis, children of Leto, slew her fourteen children. She was turned by Zeus into a stone which continually dropped tears.   150 *wants . . . reason:* lacks the faculty of reason.   155 *galled:* irritated, inflamed.   157 *incestuous:* in Shakespeare's day, the marriage of a man like Claudius to his deceased brother's wife was considered incestuous. 163 *change:* exchange (i.e., the name of friend).   164 *make:* do.   179 *hard:* close.   182 *dearest:* direst.   183 *or:* ere, before.

HORATIO.   I saw him once. 'A° was a goodly king.
HAMLET.   'A was a man, take him for all in all,
    I shall not look upon his like again.
HORATIO.   My lord, I think I saw him yesternight.
HAMLET.   Saw? Who? 190
HORATIO.   My lord, the King your father.
HAMLET.   The King my father?
HORATIO.   Season your admiration° for a while
    With an attent° ear, till I may deliver,
    Upon the witness of these gentlemen,
    This marvel to you.
HAMLET.   For God's love, let me hear! 195
HORATIO.   Two nights together had these gentlemen,
    Marcellus and Bernardo, on their watch,
    In the dead waste and middle of the night,
    Been thus encount'red. A figure like your father,
    Armed at point° exactly, cap-a-pe,° 200
    Appears before them, and with solemn march
    Goes slow and stately by them. Thrice he walk'd
    By their oppress'd and fear-surprised eyes
    Within his truncheon's° length, whilst they, distill'd
    Almost to jelly with the act° of fear, 205
    Stand dumb and speak not to him. This to me
    In dreadful secrecy impart they did,
    And I with them the third night kept the watch,
    Where, as they had delivered, both in time,
    Form of the thing, each word made true and 210
    Good, the apparition comes. I knew your father;
    These hands are not more like.
HAMLET.   But where was this?
MARCELLUS.   My lord, upon the platform where we watch.
HAMLET.   Did you not speak to it?
HORATIO.   My lord, I did.
    But answer made it none. Yet once methought 215
    It lifted up it° head and did address
    Itself to motion, like as it would speak;
    But even then the morning cock crew loud,
    And at the sound it shrunk in haste away,
    And vanish'd from our sight.
HAMLET.   'Tis very strange, 220
HORATIO.   As I do live, my honor'd lord, 'tis true,
    And we did think it writ down in our duty
    To let you know of it.
HAMLET.   Indeed, indeed, sirs. But this troubles me.
    Hold you the watch tonight?
ALL.   We do, my lord. 225

---

186 *'A:* he.   192 *season your admiration:* restrain your astonishment.   193 *attent:* attentive.
200 *at point:* completely.   *cap-a-pe:* from head to foot.   204 *truncheon:* officer's staff.
205 *act:* action, operation.   216 *it:* its.

HAMLET. Arm'd, say you?
ALL. Arm'd, my lord.
HAMLET. From top to toe?
ALL.   My lord, from head to foot.
HAMLET. Then saw you not his face?
HORATIO. O, yes, my lord. He wore his beaver° up.   230
HAMLET. What, looked he frowningly?
HORATIO.   A countenance more
  In sorrow than in anger.
HAMLET.   Pale or red?
HORATIO. Nay, very pale.
HAMLET.   And fix'd his eyes upon you?
HORATIO. Most constantly.
HAMLET.   I would I had been there.
HORATIO. It would have much amaz'd you.   235
HAMLET. Very like, very like. Stay'd it long?
HORATIO. While one with moderate haste might tell° a hundred.
MARCELLUS, BERNARDO: Longer, longer.
HORATIO. Not when I saw't.
HAMLET.   His beard was grizzl'd,—no?
HORATIO. It was, as I have seen it in his life,   240
  A sable silver'd.°
HAMLET.   I will watch tonight.
  Perchance 'twill walk again.
HORATIO.   I warr'nt it will.
HAMLET. If it assume my noble father's person,
  I'll speak to it, though hell itself should gape
  And bid me hold my peace. I pray you all,   245
  If you have hitherto conceal'd this sight,
  Let it be tenable° in your silence still,
  And whatsomever else shall hap tonight,
  Give it an understanding, but no tongue.
  I will requite your loves. So, fare you well.   250
  Upon the platform, 'twixt eleven and twelve,
  I'll visit you.
ALL.   Our duty to your honor.
HAMLET. Your loves, as mine to you. Farewell.

(Exeunt [all but Hamlet].)

My father's spirit in arms! All is not well.
I doubt° some foul play. Would the night were come!   255
Till then sit still, my soul. Foul deeds will rise,
Though all the earth o'erwhelm them, to men's eyes.

(Exit.)

---

230 *beaver:* visor on the helmet.   237 *tell:* count.   241 *sable silver'd:* black mixed with white.
247 *tenable:* held tightly.   255 *doubt:* suspect.

[Scene III]°

(Enter Laertes and Ophelia, his sister.)

LAERTES.   My necessaries are embark'd. Farewell.
And, sister, as the winds give benefit
And convoy is assistant,° do not sleep
But let me hear from you.

OPHELIA.   Do you doubt that?

LAERTES. For Hamlet, and the trifling of his favor,   5
Hold it a fashion and a toy in blood,°
A violet in the youth of primy° nature,
Forward,° not permanent, sweet, not lasting,
The perfume and suppliance° of a minute—
No more.

OPHELIA.   No more but so?

LAERTES.   Think it no more.   10
For nature crescent° does not grow alone
In thews° and bulk, but, as this temple° waxes,
The inward service of the mind and soul
Grows wide withal.° Perhaps he loves you now,
And now no soil° nor cautel° doth besmirch   15
The virtue of his will;° but you must fear,
His greatness weigh'd,° his will is not his own.
[For he himself is subject to his birth.]
He may not, as unvalued persons do,
Carve° for himself; for on his choice depends   20
The safety and health of this whole state,
And therefore must his choice be circumscrib'd
Unto the voice and yielding° of that body
Whereof he is the head. Then if he says he loves you,
It fits your wisdom so far to believe it   25
As he in his particular act and place
May give his saying deed,° which is no further
Than the main voice of Denmark goes withal.
Then weigh what loss your honor may sustain
If with too credent° ear you list° his songs,   30
Or lose your heart, or your chaste treasure open
To his unmaster'd importunity.
Fear it, Ophelia, fear it, my dear sister,
And keep you in the rear of your affection,
Out of the shot° and danger of desire.   35

I. III. *Location:* Polonius's chambers.   3 *convoy is assistant:* means of conveyance are available.
6 *toy in blood:* passing amorous fancy.   7 *primy:* in its prime, springtime.   8 *Forward:* precocious.   9 *suppliance:* supply,   filler.   11 *crescent:* growing,   waxing.   12 *thews:* bodily
strength.   *temple:* body.   14 *grows wide withal:* grows along with it.   15 *soil:* blemish.   *cau-
tel:* deceit.   16 *will:* desire.   17 *greatness weigh'd:* high position considered.   20 *carve:* choose
pleasure.   23 *voice and yielding:* assent, approval.   27 *deed:* effect.   30 *credent:* credulous.
list: listen to.   35 *shot:* range.

The chariest° maid is prodigal enough
If she unmask her beauty to the moon.
Virtue itself scapes not calumnious strokes.
The canker galls° the infants of the spring
Too oft before their buttons° be disclos'd,°   40
And in the morn and liquid dew° of youth
Contagious blastments° are most imminent.
Be wary then; best safety lies in fear.
Youth to itself rebels, though none else near.

OPHELIA.   I shall the effect of this good lesson keep   45
As watchman to my heart. But, good my brother,
Do not, as some ungracious pastors do,
Show me the steep and thorny way to heaven,
Whiles, like a puff'd° and reckless libertine,
Himself the primrose path of dalliance treads,   50
And recks° not his own rede.°

(Enter Polonius.)

LAERTES.   O, fear me not.
I stay too long. But here my father comes.
A double blessing is a double° grace;
Occasion° smiles upon a second leave.

POLONIUS.   Yet here, Laertes? Aboard, aboard, for shame!   55
The wind sits in the shoulder of your sail,
And you are stay'd for.° There—my blessing with thee!
And these few precepts in thy memory
Look thou character.° Give thy thoughts no tongue,
Nor any unproportion'd thought his° act.   60
Be thou familiar,° but by no means vulgar.°
Those friends thou hast, and their adoption tried,°
Grapple them to thy soul with hoops of steel,
But do not dull thy palm with entertainment
Of each new-hatch'd, unfledg'd courage.° Beware   65
Of entrance to a quarrel, but, being in,
Bear't that° th' opposed may beware of thee.
Give every man thy ear, but few thy voice;
Take each man's censure,° but reserve thy judgment.
Costly thy habit as thy purse can buy,   70
But not express'd in fancy; rich, not gaudy,
For the apparel oft proclaims the man,
And they in France of the best rank and station
Are of a most select and generous chief° in that.

36 *chariest:* most scrupulously modest.   39 *canker galls:* cankerworm destroys.   40 *buttons:*
buds.   *disclos'd:* opened.   41 *liquid dew:* Time when dew is fresh.   42 *blastments:*
blights.   49 *puff'd:* bloated.   51 *recks:* heeds.   *rede:* counsel.   53 *double:* i.e., Laertes
has already bidden his father good-by.   54 *occasion:* opportunity.   57 *stay'd for:* waited
for.   59 *character:* inscribe.   60 *his:* Its.   61 *familiar:* sociable.   *vulgar:* common.
62 *tried:* tested.   65 *courage:* young man of spirit.   67 *Bear't that:* manage it so that.   69 *cen-*
sure: opinion, judgment.   74 *generous chief:* noble eminence (?).

Neither a borrower nor a lender be,   75
For loan oft loses both itself and friend,
And borrowing dulleth edge of husbandry.°
This above all: to thine own self be true,
And it must follow, as the night the day,
Thou canst not then be false to any man.   80
Farewell. My blessing season° this in thee!
LAERTES.   Most humbly do I take my leave, my lord.
POLONIUS.   The time invests° you. Go, your servants tend.°
LAERTES. Farewell, Ophelia, and remember well
What I have said to you.   85
OPHELIA.   'Tis in my memory lock'd
And you yourself shall keep the key of it.
LAERTES. Farewell.   *(Exit Laertes.)*
POLONIUS.   What is 't, Ophelia, he hath said to you?
OPHELIA.   So please you, something touching the Lord Hamlet.   90
POLONIUS.   Marry,° well bethought.
'Tis told me he hath very oft of late
Given private time to you, and you yourself
Have of your audience been most free and bounteous.
If it be so—as so 'Tis put on° me,   95
And that in way of caution—I must tell you
You do not understand yourself so clearly
As it behooves my daughter and your honor.
What is between you? Give me up the truth.
OPHELIA.   He hath, my lord, of late made many tenders°   100
Of his affection to me.
POLONIUS.   Affection? Pooh! You speak like a green girl,
Unsifted° in such perilous circumstance.
Do you believe his tenders, as you call them?
OPHELIA.   I do not know, my lord, what I should think.   105
POLONIUS.   Marry, I will teach you. Think yourself a baby
That you have ta'en these tenders° for true pay,
Which are not sterling.° Tender° yourself more dearly,
Or—not to crack the wind° of the poor phrase,
Running it thus—you'll tender me a fool.°   110
OPHELIA.   My lord, he hath importun'd me with love
In honorable fashion.
POLONIUS.   Ay, fashion° you may call it. Go to, go to.
OPHELIA.   And hath given countenance° to his speech, my lord,
With almost all the holy vows of heaven.   115
POLONIUS.   Ay, springes° to catch woodcocks.° I do know,

---

77 *husbandry:* thrift.   81 *season:* mature.   83 *invests:* besieges.   *tend:* attend,
wait.   91 *Marry:* by the Virgin Mary (a mild oath).   95 *put on:* impressed on, told to.
100 *tenders:* offers.   103 *unsifted:* untried.   107 *tenders:* With added meaning here of promises
to pay.   108 *sterling:* legal currency.   *Tender:* hold.   109 *crack the wind:* run it until it is broken, winded.   110 *tender me a fool:* (1) show yourself to me as a fool; (2) show me up as a fool;
(3) present me with a grandchild (fool was a term of endearment for a child).   113 *fashion:* mere
form, pretense.   114 *countenance:* credit, support.   116 *springes:* snares.   *woodcocks:* birds
easily caught; here used to connote gullibility.

When the blood burns, how prodigal the soul
Lends the tongue vows. These blazes, daughter,
Giving more light than heat, extinct in both
Even in their promise, as it is a-making,   120
You must not take for fire. From this time
Be something scanter of your maiden presence.
Set your entreatments° at a higher rate
Than a command to parle.° For Lord Hamlet,
Believe so much in him° that he is young,   125
And with a larger tether may he walk
Than may be given you. In few,° Ophelia,
Do not believe his vows, for they are brokers,°
Not of that dye° which their investments° show,
But mere implorators° of unholy suits,   130
Breathing° like sanctified and pious bawds,
The better to beguile. This is for all:
I would not, in plain terms, from this time forth
Have you so slander° any moment leisure
As to give words or talk with the Lord Hamlet.   135
Look to 't, I charge you. Come your ways.
OPHELIA.   I shall obey, my lord.   *(Exeunt.)*

123 *entreatments:* negotiations for surrender (a military term).   124 *parle:* discuss terms with the
enemy. (Polonius urges his daughter, in the metaphor of military language, not to meet with Hamlet and consider giving in to him merely because he requests an interview.)   125 *so . . . him:* this
much concerning him.   127 *In few:* briefly.   128 *brokers:* go-betweens, procurers.   129 *dye:*
color or sort.   *investments:* clothes (i.e., they are not what they seem).   130 *mere im-
plorators:* out and out solicitors.   131 *breathing:* speaking.   134 *slander:* bring disgrace or reproach upon.

[Scene IV]°

(Enter Hamlet, Horatio, and Marcellus.)

HAMLET.   The air bites shrewdly; it is very cold.
HORATIO.   It is a nipping and an eager air.
HAMLET.   What hour now?
HORATIO.   I think it lacks of twelve.
MARCELLUS.   No, it is struck.
HORATIO.   Indeed? I heard it not.
    It then draws near the season   5
    wherein the spirit held his wont to walk.

                            *(A flourish of trumpets, and two pieces° go off
                            [within].)*

    What does this mean, my lord?
HAMLET.   The King doth wake° tonight and takes his rouse,°
    Keeps wassail,° and the swagg'ring up-spring° reels;

I. IV. *Location:* the guard platform.   6 *pieces:* i.e., of ordnance, cannon   8 *wake:* stay awake
and hold revel.   *rouse:* carouse, drinking bout.   9 *wassail:* carousal.   *up-spring:* wild German dance.

And as he drains his draughts of Rhenish° down,   10
The kettle-drum and trumpet thus bray out
The triumph of his pledge.°
HORATIO.   Is it a custom?
HAMLET.   Ay, marry, is 't,
But to my mind, though I am native here
And to the manner° born, it is a custom   15
More honor'd in the breach than the observance.°
This heavy-headed revel east and west°
Makes us traduc'd and tax'd of° other nations.
They clepe° us drunkards, and with swinish phrase°
Soil our addition;° and indeed it takes   20
From our achievements, though perform'd at height,°
The pith and marrow of our attribute.
So, oft it chances in particular men,
That for some vicious mole of nature° in them,
As in their birth—wherein they are not guilty,   25
Since nature cannot choose his° origin—
By the o'ergrowth of some complexion,°
Oft breaking down the pales° and forts of reason,
Or by some habit that too much o'er-leavens°
The form of plausive° manners, that these men,   30
Carrying, I say, the stamp of one defect,
Being nature's livery,° or fortune's star,°
Their virtues else, be they as pure as grace,
As infinite as man may undergo,
Shall in the general censure take corruption   35
From that particular fault. The dram of eale°
Doth all the noble substance of a doubt°
To his own scandal.°

(Enter Ghost.)

HORATIO.   Look, my lord, it comes!
HAMLET.   Angels and ministers of grace defend us!
Be thou a spirit of health° or goblin damn'd,   40
Bring with thee airs from heaven or blasts from hell,
Be thy intents wicked or charitable,
Thou com'st in such a questionable° shape
That I will speak to thee. I'll call thee Hamlet,

---

10 *Rhenish:* Rhine wine.   12 *triumph . . . pledge:* his feat in draining the wine in a single draught.
15 *manner:* custom (of drinking).   16 *more . . . observance:* better neglected than followed.
17 *east and west:* i.e., everywhere.   18 *tax'd of:* censured by.   19 *clepe:* call.   *with swinish
phrase:* by calling us swine.   20 *addition:* reputation.   21 *at height:* outstandingly.   24 *mole
of nature:* natural blemish in one's constitution.   26 *his:* its.   27 *complexion:* humor (i.e., one of
the four humors or fluids thought to determine temperament).   28 *pales:* palings, fences (as of a
fortification).   29 *o'er-leavens:* Induces a change throughout (as yeast works in dough).   30
plausive: Pleasing.   32 *nature's livery:* endowment from nature.   *fortune's star:* mark placed by
fortune.   36 *dram of eale:* small amount of evil (?).   37 *of a doubt:* a famous crux, sometimes
emended to *oft about* or *often dout,* i.e., "often erase" or "do out," or to *antidote,* counteract.
38 *To . . . scandal:* to the disgrace of the whole enterprise.   40 *of health:* of spiritual good.
43 *questionable:* inviting question or conversation.

King, father, royal Dane. O, answer me!   45
Let me not burst in ignorance; but tell
Why thy canoniz'd° bones, hearsed° in death,
Have burst their cerements;° why the sepulcher
Wherein we saw thee quietly interr'd
Hath op'd his ponderous and marble jaws   50
To cast thee up again. What may this mean,
That thou, dead corse, again in complete steel
Revisits thus the glimpses of the moon,°
Making night hideous, and we fools of nature°
So horridly to shake our disposition   55
With thoughts beyond the reaches of our souls?
Say, why is this? Wherefore? What should we do?

([Ghost] beckons [Hamlet].)

HORATIO.   It beckons you to go away with it,
    As if it some impartment° did desire
    To you alone.
MARCELLUS.   Look with what courteous action   60
    It waves you to a more removed ground.
    But do not go with it.
HORATIO.   No, by no means.
HAMLET.   It will not speak. Then I will follow it.
HORATIO.   Do not, my lord.
HAMLET.   Why, what should be the fear?
    I do not set my life at a pin's fee,°   65
    And for my soul, what can it do to that,
    Being a thing immortal as itself?
    It waves me forth again. I'll follow it.
HORATIO.   What if it tempt you toward the flood, my lord,
    Or to the dreadful summit of the cliff   70
    That beetles o'er° his° base into the sea,
    And there assume some other horrible form
    Which might deprive your sovereignty of reason,°
    And draw you into madness? Think of it.
    The very place puts toys of desperation,°   75
    Without more motive, into every brain
    That looks so many fathoms to the sea
    And hears it roar beneath.
HAMLET.   It waves me still.
    Go on, I'll follow thee.
MARCELLUS.   You shall not go, my lord.

[They try to stop him.]

---

47 *canoniz'd:* buried according to the canons of the church.   *hearsed:* coffined.   47 *cerements:* grave-clothes.   48 *glimpses of the moon:* earth by night.   53 *fools of nature:* mere men,
limited to natural knowledge.   59 *impartment:* communication.   65 *fee:* value.   71 *beetles o'er:* overhangs threateningly.   *his:* its.   73 *deprive . . . reason:* take away the rule of reason over your mind.   75 *toys of desperation:* fancies of desperate acts, i.e., suicide.

HAMLET.   Hold off your hands!   80
HORATIO.   Be rul'd, you shall not go.
HAMLET.   My fate cries out,
   And makes each petty artery° in this body
   As hardy as the Nemean lion's° nerve.°
   Still am I call'd. Unhand me, gentlemen.
   By heaven, I'll make a ghost of him that lets° me!   85
   I say, away! Go on. I'll follow thee.

(Exeunt Ghost and Hamlet.)

HORATIO.   He waxes desperate with imagination.
MARCELLUS.   Let's follow. 'Tis not fit thus to obey him.
HORATIO.   Have after. To what issue° will this come?
MARCELLUS.   Something is rotten in the state of Denmark.   90
HORATIO.   Heaven will direct it.°
MARCELLUS.   Nay, let's follow him.   *(Exeunt.)*

82 *artery:* sinew.   83 *nemean lion:* one of the monsters slain by hercules in his twelve labors.
nerve: sinew.   85 *lets:* hinders.   89 *issue:* outcome.   91 *it:* the outcome.

[Scene V]°

(Enter Ghost and Hamlet.)

HAMLET.   Whither wilt thou lead me? Speak. I'll go no further.
GHOST.   Mark me.
HAMLET.   I will.
GHOST.   My hour is almost come,
   When I to sulph'rous and tormenting flames
   Must render up myself.
HAMLET.   Alas, poor ghost!
GHOST.   Pity me not, but lend thy serious hearing   5
   To what I shall unfold.
HAMLET.   Speak. I am bound to hear.
GHOST.   So art thou to revenge, when thou shalt hear.
HAMLET.   What?
GHOST.   I am thy father's spirit,   10
   Doom'd for a certain term to walk the night,
   And for the day confin'd to fast° in fires,
   Till the foul crimes° done in my days of nature
   Are burnt and purg'd away. But that° I am forbid
   To tell the secrets of my prison-house,   15
   I could a tale unfold whose lightest word
   Would harrow up thy soul, freeze thy young blood,
   Make thy two eyes, like stars, start from their spheres,°
   Thy knotted and combined locks° to part,

I. v. *Location:* the battlements of the castle.   12 *fast:* do penance.   13 *crimes:* sins.   14 *but
that:* were it not that.   18 *spheres:* eye sockets, here compared to the orbits or transparent revolving spheres in which, according to Ptolemaic astronomy, the heavenly bodies were fixed.
19 *knotted . . . locks:* hair neatly arranged and confined.

And each particular hair to stand an end,°   20
Like quills upon the fearful porpentine.°
But this eternal blazon° must not be
To ears of flesh and blood. List, list, O, list!
If thou didst ever thy dear father love—
HAMLET.   O God!   25
GHOST.   Revenge his foul and most unnatural murder.
HAMLET.   Murder?
GHOST.   Murder most foul, as in the best it is,
But this most foul, strange, and unnatural.
HAMLET.   Haste me to know't, that I, with wings as swift   30
As meditation or the thoughts of love,
May sweep to my revenge.
GHOST.   I find thee apt;
And duller shouldst thou be than the fat weed
That roots itself in ease on Lethe° wharf,°
Wouldst thou not stir in this. Now, Hamlet, hear.   35
'Tis given out that, sleeping in my orchard,
A serpent stung me. So the whole ear of Denmark
Is by a forged process° of my death
Rankly abus'd.° But know, thou noble youth,
The serpent that did sting thy father's life   40
Now wears his crown.
HAMLET.   O my prophetic soul!
My uncle!
GHOST.   Ay, that incestuous, that adulterate° beast,
With witchcraft of his wits, with traitorous gifts—
O wicked wit and gifts, that have the power   45
So to seduce!—won to his shameful lust
The will of my most seeming-virtuous queen.
O Hamlet, what a falling-off was there!
From me, whose love was of that dignity
That it went hand in hand even with the vow   50
I made to her in marriage, and to decline
Upon a wretch whose natural gifts were poor
To those of mine!
But virtue, as it never will be moved,
Though lewdness court it in a shape of heaven,°   55
So lust, though to a radiant angel link'd,
Will sate itself in a celestial bed,
And prey on garbage.
But, soft, methinks I scent the morning air.
Brief let me be. Sleeping within my orchard,   60
My custom always of the afternoon,
Upon my secure° hour thy uncle stole,

---

20 *an end:* on end.   21 *fearful porpentine:* frightened porcupine.   22 *eternal blazon:* revelation
of the secrets of eternity.   34 *lethe:* the river of forgetfulness in Hades.   *wharf:* bank.
38 *forged process:* falsified account.   39 *abus'd:* deceived.   43 *adulterate:* adulterous.   55 *shape
of heaven:* heavenly form.   62 *secure:* confident, unsuspicious.

With juice of cursed hebona° in a vial,
And in the porches of my ears did pour
The leprous° distillment, whose effect   65
Holds such an enmity with blood of man
That swift as quicksilver it courses through
The natural gates and alleys of the body,
And with a sudden vigor it doth posset°
And curd, like eager° droppings into milk,   70
The thin and wholesome blood. So did it mine,
And a most instant tetter° bark'd° about,
Most lazar-like,° with vile and loathsome crust,
All my smooth body.
Thus was I, sleeping, by a brother's hand   75
Of life, of crown, of queen, at once dispatch'd,°
Cut off even in the blossoms of my sin,
Unhous'led,° disappointed,° unanel'd,°
No reck'ning made, but sent to my account
With all my imperfections on my head.   80
O, horrible! O, horrible, most horrible!
If thou hast nature° in thee, bear it not.
Let not the royal bed of Denmark be
A couch for luxury° and damned incest.
But, howsomever thou pursues this act,   85
Taint not thy mind, nor let thy soul contrive
Against thy mother aught. Leave her to heaven
And to those thorns that in her bosom lodge,
To prick and sting her. Fare thee well at once.
The glow-worm shows the matin° to be near,   90
And 'gins to pale his uneffectual fire.°
Adieu, adieu, adieu! Remember me.   [Exit.]
HAMLET. O all you host of heaven! O earth! What else?
And shall I couple° hell? O fie! Hold, hold, my heart,
And you, my sinews, grow not instant old,   95
But bear me stiffly up. Remember thee!
Ay, thou poor ghost, whiles memory holds a seat
In this distracted globe.° Remember thee!
Yea, from the table° of my memory
I'll wipe away all trivial fond° records,   100
All saws° of books, all forms,° all pressures° past
That youth and observation copied there,

---

63 *hebona:* poison. (The word seems to be a form of ebony, though it is perhaps thought to be related to henbane, a poison, or to ebenus, yew.)   65 *leprous:* causing leprosy-like disfigurement.   69 *posset:* coagulate, curdle.   70 *eager:* sour, acid.   72 *tetter:* eruption of scabs. *bark'd:* covered with a rough covering, like bark on a tree.   73 *lazar-like:* leper-like.   76 *dispatch'd:* suddenly deprived.   76 *unhous'led:* without having received the sacrament (of holy communion).   *disappointed:* unready (spiritually) for the last journey.   *unanel'd:* without having received extreme unction.   82 *nature:* the promptings of a son.   84 *luxury:* lechery. 90 *matin:* morning.   91 *uneffectual fire:* cold light.   94 *couple:* add.   98 *globe:* head.   99 *table:* writing tablet.   100 *fond:* foolish.   101 *saws:* wise sayings.   *forms:* images.   *pressures:* impressions stamped.

And thy commandment all alone shall live
Within the book and volume of my brain,
Unmix'd with baser matter. Yes, by heaven!   105
O most pernicious woman!
O villain, villain, smiling, damned villain!
My tables-meet it is I set it down,
That one may smile, and smile, and be a villain.
At least I am sure it may be so in Denmark.   110

                                              [Writing.]

So, uncle, there you are. Now to my word;
it is "Adieu, adieu! Remember me."
I have sworn 't.

(Enter Horatio and Marcellus.)

HORATIO.   My lord, my lord!
MARCELLUS.   Lord Hamlet!
HORATIO.   Heavens secure him!
HAMLET.   So be it!   115
MARCELLUS.   Illo, ho, ho, my lord!
HAMLET.   Hillo, ho, ho,° boy! Come, bird, come.
MARCELLUS.   How is 't, my noble lord?
HORATIO.   What news, my lord?
HAMLET.   O, wonderful!
HORATIO.   Good my lord, tell it.
HAMLET.   No, you will reveal it.   120
HORATIO.   Not I, my lord, by heaven.
MARCELLUS.   Nor I, my lord.
HAMLET.   How say you, then, would heart of man once think it?
    But you'll be secret?
HORATIO, MARCELLUS.   Ay, by heaven, my lord.
HAMLET.   There's never a villain dwelling in all Denmark.
    But he's an arrant° knave.   125
HORATIO.   There needs no ghost, my lord, come from the grave
    To tell us this.
HAMLET.   Why, right, you are in the right.
    And so, without more circumstances° at all,
    I hold it fit that we shake hands and part,
    You, as your business and desire shall point you—   130
    For every man hath business and desire,
    Such as it is—and for my own poor part,
    Look you, I'll go pray.
HORATIO.   These are but wild and whirling words, my lord.
HAMLET.   I am sorry they offend you, heartily;   135
    Yes, faith, heartily.
HORATIO.   There's no offense, my lord.

---

117 *hillo, ho, ho:* a falconer's call to a hawk in air. Hamlet is playing upon Marcellus's illo, i.e., hal-
loo.   125 *arrant:* thoroughgoing.   128 *circumstance:* ceremony.

HAMLET.   Yes, by Saint Patrick,° but there is, Horatio,
   And much offense too. Touching this vision here,
   It is an honest° ghost, that let me tell you.
   For your desire to know what is between us,   140
   O'ermaster 't as you may. And now, good friends,
   As you are friends, scholars, and soldiers,
   Give me one poor request.
HORATIO.   What is 't, my lord? We will.
HAMLET.   Never make known what you have seen tonight.   145
HORATIO, MARCELLUS.   My lord, we will not.
HAMLET.   Nay, but swear 't.
HORATIO.   In faith
   My lord, not I.
MARCELLUS.   Nor I, my lord, in faith.
HAMLET.   Upon my sword.°   *[Holds out his sword.]*
MARCELLUS.   We have sworn, my lord, already.
HAMLET.   Indeed, upon my sword, indeed.

(Ghost cries under the stage.)

GHOST.   Swear.   150
HAMLET.   Ha, ha, boy, say'st thou so? Art thou there, truepenny?°
   Come on, you hear this fellow in the cellarage.
   Consent to swear.
HORATIO.   Propose the oath, my Lord.
HAMLET.   Never to speak of this that you have seen,
   Swear by my sword.   155
GHOST *[beneath]*.   Swear.
HAMLET.   Hic et ubique?° Then we'll shift our ground.

                                        [He moves to another spot.]

   Come hither, gentlemen,
   And lay your hands again upon my sword.
   Swear by my sword   160
   Never to speak of this that you have heard.
GHOST *[beneath]*.   Swear by his sword.
HAMLET.   Well said, old mole! Canst work i' th' earth so fast?
   A worthy pioner!° Once more remove, good friends.

                                               [Moves again.]

HORATIO.   O day and night, but this is wondrous strange!   165
HAMLET.   And therefore as a stranger give it welcome.
   There are more things in heaven and earth, Horatio,
   Than are dreamt of in your philosophy.°
   But come;

137 *Saint Patrick:* the keeper of purgatory and patron saint of all blunders and confusion.
139 *honest:* i.e., a real ghost and not an evil spirit.   148 *sword:* the hilt in the form of a cross.
151 *truepenny:* honest old fellow.   157 *Hic et ubique:* here and everywhere (Latin).   164 *pioner:* pioneer, digger, miner.   168 *your philosophy:* this subject called "natural philosophy" or "science" that people talk about.

Here, as before, never, so help you mercy,   170
How strange or odd soe'er I bear myself—
As I perchance hereafter shall think meet
To put an antic° disposition on—
That you, at such times seeing me, never shall,
With arms encumb'red° thus, or this headshake,   175
Or by pronouncing of some doubtful phrase,
As "Well, well, we know," or "We could, an if° we would,"
Or "If we list° to speak," or "There be, an if they might,"
Or such ambiguous giving out,° to note°
That you know aught of me—this do swear,   180
So grace and mercy at your most need help you.
GHOST *[beneath].*   Swear.   *[They swear.]*
HAMLET.   Rest, rest, perturbed spirit! So, gentlemen,
With all my love I do commend me to you;
And what so poor a man as Hamlet is   185
May do, t' express his love and friending to you,
God willing, shall not lack. Let us go in together,
And still° your fingers on your lips, I pray.
The time is out of joint. O cursed spite,
That ever I was born to set it right!   190

[They wait for him to leave first.]

Nay, come, let's go together.   *(Exeunt.)*

173 *antic:* fantastic.   175 *encumb'red:* folded or entwined.   177 *an if:* if.   178 *list:* were inclined.   179 *giving out:* profession of knowledge.   *note:* give a sign, indicate.   188 *still:* always.

[ACT II

Scene I]°

(Enter old Polonius, with his man [Reynaldo].)

POLONIUS.   Give him this money and these notes, Reynaldo.
REYNALDO.   I will, my lord.
POLONIUS.   You shall do marvel's° wisely, good Reynaldo,
Before you visit him, to make inquire
Of his behavior.
REYNALDO.   My lord, I did intend it.   5
POLONIUS.   Marry, well said, very well said. Look you, sir,
Inquire me first what Danskers° are in Paris,
And how, and who, what means,° and where they keep,°
What company, at what expense; and finding
By this encompassment° and drift° of question   10

II. I. *Location:* Polonius's chambers.   3 *marvel's:* marvelous(ly).   7 *Danskers:* Danes.   8 *what
means:* what wealth (they have).   *keep:* dwell.   10 *encompassment:* roundabout talking.   *drift:*
gradual approach or course.

That they do know my son, come you more nearer
Than your particular demands will touch it.°
Take° you, as 'twere, some distant knowledge of him,
As thus, "I know his father and his friends,
And in part him." Do you mark this, Reynaldo?   15
REYNALDO. Ay, very well, my lord.
POLONIUS. "And in part him, but," you may say, "not well.
But, if 't be he I mean, he's very wild,
Addicted so and so," and there put on° him
What forgeries° you please—marry, none so rank   20
As may dishonor, him take heed of that,
But, sir, such wanton,° wild, and usual slips,
As are companions noted and most known
To youth and liberty.
REYNALDO.   As gaming, my lord.
POLONIUS. Ay, or drinking, fencing, swearing,   25
Quarreling, drabbing°—you may go so far.
REYNALDO. My lord, that would dishonor him.
POLONIUS. Faith, no, as you may season° it in the charge.
You must not put another scandal on him
That he is open to incontinency;°   30
That's not my meaning. But breathe his faults so quaintly°
That they may seem the taints of liberty,°
The flash and outbreak of a fiery mind,
A savageness in unreclaimed° blood,
Of general assault.°
REYNALDO.   But, my good lord—   35
POLONIUS. Wherefore should you do this?
REYNALDO.   Ay, my lord,
I would know that.
POLONIUS.   Marry, sir, here's my drift,
And, I believe, it is a fetch of wit.°
You laying these slight sullies on my son,
As 'twere a thing a little soil'd i' th' working,°   40
Mark you,
Your party in converse,° him you would sound,°
Having ever° seen in the prenominate crimes°
The youth you breathe° of guilty, be assur'd
He closes with you in this consequence:°   45
"Good sir," or so, or "friend," or "gentleman,"
According to the phrase or the addition°

11–12 *come . . . it:* you will find out more this way than by asking pointed questions (particular demands).   13 *take:* assume, pretend.   19 *put on:* impute to.   20 *forgeries:* invented tales.   22 *wanton:* sportive, unrestrained.   26 *drabbing:* whoring.   28 *season:* temper, soften.   30 *incontinency:* habitual loose behavior.   31 *quaintly:* delicately, ingeniously.   32 *taints of liberty:* faults resulting from freedom.   34 *unreclaimed:* untamed.   34 *general assault:* tendency that assails all unrestrained youth.   38 *fetch of wit:* clever trick.   40 *soil'd i' th' working:* shopworn.   42 *converse:* conversation.   *sound:* sound out.   43 *Having ever:* if he has ever.   *prenominate crimes:* before-mentioned offenses.   44 *breathe:* speak.   45 *closes . . . consequence:* follows your lead in some fashion as follows.   47 *addition:* title.

Of man and country.

REYNALDO.   Very good, my lord.

POLONIUS.   And then, sir, does 'a this—'a does—what was I about to say?

    By the mass, I was about to say something.   50

    Where did I leave?

REYNALDO.   At "closes in the consequence."

POLONIUS.   At "closes in the consequence," ay, marry.

    He closes thus: "I know the gentleman;

    I saw him yesterday, or th' other day,

    Or then, or then, with such, or such, and, as you say,   55

    There was 'a gaming, there o'ertook in 's rouse,°

    There falling out° at tennis," or perchance,

    "I saw him enter such a house of sale,"

    Videlicet,° a brothel, or so forth. See you now,

    Your bait of falsehood takes this carp° of truth;   60

    And thus do we of wisdom and of reach,°

    With windlasses° and with assays of bias,°

    By indirections find directions° out.

    So by my former lecture and advice

    Shall you my son. You have me, have you not?   65

REYNALDO.   My lord, I have.

POLONIUS.   God buy ye; fare ye well.

REYNALDO.   Good my lord.

POLONIUS.   Observe his inclination in yourself.°

REYNALDO.   I shall, my lord.

POLONIUS.   And let him ply° his music.

REYNALDO.   Well, my lord.   70

POLONIUS.   Farewell.   *(Exit Reynaldo.)*

                                          (Enter Ophelia.)

           How now, Ophelia, what's the matter?

OPHELIA.   O, my lord, my lord, I have been so affrighted!

POLONIUS.   With what, i' th' name of God?

OPHELIA.   My lord, as I was sewing in my closet,°

    Lord Hamlet, with his doublet° all unbrac'd,°   75

    No hat upon his head, his stockings fouled,

    Ungart'red, and down-gyved to his ankle,°

    Pale as his shirt, his knees knocking each other,

    And with a look so piteous in purport

    As if he had been loosed out of hell   80

    To speak of horrors—he comes before me.

POLONIUS.   Mad for thy love?

OPHELIA.   My lord, I do not know,

    But truly I do fear it.

---

56 *o'ertook in 's rouse:* overcome by drink.   57 *falling out:* quarreling.   59 *Videlicet:* namely.
60 *carp:* a fish.   61 *reach:* capacity, ability.   62 *windlasses:* circuitous paths (literally, circuits
made to head off the game in hunting).   *assays of bias:* attempts through indirection (like the
curving path of the bowling ball which is biased or weighted to one side).   63 *directions:* the way
things really are.   68 *in yourself:* in your own person (as well as by asking questions).   70 *let him
ply:* see that he continues to study.   74 *closet:* private chamber.   75 *doublet:* close-fitting jacket.
unbrac'd: unfastened.   77 *down-gyved to his ankle:* fallen to the ankles (like gyves or fetters).

POLONIUS.   What said he?
OPHELIA.   He took me by the wrist and held me hard.
   Then goes he to the length of all his arm,   85
   And, with his other hand thus o'er his brow,
   He falls to such perusal of my face
   As 'a would draw it. Long stay'd he so.
   At last, a little shaking of mine arm
   And thrice his head thus waving up and down,   90
   He rais'd a sigh so piteous and profound
   As it did seem to shatter all his bulk°
   And end his being. That done, he lets me go,
   And, with his head over his shoulder turn'd,
   He seem'd to find his way without his eyes,   95
   For out o' doors he went without their helps,
   And, to the last, bended their light on me.
POLONIUS.   Come, go with me. I will go seek the King.
   This is the very ecstasy° of love,
   Whose violent property° fordoes° itself   100
   And leads the will to desperate undertakings
   As oft as any passion under heaven
   That does afflict our natures. I am sorry.
   What, have you given him any hard words of late?
OPHELIA.   No, my good lord, but, as you did command,   105
   I did repel his letters and denied
   His access to me.
POLONIUS.   That hath made him mad.
   I am sorry that with better heed and judgment
   I had not quoted° him. I fear'd he did but trifle
   And meant to wrack thee; but, beshrew my jealousy!°   110
   By heaven, it is as proper to our age°
   To cast beyond° ourselves in our opinions
   As it is common for the younger sort
   To lack discretion. Come, go we to the King.
   This must be known, which, being kept close,° might move   115
   More grief to hide than hate to utter love.°
   Come.   *(Exeunt.)*

92 *bulk:* body.   99 *ecstasy:* madness   100 *property:* nature   *fordoes:* destroys   109 *quoted:* observed   110 *beshrew my jealousy:* a plague upon my suspicious nature   111 *proper . . . age:* characteristic of us (old) men   112 *cast beyond:* overshoot, miscalculate   115 *close:* secret.   115–16 *might . . . love:* might cause more grief (to others) by hiding the knowledge of Hamlet's strange behavior to Ophelia than hatred by telling it.

[Scene II]°

(Flourish. Enter King and Queen, Rosencrantz, and Guildenstern [with others].)

KING.   Welcome, dear Rosencrantz and Guildenstern.
   Moreover that° we much did long to see you,

II. II. *Location:* the castle.   2 *Moreover that:* besides the fact that.

The need we have to use you did provoke
Our hasty sending. Something have you heard
Of Hamlet's transformation—so call it,   5
Sith° nor th' exterior nor° the inward man
Resembles that° it was. What it should be,
More than his father's death, that thus hath put him
So much from th' understanding of himself,
I cannot dream of. I entreat you both   10
That, being of so young days° brought up with him,
And sith so neighbor'd to his youth and havior,
That you vouchsafe your rest° here in our court
Some little time, so by your companies
To draw him on to pleasures, and to gather   15
So much as from occasion you may glean,
Whether aught to us unknown afflicts him thus,
That, open'd,° lies within our remedy.
QUEEN.   Good gentlemen, he hath much talk'd of you,
And sure I am two men there is not living   20
To whom he more adheres. If it will please you
To show us so much gentry° and good will
As to expend your time with us awhile
For the supply and profit° of our hope,
Your visitation shall receive such thanks   25
As fits a king's remembrance.
ROSENCRANTZ: Both your Majesties
Might, by the sovereign power you have of us,
Put your dread pleasures more into command
Than to entreaty.
GUILDENSTERN: But we both obey,
And here give up ourselves in the full bent°   30
To lay our service freely at your feet,
To be commanded.
KING.   Thanks, Rosencrantz and gentle Guildenstern.
QUEEN.   Thanks, Guildenstern and gentle Rosencrantz.
And I beseech you instantly to visit   35
My too much changed son. Go, some of you,
And bring these gentlemen where Hamlet is.
GUILDENSTERN.   Heavens make our presence and our practices
Pleasant and helpful to him!
QUEEN.   Ay, amen!

(Exeunt Rosencrantz and Guildenstern [with some Attendants].)

(Enter Polonius.)

POLONIUS.   Th' ambassadors from Norway, my good lord,   40
Are joyfully return'd.

---

6 *sith:* since.   *nor . . . nor:* neither . . . nor.   7 *that:* what.   11 *of . . . days:* from such early
youth.   13 *vouchsafe your rest:* please to stay.   18 *open'd:* revealed.   24 *gentry:* courtesy.
22 *supply and profit:* aid and successful outcome.   30 *in . . . bent:* to the utmost degree of our
capacity.

KING.   Thou still° hast been the father of good news.
POLONIUS.   Have I, my lord? I assure my good liege
　I hold my duty, as I hold my soul,
　Both to my God and to my gracious king;   45
　And I do think, or else this brain of mine
　Hunts not the trail of policy so sure
　As it hath us'd to do, that I have found
　The very cause of Hamlet's lunacy.
KING.   O, speak of that! That do I long to hear.   50
POLONIUS.   Give first admittance to th' ambassadors.
　My news shall be the fruit° to that great feast.
KING.   Thyself do grace to them, and bring them in.

(Exit Polonius.)

　He tells me, my dear Gertrude, he hath found
　The head and source of all your son's distemper.   55
QUEEN.   I doubt° it is no other but the main,°
　His father's death, and our o'erhasty marriage.

(Enter Ambassadors [Voltimand and Cornelius, with Polonius].)

KING.   Well, we shall sift him.—Welcome, my good friends!
　Say, Voltimand, what from our brother Norway?
VOLTIMAND: Most fair return of greetings and desires.   60
　Upon our first,° he sent out to suppress
　His nephew's levies, which to him appear'd
　To be a preparation 'gainst the Polack,
　But, better look'd into, he truly found
　It was against your Highness. Whereat griev'd   65
　That so his sickness, age, and impotence
　Was falsely borne in hand,° sends out arrests
　On Fortinbras, which he, in brief, obeys,
　Receives rebuke from Norway, and in fine°
　Makes vow before his uncle never more   70
　To give th' assay° of arms against your Majesty.
　Whereon old Norway, overcome with joy,
　Gives him three score thousand crowns in annual fee,
　And his commission to employ those soldiers,
　So levied as before, against the Polack,   75
　With an entreaty, herein further shown,

[Giving a paper.]

　That it might please you to give quiet pass
　Through your dominions for this enterprise,
　On such regards of safety and allowance°
　As therein are set down.

42 *still:* always.   52 *fruit:* dessert.   56 *doubt:* fear, suspect.
cern.   61 *Upon our first:* at our first words on the business.
advantage of.   69 *in fine:* in the end.   71 *assay:* trial.
pledges of safety and provisos.

main: chief point, principal con-
67 *borne in hand:* deluded, taken
79 *On . . . allowance:* with such

KING.   It likes° us well;   80
   And at our more consider'd° time we'll read,
   Answer, and think upon this business.
   Meantime we thank you for your well-took labor.
   Go to your rest; at night we'll feast together.
   Most welcome home!   *(Exeunt Ambassadors.)*
POLONIUS.   This business is well ended.   85
   My liege, and madam, to expostulate°
   What majesty should be, what duty is,
   Why day is day, night night, and time is time,
   Were nothing but to waste night, day, and time.
   Therefore, since brevity is the soul of wit,°   90
   And tediousness the limbs and outward flourishes,
   I will be brief. Your noble son is mad.
   Mad call I it, for, to define true madness,
   What is 't but to be nothing else but mad?
   But let that go.
QUEEN.   More matter, with less art.   95
POLONIUS.   Madam, I swear I use no art at all.
   That he is mad, 'Tis true; 'Tis true 'Tis pity,
   And pity 'Tis 'Tis true—a foolish figure,°
   But farewell it, for I will use no art.
   Mad let us grant him, then, and now remains   100
   That we find out the cause of this effect,
   Or rather say, the cause of this defect,
   For this effect defective comes by cause.°
   Thus it remains, and the remainder thus.
   Perpend.°   105
   I have a daughter—have while she is mine—
   Who, in her duty and obedience, mark,
   Hath given me this. Now gather, and surmise.
   [Reads the letter.] "To the celestial and my soul's idol,
   The most beautified Ophelia"—   110
   That's an ill phrase, a vile phrase; "beautified" is a vile
   Phrase. But you shall hear. Thus: *[Reads.]*
   "In her excellent white bosom, these, etc."
QUEEN.   Came this from Hamlet to her?
POLONIUS.   Good madam, stay awhile; I will be faithful.   115

                                                    [Reads.]

   "Doubt° thou the stars are fire,
     Doubt that the sun doth move,
   Doubt truth to be a liar,
     But never doubt I love.
   O dear Ophelia, I am ill at these numbers.° I have   120

80 *likes:* pleases.   81 *consider'd:* suitable for deliberation.   86 *expostulate:* expound.   90 *wit:*
sound sense or judgment.   98 *figure:* figure of speech.   103 *for . . . cause:* i.e., for this defective behavior, this madness has a cause.   105 *perpend:* consider.   116 *doubt:* suspect, question.   120 *ill . . . numbers:* unskilled at writing verses.

not art to reckon° my groans. But that I love thee
best, O most best, believe it. Adieu.
   Thine evermore, most dear lady, whilst this machine° is to him,
    Hamlet.
This in obedience hath my daughter shown me,   125
And, more above,° hath his solicitings,
As they fell out° by time, by means, and place,
All given to mine ear.
KING.   But how hath she
Receiv'd his love?
POLONIUS.   What do you think of me?
KING. As of a man faithful and honorable.   130
POLONIUS. I would fain prove so. But what might you think,
When I had seen this hot love on the wing—
As I perceiv'd it, I must tell you that,
Before my daughter told me—what might you,
Or my dear Majesty your Queen here, think,   135
If I had play'd the desk or table-book,°
Or given my heart a winking,° mute and dumb,
Or look'd upon this love with idle sight?°
What might you think? No, I went round° to work,
And my young mistress thus I did bespeak:°   140
"Lord Hamlet is a prince, out of thy star;°
This must not be." And then I prescripts gave her,
That she should lock herself from his resort,
Admit no messengers, receive no tokens.
Which done, she took the fruits of my advice;   145
And he, repelled—a short tale to make—
Fell into a sadness, then into a fast,
Thence to a watch,° thence into a weakness,
Thence to a lightness,° and, by this declension,°
Into the madness wherein now he raves,   150
And all we mourn for.
KING. Do you think this?
QUEEN.   It may be, very like.
POLONIUS. Hath there been such a time—I would fain know that—
That I have positively said " 'Tis so,"
When it prov'd otherwise?
KING.   Not that I know.   155
POLONIUS *[pointing to his head and shoulder].* Take this from this, if this
  be otherwise.
If circumstances lead me, I will find
Where truth is hid, though it were hid indeed

---

121 *reckon:* (1) count, (2) number metrically, scan. 123 *machine:* body. 126 *more above:* moreover. 127 *fell out:* occurred. 136 *play'd . . . table-book:* remained shut up, concealing the information. 137 *winking:* closing of the eyes. 138 *with idle sight:* complacently or incomprehendingly. 139 *round:* roundly, plainly. 140 *bespeak:* address. 141 *out of thy star:* above your sphere, position. 148 *watch:* state of sleeplessness. 149 *lightness:* lightheadedness. *declension:* decline, deterioration.

Within the center.°
KING.   How may we try it further?
POLONIUS.   You know, sometimes he walks four hours together   160
Here in the lobby.
QUEEN.   So he does indeed.
POLONIUS.   At such a time I'll loose my daughter to him.
Be you and I behind an arras° then.
Mark the encounter. If he love her not
And be not from his reason fall'n thereon,°   165
Let me be no assistant for a state,
But keep a farm and carters.
KING.   We will try it.

(Enter Hamlet [reading on a book].)

QUEEN.   But look where sadly the poor wretch comes reading.
POLONIUS.   Away, I do beseech you both, away.
I'll board° him presently.

(Exeunt King and Queen [with Attendants].)

O, give me leave.   170
How does my good Lord Hamlet?
HAMLET.   Well, God-a-mercy.°
POLONIUS.   Do you know me, my lord?
HAMLET.   Excellent well. You are a fishmonger.°
POLONIUS.   Not I, my Lord.   175
HAMLET.   Then I would you were so honest a man.
POLONIUS.   Honest, my lord?
HAMLET.   Ay, sir. To be honest, as this world goes, is to be one man
pick'd out of ten thousand.
POLONIUS.   That's very true, my lord.   180
HAMLET.   For if the sun breed maggots in a dead dog, being a good
kissing carrion°—Have you a daughter?
POLONIUS.   I have, my lord.
HAMLET.   Let her not walk i' th' sun.° Conception° is a blessing, but
as your daughter may conceive, friend, look to 't.   185
POLONIUS *[aside].*   How say you by that? Still harping on my daughter.
Yet he knew me not at first; 'a said I was a fishmonger. 'A is far
gone. And truly in my youth I suff'red much extremity for love,
very near this. I'll speak to him again.—What do you read, my lord?
HAMLET.   Words, words, words.   190
POLONIUS.   What is the matter,° my lord?
HAMLET.   Between who?
POLONIUS.   I mean, the matter that you read, my lord.

---

159 *center:* middle point of the earth (which is also the center of the Ptolemaic universe).
163 *arras:* hanging, tapestry.   165 *thereon:* on that account.   170 *board:* accost.   172 *God-a-mercy:* thank you.   174 *fishmonger:* fish merchant (with connotation of bawd, procurer?).
181–82 *good kissing carrion:* a good piece of flesh for kissing, or for the sun to kiss.   184 *i' th' sun:* with additional implication of the sunshine of princely favors.   *conception:* (1) understanding, (2) pregnancy.   191 *matter:* substance (but Hamlet plays on the sense of basis for a dispute).

HAMLET.   Slanders, sir; for the satirical rogue says here that old men
have gray beards, that their faces are wrinkled, their eyes purging°   200
thick amber and plum-tree gum, and that they have a plentiful lack
of wit, together with most weak hams. All which, sir, though I
most powerfully and potently believe, yet I hold it not honesty°
to have it thus set down, for you yourself, sir, shall grow old as I
am, if like a crab you could go backward.   205
POLONIUS [ASIDE].   Though this be madness, yet there is method in 't.—
Will you walk out of the air, my lord?
HAMLET.   Into my grave.
POLONIUS.   Indeed, that's out of the air. *[Aside.]* How pregnant°
sometimes his replies are! A happiness° that often madness hits on,   210
which reason and sanity could not so prosperously° be deliver'd
of. I will leave him, [and suddenly contrive the means of meeting
between him] and my daughter.—My honorable lord, I will most
humbly take my leave of you.
HAMLET.   You cannot, sir, take from me any thing that I will more   215
willingly part withal—except my life, except my life, except my life.

(Enter Guildenstern and Rosencrantz.)

POLONIUS.   Fare you well, my lord.
HAMLET.   These tedious old fools!°
POLONIUS.   You go to seek the Lord Hamlet; there he is.
ROSENCRANTZ *[to Polonius].*   God save you, sir!

                                                          [Exit Polonius.]

GUILDENSTERN.   My honor'd lord!   220
ROSENCRANTZ.   My most dear lord!
HAMLET.   My excellent good friends! How dost thou, Guildenstern?
Ah, Rosencrantz! Good lads, how do you both?
ROSENCRANTZ.   As the indifferent° children of the earth.
GUILDENSTERN.   Happy in that we are not over-happy. On Fortune's cap   225
we are not the very button.
HAMLET.   Nor the soles of her shoe?
ROSENCRANTZ.   Neither, my lord.
HAMLET.   Then you live about her waist, or in the middle of her favors?
GUILDENSTERN.   Faith, her privates° we.   230
HAMLET.   In the secret parts of Fortune? O, most true; she is a strumpet.°
What news?
ROSENCRANTZ.   None, my lord, but the world's grown honest.
HAMLET.   Then is doomsday near. But your news is not true. [Let me
question more in particular. What have you, my good friends,   235
deserv'd at the hands of Fortune that she sends you to prison hither?
GUILDENSTERN.   Prison, my lord?
HAMLET.   Denmark's a prison.

200 *purging:* discharging.   203 *honesty:* decency.   209 *pregnant:* full of meaning.   *happi-*
ness: felicity of expression.   211 *prosperously:* successfully.   218 *old fools:* i.e., old men like Polonius.   224 *indifferent:* ordinary.   230 *privates:* close acquaintants (with sexual pun on private
parts).   231 *strumpet:* prostitute (a common epithet for indiscriminate fortune; see line 462).

ROSENCRANTZ.   Then is the world one.

HAMLET.   A goodly one, in which there are many confines,° wards,°   240
and dungeons, Denmark being one o' th' worst.

ROSENCRANTZ.   We think not so, my lord.

HAMLET.   Why then 'Tis none to you, for there is nothing either good
or bad but thinking makes it so. To me it is a prison.

ROSENCRANTZ.   Why then, your ambition makes it one. 'Tis too narrow   245
for your mind.

HAMLET.   O God, I could be bounded in a nutshell and count myself
a king of infinite space, were it not that I have bad dreams.

GUILDENSTERN.   Which dreams indeed are ambition, for the very
substance of the ambitious° is merely the shadow of a dream.   250

HAMLET.   A dream itself is but a shadow.

ROSENCRANTZ.   Truly, and I hold ambition of so airy and light a quality
that it is but a shadow's shadow.

HAMLET.   Then are our beggars bodies,° and our monarchs and
outstretch'd° heroes the beggars' shadows. Shall we to th' court? For,   255
by my fay,° I cannot reason.

ROSENCRANTZ, GUILDENSTERN.   We'll wait upon° you.

HAMLET.   No such matter. I will not sort° you with the rest of my servants,
for, to speak to you like an honest man, I am most
dreadfully attended.°] But, in the beaten way° of friendship, what   260
make° you at Elsinore?

ROSENCRANTZ.   To visit you, my lord, no other occasion.

HAMLET.   Beggar that I am, I am even poor in thanks; but I thank you,
and sure, dear friends, my thanks are too dear a halfpenny.° Were
you not sent for? Is it your own inclining? Is it a free visitation?   265
Come, come, deal justly with me. Come, come; nay, speak.

GUILDENSTERN.   What should we say, my lord?

HAMLET.   Why, anything, but to th' purpose. You were sent for; and
there is a kind of confession in your looks which your modesties
have not craft enough to color. I know the good King and Queen   270
have sent for you.

ROSENCRANTZ.   To what end, my lord?

HAMLET.   That you must teach me. But let me conjure° you, by the
rights of our fellowship, by the consonancy of our youth,° by the
obligation of our ever-preserv'd love, and by what more dear a   275
better proposer° could charge° you withal, be even° and direct
with me, whether you were sent for, or no?

ROSENCRANTZ *[aside to Guildenstern].*   What say you?

---

240 *confines:* places of confinement.   *wards:* cells.   249–50 *the very . . . ambitious:* that seemingly very substantial thing which the ambitious pursue.   254 *bodies:* solid substances rather
than shadows (since beggars are not ambitious).   255 *outstretch'd:* (1) far-reaching in their ambition, (2) elongated as shadows.   256 *fay:* faith.   257 *wait upon:* accompany, attend.
258 *sort:* class, associate.   260 *dreadfully attended:* waited upon in slovenly fashion.   *beaten*
way: familiar path.   261 *make:* do.   264 *dear a halfpenny:* expensive at the price of a halfpenny,
i.e., of little worth.   273 *conjure:* adjure, entreat.   274 *consonancy of our youth:* the fact that we
are of the same age.   276 *better proposer:* more skillful propounder.   *charge:* urge.   *even:*
straight, honest.

HAMLET *[aside].*   Nay then, I have an eye of° you.—If you love me,
    hold not off. 280
GUILDENSTERN.   My lord, we were sent for.
HAMLET.   I will tell you why; so shall my anticipation prevent your
    discovery,° and your secrecy to the King and Queen molt no
    feather.° I have of late—but wherefore I know not—lost all my
    mirth, forgone all custom of exercises; and indeed it goes so heavily 285
    with my disposition that this goodly frame, the earth, seems to
    me a sterile promontory; this most excellent canopy, the air, look
    you, this brave° o'erhanging firmament, this majestical roof
    fretted° with golden fire, why, it appeareth nothing to me but a
    foul and pestilent congregation of vapors. What a piece of work is 290
    a man! How noble in reason, how infinite in faculties, in form and
    moving how express° and admirable, in action how like an angel,
    in apprehension how like a god! The beauty of the world, the
    paragon of anmals! And yet, to me, what is this quintessence° of
    dust? Man delights not me—no, nor woman neither, though by 295
    your smiling you seem to say so.
ROSENCRANTZ.   My lord, there was no such stuff in my thoughts.
HAMLET.   Why did you laugh then, when I said "man delights not me"?
ROSENCRANTZ.   To think, my lord, if you delight not in man, what lenten
    entertainment° the players shall receive from you. We coted° them 300
    on the way, and hither are they coming, to offer you service.
HAMLET.   He that plays the king shall be welcome; his Majesty shall have
    tribute of me. The adventurous knight shall use his foil and target,°
    the lover shall not sigh gratis, the humorous man° shall end his part
    in peace, [the clown shall make those laugh whose lungs are tickle 305
    o' th' sere°], and the lady shall say her mind freely, or the blank verse
    shall halt° for 't. What players are they?
ROSENCRANTZ.   Even those you were wont to take such delight in, the
    tragedians of the city.
HAMLET.   How chances it they travel? Their residence,° both in 310
    reputation and profit, was better both ways.
ROSENCRANTZ.   I think their inhibition° comes by the means of the
    innovation.°
HAMLET.   Do they hold the same estimation they did when I was in the
    city? Are they so follow'd? 315
ROSENCRANTZ.   No, indeed, are they not.
HAMLET.   How comes it? Do they grow rusty?

279 *of:* on.   282–83 *prevent your discovery:* forestall your disclosure.   283–84 *molt no feather:* not
diminish in the least.   288 *brave:* splendid.   289 *fretted:* adorned (with fretwork, as in a vaulted
ceiling).   292 *express:* well-framed (?), exact (?).   294 *quintessence:* the fifth essence of ancient
philosophy, beyond earth, water, air, and fire, supposed to be the substance of the heavenly bodies and to be latent in all things.   300 *lenten entertainment:* meager reception (appropriate to
Lent).   *coted:* overtook and passed beyond.   303 *foil and target:* sword and shield.   304 *humorous man:* eccentric character, dominated by one trait or "humor."   305–6 *tickle o' th' sere:* easy
on the trigger, ready to laugh easily. (*sere* is part of a gunlock.)   307 *halt:* limp.   310 *residence:* remaining in one place, i.e., in the city.   312 *inhibition:* formal prohibition (from acting
plays in the city).   313 *innovation:* i.e., the new fashion in satirical plays performed by boy
actors in the "private" theaters; or possibly a political uprising; or the strict limitations set on the
theater in London in 1600.

ROSENCRANTZ.   Nay, their endeavor keeps in the wonted° pace. But there
is, sir, an aery° of children, little eyases,° that cry out on the top of
question,° and are most tyrannically° clapp'd for 't. These are now   320
the fashion, and so berattle° the common stages°—so they call
them—that many wearing rapiers° are afraid of goose-quills° and
dare scarce come thither.

HAMLET.   What, are they children? Who maintains 'em? How are they
escoted?° Will they pursue the quality° no longer than they can   325
sing?° Will they not say afterwards, if they should grow themselves
to common° players—as it is most like, if their means are no
better—their writers do them wrong, to make them exclaim against
their own succession?°

ROSENCRANTZ.   Faith, there has been much to do° on both sides; and   330
the nation holds it no sin to tarre° them to controversy. There was,
for a while, no money bid for argument° unless the poet and the
player went to cuffs in the question.°

HAMLET.   Is 't possible?

GUILDENSTERN.   O, there has been much throwing about of brains.   335

HAMLET.   Do the boys carry it away?°

ROSENCRANTZ.   Ay, that they do, my lord—Hercules and his load° too.°

HAMLET.   It is not very strange; for my uncle is King of Denmark, and
those that would make mouths° at him while my father liv'd, give
twenty, forty, fifty, a hundred ducats° apiece for his picture in   340
little.° 'Sblood,° there is something in this more than natural, if
philosophy could find it out.

(A flourish [of trumpets within].)

GUILDENSTERN.   There are the players.

HAMLET.   Gentlemen, you are welcome to Elsinore. Your hands, come
then. Th' appurtenance of welcome is fashion and ceremony. Let   345
me comply° with you in this garb,° lest my extent° to the players,
which, I tell you, must show fairly outwards,° should more appear
like entertainment° than yours. You are welcome. But my uncle-
father and aunt-mother are deceiv'd.

---

318 *wonted:* usual.   319 *aery:* nest.   *eyases:* young hawks.   319–20 *cry . . . question:* speak
shrilly, dominating the controversy (in decrying the public theaters).   *tyrannically:* outra-
geously.   321 *berattle:* berate.   *common stages:* public theaters.   322 *many wearing rapiers:*
many men of fashion, who were afraid to patronize the common players for fear of being satirized
by the poets who wrote for the children.   *goose-quills:* pens of satirists.   325 *escoted:* maintained.   *quality:* (acting) profession.   325–26 *no longer . . . sing:* only until their voices
change.   327 *common:* regular, adult.   329 *succession:* future careers.   330 *to do:* ado.
331 *tarre:* set on (as dogs).   332 *argument:* plot for a play.   333 *went . . . question:* came to
blows in the play itself.   336 *carry it away:* win the day.   337 *Hercules . . . load:* thought to be
an allusion to the sign of the Globe Theatre, which was Hercules bearing the world on his shoulder.   317–337 *how . . . load too:* the passage omitted from the early quartos, alludes to the so-
called War of the Theatres, 1599–1602, the rivalry between the children companies and the adult
actors.   339 *mouths:* faces.   340 *ducats:* gold coins.   340–41 *in little:* in miniature.
341 *'Sblood:* by His (God's, Christ's) blood.   346 *comply:* observe the formalities of courtesy.
garb: manner.   *my extent:* the extent of my showing courtesy.   347 *show fairly outwards:* look
cordial to outward appearances.   348 *entertainment:* a (warm) reception.

GUILDENSTERN.   In what, my dear lord?   350
HAMLET.   I am but mad north-north-west.° When the wind is southerly
    I know a hawk from a handsaw.°

(Enter Polonius.)

POLONIUS.   Well be with you, gentlemen!
HAMLET.   Hark you, Guildenstern, and you too; at each ear a hearer.
    That great baby you see there is not yet out of his swaddling-clouts.°   355
ROSENCRANTZ.   Happily° he is the second time come to them; for they
    say an old man is twice a child.
HAMLET.   I will prophesy he comes to tell me of the players; mark it.—
    You say right, sir, o' Monday morning, 'twas then indeed.
POLONIUS.   My lord, I have news to tell you.   360
HAMLET.   My lord, I have news to tell you. When Roscius° was an
    actor in Rome—
POLONIUS.   The actors are come hither, my lord.
HAMLET.   Buzz,° buzz!
POLONIUS.   Upon my honor—   365
HAMLET.   Then came each actor on his ass—
POLONIUS.   The best actors in the world, either for tragedy, comedy,
    history, pastoral, pastoral-comical, historical-pastoral, tragical-
    historical, tragical-comical-historical-pastoral, scene individable,°
    or poem unlimited.° Seneca° cannot be too heavy, nor Plautus° too   370
    light. For the law of writ and the liberty,° these are the only men.
HAMLET.   O Jephthah, judge of Israel,° what a treasure hadst thou!
POLONIUS.   What a treasure had he, my lord?
HAMLET.   Why,
    "One fair daughter, and no more,   375
    The which he loved passing° well."
POLONIUS *[aside]*.   Still on my daughter.
HAMLET.   Am I not i' th' right, old Jephthah?
POLONIUS.   If you call me Jephthah, my lord, I have a daughter that I
    love passing well.   380
HAMLET.   Nay, that follows not.
POLONIUS.   What follows, then, my lord?
HAMLET.   Why,
    "As by lot, God wot,"°
    and then, you know,"   385
    It came to pass, as most like° it was."

---

351 *north-north-west:* only partly, at times.   352 *hawk, handsaw:* mattock (or hack) and a carpenter's cutting tool, respectively; also birds, with a play on hernshaw or heron.   355 *swaddling-clouts:* cloths in which to wrap a newborn baby.   356 *happily:* haply, perhaps.   361 *Roscius:* a famous Roman actor who died in 62 B.C.   364 *Buzz:* an interjection used to denote stale news.   369 *scene individable:* a play observing the unity of place.   370 *poem unlimited:* a play disregarding the unities of time and place.   *Seneca:* writer of Latin tragedies.   *Plautus:* writer of Latin comedy.   371 *law . . . liberty:* dramatic composition both according to rules and without rules, i.e., "classical" and "romantic" dramas.   372 *Jephthah . . . Israel:* Jephthah had to sacrifice his daughter; see Judges 11. Hamlet goes on to quote from a ballad on the theme.   376 *passing:* surpassingly.   384 *wot:* knows.   386 *like:* likely, probable.

The first row° of the pious chanson° will show you more, for look
where my abridgement° comes.

(Enter the Players.)

You are welcome, masters; welcome, all. I am glad to see thee well.
Welcome, good friends. O, old friend! Why, thy face is valanc'd°   395
since I saw thee last. Com'st thou to beard° me in Denmark? What,
my young lady° and mistress? By 'r lady, your ladyship is nearer to
heaven than when I saw you last, by the altitude of a chopine.°
Pray God your voice, like a piece of uncurrent° gold, be not
crack'd within the ring.° Masters, you are all welcome. We'll e'en   400
to 't like French falconers, fly at anything we see. We'll have a
speech straight.° Come, give us a taste of your quality; come, a
passionate speech.

FIRST PLAYER.   What speech, my good lord?

HAMLET.   I heard thee speak me a speech once, but it was never acted,   405
or, if it was, not above once, for the play, I remember, pleas'd
not the million; 'twas caviary to the general.° But it was—as I
receiv'd it, and others, whose judgments in such matters cried in
the top of° mine—an excellent play, well digested in the scenes,
set down with as much modesty as cunning.° I remember one   410
said there were no sallets° in the lines to make the matter savory,
nor no matter in the phrase that might indict° the author of
affectation, but call'd it an honest method, as wholesome as sweet,
and by very much more handsome than fine.° One speech in 't
I chiefly lov'd: 'twas Aeneas' tale to Dido, and thereabout of it   415
especially when he speaks of Priam's slaughter.° If it live in your
memory, begin at this line: let me see, let me see—
"The rugged Pyrrhus,° like th' Hyrcanian beast"°—
'Tis not so. It begins with Pyrrhus:
"The rugged Pyrrhus, he whose sable° arms,   420
Black as his purpose, did the night resemble
When he lay couched in the ominous horse,°
Hath now this dread and black complexion smear'd
With heraldry more dismal.° Head to foot

---

387 *row:* stanza.   chanson: ballad, song.   388 *my abridgement:* something that cuts short my
conversation; also, a diversion.   395 *valanc'd:* fringed (with a beard).   396 *beard:* confront
(with obvious pun).   397 *young lady:* boy playing women's parts.   398 *chopine:* thick-soled
shoe of Italian fashion.   399 *uncurrent:* not passable as lawful coinage.   400 *crack'd . . .
ring:* changed from adolescent to male voice, no longer suitable for women's roles. (Coins fea-
tured rings enclosing the sovereign's head; if the coin was cracked within this ring, it was unfit for
currency.)   402 *straight:* at once.   407 *caviary to the general:* caviar to the multitude, i.e., a
choice dish too elegant for coarse tastes.   408-9 *cried in the top of:* spoke with greater authority
than.   410 *cunning:* skill.   411 *sallets:* salad, i.e., spicy improprieties.   412 *indict:* convict.
414 *fine:* elaborately ornamented, showy.   416 *Priam's slaughter:* the slaying of the rule of Troy,
when the Greeks finally took the city.   418 *Pyrrhus:* a Greek hero in the Trojan War, also known
as Neoptolemus, son of Achilles.   *Hyrcanian beast:* i.e., the tiger. (See Virgil, Aeneid IV. 266;
compare the whole speech with Marlowe's Dido Queen of Carthage II. i. 214 *ff.*)   422 *sable:* black
(for reasons of camouflage during the episode of the Trojan horse).   422 *ominous horse:* Trojan
horse, by which the Greeks gained access to Troy.   424 *dismal:* ill-omened.

Now is he total gules,° horridly trick'd° 425
With blood of fathers, mothers, daughters, sons,
Bak'd and impasted° with the parching streets,°
That lend a tyrannous and a damned light
To their lord's° murder. Roasted in wrath and fire,
And thus o'er-sized° with coagulate, gore, 430
With eyes like carbuncles, the hellish Pyrrhus
Old grandsire Priam seeks."
So proceed you.

POLONIUS. 'Fore God, my lord, well spoken, with good accent and
good discretion. 435

FIRST PLAYER.   "Anon he finds him
Striking too short at Greeks. His antique sword,
Rebellious to his arm, lies where it falls,
Repugnant° to command. Unequal match'd,
Pyrrhus at Priam drives, in rage strikes wide, 440
But with the whiff and wind of his fell° sword
Th' unnerved father falls. [Then senseless Ilium,°]
Seeming to feel this blow, with flaming top
Stoops to his° base, and with a hideous crash
Takes prisoner Pyrrhus' ear. For, lo! His sword, 445
Which was declining on the milky head
Of reverend Priam, seem'd i' th' air to stick.
So as a painted° tyrant Pyrrhus stood,
And, like a neutral to his will and matter,°
Did nothing. 450
But, as we often see, against° some storm,
A silence in the heavens, the rack° stand still,
The bold winds speechless, and the orb below
As hush as death, anon the dreadful thunder
Doth rend the region,° so, after Pyrrhus' pause, 455
Aroused vengeance sets him new a—work,
And never did the Cyclops'° hammers fall
On Mars's armor forg'd for proof eterne°
With less remorse than Pyrrhus' bleeding sword 460
Now falls on Priam.
Out, out, thou strumpet Fortune! All you gods,
In general synod,° take away her power!
Break all the spokes and fellies° from her wheel,
And bowl the round nave° down the hill of heaven,
As low as to the fiends!" 465

---

425 *gules:* red (a heraldic term).   *trick'd:* adorned, decorated.   427 *impasted:* crusted, like a
thick paste.   *with . . . streets:* by the parching heat of the streets (because of the fires everywhere).   429 *their lord's:* Priam's.   430 *o'er-sized:* covered as with size or glue.   439 *repug-
nant:* disobedient, resistant.   441 *fell:* cruel.   442 *senseless ilium:* insensate troy.   444 *his:*
its.   448 *painted:* painted in a picture.   450 *like . . . matter:* as though poised indecisively
between his intention and its fulfillment.   451 *against:* just before.   452 *rack:* mass of clouds.
455 *region:* sky.   457 *Cyclops:* giant armor-makers in the smithy of Vulcan.   458 *proof eterne:* eternal resistance to assault.   463 *synod:* assembly.   464 *fellies:* pieces of wood forming the rim of
a wheel.   465 *nave:* hub.

POLONIUS.   This is too long.

HAMLET.   It shall to the barber's with your beard.—
　　Prithee say on. He's for a jig° or a tale of bawdry,
　　Or he sleeps. Say on; come to Hecuba.°

FIRST PLAYER.   "But who, ah woe! had seen the mobled° queen"—　　　　470

HAMLET.   "The mobled queen?"

POLONIUS.   That's good. "Mobled queen" is good.

FIRST PLAYER.   "Run barefoot up and down, threat'ning the flames
　　With bisson rheum,° a clout° upon that head
　　Where late the diadem stood, and for a robe,　　　　475
　　About her lank and all o'er-teemed° loins
　　A blanket, in the alarm of fear caught up—
　　Who this had seen, with tongue in venom steep'd,
　　'Gainst Fortune's state° would treason have pronounc'd.°
　　But if the gods themselves did see her then　　　　480
　　When she saw Pyrrhus make malicious sport
　　In mincing with his sword her husband's limbs,
　　The instant burst of clamor that she made,
　　Unless things mortal move them not at all,
　　Would have made milch° the burning eyes of heaven,　　　　485
　　And passion in the gods."

POLONIUS.   Look whe'er° he has not turn'd his color and has tears in 's
　　eyes. Prithee, no more.

HAMLET.   'Tis well; I'll have thee speak out the rest of this soon. Good
　　my lord, will you see the players well bestow'd?° Do you hear, let　　　　490
　　them be well us'd, for they are the abstract° and brief chronicles
　　of the time. After your death you were better have a bad epitaph
　　than their ill report while you live.

POLONIUS.   My lord, I will use them according to their desert.

HAMLET.   God's bodkin,° man, much better! Use every man after his　　　　495
　　desert, and who shall scape whipping? Use them after your own
　　honor and dignity. The less they deserve, the more merit is in your
　　bounty. Take them in.

POLONIUS.   Come, sirs.

HAMLET.   Follow him, friends. We'll hear a play tomorrow. *[As they*　　　　500
　　start to leave, Hamlet detains the First Player.] Dost thou hear
　　me, old friend? Can you play the Murder of Gonzago?

FIRST PLAYER: Ay, my lord.

HAMLET.   We'll ha 't tomorrow night. You could, for need, study a
　　speech of some dozen or sixteen lines, which I would set down　　　　505
　　and insert in 't, could you not?

FIRST PLAYER: Ay, my lord.

HAMLET.   Very well, Follow that lord, and look you mock him not.—

---

468 *jig:* comic song and dance often given at the end of a play.　　469 *Hecuba:* wife of
Priam.　　470 *mobled:* muffled.　　474 *bisson rheum:* blinding tears.　　*clout:* cloth.　　476 *o'er-
teemed:* worn out with bearing children.　　479 *state:* rule, managing.　　*pronounc'd:* proclaimed
485 *milch:* milky, moist with tears.　　487 *whe'r:* whether.　　490 *bestow'd:* lodged.　　491 *abstract:* summary account.　　495 *God's bodkin:* by God's (Christ's) little body,　　*bodykin:* (not to
be confused with bodkin, dagger).

My good friends, I'll leave you till night. You are welcome to
Elsinore.   510

(Exeunt Polonius and Players.)

ROSENCRANTZ.   Good my lord!

(Exeunt [Rosencrantz and Guildenstern].)

HAMLET.   Ay, so, God buy you.—Now I am alone.
O, what a rogue and peasant slave am I!
Is it not monstrous that this player here,
But in a fiction, in a dream of passion,   515
Could force his soul so to his own conceit°
That from her working all his visage wann'd,°
Tears in his eyes, distraction in his aspect,
A broken voice, and his whole function suiting
With forms to his conceit?° And all for nothing!   520
For Hecuba!
What's Hecuba to him, or he to Hecuba,
That he should weep for her? What would he do,
Had he the motive and the cue for passion
That I have? He would drown the stage with tears   525
And cleave the general ear with horrid speech,
Make mad the guilty and appall the free,°
Confound the ignorant, and amaze indeed
The very faculties of eyes and ears. Yet I,
A dull and muddy-mettled° rascal, peak,°   530
Like John-a-dreams,° unpregnant of° my cause,
And can say nothing—no, not for a king
Upon whose property° and most dear life
A damn'd defeat was made. Am I a coward?
Who calls me villain? Breaks my pate across?   535
Plucks off my beard, and blows it in my face?
Tweaks me by the nose? Gives me the lie° i' th' throat,
As deep as to the lungs? Who does me this?
Ha, 'swounds, I should take it; for it cannot be
But I am pigeon-liver'd,° and lack gall   540
To make oppression bitter, or ere this
I should have fatted all the region kites°
With this slave's offal. Bloody, bawdy villain!
Remorseless, treacherous, lecherous, kindless° villain!
[O, vengeance!]   545

516 *conceit:* conception.   517 *wann'd:* grew pale.   519–20 *his whole . . . conceit:* his whole being responded with actions to suit his thought.   527 *free:* innocent.   530 *muddy-mettled:* dull-spirited.   *peak:* mope, pine.   531 *john-a-dreams:* sleepy dreaming idler.   *unpregnant of:* not quickened by.   533 *property:* the crown; perhaps also character, quality.   537 *gives me the lie:* calls me a liar.   540 *pigeon-liver'd:* the pigeon or dove was popularly supposed to be mild because it secreted no gall.   542 *region kites:* kites (birds of prey) of the air, from the vicinity.   544 *kindless:* unnatural.

Why, what an ass am I! This is most brave,
That I, the son of a dear father murder'd,
Prompted to my revenge by heaven and hell,
Must, like a whore, unpack my heart with words,
And fall a-cursing, like a very drab,°   550
A stallion!° Fie upon 't, foh! About,° my brains!
Hum, I have heard
That guilty creatures sitting at a play
Have by the very cunning of the scene
Been struck so to the soul that presently°   555
They have proclaim'd their malefactions;
For murder, though it have no tongue, will speak
With most miraculous organ. I'll have these players
Play something like the murder of my father
Before mine uncle. I'll observe his looks;   560
I'll tent° him to the quick. If 'a do blench,°
I know my course. The spirit that I have seen
May be the devil, and the devil hath power
T' assume a pleasing shape; yea, and perhaps
Out of my weakness and my melancholy,   565
As he is very potent with such spirits,°
Abuses° me to damn me. I'll have grounds
More relative° than this. The play's the thing
Wherein I'll catch the conscience of the King.

(Exit.)

550 *drab:* prostitute.   551 *stallion:* prostitute (male or female). (Many editors follow the Folio
reading of scullion.) *About:* about it, to work.   555 *presently:* at once.   561 *tent:* probe.
blench: quail, flinch.   566 *spirits:* humors (of melancholy).   567 *Abuses:* deludes.   568 *relative:* closely related, pertinent.

[ACT III

Scene I]°

(Enter King, Queen, Polonius, Ophelia, Rosencrantz, Guildenstern, Lords.)

KING.   And can you, by no drift of conference,°
    Get from him why he puts on this confusion,
    Grating so harshly all his days of quiet
    With turbulent and dangerous lunacy?
ROSENCRANTZ.   He does confess he feels himself distracted,   5
    But from what cause 'a will by no means speak.
GUILDENSTERN.   Nor do we find him forward° to be sounded,°
    But with a crafty madness keeps aloof
    When we would bring him on to some confession
    Of his true state.

III. I. *Location:* The castle.   1 *drift of conference:* direction of conversation.   7 *forward:* willing.
sounded: tested deeply.

QUEEN.   Did he receive you well?   10
ROSENCRANTZ.   Most like a gentleman.
GUILDENSTERN.   But with much forcing of his disposition.°
ROSENCRANTZ.   Niggard of question,° but of our demands
   Most free in his reply.
QUEEN.   Did you assay° him
   To any pastime?   15
ROSENCRANTZ.   Madam, it so fell out that certain players
   We o'er-raught° on the way. Of these we told him,
   And there did seem in him a kind of joy
   To hear of it. They are here about the court,
   And, as I think, they have already order   20
   This night to play before him.
POLONIUS.   'Tis most true,
   And he beseech'd me to entreat your Majesties
   To hear and see the matter.
KING.   With all my heart, and it doth much content me
   To hear him so inclin'd.   25
   Good gentlemen, give him a further edge,°
   And drive his purpose into these delights.
ROSENCRANTZ.   We shall, my lord.

(Exeunt Rosencrantz and Guildenstern.)

KING.   Sweet Gertrude, leave us too,
   For we have closely° sent for Hamlet hither,
   That he, as 'twere by accident, may here   30
   Affront° Ophelia.
   Her father and myself, [lawful espials,°]
   Will so bestow ourselves that seeing, unseen,
   We may of their encounter frankly judge,
   And gather by him, as he is behav'd,   35
   If 't be th' affliction of his love or no
   That thus he suffers for.
QUEEN.   I shall obey you.
   And for your part, Ophelia, I do wish
   That your good beauties be the happy cause
   Of Hamlet's wildness. So shall I hope your virtues   40
   Will bring him to his wonted way again,
   To both your honors.
ROSENCRANTZ.   Madam, I wish it may.

[Exit Queen.]

POLONIUS.   Ophelia, walk you here.—Gracious,° so please you,
   We will bestow ourselves. *[To Ophelia.]* Read on this book,

[Gives her a book.]

---

12 *disposition:* inclination.   13 *question:* conversation.   15 *assay:* try to win.   17 *o'er-*
raught: overtook and passed.   26 *edge:* incitement.   29 *closely:* privately.   31 *Affront:* confront, meet.   32 *espials:* spies.   43 *Gracious:* Your Grace (i.e., the King).

That show of such an exercise° may color°   45
Your loneliness. We are oft to blame in this—
'Tis too much prov'd°—that with devotion's visage
And pious action we do sugar o'er
The devil himself.
KING *[aside].*   O, 'Tis too true!   50
How smart a lash that speech doth give my conscience!
The harlot's cheek, beautied with plast'ring art,
Is not more ugly to° the thing° that helps it
Than is my deed to my most painted word.
O heavy burden!   55
POLONIUS.   I hear him coming. Let's withdraw, my lord.

[King and Polonius withdraw.°]

(Enter Hamlet. [Ophelia pretends to read a book.])

HAMLET.   To be, or not to be, that is the question:
Whether 'Tis nobler in the mind to suffer
The slings and arrows of outrageous fortune,
Or to take arms against a sea of troubles,   60
And by opposing end them. To die, to sleep—
No more—and by a sleep to say we end
The heart-ache and the thousand natural shocks
That flesh is heir to. 'Tis a consummation
Devoutly to be wish'd. To die, to sleep;   65
To sleep, perchance to dream. Ay, there's the rub,°
For in that sleep of death what dreams may come
When we have shuffled° off this mortal coil,°
Must give us pause. There's the respect°
That makes calamity of so long life.°   70
For who would bear the whips and scorns of time,
Th' oppressor's wrong, the proud man's contumely,°
The pangs of despis'd° love, the law's delay,
The insolence of office,° and the spurns°
That patient merit of th' unworthy takes,   75
When he himself might his quietus° make
With a bare bodkin?° Who would fardels° bear,
To grunt and sweat under a weary life,
But that the dread of something after death,
The undiscover'd country from whose bourn°   80
No traveler returns, puzzles the will,
And makes us rather bear those ills we have

---

45 *exercise:* act of devotion. (The book she reads is one of devotion.)   *color:* give a plausible appearance to.   47 *too much prov'd:* too often shown to be true, too often practiced.   53 *to:* compared to.   *thing:* i.e., the cosmetic.   56 *withdraw:* (The King and Polonius may retire behind
an arras. The stage directions specify that they "enter" again near the end of the scene.)
66 *rub:* literally, an obstacle in the game of bowls.   68 *shuffled:* sloughed, cast.   *coil:* turmoil.   69 *respect:* consideration.   70 *of. . . life:* so long-lived.   72 *contumely:* insolent abuse.
73 *despis'd:* rejected.   74 *office:* officialdom.   *spurns:* insults.   76 *quietus:* acquittance; here,
death.   77 *bodkin:* dagger.   *fardels:* burdens.   80 *bourn:* boundary.

Than fly to others that we know not of?
Thus conscience does make cowards of us all
And thus the native hue° of resolution   85
Is sicklied o'er with the pale cast° of thought,
And enterprises of great pitch° and moment°
With this regard° their currents° turn awry,
And lose the name of action.—Soft you now,
The fair Ophelia. Nymph, in thy orisons°   90
Be all my sins rememb'red.

OPHELIA.   Good my lord,
How does your honor for this many a day?

HAMLET. I humbly thank you; well, well, well.

OPHELIA. My lord, I have remembrances of yours,
That I have longed long to re-deliver.   95
I pray you, now receive them.   *[Offers tokens.]*

HAMLET. No, not I, I never gave you aught.

OPHELIA. My honor'd lord, you know right well you did,
And with them words of so sweet breath compos'd
As made these things more rich. Their perfume lost,   100
Take these again, for to the noble mind
Rich gifts wax poor when givers prove unkind.
There, my lord.   *[Gives tokens.]*

HAMLET. Ha, ha! Are you honest?°

OPHELIA. My lord?   105

HAMLET. Are you fair?°

OPHELIA. What means your lordship?

HAMLET. That if you be honest and fair, your honesty° should admit
    no discourse° to your beauty.

OPHELIA. Could beauty, my lord, have better commerce° than with
    honesty?   110

HAMLET. Ay, truly; for the power of beauty will sooner transform
    honesty from what it is to a bawd than the force of honesty can
    translate beauty into his likeness. This was sometime° a paradox,°
    but now the time° gives it proof. I did love you once.

OPHELIA. Indeed, my lord, you made me believe so.   115

HAMLET. You should not have believ'd me, for virtue cannot so
    inoculate° our old stock but we shall relish of it.° I lov'd you not.

OPHELIA. I was the more deceiv'd.

HAMLET. Get thee to a nunn'ry.° Why wouldst thou be a breeder of
    sinners? I am myself indifferent honest;° but yet I could accuse me   120
    of such things that it were better my mother had not borne me:
    I am very proud, revengeful, ambitious, with more offenses at my

---

85 *native hue:* natural color, complexion.   86 *cast:* shade of color.   87 *pitch:* height (as of a
falcon's flight).   *moment:* importance.   88 *regard:* respect, consideration.   *currents:* courses.
90 *orisons:* prayers.   104 *honest:* (1) truthful, (2) chaste.   106 *fair:* (1) beautiful, (2) just, honorable.   107 *your honesty:* your chastity.   108 *discourse:* familiar dealings.   109 *commerce:* dealings.   113 *sometime:* formerly.   *paradox:* a view opposite to commonly held opinion.   114 *the
time:* the present age.   117 *inoculate:* graft, be engrafted to.   *but . . . it:* that we do not still
have about us a taste of the old stock; i.e., retain our sinfulness.   119 *nunn'ry:* (1) convent, (2)
brothel.   120 *indifferent honest:* reasonably virtuous.

beck° than I have thoughts to put them in, imagination to give
them shape, or time to act them in. What should such fellows as
I do crawling between earth and heaven? We are arrant knaves, all;   125
believe none of us. Go thy ways to a nunn'ry. Where's your father?

OPHELIA.   At home, my lord.

HAMLET.   Let the doors be shut upon him, that he may play the fool
nowhere but in 's own house. Farewell.

OPHELIA.   O, help him, you sweet heavens!   130

HAMLET.   If thou dost marry, I'll give thee this plague for thy dowry:
be thou as chaste as ice, as pure as snow, thou shalt not escape
calumny. Get thee to a nunn'ry, farewell. Or, if thou wilt needs
marry, marry a fool, for wise men know well enough what
monsters° you° make of them. To a nunn'ry, go, and quickly too.   135
Farewell.

OPHELIA.   Heavenly powers, restore him!

HAMLET.   I have heard of your paintings too, well enough. God hath
given you one face, and you make yourselves another. You jig,°
and amble, and you lisp, you nickname God's creatures, and make   140
your wantonness your ignorance.° Go to, I'll no more on 't; it hath
made me mad. I say, we will have no moe° marriage. Those that
are married already—all but one—shall live. The rest shall keep as
they are. To a nunn'ry, go.   *(Exit.)*

OPHELIA.   O, what a noble mind is here o'erthrown!   145
  The courtier's, soldier's, scholar's, eye, tongue, sword,
  Th' expectancy and rose of the fair state,°
  The glass of fashion and the mold of form,°
  Th' observ'd of all observers,° quite, quite down!
  And I, of ladies most deject and wretched,   150
  That suck'd the honey of his music vows,
  Now see that noble and most sovereign reason,
  Like sweet bells jangled, out of time and harsh,
  That unmatch'd form and feature of blown°
  Youth blasted with ecstacy.° O, woe is me,   155
  T' have seen what I have seen, see what I see!

(Enter King and Polonius.)

KING.   Love? His affections do not that way tend;
  Nor what he spake, though it lack'd form a little,
  Was not like madness. There's something in his soul,
  O'er which his melancholy sits on brood,   160
  And I do doubt° the hatch and the disclose°
  Will be some danger; which for to prevent,
  I have in quick determination

123 *beck:* command.   135 *monsters:* an allusion to the horns of a cuckold.   *you:* you women.
139 *jig:* dance and sing affectedly and wantonly.   140-41 *make . . . ignorance:* excuse your affection on the grounds of your ignorance.   142 *moe:* more.   147 *Th' expectancy . . . state:* the
hope and ornament of the kingdom made fair (by him).   148 *The glass . . . form:* the mirror of
fashion and the pattern of courtly behavior.   149 *observ'd . . . observers:* the center of attention
and honor in the court.   154 *blown:* booming.   155 *ecstasy:* madness.   161 *doubt:* fear.
disclose: disclosure.

Thus set it down: he shall with speed to England,
For the demand of° our neglected tribute.   165
Haply the seas and countries different
With variable° objects shall expel
This something-settled° matter in his heart,
Whereon his brains still beating puts him thus
From fashion of himself.° What think you on 't?   170
POLONIUS.   It shall do well. But yet do I believe
The origin and commencement of his grief
Sprung from neglected love.—How now, Ophelia?
You need not tell us what Lord Hamlet said;
We heard it all.—My lord, do as you please,   175
But, if you hold it fit, after the play
Let his queen mother all alone entreat him
To show his grief. Let her be round° with him;
And I'll be plac'd, so please you, in the ear of all their conference.
If she find him not, to England send him,   180
Or confine him where your wisdom best shall think.
KING.   It shall be so.
Madness in great ones must not unwatch'd go.

(Exeunt.)

---

165 *For . . . of:* to demand.   167 *variable:* various.   168 *something-settled:* somewhat settled.
170 *from . . . himself:* out of his natural manner   178 *round:* blunt.

[Scene II]°

(Enter Hamlet and three of the Players.)

HAMLET.   Speak the speech, I pray you, as I pronounc'd it to you,
trippingly on the tongue. But if you mouth it, as many of our
players° do, I had as lief the town-crier spoke my lines. Nor do not
saw the air too much with your hand, thus, but use all gently; for
in the very torrent, tempest, and, as I may say, whirlwind of your   5
passion, you must acquire and beget a temperance that may give
it smoothness. O, it offends me to the soul to hear a robustious°
periwig-pated° fellow tear a passion to tatters, to very rags, to split
the ears of the groundlings,° who for the most part are capable of°
nothing but inexplicable dumb-shows and noise. I would have   10
such a fellow whipp'd for o'er-doing Termagant.° It out-herods Herod.°
Pray you, avoid it.
FIRST PLAYER: I warrant your honor.

III. II. *Location:* The castle.   2-3 *our players:* indefinite use; i.e., players nowadays.   7 *robus-*
tious: violent, boisterous.   8 *periwig-pated:* wearing a wig.   9 *groundlings:* spectators who paid
least and stood in the yard of the theater.   *capable of:* susceptible of being influenced by.
11 *Termagant:* a god of the Saracens; a character in the St. Nicholas play, where one of his wor-
shipers, leaving him in charge of goods, returns to find them stolen; whereupon he beats the god
or idol, which howls vociferously.   12 *Herod:* Herod of Jewry (a character in *The Slaughter of the*
Innocents and other cycle plays; the part was played with great noise and fury).

HAMLET.   Be not too tame neither, but let your own discretion be your
tutor. Suit the action to the word, the word to the action, with   15
this special observance, that you o'erstep not the modesty of
nature. For anything so o'erdone is from° the purpose of playing,
whose end, both at the first and now, was and is, to hold, as
't were, the mirror up to nature, to show virtue her feature, scorn
her own image, and the very age and body of the time his° form   20
and pressure.° Now this overdone, or come tardy off,° though it
makes the unskillful laugh, cannot but make the judicious grieve,
the censure of which one° must in your allowance o'erweigh a
whole theater of others. O, there be players that I have seen play,
and heard others praise, and that highly, not to speak it profanely,   25
that, neither having th' accent of Christians nor the gait of
Christian, pagan, nor man, have so strutted and bellow'd that I
have thought some of nature's journeymen° had made men and
not made them well, they imitated humanity so abominably.

FIRST PLAYER: I hope we have reform'd that indifferently° with us, sir.   30

HAMLET.   O, reform it altogether. And let those that play your clowns
speak no more than is set down for them; for there be of them°
that will themselves laugh, to set on some quantity of barren°
spectators to laugh too, though in the mean time some necessary
question of the play be then to be consider'd. That's villainous,   35
and shows a most pitiful ambition in the fool that uses it. Go, make
you ready.

[Exeunt Players.]

(Enter Polonius, Guildenstern, and Rosencrantz.)

How now, my lord? Will the King hear this piece of work?

POLONIUS.   And the Queen too, and that presently.°

HAMLET.   Bid the players make haste.

[Exit Polonius.]

Will you two help to hasten them?   40

ROSENCRANTZ.   Ay, my lord.

(Exeunt they two.)

HAMLET.   What ho, Horatio!

(Enter Horatio.)

HORATIO.   Here, sweet lord, at your service.

HAMLET.   Horatio, thou art e'en as just a man
as e'er my conversation cop'd withal.°

---

17 *from:* contrary to.   20 *his:* its.   21 *pressure:* stamp, impressed character.   *come tardy off:* in-
adequately done.   23 *the censure . . . one:* the judgment of even one of whom.   28 *journey-*
men: laborers not yet masters in their trade.   30 *indifferently:* tolerably.   32 *of them:* some
among them.   33 *barren:* i.e., of wit.   39 *presently:* at once.   44 *my . . . withal:* my contact
with people provided opportunity for encounter with.

HORATIO.   O, my dear lord—   45
HAMLET.   Nay, do not think I flatter;
   For what advancement may I hope from thee
   That no revenue hast but thy good spirits,
   To feed and clothe thee? Why should the poor be flatter'd?
   No, let the candied° tongue lick absurd pomp,   50
   And crook the pregnant° hinges of the knee
   Where thrift° may follow fawning. Dost thou hear?
   Since my dear soul was mistress of her choice
   And could of men distinguish her election,
   Sh'hath seal'd thee for herself, for thou hast been   55
   As one, in suff'ring all, that suffers nothing,
   A man that Fortune's buffets and rewards
   Hast ta'en with equal thanks; and blest are those
   Whose blood° and judgment are so well commeddled°
   That they are not a pipe for Fortune's finger   60
   To sound what stop° she please. Give me that man
   That is not passion's slave, and I will wear him
   In my heart's core, ay, in my heart of heart,
   As I do thee.—Something too much of this.—
   There is a play tonight before the King.   65
   One scene of it comes near the circumstance
   Which I have told thee of my father's death.
   I prithee, when thou seest that act afoot,
   Even with the very comment of thy soul°
   Observe my uncle. If his occulted° guilt
   Do not itself unkennel in one speech,   70
   It is a damned° ghost that we have seen,
   And my imaginations are as foul
   As Vulcan's stithy.° Give him heedful note,
   For I mine eyes will rivet to his face,
   And after we will both our judgments join   75
   In censure of his seeming.°
HORATIO: Well, my lord.
   If 'a steal aught the whilst this play is playing,
   and scape detecting, I will pay the theft.

([Flourish.] Enter trumpets and kettledrums, King, Queen, Polonius, Ophelia, [Rosencrantz,
Guildenstern, and other Lords, with Guards carrying torches].)

HAMLET.   They are coming to the play. I must be idle. Get you a place.

                                       [The King, Queen, and courtiers sit.]

KING.   How fares our cousin Hamlet?   80

---

50 *candied:* sugared, flattering.   51 *pregnant:* compliant.   52 *thrift:* profit.   59 *blood:* passion.   *commeddled:* commingled.   61 *stop:* hole in a wind instrument for controlling the sound.
67 *very . . . soul:* inward and sagacious criticism.   69 *occulted:* hidden.   71 *damned:* in league
with Satan.   73 *stithy:* smithy, place of stiths (anvils).   76 *censure of his seeming:* judgment of his
appearance or behavior.

HAMLET.   Excellent, i' faith, of the chameleon's dish:° I eat the air,
    promise-cramm'd. You cannot feed capons so.

KING.   I have nothing with° this answer, Hamlet. These words are not
    mine.°

HAMLET.   No, nor mine now. [To Polonius.] My lord, you played once   85
    i' th' university, you say?

POLONIUS.   That did I, my lord; and was accounted a good actor.

HAMLET.   What did you enact?

POLONIUS.   I did enact Julius Caesar. I was killed i' th' Capitol; Brutus
    kill'd me.   90

HAMLET.   It was a brute part of him to kill so capital a calf there. Be
    the players ready?

ROSENCRANTZ.   Ay, my lord; they stay upon your patience.

QUEEN.   Come hither, my dear Hamlet, sit by me.

HAMLET.   No, good mother, here's metal more attractive.   95

POLONIUS *[to the King]*.   O, ho, do you mark that?

HAMLET.   Lady, shall I lie in your lap?

                                          [Lying down at Ophelia's feet.]

ROSENCRANTZ.   No, my lord.

[HAMLET.   I mean, my head upon your lap?

ROSENCRANTZ.   Ay, my lord.]   100

HAMLET.   Do you think I meant country° matters?

ROSENCRANTZ.   I think nothing, my lord.

HAMLET.   That's a fair thought to lie between maids' legs.

ROSENCRANTZ.   What is, my lord?

HAMLET.   Nothing.   105

ROSENCRANTZ.   You are merry, my lord.

HAMLET.   Who, I?

ROSENCRANTZ.   Ay, my lord.

HAMLET.   O God, your only jig-maker.° What should a man do but be
    merry? For look you how cheerfully my mother looks, and my   110
    father died within 's° two hours.

ROSENCRANTZ.   Nay, 'Tis twice two months, my lord.

HAMLET.   So long? Nay then, let the devil wear black, for I'll have a
    suit of sables.° O heavens! Die two months ago, and not
    forgotten yet? Then there's hope a great man's memory may   115
    outlive his life half a year. But, by 'r lady, 'a must build churches,
    then, or else shall 'a suffer not thinking on,° with the hobby-horse,
    whose epitaph is "For, O, for, O, the hobby-horse is forgot."°

---

81 *chameleon's dish:* chameleons were supposed to feed on air. Hamlet deliberately misinterprets the
King's *fares* as *feeds.* By his phrase *eat the air* he also plays on the idea of feeding himself with the
promise of succession, of being the heir.   83 *have. . . with:* make nothing of.   83–84 *are not
mine:* do not respond to what I asked.   101 *country:* with a bawdy pun.   109 *only jig-maker:* very
best composer of jigs (song and dance).   111 *within 's:* within this.   114 *suit of sables:* garments trimmed with the fur of the sable and hence suited for a wealthy person, not a mourner (with
a pun on *sable* black).   117 *suffer. . . on:* undergo oblivion.   118 *"For. . . forgot":* verse of
a song occurring also in *Love's Labor's Lost* III. i. 30. The hobby-horse was a character made up to
resemble a horse, appearing in the Morris Dance and such May-game sports. This song laments the
disappearance of such customs under pressure from the Puritans.

(The trumpets sound. Dumb show follows.)

(Enter a King and a Queen [very lovingly]; the Queen embracing him, and he her. [She kneels, and makes show of protestation unto him.] He takes her up, and declines his head upon her neck. He lies him down upon a bank of flowers. She, seeing him asleep, leaves him. Anon comes in another man, takes off his crown, kisses it, pours poison in the sleeper's ears, and leaves him. The Queen returns; finds the King dead, makes passionate action. The Poisoner, with some three or four, come in again, seem to condole with her. The dead body is carried away. The Poisoner woos the Queen with gifts; she seems harsh awhile, but in the end accepts love.)

[Exeunt.]

OPHELIA.   What means this, my lord?
HAMLET.   Marry, this' miching mallecho;° it means mischief.   120
OPHELIA.   Belike° this show imports the argument° of the play.

(Enter Prologue.)

HAMLET.   We shall know by this fellow. The players cannot keep
        counsel;° they'll tell all.
OPHELIA.   Will 'a tell us what this show meant?
HAMLET.   Ay, or any show that you will show him. Be not you°   125
        asham'd to show, he'll not shame to tell you what it means.
OPHELIA.   You are naught, you are naught.° I'll mark the play.
Prologue.   For us, and for our tragedy, here stooping° to your
        clemency, we beg your hearing patiently.

[Exit.]

HAMLET.   Is this a prologue, or the posy of a ring?°   130
OPHELIA..   'Tis brief, my lord.
HAMLET.   As woman's love.

(Enter [two Players as] King and Queen.)

PLAYER KING.   Full thirty times hath Phoebus' cart° gone round
        Neptune's salt wash° and Tellus'° orbed ground,
        And thirty dozen moons with borrowed° sheen   135
        About the world have times twelve thirties been,
        Since love our hearts and Hymen° did our hands
        Unite commutual° in most sacred bands.
PLAYER QUEEN.   So many journeys may the sun and moon
        Make us again count o'er ere love be done!   140
        But, woe is me, you are so sick of late,
        So far from cheer and from your former state,
        That I distrust you. Yet, though I distrust,°
        Discomfort you, my lord, it nothing° must.

---

120 *this' miching mallecho:* this is sneaking mischief.   121 *belike:* probably.   *argument:* plot.
123 *counsel:* secret.   125 *Be not you:* if you are not.   127 *naught:* indecent.   128 *stooping:*
bowing.   130 *posy . . . ring:* brief motto in verse inscribed in a ring.   133 *Phoebus' cart:* the sun
god's chariot.   134 *salt wash:* the sea.   *Tellus:* Goddess of the earth, of the orbed ground.
135 *borrowed:* reflected.   137 *Hymen:* God of matrimony.   138 *commutual:* mutually.   143 *distrust:* am anxious about.   144 *nothing:* not at all.

For women's fear and love hold quantity;°   145
In neither aught, or in extremity.
Now, what my love is, proof° hath made you know,
And as my love is siz'd, my fear is so.
Where love is great, the littlest doubts are fear;
Where little fears grow great, great love grows there.   150
PLAYER KING.   Faith, I must leave thee, love, and shortly too;
   My operant° powers their functions leave to do.°
   And thou shalt live in this fair world behind,
   Honor'd, belov'd; and haply one as kind
   For husband shalt thou—
PLAYER QUEEN.   O, confound the rest!   155
   Such love must needs be treason in my breast.
   In second husband let me be accurst!
   None wed the second but who kill'd the first.
HAMLET.   Wormwood, wormwood.
PLAYER QUEEN.   The instances° that second marriage move°   160
   Are base respects of thrift,° but none of love.
   A second time I kill my husband dead,
   When second husband kisses me in bed.
PLAYER KING.   I do believe you think what now you speak,
   But what we do determine oft we break.   165
   Purpose is but the slave to memory,°
   Of violent birth, but poor validity,°
   Which now, like fruit unripe, sticks on the tree,
   But fall unshaken when they mellow be.
   Most necessary 'Tis that we forget   170
   To pay ourselves what to ourselves in debt.°
   What to ourselves in passion we propose,
   The passion ending, doth the purpose lose.
   The violence of either grief or joy
   Their own enactures° with themselves destroy.   175
   Where joy most revels, grief doth most lament;
   Grief joys, joy grieves, on slender accident.
   This world is not for aye,° nor 'Tis not strange
   That even our loves should with our fortunes change;
   For 'Tis a question left us yet to prove,   180
   Whether love lead fortune, or else fortune love.
   The great man down, you mark his favorite flies;
   The poor advanc'd makes friends of enemies.
   And hitherto doth love on fortune tend;
   For who not needs° shall never lack a friend,   185
   And who in want° a hollow friend doth try,°

---

145 *hold quantity:* keep proportion with one another.   147 *proof:* experience.   152 *operant:*
active.   *leave to do:* cease to perform.   160 *instances:* motives.   *move:* motivate.   161 *base
. . . thrift:* ignoble considerations of material prosperity.   166 *Purpose . . . memory:* our good
intentions are subject to forgetfulness.   167 *validity:* strength, durability.   170–71 *most . . . debt:*
it's inevitable that in time we forget the obligations we have imposed on ourselves.   175 *enac-
tures:* fulfillments.   178 *aye:* ever.   185 *who not needs:* he who is not in need (of wealth).
186 *who in want:* he who is in need.   *try:* test (his generosity).

Directly seasons him° his enemy.
But, orderly to end where I begun,
Our wills and fates do so contrary run
That our devices still° are overthrown;   190
Our thoughts are ours, their ends° none of our own.
So think thou wilt no second husband wed,
But die thy thoughts when thy first lord is dead.

PLAYER QUEEN.   Nor earth to me give food, nor heaven light,
Sport and repose lock from me day and night,   195
To desperation turn my trust and hope,
An anchor's cheer° in prison be my scope!°
Each opposite° that blanks° the face of joy
Meet what I would have well and it destroy!
Both here and hence° pursue me lasting strife,   200
If, once a widow, ever I be wife!

HAMLET.   If she should break it now!

PLAYER KING.   'Tis deeply sworn. Sweet, leave me here awhile;
My spirits grow dull, and fain I would beguile
The tedious day with sleep.   *[Sleeps.]*

PLAYER QUEEN.   Sleep rock thy brain,   205
And never come mischance between us twain!

                                                              [Exit.]

HAMLET.   Madam, how like you this play?

QUEEN.   The lady doth protest too much, methinks.

HAMLET.   O, but she'll keep her word.

KING.   Have you heard the argument?° Is there no offense in 't?

HAMLET.   No, no, they do but jest, poison in jest; no offense i' th'   210
       world.

KING.   What do you call the play?

HAMLET.   "The Mouse-trap." Marry, how? Tropically.° This play is the
       image of a murder done in Vienna. Gonzago is the Duke's name;
       his wife, Baptista. You shall see anon. 'Tis a knavish piece of work,   215
       but what of that? Your Majesty, and we that have free° souls, it
       touches us not. Let the gall'd jade° winch,° our withers° are
       unwrung.°

(Enter Lucianus.)

       This is one Lucianus, nephew to the King.

OPHELIA.   You are as good as a chorus,° my lord.   220

---

187 *seasons him:* ripens him into.   190 *devices still:* intentions continually.   191 *ends:* results.
197 *anchor's cheer:* anchorite's or hermit's fare.   *my scope:* the extent of my happiness.   198 *opposite:* adverse thing.   *blanks:* causes to blanch or grow pale.   200 *hence:* in the life hereafter.
210 *argument:* plot.   213 *Tropically:* figuratively. (The first quarto reading, *trapically,* suggests a
pun on *trap* in *Mouse-trap.*)   216 *free:* guiltless.   217 *gall'd jade:* horse whose hide is rubbed by
saddle or harness.   *Winch:* wince.   *withers:* the part between the horse's shoulder blades.
218 *unwrung:* not rubbed sore.   220 *chorus:* in many Elizabethan plays the forthcoming action
was explained by an actor known as the "chorus"; at a puppet show the actor who spoke the dialogue was known as an "interpreter," as indicated by the lines following.

HAMLET.   I could interpret between you and your love, if I could see
      the puppets dallying.°
OPHELIA.   You are keen, my lord, you are keen.
HAMLET.   It would cost you a groaning to take off mine edge.
OPHELIA.   Still better, and worse.°   225
HAMLET.   So° you mistake° your husbands. Begin, murderer; leave thy
      damnable faces, and begin. Come, the croaking raven doth
      bellow for revenge.
LUCIANUS.   Thoughts black, hands apt, drugs fit, and time agreeing,
      Confederate season,° else no creature seeing,   230
      Thou mixture rank, of midnight weeds collected,
      With Hecate's ban° thrice blasted, thrice infected,
      Thy natural magic and dire property
      On wholesome life usurp immediately.

[Pours the poison into the sleeper's ears.]

HAMLET.   'A poisons him i' th' garden for his estate. His name's   235
      Gonzago. The story is extant, and written in very choice Italian. You
      shall see anon how the murderer gets the love of Gonzago's wife.

[Claudius raises.]

OPHELIA.   The King rises.
[HAMLET.   What, frighted with false fire?°]
QUEEN.   How fares my lord?   240
POLONIUS.   Give o'er the play.
KING.   Give me some light. Away!
POLONIUS.   Lights, lights, lights!

(Exeunt all but Hamlet and Horatio.)

HAMLET.   "Why, let the strucken deer go weep,
      The hart ungalled° play.   245
    For some must watch,° while some must sleep;
      Thus runs the world away."°
    Would not this,° sir, and a forest of feathers°—
    If the rest of my fortunes turn Turk with° me—
    With two Provincial roses° on my raz'd° shoes, get   250
    Me a fellowship in a cry of players?°
HORATIO.   Half a share.

222 *dallying:* with sexual suggestion, continued in keen, i.e., sexually aroused, groaning, i.e., moaning in pregnancy, and edge, i.e., sexual desire or impetuosity.   225 *Still . . . worse:* more keenwitted and less decorous.   226 *so:* even thus (in marriage).   *mistake:* mis-take, take erringly, falseheartedly.   230 *Confederate season:* the time and occasion conspiring (to assist the murderer).   232 *Hecate's ban:* the curse of Hecate, the goddess of witchcraft.   239 *false fire:* the blank discharge of a gun loaded with powder but not shot.   245 *ungalled:* unafflicted.   246 *watch:* remain awake.   244–47 *Why . . . away:* probably from an old ballad, with allusion to the popular belief that a wounded deer retires to weep and die; cf. *As You Like It* II.i.66.   248 *this:* the play.   *feathers:* allusion to the plumes which Elizabethan actors were fond of wearing.   249 *turn Turk with:* turn renegade against, go back on.   250 *provincial roses:* rosettes of ribbon like the roses of a part of France.   *raz'd:* with ornamental slashing.   251 *fellowship . . . players:* partnership in a theatrical company.

HAMLET.   A whole one, I.
  "For thou dost know, O Damon dear,
    This realm dismantled° was   255
  Of Jove himself, and now reigns here
    A very, very-pajock."°
HORATIO.   You might have rhym'd.
HAMLET.   O good Horatio, I'll take the ghost's word for a thousand
    pound. Didst perceive?   260
HORATIO.   Very well, my lord.
HAMLET.   Upon the talk of pois'ning?
Horatio: I did very well note him.
HAMLET.   Ah, ha! Come, some music! Come, the recorders!°
  "For if the King like not the comedy,   265
  Why then, belike, he likes it not, perdy"°
  Come, some music!

(Enter Rosencrantz and Guildenstern.)

GUILDENSTERN.   Good my lord, vouchsafe me a word with you.
HAMLET.   Sir, a whole history.
GUILDENSTERN.   The King, sir—   270
HAMLET.   Ay, sir, what of him?
GUILDENSTERN.   Is in his retirement marvelous distemp'red.
HAMLET.   With drink, sir?
GUILDENSTERN.   No, my lord, with choler.°
HAMLET.   Your wisdom should show itself more richer to signify this   275
    to the doctor, for for me to put him to his purgation would
    perhaps plunge him into more choler.
GUILDENSTERN.   Good my lord, put your discourse into some frame°
    and start not so wildly from my affair.
HAMLET.   I am tame, sir. Pronounce.   280
GUILDENSTERN.   The Queen, your mother, in most great affliction of
    spirit, hath sent me to you.
HAMLET.   You are welcome.
GUILDENSTERN.   Nay, good my lord, this courtesy is not of the right
    breed. If it shall please you to make me a wholesome answer, I will   285
    do your mother's commandment; if not, your pardon° and my
    return shall be the end of my business.
HAMLET.   Sir, I cannot.
ROSENCRANTZ.   What, my lord?
HAMLET.   Make you a wholesome answer; my wit's diseas'd. But, sir,   290
    such answer as I can make, you shall command, or rather, as you
    say, my mother. Therefore no more, but to the matter. My mother,
    you say—

---

255 *dismantled:* stripped, divested.   257 *pajock:* peacock, a bird with a bad reputation (here substituted for the obvious rhyme-word *ass*).   264 *recorders:* wind instruments of the flute kind.   266 *perdy:* a corruption of the French *par dieu,* "by God."   274 *choler:* anger. (But Hamlet takes the word in its more basic humors sense of *bilious disorder.*)   278 *frame:* order. 286 *pardon:* permission to depart.

ROSENCRANTZ.   Then thus she says: your behavior hath struck her into
    amazement and admiration.° 295

HAMLET.   O wonderful son, that can so stonish a mother! But is there
    no sequel at the heels of this mother's admiration? Impart.

ROSENCRANTZ.   She desires to speak with you in her closet,° ere you go
    to bed.

HAMLET.   We shall obey, were she ten times our mother. Have you any 300
    further trade with us?

ROSENCRANTZ.   My lord, you once did love me.

HAMLET.   And do still, by these pickers and stealers.°

ROSENCRANTZ.   Good my lord, what is your cause of distemper? You do
    surely bar the door upon your own liberty, if you deny your griefs 305
    to your friend.

HAMLET.   Sir, I lack advancement.

ROSENCRANTZ.   How can that be, when you have the voice of the King
    himself for your succession in Denmark?

HAMLET.   Ay, sir, but "While the grass grows"°—the proverb is 310
    something° musty.

(Enter the Players with recorders.)

    O, the recorders! Let me see one. [He takes a recorder.] To
    withdraw° with you: why do you go about to recover the wind°
    of me, as if you would drive me into a toil?°

GUILDENSTERN.   O, my lord, if my duty be too bold, my love is too 315
    unmannerly.°

HAMLET.   I do not well understand that. Will you play upon this pipe?

GUILDENSTERN.   My lord, I cannot.

HAMLET.   I pray you.

GUILDENSTERN.   Believe me, I cannot 320

HAMLET.   I do beseech you.

GUILDENSTERN.   I know no touch of it, my lord.

HAMLET.   It is as easy as lying. Govern these ventages° with your
    fingers and thumb, give it breath with your mouth, and it will
    discourse most eloquent music. Look you, these are the stops. 325

GUILDENSTERN.   But these cannot I command to any utt'rance of
    harmony; I have not the skill.

HAMLET.   Why, look you now, how unworthy a thing you make of me!
    You would play upon me, you would seem to know my stops, you
    would pluck out the heart of my mystery, you would sound me 330
    from my lowest note to the top of my compass,° and there is much
    music, excellent voice, in this little organ,° yet cannot you make
    it speak. 'Sblood, do you think I am easier to be play'd on than a

---

295 *admiration:* wonder.   298 *closet:* private chamber.   303 *pickers and stealers:* hands (so called
from the catechism, "to keep my hands from picking and stealing").   310 *"While . . . grows":* the
rest of the proverb is "the silly horse starves"; Hamlet may not live long enough to succeed to the
kingdom.   311 *something:* somewhat.   313 *withdraw:* speak privately.   *recover the wind:* get
the windward side.   314 *toil:* snare.   315–16 *if. . . unmannerly:* if I am using an unmannerly
boldness, it is my love which occasions it.   323 *ventages:* stops of the recorder.   331 *compass:* range (of voice).   332 *organ:* musical instrument.

pipe? Call me what instrument you will, though you can fret° me,
you cannot play upon me. 335

(Enter Polonius.)

    God bless you, sir!
POLONIUS. My lord, the Queen would speak with you, and presently.°
HAMLET. Do you see yonder cloud that's almost in shape of a camel?
POLONIUS. By th' mass, and 'Tis like a camel, indeed.
HAMLET. Methinks it is like a weasel. 340
POLONIUS. It is back'd like a weasel.
HAMLET. Or like a whale?
POLONIUS. Very like a whale.
HAMLET. Then I will come to my mother by and by.° *[Aside.]* They
    fool me° to the top of my bent.°—I will come by and by. 345

    POLONIUS. I will say so.

                                    [Exit.]

HAMLET. "By and by" is easily said. Leave me, friends.

                           [Exeunt all but Hamlet.]

'Tis now the very witching time° of night,
When churchyards yawn and hell itself breathes out
Contagion to this world. Now could I drink hot blood, 350
And do such bitter business as the day
Would quake to look on. Soft, now to my mother.
O heart, lose not thy nature! Let not ever
The soul of Nero° enter this firm bosom. Let me be cruel,
not unnatural; I will speak daggers to her, but use none. 355
My tongue and soul in this be hypocrites:
How in my words somever° she be shent,°
To give them seals° never, my soul, consent!

                                    (Exit.)

334 *fret:* irritate (with a quibble on fret meaning the piece of wood, gut, or metal which regulates the fingering on an instrument). 337 *presently:* at once. 344 *by and by:* immediately. 345 *fool me:* make me play the fool. *top of my bent:* limit of my ability or endurance (literally, the extent to which a bow may be bent). 348 *witching time:* time when spells are cast and evil is abroad. 354 *Nero:* murderer of his mother, Agrippina. 357 *How . . . somever:* however much by my words. *shent:* rebuked. 358 *give them seals:* confirm them with deeds.

[Scene III]°

(Enter King, Rosencrantz, and Guildenstern.)

KING. I like him not, nor stands it safe with us
    To let his madness range. Therefore prepare you.
    I your commission will forthwith dispatch,°

III. III. *Location:* the castle. 3 *dispatch:* prepare, cause to be drawn up.

And he to England shall along with you.
The terms° of our estate° may not endure   5
Hazard so near 's as doth hourly grow
Out of his brows.°
GUILDENSTERN.   We will ourselves provide.
Most holy and religious fear it is
To keep those many many bodies safe
That live and feed upon your Majesty.   10
ROSENCRANTZ.   The single and peculiar° life is bound
With all the strength and armor of the mind
To keep itself from noyance,° but much more
That spirit upon whose weal depends and rests
The lives of many. The cess° of majesty   15
Dies not alone, but like a gulf° doth draw
What's near it with it; or it is a massy wheel
Fix'd on the summit of the highest mount,
To whose huge spokes ten thousand lesser things
Are mortis'd and adjoin'd, which, when it falls,   20
Each small annexment, petty consequence,
Attends° the boist'rous ruin. Never alone
Did the King sigh, but with a General groan.
KING.   Arm° you, I pray you, to this speedy voyage,
For we will fetters put about this fear,   25
Which now goes too free-footed.
ROSENCRANTZ.   We will haste us.

(Exeunt Gentlemen [Rosencrantz and Guildenstern].)

(Enter Polonius.)

POLONIUS.   My lord, he's going to his mother's closet.
Behind the arras° I'll convey myself
To hear the process.° I'll warrant she'll tax him home,°
And, as you said, and wisely was it said,   30
'Tis meet that some more audience than a mother,
Since nature makes them partial, should o'erhear
The speech, of vantage.° Fare you well, my liege.
I'll call upon you ere you go to bed,
And tell you what I know. Thanks, dear my lord.   35

(Exit [Polonius].)

KING.   O, my offense is rank, it smells to heaven;
It hath the primal eldest curse° upon 't,
A brother's murder. Pray can I not,

---

5 *terms:* condition, circumstances.   *our estate:* my royal position.   7 *brows:* effronteries, threatening frowns (?), brain (?).   11 *single and peculiar:* individual and private.   13 *noyance:* harm.
15 *cess:* decease.   16 *gulf:* whirlpool.   22 *Attends:* participates in.   24 *Arm:* prepare.   28 *arras:* screen of tapestry placed around the walls of household apartments. (On the Elizabethan stage, the arras was presumably over a door or discovery space in the tiring house facade.)   29 *process:* proceedings.   *tax him home:* reprove him severely.   33 *of vantage:* from an advantageous place.   37 *primal eldest curse:* the curse of Cain, the first murderer; he killed his brother Abel.

Though inclination be as sharp as will.°
My stronger guilt defeats my strong intent,   40
And, like a man to double business bound,
I stand in pause where I shall first begin,
And both neglect. What if this cursed hand
Were thicker than itself with brother's blood,
Is there not rain enough in the sweet heavens   45
To wash it white as snow? Whereto serves mercy
But to confront the visage of offense?°
And what's in prayer but this twofold force,
To be forestalled° ere we come to fall,
Or pardon'd being down? Then I'll look up;   50
My fault is past. But, O, what form of prayer
Can serve my turn? "Forgive me my foul murder"?
That cannot be, since I am still possess'd
Of those effects for which I did the murder,
My crown, mine own ambition, and my queen.   55
May one be pardon'd and retain th' offense?
In the corrupted currents° of this world
Offense's gilded hand° may shove by justice,
And oft 'Tis seen the wicked prize° itself
Buys out the law. But 'Tis not so above.   60
There is no shuffling,° there the action lies°
In his° true nature, and we ourselves compell'd,
Even to the teeth and forehead° of our faults,
To give in evidence. What then? What rests?°
Try what repentance can. What can it not?   65
Yet what can it, when one cannot repent?
O wretched state! O bosom black as death!
O limed° soul, that, struggling to be free,
Art more engag'd!° Help, angels! Make assay.°
Bow, stubborn knees, and heart with strings of steel,   70
Be soft as sinews of the new-born babe!
All may be well.

                                                              [He kneels.]

(Enter Hamlet [with sword drawn].)

HAMLET.   Now might I do it pat,° now 'a is apraying;
          And now I'll do 't. And so 'a goes to heaven;
          And so am I reveng'd. That would be scann'd:°   75
          A villain kills my father, and for that,

---

39 *Though . . . will:* though my desire is as strong as my determination.   46–47 *Whereto . . . offense:* for what function does mercy serve other than to undo the effects of sin?   49 *forestalled:*
prevented (from sinning).   57 *currents:* courses.   58 *gilded hand:* hand offering gold as a
bribe.   59 *wicked prize:* prize won by wickedness.   61 *shuffling:* escape by trickery.   *the action lies:* the accusation is made manifest, comes up for consideration (a legal metaphor).   62 *his:*
its.   63 *teeth and forehead:* face to face, concealing nothing.   64 *rests:* remains.   68 *limed:*
caught as with birdlime, a sticky substance used to ensnare birds.   69 *engag'd:* embedded.
assay: trial.   73 *pat:* opportunely.   75 *would be scann'd:* needs to be looked into.

I, his sole son, do this same villain send
To heaven.
Why, this is hire and salary, not revenge.
'A took my father grossly,° full of bread,°   80
With all his crimes broad blown,° as flush° as May;
And how his audit° stands who knows save heaven?
But in our circumstance and course° of thought,
'Tis heavy with him. And am I then reveng'd,
To take him in the purging of his soul,   85
When he is fit and season'd for his passage?
No!
Up, sword, and know thou a more horrid hent.°

                                                            [Puts up his sword.]

When he is drunk asleep, or in his rage,
Or in th' incestuous pleasure of his bed,   90
At game a-swearing, or about some act
That has no relish of salvation in 't—
Then trip him, that his heels may kick at heaven,
And that his soul may be as damn'd and black
As hell, whereto it goes. My mother stays.   95
This physic° but prolongs thy sickly days.

                                                                        (Exit.)

KING.   My words fly up, my thoughts remain below.
        Words without thoughts never to heaven go.

                                                                        (Exit.)

80 *grossly:* not spiritually prepared.   *full of bread:* enjoying his worldly pleasures (see Ezek. 16:49.)
81 *crimes broad blown:* sins in full bloom.   *flush:* lusty.   82 *audit:* account.   83 *in . . . course:* as
we see it in our mortal situation.   88 *know . . . hent:* await to be grasped by me on a more horrid occasion.   96 *physic:* purging (by prayer).

[Scene IV]°

(Enter [Queen] Gertrude and Polonius.)

POLONIUS.   'A will come straight. Look you lay° home to him.
        Tell him his pranks have been too broad° to bear with,
        And that your Grace hath screen'd and stood between
        Much heat° and him. I'll sconce° me even here.
        Pray you, be round° [with him.
HAMLET *(within).*   Mother, mother, mother!]   5
QUEEN.   I'll warrant you, fear me not.
        Withdraw, I hear him coming.

                                                    [Polonius hides behind the arras.]

III. IV. *Location:* the queen's private chamber.   1 *lay:* thrust (i.e., reprove him soundly).
2 *broad:* unrestrained.   4 *Much heat:* the king's anger.   *sconce:* ensconce, hide.   5 *round:* blunt.

(Enter Hamlet.)

HAMLET.   Now, mother, what's the matter?
QUEEN.   Hamlet, thou hast thy father° much offended.
HAMLET.   Mother, you have my father much offended.
QUEEN.   Come, come, you answer with an idle° tongue.   10
HAMLET.   Go, go, you question with a wicked tongue.
QUEEN.   Why, how now, Hamlet?
HAMLET.   What's the matter now?
QUEEN.   Have you forgot me?
HAMLET.   No, by the rood,° not so:
    You are the Queen, your husband's brother's wife,   15
    And—would it were not so!—you are my mother.
QUEEN.   Nay, then, I'll set those to you that can speak.
HAMLET.   Come, come, and sit you down; you shall not budge.
    You go not till I set you up a glass
    Where you may see the inmost part of you.   20
QUEEN.   What wilt thou do? Thou wilt not murder me? Help, ho!
POLONIUS *[behind].*   What, ho! Help!
HAMLET *[drawing].*   How now? A rat? Dead, for a ducat, dead!

                         [Makes a pass through the arras.]

POLONIUS *[behind].*   O, I am slain!   *[Falls and dies.]*
QUEEN.   O me, what hast thou done?
HAMLET.   Nay, I know not. Is it the King?   25
QUEEN.   O, what a rash and bloody deed is this!
HAMLET.   A bloody deed—almost as bad, good mother,
    As kill a king, and marry with his brother.
QUEEN.   As kill a king!

              [Parts the arras and discovers Polonius.]

HAMLET.   Ay, lady, it was my word.
    Thou wretched, rash, intruding fool, farewell!   30
    I took thee for thy better. Take thy fortune.
    Thou find'st to be too busy is some danger.—
    Leave wringing of your hands. Peace, sit you down,
    And let me wring your heart, for so I shall,
    If it be made of penetrable stuff,   35
    If damned custom° have not braz'd° it so
    That it be proof° and bulwark against sense.°
QUEEN.   What have I done, that thou dar'st wag thy tongue
    In noise so rude against me?
HAMLET.   Such an art
    That blurs the grace and blush of modesty,   40
    Calls virtue hypocrite, takes off the rose
    From the fair forehead of an innocent love
    And sets a blister° there, makes marriage-vows

---

9 *thy father:* your stepfather, Claudius.   11 *idle:* foolish.   14 *rood:* cross.   36 *damned custom:* habitual wickedness.   *braz'd:* brazened, hardened.   37 *proof:* armor.   *sense:* feeling.
43 *sets a blister:* brands as a harlot.

As false as dicers' oaths. O, such a deed
As from the body of contraction° plucks   45
The very soul, and sweet religion° makes
A rhapsody° of words. Heaven's face does glow
O'er this solidity and compound mass
With heated visage, as against the doom,
Is thought-sick at the act.°
QUEEN.   Ay me, what act,   50
That roars so loud and thunders in the index?°
HAMLET.   Look here, upon this picture, and on this, the counterfeit
presentment° of two brothers.

[Shows her two likenesses.]

See, what a grace was seated on this brow:
Hyperion's° curls, the front° of Jove himself,   55
An eye like Mars, to threaten and command,
A station° like the herald Mercury
New-lighted on a heaven-kissing hill—
A combination and a form indeed,
Where every god did seem to set his seal,   60
To give the world assurance of a man.
This was your husband. Look you now, what follows:
Here is your husband, like a mildew'd ear,°
Blasting his wholesome brother. Have you eyes?
Could you on this fair mountain leave to feed,   65
And batten° on this moor?° Ha, have you eyes?
You cannot call it love, for at your age
The heyday° in the blood is tame, it's humble,
And waits upon the judgment, and what judgment
Would step from this to this? Sense,° sure, you have,   70
Else could you not have motion, but sure that sense
Is apoplex'd,° for madness would not err,
Nor sense to ecstasy was ne'er so thrall'd
But it reserv'd some quantity of choice
To serve in such a difference. What devil was 't   75
That thus hath cozen'd° you at hoodman-blind?°
Eyes without feeling, feeling without sight,
Ears without hands or eyes, smelling sans° all,
Or but a sickly part of one true sense

45 *contraction:* the marriage contract.   46 *religion:* riligious vows.   47 *rhapsody:* senseless
string.   47–50 *Heaven's . . . act:* Heaven's face flushes with anger to look down upon this solid
world, this compound mass, with hot face as though the day of doom were near, and is thought-
sick at the deed (i.e., Gertrude's marriage)   51 *index:* table of contents, prelude, or preface.   52–53 *counterfeit presentment:* portrayed representation.   55 *Hyperion:* the sun god.
front: brow.   57 *station:* manner of standing   63 *ear:* i.e., of grain.   66 *batten:* gorge.
moor: barren upland.   68 *heyday:* state of excitement.   70 *Sense:* perception through the five
senses (the functions of the middle or sensible soul).   72 *apoplex'd:* paralyzed. (Hamlet goes on
to explain that without such a paralysis of will, mere madness would not so err, nor would the five
senses so enthrall themselves to *ecstasy* or lunacy; even such deranged states of mind would be able
to make the obvious choice between Hamlet Senior and Claudius.)   76 *cozen'd:* cheated.
hoodman-blind: blindman's buff.   78 *sans:* without.

Could not so mope.°   80
O shame, where is thy blush? Rebellious hell,
If thou canst mutine° in a matron's bones,
To flaming youth let virtue be as wax,
And melt in her own fire. Proclaim no shame
When the compulsive ardor gives the charge,   85
Since frost itself as actively doth burn,
And reason panders will.°

QUEEN. O Hamlet, speak no more!
Thou turn'st mine eyes into my very soul,
And there I see such black and grained° spots   90
As will not leave their tinct.°

HAMLET.   Nay, but to live
In the rank sweat of an enseamed° bed,
Stew'd in corruption, honeying and making love
Over the nasty sty-

QUEEN. O, speak to me no more.   95
These words, like daggers, enter in my ears.
No more, sweet Hamlet!

HAMLET.   A murderer and a villain,
A slave that is not twentieth part the tithe°
Of your precedent° lord, a vice° of kings,
A cutpurse of the empire and the rule,   100
That from a shelf the precious diadem stole,
And put it in his pocket!

QUEEN. No more!

(Enter Ghost [in his nightgown].)

HAMLET. A king of shreds and patches°
Save me, and hover o'er me with your wings,   105
You heavenly guards! What would your gracious figure?

QUEEN. Alas, he's mad!

HAMLET. Do you not come your tardy son to chide,
That, laps'd in time and passion,° lets go by
Th' important° acting of your dread command? O, say!   110

GHOST. Do not forget. This visitation
Is but to whet thy almost blunted purpose.
But, look, amazement° on thy mother sits.
O, step between her and her fighting soul!
Conceit° in weakest bodies strongest works.   115
Speak to her, Hamlet.

---

80 *mope:* be dazed, act aimlessly.   82 *mutine:* mutiny.   84–87 *Proclaim . . . will:* call it no shameful business when the compelling ardor of youth delivers the attack, i.e., commits lechery, since the
frost of advanced age burns with as active a fire of lust and reason perverts itself by fomenting lust
rather than restraining it.   90 *grained:* dyed in grain, indelible.   91 *tinct:* color.   92 *en-
seamed:* laden with grease.   98 *tithe:* tenth part.   99 *precedent:* former (i.e., the elder Hamlet).   *vice:* buffoon (a reference to the vice of the morality plays).   104 *shreds and
patches:* motley, the traditional costume of the clown or fool.   109 *laps'd . . . passion:* having allowed time to lapse and passion to cool.   110 *important:* importunate, urgent.   113 *amazement:* distraction.   115 *Conceit:* imagination.

HAMLET.   How is it with you, lady?
QUEEN.   Alas, how is 't with you,
       That you do bend your eye on vacancy,
       And with th' incorporal° air do hold discourse?
       Forth at your eyes your spirits wildly peep,   120
       And, as the sleeping soldiers in th' alarm,
       Your bedded° hair, like life in excrements,°
       Start up and stand an° end. O gentle son,
       Upon the heat and flame of thy distemper
       Sprinkle cool patience. Whereon do you look?   125
HAMLET.   On him, on him! Look you how pale he glares!
       His form and cause conjoin'd,° preaching to stones,
       Would make them capable.°—Do not look upon me,
       Lest with this piteous action you convert
       My stern effects.° Then what I have to do   130
       Will want true color°—tears perchance for blood.
QUEEN.   To whom do you speak this?
HAMLET.   Do you see nothing there?
QUEEN.   Nothing at all; yet all that is I see.
HAMLET.   Nor did you nothing hear?   135
QUEEN.   No, nothing but ourselves.
HAMLET.   Why, look you there, look how it steals away!
       My father, in his habit° as he lived!
       Look, where he goes, even now, out at the portal!

                                                              (Exit Ghost.)

QUEEN.   This is the very coinage of your brain.   140
       This bodiless creation ecstasy°
       Is very cunning in.
HAMLET.   Ecstasy?
       My pulse, as yours, doth temperately keep time,
       And makes as healthful music. It is not madness
       That I have utter'd. Bring me to the test,   145
       And I the matter will reword, which madness
       Would gambol° from. Mother, for love of grace,
       Lay not that flattering unction° to your soul
       That not your trespass but my madness speaks.
       It will but skin and film the ulcerous place,   150
       Whiles rank corruption, mining° all within,
       Infects unseen. Confess yourself to heaven,
       Repent what's past, avoid what is to come,
       And do not spread the compost° on the weeds
       To make them ranker. Forgive me this my virtue;°   155

---

119 *incorporal:* immaterial.   122 *bedded:* laid in smooth layers.   *excrements:* outgrowths.
123 *an:* on.   127 *His . . . conjoin'd:* his appearance joined to his cause for speaking.   128 *capable:* receptive.   129-30 *convert . . . effects:* divert me from my stern duty.   131 *want true color:* lack plausibility so that (with a play on the normal sense of *color*) I shall shed tears instead of blood.   138 *habit:* dress.   141 *ecstasy:* madness.   147 *gambol:* skip away.   148 *unction:* ointment.   151 *mining:* working under the surface.   154 *compost:* manure.   155 *this my virtue:* my virtuous talk in reproving you.

For in the fatness° of these pursy° times
Virtue itself of vice must pardon beg,
Yea, curb° and woo for leave° to do him good.
QUEEN.   O Hamlet, thou hast cleft my heart in twain.
HAMLET.   O, throw away the worser part of it,   160
And live the purer with the other half.
Good night. But go not to my uncle's bed;
Assume a virtue, if you have it not.
That monster, custom, who all sense doth eat,°
Of habits devil,° is angel yet in this,   165
That to the use of actions fair and good
He likewise gives a frock or livery°
That aptly is put on. Refrain tonight,
And that shall lend a kind of easiness
To the next abstinence; the next more easy;   170
For use° almost can change the stamp of nature,
And either° ... the devil, or throw him out
With wondrous potency. Once more, good night;
And when you are desirous to be bless'd,°
I'll blessing beg of you, For this same lord,   175

                                            [Pointing to Polonius.]

I do repent; but heaven hath pleas'd it so
To punish me with this, and this with me,
That I must be their scourge and minister.°
I will bestow° him, and will answer well
The death I gave him. So, again, good night.   180
I must be cruel only to be kind.
Thus bad begins and worse remains behind.°
One word more, good lady.
QUEEN.   What shall I do?
HAMLET.   Not this, by no means, that I bid you do:
Let the bloat° king tempt you again to bed,   185
Pinch wanton on your cheek, call you his mouse,
And let him, for a pair of reechy° kisses,
Or paddling in your neck with his damn'd fingers,
Make you to ravel all this matter out,
That I essentially am not in madness,   190
But mad in craft. 'Twere good° you let him know,
For who that's but a queen, fair, sober, wise,

156 *fatness:* grossness.   *pursy:* short-winded, corpulent.   158 *curb:* bow, bend the knee.
leave: permission.   164 *who . . . eat:* who consumes all proper or natural feeling.   165 *Of
habits devil:* devil-like in prompting evil habits.   167 *livery:* an outer appearance, a customary
garb (and hence a predisposition easily assumed in time of stress).   171 *use:* habit.   172 *And
either:* a defective line usually emended by inserting the word *master* after *either,* following the fourth
quarto and early editors.   174 *be bless'd:* become blessed, i.e., repentant.   178 *their scourge
and minister:* agent of heavenly retribution. (By *scourge,* Hamlet also suggests that he himself will eventually suffer punishment in the process of fulfilling heaven's will.)   179 *bestow:* stow, dispose
of.   182 *behind:* to come.   185 *bloat:* bloated.   187 *reechy:* dirty, filthy   191 *good:* said
ironically; also the following eight lines.

Would from a paddock,° from a bat, a gib,°
Such dear concernings° hide? Who would do so?
No, in despite of sense and secrecy,   195
Unpeg the basket° on the house's top,
Let the birds fly, and, like the famous ape,°
To try conclusions,° in the basket creep
And break your own neck down.

QUEEN.   Be thou assur'd, if words be made of breath,   200
And breath of life, I have no life to breathe
What thou hast said to me.

HAMLET.   I must to England; you know that?

QUEEN.   Alack, I had forgot. 'Tis so concluded on.

HAMLET.   There's letters seal'd, and my two school—fellows,   205
Whom I will trust as I will adders fang'd,
They bear the mandate; they must sweep my way,°
And marshal me to knavery. Let it work.
For 'Tis the sport to have the enginer°
Hoist with° his own petar,° and 't shall go hard   210
But I will delve one yard below their mines,°
And blow them at the moon. O, 'Tis most sweet,
When in one line two crafts° directly meet.
This man shall set me packing,°
I'll lug the guts into the neighbor room.   215
Mother, good night indeed. This counselor
Is now most still, most secret, and most grave,
Who was in life a foolish prating knave.
Come, sir, to draw toward an end° with you.
Good night, mother.

(Exeunt [severally, Hamlet dragging in Polonius].)

193 *paddock:* toad.   *gib:* tomcat.   194 *dear concernings:* important affairs.   196 *Unpeg the basket:* open the cage, i.e., let out the secret.   197 *famous ape:* in a story now lost   198 *conclusions:* experiments (in which the ape apparently enters a cage from which birds have been released and then tries to fly out of the cage as they have done, falling to his death).   207 *sweep my way:* go before me.   209 *enginer:* constructor of military contrivances.   210 *Hoist with:* blown up by.   *petar:* petard, an explosive used to blow in a door or make a breach.   211 *mines:* tunnels used in warfare to undermine the enemy's emplacements; Hamlet will countermine by going under their mines.   213 *crafts:* acts of guile, plots.   214 *set me packing:* set me to making schemes, and set me to lugging (him) and, also, send me off in a hurry.   219 *draw . . . end:* finish up (with a pun on *draw,* pull).

[ACT IV

Scene I]°

(Enter King and Queen, with Rosencrantz and Guildenstern.)

KING.   There's matter in these sighs, these profound heaves
You must translate; 'Tis fit we understand them. Where is your son?

I. I. *Location:* the castle.

QUEEN.   Bestow this place on us a little while.

[Exeunt Rosencrantz and Guildenstern.]

    Ah, mine own lord, what have I seen tonight!   5
KING.   What, Gertrude? How does Hamlet?
QUEEN.   Mad as the sea and wind when both contend
    Which is the mightier. In his lawless fit,
    Behind the arras hearing something stir,
    Whips out his rapier, cries, "A rat, a rat!"   10
    And, in this brainish apprehension,° kills
    The unseen good old man.
KING.   O heavy deed!
    It had been so with us, had we been there.
    His liberty is full of threats to all—
    To you yourself, to us, to everyone.   15
    Alas, how shall this bloody deed be answer'd?
    It will be laid to us, whose providence°
    Should have kept short,° restrain'd, and out of haunt°
    This mad young man. But so much was our love
    We would not understand what was most fit,   20
    But, like the owner of a foul disease,
    To keep it from divulging,° let it feed
    Even on the pith of life. Where is he gone?
QUEEN.   To draw apart the body he hath kill'd,
    O'er whom his very madness, like some ore°   25
    Among a mineral° of metals base,
    Shows itself pure: 'a weeps for what is done.
KING.   O Gertrude, come away!
    The sun no sooner shall the mountains touch
    But we will ship him hence; and this vile deed   30
    We must, with all our majesty and skill,
    Both countenance and excuse. Ho, Guildenstern!

(Enter Rosencrantz and Guildenstern.)

    Friends both, go join you with some further aid.
    Hamlet in madness hath Polonius slain,
    And from his mother's closet hath he dragg'd him.   35
    Go seek him out; speak fair, and bring the body
    Into the chapel. I pray you, haste in this.

[Exeunt Rosencrantz and Guildenstern.]

    Come, Gertrude, we'll call up our wisest friends
    And let them know both what we mean to do
    And what's untimely done°.   40

---

11 *brainish apprehension:* headstrong conception..   17 *providence:* foresight.   18 *short:* on a
short tether.   *out of haunt:* secluded   22 *divulging:* becoming evident.   25 *ore:* vein of
gold   26 *mineral:* mine.   40 *And . . . done:* a defective line; conjectures as to the missing
words include *so, haply, slander* (Capell and others); *for, haply, slander* (Theobald and others).

Whose whisper o'er the world's diameter,°
As level° as the cannon to his blank,°
Transports his pois'ned shot, may miss our name,
And hit the woundless° air. O, come away!
My soul is full of discord and dismay.   *(Exeunt.)*   45

41 *diameter:* extent from side to side.   42 *As level:* with as direct aim.   *blank:* white spot in the center of a target.   44 *woundless:* invulnerable.

[Scene II]°

(Enter Hamlet.)

HAMLET.   Safely stow'd.
[ROSENCRANTZ, GUILDENSTERN *(within)*: Hamlet! Lord Hamlet!]
HAMLET.   But soft, what noise? Who calls on Hamlet? O, here they
            come.

(Enter Rosencrantz and Guildenstern.)

ROSENCRANTZ.   What have you done, my lord, with the dead body?   5
HAMLET.   Compounded it with dust, whereto 'Tis kin.
ROSENCRANTZ.   Tell us where 'Tis, that we may take it thence and
            bear it to the chapel.
HAMLET.   Do not believe it.
ROSENCRANTZ.   Believe what?   10
HAMLET.   That I can keep your counsel and not mine own. Besides, to
            be demanded of° a sponge, what replication° should be made by
            the son of a king?
ROSENCRANTZ.   Take you me for a sponge, my lord?
HAMLET.   Ay, sir, that soaks up the King's countenance,° his rewards, his   15
            authorities. But such officers do the King best service
            in the end. He keeps them, like an ape an apple, in the corner of
            his jaw, first mouth'd, to be last swallow'd. When he needs what
            you have glean'd, it is but squeezing you, and, sponge, you shall
            be dry again.   20
ROSENCRANTZ.   I understand you not, my lord.
HAMLET.   I am glad of it. A knavish speech sleeps in° a foolish ear.
ROSENCRANTZ.   My lord, you must tell us where the body is, and go with
            us to the King.
HAMLET.   The body is with the King, but the King is not with the   25
            body.° The King is a thing—
GUILDENSTERN.   A thing, my lord?
HAMLET.   Of nothing.° Bring me to him. [Hide fox, and all after.°]

                                                                          (Exeunt.)

IV. II. *Location:* the castle.   12 *demanded of:* questioned by.   *replication:* reply.   15 *countenance:* favor   22 *sleeps in:* has no meaning to.   25-26 *The . . . body:* perhaps alludes to the
legal commonplace of "the king's two bodies," which drew a distinction between the sacred office
of kingship and the particular mortal who possessed it at any given time.   28 *Of nothing:* of no
account.   *Hide . . . after:* an old signal cry in the game of hide-and-seek, suggesting that Hamlet now runs away from them.

[Scene III]°

(Enter King, and two or three.)

KING. I have sent to seek him, and to find the body.
　　How dangerous is it that this man goes loose!
　　Yet must not we put the strong law on him.
　　He's lov'd of the distracted° multitude,
　　Who like not in their judgment, but their eyes,　　　　　　　　5
　　And where 'Tis so, th' offender's scourge° is weigh'd,°
　　But never the offense. To bear° all smooth and even,
　　This sudden sending him away must seem
　　Deliberate pause.° Diseases desperate grown
　　By desperate appliance are reliev'd,　　　　　　　　　　　10
　　Or not at all.

(Enter Rosencrantz, [Guildenstern,] and all the rest.)

　　　　　　　　How now? What hath befall'n?
ROSENCRANTZ. Where the dead body is bestow'd, my lord,
　　We cannot get from him.
KING.　　　　　　　　　But where is he?
ROSENCRANTZ. Without, my lord; guarded, to know your pleasure.
KING. Bring him before us.
ROSENCRANTZ.　　　　　Ho! Bring in the lord.　　　　　　　15

(They enter [with Hamlet].)

KING. Now, Hamlet, where's Polonius?
HAMLET. At supper.
KING. At supper? Where?
HAMLET. Not where he eats, but where 'a is eaten. A certain
　　convocation of politic worms° are e'en at him. Your worm is your　　20
　　only emperor for diet.° We fat all creatures else to fat us, and we
　　fat ourselves for maggots. Your fat king and your lean beggar is
　　but variable service,° two dishes, but to one table—that's the end.
KING. Alas, alas!
HAMLET. A man may fish with the worm that hath eat° of a king, and　　25
　　eat of the fish that hath fed of that worm.
KING. What dost thou mean by this?
HAMLET. Nothing but to show you how a king may go a progress°
　　through the guts of a beggar.
KING. Where is Polonius?　　　　　　　　　　　　　　　　30
HAMLET. In heaven. Send thither to see. If your messenger find him
　　not there, seek him i' th' other place yourself. But if indeed you

---

IV. III. *Location:* the castle.　　4 *distracted:* fickle, unstable.　　6 *scourge:* punishment.　　*weigh'd:*
taken into consideration.　　7 *bear:* manage　　9 *Deliberate pause:* carefully considered action.
20 *politic worms:* crafty worms (suited to a master spy like Polonius).　　21 *diet:* food, eating (with
perhaps a punning reference to the Diet of Worms, a famous *convocation* held in 1521).　　23
variable service: different courses of a single meal.　　25 *eat:* eaten (pronounced *et*).　　28 *progress:*
royal journey of state.

find him not within this month, you shall nose him as you go up
the stairs into the lobby.

KING *[to some Attendants]:* Go seek him there. 35

HAMLET. 'A will stay till you come.

[*Exit Attendants.*]

KING. Hamlet, this deed, for thine especial safety.—
Which we do tender,° as we dearly° grieve
For that which thou hast done—must send thee hence
[With fiery quickness.] Therefore prepare thyself 40
The bark° is ready, and the wind at help,
Th' associates tend,° and everything is bent°
For England.

HAMLET. For England!

KING. Ay, Hamlet. 45

HAMLET. Good.

KING. So is it, if thou knew'st our purposes.

HAMLET. I see a cherub° that sees them. But, come, for England!
Farewell, dear mother.

KING. Thy loving father, Hamlet. 50

HAMLET. My mother. Father and mother is man and wife, man and
wife is one flesh, and so, my mother. Come, for England!

(*Exit.*)

KING. Follow him at foot;° tempt him with speed aboard.
Delay it not; I'll have him hence tonight.
Away! For everything is seal'd and done 55
That else leans on° th' affair. Pray you, make haste.

[*Exeunt all but the King.*]

And, England,° if my love thou hold'st at aught—
As my great power thereof may give thee sense,
Since yet thy cicatrice° looks raw and red
After the Danish sword, and thy free awe° 60
Pays homage to us—thou mayst not coldly set°
Our sovereign process,° which imports at full,
By letters congruing° to that effect,
The present° death of Hamlet. Do it, England,
For like the hectic° in my blood he rages, 65
And thou must cure me. Till I know 'Tis done,
Howe'er my haps,° my joys were ne'er begun.

(*Exit.*)

---

38 *tender:* regard, hold dear.   *dearly:* intensely.   41 *bark:* sailing vessel.   42 *tend:* wait.
bent: in readiness   48 *cherub:* cherubim are angels of knowledge.   53 *at foot:* close behind, at
heel.   56 *leans on:* bears upon, is related to.   57 *England:* king of England.   59 *cicatrice:* scar.
60 *free awe:* voluntary show of respect.   61 *set:* esteem.   62 *process:* command.   63 *congru-
ing:* agreeing.   64 *present:* immediate.   65 *hectic:* persistent fever.   67 *haps:* fortunes.

[Scene IV]°

(*Enter Fortinbras with his Army over the stage.*)

FORTINBRAS.   Go, captain, from me greet the Danish king.
  Tell him that, by his license,° Fortinbras
  Craves the conveyance° of a promis'd march
  Over his kingdom. You know the rendezvous.
  If that his Majesty would aught with us,   5
  We shall express our duty in his eye;°
  And let him know so.
CAPTAIN.   I will do 't, my lord.
FORTINBRAS.   Go softly° on.

                                   [Exeunt all but the Captain.]

(*Enter Hamlet, Rosencrantz, [Guildenstern,] etc.*)

HAMLET.   Good sir, whose powers° are these?
CAPTAIN.   They are of Norway, sir   10.
HAMLET.   How purposed, sir, I pray you?
CAPTAIN.   Against some part of Poland.
HAMLET.   Who commands them, sir?
CAPTAIN.   The nephew to old Norway, Fortinbras.
HAMLET.   Goes it against the main° of Poland, sir,   15
  Or for some frontier?
CAPTAIN.   Truly to speak, and with no addition,°
  We go to gain a little patch of ground
  That hath in it no profit but the name.
  To pay° five ducats, five, I would not farm it;°   20
  Nor will it yield to Norway or the Pole
  A ranker° rate, should it be sold in fee.°
HAMLET.   Why, then the Polack never will defend it.
CAPTAIN.   Yes, it is already garrison'd.
HAMLET.   Two thousand souls and twenty thousand ducats   25
  Will not debate the question of this straw.°
  This is th' imposthume° of much wealth and peace,
  That inward breaks, and shows no cause without
  Why the man dies. I humbly thank you, sir.
CAPTAIN.   God buy you, sir.   *[Exit.]*
ROSENCRANTZ.   Will 't please you go, my lord?   30
HAMLET.   I'll be with you straight. Go a little before.

                                   [Exit all except Hamlet.]

  How all occasions do inform against° me,
  And spur my dull revenge! What is a man,

IV. IV. *Location:* the coast of Denmark.   2 *license:* permission.   3 *conveyance:* escort, convoy.   6 *eye:* presence.   8 *softly:* slowly.   9 *powers:* forces.   15 *main:* main part.   17 *addition:* exaggeration.   20 *To pay:* i.e., for a yearly rental of.   *farm it:* take a lease of it.   22 *ranker:* higher.   *in fee:* fee simple, outright.   26 *debate . . . straw:* settle this trifling matter.   27 *imposthume:* abscess.   32 *inform against:* denounce, betray; take shape against.

If his chief good and market of° his time
Be but to sleep and feed? A beast, no more.   35
Sure he that made us with such large discourse,°
Looking before and after, gave us not
That capability and god-like reason
To fust° in us unus'd. Now, whether it be
Bestial oblivion,° or some craven scruple   40
Of thinking too precisely on th' event°—
A thought which, quarter'd, hath but one part wisdom
And ever three parts coward—I do not know
Why yet I live to say "This thing's to do,"
Sith° I have cause and will and strength and means   45
To do 't. Examples gross° as earth exhort me:
Witness this army of such mass and charge°
Led by a delicate and tender prince,
Whose spirit, with divine ambition puff'd
Makes mouths° at the invisible event,   50
Exposing what is mortal and unsure
To all that fortune, death, and danger dare,
Even for an egg-shell. Rightly to be great
Is not to stir without great argument,
But greatly to find quarrel in a straw   55
When honor's at the stake. How stand I then,
That have a father kill'd, a mother stain'd,
Excitements of° my reason and my blood,
And let all sleep, while, to my shame, I see
The imminent death of twenty thousand men,   60
That, for a fantasy° and trick° of fame,
Go to their graves like beds, fight for a plot°
Whereon the numbers cannot try the cause,°
Which is not tomb enough and continent°
To hide the slain? O, from this time forth,   65
My thoughts be bloody, or be nothing worth!

(Exit.)

34 market of: profit of, compensation for.   *36 discourse:* power of reasoning.   *39 fust:* grow moldy.   *40 oblivion:* forgetfulness.   *41 event:* outcome.   *45 sith:* since.   *46 gross:* obvious.   *47 charge:* expense.   *50 Makes mouths:* makes scornful faces.   *58 Excitements of:* promptings by.   *61 fantasy:* fanciful caprice.   *trick:* trifle.   *62 plot:* i.e., of ground.   *63 Whereon . . . cause:* on which there is insufficient room for the soldiers needed to engage in a military contest.   *64 continent:* receptacle, container.

[Scene V]°

(Enter Horatio, [Queen] Gertrude, and a Gentleman.)

QUEEN.   I will not speak with her.
GENTLEMAN.   She is importunate, indeed distract.

V. *Location:* the castle.

Her mood will needs be pitied.

QUEEN.   What would she have?

GENTLEMAN. She speaks much of her father, says she hears

    There's tricks° i' th' world, and hems, and beats her heart,°   5

    Spurns enviously at straws,° speaks things in doubt°

    That carry but half sense. Her speech is nothing,

    Yet the unshaped use° of it doth move

    The hearers to collection;° they yawn° at it,

    And botch° the words up fit to their own thoughts,   10

    Which, as her winks and nods and gestures yield° them,

    Indeed would make one think there might be thought,°

    Though nothing sure, yet much unhappily.

HORATIO. 'Twere good she were spoken with, for she may strew

    Dangerous conjectures in ill-breeding° minds.   15

QUEEN. Let her come in.

                                [Exit Gentlemen.]

    [Aside.] To my sick soul, as sin's true nature is,

    Each toy° seems prologue to some great amiss.°

    So full of artless jealousy is guilt,

    It spills itself in fearing to be spilt.°   20

(Enter Ophelia [distracted].)

OPHELIA. Where is the beauteous majesty of Denmark?

QUEEN. How now, Ophelia?

OPHELIA *(she sings)*. "How should I your true love know

      From another one?

    By his cockle hat° and staff,   25

    And his sandal shoon."°

QUEEN. Alas, sweet lady, what imports this song?

OPHELIA. Say you? Nay, pray you, mark.

    "He is dead and gone, lady,   *(Song.)*

      He is dead and gone;   30

    At his head a grass-green turf

      At his heels a stone."

    O, ho!

QUEEN. Nay, but Ophelia—

OPHELIA. Pray you mark.   35

    [Sings.] "White his shroud as the mountain snow"—

(Enter King.)

QUEEN. Alas, look here, my lord.

---

5 *tricks:* deceptions.   *heart:* breast   7 *Spurns . . . straws:* kicks spitefully, takes offense at trifles.   *in doubt:* obscurely.   8 *unshaped use:* distracted manner.   9 *collection:* inference, a guess
at some sort of meaning.   *yawn:* wonder, grasp.   10 *botch:* patch   11 *yield:* deliver, bring
forth (her words).   12 *thought:* conjectured.   15 *ill-breeding:* prone to suspect the worst.   18 *toy:*
trifle.   *amiss:* calamity.   19–20 *So . . . spilt:* Guilt is so full of suspicion that it unskillfully betrays itself in fearing betrayal.   25 *cockle hat:* hat with cockleshell stuck in it as a sign that the
wearer had been a pilgrim to the shrine of St. James of Compostela in Spain.   26 *shoon:* shoes.

OPHELIA.   "Larded° all with flowers   *(Song.)*
  Which bewept to the ground did not go
   With true-love showers."   40
KING.   How do you, pretty lady?
OPHELIA.   Well, God 'ild° you! They say the owl° was a baker's
   daughter. Lord, we know what we are, but know not what
   we may be. God be at your table!
KING.   Conceit° upon her father.   45
OPHELIA.   Pray let's have no words of this; but when they ask you
  what it means, say you this:
  "Tomorrow is Saint Valentine's° day.   *(Song.)*
   All in the morning betime,
  And I a maid at your window,   50
   To be your Valentine.
  Then up he rose, and donn'd his clo'es,
   And dupp'd° the chamber-door,
  Let in the maid, that out a maid
   Never departed more."   55
KING.   Pretty Ophelia!
OPHELIA.   Indeed, la, without an oath, I'll make an end on 't:
  [Sings.] "By Gis° and by Saint Charity,
   Alack, and fie for shame!
  Young men will do 't, if they come to 't;   60
   By Cock,° they are to blame.
  Quoth she, 'Before you tumbled me,
   You promised me to wed.' "
  He answers:
  " 'So would I ha' done, by yonder sun,   65
   An thou hadst not come to my bed.' "
KING.   How long hath she been thus?
OPHELIA.   I hope all will be well. We must be patient, but I cannot
   choose but weep, to think they would lay him i' th' cold ground.
   My brother shall know of it; and so I thank you for your good   70
   counsel. Come, my coach! Good night, ladies; good night, sweet
   ladies; good night, good night.

                       [Exit.]

KING.   Follow her close; give her good watch, I pray you.

                    [Exit Horatio.]

  O, this is the poison of deep grief; it springs
  All from her father's death—and now behold!   75
  O Gertrude, Gertrude,
  When sorrows come, they come not single spies,°

---

38 *Larded:* decorated. 42 *God 'ild:* god yield or reward. *owl:* refers to a legend about a baker's
daughter who was turned into an owl for refusing Jesus bread. 45 *Conceit:* brooding. 48 *Valentine's:* this song alludes to the belief that the first girl seen by a man on the morning of this day was his valentine or true love. 53 *dupp'd:* opened. 58 *Gis:* Jesus.
61 *Cock:* aperversion of *God* in oaths. 77 *spies:* scouts sent in advance of the main force.

But in battalions. First, her father slain;
Next, your son gone, and he most violent author
Of his own just remove; the people muddied,° 80
Thick and unwholesome in their thoughts and whispers,
For good Polonius' death; and we have done but greenly,°
In hugger-mugger° to inter him; poor Ophelia
Divided from herself and her fair judgment,
Without the which we are pictures, or mere beasts; 85
Last, and as much containing as all these,
Her brother is in secret come from France,
Feeds on his wonder, keeps himself in clouds,°
And wants° not buzzers° to infect his ear
With pestilent speeches of his father's death, 90
Wherein necessity, of matter beggar'd,°
Will nothing stick our person to arraign
In ear and ear.° O my dear Gertrude, this,
Like to a murd'ring-piece,° in many places
Gives me superfluous death. *(A noise within.)* 95
[QUEEN   Alack, what noise is this?]
KING.   Attend!
Where are my Switzers?° Let them guard the door.

(Enter a Messenger.)

What is the matter?
MESSENGER.   Save yourself, my lord!
The ocean, overpeering of his list,° 100
Eats not the flats° with more impiteous° haste
Than young Laertes, in a riotous head,°
O'erbears your officers. The rabble call him lord,
And, as° the world were now but to begin,
Antiquity forgot, custom not known, 105
The ratifiers and props° of every word,°
They cry, "Choose we! Laertes shall be king!"
Caps, hands, and tongues applaud it to the clouds,
"Laertes shall be king, Laertes king!"

(A noise within.)

QUEEN.   How cheerfully on the false trail they cry! 110
O, this is counter,° you false Danish dogs!

(Enter Laertes with others.)

---

80 *muddied:* stirred up, confused.   82 *greenly:* imprudently, foolishly.   89 *hugger-mugger:* secret haste.   88 *in clouds:* i.e., of suspicion and rumor.   89 *wants:* lacks.   *buzzers:* gossipers, informers.   91 *of matter beggar'd:* unprovided with facts.   92–93 *Will. . . . ear:* will not hesitate to accuse my (royal) person in everybody's ears.   94 *murd'ring-piece:* cannon loaded so as to scatter its shot.   97 *Switzers:* Swiss guards, mercenaries.   100 *overpeering of his list:* overflowing its shore.   101 *flats:* flatlands near shore.   *impiteous:* pitiless.   102 *head:* armed force.   104 *as:* as if.   106 *ratifiers and props:* refer to *antiquity* and *custom.*   *word:* promise.   111 *counter:* a hunting term meaning to follow the trail in a direction opposite to that which the game has taken.

KING. The doors are broke.

LAERTES. Where is this King? Sirs, stand you all without.

ALL. No, let's come in.

LAERTES.   I pray you, give me leave.

ALL. We will, we will.   115

[They retire without the door.]

LAERTES. I thank you. Keep the door. O thou vile king,
    Give me my father!

QUEEN.   Calmly, good Laertes.

[She tries to hold him back.]

LAERTES. That drop of blood that's calm proclaims me bastard,
    Cries cuckold to my father, brands the harlot
    Even here, between the chaste unsmirched brow   120
    Of my true mother.

KING.   What is the cause, Laertes,
    That thy rebellion looks so giant-like?
    Let him go, Gertrude. Do not fear our° person.
    There's such divinity doth hedge a king
    That treason can but peep to what it would,°   125
    Acts little of his will.° Tell me, Laertes,
    Why thou art thus incens'd. Let him go, Gertrude.
    Speak, man.

LAERTES.   Where is my father?

KING.   Dead.

QUEEN. But not by him.

KING.   Let him demand his fill.

LAERTES. How came he dead? I'll not be juggled with.   130
    To hell, allegiance! Vows, to the blackest devil!
    Conscience and grace, to the profoundest pit!
    I dare damnation. To this point I stand,
    That both the worlds I give to negligence,°
    Let come what comes, only I'll be reveng'd   135
    Most throughly° for my father.

KING. Who shall stay you?

LAERTES.   My will, not all the world's.°
    And for my means, I'll husband them so well,
    They shall go far with little.

KING.   Good Laertes,   140
    If you desire to know the certainty
    Of your dear father, is 't writ in your revenge
    That, swoopstake,° you will draw both friend and foe,

---

123 *fear our:* fear for my.   125 *can . . . would:* can only glance; as from far off or through a barrier, at what it would intend.   126 *Acts . . . will:* (but)performs little of what it intends. 134 *both . . . negligence:* both this world and the next are of no consequence to me.   136 *throughly:* thoroughly.   138 *My will . . . world's:* I'll stop (*stay*) when my will is accomplished, not for anyone else's.   143 *swoopstake:* literally, taking all stakes on the gambling table at once, i.e., indiscriminately; *draw* is also a gambling term.

Winner and loser?
LAERTES.   None but his enemies.
KING.   Will you know them then?   145
LAERTES.   To his good friends thus wide I'll ope my arms,
    And, like the kind life-rend'ring pelican,°
    Repast° them with my blood.
KING.   Why, now you speak
    Like a good child and a true gentleman.
    That I am guiltless of your father's death,   150
    And am most sensibly° in grief for it,
    It shall as level° to your judgment 'pear
    As day does to your eye.
                              (A noise within:)   "Let her come in."
LAERTES.   How now? What noise is that?

(Enter Ophelia.)

    O heat, dry up my brains! Tears seven times salt   155
    Burn out the sense and virtue° of mine eye!
    By heaven, thy madness shall be paid with weight°
    Till our scale turn the beam.° O rose of May!
    Dear maid, kind sister, sweet Ophelia!
    O heavens, is 't possible a young maid's wits   160
    Should be as mortal as an old man's life?
    [Nature is fine in° love, and where 'Tis fine,
    It sends some precious instance°of itself
    After the thing it loves.°]
OPHELIA.   "They bore him barefac'd on the bier;   165
                                      (Song.)

    [Hey non nonny, nonny, hey nonny,]
    And in his grave rain'd many a tear"—
    Fare you well, my dove!
LAERTES.   Hadst thou thy wits, and didst persuade° revenge,
    It could not move thus.   170
OPHELIA.   You must sing "A-down a-down,
    And you call him a-down-a."
    O, how the wheel° becomes it! It is the false steward°
    That stole his master's daughter.
LAERTES.   This nothing's more than matter.°   175
OPHELIA.   There's rosemary,° that's for remembrance; pray you, love,
    remember. And there is pansies,° that's for thoughts.

---

147 *pelican:* refers to the belief that the female pelican fed its young with its own blood.   148 *Repast:* feed.   151 *sensibly:* feelingly.   152 *level:* plain.   156 *virtue:* faculty, power.   157 *paid with weight:* repaid, avenged equally or more.   158 *beam:* crossbar of a balance.   162 *fine in:* refined by.   163 *instance:* token   164 *After. . loves:* into the grave, along with Polonius.   169 *persuade:* argue cogently for.   173 *wheel:* spinning wheel as accompaniment to the song, or refrain   *false steward:* the story is unknown.   175 *This . . matter:* This seeming nonsense is more meaningful than sane utterance.   176 *rosemary:* used as a symbol of remembrance both at weddings and at funerals.   177 *pansies:* emblems of love and courtship; perhaps from French *pensées,* thoughts.

LAERTES.   A document° in madness, thoughts and remembrance fitted.

OPHELIA.   There's fennel° for you, and columbines.° There's rue° for
    you, and here's some for me; we may call it herb of grace o' Sundays.   180
    You may wear your rue with a difference.° There's a daisy.° I would
    give you some violets,° but they wither'd all when my father died.
    They say 'a made a good end—
    [Sings.] "For bonny sweet Robin is all my joy."

LAERTES.   Thought° and affliction, passion, hell itself,   185
    She turns to favor° and to prettiness.

OPHELIA.   "And will 'a not come again?   *(Song.)*
    And will 'a not come again?
      No, no, he is dead,
      Go to thy death-bed,   190
    He never will come again.
    "His beard was as white as snow,
    All flaxen was his poll.°
      He is gone, he is gone,
      And we cast away moan.   195
    God 'a' mercy on his soul!
    And of all Christians' souls, I pray God. God buy you.

                                                                     [Exit.]

LAERTES.   Do you see this, O God?

KING.   Laertes, I must commune with your grief,
    Or you deny me right. Go but apart,   200
    Make choice of whom your wisest friends you will,
    And they shall hear and judge 'twixt you and me.
    If by direct or by collateral° hand
    They find us touch'd,° we will our kingdom give,
    Our crown, our life, and all that we call ours,   205
    To you in satisfaction; but if not,
    Be you content to lend your patience to us,
    And we shall jointly labor with your soul
    To give it due content.

LAERTES.   Let this be so.
    His means of death, his obscure funeral—   •   210
    No trophy,° sword, nor hatchment° o'er his bones,
    No noble rite nor formal ostentation°—
    Cry to be heard, as 'twere from heaven to earth,
    That I must call 't in question.

---

178 *document:* instruction, lesson.   179 *fennel:* emblem of flattery.   *columbines:* emblems of
unchastity (?) or ingratitude (?).   *rue:* emblem of repentance; when mingled with holy water,
it was known as *herb of grace.*   181 *with a difference:* suggests that Ophelia and the Queen have different causes of sorrow and repentance; perhaps with a play on *rue* in the sense of ruth, pity.
daisy: emblem of dissembling, faithlessness.   182 *violets:* emblems of faithfulness.   185 *Thought:*
melancholy.   186 *favor:* grace.   193 *poll:* head.   203 *collateral:* indirect.   204 *us
touch'd:* me implicated.   211 *trophy:* memorial.   *hatchment:* tablet displaying the armorial bearings of a deceased person.   212 *ostentation:* ceremony.

KING.   So you shall;
   And where th' offense is, let the great ax fall.   215
   I pray you go with me.

                                          (Exeunt.)

[Scene VI]°

(Enter Horatio and others.)

HORATIO.   What are they that would speak with me?
GENTLEMAN.   Seafaring men, sir. They say they have letters for you.

                                    [Exit Gentleman.]

HORATIO.   Let them come in. I do not know from what part of the
   world I should be greeted, if not from lord Hamlet.

(Enter Sailors.)

FIRST SAILOR.   God bless you sir.   5
HORATIO.   Let him bless thee too.
FIRST SAILOR.   'A shall, sir an't please him. There's a letter for you, sir—
   it came from th' ambassador that was bound for England—if your
   name be Horatio, as I am let to know it is.

                                      [Gives letter.]

HORATIO [reads]: "Horatio, when thou shalt have overlook'd this, give   10
   these fellows some means° to the King; they have letters for him.
   Ere we were two days old at sea, a pirate of very warlike
   appointment° gave us chase. Finding ourselves too slow of sail, we
   put on a compell'd valor, and in the grapple I boarded them. On
   the instant they got clear of our ship, so I alone became their   15
   prisoner. They have dealt with me like thieves of mercy,° but they
   knew what they did: I am to do a good turn for them. Let the King
   have the letters I have sent, and repair thou to me with as much
   speed as thou wouldest fly death. I have words to speak in thine
   ear will make thee dumb; yet are they much too light for the bore°   20
   of the matter. These good fellows will bring thee where I am.
   Rosencrantz and Guildenstern hold their course for England.
   Of them I have much to tell thee. Farewell.
      He that thou knowest thine, Hamlet." Come, I will give you
   way for these your letters, and do 't the speedier that you may   25
   direct me to him from whom you brought them.

                                          (Exeunt.)

IV. VI.   *Location:* the   castle.   11 *means:* means   of   access.   13 *appointment:* equipage.
16 *thieves of mercy:* merciful thieves.   23 *bore:* caliber, i.e., importance.

[Scene VII]°

(Enter King and Laertes.)

KING.   Now must your conscience my acquittance seal,°
        And you must put me in your heart for friend,
        Sith you have heard, and with a knowing ear,
        That he which hath your noble father slain
        Pursued my life.
LAERTES.   It well appears. But tell me   5
        Why you proceeded not against these feats°
        So criminal and so capital° in nature,
        As by your safety, greatness, wisdom, all things else,
        You mainly° were stirr'd up.
KING.   O, for two special reasons,
        Which may to you, perhaps, seem much unsinew'd,°   10
        But yet to me th' are strong.
        The Queen his mother
        Lives almost by his looks, and for myself—
        My virtue or my plague, be it either which—
        She's so conjunctive° to my life and soul
        That, as the star moves not but in his sphere,°   15
        I could not but by her. The other motive,
        Why to a public count° I might not go,
        Is the great love the general gender° bear him,
        Who, dipping all his faults in their affection,
        Would, like the spring° that turneth wood to stone,   20
        Convert his gyves° to graces, so that my arrows,
        Too slightly timber'd° for so loud° a wind,
        Would have reverted to my bow again
        And not where I had aim'd them.
LAERTES.   And so have I a noble father lost,   25
        A sister driven into desp'rate terms,°
        Whose worth, if praises may go back° again,
        Stood challenger on mount° of all the age
        For her perfections. But my revenge will come.
KING.   Break not your sleeps for that. You must not think   30
        That we are made of stuff so flat and dull
        That we can let our beard be shook with danger
        And think it pastime. You shortly shall hear more.
        I lov'd your father, and we love ourself;
        And that, I hope, will teach you to imagine—   35

IV. VII. *Location:* the castle.   1 *my acquittance seal:* confirm or acknowledge my innocence.
6 *feats:* acts.   7 *capital:* punishable by death.   9 *mainly:* greatly.   10 *unsinew'd:* weak   14 *conjunctive:* closely united.   15 *sphere:* the hollow sphere in which, according to Ptolemaic astronomy, the planets moved.   17 *count:* account, reckoning.   18 *general gender:* common people.   20 *spring:* aspring with such a concentration of line that it coats a piece of wood with limestone, in effect gilding it.   21 *gyves:* fetters (which, gilded by the people's praise, would look like badges of honor).   22 *slightly timber'd:* light.   *loud:* strong.   26 *terms:* state, condition.   27 *go back:* recall Ophelia's former virtues.   28 *mount:* on high.

(Enter a Messenger with Letters.)

[How now? What news?]
MESSENGER.   [Letters, my lord, from Hamlet:]
   These to your Majesty, this to the Queen.

                                                     [Gives letters.]

KING.   From Hamlet? Who brought them?
MESSENGER.   Sailors, my lord, they say; I saw them not.
   They were given me by Claudio. He receiv'd them   40
   Of him that brought them.
KING.   Laertes, you shall hear them.
   Leave us.   *[Exit Messenger.]*
   [Reads.] "High and mighty, you shall know I am set naked°
   on your kingdom. Tomorrow shall I beg leave to see your kingly eyes,
   when I shall, first asking your pardon° thereunto, recount the   45
   occasion of my sudden and more strange return. Hamlet." What
   should this mean? Are all the rest come back? Or is it some abuse,°
   and no such thing?
LAERTES.   Know you the hand?
KING.   'Tis Hamlet's character.° "Naked!"
   And in a postscript here, he says "alone."   50
   Can you devise° me?
LAERTES.   I am lost in it, my lord. But let him come.
   It warms the very sickness in my heart
   That I shall live and tell him to his teeth,
   "Thus didst thou."
KING.   If it be so, Laertes—   55
   As how should it be so? How otherwise?°—
   Will you be ruled by me?
LAERTES.   Ay, my lord,
   So° you will not o'errule me to a peace.
KING.   To thine own peace. If he be now returned,
   As checking at° his voyage, and that he means   60
   No more to undertake it, I will work him
   To an exploit, now ripe in my device,
   Under the which he shall not choose but fall;
   And for his death no wind of blame shall breathe,
   But even his mother shall uncharge the practice°   65
   And call it accident.
LAERTES.   My lord, I will be rul'd,
   The rather if you could devise it so
   That I might be the organ.°

---

43 *naked:* destitute, unarmed, without following.   45 *pardon:* permission.   47 *abuse:* deceit.
49 *character:* handwriting.   51 *Devise:* explain to.   56 *As . . . otherwise:* How can this (Hamlet's return) be true? Yet how otherwise than true (since we have the evidence of his letter)?
58 *So:* provided that.   60 *checking at:* turning aside from (like a falcon leaving the quarry to fly
at a chance bird).   65 *uncharge the practice:* acquit the stratagem of being a plot.   68 *organ:*
agent, instrument.

KING.   It falls right.
   You have been talk'd of since your travel much,
   And that in Hamlet's hearing, for a quality   70
   Wherein, they say, you shine. Your sum of parts°
   Did not together pluck such envy from him
   As did that one, and that, in my regard,
   Of the unworthiest siege.°
LAERTES.   What part is that, my lord?   75
KING.   A very riband in the cap of youth,
   Yet needful too, for youth no less becomes
   The light and careless livery that it wears
   Than settled age his sables° and his weeds,°
   Importing health° and graveness. Two months since   80
   Here was a gentleman of Normandy.
   I have seen myself, and serv'd against, the French,
   And they can well° on horseback, but this gallant
   Had witchcraft in 't; he grew unto his seat,
   And to such wondrous doing brought his horse   85
   As had he been incorps'd and demi-natured°
   With the brave beast. So far he topp'd° my thought
   That I, in forgery° of shapes and tricks,
   Come short of what he did.
LAERTES.   A Norman was 't?
KING.   A Norman.
LAERTES.   Upon my life, Lamord.
KING.   The very same.   90
LAERTES.   I know him well. He is the brooch° indeed
   And gem of all the nation.
KING.   He made confession° of you,
   And gave you such a masterly report
   For art and exercise in your defense,   95
   And for your rapier most especial,
   That he cried out, 'twould be a sight indeed,
   If one could match you. The scrimers° of their nation,
   He swore, had neither motion, guard, nor eye,
   If you oppos'd them. Sir, this report of his   100
   Did Hamlet so envenom with his envy
   That he could nothing do but wish and beg
   Your sudden coming o'er to play° with you.
   Now, out of this—
LAERTES.   What out of this, my lord?
KING.   Laertes, was your father dear to you?   105
   Or are you like the painting of a sorrow,
   A face without a heart?

---

71 *Your . . . parts:* all your other virtues.   74 *unworthiest siege:* least important rank.   79 *sables:* rich robes furred with sable.   *weeds:* garments.   80 *importing health:* indicating prosperity.   83 *can well:* are skilled.   86 *incorps'd and demi-natur'd:* of one body and nearly of one nature (like the centaur).   87 *topp'd:* surpassed.   88 *forgery:* invention.   91 *brooch:* ornament.   93 *confession:* admission of superiority.   98 *scrimers:* fencers.   103 *play:* fence.

LAERTES.   Why ask you this?
KING.   Not that I think you did not love your father,
        But that I know love is begun by time,°
        And that I see, in passages of proof,°   110
        Time qualifies° the spark and fire of it.
        There lives within the very flame of love
        A kind of wick or snuff° that will abate it,
        And nothing is at a like goodness still,°
        For goodness, growing to a plurisy,°   115
        Dies in his own too much.° That° we would do,
        We should do when we would; for this "would" changes
        And hath abatements° and delays as many
        As there are tongues, are hands, are accidents,°
        And then this "should" is like a spendthrift's sigh,°   120
        That hurts by easing.° But, to the quick o' th' ulcer;
        Hamlet comes back. What would you undertake
        To show yourself your father's son in deed
        More than in words?
LAERTES.   To cut his throat i' th' church!
KING.   No place, indeed, should murder sanctuarize;°   125
        Revenge should have no bounds. But, good Laertes,
        Will you do this,° keep close within your chamber.
        Hamlet return'd shall know you are come home.
        We'll put on those° shall praise your excellence
        And set a double varnish on the fame   130
        The Frenchman gave you, bring you in fine° together,
        And wager on your heads. He, being remiss,°
        Most generous,° and free from all contriving,
        Will not peruse the foils, so that, with ease,
        Or with a little shuffling, you may choose   135
        A sword unbated,° and in a pass of practice°
        Requite him for your father.
LAERTES.   I will do 't.
        And for that purpose I'll anoint my sword.
        I bought an unction° of a mountebank°
        So mortal that, but dip a knife in it,   140
        Where it draws blood no cataplasm° so rare,
        Collected from all simples° that have virtue
        Under the moon, can save the thing from death

---

109 *begun by time:* subject to change.   110 *passages of proof:* actual instances.   111 *qualifies:* weakens.   113 *snuff:* the charred part of a candlewick.   114 *nothing . . . still:* nothing remains at a constant level of perfection.   115 *plurisy:* excess, plethora.   116 *in . . . much:* of its own excess.   *That:* that which.   118 *abatements:* diminutions.   119 *accidents:* occurrences, incidents.   120 *spendthrift's sigh:* an allusion to the belief that each sigh cost the heart of a drop of blood.   121 *hurts by easing:* costs the heart blood even while it affords emotional relief.   125 *sanctuarize:* protect from punishment (alludes to the right of sanctuary with which certain religious places were invested).   127 *Will you do this:* if you wish to do this.   129 *put on those:* instigate those who.   131 *in fine:* finally.   132 *remiss:* negligently unsuspicious.   133 *generous:* nobleminded   136 *unbated:* not blunted, having no button.   *pass of practice:* treacherous thrust.   139 *unction:* ointment.   *mountebank:* quack doctor.   141 *cataplasm:* plaster or poultice.   142 *simples:* herbs.

That is but scratch'd withal. I'll touch my point
With this contagion, that, if I gall° him slightly,   145
It may be death.

KING.   Let's further think of this,
Weigh what convenience both of time and means
May fit us to our shape.° If this should fail,
And that our drift look through our bad performance,°
'Twere better not assay'd. Therefore this project   150
Should have a back or second, that might hold
If this did blast in proof.° Soft, let me see.
We'll make a solemn wager on your cunnings—I ha 't!
When in your motion you are hot and dry—
As° make your bouts more violent to that end—   155
And that he calls for drink, I'll have prepar'd him
A chalice for the nonce,° whereon but sipping,
If he by chance escape your venom'd stuck,°
Our purpose may hold there. [*A cry within.*]
But stay, what noise?   160

(*Enter Queen.*)

QUEEN.   One woe doth tread upon another's heel,
So fast they follow. Your sister's drowned, Laertes.
LAERTES.   Drown'd! O, where?
QUEEN.   There is a willow grows askant° the brook,
That shows his hoar° leaves in the glassy stream;   165
Therewith fantastic garlands did she make
Of crow-flowers, nettles, daisies, and long purples°
That liberal° shepherds give a grosser name,
But our cold° maids do dead men's fingers call them.
There on the pendent boughs her crownet° weeds   170
Clamb'ring to hang, an envious sliver° broke,
When down her weedy° trophies and herself
Fell in the weeping brook. Her clothes spread wide,
And mermaid—like awhile they bore her up,
Which time she chanted snatches of old lauds,°   175
As one incapable° of her own distress,
Or like a creature native and indued°
Unto that element. But long it could not be
Till that her garments, heavy with their drink,
Pull'd the poor wretch from her melodious lay   180
To muddy death.
LAERTES.   Alas, then she is drown'd?
QUEEN.   Drown'd, drown'd.

145 *gall:* graze, wound.   148 *shape:* part that we propose to act.   149 *drift . . . performance:* i.e.,
intention be disclosed by our bungling.   152 *blast in proof:* burst in the test (like a cannon).
155 *As:* and you should.   157 *nonce:* occasion.   158 *stuck:* thrust (from stoccado, a fencing
term).   164 *askant:* aslant.   165 *hoar:* white or gray.   167 *long purples:* early purple orchids.
168 *liberal:* free-spoken.   169 *cold:* chaste.   170 *crownet:* made into a chaplet or coronet.
171 *envious sliver:* malicious branch.   172 *weedy:* i.e., of plants.   175 *lauds:* hymns.   176 *incapable:* lacking capacity to apprehend.   177 *indued:* adapted by nature.

LAERTES.   Too much of water hast thou, poor Ophelia,
    And therefore I forbid my tears.
    But yet It is our trick;° nature her custom holds,   185
    Let shame say what it will. [*He weeps.*] When these are gone,
    The woman will be out.° Adieu, my lord.
    I have a speech of fire, that fain would blaze,
    But that this folly drowns it.   (*Exit.*)
KING.   Let's follow, Gertrude.
    How much I had to do to calm his rage!   195
    Now fear I this will give it start again;
    Therefore let's follow.

                                                        (*Exeunt.*)

---

185 *It is our trick:* weeping is our natural way (when sad).   186–87 *When . . . out:* When my tears
are all shed, the woman in me will be expended, satisfied.

[ACT V

Scene I]°

(*Enter two Clowns.° [with spades, etc.])*)

FIRST CLOWN.   Is she to be buried in Christian burial when she willfully
    seeks her own salvation?
SECOND CLOWN.   I tell thee she is; therefore make her grave straight.°
    The crowner° hath sat on her, and finds it Christian burial.
FIRST CLOWN.   How can that be, unless she drown'd herself in her own   5
    defense?
SECOND CLOWN.   Why, 'Tis found so.
FIRST CLOWN.   It must be "se offendendo";° it cannot be else. For here
    lies the point: if I drown myself wittingly, it argues an act, and
    an act hath three branches—it is to act, to do, and to perform. Argal,°   10
    she drown'd herself wittingly.
SECOND CLOWN.   Nay, but hear you, goodman delver—
FIRST CLOWN.   Give me leave. Here lies the water; good. Here stands
    the man; good. If the man go to this water, and drown himself, it
    is, will he,° nill he, he goes, mark you that. But if the water come   15
    to him and drown him, he drowns not himself. Argal, he that is
    not guilty of his own death shortens not his own life.
SECOND CLOWN.   But is this law?
FIRST CLOWN.   Ay, marry, is 't-crowner's quest° law.
SECOND CLOWN.   Will you ha' the truth on 't? If this had not been a   20
    gentlewoman, she should have been buried out o' Christian burial.

V. I. *Location:* a churchyard.   *clowns:* rustics.   3 *straight:* straightway, immediately.   4 *crowner:*
coroner.   8 *se offendendo:* a comic mistake for *se defendendo,* term used in verdicts of justifiable
homicide.   10 *Argal:* corruption of *ergo,* therefore.   15 *will he, nill he:* willy-nilly, whether he
wants to or not.   19 *quest:* inquest.

FIRST CLOWN.   Why, there thou say'st.° And the more pity that great
    folk should have count'nance° in this world to drown or hang
    themselves, more than their even-Christen.° Come, my spade.
    There is no ancient gentlemen but gard'ners, ditchers, and   25
    gravemakers. They hold up Adam's profession.
SECOND CLOWN.   Was he a gentleman?
FIRST CLOWN.   'A was the first that ever bore arms.
[SECOND CLOWN.   Why, he had none.
FIRST CLOWN.   What, art a heathen? How dost thou understand the   30
    Scripture? The Scripture says "Adam digg'd." Could he dig
    without arms?] I'll put another question to thee. If thou
    answerest me not to the purpose, confess thyself°—
SECOND CLOWN.   Go to.
FIRST CLOWN.   What is he that builds stronger than either the mason,   35
    the shipwright, or the carpenter?
SECOND CLOWN.   The gallows-maker, for that frame outlives a thousand
    tenants.
FIRST CLOWN.   I like thy wit well, in good faith. The gallows does well;
    but how does it well? It does well to those that do ill. Now thou   40
    dost ill to say the gallows is built stronger than the church. Argal,
    the gallows may do well to thee. To 't again, come.
SECOND CLOWN.   "Who builds stronger than a mason, a shipwright, or
    a carpenter?"
FIRST CLOWN.   Ay, tell me that, and unyoke.°   45
SECOND CLOWN.   Marry, now I can tell.
FIRST CLOWN.   To 't.
SECOND CLOWN.   Mass,° I cannot tell.

Enter Hamlet and Horatio [at a distance].)

FIRST CLOWN.   Cudgel thy brains no more about it, for your dull ass will
    not mend his pace with beating; and, when you are ask'd this   50
    question next, say "a grave-maker." The houses he makes lasts till
    doomsday. Go, get thee in, and fetch me a stoup° of liquor.

                                   [Exit Second Clown. First Clown digs.]

(Song.)

    "In youth, when I did love, did love,°
      Methought it was very sweet,
    To contract—O—the time for—a—my behove,°   55
      O, methought there—a—was nothing—a—meet."°
HAMLET.   Has this fellow no feeling of his business, that a sings at
    grave-making?

---

22 *there you say'st:* that's right.   23 *count'nance:* privilege.   24 *even-Christen:* fellow
Christian.   33 *confess thyself:* The saying continues, "and be hanged."   45 *Unyoke:* After this
great effort you may unharness the team of your wits.   48 *Mass:* by the Mass.   52 *stoup:* two-
quart measure.   53 *In . . . love:* This and the two following stanzas, with nonsensical variations,
are from a poem attributed to Lord Vaux and printed in *Tottel's Miscellany,* 1557. The *O* and *a* (for
"ah") seemingly are the grunts of the digger.   55 *To contract . . . behoove:* to make a betrothal
agreement for my benefit (?).   56 *meet:* suitable, i.e., more suitable.

HORATIO.   Custom hath made it in him a property of easiness.°
HAMLET.   'Tis e'en so. The hand of little employment hath the   60
    daintier sense.°

(Song.)

FIRST CLOWN.   "But age, with his stealing steps,
      Hath claw'd me in his clutch,
    And hath shipped me into the land,°
      As if I had never been such."   65

[Throws up a skull.]

HAMLET.   That skull had a tongue in it, and could sing once. How the
    knave jowls° it to the ground, as if 'twere Cain's jaw-bone, that
    did the first murder! This might be the pate of a politician,° which
    this ass now o'erreaches,° one that would circumvent God, might
    it not?   70
HORATIO.   It might, my lord.
HAMLET.   Or of a courtier, which could say "Good morrow, sweet lord!
    How dost thou, sweet lord?" This might be my Lord Such-a-one,
    that prais'd my Lord Such-a-one's horse when 'a meant to beg it, might
    it not?   75
HORATIO.   Ay, my lord.
HAMLET.   Why, e'en so, and now my Lady Worm's, chapless,° and
    knock'd about the mazzard° with a sexton's spade. Here's fine
    revolution,° an° we had the trick to see 't. Did these bones cost
    no more the breeding,° but to play at loggats° with them? Mine   80
    ache to think on 't.

(Song.)

FIRST CLOWN   "A pick-axe, and a spade, a spade,
      For and° a shrouding sheet;
    O, a pit of clay for to be made
      For such a guest is meet."   85

[Throws up another skull.]

HAMLET.   There's another. Why may not that be the skull of a lawyer?
    Where be his quiddities° now, his quillities,° his cases, his tenures,°
    and his tricks? Why does he suffer this mad knave now to knock
    him about the sconce° with a dirty shovel, and will not tell him of
    his action of battery? Hum! This fellow might be in 's time a great   90

---

59 *property of easiness:* something he can do easily and without thinking.   61 *daintier sense:* more
delicate sense of feeling.   64 *into the land:* toward my grave (?) (but note the lack of rhyme in
steps, land).   67 *jowls:* dashes.   68 *politician:* schemer, plotter.   69 *o'erreaches:* circumvents,
gets the better of (with a quibble on the literal sense).   77 *chapless:* having no lower jaw.   78 *maz-
zard:* head (literally, a drinking vessel).   79 *revolution:* change.   *an:* if   80 *the breeding:* in
the breeding, raising.   *loggats:* a game in which pieces of hard wood are thrown to lie as near
as possible to a stake.   83 *For and:* and moreover.   87 *quiddities:* subtleties, quibbles (from
Latin *quid,* a thing).   *quillities:* verbal niceties, subtle distinctions (variation of *quiddities*).
tenures: the holding of a piece of property or office, or the conditions of period of such holding.
89 *sconce:* head.

buyer of land, with his statutes, his recognizances,° his fines, his
double° vouchers,° his recoveries.° [Is this the fine of his fines, and
the recovery of his recoveries,] to have his fine pate full of fine
dirt?° Will his vouchers vouch him no more of his purchases, and
double [ones too], than the length and breadth of a pair of   95
indentures?° The very conveyances° of his lands will scarcely lie in
this box,° and must th' inheritor° himself have no more, ha?

HORATIO.   Not a jot more, my lord.

HAMLET.   Is not parchment made of sheep-skins?

HORATIO.   Ay, my lord, and of calf-skins too.   100

HAMLET.   They are sheep and calves which seek out assurance in that.°
I will speak to this fellow.—Whose grave's this, sirrah?°

FIRST CLOWN.   Mine, sir. [*Sings.*] "O, a pit of clay for to be made [For
such a guest is meet]."

HAMLET.   I think it be thine, indeed, for thou liest in 't.   110

FIRST CLOWN.   You lie out on 't, sir, and therefore 'Tis not yours. For
my part, I do not lie in 't, yet it is mine.

HAMLET.   Thou dost lie in 't, to be in 't and say it is thine. 'Tis for the
dead, not for the quick;° therefore thou liest.

FIRST CLOWN.   'Tis a quick lie, sir; 'twill away again from me to you.   115

HAMLET.   What man dost thou dig it for?

FIRST CLOWN.   For no man, sir.

HAMLET.   What woman, then?

FIRST CLOWN.   For none, neither.

HAMLET.   Who is to be buried in 't?   120

FIRST CLOWN.   One that was a woman, sir, but, rest her soul, she's dead.

HAMLET.   How absolute° the knave is! We must speak by the card,° or
equivocation° will undo us. By the Lord, Horatio, this three years
I have taken note of it: the age is grown so pick'd° that the toe
of the peasant comes so near the heel of the courtier, he galls his   125
kibe.° How long hast thou been a gravemaker?

FIRST CLOWN.   Of all the days i' th' year, I came to 't that day that our
last king Hamlet overcame Fortinbras.

HAMLET.   How long is that since?

FIRST CLOWN.   Cannot you tell that? Every fool can tell that. It was that   130
very day that young Hamlet was born—he that is mad, and sent
into England.

HAMLET.   Ay, marry, why was he sent into England?

---

90 *statutes, recognizance:* legal documents guaranteeing a debt by attaching land and property.
92–93 *fines, recoveries:* ways of converting entailed estates into "fee simple" or freehold.   92 *double:*
signed by two signatories.   *vouchers:* guarantees of the legality of a title to real estate.   92–94 *fine
of his fines . . . fine pate . . . fine dirt:* end of his legal maneuvers . . . elegant head . . . minutely
sifted dirt.   95–96 *a pair of indentures:* legal document drawn up in duplicate on a single sheet
and then cut apart on a zigzag line so that each pair was uniquely matched. (Hamlet may refer to
two rows of teeth, or dentures.)   96 *conveyances:* deeds.   97 *this box:* the skull.   *inheri-
tor:* possessor, owner.   101 *assurance in that:* safety in legal parchments.   102 *sirrah:* term of address to inferiors.   114 *quick:* living.   122 *absolute:* positive, decided.   *by the card:* by the
mariner's card on which the points of the compass were marked, i.e., with precision.   123 *equiv-
ocation:* ambiguity in the use of terms.   124 *pick'd:* refined fastidious.   125–26 *galls his
kibe:* chafes the courtier's chilblain (a swelling or sore caused by cold).

FIRST CLOWN. Why, because 'a was mad. 'A shall recover his wits there,
    or, if 'a do not, 'Tis no great matter there.   135
HAMLET. Why?
FIRST CLOWN. Twill not be seen in him there. There the men are as
    mad as he.
HAMLET. How came he mad?
FIRST CLOWN. Very strangely, they say.   140
HAMLET. How strangely?
FIRST CLOWN. Faith, e'en with losing his wits.
HAMLET. Upon what ground?
FIRST CLOWN. Why, here in Denmark. I have been sexton here, man
    and boy, thirty years.   145
HAMLET. How long will a man lie i' th' earth ere he rot?
FIRST CLOWN. Faith, if 'a be not rotten before 'a die—as we have many
    pocky° corses [now-a-days], that will scarce hold the laying in—
    'a will last you some eight year or nine year. A tanner will last you
    nine year.   150
HAMLET. Why he more than another?
FIRST CLOWN. Why, sir, his hide is so tann'd with his trade that 'a will
    keep out water a great while, and your water is a sore decayer of
    your whoreson dead body. [Picks up a skull.] Here's a skull now
    hath lain you° i' th' earth three and twenty years.   155
HAMLET. Whose was it?
FIRST CLOWN. A whoreson mad fellow's it was. Whose do you think it
    was?
HAMLET. Nay, I know not.
FIRST CLOWN. A pestilence on him for a mad rogue! 'A pour'd a flagon   160
    of Rhenish° on my head once. This same skull, sir, was Yorick's
    kull, the King's jester.
HAMLET. This?
FIRST CLOWN. E'en that.
HAMLET. [Let me see.] [Takes the skull.] Alas, poor Yorick! I knew   165
    him, Horatio, a fellow of infinite jest, of most excellent fancy. He
    hath borne me on his back a thousand times; and now, how
    abhorr'd in my imagination it is! My gorge rises at it. Here hung
    those lips that I have kiss'd I know not how oft. Where be your
    gibes now? Your gambols, your songs, your flashes of merriment   170
    that were wont to set the table on a roar? Not one now, to mock
    your own grinning? Quite chap-fall'n?° Now get you to my lady's
    chamber, and tell her, let her paint an inch thick, to this favor° she
    must come; make her laugh at that. Prithee, Horatio, tell me one
    thing.   175
HORATIO. What's that, my lord?
HAMLET. Dost thou think Alexander look'd o' this fashion i' th' earth?
HORATIO. E'en so.
HAMLET. And smelt so? Pah! [*Puts down the skull.*]

148 *pocky:* rotten, diseased (literally, with the pox, or syphilis).   155 *lain you:* lain.
161 *Rhenish:* Rhine wine.   172 *chap-fall'n:* (1) lacking the lower jaw, (2) dejected.   173 *favor:* aspect, appearance.

HORATIO.   E'en so, my lord.   180

HAMLET.   To what base uses we may return, Horatio! Why may not
    imagination trace the noble dust of Alexander, till a' find it
    stopping a bung-hole?

HORATIO.   'Twere to consider too curiously,° to consider so.

HAMLET.   No, faith, not a jot, but to follow him thither with modesty°   185
    enough, and likelihood to lead it. [As thus]: Alexander died,
    Alexander was buried, Alexander returneth to dust; the dust is
    earth; of earth we make loam;° and why of that loam, whereto he
    was converted, might they not stop a beer-barrel?
    Imperious° Caesar, dead and turn'd to clay,   190
    Might stop a hole to keep the wind away.
    O, that that earth which kept the world in aw
    Should patch a wall t' expel the winter's flaw!°
    But soft, but soft awhile! Here comes the King.

(Enter King, Queen, Laertes, and the Corse [of Ophelia,
in procession, with Priest, Lords etc.].)

    The Queen, the courtiers. Who is this they follow?   195
    And with such maimed rites? This doth betoken
    The corse they follow did with desp'rate hand
    Fordo it° own life. 'Twas of some estate.°
    Couch° we awhile, and mark.

                            [He and Horatio conceal themselves.
                            Ophelia's body is taken to the grave.]

LAERTES.   What ceremony else?   200

HAMLET *[to Horatio]*.   That is Laertes, a very noble youth. Mark.

LAERTES.   What ceremony else?

PRIEST.   Her obsequies have been as far enlarg'd
    As we have warranty. Her death was doubtful,
    And, but that great command o'ersways the order   205
    She should in ground unsanctified been lodg'd
    Till the last trumpet. For° charitable prayers,
    Shards,° flints, and pebbles should be thrown on her.
    Yet here she is allow'd her virgin crants,°
    Her maiden strewments,° and the bringing home   210
    Of bell and burial.°

LAERTES.   Must there no more be done?

PRIEST: No more be done.
    We should profane the service of the dead
    To sing a requiem and such rest to her
    As to peace-parted souls.

LAERTES.   Lay her i' th' earth,   215

---

184 *curiously:* minutely.   185 *modesty:* moderation.   188 *loam:* clay mixture for brickmaking
or other clay use.   190 *Imperious:* imperial.   193 *flaw:* gust of wind.   198 *Fordo it:* destroy
its.   *estate:* rank   199 *Couch:* hide, lurk.   207 *For:* in place of.   208 *Shards:* broken bits
of pottery.   209 *crants:* garland.   210 *strewments:* traditional stewing of flowers.   210–11 *bringing . . . burial:* laying to rest of the body in consecrated ground, to the sound of the bell.

And from her fair and unpolluted flesh
May violets° spring! I tell thee, churlish priest,
A minist'ring angel shall my sister be
When thou liest howling!

HAMLET *[To Horatio].*   What, the fair Ophelia!

QUEEN *[Scattering flowers].*   Sweets to the sweet! Farewell.   220
   I hoped thou shouldst have been my Hamlet's wife.
   I thought thy bride-bed to have deck'd, sweet maid,
   And not have strew'd thy grave.

LAERTES.   O, treble woe
   Fall ten times treble on that cursed head
   Whose wicked deed thy most ingenious sense°   225
   Depriv'd thee of! Hold off the earth awhile,
   Till I have caught her once more in mine arms.

[Leaps into the grave and embraces Ophelia.]

   Now pile your dust upon the quick and dead,
   Till of this flat a mountain you have made
   T' o'ertop old Pelion,° or the skyish head   230
   Of blue Olympus.°

HAMLET *[coming forward].*   What is he whose grief
   Bears such an emphasis, whose phrase of sorrow
   Conjures the wand'ring stars,° and makes them stand
   Like wonder-wounded hearers? This is I,
   Hamlet the Dane.°   235

LAERTES.   The devil take thy soul!

[Grappling with him.]

HAMLET.   Thou pray'st not well.
   I prithee, take thy fingers from my throat;
   For, though I am not splenitive° and rash,
   Yet have I in me something dangerous,
   Which let thy wisdom fear. Hold off thy hand.   240

KING.   Pluck them asunder.

QUEEN.   Hamlet, Hamlet!

ALL: Gentlemen!

HORATIO.   Good my lord, be quiet.

[Hamlet and Laertes are parted.]

HAMLET.   Why, I will fight with him upon this theme
   Until my eyelids will no longer wag.

QUEEN.   O my son, what theme?   245

HAMLET.   I lov'd Ophelia. Forty thousand brothers
   Could not with all their quantity of love
   Make up my sum. What wilt thou do for her?

---

217 *violets:* see IV. v. 182 and note.   225 *ingenious sense:* mind endowed with finest qualities.
230–31 *Pelion, Olympus:* mountains in the north of Thessaly; see also Ossa, at line 260.   233 *wand'ring stars:* planets.   235 *the Dane:* this title normally signifies the king; see I.i.15 and note.   238 *splenitive:* quick-tempered.

KING.   O, he is mad, Laertes.

QUEEN.   For love of God, forbear him.   250

HAMLET.   'Swounds,° show me what thou't do.
    Woo 't° weep? Woo 't fight? Woo 't fast?
    Woo 't tear thyself? Woo 't drink up eisel?°
    Eat a crocodile? I'll do 't. Dost thou come here to whine?
    To outface me with leaping in her grave?   255
    Be buried quick° with her, and so will I.
    And, if thou prate of mountains, let them throw
    Millions of acres on us, till our ground,
    Singeing his pate° against the burning zone,°
    Make Ossa° like a wart! Nay, an thou 'lt mouth,°   260
    I'll rant as well as thou.

QUEEN.   This is mere° madness,
    And thus a while the fit will work on him;
    Anon, as patient as the female dove
    When that her golden couplets° are disclos'd,°
    His silence will sit drooping.

HAMLET.   Hear you, sir.   265
    What is the reason that you use me thus?
    I lov'd you ever. But it is no matter.
    Let Hercules himself do what he may,
    The cat will mew, and dog will have his day.°

KING.   I pray thee, good Horatio, wait upon him.   270

                                         (Exit Hamlet and Horatio.)

    [*To Laertes.*] Strengthen your patience in° our last night's speech;
    We'll put the matter to the present push.°—
    Good Gertrude, set some watch over your son.—
    This grave shall have a living° monument.
    An hour of quiet shortly shall we see;   275
    Till then, in patience our proceeding be.   *(Exeunt.)*

251 *'swounds:* by His (Christ's) wounds.   252 *Woo's:* wilt thou.   253 *eisel:* vinegar.   256 *quick:* alive.   259 *his pate:* its head, i.e., top.   *burning zone:* sun's orbit.   260 *Ossa:* another mountain in Thessaly. (In their war against the Olympian gods, the giants attempted to heap Ossa, Pelion, and Olympus on one another to scale heaven.)   *mouth:* rant.   261 *mere:* utter.   264 *golden couplets:* two baby pigeons, covered with yellow down.   *disclos'd:* hatched.   268–69 *Let . . . day:* Despite any blustering attempts at interference every person will sooner or later do what he must do.   271 *in:* by recalling.   272 *present push:* immediate test.   274 *living:* lasting; also refers (for Laertes' benefit) to the plot against Hamlet.

[Scene II]°

(Enter Hamlet and Horatio.)

HAMLET.   So much for this, sir; now shall you see the other.°
    You do remember all the circumstance?

HORATIO.   Remember it, my lord!

V.II. *Location:* the castle.   1 *see the other:* hear the other news.

HAMLET.   Sir, in my heart there was a kind of fighting
    That would not let me sleep. Methought I lay   5
    Worse than the mutines° in the bilboes.° Rashly,°
    And prais'd be rashness for it—let us know,°
    Our indiscretion sometime serves us well
    When our deep plots do pall,° and that should learn° us
    There's a divinity that shapes our ends,   10
    Rough-hew° them how we will—
HORATIO.   That is most certain.
HAMLET.   Up from my cabin,
    My sea-gown scarf'd about me, in the dark
    Grop'd I to find out them, had my desire,
    Finger'd° their packet, and in fine° withdrew   15
    To mine own room again, making so bold,
    My fears forgetting manners, to unseal
    Their grand commission; where I found, Horatio—
    Ah, royal knavery!—an exact command,
    Larded° with many several sorts of reasons   20
    Importing° Denmark's health and England's too,
    With, ho, such bugs° and goblins in my life,°
    That, on the supervise,° no leisure bated,°
    No, not to stay the grinding of the axe,
    My head should be struck off.
HORATIO.   Is 't possible?   25
HAMLET.   Here's the commission; read it at more leisure.

                                 [Gives document.]

    But wilt thou hear now how I did proceed?
HORATIO.   I beseech you.
HAMLET.   Being thus benetted round with villainies,
    Or I could make a prologue to my brains,   30
    They had begun the play.° I sat me down,
    Devis'd a new commission, wrote it fair.°
    I once did hold it, as our statists° do,
    A baseness° to write fair, and labor'd much
    How to forget that learning, but, sir, now   35
    It did me yeoman's° service. Wilt thou know
    Th' effect° of what I wrote?
HORATIO.   Ay, good my lord.
HAMLET.   An earnest conjuration from the King,
    As England was his faithful tributary,
    As love between them like the palm might flourish,   40

---

6 *mutines:* mutineers.   *bilboes:* shackles.   *Rashly:* on impulse (this adverb goes with lines 12 ff.)   7 *know:* acknowledge.   9 *pall:* fail.   *learn:* teach.   11 *Rough-hew:* shape roughly.   15 *Finger'd:* pilfered, pinched.   *in fine:* finally, in conclusion.   20 *Larded:* enriched.   21 *Importing:* relating to.   22 *bugs:* bugbears, hobgoblins.   *in my life:* to be feared if I were allowed to live.   23 *supervise:* reading.   *leisure bated:* delay allowed.   30–31 *Or . . . play:* Before I could consciously turn my brain to the matter, it had started working on a plan. (*Or* means *ere.*)   32 *fair:* in a clear hand.   33 *statists:* statesmen.   34 *baseness:* lower-class trait.   36 *yeoman's:* substantial, workmanlike.   37 *effect:* purport.

As peace should still her wheaten garland° wear
And stand a comma° 'tween their amities,
And many such-like as's° of great charge,°
That, on the view and knowing of these contents,
Without debatement further, more or less,   45
He should those bearers put to sudden death,
Not shriving time° allow'd.
HORATIO.   How was this seal'd?
HAMLET.   Why, even in that was heaven ordinant.°
I had my father's signet° in my purse,
Which was the model of that Danish seal;   50
Folded the writ up in the form of th' other,
Subscrib'd° it, gave 't th' impression,° plac'd it safely,
The changeling° never known. Now, the next day
Was our sea-fight, and what to this was sequent
Thou knowest already.   55
HORATIO.   So Guildenstern and Rosencrantz go to 't.
HAMLET.   [Why, man, they did make love to this employment.]
They are not near my conscience. Their defeat
Does by their own insinuation° grow.
'Tis dangerous when the baser nature comes   60
Between the pass° and fell° incensed points
Of mighty opposites.
HORATIO.   Why, what a king is this!
HAMLET.   Does it not, think thee, stand° me now upon—
He that hath killed my king and whor'd my mother,
Popp'd in between th' election° and my hopes,   65
Thrown out his angle° for my proper° life,
And with such coz'nage°—is 't not perfect conscience
[To quit° him with this arm? And is 't not to be damn'd
To let this canker° of our nature come in further evil?
HORATIO.   It must be shortly known to him from England   70
What is the issue of the business there.
HAMLET.   It will be short. The interim is mine,
And a man's life's no more than to say "One."°
But I am very sorry, good Horatio,
That to Laertes I forgot myself,   75
For by the image of my cause I see
The portraiture of his. I'll court his favors.
But, sure, the bravery° of his grief did put me

---

41 *wheaten garland:* symbolic of fruitful agriculture, of peace.   42 *comma:* indicating continuity,
link.   43 *as's:* (1) the "whereases" of formal document, (2) asses.   *charge:* (1) import, (2) burden.   47 *shriving-time:* time for confession and absolution.   48 *ordinant:* directing.   49 *signet:*
small seal.   52 *Subscrib'd:* signed.   *impression:* with a wax seal.   53 *changeling:* the substituted letter (literally, a fairy child substituted for a human one).   59 *insinuation:* interference.   61 *pass:* thrust.   *fell:* fierce.   63 *stand:* become incumbent.   65 *election:* the
Danish monarch was "elected" by a small number of high-ranking electors.   66 *angle:* fishing line.
proper: very.   67 *coz'nage:* trickery.   68 *quit:* repay.   69 *canker:* ulcer.   73 *a man's . . .*
"One": To take a man's life requires no more than to count to one as one duels.   78 *bravery:* bravado.

Into a tow'ring passion.

HORATIO.   Peace, who comes here?]

(Enter a Courtier [Osric].)

OSRIC. Your lordship is right welcome back to Denmark.   80

HAMLET. I humbly thank you, sir. [*To Horatio.*] Dost know this
    water-fly?

HORATIO. No, my good lord.

HAMLET. Thy state is the more gracious, for 'Tis a vice to know him.
    He hath much land, and fertile. Let a beast be lord of beasts, and
    his crib shall stand at the King's mess.° 'Tis a chough,° but, as I   85
    say, spacious in the possession of dirt.

OSRIC. Sweet lord, if your lordship were at leisure, I should impart a
    thing to you from his Majesty.

HAMLET. I will receive it, sir, with all diligence of spirit. Put your
    bonnet to his right use; 'Tis for the head.   90

OSRIC. I thank your lordship, it is very hot.

HAMLET. No, believe me, 'Tis very cold; the wind is northerly.

OSRIC. It is indifferent° cold, my lord, indeed.

HAMLET. But yet methinks it is very sultry and hot for my
    complexion.°   95

OSRIC. Exceedingly, my lord; it is very sultry, as 'twere-I cannot tell
    how. My lord, his Majesty bade me signify to you that 'a has laid
    a great wager on your head. Sir, this is the matter-

HAMLET. I beseech you, remember-

[Hamlet moves him to put on his hat.]

OSRIC. Nay, good my lord; for my ease,° in good faith. Sir, here is   100
    newly come to court Laertes—believe me, an absolute gentleman,
    full of most excellent differences,° of very soft society° and great
    showing.° Indeed, to speak feelingly° of him, he is the card° or
    calendar° of gentry,° for you shall find in him the continent of
    what part° a gentleman would see.   105

HAMLET. Sir, his definement° suffers no perdition° in you, though, I
    know, to divide him inventorially° would dozy° th' arithmetic of
    memory, and yet but yaw° neither° in respect of° his quick sail.
    But, in the verity of extolment,° I take him to be a soul of great
    article,° and his infusion° of such dearth and rareness,° as, to make   110

84–85 *Let . . . mess:* if a man, no matter how beastlike, is as rich in possessions as Osric, he may
eat at the king's table.   85 *chough:* chattering jackdaw.   93 *indifferent:* somewhat.   95 *complexion:* temperament.   100 *for my ease:* a conventional reply declining the invitation to put his
hat back on.   102 *differences:* special qualities.   *soft society:* agreeable manners.   102–3 *great
showing:* distinguished appearance.   103 *feelingly:* with just perception.   *card:* chart, map
104 *calendar:* guide.   *gentry:* good breeding.   104–5 *the continent . . . part:* one who contains
in him all the qualities (a *continent* is that which contains).   106 *definement:* definition: loss,
diminution.   107 *divide him inventorially:* enumerate his graces.   *dozy:* dizzy.   108 *yaw:* to move
unsteadily (said of a ship).   *neither:* for all that.   *in respect of:* in comparison with.
109 *in . . . extolment:* in true praise (of Him).   110 *article:* moment or importance.   *infusion:*
essence, character imparted by nature.   *dearth and rareness:* rarity.

true diction° of him, his semblable° is his mirror, and who else
would trace° him, his umbrage,° nothing more.

OSRIC.   Your lordship speaks most infallibly of him.

HAMLET.   The concernancy,° sir? Why do we wrap the gentleman in
our more rawer breath?°   115

OSRIC.   Sir?

HORATIO.   Is 't not possible to understand in another tongue?° You will
do 't,° sir, really.

HAMLET.   What imports the nomination° of this gentleman?

OSRIC.   Of Laertes?   120

Horatio *[to Hamlet]*:   His purse is empty already; all 's golden words
are spent.

HAMLET.   Of him, sir.

OSRIC.   I know you are not ignorant—

HAMLET.   I would you did, sir; yet, in faith, if you did, it would not   125
much approve° me. Well, sir?

OSRIC.   You are not ignorant of what excellence Laertes is—

HAMLET.   I dare not confess that, lest I should compare° with him in
excellence; but to know a man well were to know himself.°

OSRIC.   I mean, sir, for his weapon; but in the imputation laid on him   130
by them,° in his meed° he's unfellow'd.°

HAMLET.   What's his weapon?

OSRIC.   Rapier and dagger.

HAMLET.   That's two of his weapons-but well.

OSRIC.   The King, sir, hath wager'd with him six Barbary horses, against   135
the which he has impawn'd,° as I take it, six French rapiers and
poniards, with their assigns,° as girdle, hangers,° and so. Three of
the carriages,° in faith, are very dear to fancy,° very responsive° to
the hilts, most delicate° carriages, and of very liberal conceit.°

HAMLET.   What call you the carriages?   140

HORATIO *[to Hamlet]*.   I knew you must be edified by the margent° ere
you had done.

OSRIC.   The carriages, sir, are the hangers.

HAMLET.   The phrase would be more germane to the matter if we could
carry a cannon by our sides; I would it might be hangers till then.   145
But, on: six Barb'ry horses against six French swords, their assigns,
and three liberal-conceited carriages; that's the French bet against
the Danish. Why is this impawn'd, as you call it?

110–11 *make true diction:* speak truly.   111 *semblable:* only true likeness.   111–12 *who . . .
trace:* any other person who would wish to follow.   112 *umbrage:* shadow.   114 *concernancy:* import, relevance.   115 *breath:* speech.   117 *to understand . . . tongue:* for Osric to understand
when someone else speaks in his manner. (Horatio twits Osric for not being able to understand the
kind of flowery speech he himself uses when Hamlet speaks in such a vein.)   117–18 *You will
do 't:* you can if you try.   119 *nomination:* naming   126 *approve:* commend.   128 *compare:*
seem to compete.   129 *but . . . himself:* for, to recognize excellence in another man, one must
know oneself.   130–31 *imputation . . . them:* reputation given him by others.   131 *meed:*
merit.   *unfellow'd:* unmatched.   136 *impawn'd:* staked, wagered.   137 *assigns:* appurte-
nances.   *hangers:* straps on the sword belt (*girdle*) from which the sword hung.   138 *carriages:* an affected way of saying *hangers;* literally, gun-carriages.   *dear to fancy:* fancifully designed,
tasteful.   *responsive:* corresponding closely, matching.   139 *delicate:* i.e., in workmanship.
liberal conceit: elaborate design.   141 *margent:* margin of a book, place for explanatory notes.

OSRIC. The King, sir, hath laid,° sir, that in a dozen passes° between
yourself and him, he shall not exceed you three hits. He hath laid 150
on twelve for nine, and it would come to immediate trial, if your
lordship would vouchsafe the answer.

HAMLET. How if I answer no?

OSRIC. I mean, my lord, the opposition of your person in trial.

HAMLET. Sir, I will walk here in the hall. If it please his Majesty, it is the 155
breathing time° of day with me. Let the foils be brought, the
gentleman willing, and the King hold his purpose, I will win for him
an I can; if not, I will gain nothing but my shame and the odd hits.

OSRIC. Shall I deliver you so?

HAMLET. To this effect, sir—after what flourish your nature will. 160

OSRIC. I commend my duty to your lordship.

HAMLET. Yours, yours. [*Exit Osric.*] He does well to commend it
himself; there are no tongues else for 's turn.

HORATIO. This lapwing ° runs away with the shell on his head.

HAMLET. 'A did comply, sir, with his dug,° before 'a suck'd it. Thus 165
has he-and many more of the same breed that I know the drossy°
age dotes on—only got the tune° of the time and, out of an habit
of encounter,° a kind of yesty° collection,° which carries them
through and through the most fann'd and winnow'd° opinions;
and do but blow them to their trial, the bubbles are out.° 170

(*Enter a Lord.*)

LORD. My lord, his Majesty commended him to you by young Osric,
who brings back to him that you attend him in the hall. He sends
to know if your pleasure hold to play with Laertes, or that you will
take longer time.

HAMLET. I am constant to my purposes; they follow the King's 175
pleasure. If his fitness speaks,° mine is ready; now or whensoever,
provided I be so able as now.

LORD. The King and Queen and all are coming down.

HAMLET. In happy time.°

LORD. The Queen desires you to use some gentle entertainment° to 180
Laertes before you fall to play.

HAMLET. She well instructs me. [*Exit Lord.*]

HORATIO. You will lose, my lord.

HAMLET. I do not think so. Since he went into France, I have been in
continual practice; I shall win at the odds. But thou wouldst not 185
think how ill all's here about my heart; but it is no matter.

149 *laid:* wagered. *passes:* bouts. (The odds of the betting are hard to explain. Possibly the
King bets that Hamlet will win at least five out of twelve, at which point Laertes raises the odds
against himself by betting he will win nine.) 156 *breathing time:* exercise period. 164 *lapwing:* a bird that draws intruders away from its nest and was thought to run about when newly
hatched with its head in the shell; a seeming reference to Osric's hat. 165 *comply . . . dug:* observe ceremonious formality toward his mother's teat. 166 *drossy:* frivolous. 167 *tune:* temper, mood, manner of speech. 167–79 *habit of encounter:* demeanor of social intercourse.
168 *yesty:* yeasty, frothy. *collection:* i.e., of current phrases. 169 *fann'd and winnow'd:* select and
refined. 170 *blow . . . out:* put them to the test, and their ignorance is exposed. 176 *If . . .
speaks:* if his readiness answers to the time. 179 *In happy time:* a phrase of courtesy indicating acceptance. 180 *entertainment:* greeting.

HORATIO. Nay, good my lord—

HAMLET. It is but foolery, but it is such a kind of gain-giving,° as would
perhaps trouble a woman.

HORATIO. If your mind dislike anything, obey it. I will forestall their   190
repair hither, and say you are not fit.

HAMLET. Not a whit, we defy augury. There is special providence in
the fall of a sparrow. If it be now, 'Tis not to come; if it be not to
come, it will be now; if it be not now; yet it will come. The
readiness is all. Since no man of aught he leaves knows what is 't   195
to leave betimes,° let be.

*(A table prepar'd. [Enter] trumpets, drums, and Officers with cushions; King, Queen,
[Osric,] and all the State; foils, daggers, [and wine borne in;] and Laertes.)*

KING. Come, Hamlet, come, and take this hand from me.

[The King puts Laertes' hand into Hamlet's.]

HAMLET. Give me your pardon, sir. I have done you wrong,
But pardon 't , as you are a gentleman.
This presence° knows,   200
And you must needs have heard, how I am punish'd
With a sore distraction. What I have done
That might your nature, honor, and exception°
Roughly awake, I here proclaim was madness.
Was 't Hamlet wrong'd Laertes? Never Hamlet.   205
If Hamlet from himself be ta'en away,
And when he's not himself does wrong Laertes,
Then Hamlet does it not, Hamlet denies it.
Who does it, then? His madness. If 't be so,
Hamlet is of the faction that is wrong'd;   210
His madness is poor Hamlet's enemy.
[Sir, in this audience,]
Let my disclaiming from a purpos'd evil
Free me so far in your most generous thoughts
That I have shot my arrow o'er the house   215
And hurt my brother.

LAERTES.   I am satisfied in nature,°
Whose motive in this case should stir me most
To my revenge. But in my terms of honor
I stand aloof, and will no reconcilement
Till by some elder masters of known honor   220
I have a voice° and precedent of peace
To keep my name ungor'd. But till that time,
I do receive your offer'd love like love,
And will not wrong it.

HAMLET.   I embrace it freely,
And will this brothers' wager frankly play.   225

188 *gain-giving:* misgiving.   195–96 *what . . . betimes:* what is the best time to leave it.   200 *presence:* royal assembly.   203 *exception:* disapproval.   216 *in nature:* as to my personal feelings.   221 *voice:* authoritative pronouncement.

Give us the foils. Come on.

LAERTES.   Come, one for me.

HAMLET.   I'll be your foil,° Laertes. In mine ignorance
Your skill shall, like a star i' th' darkest night,
Stick fiery off° indeed.

LAERTES.   You mock me, sir.

HAMLET.   No, by this hand.   230

KING.   Give them the foils, young Osric. Cousin Hamlet,
You know the wager?

HAMLET.   Very well, my lord.
Your Grace has laid the odds o' th' weaker side.

KING.   I do not fear it; I have seen you both.
But since he is better'd,° we have therefore odds.   235

LAERTES.   This is too heavy, let me see another.

[Exchanges his foil for another.]

HAMLET.   This likes me well. These foils have all a length?

[They prepare to play.]

OSRIC.   Ay, my good lord.

KING.   Set me the stoups of wine upon that table.
If Hamlet give the first or second hit,   240
Or quit° in answer of the third exchange,
Let all the battlements their ordnance fire.
The King shall drink to Hamlet's better breath,
And in the cup an union° shall he throw,
Richer than that which four successive kings   245
In Denmark's crown have worn. Give me the cups,
And let the kettle° to the trumpet speak,
The trumpet to the cannoneer without,
The cannons to the heavens, the heaven to earth,
"Now the King drinks to Hamlet." Come, begin.   250

(Trumpets the while.)

And you, the judges, bear a wary eye.

HAMLET.   Come on sir.

LAERTES.   Come, my lord.

[They play. Hamlet scores a hit.]

HAMLET.   One.

LAERTES.   No.   255

HAMLET.   Judgment.

OSRIC.   A hit, a very palpable hit.

*(Drum, trumpets, and shot. Flourish.
A piece goes off.)*

227 *foil:* thin metal background that sets a jewel off (with pun on the blunted rapier for fencing).   229 *Stick fiery off:* stand out brilliantly.   235 *is better'd:* has improved; is the odds-on-fa-
vorite.   241 *quit:* repay (with a hit).   244 *union:* pearl (so called, according to Pliny's *Natural
History,* IX, because pearls are *unique,* never identical.)   247 *kettle:* kettledrum.

LAERTES. Well, again.
KING. Stay, give me drink. Hamlet, this pearl is thine.

> *[He throws a pearl in Hamlet's cup, and drinks.]*

Here's to thy health. Give him the cup.
HAMLET. I'll play this bout first; set it by awhile. Come.   *[They play.]*   260
    Another hit; what say you?
LAERTES. A touch, a touch, I do confess 't.
KING. Our son shall win.
QUEEN.   He's fat,° and scant of breath.
    Here, Hamlet, take my napkin,° rub thy brows.
    The Queen carouses° to thy fortune, Hamlet.   265
HAMLET. Good madam!
KING. Gertrude, do not drink.
QUEEN. I will, my lord; I pray you pardon me.

> *[Drinks.]*

KING *[aside].* It is the pois'ned cup. It is too late.
HAMLET. I dare not drink yet, madam; by and by.   270
QUEEN. Come, let me wipe thy face.
LAERTES *[to King].* My lord, I'll hit him now.
KING.   I do not think 't.
LAERTES *[aside].* And yet it is almost against my conscience.
HAMLET. Come, for the third, Laertes. You do but dally.
    I pray you, pass with your best violence;   275
    I am afeard you make a wanton of me.°
LAERTES. Say you so? Come on.   *[They play.]*
OSRIC. Nothing, neither way.
LAERTES. Have at you now!

> *[Laertes wounds Hamlet; then, in scuffling,*
> *they change rapiers,° and Hamlet wounds Laertes.]*

KING.   Part them! They are incens'd.   280
HAMLET. Nay, come, again.

> *[The Queen falls.]*

OSRIC.   Look to the Queen there, ho!
HORATIO. They bleed on both sides. How is it, my lord?
OSRIC. How is 't, Laertes?
LAERTES. Why, as a woodcock° to mine own springe,° Osric;
    I am justly kill'd with mine own treachery.   290
HAMLET. How does the Queen?
KING.   She swoons to see them bleed.

---

263 *fat:* not physically fit, out of training.   264 *napkin:* handkerchief: 265 *carouses:* drinks a toast.   276 *make . . . me:* treat me like a spoiled child, holding back to give me an advantage.   279 *in scuffling, they change rapiers:* this stage direction occurs in the Folio. According to a widespread stage tradition, Hamlet receives a scratch, realizes that Laertes's sword is unbated, and accordingly forces an exchange.   289 *woodcock:* a bird, a type of stupidity or as a decoy. *springe:* trap, snare.

QUEEN. No, no, the drink, the drink—O my dear Hamlet—
    The drink, the drink! I am pois'ned.   *[Dies.]*
HAMLET. O villainy! Ho, let the door be lock'd!
    Treachery! Seek it out.   *[Laertes falls.]* 295
LAERTES. It is here, Hamlet. Hamlet, thou art slain.
    No med'cine in the world can do thee good;
    In thee there is not half an hour's life.
    The treacherous instrument is in thy hand,
    Unbated° and envenom'd. The foul practice   300
    Hath turn'd itself on me. Lo, here I lie,
    Never to rise again. Thy mother's pois'ned.
    I can no more. The King, the King's to blame.
HAMLET. The point envenom'd too? Then, venom, to thy work.

                                        [Stabs the King.]

ALL. Treason! Treason!   305
KING. O, yet defend me, friends; I am but hurt.
HAMLET. Here, thou incestuous, murd'rous, damned Dane,

                            *[He forces the King to drink
                                    the poisoned cup.]*

    Drink off this potion. Is thy union° here?
    Follow my mother.   *[King dies.]*
LAERTES.   He is justly serv'd.
    It is a poison temper'd° by himself.   310
    Exchange forgiveness with me, noble Hamlet.
    Mine and my father's death come not upon thee,
    Nor thine on me!   *[Dies.]*
HAMLET. Heaven make thee free of it! I follow thee.
    I am dead, Horatio. Wretched Queen, adieu!   315
    You that look pale and tremble at this chance,
    That are but mutes° or audience to this act,
    Had I but time—as this fell° sergeant,° Death,
    Is strict in his arrest—O, I could tell you—
    But let it be. Horatio, I am dead;   320
    Thou livest. Report me and my cause aright
    To the unsatisfied.
HORATIO.   Never believe it.
    I am more an antique Roman° than a Dane.
    Here's yet some liquor left.

                        *[He attempts to drink from the poisoned cup.
                                    Hamlet prevents him.]*

HAMLET.   As th' art a man,
    Give me the cup! Let go! By heaven, I'll ha 't.   325

---

300 *Unbated:* not blunted with a button.   308 *union:* pearl (see line 258; with grim puns on the
word's other meanings: marriage, shared death?).   310 *temper'd:* mixed.   317 *mutes:* silent
observers.   318 *fell:* cruel.   *sergeant:* sheriff's officer.   323 *Roman:* It was the Roman custom to follow masters in death.

O God, Horatio, what a wounded name,
Things standing thus unknown, shall I leave behind me!
If thou didst ever hold me in thy heart,
Absent thee from felicity awhile,
And in this harsh world draw thy breath in pain   330
To tell my story.

(A march afar off [and a volley within].)

OSRIC.   What warlike noise is this?
    Young Fortinbras, with conquest come from Poland,
    To the ambassadors of England gives
    This warlike volley.
HAMLET.   O, I die, Horatio!
    The potent poison quite o'ercrows° my spirit.   335
    I cannot live to hear the news from England,
    But I do prophesy th' election lights
    On Fortinbras. He has my dying voice.°
    So tell him, with th' occurrents° more and less
    Which have solicited°—the rest is silence.   *[Dies.]*   340
HORATIO.   Now cracks a noble heart. Good night, sweet prince;
    And flights of angels sing thee to thy rest!

[March within.]

    Why does the drum come hither?

*(Enter Fortinbras, with the [English] Ambassadors [with
drum, colors, and attendants].)*

FORTINBRAS.   Where is this sight?
HORATIO.   What is it you would see?
    If aught of woe or wonder, cease your search.   345
FORTINBRAS.   This quarry° cries on havoc.° O proud Death,
    What feast is toward° in thine eternal cell,
    That thou so many princes at a shot
    So bloodily hast struck?
FIRST AMBASSADOR.   The sight is dismal;
    And our affairs from England come too late.   350
    The ears are senseless that should give us hearing,
    To tell him his commandment is fulfill'd,
    That Rosencrantz and Guildenstern are dead.
    Where should we have our thanks?
HORATIO.   Not from his° mouth,
    Had it th' ability of life to thank you.   355
    He never gave commandment for their death.
    But since, so jump° upon this bloody question,°
    You from the Polack wars, and you from England,
    Are here arriv'd, give order that these bodies

---

335 *o'ercrows:* triumphs over.   338 *voice:* vote.   339 *occurrents:* events, incidents.   340 *so-
licited:* moved, urged.   346 *quarry:* heap of dead.   *cries on havoc:* proclaims a general *slaughter.*
347 *toward:* in preparation.   354 *his:* Claudius's.   357 *jump:* precisely.   *question:* dispute.

High on a stage° be placed to the view,   360
And let me speak to th' yet unknowing world
How these things came about. So shall you hear
Of carnal, bloody, and unnatural acts,
Of accidental judgments,° casual° slaughters,
Of deaths put on° by cunning and forc'd cause,   365
And, in this upshot, purposes mistook
Fall'n on th' inventors' heads. All this can
I Truly deliver.
FORTINBRAS.   Let us haste to hear it,
And call the noblest to the audience.
For me, with sorrow I embrace my fortune.   370
I have some rights of memory° in this kingdom,
Which now to claim my vantage° doth invite me.
HORATIO.   Of that I shall have also cause to speak,
And from his mouth whose voice will draw on more.°
But let this same be presently° perform'd,   375
Even while men's minds are wild, lest more mischance
On° plots and errors happen.
FORTINBRAS.   Let four captains
Bear Hamlet, like a soldier, to the stage,
For he was likely, had he been put on,°
To have prov'd most royal; and, for his passage,°   380
The soldiers' music and the rite of war
Speak loudly for him. Take up the bodies.
Such a sight as this
Becomes the field,° but here shows much amiss.
Go, bid the soldiers shoot.   390

(Exeunt [marching, bearing off the dead bodies;
a peal of ordnance is shot off].)

360 *stage:* platform.   364 *judgments:* retributions.   *casual:* occuring by chance.   365 *put on:* instigated.   371 *of memory:* traditional, remembered.   372 *vantage:* presence at this opportune moment.   374 *voice . . . more:* vote will influence still others.   375 *presently:* immediately.   377 *On:* on the basis of.   379 *put on:* invested in royal office, and so put to the test.   380 *passage:* death.   389 *field:* i.e., of battle.

TENNESSEE WILLIAMS   (1911–1983)

Born in Missisippi, Tennessee Williams was raised in St. Louis and attended the University of Missouri and Washington University in St. Louis. Eventually, he got his degree at the State University of Iowa. Some of his plays were produced while he was an undergraduate, but when his first commercially produced play, Battle of Angels *(1940), failed in Boston, he feared he had no future as a playwright. While living on foundation grants he wrote* The Glass Menagerie, *which opened in Chicago in 1944 and in New York in 1945. It was his first success, winning the New York Drama Critic's Circle Award for best play. It ran for 561 performances.* A Streetcar Named Desire *(1947) established him as one of the most important American postwar playwrights. The play ran for 855 performances and won the Pulitzer Prize. Williams was a poetic writer, and his stage directions have a special lyrical quality.*

Some circumstances in The Glass Menagerie *were drawn from Williams's own life. Laura Wingfield resembles his sister, Rose, who also took consolation from a collection of glass animals. She was a psychologically troubled woman whose condition worsened when Williams was young. The family decided to have Rose undergo a lobotomy—an operation in which a portion of the frontal lobe of the brain is cut away. The operation was unsuccessful, and Rose spent most of her life in an institution. Williams felt a lifelong sense of guilt and failure over his family's decision.*

Williams solidified his position as a major playwright with Summer and Smoke *(1948),* The Rose Tattoo *(1951),* Camino Real *(1953),* Cat on a Hot Tin Roof *(1955), and* Night of the Iguana *(1961).* The Glass Menagerie *is a "memory play," exploring complex psychological issues operating in the minds of all the characters. The production notes to this play explain many of the approaches to drama that characterize Williams's work. He thought carefully about all phases of the production, including the music.*

The Glass Menagerie —————————————————————————— *1944*

"Nobody, not even the rain, has such small hands."

—*E. E. Cummings*

Production Notes by Tennessee Williams

Being a "memory play," The Glass Menagerie can be presented with unusual freedom of convention. Because of its considerably delicate or tenuous material, atmospheric touches and subtleties of direction play a particularly important part. Expressionism and all other unconventional techniques in drama have only one valid aim, and this is a closer approach to truth. When a play employs unconventional techniques, it is not, or certainly shouldn't be, trying to escape its responsibility of dealing with reality, or interpreting experience, but is actually or should be attempting to find a closer approach, or more penetrating and vivid expression of things as they are. The straight realistic play with its genuine frigidaire and authentic ice cubes, its characters that speak exactly as its audience speaks, corresponds to the academic landscape and has the same virtue of a photographic likeness. Everyone should know nowadays the unimportance of the photographic in art: that truth, life, or reality is an organic thing which the poetic imagination can represent or suggest, in essence, only through transformation, through changing into other forms than those which were merely present in appearance.

These remarks are not meant as a preface only to this particular play. They have to do with a conception of a new, plastic theatre which must take the place of the exhausted theatre of realistic conventions if the theatre is to resume vitality as a part of our culture.

THE SCREEN DEVICE. *There is only one important difference between the original and acting version of the play* and that is the *omission* in the latter of the device which I tentatively included in my *original* script. This device was the use of a screen on which were projected magic-lantern slides bearing images or titles. I do not regret the omission of this device from the present Broadway production.

The extraordinary power of Miss Taylor's° performance made it suitable to have the utmost simplicity in the physical production. But I think it may be interesting to some readers to see how this device was conceived. So I am putting it into the published manuscript. These images and legends, projected from behind, were cast on a section of wall between the front-room and dining-room areas, which should be indistinguishable from the rest when not in use.

The purpose of this will probably be apparent. It is to give accent to certain values in each scene. Each scene contains a particular point (or several) which is structurally the most important. In an episodic play, such as this, the basic structure or narrative line may be obscured from the audience; the effect may seem fragmentary rather than architectural. This may not be the fault of the play so much as a lack of attention in the audience. The legend or image upon the screen will strengthen the effect of what is merely allusion in the writing and allow the primary point to be made more simply and lightly than if the entire responsibility were on the spoken lines. Aside from this structural value, I think the screen will have a definite emotional appeal, less definable but just as important. An imaginative producer or director may invent many other uses for this device than those indicated in the present script. In fact the possibilities of the device seem much larger to me than the instance of this play can possibly utilize.

THE MUSIC.   Another extraliterary accent in this play is provided by the use of music. A single recurring tune, "The Glass Menagerie," is used to give emotional emphasis to suitable passages. This tune is like circus music, not when you are on the grounds or in the immediate vicinity of the parade, but when you are at some distance and very likely thinking of something else. It seems under those circumstances to continue almost interminably and it weaves in and out of your preoccupied consciousness; then it is the lightest, most delicate music in the world and perhaps the saddest. It expresses the surface vivacity of life with the underlying strain of immutable and inexpressible sorrow. When you look at a piece of delicately spun glass you think of two things: how beautiful it is and how easily it can be broken. Both of those ideas should be woven into the recurring tune, which dips in and out of the play as if it were carried on a wind that changes. It serves as a thread of connection and allusion between the narrator with his separate point in time and space and the subject of his story. Between each episode it returns as reference to the emotion, nostalgia, which is the first condition of the play. It is primarily Laura's music and therefore comes out most clearly when the play focuses upon her and the lovely fragility of glass which is her image.

THE LIGHTING.   The lighting in the play is not realistic. In keeping with the atmosphere of memory, the stage is dim. Shafts of light are focused on selected areas or actors, sometimes in contradistinction to what is the apparent center.

Miss Taylor: The actress Laurette Taylor (1884–1947), who played Amanda.

For instance, in the quarrel scene between Tom and Amanda, in which Laura has no active part, the clearest pool of light is on her figure. This is also true of the supper scene, when her silent figure on the sofa should remain the visual center. The light upon Laura should be distinct from the others, having a peculiar pristine clarity such as light used in early religious portraits of female saints or madonnas. A certain correspondence to light in religious paintings, such as El Greco's, where the figures are radiant in atmosphere that is relatively dusky, could be effectively used throughout the play. (It will also permit a more effective use of the screen.) A free, imaginative use of light can be of enormous value in giving a mobile, plastic quality to plays of a more or less static nature.

Characters

> Amanda Wingfield, *the mother. A little woman of great but confused vitality clinging frantically to another time and place. Her characterization must be carefully created, not copied from type. She is not paranoiac, but her life is paranoia. There is much to admire in Amanda, and as much to love and pity as there is to laugh at. Certainly she has endurance and a kind of heroism, and though her foolishness makes her unwittingly cruel at times, there is tenderness in her slight person.*
> Laura Wingfield, *her daughter. Amanda, having failed to establish contact with reality, continues to live vitally in her illusions, but Laura's situation is even graver. A childhood illness has left her crippled, one leg slightly shorter than the other, and held in a brace. This defect need not be more than suggested on the stage. Stemming from this, Laura's separation increases till she is like a piece of her own glass collection, too exquisitely fragile to move from the shelf.*
> Tom Wingfield, *her son. And the narrator of the play. A poet with a job in a warehouse. His nature is not remorseless, but to escape from a trap he has to act without pity.*
> Jim O'Connor, *the gentleman caller. A nice, ordinary, young man.*

Scene: An alley in St. Louis.
Part I: Preparation for a Gentleman Caller.
Part II: The Gentleman Calls.
Time: Now and the Past.

SCENE I

> *(The Wingfield apartment is in the rear of the building, one of those vast hivelike conglomerations of cellular living-units that flower as warty growths in overcrowded urban centers of lower middle-class population and are symptomatic of the impulse of this largest and fundamentally enslaved section of American society to avoid fluidity and differentiation and to exist and function as one interfused mass of automatism.)*
> *(The apartment faces an alley and is entered by a fire escape, a structure whose name is a touch of accidental poetic truth, for all of these huge buildings are always burning with the slow and implacable fires of human desperation. The fire escape is included in the set—that is, the landing of it and steps descending from it.)*
> *(The scene is memory and is therefore nonrealistic. Memory takes a lot of poetic license. It omits some details; others are exaggerated, according to the emotional value of*

*the articles it touches, for memory is seated predominantly in the heart. The interior is
therefore rather dim and poetic.)*

*(At the rise of the curtain, the audience is faced with the dark, grim rear wall of
the Wingfield tenement. This building, which runs parallel to the footlights, is flanked
on both sides by dark, narrow alleys which run into murky canyons of tangled
clotheslines, garbage cans, and the sinister latticework of neighboring fire escapes. It is
up and down these side alleys that exterior entrances and exits are made, during the
play. At the end of Tom's opening commentary, the dark tenement wall slowly reveals
(by means of a transparency) the interior of the ground floor Wingfield apartment.)*

*(Downstage is the living room, which also serves as a sleeping room for Laura,
the sofa unfolding to make her bed. Upstage, center, and divided by a wide arch or
second proscenium with transparent faded portieres (or second curtain), is the dining
room. In an old-fashioned what-not in the living room are seen scores of transparent
glass animals. A blown-up photograph of the father hangs on the wall of the living
room, facing the audience, to the left of the archway. It is the face of a very handsome
young man in a doughboy's First World War cap. He is gallantly smiling, ineluctably
smiling, as if to say, "I will be smiling forever.")*

*(The audience hears and sees the opening scene in the dining room through both
the transparent fourth wall of the building and the transparent gauze portieres of the
dining room arch. It is during this revealing scene that the fourth wall slowly ascends,
out of sight. This transparent exterior wall is not brought down again until the very
end of the play, during Tom's final speech.)*

*(The narrator is an undisguised convention of the play. He takes whatever
license with dramatic convention as is convenient to his purposes.)*

*(Tom enters dressed as a merchant sailor from alley, stage left, and strolls across
the front of the stage to the fire escape. There he stops and lights a cigarette. He
addresses the audience.)*

TOM.   Yes, I have tricks in my pocket, I have things up my sleeve. But I am the opposite of a stage magician. He gives you illusion that has the appearance of truth. I give
you truth in the pleasant disguise of illusion. To begin with, I turn back time. I reverse
it to that quaint period, the thirties, when the huge middle class of America was ma-
triculating in a school for the blind. Their eyes had failed them, or they had failed their
eyes, and so they were having their fingers pressed forcibly down on the fiery Braille alphabet of a dissolving economy. In Spain there was revolution. Here there was only
shouting and confusion. In Spain there was Guernica.° Here there were disturbances of
labor, sometimes pretty violent, in otherwise peaceful cities such as Chicago, Cleveland,
Saint Louis. . . . This is the social background of the play.

(Music.)

The play is memory. Being a memory play, it is dimly lighted, it is sentimental, it is not
realistic. In memory everything seems to happen to music. That explains the fiddle in
the wings. I am the narrator of the play, and also a character in it. The other characters
are my mother, Amanda, my sister, Laura, and a gentleman caller who appears in the
final scenes. He is the most realistic character in the play, being an emissary from a
world of reality that we were somehow set apart from. But since I have a poet's weakness
for symbols, I am using this character also as a symbol; he is the long delayed but always

Guernica: Spanish town destroyed by aerial bombardment as an "experiment" during the Spanish
Civil War.

expected something that we live for. There is a fifth character in the play who doesn't appear except in this larger-than-life photograph over the mantel. This is our father who left us a long time ago. He was a telephone man who fell in love with long distances; he gave up his job with the telephone company and skipped the light fantastic out of town . . . The last we heard of him was a picture postcard from Mazatlan, on the Pacific coast of Mexico, containing a message of two words—"Hello—Good-bye!" and no address. I think the rest of the play will explain itself. . . .

(Amanda's voice becomes audible through the portieres.)

(Legend on Screen: "Où Sont les Neiges.")°

(He divides the portieres and enters the upstage area.)

(Amanda and Laura are seated at a drop-leaf table. Eating is indicated by gestures without food or utensils. Amanda faces the audience. Tom and Laura are seated in profile.)

(The interior has lit up softly and through the scrim we see Amanda and Laura seated at the table in the upstage area.)

AMANDA *(calling)*.   Tom?

TOM.   Yes, Mother.

AMANDA.   We can't say grace until you come to the table!

TOM.   Coming, Mother. *(He bows slightly and withdraws, reappearing a few moments later in his place at the table.)*

AMANDA *(to her son)*.   Honey, don't push with your fingers. If you have to push with something, the thing to push with is a crust of bread. And chew—chew! Animals have sections in their stomachs which enable them to digest food without mastication, but human beings are supposed to chew their food before they swallow it down. Eat food leisurely, son, and really enjoy it. A well-cooked meal has lots of delicate flavors that have to be held in the mouth for appreciation. So chew your food and give your salivary glands a chance to function!

(Tom deliberately lays his imaginary fork down and pushes his chair back from the table.)

TOM.   I haven't enjoyed one bite of this dinner because of your constant directions on how to eat it. It's you that makes me rush through meals with your hawklike attention to every bite I take. Sickening—spoils my appetite—all this discussion of animals' secretion—salivary glands—mastication!

AMANDA *(lightly)*.   Temperament like a Metropolitan° star! *(He rises and crosses downstage.)* You're not excused from the table.

TOM.   I'm getting a cigarette.

AMANDA.   You smoke too much.

(Laura rises.)

LAURA.   I'll bring in the blancmange.

(He remains standing with his cigarette by the portieres during the following.)

AMANDA *(rising)*.   No, sister, no, sister—you be the lady this time and I'll be the darky.

LAURA.   I'm already up.

AMANDA.   Resume your seat, little sister—I want you to stay fresh and pretty— for gentlemen callers!

Où Sont les Neiges: Where are the snows [of yesteryear]?   *Metropolitan:* the Metropolitan Opera in New York City.

LAURA.   I'm not expecting any gentlemen callers.

AMANDA.   *(crossing out to kitchenette. Airily)*. Sometimes they come when they are least expected! Why, I remember one Sunday afternoon in Blue Mountain—*(Enters kitchenette.)*

TOM.   I know what's coming!

LAURA.   Yes. But let her tell it.

TOM.   Again?

LAURA.   She loves to tell it.

(Amanda returns with bowl of dessert.)

AMANDA.   One Sunday afternoon in Blue Mountain—your mother received—*seventeen!*—gentlemen callers! Why, sometimes there weren't chairs enough to accommodate them all. We had to send the nigger over to bring in folding chairs from the parish house.

TOM *(remaining at portieres)*.   How did you entertain those gentlemen callers?

AMANDA.   I understood the art of conversation!

TOM.   I bet you could talk.

AMANDA.   Girls in those days knew how to talk, I can tell you.

TOM.   Yes?

(Image: Amanda as a girl on a porch greeting callers.)

AMANDA.   They *knew* how to entertain their gentlemen callers. It wasn't enough for a girl to be possessed of a pretty face and a graceful figure—although I wasn't slighted in either respect. She also needed to have a nimble wit and a tongue to meet all occasions.

TOM.   What did you talk about?

AMANDA.   Things of importance going on in the world! Never anything coarse or common or vulgar.*(She addresses Tom as though he were seated in the vacant chair at the table though he remains by portieres. He plays this scene as though he held the book.)* My callers were gentlemen—all! Among my callers were some of the most prominent young planters of the Mississippi Delta—planters and sons of planters!

(Tom motions for music and a spot of light on Amanda.)

(Her eyes lift, her face glows, her voice becomes rich and elegiac.)

(Screen legend: "Où Sont les Neiges.")

There was young Champ Laughlin who later became vice-president of the Delta Planters Bank. Hadley Stevenson who was drowned in Moon Lake and left his widow one hundred and fifty thousand in Government bonds. There were the Cutrere brothers, Wesley and Bates. Bates was one of my bright particular beaux! He got in a quarrel with that wild Wainright boy. They shot it out on the floor of Moon Lake Casino. Bates was shot through the stomach. Died in the ambulance on his way to Memphis. His widow was also well-provided for, came into eight or ten thousand acres, that's all. She married him on the rebound—never loved her—carried my picture on him the night he died! And there was that boy that every girl in the Delta had set her cap for! That beautiful, brilliant young Fitzhugh boy from Greene County!

TOM.   What did he leave his widow?

AMANDA.   He never married! Gracious, you talk as though all of my old admirers had turned up their toes to the daisies!

TOM.   Isn't this the first you mentioned that still survives?

AMANDA.   That Fitzhugh boy went North and made a fortune—came to be known as the Wolf of Wall Street! He had the Midas touch, whatever he touched turned to gold! And I could have been Mrs. Duncan J. Fitzhugh, mind you! But—I picked your *father!*

LAURA *(rising).*   Mother, let me clear the table.

AMANDA.   No, dear, you go in front and study your typewriter chart. Or practice your shorthand a little. Stay fresh and pretty!—It's almost time for our gentlemen callers to start arriving.*(She flounces girlishly toward the kitchenette.)* How many do you suppose we're going to entertain this afternoon?

(Tom throws down the paper and jumps up with a groan.)

LAURA *(alone in the dining room).*   I don't believe we're going to receive any, Mother.

AMANDA *(reappearing, airily).*   What? No one—not one? You must be joking!*(Laura nervously echoes her laugh. She slips in a fugitive manner through the half-open portieres and draws them gently behind her. A shaft of very clear light is thrown on her face against the faded tapestry of the curtains. Music: "The Glass Menagerie" under faintly. Lightly.)* Not one gentleman caller? It can't be true! There must be a flood, there must have been a tornado!

LAURA.   It isn't a flood, it's not a tornado, Mother. I'm just not popular like you were in Blue Mountain. . . . *(Tom utters another groan. Laura glances at him with a faint, apologetic smile. Her voice catching a little.)* Mother's afraid I'm going to be an old maid.

(The scene dims out with "Glass Menagerie" music.)

SCENE II

("Laura, Haven't You Ever Liked Some Boy?")

(On the dark stage the screen is lighted with the image of blue roses.)

(Gradually Laura's figure becomes apparent and the screen goes out.)

(The music subsides.)

(Laura is seated in the delicate ivory chair at the small clawfoot table.)

(She wears a dress of soft violet material for a kimono—her hair tied back from her forehead with a ribbon.)

(She is washing and polishing her collection of glass.)

(Amanda appears on the fire escape steps. At the sound of her ascent, Laura catches her breath, thrusts the bowl of ornaments away and seats herself stiffly before the diagram of the typewriter keyboard as though it held her spellbound. Something has happened to Amanda. It is written in her face as she climbs to the landing: a look that is grim and hopeless and a little absurd.)

(She has on one of those cheap or imitation velvety-looking cloth coats with imitation fur collar. Her hat is five or six years old, one of those dreadful cloche hats that were worn in the late twenties, and she is clasping an enormous black patent-leather pocketbook with nickel clasp and initials. This is her full-dress outfit, the one she usually wears to the D.A.R.°)

(Before entering she looks through the door.)

(She purses her lips, opens her eyes wide, rolls them upward and shakes her head.)

(Then she slowly lets herself in the door. Seeing her mother's expression Laura touches her lips with a nervous gesture.)

D.A.R.: Daughters of the American Revolution, a conservative, patriotic organization for women whose ancestors were involved in the American Revolutionary War.

LAURA. Hello, Mother, I was—*(She makes a nervous gesture toward the chart on the wall. Amanda leans against the shut door and stares at Laura with a martyred look.)*

AMANDA. Deception? Deception? *(She slowly removes her hat and gloves, continuing the swift suffering stare. She lets the hat and gloves fall on the floor—a bit of acting.)*

LAURA *(shakily).* How was the D.A.R. meeting? *(Amanda slowly opens her purse and removes a dainty white handkerchief which she shakes out delicately and delicately touches to her lips and nostrils.)* Didn't you go to the D.A.R. meeting, Mother?

AMANDA *(faintly, almost inaudibly).* —No.—No. *(Then more forcibly.)* I did not have the strength—to go to the D.A.R. In fact, I did not have the courage! I wanted to find a hole in the ground and hide myself in it forever! *(She crosses slowly to the wall and removes the diagram of the typewriter keyboard. She holds it in front of her for a second, staring at it sweetly and sorrowfully—then bites her lips and tears it in two pieces.)*

LAURA *(faintly).* Why did you do that, Mother? *(Amanda repeats the same procedure with the chart of the Gregg Alphabet.)* Why are you—

AMANDA. Why? Why? How old are you, Laura?

LAURA. Mother, you know my age.

AMANDA. I thought that you were an adult; it seems that I was mistaken. *(She crosses slowly to the sofa and sinks down and stares at Laura.)*

LAURA. Please don't stare at me, Mother.

(Amanda closes her eyes and lowers her head. Count ten.)

AMANDA. What are we going to do, what is going to become of us, what is the future?

(Count ten.)

LAURA. Has something happened, Mother? *(Amanda draws a long breath and takes out the handkerchief again. Dabbing process.)* Mother, has—something happened?

AMANDA. I'll be all right in a minute. I'm just bewildered—*(Count five.)*—by life. . . .

LAURA. Mother, I wish that you would tell me what's happened.

AMANDA. As you know, I was supposed to be inducted into my office at the D.A.R. this afternoon. *(Image: a swarm of typewriters.)* But I stopped off at Rubicam's Business College to speak to your teachers about your having a cold and ask them what progress they thought you were making down there.

LAURA. Oh. . . .

AMANDA. I went to the typing instructor and introduced myself as your mother. She didn't know who you were. Wingfield, she said. We don't have any such student enrolled at the school! I assured her she did, that you had been going to classes since early in January. "I wonder," she said, "if you could be talking about that terribly shy little girl who dropped out of school after only a few days' attendance?" "No," I said, "Laura, my daughter, has been going to school every day for the past six weeks!" "Excuse me," she said. She took the attendance book out and there was your name, unmistakably printed, and all the dates you were absent until they decided that you had dropped out of school. I still said, "No, there must have been some mistake! There must have been some mix-up in the records!" And she said, "No—I remember her perfectly now. Her hands shook so that she couldn't hit the right keys! The first time we gave a speed test, she broke down completely—was sick at the stomach and almost had to be carried into the wash-room! After that morning she never showed up any more. We phoned the house but never got any answer"—while I was working at Famous and Barr, I suppose, demonstrating those—Oh! I felt so weak I could barely keep on my feet. I had to sit down while they got me a glass of water! Fifty dollars' tuition, all of our plans—my hopes and ambitions for you—just gone up the spout, just gone up the spout like that.*(Laura draws a long breath and gets awkwardly to her feet. She crosses to the victrola and winds it up.)* What are you doing?

LAURA.   Oh! *(She releases the handle and returns to her seat.)*

AMANDA.   Laura, where have you been going when you've gone out pretending that you were going to business college?

LAURA.   I've just been going out walking.

AMANDA.   That's not true.

LAURA.   It is. I just went walking.

AMANDA.   Walking? Walking? In winter? Deliberately courting pneumonia in that light coat? Where did you walk to, Laura?

LAURA.   All sorts of places—mostly in the park.

AMANDA.   Even after you'd started catching that cold?

LAURA.   It was the lesser of two evils, Mother. *(Image: winter scene in park.)* I couldn't go back up. I—threw up—on the floor!

AMANDA.   From half past seven till after five every day you mean to tell me you walked around in the park, because you wanted to make me think that you were still going to Rubicam's Business College?

LAURA.   It wasn't as bad as it sounds. I went inside places to get warmed up.

AMANDA.   Inside where?

LAURA.   I went in the art museum and the bird houses at the Zoo. I visited the penguins every day! Sometimes I did without lunch and went to the movies. Lately I've been spending most of my afternoons in the Jewel-box, that big glass house where they raise the tropical flowers.

AMANDA.   You did all this to deceive me, just for the deception?*(Laura looks down.)* Why?

LAURA.   Mother, when you're disappointed, you get that awful suffering look on your face, like the picture of Jesus' mother in the museum!

AMANDA.   Hush!

LAURA.   I couldn't face it.

(Pause. A whisper of strings.)

(Legend: "The Crust of Humility.")

AMANDA *(hopelessly fingering the huge pocketbook).*   So what are we going to do the rest of our lives? Stay home and watch the parades go by? Amuse ourselves with the glass menagerie, darling? Eternally play those worn-out phonograph records your father left as a painful reminder of him? We won't have a business career—we've given that up because it gave us nervous indigestion!*(Laughs wearily.)* What is there left but dependency all our lives? I know so well what becomes of unmarried women who aren't prepared to occupy a position. I've seen such pitiful cases in the South—barely tolerated spinsters living upon the grudging patronage of sister's husband or brother's wife!—stuck away in some little mousetrap of a room—encouraged by one in-law to visit another—little birdlike women without any nest—eating the crust of humility all their life! Is that the future that we've mapped out for ourselves? I swear it's the only alternative I can think of! It isn't a very pleasant alternative, is it? Of course—some girls do marry. *(Laura twists her hands nervously.)* Haven't you ever liked some boy?

LAURA.   Yes. I liked one once.*(Rises.)* I came across his picture a while ago.

AMANDA *(with some interest).*   He gave you his picture?

LAURA.   No, it's in the yearbook.

AMANDA *(disappointed)*.   Oh—a high-school boy.

(Screen image: Jim as high school hero bearing a silver cup.)

LAURA.   Yes. His name was Jim. *(Laura lifts the heavy annual from the clawfoot table.)* Here he is in *The Pirates of Penzance.*

AMANDA *(absently)*.   The what?

LAURA.   The operetta the senior class put on. He had a wonderful voice and we sat across the aisle from each other Mondays, Wednesdays, and Fridays in the Aud. Here he is with the silver cup for debating! See his grin?

AMANDA *(absently)*.   He must have had a jolly disposition.

LAURA.   He used to call me—Blue Roses.

(Image: blue roses.)

AMANDA.   Why did he call you such a name as that?

LAURA.   When I had that attack of pleurosis—he asked me what was the matter when I came back. I said pleurosis—he thought that I said Blue Roses! So that's what he always called me after that. Whenever he saw me, he'd holler, "Hello, Blue Roses!" I didn't care for the girl that he went out with. Emily Meisenbach. Emily was the best-dressed girl at Soldan. She never struck me, though, as being sincere . . . It says in the Personal Section—they're engaged. That's—six years ago! They must be married by now.

AMANDA.   Girls that aren't cut out for business careers usually wind up married to some nice man. *(Gets up with a spark of revival.)* Sister, that's what you'll do!

(Laura utters a startled, doubtful laugh. She reaches quickly for a piece of glass.)

LAURA.   But, Mother—

AMANDA.   Yes? *(Crossing to photograph.)*

LAURA *(in a tone of frightened apology)*.   I'm—crippled!

(Image: screen.)

AMANDA.   Nonsense! Laura, I've told you never, never to use that word. Why, you're not crippled, you just have a little defect—hardly noticeable, even! When people have some slight disadvantage like that, they cultivate other things to make up for it— develop charm—and vivacity—and—charm! That's all you have to do! *(She turns again to the photograph.)* One thing your father had plenty of—was charm!

(Tom motions to the fiddle in the wings.)

(The scene fades out with music.)

SCENE III

(Legend on screen: "After the Fiasco—")

(Tom speaks from the fire escape landing.)

TOM.   After the fiasco at Rubicam's Business College, the idea of getting a gentleman caller for Laura began to play a more important part in Mother's calculations. It became an obsession. Like some archetype of the universal unconscious, the image of the gentleman caller haunted our small apartment. . . . *(Image: young man at door with flowers.)* An evening at home rarely passed without some allusion to this image, this specter, this hope. . . . Even when he wasn't mentioned, his presence hung in Mother's preoccupied look and in my sister's frightened, apologetic manner—hung like a sentence passed upon the Wingfields! Mother was a woman of action as well as words. She began to take logical steps in the planned direction. Late that winter and in the early spring—realizing that extra money would be needed to properly feather the nest and plume the bird—she conducted a vigorous campaign on the telephone, roping in subscribers to one of those magazines for matrons called *The Home-maker's Companion,* the type of journal that features the serialized sublimations of ladies of letters who think in terms of delicate cuplike breasts, slim, tapering waists, rich, creamy thighs, eyes like wood smoke in autumn, fingers that soothe and caress like strains of music, bodies as powerful as Etruscan sculpture.

(Screen image: glamor magazine cover.)

(Amanda enters with phone on long extension cord. She is spotted in the dim stage.)

AMANDA.   Ida Scott? This is Amanda Wingfield! We *missed* you at the D.A.R. last Monday! I said to myself: She's probably suffering with that sinus condition! How is that sinus condition? Horrors! Heaven have mercy!—You're a Christian martyr, yes, that's what you are, a Christian martyr! Well, I just now happened to notice that your subscription to the *Companion's* about to expire! Yes, it expires with the next issue, honey!— just when that wonderful new serial by Bessie Mae Hopper is getting off to such an exciting start. Oh, honey, it's something that you can't miss! You remember how *Gone with the Wind* took everybody by storm? You simply couldn't go out if you hadn't read it. All everybody *talked* was Scarlett O'Hara. Well, this is a book that critics already compare to *Gone with the Wind.* It's the *Gone with the Wind* of the post–World War generation!—What?—Burning?—Oh, honey, don't let them burn, go take a look in the oven and I'll hold the wire! Heavens—I think she's hung up!

(Dim out.)

(Legend on screen: "You Think I'm in Love with Continental Shoemakers?")

(Before the stage is lighted, the violent voices of Tom and Amanda are heard.)

(They are quarreling behind the portieres. In front of them stands Laura with clenched hands and panicky expression.)

(A clear pool of light on her figure throughout this scene.)

TOM.   What in Christ's name am I—
AMANDA *(shrilly).*   Don't you use that—
TOM.   Supposed to do!
AMANDA.   Expression! Not in my—
TOM.   Ohhh!
AMANDA.   Presence! Have you gone out of your senses?
TOM.   I have, that's true, *driven* out!
AMANDA.   What is the matter with you, you—big—big—idiot!
TOM.   Look—I've got *no thing,* no single thing—
AMANDA.   Lower your voice!
TOM.   In my life here that I can call my OWN! Everything is—
AMANDA.   Stop that shouting!
TOM.   Yesterday you confiscated my books! You had the nerve to—
AMANDA.   I took that horrible novel back to the library—yes! That hideous book by that insane Mr. Lawrence.° *(Tom laughs wildly.)* I cannot control the output of diseased

Mr. Lawrence: D. H. Lawrence (1885–1930), in this collection. His sexual explicitness was shocking to many.

minds or people who cater to them—*(Tom laughs still more wildly.)* BUT I WON'T ALLOW
SUCH FILTH BROUGHT INTO MY HOUSE! No, no, no, no, no!

TOM.   House, house! Who pays rent on it, who makes a slave of himself to—

AMANDA *(fairly screeching).*   Don't you DARE to—

TOM.   No, no, *I* mustn't say things! *I've* got to just—

AMANDA.   Let me tell you—

TOM.   I don't want to hear any more! *(He tears the portieres open. The upstage area is
lit with a turgid smoky red glow.)*

*(Amanda's hair is in metal curlers and she wears a very old bathrobe, much too large for her slight
figure, a relic of the faithless Mr. Wingfield.)*

*(An upright typewriter and a wild disarray of manuscripts are on the dropleaf table. The quarrel
was probably precipitated by Amanda's interruption of his creative labor. A chair lying overthrown
on the floor.)*

(Their gesticulating shadows are cast on the ceiling by the fiery glow.)

AMANDA.   You *will* hear more, you—

TOM.   No, I won't hear more, I'm going out!

AMANDA.   You come right back in—

TOM.   Out, out out! Because I'm—

AMANDA.   Come back here, Tom Wingfield! I'm not through talking to you!

TOM.   Oh, go—

LAURA *(desperately).*   Tom!

AMANDA.   You're going to listen, and no more insolence from you! I'm at the
end of my patience! *(He comes back toward her.)*

TOM.   What do you think I'm at? Aren't I supposed to have any patience to reach
the end of, Mother? I know, I know. It seems unimportant to you, what I'm *doing*—what
I *want* to do—having a little *difference* between them! You don't think that—

AMANDA.   I think you've been doing things that you're ashamed of. That's why
you act like this. I don't believe that you go every night to the movies. Nobody goes to
the movies night after night. Nobody in their right minds goes to the movies as often as
you pretend to. People don't go to the movies at nearly midnight, and movies don't let
out at two A.M. Come in stumbling. Muttering to yourself like a maniac! You get three
hours' sleep and then go to work. Oh, I can picture the way you're doing down there.
Moping, doping, because you're in no condition.

TOM *(wildly).*   No, I'm in no condition!

AMANDA.   What right have you got to jeopardize your job? Jeopardize the security of us all? How do you think we'd manage if you were—

TOM.   Listen! You think I'm crazy *about* the *warehouse? (He bends fiercely toward her
slight figure.)* You think I'm in love with the Continental Shoemakers? You think I want
to spend fifty-five years down there in that—*celotex interior!* with—*fluorescent*—*tubes!* Look!
I'd rather somebody picked up a crowbar and battered out my brains—than go back
mornings! I go! Every time you come in yelling that God damn *"Rise and Shine!" "Rise
and Shine!"* I say to myself, *"How lucky dead* people are!" But I get up. I *go!* For sixty-five
dollars a month I give up all that I dream of doing and being ever! And you say self—
self's all I ever think of. Why, listen, if self is what I thought of, Mother, I'd be where he
is—gone! *(Pointing to father's picture.)* As far as the system of transportation reaches! *(He
starts past her. She grabs his arm.)* Don't grab at me, Mother!

AMANDA.   Where are you going?

TOM.   I'm going to the *movies!*

AMANDA.   I don't believe that lie!

TOM *(crouching toward her, overtowering her tiny figure. She backs away, gasping).*   I'm going to opium dens! Yes, opium dens, dens of vice and criminals' hangouts, Mother. I've joined the Hogan gang, I'm a hired assassin, I carry a tommy-gun in a violin case! I run a string of cathouses in the Valley! They call me Killer, Killer Wingfield, I'm leading a double life, a simple, honest warehouse worker by day, by night, a dynamic *czar* of the *underworld, Mother.* I go to gambling casinos, I spin away fortunes on the roulette table! I wear a patch over one eye and a false mustache, sometimes I put on green whiskers. On those occasions they call me—*El Diablo!°* Oh, I could tell you things to make you sleepless! My enemies plan to dynamite this place. They're going to blow us all sky-high some night! I'll be glad, very happy, and so will you! You'll go up, up on a broomstick, over Blue Mountain with seventeen gentlemen callers! You ugly—babbling old—witch. . . . *(He goes through a series of violent, clumsy movements, seizing his overcoat, lunging to the door, pulling it fiercely open. The women watch him, aghast. His arm catches in the sleeve of the coat as he struggles to pull it on. For a moment he is pinioned by the bulky garment. With an outraged groan he tears the coat off again, splitting the shoulders of it, and hurls it across the room. It strikes against the shelf of Laura's glass collection, there is a tinkle of shattering glass. Laura cries out as if wounded.)*

(Music legend: "The Glass Menagerie.")

LAURA *(shrilly).*   My glass!—menagerie. .. .   *(She covers her face and turns away.)*

(But Amanda is still stunned and stupefied by the "ugly witch" so that she barely notices this occurrence. Now she recovers her speech.)

AMANDA *(in an awful voice).*   I won't speak to you—until you apologize! *(She crosses through portieres and draws them together behind her. Tom is left with Laura. Laura clings weakly to the mantel with her face averted. Tom stares at her stupidly for a moment. Then he crosses to shelf. Drops awkwardly to his knees to collect the fallen glass, glancing at Laura as if he would speak but couldn't.)*

("The Glass Menagerie" steals in as the scene dims out.)

El Diablo: The devil (Spanish).

SCENE IV

(The interior is dark. Faint light in the alley.)

(A deep-voiced bell in a church is tolling the hour of five as the scene commences.)

(Tom appears at the top of the alley. After each solemn boom of the bell in the tower, he shakes a little noisemaker or rattle as if to express the tiny spasm of man in contrast to the sustained power and dignity of the Almighty. This and the unsteadiness of his advance make it evident that he has been drinking.)

(As he climbs the few steps to the fire escape landing light steals up inside. Laura appears in nightdress, observing Tom's empty bed in the front room.)

(Tom fishes in his pockets for the door key, removing a motley assortment of articles in the search, including a perfect shower of movie ticket stubs and an empty bottle. At last he finds the key, but just as he is about to insert it, it slips from his fingers. He strikes a match and crouches below the door.)

Tom (bitterly).   One crack—and it falls through!

(Laura opens the door.)

Laura.   Tom! Tom, what are you doing?

Tom.   Looking for a door key.

Laura.   Where have you been all this time?

Tom.   I have been to the movies.

Laura.   All this time at the movies?

Tom.   There was a very long program. There was a Garbo picture and a Mickey Mouse and a travelogue and a newsreel and a preview of coming attractions. And there was an organ solo and a collection for the milk fund—simultaneously—which ended up in a terrible fight between a fat lady and an usher!

Laura *(innocently).*   Did you have to stay through everything?

Tom.   Of course! And, oh, I forgot! There was a big stage show! The headliner on this stage show was Malvolio the Magician. He performed wonderful tricks, many of them, such as pouring water back and forth between pitchers. First it turned to wine and then it turned to beer and then it turned to whiskey. I know it was whiskey it finally turned into because he needed somebody to come up out of the audience to help him, and I came up—both shows! It was Kentucky Straight Bourbon. A very generous fellow, he gave souvenirs. *(He pulls from his back pocket a shimmering rainbow-colored scarf.)* He gave me this. This is his magic scarf. You can have it, Laura. You wave it over a canary cage and you get a bowl of goldfish. You wave it over the goldfish bowl and they fly away canaries. . . . But the wonderfullest trick of all was the coffin trick. We nailed him into a coffin and he got out of the coffin without removing one nail. *(He has come inside.)* There is a trick that would come in handy for me—get me out of this 2 by 4 situation! *(Flops onto bed and starts removing shoes.)*

Laura.   Tom—Shhh!

Tom.   What you shushing me for?

Laura.   You'll wake up Mother.

Tom.   Goody, goody! Pay 'er back for all those "Rise an' Shines." *(Lies down, groaning.)* You know it don't take much intelligence to get yourself into a nailed-up coffin, Laura. But who in hell ever got himself out of one without removing one nail?

(As if in answer, the father's grinning photograph lights up.)

(Scene dims out.)

(Immediately following: The church bell is heard striking six. At the sixth stroke the alarm clock goes off in Amanda's room, and after a few moments we hear her calling: "Rise and Shine! Rise and Shine! Laura, go tell your brother to rise and shine!")

Tom *(sitting up slowly).*   I'll rise—but I won't shine.

(The light increases.)

Amanda   Laura, tell your brother his coffee is ready.

(Laura slips into front room.)

Laura.   Tom! it's nearly seven. Don't make Mother nervous. *(He stares at her stupidly. Beseechingly.)* Tom, speak to Mother this morning. Make up with her, apologize, speak to her!

Tom.   She won't to me. It's her that started not speaking.

Laura.   If you just say you're sorry she'll start speaking.

Tom.   Her not speaking—is that such a tragedy?

LAURA. Please—please!

AMANDA (*calling from kitchenette*). Laura, are you going to do what I asked you to do, or do I have to get dressed and go out myself?

LAURA. Going, going—soon as I get on my coat! (*She pulls on a shapeless felt hat with nervous, jerky movement, pleadingly glancing at Tom. Rushes awkwardly for coat. The coat is one of Amanda's, inaccurately made over, the sleeves too short for Laura.*) Butter and what else?

AMANDA. (*entering upstage*). Just butter. Tell them to charge it.

LAURA. Mother, they make such faces when I do that.

AMANDA. Sticks and stones may break my bones, but the expression on Mr. Garfinkel's face won't harm us! Tell your brother his coffee is getting cold.

LAURA (*at door*). Do what I asked you, will you, will you, Tom?

(*He looks sullenly away.*)

AMANDA. Laura, go now or just don't go at all!

LAURA (*rushing out*). Going—going! (*A second later she cries out. Tom springs up and crosses to the door. Amanda rushes anxiously in. Tom opens the door.*)

TOM. Laura?

LAURA. I'm all right. I slipped, but I'm all right.

AMANDA (*peering anxiously after her*). If anyone breaks a leg on those fire escape steps, the landlord ought to be sued for every cent he possesses! (*She shuts door. Remembers she isn't speaking and returns to other room.*)

(*As Tom enters listlessly for his coffee, she turns her back to him and stands rigidly facing the window on the gloomy gray vault of the areaway. Its light on her face with its aged but childish features is cruelly sharp, satirical as a Daumier° print.*)

(*Music under: "Ave Maria."*)

(*Tom glances sheepishly but sullenly at her averted figure and slumps at the table. The coffee is scalding hot; he sips it and gasps and spits it back in the cup. At his gasp, Amanda catches her breath and half turns. Then catches herself and turns back to window.*)

(*Tom blows on his coffee, glancing sidewise at his mother. She clears her throat. Tom clears his. He starts to rise. Sinks back down again, scratches his head, clears his throat again. Amanda coughs. Tom raises his cup in both hands to blow on it, his eyes staring over the rim of it at his mother for several moments. Then he slowly sets the cup down and awkwardly and hesitantly rises from the chair.*)

TOM (*hoarsely*). Mother, I—I apologize. Mother. (*Amanda draws a quick, shuddering breath. Her face works grotesquely. She breaks into childlike tears.*) I'm sorry for what I said, for everything that I said, I didn't mean it.

AMANDA (*sobbingly*). My devotion has made me a witch and so I make myself hateful to my children!

TOM. No, you *don't*.

AMANDA I worry so much, don't sleep, it makes me nervous!

TOM (*gently*). I understand that.

AMANDA. I've had to put up a solitary battle all these years. But you're my right-hand bower!° Don't fall down, don't fail!

TOM (*gently*). I try, Mother.

Daumier: Honoré Daumier (1808–1879), a French painter known for his satirical art. *right-hand bower:* reference to a card game in which the Jack of trump is the second-highest card.

AMANDA *(with great enthusiasm)*. Try and you will SUCCEED! *(The notion makes her breathless.)* Why, you—you're just *full* of natural endowments! Both of my children— they're *unusual* children! Don't you think I know it? I'm so—*proud!* Happy and—feel I've—so much to be thankful for but—Promise me one thing, son!

TOM. What, Mother?

AMANDA. Promise, son, you'll—never be a drunkard!

TOM *(turns to her grinning)*. I will never be a drunkard, Mother.

AMANDA. That's what frightened me so, that you'd be drinking! Eat a bowl of Purina!

TOM. Just coffee, Mother.

AMANDA. Shredded wheat biscuit?

TOM. No, no, Mother, just coffee.

AMANDA You can't put in a day's work on an empty stomach. You've got ten minutes—don't gulp! Drinking too-hot liquids makes cancer of the stomach. . . . Put cream in.

TOM. No, thank you.

AMANDA. To cool it.

TOM. No! No, thank you, I want it black.

AMANDA. I know, but it's not good for you. We have to do all that we can to build ourselves up. In these trying times we live in, all that we have to cling to is—each other. .. . That's why it's so important to—Tom, I—I sent out your sister so I could discuss something with you. If you hadn't spoken I would have spoken to you. *(Sits down.)*

TOM *(gently)*. What is it, Mother, that you want to discuss?

AMANDA Laura!

(Tom puts his cup down slowly.)

(Legend on screen: "Laura.")

(Music: "The Glass Menagerie.")

TOM. —Oh.—Laura . . .

AMANDA *(touching his sleeve)*. You know how Laura is. So quiet but—still water runs deep! She notices things and I think she—broods about them. *(Tom looks up.)* A few days ago I came in and she was crying.

TOM. What about?

AMANDA. You.

TOM. Me?

AMANDA. She has an idea that you're not happy here.

TOM. What gave her that idea?

AMANDA. What gives her any idea? However, you do act strangely. I—I'm not criticizing, understand that! I know your ambitions do not lie in the warehouse, that like everybody in the whole wide world—you've had to—make sacrifices, but—Tom— Tom—life's not easy, it calls for—Spartan endurance! There's so many things in my heart that I cannot describe to you! I've never told you but I—*loved your father.* . . .

TOM *(gently)*. I know that, Mother.

AMANDA. And you—when I see you taking after his ways! Staying out late— and—well, you *had* been drinking the night you were in that—terrifying condition! Laura says that you hate the apartment and that you go out nights to get away from it! Is that true, Tom?

TOM. No. You say there's so much in your heart that you can't describe to me. That's true of me, too. There's so much in my heart that I can't describe to you! So let's respect each other's—

AMANDA.   But, why—*why*, Tom—are you always so *restless?* Where do you go to, nights?

TOM.   I—go to the movies.

AMANDA.   Why do you go to the movies so much, Tom?

TOM.   I go to the movies because—I like adventure. Adventure is something I don't have much of at work, so I go to the movies.

AMANDA.   But, Tom, you go to the movies entirely too much!

TOM.   I like a lot of adventure.

(Amanda looks baffled, then hurt. As the familiar inquisition resumes he becomes hard and impatient again. Amanda slips back into her querulous attitude toward him.)

(Image on screen: sailing vessel with Jolly Roger.°)

AMANDA.   Most young men find adventure in their careers.

TOM.   Then most young men are not employed in a warehouse.

AMANDA.   The world is full of young men employed in warehouses and offices and factories.

TOM.   Do all of them find adventure in their careers?

AMANDA.   They do or they do without it! Not everybody has a craze for adventure.

TOM.   Man is by instinct a lover, a hunter, a fighter, and none of those instincts are given much play at the warehouse!

AMANDA.   Man is by instinct! Don't quote instinct to me! Instinct is something that people have got away from! It belongs to animals! Christian adults don't want it!

TOM.   What do Christian adults want, then, Mother?

AMANDA.   · Superior things! Things of the mind and the spirit! Only animals have to satisfy instincts! Surely your aims are somewhat higher than theirs! Than monkeys— pigs—

TOM.   I reckon they're not.

AMANDA.   You're joking. However, that isn't what I wanted to discuss.

TOM *(rising).*   I haven't much time.

AMANDA. *(pushing his shoulders).*   Sit down.

TOM.   You want me to punch in red° at the warehouse, Mother?

AMANDA.   You have five minutes. I want to talk about Laura.

(Legend: "Plans and Provisions.")

TOM.   All right! What about Laura?

AMANDA.   We have to be making plans and provisions for her. She's older than you, two years, and nothing has happened. She just drifts along doing nothing. It frightens me terribly how she just drifts along.

TOM.   I guess she's the type that people call home girls.

AMANDA.   There's no such type, and if there is, it's a pity! That is unless the home is hers, with a husband!

TOM.   What?

AMANDA.   Oh, I can see the handwriting on the wall as plain as I see the nose in front of my face! It's terrifying! More and more you remind me of your father! He was out all hours without explanation—Then *left! Goodbye!* And me with a bag to hold. I saw that letter you got from the Merchant Marine. I know what you're dreaming of. I'm not

---

Jolly Roger: the black flag with white skull and crossbones used by pirates.   *punch in red:*   be late.

standing here blindfolded. Very well, then. Then *do* it! But not till there's somebody to take your place.

TOM.   What do you mean?

AMANDA.   I mean that as soon as Laura has got somebody to take care of her, married, a home of her own, independent—why, then you'll be free to go wherever you please, on land, on sea, whichever way the wind blows you! But until that time you've got to look out for your sister. I don't say me because I'm old and don't matter! I say for your sister because she's young and dependent. I put her in business college—a dismal failure! Frightened her so it made her sick to her stomach. I took her over to the Young People's League at the church. Another fiasco. She spoke to nobody, nobody spoke to her. Now all she does is fool with those pieces of glass and play those worn-out records. What kind of a life is that for a girl to lead!

TOM.   What can I do about it?

AMANDA.   Overcome selfishness! Self, self, self is all that you ever think of! *(Tom springs up and crosses to get his coat. It is ugly and bulky. He pulls on a cap with earmuffs.)* Where is your muffler? Put your wool muffler on! *(He snatches it angrily from the closet and tosses it around his neck and pulls both ends tight.)* Tom! I haven't said what I had in mind to ask you.

TOM.   I'm too late to—

AMANDA *(catching his arms—very importunately. Then shyly).*   Down at the ware-house, aren't there some—nice young men?

TOM.   No!

AMANDA.   There *must* be—*some . . .*

TOM.   Mother—

(Gesture.)

AMANDA.   Find out one that's clean-living—doesn't drink and—ask him out for sister!

TOM.   What?

AMANDA.   For *sister!* To *meet!* Get *acquainted!*

TOM *(stamping to door).*   Oh, my go-osh!

AMANDA.   Will you? *(He opens door. Imploringly.)* Will you? *(He starts down.)* Will you? *Will* you, dear?

TOM *(calling back).*   YES!

(Amanda closes the door hesitantly and with a troubled but faintly hopeful expression.)

(Screen image: glamor magazine cover.)

(Spot° Amanda at phone.)

AMANDA.   Ella Cartwright? This is Amanda Wingfield! How are you, honey? How is that kidney condition? *(Count five.)* Horrors! *(Count five.)* You're a Christian martyr, yes, honey, that's what you are, a Christian martyr! Well, I just happened to notice in my lit-tle red book that your subscription to the *Companion* has just run out! I knew that you wouldn't want to miss out on the wonderful serial starting in this new issue. It's by Bessie Mae Hopper, the first thing she's written since *Honeymoon for Three.* Wasn't that a strange and interesting story? Well, this one is even lovelier, I believe. It has a sophisticated so-ciety background. It's all about the horsey set on Long Island!

(Fade out.)

Spot: Spotlight.

SCENE V

(Legend on screen: "Annunciation." Fade with music.)

(It is early dusk of a spring evening. Supper has just been finished in the Wingfield apartment. Amanda and Laura in light colored dresses are removing dishes from the table, in the upstage area, which is shadowy, their movements formalized almost as a dance or ritual, their moving forms as pale and silent as moths.)

(Tom, in white shirt and trousers, rises from the table and crosses toward the fire escape.)

AMANDA *(as he passes her)*.   Son, will you do me a favor?

TOM.   What?

AMANDA.   Comb your hair! You look so pretty when your hair is combed! *(Tom slouches on sofa with evening paper. Enormous caption "Franco° Triumphs.")* There is only one respect in which I would like you to emulate your father.

TOM.   What respect is that?

AMANDA.   The care he always took of his appearance. He never allowed himself to look untidy. *(He throws down the paper and crosses to fire escape.)* Where are you going?

TOM.   I'm going out to smoke.

AMANDA.   You smoke too much. A pack a day at fifteen cents a pack. How much would that amount to in a month? Thirty times fifteen is how much, Tom? Figure it out and you will be astounded at what you could save. Enough to give you a night school course in accounting at Washington U! Just think what a wonderful thing that would be for you, son!

(Tom is unmoved by the thought.)

TOM.   I'd rather smoke. *(He steps out on landing, letting the screen door slam.)*

AMANDA *(sharply)*.   I know! That's the tragedy of it. . . . *(Alone, she turns to look at her husband's picture.)*

(Dance music: "All the World IS Waiting for the Sunrise!")

TOM *(to the audience)*.   Across the alley from us was the Paradise Dance Hall. On evenings in spring the windows and doors were open and the music came outdoors. Sometimes the lights were turned out except for a large glass sphere that hung from the ceiling. It would turn slowly about and filter the dusk with delicate rainbow colors. Then the orchestra played a waltz or a tango, something that had a slow and sensuous rhythm. Couples would come outside, to the relative privacy of the alley. You could see them kissing behind ash-pits and telephone poles. This was the compensation for lives that passed like mine, without any change or adventure. Adventure and change were immi-•nent in this year. They were waiting around the corner for all these kids. Suspended in the mist over Berchtesgaden, caught in the folds of Chamberlain's° umbrella—In Spain there was Guernica! But here there was only hot swing music and liquor, dance halls, bars, and movies, and sex that hung in the gloom like a chandelier and flooded the world with brief, deceptive rainbows. . . . All the world was waiting for bombardments!

(Amanda turns from the picture and comes outside.)

Franco: Generalissimo Franco's Fascist army won the Spanish Civil War in 1939.   *Berchtesgaden . . . Chamberlain:*   References to the approach of World War II in Europe. Berchtesgaden was Hitler's summer home; Neville Chamberlain was the prime minister of England who signed the Munich Pact, 1938, which was regarded as a capitulation to Hitler.

AMANDA *(sighing).* A fire escape landing's a poor excuse for a porch. *(She spreads a newspaper on a step and sits down, gracefully and demurely as if she were settling into a swing on a Mississippi veranda.)* What are you looking at?

TOM. The moon.

AMANDA. Is there a moon this evening?

TOM. It's rising over Garfinkel's Delicatessen.

AMANDA. So it is! A little silver slipper of a moon. Have you made a wish on it yet?

TOM. Um-hum.

AMANDA. What did you wish for?

TOM. That's a secret.

AMANDA. A secret, huh? Well, I won't tell mine either. I will be just as mysterious as you.

TOM. I bet I can guess what yours is.

AMANDA. Is my head so transparent?

TOM. You're not a sphinx.

AMANDA. No, I don't have secrets. I'll tell you what I wished for on the moon. Success and happiness for my precious children! I wish for that whenever there's a moon, and when there isn't a moon, I wish for it, too.

TOM. I thought perhaps you wished for a gentleman caller.

AMANDA. Why do you say that?

TOM. Don't you remember asking me to fetch one?

AMANDA. I remember suggesting that it would be nice for your sister if you brought home some nice young man from the warehouse. I think I've made that suggestion more than once.

TOM. Yes, you have made it repeatedly.

AMANDA. Well?

TOM. We are going to have one.

AMANDA. *What?*

TOM. A gentleman caller!

(The annunciation is celebrated with music.)

(Amanda rises.)

(Image on screen: caller with bouquet.)

AMANDA. You mean you have asked some nice young man to come over?

TOM. Yep. I've asked him to dinner.

AMANDA. You really did?

TOM. I did!

AMANDA. You did, and did he—*accept?*

TOM. He did!

AMANDA. Well, well—well, well! That's—lovely!

TOM. I thought that you would be pleased.

AMANDA. It's definite, then?

TOM. Very definite.

AMANDA. Soon?

TOM. Very soon.

AMANDA. For heaven's sake, stop putting on and tell me some things, will you?

TOM. What things do you want me to tell you?

AMANDA. *Naturally* I would like to know when he's *coming!*

TOM. He's coming tomorrow.

AMANDA. *Tomorrow?*

TOM. Yep. Tomorrow.

AMANDA. But, Tom!

TOM. Yes, Mother?

AMANDA. Tomorrow gives me no time!

TOM. Time for what?

AMANDA. Preparations! Why didn't you phone me at once, as soon as you asked him, the minute that he accepted? Then, don't you see, I could have been getting ready!

TOM. You don't have to make any fuss.

AMANDA. Oh, Tom, Tom, Tom, of course I have to make a fuss! I want things nice, not sloppy! Not thrown together. I'll certainly have to do some fast thinking, won't I?

TOM. I don't see why you have to think at all.

AMANDA. You just don't know. We can't have a gentleman caller in a pigsty! All my wedding silver has to be polished, the monogrammed table linen ought to be laundered! The windows have to be washed and fresh curtains put up. And how about clothes? We have to wear something, don't we?

TOM. Mother, this boy is no one to make a fuss over!

AMANDA. Do you realize he's the first young man we've introduced to your sister? It's terrible, dreadful, disgraceful that poor little sister has never received a single gentleman caller! Tom, come inside! *(She opens the screen door.)*

TOM. What for?

AMANDA. I want to ask you some things.

TOM. If you're going to make such a fuss, I'll call it off, I'll tell him not to come.

AMANDA. You certainly won't do anything of the kind. Nothing offends people worse than broken engagements. It simply means I'll have to work like a Turk! We won't be brilliant, but we'll pass inspection. Come on inside. *(Tom follows, groaning.)* Sit down.

TOM. Any particular place you would like me to sit?

AMANDA. Thank heavens I've got that new sofa! I'm also making payments on a floor lamp I'll have sent out! And put the chintz covers on, they'll brighten things up! Of course I'd hoped to have these walls repapered. . . . What is the young man's name?

TOM. His name is O'Connor.

AMANDA. That, of course, means fish—tomorrow is Friday!° I'll have that salmon loaf—with Durkee's dressing! What does he do? He works at the warehouse?

TOM. Of course! How else would I—

AMANDA. Tom, he—doesn't drink?

TOM. Why do you ask me that?

AMANDA. Your father *did!*

TOM. Don't get started on that!

AMANDA. He *does* drink, then?

TOM. Not that I know of!

AMANDA. Make sure, be certain! The last thing I want for my daughter's a boy who drinks!

TOM. Aren't you being a little premature? Mr. O'Connor has not yet appeared on the scene!

AMANDA. But will tomorrow. To meet your sister, and what do I know about his character? Nothing! Old maids are better off than wives of drunkards!

TOM. Oh, my God!

fish . . . Friday: Until recent decades, Catholics were prohibited from eating meat on Fridays.

AMANDA. Be still!

TOM *(leaning forward to whisper).* Lots of fellows meet girls whom they don't marry!

AMANDA. Oh, talk sensibly, Tom—and don't be sarcastic! *(She has gotten a hairbrush.)*

TOM. What are you doing?

AMANDA. I'm brushing that cowlick down! What is this young man's position at the warehouse?

TOM *(submitting grimly to the brush and the interrogation).* This young man's position is that of a shipping clerk, Mother.

AMANDA. Sounds to me like a fairly responsible job, the sort of a job you would be in if you just had more *get-up*. What is his salary? Have you got any idea?

TOM. I would judge it to be approximately eighty-five dollars a month.

AMANDA. Well—not princely, but—

TOM. Twenty more than I make.

AMANDA. Yes, how well I know! But for a family man, eighty-five dollars a month is not much more than you can just get by on. . . .

TOM. Yes, but Mr. O'Connor is not a family man.

AMANDA. He might be, mightn't he? Some time in the future?

TOM. I see. Plans and provisions.

AMANDA. You are the only young man that I know of who ignores the fact that the future becomes the present, the present the past, and the past turns into everlasting regret if you don't plan for it!

TOM. I will think that over and see what I can make of it.

AMANDA. Don't be supercilious with your mother! Tell me some more about this—what do you call him?

TOM. James D. O'Connor. The D. is for Delaney.

AMANDA. Irish on *both* sides! *Gracious!* And doesn't drink?

TOM. Shall I call him up and ask him right this minute?

AMANDA. The only way to find out about those things is to make discreet inquiries at the proper moment. When I was a girl in Blue Mountain and it was suspected that a young man drank, the girl whose attentions he had been receiving, if any girl *was*, would sometimes speak to the minister of his church, or rather her father would if her father was living, and sort of feel him out on the young man's character. That is the way such things are discreetly handled to keep a young woman from making a tragic mistake!

TOM. Then how did you happen to make a tragic mistake?

AMANDA. That innocent look of your father's had everyone fooled! He *smiled*—the world was *enchanted!* No girl can do worse than put herself at the mercy of a handsome appearance! I hope that Mr. O'Connor is not too good-looking.

TOM. No, he's not too good-looking. He's covered with freckles and hasn't too much of a nose.

AMANDA. He's not right-down homely, though?

TOM. Not right-down homely. Just medium homely, I'd say.

AMANDA. Character's what to look for in a man.

TOM. That's what I've always said, Mother.

AMANDA. You've never said anything of the kind and I suspect you would never give it a thought.

TOM. Don't be suspicious of me.

AMANDA. At least I hope he's the type that's up and coming.

TOM. I think he really goes in for self-improvement.

AMANDA. What reason have you to think so?

TOM.   He goes to night school.

AMANDA *(beaming)*.   Splendid! What does he do, I mean study?

TOM.   Radio engineering and public speaking!

AMANDA.   Then he has visions of being advanced in the world! Any young man who studies public speaking is aiming to have an executive job some day! And radio engineering? A thing for the future! Both of these facts are very illuminating. Those are the sort of things that a mother should know concerning any young man who comes to call on her daughter. Seriously or—not.

TOM.   One little warning. He doesn't know about Laura. I didn't let on that we had dark ulterior motives. I just said, why don't you come have dinner with us? He said okay and that was the whole conversation.

AMANDA.   I bet it was! You're eloquent as an oyster. However, he'll know about Laura when he gets here. When he sees how lovely and sweet and pretty she is, he'll thank his lucky stars he was asked to dinner.

TOM.   Mother, you mustn't expect too much of Laura.

AMANDA.   What do you mean?

TOM.   Laura seems all those things to you and me because she's ours and we love her. We don't even notice she's crippled anymore.

AMANDA.   Don't say crippled! You know that I never allow that word to be used!

TOM.   But face facts, Mother. She is and—that's not all—

AMANDA.   What do you mean "not all"?

TOM.   Laura is very different from other girls.

AMANDA.   I think the difference is all to her advantage.

TOM.   Not quite all—in the eyes of others—strangers—she's terribly shy and lives in a world of her own and those things make her seem a little peculiar to people outside the house.

AMANDA.   Don't say peculiar.

TOM.   Face the facts. She is.

(The dance-hall music changes to a tango that has a minor and somewhat ominous tone.)

AMANDA.   In what way is she peculiar—may I ask?

TOM *(gently)*.   She lives in a world of her own—a world of—little glass ornaments, Mother. .. . *(Gets up. Amanda remains holding brush, looking at him, troubled.)* She plays old phonograph records and—that's about all—*(He glances at himself in the mirror and crosses to door.)*

AMANDA *(sharply)*.   Where are you going?

TOM.   I'm going to the movies. *(Out screen door.)*

AMANDA..   Not to the movies, every night to the movies! *(Follows quickly to screen door.)* I don't believe you always go to the movies! *(He is gone. Amanda looks worriedly after him for a moment. Then vitality and optimism return and she turns from the door. Crossing to portieres.)* Laura! Laura! *(Laura answers from kitchenette.)*

LAURA.   Yes, Mother.

AMANDA.   Let those dishes go and come in front! *(Laura appears with dish towel. Gaily.)* Laura, come here and make a wish on the moon!

LAURA *(entering)*.   Moon—moon?

AMANDA.   A little silver slipper of a moon. Look over your left shoulder, Laura, and make a wish! *(Laura looks faintly puzzled as if called out of sleep. Amanda seizes her shoulders and turns her at an angle by the door.)* Now! Now, darling, wish!

LAURA.   What shall I wish for, Mother?

AMANDA *(her voice trembling and her eyes suddenly filling with tears).* Happiness! Good Fortune!

(The violin rises and the stage dims out.)

SCENE VI

(Image: high school hero.)

TOM. And so the following evening I brought Jim home to dinner. I had known Jim slightly in high school. In high school Jim was a hero. He had tremendous Irish good nature and vitality with the scrubbed and polished look of white chinaware. He seemed to move in a continual spotlight. He was a star in basketball, captain of the debating club, president of the senior class and the glee club and he sang the male lead in the annual light operas. He was always running or bounding, never just walking. He seemed always at the point of defeating the law of gravity. He was shooting with such velocity through his adolescence that you would logically expect him to arrive at nothing short of the White House by the time he was thirty. But Jim apparently ran into more interference after his graduation from Soldan. His speed had definitely slowed. Six years after he left high school he was holding a job that wasn't much better than mine.

(Image: clerk.)

He was the only one at the warehouse with whom I was on friendly terms. I was valuable to him as someone who could remember his former glory, who had seen him win basketball games and the silver cup in debating. He knew of my secret practice of retiring to a cabinet of the washroom to work on poems when business was slack in the warehouse. He called me Shakespeare. And while the other boys in the warehouse regarded me with suspicious hostility, Jim took a humorous attitude toward me. Gradually his attitude affected the others, their hostility wore off and they also began to smile at me as people smile at an oddly fashioned dog who trots across their path at some distance.

I knew that Jim and Laura had known each other at Soldan, and I had heard Laura speak admiringly of his voice. I didn't know if Jim remembered her or not. In high school Laura had been as unobtrusive as Jim had been astonishing. If he did remember Laura, it was not as my sister, for when I asked him to dinner, he grinned and said, "You know, Shakespeare, I never thought of you as having folks!"

He was about to discover that I did. .. .

(Light up stage.)

(Legend on screen: "The Accent of a Coming Foot.")

(Friday evening. It is about five o'clock of a late spring evening which comes "scattering poems in the sky.")

(A delicate lemony light is in the Wingfield apartment.)

(Amanda has worked like a Turk in preparation for the gentleman caller. The results are astonishing. The new floor lamp with its rose-silk shade is in place, a colored paper lantern conceals the broken light fixture in the ceiling, new billowing white curtains are at the windows, chintz covers are on chairs and sofa, a pair of new sofa pillows make their initial appearance.)

(Open boxes and tissue paper are scattered on the floor.)

(Laura stands in the middle with lifted arms while Amanda crouches before her, adjusting the hem of the new dress, devout and ritualistic. The dress is colored and designed by memory. The arrangement of Laura's hair is changed; it is softer and more becoming. A fragile, unearthly prettiness has come out in Laura: she is like a piece of translucent glass touched by light, given a momentary radiance, not actual, not lasting.)

AMANDA *(impatiently)*.   Why are you trembling?
LAURA.   Mother, you've made me so nervous!
AMANDA.   How have I made you nervous?
LAURA.   By all this fuss! You make it seem so important!
AMANDA.   I don't understand you, Laura. You couldn't be satisfied with just sitting home, and yet whenever I try to arrange something for you, you seem to resist it. *(She gets up.)* Now take a look at yourself. No, wait! Wait just a moment—I have an idea!
LAURA.   What is it now?

(Amanda produces two powder puffs which she wraps in handkerchiefs and stuffs in Laura's bosom.)

LAURA.   Mother, what are you doing?
AMANDA.   They call them "Gay Deceivers"!
LAURA.   I won't wear them!
AMANDA.   You will!
LAURA.   Why should I?
AMANDA.   Because, to be painfully honest, your chest is flat.
LAURA.   You make it seem like we were setting a trap.
AMANDA.   All pretty girls are a trap, a pretty trap, and men expect them to be. *(Legend: "A Pretty Trap.")* Now look at yourself, young lady. This is the prettiest you will ever be! I've got to fix myself now! You're going to be surprised by your mother's appearance! *(She crosses through portieres, humming gaily.)*

(Laura moves slowly to the long mirror and stares solemnly at herself.)

(A wind blows the white curtains inward in a slow, graceful motion and with a faint, sorrowful sighing.)

AMANDA *(offstage)*.   It isn't dark enough yet. *(She turns slowly before the mirror with a troubled look.)*

(Legend on screen: "This Is My Sister: Celebrate Her with Strings!" Music.)

AMANDA *(laughing, off)*.   I'm going to show you something. I'm going to make a spectacular appearance!
LAURA.   What is it, Mother?
AMANDA.   Possess your soul in patience—you will see! Something I've resurrected from that old trunk! Styles haven't changed so terribly much after all. . . . *(She parts the portieres.)* Now just look at your mother! *(She wears a girlish frock of yellowed voile with a blue silk sash. She carries a bunch of jonquils—the legend of her youth is nearly revived. Feverishly.)* This is the dress in which I led the cotillion. Won the cakewalk twice at Sunset Hill, wore one spring to the Governor's ball in Jackson! See how I sashayed around the ballroom, Laura? *(She raises her skirt and does a mincing step around the room.)* I wore it on Sundays for my gentlemen callers! I had it on the day I met your father—I had malaria fever all that spring. The change of climate from East Tennessee to the Delta—weakened resistance— I had a little temperature all the time—not enough to be serious—just enough to make me restless and giddy! Invitations poured in—parties all over the Delta!—"Stay in bed,"

said Mother, "you have fever!"—but I just wouldn't.—I took quinine but kept on going, going!—Evenings, dances!—Afternoons, long, long rides! Picnics—lovely!—So lovely, that country in May.—All lacy with dogwood, literally flooded with jonquils!—That was the spring I had the craze for jonquils. Jonquils became an absolute obsession. Mother said, "Honey, there's no more room for jonquils." And still I kept on bringing in more jonquils. Whenever, wherever I saw them, I'd say, "Stop! Stop! I see jonquils!" I made the young men help me gather the jonquils! It was a joke, Amanda and her jonquils! Finally there were no more vases to hold them, every available space was filled with jonquils. No vases to hold them? All right, I'll hold them myself! And then I—*(She stops in front of the picture. Music.)* met your father! Malaria fever and jonquils and then—this—boy. .. . *(She switches on the rose-colored lamp.)* I hope they get here before it starts to rain. *(She crosses upstage and places the jonquils in bowl on table.)* I gave your brother a little extra change so he and Mr. O'Connor could take the service car home.

LAURA *(with altered look).*   What did you say his name was?

AMANDA.   O'Connor.

LAURA.   What is his first name?

AMANDA.   I don't remember. Oh, yes, I do. It was—Jim!

(Laura sways slightly and catches hold of a chair.)

(Legend on screen: "Not Jim!")

LAURA *(faintly).*   Not—Jim!

AMANDA.   Yes, that was it, it was Jim! I've never known a Jim that wasn't nice!

(Music: ominous.)

LAURA.   Are you sure his name is Jim O'Connor?

AMANDA.   Yes. Why?

LAURA.   Is he the one that Tom used to know in high school?

AMANDA.   He didn't say so. I think he just got to know him at the warehouse.

LAURA.   There was a Jim O'Connor we both knew in high school—*(Then, with effort.)* If that is the one that Tom is bringing to dinner—you'll have to excuse me, I won't come to the table.

AMANDA.   What sort of nonsense is this?

LAURA.   You asked me once if I'd ever liked a boy. Don't you remember I showed you this boy's picture?

AMANDA.   You mean the boy you showed me in the yearbook?

LAURA.   Yes, that boy.

AMANDA.   Laura, Laura, were you in love with that boy?

LAURA.   I don't know, Mother. All I know is I couldn't sit at the table if it was him!

AMANDA.   It won't be him! It isn't the least bit likely. But whether it is or not, you will come to the table. You will not be excused.

LAURA.   I'll have to be, Mother.

AMANDA.   I don't intend to humor your silliness, Laura. I've had too much from you and your brother, both! So just sit down and compose yourself till they come. Tom has forgotten his key so you'll have to let them in, when they arrive.

LAURA *(panicky).*   Oh, Mother—*you* answer the door!

AMANDA *(lightly).*   I'll be in the kitchen—busy!

LAURA.   Oh, Mother, please answer the door, don't make me do it!

AMANDA *(crossing into kitchenette).*   I've got to fix the dressing for the salmon. Fuss, fuss—silliness!—over a gentleman caller!

(Door swings shut. Laura is left alone.)

(Legend: "Terror!")

(She utters a low moan and turns off the lamp—sits stiffly on the edge of the sofa, knotting her fingers together.)

(Legend on screen: "The Opening of a Door!")

(Tom and Jim appear on the fire escape steps and climb to landing. Hearing their approach, Laura rises with a panicky gesture. She retreats to the portieres.)

(The doorbell. Laura catches her breath and touches her throat. Low drums.)

AMANDA *(calling).*   Laura, sweetheart! The door!

(Laura stares at it without moving.)

JIM.   I think we just beat the rain.

TOM.   Uh-huh. *(He rings again, nervously. Jim whistles and fishes for a cigarette.)*

AMANDA. *(very, very gaily).*   Laura, that is your brother and Mr. O'Connor! Will you let them in, darling?

(Laura crosses toward kitchenette door.)

LAURA *(breathlessly).*   Mother—you go to the door!

(Amanda steps out of kitchenette and stares furiously at Laura. She points imperiously at the door.)

LAURA.   Please, please!

AMANDA *(in a fierce whisper).*   What is the matter with you, you silly thing?

LAURA *(desperately).*   Please, you answer it, *please!*

AMANDA.   I told you I wasn't going to humor you, Laura. Why have you chosen this moment to lose your mind?

LAURA.   Please, please, please, you go!

AMANDA.   You'll have to go to the door because I can't!

LAURA *(despairingly).*   I can't either!

AMANDA.   *Why?*

LAURA.   I'm *sick!*

AMANDA.   I'm sick, too—of your nonsense! Why can't you and your brother be normal people? Fantastic whims and behavior! *(Tom gives a long ring.)* Preposterous goings on! Can you give me one reason—*(Calls out lyrically.)* COMING! JUST ONE SECOND!— why should you be afraid to open a door? Now you answer it, Laura!

LAURA.   Oh, oh, oh . . . *(She returns through the portieres. Darts to the victrola and winds it frantically and turns it on.)*

AMANDA.   Laura Wingfield, you march right to that door!

LAURA.   Yes—yes, Mother!

(A faraway, scratchy rendition of "Dardanella" softens the air and gives her strength to move through it. She slips to the door and draws it cautiously open.)

(Tom enters with the caller, Jim O'Connor.)

TOM.   Laura, this is Jim. Jim, this is my sister, Laura.

JIM *(stepping inside).*   I didn't know that Shakespeare had a sister!

LAURA *(retreating stiff and trembling from the door).*   How—how do you do?

JIM *(heartily extending his hand).*   Okay!

(Laura touches it hesitantly with hers.)

JIM.   Your hand's *cold,* Laura!

LAURA.   Yes, well—I've been playing the victrola. . . .

JIM.   Must have been playing classical music on it! You ought to play a little hot swing music to warm you up!

LAURA.   Excuse me—I haven't finished playing the victrola. . . .

(She turns awkwardly and hurries into the front room. She pauses a second by the victrola. Then catches her breath and darts through the portieres like a frightened deer.)

JIM *(grinning).*   What was the matter?

TOM.   Oh—with Laura? Laura is—terribly shy.

JIM.   Shy, huh? It's unusual to meet a shy girl nowadays. I don't believe you ever mentioned you had a sister.

TOM.   Well, now you know. I have one. Here is the *Post Dispatch.* You want a piece of it?

JIM.   Uh-huh.

TOM.   What piece? The comics?

JIM.   Sports! *(Glances at it.)* Ole Dizzy Dean° is on his bad behavior.

TOM *(disinterest).*   Yeah? *(Lights cigarette and crosses back to fire escape door.)*

JIM.   Where are *you* going?

TOM.   I'm going out on the terrace.

JIM *(goes after him).*   You know, Shakespeare—I'm going to sell you a bill of goods!

TOM.   What goods?

JIM.   A course I'm taking.

TOM.   Huh?

JIM.   In public speaking! You and me, we're not the warehouse type.

TOM.   Thanks—that's good news. But what has public speaking got to do with it?

JIM.   It fits you for—executive positions!

TOM.   Awww.

JIM.   I tell you it's done a helluva lot for me.

(Image: executive at desk.)

TOM.   In what respect?

JIM.   In every! Ask yourself what is the difference between you an' me and men in the office down front? Brains?—No!—Ability?—No! Then what? Just one little thing—

TOM.   What is that one little thing?

JIM.   Primarily it amounts to—social poise! Being able to square up to people and hold your own on any social level!

AMANDA *(offstage).*   Tom?

TOM.   Yes, Mother?

AMANDA.   Is that you and Mr. O'Connor?

TOM.   Yes, Mother.

AMANDA.   Well, you just make yourselves comfortable in there.

TOM.   Yes, Mother.

AMANDA.   Ask Mr. O'Connor if he would like to wash his hands.

JIM.   Aw,—no—no—thank you—I took care of that at the warehouse. Tom—

TOM.   Yes?

JIM.   Mr. Mendoza was speaking to me about you.

TOM.   Favorably?

JIM.   What do you think?

Dizzy Dean: baseball "bad boy" of the 1930s.

TOM. Well—

JIM. You're going to be out of a job if you don't wake up.

TOM. I am waking up—

JIM. You show no signs.

TOM. The signs are interior.

(Image on screen: the sailing vessel with Jolly Roger again.)

TOM. I'm planning to change. *(He leans over the rail speaking with quiet exhilaration. The incandescent marquees and signs of the first-run movie houses light his face from across the alley. He looks like a voyager.)* I'm right at the point of committing myself to a future that doesn't include the warehouse and Mr. Mendoza or even a night school course in public speaking.

JIM. What are you gassing about?

TOM. I'm tired of the movies.

JIM. Movies!

TOM. Yes, movies! Look at them—*(A wave toward the marvels of Grand Avenue.)* All of those glamorous people—having adventures—hogging it all, gobbling the whole thing up! You know what happens? People go to the *movies* instead of *moving!* Hollywood characters are supposed to have all the adventures for everybody in America, while everybody in America sits in a dark room and watches them have them! Yes, until there's a war. That's when adventure becomes available to the masses! *Everyone's* dish, not only Gable's! Then the people in the dark room come out of the dark room to have some adventures themselves—Goody, goody!—It's our turn now, to go to the South Sea Island—to make a safari—to be exotic, far-off!—But I'm not patient. I don't want to wait till then. I'm tired of the *movies* and I am *about* to *move!*

JIM *(incredulously)*. Move?

TOM. Yes.

JIM. When?

TOM. Soon!

JIM. Where? Where?

(Theme three music seems to answer the question, while Tom thinks it over. He searches among his pockets.)

TOM. I'm starting to boil inside. I know I seem dreamy, but inside—well, I'm boiling! Whenever I pick up a shoe, I shudder a little thinking how short life is and what I am doing!—Whatever that means. I know it doesn't mean shoes—except as something to wear on a traveler's feet! *(Finds paper.)* Look—

JIM. What?

TOM. I'm a member.

JIM *(reading)*. The Union of Merchant Seamen.

TOM. I paid my dues this month, instead of the light bill.

JIM. You will regret it when they turn the lights off.

TOM. I won't be here.

JIM. How about your mother?

TOM. I'm like my father. The bastard son of a bastard! See how he grins? And he's been absent going on sixteen years!

JIM. You're just talking, you drip. How does your mother feel about it?

TOM. Shhh!—Here comes Mother! Mother is not acquainted with my plans!

AMANDA *(enters portieres)*. Where are you all?

TOM. On the terrace, Mother.

(They start inside. She advances to them. Tom is distinctly shocked at her appearance. Even Jim blinks a little. He is making his first contact with girlish Southern vivacity and in spite of the night school course in public speaking is somewhat thrown off the beam by the unexpected outlay of social charm.)

(Certain responses are attempted by Jim but are swept aside by Amanda's gay laughter and chatter. Tom is embarrassed but after the first shock Jim reacts very warmly. Grins and chuckles, is altogether won over.)

(Image: Amanda as a girl.)

AMANDA *(coyly smiling, shaking her girlish ringlets).*   Well, well, well, so this is Mr. O'Connor. Introductions entirely unnecessary. I've heard so much about you from my boy. I finally said to him, Tom—good gracious!—why don't you bring this paragon to supper? I'd like to meet this nice young man at the warehouse!—Instead of just hearing him sing your praises so much! I don't know why my son is so standoffish—that's not Southern behavior! Let's sit down and—I think we could stand a little more air in here! Tom, leave the door open. I felt a nice fresh breeze a moment ago. Where has it gone to? Mmm, so warm already! And not quite summer, even. We're going to burn up when summer really gets started. However, we're having—we're having a very light supper. I think light things are better fo' this time of year. The same as light clothes are. Light clothes an' light food are what warm weather calls fo'. You know our blood gets so thick during th' winter—it takes a while fo' us to *adjust* ou'selves!—when the season changes . . . It's come so quick this year. I wasn't prepared. All of a sudden—heavens! Already summer!— I ran to the trunk an' pulled out this light dress—Terribly old! Historical almost! But feels so good—so good an' co-ol, y'know. . . .

TOM.   Mother—

AMANDA.   Yes, honey?

TOM.   How about—supper?

AMANDA.   Honey, you go ask Sister if supper is ready! You know that Sister is in full charge of supper! Tell her you hungry boys are waiting for it. *(To Jim.)* Have you met Laura?

JIM.   She—

AMANDA.   Let you in? Oh, good, you've met already! It's rare for a girl as sweet an' pretty as Laura to be domestic! But Laura is, thank heavens, not only pretty but also very domestic. I'm not at all. I never was a bit. I never could make a thing but angel food cake. Well, in the South we had so many servants. Gone, gone, gone. All vestiges of gracious living! Gone completely! I wasn't prepared for what the future brought me. All of my gentlemen callers were sons of planters and so of course I assumed that I would be married to one and raise my family on a large piece of land with plenty of servants. But man proposes—and woman accepts the proposal!—To vary that old, old saying a little bit—I married no planter! I married a man who worked for the telephone company!—That gallantly smiling gentleman over there! *(Points to the picture.)* A telephone man who—fell in love with long distance!—Now he travels and I don't even know where!—But what am I going on for about my—tribulations! Tell me yours—I hope you don't have any! Tom?

TOM *(returning).*   Yes, Mother?

AMANDA.   Is supper nearly ready?

TOM.   It looks to me like supper is on the table.

AMANDA.   Let me look—*(She rises prettily and looks through portieres.)* Oh, lovely!— But where is Sister?

TOM.   Laura is not feeling well and she says that she thinks she'd better not come to the table.

AMANDA. What?—Nonsense!—Laura? Oh, Laura!

LAURA (*offstage, faintly*). Yes, Mother.

AMANDA. You really must come to the table. We won't be seated until you come to the table! Come in, Mr. O'Connor. You sit over there, and I'll—Laura? Laura Wingfield! You're keeping us waiting, honey! We can't say grace until you come to the table!

(*The back door is pushed weakly open and Laura comes in. She is obviously quite faint, her lips trembling, her eyes wide and staring. She moves unsteadily toward the table.*)

(*Legend: "Terror!"*)

(*Outside a summer storm is coming abruptly. The white curtains billow inward at the windows and there is a sorrowful murmur and deep blue dusk.*)

(*Laura suddenly stumbles—she catches at a chair with a faint moan.*)

TOM. Laura!

AMANDA. Laura! (*There is a clap of thunder.*) (*Legend: "Ah!"*) (*Despairingly.*) Why, Laura, you are sick, darling! Tom, help your sister into the living room, dear! Sit in the living room, Laura—rest on the sofa. Well! (*To the gentleman caller.*) Standing over the hot stove made her ill!—I told her that it was just too warm this evening, but—(*Tom comes back in. Laura is on the sofa.*) Is Laura all right now?

TOM. Yes.

AMANDA. What is that? Rain? A nice cool rain has come up! (*She gives the gentleman caller a frightened look.*) I think we may—have grace—now . . . (*Tom looks at her stupidly.*) Tom, honey—you say grace!

TOM. Oh . . . "For these and all thy mercies—" (*They bow their heads, Amanda stealing a nervous glance at Jim. In the living room Laura, stretched on the sofa, clenches her hand to her lips, to hold back a shuddering sob.*) God's Holy Name be praised—

(*The scene dims out.*)

SCENE VII

(*A Souvenir*)

(*Half an hour later. Dinner is just being finished in the upstage area which is concealed by the drawn portieres.*)

(*As the curtain rises Laura is still huddled upon the sofa, her feet drawn under her, her head resting on a pale blue pillow, her eyes wide and mysteriously watchful. The new floor lamp with its shade of rose-colored silk gives a soft, becoming light to her face, bringing out the fragile, unearthly prettiness which usually escapes attention. There is a steady murmur of rain, but it is slackening and stops soon after the scene begins; the air outside becomes pale and luminous as the moon breaks out.*)

(*A moment after the curtain rises, the lights in both rooms flicker and go out.*)

JIM. Hey, there, Mr. Light Bulb!

(*Amanda laughs nervously.*)

(*Legend: "Suspension of a Public Service."*)

AMANDA. Where was Moses when the lights went out? Ha-ha. Do you know the answer to that one, Mr. O'Connor?

JIM. No, Ma'am, what's the answer?

AMANDA.   In the dark! *(Jim laughs appreciably.)* Everybody sit still. I'll light the candles. Isn't it lucky we have them on the table? Where's a match? Which of you gentlemen can provide a match?

JIM.   Here.

AMANDA.   Thank you, sir.

JIM.   Not at all, Ma'am!

AMANDA.   I guess the fuse has burnt out. Mr. O'Connor, can you tell a burnt-out fuse? I know I can't and Tom is a total loss when it comes to mechanics. *(Sound: getting up: voices recede a little to kitchenette.)* Oh, be careful you don't bump into something. We don't want our gentleman caller to break his neck. Now wouldn't that be a fine howdy-do?

JIM.   Ha-ha! Where is the fuse box?

AMANDA.   Right here next to the stove. Can you see anything?

JIM.   Just a minute.

AMANDA.   Isn't electricity a mysterious thing? Wasn't it Benjamin Franklin who tied a key to a kite? We live in such a mysterious universe, don't we? Some people say that science clears up all the mysteries for us. In my opinion it only creates more! Have you found it yet?

JIM.   No, Ma'am. All these fuses look okay to me.

AMANDA.   Tom!

TOM.   Yes, Mother?

AMANDA.   That light bill I gave you several days ago. The one I told you we got the notices about?

TOM.   Oh.—Yeah.

(Legend: "Ha!")

AMANDA.   You didn't neglect to pay it by any chance?

TOM.   Why, I—

AMANDA.   Didn't! I might have known it!

JIM.   Shakespeare probably wrote a poem on that light bill, Mrs. Wingfield.

AMANDA.   I might have known better than to trust him with it! There's such a high price for negligence in this world!

JIM.   Maybe the poem will win a ten-dollar prize.

AMANDA.   We'll just have to spend the remainder of the evening in the nineteenth century, before Mr. Edison made the Mazda lamp!

JIM.   Candlelight is my favorite kind of light.

AMANDA.   That shows you're romantic! But that's no excuse for Tom. Well, we got through dinner. Very considerate of them to let us get through dinner before they plunged us into everlasting darkness, wasn't it, Mr. O'Connor?

JIM.   Ha-ha!

AMANDA.   Tom, as a penalty for your carelessness you can help me with the dishes.

JIM.   Let me give you a hand.

AMANDA.   Indeed you will not!

JIM.   I ought to be good for something.

AMANDA.   Good for something? *(Her tone is rhapsodic.)* You? Why, Mr. O'Connor, nobody, *nobody's* given me this much entertainment in years—as you have!

JIM.   Aw, now, Mrs. Wingfield!

AMANDA.   I'm not exaggerating, not one bit! But Sister is all by her lonesome. You go keep her company in the parlor! I'll give you this lovely old candelabrum that used

Mazda lamp: the first incandescent lamp.

to be on the altar at the church of the Heavenly Rest. It was melted a little out of shape when the church burnt down. Lightning struck it one spring. Gypsy Jones was holding a revival at the time and he intimated that the church was destroyed because the Episcopalians gave card parties.

JIM.   Ha-ha.

AMANDA.   And how about coaxing Sister to drink a little wine? I think it would be good for her! Can you carry both at once?

JIM.   Sure. I'm Superman!

AMANDA.   Now, Thomas, get into this apron!

(The door of kitchenette swings closed on Amanda's gay laughter; the flickering light approaches the portieres.)

(Laura sits up nervously as he enters. Her speech at first is low and breathless from the almost intolerable strain of being alone with a stranger.)

(The legend: "I Don't Suppose You Remember Me at All!")

(In her first speeches in this scene, before Jim's warmth overcomes her paralyzing shyness, Laura's voice is thin and breathless as though she has just run up a steep flight of stairs.)

(Jim's attitude is gently humorous. In playing this scene it should be stressed that while the incident is apparently unimportant, it is to Laura the climax of her secret life.)

JIM.   Hello, there, Laura.

LAURA *(faintly)*.   Hello. *(She clears her throat.)*

JIM.   How are you feeling now? Better?

LAURA.   Yes. Yes, thank you.

JIM.   This is for you. A little dandelion wine. *(He extends it toward her with extravagant gallantry.)*

LAURA.   Thank you.

JIM.   Drink it—but don't get drunk! *(He laughs heartily. Laura takes the glass uncertainly; laughs shyly.)* Where shall I set the candles?

LAURA.   Oh—oh, anywhere . . .

JIM.   How about here on the floor? Any objections?

LAURA.   No.

JIM.   I'll spread a newspaper under to catch the drippings. I like to sit on the floor. Mind if I do?

LAURA.   Oh, no.

JIM.   Give me a pillow?

LAURA.   What?

JIM.   A pillow!

LAURA.   Oh . . . *(Hands him one quickly.)*

JIM.   How about you? Don't you like to sit on the floor?

LAURA.   Oh—yes.

JIM.   Why don't you, then?

LAURA.   I—will.

JIM.   Take a pillow! *(Laura does. Sits on the other side of the candelabrum. Jim crosses his legs and smiles engagingly at her.)* I can't hardly see you sitting way over there.

LAURA.   I can—see you.

JIM.   I know, but that's not fair, I'm in the limelights. *(Laura moves her pillow closer.)* Good! Now I can see you! Comfortable?

LAURA.   Yes.

JIM.   So am I. Comfortable as a cow. Will you have some gum?

LAURA.   No, thank you.

JIM.   I think that I will indulge, with your permission. *(Musingly unwraps it and holds it up.)* Think of the fortune made by the guy that invented the first piece of chewing gum. Amazing, huh? The Wrigley Building is one of the sights of Chicago.—I saw it summer before last when I went up to the Century of Progress. Did you take in the Century of Progress?

LAURA.   No, I didn't.

JIM.   Well, it was quite a wonderful exposition. What impressed me most was the Hall of Science. Gives you an idea of what the future will be in America, even more wonderful than the present time is! *(pause. Smiling at her.)* Your brother tells me you're shy. Is that right, Laura?

LAURA.   I—don't know.

JIM.   I judge you to be an old-fashioned type of girl. Well, I think that's a pretty good type to be. Hope you don't think I'm being too personal—do you?

LAURA *(hastily, out of embarrassment).*   I believe I *will* take a piece of gum, if you— don't mind. *(Clearing her throat.)* Mr. O'Connor, have you—kept up with your singing?

JIM.   Singing? Me?

LAURA.   Yes. I remember what a beautiful voice you had.

JIM.   When did you hear me sing?

(Voice offstage in the pause.)

VOICE *(offstage).*   O blow, ye winds, heigh-ho,
        A-roving I will go!
           I'm off to my love
           With a boxing glove—
           Ten thousand miles away!

JIM.   You say you've heard me sing?

LAURA.   Oh, yes! Yes, very often .. . I—don't suppose you remember me—at all?

JIM *(smiling doubtfully).*   You know I have an idea I've seen you before. I had that idea soon as you opened the door. It seemed almost like I was about to remember your name. But the name that I started to call you—wasn't a name! And so I stopped myself before I said it.

LAURA.   Wasn't it—Blue Roses?

JIM *(springs up. Grinning).*   Blue Roses! My gosh, yes—Blue Roses! That's what I had on my tongue when you opened the door! Isn't it funny what tricks your memory plays? I didn't connect you with the high school somehow or other. But that's where it was; it was high school. I didn't even know you were Shakespeare's sister! Gosh, I'm sorry.

LAURA.   I didn't expect you to. You—barely knew me!

JIM.   But we did have a speaking acquaintance, huh?

LAURA.   Yes, we—spoke to each other.

JIM.   When did you recognize me?

LAURA.   Oh, right away!

JIM.   Soon as I came in the door?

LAURA.   When I heard your name I thought it was probably you. I knew that Tom used to know you a little in high school. So when you came in the door—Well, then I was—sure.

JIM.   Why didn't you say something, then?

LAURA *(breathlessly).*   I didn't know what to say, I was—too surprised!

JIM.   For goodness' sakes! You know, this sure is funny!

LAURA.   Yes! Yes, isn't it, though . . .

JIM.   Didn't we have a class in something together?

LAURA.   Yes, we did.

JIM.   What class was that?

LAURA.   It was—singing—Chorus!

JIM.   Aw!

LAURA.   I sat across the aisle from you in the Aud.

JIM.   Aw.

LAURA.   Mondays, Wednesdays, and Fridays.

JIM.   Now I remember—you always came in late.

LAURA.   Yes, it was so hard for me, getting upstairs. I had that brace on my leg—it clumped so loud!

JIM.   I never heard any clumping.

LAURA *(wincing at the recollection)*.   To me it sounded like—thunder!

JIM.   Well, well, well, I never even noticed.

LAURA.   And everybody was seated before I came in. I had to walk in front of all those people. My seat was in the back row. I had to go clumping all the way up the aisle with everyone watching!

JIM.   You shouldn't have been self-conscious.

LAURA.   I know, but I was. It was always such a relief when the singing started.

JIM.   Aw, yes, I've placed you now! I used to call you Blue Roses. How was it that I got started calling you that?

LAURA.   I was out of school a little while with pleurosis. When I came back you asked me what was the matter. I said I had pleurosis—you thought I said Blue Roses. That's what you always called me after that!

JIM.   I hope you didn't mind.

LAURA.   Oh, no—I liked it. You see, I wasn't acquainted with many—people. . . .

JIM.   As I remember you sort of stuck by yourself.

LAURA.   I—I—never had much luck at—making friends.

JIM.   I don't see why you wouldn't.

LAURA.   Well, I—started out badly.

JIM.   You mean being—

LAURA.   Yes, it sort of—stood between me—

JIM.   You shouldn't have let it!

LAURA.   I know, but it did, and—

JIM.   You were shy with people!

LAURA.   I tried not to be but never could—

JIM.   Overcome it?

LAURA.   No, I—I never could!

JIM.   I guess being shy is something you have to work out of kind of gradually.

LAURA *(sorrowfully)*.   Yes—I guess it—

JIM.   Takes time!

LAURA.   Yes—

JIM.   People are not so dreadful when you know them. That's what you have to remember! And everybody has problems, not just you, but practically everybody has got some problems. You think of yourself as having the only problems, as being the only one who is disappointed. But just look around you and you will see lots of people as disappointed as you are. For instance, I hoped when I was going to high school that I would be further along at this time, six years later, than I am now—You remember that wonderful write-up I had in *The Torch?*

LAURA.   Yes! *(She rises and crosses to table.)*

JIM.   It said I was bound to succeed in anything I went into! *(Laura returns with the annual.)* Holy Jeez! *The Torch!*(He accepts it reverently. They smile across it with mutual wonder. Laura crouches beside him and they begin to turn through it. Laura's shyness is dissolving in his warmth.)*

LAURA.   Here you are in *Pirates of Penzance!*

JIM *(wistfully).*   I sang the baritone lead in that operetta.

LAURA *(rapidly).*   So—*beautifully!*

JIM *(protesting).*   Aw—

LAURA.   Yes, yes—beautifully—beautifully!

JIM.   You heard me?

LAURA.   All three times!

JIM.   No!

LAURA.   Yes!

JIM.   All three performances?

LAURA *(looking down).*   Yes.

JIM.   Why?

LAURA.   I—wanted to ask you to—autograph my program.

JIM.   Why didn't you ask me to?

LAURA.   You were always surrounded by your own friends so much that I never had a chance to.

JIM.   You should have just—

LAURA.   Well, I—thought you might think I was—

JIM.   Thought I might think you was—what?

LAURA.   Oh—

JIM *(with reflective relish).*   I was beleaguered by females in those days.

LAURA.   You were terribly popular!

JIM.   Yeah—

LAURA.   You had such a—friendly way—

JIM.   I was spoiled in high school.

LAURA.   Everybody—liked you!

JIM.   Including you?

LAURA.   I—yes, I—I did, too—*(She gently closes the book in her lap.)*

JIM.   Well, well, well!—Give me that program, Laura. *(She hands it to him. He signs it with a flourish.)* There you are—better late than never!

LAURA.   Oh, I—what a—surprise!

JIM.   My signature isn't worth very much right now. But some day—maybe—it will increase in value! Being disappointed is one thing and being discouraged is something else. I am disappointed but I am not discouraged. I'm twenty-three years old. How old are you?

LAURA.   I'll be twenty-four in June.

JIM.   That's not old age!

LAURA.   No, but—

JIM.   You finished high school?

LAURA *(with difficulty).*   I didn't go back.

JIM.   You mean you dropped out?

LAURA.   I made bad grades in my final examinations. *(She rises and replaces the book and the program. Her voice strained.)* How is—Emily Meisenbach getting along?

JIM.   Oh, that kraut-head!

LAURA.   Why do you call her that?

JIM.   That's what she was.

LAURA.   You're not still—going with her?

JIM.   I never see her.

LAURA.   It said in the Personal Section that you were—engaged!

JIM.   I know, but I wasn't impressed by that—propaganda!

LAURA.   It wasn't—the truth?

JIM.   Only in Emily's optimistic opinion!

LAURA.   Oh—

(Legend: "What Have You Done since High School?")

(Jim lights a cigarette and leans indolently back on his elbows smiling at Laura with a warmth and charm which lights her inwardly with altar candles. She remains by the table and turns in her hands a piece of glass to cover her tumult.)

JIM *(after several reflective puffs on a cigarette).*   What have you done since high school? *(She seems not to hear him.)* Huh? *(Laura looks up.)* I said what have you done since high school, Laura?

LAURA.   Nothing much.

JIM.   You must have been doing something these six long years.

LAURA.   Yes.

JIM.   Well, then, such as what?

LAURA.   I took a business course at business college—

JIM.   How did that work out?

LAURA.   Well, not very—well—I had to drop out, it gave me—indigestion—

(Jim laughs gently.)

JIM.   What are you doing now?

LAURA.   I don't do anything—much. Oh, please don't think I sit around doing nothing! My glass collection takes up a good deal of my time. Glass is something you have to take good care of.

JIM.   What did you say—about glass?

LAURA.   Collection I said—I have one—*(She clears her throat and turns away again, acutely shy.)*

JIM *(abruptly).*   You know what I judge to be the trouble with you? Inferiority complex! Know what that is? That's what they call it when someone low-rates himself! I understand it because I had it, too. Although my case was not so aggravated as yours seems to be. I had it until I took up public speaking, developed my voice, and learned that I had an aptitude for science. Before that time I never thought of myself as being outstanding in any way whatsoever! Now I've never made a regular study of it, but I have a friend who says I can analyze people better than doctors that make a profession of it. I don't claim that to be necessarily true, but I can sure guess a person's psychology, Laura! *(Takes out his gum.)* Excuse me, Laura. I always take it out when the flavor is gone. I'll use this scrap of paper to wrap it in. I know how it is to get it stuck on a shoe. Yep—that's what I judge to be your principal trouble. A lack of confidence in yourself as a person. You don't have the proper amount of faith in yourself. I'm basing that fact on a number of your remarks and also on certain observations I've made. For instance that clumping you thought was so awful in high school. You say that you even dreaded to walk into class. You see what you did? You dropped out of school, you gave up an education because of a clump, which as far as I know was practically nonexistent! A little physical defect is what you have. Hardly noticeable even! Magnified thousands of times by imagination! You know what my strong advice to you is? Think of yourself as *superior* in some way!

LAURA. In what way would I think?

JIM. Why, man alive, Laura! Just look about you a little. What do you see? A world full of common people! All of 'em born and all of 'em going to die! Which of them has one-tenth of your good points! Or mine! Or anyone else's, as far as that goes—Gosh! Everybody excels in some one thing. Some in many! *(Unconsciously glances at himself in the mirror.)* All you've got to do is discover in what! Take me, for instance. *(He adjusts his tie at the mirror.)* My interest happens to lie in electrodynamics. I'm taking a course in radio engineering at night school, Laura, on top of a fairly responsible job at the warehouse. I'm taking that course and studying public speaking.

LAURA. Ohhhh.

JIM. Because I believe in the future of television! *(Turning back to her.)* I wish to be ready to go up right along with it. Therefore I'm planning to get in on the ground floor. In fact, I've already made the right connections and all that remains is for the industry itself to get under way! Full steam—*(His eyes are starry.)* Knowledge—Zzzzzp! Money—Zzzzzp!—*Power!* That's the cycle democracy is built on! *(His attitude is convincingly dynamic. Laura stares at him, even her shyness eclipsed in her absolute wonder. He suddenly grins.)* I guess you think I think a lot of myself!

LAURA. No—o-o-o, I—

JIM. Now how about you? Isn't there something you take more interest in than anything else?

LAURA. Well, I do—as I said—have my—glass collection—

(A peal of girlish laughter from the kitchen.)

JIM. I'm not right sure I know what you're talking about. What kind of glass is it?

LAURA. Little articles of it, they're ornaments mostly! Most of them are little animals made out of glass, the tiniest little animals in the world. Mother calls them a glass menagerie! Here's an example of one, if you'd like to see it! This one is one of the oldest. It's nearly thirteen. *(He stretches out his hand.)* *(Music: "The Glass Menagerie.")* Oh, be careful—if you breathe, it breaks!

JIM. I'd better not take it. I'm pretty clumsy with things.

LAURA. Go on, I trust you with him! *(Places it in his palm.)* There now—you're holding him gently! Hold him over the light, he loves the light! You see how the light shines through him?

JIM. It sure does shine!

LAURA. I shouldn't be partial, but he is my favorite one.

JIM. What kind of a thing is this one supposed to be?

LAURA. Haven't you noticed the single horn on his forehead?

JIM. A unicorn, huh?

LAURA. Mmm-hmmm!

JIM. Unicorns, aren't they extinct in the modern world?

LAURA. I know!

JIM. Poor little fellow, he must feel sort of lonesome.

LAURA *(smiling).* Well, if he does he doesn't complain about it. He stays on a shelf with some horses that don't have horns and all of them seem to get along nicely together.

JIM. How do you know?

LAURA *(lightly).* I haven't heard any arguments among them!

JIM *(grinning).* No arguments, huh? Well, that's a pretty good sign! Where shall I set him?

LAURA. Put him on the table. They all like a change of scenery once in a while!

JIM *(stretching)*. Well, well, well, well—Look how big my shadow is when I stretch!

LAURA. Oh, oh, yes—it stretches across the ceiling!

JIM *(crossing to door)*. I think it's stopped raining. *(Opens fire escape door.)* Where does the music come from?

LAURA. From the Paradise Dance Hall across the alley.

JIM. How about cutting the rug a little, Miss Wingfield?

LAURA. Oh, I—

JIM. Or is your program filled up? Let me have a look at it. *(Grasps imaginary card.)* Why, every dance is taken! I'll just have to scratch some out. *(Waltz music: "La Golondrina.")* Ahhh, a waltz! *(He executes some sweeping turns by himself then holds his arms toward Laura.)*

LAURA *(breathlessly)*. I—can't dance!

JIM. There you go, that inferiority stuff!

LAURA. I've never danced in my life!

JIM. Come on, try!

LAURA. Oh, but I'd step on you!

JIM. I'm not made out of glass.

LAURA. How—how—how do we start?

JIM. Just leave it to me. You hold your arms out a little.

LAURA. Like this?

JIM. A little bit higher. Right. Now don't tighten up, that's the main thing about it—relax.

LAURA *(laughing breathlessly)*. It's hard not to.

JIM. Okay.

LAURA. I'm afraid you can't budge me.

JIM. What do you bet I can't? *(He swings her into motion.)*

LAURA. Goodness, yes, you can!

JIM. Let yourself go, now, Laura, just let yourself go.

LAURA. I'm—

JIM. Come on!

LAURA. Trying!

JIM. Not so stiff—Easy does it!

LAURA. I know but I'm—

JIM. Loosen th' backbone! There now, that's a lot better.

LAURA. Am I?

JIM. Lots, lots better! *(He moves her about the room in a clumsy waltz.)*

LAURA. Oh, my!

JIM. Ha-ha!

LAURA. Oh, my goodness!

JIM. Ha-ha-ha! *(They suddenly bump into the table. Jim stops.)* What did we hit on?

LAURA. Table.

JIM. Did something fall off it? I think—

LAURA. Yes.

JIM. I hope that it wasn't the little glass horse with the horn!

LAURA. Yes.

JIM. Aw, aw, aw. Is it broken?

LAURA. Now it is just like all the other horses.

JIM. It's lost its—

LAURA. Horn! It doesn't matter. Maybe it's a blessing in disguise.

JIM. You'll never forgive me. I bet that that was your favorite piece of glass.

LAURA. I don't have favorites much. It's no tragedy, Freckles. Glass breaks so easily. No matter how careful you are. The traffic jars the shelves and things fall off them.

JIM. Still I'm awfully sorry that I was the cause.

LAURA *(smiling)*. I'll just imagine he had an operation. The horn was removed to make him feel less—freakish! *(They both laugh.)* Now he will feel more at home with the other horses, the ones that don't have horns . . .

JIM. Ha-ha, that's very funny! *(Suddenly serious.)* I'm glad to see that you have a sense of humor. You know—you're—well—very different! Surprisingly different from anyone else I know! *(His voice becomes soft and hesitant with a genuine feeling.)* Do you mind me telling you that? *(Laura is abashed beyond speech.)* I mean it in a nice way . . . *(Laura nods shyly, looking away.)* You make me feel sort of—I don't know how to put it! I'm usually pretty good at expressing things, but—This is something that I don't know how to say! *(Laura touches her throat and clears it—turns the broken unicorn in her hands. Even softer.)* Has anyone ever told you that you were pretty? *(Pause: Music. Laura looks up slowly, with wonder, and shakes her head.)* Well, you are! In a very different way from anyone else. And all the nicer because of the difference, too. *(His voice becomes low and husky. Laura turns away, nearly faint with the novelty of her emotions.)* I wish that you were my sister. I'd teach you to have some confidence in yourself. The different people are not like other people, but being different is nothing to be ashamed of. Because other people are not such wonderful people. They're one hundred times one thousand. You're one times one! They walk all over the earth. You just stay here. They're common as—weeds, but—you—well, you're—*Blue Roses!*

(Image on screen: blue roses.)

(Music changes.)

LAURA. But blue is wrong for—roses . . .

JIM. It's right for you—You're—pretty!

LAURA. In what respect am I pretty?

JIM. In all respects—believe me! Your eyes—your hair—are pretty! Your hands are pretty! *(He catches hold of her hand.)* You think I'm making this up because I'm invited to dinner and have to be nice. Oh, I could do that! I could put on an act for you, Laura, and say lots of things without being very sincere. But this time I am. I'm talking to you sincerely. I happened to notice you had this inferiority complex that keeps you from feeling comfortable with people. Somebody needs to build your confidence up and make you proud instead of shy and turning away and—blushing—Somebody ought to—Ought to—kiss you, Laura! *(His hand slips slowly up her arm to her shoulder. Music swells tumultuously. He suddenly turns her about and kisses her on the lips. When he releases her Laura sinks on the sofa with a bright, dazed look. Jim backs away and fishes in his pocket for a cigarette.) (Legend on screen: "Souvenir.")* Stumble-john! *(He lights the cigarette, avoiding her look. There is a peal of girlish laughter from Amanda in the kitchen. Laura slowly raises and opens her hand. It still contains the little broken glass animal. She looks at it with a tender, bewildered expression.)* Stumble-john! I shouldn't have done that—That was way off the beam. You don't smoke, do you? *(She looks up, smiling, not hearing the question. He sits beside her a little gingerly. She looks at him speechlessly—waiting. He coughs decorously and moves a little farther aside as he considers the situation and senses her feelings, dimly, with perturbation. Gently.)* Would you—care for a—mint? *(She doesn't seem to hear him but her look grows brighter even.)* Peppermint—Life Saver? My pocket's a regular drugstore—wherever I go . . . *(He pops a mint in his mouth. Then gulps and decides to make a clean breast of it. He speaks slowly and gingerly.)* Laura, you know, if I had a sister like you, I'd do the same thing as Tom. I'd bring out fellows and—introduce her to them. The right type of boys of a type to—appreciate her. Only—well—he made a mistake about me. Maybe I've got no call to be saying this. That may not have been the idea in having me over. But what if it was? There's nothing wrong about that. The only trouble is that in my case—I'm not in a situation to—do the right thing. I can't take down your number and say I'll phone. I can't call up next week and—ask for a date. I thought I had better explain the situation in case you misunderstood it and—hurt your feelings. . . . *(Pause. Slowly, very slowly, Laura's look changes, her eyes returning slowly from his to the ornament in her palm.)*

(Amanda utters another gay laugh in the kitchen.)

LAURA *(faintly).* You—won't—call again?

JIM. No, Laura, I can't. *(He rises from the sofa.)* As I was just explaining, I've—got strings on me, Laura, I've—been going steady! I go out all the time with a girl named Betty. She's a home-girl like you, and Catholic, and Irish, and in a great many ways we—get along fine. I met her last summer on a moonlight boat trip up the river to Alton, on the *Majestic*. Well—right away from the start it was—love! *(Legend: Love!) (Laura sways slightly forward and grips the arm of the sofa. He fails to notice, now enrapt in his own comfortable being.)* Being in love has made a new man of me! *(Leaning stiffly forward, clutching the arm of the sofa, Laura struggles visibly with her storm. But Jim is oblivious, she is a long way off.)* The power of love is really pretty tremendous! Love is something that—changes the whole world, Laura! *(The storm abates a little and Laura leans back. He notices her again.)* It happened that Betty's aunt took sick, she got a wire and had to go to Centralia. So Tom—when he asked me to dinner—I naturally just accepted the invitation, not knowing that you—that he—that I—*(He stops awkwardly.)* Huh—I'm a stumble-john! *(He flops back on the sofa. The holy candles in the altar of Laura's face have been snuffed out! There is a look of almost infinite desolation. Jim glances at her uneasily.)* I wish that you would—say something. *(She bites her lip which was trembling and then bravely smiles. She opens her hand again on the broken glass ornament. Then she gently takes his hand and raises it level with her own. She carefully places the unicorn in the palm of his hand, then pushes his fingers closed upon it.)* What are you—doing that for? You want me to have him?—Laura? *(She nods.)* What for?

LAURA. A—souvenir . . .

(She rises unsteadily and crouches beside the victrola to wind it up.)

(Legend on screen: "Things Have a Way of Turning out so Badly.")

(Or Image: "Gentleman Caller Waving Good-bye!—Gaily.")

(At this moment Amanda rushes brightly back in the front room. She bears a pitcher of fruit punch in an old-fashioned cut-glass pitcher and a plate of macaroons. The plate has a gold border and poppies painted on it.)

AMANDA. Well, well, well! Isn't the air delightful after the shower? I've made you children a little liquid refreshment. *(Turns gaily to the gentleman caller.)* Jim, do you know that song about lemonade?

"Lemonade, lemonade
Made in the shade and stirred with a spade—
Good enough for any old maid!"

JIM *(uneasily).* Ha-ha! No—I never heard it.

AMANDA. Why, Laura! You look so serious!

JIM. We were having a serious conversation.

AMANDA. Good! Now you're better acquainted!

JIM (*uncertainly*).   Ha-ha! Yes.

AMANDA.   You modern young people are much more serious-minded than my generation. I was so gay as a girl!

JIM.   You haven't changed, Mrs. Wingfield.

AMANDA.   Tonight I'm rejuvenated! The gaiety of the occasion, Mr. O'Connor! (*She tosses her head with a peal of laughter. Spills lemonade.*) Oooo! I'm baptizing myself!

JIM.   Here—let me—

AMANDA (*setting the pitcher down*).   There now. I discovered we had some maraschino cherries. I dumped them in, juice and all!

JIM.   You shouldn't have gone to that trouble, Mrs. Wingfield.

AMANDA.   Trouble, trouble? Why it was loads of fun! Didn't you hear me cutting up in the kitchen? I bet your ears were burning! I told Tom how outdone with him I was for keeping you to himself so long a time! He should have brought you over much, much sooner! Well, now that you've found your way, I want you to be a very frequent caller! Not just occasional but all the time. Oh, we're going to have a lot of gay times together! I see them coming! Mmm, just breathe that air! So fresh, and the moon's so pretty! I'll skip back out—I know where my place is when young folks are having a—serious conversation!

JIM.   Oh, don't go out, Mrs. Wingfield. The fact of the matter is I've got to be going.

AMANDA.   Going, now? You're joking! Why, it's only the shank of the evening, Mr. O'Connor!

JIM.   Well, you know how it is.

AMANDA.   You mean you're a young workingman and have to keep workingmen's hours. We'll let you off early tonight. But only on the condition that next time you stay later. What's the best night for you? Isn't Saturday night the best night for you workingmen?

JIM.   I have a couple of time clocks to punch, Mrs. Wingfield. One at morning, another one at night!

AMANDA.   My, but you *are* ambitious! You work at night, too?

JIM.   No, Ma'am, not work but—Betty! (*He crosses deliberately to pick up his hat. The band at the Paradise Dance Hall goes into a tender waltz.*)

AMANDA.   Betty? Betty? Who's—Betty! (*There is an ominous cracking sound in the sky.*)

JIM.   Oh, just a girl. The girl I go steady with! (*He smiles charmingly. The sky falls.*)

(*Legend: "The Sky Falls."*)

AMANDA (*a long-drawn exhalation*).   Ohhhh . . . Is it a serious romance, Mr. O'Connor?

JIM.   We're going to be married the second Sunday in June.

AMANDA.   Ohhhh—how nice! Tom didn't mention that you were engaged to be married.

JIM.   The cat's not out of the bag at the warehouse yet. You know how they are. They call you Romeo and stuff like that. (*He stops at the oval mirror to put on his hat. He carefully shapes the brim and the crown to give a discreetly dashing effect.*) It's been a wonderful evening, Mrs. Wingfield. I guess this is what they mean by Southern hospitality.

AMANDA.   It really wasn't anything at all.

JIM.   I hope it don't seem like I'm rushing off. But I promised Betty I'd pick her up at the Wabash depot, an' by the time I get my jalopy down there her train'll be in. Some women are pretty upset if you keep 'em waiting.

AMANDA.   Yes, I know—The tyranny of women! (*Extends her hand.*) Good-bye, Mr. O'Connor. I wish you luck—and happiness—and success! All three of them, and so does Laura!—Don't you, Laura?

LAURA. Yes!

JIM *(taking her hand).* Good-bye, Laura. I'm certainly going to treasure that souvenir. And don't you forget the good advice I gave you. *(Raises his voice to a cheery shout.)* So long, Shakespeare! Thanks again, ladies—Good night!

(He grins and ducks jauntily out.)

(Still bravely grimacing, Amanda closes the door on the gentleman caller. Then she turns back to the room with a puzzled expression. She and Laura don't dare to face each other. Laura crouches beside the victrola to wind it.)

AMANDA *(faintly).* Things have a way of turning out so badly. I don't believe that I would play the victrola. Well, well—well—Our gentleman caller was engaged to be married! Tom!

TOM *(from back).* Yes, Mother?

AMANDA. Come in here a minute. I want to tell you something awfully funny.

TOM *(enters with macaroon and a glass of the lemonade).* Has the gentleman caller gotten away already?

AMANDA. The gentleman caller has made an early departure. What a wonderful joke you played on us!

TOM. How do you mean?

AMANDA. You didn't mention that he was engaged to be married.

TOM. Jim? Engaged?

AMANDA. That's what he just informed us.

TOM. I'll be jiggered! I didn't know about that.

AMANDA. That seems very peculiar.

TOM. What's peculiar about it?

AMANDA. Didn't you call him your best friend down at the warehouse?

TOM. He is, but how did I know?

AMANDA. It seems extremely peculiar that you wouldn't know your best friend was going to be married!

TOM. The warehouse is where I work, not where I know things about people!

AMANDA. You don't know things anywhere! You live in a dream; you manufacture illusions! *(He crosses to door.)* Where are you going?

TOM. I'm going to the movies.

AMANDA. That's right, now that you've had us make such fools of ourselves. The effort, the preparations, all the expense! The new floor lamp, the rug, the clothes for Laura! All for what? To entertain some other girl's fiancé! Go to the movies, go! Don't think about us, a mother deserted, an unmarried sister who's crippled and has no job! Don't let anything interfere with your selfish pleasure! Just go, go, go—to the movies!

TOM. All right, I will! The more you shout about my selfishness to me the quicker I'll go, and I won't go to the movies!

AMANDA. Go, then! Then go to the moon—you selfish dreamer!

(Tom smashes his glass on the floor. He plunges out on the fire escape, slamming the door. Laura screams—cut by door.)

(Dance-hall music up. Tom goes to the rail and grips it desperately, lifting his face in the chill white moonlight penetrating the narrow abyss of the alley.)

(Legend on screen: And so Good-bye . . .")

(Tom's closing speech is timed with the interior pantomime. The interior scene is played as though viewed through soundproof glass. Amanda appears to be making a comforting speech to Laura who is huddled upon the sofa. Now that we cannot hear the mother's speech, her silliness is gone and she has dignity and tragic beauty. Laura's dark hair hides her face until at the end of the speech she lifts it to smile at her mother. Amanda's gestures are slow and graceful, almost dancelike, as she comforts the daughter. At the end of her speech she glances a moment at the father's picture— then withdraws through the portieres. At close of Tom's speech, Laura blows out the candles, ending the play.)

TOM.   I didn't go to the moon, I went much further—for time is the longest distance between two places—Not long after that I was fired for writing a poem on the lid of a shoebox. I left Saint Louis. I descended the steps of this fire escape for a last time and followed, from then on, in my father's footsteps, attempting to find in motion what was lost in space—I traveled around a great deal. The cities swept about me like dead leaves, leaves that were brightly colored but torn away from the branches. I would have stopped, but I was pursued by something. It always came upon me unawares, taking me altogether by surprise. Perhaps it was a familiar bit of music. Perhaps it was only a piece of transparent glass—Perhaps I am walking along a street at night, in some strange city, before I have found companions. I pass the lighted window of a shop where perfume is sold. The window is filled with pieces of colored glass, tiny transparent bottles in delicate colors, like bits of a shattered rainbow. Then all at once my sister touches my shoulder. I turn around and look into her eyes . . . Oh, Laura, Laura, I tried to leave you behind me, but I am more faithful than I intended to be! I reach for a cigarette, I cross the street, I run into the movies or a bar, I buy a drink, I speak to the nearest stranger—anything that can blow your candles out! *(Laura bends over the candles.)*—for nowadays the world is lit by lightning! Blow out your candles, Laura—and so good-bye. . . .

(She blows the candles out.)

(The scene dissolves.)

AUGUST WILSON   (b. 1945)

*August Wilson spent much of the period of the 1960s and 1970s in civil rights activities, during which time he described himself as a black nationalist. He began writing plays in his native Pittsburgh and continued when he moved to St. Paul to work for the Science Museum of Minnesota. Many of his dramatic skits were performed at the museum. He joined the Playwrights Center in Minneapolis and began a professional career writing plays for performance there. *Jitney, about gypsy cabs, was produced in 1982. His first Broadway play was* Ma Rainey's Black Bottom *(1984), which won the New York Drama Critics' Circle Award.* Fences *followed in 1985, winning the Drama Critics' Circle Award and the Pulitzer Prize. Wilson won the Drama Critics' Circle Award again in 1988 for* Joe Turner's Come and Gone. *These have been followed by two highly successful plays,* The Piano Lesson *(1987) and* Two Trains Running *(1992). The last five plays all premiered earlier at the Yale Repertory Theatre under the direction of Lloyd Richards, and then moved to Broadway. The plays are part of a large cycle projected by Wilson to cover the experience of African-Americans. Wilson has said, "I think the black Americans have the most dramatic story of all mankind to tell."* Seven Guitars *(1994) and* King Hedley II *(2001) are his most recent plays.*

Fences ———————————————————————————— *1987*

Characters

Troy Maxson

Jim Bono, *Troy's friend*

Rose, *Troy's wife*

Lyons, *Troy's oldest son by previous marriage*

Gabriel, *Troy's brother*

Cory, *Troy and Rose's son*

Raynell, *Troy's daughter*

*(**Setting:** The setting is the yard which fronts the only entrance to the Maxson household, an ancient two-story brick house set back off a small alley in a big-city neighborhood. The entrance to the house is gained by two or three steps leading to a wooden porch badly in need of paint.)*

(A relatively recent addition to the house and running its full width, the porch lacks congruence. It is a sturdy porch with a flat roof. One or two chairs of dubious value sit at one end where the kitchen window opens onto the porch. An old-fashioned icebox stands silent guard at the opposite end.)

*(The yard is a small dirt yard, partially fenced, except for the last scene, with a wooden sawhorse, a pile of lumber, and other fence-building equipment set off to the side. Opposite is a tree from which hangs a ball made of rags. A baseball bat leans against the tree. Two oil drums serve as garbage receptacles and sit near the house at right to complete the setting.) (**The Play:** Near the turn of the century, the destitute of Europe sprang on the city with tenacious claws and an honest and solid dream. The city devoured them. They swelled its belly until it burst into a thousand furnaces and sewing machines, a thousand butcher shops and bakers' ovens, a thousand churches and hospitals and funeral parlors and money-lenders. The city grew. It nourished itself and offered each man a partnership limited only by his talent, his guile, and his willingness and capacity for hard work. For the immigrants of Europe, a dream dared and won true.)*

(The descendants of African slaves were offered no such welcome or participation. They came from places called the Carolinas and the Virginias, Georgia, Alabama, Mississippi, and Tennessee. They came strong, eager, searching. The city rejected them and they fled and settled along the riverbanks and under bridges in shallow, ramshackle houses made of sticks and tarpaper. They collected rags and wood. They sold the use of their muscles and their bodies. They cleaned houses and washed clothes, they shined shoes, and in quiet desperation and vengeful pride, they stole, and lived in pursuit of their own dream. That they could breathe free, finally, and stand to meet life with the force of dignity and whatever eloquence the heart could call upon.)

(By 1957, the hard-won victories of the European immigrants had solidified the industrial might of America. War had been confronted and won with new energies that used loyalty and patriotism as its fuel. Life was rich, full, and flourishing. The Milwaukee Braves won the World Series, and the hot winds of change that would make the sixties a turbulent, racing, dangerous, and provocative decade had not yet begun to blow full.)

ACT I

Scene I

(It is 1957. Troy and Bono enter the yard, engaged in conversation. Troy is fifty-three years old, a large man with thick, heavy hands; it is this largeness that he strives to fill out and make an

accommodation with. Together with his blackness, his largeness informs his sensibilities and the choices he has made in his life.)

(Of the two men, Bono is obviously the follower. His commitment to their friendship of thirty-odd years is rooted in his admiration of Troy's honesty, capacity for hard work, and his strength, which Bono seeks to emulate.)

(It is Friday night, payday, and the one night of the week the two men engage in a ritual of talk and drink. Troy is usually the most talkative and at times he can be crude and almost vulgar, though he is capable of rising to profound heights of expression. The men carry lunch buckets and wear or carry burlap aprons and are dressed in clothes suitable to their jobs as garbage collectors.)

BONO.   Troy, you ought to stop that lying!

TROY.   I ain't lying! The nigger had a watermelon this big. *(He indicates with his hands.)* Talking about . . . "What watermelon, Mr. Rand?" I liked to fell out! "What watermelon, Mr. Rand?" . . . And it sitting there big as life.

BONO.   What did Mr. Rand say?

TROY.   Ain't said nothing. Figure if the nigger too dumb to know he carrying a watermelon, he wasn't gonna get much sense out of him. Trying to hide that great big old watermelon under his coat. Afraid to let the white man see him carry it home.

BONO.   I'm like you . . . I ain't got no time for them kind of people.

TROY.   Now what he look like getting mad cause he see the man from the union talking to Mr. Rand?

BONO.   He come to me talking about . . . "Maxson gonna get us fired." I told him to get away from me with that. He walked away from me calling you a troublemaker. What Mr. Rand say?

TROY.   Ain't said nothing. He told me to go down the Commissioner's office next Friday. They called me down there to see them.

BONO.   Well, as long as you got your complaint filed, they can't fire you. That's what one of them white fellows tell me.

TROY.   I ain't worried about them firing me. They gonna fire me cause I asked a question? That's all I did. I went to Mr. Rand and asked him, "Why? Why you got the white mens driving and the colored lifting?" Told him, "what's the matter, don't I count? You think only white fellows got sense enough to drive a truck. That ain't no paper job! Hell, anybody can drive a truck. How come you got all whites driving and the colored lifting?" He told me "take it to the union." Well, hell, that's what I done! Now they wanna come up with this pack of lies.

BONO.   I told Brownie if the man come and ask him any questions . . . just tell the truth! It ain't nothing but something they done trumped up on you cause you filed a complaint on them.

TROY.   Brownie don't understand nothing. All I want them to do is change the job description. Give everybody a chance to drive the truck. Brownie can't see that. He ain't got that much sense.

BONO.   How you figure he be making out with that gal be up at Taylors' all the time . . . that Alberta gal?

TROY.   Same as you and me. Getting just as much as we is. Which is to say nothing.

BONO.   It is, huh? I figure you doing a little better than me . . . and I ain't saying what I'm doing.

TROY.   Aw, nigger, look here . . . I know you. If you had got anywhere near that gal, twenty minutes later you be looking to tell somebody. And the first one you gonna tell . . . that you gonna want to brag to . . . is gonna be me.

BONO.   I ain't saying that. I see where you be eyeing her.

TROY.   I eye all the women. I don't miss nothing. Don't never let nobody tell you Troy Maxson don't eye the women.

BONO.   You been doing more than eyeing her. You done bought her a drink or two.

TROY.   Hell yeah, I bought her a drink! What that mean? I bought you one, too. What that mean cause I buy her a drink? I'm just being polite.

BONO.   It's all right to buy her one drink. That's what you call being polite. But when you wanna be buying two or three . . . that's what you call eyeing her.

TROY.   Look here, as long as you known me . . . you ever known me to chase after women?

BONO.   Hell yeah! Long as I done known you. You forgetting I knew you when.

TROY.   Naw, I'm talking about since I been married to Rose?

BONO.   Oh, not since you been married to Rose. Now, that's the truth, there. I can say that.

TROY.   All right then! Case closed.

BONO.   I see you be walking up around Alberta's house. You supposed to be at Taylors' and you be walking up around there.

TROY.   What you watching where I'm walking for? I ain't watching after you.

BONO.   I seen you walking around there more than once.

TROY.   Hell, you liable to see me walking anywhere! That don't mean nothing cause you see me walking around there.

BONO.   Where she come from anyway? She just kinda showed up one day.

TROY.   Tallahassee. You can look at her and tell she one of them Florida gals. They got some big healthy women down there. Grow them right up out the ground. Got a little bit of Indian in her. Most of them niggers down in Florida got some Indian in them.

BONO.   I don't know about that Indian part. But she damn sure big and healthy. Woman wear some big stockings. Got them great big old legs and hips as wide as the Mississippi River.

TROY.   Legs don't mean nothing. You don't do nothing but push them out of the way. But them hips cushion the ride!

BONO.   Troy, you ain't got no sense.

TROY.   It's the truth! Like you riding on Goodyears!

(Rose enters from the house. She is ten years younger than Troy, her devotion to him stems from her recognition of the possibilities of her life without him: a succession of abusive men and their babies, a life of partying and running the streets, the Church, or aloneness with its attendant pain and frustration. She recognizes Troy's spirit as a fine and illuminating one and she either ignores or forgives his faults, only some of which she recognizes. Though she doesn't drink, her presence is an integral part of the Friday night rituals. She alternates between the porch and the kitchen, where supper preparations are under way.)

ROSE.   What you all out here getting into?

TROY.   What you worried about what we getting into for? This is men talk, woman.

ROSE.   What I care what you all talking about? Bono, you gonna stay for supper?

BONO.   No, I thank you, Rose. But Lucille say she cooking up a pot of pigfeet.

TROY.   Pigfeet! Hell, I'm going home with you! Might even stay the night if you got some pigfeet. You got something in there to top them pigfeet, Rose?

ROSE.   I'm cooking up some chicken. I got some chicken and collard greens.

TROY.   Well, go on back in the house and let me and Bono finish what we was talking about. This is men talk. I got some talk for you later. You know what kind of talk I mean. You go on and powder it up.

ROSE.   Troy Maxson, don't you start that now!

TROY (*puts his arm around her*).   Aw, woman . . . come here. Look here, Bono . . . when I met this woman . . . I got out that place, say, "Hitch up my pony, saddle up my mare . . . there's a woman out there for me somewhere. I looked here. Looked there. Saw Rose and latched on to her." I latched on to her and told her-I'm gonna tell you the truth-I told her, "Baby, I don't wanna marry, I just wanna be your man." Rose told me . . . tell him what you told me, Rose.

ROSE.   I told him if he wasn't the marrying kind, then move out the way so the marrying kind could find me.

TROY.   That's what she told me. "Nigger, you in my way. You blocking the view! Move out the way so I can find me a husband." I thought it over two or three days. Come back—

ROSE.   Ain't no two or three days nothing. You was back the same night.

TROY.   Come back, told her . . . "Okay, baby . . . but I'm gonna buy me a banty rooster and put him out there in the backyard . . . and when he see a stranger come, he'll flap his wings and crow . . ." Look here, Bono, I could watch the front door by myself . . . it was that back door I was worried about.

ROSE.   Troy, you ought not talk like that. Troy ain't doing nothing but telling a lie.

TROY.   Only thing is . . . when we first got married . . . forget the rooster . . . we ain't had no yard!

BONO.   I hear you tell it. Me and Lucille was staying down there on Logan Street. Had two rooms with the outhouse in the back. I ain't mind the outhouse none. But when that goddamn wind blow through there in the winter . . . that's what I'm talking about! To this day I wonder why in the hell I ever stayed down there for six long years. But see, I didn't know I could do no better. I thought only white folks had inside toilets and things.

ROSE.   There's a lot of people don't know they can do no better than they doing now. That's just something you got to learn. A lot of folks still shop at Bella's.

TROY.   Ain't nothing wrong with shopping at Bella's. She got fresh food.

ROSE.   I ain't said nothing about if she got fresh food. I'm talking about what she charge. She charge ten cents more than the A&P.

TROY.   The A&P ain't never done nothing for me. I spends my money where I'm treated right. I go down to Bella, say, "I need a loaf of bread, I'll pay you Friday." She give it to me. What sense that make when I got money to go and spend it somewhere else and ignore the person who done right by me? That ain't in the Bible.

ROSE.   We ain't talking about what's in the Bible. What sense it make to shop there when she overcharge?

TROY.   You shop where you want to. I'll do my shopping where the people been good to me.

ROSE.   Well, I don't think it's right for her to overcharge. That's all I was saying.

BONO.   Look here . . . I got to get on. Lucille going be raising all kind of hell.

TROY.   Where you going, nigger? We ain't finished this pint. Come here, finish this pint.

BONO.   Well, hell, I am . . . if you ever turn the bottle loose.

TROY (*hands him the bottle*).   The only thing I say about the A&P is I'm glad Cory got that job down there. Help him take care of his school clothes and things. Gabe done moved out and things getting tight around here. He got that job. . . . He can start to look out for himself.

ROSE.   Cory done went and got recruited by a college football team.

TROY.   I told that boy about that football stuff. The white man ain't gonna let him get nowhere with that football. I told him when he first come to me with it. Now you come telling me he done went and got more tied up in it. He ought to go and get recruited in how to fix cars or something where he can make a living.

ROSE.   He ain't talking about making no living playing football. It's just something the boys in school do. They gonna send a recruiter by to talk to you. He'll tell you he ain't talking about making no living playing football. It's a honor to be recruited.

TROY.   It ain't gonna get him nowhere. Bono'll tell you that.

BONO.   If he be like you in the sports . . . he's gonna be all right. Ain't but two men ever played baseball as good as you. That's Babe Ruth and Josh Gibson.° Them's the only two men ever hit more home runs than you.

TROY.   What it ever get me? Ain't got a pot to piss in or a window to throw it out of.

ROSE.   Times have changed since you was playing baseball, Troy. That was before the war. Times have changed a lot since then.

TROY.   How in hell they done changed?

ROSE.   They got lots of colored boys playing ball now. Baseball and football.

BONO.   You right about that, Rose. Times have changed, Troy. You just come along too early.

TROY.   There ought not never have been no time called too early! Now you take that fellow . . . what's that fellow they had playing right field for the Yankees back then? You know who I'm talking about, Bono. Used to play right field for the Yankees.

ROSE.   Selkirk?

TROY.   Selkirk! That's it! Man batting .269, understand? .269. What kind of sense that make? I was hitting .432 with thirty-seven home runs! Man batting .269 and playing right field for the Yankees! I saw Josh Gibson's daughter yesterday. She walking around with raggedy shoes on her feet. Now I bet you Selkirk's daughter ain't walking around with raggedy shoes on her feet! I bet you that!

ROSE.   They got a lot of colored baseball players now. Jackie Robinson was the first. Folks had to wait for Jackie Robinson.

TROY.   I done seen a hundred niggers play baseball better than Jackie Robinson. Hell, I know some teams Jackie Robinson couldn't even make! What you talking about Jackie Robinson. Jackie Robinson wasn't nobody. I'm talking about if you could play ball then they ought to have let you play. Don't care what color you were. Come telling me I come along too early. If you could play . . . then they ought to have let you play.

(Troy takes a long drink from the bottle.)

ROSE.   You gonna drink yourself to death. You don't need to be drinking like that.

TROY.   Death ain't nothing. I done seen him. Done wrassled with him. You can't tell me nothing about death. Death ain't nothing but a fastball on the outside corner. And you know what I'll do to that! Lookee here, Bono . . . am I lying? You get one of them fastballs, about waist high, over the outside corner of the plate where you can get the meat of the bat on it . . . and good god! You can kiss it goodbye. Now, am I lying?

BONO.   Naw, you telling the truth there. I seen you do it.

TROY.   If I'm lying . . . that 450 feet worth of lying! *(Pause.)* That's all death is to me. A fastball on the outside corner.

ROSE.   I don't know why you want to get on talking about death.

TROY.   Ain't nothing wrong with talking about death. That's part of life. Everybody gonna die. You gonna die, I'm gonna die. Bono's gonna die. Hell, we all gonna die.

ROSE.   But you ain't got to talk about it. I don't like to talk about it.

Josh Gibson 1911–1947: powerful, black baseball player known in the 1930s as the Babe Ruth of the Negro Leagues.

TROY.   You the one brought it up. Me and Bono was talking about baseball . . . you tell me I'm gonna drink myself to death. Ain't that right, Bono? You know I don't drink this but one night out of the week. That's Friday night. I'm gonna drink just enough to where I can handle it. Then I cuts it loose. I leave it alone. So don't you worry about me drinking myself to death. 'Cause I ain't worried about Death. I done seen him. I done wrestled with him.

Look here, Bono . . . I looked up one day and Death was marching straight at me. Like Soldiers on Parade! The Army of Death was marching straight at me. The middle of July, 1941. It got real cold just like it be winter. It seem like Death himself reached out and touched me on the shoulder. He touch me just like I touch you. I got cold as ice and Death standing there grinning at me.

ROSE.   Troy, why don't you hush that talk.

TROY.   I say . . . What you want, Mr. Death? You be wanting me? You done brought your army to be getting me? I looked him dead in the eye. I wasn't fearing nothing. I was ready to tangle. Just like I'm ready to tangle now. The Bible say be ever vigilant. That's why I don't get but so drunk. I got to keep watch.

ROSE.   Troy was right down there in Mercy Hospital. You remember he had pneumonia? Laying there with a fever talking plumb out of his head.

TROY.   Death standing there staring at me . . . carrying that sickle in his hand. Finally he say, "You want bound over for another year?" See, just like that . . . "You want bound over for another year?" I told him, "Bound over hell! Let's settle this now!"

It seem like he kinda fell back when I said that, and all the cold went out of me. I reached down and grabbed that sickle and threw it just as far as I could throw it . . . and me and him commenced to wrestling.

We wrestled for three days and three nights. I can't say where I found the strength from. Every time it seemed like he was gonna get the best of me, I'd reach way down deep inside myself and find the strength to do him one better.

ROSE.   Every time Troy tell that story he find different ways to tell it. Different things to make up about it.

TROY.   I ain't making up nothing. I'm telling you the facts of what happened. I wrestled with Death for three days and three nights and I'm standing here to tell you about it. *(Pause.)* All right. At the end of the third night we done weakened each other to where we can't hardly move. Death stood up, throwed on his robe . . . had him a white robe with a hood on it. He throwed on that robe and went off to look for his sickle. Say, "I'll be back." Just like that. "I'll be back." I told him, say, "Yeah, but . . . you gonna have to find me!" I wasn't no fool. I wan't going looking for him. Death ain't nothing to play with. And I know he's gonna get me. I know I got to join his army . . . his camp followers. But as long as I keep my strength and see him coming . . . as long as I keep up my vigilance . . . he's gonna have to fight to get me. I ain't going easy.

BONO.   Well, look here, since you got to keep up your vigilance . . . let me have the bottle.

TROY.   Aw hell, I shouldn't have told you that part. I should have left out that part.

ROSE.   Troy be talking that stuff and half the time don't even know what he be talking about.

TROY.   Bono know me better than that.

BONO.   That's right. I know you. I know you got some Uncle Remus° in your blood. You got more stories than the devil got sinners.

Uncle Remus: black storyteller who recounts traditional black tales in the book by Joel Chandler Harris.

TROY.   Aw hell, I done seen him too! Done talked with the devil.

ROSE.   Troy, don't nobody wanna be hearing all that stuff.

(Lyons enters the yard from the street. Thirty-four years old, Troy's son by a previous marriage, he sports a neatly trimmed goatee, sport coat, white shirt, tieless and buttoned at the collar. Though he fancies himself a musician, he is more caught up in the rituals and "idea" of being a musician than in the actual practice of the music. He has come to borrow money from Troy, and while he knows he will be successful, he is uncertain as to what extent his lifestyle will be held up to scrutiny and ridicule.)

LYONS.   Hey, Pop.

TROY.   What you come "Hey, Popping" me for?

LYONS.   How you doing, Rose? *(He kisses her.)* Mr. Bono. How you doing?

BONO.   Hey, Lyons . . . how you been?

TROY.   He must have been doing all right. I ain't seen him around here last week.

ROSE.   Troy, leave your boy alone. He come by to see you and you wanna start all that nonsense.

TROY.   I ain't bothering Lyons. *(Offers him the bottle.)* Here . . . get you a drink. We got an understanding. I know why he come by to see me and he know I know.

LYONS.   Come on, Pop . . . I just stopped by to say hi . . . see how you was doing.

TROY.   You ain't stopped by yesterday.

ROSE.   You gonna stay for supper, Lyons? I got some chicken cooking in the oven.

LYONS.   No, Rose . . . thanks. I was just in the neighborhood and thought I'd stop by for a minute.

TROY.   You was in the neighborhood all right, nigger. You telling the truth there. You was in the neighborhood cause it's my payday.

LYONS.   Well, hell, since you mentioned it . . . let me have ten dollars.

TROY.   I'll be damned! I'll die and go to hell and play blackjack with the devil before I give you ten dollars.

BONO.   That's what I wanna know about . . . that devil you done seen.

LYONS.   What . . . Pop done seen the devil? You too much, Pops.

TROY.   Yeah, I done seen him. Talked to him too!

ROSE.   You ain't seen no devil. I done told you that man ain't had nothing to do with the devil. Anything you can't understand, you want to call it the devil.

TROY.   Look here, Bono . . . I went down to see Hertzberger about some furniture. Got three rooms for two-ninety-eight. That what it say on the radio. "Three rooms . . . two-ninety-eight." Even made up a little song about it. Go down there . . . man tell me I can't get no credit. I'm working every day and can't get no credit. What to do? I got an empty house with some raggedy furniture in it. Cory ain't got no bed. He's sleeping on a pile of rags on the floor. Working every day and can't get no credit. Come back here—Rose'll tell you—madder than hell. Sit down . . . try to figure what I'm gonna do. Come a knock on the door. Ain't been living here but three days. Who know I'm here? Open the door . . . devil standing there bigger than life. White fellow . . . got on good clothes and everything. Standing there with a clipboard in his hand. I ain't had to say nothing. First words come out of his mouth was . . . "I understand you need some furniture and can't get no credit." I liked to fell over. He say, "I'll give you all the credit you want, but you got to pay the interest on it." I told him, "Give me three rooms worth and charge whatever you want." Next day a truck pulled up here and two men unloaded them three rooms. Man what drove the truck give me a book. Say send ten dollars, first of every month to the address in the book and everything will be all right. Say if I miss a payment the devil was coming back and it'll be hell to pay. That was fifteen years ago. To this day . . . the first of the month I send my ten dollars, Rose'll tell you.

ROSE. Troy lying.

TROY. I ain't never seen that man since. Now you tell me who else that could have been but the devil? I ain't sold my soul or nothing like that, you understand. Naw, I wouldn't have truck with the devil about nothing like that. I got my furniture and pays my ten dollars the first of the month just like clockwork.

BONO. How long you say you been paying this ten dollars a month?

TROY. Fifteen years!

BONO. Hell, ain't you finished paying for it yet? How much the man done charged you.

TROY. Ah hell, I done paid for it. I done paid for it ten times over! The fact is I'm scared to stop paying it.

ROSE. Troy lying. We got that furniture from Mr. Glickman. He ain't paying no ten dollars a month to nobody.

TROY. Aw hell, woman. Bono know I ain't that big a fool.

LYONS. I was just getting ready to say . . . I know where there's a bridge for sale.

TROY. Look here, I'll tell you this . . . it don't matter to me if he was the devil. It don't matter if the devil give credit. Somebody has got to give it.

ROSE. It ought to matter. You going around talking about having truck with the devil . . . God's the one you gonna have to answer to. He's the one gonna be at the Judgment.

LYONS. Yeah, well, look here, Pop . . . let me have that ten dollars. I'll give it back to you. Bonnie got a job working at the hospital.

TROY. What I tell you, Bono? The only time I see this nigger is when he wants something. That's the only time I see him.

LYONS. Come on, Pop, Mr. Bono don't want to hear all that. Let me have the ten dollars. I told you Bonnie working.

TROY. What that mean to me? "Bonnie working." I don't care if she working. Go ask her for the ten dollars if she working. Talking about "Bonnie working." Why ain't you working?

LYONS. Aw, Pop, you know I can't find no decent job. Where am I gonna get a job at? You know I can't get no job.

TROY. I told you I know some people down there. I can get you on the rubbish if you want to work. I told you that the last time you came by here asking me for something.

LYONS. Naw, Pop . . . thanks. That ain't for me. I don't wanna be carrying nobody's rubbish. I don't wanna be punching nobody's time clock.

TROY. What's the matter, you too good to carry people's rubbish? Where you think that ten dollars you talking about come from? I'm just supposed to haul people's rubbish and give my money to you cause you too lazy to work. You too lazy to work and wanna know why you ain't got what I got.

ROSE. What hospital Bonnie working at? Mercy?

LYONS. She's down at Passavant working in the laundry.

TROY. I ain't got nothing as it is. I give you that ten dollars and I got to eat beans the rest of the week. Naw . . . you ain't getting no ten dollars here.

LYONS. You ain't got to be eating no beans. I don't know why you wanna say that.

TROY. I ain't got no extra money. Gabe done moved over to Miss Pearl's paying her the rent and things done got tight around here. I can't afford to be giving you every payday.

LYONS.   I ain't asked you to give me nothing. I asked you to loan me ten dollars. I know you got ten dollars.

TROY.   Yeah, I got it. You know why I got it? Cause I don't throw my money away out there in the streets. You living the fast life . . . wanna be a musician . . . running around in them clubs and things . . . then, you learn to take care of yourself. You ain't gonna find me going and asking nobody for nothing. I done spent too many years without.

LYONS.   You and me is two different people, Pop.

TROY.   I done learned my mistake and learned to do what's right by it. You still trying to get something for nothing. Life don't owe you nothing. You owe it to yourself. Ask Bono. He'll tell you I'm right.

LYONS.   You got your way of dealing with the world . . . I got mine. The only thing that matters to me is the music.

TROY.   Yeah, I can see that! It don't matter how you gonna eat . . . where your next dollar is coming from. You telling the truth there.

LYONS.   I know I got to eat. But I got to live too. I need something that gonna help me to get out of the bed in the morning. Make me feel like I belong in the world. I don't bother nobody. I just stay with my music 'cause that's the only way I can find to live in the world. Otherwise there ain't no telling what I might do. Now I don't come criticizing you and how you live. I just come by to ask you for ten dollars. I don't wanna hear all that about how I live.

TROY.   Boy, your mamma did a hell of a job raising you.

LYONS.   You can't change me, Pop. I'm thirty-four years old. If you wanted to change me, you should have been there when I was growing up. I come by to see you . . . ask for ten dollars and you want to talk about how I was raised. You don't know nothing about how I was raised.

ROSE.   Let the boy have ten dollars, Troy.

TROY *(to Lyons)*.   What the hell you looking at me for? I ain't got no ten dollars. You know what I do with my money. *(To Rose.)* Give him ten dollars if you want him to have it.

ROSE.   I will. Just as soon as you turn it loose.

TROY *(handing Rose the money)*.   There it is. Seventy-six dollars and forty-two cents. You see this, Bono? Now, I ain't gonna get but six of that back.

ROSE.   You ought to stop telling that lie. Here, Lyons. *(She hands him the money.)*

LYONS.   Thanks, Rose. Look . . . I got to run . . . I'll see you later.

TROY.   Wait a minute. You gonna say, "thanks, Rose" and ain't gonna look to see where she got that ten dollars from? See how they do me, Bono?

LYONS.   I know she got it from you, Pop. Thanks. I'll give it back to you.

TROY.   There he go telling another lie. Time I see that ten dollars . . . he'll be owing me thirty more.

LYONS.   See you, Mr. Bono.

BONO.   Take care, Lyons!

LYONS.   Thanks, Pop. I'll see you again.

(Lyons exits the yard.)

TROY.   I don't know why he don't go and get him a decent job and take care of that woman he got.

BONO.   He'll be all right, Troy. The boy is still young.

TROY.   The *boy* is thirty-four years old.

ROSE.   Let's not get off into all that.

BONO.   Look here . . . I got to be going. I got to be getting on. Lucille gonna be waiting.

TROY *(puts his arm around Rose).*   See this woman, Bono? I love this woman. I love this woman so much it hurts. I love her so much . . . I done run out of ways of loving her. So I got to go back to basics. Don't you come by my house Monday morning talking about time to go to work . . . 'Cause I'm still gonna be stroking!

ROSE.   Troy! Stop it now!

BONO.   I ain't paying him no mind, Rose. That ain't nothing but gin-talk. Go on, Troy. I'll see you Monday.

TROY.   Don't you come by my house, nigger! I done told you what I'm gonna be doing.

(The lights go down to black.)

Scene II

(The lights come up on Rose hanging up clothes. She hums and sings softly to herself. It is the following morning.)

ROSE (SINGS).   Jesus, be a fence all around me every day Jesus, I want you to protect me as I travel on my way. Jesus, be a fence all around me every day.

(Troy enters from the house.)

Jesus, I want you to protect me
as I travel on my way.

(To Troy.) 'Morning. You ready for breakfast? I can fix it soon as I finish hanging up these clothes?

TROY.   I got the coffee on. That'll be all right. I'll just drink some of that this morning.

ROSE.   That 651 hit yesterday. That's the second time this month. Miss Pearl hit for a dollar . . . seem like those that need the least always get lucky. Poor folks can't get nothing.

TROY.   Them numbers don't know nobody. I don't know why you fool with them. You and Lyons both.

ROSE.   It's something to do.

TROY.   You ain't doing nothing but throwing your money away.

ROSE.   Troy, you know I don't play foolishly. I just play a nickel here and a nickel there.

TROY.   That's two nickels you done thrown away.

ROSE.   Now I hit sometimes . . . that makes up for it. It always comes in handy when I do hit. I don't hear you complaining then.

TROY.   I ain't complaining now. I just say it's foolish. Trying to guess out of six hundred ways which way the number gonna come. If I had all the money niggers, these Negroes, throw away on numbers for one week—just one week—I'd be a rich man.

ROSE.   Well, you wishing and calling it foolish ain't gonna stop folks from playing numbers. That's one thing for sure. Besides . . . some good things come from playing numbers. Look where Pope done bought him that restaurant off of numbers.

TROY.   I can't stand niggers like that. Man ain't had two dimes to rub together. He walking around with his shoes all run over bumming money for cigarettes. All right. Got lucky there and hit the numbers . . .

ROSE.   Troy, I know all about it.

TROY.   Had good sense, I'll say that for him. He ain't throwed his money away. I seen niggers hit the numbers and go through two thousand dollars in four days. Man bought him that restaurant down there . . . fixed it up real nice . . . and then didn't want nobody to come in it! A Negro go in there and can't get no kind of service. I seen a white fellow come in there and order a bowl of stew. Pope picked all the meat out the pot for him. Man ain't had nothing but a bowl of meat! Negro come behind him and ain't got nothing but the potatoes and carrots. Talking about what numbers do for people, you picked a wrong example. Ain't done nothing but make a worser fool out of him than he was before.

ROSE.   Troy, you ought to stop worrying about what happened at work yesterday.

TROY.   I ain't worried. Just told me to be down there at the Commissioner's office on Friday. Everybody think they gonna fire me. I ain't worried about them firing me. You ain't got to worry about that. *(Pause.)* Where's Cory? Cory in the house? *(Calls.)* Cory?

ROSE.   He gone out.

TROY.   Out, huh? He gone out 'cause he know I want him to help me with this fence. I know how he is. That boy scared of work.

(Gabriel enters. He comes halfway down the alley and, hearing Troy's voice, stops.)

TROY *(continues)*.   He ain't done a lick of work in his life.

ROSE.   He had to go to football practice. Coach wanted them to get in a little extra practice before the season start.

TROY.   I got his practice . . . running out of here before he get his chores done.

ROSE.   Troy, what is wrong with you this morning? Don't nothing set right with you. Go on back in there and go to bed . . . get up on the other side.

TROY.   Why something got to be wrong with me? I ain't said nothing wrong with me.

ROSE.   You got something to say about everything. First it's the numbers . . . then it's the way the man runs his restaurant . . . then you done got on Cory. What's it gonna be next? Take a look up there and see if the weather suits you . . . or is it gonna be how you gonna put up the fence with the clothes hanging in the yard.

TROY.   You hit the nail on the head then.

ROSE.   I know you like I know the back of my hand. Go on in there and get you some coffee . . . see if that straighten you up. 'Cause you ain't right this morning.

(Troy starts into the house and sees Gabriel. Gabriel starts singing. Troy's brother, he is seven years younger than Troy. Injured in World War II, he has a metal plate in his head. He carries an old trumpet tied around his waist and believes with every fiber of his being that he is the Archangel Gabriel. He carries a chipped basket with an assortment of discarded fruits and vegetables he has picked up in the strip district and which he attempts to sell.)

GABRIEL *(singing)*.   Yes, ma'am, I got plums
You ask me how I sell them
Oh ten cents apiece
Three for a quarter
Come and buy now
'Cause I'm here today
And tomorrow I'll be gone

(Gabriel enters.)

Hey, Rose!

ROSE.   How you doing, Gabe?

GABRIEL.   There's Troy . . . Hey, Troy!

TROY.   Hey, Gabe.

(Exit into kitchen.)

ROSE *(to Gabriel).*   What you got there?

GABRIEL.   You know what I got, Rose. I got fruits and vegetables.

ROSE *(looking in basket).*   Where's all these plums you talking about?

GABRIEL.   I ain't got no plums today, Rose. I was just singing that. Have some to-morrow. Put me in a big order for plums. Have enough plums tomorrow for St. Peter and everybody. *(Troy reenters from kitchen, crosses to steps. To Rose.)* Troy's mad at me.

TROY.   I ain't mad at you. What I got to be mad at you about? You ain't done nothing to me.

GABRIEL.   I just moved over to Miss Pearl's to keep out from in your way. I ain't mean no harm by it.

TROY.   Who said anything about that? I ain't said anything about that.

GABRIEL.   You ain't mad at me, is you?

TROY.   Naw . . . I ain't mad at you, Gabe. If I was mad at you I'd tell you about it.

GABRIEL.   Got me two rooms. In the basement. Got my own door too. Wanna see my key? *(He holds up a key.)* That's my own key! Ain't nobody else got a key like that. That's my key! My two rooms!

TROY.   Well, that's good, Gabe. You got your own key . . . that's good.

ROSE.   You hungry, Gabe? I was just fixing to cook Troy his breakfast.

GABRIEL.   I'll take some biscuits. You got some biscuits? Did you know when I was in heaven . . . every morning me and St. Peter would sit down by the gate and eat some big fat biscuits? Oh, yeah! We had us a good time. We'd sit there and eat us them biscuits and then St. Peter would go off to sleep and tell me to wake him up when it's time to open the gates for the judgment.

ROSE.   Well, come on . . . I'll make up a batch of biscuits.

(Rose exits into the house.)

GABRIEL.   Troy . . . St. Peter got your name in the book. I seen it. It say . . . Troy Maxson. I say . . . I know him! He got the same name like what I got. That's my brother!

TROY.   How many times you gonna tell me that, Gabe?

GABRIEL.   Ain't got my name in the book. Don't have to have my name. I done died and went to heaven. He got your name though. One morning St. Peter was look-ing at his book . . . marking it up for the judgment . . . and he let me see your name. Got it in there under M. Got Rose's name . . . I ain't seen it like I seen yours . . . but I know it's in there. He got a great big book. Got everybody's name what was ever been born. That's what he told me. But I seen your name. Seen it with my own eyes.

TROY.   Go on in the house there. Rose going to fix you something to eat.

GABRIEL.   Oh, I ain't hungry. I done had breakfast with Aunt Jemimah. She come by and cooked me up a whole mess of flapjacks. Remember how we used to eat them flapjacks?

TROY.   Go on in the house and get you something to eat now.

GABRIEL.   I got to go sell my plums. I done sold some tomatoes. Got me two quar-ters. Wanna see? *(He shows Troy his quarters.)* I'm gonna save them and buy me a new horn so St. Peter can hear me when it's time to open the gates. *(Gabriel stops suddenly. Listens.)* Hear that? That's the hellhounds. I got to chase them out of here. Go on get out of here! Get out! *(Gabriel exits singing.)* Better get ready for the judgment better get ready for the judgment my Lord is coming down

(Rose enters from the house.)

> TROY.   He gone off somewhere.
>
> GABRIEL *(offstage)*.   Better get ready for the judgment
> Better get ready for the judgment morning
> Better get ready for the judgment
> My God is coming down
>
> ROSE.   He ain't eating right. Miss Pearl say she can't get him to eat nothing.
>
> TROY.   What you want me to do about it, Rose? I done did everything I can for the man. I can't make him get well. Man got half his head blown away . . . what you expect?
>
> ROSE.   Seem like something ought to be done to help him.
>
> TROY.   Man don't bother nobody. He just mixed up from that metal plate he got in his head. Ain't no sense for him to go back into the hospital.
>
> ROSE.   Least he be eating right. They can help him take care of himself.
>
> TROY.   Don't nobody wanna be locked up, Rose. What you wanna lock him up for? Man go over there and fight the war . . . messin' around with them Japs, get half his head blown off . . . and they give him a lousy three thousand dollars. And I had to swoop down on that.
>
> ROSE.   Is you fixing to go into that again?
>
> TROY.   That's the only way I got a roof over my head . . . 'cause of that metal plate.
>
> ROSE.   Ain't no sense you blaming yourself for nothing. Gabe wasn't in no condition to manage that money. You done what was right by him. Can't nobody say you ain't done what was right by him. Look how long you took care of him . . . till he wanted to have his own place and moved over there with Miss Pearl.
>
> TROY.   That ain't what I'm saying, woman! I'm just stating the facts. If my brother didn't have that metal plate in his head . . . I wouldn't have a pot to piss in or a window to throw it out of. And I'm fifty-three years old. Now see if you can understand that!

(Troy gets up from the porch and starts to exit the yard.)

> ROSE.   Where you going off to? You been running out of here every Saturday for weeks. I thought you was gonna work on this fence?
>
> TROY.   I'm gonna walk down to Taylors'. Listen to the ball game. I'll be back in a bit. I'll work on it when I get back.

(He exits the yard. The lights go to black.)

SCENE III

(The lights come up on the yard. It is four hours later. Rose is taking down the clothes from the line. Cory enters carrying his football equipment.)

> ROSE.   Your daddy like to had a fit with you running out of here this morning without doing your chores.
>
> CORY.   I told you I had to go to practice.

ROSE.   He say you were supposed to help him with this fence.

CORY.   He been saying that the last four or five Saturdays, and then he don't never do nothing, but go down to Taylors'. Did you tell him about the recruiter?

ROSE.   Yeah, I told him.

CORY.   What he say?

ROSE.   He ain't said nothing too much. You get in there and get started on your chores before he gets back. Go on and scrub down them steps before he gets back here hollering and carrying on.

CORY.   I'm hungry. What you got to eat, Mama?

ROSE.   Go on and get started on your chores. I got some meat loaf in there. Go on and make you a sandwich . . . and don't leave no mess in there. *(Cory exits into the house. Rose continues to take down the clothes. Troy enters the yard and sneaks up and grabs her from behind.)* Troy! Go on, now. You liked to scared me to death. What was the score of the game? Lucille had me on the phone and I couldn't keep up with it.

TROY.   What I care about the game? Come here, woman. *(He tries to kiss her.)*

ROSE.   I thought you went down Taylors' to listen to the game. Go on, Troy! You supposed to be putting up this fence.

TROY *(attempting to kiss her again).*   I'll put it up when I finish with what is at hand.

ROSE.   Go on, Troy. I ain't studying you.

TROY *(chasing after her).*   I'm studying you . . . fixing to do my homework!

ROSE.   Troy, you better leave me alone.

TROY.   Where's Cory? That boy brought his butt home yet?

ROSE.   He's in the house doing his chores.

TROY *(calling).*   Cory! Get your butt out here, boy! *(Rose exits into the house with the laundry. Troy goes over to the pile of wood, picks up a board, and starts sawing. Cory enters from the house.)* You just now coming in here from leaving this morning?

CORY.   Yeah, I had to go to football practice.

TROY.   Yeah, what?

CORY.   Yessir.

TROY.   I ain't but two seconds off you noway. The garbage sitting in there overflowing . . . you ain't done none of your chores . . . and you come in here talking about "Yeah."

CORY.   I was just getting ready to do my chores now, Pop . . .

TROY.   Your first chore is to help me with this fence on Saturday. Everything else come after that. Now get that saw and cut them boards.

(Cory takes the saw and begins cutting the boards. Troy continues working. There is a long pause.)

CORY.   Hey, Pop . . . why don't you buy a TV?

TROY.   What I want with a TV? What I want one of them for?

CORY.   Everybody got one. Earl, Ba Bra . . . Jesse!

TROY.   I ain't asked you who had one. I say what I want with one?

CORY.   So you can watch it. They got lots of things on TV. Baseball games and everything. We could watch the World Series.

TROY.   Yeah . . . and how much this TV cost?

CORY.   I don't know. They got them on sale for around two hundred dollars.

TROY.   Two hundred dollars, huh?

CORY.   That ain't that much, Pop.

TROY.   Naw, it's just two hundred dollars. See that roof you got over your head at night? Let me tell you something about that roof. It's been over ten years since that roof was last tarred. See now . . . the snow come this winter and sit up there on that roof like it is . . . and it's gonna seep inside. It's just gonna be a little bit . . . ain't gonna hardly notice it. Then the next thing you know, it's gonna be leaking all over the house. Then the wood rot from all that water and you gonna need a whole new roof. Now, how much you think it cost to get that roof tarred?

CORY.   I don't know.

TROY.   Two hundred and sixty-four dollars . . . cash money. While you thinking about a TV, I got to be thinking about the roof . . . and whatever else go wrong around here. Now if you had two hundred dollars, what would you do . . . fix the roof or buy a TV?

CORY.   I'd buy a TV. Then when the roof started to leak . . . when it needed fixing . . . I'd fix it.

TROY.   Where you gonna get the money from? You done spent it for a TV. You gonna sit up and watch the water run all over your brand new TV.

CORY.   Aw, Pop. You got money. I know you do.

TROY.   Where I got it at, huh?

CORY.   You got it in the bank.

TROY.   You wanna see my bankbook? You wanna see that seventy-three dollars and twenty-two cents I got sitting up in there.

CORY.   You ain't got to pay for it all at one time. You can put a down payment on it and carry it on home with you.

TROY.   Not me. I ain't gonna owe nobody nothing if I can help it. Miss a payment and they come and snatch it right out your house. Then what you got? Now, soon as I get two hundred dollars clear, then I'll buy a TV. Right now, as soon as I get two hundred and sixty-four dollars, I'm gonna have this roof tarred.

CORY.   Aw . . . Pop!

TROY.   You go on and get you two hundred dollars and buy one if ya want it. I got better things to do with my money.

CORY.   I can't get no two hundred dollars. I ain't never seen two hundred dollars.

TROY.   I'll tell you what . . . you get you a hundred dollars and I'll put the other hundred with it.

CORY.   All right, I'm gonna show you.

TROY.   You gonna show me how you can cut them boards right now.

(Cory begins to cut the boards. There is a long pause.)

CORY.   The Pirates won today. That makes five in a row.

TROY.   I ain't thinking about the Pirates. Got an all-white team. Got that boy . . . that Puerto Rican boy . . . Clemente. Don't even half-play him. That boy could be something if they give him a chance. Play him one day and sit him on the bench the next.

CORY.   He gets a lot of chances to play.

TROY.   I'm talking about playing regular. Playing every day so you can get your timing. That's what I'm talking about.

CORY.   They got some white guys on the team that don't play every day. You can't play everybody at the same time.

TROY.   If they got a white fellow sitting on the bench . . . you can bet your last dollar he can't play! The colored guy got to be twice as good before he get on the team. That's why I don't want you to get all tied up in them sports. Man on the team and what it get him? They got colored on the team and don't use them. Same as not having them. All them teams the same.

CORY.   The Braves got Hank Aaron and Wes Covington. Hank Aaron hit two home runs today. That makes forty-three.

TROY.   Hank Aaron ain't nobody. That's what you supposed to do. That's how you supposed to play the game. Ain't nothing to it. It's just a matter of timing . . . getting the right follow-through. Hell, I can hit forty-three home runs right now!

CORY.   Not off no major-league pitching, you couldn't.

TROY.   We had better pitching in the Negro leagues. I hit seven home runs off of Satchel Paige.° You can't get no better than that!

CORY.   Sandy Koufax. He's leading the league in strikeouts.

TROY.   I ain't thinking of no Sandy Koufax.

CORY.   You got Warren Spahn and Lew Burdette. I bet you couldn't hit no home runs off of Warren Spahn.

TROY.   I'm through with it now. You go on and cut them boards. *(Pause.)* Your mama tell me you done got recruited by a college football team? Is that right?

CORY.   Yeah. Coach Zellman say the recruiter gonna be coming by to talk to you. Get you to sign the permission papers.

TROY.   I thought you supposed to be working down there at the A&P. Ain't you suppose to be working down there after school?

CORY.   Mr. Stawicki say he gonna hold my job for me until after the football season. Say starting next week I can work weekends.

TROY.   I thought we had an understanding about this football stuff? You suppose to keep up with your chores and hold that job down at the A&P. Ain't been around here all day on a Saturday. Ain't none of your chores done . . . and now you telling me you done quit your job.

CORY.   I'm gonna be working weekends.

TROY.   You damn right you are! And ain't no need for nobody coming around here to talk to me about signing nothing.

CORY.   Hey, Pop . . . you can't do that. He's coming all the way from North Carolina.

TROY.   I don't care where he coming from. The white man ain't gonna let you get nowhere with that football noway. You go on and get your book-learning so you can work yourself up in that A&P or learn how to fix cars or build houses or something, get you a trade. That way you have something can't nobody take away from you. You go on and learn how to put your hands to some good use. Besides hauling people's garbage.

CORY.   I get good grades, Pop. That's why the recruiter wants to talk with you. You got to keep up your grades to get recruited. This way I'll be going to college. I'll get a chance . . .

TROY.   First you gonna get your butt down there to the A&P and get your job back.

CORY.   Mr. Stawicki done already hired somebody else 'Cause I told him I was playing football.

TROY.   You a bigger fool than I thought . . . to let somebody take away your job so you can play some football. Where you gonna get your money to take out your girlfriend and whatnot? What kind of foolishness is that to let somebody take away your job?

CORY.   I'm still gonna be working weekends.

TROY.   Naw . . . naw. You getting your butt out of here and finding you another job.

Satchel Paige (1906?–1982): legendary black pitcher in the Negro leagues.

CORY.   Come on, Pop! I got to practice. I can't work after school and play football too. The team needs me. That's what Coach Zellman say . . .

TROY.   I don't care what nobody else say. I'm the boss . . . you understand? I'm the boss around here. I do the only saying what counts.

CORY.   Come on, Pop!

TROY.   I asked you . . . did you understand?

CORY.   Yeah . . .

TROY.   What?!

CORY.   Yessir.

TROY.   You go on down there to that A&P and see if you can get your job back. If you can't do both . . . then you quit the football team. You've got to take the crookeds with the straights.

CORY.   Yessir. *(Pause.)* Can I ask you a question?

TROY.   What the hell you wanna ask me? Mr. Stawicki the one you got the questions for.

CORY.   How come you ain't never liked me?

TROY.   Liked you? Who the hell say I got to like you? What law is there say I got to like you? Wanna stand up in my face and ask a damn fool-ass question like that. Talking about liking somebody. Come here, boy, when I talk to you. *(Cory comes over to where Troy is working. He stands slouched over and Troy shoves him on his shoulder.)* Straighten up, goddammit! I asked you a question . . . what law is there say I got to like you?

CORY.   None.

TROY.   Well, all right then! Don't you eat every day? *(Pause.)* Answer me when I talk to you! Don't you eat every day?

CORY.   Yeah.

TROY.   Nigger, as long as you in my house, you put that sir on the end of it when you talk to me!

CORY.   Yes . . . sir.

TROY.   You eat every day.

CORY.   Yessir!

TROY.   Got a roof over your head.

CORY.   Yessir!

TROY.   Got clothes on your back.

CORY.   Yessir.

TROY.   Why you think that is?

CORY.   Cause of you.

TROY.   Ah, hell I know it's 'cause of me . . . but why do you think that is?

CORY *(hesitant)*.   Cause you like me.

TROY.   Like you? I go out of here every morning . . . bust my butt . . . putting up with them crackers° every day . . . cause I like you? You about the biggest fool I ever saw. *(Pause.)* It's my job. It's my responsibility! You understand that? A man got to take care of his family. You live in my house . . . sleep you behind on my bed-clothes . . . fill you belly up with my food . . . cause you my son. You my flesh and blood. Not 'cause I like you! Cause it's my duty to take care of you. I owe a responsibility to you! Let's get this straight right here . . . before it go along any further . . . I ain't got to like you. Mr. Rand don't give me my money come payday cause he likes me. He gives me cause he owe me. I done give you everything I had to give you. I gave you your life! Me and your

---

crackers: white people, often used to refer disparagingly to whites.

mama worked that out between us. And liking your black ass wasn't part of the bargain. Don't you try and go through life worrying about if somebody like you or not. You best be making sure they doing right by you. You understand what I'm saying, boy?

CORY. Yessir.

TROY. Then get the hell out of my face, and get on down to that A&P.

(Rose has been standing behind the screen door for much of the scene. She enters as Cory exits.)

ROSE. Why don't you let the boy go ahead and play football, Troy? Ain't no harm in that. He's just trying to be like you with the sports.

TROY. I don't want him to be like me! I want him to move as far away from my life as he can get. You the only decent thing that ever happened to me. I wish him that. But I don't wish him a thing else from my life. I decided seventeen years ago that boy wasn't getting involved in no sports. Not after what they did to me in the sports.

ROSE. Troy, why don't you admit you was too old to play in the major leagues? For once . . . why don't you admit that?

TROY. What do you mean too old? Don't come telling me I was too old. I just wasn't the right color. Hell, I'm fifty-three years old and can do better than Selkirk's .269 right now!

ROSE. How's was you gonna play ball when you were over forty? Sometimes I can't get no sense out of you.

TROY. I got good sense, woman. I got sense enough not to let my boy get hurt over playing no sports. You been mothering that boy too much. Worried about if people like him.

ROSE. Everything that boy do . . . he do for you. He wants you to say "Good job, son." That's all.

TROY. Rose, I ain't got time for that. He's alive. He's healthy. He's got to make his own way. I made mine. Ain't nobody gonna hold his hand when he get out there in that world.

ROSE. Times have changed from when you was young, Troy. People change. The world's changing around you and you can't even see it.

TROY *(slow, methodical)*. Woman . . . I do the best I can do. I come in here every Friday. I carry a sack of potatoes and a bucket of lard. You all line up at the door with your hands out. I give you the lint from my pockets. I give you my sweat and my blood. I ain't got no tears. I done spent them. We go upstairs in that room at night . . . and I fall down on you and try to blast a hole into forever. I get up Monday morning . . . find my lunch on the table. I go out. Make my way. Find my strength to carry me through to the next Friday. *(Pause.)* That's all I got, Rose. That's all I got to give. I can't give nothing else.

(Troy exits into the house. The lights go down to black.)

Scene IV

(It is Friday. Two weeks later. Cory starts out of the house with his football equipment. The phone rings.)

CORY *(calling)*. I got it! *(He answers the phone and stands in the screen door talking.)* Hello? Hey, Jesse. Naw . . . I was just getting ready to leave now.

ROSE *(calling)*. Cory!

CORY.   I told you, man, them spikes is all tore up. You can use them if you want, but they ain't no good. Earl got some spikes.

ROSE *(calling)*.   Cory!

CORY *(calling to Rose)*.   Mam? I'm talking to Jesse. *(Into phone.)* When she say that? *(Pause.)* Aw, you lying, man. I'm gonna tell her you said that.

ROSE *(calling)*.   Cory, don't you go nowhere!

CORY.   I got to go to the game, Ma! *(Into the phone.)* Yeah, hey, look, I'll talk to you later. Yeah, I'll meet you over Earl's house. Later. Bye, Ma.

(Cory exits the house and starts out the yard.)

ROSE.   Cory, where you going off to? You got that stuff all pulled out and thrown all over your room.

CORY *(in the yard)*.   I was looking for my spikes. Jesse wanted to borrow my spikes.

ROSE.   Get up there and get that cleaned up before your daddy get back in here.

CORY.   I got to go to the game! I'll clean it up when I get back. *(Cory exits.)*

ROSE.   That's all he need to do is see that room all messed up.

(Rose exits into the house. Troy and Bono enter the yard. Troy is dressed in clothes other than his work clothes.)

BONO.   He told him the same thing he told you. Take it to the union.

TROY.   Brownie ain't got that much sense. Man wasn't thinking about nothing. He wait until I confront them on it . . . then he wanna come crying seniority. *(Calls.)* Hey, Rose!

BONO.   I wish I could have seen Mr. Rand's face when he told you.

TROY.   He couldn't get it out of his mouth! Liked to bit his tongue! When they called me down there to the Commissioner's office . . . he thought they was gonna fire me. Like everybody else.

BONO.   I didn't think they was gonna fire you. I thought they was gonna put you on the warning paper.

TROY.   Hey, Rose! *(To Bono.)* Yeah, Mr. Rand like to bit his tongue.

(Troy breaks the seal on the bottle, takes a drink, and hands it to Bono.)

BONO.   I see you run right down to Taylors' and told that Alberta gal.

TROY *(calling)*.   Hey Rose! *(To Bono.)* I told everybody. Hey, Rose! I went down there to cash my check.

ROSE *(entering from the house)*.   Hush all that hollering, man! I know you out here. What they say down there at the Commissioner's office?

TROY.   You supposed to come when I call you, woman. Bono'll tell you that. *(To Bono.)* Don't Lucille come when you call her?

ROSE.   Man, hush your mouth. I ain't no dog . . . talk about "come when you call me."

TROY *(puts his arm around Rose)*.   You hear this, Bono? I had me an old dog used to get uppity like that. You say, "C'mere, Blue!" . . . and he just lay there and look at you. End up getting a stick and chasing him away trying to make him come.

ROSE.   I ain't studying you and your dog. I remember you used to sing that old song.

TROY *(he sings)*.   Hear it ring! Hear it ring! I had a dog his name was Blue.

ROSE.   Don't nobody wanna hear you sing that old song.

TROY *(sings)*.   You know Blue was mighty true.

ROSE.   Used to have Cory running around here singing that song.

BONO. Hell, I remember that song myself.

TROY *(sings)*. You know Blue was a good old dog. Blue treed a possum in a hollow log. That was my daddy's song. My daddy made up that song.

ROSE. I don't care who made it up. Don't nobody wanna hear you sing it.

TROY *(makes a song like calling a dog)*. Come here, woman.

ROSE. You come in here carrying on, I reckon they ain't fired you. What they say down there at the Commissioner's office?

TROY. Look here, Rose . . . Mr. Rand called me into his office today when I got back from talking to them people down there . . . it come from up top . . . he called me in and told me they was making me a driver.

ROSE. Troy, you kidding!

TROY. No I ain't, Ask Bono.

ROSE. Well, that's great, Troy. Now you don't have to hassle them people no more.

(Lyons enters from the street.)

TROY. Aw hell, I wasn't looking to see you today. I thought you was in jail. Got it all over the front page of the Courier about them raiding Sefus' place . . . where you be hanging out with all them thugs.

LYONS. Hey, Pop . . . that ain't got nothing to do with me. I don't go down there gambling. I go down there to sit in with the band. I ain't got nothing to do with the gambling part. They got some good music down there.

TROY. They got some rogues . . . is what they got.

LYONS. How you been, Mr. Bono? Hi, Rose.

BONO. I see where you playing down at the Crawford Grill tonight.

ROSE. How come you ain't brought Bonnie like I told you. You should have brought Bonnie with you, she ain't been over in a month of Sundays.

LYONS. I was just in the neighborhood . . . thought I'd stop by.

TROY. Here he come . . .

BONO. Your daddy got a promotion on the rubbish. He's gonna be the first colored driver. Ain't got to do nothing but sit up there and read the paper like them white fellows.

LYONS. Hey, Pop . . . if you knew how to read you'd be all right.

BONO. Naw . . . naw . . . you mean if the nigger knew how to drive he'd be all right. Been fighting with them people about driving and ain't even got a license. Mr. Rand know you ain't got no driver's license?

TROY. Driving ain't nothing. All you do is point the truck where you want it to go. Driving ain't nothing.

BONO. Do Mr. Rand know you ain't got no driver's license? That's what I'm talking about. I ain't asked if driving was easy. I asked if Mr. Rand know you ain't got no driver's license.

TROY. He ain't got to know. The man ain't got to know my business. Time he find out, I have two or three driver's licenses.

LYONS *(going into his pocket)*. Say, look here, Pop . . .

TROY. I knew it was coming. Didn't I tell you, Bono? I know what kind of "Look here, Pop" that was. The nigger fixing to ask me for some money. It's Friday night. It's my payday. All them rogues down there on the avenue . . . the ones that ain't in jail . . . and Lyons is hopping in his shoes to get down there with them.

LYONS. See, Pop . . . if you give somebody else a chance to talk sometime, you'd see that I was fixing to pay you back your ten dollars like I told you. Here . . . I told you I'd pay you when Bonnie got paid.

TROY.   Naw . . . you go ahead and keep that ten dollars. Put it in the bank. The next time you feel like you wanna come by here and ask me for something . . . you go on down there and get that.

LYONS.   Here's your ten dollars, Pop. I told you I don't want you to give me nothing. I just wanted to borrow ten dollars.

TROY.   Naw . . . you go on and keep that for the next time you want to ask me.

LYONS.   Come on, Pop . . . here go your ten dollars.

ROSE.   Why don't you go on and let the boy pay you back, Troy?

LYONS.   Here you go, Rose. If you don't take it I'm gonna have to hear about it for the next six months.

(He hands her the money.)

ROSE.   You can hand yours over here too, Troy.

TROY.   You see this, Bono. You see how they do me.

BONO.   Yeah, Lucille do me the same way.

(Gabriel is heard singing offstage. He enters.)

GABRIEL.   Better get ready for the Judgment! Better get ready for . . . Hey! . . . Hey! . . . There's Troy's boy!

LYONS.   How are you doing, Uncle Gabe?

GABRIEL.   Lyons . . . The King of the Jungle! Rose . . . hey, Rose. Got a flower for you. *(He takes a rose from his pocket.)* Picked it myself. That's the same rose like you is!

ROSE.   That's right nice of you, Gabe.

LYONS.   What you been doing, Uncle Gabe?

GABRIEL.   Oh, I been chasing hellhounds and waiting on the time to tell St. Peter to open the gates.

LYONS.   You been chasing hellhounds, huh? Well . . . you doing the right thing, Uncle Gabe. Somebody got to chase them.

GABRIEL.   Oh, yeah . . . I know it. The devil's strong. The devil ain't no pushover. Hellhounds snipping at everybody's heels. But I got my trumpet waiting on the Judgment time.

LYONS.   Waiting on the Battle of Armageddon, huh?

GABRIEL.   Ain't gonna be too much of a battle when God get to waving that Judgment sword. But the people's gonna have a hell of a time trying to get into heaven if them gates ain't open.

LYONS *(putting his arm around Gabriel).*   You hear this, Pop. Uncle Gabe, you all right!

GABRIEL *(laughing with Lyons).*   Lyons! King of the Jungle.

ROSE.   You gonna stay for supper, Gabe. Want me to fix you a plate?

GABRIEL.   I'll take a sandwich, Rose. Don't want no plate. Just wanna eat with my hands. I'll take a sandwich.

ROSE.   How about you, Lyons? You staying? Got some short ribs cooking.

LYONS.   Naw, I won't eat nothing till after we finished playing. *(Pause.)* You ought to come down and listen to me play, Pop.

TROY.   I don't like that Chinese music. All that noise.

ROSE.   Go on in the house and wash up, Gabe . . . I'll fix you a sandwich.

GABRIEL *(to Lyons, as he exits).*   Troy's mad at me.

LYONS.   What you mad at Uncle Gabe for, Pop.

ROSE.   He thinks Troy's mad at him cause he moved over to Miss Pearl's.

TROY.   I ain't mad at the man. He can live where he want to live at.

LYONS.   What he move over there for? Miss Pearl don't like nobody.

ROSE.   She don't mind him none. She treats him real nice. She just don't allow all that singing.

TROY.   She don't mind that rent he be paying . . . that's what she don't mind.

ROSE.   Troy, I ain't going through that with you no more. He's over there 'cause he want to have his own place. He can come and go as he please.

TROY.   Hell, he could come and go as he please here. I wasn't stopping him. I ain't put no rules on him.

ROSE.   It ain't the same thing, Troy. And you know it. *(Gabriel comes to the door.)* Now, that's the last I wanna hear about that. I don't wanna hear nothing else about Gabe and Miss Pearl. And next week . . .

GABRIEL.   I'm ready for my sandwich, Rose.

ROSE.   And next week . . . when that recruiter come from that school . . . I want you to sign that paper and go on and let Cory play football. Then that'll be the last I have to hear about that.

TROY *(to Rose as she exits into the house)*.   I ain't thinking about Cory nothing.

LYONS.   What . . . Cory got recruited? What school he going to?

TROY.   That boy walking around here smelling his piss . . . thinking he's grown. Thinking he's gonna do what he want, irrespective of what I say. Look here, Bono . . . I left the Commissioner's office and went down to the A&P . . . that boy ain't working down there. He lying to me. Telling me he got his job back . . . telling me he working weekends . . . telling me he working after school . . . Mr. Stawicki tell me he ain't working down there at all!

LYONS.   Cory just growing up. He's just busting at the seams trying to fill out your shoes.

TROY.   I don't care what he's doing. When he get to the point where he wanna disobey me . . . then it's time for him to move on. Bono'll tell you that. I bet he ain't never disobeyed his daddy without paying the consequences.

BONO.   I ain't never had a chance. My daddy came on through . . . but I ain't never knew him to see him . . . or what he had on his mind or where he went. Just moving on through. Searching out the New Land. That's what the old folks used to call it. See a fellow moving around from place to place . . . woman to woman . . . called it searching out the New Land. I can't say if he ever found it. I come along, didn't want no kids. Didn't know if I was gonna be in one place long enough to fix on them right as their daddy. I figured I was going searching too. As it turned out I been hooked up with Lucille near about as long as your daddy been with Rose. Going on sixteen years.

TROY.   Sometimes I wish I hadn't known my daddy. He ain't cared nothing about no kids. A kid to him wasn't nothing. All he wanted was for you to learn how to walk so he could start you to working. When it come time for eating . . . he ate first. If there was anything left over, that's what you got. Man would sit down and eat two chickens and give you the wing.

LYONS.   You ought to stop that, Pop. Everybody feed their kids. No matter how hard times is . . . everybody care about their kids. Make sure they have something to eat.

TROY.   The only thing my daddy cared about was getting them bales of cotton in to Mr. Lubin. That's the only thing that mattered to him. Sometimes I used to wonder why he was living. Wonder why the devil hadn't come and got him. "Get them bales of cotton in to Mr. Lubin" and find out he owe him money . . .

LYONS.   He should have just went on and left when he saw he couldn't get nowhere. That's what I would have done.

TROY.   How he gonna leave with eleven kids? And where he gonna go? He ain't knew how to do nothing but farm. No, he was trapped and I think he knew it. But I'll say this for him . . . he felt a responsibility toward us. Maybe he ain't treated us the way I felt he should have . . . but without that responsibility he could have walked off and left us . . . made his own way.

BONO.   A lot of them did. Back in those days what you talking about . . . they walk out their front door and just take on down one road or another and keep on walking.

LYONS.   There you go! That's what I'm talking about.

BONO.   Just keep on walking till you come to something else. Ain't you never heard of nobody having the walking blues? Well, that's what you call it when you just take off like that.

TROY.   My daddy ain't had them walking blues! What you talking about? He stayed right there with his family. But he was just as evil as he could be. My mama couldn't stand him. Couldn't stand that evilness. She run off when I was about eight. She sneaked off one night after he had gone to sleep. Told me she was coming back for me. I ain't never seen her no more. All his women run off and left him. He wasn't good for nobody.

When my turn come to head out, I was fourteen and got to sniffing around Joe Canewell's daughter. Had us an old mule we called Greyboy. My daddy sent me out to do some plowing and I tied up Greyboy and went to fooling around with Joe Canewell's daughter. We done found us a nice little spot, got real cozy with each other. She about thirteen and we done figured we was grown anyway . . . so we down there enjoying ourselves . . . ain't thinking about nothing. We didn't know Greyboy had got loose and wandered back to the house and my daddy was looking for me. We down there by the creek enjoying ourselves when my daddy come up on us. Surprised us. He had them leather straps off the mule and commenced to whupping me like there was no tomorrow. I jumped up, mad and embarrassed. I was scared of my daddy. When he commenced to whupping on me . . . quite naturally I run to get out of the way. *(Pause.)* Now I thought he was mad 'cause I ain't done my work. But I see where he was chasing me off so he could have the gal for himself. When I see what the matter of it was, I lost all fear of my daddy. Right there is where I become a man . . . at fourteen years of age. *(Pause.)* Now it was my turn to run him off. I picked up them same reins that he had used on me. I picked up them reins and commenced to whupping on him. The gal jumped up and run off . . . and when my daddy turned to face me, I could see why the devil had never come to get him . . . 'cause he was the devil himself. I don't know what happened. When I woke up, I was laying right there by the creek, and Blue . . . this old dog we had . . . was licking my face. I thought I was blind. I couldn't see nothing. Both my eyes were swollen shut. I layed there and cried. I didn't know what I was gonna do. The only thing I knew was the time had come for me to leave my daddy's house. And right there the world suddenly got big. And it was a long time before I could cut it down to where I could handle it.

Part of that cutting down was when I got to the place where I could feel him kicking in my blood and knew that the only thing that separated us was the matter of a few years.

(Gabriel enters from the house with a sandwich.)

LYONS.   What you got there, Uncle Gabe?

GABRIEL.   Got me a ham sandwich. Rose gave me a ham sandwich.

TROY.   I don't know what happened to him. I done lost touch with everybody except Gabriel. But I hope he's dead. I hope he found some peace.

LYONS. That's a heavy story, Pop. I didn't know you left home when you was fourteen.

TROY. And didn't know nothing. The only part of the world I knew was the forty-two acres of Mr. Lubin's land. That's all I knew about life.

LYONS. Fourteen's kinda young to be out on your own. *(Phone rings.)* I don't even think I was ready to be out on my own at fourteen. I don't know what I would have done.

TROY. I got up from the creek and walked on down to Mobile. I was through with farming. Figured I could do better in the city. So I walked the two hundred miles to Mobile.

LYONS. Wait a minute . . . you ain't walked no two hundred miles, Pop. Ain't nobody gonna walk no two hundred miles. You talking about some walking there.

BONO. That's the only way you got anywhere back in them days.

LYONS. Shhh. Damn if I wouldn't have hitched a ride with somebody!

TROY. Who you gonna hitch it with? They ain't had no cars and things like they got now. We talking about 1918.

ROSE *(entering)*. What you all out here getting into?

TROY *(to Rose)*. I'm telling Lyons how good he got it. He don't know nothing about this I'm talking.

ROSE. Lyons, that was Bonnie on the phone. She say you supposed to pick her up.

LYONS. Yeah, okay, Rose.

TROY. I walked on down to Mobile and hitched up with some of them fellows that was heading this way. Got up here and found out . . . not only couldn't you get a job . . . you couldn't find no place to live. I thought I was in freedom. Shhh. Colored folks living down there on the riverbanks in whatever kind of shelter they could find for themselves. Right down there under the Brady Street Bridge. Living in shacks made of sticks and tarpaper. Messed around there and went from bad to worse. Started stealing. First it was food. Then I figured, hell, if I steal money I can buy me some food. Buy me some shoes too! One thing led to another. Met your mama. I was young and anxious to be a man. Met your mama and had you. What I do that for? Now I got to worry about feeding you and her. Got to steal three times as much. Went out one day looking for somebody to rob . . . that's what I was, a robber. I'll tell you the truth. I'm ashamed of it today. But it's the truth. Went to rob this fellow . . . pulled out my knife . . . and he pulled out a gun. Shot me in the chest. It felt just like somebody had taken a hot branding iron and laid it on me. When he shot me I jumped at him with my knife. They told me I killed him and they put me in the penitentiary and locked me up for fifteen years. That's where I met Bono. That's where I learned how to play baseball. Got out that place and your mama had taken you and went on to make life without me. Fifteen years was a long time for her to wait. But that fifteen years cured me of that robbing stuff. Rose'll tell you. She asked me when I met her if I had gotten all that foolishness out of my system. And I told here, "Baby, it's you and baseball all what count with me." You hear me, Bono? I meant it too. She say, "Which one comes first?" I told her, "Baby, ain't no doubt it's baseball . . . but you stick and get old with me and we'll both outlive this baseball." Am I right, Rose? And it's true.

ROSE. Man, hush your mouth. You ain't said no such thing. Talking about, "Baby, you know you'll always be number one with me." That's what you was talking.

TROY. You hear that, Bono. That's why I love her.

BONO. Rose'll keep you straight. You get off the track, she'll straighten you up.

ROSE. Lyons, you better get on up and get Bonnie. She waiting on you.

LYONS *(gets up to go)*.   Hey, Pop, why don't you come on down to the Grill and hear me play?

TROY.   I ain't going down there. I'm too old to be sitting around in them clubs.

BONO.   You got to be good to play down at the Grill.

LYONS.   Come on, Pop . . .

TROY.   I got to get up in the morning.

LYONS.   You ain't got to stay long.

TROY.   Naw, I'm gonna get my supper and go on to bed.

LYONS.   Well, I got to go. I'll see you again.

TROY.   Don't you come around my house on my payday.

ROSE.   Pick up the phone and let somebody know you coming. And bring Bonnie with you. You know I'm always glad to see her.

LYONS.   Yeah, I'll do that, Rose. You take care now. See you, Pop. See you, Mr. Bono. See you, Uncle Gabe.

GABRIEL.   Lyons! King of the Jungle!

(Lyons exits.)

TROY.   Is supper ready, woman? Me and you got some business to take care of. I'm gonna tear it up too.

ROSE.   Troy, I done told you now!

TROY *(puts his arm around Bono)*.   Aw hell, woman . . . this is Bono. Bono like family. I done known this nigger since . . . how long I done know you?

BONO.   It's been a long time.

TROY.   I done known this nigger since Skippy was a pup. Me and him done been through some times.

BONO.   You sure right about that.

TROY.   Hell, I done know him longer than I known you. And we still standing shoulder to shoulder. Hey, look here, Bono . . . a man can't ask for no more than that. *(Drinks to him.)* I love you, nigger.

BONO.   Hell, I love you too . . . but I got to get home see my woman. You got yours in hand. I got to go get mine.

(Bono starts to exit as Cory enters the yard, dressed in his football uniform. He gives Troy a hard, uncompromising look.)

CORY.   What you do that for, Pop?

(He throws his helmet down in the direction of Troy.)

ROSE.   What's the matter? Cory . . . what's the matter?

CORY.   Papa done went up to the school and told Coach Zellman I can't play football no more. Wouldn't even let me play the game. Told him to tell the recruiter not to come.

ROSE.   Troy . . .

TROY.   What you Troying me for. Yeah, I did it. And the boy know why I did it.

CORY.   Why you wanna do that to me? That was the one chance I had.

ROSE.   Ain't nothing wrong with Cory playing football, Troy.

TROY.   The boy lied to me. I told the nigger if he wanna play football . . . to keep up his chores and hold down that job at the A&P. That was the conditions. Stopped down there to see Mr. Stawicki . . .

CORY.   I can't work after school during the football season, Pop! I tried to tell you that Mr. Stawicki's holding my job for me. You don't never want to listen to nobody. And then you wanna go and do this to me!

TROY.   I ain't done nothing to you. You done it to yourself.

CORY.   Just cause you didn't have a chance! You just scared I'm gonna be better than you, that's all.

TROY.   Come here.

ROSE.   Troy . . .

(Cory reluctantly crosses over to Troy).

TROY.   All right! See. You done made a mistake.

CORY.   I didn't even do nothing!

TROY.   I'm gonna tell you what your mistake was. See . . . you swung at the ball and didn't hit it. That's strike one. See, you in the batter's box now. You swung and you missed. That's strike one. Don't you strike out!

(Lights fade to black).

ACT II

Scene I

(The following morning. Cory is at the tree hitting the ball with the bat. He tries to mimic Troy, but his swing is awkward, less sure. Rose enters from the house.)

ROSE.   Cory, I want you to help me with this cupboard.

CORY.   I ain't quitting the team. I don't care what Poppa say.

ROSE.   I'll talk to him when he gets back. He had to go see about your Uncle Gabe. The police done arrested him. Say he was disturbing the peace. He'll be back directly. Come on in here and help me clean out the top of this cupboard. *(Cory exits into the house. Rose sees Troy and Bono coming down the alley.)* Troy . . . what they say down there?

TROY.   Ain't said nothing. I give them fifty dollars and they let him go. I'll talk to you about it. Where's Cory?

ROSE.   He's in there helping me clean out these cupboards.

TROY.   Tell him to get his butt out here.

(Troy and Bono go over to the pile of wood. Bono picks up the saw and begins sawing).

TROY *(to Bono).*   All they want is the money. That makes six or seven times I done went down there and got him. See me coming they stick out their *hands.*

BONO.   Yeah. I know what you mean. That's all they care about . . . that money. They don't care about what's right. *(Pause.)* Nigger, why you got to go and get some hard wood? You ain't doing nothing but building a little old fence. Get you some soft pine wood. That's all you need.

TROY.   I know what I'm doing. This is outside wood. You put pine wood inside the house. Pine wood is inside wood. This here is outside wood. Now you tell me where the fence is gonna be?

BONO.   You don't need this wood. You can put it up with pine wood and it'll stand as long as you gonna be here looking at it.

TROY.   How you know how long I'm gonna be here, nigger? Hell, I might just live forever. Live longer than old man Horsely.

BONO.   That's what Magee used to say.

TROY. Magee's a damn fool. Now you tell me who you ever heard of gonna pull their own teeth with a pair of rusty pliers.

BONO. The old folks . . . my granddaddy used to pull his teeth with pliers. They ain't had no dentists for the colored folks back then.

TROY. Get clean pliers! You understand? Clean pliers! Sterilize them! Besides we ain't living back then. All Magee had to do was walk over to Doc Goldblum's.

BONO. I see where you and that Tallahassee gal . . . that Alberta . . . I see where you all done got tight.

TROY. What you mean "got tight"?

BONO. I see where you be laughing and joking with her all the time.

TROY. I laughs and jokes with all of them, Bono. You know me.

BONO. That ain't the kind of laughing and joking I'm talking about.

(Cory enters from the house.)

CORY. How you doing, Mr. Bono?

TROY. Cory? Get that saw from Bono and cut some wood. He talking about the wood's too hard to cut. Stand back there, Jim, and let that young boy show you how it's done.

BONO. He's sure welcome to it. *(Cory takes the saw and begins to cut the wood.)* Whew-e-e! Look at that. Big old strong boy. Look like Joe Louis. Hell, must be getting old the way I'm watching that boy whip through that wood.

CORY. I don't see why Mama want a fence around the yard noways.

TROY. Damn if I know either. What the hell she keeping out with it? She ain't got nothing nobody want.

BONO. Some people build fences to keep people out . . . and other people build fences to keep people in. Rose wants to hold on to you all. She loves you.

TROY. Hell, nigger, I don't need nobody to tell me my wife loves me, Cory . . . go on in the house and see if you can find that other saw.

CORY. Where's it at?

TROY. I said find it! Look for it till you find it! *(Cory exits into the house.)* What's that supposed to mean? Wanna keep us in?

BONO. Troy . . . I done known you seem like damn near my whole life. You and Rose both. I done know both of you all for a long time. I remember when you met Rose. When you was hitting them baseball out the park. A lot of them old gals was after you then. You had the pick of the litter. When you picked Rose, I was happy for you. That was the first time I knew you had any sense. I said . . . My man Troy knows what he's doing . . . I'm gonna follow this nigger . . . he might take me somewhere. I been following you too. I done learned a whole heap of things about life watching you. I done learned how to tell where the shit lies. How to tell it from the alfalfa. You done learned me a lot of things. You showed me how to not make the same mistakes . . . to take life as it comes along and keep putting one foot in front of the other. *(Pause.)* Rose a good woman, Troy.

TROY. Hell, nigger, I know she a good woman. I been married to her for eighteen years. What you got on your mind, Bono?

BONO. I just say she a good woman. Just like I say anything. I ain't got to have nothing on my mind.

TROY. You just gonna say she a good woman and leave it hanging out there like that? Why you telling me she a good woman?

BONO. She loves you, Troy. Rose loves you.

TROY. You saying I don't measure up. That's what you trying to say. I don't measure up 'cause I'm seeing this other gal. I know what you trying to say.

BONO. I know what Rose means to you, Troy. I'm just trying to say I don't want to see you mess up.

TROY. Yeah, I appreciate that, Bono. If you was messing around on Lucille I'd be telling you the same thing.

BONO. Well, that's all I got to say. I just say that because I love you both.

TROY. Hell, you know me . . . I wasn't out there looking for nothing. You can't find a better woman than Rose. I know that. But seems like this woman just stuck onto me where I can't shake her loose. I done wrestled with it, tried to throw her off me . . . but she just stuck on tighter. Now she's stuck on for good.

BONO. You's in control . . . that's what you tell me all the time. You responsible for what you do.

TROY. I ain't ducking the responsibility of it. As long as it sets right in my heart . . . then I'm okay. Cause that's all I listen to. It'll tell me right from wrong every time. And I ain't talking about doing Rose no bad turn. I love Rose. She done carried me a long ways and I love and respect her for that.

BONO. I know you do. That's why I don't want to see you hurt her. But what you gonna do when she find out? What you got then? If you try and juggle both of them . . . sooner or later you gonna drop one of them. That's common sense.

TROY. Yeah, I hear what you saying, Bono. I been trying to figure a way to work it out.

BONO. Work it out right, Troy. I don't want to be getting all up between you and Rose's business . . . but work it so it come out right.

TROY. Ah hell, I get all up between you and Lucille's business. When you gonna get that woman that refrigerator she been wanting? Don't tell me you ain't got no money now. I know who your banker is. Mellon don't need that money bad as Lucille want that refrigerator. I'll tell you that.

BONO. Tell you what I'll do . . . when you finish building this fence for Rose . . . I'll buy Lucille that refrigerator.

TROY. You done stuck your foot in your mouth now! *(Troy grabs up a board and begins to saw. Bono starts to walk out the yard.)* Hey, nigger . . . where you going?

BONO. I'm going home. I know you don't expect me to help you now. I'm protecting my money. I wanna see you put that fence up by yourself. That's what I want to see. You'll be here another six months without me.

TROY. Nigger, you ain't right.

BONO. When it comes to my money . . . I'm right as fireworks on the Fourth of July.

TROY. All right, we gonna see now. You better get out your bankbook.

(Bono exits, and Troy continues to work. Rose enters from the house.)

ROSE. What they say down there? What's happening with Gabe?

TROY. I went down there and got him out. Cost me fifty dollars. Say he was disturbing the peace. Judge set up a hearing for him in three weeks. Say to show cause why he shouldn't be recommitted.

ROSE. What was he doing that cause them to arrest him?

TROY. Some kids was teasing him and he run them off home. Say he was howling and carrying on. Some folks seen him and called the police. That's all it was.

ROSE. Well, what's you say? What'd you tell the judge?

TROY.   Told him I'd look after him. It didn't make no sense to recommit the man. He stuck out his big greasy palm and told me to give him fifty dollars and take him on home.

ROSE.   Where's he at now? Where'd he go off to?

TROY.   He's gone on about his business. He don't need nobody to hold his hand.

ROSE.   Well, I don't know. Seem like that would be the best place for him if they did put him into the hospital. I know what you're gonna say. But that's what I think would be best.

TROY.   The man done had his life ruined fighting for what? And they wanna take and lock him up. Let him be free. He don't bother nobody.

ROSE.   Well, everybody got their own way of looking at it I guess. Come on and get your lunch. I got a bowl of lima beans and some cornbread in the oven. Come on get something to eat. Ain't no sense you fretting over Gabe.

(Rose turns to go into the house.)

TROY.   Rose . . . got something to tell you.

ROSE.   Well, come on . . . wait till I get this food on the table.

TROY.   Rose! *(She stops and turns around.)* I don't know how to say this. *(Pause.)* I can't explain it none. It just sort of grows on you till it gets out of hand. It starts out like a little bush . . . and the next thing you know it's a whole forest.

ROSE.   Troy . . . what is you talking about?

TROY.   I'm talking, woman, let me talk. I'm trying to find a way to tell you . . . I'm gonna be a daddy. I'm gonna be somebody's daddy.

ROSE.   Troy . . . you're not telling me this? You're gonna be . . . what?

TROY.   Rose . . . now . . . see . . .

ROSE.   You telling me you gonna be somebody's daddy? You telling your wife this?

(Gabriel enters from the street. He carries a rose in his hand.)

GABRIEL.   Hey, Troy! Hey, Rose!

ROSE.   I have to wait eighteen years to hear something like this.

GABRIEL.   Hey, Rose . . . I got a flower for you. *(He hands it to her.)* That's a rose. Same rose like you is.

ROSE.   Thanks, Gabe.

GABRIEL.   Troy, you ain't mad at me is you? Them bad mens come and put me away. You ain't mad at me is you?

TROY.   Naw, Gabe, I ain't mad at you.

ROSE.   Eighteen years and you wanna come with this.

GABRIEL *(takes a quarter out of his pocket)*.   See what I got? Got a brand new quarter.

TROY.   Rose . . . it's just . . .

ROSE.   Ain't nothing you can say, Troy. Ain't no way of explaining that.

GABRIEL.   Fellow that give me this quarter had a whole mess of them. I'm gonna keep this quarter till it stop shining.

ROSE.   Gabe, go on in the house there. I got some watermelon in the frigidaire. Go on and get you a piece.

GABRIEL.   Say, Rose . . . you know I was chasing hellhounds and them bad mens come and get me and take me away. Troy helped me. He come down there and told them they better let me go before he beat them up. Yeah, he did!

ROSE.   You go on and get you a piece of watermelon, Gabe. Them bad mens is gone now.

GABRIEL.   Okay, Rose . . . gonna get me some watermelon. The kind with the stripes on it.

(Gabriel exits into the house.)

ROSE.   Why, Troy? Why? After all these years to come dragging this in to me now. It don't make no sense at your age. I could have expected this ten or fifteen years ago, but not now.

TROY.   Age ain't got nothing to do with it, Rose.

ROSE.   I done tried to be everything a wife should be. Everything a wife could be. Been married eighteen years and I got to live to see the day you tell me you been seeing another woman and done fathered a child by her. And you know I ain't never wanted no half nothing in my family. My whole family is half. Everybody got different fathers and mothers . . . my two sisters and my brother. Can't hardly tell who's who. Can't never sit down and talk about Papa and Mama. It's your papa and your mama and my papa and my mama . . .

TROY.   Rose . . . stop it now.

ROSE.   I ain't never wanted that for none of my children. And now you wanna drag your behind in here and tell me something like this.

TROY.   You ought to know. It's time for you to know.

ROSE.   Well, I don't want to know, goddamn it!

TROY.   I can't just make it go away. It's done now. I can't wish the circumstance of the thing away.

ROSE.   And you don't want to either. Maybe you want to wish me and my boy away. Maybe that's what you want? Well, you can't wish us away. I've got eighteen years of my life invested in you. You ought to have stayed upstairs in my bed where you belong.

TROY.   Rose . . . now listen to me . . . we can get a handle on this thing. We can talk this out . . . come to an understanding.

ROSE.   All of a sudden it's "we." Where was "we" at when you was down there rolling around with some godforsaken woman? "We" should have come to an understanding before you started making a damn fool of yourself. You're a day late and a dollar short when it comes to an understanding with me.

TROY.   It's just . . . She gives me a different idea . . . a different understanding about myself. I can step out of this house and get away from the pressures and problems . . . be a different man. I ain't got to wonder how I'm gonna pay the bills or get the roof fixed. I can just be a part of myself that I ain't never been.

ROSE.   What I want to know . . . is do you plan to continue seeing her. That's all you can say to me.

TROY.   I can sit up in her house and laugh. Do you understand what I'm saying. I can laugh out loud . . . and it feels good. It reaches all the way down to the bottom of my shoes. *(Pause.)* Rose, I can't give that up.

ROSE.   Maybe you ought to go on and stay down there with her . . . if she's a better woman than me.

TROY.   It ain't about nobody being a better woman or nothing. Rose, you ain't the blame. A man couldn't ask for no woman to be a better wife than you've been. I'm responsible for it. I done locked myself into a pattern trying to take care of you all that I forgot about myself.

ROSE.   What the hell was I there for? That was my job, not somebody else's.

TROY.   Rose, I done tried all my life to live decent . . . to live a clean . . . hard . . . useful life. I tried to be a good husband to you. In every way I knew how. Maybe I come into the world backwards, I don't know. But . . . you born with two strikes on you before you come to the plate. You got to guard it closely . . . always looking for the curve ball on the inside corner. You can't afford to let none get past you. You can't afford a call strike. If you going down . . . you going down swinging. Everything lined up against you. What you gonna do. I fooled them, Rose. I bunted. When I found you and Cory and a halfway decent job . . . I was safe. Couldn't nothing touch me. I wasn't gonna strike out no more. I wasn't going back to the penitentiary. I wasn't gonna lay in the streets with a bottle of wine. I was safe. I had me a family. A job. I wasn't gonna get that last strike. I was on first looking for one of them boys to knock me in. To get me home.

    ROSE.   You should have stayed in my bed, Troy.

    TROY.   Then when I saw that gal . . . she firmed up my backbone. And I got to thinking that if I tried . . . I just might be able to steal second. Do you understand after eighteen years I wanted to steal second.

    ROSE.   You should have held me tight. You should have grabbed me and held on.

    TROY.   I stood on first base for eighteen years and I thought . . . well, goddamn it . . . go on for it!

    ROSE.   We're not talking about baseball! We're talking about you going off to lay in bed with another woman . . . and then bring it home to me. That's what we're talking about. We ain't talking about no baseball.

    TROY.   Rose, you're not listening to me. I'm trying the best I can to explain it to you. It's not easy for me to admit that I been standing in the same place for eighteen years.

    ROSE.   I been standing with you! I been right here with you, Troy. I got a life too. I gave eighteen years of my life to stand in the same spot with you. Don't you think I ever wanted other things? Don't you think I had dreams and hopes? What about my life? What about me. Don't you think it ever crossed my mind to want to know other men? That I wanted to lay up somewhere and forget about my responsibilities? That I wanted someone to make me laugh so I could feel good? You not the only one who's got wants and needs. But I held on to you, Troy. I took all my feelings, my wants and needs, my dreams . . . and I buried them inside you. I planted a seed and watched and prayed over it. I planted myself inside you and waited to bloom. And it didn't take me no eighteen years to find out the soil was hard and rocky and it wasn't never gonna bloom.

    But I held on to you, Troy. I held you tighter. You was my husband. I owed you everything I had. Every part of me I could find to give you. And upstairs in that room . . . with the darkness falling in on me . . . I gave everything I had to try and erase the doubt that you wasn't the finest man in the world. And wherever you was going . . . I wanted to be there with you. Cause you was my husband. Cause that's the only way I was gonna survive as your wife. You always talking about what you give . . . and what you don't have to give. But you take too. You take . . . and don't even know nobody's giving!

(Rose turns to exit into the house; Troy grabs her arm.)

    TROY.   You say I take and don't give!
    ROSE.   Troy! You're hurting me!
    TROY.   You say I take and don't give.
    ROSE.   Troy . . . you're hurting my arm! Let go!
    TROY.   I done give you everything I got. Don't you tell that lie on me.
    ROSE.   Troy!
    TROY.   Don't you tell that lie on me!

(Cory enters from the house.)

    CORY.   Mama!

ROSE.   Troy. You're hurting me.

TROY.   Don't you tell me about no taking and giving.

(Cory comes up behind Troy and grabs him. Troy, surprised, is thrown off balance just as Cory throws a glancing blow that catches him on the chest and knocks him down. Troy is stunned, as is Cory.)

ROSE.   Troy. Troy. No! *(Troy gets to his feet and starts at Cory.)* Troy . . . no. Please! Troy!

(Rose pulls on Troy to hold him back. Troy stops himself.)

TROY *(to Cory)*.   All right. That's strike two. You stay away from around me, boy. Don't you strike out. You living with a full count. Don't you strike out.

(Troy exits out the yard as the lights go down.)

Scene II

(It is six months later, early afternoon. Troy enters from the house and starts to exit the yard. Rose enters from the house.)

ROSE.   Troy, I want to talk to you.

TROY.   All of a sudden, after all this time, you want to talk to me, huh? You ain't wanted to talk to me for months. You ain't wanted to talk to me last night. You ain't wanted no part of me then. What you wanna talk to me about now?

ROSE.   Tomorrow's Friday.

TROY.   I know what day tomorrow is. You think I don't know tomorrow's Friday? My whole life I ain't done nothing but look to see Friday coming and you got to tell me it's Friday.

ROSE.   I want to know if you're coming home.

TROY.   I always come home, Rose. You know that. There ain't never been a night I ain't come home.

ROSE.   That ain't what I mean . . . and you know it. I want to know if you're coming straight home after work.

TROY.   I figure I'd cash my check . . . hang out at Taylors' with the boys . . . maybe play a game of checkers . . .

ROSE.   Troy, I can't live like this. I won't live like this. You livin' on borrowed time with me. It's been going on six months now you ain't been coming home.

TROY.   I be here every night. Every night of the year. That's 365 days.

ROSE.   I want you to come home tomorrow after work.

TROY.   Rose . . . I don't mess up my pay. You know that now. I take my pay and I give it to you. I don't have no money but what you give me back. I just want to have a little time to myself . . . a little time to enjoy life.

ROSE.   What about me? When's my time to enjoy life?

TROY.   I don't know what to tell you, Rose. I'm doing the best I can.

ROSE.   You ain't been home from work but time enough to change your clothes and run out . . . and you wanna call that the best you can do?

TROY.   I'm going over to the hospital to see Alberta. She went into the hospital this afternoon. Look like she might have the baby early. I won't be gone long.

ROSE.   Well, you ought to know. They went over to Miss Pearl's and got Gabe today. She said you told them to go ahead and lock him up.

TROY.   I ain't said no such thing. Whoever told you that is telling a lie. Pearl ain't doing nothing but telling a big fat lie.

ROSE.   She ain't had to tell me. I read it on the papers.

TROY.   I ain't told them nothing of the kind.

ROSE.   I saw it right there on the papers.

TROY.   What it say, huh?

ROSE.   It said you told them to take him.

TROY.   Then they screwed that up, just the way they screw up everything. I ain't worried about what they got on the paper.

ROSE.   Say the government send part of his check to the hospital and the other part to you.

TROY.   I ain't got nothing to do with that if that's the way it works. I ain't made up the rules about how it work.

ROSE.   You did Gabe just like you did Cory. You wouldn't sign the paper for Cory . . . but you signed for Gabe. You signed that paper.

(The telephone is heard ringing inside the house.)

TROY.   I told you I ain't signed nothing, woman! The only thing I signed was the release form. Hell, I can't read, I don't know what they had on that paper! I ain't signed nothing about sending Gabe away.

ROSE.   I said send him to the hospital . . . you said let him be free . . . now you done went down there and signed him to the hospital for half his money. You went back on yourself, Troy. You gonna have to answer for that.

TROY.   See now . . . you been over there talking to Miss Pearl. She done got mad cause she ain't getting Gabe's rent money. That's all it is. She's liable to say anything.

ROSE.   Troy, I seen where you signed the paper.

TROY.   You ain't seen nothing I signed. What she doing got papers on my brother anyway? Miss Pearl telling a big fat lie. And I'm gonna tell her about it too! You ain't seen nothing I signed. Say . . . you ain't seen nothing I signed.

(Rose exits into the house to answer the telephone. Presently she returns.)

ROSE.   Troy . . . that was the hospital. Alberta had the baby.

TROY.   What she have? What is it?

ROSE.   It's a girl.

TROY.   I better get on down to the hospital to see her.

ROSE.   Troy . . .

TROY.   Rose . . . I got to go see her now. That's only right . . . what's the matter . . . the baby's all right, ain't it?

ROSE.   Alberta died having the baby.

TROY.   Died . . . you say she's dead? Alberta's dead?

ROSE.   They said they done all they could. They couldn't do nothing for her.

TROY.   The baby? How's the baby?

ROSE.   They say it's healthy. I wonder who's gonna bury her.

TROY.   She had family, Rose. She wasn't living in the world by herself.

ROSE.   I know she wasn't living in the world by herself.

TROY.   Next thing you gonna want to know if she had any insurance.

ROSE.   Troy, you ain't got to talk like that.

TROY.   That's the first thing that jumped out your mouth. "Who's gonna bury her?" Like I'm fixing to take on that task for myself.

ROSE.   I am your wife. Don't push me away.

TROY.   I ain't pushing nobody away. Just give me some space. That's all. Just give me some room to breathe.

(Rose exits into the house. Troy walks about the yard.)

TROY *(with a quiet rage that threatens to consume him).*   All right . . . Mr. Death. See now . . . I'm gonna tell you what I'm gonna do. I'm gonna take and build me a fence around this yard. See? I'm gonna build me a fence around what belongs to me. And then I want you to stay on the other side. See? You stay over there until you're ready for me. Then you come on. Bring your army. Bring your sickle. Bring your wrestling clothes. I ain't gonna fall down on my vigilance this time. You ain't gonna sneak up on me no more. When you ready for me . . . when the top of your list say Troy Maxson . . . that's when you come around here. You come up and knock on the front door. Ain't nobody else got nothing to do with this. This is between you and me. Man to man. You stay on the other side of that fence until you ready for me. Then you come up and knock on the front door. Anytime you want. I'll be ready for you.

(The lights go down to black.)

Scene III

(The lights come up on the porch. It is late evening three days later. Rose sits listening to the ball game waiting for Troy. The final out of the game is made and Rose switches off the radio. Troy enters the yard carrying an infant wrapped in blankets. He stands back from the house and calls.)

(Rose enters and stands on the porch. There is a long, awkward silence, the weight of which grows heavier with each passing second.)

TROY.   Rose . . . I'm standing here with my daughter in my arms. She ain't but a wee bittie little old thing. She don't know nothing about grownups' business. She innocent . . . and she ain't got no mama.

ROSE.   What you telling me for, Troy? *(She turns and exits into the house.)*

TROY.   Well . . . I guess we'll just sit out here on the porch. *(He sits down on the porch. There is an awkward indelicateness about the way he handles the baby. His largeness engulfs and seems to swallow it. He speaks loud enough for Rose to hear.)* A man's got to do what's right for him. I ain't sorry for nothing I done. It felt right in my heart. *(To the baby.)* What you smiling at? Your daddy's a big man. Got these great big old hands. But sometimes he's scared. And right now your daddy's scared cause we sitting out here and ain't got no home. Oh, I been homeless before. I ain't had no little baby with me. But I been homeless. You just be out on the road by your lonesome and you see one of them trains coming and you just kinda go like this . . .

(He sings as a lullaby.) Please, Mr. Engineer let a man ride the line Please, Mr. Engineer let a man ride the line I ain't got no ticket please let me ride the blinds

(Rose enters from the house. Troy hearing her steps behind him, stands and faces her.) She's my daughter, Rose. My own flesh and blood. I can't deny her no more than I can deny them boys. *(Pause.)* You and them boys is my family. You and them and this child is all I got in the world. So I guess what I'm saying is . . . I'd appreciate it if you'd help me take care of her.

ROSE.   Okay, Troy . . . you're right. I'll take care of your baby for you . . . cause . . . like you say . . . she's innocent . . . and you can't visit the sins of the father upon the child. A motherless child has got a hard time. *(She takes the baby from him.)* From right now . . . this child got a mother. But you a womanless man.

(Rose turns and exits into the house with the baby. Lights go down to black.)

Scene IV

(It is two months later. Lyons enters from the street. He knocks on the door and calls.)

LYONS.   Hey, Rose! *(Pause.)* Rose!

ROSE *(from inside the house).*   Stop that yelling. You gonna wake up Raynell. I just got her to sleep.

LYONS.   I just stopped by to pay Papa this twenty dollars I owe him. Where's Papa at?

ROSE.   He should be here in a minute. I'm getting ready to go down to the church. Sit down and wait on him.

LYONS.   I got to go pick up Bonnie over her mother's house.

ROSE.   Well, sit it down there on the table. He'll get it.

LYONS *(enters the house and sets the money on the table).*   Tell Papa I said thanks. I'll see you again.

ROSE.   All right, Lyons. We'll see you.

(Lyons starts to exit as Cory enters.)

CORY.   Hey, Lyons.

LYONS.   What's happening, Cory. Say man, I'm sorry I missed your graduation. You know I had a gig and couldn't get away. Otherwise, I would have been there, man. So what you doing?

CORY.   I'm trying to find a job.

LYONS.   Yeah I know how that go, man. It's rough out here. Jobs are scarce.

CORY.   Yeah, I know.

LYONS.   Look here, I got to run. Talk to Papa . . . he know some people. He'll be able to help get you a job. Talk to him . . . see what he say.

CORY.   Yeah . . . all right, Lyons.

LYONS.   You take care. I'll talk to you soon. We'll find some time to talk.

(Lyons exits the yard. Cory wanders over to the tree, picks up the bat, and assumes a batting stance. He studies an imaginary pitcher and swings. Dissatisfied with the result, he tries again. Troy enters. They eye each other for a beat. Cory puts the bat down and exits the yard. Troy starts into the house as Rose exits with Raynell. She is carrying a cake.)

TROY.   I'm coming in and everybody's going out.

ROSE.   I'm taking this cake down to the church for the bake sale. Lyons was by to see you. He stopped by to pay you your twenty dollars. It's laying in there on the table.

TROY *(going into his pocket).*   Well . . . here go this money.

ROSE.   Put it in there on the table, Troy. I'll get it.

TROY.   What time you coming back?

ROSE.   Ain't no use in you studying me. It don't matter what time I come back.

TROY.   I just asked you a question, woman. What's the matter . . . can't I ask you a question?

ROSE.   Troy, I don't want to go into it. Your dinner's in there on the stove. All you got to do is heat it up. And don't you be eating the rest of them cakes in there. I'm coming back for them. We having a bake sale at the church tomorrow.

(Rose exits the yard. Troy sits down on the steps, takes a pint bottle from his pocket, opens it, and drinks. He begins to sing.)

TROY.   Hear it ring! Hear it ring!
Had an old dog his name was Blue
You know Blue was mighty true
You know Blue was a good old dog
Blue treed a possum in a hollow log
You know from that he was a good old dog

(Bono enters the yard.)

BONO.   Hey, Troy.

TROY.   Hey, what's happening, Bono?

BONO.   I just thought I'd stop by to see you.

TROY.   What you stop by and see me for? You ain't stopped by in a month of Sundays. Hell, I must owe you money or something.

BONO.   Since you got your promotion I can't keep up with you. Used to see you every day. Now I don't even know what route you working.

TROY.   They keep switching me around. Got me out in Greentree now . . . hauling white folks' garbage.

BONO.   Greentree, huh? You lucky, at least you ain't got to be lifting them barrels. Damn if they ain't getting heavier. I'm gonna put in my two years and call it quits.

TROY.   I'm thinking about retiring myself.

BONO.   You got it easy. You can drive for another five years.

TROY.   It ain't the same, Bono. It ain't like working the back of the truck. Ain't got nobody to talk to . . . feel like you working by yourself. Naw, I'm thinking about retiring. How's Lucille?

BONO.   She all right. Her arthritis get to acting up on her sometime. Saw Rose on my way in. She going down to the church, huh?

TROY.   Yeah, she took up going down there. All them preachers looking for somebody to fatten their pockets. *(Pause.)* Got some gin here.

BONO.   Naw, thanks. I just stopped by to say hello.

TROY.   Hell, nigger . . . you can take a drink. I ain't never known you to say no to a drink. You ain't got to work tomorrow.

BONO.   I just stopped by. I'm fixing to go over to Skinner's. We got us a domino game going over his house every Friday.

TROY.   Nigger, you can't play no dominoes. I used to whup you four games out of five.

BONO.   Well, that learned me. I'm getting better.

TROY.   Yeah? Well, that's all right.

BONO.   Look here . . . I got to be getting on. Stop by sometime, huh?

TROY.   Yeah, I'll do that, Bono. Lucille told Rose you bought her a new refrigerator.

BONO.   Yeah, Rose told Lucille you had finally built your fence . . . so I figured we'd call it even.

TROY.   I knew you would.

BONO.   Yeah . . . okay. I'll be talking to you.

TROY.   Yeah, take care, Bono. Good to see you. I'm gonna stop over.

BONO.   Yeah. Okay, Troy.

(Bono exits. Troy drinks from the bottle.)

TROY.   Old Blue died and I dig his grave
Let him down with a golden chain
Every night when I hear old Blue bark

I know Blue treed a possum in Noah's Ark.
Hear it ring! Hear it ring!

(Cory enters the yard. They eye each other for a beat. Troy is sitting in the middle of the steps. Cory walks over.)

CORY.   I got to get by.

TROY.   Say what? What's you say?

CORY.   You in my way. I got to get by.

TROY.   You got to get by where? This is my house. Bought and paid for. In full. Took me fifteen years. And if you wanna go in my house and I'm sitting on the steps . . . you say excuse me. Like your mama taught you.

CORY.   Come on, Pop . . . I got to get by.

(Cory starts to maneuver his way past Troy. Troy grabs his leg and shoves him back.)

TROY.   You just gonna walk over top of me?

CORY.   I live here too!

TROY *(advancing toward him).*   You just gonna walk over top of me in my own house?

CORY.   I ain't scared of you.

TROY.   I ain't asked if you was scared of me. I asked you if you was fixing to walk over top of me in my own house? That's the question. You ain't gonna say excuse me? You just gonna walk over top of me?

CORY.   If you wanna put it like that.

TROY.   How else am I gonna put it?

CORY.   I was walking by you to go into the house cause you sitting on the steps drunk, singing to yourself. You can put it like that.

TROY.   Without saying excuse me??? (Cory doesn't respond.) I asked you a question. Without saying excuse me???

CORY.   I ain't got to say excuse me to you. You don't count around here no more.

TROY.   Oh, I see . . . I don't count around here no more. You ain't got to say excuse me to your daddy. All of a sudden you done got so grown that your daddy don't count around here no more . . . Around here in his own house and yard that he done paid for with the sweat of his brow. You done got so grown to where you gonna take over. You gonna take over my house. Is that right? You gonna wear my pants. You gonna go in there and stretch out on my bed. You ain't got to say excuse me cause I don't count around here no more. Is that right?

CORY.   That's right. You always talking this dumb stuff. Now, why don't you just get out my way.

TROY.   I guess you got someplace to sleep and something to put in your belly. You got that, huh? You got that? That's what you need. You got that, huh?

CORY.   You don't know what I got. You ain't got to worry about what I got.

TROY.   You right! You one hundred percent right! I done spent the last seventeen years worrying about what you got. Now it's your turn, see? I'll tell you what to do. You grown . . . we done established that. You a man. Now, let's see you act like one. Turn your behind around and walk out this yard. And when you get out there in the alley . . . you can forget about this house. See? 'Cause this is my house. You go on and be a man and get your own house. You can forget about this. 'Cause this is mine. You go on and get yours 'cause I'm through with doing for you.

CORY.   You talking about what you did for me . . . what'd you ever give me?

TROY.   Them feet and bones! That pumping heart, nigger! I give you more than anybody else is ever gonna give you.

CORY.   You ain't never gave me nothing! You ain't never done nothing but hold me back. Afraid I was gonna be better than you. All you ever did was try and make me scared of you. I used to tremble every time you called my name. Every time I heard your footsteps in the house. Wondering all the time . . . what's Papa gonna say if I do this? . . . What's he gonna say if I do that? . . . What's Papa gonna say if I turn on the radio? And Mama, too . . . she tries . . . but she's scared of you.

TROY.   You leave your mama out of this. She ain't got nothing to do with this.

CORY.   I don't know how she stand you . . . after what you did to her.

TROY.   I told you to leave your mama out of this!

(He advances toward Cory.)

CORY.   What you gonna do . . . give me a whupping? You can't whup me no more. You're too old. You just an old man.

TROY *(shoves him on his shoulder)*.   Nigger! That's what you are. You just another nigger on the street to me!

CORY.   You crazy! You know that?

TROY.   Go on now! You got the devil in you. Get on away from me!

CORY.   You just a crazy old man . . . talking about I got the devil in me.

TROY.   Yeah, I'm crazy! If you don't get on the other side of that yard . . . I'm gonna show you how crazy I am! Go on . . . get the hell out of my yard.

CORY.   It ain't your yard. You took Uncle Gabe's money he got from the army to buy this house and then you put him out.

TROY *(Troy advances on Cory)*.   Get your black ass out of my yard!

(Troy's advance backs Cory up against the tree. Cory grabs up the bat.)

CORY.   I ain't going nowhere! Come on . . . put me out! I ain't scared of you.

TROY.   That's my bat!

CORY.   Come on!

TROY.   Put my bat down!

CORY.   Come on, put me out. *(Cory swings at Troy, who backs across the yard.)* What's the matter? You so bad . . . put me out! *(Troy advances toward Cory.)*

CORY *(backing up)*.   Come on! Come on!

TROY.   You're gonna have to use it! You wanna draw that bat back on me . . . you're gonna have to use it.

CORY.   Come on! . . . Come on!

(Cory swings the bat at Troy a second time. He misses. Troy continues to advance toward him.)

TROY.   You're gonna have to kill me! You wanna draw that bat back on me. You're gonna have to kill me. *(Cory, backed up against the tree, can go no farther. Troy taunts him. He sticks out his head and offers him a target.)* Come on! Come on!

(Cory is unable to swing the bat. Troy grabs it.)

TROY.   Then I'll show you. *(Cory and Troy struggle over the bat. The struggle is fierce and fully engaged. Troy ultimately is the stronger and takes the bat from Cory and stands over him ready to swing. He stops himself.)* Go on and get away from around my house.

(Cory, stung by his defeat, picks himself up, walks slowly out of the yard and up the alley.)

CORY.   Tell Mama I'll be back for my things.

TROY. They'll be on the other side of that fence. *(Cory exits.)* I can't taste nothing. Hallelujah! I can't taste nothing no more. *(Troy assumes a batting posture and begins to taunt Death, the fastball on the outside corner.)* Come on! It's between you and me now! Come on! Anytime you want! Come on! I be ready for you . . . but I ain't gonna be easy.

(The lights go down on the scene.)

Scene V

(The time is 1965. The lights come up in the yard. It is the morning of Troy's funeral. A funeral plaque with a light hangs beside the door. There is a small garden plot off to the side. There is noise and activity in the house as Rose, Gabriel, and Bono have gathered. The door opens and Raynell, seven years old, enters dressed in a flannel nightgown. She crosses to the garden and pokes around with a stick. Rose calls from the house.)

ROSE. Raynell!
RAYNELL. Mam?
ROSE. What you doing out there?
RAYNELL. Nothing.

(Rose comes to the door.)

ROSE. Girl, get in here and get dressed. What you doing?
RAYNELL. Seeing if my garden growed.
ROSE. I told you it ain't gonna grow overnight. You got to wait.
RAYNELL. It don't look like it never gonna grow. Dag!
ROSE. I told you a watched pot never boils. Get in here and get dressed.
RAYNELL. This ain't even no pot, Mama.
ROSE. You just have to give it a chance. It'll grow. Now you come on and do what I told you. We got to be getting ready. This ain't no morning to be playing around. You hear me?
RAYNELL. Yes, mam.

(Rose exits into the house. Raynell continues to poke at her garden with a stick. Cory enters. He is dressed in a Marine corporal's uniform, and carries a duffel bag. His posture is that of a military man, and his speech has a clipped sternness.)

CORY *(to Raynell)*. Hi. *(Pause.)* I bet your name is Raynell.
RAYNELL. Uh huh.
CORY. Is your mama home?

(Raynell runs up on the porch and calls through the screendoor.)

RAYNELL. Mama . . . there's some man out here. Mama?

(Rose comes to the door.)

ROSE. Cory? Lord have mercy! Look here, you all!

(Rose and Cory embrace in a tearful reunion as Bono and Lyons enter from the house dressed in funeral clothes.)

BONO. Aw, looka here . . .
ROSE. Done got all grown up!
CORY. Don't cry, Mama. What are you crying about?
ROSE. I'm just so glad you made it.

CORY.   Hey Lyons. How you doing, Mr. Bono.

(Lyons goes to embrace Cory.)

LYONS.   Look at you, man. Look at you. Don't he look good, Rose. Got them Corporal stripes.

ROSE.   What took you so long.

CORY.   You know how the Marines are, Mama. They got to get all their paperwork straight before they let you do anything.

ROSE.   Well, I'm sure glad you made it. They let Lyons come. Your Uncle Gabe's still in the hospital. They don't know if they gonna let him out or not. I just talked to them a little while ago.

LYONS.   A Corporal in the United States Marines.

BONO.   Your daddy knew you had it in you. He used to tell me all the time.

LYONS.   Don't he look good, Mr. Bono?

BONO.   Yeah, he remind me of Troy when I first met him. *(Pause.)* Say, Rose, Lucille's down at the church with the choir. I'm gonna go down and get the pallbearers lined up. I'll be back to get you all.

ROSE.   Thanks, Jim.

CORY.   See you, Mr. Bono.

LYONS *(with his arm around Raynell)*.   Cory . . . look at Raynell. Ain't she precious? She gonna break a whole lot of hearts.

ROSE.   Raynell, come and say hello to your brother. This is your brother, Cory. You remember Cory.

RAYNELL.   No, Mam.

CORY.   She don't remember me, Mama.

ROSE.   Well, we talk about you. She heard us talk about you. *(To Raynell.)* This is your brother, Cory. Come on and say hello.

RAYNELL.   Hi.

CORY.   Hi. So you're Raynell. Mama told me a lot about you.

ROSE.   You all come on into the house and let me fix you some breakfast. Keep up your strength.

CORY.   I ain't hungry, Mama.

LYONS.   You can fix me something, Rose. I'll be in there in a minute.

ROSE.   Cory, you sure you don't want nothing. I know they ain't feeding you right.

CORY.   No, Mama . . . thanks. I don't feel like eating. I'll get something later.

ROSE.   Raynell . . . get on upstairs and get that dress on like I told you.

(Rose and Raynell exit into the house.)

LYONS.   So . . . I hear you thinking about getting married.

CORY.   Yeah, I done found the right one, Lyons. It's about time.

LYONS.   Me and Bonnie been split up about four years now. About the time Papa retired. I guess she just got tired of all them changes I was putting her through. *(Pause.)* I always knew you was gonna make something out yourself. Your head was always in the right direction. So . . . you gonna stay in . . . make it a career . . . put in your twenty years?

CORY.   I don't know. I got six already, I think that's enough.

LYONS.   Stick with Uncle Sam and retire early. Ain't nothing out here. I guess Rose told you what happened with me. They got me down the workhouse. I thought I was being slick cashing other people's checks.

CORY.   How much time you doing?

LYONS.   They give me three years. I got that beat now. I ain't got but nine more months. It ain't so bad. You learn to deal with it like anything else. You got to take the crookeds with the straights. That's what Papa used to say. He used to say that when he struck out. I seen him strike out three times in a row . . . and the next time up he hit the ball over the grandstand. Right out there in Homestead Field. He wasn't satisfied hitting in the seats . . . he want to hit it over everything! After the game he had two hundred people standing around waiting to shake his hand. You got to take the crookeds with the straights. Yeah, Papa was something else.

CORY.   You still playing?

LYONS.   Cory . . . you know I'm gonna do that. There's some fellows down there we got us a band . . . we gonna try and stay together when we get out . . . but yeah, I'm still playing. It still helps me to get out of bed in the morning. As long as it do that I'm gonna be right there playing and trying to make some sense out of it.

ROSE *(calling)*.   Lyons, I got these eggs in the pan.

LYONS.   Let me go on and get these eggs, man. Get ready to go bury Papa. *(Pause.)* How you doing? You doing all right?

(Cory nods. Lyons touches him on the shoulder and they share a moment of silent grief. Lyons exits into the house. Cory wanders about the yard. Raynell enters.)

RAYNELL.   Hi.

CORY.   Hi.

RAYNELL.   Did you used to sleep in my room?

CORY.   Yeah . . . that used to be my room.

RAYNELL.   That's what Papa call it. "Cory's room." It got your football in the closet.

(Rose comes to the door.)

ROSE.   Raynell, get in there and get them good shoes on.

RAYNELL.   Mama, can't I wear these. Them other one hurt my feet.

ROSE.   Well, they just gonna have to hurt your feet for a while. You ain't said they hurt your feet when you went down to the store and got them.

RAYNELL.   They didn't hurt then. My feet done got bigger.

ROSE.   Don't you give me no backtalk now. You get in there and get them shoes on. *(Raynell exits into the house.)* Ain't too much changed. He still got that piece of rag tied to that tree. He was out here swinging that bat. I was just ready to go back in the house. He swung that bat and then he just fell over. Seem like he swung it and stood there with this grin on his face . . . and then he just fell over. They carried him on down to the hospital, but I knew there wasn't no need . . . why don't you come on in the house?

CORY.   Mama . . . I got something to tell you. I don't know how to tell you this . . . but I've got to tell you . . . I'm not going to Papa's funeral.

ROSE.   Boy, hush your mouth. That's your daddy you talking about. I don't want hear that kind of talk this morning. I done raised you to come to this? You standing there all healthy and grown talking about you ain't going to your daddy's funeral?

CORY.   Mama . . . listen . . .

ROSE.   I don't want to hear it, Cory. You just get that thought out of your head.

CORY.   I can't drag Papa with me everywhere I go. I've got to say no to him. One time in my life I've got to say no.

ROSE.   Don't nobody have to listen to nothing like that. I know you and your daddy ain't seen eye to eye, but I ain't got to listen to that kind of talk this morning. Whatever was between you and your daddy . . . the time has come to put it aside. Just take it and set it over there on the shelf and forget about it. Disrespecting your daddy ain't gonna make you a man, Cory. You got to find a way to come to that on your own. Not going to your daddy's funeral ain't gonna make you a man.

CORY. The whole time I was growing up . . . living in his house . . . Papa was like a shadow that followed you everywhere. It weighed on you and sunk into your flesh. It would wrap around you and lay there until you couldn't tell which one was you anymore. That shadow digging in your flesh. Trying to crawl in. Trying to live through you. Everywhere I looked, Troy Maxson was staring back at me . . . hiding under the bed . . . in the closet. I'm just saying I've got to find a way to get rid of that shadow, Mama.

ROSE. You just like him. You got him in you good.

CORY. Don't tell me that, Mama.

ROSE. You Troy Maxson all over again.

CORY. I don't want to be Troy Maxson. I want to be me.

ROSE. You can't be nobody but who you are, Cory. That shadow wasn't nothing but you growing into yourself. You either got to grow into it or cut it down to fit you. But that's all you got to make life with. That's all you got to measure yourself against that world out there. Your daddy wanted you to be everything he wasn't . . . and at the same time he tried to make you into everything he was. I don't know if he was right or wrong . . . but I do know he meant to do more good than he meant to do harm. He wasn't always right. Sometimes when he touched he bruised. And sometimes when he took me in his arms he cut.

When I first met your daddy I thought . . . Here is a man I can lay down with and make a baby. That's the first thing I thought when I seen him. I was thirty years old and had done seen my share of men. But when he walked up to me and said, "I can dance a waltz that'll make you dizzy," I thought, Rose Lee, here is a man that you can open yourself up to and be filled to bursting. Here is a man that can fill all them empty spaces you been tipping around the edges of. One of them empty spaces was being somebody's mother.

I married your daddy and settled down to cooking his supper and keeping clean sheets on the bed. When your daddy walked through the house he was so big he filled it up. That was my first mistake. Not to make him leave some room for me. For my part in the matter. But at that time I wanted that. I wanted a house that I could sing in. And that's what your daddy gave me. I didn't know to keep up his strength I had to give up little pieces of mine. I did that. I took on his life as mine and mixed up the pieces so that you couldn't hardly tell which was which anymore. It was my choice. It was my life and I didn't have to live it like that. But that's what life offered me in the way of being a woman and I took it. I grabbed hold of it with both hands.

By the time Raynell came into the house, me and your daddy had done lost touch with one another. I didn't want to make my blessing off of nobody's misfortune . . . but I took on to Raynell like she was all them babies I had wanted and never had. *(The phone rings.)* Like I'd been blessed to relive a part of my life. And if the Lord see fit to keep up my strength . . . I'm gonna do her just like your daddy did you . . . I'm gonna give her the best of what's in me.

RAYNELL *(entering, still with her old shoes).* Mama . . . Reverend Tollivier on the phone. *(Rose exits into the house.)* Hi.

CORY. Hi.

RAYNELL. You in the Army or the Marines?

CORY. Marines.

RAYNELL. Papa said it was the Army. Did you know Blue?

CORY. Blue? Who's Blue?

RAYNELL. Papa's dog what he sing about all the time.

CORY *(singing)*. Hear it ring! Hear it ring!
I had a dog his name was Blue
You know Blue was mighty true
You know Blue was a good old dog
Blue treed a possum in a hollow log
You know from that he was a good old dog.
Hear it ring! Hear it ring!

(Raynell joins in singing.)

CORY AND RAYNELL. Blue treed a possum out on a limb
Blue looked at me and I looked at him
Grabbed that possum and put him in a sack
Blue stayed there till I came back
Old Blue's feets was big and round
Never allowed a possum to touch the ground.
Old Blue died and I dug his grave
I dug his grave with a silver spade
Let him down with a golden chain
And every night I call his name
Go on Blue, you good dog you
Go on Blue, you good dog you

RAYNELL. Blue laid down and died like a man
Blue laid down and died . . .

BOTH. Blue laid down and died like a man
Now he's treeing possums in the Promised Land
I'm gonna tell you this to let you know
Blue's gone where the good dogs go
When I hear old Blue bark
When I hear old Blue bark
Blue treed a possum in Noah's Ark
Blue treed a possum in Noah's Ark.

(Rose comes to the screen door.)

ROSE. Cory, we gonna be ready to go in a minute.

CORY *(to Raynell)*. You go on in the house and change them shoes like Mama told you so we can go to Papa's funeral.

RAYNELL. Okay, I'll be back.

(Raynell exits into the house. Cory gets up and crosses over to the tree. Rose stands in the screen door watching him. Gabriel enters from the alley.)

GABRIEL *(calling)*. Hey, Rose!

ROSE. Gabe?

GABRIEL. I'm here, Rose. Hey Rose, I'm here!

(Rose enters from the house.)

ROSE. Lord . . . Look here, Lyons!

LYONS. See, I told you, Rose . . . I told you they'd let him come.

CORY. How you doing, Uncle Gabe?

LYONS. How you doing, Uncle Gabe?

GABRIEL.   Hey, Rose. It's time. It's time to tell St. Peter to open the gates. Troy, you ready? You ready, Troy. I'm gonna tell St. Peter to open the gates. You get ready now.

(Gabriel, with great fanfare, braces himself to blow. The trumpet is without a mouthpiece. He puts the end of it into his mouth and blows with great force, like a man who has been waiting some twenty-odd years for this single moment. No sound comes out of the trumpet. He braces himself and blows again with the same result. A third time he blows. There is a weight of impossible description that falls away and leaves him bare and exposed to a frightful realization. It is a trauma that a sane and normal mind would be unable to withstand. He begins to dance. A slow, strange dance, eerie and life-giving. A dance of atavistic signature and ritual. Lyons attempts to embrace him. Gabriel pushes Lyons away. He begins to howl in what is an attempt at song, or perhaps a song turning back into itself in an attempt at speech. He finishes his dance and the gates of heaven stand open as wide as God's closet.)

That's the way that go!

VIII
*W*RITING
ABOUT
*L*ITERATURE

21

The *I*mportance of *W*riting about *L*iterature

Writing helps you establish, clarify, and communicate your interpretations of literature. Not all readers of Faulkner's "A Rose for Emily," Frost's "Birches," or Glaspell's *Suppressed Desires* would have developed the interpretations you have seen in earlier pages. Such interpretations developed from personal points of view naturally expand everyone's sensitivity to the function of various issues in the poem. Your writing will, in turn, do that for others. In addition, it will clarify your own ideas and insights and make them more useful to you.

DEVELOPING INSIGHTS

Writing about literature begins with finding critical insights to help make your interpretation original and useful. One such insight might be the sudden awareness that Robert Frost's "Fire and Ice" is not a poem about the natural physics of hot and cold but about the human emotions of anger and hatred, which we associate with hot and cold. Insights begin with questions developed from a close reading. As you ask questions about details, your insights will lead you to a deeper understanding of the piece of literature and signal the possibility that you are on to something.

Sometimes you develop insights almost automatically when you read a piece of literature. But other times, a story, play, or poem will be resistant to your reading. The following tips can help in either case because they give you a system for freeing up your powers of observation.

- Assume that most details in the work will add up to a meaning that may not be obvious. Ask questions about each detail: How does it relate to details that follow it or details that come before? What significance do the details seem to have? What effect do the details have on you?

- Look for repeated words, phrases, or actions. Ask yourself: Why do these details repeat themselves? What possible meanings could they have?
- Note patterns of repetition: of similar characters, similar behavior, imagery, language, and action. Ask yourself if the patterns could add up to something meaningful.
- Examine your responses and trust them. Why do certain characters make you feel uneasy? Why do others win your sympathy?
- Study details or situations that you do not immediately understand and note what they might possibly mean to the overall work.
- Learn by watching and listening. In your discussions about literature, notice what kinds of insights other people develop and what they make of them. Keep track of the kinds of questions they seem to ask and ask them yourself.

Beginning with Close Reading

The insights that will guide you toward your interpretation of a work begin with close reading, through which you try to account for the details within the literary text. To demonstrate, let's consider the following poem.

PERCY BYSSHE SHELLEY   (1792–1822)

Ozymandias ———————————————————————— *1818*

I met a traveller from an antique land
Who said: Two vast and trunkless legs of stone
Stand in the desert . . . Near them, on the sand,
Half sunk, a shattered visage lies, whose frown,
And wrinkled lip, and sneer of cold command,   5
Tell that its sculptor well those passions read
Which yet survive, stamped on these lifeless things,
The hand that mocked them, and the heart that fed:
And on the pedestal these words appear:
"My name is Ozymandias, king of kings: 10
Look on my works, ye Mighty, and despair!"
Nothing beside remains. Round the decay
Of that colossal wreck, boundless and bare
The lone and level sands stretch far away.

Questions for close reading depend on the poem, not on background or other considerations. You should formulate these questions as you read and reread. Later, you can learn the background of the poem.

QUESTIONS FOR CLOSE READING

1.   What is "Ozymandias"? Is it a person or a place?
2.   Who is speaking in the poem?

3. What antique land is being spoken about?

4. What does the traveler describe? Why are the legs "trunkless"? Why is the visage shattered?

5. The expression on the face is a sneer. What does that tell us about the person?

6. Whose is the "hand that mocked them"? What did it mock?

7. What is the meaning of the words on the pedestal? Is there a difference in their meaning today and when they were originally written?

8. Why is there nothing around the "colossal wreck"? Why is important to know that the "sands stretch far away"?

Not all these questions may be answered right away. They come from a line-by-line reading of the poem that tries to puzzle out the main issues. Some of the questions can be answered relatively easily. For example, the name Ozymandias refers to a person. The pedestal tells us that he was a mighty king, but the fact that the statue that was on the pedestal lies shattered on the ground also tells us that the greatness of the king did not live after him. The king's power, implied in the sneer of command that the sculptor carved into the stone of the statue, has disappeared. He was not as powerful as he thought. The statue is colossal, but it is a wreck, and the works of the king have long since gone. Certain other questions, such as what antique land is referred to and who is speaking, may be held off until more work is done on the poem. Close reading is only a beginning in interpreting literature.

Taking Notes and Summarizing

During your first readings of a work such as "Ozymandias," your best preparation for writing is to underline the key phrases and words and jot down questions or observations in the margins. Use the margins to keep track of what you think is important for understanding. Once you have underlined key passages, you can then make notes and summarize the work's main ideas. Here is a sample summary with notes about what the reader needs to do to make fuller sense of the poem.

> What seems to be going on here is that the poet heard about an "antique land--probably Egypt--where there's a broken Statue. The word <u>visage</u> is interesting--means face. Look it up. This is a tough face, like a dictator or something. It sounds as if he looks mean. But it's broken now. The statue is shattered and "nothing . . . remains." All you see is desert. So this guy's empire is wasted. But there's that inscription where he says he's "king of kings." So there's a contradiction here and that's probably the point of the poem. Time destroys things, even when they're made out of stone--even big stone, like this, which is supposed to be colossal. But that's all there is to it. This guy tells the poet he saw the broken statue and then the empty sand. I guess that's the point. I should look up Ozymandias in an encyclopedia. What I don't understand is what the line means, "The hand that mocked them, and the heart that fed." I also wonder what the things are that "yet survive."

Keeping a Response Journal

One way to track the responses you give to a literary work is to use a response journal. For best results, date the journal entries so you can see what happens when you go over the work again. Here is a sample from a **response journal** on "Ozymandias." Notice that one of the responses comes after a class discussion of the poem.

Sept. 22. This poem makes me a little scared because it talks about the way things get ruined. Like whole cultures. If this is about Egypt, then it makes sense. There are these great statues in the desert there and once the Egyptians dominated the world. But that's all gone. And the point of this seems to be that if they can be destroyed, so can we. Or at least that's what it says to me. It's scary.

Sept. 24. We talked about the poem in class. I was surprised because one person said the poem made her feel relieved. That didn't make sense to me, but she said she was relieved because the king was probably a bad guy. She got that from the sneer and the frown on his face. Anyone who would leave a monument behind like that to tell everyone how great he was has to be strange. Anyway, she was relieved because the poem made her realize that people like that are wrong when they think their empire will last forever. Better things take its place. We didn't talk about the hand and the heart. I should have asked.

Sept. 27. I want to write about this one. I don't feel relieved. Or maybe in a way I do, about the tyrant being destroyed. In class we said his real name is Ramses II and he's supposed to be the pharaoh who booted out Moses in Exodus in the Bible. In those days they didn't have nuclear weapons. We do. We could destroy our civilization in an instant. Ozymandias. The point is that you feel secure when your society seems dominant, like now for us. But nothing lasts forever. Like we said in class, the Egyptians, then the Greeks, then the Romans, every empire goes down the tubes. What we said, it's kind of ironic. That's what I realized, that the whole point of the poem was ironic. Here's this big deal pharaoh, or whatever, saying his works are fantastic, when they are totally blown away. It's a tough poem when you break it down.

Whether extensive or brief, a response can be a starting point for writing about a work of literature. The focus of the last journal entry above is on irony, a contrast between what is said and what is understood: Ozymandias's boast echoes uselessly in the middle of a wasteland. Because irony is one of the favorite topics of modern critics, this journal already gives the writer a hint about one critical strategy that would be appropriate for the poem. The writer's concern about the destruction of civilization also provides an excellent beginning for a reader response approach. And talking about Egypt and wondering about the reign of Ozymandias suggest a historical approach. Studying the history of that age might produce many critical insights for interpreting this poem. Thus already three possible approaches spring to mind from these journal entries.

THE PROCESS OF WRITING AN INTERPRETIVE ESSAY: PREWRITING

Writing implies a process of discovering material and gathering, organizing, and polishing it until you have a presentable essay. Underlining, taking notes, summarizing, and keeping a response journal to generate ideas to come back to later are prewriting techniques. Others include freewriting, brainstorming, and listing, which also produce useful insights, often so much material that you may need to discard several promising topics as you focus on one.

Freewriting, Brainstorming, and Listing

Freewriting, brainstorming, and listing work best at high speed because speed neutralizes the normal self-censorship that can make writing difficult. In these stages of the writing process you can forget about punctuation, spelling, accuracy, and all the details that count in your final essay. The less you censor, the more you will find that ideas emerge, ideas you didn't know you had.

- Prewriting techniques work best right after you have read or reread the work you wish to write about.
- Speed is an essential part of these techniques because it frees up the normal restrictions we place on ourselves.
- These techniques produce garbage as well as diamonds. After freewriting or listing, sift through and pick out the diamonds—the most useful critical insights.
- Don't censor yourself. Anything you produce in the prewriting stage is potentially valuable. Remember, at this stage be totally open-minded.

Freewriting is best done with a time limit. The following example was produced with a stopwatch in one minute. The writer wrote as fast as possible. The mistakes were left as is.

> wrinkled lip gross. this visage thing. then trunkless what is trunkless about the legs. how can the legs standt isf they are brokenwreck and sand plenty of sand the sculptor must have had to deal with this guy he sculpted maybe he got killed in the act but he saw something did Oz. like this sculpture maybe would I like it

Brainstorming implies speed, too. But it also implies saying anything, no matter how unrelated it may seem at the time. Brainstorming was first used in industry: people sat around a table saying the first thing that came to their mind, usually in response to what was said by someone else. That method works. It also works when one person does it, bouncing one insight off another. After the session you sift through to find the most useful insights. Here are the results of a one-minute brainstorming on "Ozymandias."

> travelers cover a big distance
> they see places we can't

bring back ideas
expand horizons
innovation
do they tell the truth?
they like to tell stories
the thing is that nothing is here
this traveler was going where?
people travel in Egypt even today
people see ruins all the time there
ruins tell us about ourselves
ruins are always broken
that makes them interesting
who broke these statues
were they people who knew Ozymandias?
statue breakers are iconoclasts
the traveler is an iconoclast maybe
not just broken, but decayed
decay means something special
stone doesn't decay
what decays?

The brainstorming session begins with a concern for the traveler, then moves to a concern for the statues and how they got broken. This session produced different material than the response journal or the freewriting session. It also produced apparently unrelated ideas, such as the reflection on decay, which at first seems irrelevant because stone does not decay. But that raises the question: What decays? Answering that question could provide the focus of an interpretive essay.

A third prewriting method, listing, connects or collects ideas together. As in freewriting and brainstorming, work fast, do not censor yourself, and let the ideas flow freely. Aim to list all related ideas that you develop in response to the work. Begin with a word or phrase from the poem. List everything you can think of that relates to it, and when you see that you have begun another "subject," start a new list. If you need to go back to the poem for a new word or phrase to start a new list with, then do it. The list here was generated in two minutes.

1	2
pedestal	colossal
standing	huge, so vast
nothing stands	the waste is huge
falling from a pedestal	sand stretches forever
a crash	nothing
a collapse	vast nothingness
a cracking up	
smashing from a height	

3
frown is a sneer
wrinkled lip, a sneer
Oz. sneered at the gods
He's like the Greeks who sneered
    at the gods and fell
Oz. deserves his fate

4
despair
this is the point: give up hope
ironic--who has hope?

Oz. had hope, maybe faith
faith in his empire
to lose faith = despair

Narrowing the Topic

These prewriting techniques have produced more than enough material to begin shaping an interpretive essay. Each technique has provided material that can be narrowed down to a useful topic. Here are the possibilities that have been suggested by the prewriting.

Taking Notes and Summarizing.   The best focus is on the contradiction built into the inscription in contrast with the emptiness of the sand stretching around. The questions concerning what "yet survive[s]" and what the hand and heart mean are good points to develop.

Keeping a Response Journal.   The response journal focuses on the fate of Ozymandias's huge empire as a model for the fate of our own society. Empires do not live forever, even those carved in stone. Whether the world should be glad or sad about the destruction of the empire of Ozymandias is also important.

Freewriting.   The freewriting centers on the role of the sculptor. Did he purposely reveal Ozymandias's weaknesses of character? What did Ozymandias's own people know about him?

Brainstorming.   A concern for the statue breakers links with a concern for the stories travelers tell. The traveler is a historian whose tale of broken statues makes him an *iconoclast* ("breaker of statues"). An iconoclast, according to the dictionary, has no respect for authority, and this traveler has no respect for Ozymandias's.

Listing.   New issues come into play with listing. The pedestal suggests an elevation, and one cannot have a fall without an elevation. Therefore, the pedestal is a symbol. The wrinkled lips suggest disdainful sneering, a challenging of the gods, which usually comes before a tragic fall. Did Ozymandias insult the gods and tempt fate by making colossal statues of himself?

Various Interpretive Strategies

One approach is to focus on tensions within the poem, such as those relating to the ironic contrast of the boastful inscription on the pedestal and the level sands that stretch far away. This interpretation would then focus on such contrasts, a number of which have been discovered in the prewriting stages: the traveler and the listener; hope and despair; the surviving passions on "lifeless things"; the nothingness that the traveler saw and the empire that was supposed to be there.

The response journal could help us focus on the way the poem makes us uneasy about the survival of our own culture. Shelley might be trying to tell us that we have less reason to be confident that our culture will survive than Ozymandias did. Like his, our culture could be swallowed up by the sands of time. The reader response interpretation would use as support details in the poem that intensify such a response. It could also describe the feelings that the poem draws on for its power.

A psychological interpretation might begin with biographical information about the issues that were pressing on Shelley in 1817–1818 when the poem was written. For one thing, Harriet, his first wife, whom he married in 1811, committed suicide in London on December 10, 1816. Shelley had run off with Mary Wollstonecraft in 1814, and he married her on December 30, 1816. Another close friend, Fanny Imlay, killed herself in 1816 as well. Around the time the poem was written, Shelley was sick and a daughter died in infancy. Shelley was worried that his work was a failure and that he would leave nothing to posterity. Such anxieties could express themselves in this poem. The best biography of Shelley, by Newman Ivey White, discusses these issues in depth. Biographical details could produce insights into the significance of the poem.

Since history is, in a way, part of the subject of the poem, an historical approach is possible. The first thing to do, in addition to the prewriting exercise, is to look up the history of this poem in a biography of Shelley or in Thomas Hutchinson's notes in the Oxford edition of Shelley's poetry. Hutchinson's notes reveal that Shelley found the quoted inscription in *The Historical Library* by Greek historian Diodorus Siculus, who lived near the time of Christ. Diodorus said that the largest statue he saw in Egypt had the inscription "I am Ozymandias, king of kings; if anyone wishes to know what I am and where I lie, let him surpass me in some of my exploits." The Egyptian name for Ozymandias was Ramses, who was a hard-bitten warrior and part of a dynasty of eleven Egyptian pharaohs. Research into the social assumptions of Egypt of the time of Ramses II (1200 B.C.) could help an interpretation using historical techniques. Research into the recent defeat of Napoleon in 1814 would also bring useful insights into Shelley's political fears of a modem tyranny in Europe.

Other critical strategies might be used to interpret this poem, but these four approaches arc probably the most useful ones, given the poem and the material that prewriting has developed.

Developing a Thesis

A thesis states the position you propose to argue in your essay. It helps you clarify your thinking. You can develop it in the prewriting stage, in your first draft, or even later.

* A thesis makes an interpretive claim that needs to be defended.
* You can find the subject of your claim in your prewriting materials.
* Examine them for insights that could be the core of your essay. Determine your best argument by observing what you say about the literary work throughout your prewriting. Choose among your observations for the position you can best defend.

⚬ In your thesis state a position that you will defend by a close reading of the text.

Here are some sample theses built from the prewriting material gathered above and keyed to interpretive strategies:

Focus on Irony. The power of "Ozymandias" depends on irony. Ozymandias's boastful claim contrasts ironically with the reality of his broken statue lying in a desert wasteland.

Focus on Reader Response. "Ozymandias" is frightening because the same destruction of a civilization described in the poem can take place now to our own civilization.

Focus on Psychology. Shelley may have been unconsciously fretting over sexual guilt and his own potential failure as a poet when he wrote this poem.

Focus on History. Shelley's poem criticizes the staying power and influence of Ozymandias, a real king whose empire was built on terror and fear.

Theses like these samples help define the limits of your essay. They also clarify your purposes and reveal your direction in interpreting the poem. They clarify your aim because they give you something to prove. A good thesis states your purpose and implies how you are going to achieve it.

PRINCIPLES OF EVIDENCE

Backing Up Your Thesis with Details from the Text

A thesis is one thing; backing it up is another. If you say, for instance, that the most significant element in "Ozymandias" is the irony implied in the boast on a pedestal of a destroyed statue of a destroyed king, then your obligation is to back up that thesis. You do so by referring to the text of the poem and interpreting it to show how it emphasizes irony. The text is the most important source of evidence for an interpretive claim. For example, you can point to these instances of irony in the poem.

The legs "Stand in the desert," but ironically there is no body on them
The "visage" of the statue has a "sneer of cold command," but it is "shattered"
"Passions" survive on "lifeless things"
The statue is gigantic but totally alone in the desert
The inscription "on the pedestal" makes a claim that is mocked by the emptiness of the "lone and level sands"

The greatest irony is that there are no "works" to "look on" except for the gigantic statue broken into fragments. Making a claim for the importance of irony in the poem will best be defended by going to the text and finding instances of irony and analyzing them.

Assume, for example, that you begin with the following thesis.

> Shelley emphasizes the irony of finding such a colossal statue on the empty desert by focusing on the "visage" in a kind of movie close-up.

A sample interpretation beginning with the above statement and centering on its irony follows.

> Shelley emphasizes the irony of finding such a colossal statue on the empty desert by focusing on the "visage" in a kind of movie close-up. He says the "visage" of the statue has a "sneer of cold command," and then says it is "shattered." Calling it a visage is especially ironic. A king would have a visage, for instance. So when he says visage, we get the picture of something that is really great and impressive. But this visage is shattered, and Shelley is telling us that everything Ozymandias stood for is shattered, too. There is nothing left of all the greatness that he boasts about. The terrific frown that everybody feared is broken down, just like his whole empire.

The quoted words in the paragraph above are details drawn from the text. An interpretation usually uses quotations sparingly, but such details communicate your ideas and keep you close to the text and its issues. If you do not account for details in the text, you risk the possibility of wandering off in a general ramble. Keep your attention on the poem by showing how the details clarify your thesis.

Finding Patterns, Implications, Silent Gestures, Codes, and Subtleties

Underlining and taking notes as you read a poem or other piece of literature help keep track of details that should eventually suggest a pattern. Patterns usually add up to meaning and provide material to interpret. But the details imply more than they say outright. The shattering of the visage implies a loss of face, just as the "trunkless legs" imply that no body is there: nobody is visible here, only a gesture. The shards of the statue are silent gestures telling us that Ozymandias's ambition was thwarted by history. We cannot actually look at his works anymore, but we can think that our own cultural achievements may be destroyed as Ozymandias's were.

The "frown," "wrinkled lip," and "sneer" on the face are codes for tyranny. The tyrant or dictator rarely smiles. Usually the dictator shows displeasure and maintains a look designed to instill fear in people. The words vast and colossal are codes for the scope of Ozymandias's rule, but they are neutralized by the equally powerful code words for nothingness: *boundless and bare* and *lone and level*. These codes need interpretation. They suggest that natural forces somehow destroyed the unnatural tyranny of Ozymandias and, along with it, his empire. Those who fear that our culture may perish as did Ozymandias's can take heart from these codes. They seem to imply that as long as our culture avoids tyranny and the sneering power of the dictator, we may avoid the fate of destruction.

However, none of this is said directly in the poem. In order to say it, you need to fill in the poem's silences. The poem gives you the code for tyranny, then shows you the boast of the tyrant, then points to the barren landscape. But it does no more. It does not tell you that you must beware or that tyrants come to a bad end. You sense those things from interpreting the details and seeing how they form patterns. Filling in the silences is the most interesting part of the job of interpretation.

USING OUTSIDE SOURCES

Ordinarily, your only source will be the work of literature you are interpreting. For a research essay, however, critical essays, letters or journal entries from your author, a biography, or historical documents can all be important sources. In this book, you will find critical and biographical sources about the authors who are treated in depth. These sources of information can place a work in a new light to help you interpret it in new ways.

Finding Available Sources

Background sources are available for most authors. Many biographies center on economic or psychological issues and could be useful for political-economic or psychoanalytic interpretations. Some authors wrote extensive journals or letters that have been collected and published. These may provide insight into the circumstances under which a work was written. Some writers have commented on their work in interviews. The *Paris Review Interviews* (available in most libraries) includes many modern writers, beginning in the 1960s. All these can help in the study of any work of literature.

Your library will be the best source for available biographies of your author. Look up your author's name in the catalog for holdings, especially journals or letters. Also go to the shelves where your author's works are held, and study the books there. First you will find works by your author, then next to them critical and biographical discussions. Browsing on the shelves supplements the computer or card catalog, which does not always tell everything important about your author.

More specific studies can help you focus on a work such as "Ozymandias." The Modern Language Association publishes an *Annual Bibliography* keyed to literature according to its language, its nation, its historical period, its author, and then its title. You can look up *English, England, Nineteenth Century, Shelley,* and *Ozymandias* to find out what has been written in a given year on the poem. Or you can go to a library that subscribes to the *MLA Bibliography* on CD-ROM and do a computer search that will list all that has been written since 1963. The search will produce a list of critical essays, some of which may be available in your library's holdings of critical journals. You would not need to read more than a few of those available, and your best strategy is to read the most modern essay first, then read back in time. The following example is the result of a search that specified two fields: Author: Shelley; Title: Ozymandias.

1 HUM
Nablow, Ralph A.
Shelley, Ozymandias, and Volney's Les ruines
Notes and Queries v36 p172-3 June '89

SUBJECTS COVERED'
Antiquities in literature
Shelley, Percy Bysshe: 1792-1822/Sources
Volney, Constantin Francois de Chasseboeuf:comte de:
1757-1820/Influence

2 HUM
Fruman, Norman
Ozymandias and the reconciliation of opposites
Studies in the Literary Imagination v19 p71-87 Fall '86

SUBJECTS COVERED:
Imagination
Criticism
Polarity in literature
Coleridge, Samual Taylor:1772-1834

3 HUM Freedman, William
Postponement and perspectives in Shelley's Ozymandias
Studies in Romanticism v25 p63-73 Spring '86

SUBJECTS COVERED:
Travel in literature
Perspective (Philosophy)
Sculpture in literature
Shelley, Percy Bysshe:1792-1822

4 HUM
Siegel, Mark
Ozymandias melancholia: the nature of parody in Woody Allen's
Stardust memories
Literature/Film Quarterly v13 no 2 p77-84 '85
i'l

SUBJECTS COVERED:
Parody
Allen, Woody

5 HUM
Janowitz, Anne
Shelley's monument to Ozymandias
Philological Quarterly v63 p477-91 Fall '84

SUBJECTS COVERED:
Sonnets, English
Antiquities in literature
Sculpture in literature
Egypt/Antiquities
Egypt in literature
Monuments
Shelley, Percy Bysshe:1792-1822

6 HUM
Quinn, Mary A.
Ozymandias as Shelley's rejoinder to Peacock's Palmyra
English Language Notes v21 p48-56 June '84

SUBJECTS COVERED:
Antiquities in literature
Shelley, Percy Bysshe:1792-1822/Sources
Peacock, Thomas Love:1785-1866/Influence

7 HUM
Marks, Sally
My name is Ozymandias: the Kaiser in exile
Central European History vl6 p122-70 June '83

SUBJECTS COVERED:
World War,   1914-1918/Peace
World War,   1914-1918/Netherlands
Exiles
William: II:German Emperor:1859-1941

Gathering and Using Sources

As you conduct research, be sure to record in a research notebook all the sources you want to consult. Include in each entry the information you will need when you compile a Works Cited list for your essay. (See p. 1366 in this book or refer to the *MLA Handbook for Writers of Research Papers*, 5th ed., by Joseph Gibaldi and Walter S. Achtert for more about creating a Works Cited list of sources.) Here is an example of how to write an entry for an article in your research notebook.

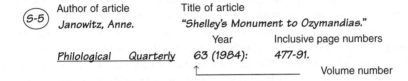

Here is an example of how to write an entry for a book in your research notebook.

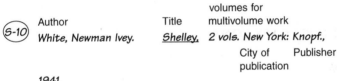

When you find an article you want to read, photocopy it, and then assign it and its listing in your research notebook a number or letter (S-5 and S-10 in the examples). Write this source identification code on every page of the photocopy. Make sure the article's page numbers show up on the photocopy; if they don't, write them in. When you read the photocopy, you can underline the important passages. (Never underline the library's copy of an article.)

When you use a book source, you will probably have to take notes, as opposed to photocopying. Use the identification number (or letter) you assign to the source on every note card or page of notes you take. Also put the source's page number(s) for the material covered on each page of notes or every note card that you write. For a multivolume work, like the White source above, include the volume number too.

Perhaps most important, *always* put quotation marks around the source's words in your notes. Write the page number in the source right after the closing quotation mark.

All these details about the identification-number system, taking notes, clearly noting page and volume numbers, and carefully distinguishing a source's words from yours will help you document the use you make of sources' words and ideas in your essay.

If your library does not have a source you want, interlibrary loan can often supply it. You can underline these articles (they are photocopies) and take notes from loaned books.

Make every effort to consult worthwhile sources. When using a book written about your author, make sure it was published by a reliable university or commercial press and that it is up to date. Look for a balanced view, one that is not obviously biased and that supports its argument with logically sound evidence. Although most sources you find will be reliable, occasionally one may be eccentric. If in doubt, ask your instructor's opinion. Be moderate in quoting from your sources. If you quote extensively, you will reduce the room available for your own interpretation. Quote the most telling comment, the most important issue. You can always explain a critic's opinion in your own words, quoting only when the critic's words are particularly economical or worthwhile. You must always establish the importance of a citation. Even the critic will need some interpretation. One mistake some writers make is leaving the critic's words there without comment, as if they settled everything. In fact, they rarely do. Your commentary and explanation are essential. (See p. 1362 for advice on handling punctuation, format, and documentation of source material in your essays.)

THE WRITING PROCESS CONTINUED

Outlining

The prewriting stage—brainstorming, listing, freewriting, and other methods—helps you free yourself up to produce a first draft of an essay. If you produce a useful list or if you see that your freewriting is taking you in a useful direction, one of the best things you can do early on is prepare an outline. It need not be absolutely detailed, but it should guide you in structuring the essay. Decide what goes where: what parts of a story, poem, or play will be discussed, and what your discussion angle will be.

The following brief outline depends on the response journal and prewriting assignments that directed the writer to combine formalist and historicist interpretive strategies.

The Shattered Visage: Irony in "Ozymandias"

   I. Background: who Ozymandias was
      A. Ramses II
         1. Statue in the British Museum
         2. Taken from Napoleon after Waterloo
      B. Current politics (maybe)
  II. Competition to write a sonnet
      A. Horace Smith
      B. Shelley's best sonnet
 III. Shelley emphasizes irony

    A. Ironic boast of Ozymandias
    B. The sneer on the broken face
IV. How irony fits in with current affairs
    A. Napoleon defeated
    B. Maybe an end to tyranny

Since it is "approximate," this outline can be kept flexible. It does not have too much detail, and it can change as you write drafts. When you read the essay (at the end of this chapter), you will see that this outline is dynamic and that it changed with the essay. Most of the material in the outline appears in the essay, but not all of it is where the author thought it would go when she constructed the outline. Your own style will dictate how you may want to outline your essay; just remember that an outline is a guide intended to change. Think of an outline as a form of planning. Make it as detailed as you need it, but do not let it constrain your imagination.

Drafting and Revising

Once you have settled on the best approach and have set up an outline that will serve you, the next step is to begin drafting. Drafting means writing an early version of the essay. Generally, writers try to get a rough draft at first so that they can rethink their purposes and strategies. If you do your planning well, your rough draft may be close to your final version. However, you must not miss the opportunity to rearrange sentences or sections of your first draft. Whether you use a computer or a ballpoint pen, you can always profit from **revising:** rethinking your organization and looking for ways to sharpen your focus and put the emphasis where it belongs.

REVISION ISSUES

- Check to see if your overall argument needs revision. You may find yourself beginning with one thesis but discovering that the evidence points you in a new direction. If that happens, revise your first draft to take your revised thesis into account. Revise your thesis statement.
- Outline your first draft to discover what additions you will need. Compare the new outline with the old to see if you have accounted for everything you wanted to.
- Before writing the final draft, make a new outline. Try to follow it closely and profit from the discoveries you made in your first draft.
- Do not let your first draft cramp your style. If you are writing a short essay, do not be afraid to discard sections and redo them. Remember that a second draft has the advantage of the first: you know more about what you want to say and how to say it.

Drafting and revising present important opportunities for making your essay strong and effective. Do not hand in a retyped first draft. Even excellent essays profit from revision.

Editing

Editing an essay is different from revising it. Revision implies making major, structural changes; editing implies making stylistic changes. When editing your essay, whether the first, second, or later draft, aim for establishing your authority as a writer. Look for chances to use the strongest verbs, the clearest sentences, the best-organized paragraphs possible. Always avoid jargon, overly technical language designed to impress somebody. Look for the simplest way to say what you mean. Test sentences by saying them out loud. Ask yourself if this is the way you would express this sentence to a parent or to a friend. Think of your audience when you write. Ask yourself whether a willing reader can hope to understand your points. If possible, have a friend read your essay and comment on it.

EDITING ISSUES

- Strengthen verbs. Usually a first draft overdoes the verb *to be*. Look for and highlight all occurrences of *is, are, was, will be,* and *were.* When you revise each sentence, find ways to eliminate those weak verbs and substitute action verbs. Use *to be* only when it presents the simplest, most essential way to say what you want. Eliminate weak verbs in this way: *Original:* "Calling it a visage is especially ironic. A king would have a visage, for instance. So when he says 'visage,' we get the picture of something that is really great and impressive. But this visage is shattered." *Revision:* "Because of the use of the word *visage,* we picture the face of a king, not the shattered remains Shelley describes."

- Avoid passive voice. First drafts often suffer from this problem. Here is a common example of passive voice: "In Wasserman's article, **it is stated** that Shelley was depressed in 1816." A revision to active tense is shorter and stronger: "Wasserman *says* that Shelley was depressed in 1816."

- Avoid redundancy. First-draft jitters may make you say the same thing twice. Expressions such as "the poet Shelley" or "the literary critic Earl Wasserman" are all too common. Context makes clear that one is a poet and the other a critic. The same is true of an expression such as "in the play *Hamlet.*" You can just write "in *Hamlet*" and be well understood. Search for redundancies and root them out.

- Shorten sentences and say things clearly. First drafts often produce long, tangled sentences because they try to say too many things at once. Break down long sentences and revise them for clarity. Vary sentence lengths in your final draft, but avoid overloading sentences with more than one topic.

- Double-check spelling, look for typos, and repair basic grammatical glitches such as faulty subject-verb agreement, sentence fragments, dangling references, and unnecessary shifts of tense, person, or perspective. Remember to use the present tense when you write about a literary *text* ("Shelley **says** the 'visage' of the statue **has** a 'sneer of cold command' ").

- Prepare a clean copy of this final, edited draft, and proofread it carefully. Uncorrected typos, misspellings, and other careless errors drain away some of your authority as a writer and critic.

The Interpretive Essay's Structure

Interpretive essays come in many sizes. Usually, an essay will be three, five, or sometimes even ten pages long. For the sake of this discussion, we have assumed an essay of three typed pages, the size of the sample essays at the end of this chapter. In typescript that would be about seven hundred fifty words. But no matter how long the essay is, its structure will conform to most of the following requirements.

- The essay begins with a title that indicates your subject.
- The first paragraph presents your thesis (argument) and reveals the direction your essay will take.
- The body of the essay contains the bulk of your interpretation. Each paragraph develops an aspect of your main thesis and works out the details of the argument.
- Quotations from the text of the story, play, or poem establish your views and give you a chance for interpretive commentary.
- Sources, either quoted or alluded to, may back up your position and allow you opportunity for interpretation and further commentary.
- Your last paragraph or paragraphs are your conclusion. They draw your argument to a close and sum up or restate your position.

These suggestions can help you fashion a strong essay. But they are only suggestions and should not be regarded as absolute. Your ultimate goal is always to offer an original and interesting interpretation of a text *that engages your attention*. There will be times when you will follow the suggestions above closely, and other times when you will veer from them. Your judgment and the suggestions of your instructor will guide you.

THE MECHANICS OF QUOTATION AND DOCUMENTATION

When you write about a literary text, one of the main strategies you use to provide evidence for your interpretation is quoting the text itself. When you use sources in addition to the literary text, you incorporate some of their ideas into your essay, quoting, paraphrasing, or summarizing them. In this section you will find advice about the mechanics of quotation, as well as MLA guidelines for documenting the uses you make of other writers' words and ideas.

Quoting from a Literary Text

In writing about a work of literature, you usually need to quote words, phrases, passages, or lines of verse from it. These quotations represent a portion of your evidence and offer you the opportunity to make your own commentary and analysis—two aspects of your interpretation.

INCORPORATING SHORT QUOTATION.   Quotations shorter than forty words of prose and four lines of poetry can be put in quotation marks and incorporated into your own sentences.

> When Shelley said, "I met a traveller from an antique land," he implied that the traveller was also old.

Separate two or three lines of quoted poetry with a slash mark. Type a space on each side of this line-dividing slash.

> With its first words, "I met a traveller from an antique land / Who said: Two vast and trunkless legs of stone / Stand in the desert," the poem conveys an impersonal, faceless impression.

SETTING OFF LONG QUOTATIONS.   Quotations of more than forty words of prose and quotations of four or more lines of poetry should be visually set off from your words. Start a new line for the quotation, and, if your instructor wants you to follow MLA style guidelines, indent each line ten spaces from the left. Then start another new line for your own words after the end of the quotation. Don't use quotation marks around a set-off quotation.

> With its first words, the poem creates an impersonal, faceless impression:
>
> > I met a traveller from an antique land
> > Who said: Two vast and trunkless legs of stone
> > Stand in the desert . . . Near them, on the sand,
> > Half sunk, a shattered visage lies, . . .
>
> But the appearance of a "face" immediately changes the mood from impersonal to ominous.

Documenting Quotations from a Literary Text

Unless your instructor gives you other instructions, you don't have to give publication information about a literary text you are writing about. If you are quoting from a long poem or play, however, giving location information for the quotation itself can be a courtesy to your readers. When omitting words from a quotation, use an ellipsis, three periods with a space separating each:

> " 'My name is Ozymandias . . . Look on my works, . . . and despair!'

When omitting a sentence in an ellipsis, use four periods with a space separating each. The fourth period is the final punctuation mark:

> "in the desert. . . . these lifeless things."

When ending a quotation with an omission, also use four periods:

> "in the desert. . . ."

When quoting poetry and omitting a line or more, use a full line of spaced periods:

I met a traveller from an ancient land
. . . .
The lone and level sands stretch far away.

When quoting from a long poem, put the line numbers in parentheses—two spaces from the last word in a set-off quotation or one space after the closing quotation mark of a short quotation. For *Paradise Lost* by John Milton, for example, (X. 123–37) at the end of a quotation means that the quoted material is lines 123 to 137 in Book X.

Quoting from a play usually involves citing the act, scene, and line numbers, especially in the works of Shakespeare or other verse playwrights. Here is that famous line from *Hamlet:* "To be, or not to be—that is the question" (III.i.57). The parenthetical information means that the quotation is from Act III, Scene i, line 57. In prose plays, give act, scene, and page number. Note that the parenthetical information for this short quotation comes after the quotation marks but *before* the closing period. If this were a set-off quotation, the parentheses would follow the concluding period as well.

To be. or not to be--that is the question:
Whether 'tis nobler in the mind to suffer
The slings and arrows of outrageous fortune
Or to take arms against a sea of troubles
And by opposing end them. . . . (III.i.57–61)

Compiling a Works Cited List

MLA (Modern Language Association) documentation format is standard for all student research papers on literature.[1] The main purpose of this format is to provide a simple, reliable method for citing sources that you rely on when writing an interpretive essay. The method uses references, often parenthetical, that direct readers to a list that appears at the end of your essay, on a separate page, usually headed *Works Cited*. These are the articles and books that you actually quote, paraphrase, or summarize in your text, apart from the literary text you are interpreting. If you read articles or books that you do not refer to but feel your reader should know about, you include them in a separate list named *Works Consulted*. That list comes after the Works Cited list. The Works Cited list makes it possible for you to refer to a book or article in a parenthetical shorthand of the kind illustrated in examples in the next section and in the student papers on "Ozymandias." Here is a Works Cited list for an essay on "Ozymandias."

[1]Published books, including this one, often follow the style outlined by the *Chicago Manual of Style*.

Works Cited

Holmes, Richard. <u>Shelley: The Pursuit</u>. London: Weidenfeld, 1974.

Janowitz, Anne. "Shelley's Monument to Ozymandias. <u>Philological Quarterly</u> 63 (1984) : 477–91.

"Ramses." <u>Encyclopaedia Britannica: Macropaedia</u>. 1986 ed.

"Shelley in Bloomsbury." <u>Smithsonian Magazine</u> June 1988: 64–73.

Thomas Hutchinson, ed. <u>Poems of Percy Bysshe Shelley</u>. Rev. G. M. Matthews. Oxford: Oxford UP, 1970.

Wasserman, Earl. "Shelley's Crisis." <u>Shelley: A Collection of Critical Essays</u>. Ed. George Ridenour. Englewood Cliffs: Prentice, 1965. 77–80.

White, Newman Ivey. <u>Shelley</u>. 2 vols. New York: Knopf, 1941.

Works Consulted

Fruman, Norman. "Ozymandias and the Reconciliation of Opposites." <u>Studies in the Literary Imagination</u> 19.3 (1986): 71–87.

Yeats, W. B. "The Philosophy of Shelley's Poetry." <u>Essays</u>. London: Macmillan, 1924.

IMPORTANT FEATURES OF WORKS CITED LISTS

* Works are alphabetized, by the last name of the author. If the author's name is unknown, use the title of the work.

* Each entry uses a hanging indentation: the first line is flush left, and every succeeding line is indented five spaces.

* Periods end each segment of the citation: Author (or editor). Title of book or article. Journal title. Volume number and other information (if an article). Place of publication: Publisher, date (if a book). Date is in parentheses if you cite an article, followed by colon (:) and pages (see Janowitz entry above).

* Book titles are underlined; names of journals are underlined. Articles are in quotation marks. The general rule is that anything of book length is underlined, whereas anything normally included in a book (such as a chapter) uses quotation marks (see Wasserman entry above: note both article and book titles).

* Short forms and abbreviations are used for publishers' names, such as Simon for *Simon & Schuster* and UP for *University Press*.

* When a second work by an author is listed, three hyphens and a period: --- are used instead of repeating the name.

Holmes, Richard. <u>Shelley: The Pursuit</u>. London: Weidenfeld, 1974.
---. <u>Coleridge: Early Visions</u>. New York: Viking, 1990.

* For magazines, include month of publication (see "Shelley in Bloomsbury" above), not the volume number.

* When a journal paginates continuously throughout a given year—as when, for example, volume 15, number 1 (1993), begins with page 1; volume 15, number 2 (1993), with page 221; and volume 15, number 3 (1993), with page 345—you need not cite the individual issue number (see Janowitz entry above).

* When the journal begins new pagination with each issue within a volume, then cite the volume, issue number, and pagination (see Fruman entry above).

For encyclopedia articles, include the date of the edition (see "Ramses" entry on p. 1366).

A fuller discussion of these details is available in the *MLA Handbook for Writers of Research Papers,* 5th ed., by Joseph Gibaldi and Walter S. Achtert, published by the Modern Language Association of America in 1999 and widely available in college bookstores. It covers all the possible problems you might face in citing any sources.

Citing Works in Your Essay in MLA Style

A few examples here and the student papers on "Ozymandias" show the basic principles of citing works in your own essays to support your points as you write. The rule is, keep it simple. Use parentheses to supply the important information that will allow readers to find the source in your Works Cited list. The following examples rely on the Works Cited list in the preceding section.

When you mention the author's name in your text, include volume (if necessary) and page reference in parentheses:

Newman Ivey White says that Shelley had eye trouble when he wrote "Ozymandias" (2: 321).

When you do not mention the author's name in your text, include it in parentheses along with the volume and page reference:

Apparently, Shelley played a great deal of chess around the time he wrote "Ozymandias" (White 2: 323).

Note that no comma comes after the author's name, the colon separates volume and page number, and you do not need "p." to indicate the page reference.

When you want to note that more than one author cites an important detail, use this form:

(Holmes 316; Yeats 110)

And if you need to refer to an author who has more than one title in your Works Cited list, use a short form of the title to indicate which book you are referring to:

(Hutchinson. <u>Poem</u> 331).

(If you used the author's name in your sentence, then you need only the title and page number.)

When in doubt, be sure to use the simplest, most economical means of citing a reference. Thus if there is no author of a piece, use the key word of the title:

("Shelley" 15).

Similarly, for an encyclopedia article, use the key term of the article as you would the author's name, and no page numbers:

("Ramses").

When you need to consult outside sources in your interpretive essays, use the clearest and most reliable method. Do not let your sources overwhelm you. Question them, use them sparingly, and be sure to go beyond them with your own commentary. Do not let them limit your imagination in regard to the work you interpret.

DETAILS OF MANUSCRIPT PREPARATION

A well-presented manuscript is more important than you may realize. When you demonstrate that you understand the formalities and conventions of an essay that needs sources, you convince your instructor of your seriousness. If you do not use sources, then a neatly typed—or carefully handwritten—essay makes the job of reading and commenting on your work much easier. If your instructor doesn't give you special manuscript format guidelines, you can safely follow these.

- Begin the first page about one-third down, with your name, course name, and instructor's name at the left. Your instructor's name is important because if the paper is lost it will be returned more quickly to your instructor than to you. In order to minimize the risk of loss, be sure to photocopy or print a second copy of any essay you hand in. A typical first page would begin something like this.

Bisberg 1

Betsy Bisberg
English 109–07
Mr. Jacobus

The Shattered Visage: Irony in "Ozymandias"

Percy Bysshe Shelley's "Ozymandias," the finest sonnet he ever wrote' (Holmes 410), is ironic in many ways. One of the most interesting things about Shelley's poem is that it was written in a competition with another poet. Horace Smith (Reiman 47–49). Both had been to the British Museum to see the Egyptian statues

- Leave margins of approximately 1 to 1 1/2 inches on the left so that your instructor can offer useful comments.
- Number each page with your last name in the upper right corner.
- When you type, double-space all your text (not single-spaced as shown here) so that comments and corrections can be inserted between the lines. If you handwrite, ask your instructor whether the essay should be single- or double-spaced.
- Do not crowd your pages. Leave comfortable margins of one inch on the top, bottom, and right.
- Proofread your essays before handing them in. Make sure that you have done everything to avoid handing in essays with typos, with misspellings (especially of

the names of your author or instructor), or with omissions that you could have caught if you were vigilant.

SAMPLE ESSAYS

Both of the following essays on Shelley's "Ozymandias" were developed from the prewriting and planning efforts shown above. The first essay uses outside sources and joins a close reading method with an historical approach. The second, which did not consult outside sources except for class discussion, uses a reader response approach. Both essays offer a distinct interpretation of the poem.

A Close Reading/Historical Interpretation Using Sources

Bisberg 1

Betsy Bisberg
English 109-07
Mr. Jacobus

The Shattered Visage: Irony in "Ozymandias"

The power of Percy Bysshe Shelley's "Ozymandias," "the finest sonnet he ever wrote" (Holmes 410), depends on irony. The boast "Look on my works, ye Mighty, and despair!" contrasts ironically with the reality of his broken statue lying in a desert wasteland. Shelley's poem was written in a competition with another poet, Horace Smith (Reiman 47-49). Both had been to the British Museum to see the Egyptian statues brought there in 1817 by the British after the defeat of Napoleon in Egypt. "Among these . . . the massive figure of Ramses II . . . perhaps the most famous of all Egyptian fragments . . ." (Holmes 410). Holmes tells us that Shelley imagined the traveler and the setting for his poem. But he did not have to imagine the statue, since its fragments rested near where he lived and he saw them whenever he wanted. In its way that was also an irony. Ramses II could not prevent these huge statues from being carted off like souvenirs. Ozymandias would not have been able to imagine a time when his statue could be carted away.

Shelley did not like tyrants, and Ramses II was a tyrant in ancient Egypt. A warlike general, he caused great turmoil in the world. According to the Encyclopaedia Britannica he was probably the pharaoh who caused Moses to leave on the exodus from Egypt. Ironically, the statue of Ramses was brought to London after the British defeated a modern tyrant, Napoleon, at Waterloo. In 1817, when Shelley saw the fragments of this huge statue, the world could breathe easier because both tyrants were defeated (Holmes 409).

Shelley really focused on the ironic boasts of all tyrants when he wrote his poem. Shelley says the "visage" of the statue has a "sneer of cold command," and then says it is "shattered." He emphasizes the irony of finding such a colossal statue on the empty desert by focusing on the "visage" in a kind of movie close-up. Calling it a visage is especially ironic. A king would have a visage, for instance. So when he says "visage," we get the picture of something that is really great and impressive. But this visage is shattered and Shelley says everything Ozymandias stood for is shattered, too. There is nothing left of all the greatness that he boasts about. The terrific frown that everybody feared is broken down, just like his whole empire.

The writing on the pedestal is: "My name is Ozymandias, king of kings: / Look on my works, ye Mighty, and despair!" The irony here is plain. There are no works, except for the statue, and it is broken. Everything else is gone. The writing on the real statue Shelley saw is pretty much the same: "I am Ozymandias, king of kings; if anyone wishes to know what I am and where I lie, let him surpass me in some of my exploits" (Hutchinson 121). Hutchinson says Shelley probably got this from reading the Greek historian Diodorus Siculus, who was probably the model for the "ancient traveller" of the first line. In either case, the writing adds to the irony, especially the way Shelley changes it. He changes it to include the idea of despair. We are supposed to look on all these mighty works and despair.

Telling us to despair means we should automatically give up hope. Well, maybe we would have when this statue was standing. And maybe that is what Ramses II wanted Moses and the Hebrews to do in the Bible. The only way not to give up hope, though, is to have faith. Moses had faith. Ozymandias had faith in his empire, but it was like his statue. It was built out of stone and it broke.

Works Cited

Holmes, Richard. <u>Shelley: The Pursuit</u>. London: Weidenfeld, 1974.

Hutchinson, Thomas, ed. <u>Poems of Percy Bysshe Shelley</u>. Rev. G. M. Matthews. Oxford: Oxford UP, 1970.

"Ramses." <u>Encyclopaedia Britannica: Macropaedia</u>. 1986 ed.

Reiman, Donald. <u>Percy Bysshe Shelley</u>. New York: Twayne, 1969.

Works Consulted

Janowitz, Anne. "Shelley's Monument to Ozymandias." <u>Philological Quarterly</u> 63 (1984): 477–91.

Ridenour, George, ed. <u>Shelley: A Collection of Critical Essays</u>. Englewood Cliffs: Prentice, 1965.

White, Newman Ivey. <u>Shelley</u>. 2 vols. New York: Knopf, 1941.

Yeats, W. B. "The Philosophy of Shelley's Poetry." <u>Essays</u>. London: Macmillan, 1924.

A Reader Response Interpretation

Louis Mendes
English 109–07
Mr. Jacobus

"Ozymandias": What the Future Holds

When I first read this poem I could not help but feel a little frightened for the future. Shelley tells us about a "king of kings" whose great empire now lies around in ruins. I have seen pictures of the sphinx and the pyramids and some of the big statues still in the desert in Egypt, and the way Shelley describes things, "The lone and level sands stretch far away," gives you the feeling that there is nothing here but emptiness where there was once a gigantic civilization.

In class, when we talked about it I could not agree that the poem should make us feel better because Ozymandias is dead and gone. I agree that the sneer on the "visage" means he was a tough guy, a mean ruler. And maybe it is true that the empire he led was cruel in a lot of ways. But you also have to admit that those great things they built, and the good things they had, like cities and high culture, were impressive. Even now the pyramids impress people from around the world, so the ancient Egyptians must have had a fantastic organization to get them built. Someone said that the culture the Egyptians put together was imitated by the Greeks and even the Romans and maybe some of what they were doing is even still being done by our culture. But in a way that makes me worried.

I am not sure Shelley wanted me to worry about civilization going under, but I think it is possible. I mean, he uses words like <u>decay</u>, <u>wreck</u>, <u>bare</u>, and <u>lifeless</u> for a reason. He wants to get us worked up about this statue. The notes to the poem say that "the hand that mocked them" refers to the hand of the sculptor who made the lips into a sneer and the expression into a frown. "The heart that fed" is supposed to be the heart of Ozymandias because he ate it all up as if it was praise. Here Ozymandias thought he was leader of an empire that was going to be around forever. But it is gone.

That scares me. The Egyptians are gone, and they were once mighty. The Greeks were great and so were the Romans. They all conquered the world but everything they built is more or less gone. Look at Greece and Italy today. And what about our culture? We build a lot of monuments, too. The Statue of Liberty, the Sears Tower, and the Space Needle, to mention only three pretty big things. You could include the Golden Gate Bridge in San Francisco, and the new tunnel from England to France. These are great monuments and you could write the same kind of thing on them that Ozymandias wrote on his statue. You can imagine all of them "half sunk" and "shattered."

What the poem makes me think of is the possibility that our civilization will destroy itself. With the threats of global warming, general pollution, the ozone layer depletion, and nuclear war, we could probably destroy our civilization much faster than Ozymandias's civilization went. We could wipe ourselves out in an instant. That is scary. In ancient Egypt it was a big operation to break up statues that were gigantic like the one Shelley describes. They did it, but it took lots of time. We can do it too, and it would take no time at all. Then, when you think of it, how could there be "a traveller from an antique land" telling anyone about us? There would be no way. There could never be another Shelley, any more than there could be a poem like this written in the future.

So what gets me worried is the thought that if we let our civilization disappear the way Ozymandias did, there will be no way anyone would hear about it. There would be no future if we destroy life on the planet. The sands that stretch away in this poem will stretch away on the earth, but there will not be anyone to see them and report back. That is the bottom line in this poem, and it is one of the scariest poems I have read.

IX

INTERPRETIVE
STRATEGIES

22

*I*NTRODUCTION
TO *I*NTERPRETATION

Most interpretations are primarily text based, reader based, or context based. **Formalist interpretations** assume that the meaning is "in" the text and that the critic's job is to find it. **Reader response interpretation** assumes that the meaning of the text is created by the reader in the act of reading. **Contextual interpretations** consider the text in relation to biographical, historical, and cultural information. They assume that the meaning of the text is not exclusively in the text or in the reader but is affected by the relationship of text and reader to the cultural issues surrounding the creation of the text, its present circumstances, or the cultural circumstances of the reader.

FORMALIST INTERPRETATIONS

The text-based strategy of formalism examines the interrelationship of the formal elements of a text, such as theme, plot, setting, characterization, the expression of ideas, special use of language, metaphor, tone, rhyme, meter, and all other stylistic qualities. The formalist is especially interested in irony, the use of language that says one thing but means another. Sarcasm is one form of irony. In literature, we often see tragic irony, in which characters sometimes achieve their dearest wish only to find that it destroys them. For example, Oedipus discovers that the killer of Laios is himself.

A widely known formalist method is New Criticism, which examines texts for their unity and tries to show how each detail contributes to a unified overall meaning. **Psychoanalytic criticism** is also text based when it centers on an examination of symbols, including symbolic relationships between characters, such as those that resemble mother and son or father and daughter. (Psychoanalytic interpretations become context based when they begin to focus on the author's life, which is outside the text, not in it.)

The Formalist Approach: New Criticism

Developed in the 1940s, **New Criticism** continues to be one of the strong intellectual forces in modern thought. The following list describes some of its purer forms.

ISSUES OF NEW CRITICISM

- A work of literature should be considered as an object independent of the author's intention or biography.
- The response of the reader is not part of the work of literature and therefore should not figure in its interpretation.
- Political, sociological, religious, or moral issues outside the work do not affect its meaning. Therefore, they do not enter into the act of interpretation.
- Because works of literature aim for organic unity, one goal of interpretation is demonstrating how every element and detail helps achieve that unity.
- Patterns of imagery, such as light and dark, sun and moon, and other repetition of details observed during close reading, often provide the basis of interpretation.
- The most interesting literary effects usually involve tension produced by irony, ambiguity, paradox, and wit.

Today, most practitioners relax enough to admit that history and ideas outside the work can sometimes influence our reading. However, the ideal of the work as an object separate from the reader's apprehension remains. In New Criticism, it is especially important to separate the reader's response from the work. For example, that you may be saddened or frightened by a poem is irrelevant to an interpretation of its unity or the relationship of its imagery to its theme.

Psychoanalytic Criticism

Literature has always had a psychological dimension, and **psychoanalytic criticism** pays special attention to it. Hamlet's psychology has fascinated audiences for four hundred years. Relations between parents and children have always been important in both psychology and literature. The way characters cope with sexual awareness, an important stage in psychological development, is a major theme in most stories of growing up. Even the most ancient epic literature has revealed insights into personality and psychology for almost every generation of readers. Literature and psychology were connected before psychology became a science.

Acknowledging this significant connection in *The Interpretation of Dreams,* Sigmund Freud (1856–1939), the founder of psychoanalysis, explained that literature such as the story of Oedipus in *Oedipus Rex* gives insights into the subconscious, the aspect of the mind that speaks to us in dreams.

The foundation of Freud's theories about human psychology is that the mind has three parts: the ego, or conscious personality; the superego, which monitors and censors desires unacceptable to the ego; and the id, which contains dark sexual desires that would destroy society if they were let loose. Sexuality, according to Freud, is at the heart of most human behavior, whether the individual is conscious or unconscious of this motivation. The ego, the conscious part of the mind, communicates in language. The subconscious mind, the super-ego and the id, communicates only in symbols. Freudian psychoanalysis puts important emphasis on the symbols of dreams as clues to an individual's psychology.

Many psychoanalytic critics apply Freudian theory to literary works. Looking for a work's repressed sexual content, for example, such critics consider telephone poles, steeples, rifles, pencils, cigars, and zeppelins to be symbols for the penis, and dark, damp caves, forests, interiors of houses, unknown locations on a map, and the unknown in general to be symbols of the vagina.

ISSUES OF PSYCHOANALYTIC CRITICISM

- Part of the critic's job is to reconcile sexual symbols with the theme of the work.
- A central concern is to find signs of restricted emotional development.
- A close reading takes special interest in recurrent sexual symbols, dreams, and evidence of repressed feelings directing the action of characters or the author.
- A close reading examines the narrative for its manifest meaning—what it apparently means—and its latent meaning—what it really means to the subconscious. Casual accidents, such as mistakes in language, therefore take on important significance.
- An important function is to discover patterns of behavior central to Freudian theory, such as complexes and neuroses. The critic tries to reveal subconscious motivations that characters (and untrained readers) do not notice.

Psychoanalytic criticism has been applied most to works written after 1910, the authors of which were likely to have absorbed some of Freud's ideas even though they may not have read his works. At first glance it may seem inappropriate to apply Freudian theory to works by writers who predated Freud. However, if Freud's ideas accurately describe human psychology, their relevance is not time bound. If Freud was right, a Freudian interpretation of Shakespeare's *Hamlet* is as legitimate as one of Susan Glaspell's play *Suppressed Desires*.

READER RESPONSE INTERPRETATION

Reader Response Criticism

Response criticism is based on the reactions of the reader to the work of literature. Because the work causes responses, examining those responses delivers insight into the work. The reader's accumulated experience always affects his or her response. For instance, someone who has never seen a Frankenstein movie will respond very differently to Mary Shelley's novel *Frankenstein* than will a person who has seen the films with Boris Karloff.

ISSUES OF READER RESPONSE CRITICISM

- The work of literature is not an object separate from the reader; in a sense it does not exist until it is read. The reader's response is the most important part of the interpretive act.

- We can learn about a work of literature by seeing how readers in different ages responded to it. The history of the work includes a history of readers' responses.

- The reader supplies what the literary text omits, which can include the physical appearance of characters, the sensory experience of events, and a variety of unspoken background information, such as what it means to be male, female, young, old, sick, or well. The ability of the reader to supply that information affects the interpretation.

- Because readers are different, there are many responses to the same work of literature, each valuable because each provides insights for interpreting a literary work.

- Readers tend to fall into what reader response critic Stanley Fish calls "interpretive communities," groups of people who respond similarly. For example, readers who respond to the cosmic issues in Frost's "Fire and Ice" constitute one community, and those who do not perceive the cosmic issues form another community.

- A close reading notes the kinds of reactions the author seems to expect from the reader, and the kinds that the reader really gives.

- A close reading also takes into account what changes in attitude the author has caused in the reader as the reader progresses through the work. To what use does the author put those changes?

Since specific elements in a work of literature—such as metaphors, word choice, and images—affect readers in specific ways, the reader response critic examines the elements for the response they demand. One obvious value of the reader response strategy is that, since virtually all readers have some response to a work of literature, everyone has a place from which to begin an interpretation. In addition, this interpretive strategy helps explain why the meanings of texts—whose words remain the same—change over the years.

CONTEXTUAL INTERPRETATIONS

The contexts in which a literary text's author, the text itself, and/or its reader exist can inform context-based interpretations. **Feminist criticism** examines gender issues within and outside texts; **political-economic criticism** examines economic and political issues; **cultural criticism** examines African-American, Asian-American, native American, Hispanic, and other cultural issues. **Historicism** and **New Historicism** aim to place the text in a historical context, thereby showing its meaning in a new light.

Close reading by context-based critics is often preceded by special preparation, such as collecting historical or political information or information about ethnic groups, cultural values, or other cultural issues.

Feminist Criticism

Interpretive strategies developed by feminist critics are context based since they take into consideration the social circumstances surrounding the creation and the reading of a text. **Feminist criticism** focuses on aspects of literature that have often been ignored by male authors, male readers, or male critics. The feminist interpretation examines gender distinctions implied in the roles that women play or are expected to play. The extent to which women have been oppressed by the expectations of a society—illustrated, for example, in Charlotte Perkins Gilman's story "The Yellow Wallpaper"—becomes a major interpretive issue.

Certain feminist critics have argued that the ways in which men and women use language differ. Some of them suggest that men perceive women's language as being less logical, more intuitive, and more difficult to follow. Therefore, men do not credit women's use of language and force women either to adopt the masculine use of language or be ignored. Feminist critics, whatever their special interest, examine literature for language that oppresses women. Because feminists assume that society is patriarchal (male-dominated), they also look for assumptions of male dominance in works of literature.

ISSUES OF FEMINIST CRITICISM

* One function of close reading is to find language oppositions: *sun/moon; powerful/weak; light/dark; logical/intuitive; calm/hysterical; active/passive; rational/emotional master/slave; intellectuality/sensitivity; dominating/nurturing; self/other.* The first word in each of these pairings is culturally associated with male dominance; the second is associated with female passivity.

* Exposing subconscious patriarchal assumptions in literature reveals hitherto unexpected themes in a work.

* Features such as unusual awareness of the female body, maternity, natural cycles, madness, witchery, the demonic, and disease are important to explore.

* A reevaluation of literature written when male dominance was taken for granted is implicit.

Like most current schools of criticism, feminist criticism "borrows" from other interpretive strategies. For example, feminist critics are interested in a reader's responses. They also use techniques of New Criticism to connect patterns that produce meanings that might be otherwise unnoticed. However, unlike New Critics, they do not insist that the work must be read alone, without reference to anything outside itself. Feminist critics value psychoanalytic techniques as well as those of the historical critic, particularly in regard to examining the condition of women when a work was written.

Political-Economic Criticism

Although not every piece of literature highlights political and economic issues, every piece of literature does reflect a certain political economy, and this is the focus of **political-economic criticism.** This approach is especially interested in the relation of individual characters to their society, especially the class system that holds their society together. **Marxist criticism** focuses on the class struggle between the bourgeoisie, those who control capital and the means of production, and the proletariat, those who do the work. Marxists examine literature for its position on the exploitation of the poor by the rich. Often that means looking for signs of indifference on the part of the author or the characters.

Generally, the interpretive strategy emphasizing political and economic issues looks closely at the level of awareness shown by the literature. For example, in many plays the characters may have no observable occupation—one wonders how they can live in comfort and yet do nothing to earn their position. Comedies often ignore the basic issues of making a living because they seem insignificant in relation to the action of the drama. But the political and economic perspective attempts to establish a balance and produce an interpretation sensitive to the realities that most people have to face.

ISSUES OF POLITICAL-ECONOMIC CRITICISM

- Economic circumstances in a work of literature receive close scrutiny for signs of economic exploitation.
- The literary work reflects the economic social order that produces it; therefore, writers are expected to reflect their class concerns.
- The text, the author, and the reader's responses are all susceptible to analysis because all three reveal attitudes toward the bourgeoisie (upper-middle class) and the proletariat (workers).
- Contradictions and exaggerations of character, description, or language in a piece of literature are sometimes taken as implied critiques of the economic order.
- Colonialism, whether implicit or overt, becomes a significant subject of analysis.
- The study of the class struggle reveals itself in literature.

Because most literature assumes the appropriateness of the economic circumstances of its time, political and economic interpretations often come up with surprises. For example, in *Robinson Crusoe* Daniel Defoe does not comment on the exploitation of Crusoe's servant, Friday. From the political perspective, however, exploitation is a key issue because Crusoe represents the colonial European who lands on a foreign shore and forces the native population to support and serve while learning the exploiter's language. Crusoe makes no effort to learn Friday's language—nor does he even bother to learn his name—because there is no economic advantage in doing so. Perhaps without intending to, Defoe has represented the general attitude of English society in his own time toward colonial exploitation of people in other countries. This kind of political-economic criticism calls our attention to politics and economics as moral issues in literature.

Cultural Criticism

Since the 1960s **cultural criticism** has called attention to issues involving the special provinces of Asian, Latino, Chicano, and African-American literary experience that are not taken into account by traditional critical methods. For example, the rhythms and styles of American jazz have influenced poets such as Langston Hughes and Nikki Giovanni. Themes of nostalgia for the loss of older ways of life inform Chicano literature. For Chicanos, Aztlán (northern Mexico and southwestern United States) is the homeland. Asian writers have explored family structures, traditions, and other distinguishing features that mark their culture. Louise Erdrich, Carter Revard, and other native Americans sometimes focus on their knowledge of life both within and apart from the larger American culture.

Like feminist criticism, cultural criticism focuses on a specific segment of society. For example, it often examines works by writers of a particular ethnic group. Larger cultural issues such as apartheid, prejudice, and the effects of colonialism on the colony and the colonizer are also considered important.

Likewise, lesbian and homosexual criticism examines issues relating to lesbians and homosexuals that might otherwise be unnoticed, such as prejudice against their lifestyles. In addition, certain works, such as Becky Birtha's short story "Johnnieruth," contain explicit lesbian themes, which need examination on their own terms rather than on terms dictated by the assumptions of a heterosexual majority.

ISSUES OF CULTURAL CRITICISM

- Both stated and unstated cultural issues in literature are to be examined.
- Black English, Latino bilingualism, and the special uses of language by ethnic groups are examined as special sources of literary power.
- The role of art and music in literature is of special importance.
- Folk tales have a special cultural significance in many works.
- Gender roles and gender expectations relevant to gay and lesbian characters can be the focus of interpretation.

Cultural criticism shares many interests with other critical schools, such as the political-economic concern for oppression and the feminist concern for male domination. However, you need not be a member of a specific cultural group to use cultural interpretive strategies any more than you need to be a feminist, Marxist, or psychoanalyst to use those interpretive strategies. Although the methods of cultural criticism are context based, since they examime the cultural context of the literature, the text is very important in itself. Thus the cultural critic often uses formalist interpretive strategies, such as searching for irony, patterns of imagery, and revealing uses of language within the cultural context.

Historicism and New Historicism

Before the 1940s, historical criticism, or **historicism,** was concerned with factual historical matters surrounding the literary text: When was the work written? What are the author's dates? What sovereigns or political leaders were in place when the work was published? This school of thought was a prime target of the New Critics, who led a revolt in literature in the 1930s and 1940s to encourage study of the work of literature, not its historical period.

New Historicism shows how a greater understanding of a work can develop when its cultural, political, sociological, and ideological context—in effect, its cultural history—is known. The New Historicist might search out the general writings prevalent in 1923, when Frost's "Fire and Ice" was published. In 1923, five years after the end of World War I, the world was still reeling from the destruction of war and the deaths of many millions. The extent to which "Fire and Ice" was affected by the mood of the times could be an interesting clue to its meaning. The New Historicist links a work to the culture of its time.

ISSUES OF HISTORICAL APPROACHES TO CRITICISM

- Every work of literature profits from being read in a context of its own historical culture.
- A social era—its assumptions, limitations, aspirations, and values—affects its literature, becoming part of its meaning, and therefore affects our interpretation.
- Understanding inteliectual trends and scientific, psychological, economic, and political theories of the time is essential to interpretation.
- Details about the life of the author can be relevant to an interpretation.
- The study of history is a primary preparation for interpreting any work of literature.

Historical approaches to literature involve and reward research and reading in the period associated with the work of literature. If, for example, you have studied the history of the court of Queen Elizabeth in 1600–1601, when *Hamlet* was produced, knowing that it was filled with intrigue and uncertainty because Elizabeth was old, frail, quarrelsome, and threatened by rebellion, you would interpret Hamlet much differently than someone who lacks this historical knowledge. Instead of appearing to be only about revenge, the play opens up to reveal a layer of meaning about royal succession, Shakespeare perhaps reflecting England's uncertainty as to who would succeed Queen Elizabeth.

Combining Interpretive Strategies

Methods of interpretation are not always absolutely distinct from one another. In practice, feminist critics often use psychoanalytic techniques, and political-economic critics may rely on formalist New Critical techniques for support. Interestingly, these interpretive strategies feed one another. A text-based reading will find elements in the text that need to be accounted for in a formalist strategy and then interpret those elements. A reader-based approach will find details in the text to which the reader must respond and then interpret the responses. A context-based approach will find biographical, cultural, or historical details in and relating to the text and then interpret them. No one of these approaches needs to be kept separate from others that may be useful to you.

USING INTERPRETING STRATEGIES

The following brief interpretations of Nikki Giovanni's "Master Charge Blues" show the extraordinary resources of the poem and the interests and outcomes of various interpretive strategies. The interpretations result from the different kinds of questions that are implied in each strategy. All strategies begin with a close reading of the text; some add the reader's response; others add cultural considerations. As you read this section, you will discover that your own interpretation of the poem differs from these because you bring a different experience to Nikki Giovanni's poem.

For the sake of illustration, these interpretations make an effort to avoid combining strategies. In practice, however, you can and will mix the strategies to produce a personal interpretation.

NIKKI GIOVANNI   (b. 1943)

Master Charge Blues _____ *1970*

its wednesday night baby
and i'm all alone
wednesday night baby
and i'm all alone
sitting with myself   5
waiting for the telephone

wanted you baby
but you said you had to go
wanted you yeah
but you said you had to go   10
called your best friend
but he can't come 'cross no more

did you ever go to bed
at the end of a busy day
look over and see the smooth   15
where your hump usta lay
feminine odor and no reason why
asked the lord to help me
he shook his head "not i"

but i'm a modern woman baby   20
ain't gonna let this get me down
i'm a modern woman
ain't gonna let this get me down
gonna take my master charge
and get everything in town   25

A Formalist Interpretation: New Criticism

The repetition of phrases, such as "wanted you baby / but you said you had to go / wanted you yeah / but you said you had to go," identifies the form of the poem as a song. The title tells us that it is a blues song, which means that it will focus on some kind of personal complaint. However, the blues usually expresses a personal slight, and sometimes the slight is the result of deeper social injustice. Here, the complaint is that "a modern woman" has been rebuffed by her man, and she wants to do something about it.

The New Critic, who often searches for irony, will find it in this poem in a number of ways. For example, this modern woman uses a modern aggressive approach and a modern instrument, the telephone, but she still cannot get what she needs. After being disappointed by her lover, she is modern enough to call her absent lover's best friend, only to find "he can't come 'cross no more." (She has apparently called him before.) The irony lies in the failure of the woman's modernity: It does not produce sexual satisfaction. She has gone so far as to ask "the lord to help me," but he does nothing. She has got herself sexually excited (or perfumed): "feminine odor and no reason why." Ironically, this modern woman, if she cannot get what she really wants, can take out her sexual frustration in a bout of shopping: "get everything in town." But again ironically, buying everything in town is not going to solve her problem or give her anything more than temporary satisfaction. In this sense, the poem is an appropriate blues song: Her actions may increase the modern woman's unhappiness.

A Psychoanalytic Interpretation

The psychoanalytic critic finds this a congenial poem because it focuses on the basic Freudian question of channeling the sexual drive in ways that are acceptable to society. This poem is sexual, and the rhythms of sex are implied in the chanted repetition of critical lines like "wanted you baby." Even the word baby has a sexual value in this poem. The allusion to the bed and "where your hump usta lay" contains obvious sexual meaning. The bed is there, but the bed is painfully empty. All that is left is the imprint of a body, a memory of sexuality.

This "modern woman" has no channel for these powerful sexual energies. We know she must repress her energies because "you said you had to go." Yet we know that such energies cannot long remain unexpressed, or else she will become neurotic. Therefore, she emblematically seizes a phallic instrument: the master charge with (if it is a MasterCard) its emblem of male sex. Finally, she finds an acceptable channel for sexual energies in shopping.

A Reader Response Interpretation

A blues song often invites the listener to share the emotional mood associated with the blues. In order to do the same, this poem must establish the narrator as someone who is worthy of the reader's sympathy. A reader who is not sympathetic will respond differently than a reader who is. Thus a reader's personal values may become involved in a response to the poem. For example, a reader who does not approve of the narrator's being sexually assertive might want to interpret this poem in terms of what it lacks: a stable relationship with a man, for example. The detail of calling "your best friend" implies that at this point any man will do. Some readers may be shocked by this detail, and their interpretation of the poem will emphasize that shock. Another response might be to compare a personal recollection of romantic disappointment with the feelings expressed in this poem. It is possible that many readers have gone shopping as a substitute for romance. Is this a triumph over adversity, or a surrender to the materialism of shopping? A reader's response to the situation explored in the poem will affect his or her interpretation of this point. Important questions to explore include: How does Nikki Giovanni present this woman? Does she seem like a loser or a winner? How many responses are possible?

A Feminist Interpretation

A feminist interpretation would see this unnamed woman as a victim of a male-dominated social order that forces her to question her self sufficiency. Her culture has lied to her by making her think that as a modern woman she is incomplete without a man. The telephone's failure to produce a lover produces instead an expression of feminine willpower: "ain't gonna let this get me down." She has been let down by men, including the patriarchal "lord" who "shook his head 'not i'" when she asked for help. The male world has turned against her in a big way.

The modern woman's decision to turn this moment into a triumph even after the Lord turns her down is a testament to the power of woman. She takes special pleasure in her "feminine odor" and turns the emblem of male domination—"*master* charge"—into an instrument to get back at the men who let her down.

A Political-Economic Interpretation

The political-economic critic sees economic issues at the center of the poem. The master charge is a symbol of oppression because it invites the proletariat, including this woman, to spend money it does not have. Then, once the money has been spent, those who control its source demand repayment with interest, a typical capitalist strategy. The capitalist has the money and lends it to the woman so she can "get everything in town." But soon a reckoning will come. Society, by encouraging her to spend her money impetuously in response to her frustration, exploits this "modern woman." Her master card is an all too convenient instrument of exploitation. Those who control the master charge do not work: their capital earns money for them. The woman, on the other hand, does work (she comes home "at the end of a busy day") but does not get the satisfaction she needs. Ironically, she thinks that by using a credit card she will get back at the men in her life, but the reality is that society exploits her by providing her with this dangerous instrument of self-oppression.

A Cultural Interpretation

The *master* in *master charge* has obvious negative connotations for any cultural critic sensitive to issues of slavery and domination. This woman, whether she knows it or not, is dominated by the economic realities of her life. The blues is a form developed by African-American musicians, and Nikki Giovanni is African-American. The modern woman in the poem sounds like Bessie Smith, a famous African-American blues singer (see her poem "Empty Bed Blues" in the Poetry section), and may be herself African-American. The blues, which often portrays disappointment, is an African-American art describing the African-American experience, and this poem celebrates this woman's victory of character, something common to most blues tunes.

A Historical Interpretation

The emphasis on the concept of "modern" immediately tips off the historical critic. This poem establishes a New Historicist position regarding romance and courtship by referring to modern instruments such as the telephone and the Master Charge. Understanding the poem may well depend on understanding what the credit card permits the woman in the poem to do. For example, if it is her own credit card and she has earned enough money to pay for her bills, then the card will give her pleasure. If, on the other hand, she is borrowing on the card, then she may have the later grief associated with debt. Finally, if the card is owned by the man she cannot contact, then her purchases may be a form of revenge.

On the other hand, the historicist may also wish to probe into the personal history of Nikki Giovanni. If her biography were available, and she or her biographer were able to supply enough details about this poem to show that it is a personal statement, the poem could be interpreted in relation to a specific event in her life.

A Final Point

The short stories, poems, plays, and essays you read in this book can be interpreted using most of the strategies introduced in this chapter. Your choice will depend on the individual work and on your personal experience. However, keep in mind that it is possible to combine these strategies and produce an interesting interpretation. The approach you use will depend on what you bring to the work and what interpretive strategies you find most congenial to your thinking.

$\mathcal{A}$CKNOWLEDGMENTS

Critical Reading

Robert Frost. "Fire and Ice" from THE POETRY OF ROBERT FROST edited by Edward Connery Lathem, Copyright 1923, © 1969 by Henry Holt and Co., copyright 1936, 1951, 1956, 1960, 1962 by Robert Frost, © 1964 by Lesley Frost Ballantine, © 1988 by Alfred Edwards. Reprinted by permission of Henry Holt and Company, LLC.

Interpreting Short Fiction and Critical Approaches to Short Fiction

Toni Cade Bambara. "The Lesson." From GORILLA, MY LOVE by Toni Cade Bambara. Copyright © 1972 by Toni Cade Bambara. Reprinted by permission of Random House, Inc.

Charles Baxter. "Gryphon" from THROUGH THE SAFETY NET by Charles Baxter. Copyright © 1985 by Charles Baxter. Used by permission of Viking Penguin, a division of Penguin Books USA.

Ann Beattie. "Cinderella Waltz: from THE BURNING HOUSE by Ann Beattie. Copyright © 1979, 1980, 1981, 1982 by Irony and Pity, Inc. Reprinted by permission of Random House, Inc.

Becky Birtha. "Johnnieruth" from LOVER'S CHOICE. Copyright © 1981, 1987 by Becky Birtha. Reprinted by permission of Seal Press.

Giovanni Boccaccio. "Pot of Basil" from THE DECAMERON by Giovanni Boccaccio, translated by G. H. McWilliam (Penguin Classics, 1972). Copyright © G. H. McWilliam, 1972. Reproduced by permission of Penguin Books Ltd.

Raymond Carver. "Night School" from WILL YOU PLEASE BE QUIET, PLEASE. Copyright 1971 by Tess Gallagher. Reprinted by permission of Tess Gallagher.

John Cheever. "The Swimmer" from THE STORIES OF JOHN CHEEVER by John Cheever. Copyright © 1964 by John Cheever. Reprinted by permission of Alfred A. Knopf, Inc.

Ralph Ellison. "Battle Royal" from INVISIBLE MAN by Ralph Ellison. Copyright 1948 by Ralph Ellison. Reprinted by permission of Random House, Inc.

William Faulkner. "A Rose for Emily" from COLLECTED STORIES OF WILLIAM FAULKNER by William Faulkner. Copyright 1930 and renewed 1958 by William Faulkner. Reprinted by permission of Random House, Inc.

Richard Ford. "Communist" from the book ROCK SPRINGS by Richard Ford. Copyright © 1987 by Richard Ford. Used with the permission of Grove/Atlantic Monthly Press.

Ernest Hemingway. "Hills Like White Elephants" is reprinted with permission of Scribner, a Division of Simon & Schuster, from MEN WITHOUT WOMEN by Ernest Hemingway. Copyright 1927 by Charles Scribners Sons. Copyright renewed 1955 by Ernest Hemingway.

Suzanne Jacob. "Two Cents" from LIFE AFTER ALL, Tr. by Susanna Finnell. Reprinted by permission of Press Gang Publishers.

Franz Kafka. "The Hunger Artist" from THE METAMORPHOSIS, THE PENAL COLONY, AND OTHER STORIES by Franz Kafka, Translated by Willa and Edwin Muir. Copyright © 1948 by Schocken Books. Copyright renewed 1975 by Schocken Books. Reprinted by permission of Schocken Books, a division of Random House, Inc.

Jhumpa Lahiri. "Interpreter of Maladies" from INTERPRETER OF MALADIES by Jhumpa Lahiri. Copyright © 1999 by Jhumpa Lahiri. Reprinted by permission of Houghton Mifflin Company. All rights reserved.

Mary Lavin. "Happiness" from HAPPINESS. Copyright © 1969 by Mary Lavin. Reprinted by permission of the author's daughter, Caroline Walsh.

D. H. Lawrence. "The Horse Dealer's Daughter" from COMPLETE SHORT STORIES OF D. H. LAWRENCE. Copyright 1922 by Thomas H. Seltzer, Inc., renewed 1950 by Frieda Lawrence. Used by permission of Viking Penguin, a division of Penguin Books USA Inc.

Ursula K. Le Guin. "Sur" by Ursula K. Le Guin first appeared in THE NEW YORKER. Copyright © 1982 by Ursula K. Le Guin. Reprinted by permission of the author and the author's agent, Virginia Kidd.

Doris Lessing. "To Room 19" from THE DORIS LESSING READER by Doris Lessing. Copyright © 1988 by Doris Lessing. Reprinted by permission of Alfred A. Knopf, Inc.

Doris Lessing. "To Room Nineteen" from A MAN AND TWO WOMEN by Doris Lessing. Copyright © 1963 by Doris Lessing. Reprinted by kind permission of Jonathan Clowes Ltd., London, on behalf of Doris Lessing.

David Wong Louie. "Pangs of Love" from PANGS OF LOVE AND OTHER STORIES by David Wong Louie. Copyright © 1991 by David Wong Louie. Reprinted by permission of Alfred A. Knopf, a Division of Random House Inc.

Gabriel García Márquez. "Eyes of a Blue Dog" from INNOCENT ERENDIRA AND OTHER STORIES by Gabriel García Márquez. Copyright © 1978 by Harper & Row, Publishers, Inc. Reprinted by permission of HarperCollins, Publishers, Inc. This story originally appeared in THE NEW YORKER.

Bharati Mukerjee. "Jasmine" from the book THE MIDDLEMAN & OTHER STORIES by Bharati Mukerjee. Copyright © 1988 by Bharati Mukerjee. Used with the permission of Grove/Atlantic Monthly Press. To order call 800-937-5557.

Alice Munro. "The Moons of Jupiter" from THE MOONS OF JUPITER AND OTHER STORIES by Alice Munro. Copyright © 1982 by Alice Munro. Reprinted by permission of Alfred A. Knopf, Inc. and The Writers Shop.

Tim O'Brien. "Sweetheart of the Song Tra Bong", from THE THINGS THEY CARRIED by Tim O'Brien. Copyright © 1990 by Tim O'Brien. Reprinted by permission of Houghton Mifflin Company. All rights reserved.

Katherine Anne Porter. "The Jilting of Granny Weatherall" from FLOWERING JUDAS AND OTHER STORIES, copyright 1930 and renewed 1958 by Katherine Anne Porter, reprinted by permission of Harcourt, Inc.

William Trevor. "The Ballroom of Romance" from THE BALLROOM OF ROMANCE by William Trevor. Copyright © 1965, 1966, 1969, 1971, 1972 by William Trevor. Used by permission of Viking Penguin, a division of Penguin Books USA Inc.

Fay Weldon. "Weekend" from WATCHING ME, WATCHING YOU. Copyright © Fay Weldon 1981. Reprinted by permission of Sheil Land Associates Ltd.

Reading Anton Chekhov in Depth

Anton Chekhov. "Concerning Love" from THE RUSSIAN MASTER AND OTHER STORIES by Anton Chekhov, translated by Ronald Hingley (1984). © Oxford University Press 1975. Reprinted by permission of Oxford University Press, England.

Charles E. May. From "Chekhov and the Modern Short Story" in A CHEKHOV COMPANION, ed. Toby W. Clyman. Copyright © 1985 by Toby W. Clyman. Reproduced with permission of Greenwood Publishing Group, Inc., Westport, CT.

Vladimir Nabokov. "The Lady with the Little Dog" from LECTURES ON RUSSIAN LITERATURE, copyright © 1981 by the Estate of Vladimir Nabokov, reprinted by permission of Harcourt, Inc.

Anton Chekhov. Excerpts from THE PORTABLE CHEKHOV by Anton Chekhov, translated by Avram Yarmolinsky. Translation copyright 1947, © 1968 by Viking Penguin Inc. Renewed © 1975 by Avram Yarmolinsky. Reprinted by Viking Penguin, a division of Penguin Putnam Inc.

Eudora Welty. "Reality in Chekhov's Stories." (Originally titled "Chekhov's 'The Darling' ") from THE EYE OF THE STORY by Eudora Welty. Copyright © 1978 by Eudora Welty. Reprinted by permission of Random House, Inc.

Reading Eudora Welty in Depth

Peter Schmidt. "Lily Daw and the Three Ladies," a passage from THE HEART OF THE STORY, EUDORA WELTY'S SHORT FICTION. Reprinted by permission of the University Press of Mississippi.

Eudora Welty. "A Worn Path" from A CURTAIN OF GREEN AND OTHER STORIES, copyright © 1941 and renewed 1969 by Eudora Welty, reprinted by permission of Harcourt, Inc.

Eudora Welty. "Livvie" from THE WIDE NET AND OTHER STORIES, copyright 1942 and renewed 1970 by Eudora Welty, reprinted by permission of Harcourt, Inc.

Eudora Welty. "Lily Daw and the Three Ladies" from A CURTAIN OF GREEN AND OTHER STORIES, copyright 1937 and renewed 1965 by Eudora Welty, reprinted by permission of Harcourt, Inc.

Eudora Welty. Passage from ONE WRITER'S BEGINNINGS is reprinted by permission of the publisher from pp. 14–15 in ONE WRITER'S BEGINNINGS by Eudora Welty, Cambridge, MA: Harvard University Press, Copyright © 1983–1984 by Eudora Welty.

Eudora Welty. "Is Phoenix Jackson's Grandson Really Dead?" from THE EYE OF THE STORY: SELECTED ESSAYS & REVIEWS by Eudora Welty. Copyright © 1978 by Eudora Welty. Reprinted by permission of Random House, Inc.

Ruth M. Vande Kieft. "Technique in 'Livvie'" from EUDORA WELTY, Revised Edition by Ruth M. Vande Kieft. Copyright © 1987 by G. K. Hall & Co. Reprinted by permission of The Gale Group.

Ruth D. Weston. Excerpt from "American Folk Art, Fine Art and Eudora Welty" from EUDORA WELTY: EYE OF THE STORYTELLER, edited by Dawn Trouard. Reprinted by permission of Kent State University Press.

Interpreting Poetry and Critical Approaches to Poetry

Emily Dickinson. "A Narrow Fellow in the Grass" is reprinted by permission of the publishers and the Trustees of Amherst College from THE POEMS OF EMILY DICKINSON, Thomas H. Johnson, ed. Cambridge, MA: The Belknap Press of Harvard University Press, Copyright © 1951, 1955, 1979 by the President and Fellows of Harvard College.

John Masefield. "Cargoes." Copyright 1912 by The Macmillan Company, renewed 1940 by John Masefield. Reprinted by permission of The Society of Authors as the literary representative of the Estate of John Masefield.

W. S. Merwin. "Fly" from THE LICE by W. S. Merwin. Copyright © 1963, 1964, 1965, 1966, 1967 by W. S. Merwin. Reprinted by permission of The Wylie Agency.

Maya Angelou. "These Yet To Be United States" from I SHALL NOT BE MOVED by Maya Angelou. Copyright © 1990 by Maya Angelou. Reprinted by permission of Random House, Inc.

William Carpenter. "Fire" from RAIN by William Carpenter. Reprinted by permission of Northeastern University Press.

Marilyn Chin. "How I Got That Name" from THE IOWA REVIEW, Spring/Summer 1990. Reprinted by permission of Marilyn Chin.

Gerald Costanzo. "At Irony's Picnic" from IN THE AVIARY. Originally published by University of Missouri Press. Reprinted by permission of the author.

Henri Coulette. "Correspondence" from POETRY, June 1990. Reprinted by permission of POETRY and Robert Mezey.

Countee Cullen. "Heritage" from COLOR by Countee Cullen. Copyright 1925 by Harper & Brothers; copyright renewed 1953 by Ida M. Cullen. Reprinted by permision of GRM Associates, Inc., as agents for the Estate of Ida M. Cullen.

E. E. Cummings. "POEM, OR BEAUTY HURTS MR. VINAL," "she being brand new," "anyone lived in a pretty how town" and "l(a" reprinted from COMPLETE POEMS, 1904–1962, by E. E. Cummings, edited by George J. Firmage, by permission of Liveright Publishing Corporation. Copyright © 1923, 1925, 1926, 1931, 1935, 1938, 1939, 1940, 1944, 1945, 1946, 1947, 1948, 1949, 1950, 1951, 1952, 1953, 1954, 1955, 1956, 1957, 1958, 1959, 1960, 1961, 1962 by E. E. Cummings. Copyright © 1961, 1963, 1966, 1967, 1968 by Marion Morehouse Cummings. Copyright © 1972, 1973, 1974, 1975, 1976, 1977, 1978, 1979, 1980, 1981, 1982, 1983, 1984, 1985, 1986, 1987, 1988, 1989, 1990, 1991 by the Trustees for the E. E. Cummings Trust.

Carolyn Forché. "The Colonel" from THE COUNTRY BETWEEN US by Carolyn Forché. Copyright © 1982 by Carolyn Forché. Reprinted by permission of HarperCollins, Publishers, Inc.

Louise Glück. "Vespers" from THE WILD IRIS by Louise Glück. Copyright © 1993 by Louise Glück. Reprinted by permission of HarperCollins Publishers, Inc.

Patricia Goedicke. "Wise Owl," first published in THE SATURDAY REVIEW OF LITERATURE, then in BETWEEN OCEANS by Patricia Goedicke, published by Harcourt, Brace & World, Inc., Copyright © 1968 by Patricia Goedicke. Reprinted by permission of the author.

Edward Hirsch. "Fast Break" from WILD GRATITUDE by Edward Hirsch. Copyright © 1985 by Edward Hirsch. Reprinted by permission of Alfred A. Knopf, Inc.

Edwin Honig. "As a Great Prince" by Edwin Honig from THE GAZABOS: FORTY-ONE POEMS published by Clark & Way, Inc., NY, 1959. Reprinted by permission of Edwin Honig.

Andrew Hudgins. "Gauguin: The Yellow Christ" by Andrew Hudgins. Reprinted by permission from THE HUDSON REVIEW, Vol XLIII, No. 1 (Spring 1990). Copyright © 1990 by Andew Hudgins

Randall Jarrell. "The Death of the Ball Turrett Gunner" from THE COMPLETE POEMS OF RANDALL JARRELL. Copyright © 1969, renewed 1997 by Mary von S. Jarrell. Reprinted by permission of Farrar, Straus and Giroux, LLC.

Patrick Kavanagh. "To the Man after the Harrow" is reprinted by permission from THE COMPLETE POEMS OF PATRICK KAVANAGH, New York, 1996, edited and with commentary by Peter Kavanagh. Copyright 1972, 1996 Peter Kavanagh.

Denise Levertov. "Cancion" from THE FREEING OF THE DUST by Denise Levertov. Copyright © 1975 by Denise Livertov. First published in POETRY. Reprinted by permission of New Directions Publishing Corporation.

Walter McDonald. "The Food Pickers of Saigon" is reprinted from AFTER THE NOISE OF SAIGON, by Walter McDonald (Amherst: University of Massachusetts Press, 1988), copyright © 1988 by Walter McDonald.

Peter Meinke. "Miss Arbuckle" by Peter Meinke from THE EDUCATIONAL FORUM, Volume 33, Number 1, Nov. 1968, Page 26. Reprinted by permission of Kappa Delta Pi, and International Honor Society in Education.

Peter Meinke. "The Poet, Trying to Surprise God" from TRYING TO SURPRISE GOD by Peter Meinke © 1981. Reprinted by permission of the University of Pittsburgh.

Howard Nemerov. "Because You Asked About the Line Between Prose and Poetry" from SENTENCE. Reprinted by permission of Margaret Nemerov, Trustee of the Howard Nemerov Trust.

Sharon Olds. "The Death of Marilyn Monroe" from THE DEAD AND THE LIVING by Sharon Olds. Copyright © 1983 by Sharon Olds. Reprinted by permission of Alfred A. Knopf, Inc.

Ezra Pound. "In a Station of the Metro" from EZRA POUND: PERSONAE. Copyright 1926 by Ezra Pound. Reprinted by permission of New Directions Publishing Corporation.

Ishmael Reed. "Beware: Do Not Read This Poem" by Ishmael Reed. Reprinted by permission of Whitman, Breed, Abbot & Morgan.

Judith Rodriquez. "Eskimo occasion" from JUDITH RODRIQUEZ: NEW AND SELECTED POEMS, University of Queensland Press, St. Lucia, 1988. Reprinted with permission.

Muriel Rukeyser. "From Letter to the Front: To Be a Jew in the Twentieth Century" from OUT OF SILENCE by Muriel Rukeyser, 1992. Reprinted by permission of International Creative Management, Inc. Copyright © 1992 by William Rukeyser.

Carol Rumens. "An Easter Garland" from THINKING OF SKINS: NEW AND SELECTED POEMS by Carol Rumens, Bloodaxe Books, 1993. Reprinted by permission.

Edith Sitwell. "Sir Beelzebub" from COLLECTED POEMS by Edith Sitwell, published by Sinclair Stevenson. Reprinted by permission of David Higham Associates.

Stevie Smith. "Mother among the Dustbins" from COLLECTED POEMS OF STEVIE SMITH by Stevie Smith. Copyright © 1972 by Stevie Smith. Reprinted by permission of New Directions Publishing Corporation.

James Stephens. "A Glass of Beer" from COLLECTED POEMS OF JAMES STEPHENS. Reprinted by permission of The Society of Authors as the literary representative of the Estate of James Stephens.

Anne Stevenson. "The Fiction-Makers" from SELECTED POEMS 1955–1995, Bloodaxe Books, 2000. Reprinted by permission of Bloodaxe Books.

Dylan Thomas. "Do Not Go Gentle into That Good Night" from POEMS OF DYLAN THOMAS by Dylan Thomas. Copyright 1939 by New Directions Publishing Corporation, 1945 by The Trustees for the Copyrights of Dylan Thomas, 1952 by Dylan Thomas. Reprinted by permission of New Directions Publishing Corporation and David Higham Associates.

Candice Warne. "Blackbird Sestina" by Candice Warne. Reprinted by permission of the author.

Reading John Keats in Depth

Walter Jackson Bate. "The Odes of April and May, 1819" is reprinted by permission of the publishers from JOHN KEATS, by Walter Jackson Bate, Cambridge, MA: The Belknap Press of Harvard University Press, Copyright © 1963 by the President and Fellows of Harvard College, Copyright © renewed 1991 by Walter Jackson Bate.

Aileen Ward. Excerpt from "The Melancholy Storm" from JOHN KEATS: THE MAKING OF A POET by Aileen Ward. Copyright 1963, renewed 1991 by Aileen Ward. Reprinted by permission of Farrar, Straus and Giroux, LLC.

Reading Robert Frost in Depth

Robert Frost. THE POETRY OF ROBERT FROST edited by Edward Connery Lathem, Copyright 1923, © 1969 by Henry Holt and Co., copyright 1936, 1951, 1956, 1960, 1962 by Robert Frost, © 1964 by Lesley Frost Ballantine, © 1988 by Alfred Edwards. Reprinted by permission of Henry Holt and Company, LLC.

Robert Frost. THE LETTERS OF ROBERT FROST TO LOUIS UNTERMEYER by Robert Frost, Copyright 1963 by Louis Untermeyer, © 1991 by Laurence S. Untermeyer. Reprinted by permission of Henry Holt and Company, LLC.

Reading Sylvia Plath in Depth

Sylvia Plath. "Daddy" from ARIEL by Sylvia Plath. Copyright © 1963 by Ted Hughes. Copyright renewed. "Ariel" from ARIEL by Sylvia Plath. Copyright © 1965 by Ted Hughes. "Elm" from ARIEL by Sylvia Plath. Originally appeared in The New Yorker. Copyright © 1963 by Ted Hughes. Copyright renewed. "Morning Song" from ARIEL by Sylvia Plath. Copyright © 1961 by Ted Hughes. Copyright renewed. "Tulips" from ARIEL by Sylvia Plath. Copyright © 1962 by Ted Hughes. Copyright renewed. "Mary's Song" from ARIEL by Sylvia Plath. Copyright © 1963 by Ted Hughes. Copyright renewed. "Paralytic" from ARIEL by Sylvia Plath. Copyright © 1965 by Ted Hughes. Copyright renewed. "Lady Lazarus" from ARIEL by Sylvia Plath. Copyright © 1963 by Ted Hughes. Copyright renewed. "Metaphors" from THE COLOSSUS by Sylvia Plath. Copyright © 1960 by Ted Hughes. Copyright renewed. "Mirror" from THE COLOSSUS by Sylvia Plath. Copyright © 1963 by Ted Hughes. Copyright renewed. "The Moon and the Yew Tree" from ARIEL by Sylvia Plath. Copyright © 1963 by Ted Hughes. Copyright renewed. Reprinted by permission of Harper Collins Publishers, Inc. and Faber and Faber Limited. "The Colossus" from THE COLOSSUS AND OTHER POEMS by Sylvia Plath. Copyright © 1960 by Sylvia Plath. Reprinted by permission of Alfred A. Knopf, Inc. and Faber and Faber Limited.

Sylvia Plath. "On Suicide" from Her Journal from THE JOURNALS OF SYLVIA PLATH by Ted Hughes (ed.). Copyright © 1982 by Ted Hughes as Executor of the Estate of Sylvia Plath. Used by permission of Doubleday, a division of Bantam Doubleday Dell Publishing Group, Inc.

Sylvia Plath. Pages 86–88 from LETTERS HOME by Sylvia Plath. Copyright © 1975 by Aurelia Schober Plath. Reprinted by permission of HarperCollins Publishers, Inc.

An Album of Poems

Diane Ackerman. "On Looking into Sylvia Plath's Copy of Goethe's *Faust.*" "Letter to Wallace Stevens," and "Anne Donne to Her Husband" form JAGUAR OF SWEET LAUGHTER by Diane Ackerman. Copyright © 1991 by Diane Ackerman. Reprinted by permission of Random House, Inc.

Bella Akhmadulina. "Volcanoes" Bella Akhmadulina, 32 11 from ABOUT THE HOUSE by W. H. Auden. Copyright © 1963 by W. H. Auden. Reprinted by permission of Random House, Inc.

Agha Shahid Ali. "Homage to Faiz" from THE HALF-INCH HIMALAYAS © 1987 by Ali Agha Shahid, Wesleyan University Press by permission of the University Press of New England.

Auden, W. H. "Musee des Beaux Arts" and "In Memory of W. B. Yeats" from W. H. AUDEN: COLLECTED POEMS, edited by E. Mendelson. Copyright 1940 and renewed 1968 by W. H. Auden. Reprinted by permission of Random House and Faber and Faber Ltd.

Imamu Amiri Baraka. "In Memory of Radio" from PREFACE TO A TWENTY VOLUME SUICIDE NOTE by Amiri Baraka. Copyright © 1961 by Amiri Baraka. Reprinted by permission of Sterling Lord Literistic, Inc.

Grace Bauer. "Eve Recollecting the Garden" from POETRY, April 1990. Copyright 1990 by The Modern Poetry Association. Reprinted by permission of the Editor of POETRY and Grace Bauer.

Elizabeth Bishop. "Poem" from THE COMPLETE POEMS 1927–1979 by Elizabeth Bishop. Copyright 1979, 1983 by Alice Helen Methfessell. Reprinted by permission of Farrar, Straus and Giroux, LLC.

Louise Bogan. "Medusa" and "Women" from THE BLUE ESTUARIES: POEMS 1923–1968 by Louise Bogan. Copyright © 1968 by Louise Bogan. Copyright renewed 1996 by Ruth Limmer. Reprinted by permission of Farrar, Straus and Giroux, LLC.

Arna Bontemps. "A Black Man Talks of Reaping." Reprinted by permission of Harold Ober Associates, Inc. Copyright © 1963 by Arna Bontemps.

Gwendolyn Brooks. "the mother" and "We Real Cool" from BLACKS by Gwendolyn Brooks. Copyright © 1991 by Gwendolyn Brooks. Published by Third World Press, Chicago, 1991. Reprinted by permission of the author.

Jose Antonio Burciago. "World Premiere" from RESTLESS SERPENTS. Reprinted by permission of the author.

Kathryn Stripling Byer. "Chestnut Flat Mine" from WILDWOOD FLOWER by Kathryn Stripling Byer, published by LSU Press, Baton Rouge, LA. Copyright © Kathryn Stripling Beer.

Juanita Casey. "Pegasus" from HORSE BY THE RIVER. Reprinted by permission of Colin Smythe, Ltd.

Amy Clampitt. "Beach Glass" from THE KINGFISHER by Amy Clampitt. Copyright © 1983 by Amy Clampitt. Reprinted by permission of Alfred A. Knopf, Inc.

John Cotton. "Report Back" from OLD MOVIES AND OTHER POEMS by John Cotton. Reprinted by permission of the author.

Robert Creeley. "Ballad of the Despairing Husband" from COLLECTED POEMS OF ROBERT CREELEY, 1945–1975. Reprinted by permission of University of California Press.

E. E. Cummings. "Buffalo Bill's Defunct" and "my sweet old etcetera" reprinted from COMPLETE POEMS, 1904–1962, by E. E. Cummings, Edited by George J. Firmage, by permission of Liveright Publishing Corporation. Copyright © 1923, 1925, 1926, 1931, 1935, 1938, 1939, 1940, 1944, 1945, 1946, 1947, 1948, 1949, 1950, 1951, 1952, 1953, 1954, 1955, 1956, 1957, 1958, 1959, 1960, 1961, 1962 by E. E. Cummings. Copyright © 1961, 1963, 1966, 1967, 1968 by Marion Morehouse Cummings. Copyright © 1972, 1973, 1974, 1975, 1976, 1977, 1978, 1979, 1980, 1981, 1982, 1983, 1984, 1985, 1986, 1987, 1988, 1989, 1990, 1991 by the Trustees for the E. E. Cummings Trust.

Philip Dacey. "Jack, Afterwards" and "Jill, Afterwards" from HOW I ESCAPED FROM THE LABYRINTH AND OTHER POEMS. Reprinted by permission of Carnegie Mellon University Press, © 1977 by Philip Dacey.

Bernard Dadié. "In Memoriam" from the NEGRITUDE POETS, edited by Ellen Conroy Kennedy. Reprinted by permission of Thunder's Mouth Press.

Carl Dennis. "Oedipus the King" from MEETINGS WITH TIME (Viking Penguin, 1992). Reprinted by permission of Carl Dennis.

James Dickey. "On the Hill Below the Lighthouse" from THE WHOLE MOTION: collected poems, 1945–1992. © 1992 by James Dickey, Wesleyan University Press by permission of University Press of New England.

Emily Dickinson. "After Great Pain, a Formal Feeling" (Poem #341) from THE COMPLETE POEMS OF EMILY DICKINSON, edited by Thomas H. Johnson. Copyright 1929 by Martha Dickinson Bianchi; copyright © renewed 1957 by Mary L. Hampson. By permission of Little, Brown and Company.

Emily Dickinson. "Success is Countest Sweetest"; "I Taste a Liquor Never Brewed"; "I Felt a Funeral, in My Brain"; "Tell the Truth, But Tell It Slant"; "Because I Could Not Stop for Death"; and "I Heard a Fly Buzz When I Died" are reprinted by permission of the publishers and the Trustees of Amherst College from THE POEMS OF EMILY DICKINSON, Thomas H. Johnson, ed, Cambridge, MA: The Belknap Press of Harvard University Press, Copyright © 1951, 1955, 1979 by the President and Fellows of Harvard College.

Sheila Dietz. "Not Remembering More" by Sheila Dietz. Reprinted by permission of the author.

Birago Diop. "Viaticum" from THE NEGRITUDE POETS, edited by Ellen Conroy Kennedy. Reprinted by permission of Thunder's Mouth Press.

H. D. (Hilda Doolittle). "Heat, part II of Garden" and "Helen" by H. D. Doolittle, from COLLECTED POEMS, 1912–1944, copyright © 1982 by The Estate of Hilda Doolittle. Reprinted by permission of New Directions Publishing Corp.

Rita Dove. "Used" was first published in THE ATLANTIC MONTHLY. Copyright 1989 by Rita Dove. Reprinted by permission of the author.

Gretel Ehrlich. "The Orchard" © Gretel Ehrlich. Published in 1980 by Ahsahta Press, Boise State University, Boise, Idaho. Reprinted by permission of Gretel Ehrlich and Ahsahta Press.

Faiz Ahmed Faiz. "Before You Came" by Faiz Ahmed Faiz, translated by Agha Shahid Ali. Published in the new renaissance, Vol. VIII, No. 2—Spring 1988. Reprinted by permission of the new renaissance.

Margaret Gibson. "Out in the Open" from OUT IN THE OPEN by Margaret Gibson. Copyright © 1989 by Margaret Gibson. "Unborn Child" from LONG WALKS IN THE AFTERNOON by Margaret Gibson. Copyright © 1982 by Margaret Gibson. Both reprinted by permission of Louisiana State University Press.

Louise Glück. "Matins" from THE WILD IRIS by Louise Glück. Copyright © 1993 by Louise Glück. Reprinted by permission of HarperCollins Publishers, Inc.

Louise Glück. "Brooding Likeness" from THE TRIUMPH OF ACHILLES from THE FIRST FOUR BOOKS OF POEMS by Louise Glück. Copyright © 1968, 1971, 1972, 1973, 1974, 1975, 1976, 1977, 1978, 1979, 1980, 1985, 1995 by Louise Glück. Reprinted by permission of HarperCollins Publishers, Inc.

Louise Glück. "Brown Circle" from ARARAT by Louise Glück. Copyright © 1990 by Louise Glück. Reprinted by permission of HarperCollins Publishers, Inc.

Lorna Goodison. "Jamaica 1980" and "My Last Poem" from I AM BECOMING MY MOTHER by Lorna Goodison, published by New Beacon Books 1986; "My Last Poem (Again)" from HEART-EASE by Lorna Goodison, published by New Beacon Books 1988. Reprinted by permission of New Beacon Books.

Jorie Graham. "The Hiding Place" from REGION OF UNLIKENESS by Jorie Graham. Copyright © 1991 by Jorie Graham. Reprinted by permission of HarperCollins Publishers, Inc.

Jorie Graham. "History" by Jorie Graham from EROSION. Copyright © 1983 by Princeton University Press. Reprinted by permission of Princeton University Press.

Linda Gregg. "Whole and without Blessing" copyright 1981 by Linda Gregg. Reprinted from TOO BRIGHT TO SEE with the permission of Graywolf Press, Saint Paul, Minnesota.

Marilyn Hacker. "Did you love well what very soon you left?" from LOVE, DEATH AND THE CHANGING OF THE SEASONS. Copyright © 1986 by Marilyn Hacker. "Sonnet Ending with a Film Subtitle" from TAKING NOTICE by Marilyn Hacker. Copyright © 1976, 1978, 1979, 1980 by Marilyn Hacker. Reprinted by permission of Frances Collin, Literary Agent.

Thomas Hardy. "The Darkling Thrush" is reprinted with the permission of Scribner, a Division of Simon & Schuster from THE COMPLETE POEMS OF THOMAS HARDY, edited by James Gibson (New York: MacMillan, 1976).

Joy Harjo. "Sante Fe" and "Nine Lives" from IN MAD LOVE AND WAR © 1990 by Joy Harjo, Wesleyan University Press, reprinted by permission of the author and University Press of New England.

Michael Harper. "Last Affair: Bessie's Blues Song" is reprinted from SONG: I WANT A WITNESS by Michael S. Harper. © Michael S. Harper, 1972. Reprinted by permission of the author.

Seamus Heaney. "Punishment" from OPENED GROUND: SELECTED POEMS 1966–1996 by Seamus Heaney. Copyright © 1998 by Seamus Heaney. "The Tollund Man" from SELECTED POEMS 1966–1987 by Seamus Heaney. Copyright © 1990 by Seamus Heaney. Reprinted by permission of Farrar, Straus and Giroux, LLC and Faber and Faber Ltd.

Geoffrey Hill. "September Song" from NEW AND COLLECTED POEMS 1952–1992. Copyright © 1994 by Geoffrey Hill. Reprinted by permission of Houghton Mifflin Co. and Penguin Books. All rights reserved. Previously published in KING LOG (1968).

Christine Holbo. "Gomorrah," originally in THE NEW YORKER, © 1992 by Christine Holbo. Reprinted by permission of the author.

Langston Hughes. "The Negro Speaks of Rivers" and "The Weary Blues" from SELECTED POEMS by Langston Hughes. Copyright 1926 by Alfred A. Knopf, Inc. and renewed 1954 by Langston Hughes. "Madam and the Rent Man" from SELECTED POEMS by Langston Hughes. Copyright 1948 by Alfred A. Knopf, Inc. Reprinted by permission of Alfred A. Knopf, Inc.

Langston Hughes. "Theme for English B" from COLLECTED POEMS by Langston Hughes. Copyright © 1994 by the Estate of Langston Hughes. Reprinted by permission of Alfred A. Knopf, a division of Random House Inc.

Ted Hughes. "Crow's First Lesson" and "Examination at the Womb Door" copyright © 1971 by Ted Hughes. Originally appeared in CROW by Ted Hughes. From NEW SELECTED POEMS by Ted Hughes. Reprinted by permission of HarperCollins Publishers and Faber and Faber Ltd.

Lynda Hull. "Midnight Reports" by Lynda Hull reprinted from STAR LEDGER by Lynda Hull by permission of the University of Iowa Press. Copyright 1991 by Lynda Hull.

T. R. Hummer. "The Rural Carrier Stops to Kill a Nine-Foot Cottonmouth" by T. R. Hummer. Reprinted by permission of Louisiana State University Press from THE ANGELIC ORDERS by T. R. Hummer. Copyright © 1982 by T. R. Hummer.

T. R. Hummer. "The Rural Carrier Discovers That Love Is Everywhere" by T. R. Hummer, Copyright © Commonweal 1980. Reprinted by permission of COMMONWEAL.

Elizabeth Jennings. "Fragment for the Dark," "The Child's Story" from COLLECTED POEMS by Elizabeth Jennings, published by Carcanet Press Ltd. Reprinted by permission of David Higham Associates.

June Jordan. "Letter to the Local Police" from PASSION: NEW POEMS 1977–1980 by June Jordan. Reprinted by permission of June Jordan.

Jenny Joseph. "Warning" from SELECTED POEMS published by Bloodaxe Books. © Jenny Joseph 1992. Reprinted by permission of the author and the author's agent, John Johnson Ltd.

Donald Justice. "A Map of Love" from NEW AND SELECTED POEMS by Donald Justice. Copyright © 1995 by Donald Justice. Reprinted by permission of Alfred A. Knopf, a division of Random House, Inc.

Brigit Pegeen Kelly. "Young Wife's Lament" reprinted from TO THE PLACE OF TRUMPETS by permission of Yale University Press, copyright 1983.

Dolores Kendrick. "Leah: in Freedom" from THE WOMEN OF PLUMS: POEMS IN THE VOICES OF SLAVE WOMEN. Copyright © 1989 by Dolores Kendrick, William Morrow and Company, Inc., NY, Publisher, Phillips Exeter Academy Press Edition, Exeter, NH. 1991. Reprinted by permission of the author.

Rachel Korn. "Keep Hidden from Me" by Rachel Korn from A TREASURY OF YIDDISH POETRY, edited by Irving Howe and Eliezer Greenberg. Copyright © 1969 by Irving Howe and Eliezer Greenberg. Reprinted by permission of Henry Holt and Company, LLC.

Mazisi Kunene. "From the Ravages of Life We Create," "The Political Prisoner," and "Place of Dreams" from ZULU POEMS by Mazisi Kunene (New York: Africana Publishing Co., 1970). Copyright © 1970 by Mazisi Kunene. Reprinted by permission of the Publisher, Africana Publishing Co., a division of Holmes & Meier Publishers, Inc.

Philip Larkin. "Faith Healing" from COLLECTED POEMS by Philip Larkin. Copyright © 1988, 1989 by the Estate of Philip Larkin. Reprinted by permission of Farrar, Straus and Giroux, LLC and Faber and Faber Ltd.

Philip Larkin. "Church Going" by Philip Larkin is reprinted from THE LESS DECEIVED by permission of The Marvell Press, England and Australia.

Denise Levertov. "O Taste and See" and "Matins" from DENISE LEVERTOV: POEMS 1960–1967. Copyright © 1961, 1964 by Denise Levertov Goodman. Reprinted by permission of New Directions Publishing Corporation.

Jan Heller Levi. "Sex Is Not Important" from ONCE I GAZED AT YOU IN WONDER (Louisiana State University Press, 1999). Originally appeared in THE ANTIOCH REVIEW.

Robert Lowell. "Robert Frost" from SELECTED POEMS by Robert Lowell. Copyright © 1976 by Robert Lowell. Reprinted by permission of Farrar, Straus and Giroux, LLC.

Wing Tek Lum. "At a Chinaman's Grave" and "Minority Poem" by Wing Tek Lum from EXPOUNDING DOUBTFUL POINTS. Reprinted by permission of the author.

George Ella Lyon. "Salvation" copyright 1982 by Appalachian State University/Appalachian Journal. "Progress" copyright 1984 by Appalachian State University/Appalachian Journal. Both used with permission of Appalachian Journal.

Naomi Long Madgett. "The Race Question" from STAR BY STAR by Naomi Long Madgett, 1970. By permission of the author.

Naomi Long Madgett. "Midway" from STAR BY STAR by Naomi Long Madgett, 1965. By permission of the author.

Mekeel McBride. "If I'd Been Born in Tennessee" reprinted from RED LETTER DAYS by Mekeel McBride by permission of Carnegie Mellon University Press, © 1986 by Mekeel McBride.

Walter McDonald. "Father's Straight Razor" first appeared in POETRY, June 1990. Copyright © 1990 by The Modern Poetry Association. Reprinted by permission of the editor of POETRY and Walter McDonald.

W. S. Merwin. "For a Coming Extinction" from THE LICE by W. S. Merwin. Copyright © 1963, 1964, 1965, 1966, 1967 by W. S. Merwin. Reprinted by permission of The Wylie Agency.

Edna St. Vincent Millay. "Childhood Is the Kingdom Where Nobody Dies" by Edna St. Vincent Millay. From COLLECTED POEMS, HarperCollins. Copyright © 1934, 1962 by Edna St. Vincent Millay and Norma Millay Ellis. All rights reserved. Reprinted by permission of Elizabeth Barnett, literary executor.

Cheng Min. "Student" from WOMEN POETS OF CHINA by Kenneth Rexroth. Copyright © 1972 by Kenneth Rexroth and Ling Chung. Reprinted by permission of New Directions Corporation.

N. Scott Momaday. "Comparatives" from THE GOURD DANCER by N. Scott Momaday. Reprinted by permission of the author.

Marianne Moore. "Poetry" is reprinted with the permission of Scribner, a division of Simon & Schuster, from COLLECTED POEMS OF MARIANNE MOORE. Copyright 1935 by Marianne Moore; copyright renewed © 1963 by Marianne Moore and T. S. Eliot.

Larry Neal. "Ghost Poem #1" from VISION OF A LIBERATED FUTURE by Larry Neal. Reprinted by permission of Evelyn Neal.

Sharon Olds. "Things That Are Worse Than Death" and "The One Girl at the Boy's Party" from THE DEAD AND THE LIVING by Sharon Olds. Copyright © 1983 by Sharon Olds. Reprinted by permission of Alfred A. Knopf, Inc.

Mary Oliver. "Some Questions You Might Ask" and "The Summer Day" from HOUSE OF LIGHT by Mary Oliver. Copyright © 1990 by Mary Oliver. Reprinted by permission of Beacon Press, Boston.

Simon Ortiz. "Juanita, Wife of Manuelito" by Simon J. Ortiz from GOING FOR THE RAIN. Reprinted by permission of the author, Simon J. Ortiz.

Dorothy Parker. "General Review of the Sex Situation," copyright 1926, renewed © 1954 by Dorothy Parker, "Men," copyright 1928, renewed © 1956 by Dorothy Parker, "Observation," copyright 1928, renewed © 1956 by Dorothy Parker, "Incurable," copyright 1928, renewed © 1956 by Dorothy Parker, "Symptom Recital," copyright 1928, renewed © 1956 by Dorothy Parker, from THE PORTABLE DOROTHY PARKER by Dorothy Parker, Introduction by Brendan Gill. Used by permission of Viking Penguin, a division of Penguin Books USA Inc.

Marge Piercy. "Secretary Chant" from CIRCLES ON THE WATER by Marge Piercy. Copyright © 1982 by Marge Piercy. Reprinted by permission of Alfred A. Knopf, Inc.

Katha Pollitt. "Old Neighbors" by Katha Pollitt. Originally published in SOUTHWEST REVIEW, Winter 1990. Reprinted by permission of the author. "In Memory" from ANTARTIC TRAVELLER by Katha Pollitt. Copyright © 1981 by Katha Pollitt. Reprinted by permission of Alfred A. Knopf, Inc.

Alexander Pope. "Ode on Solitude" from POEMS OF ALEXANDER POPE. Reprinted by permission of Methuen & Co.

Henry Reed. "The Naming of Parts" from A MAP OF VERONA. Reproduced with permission of Curtis Brown Group Ltd. London on behalf of the Estate of Henry Reed. Copyright Henry Reed.

Carter Revard. "What the Eagle Fan Says" from COWBOYS AND INDIANS. Also, reprinted in AN EAGLE NATION. Reprinted by permission of Carter Revard.

Adrienne Rich. "Trying to Talk With a Man" and "Diving Into the Wreck" from THE FACT OF A DOORFRAME. Poems Selected and New, 1950–1984 by Adrienne Rich. Copyright © 1984 by Adrienne Rich. Copyright © 1984 by Adrienne Rich. Copyright © 1975, 1978 by W. W. Norton & Company, Inc. Copyright © 1981 by Adrienne Rich. Used by permission of W. W. Norton & Company, Inc.

Theodore Roethke. "Elegy for Jane," copyright 1950 by Theodore Roethke. "My Papa's Waltz," copyright 1942 by Hearst Magazines, Inc. from THE COLLECTED POEMS OF THEODORE ROETHKE by Theodore Roethke. Used by permission of Doubleday, a division of Bantam Doubleday Dell Publishing Group, Inc.

Muriel Rukeyser. "Myth" from OUT OF SILENCE by Muriel Rukeyser, 1992. Reprinted by permission of International Creative Management, Inc. Copyright © 1992 by William Rukeyser.

Léopold Senghor. "Night of Sine" from THE NEGRITUDE POETS, edited by Ellen Conroy Kennedy. Reprinted by permission of Thunder's Mouth Press.

Anne Sexton. "Red Riding Hood" from TRANSFORMATIONS. Copyright © 1971 by Anne Sexton. Reprinted by permission of Houghton Mifflin Company. All rights reserved.

Fily-Dabo Sissoko. "Brush Fire" from THE NEGRITUDE POETS, edited by Ellen Conroy Kennedy. Reprinted by permission of Thunder's Mouth Press.

Stevie Smith. "The Galloping Cat," "Scorpion," and "Away, Melancholy" from COLLECTED POEMS OF STEVIE SMITH by Stevie Smith. Copyright © 1972 by Stevie Smith. Reprinted by permission of New Directions Publishing Corporation.

Gary Snyder. "Riprap" from RIPRAP AND COLD MOUNTAIN POEMS by Gary Snyder. Copyright © 1990 by Gary Snyder. Reprinted by permission of North Point Press, a division of Farrar, Straus and Giroux, LLC.

Cathy Song. "The Youngest Daughter" from PICTURE BRIDE by Cathy Song. Copyright © 1983 by Cathy Song. Reprinted by permission of the publisher, Yale University Press.

Marcia Southwick. "Owning a Dead Man" from THE NIGHT WON'T SAVE ANYONE by Marcia Southwick. Copyright © 1980 by the University of Georgia Press. Reprinted by permission of the University of Georgia Press.

Maura Stanton. "Childhood" from CRIES OF SWIMMERS by Maura Stanton. Copyright © 1984 by Maura Stanton. Reprinted by permission of Carnegie Mellon University Press.

George Starbuck. "On First Looking in on Blodgett Keats's Chapman's Homer" from BONE THOUGHTS by George Starbuck. Copyright © 1960 by George Starbuck. Reprinted by permission of Yale University Press.

Wallace Stevens. "The Emperor of Ice Cream," copyright 1923 and renewed 1951 by Wallace Stevens. "The Idea of Order at Key West," copyright 1936 by Wallace Stevens and renewed 1964 by Holly Stevens. From COLLECTED POEMS by Wallace Stevens. Reprinted by permission of Alfred A. Knopf, Inc.

Anne Stevenson. "Cain" and "By the Boat House, Oxford" from SELECTED POEMS 1955–1995, Bloodaxe Books, 2000. Reprinted by permission of Bloodaxe Books.

Ruth Stone. "Where I Came From," copyright © 1987 by Ruth Stone. Reprinted by permission of Yellow Moon Press, P.O. Box 3816, Cambridge, MA 02238.

Mark Strand. "Where Are the Waters of Childhood?" from SELECTED POEMS by Mark Strand. Copyright © 1979, 1980 by Mark Strand. Reprinted by permission of Alfred A. Knopf, Inc.

Dylan Thomas. "Fern Hill" and "Poem in October" from POEMS OF DYLAN THOMAS by Dylan Thomas. Copyright 1939 by New Directions Publishing Corporation, 1945 by the Trustees for the Copyrights of Dylan Thomas, 1952 by Dylan Thomas. "Poem in October" was first published in POETRY. Reprinted by permission of New Directions Publishing Corporation and David Higham Associates.

David Wagoner. "The Shooting of John Dillinger Outside the Biograph Theater, July 22, 1934" from NEW AND SELECTED POEMS by David Wagoner. Copyright © 1976 by David Wagoner. Reprinted by permission of the author.

Marilyn Nelson Waniek. "Emily Dickinson's Defunct." Reprinted by permission of Louisiana State University Press from FOR THE BODY by Marilyn Nelson Waniek. Copyright © 1978 by Marilyn Nelson Waniek.

Belle Waring. "What Hurts" and "Children Must Have Manners" are from REFUGE, by Belle Waring, © 1990. Reprinted by permission of the University of Pittsburgh Press.

John Wieners. "The Eagle Bar," copyright © 1986 by John Wieners. Reprinted from SELECTED POEMS 1958–1984 with the permission of Black Sparrow Press.

William Carlos Williams. "The Red Wheelbarrow" and "Danse Russe" from COLLECTED POEMS OF WILLIAM CARLOS WILLIAMS, 1909–1939, Vol. I by William Carlos Williams. Copyright 1938 by New Directions Publishing Corporation. Reprinted by permission of New Directions Publishing Corporation.

Terence Winch. "The Meanest Gang in the Bronx" and "Six Families of Puerto Ricans" from IRISH MUSICIANS AMERICAN FRIENDS by Terence Winch, Coffee House Press, 1985. Reprinted by permission of the author.

James Wright. "At the Executed Murderer's Grave" from ABOVE THE RIVER: THE COMPLETE POEMS © 1990 by Anne Wright, Wesleyan University Press, by permission of University Press of New England.

William Butler Yeats. "Sailing to Byzantium" is reprinted with the permission of Scribner, a Division of Simon & Schuster from THE COLLECTED POEMS OF W. B. YEATS: Revised Second Edition, edited by Richard J. Finneran. Copyright 1928 by MacMillan Publishing Company; copyright renewed © 1956 by Georgie Yeats.

William Butler Yeats. "The Lake Isle of Innisfree" is reprinted with the permission of Scribner, a Division of Simon & Schuster, from THE COLLECTED POEMS OF W. B. YEATS, Revised Second Edition edited by Richard J. Finneran (New York: Scribner, 1996).

Interpreting Drama and Critical Approaches to Drama

Mariá Irene Fornés. CONDUCT OF LIFE from MARIÁ IRENE FORNÉS: PLAYS © copyright 1986 by PAJ Publications. Reprinted by permission of PAJ Publications.

Athol Fugard. "MASTER HAROLD" . . . AND THE BOYS by Athol Fugard. Copyright © 1982 by Athol Fugard. Reprinted by permission of Alfred A. Knopf, Inc.

Arthur Miller. Entire Play DEATH OF A SALESMAN by Arthur Miller. Copyright 1949, renewed © 1977 by Arthur Miller. Used by permission of Viking Penguin, a division of Penguin Books USA Inc.

William Shakespeare. A MIDSUMMER NIGHT'S DREAM. Footnotes for A MIDSUMMER NIGHT'S DREAM from THE COMPLETE WORKS OF SHAKESPEARE, 3rd ed. by David M. Bevington. Copyright © 1980 by Scott, Foresman and Company. Reprinted by permission of Addison-Wesley Educational Publishers, Inc.

William Shakespeare. HAMLET. Footnotes for HAMLET from THE COMPLETE WORKS OF SHAKESPEARE, 3rd ed. by David M. Bevington. Copyright © 1980 by Scott, Foresman and Company. Reprinted by permission of Addison-Wesley Educational Publishers, Inc.

Sophocles. "Oedipus Rex" from SOPHOCLES, THE OEDIPUS CYCLE: AN ENGLISH VERSION by Dudley Fitts and Robert Fitzgerald, copyright 1949 by Harcourt, Inc. and renewed 1977 by Cornelia Fitts and Robert Fitzgerald, reprinted by permission of the publisher. CAUTION: All rights, including professional, amateur, motion picture, recitation, lecturing, public reading, radio broadcasting, and television are strictly reserved. Inquiries on all rights should be addressed to Harcourt, Inc., Permissions Department, Orlando, FL, 32887-6777.

Tennessee Williams. Entire play THE GLASS MENAGERIE by Tennessee Williams. Copyright 1945 by Tennessee Williams and Edwina C. Williams and renewed 1973 by Tennessee Williams. Reprinted by permission of Random House, Inc.

August Wilson. Entire play FENCES by August Wilson. Copyright © 1986 by August Wilson. Used by permission of New American Library, a division of Penguin Books USA Inc.

Interpretive Strategies

Nikki Giovanni. "Master Charge Blues" from RE: CREATION by Nikki Giovanni. Reprinted by permission of the author. © 1970.

INDEX

Indexing is of authors, titles, and, where there is no title, first lines. Authors' names are in bold type, titles are in italic type, and first lines are in roman type.